CAMRA'S GOOD BEER GUIDE 2020

EST 1972

MANAGING EDITOR
Emma Haines

EDITORIAL PROJECT MANAGER
Claire-Michelle Taverner-Pearson

EDITORS
Ione Brown, Claire-Michelle Taverner-Pearson, Simon Tuite

PROJECT ASSISTANCE
Katie Button, Stewart Campbell

SALES & MARKETING
Toby Langdon

CAMRA BOOKS

www.camra.org.uk

Laughing Fish, Isfield, East Sussex, p462

Special thanks to 190,000+ CAMRA members who carried out research for the pub entries; the Campaign's Regional Directors and Area Organisers, who co-ordinated the pub entries; the Campaign's Brewery Liaison Co-ordinators and Brewery Liaison Officers, who carried out research for the brewery entries; Rick Pickup for assistance co-ordinating the brewery entries; Alex Presland for technical support; Iain Barker and Christine Beatty at AMA Dataset; Michael Slaughter for advising on heritage pubs; Nick Boley, Professor Brian Cox, Christine Cryne, Tim Hampson, Emma Inch, Jodie Kidd, Roger Protz and Ben Wilkinson for supplying articles for the Guide; Jonathan Lloyd at JW Lees and David Cunningham at Long Live the Local; all CAMRA's staff and CAMRA's National Executive for their help and support.

Thanks also to the publicans, breweries and others who have kindly contributed their photographs.

Photo credits: [Key: t = top; b = bottom; c = centre; l = left; r = right] p2 Britain - buildings and ruins / Alamy Stock Photo; p4 Maria Jefferis / Alamy Stock Photo; p5 Mike Frisbee; p10 World Image Archive / Alamy Stock Photo; p11 (t) Rod Davis; (b) Washington Imaging / Alamy Stock Photo; p13 Bob Steel; p14 (l) Roger Bamber / Alamy Stock Photo; p16 (r) Cath Harries; p26 (r) Cath Harries; (b) Wild Beer Co; p1054 (bl) David Cassidy (br) George Howie.

Design: Page design: Jack Pemberton, Keith Holmes (Thames Street Studio); cover design: Jack Pemberton.

Maps & illustrations: Pubs section maps: David and Morag Perrot, PerroCarto; Illustrations Keith Holmes and Jack Pemberton.

Production: Database, typesetting of listings and indexes: AMA Dataset Ltd, Preston.

Printing: Printed and bound in the UK by CPI William Clowes, Beccles, Suffolk.

Published by the Campaign for Real Ale Ltd, 230 Hatfield Road, St Albans, Herts, AL1 4LW. www.camra.org.uk

ISBN 978-1-85249-358-5

CONTENTS

PEFC
BMT-PEFC-0826
All of the papers used in this book are recyclable and made from wood grown in managed, sustainable forests. They are manufactured at mills certified to ISO 14001 and/or EMAS.

ABOUT THE GOOD BEER GUIDE

Your guide to the best pubs & beer in the UK.

For nearly five decades, the *Good Beer Guide* has been a comprehensive guide to the UK's breweries, their ales, and the best outlets to find them in around the country.

There may be other pub guides out there, but this book is different; better even. Where other guides might have a small editorial board pulling together entries, the *Good Beer Guide* has a huge volunteer team, based around the country. All regularly using their local pubs, trying out the beers on offer, and recommending the best of them to other beer- and pub-lovers.

We strive hard to ensure that all areas of the country are covered. Each county or region has a listing allocation based on a scientific calculation of its population, number of licensed premises, and levels of tourism. As a result, the Guide's reach is unparalleled.

The *Good Beer Guide* is also proudly independent. Unlike some competitor titles inclusion in this book is dependent on merit, not on payment. No pubs paid to be in this book.

PUBS SECTION

CAMRA has more than 190,000 members across more than 200 branches around the UK. It's within these branches that entries are democratically selected. All members are invited to rate beers served to them via the National Beer Scoring System (see p1058). These scores are used by branches to identify pubs consistently serving the best real ale. Not only is the quality of the cask beer monitored, but also factors that could affect the range on offer, and the overall standard of the pub, such as change of ownership or management.

While the core purpose of the Guide is to seek out quality real ale, it also takes into account other things a pub might have to offer, such as history, architecture, food, family and disabled facilities, gardens, and special events (such as beer festivals). The pub listings you find in these pages paint a full picture of what you can expect before you embark on a trip to visit them.

The listings are checked many times before publication, to ensure they are accurate and up-to-date.

Many pubs, such as the Dolphin in Hastings (p461), hold regular events

COMPREHENSIVE BREWERIES SECTION

The *Good Beer Guide* includes a comprehensive listing of the more than 1,800 breweries currently operating in the UK – not just those producing real ale – and their core beers available.

Each one is appointed a local CAMRA volunteer, as soon as they come on stream. These volunteer officers will regularly keep in touch with the brewery to stay abreast of what's being brewed, and developments that may be taking place – such as new equipment, increased production capacity, a change in ingredients (such as vegan or gluten free), or even a site move.

FEATURED ARTICLES

In addition to the pub and brewery listings, the Guide also includes a selection of entertaining and informative features. This year's Guide includes a look at how CAMRA is campaigning to protect pubs, from editor of CAMRA's *What's Brewing* Tim Hampson (p6), and an article on diversity in the beer industry by Emma Inch, the British Guild of Beer Writers' Beer Writer of the Year (p14).

ADDITIONAL RESOURCES

The *Good Beer Guide* is complemented by a host of other resources for you to make the most of it throughout the year:

- Updates to the Guide appear in members' newspaper *What's Brewing*, and in the *Good Beer Guide* mobile app (see p1058)
- Many CAMRA branches produce local guides, available through beer festivals and local outlets
- CAMRA's **whatpub.com** is a useful online resource for licensed premises in the UK
- CAMRA produces a constantly expanding range of other books on the subjects of beer, cider and perry, pubs, clubs and brewing. The full list of titles can be found at **shop.camra.org.uk**
- Want to recommend a pub, or feel one you visited fell below par? Please use the readers' recommendations forms on p1055-1056, or email **gbgeditor@camra.org.uk** and these will be forwarded to branches to take into account during surveying

A JOURNEY OF DISCOVERY

I grew up within a mile of JW Lees' Greengate Brewery and remember vividly the malt aromas in the air and steam billowing above the 150-year-old 'new' brewhouse. What are they brewing in there? What exotic liquids reside in those tanks? I discovered the answer at (roughly) 18 years of age in the Horton Arms in Chadderton, spending dark Oldham evenings drinking Lees' Bitter, still a favourite. After almost 50 years of curiosity, I discovered what really happens inside after a chance meeting with a member of the Lees-Jones family, and Cosmic Brew was born.

Today, brewing at Greengate is a fascinating mixture of technology and tradition. I learned that JW Lees' yeast is legendary in the industry; at least 5,000 generations old, having been re-pitched time and again over half a century. I discovered that there are between 0.25 and 2.5 million yeast cells per ml, and therefore in a 200 barrel brew length there will be trillions of yeast cells; one for every galaxy in the observable universe.

After some magnificent lessons on brewing, and fascinating tasting sessions, we settled on a hoppy, amber ale for Cosmic Brew. But there is a secret I'd like to share. The star pattern on the label is the sky over Greengate Brewery on the evening I was born, just a couple of miles away at Oldham Royal Hospital on 3rd March 1968. I love the thought that the yeast is as old as me.

JW Lees is not alone in the beery cosmos. There are now more than 1,850 breweries in the UK offering a scintillating choice for beer lovers. CAMRA has contributed to this rejuvenation over the past 48 years and the *Good Beer Guide* points you in the direction of where to find, and more importantly drink, those beers.

Professor Brian Cox
July 2019

Professor Brian Cox, OBE, FRS is a physicist and professor of particle physics at the University of Manchester. He has brewed his first beer, Cosmic Brew, with JW Lees at Greengate Brewery, Middleton Junction, Greater Manchester.

INTRODUCTION

Campaigning is the very essence of CAMRA's DNA. Tim Hampson explores the threats to the British pub and how CAMRA is working to effect change.

More than a quarter of the UK's pubs have closed their doors since the turn of the turn of the century, according to official figures published at the start of 2019. But CAMRA's pub campaigns are hoping to stem this tide by both calling for legislation reform and by encouraging drinkers to support their local.

CAMRA continues to fight for pubs to help save them from extinction

Since the publication of the last *Good Beer Guide*, CAMRA has been successful in a number of important campaigns. The Budget saw a freeze in beer duty and a further package of business rate relief for some pubs. This goes some way to relieving the tax burden on our pubs, but major reform is needed to bring some back from the brink.

For this reason, CAMRA launched its Save Our Pubs campaign. The Campaign is calling for a lower rate of duty for draught beer, a complete review of business rates for pubs and key changes to the Pubs Code to make it work for tenants.

Reform is needed. According to the Office for National Statistics (ONS) the number of pubs in the UK had fallen from 52,500 in 2001 to 38,815 in 2018, with pubs on the outskirts of major cities most likely to have called last orders for the final time. And it is the smaller, community, pubs which have borne the brunt of this mass extinction. Analysis shows that it's small pubs that are disappearing, as the big pub chains consolidate their businesses around bigger bars.

CAMRA's chief executive Tom Stainer said: "These shocking new figures show the huge loss that has been felt by communities up and down the country as beloved locals have closed down."

Brigid Simmonds, the chief executive of the British Beer and Pub Association (BBPA), said: "Pubs face a number of cost pressures, from high taxes in the form of beer duty, VAT and business rates, to wage increases and food inflation. This means they are under increasing financial pressure from every angle, which is driving closures. Unless more is done to help alleviate the cost pressures pubs face however, they will continue to close and jobs will be lost."

COMMUNITY PUBS

But it is not all gloom for smaller pubs. Community-run pubs are stronger than ever and people's enthusiasm for running one is growing finds a new report. The Plunkett Foundation's report discovered that pubs owned as community businesses are continuing to thrive where private enterprise has failed.

CAMRA welcomed the report, which finds the community pub sector is continuing to grow. No community pubs ceased trading during 2018,

Drovers Inn, Gussage All Saints, celebrating community acquisition

The Packhorse, South Stoke

maintaining an impressive 100 per cent survival rate. CAMRA's own figures show more than 120 pubs across the UK owned by a local community group, including the Drovers Inn, Gussage All Saints, Dorset, which reopened, after a long battle, in 2016. Locals fought to have the pub listed as an Asset of Community Value (ACV), campaigning against a Change of Use planning application to convert the pub into a house, before setting up a community share offering in order to buy and refurbish the pub. The pub is now a thriving heart of the local community.

CAMRA recognises the hard work by many communities to save their local with its Pub Saving Award. The most recent award was made to campaigners in Somerset who saved a 150-year-old village pub from closure.

The Save the Packhorse Project was set up by residents of South Stoke, Bath, in May 2012, in response to the much-loved Packhorse Inn being sold to new owners, who planned to convert it into a residence with ground floor office space. By the end of May, the Save the Packhorse Project had acquired the support of Bath and North East Somerset Council, achieved national news coverage, and secured backing from nearly 1,500 signatories on an online petition.

In February 2013 after a wave of local support and campaigning, the Packhorse Inn was added to the Council's Assets of Community Value list, giving the local community six months to raise funds to buy it.

The community organised a Save the Packhorse pop-up bar in South Stoke in May 2013, which has become a well-attended annual event with entertainment, flowing drinks, and press coverage. After a long stalemate with the pub's new owner, the team were told in June 2016 that they had less than 100 days to raise the £500,000 plus legal costs to secure the pub. Within three weeks, £287,000 had been raised. By September 2016, they had raised £601,000 with the help of 200 investors. CAMRA's Pub Saving Award organiser Paul Ainsworth said: "I hope that success stories such as this of the Packhorse Community Pub encourage other communities to fight for their local pub. The Packhorse has served the village of South Stoke for centuries now – to have lost it would have been devastating, and I am delighted that the team have been rewarded for their unyielding persistence and effort."

PUBS CODE

Another issue faced by many pubs is legal wrangling with the big national pub-owning companies (pubcos) about where they can buy their beer from.

In 2016 the Pubs Code regulations came into force, it included changes to the beer tie – an arrangement under which tenants buy beer exclusively from the company that owns their pub, in exchange for lower rent.

The Code gives tied tenants certain rights, including the right at certain times to exercise a 'Market Rent Only' (MRO) option, under which their rent is set at the market level and, in return, they are no longer required to buy products from their pub-owning business.

The introduction of the Code was expected to mark a turning point for many of England's community pubs, but that simply hasn't happened. CAMRA research has found that pubcos are riding roughshod over the provisions of the Code. Evidence is growing that pub companies are using every trick in the book to stop tied tenants taking advantage of the Code. Now, CAMRA is calling for profound changes to the Code as it says the large national pub companies are preventing meaningful reforms.

RATES REFORM

Another threat to pubs is changes to the way in which business rates are calculated. Business rates are a major cost to pubs, who pay a disproportionate amount compared to other businesses. In April 2017 there was a revaluation of rates across the UK, with many pubs seeing further significant increases. More than 40 per cent of pubs were handed an increase in their rates bill – the result of which is that many have had to put up their prices for drinkers to cover their increases,

Olde Fighting Cocks, St Albans, is threatened by excessive business rates

Craven Arms, Enborne, is one of many that participated in CAMRA's Summer of Pub

or in some cases close for good. Pubs currently pay 2.8 per cent of the business rates bill but only account for 0.5 per cent of total business turnover, which is an overpayment of around £500 million by the sector each year.

Now CAMRA has recognised the campaigning efforts of two St Albans licensees, whose local campaign against excessive business rates has gone national. The Boot's Sean Hughes and Christo Tofalli of Olde Fighting Cocks were named the Campaign's campaigners of the year. The pair's local campaigning efforts, which included an online petition against the rates rise had now become a national campaign against punitive business rates. Hughes and Tofalli launched Save St Albans Pubs as a result of fears that many of the city's 50 pubs could close as a result of the rates increases. The pair faced a combined rates rise of more than £80,000, which they calculated would mean they would have to sell an additional 180,000 pints to pay for it.

Save St Albans Pubs started as on online petition in the two pubs and was taken up by other pubs in the city. Following a meeting between the licensees and St Albans MP Anne Main, she arranged a meeting with publicans and Treasury officials where the publicans argued the case for a review of business rates for pubs.

Since then, Treasury minister Robert Jenrick has asked the publicans to provide an analysis of the national impact of business rates for pubs.

As a result, Save St Albans Pubs has broadened out into a national campaign called Save UK Pubs.

CAMRA is calling on the Government to conduct a full review of how the system works – as promised in their manifesto. This needs to look at how to address the current system where pubs are unfairly burdened.

SUMMER OF PUB

Alongside supporting community groups and campaigners, CAMRA is also working to encourage the most simple form of grassroots action. The Campaign's most recent campaigning initiative is the Summer of Pub. Its essence is straightforward, but ambition is big – to get more people down to the pub.

In June 2019 CAMRA wrote to thousands of pubs across the country encouraging them to host celebratory events to help more people rediscover their love for the great British local.
Cause for celebration included the 'PUBlic' bank holiday weekends when pub-goers were encouraged to tweet photos of themselves using the hashtag #SummerofPub. Events included special screenings of the Women's World Cup, a toast for Beer Day Britain (15 June), and beer and cider tasting events showcasing local producers. There were also a number of fringe events across London to coincide with the Great British Beer Festival.

The Craven Arms, in the small village of Enborne close to Newbury in West Berkshire took up the call. Determined to keep the tradition of pub going alive by reminding the public how important their local is to community, staff organised a number of events to encourage locals and visitors alike to head down to their pub this summer, including a garden party, a music night and an eight mile ramble through the countryside.

The pub is a unique Great British institution, and CAMRA is committed through its political and consumer campaigns undertaken by its thousands of hard-working volunteers to ensure that community pubs survive as the place where people can go out to and socialise.

Tim Hampson is the editor of CAMRA's *What's Brewing* newspaper and *BEER* magazine, and author of books about pubs and beer, including *101 Beer Days Out*. Follow him on Twitter **@beerhero**

LONG LIVE THE LOCAL

Pubs are at the heart of communities, towns and villages. Publican Jodie Kidd tells us why she's championing the local.

The Half Moon has always held a special place in my heart. It's a pub that I've grown up in, one that has been home to countless celebrations and fond memories. When I heard it was up for sale and earmarked for residential conversion, I had to step in to save it.

As a new publican, I know that my pub is one of the lucky ones. Across the UK, three pubs a day are closing their doors for good. Pub closures are fast becoming a familiar story to us all, and the impact is never greater than on the local communities of which they are a part.

It's an issue that resonates with me now more than ever. That's why I helped to launch Long Live The Local, a campaign that celebrates the positive role pubs play in our community, culture, and economy; and highlights the jeopardy that pubs face from a range of tax pressures.

In 2018, more than 116,000 people signed Long Live the Local's petition to the government to cut beer tax, and almost 50,000 people wrote to their MP. This helped secure a vital freeze to beer duty, protecting thousands of jobs.

Pubs are at the heart of communities, towns and villages. At The Half Moon, I see people from all around coming in, enjoying themselves and making memories. For example, we sponsor our local cricket team... although they haven't been that successful this season!

We hold lots of events from Summer Solstice parties to BBQs, and we have weddings and events all year round – such as curry nights and quiz nights. The WI (Women's Institute) have their meetings there as well. Charities will often use the pub as a central meeting point and we also use the pub as a great place to start off charity bikes rides and fundraising events.

Lastly but by no means least – pubs are proven to boost local economies by £100,000. At The Half Moon, one of the ways we do this is by only using produce and suppliers from within a 25 mile radius of the pub. It is something that I'm incredibly passionate about.

It's up to us to help protect pubs like this. Sign the petition to ask for a cut to beer duty at **longlivethelocal.pub**.

Jodie Kidd behind the bar at the Half Moon, Kirdford

Jodie Kidd is the licensee of the Half Moon in Kirdford, Sussex **halfmoonkirdford.co.uk**. A former model, racing driver and television presenter, in 2017 she and her two partners bought her local pub, which was earmarked for residential conversion, and turned it into a thriving community local. In 2019 she was named Beer Drinker of the Year by the All-Party Parliamentary Beer Group.

STATE OF THE NATION'S PUBS

With pubs still closing year-on-year, is it all doom and gloom for the nation's pubs? Ben Wilkinson explains.

Some 47 years after it first arrived, the *Good Beer Guide* continues to do what it always has – showcase the best real ale the UK has to offer.

When that first edition came – a fraction of its modern-day size – it was a godsend to beer enthusiasts. Good-quality ale had been all-but obliterated from some parts of the country and – where it remained – its existence was under perilous threat.

Despite the destruction of the brewing industry, the 1970s was a golden age of pub-going

It's no exaggeration to suggest that, without CAMRA, real ale might not exist today. Certainly the term wouldn't – our founders coined it, in the process capturing and unleashing a previously inhibited outrage at the theft of Britain's national drink.

It all feels like a very long time ago. And haven't we come a long way, in beer just as in cultural life generally? But while those of us from a younger generation might feel a justified smugness at living in a time without Watney's Red, industrial strife and Bri-nylon shirts, there is another aspect of those days we can look back on only longingly. Because despite the early '70s being an era that saw the heart ripped out of Britain's brewing heritage, for something else it was a golden age: the simple tradition of pub-going.

The much maligned 'big six' firms that dominated the industry at the time might not have shown much interest in the quality of their ale, but they certainly did care about having places to sell it.

Yes, philistinism was rife with many traditional and historic pubs seeing their bars knocked through and original features chucked in the skip. But as misguided – and in some cases heartbreaking – as such material vandalism was, it did not happen for want of investment. If anything, breweries were throwing around too much cash, with needless refurbishments and modernisations showing, footballer's mansion-style, what happens when money exceeds taste.

Unlike their modern-day, non-brewing successors, more likely to spend the bare minimum on upkeep and flog sites off for development if made the right offer, to the firms that controlled pubs back then, keeping people coming through the doors was of paramount importance. And in spite of everything, keep coming through the doors people did. A smaller UK population than today's, drank millions of pints more beer, and the vast majority of it was served on draught across bars. Taking home bottles from the supermarket with the weekly shop was just not a thing. Going to the pub after work on a regular basis was though; as was, for many, calling in for a swift pint or two in the lunch hour. Return to work after lunch with ale on your breath these days and, in some workplaces, you might as well have left a signed print out of your bottom on the office photocopier.

So what has caused society to change its view of pub-going so markedly over that time? Inconveniently for those of us who consider ourselves discerning beer drinkers, improvements in the quality of ale in pubs have been matched by a decline in custom. If the misery of having to drink Double Diamond wasn't enough to make people fall out of love with pubs, what on Earth is keeping people away now, at a time when quality brews (of traditional and modern varieties) are far more readily available?

One theory, and perhaps the most obvious, is cost. People tend to think house prices have seen eyewatering inflation, but since the early '70s the price of a pint in the pub has risen by an even higher percentage. And for all the recent talk of the 'climate emergency', beer has gone up more than petrol too.

"Perhaps we just have to accept the hard truth that the biggest threat to the pub is the pub itself."

Pubs in some areas face crippling costs and CAMRA strongly believes these pressures need to be alleviated. But on a nationwide level, are prices the key reason for people shunning the local? Over the same period, disposable incomes have risen significantly as well. And in reality, pricing spans a big range, from ostentatious city centre establishments where folk wave Amex cards

The Blisland Inn in Cornwall (p80) offers a warm welcome to all comers

with abandon, to unassuming locals on Yorkshire housing estates where thou can still order half a mild and pay for it in pence.

Could it be that home comforts have improved? Has central heating, better TV sets (and more channels), computer games and the like, made the front room more appealing than the lounge bar? Perhaps – but while modern houses might be warmer and boast more sophisticated entertainment than a piano in the corner, more and more people, particularly the under 40s, are unable to afford them. Many remain in cramped flats or house shares beyond an age by which their parents might have bought their lifelong home.

Some say that the smoking ban continues to damage pubs. At a time when less than 20 per cent of adults still puff? Unlikely.

Perhaps we just have to accept the hard truth that the biggest threat to the pub is the pub itself. Or rather, the perception of the pub. We know how one bad pint of cask ale can put someone off for life, but perhaps we're less ready to consider the equivalent risk with pubs. You go in one where the welcome is unfriendly, the beer is stale, the tables are sticky and an insufferable bore persists in engaging you in conversation, and maybe staying at home with the TV wins out for evermore. And sadly, at times over the past four decades, that was not an uncommon experience.

Of course, just as the enlightened know that not every pint of cask ale tastes like the unlucky bad one, we also know the overall quality of pubs today is good and improving. But the battle now is getting people who have fallen out of the pub-going habit to give them another chance. That's why, for the first time, CAMRA launched a new campaign which declared 2019 the 'Summer of Pub', and supported events across the UK to get new people to rediscover their local.

You don't have to go on a march or demonstration to be a pub campaigner. A big part of keeping pubs open is as simple as heading out for a pint and encouraging your friends to join you. Most of us recognise that the local pub is part of what makes the UK the country it is. What we don't recognise enough is that to survive, they need us. The clearest way we can all demonstrate how much we value our community pubs isn't to shout about them, it's to use them.

Unwelcoming pubs can bring down the reputation of the whole industry

Ben Wilkinson is a National Director of CAMRA. A lifelong resident of St Albans, CAMRA's base, his love of pubs began at the age of 16 when he found his first employment as a glass collector. He went on to become a newspaper journalist and PR specialist and is a father of one.

WHY BE A CAMRA MEMBER?

The Campaign for Real Ale (CAMRA) has so much to offer you in so many different ways, each and every year. Discover your reason to join us. Here are just ten great reasons to tempt you.

1 CAMPAIGN for great beer, cider and perry

As a member of CAMRA, you help to promote and protect real ale, cider and perry by actively supporting Britain's pubs, breweries, and producers to get a better deal for drinkers. In fact, its membership is why CAMRA is one of the most successful consumer rights organisations in Europe.

See **camra.org.uk/pubs/campaigns** for more information.

2 Become a BEER EXPERT

With a wealth of information available to members, you can discover everything you need to learn about beer, cider and perry. From the history, the range of styles, or how it's made.

Resources include branch events, tutored tastings and training, and our award-winning *BEER* magazine and *What's Brewing* newspaper, packed with news and features from industry insiders and experts, throughout the year. See **camra.org.uk/learn-discover** for details.

3 Enjoy BEER FESTIVALS in front of or behind the bar

You can gain free or discounted entry to more than 180 beer festivals around the country, every year. There's plenty of beer and camaraderie you can benefit from by attending a CAMRA beer festival, or you can volunteer to be a festival staff member and gain some hands-on experience. There are plenty of things to do if you don't fancy being behind the bar, from stewarding, to admin. Go to **camra.org.uk/beer-festivals-events** to learn more.

4 GET INVOLVED and make new friends

As a CAMRA member you automatically join the CAMRA branch in your local area. By attending meetings and socials you can make new friends, get actively involved as a beer scorer (which helps selection for this very Guide), or volunteer to be a branch committee member or festival worker. Most branches hold a variety of social events, and branch meetings are a great way to keep up-to-date with what's going on in the Campaign.

Visit **camra.org.uk/about/work-with-us/volunteering-opportunities** for more information and latest roles.

5 Help SAVE YOUR LOCAL

Fourteen pubs close every week. Becoming a member means you can help save the great British pub from extinction. The pub and beer industry supports nearly 900,000 jobs in the UK and contributes £23.6bn to the UK economy annually. The pub is also an asset to its community, providing a place to meet friends and social groups, a place for sports teams to compete, to buy local produce, and in some instances access local services like a post office. Go to **camra.org.uk/pubs/save-our-pubs-campaign** to find out how you can get involved.

6 Find the BEST PUBS IN BRITAIN

Members can purchase the *Good Beer Guide* at a reduced rate, or subscribe to the Good Beer Guide Privilege Club for additional discounts. A Good Beer Guide app is also available to help you find the best pubs and clubs around the country serving real ale, cider and perry, individually selected by local CAMRA members. You will also be the first to hear about our national Pub of the Year and Club of the Year winners! **gbgapp.camra.org.uk**.

7 Get great VALUE FOR MONEY

CAMRA offers a great membership deal at just £26.50* for a single membership. Receive a welcome pack, £30 worth of CAMRA beer vouchers**, plus discounts at over 3,500 pubs nationwide via our Real Ale Discount Scheme, and so much more. **www.camra.org.uk/benefits**

8 DISCOVER pub heritage and the great outdoors

Get out, get active and get exploring our great British pubs – enjoy a pub walk across the wild terrain of Scotland, discover historic pub interiors in the Midlands or find the perfect pub garden near you. Whatever your interest, check out the CAMRA shop for a book to complement it, and enjoy exclusive member discounts. Go to **shop.camra.org.uk** to see what's on offer.

Some branches hold walking or cycling socials, and some will run bus tours to more out of the way, rural gems.

9 Enjoy great HEALTH BENEFITS (really!)

We champion pubs and wellbeing – your local is at the heart of the communit. Research shows that having a local pub can make you happier and healthier, and helps local communities to tackle loneliness and isolation. So make the most of your local using our online pubs database **whatpub.com** to discover pubs and real ale discounts in your area.

10 HAVE YOUR SAY

As a volunteer-led organisation, each and every member has a say in the future direction of the Campaign. Join the annual Members' Weekend, AGM and Conference to have your say on the issues that matter to you, and influence CAMRA policy. Go to the **agm.camra.org.uk** website for more details.

So, go to **camra.org.uk/join** for information on becoming a member, or to buy a gift membership.
Alternatively call **01727 798440**.

*Rates and benefits are subject to change. **Real ale, cider and perry, subject to terms and conditions.

THE USUAL

Long-gone are the days of limited choice. Emma Inch tells us why diversity enriches the beer world.

"A pint of the usual, please."

It's been a good few years since I last walked into a pub and said that.

It's not that I think there's anything wrong with finding something you like and sticking with it. On the contrary, I value loyalty so much that I possess six identical pairs of jeans, I've used the same brand of toothpaste for my entire life and, if I find a meal I enjoy on a restaurant's menu, it's unlikely I'll ever choose anything different again.

I came of drinking age in the late 1980s in the heart of Greene King country and, until I left home, I wasn't even aware there were alternatives to their IPA. When I moved to London I worked in Wandsworth and became fiercely devoted to Young's Bitter. Then, when I relocated to Brighton some twenty-five years ago, Harvey's Best quickly became my drink of choice. I haven't turned my back on these beers; each still resides in a special corner of my heart. In fact, at the last CAMRA festival I attended – the wonderful Cambridge Beer Festival – I chose a copper-coloured pint of Harvey's Best as my opening drink. But there's no denying the beer world has changed, and – in common with many people – I have changed along with it.

Beers like Young's Bitter and Harvey's Best are stalwarts on the bar and hold a special place in our hearts

A decade ago, there were just a few hundred breweries in the UK; today there are nearly two thousand. This rapid growth has brought with it more choice than most British beer drinkers have ever known. From traditional English bitters to American-influenced IPAs, from pin-bright ales to hazy juice-bombs, from rich milk stouts to ancient farmhouse sours, in most UK cities and towns – and increasingly in rural pockets – the range of available beers is now immense. In defiance of anyone who ever doubted it, beer has emphatically proved itself to be so much more versatile than wine, gin, cider, or pretty much any other drink on the bar and, as a long-term advocate of British beer, this leaves me feeling incredibly proud.

THE CHANGING WORLD OF BEER

Beer has embraced diversity, and I'm not just talking about the liquid in your glass. Over the past few years the way we discuss beer, the aesthetic surrounding it, the people who brew it, and even the people who drink it have begun to change. In November 2018 I became the first solo woman to be named 'Beer Writer of the Year' by the British Guild of Beer Writers and women like me are now represented in every sector of the beer world. They are brewery owners, brewers, dray drivers, lab technicians, marketing executives, sales people, writers, educators and more.

"this blending of tradition and modernity, the past and the future, will propel us forward towards an even more interesting chapter in the history of brewing, one in which all ideas are valued, and every person is welcomed"

Women such as Jaega Wise, head brewer at Wild Card Brewery in Walthamstow and an elected director of the Society of Independent Brewers. Or Sara Barton, founder of Brewster's Brewery, instigator of Project Venus – a collaborative group for female brewers – and the first woman to be named Brewer of the Year by the British Guild of Beer Writers. Or drinks educator, Jane Peyton, who, in 2018, was given a Lifetime Achievement Award by the All-Party Parliamentary Beer Group, in large part for her work as founder of Beer Day Britain, the country's national beer day. Or Sophie de Ronde, head brewer at the award-winning Burnt Mill Brewery and instigator of International Women's Collaboration Brew Day. Or Lily Waite, artist, writer and driving force behind the Queer Brewing Project, a charitable collaborative brewing venture designed to raise the awareness of LGBTQ+ people in the beer and hospitality industry.

Queer Brewing Project founder Lily Waite, with collaboration beer Queer Royale

These women – and many more like them – represent the evolution of the beer industry. Thousands of years ago, women were the first brewers. Now, their descendants have held a magnifying mirror up to the world of beer, asked questions, sought solutions, and ultimately enriched the environment in which we enjoy a pint. Through them – and many other people of all genders – the British beer scene is slowly becoming as diverse as the drink we all adore.

We lose nothing by embracing this diversity. In the same way that my cocoa nib Belgian-style sour doesn't make your pint of bitter taste any less appealing, and your raspberry milkshake IPA doesn't affect my enjoyment of a glass of mild, the diversity of people now actively involved in the UK beer scene in no way undermines the brewing and drinking tradition of the past. Quite the opposite, it serves to strengthen it. Just like the liquid itself, this blending of tradition and modernity, the past and the future, will propel us forward towards an even more interesting chapter in the history of brewing, one in which all ideas are valued, and every person is welcomed.

Camden Town's brewery tap showcases a diverse range of beers

FREEDOM TO CHOOSE

I'll admit that, just occasionally, I miss the easy familiarity that came with asking for 'the usual'. I sometimes yearn for the simplicity of the days when I was consistently rewarded with a great pint without even having to think. But then I remember the liberty I now possess to choose – not only from timeless favourites but from new beers that I might grow to love just as much – and I understand that what makes things better for other people equally enriches my own life. In this world of the unexplored, the unexpected and sometimes the unusual, beer and pubs still possess the power to bring us together. Let's allow them to do that.

Jaega Wise, head brewer at Wild Card Brewery

Emma Inch is an award-winning freelance beer writer and audio-maker, and the current British Guild of Beer Writers' Beer Writer of the Year. She has written for a number of national and international publications and also produces creative audio and podcasts for the beer and pub trade. Emma produces and presents *Fermentation Beer & Brewing Radio* – one of the UK's leading beer and brewing podcasts, and is the founder of Brighton & Hove Beer Week. Find out more at **fermentationonline.com** or follow her **@fermentradio** on Twitter.

CASK MARQUE — WHO ARE WE?

Last year Cask Marque celebrated its 20th year. It is a not-for-profit organisation set up to 'ensure an exceptional drinking experience is available to every drinker'.

What have we achieved over that period?

- Accredited over 10,000 pubs for the quality of their beer.
- Improved standards of cellarmanship by developing a cellar management qualification.
- Placed quality on the agenda.
- Installation of cooling from cellar to glass.
- Championed cask ales through the annual cask report.
- 77% of consumers recognize the Cask Marque plaque (YouGov 2018).
- More recently a star rating for cellars.
- The CaskFinder app used up to 60,000 times a month to find Cask Marque pubs.

CASK MARQUE PUBS

The pubs who apply for a Cask Marque award have two unannounced visits per year from one of our 55 assessors who are qualified brewers or senior technical services personnel. On a visit they check up to six cask ales in the glass and check for temperature, aroma, appearance and taste. A beer failing on any one of these criteria fail their assessment.

Any new pubs applying for the award have to pass an 11 point check list on the cellar. Our results, not surprisingly, show a correlation between cellar practices and beer quality in the glass.

You will begin to see a beer cellar rating appear in pubs. We call this Scores on the Cellar Doors. The kitchen is to food as the cellar is to beer.

Cask Marque assessors will check up to six cask ales in the glass

TEMPERATURE

Frequently an emotive topic. The industry recommends that cask ale is served cellar cool at 11–13°C. Cask Marque on their inspections allow a 1°C variant either way. Pubs should now have a separate cooling system called an ale python. It is most important that licensees check beer in glass at least once a week to see that the equipment is working effectively.

Consumer research shows that when beer is served at above 14°C the majority of drinkers say that it is too warm. This is particularly important as in the summer you need refreshment value. Sadly, in summer 1 in 3 beers are still served too warm. Demand a cool pint.

MAKE CASK COOL

CELLAR MANAGEMENT

We have, with industry support, developed a cellar management qualification. The Scores on the Cellar Doors scheme measures the use of these best practices. To gain the qualification you need to attend a one day training course which is accredited by the British Institute of Innkeepers (Bii). Cask Marque runs courses at breweries throughout the country. As an additional training option Cask Marque also offers 1-2-1 training at a licensees pub.

All pubs should have a trained cellar manager as it helps to improve yields, quality and rate of sale.

BII

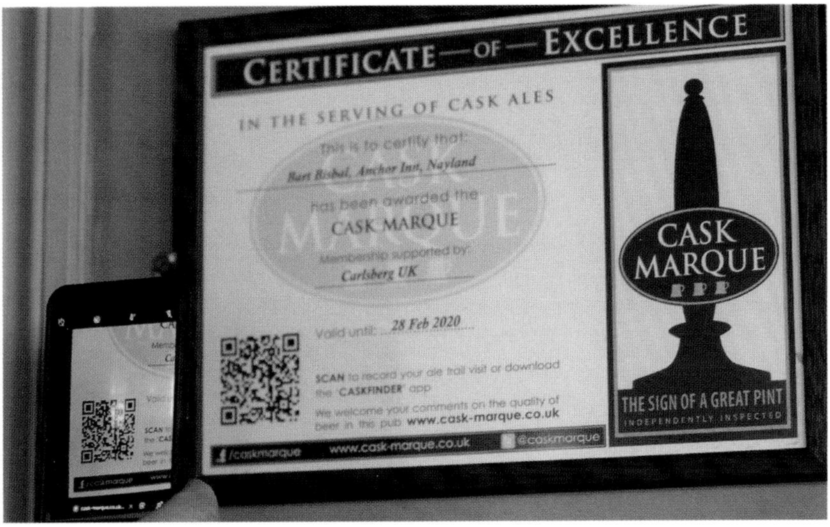

Scan pub certificates to join in the world's biggest ale trail

CASKFINDER APP

An updated version of the free CaskFinder app is now available on both iPhone and Android.
The new app has:

- Map and directions to Cask Marque pubs.
- The World's Biggest Ale Trail - 3,500 scans of the pubs QR codes happen each week.
- 7 National Walking Ale Trails plus many more.
- Pump clip recognition.
- Beer festivals near you.
- Details on 10,000 beers and 1,000 breweries.

An encyclopedia of beer in the palm of your hand.

PUMP CLIP RECOGNITION

Today, with so many brewer's beers to choose from you can just scan the pumpclip and the app will tell you the Cyclops descriptor (as below) and the details of the brewery.

All part of beer education!

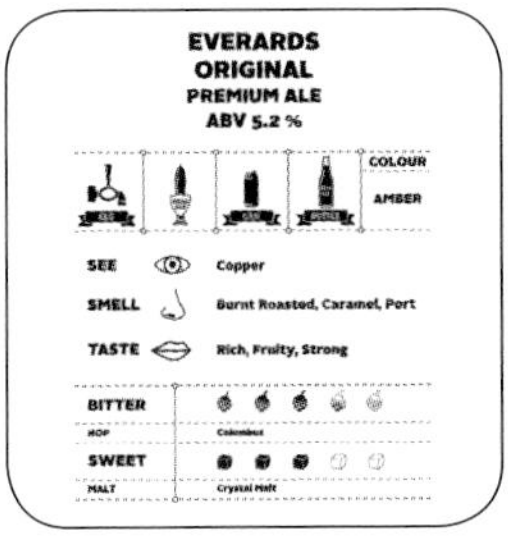

ALE TRAILS

The World's Biggest Ale Trail has all 10,000 Cask Marque pubs and you receive prizes as you scan more and more pub certificates. The app gives you the opportunity to join other ale trails.

The Seven National Walking Ale Trails have been developed in conjunction with Visit England. Why not complete the ale trails over a number of visits. You can also stay in a pub close to the trail **stayinapub.co.uk/ThingsToDo/Activities/Walking**

There is more to Cask Marque than people think!

A FINAL WORD
To find out more about Cask Marque, please do visit our website at cask-marque.co.uk and we hope you will join with us in championing beer quality in the glass to make sure you get served the perfect pint every time.

A CELEBRATION OF BEER, FOOD AND FUN

For a true showcase of British beer, head to one of the many CAMRA festivals around the country.

CAMRA beer festivals come in all shapes and sizes; from large nationals with hundreds of beers to try, to quiet events with a small selection of locally-brewed beers. So whether you're hunting out a rare collaboration brew or looking for a friendly venue where families are welcome, you can be confident that CAMRA has a festival that will suit you.

CAMRA festivals offer a huge choice of beer

There are around 200 CAMRA festivals – local, regional and national – held throughout the country. Organised, staffed and run by talented, dedicated volunteers, beer festivals play a key role in spreading the message about good beer in Britain. They have played an important role in the long campaign to offer a wider choice of beer for consumers. In the early days of CAMRA, when outlets for real ale were diminishing, festivals proved that good beer was still alive and well.

Britain has a rich beer heritage and CAMRA celebrates that by featuring a wide range of styles at its festivals, including mild, porter, stout, and barley wine. Festivals also feature innovative new styles of beer, including those aged in wood or made with the addition of fruit, herbs and spices. Beers suitable for vegans and vegetarians, as well as beers that are gluten-free are also often available. Most festivals will feature cider and perry.

There's no hard sell at a CAMRA event. The atmosphere is relaxed, and many will offer tasters of beer so you can sample before buying. Prices for both entry and beer are kept as low as possible, with many festivals offering free entry for CAMRA members. Wherever possible, there will be ample seating provided along with family rooms for visitors with children. Beer's diversity is stressed by talks and tastings while live entertainment ranges from jazz, folk, rock and blues to light classical.

NATIONAL FESTIVALS

CAMRA has several large-scale festivals that, between them, boast an incredible beer, cider and perry offering, as well as playing host to key beer award judging, including the Champion Beer of Wales, Scotland, Winter and Britain.

Darker beers come into their own during the colder months and many CAMRA events will feature seasonal ales, culminating in the Great British Beer Festival – Winter, held in Birmingham in February 2020. This is where several categories of the Champion Beer of Britain are judged (including the Barley Wines & Strong Old Ales, and Porters divisions), and the Champion Winter Beer of Britain is decided. Go to **winter.gbbf.org.uk** for more information.

The Champion Beer of Britain competition concludes in the summer at the Great British Beer Festival, held in London in August. Winning the top prize can change the life of a smaller brewery as drinkers clamour to sample the best in the country. Go to **gbbf.org.uk** for more information, and see p32 for the results of the 2019 Champion Beer of Britain competition.

For a showcase of beers from Wales and the Borders, you must head to the Great Welsh Beer & Cider Festival. This is where the Champion Beer of Wales is decided. Head to **gwbcf.info** for more information.

Sadly the Scottish Real Ale Festival was without a venue in 2019 so it didn't take place. However, a new home was being scouted for 2020 – keep an eye on **sraf.camra.org.uk** for updates.

CIDER AND PERRY

The Campaign for Real Ale has campaigned for two of the UK's other traditional drinks – cider and perry – for more than 25 years. Both have a long, rich history in Britain, and this is celebrated at many CAMRA festivals.

One of the best to enjoy cider and perry is the Reading Beer & Cider Festival, which takes place around May each year. It features 150 ciders and perries, alongside 550 different beers, and it's here that the annual Cider of the Year, and Perry of the Year judging takes place. Head to **readingbeerfestival.org.uk** for the details.

Come to a CAMRA festival for a great day out with friends

NOT JUST HERE FOR THE BEER

As well as other drinks offerings, many CAMRA festivals make it a point to offer a full day of fun. Some offer family facilities, live music and performances, traditional pub games, and camping so the fun can last all weekend. Food is a key element of most, often including 'street food' and offerings from local artisans who share the ideals of craft brewers.

CAMRA also holds discussion groups, and Learning and Discovery booths at selected festivals. See **camra.org.uk/learn-discover** for more information.

Cheers to beer, at the Great British Beer Festival

MEMBERS' WEEKEND, AGM & CONFERENCE

Every year CAMRA holds its annual meeting in a different part of the country, and this includes an on-site beer festival – the Member's Bar. The Members' Bar is open to every member attending, and also helps support local breweries and cider and perry producers, as well as giving visiting members a chance to sample a wide range of local drinks. The Members' Weekend also usually includes cider- and beer-related organised trips to local producers. Head to **agm.camra.org.uk** for more information.

VOLUNTEERING

CAMRA festivals, big and small are run and staffed by an army of talented, dedicated volunteers. From ordering the beers, food and live music, designing marketing material, building the bars and stages, to working the bars and games, and helping keep everyone safe during the event – none of it would be possible without them. Cheers to the volunteers! #thankavolunteer

Go to **camra.org.uk/volunteer** if you're interested in lending a hand, building your CV, and making friends while you're at it.

FANCY SOMETHING A BIT DIFFERENT? TRY ONE OF THESE:

Vintage transport: Woodcote Festival of Ales takes place during the Woodcote Rally and features over 600 vehicles, including vintage cars and motorbikes. Go to **soxon.camra.org.uk** for information.

Food: Manchester – A wide range of food stalls provide everything from snacks and sweets to tacos, burgers and hearty meals. Enter **mancbeerfest.uk** for details.

Family-friendly: Canterbury – An outdoor festival that welcomes families, with children's entertainers on the Saturday. Go to **kentbeerfestival.com** to find out more.

Make a weekend of it: Noted as one of the most picturesque beer festivals by the *Guardian*, the Cotswold Beer Festival takes place in a medieval Tithe Barn at Postlip Hall, surrounded by the beautiful British countryside See **postlip.camra.org.uk** for details.

Live music: Robin Hood Beer Festival, Nottingham – There is live entertainment throughout the festival, with a varied selection of music styles. Head to **beerfestival.nottinghamcamra.org** for more.

Beers by the sea: Eastbourne – Held on Eastbourne seafront, you can enjoy your beer at outside tables with fine sea views. Enter **eastbournebeerfestival.co.uk** for the latest.

Service with a smile at the Hitchin beer festival

Beer Festivals come in all shapes and sizes and offer a wide choice for discerning drinkers around the country throughout the year. Whether it be winter warmers, or cider in the sunshine, all offer a warm welcome, and in many cases added extras such as street food, family facilities, and live entertainment.
Go to **camra.org.uk/events** for up-to-date information about planned festivals and events around the UK.

AWARD-WINNING PUBS AND CLUBS

Each year CAMRA celebrates the best of the best with its pub and club awards. Find out more about this year's winners and finalists.

PUB OF THE YEAR

WINNER

A pub that stood empty and derelict just four years ago has proved that with a will and a way, it can become not just a local favourite, but the best in the country. Nestled in the heart of a Hampshire village, the **Wonston Arms in Wonston**, near Winchester (see p200) was taken on and revitalised by owner and landlord Matt Todd, who focusses heavily on serving the community.

The Wonston Arms, Winchester was crowned top pub in 2019

"I'm overwhelmed that our little pub – which had been handed a death sentence four years ago - has now been named the very best in the country," said Matt.

"I have strived to recreate the kind of wet pub I went to in the 1970s with my dad when I was a young boy in the north of England. The support from the local community and beyond has been overwhelming, helping to propel us forward despite these testing times."

As a result, the pub has become an important asset for local residents. Alongside a selection of carefully kept cask ales and a gin bar with 180 varieties, the Wonston Arms boasts a range of pop-up foodie nights (local food vendors are invited for special fish and chip, pizza, and curry nights). Social events are carefully selected to meet local demand, including darts matches, folk music, jazz sessions, quizzes and a photography club all regularly taking place.

The Wonston Arms is also the heart of fundraising for the local area. To date, it has raised in excess of £25,000. Its monthly pop-up cafe, has raised over £7,000 for local charitable causes.

"Matt and his team have created a fantastic rural village pub with a great atmosphere by shaping it around the community and its needs. The Wonston Arms serves excellent cask ales and is a great social environment for all," said National Pub of the Year Coordinator Ben Wilkinson.

He added: "Pubs like the Wonston Arms highlight what communities stand to lose if their local closes – something being experienced in all too many places. These types of pubs are more than just businesses, they are the heart of our local communities and part of what makes the UK the country it is." See page 10 for Ben's take on challenges facing the pub industry.

FINALISTS

The three other finalists in the Pub of the Year competition are:

Cricketers Arms, St Helens, Merseyside
(see p349)

Last year's winner proves its still doing something right, making it to the final stages of the competition. This is another pub that has had its fortunes turned around. When owners Andy and Denise Evans took it on in 2013 it was boarded up, and cask beer hadn't graced the bar since the 1980s. It is now a thriving community local with an excellent selection of 13 locally-sourced cask ales.

Chequers, Little Gransden, Cambridgeshire
(see p65)

Another highly-decorated pub and CAMRA favourite. This charming village pub has been run by the same family for more than 60 years and it's a long-running Guide entry, having featured for 25 years. Its roaring fire is the perfect spot for the community to gather for events.

Volunteer Arms (Staggs), Musselburgh, Edinburgh & the Lothians
(see p651)

This award-winning Scottish pub has been in the same family for more than 160 years. Its traditional features, coupled with a modern lounge area make it the perfect place for visitors to enjoy the range of ales on the bar.

CAMRA's National Pub of the Year competition considers all the criteria that make for a good pub. The competition is judged by the Campaign's 190,000-plus members. Each branch selects its top pub. The branch winners are entered into 16 regional competitions, with the winners battling it out to reach the final stages of the competition. Look out for the 🏆 symbol against pub entries in the Guide and see 'Award-winning pubs' on pages 1051–1054 for the full list of winners.

CLUB OF THE YEAR

WINNER

The 2019 winner of CAMRA's Club of the Year award is no stranger to the top prize, having won 10 years ago, almost to the day.

The **Appleton Thorn Village Hall near Warrington** (see p71) has once again wowed the judges with its bonhomie and beer range.

Chris Massey, Steward of the club said: "It is a huge honour to not only win the Club of the Year title once – but twice! We are a true community club and take pride in hosting a range of activities and events for our locals and serving great beers as well."

The club – housed in an attractive sandstone building – features an ever-changing range of seven beers from regional and micro-breweries. The hub of its community, it houses a comfortable bar area, small pool room, enclosed garden area and bowling green. Home cooked food is served at Sunday lunchtime and the function room hosts quizzes, live music and an annual beer festival in October. The recent addition of a gin bar has also proved popular with the club's members.

Club of the Year organiser, Keith Spencer, said: "This club is the very hub of the community, from hosting pre-school events to yoga, dance, Guides and rehearsals for the Vale Royal String Orchestra! It is a very deserving winner of this year's Club of the Year competition and a shining example of the intrinsic role that clubs can play in their local areas."

The Club of the Year competition is run in conjunction with *Club Mirror* magazine, with the simple aim of finding the clubs with the greatest commitment to quality real ale – those which offer a fantastic atmosphere, welcoming surroundings and most importantly, top quality real ale served in great condition.

FINALISTS

The three other finalists in the Club of the Year competition are:

Real Ale Farm (RAF), Gilfach Fargoed, Glamorgan

Housed in the former Gilfach Fargoed Fawr Farm – built in the 17th century and the oldest surviving building in Fargoed – the Real Ale Farm offers the best range and quality of beer for miles. Beers from breweries both local and further afield, are selected for flavour and interest. Numerous charity events and the occasional beer festival are hosted. Visitors are welcome but must be signed in. The short walk from Gilfach Fargoed station presents a modest but energetic climb.

Canine Club, Accrington, Lancashire
(see p239)

Located on a bustling street in an area known for its many independent retailers, this large street corner club offers visitors a comfortable place to pause in its lounge area. A traditional games room can be found at the rear, where snooker, pool and darts are played, and an upstairs function room hosts live entertainment most weekends. The beer range is ever-changing and usually includes some from the East Lancashire area.

Egham United Services Club, Egham, Surrey
(see p449)

Award-winning Guide stalwart, the Egham United Services Club offers a changing range of beers always including at least one dark beer, and cider is also available. The club also hosts several annual beer festivals, championing many new, small breweries. Show a copy of this Guide for entry.

The picturesque Appleton Thorn Village Hall, near Warrington has again been ranked as best club in the country

The Club of the Year competition is run by CAMRA in conjunction with the magazine *Club Mirror* to find the best real ale clubs in the country. One of the criteria for entry into the competition is that the clubs must admit any CAMRA member, of any gender. Many will also admit non-CAMRA members, if they are carrying a copy of this Guide. A number of the best real ale clubs feature in the *Good Beer Guide* alongside recommended pubs. See individual listings for information.

PUB DESIGN AWARDS

In 2019, there were five winners in CAMRA's prestigious Pub Design Awards, which recognises the most stunning feats of architecture, design and conservation in pubs across the UK.

THE WINNERS

The **Pilot Boat in Lyme Regis**, Dorset, won the coveted Refurbishment award after owners Palmers Brewery decided the dated pub needed refreshing. The brewery made the pub into a fresh, modern space, while retaining old charms. A new restaurant and open kitchen were created, tastefully connected to the pub area by utilising reclaimed ship timber and a new bi-folding glass wall to create an 'inside-outside' feel.

The majestic Royal Victoria Pavilion with its beautiful views out to sea

A striking example of seaside architecture, the Grade II-listed **Royal Victoria Pavilon, Ramsgate**, Kent had been one of the most at-risk Victorian/Edwardian buildings in Kent. Built in 1903 as a concert hall and assembly rooms, and later a casino, it fell into disrepair after closing in 2008. The interior and exterior have been smartened up by owner Wetherspoon, leading to the Conversion to Pub Use award. Joint winner of the same award was the **Slaughterhouse, St Peter Port**, Guernsey. Originally built in 1887, the Slaughterhouse is a protected building occupying a prominent position on the seafront. It served Guernsey for over 125 years as a slaughterhouse until 2013 when it was bought by RW Randall Ltd. It reopened in 2017.

The **Coopers Tavern, Burton upon Trent**, Staffordshire (see p425) won the Historic England Award for Conservation. It operated as a brewer's house and a malt store, and was the shopfront for Bass Imperial Stout in the 1800s. Later, it became the Bass Brewery tap. When Joule's Brewery took on ownership, it carried out careful refurbishment of the run down pub. The simply furnished interior has been conserved with appropriate materials, and has new public areas.

A substantial late Victorian pub, the **Cardigan Arms, Leeds**, West Yorkshire (see p569) was designed by Leeds architect Thomas Winn and boasts an impressive multi-room interior. However, it has struggled in recent years due to lack of investment and a changing demographic in the area. It was saved from closure by Steve Holt of Kirkstall Brewery, and the brewery's work has been rewarded with the Joe Goodwin Award for best street corner local.

Andrew Davidson, chair of CAMRA's judging panel said: "The work has been done with great care, using historic colour schemes and matching historic finishes. The pub has truly been restored to something approaching its former glory."

CIDER PUB OF THE YEAR

WINNER

A former shop turned independent micropub was named CAMRA's National Cider Pub of Year 2018. The **Firkin Shed in Bournemouth**, Dorset (see p134), opened its doors as the first micropub in Bournemouth, in 2015.

"We're truly thrilled to receive this award. We know we have a great range of locally produced real cider, but to be recognised as the National Cider Pub of the Year is more than we ever imagined," said Paul Gray, who runs the pub with his wife, Lisa.

"We actively buy from traditional cider makers and small producers, many of whom have cultivated their own orchards and share the same ethos. We hope that has been reflected in this award and that our success has shown there is a place for real cider in all pubs," he added.

Competition organiser Sarah Newson said: "Paul Gray and his team have done brilliantly to convert a former video shop into a national award-winning and very popular micropub in such a short time."

The Firkin Shed is housed in a former Blockbuster

CAMRA's annual Pub Design Awards aim to find the most stunningly designed pubs in the UK. The awards, held in association with Historic England, recognise the highest standards of architecture in the refurbishment and conservation of existing pubs as well as in the construction of new ones. Go to **camra.org.uk/pub-design-awards** for more information. The National Cider Pub of the Year recognises the best pub or club that promotes and encourages the sale of quality real cider and perry. The winner is announced on 1st October to start Cider & Perry Month.

HOW BEER IS BREWED

The brewer's art sees raw ingredients transformed into a wide variety of styles of beer. Follow their journey from field to glass with this general look at how beer is brewed.

THE KEY INGREDIENTS OF BEER

While brewers will experiment and make use of the cornucopia of ingredients available to them, there are four key elements most beers have in common: water, yeast, malt and hops, although, increasingly brewers are playing with extra ingredients that impart unusual and exciting flavours, aromas or consistency into a beer. Lactose, and heather, for example, have historically been used as additions, but more and more brewers are now employing honey, flowers, spices, fruits, and even meat in specialty ales.

Differing preparation methods, and varietals can create a spectrum of beer – from the very pale, to the near black; from clean, simple aromas, to deep coffee notes, or a fruity punch on the nose; and gentle, sessionable flavours that comfort the palate, to those that assault and challenge your taste buds.

Some breweries will have their own specific way of doing things, and each brewery set-up is individual, but the process is broadly the same. Use the flow chart overleaf to discover how brewers take the four key ingredients below and use them to create one of the most diverse drinks on the planet.

MALT

The mix of malts used in making a beer contribute to the colour, flavour and strength of the beer. Malted barley is most common, but other grains, such as wheat, oats, or rye can be used. Once harvested, maltsters steep barley in water to absorb moisture, then spread it on heated floors or inside rotating drums where it will start to germinate.
It is then kilned to dry. The temperature determines the type of malt produced – from pale, through to black. Common flavours and aromas derived include Ovaltine, oatmeal biscuits, Ryvita, almonds/nuts, honey, butterscotch, caramel, tobacco and vanilla.

HOPS

Hops can be used either as dried whole flowers or ground and compressed into pellets. Hops – via their oils and resins – impart aroma and flavour (including bitterness) into a beer, and are added into the copper/kettle, but can also be added later in the process. 'Dry-hopping', for example, is the process of adding a small amount of hops to a cask before it leaves the brewery en route to the pub, for additional aroma. Delicate aromas that can be destroyed during the boil can be retained in this way. While New World hops have become increasingly popular for their tropical fruit explosion in the last few years, UK hops provide the basis of more traditional beers.

WATER

Water used for the brewing process is called liquor. Pure water can come from springs, bore holes or from the public supply. And while some breweries will treat their water to achieve a certain profile (adding sulphates such as gypsum and magnesium), or to remove potential off-flavour-causing compounds, others have embraced the natural, distinct quality of the local water – such as world-renowned Burton water. This water trickles through bands of gypsum and gives the resulting beer the world-famous, sought-after 'Burton snatch'.

YEAST

Every brewery will have its own yeast culture and often this will be a closely guarded asset. Yeast are living organisms that consume sugars, turning them in to alcohol and carbon dioxide. Traditionally most yeast used in UK beer production would have been 'ale yeast' which rises to the surface during fermentation and is therefore known as 'top-fermenting'. Other commonly-used yeasts are lager yeast, known as 'bottom-fermenting', and wild yeasts which create 'spontaneous fermentation', when beer in open vats is exposed to wild yeast in the air. Yeast produces natural chemical compounds called esters that give off aromas reminiscent of apples, oranges, pear drops, banana, liquorice, molasses and, in especially strong beers, fresh leather.

START

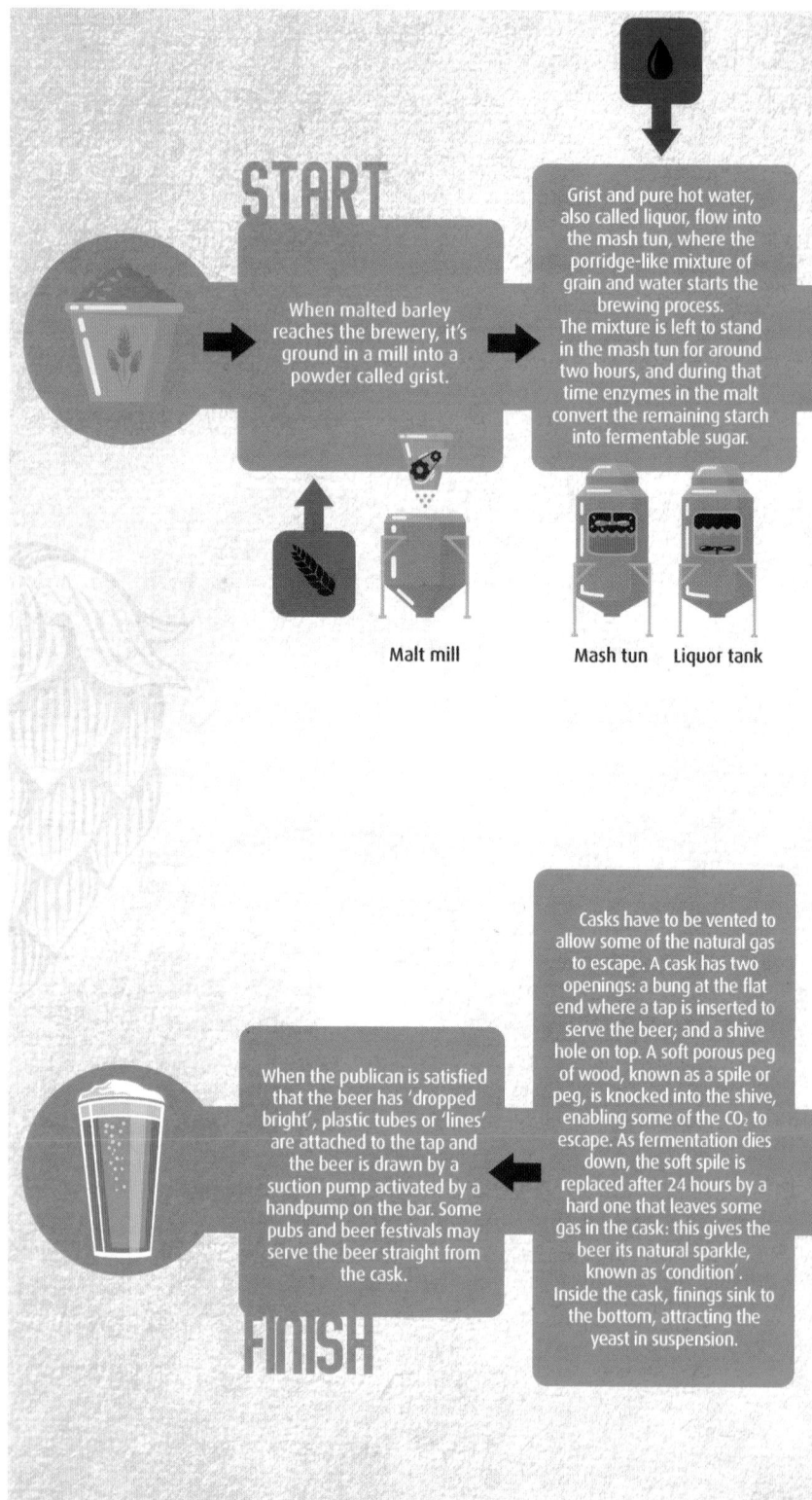

When malted barley reaches the brewery, it's ground in a mill into a powder called grist.

Grist and pure hot water, also called liquor, flow into the mash tun, where the porridge-like mixture of grain and water starts the brewing process.
The mixture is left to stand in the mash tun for around two hours, and during that time enzymes in the malt convert the remaining starch into fermentable sugar.

Malt mill

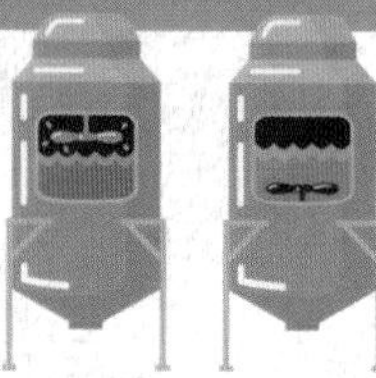

Mash tun Liquor tank

Casks have to be vented to allow some of the natural gas to escape. A cask has two openings: a bung at the flat end where a tap is inserted to serve the beer; and a shive hole on top. A soft porous peg of wood, known as a spile or peg, is knocked into the shive, enabling some of the CO_2 to escape. As fermentation dies down, the soft spile is replaced after 24 hours by a hard one that leaves some gas in the cask: this gives the beer its natural sparkle, known as 'condition'.
Inside the cask, finings sink to the bottom, attracting the yeast in suspension.

When the publican is satisfied that the beer has 'dropped bright', plastic tubes or 'lines' are attached to the tap and the beer is drawn by a suction pump activated by a handpump on the bar. Some pubs and beer festivals may serve the beer straight from the cask.

FINISH

When starch conversion is complete, the brewer and their team will run the sweet extract (called wort) to a second vessel – the copper/ kettle – where it's vigorously boiled with hops.

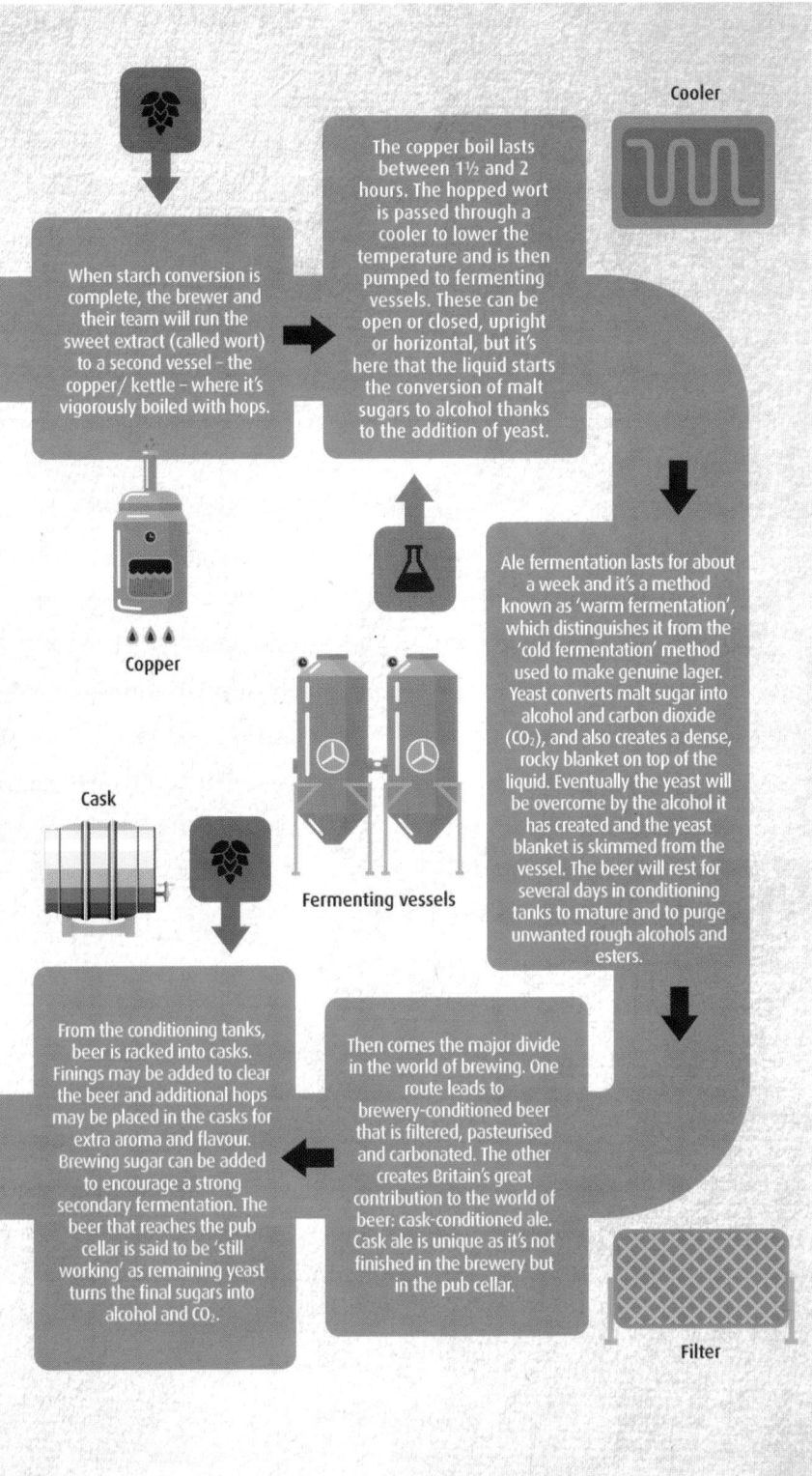

The copper boil lasts between 1½ and 2 hours. The hopped wort is passed through a cooler to lower the temperature and is then pumped to fermenting vessels. These can be open or closed, upright or horizontal, but it's here that the liquid starts the conversion of malt sugars to alcohol thanks to the addition of yeast.

Cooler

Copper

Fermenting vessels

Ale fermentation lasts for about a week and it's a method known as 'warm fermentation', which distinguishes it from the 'cold fermentation' method used to make genuine lager. Yeast converts malt sugar into alcohol and carbon dioxide (CO_2), and also creates a dense, rocky blanket on top of the liquid. Eventually the yeast will be overcome by the alcohol it has created and the yeast blanket is skimmed from the vessel. The beer will rest for several days in conditioning tanks to mature and to purge unwanted rough alcohols and esters.

Then comes the major divide in the world of brewing. One route leads to brewery-conditioned beer that is filtered, pasteurised and carbonated. The other creates Britain's great contribution to the world of beer: cask-conditioned ale. Cask ale is unique as it's not finished in the brewery but in the pub cellar.

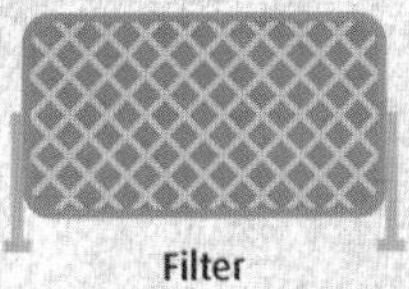

Filter

Cask

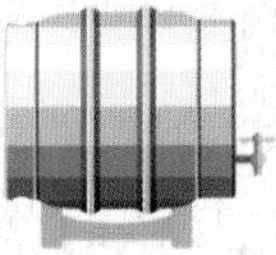

From the conditioning tanks, beer is racked into casks. Finings may be added to clear the beer and additional hops may be placed in the casks for extra aroma and flavour. Brewing sugar can be added to encourage a strong secondary fermentation. The beer that reaches the pub cellar is said to be 'still working' as remaining yeast turns the final sugars into alcohol and CO_2.

BEER APPRECIATION

Beer is not just fluid in a glass. A good beer is enjoyable, but a great beer is liquid art. With a bit of know-how, you can get the most out of one of Britain's crowning glories.

The best way to enjoy a beer is as a shared experience, in the pub, your local club, or a brewery tasting room. The breadth of choice of beers in the UK, means there's plenty to talk about. Don't know your mouthfeel from your malted barley? Read on for some tips to getting the most from your tipple.

Beer is best enjoyed as a shared experience

TEMPERATURE

To enjoy the aromas and flavours of a beer, cask ale should be served at the correct temperature. Too warm and unwanted aromas will be released. Too cold and the clean, fresh vibrancy of the beer could be lost. A very low temperature could make the beer cloudy (chill haze).

The ideal serving temperature for most cask-conditioned ale is between 11 and 13°C. Stronger ales can be served slightly warmer: the higher temperature releases fruity aromas and esters, enhancing the flavour. Likewise, a cool, crisp golden ale can be served slightly colder. Cask Marque (see p16–17) audits to a required range of 10–14°C allowing a little leeway.

Some cask ales are meant to be dispensed at lower temperatures, particularly summer beers. These have been specially brewed in order that no chill haze occurs at temperatures where other cask ales might be affected. Other draught beers (lagers and keg) are usually served between 5 and 8°C. Some draught beers are served even colder using glycol cooling systems and flash coolers. Such beers are normally poured between 0 and 5°C. Most bottle-conditioned real ales should be served at between 8 and 12°C. Other bottled beers are served colder.

GLASSWARE

The choice of glassware can have a significant effect on appreciation of beer. Brewers in Belgium go to great lengths and expense designing specific glasses to best enhance (and market) their beers, and the shape of a glass can affect head creation or allow aromas to be appreciated. Pubs in the UK are increasingly embracing stemmed glasses alongside standard nonic pint glasses, and research shows that beer served in a tankard stays at the best drinking temperature for longer because It isn't warmed by the drinker's hand.

CLOUDY OR CLEAR?

For many years, a lot of beer drinkers believed the perfect pint should be crystal clear. But times are changing, after the trend began in the States, and some perfectly good beers are being served cloudy (in the capital they are known as 'London murky'). In some beer bars, murk is the new normal and quite acceptable.

German-style weiss beers have traditionally been served cloudy, but today some of the UK's best brewers, including Kernel, Fuller's and Moor, are serving some of their beers unfined and unfiltered.

Supporters of the hazy brews say they are packed with tropical fruit and protein flavours which filtering takes out. Historically, cloudy real ale was a sign that the beer had not been conditioned properly, and that can still be true. A good rule of thumb is, if it doesn't smell right it is probably off.

So, before you send a cloudy beer back check with the bar staff. If they are on top of their game they will know if its intentional.

Pubs and bars are increasingly embracing stemmed glasses alongside more traditional drinking vessels

HOW TO TASTE BEER

SIGHT

We drink with our eyes, and our first impression is its visual appearance. How does the beer look? Is it pale, almost black, cloudy or ruby-hued? Does it have a large head of foam on top? Or is it tight, discrete and somewhat more restrained? Are there bubbles of carbon dioxide rising up the beer? The answers can be an indicator to the beer's style and also of its condition.

AROMA

Our noses can detect more than 1,000 aromas. Gently swirl the liquid in the glass to release the aroma or the 'nose' and discover the malt, hop and fruit notes that emerge. Can you discern notes of citrus fruit? If it's a rich, dark stout, do you get a hint of coffee? In a barley wine you might detect some wine, almost sherry-like, aromas. In a German-style wheat beer, you might find a flourish of bubblegum.

The malts used can give a beer a rich biscuit or Ovaltine-like character. Hops will also add their own distinctive note. Traditional English hops deliver a restrained spicy, peppery, earthy, wood and resinous note. American hops (and more recent English varieties such as Jester) are famous for punchy, pronounced citrus notes, with grapefruit to the fore. Traditional European hops are called 'noble', and varieties offer cedar wood, mint, pine kernels and lemon zest. New Zealand hops have a vinous fruit character. One popular variety, Nelson Sauvin, is so called as a result of flavours similar to Sauvignon wine.

The trend in using aroma hop varieties continues. Some of the hops with the most intense aromas are grown in the New World, just like with wine. North America, New Zealand and even Eastern Europe are producing hops with some very distinct citrus, floral and fruit-like aromas. Traditional British hops are unique due to the latitude of the UK, the climate, the soil, the hours of sunshine and the breeding history. It is this unique and sustainable terroir that gives British hops a lower level of myrcene than hops grown elsewhere in the world, producing hop aromas which are much more delicate and complex.

SENSATION

What temperature is the glass? Each beer has an optimal serving temperature – has yours been served in the ideal condition for its style? How does the beer feel on your palate (mouthfeel)? Aside from temperature, does it feel thick and syrupy, thin and watery, creamy, or smooth? And don't forget to swallow. Ideally there should be a slow, warming feeling, which should linger, but not for too long, in the back of the throat?

TASTE

Anticipate the first sip and then enjoy it. Let it caress your tongue. Our mouths have thousands of taste buds, which can detect salt, sweet, bitter, sour and umami.

Many mistakenly believe certain parts of the tongue are exclusively designed to detect a certain taste. Not so, though certain areas may be more susceptible to certain sensations than others. Some beer can play tricks: a hoppy aroma, may not always follow through in the taste. Is the beer fruity? Can you detect dark fruit flavours or even a hint of malted biscuits? Is there a satisfying level of bitterness to your beer?

INSIST ON QUALITY BEER

Real ale, when it's conditioned with care, should be bright, sparkling, with a lively head and served cool and refreshing (note – some beers, such as wheat beers, may be intentionally cloudy). As a paying consumer, don't be afraid to take your pint back to the bar if it is not in good condition. Bar staff should replace it and might not be aware of an issue unless you tell them.

Take your pint back to the bar if:

- Your beer is served either too warm or too cold. Real ale should be served cool – around 11–13°C. It's a myth that it should be served at room temperature. Warm beer tastes bad. But bear in mind that some golden ales are meant to be served cooler than other styles.
- Your beer smells of acetone, vinegar or stale bread.
- The pint has no head, is totally flat and out of condition.
- It's not only flat but hazy and has yeast particles or protein floating in the liquid.

BRITISH BEER STYLES

With the help of Christine Cryne, we explore some of the beer styles you'll find in the British Isles.

While Britain may have its stable of beer styles – such as the enduring bitter style for which it is probably best known – increasingly brewers are looking for inspiration elsewhere.

It's now more common to see British brewers dabbling with wheat beers, lambics and saisons to name a few.

That's not to say the more traditional British styles are dying out. In fact it's now easier to find beer styles that almost disappeared in the last century, such as mild and porter.

But with so much choice at the bar, how do you navigate the baffling array of beers on offer?

CHARTING BEER STYLES

Use this chart to find the right type of beer style for you.

Start with the simple flavour options given and follow from there to find the beer style most suited to your tastes.

We have broken beer flavours down in to six broad flavour options. Think about the flavours you enjoy in beer or other drinks such as cider, wine or coffee. Each of the broad elements is then broken down again, to enable you to identify the aspects of the flavour you prefer. We then suggest some beer styles to try.

Different people will pick up on different aspects of a beer, and one person's refreshing is another's bitter, but by exploring different beer styles and tasting widely you will soon become more confident in your palate, and hopefully discover some fascinating beers in the process.

See pages 30–31 for more information and description of the beer styles.

Christine Cryne loves educating people about beer. A master trainer and an accredited European Beer Consumers Union judge, she has judged at many events. Alongside training volunteers for CAMRA's tasting panels, Christine has led tutored tastings at many events, including the BBC Good Food Show, and offers a variety of training courses for both the trade and individuals. Go to **cryneinyourbeer.sitelio.me** for details.

Thank you to Christine Cryne for supplying the beer styles chart.

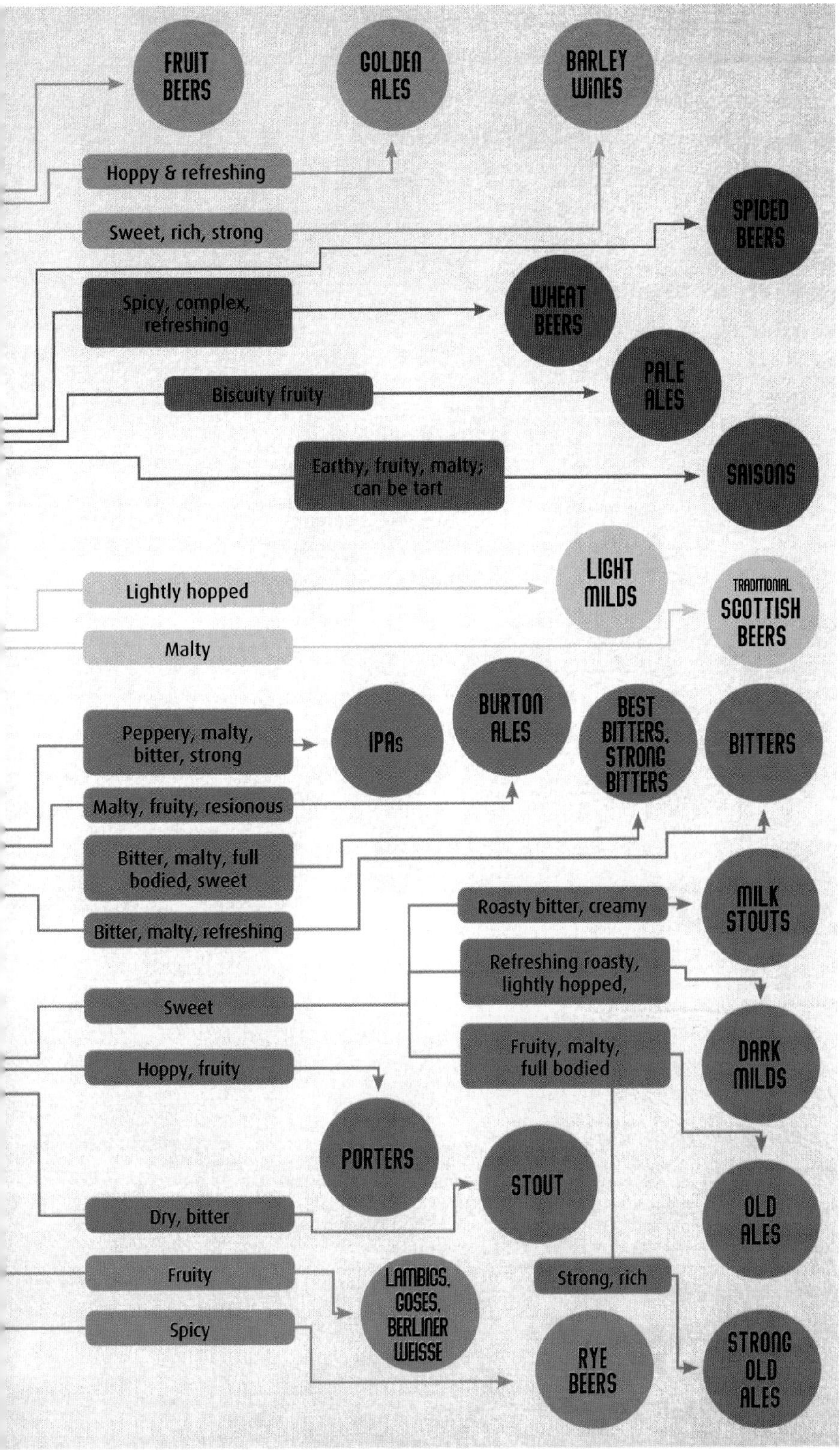
FRUIT BEERS
GOLDEN ALES
BARLEY WINES
Hoppy & refreshing
Sweet, rich, strong
SPICED BEERS
Spicy, complex, refreshing
WHEAT BEERS
Biscuity fruity
PALE ALES
Earthy, fruity, malty; can be tart
SAISONS
Lightly hopped
LIGHT MILDS
TRADITIONAL SCOTTISH BEERS
Malty
Peppery, malty, bitter, strong
IPAs
BURTON ALES
BEST BITTERS, STRONG BITTERS
BITTERS
Malty, fruity, resionous
Bitter, malty, full bodied, sweet
Bitter, malty, refreshing
Roasty bitter, creamy
MILK STOUTS
Refreshing roasty, lightly hopped,
Sweet
Fruity, malty, full bodied
DARK MILDS
Hoppy, fruity
PORTERS
STOUT
OLD ALES
Dry, bitter
Fruity
LAMBICS, GOSES, BERLINER WEISSE
Strong, rich
Spicy
RYE BEERS
STRONG OLD ALES

BARLEY WINE ●

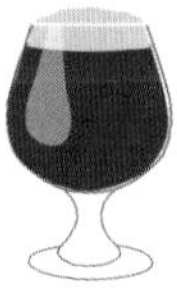

Dating back to the 18th century, barley wine was a way of thumbing one's nose at France (who we were often at war with) and its wine. This patriot's tipple usually comes in around 10–14 per cent ABV, and its usually aged for up to two years. Expect Christmas cake sweetness and fruit (including pear drops, mandarin orange and lemon peel). If darker malts are used, also anticipate chocolate and coffee. Generous hopping also gives bitterness, and peppery, grassy and floral notes.

BITTER/ BEST BITTER/ STRONG BITTER ●

As more pub estates sprung up in the 19th and 20th centuries, breweries needed beers with a quicker turn around than those that required storing for months, if not years. These 'running beers', including bitter, could be stored in the pub cellar for a few days before serving. Usually copper-coloured or deep bronze due to the use of slightly darker malts, bitters usually fall between 3.4–3.9 per cent. Look for spicy, peppery and grassy hop character, a powerful bitterness, tangy fruit and juicy/nutty malt.

Variations are 'best bitter' – a stronger version at 4 per cent upwards – and 'strong bitter' which usually starts at 5 per cent. In both, malt and fruit character tend to dominate but hop aroma and bitterness are still crucial.

BURTON ALE ●

Hailing from Burton upon Trent, the style became popular in the 18th and 19th centuries with many brewers around the country imitating the style. Falling out of popularity, in favour of pale ale and bitter, the style saw a temporary change in fortune in the 1970s with the introduction of the popular Ind Coope Draught Burton Ale, before new owner Carlsberg stopped production in 2015.

Burton Bridge Brewery has recreated the style, and it can be found in other versions including Young's Winter Warmer.

Look for a amber colour, a rich malt and fruit character underscored by a solid resinous and cedar wood hop note.

FRUIT/SPECIALITY BEERS ● ● ●

Just as the British desire for exciting flavour combinations in food has increased in recent years, so has the excitement for flavoured beers. Many British brewers have tried their hand at a Belgian-style fruit beer, or looked in the kitchen cupboard for inspiration, including honey, spices, chilli, even meat. Some brewers will use bourbon, whisky and Cognac casks to mature beer and impart flavours. Other grains, such as rye are also used in speciality beers. Fruit and honey beers aren't always sweet. While some can be jam-like, others are dry and quenching.

GOLDEN ALE ●

With the introduction of the style in the 1980s, its popularity quickly rose, as cask brewers saw golden ale as the answer to draw younger drinkers to cask and away from mass-produced keg lagers.

The style is different to pale ale: golden ale is paler, with hops allowed to give full expression, balancing sappy malt with luscious fruit, floral, herbal, spicy and resinous notes. While brewers of pale ale tend to use such traditional English hop varieties, imported hops give radically different notes to golden ale. They are often served colder than draught bitter.

IPA ●

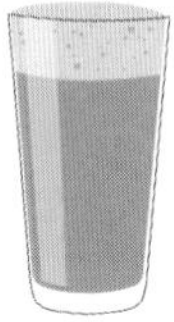

India Pale Ale (IPA) changed the face of brewing in the 19th century, when new technologies of the Industrial Revolution enabled brewers to use pale malts to produce paler beers. The first 'India Ales' were brewed in London and were ideally suited – due to the high alcohol and hopping – to a long sea journey to India. The style found a home in Burton upon Trent were its mineral-rich spring waters brought out the fullest flavours. It fell out of favour in place of German lager beer, but made a big comeback around the world in the past decade.

Look for a big peppery hop aroma and palate balanced by juicy malt and tart citrus fruit.

MILD ● ●

Mild ale was drunk primarily by industrial and agricultural workers in the 18th and 19th centuries, who needed to refresh themselves after long hours of arduous labour. Early milds were much stronger than modern versions, which tend to fall around 3–3.5 per cent. Usually dark brown in colour, due to the well-roasted malts, there are a few paler versions such as Banks's Mild and Timothy Taylor's Golden Best. Look for a rich malty aroma and flavour, with hints of dark fruit, chocolate, coffee and caramel, with a gentle underpinning of hop bitterness.

OLD ALE ●

Another style that grew in prominence in the 18th century, old ale was a beer stored for months, if not years and owed its taste to the barrels it was stored in. Lactic sourness from wild yeast and tannins in the wood meant drinkers gave the beer the moniker 'stale'. The style has returned to popularity in recent years.

Contrary to expectations, old ales do not have to be strong (they can be no more than 4 per cent), or dark. Pale old ale can be bursting with lush malt, tart fruit and spicy hops. Darker versions will have a more profound malt character, with powerful hints of roasted grain, dark fruit, polished leather and fresh tobacco. The hallmark of the style is a lengthy period of maturation, often in bottle rather than cask.

PALE ALE

Burton brewers were keen to produce versions of IPA with lower alcohol and hop rates that didn't require months to mature. The clamour for pale ale was so great that brewers from elsewhere opened second breweries in Burton to make use of the mineral-rich water to make their own versions of the style. From the early 20th century, bitter began to overtake pale ale in popularity and as a result it became mainly a bottled product. It is seeing a resurgence in popularity in recent years. A true pale ale should be different to bitter, similar in colour and style to IPA and brewed without the addition of coloured malts. It should have a spicy/resinous aroma and palate with biscuit malt and tart fruit from the hops.

PORTER & STOUT

Porter originated in London in the early 18th century, heralding in the commercial brewing industry. During World War One the government restricted the use of malt, particularly dark, and Irish brewers came to dominate the market. In recent years, porter and stout have returned to popularity.

For stouts look for a jet-black colour and expect a dark and roasted grain character with burnt fruit, espresso or cappuccino coffee, liquorice and molasses. The beer should have a deep bitterness to balance the richness of malt and fruit. Milk Stout, made by a few brewers, uses lactose or 'milk sugar' to give a creamy character to the beer. A few examples also have fruit (such as cherries) or chocolate added. Porters tend to be dark brown in colour, and are sweeter than stouts, often with fruity, and chocolate notes.

SAISON

Saison is a Belgian beer style now finding favour in Britain and other countries. Originating in Wallonia, it was a seasonal beer brewed by farmers to refresh labourers during the harvest. Saison should have a rich malty/fruity palate balanced by earthy, spicy and peppery hops. Some are made with the addition of 'botanicals' such as ginger, black pepper and aniseed. British interpretations include those from Adnams, Brew By Numbers, Partizan and Poppyland.

SCOTTISH BEERS

Historically, Scottish beers tend to be darker and maltier than beers south of the border, the reflection of a colder climate where beer needs to be nourishing. It's an urban myth, though, that Scottish beers are less heavily hopped than English ones. Traditional styles are light, heavy and export (not dissimilar to mild, bitter and IPA). They are also known as 60, 70 and 80 shilling ales from a 19th century system of invoicing beers according to strength. A 'Wee Heavy'/90 shilling ale is the (rare) Scottish equivalent of barley wine.

SOUR BEER/ LAMBIC

Also known simply as 'sours', this is a style brewed in both the UK and US by brewers fascinated by Belgian lambics (spontaneously fermented beers). Instead of cultivated brewer's yeast, lambic is left open to the atmosphere to allow wild yeasts into the beer. Following the first fermentation, true lambics are stored in wooden casks for a year or more.

Variations include: 'Faro' – lambics with the addition of sugar in the cask; 'Krieks' – cherry-steeped lambics; 'framboise' – raspberry lambic; and 'gueuze' – a blend of two or more 100 per cent lambics.

Look for rich, complex beer with lemony notes, old paper, aged red wine, and phenolic whisky hints. Examples of British sours come from Elgoods, Wild Beer, Kernel and Burning Sky.

WHEAT BEER/ BERLINER WEISSE

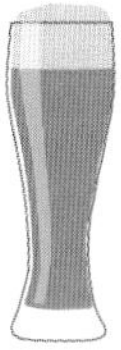

Wheat beer is a style most commonly associated with Bavaria and Belgium and its popularity in Britain has encouraged many brewers to add wheat beers to their portfolios. The title is something of a misnomer as all 'wheat beers' are a blend of malted barley as well as wheat, as the latter grain is difficult to brew with and needs the addition of barley, which acts a natural filter during the mashing stage. Wheat, if used with appropriate yeast, gives distinctive aromas and flavours, such as clove, banana and bubblegum, making it a complex, refreshing beer. Belgian versions often contain herbs and spices, such as milled coriander seeds and orange peel – a habit dating back to medieval times.

LEARNING & DISCOVERY

CAMRA's learning and discovery programme aims to support all those with an interest in beer, cider and perry of any type to learn more about them via our books, publications, festivals and online at the CAMRA website. An important step towards learning more about your favourite drinks is developing your tasting skills. Learn with CAMRA at our festivals across the country by attending tutored tastings or exploring our learning and discovery spaces where you can meet brewers, cider and perry makers and learn more about the ingredients and techniques that go into each drink. Individual beer and cider styles exhibits signature characteristics that once learnt can be drawn upon to identify and describe drinks in the future. If you come across a novel or unfamiliar brew you'll have the sensory and verbal repertoire to articulate how it tastes and smells and precisely why you do or don't like it.

CAMRA'S BEERS OF THE YEAR

The beers below were short-listed for the 2019 Champion Beer of Britain competition, held at the Great British Beer Festival in August, and the Champion Winter Beer of Britain competition, held in the February. Each beer was found to be consistently outstanding in its category by a panel of trained CAMRA judges. In the finals, the best from each category are judged together to decide the overall national winner. All receive a ■ against their entry in the Breweries section. Go to **camra.org.uk/beer/awards** for the full results.

GOLDEN ALES

Bakers Dozen, Magic Potion
Bays, Gold
Big Lamp, Prince Bishop Ale
Black Isle, Yellowhammer
Blue Monkey, Infinity
Byatt's, Regal Blonde
Crouch Vale, Brewers Gold
Five Points, Pale
Fyne Ales, Jarl
Grey Trees, Diggers Gold
Kent, Prohibition
Monty's, Sunshine
Moor, Nor'Hop
Oakham, Citra
Pictish, Talisman IPA
RedWillow, Headless
Salopian, Oracle
Vocation, Heart & Soul

BITTERS

Acorn, Barnsley Bitter
Batemans, XB
Bays, Topsail
Bishop Nick, Ridley's Rite
Brimstage, Trapper's Hat Bitter
Butcombe, Original
Cromarty, Atlantic Drift
Dancing Duck, Ay up
Holden's, Black Country Bitter
Irving, Frigate
Loch Lomond, Southern Summit
Purple Moose, Cwrw Madog/Madog's Ale
Rhymney, Hobby Horse
Timothy Taylor, Boltmaker
Ulverston, Laughing Gravy
West Berkshire, Good Old Boy
Wolf, Edith Cavell
Wye Valley, HPA

MILDS

Belhaven, 60/- Ale
Church End, Gravediggers Ale
Coniston, Oliver's Light Ale
Fernandes, Malt Shovel Mild
Grainstore, Rutland Panter
Penzance, Mild
Rhymney, Dark
Shortts, Two Tone
West Berkshire, Maggs' Magnificent Mild

BEST BITTERS

Abbeydale, Deception
Bath, Gem
Bishop Nick, 1555
Blue Monkey, Funky Gibbon
Castle Rock, Preservation Fine Ale
Conwy, Rampart
Bristol Beer Factory, Independence
Fuller's, London Pride
Green Jack, Trawlerboys Best Bitter
Marble, Manchester Bitter
Salopian, Darwins Origin
Surrey Hills, Shere Drop
Swannay, Scapa Special
Three Tuns, XXX
Timothy Taylor, Landlord
Tiny Rebel, Cwtch
Tryst, Carronade Pale Ale
Weetwood, Eastgate

PORTERS

Calverley's, Porter
Conwy, Telford Porter
Dancing Duck, Indian Porter
Driftwood Spars, Bolster's Blood
Enville, Old Porter
Harviestoun, Old Engine Oil
Hawkshead, Brodie's Prime
Kirkstall, Black Band Porter
Red Cat, Mr M's Porter

STRONG BITTERS

Batemans, XXXB
Church End, Fallen Angel
Grey Trees, Afghan Pale
Irving, Iron Duke
Little Valley, Python IPA
Otter, Head
S&P, NASHA IPA
South Lakes, Rakau
Swannay, Orkney IPA

STRONG MILDS & OLD ALES

Bampton, Mild
Beckstones, Hematite
Beowulf, Dark Raven
Harvey's, Old Ale
Theakston, Old Peculier
Tintagel, Excalibur
Untapped, Ember
Wibblers, Winter Wibble
Windswept, Wolf

STOUTS

Acorn, Gorlovka Imperial Stout
Boss, Black
Cairngorm, Black Gold
Coniston, Special Oatmeal Stout
Dancing Duck, Dark Drake
Dark Star, Imperial
Fixed Wheel, Blackheath Stout
Mersea Island, Oyster Stout
Plain Ales, Inncognito

BARLEY WINES & STRONG OLD ALES

Broughton, Old Jock
Heart of Wales, High as a Kite
Kinver, Over the Edge
Lacons, Audit
Moor, Old Freddy Walker
Parish, Baz's Bonce Blower
Robinsons, Old Tom
Tring, Death or Glory
Vocation, Life & Death

SPECIALITY BEERS

Bank Top, Port O Call
Binghams, Vanilla Stout
Blue Monkey, Chocolate Guerilla
Brass Castle, Bad Kitty
Colchester, Brazilian Coffee & Vanilla Porter
Hanlons, Port Stout
Titanic, Chocolate & Vanilla Stout
Untapped, Crystal
Windswept, Weizen

CHAMPION WINTER BEER OF BRITAIN 2019
LACONS, AUDIT

CHAMPION BEER OF BRITAIN 2019
SURREY HILLS, SHERE DROP

The Pubs

Wonston Arms, Wonston, Hampshire (p200)

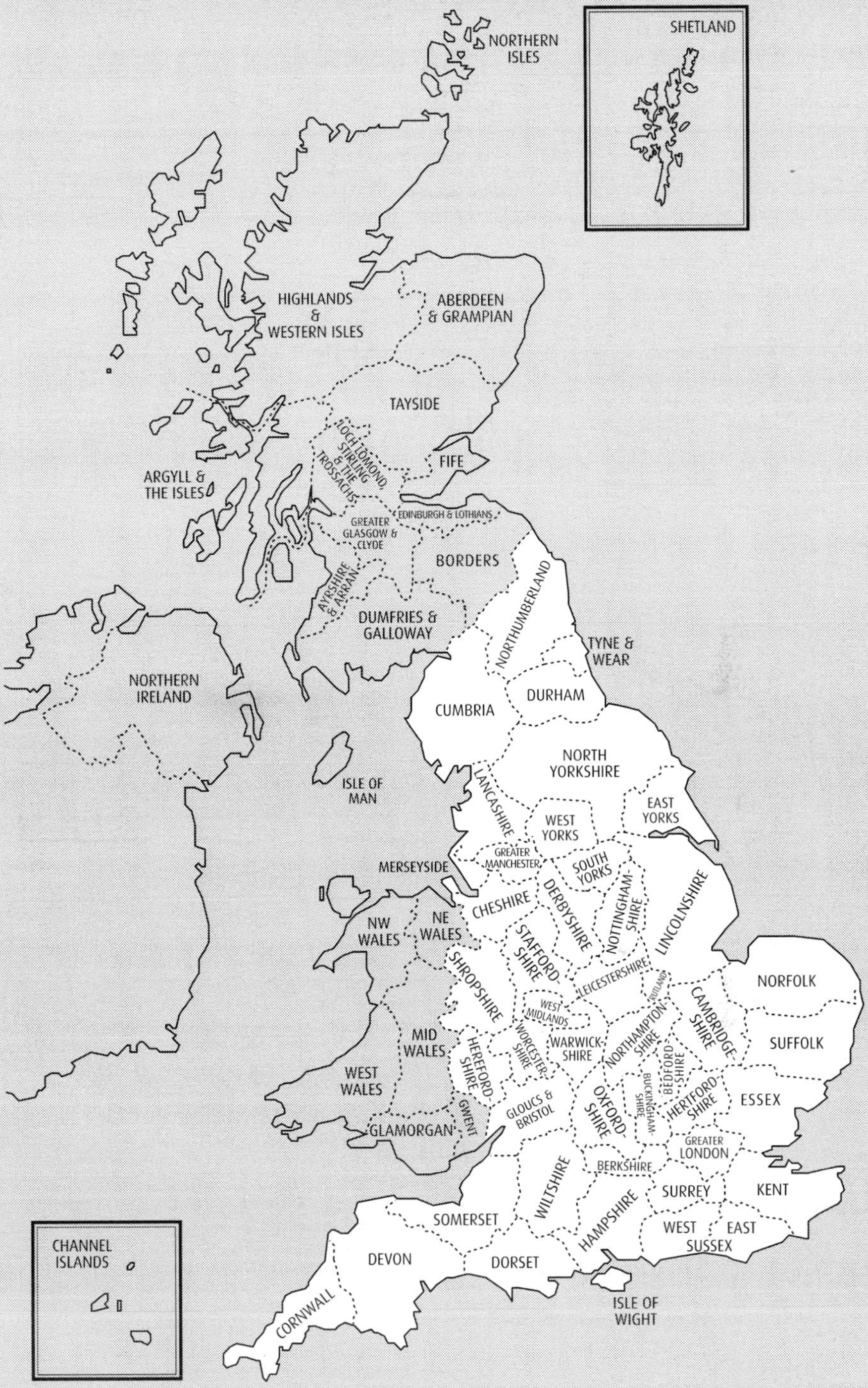

SHETLAND
NORTHERN ISLES
HIGHLANDS & WESTERN ISLES
ABERDEEN & GRAMPIAN
TAYSIDE
LOCH LOMOND, STIRLING & THE TROSSACHS
FIFE
ARGYLL & THE ISLES
EDINBURGH & LOTHIANS
GREATER GLASGOW & CLYDE
BORDERS
AYRSHIRE & ARRAN
DUMFRIES & GALLOWAY
NORTHUMBERLAND
TYNE & WEAR
NORTHERN IRELAND
CUMBRIA
DURHAM
NORTH YORKSHIRE
ISLE OF MAN
LANCASHIRE
WEST YORKS
EAST YORKS
GREATER MANCHESTER
SOUTH YORKS
MERSEYSIDE
CHESHIRE
DERBYSHIRE
NOTTINGHAMSHIRE
LINCOLNSHIRE
NW WALES
NE WALES
STAFFORDSHIRE
SHROPSHIRE
LEICESTERSHIRE
RUTLAND
NORFOLK
WEST MIDLANDS
CAMBRIDGESHIRE
NORTHAMPTONSHIRE
MID WALES
HEREFORDSHIRE
WORCESTERSHIRE
WARWICKSHIRE
SUFFOLK
BEDFORDSHIRE
BUCKINGHAMSHIRE
WEST WALES
OXFORDSHIRE
HERTFORDSHIRE
ESSEX
GLOUCS & BRISTOL
GWENT
GLAMORGAN
GREATER LONDON
BERKSHIRE
WILTSHIRE
SURREY
KENT
CHANNEL ISLANDS
SOMERSET
HAMPSHIRE
WEST SUSSEX
EAST SUSSEX
DEVON
DORSET
CORNWALL
ISLE OF WIGHT

England

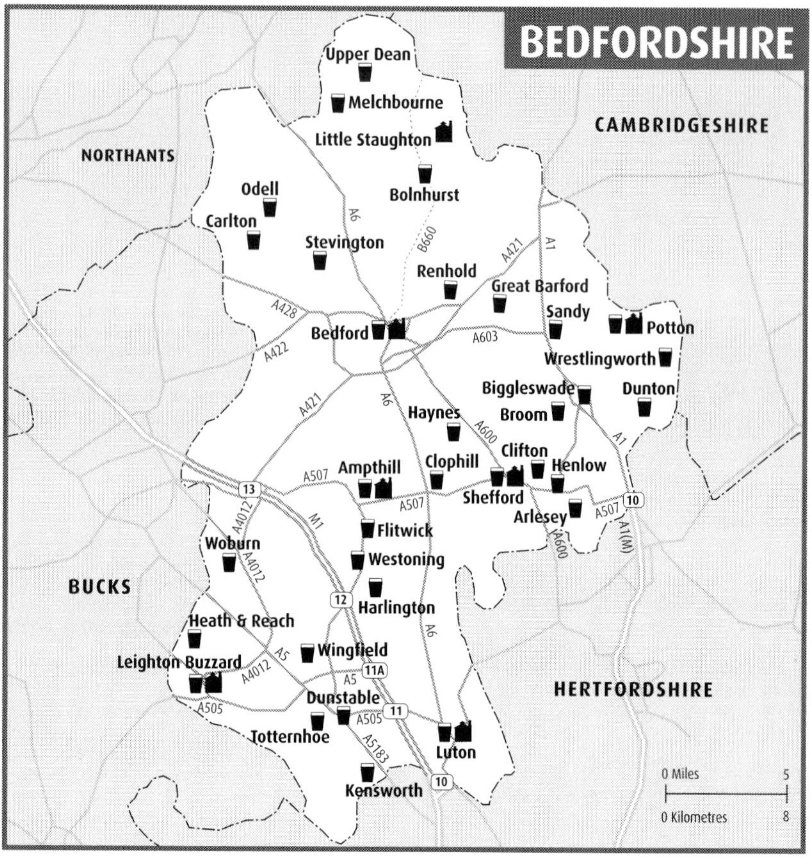

Ampthill

Albion

36 Dunstable Street, MK45 2JT
11.30-11 (midnight Fri & Sat); 12-10.30 Sun
(01525) 634857
B&T Shefford Bitter, Golden Fox, Dragon Slayer; Everards Tiger; 8 changing beers Ⓗ
An award-winning, proper, narrow-fronted Victorian pub with one large bar and 12 handpumps offering a range of the local B&T beers as well as Everards Tiger and eight constantly changing ales mainly from microbreweries. Two real regular ciders and a guest are also served. Beer and cider festivals are held at least annually. There is a meeting room and a secluded patio garden towards the rear. English music nights feature once a month on a Wednesday. Twice CAMRA Bedfordshire Pub of the Year.

Arlesey

Vicars Inn

68 Church Lane, SG15 6UX
5-midnight; 12-4, 7-midnight Sat; 12-4, 7-11 Sun
(01462) 731215
Eagle IPA; 1 changing beer (sourced nationally) Ⓗ
Situated in Church End and handy for the railway station, the pub can be traced back to the 1860s, when it was known as the Steam Engine. It has two distinct bars – a large lounge and a smaller public bar where cribbage and dominoes players can regularly be found. Complimentary cheese and biscuits are often provided on both bars. Historical local pictures feature, together with other memorabilia in the public bar. Outside is a practical patio area. **Q P** (9A,96)

Bedford

Brewhouse & Kitchen Bedford

115 High Street, MK40 1NU
11-11 (midnight Fri & Sat); 12-10.30 Sun
(01234) 342931
Brewhouse & Kitchen Banker's Draught, Intrepid, Braxator, Invarsity Ⓗ
A former bank then Wetherspoon pub relaunched by Brewhouse & Kitchen in 2016. The microbrewery is located within the main bar area, alongside different seating areas separated by half-height dividers that are features in themselves. Orders can be placed at the table or at the bar, the menu containing an extensive range of drinks as well as food. Seasonal and special ales are available but only in KeyKeg.

Castle

17 Newnham Street, MK40 3JR
12-11 (midnight Thu); 11.30-midnight Fri; 11-midnight Sat
(01234) 353295 castlebedford.co.uk
Courage Directors; Eagle IPA; Young's Bitter, Special; 2 changing beers (sourced nationally) Ⓗ
Lively town pub with a pleasant walled patio garden, five minutes from the town centre and

convenient for the Bedford Blues rugby ground. Lunches are served daily and evening meals weekdays only. Current guest beers with tasting notes are listed on the website and social media. A guesthouse behind the pub provides five en-suite bedrooms. Open mic features on a Monday evening. A former local CAMRA Pub of the Year.

Devonshire Arms

32 Dudley Street, MK40 3TB (1 mile E of town centre S of A4280)

5 (4 Fri)-11; 12-11 Sat; 12-10.30 Sun ☎ (01234) 301170

devonshirearmsbedford.co.uk

Courage Directors; Eagle IPA; 4 changing beers (sourced regionally) H

Pleasant Victorian pub in a residential area. Guest and seasonal ales are mainly from Marston's, the ciders are from Westons. Beer and cider festivals are held twice a year. The front bar has bare floorboards and an open fire, while there is a separate rear bar. The garden has a gazebo for smokers and a no-smoking paved area. A range of wines is sold by the glass or bottle. Local CAMRA Cider Pub of the Year 2018 and Town Pub of the Year 2019. Q (4)

Pilgrim's Progress

42 Midland Road, MK40 1QB

10am-midnight (1am Fri & Sat) ☎ (01234) 363751

Greene King Abbot; Ruddles Best Bitter; 8 changing beers (sourced nationally) H

Remodelled as a Wetherspoon hotel in 2016, the pub now has five internal areas and two outdoor seating areas, one of them no-smoking. The bar is popular with all ages but doesn't usually get overcrowded, even on weekend evenings. There are views into the kitchen, and the varied food menu specifies allergens and low-calorie options. Wetherspoon Club offers are available. The location is convenient for public transport and offers a good view of the town centre. Q

Wellington Arms

40-42 Wellington Street, MK40 2JX (N of town centre)

12-11; 12-10.30 Sun ☎ (01234) 308033

Adnams Southwold Bitter; B&T Shefford Bitter; Draught Bass; 9 changing beers (sourced nationally; often B&T) H

A traditional street-corner pub and a key part of the Bedford real ale scene for 20 years. There is always an interesting selection of 12 ales and two real ciders on handpump. Draught continental beers and a range of bottled Belgian beers are also available. There is a courtyard for drinkers and smokers. A friendly pub with a mixed clientele, it can get busy on Friday and Saturday evenings. Winner of a local CAMRA special real ale award in 2017.

White Horse

84 Newnham Avenue, MK41 9PX

12 (4 Mon)-11.30; 12-midnight Fri & Sat; 12.30-11 Sun ☎ (01234) 409306 thewhitehorsebedford.co.uk

Courage Directors; Eagle IPA; 3 changing beers (sourced regionally) H

Three seating areas, each with its own style, are served from a single bar. The smartphone quiz on Sunday and regular Tuesday quiz are popular, as is the Monday evening jazz. Other musical events are advertised on Facebook. Food is freshly cooked to order, with a choice of roasts on Sunday (book ahead on Sunday and Tuesday evening). The beer and wine selection is complemented by a wide choice of gins. Afternoon tea can be ordered for groups. P (4)

Biggleswade

Golden Pheasant

71 High Street, SG18 0JH

12-11.30; 11-1am Fri & Sat ☎ (01767) 313653

goldenpheasantpub.co.uk

Eagle IPA; 5 changing beers (sourced nationally) H

Town-centre pub renowned for its six well-kept ales and four real ciders. It has recently undergone a sympathetic makeover and has a single room with corner bar, furnished with tables and seating that can be moved around to accommodate local organisations and the darts team. The pub has a strong community focus and holds regular live music charity fundraising events on the spacious patio area when the weather permits.

Q

Bolnhurst

Plough

Kimbolton Road, MK44 2EX (on W side of B660 S of turning to Thurleigh) TL088587

closed Mon; 12-3, 6.30-11; 12-3 Sun ☎ (01234) 376274

bolnhurst.com

Adnams Southwold Bitter; 2 changing beers (sourced regionally) H

Award-winning pub restaurant dating in part from the Tudor period, serving excellent food and beer. The main bar has a wood-burning stove and a second room is used for dining and functions. There is a large garden with decking beside a small pond. The pub has no prominent signage, just a modest hanging sign on a post by the road entrance. Closed from Christmas until the second week of January each year. Wheelchair users should contact the pub in advance. Q P

Broom

Cock ★

23 High Street, SG18 9NA

12-11; 12-8 Sun ☎ (01767) 314411

thecockatbroom.co.uk

Greene King Abbot; 3 changing beers (sourced nationally; often Caledonian, Tring, Wychwood) G

The entrance from the street opens onto a corridor the length of the pub – off that is a room for skittles and darts and two other rooms with tables, chairs, benches and fireplaces. Four beers are served by gravity from the cellar along with three or four ciders typically from Apple Cottage. Food is freshly prepared and mostly local. Outside is a large seating area and a field for camping where the annual Broomstock charity music festival takes place. Q P (200)

REAL ALE BREWERIES

B&T Shefford
Brewhouse & Kitchen Bedford
Crown Little Staughton
Eagle Bedford
Kelchner Ampthill
Leighton Buzzard Leighton Buzzard
Potton Potton (NEW)
Rockhopper Luton

Carlton

Fox

High Street, MK43 7LA (off Turvey Rd S of village centre)
12-11 (10 Mon & Tue); 12-9.30 Sun (01234) 720235
thefoxatcarlton.pub
Eagle IPA; Fuller's London Pride; 2 changing beers (sourced regionally) H
A charming thatched community pub with a warm welcome and an attractive garden popular with families. Guest beers are often from local microbreweries. Good-value, home-cooked lunches are served daily except Monday and evening meals Tuesday to Saturday. There is a regular quiz on Thursday evening. Spring and summer bank holiday festivals are held using an outbuilding as an additional bar, plus a one-day gin festival in June. Local CAMRA Country Pub of the Year 2017. Q P (25)

Clifton

Admiral

1 Broad Street, SG17 5RJ
3-11; 11-1am Fri & Sat; 11-11 Sun (01462) 811069
5 changing beers (sourced nationally; often Brains, Harvey's, Robinsons) H
A small pub with friendly staff, serving five ales often including Brains Rev James, St Austell Trelawny, Harvey's Sussex Best and Robinsons Double Hop, plus one real cider on handpump. The interior of this Original Beer House complements its nautical name, featuring maritime pictures and model ships. Darts and board games are available, plus monthly live music, quizzes and an annual beer festival. Food is served daily including Friday fish and chips, weekend breakfasts, Sunday roasts, Monday steak night plus stone-baked pizzas on summer weekends. (9A,9B)

Clophill

Stone Jug

10 Back Street, MK45 4BY (500yds off A6 at N end of village) TL083381
12-3.30 (not Mon), 6-11; 12-midnight Fri & Sat; 12-10.30 Sun (01525) 860526 stonejug.co.uk
Otter Amber; St Austell Trelawny; 3 changing beers (sourced nationally) H
Originally three 16th-century cottages, this popular village local has an L-shaped bar serving two drinking areas and a family/function room. Excellent home-made lunches are available Tuesday to Saturday. The guest beers are often from local microbreweries, the cider is Westons Old Rosie. Picnic benches at the front and a rear patio garden offer outdoor drinking space in fine weather. Parking can be difficult at busy times. A good pit stop for the Greensand Ridge Walk and a former CAMRA Pub of the Year.
Q P (44,81)

Dunstable

Gary Cooper

Grove Park, Court Drive, LU5 4GP
8am-midnight (1am Fri & Sat) (01582) 471452
Greene King Abbot; Ruddles Best Bitter; Sharp's Doom Bar; 7 changing beers H
A large, airy, modern Wetherspoon bar serving a selection of up to seven guest ales, often local. The usual range of JDW craft beer is also well stocked. Situated in Grove Park leisure area, the patio overlooks the Grove House gardens, with many bus routes stopping outside. It gets busy on Friday and Saturday nights. The pub is named after the famous Hollywood star, Gary Cooper, who attended the local grammar school 1910-13.

Globe

43 Winfield Street, LU6 1LS
12-11 (midnight Fri & Sat); 12-10.30 Sun
(01582) 512300
B&T Shefford Bitter, Edwin Taylor's Extra Stout; Everards Tiger; 7 changing beers H
Popular beer destination and community local where 13 handpumps boast a good range of regular B&T beers, five ever-changing microbrewery beers, a real cider and a perry. More than 20 Belgian beers are also available. Bare boards, bar stools, breweriana and a famous plank at the end of the bar create a traditional town pub atmosphere buzzing with conversation. Acoustic music night is Tuesday. Regular beer festivals are held. A former CAMRA Bedfordshire and South Bedfordshire Pub of the Year. Q (70)

Pheasant Inn

208 West Street, LU6 1NX
11-11 (11.30 Fri & Sat); 12-11 Sun (01582) 662706
the-pheasant-inn-dunstable.co.uk
Mad Squirrel Hopfest; Sharp's Doom Bar; 4 changing beers (sourced nationally) H
A just-out-of-town-centre pub and hotel/B&B (with en-suite, basic and family rooms) on a bus route. It has a large main bar and function room selling six real ales, and screens all major sports. Traditional pub games are played. Real ales are available to take away, often from local breweries. Outside is a covered and heated smoking area at the front, a garden to the rear, large umbrellas and a car park. P

Victoria

69 West Street, LU6 1ST
11-11.30 (midnight Fri & Sat); 12-midnight Sun
(01582) 662682
House beer (by Tring); 3 changing beers H
The Victoria is a popular town-centre pub on West Street. It usually offers three varying ales from microbreweries plus a house beer from the local Tring brewery. Darts, dominoes and crib are popular as well as televised sports in the bar. There is a separate function room next to the rear courtyard.

Dunton

March Hare

34 High Street, SG18 8RN
6-11 (midnight Thu); 3-midnight Fri & Sat; 12-10.30 Sun
(01767) 600258 themarchharedunton.co.uk
6 changing beers (sourced nationally; often Digfield, Nobby's) H
The pub is renowned for an eclectic range of well-kept beers of varying strengths and styles. Cribbage and quiz nights, occasional live music, wassailing and two beer festivals provide plenty of diversion, as does the welcoming fire in winter and the garden area next to the churchyard in summer. Jigsaw puzzles depicting historic pub scenes decorate the walls in the open-plan interior. Opens at noon on summer Saturdays. CAMRA branch Rural Pub of the Year 2019. Q (188)

Flitwick

Crown
Station Road, MK45 1LA
☼ 11.30-3, 5.30-11; 11.30-midnight Fri & Sat; 12-11 Sun
☎ (01525) 713737 ⊕ crownflitwick.co.uk
Sharp's Doom Bar; 3 changing beers (sourced nationally) ℍ
This large and tidy thriving estate pub was successfully rescued by the current tenants who are keen on their real ales, with interesting guest beers common. Varying craft keg beers are also sold. There is a games room with TV, jukebox and pool. Saturday music nights are popular. It has a large garden with patio and children's play area. Traditional pub food is served lunchtimes and evenings (lunches only on Sunday).
☼☺◑ⅉ≒♣Pⅎ(42,C2)🐾🛜

Great Barford

Anchor Inn 🅛 ✅
High Street, MK44 3LF (by river 1 mile S of village centre) TL134517
☼ 12-3, 6.30 (5.30 Fri)-11; 12-11 Sat; 12-10.30 Sun
☎ (01234) 870364 ⊕ anchorinngreatbarford.co.uk
Eagle IPA; Young's Bitter; 4 changing beers (sourced nationally) ℍ
Busy inn next to the church, overlooking a medieval bridge across the River Great Ouse. At least two guest beers are usually available from an extensive range offered by the pub company. Good home-cooked food is available in the bar and restaurant, as well as a fine selection of wines. The pub is popular with river users in the summer. Occasional themed food nights are held, mainly during the winter months. Q☼☺◑ⅉ♣Pⅎ(27)🛜

Harlington

Carpenters Arms
Sundon Road, LU5 6LS
☼ 12-3.30, 6-midnight; 12-midnight Fri & Sat; 12-11 Sun
☎ (01525) 872384 ⊕ thecarpentersarmsharlington.com
Greene King IPA; Wainwright; Woodforde's Wherry; 1 changing beer (sourced nationally; often Purity) ℍ
Situated in the heart of Harlington, this low-beamed watch-your-head traditional village inn was first licensed in 1790 and has listings of landlords from then until the present. Three regular ales and one changing guest are available. Food is reasonably priced with good helpings – Monday is burger night. The railway station and bus service along with a range of country walks make this a popular stop-off. Q☼☺◑ⅉ≒♣Pⅎ(42)🐾🛜

Haynes

Greyhound ✅
68 Northwood End Road, MK45 3QD (at Northwood End)
☼ 12-11.30 (midnight Fri & Sat); 12-8 Sun
☎ (01234) 381239 ⊕ thegreyhoundhaynes.co.uk
Greene King IPA, Abbot; 2 changing beers (sourced regionally) ℍ
A family-run village pub on the John Bunyan Trail close to the Greensand Ridge Walk, with a large garden offering play equipment and a pétanque court. Families are welcome in the spacious lounge and dining area until 9pm. The dog-friendly public bar area hosts darts and other village teams, with four changing beers in summer. The fortnightly

quiz is a popular event. Sunday lunch is a carvery (there is no food Sun eve or Mon). Open until 10pm on Sunday in summer. ☼☺◑ⅉ≒♣Pⅎ(9B)🐾🛜

Heath & Reach

Axe & Compass
Leighton Road, LU7 0AA
☼ 12-midnight ☎ (01525) 237394
⊕ theaxeandcompass.pub
3 changing beers ℍ
This village community pub has been a free house since 2014. The older front bar, with its low beams, is a lounge and dining area, while the rear public bar has gaming machines, pool table and a TV screen. The large garden includes a children's play area. Regular guest beers often come from local breweries such as Hornes, Tring and Leighton Buzzard. Accommodation is available in a separate lodge. ☼☺🛏◑♣Pⅎ(150)🐾🛜

Henlow

Engineers Arms 🍺 🅛 ✅
68 High Street, SG16 6AA
☼ 12-11 (1am Fri & Sat); 12-10.30 Sun ☎ (01462) 812284
⊕ engineersarms.co.uk
10 changing beers (sourced nationally; often Leighton Buzzard, Tring) ℍ
A haven for ale lovers and sports fans, the Engineers has 10 changing ales, two guests from the wood and eight ciders including some from Potton Press. The front bar has a real fire, local history photos and a fine collection of water jugs. The rear space has two large-screen TVs and an array of sporting pictures. The pub hosts weekly darts and poker nights, occasional discos and live music, plus annual beer and cider festivals. County CAMRA Pub of the Year for 2019.
☼☺🅰♣●🖥🐾🛜

Old Transporter Ale House 🅛
300 Hitchin Road, SG16 6DP
☼ closed Mon; 4-10.30 Tue-Thu; 2-11 Fri & Sat; 2-9 Sun
☎ (01462) 817410 ⊕ theoldtransporter.co.uk
4 changing beers (sourced nationally; often Potbelly, Tring) 🅖
Single-room beer house near RAF Henlow offering up to four ales direct from the cask, often from local and regional breweries. A range of traditional and fruit ciders is available, mainly from Lilley's, plus a variety of small snacks. There is a regular darts team, monthly live music events, occasional raffles and mini beer festivals. A large TV screen caters for live rugby matches. Closed Sunday and Monday bank holiday weekends.
☼♣●ⅎ(9B,188)🐾🛜

Kensworth

Farmer's Boy ✅
216 Common Road, LU6 2PJ
☼ 12-11; 11-11 Sat & Sun ☎ (01582) 872207
⊕ farmersboykensworth.co.uk
Fuller's London Pride, ESB; Gale's Seafarers Ale; 1 changing beer (sourced nationally) ℍ
Located on the main road between the A5 and Whipsnade, this 19th-century village pub offers the usual Fuller's favourites plus changing guest ales. The interior is very much in keeping with a building of its era, featuring original windows from when it was owned by the Mann, Crossman & Paulin

Brewery. The varied menu includes all manner of steaks as well as vegetarian and gluten-free options. (X31)

Leighton Buzzard

Bald Buzzard Alehouse

6 Hockliffe Street, LU7 1HJ

12-9 (10 Fri & Sat); closed Sun & Mon 07484 896131
baldbuzzard.co.uk

5 changing beers (sourced locally; often Chiltern, Oakham)

This award-winning micropub opened its doors in 2015. A small but perfectly formed premises, it has a clever bespoke chiller room with sliding glass doors behind the bar containing 12 casks on stillage and three or four ciders. Five ever-changing beers are usually from the Oakham and Chiltern breweries. As well as the cask ales and ciders there is a selection of bottled beers, weiss beer, wines and more. The generous pork pies are popular. (70,150)

Black Lion

20 High Street, LU7 1EA

12-11 (midnight Fri & Sat); 12-10.30 Sun
(01525) 853725 blacklionlb.com

Draught Bass; Nethergate Suffolk County Best Bitter; Oakham Bishops Farewell; 5 changing beers (sourced nationally)

This traditional alehouse with 17th-century origins features exposed beams, wooden floors and an open fire. Eight handpumps dispense beers from the likes of Hook Norton, North Cotswold, Hornes and Purity. Eight changing real ciders are also available and an impressive bottled and canned beer menu lists over 100 continental and British beers. There is a large paved garden. Bar snacks are served and bring-your-own cold lunches are welcome. Local CAMRA Pub of the Year 2015 to 2019. Q (70,150)

Leighton Buzzard Brewing Company Brewery Tap

Unit 31, Harmill Industrial Estate, Grovebury Road, LU7 4FF (2nd left from Grovebury Rd)

12-8 Fri; 10-8 Sat; closed Sun-Thu 07538 903753
leightonbuzzardbrewing.co.uk

Leighton Buzzard Cuckoo, Narrow Gauge, Restoration Ale, Black Buzzard; 2 changing beers (sourced locally; often Leighton Buzzard)

The tap for the Leighton Buzzard Brewing Company, offering a core range of the brewery's ales plus some varying beers from the bar. There is also a good selection of bottled and canned artisan beers from other like-minded breweries plus real cider. Beers are available to drink on the premises and to take home. Open days are held one Saturday per month in the spring and summer (check the website for dates), with various local food offerings and occasional live music. P

Red Lion

1 North Street, LU7 1EF

10-11 (midnight Fri & Sat); 11-11 Sun (01525) 374350

Greene King Abbot; 2 changing beers (sourced nationally)

This 17th-century building is a town centre institution. An old-fashioned pub with old-fashioned values, the manager of over 20 years offers a warm welcome. The public bar has all the traditional pub games; the main bar resembles a living room with comfy chairs, a large fish tank, TV and the pub's dog wandering around. As well as the well-kept ales there is a choice of 21 Irish and Scottish single malt whiskies. (70,150)

Swan Hotel

50 High Street, LU7 1EA

6am (7am Mon)-midnight; 7am-midnight Sat; 7am-11.30 Sun (01525) 380170

Greene King Abbot; Rebellion IPA; Ruddles Best Bitter; Sharp's Doom Bar; 6 changing beers (sourced nationally)

Dating from the 17th century, this former coaching inn was renovated by Wetherspoon. With good-value food and 39 guest rooms, the Swan is busy and bustling for much of the week. One long bar provides friendly service to two rooms, a conservatory and a courtyard. Guest beers may come from local microbreweries such as Chiltern, Mad Squirrel, Tring and Vale, and real cider is available in the summer months. Families are welcome until 11pm. Events include biannual beer festivals. Q (70,150)

Luton

Black Horse

23 Hastings Street, LU1 5BE

3-11; 1-11 Sat & Sun (01582) 965290

3 changing beers (sourced nationally; often Leighton Buzzard, Oakham, Tring)

Back-street pub near Luton town centre where there is always an interesting range of up to three changing real ales, often from local breweries. The entertainment includes a popular jukebox, dartboard, pool table and a stage for the live music events hosted here. There is a covered outdoor seating area for smokers. P

Bricklayers Arms

High Town Road, LU2 0DD

12-11 (midnight Fri & Sat); 12-10.30 Sun
(01582) 611017 bricklayersarmsluton.co.uk

6 changing beers (sourced nationally; often Oakham)

This quirky High Town pub, run by the same landlady for over 30 years, is busy with Hatters fans on match days. It has TVs in both bars and a popular quiz night every Monday. Six handpumps serve a variety of guest beers from breweries all over the nation, including a choice of light, amber and usually a mild. Draft Belgian beers and two real ciders are also available.

Great Northern

63 Bute Street, LU1 2EY

11-11 (midnight Fri & Sat) (01582) 729311

St Austell Tribute; Sharp's Doom Bar

This may be the smallest pub in Luton. Its name was changed in the 1860s when the Great Northern Railway was built right on its doorstep. It still retains Victorian green wall tiles and a table featuring quirky brass pint glass holders at each corner. Sports are shown on TV. There is a smoking area at the rear.

White House

1 Bridge Street, LU1 2NB

8am-midnight (1am Fri & Sat) (01582) 454608

Greene King Abbot; Ruddles Best Bitter; Sharp's Doom Bar; 6 changing beers (sourced nationally)

The White House is a large two-bar town-centre Wetherspoon pub with the usual keenly priced food and drinks. Following a refurbishment in 2017 it now offers six different guest ales split across two bars. Local beers often come from the Vale and Tring breweries. This is a bright and clean pub in the Galaxy Centre, conveniently located for several bus routes. Q ☾ ⑳ ◑ ❶ ᕐ ᕁ ⚌ 呂

Melchbourne

St John's Arms Ⓛ

Knotting Road, MK44 1BG (at jct on Yelden to Swineshead road) TL030662

☼ 4-11; 12-11 Sat; 12-8 Sun ☎ (01234) 708238

⊕ stjohnsarms.co.uk

3 changing beers (sourced nationally; often Marston's) Ⓗ

Originally built as a hunting lodge, it was then used as a pub for workers on the Melchbourne estate. The L-shaped bar opens into a conservatory and large garden. A second room is used for dining and for skittles and darts. There are camping facilities in the field to the rear. Entertainment includes occasional live music, a quiz on Tuesday and an annual summer beer festival. Beers are mainly from Marston's and local microbreweries. Opens at 3pm on Saturday in winter. ☾ ⑳ ◑ Ⓐ ♣ P ❀ ☗ ≋

Odell

Bell

81 High Street, MK43 7AS

☼ 11.30-11; 12-10.30 Sun ☎ (01234) 910850

⊕ thebellinodell.co.uk

Greene King IPA, Abbot; 4 changing beers (sourced nationally) Ⓗ

Handsome thatched village pub with a large garden near the River Great Ouse. With the Harrold-Odell Country Park just down the lane, this is a popular stop for walkers. Sympathetic refurbishment and a series of linked but distinct seating areas help retain a traditional pub atmosphere. Good-value, quality food includes a Sunday roast, steak and chips night Monday and pie and chips night Tuesday. Tea and cakes are served all day. Q ☾ ⑳ ◑ P 呂 (25,26) ❀ ≋

Potton

George & Dragon

2 King Street, SG19 2QT

☼ 12-3, 4.45-11.30 Mon & Tue; 12-11.30 Wed & Thu; 12-midnight Fri & Sat; 12-11.30 Sun ☎ (01767) 260227

Greene King IPA, Abbot; 3 changing beers (sourced nationally; often Greene King) Ⓗ

Small, traditional, Grade II-listed pub. The lively public bar has a pool table, dartboard, jukebox and large-screen TV for sports. The lounge bar is smaller, quieter, cosy and comfortable with old photos, horse brasses and other memorabilia. At the back there is a family-friendly garden with bench tables and a climbing frame. The beer in this welcoming pub is well kept and varied. Seating throughout is a mix of tables, chairs, stools and pews. ☾ ⑳ ♣ P 呂 (188,190) ❀ ≋

Rising Sun Ⓛ ✅

11 Everton Road, SG19 2PA

☼ 12-3, 5-11 (midnight Fri); 12-midnight Sat; 12-11 Sun

☎ (01767) 260231 ⊕ risingsunpotton.co.uk

Bombardier; Woodforde's Wherry; 5 changing beers (sourced nationally; often Oakham, Potton) Ⓗ

Part 16th-century pub with a covered well in the bar where seven well-kept ales – including reliably excellent guests – and a regularly changing real cider are served. Various small seating areas afford privacy if desired. The pub is popular for its good-value food. There is a patio area outside and the upstairs function room has an outdoor terrace. Live music features every couple of months. There are beer festivals annually in May and every two years in August, each listing 40-50 beers. ☾ ⑳ ◑ Ⓐ ♣ P 呂 (188,190) ❀ ≋

Renhold

Polhill Arms ♈ ✅

25 Wilden Road, MK41 0JP (at Salph End)

☼ 4.30-10 Mon; 12-11; 12-10 Sun ☎ (01234) 771398

⊕ polhillarms.co.uk

Hardys & Hansons Bitter; 5 changing beers (sourced nationally; often Greene King) Ⓗ

Family-friendly village local with a welcoming atmosphere and a large garden, play area and restaurant. An interesting collection of pub and brewery artefacts and airship memorabilia is displayed. Traditional pub food is served including fish and chips (no food Sun or Mon eves). There are regular quiz nights and live music, and darts and skittles are popular. Two real ciders are available in the winter months, four in summer. Local CAMRA Pub of the Year 2018 and 2019. ☾ ⑳ ◑ ♣ ● P 呂 (27) ❀ ≋

Sandy

Sir William Peel ✅

39 High Street, SG19 1AG

☼ 12-11; 12-10.30 Sun ☎ (01767) 680607

⊕ sirwilliampeel.webs.com

Batemans XB; 3 changing beers (sourced nationally; often Oakham) Ⓗ

A traditional pub with a dark exterior, the history of which can be traced to 1838 when it was converted from two cottages. A U-shaped bar has, to the left, access to the rear patio and old stables, both of which are fully utilised during the April beer and July cider festivals, with a digital jukebox and library to the right. Inside are tables, chairs and padded benches, and the exterior front seating faces the sunset. There is a regular cheeseboard on Sundays. ☾ ⑳ ᕐ ♣ ● P 呂 (73,188) ❀ ≋

Shefford

Brewery Tap Ⓛ

14 Northbridge Street, SG17 5DH

☼ 11.30-11; 12-10.30 Sun ☎ (01462) 628448

B&T Shefford Bitter, Dragon Slayer; Everards Tiger; 3 changing beers (sourced nationally) Ⓗ

The Tap is primarily a drinkers' pub, offering three regular beers and three, usually stronger, guest ales. Breweriana decorates an open-plan interior divided into two distinct areas, plus a family room at the rear. Lunchtime rolls are available. Darts, dominoes and cribbage teams are supported, as is a golf society. The rear patio garden is heated on cool evenings. Car park access is through an archway beside the pub. ☾ ⑳ ♣ P 呂 (9A,9B) ❀

Stevington

Royal George

8-10 Silver Street, MK43 7QP

5-11 Mon-Wed; 12-midnight Thu-Sun ☎ (01234) 822184

Eagle IPA; 2 changing beers (sourced nationally; often Adnams, Timothy Taylor)

A lively community pub created from two old buildings joined together. London commuters will appreciate the hanging straps over the bar. Live bands play occasionally at weekends. Lunchtime and evening meals with weekly specials are served Thursday to Saturday, and cream teas with home-made cakes are available on Thursday afternoon. A key to the 18th-century Stevington Windmill museum may be borrowed for a £10 deposit. Q P (25)

Totternhoe

Old Farm Inn

16 Church Road, LU6 1RE

5-midnight Mon; 12-3, 5-11 Tue-Thu; 12-midnight Fri & Sat; 12-11 Sun ☎ (01582) 674053 oldfarminndunstable.co.uk

Fuller's London Pride, ESB; 2 changing beers

Located in the conservation area of Church End, this charming village pub boasts two inglenooks. The public bar with its low boarded ceiling is where you will find good conversation and traditional pub games. Dogs are welcome in the front bar and there is a child-friendly garden. Quizzes are held on alternate Thursday nights. Tasty home-cooked food is served including popular Sunday roasts (no food Mon or Sun eves). Beer festivals are held in May and August. Q P (61)

Upper Dean

Three Compasses

High Street, PE28 0NE (S of village on road to Melchbourne) TL043677

4-11; 12-11 Sat & Sun ☎ (01234) 708346

thethreecompasses.co.uk

Greene King IPA; St Austell Tribute; Timothy Taylor Landlord

Attractive thatched and partly boarded pub on the southern edge of the village. The main bar is to the left of the entrance with a games area behind. There is a small lounge bar on the right which is used mainly for dining. A large garden is to the rear. Since reopening in 2013 after a period of closure, the new owners have made great efforts to enhance the pub. Local CAMRA Most Improved Pub 2019. P (28)

Westoning

Chequers

Park Road, MK45 5LA

9am-11 (midnight Fri); 10-midnight Sat; 10-11 Sun ☎ (01525) 712967 thechequerswestoning.co.uk

Otter Bitter; Purity Pure UBU; 1 changing beer (sourced nationally)

This highly attractive pub in the very heart of the village originates from the 17th century, with a large extension. There are various drinking and dining areas throughout the building as well as a large enclosed patio area with heating. Popular for dining, with an emphasis on a high standard of service, good food includes breakfast every morning. Two regular ales are available plus a changing guest. P

Wingfield

Plough

Tebworth Road, LU7 9QH

12-3 (not Mon), 5.30-11; 12-11 Sat; 12-10.30 Sun ☎ (01525) 873077 theploughinn.com

Fuller's London Pride; Gale's HSB; 2 changing beers (sourced nationally)

Charming thatched village inn dating from the 17th century, decorated with paintings of rural scenes and ploughs. Beware the low beams! Good home-cooked food is served lunchtimes and evenings Tuesday to Sunday except after 4pm on Sunday evening when a quiz is held fortnightly. There are tables outside at the front and a conservatory to the rear which can be booked as a function room. The pub has a lovely garden. P

Woburn

Woburn Ale House

11 Market Place, MK17 9PZ

5 (3 Fri)-11; 12-11 Sat; 12-10.30 Sun ☎ (01525) 290142 woburnalehouse.com

Hornes Triple Goat Porter; Leighton Buzzard Restoration Ale; 4 changing beers (sourced locally; often Hornes, Tring)

This charming bar in a former flower shop has six handpumps for cask ales and two for varying ciders and perries. Local beers feature heavily, in particular from Hornes Brewery and Leighton Buzzard Brewing Company. A wide variety of up to 40 different and interesting artisan keg, canned and bottled beers is also available. There is comfortable seating towards the rear. (49)

Wrestlingworth

Chequers

43 High Street, SG19 2EP

5-10.30 Mon; 12-3, 5-11 Tue-Thu; 12-midnight Fri & Sat; 12-10.30 Sun ☎ (01767) 631818 chequersfreehouse.co.uk

Adnams Southwold Bitter; 5 changing beers (sourced nationally; often Adnams, Woodforde's, Young's)

This sand-coloured Grade II-listed pub is the meeting place for several local community groups. Outside is a south-facing patio and a garden on the opposite side of the car park. Inside is a large bar area with a free jukebox and real fire in winter, with space for dining at one end. The entrance corridor leads to a room for darts with wide-screen TV for major sporting events. Freshly prepared meals feature meats from local butchers. Real cider is available in summer. P (188)

Good ale is the true and proper drink of Englishmen. He is not deserving of the name of Englishman who speaketh against ale, that is good ale.
George Borrow, Lavengro

Public transport information

Leave the car behind and travel to the pub by bus, train, tram or even ferry...

Using public transport is an excellent way to get to the pub, but many people use it irregularly, and systems can be slightly different from place to place. So, below are some useful websites and phone numbers where you can find all the information you might need.

Combined travel information

The national **Traveline** system gives information on all rail and local bus services throughout England, Scotland and Wales. Calls are put through to a local call centre and if necessary your call will be switched through to a more relevant one. There are also services for mobiles, including a next-bus text service and smart-phone app. The website offers other services including timetables and a journey planner with mapping:

- 0871 200 22 33
  www.traveline.info

LONDON

In London use Traveline or **Transport for London (TfL)** travel services. TfL provides information and route planning for all of London's transport networks, including London Underground and Overground, Docklands Light Railway, National Rail, buses, River Buses, Tramlink, Barclays Cycles and cycle routes. Detailed ticketing information helps you find the most cost-effective ways to travel in London. There are also live departure boards, service and traffic updates; mobile services and more:

- 0343 222 1234
  www.tfl.gov.uk

Train travel

National Rail Enquiries covers the whole of Great Britain's rail network and provides service information, ticketing, online journey planning and other information.

- 03457 48 49 50
  www.nationalrail.co.uk

Coach travel

The two main UK coach companies are **National Express** and **Scottish Citylink**. Between them, they serve everywhere from Cornwall to the Highlands. Their websites offer timetables, journey planning, ticketing, route mapping, and other useful information. CAMRA members can benefit from 20% off travel with National Express*. See **camra.org.uk/benefits** for details.

- National Express: 08717 81 81 81
  www.nationalexpress.com
- Scottish Citylink: 0141 352 4444
  www.citylink.co.uk

Scottish ferries

Caledonian MacBrayne (CalMac) operate throughout Scotland's Hebridean and Clyde islands, stretching from Arran in the south to Lewis in the north. They run 475 sailings per day in summer and around 350 per day in winter.

- 0800 066 5000
  www.calmac.co.uk

Northern Ireland & islands

For travel outside mainland Britain but within the area of this Guide, information is available from the following companies:

NORTHERN IRELAND

- Translink: 028 9066 6630
  www.translink.co.uk

ISLE OF MAN

- Isle of Man Transport: 01624 662 525
  www.iombusandrail.info

JERSEY

- Liberty Bus: 01534 828 555
  www.libertybus.je

GUERNSEY

- Island Coachways: 01481 720 210
  www.buses.gg

Public transport symbols in the Guide

Pub entries in the Guide include helpful symbols to show if there are stations and/or bus routes close to a pub. There are symbols for railway stations (⇌); tram or light rail stations (tram symbol); London Underground, Overground or DLR stations (⊖); and bus routes (bus symbol). See the 'Key to symbols' on the inside front cover for more details.

**Membership benefits are subject to change.*

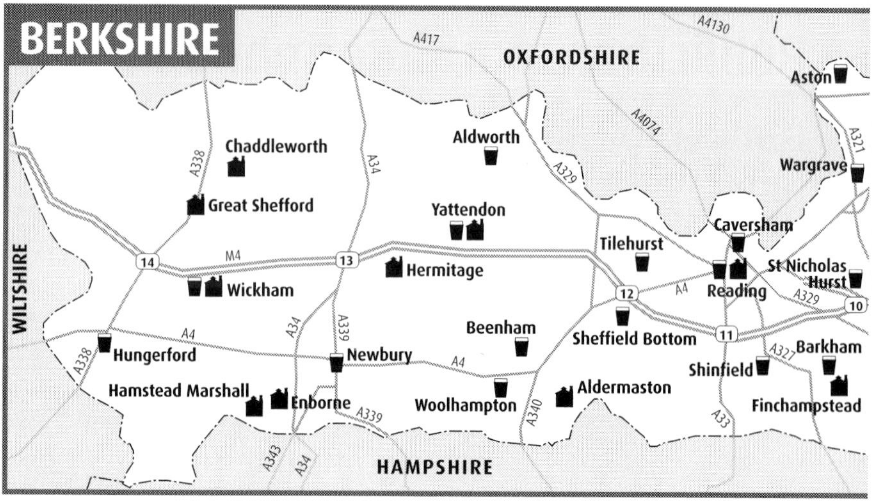

Aldworth

Bell Inn

Bell Lane, RG8 9SE (off Bell Lane)
closed Mon; 11-3, 6-11; 12-3, 7-10.30 Sun
(01635) 578272
Arkell's 3B; West Berkshire Maggs' Magnificent Mild; house beer (by West Berkshire); 2 changing beers (sourced locally; often Loose Cannon, Rebellion, West Berkshire)
A long-standing Guide entry, this traditional inn has been owned by the same family for 130 years, and has been recognised by CAMRA as a having a nationally important historic pub interior. Locals, walkers, cyclists and visitors rub shoulders and share tables to enjoy not only great beer but also an extensive menu of filled rolls, hot soups and proper puddings. It has a large, secluded garden. Local CAMRA Pub of the Year and a former National Pub of the Year. QP

Aston

Flower Pot

Ferry Lane, RG9 3DG (jct with Remenham Lane)
SU784842
11-3, 6-11; 11-11 Sat; 12-11 Sun (01491) 574721
Brakspear Bitter; Ringwood Boondoggle; 2 changing beers
Charming rural country inn set in the heart of the village. It has an enviable position close to the River Thames with beautiful views of the countryside. The large, popular garden is a picture in summer, providing a welcoming place to enjoy food and well-kept beers. In the public bar and restaurant you will find an eclectic collection of aquatic taxidermy. Licensees Tony and Pat have been here over 28 years and are Brakspear's longest-serving tenants in a single pub.
QP

Barkham

Bull

Barkham Road, RG41 4TL (on B3349 jct with Barkham St)
12-11 (8 Sun) (0118) 976 2816 thebullbarkham.com
Gale's HSB; Rebellion Smuggler; Sharp's Doom Bar; Timothy Taylor Landlord; 2 changing beers (sourced locally; often Rebellion, Siren)
Grade II-listed pub and restaurant, featuring etched glass windows and a working inglenook fireplace. Formerly a brewhouse, then a smithy, the old forge can still be seen. Up to six real ales are served, including some from local breweries. Authentic Thai dishes are a speciality, with food freshly prepared from ingredients mostly sourced locally (no food Sun eve). The garden hosts three beer festivals and other events during the year. Quiz night is Monday. Dogs are welcome in the bar only.
QP(3)

Beenham

Six Bells

The Green, RG7 5NX (at Bucklebury end of main road through village)
12-2.30 (not Mon), 6-11; 12-2.30, 6.30-11 Sat; 12-3 Sun
(0118) 971 3368 thesixbells.co.uk
West Berkshire Good Old Boy; 2 changing beers (sourced locally; often Loddon, Vale, West Berkshire)
A well-deserved entry in the Guide for the 12th consecutive year for this welcoming country pub. Outside there is a pretty summer patio and inside there are two cosy areas adorned with various collectables: key rings, coins and fishing flies. Open fires provide comfort for chilly days. All the food is home cooked; pie and pudding night is a highlight on Wednesday. Community meetings are held here and the pub is a popular waypoint for walkers and cyclists. QP(41,44)

Binfield

Binfield Club

Forest Road, RG42 4HP (at mini roundabout jct with Terrace Rd S)
11-11; 12-10.30 Sun (01344) 420690
binfieldclub.com
Courage Best Bitter; Fuller's London Pride; Sharp's Doom Bar; 1 changing beer (sourced nationally; often Wadworth)
This community club is a keen supporter of CAMRA and offers its facilities to many local organisations

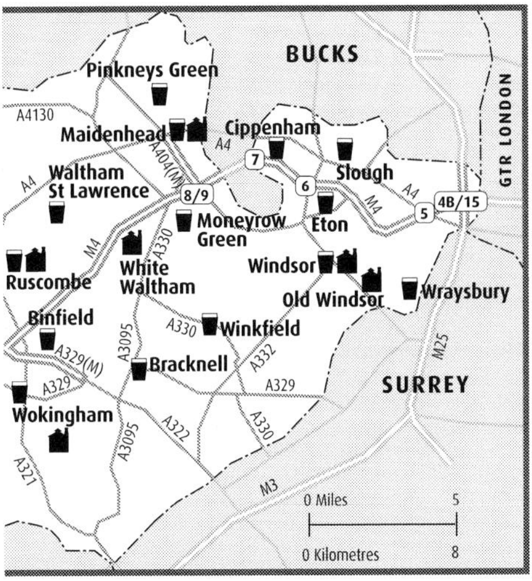

and community groups. It has an informative website and hosts a whole range of activities including snooker, pool and darts, plus sports TV. Four handpumps on the bar provide one ever-changing guest ale along with three club favourites. A warm, friendly welcome is offered to visitors and CAMRA members – show your membership card to gain entry.
♘❀◑♿♣P🚌(150,151)📶

Jack o' Newbury 🄻

Terrace Road North, RG42 5PH (200yds S of jct with B3018)
⏲ 11-11 (midnight Sat); 11-6 Sun ☎ (01344) 454881
🌐 jackonewbury.co.uk
Brains SA; Greene King Abbot; Rebellion IPA; Young's Special; 1 changing beer (sourced nationally; often Greene King) 🄷
Victorian free house usually with four permanent and one changing real ale. There is an eclectic mix of lamps on display throughout the bar, and a real fire provides a cosy atmosphere on cooler days. The garden includes a newly constructed decking area for summer use. Home-cooked meals are served lunchtimes and evenings, and families are welcome (no food Sun eve). The refurbished skittle alley outside is available to book. ♘❀◑P🐾📶

Victoria Arms

Terrace Road North, RG42 5JA (100yds S of jct with Tilehurst Lane)
⏲ 11.30-11 (midnight Fri & Sat) ☎ (01344) 483856
🌐 victoriaarmsbinfield.co.uk
Fuller's Oliver's Island, London Pride, ESB; 1 changing beer (sourced nationally) 🄷
Cosy village pub with a central bar warmed by a real fire in winter months. A large array of beer bottles adorns the walls and beams. There is a terraced garden down steps to enjoy in summer, with fleeces available for chillier evenings. Food is served lunchtimes and evenings, with a separate children's menu. Burger night is Thursday and traditional roasts are served on Sunday, followed by a quiz night in the evening.
♘❀◑♣P🚌(150,151)🐾📶

Bracknell

Cannie Man 🄻 ✔

Bywood, RG12 7RF
⏲ 12-11 (11.30 Fri & Sat); 12-10.30 Sun ☎ (01344) 307620
🌐 cannieman.co.uk
Fuller's London Pride; Sharp's Doom Bar; 2 changing beers (sourced nationally; often Brains, West Berkshire) 🄷
An estate pub at the heart of the local community in every sense of the word, with a good cross-section of customers. Up to four well-kept real ales are always available. Support is offered to a myriad of local teams including darts, pool and the football team. The pub raises thousands of pounds through events for local charities and stages live music, with entertainment at least one night a week.
❀♣P🚌(4,171)📶

Old Manor 🄻 ✔

Grenville Place, RG12 1BP (at College roundabout jct with Church Rd)
⏲ 8am-midnight (1am Fri & Sat) ☎ (01344) 304490
Greene King Abbot; Ruddles Best Bitter; Sharp's Doom Bar; 6 changing beers (sourced nationally; often Binghams, Loddon, Windsor & Eton) 🄷
Wetherspoon pub set in a former 17th-century Tudor manor house and one of the oldest buildings in Bracknell. It has several drinking and dining areas including the Monk's Room where a priest's hole dating from 1682 can be seen. Real ales are available in two separate bars, plus Old Rosie and Black Dragon ciders. Extensive gardens and patio areas surround the pub, which is always busy with a mixed clientele. Current local CAMRA Cider Pub of the Year. **Q**♘❀◑♿⇄🍎P🚌(4,53)🐾📶

Caversham

Fox & Hounds 🄻

51 Gosbrook Road, RG4 8BN
⏲ 12-midnight (11 Sun) ☎ 07540 816293
8 changing beers (often Oakham, Siren, Wild Weather Ales) 🄷
A regular winner or runner-up in local CAMRA Pub of the Year awards. This popular and lively community hub offers eight regularly changing beers, six craft keg lines, six or more ciders and perries, plus a good selection of bottles. A blue plaque commemorates the day in 1960 that John Lennon and Paul McCartney performed a gig here

REAL ALE BREWERIES

Binghams Ruscombe
Bond Brews Wokingham
Butts Great Shefford
Double-Barrelled Reading
Elusive Finchampstead
Hermitage Hermitage
Indigenous Chaddleworth
INNformal ▤ Wickham
New Wharf Maidenhead
Old Windsor Old Windsor (NEW)
Saviour ▤ Hamstead Marshall (NEW)
Siren Craft Finchampstead
Stardust White Waltham
Two Cocks Enborne
West Berkshire Yattendon
Wild Weather Aldermaston
Windsor & Eton Windsor
Zerodegrees ▤ Reading

as the Nerk Twins. A quiz night every second Wednesday is always well attended. Food includes excellent pizzas and Sunday roasts.
🐴❀◑♣🍎P🚌(25)🐾📶

Cippenham

Barleycorn 𝕃

151 Lower Cippenham Lane, SL1 5DS
⏲ 12-midnight (12.30am Fri & Sat); 12-11.30 Sun
☎ (01628) 603115
7 changing beers (sourced nationally) 🄷
A traditional single-bar pub, now refurbished, with seating on one side and a pool table on the other. It caters well for a strong local following. Around the walls are a large number of bottles and jugs. Of the seven guest ales there is always one from Rebellion and a strong ale. The remaining guests come from near and far. There are a couple of sports TVs and occasional live music. The nearby public car park is free. Q❀♣🍎P🚌(5)🐾📶

Eton

George Inn 𝕃 ✔

77 High Street, SL4 6AF
⏲ 8am-11 (10 Sun) ☎ (01753) 861797
🌐 georgeinn-eton.co.uk
Windsor & Eton ParkLife, Windsor Knot, Guardsman, Conqueror; 2 changing beers (often Windsor & Eton) 🄷
Windsor & Eton Brewery's first pub, facing Eton bridge. The refurbishment is now complete, including a new bar with six ales all from the brewery. Breakfast is served daily 8-10am. The wooden floors, carriage lamps and candles help to create a warm atmosphere. Please note the range of Windsor & Eton beers can change depending on the number of specials/seasonals on the bar. Real cider is sold in summer. The Hop House is available for private parties. Q🐴❀🛏◑🚆🍎🚌(10)🐾📶

Hungerford

Hungerford Club ✔

3 The Croft, RG17 0HY (on foot via Church Lane)
⏲ 12-3, 7-11; 12-5 Sun ☎ (01488) 682357
Fuller's London Pride; 1 changing beer (sourced nationally) 🄷
A warm welcome is assured at this comfortable bowls, tennis and social club, situated in the quiet Croft, just a few yards from the High Street. Indoor games such as billiards and snooker are also played here. The changing guest beer, sourced nationally, is often chosen by club members. Look out for the annual beer festival over the August bank holiday. CAMRA members are welcome – show a copy of this Guide or membership card for entry.
Q🐴❀🚆♣P🚌(3,20)🐾📶

John O' Gaunt ✔

21 Bridge Street, RG17 0EG (N of canal bridge)
⏲ 11-11 (midnight Fri & Sat); 12-10.30 Sun
☎ (01488) 683535 🌐 john-o-gaunt-hungerford.co.uk
6 changing beers (sourced nationally) 🄷
Historic 16th-century town-centre pub named after the Duke of Lancaster. This Grade II-listed building has been restored, keeping many original features. The range of ales changes constantly, with no beer repeated in a six month period, complemented by a large selection of real ciders and around 80 bottled beers from around the world. One of the beers usually comes from the house brewery, INNformal, situated at the Five Bells at Wickham – the sister pub to this one.
Q🐴❀◑🚆♣🍎P🚌(46,X22)🐾📶

Maidenhead

Bear 𝕃 ✔

8-10 High Street, SL6 1QJ
⏲ 8am-midnight (1am Fri & Sat) ☎ (01628) 763030
Greene King IPA, Abbot; Sharp's Doom Bar; 6 changing beers 🄷
A short walk from the Town Hall, this former coaching inn became a Wetherspoon in 2009 and has an open-plan bar with several different seating areas, including an outside area to the front of the building. A spiral staircase leads to an upper floor with additional seating. Ten handpumps dispense up to six guest ales, many from local breweries. Two or three ciders are often available, including Old Rosie and Black Dragon. 🐴❀◑🚆🍎🚌📶

Craufurd Arms 🏆 𝕃

15 Gringer Hill, SL6 7LY
⏲ 12-midnight (1am Fri & Sat) ☎ (01628) 675410
🌐 craufurdarms.com
Rebellion IPA; West Berkshire Good Old Boy; Windsor & Eton Knight of the Garter; 2 changing beers (sourced locally; often Stardust, Windsor & Eton) 🄷
The pub was registered as an Asset of Community Value and is now owned by the community. The building dates back to the late 1800s and was close to Craufurd College, a private school for boys, hence the unusual spelling. A cosy single bar hosts a multitude of activities – crib on Monday, ladies' darts Tuesday, gents' darts Wednesday and Thursday quiz night. Two large screens show Sky and BT sports. Live music features on occasion.
🐴❀🚆♣P🚌(5,8)🐾📶

Maiden's Head 𝕃

34 High Street, SL6 1QE
⏲ 12-11 (midnight Fri & Sat) ☎ (01628) 784786
🌐 themaidenshead.co.uk
St Austell Tribute; 3 changing beers (often Rebellion) 🄷
Large single-room high-street bar offering four real ales and four keg craft beers, two American, plus Weissbier and Grimbergen Blonde, as well as a range of world bottled beers. The guest beers are constantly rotating. Food is served, with a roast on Sunday. Outside, there is a large beer garden at the back. Live music is hosted at the weekend.
🐴❀◑♿🚆♣P🚌🐾📶

Maidenhead Conservative Club 𝕃

32 York Road, SL6 1SF
⏲ 11-11 (midnight Fri & Sat); 11-7 Sun ☎ (01628) 620579
🌐 maidenheadconclub.co.uk
Fuller's London Pride; 4 changing beers 🄷
A friendly real ale outlet close to the station, awarded CAMRA branch Club of the Year 2017 and 2018. The four guests ales come from mainly local independent breweries, and a selection of bottle-conditioned beers is available. Crib nights are held during the week and a quiz night on the last Wednesday of the month. The TV lounge has been refurbished. Your CAMRA membership card allows entry for a minimal fee. Public parking is nearby.
🐴◑♿🚆♣P🚌(4)📶

Moneyrow Green

White Hart

SL6 2ND

12-10 Mon; 12-11 (11.30 Fri); 12-9 Sun ☎ (01628) 621460

thewhitehartholyport.co.uk

Greene King IPA; 3 changing beers [H]

A welcoming, traditional two-bar pub half a mile south of the village. The wood-panelled lounge features leather sofas and log fires in winter. The larger public bar has wooden flooring, a TV and traditional pub games including bar billiards. There is a quiz night Monday, open mic on Tuesday and Joker Jackpot on Sunday. Outside is a large, fenced beer garden with a pétanque pitch and children's play area. ♣P

Newbury

Catherine Wheel

35 Cheap Street, RG14 5DB

12-11 (1am Thu; 2am Fri & Sat) ☎ (01635) 569897

thecatherinewheel.com

West Berkshire Good Old Boy; 4 changing beers (often Binghams, Longdog, Wild Weather Ales) [H]

Refurbished in 2014, this town-centre pub serves a changing selection of beers from six handpumps on the main bar. Additionally, over 100 UK and international beers are available in chilled bottles. A gin bar is housed in the covered courtyard. Winner of the CAMRA branch's 2017 Cider Pub of the Year award, it also offers 18 boxed ciders and local bottled ciders. The landlord arranges beer festivals, Meet the Brewer events and trips. The food menu, based around Pieminister pies, satisfies customers' appetites.
♣ (1,2)

Cow & Cask

1 Inches Yard, Market Street, RG14 5DP

12-2 (not Tues & Wed), 5-9; 12-2, 4.30-10 Fri; 12-9 Sat; closed Sun & Mon ☎ 07517 658071 cowandcask.co.uk

3 changing beers (sourced regionally; often Loose Cannon, Two Cocks, XT) [G]

The compact nature of this micropub helps to create a friendly atmosphere where conversation flourishes. The landlord usually offers three different locally sourced real ales on stillage, along with three or four varieties of real cider from bag-in-box containers. Snacks include pork pies, cheese rolls and various crisps and nuts. The pub is within town and has easy access to public transport and car parks. Quiz night is the third Wednesday of the month. Q♣ (2,2A)

Hatchet Inn

12 Market Place, RG14 5BD

7am-midnight (1am Fri & Sat) ☎ (01635) 277560

Greene King Abbot; Ruddles Best Bitter; Sharp's Doom Bar; 5 changing beers (sourced nationally; often Loddon, Ramsbury, Two Cocks) [H]

Newbury's Grade II-listed Wetherspoon hotel is ideally situated in the pedestrianised Market Place. Since opening in 2011, a dining area extension has added plenty of extra space. Outside seating at the front and rear is popular all year, especially on sunny days. The long bar offers three regular and five changing real ales, with a real cider in the fridge. Beer and cider festivals are held regularly. Food is available daily, from breakfast time to 11pm. Q P (4B,124)

King Charles Tavern

54 Cheap Street, RG14 5BX

11.30-midnight (1am Thu-Sat); 12-midnight Sun

☎ (01635) 36695 kctavern.com

West Berkshire Good Old Boy; house beer (by Greene King); 6 changing beers (sourced nationally) [H]

Town-centre pub and a former CAMRA branch Pub of the Year, close to the railway station. It serves up to eight beers, sourced nationally, often from XT, Saltaire and Hop Back breweries. The freshly made food is sourced locally. Two front bars feature open fireplaces and are complemented by a rear room that can be hired for events. Note the old map of Newbury on the ceiling in the right-hand bar. (2,2A)

Pinkneys Green

Boundary Arms

112 Pinkneys Road, SL6 5DN

12-11 (midnight Fri & Sat) ☎ (01628) 629667

Rebellion IPA, Roasted Nuts; 1 changing beer [H]

This large pub opposite the green has recently been bought by a private buyer and refurbished. It has two bars, both with real fires – the public bar at the front and a pleasant lounge bar at the back with doors out to the garden, where there is a secure children's play area. There are also a couple of tables outside at the front where you can watch the world go by. Q♣P (9)

Reading

Alehouse

2 Broad Street, RG1 2BH

11-11 (midnight Fri); 12-10.30 Sun ☎ (0118) 950 8119

9 changing beers (often West Berkshire) [H]

Popular drinking establishment which always leaves an impression on visitors with its quirky wooden fixtures and reclaimed wooden floor. As a champion of microbreweries, both local and further afield, rare and unusual ales are frequently found on the pumps. A selection of real ciders and perries is also available. Often busy around the bar area, those wishing for a more peaceful drink can take advantage of the secluded cubbyholes at the back of the pub. ♣ (4,X4)

Allied Arms

57 St Mary's Butts, RG1 2LG

12 (5 Mon)-11; closed Sun ☎ (0118) 958 3323

allied-arms.co.uk

Loddon Hullabaloo; 9 changing beers [H]

Town-centre pub situated near the bus terminus, dating from around 1828, with two cosy bars that are best entered via the side passage, not the front door. The wide range of ales on offer goes up to 10 at the weekend. The jukebox features an interesting and varied selection of songs. A regular charity pub quiz is hosted. The large walled garden is a popular refuge from the chaos of the town, with patio heaters for colder nights.

Butler

85-91 Chatham Street, RG1 7DS

4 (12 Thu)-11; 12-midnight Fri & Sat; 12-11 Sun

☎ (0118) 959 5500 thebutlerreading.co.uk

St Austell Proper Job; Timothy Taylor Landlord; West Berkshire Mr Chubb's Lunchtime Bitter; 2 changing beers [H]

Named after Butler's Wine Merchants, who operated from these premises many years ago, this is very much a community pub in the heart of town. Taken over by a local consortium after a long period of Fuller's stewardship, there has been an ongoing process of upgrading both inside and out. Ales are sourced from regionals and local breweries, with some often unusual choices for the area. Live music is a weekly feature and draws large crowds. ❀◐≠(West)♣P🚌(17)🐾📶

Castle Tap 🄻

120 Castle Street, RG1 7RJ
11-11.30 (midnight Fri & Sat); 12-10.30 Sun
☎ (0118) 958 0473 🌐 thecastletap.co.uk
4 changing beers 🄷
Alongside its varied selection of real ales and ciders, the Castle Tap boasts an excellent range of bottled and canned beers. While offering a warm welcome to visiting real ale aficionados and craft beer fans, it maintains a friendly local atmosphere. The frequent live music and other events are well worth checking out. And for those feeling peckish, cheeseboards are available. The back room can be booked for functions. ❀♣●P🚌(1,2)🐾📶

Greyfriar 🄻

53 Greyfriars Road, RG1 1PA
11.30-11 (midnight Thu-Sat); 12.30-7 Sun
☎ (0118) 958 0560 🌐 thegreyfriarreading.co.uk
Hogs Back HBB; 7 changing beers (often Elusive, Siren, Wild Weather Ales) 🄷
A modern-looking yet traditional pub with eight handpumps and 14 keg lines, all offering beers from independent breweries. Tap takeovers are held on occasion, which are proving popular, as are Meet the Brewer evenings. A small range of paninis is available lunchtime to early evening. A regular quiz night is held every other Monday. Convenient for the railway station and popular with the after-work crowd. ◐≠♣🚌(3,3B)🐾📶

Moderation

213 Caversham Road, RG1 8BB
12-11 (midnight Fri & Sat) ☎ (0118) 375 0767
🌐 themodreading.com
4 changing beers 🄷
A smart pub popular with local residents and office workers alike. Decor in the airy interior is a fusion of East meets West, with comfy sofas and wooden tables. There is a large decked garden and smoking area to the rear, plus roadside tables at the front. Food is a mixture of English and Thai cuisines, with regular offers including steak night and two-for-one on main courses on Monday. A pub quiz is held on Sunday night. ❀◐◑≠♣🚌(22,27)📶

Nag's Head 🏆 🄻

5 Russell Street, RG1 7XD
12-11 (midnight Fri); 11-midnight Sat ☎ 07765 880137
🌐 thenagsheadreading.co.uk
12 changing beers 🄷
With a wide range of real ales, real cider and perry always on offer, visitors are sure to find something to their taste here. Craft beers have vessel and dispense type shown on an adjacent blackboard. A selection of board games is available for those wanting to while away a few sociable hours. The pub gets busy on Reading FC match days. A regular in the CAMRA National Pub of the Year awards. ❀◐◑≠(West)♣●P🚌(1,2)🐾📶

Park House (University of Reading)

Park House, Whiteknights Campus, RG6 6UR
12-11; closed Sat & Sun ☎ (0118) 378 5097
5 changing beers (often Rebellion, Siren, Titanic) 🄷
The university's old Senior Common Room is open to the public. Five ales, mostly LocAle, are usually available in an array of styles. It is a popular venue for the mature university community and can get busy in the early evening. Open from 4pm during the Christmas and Easter holidays. Note, the bar is cashless. Non-accredited vehicles are not allowed on campus until after 5pm but a regular bus service drops off inside the campus.
Q❀◐◑♿●🚌(21,21A)🐾📶

Retreat

8 St John's Street, RG1 4EH
4.30-11; 12-11.30 Fri & Sat; 12-11 Sun
☎ (0118) 9376 9159 🌐 theretreat.pub
6 changing beers (often Butcombe, Harvey's, Sharp's) 🄷
A well-loved back-street boozer with a traditional layout and feel. A good range of real ales is squeezed into the small bar. The landlord tends to concentrate on well-known regional brands; however, there is a selection of more eclectic choices available in bottles, as well as a number of ciders. The pub is locally renowned for regular live music and hosting community events. A quiz night is held every second Wednesday of the month.
Q♣🚌(4,17)🐾

Three Guineas

Station Approach, RG1 1LY
8am-11 (midnight Fri & Sat); 9am-10.30 Sun
☎ (0118) 957 2743 🌐 three-guineas.co.uk
Fuller's Oliver's Island, London Pride, ESB; Gale's Seafarers Ale; 4 changing beers (often Butcombe, Windsor & Eton) 🄷
A welcome addition to the pubs in the area, this building in the old ticket hall of Reading's Grade II-listed railway station has a large seating area outside at the front. Recently refurbished, the ground floor is greatly improved and the cellar bar, named Firefly after the first train to leave Reading station, has a vaulted ceiling and bare brick walls. There is no access to the platforms directly, so passengers are advised to allow plenty of time to catch their train. ❀◐◑♿≠🚌(21,702)🐾📶

Ruscombe

Royal Oak 🄻

Ruscombe Lane, RG10 9JN (on B3024 E out of Twyford)
12-3 Mon; 12-3, 6-11; 12-4 Sun ☎ (0118) 934 5190
🌐 burattas.co.uk
Fuller's London Pride; 2 changing beers (often Binghams) 🄷
Across the road from Binghams Brewery, the pub's open-plan area is divided between cosy seating areas and a dining space. Through the restaurant is a bright conservatory overlooking the beautifully kept garden, excellent for families in summer. The interior is comfortably furnished and decorated with quirky objects and antiques – many are for sale. Also known as Buratta's, the pub is noted for its food, but welcomes drinkers with up to three real ales including one from Binghams, and a range of wines. Q❀◐◑♿≠(Twyford)P🚌(127)🐾📶

St Nicholas Hurst

Wheelwrights Arms
Davis Way, RG10 0TR (off B3030 opp entrance to Dinton Pastures)
11-11 (10.30 Sun) (0118) 934 4100
thewheelwrightsarms.co.uk
Wadworth IPA, Horizon, 6X, Swordfish; 2 changing beers (sourced nationally; often Wadworth)
Welcoming family-run country pub and restaurant with a main bar serving up to six real ales and two ciders, including Westons Old Rosie. The bar is warmed by two log fires in colder months, and the garden accommodates dining, sporting and music events in summer. Dogs are encouraged, and the pub is a popular stop off for walkers and cyclists. Local club and community events are held along with a quiz night on Monday and music night on the last Friday of the month.
P (128,129)

Sheffield Bottom

Fox & Hounds
Deans Copse Road, RG7 4BE (80yds E of jct with Hangar Rd roundabout)
11-11 (10.30 Sun) (0118) 930 2295
foxandhoundstheale.co.uk
Wadworth IPA, 6X, Bishops Tipple; 2 changing beers (often Wadworth)
Worth the walk from the village, station or canal. Formerly known as the Drum & Monkey when it was used by local farmers, it is now an efficiently run and comfortable Wadworth house (with some of its old signs adorning the walls), catering for a wide range of customers. There is an emphasis on food, although you are welcome to come in just for a drink. The garden and patio areas to the front and side make for a comfortable summer setting.
P

Shinfield

Magpie & Parrot
Arborfield Road, RG2 9EA (on A327, 100yds E of Arborfield Rd roundabout)
closed Mon; 12-7.30; 12-4 Sun (0118) 988 4130
Fuller's London Pride
A delightful pub in a rural setting, just past the eastern edge of the village. The cosy interior was recently expanded; there are now two small, quiet rooms, both festooned with an eclectic selection of memorabilia. A small food menu is available weekday lunchtimes – it is advisable to book for the popular Friday fish and chips. Opening hours are limited so check ahead to avoid disappointment. Q P (3,3B)

Slough

Moon & Spoon
86 High Street, SL1 1EL
9am-midnight; 8am-midnight Fri & Sat; 8am-11 Sun
(01753) 531650
Greene King Abbot; Ruddles Best Bitter; Sharp's Doom Bar; 4 changing beers
This Wetherspoon establishment has 12 handpumps offering three regulars beers accompanied by up to four constantly changing guest ales, always including one from a local brewery. A couple of ciders are also usually available, often Old Rosie and Black Dragon. At the entrance is an eye-catching sculpture made of 1,148 spoons. The usual Wetherspoon extensive all-day food menu is served. Soft lighting gives the pub a cosy feel, especially at quieter times.
(8,2)

Tilehurst

Fox & Hounds
116 City Road, RG31 5SB
11.30 (3 Mon)-11; 12-10.30 Sun (0118) 942 2982
thefoxandhoundstilehurst.co.uk
Fuller's London Pride; Sharp's Doom Bar; 1 changing beer
A thriving local with a genuine country-pub atmosphere near the western edge of Tilehurst. This Courage-badged, low-beamed inn is a short walk from open fields and Sulham Woods. Originally cottage sized, a large conservatory extension at the rear has added a light and airy space for eating and drinking. A bricked-in open fireplace, recently uncovered by the entrance, now houses a wood-burning stove.
P (33)

Waltham St Lawrence

Bell
The Street, RG10 0JJ
12-3, 5-11; 12-11 Sat & Sun (0118) 934 1788
thebellwalthamstlawrence.co.uk
Loddon Hoppit; 4 changing beers (often Binghams, Butts, Stardust)
Classic half-timbered 15th-century pub bequeathed to the village in 1608 by Sir Ralph Newbury and identified by CAMRA as having a regionally important historic pub interior. Well worth seeking out, it serves as the village local, promoting real ales from small, independent breweries, while offering exceptionally good food from fresh, seasonal ingredients. Up to eight ciders and perries are served from the cellar. You will find log fires in the winter and a good-sized beer garden for sunny summer days. Q (4,4A)

Wargrave

Wargrave & District Snooker Club
Woodclyffe Hostel, Church Street, RG10 8EP
7-11; closed Sat & Sun wargravesnooker.co.uk
2 changing beers
The club opens weekday evenings and shares the building with the local library. The regularly changing beers reflect members' recommendations, with two on in the winter months and one in the summer. The TV's default is off, though the Six Nations and Rugby World Cup are an exception. Visitors may show this Guide or CAMRA membership card for entry (£3 fee to use the snooker tables). Winner of CAMRA branch Club of the Year for several years. (850)

Wickham

Five Bells
Baydon Road, RG20 8HH (N side of B4000)
12-3, 5-10 (11 Fri); 12-11 Sat; 12-10 Sun
(01488) 657300 fivebellswickham.co.uk
INNformal INNHouse Bitter; 9 changing beers (sourced regionally; often Mad Squirrel, Siren, Wild Weather Ales)

Seventeeth-century thatched pub in a popular rural destination. The large single-room layout has an open fire at one end and steps to a large garden at the other. In between is a long bar offering 10 real ales, four from the on-site INNformal Brewery, plus three real ciders. Four more bag-in-box real ciders are kept in the fridge. A range of bottled Belgian beers is also available. A changing menu of excellent home-cooked food attracts passers-by and locals alike. Q🐴❀🛏◐◑♿♣●P🚌(4A)🐾📶

Windsor

Acre 𝕃 ✔

Donnelly House, Victoria Street, SL4 1EN
⏲ 11-11 (midnight Fri & Sat); 12-10.30 Sun
☎ (01753) 841083 🌐 theacrewindsor.com
Windsor & Eton Guardsman; 2 changing beers Ⓗ
Formerly the Liberal Club, now a free house open to all. The name refers to the adjacent Bachelors Acre. Three ales are on offer, with Windsor & Eton's Guardsman a permanent feature and two regularly changing guests, often from local breweries. Freshly made rolls, pies and pasties are available daily. Live music is hosted every Saturday night. Two screens show live sporting events and there are excellent facilities for darts. Now with a cellar bar. 🐴⇶♣🚌(2)📶

Corner House 𝕃

22 Sheet Street, SL4 1BG
⏲ 11-11 (midnight Thu; 1am Fri & Sat); 12-11 Sun
☎ (01753) 862031 🌐 thecornerhousepub.co.uk
Big Smoke Solaris Session Pale Ale; 9 changing beers Ⓗ
This Grade II-listed building was completely refurbished in a traditional style by new owners in 2017 and designated as an ale and cider house. Fifteen handpumps serve 10 regularly changing real ales, five ciders and 10 keg lines. A good selection of traditional pub food is available. Upstairs is a function room. Unusually, there is a small, partly covered roof terrace, catering for smokers and those wishing to savour the air. Pub quiz night is Monday. ❀◐◑⇶●🚌🐾📶

Queen Charlotte 𝕃 ✔

6 Church Lane, SL4 1PA
⏲ 12-11 (midnight Fri & Sat); 12-10.30 Sun
☎ (01753) 859268 🌐 queencharlottewindsor.co.uk
6 changing beers Ⓗ
The pub takes its name from the nearby Queen Charlotte Street which is listed as the shortest street in Britain. There are good views of Windsor Castle's Henry VIII Gate from the outside seating area. The local community is well represented among the clientele and the vicar from the nearby parish church can sometimes be seen working behind the bar. An extensive drinks menu includes six constantly changing cask beers, with several from local breweries. Q🛏◐◑⇶🚌📶

Windsor & Eton Brewery Taproom 𝕃

1 Vansittart Estate, Duke Street, SL4 1SE
⏲ 10-9 (7 Mon); closed Sun ☎ (01753) 854075
🌐 webrew.co.uk
6 changing beers (often Windsor & Eton) Ⓗ
The brewery taproom opened in 2016. It offers six cask beers from the Windsor & Eton range and four keg beers on tap. Two or three Uprising beers are also on keg. Tasting trays are served with three third-pints. The full range of bottled beers including some vintage bottles is available for take-out. As a bonus you can view the brewery from the bar via glass doors, and there are regular tours – see the website for details. ⇶P🚌

Winkfield

White Hart 𝕃

Church Road, SL4 4SE (on A330 opp St Mary's Church)
⏲ 12-11 ☎ (01344) 882415 🌐 thewhitehartwinkfield.co.uk
Rebellion IPA; Sharp's Doom Bar; 1 changing beer (sourced locally; often Rebellion) Ⓗ
Former parish courthouse, now a genuine village community pub with a large bar, paved stone floor and sofas close to the real fire. The kitchen prepares locally sourced home-made food (children's menu available), served in the separate dining room/function room, which can be hired. Quiz night on Wednesday and fish and chips night on Friday are popular. The extensive garden can be enjoyed in warmer weather. Dogs are allowed in the bar area only. Q🐴❀◐◑♣P🚌(162,162A)🐾📶

Winning Post ✔

Winkfield Street, SL4 4SW (200yds S jct with Winkfield Lane)
⏲ 7am-11; 8am-11 Sat; 8am-10.30 Sun ☎ (01344) 882242
🌐 winningpostwinkfield.co.uk
Ascot Final Furlong, Gold Cup Ⓗ
Eighteenth-century rural dining pub refurbished in 2011 to a high standard. Exposed brick and timber beams accentuate the racing-themed formal dining areas, while a stone-paved floor and a real fire add character to the small, cosy front bar. Food is freshly prepared on the premises with a mixture of traditional and more imaginative dishes, often featuring game. Breakfast is served from 7.30am on weekdays and 8am at weekends. Ten B&B rooms and a private dining area are also available. ❀🛏◐◑P🐾📶

Wokingham

Crispin 🏆 𝕃

45 Denmark Street, RG40 2AY (opp Denmark St car park)
⏲ 12-11 (midnight Thu-Sat); 12-10.30 Sun
☎ (0118) 978 0309 🌐 crispinpub.co.uk
Hogs Back HBB; 4 changing beers (sourced regionally; often Loddon, Rebellion, Siren) Ⓗ
Named after St Crispin, the patron saint of cobblers, this was originally a 15th-century hall house. Up to five real ales, mostly local, and six real ciders (mainly from Lilley's) are available. No food is served but you can bring your own, with plates and cutlery provided, to enjoy with a drink from the bar. The garden includes an Aunt Sally pitch and gazebo smoking area. Regular poker nights are held plus occasional beer and cider festivals. Local CAMRA Pub of the Year 2019. ❀⇶♣●🍺🚌(4,X4)🐾📶

Queen's Head 𝕃 ✔

23 The Terrace, RG40 1BP
⏲ 12-11 (12.30am Fri & Sat); 12-10.30 Sun
☎ (0118) 978 1221 🌐 queensheadwokingham.co.uk
Greene King Yardbird, Abbot; house beer (by Hardys & Hansons); 3 changing beers (sourced locally; often Binghams, Hogs Back, Loddon) Ⓗ
A 15th-century timber cruck-framed building on a terrace in the old town, with a real fire in the bar creating a cosy atmosphere in winter. A Greene King Local Heroes pub, it serves three local ales

alongside three from the brewery. Third-pint beer paddles are available to try a selection. There is limited seating on the south-facing terrace plus a garden to the rear with an Aunt Sally pitch.
❀⇌♣🚌(4,X4)🐾📶

Woolhampton

Rowbarge 🄻
Station Road, RG7 5SH
10-11 (10.30 Sun) ☎ (0118) 971 2213
House beer (by St Austell); 5 changing beers (sourced nationally; often Indigenous, Loddon, Wild Weather Ales) Ⓗ
Traditional pub, owned by Brunning & Price, on the towpath of the Kennet & Avon Canal, two minutes' walk from Midgham train station. The pub has three main areas: the bar, a drinking space and a hidden room behind the real fire, with food served throughout. The Rowbarge is ideally placed for both walkers and cyclists to take a break from exploring the area. Close by are mooring spots for canal users.
Q❀◑♿⇌(Midgham)♣●P🚌(1,F20)🐾📶

Wraysbury

Perseverance ✔
2 High Street, TW19 5DB
12-11 (8 Sun) ☎ (01784) 482375 🌐 thepercy.co.uk
Otter Ale; 3 changing beers Ⓗ
Comfortable pub with several seating areas. The larger front room has soft sofas, a piano and a large inglenook fireplace, with a real log fire. Another seating area with an open fire leads to the rear dining area, which has well-stocked bookshelves. The rear garden is delightful. Three guest ales are always varied and from some of the more interesting breweries, both LocAle and around the country. Regular beer festivals are held. Quiz night is Thursday, steak night is Wednesday and live music on Sunday afternoon.
Q❀◑♣●P🚌(10,305)🐾📶

Yattendon

Taproom & Kitchen at West Berkshire Brewery 🄻
The Old Dairy, RG18 0XT
11-11 (6 Sun-Tue) ☎ (01635) 767090 🌐 wbbrew.com
West Berkshire Mr Chubb's Lunchtime Bitter, Maggs' Magnificent Mild, Good Old Boy, Mr Swift's Pale Ale, Tamesis Extra Stout, Dr Hexter's Healer; 1 changing beer (sourced locally; often West Berkshire) Ⓗ
This expansive taproom occupies the east side of the new brewery development. The family-, dog- and welly-friendly space hosts a monthly quiz, film nights, brewery tours and live screening of major international sporting events. Tryanuary and OctoberWest beer festivals add live music to the mix. The complete WBB range of cask beers, draught beers and lagers is usually available. An open kitchen offers explorations into food and beer matching across a range of freshly cooked dishes.
❀◑♿P🐾📶

Flower Pot, Aston (Photo: Andrew Bowden/Flickr CC BY-SA 2.0)

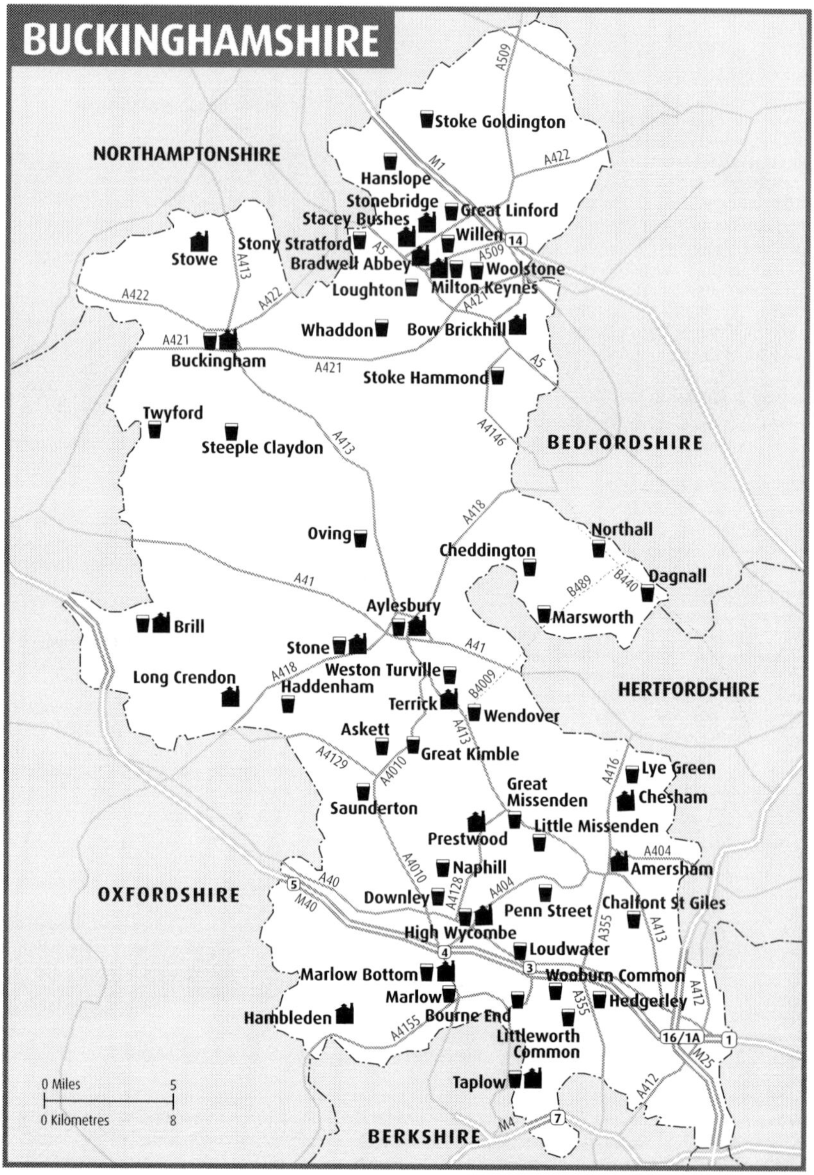

Askett

Stable Bar at the Three Crowns L

HP27 9LT (150yds W of A4010)

12-8.30 Mon & Tue (9.30 Wed & Thu; 10 Fri & Sat); 12-8 Sun ☎ (01844) 347166 thethreecrownsaskett.co.uk

Shepherd Neame Spitfire; 1 changing beer H

The Stable Bar is a welcome extension to its more food-oriented parent pub, the Three Crowns. Aimed at drinkers and arguably the area's first micropub, it is a cosy and welcoming conversion of the main pub's outbuilding. At the heart of the local community, the bar hosts events such as weekly film nights. It is easily accessible by public transport despite its location in a chocolate-box village in deepest Midsomer Murders country.
Q P (300)

Aylesbury

Bricklayers Arms

Walton Terrace, HP21 7QY

3.30-11 (midnight Fri); 12-midnight Sat; 12-11 Sun ☎ (01296) 482930 bricklayersarmsaylesbury.co.uk

Fuller's London Pride; 2 changing beers (sourced regionally) H

Originally part of the hamlet of Walton, this 17th-century pub is situated on a crossroads around the corner from Walton pond, once a centre for breeding the famous Aylesbury ducks. The pub has an attractive timber-beamed interior on several levels, with a function room at the rear. A large fire provides a warm welcome in winter; the sizeable enclosed beer garden at the back is a suntrap in summer. P

Hop Pole Inn 𝕃

83 Bicester Road, HP19 9AZ (near Gatehouse Industrial Area)

4.30-10.30 Mon; 12-2.30, 4.30-11 Tue-Thu; 12-midnight Fri & Sat; 12-10.30 Sun ☎ (01296) 482129

Vale Best IPA, Gravitas; 7 changing beers Ⓗ

Well worth a short stroll out of the town centre, this is Vale Brewery's flagship pub, complete with its own brewhouse. It regularly offers nine cask ales including three or four guests among the Vale and brewhouse beers. There is also a good range of mostly Belgian bottled beers. It hosts a long-running quiz on Tuesday and a ukulele night on the second and fourth Wednesday of each month. Occasional live music features at the weekend. ❀◑●🚌🐾📶

King's Head 𝕃

Market Square, HP20 2RW

11-11; 12-10.30 Sun ☎ (01296) 718812

🌐 farmersbar.co.uk

Chiltern Pale Ale, Beechwood Bitter; 2 changing beers Ⓗ

A National Trust pub run by the Chiltern Brewery for many years, the King's Head is the oldest courtyard inn in England, complete with cobbles and with the converted stables occupying one side. It has no TV or piped music. The bar has up to four Chiltern ales and a guest beer; often a stout or porter in winter. A cider is often stocked. A chalkboard notes current beers and those to come. The ales are often used in the pub's cooking and in its cheeses and chutneys. Q❀◑♿⇌●🚌📶

Old Millwrights Arms 𝕃 ✔

83 Walton Road, HP21 7SN

12-midnight (1am Sat); 12-11 Sun ☎ (01296) 488161

🌐 barrelandstone.co.uk

Greene King IPA; 8 changing beers Ⓗ

Vibrant community pub with much to interest all including an open mic night, comedy night, Dungeons & Dragons night and board games night. The Thursday quiz is well attended. A selection of up to nine real ales helps make the pub a popular venue. Food is served daily with pizzas a speciality. ❀◑⇌P🚌🐾

Bourne End

Black Lion 𝕃

Marlow Road, Well End, SL8 5PL

12-11 ☎ (01628) 520421

Butcombe Original; 4 changing beers (sourced locally; often Rebellion) Ⓗ

A cosy establishment with a real coal fire, this is the only pub in the area with a pool table. There is a small bar and the interior is split into three areas, one mainly for food. At least two ever-changing real ciders are served. The entrance to the car park is down the side of the pub and is not large but spaces are normally available. Q❀◑P

KEG Craft Beer Tasting Bar

12 Oakfield Road, SL8 5QN

11-9 (10 Fri; 11 Sat); 12-6 Sun ☎ (01628) 529369

🌐 kegcraftbeer.co.uk

2 changing beers

Opened in November 2016, this is a small, comfortable micropub with a warm welcome for all. Named KEG after its owner Kim E Georgiou, the bar offers two regularly changing cask ales, six craft keg beers and four or five real ciders. The music is from the owner's vast collection of vinyl records. Parking is available either in front of the shops or in a nearby car park. ⇌●🚌(36)🐾📶

Brill

Pheasant Inn 𝕃

39 Windmill Street, HP18 9TG

12-11 (midnight Fri & Sat) ☎ (01844) 239370

🌐 thepheasant.co.uk

Fuller's London Pride; Vale Brill Gold; 2 changing beers (sourced nationally) Ⓗ

Popular with walkers, this picturesque pub is in the village that was the inspiration for the fictional Bree in The Lord of the Rings. Refurbishment has opened up the interior to create a large, airy bar with plenty of seating. The outside dining area gives a spectacular view past Brill Windmill towards Oxford. Four rooms offer B&B accommodation. Q❀🛏◑♣●P🚌

Buckingham

Mitre

2 Mitre Street, MK18 1DW

5-11 (midnight Thu & Fri); 12-midnight Sat; 12-10.30 Sun ☎ (01280) 813080 🌐 themitrepub.co.uk

Harvey's Sussex Best Bitter; St Austell Trelawny; 3 changing beers (sourced nationally; often Kelham Island, North Cotswold, Thornbridge) Ⓗ

Buckingham's oldest pub is a 10-minute walk from the town centre. A free house, it offers changing and interesting beers, often featuring guests from local breweries. Attractions include darts and board games, plus books that can be borrowed from the shelves. The cosy atmosphere is enhanced by an open fire in winter. Five large-screen TVs show major events. The pub hosts wine and whisky tasting events, and live music once or twice monthly. ❀♣P🐾📶

Chalfont St Giles

Merlin's Cave

Village Green, HP8 4QF

12-11; 9am-11 Sat; 9am-10.30 Sun ☎ (01494) 871072

🌐 merlins-cave.com

REAL ALE BREWERIES

Abington Buckingham
Aylesbury ▮ Aylesbury
Bad Joke Amersham (NEW)
Blackened Sun Milton Keynes: Stacey Bushes
Blackpit Stowe
Brewhouse & Kitchen ▮ Milton Keynes
Bucks Star Milton Keynes: Stonebridge
Chiltern Terrick
Concrete Cow Milton Keynes: Bradwell Abbey
Fisher's High Wycombe
Haresfoot Chesham
Hillfire Aylesbury
Hornes Milton Keynes: Bow Brickhill
Malt Prestwood
moogBREW Taplow
Old Luxters Hambleden
Rebellion Marlow Bottom
Vale Brill
Willy's Brew ▮ Stone
XT Long Crendon

Bombardier Burning Gold; Eagle IPA; 2 changing beers (sourced nationally; often Adnams, St Austell) H

A Charles Wells pub, part of its Apostrophe Pubs group, in the heart of the village. This popular hostelry has been extended in recent years to cater for diners and drinkers, and features a large garden to the rear between the church and River Misbourne. Four draught beers are on offer, one from the Wandering Brewer, along with numerous bottled beers and excellent food. There is easy wheelchair access and a parking bay.
🏠🛏🏢🕮💷♿♣🚌(580,105)🐾🛜

Cheddington

Three Horseshoes ✓

13 Mentmore Road, LU7 0SD

☼ closed Mon; 12-11 (midnight Fri & Sat); 12-10.30 Sun

☎ (01296) 668367

Bombardier Pale Ale; Greene King IPA; Sharp's Doom Bar; 1 changing beer (sourced nationally) H

This friendly two-bar pub, over 200 years old, is popular with walkers and cyclists. The larger bar to the right has a step down and an open fireplace. The pub is the centre of village life, hosting a Sunday afternoon wine club and quarterly quiz night. Food is traditional pub grub, with an interesting menu. Friday is pizza night 7-9pm. Cheddington railway station is a 15-minute walk away. Q🏠🛏🕮P🚌(164)🐾🛜

Dagnall

Red Lion L ✓

21 Main Road, HP4 1QZ

☼ 12 (5 Mon)-11; 12-10.30 Sun ☎ (01442) 843020

⊕ theredliondagnall.co.uk

Greene King IPA; Sharp's Doom Bar; 2 changing beers (sourced locally) H

A warm welcome awaits at this cosy free house, offering well-kept beers and home-made food using fresh ingredients. A wood-burning stove and a rear dining room with paintings by local artists add to the homely atmosphere. A quiz night every second Monday and a Tuesday curry night (booking advised) are popular. Children are welcome, as are dogs in the bar. Whipsnade Zoo is three miles to the north east. 🏠🛏🕮♣P🐾🛜

Downley

De Spencer Arms

The Common, HP13 5YQ (across common from village on flint track beyond the end of Plomer Green Lane)

☼ 12-11 (midnight Fri & Sat); 11.30-10 Sun

☎ (01494) 535317 ⊕ ledespencersarms.co.uk

Fuller's London Pride, ESB; 2 changing beers (sourced nationally) H

The pub, named after the notorious 15th Baron le Despencer, whose family still owns the surrounding estate, is a busy, traditional village inn offering four real ales, good wines and home-cooked food. It is popular with walkers (dogs welcome too) and cyclists, and just a quarter of a mile by road or across the common from the village hall bus stop. Quiz nights, music nights, beer and food events add to the attraction of this cosy flint pub on Downley Common.
🏠🛏🕮♣P🚌🐾🛜

Great Kimble

Swan L

Lower Icknield Way, HP17 9TR

☼ 12-3, 5-11 (9 Mon & Tue; 10 Wed); 12-7 Sun

☎ (01844) 275288 ⊕ kimbleswan.co.uk

Tring Moongazing; 2 changing beers (sourced locally; often Hillfire, Tring) H

Situated in a village at the foot of the Chiltern Hills in excellent hiking, horse riding and cycling country, the Swan is a genuine, family-owned free house with a warm welcome. The building dates back to the 18th century and is reputedly haunted by a former landlady. Ales from local breweries such as Hillfire are championed by the pub. Good pub food is available, with Sunday lunchtimes particularly well attended. Late evening opening hours can vary, especially in winter.
🏠🛏🏢🕮💷♿♣P🚌(300)🐾🛜

Great Linford

Nag's Head ✓

30 High Street, MK14 5AX

☼ 12-11 (11.30 Fri & Sat) ☎ (01908) 607449

⊕ thenagsheadmk.co.uk

Greene King IPA; St Austell Tribute; Timothy Taylor Landlord; 1 changing beer H

A pretty thatched pub at the heart of Great Linford village, believed to date from the 16th century. Refurbished in 2018, it has two bars whose low ceilings and exposed beams give a cosy feel, especially in the saloon bar when the log-burning stove is lit. There is also a large rear courtyard. The pub holds a monthly quiz night and regular live music events. Close to Linford Manor Park and the Grand Union Canal, it is popular with ramblers and narrow-boaters. Q🏠🛏🕮♣🐾🛜

Great Missenden

Cross Keys ✓

40 High Street, HP16 0AU

☼ 11-11 (midnight Fri & Sat); 11-10.30 Sun

☎ (01494) 865373 ⊕ thecross-keys.com

Dark Star Hophead; Fuller's London Pride, ESB H /G; 1 changing beer (sourced regionally; often Fuller's) H

A wonderful 16th-century pub that has been sensitively refurbished in recent years, bringing the decor up to date while preserving the building's historic character. The interior is divided into two. To the right is the bar, with low-beamed ceilings and cosy tables grouped around an enormous wood-burning stove. The smart restaurant to the left offers an adventurous choice of high-quality cuisine. The well-kept ales come from the Fuller's range, including Dark Star and Gale's.
Q🏠🛏🕮♣P🚌(41)🐾🛜

Haddenham

Rising Sun ♟ L ✓

9 Thame Road, HP17 8EN

☼ 12-2.30, 5-11; 12-midnight Fri & Sat; 12-10.30 Sun

☎ (01844) 291744 ⊕ risingsunhaddenham.co.uk

XT Four; 5 changing beers (sourced locally) H

This bustling village pub boasts six real ales on handpump, with favourites from XT Brewing as well as unusual new Animal Brewing Co creations, plus a selection of guest ales, craft beers and ciders. With a newly landscaped garden and treats on tap for canine companions, this family and pooch-friendly pub blends the best of old and new seamlessly. Local CAMRA Pub of the Year 2019. Q (280)

Hanslope

Club

28 High Street, MK19 7LQ
12-2.30, 6-11 Mon; 6-11 Tue-Thu; 5-11 Fri; 12-11 Sat & Sun
(01908) 510337
Adnams Ghost Ship; Draught Bass; Shepherd Neame Bishops Finger; 1 changing beer H
The Club (formerly Hanslope Working Men's Club) welcomes non-members at all times for a nominal fee. Its two rooms, designated the Bar and the Lounge, serve three regular beers and a weekly changing guest ale. The Club offers a wide range of community activities including darts, skittles, pool, cards, quizzes and monthly bingo. It also hosts discos, film nights and children's events. A beer festival is held over the Easter weekend. Local CAMRA Club of the Year 2017. P

Cock Inn

35 High Street, MK19 7LQ
4-11; 12-11 Sat & Sun (01908) 510553
Great Oakley Wagtail; Greene King IPA; 1 changing beer (sourced regionally; often Great Oakley, Magpie) H
A local pub comprising one large, L-shaped room with a pool table, dartboard and large-screen TV at one end and a real fire at the other. The bar is directly in front of you as you enter and serves Greene King IPA, Great Oakley Wagtail and a guest ale. There is BT Sport on the TV, live music is staged once a month and the pub also hosts themed events including a Halloween fancy dress party. P

Hedgerley

White Horse L

Village Lane, SL2 3UY (in old village, near church)
11-2.30, 5-11; 11-11 Sat; 12-10.30 Sun (01753) 643225
thewhitehorsehedgerley.co.uk
Rebellion IPA; 7 changing beers (often Mallinsons, Mighty Oak, Oakham) G
Local CAMRA Pub of the Year on numerous occasions, this village pub offers an impressive range of real ales. New breweries often feature, as well as favourite beers from Oakham, Mallinsons and Mighty Oak. A draught Belgian beer and three real ciders are also available. This classic pub has a well-tended garden and the heated, covered patio area provides additional seating all year round. Regular beer festivals are held, the largest of which is over the Whitsun weekend and is a must for real ale enthusiasts. Q P

High Wycombe

Belle Vue

45 Gordon Road, HP13 6EQ
4.30-11; 3.30-midnight Fri; 12-1am Sat; 12-10.30 Sun
(01494) 524728 thebv.pub
Adnams Ghost Ship, Broadside; 4 changing beers H
A Guide regular with a community atmosphere, this friendly, traditional pub has an open fire in winter, five real ciders from Westons and hosts regular music events and occasional beer festivals. It is situated next to the railway line (take the north exit from the station). The name is a mystery as the only view from the pub is of the brick wall enclosing the railway. It was once the corner building of a terrace of workers' houses but they have now all gone.

Heidrun L

14 Paul's Row, HP11 2HQ
11-midnight (10.30 Sun) (01494) 449692
heidrun.bar
6 changing beers (sourced nationally) H
Craft beer bar in the centre of High Wycombe, convenient for the Eden shopping centre. The American-style bar is dominated by a long, stainless-steel counter in the shape of a horseshoe, with plentiful bar stools. Wooden booths are provided for more traditional drinking. Beers are listed on a printed menu and always feature a good selection of cask ales, many from interesting microbreweries. Food is served from a kitchen that can be viewed via an open window.

Mad Squirrel Brewery Shop Emporium

4-5 Church Street, HP11 2DE
11-9.30 (10 Fri & Sat); 11-9 Sun (01494) 395980
redsquirrelbrewery.co.uk
Mad Squirrel Mister Squirrel H**, London Porter** H/A**; 4 changing beers (sourced nationally)** A
The tasting bar and bottle shop opened in 2016 and has a downstairs bar with seating as well as more upstairs. At least two cask ales are offered alongside a range of craft keg beers, plus plenty of beers to take away. There is a walk-in chiller with a selection of real ale in a bottle plus cans, some of which are real ale in a can. You can enjoy a pizza with your favourite beer. P

Little Missenden

Crown Inn

HP7 0RD (off A413, between Amersham and Gt Missenden)
11-2.30, 6-11; 12-3 Sun (01494) 862571
thecrownlittlemissenden.co.uk
St Austell Tribute; 3 changing beers (sourced nationally; often Oakham, Otter, Rebellion) H
This lovely old village pub is a Guide regular and was a former local CAMRA Pub of the Year. Situated in the Chilterns Area of Outstanding Natural Beauty, it is ideally placed as a start or end point for a walk or cycle. The landlord is a real ale enthusiast and often rotates his beer, so it is a good idea to check if you are after a particular pint. Three en-suite rooms are available and there is a large garden behind the pub.
Q P (55)

Littleworth Common

Blackwood Arms

Common Lane, SL1 8PP SU937863
closed Mon; 12-11; 12-7.30 Sun (01753) 645672
theblackwoodarms.net
Brakspear Bitter, Oxford Gold; 4 changing beers (sourced locally) H
A delightful Victorian country pub brought back to life by an enthusiastic couple after a long period of closure. Close to Burnham Beeches nature reserve, it is popular with walkers and diners. An attractive garden with plenty of seating is a feature in summer, as is the roaring fire in winter. Four guest ales are offered, two from the Marston's group plus

two free of tie. Dog- and horse-friendly – hay can be provided. Cider is available in summer only.
Q❀☺🚫◑♣♦P🐾❀🛜

Jolly Woodman 🅛
Littleworth Road, SL1 8PF
🕙 11-10; 12-8 Sun ☎ (01753) 644350
🌐 thejollywoodman.com
Rebellion IPA; 5 changing beers 🅗
Attractive country pub close to the northern edge of Burnham Beeches. It has been fully refurbished by new management who already run two Guide-listed pubs. Rebellion IPA is augmented by five changing beers from LocAle and regional microbreweries. The spacious garden is popular in fine weather. A jazz evening is held on the first Monday in the month. The pub is dog- and horse-friendly. Q❀☺🚫◑P🐾🛜

Loudwater

Derehams Inn
5 Derehams Lane, HP10 9RH
🕙 11.30-3.30, 5.30-11; 11-midnight Fri & Sat; 12-11 Sun
☎ (01494) 530965 🌐 derehamsinn.co.uk
5 changing beers 🅗
A friendly local up a lane off the London Road, with a car park at the rear. Outside is a covered smoking area with a pool table and a garden space. An annual beer festival is held at the beginning of July. This is a traditional pub where families and dogs are welcome. Formerly known as the Bricklayers Arms, it has been run by the same couple for close to 20 years. Q☺◑P🚃🐾

General Havelock
114 Kingsmead Road, HP11 1HZ
🕙 12-3, 5-11.30; 12-11.30 Fri-Sun ☎ (01494) 520391
🌐 generalhavelock.co.uk
Fuller's London Pride, ESB; Gale's Seafarers Ale; 3 changing beers 🅗
The General Havelock was purchased by Fuller's in 1986 and has been run by the same family since then. It was originally farm buildings before conversion to a pub. The decor is an eclectic mix of antiques and bric-a-brac. Six ales are available at all times, mostly from Fuller's. TVs are brought out for England football matches and some other events. There is an open fire in the winter and the garden is a peaceful haven in the summer.
☺◑♣P🚃(35)🐾🛜

Loughton

Talbot ✅
33 London Road, MK5 8AB
🕙 11.30-11 (midnight Fri); 10-midnight Sat; 10-11 Sun
☎ (01908) 827296
Fuller's London Pride; Purity Pure UBU; Thornbridge Jaipur IPA; house beer (by Black Sheep); 7 changing beers 🅗
A large pub with a single bar and the room divided into several seating areas. The main bar area is for adults only but under-18s are welcome if dining. Monday is cask ale day, with all real ales £2.49 per pint. Wednesday is quiz night. Food is served all day every day, including brunch at the weekend. The large garden is popular in summer.
❀☺◑&♦P🚃(24,25)🛜

Lye Green

Black Cat
Lycrome Road, HP5 3LF (off A413)
🕙 11-2.30, 5-11 (7 Mon); 11-11 Sat; 12-10.30 Sun
☎ (01494) 773966 🌐 blackcatchesham.co.uk
Timothy Taylor Landlord; Young's Bitter; 1 changing beer (sourced nationally) 🅗
A warm and welcoming community pub with a log fire. A regular Guide entry, it serves well-kept beers and has been awarded Timothy Taylor's Champion Club status. Home-cooked food is on the menu at good-value prices, including breakfast (9am-noon Mon-Sat). The pub holds a weekly quiz night and hosts darts, cribbage and dominoes matches. There is an attractive fenced garden with children's games. ☺◑♣P🚃(105)🐾🛜

Marlow

Royal British Legion 🅛 ✅
Station Approach, SL7 1NT
🕙 7-11 (midnight Fri & Sat); 11-4 Sun ☎ (01628) 486659
🌐 rblmarlow.co.uk
Jennings Bitter; 5 changing beers 🅗
The Royal British Legion club, situated next to Marlow railway station, is a friendly venue holding two beer festivals a year. A wide range of cask ales is available. Although a private members' club, guests are welcome – show a copy of this Guide or a CAMRA membership card for entry. Various events are held including jazz and music nights. This venue has been a local CAMRA Club of the Year and regional Club of the Year for the past five years. ☺&🚆♣♦P🚃🛜

Marlow Bottom

Three Horseshoes 🅛 ✅
Burroughs Grove Hill, SL7 3RA
🕙 11.30-11; 12-6 Sun ☎ 0800 612 5564
🌐 3horseshoesmarlow.co.uk
Rebellion IPA, Smuggler, Zebedee; 1 changing beer (sourced locally) 🅗
Recently refurbished, this large open-plan pub is a short bus ride from both High Wycombe and Marlow. Popular with diners, the pub has an extensive specials board, open fires and a pleasant garden. Drinkers are welcome too, as are well-behaved children and dogs, and the close proximity of the Rebellion Beer Company means the six Rebellion ales on offer are always in great condition. Q❀☺🚫◑♦P🚃(800,850)🐾🛜

Marsworth

Red Lion 🅛 ✅
90 Vicarage Road, HP23 4LU (opp church)
🕙 11-3, 5-11; 11-11 Sat; 12-10.30 Sun ☎ (01296) 668366
🌐 redlionmarsworth.co.uk
Fuller's London Pride; Harvey's Sussex Best Bitter; 5 changing beers (sourced locally) 🅗
Genuine 17th-century village pub close to the Grand Union Canal. A central bar serves three areas: an upstairs lounge bar with comfortable sofas, a small snug, and a public bar with an open coal-burning fire. A separate games area hosts bar billiards, darts and shove-ha'penny. Five or more well-kept beers, some from local breweries, are on handpump and the kitchen serves generous portions of home-cooked food. There is a beautiful garden to the rear. Q❀☺🚫◑♣♦P🚃(164)🐾🛜

Milton Keynes

Brewhouse & Kitchen 🄻 ✔

7 Savoy Crescent, MK9 3PU

🕘 11-11 (1am Fri & Sat); 11-10.30 Sun ☎ (01908) 049032

Brewhouse & Kitchen 12th Street, Leaping Man, Webber's Vision, Colossus 🄷

Brewpub boasting a microbrewery in the round, and offering a good range of real ales, craft and other beers brewed on-site. Seating is available on several levels including a mezzanine floor and front terrace. Various private areas can be hired for weddings – the pub is a licensed marriage venue – and conferences, including a large top-floor room. Food is freshly cooked to order; each dish has a recommended beer to match. Events hosted include beer tastings and a day spent with the brewer. ❀◑♿P🚌🐾

Wetherspoons 🄻 ✔

201 Midsummer Boulevard, MK9 1EA

🕘 7am-midnight (1am Fri & Sat) ☎ (01908) 606074

Greene King Abbot; Ruddles Best Bitter; Sharp's Doom Bar; 9 changing beers (sourced nationally; often Concrete Cow, Hornes, Oakham) 🄷

A busy pub, popular with CAMRA members and unbeatable for its prices and range of cask ales. The 12 handpumps dispense several local beers; real ciders are also available. There is a large single-room bar with tables and chairs outside. A beer shop offers a wide range of canned and bottled craft ales. Food is from the usual Wetherspoon menu, served early morning until late evening. Local CAMRA Pub of the Year 2017.
🐴❀◑♿≋🍎P🚌📶

Naphill

Wheel ✔

100 Main Road, HP14 4QA

🕘 12 (4.30 Mon)-11; 12-10.30 Sun ☎ (01494) 562210

🌐 thewheelnaphill.com

Greene King IPA Reserve; Ruddles Best Bitter; 2 changing beers 🄷

Popular with locals and visitors alike, this traditional village local has a cosy atmosphere, with two bar areas, one of which leads to the dining space. There is a large garden which is ideal on summer days. A warm welcome is extended to all – including ramblers in muddy boots enjoying the nearby walks. This pub has been in the Guide for a number of years and prides itself on serving good cask ale. Q❀🛏◑♣P🚌🐾📶

Northall

Swan

Leighton Road, LU6 2EY

🕘 12-midnight ☎ (01525) 220444

Fuller's London Pride; Greene King Abbot; Sharp's Doom Bar; Timothy Taylor Landlord; 1 changing beer (sourced nationally) 🄷

The only pub in the village, this old wayside building features beamed ceilings, two bars and multiple seating areas, including a restaurant and games room. Outside is a children's play area and a patio that catches the sun in fine weather. An extensive menu helps make the Swan as renowned for its food as for its beer. Entertainment includes quiz night every other Monday, open mic night on the first Sunday of the month, and occasional beer festivals.
Q🐴❀◑♣P🚌(162)🐾📶

Oving

Black Boy 🄻

Church Lane, HP22 4HN

🕘 12-11 (6 Sun) ☎ (01296) 641258

🌐 theblackboyoving.co.uk

XT Four; 3 changing beers (sourced locally; often Chiltern, Leighton Buzzard, XT) 🄷

Delightful 17th-century inn with a roaring fire in winter. Summer visits are also a treat, with wonderful views across the local countryside from the huge beer garden. The restaurant opposite the bar is separated from the drinking area by a wooden mesh around the archway. The drinking areas offer flagstone floors and wooden beams. With good food, friendly staff and a great atmosphere, this is a cosy pub and a pleasure to visit. 🐴❀◑🍎P🐾📶

Penn Street

Squirrel 🄻 ✔

HP7 0PX

🕘 12 (4 Mon)-11; 12-1am Fri; 12-10.30 Sun

☎ (01494) 711291 🌐 thesquirrelpub.co.uk

5 changing beers (sourced locally; often Rebellion, Tring, Vale) 🄷

A delightful pub by the village green where the local cricket team plays. Three to five real ales are available plus a cider. Good food is on offer and families are welcome, with a fenced garden and play equipment outside. There is also an outdoor decked heated area with comfy chairs. Inside, logburners warm the bar and comfortable seating spaces. Themed quiz nights with food are held monthly on a Monday, and live music on Friday evening. 🐴❀◑♣🍎P🚌(1)🐾📶

Saunderton

Golden Cross

Wycombe Road, HP14 4HU

🕘 12-11 ☎ (01494) 565974 🌐 goldencrosspub.co.uk

Greene King IPA; 2 changing beers (sourced nationally) 🄷

A family pub, popular for food as well as real ale, that has won awards both locally and nationally. It offers one regular beer, Greene King IPA, plus two changing national ales, along with a selection of bottled beers and ciders. The large enclosed garden features a marquee and children's play area.
🐴❀◑≋♣P🚌(X30)🐾📶

Steeple Claydon

Fountain

10 West Street, MK18 2NT

🕘 4-11; 11-1, 4-12.30am Fri; 12-12.30am Sat; 12-10 Sun

☎ (01296) 730286

Fuller's London Pride; St Austell Tribute; 2 changing beers (sourced regionally; often Fuller's) 🄷

A free house that is divided into two areas – a main bar with flat-screen TV and a games bar featuring a dartboard and pool table. The busy Fountain gives active support to charities and the local community. It has car parking at the front, and a garden with a covered smoking area to the side. Food is not sold in the pub but a popular fish and chips van visits on Saturday evening.
🐴❀♣P🚌(16,18)🐾

Stoke Goldington

Lamb 🏆 L

16-20 High Street, MK16 8NR

12 (5 Mon)-11; 12-7 Sun ☎ (01908) 551233

thelambatstokegoldington.co.uk

Tring Brock Bitter, Death or Glory; 2 changing beers (sourced regionally) H

Located in a peaceful village midway between Milton Keynes and Northampton on the B526, the Lamb features an intimate bar, a large separate restaurant and a less formal dining room. It has a dartboard and a Northamptonshire skittles table. The pub serves home-cooked food, including award-winning pies, using local seasonal produce. The large garden has a stage for music events. There is ample parking and walking groups are encouraged to park early and order food before their walk to enjoy on their return. Two en-suite bedrooms are available. Local CAMRA Pub of the Year 2019. Q P (37)

Stoke Hammond

Three Locks L

Leighton Road, MK17 9DD

11.30-11; 9am-11 Sat & Sun ☎ (01525) 270214

thethreelocksstokehammond.com

5 changing beers (sourced regionally; often Hornes, Leighton Buzzard, Tring) H

Canalside pub that supports local breweries. Usually three or four changing beers are local, as is some of the cider, with other ciders coming from traditional producers elsewhere. There is a beer festival over the May bank holiday weekend, live music every Friday, and monthly themed nights. The pub is particularly popular in summer, with customers arriving by road and by narrowboat. A 10% food discount is offered to card-carrying Inland Waterways Association members. There is plenty of outdoor seating alongside the lock. P (70)

Stone

Rose & Crown L

2 Oxford Road, HP17 8PB (on Oxford Rd at jct with Upper Hartwell)

12-11; 11-9.30 Sun ☎ (01296) 749160

roseandcrownstone.co.uk

2 changing beers (sourced locally) H

A recent refurbishment has given the pub a stylish feel. The Willy's Brew microbrewery has been installed at the rear and provides all the ales on offer. Food includes home-made traditional pub classics alongside Jamaican dishes made to the landlady's family recipes. The Sunday carvery and seniors' menu on weekday lunchtimes are popular. There is a lovely beer garden area to the rear. P (280,110)

Stony Stratford

Fox & Hounds ✔

87 High Street, MK11 1AT

11-11 (12.30am Sat); 12-11 Sun ☎ (01908) 260604

Fuller's London Pride; Hawkshead Bitter; Purity Mad Goose; St Austell Tribute; Sharp's Doom Bar H

The Fox & Hounds has two bars, one quiet and one with regular live bands and music plus sports TV, a dartboard and Northamptonshire skittles table. There is also a separate restaurant. The pub has women's and men's darts teams and a mixed skittles team. Outside is a garden with wooden tables and benches plus two Scandinavian-style partially open cabins, one with a log fire, where smoking is permitted. The car park is beyond the garden and accessed from Prospect Road. P

Taplow

Oak & Saw L

Rectory Road, SL6 0ET

4.30-10 Mon; 12-11; 12-midnight Fri ☎ (01628) 604074

oakandsaw.co.uk

Fuller's Oliver's Island; Rebellion IPA, Monthly Special H

Opposite the village green and church in an idyllic setting, this pub offers good pub food and three real ales, including the Rebellion monthly. The food is home made and features local produce. The meat, including venison, comes from a farm and butchery just 20 miles away. The large decked patio is great for summer and includes a covered smoking area. Dogs are allowed in non-dining areas. Q P

Twyford

Crown Inn

The Square, MK18 4EG

12-2.30, 4-11; 12-midnight Fri-Sun ☎ (01296) 730216

thecrowntwyford.co.uk

Sharp's Doom Bar; 1 changing beer H

This freehold inn is central to the life of the village. The landlady has seen the other local pubs decline and close, and has increased opening hours and food provision with the help of her family. The Crown is a deceptively large brick building opposite the village hall. A spacious bar area leads to an even larger lounge/function area on the left. Serving one frequently changing beer from the barrel, it is usual to have seven different beers on during the week. (16)

Wendover

King & Queen ✔

17 South Street, HP22 6EF

11 (3 Mon)-11; 11-midnight Fri & Sat; 12-11 Sun ☎ (01296) 696872 thekingandqueen.squarespace.com

Young's Special; 3 changing beers H

The pub is situated just off the High Street within easy reach of the station. It has three rooms, one a restaurant serving good food. The interior has been refurbished without losing its ambience and there is an impressive wall map of the local countryside in one room. A wood fire helps to provide a warm winter welcome for walkers returning from the nearby Chiltern Hills. Q P

Pack Horse

29 Tring Road, HP22 6NR

12-11 (midnight Fri & Sat) ☎ (01296) 622075

Fuller's London Pride; 2 changing beers (often Fuller's) H

A small, friendly village inn serving a varied range of beers from the Fuller's portfolio. The building dates from 1769 and is on the Ridgeway path, at the end of a terrace of thatched cottages named after Anne Boleyn, said to have been a gift from Henry VIII to Anne. The pub has been owned for more than 50 years by the family that also runs the

White Swan, another Fuller's pub in the village that deserves a visit. The Pack Horse has connections with nearby RAF Halton. ≷♣🚌

Weston Turville

Chandos Arms ✔

1 Main Street, HP22 5RR

12-11 (midnight Fri & Sat); 12-10.30 Sun

☎ (01296) 613532 thechandosarms.co.uk

Eagle IPA; 2 changing beers H

A friendly Charles Wells pub in the heart of a village just outside Aylesbury. It offers something for all the family, including freshly cooked food, and is noted for being dog-friendly. The pleasantly decorated interior contains a public bar and relaxing lounge. Outside to the front is a large beer garden. ❀◑P🚌🐾

Whaddon

New Lowndes Arms L

4 High Street, MK17 0NA

closed Mon; 5-10 Tue; 12-10 Wed & Thu (midnight Fri & Sat); 12-6 Sun ☎ (01908) 508373

thenewlowndesarms.co.uk

Adnams Ghost Ship; St Austell Tribute; 2 changing beers (sourced locally; often Hornes, Tring) H

Reopened in March 2017 after a long closure, this village pub has a single-room bar split into two areas, with additional restaurant seating and a marquee at the back. Two of the four cask beers are usually local. Wednesday is quiz night. This dog-friendly pub is popular with walkers at weekends. There is a small car park at rear. The large garden has panoramic views of the countryside bordering the western edge of Milton Keynes. Accommodation is in 10 en-suite rooms in converted outbuildings. Q❀🛏◑♣P🐾

Willen

Ship Ashore ✔

Granville Square, MK15 9JL

11.30-11 (midnight Fri); 10-midnight Sat; 10-11 Sun

☎ (01908) 694360

House beer (by Black Sheep); 4 changing beers H

A smart, modern pub on a residential estate not far from Willen Lake and its recreational facilities. The pub comprises one large bar but pillars and half walls break up the area to give a more intimate feel. Real ales include the Black Sheep-brewed house beer plus three changing beers. On Monday all real ales are £2.49 per pint. Food is served all day and includes dedicated vegetarian/vegan menus. Attractions include weekly quizzes, a small garden and ample parking. ❀◑♿●P🚌(2)🐾

Wooburn Common

Royal Standard L

Wooburn Common Lane, HP10 0JS (follow signs to Odds Farm)

12-11 (10.30 Sun) ☎ (01628) 521121

theroyalstandard.biz

Hop Back Summer Lightning H**; St Austell Tribute** G**; 7 changing beers** H

A regular in the Guide, this is a traditional rural pub, convenient for Odds Farm Park. Its changing guest ales include one dark beer of a higher ABV. Up to eight real ciders are also usually available. Dogs and families are welcome and it is a popular stopping-off point for walkers. There is ample parking in the car park at the side of the pub. Well worth seeking out. Q❀◑♿●P🐾

Woolstone

Cross Keys

34 Newport Road, MK15 0AA

11-11 ☎ (01908) 528145 crosskeysmiltonkeynes.co.uk

Courage Directors; Young's Bitter; 4 changing beers (sourced nationally; often St Austell, Wadworth) H

Set in a period building with a thatched roof, this pub is close to the Grand Union Canal and local parkland, so is popular with walkers. It comprises a bar and separate restaurant, refurbished in 2018. The home-made food uses fresh local produce and is served all day. A large-screen TV in the bar shows terrestrial channels with subtitles. A quiz is held on Tuesday. The patio and garden to the rear are attractions in summer. Q❀◑♿P🚌(18)🐾

Merlin's Cave, Chalfont St Giles (Photo: David Short/Flickr CC BY 2.0)

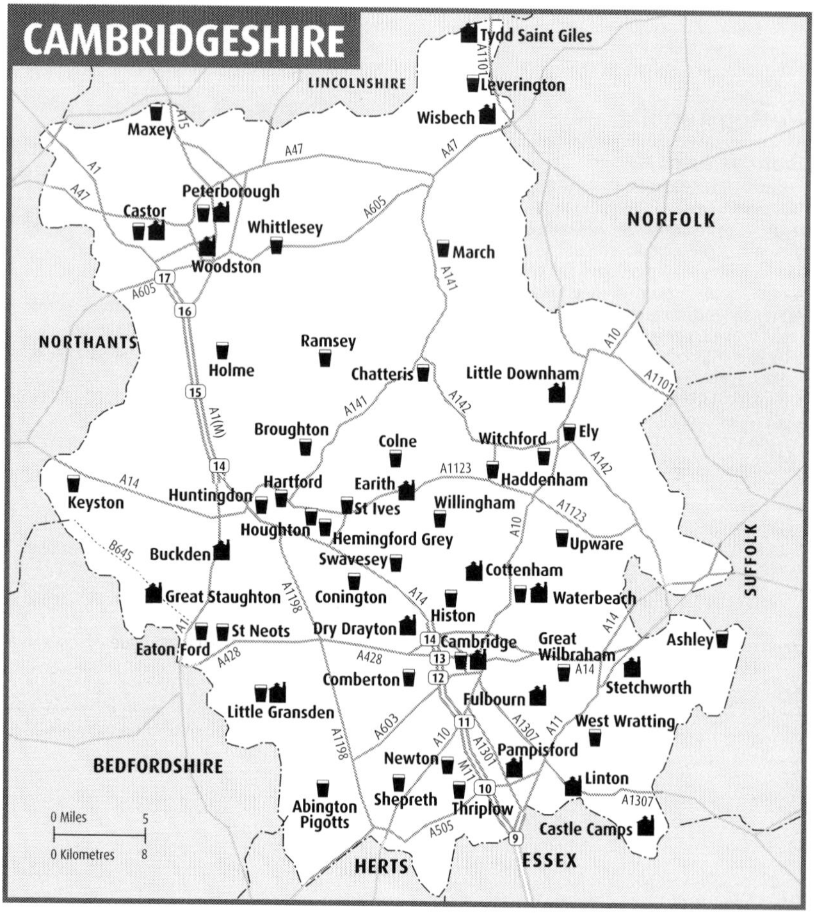

Abington Pigotts

Pig & Abbot

High Street, SG8 0SD (off A505 through Litlington)
12-3, 6-11; 12-11 Sat; 12-10.30 Sun ☎ (01763) 853515
pigandabbot.co.uk
Adnams Southwold Bitter; Fuller's London Pride; 2 changing beers (often Mighty Oak, Oakham, Woodforde's) [H]

Located in a surprisingly remote part of the south Cambridgeshire countryside, this Queen Anne-period pub offers a warm welcome. The interior has exposed oak beams and a large inglenook featuring a wood-burning stove. A comfortable restaurant serves home-made traditional pub food and specialises in fresh fish and chips, steak and kidney puddings, and pies. Two guest beers are stocked, often from Burton Bridge, Humpty Dumpty, Mighty Oak, Timothy Taylor or Woodforde's. A former CAMRA branch Pub of the Year. Q♣P

Ashley

Crown Inn

24 Newmarket Road, CB8 9DR
3-11 (9 Mon); 12-11 Sat; 12-10 Sun ☎ (01638) 730117
thecrowninnashley.co.uk
Mighty Oak Captain Bob; 3 changing beers [H]

This family- and dog-friendly community hub was first recorded as an inn in 1712, though parts of the imposing building are earlier. A former Greene King

REAL ALE BREWERIES

Bexar County Peterborough
Calverley's Cambridge
Cambridge Cambridge
Castor Castor
Crafty Beers Stetchworth
Downham Isle Little Downham
Draycott Buckden
Elgood's Wisbech
Fellows Cottenham
Lord Conrad's Dry Drayton
Mile Tree Peterborough
Milton Waterbeach
Moonshine Fulbourn
Oakham Peterborough
Papworth Earith
Rocket Great Staughton
Roughacre Castle Camps (NEW)
Son of Sid Little Gransden
Three Blind Mice Little Downham
Turpin's Pampisford
Tydd Steam Tydd Saint Giles
Wylde Sky Linton (NEW)
Xtreme Peterborough: Woodston

pub, the Crown became free of tie in 2014. It has a bright bar area with a cosy back room. Real ciders, direct from the box, are stocked. Pub games include darts, pool and, in the enclosed rear garden, pétanque. P

Broughton

Crown Inn

Bridge Road, PE28 3AY

closed Mon; 11.30-3, 6.30-11; 11.30-6 Sun
(01487) 824428 thecrowninnrestaurant.co.uk

3 changing beers (sourced locally) [H]

An idyllic 19th-century pub opposite the village church. The decor is modern yet comfortable with scrubbed pine tables and a stone floor. There is a separate area for private use. Three changing beers are offered, always from small, often local, breweries. Gastro-pub food is served, with seasonally changing menus. There is a large beer garden where a beer festival is held in May.
Q P

Cambridge

Alexandra Arms

22 Gwydir Street, CB1 2LL (300yds from Mill Rd)

12-11.30 (midnight Fri & Sat); 12-11 Sun
(01223) 324441 thealexcambridge.com

7 changing beers [H]

Refurbished in 2014 in a modern kitchen style, the pub has three distinct areas on two levels with wooden flooring and plenty of tables. The attractive enclosed garden has a newly built garden room. A Greene King Local Hero pub, it is mainly free of tie, with guest ales frequently from Oakham alongside the Greene King beers. Food is home made and includes burgers, with bread from a local bakery. Local CAMRA Most Dog-Friendly Pub 2018.

Calverley's Brewery Tap

23A Hooper Street, CB1 2NZ

5-10.30 Thu & Fri; 11-10.30 Sat; closed Sun-Wed
07769 537342 calverleys.com

Calverley's Porter [G]

Close to Mill Road, the brewery was established in a former stable in 2013. It is open for on-sales on Thursday and Friday evenings and all day Saturday. Up to two beers are served direct from the cask plus others from kegs. The bar is in the same room as the brewing equipment, with tables in a side room and more outside, plus additional seating in one of the outbuildings. Gourmet food vans provide snacks at all sessions. Local CAMRA Young Members Pub of the Year 2019. Q

Cambridge Blue

85-87 Gwydir Street, CB1 2LG

12-11; 11-11 Sat; 12-10.30 Sun (01223) 471680
cambridge.pub/the-blue

Changing beers [H]/[G]

Ever popular side-street pub close to Mill Road. A large rear extension leads to its garden, which frequently contains a marquee. Breweriana and pumpclips provide much of the decoration. Up to 14 ales from microbreweries nationwide are dispensed by handpump or by gravity from the tap room, often including Animal beers. Up to seven real ciders and perries and a large selection of international bottled beers are also kept. The main beer festival is held in June.

Champion of the Thames

68 King Street, CB1 1LN

12-11 (01223) 351464
thechampionofthethames.com

Greene King IPA, Abbot; 3 changing beers [H]

Small, two-room city-centre pub with a welcoming atmosphere; the chatter of customers predominates. Wood-panelled with fixed benches and a part-glazed partition between the rooms, it is one of the four remaining pubs on the King Street Run pub crawl, which involved a pint in each of the eight pubs. The oarsman of the name is commemorated in the etched windows and the pub is identified by CAMRA as having a regionally important historic interior. Pub snacks are available. Local CAMRA City Community Pub of the Year 2018.

Elm Tree

16A Orchard Street, CB1 1JT

11-11; 12-10.30 Sun (01223) 502632
theelmtreecambridge.co.uk

7 changing beers (sourced nationally; often B&T) [H]

Back-street pub close to Parker's Piece, decorated with breweriana, quirky bric-a-brac, photos and Belgian flags. The short bar is near the entrance with seating around and beyond. Jointly owned by B&T and Wells, they have three handpumps each. Six other pumps offer changing guest ales. A real cider or perry is also served. Complementing these is a menu of around 100 bottled Belgian beers – the landlord has written a book on the subject and is happy to advise. Regular live music features.
(PR3,X5)

Flying Pig

106 Hills Road, CB2 1LQ

12-11 (midnight Fri); 7-11 Sat & Sun (01223) 354623
theflyingpigpub.wordpress.com

Crouch Vale Brewers Gold; Rudgate Ruby Mild; 4 changing beers [H]

Much-loved, cosy and friendly pub with a local feel that defies its main road location. A beer and music venue, its walls and ceiling are adorned with an eclectic collection of old posters and pig paraphernalia. In the evenings the intimate lighting is enhanced by candles. Ales usually include some from local breweries, and craft keg beers are also available. Basic pub grub is served weekday lunchtimes only. Live music plays on Tuesday, Thursday, Saturday and some Fridays. The pub hosts an annual Pigfest charity music festival.

Free Press

7 Prospect Row, CB1 1DU

12-11 (midnight Fri & Sat) (01223) 368337
freepresscambridge.com

Greene King XX Mild, IPA, Abbot; 4 changing beers (often Greene King) [H]

Close to Parker's Piece, this intimate, friendly pub serves high-quality food and great beer. Greene King-tied, the rare XX Mild is a regular, alongside three guest ales. A pub for over 120 years, it just avoided the 1970s Kite area redevelopment, and is identified by CAMRA as having a regionally important historic pub interior. Only the tiny snug is original – the rest is a loving reconstruction. There is a walled garden at the rear. Named after a Temperance movement newspaper that lasted for just one edition. Q

Geldart ✔

1 Ainsworth Street, CB1 2PF (off Mill Rd)
⏲ closed Mon; 5-11 (1am Fri); 12-1am Sat; 12-midnight Sun
☎ (01223) 314264 🌐 the-geldart.co.uk
Adnams Ghost Ship; Caledonian Deuchars IPA; Oakham Citra; St Austell Tribute; 4 changing beers (sourced nationally) Ⓗ
Large two-bar back-street corner pub with an enclosed patio garden behind. It is decorated throughout with film and music memorabilia. The pub has a good reputation for its home-made food – including 'hot rocks' – and its beers, with a restaurant area to the right of the entrance and a bar area to the left. Eight ales and a wide selection of malt whiskies and rums are available. The changing guest beers always include a dark one. Frequent live music is hosted. 🐴❀◐🐾📶

Haymakers 𝕃

54 High Street, CB4 1NG
⏲ 12-11 (midnight Fri & Sat); 12-10.30 Sun
☎ (01223) 311077
Milton Pegasus; 7 changing beers (often Milton) Ⓗ
Milton Brewery's second of three Cambridge pubs, popular with locals and employees from the nearby science park. There are drinking areas either side of the door and a snug with its own bar access. Dark wood and warm colours abound. A good-sized beer garden is to the rear. The car park contains the largest pub cycle park in Cambridge. Eight real ales, including one dark and three guests, are on offer plus four real ciders or perries and Moravka unpasteurised lager. Local CAMRA City LocAle Pub of the Year 2019. 🐴❀◐♣🍎P🚌🐾📶

Kingston Arms ✔

33 Kingston Street, CB1 2NU
⏲ 12-3, 5-11 Mon; 5-11 Tue-Thu; 12-midnight Fri; 11-midnight Sat; 12-11 Sun ☎ (01223) 319414
Crouch Vale Brewers Gold; Hop Back Summer Lightning; Mighty Oak Oscar Wilde; Oakham JHB; Thornbridge Jaipur IPA; Woodforde's Wherry; 4 changing beers Ⓗ
A classic, cosy, side-street pub close to Mill Road that is equally popular with drinkers and diners. Windows and mirrors keep the interior light and welcoming. Its rear walled garden, complete with canopies and heaters, is popular all year round. Twelve handpumps offer regular and changing beers, usually two dark ales, as well as two changing ciders or perries. A selection of Belgian and other bottled beers is stocked. Home-cooked food is available at all sessions including Saturday breakfast. Q🐴❀◐⇌♣🍎🚌🐾📶

Live & Let Live

40 Mawson Road, CB1 2EA
⏲ 11.30-2.30 (not Wed & Thu), 5.30-11; 11.30-2.30, 6-11 Sat; 12-2.30, 7-11 Sun ☎ (01223) 460261
Nethergate Umbel Ale; Oakham Citra; 3 changing beers Ⓗ
A discreet corner local, just off Mill Road, with roadside cycle parking. It has a simply furnished single bar and a small snug to the rear. Wood panelling plus railway and beer memorabilia add to a yesteryear atmosphere. It is a pub for contemplation, conversation and ale and cider consumption. Five beers cover a range of styles and strengths, alongside three changing ciders or perries. Rum festivals feature twice a year. Local CAMRA Dark Beer Pub of the Year 2019. Q⇌♣🍎🚌🐾

Maypole 𝕃

20A Portugal Place, CB5 8AF
⏲ 11.30-midnight (1am Fri & Sat); 12-11.30 Sun
☎ (01223) 352999 🌐 maypolefreehouse.co.uk
Changing beers Ⓗ
The Maypole has been in the capable hands of the Castiglione family since 1982, initially as tenants, latterly as owners. Showcasing quality beers won the landlord the branch's first Real Ale Champion award. Up to 16 ever-changing beers are kept, more during festivals, including LocAles, with micros predominating. The keg beers include several of interest. It has a busy front bar, quieter back bar downstairs, function room upstairs and a large covered patio. Food focuses on home-cooked Italian dishes and English pub classics. Local CAMRA Pub of the Year 2018. ❀◐♿🍎🚌📶

Mill 𝕃 ✔

14 Mill Lane, CB2 1RX
⏲ 11-11 (midnight Thu-Sat) ☎ (01223) 311829
🌐 themillpubcambridge.co.uk
7 changing beers (sourced locally; often Cambridge Brew House) Ⓗ
Set in a honeypot riverside location across from Laundress Green, the building was refurbished and reopened in 2012 – improvements include an attractive wood-panelled side room. A vintage radiogram plays vinyl records. The curved wooden bar has eight handpumps, including one for cider. The beer range shows a strong commitment to local ales, including those brewed at sister pub the Cambridge Brew House. Tasty food is made with locally sourced ingredients. Local CAMRA Young Members Pub of the Year 2018. 🐴◐🍎🐾📶

Old Ticket Office 𝕃 ✔

Station Square, CB1 2JW
⏲ 12-11 Mon-Wed (midnight Thu & Fri); 10-midnight Sat; 10-11 Sun ☎ (01223) 859017 🌐 oldticketoffice.com
5 changing beers (sourced regionally; often Adnams, Cambridge Brew House) Ⓗ
Cambridge's newest pub (opened June 2018) is housed in part of the train station complex, with tables outside on Station Square. Its attractive interior, painted in GNER green, gives it the feel of a traditional station bar despite it only recently becoming one. There are five handpumps and a range of taps. Ales include those brewed by the Cambridge Brewing Company at its sister pub the Cambridge Brew House, plus others from regional small breweries. Local CAMRA New/Most Improved Pub of the Year 2019. ◐♿⇌🚌🐾📶

Castor

Prince of Wales Feathers 𝕃

38 Peterborough Road, PE5 7AL
⏲ 12-11 (1am Fri & Sat); 12-midnight Sun
☎ (01733) 380222 🌐 princeofwalesfeathers.co.uk
Adnams Broadside; Castor Ales Hopping Toad Ⓗ**; 3 changing beers** Ⓗ/Ⓖ
This village corner pub is about 300 years old and built of stone with stained-glass windows, with two patios. Originally a boot and shoe shop, the pub has one main bar area, divided into two by the fire. There are two smaller rooms for pool and darts; dominoes and crib are also played. Four real ales are usually served. Entertainment includes Sky Sports, plus live music every Saturday. Away football fans visiting Peterborough are warmly welcomed. 🐴❀◐♣🍎▯🚌🐾📶

Chatteris

Ship ✔

34 Bridge Street, PE16 6RN

5-11; 4-11 Fri; 1-11 Sat; 12-11 Sun ☎ 07880 326263

Belhaven 80/- Ale; Timothy Taylor Landlord; 2 changing beers H

A community free house dating from the 1850s. The main bar area is a single L-shaped room, with a separate back room featuring a pool table. There are plans for a new rear extension. Of the four real ales on handpump, one is always a little out of the ordinary and one is a dark beer. A quiz is held once a month. The pub supports two charities, Macmillan and the Stroke Association, plus a local cricket team. Q♣P (33)

Colne

Green Man L

1 East Street, PE28 3LZ

12-2.30 (not Mon), 5-11; 12-11 Fri-Sun ☎ (01487) 840368

greenmancolne.co.uk

Adnams Ghost Ship; Milton Justinian; Papworth Half Nelson; 1 changing beer (sourced regionally) H

A picturesque, 17th-century village local in an old Fenland fruit-growing area. The corrugated roof covers an original thatch. This busy, friendly pub provides a public bar with pool, darts and TV, plus a warm, sociable lounge with a modern dining extension serving good food. A quiz night is held fortnightly. The garden has a children's play area and hosts barbecues in summer. Camping is available nearby at Earith Lakes.

♣P (21,22)

Comberton

Three Horseshoes

22 South Street, CB23 7DZ

closed Mon; 12-2.30, 5.30-11 (midnight Fri); 12-midnight Sat; 12-11 Sun ☎ (01223) 262252

Adnams Lighthouse; Greene King IPA; 3 changing beers H

Hanging baskets adorn this red-roofed village pub. Popular with local clubs and societies, it sponsors football and cricket teams. Historical photographs of the village and its sports players adorn the walls. The long, low-ceilinged main bar has a cosy alcove at one end and a small raised area at the other, with a games room off to the left. The brick-fronted bar takes up much of the central section. An extensive garden features children's play equipment. ♣P (18)

Conington

White Swan

Elsworth Road, CB23 4LN

12-11; 12-10.30 Sun ☎ (01954) 267251

thewhiteswanconington.co.uk

Adnams Southwold Bitter, Ghost Ship; 1 changing beer G

Sturdy 18th-century brick building fronted by an impressive sward for outside drinking. The main bar has a tiled floor and a brick fireplace occupied by a fine cast-iron stove. The former cellar is now in use again, with the real ales served by gravity from behind the new low (wheelchair-friendly) bar. Freshly cooked food offers quality and value (no meals Sun eve). Purchased from Greene King in 2013 by a village resident. Q♣P

Eaton Ford

Barley Mow ✔

27 Crosshall Road, PE19 7AB

11.30-11 (midnight Thu-Sat); 12-11 Sun

☎ (01480) 474435

Greene King IPA, Abbot; 2 changing beers H

Simple one-bar community pub with a wide variety of activities focused on the regulars, plus live music events and seasonal celebrations. The decor is a mix of plaster, brick and wood panelling, and a long service counter dominates the centre of the bar. Images of past pub social events adorn the walls, some dating back to the early part of the last century. There is a large beer garden with an extensive children's play area. ♣P (X5)

Ely

3At3 Real Ale & Craft Beer Café

3 Three Cups Walk, CB7 4AN

9am-5 (10 Fri & Sat); 9am-4 Sun ☎ (01353) 659916

3at3craftbeer.co.uk

6 changing beers (sourced locally) H

The 3At3 is in a small passageway off the top end of Fore Hill. The terraced café offers six regularly changing draught craft beers, local ciders and wines paired with a rustic sharing menu. The bottle shop stocks over 150 different bottled real ales from local microbreweries as well as local ciders and wines from the nearby Elysian Fields Vineyard. Brewery tap takeovers and Meet the Brewer sessions feature regularly.

Drayman's Son L

29A Forehill, CB7 4AA

5-10.30 Mon-Wed; 11-11 Thu-Sat; 12-10.30 Sun

☎ (01353) 662920

10 changing beers (sourced nationally; often Three Blind Mice) G

Small micropub nostalgically themed with old signs, posters and music scores. Ten real ales are usually served, mostly sourced from nearby micro and small breweries. More than 20 often local ciders are also available. The pub supports local producers including Ely Gin. The cellar is in a temperature-controlled back room and drinks are delivered to your table. Quiz nights and music nights are regular events. ♣

Great Wilbraham

Carpenters Arms L

10 High Street, CB21 5JD

closed Mon & Tue; 11.30-3, 6.30-11; 11.30-3 Sun

☎ (01223) 882093 carpentersarmsgastropub.co.uk

Crafty Beers Carpenter's Cask; 2 changing beers (often Crafty Beers) H

The rustic public bar to the right offers up to three real ales, mostly from Crafty Beers, and occasional guest ales. Crafty Beers originated in the rear stables before moving to larger premises in Stetchworth in 2016. The dining room offers both traditional pub food and a menu reflecting the owners' previous experience running an award-winning restaurant in France. Parts of the building date back to the 17th century. The bar billiards table is in regular use. Local CAMRA Rural LocAle Pub of the Year 2018. ♣P

Haddenham

Three Kings 🄻 ✓

1 Station Road, CB6 3XD
11-11; 11.30-10 Sun ☎ (01353) 749080
threekingsely.co.uk
Greene King IPA; 2 changing beers (sourced nationally) Ⓗ
This 17th-century building has been updated over time but retains its rustic framework and charm with plenty of exposed old beams, cosy spaces and an inglenook fireplace. While this village pub focuses on fine food, it is also keen to promote high-quality ales and cider and is well supported by local drinkers. At the rear is a relaxing courtyard drinking area and a large car park.
Q❀◐♿●P

Hartford

King of the Belgians 🄻

27 Main Street, PE29 1XU (on old village high street)
11-11 (midnight Fri & Sat); 12-10.30 Sun
☎ (01480) 52030 kingofthebelgians.com
4 changing beers (sourced locally; often Digfield, Elgood's, Nene Valley)
This 16th-century pub at the heart of the community actively supports local charities. It hosts a beer festival in May and another in late August. An ever-changing selection of four real ales, ciders and good-value food is served every day. The public bar is characterised by its low oak beams and a copper-topped bar, and there is a peaceful separate dining area. Entertainment includes regular quizzes, games nights and an open mic night on the first Monday of each month.
Q❀◐♣●P

Hemingford Grey

Cock 🄻

47 High Street, PE28 9BJ (off A14, SE of Huntingdon)
12-3, 6 (5 Fri)-11; 12-11 Sat; 12-10.30 Sun
☎ (01480) 463609 thecockhemingford.co.uk
Adnams Southwold Bitter; Brewsters Hophead; 1 changing beer Ⓗ
This village inn has won local, regional and national awards. The cosy pub has recently been refurbished to provide more comfortable facilities, and locals enjoy the well-kept locally sourced beers and real Cromwell cider produced in the village. The separate restaurant features an extensive fish board, meat, game and excellent home-made sausages (booking essential at all times). During the summer, occasional beer festivals are held in the beer garden. Q❀◐♿ÅP(5)

Histon

Red Lion

27 High Street, CB24 9JD
10.30-11 (midnight Fri); 12-11 Sun ☎ (01223) 564437
theredlionhiston.co.uk
Adnams Ghost Ship; Tring Side Pocket for a Toad; 6 changing beers (often Batemans, Lacons) Ⓗ
Free house with two bars adorned with a wonderful collection of breweriana and historical photographs. The left-hand bar features the TV, while the nine handpumps are in the right-hand bar which is quieter and child-free. Guest beers always include a mild. There are also Belgian and German beers on draught, a range of continental bottled beers, two ciders and a perry. Two beer festivals are held each year – the Easter aperitif and the main event in September. Local CAMRA Pub of the Year 2017 and Dark Ale Pub of the Year 2018.
❀◐♿♣●P

Holme

Admiral Wells 🄻

41 Station Road, PE7 3PH (jct of B660 and Yaxley Rd)
12-2.30, 5-11; 11.30-11 Sat; 11.30-10.30 Sun
☎ (01487) 831214 admiralwells.co.uk
Adnams Southwold Bitter, Broadside; Oakham JHB; 2 changing beers (often Digfield) Ⓗ
Officially the lowest-level pub in the UK. This Victorian inn was named after one of Nelson's pallbearers, William Wells, by its builder. Following a recent facelift it has two bar/lounge areas in a modern contemporary style, a conservatory and a function room at the rear. Outside there is a beer garden at the front, a large car park to the side and a children's play area. Five ales are usually available including two sourced locally, and a cider in summer. Quiz night is Tuesday.
Q❀◐♣●P

Houghton

Three Horseshoes

St Ives Road, PE28 2BE (off A1123)
12-11.30; 12-10.30 Sun ☎ (01480) 462410
threehorseshoesinnhoughton.co.uk
Greene King IPA Ⓗ/Ⓖ**; Sharp's Doom Bar; 2 changing beers** Ⓖ
Characterful Grade II-listed 17th-century building in a picturesque village. Popular with locals, it also gets lots of passing trade in the summer months. The lane opposite leads to the river and the historic Houghton Mill. There are two bar areas and plenty of space for diners. The real ales, usually including one from a local brewery, are served by gravity dispense from a taproom behind the bar. Three en-suite letting rooms are available.
Q❀◐Å♣P

Huntingdon

Falcon 🄻

Market Hill, PE29 3NR
10-midnight (1am Fri & Sat); 12-11 Sun
☎ (01480) 457416 falconhuntingdon.co.uk
Potbelly Best; Wychwood Hobgoblin Gold, Hobgoblin; 12 changing beers (often Great Oakley) Ⓗ
An established venue steeped in local history. This former coaching inn used to be Oliver Cromwell's recruiting station and the gates from the market square were once the entrance to Huntingdon prison. Choose from a selection of up to 18 beers, many from Northamptonshire breweries, and a range of real ciders. Good-value food is available every day. CAMRA branch Mild and Dark Ales Pub of the Year 2017. Q❀◐♣●

Old Bridge Hotel 🄻 ✓

1 High Street, PE29 3TQ (at S end of High St on ring road, by river)
11-11; 11-10.30 Sun ☎ (01480) 424300
huntsbridge.com
3 changing beers (sourced locally; often Hart Family, Nene Valley) Ⓗ
An ivy-clad hotel in an 18th-century former private bank at the southern end of the High Street with a

prominent position on the banks of the River Great Ouse. Enjoy imaginative and high-quality food in the Terrace Restaurant, the covered patio and the garden area or simply relax with a drink in the bar or lounge. The award-winning Old Bridge Wine Shop offers wine tasting. The bus station is a short walk away. Q🐴❀🛏◑◗♿⛺P🚌🐾📶

Sandford House ✔

George Street, PE29 3AD

⏲ 7am-midnight (1am Fri & Sat) ☎ (01480) 432402

Greene King IPA, Abbot; Sharp's Doom Bar; 3 changing beers (sourced nationally; often B&T, Oakham, Saffron) 🄷

A stylish conversion of two Victorian buildings by Wetherspoon which offers several different drinking and dining areas. Sandford House is built on the site of the original Huntingdon Theatre, a chapel dating from 1848, and was the home of the local Victorian industrialist Charles Sandford Windover. More recent uses include as the town's post office and as a furniture retailer. Wetherspoon's standard wide range of good-value food and drink is available. A 22-room hotel is at the rear of the pub. Q🐴❀🛏◑◗♿⇌🍎P🚌📶

Keyston

Pheasant 🄻

Loop Road, PE28 0RE (on B663, 1 mile S of A14, E of Thrapston)

⏲ closed Mon; 12-3, 6-11 Tue-Thu; 12-11 Fri & Sat; 12-5 Sun

☎ (01832) 710241 🌐 thepheasant-keyston.co.uk

Adnams Southwold Bitter; 2 changing beers 🄷

The village is named after Ketil's Stone, probably an Anglo-Saxon boundary marker. Created from a row of thatched cottages in an idyllic setting, the pub offers high-quality food, fine wines and well-kept cask ales. There is a splendid lounge bar and three dining areas. Regularly changing guest beers are offered, usually from Nene Valley or Digfield. Food is served lunchtimes and evenings Tuesday to Saturday, lunchtime only on Sunday. One of the few pubs included in the 1972 Good Beer Guide. Q🐴❀◑◗P🐾📶

Leverington

Rising Sun Inn 🄻

Dowgate Road, PE13 5DH

⏲ 6-11 Mon; 12-2, 6-11; 12-11 Fri; 12-4 Sun

☎ (01945) 583754

Elgood's Cambridge Bitter; 2 changing beers (often Elgood's) 🄷

Comfortably furnished pub with an enclosed garden. It dates back to at least 1872 and was refurbished a few years ago but the bar retains the feel of a true village local. It serves Cambridge Bitter and two changing beers including Elgood's seasonals and guest beers. Well known for good-value quality food, the restaurant hosts regular themed nights. Wednesday is steak night. Dogs and children are welcome. Closing time may be earlier than listed if there is no trade. A former CAMRA branch Gold Award winner.
❀◑◗♣P🚌(50)🐾📶

Little Gransden

Chequers 🄻

71 Main Road, SG19 3DW

⏲ 12-4, 7-11; 12-11 Fri & Sat; 12-4.30, 7-10.30 Sun

☎ (01767) 677348 🌐 chequersgransden.co.uk

4 changing beers (sourced locally) 🄷

Village pub owned and run by the same family for over 60 years and in this Guide for 25. The unspoilt middle bar, with its wooden benches, roaring fire and collection of decoy birds gathering on the beam over the bar, is a favourite spot to pick up on the local gossip. The Chequers' Son of Sid brewhouse supplies the pub and local beer festivals. Fish and chips are a highlight on Friday night (booking essential). A winner of numerous CAMRA awards, and Pub of the Year finalist in 2018. Q❀◗⛺🍎P🚉🚌🐾📶

March

Rose & Crown 🄻 ✔

41 St Peters Road, PE15 9NA

⏲ 12-11 (midnight Fri & Sat) ☎ (01354) 652077

St Austell Cornish Best Bitter; 6 changing beers (often Oakham, Tydd Steam) 🄷

Traditional community pub, over 150 years old, with two carpeted rooms and low-beamed ceilings. There is a real fire in the main bar and a pool table in the smaller bar. Six real ales are usually on offer, mainly from microbreweries, including one from Oakham, and up to seven traditional ciders. A mini beer festival is held at Easter. Good-quality food is served lunchtimes and evenings. Quiz night is Thursday. Q❀◑◗🍎P🚌📶

Ship Inn 🄻

1 Nene Parade, PE15 8TD

⏲ 12-11 Mon & Tue; 9am-midnight Wed & Thu (12.30am Fri & Sat); 9am-10.30 Sun ☎ (01354) 607878

Woodforde's Wherry; 4 changing beers (often Church End, Tydd Steam) 🄷

Thatched Grade II-listed riverside pub, built in 1680, with extensive riverside moorings. Its unusual carved beams are said to have 'fallen off a barge' during the building of Ely Cathedral. A quaint wobbly floor and wall lead to the toilets and a small games room. A free house since March 2010, when it reopened after a major refit, the Ship has a friendly and welcoming atmosphere. Attractions include monthly music from local bands and an annual beer festival in September.
Q🐴❀◑♣🚌🐾📶

Maxey

Blue Bell 🄻

39 High Street, PE6 9EE

⏲ 1-11; 1.30-11.30 Sat; 12-6 Sun ☎ (01778) 348182

Abbeydale Absolution; Fuller's London Pride, ESB; Oakham Bishops Farewell; 5 changing beers (sourced regionally; often Grainstore, Oakham, Woodforde's) 🄷

Originally a limestone barn, the building was converted many years ago and reflects the rural setting in which it is found. Paraphernalia of country life adorn the stone walls and shelves of the two-roomed interior. Nine handpumps dispense a range of quality ales from large and small breweries far and wide. The Blue Bell is a popular meeting place for groups including birdwatchers and golfers. A former local CAMRA Pub of the Year and Gold Award winner.
Q❀♣P🚌(22,413)🐾📶

Newton

Queen's Head
CB22 7PG
⏲ 11.30-2.30, 6-11 (10 Mon); 11.30-2.30, 5-11 Fri; 11.30-11 Sat; 12-10 Sun ☎ (01223) 870436
Adnams Southwold Bitter, Broadside; 2 changing beers Ⓖ
This village local is one of a handful of pubs to have appeared in every edition of the Guide. The list of landlords since 1729, displayed on the wall in the simply furnished public bar, has just 18 entries. The cosy lounge is warmed by a welcoming fire in the colder months. Guest beers are often Adnams seasonals. Simple but excellent food centres on soup and sandwiches. The King and Kaiser are reputed to have stopped here for a pint in the early 1900s. Q◑♣●P🚌(31)🐾

Peterborough

Bumble Inn
46 Westgate, PE1 1RE
⏲ 12-10 (8 Mon); 12-11 Fri & Sat; 12-6 Sun
🌐 thebimbleinn.wordpress.com
5 changing beers (often Axholme, North Riding, Tyne Bank) Ⓗ
Local CAMRA Pub of the Year for 2018, this micropub opened in 2016 in what was a chemist's shop. Minimalist in style, it has five handpumps dispensing quality ales from far and wide – expect the unusual. Order a taster paddle of three third-pints if you want to try a selection. Rare bottled and canned beers are also stocked plus two craft keg beers and Korev Cornish keg lager. Regular tap takeovers and food nights add to the attraction. Tea, coffee, soft drinks, home-made pasties, pies and Scotch eggs are available. ≥●🚌📶

Charters Ⓛ ✔
Town Bridge, PE1 1FP (down steps at Town Bridge)
⏲ 12-11 (midnight Fri & Sat); 12-10.30 Sun
☎ (01733) 315700 🌐 charters-bar.co.uk
Oakham JHB, Inferno, Citra, Bishops Farewell; 3 changing beers (often Nene Valley) Ⓗ/Ⓖ
The converted Dutch grain barge from circa 1907 sits on the River Nene near the city centre. An oriental restaurant is on the upper deck and food is also served in the bar. Up to 12 beers are on offer plus cider. The large garden with a marquee, bar and landing stage for boats is popular in summer. Live music plays some weekends and in summer outside the pub. It gets busy on football match days. Close to the Nene Valley Railway.
🐴❀◑♣●P🚌🐾📶

Coalheavers Arms
5 Park Street, Woodston, PE2 9BH
⏲ 3.30-11; 12-11 Fri & Sat; 12-10.30 Sun ☎ (01733) 565664
Greene King IPA; house beer (by Morland); 6 changing beers (sourced locally; often Hop Back, Lacons, Oldershaw) Ⓗ
This one-roomed back-street community pub dates back to the 1850s and was the only Peterborough pub to be bombed in World War II. A couple of Greene King ales are usually available, along with up to six guests, plus cider. Beer festivals are held four times a year, and the large garden is popular with families in summer. You can bring in your own food – plates provided. This small, friendly pub can be busy on football match days.
Q🐴❀♣●P🚌🐾📶

Draper's Arms Ⓛ
29-31 Cowgate, PE1 1LZ
⏲ 8am-midnight (1am Fri & Sat) ☎ (01733) 847570
Brewsters Hophead; Grainstore Ten Fifty; Greene King Abbot; Ruddles Best Bitter; Sharp's Doom Bar; 5 changing beers (often Oakham, Xtreme Ales) Ⓗ
A converted draper's shop, built in 1899 and one of two Wetherspoon pubs in the city. The beer range, with many from local microbreweries, is dispensed through 10 handpumps. The interior is broken up with dividers and wood-panelled intimate drinking and dining areas. Good value food is served all day and regular beer and cider festivals are held throughout the year. Quiz night is Wednesday. A regular top 10 real ale pub within the company's chain. Close to bus and railway stations.
Q🐴◑♿≥●🚌📶

Frothblowers 🏆 Ⓛ
78 Storrington Way, Werrington, PE4 6QP
⏲ closed Mon; 3-9 Tue-Thu (10 Fri); 12-10 Sat; 12-6 Sun
☎ 07765 066503 🌐 frothblowers.site
5 changing beers (often Froth Blowers, Hopshackle, Mile Tree) Ⓗ/Ⓖ
Formerly a tanning parlour, this micropub is set in a row of small shops on a housing estate in the north of the city, easily accessed by bus. It has five handpumps plus more beers in the cellar, six real ciders and a selection of bottled beers. Various activities and events include neighbour nights with board games, quizzes, acoustic music, a wine festival and a cider festival. It can get crowded on Friday and Saturday evenings. Local CAMRA Cider Pub of the Year 2018 and Pub of the Year 2019.
🐴♿♣●P🚆🚌(1)

Hand & Heart ★ Ⓛ
12 Highbury Street, PE1 3BE
⏲ 3-11.30 (midnight Fri); 12-midnight Sat; 12-11.30 Sun
☎ (01733) 564653 🌐 thehandandheart.com
5 changing beers (sourced regionally; often Brewsters, Rockingham, Tydd Steam) Ⓗ/Ⓖ
This 1930s back-street pub is on CAMRA's National Inventory of Historic Pub Interiors. The separate bar and quiet back room are connected by a drinking corridor. Beers are from five handpumps and the cellar, often including some hard-to-find ales. Live music plays on the second Thursday of the month and a cheese club is held on the last Thursday. Home-made Scotch eggs and rolls are usually available. The large garden has an outside bar and stage used for beer festivals and music events. A former local CAMRA Pub of the Year, it became free of tie in 2016. Q🐴❀♣●🚌(1)🐾📶

Ostrich Inn Ⓛ
17 North Street, PE1 2RA
⏲ 12-11; 11-1am Fri & Sat ☎ 07718 912271
Oakham JHB; house beer (by King's Cliffe); 3 changing beers (sourced locally) Ⓗ
Refurbished in 2009, this relaxing side-street pub reopened with its original name restored. The single-room interior has a U-shaped bar featuring many pictures for sale by local artists, which change monthly. Up to five varying real ales are on offer, many from local breweries, alongside a few craft keg lines. A large gin selection is also stocked. Live music plays most weekends. The small enclosed patio is a suntrap. Popular on football match days. Close to bus and rail stations.
🐴❀♿≥♣●🚌🐾

Palmerston Arms

82 Oundle Road, PE2 9PA
3-11.30; 2-midnight Fri; 12-midnight Sat; 12-11.30 Sun
(01733) 565865
Batemans Gold, XXXB G; Castle Rock Harvest Pale; Oakham Citra H/G; 10 changing beers (sourced regionally; often Lacons, Ossett, St Austell) G
Popular 400-year-old listed stone-built locals' pub. Owned by Batemans, three of its beers are rotated alongside nine or more other real ales, including some from Oakham. Traditional cider, perry and an extensive range of malt whiskies are also available. Most beers are served straight from the cellar, which can be seen through a large glass screen. Rolls and a variety of snacks tempt customers. Live music features most weekends and philosophy nights on occasion. Busy on football match days. (1,24)

Ploughman

1 Staniland Way, Werrington, PE4 6NA
3-11; 2-11.30 Fri; 12-midnight Sat & Sun
(01733) 327696
6 changing beers (sourced regionally; often Castor Ales, Hopshackle, Tiny Rebel) H
A rejuvenated two-roomed community pub brought to the forefront of the city's real ale outlets by the enthusiastic licensee. Six handpumps serve beers from local breweries and further afield. Many activities and charity events are held regularly as well as live music at weekends. A well-supported annual beer festival is hosted in early July. A former local CAMRA Pub of the Year. P (1,22)

Yard of Ale

72 Oundle Road, PE2 9PA
12-11 (1am Fri & Sat) (01733) 348000
theyardofalepub.co.uk
Digfield Fools Nook; Oakham Bishops Farewell; Sharp's Doom Bar; Tydd Steam Barn Ale; 2 changing beers (often Hop Back, Lacons, Rooster's) H
Built on land that was part of the Palmerston Arms stable yard and originally called the New Inn, this 120-year-old pub was refurbished and reopened in early 2017 by an experienced husband and wife team from the nearby Swiss Cottage. Decorated in shades of grey with a warm wooden bar and surround, the large open-plan single room is divided into four distinct areas by the central supporting structure. Entertainment includes live sports TV, darts and pool. Outside is a large beer garden. (1)

Ramsey

Angel

76 High Street, PE26 1BS
12-11 (midnight Fri & Sat); 12-10.30 Sun
(01487) 711968
Adnams Ghost Ship; 3 changing beers (sourced locally; often Adnams, Lacons, Tydd Steam) H
This traditional brick-built pub consists of a bar area and country-style restaurant that doubles up as a function room. The front of the building still retains the original serving hatch and stained-glass windows. There is a pool table and dartboard in the main bar. Reopened in 2016 after extensive refurbishment by the new owner. Friendly staff and locals provide a great venue to enjoy a drink or two with a LocAle always being available, usually from Tydd Steam. Q P (31)

St Ives

Nelson's Head

Merryland, PE27 5ED
11.30-11 (midnight Fri & Sat); 12-9 Sun
(01480) 494454 nelsonsheadstives.pub
Greene King IPA, Abbot; Morland Old Speckled Hen; 2 changing beers (sourced locally; often Grainstore, Nene Valley, Oakham) H
Lively Greene King pub in a picturesque narrow street in St Ives town centre. Formerly the Three Tuns, the pub name provides an unusual local reference to the maritime hero, more common around his Norfolk birthplace. The four real ales include two from local breweries, and a local cider is sold. Lunchtime food is served daily, plus pizza in the evening. The pub gets busy on Sunday afternoons when there are live bands.

Royal Oak

13 Crown Street, PE27 5EB
11-11 (2am Fri & Sat); 12-midnight Sun (01480) 462586
Oakham Inferno; 5 changing beers (sourced locally; often Nobby's, Oakham, Tydd Steam) H
One of a number of historic listed pubs in St Ives. Despite the date 1502 over the door, most of the building dates from the 18th century. The multi-room layout has been preserved. Changing beers are from local SIBA breweries and often include a porter. Live sporting events are shown on several TV screens, and live music plays on Saturday nights. A locals' pub, but visitors are always made to feel welcome.

St Neots

Ale Taster

25 Russell Street, PE19 1BA
4-11; 12-11 Sat; 12-6 Sun (01480) 581368
6 changing beers (sourced locally) G
A small, traditional, back-street pub operated in the style of a micropub. It features up to three changing ales served from stillage behind the bar, and up to nine real ciders and perries. The owners source beer and cider from local producers as much as possible, and are happy to chat about their beers. Three large fridges display a wide selection of bottled beers from around the world. The pub encourages conversation, with quiet background music and no electronic machines. Traditional bar games are played here. Q P (X5)

Olde Sun

11 Huntingdon Street, PE19 1BL
12-11 (01480) 216863 yeoldesun.moonfruit.com
Adnams Ghost Ship; Woodforde's Wherry; house beer (by Woodforde's); 2 changing beers (sourced regionally; often Adnams, Elgood's, Woodforde's) H
Low-beamed and cosy traditional town-centre pub with two large inglenook fireplaces, three bar areas and a secluded patio. The jukebox is zoned, allowing quiet areas for conversation. Shove-ha'penny and bar billiards are played. Five constantly changing guest beers come from various regional breweries including Adnams, Elgood's, Marston's, Thwaites and Woodforde's. A mild and other dark beers are usually among the range. A former local CAMRA Mild/Dark Ales Pub of the Year. (X5)

Pig 'n' Falcon

9 New Street, PE19 1AE (behind Barretts department store)

6-midnight Mon; 11.30-midnight Tue & Wed; 11-midnight Thu (2.30am Fri & Sat); 11-midnight Sun ☎ 07951 785678

pignfalcon.co.uk

Greene King IPA H, Abbot G; Potbelly Best H; 5 changing beers (sourced locally; often Potbelly, Three Blind Mice) G

This busy town-centre free house has up to six real ales and five real ciders, focusing on beers from microbreweries and unusual choices including milds, porters and stouts. A good range of bottled ciders, UK and foreign bottled beers includes Trappist ales. Beer festivals are held throughout the year. Live music nights are hosted on Wednesday, Friday, Saturday and Sunday. Outside is a large, imaginative, covered and heated beer garden. Three Blind Mice beers are real ale served in KeyKegs. (X5)

Shepreth

Plough

12 High Street, SG8 6PP

11-11; 12-9 Sun ☎ (01763) 290348

theploughshepreth.co.uk

4 changing beers (sourced regionally) H

Saved from conversion to residential use and reopened in 2014 after extensive renovation, the Plough has a large L-shaped bar facing the entrance, with a drinking area to the right themed on the Spitfire. To the left is a larger seating area. Doors lead to a spacious patio and garden. Cask beers come from local or regional breweries, and craft keg beers include some from BrewBoard Brewery. An extensive range of mostly local real ciders is also available. Frequent live music, comedy and quiz nights are hosted. County CAMRA Cider Pub of the Year 2019. P

Swavesey

White Horse

1 Market Street, CB24 4QG

12 (5 Mon)-11; 12-midnight Fri; 12-10.30 Sun

☎ (01954) 231665 thewhitehorseswavesey.com

4 changing beers H

The White Horse occupies a fine old building in the village's former market area. The public bar is a true classic with its polished, tiled floor, beamed ceiling, wood panelling and elevated fireplace. The large lounge bar with dining area was once a separate property, and the pool and function rooms behind the public are also later additions. Beyond them is a large garden with play equipment. The food is hearty, home-cooked pub grub with daily specials.

Thriplow

Green Man

2 Lower Street, SG8 7RJ

11-11; 12-9.30 Sun ☎ (01763) 208855

thegreenmanthriplow.co.uk

4 changing beers (sourced regionally) H

Purchased by villagers in 2013, the bright interior is divided in two. To the left is an area with a village-pub feel, complete with open fire, and to the right is a larger area mostly used for dining. The pub has a reputation for good food and beer – the ales tend to come from smaller regional breweries. There is outside seating both on the green in front and in the pleasant garden. Local CAMRA Rural LocAle Pub of the Year 2019. Q P (31)

> Give my people plenty of beer, good beer and cheap beer, and you will have no revolution among them.
> **Queen Victoria**

Upware

Five Miles Inn

Old School Lane, CB7 5ZR

11-11 (midnight Fri & Sat) ☎ (01353) 721654

fivemilesinn.com

Morland Old Speckled Hen; 3 changing beers (sourced nationally) H

The pub's full name is The Five Miles From Anywhere No Hurry Inn. It is located off the beaten track, next to the River Cam, overlooking part of the Fens. Four ales are on handpump with an occasional fifth beer direct from the cask during the summer, along with one real cider. A selection of food is available in the bar and separate restaurant. The pub has recently been extended. It offers visitor moorings and services for narrowboats and motor cruisers, and there is a large car park for those arriving by land. P

Waterbeach

Sun Inn

Chapel Street, CB25 9HR

5-11; 12-midnight Fri-Sun ☎ (01223) 861254

Woodforde's Wherry; 3 changing beers H

The small, cosy lounge is dominated by a huge fireplace, while the simply appointed public bar, with its woodblock floor, is always lively. There is a small meeting room and a function room upstairs where regular gigs are held. An annual beer and music festival features over the early May bank holiday weekend. There is no food on Monday or Sunday evening. The pub hosts the local CJ's café from 9am Friday and Saturday.

(9)

West Wratting

Chestnut Tree

1 Mill Road, CB21 5LT

12-3 (not Mon), 5.30-11.30; 12-midnight Fri & Sat; 12-10.30 Sun ☎ (01223) 290384 chestnuttreepub.co.uk

Greene King IPA; 3 changing beers H

Impressive two-bar Victorian-style pub with modern extensions creating a roomy, comfortable interior. The lounge to the right is mainly set out for dining. To the left is a nicely furnished public bar with a pool table. This friendly pub hosts darts, pool and pétanque teams, and a small lending library. It has been free of tie since the present owners bought it in 2012. Its three changing beers are mainly from micros, often local. Local CAMRA Pub of the Year 2019 and Rural Community Pub of the Year 2019. Q P (19)

Whittlesey

Boat Inn

2 Ramsey Road, PE7 1DR

4-midnight; 11-midnight Fri-Sun ☎ (01733) 202488
quinnboatinn.wordpress.com
Pitchfork Ⓗ; 4 changing beers (sourced regionally; often Grainstore) Ⓗ/Ⓖ
This corner pub has two rooms, a public bar with sports TV and a cosy lounge. Up to 17 traditional ciders and perries supplement the real ales, some of which are served direct from the cask. It hosts a whisky club on the second Friday of the month and organises regular trips to tasting events. Outside is a pétanque terrain which is also used by dancers at the Straw Bear Festival in January each year. Closing times can be flexible as the pub has a 24-hour licence. P (31)

Falcon Hotel
London Street, PE7 1BH
12-11 (midnight Fri & Sat) ☎ (01733) 351001
falconwhittlesey.com
Adnams Southwold Bitter; 2 changing beers Ⓗ
Old coaching inn and hotel built around 1600 with a number of rooms including a large function room, snug and a bar area on two levels. Three beers are offered, with at least one local ale. There is a courtyard and several outhouses to the rear which host outside bars and dancers during the Straw Bear Festival in January each year. Lunchtime and evening meals are served every day (except Sun eve). QP

George Hotel
10 Market Place, PE7 1AB
8am-midnight (1am Fri & Sat) ☎ (01733) 359970
Adnams Ghost Ship; Greene King Abbot; Oakham Bishops Farewell; Ruddles Best Bitter; Sharp's Doom Bar; 5 changing beers Ⓗ
Built in the town square in the late 1700s, this building was significantly altered in the mid-19th century before getting a Grade II listing in 1974. A busy Wetherspoon pub since 2010, it offers a large selection of real ales and ciders alongside the typical well-priced food menu. There are many pictures around the walls showing local historic figures and places, including how the town gained its name, and details about the extensive drainage work that created the East Anglian Fens.
P

Letter B
53-57 Church Street, PE7 1DE
5-11; 3.30-midnight Fri; 12-midnight Sat; 12-11 Sun
☎ (01733) 206975 theletterb.co.uk
Sharp's Doom Bar; 4 changing beers (sourced locally; often Digfield, Tydd Steam) Ⓗ
The Letter B is over 200 years old, with two bars, a small side room and a decked rear patio area. A beer festival is held in January during the Straw Bear Festival weekend, which is popular with locals and visitors. Over recent years the cider range has expanded rapidly to complement the five real ales. A winner of numerous local CAMRA awards including County Pub of the Year and County Cider Pub of the Year. Q (31,33)

Willingham

Bank Micropub
9 High Street, CB24 5ES
6-10 Mon; 5.30-10 Tue; 5-10 Wed; 5.30-11 Thu-Sat; closed Sun ☎ (01954) 200045 thebankmicropub.co.uk
5 changing beers Ⓖ
Formerly a bank, this micropub opened in 2012. The single room has a bar rescued from a closed Cambridge pub. The walls are decorated with photos of local interest. Up to five real ales are available direct from the cask, with regional and local beers featuring strongly. A range of craft ales includes three served from kegs. The Bank offers a warm welcome and the casual visitor is certain to be included in local conversation. Q

Witchford

Village Inn
80 Main Street, CB6 2HQ
11-11; 12-10.30 Sun ☎ (01353) 663763
2 changing beers (sourced nationally) Ⓗ
A friendly village inn offering a choice of two regularly changing real ales. The food menu includes traditional pub meals, pizza and blackboard specials, with themed events such as steak night. Food service is 12-3pm, 5.30-8.30pm Wednesday to Friday, 12-8pm Saturday, 12-3pm Sunday. Entertainment includes live music, quiz nights, disco nights and major sporting events on TV.

Definitions

bivvy – beer
bumclink – inferior beer
bunker – beer
cooper – half stout, half porter
gatters – beer
shant of gatter – glass of beer
half and half – mixture of ale and porter, much favoured by medical students
humming – strong (as applied to drink)
ponge or pongelow – beer, half and half
purl – mixture of hot ale and sugar, with wormwood infused
rot-gut – bad
small beer shandy – gaffs ale and gingerbeer
shant – pot or quart (shant of bivvy – quart of beer)
swipes – soup or small beer
wobble-shop – shop where beer sold without a licence
J C Hotten, The Slang Dictionary, 1887

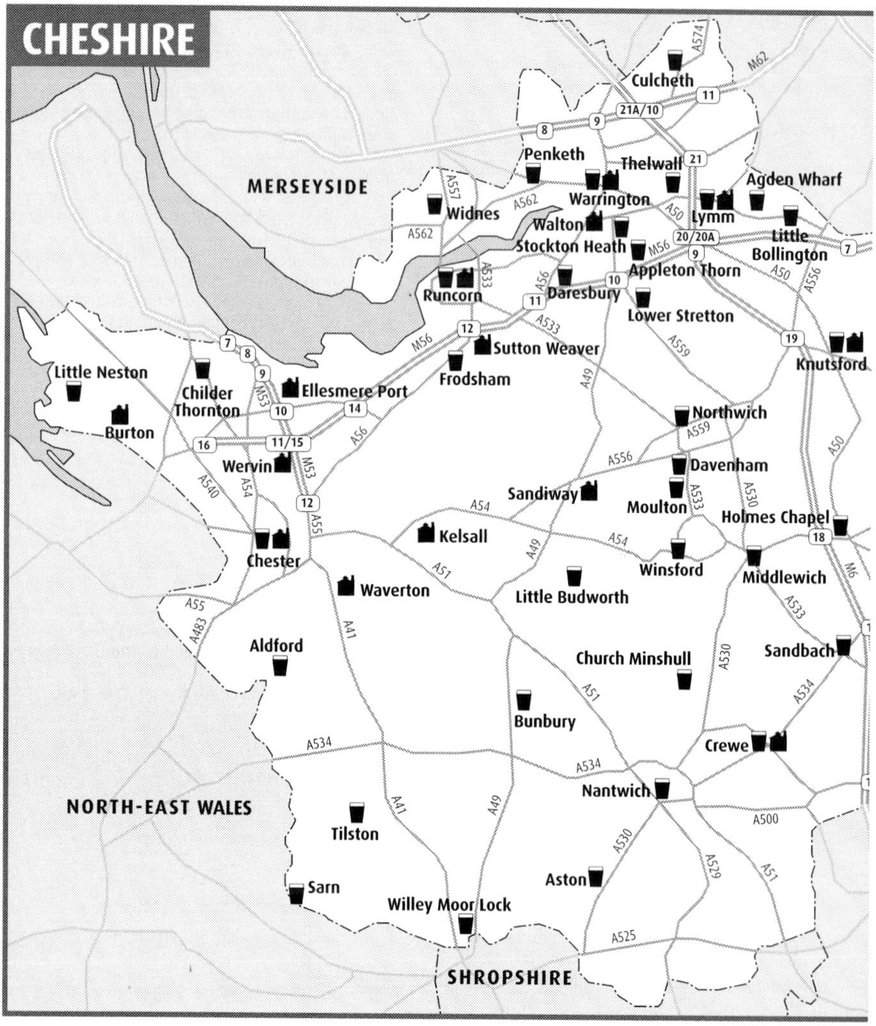

Agden Wharf

Barn Owl L

Warrington Lane, WA13 0SW (on Bridgewater Canal, off A56)

12-11 ☎ (01925) 752020 thebarnowlinn.co.uk

Lancaster Bomber; Moorhouse White Witch; Wainwright; 3 changing beers (sourced locally; often Pictish, Storm) H

Situated alongside the Bridgewater Canal, the Barn Owl offers fine views across the Cheshire countryside and has a canalside patio for use in summer. The three regular beers are complemented by up to three guest ales, sourced mainly from independent breweries, including at least one LocAle. Renowned for its food, which is freshly cooked using mainly local produce. Check out the wood carvings that front the building.

P

Aldford

Grosvenor Arms L

Chester Road, CH3 6HJ (on B5130)

11.30-11; 12-10.30 Sun ☎ (01244) 620228

grosvenorarms-aldford.co.uk

Timothy Taylor Landlord; Weetwood Eastgate; house beer (by Phoenix); 4 changing beers (sourced nationally) H

A spacious, stylish and unashamedly upmarket pub. It is multi-roomed with a pleasant garden room leading to an outside terrace and lawn with picnic tables. The interior features lots of bare wood, bookcases, pictures and chalkboards. Four guest ales complement the house offerings brewed by Phoenix, plus beers from Weetwood and Timothy Taylor. High-quality food from an imaginative menu is available all day. Dogs are welcome away from dining areas.

Q P (C56)

Alsager

Lodge L

88 Crewe Road, ST7 2JA (jct Crewe Rd and Station Rd, opp Church Rd)

4-11 (midnight Fri); 2-midnight Sat; 2-11 Sun

☎ (01270) 873669

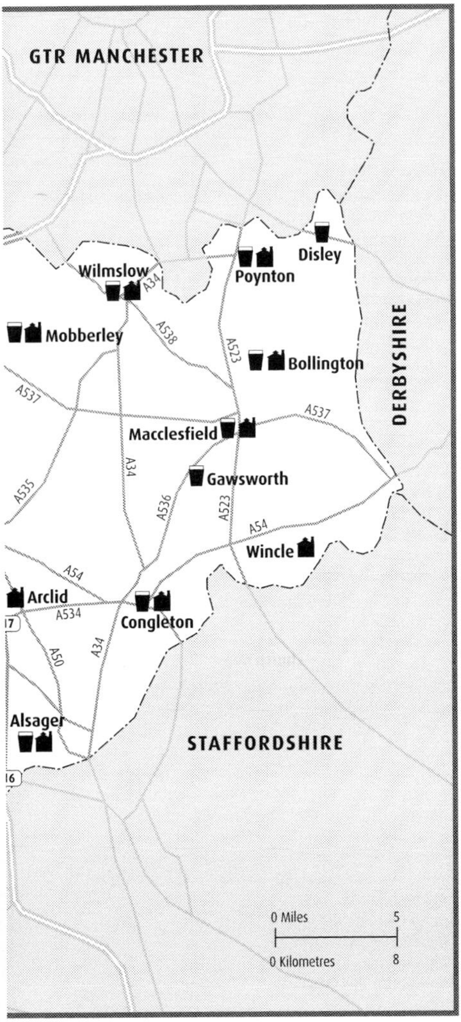

House beer (by Marston's); 7 changing beers (sourced nationally; often Dark Star, Oakham) H
A spacious pub with two rooms – one featuring an open fire with many CAMRA publications available on a ledge above – plus a large beer garden at the rear. Ales from the Lodge's own two-barrel brewery occasionally add further variety. Three real ciders are available in the bar. Q P

Appleton Thorn

Appleton Thorn Village Hall

Stretton Road, WA4 4RT
closed Mon-Wed; 7.30-11.30 Thu-Sat; 1-4; 7.30-10.30 Sun
(01925) 261187 appletonthornvillagehall.co.uk
8 changing beers (sourced nationally; often Castle Rock, Facer's, Mallinsons) H
CAMRA National Club of the Year 2019, this excellent, multi award-winning village hall is the hub of the local community. A central bar serves a large function room and smaller lounge. An ever-changing range of beer is on offer, with paddles of thirds available. Five real ciders are also stocked. An annual beer festival is held in October. Quizzes and regular live music nights also feature. Non-members pay a minimal fee for admission.
Q P (8,8E)

Aston

Bhurtpore

Wrenbury Road, CW5 8DQ (on Wrenbury Rd, just off A530)
12-11.30 (midnight Fri & Sat); 12-11 Sun
(01270) 780917 bhurtpore.co.uk
11 changing beers (sourced nationally) H
With 27 consecutive years in the Guide, this friendly country pub has it all: a relaxing bar area with separate room containing pool table and TV; a restaurant serving locally sourced food, with curries a speciality; and an excellent garden in which to sample some of the 11 changing ales, plus Belgian beers and ciders. The pub hosts regular vintage transport meetings, cycling events and folk nights as well as many local community events.
Q P (72)

Bollington

Poachers Inn

95 Ingersley Road, SK10 5RE
5.30-11 Mon; 12-2, 5.30-11 Tue-Thu; 12-midnight Fri & Sat; 12-11 Sun (01625) 572086 thepoachers.org
Storm Beauforts Ale; Weetwood Old Dog; 3 changing beers (sourced locally) H
Family-run, community free house generating a friendly atmosphere, with a lovely suntrap garden for summer and a coal fire in winter, near Gritstone Trail and Peak District National Park. The Poachers enthusiastically supports local breweries. Many of its three rotating guest beers are locally sourced, as is the food, which is home-prepared and good value. Bottled beers and real cider are also available. The pub is popular with ramblers, cyclists and dog walkers. Events include Wednesday pie night, monthly quizzes and golf days.
P

Vale Inn

29-31 Adlington Road, SK10 5JT
12-11; 12-10.30 Sun (01625) 575147 valeinn.co.uk
Bollington White Nancy, Long Hop, Best, Dinner Ale, Oat Mill Stout, Eastern Nights H
Close to the Macclesfield Canal and Middlewood Way, this mid-terraced, single-room pub is the tap for the nearby Bollington Brewing Co. It features up to six of the brewery's own beers, plus two guest ciders. Keg lines have also been installed. The renovated beer garden (separate from the pub) overlooking the recreation ground is ideal for a lazy summer evening watching the cricket. Good home-cooked food is available – booking recommended at busy times. P

Bunbury

Dysart Arms

Bowe's Gate Road, CW6 9PH (at jct of Bowe's Gate Rd, College Lane and Wyche Lane)
11.30-11; 12-10.30 Sun (01829) 260183
dysartarms-bunbury.co.uk
House beer (by Phoenix); 5 changing beers (sourced regionally; often Salopian, Storm, Weetwood) H
Situated opposite the imposing St Boniface Church, the pub takes its name from the Tollemache family who were the Earls of Dysart and local landowners.

The original building was a farmhouse dating from the mid 18th century; a tasteful modern extension was added in 1996. An interior with wooden beams, extensive bookcases and tiled floors conveys a pleasant and homely atmosphere. The excellent and varied fresh food menu features many locally sourced ingredients.

Chester

Big Hand Alehouse

85 Watergate Street, CH1 2LF
12-11 (midnight Fri & Sat) (01244) 313276
alehousechester.pub
7 changing beers (sourced nationally; often Big Hand)
This pub previously comprised various restaurants and bars, before being taken on by Wrexham-based Big Hand Brewery and transformed into a relaxed alehouse. Its main bar area leads to a comfortable side room; to the rear is a quirky basement containing a bagatelle table. Three Big Hand beers are available, along with four guest ales and a real cider on handpump. Conveniently located for thirsty racegoers and tourists visiting Chester's Roman city walls.

Cellar

19-21 City Road, CH1 3AE
3-12.30am; 12-1.30am Fri & Sat; 12-12.30am Sun
(01244) 318950 thecellarchester.co.uk
Timothy Taylor Landlord; 5 changing beers (sourced nationally; often Burning Sky, Hammerton, Hawkshead)
Friendly, modern bar at street level with a cellar also available for functions. The pub is renowned for its excellent selection of cask ales, complemented by at least three real ciders plus a wide variety of keg, bottled and canned beers. Sport features on three TV screens. The Cellar offers bar snacks, free bacon sandwiches on Sunday and free food during major sporting events. Dogs are welcome at all times. Twice CAMRA local Pub of the Year.

Cornerhouse

4-8 City Road, CH1 3AE
12-midnight (1.30am Fri & Sat); 12-11.30 Sun
(01244) 347518 cornerhousechester.com
Salopian Oracle; Timothy Taylor Landlord; 2 changing beers (sourced nationally; often Big Hand)
Attractive candlelit mock-Tudor building featuring lots of bare brick and wood flooring. It offers two regular beers and two changing ales, one of which is usually dark, plus a selection of bottled beers and an extensive wine list. Live music is hosted Thursday to Saturday and a quiz on Sunday. There is a free-to-hire function room upstairs. Outdoor seating is at the front of the pub. Food is of the platter variety (cheeses and meats) plus snacks.

Cross Keys

2 Duke Street, CH1 1RP
closed Mon & Tue; 12-11; 12-10.30 Sun (01244) 344460
Joule's Blonde, Pale Ale, Slumbering Monk; 3 changing beers (sourced nationally; often Joule's)
Attractive red-brick building with a stylish interior featuring oak floors, wood panelling and stained-glass windows depicting other Joule's hostelries. Three regular Joule's beers and a seasonal Joule's are complemented by two changing guests and up to four real ciders. A large upstairs room is available for hire. The small terrace beer garden catches afternoon sunshine. A choice of pies is always available and a traditional roast on Sunday. The pub hosts a quiz on Thursdays and live Irish music on the second and fourth Wednesdays of the month.

Deva Tap

121 Brook Street, CH1 3DU (at city end of Hoole Bridge close to railway station)
4-9 (closed winter) Mon; 4-10 Tue; 4-11 Wed & Thu; 3-midnight Fri; 12-midnight Sat; 2-10 Sun (01244) 314440
5 changing beers (sourced regionally)
The Deva Tap's long, narrow interior is divided into three: a small seating area by the entrance, a larger central space and a bar at the far end. The pub offers up to five rotating beers, usually including a light session ale and a stout, plus four ciders and up to 10 keg, KeyKeg and continental beers. There is outside seating in a small courtyard. Food is served daily, with meal offers of pizza on Wednesday and burgers on Thursday.

Goat & Munch

52 Garden Lane, CH1 4EW
closed Mon; 2-10 Tue-Thu (10.30 Fri & Sat); 2-7.30 Sun
07807 198267 goatandmunch.com
4 changing beers (sourced regionally; often Chapter, RedWillow, Salopian)
Chester's first micropub occupies a former electrical appliance repair shop in the Garden Quarter – an area heavily populated by students. The front room features a blue-painted bar with the bar front made from old pallets; furniture includes Swedish high tables and chairs plus some bench seating. There is also a brighter side room with additional seating. The four real ales tend to be from

REAL ALE BREWERIES

4Ts Warrington
Beartown Congleton
Beer Refinery Wervin
Blueball Runcorn
Bollington Bollington
Borough Crewe
Brewhouse & Kitchen Chester
Brewhouse & Kitchen Wilmslow
Britman Burton (brewing suspended)
Buccaneer Sutton Weaver
Chapter Sutton Weaver
Cheshire Brewhouse Congleton
Coach House Warrington
Goodalls Alsager
Happy Valley Macclesfield
Lymm Lymm
Manning Congleton
Merlin Arclid
Mobberley Mobberley
Norton Runcorn
Oaks Ellesmere Port
Pied Bull Chester
Poynton Poynton
RedWillow Macclesfield
Sandiway Sandiway (brewing suspended)
Spitting Feathers Waverton
Stag Walton
Storm Macclesfield
Tatton Knutsford
Tom's Tap Crewe (NEW)
Weetwood Kelsall
Wincle Wincle

independent breweries, generally sourced relatively locally. Discounted beers are available on Tuesday. (1,1A)

Old Harkers Arms

1 Russell Street, CH3 5AL (down steps off City Rd to canal towpath)
10.30-11 (11 Sat & Sun) (01244) 344525
harkersarms-chester.co.uk
Weetwood Cheshire Cat, Eastgate; house beer (by Phoenix); 6 changing beers (sourced nationally; often Derby, Hawkshead) H
Upmarket pub converted from the ground floor of a former Victorian canalside warehouse. Timber flooring, traditional wooden furniture and cast-iron pillars provide an insight to its history. Blackboards show tasting notes for up to six guest ales, which include bitters, stouts, milds or porters, many from local breweries. Ciders and perries are listed separately and served from the cellar. Food is available all day (booking advised for busy weekend periods). Outside seating offers views of the canal. Q P

Olde Cottage

34-36 Brook Street, CH1 3DZ
4-11 (midnight Fri); 2-midnight Sat; 2-11 Sun
(01244) 324065 oldecottagechester.co.uk
4 changing beers (sourced nationally; often Otter, Sharp's) H
Welcoming and traditional community hostelry, close to the railway station and Brook Street's many places to eat. It is known for pub games including darts, pool and bagatelle (a game similar to bar billiards and popular in the Chester area). The regular beer is supplemented by three guests, one free of tie.

Telford's Warehouse

Canal Basin, Tower Wharf, CH1 4EZ (just off city walls)
12-1am (11 Mon & Tue; 12.30am Wed & Thu)
(01244) 390090 telfordswarehousechester.com
Salopian Oracle; Weetwood Cheshire Cat; Young's Bitter; 3 changing beers (sourced nationally; often Hawkshead, Tatton, Three Tuns) H
Converted warehouse featuring a glass frontage overlooking the Shropshire Union Canal basin, with an interior adorned with industrial artefacts. Its three changing beers are often from microbreweries, including local ones. The pub is a popular live music venue, charging admission on some evenings. Children are welcome in the upstairs restaurant, which serves good-quality food and can be hired. The annual beer festival is usually held in October. P (1A)

Childer Thornton

Halfway House

New Chester Road, CH66 1QN (on A41 close to M53 jct 5)
3-11.30; 12-midnight Sat; 12-11 Sun (0151) 339 2202
4 changing beers (sourced nationally; often First Chop, Ringwood, Weetwood) H
Friendly, traditional former coaching inn dating from the 1770s, based at the midpoint between Chester and New Ferry. The building retains much of its original character, with several drinking areas offering smart, comfortable seating. A community feel is evident, with darts and dominoes teams plus a golf society. The pub can be busy when sporting events are on TV. Quiz night is Thursday. P

Church Minshull

Badger

Cross Lane, CW5 6DY (on B5074 in village centre beside St Bartholomew's church)
10-11 (10.30 Sun) (01270) 522348 badgerinn.co.uk
Titanic Anchor Bitter; house beer (by Tatton); 2 changing beers (sourced locally; often Weetwood) H
Set amid rolling Cheshire countryside, this 18th-century former coaching inn has gone from strength to strength since reopening a few years ago. Its central bar is flanked by two contrasting rooms, one of which blends seamlessly into the dining area. Four beers are served from smaller established local breweries. Food includes breakfast from 10am and a main menu from noon, with takeaways also available. The accommodation comprises five comfortable bedrooms. P

Congleton

Barley Hops

2 Swan Bank, CW12 1AH
closed Mon; 9am-5 Tue; 4-8 Wed & Thu; 4-10 Fri; 12-10 Sat; 2-6 Sun (01260) 270164 barleyhops.co.uk
3 changing beers (sourced locally) H
In an impressive street-corner location, this is a micropub and well-stocked bottled beer specialist. Three handpumps dispense predominantly local ales, with local cider available in summer. The bottled beer selection focuses on British produce but there are well-chosen foreign options too. Attractions include occasional Meet the Brewer events and specialist spirit evenings. Closing times may vary according to demand.
Q (38,42)

Beartown Tap

18 Willow Street, CW12 1RL
4-11; 12-11 Fri-Sun (01260) 270775
Beartown Kodiak Gold, Bearskinful; 4 changing beers (sourced locally; often Beartown, Manning) H
This is the outlet for Congleton's Beartown Brewery, now merged with Manning Brewers, which has long been a leading real ale producer in the area. At least five real ales are always available. The traditional, opened-out pub layout has several separate areas. There is also an upstairs function room that can be booked for meetings, and a secluded outdoor beer terrace. A community pub for conversation, games and occasional music, it also offers regular brewery tours.
(92)

Prince of Wales

4-6 Lawton Street, CW12 1RP
4 (12 Thu)-11; 12-midnight Fri & Sat; 12-10.30 Sun
(01260) 280714
Joule's Blonde, Pale Ale, Slumbering Monk; 3 changing beers (sourced regionally; often Joule's) H
The pub is divided into three areas, creating snug corners warmed by a logburner. The decor is interesting, featuring green-tiled walls, enamel signs and numerous artefacts. Now owned by Joule's brewery, the Prince of Wales sells four of the firm's beers plus two well-chosen guest ales, one often local, and a cider. Occasional music nights are feature as well as quiz nights. There is a substantial outside drinking area behind the pub. Local CAMRA Pub of the Year 2018.

Young Pretender

30-34 Lawton Street, CW12 1RS
4-11; 12-1am Fri & Sat; 12-11 Sun (01260) 273277
thebeerparlours.co.uk
Wincle Sir Philip; 5 changing beers
Bonnie Prince Charlie allegedly slept here, hence the name. Set within a partly Grade II-listed building, this large one-room bar is split into several areas. Five changing real ales and one cider are available, with food served during the day. Activities include a weekly quiz and movie night. The pub is also a meeting point for several local community groups. P

Crewe

Borough Arms

33 Earle Street, CW1 2BG (on Earle St railway bridge, with entrance up steps in adjoining Thomas St)
5-11; 12-midnight Fri & Sat; 12-11 Sun
10 changing beers (sourced nationally; often Fyne Ales, Oakham, Salopian)
Popular pub close to the town centre. Ten handpumps supply an excellent range of beers from all over the UK, with a preference for pale and golden ales. Three distinct seating areas on split levels surround the L-shaped bar, with a further seating area downstairs that can double as a function room. A pleasant and secluded beer garden is accessed through the downstairs room.
Q P (8)

Hops

Prince Albert Street, CW1 2DF (opp Lifestyle Centre at southern end of Prince Albert St)
11 (5 Mon)-11.30; 12-11.30 Sun (01270) 211100
6 changing beers (sourced nationally; often Townhouse)
A multi award-winning café bar in a secluded spot close to the town centre. It offers a varied selection of six cask ales, including at least one dark beer. It has an extensive range of bottled beers, mainly from Belgium, and is among the UK's few official Orval Ambassadors. Up to six real ciders and perries are also served. Light meals are available at lunchtime Wednesday to Saturday.
Q

Raven

Brookhouse Drive, CW2 6NA (jct Brookhouse Drive and Davenport Avenue/Broadleigh Way)
3.30-midnight (1am Fri); 12-1am Sat; 12-midnight Sun
(01270) 482576
Sharp's Doom Bar; 4 changing beers (sourced regionally; often Salopian, Titanic)
Large community pub with a separate bar and lounge, located in a modern housing estate area. As well as beers, it offers a large range of gins and vodkas. The bar, which can be lively, hosts pool, darts and dominoes. The lounge doubles as a concert room – featuring open-mic sessions on Wednesday evening and live music most weekends – and as a function room for many other events. On spring bank holiday there is a music extravaganza with additional beers on offer.
P

Culcheth

Cherry Tree

35 Common Lane, WA3 4EX (on B5207, 400yds from A574)
11-11 (1am Fri & Sat) (01925) 762624
Sharp's Doom Bar; Tetley Bitter; Timothy Taylor Landlord; 4 changing beers (sourced nationally)
Large open-plan pub near the village centre, popular with families and sports fans. It offers three regular ales plus four changing guest beers, and serves good-value food all day. A quiz night is held on Wednesday. The car park fee is refunded with purchases at the bar. Part of the Mitchells & Butlers Sizzling Pubs chain, the Cherry Tree is a former local CAMRA Community Pub of the Year.
P (19,28,28E)

Daresbury

Ring o' Bells

Chester Road, WA4 4AJ (just off A56 in centre of village)
12-11; 12-10.30 Sun (01925) 740256
Greene King IPA; 4 changing beers (sourced locally; often Weetwood)
Once the village courthouse, this 19th-century pub still retains many original features, including a horse trough. Although food-oriented, this Chef & Brewer hostelry has five handpumps, serving beers mainly from the local Weetwood range. Outside the pub is Daresbury parish church which was once officiated over by The Rev Charles Dodgson, better known by his pen name Lewis Carroll – many of the author's sayings and characters are dotted around the pub. P (X30)

Davenham

Davenham Cricket Club

Butchers Stile, Hartford Road, CW9 8JG (down a narrow driveway after Mount Pleasant Rd)
closed Mon; 4.30-8.30 (10.30 Fri); 4-11 Sat
(01606) 48922 davenham.play-cricket.com
4 changing beers (sourced locally; often Beartown, Brimstage, Mobberley)
This family-oriented club is a community facility in an idyllic village setting. Extensive seating in front of the pavilion makes it a perfect place to enjoy beer, cricket and the summer warmth. The local football club is made welcome, and sporting events are shown on TV. Four handpumps serve real ale mainly from local breweries. During the cricket season the opening hours are extended. Show your CAMRA membership card for admission.
P

Disley

Malt Disley

22 Market Street, SK12 2AA (on A6)
4-11 (9 Mon); 2-11 Fri; 12-11 Sat; 12-10 Sun
(01663) 308020 maltdisley.co.uk
5 changing beers (sourced locally)
This vibrant and friendly converted shop is located in the village centre. It is spacious for a micropub and includes a downstairs room. Five regular changing cask beers are available, some from local microbreweries, along with a cask cider. KeyKeg beers, a further cider and a range of British and continental bottled beers are also on offer. Live music is played on the last Sunday afternoon of each month. Q (199)

Frodsham

Helter Skelter

31 Church Street, WA6 6PN

11-11 (11.30 Fri & Sat); 12-11 Sun (01928) 733361
thehelterskelter.net
Oakham Bishops Farewell; Salopian Oracle; Weetwood Bitter; 7 changing beers (sourced nationally; often Ossett, Thornbridge) H
Local CAMRA Pub of the Year 2019, this multi award-winner offers three regular cask ales plus a further seven constantly changing guest beers from local and national micros. Two rotating guest ciders and a variety of imported bottled beers are also available. The single-room bar has a friendly, relaxed atmosphere attracting both locals and travellers. Excellent food is served in the bar and upstairs restaurant. Dogs are welcome and there are water bowls aplenty. (21,48)

Kash 22
22 Church Street, WA6 6QW
4 (12 Thu)-11; 12-midnight Fri & Sat; 12-10.30 Sun
(01928) 733116
4 changing beers (sourced regionally) H
A friendly, two-storey bar in the town centre which specialises in live music. Its four real ales are from independent breweries. Hot food is available every day from a popular and varied menu using locally sourced ingredients. The pub is busy at weekends and on music nights, but offers a quieter lounge upstairs. (21,48)

Gawsworth

Harrington Arms ★
Church Lane, SK11 9RJ (off A536)
12-3, 5-11; 12-3, 4.30-midnight Fri; 12-11 Sat; 12-10.30 Sun (01260) 223325
Robinsons Wizard, Dizzy Blonde, Unicorn; 1 changing beer (sourced locally; often Robinsons) H
A Grade II-listed building dating from the late 17th century and has been identified by CAMRA as having a nationally important historic pub interior. There is a small bar area with separate rooms off, including open fires and woodburners. A good selection of beers is available from the Stockport-based Robinsons brewery, to enjoy for themselves or to accompany the lunchtime and evening menus. For summer days, there is a large outdoor area. Q (38)

Holmes Chapel

Bottle Bank
24-26 London Road, CW4 7AL
2-10.30 (11.30 Thu-Sat) (01477) 534380
4 changing beers (sourced locally; often Merlin, Mobberley) H
Recently established bar and off-licence in the former NatWest bank building – hence the name. There are two rooms behind the front bar, one of which is the former strong room and can be reserved for functions. Four changing cask ales are supplemented by eight other draught beers, and you can get third-pints. A large range of British and foreign bottled beers is also stocked to drink or take away. Bar snacks are available.
(42,316)

Knutsford

Wine & Wallop
76 King Street, WA16 6ED
11-10 (midnight Fri & Sat) (01565) 228429
wineandwallop.co.uk
4 changing beers (sourced locally)
This welcome addition to Knutsford's eclectic range of bars looks narrow at first glance but is deceptively spacious, yet cosy and comfortable. The bar offers interesting styles such as unfiltered beer, and its friendly and helpful staff are happy to provide information. There is also a try-before-you-buy option. (88,188)

Little Bollington

Swan with Two Nicks
Park Lane, WA14 4TJ (signposted off A56)
12-11 (10.30 Sun) (0161) 928 2914
swanwithtwonicks.co.uk
Black Sheep Best Bitter; Dunham Massey Big Tree Bitter; Timothy Taylor Landlord; house beer (by Coach House); 2 changing beers (sourced locally) H
Spacious, traditionally styled country pub. To the front is the drinking area warmed by two large fires in chilly weather. In the middle is the bar and beyond that the restaurant. The house beer, Swan with Two Nicks, is typically accompanied by at least two local and two national ales. There is a varied food offering including gluten-free dishes.
P (5,35,289)

Little Budworth

Egerton Arms
Pinfold Lane, CW6 9BS (on edge of village)
closed Mon; 3-11 Tue-Thu; 12-midnight Fri & Sat; 12-11 Sun
(01829) 760424 egerton-arms.co.uk
Timothy Taylor Landlord; 5 changing beers (sourced regionally; often Marble, Pennine, Tatton) H
This traditional, unspoilt and friendly pub offers a range of continental lagers and bottled world beers in addition to cask ales. A woodburner creates a warm, cosy atmosphere in winter. The beer garden is a sunny place to watch cricket in summer. The pub hosts a summer beer festival and winter Oktoberfest. Regular live music and themed events also feature. P

Little Neston

Harp
19 Quayside, CH64 0TB (turn left at bottom of Marshlands Rd, pub is 300yds on left)
12-midnight (12.30am Fri & Sat); 12-11 Sun
(0151) 336 6980
Joseph Holt Bitter; Peerless Triple Blonde; Timothy Taylor Landlord; 2 changing beers (sourced nationally) H
A former coal miners' inn, converted from two cottages, the Harp has a basic lounge plus a public bar with a real fire in winter. In a glorious location on the Deeside to Neston stretch of the National Cycle Network, the pub and its recently enlarged garden overlook the Dee Marshes and North Wales. Evening food is available on Tuesday only, with a popular curry night. Q P (22,487)

Lower Stretton

Ring o' Bells
Northwich Road, WA4 4NZ (200yds from M56 jct 10)
5.30-11 (midnight Fri); 4.30-10.30 Sun 07791 572555
Coach House Gunpowder Mild; Merlin Dark Magic; Wood Shropshire Lad; 3 changing beers (sourced locally; often Merlin) H

A small village local with no music or games machines. The main room, served by a single bar, leads to two smaller rooms for quieter drinking. Up to three rotating guest beers are available, often from local microbreweries. A quiz night is held on the second and fourth Tuesdays of the month, and a folk session on the first Tuesday of most months. Q P

Lymm

Brewery Tap

18 Bridgewater Street, WA13 0AB
12-11 (midnight Thu; 11.30 Fri & Sat) (01925) 755451
lymmbrewing.co.uk
Dunham Massey Dunham Dark; Lymm Bitter, Bridgewater Blonde; 4 changing beers (sourced locally; often Dunham Massey, Lymm) H
Modern venue situated in a red-brick former post office, a stone's throw from the Bridgewater Canal. The well-lit bar is complemented by a tastefully decorated front room with subdued lighting, comfy armchairs and a wood-fired stove. Four changing ales are either from the microbrewery under the pub or nearby Dunham Massey Brewery. One rotating real cider is also available. An open mic night is held twice a month.

Macclesfield

Bull's Head

155-157 Broken Cross, SK11 8TU (1½ miles W of town centre on A537)
12-midnight (1am Fri & Sat); 12-11 Sun (01625) 421117
5 changing beers (sourced nationally) H
This welcoming, traditional community local is over 200 years old and serves the area of Broken Cross on the outskirts of Macclesfield. The landlord takes pride in his real ale, offering up to five beers at weekends. The main room houses the bar and includes a cosy area around a corner. A separate taproom hosts darts matches. There is also an outdoor drinking area for the warmer months. P

Park Tavern

158 Park Lane, SK11 6UB
4-11; 12-midnight Fri & Sat; 12-11 Sun (01625) 667846
park-tavern.co.uk
Bollington White Nancy, Long Hop, Best, Dinner Ale, Oat Mill Stout H
Dating from around 1825, this popular community local showcases the range of local Bollington Brewery beers plus two real ciders. A 10-minute walk from the town centre, it features an open-plan area around the bar plus a separate panelled room to enjoy a pint with the paper. Regular events include quizzes and science evenings, plus film nights in a mini cinema and function room upstairs.

RedWillow

32A Park Green, SK11 7NA
closed Mon; 4-11 Tue & Wed (midnight Thu); 12-midnight Fri & Sat; 12-10.30 Sun (01625) 830718
redwillowbar.com
5 changing beers (often RedWillow) H
The RedWillow Brewery's local tap was converted from a former shop. Its beer selection includes RedWillow's cask and keg offerings plus guests from national microbrewers. Fresh pizza is offered to complement the ales. The pub can get busy at weekends so visit during the day if you are looking for a quiet drink. At least one dark beer is always available.

Waters Green Tavern

96 Waters Green, SK11 6LH
12-3, 5-11; 12-11 Sat; 12-10.30 Sun (01625) 422653
7 changing beers (sourced regionally; often Abbeydale, Acorn, Elland) H
A mainstay in the Guide for over 20 years, this gem of a traditional free house benefits from the vast experience of the long-serving landlord. One of the beers is always dark. The open, L-shaped layout provides two seating areas, one with a real fire. Other attractions include a pool room and a great jukebox. Home-cooked meals, served Monday to Saturday lunchtimes, provide good value.

Wharf

107 Brook Street, SK11 7AW
12-2.30 Mon; 4.30-11.30 Tue-Thu; 12-2.30, 4.30-midnight Fri; 3-midnight Sat; 3-11.30 Sun (01625) 261879
thewharfmacc.co.uk
Oakham JHB; Tetley Bitter; 3 changing beers (sourced nationally) H
Traditional community local whose bar features narrowboat decoration, reflecting its name and the nearby canal. A former Cheshire CAMRA Pub of the Year, this one-room free house has a cosy lounge area with a real fire on one side and a pool table on the other. It offers a superb range of regular and changing cask ales, including a dark beer. Live music is often performed at weekends. (58)

Middlewich

White Bear Hotel

Wheelock Street, CW10 9AG (on lower end of Wheelock St, just off A54 St Michael's Way)
11-11 (midnight Fri & Sat); 12-10.30 Sun
(01606) 837666 thewhitebearmiddlewich.co.uk
4 changing beers (sourced locally) H
Friendly free house with five handpumps on the bar dispensing a rotating range of beers in various styles. One dark ale, porter or stout always features, with a handpump dedicated to real cider. The interior includes open-plan drinking areas, a dining room and a rear room with a solid-fuel stove. A selection of newspapers is provided. The pub is near moorings on the Trent and Mersey Canal. P (37,42)

Mobberley

Church Inn

Church Lane, WA16 7RD (opp church, signposted from local roads)
12-10.30 (11 Fri & Sat) (01565) 873178
churchinnmobberley.co.uk
House beer (by Tatton); 2 changing beers (sourced regionally) H
Up a lane from the MCC (Mobberley Cricket Club), this sister to the nearby Bull's Head is an upmarket dining pub with a cricket-themed bar. Its 300-year-old, Grade II-listed building retains vestiges of a former multi-room layout. A snug, a characterful boot room and two dining rooms are supplemented by private dining rooms upstairs, a beer garden to the rear and a partly covered patio. P (88,88A)

Moulton

Lion

74 Main Road, CW9 8PB
5-11; 4-midnight Fri; 2-midnight Sat; 2-10.30 Sun
(01606) 606049
Wainwright; 4 changing beers (sourced locally; often Cheshire Brewhouse, RedWillow, Tatton)
In the centre of the village, this is a welcoming community-focused pub. Its handpumps dispense numerous ales and ciders, mainly from local breweries. Quiz nights and themed music events are always popular. A complimentary cheeseboard is offered on Friday evening. A beer garden to the side and decking to the front enable customers to take advantage of the warm summer months. A new function room is also available.
P

Nantwich

Black Lion

29 Welsh Row, CW5 5ED (opp Cheshire Cat)
12-3 (not Mon), 5-11; 12-11 Sat; 12-10.30 Sun
(01270) 628711 blacklion-nantwich.co.uk
Weetwood Bitter, Cheshire Cat, Eastgate, Old Dog; 3 changing beers (sourced regionally)
A traditional black-and-white-fronted inn dating from the 17th century, standing among historic buildings. Its beautiful plaster and wood-beamed interior retains the expected bowed walls and creaking floorboards. An open fire welcomes you into an open-plan area. The small Hop Room features hop bines on the ceiling and a pot-bellied stove for heating. There is a restaurant upstairs and a covered beer garden to the side.
Q (84,85)

Crown

High Street, CW5 5AS
11-11.30 (midnight Fri & Sat); 11-11 Sun
(01270) 625283 crownhotelnantwich.com
5 changing beers (sourced regionally)
Recently refurbished, this three-storey building was burned down in the Fire of Nantwich in 1583 and quickly rebuilt using timbers from Delamere Forest. Now Grade I-listed, it features an abundance of old beams, wattle and daub walls, roaring fires and the strangest uneven bespoke flooring to be found in Cheshire. The bar offers a selection of real ales including one from the Salopian Brewery plus three rotating guests. Live music plays on Thursday nights.
P (84,85)

Vine Inn

42 Hospital Street, CW5 5RP (near St Mary's Church)
12-midnight (01270) 619055 vineinnnantwich.co.uk
Hydes Old Indie, Original, Lowry; 3 changing beers (sourced regionally)
A 17th-century two-storey building with its floor below street level and an open-plan interior with distinct levels. Beers are from the full Hydes range, often complemented by guest ales. Attractions include sports channels on TV in all rooms, and dominoes league games on Monday – normally three teams, with new members welcome. This family- and dog-friendly pub has a rear room heated by a logburner, plus a small garden behind. On Monday there is a 50p discount on a pint of real ale.

Northwich

Baron's Lounge

13 Witton Street, CW9 5DE (in pedestrianised town centre)
4-10 Mon; 3-11 Tue-Thu; 2-11 Fri; 12-11 Sat; 2-10 Sun
(01606) 212443
4 changing beers (sourced locally; often 4Ts, Beartown, Merlin)
Situated close to the new Barons Quay development, the Baron's Lounge opened in late 2017 in a former Red Cross shop and converted into a two-storey microbar in 2018. Although small, the pub offers plenty of entertainment including quiz evenings, acoustic open mic sessions, weekly retro games nights and live music events. A suntrap patio perfect for summer evenings is to the rear.
Q

Salty Dog

21-23 High Street, CW9 5BY (in pedestrianised town centre)
11-11; 12-10.30 Sun salty-dog.co.uk
4 changing beers (sourced locally; often Bollington, RedWillow, Tatton)
This former shop retains its picturesque black-and-white exterior. The landlord and co-owner played drums in punk band The Business. Live music features along with comedy nights. A room at the rear has a jukebox, table football, retro arcade and quiz machine. An extensive range of bottled British and European beers is available. The staff are particularly knowledgeable about their beers.

Penketh

Ferry Tavern

Station Road, WA5 2UJ
5.30-9.30 Mon; 12-11 Tue-Thu (midnight Fri & Sat); 12-10.30 Sun (01925) 791117 theferrytavern.com
Jennings Cumberland Ale; 9 changing beers (sourced nationally)
Nestling between the River Mersey and St Helens Canal, this place holds brewery tap takeovers, and offers a wide range of whiskies and gins. Food includes the famous fish and chips plus locally made pies at the weekend. The large beer garden is popular with locals as well as walkers, and cyclists using the Trans Pennine Trail. Local CAMRA Community Pub of the Year 2019.
P (32)

Poynton

Flute & Firkin

51 Park Lane, SK12 1RD
closed Mon; 3-11 Tue-Thu; 12-11.30 Fri & Sat; 12-10.30 Sun
(01625) 879181
Poynton Vulcan; 5 changing beers (sourced locally; often Poynton, RedWillow)
Poynton Brewery's tap is a converted shop in the centre of town. Its contemporary bar area is supplemented by a small wooden cabin-style outbuilding to the rear and an upstairs function room that shows sport on TV. Six handpumps dispense several ales from the Poynton range, with Vulcan a regular. The other changing offerings usually include one dark beer. There are also one or two guest ales and six KeyKeg beers plus an occasional cask cider.

Runcorn

Ferry Boat

10 Church Street, WA7 1LR

8am-midnight (1am Fri & Sat) (01928) 583380

Greene King Abbot; Ruddles Best Bitter; Sharp's Doom Bar; 2 changing beers (sourced nationally)

Large, busy Wetherspoon pub opposite Runcorn old town bus station in the town centre. As well as the standard Wetherspoon offerings there are usually another two or three beers of ever-changing type and origin plus a real cider. The pub's name derives from the river crossing that used to operate between the towns of Runcorn and Widnes (on the opposite bank of the River Mersey) before the building of the Manchester Ship Canal in the 1890s. The Brindley Theatre is 200 yards away.

Norton Arms

125-127 Main Street, WA7 2AD

12-11 (midnight Fri & Sat); 12-10 Sun (01928) 567642
thenortonarms.co.uk

Greene King IPA; 3 changing beers (sourced nationally)

Another year in the Guide for this Grade II-listed, traditional, two-roomed, oak-beamed pub in the centre of Halton Village. The building has existed since 1758. Beers are on four handpumps. Among the many attractions are sport shown on three TV screens, open mic nights, live music, quiz evenings, a bowling green and the local Laurel and Hardy Appreciation Society. The pub can get busy at weekends, and access is tricky due to its age – the door is up a flight of stone steps.

Society Tap Rooms

33 Ashridge Street, WA7 1HU (5 mins' walk from Runcorn Station, 10 mins' walk from Old Town)

closed Mon-Wed; 4-midnight Thu; 3-midnight Fri; 12-midnight Sat; 12-11 Sun (01928) 775628
societyltd.co.uk

4 changing beers (sourced locally; often Blueball, Heavy Industry)

An unusual find in Runcorn, this brewery and tap was once a Co-operative building, then a bakery. Its beers are from Blueball Brewery, which is attached to the building, plus others including Heavy Industry and Chapter. KeyKeg craft ale is also served. The STR is hidden away in the Dukesfield area of the town, with an entrance under the arches of the railway between Runcorn station and Ethelfleda Bridge, which carries the line over the Mersey.

Sandbach

Beer Emporium

8 Welles Street, CW11 1GT (off Hightown roundabout, down one-way street)

12-8 (10 Thu-Sat); 2-10 Sun (01270) 760113
thebeeremporium.com

5 changing beers

The first micropub in south Cheshire, opened in 2009, has gone from strength to strength, changing hands seamlessly in 2016. Beers include five ever-changing real ales and a KeyKeg, some of which are sourced locally. The management know their stuff and also supply a huge range of bottled beers. This is a compact venue, popular with locals and visitors. Its home brewers' night is well attended on the first Thursday of the month. Located in central Sandbach, it is easily reachable by bus.

Sarn

Queen's Head

SY14 7LN (off B5069)

closed Mon; 6-midnight Tue-Thu; 5-midnight Fri & Sat; 12-11 Sun (01948) 770244 queensheadsarn.co.uk

Timothy Taylor Golden Best; 1 changing beer (often Marston's)

Known locally as the Sarn, this cosy rural pub sits right on the border with Wales. Regular ale Timothy Taylor Golden Best is complemented by a guest beer. The lounge has a real fire and a former taproom features darts and pool. Home-made food is served in the dining room. The patio garden is partly covered and overlooks the lovely Wych Brook, which has a fish ladder and converted cornmill. Opens bank holiday Mondays.

Stockton Heath

Costello's Bar

23 Walton Road, WA4 6NJ

12-11 (midnight Thu; 12.30am Fri & Sat)
(01925) 600910 costellosbar.co.uk

Dunham Massey Big Tree Bitter; Lymm Bridgewater Blonde; 5 changing beers (sourced locally; often Dunham Massey, Lymm)

A welcoming and friendly modern real ale bar owned and run by Dunham Massey Brewing. There are seven handpumps, with five cask ales on rotation and two mainstays, always including at least one dark beer, one mild and one strong ale. Real cider is also sold. All cask ale is provided by Dunham Massey and Lymm. Live music features every other Tuesday and Sunday. Local CAMRA Pub of the Year 2018.

Thelwall

Little Manor

Bell Lane, WA4 2SX

10.30-11 (10.30 Sun) (01925) 212070
littlemanor-thelwall.co.uk

Coach House Cromwells Best Bitter; house beer (by Phoenix); 6 changing beers (sourced regionally)

A large upmarket food-based pub with a changing range of local and regional cask ales. The pub is tastefully furnished and has attractive garden areas for dining alfresco in the summer. A regularly changing food menu suits all tastes and is served throughout the day. Details of country walks around the pub are available from the website or bar.

Tilston

Carden Arms

Mount View, Church Road, SY14 7HB

12-11 (01829) 250900 cardenarms.co.uk

Coach House Gunpowder Mild; Salopian Shropshire Gold; Weetwood Eastgate; 2 changing beers (sourced locally; often Peerless, Spitting Feathers, Wincle)

Stylish rural free house situated at the crossroads in the village. The interior has rug-covered wood and tiled floors, two real fires, traditional furniture and attractive framed pictures on the plain white walls. In addition to three regular beers are two guests, often from local microbreweries. There is a separate dining room and the adjoining old stable is available for groups of up to eight people. Outside there are seating areas to both the front and rear. Q P (41)

Warrington

Albion

94 Battersby Lane, WA2 7EG (200yds N of A57/A49 jct)
12-midnight (1am Fri & Sat) ☎ (01925) 231820
4 changing beers (sourced locally; often Merlin)
A large Victorian pub with an outside courtyard surrounded by the original stables. Inside there are distinctly separate rooms with two of them still retaining real fires. This is a true community pub with a games room including a pool table. It features regular live bands and varying entertainment, often in support of local charities. The four real ales are sourced mainly from local independent breweries.

Lower Angel

27 Buttermarket Street, WA1 2LY (in pedestrianised town centre)
11-11 (midnight Sat); 12-10 Sun ☎ (01925) 653326
Weetwood Bitter; 8 changing beers (sourced nationally)
Enjoy a step back in time here, with a traditional vault and lounge layout, and sheltered beer garden. Memorabilia from the former Walker's Brewery and stained-glass windows remain. The summer room to the rear is adorned with hundreds of pumpclips. The pub supports local charities and a visit at Halloween or Christmas is a must to see the decorations. The eight changing beers are mainly from independent breweries.

Tavern

25 Church Street, WA1 2SS
4-midnight Mon (11 Tue); 3-11 Wed (midnight Thu); 12-midnight Fri-Sun ☎ 07747 668817
8 changing beers (sourced nationally; often Fyne Ales, Mallinsons, Oakham)
A regular Guide entry, this single-room pub has eight varying beers – two from local 4Ts, one bitter, one dark, one session and three pale choices providing a good range for the discerning drinker. There is a board by the bar which is religiously updated to show beer name, price, style and strength. Multiple TVs allow different sporting events to be shown simultaneously. The large covered smoking area at the rear offers seating and TV.

Widnes

Premier

93-99 Albert Road, WA8 6JS
8am-midnight (12.30am Fri & Sat) ☎ (0151) 422 4920
Greene King Abbot; Ruddles Best Bitter; 3 changing beers
First the Premier cinema, then Carpenters bottling plant, and now a Wetherspoon, on the edge of the shopping centre. It has a pleasant atmosphere and a changing clientele depending on the time of day. Sgt Mottershead VC, who died in 1917 while serving on the Western Front with the Royal Flying Corps, used to visit when it was a cinema and the Sgt Mottershead VC statue appeal was launched here.

Willey Moor Lock

Willey Moor Lock Tavern

Tarporley Road, SY13 4HF (400yds off A49, around 1½ miles N of Whitchurch)
12-2.30, 6-10.30; 12-3, 6-11 Sat; 12-3, 6-10.30 Sun
☎ (01948) 663274 🌐 willeymoorlock.co.uk
6 changing beers (sourced nationally)
This former lock-keeper's cottage is now a family-run free house. Access from the car park is via a footbridge over the Llangollen Canal. The pub is very popular with boaters and also walkers on the Sandstone Trail, especially in the summer. Choose your outside seating either next to the lock or in the attractive garden. Three changing beers, many from local brewers, increase to six in summer. Good-value meals are available during lunchtime and evening sessions. There is a campsite next door. Q ΛP

Wilmslow

Brewhouse & Kitchen

6-12 Swan Street, SK9 1HE
11-11 (midnight Fri & Sat); 12-11 Sun ☎ (01625) 441850
Brewhouse & Kitchen Bollin Ruby, Fustian Cut, Secret Genius, Lucky Sam
Opened in 2016, this brewery diner is a new concept to the area. The decor is unsurprisingly beer-related, with lamps made from beer glasses and bottles. Brewed on the premises, the four cask ales all have locally themed names. Food focuses on steaks and burgers, but there is also a selection of vegetarian and vegan dishes. The menu gives suggested beer pairings for most dishes. See the website for the current beer selection and menus.

Old Dancer

16 Grove Street, SK9 1DR
12-midnight (1am Fri & Sat) ☎ (01625) 530775
🌐 theolddancer.co.uk
5 changing beers
Lively café-bar on the main pedestrian shopping street. Furnished mainly with simple wooden tables on boarded floors, the walls are decorated with striking hand-painted murals on a dance theme. Six handpumps serve an interesting range of beers, often local, and a cask cider. Teas, coffees and food are available until 9pm including bar snacks, sandwiches, burgers and salads. The pub hosts live music on Saturday, film, quiz and science nights, a writers' group and a book club.

Winsford

Queen's Arms

Dene Drive, CW7 1AT (opp Winsford Cross shopping centre)
8am-midnight (1am Fri & Sat) ☎ (01606) 595350
Greene King Abbot; Ruddles Best Bitter; Sharp's Doom Bar; Wychwood Hobgoblin Gold; 4 changing beers (sourced regionally)
Modern open-plan Wetherspoon pub with a loyal following of regulars due to the varying range of beers on offer, often with a focus on the stronger and darker ones. Regular Meet the Brewer evenings are hosted. A conversational and busy pub, with muted TV screens, the patio area with decking outside is popular in summer. Access is easy, with a bus stop and taxi rank close by. Q P

CORNWALL

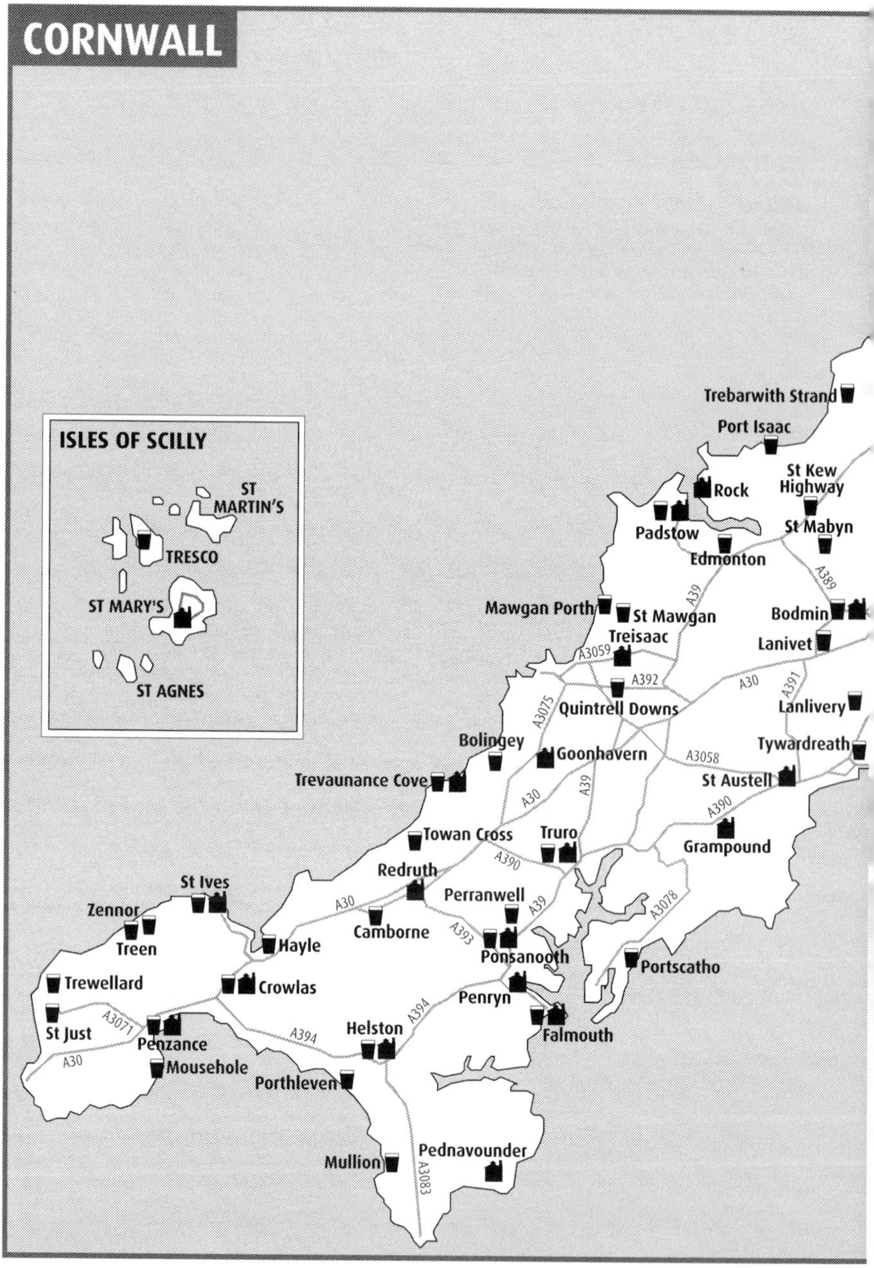

Altarnun

Rising Sun

PL15 7SN (NW of Altarnun village) SX215825

12-2.30, 5-11; 12-11 Sat; 12-10.30 Sun ☎ (01566) 86636
therisingsuninn.co.uk

Altarnun St Nonna's; Skinner's Lushingtons; 3 changing beers (sourced nationally)

A thriving 150-year-old community pub and tap for nearby Altarnun Brewery on the outskirts of town. The interior of this characterful building is cosy and warm, with beamed ceilings and an open fireplace, and antique guns and various pictures on the walls. Deceptively spacious, the pub offers ample seating in the bar, two small annexes for pool and drinkers, and a separate restaurant. Outside, there is a large patio and grassed area for games. Food always uses locally sourced ingredients.
Q P

Blisland

Blisland Inn

The Green, PL30 4JF (off A30 NE of Bodmin) SX100732

11.30-11; 12-10.30 Sun ☎ (01208) 850739

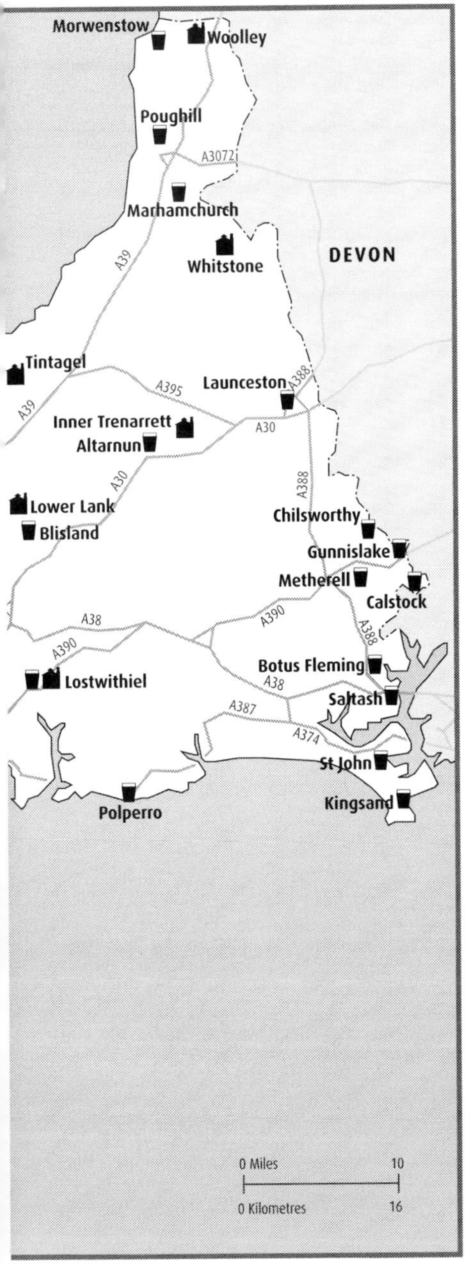

Dowr Kammel Blisland Gold; house beer (by Sharp's) [H]; 4 changing beers (sourced nationally) [H]/[G]
A friendly rural community pub by the village green, the Blisland retains its reputation as a real ale destination on the edge of Bodmin Moor. Having served more than 3,000 different real ales, it usually has at least five or six beers available with several brewed locally, plus frequently changing draught ciders including some unusual varieties. Food is freshly prepared using local produce. Popular with walkers and cyclists, the pub also welcomes well-behaved children and dogs. Winner of many local CAMRA awards it is also a former CAMRA National Pub of the Year.
Q🐴❀◐◑♣🍎🥛🐾

Bodmin

Hole in the Wall Ŀ ✔

16 Crockwell Street, PL31 2DS
⏲ 12-11 (9 Sun) ☎ (01208) 72397
Butcombe Original; Sharp's Doom Bar, Atlantic, Sea Fury; 2 changing beers (sourced nationally; often Draught Bass, Timothy Taylor) [H]
Popular locals' pub built in the 18th century as a debtors' prison. The building can be accessed direct from the public car park or through a secluded, leafy garden containing its own hop bine and stream, and presided over by a rather bleached stuffed lion. The single bar, which is subdivided by archways, contains a large and eclectic collection of antiques and military memorabilia. Upstairs is a separate function room. The pub has twice won local CAMRA Pub of the Year.
Q🐴❀◐◑♿🚆♣🍎🚌(27,11A)🐾📶

Bolingey

Bolingey Inn Ŀ

Penwartha Road, TR6 0DH (near B3284) SW763531
⏲ 11-midnight; 12-11 Sun ☎ (01872) 571626
Sharp's Doom Bar; 3 changing beers (sourced nationally; often Dynamite Valley, St Austell, Wadworth) [H]
Tucked away in a small hamlet approached by narrow, hilly lanes, this attractive wisteria-clad 17th-century pub has two bars. One is primarily used as a restaurant area; the other, with wooden floor and open fire, is popular with local drinkers and dog owners. One of the four handpumps is free of tie and usually offers a local brew. Beer festivals are held in April and October. Parking is limited but the pub has a hitching rail for equestrian patrons.
Q🐴❀◐◑⛺♣P🐾📶

Botus Fleming

Rising Sun Inn

PL12 6NJ SX405613
⏲ 6-midnight; 12-midnight Sat & Sun ☎ (01752) 842792
Skinner's Betty Stogs; 3 changing beers (sourced nationally; often Dartmoor, Everards, Greene King) [H]
Tastefully refurbished after remaining largely unaltered for years, this rural gem with low ceilings and well-trodden wooden floors is tucked away in a quiet village near Saltash, just off the beaten track. The three real ales are regularly and imaginatively changed; there is, however, no food. Draught cider is generally from Westons. The pub is dog-friendly, supports darts and euchre teams and hosts occasional live music. Regular buses pass on the A388, roughly a 20-minute walk away.
Q❀♣🍎P🐾📶

Calstock

Tamar Inn ✔

The Quay, PL18 9QA SX436686
⏲ 12-midnight summer; 12-2, 4.30-11 Mon-Thu; 12-midnight Fri & Sat; 12-10.30 Sun winter ☎ (01822) 832487
🌐 tamarinn.com
Sharp's Doom Bar; 4 changing beers (sourced regionally; often Exeter, Hanlons, Tintagel) [H]

This split-level 17th-century granite village pub is right beside the River Tamar. Its beamed interior is divided into distinct drinking areas, with well-worn floorboards, slate flagstones and paintings on the walls. The rear bar is more airy and leads to the courtyard. The changing beers are usually from Cornwall and Devon; cider is Westons Old Rosie. Good home-cooked traditional food is served. Live entertainment takes place on Friday or Saturday evening. ⏰❀❍➡●🖵(79)❀ 🛜

Camborne

John Francis Basset ✓
21 Commercial Street, TR14 8JZ
☼ 9am-midnight (1am Fri & Sat) ☎ (01209) 721720
Greene King IPA, Abbot; Sharp's Doom Bar; 5 changing beers Ⓗ
Wetherspoon pub in the former market house built by architect William Bond in 1866. Previous uses of the building have included as a cinema, night club and a pub called the Corn Exchange. Named after a prominent former local mine owner, it is a large, airy, open-plan venue with high ceilings and tall windows. Its single long bar offers an impressive selection of varying beers, many locally brewed. A real ale oasis in the town, well worth a visit.
Q⏰❀🚲❍🖶➡●🖵❀🛜

Chilsworthy

White Hart 🍺 ✓
PL18 9PB (signposted from A390) SX416721
☼ 12-11 (midnight Fri & Sat); 12-10 Sun ☎ (01822) 833876
⊕ whitehartchilsworthy.com
Butcombe Original; 4 changing beers (sourced regionally) Ⓗ
Cornwall CAMRA Pub of the Year 2019, this solid and cosy rural community free house is tucked into the steep northern slopes of the Tamar Valley near the prominent landmark of Kit Hill. The drinking area is carpeted throughout and simply furnished with wooden tables and chairs. It is warmed in winter by wood-burning stoves set in two stone chimney breasts. Horse brasses and other pub artefacts decorate the bar. Good food is made with fresh ingredients sourced locally wherever possible. ⏰❀❍♣●P❀🛜

Crowlas

Star Inn Ⓛ
TR20 8DX (on A30, 3 miles E of Penzance)
☼ 11.30-11; 12-10.30 Sun ☎ (01736) 740375
Penzance Mild, Crowlas Bitter, Potion No.9; 4 changing beers (sourced nationally) Ⓗ
Roadside free house and former local CAMRA Pub of the Year, home to the Penzance Brewery. The long U-shaped bar dispenses real ales from the pub's own brewhouse and two or three from other microbreweries. There is a pool table to the right, a comfy raised seating area, a cosy lounge area with leather sofas and chairs, and an adjacent meeting room. This is essentially a beer-drinkers' local where conversation is the main entertainment, with no noisy machines to distract. ❀♣P🖵❀🛜

Edmonton

Quarryman Inn Ⓛ
PL27 7JA (just off A39 near Royal Cornwall showground)
☼ 12-11 (11.30 Sun) ☎ (01208) 816444
⊕ thequarryman.co.uk
Otter Bitter; Skinner's Lushingtons; 2 changing beers (sourced regionally; often Padstow) Ⓗ
A highly popular traditional free house well worth seeking out. Its quiet, comfortable interior features a slate-floored public bar and carpeted lounge, both with dining areas. The light, airy and eclectic decor includes sporting memorabilia and local art. The ever-changing beer menu offers up to four quality ales, generally local. Local produce is used for the food menu. The atmosphere is convivial and family-friendly, and conversation flourishes – but mobile phone usage is prohibited.
Q⏰❀❍▲♣P🖵(11A,95)❀🛜

Falmouth

'Front Ⓛ
Custom House Quay, TR11 3JT
☼ 11-11 (midnight Fri & Sat); 11-10.30 Sun ☎ 07977 813494
Sharp's Sea Fury; 13 changing beers (sourced nationally; often Skinner's, Tintagel, Treen's) Ⓗ
A warm welcome awaits at this quayside cellar-style bar. Its wide range of ales caters for all tastes and there is also plenty of choice for the cider drinker – a fact recognised when the 'Front became the first Cornish pub to win both beer and cider local CAMRA Pub of the Year awards in 2018. There is a popular Sunday quiz and other evening entertainment. No food is available but you may bring your own. The pub offers a 10 per cent discount on real ales and ciders before 6pm.
Q⏰❀➡♣●❀🛜

Beerwolf Books
3-4 Bells Court, TR11 3AZ (up side alley off main shopping street)
☼ 10-midnight; 12-11 Sun ☎ (01326) 618474
⊕ beerwolfbooks.com

REAL ALE BREWERIES

Ales of Scilly St Mary's: Isles of Scilly
Altarnun Inner Trenarrett
Atlantic Treisaac
Black Flag Goonhavern
Black Rock Falmouth (brewing suspended)
Blue Anchor 🍺 Helston
Castle Lostwithiel
Cornish Crown Penzance
Dowr Kammel Lower Lank
Driftwood Spars 🍺 Trevaunance Cove
Dynamite Valley Ponsanooth
Forge Woolley
Fowey Lostwithiel
Granite Rock Penryn
Harbour Bodmin
Keltek Redruth
Lizard Pednavounder
Longhill Whitstone
Padstow Padstow
Penzance 🍺 Crowlas
Sharp's Rock
Skinner's Truro
St Austell St Austell
St Ives St Ives
Tintagel Tintagel
Treen's Ponsanooth
Tremethick Grampound
Woodman's Ponsanooth

6 changing beers (sourced nationally; often Blackjack, Penzance, Shiny) H
Pub or bookshop? Actually, it's both! Popular with all ages, this former maritime storage loft and pleasant outside courtyard is tucked away off Market Street. It is accessed via a steep flight of stairs, at the top of which is the bookshop, while to the right is the bar, dispensing an adventurous selection of constantly changing beers. Four further handpumps ensure that cider lovers are not forgotten. No food, but you may bring your own.

Boathouse L

Trevethan Hill, TR11 2AG (top of High St)
12-11 (midnight Fri & Sat) summer; 5-11 Mon-Thu; 4-midnight Fri; 12-midnight Sat; 12-11 Sun winter
(01326) 315425 theboathousefalmouth.co.uk
4 changing beers (sourced regionally; often Skinner's) H
This popular two-storey pub can be found up a short but steep hill on the edge of the town centre. The two-roomed interior is nautically themed, with distinct drinking and dining areas and a decked outdoor drinking balcony affording spectacular views across the river towards Flushing. Four handpumps dispense regularly changing regional and local brews, usually including a Skinner's Brewery beer. Food is locally sourced where possible, and freshly cooked; booking is advisable for the popular Sunday lunch.

Oddfellows Arms

Quay Hill, TR11 3HA
12-11 (10.30 Sun) (01326) 218611
Sharp's Sea Fury H**; 2 changing beers (sourced locally; often Skinner's)** H/G
A small, unpretentious single-bar community pub tucked up a hilly side street off the town centre and is popular with locals and visitors alike. Decorated with old photographs, it has a convivial atmosphere in which to enjoy the three beers normally on offer, with sometimes a fourth racked up at the back of the bar. A small room to the rear hosts the dartboard, pool table and real fire. The pub organises various festivals throughout the year, often involving food made by the locals.
Q

Seaview Inn

Wodehouse Terrace, TR11 3EP
5-11 (11.30 Wed); 12-2, 5-midnight Fri; 12-midnight Sat; 12-11 Sun (01326) 311359 seaviewinnfalmouth.co.uk
Sharp's Doom Bar; 2 changing beers (sourced nationally; often Treen's) H
A traditional and comfortable town pub with a large, beamed, open-plan island bar. As the name suggests, it provides excellent views over Falmouth harbour and the Carrick Roads estuary with their abundant maritime activity. The locals are a friendly mix of all ages, and the pub welcomes children and dogs. A games area to the rear hosts darts and pool. Accommodation is in three rooms. Q

Seven Stars ★

The Moor, TR11 3QA
11-11; 12-10.30 Sun (01326) 312111
thesevenstarsfalmouth.com
Draught Bass; Sharp's Atlantic, Sea Fury; 2 changing beers (sourced locally; often Skinner's, Treen's) G
This timeless and unspoilt town-centre local has been in the same family for nearly 170 years and features on CAMRA's National Inventory of Historic Pub Interiors. It has a lively, narrow taproom where beers are served on gravity from a unique, eccentrically designed stillage. There are two quiet snugs at the back. The old bottle-and-jug hatch still remains for outdoor drinkers. Bass is ever-present, as are beers from Sharp's Brewery. A real gem that should not be missed. Q

Gunnislake

Rising Sun Inn

Calstock Road, PL18 9BX (off A390) SX432711
12-midnight (11 Sun) (01822) 832201
therisingsungunnislake.com
Dartmoor Legend, Jail Ale; Exmoor Ale; Otter Bitter; 2 changing beers (sourced regionally) H
Friendly oak-beamed country inn dating from the 17th century, lying in a conservation area in a rural setting off the beaten track. It has much charm and character, and serves a good choice of up to six varying real ales, normally from Cornish or other West Country breweries. Exposed stone walls and wooden beams display an extensive collection of chinaware. Outside, the beautiful terraced garden affords views of the Tamar Valley. A true community pub hosting various local activities.
Q P (79)

Hayle

Bird in Hand

Trelissick Road, TR27 4HY
12-11 (01736) 753974
Exeter Avocet; 2 changing beers (sourced regionally; often Bays, Dartmoor) H
Families are welcome in this spacious pub converted from Victorian stables, adjacent to Paradise Park wildlife sanctuary. The decor in the one-room bar is a mix of local industrial paraphernalia and horse paintings on the walls, painted casks over the bar, and an end wall decorated with a frieze depicting scenes from Cornwall's industrial past. Outside is a large seating area; parking is shared with the wildlife sanctuary.
P (T1,T2)

Helston

Blue Anchor

50 Coinagehall Street, TR13 8EL
10-midnight (1am Fri & Sat) (01326) 562821
spingoales.com
Blue Anchor Jubilee IPA, Middle, Special; 1 changing beer (sourced locally; often Blue Anchor) H
A former monks' rest, this 15th-century brewpub is one of the oldest in Britain, changing little over the years and retaining much of its original character. Two separate small bars are found to the right of the central passageway, one with an open fire, and two sitting rooms to the left, all with slate floors. To the rear are a skittle alley and partly covered garden area with its own bar and barbecue. An anchor is visible on the thatched roof.
Q

Coinage Hall

9-11 Coinagehall Street, TR13 8ER
8am-midnight (1am Fri & Sat) (01326) 565344
Ruddles Best Bitter; Sharp's Doom Bar; 4 changing beers (sourced locally; often Cornish Chough, Skinner's) H

This pub in a former furniture store takes its name from when locally mined tin was assayed in the coinage hall. Surprisingly large and deep inside, it spans four separate levels, with steps between them and a number of distinct drinking or dining spaces all the way through. The single long bar usually offers up to four changing local microbrewery beers. The lowest level at the rear leads out to a patio for alfresco drinking. There is also a roof terrace. Q

Kingsand

Devonport Inn

The Cleave, PL10 1NF
11-11 summer; closed Tue winter (01752) 822869
devonportinn.com
Dartmoor Legend; 2 changing beers (sourced locally; often Bays, Otter)
Set between a narrow lane and the sea, this old pub was formerly divided into two bars but is now partly opened out to one, albeit still with distinct drinking areas. The small, wooden-floored bar has snug recesses and is ship themed. It serves up to two constantly changing real ales, mostly from Devon. Live bands perform monthly in winter and more frequently in summer. The pub provides a welcome halt, both for walkers on the Cornwall coast path and the less energetic.
(70,71)

Lanivet

Lanivet Inn

PL30 5ET (on A389)
11-11; 12-11 Sun (01208) 831212 lanivetinn.co.uk
St Austell Trelawny, Tribute, HSD; 2 changing beers (sourced nationally; often Greene King, Timothy Taylor)
Traditional Cornish pub in the village centre offering something for the whole community. The spacious open-plan bar has a large stone inglenook fireplace. The layout is food-oriented and an extended restaurant hosts weekly theme nights. Games, quizzes and music provide entertainment. Outside is a beer garden and large car park. The panda on the pub sign dates from 1937, when a Lanivet bamboo grove supplied the food for London Zoo's first such animal.
P (27)

Lanlivery

Crown Inn

PL30 5BT
11.30-11; 12-10.30 Sun (01208) 872707
thecrowninncornwall.co.uk
Sharp's Doom Bar; 2 changing beers (sourced locally; often Fowey, St Austell)
Picturesque pub in a long farmhouse style, with the main bar and snug at one end. The rest of the interior comprises a comfortable lounge with an inglenook fireplace, containing a huge wood-burning stove, and the restaurant. There has been an inn on the site since the 12th century. An old well in the conservatory can be viewed through its glass cover. Food is available daily, with most of the ingredients sourced locally. Snacks are served all day in summer. Accommodation is in the former piggery, and wheelchair-accessible.
Q P

Launceston

Bell Inn

1 Tower Street, PL15 8BQ (next to church tower)
12-11 (10.30 Sun) (01566) 779970
House beer (by Holsworthy Ales); 5 changing beers (sourced regionally)
Cosy 14th-century town hostelry originally built to house stonemasons erecting the nearby church. Conversation rules in this locals' pub, with a changing range of mostly local beers and two ciders, although the selection may be reduced out of season. A separate family room, available for groups to use, contains ancient frescoes uncovered when previous owners stripped away decades of modernisation. Cribbage and other pub games are played. Food is limited to a pasty or pork pie.
Q

Lostwithiel

Globe Inn

3 North Street, PL22 0EG (near railway station, town side of river bridge)
12-11 (midnight Fri & Sat) (01208) 872501
Sharp's Original; Skinner's Betty Stogs; 2 changing beers (sourced regionally)
Cosy 13th-century pub in the narrow streets of an old stannary (tin-mining) town, close to the station and medieval stone river bridge. The welcoming, rather rambling interior accommodates a single bar with several drinking/dining spaces, a restaurant and a suntrap patio at the rear. The beer range increases to four in summer. An extensive home-cooked menu features fish and game. The pub is named after a ship that took part in a sea battle in 1813, when a member of the family that owned it at the time was killed. Q

Royal Oak

Duke Street, PL22 0AG
11-11 (midnight Fri & Sat); 12-10.30 Sun
(01208) 872552
St Austell Tribute, Proper Job; Sharp's Doom Bar; 1 changing beer
This historic 13th-century inn lies just off the main road through Cornwall's old capital. A traditional, stone-floored public bar contrasts with a comfortable lounge and attached restaurant; there is a patio outside. The pub has a dartboard and pool table, and hosts occasional quiz nights and live entertainment. Accommodation is in six en-suite rooms. There is reputedly a mile-long tunnel, once used by smugglers, from the pub cellar to the dungeons of Restormel Castle.
Q P

Marhamchurch

Buller's Arms Hotel

Helebridge Road, EX23 0HB (off A39 S of Bude)
12-11 summer; closed Mon; 4-11 Tue-Fri; 12-11 Sat & Sun winter (01288) 361277 thebullersarmshotel.com
Sharp's Atlantic; Tintagel Arthur's Ale; house beer (by Tintagel); 1 changing beer (sourced locally; often Longhill)
Large community-oriented village hotel with a spacious beamed and slate-flagged bar room. Decorative bric-a-brac includes buffalo horns, a stuffed fox and a badger at one end of the room, while the other end hosts a dartboard, pool table and an upright piano. The beers may vary occasionally but are generally from local breweries.

The pub holds quiz nights and monthly live weekend entertainment. An under-fives soft play area is available most afternoons, and birthday party hosting on Saturday. Q ☆🐕🛏️🕧🚻♣🚆(218)🦮 📶

Mawgan Porth

Merrymoor 🄻 ✅

TR8 4BA (beside B3276 coast road)
🕧 10-midnight (11 Sun) ☎ (01637) 860258
🌐 merrymoorinn.com
St Austell Tribute; Sharp's Doom Bar, Original; 1 changing beer (sourced locally; often Bath Ales) Ⓗ
Originally a café whose owner served in the North African Campaign, hence the name. Now an atmospheric pub run by the same family since 1961, it is very much at the heart of the local community and raises huge sums for charity every year. Large picture windows overlook the sandy beach just 50 yards away. It is naturally busy in the season, and has a large beer garden, a spacious main bar and a separate family room.
☆🐕🛏️🕧🅿️🚆(A5)🦮 📶

Metherell

Carpenters Arms

Lower Metherell, PL17 8BJ SX408695
🕧 12-10 (midnight Fri & Sat) ☎ (01579) 351148
Sharp's Doom Bar; 2 changing beers (sourced locally) Ⓗ
Hard to find down a network of country lanes, this timeless, friendly, 15th-century pub is full of character and atmosphere. The public bar is flagged with slate, while heavy black beams are held in place by massive exposed stone walls, in contrast to the larger lounge, which also functions as a dining area. All food is freshly cooked on-site. The guest ales change constantly. Outdoor seating is on the suntrap terrace and the pub hosts a monthly local produce market. Q 🐕☆🕧🅿️🚆(79)🦮 📶

Morwenstow

Bush Inn

Crosstown, EX23 9SR (off A39, N of Kilkhampton)
SS208150
🕧 12-midnight (11 Sun) ☎ (01288) 331242
🌐 thebushinnmorwenstow.com
St Austell Tribute, HSD; 1 changing beer (sourced locally; often Forge, Tintagel) Ⓗ
Unassuming from the outside, this little gem is an ancient former chapel, dating in parts back to 950AD. Inside, it is simply furnished, with slate floors, granite walls and exposed beams in two small bar rooms, one of which is subdivided into separate drinking areas. Conversation is the main entertainment, although there is occasional live music. A large garden offers outstanding views over the Tidna Valley and out to sea. Four en-suite rooms and a two-person holiday cottage are available. Q ☆🐕🛏️🕧♣●🅿️🚆(217,219)🦮 📶

Mousehole

Old Coastguard Hotel

The Parade, TR19 6PR
🕧 10.30-11.30 ☎ (01736) 731222
🌐 oldcoastguardhotel.co.uk
Padstow Windjammer; St Austell Tribute; 1 changing beer (sourced locally; often Padstow) Ⓗ

An interesting hotel at the top of the village, entered down a steep flight of stairs. Constructed on different levels on the cliffside and with mostly wooden floors, it offers plenty of drinking and dining space. There are stunning views over the rocky St Clement's Isle and Mount's Bay, notably from a large, tropical-style garden that slopes down to the shore. Beers are from Cornish breweries and may be reduced to two at quiet times of the year. Q ☆🐕🛏️🕧Å●🚆(M6)🦮 📶

Mullion

Old Inn ✅

Churchtown, TR12 7HN
🕧 12-11; 12-midnight Fri & Sat ☎ (01326) 240240
🌐 oldinnmullion.co.uk
St Austell Tribute, Proper Job; 2 changing beers (sourced regionally) Ⓗ
This 16th-century partly-thatched and low-beamed village inn sits next to the church. A tiled passage from the main entrance leads to the bar room, which has parquet flooring and several distinct drinking spaces, although the former public bar area itself is quite small. More seating is available on the upper level further in. The interior is well-decorated with numerous antiques, mirrors, prints and cartoons and other interesting items. The pub is well-established locally as a favourite for drinking and dining. 🐕☆🛏️🕧♣🅿️🚆(37)🦮 📶

Padstow

Golden Lion Hotel

Lanadwell Street, PL28 8AN
🕧 11-11; 12-11 Sun ☎ (01841) 532797
🌐 goldenlionpadstow.co.uk
Padstow Windjammer; Sharp's Doom Bar; Tintagel Castle Gold Ⓗ
Padstow's oldest pub, dating back well over 400 years, and still used for stabling the famous red 'oss which makes its energetic appearance every May Day during the famous 'obby-'oss celebrations. The busy low-beamed and slate-flagged public bar is partitioned to create a family dining area; the quieter lounge is spacious and comfortable. There is also a seated patio outside. The pub is situated a little way from the bustling harbour area but can get crowded during the summer season. 🐕☆🛏️🕧🚻Å🚆(A5,11A)🦮 📶

Penzance

Crown 🄻

Victoria Square, TR18 2EP
🕧 12-midnight (11.30 Fri & Sat); 12-10.30 Sun
☎ (01736) 351070 🌐 thecrownpenzance.co.uk
5 changing beers (sourced locally; often Cornish Crown) Ⓗ
Close to the railway and bus stations, and brewery tap for Cornish Crown, this small, traditional community local is tucked away behind the main shopping street. Offering a relaxed, friendly atmosphere, it has a tidily furnished bar with upholstered window seats and a huge mirror covering one wall, and a cosy two-table snug at the rear. The real ales are usually from Crown, although an occasional guest brew appears. You may bring your own food, with plates provided. 🐕☆🚈♣●🚆🦮 📶

Dock Inn

17 Quay Street, TR18 4BD
11-11 summer; 12-10.30 winter (01736) 362833
thedockinnpenzance.co.uk
Blue Anchor Middle; Penzance Potion No.9; Sharp's Doom Bar; 1 changing beer (sourced locally; often Skinner's)
Old and traditional one-time fishermen's pub near the dockside, close to the Scilly ferry pier. The pub extends through two old cottages, with the bar in the upper level, and a comfortable lounge next door also serving as a dining area. The decor includes a large picture mirror, nautical and mining pictures, and bric-a-brac including a stuffed bird in a cage. A ship's figurehead oversees proceedings in the bar. Q P

Perranwell

Royal Oak

TR3 7PX
11.30-3, 6-midnight; 11.30-midnight Fri & Sat; 12-11.30 Sun (01872) 863175
theroyaloakperranwellstation.co.uk
Sharp's Doom Bar; Skinner's Lushingtons; 2 changing beers (sourced nationally; often Harbour, Padstow)
Small 18th-century cottage-style village community pub with an emphasis on good food – most of the tables are set for meals, but drinkers are equally welcome, as the many locals at the bar will testify. Booking for meals is advisable however, especially evenings. The beers vary frequently and are often from local breweries. The pub holds monthly quiz nights and fundraising events for local charities.
Q P (L2,46)

Polperro

Blue Peter Inn

Quay Road, PL13 2QZ (far end of W side of harbour)
11-11; 12-10.30 Sun (01503) 272743
thebluepeterinn.com
St Austell Tribute; Sharp's Original; 4 changing beers (sourced regionally; often Bays, Cornish Crown, Harbour)
Named after the naval flag, this friendly inn is reached up a flight of steps near the quay, and is the only pub with a sea view in the village. In summer it offers up to five ales from Cornwall and Devon, and a varied menu of home-cooked dishes served all day. Featuring low beams, wooden floors, unusual souvenirs and work by local artists, the pub is popular with locals, fishermen, visitors – and their dogs.

Crumplehorn Inn

The Old Mill, Crumplehorn, PL13 2RJ (on A387, top of town near coach park)
10.30-midnight (01503) 272348
thecrumplehorninn.co.uk
St Austell Tribute, Proper Job; Tintagel Castle Gold, Harbour Special; 2 changing beers (sourced locally)
Once a mill and mentioned in the Domesday Book, this 14th-century inn at the entrance to the village still has a working waterwheel. The split-level bar has three comfortable areas with low ceilings and slate flagstone floors. Outside, the pleasant, spacious patio by the millstream offers large umbrellas as sunshades. A varied menu includes locally sourced food. Accommodation is B&B or self-catering. In summer, catch the electric milk float tram down to the harbour from the nearby public car park. Children and dogs welcome.
P

Ponsanooth

Stag Hunt

20 St Michael's Road, TR3 7EE (on A393)
5-11 (11.30 Thu; midnight Fri & Sat); 12-3, 7-11 Sun
(01872) 863046
St Austell Tribute; Treen's Classic; 1 changing beer (sourced locally; often Treen's)
Traditional Cornish granite community pub on the main Falmouth to Redruth road. The front bar leads up to a raised back room. The downstairs drinking area is carpeted throughout and decorated with photos depicting scenes from the area. An upstairs room, with its own small bar, can act as a function room or host the Thursday evening jam session. The real ales are mostly locally brewed. Food times vary; Indian cuisine is a speciality.
Q P (U2)

Port Isaac

Golden Lion

13 Fore Street, PL29 3RB
12-11 (midnight Fri & Sat); 12-10.30 Sun
(01208) 880336 thegoldenlionportisaac.co.uk
St Austell Trelawny, Tribute, Proper Job; 1 changing beer (sourced locally; often St Austell)
This fine old 18th-century pub in the heart of Port Isaac has several drinking areas and a small balcony overlooking the harbour. Beware the slightly uneven bare-boarded floors, which, together with Victorian cast-iron fireplaces means it has been identified by CAMRA as having a regionally important historic pub interior. The games room downstairs was originally the Bloody Bones locals' bar, and boasts a smugglers' tunnel down to a causeway on the beach. A small flagstoned courtyard at the rear offers alfresco drinking. (96)

Porthleven

Ship Inn

Mount Pleasant Road, TR13 9JS
11-midnight (01326) 564204
theshipinnporthleven.co.uk
Sharp's Cornish Coaster, Doom Bar; Skinner's Porthleven; Tintagel Harbour Special; 1 changing beer (sourced locally)
Seventeeth-century fishermen's inn perched on the south-west corner of the harbour, accessed up a steep flight of steps. It enjoys a commanding view over the harbour; here you can sit comfortably and watch the rough seas on stormy days. The rambling split-level interior has wooden and slated floors, beams decorated with an eclectic mix of coins, banknotes, beermats and brass artefacts, and sketches of local characters. A large log fire warms the pub in winter. (U4)

Portscatho

Plume of Feathers

The Square, TR2 5HW
11-11; 12-10.30 Sun (01872) 580321
plumeoffeathers-roseland.com
St Austell Tribute, Proper Job; 2 changing beers (often St Austell, Timothy Taylor)

Built in 1756, the Plume is one of the oldest buildings in the village, and the hub of the local community. Its contemporary exterior hides a traditional wood-beamed, slate-walled interior with cosy nooks, a split-room bar and separate restaurant. The selection of St Austell ales may be supplemented by a changing beer from elsewhere. The pub is focused on home-cooked and locally sourced food, and hosts charity nights and other community events. You will receive a warm welcome here. **Q** (50)

Poughill

Preston Gate Inn

Poughill Road, EX23 9ET (just outside Bude, on Sandymouth Bay road) SS224077

11-11 (01288) 354017 prestongateinn.co.uk

Sharp's Original; Skinner's Lushingtons; 2 changing beers (sourced locally; often Holsworthy Ales, Tintagel) H

This cosy 16th-century building, originally two cottages, has been a village pub since 1983. The spacious U-shaped room hosts a dartboard at one end of the bar; the other end is roomier with more seating and a roaring log fire in winter. Conversation rules here, and the pub is home to darts and quiz teams. Meals include monthly theme nights (booking advised). The beer range may reduce in winter and the cider varies. The name Preston comes from the Cornish word for priest. **Q** **P** (128)

Quintrell Downs

Two Clomes

East Road, TR8 4PD (on A392)

11.30-11 (01637) 879737

Sharp's Doom Bar; 2 changing beers (sourced locally; often Harbour, Padstow) H

Named after the two ovens situated either side of the open fireplace – which is now fitted with a wood-burning stove – this 18th-century free house is popular for dining out. Various extensions to the original building have added a large restaurant (booking is advisable, even in winter). Background music plays and a TV shows sporting events. The pub is conveniently situated on a main route into Newquay, and close to campsites. **P** (21,92)

St Ives

Kettle & Wink Bar (Western Hotel)

Gabriel Street, TR26 2LU

12-1am (01736) 795277 hotelstives.com

St Austell Tribute, Proper Job; 1 changing beer H

This small drinkers' pub is part of the Western Hotel with its own street entrance and a courtyard garden to the rear. The ale range may increase to three during busy summer periods, with changing beers from Bath Ales or St Austell's main and small batch ranges. Food is available only on weekdays in high season. A large function room in the hotel can also supply real ale. This is the town's main venue for live entertainment, featuring music every evening. **Q**

Pilchard Press Alehouse

Wharf Road, TR26 1LF

4-11 summer; closed Mon-Wed; 4-10 Thu-Sun winter (01736) 791665

6 changing beers (sourced locally; often Altarnun, St Ives, Treen's) H/G

Cornwall's first micropub, the Pilchard Press opened in 2016, with space for around 25 people. Situated up an alley off the harbour front, it offers a friendly atmosphere and up to six real ales from casks racked up on an interesting wooden stillage. There are a few bar stools, plus two tables with chairs and a smaller chessboard table. Note that the pub may close early if the beer runs out. **Q**

St John

St John Inn

PL11 3AW

closed Mon-Wed; 5-11 Thu (midnight Fri); 12-midnight Sat; 12-10.30 Sun (01752) 829299

Draught Bass; 2 changing beers (sourced nationally; often Exmoor, Woodforde's) H

This picturesque and welcoming 16th-century village pub is constructed from two former cottages. Reached down narrow country lanes, it has a pleasant, cosy ambience. The L-shaped bar room features a beamed ceiling, red-tiled floor, wooden furniture and a warming open fire in winter. A cosy snug opposite the bar, a patio with seating at the front and an attractive beer garden add to the appeal. Live events are hosted in a semi-permanent marquee. **Q** **P**

St Just

Star Inn ✔

1 Fore Street, TR19 7LL

11.30-midnight (11.30 Sun) (01736) 788767

thestarinn-stjust.co.uk

Bath Ales Gem; St Austell Cornish Best Bitter, Proper Job; 2 changing beers (sourced regionally; often Bath Ales, St Austell) H

Banter is guaranteed at this simple 18th-century granite inn, where good ale and conversation rule. The pub has changed little over time, its atmospheric interior, with wooden furnishings and an open fire, generating a traditional ambience. Celtic flags adorn the beamed ceiling, and artefacts of former mining and maritime activities are displayed on the walls. An adjacent snug is used for various activities, and there is a walled beer garden. Up to five ales are offered, but no food is available.

St Kew Highway

Red Lion Inn L

PL30 3DN (just off A39)

12-3 (not Mon-Thu), 5.30-11; 12-11 (4 winter) Sun

(01208) 841271 redlionstkew.com

3 changing beers (sourced regionally; often Padstow) H

Fully community-oriented, this picturesque family-run 17th-century pub is central to village activities. Its L-shaped single-bar interior divides distinctly in two – the front area mainly for drinking, though it includes an elevated dining space, and the rear a restaurant for more leisurely dining. Comfortable furnishings and open fires contribute to the cosy, relaxed ambience. Up to three ales are offered, mostly from Cornwall or Devon breweries. Interesting freshly cooked meals feature local produce. Well worth a visit.

Q **P** (95)

St Mabyn

St Mabyn Inn

Churchtown, PL30 3BA
12-midnight (11 Sun) (01208) 841266
stmabyninn.com
Sharp's Doom Bar, Sea Fury; Tintagel Cornwall's Pride; 1 changing beer (sourced locally) H
Near the church stands this popular, attractive, 17th-century free house, a village local where conversation thrives. It features a single bar with adjoining snug, games room and stylish well-appointed restaurant, and an attractive beer garden outside. Open fires, wood furnishings including settles, stained-glass partitions and windows add character, complemented by an interesting collection of toby jugs, horse brasses and vintage advertising. With four quality ales and an ever-changing menu specialising in local produce, this pub is one to seek out.
Q P (55)

St Mawgan

Falcon Inn L

TR8 4EP
11-11 (midnight Fri & Sat); 12-11 Sun summer; 11-3, 5.30-11; 11-midnight Fri & Sat; 12-11 Sun winter
(01637) 860225 thefalconinnstmawgan.co.uk
Dartmoor IPA, Legend; 2 changing beers (sourced locally; often Harbour, Padstow) H
Attractive community pub in the idyllic setting of the Lanherne Valley; a quiet retreat only a few miles from the bustle of Newquay and the airport. The single bar exudes a warm, welcoming atmosphere and offers three real ales, one of which changes regularly. A beer festival with gin bar is held every July. The Falcon is popular for meals. It also has a games room and a large garden; dogs are welcome here and in the pub.
Q P (A5)

Saltash

Union Inn

Tamar Street, PL12 4EL (on waterfront, beneath bridges)
11-11; 12-10.30 Sun (01752) 844770
Dartmoor Legend, Jail Ale; Sharp's Doom Bar H**; 2 changing beers (sourced regionally; often Bays, Cornish Crown)** G
The frontage of this riverside local, overlooked by the Tamar bridges, is strikingly painted as a union flag. The single bar offers a selection of real ales and a varying guest beer, usually on gravity in the cellar. The draught cider is Sam's Devon Dry. Outside drinking is at tables overlooking the river. Live music features on Tuesday or weekend evenings. Tamar Street, the pub's location, used to be known as Pickle Cock Alley as shellfish were sold through open windows. Q P

Towan Cross

Victory Inn L

TR4 8BN
12-11.30 (01209) 890359
Skinner's Betty Stogs, Lushingtons; St Austell Tribute; 1 changing beer (sourced locally; often Dynamite Valley) H
Built in 1605, this clifftop former coaching inn was originally opened to quench the thirst of local miners. Welcoming and family-run, it offers impressive sea views – and breezes – to enjoy alongside Cornish ales and locally sourced quality food. The open plan single bar separates into drinking and dining areas, extending to the conservatory and spacious beer garden. In former times, pedestrian funeral corteges would stop outside, rest the coffin on the nearby horizontal Towan Cross, and take refreshment within.
Q P (304,315)

Trebarwith Strand

Mill House Inn

PL34 0HD (off B3263, near Tintagel) SX058865
11-11 (midnight Fri & Sat); 12-10.30 Sun
(01840) 770200 themillhouseinn.co.uk
Tintagel Castle Gold; house beer (by Tintagel); 1 changing beer (sourced locally; often Tintagel) H
Converted 16th-century corn mill and waterwheel set beside a stream in a deep wooded valley. This friendly inn has a stone-flagged bar area accessible up a flight of steps by the adjacent drinking terrace. The restaurant is in an extension, offering an imaginative, daily changing food menu. While the Mill House is primarily a food and accommodation establishment, drinkers are nevertheless welcome in the bar, with a mix of local beers from nearby Tintagel Brewery. Q P

Treen

Gurnard's Head Hotel L

TR26 3DE (on B3306, Lands End-St Ives coast road)
10-11 (11.30 Sun) (01736) 796928
gurnardshead.co.uk
St Austell Tribute; 3 changing beers (sourced locally; often Cornish Crown, Padstow, Skinner's) H
Named after the nearby headland, this striking yellow-coloured inn stands near the coastal path on the rugged and beautiful granite moorland. Its wood-floored interior comprises a large bar, cosy snug and stylish restaurant. Wooden furnishings, comfy sofas and open fires create a relaxed atmosphere, with local art adorning the walls. The changing beer range features Cornish microbreweries. Daily variations to the food menu reflect availability of local produce.
Q P (7,16A)

Tresco (Isles of Scilly)

New Inn

Townshill, TR24 0QG
11-11 summer; closed Mon & Wed; 6-11 Tue; 11-3, 6-11 Thu-Sat; 11-10.30 Sun winter (01720) 423006
Sharp's Doom Bar; 3 changing beers (sourced locally; often Ales of Scilly, St Austell, Skinner's) H
Excellent old pub near New Grimsby harbour, a haven between demanding coastal walks and the boat to St Mary's. Extensions to the garden and a covered pavilion have added to the attractions of this popular real ale outlet. The varying beers are mostly from Cornish breweries, often Skinner's and St Austell, and local brewer Ales of Scilly is frequently represented. Beer festivals are held over the spring and late summer bank holidays.
Q

Trevaunance Cove

Driftwood Spars [L]

Quay Road, TR5 0RT
11-11 (midnight Fri & Sat) (01872) 552428
driftwoodspars.com
6 changing beers (sourced locally; often Atlantic, Driftwood, Harbour) [H]
This friendly brewpub has it all. A former 17th-century sail loft and mine warehouse, it features three wood-beamed bars, lead-light windows and open granite fireplaces. The decor is mainly smuggling- and shipwreck-themed. Upstairs, the restaurant affords panoramic views across the bay, while over the road the beer garden adjoins the Driftwood Brewery, whose beers are always on the bar alongside regional guests. The pub holds three beer festivals a year, and occasional tutored tastings. Q P (57,87)

Trewellard

Trewellard Arms [L]

Trewellard Road, TR19 7TA (on B3318/B3306 jct)
12-11 (midnight Sat); 12-10.30 Sun (01736) 788634
5 changing beers (sourced regionally; often Bays, Brains, Tintagel) [H]
Formerly the nearby Geevor mine owner's residence, this is now a thriving family-run free house, where a warm welcome is assured. Its cosy interior accommodates a spacious open-beamed single bar and pleasant restaurant with secluded dining space. Open fires enhance the atmosphere. A varying beer menu offers up to five ales and two ciders, and good-value home-cooked food is available. The south-facing exterior includes a paved patio area and an extensive car park. A beer festival is held each May. Q P

Truro

Old Ale House

7 Quay Street, TR1 2HD (near bus station)
11-11 (11.30 Fri; midnight Sat); 12-10.30 Sun
(01872) 271122 old-ale-house.co.uk
Skinner's Betty Stogs, Hops 'n Honey, Lushingtons, Porthleven [H]**; 4 changing beers (sourced regionally; often Skinner's)** [H]/[G]
A friendly and lively city-centre pub that is Skinner's brewery tap. The main bar is atmospheric, with subtle lighting, wooden floors, beamed ceiling, scattered artefacts and a barrel of free monkey nuts. Seating is plentiful, while upstairs is a quieter drinking area and function room. Up to 13 real ales and six real ciders are on offer, as well as an impressive range of up to 40 craft keg and foreign beers. Customers may bring in their own food. Q

Rising Sun

Mitchell Hill, TR1 1ED
11.30 (12 Sun)-midnight; closed Mon winter
(01872) 240003 risingsuntruro.co.uk
Fuller's London Pride; Skinner's Betty Stogs; 2 changing beers (sourced locally; often Skinner's) [G]
Near the city centre up a steep hill, this award-winning pub is worth seeking out. Its narrow frontage belies a spacious interior featuring a lounge bar and a small public bar with adjacent dining area. A raised restaurant area leads to the sheltered patio where periodic beer festivals are held. The pub is comfortably furnished throughout, its decor including old Truro scenes. The varied beer menu offers up to four ales dispensed straight from casks. The locally sourced food menu is popular – booking is advised. Q P

Tywardreath

New Inn [L]

Fore Street, PL24 2QP
12-11 (01726) 813901
Draught Bass [G]**; St Austell Cornish Best, Tribute, Proper Job; 1 changing beer (sourced nationally)** [H]
Built in the mid-18th century by mine owners, this classic village pub is a perfect example of a community local and the hub of village life. Groups meet here regularly, and fêtes are held in the extensive gardens. Although tied to a brewery, the landlord serves a guest beer and Draught Bass, which the pub is covenanted to sell in perpetuity. Pub games, good conversation and regular live music provide the entertainment. There is a separate restaurant area to the rear.
Q P (24)

Zennor

Tinner's Arms

TR26 3BY (off B3306 St Ives-St Just coast road)
11-11; 12-10.30 Sun (01736) 796927
tinnersarms.com
House beer (by St Austell); 2 changing beers (sourced locally; often Skinner's) [H]
Popular with walkers and tourists drawn by a local mermaid legend, this ancient granite village pub lies on the north coast of the Penwith peninsula. An atmospheric interior accommodates a single bar and adjacent restaurant, the ambience enhanced by exposed granite walls and wood beams, open fires, wall panels and rustic furnishings. The food menu features local produce, but best to phone the pub first if planning to eat here. Folk music on Thursday evenings; Sunday is quiz night.
Q P

Cask beer

Real ale is often described as 'beer from a barrel' and pubs are said to have 'barrels behind the bar'. In fact, barrels are large containers, too big for most bars. The correct generic term for the containers for real ale is cask and casks come in the following sizes:

Pin – 4.5 gallons
Firkin (from old Dutch word meaning 'fourth') – 9 gallons
Kilderkin (from old Dutch word meaning 'small cask') – 18 gallons
Barrel – 36 gallons
Hogshead – 54 gallons

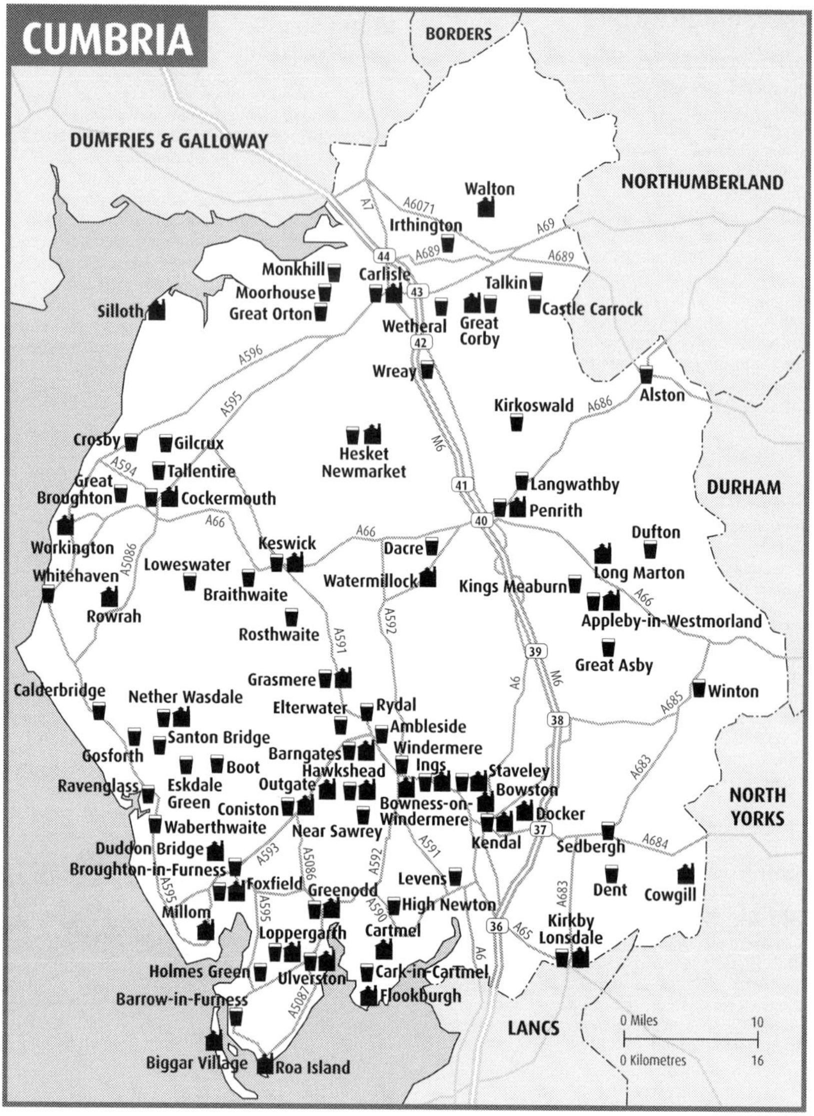

Alston

Cumberland Inn L

Townfoot, CA9 3HX

12-11 ☎ (01434) 381875 cumberlandalston.co.uk

Firebrick Blaydon Brick; 3 changing beers H

A family-run 19th-century inn overlooking the South Tyne river, the Cumberland is a regular in the Guide. Close to the Coast-to-Coast cycle route and Pennine Way, it is an ideal base to explore the highest market town in England. Guest beers are dispensed from four handpumps. They have included brews from Hesket Newmarket, Consett Ale Works, Allendale, High House Farm, Mordue breweries and further afield. Old Rosie is a regular real cider, alongside two or three changing ciders and perries. Freshly cooked food is served in the bar and restaurant, including a traditional Sunday roast. The patio overlooks the South Tyne Valley. **Q❀🛏◑●P🚌🐾📶**

Ambleside

Golden Rule ✔

Smithy Brow, LA22 9AS

11-midnight ☎ (015394) 32257

Robinsons Cumbria Way, Dizzy Blonde, Double Hop, Wizard; 3 changing beers (sourced regionally; often Robinsons) H

A good range of well-kept and well-served Robinsons ales is available at this exceptionally high-quality traditional pub, tucked away off the main road in the town. The bar has a cosy feel with a real fire, bench seating and historical rock-climbing photos decorating the walls. An attractive snug with a dartboard is popular for families with children. The pub is regularly packed with jolly locals and students from the nearby Cumbria university, mingling with visiting walkers and climbers. The Rule has featured in the Guide since 1977 as a local fixture. **Q❀♿♣●P🚌🐾📶**

Royal Oak
Lake Road, LA22 9BU
12-11 (11.30 Fri & Sat) (015394) 33382
Greene King IPA, Abbot; Kirkby Lonsdale Monumental Blonde, Radical Red, Pennine Ambler, Singletrack; 1 changing beer (sourced locally; often Kirkby Lonsdale, Coniston, Old School)
A vastly improved outlet since it became a Greene King Local Hero offering local ales. Beers from Kirkby Lonsdale are currently featured but other local brews may be available. Its central position in the Ambleside honeypot encourages a busy trade of visitors and regulars – the outside covered seating is often full even in winter rain. The bar is efficiently run by friendly staff to avoid a bottleneck, other areas focus on dining. Hungarian goulash is a speciality. Old Lake District photos are on display.

Appleby-in-Westmorland

Midland Hotel
25 Clifford Street, CA16 6TS
2-11; 11.30-11 Sat & Sun (017683) 51524
themidlandhotelappleby.co.uk
3 changing beers (sourced nationally; often Cross Bay, Eden River, Malvern Hills)
The Midland has three handpumps showcasing mainly local ales with interesting additions from further afield, including Worcestershire. Cider and perry are usually on offer. An acclaimed three-day beer festival takes place in September. The pub's two rooms have a light, modern decor and wooden floors. Upstairs accommodation is popular all year round, especially with steam train fans.
Q P (563)

Barngates

Drunken Duck Inn
LA22 0NG (signed off the B5286 Hawkshead to Ambleside road)
11.30-11; 12-10.30 Sun (015394) 36347
drunkenduckinn.co.uk
Barngates Cat Nap, Cracker, Tag Lag; 3 changing beers (sourced locally; often Barngates)
The Drunken Duck stands high above Ambleside, a traditional Lakeland dwelling reflecting the simplicity, beauty and longevity of its natural environment. From the fells, it draws water for the beers brewed on-site by Barngates Brewery. The bar has six handpumps and serves all the Barngates beers on rotation. The outside seating area at the front offers dramatic views of the fells to the north-east. Dogs are allowed except in the dining room. Q P

Barrow-in-Furness

Duke of Edinburgh
Abbey Road, LA14 5QR
11-midnight (01229) 821039
dukeofedinburghhotel.co.uk
Lancaster Amber, Blonde, Red; Wainwright; 4 changing beers (sourced regionally)
On the edge of the town centre near the station, the Duke is not as noisy as similar bars in the town. It has an airy feel with modern, comfortable furniture and a fine open fire. Paintings by local artists are displayed. Good-quality, reasonably priced bar meals are served, with a separate restaurant and large function room. Beers are mainly from Lancaster, with guest ales plus three craft keg ales and bottled beers from around the world. P

King's Arms
Quarry Brow, Hawcoat, LA14 4HY
5.30-11; 4-midnight Fri; 12.30-midnight Sat; 1-midnight Sun (01229) 828137
Cumbrian Legendary Ales Loweswater Gold; Kirkby Lonsdale Monumental Blonde; 4 changing beers (sourced locally; often Barngates, Bowness Bay, Cross Bay)
Popular local pub selling ales mainly from local micros, including Barngates, Bowness Bay, Cross Bay, Cumberland, Cumbrian Legendary Ales and Kirkby Lonsdale. A beer menu on a chalkboard lists forthcoming attractions. The pub, which has been on these premises since the 1860s, has been extensively extended and renovated, and features an open bar with adjacent separate rooms. Friendly staff give a warm welcome. Well-behaved dogs are allowed in one of the rooms. Q

REAL ALE BREWERIES

Appleby Kendal
Barngates Barngates
Beckstones Millom
Biggar Biggar Village
Bowness Bay Kendal
Brack'N'Brew Watermillock
Carlisle Carlisle
Coniston Coniston
Cumbrian Legendary Hawkshead
Dent Cowgill
Derwent Silloth
Eden River Penrith
Ennerdale Craft Rowrah
Fell Flookburgh
Foxfield Foxfield
Grasmere Grasmere
Great Corby Great Corby
Greenodd Greenodd
Handsome Bowston
Hawkshead Flookburgh/Staveley
Healey's Loppergarth
Helm Bar Appleby-in-Westmorland
Hesket Newmarket Hesket Newmarket
Jennings Cockermouth
Keswick Keswick
Kirkby Lonsdale Kirkby Lonsdale
Langdale Docker (NEW)
Logan Beck Duddon Bridge (NEW)
Old Friends Ulverston (NEW)
Old Vicarage Walton (NEW)
Roa Island Roa Island (NEW)
South Lakes Ulverston
Strands Nether Wasdale
Stringers Ulverston
Tarn Hows Outgate
Tirril Long Marton
Tractor Shed Workington
Ulverston Ulverston
Unsworth's Yard Cartmel
Watermill Ings
Westmorland Kendal
Wild Boar Bowness-on-Windermere

Boot

Brook House Inn

CA19 1TG (200yds walk from Dalegarth Station – La'al Ratty)

9am-11 ☎ (019467) 23288 brookhouseinn.co.uk

Cumbrian Legendary Ales Langdale; Ennerdale Craft Blonde, Wild; 6 changing beers (sourced nationally)

In the heart of the western Lake District in beautiful Eskdale, close to the terminus of the Ravenglass and Eskdale miniature railway, this popular family-run tourist pub is renowned for good food and a wide range of well-kept cask ales. Together with other nearby pubs in the Eskdale valley, the Brook House Inn provides the focal point for an annual beer festival held in June. Local CAMRA Pub of the Year finalist 2019. Q P

Woolpack Inn

CA19 1TH (¾ mile E of Boot village)

8am-11 ☎ (019467) 23230 woolpack.co.uk

Barngates Cracker; Bowness Bay Lakeland Blonde; 10 changing beers (sourced nationally)

Iconic Lakeland pub on the approach to Hardknott Pass, surrounded by stunning scenery. This family-run tourist pub is renowned for good food and well-kept cask ales. The lounge and walkers' bars offer an attractive mix of traditional and modern styles, with wood-burning stoves in both areas. It is popular with families. Together with other nearby pubs in the Eskdale valley, the Woolpack Inn participates in the annual Eskdale beer festival in June. It also holds a cider festival.
Q (Dalegarth) P

Braithwaite

Middle Ruddings Country Inn

CA12 5RY (N side of Braithwaite village, on jct for Thornthwaite and A66)

10.30-11; 12.30-10.30 Sun ☎ (017687) 78436

middle-ruddings.co.uk

3 changing beers (sourced nationally)

Comfortable family-run country inn with two rooms and a lounge. A separate conservatory restaurant serves good home-made food using locally sourced produce. Passionate about real ale, usually brewed in Cumbria, the pub also serves real ciders and an increasing range of bottle-conditioned ales, hosts an annual beer lovers' dinner, and is a winner of a number of CAMRA awards. Well-behaved dogs are allowed in the bar areas.
Q P (X5)

Broughton-in-Furness

Manor Arms

The Square, LA20 6HY

12-11.30 (midnight Fri & Sat); 12-11 Sun

☎ (01229) 716286 manorarmsthesquare.co.uk

Great Corby Blonde; Hawkshead Windermere Pale; 6 changing beers (sourced regionally)

An outstanding free house owned by the Varty family for more than 30 years. Set in an attractive Georgian square, it has received many CAMRA awards, including Furness Pub of the Year 2018 and 2019. Real ale dominates and usually includes a dark beer, along with traditional cider and perry. A mini beer festival is held every day. Two fires keep the pub warm and the bar staff are always friendly.
Q

Calderbridge

Stanley Arms Hotel

CA20 1DN

12-11.30 ☎ (01946) 841235 stanleyarmshotel.com

Timothy Taylor Landlord; Wychwood Hobgoblin Gold; 4 changing beers (sourced nationally)

This small family-run village hotel, just outside the Lake District National Park, has a delightful beer garden beside the River Calder. It has full fishing rights. The hotel is on the A595 which gives easy access to the western lakes, fells and valleys. Hearty meals, using locally sourced produce, are served in the two-room bar and restaurant. A well-equipped function/conference room is available. Local attractions include the riverside walk along the Calder, past the ruined 12th-century Calder abbey. Q P

Cark-in-Cartmel

Engine Inn

LA11 7NZ

12-11 (10.30 Mon); 12-10.30 Sun ☎ (015395) 58341

theengineinncartmel.co.uk

Lancaster Blonde; Timothy Taylor Landlord; 2 changing beers (sourced regionally; often Unsworth's Yard)

This 17th-century inn, refurbished in 2010, is a short walk from the station and makes an excellent end to the walk from Grange, as described in CAMRA's Lake District Pub Walks. Beers are selected to provide a range of styles. There is an open bar area with a cosy fire, separate rooms away from the bar, and a riverside beer garden. Regular live music plays on Saturday evenings. Five en-suite rooms are available. Winter hours, especially for food, may vary.
P (531,530)

Carlisle

Beehive

Warwick Road, CA1 1LH

11.30-11 (midnight Fri & Sat); 12-11 Sun

☎ (01228) 549731

Morland Old Golden Hen; 3 changing beers (often Greene King, Marston's)

Large, popular pub opposite Carlisle football and rugby grounds on the A69 leading into town (home fans only for some games). There are lots of TV screens for Sky sports, showing multiple channels at the same time when necessary. Food is served all day. There is a quiz on Thursday night, and a covered outdoor smoking area. Live music features most Friday evenings. The pub was refurbished following flooding in 2015. P

Fat Gadgie

5 Devonshire Street, CA3 8LG

3-midnight; 12-1am Sat & Sun ☎ (01228) 812880

thefatgadgie.co.uk

6 changing beers

Opened in May 2017 after the closure of a specialist ale bar in the same premises, the new owner has refurbished the space to provide a pleasant, quiet drinking environment without the distraction of television or gaming machines. This city-centre bar serves a choice of beers from far and wide, changing the range frequently and targeting the discerning drinker. The Fat Gadgie adds to a series of unusual bar names in this area of the city.

King's Head Inn 🄻

Fisher Street, CA3 8RF

🕘 10-11; 11-midnight Sat; 12-11 Sun
🌐 kingsheadcarlisle.co.uk

4 changing beers 🄷

An excellent city-centre pub, winner of many CAMRA awards, serving a range of guest ales from four handpumps. Pictures of old Carlisle adorn the internal walls, and outside is an explanation of why the city is not in the Domesday Book. Good-value meals are served at lunchtime. The covered outdoor courtyard has a large-screen TV and regularly features live music. CAMRA City Pub of the Year 2015-17. Children and dogs are not allowed. ❀◐≈♣●🚌🐾📶

Spinners Arms 🄻

Cummersdale, CA2 6BD

🕘 6-midnight; 5-midnight Fri; 12-midnight Sat & Sun
☎ (01228) 532928 🌐 thespinnersarms.org.uk

Carlisle Spun Gold, Flaxen, Magic Number 🄷

Cosy family-friendly hostelry, an original Redfern pub with unique and original features. It is less than half a mile from Carlisle's south-western boundary, close to the Cumbrian Way and National Cycle Route 7, which run alongside the picturesque River Caldew. There is regular live music, with Irish music sessions every first and third Wednesday. Children are welcome until 9pm and well-behaved dogs are permitted. The pub is the tap for Carlisle Brewing Co, showcasing the brewery's beers on five pumps. 🐴❀♿♣P🚌(75)🐾

Woodrow Wilson 🄻 ✔

48 Botchergate, CA1 1QS

🕘 8am-midnight (1am Fri & Sat) ☎ (01228) 819942

Great Corby Ale, Blonde; Greene King Abbot; Marston's Old Empire; Ruddles Best Bitter; Sharp's Doom Bar; 6 changing beers (sourced nationally) 🄷

One of two almost adjacent Wetherspoon pubs, this refurbished Co-op building is named after the former US president, whose mother was born in Carlisle. Up to 14 handpumps offer the largest range of real ales to be found in town. Food is served all day till 11pm. At the rear there is a spacious outdoor seating area, a heated patio and a smokers' area. Children are welcome in some parts of the pub until 8pm. 🐴❀◐◑♿≈●P🚌📶

Castle Carrock

Duke of Cumberland 🄻

CA8 9LU

🕘 closed Mon & Tue; 12-midnight ☎ (01228) 670341
🌐 the-dukeofcumberlandinn.com

2 changing beers (often Derwent, Hesket Newmarket) 🄷

At the heart of this charming village, the Duke reopened in 2009 and is now successfully re-established. A local following also sees it as the centre for the annual Marr Folk Festival in July. At the foot of the northern Pennines, it is ideally located for outdoor activity enthusiasts, who can enjoy real ale and sample the home-made food, which has a growing reputation. The layout separates the games/TV area from the dining area. Dogs are not allowed inside the pub.
🐴❀◐◑♿♣●P📶

Cockermouth

Castle Bar ✔

14 Market Place, CA13 9NQ

🕘 11-11 (midnight Fri & Sat); 12-10.30 Sun
☎ (01900) 829904 🌐 cockermouth.org.uk/castlebar

Cumbrian Legendary Ales Loweswater Gold; Jennings Cumberland Ale, Bitter; Titanic Plum Porter; 2 changing beers (sourced nationally) 🄷

Located in the town's Market Place with a refurbished interior that retains many historic features, this often-busy pub has three floors, with the main bar on the ground floor, restaurant on the first floor, and a relaxing room with comfortable leather sofas on the second. Popular with diners, booking for food is recommended at weekends. Several TV screens on the ground floor cater for the sports enthusiast, and a terraced beer garden proves popular with drinkers in summer.
🐴❀◐◑●🚌🐾📶

New Cock & Bull

7 South Street, CA13 9RT (centre of town opp Sainsbury's)

🕘 3-11 ☎ (01900) 827999 🌐 thenewcockandbull.co.uk

Coniston Bluebird Bitter; Great Corby Blonde, Fox; 5 changing beers (sourced nationally) 🄷

A popular town community pub that charges reasonable prices and offers a consistently good range of cask beers. The venue is on three levels and is sensitively modernised, with quieter, more comfortable surroundings if required. It hosts occasional live music. No meals are served but it does have a range of bar snacks. With up to five real ales on offer, including some from Cumbrian breweries, this pub is usually lively, attracting locals and visitors alike. 🐴❀🚌🐾📶

Swan Inn 🄻

52-56 Kirkgate, CA13 9PH

🕘 5-11.30 (midnight Fri); 12-midnight Sat; 12-11 Sun
☎ (01900) 822425 🌐 swaninncockermouth.com

Fyne Ales Jarl; Jennings Bitter, Cocker Hoop, Cumberland Ale; 1 changing beer (sourced nationally) 🄷

A true community venue well supported by locals, this 17th-century pub has flagged floors, exposed beams, a real fire and quiet nooks and crannies. It hosts a monthly whisky club and folk music sessions. There are six handpumps with three of the beers served from the local Jennings Brewery. There is a large-screen TV at the back that is used for showing sports. The pub is situated a short walk from the centre of town. 🐴♣🚌🐾📶

Coniston

Black Bull Inn & Hotel 🄻

LA21 8DU

🕘 10-11 (10.30 winter) ☎ (015394) 41335
🌐 blackbullconiston.co.uk

Coniston Bluebird Bitter, Bluebird Premium XB, No.9 Barley Wine, Old Man Ale, Oliver's Light Ale, Special Oatmeal Stout; 3 changing beers (sourced locally; often Coniston) 🄷

A 16th-century coaching inn, this is Coniston Brewing Company's on-site taphouse, also serving good food in traditional, comfortable surroundings. Six regular beers are supplemented by other beers from the brewery on a rotation basis – try a tasting paddle. The spacious bar and lounge are well frequented by tourists in this hugely popular, spectacular location near Coniston Old Man. The outside seating area is perfect in summer. Dogs are not allowed in the restaurant. A full menu is served from noon. P (X12,505)

Sun

LA21 8HQ

11-11 (015394) 41248 thesunconiston.com

Coniston Bluebird Premium XB; Cumbrian Legendary Ales Loweswater Gold; 6 changing beers (sourced locally)

Take the Walna Scar road up from Coniston village, or down from Coniston Old Man, to visit this 16th-century pub and hotel. The deliberately unmodernised dual-level bar has atmosphere and character, with slate flooring, exposed beams and stone walls, heated by a large open range. The slate-topped bar offers up to eight cask ales, mostly from local brewers. The conservatory and terrace complete the picture, with delightful views over the garden. Dogs are not allowed in the conservatory. Winter opening hours vary.

Q P (505,X12)

Yewdale Inn

2 Yewdale Road, LA21 8DU

12-11 (015394) 41280 yewdaleinn.com

Barngates Tag Lag; Cumbrian Legendary Ales Loweswater Gold; Theakston Old Peculier; 2 changing beers (sourced locally)

A welcoming village inn in the centre of Coniston attracting locals and visitors alike. In winter a cosy fire and jovial atmosphere prevail; in summer enjoy a drink on the terrace with stunning views of the Old Man of Coniston and surrounding fells, and Church Beck, a babbling brook running through the village. Opening hours and the availability of food are reduced in winter but details are maintained on the website. Breakfast is available 9-11am.

(505,X12)

Crosby

Stag Inn

Lowside, CA15 6SH

11.30 (3 Tue)-11; 12-11 Sun (01900) 812549

staginncrosby.com

Jennings Cumberland Ale; 3 changing beers (sourced nationally)

Welcoming and popular with locals and visitors, the Stag is in a great location, with views over the Solway Firth to Scotland. The pub has a large bar with two serving points and quiet corners, plus a dining area with an extensive menu to suit all tastes. Beer is from the Marston's range and usually includes an ale from the local Jennings Brewery. P (300)

Dacre

Horse & Farrier

CA11 0HL (1 mile S of A66)

closed Mon; 12-11 (10.30 Sun) (017684) 86022

horseandfarrier.com

3 changing beers (sourced locally; often Allendale, Eden River, Hesket Newmarket)

Welcoming old Cumbrian pub saved from closure and lovingly refurbished by friendly young enthusiasts. In the bar, a woodburner has been cleverly housed in the original black range. You will find good craic from friendly locals, wholesome food and interesting and varied styles of guest beers. It has an unusual range of keg products including local real lagers. Beer festivals are held at the end of May and the end of July. For tempting regular events see Facebook. Dacre is a lovely quiet village on the new Ullswater round walk.

Q P

Dent

Sun Inn

Main Street, LA10 5QL

11-11; 12-10.30 Sun (015396) 25208

suninndent.co.uk

Kirkby Lonsdale Monumental Blonde, Tiffin Gold; 2 changing beers (sourced regionally)

Standing proudly at the top of Dent's cobbled main street for more than 300 years, the Sun Inn is the archetypal Dales village inn. It is a true pub unspoilt by modern distractions – no TV, no jukebox and no fruit machines, instead just great-value food and drink, an open fire, original coin-studded beams, and some good cheer to be had with the folk around the bar. With local ales from Kirkby Lonsdale and additional guest beers, there is always something to savour.

Q P

Dufton

Stag Inn

CA16 6DB

5 (6 Mon)-11; 12-11 Fri & Sat; 12-10.30 Sun

(017683) 51608 thestagdufton.co.uk

3 changing beers (sourced regionally)

Charming old pub facing the village green. It has a small bar with an old black range, a snug with a woodburner, and a dining room to the rear with views over the beer garden to the North Pennines. One of the last Fellside pubs, the Pennine Way runs through the village. Good craic and banter with the locals is to be had. The beers change, often featuring a dark or strong ale. All food is locally sourced and served in good hearty portions. Camping, a YHA and a caravan site are all close by. It stages a summer beer festival in August.

Q P

Elterwater

Britannia Inn

LA22 9HP

10.30-11 (015394) 37210 britinn.co.uk

Coniston Bluebird Bitter; Jennings Sneck Lifter; house beer (by Coniston); 2 changing beers (sourced locally; often Eden River)

A famous watering hole in the heart of the Langdale valley, this cosy pub is always popular with walkers – which is fortunate as the five rooms get very busy, so outdoor clothing helps ensure a seat! The narrow bar room dictates efficient service. It has a great atmosphere and stocks ales from local breweries including Langdale. Hearty Lakeland food is served and evening booking is advisable. A large annual beer festival prompts a local stay if you want to fully enjoy it. Residents have use of the Langdale Spa complex nearby.

P (516)

Eskdale Green

Bower House Inn

CA19 1TD (short walk from Irton Road station – La'al Ratty)

9am-11 ☎ (019467) 23244 ⊕ bowerhouseinn.com
Cumbrian Legendary Ales Loweswater Gold; Timothy Taylor Landlord; 2 changing beers (sourced nationally) Ⓗ
On the edge of the village and close to the famous Outward Bound school, this popular tourist hostelry is renowned for good food and a wide range of well-kept ales. The dining room has oak-panelled seating and beamed ceilings, and there is a real fire in the bar. The pub is a community focal point with a local cricket team and darts, and hosts quizzes for charities and themed food evenings.
Q ☆ ❀ ⟁ ◖ ▲ ≉ ♣ ● P ❀ ❧ ☞

Foxfield

Prince of Wales Ⓛ
LA20 6BX
✪ closed Mon & Tue; 2.45-11 Wed & Thu; 11.45-11 Fri & Sat; 12-10.30 Sun ☎ (01229) 716238
⊕ princeofwalesfoxfield.co.uk
6 changing beers (sourced nationally; often Foxfield) Ⓗ
Stuart and Lynda are testament to what is achievable through passion and hard work at this splendid pub, which has been presented with numerous awards over the years. Guest ales come from the pub's two house breweries, Foxfield and Tigertops, plus others from carefully selected nationwide breweries. Beers will always include a mild. Check the website for various events throughout the year. Excellent accommodation includes superb breakfast. It is a cash-only pub, with no card facilities. The railway stops outside. Food is served; telephone for details.
Q ☆ ❀ ⟁ ◖ ♿ ≉ ♣ ● P ◨ ❀ ☞

Gilcrux

Barn Bistro
CA7 2QX (4 miles S of Aspatria via A596, and 5 miles N of Cockermouth via A5086, near A594 and A595) NY114380
✪ closed Mon; 12 (5 Tue)-11 ☎ (016973) 23289
⊕ barnbistro.co.uk
Jennings Bitter; 2 changing beers (sourced nationally) Ⓗ
Sensitively converted barn with a bar and restaurant, set in the centre of the village next door to the Beeches caravan site, with an extra seating area in a gallery above. The beer offered is frequently Cumbrian. There is an extensive range of malt whiskies and gins. The restaurant serves locally sourced produce. A beer festival is held each July. Q ☆ ❀ ◖ P ❀ ☞

Gosforth

Gosforth Hall Inn
Wasdale Road, CA20 1AZ (from A595 follow road signed to Wasdale)
9am-11 ☎ (019467) 25322 ⊕ gosforthhall.co.uk
4 changing beers (sourced nationally) Ⓗ
On the edge of an attractive village, this ancient, popular locals and tourists pub offers food and a wide range of cask ales. It has interesting Elizabethan architecture, is Grade II listed and was formerly a farmhouse. An annual beer festival is held in August. Next to the pub is St Mary's church, which has a cross dating from 950AD. Local CAMRA Pub of the Year 2017. Q ☆ ❀ ⟁ ◖ ♿ ♣ ● P ❀ ☞

Grasmere

Tweedies Bar (Dale Lodge Hotel) Ⓛ
Red Bank Road, LA22 9SW
12-11 (midnight Fri & Sat) ☎ (015394) 35300
⊕ tweediesgrasmere.com
Coniston Old Man Ale; Cumbrian Legendary Ales Loweswater Gold; Hawkshead Bitter; 8 changing beers (sourced nationally; often Arbor, Brewsmith, Hawkshead) Ⓗ
Part of the Dale Lodge Hotel but operating separately, this acclaimed pub is used mainly by visitors - especially walkers – and caters well to this market. It focuses on quality beer and ciders and always has an interesting and varied range. Third-pint bats enable sampling. The bar lists helpful beer and food pairing suggestions and gives maximum information on current beers. The famous Grasmere Guzzler festival is held on the first weekend in September. Visit and enjoy.
☆ ❀ ⟁ ◖ ♿ ● P ⟐ (555,599) ❀ ❧ ☞

Great Asby

Three Greyhounds Ⓛ
CA16 6EX
✪ closed Mon; 11-3, 6-10 (11 Fri); 12-11 Sat; 12-9 Sun
☎ (017683) 51428 ⊕ asbyparish.org.uk/the-three-greyhounds
2 changing beers (sourced locally; often Allendale, Derwent, Hawkshead) Ⓗ
A former hunting lodge in Ormside valley five miles south-west of Appleby, built in 1707 and overlooked by St Peter's church on the charming Asby beck and village green. This is an unspoilt pub with beamed ceiling, flagstone floor and iron range fireplace. It serves two rotating ales, mostly local, and home-made food in the evening including stone-baked pizzas. It is a popular stop on the Pennine Route 68 cycleway, with Rutter Force waterfall within two miles. Closed Monday and Tuesday in winter. Q ☆ ❀ ⟁ ◖ ♿ ▲ ♣ ❀ ☞

Great Broughton

Punch Bowl Inn
19 Main Street, CA13 0YJ
✪ closed Mon-Wed; 8-11 Thu; 5-11 Fri & Sat; 12-3, 6-10.30 Sun ☎ (01900) 267070
3 changing beers (sourced nationally) Ⓗ
A community establishment run by a committee of local volunteers, which was saved from closure in 2012. It always offers two locally sourced beers which constantly change. Although it has limited opening hours, this is more than compensated for by the quality and variation of the real ale it serves – usually Cumbrian. Originally a 17th-century coaching inn, this is very much a locals' pub.
Q ☆ ♣ P ❀ ☞

Great Corby

Queen Inn Ⓛ
The Green, CA4 8LR
4-10 Mon; 12-11; 12-10.30 Sun ☎ (01228) 561592
Great Corby Ale, Blonde; 1 changing beer (sourced locally) Ⓗ
Refurbished village pub that uses two storeys and provides two restaurant areas. There is a separate room for Sky Sports. A conference room is also available and a private dining room. This is a pub posing as a restaurant, so booking is essential if

you wish to eat. It serves a range of ales from the next door Great Corby Brewery and occasionally hosts live music. Q❀◑♿P🐾ᯤ

Great Orton

Wellington Inn

CA5 6LZ

closed Mon & Tue; 12-2, 6-11 Wed-Fri; 12-3, 6-midnight Sat; 12-3, 6-10.30 Sun ☎ (01228) 710775

3 changing beers (sourced locally; often Derwent, Keswick) 🄷

Set in a quiet village, this is an attractive country inn, with good-value meals using ingredients sourced locally, including meat from the renowned local butcher. Three handpumps serve ales from mainly local breweries like Derwent and Keswick. Live music is being reintroduced here, with open mic nights on an occasional basis. There is space for 10 touring caravans on the adjacent campsite. Q❀◑♿♣P

Greenodd

Ship 🄻

Main Street, LA12 7QZ

closed Mon & Tue; 5-11 Wed-Fri; 12-11 Sat; 12-10.30 Sun ☎ (01229) 861553 🌐 theshipinngreenodd.co.uk

Greenodd Citra, Roundabout; 3 changing beers (sourced locally; often Greenodd) 🄷

A traditional village inn, just off the A590, attracting a good mix of locals and visitors. Five handpumps serve beers selected from a range of over 20 brewed by the on-site Greenodd Brewery. The pub has recently been refurbished and its open-plan interior features slate floors, stone walls, exposed beams and open fires, with a separate quiet room to the rear. Good-quality locally produced food is served. ◑♣P🚌(X6)🐾ᯤ

Hawkshead

King's Arms Hotel 🄻 ✔

The Square, LA22 0NZ

11-midnight ☎ (015394) 36372

🌐 kingsarmshawkshead.co.uk

Cumbrian Legendary Ales Loweswater Gold; Hawkshead Bitter; 2 changing beers (sourced locally) 🄷

Characterful 500-year-old village inn on the square of this historic settlement. Its traditional interior features beamed ceilings, an open fire and a hand-carved king in the bar supporting the floor above. Good food is available in the bar and dining area and there is frequent live music. The patio is south-facing on the edge of the square. It is family-friendly and dogs are welcome in the bar area. There is plenty of parking available in the central village car park. Winter hours vary. Q❀🛏◑⛺🚌(505)🐾ᯤ

Hesket Newmarket

Old Crown 🄻 ✔

CA7 8JG

5.30-11; 12-2.30, 5-11 Fri; 12-11 Sat & Sun ☎ (016974) 78288 🌐 theoldcrownpub.co.uk

Hesket Newmarket Haystacks, Black Sail, Helvellyn Gold, High Pike, Doris' 90th Birthday Ale, Brim Fell; 4 changing beers (sourced locally; often Hesket Newmarket) 🄷

Sitting in the heart of this lovely fellside village, the Old Crown is a showcase for the Hesket Newmarket brewery, which is immediately behind the pub. It is well known as the first co-operatively owned pub in the country and is popular with locals and visitors alike, with Prince Charles and Sir Chris Bonington among its supporters. Opening hours are subject to change; please check the pub website before travelling. Q❀◑♣●🐾ᯤ

High Newton

Crown Inn 🄻

Newton in Cartmel, LA11 6JH (in centre of village) SD402829

12-11 ☎ (015395) 30017

Bowness Bay Swan Blonde; Cumbrian Legendary Ales Loweswater Gold; Hawkshead Bitter; 2 changing beers (sourced locally) 🄷

Village local with a large restaurant area, worth a detour off the A590 High Newton bypass or a stop off the X6 bus from Kendal to Barrow-in-Furness. The three regular local beers are complemented by a varied selection of beers both local and from further afield, in a range of styles. An excellent choice of locally produced food is also served. The restaurant area can be reached by a door to the rear of the pub which has disabled access. Q❀🛏◑♿⛺♣P🚌(X6)🐾ᯤ

Holmes Green

Black Dog Inn 🄻

Broughton Road, LA15 8JP (1½ miles from Dalton-in-Furness – Tudor Square – on Broughton Rd towards Askam) SD233761

closed Mon-Wed; 3-11 Thu-Sat; 3-9 Sun ☎ (01229) 462975

Cumbrian Legendary Ales Esthwaite Bitter, Loweswater Gold; 3 changing beers (sourced nationally; often Abbeydale, Cumbrian Legendary Ales, Oakham) 🄷

With five real ales on offer, a warm welcome awaits from the landlord and locals alike. This former coaching inn, with two real fires, quarry-tiled floor and rustic beams, was recently refurbished but retains plenty of character. There is live music monthly, usually the last Saturday, plus open mic nights and music festivals. Dog Fest is normally on the August bank holiday Sunday. There is an outdoor decked seating area. Q❀P🐾ᯤ

Ings

Watermill Inn 🄻

LA8 9PY

11-11 (10.30 Sun) ☎ (01539) 821309

🌐 watermillinn.co.uk

Watermill Collie Wobbles, A Bit'er Ruff, Windermere Blonde; 9 changing beers (sourced locally; often Keswick, Kirkby Lonsdale, Watermill) 🄷

A multi award-winning inn with 12 handpulls, owned and run by the same family for 28 years. It has consistently maintained CAMRA aims and objectives. As the name indicates, it is a former watermill with several rooms – one with a window into the brewery – all served by a central bar area. Watermill beers all have doggy themes – regular canines have their own web page! The monthly Lakeland Storytelling Club is now 25 years old. Landlord Brian is sadly missed. Q❀🛏◑♿⛺♣P🚌🐾ᯤ

Irthington

Sally

CA6 4NJ

12-11 ☎ (016977) 42954 thesallyirthington.co.uk

Wainwright; 1 changing beer (sourced nationally; often Thwaites) H

Fully refurbished and extended former coaching inn in a village popular as a rest stop for Hadrian's Wall walkers. It has a superb slate fireplace in the dining area with a roaring fire in colder weather. Food is served daily and booking is recommended. This is very much a gastro-pub and boutique hotel, but all are welcome to enjoy real ales from the Thwaites range. The unusual name is a diminutive of the original Salutation Inn. P

Kendal

Fell Bar L

3 Lowther Street, LA9 4DH

4-11 (midnight Fri); 12-midnight Sat & Sun

☎ 07725 987600 fellbrewery.co.uk

Fell Ghyll H**, Tinderbox IPA, Crag** A**; 11 changing beers (sourced regionally; often Chapter, Flagship, Fyne Ales)** H/A

This exciting modern bar in a former town-centre shop is a recent addition to the Kendal pub scene. A tap for the nearby Fell Brewery, the bar serves four of its own cask beers with guests from other northern breweries and up to six top-quality real keg lines from Fell and elsewhere, as well as rotating guest ciders. It also has an interesting selection of UK and foreign bottled beers. Regular live music and innovative brewery collaboration events are held. It is the sister pub to Fell Bar, Penrith.

New Union L

Stricklandgate, LA9 4RF

closed Mon; 4.30-11 Tue-Thu; 3-midnight Fri & Sat; 12-9 Sun ☎ (01539) 724004 thenewunion.co.uk

Hawkshead Windermere Pale; 3 changing beers (sourced regionally; often Cumbrian Legendary Ales, Hawkshead, Kirkby Lonsdale) H

A CAMRA award winner within two years of opening by a CAMRA enthusiast, this town local has seen a complete turnaround in trade. Four quality handpulls catering for all tastes are complemented by three real keg lines for the more adventurous. An onsite microbrewery is now up and running. Unusual real ciders and perries also feature, alongside a wide range of European bottled beers, with an annual festival in July. The pub hosts frequent community events – see Facebook for updates. Cumbria Pub of the Year and Regional Cider Pub of the Year 2019.

P (555)

Ring o' Bells L

37-39 Kirkland, LA9 5AF

12 (6 Thu)-11; 12-midnight Fri & Sat ☎ (01539) 720326

ringobellskendal.webs.com

Coniston Bluebird Bitter; 2 changing beers (sourced nationally; often Beckstones, Cross Bay, Eden River) H

The little pub with the big heart! Everyone is warmly welcome to join in the bar-room banter or meet friends and colleagues in the lounge. A great range of beers is skilfully served and features popular favourites from the locality. Unusual cider, perry and gin are also stocked. Tasty home-cooked food is available, and functions can be catered for in a private lounge. Regular community events and live Sunday music, including karaoke, are staged. It has a roaring fire for winter, sunny tables for summer. Q P

Keswick

Pheasant Inn

Crosthwaite Road, CA12 5PP

12.30-11 ☎ (017687) 72219

thepheasantinnkeswick.co.uk

Jennings Bitter, Cocker Hoop, Cumberland Ale; 5 changing beers (sourced nationally) H

This edge-of-town pub is popular with diners and drinkers. It has two areas, one primarily for dining, the other, in front of the bar, is suitable for drinkers and bar meals. It has low beams and a flagged floor and offers a welcoming open fire for the cooler months. A number of original Wilks (John Wilkinson) works adorn the walls. Ladyside Pike Alpine Club meet here. It offers a selection of Jennings beers and guests from Marston's.

Q

Wainwright

Lake Road, CA12 5BZ

11-11.30 (12.30am Fri & Sat); 11-11 Sun

☎ (017687) 44927 thewainwright.pub

Fell Tinderbox IPA; Wainwright; 5 changing beers (sourced nationally) H

With a distinctive black and white frontage, this pub is readily identifiable. Inside, it has oak floors throughout and comprises two drinking areas served by an L-shaped bar. The interior is mountain-themed and has a cosy ambience. It has a good reputation for food in terms of quality, quantity and price. The beers and the food mostly come from in and around Cumbria. Readily welcomes dogs. Q

Kings Meaburn

White Horse Inn L

CA10 3BU

5-11.45; 12-11.45 Sat; 12-10.30 Sun ☎ (01931) 714256

3 changing beers (sourced nationally; often Bowness Bay, Eden River, Fell) H

A welcoming 17th-century inn that is still the hub of the community – this is a proper local with a relaxing atmosphere and a real fire. Quality local ales are sold as well as justifiably famous pies, which also feature at the annual pie-making competition. Visitors flock from afar to the summer Music and Beer Festival and there are regular music events throughout the year, advertised on Facebook. A pub that is well worth seeking out if you are in the area. Q

Kirkby Lonsdale

Royal Barn L

New Road, LA6 2AB

10-9.30 (11 Thu-Sat); 11-10 Sun ☎ (015242) 71918

kirkbylonsdalebrewery.com

Kirkby Lonsdale Jubilee Stout, Monumental Blonde, Ruskins Bitter, Singletrack, Stanley's Pale Ale, Tiffin Gold; 4 changing beers (sourced locally; often Kirkby Lonsdale) H

The name says it all for the Kirkby Lonsdale taphouse known as The Barn. The long bar has 12 handpumps, eight real keg taps, real cider and a large selection of international craft beers, plus home-roasted coffee. A large stove is welcoming and warming. There are tasty bites and hot pies to accompany the beers, and cakes too. A pianist, Archie, entertains customers with songs from the shows every afternoon – requests possible.

Kirkoswald

Crown Inn

CA10 1DQ

6-11.45; 12-4, 6-11.45 Fri-Sun ☎ (01768) 870410

Jennings Bitter; 2 changing beers H

Friendly village pub situated in the main street and well supported by locals. A traditional coal fire helps create a warm atmosphere on cold winter nights. There is a pool table upstairs. Visitors travel from some distance for the excellent food, which includes Italian specialities, and is freshly prepared to order (booking advisable). Two guest real ales are usually available along with the regular Jennings Bitter.

Fetherston Arms

The Square, CA10 1DQ

4-11; 12-midnight Sat & Sun ☎ (01768) 898284

fetherston-arms.co.uk

Theakston Best Bitter; 3 changing beers (often Allendale, Hesket Newmarket) H

The Fethers is in the centre of this historic village. Extensive alterations and the friendly enthusiasm of the owners have helped convert it into a truly outstanding pub, also well known for its food. Three changing real ales are available from breweries such as Allendale and Hesket Newmarket. Check hours in winter. Although Kirkoswald is not on a bus route, it is a 20-minute stroll from Lazonby station on the Carlisle-Settle line. Q

Langwathby

Shepherds Inn

The Village Green, CA10 1LW

12-11 ☎ (01768) 881463 shepherds-inn.co.uk

3 changing beers H

A welcoming country pub at the heart of the community. This 18th-century inn was totally refurbished in 2012. The bar is made of local stone to resemble a sheep fold. The lounge is bright and comfortable and there is a games area in the snug. Real cider is available. The Shepherds has a well-deserved reputation for excellent food. Booking is advised, but not essential. P

Levens

Hare & Hounds Inn

Causeway End, LA8 8PN

12-11 (11.30 Fri & Sat); 12-10.30 Sun ☎ (015395) 60004

hareandhoundslevens.co.uk

Bowness Bay Swan Blonde; 4 changing beers (sourced regionally; often Barngates, Handsome, Kirkby Lonsdale) H

This cosy village pub is going from strength to strength. A popular community local, it offers great beer, quality accommodation and good food that includes among the best pizzas in the area. It serves four well-kept casks plus craft ales that cover a range of styles, mostly from local and regional breweries. The pub offers a friendly welcome and hosts a number of community groups. There are great views of Morecambe Bay and Lyth Valley from the top terrace.

Q P

Loppergarth

Wellington Inn

Main Street, LA12 0JL (1 mile from A590 between Lindal and Pennington)

closed Sun & Mon; 6-11 (midnight Fri & Sat)

☎ (01229) 582388

Healey's Blonde, Dark Mild, Golden; 2 changing beers (sourced locally; often Healey's) H

Superb village local with its own microbrewery (Healey's), a custom-made stainless steel plant which is viewable from the snug. Four handpumps, occasionally five, primarily dispense Healey's beers. These include an award-winning blonde, a golden bitter, a traditional darker best bitter, a superb mild, and occasional specials. Wood-burning stoves make this a cosy pub with games, books and good conversation. There is a quiz on alternate Saturdays. Well-behaved dogs on leads are welcome.

Loweswater

Kirkstile Inn

CA13 0RU (off B5289, 7 miles S from Cockermouth) NY140210

11-11; 12-10.30 Sun ☎ (01900) 85219 kirkstile.com

Cumbrian Legendary Ales Esthwaite Bitter, Grasmoor Dark Ale, Langdale, Loweswater Gold; 3 changing beers (sourced nationally) H

CAMRA award-winning 16th-century Lakeland coaching inn, scenically located below Melbreak, Crummock Water and Loweswater. It features low-beamed ceilings, solid wood tables, chairs and settles in three bar areas. There is an open fire for chilly days. Substantial bar meals are served from midday and there is a well-established restaurant (requires booking). The original home of Loweswater Brewery, it is now the brewery tap for Cumbrian Legendary Ales. There is an outdoor drinking area in stunning surroundings. Dogs are welcome up to 6pm. Local CAMRA branch Pub of the Year for 2019. Q P

Monkhill

Drovers Rest

CA5 6DB

12 (5 Mon-Wed)-11 ☎ (01228) 576141

4 changing beers H

A traditional country pub close to the popular Hadrian's Wall path, with a strong community focus. Although opened up, the interior still has the feel of three distinct rooms. The bar area is cosy and welcoming, with a roaring fire in winter. Some interesting historical State Management Scheme documents adorn the walls. The Drovers is an oasis for lots of different and sometimes obscure (for the area) real ales. A winner of multiple CAMRA awards including at regional level.

P (93)

Moorhouse

Royal Oak

CA5 6EZ

5-11 Mon, Wed & Thu; closed Tue; 4-11 Fri; 12-11 Sat & Sun

☎ (01228) 576475

2 changing beers (sourced locally)
This is a small country pub on the outskirts of Carlisle. It is over 250 years old, so be prepared to duck as you go through some of the doors. Log-burning stoves help provide a rustic atmosphere. A traditional home-cooked menu is available along with real ale from local breweries. Regular updates are on Facebook.

Near Sawrey

Tower Bank Arms

LA22 0LF (on B5285 2 miles S of Hawkshead)
12-11 (10.30 Sun) (015394) 36334
towerbankarms.co.uk
Barngates Tag Lag; Cumbrian Legendary Ales Loweswater Gold; Hawkshead Bitter; 3 changing beers (sourced locally)
A 17th-century Lakeland inn with slate floors, oak beams and a cast-iron range with an open fire, next to the National Trust's Hill Top (Beatrix Potter's home). It delivers great local flavours in food, beer and atmosphere. Five handpumps serve very local beer plus cider and perry. Families and dogs are welcomed. There is a seasonal bus service connecting to the Windermere ferry and Hawkshead. Closed Mondays in winter. Booking is essential for evening meals.
Q P

Nether Wasdale

Strands Inn

CA20 1ET
12-11; 12-10.30 Sun (019467) 26237
thestrandsinn.com
Strands Brown Bitter, Errmmm...; 6 changing beers (sourced nationally)
This inn, originally a 17th-century post house, sits at the entrance to Wasdale, famed for its view of England's deepest lake and highest mountains. Six beers are regularly offered, chosen from the 30 produced by the inn's microbrewery. Most of these are available bottle-conditioned and also at the annual beer festival in May, which is popular for morris dances and folk musicians, walkers, drinkers and everyone else too! The pub also brews its own cider and has won frequent local CAMRA branch awards. Q P

Penrith

Agricultural Hotel

Castlegate, CA11 7JE
11-11 (midnight Fri & Sat); 12-10.30 Sun
(01768) 862622 agricultural-cavern.co.uk/the-agricultural-hotel
6 changing beers
The hotel is built from local sandstone and the bar and dining room are open plan, with steps from one to the other. There is also a small reception area. It has a Victorian shuttered bar of sash screens with six handpumps. Food is served in the large dining area, as well as in the bar at quiet times. Convenient for the railway station and nearby bus stops. P

Fell Bar

52 King Street, CA11 7AY
4-midnight; 1-midnight Sat & Sun (01768) 866860
6 changing beers
A small and intimate pub in the centre of Penrith on three floors, which was only turned into a pub in 2012. It is the tap pub for Fell Brewery but also serves a range of other cask ales and craft beers as detailed on the blackboard near the bar. The Fell holds regular quiz, comedy and music nights, which are advertised on its Facebook page.

Royal

Wilson Row, CA11 7PZ
12-midnight (2am Fri & Sat) (01768) 862670
3 changing beers
Traditional pub on the edge of the town centre, with tiled walls and lots of mellow wood. It has three separate areas served by one bar. Two handpumps offer beers from all over the UK including LocAles. It is home to darts, dominoes and pool teams, and there is full sports TV coverage. Live music sessions with a broad appeal are held on Sunday afternoons outwith the football season. Food is served weekday evenings but not Friday and weekend afternoons.

Ravenglass

Inn at Ravenglass

Main Street, CA18 1SQ (N end, overlooking Irish Sea)
4-10 Mon, Tue & Thu; closed Wed; 3-11.30 Fri; 2-11.30 Sat; 12-9 Sun (01229) 717230 theinnatravenglass.co.uk
Bowness Bay Swan Blonde; Hawkshead Bitter; 3 changing beers (sourced nationally)
A 17th-century inn set in a hamlet that was once a Roman port, at the junction of the rivers Esk, Irt and Mite in the Lake District National Park. There is a choice of real ales that are especially enjoyable after a day on the fells, messing about in boats, or just when relaxing by the woodburning stove in winter. There are great sunset views over the estuary. Close to Ravenglass stations for mainline and L'aal Ratty trains.
Q P (6)

Rosthwaite

Scafell Hotel

Borrowdale, CA12 5XB (on B5289)
12-11; 12-10.30 Sun (017687) 77208 scafell.co.uk
Jennings Bitter; 6 changing beers (sourced nationally)
Located in beautiful Borrowdale, in the heart of the Lake District, the Riverside Bar at the Scafell Hotel welcomes walkers, cyclists and all those who enjoy the outdoor life. It is the home of the annual Borrowdale Fell Race, and the River Derwent rushes past the windows of the bar. Good food is served and a selection of malt whiskies is available. Open fires create a homely atmosphere.
P (78)

Rydal

Badger Bar (Glen Rothay Hotel)

LA22 9LR
10-10.45 (10.15 Sun) (015394) 34500
theglenrothay.co.uk
Barngates Goodhew's Dry Stout; house beer (by Old School); 4 changing beers (sourced locally; often Fox, Great Corby, Hawkshead)
This excellent local bar forms part of the larger hotel overlooking tranquil Rydal Water between

Windermere and Grasmere. A good selection of local ales is headed up by Badger Bar Ale from Old School Brewery and features Barngates Goodhew's Stout as a tasty change from the brand leader. Several small old rooms lead off the main bar and a large restaurant serving local food. It has feature toilets and a popular Badgercam. A welcome stop for walkers and bus riders, with a popular garden.
Q❀ ⛺♣P (555,599)

Santon Bridge

Bridge Inn ✔

CA19 1UX (on road from Gosforth to Eskdale)
11-11 ☎ (019467) 26221 santonbridgeinn.com
Jennings Cumberland Ale, Bitter, Sneck Lifter; Adnams Mosaic; 6 changing beers (sourced nationally) [H]
The Bridge Inn, once a modest mail coach halt, is now a fine, comfortable country inn well located at a junction of the roads into Wasdale and Eskdale. It is cosy, with low beams, creaking floors and a log fire. The seven beers are from local, regional and national breweries, and a local CAMRA award was presented in 2017. The World's Biggest Liar competition is held here every November. The food is sourced locally. The clientele is a mix of guests, tourists and locals. The inn is licensed for civil marriage ceremonies.
Q❀♿⛺♣P

Sedbergh

Dalesman L

Main Street, LA10 5BN
11-11; 12-10.30 Sun ☎ (015396) 21183
thedalesman.co.uk
5 changing beers (sourced regionally; often Barngates, Box Steam, Black Sheep) [H]
Comfortable and welcoming family-run pub in the book town of Sedbergh on the Dalesway Walk and Cumbria Cycleway. This is a free house with a frequently changing selection of well-kept ales in different styles. It has a large bar with a wood-burning stove plus two separate dining areas suitable for families. The menus are well thought-out and the brunch selection is mouthwatering. The rooms are furnished to a high standard and make a good base for exploring the Howgill Fells and the Lake District. ❀⛺P

Staveley

Beer Hall L ✔

Hawkshead Bewery, Mill Yard, LA8 9LR
12-7 (11 Fri & Sat); 12-8 Sun ☎ (01539) 825260
hawksheadbrewery.co.uk
Hawkshead Bitter, Brodie's Prime, Cumbrian Five Hop, Lakeland Gold, Red, Windermere Pale; 16 changing beers (sourced locally; often Hawkshead) [H]
This is still the Hawkshead Brewery tap, although main production has moved to the Flookburgh site. It always offers a selection from the 11 core beers, plus a varying choice from the small-batch range and real keg specials. Large spring and summer beer festivals are hosted. Tasty snacks are served and there is varied live music every Saturday; Friday is folk and acoustic night. There are uplifting fell views from the glazed top lounge which also gives access to the brewery viewing area. Brewery tours are bookable and there are rail-user discounts. Q❀♿⛺P (555)

Eagle & Child Hotel L

Kendal Road, LA8 9LP
11.30-11 (11.30 Fri & Sat); 12-10.30 Sun
☎ (01539) 821320 eaglechildinn.co.uk
Hawkshead Bitter; 5 changing beers (sourced locally; often Barngates, Cumbrian Legendary Ales, Hawkshead) [H]
An outstanding example of a traditional village inn, which is always open to the new where beer is concerned. Popular with Lakeland visitors, those who like eating out with good beer and ambience, and connoisseurs of interesting local ales, it is also a hub for its community, with Thursday quiz nights locally famous. In summer the delightful riverside garden hosts beer festivals, and in winter the cosy log fires are a welcoming draw. Convenient for travellers by bus and train.
Q❀♣P (555)

Talkin

Blacksmiths Arms L

CA8 1LE
12-midnight ☎ (016977) 3452 blacksmithstalkin.co.uk
Black Sheep Ale; 2 changing beers [H]
Since taking over in 1997, the present owners have made this probably the most popular pub in the vicinity. The winning formula includes four real ales, a superbly stocked bar, friendly efficient staff, no TV and meticulous attention to detail. With a golf course and country park within two miles and plenty of other outdoor activities locally, it attracts visitors from far outside north Cumbria to this Area of Outstanding Natural Beauty.
Q❀♿♣P

Tallentire

Bush Inn

Tallentire, CA13 0PT
closed Mon; 6 (6.30 Thu; 5 Fri)-midnight; 12-2, 7-11 Sun
☎ (01900) 823707
3 changing beers (sourced nationally) [H]
A genuine, old-fashioned, Grade II-listed pub, with exposed beams, stone floors and a wood-burning stove. A changing selection of ales is stocked, usually including at least one from a Cumbrian brewery. It is home to the local cricket and darts teams. Folk music is hosted on the last Wednesday of the month. Well-behaved dogs are welcome. Food is served in the bar and in the separate dining room Thursday to Saturday, March to December.
Q❀♣

Ulverston

Beerwolf L

7 Market Street, LA12 7AY
closed Mon & Tue; 12-9.30 Wed & Thu; 12-11 Fri; 11-11 Sat; 1-9 Sun wearebeerwolf.com
2 changing beers (sourced nationally) [H]
Micropub and bottle shop owned by an enthusiastic CAMRA member, with two handpumps plus eight KeyKeg beers, an extensive range of interesting local, national and international bottled and canned beers and ciders, plus growler fills in cans to take away. Tap takeovers have included Cloudwater and Tiny Rebel, and other events are occasionally held. Additional seating upstairs helps make for a pleasant and relaxing atmosphere.

Devonshire Arms

Braddyll Terrace, Victoria Road, LA12 0DH (next to railway bridge in town centre)

4-11; 12-midnight Fri & Sat; 12-10.30 Sun

(01229) 582537

Abbeydale Moonshine; 4 changing beers (sourced regionally; often Abbeydale, Cross Bay, Moorhouse's)

Conveniently situated between the bus and train stations, the Dev is a real locals' pub with a welcoming atmosphere. Four TVs provide comprehensive sports coverage, and it also has two dartboards and a pool table. Five constantly changing cask ales and a real cider are all dispensed from handpump. The pub has received numerous awards from CAMRA over the years. The outside seating area is popular in summer. The Sunday meat raffle is drawn at 6pm.
♿ ♣ P

Mill

Mill Street, LA12 7EB

11-11 (1am Fri & Sat); 11-10.30 Sun (01229) 581384

mill-at-ulverston.co.uk

Lancaster Amber, Black, Blonde, Red; 6 changing beers (sourced nationally)

A converted flour mill in the town centre with an interesting, characterful layout. The original waterwheel is central to the ground floor, fed from the stream channelled alongside the first-floor outdoor terrace. The main bar has ten handpumps, serving six guest beers alongside the Lancaster Brewery range. Food is served in both the bar and, at the weekend, in the upstairs restaurant (booking recommended). Tuesday is quiz night and open mic session is Wednesday. A recently opened loft bar/function suite serves wine and cocktails on Friday and Saturday evenings. Dogs are welcome in the bar area. ♿ (6,X6)

Old Friends

49 Soutergate, LA12 7ES

4 (2 Thu)-11; 2-midnight Fri; 12-midnight Sat; 12-10.30 Sun (01229) 208195 oldfriendsulverston.co.uk

6 changing beers (sourced locally)

Welcoming old-fashioned locals' pub about 200 yards uphill from the town centre. There is a cosy snug in front of the bar with an open fire; another seating area with TV is separated by a passageway with a hatch to the bar. Beers are mostly from local brewers plus two brewed by the Old Friends. A popular quiz night is held every Tuesday and there is a wonderful beer garden at the back with heating in the winter.

Stan Laurel Inn

31 The Ellers, LA12 0AB

7-11 Mon; 12-2.30, 6-11 (midnight Fri & Sat); 12-11.30 Sun

(01229) 582814 thestanlaurel.co.uk

House beer (by Marston's); 5 changing beers (sourced regionally)

Just off the centre of Stan Laurel's home town, the Stan offers a warm welcome to locals and visitors alike. Six handpulls serve a variety of mainly locally brewed beers, always featuring Ulverston Brewing Co. Excellent-value quality food is available (no food Mon). Adjacent to the bar is a large room with pool and darts and a smaller room primarily used by diners. In winter a log-burning stove adds to the comfortable ambience. Well-behaved dogs are welcome in the bar.
Q ♣ P (6,X6)

> Beer makes you feel the way you ought to feel without beer. **Henry Lawson**

Sun Inn

6-14 Market Street, LA12 7AY

10-1am (3am Fri & Sat) (01229) 585044

thesuninnulverston.co.uk

6 changing beers (sourced nationally)

Tastefully refurbished Grade II-listed coaching inn in the heart of Ulverston town centre. The bar carries a selection of six guest ales, ranging from beers from small local breweries to the larger more well-known names. Along with a warm welcome, you can expect a number of screens for watching sports, a large heated beer garden, en-suite hotel rooms and delicious food served daily. There will always be at least one beer from Stringers Brewery. ♿ P (6,X6)

Swan Inn

Swan Street, LA12 7JX

2.30-11; 2-midnight Fri; 12-midnight Sat; 12-11 Sun

(01229) 582519

9 changing beers (sourced nationally)

On the edge of the town centre, overlooking the A590, there is an open-plan feel here, yet there are three distinct drinking areas. Premier League football and major sports events are screened. Live music features occasionally, and a jukebox allows for all genres of music. A Sunday night quiz rounds off the entertainment. The beer garden is popular, especially in summer. Children are allowed until 8pm. Cash only – no cards. ♿ ♣ (6,X6)

Waberthwaite

Brown Cow Inn

LA19 5YJ

4-11 Mon & Tue; 12-midnight Wed-Sun

(01229) 717243 thebrowncow-inn.simplesite.com

Hawkshead Bitter; 7 changing beers (sourced locally)

This 100-year-old family-run pub is the centre of activity in the village and has recently undergone extensive refurbishment. It serves guest ales that regularly change with the support of its Waberthwaite ale-tasting society. Cider is also available in summer and there is an annual beer festival. The three family chefs produce pub food made with local ingredients. Live music features occasionally at weekends and there are regular quiz nights. A conference room is available. It is on the A595, offering easy access to the Western Fells, the coast and Eskmeals nature reserve.
♿ ♣ P

Wetheral

Wheatsheaf Inn

CA4 8HD

12-11 (Fri & Sat); 12-11.30 Sun (01228) 560686

wheatsheafwetheral.co.uk

Great Corby Ale; 2 changing beers

An early 19th-century village pub, just a few minutes' walk from the village green and railway station, deservedly popular with locals and visitors. Along with Corby Ale from the local Great Corby Brewery there are two changing ales from local breweries. Good-value bar meals are served Wednesday to Sunday. Booking is advisable at weekends. It was a CAMRA award-winner again in 2018. The regular Tuesday quiz nights are well supported. (75)

Whitehaven

Vagabond

9 Marlborough Street, CA28 7LL

5-9.30 ☎ (01946) 66653 thevagabondpub.co.uk

4 changing beers (sourced nationally) H

The Vagabond is just off the historic harbourside of this Georgian town. The present and former name (American Connection) commemorate the pirate raid of John Paul Jones in 1778. It is a traditional two-storey, wooden-floored pub with a welcoming atmosphere. Food includes stone-baked pizzas, while the beers are changed constantly, with choices and styles from Cumbrian, Scottish and national micros.

Windermere

Crafty Baa L

21 Victoria Street, LA23 1AB

11-11 ☎ (015394) 88002 thecraftybaa.business.site

10 changing beers (sourced nationally; often Fell, Handsome, Keswick) A

A fascinating themed family enterprise constructed over two floors using recycled materials, with a small patio in front. Quirky and fun, the Baa is a craft ale mecca featuring 10 changing real keg taps and eight ciders and perries plus nearly 200 worldwide bottled beers – many bottle-conditioned. Awarded AA Pub of the Year 2018, it is also famous for its baked camembert and specialises in charcuterie and grilled sandwiches. Small but intriguing, the tiny empire has expanded with Pie and Pint. (555)

Winton

Bay Horse Inn L

CA17 4HS

12-2, 6-11 ☎ (017683) 71451

thebayhorsewinton.co.uk

Cumbrian Legendary Ales Loweswater Gold; 2 changing beers (sourced nationally; often Cross Bay, Hawkshead, Marston's) H

A traditional hostelry facing the village green in a picturesque setting, within easy walking distance of Kirkby Stephen. Popular with visitors of all ages, it is often comfortably busy and has a bar area, dining room, family room and pleasing rural beer garden. Cosy on a cold day with a logburner in the bar, it is friendly both to dogs and customers. It offers a good choice of locally sourced food and well-kept – mostly local – beers. Definitely worth visiting. **Q** **P**

Wreay

Plough Inn L

CA4 0RL

7-11 Mon; closed Tue; 12-3, 5.30-11 Wed-Sun

☎ (016974) 75770 theploughwreay.co.uk

Hawkshead Lakeland Gold; 2 changing beers (sourced locally) H

Tastefully modernised pub dating back to 1786, in the heart of this picturesque village just five miles south of Carlisle. Locally sourced, excellent food is served in the split-level bar and dining area, with two cask ales from Cumbrian breweries usually available. The village guardians continue to use the Plough as their meeting place and their display of clay pipes can be seen inside. Quiz night is Monday from 8pm. **Q** **P**

Sun Inn, Ulverston (Photo: Reading Tom/Flickr CC BY 2.0)

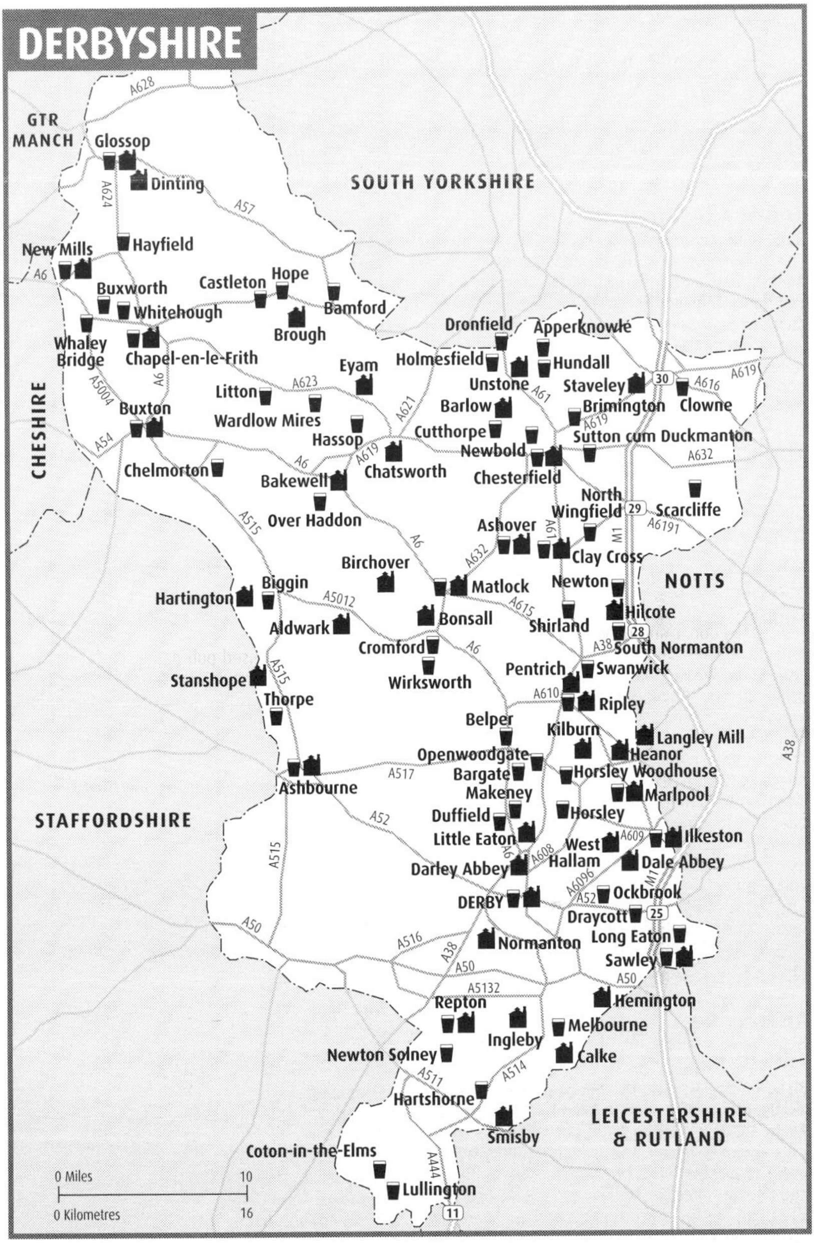

Apperknowle

Traveller's Rest 🄻

High Street, S18 4BD SK384782

✪ 12-11 ☎ (01246) 460169

Neepsend Blonde; Timothy Taylor Landlord Ⓗ; 4 changing beers (sourced nationally; often Church End, Coastal, Welbeck Abbey) Ⓗ/Ⓖ

The Traveller's Rest is a regular winner of CAMRA branch awards. It is a traditional country pub at the edge of the village, serving a good range of beers, cider and perries. The outdoor drinking area provides sweeping views over the Drone Valley – one of the best views in Derbyshire. Good-quality food is available much of the time; the cheese platters and pork pies are particularly popular. Live music features strongly, with jazz every other Monday night. **Q🐎❀◑ Å♣●P🚌**(14,15)🐾📶

Ashbourne

Maison du Biere

28B Church Street, DE6 1EA

✪ closed Mon; 11-9; 12-7 Sun ☎ (01335) 343669

10 changing beers

Opened summer 2018, this is a combined bottle shop and craft ale taproom in a former antique shop. It has 10 KeyKeg taps for three permanent and seven changing ales. The front area contains 400 world beers and ciders, including a good selection from British breweries, both local and nationwide. It also has many examples of Real Ale in a Bottle, as well as mini-pins. Locally sourced pies are sold at the bar, and free coffee for the designated driver. Four cider taps were introduced in 2018.

Smith's Tavern

36 St John Street, DE6 1GH
12-11 (midnight Fri & Sat) (01335) 300809
Banks's Sunbeam; Brakspear Bitter; Marston's Pedigree; Ringwood Fortyniner; 3 changing beers (sourced regionally) H
Small, highly traditional town-centre pub, with as many as seven real ales on. It sells the Marston's portfolio of beers, from which the landlord selects the widest possible choice. He is also allowed one free choice guest ale to be served at weekends, usually from a local brewery. Locally sourced pork pies are normally available. The pub has a good selection of around 40 malt whiskies, and hosts tutored tastings regularly throughout the year. Q

Ashover

Old Poets' Corner L

Butts Road, S45 0EW (downhill from church)
12-11 (01246) 590888
Ashover Poets' Tipple, Butts Pale Ale; 8 changing beers H
The original home of the award-winning Ashover Brewery, this large Brewers' Tudor pub is a frequent CAMRA award winner for ale and cider. The staff welcome walkers and dogs, and provide excellent food and drink. Choose from up to 10 beers, some from Ashover, along with a range of guest ales, traditional ciders, bottled Belgian beers and country wines. The pub hosts three beer festivals a year, plus weekly quizzes and live music. Q P (63,64)

Bamford

Anglers Rest L

Taggs Knoll, S33 0DY
11-11; 12-11 Sun (01433) 659317 anglers.rest
Black Sheep Best Bitter; 5 changing beers (sourced locally; often Abbeydale, Bradfield, Little Critters) H
At the heart of Bamford and not far from Ladybower Reservoir, this is a community hub in every sense; the locals have been running the pub, and its associated post office and café, since 2013. The main bar is the focal point and is extremely popular with families, walkers and especially cyclists, who have access to dedicated bike parking and a DIY repair shop. There is also a quieter snug. Good-value, rustic bar food is served Wednesday to Sunday. Q P (273,274)

Bargate

White Hart

Sandbed Lane, DE56 0JA
5-11; 3-11 Fri; 12-11 Sat & Sun (01773) 827397
Fuller's London Pride; Hardys & Hansons Bitter; 4 changing beers (sourced nationally; often Oakham) H
The White Hart is a cosy two-roomed pub in the heart of Bargate, above the town of Belper. With a reputation for friendly staff and good beer, it is popular with locals and has an excellent selection of changing cask ales. Bar snacks are usually available. There is large beer garden to the rear. Walkers are always welcome. Local CAMRA Pub of the Year 2017 and 2018, and winner of the East Midlands award in 2018. P (7.1)

REAL ALE BREWERIES

Abstract Jungle Langley Mill
Aldwark Artisan Aldwark
Amber Ripley
Ashover Ashover/Clay Cross
Aurora Ilkeston
Bentley Brook Matlock (NEW)
Birch Cottage Sawley
Birchover Birchover
Black Hole Little Eaton
Boot Repton
Bottle Brook Kilburn
Brampton Chesterfield
Brunswick Derby
Buxton Buxton
Chapel-en-le-Frith Chapel-en-le-Frith
Chickenfoot Bonsall (NEW)
Collyfobble Barlow
Dancing Duck Derby
Derby Derby
Derventio Darley Abbey
Dovedale Stanshope (NEW)
Draycott Dale Abbey
Drone Valley Unstone
Eyam Eyam
Falstaff Derby: Normanton
Furnace Derby (NEW)
Globe Glossop
Grasshopper Langley Mill
Hartshorns Derby
Haywood Bad Ram Ashbourne
Hemlock Hemington
High Peak Chapel-en-le-Frith
Howard Town Glossop
Instant Karma Clay Cross
Intrepid Brough
John Thompson Ingleby
Leadmill Heanor
Leatherbritches Smisby
Littleover Derby
Marlpool Marlpool
Matlock Wolds Farm Matlock
Middle Earth Derby (brewing suspended)
Moody Fox Hilcote
Moot Oak Matlock (NEW)
Mouselow Farm Dinting
Mr Grundy's Derby
Muirhouse Ilkeston
Nutbrook West Hallam
Old Sawley Sawley
Peak Chatsworth
Pentrich Pentrich
Rock Mill New Mills
Rowditch Derby
Shiny Little Eaton
Silver Staveley (NEW)
Thorley & Sons Ilkeston
Thornbridge Bakewell
Tollgate Calke
Torrside New Mills
Townes Staveley
Urban Chicken Ilkeston
Whim Hartington

Belper

Angels Micro Pub

Market Place, DE56 1FZ (top right-hand side of Market Place)

closed Mon-Wed; 12-10

Oakham Citra; Thornbridge Jaipur IPA; Titanic Plum Porter; 5 changing beers (sourced nationally) G

A small, friendly bar offering real ales, plus an excellent choice of real ciders, wines, gin and juices; more like a mini beer festival than a pub. It offers a full selection of beer (up to eight, plus eight ciders at times) from Thursday onwards, gradually decreasing as Sunday approaches and the ale is drunk! Locally sourced pork pies and cheeses are served. Live artists feature most Sunday afternoons. A quirky and popular micropub.

Arkwright's Real Ale Bar L

5 Campbell Street, DE56 1AP

4-11; 12-11 Sat & Sun ☎ (01773) 823117

Marston's Pedigree G**; 6 changing beers (sourced nationally)** H

Situated below the Strutt Club in the centre of Belper, Arkwright's is a modern, friendly one-roomed bar regularly serving six real ales plus ciders and perry. Named after Sir Richard Arkwright, an important 18th-century mill owner, this is a popular pub with local drinkers. Bar snacks are always available. Live acoustic music is often performed, and some sporting events are shown on terrestrial TV, but a no-under-14s rule helps provide a relaxing environment for adults to enjoy a pint or two.

Biggin

Waterloo Inn

Main Street, Biggin by Hartington, SK17 0DH

12-3, 6-11; 12-11 Fri & Sat; 12-10.30 Sun

☎ (01298) 84284 waterlooinnbiggin.com

Black Sheep Best Bitter; Wychwood Hobgoblin; 3 changing beers H

A traditional country pub in a Peak District village, featuring log fires, a beer garden and a caravan/campsite. Adjacent to the Tissington Trail, it is ideal for those exploring this beautiful part of the country. Home-cooked meals and snacks are served. The pub is at the heart of the village community, with teams playing darts, dominoes and football; it also hosts quizzes and live music. The adjoining campsite has electric hook-ups, and hard standings for tourers. Closed Mondays in winter, except bank holidays. P

Brimington

Brimming with Beer

Patrick Hinds House, Chesterfield Road, S43 1AD (adjacent to Ark Tavern pub)

12-9 (10 Thu); 11-11 Fri; 10-11 Sat; 11-12 Sun

☎ (01246) 278888

3 changing beers H

A beer shop with an on-licence, open since 2016. It stocks a vast range of bottled beers from around the world, plus the shop's own British bottled beers. Between three and five cask ales are served on the bar, along with three permanent and two changing keg beers and some ciders. A selection of advertising signs and presentation packs is usually available. Q

Buxton

Cheshire Cheese

37-39 High Street, SK17 6HA

12-11 (midnight Fri & Sat) ☎ (01298) 212453

Everards Tiger; Titanic Steerage, Iceberg, White Star, Plum Porter, Captain Smith's Strong Ale; 4 changing beers H

A double-fronted building of considerable age, which was refurbished before reopening under the management of Titanic in 2013. The pub is essentially open plan but is split into several distinct areas. Low ceilings with original beams add to the cosy atmosphere. There is a quiet area at one end featuring an open fire. The bar boasts an array of 10 handpulls serving a range of Titanic beers and guests. Thursday is pie night, and there is a quiz on Sundays. Q P

RedWillow Buxton

1 Cavendish Circus, SK17 6AT

4-11; 12-midnight Fri & Sat; 12-10.30 Sun

RedWillow Wreckless; 4 changing beers (sourced locally) H

Opened in late 2017 in a former bank in the centre of Buxton, this is the RedWillow Brewery's second bar. Original features, including etched windows and the mahogany and glass office, have been retained alongside a new bar and smaller mezzanine area. The five cask ales comprise four RedWillow beers and a guest. Small plates and stone-baked pizzas are served. Live music features monthly, and private beer tastings can be arranged.

Buxworth

Navigation Inn

Brookside, SK23 7NE (off B6062)

11-midnight; 11-11 Sun ☎ (01663) 732072

navigationinn.co.uk

Black Sheep Best Bitter; Timothy Taylor Landlord; 3 changing beers H

Multi-roomed 18th-century village pub in attractive countryside. It caters for all tastes; families, walkers and dogs are welcome. There is a pleasant outdoor drinking area. Good-value food and real fires contribute to a warm and welcoming atmosphere. The guest beers tend to come from micros. The pub stands alongside the magnificent renovated Peak Forest canal basin, once the terminus of the limestone-carrying Peak Forest tramway from the quarries high up at Dove Holes.

P (190)

Castleton

Olde Nag's Head L

Cross Street, S33 8WH

12-11 (midnight Fri & Sat) ☎ (01433) 620248

yeoldenagshead.co.uk

Bradfield Farmers Blonde; Sharp's Doom Bar; 6 changing beers (sourced locally; often Abbeydale, Bradfield, Intrepid) H

The bar area of this busy family-run 17th-century coaching inn has a feature fireplace, exposed stone walls and carved wooden chairs, and is adjacent to the stylish restaurant. The impressive array of handpumps dispenses what is possibly the largest range of cask beers in the Hope Valley, mainly from local breweries. There is a quiz on Friday night and live music on Saturday night.

P (173,272)

Chapel en le Frith

Old Cell Ale Bar
10-12 Market Place, SK23 0EN
🕓 4 (5 Wed)-11; closed Tue; 12-11 Sat; 12-11 Sun
☎ 07709 163316 ⊕ theoldcell.co.uk
3 changing beers (sourced locally) Ⓗ
The Old Cell is a micropub on the historic marketplace, situated in what was originally the local lock-up. Its cosy bar area is well furnished with benches, tables, chairs and stools. Three changing beers are served, many sourced from local micros. A range of bottled beers is also available, some coming from the town's local brewery. Gins also feature. A warm welcome for all helps make this a pub not to be missed.
Q ⏰ ♿ P 🚃 ❀

Chelmorton

Church Inn
Main Street, SK17 9SL
🕓 12-3, 6-11; 12-11 Fri-Sun ☎ (01298) 85319
⊕ thechurchinn.co.uk
Adnams Southwold Bitter; Marston's 61 Deep, Pedigree; 2 changing beers (sourced locally; often Abbeydale, Thornbridge) Ⓗ
Set in beautiful surroundings opposite the local church (look for the unusual weathervane), this traditional village pub caters both for locals and walkers. Its main room is laid out for dining, with good home-cooked food on offer. A low ceiling and real fire help maintain a cosy pub atmosphere. Guest beers are usually from local micros. There is an excellent patio area outside. Parking is on the road in front of the pub. Monday is quiz night.
Q ✿ 🚃 ◑ ▲ ❀ 🛜

Chesterfield

Beer Parlour Ⓛ
1 King Street North, Whittington Moor, S41 9BA
🕓 4-11; 12-midnight Sat; 1-10 Sun ☎ 07870 693411
⊕ the-beer-parlour.co.uk
8 changing beers (often Double Top, Thornbridge, Timothy Taylor) Ⓗ
A compact, rustic one-roomed bar with a friendly welcome, close to Chesterfield FC's stadium. Its relaxed atmosphere and comfy seating help to give a genuine micropub feel. There is a choice of up to eight real ales, plus keg, real cider, Belgian and continental beers. Customers can opt to take a beer home from the varied range of bottled ales available. A winner of CAMRA awards. Q ♿ ● 🚃 ❀

Chesterfield Alehouse
37 West Bars, S40 1AG
🕓 3-10; 12-10 Thu-Sat; 12-8 Sun
⊕ chesterfieldalehouse.co.uk
6 changing beers Ⓗ
Chesterfield's first micropub is a few minutes' walk from the historic marketplace. Previously a furniture shop, the split-level room has a small lower seating area leading up a few steps to the serving area. Here you will find six regularly changing cask beers; a stout or a porter is ever-present alongside 12 keg ales. A popular free cheese night takes place every Wednesday. A range of ciders, perries, local gins and wines is also stocked. Major free-to-air sporting events are shown upstairs. Q ♿ ♣ ● 🚃 🚃 ❀ 🛜

Chesterfield Arms Ⓛ
Newbold Road, S41 7PH
🕓 3 (12 Thu)-11; 12-midnight Fri & Sat; 12-11 Sun
☎ (01246) 236634
Everards Beacon Hill; 10 changing beers (often Abbeydale, Thornbridge) Ⓗ
Oak-clad walls, open fires and hop-strewn bars create a relaxing ambience. Conservatory doors open up on a warm evening, extending the outdoor seating area. Up to 10 real ales are available, often from microbreweries. The barn, warmed by a log-burning stove, opens at weekends, with additional beers and beer festivals. A former two-times local CAMRA Pub of the Year. Q ⏰ ✿ ♿ ● 🚃 (10) ❀

Neptune Beer Emporium Ⓛ
46 St Helen's Street, S41 7QD
🕓 4-9 Mon; 4-11 Tue-Thu; 4-midnight Fri; 12-midnight Sat; 3-11 Sun ☎ (01246) 220146
8 changing beers (sourced locally) Ⓗ
Now a free house and a self-styled beer emporium, this is a compact back-street local, serving excellent beer in two drinking areas either side of a central bar. The list of real ales is always changing and includes local breweries. The real ales are complemented by an extensive range of continental and craft beers on draught and in bottles, all displayed on a very descriptive chalkboard. 🚃 ♣ ● 🚃 ❀

Rose & Crown 🍷 Ⓛ ⊘
104 Old Road, Brampton, S40 2QT
🕓 12 (3 Mon & Tue)-11; 12-midnight Fri & Sat; 12-11 Sun
☎ (01246) 563750 ⊕ roseandcrownbrampton.co.uk
Brampton Golden Bud, Best; Everards Tiger; 6 changing beers (often Brampton) Ⓗ
Brampton Brewery's first tied house as part of Everards' Project William. A compact snug provides room for group meetings; the main room has plenty of quiet corners. Mementos from the original Brampton Brewery are displayed on the walls. Four Brampton beers are always on, including a dark ale. Sunday lunches are available. There are outdoor drinking areas to the front and rear. An annual beer festival is held to mark St George's Day. Quiz night is Tuesday. Local CAMRA Pub of the Year 2018 and Cider Pub of the Year 2019. ⏰ ✿ ◑ ♣ ● P 🚃 (170) ❀ 🛜

Clay Cross

Rykneld Turnpyke Ⓛ
4 John Street, S45 9NQ
🕓 3-11.30 (midnight Fri); 12-midnight Sat; 12-11.30 Sun
☎ (01246) 250366
12 changing beers Ⓗ
Formerly the Egstow Working Men's Club, this place (named after Rykneld Street, the old road between Chesterfield and Derby) has one large room divided into various areas, with comfortable seating. There is an excellent choice of up to 12 reasonably-priced beers from the on-site Instant Karma Brewery, plus local guests. Keg and ciders are also served. Cribbage, dominoes and board games are always available. The brewery can be seen through a viewing panel at the rear. ♣ ● (51,54) ❀

Clowne

Centre Ⓛ
Recreation Close, S43 4PL

7-11; 5-11 Sat & Sun ☎ (01246) 819546
4 changing beers (often Timothy Taylor) H
A council-run community centre widely used by the locals for functions. The place is well cared for, with a relaxed and friendly atmosphere. It serves a changing Timothy Taylor house beer plus guests. The Rock and Blues Club puts on live bands every Sunday and there is a popular quiz night on Tuesday, with free food. A beer festival is held in May. Ample car parking is available. P

Coton-in-the-Elms

Black Horse
17 Burton Road, DE12 8HJ (in centre of village)
4-11 (midnight Fri); 1-midnight Sat; 12-10.30 Sun
☎ (01283) 762947 theblackhorsederbyshire.co.uk
Draught Bass; Joule's Pale Ale; Marston's Pedigree; 1 changing beer (sourced regionally) H
Lively and popular free house, owned by the licensee, with a bright and airy main room divided into bar and lounge areas by glass-topped wood partitions. A small snug, served through a hatch, features a bar billiards table. The guest beer, often from a local microbrewery, is dispensed alongside over 30 ciders and perries. A free cheeseboard is provided for weekday evenings and weekend lunchtimes. Quiz night is Tuesday; live music is played monthly on Sunday. Accommodation is a two-person self-catering flat.
Q P (22)

Cromford

Boat Inn
Scarthin, DE4 3QF
12-midnight (11.30 Sun) ☎ (01629) 258083
the-boat-inn.co.uk
4 changing beers (sourced locally; often Abbeydale, Dancing Duck, Whim) H
Built in 1772, beamed ceilings, exposed stone walls and an open fire give the main bar a cosy atmosphere. A small snug area, dining room and cellar bar with Sky and BT Sport cater for most, if not all, needs. Award-winning home-cooked meals are served every day until 9pm. Live music plays every Friday and Saturday night. The beer garden overlooks a large mill pond. Cromford is in the Derwent Valley Mills World Heritage Site.
(6.1)

Cutthorpe

Gate Inn
Overgreen, S42 7BA
11.30-11; 12-11 Sun ☎ (01246) 276923
Black Sheep Best Bitter; Fuller's London Pride; 4 changing beers H
This venue is in a great scenic location, with views overlooking two counties. Its large dining areas, to the left and rear of the main bar area, serve meals all day until 9pm. The pub usually sells two beers from local breweries such as Peak, Bradfield and Thornbridge. Although in a remote location, it is only a 10-minute walk from the nearest bus stop at Linacre Reservoir. Q P

Derby

Alexandra Hotel
203 Siddals Road, DE1 2QE
12-11 (midnight Fri); 11-midnight Sat ☎ (01332) 293993
alexandrahotelderby.co.uk
Castle Rock Harvest Pale; 7 changing beers (sourced nationally) H
A Castle Rock pub serving the brewery's own beers and up to five guest ales, including a mild and a stout or porter. It also offers more than 50 UK and continental bottled beers of varying styles. Themed food nights are held approximately monthly. The lounge is adorned with breweriana and the bar with railway memorabilia. A Class 37 locomotive cab resides in the car park. The birthplace of Derby CAMRA in 1974. Q P

Babington Arms
11-13 Babington Lane, DE1 1TA
8am-midnight ☎ (01332) 383647
Draught Bass; Greene King Abbot; Marston's Pedigree; Ruddles Best Bitter; Small World Thunderbridge Stout, Twin Falls; 11 changing beers (sourced nationally) H
This Wetherspoon pub is a converted furniture showroom close to the city centre. It boasts a huge range of real ales, many from local microbreweries, and typically has six ciders on handpump or gravity dispense. The rear end of the large bar has some half-partitioned banquette seating and caters for family eating. At the front of the pub there is a small fenced-off area where outdoor drinkers can smoke.

Brunswick Inn
1 Railway Terrace, DE1 2RU
11-11 (11.30 Fri & Sat); 12-10.30 Sun ☎ (01332) 290677
brunswickderby.co.uk
Brunswick White Feather, Triple Hop, The Usual; Everards Beacon Hill, Tiger; Timothy Taylor Landlord; 10 changing beers (sourced nationally) H
Originally part of the railway village, this multi-roomed pub was restored and opened as Derby's first multiple-choice real ale house in 1987. Owned by Everards, it has since become one of the best known free houses in the country. The range of up to 16 real ales includes at least six from Brunswick, the in-house brewery, which was added in 1991. The pub gets busy on Derby County match days. Local CAMRA Cider Pub of the Year 2019.
Q P

Exeter Arms
13 Exeter Place, DE1 2EU
12-11 (11.30 Wed & Thu; midnight Fri & Sat); 12-10.30 Sun
☎ (01332) 605323 exeterarms.co.uk
Dancing Duck Ay Up, Dark Drake; Marston's Pedigree; 3 changing beers H
A joint venture between Dancing Duck Brewery and a local food and drink entrepreneur has resulted in a fine range of beers and an excellent dining experience, all put together in a pub with old-world charm. The small bar has an open fire and leads to several other rooms, including a wooden-settled snug with an old-fashioned range. The adjoining atmospheric cottage, dating from about 1815, has been incorporated into the pub. A popular and quirky quiz is held on Monday evening. P

Falstaff
74 Silverhill Road, DE23 6UJ
12-11 (midnight Fri & Sat) ☎ (01332) 342902
falstaffbrewery.co.uk
Falstaff Fist Full of Hops, Phoenix, Smiling Assassin; 1 changing beer H

A 20-minute walk from the city centre into the Normanton district rewards you with this atmospheric and reputedly haunted free house. Originally a coaching inn before the neighbourhood was built up, it is now the Falstaff Brewery tap and has long been the best real ale house in the area. The rear lounge is a shrine to Offilers' Brewery, with a display of memorabilia. Other collectables can be viewed throughout the games room and second bar room. Q (4,7)

Five Lamps

25 Duffield Road, DE1 3BH

12-11 (midnight Fri & Sat) (01332) 348730

fivelampsderby.co.uk

Draught Bass; Everards Tiger; Peak Ales Chatsworth Gold; St Austell Proper Job; Thornbridge Jaipur IPA; house beer (by Derby); 8 changing beers (sourced regionally) H

Since reopening in 2010, this pub has gone from strength to strength thanks to the dedication of its licensees and staff. Its 14 handpumps showcase many local ales from breweries such as Derby, Peak and Whim. The Lamps is essentially open plan, but has many little nooks and crannies, giving it a homely feel. It has been tastefully refurbished with wood panelling and leather seating in a traditional style. P

Flowerpot

23-25 King Street, DE1 3DZ

12-11 (11.30 Wed & Thu; 12.30am Fri & Sat)

(01332) 204955 rawpromo.co.uk

Marston's Pedigree; Oakham Bishops Farewell; Sharp's Doom Bar H**; Whim Hartington IPA** H/G**, Flower Power** H**; 9 changing beers (sourced nationally)** H/G

Dating from around 1800 but much expanded from its original premises, this vibrant pub reaches back from the roadside frontage and divides into several interlinking rooms. One room provides the stage for regular live bands; another has a glass cellar wall revealing rows of stillaged firkins, which can be seen from the bar and from the road outside. Up to 14 real ales and two ciders are offered. Good en-suite accommodation is available.

Furnace Inn

Duke Street, DE1 3BX

2-11; 11-midnight Fri & Sat; 11-11 Sun (01332) 385981

shinybrewing.com/the-furnace-inn

8 changing beers (sourced nationally) H

The Furnace has been transformed into a real ale mecca since reopening in 2012. A former Hardys and Hansons pub, it is now the tap for Furnace Brewery. Up to eight real ales and three ciders/perries are served, complemented by a variety of UK craft beers. There are two distinct open-plan rooms with a central bar. Poker and cheese nights feature weekly, with regular beer festivals held throughout the year. P

Last Post

1 Uttoxeter Old Road, DE1 1GA

11-11 (8 Mon-Wed) (01332) 296737

thelastpostderbylt.wixsite.com/thelastpostderbyltd

4 changing beers (sourced nationally) H

This former post office in the West End area of Derby was the town's second micropub, and consists of a large single room with the bar towards the rear. Its four changing beers vary continuously; one is usually dark. An interesting variety of whiskies is also on offer. Live acoustic music is performed every evening from Thursday to Sunday. The small rear yard is a dedicated smoking area. Beer festivals coincide with those of the local CAMRA branch. (8)

Old Bell Hotel

51 Sadler Gate, DE1 3NQ

12-11 (1am Fri & Sat) (01332) 723090

bellhotelderby.co.uk

Dancing Duck Dark Drake; Draught Bass; 6 changing beers (sourced locally) H

One of Derby's best-loved pubs continues to be restored to its former magnificence. The front Tavern Bar features a range of real ale and craft kegs, but discerning drinkers should seek out the Tudor Bar to the rear, which did not admit women until 1975. This 18th-century coaching inn is a welcome oasis in Sadler Gate, a premier shopping street in the Cathedral Quarter. The exterior's Tudor-style half-timbering was added in 1929.

Olde Dolphin Inne ★

5a Queen Street, DE1 3DL (close to cathedral)

11.30-11 (midnight Fri & Sat); 12-11 Sun

(01332) 267711 yeoldedolphin.co.uk

Draught Bass; Greene King Abbot; Marston's Pedigree; Sharp's Doom Bar; 4 changing beers (sourced nationally) H

Claimed to be Derby's oldest pub, it certainly looks the part. It has a number of small rooms, including a traditional snug which has a real fire in winter and conversation all year round. Food is provided in the bar areas, complemented by the upstairs steak restaurant, open Thursday to Saturday evening. A music quiz is held on Tuesday evening and a general knowledge quiz on Sunday evening. Live music features regularly on the large outdoor patio.

Q P

Peacock Inn

87 Nottingham Road, DE1 3QS

11 (3 Mon)-11; 11-midnight Fri & Sat; 12-10.30 Sun

(01332) 583308

Draught Bass; Marston's Pedigree; Whim Arbor Light, Hartington IPA; house beer (by Leatherbritches); 4 changing beers (sourced nationally) H

This attractive 18th-century stone-built roadside pub used to be a staging post on the main coach road out of Derby, which ran alongside the old Derby Canal. Two rooms on different levels are divided by a central bar and feature wooden floors, stove burners, Derby County memorabilia and photos of the old town. Up to nine real ales and two ciders and/or perries feature. Beer festivals are held in the large, covered garden area to the rear. Q

Pot Hole

Unit 17, Park Farm Shopping Centre, Park Farm Drive, Allestree, DE22 2QQ

closed Mon-Wed; 2-9 Thu; 2-10 Fri; 12-10 Sat; 12-6 Sun

07749 857879

Littleover Epiphany Pale Ale; 5 changing beers (sourced nationally) H

Formerly a dry cleaners, the premises was transformed into Allestree's first micropub in 2017; a welcome return of a licensed venue in the Park Farm shopping area. This friendly single-roomed pub serves six real ales including at least one from the local Littleover Brewery. Beers from near and far constantly change week on week, complemented by real cider. There is plentiful seating both inside and to the front of the pub. Q❀♣●P🚌

Rowditch Inn
246 Uttoxeter New Road, DE22 3LL
7-11; 12-2, 7-11 Sat & Sun ☎ (01332) 343123
Marston's Pedigree; Rowditch St Stephens, St Andrews; 1 changing beer (sourced locally) H
A welcoming roadside hostelry with an unexpectedly deep interior which divides into two bar areas and a small snug. There is a display cabinet of pub memorabilia, and the pumpclips adorning the walls testify to the myriad guest ales. Downstairs, at the rear, the garden is a peaceful haven. The output of the pub's brewery is exclusively consumed on the premises. Well worth the walk or five-minute bus ride from the city centre. Q❀♣●🚌🐾

Smithfield 🏆 L
Meadow Road, DE1 2BH
12-10.30; 12-midnight Fri-Sun ☎ (01332) 986601
smithfieldderby.co.uk
Draught Bass; 7 changing beers (sourced nationally) H
The Smithfield sits near the town centre, on the banks of the River Derwent opposite Bass's Rec. The large main bar boasts an eclectic range of new and interesting beers supported by Draught Bass. A separate quiet room with a real fire overlooks the patio, itself against the river. The pub has regular live music and many beer-related activities. Local CAMRA Pub of the Year 2019. ❀◐♣●P🚌🐾

Standing Order ✔
28-32 Iron Gate, DE1 3GL
7am-12.30am (2am Fri & Sat); 7am-midnight Sun
☎ (01332) 207591
Draught Bass; Greene King Abbot; Kelham Island Pale Rider; Marston's Pedigree; Ruddles Best Bitter; Sharp's Doom Bar; 12 changing beers H
This first, grandest and certainly tallest of the three Wetherspoon outlets in Derby is wittily named after its former role as a bank. It features full-size reproductions of paintings of local worthies from the time of the Industrial Revolution. There are a few quieter corners but the atmosphere is generally of a busy city-centre pub. A good changing selection of guest ales is offered, with alcohol served from 9am. Q◐♿●

Tap L
1 Derwent Street, DE1 2ED
12-11 (midnight Thu; 1am Fri); 11-1am Sat; 11-11 Sun
☎ (01332) 366283 brewerytap-dbc.co.uk
Derby Business As Usual, Dashingly Dark; 4 changing beers (sourced nationally) H
A flat-iron-shaped building on the banks of the Derwent with a roof terrace overlooking the river. Two bars sit either side of the main entrance, and there is a small courtyard. Exposed brickwork and wooden flooring give a contemporary feel, added to by modern and eclectic food offerings. Patrons may choose from six handpumps and a wide range of foreign beers from tap or bottle. A rack of ale, accompanied by local cheese, is also available. ❀◐♿●🚌🐾

Draycott

Coach & Horses ✔
1 Victoria Road, DE72 3PS
4-11 (7 Mon); 3-11.30 Fri; 12-11.30 Sat; 12-11 Sun
☎ (01332) 874636 thecoachdraycott.co.uk
Blue Monkey BG Sips; Greene King Abbot; Sharp's Doom Bar; 1 changing beer (sourced locally) H
Large, two-roomed village pub and part of the local Draycott heritage area. Friendly and informal, it offers a well-kept pint and periodic entertainment in the large bar area. There is ample parking and a large outside smoking area at the rear of the pub. Events at the weekend include karaoke on Saturday night and occasional gigs. Q❀◐♿♣P🚌🐾

Dronfield

Coach & Horses L ✔
Sheffield Road, S18 2GD
4-10.30 Mon; 12-11 Tue-Thu; 12-midnight Fri & Sat; 12-10.30 Sun ☎ (01246) 413269 mycoachandhorses.co.uk
Thornbridge Wild Swan, Brother Rabbit, Lord Marples, Ashford, Kipling, Saint Petersburg Imperial Russian Stout; 1 changing beer (sourced nationally; often Drone Valley, Mallinsons) H
The pub is next to Sheffield FC's ground on the northern edge of Dronfield. It is operated by Thornbridge Brewery and showcases a good choice of beers, with guest ales across a wide range of styles. The large outdoor drinking area is particularly popular. Good-value meals are served from Chariot's Kitchen (no food Mon). The pub hosts a quiz night on Sunday and an open mic acoustic evening on Monday. Q❀◐●P🚌(43)🐾

Duffield

Town Street Tap L
17 Town Street, DE56 4EH
closed Mon; 4-10 Tue-Thu; 3-10.30 Fri; 12-10.30 Sat; 12-5 Sun ☎ 07925 461706 thetownstreettap.co.uk
6 changing beers (sourced nationally) G
On the main road through Duffield, this micropub for Tollgate Brewery has been converted into a modern, uncluttered drinking space with table service. Of the six changing real ales, two are from the Tollgate range and at least one is dark. Four ciders are served; takeouts come in containers or from the bottle shop. Pork pies and Scotch eggs are available for the hungry, with free tea and coffee for drivers. Walkers with boots are welcome. Local CAMRA Country Pub of the Year 2018. Q⇌♣●P🚌🐾

Glossop

Crown Inn ★
142 Victoria Street, SK13 8JF (on Hayfield Rd out of town centre)
5-11; 12-11 Fri & Sat; 12-10.30 Sun ☎ (01457) 862824
Samuel Smith Old Brewery Bitter H
Stone-built end-of-terrace locals' pub, a few minutes from the town centre and railway station. It was built in 1846 and acquired by the brewery in 1977. The pub features on CAMRA's National Inventory of Historic Pub Interiors. A curved bar serves two snugs, each with a real fire in winter, and a pool/games room. Pictures of bygone Glossop add to the traditional character. An enclosed outdoor drinking area is provided in the rear yard. Q❀♿⇌♣🚌(390)🐾

Queen's Arms
1 Shepley Street, SK13 7RZ
10.30-midnight ☎ (01457) 853005
queens-arms-hotel-old-glossop.co.uk
Joseph Holt Bitter; Morland Old Speckled Hen; Oakham Citra; Thornbridge Jaipur IPA; Wainwright; 3 changing beers (sourced locally; often Peak Ales, Sharp's) H
In Old Glossop, below the Bleaklow hills, this place is a pleasant 15-minute walk from the town centre through Manor Park. Popular with locals, visitors and hikers, it serves breakfast from 10.30am. Food is available from a standard pub menu downstairs and from the Queen Spice Indian restaurant on the first floor. Live entertainment features on Tuesday and Saturday; Thursday is quiz night. Local CAMRA Pub of the Year 2017. (390)

Star Inn
2 Howard Street, SK13 7DD (next to railway station)
2-11 (midnight Fri); 12-midnight Sat; 12-10.30 Sun
☎ (01457) 853072
4 changing beers (sourced regionally; often Abbeydale, Howard Town, Pictish) H
A popular town-centre pub, run by a dedicated CAMRA member. Conversation dominates in the large, comfortable main room with its wooden panelling. One wall in the smaller rear room features a large map of part of the Peak District National Park. Guest beers are mainly from local microbreweries. Located very close to the railway station, the pub is an ideal starting or finishing point for walking and cycling in the Dark Peak area.
QP

Hartshorne

Admiral Rodney Inn
65 Main Street, DE11 7ES (on A514)
5-11 Mon-Fri; 4.30 (1.30 summer)-11 Sat; 3.30-11 Sun
☎ (01283) 227771 theadmiralrodney.uk
Exmoor Gold; 5 changing beers (sourced nationally) H
Traditional village local dating back to the early 19th century. The pub was rebuilt and extended in the late 20th century to provide an open-plan, L-shaped drinking area while retaining the original oak beams in the former snug. There is also a secluded raised area tucked away behind the bar. Cheese tasting takes place on the first Monday of the month, open mic night is the third Tuesday, and quiz night every Sunday. A changing real cider is available at weekends. The grounds include a cricket pitch, home of Hartshorne Cricket Club.
P (2)

Hassop

Eyre Arms ★
DE45 1NS
12-11 ☎ (01629) 640390
Peak Ales Swift Nick; 3 changing beers (sourced locally; often Abbeydale, Bradfield, Kelham Island) H
A 300-year-old country pub with two comfortably furnished rooms and a small snug squeezed between, watched over by an imposing grandfather clock. The impressive Eyre family coat of arms is displayed above the fireplace. Excellent, good-value home-cooked food is served 12-3pm and 6-9pm, with bar snacks available between those times. You can expect friendly service in this characterful, unspoilt pub. QP

Hayfield

Royal Hotel
Market Street, SK22 2EP
11-11 ☎ (01663) 742721 theroyalhayfield.co.uk
5 changing beers (sourced locally) H
An imposing stone pub, built as a coaching inn in the 18th century, close to the church, cricket ground and River Sett. The interior boasts oak panels and pews creating a relaxing atmosphere, enhanced by real fires in winter. Guest beers from local micros are always on tap. A function room and restaurant complete the facilities; food is available all day in summer. The village is the base for many leisure activities in the Dark Peak and was the birthplace of actor Arthur Lowe.
QP

Holmesfield

Rutland Arms
96 Main Road, S18 7WT
12-11.30 ☎ (0114) 289 0374
Black Sheep Best Bitter; Bradfield Farmers Blonde; Castle Rock Harvest Pale; Theakston Best Bitter; 2 changing beers (often Bradfield, Everards, Pheasantry) H
A traditional and popular village pub offering a relaxing, warm and snug atmosphere, with open fires and low wooden beams. The beer range has increased steadily over the years to six handpulled cask ales. The extensive outdoor seating area with grassed children's play section is idyllic in late spring and summer. A collection of books and magazines of local interest is available for customers' use. QP (15)

Hope

Cheshire Cheese Inn
Edale Road, S33 6ZF
closed Mon; 12-3, 6-11; 12-11.30 Sat; 12-10 Sun
☎ (01433) 620381 thecheshirecheeseinn.co.uk
Bradfield Farmers Blonde; 3 changing beers (sourced locally; often Bradfield, Peak Ales) H
A cosy country inn dating from 1578, with an open-plan bar area. A smaller room at a lower level, probably originally used to house animals, is now mainly a dining area. Home-cooked meals featuring local produce are served lunchtimes and evenings. The pub is in good walking country but parking is limited as the road outside is narrow.
QP

Horsley

Coach & Horses
47 Church Street, DE21 5BQ
12-11 ☎ (01332) 988064
Marston's Pedigree; Wychwood Hobgoblin Gold; 2 changing beers (sourced nationally) H
This traditional country pub sits at the triangle junction on the edge of the village of Horsley. Following a full refurbishment it has two lounges, one large and the other small, both well presented and served by a single bar. There is also a conservatory to the side, which allows the rural location to be appreciated. Food is served daily.
QP

Horsley Woodhouse

Old Oak Inn

176 Main Street, DE7 6AW

4 (3 Thu & Fri; 12 Sat)-11; 12-10.30 Sun ☎ (01332) 881299

Changing beers (sourced nationally; often Bottle Brook, Leadmill) H

As the taphouse for the Leadmill Brewery, the Old Oak features an extensive variety of the firm's beers, plus a couple of guests. It is a traditional pub boasting four rooms of differing character, some with open fires. At weekends drinkers can enjoy the RURAD (rural real ale drinkers) bar – effectively a mini beer festival offering gravity-dispensed ales from craft brewers near and far, alongside the more local Leadmill and Bottle Brook beers. Homely and welcoming. Q

Hundall

Miners Arms

Hundall Lane, S18 4BP

12-midnight ☎ (01246) 414505

Drone Valley Dronny Bottom Bitter; Pictish Alchemists Ale; 3 changing beers (sourced nationally) H

On the high ridge above Unstone, this is a traditional village local which has thrived since its change of ownership in 2015. The beer garden provides an excellent alternative space in which to enjoy the wide range of beers and ciders that are always available. The Miners operates a Monday Club, when real ales are discounted for all customers. A multiple award-winning pub both for ales and cider, and CAMRA local Pub of the Year from 2016 to 2019. Q P (14)

Ilkeston

Burnt Pig

53 Market Street, DE7 5RB

closed Mon-Wed; 11-11 ☎ 07538 723722

5 changing beers H/G

A well-established and popular local micropub, extended over three rooms and with a collection of historical pub memorabilia. Hosted by its welcoming and enthusiastic owner, Simon, it dispenses five changing ales and a good selection of real ciders and continental bottled beers. The Burnt Pig's famous pork scratchings are on offer along with tasty cheeses to take away. This is a pub not to be missed. Q

Dewdrop

24 Station Road, DE7 5TE

4-11; 3-11 Fri; 12-11 Sat; 12-10.30 Sun ☎ (0115) 932 9684

Oakham Bishops Farewell; house beer (by Oakham); changing beers (often Acorn, Blue Monkey, Castle Rock) H

Victorian pub with a regionally important historic interior next to the new Ilkeston railway station on the outskirts of town. It is ideal as a first port of call on the real ale scene in Ilkeston, or for a relaxed visit before returning to the train. The interior comprises three rooms, with the bar and lounge separated by the serving area. A small room offset from the entrance provides a quiet area to sit. Eight beers plus three ciders are served, with pub food available. Q (27)

Prince of Wales

69 South Street, DE7 5QQ

3-11; 12-11.30 Fri & Sat; 12-11 Sun ☎ (0115) 932 5452

3 changing beers H

A recent addition to the Guide, this is a two-roomed ex-Shipstone's pub, with a smaller lounge to the left and a popular bar to the right. The serving area is central to both and dispenses ales from three handpumps, supporting local breweries such as Falstaff and Blue Monkey. The pub offers brewery takeovers throughout the year, increasing the number of beers available.

Litton

Red Lion

Church Lane, SK17 8QU

12-11 (midnight Fri & Sat); 12-10.30 Sun ☎ (01298) 871458 theredlionlitton.co.uk

Abbeydale Absolution; Peak Ales Bakewell Best Bitter; 2 changing beers (sourced locally; often Abbeydale, Peak Ales) H

Nestling on the green and the only pub in the village, the Red Lion is a welcome refuge for locals and visitors alike. Its large fireplace provides warmth to several rooms off a central passageway. Fresh food is served all day, every day. The pub holds a beer festival at the end of June during the annual wakes week, which features events including a well dressing on the village green, and is not to be missed. (65,173)

Long Eaton

Hole in the Wall

Regent Street, NG10 1JX

4-11 Mon, Tue & Thu; closed Wed; 11-11 Fri & Sat; 12-11 Sun ☎ (0115) 973 4920

Draught Bass; Nottingham Extra Pale Ale; Oakham Citra, Bishops Farewell; 1 changing beer H

This unchanged two-roomed local has retained its charm and is a regular Guide entry. The walls of both bar rooms are covered with pub memorabilia collected by the landlord of more than 30 years. The pub has maintained a high standard of beer quality over the years and now offers a choice of four regular ales plus one guest. Wheelchair access is via the rear entrance. Q

Lullington

Colvile Arms

Main Street, DE12 8EG (centre of village)

5-11 (9 Mon); 12-10 Sun summer; 6-11 (9 Mon); 5-11 Fri & Sat; 12-2.30, 6-10 Sun winter ☎ 07510 870980

thecolvilearms.com

Draught Bass; Marston's Pedigree; 2 changing beers (sourced regionally) H

Leased from the Lullington Estate, seat of the Colvile family until the early 1900s, this popular 18th-century free house is at the heart of an attractive hamlet at the southern tip of the county. The public bar comprises an adjoining hallway and snug, each featuring high-backed settles with wood panelling. The bar and a comfortable lounge are on opposite sides of a central serving area. A second lounge/function room overlooks the beer garden and lawn. Pop-up food is available Wednesday and Friday evenings. Q P

Makeney

Holly Bush ★

Holly Bush Lane, DE56 0RX

12-11; 12-10.30 Sun ☎ (01332) 841729

hollybushinnmakeney.co.uk

Fuller's London Pride; Greene King Abbot; Marston's Pedigree; Timothy Taylor Landlord; 4 changing beers (sourced nationally) [H]
The Holly Bush is an excellent, late 17th-century Grade II-listed pub with great character. Once a farmhouse and brewery on the Strutt Estate, it stood on the main Derby turnpike before the new road (now the A6) opened in 1818. Dick Turpin reputedly drank here, and the pub, recognised by CAMRA as having a nationally important historic interior, has various stone-flagged hideaways. Welcoming fires burn in winter. A home-cooked lunchtime menu is offered and bar snacks are always available. Regular beer festivals take place. Walkers, families and dogs are all welcome.
Q🐎❀◐♿♣●P🚌🐾

Marlpool

Marlpool Ale House 𝕃

5 Breach Road, DE75 7NJ
❂ closed Mon-Thu; 2-11 Fri; 12-11 Sat; 12-10 Sun
☎ 07963 511855 🌐 marlpoolbrewing.co.uk
Marlpool Blind Boris, Otters Pocket, Scratty Ratty, Frank [H]**; 5 changing beers (sourced regionally)** [H]/[G]
The Ale House is one of the smallest pubs in Derbyshire; a welcoming and cosy place in which to meet friends and strangers. Its staff are cheery and informative. The bar is an old Methodist chapel pulpit. A rear room features a wood-burning stove. Beers come on handpump or from the cellar, and there is a two-barrel brewery in the rear yard. Apart from the tap beers, the selection on offer is usually from smaller breweries around the country.
Q❀●🚌🐾

Matlock

MoCa Bar 𝕃

77 Dale Road, DE4 3LT
❂ 11-11 (1am Fri & Sat) ☎ (01629) 583973
7 changing beers (sourced locally; often Abbeydale, Blue Monkey, Thornbridge) [H]
This modern single-room bar has a sophisticated city café feel, with wooden floors and chunky pine furniture. It is open plan and urbane, with music memorabilia adorning the walls. Comfortable seating includes a large window area and a decked terrace at the rear. Seven handpulls dispense ales from dedicated breweries Abbeydale, Blue Monkey, Totally Brewed, Dancing Duck, Pentrich, Oakham and Thornbridge. There is a reduction in the price of real ales (except premium beers) Monday-Wednesday. 🐎❀◐⇌🚌(6.1,141)🐾📶

Newsroom (Armitts) 𝕃

75-77 Smedley Street East, DE4 3FQ
❂ 12 (6 Mon)-11; 12-midnight Fri & Sat; 12-11 Sun
☎ (01629) 583625
4 changing beers (sourced regionally)
This smart conversion from newsagent to micropub is an L-shaped room with exposed brickwork and renovated sash windows. It serves four real ales from interesting local and sometimes national microbreweries. The half-dozen craft ales normally include a stout and a lager; at least one will be KeyKeg. More than 60 bottled and canned beers are currently stocked, to drink in or take away. A good range of gins and wines is also sold. ♿⇌🚌🐾

Thorn Tree Inn 🏆

48 Jackson Road, DE4 3JQ (up Bank Rd, left into Smedley St, 2nd right up Smith Rd, 1st left)
❂ 12-2 (not Mon), 5-11; 12-midnight Fri & Sat; 12-11 Sun
☎ (01629) 580295
Draught Bass; Nottingham Extra Pale Ale; Timothy Taylor Landlord; 4 changing beers (sourced nationally) [H]
Perched high above Matlock, this compact and traditional two-roomed pub provides beautiful views from its heated patio area. A haunted wall clock hangs in the lounge where regulars, ramblers and real ale enthusiasts convene to enjoy the atmosphere. Three permanent real ales are complemented by four changing guests. Home-made food is served Tuesday-Friday lunchtime, pie night is Wednesday, Sunday lunch is on offer, and bar snacks are available all day. Children and dogs are welcome. Local CAMRA Pub of the Year 2018 and 2019. Q❀◐♣▯🚌(M2)🐾📶

Twenty Ten 𝕃

16 Dale Road, DE4 3LT
❂ closed Mon; 5-10 Tue; 12-10 Wed & Thu; 12-midnight Fri & Sat; 12-7 Sun ☎ 07710 427442 🌐 twentytenmatlock.co.uk
4 changing beers (sourced locally; often Thornbridge) [H]
A stone's throw from the local train station, Twenty Ten nestles among the antique shops of Dale Road. It serves four real ales and focuses on LocAle, with Thornbridge and Matlock Wolds Farm regularly on the handpulls. These are complemented by 16 draught craft beers of which at least eight are KeyKeg. Food is served at lunchtime, followed by a Light Bites menu until 7pm. Live music is performed on Friday and Saturday evening.
🐎❀◐⇌🚌(6.1,141)🐾📶

Melbourne

Chip & Pin 𝕃

8-10 High Street, DE73 8GJ
❂ closed Mon; 4.30-9.30 Tue-Thu; 12-9.30 Fri & Sat; 12-2.30 Sun ☎ 07957 806454 🌐 chipandpinpub.com
4 changing beers (sourced regionally) [G]
This micropub is centrally located in former Midland Bank premises. It is owned by a group of local real ale enthusiasts who serve you at your table. The building has been sympathetically restored and has two rooms: a main drinking area and a meeting room for local groups. Real ales are available in third-of-a-pint taster racks. Real cider, wine, soft drinks and snacks are also on sale. Sunday opening hours apply on bank holidays. Q●▯🚌(2)🐾

New Mills

Beer Shed

47B Market Street, SK22 4AA
❂ closed Mon & Tue; 4-10.30 Wed & Thu; 2-10.30 Fri-Sun
☎ (01663) 742005
House beer (by Fool Hardy Ales); 3 changing beers (sourced locally; often Rock Mill, Torrside) [H]
New Mills' first micropub, handily situated in the town centre close to New Mills Central railway station and bus station. The layout is slightly unusual, comprising a small frontage and a long narrow bar, which serves its purpose well. There is also a small downstairs room. The three changing beers com from local micros. A cheerful, intimate atmosphere makes for a pleasant drinking experience. Q⇌●🚌🐾

Masons Arms
High Street, SK22 4BR
⏲ 12-11 (midnight Fri & Sat) ☎ (01663) 635466
Robinsons Unicorn; 4 changing beers (sourced regionally) 🄷
Located close to the Sett River Valley and Torrs Millennium Walkway in the centre of town, this former Robinsons pub is now a free house following a local campaign to save it. Very much a community asset, it is a lively, friendly pub offering a changing range of beers. It has a strong sports orientation and also hosts regular live music featuring local bands. There is a small outside drinking area. ⇌P🚌🐾📶

Newbold

Nag's Head Inn 🄻
37 Newbold Village, S41 8RJ (about 2 miles from Chesterfield town centre)
⏲ 4-11; 12-midnight Sat; 12-11 Sun ☎ (01246) 297446
Sharp's Doom Bar; 5 changing beers (often Peak Ales, Pentrich) 🄷
Built in 1760, the pub is Grade II listed. It retains its central bar layout, surrounded by four separate rooms, one of them with an open fire. Another historic building lies directly behind: the medieval Eyre Chapel is accessed through the pub car park. Adjoining this is the Newbold Observatory, which has public open evenings. On Tuesday there is a discount on cask ales. Traditional cider is available in summer. ♨❀♣🍎P🚌(10)🐾📶

Newton

New Inn
80 Main Street, DE55 5TE
⏲ closed Mon; 4-midnight (1am Fri); 12-1am Sat; 12-midnight Sun ☎ (01773) 873944
Dukeries A Ray of Sunshine, Farmers Branch; 1 changing beer (sourced locally) 🄷
Two Dukeries beers and a guest ale are served in this welcoming village pub, along with a cider or perry. The L-shaped bar has comfortable seating with a real fire. The outdoor area has had an impressive makeover and is popular in summer. Thursday is steak night, followed by a quiz and 13-card bingo. Live music features most Saturdays. Five en-suite rooms are available for booking. Q♨❀◗♣🍎P🚌🐾📶

Newton Solney

Brickmakers Arms
9-11 Main Street, DE15 0SJ (on B5008, opp jct with Trent Lane)
⏲ 5-11; 4-11 Fri; 1-11 Sat; 12-11 Sun ☎ 07525 220103
🌐 brickmakersarms.pub
Burton Bridge Sovereign Gold, Bitter, Porter, Stairway to Heaven; 1 changing beer (sourced regionally) 🄷
This cosy local at the end of an 18th-century terrace of cottages was converted into a pub in the early 19th century for workers at a nearby brickworks. It features a narrow central bar leading at one end to a room served through a hatch, and at the other to an impressive oak-panelled room. The street entrance hallway houses a small bring and take library, beyond which is a function/meeting room. Quiz night is Monday, bingo Tuesday and poker Thursday. Q♨❀♣🍎P🚌(V3)🐾📶

North Wingfield

Shinnon
99 Station Road, S42 5JJ
⏲ 4-11; 2-midnight Fri; 12-midnight Sat; 2-midnight Sun
☎ 07983 503932
2 changing beers (sourced regionally) 🄷
Traditional two-roomed village community local with a friendly welcome. Formerly the Midland Hotel, it takes its name from an early 20th-century landlady who wore her hair in a chignon. Two handpumps serve regularly changing beers from local and regional breweries, usually one lighter and one darker option. The pub is family friendly, and allows dogs in the taproom only. Music features at weekends; Wednesday is quiz night.
♨♣P🚌(54)🐾📶

Ockbrook

Royal Oak 🄻
55 Green Lane, DE72 3SE
⏲ 11.30-3, 5-11; 11.30-11.30 Fri & Sat; 12-11 Sun
☎ (01332) 662378 🌐 royaloakockbrook.com
Draught Bass; 4 changing beers 🄷
Attractive 18th-century pub with a number of small rooms. Since 1953 it has been run by the Wilson family, who have implemented many improvements while retaining the original character and features. Excellent home-cooked food is served Monday to Saturday lunchtime and early evening, with two sittings for Sunday lunch. A large function room hosts many community and public events, including live music and open mic nights. There are two pleasant gardens, one with an enclosed play area for children. Local CAMRA Country Pub of the Year 2017.
Q♨❀◖◗♿♣🍎P🚌(9,9A)🐾📶

Openwoodgate

Black Bull's Head
2 Kilburn Lane, DE56 0SF
⏲ 12-11; 12-10.30 Sun ☎ 07860 757741
Draught Bass; Greene King Abbot; Oakham Bishops Farewell; 6 changing beers (sourced nationally; often Blue Monkey, Castle Rock, Dancing Duck) 🄷
A two-roomed former Greene King pub, now a free house, offering a warm welcome in comfortable surroundings, with real fires in the winter. The walls are adorned with historic photographs and newspaper clippings of local and national interest, with one wall dedicated to the RAF. The pub serves many real ales and ciders. Q❀♣P🚌🐾

Over Haddon

Lathkil Hotel 🄻
School Lane, DE45 1JE
⏲ 11-11; 12-10.30 Sun ☎ (01629) 812501 🌐 lathkil.co.uk
Whim Hartington Bitter; 4 changing beers 🄷
This pub overlooks a masterpiece of Peak District scenery, marvellous in any weather. Walking in, on one side is an old-fashioned bar room with a real fire and oak beams, while opposite is a larger room where diners enjoy superb home-cooked meals, again with a log-burning fire. The covered beer garden is the perfect place to while away a summer evening with a pint. Dogs are welcome in the bar, but walkers should remove their boots at the door. Q♨❀🛏◖◗⛺P🚆🚌(178)🐾📶

Repton

Boot ⬡ ✓
12 Boot Hill, DE65 6FT (from Repton Cross head down Brook End; pub is on right as road is joined by Boot Hill)
✦ 11-11.45 ☎ (01283) 346047 ⬡ thebootatrepton.co.uk
Boot Clod Hopper, Bitter, ESB; 4 changing beers (sourced regionally) Ⓗ
Close to the Repton Cross at the centre of the village, the Boot has been brought back to life by the local Bespoke pub company with a refurbishment and the addition of an on-site microbrewery supplying up to six of the real ales on the bar. The pub has two main rooms, one devoted to dining. Food and accommodation are also available. 🛏🍴♿◑● P🚆(V3)🐾 ☂

Ripley

Beehive Inn
151 Peasehill, DE5 3JN
✦ 4-11; 3-midnight Wed; 6-11 Thu; 6-midnight Fri; 3-1am Sat
☎ (01773) 749593
6 changing beers (sourced nationally) Ⓗ
Half a mile from the town centre, this three-roomed free house is a hub for local rugby and pub league teams. The pub has welcoming fires in winter, Sky TV in the public bar, and a large, pleasant beer garden. The Honeypot Bar in a building at the top of the garden is popular, with up to six real ales and several ciders always available. (Honeypot Bar opening times: closed Mon-Wed; 4-10 Thu & Fri; 2-10 Sat; 12-8 Sun.)
Q🛏🍴♿&♣●P🚆(9.1,9.3)🐾☂

Red Lion ✓
Market Place, DE5 3BS
✦ 8am-midnight (1am Fri & Sat) ☎ (01773) 512875
Greene King Abbot; Ruddles Best Bitter; Sharp's Doom Bar; 8 changing beers (sourced nationally; often Exmoor, Thornbridge) Ⓗ
A former Home Brewery pub built in the 1960s and easily identified by the large red lion rampant on its frontage. The building faces Ripley's Victorian town hall and marketplace at the centre of a vibrant, well-pubbed market town. A busy Wetherspoon's outlet, it serves a large selection of guest beers and good-quality wines. Food is available all day. 🛏🍴◑&●P🚆☂

Talbot 🏆
1 Butterley Hill, DE5 3LT
✦ 2-10.30; 12-11.30 Fri & Sat; 12-10.30 Sun
☎ (01773) 742382
8 changing beers (sourced nationally) Ⓗ
A classic Victorian flat-iron-shaped pub, the Talbot is blissfully free of music, instead offering the sounds of conversation, laughter and traditional games. It features a real fire in winter and stocks an excellent selection of real ales pulled from casks stored on an original stone stillage. Bar snacks are usually available. Locally turned pump handles in various designs add to the appeal of this welcoming and friendly pub. Local CAMRA Cider Pub of the Year 2018 and Pub of the Year 2019.
Q🛏●P🚆🐾

Sawley

White Lion ⬡ ✓
Tamworth Road, NG10 3AT
✦ 12-11.30 ☎ (0115) 946 3061 ⬡ oldsawley.com

Old Sawley Jobber, Little Jack, Tollbridge Porter; 3 changing beers Ⓗ
Well established as the Old Sawley Brewery taphouse, this venue normally has four of the brewery's own beers on offer alongside two or three guest ales. The pub dates back to the 18th century and is close to the River Trent and Sawley Marina. It is a two-roomed premises, with both rooms warmed by real fires in the colder months. The expanding microbrewery is at the rear. The large beer garden often features live music during the summer months. 🛏🍴♣●P🚆🐾☂

Scarcliffe

Horse & Groom
Mansfield Road, S44 6SU
✦ 12-11 ☎ (01246) 823152
Black Sheep Best Bitter; Greene King Abbot; Morland Old Golden Hen; Sharp's Doom Bar; 3 changing beers Ⓗ
Up to seven beers are served from this charming two-roomed rural pub, along with a cider. The pub is over 500 years old and has been owned and run by the same family for the last 19 years. Its main bar is mobile phone free. The locally made pork pies should be tried. Dogs and young families are welcome in the large conservatory. There is a large car park to the front, and a bus stop right outside the pub. Accommodation is available on-site in a couple of cottages. Q🛏🍴♿●P🚆(53)🐾

Shirland

Shoulder of Mutton ⬡
Hallfieldgate Lane, DE55 6AA (on B6013, Wessington-Shirland crossroads)
✦ 5-11 (closed Tue); 12-11 Fri & Sat; 12-10.30 Sun
☎ (01773) 834992
3 changing beers Ⓗ
Eclectic, 16th-century traditional drinking den, nestling on the edge of Amber Valley. This is a true free house, where customers enjoy real ale from small breweries. The regulars are drawn from far and wide, fuelling the unique, easy atmosphere created by the irrepressible landlord and landlady. There is no beer list on the wall because the ales change daily. Dogs and hikers are welcome. The beer garden offers spectacular views and sunsets. Check out the teacups. Q🍴♣P🐾☂

South Normanton

Devonshire Arms 🏆
137 Market Street, DE55 2AA (at M1 jct 28 take B6019; at 1st mini-roundabout turn right into Market St)
✦ 12-midnight ☎ (01773) 810748
⬡ thedevonshirearms.pub
Sarah Hughes Dark Ruby Mild; Theakston XB; 4 changing beers (often Little Critters, Moody Fox, Thornbridge) Ⓗ
A genuine free house which offers up to six real ales and two real ciders or perries. Sarah Hughes Dark Ruby is the house beer along with Theakston's XB. The other guests vary and are often customers' requests. Home-cooked food is available until 8pm every day except Sunday, when a popular carvery is offered. Vegetarians, vegans and coeliacs are all catered for. Winner of many CAMRA awards including branch Pub of the Year for an impressive 12 years running from 2008 to 2019.
🛏◑&♣●P🚆(9.1)🐾☂

Sutton cum Duckmanton

Arkwright Arms 🄻

Chesterfield Road, S44 5JG (on A632 between Chesterfield and Bolsover)
11-11 (midnight Fri & Sat); 11-10.30 Sun
☎ (01246) 232053 🌐 arkwrightarms.co.uk
Greene King Abbot; Whim Arbor Light; 8 changing beers 🄷
A Brewers' Tudor-fronted free house. A changing range of up to 10 guest ales, many from local micros, is complemented by 12 ciders and four perries. Beer festivals are held at Easter and bank holidays, with mini events throughout the year. Quality food is served until 8pm Monday to Saturday, and until 3pm Sunday. The spacious beer garden has play equipment for children. A winner of numerous CAMRA awards, including East Midlands Cider Pub of the Year and local branch Pub of the Year. P

Swanwick

Steampacket Inn

Derby Road, DE55 1AB
2-11; 12-midnight Sat & Sun ☎ (01773) 607771
House beer (by Nottingham); 5 changing beers (sourced nationally; often Blue Monkey, Derby, Nottingham) 🄷
A friendly and welcoming Pub People Company establishment in the centre of Swanwick, boasting an excellent and constantly changing range of well-kept real ales and ciders, many from local microbreweries. It regularly serves Nottingham Packet Pale, which is brewed specially for the pub. The Steampacket is lively at weekends, with regular live music, and hosts summer and winter beer festivals. Tuesday is quiz night. There are outdoor tables in summer and a welcoming fire in winter. Q P

Thorpe

Old Dog

Spend Lane, DE6 2AT
11.30-10.30 ☎ (01335) 350990 🌐 theolddog.co.uk
4 changing beers (sourced locally; often Dancing Duck, Derby, Titanic) 🄷
A brilliantly revived pub that rose again at the end of 2014 after a lengthy closure. Four real ales including a dark beer are always available, usually sourced from local breweries. Excellent food is served at most times. Set alone outside the village, within easy walking distance of the Tissington Trail and Dovedale, the pub is welcoming to walkers and dogs. P

Wardlow Mires

Three Stags' Heads ★ 🄻

Mires Lane, SK17 8RW (jct A623/B6465)
closed Mon-Thu; 7-11 Fri; 11-11 Sat; 12-10.30 Sun
☎ (01298) 872268
Abbeydale Deception, Absolution; house beer (by Abbeydale); 1 changing beer (sourced regionally) 🄷
A quaint 300-year-old pub with two small rooms, stone-flagged floors and low ceilings. Unspoilt, it is one of the few hostelries in the area identified by CAMRA as having a nationally important historic pub interior. An ancient range warms the bar and the pub's dogs, one of which inspired the name of the house beer – Black Lurcher. Traditional cider is available only in summer. Q P (173)

Whaley Bridge

Goyt Inn

8 Bridge Street, SK23 7LR
4.30-11.30; 2-11.30 Sat & Sun ☎ (01663) 732710
5 changing beers (sourced nationally) 🄷
Tucked away in the centre of Whaley Bridge and close to the historic Peak Forest Whaley Bridge Canal Basin, which once was the northern end of the Cromford and High Peak Railway, this end-of-terrace pub is a true local and fulfils its role well. Characterful, dog-friendly and welcoming, it serves a changing range of real ales and is well worth a visit. Features include a small but attractive patio/beer garden. Q

Whitehough

Old Hall Inn 🄻

Chinley, SK23 6EJ (in village, 750yds off B6062)
12-11 ☎ (01663) 750529 🌐 old-hall-inn.co.uk
Marston's Saddle Tank; 8 changing beers 🄷
The 14th-century Whitehough Hall forms part of this quintessential country inn, which has won the Great British Pub award for best cask pub in the region for several years and is a regular entry in this Guide. Up to eight real ales, including seven regularly changing guests from quality local micros, complement those available at the adjacent Paper Mill Inn (under the same ownership). The popular food menu features dishes using local produce. A well-attended beer festival runs in September. P (189,190)

Wirksworth

Feather Star 🄻

15 St Johns Street, DE4 4DR
12-10.30 (11 Fri & Sat); 4-10 Sun ☎ 07931 424117
🌐 thefeatherstar.co.uk
4 changing beers (sourced nationally) 🄷
Opened in 2016 in a former antiques shop, this small and cosy micropub is full of character. The main room has a logburner and wooden beams. There is further seating upstairs. Four beers are served on handpump, alongside four taps for craft beers, plus a keg cider. Crisps and nuts are always available; pork pies and cheese platters are usually an option. Customers may take their own food to eat in the pub. Q (6.1)

By George!

It was my Uncle George who discovered that alcohol was a food well in advance of modern medical thought.

P G Wodehouse, The Inimitable Jeeves

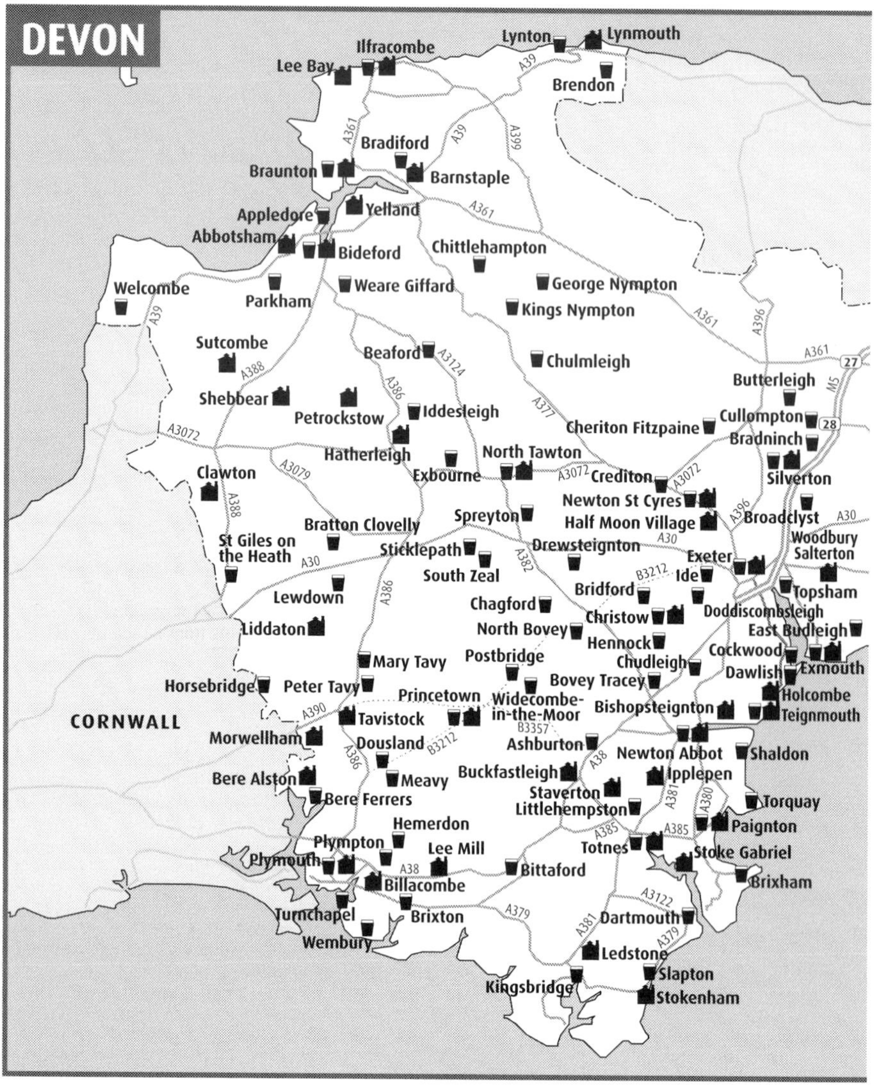

Appledore

Champ

Meeting Street, EX39 1RJ (just off Appledore quay)

closed Mon; 5-midnight ☎ (01237) 421662

champappledore.co.uk

Clearwater Expedition Ale; 3 changing beers (sourced locally) H

The brewery tap for nearby Clearwater Brewery, this cosy, traditional evening pub is set in a picturesque coastal village. It keeps real ale on four pumps as well as real cider. The Champ is renowned for live music which features regularly on Friday and Saturday, together with popular open mic folk and blues evenings Tuesday to Thursday. It has an interesting and eclectic decor, with a predominant boxing theme. Customers are welcome to bring in food for consumption on the premises – there is a fish and chips shop next door – while a nearby public car park accommodates camper vans overnight for a modest fee.

Ashburton

Exeter Inn

26 West Street, TQ13 7DU (on main road through centre of Ashburton opp church)

11-11 (10.30 Sun) ☎ (01364) 652013

Dartmoor IPA, Legend; 1 changing beer H

The oldest pub in Ashburton. Seated drinking areas either side of the entrance lead to a wood-panelled, L-shaped and canopy-covered bar to the right. The rear bar has a seating area and small serving counter. Built in 1131, with additions in the 17th century, this friendly local's original purpose was to house the workers building the nearby church. There is a lovely secluded walled garden at the back. Local Thompstone's cider is sold.

Q

Victoria Inn

77 North Street, TQ13 7QH

11-11; 12-10.30 Sun ☎ (01364) 653333

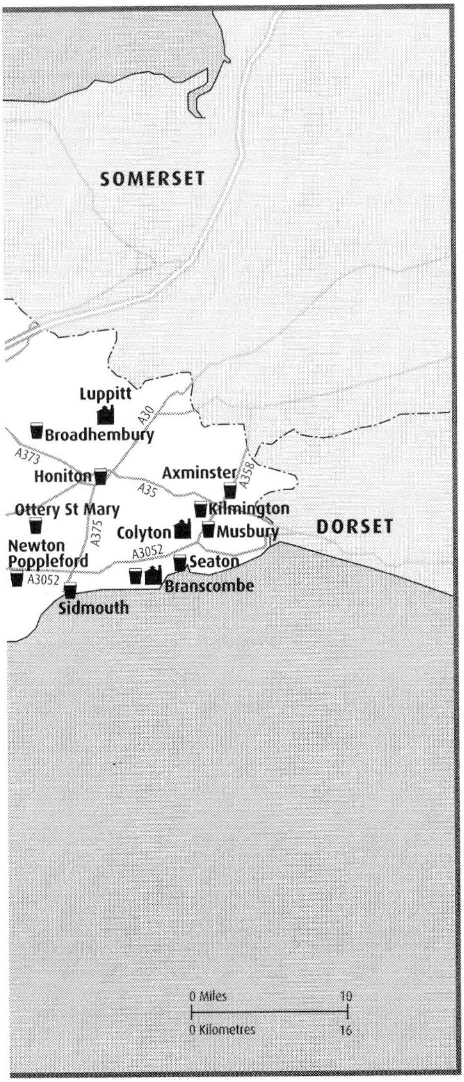

Dartmoor Legend, Jail Ale; 1 changing beer (sourced locally) H
Originally a coaching inn, it has a single-room L-shaped bar area with a separate dining area. The interior is traditional, with black timber beams, nooks, painted stone and half timber-panelled walls, and two welcoming logburners. The beer garden, with its sheltered smokers' retreat, is accessed from the rear of the premises via a footbridge over the River Ashburn. The menu features simple traditional British pub classics at affordable prices. P

Axminster

Axminster Inn

Silver Street, EX13 5AH
10.30-midnight (12.30am Thu; 1am Fri & Sat); 11-midnight Sun ☎ (01297) 34947 axminsterinn.pub
Palmers Copper Ale, IPA, Dorset Gold, 200; 1 changing beer (sourced locally) H
A friendly, traditional pub, lying just off the town centre, with a real log fire for the winter months and a lovely enclosed beer garden to enjoy in the warmer weather. It is a Palmers house, offering a good range of the brewery's real ales. Live music is featured. Free Wi-Fi is available, and there is a skittle alley and dartboard. The pub is dog-friendly. Sorry, no under-18s after 7pm.
P

Beaford

Globe Inn L

Exeter Road, EX19 8LR (on main Exeter Rd in centre of village)
closed Mon; 5-11 Tue-Thu; 12-11.30 Fri-Sun
☎ (01805) 603920 globeinnpub.co.uk
3 changing beers (sourced regionally) H
Reopened by the new owners in 2017, this cosy traditional country pub has quickly established itself as something of an oasis for beer lovers of all tastes. Three changing and predominantly local real ales are usually on the bar, alongside a comprehensive drinks menu that includes more than 40, often legendary, bottled and bottle-conditioned beers from around the globe. A seasonal and attractively priced food menu uses the best of ingredients from local producers.
Q

Bere Ferrers

Olde Plough Inn L

Fore Street, PL20 7JG (close to church and river)
11-3, 6-11; 11-11 Sun ☎ (01822) 840358
theoldeploughinn.co.uk
Sharp's Doom Bar; 2 changing beers (sourced locally; often Roam, Salcombe, Summerskills) H
A 16th-century village inn that has outstanding views over the River Tavy from the beer garden and is only a 15-minute walk from the station on the picturesque Tamar Valley line. Two guest beers come from both local and popular national breweries. Inside, there are flagstone floors, exposed stonework walls, beamed ceilings, real fires and a welcoming atmosphere. Live music, acoustic nights and jam sessions feature, along with themed food nights. Food is served to suit all ages, tastes and appetites.
Q (87)

Bideford

Appledore Inn L

Chingswell Street, EX39 2NF
11-11; 12-10.30 Sun ☎ (01237) 476956
appledoreinnbideford.co.uk
Sharp's Doom Bar, Original; Jollyboat Grenville's Renown; 1 changing beer (sourced regionally) H
One of the oldest inns in Bideford, dating from the 15th century, this friendly family-run pub lies close to Bideford football ground. There is a single bar, with a restaurant area to the side and a paved beer garden at the rear. Four real ales are generally offered, sometimes joined by a fifth served from the cask. The pub is renowned for high-quality authentic Thai food, served daily 12-9pm.
Q

Bittaford

Horse & Groom

Exeter Road, PL21 0EL

12-11 (midnight Fri & Sat) ☎ (01752) 892358

Dartmoor Jail Ale; house beer (by Hunters); 4 changing beers (sourced locally; often Roam, South Hams, Summerskills) H

A family-owned pub run by a keen real ale enthusiast, with six pumps, two dedicated to real cider, the others offering predominantly ales from local breweries in south Devon and Cornwall. Third-pint tapas are available. It has a long bar and a separate dining area serving good home-cooked food, with pictures of the former Moorhaven Hospital on the wall. A monthly quiz night is held. A beer festival and a cider and sausage festival are staged, supporting local charities.

P (X38,Gold)

Bovey Tracey

Cromwell Arms ✔

Fore Street, TQ13 9AE

11-11 (11.30 Fri & Sat); 12-11 Sun ☎ (01626) 833473

thecromwellarms.co.uk

4 changing beers (sourced regionally; often St Austell) H

A 17th-century pub on the main square in this gateway town to Dartmoor. There is a dominant central bar with adjoining drinking areas and a separate restaurant, together with 14 letting rooms. Beers are from St Austell, but constantly rotated with many seasonals and guests. To the rear a wisteria-covered smokers' area leads onto an elongated outside drinking area and pagoda adjoining the car park. An excellent 39 bus service runs from Newton Abbot and Exeter with a nearby stop. Q P

Bradiford

Windsor Arms

55 Bradiford, EX31 4AD (on main road through village, approximately ½ mile N of Pilton)

5-11 Mon & Tue; 12-11 Wed; 12-2, 5-11 Thu; 12-11.30 Fri & Sat; 12-10 Sun ☎ (01271) 343583

GT Ales Thirst of Many; 1 changing beer (sourced nationally; often Greene King, Wadworth) H

A friendly welcome is assured to all who visit this community-oriented village pub. Two changing real ales are kept, with one of these invariably from local GT Ales. Good, freshly cooked and locally sourced food is served Friday to Sunday in the separate lounge bar. A function room, with skittle alley, pool table and dartboard, lies to the rear of the pub.

Bradninch

Olde White Lion

26 High Street, EX5 4QL

4-midnight; 12-midnight Fri; 12-1am Sat; 12-midnight Sun ☎ (01392) 881263

Butcombe Original; Otter Ale; 1 changing beer (sourced regionally) H

A friendly, family-run locals' pub that caters for everyone including TV sports fans. It has one large room with many dark oak beams, plus a large fireplace and wood-burning stove. Food is limited to fish and chips on Friday evening. The folk club meets here on the first Tuesday of each month. The pub is involved with the annual town music festival. One real cider is available alongside the three real ales. Q

Branscombe

Fountain Head Inn

EX12 3BG (in main street 1 mile S of A3052)

10-3, 6-11; 12-10.30 Sun ☎ (01297) 680359

fountainheadinn.com

Branscombe Vale Branoc, Golden Fiddle; 1 changing beer (sourced locally) H

Set in a beautiful coastal valley, this walker-friendly hostelry is at the west end of one of England's longest villages. Ancient features in this old pub such as the inglenook fireplace, wood panelling and flagstone floors greet the visitors and

REAL ALE BREWERIES

Art Brew Sutcombe
Bale Liddaton
Barnaby's Staverton
Barum Barnstaple
Bays Paignton
Beer Engine Newton St Cyres
Bere Bere Alston
Black Tor Christow
Branscombe Vale Branscombe
Bridgetown Totnes
Buckland Bideford
Checkstone Exmouth
Clearwater Bideford
Country Life Abbotsham
Crossed Anchors Exmouth
Darkplace Colyton
Dartmoor Princetown
Devon Earth Buckfastleigh
Exe Valley Silverton
Exeter Exeter
Fat Belly Ilfracombe
Fat Pig Exeter
Grampus Lee Bay
GT Braunton
Hanlons Half Moon Village
Holsworthy Clawton
Hunters Ipplepen
Isca Holcombe
Jollyboat Bideford
Madrigal Lynmouth
Moonchild Petrockstow
Morwell Morwellham
New Lion Totnes
Noss Beer Works Lee Mill
Otter Luppitt
Platform 5 Newton Abbot
Powderkeg Woodbury Salterton
Red Rock Bishopsteignton
Riviera Stoke Gabriel
Roam Plymouth
Salcombe Ledstone
South Hams Stokenham
Sprey Point Teignmouth (brewing suspended)
Stannary Tavistock
Summerskills Billacombe
Tally Ho! Hatherleigh
Taw Valley North Tawton (NEW)
Teignworthy Newton Abbot
Topsham Exeter (NEW)
Totnes Totnes
Two Tone Shebbear
Wizard Ilfracombe
Yelland Manor Yelland

locals, while the bar offers Branscombe Vale ales and ciders. Good-value home-cooked food is served and the pub opens for breakfast at 10am Monday to Saturday. A beer festival is held on the closest weekend to the longest day.
Q P (899)

Bratton Clovelly

Clovelly Inn L ✔

EX20 4JZ (between A30 and A3079) SX464919
12-3, 6-11; 12-11 Sat & Sun ☎ (01837) 871447
clovellyinn.co.uk
Dartmoor IPA, Jail Ale; Sharp's Doom Bar; 1 changing beer (sourced nationally) H
Traditional village pub on the edge of Dartmoor National Park and dating back to the 18th century. The cosy main bar, with a large wood-burning stove, is complemented by two separate dining areas (advisable to book in evenings) and a games room. Three real ales are kept, with Sam's Medium cider also sold in summer. Good home-cooked food is served seven days a week. Jazz sessions take place on the second Monday of each month.
P (633)

Braunton

White Lion Inn ✔

1 North Street, EX33 1AJ
3-11 (midnight Fri); 12-midnight Sat; 12-11 Sun
☎ (01271) 813085 thewhitelionbraunton.co.uk
Otter Amber; 2 changing beers (sourced nationally) H
A locals' pub usually selling three well-chosen real ales, together with a good selection of bottle-conditioned beers. Good-value pub food, often with an interesting twist, is served throughout the year, but please note that the kitchen is normally closed on Mondays in January and February. Outside there is an attractive beer garden. There is a nearby bus stop and the main Braunton campsite is close by. Q P

Brendon

Staghunters Inn L

EX35 6PS SS767481
12-11 ☎ (01598) 741222 staghunters.com
Exmoor Ale; St Austell Trelawny; 1 changing beer (sourced regionally) G
Family-owned hotel on the River Lyn, set in a picturesque valley within Exmoor National Park. An ideal base for those exploring the local area, there are 14 well-appointed rooms, and dogs can also stay overnight for a nominal charge. Up to four real ales are served on gravity, with the regulars from Exmoor and St Austell accompanied by guests from other local breweries. Good, locally sourced food can be enjoyed in the attractive restaurant.
Q P

Bridford

Bridford Inn L

EX6 7HT
12-11 (midnight Fri & Sat) ☎ (01647) 252250
bridfordinn.co.uk
Dartmoor Jail Ale; 3 changing beers (sourced regionally; often Brains, Inveralmond, Morland) H
Local CAMRA Pub of the Year twice in recent years. Jail Ale is the permanent beer, while the others change all the time. This place is a 17th-century Devon longhouse, within the Dartmoor National Park, converted to a pub in 1968. The layout is spacious and open plan, with oak beams, an inglenook fireplace complete with bread oven, and a woodburner. Freshly cooked food, using local produce, is served. It has a beer garden out front with benches and a view to die for. It also stocks around 20 local ciders. P (360)

Brixham

Queen's Arms L ✔

31 Station Hill, TQ5 8BN (from Brixham library go up Church Hill East, then Station Hill)
4-11; 2-midnight Fri; 12-midnight Sat; 12-11 Sun
☎ (01803) 852074 thequeensarmsbrixham.co.uk
House beer (by Teignworthy); 6 changing beers (sourced nationally; often Oakham, Teignworthy) H
A single-bar, end-of-terrace pub with a well-deserved reputation for the quality of its six beers and seven real ciders. The venue has a strong community ethos, a friendly atmosphere and, on cold winter nights, wood-burning stoves. Live music at weekends and good-value Sunday lunches feature. In early December it hosts a charity beer festival with over 30 ales and ciders.
P

Vigilance L ✔

5 Bolton Street, TQ5 9DE
8am-midnight ☎ (01803) 850489
Dartmoor Jail Ale; Greene King Abbot; Ruddles Best Bitter; Sharp's Doom Bar; 4 changing beers (sourced nationally) H
This Wetherspoon establishment is in the town centre with the largest choice of ales – eight in total. The pub is named after the last sailing trawler now moored in the town's harbour, originally built in Uphams's shipyard in 1926. An old ship's figurehead looks down on customers from its wall mounting. Regular beer, cider, wine and gin festivals are held throughout the year. Traditional Welsh cider and Devon perry are available, and food is served 8am-11pm. P

Brixton

Foxhound Inn L

Kingsbridge Road, PL8 2AH
11-11 (midnight Fri & Sat); 12-11 Sun ☎ (01752) 880271
foxhoundinn.co.uk
Courage Directors; house beer (by Summerskills); 3 changing beers (sourced nationally; often Caledonian, Courage, Summerskills) H
An 18th-century former coaching house in a rural village just east of Plymouth which is well served by a frequent daytime bus service. The pub has two separate bars and a small restaurant. Traditional English meals are available daily, made with locally sourced ingredients. Look out for Red Coat, an ale crafted by the landlord, among four guest beers. A monthly charity quiz night is held. Local CAMRA branch Country Pub of the Year runner-up 2019.
Q P

Broadclyst

New Inn L

Whimple Road, EX5 3BX (½ mile E of village)
11-11 ☎ (01392) 461312 newinnbroadclyst.co.uk
Dartmoor Jail Ale; Exmoor Gold; Otter Bitter; Sharp's Doom Bar H

Large, traditional 17th-century inn with a recently extended car park to the rear, and a large beer garden and play area. Freshly cooked food is served lunchtimes and evenings. The skittle alley can double as a function room, and regular events are held (see website for details). Will close earlier if empty in late evening. Q ♿ ♣ P

Broadhembury

Drewe Arms

EX14 3NF

12-11 (midnight Fri & Sat); 12-9 Sun ☎ (01404) 841267
drewearmsinn.co.uk

Bays Devon Dumpling; Exeter Avocet; Otter Amber, Ale; 1 changing beer (sourced regionally) [H]

A Grade II-listed 16th-century thatched pub with a secluded garden, set in a picturesque estate village of cob and limewashed cottages within the Blackdown Hills. There are low-beamed ceilings and uneven floor levels throughout the many rooms. This is a friendly and welcoming family-run venue with the emphasis on local real ales and produce. Good-value food is served from Tuesday to Saturday and lunchtimes on Sunday; a takeaway menu is also available. Q ♣ P

Butterleigh

Butterleigh Inn

The Green, EX15 1PN (opp church) SS9746108212

12-2.30 (not Mon), 6-11; 12-2.30, 6-midnight Fri & Sat; 12-3 Sun ☎ (01884) 855433 butterleighinn.co.uk

Cotleigh Tawny Owl; Dartmoor Jail Ale; Otter Ale; 1 changing beer (sourced locally) [H]

In a small, quaint village, hidden along narrow country lanes, this is an excellent country pub with a mixed clientele creating a great atmosphere with diverse conversation. There are two rooms around the bar with a modern dining room at the back, and a covered patio outside with grapevines in summer. Good-value home-cooked food is served lunchtimes and evenings Tuesday to Saturday, with a carvery Sunday lunchtime. The bar offers a choice of up to four real ales and three ciders.
Q ♣ P

Chagford

Globe Inn

9 High Street, TQ13 8AJ

11-11.30 (midnight Fri & Sat); 12-11 Sun
☎ (01647) 433485 theglobeinnchagford.co.uk

Dartmoor IPA; Otter Bitter [H]**; 1 changing beer (sourced locally)** [H]/[G]

The Globe overlooks the parish church and was once a coaching inn and coopery. The evolution of the pub has led to it becoming a focal point of this historic stannary town, providing good food, music, a cinema club and many other events. There is a splendid public bar and a separate lounge bar and restaurant, both with large open fires. A small courtyard garden is at the rear and parking is nearby. Ciders sold are Sam's and Westons Old Rosie. (173,178)

Ring o' Bells

44 The Square, TQ13 8AH

10-midnight ☎ (01647) 432466
ringobellschagford.co.uk

Dartmoor IPA, Jail Ale; Teignworthy Reel Ale; 1 changing beer (sourced locally) [H]

In the centre of the town lies this 16th-century inn; however, archives reveal there had been an inn on this site well before this. The bar is comfortably furnished with bench and booth seating, and has a large open fireplace. To the rear is a separate dining room, again with an open fireplace. A passageway leads to a pretty walled garden with plenty of seating and a covered smokers' area.
♣ (173,178)

Cheriton Fitzpaine

Ring of Bells

EX17 4JG

closed Mon; 12-2.30, 5.30-11; 12-7 Sun
☎ (01363) 860111 theringofbells.com

2 changing beers [H]

A Grade II-listed pub set in the heart of mid-Devon in a tranquil and picturesque village. It has something for everyone, whether you are looking for a quiet pint and the crossword, a cheese and pickle sandwich, a refined three-course meal, a few drinks with friends or somewhere to bring the kids. David and Binka have made it their mission to create a pub for all. ♣ P

Chittlehampton

Bell Inn

The Square, EX37 9QL (opp St Hieritha's parish church) SS636254

11-3, 6-11; 11-11 Fri-Sun ☎ (01769) 540368
thebellatchittlehampton.co.uk

Exmoor Ale; 6 changing beers (sourced nationally) [H]

Large, comfortable and homely village local which has been in the same family since 1975 and celebrated 20 continuous years of Guide inclusion in 2016. A good selection of real ales is kept, with up to eight regularly available. The bar area is notable for its sporting memorabilia, with good-value home-cooked food being served both here and in the adjoining restaurant. Well-behaved children and dogs are welcome. Local CAMRA branch Pub of the Year 2018 and 2019.
♿ ♣ P (658,859)

Christow

Teign House Inn

Teign Valley Road, EX6 7PL

12-11 (midnight Fri & Sat) ☎ (01647) 252286
teignhouseinn.co.uk

Otter Bitter; 2 changing beers (sourced regionally; often Black Tor, Hunters) [H]

On the edge of Dartmoor in the scenic Teign Valley you will find this welcoming, atmospheric country pub with exposed beams and a warming log fire in winter. The pub is supported strongly by the locals, with a large garden attracting families; the adjoining field has space for caravans, camper vans and campers. There is live music every third Wednesday evening and every fourth Sunday afternoon. It serves great pub food, all home-cooked, with a special Thai menu which is also available to take away.
Q ♿ ♣ P (360)

Chudleigh

Bishop Lacy Inn

52-53 Fore Street, TQ13 0HY

12-midnight (1am Fri & Sat) ☎ (01626) 854585

3 changing beers (sourced regionally; often Black Tor, Hanlons, Hunters) Ⓗ/Ⓖ
Grade II-listed building dating back to 1807, previously the Plymouth Inn and run by the same landlords since 1994. Two separate drinking areas are dominated by the left-hand locals' bar with its magnificent fireplace once used to cure ham, while to the right is an area used for dining. Local beers predominate including those from Hunters, Black Tor or Hanlons. Despite the witches hanging over the bar, the welcome is very friendly.
Q❀◑♿⛺♣P🚌(39,182)🐾📶

Chulmleigh

Old Court House

South Molton Street, EX18 7BW
🕒 11-11 ☎ (01769) 580045 🌐 oldcourthouseinn.co.uk
Exmoor Ale; Dartmoor IPA; Butcombe Original; 1 changing beer (sourced nationally) Ⓗ
This friendly, cosy local is a Grade II-listed thatched inn where Charles I held court in 1634. A huge coat of arms commemorating the event dominates one of the bedrooms, while a replica hangs above the fireplace in the main bar. Three regular real ales are often joined by a guest beer in summer. Good home-cooked food can be enjoyed in the bar area, the separate dining room or in the pretty cobbled courtyard garden. ❀🛏◑♿♣🚌(377)🐾📶

Cockwood

Ship Inn 🄻 ✔

Church Road, EX6 8NU (just off A379, outside Starcross, close to Cockwood harbour)
🕒 11-11 (11.30 Fri & Sat); 12-10.30 Sun ☎ (01626) 890373
🌐 shipinncockwood.co.uk
Black Sheep Best Bitter; Dartmoor Jail Ale; St Austell Tribute, Proper Job; 1 changing beer (sourced locally) Ⓗ
A busy family-run pub, close to the picturesque harbour at Cockwood, with a large beer garden with views of the estuary, and a log fire in winter. Popular with drinkers and diners alike, it offers a choice of four regular ales and usually one rotating guest, and has an excellent food menu. Meals are prepared with local produce where possible including a varied choice of locally caught fish. The bus stops 100 yards across the bridge.
Q❀◑⛺♣🍎P🚌(2)🐾📶

Crediton

Crediton Inn 🄻

28a Mill Street, EX17 1EZ
🕒 12-11; 12-4, 7-10.30 Sun ☎ (01363) 772882
🌐 crediton-inn.co.uk
5 changing beers (sourced nationally) Ⓗ
The framed deeds date this inn to 1878, with windows etched with the ancient town seal. It is a genuine free house with a welcoming landlady, and has been in the Guide for 32 consecutive years. There is normally a Branscombe beer on. The skittle alley doubles as a function room. Good home-cooked food is served at weekends, with snacks and renowned Scotch eggs at other times. A beer festival is held in mid-November.
❀◑≠♣🍎P🚌(5)🐾📶

Mitre

9 High Street, EX17 3AE (on A377 in town centre opp Co-op)
🕒 1-1am; 12-1am Sat & Sun ☎ (01363) 772508
3 changing beers (sourced regionally) Ⓗ
A Grade II-listed free house, fondly known by older locals as Number Nine. It has interesting pub decor, with beer-originated curios and other knick-knacks, and is well supported by local rugby, football and darts teams. Live music plays every Saturday evening. The terraced garden, which is south-facing, is great for warmer months, and serves as a smoking area in all weathers. You can always depend on well-kept ales and good conversation.
❀♿♣🚌🐾📶

Cullompton

Pony & Trap 🄻 ✔

10 Exeter Hill, EX15 1DJ (on B3181 S of town)
🕒 12-2 (3 Fri & Sat), 5-11; 12-5, 8-11 Sun ☎ (01884) 34182
Branscombe Vale Golden Fiddle; Dartmoor Jail Ale; Draught Bass; Exmoor Ale; Skinner's Betty Stogs; 2 changing beers (sourced regionally) Ⓗ
A traditional local with a good atmosphere and a mixed clientele. Many local darts and skittles teams are based here. It has a smart interior featuring a logburner, making it cosy in winter; flowers and ornaments give it a homely feel. Up to seven real ales could be on offer, plus four real ciders. There is a garden and seating area. Live music features once a month and pub games are played. Q❀◑♣🍎🚌(1)🐾

Dartmouth

Cherub Inn ✔

13 Higher Street, TQ6 9RB
🕒 11-11; 12-10.30 Sun ☎ (01803) 832571
🌐 the-cherub.co.uk
Exeter Ferryman; St Austell Proper Job; South Hams Devon Pride; house beer (by St Austell); 1 changing beer (sourced locally) Ⓗ
This 14th-century merchant's home is the oldest house in a nautical town famous for its Tudor buildings; the Grade II*-listed Cherub is one of the best. Three cask ales are on handpump. The bar has many original features, with beams made from old ship's timbers. An intricate winding staircase leads to a restaurant and facilities on the upper two floors. Q◑⛺≠🍎P🚌🐾

Dawlish

Swan Inn

94 Old Town Street, EX7 9AT
🕒 3-midnight; 12-midnight Sat; 12-11 Sun
☎ (01626) 863677
St Austell Proper Job; 2 changing beers (sourced regionally) Ⓗ
A friendly locals' pub, reputedly the oldest of Dawlish's pubs, dating from 1642, and in the old part of town. It has a large patio and garden, and a covered heated smoking area. It does not serve food. Dogs are welcome. One regular real ale is on tap, plus two changing beers, usually from St Austell or Dartmoor breweries. Q❀♣P🚌🐾

White Hart

6 Albert Street, EX7 9JY
🕒 12-midnight ☎ (01626) 866476
Teignworthy Gun Dog; 2 changing beers Ⓗ
Popular with ale drinkers, offering two or three changing beers, including one from Teignworthy Brewery. This is a single-room local, and a friendly

welcome awaits old and new visitors. Local licensees have produced a Dawlish Ale Trail leaflet that has 10 pubs within walking distance of each other, and all based around the beautiful Dawlish Water and central area. It has a welcoming winter fire. No food is served. ❀⇌▭(2)🐾

Doddiscombsleigh

NoBody Inn ✔

EX6 7PS (best approached from A38 at top of Haldon Hill)
☼ 11-11; 12-10.30 Sun ☎ (01647) 252394
🌐 nobodyinn.co.uk
House beer (by St Austell); 2 changing beers (sourced locally) Ⓗ
A venerable village inn, mainly 15th century with some later additions, full of old beams and antique furniture. Part of the bar is used for meals, and a separate restaurant is open Tuesday to Saturday evenings. It has an extensive whisky list (240 plus) and wine list (250 plus). Five comfortable bedrooms are available, and high-quality food is served every lunchtime and evening.
Q❀🛏◐P▭(360)🐾📶

Dousland

Burrator Inn 🄻 ✔

PL20 6NP
☼ 12-11 (12.30am Sat); 12-10.30 Sun ☎ (01822) 853121
🌐 theburratorinn.com
Dartmoor Jail Ale; Otter Amber; St Austell Tribute; Sharp's Doom Bar Ⓗ
A substantial pub on the road between Yelverton, Burrator Reservoir and Princetown. Inside, there is a large bar area with space for a pool table and two dartboards, along with various other rooms including a separate dining room. Food is served all day. Outside, there is ample parking and a garden incorporating a children's play area. The pub is frequented by locals and visited by those living in the surrounding towns and city. A September beer festival is held. Q🐴❀🛏◐♿♣P▭🐾📶

Drewsteignton

Drewe Arms ★

The Square, EX6 6QN
☼ 5-11 Mon; 12-3, 5-11 (midnight Fri); 12-6 Sun
☎ (01647) 281409 🌐 drewearms.com
St Austell Tribute; 2 changing beers (sourced nationally) Ⓖ
Set in a picturesque village square, this attractive thatched pub has an interior of historic importance. It was famously run for a record-breaking 75 years by Aunt Mabel, who only retired when aged 96. Between two and four ales are dispensed directly from the cask, just as Aunt Mabel did. The pub serves excellent food using local ingredients and hosts a series of events such as quizzes, live music (in the separate function room) and a beer festival.
Q🐴❀🛏◐♿⛺♣🍎P▭(173)🐾📶

East Budleigh

Sir Walter Raleigh Inn 🄻

22 High Street, EX9 7ED (off B3178 opp Hayes Lane)
☼ 12-2.30 (3 Sat), 6-11; 12-3, 7-11 Sun ☎ (01395) 442510
4 changing beers (sourced regionally) Ⓗ
In the middle of a delightful village, the birthplace of Sir Walter Raleigh, this free house is a truly welcoming 16th-century country inn. Good-quality local pub food is served lunchtimes and evenings in addition to four varying real ales, and up to six real ciders. Originally two cottages, the buildings were converted into a Jacobean-style pub, retaining the original wooden beams throughout. This gem is well worth a visit for good-quality real ale, cider, pub food and friendly service.
Q🐴❀◐🍎▭(157)🐾

Exbourne

Red Lion 🄻 ✔

High Street, EX20 3RY (200yds N of jct with A3072)
SS602018
☼ 4-11 (7 Mon); 12-11 Sat & Sun ☎ (01837) 851551
🌐 theredlionexbourne.co.uk
Dartmoor IPA, Jail Ale; 1 changing beer (sourced nationally) Ⓖ
Casks are set on stillage at the end of the L-shaped bar, which is notable for the absence of handpumps, as the landlord refuses to serve draught lager. This 16th-century village local has an excellent reputation for the quality and consistency of its ales and has been local CAMRA branch Pub of the Year several times in recent years. There is always good conversation around the bar. Live music also features regularly. Q🐴❀P▭🐾📶

Exeter

Bowling Green 🄻 ✔

29-30 Blackboy Road, EX4 6ST
☼ 12-11 (midnight Fri & Sat) ☎ (01392) 678962
Sharp's Doom Bar; 3 changing beers (sourced locally) Ⓗ
Originally an 18th-century pub called the Ropemakers, the Bowling Green is a cosy local away from the main city centre, close to Exeter City football club at St James Park. It offers an extensive selection of reasonably priced pub food including pizzas and gluten-free and vegetarian options. Four real ales are stocked; three are rotating and supporting local breweries. Live music plays every Saturday night and Sunday afternoon followed by a quiz in the evening.
Q🐴❀◐♿⇌(St James Park)♣🍎▭🐾📶

George's Meeting House ✔

38 South Street, EX1 1ED (near bottom of South St)
☼ 8am-midnight (1am Fri & Sat) ☎ (01392) 454250
Greene King Abbot; Ruddles Best Bitter; Sharp's Doom Bar; 6 changing beers Ⓗ
This Wetherspoon opened in January 2005 having been sympathetically converted from a Unitarian Chapel dating from 1760. Many of the original features remain unaltered; these include two upstairs galleries, a pulpit and stained-glass windows. A range of national, regional and local real ales and five real ciders is served. Food is available throughout the day until 10pm. A newer extension, which is at the rear of the main building, leads to more seating outdoors.
Q🐴❀◐♿⇌🍎▭📶

Great Western Hotel 🄻

St David's Station, EX4 4NU
☼ 10-midnight (1am Fri & Sat) ☎ (01392) 274039
🌐 greatwesternhotel.co.uk
9 changing beers Ⓗ
The Great Western Hotel dates from 1840, and is close to St David's railway station. A range of up to nine ales is offered from around the country. It has

a good community atmosphere, with wheelchair users most welcome and easy access to the bar and toilet. Ideal for stopovers, the hotel offers a variety of 35 en-suite rooms. It has won CAMRA branch Pub of the Year twice. The Karma restaurant serves traditional bar snacks as well as an exclusive Indian cuisine. Q🕽⌖🏠✎◑①♿✖️🚌🐾🛜

Imperial L ✔

New North Road, EX4 4AH

🕽 8am-midnight; 9am-1am Fri & Sat ☎ (01392) 434050

Greene King Abbot Ⓗ; Ruddles Best Bitter Ⓗ/Ⓖ; changing beers Ⓗ

This pub features a range of beers from local and national breweries. It was built in 1810 as a private house, converted to a hotel and opened as a Wetherspoon pub in 1996. It has an orangery and a large beer garden. Regular beer festivals are held, featuring local, national and international breweries. Food is served all day. Close to the university, there is a bus stop directly outside the premises. Q🕽⌖✎◑①♿≠(St David's)♿P🚌🛜

Little Drop of Poison

154-155 Fore Street, EX4 3AT

🕽 closed Mon; 4-11 (midnight Fri); 11-midnight Sat; closed Sun ☎ (01392) 757570

6 changing beers (sourced regionally; often Bristol Beer Factory, GT Ales, Tapstone) Ⓗ

After several years of closure, this city centre pub reopened in 2018. A single large room with one bar, it serves between three and six cask ales. There are three changing gravity-dispensed ciders on the back of the bar along with a vast amount of taps serving keg/craft beer. Entertainment-wise there is live music on Friday and a quiz on Tuesday, as well as a free-to-use pool table. ♿≠♣🐾🛜

Pursuit of Hoppiness

42 Longbrook Street, EX4 6AE

🕽 12-11 (midnight Fri & Sat); 12-10 Sun ☎ 07506 417729

⊕ hoppiness.co.uk

6 changing beers Ⓗ

Friendly new-style city-centre micropub under the same ownership as the original in Bridport and popular with all age groups. This free house serves up to six changing real ales plus four craft kegs. There is background music and high-level wooden seating. Light snacks are available. Real cider from boxes is served and there is a good selection of bottled beers. ≠♿🚌🛜

Thatched House Inn ✔

Exwick Road, EX4 2BQ

🕽 12-10.30 (11.30 Fri & Sat); 12-7 Sun ☎ (01392) 272920

⊕ thatchedhouse.net

Greene King Abbot; 6 changing beers (sourced locally; often Dartmoor, Hanlons, Salcombe) Ⓗ

A thatched building dating from the 1600s, this is a community pub next to the Exwick playing fields, opposite the Exeter College Sports Hub. It is close to the river, convenient for dog walkers, cyclists and sightseers. Seven real ales and one real cider are usually on sale, with great-value home-cooked food sourced from local ingredients and producers. On-street parking is available nearby, and the pub is on the Stagecoach F1 and F2 bus route. Q🕽⌖✎◑①♿≠♿🚌🐾🛜

Exmouth

Bicton Inn L ✔

5 Bicton Street, EX8 2RU

🕽 11-midnight ☎ (01395) 272589 ⊕ bictoninn.co.uk

Dartmoor Jail Ale; Hanlons Port Stout; 6 changing beers Ⓗ

A friendly and popular back-street local, offering good beer and chat. This is a community hub where traditional games are played such as darts, pool and euchre, and regular live music events are featured. Up to eight real ales and one cider are normally on offer, usually including several LocAles. The snug is available for small gatherings and meetings. There is a logburner in the main bar. Two beer festivals are held during the year. 🕽≠♣♿🚌🐾🛜

First & Last Inn L

10 Church Street, EX8 1PE (off B3178 Rolle St)

🕽 11-midnight; 12-11 Sun ☎ (01395) 263275

Dartmoor Jail Ale; Otter Ale; Teignworthy Neap Tide Ⓗ; 2 changing beers (sourced locally; often Checkstone) Ⓖ

Victorian pub near the town centre with a public car park opposite. This is a genuine free house; the Checkstone Brewery started here in 2016 and supplies the pub with changing ales from an increasing range. It has three distinct areas and a courtyard patio with heated awnings. Games include pool and darts, and there is a skittle alley. Televised sport is prominent and regular live music is hosted. Up to nine ciders are on offer including Westons Old Rosie and Thatchers Traditional. ⌖♿≠♣♿(57)🐾

Grapevine

2 Victoria Road, EX8 1DL

🕽 12-11 (midnight Fri & Sat); 12-10 Sun ☎ (01395) 222208

⊕ thegrapevineexmouth.com

6 changing beers Ⓗ

The Grapevine brewhouse is a stylish Victorian free house in the centre of Exmouth. It is home to Crossed Anchors Brewing and Ruby Diner burger specialists. As well as serving up to four Crossed Anchors beers there is always a wide selection of guest ales, craft beers from the UK and around the world, and Green Valley Cyder. You will find a pub quiz on Monday, live music at the weekends and a good selection of board games. 🕽⌖◑①♿≠♣♿🚌(57)🐾🛜

George Nympton

Castle Inn L

EX36 4JE (1 mile S of South Molton on the Chulmleigh road)

🕽 6-10 Mon & Tue; 12-3, 6-11 Wed-Fri; 12-11 Sat; 12-10 Sun ☎ (01769) 574945

Exmoor Ale; 1 changing beer (sourced regionally) Ⓗ

Traditional Devon country pub, within easy reach of Exmoor. The main bar has a pleasant eating area offset, while the lounge bar can at times be used as a family room. Two real ales are kept, together with a local cider. The pub has gained a good local reputation for the quality and value of its freshly prepared food, with a menu to cater for all tastes and dietary requirements. Three well-appointed rooms for overnight stays are also available. Q🕽⌖🏠◑①♿▲♣♿P🚌🐾🛜

Hemerdon

Miners Arms L

PL7 5BU

🕽 11-11 ☎ (01752) 336040 ⊕ theminersarmspub.co.uk

Dartmoor Jail Ale; Draught Bass; house beer (by Dartmoor) Ⓗ; 2 changing beers (sourced locally; often Dartmoor, Fuller's, Greene King) Ⓗ/Ⓖ
Dating from 1783, this pub is rich in history with its association with the close-by Drakelands mine. The friendly atmosphere and delightful location make it popular. Three regular beers are supplemented by at least one other local ale. There is a conservatory dining area, and alfresco meals can also be enjoyed on the terrace on a summer's day. The pub welcomes families and the extensive garden has a children's play area. Regular beer and cider festivals are held, as are regular quiz nights and other events. Q❀◑♣P🚌(59)🐾

Hennock

Palk Arms

Church Road, TQ13 9QB (take B3344 from A38 to Chudleigh Knighton; follow Hennock signs)
closed Mon; 12-3 (not Tue), 5-11; 12-11 Sat & Sun
☎ (01626) 836584 theonlypalkarms.co.uk
3 changing beers (often Dartmoor, Otter, Teignworthy) Ⓗ
A 16th-century free house on the edge of Dartmoor national park, rumoured to be haunted, and boasting spectacular views of Haldon moor from the dining room. The pub is also a regular destination for walkers, cyclists and campers, who all enjoy the welcoming, cosy atmosphere – including two wood-burning stoves – of this community-minded pub. The beer selection focuses on locally sourced products. One cider is also available. Visitors should also investigate the local library and mining heritage, which add to the charm of the pub and village.
Q❀◑♿▲♣P🚌🐾

Honiton

Holt

178 High Street, EX14 1LA
11-3, 5.30-11; closed Sun & Mon ☎ (01404) 47707
theholt-honiton.com
Otter Bitter, Amber, Bright, Ale, Head Ⓗ
The Holt has a cosy bar at street level and a fine-dining restaurant upstairs, both smartly decorated. The kitchen is in full view of the clientele. A lunch menu of tapas and home-smoked food is served in the bar. Independently owned by two sons of the Otter Brewery family, the pub has won awards including Gastro-Pub of the Year and Taste of the West, and currently holds two AA rosettes. The head chef also runs popular bread-making and cookery courses. Q◑♿♣🚌🐾

Horsebridge

Royal Inn

PL19 8PJ (off A384 Tavistock-Launceston road) SX401748
12-3, 6.30-11 (10.30 Sun) ☎ (01822) 870214
royalinn.co.uk
Draught Bass; Otter Ale; St Austell Proper Job Ⓗ; 3 changing beers (sourced regionally; often Skinner's, Tintagel) Ⓖ
Originally built as a nunnery in 1437 by French Benedictine monks, the inn is reported to have been visited by Charles I. The building overlooks an old bridge on the River Tamar, connecting Devon to Cornwall, and features half-panelling, stone floors, log fires and traditional styling in the bar and lounge, with another larger room off the lounge. It has a terraced garden with sheltered seating and free Wi-Fi. Guest beers are usually served on gravity; the locally sourced food is recommended.
Q❀◑P🚌(115)🐾

Iddesleigh

Duke of York

EX19 8BG (off B3217 next to church) SS570083
11-11; 12-10.30 Sun ☎ (01837) 810253
dukeofyorkdevon.co.uk
Adnams Broadside; Bays Topsail; 1 changing beer (sourced nationally) Ⓖ
Popular with locals and visitors alike, this iconic, thatched 15th-century village inn has a welcoming open fire in the bar, where the ales are dispensed on gravity. The pub is renowned for its generous portions of locally sourced, home-cooked food. A popular beer festival is held every August bank holiday weekend. There are seven en-suite rooms available, and a courtesy bus to and from the pub for those living in surrounding villages.
Q❀◑♿▲♣🚌🐾

Ide

Poachers Inn

55 High Street, EX2 9RW (3 miles from M5 jct 31, via A30)
12-midnight (1am Fri & Sat) ☎ (01392) 273847
poachersinn.co.uk
Branscombe Vale Branoc; Exeter Tomahawk; 4 changing beers (sourced regionally; often Exeter, Palmers, Sharp's) Ⓗ
Typical busy village pub, with a friendly atmosphere, serving a varied menu of home-made locally sourced produce, including excellent-value fish and chips to eat in or take away on Wednesday evenings. Dogs are welcome in the comfortably furnished bar, with old sofas, chairs and a big log fire in winter. There is also a large beer garden overlooking the glorious Devon countryside. Usually five or six ales are on tap, with various guest beers from the West Country.
Q❀◑▲P🚌(360)🐾

Ilfracombe

Admiral Collingwood

Wilder Road, EX34 9AP
8am-midnight (1am Fri & Sat); 8am-11 Sun
☎ (01271) 862373
Greene King Abbot; Ruddles Best Bitter; Sharp's Doom Bar; 3 changing beers (sourced nationally) Ⓗ
Built on the site of the old Collingwood Hotel, this purpose-built Wetherspoon pub was voted the best new build at the National Pub Design Awards in 2015. Situated on Ilfracombe's seafront, there are stunning views from the roof terrace, which is open March to October. Since opening its doors, the pub has earned a well-deserved reputation for its range of well-kept ales, many of which are brewed locally. ❀◑♿P🚌(21A)

Hip & Pistol

8 St James Place, EX34 9BH
11-11 (11.30 Fri & Sat); 12-10.30 Sun ☎ (01271) 549651
Exmoor Stag; GT Ales North Coast IPA, Thirst of Many; 2 changing beers (sourced nationally) Ⓗ
Converted from an old Georgian house and opened as a pub in 2017, the building has been extensively modernised and has a timber-fronted bar with a

nautical theme. The flooring is a special feature, showing the bay around Ilfracombe in pictorial form, with local landmarks and shipwrecks from the past together with an impressive pub logo in an image of a compass. A minimum of four real ales and six ciders is always sold.
(21)

Wellington Arms

66-67 High Street, EX34 9QE
11-midnight; 10-midnight Sun ☎ (01271) 864720
St Austell Tribute; Sharp's Doom Bar; 3 changing beers (sourced nationally) H
Grade II-listed, this friendly town local was originally two pubs. It has a separate public bar, lounge bar and games room, and a cosy lounge retaining its original beams and large open fire. TVs and music sound systems enable different channels to be shown in each area, making the pub popular with sports enthusiasts. Up to five competitively priced ales are usually on the bar. Regular live music sessions, quiz nights and beer festivals are held. P

Kilmington

New Inn

The Hill, EX13 7SF (in village, S of A35)
12-3 (not Mon), 6-11; 12-8 Sun ☎ (01297) 33376
newinnkilmington.com
Palmers Copper Ale, IPA, 200; 1 changing beer (sourced locally) H
This thatched Devon longhouse became a pub in the early 1800s. It was rebuilt after a major fire in 2004, retaining the welcoming atmosphere and gaining excellent toilets with wheelchair access. There is a large, safe garden, and a well-used skittle alley. A quiz night is held monthly on the first Sunday, with other events that maintain the pub's position as an important part of village life. A meat draw is held on Friday. QP

Kings Nympton

Grove Inn

EX37 9ST (in centre of village) SS683194
closed Mon; 12-3, 6-11; 12-4, 7-10 Sun ☎ (01769) 580406
thegroveinn.co.uk
Exmoor Ale G**; 3 changing beers (sourced nationally)** H
A 17th-century Grade II-listed thatched inn set in a picturesque village. It has low beams, flagstone floors and an open fire in winter, while outside there is a pretty enclosed terrace to enjoy in summer. Four real ales are normally on tap, alongside a good range of ciders. Award-winning food is served in the dining area, which is adjacent to the bar. Local CAMRA Cider Pub of the Year 2017.
QP

Kingsbridge

Hermitage Inn

8 Mill Street, TQ7 1ED
2-11 (midnight Fri); 12-1am Sat; 12-11 Sun
☎ (01548) 853234
2 changing beers (sourced regionally; often Cotleigh, Teignworthy) H
A new entry of late, popular with locals to Kingsbridge, this is an extremely friendly pub with log fires and a traditional interior. It has an enclosed pleasant beer garden to the rear. An eclectic range of local beers is served, normally two at any given time, with bar snacks and basket meals on Friday nights and lunchtimes during the summer. Live music is hosted regularly, which proves popular. Facebook is a key source of information if you are planning a visit.
QP

Lewdown

Blue Lion Inn

EX20 4DL
5 (6 Tue & Thu)-11; 12-midnight Sat; 12-3.30 Sun
☎ (01566) 783238
Dartmoor Jail Ale; Otter Amber; Sharp's Doom Bar; 1 changing beer (sourced regionally) H
Originally a 17th-century farmhouse, this family-run pub is an interesting building with beautiful views of the surrounding countryside. Extended and developed in the early 20th century as part of the Lewtrenchard Estate, it is home to numerous local groups and supports several pub teams. Predominantly wet-sales oriented, it is also dog-friendly. An annual beer and music festival is held in late July/early August. P

Littlehempston

Tally Ho

TQ9 6LY SX813627
closed Mon; 11-3, 5.30-11; 12-10.30 Sun
☎ (01803) 862316 tallyhoinn.co.uk
Dartmoor Legend; 1 changing beer (sourced locally; often Teignworthy) H
Charming 14th-century stone-built pub saved by the local community from closure in 2014. The single-roomed bar with timber beams has a cosy feel, complemented by two woodburners, and is furnished with pews and wooden settles. Guest beers are from local breweries alongside a real cider. The pub hosts numerous events including an annual beer festival, occasional local live music, and a regular Sunday night quiz. The enclosed beer garden is to the rear of the pub.
QP(X64,177)

Lynton

Cottage Inn

Lynbridge, EX35 6NR (on B3234 between Barbrook and Lynton)
12-11 ☎ (01598) 753496 thecottageinnlynton.co.uk
Fat Belly Carver Doone, Crafty, Lyn Valley; 2 changing beers (sourced nationally) H
Spacious 17th-century riverside inn and authentic Thai restaurant, overlooked by National Trust woodlands. Fat Belly ales were originally brewed on the premises and are part of the business. Now brewed at nearby Mullacott, at least three of the beers are always available, together with a local guest ale and a selection of craft beers which are poured through a US-style craft beer dispenser. Please note that winter hours may vary.
P

Sandrock Hotel

Longmead, EX35 6DH
11-11 (midnight Fri & Sat); 12-11 Sun ☎ (01598) 752000
sandrockhotel.co.uk
3 changing beers (sourced nationally) H
An Edwardian hotel and pub nestled between the wildly rugged Valley of the Rocks and the

picturesque village of Lynton. Many of the original features have been retained and the large wood-burning stove adds to the cosy and welcoming atmosphere in the bar. The pub is well known for good-quality, value-for-money food, while there is a pleasant beer garden to enjoy in summer. Closed weekday lunchtimes during quieter winter months. Q🐴❀🛏◐◑♿⛺♣🍎P🚌🐾📶

Mary Tavy

Mary Tavy Inn

Lane Head, PL19 9PN

⏲ closed Mon; 12-2.30, 6-11; 12-2.30, 5-midnight Fri & Sat; 12-3, 6-11 Sun ☎ (01822) 810326 🌐 marytavyinn.com

Dartmoor IPA, Jail Ale; St Austell Tribute; 2 changing beers (sourced regionally; often Exeter, St Austell) Ⓗ

A traditional roadside inn where families, visitors and locals are welcome. The popular bar area accommodates pool, darts, TV, a large fire and up to five real ales and a cider. This is complemented by a spacious restaurant and garden with views to Dartmoor. Music nights, charity events, a Sunday carvery and a bank holiday beer festival feature in the pub's calendar. Modern B&B accommodation is provided in adjacent buildings, with camping available in the pub grounds and motorhomes by prior arrangement. The pub is open 12-11pm daily in summer. Q🐴❀🛏◐◑⛺♣🍎P🚌(46)🐾📶

Meavy

Royal Oak Inn

PL20 6PJ (on village green)

⏲ 11-11; 11-10.30 Sun ☎ (01822) 852944 🌐 royaloakinn.org.uk

Dartmoor Jail Ale; Otter Amber; St Austell Proper Job; house beer (by Black Tor); 1 changing beer (sourced regionally; often Otter) Ⓗ

People come from miles around to enjoy the food and drink at this tucked-away, civilised but unpretentious 16th-century pub. In the summer, sit at one of the outside benches by the legendary tree and watch children play on the village green. In winter, relax in the public bar and enjoy the conversation, dogs and roaring fire. There is an interesting range of cider, with a festival in August and occasional live music. Local CAMRA branch Country Pub of the Year 2019. Q🐴❀◐◑⛺🍎🚌(56)🐾📶

Musbury

Hind

The Street, EX13 8AU

⏲ 5-9.30 Mon; 12-2.30, 5-11; 12-11.30 Sat; 12-9.30 Sun ☎ (01297) 553553 🌐 thegoldenhindmusbury.co.uk

3 changing beers Ⓗ

A free house on the crossroads of the A358, between Seaton and Axmouth. It has a public bar and a lounge/restaurant where good-value home-cooked food is served lunchtimes and evenings (no food Mon or Sun eve). There are two outside areas: a front courtyard with stunning views over the Axe Valley and a rear beer garden which is lawned and enclosed. Dogs are welcome. Q🐴❀◐◑♣P🚌(885)🐾📶

Newton Abbot

Taphouse & Bottle Shop

Tuckers Maltings, Teign Road, TQ12 4AA (500yds from Newton Abbot railway station)

⏲ closed Mon-Wed; 5-11 Thu; 4-11 Fri; 12-11 Sat; 2-9 Sun ☎ (01626) 334734 🌐 themaltingstaphouse.co.uk

Edwin Tucker's Devonshire Prize Ale; 2 changing beers (sourced nationally; often New Lion) Ⓗ

In the old Tuckers Maltings, which also houses the Teignworthy Brewery. The interior reflects the maltings' heritage; the furniture, made with recycled wood from the old barley storage bins, still exudes the aroma of its original function. The walls are draped with images reflecting the history of the maltings, railway and town. A vast range of bottled beers and several craft beers is also available. No jukebox, TV or fruit machines here; beer and conversation prevail. Local CAMRA Pub of the Year 2019. Q❀♿⇌🍎P🚌(12)🐾📶

Newton Poppleford

Cannon Inn

High Street, EX10 0DW

⏲ 11-2.30, 5.30-11 (midnight Thu & Fri); 11-midnight Sat; 12-11 Sun ☎ (01395) 568266 🌐 pubindevon.com

Exmoor Gold; 1 changing beer (sourced nationally) Ⓖ

Cheery, welcoming, two-bar pub with tables for dining in the lounge bar and restaurant area. Real ales are served by gravity from stillage behind the bar. This is a friendly locals' pub with busy passing trade. Good-value home-cooked food, served lunchtimes and evenings, covers most traditional pub favourites and, locals say, is of a tasty standard. Well-behaved dogs are allowed. There are two large gardens and a skittle alley. The only pub in the village, and a community hub. Q🐴❀🛏◐◑♿⛺♣P🚌(52,157)🐾📶

Newton St Cyres

Beer Engine

EX5 5AX (beside railway station, ½ mile N of A377)

⏲ 11-11; 12-9 Sun ☎ (01392) 851282 🌐 thebeerengine.co.uk

Beer Engine Rail Ale, Piston Bitter, Sleeper Heavy; 2 changing beers Ⓗ

A Victorian pub, built in 1850, on the Exeter to Barnstaple Tarka Line. Popular with drinkers and diners alike, it is well frequented by locals, visitors and its own cricket team. Home-cooked food is served lunchtimes and evenings made with locally sourced produce. The pub brews its own ales including four regulars and a seasonal one which, like the village pictures and old pub signs, reflect a railway theme. Q🐴❀◐◑♿⇌P🐾

North Bovey

Ring of Bells Inn

TQ13 8RB

⏲ 10-11 ☎ (01647) 440375 🌐 ringofbells.net

Dartmoor IPA; Teignworthy Reel Ale Ⓖ

The inn had a devastating fire three years ago and was rebuilt to a high standard with a new thatched roof. In the heart of Dartmoor, it is in an idyllic village with an ancient parish church and a tree-lined village green. The beer is dispensed straight from the barrel here and good locally produced food is served. With 15th-century origins, the pub has low ceilings and arched door frames plus open

fireplaces and a grandfather clock. The enclosed courtyard is a delight in the summer. Quality accommodation is available, too.
Q❀🛏◑🚌(671)🐾

North Tawton

Railway Inn 𝕃

Whiddon Down Road, EX20 2BE (1 mile S of town, just off A3124 and next to old North Tawton railway station) SS666000
⏲ 6-11; 12-3, 6-11 Fri & Sat; 12-3, 7-10.30 Sun
☎ (01837) 82789
Teignworthy Reel Ale; 1 changing beer (sourced nationally) [H]
There is always a warm welcome and good value to be found at this popular family-run local. The bar features railway memorabilia and old photos of the adjacent railway station, which closed in 1971. Reel Ale from Teignworthy is normally joined by a guest ale from one of the other West Country breweries, together with a real cider in summer. The dining room is popular in the evening (no food Thu), with light meals served at lunchtime. No dogs allowed except guide dogs.
Q🐴❀◑♣🍎P🚌📶

Ottery St Mary

London Inn

4 Gold Street, EX11 1DG
⏲ 12 (4 Mon)-11; 12-midnight Fri & Sat; 12-10 Sun
☎ (01404) 812045 🌐 londoninn.net
6 changing beers (sourced nationally) [H]
A 17th-century coaching inn close to the historic 14th-century parish church. This friendly locals' pub has two separate bars offering six changing real ales from breweries near and far, with a good range of styles and strengths, all at the same price. Good-value home-cooked food, including a roast on Sunday, is served. There is a pool room and a function room, and live music is regularly promoted. Four B&B rooms are available.
Q🐴❀🛏◑♣🍎P🚌🐾📶

Volunteer Inn

Broad Street, EX11 1BZ
⏲ 12-midnight ☎ (01404) 814060
🌐 volunteerinnottery.co.uk
Otter Bitter; 4 changing beers (sourced regionally) [G]
The pub has been part of Ottery St Mary's history since 1810, when it opened as a dwelling, hostelry and recruitment centre for the Napoleonic War. In the centre of the town, it is popular. The front bar has been kept traditional and the rear bar is more modern. All real ales, mainly from local breweries, are delivered by gravity. Food is served seven days a week, including traditional Sunday roast, in the recently refurbished and extended restaurant.
🐴❀◑♿♣🍎🚌(4)🐾📶

Paignton

Henry's Bar 𝕃 ✔

53 Torbay Road, TQ4 6AJ
⏲ 11-11 (midnight Fri & Sat) ☎ (01803) 551190
🌐 henrysbarpaignton.co.uk
Sharp's Doom Bar; 3 changing beers (sourced nationally; often Exmoor) [H]
Traditional-style town pub with plenty of character and a keen interest in real ale and cider including local suppliers. The long bar boasts four handpumps with three regular beers and one guest, a cider on the fifth, and various bottles/polyboxes. This warm and welcoming pub is on the main street close to train and bus stations, and has ties to the local surfing community and many local events. Home-cooked food is served daily with a roast on Sunday, and families are welcome to 10pm. 🐴❀◑⇌🍎P🚌🐾📶

Isaac Merritt 𝕃 ✔

54-58 Torquay Road, TQ3 3AA
⏲ 8am-midnight ☎ (01803) 556066
Dartmoor Jail Ale; Greene King Abbot; Ruddles Best Bitter; Sharp's Abbey Christmas; changing beers (sourced nationally; often Bays, Hanlons, Teignworthy) [H]
A Wetherspoon pub, the longest-standing in Torbay, with a well-deserved reputation for its fine quality and extensive range of handpumped real ales and ciders. The décor is traditional and wood-clad, with alcoves, and families are welcome. There is a covered and heated smokers' patio to the rear. The interior is themed around Isaac Merritt Singer, inventor of the Singer sewing machine, plus it has many vintage shots of Paignton. The pub is towards the edge of town, minutes from train and bus stations. It has wheelchair access for the bar and toilets.
Q🐴❀◑♿⇌🍎P🚌📶

Parkham

Bell Inn ✔

Rectory Lane, EX39 5PL (½ mile S of A39 at Horns Cross, on opp corner to village primary school) SS387212
⏲ 5.30-11 Mon; closed Tue; 12-3, 5.30-midnight Wed, Thu & Sat; 12-3, 5-midnight Fri; 12-4 Sun ☎ (01237) 451201
🌐 thebellinnparkham.co.uk
3 changing beers (sourced regionally) [H]
Originally a forge and two farmworkers' cottages, this 13th-century inn has been tastefully and sympathetically restored following a serious fire in 2017. Retaining its old-world charm, with cob walls, oak beams and woodburner fires all housed under a traditional newly thatched roof, the pub reopened in October 2018. As before, four changing real ales are usually on tap, while good home-cooked food is served either in the bar or in the adjacent raised restaurant area.
Q🐴❀◑♣🍎P🚌(372)🐾📶

Peter Tavy

Peter Tavy Inn

Lane Head, PL19 9NN
⏲ 12-11 (10.30 Sun) summer; 12-3, 6-11; 12-3, 6.30-10.30 Sun winter ☎ (01822) 810348 🌐 petertavyinn.com
Dartmoor Jail Ale; 4 changing beers (sourced regionally; often Black Tor, Roam, Salcombe) [H]
In a quiet village on the edge of Dartmoor, the inn has a small central bar offering Dartmoor Jail Ale supplemented by a varying range of up to four local guest beers. Traditionally attired throughout, there are also two larger rooms. A patio and hidden garden are added attractions. The pub is renowned for its food, but drinkers are made welcome. Situated on the No.27 cycle route, near a caravan and camping site.
Q🐴❀◑⛺♣P🚌(46,95)🐾📶

Plymouth

Artillery Arms 🄻

6 Pound Street, Stonehouse, PL1 3RH (behind Stonehouse Barracks and Millbay Docks)
4-11; 12-11 Fri-Sun ☎ (01752) 262515
Draught Bass; 2 changing beers (sourced locally; often Black Tor, Dartmoor, Summerskills) 🄷
Cracking back-street local tucked away in the old quarter of Stonehouse, close to the magnificent Grade I-listed Royal William Yard, and maintaining the area's military connections. Two South-West guest beers and Thatchers Heritage cider are normally stocked. An out-of-season beach party takes place on the last weekend of February, and charity monkey racing also features. This place is a real find and is popular with local hockey teams. (34,34A)

Bread & Roses 🄻

62 Ebrington Street, PL4 9AF
4-1am; 12-1am Fri & Sat; 12-11 Sun ☎ (01752) 659861
breadandrosesplymouth.co.uk
Exeter Avocet; 3 changing beers (sourced regionally; often Altarnun, Bude, Red Rock) 🄷
This friendly and sympathetically restored late-Victorian pub is popular with university staff, but has a mixed clientele. Up to three varied real ales are sold, which are organic/Fairtrade wherever possible, just like the snacks. The beers are selected from local and regional breweries, including small-batch and speciality beers unusual for the area. The pub promotes artistic and musical creativity, and is a vibrant music hub for local talent. (23,24)

Britannia Inn 🄻 ✔

2 Wolesely Road, Milehouse, PL2 3BH
8am-midnight (1am Fri & Sat) ☎ (01752) 607596
Dartmoor Jail Ale; Greene King Abbot; Ruddles Best Bitter; Sharp's Doom Bar; changing beers (sourced nationally; often Bays, Fuller's, Summerskills) 🄷
An Edwardian pub, built in the 1830s, situated opposite the Plymouth City bus depot, Central Park and the Life Centre, and a short walk from Home Park, Plymouth Argyle FC. The pub itself was built by the grandfather of Captain Scott (of the Antarctic fame). Ten handpumps dispense at least one real cider, with Westons and other local ciders appearing regularly. Since becoming a Wetherspoon establishment in 1999, the pub has established a well-earned reputation for its beer.

Dolphin Hotel ✔

14 The Barbican, Barbican, PL1 2LS
10-11 (midnight Thu-Sat); 11-11 Sun ☎ (01752) 660876
Dartmoor Jail Ale; Draught Bass; Otter Ale; St Austell Tribute; Sharp's Doom Bar; Skinner's Betty Stogs; 2 changing beers (sourced regionally; often St Austell, Sharp's) 🄶
A Plymouth institution, this unpretentious hostelry is steeped in history. Up to eight ales are all dispensed by gravity from the cask. The character of this establishment is charming, with tiled floors, well-used wooden benches and a traditional open fire all creating the perfect ambience. The walls are adorned with paintings by a local artist, the late Beryl Cook, who depicted many of the characters she encountered in the Dolphin. Local CAMRA City Pub of the Year runner-up 2019. (25)

Fareham Inn

6 Commercial Road, Coxside, PL4 0LD
11-11; 12-10.30 Sun ☎ (01752) 651897
1 changing beer (sourced regionally; often Bath Ales, St Austell) 🄷
A corner terrace, older pub with a slate-floored single room, close to Sutton Harbour and the Barbican Leisure Complex. It is a favourite haunt of local fishermen and the people who live close by. Paintings of fishing trawlers from the area adorn the walls, as do old photographs of the pub in days gone by. The single well-kept rotating ale on offer generally comes from St Austell or Bath Ales breweries. (14)

Fawn Private Members Club 🄻

39 Prospect Street, Greenbank, PL4 8NY
3-11; 2-11 Fri; 12-11 Sat & Sun ☎ (01752) 226385
Bays Topsail; 4 changing beers (sourced regionally; often St Austell, Sharp's, Teignworthy) 🄷
This mid 19th-century establishment was originally the Fawn Inn/Hotel, prior to converting to a club. CAMRA members are welcome with a valid membership card; regular visitors will be required to join. Four guest ales from the surrounding area are generally served, as well as a rotating range of local cider from Countryman. The club is popular for rugby and other televised sports, and supports multiple darts and euchre teams. Local CAMRA branch Club of the Year 2019, and former regional Club of the Year runner-up.

Ferry House Inn ✔

888 Wolseley Road, Saltash Passage, PL5 1LA
12-11.30 ☎ (01752) 361063 ferryhouseinn.com
Dartmoor Jail Ale; Sharp's Doom Bar, Atlantic 🄷
A warm welcome awaits you and your dog from the landlord and locals at this picturesque riverside pub on the River Tamar. Three regular West Country ales are served, as well as good home-cooked food. A decking area on the edge of the river gives spectacular views of both the road bridge and Brunel's iconic 1859 railway bridge. Photos, some dating back to the turn of the 20th century, adorn the walls. Accommodation is available, and there is a regular Sunday quiz.
(St Budeaux Victoria Rd) (13)

Fisherman's Arms 🄻

31 Lambhay Street, Barbican, PL1 2NN
12-11 (midnight Fri & Sat); 11-midnight Sun
☎ (01752) 268243 fishermansarms.co.uk
Dartmoor Jail Ale; house beer (by Summerskills); 1 changing beer (often Otter) 🄷
Owner Donna, her partner Lee, and his family have turned this former St Austell pub back into a traditional free house. The interior is welcoming, with several distinctly decorated areas. The dartboard has returned alongside a variety of games and puzzles. Ale and cider festivals are held twice a year. Traditional pub grub at affordable prices is supplemented by specials, while only the famous roast is available on Sundays. Close to the Royal Citadel and the Barbican.
(25)

Fortescue Hotel 🄻 ✔

37 Mutley Plain, PL4 6JQ
11-midnight; 12-11 Sun ☎ (01752) 660673
Bays Devon Dumpling; Dartmoor Legend; Roam Tavy IPA; St Austell Proper Job; Skinner's Betty Stogs; Summerskills Devon Dew; 4 changing beers (sourced

nationally; often Cornish Crown, Hunters, South Hams)
This multi award-winning and lively local is frequented by a broad section of the community and conversation flourishes. Nine real ales are usually on tap and up to six real ciders. A perfect Sunday can be spent here - a good-value home-cooked roast washed down with a pint of Spingo Special, followed by a brain-teasing quiz in the evening. The patio beer garden draws crowds in the summer and is heated in winter. Note the interesting cricket memorabilia adorning the walls.

Mannamead

61 Mutley Plain, PL4 6JH
8am-midnight (1am Fri & Sat) (01752) 825610
Dartmoor Jail Ale; Greene King Abbot; Ruddles Best Bitter; Sharp's Doom Bar; changing beers (sourced nationally; often Dartmoor, Roam, Summerskills)
A Wetherspoon establishment converted from a former NatWest Bank. A wide range of ales from near and far can be found, with at least two local brews usually on the pumps. There is also a good range of real cider and perry. Beer and cider festivals take place several times a year. Brewery showcase events are also held, featuring a large number of beers from local breweries, as well as a Devon ale festival.

Minerva Inn

31 Looe Street, Barbican, PL4 0EA
11.30-11.30 (midnight Wed; 12.30am Thu & Fri); 12-12.30am Sat; 1-10.30 Sun (01752) 223047
minervainn.co.uk
St Austell Trelawny, Tribute; 2 changing beers (sourced locally; often Dartmoor, Roam, Summerskills)
Plymouth's oldest pub, dating from about 1540, is within easy walking distance of the city centre and the historic Barbican. The pub has a long and narrow bar, leading through to a cosy seating area at the rear. Two guest beers are always available and beer festivals are held in spring and autumn, where beer could, and does, come from all over the country. Live music takes place Thursday to Sunday evenings, and Sunday lunchtime. The pub benefits from a varied clientele.

Nowhere Inn

21 Gilwell Street, PL4 8BU
4-1am (3am Fri); 6-3am Sat; closed Sun
(01752) 670592
4 changing beers (sourced locally; often Bridgetown, Roam, Summerskills)
Old-fashioned back-street pub tucked away in the midst of the student campus. It is close to the city centre and easily accessible by public transport, and is frequented by an eclectic variety of patrons, from students to elderly locals. A quiz night is held on Monday and live music plays on Thursday. A changing selection of local ales draws in visitors hoping to catch a glimpse both of favourite brews and those hard to find. A black beer is usually on.

Prince Maurice

3 Church Hill, Eggbuckland, PL6 5RJ
11-3, 6-11; 11-11 Fri-Sun (01752) 771515
Dartmoor Jail Ale; St Austell Tribute, Proper Job, HSD; South Hams Eddystone; Summerskills Whistle Belly Vengeance; 2 changing beers (sourced locally; often Hunters, Roam)
There is very much a village feel to this four-times local CAMRA Pub of the Year, which sits between the church and village green. Seven regular ales are supplemented by a changing guest ale. The pub is named after the Royalist general, the King's nephew, who had his headquarters nearby during the siege of Plymouth in the Civil War. Two log fires keep you warm in winter, adding to the ambience. Food is not available at weekends.
P (28A)

Pub on the Hoe

159 Citadel Road, The Hoe, PL1 2HU
10-midnight (01752) 202405 thepubonthehoe.co.uk
House beer (by Hunters); 5 changing beers (sourced locally; often Bays, Noss Beer Works, Roam)
A busy street-corner pub serving a mixed clientele and near Plymouth Hoe, where Sir Francis Drake famously played bowls. Up to five varying real ales supplement the house beer, Drunken Hoe, and two local real ciders. Good home-cooked food is served all day. The wood-panelled raised and lower deck seating areas add to the nautical theme. It is just a short walk from the historic Barbican and is well worth a visit. (25)

Vessel Beer Shop

184 Exeter Street, St Jude's, PL4 0NQ
closed Mon; 11-8 (10 Fri & Sat); 1-8 Sun 07796 667449
vesselbeer.co.uk
Changing beers (sourced nationally)
An independent bar and beer shop a few minutes' walk from Plymouth city centre and opposite St Jude's retail park. It stocks over 180 different beers from some of the best breweries in Britain and around the world. Beers are available in bottles, cans and on draught, and can now be enjoyed in the bar. Light snacks may be available. Regular events include Meet the Brewer or Food Producers, beer tastings and beer styles (see social media for up-to-date activities).

Plympton

Union Inn

17 Underwood Road, PL7 1SY
4-11 (11.30 Fri); 2-midnight Sat; 12-11 Sun
(01752) 336756 unioninnplympton.com
4 changing beers (sourced regionally; often Exeter, Summerskills, Tintagel)
The landlord is a beer hunter, tracking down changing brews to charm his regulars' palates, and to create a year-round beer festival. The four beers on offer are regional, but could be from almost anywhere. It is the same with the cider selection, with Old Rosie a regular. This early 19th-century award-winning pub is a family-run community venue that offers a warm welcome to all who enter. A local CAMRA branch former Cider Pub of the Year runner-up. Q P

Postbridge

Warren House Inn

PL20 6TA (on B3212 between Postbridge and Bennett's Cross)
11-10 (3 Mon & Tue); 12-10.30 Sun (01822) 880208
warrenhouseinn.co.uk
Otter Ale; 3 changing beers (sourced regionally; often Black Tor, Exeter, Summerskills)
Isolated and exposed at 1,425 feet above sea level, this is one of England's highest pubs. Countryman

cider features regularly, with up to three varying guest beers mainly from the West Country. The characterful main bar boasts two log fires – one never goes out. Excellent-value home-made food includes the famous rabbit pie, local lamb and delicious puddings with clotted cream. There is a large family room and tables outside with breathtaking views over the moors. Open all day in summer. Q

Princetown

Plume of Feathers Inn

Plymouth Hill, PL20 6QQ
10.30-11 (midnight Fri & Sat) ☎ (01822) 890240
theplumeoffeathersdartmoor.co.uk
Dartmoor Jail Ale; St Austell Tribute; Sharp's Doom Bar; 3 changing beers (sourced regionally; often Dartmoor) H
Whatever the season, the Plume is a fine destination. Built in 1785, it retains many original features and has a traditional country feel. There are four separate areas – the cosy main bar, the booths, the rear bar and the back room – ensuring you will usually find a seat. In addition there is a function room and plenty of garden seating. The pub also offers a children's play area, extensive parking and a wide variety of accommodation including camping facilities.
Q P (98)

St Giles on the Heath

Pint & Post

PL15 9SA (just off main road through village)
6-11 Mon; 12-3, 6-11 Tue-Thu; 12-3, 6-midnight Fri & Sat; 12-6 Sun ☎ (01566) 779933
Holsworthy Ales Muck 'n' Straw; 1 changing beer (sourced nationally) H
A cob and timber-framed thatched inn close to the Devon and Cornwall county border. Once two cottages and then the village post office, it eventually became a pub and post office, thereby acquiring its name. Today, although no longer housing the post office, this friendly family-run pub remains at the heart of the community. The regular Muck 'n' Straw from Holsworthy is usually joined by another local guest ale. Q P

Seaton

All Hat But No Cattle

34 Queen Street, EX12 2RB
closed Mon; 5-11; 5-10.30 Sun ☎ 07912 242385
4 changing beers H
Known as the Hat, this micropub is in an old butcher's shop. There are four real ales and four real ciders served straight from the casks, which are stored in the old cold room. There is no fizzy beer or lager and no music. The emphasis is on conversation but not on mobile phones. The landlord always wears a hat, hence the pub's unusual name. Snacks such as pork pies, Scotch eggs and cheese and biscuits are available.
Q

Shaldon

London Inn

The Green, TQ14 0DN
11-11.30 ☎ (01626) 872453 londoninnshaldon.co.uk
Otter Bitter; St Austell Proper Job; 1 changing beer H
Attractive white-fronted building dating from 1790 near the Teignmouth foot ferry. Internally, there are two areas with a small, more local public bar and a larger area more likely to be used by diners and dominated by large scrubbed tables. To the rear are photos of old Shaldon depicting life on the estuary from a bygone age. Externally, there is an attractive front drinking area surrounded by flowerbeds overlooking the bowling green. Quiz night is Tuesday and live music plays on the last Sunday in the month. Q (22)

Shaldon Conservative Club

Dagmar Street, TQ14 0DU
12-3, 5-11; 12-11 Sat & Sun ☎ (01626) 873667
St Austell Tribute; Teignworthy Reel Ale; 1 changing beer (sourced nationally) H
Hidden in the back streets of this picture-postcard village is a modern single-room club where card-carrying CAMRA members and temporary members are welcomed. Three handpumps serve real ale and one a cider, while snooker, darts, bingo, live music, a weekly meat draw and card games attract all ages. Televised sporting events can also be enjoyed in the comfortable spacious surroundings. A mini beer festival is usually held in August.
(22)

Sidmouth

Sidmouth Conservative Club

Radway Place, EX10 8TL
10-2.30, 6-11; 10-2.30, 7-11.30 Sat; 12-3.30, 7-10.30 Sun
☎ (01395) 514311 sidmouthconservativeclub.co.uk
3 changing beers H
Close to the town centre, this warm and friendly club was formed in 1906. It is open to its members and their guests, but card-carrying CAMRA members are also welcome at all times. Regular visitors will be asked to join. Beers are mainly from Otter Brewery and Greene King, but there is also a good variety of ales, rotated regularly. The club has a beer festival during Sidmouth Folk Festival which is open to everyone, all day, every day.
Q P

Silverton

Lamb Inn

Fore Street, EX5 4HZ
12-2.30, 6-11; 12-11 Sat & Sun ☎ (01392) 860272
thelambinnsilverton.co.uk
Otter Ale; 2 changing beers (sourced regionally) G
Popular family-run village pub with stone floors, stripped timber, old pine furniture and a large open real fire. A fine display of old pumpclips is a reminder of the long list of previous guest beers. Three ales are served by gravity from a temperature-controlled stillage behind the bar, at competitive prices. There is a function room and skittle alley. Good-value home-cooked food is served lunchtimes and evenings, plus a popular Sunday roast. Q (55B)

Slapton

Queen's Arms

TQ7 2PN
12-3, 5.30-11; 12-3, 6-10.30 Sun ☎ (01548) 580800
queensarmsslapton.co.uk

Dartmoor Jail Ale; Otter Bitter; South Hams Wild Blonde; 1 changing beer (sourced regionally; often Salcombe) H

Deep in the South Hams countryside you will find this splendid 14th-century village pub, half a mile from Slapton beach, boasting a flower-filled garden in summer, patios at the rear and an open fire in winter. The walls are adorned with WWII evacuation photographs depicting local life and history. The food menu is extensive, with daily specials, and the chef is known for his home-made pies in winter; Sunday roasts are popular (booking advised). Takeaway meals are available and children and dogs are welcome.
Q P

South Zeal

King's Arms

EX20 2JP (centre of village) SX649936
12-11 (01837) 840300 thekingsarmssouthzeal.com
Dartmoor IPA, Legend; 1 changing beer (sourced regionally) H

A former cider house, this thatched 14th-century village local is now the hub of the local community. The long single bar has two regular Dartmoor beers together with a changing guest ale from another local brewery and a local cider. Good food is served lunchtimes and evenings every day. Regular live music sessions are held throughout the year and the pub plays a central role during the Dartmoor Folk Festival in August. Q P

Spreyton

Tom Cobley Tavern

EX17 5AL (off A3124 in village) SX6986096761
6-10 Mon; 12-3, 6-11 (midnight Fri & Sat); 12-4, 7-10 Sun
(01647) 231314 tomcobleytavern.co.uk
14 changing beers (sourced regionally) H/G

Up to 14 West Country ales, some straight from the cask, plus about 18 real ciders and perries, are on offer in this traditional 16th-century village pub. A wide range of bar snacks and an extensive menu are available lunchtimes and evenings. The pub has won a multitude of CAMRA awards at local level. Darts, quizzes and social events are promoted and there are five en-suite guest rooms.
Q P

Sticklepath

Devonshire Inn

EX20 2NW (in centre of village)
12-2.30, 6-11 Mon; 6-11 Tue; 12-3, 6-11 Wed & Thu; 11.30-10.30 Fri & Sat; 12-3 Sun (01837) 840626
Dartmoor IPA; Holsworthy Ales Muck 'n' Straw, Sunshine; 1 changing beer (sourced locally) G

Unspoilt thatched local, with low ceilings and an open fire, originally at the end of a terrace of Elizabethan cottages in this Dartmoor village. Entering it today is to experience an atmospheric step back in time. There is a leat running past the rear wall of the pub which helps cool the three real ales on stillage, as well as powering the waterwheel of the Finch Foundry Museum (NT) next door. Q P

Taw River Inn

Sticklepath, EX20 2NW (on main road, old A30, through village) SX642941
12-midnight; 12-11 Sun (01837) 840377
tawriver.co.uk
St Austell Tribute; Sharp's Doom Bar; Dartmoor Jail Ale; 1 changing beer (sourced regionally) H

Dating from the 17th century and set in an active village on the edge of Dartmoor, this venue is popular with visitors and locals alike. The real ales are attractively priced, while the cider is made in the village. Good-value pub food is served in both the bar area and adjacent dining room. There is a TV in the large single bar, where numerous sports and pub games are played by friendly locals.
P

Teignmouth

Blue Anchor Inn

Teign Street, TQ14 8EG
12-midnight (01626) 772741
6 changing beers (sourced regionally; often Exeter, Summerskills, Teignworthy) H

Situated on the edge of town, a warm and friendly atmosphere awaits you here. This single-room pub boasts eight handpumps serving cider and real ale; a dark beer is often available. Outside seating areas are a flourish of floral delight in spring and summer, becoming a winter wonderland at Christmas. As well as being a great supporter of local events and charities, the pub hosts a beer festival on the Easter and August bank holidays. Live music, pool and darts are also popular attractions. (2,22)

Brass Monkey

Hollands Road, TQ14 8SR
11-midnight; 12-11 Sun 07708 910144
St Austell Tribute H

A simple and straightforward one-bar community pub with a pool table and two TV screens. Just off the town centre, it is somewhat dwarfed by much larger and more exuberant nearby establishments. During the day the pub is an ideal retreat for a peaceful pint and a read of the newspaper, very much in contrast to the lively, enjoyable and potentially crowded karaoke on offer at weekends. It is also an excellent waiting room for local transport, situated 150 yards from the railway station and 50 yards from bus stops. Quiz night is Tuesday. Q (2,22)

Topsham

Bridge Inn ★

Bridge Hill, EX3 0QQ
12-2, 6-10.30 (11 Fri & Sat); 12-2, 7-10.30 Sun
(01392) 873862 cheffers.co.uk/bridge.html
Branscombe Vale Branoc; changing beers G

A historic, cosy, 16th-century inn beautifully positioned overlooking the River Clyst and meadows. Run by six generations of the same family (they celebrated 121 years in 2018), this hostelry is a delight to fans of real ale and was even visited by the Queen in 1998. A varying range of seven to nine ales, local and from further afield, are dispensed by gravity directly from the cellar. Traditional pub lunches such as ploughman's and sandwiches are offered. Q P (57,T)

Exeter Inn

68 High Street, EX3 0DY
4-11; 12-midnight Fri & Sat; 12-10.30 Sun
(01392) 873131

Teignworthy Beachcomber; 3 changing beers (sourced regionally)
A pub since at least 1860, some of this partially thatched building dates from the 17th century when it was a coaching inn and blacksmith's. It is a friendly local serving Teignworthy Beachcomber, three guest ales and two ciders plus, occasionally, snacks such as rolls. Three TVs show various sports, while the front area is devoted to pool and darts. There is a small sheltered garden and smoking area at the side. Dogs are welcome.

Torquay

Crown & Sceptre

2 Petitor Road, St Marychurch, TQ1 4QA
6-11 Mon; 12 (1 Tue)-4, 6-11; 12-4, 7-11 Sun
(01803) 328290
Butcombe Gold; Courage Best Bitter, Directors; Dartmoor Jail Ale; Hanlons Yellow Hammer; 3 changing beers (sourced nationally)
This lovely old-fashioned local is on the outskirts of St Marychurch not far from the shopping precinct, and has been run by the same family for over 40 years. The lounge has bare stone walls, a logburner, and bench and stool seating. The public bar has tables and bench seating, lots of chamber pots, hats and interesting knick-knacks hanging from the ceiling. There are two garden areas and a small car park. Live music takes place at least three times a week. Everyone is welcome including families and dogs. P

Totnes

Albert Inn

32 Bridgetown, TQ9 5AD (from Totnes centre cross river, 100yds on left)
12-11 (midnight Fri & Sat) (01803) 863214
albertinntotnes.com
Bridgetown Albert Ale, Shark Island Stout, West Coast IPA; 2 changing beers (sourced locally)
Named after Albert Einstein, this pub is the brewery tap for Bridgetown Brewery. It is a classic community local, hosting pub teams, live music, quizzes and culinary evenings, as well as regular beer and cider festivals throughout the year. The only pub on the Bridgetown side of the river that divides Totnes, it has a cosy beer garden to the rear which affords views of the River Dart.
Q P

Bay Horse Inn

8 Cistern Street, TQ9 5SP (on right at top of main shopping street in Totnes)
12-11.30 (01803) 862088 bayhorsetotnes.com
New Lion Mane Event, Totnes Stout, Pandit IPA; 2 changing beers (sourced locally; often Noss Beer Works, Salcombe, Teignworthy)
This friendly, traditional – but not old-fashioned – pub boasts a large, stylish beer garden in which many events are held, including beer festivals on the Easter and August bank holidays. The community feel of the pub is enhanced by quiz nights and live music nights including jazz and open mic, and it hosts various societies including the Purl and Pint local knitting circle. Evening food is not available but patrons are welcome to bring in their takeaways.
Q P (X64,164)

Royal Seven Stars Hotel

The Plains, TQ9 5DD
8am-11 (11.30 Fri & Sat) (01803) 862125
royalsevenstars.co.uk
Dartmoor Jail Ale; Sharp's Doom Bar; 2 changing beers (sourced locally; often Bays, New Lion, Salcombe)
Prominently sited at the bottom of the main shopping street, this former coaching house welcomes families and dogs. It has 21 rooms, an excellent à la carte restaurant, and is a wedding venue with two function rooms. The hotel hosts live music and also has plenty of seating outside at the front, where events are held in the warmer months. Q P

Totnes Brewing Company

59a High Street, TQ9 5PB (at top of High St by market square)
5-midnight; 12-midnight Fri & Sat; 12-11.30 Sun
thetotnesbrewingco.co.uk
8 changing beers (sourced nationally; often Totnes)
Popular and quirky brewpub serving a broad and diverse range of beers, with staff who are enthusiastic and knowledgeable about beer. The changing ales generally include at least one brewed on the premises, alongside other guests on up to seven more handpumps. A good range of KeyKeg ales is also available. Takeaway food may be brought in. There is a Saxon castle at the rear of the premises. Q

Turnchapel

Boringdon Arms

13 Boringdon Terrace, PL9 9TQ
12-11 (midnight Fri & Sat); 12-10.30 Sun
(01752) 402053 boringdon-arms.net
Dartmoor Jail Ale; Fuller's London Pride; Sharp's Atlantic, Sea Fury
The Bori is a traditional and dog-friendly former CAMRA Regional Pub of the Year, with six letting rooms. It sits in this waterside village on the South-West Coastal Footpath, and benefits from a regular bus service from Plymouth, or a water taxi from the Barbican. The four regular ales are supplemented by four beer festivals a year. Good-value, home-cooked food is served daily. There are two secluded gardens to the rear.
Q (2,2A)

Weare Giffard

Cyder Presse

EX39 4QR
5-11 (01237) 425517
Timothy Taylor Landlord; 3 changing beers (sourced nationally)
Family-friendly village local with cosy bar and restaurant areas, two en-suite twin rooms and a beer garden. Up to four real ales are regularly dispensed, alongside at least nine well-kept real ciders. Home-cooked food from local produce is served Wednesday to Saturday and Sunday lunchtime. Tuesday is live folk music night, with new musicians always welcome. Local CAMRA Cider Pub of the Year 2018 and 2019.
Q P (7A)

Welcombe

Old Smithy Inn 🄻

EX39 6HG (turn off A39 Bideford to Kilkhampton road at Welcombe Cross, follow signs to Welcombe and then to pub)
12 (5 Mon)-midnight; 12-5 Sun ☎ (01288) 331305
theoldsmithyinn.co.uk
3 changing beers (sourced regionally) 🄷
A 13th-century thatched inn, nestled at the top of the Welcombe Valley and just a mile from the sea near the Cornish border. Appropriately, the landlord and landlady provide a warm welcome while offering a wide range of excellent locally sourced food, along with quality ales from nearby Forge and other fairly local breweries. There is also a pleasant garden and a separate function room. A four-bed backpackers' hostel is available for hire.
P

Wembury

Odd Wheel 🄻

Knighton Road, PL9 0JD
12-3, 5-midnight; 12-midnight Sat & Sun
☎ (01752) 863052 theoddwheel.co.uk
Dartmoor Jail Ale; St Austell Tribute; 4 changing beers (sourced regionally) 🄷
Friendly country pub which was tastefully refurbished several years ago, at the northern end of this picturesque village. The two regular beers are supplemented by up to four guest beers, sourced mainly from Devon and Cornwall breweries. Regular beer festivals are held. It is only a short distance from many walking routes, including the South-West Coast Path. Food is served daily, with ingredients from local suppliers. Outside, there is a terraced garden and play area for children. Dogs are welcome in the lounge bar only. P (48)

Widecombe-in-the-Moor

Rugglestone Inn 🄻

TQ13 7TF (¼ mile from centre of village)
11.30-3, 6-11.30; 11.30-3, 5-midnight Fri; 11.30-midnight Sat; 12-11 Sun ☎ (01364) 621327 rugglestoneinn.co.uk
Dartmoor Legend; house beer (by Teignworthy); 2 changing beers (sourced regionally) 🄶
The Rugglestone is a Grade II-listed unspoilt Dartmoor building converted to an inn in 1832. There is a cosy bar room with a woodburner and two further rooms, one with an open fire. Beer is also served through a hatch in the passageway. A wide selection of home-cooked food is available. Across the stream is a large grassed seating area with the car park just down the road. Local farm Ashridge real cider is sold plus additional real cider and perry. Q P (271,672)

Albert Inn, Totnes (Photo: Phil Gayton/Flickr CC BY 2.0)

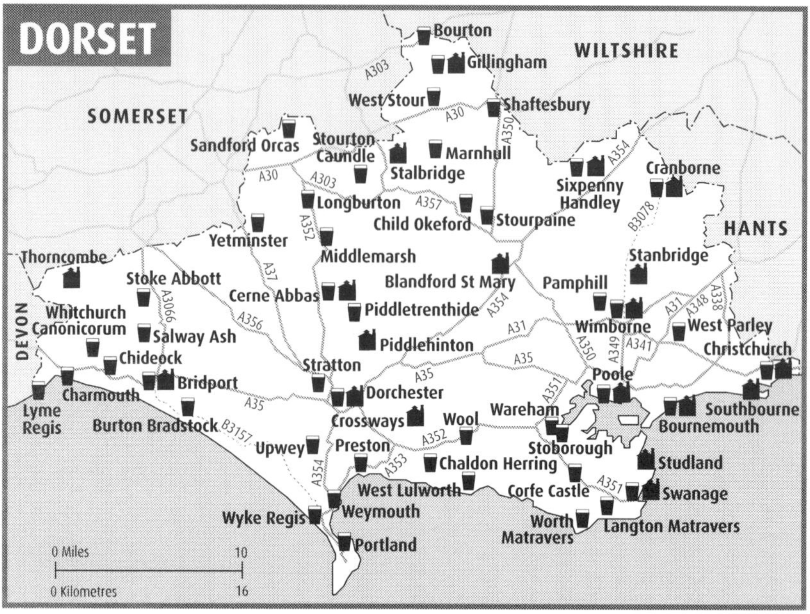

Bournemouth

All Hail Ale

10 Queens Road, Westbourne, BH2 6BE

12 (5 Mon)-10.30 ☎ 07786 045996

4 changing beers (sourced nationally) H

A vibrant micropub and bottle shop, this former restaurant has been skilfully converted, with wooden flooring and a polished-wood bar and tables. Four handpumps serve a wide range of ales from independent breweries nationwide, alongside 10 keg pumps offering a varied and well-chosen selection of beer, lager and cider. Popular tap takeovers are held to showcase some of the major new craft ales available. Beer-related slogans adorn the walls and a large blackboard lists the beers available.

Cricketers ✔

41 Windham Road, Springbourne, BH1 4RN

11-11; 12-10.30 Sun ☎ (01202) 551589

Fuller's London Pride; 2 changing beers (sourced nationally) H

Set on two levels, this imposing Victorian local retains many original features and is rich in mahogany and stained glass. The vaulted upper section of the main bar was converted from the gym where world champion boxer Freddie Mills once trained. Close to Bournemouth football ground and popular with fans from both home and away, sporting matches are televised. Lunches are served at weekends and the Sunday roasts are reasonably priced. Quiz night on Tuesday, pool, darts and other in-house games give this pub an excellent vibe. P (2)

Firkin Shed 🏆

279 Holdenhurst Road, Springbourne, BH8 8BZ

closed Mon & Tue; 4-11 Wed; 3-11 Thu (midnight Fri); 12-midnight Sat; 3-10 Sun ☎ (01202) 302340

6 changing beers (sourced nationally; often Cerne Abbas, Farmageddon, Vibrant Forest) G

Winner of CAMRA National Cider Pub and East Dorset Pub of the Year in 2018, the Shed is a quirky, friendly, family-run micropub. Tables and benches hug the walls, which are decorated with flags, musical instruments, puppets and skulls. A shed is used as the bar, with 10 changing ales and 14 or more ciders from around the country. Beers are served straight from the cellar, viewable through the window in the corridor. There is occasional live music and quality bar snacks are available. (2,6A)

Micro Moose

326 Wimborne Road, Winton, BH9 2HH

4-11; 12-11 Fri & Sat; 3-8 Sun ☎ (01202) 538542

micromoose.co.uk

6 changing beers (sourced nationally) H/G

Established when the Canadian owner decided to convert her coffee shop into a micropub offering 'Great British Ales with Canadian Hospitality'. This friendly and cosy bar serves a selection of local and regional ales on both handpump and gravity. The bottled beer selection is Canadian themed, as is the decor, complete with fluffy moose head. In common with other micropubs, sharing tables is encouraged. Local cider is also available, and a good selection of bar snacks. Q

Silverback Alehouse

518 Wimborne Road, Winton, BH9 2EX

2-10 Mon; 4-11 Tue-Thu; 12-11 Fri & Sat; 12-10 Sun ☎ 07999 586730 silverbackalehouse.co.uk

4 changing beers G

Set on Winton's bustling high street, this micropub offers a welcome respite from the weekly shop. Four carefully chosen real ales are served on gravity, often including ales from the Nottinghamshire area. Four ciders from small independent cider makers are also on offer. Benches and tables line the perimeter, with table service by friendly staff. Light snacks are available and you are welcome to bring in your takeaway. The Silverback has a relaxed and friendly atmosphere, making it popular with locals and visitors alike. Q

ENGLAND

Bourton

White Lion
High Street, SP8 5AT
12-11 (10.30 Sun) ☎ (01747) 840866
whitelionbourton.co.uk
Otter Amber; 2 changing beers (often Exmoor, Keystone, Wessex) Ⓗ
The White Lion is a traditional inn dating from 1763. Originally separate rooms, the cosy bar with stone-flagged floor has been opened out but there is always a quiet corner to be found. It has a cosy, intimate restaurant and a large beer garden. The pub is set back from the road with parking opposite as well as in the car park. Either Thatchers Original or Rich's Cider is served on handpump.
Q❀🛏◑◗●P🚌(X4)🛜

Bridport

Pursuit of Hoppiness
15 West Street, DT6 3QJ
12-11 (midnight Fri & Sat); 12-10 Sun ☎ (01308) 427111
hoppiness.co.uk
6 changing beers (sourced nationally; often Eight Arch, Tapstone) Ⓗ
Popular town-centre micropub with a single room which accommodates up to 25 people. There are six handpumps serving beers of all styles, changing regularly every few days – over 500 different beers from all over the UK were served in the first 15 months the pub was open. Six ciders are normally available including regulars Dorset Nectar and West Milton. Outdoor seating is at the front.
Q♣●🚌🐾🛜

Ropemakers Arms Ⓛ ✔
36 West Street, DT6 3QP
10-11 (12.30am Fri & Sat); 12-4 Sun ☎ (01308) 421255
theropemakers.com
Palmers Copper Ale, IPA, Dorset Gold, 200, Tally Ho!; 1 changing beer (often Palmers) Ⓗ
Deceptively large pub situated in the centre of town serving the full Palmers range of beers. The interior is divided into lots of separate themed areas decorated with memorabilia and local history. There is a large partially covered courtyard at the rear and wheelchair access via the back door. Quality home-cooked food is from local suppliers. Music features on Friday and Saturday evenings. The pub closes around 4pm on Sundays in the winter (later on bank holiday weekends or if there is live music). **❀◑◗Ⲁ♣●🚌🐾**🛜

Burton Bradstock

Anchor Inn
High Street, DT6 4QF
12-3, 6-10.30 Mon; 12-10.30 Tue-Thu (11 Fri & Sat); 12-7 Sun ☎ (01308) 897228 anchorinnburtonbradstock.co.uk
4 changing beers (sourced regionally) Ⓗ
One of the few free houses in this part of Dorset, the Anchor is in a pretty village with an excellent beach nearby. Inside, the Stables Bar has a traditional pub feel (and bar food) and there is also a larger restaurant area with an extensive menu. Local shellfish and seafood is the speciality. Up to four beers are selected from Dartmoor Jail Ale, Dorset Jurassic, Exmoor Gold, Sharp's Cornish Coaster or Doom Bar and St Austell Tribute. The accommodation consists of two recently refurbished rooms. **Q❀🛏◑◗Ⲁ♣P🚌**(C1,X53)🐾

Cerne Abbas

New Inn Ⓛ ✔
14 Long Street, DT2 7JF
12-11; 12-10 Sun ☎ (01300) 341274
thenewinncerneabbas.co.uk
Palmers Copper Ale, IPA, Dorset Gold, 200 Ⓗ
This stone and flint coaching inn dating from 1855 has been extensively refurbished to a very high standard while retaining its country feel, with an open fire and comfortable decor. The New Inn has friendly, welcoming staff, and 10 well-equipped luxury rooms named after local rivers. The bar and separate dining room serve seasonal local produce. Outside to the rear is a secluded courtyard. Dorset Orchards First Press Cider is available in the summer. **Q❀🛏◑◗♿Ⲁ●P🚌**(X11)🐾🛜

Chaldon Herring

Sailor's Return Ⓛ
DT2 8DN
closed Mon; 6-11 Tue; 12-2.30, 6-11 Wed-Fri; 12-11 Sat; 12-10.30 Sun ☎ (01305) 854441 sailorsreturnpub.com
Otter Ale; Palmers Copper Ale; 1 changing beer (sourced regionally; often Cerne Abbas, Sharp's) Ⓗ
Historic thatched inn situated on the edge of a small village a few miles from the Jurassic Coast. The pub dates from the 1860s but the buildings are from much earlier. There are several dining and drinking areas with flagstone floors. An original inn sign hangs in the main bar. Food comes mainly from local suppliers with seasonal variations. Wednesday is pie night. The restaurant is popular so booking is highly advisable. **Q❀◑◗●P🐾**🛜

Charmouth

Royal Oak Inn Ⓛ ✔
The Street, DT6 6PE
11-10.30 (11 Fri & Sat); 11-6 Sun ☎ (01297) 560277
royaloakcharmouth.co.uk
Palmers Copper Ale, IPA, Dorset Gold, 200; 1 changing beer (often Palmers) Ⓗ

REAL ALE BREWERIES
Barefaced Bournemouth
Brew Shack Sixpenny Handley
Brewers Folly Stanbridge
Brewhouse & Kitchen ▤ Bournemouth
Brewhouse & Kitchen ▤ Dorchester
Brewhouse & Kitchen ▤ Poole
Brewhouse & Kitchen ▤ Southbourne
Cerne Abbas Cerne Abbas
Copper Street Dorchester (NEW)
Dorset (DBC) Crossways
Drop The Anchor Christchurch
Eight Arch Wimborne
Gyle 59 Thorncombe
Hall & Woodhouse (Badger) Blandford St Mary
Hattie Brown's Swanage
Isle of Purbeck ▤ Studland
Palmers Bridport
Piddle Piddlehinton
Sandbanks Poole
Sixpenny Cranborne
Small Paul's Gillingham
Southbourne Bournemouth
Stripey Cat ▤ Bridport
Way Outback Southbourne
Wriggle Valley Stalbridge

A family-run traditional village pub a short walk from the beach on the Jurassic Coast. The friendly staff are welcoming of locals and visitors alike. It serves locally brewed Palmers beers, including the seasonal ales, and a local real cider. Dogs are allowed in the lower bar area. Food is freshly cooked from locally sourced produce (no food all day Tue and Sun eve).
(X51,X53)

Chideock

Clock Inn

Main Street, DT6 6JW
12-3, 6-11 (01297) 489423 clockchideock.co.uk
Branscombe Vale Summa That; Otter Bitter, Ale; 1 changing beer (sourced nationally; often Butcombe, Marston's, Morland)
The Clock, as it is known locally, is a traditional family-run free house. It is currently home to around 30 teams, with eight dartboards, table skittles, long alley skittles, table football and table tennis. There is a fantastic choice of home-made dishes on the menu as well as daily specials and Sunday roasts. The pub also features some 150 clocks and around 500 books on the charity bookshelves. During school holidays, opening hours are extended.
Q P (X51,X53)

Child Okeford

Saxon Inn

Gold Hill, DT11 8HD
12-3 (not Tue), 6-11 (01258) 860310 saxoninn.co.uk
Butcombe Original; Otter Bitter; 1 changing beer (sourced regionally; often Flack Manor, Goddards, Otter)
This 300-year-old inn retains its rustic charm despite significant extension following conversion from cottages in the 1950s. The bar area is cosy, with tables and chairs around the log fire. There are two distinct dining areas, and a garden for alfresco drinking, where a September beer festival is held. A varied menu of quality home-cooked food is available. The pub also does B&B and is an ideal base for exploring rural Dorset.
P

Christchurch

Saxon Bar

5 The Saxon Centre, Fountain Way, BH23 1QN
11-8 Mon; 4-10 Tue & Wed; 12-10 Thu (11 Fri & Sat); 12-10.30 Sun (01202) 488931
4 changing beers (sourced nationally; often Downton, Sixpenny, Vibrant Forest)
This friendly, single-room micropub, close to the town centre, has perimeter seating and high tables made from reclaimed wood that was once part of Bournemouth Pier. It offers a variety of well-chosen ales, direct from the cask, as well as up to 10 real ciders, all served direct to your table. Speciality bar snacks, local and international spirits along with four KeyKeg beers are also available. Look out for the Carlsbog urinal, not to be missed! Please note winter hours vary. Q

Thomas Tripp

10 Wick Lane, BH23 1HX
11-midnight (01202) 490498 thomastripp.co.uk
Ringwood Razorback, Fortyniner; 2 changing beers (sourced regionally; often Cerne Abbas, Southbourne Ales, Vibrant Forest)
This was formerly the Plumbers Arms, renamed after a legendary local smuggler, and in the historic town centre near the Priory Church and Castle. Continuing the theme, it features paintings of locals throughout the smuggling era. It is rugby union-oriented and supports East Dorset RFC. Great bar food is available lunchtimes and evenings, with speciality fish dishes served in the adjoining shack. The large paved patio area with sheltered alcoves is a must in the summer. Live music plays several nights a week.

Corfe Castle

Corfe Castle Club

70 East Street, BH20 5EQ (off A351)
12-2.30, 6-11; 12-11 Sat & Sun (01929) 480591
Ringwood Razorback; Timothy Taylor Landlord; 1 changing beer (sourced nationally)
Friendly club in the village centre, formerly a school and built in Purbeck stone. The main bar has upholstered bench seating, TV for major sporting events, darts and Purbeck longboard shove-ha'penny. An upstairs room has a pool table and can be hired for meetings. Filled rolls are available all day. The spectacular garden boasts a boules court and views over the Purbeck hills. Convenient for the castle or steam railway, visitors are welcome with a CAMRA membership card or copy of the Guide. P (40)

Cranborne

Sixpenny Tap

Holwell Farm, Holwell, BH21 5QP (1 mile from village centre on B3078)
4-7.30; 11.30-7.30 Fri; 11.30-4 Sat & Sun
(01725) 762006 sixpennybrewery.co.uk
Sixpenny Best Bitter, Gold, IPA; 1 changing beer (often Sixpenny)
Housed in a converted Victorian stables and packed full of quirky miscellaneous items, the Sixpenny Tap has established itself at the heart of the local community. With the brewery located next door, its popular range of ales is served with pride and enthusiasm. The pub hosts many successful and colourful community and charity events in the extensive courtyard, with a warm welcome for all who visit. This is a real countryside gem set within picturesque farmland, and even has its own Tardis.
Q P

Dorchester

Blue Raddle

9 Church Street, DT1 1JN
12-3 (not Mon), 6.30-11; 12-11 Sat; 12-10.30 Sun
(01305) 267762 blueraddle.co.uk
Dartmoor Jail Ale; Otter Bitter; St Austell Tribute; 2 changing beers (sourced regionally; often Bristol Beer Factory, Flowerpots)
Town-centre pub with a comfortable and cosy ambience and a friendly and enthusiastic landlord and staff, popular with a wide age range. Well-kept beers and a good selection of guest ales are complemented by a range of ciders. Locally sourced food is cooked and served to order lunchtimes Wednesday to Saturday and evenings Thursday to Saturday. The walls are covered in

interesting and quirky pictures including Private Eye covers in the Gents. Folk music sessions feature regularly. No children are allowed but dogs are welcome. Q

Convivial Rabbit

Trinity House, Trinity Street, DT1 1TT

closed Mon & Tue; 12-10 Wed & Thu; 12-11 Fri & Sat; 3-10.30 Sun convivialrabbit.co.uk

6 changing beers (sourced nationally)

Popular cosy and convivial pop-up micropub with a changing choice of around six real ales of varying styles on gravity from micro and independent British breweries, as well as local ciders, wines and spirits. Run by friendly and knowledgeable licensees, the pub is tucked away down an alley to the left of Pennywise, but is well worth seeking out when visiting Dorchester town centre. It hosts folk music sessions on Sunday evenings.

Q

Duchess of Cornwall

12 Queen Mother Square, Poundbury, DT1 3BW

8am-11.30; 9am-10.30 Sun (01305) 757569

duchessofcornwall.co.uk

Hall & Woodhouse Badger Best Bitter, Fursty Ferret, Tanglefoot

Built in 2016 by the Duchy of Cornwall but operated by Hall & Woodhouse, this pub in the heart of Poundbury is named after the Duchess of Cornwall at the request of the Prince of Wales and was opened by the Prince and Duchess. The pub is split across three floors with areas incorporating different styles called the dining room, pantry, common room and bar. The pub also has 20 Georgian-style rooms.

Royal Oak

20 High West Street, DT1 1UW

8am-midnight (1am Fri & Sat) (01305) 755910

Greene King Abbot; Ruddles Best Bitter; Sharp's Doom Bar; 6 changing beers (sourced nationally; often Dorset, Otter, Wychwood)

A busy town-centre Wetherspoon pub offering a wide selection of frequently changing local and national ales on handpump, with regular beer festivals adding to the range. The pub offers a full food menu and is open for breakfast daily, welcoming children and families. It has a number of separate areas for both diners and drinkers. To the rear is a sunny patio area with wheelchair access to the main internal area.

Q

Gillingham

Buffalo

2 Lydford Lane, SP8 4NJ (100yds S of B3081)

12-3 (not Mon), 5.30-11; 12-7.30 Sun (01747) 823759

ristorantedamassimo.co.uk

Hall & Woodhouse Fursty Ferret, Tanglefoot; 1 changing beer (often Hall & Woodhouse)

This traditional old stone pub was formerly the Drum & Monkey. It is tucked away on a side road opposite the old Matthews Brewery which closed in the 1960s. The pub has been extended and refurbished to capitalise on the large car park, beautiful garden and patio areas, and now caters for up to 60 diners while retaining a well-used public bar. The restaurant trades as Ristorante Da Massimo. P

Phoenix

High Street, SP8 4AY

10-11; 11-midnight Sat; 11-11 Sun (01747) 823277

Bath Ales Gem; St Austell Proper Job; Sharp's Doom Bar

Originally a 15th century coaching inn when it had its own brewery and stables. Following a fire in the 17th century it was rebuilt and renamed the Phoenix. It has an open-plan layout with a dining area to one side and an open fire. Good-value pub grub plus specials are served lunchtimes Monday to Friday, plus a breakfast menu and traditional Sunday lunch. There is a small car park to the rear and two public car parks within walking distance.

P (X2,X4)

Langton Matravers

King's Arms

27 High Street, BH19 3HA

12-11 (01929) 422979

Ringwood Razorback; 3 changing beers (sourced nationally)

Dating back to 1743, this Purbeck stone-built pub, with original flagstone floors, has many quirky little rooms off a central bar area, and a suntrap rear garden. The seaside town of Swanage with its steam railway is close by, as are many fine walks where you can explore the Purbecks and the South West Coast Path. A dog- and family-friendly pub serving fine pub food and well chosen ales, this is a magnet both for locals and visitors.

Q (40)

Longburton

Rose & Crown

DT9 5PD

12-3 (not Mon), 6-11; 12-3, 6-10.30 Sun

(01963) 210202 roseandcrownlongburton.com

5 changing beers (often Sharp's)

This lovely thatched 17th-century coaching inn is a fascinating blend of traditional beams, stone flags and open fireplaces, set off by contemporary decor. A free house, it offers one beer from Sharp's and four constantly rotating regional and local beers. Traditional pub food is served in the bar and restaurant (booking essential on Sundays). There is a large beer garden plus two B&B rooms in a separate building. Real cider is available in summer. Open all day on bank holidays.

Q P (X11)

Lyme Regis

Cellar 59

57/58 Broad Street, DT7 3QF

closed Mon & Tue; 4-10 Wed & Thu; 12-11 Fri & Sat; 12-8.30 Sun (01297) 445086 cellar59.co.uk

4 changing beers (sourced nationally; often Gyle 59)

The beer house and brewery tap for the Gyle 59 brewery, situated 10 miles away. Beers from Gyle 59 and guests are unfined and joined by real cider and craft keg ales. Check the website for beer lists, tasting notes and events or, better still, just visit. There is a bottle shop on-site selling beers from around the world. The bar stays open longer when busy and is open on Tuesdays in summer. Children are welcome before 7pm.

Nag's Head L

32 Silver Street, DT7 3HS
11.30-11 (midnight Fri); 11-midnight Sat; 11-10.30 Sun
☎ (01297) 442312 nagsheadlymeregis.com
Otter Bitter, Ale; 2 changing beers (sourced regionally; often Exeter, Hanlon's, Yeovil Ales) [H]
Popular community-focused locals' pub away from the seafront. Two changing guest ales are usually LocAle and pale and hoppy in style. A woodburner makes it cosy in winter, and the large patio and garden are busy in summer. Live music is hosted most Saturdays and a big screen shows most major sporting events. There is a meat raffle on a Friday night. ❀ ♣

Marnhull

Blackmore Vale Inn

Burton Street, DT10 1JJ
closed Mon; 12-2.30, 6-10.30; 11.30-10.30 Sat; 12-3, 7-10.30 Sun ☎ (01258) 820701
St Austell Tribute; 1 changing beer (sourced regionally; often Bath Ales, Otter, Wriggle Valley) [H]
Refurbished in 2018, this 15th-century building retains some character features and has a spacious bar area with a woodburner stove and low beams. A separate dining area leads off the bar. A Wriggle Valley beer is always available. Outside there is a stable block which has space for camp beds in the loft. An extension is being built, with plans for a bottle store and microbrewery. Music night is Friday, quiz night is Sunday. Q❀ ♣P (X4)

Middlemarsh

Hunter's Moon

DT9 5QN
10.30-2.30, 6-10.30; 10.30-11 Sat; 10.30-10.30 Sun
☎ (01963) 210966 hunters-moon.org.uk
Butcombe Original; Cerne Abbas Ale; 1 changing beer (sourced nationally; often Sandbanks, Timothy Taylor) [H]
Welcoming mid 8th-century former coaching inn roughly halfway between Sherborne and Dorchester, serving locally sourced home-cooked food and regional real ales. The guest ale changes every week (every few days in summer). There is an enclosed garden with ample seating next to the large car park. Eight en-suite bedrooms are available, mainly on the ground floor. Closing time may vary depending on custom.
Q❀ ♣P (X11)

Pamphill

Vine Inn ★

Vine Hill, BH21 4EE (off B3082)
11-3, 7-10.30 (11 Thu-Sat); 12-3, 7-10.30 Sun
☎ (01202) 882259
2 changing beers (sourced regionally; often Plain, Sixpenny) [H]/[G]
Quintessential country pub owned by the National Trust and managed by the same family for 119 years – the current landlady has been here for over 30 years. The small bar nestles between two cosy rooms and offers a welcoming atmosphere. Outside, the large suntrap patio and garden provide a relaxing place to enjoy a drink. Ploughman's and sandwiches are served at lunchtime. This multi award-winning rural gem features in CAMRA's National Inventory of Historic Pub Interiors. Q❀ ♣P

Piddletrenthide

Poachers Inn

DT2 7QX
12-11.30 ☎ (01300) 348358 thepoachersinn.co.uk
Morland Old Speckled Hen; Ruddles County [H]
A quiet family pub with a friendly welcome and two permanent real ales, renowned for its good food sourced from local suppliers. The bar is a mix of traditional and modern, set on split levels. There is a 17th-century restaurant, plus accommodation in 21 rooms arranged around a central courtyard, with a pool for the summer months. Outside, there is a riverside garden and plenty of parking.
Q❀ ♣P

Poole

Barking Cat Alehouse

184 Ashley Road, Upper Parkstone, BH14 9BY
12 (5 Mon)-11; 12-midnight Fri & Sat ☎ (01202) 258465
8 changing beers (sourced regionally) [H]
A bustling alehouse serving an interesting range of eight ales from local and national microbreweries alongside six ciders, all on handpull. There are also 10 craft keg lines, providing an excellent range for all beer tastes. Customers are welcome to bring in a takeaway – there is a Chinese next door. The large function room has a pool table and dartboards. Entertainment includes a quiz night on alternate Thursdays, Scalextric racing night on the first Friday of the month, and live music on Saturday night. ♣

Bermuda Triangle

10 Parr Street, Lower Parkstone, BH14 0JY
12-11 (midnight Fri & Sat) ☎ (01202) 748047
bermudatrianglepub.com
4 changing beers (sourced nationally; often Dark Star, Oakham, Sharp's) [H]
This vibrant, busy pub is decorated to reflect the Bermuda Triangle story. The single-room bar is on three levels, but look out for the hidden stairway leading to the snug upstairs, open at weekends. The bar has four handpumps offering an ever-changing range of ales sourced locally and throughout the UK, alongside speciality lagers and foreign beers. The covered patio area is occasionally used for barbecues in summer. Live music often features at weekends. ❀

Brewhouse

68 High Street, BH15 1DA
11-11; 11.30-11 Sun ☎ (01202) 685288
Frome Same Again, Beer; 3 changing beers (sourced nationally; often Dark Star, Oakham, VOG) [H]
This multi award-winning pub is a long-established feature of Poole High Street, and a reliable source of interesting ales from Frome Brewery and well-chosen ales from national microbreweries. Real cider is also available. Entering from the High Street you find tables in the window, and past the busy bar area is a space for pool and darts. Dogs are welcome in this no-frills traditional community pub, which offers a warm welcome to locals and visitors alike. ❀ ♣

Poole Arms ✔

19 The Quay, BH15 1HJ
11-11; 12-11 Sun ☎ (01202) 673450 poolearms.co.uk
Dorset Jurassic; Flack Manor Flack's Double Drop; Ringwood Fortyniner; St Austell Proper Job; 1 changing beer (sourced regionally) [H]

Originating from 1635 and steeped in history, this distinctive green-tiled pub on the quayside is popular with locals and tourists alike. Pews, the bar and wood-panelled walls adorned with old Poole photographs dominate the cosy single-room interior, while bench seating at the front provides a great place to watch activities taking place on the quay. A fifth beer is available during the busier summer months. This is one of the best places in the area to enjoy locally sourced seafood.
Q❀◐◑≹🚌

Portland

Britannia

17 Fortuneswell, DT5 1LP
⏲ 11-11 (2am Fri & Sat); 12-11 Sun ☎ (01305) 820159
2 changing beers (sourced regionally; often Bath Ales, Branscombe Vale, St Austell) Ⓗ
Small one-bar pub frequented by locals, situated at the top end of Fortuneswell. The two changing beers are accompanied by a real cider, usually from Cheddar Valley. Food is served 11-5pm Monday to Saturday. Live music plays on Friday evening and Sunday afternoon, and a meat raffle is held on Sunday evening. There is a beer garden at the rear of the bar. Free public car parks are nearby.
❀◐Λ♣●🚌(1,701)🐾

George Inn ✔

133 Reforne, Easton, DT5 2AP
⏲ 12 (3 Mon & Tue)-11; 12-10 Sun ☎ (01305) 820011
Greene King Abbot; 3 changing beers (sourced nationally; often Otter, Sharp's, Timothy Taylor) Ⓗ
A friendly, family-oriented local dating from the mid-18th century. It has four separate bar and dining areas, and a large enclosed beer garden. Food is available daily Thursday to Sunday – Sunday roasts are popular, as is the Thursday evening curry and quiz. There are usually three constantly rotated guest ales on offer. Live music plays on some Saturday evenings and Sunday afternoons. A popular beer festival is held annually around St George's Day. 🐴❀◐◑●🚌(1,701)🐾📶

Preston

Bridge Inn

Bridge Inn Lane, DT3 6BD (in a valley just off A353)
⏲ 12-midnight ☎ (01305) 833380
Dartmoor Jail Ale; 2 changing beers (often Jennings, Ringwood) Ⓗ
Traditional village inn built in the 18th century alongside the River Jordan, surrounded by stone cottages. The entrance leads to the lounge with its single bar; to the left is a snug with dartboard, to the right is a pool table. The separate restaurant serves traditional pub fare. Outside, the extensive beer garden has a children's play area. There is a paved path from the car park providing level access to the pub. Q🐴❀◐◑Λ♣P🚌🐾📶

Salway Ash

Anchor Inn Ⓛ

DT6 5HU (on B3162)
⏲ 7-11 Mon & Tue; 12-2, 7-11 Wed, Thu & Sat; 12-2, 7-midnight Fri; 12-4, 7-11 Sun ☎ (01308) 488398
Otter Bitter; 1 changing beer (sourced regionally; often Black Tor, St Austell, Sharp's) Ⓗ
Located in rural Dorset walking country, yet just four miles from the sea, this village pub has a bar and separate lounge warmed by real fires. Traditional pub games include darts, table skittles and cribbage. A folk sing-around is held on the fourth Tuesday of the month. At least three real ciders are available in the summer.
Q❀🛏♿Λ♣●P🚌(CB3,6A)🐾📶

Sandford Orcas

Mitre Inn

DT9 4RU
⏲ 11.30-2.30 (not Mon), 7-11; 12-3, 7-10.30 Sun
☎ (01963) 220271 🌐 mitreinn.co.uk
Sharp's Doom Bar; 2 changing beers (sourced nationally; often Church End) Ⓗ
Run by the same couple since 1992, the Mitre is a homely, family-friendly pub with a cosy bar and separate restaurant area. There are flagstoned floors throughout, but mind your head on the door lintels. The guest beers are well kept and change regularly. Beer festivals take place twice a year. Booking is recommended for Sunday lunch. The pretty elevated garden at the rear is accessed via steps. Q🐴❀🛏◐◑♣P🚌(19)🐾📶

Shaftesbury

Ship Inn 🏆 ✔

24 Bleke Street, SP7 8JZ
⏲ 1-midnight (1am Fri); 12-1am Sat; 12-midnight Sun
☎ (01747) 853219
Butcombe Original; Sixpenny IPA; 2 changing beers Ⓗ
Stone-built town pub at the top of the steep Tout Hill. The single bar serves four different areas – the main bar, a games room with pool, darts, fruit machine and jukebox, a snug with an open fire, and a newly refurbished lounge bar. Outside there is a sunny patio and covered smoking area. No cooked food is available but you can order from local takeaways or bring your own. Local CAMRA Pub of the Year 2019. ❀●🚌🐾📶

Sixpenny Handley

Penny Tap

The Sports Pavilion, SP5 5NJ
⏲ closed Sun-Tue; 4.30-7 Wed & Thu (7.30 Fri); 2-6 Sat
🌐 thepennytap.co.uk
4 changing beers (often Brew Shack, Sixpenny, Wriggle Valley) Ⓖ
When the Sixpenny Brewery moved out of the village to larger premises elsewhere, the brewery tap also closed. A group of locals worked hard to establish a suitable outlet to fill the void and opted for the sports pavilion, creating a bar and cellar. It provides a focus for village sports and social events. A wide range of beer from local microbreweries is on offer. Opening times may be extended when events are held locally. Λ●P

Stoborough

King's Arms

3 Corfe Road, BH20 5AB (on B3075)
⏲ 11-3, 5.30-midnight; 11-midnight Fri & Sat; 12-midnight Sun ☎ (01929) 552705 🌐 thekingsarms-stoborough.co.uk
Isle of Purbeck Best Bitter; Ringwood Razorback; 2 changing beers (sourced nationally; often Plain) Ⓗ
This attractive, historic thatched pub stands at the gateway to the Isle of Purbeck. Formerly a butcher's shop, the 17th-century village inn hosted Cromwell's troops in 1642. An excellent menu of

both modern and traditional classics is served in the beamed bar and restaurant. Four handpumps dispense two regular beers and two well-chosen guests. The garden and patio area are a fantastic place to relax and enjoy the summer sunshine, and host the annual beer festivals and bonfire party. Q🐴❀◑♿▲P🚌(40)🐾📶

Stoke Abbott

New Inn Ⓛ ✔
DT8 3JW
⏲ closed Mon; 12-3 (not Tue), 6-11; 12-3 Sun
☎ (01308) 868333 🌐 newinnstokeabbott.co.uk
Palmers Copper Ale, Dorset Gold Ⓗ
Comfortable 17th-century inn with an impressive fireplace, in the heart of a picturesque village. The bar's unusual thatched roof reflects the thatch covering the building outside. Good-quality freshly cooked food is offered, with ingredients sourced locally where possible. The pub hosts themed events throughout the month including a quiz night, pie and a pint night and steak night. It can get busy during the tourist season. Q🐴❀◑♣P🐾

Stourpaine

White Horse Inn ✔
Shaston Road, DT11 8TA
⏲ 12-11 (midnight Fri); 10.30-midnight Sat
☎ (01258) 453535 🌐 whitehorse-stourpaine.co.uk
5 changing beers (sourced regionally; often Flack Manor, Gritchie, Sixpenny) Ⓗ
Dating back to the early 18th century, two cottages were joined to make this attractive open-plan pub in the heart of the community. It contains the local shop and post office. Five changing beers, mainly sourced locally, and three Cranborne Chase ciders, are available alongside an excellent, reasonably priced food menu. This atmospheric country gem has a cosy interior, with woodburners adding warmth in winter. In summer the attractive garden and outside drinking areas are popular. Live music features occasionally. Dogs are welcome and have their own firkin of water. 🐴❀◑♣🍎P🚌(X3)🐾

Stourton Caundle

Trooper
Golden Hill, DT10 2JW (½ mile E of A357) ST71491495
⏲ closed Mon; 12-2 (2.30 Sat), 7-11; 12-3.30, 7-11 Sun
☎ (01963) 362405 🌐 thetrooperinn.co.uk
3 changing beers Ⓗ
Stone-built, single-room community pub with a separate function room/skittle alley. There is an attached camping and caravan site and children's play area next to the beer garden. Good food is served lunchtimes and early evenings including a popular Friday fish and chips night. There are two guest ales and a farmhouse cider. An annual beer festival is held in the spring. Dogs and walkers are welcome. A former CAMRA Regional Pub of the Year. Q❀◑▲♣🍎P🐾

Stratton

Saxon Arms
20 The Square, DT2 9WG
⏲ 11-2.30, 5.30-11; 11-midnight Fri & Sat; 12-midnight Sun
☎ (01305) 260020 🌐 thesaxon-stratton.co.uk
Butcombe Original; Timothy Taylor Landlord; 2 changing beers (sourced nationally; often Otter, St Austell) Ⓗ
A thatched inn built of stone and flint in 2001. Set in the village square, with the church and village hall nearby, it is the hub of the community and offers a warm, friendly welcome. Four ales are available plus cider and a decent wine list. There is locally sourced food and a real fire in winter. Dogs are welcome, but not in the restaurant area. During August it stays open all day from 11.30am. Q🐴❀◑♿♣🍎P🐾📶

Swanage

Black Swan Ⓛ ✔
159-161 High Street, BH19 2NE
⏲ 5.30-11; 12-11 Sun ☎ (01929) 423846
🌐 blackswanswanage.co.uk
Dorset Knob; 2 changing beers (often Sharp's, Skinner's, Timothy Taylor) Ⓗ
Traditional Grade II-listed pub on the historic High Street in the heart of Swanage. It has two bars with stone floors and log fires, and serves three well-kept ales – the locally produced Dorset Knob is named after a local biscuit. The pub is renowned for its quality food and booking is recommended. The suntrap garden is the perfect place to enjoy the last of the evening sunshine. Swanage station is the terminus of the steam railway. Q🐴❀◗⇌🚌(40,50)🐾

Red Lion
63 High Street, BH19 2LY
⏲ 11-11; 12-11 Sun ☎ (01929) 423533
🌐 redlionswanage.co.uk
Hop Back GFB; Otter Bitter; Sharp's Doom Bar; Timothy Taylor Landlord; 2 changing beers (sourced nationally) Ⓖ
Traditional 17th-century inn in the heart of the town, serving up to six ales on gravity from the ground-floor cellar behind the public bar. A large selection of real ciders and perries is a big draw, with the range displayed on blackboards in both bars. The lounge has a restaurant area where quality food is served, with curry and steak nights always popular. The large, partly covered garden is busy throughout the year. Q🐴❀🛏◑⇌♣🍎P🚌(40,50)🐾📶

Upwey

Royal Standard
700 Dorchester Road, DT3 5LA
⏲ 12-3, 5.30-11; 12-11 Sat & Sun ☎ (01305) 812558
🌐 theroyalstandardupwey.co.uk
Butcombe Original; 3 changing beers (sourced nationally; often Bath Ales, Fine Tuned, Yeovil Ales) Ⓗ
Situated on the outskirts of Weymouth, the pub is popular with locals and visitors for its excellent real ales and food. The U-shaped wood-panelled bar has a cosy lounge on one side and a tall table and stool arrangement on the other. There is an outdoor seating area and a car park to the rear. The pub hosts an annual beer festival and a sausage and cider festival. Occasionally a real cider in a box is available. Opening times are extended during the summer holidays. 🐴❀◑♣🍎P🚌(10)🐾📶

Wareham

Horse & Groom ✓
St John's Hill, BH20 4LZ
🕓 11-11; 12-10.30 Sun ☎ (01929) 552222
3 changing beers (sourced regionally; often Palmers) Ⓗ
Situated in the heart of historic Wareham, this comfortable, airy, open-plan pub has two real fires. A free house, it offers customers a range of three ales plus real ciders, sourced both locally and regionally, with Palmers ales among the favourites. Traditional, well-cooked pub food is served every day. A pleasant garden area can be found tucked away at the rear. Live music plays occasionally, making this a pub for all.
🛏️❀🌙◑●🚬(40,X54)🐾🐾 🛜

King's Arms ✓
41 North Street, BH20 4AD
🕓 12-11 (10.30 Sun) ☎ (01929) 552503
⊕ kingsarmswareham.co.uk
5 changing beers (sourced nationally; often Exmoor, Otter, St Austell) Ⓗ
This traditional thatched inn has its roots in the 1500s and survived the Great Fire of 1762. The flagstone-floored public bar is adorned with interesting artefacts including old armament shell casings. There is a dedicated dining area with an excellent range of home-cooked food on offer (served daily), a drinking corridor and a large garden to the rear with a covered area for smokers. The five ever-changing guest beers are usually from the West Country. Live music often features at weekends. Q🛏️❀🌙◑≥●🚬(40,X54)🐾🐾 🛜

West Lulworth

Lulworth Cove Inn ⓛ
Main Road, BH20 5RQ
🕓 11-10.30 ☎ (01929) 400333 ⊕ lulworth-coveinn.co.uk
Badger Best Bitter, Tanglefoot; 2 changing beers (often Badger) Ⓗ
Set in the Natural World Heritage Site of Lulworth Cove on the Jurassic Coast, the pub is almost 400 years old and has links to King Henry VIII, Napoleon and Thomas Hardy. Originally a mail stagecoach stop on the road from Wareham, it was later a haven for smugglers who brought ashore French lace, brandy and other contraband. It now has a comfortable, contemporary interior with large windows overlooking an attractive seating area outside, with views towards the cove. Accommodation is in 12 nautical-themed rooms.
🛏️❀🛏️◑🐾 🛜

West Parley

Owl's Nest
196 Christchurch Road, BH22 8SS
🕓 11.30-2.30 (not Mon), 5-11; 11.30-2.30, 6-midnight Sat; 12-3, 6-10 Sun ☎ (01202) 572793
⊕ theowlsnest-westparley.com
4 changing beers (sourced regionally) Ⓗ
Charming and welcoming, this Tudor-style building with beamed ceilings and a woodburner has a comfortable vibe. Decorated with numerous adornments, owls feature heavily among miniatures, jugs and plates. Four handpumps dispense well-chosen local and regional ales. A beer and home-made pie festival has become an early-in-the-year favourite. There is occasional live music, with an Irish session on the first Thursday of the month. Popular for its excellent home-made food, booking is recommended for diners.
🛏️◑👤P🚬(13,X6)🐾 🛜

West Stour

Ship Inn
SP8 5RP
🕓 12-3, 6-11; 12-midnight Sat; 12-11 Sun
☎ (01747) 838640 ⊕ shipinn-dorset.com
3 changing beers Ⓗ
Once a coaching inn, this popular roadside pub has views across the Blackmore Vale. The public bar features a flagstone floor and the separate light and airy restaurant area has stripped oak floorboards. There is a patio and large garden at the rear. This friendly pub is renowned for superb home-cooked food (no meals Sun eve) and comfortable accommodation. Six local ciders usually sit alongside the three ales. Dogs are welcome in the bar. An annual beer festival is held in the summer. Q❀🛏️◑♣●P🐾 🛜

Weymouth

Dolphin Hotel
67 Park Street, DT4 7DE
🕓 10-midnight (2am Sat); 11-midnight Sun
☎ (01305) 786751 ⊕ dolphinhotelweymouth.co.uk
Hop Back Crop Circle, Summer Lightning Ⓗ
A Hop Back Brewery pub close to the railway station, local bus routes and only a few minutes' walk from the beach. The pub is light and airy, divided into two rooms – the rear is a family room with a pool table and a large TV screen for sports. Live music plays on Sunday. 🛏️🛏️≥♣🚬🐾 🛜

Globe Inn
24 East Street, DT4 8BN
🕓 11-1am ☎ (01305) 786061
Dartmoor Jail Ale; St Austell Cornish Best Bitter, Proper Job; Sharp's Doom Bar; 2 changing beers (sourced regionally; often Cerne Abbas, Palmers) Ⓗ
Free house with a friendly welcome, tucked away on a street corner just 30 yards from the iconic harbourside. The Globe is only a short distance from the town centre, the beach and the esplanade, and offers a distinct change from the packed waterside. There is a jukebox and a separate games room with pool table, darts and pub games. A fun quiz is held on Sunday afternoon. Guest ales are not always available in the low season. The cider is Thatchers Cheddar Valley.
🛏️♣●🚬🐾 🛜

William Henry ✓
1 Frederick Place, DT4 8HQ
🕓 7am-midnight (1am Fri & Sat) ☎ (01305) 763730
Greene King Abbot; Ruddles Best Bitter; Sharp's Doom Bar; 5 changing beers (sourced nationally; often Dorset, Piddle, Thornbridge) Ⓗ
A popular Wetherspoon pub with enthusiastic management, conveniently located in the town centre close to main transport links. There is an excellent range of ales, with three regulars and at least five guests, plus ciders. The bars are on two levels but accessibility is good, including toilets. Family-friendly and appealing to all ages, the pub was built in the gardens of the summer residence of Prince William Henry, Duke of Gloucester, and brother of George III, hence the name.
🛏️◑👤≥●🚬🐾 🛜

Whitchurch Canonicorum

Five Bells Inn 🄻 ✔
DT6 6RH
✪ closed Mon; 6.30-11 Tue; 12-2.30, 7-11
☎ (01297) 489262
Palmers Copper Ale, IPA, 200; 1 changing beer (sourced locally; often Palmers) 🄷
A hidden gem nestled in the stunning Marshwood Vale, the pub gets its name from the church which originally had a five-bell peal. Traditional food is served, prepared using locally sourced produce. The pub is children- and dog-friendly, with a large beer garden and a seven-acre campsite with shower and toilet block. Winter opening times are listed above, but the pubs opens all day every day in summer. However, times can vary so please call ahead. Q🐴❀◖◗⛺♣🍎P🐾📶

Wimborne

Green Man ✔
1 Victoria Road, BH21 1EN
✪ 11-11 Mon; 10-11 (midnight Fri & Sat); 10-10.30 Sun
☎ (01202) 881021 🌐 greenmanwimborne.com
Wadworth IPA, 6X, Swordfish 🄷
An 18th-century one-bar inn with open-plan drinking areas, a cosy woodburner and a separate restaurant, ideally located within easy walking distance of the centre of Wimborne. Excellent food, including breakfast, is served until 4pm, with a roast on Sunday. The garden has a marvellous floral display in summer, and a partially covered patio leading to the barn where pool and pub games are played. Please step over the green man when entering the pub. 🐴❀◖♣🍎P🚌(3,13)🐾📶

Taphouse Wimborne
11 West Borough, BH21 1LT
✪ 11-11 ☎ (01202) 911200 🌐 thetaphousewimborne.co.uk
Sharp's Doom Bar; 6 changing beers (sourced nationally; often Brew Shack, Eight Arch, Sixpenny) 🄶
Close to the historic town centre, the centrepiece of this narrow wood-panelled pub is the long hardwood bar, with beers served from the stillage behind. The pub offers up to 12 well-chosen real ales from local, regional and national breweries, including some popular favourites. Always a bustling community pub full of atmosphere, conversation rules in the cosy window seating area and the suntrap patio outside. Live acoustic music features on Sunday. ❀♣🍎🚌(3,13)🐾📶

Wool

Black Bear Inn
High Street, BH20 6BP
✪ 10.30-11 (midnight Fri & Sat); 10.30-10.30 Sun
☎ (01929) 405541 🌐 blackbear.website
House beer (by Flack Manor); 3 changing beers (sourced nationally) 🄷
Local CAMRA Rural Pub of the Year in 2018, the inn is located in the heart of Wool village and close to the many attractions of the Purbecks. It offers so much more than its four well-kept cask ales. Hearty home-cooked food is available in the front bar and in the restaurant area to the rear. Curry nights, quizzes, pub walks and a breakfast club all contribute to the Black Bear being a real community asset. The outside seating area is perfect for enjoying the summer sun. Q🐴❀◖◗⇌P🚌(X54)🐾📶

Worth Matravers

Square & Compass ★ 🄻
Weston Road, BH19 3LF (off B3069)
✪ 12-11 ☎ (01929) 439229 🌐 squareandcompasspub.co.uk
Hattie Brown's HBA, Moonlite; 3 changing beers (sourced regionally) 🄶
A real gem, this multi award-winning pub is on CAMRA's National Inventory of Historic Pub Interiors and has appeared in every edition of the Guide. It has been in the same family since 1907. Two rooms either side of a serving hatch convey an impression that little has changed over the years. The sea-facing garden offers fantastic views across the Purbecks, and fossils are displayed in the small adjacent museum. Pasties are available. Beer and cider festivals are held in October and November respectively. Local CAMRA Cider Pub of the Year 2018 for landlord Charlie's home-pressed cider.
Q🐴❀♿🍎🐾

Wyke Regis

Wyke Smugglers ✔
76 Portland Road, DT4 9AB
✪ 11-11 Mon-Wed; 12-midnight Thu & Sun; 12-1am Fri & Sat
☎ (01305) 760010 🌐 thewykesmugglers.com
St Austell Proper Job; 3 changing beers (sourced nationally; often Dorset, Marston's, Sharp's) 🄷
A large, lively local hosting many community events. Regional guest beers often come from the SIBA south-west region. Good food is served six days a week (no food Mon). In winter, the dining area is set around the woodburner. There are racks for bicycles at the front and the skittle alley doubles as a function room. Dogs are welcome. There is live music at weekends, a Sunday quiz night, and a beer and cider festival in the summer.
🐴❀◖◗♿⛺♣🍎P🚌(1,701)🐾📶

Yetminster

White Hart Inn 🍷 🄻
High Street, DT9 6LF
✪ 12-2.30 (not Mon), 5.30-11; 12-11 Fri & Sat; 12-6 Sun
☎ (01935) 872338 🌐 yetminsterwhitehart.pub
House beer (by Fine Tuned); 2 changing beers (sourced locally; often Piddle, Wriggle Valley, Yeovil Ales) 🄷
A 16th-century, Grade II-listed thatched free house in the middle of the village. The building is stone-built with mullion windows. Inside, the single-room bar area has low beams and an inglenook fireplace. Four ciders are served along with the beers, all from within a 20-mile radius of the pub. The skittle alley is themed after local band The Yetties. Local CAMRA Pub of the Year 2019.
Q🐴❀◖◗♿⛺⇌♣🍎P🐾📶

The Campaign for Real Ale has been fighting for nearly 50 years to save Britain's proud heritage of cask-conditioned ales, independent breweries, and pubs that offer a good choice of beer. You can help that fight by joining the campaign: see **www.camra.org.uk**

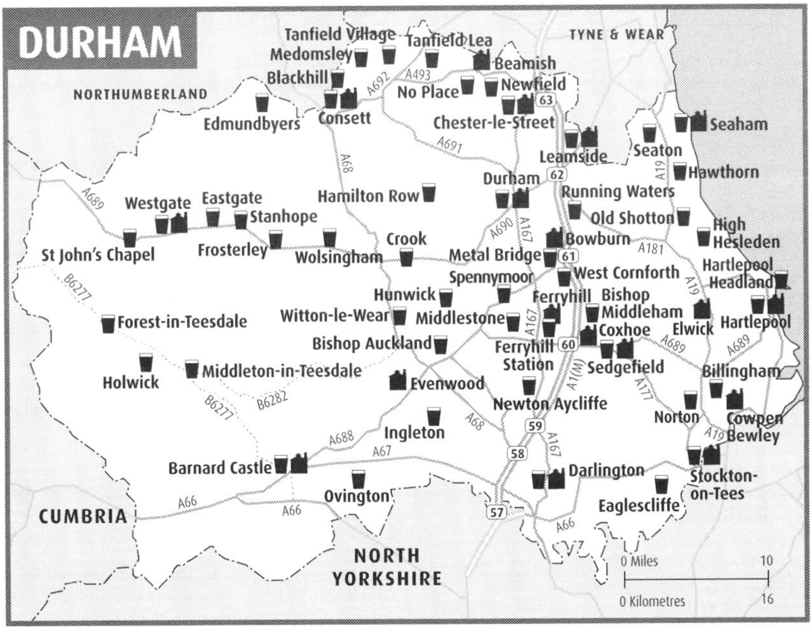

Co Durham incorporates part of the former county of Cleveland

Barnard Castle

Firkin Alley 🄻

2 Bakery Mews, DL12 8LZ (behind 20 Horsemarket, down alleyway next to YMCA charity shop)

⏲ closed Mon & Tue; 4-10.30 Wed-Fri; 2-10.30 Sat; 1-8 Sun
☎ 07825 727660

5 changing beers (sourced nationally) 🄷

A new micropub established in 2016 housed in an ex-bakery storeroom, difficult to find down an alley off the main street. It has a bar downstairs and a spacious and comfortable room upstairs, tastefully fitted with warm wood surrounds. It offers a good and ever-changing ale selection, mainly from the region, plus a changing choice of cider. Well worth a visit, with hospitable licensees and a friendly, regular and local clientele. Q❀🍏🚌(75,76)🐾

Old Well Inn 🄻 ✔

21 The Bank, DL12 8PH

⏲ 12-11 ☎ (01833) 690130 🌐 theoldwellinn.co.uk

Timothy Taylor Landlord; 4 changing beers (sourced locally) 🄷

The boundary of this 17th-century town-centre inn incorporates part of the medieval castle wall. The pub has a cosy front bar and a comfortable lounge, a separate restaurant and an airy conservatory, plus an enclosed beer garden. At least five well-kept beers are available including four guests from local micros, usually including Mithril. Excellent food is served daily, and there is accommodation in 10 rooms. Five-day beer festivals are held at Easter, October and Christmas. The Castle Players meet here. Q❀🛏◐♿🚌(75,76)🐾

Billingham

Billingham Catholic Club 🄻

37 Wolviston Road, TS23 2RU (on E side of old A19, just S of Roseberry Road roundabout, next to bus stop)

⏲ 7-midnight (1am Fri); 3-2am Sat; 12-midnight Sun
☎ (01642) 901143 🌐 billinghamcatholicclub.webs.com

3 changing beers 🄷

Now in its 11th year of continuous Guide recognition, this Victorian mansion and former school is a friendly club, renowned for its real beers and R&B/rock bands, where a genuine welcome awaits CAMRA members. Dedicated and enthusiastic volunteers ensure that the club's reputation for serving 150 different beers annually continues. Three beers and two ciders are normally on offer, with eight beers available throughout the popular bank holiday beer and music festivals. Local CAMRA Community Pub of the Year 2019. ❀♿♣🍏P🚌(35,36)🐾

Crafty Cock 🄻

113 Station Road, TS23 2RL (at N end of Station Rd among a row of shops)

⏲ 4-11; 12-11 Sat & Sun ☎ (01642) 881478

3 changing beers 🄷

This small, cosy bar is one of several recently opened micropub-style outlets in Old Billingham. Friendly and knowledgeable bar staff serve three beers, including offerings from local breweries, as well as real cider. Third-pint tasting bats are available. There is also an extensive gin menu. This increasingly popular bar has now become renowned locally for its varied live bands. Sunday lunches are served, with a takeaway and a local delivery service also available. ◐♿🍏P🚌(36,X9)

Bishop Auckland

Bay Horse

38-40 Fore Bondgate, DL14 7PE (just N of bus station)

⏲ 11-11 (1am Fri & Sat); 12-11 Sun ☎ (01388) 609765
🌐 dorbiere.co.uk/bay-horse

3 changing beers (sourced nationally; often Camerons) 🄷

There has been a pub on this site since 1530, and this lively, open-plan bar is a quiet relief from shopping during the week. With live music on Friday and Sunday and karaoke on Saturday, it becomes joyfully boisterous at the weekend, and is popular for televised sport. It retains its roots as a long-established, proper pub, with pub games teams, and an eclectic choice of ales.

Green Tree

Cockton Hill Road, DL14 6EN (close to Station Bridge)
4-midnight (1am Thu); 12-1am Fri & Sat; 12-midnight Sun
(01388) 663249
2 changing beers (sourced nationally) H
A large pub at the south end of the shopping street. It has a bar with pool table area, a spacious lounge, and a big garden patio with a covered smoking area to the rear. Popular for TV sport and the Tuesday quiz, it hosts occasional live music. Interesting football and music memorabilia adorn the walls alongside paintings of the town by local artist Gaz Miller.

Pollards L

104 Etherley Lane, DL14 6TU (just W of railway station)
6-midnight Mon; 12-1.30, 5-midnight; 12-3, 7-midnight Sun (01388) 603539 pollardsinn.business.site
Wainwright; 4 changing beers (sourced nationally; often Allendale, Consett, Marston's) H
This comfortable and busy establishment is a great combination of traditional pub and pleasant diner, 10-minutes' stroll from the town centre. Two of the four original areas, including the bar, boast open fires or logburners, while there is a spacious restaurant to the rear where the famous Sunday carvery can be enjoyed. A popular quiz on Sunday evening, good conversation and five well-kept ales top things off. QP

Bishop Middleham

Cross Keys L

9 High Street, DL17 9AR (1 mile from A177)
12 (2.30 Mon)-11 (01740) 651231 crosskeysbm.com
2 changing beers (sourced nationally) H
A busy family-run village inn with a good reputation for its food. It has a bar with a real fire, a lounge and a large restaurant at the back. The pub is opposite the remains of Forsters Brewery which closed in 1913 and it may well have been the tap house. The village has a series of walks exploring beautiful countryside and the remains of Bishop Middleham Castle. Q

Blackhill

Scotch Arms L

48 Derwent Street, DH8 8LZ
4-11; 1-1am Fri; 12-1am Sat; 10.30-10.30 Sun
(01207) 593709
Sharp's Atlantic; 3 changing beers (sourced nationally; often Big Lamp, Blackhill, Caledonian) H
A traditional community hostelry off the main street in Blackhill with a large L-shaped bar. The interior was freshened up to celebrate the licensee's 10-year anniversary in 2018. Up to four cask ales are on offer, always including local beers. The welcoming pub is home to pool and darts teams, and a local football team, and popular for sports TV. Charity nights and other live events often feature. Toasted sandwiches are available.

Chester-le-Street

Butchers Arms

Middle Chare, DH3 3QD (off Front St on left from Market Place)
11-11 (midnight Fri & Sat) (0191) 388 3605
butchersarms.org.uk
Jennings Cumberland Ale; Marston's Pedigree; 5 changing beers (sourced nationally; often Ringwood, Wainwright, Wychwood) H
A cosy pub acknowledged for the quality and quantity of its beers, selling seven cask ales from the Marston's range. The pub is also noted for its food, with home-cooking a speciality; Sunday lunches are popular and good value. Teas and coffees are also served. Dogs are welcome and it is convenient for the railway station and all buses through the town. Quiz night is Tuesday.
Q(21)

Masonic Centre

Station Road, DH3 3DU
7.30-11 (midnight Wed); 3.45-midnight Fri; 7.30-midnight Sat; 11.30-3.30, 7-11 Sun (0191) 388 4905
3 changing beers (sourced nationally; often Blackhill, Oakham, Roundhill) H
Guests are more than welcome at the Masonic Centre just off Front Street in the heart of the town. Press the buzzer on the front door and walk in. As well as three changing real ales, you will also find one of the biggest selections of single malt whisky in the area. Sunday lunches and Friday fish suppers are popular. P(21)

Smiths Arms L

Forge Lane, Castle Dene, DH3 4HE NZ299507
3-11; 12-11 Fri & Sat; 12-10.30 Sun (0191) 385 7559
7 changing beers (sourced nationally; often Dark Star, Maxim) H
Somewhat off the beaten track, this traditional pub has a small, cosy bar and a larger lounge, both with open fires. The beers are sourced by the landlord, with up to seven cask ales and a real cider, always including LocAle. A beer festival is held in May. The pub is reputed to be haunted. Voted local CAMRA branch Country Pub of the Year in 2017.
P(71,78)

REAL ALE BREWERIES

Barnard Castle Barnard Castle
Blackhill Chester-le-Street
Camerons Hartlepool
Castle Eden Seaham
Consett Ale Works Consett
Crafty Monkey Elwick
Crafty Pint Darlington
Durham Bowburn
Hill Island Durham
Hopburst Darlington
Hopper House Brew Farm Sedgefield (NEW)
Mad Scientist Darlington
McColl's Evenwood
Roundhill Cowpen Bewley
S43 Coxhoe
Saint's Row Darlington
Stables Beamish
Stockton Stockton on Tees
Three Brothers Stockton on Tees
Village Brewer: Brew 22 Darlington
Weard'ALE Westgate
Working Hand Leamside
Yard of Ale Ferryhill

Wicket Gate L ✓
193 Front Street, DH3 3AX
8am-midnight (2.30am Fri & Sat) ☎ (0191) 387 2960
Greene King Abbot; Ruddles Best Bitter; 5 changing beers (sourced nationally) Ⓗ
This modern Wetherspoon Lloyds No.1 bar's name acknowledges the strong connection the town has with cricket. Situated close to the town club and the county club ground at the Riverside, various items of cricket memorabilia decorate the walls. It is roomy inside, with a central oval-shaped bar with service on both sides, championing local beers. ★◖◗&≠♣●⌂(21)☎

Consett

Company Row L ✓
Victoria Road, DH8 5BQ
8am-midnight ☎ (01207) 585600
Greene King Abbot; Ruddles Best Bitter; 3 changing beers (sourced nationally) Ⓗ
Modern pub named after the rows of houses built by the Derwent Iron Company for its workers, which were mostly demolished in the mid-1920s. This spacious and well-decorated Wetherspoon establishment is a real asset to Consett town centre. An excellent beer selection, including local ales, and good food make this social pub popular with a wide clientele of all ages. ★❀◖◗&♣●⌂☎

Grey Horse ♔ L ✓
115 Sherburn Terrace, DH8 6NE
12-11 (11.30 Wed & Thu; midnight Fri & Sat)
☎ (01207) 502585 ⊕ consettaleworks.co.uk/the-grey-horse
Consett Red Dust, Steel Town Bitter, White Hot, Steelworkers Blonde; 5 changing beers (sourced nationally) Ⓗ
Traditional pub dating back to 1848. The interior comprises a lounge and L-shaped bar, with a wood-beamed ceiling. Consett Ale Works Brewery is located at the rear. Beer festivals are held twice a year, live entertainment is hosted on Thursday and a quiz on Wednesday. The coast-to-coast cycle route is close by. There is some bench seating outside at the front of the pub. Local CAMRA Town Pub of the Year 2019. ❀&●❀☎

Crook

Copper Mine L
26 High Jobs Hill, DL15 0UL
closed Mon; 12-2, 5-10.30 Tue-Thu; 12-2.30, 4.30-11 Fri; 12-11.30 Sat; 12-6 Sun ☎ (01388) 763333
⊕ copperminecrook.com
3 changing beers (sourced locally; often Allendale, Yard of Ale) Ⓗ
A comfortable family-run local on the edge of Weardale up the hill from Crook towards Durham. The refurbished interior is open plan but with distinct drinking and dining areas. Home-cooked quality food is available to cater for all tastes. The beers are nearly always from local breweries. ★❀◖P⌂(X46)❀☎

Horse Shoe L ✓
4 Church Street, DL15 9BG
8am-midnight (1am Fri & Sat) ☎ (01388) 744980
Greene King Abbot; Maxim Double Maxim; Ruddles Best Bitter; 6 changing beers (sourced nationally) Ⓗ
This busy and tasteful refurbishment has four interlinked drinking areas making up the main part

of the pub, with a pleasant sheltered patio to the side. There is the usual Wetherspoon acknowledgement of previous use, in this case a butcher's, in the metal bar top. Local history is reflected in the decor, with a surprise at the top of the stairs in the shape of old mining equipment. ★❀◖◗●⌂(X1,X46)☎

Darlington

Britannia L ✓
1 Archer Street, DL3 6LR (next to ring road W of town centre)
12-11 (9 Sun) ☎ (01325) 463787
Camerons Strongarm; Draught Bass; John Smith's Bitter; 3 changing beers (sourced nationally) Ⓗ
Warm, friendly, local CAMRA award-winning inn – a bastion of cask beer since 1859. The comfortable, traditional pub retains much of the appearance and layout of the private house it once was – a modestly enlarged bar and small parlour sit either side of a central corridor. Grade II-listed for its historic association, it was the birthplace of teetotal 19th-century publisher JM Dent. Three changing guest ales complement the three regular ales. ≠♣●P❀☎

Darlington Snooker Club L
1 Corporation Road, DL3 6AE (corner of Northgate)
12-11 (1am Sat) ☎ (01325) 241388
4 changing beers (sourced nationally) Ⓗ
First-floor, family-run and family-oriented private snooker club which in 2015 celebrated its centenary. A cosy, comfortable TV lounge is available for those not playing on one of the 10 top-quality snooker tables. Twice yearly, the club hosts a professional celebrity. Four guest beers from micros countrywide are stocked and two beer festivals are held annually. Frequently voted CAMRA Regional Club of the Year and a former National finalist, it welcomes CAMRA members on production of a membership card or copy of this Guide. ★◖≠●

Half Moon L
130 Northgate, DL1 1QS
12 (5 Wed)-11 ☎ (01325) 469965 ⊕ thecraftypint.co.uk
7 changing beers (sourced nationally) Ⓗ
Old-school pub just across the ring road from the town centre with friendly staff and customers creating a relaxed atmosphere. This local reopened in 2013 as a real ale pub following a long period of closure. It offers seven changing cask ales including brews from micros unusual for the area and occasional ales from the on-site Crafty Pint nano brewery. There is a library area to borrow and exchange books. ★❀&♣●❀☎

Hole in the Wall ✓
14-15 Horsemarket, DL1 5PT
11-11.30 (midnight Fri & Sat); 12-11 Sun
☎ (01325) 466720
7 changing beers (sourced nationally) Ⓗ
Recently refurbished pub with a fine Edwardian frontage, smart wooden interior and large windows overlooking the town's Market Place. Seating outside is pleasant for relaxing with a drink in the summer. A wide range of ales is stocked alongside a variety of spirits. There is a full menu of traditional pub food, with a big emphasis on pies. ★◖◗&≠❀☎

Number Twenty 2 Ⓛ ✔

22 Coniscliffe Road, DL3 7RG

🕐 12-11 (9 Mon); closed Sun ☎ (01325) 354590

Village Bull, Old Raby, White Boar; 7 changing beers (sourced nationally) Ⓗ

Town-centre ale house with a passion for cask beer and a winner of many CAMRA awards. Ales are dispensed from up to 16 handpumps, including a stout or porter, plus two real ciders and 10 draught European beers. Huge curved windows, stained-glass panels and a high ceiling give the interior an airy, spacious feel. To the rear is the in-house nano distillery and microbrewery producing gin, vodka and ale. Sandwiches and snacks are available at lunchtime. Home of Village Brewer beers, commissioned from Hambleton by the licensee. Q♞♿📶

ORB Micropub 🏆 Ⓛ

28 Coniscliffe Road, DL3 7RG

🕐 closed Mon & Tue; 5-10 Wed & Thu; 3-10.30 Fri; 12-10.30 Sat; 3-8 Sun ☎ 07903 237246

6 changing beers (sourced nationally) Ⓗ

Traditional micropub in a former beauty salon with no TV or loud music, the first of its kind in Darlington. This is a place to relax and engage in conversation, with friendly, knowledgeable staff. It provides six local real ales, two craft beers, two real ciders and a large range of single malt whiskies. ORB stands for Orchard Road Brewery. Local CAMRA Pub of the Year in 2018 & 2019. Q🍏🐾

Quakerhouse Ⓛ

2 Mechanics Yard, DL3 7QF (off High Row)

🕐 11-11 (midnight Fri & Sat) ☎ (01325) 245052

🌐 quakerhouse.co.uk

8 changing beers (sourced nationally) Ⓗ

Sixteen times local CAMRA Town Pub of the Year, and a former North-East Pub of the Year, this gem of a pub is located in one of the town's historic Yards. The lively bar offers eight handpulled guest beers from local and regional breweries and three changing real ciders. Friendly and welcoming, the pub is a popular music venue, catering for all tastes from acoustic to rock, with live music every Wednesday, as well as other nights, with free entry. Home to the Mad Scientist microbrewery. ✿♿♣🍏P🚌🐾📶

Durham

Colpitts Hotel

Colpitts Terrace, DH1 4EG

🕐 11-11; 12-10.30 Sun ☎ (0191) 386 9913

Samuel Smith Old Brewery Bitter Ⓗ

A refurbishment has given this late-Victorian pub a smart makeover, but it remains little changed from when it was first built and continues to thrive on its traditional charm. As with all Samuel Smith's pubs, the noise comes from the chatter of conversation rather than from music or TV. The unusual A-shaped building comprises a cosy snug, a pool room and the main bar area partially divided by a fireplace. If you want to take a step back in time, this is the pub for you. Q♞≢♣🚌🐾

Court Inn Ⓛ

Court Lane, DH1 3AW

🕐 11-11 (midnight Fri & Sat) ☎ (0191) 384 7350

🌐 courtinn.co.uk

Timothy Taylor Landlord; 5 changing beers (sourced nationally; often Maxim) Ⓗ

A busy venue with decor that reflects the location near the city's Crown Courts. Up to six real ales are on offer at any one time as well as two real ciders. A wide selection of food is served until 10.15pm daily. The pub is popular with locals and students alike, and offers a warm welcome to all visitors. ♞✿◐◑🍏🚌(6)🐾📶

Dun Cow Ⓛ ✔

37 Old Elvet, DH1 3HN

🕐 11.30-10.30 (11 Wed & Thu); 11-11 Fri & Sat; 12-9.45 Sun ☎ (0191) 386 9219 🌐 duncowdurham.com

Black Sheep Best Bitter; Castle Eden Ale; Moorhouse's White Witch Ⓗ

A Grade II-listed pub, parts of which date back to the 15th century. In 995AD, Lindisfarne monks searching for a resting place for the body of St Cuthbert came across a milkmaid looking for her lost cow. She directed them to Dun Holm (Durham), and the pub is named after the historic animal. There is a friendly front snug with a larger lounge to the rear. Three real ales are on offer. Q♞◐🚌(58,59)🐾📶

Half Moon Inn Ⓛ ✔

86 New Elvet, DH1 3AQ

🕐 11-11 (midnight Fri & Sat); 12-11 Sun ☎ (0191) 374 1918

🌐 thehalfmooninndurham.co.uk

Draught Bass; Durham White Gold; Sharp's Doom Bar; Timothy Taylor Landlord Ⓗ

Popular city-centre pub, reputedly named after the crescent-shaped bar that runs through it. It has traditional decor throughout, with photos of the pub at the beginning of the 20th century, including many from the Miners' Gala. The large beer garden overlooks the river. A friendly venue with a relaxed atmosphere, it offers a good selection of ales to locals and visitors to the city. ✿♿🚌(6)🐾📶

Head of Steam Ⓛ

Reform Place, DH1 4RZ (through archway from North Rd)

🕐 12-11 (midnight Fri & Sat) ☎ (0191) 383 2173

5 changing beers (sourced nationally; often Camerons, Leeds) Ⓗ

This recently refurbished, vibrant pub has a continental feel, attracting beer lovers of all ages. As well as five real ales, it offers an extensive choice of bottled beers from around the world and a range of real ciders. Tasting events are often held featuring a wide choice of ales and ciders. Excellent, good-value food is available and families are welcome during the day. ♞✿◐◑♿≢🍏🚌📶

Market Tavern Ⓛ ✔

27 Market Place, DH1 3NJ

🕐 11-midnight (12.30am Sat); 11-11 Sun ☎ (0191) 386 2069

Greene King IPA; 4 changing beers (sourced nationally; often Greene King, Maxim) Ⓗ

A busy city-centre pub in Durham's historic marketplace, offering a good selection of five local and national cask ales and one real cider. Despite refurbishments, the pub has managed to keep its traditional wooden alehouse appearance, and pictures of miners' banners take pride of place. Locals and visitors to the city are given a warm welcome, and good food based on pub classics is served until 9.30pm. Quiz night is Thursday. ♞✿◐◑≢🍏🚌📶

Old Elm Tree L
12 Crossgate, DH1 4PS
⏲ 11.30-11 (midnight Fri & Sat) ☎ (0191) 386 4621
Wychwood Hobgoblin; 5 changing beers (sourced nationally; often Great Corby, Marston's) H
One of Durham's oldest inns, dating back to at least 1600, with a friendly atmosphere attracting a good mix of locals, students and visitors to the city. The interior comprises an L-shaped bar and a top room linked by stairs. A good range of ales and home-cooked food is available. The pub hosts a Wednesday quiz (arrive early), and a folk group on Monday and Tuesday. A former local CAMRA Town Pub of the Year. ♞✿◐⇌●P⊟🐾≋

Station House L
North Road, DH1 4SE
⏲ 4-10.30; 12-11 Fri & Sat; 2-10.30 Sun
🌐 stationhousedurham.co.uk
4 changing beers (sourced nationally; often Abbeydale, Almasty, North Riding) G
An ever-changing range of local and national real ales and ciders is served straight from the cask directly through a hatch from the cold room. A dark beer is always available and a fifth ale is added at weekends. This is a quirky, friendly pub with a back-to-basics approach and an emphasis on conversation. The two rocking chairs in the window are highly sought after. Beer festivals are held in March and October. A regular CAMRA award winner and North-East Regional Cider Pub of the Year in 2017. Q♞♿⇌●▯⊟🐾≋

Tap & Spile L ✔
Front Street, Framwellgate Moor, DH1 5EE
⏲ 6-11; 5-11 Fri; 12-3, 6-11 Sat; 12-3, 7-10.30 Sun
☎ (0191) 386 5451
8 changing beers (sourced nationally; often Abbeydale, Adnams, Cullercoats) H
Offering an excellent range of eight constantly changing real ales, this is a popular pub for beer drinkers. There are two bars at one side while the other side can be partitioned into two —families are welcome in the side room until 9pm. Quiz night is Wednesday and folk music night is Thursday. The pub has a relaxed atmosphere with a warm welcome for locals and visitors from further afield. ♞●P⊟(21)🐾

Victoria Inn 🏆 ★ L
86 Hallgarth Street, DH1 3AS
⏲ 11.45-11; 12-10.30 Sun ☎ (0191) 386 5269
🌐 victoriainn-durhamcity.co.uk
Big Lamp Bitter; 4 changing beers (sourced nationally; often Durham, Fyne Ales, Wylam) H
This family-run Grade II-listed Victorian pub has remained almost unchanged since it was built in 1899, and the quaint decor, coal fires, cosy snug and genuine Victorian cash drawer help create an old-world feel. Ales are mainly from local breweries, with a wide selection of single malts also on offer. No meals are served but toasties are available. Voted local CAMRA City Pub of the Year for the 12th time in 2019, the Victoria is popular with locals, students and visitors to the city. Q♞🛏♣●⊟(6,PR2)🐾≋

Waiting Room L
Northbound Platform, Durham Railway Station, DH1 4RB
⏲ 11-10; 10-10 Fri-Sun ☎ (0191) 386 7773
Durham Magus; 2 changing beers (sourced locally; often Allendale, Durham, Yard of Ale) H
This attractive venue on Durham northbound platform is an interesting relaunch of the original 1872 Ladies' Waiting Room, out of use for many years other than as a storage facility. In keeping with the Grade II-listed status of the building, the design is traditional, with Chesterfield-style seating, original floorboards and fireplaces, wood panelling and a dark-wood bar. Three handpumps showcase local beers. Q♿⇌P⊟(40)🐾

Eaglescliffe

Cleveland Bay
718 Yarm Road, TS16 0JE (jct of A67 and A135, N of Tees bridge)
⏲ 11-1am ☎ (01642) 780275 🌐 clevelandbay.co.uk
Timothy Taylor Landlord; Wainwright; 2 changing beers H
A large three-roomed locals' pub under the stewardship of an enthusiastic licensee with an enviable reputation for serving fine premium bitters. Third-pint glasses and tasting notes are available for the four handpumps. On Fridays, the increasingly popular Blues at the Bay live music evenings feature a wide variety of bands of national and international repute. A free buffet lunch is served on Sunday. A former CAMRA branch Community Pub of the Year.
Q✿♿♣P⊟(7,17)🐾≋

Eastgate

Cross Keys L
DL13 2HW
⏲ 5-midnight; 12-midnight Sat & Sun ☎ (01388) 517234
🌐 crosskeyseastgate.co.uk
2 changing beers (sourced nationally; often Allendale) H
A proper family-run Weardale pub, popular with holidaymakers and locals. The ancient 17th-century building has a pleasant interior with a lively, welcoming bar and a restaurant providing relaxed dining. Allendale Brewery beers feature regularly. There is a beer garden to the rear. Comfortable B&B accommodation is available for those wishing to explore the beautiful surrounding countryside.
Q♞✿🛏◐▲♣P⊟(101)🐾

Edmundbyers

Baa L
Low House Haven, DH8 9NL
⏲ 4.30-10; 12-midnight Fri & Sat; 12-10 Sun
☎ (01207) 255651 🌐 thebaabar.com/thebaa
2 changing beers (sourced nationally; often Cullercoats) H
Former Youth Hostel Association building and now an independent hostel close to Derwent Reservoir, dating back to 1600 when it began life as an inn. The cycle sheds have been converted into a welcoming stone-floored micropub-style bar, offering two well-kept ales, invariably from local breweries and often produced especially for the pub. Opening hours may vary so check before travelling to avoid disappointment. Q♞🛏▲⊟🐾

Ferryhill Station

Surtees Arms L ✔
Chilton Lane, DL17 0DH
⏲ closed Mon; 4-11 Tue-Fri; 12-midnight Sat; 12-11 Sun
☎ (01740) 655724 🌐 thesurteesarms.co.uk

Yard of Ale One Foot in the Yard; 4 changing beers (sourced nationally) Ⓗ
Traditional pub serving local and national ales and ciders as well as beers from the on-site Yard of Ale Brewery (est 2008). Annual beer festivals are held in the summer and at Halloween. Live music and charity nights are regular events. Lunches are served on Sunday only. A large function room is available. A former regional CAMRA Pub of the Year and local branch Country Pub of the Year.
Q

Forest-in-Teesdale

Langdon Beck Hotel

DL12 0XP (on B6277, 8 miles NW of Middleton in Teesdale)
11-10.30 (closed winter Mon); 12-10.30 Sun
☎ (01833) 622267 langdonbeckhotel.com
Great North Eastern Rivet Catcher; Wainwright; 1 changing beer (sourced nationally) Ⓗ
Known as the Sportsman's Rest in the early 1800s, this pub is situated in the North Pennines, three miles from the spectacular High Force and Cauldron Snout waterfalls and close to the Pennine Way. The welcoming inn has long been a destination for walkers, fishermen and those seeking hospitality in scenic and peaceful surroundings, whether staying overnight or just long enough to enjoy the excellent food and drink. A beer festival is held over the late May bank holiday weekend.
Q♣P

Frosterley

Black Bull

Bridge End, DL13 2SL
closed Mon-Wed; 11-11 Thu-Sat; 11-5 Sun
☎ (01388) 527784 blackbullfrosterley.com
4 changing beers (sourced regionally; often Allendale, Wylam) Ⓗ
A truly unique, family-run pub next to the Weardale Railway and river, with four ales usually from local brewers, and up to four ciders and perries. Bare boards, stone flags featuring Frosterley marble, all manner of artefacts and antique furniture create a wonderful ambience. It offers high-quality, locally sourced food, and music, plays and story-telling. The outbuilding houses a peal of bells, visited by enthusiasts from across the country. Local CAMRA Country Cider Pub of the Year 2019. Q(Weardale)♣P(101)

Hamilton Row

Black Horse

DH7 9AU
3-10; 2-11 Fri; 12-11 Sat; 11-10 Sun ☎ (0191) 373 4576
2 changing beers (sourced nationally; often Castle Rock, Sonnet 43) Ⓗ
A friendly local with an open fire at one end and a glass-fronted fire at the other helping to create a warm, cosy atmosphere. Two well-kept real ales always include one from a local brewery. Good-value Sunday lunches are served. There is a pool table. An excellent pub for walkers, it is handily situated adjacent to the Deerness Valley Way.
Q♣P(52,725)

Hartlepool

Anchor Tap Room & Bottle Shop

Stockton Street, TS24 7QY (on A689, in front of Camerons Brewery) ☎ (01429) 868686
Camerons Strongarm; 2 changing beers Ⓗ
When Camerons Brewery discovered that it owned an adjacent derelict pub, they converted it into the brewery's tap and visitor centre. Now in its 16th successful year, after an extensive refurbishment it has been rebranded as a bar and bottle shop. Strongarm and the brewery's monthly specials are always available, together with an array of limited edition and continental bottled beers. Meetings, conferences and social events, as well as superb buffets, can all be arranged. P(1,36)

Causeway

Vicarage Gardens, Stranton, TS24 7QT (between Stranton Church and Camerons Brewery)
12-11 (midnight Thu & Fri); 11-midnight Sat
☎ (01429) 263000
Camerons Strongarm; 4 changing beers Ⓗ
Marvellous multi-roomed, red-brick Victorian building, dating from 1862, and Camerons' unofficial brewery tap for more than a century. The Causeway is now owned by Marston's, though the sales of Camerons Strongarm remain huge. Guest beers are Marston's monthly specials. Good-value bar snacks are available. The licensees host an eclectic mix of live music most evenings and on Sunday afternoon, while the local Arts Association meets here on Tuesday evening. A local CAMRA multi award winner. (1,36)

Hops & Cheese

9-11 Tower Street, TS24 7HH (100yds S of bus interchange/railway station)
closed Mon & Tue; 2-10 Wed & Thu; 12-11 Fri & Sat; 2-8 Sun
☎ 07704 660417 hopsandcheese.co.uk
3 changing beers Ⓗ
Run by enthusiastic hosts fulfilling a vision of bringing home a flavour of the contemporary tapas-style bars experienced on their continental holidays, this welcoming bar represents something modern, original and different. Three interesting beers and a real cider are available together with artisan cheeses and charcuterie, all served in a relaxed atmosphere. Meet the Brewer and Meet the Cheesemaker evenings are hosted, while newspapers, a book club, off-sales and low-key background music all enhance the experience.
(1,36)

Rat Race Ale House

Station Approach, Hartlepool Railway Station, TS24 7ED (on Platform 1)
12.02-2.15, 4.02-8.15; 12.02-9 Sat; closed Sun & Mon
☎ 07903 479378 ratracealehouse.co.uk
4 changing beers Ⓗ
The second micropub in the country, now celebrating 10 years of continuous Guide recognition, adheres to the original micropub norms – no fizzy lager or beer, no spirits or alcopops, no TV or jukebox, no one-arm bandit, and even no bar! Since opening in 2009, more than 1,800 beers, sourced from over 500 breweries, have been served direct to the table by the landlord himself. Two real ciders are also on offer, as well as top-quality crisps, nuts and scratchings. Reusable beer cartons are available for takeaways.
Q♣(1,36)

ENGLAND

Hartlepool Headland

Fisherman's Arms

Southgate, TS24 0JJ (on headland close to Fish Quay)
closed Mon; 2 (7 Wed)-11; 2-midnight Fri & Sat
07847 208599 thefishhartlepool.co.uk
Maxim Double Maxim; 3 changing beers
The Fish, a local CAMRA multi award-winner, is a friendly one-room locals' pub. Now free of tie, up to four beers are available, while a cider is served during the summer months. The pub's theme is Keeping Music Alive – it hosts well-supported open mic nights together with live music on Saturday. A popular quiz is held on Sunday. No jukebox, no TV, no one-armed-bandit. Two beer festivals, also with live music, are held annually. Winter opening hours may vary. Q (7)

Globe

26 Northgate, TS24 0LJ (on headland, towards Fish Quay)
11.30-11; 11-11 Sun (01429) 860097
Camerons Strongarm
Opposite the port that was once bustling with shipbuilding, fishing boats, coal staithes and pit props, this typical two-roomed local is under the stewardship of a friendly and experienced licensee with over 25 years of service to the trade. The price of Strongarm (ask for a Hartlepool Head) still represents remarkable value, reflecting the pub's freehold status, with savings negotiated with Camerons passed on to customers. A recent local CAMRA Community Pub of the Year. Q (7)

Hawthorn

Stapylton Arms

Village Green, SR7 8SD
11-3, 5.30-11; 11-11 Fri & Sat; 12-5 Sun
(0191) 527 0778
3 changing beers (sourced regionally; often Maxim, Mordue, Sonnet 43)
Delightfully welcoming, locally owned village pub serving excellent food. It has two comfortable well-appointed rooms – one a bar and the other a lounge/restaurant. Three well-kept cask ales showcase the best of North-East breweries. The weekly quiz is well attended and contested on Monday evening. This hidden-away pub is in an ideal location for walkers exploring the nearby Hawthorn Dene. QP

High Hesleden

Ship Inn

Mickle Hill Road, TS27 4QD (between A19 and Blackhall, signed from B1281)
closed Mon; 6-11 Tue-Fri; 12-3, 6-11 Sat; 12-8 Sun
(01429) 836453 theshipinn.net
7 changing beers
Now in its 19th year of family ownership, complete satisfaction is guaranteed at this rural gem. The landlord serves seven beers, most locally sourced, as well as real cider. His wife runs the superb restaurant, offering top-quality food at reasonable prices, including mid-week early-doors two-course specials. There are stupendous coastal views from the well-kept gardens. Six motel-style chalets provide good-value accommodation. The pub closes during the owners' annual holidays, so check before making a long journey. A former CAMRA Regional Pub of the Year.
QP (206)

Holwick

Strathmore Arms

DL12 0NJ (just outside Middleton-in-Teesdale)
closed Tue; 12-midnight (01833) 640362
strathmoregold.co.uk
Mithril A66; Wainwright; 3 changing beers (sourced nationally)
Three miles off the B6277 at Middleton-in-Teesdale, this 17th-century stone and buttressed roadside pub has a welcoming bar with a stone flag floor, beams and real fire, and a separate lounge with a tiled floor and pool table. Outside is a beer garden. It offers a house beer from Mithril, Strathmore Gold, four guest ales (six in summer) and up to 20 ciders. A beer festival is held at the end of July. Food is served during all sessions. Regular live music plays on Fridays. Four en-suite letting rooms are available. CAMRA Country Cider Pub 2016-19. P

Hunwick

Joiners Arms

13 South View, DL15 0JW
6-11; 12-3, 5-11 Fri; 12-11 Sat; 12-10.30 Sun
(01388) 417878 thejoinersarms.webnode.com
Timothy Taylor Boltmaker, Landlord; 1 changing beer (sourced nationally; often Timothy Taylor)
Family-run village local with a welcoming bar, restaurant, tiny snug and covered yard/pool room. The bar is the place for proper conversation, along with three handpumps featuring a changing selection. Quality locally sourced food is served Wednesday to Saturday evenings, and Sunday lunchtime in the restaurant. On Monday evening the pub hosts a cheese night.
P (108,109)

Ingleton

Black Horse

Front Street, DL2 3HS
5-11; 12-11 Sat & Sun (01325) 730374
blackhorseingleton.co.uk
Camerons Strongarm; 3 changing beers (sourced nationally)
Free house and restaurant set back from the road with a large car park, situated in a picturesque village. The friendly bar runs into the dining area. This is a popular community hostelry with a relaxed atmosphere. Three guest ales come from local micros within a 30-mile radius of the pub. Excellent Italian food is served in the restaurant Wednesday to Sunday. Local darts teams are supported. The weekly quiz night is on a Sunday.
QP (84)

Leamside

Three Horseshoes

Pit House Lane, DH4 6QQ (½ mile N of A690, just outside West Rainton)
11-11 (0191) 584 2394
threehorseshoesleamside.co.uk
Timothy Taylor Landlord; 5 changing beers (sourced nationally; often Working Hand)
A country pub with an excellent restaurant, the Back Room (booking advisable). The traditional bar has open fires in winter and a large TV for sport. The attached Working Hand Brewery provides up to four real ales with names all linked to characters

from the pub with a story to tell. Timothy Taylor Landlord is always available. The pub is home to a local cycle club and hosts a quiz on Sunday evening. Voted CAMRA branch Country Pub of the Year 2018 and 2019. Q🐴❀◑♿🍎P🐾📶

Medomsley

Royal Oak 🄻
7 Manor Road, DH8 6QN
🕔 11.30-3, 5.30-11; 11-11 Sat; 12-11 Sun ☎ (01207) 560336
Hadrian Border Tyneside Blonde; Mordue Workie Ticket; 1 changing beer (sourced nationally; often Hadrian Border) 🄷
The Royal Oak is a traditional country-style pub with a warm, welcoming country feel. It has a large bar with a selection of seating including soft sofas and leather chairs, and plenty of dining space. Outside, there is a large, attractive garden at the back and ample parking to the front. An excellent, friendly local, it offers a rotation of quality beers as well as good food. Quiz night is Sunday. Q🐴❀◑♿P🚌🐾📶

Metal Bridge

Old Mill 🄻
Thinford Road, DH6 5NX (off A1M jct 61, follow signs on A177)
🕔 12-11 (10.30 Sun) ☎ (01740) 652928
🌐 oldmilldurham.co.uk
4 changing beers (sourced nationally) 🄷
Originally a paper mill in 1813, the pub offers good-quality food and well-kept ales – four handpumps serve a diverse range, with local breweries supplying at least one of the beers. The food menu is extensive, with daily specials written on a board above the bar. Larger groups are welcome in the conservatory. Accommodation is of a high standard, with all rooms en-suite. Q🐴🛏◑P

Middlestone

Ship Inn 🄻
Low Road, DL14 8AB (between Coundon and Kirk Merrington)
🕔 4-11.30; 12-11.30 Fri-Sun ☎ (01388) 810904
🌐 theshipinnmiddlestonevillage.co.uk
6 changing beers (sourced nationally) 🄷
Regular drinkers come from far and wide to the Ship. It has a bar divided into three distinct areas with an open fire, and a large function room upstairs which is the location for occasional beer festivals. The rooftop patio has spectacular views, and there is always an event either taking place or imminent. Various pieces of Vaux memorabilia are on display – one of the many subjects of conversation. Sunday lunches are popular. A former Durham CAMRA Country Pub winner. Q🐴❀◑♿♣🍎P🚌(56,99)🐾

Middleton-in-Teesdale

Teesdale Hotel
Market Place, DL12 0QG
🕔 11-11; 12-11 Sun ☎ (01833) 640264
🌐 teesdalehotel.co.uk
Black Sheep Best Bitter; 2 changing beers (sourced nationally) 🄷
A former coaching inn updated to provide excellent accommodation. This is a popular village local as well as a resting place for Pennine walkers. Middleton-in-Teesdale is often referred to as the capital of Upper Teesdale, with High Force and Cauldron Snout nearby. Up to two guest beers, often from local micros, are served. Meals can be enjoyed in the main bar and the comfortable restaurant. A farmers' market is held on the last Sunday of the month. Q🐴🛏◑P🚉🚌(95,96)🐾

Newfield

Newfield Inn 🄻
Front Street, DH2 2SP
🕔 6-11.30; 12-11.30 Sat & Sun ☎ (0191) 370 0565
Maxim Double Maxim; 1 changing beer (sourced nationally; often Maxim, Welbeck Abbey) 🄷
A friendly two-roomed pub in the centre of the village, known locally simply as The Inn. It is owned by Maxim Brewery from nearby Houghton-le-Spring, with one of its beers and a guest on the bar. The pub offers accommodation, monthly live music, a regular Tuesday night quiz and football on TV. Families are welcome and there is a pleasant beer garden. 🐴🛏♿P🚌(78)🐾

Newton Aycliffe

Turbinia 🄻
Parsons Centre, Sid Chaplin Drive, DL5 7PA (off Burnhill Way, next to Methodist church)
🕔 1-midnight (1am Fri & Sat) ☎ (01325) 313034
🌐 turbiniapub.co.uk
4 changing beers (sourced nationally; often Mithril, Revolutions, Three Brothers) 🄷
Named after the famous Tyneside ship, this friendly free house comprises a large lounge and function room, with traditional pub decor featuring a pictorial history of the Turbinia ship throughout. This local favourite serves an ever-changing variety of beers sourced locally and nationally, as well as craft gins. It hosts a beer and cider festival twice yearly. Darts, dominoes and pool can be found in the main bar during the week and live music at the weekend. 🐴❀♿♣🍎P🚌(7)🐾📶

No Place

Beamish Mary Inn 🄻
DH9 0QH (follow signs to No Place off A693 from Chester-le-Street to Stanley)
🕔 12-11 (10.30 Sun) ☎ (0191) 370 0237
5 changing beers (sourced nationally; often Big Lamp, Consett) 🄷
Full of character, this pub is well respected for its warm welcome, generously portioned pub grub and ample selection of well-kept real ale. The location is handy for visitors to the nearby world-renowned Beamish Open Air Museum. Consett Ale Works and Big Lamp beers are usually included among the range of LocAles on offer. Accommodation is available including twin, double and family rooms. Q🐴❀🛏◑♿🍎P🚌🐾📶

Norton

Hyde's Bar 🄻
Rowan Yard, Billingham Road, TS20 2RZ (in a former builder's yard, at S end of High St)
🕔 12-11.30 Mon (midnight Tue & Wed; 11.30 Thu; midnight Fri & Sat); 12-11 Sun ☎ (01642) 550662
4 changing beers 🄷

Comfortable, contemporary, friendly bar, located in the former workshop of John Hyde, a family-run joiner and builder's merchant for more than 50 years. The workshop was refurbished in 2016, making use of items recovered during the work, with its former use still readily apparent. Photographs from its heyday adorn the walls. Large patio doors open onto a south-facing courtyard area. Four guest beers and four ciders are served. Music nights feature throughout the week.
(36,37)

Old Shotton

Royal George

The Village, SR8 2ND
11-11 (midnight Fri & Sat); 11-10.30 Sun
(0191) 586 6500 royalgeorgeoldshotton.co.uk
Timothy Taylor Landlord; 2 changing beers (sourced nationally; often Harviestoun, Working Hand)
Pub and restaurant situated on the old village green, reopened after a major refurbishment of a virtually derelict establishment in 2014. The bar has been reinstated, as well as a larger lounge and restaurant area. Owned by Working Hand Brewery, its beers are among the changing range of ales. Handpulled cider is always on offer. Traditional pub grub and bar snacks are available. Dogs are welcome, with treats on the bar.
QP

Ovington

Four Alls

The Green, DL11 7BP (2 miles S of Winston)
closed Mon & Tue; 7-11 Wed; 11-3, 7-11 Thu & Sat; 11-3, 6-11 Fri; 11-5 Sun (01833) 627302
thefouralls-ovington.co.uk
2 changing beers (sourced locally)
Friendly stone-built 18th-century inn opposite the village green in what is known as 'the maypole village'. A Victorian sign denotes the four alls: 'I govern all (queen), I fight for all (soldier), I pray for all (parson), I pay for all (farmer).' The single room interior has an 'upstairs' snug serving excellent, good-value food made with local ingredients. Two real ales are available – a dark and a light from local Mithril Ales. There is seating outside at the front and the rear beer garden is perfect on sunny days. QP

Running Waters

Three Horseshoes

Sherburn House, DH1 2SR
7am-10.30; 8am-10.30 Sat & Sun (0191) 372 0286
threehorseshoesdurham.co.uk
3 changing beers (sourced nationally)
A nicely situated country inn only a few miles from Durham City, extensively refurbished in 2016. It offers comfortable accommodation, good food and drink. Three cask ales are available, usually at least one sourced locally. There are excellent rural views over open countryside from the beer garden to the rear. Alcohol is served from noon.
QP

St John's Chapel

Blue Bell Inn

Hood Street, DL13 1QJ
5-1am; 12-1am Sat & Sun (01388) 537256
2 changing beers (sourced nationally)
Originally a pair of terraced cottages, the Blue Bell is a friendly and cosy pub with a bar across the front of the building leading to a small pool room, and garden to the rear. Situated on the A689, it serves the local community and those who holiday in Upper Weardale. Popular for pub games, it also doubles as a library. Q(101)

Seaham

Coalhouse

39 Church Street, SR7 7EJ
4-10; 12-10 Fri & Sat; 2-10 Sun (0191) 581 6235
4 changing beers (sourced locally; often Cullercoats, Yard of Ale)
A former bookmakers', refurbished in 2018 using 100-year-old timbers salvaged from the demolished Co-op building in the town, with decor celebrating the coal-mining heritage of the area. An impressive mural depicting Seaham pits adorns one wall. Four changing cask beers are offered along with two real ciders and five keg taps. A welcome addition to the licensed trade in Seaham.
(265,60)

Seaton

Dun Cow

The Village, SR7 0NA
4 (5 winter)-midnight; 12-midnight Fri-Sun
(0191) 513 1133
4 changing beers (sourced nationally; often Jennings, Maxim, Wainwright)
Excellent, friendly, unspoilt inn on the village green with public bar and lounge areas. A pub for good conversation or a game of darts, the TV is only turned on for special events. No meals are served but toasties are always available. The guest beer selection changes but usually comprises two light and two dark beers to satisfy all tastes. Regular busker and acoustic music nights are hosted. A former CAMRA branch Country Pub of the Year.
P(238)

Sedgefield

Dun Cow

43 Front Street, TS21 3AT
12-11 (01740) 620894 duncowinn.co.uk
Black Sheep Best Bitter; Theakston Best Bitter; 2 changing beers (sourced nationally; often Caledonian)
Run by the same landlord for over 40 years, this large and comfortable 18th-century inn has an excellent county-wide reputation for good food using locally sourced produce as much as possible. It was the scene of a historic George Bush and Tony Blair lunch in 2003. There are three bars including a farmers' bar-cum-snug and restaurant. Four real ales are always available including at least one local beer. QP

Spennymoor

Frog & Ferret

Coulson Street, DL16 7RS
12-11 (midnight Sat); 12-8 Sun (01388) 815840
thefrogandferretspennymoor.co.uk
4 changing beers (sourced nationally; often Consett)

Friendly, traditional family-run free house offering four constantly changing real ales, sourced from far and wide, with local and northern microbreweries well represented. The comfortably furnished lounge has a three-sided bar with brick, stone and wood cladding and a solid fuel burner. Sports TV is featured and well-behaved children are welcome until 9pm. Live music is hosted on a Saturday night. ♣(6,21)

Grand Electric Hall 🄻 ✔

Cheapside, DL16 6DJ

8am-midnight (1am Fri & Sat) ☎ (01388) 825470

Greene King Abbot; Ruddles Best Bitter; Sharp's Doom Bar; 3 changing beers (sourced nationally; often Maxim) 🄷

Formerly a cinema and bingo hall, this is a bright and airy Wetherspoon conversion, with film-themed decor and fittings. The main area is spacious with a high ceiling, and there is a smaller room on a lower level. Set in the centre of town, it boasts a large patio drinking area to the front which can be quite a suntrap in the summer months. Alcohol is served from 9am. (6,21)

Stanhope

Grey Bull

17 West Terrace, DL13 2PB

12-midnight; 11.45-midnight Sat ☎ (01388) 529428

3 changing beers (sourced nationally) 🄷

At the foot of Crawleyside Bank at the west end of town, the pub has a busy bar area across the front and a lounge to the rear, served by a central bar, with three cask beers available. A community-focused hostelry with a warm welcome, it is convenient for the coast-to-coast cycle route. The tables to the front are popular in good weather. **Q**♣(101)

Stockton-on-Tees

Golden Smog 🏆

1 Hambletonian Yard, TS18 1DS (in a ginnel between High St and West Row)

2-10 ☎ (01642) 385022

4 changing beers 🄷

The town's original micropub, a multi-award winner and 2018 CAMRA Regional Pub of the Year, is named after the environmental conditions that formerly prevailed on Teesside. Four real beers and two real ciders are on handpump alongside an impressive range of Belgian beers, some familiar, most not so familiar, but all served in matching glasses in the continental fashion. Third-pints, served on bespoke Smog tasting tables, are also available. An extensive selection of free bar snacks is offered on Sunday. Local CAMRA Pub of the Year 2019. **Q**

Hope & Union 🄻

9-10 Silver Court, TS18 1SL (E of High St, through a ginnel off Silver St)

11-11 (12.30am Sat); 12-11 Sun ☎ (01642) 385022

4 changing beers 🄷

Tucked away in a quiet square in the town's cultural quarter, Hope was Stephenson's second locomotive while Union was a horse-drawn coach, both operated by the world's first passenger railway, the Stockton & Darlington. This bright, modern pub serves four interesting beers, real cider and a large selection of gins and whiskies. The cellar is on open display, as is the kitchen, offering locally sourced, freshly cooked and good-value dishes all day, every day.

Thomas Sheraton 🄻 ✔

4 Bridge Road, TS18 3BW (at S end of High St)

8am-midnight; 8am-11 Sun ☎ (01642) 606134

7 changing beers 🄷

This Grade II-listed Victorian building is a fine conversion of the town's law courts and named after one of the country's great Georgian cabinet makers, born in the town in 1751. The large, airy interior comprises several separate drinking and dining areas, together with a pleasant balcony and an outdoor terrace upstairs. The guest beers are usually locally sourced, while an extensive and varied range of real ciders is available. Local CAMRA Pub of the Year 2018 and Cider Pub of the Year 2019. **Q**♣

Wasps Nest 🄻

Wasps Nest Yard, 1 Calvert's Square, TS18 1TB (E of High St, through a ginnel off Silver St)

11-11 (midnight Fri & Sat); 12-11 Sun ☎ 07789 277364

3 changing beers 🄷

This venue, between the Grade II-listed Georgian Theatre and the River Tees, is now firmly established as a welcome addition to the town's social life. It is a modern and lively pub serving a selection of local beers, real cider and perry. Third-pint bats are available. The pub's claim to fame is that it has the town's only outdoor courtyard patio drinking area. **Q**

Tanfield Lea

Tanfield Lea Working Men's Club

West Street, DH9 9NA

2-4, 7-11; 12-11.30 Fri & Sat; 12-2, 7-11 Sun

☎ (01207) 238783

2 changing beers (sourced nationally) 🄷

The village has no pub, reflecting its strong Methodist history, but guests are most welcome in this CIU-affiliated club, which has become something of a flagship for real ale in the area after a diet of keg beer for many years. TV sport is shown in the bar and there is a quiet, comfortable lounge. Traditional club activities such as bingo take place and there is usually a live act on Sunday when nibbles are provided on the bar. Local CAMRA Club of the Year 2016-2019. ♣**P**(V7,V8)

Tanfield Village

Peacock ✔

Front Street, DH9 9PX

4.30-10.30 Mon; 3-11 Tue-Fri; 12-midnight Sat & Sun

☎ (01207) 232720

Black Sheep Best Bitter; 1 changing beer (sourced nationally) 🄷

A warm welcome is guaranteed in this friendly, traditional, two-bar pub in a pretty village, popular with locals and visitors alike – including bell-ringers from the church opposite. Lovely home-cooked meals are served Wednesday to Saturday evenings and Sunday lunchtime – the portions are generous and great value for money. There is a small beer garden and ample parking. Black Sheep is always available plus a changing guest beer. **Q**♣**P**(V8)

West Cornforth

Square & Compass

7 The Green, DL17 9JQ (off Coxhoe-W Cornforth road)
5-11; 4-11 Fri; 12-11 Sat & Sun
3 changing beers (sourced nationally)
A proper drinking pub and friendly local on the village green in the old part of Doggy (the village's local nickname). It has sold real ale for more than 40 years and usually offers at least one local beer among its three guests. It is home to darts and dominoes clubs and hosts a well-attended Thursday night quiz. The pub has good views over to Wear Valley and Durham City.
QP(56)

Westgate

Hare & Hounds

24 Front Street, DL13 1RX
closed Mon; 6.30-11; 3-11 Sat; 12-3, 6.30-9.30 Sun
(01388) 517212
hareandhoundswestgate.blogspot.co.uk
Weard'ALE Chilled Nights, Dark Nights, Gold, Pilsner
On the banks of the Wear, on the A689. The spacious stone-flagged bar is partially fitted out with items salvaged from the former village chapel, and is a great place to catch up on local news. The restaurant has a patio overlooking the river, while the beer is brewed beneath your feet. Food, including the famous Sunday carvery, is locally sourced. A former local CAMRA Country Pub of the Year runner-up. **QP**(101)

Witton-le-Wear

Dun Cow

19 High Street, DL14 0AY
6-11; 1-11 Sat; 12-11 Sun (01388) 488294
3 changing beers (sourced nationally; often Timothy Taylor)
A welcoming local set back from the road through the village, with a single L-shaped room warmed by open fires at both ends. Dating from 1799, the bar is guarded by a sleeping fox who always seems to have just closed his eyes. There are benches to the left of the bar, and seating outside offering pleasant views over the Wear Valley. The decor includes some interesting football memorabilia.
QP

Wolsingham

Black Lion

21 Meadhope Street, DL13 3EN (50yds N of market place)
12 (4 Tue & Thu)-11; 12-10.30 Sun (01388) 527772
5 changing beers (sourced nationally)
Nationally recognised for its commitment to real cider, hidden away a minute from the Market Place, this welcoming, comfortable gem is a great place to relax. An open fire features in the single open-plan room, with a pool table to the rear and TV sport to the front. Local charities benefit from the efforts of the pub. Six or more ciders can be on offer. A former CAMRA North-East Region Cider Pub of the Year and local branch Country Cider Pub of the Year 2013-2018. **Q**(101)

Causeway, Hartlepool (Photo: Reading Tom/Flickr CC BY 2.0)

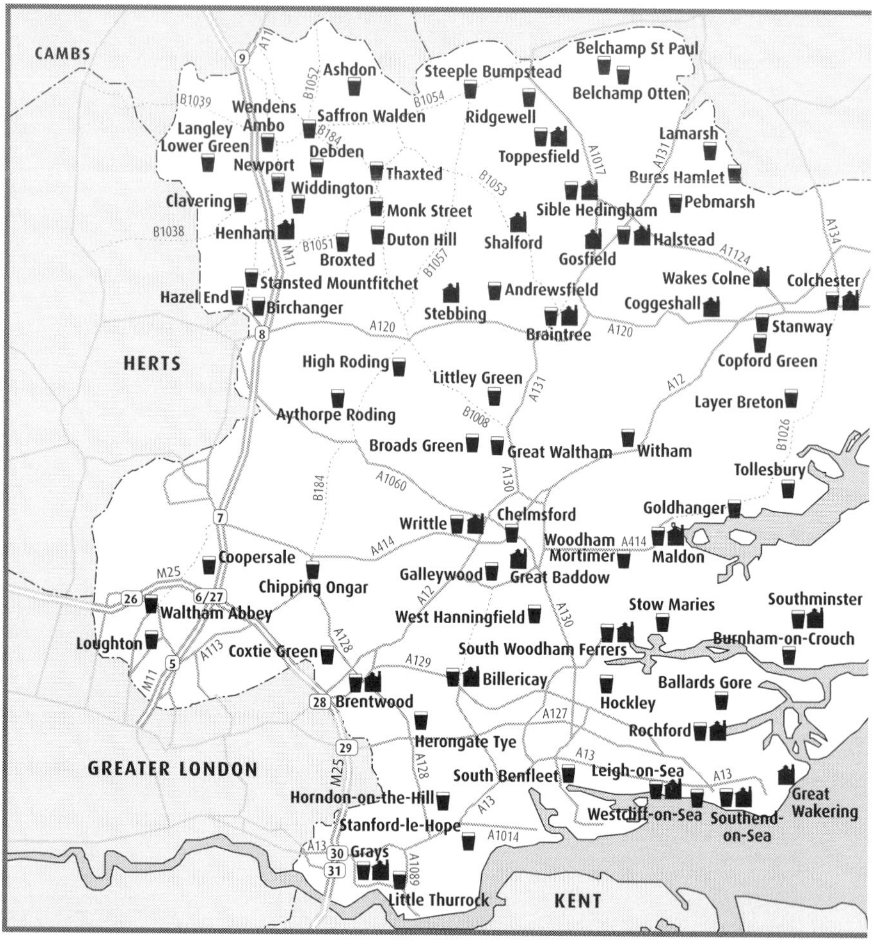

Andrewsfield

Millibar 𝕃

Stebbing Airfield, New Pasture Lane, CM6 3TH (accessed by a track beside runway, near Stebbing Green) TL689248

✪ 11-9 ☎ 07923 981900 🌐 andrewsfield.com/andrewsfield-millibar

Bishop Nick Ridley's Rite Ⓗ

The manager of the bar at this local flying school is keen on local supply and has installed Ridley's Rite from Bishop Nick Brewery as his sole ale. There is also a range of Bishop Nick bottled beers. The training airfield is a small grass strip dominated by single-engine Cessna aircraft, a Mustang III and B17 Meteor IIIs, and trial flying lessons are available. The public are welcome in the bar and it stays open until 11pm if there are customers.

Q❀◐●P🐾ᯤ

Ashdon

Rose & Crown 𝕃

Crown Hill, CB10 2HA

✪ closed Mon; 12-2.30, 5.30 (5 Fri)-11; 12-11 Sat; 12-7 Sun

☎ (01799) 584337

Woodforde's Wherry; 4 changing beers (sourced nationally) Ⓗ

The last remaining pub in this village which once had five more. It has an unusual layout, and a room named after Oliver Cromwell where he is reputed to have kept prisoners, who illustrated the walls with their feelings at the time! This is now hidden behind removable panels. Guest ales often include Nethergate and Essex-brewed beers. This pub is the focus of village social activities.

Q❀◐◑P⛟🐾ᯤ

Aythorpe Roding

Axe & Compasses 𝕃

Dunmow Road, CM6 1PP (on B1845 5 miles SW of Dunmow) TL594154

✪ 9am-11 ☎ (01279) 876648 🌐 theaxeandcompasses.co.uk

Fuller's London Pride; 2 changing beers (sourced locally; often Bishop Nick) Ⓗ

An 18th-century building, recently extensively refurbished. Drinkers are welcome, as are a mixed clientele of walkers, locals and farming folk. The award-winning food consists of pub classics with a modern twist, all locally sourced, and the service is efficient and friendly. The pub hosts quiz and themed nights. On a sunny day it is a pleasant place to view the beautiful countryside and the nearby windmill. Q❀◐◑♿●P⛟(17,18)🐾ᯤ

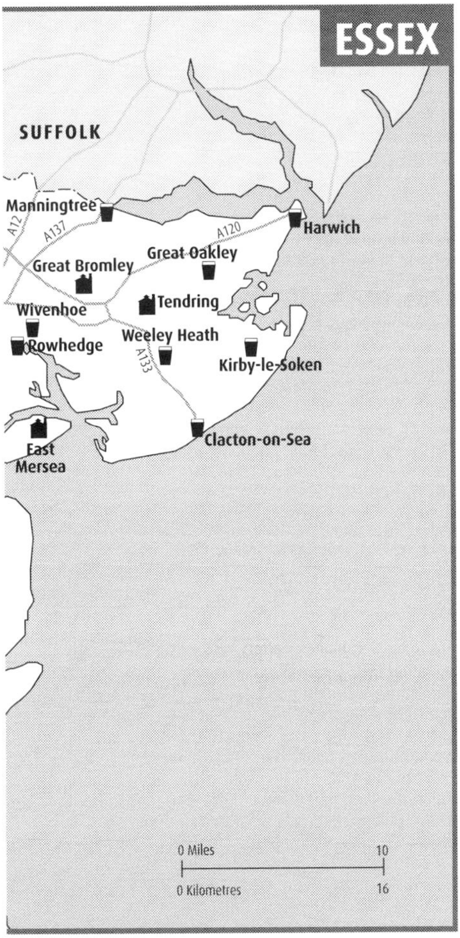

Ballards Gore (Stambridge)

Shepherd & Dog

Gore Road, SS4 2DA (between Rochford and Paglesham)
✪ 12-11; 12-10.30 Sun ☎ (01702) 258658
🌐 shepherdanddog.co.uk
6 changing beers (sourced locally; often George's) Ⓗ
A traditional country pub with beams throughout and a real fire, a regular winner of local CAMRA awards. It is L-shaped, with the bar at the front serving six changing real ales – with at least two being from local breweries – plus a range of real ciders. Towards the back is the restaurant serving home-cooked food using local produce. It has seating outside at the front and in a beer garden to the rear, with an outside bar. Regular music events are popular. ❀◑●P🚌(60)🐾

Belchamp Otten

Red Lion Ⓛ

Fowes Lane, CO10 7BQ (on very small single track lane, signed by duck pond) TL799415
✪ 12-3, 5.30-11; closed Tue; 12-6 Sun ☎ (01787) 278301
Adnams Southwold Bitter; 2 changing beers (sourced nationally) Ⓗ
A lovely local pub, hidden away in the smallest of the Belchamps. The owner provides a warm welcome, with an open fire in winter. It has darts, a pool table and runs occasional events. There are excellent views, good walks and cycle rides from here. It is currently not serving food but has delivery arrangements with local takeaway restaurants. There is a friendly labrador to welcome you when you arrive. ❀♣●P🐾

Belchamp St Paul

Half Moon ✔

Cole Green, CO10 7DP TL792423
✪ 12-3, 6-midnight (11 Mon); 12-midnight Sat & Sun
☎ (01787) 277402 🌐 halfmoonbelchamp.co.uk
Greene King IPA; 2 changing beers (sourced nationally) Ⓗ
Beautiful, warm and friendly establishment dating from about 1685, opposite the village green. Three beers are available and guest beers change regularly. This thatched rural pub is popular with locals and has an excellent choice of bar and restaurant meals (no food on Sun eve or Mon). In the past, the pub provided one of the locations for the first Lovejoy TV Series, and has original wooden beams and low ceilings in places.
Q❀◑♿♣P

Billericay

Billericay Brewing Co Shop & Micropub

52 Chapel Street, CM12 9LS
✪ 10-6 Mon-Wed; 9am-9 Thu-Sat; 11-5 Sun
☎ (01277) 500121 🌐 billericaybrewing.co.uk
Billericay Zeppelin, Blonde, Dickie; 4 changing beers (sourced locally; often Billericay) Ⓖ
Brewery tap micropub next door to the brewery. It serves up to four ales on gravity, mostly from Billericay Brewery, plus two other beers on

REAL ALE BREWERIES

Billericay Billericay
Bishop Nick Braintree
Brentwood Brentwood
Chelmsford Great Baddow
Colchester Wakes Colne
Courtyard Gosfield (NEW)
Crouch Vale South Woodham Ferrers
Fallen Angel Writtle
Fox Meadow Braintree (brewing suspended)
George's Great Wakering
Hart of Stebbing ▤ Stebbing
Keppels Rochford
Leigh on Sea Leigh-on-Sea
Maldon Maldon
Mersea Island East Mersea
Mighty Oak Maldon
Moody Goose ▤ Braintree
Mr Majolica Grays (brewing suspended)
Other Monkey Colchester
Pumphouse Community Toppesfield
Red Fox Coggeshall
Saeburh Tendring
Saffron Henham
Shalford Shalford
Silks Sible Hedingham
Sticklegs Great Bromley (brewing suspended)
Vendetta Southend-on-Sea (NEW)
Watson's Colchester
White Hart ▤ Halstead
Wibblers Southminster

KeyKeg. The micropub is also a beer shop, with bottles from Billericay plus other breweries, as well as foreign beers. Four beer festivals are held each year in March, June, September and December. It has seating on high stools next to solid wooden tables, and an extra pop-up bar in the brewery at busy times. ⌂❀≋♣●🖳(100,222)❀🛜

Coach & Horses 🅛
36 Chapel Street, CM12 9LU
✪ 11-11; 12-10 Sun ☎ (01277) 622873
⊕ thecoachandhorses.org
Adnams Broadside; Mighty Oak Captain Bob; Oakham Citra; Wibblers Dengie IPA; 2 changing beers (sourced nationally) 🅗
Close to the High Street, this welcoming pub with an inviting atmosphere has appeared in this Guide for over 20 years. Six ales are served, with one always from Oakham. Good-quality, home-made food is available lunchtimes and evenings, with a popular Sunday roast, plus themed menus including curry nights. The bar service is efficient and friendly. The walls are adorned with prints and decorative plates, and a collection of tankards hangs from the ceiling. It has a cosy and attractive courtyard garden. ❀🕽♿≋●P🖳(100)🛜

Railway
1 High Street, CM12 9BE
✪ 12-11 (10 Mon); 12-midnight Fri & Sat ☎ (01277) 652173
Dark Star Hophead; Wibblers Dengie IPA; 3 changing beers (sourced nationally) 🅗
Friendly pub with a welcoming atmosphere which earns the tag line 'No.1 in the High Street'. It has served over 700 different real ales and won several local CAMRA awards. Guest beers are updated on social media. Regular events include a quiz, live music and charity days. This community-oriented pub has two darts teams and sponsors a local rugby team. Traditional bar games include shove-ha'penny with real ha'pennies. A beer garden is outside, and an open fire indoors during winter. ⌂❀♿≋♣P🖳❀🛜

Birchanger

Birchanger Sports & Social Club
229 Birchanger Lane, CM23 5QJ
✪ 7 (12 Wed)-11; 12-11 Fri & Sat; 12-10.30 Sun
☎ (01279) 813441 ⊕ birchangerclub.com
Greene King IPA; 2 changing beers (sourced nationally) 🅗
A friendly local social club where CAMRA members are welcome as guests. Many matches and events take place here, so it can get very busy. Beers change frequently as the turnover is high. The club has football, cricket, bowls, darts, crib and snooker teams, regular quizzes, plus bingo and bottle draws. It has won CAMRA branch Club of the Year on several occasions. ⌂❀🕽♿♣●P🖳(7,7A)🛜

Braintree

King William IV 🅛
114 London Road, CM77 7PU
✪ 3-11; 12-midnight Fri-Sun ☎ (01376) 567755
⊕ kingwilliamiv.co.uk
4 changing beers (sourced nationally) 🅖
Friendly free house serving a changing range of real ales, usually featuring Essex microbreweries and at least one from the Moody Goose Brewery, located in the grounds of the pub. An interesting

selection of ciders is also on offer. There is a main bar and a small back bar with a dartboard. Outside, a large patio area and extensive gardens host beer festivals and other events. This is a traditional drinking pub that does not offer cooked meals. Q❀♣●P🖳❀🛜

Brentwood

Victoria Arms
50 Ongar Road, CM15 9AX (on A128)
✪ 11-11 (midnight Fri & Sat); 12-10.30 Sun
☎ (01277) 223371
Adnams Ghost Ship; Harvey's IPA, Sussex Best Bitter; 3 changing beers (sourced nationally) 🅗
Pleasant and comfortable Gray & Sons pub with a friendly atmosphere. Unusually for the area, there are normally two Harvey's beers available, as well as Ghost Ship and three changing beers. There are several TV screens, mostly showing sport, and an outside smoking area. Cribbage and other card games are available. Local CAMRA Pub of the Year 2018. ❀🕽♣P🖳(498,21)

Broads Green

Walnut Tree 🅛 ✓
CM3 1DT
✪ 12-11 ☎ (01245) 360222
Bishop Nick Ridley's Rite; Timothy Taylor Landlord; 1 changing beer (sourced nationally) 🅖
Handsome Victorian pub overlooking the green. The front door opens into what was the bottle and jug, but is now a small snug. To the left is the wood-panelled public bar, little changed since it was built in 1888. To the right is the slightly more modern saloon bar. Outside there is seating in front of the pub, a children's play area and a large garden. There is no food, the landlord preferring to concentrate on his beers and maintaining a traditional atmosphere. Q⌂❀♠♣●P❀🛜

Broxted

Prince of Wales 🅛 ✓
Brick End, CM6 2BJ
✪ closed Mon; 11.30-11 (midnight Fri & Sat); 12-10 Sun
☎ (01279) 850256 ⊕ princeofwalesbroxted.co.uk
Greene King IPA; 5 changing beers (sourced nationally) 🅗
A spacious former Charrington's pub transformed into a welcoming community venue after the current landlords took over in late 2011. It has a comfortable split-level bar, an adjoining room with two woodburners and a conservatory. Generously portioned pub grub, mostly locally sourced, will satisfy the most demanding appetite. A small garden is to the rear. Up to five guest beers are available, with LocAle from Bishop Nick. ⌂❀🕽P🖳(6)❀🛜

Bures Hamlet

Eight Bells
6 Colchester Road, CO8 5AE
✪ 12-3, 5-11.30; 12-11 Sat & Sun ☎ (01787) 227354
Greene King IPA, Abbot; 4 changing beers (sourced nationally) 🅗
A five-minute walk from Bures station, this is a traditional village pub with a long-serving landlord in his 38th year here. It has three separate drinking and dining areas, served by a large bar, and a

separate function area. Monthly open mic nights are hosted and the pub is home to a steel quoits team. Traditional pub food is served daily, with a roast on Sunday. Walkers and cyclists are always welcome. Q P

Burnham-on-Crouch

Queen's Head

26 Providence, CM0 8JU

2 (4 Mon)-11; 12-11 Fri-Sun (01621) 784825

Wibblers Dengie IPA; 3 changing beers (sourced nationally) [H]

A true locals' pub just off the High Street, owned by Gray & Sons. It is frequently busy, with a good and varied range of beers and ciders. The basic no-frills interior is warmed in winter by a log-burning stove. The pool table is a popular feature. A small sheltered garden to the rear provides a delightful outside space, with a heated smoking area. Beer festivals are hosted. The railway station is 15 minutes' walk away. ♣ (31X)

Chelmsford

Ale House

24-26 Viaduct Road, CM1 1TS

11-11 (midnight Fri & Sat); 12-10.30 Sun (01245) 260535 the-ale-house-chelmsford.co.uk

12 changing beers (sourced nationally) [H]

A unique bar in Chelmsford, under the arches at the railway station, with one of the widest ranges of continuously changing beers in Essex, always including dark and stronger beers, plus eight craft keg beers and 12 real ciders. There are also imported beers on tap and a wide range of bottled beers from around the world. No food is served, but customers are welcome to bring their own. A quiz is held on the last Sunday of each month. ♣

Endeavour

351 Springfield Road, CM2 6AW

11-11; 12-11 Sun (01245) 257717

Adnams Ghost Ship; Harvey's Sussex Best Bitter; Mighty Oak Maldon Gold; Wibblers Dengie IPA; 1 changing beer (sourced nationally) [H]

Busy and friendly pub, comprising three rooms. Home-cooked meals are served at lunchtimes and evenings, while sandwiches are available all day (Mon-Sat). Please book for the roast dinner on Sunday. All food is good value and locally sourced. This is a true community pub, with darts and crib teams and regular charity events. It also shows BT Sports. There is a new attractive courtyard garden. ♣

Hop Beer Shop

173 Moulsham Street, CM2 0LD

closed Sun & Mon; 12-9 Tue-Sat (01245) 353570

4 changing beers (sourced nationally) [G]

Essex's first micropub, offering four beers served by gravity, with local breweries always represented, as well as interesting beers from around the country, usually including a stout or porter and a golden beer. There are also craft keg beers, around 100 bottled beers from local and international breweries, and bottled cider, which may be drunk here or purchased to take home. Local CAMRA Pub of the Year 2017 and Cider Pub of the Year 2018 and 2019. Q

Oddfellows Arms Smokehouse

195 Springfield Road, CM2 6JP

12-11 (midnight Thu-Sat) (01245) 490514

theoddfellowsarms.com

Bishop Nick 1555; Dark Star Hophead; St Austell Tribute; Wibblers Dengie IPA; 1 changing beer (sourced nationally) [H]

A pub with a modern wood interior, but maintaining the feel of a local. There is a large U-shaped bar area, with a back room containing a pool table leading out to the attractive decked garden/smoking area. Extensive home-made food is served weekday lunchtimes and evenings, and all day at weekends. It has a new barbecue real-wood smoker serving brisket, ribs and pulled pork. There are poker nights twice a week, monthly live music and an annual beer festival. ♣P

Orange Tree

6 Lower Anchor Street, CM2 0AS

12-11 (midnight Fri; 11.30 Sat) (01245) 262664

the-ot.com

Mighty Oak Oscar Wilde; 7 changing beers (sourced nationally) [H]

The Orange Tree is one of the best real ale pubs in Chelmsford and has been local CAMRA Pub of the Year in recent years. It is a place for conversation and meeting friends, with separate public and saloon bars. A great range of real ales is on tap, always including something dark, plus craft keg beers. Food is served at lunchtimes, including a roast on Sunday, with a steak and curry night on Thursday evening. Quiz night is Tuesday. Q ♣ P

Queen's Head

30 Lower Anchor Street, CM2 0AS

12-11 (11.30 Fri & Sat) (01245) 265181

Crouch Vale Essex Boys Best Bitter, Brewers Gold; 5 changing beers (sourced nationally) [H]

Crouch Vale Brewery's first pub, this venue sells three of its beers permanently, with four guests which may include a Crouch Vale seasonal and always include a dark beer. The Victorian L-shaped pub has bare-board flooring and comfortable bench seating. Two fires make it cosy in winter. This popular local can be busy when there is a match at the nearby county cricket ground. The Essex Beard Club meets here once a year in February. Q ♣P

Railway Tavern

63 Duke Street, CM1 1LW

10-11 (11.30 Fri & Sat); 12-8 Sun (01245) 280679

Greene King Abbot; Red Fox IPA; 5 changing beers (sourced nationally) [H]

A Tardis-like corner pub, right outside Chelmsford station. Not surprisingly, a railway theme dominates. It is long and narrow, with banks of handpumps at opposite ends of the central bar counter. There is a small enclosed garden where you can listen to the station announcements and marvel at the ever-changing mural. It may stay open later on Sundays in the summer. This traditional pub also sells craft beers and over 50 different gins. Local CAMRA Pub of the Year 2018. ♣

Ship

18 Broomfield Road, CM1 1SW

10-11 (1am Fri & Sat); 12-11 Sun (01245) 265961

theshipchelmsford.co.uk

Greene King IPA, Abbot; 5 changing beers (sourced nationally; often Bishop Nick) Ⓗ
A traditional medium-sized pub with a comfortable interior and some outside seating in front. The decor is nautical with dark-brown panelling, portholes, masts, rope, rigging and other maritime artefacts. It is close to rail and bus stations, with a public car park at the rear. A wide range of food is offered, with daily specials. There is a jukebox, but no live music on a regular basis. Sport is shown on the TV. 🛏◐◑≠🚌📶

Woolpack 🏆 ✔
23 Mildmay Road, CM2 0DN
⏲ 4-11; 12-midnight Fri & Sat; 12-11 Sun ☎ (01245) 259295
🌐 thewoolpack.wix.com/woolpackchelmsford
Greene King XX Mild; Hardys & Hansons Bitter; 7 changing beers (sourced nationally) Ⓗ
It is an easy walk from the town centre to this award-winning and friendly Victorian local. There are three rooms with a lounge area overlooking the large garden. Darts and a pool table are in a smaller room. Pub grub is served, with light snacks until 11pm. There is music on Sundays, a quiz on Tuesdays. Beer festivals are held at Easter and the first weekend in September, with up to 80 beers, ciders and perries. Local CAMRA Pub of the Year 2019. ❀◐◑♿♣P🚌

Chipping Ongar

Cock Tavern 🄻
218 High Street, CM5 9AB (on A128)
⏲ 11-11 (midnight Fri & Sat) ☎ (01277) 365261
🌐 thecocktavern.com
Harvey's IPA; 3 changing beers (sourced regionally) Ⓗ
The Cock is an old-fashioned, welcoming pub in the centre of the attractive town of Ongar. It serves mostly local ales on handpumps and has a good selection of traditional pub food including a Sunday roast. Parking is available in the public car park by the library and it is close to the heritage Epping and Ongar Railway. Live music is played fortnightly.
❀◐◑≠(Ongar)♣🍎🚌🐾📶

Clacton-on-Sea

Moon & Starfish
1 Marine Parade East, CO15 1PT
⏲ 8am-11.30 (1am Fri & Sat) ☎ (01255) 222998
Greene King Abbot; Ruddles Best Bitter; Sharp's Doom Bar; 6 changing beers (sourced nationally) Ⓗ
This Wetherspoon pub has been a regular entry in the Guide since 2014. It is in one of the oldest buildings in Clacton-on-Sea, built in 1872 when Clacton was only around a year old. Situated opposite Clacton's Pavilion Fun Park and historic pier, the outside area to the front offers excellent views of the Clacton Airshow and the Clacton carnival street procession in August. It holds two beer festivals and one cider festival each year.
Q❀◐◑♿≠🍎🚌📶

Old Lifeboat House
39 Marine Parade East, CO15 6AD
⏲ 12-10 ☎ (01255) 476799
Greene King Abbot; St Austell Proper Job; 3 changing beers (sourced nationally; often Colchester, Greene King, St Austell) Ⓗ
A regular in this Guide since 2011, the pub is frequented by locals and visitors alike and regularly has up to five ales available. The outdoor patio is a pleasant place to enjoy a summer pint near Clacton seafront. Food is available on Wednesday evening. The pub hosts four darts teams: two play on Monday and two on Thursday. ❀◑≠♣🍎P🥛🚌📶

Clavering

Fox & Hounds ✔
High Street, CB11 4QR
⏲ 4-11 (midnight Fri); 12-midnight Sat; 12-11 Sun
☎ (01799) 550321 🌐 foxandhoundsclavering.co.uk
Adnams Ghost Ship; house beer (by Marston's); 1 changing beer (sourced nationally) Ⓗ
A friendly local drinkers' pub, the oldest licensed premises in Clavering still open, and with a large car park. It is a good place to start walks from, set in the middle of this village close to the River Stort. The pub runs events supporting the local school and charities, with a regular quiz on the second Thursday of the month. ❀♣P🐾📶

Colchester

Abbey Arms
St Johns Green, CO2 7HA
⏲ 12-11 (1am Fri & Sat) ☎ (01206) 579884
3 changing beers (sourced nationally) Ⓗ
Recently refurbished pub within sight of a historic Abbey gate, serving three changing real ales, two changing real ciders and a selection of keg beers and gins. The pub has a bright single bar with a pool table and dartboard, as well as a large patio area at the side with picnic tables. BT Sports and Sky are available on three TVs and a big screen showing all major sports events. Near the town bus station. ❀≠(Town)♣🍎🚌📶

Ale House 🄻
82 Butt Road, CO3 3DA
⏲ 3-11; 12-midnight Fri; 12-11 Sat; 12-10 Sun
☎ (01206) 573464 🌐 thealehousecolchester.co.uk
10 changing beers (sourced nationally) Ⓗ
Free house with a friendly landlady and staff, relaxing decor and comfortable seating. This award-winning pub offers a wide range of ales, served both from handpump and on gravity (including at least one dark beer), as well as real cider. A quiz night is held every third Wednesday; a folk music session on the fourth Tuesday of the month. Darts, bar billiards and BT sports are available. There is a large secluded walled garden at the rear. The nearest car park is in Roman Circus Walk (CO3 3DG). ❀≠(Town)♣🍎🚌(64)📶

British Grenadier 🄻
67 Military Road, CO1 2AP
⏲ 5-11.45; 4-midnight Fri; 12-midnight Sat; 7-11.45 Sun
☎ 07832 215118
4 changing beers (sourced nationally) Ⓗ
This welcoming local hostelry, run by a knowledgeable publican, has featured in the Guide for more than 10 years. It is a traditional Victorian two-bar pub with a pool table in the small rear bar and a dartboard in the main bar, heated by an open fire in the winter months. LocAle accredited, it serves a changing range of local, regional and nationally sourced beers and ciders via handpump. Card payments are not accepted here.
❀♿≠(Town)♣🍎🥛🚌🐾📶

New Inn

36 Chapel Street South, CO2 7AX

12-11 (midnight Fri & Sat) (01206) 575277

theoldnewinnpub.co.uk

Bishop Nick Ridley's Rite; 7 changing beers (sourced nationally)

Local CAMRA Pub of the Year 2019 and 2018, serving up to eight handpulled real ales, seven craft keg and five box ciders. It is a community pub with a garden and free-to-hire function room. The saloon bar focuses on comfort and relaxation while the public bar has music, TV sport and friendly conversation. Traditional pub food is served Tuesday-Saturday 12-8.45pm and Sunday 12-5pm. Regular beer events including tap takeovers are held – over 14 in 2019. A plethora of board games is on offer. Free parking is available.
Q (Town) P (64)

Odd One Out

28 Mersea Road, CO2 7ET

4.30-11; 12-11 Fri & Sat; 12-10.30 Sun (01206) 615102

Colchester Metropolis, No.1; 7 changing beers (sourced nationally)

A welcoming beer and cider house with three distinct seating areas, plus a function room for local community meetings which looks out onto the garden. There are always at least two beers from Colchester Brewery and up to six more changing guest ales, and at least three real ciders. To the rear, the secluded garden allows for a quiet pint away from the busy road. The pub is only a short walk from Colchester Town railway station and the historic town. Q (Town)

Purple Dog

42 Eld Lane, CO1 1LS

11-11 (midnight Thu); 10-1am Fri; 10-1.30am Sat; 11.30-10.30 Sun (01206) 564995

thepurpledogpub.co.uk

Adnams Ghost Ship; Sharp's Doom Bar; 4 changing beers (sourced nationally)

One of the oldest pubs in Colchester, dating back to 1647. This is a wooden-beamed corner building in the town centre with an outdoor drinking area. Six handpumps provide mainly regional beers alongside the usual town-centre pub offerings. An extensive menu, complemented by changing special dishes, is available daily. The pub hosts regular music events (DJs with occasional bands) and a monthly quiz night. (Town)

Three Wise Monkeys

60 High Street, CO1 1DN

11-midnight (1am Fri & Sat); 11-10.30 Sun

(01206) 543014 threewisemonkeyscolchester.com

Colchester No.1; 5 changing beers (sourced nationally)

Centrally located, multi-level brew bar near Colchester Castle. The ground floor houses a spacious taproom, serving a range of local and national beers (including beers from its own brewery) via both handpump and keg lines. Regular beer festivals and brewery takeovers are hosted. Meals are served daily, with a focus on American-style food. Live music and club nights take place on the top floor. There is also a basement gin bar. (Town)

Victoria Inn

10 North Station Road, CO1 1RB

12-11 (midnight Fri & Sat); 2-11 Sun (01206) 514510

victoriainncolchester.co.uk

5 changing beers (sourced nationally)

Popular pub serving two house beers and three guests. Nine real ciders, kegged beers plus a selection of bottled and canned craft beers are also available. Live music features on Sunday afternoons, sometimes taking place in the courtyard garden in summer. It also holds a monthly cheese club, a wine club and coffee mornings. Themed beer events are hosted throughout the year. A previous local, county and regional CAMRA Pub of the Year, and local Cider Pub of the Year for the past two years.

Coopersale

Theydon Oak

9 Coopersale Street, CM16 7QJ

11-11; 12-8.30 Sun (01992) 572618

thetheydonoak.co.uk

Adnams Ghost Ship; Fuller's London Pride; St Austell Tribute; Woodforde's Wherry

An ancient pub, dating back 400 years in parts, with logburners and comfortable seating, lots of exposed beams, horse brasses and antiques. A wide assortment of home-cooked food is served, for which the pub has a good reputation. It is in beautiful countryside, not far from Epping – follow the footpath from Epping Underground station. A beer festival is held in May and other events throughout the year. Q P (381)

Copford Green

Alma

School Road, CO6 1BZ (signed from London Road)

12-3, 5-11; 12-midnight Fri & Sat; 12-11 Sun

(01206) 210607 thealma.org.uk

Greene King IPA, Abbot; Red Fox Hunter's Gold; 1 changing beer (sourced nationally)

This is the eighth consecutive year in the Guide for this picturesque 16th-century village pub at the heart of the local community. The spring bank holiday beer festival showcases over 20 different ales. Lunchtime and evening home-cooked meals are available daily, plus roast dinners on Sunday. There is an open fire, TV sport, outdoor crazy golf, darts and pool, which complement classic motor vehicle meetings and a quiz night on the first Thursday of every month. Q P

Coxtie Green

White Horse

173 Coxtie Green Road, CM14 5PX (1 mile W of A128, at jct with Mores Lane) TQ564959

11.30-11 (midnight Fri & Sat); 12-11 Sun

(01277) 372410 whitehorsebrentwood.co.uk

Fuller's London Pride; Greene King Abbot; house beer (by Brentwood); 6 changing beers (sourced nationally)

Pleasant country free house with an extended comfortable saloon bar. The 10 handpumps normally dispense four regular beers and six guests, of which three are usually from Brentwood Brewery and the rest are from anywhere. The pub is badged as the Brentwood Brewery tap. There is a large play area in the garden to keep the children happy. The local bus service is limited but reliable.
P (71,72)

Debden

Plough

High Street, CB11 3LE

closed Mon; 12-3 (not Tue), 5-11; 12-midnight Fri & Sat; 12-10 Sun ☎ (01799) 541899 theploughatdebden.co.uk

Greene King IPA; 3 changing beers (sourced nationally) H

The sole remaining village pub, with a restaurant and garden, now revitalised by a young, energetic couple. This warm and welcoming pub offers an extensive menu and runs beer festivals, events and other local celebrations. The changing beer range includes an interesting and varied choice of local ales. The pub is now an important social centre for the village and surrounding area, and a good base for walkers and cyclists. A monthly quiz night is normally held on the third Wednesday.
Q ❀ ♣ P (6,313)

Duton Hill

Three Horseshoes

CM6 2DX (1 mile W of B184) TL606268

6-11; 12-2.30, 6-11 Fri; 12-3, 6-11 Sat; 12-3, 7-10.30 Sun ☎ (01371) 870681

Mighty Oak Maldon Gold; 2 changing beers (sourced nationally) H

Outstanding village local with a garden, wildlife pond and terrace overlooking the Chelmer Valley and farmland. The landlord often hosts a weekend of open-air theatre in July. A millennium beacon in the garden, breweriana, and a remarkable collection of Butlin's memorabilia are pub features. A beer festival is held on the late spring bank holiday in the Duton Hill Den. Look for the pub sign depicting a famous painting, Our Blacksmith, by a former local resident, Sir George Clausen. Local and parish newspapers are available.
❀ ♿ ♣ P (313)

Galleywood

Eagle

Stock Road, CM2 8PS

12-11 (8 Mon; midnight Fri & Sat); 12-8 Sun ☎ (01245) 269361

2 changing beers (sourced nationally) H

A Grade II-listed building, recently refurbished, with the cellar and kitchen also updated. The L-shaped wooden-floored bar room has seating at the bar, at tables and in alcoves. There is a separate pool room. Freshly prepared home-cooked food is served, with a seniors' lunch club on Thursday. Children eat free at Sunday lunchtime. Quiz evening is every Thursday, karaoke on Friday, and singers/groups on Saturday. Voted local CAMRA most improved pub in 2017.
Q ❀ ♣ P

Goldhanger

Chequers

Church Street, CM9 8AS

11-11; 12-10.30 Sun ☎ (01621) 788203 thechequersgoldhanger.co.uk

Adnams Ghost Ship; St Austell Proper Job; Sharp's Atlantic; Woodforde's Wherry; 2 changing beers (sourced nationally) H

Historic 15th-century village inn with several timbered rooms, including a games room with bar billiards and a snug. There is an extensive food menu and the pub takes pride in sourcing local ingredients where possible. There are open fires in two of the bars and the rear courtyard is a suntrap in warmer weather. A small beer festival is held in September. Four ciders are usually available on draught. Excellent footpaths along the River Blackwater are close by.
Q ❀ ♣ P (95)

Grays

Theobald Arms

141 Argent Street, RM17 6HR

12-11 (midnight Fri & Sat) ☎ (01375) 372253 theosarms.co.uk

4 changing beers (sourced nationally) H

Genuine, traditional pub with a public bar that has an unusual hexagonal pool table. The changing selection of four guest beers features local independent breweries, and a range of British bottled beers is also stocked. Regular St George's weekend and summer beer festivals are held in the old stables and on the rear enclosed patio. Lunchtime meals are served Monday to Friday. Darts and cards are played. ❀ ♿ ♣ P

White Hart

Kings Walk, RM17 6HR

12-11.30 (midnight Fri & Sat); 12-11 Sun ☎ (01375) 373319 whitehartgrays.co.uk

Dartmoor Best; Wibblers Dengie Gold; 3 changing beers (sourced nationally) H

Traditional, rejuvenated local just outside the town centre. The regular beers are supplemented by three guests, one usually dark, and a selection of over 30 bottled Belgian beers. Good-value meals are served weekday lunchtimes. There is a meeting/function room and a large, secluded beer garden. Live music features on Saturday. A collection of old-fashioned soft toys is displayed on the historic bar-back. The pub supports pool and darts teams, while sport is screened on TV. Local CAMRA Pub of the Year 2017 and 2019.
❀ ♿ ♣ P

Great Oakley

Maybush Inn

Farm Road, CO12 5AL

12-11 (1am Fri & Sat); 12-10.30 Sun ☎ (01255) 880123 maybushinn.co.uk

Courage Directors; house beer (by Eagle); 2 changing beers (sourced nationally) H

A great community-owned pub, entirely staffed and managed by volunteers and now in its fourth year of successful operation. An exceptionally community-focused pub, it hosts various activities such as quizzes, bingo, crib, music, and so on, every week. After purchasing the building next door, an excellent quiet beer garden has been opened at the rear, and work is progressing on a new car park. Plans for a restaurant are also in hand. An extremely welcoming and friendly village local. Q ❀ ♣

Great Waltham

Rose & Crown

Minnows End, Chelmsford Road, CM3 1AG

11.30-midnight; 12-1am Fri & Sat; 12-midnight Sun ☎ (01245) 360359 roseandcrowngreatwaltham.co.uk

Bishop Nick 1555; Fuller's London Pride; Greene King IPA [H]
A rural pub with a traditional bar, a separate snug seating 10 people and a small function room. It also has a restaurant serving home cooking from mainly local produce, with a 10 per cent discount on food for NHS workers. Outside, there is a patio area and new decking with themed table tops. Piano Girl features on the second Wednesday and a jazz night on the last Wednesday of each month.
Q P

Halstead

White Hart Inn L
15 High Street, CO9 2AA
12-11 (10 Mon); 12-10 Sun ☎ (01787) 475657
whitehartinnhalstead.co.uk
White Hart Halstead Bitter, Golden Hart; 2 changing beers (sourced nationally) [H]
Believed to have been built in the 15th century, this traditional inn has a drinking area with a fire, beams and comfy seating and a separate dining area. It started brewing its own beers in the old stables at the rear of the pub in 2017 and now also boasts its own gin distillery. The pub rotates its own beers with, often, a mild or stout alongside a guest. P (88)

Harwich

Alma Inn L ✔
25 Kings Head Street, CO12 3EE
12-11 (midnight Fri & Sat) ☎ (01255) 318681
almaharwich.co.uk
Adnams Southwold Bitter, Broadside; 4 changing beers (sourced regionally) [H]
The Alma always has two Adnams ales available, with four changing guest ales from around East Anglia. The 16th-century building has been trading as an inn since 1859, and has overnight accommodation upstairs. Food is served daily, often including locally caught seafood. The two real ciders, whenever possible, are from Herefordshire as they remind the landlord, Nick, of home.
≋(Town) ●

Hanover Inn 🏆
65 Church Street, CO12 3DR
12-11; 11.30-10.30 Sun ☎ (01255) 502927
hanoverinn.co.uk
Green Jack Trawlerboys Best Bitter [H]**; 3 changing beers (sourced nationally)** [H]/[G]
Taken over in 2016 by the current owners, gradual yet sympathetic improvements continue to take place. The cosy front bar has now been refurbished, enlarging it slightly, while remaining a welcoming place for conversation. The dining area to the rear offers hearty, traditional food lunchtimes and evenings. This buzzing community pub can be found in the heart of Old Harwich next to the church. Local CAMRA Pub of the Year 2019.
≋(Town) ♣●

New Bell Inn L
Outpart Eastward, CO12 3EN
11-3, 7-midnight; 11-1am Fri & Sat; 12-midnight Sun
☎ (01255) 503545 thenewbell.co.uk
Greene King IPA; Mighty Oak Oscar Wilde; 2 changing beers (sourced regionally) [H]
Known to many visitors to Harwich, the New Bell continues to be a real ale destination pub after changing hands in 2015. Two real ciders are usually available, often chosen by one of the pub's cider-drinking regulars – be warned, though, that they can be on the strong side. A lunch menu is served (except Mon); in the evening, menus, cutlery and crockery are available for those ordering in takeaways from local outlets.
Q ≋(Town) ♣●P

Hazel End

Three Horseshoes
CM23 1HB
12-3, 6-11; 12-3 Sun ☎ (01279) 813429
threehorseshoeshazelend.co.uk
Adnams Southwold Bitter; Sharp's Doom Bar; 1 changing beer (sourced nationally) [H]
A clean and friendly pub, opposite the cricket green at Hazel End. It has been completely renovated, and a large extension added later has created more space to eat and drink here very comfortably. This is a good example of a once run-down premises transformed into a thriving, successful pub. It has low ceilings, black wooden beams and two wood-burning stoves. The food menu includes an impressive choice of fish. P

Herongate Tye

Olde Dog Inn L
129 Billericay Road, CM13 3SD (¾ mile E of A128)
TQ641909
11.30-11; 12-11 Sat; 12-8.30 Sun ☎ (01277) 810337
theoldedoginn.co.uk
Crouch Vale Brewers Gold; Greene King Abbot [H]**; 2 changing beers (sourced nationally)** [G]
This 17th-century weatherboarded inn is a privately owned and run free house with traditional decor. It offers a variety of real ales including two regularly changing guests and a craft beer from countrywide microbreweries, along with more established national brands and its own locally brewed Olde Dog IPA. Two traditional ciders are also available. Food is served at the bar or in the separate restaurant area lunchtimes and evenings. Dogs are welcome in the area at the end of the bar known as the Dog House.
●P

High Roding

Black Lion L
3 The Street, CM6 1NT (on B184 Dunmow to Ongar road)
12-3, 5-11; 12-11 Fri-Sun ☎ (01371) 872847
theblacklionhighroding.co.uk
Greene King IPA; 4 changing beers (sourced locally; often Colchester, Hadham) [H]
A striking half-timbered 14th-century building, formerly a coaching inn, on the London-Norwich road, with low ceilings, oak beams and a huge fire in winter. The restaurant serves good locally sourced food, with a popular roast on Sunday. There is a TV in the end bar, usually showing rugby on Saturday. Outside is a pleasant courtyard garden. The pub runs tasting evenings throughout the year. Q P (17,18)

Hockley

White Hart
274 Main Road, SS5 4NS

⏲ 11-11; 12-10.30 Sun ☎ (01702) 203438
🌐 whitehartthockley.co.uk
House beer (by Caledonian); 2 changing beers (sourced nationally) Ⓗ
Friendly village pub facing Hawkwell village green. The housing surrounding this hostelry has made it the centre of village life for over 200 years. The old coaching inn now has a modern, comfortable interior, while retaining the original sash windows, a central open fire and horse brasses. It holds a popular quiz night on the first Monday of the month. One house beer and two changing guest ales are served. There is a large rear garden with seating and a patio area, plus picnic tables at the front. 🐴❀◐♿⇌♣P🚌(7,8)📶

Horndon-on-the-Hill

Bell Inn

High Road, SS17 8LD
⏲ 11-11; 12-10.30 Sun ☎ (01375) 642463 🌐 bell-inn.co.uk
Crouch Vale Brewers Gold; Greene King IPA; Sharp's Doom Bar; 2 changing beers (sourced nationally) Ⓗ
Popular 15th-century coaching inn, with beamed bars featuring wood panelling and carvings, run by the same family since 1938. Note the hot cross bun collection; a bun has been added every Good Friday for more than 100 years. Three regular beers plus two guests are served, including ales from Essex breweries. The award-winning restaurant is open daily, lunchtimes and evenings (booking is advisable). Gourmet nights are held – see the website for details. Accommodation is available in 27 bedrooms. Q🐴❀🛏◐♿P🚌(11)🐾📶

Kirby-le-Soken

Red Lion Ⓛ ✔

32 The Street, CO13 0EF (on B1034)
⏲ 11-11; 12-10.30 Sun ☎ (01255) 674832
🌐 redlionkirby.co.uk
Colchester No.1; Courage Directors; Fuller's London Pride; 1 changing beer (sourced nationally) Ⓗ
A 14th-century beamed public house with a welcoming atmosphere, and a large garden with a patio and children's play areas. Inside in the dining area, boards reveal the current specials as well as the regular home-cooked meal options. At the bar, the real ale board includes details such as beer miles for the ales available. Regular events include a monthly quiz, themed evenings and a monthly acoustic showcase. Real cider is sold in the summer months. Q🐴❀◐🍎P🚌(8,98)🐾📶

Ship

35 Walton Road, CO13 0DT
⏲ 11-11 ☎ (01255) 679149 🌐 theshipkirbylesoken.co.uk
Adnams Southwold Bitter, Ghost Ship, Broadside; 3 changing beers (sourced nationally) Ⓗ
The Ship is a free house, popular with locals and visitors from further afield, with a restaurant area, an outside seating area to the front and a large beer garden to the rear. The garden contains a marquee that is used for various events throughout the year. The restaurant offers a wide selection of menus. Local CAMRA Cider Pub of the Year in 2017 and 2018, with trays of three thirds of cider available. Well-behaved dogs are welcome.
Q🐴❀◐♣🍎P🚌(8,98)🐾📶

Lamarsh

Lamarsh Lion

Bures Road, CO8 5EP (1¼ miles NW of Bures) TL892355
⏲ 10.30-11 ☎ (01787) 227007 🌐 lamarshlion.co.uk
4 changing beers (sourced nationally) Ⓗ
A recently reopened, rural, 14th-century community pub with outstanding views across the Stour Valley. The Independent newspaper voted it as one of the top 20 new pubs in 2019. The beautifully renovated interior showcases a wide range of social events including music nights. A separate dining area offers a varied menu, with food served lunchtimes and evenings every day. Cyclists and ramblers are welcome, as are dogs.
Q🐴❀◐♿♣P🚌(754)🐾📶

Langley Lower Green

Bull

Park Lane, CB11 4SB TL437345
⏲ 5-11; 12-2, 4-11 Fri; 12-11 Sat & Sun ☎ (01279) 777307
🌐 thebullpub.co.uk
Adnams Mosaic; Greene King IPA; 2 changing beers (sourced regionally) Ⓗ
Classic Victorian village local with original cast-iron lattice windows, in a tiny isolated hamlet close to both Hertfordshire and Cambridgeshire. The pub has a band of local regulars. Open mic night is the last Tuesday of the month and there are occasional quiz nights. An annual beer festival takes place in September. There is an aquarium in the lounge bar. If you plan ahead, you can order food before your visit. 🐴❀◐♣P🐾📶

Layer Breton

Hare & Hounds

Crayes Green, CO2 0PN
⏲ 11-11.30; 11.30-11.30 Sun ☎ (01206) 330459
🌐 thehareandhound.co.uk
3 changing beers (sourced nationally) Ⓗ
Attractive country pub with a single bar and a separate room for dining and functions. It has cosy logburners, and a garden with a pergola for al fresco eating and drinking. Three beer festivals are held a year including a St George's Day festival. The community shop sells newspapers, and operates a post office Tuesday morning and Thursday afternoon. It is a regional finalist in the Countryside Alliance Awards, and has a good-quality food menu. Quiz night is the first Wednesday of the month. 🐴❀🛏◐♿⛺♣🍎P🚌(92)🐾📶

Leigh-on-Sea

Crooked Billet ✔

51 High Street, Old Leigh, SS9 2EP
⏲ 12-11 (11.30 Fri); 11-10.30 Sun ☎ (01702) 480289
Adnams Southwold Bitter; St Austell Nicholson's Pale Ale; Sharp's Doom Bar; 3 changing beers (sourced regionally) Ⓗ
In Old Leigh fishing village, overlooking the Thames Estuary, this 16th-century pub has two small bars with bare floorboards and beamed ceilings. The walls are decorated with local village and fishing pictures. It has a small garden to one side and a larger seating area at the front shared with a seafood merchant. Up to six real ales are on offer, with three regulars and three guests from the Nicholson's list. A short walk from Leigh-on-Sea station. 🐴❀◐⇌P🚌(21,26)🐾📶

Leigh-on-Sea Brewery Tap

35 Progress Road, SS9 5PR

closed Sun-Wed; 4-8 Thu & Fri; 1-5 Sat ☎ (01702) 817255

leighonseabrewery.co.uk

8 changing beers (sourced locally; often Leigh-on-Sea) H

The Leigh-on-Sea Brewery taproom is in the Progress Road Industrial Estate. The beer range is a rotation of core beers on either handpump or KeyKeg dispense, with one or two guest beers. The decor features exposed brickwork, tall tables and stools, industrial lighting and a bar top of cockleshells. Opening hours can vary; please check the website or social media (updated frequently). International rugby is shown, and other major sporting events on terrestrial TV. Regular music events take place.

Mayflower

5-6 High Street, Old Leigh, SS9 2EN

11-11 (midnight Fri & Sat); 12-11 Sun ☎ (01702) 478535

mayfloweroldleigh.com

Crouch Vale Brewers Gold; George's Cockleboats; St Austell Proper Job; 3 changing beers (sourced regionally) H

A pleasant pub, situated at the rear of a fish and chips restaurant at the far end of Old Leigh. The outdoor terrace has views across the Thames Estuary. LocAle is available from both George's and Crouch Vale, and there is usually a dark beer. Food is mainly fish dishes from the restaurant. One wall depicts the Pilgrim Fathers' passenger manifest of those who sailed on the Mayflower. A three-times local CAMRA Pub of the Year.
P (26)

Little Thurrock (Grays)

Traitors' Gate

40-42 Broadway, RM17 6EW (on A126)

12-11.30 (11.45 Fri & Sat) ☎ (01375) 372628

traitorsgatepub.wordpress.com

Greene King Abbot; 5 changing beers (sourced locally) H

Taken over by the current operator in 2013, this pub has established a reputation for live bands on Friday and Saturday and open mic sessions on Thursday. It has six handpumps, with five dispensing a rotating selection of guest beers from Essex breweries and further afield. Look for the chalkboards above the bar listing current and forthcoming beers. (66,66A)

Littley Green

Compasses

CM3 1BU

12-3, 5.30-11.30; 12-11.30 Thu-Sun ☎ (01245) 362308

compasseslittleygreen.co.uk

Bishop Nick Ridley's Rite; Crouch Vale Essex Boys Best Bitter; 3 changing beers (sourced nationally) G

Formerly Ridley's Brewery tap, this is a picturesque Victorian country pub in a quiet hamlet. A wood-panelled bar has benches around the walls and a tiled floor. Beers are drawn directly from casks. It has an interesting range of three ciders and a perry. Renowned filled huffers (giant baps) are available lunchtimes and evenings, plus other traditional dishes. There are seats and tables outside and in the large gardens. Regular beer festivals are held. Accommodation comprises five high-quality rooms. QP

Loughton

Victoria Tavern

165 Smarts Lane, IG10 4BP

11-11; 12-10.30 Sun ☎ (020) 8508 1779

victoriatavern.co.uk

Adnams Southwold Bitter; Greene King IPA; Sharp's Doom Bar; Timothy Taylor Landlord; 2 changing beers H

An old-fashioned pub that prides itself on real ale and inclusive conversation. It lies between Loughton and Epping Forest and is a 10-15 minute walk from Loughton Tube station. With a pleasant gated garden, the pub is used by locals and walkers; well-behaved dogs are welcome. It serves generous portions of fresh seasonal food.
QP

Maldon

Carpenters Arms

33 Gate Street, CM9 5QF

11-11 ☎ (01621) 859896 carpentersarmsmaldon.com

Adnams Southwold Bitter; Mighty Oak Kings; Sharp's Sea Fury; 3 changing beers (sourced nationally; often Skinner's, Timothy Taylor) H

This friendly back-street community Gray & Sons pub, with its ancient beams, is the local CAMRA Cider Pub of the Year for 2019. A superb selection of over 20 ciders from around the UK is served. The beer range is fairly consistent although changing ales may come from anywhere in the UK. There is an outside seating area at the front as well as a rear patio area. The pub actively supports darts, dominoes and cribbage teams. Off-street parking is limited. P

Farmers Yard

140 High Street, CM9 5BX

closed Mon; 12 (5 Tue)-9 ☎ (01621) 854202

maldonmicropub.co.uk

4 changing beers (sourced locally; often Maldon) G

In a characterful Grade II-listed building, Maldon Brewing Company's micropub and bottle shop is the local CAMRA Pub of the Year for 2019. The compact, timbered room provides seating around the walls for a dozen people and has a similar number of standing places, encouraging locals and visitors to mingle. The complete range of Maldon's bottled ales, an expanding selection of bottles and cans from other breweries, two draught Belgian ales and three real ciders are sold. Q

Mighty Oak Tap Room

10 High Street, CM9 5PJ

closed Mon; 4-10 Tue & Wed; 4-11 Thu; 12-11 Fri & Sat; 12-10 Sun ☎ (01621) 853892 micropubmaldon.uk

Mighty Oak Oscar Wilde, Captain Bob, Maldon Gold, Kings; 2 changing beers (sourced locally) G

Set in a 500-year-old beamed building, Mighty Oak Brewery's taproom showcases its award-winning range of beers, served direct from the cask from a cooled ground-floor cellar. The friendly atmosphere in the comfortable downstairs bar, with its bench seating, encourages conversation. There is a quiet and relaxing reading room upstairs, furnished with leather sofas and chairs. Ciders are from Westons and Aspall's. Unplugged acoustic music sessions feature most Sundays. Q

Rose & Crown

109 High Street, CM9 5EP

8am-midnight (1am Fri & Sat) ☎ (01621) 852255

Greene King Abbot; Ruddles Best Bitter; Sharp's Doom Bar; 4 changing beers (sourced nationally) [H]
Wetherspoon revitalised this historic 16th-century pub in 2015, adding an attractive, airy extension to the rear, which houses a long marble bar with ample seating and an outside courtyard. The old building has been opened up and is attractively furnished, with many pictures of historic Maldon adorning the walls. Food is served all day from opening until 11pm. Children accompanied by an adult are welcome until 9pm. Q🐴❀◑●🍎P🚌📶

Manningtree

Red Lion

42 South Street, CO11 1BG
⏲ 12-11 (midnight Fri & Sat) ☎ (01206) 391880
🌐 redlionmanningtree.co.uk
Adnams Southwold Bitter; 2 changing beers (sourced regionally; often Colchester, Mighty Oak, Woodforde's) [H]
This gem of a pub has recently benefited from a refurbishment and the addition of a pizzeria. Customers can still bring their own food or have a takeaway delivered to the pub, but can now have a pizza freshly cooked on-site. To keep customers and staff entertained there are regular music events on Friday and/or Saturday, pub quizzes on the second and last Sundays of the month, and comedy nights on random Thursdays throughout the year. 🐴❀♣🍎🚌🐾📶

Monk Street

Farmhouse Inn [L]

CM6 2NR (off B184, 2 miles S of Thaxted) TL614288
⏲ 11-11 (10 Mon; midnight Fri & Sat); 11-10 Sun
☎ (01371) 830864 🌐 farmhouseinn.org
Greene King IPA; 2 changing beers (sourced locally) [H]
Built in the 16th century, this former Dunmow Brewery pub has been enlarged to incorporate a restaurant and accommodation; the bar is in the original part of the building. The quiet hamlet of Monk Street overlooks the Chelmer Valley, two miles from historic Thaxted. A disused well in the garden supplied the hamlet with water during World War II. The pub has a rear patio, front garden and a top field. Draught cider from Westons is usually sold. 🐴❀🛏◑●🍎P🚌(313)🐾📶

Newport

White Horse Inn

Belmont Hill, CB11 3RF
⏲ 12 (3 Mon & Tue)-11.30; 12-1am Fri & Sat
☎ (01799) 540002 🌐 whitehorsenewport.co.uk
3 changing beers (sourced nationally) [H]
On the main road in the middle of Newport, this is a friendly drinkers' local, serving three changing ales. An ex-Greene King house purchased by a local business, extensive repair work has been carried out on the building and it has been transformed into a pub focused on the community. The change of ownership, with a new enthusiastic licensee, has raised its popularity as a beer drinkers' pub. Food is served on Tuesday evening only.
❀≠♣🚌(301)🐾📶

Pebmarsh

King's Head

The Street, CO9 2NH
⏲ closed Mon; 12-11 (11.30 Fri & Sat); 12-9 Sun
☎ (01787) 267942 🌐 kingsheadpebmarsh.co.uk
Adnams Ghost Ship; 3 changing beers (sourced nationally) [H]
This pub was saved by the community and reopened in 2017, after an extensive refurbishment, while maintaining its traditional character. A plaque is displayed showing its many shareholders' names on the wall. There is a single bar serving three areas: one for drinking, one with comfy seating, and another for dining. There is a real fire in the main bar. It has benches outside and a large garden. 🐴❀◑●P🚌🐾📶

Ridgewell

White Horse Inn [L]

Mill Road, CO9 4SG (on A1017) TL735408
⏲ 5-11 Mon; 12-2, 5-11 Tue; 12-11 Wed-Sun
☎ (01440) 785532 🌐 ridgewellwhitehorse.com
3 changing beers (sourced nationally) [G]
Set in a pretty village, which was home to the American 381st Heavy Bomb Group during WWII. A dark beer is often available here. Annual beer festivals are held in summer on the patio behind the pub. As well as a choice of excellent real ale and food, this pub offers an interesting selection of good-quality wines and 4-star accommodation.
🐴❀🛏◑●♿♣🍎P🗍🚌📶

Rochford

Golden Lion [L]

35 North Street, SS4 1AB
⏲ 11-midnight (1am Fri & Sat) ☎ (01702) 545487
🌐 goldenlionrochford.co.uk
Adnams Southwold Bitter; Greene King Abbot; Keppels Golden Crow; 4 changing beers (sourced nationally) [H]
This Grade II-listed, 16th century weatherboarded free house is a long-standing Guide entry and has won many local CAMRA awards including Pub of the Year. In addition to the three regular ales, four nationally sourced beers (one each from Tring, Cotleigh, Irwell Works and Mighty Oak) are available, along with real cider. A beer festival is held in autumn in the attractive patio-style garden. Live sports are occasionally shown on large-screen TV. A wood-burning stove and a comprehensive jukebox add to the atmosphere.
❀♿≠♣🍎P🚌🐾📶

Miley

1 Union Lane, SS4 1AP
⏲ 12-midnight (1am Fri & Sat) ☎ (01702) 544229
4 changing beers (sourced nationally) [H]
A family-owned, friendly community local selling four changing ales. Some are from the wider Greene King stable, but others are from smaller breweries such as Billericay, Milestone and Tombstone. Live bands play most weekends (on the outside stage in the summer) and there are monthly karaoke and quiz nights. It is sports-oriented, with two dartboards and large-screen TVs showing rugby and football. The annual three-legged race is a fixture. Ales are £2.50 a pint on Monday. ❀♿≠♣🍎P🚌🐾📶

Rose & Crown

45 North Road, SS4 1AD
🕑 11-midnight (1am Fri & Sat); 12-midnight Sun
☎ (01702) 530112
3 changing beers (sourced nationally) Ⓗ
A 1920s roadhouse-style corner pub in the Rochford conservation area. The single bar serves two distinct areas: a lively public bar with a pool table, and a quieter saloon bar with a dartboard. The large patio area to the side and rear has a bar serving cocktails and cider in the summer. Regular events are held such as curry and quiz nights, and live bands often play at the weekend. Happy hours feature on Monday, Tuesday and Friday at various times. ❀⇌♣🍎P🚌🐾📶

Rowhedge

Olde Albion Ⓛ

High Street, CO5 7ES
🕑 5-11 Mon; 12-3, 5-11 Tue & Wed; 12-11 Thu-Sat; 12-10.30 Sun ☎ (01206) 728972
4 changing beers (sourced nationally) Ⓗ
A free house on the waterfront, playing a substantial role in local village life. The pub serves several hundred different ales each year – the choice is always interesting, with many new and rarely seen beers from a wide range of small breweries, sourced nationally. In warmer weather there are tables and chairs on the greensward overlooking the River Colne. Beer festivals are held on St George's Day and during the Rowhedge Regatta. ❀♣🍎🚌(66)🐾📶

Saffron Walden

King's Arms Ⓛ ✔

10 Market Hill, CB10 1HQ
🕑 11 (12 Mon)-11; 11-12.30am Sat; 11-10 Sun
☎ (01799) 522768
Adnams Southwold Bitter; Oakham JHB; Woodforde's Wherry; 2 changing beers (sourced nationally) Ⓗ
Wooden-beamed, multi-roomed pub, just off the market square (market days are Tuesday and Saturday). A dark beer is often served in winter. There is live music at weekends, acoustic music on Thursday and a monthly quiz. Welcoming log fires in the winter and a pleasant patio for alfresco eating and drinking are particular features. Food is served at lunchtimes. Q🐴❀☾P🚌🐾📶

Old English Gentleman ✔

11 Gold Street, CB10 1EJ (E of B184/B1052 jct)
🕑 11-midnight (11 Mon; 1am Fri & Sat); 12-11 Sun
☎ (01799) 523595 🌐 oldenglishgentleman.com
Adnams Southwold Bitter; Woodforde's Wherry; 2 changing beers (sourced regionally) Ⓗ
An 18th-century town-centre pub with log fires and a welcoming atmosphere. It serves a selection of guest ales and an extensive menu of regularly changing bar food and sandwiches. Traditional roasts and chef's specials are available on Sunday in the bar or dining area, where a variety of works of art is displayed. There is a heated patio at the rear and a wood-burning stove too. 🐴❀☾🚌🐾📶

Sible Hedingham

White Lion Ⓛ

6 Church Street, CO9 3NS
🕑 11-11 (midnight Fri & Sat); 12-11 Sun ☎ (01787) 462534
3 changing beers (sourced nationally) Ⓗ
The last remaining pub in Sible Hedingham, proving popular with locals and visitors, featuring regular events and live music. Friendly and hospitable, it offers home-made lunches, afternoon teas by appointment, and a good range of bar snacks. Sunday lunch is served 12-4pm in the function room, which has a small stage and is available for private hire. The bar has numerous wines and spirits. There is an attractive beer garden and games room with darts, pool and sports TV. 🐴❀♣P🐾📶

South Benfleet

South Benfleet Social Club Ⓛ

8 Vicarage Hill, SS7 1PB (on B1006 High Rd)
🕑 12-11 (midnight Fri & Sat) ☎ (01268) 206159
6 changing beers Ⓗ/Ⓖ
This popular social club is a huge asset to the community. It holds two beer festivals in May and December, with a good range of beers and ciders always available. Games include pool, poker and quiz nights, with sport on TV and live music at weekends, which all add to the feel-good factor. Show a CAMRA membership card or a copy of this Guide for entry. East Anglia CAMRA regional Club of the Year 2018 and branch winner for six successive years. 🐴❀☾♿⇌♣🍎P🚌🐾📶

South Woodham Ferrers

Tap Room 19

19 Haltwhistle Road, CM3 5ZA
🕑 closed Mon; 4-9 (11 Fri); 2-11 Sat; 2-5 Sun
☎ (01245) 322744
Crouch Vale Blackwater Mild, Essex Boys Best Bitter, Brewers Gold, Yakima Gold, Amarillo; 2 changing beers (sourced locally; often Crouch Vale) Ⓖ
Tucked away on the town's Western Industrial Estate, in front of the Crouch Vale Brewery, the pub is a 10-minute walk through side streets from the railway station. It is simply furnished with an understated decor – a welcome real ale oasis in a town with few other outlets. Beers are served from a taproom, visible through windows at the rear of the bar. Up to six ciders are on offer. There is a small outdoor seating area to the front. Q❀⇌♣🍎P🚏🚌(36)🐾📶

Southend-on-Sea

Mawson's Ⓛ

781 Southchurch Road, SS1 2PP (on A13)
🕑 4-11; 2-12.30am Fri; 12-12.30am Sat; 12-10 Sun
☎ (01702) 601781
George's Wallasea Wench, Cockleboats; 4 changing beers (sourced nationally) Ⓗ
A converted shop, this is Southend's first micropub, and currently local CAMRA Cider Pub of the Year. It has six ciders and a large selection of foreign and craft bottles, plus up to six ales, with a least two from the local George's Brewery. It is in the Southchurch village area, and has a large gallery of Laurel and Hardy pictures. Quiet music adds to happy conversation and there are occasional live music and quiz nights. 🐴♿⇌(East)🍎🚏🚌(1,14)🐾📶

Railway Hotel Ⓛ ✔

32 Clifftown Road, SS1 1AJ
🕑 5-11 (10 Tue); 12-11 Fri; 12-1am Sat; 2-10 Sun
☎ (01702) 343194 🌐 railwayhotelsouthend.co.uk

Adnams Southwold Bitter, Mosaic, Ghost Ship, Broadside; Crouch Vale Brewers Gold; 1 changing beer (sourced locally) [H]
Striking Victorian railway hotel, unique and quirky inside, recognised by CAMRA as having a historic interior of some regional importance. There are usually five ales on sale from Adnams and Crouch Vale. It is a music-oriented pub, with live bands most nights and an interesting collection of vinyl records at other times. Vegan pizzas are available at the weekends and there is a large beer garden with decking at the rear. ❀◐♿≋(Central)🚌ᯤ

Southminster

Station Arms
39 Station Road, CM0 7EW
12-2.30, 6 (5.30 Fri)-11; 2-11 Sat; 12-10.30 Sun
☎ (01621) 772225 🌐 thestationarms.co.uk
Adnams Southwold Bitter; 4 changing beers (sourced regionally; often Bishop Nick, George's, Mighty Oak) [H]
A traditional Essex weatherboarded pub which has featured in this Guide for over 25 years, a friendly and often busy community local. Live blues and folk music is hosted monthly. Annually, a harvest festival charity auction and a conker championship are held. The comfortable bare-boarded bar, with its open log fire, is decorated with railway and brewery memorabilia. An attractive courtyard is popular in fine weather and a barn with a wood-burning stove provides shelter if required.
Q❀≋♣🍎🚌

Wibblers Brewery Taproom & Kitchen
Goldsands Road, CM0 7JW
closed Mon-Wed; 12-8 Thu; 12-10 Fri & Sat; 12-6 Sun
☎ (01621) 772044 🌐 wibblers.co.uk/taproomkitchen
Wibblers Dengie IPA [H]**; 5 changing beers (sourced locally; often Wibblers)** [H]/[G]
The recently expanded taproom is attached to the beautifully restored medieval tithe barn housing Wibblers Brewery. The spacious bar is attractively furnished and in the summer you can sit outside and take in the rural setting. Excellent home-cooked food is served using mostly local produce. The brewery and taproom host open days and various other events throughout the year, including televised rugby and themed food evenings. Southminster railway station is only five minutes' walk away. Q❀◑♿≋🍎P🚌(31X)🐾ᯤ

Stanford-le-Hope

Rising Sun [L]
Church Hill, SS17 0EU (opp church and near A1014)
3-10.30 Mon; 12-10.30 Tue; 12-11 Wed; 12-11.30 Thu; 12-midnight Fri & Sat; 11-10.30 Sun ☎ (01375) 671097
5 changing beers [H]
Much-improved, two-bar, traditional town pub in the shadow of the church. The five guest beers are mainly from independent breweries, including LocAle beers, and up to three ciders or perries are stocked. Regular monthly live music is a feature. Beer festivals are held three times a year, in spring, summer and winter, with the summer festival taking place in the pub's large rear garden. The back bar is available for private functions.
❀≋♣🍎P🚌🐾ᯤ

Stansted Mountfitchet

Rose & Crown [L]
31 Bentfield Green, CM24 8HX (1 mile W of B1383) TL505256
closed Mon; 6-10 Tue; 12-3, 6-11 Wed & Thu; 12-midnight Fri & Sat; 12-9 Sun ☎ (01279) 812107
🌐 roseandcrownstansted.co.uk
3 changing beers (sourced regionally) [H]
Family-run Victorian pub near a duckpond, on the edge of a small hamlet. This free house has been modernised to provide one large bar, but retains the welcoming atmosphere of an active village local. The bar has been extended to include a new largish snug, and has an old seven-inch singles jukebox on which you can play your own records. Food is home cooked and made from locally sourced produce. A large variety of gins is available. ❀◑♣P🚌(7,7A)🐾ᯤ

Stanway

Live & Let Live [L]
12 Millers Lane, CO3 0PS
12-11 (midnight Fri & Sat) ☎ (01206) 574071
🌐 theliveandletlive.co.uk
4 changing beers (sourced nationally) [H]
The Live's reputation continues to grow thanks to the publicans' great pride in the condition of their real ales, and regular beer and sausage/pie festivals. The welcoming pub has a quiet, homely saloon bar, a public bar offering sports TV, darts, pool and a comprehensive jukebox, and a beer garden. The beers are competitively priced, as is the traditional home-cooked food, served lunchtimes daily and Friday and Saturday evenings. Runner-up local CAMRA Pub of the Year 2019.
Q❀◑♿♣🍎P🚌🐾ᯤ

Steeple Bumpstead

Fox & Hounds [L]
3 Chapel Street, CB9 7DQ (on B1054 at jct with B1057)
12-3, 5-11; 12-midnight Fri & Sat; 12-11 Sun
☎ (01440) 731810 🌐 foxinsteeple.co.uk
Greene King IPA; 3 changing beers (sourced nationally) [H]
A 500-year-old friendly local near the Suffolk border, featuring a main bar with an open fire, two further rooms, seating outside at the front and a courtyard garden. Four beers are on offer from local and national breweries. No food is available but a guest chef makes a monthly appearance. On Wednesday evening there is a free cheeseboard and wine and beer prices are reduced. An annual beer festival takes place in May, and there are pub games and occasional live music.
Q❀◑♣🚌(18)🐾ᯤ

Stow Maries

Prince of Wales
Woodham Road, CM3 6SA
11-11 (midnight Fri & Sat); 12-10.30 Sun
☎ (01621) 828971 🌐 prince-stowmaries.net
Titanic Plum Porter; 6 changing beers (sourced nationally; often Dark Star, Titanic) [H]
A classic weatherboarded pub with several characterful drinking areas, open fires and an old bread oven used for baking pizzas in the winter. The extensive garden and courtyards provide plenty of options for outside drinking. Good food is

available, made with local produce where possible. Many special events are held including Burns night, a firework display on the last Saturday in October, and live music. The historic Stow Maries World War I airfield is nearby. Q♘❀🛏◖◗♿P🚆🚌(593)🐾📶

Thaxted

Maypole ✔

Orange Street, CM6 2LT

⏲ 12-11; 12-10.30 Sun ☎ (01371) 831599

🌐 maypolethaxted.com

Greene King IPA; 4 changing beers (sourced nationally) Ⓗ

A renamed ex-Ridley's pub, all in one room with a games/TV area, sofas, chairs and an area with tables. There is a pleasant patio garden and a car park at the rear. A hospitable beer drinkers' local, up to four guest ales are on tap. The pub holds musical events and runs beer festivals. ♘❀◖♣P🚌(6,312)🐾📶

Tollesbury

King's Head

1 High Street, CM9 8RG (on B1023)

⏲ 12-11 (midnight Fri & Sat); 12-10 Sun ☎ (01621) 869203

Bishop Nick Ridley's Rite; house beer (by Colchester); 3 changing beers (sourced nationally) Ⓗ

A welcoming village pub, in the same ownership for over 25 years, which offers great-value beer. The public bar contains a pool table and dartboard while the lounge bar boasts many historic yachting photographs and paintings. There is a small patio to the rear. The pub is popular with walkers and birdwatchers. Excellent home-cooked food is served Friday lunchtime only. During the week you can bring in pies, pasties or sandwiches from the bakery opposite. Q♘❀◖♿♣🍎P🚌🐾

Toppesfield

Green Man 🄻

Church Lane, CO9 4DR

⏲ 5-10 Mon; 5-11 Tue & Wed; 12-3, 5-11 Thu; 2-11 Fri; 10-11 Sat; 12-10 Sun ☎ (01787) 237418

🌐 thegreenmantoppesfield.com

Pumphouse Community Golden Duck IPA, Pumphouse Gold; 2 changing beers (sourced regionally) Ⓗ

Community-owned pub with a community-owned brewery next door, the Pumphouse Brewery – this village is the only one in the UK to have a pub, brewery and shop all owned by the community. Beer festivals and events are held throughout the year. The pub has two pool teams, and darts is played in the public bar. A range of food is available including Sunday lunch, fish and chips (including takeaways) on Friday, and bacon rolls on Saturday. Meals may need pre-booking. ♘❀◖◗♿♣🍎P🐾📶

Waltham Abbey

Woodbine Inn 🏆 🄻 ✔

Honey Lane, EN9 3QT (on A121 near M25 jct 26)

⏲ 11.30-11 (1am Fri & Sat); 11.30-10.30 Sun

☎ (01992) 713050 🌐 thewoodbine.co.uk

Adnams Ghost Ship Ⓗ**; Bishop Nick Divine** Ⓗ/Ⓖ**; Mighty Oak Oscar Wilde** Ⓖ**, Captain Bob** Ⓗ**; 3 changing beers (sourced locally)** Ⓗ/Ⓖ

The Woodbine is situated in Epping Forest. It has a separate restaurant but concentrates on real ales and over 40 small-producer ciders, including production of London Glider. Food is home-made, with local sausages, ham and steak as specialities. The ale sampling society and comedy club meet monthly; bar billiards is played. Dogs are welcome in the main bar. Local CAMRA Pub of the Year 2018 and 2019, East Anglian and national finalist Cider Pub of the Year 2018. ♘◖◗♣🍎P🚌(66,66A)🐾📶

Weeley Heath

White Hart

Clacton Road, CO16 9ED (on B1441) TM153208

⏲ 12-2.30, 4-11 (10 Mon); 12-11 Fri & Sat; 12-8 Sun

☎ (01255) 830384

2 changing beers (sourced nationally; often Greene King, Mauldons, Woodforde's) Ⓗ

A typical village local, this free house is a regular Guide entry and local CAMRA Pub of the Year 2017 and 2018. Run by the same owner/landlord for many years, it is community focused, hosting pool and darts teams and holding occasional music and quiz evenings. The garden has a covered patio for smokers. This is a great sports fan's pub, with Sky TV and BT Sport. ❀⛺♣🍎P🚌📶

Wendens Ambo

Bell 🄻

Royston Road, CB11 4JY (on B1039)

⏲ 12-11 ☎ (01799) 540382 🌐 thebellinnpub.co.uk

Adnams Ghost Ship; Woodforde's Wherry; 2 changing beers (sourced regionally; often Oakham) Ⓗ

Lovely country pub in a picturesque village, with a large garden, a terrace with seating, a pétanque pitch and children's play apparatus. Traditional locally sourced pub food is served. A chalkboard displays forthcoming guest ales. A folk open evening is held on the first Wednesday of the month. A charity fundraising event is held with a beer festival over the summer bank holiday weekend, known as the Bell Bash. Dogs, walkers and cyclists are welcome here. ♘❀◖◗🚆(Audley End)♣🍎P🚌(59,301)🐾📶

West Hanningfield

Three Compasses 🄻

Church Road, CM2 8UQ

⏲ 11.30-3 Mon; 11.30-3, 6-11; 12-3 Sun ☎ (01245) 400447

Bishop Nick Ridley's Rite; 1 changing beer (sourced nationally) Ⓗ

A delightful small country pub dating from 1425 (the landlords from 1758 are listed inside), ideally situated for country walkers and cyclists. A free house, the current landlady has been here since 1971 and her son is now joint licensee. The timber-framed and plastered Grade II-listed building has many low beams, two bars and bench seats in front of the windows. Home-cooked food is served every lunchtime and some evenings. Q♘❀◖◗P🚌(13,13A)🐾📶

Westcliff-on-Sea

Cricketers

228 London Road, SS0 7JG (on A13 London Rd)

⏲ 12-midnight (11 Tue & Wed); 12-1am Fri & Sat; 12-10.30 Sun ☎ (01702) 345053 🌐 thecricketersbarandfood.co.uk

Dark Star Hophead; Greene King Abbot; Mighty Oak Oscar Wilde, Maldon Gold; Sharp's Doom Bar; 1 changing beer (sourced regionally) [H]
A Gray & Sons pub with well-kept beer, not far from Southend town centre. A music venue adjoins the pub so it can get busy on music nights. A jazz night featuring Digby Fairweather and guests is held every second Wednesday of the month, and a pub quiz on Monday. The five regular beers, one of which is dark, are joined by an extra one on days when Southend United are playing at home.
🐎✿◐◑♿⇌🚌🐾📶

West Road Tap 🏆
2 West Road, SS0 9DA (on B1015, near A13)
⏲ closed Mon; 12-9 (10.30 Fri & Sat); 12-7 Sun
☎ (01702) 330647 🌐 westroadtap.com
3 changing beers (sourced nationally) [G]
Located near the Palace Theatre in Westcliff, this is a micropub and bottle shop serving up to three cask ales on gravity. The cask ale range is sourced nationally. Beer is also served from six KeyKeg taps, and an extensive fridge selection of craft beer in bottles and cans is also available to drink on the premises or to take home. Two real ciders in boxes are available. Children are welcome until 7pm. Local CAMRA Pub of the Year 2019.
Q🐎✿⇌🍎🚌(1,27)🐾

Widdington

Fleur de Lys 🏆 [L] ✔
High Street, CB11 3SG TL538316
⏲ 6.30-11 Mon & Tue; 12-3, 6-11 Wed & Thu; 12-11.30 Fri & Sat; 12-10 Sun ☎ (01799) 543280 🌐 thefleurdelys.co.uk
Adnams Southwold Bitter, Broadside; Woodforde's Wherry; 2 changing beers (sourced nationally) [H]
Rumours of a ghost abound at this welcoming 400-year-old village local, which boasts a large open fireplace and beams. This was the first pub to be saved from closure by the local branch of CAMRA after the branch's formation. Quality meals are offered with fresh local ingredients. The source of the River Cam and Prior's Hall Barn, an English Heritage site, are both nearby. A bridge club is held here on Monday night. Local CAMRA Pub of the Year 2019. 🐎✿◐◑♿♣🍎**P**🚌(301)🐾

Witham

Battesford Court [L] ✔
100-102 Newland Street, CM8 1AH (on B1389)
⏲ 8am-midnight (1am Fri & Sat); 8am-11 Sun
☎ (01376) 504080
Greene King Abbot; Ruddles Best Bitter; Sharp's Doom Bar; 5 changing beers (sourced nationally) [H]
A large Wetherspoon conversion of a former hotel of the same name. The 16th-century building was previously the courthouse of the manor of Battesford. It has distinct areas with wood panelling and oak beams, including a family area. Up to five regional beers are served, including something local, usually from Bishop Nick or Wibblers, plus up to two ciders and perries, normally from Westons and Gwynt y Ddraig. The standard Wetherspoon food offering is available.
Q🐎✿◐◑♿🍎🚌📶

Wivenhoe

Black Buoy ✔
Black Buoy Hill, CO7 9BS
⏲ 11-11; 12-9.30 Sun ☎ (01206) 822425 🌐 blackbuoy.co.uk
Adnams Southwold Bitter; 5 changing beers (sourced nationally) [H]
A popular and friendly community-owned free house and a regular winner of local CAMRA Rural Pub of the Year, with a changing range of ales. It has a drinking area and further spaces for drinking and dining, with a range of good-value home-cooked food on offer. The courtyard hosts beer festivals, usually around the late May and August bank holidays. Open mic, live music and quiz nights feature regularly. 🐎✿🛏◐◑⇌**P**🚌🐾📶

Horse & Groom ✔
55 The Cross, CO7 9QL (on B1028)
⏲ 10.30-3, 5.30-11; 10.30-2, 6-11 Sat; 12-4.30, 7-11 Sun
☎ (01206) 824928
Adnams Southwold Bitter, Ghost Ship, Broadside; 3 changing beers (sourced nationally) [H]
A genuine local pub at the top end of Wivenhoe, with two bars: a comfortable lounge bar and a friendly public bar. Various traditional pub games including darts and dominoes are played. Children and dogs are welcome, and there is a play area in the beer garden, which also has ample seating. A good home-cooked menu includes a Thursday roast and a regular curry club (no food on Sun). There are excellent bus links from Colchester to the pub.
Q🐎✿◐♿♣**P**🚌🐾📶

Woodham Mortimer

Hurdlemakers Arms
Post Office Road, CM9 6ST
⏲ 12-11; 12-9 Sun ☎ (01245) 225169
🌐 hurdlemakersarms.co.uk
5 changing beers (sourced locally; often Maldon, Mighty Oak, Wibblers) [H]
Traditional, welcoming Gray's pub just off the main A414 road, between Danbury and Maldon. The large garden and children's play area are ideal in summer. The pub also boasts a barn and marquee where the annual beer festival and barbecue is held on the last weekend in June. Hearty portions of superb home-cooked food are served daily and can be washed down with excellent local ales and up to six ciders. Monthly quiz nights are always popular. **Q**🐎✿◐◑♿♣🍎**P**🥛🚌🐾📶

Writtle

Wheatsheaf [L]
70 The Green, CM1 3DU
⏲ 11-11.30 (midnight Fri & Sat); 12-11 Sun
☎ (01245) 420672 🌐 thewheatsheafwrittle.co.uk
Adnams Southwold Bitter, Broadside; Maldon Drop of Nelson's Blood [H]**; Mighty Oak Oscar Wilde** [G]**, Maldon Gold; Wibblers Dengie IPA** [H]**; 2 changing beers (sourced nationally)** [G]
Traditional village pub built in 1813, with a small public bar, an equally compact lounge, and a covered patio by the road. It is a long-time favourite of the local CAMRA branch. The atmosphere is generally quiet, with the TV switched on only for occasional sporting events. Traditional pub food is served Tuesday to Saturday lunchtimes. Note the old Gray's sign in the public bar. **Q**◐♣**P**🚌

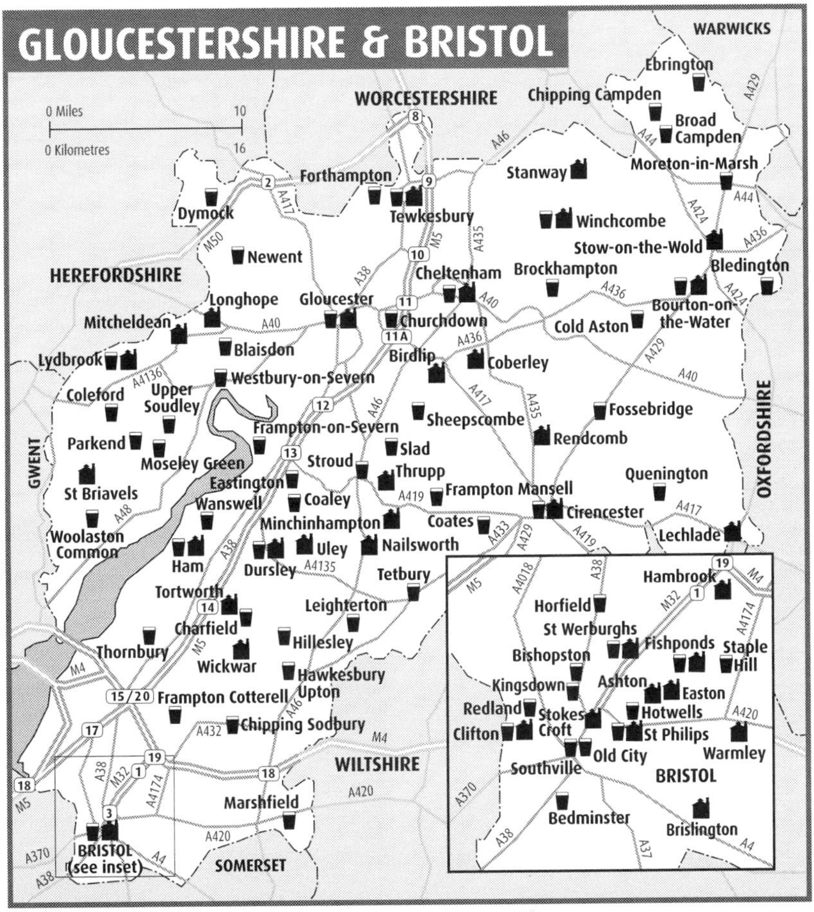

Blaisdon

Red Hart 𝕃

GL17 0AH (centre of village; signed from A4136 E of Longhope or N of A48)

12-3, 6-11; 12-3, 7-11 Sun ☎ (01452) 830477

redhartinn.co.uk

4 changing beers (sourced nationally; often Bespoke, Kingstone, Wye Valley) Ⓗ

A lovely award-winning old pub with worn flagstones in the bar, a welcoming fireplace and a veritable plethora of memorabilia as decoration. Guest ales are usually LocAle, alongside a local cider or perry from Severn Cider. The cracking restaurant means that the pub can get busy, so be prepared to mix it with a rack of lamb, not to mention free-range children, if the meals encroach into the bar area. Families are welcome to use the well-tended garden. **P**

Bledington

King's Head 𝕃 ✔

The Green, OX7 6XQ (off B4450 on village green)

11-11 ☎ (01608) 658365 kingsheadinn.net

Flying Monk Elmers; Hook Norton Hooky; 3 changing beers (sourced regionally; often Wye Valley) Ⓗ

Delightful 16th-century stone-built inn overlooking the village green. The pub has original old beams, an open inglenook log fire and high-back settles. This free house, with 12 comfortable letting rooms, is renowned for its wide range of ale and food. Bledington is about four miles from Stow-on-the-Wold, and has good local walks to nearby villages, with Kingham station close by. The two guest beers are selected from local brewers in Gloucestershire and Oxfordshire. A CAMRA award-winner and finalist for 2017 Pub of the Year. **QP**

Bourton-on-the-Water

Mousetrap Inn 𝕃

Lansdowne, GL54 2AR (300yds W of village centre)

11.30-11; 12-11 Sun ☎ (01451) 820579

themousetrapinn.co.uk

3 changing beers (sourced locally) Ⓗ

Traditional Cotswold stone free house, recently refurbished, in the Lansdowne part of Bourton close to the centre. Three changing local beers are on offer. The pub welcomes locals, tourists, children and dogs with friendly service. Food ranges from breakfasts and snacks to three-course meals. A patio area in front of the pub, with tables and hanging baskets, provides a suntrap in the summer. Local CAMRA Pub of the Year runner-up 2019. **QP**(801,855)

Bristol: Bedminster

Bristol Beer Factory Tap Room

291 North Street, BS3 1JP
⊕ 12-9 (11 Fri); 10-11 Sat; 12-7 Sun ☎ (0117) 902 6317
Bristol Beer Factory Fortitude; 3 changing beers
(often Bristol Beer Factory) Ⓗ
A short walk from Ashton Gate Stadium, and busy
on match days, this comfortable brewery taproom
showcases four rotating real ales from Bristol Beer
Factory. Visitors are welcome to bring in food from
local North Street bakeries and shops; the taproom
provides both on- and off-sales. Regular beer
events are held, both for the Bristol Beer Club and
the general public. There is a small outdoor seating
area on the pavement. ❀●🖥(24)❀

Tobacco Factory Café Bar

Raleigh Road, BS3 1TF
⊕ 10-11 (midnight Fri & Sat) ☎ (0117) 902 0060
⊕ tobaccofactory.com/cafe-bar
Bristol Beer Factory Notorious, Fortitude; 4 changing
beers (often Bristol Beer Factory) Ⓗ
The strikingly industrial interior of this former
factory makes the most of the bare brick, metal
pipework and pillars, and paved the way for many
imitators. There is a snug with a cosier feel and a
recently expanded yard providing a convivial
environment for alfresco eating and drinking.
Popular with all ages, especially when rugby or
football are on at nearby Ashton Gate, the Tobacco
Factory is proudly independent and champions
sustainable, local, high-quality food and drink, with
changing guest beers, alongside the permanent
Bristol Beer Factory range. ❀❀◑🚗🖥(24)📶

Bristol: Bishopston

Annexe

Seymour Road, BS7 9EQ (directly behind Sportsman
pub)
⊕ 11.30-3, 5-11.30; 11.30-11.30 Sat; 12-11 Sun
☎ (0117) 949 3931 ⊕ the-annexe.co.uk
Dark Star Hophead; Fuller's London Pride; Otter
Amber; Skinner's Betty Stogs; Timothy Taylor
Landlord; Wickwar BOB; 2 changing beers Ⓗ
Community pub close to Gloucestershire county
cricket ground and not far from the Memorial
Stadium, which means it can be busy on match
days. The spacious interior also has a large
conservatory/family room to one side. Several TVs
show live sport, including one on the partially
covered patio outside. One or two of the guest
beers can be fairly adventurous. Good-value
wholesome food is served lunchtime, plus pizzas in
the evening. No dogs allowed – even on the patio.
❀❀◑🖥📶

Bristol: City Centre

Bank Tavern ✔

8 John Street, BS1 2HR (take lane next to arcade on All
Saints St)
⊕ 12-midnight (1am Thu-Sat) ☎ (0117) 930 4691
⊕ banktavern.com
4 changing beers (often Cheddar Ales, Plain,
Prescott) Ⓗ
Popular and compact one-bar pub, hidden away
near the old city wall. The four beers are often from
microbrewers from the South-West or further
afield, and can be of any style. Two real ciders
change constantly. Quirky humour and many
varied events define the pub and it is a great

alternative to the more predictable establishments
all around. It has a quiz on Tuesday and live music
on Thursday. Quality food is served 12-4pm, with
booking essential for the award-winning Sunday
lunch. ❀❀◑♣●🖥❀📶

Beer Emporium

13-15 King Street, BS1 4EF
⊕ 12-2am; 1-midnight Sun ☎ (0117) 379 0333
⊕ thebeeremporium.net
12 changing beers Ⓗ
Historic King Street is home to this cellar bar set in
three tunnels – one containing the bar and seating
and a modern stained-glass window skylight, one
for dining, and a third housing the kitchens. A lift
makes it accessible to all. Up to 12 changing cask
ales are served and a wide range of world bottled
beers. There is also a bottle shop just inside the
entrance. The food is authentic Italian pizza and
pasta, with vegetarian and vegan options.
❀❀◑♣●🖥📶

REAL ALE BREWERIES

Arbor Bristol
Artisan Minchinhampton (NEW)
Bath Ales Bristol: Warmley
Battledown Cheltenham
Bespoke Mitcheldean
Brewhouse & Kitchen ▇ Bristol: Clifton
Brewhouse & Kitchen ▇ Cheltenham
Brewhouse & Kitchen ▇ Gloucester
Bristol Beer Factory Bristol: Ashton
Brythonic Beer St Briavels
Clavell & Hind Birdlip
Cocksure Bristol: St Philips
Corinium Cirencester
Cosmic Bristol: Fishponds
Cotswold Bourton-on-the-Water
Cotswold Lion Coberley
Croft Bristol: Stokes Croft
Dawkins Bristol: Easton
DEYA Cheltenham
Donnington Stow-on-the-Wold
Fierce & Noble Bristol: St Werburgh's
Fishponds Bristol: Fishponds (NEW)
Gloucester Gloucester
Goff's Winchcombe
Good Chemistry Bristol: St Philips
Great Western Bristol: Hambrook
Hal's Dursley
Halfpenny ▇ Lechlade
Hillside Longhope
Incredible Bristol: Brislington
Inferno Tewkesbury (NEW)
Keep ▇ Nailsworth
King Street ▇ Bristol
Left Handed Giant Bristol: St Philip's
Lydbrook Valley ▇ Lydbrook
Masquerade Bristol: St Werburgh's (NEW)
Moor Bristol
New Bristol Bristol
Prescott Cheltenham
Severn Tortworth
Stanway Stanway
Stroud Thrupp
TAP Rendcomb
Tiley's ▇ Ham
Uley Uley
Wickwar Wickwar
Wiper and True Bristol: St Werburghs
Zerodegrees ▇ Bristol

Bridge Inn

16 Passage Street, BS2 0JF

12-11 (1am Fri & Sat); 1.30-11 Sun (0117) 929 0942
bridgeinnbristol.co.uk

Dark Star Hophead; 4 changing beers H

This small, friendly pub is a good place to start a visit to Bristol. Close to many other good pubs, it is a short waterside stroll from Temple Meads station. The Bridge offers an adventurous choice of ales, weekday lunches, and free cheese & cracker feasts on Sunday evening. Musical memorabilia adorn the walls and board games are available to play. Thirty malt whiskies and selected vodkas, gins and rums are also served, together with Belgian bottled beers. Outside tables increase capacity during good weather.

Christmas Steps

2 Christmas Steps, BS1 5BS

12-midnight (1am Fri & Sat); 12-11 Sun
(0117) 925 3077 thechristmassteps.com

5 changing beers (often Arbor, Bristol Beer Factory, Twisted Oak) H

Just off the city centre, this fascinating pub has welcomed drinkers since the 17th century and is one of Bristol's heritage treasures. The compact, cosy drinking areas reveal many original features and the top level includes a dining area. The food and drink are sourced locally where possible. Five real ales in a variety of styles are served including Crack ales brewed locally for the pub, as well as two real ciders.

Commercial Rooms

43-45 Corn Street, BS1 1HT

8am-midnight (1am Fri & Sat) (0117) 927 9681

Greene King Abbot; Ruddles Best Bitter; 10 changing beers (often Bath Ales, Butcombe, Great Western) H

A centrally located, Grade II-listed building dating from 1810 that was Bristol's first Wetherspoon pub. It offers up to 10 guest beers, and food served from 8am until 11pm. The main bar gets busy at peak times but there is a quieter galleried room at the rear. The interior features Greek revival-style decor, a stunning ceiling with dome, portraits and memorabilia from the time as a businessmen's club. Wheelchair access is via the side entrance in Small Street.

Cornubia

142 Temple Street, BS1 6EN

12-11; 12-6 Sun (0117) 925 4415 thecornubia.co.uk

8 changing beers H

A small, cosy pub with two linked rooms adorned with much patriotic memorabilia as well as countless pumpclips. Eight changing real ales are served, plus varying ciders in spring and summer. Pork pies and pasties are usually available. You can also enjoy a wide range of board games and books here. Live blues takes place on Thursday evenings, when anyone can come along and jam, and live bands play some Saturdays. The outside area has seating and a boules piste.

Famous Royal Navy Volunteer

17-18 King Street, BS1 4EF

12-midnight (1am Fri & Sat) (0117) 316 9237
navyvolunteer.co.uk

8 changing beers H

The Volley, on historic King Street, is a much-loved part of Bristol's heritage. This Grade II*-listed 17th-century building has four bar areas, one of which is for dining. Its beers are available in third, half, two third and pint measures from unmarked pumps. The wooden boards to the right of the bar show the current selection, with the eight ales at the far right-hand side of the boards served from the cask. Wheelchair access is at the rear entrance.

Gryphon

41 Colston Street, BS1 5AP

4-11.30 (1am Fri); 1-1am Sat; 6-11 Sun 07894 239567

6 changing beers H

A shrine to dark beer and to great rock and heavy metal music. Posters, guitars and many pumpclips adorn the walls. Triangular in shape due to its corner plot, and just a few yards uphill from the Colston Hall, the Gryphon has six handpumps dispensing rapidly changing brews, many dark and often strong. Live bands sometimes play upstairs, and beer festivals are held in March and September. Food is served evenings Wednesday to Saturday. The pub may open earlier on Sundays. Children and dogs are admitted at the licensee's discretion.

Lime Kiln

17 St Georges Road, BS1 5UU (behind City Hall)

12-11; 12-10.30 Sun 07903 068256

6 changing beers H

Located directly behind City Hall on College Green, this cosy free house has a small outdoor drinking area at the front. The six handpumps dispense a range of beers in a variety of styles. Many of the breweries featured are seldom seen in Bristol, but local beers are also often stocked, along with one or more traditional cider. You are welcome to bring your own food. The pub hosts several beer festivals throughout the year, some in conjunction with other pubs nearby.

No.1 Harbourside

1 Canons Road, BS1 5UH

11-11 (midnight Wed & Thu; 1am Fri & Sat); 12-10 Sun
(0117) 929 1100 no1harbourside.co.uk

Bristol Beer Factory Notorious, Fortitude; Sharp's Atlantic; 2 changing beers (often Arbor, New Bristol) H

Modern pub/diner on the busy covered walkway on the quayside of the floating harbour, handy for city-centre buses. Five handpumps usually feature beers from local breweries, supplemented by a good selection of bottled beers and changing ciders. There are tables outside from where you can watch the ferry boats arriving and departing. At weekends a craft market takes place right outside. Live music is played late evening Wednesday to Saturday.

Seven Stars

1 Thomas Lane, BS1 6JG (just off Victoria St)

12-11; 12-10.30 Sun (0117) 927 2845 7stars.co.uk

8 changing beers H

Popular free house tucked away in a lane 10 minutes' walk from the city centre and Temple Meads station. For many years one of Bristol's premier alehouses, it serves eight beers of all styles and strengths plus ciders and perries. There is an outdoor seating area, a rock-oriented jukebox and a pool table. Weekend afternoons feature quality live acoustic music. No food is served but you may bring in your own. There is an informative plaque outside detailing how the pub featured in the 18th-century anti-slavery campaign.

Three Tuns

78 St George's Road, BS1 5UR (300yds from Bristol cathedral towards Hotwells)
12-11 (midnight Thu-Sat); 12-10.30 Sun
(0117) 329 4310 the3tuns.com
7 changing beers H
An independent pub with seven handpumps dispensing the full range of beer styles from top-rated British brewers, as well as many unusual bottled beers and several ciders. The L-shaped interior has scrubbed wooden tables and mixed seating, plus a covered heated rear patio featuring an impressive mural by artist Silent Hobo. A small range of quality bar food is served. Events include beer festivals, regular quizzes, magic shows, movies and live Irish music.

Volunteer Tavern

9 New Street, BS2 9DX (close to main Cabot Circus car park across carriageway from shops)
4 (12 Thu)-11; 12-midnight Fri & Sat; 1-11 Sun
(0117) 955 8498 volunteertavern.co.uk
6 changing beers H
A 17th-century pub tucked away in a quiet side street, close to Cabot Circus shops and convenient for Old Market and its bus interchange. As well as six changing beers from near and far, usually including a dark one, there are two changing ciders, one medium and one dry. Regular beer festivals are held in the large fully enclosed, paved and heated rear garden. Food comprises regular pop-up kitchens from local chefs, plus Sunday roasts.

Bristol: Clifton

Brewhouse & Kitchen

31-35 Cotham Hill, BS6 6JY
11-11 (midnight Fri & Sat); 11-10.30 Sun
(0117) 973 3793
Brewhouse & Kitchen Crockers, Hornigold, Ameryck, Yankee Cabot; 1 changing beer (often Brewhouse & Kitchen – Bristol) H
Popular brewpub and dining spot reopened in 2015, on the site of the 18th-century Whiteladies Tavern. The brewery is at one end of the large bar and catches the eye (and nose, on brewing days) upon entry to the pub. The in-house brewed beers are all suitable for vegans, except Treason milk stout. Brewery experience days can be booked throughout the year. A function room is available upstairs and a patio area is located just across the road from the pub.

Eldon House

6 Lower Clifton Hill, BS8 1BT (off top of Jacobs Wells Rd)
4 (12 Thu)-11; 12-midnight Fri; 2-midnight Sat; 12-11 Sun
(0117) 922 1271 theeldonhouse.com
Bath Ales Gem; 4 changing beers (often Arbor, Bath Ales, St Austell) H
Cosy end-of-terrace pub close to the busy Clifton Triangle area. Get off a bus near the top of Park Street and head a short way down Jacobs Wells Road. Four or five real ales are sold, including guests from well-chosen independent brewers, often local, and occasionally from further afield. Good food including pizza is served daily and Sunday roasts are popular. Many events are hosted, including a Monday quiz and live music every Sunday and occasional Saturdays. The pub sometimes stays open later than advertised at weekends.

Lansdown

8 Clifton Road, BS8 1AF
4-11; 12-midnight Fri & Sat; 12-10.30 Sun
(0117) 973 4949 thelansdown.com
House beer (by Otter); 5 changing beers (sourced regionally; often Cheddar Ales, Great Western, St Austell) H
Traditional pub with a strong real ale offering, mainly from South-West breweries. Guest beers change regularly, with five or six on the bar, and there is usually a good mix of styles. An upstairs lounge/dining room is available for functions. Good food is served weekend lunchtimes and every evening. The courtyard garden, which is heated and covered in winter, shows rugby (Freeview) on a big screen and is the venue for occasional beer festivals. (8,9)

Portcullis

3 Wellington Terrace, BS8 4LE (close to Clifton side of suspension bridge)
4-11; 12-11 Sat; 12-10.30 Sun (0117) 973 0270
Dawkins Bristol Blonde, Bristol Best; 4 changing beers H
A pub since 1821, rescued by Dawkins in 2008, featuring a downstairs bar and an upstairs lounge that is also used for functions. The Portcullis is part of a Georgian terrace close to Clifton suspension bridge, and has a cosy décor with many photos of film stars. Two Dawkins beers and guests from other microbreweries nationwide are served, plus a traditional cider. Cooked meals are available Monday, Tuesday, Friday and Saturday evenings, with traditional roasts Sunday afternoon. The rear garden is accessed from upstairs.
(8,505)

Victoria Ale House

2 Southleigh Road, BS8 2BH (off St Pauls Rd)
4 (3 winter)-11; 1-11 Sat; 12.30-10.30 Sun
(0117) 974 5675
Dawkins Bristol Blonde, Bristol Best, Easton IPA; 3 changing beers (often Dawkins, Tiny Rebel) H
A cosy, 19th-century, Grade II-listed Dawkins tavern tucked away just off the bottom of Whiteladies Road, next door to the Clifton Lido. Seven handpumps offer beers from Dawkins Brewery and changing guests from independent breweries, often including a dark beer. Two real ciders are also sold. Two beer festivals are held annually. Tuesday is quiz night. Parking close by can be difficult. Summer hours apply out of university terms, when the pub opens an hour later.

Bristol: Fishponds

Snuffy Jack's

800 Fishponds Road, BS16 3TE
closed Mon; 5-10 Tue-Thu; 3-11 Fri & Sat; 12-5 Sun
8 changing beers G
The name of Bristol's third micropub, opened in June 2017, relates to a former head miller at the nearby Snuff Mills. Between four and eight real ales are served on gravity from a chilled cabinet, plus two or more changing real ciders. Local beers feature alongside some from further afield, with all styles offered. Food is limited to bar snacks. The pub is close to multiple bus routes with direct links to many areas. A quiz is held on the first Wednesday of the month. Q

Bristol: Horfield

Drapers Arms L

447 Gloucester Road, BS7 8TZ
5-9.30; 4-9.30 Fri & Sun; 12-9.30 Sat
thedrapersarms.co.uk
5 changing beers G
Bristol's first micropub, opened in December 2015, close to the Memorial Stadium and county cricket ground. It prides itself on an interesting and changing beer selection from in and around Bristol, with up to eight real ales served by gravity, frequently including a dark beer, and three real ciders. Gin, wine and bar snacks are also sold. There is no music or TV, but the pub offers a warm welcome and a convivial, cosy atmosphere with a focus on conversation. Two beer festivals are held each year. Q

Bristol: Hotwells

Bag of Nails

141 St Georges Road, BS1 5UW (5 mins' walk from cathedral towards Hotwells)
12-11; 12-10.30 Sun
9 changing beers H
Close to the floating harbour, this small terraced free house dates from the 1860s and serves up to 10 changing cask ales, mainly from microbreweries, as well as a real cider. An eccentric list of pub policies includes no children or idiot pub crawls. The interior features terracotta colours, portholes in the floor, many pub cats roaming free, and eclectic music from a proper record player. There are board games for the customers and toys for the cats. A quiz takes place every Thursday.

Grain Barge

Mardyke Wharf, Hotwell Road, BS8 4RU (moored by Hotwell Rd, opp Baltic Wharf marina)
10-11 (11.30 Thu-Sat) (0117) 929 9347
Bristol Beer Factory Notorious, Fortitude; 2 changing beers (sourced locally; often Bristol Beer Factory) H
This moored barge, built in 1936 and converted into a floating pub by Bristol Beer Factory in 2007, boasts great views of the SS Great Britain, the floating harbour and passing boats. There is seating with wooden tables at either end of the central bar, an extended shelf by the window overlooking the water, and an outdoor drinking area on the top deck. The pub hosts regular themed food nights, a quiz on Monday, open mic on Tuesday and live music on Thursday.

Merchants Arms

5 Merchants Road, BS8 4PZ
4-11; 12-11 Fri-Sun (0117) 907 3047
4 changing beers H
Free-of-tie traditional pub close to the Cumberland Basin, selling mainly South-West cask-conditioned ales. It is famous for home-made Scotch eggs, hand-finished pork pies and real Cornish pasties. The pub has been completely refurbished after a car entered the bar! Both rooms are furnished with dark-wood seating and there is a real log fire in the front room. Sport is shown on the TV and a range of board games is available. Regular poetry nights take place. QP

Bristol: Kingsdown

Hillgrove Porter Stores

53 Hillgrove Street North, BS2 8LT
4-midnight (1am Fri); 2-1am Sat; 2-midnight Sun
(0117) 924 9818
Dawkins Bristol Blonde, Bristol Best; 12 changing beers (sourced regionally) H
This traditional community pub is one of several across the city owned by Dawkins Brewery. The interior is horseshoe-shaped, with a lounge area behind the bar and a pleasant patio. Alongside the two regular Dawkins beers there are up to 12 guests, including dark ales and rare styles, many from South-West breweries, plus a real cider. Japanese meals and bar snacks are available, as well as a popular Sunday roast from 4pm. The style is eclectic and relaxed, with a lively atmosphere and a wide range of customers.

Robin Hood

56 St Michael's Hill, BS2 8DX
4 (12 Wed & Thu)-11; 12-1am Fri & Sat; 12-10 Sun
(0117) 983 1489 robinhoodbristol.co.uk
6 changing beers (sourced regionally; often Bristol Beer Factory, Cheddar Ales, Moor Beer) H
Originally a grocer's but a licensed premises since 1841, this Grade II-listed pub has a lovely arched-window frontage. Inside are pale magnolia walls, wooden flooring and furniture, and a pull-down screen at the back of the pub showing sports events. There are six handpumps serving brews from local breweries and from further afield, plus a traditional cider. Weekly events include a Wednesday quiz and live music on Thursday. Food offerings come from pop-up kitchens in the evening. (9,72)

Bristol: Old City

Old Fish Market

59-63 Baldwin Street, BS1 1QZ (200yds from city centre)
11-11 (midnight Fri & Sat); 12-10 Sun (0117) 921 1515
Fuller's Oliver's Island, London Pride, ESB; Moor Beer Nor'Hop; 1 changing beer (sourced nationally; often Fuller's) H
There is something for everyone at this Fuller's pub, which was refurbished in 2014 with decor, seating and lighting in the style of a relaxed lounge. There is a stadium-like atmosphere when major sporting events are shown on the big screen. Live jazz music features every Sunday evening. Between 20 and 30 gins are a great attraction for any fan of the spirit. Food includes a range of chowders, stone-baked pizzas and Sunday roasts. Dogs are welcomed with treats and water bowls.

Bristol: Redland

Chums

22 Chandos Road, BS6 6PF
4-10.30; 12-11 Fri & Sat; 12-10 Sun (0117) 973 1498
chumsmicropub.co.uk
6 changing beers (often Butcombe, Cheddar Ales, Plain) H
A micropub in a converted shop, opened in April 2016. Conversation rules and electronic communication devices should be used with discretion. Real ales are dispensed from six handpumps – two from regular breweries – and a dark ale is always available. Six traditional ciders

are also served as well as a selection of wines and spirits. Food consists of simple bar snacks including filled rolls. Local CAMRA Pub of the Year 2018.
Q

Bristol: St Philips

Barley Mow

39 Barton Road, BS2 0LF (400yds from rear exit of Temple Meads station over footbridge)
12-11 (11.30 Fri & Sat); 12-10 Sun (0117) 930 4709
Bristol Beer Factory Notorious, Fortitude; 6 changing beers (often Bristol Beer Factory) H
Bristol Beer Factory's flagship pub has eight handpumps offering three beers from the brewery plus five constantly changing guests of varying styles from all over the UK. There is also an extensive bottled beer selection from around the world. Occasional beer-related events are held, along with a regular Monday night quiz. A small menu of quality food changes frequently and includes vegan dishes. Dogs are welcome in the beer garden. (506)

Bristol: St Werburghs

Duke of York

2 Jubilee Road, BS2 9RS (S side of Mina Rd park)
5-11; 4-midnight Fri; 3-midnight Sat; 3-11 Sun
(0117) 941 3677
4 changing beers (sourced locally; often Arbor, Electric Bear, Moor Beer) H
Tucked away in a side street, this popular local has an eclectic clientele and decor to match. The wooden floors, coloured fairy lights and an intriguing range of memorabilia and artefacts create a welcoming, grotto-like atmosphere. Notable features include a rare refurbished skittle alley, carved wooden mirrors and a Grand Old Duke of York exterior mural painted by a local artist. Upstairs is a room with sofas to lounge on. Four changing beers are served, mostly from breweries in Bristol and the surrounding area.
(5)

Miners Arms

136 Mina Road, BS2 9YQ (600yds from M32 jct 3)
4-11 (midnight Fri); 2-midnight Sat; 2-11 Sun
(0117) 907 9874
Dawkins Bristol Blonde, Easton IPA; house beer (by Dawkins); 3 changing beers H
Close to St Werburghs city farm, this popular street-corner local still has some original features, including Bottle and Jug glass door panels. There are usually three guest beers and three from Dawkins, along with a cider. A small, quiet bar lies to the side of the main bar, with a larger pool room to the rear. An upstairs room can be booked for functions. Sunday roasts are served from 2pm. Well-behaved children are welcome, as are dogs if on a lead. (5)

Bristol: Southville

Coronation

18 Dean Lane, BS3 1DD
12-11 (midnight Thu-Sat) (0117) 940 9044
Bath Ales Gem; Butcombe Original; Hop Back Summer Lightning; Wickwar Falling Star; 1 changing beer (often Bristol Beer Factory, Twisted) H
Popular traditional local in a residential area a short walk from Gaol Ferry bridge. Five reasonably priced real ales are served, with the guest often from Twisted Brewery, and there is a good range of beer in cans and bottles. Monday is quiz night. Food is limited to Sunday lunch, served from midday until sold out. Furnishings are simple and comfortable. The licensee is the creator of the eclectic artwork that decorates the walls. (24)

Broad Campden

Bakers Arms

GL55 6UR (signed off B4081, at NW end of village)
12-3, 6-11; 12-11 Sat & Sun (01386) 840515
bakersarmscampden.com
Prescott Hill Climb; Stanway Stanney Bitter; Wickwar BOB; Wye Valley HPA; 1 changing beer (sourced locally) H
Fine old village local and genuine free house, first licensed as a public house in 1724. A photograph of the building in 1905 shows it as the village bakery and grain store. It boasts Cotswold stone walls, exposed beams and a fine inglenook. Local guest beers and regular ales are served from the handsome oak bar. Excellent food is available in the bar and dining room extension and there is a large garden and children's play area. Local CAMRA Pub of the Year 2017. Q P

Brockhampton

Craven Arms

Kingsbury Street, GL54 5XQ (off A436 in centre of village in a cul-de-sac)
closed Mon; 12-3, 6-11; 12-11 Sat; 12-5 Sun
(01242) 820410 thecravenarms.co.uk
Otter Bitter; 3 changing beers (sourced regionally; often Butcombe, XT) H
A 17th-century free house set in an attractive hillside village with outstanding views and walks. It has a cosy bar area with an open fire and a dining room separated by church-style stone windows. Three carefully selected beers are well kept by the owner chef. The pub features regularly in the Guide and is a gem, well managed by a friendly family who organise functions for locals each month plus a summer beer festival. A former local CAMRA Pub of the Year. Q P

Charfield

Pear Tree Micro Pub

6 Wotton Road, GL12 8TP (on B4058 1½ miles from jct 14 on M5)
5 (2 Thu & Fri)-9.30; 2-10.30 Sat; 12-9.30 Sun
(01454) 260663
Great Western Maiden Voyage; 3 changing beers (sourced regionally; often Abbey, Cheddar Ales, St Austell) G
A small one-roomed pub popular with locals and visitors alike. It is a most attractive location for drinkers, due to the restored tiled flooring, small wooden bar, the way the beers are dispensed through wooden casks mounted in an old fireplace, and the humorous murals covering most of the walls. Up to four beers are offered at busy times, usually from local and regional breweries. There is a large fenced outdoor seating area at the front.
Q P

Cheltenham

Charlton Kings Club

21 Church Street, Charlton Kings, GL53 8AP (opp church)
12-3, 6-11; 11.30-3, 6-midnight Fri; 12-midnight Sat; 12-11 Sun ☎ (01242) 525511 charltonkingsclub.co.uk
4 changing beers (often Butcombe) H
Popular village club in the heart of Charlton Kings, with a large lounge, a separate sports bar and a skittle alley on the ground floor, plus a large function room and snooker room upstairs. Regular live music is played upstairs (Vonnies Blues Club) and also in the main lounge. Four regularly changing beers are on the bar, generally at least one from Butcombe, with guests sourced nationally. A beer festival is held in November. Occasional visits by card-carrying CAMRA members are free (others pay a small fee). Bar snacks are available. P

Cheltenham Motor Club L

Upper Park Street, GL52 6SA (first right off Hales Rd from London Rd lights, 100yds on right; pedestrian access from A40 via Crown Passage opp Sandford Mill Rd jct)
6-midnight; 12-midnight Sat; 12-3, 7-midnight Sun
☎ (01242) 522590 cheltmc.com
6 changing beers (often Moor Beer, Tiley's) H
Friendly club just off London Road that won CAMRA National Club of the Year honours in 2013 and 2017, among other awards. It serves five regularly changing ales from across the country alongside a regular local beer, often from Tileys at the Salutation, Ham. At least one KeyKeg, three real ciders and a range of bottled Belgian ales are also offered. Events include Meet the Brewer and Tap Takeover evenings and an annual beer festival. The club hosts local darts and pool teams. Non-members are welcome to make occasional free visits. QP(B,51)

Jolly Brewmaster L

39 Painswick Road, GL50 2EZ (off A40 Suffolk Rd, between Suffolks and Tivoli, 200yds S along Painswick Rd)
2.30-11 (midnight Fri); 12-midnight Sat; 12-10.30 Sun
☎ (01242) 772261
7 changing beers (often Arbor, Bespoke, Moor Beer) H
Thirteen handpumps feature a changing range of seven or eight ales sourced nationally, and five or six ciders. This busy and friendly community hub features original etched windows, a horseshoe bar and open fire. It is a traditional drinking pub with no food menu, but hot bar snacks such as pasties and pies are generally available later in the week. The attractive courtyard garden is popular in the summer, with regular Friday barbecues. Weekday opening is 3.30pm January-March.
Q(10,94U)

Kemble Brewery L

27 Fairview Street, GL52 2JF (off Northern ring road, jct of Fairview Rd/St Johns Ave, turn left into Fairview St beside Machine Mart; pub is 100yds on right)
11-11 (midnight Fri & Sat); 12-11 Sun ☎ (01242) 701053
Wye Valley HPA, Butty Bach; 4 changing beers H
Small popular back-street local, refurbished in 2016, hard to find but well worth the effort. Originally a butcher's shop in 1845, it became a pub two years later and was soon brewing ciders, hence the name, but no brewing has taken place in recent times. Six ales from near and far are generally available. There is a small attractive walled garden to the rear featuring a new servery for summer barbecues and pizzas.
Q

Moon under Water L

16-28 Bath Road, GL53 7HA (from the Strand, E end of High St, take Bath Rd; pub is 100yds on left)
8-midnight (1am Fri & Sat) ☎ (01242) 583945
Greene King Abbot; Ruddles Best Bitter; Sharp's Doom Bar; 5 changing beers H
Open-plan Lloyds No.1 just off the east end of the pedestrianised high street (Strand). A decked area at the back overlooks the River Chelt and Sandford Park. Five changing guest ales supplement the regular beers, plus Gwynt y Ddraig Black Dragon and Old Rosie ciders. The dance floor is only used Friday and Saturday evening, allowing a generally quiet atmosphere at other times. Food is served 8am to 11pm. An interactive quiz night is held on Monday.

Royal

54 Horsefair Street, Charlton Kings, GL53 8JH (in centre of village opp church)
10-11 (midnight Fri & Sat); 12-10.30 Sun
☎ (01242) 228937 royalpub.co.uk
4 changing beers (often Bath Ales, Dartmoor, Otter) H
A large, popular village pub and restaurant on the eastern fringe of town, the Royal underwent a major refurbishment a few years ago in a contemporary style. Its central bar has comfy sofas, and there is a lounge area adjacent. Guest ales are typically from Hogs Back and Bath breweries. There is no food Sunday evening. The pub has a large garden and patio areas, and hosts regular live music, quizzes and Meet the Brewer evenings. Beer festivals with live music are held on most bank holidays. QP

Sandford Park Alehouse L

20 High Street, GL50 1DZ (E end of High St, past Strand on right)
1-11 (midnight Wed & Thu); 12-midnight Fri & Sat
☎ (01242) 574517
Oakham Citra; 8 changing beers (often Oakham) H
CAMRA National Pub of the Year 2015 and local winner in recent years, this contemporary alehouse has a U-shaped main bar area complete with bar billiards, a cosy front snug with wood-burning stove and a large south-facing patio and garden. A function room/lounge is on the first floor. Ten handpumps dispense a variety of ales from microbreweries sourced nationally and locally, plus at least one cider and 16 speciality lagers and craft beers. Q

Whittle Taps

1-3A Regent Street, GL50 1HE (near Everyman theatre)
10-11 (midnight Fri & Sat) ☎ (01242) 222989
whittletaps.co.uk
4 changing beers (sourced nationally; often Purity, St Austell, Titanic) H
Modern, open-plan, stylish pub (formerly the Slug & Lettuce), refurbished in 2017 in rustic style. Up to four real ales plus seven craft kegs and three ciders are stocked. The menu features an impressive range of pizzas, tapas and burgers plus many other choices. There is good wheelchair access (one small step). Handy for pre- or post-theatre drinks or even the interval. May stay open later Friday or Saturday if busy.

Chipping Campden

Eight Bells

Church Street, GL55 6JG
12-11; 12-10.30 Sun (01386) 840371
eightbellsinn.co.uk
Hook Norton Hooky; North Cotswold Best; Purity Pure UBU; Wye Valley HPA
The Eight Bells was originally built in the 14th century to house the stonemasons who constructed St James's church, and was later used to store the eight bells that were hung in the church tower. The inn was rebuilt using most of the original stone and timbers during the 17th century. What exists today is an outstanding example of a traditional Cotswolds inn, featuring a cobbled courtyard with an underground priest passage. Local CAMRA Pub of the Year runner-up 2018.
Q (21)

Chipping Sodbury

Horseshoe

2 High Street, BS37 6AH
10-11 (midnight Fri & Sat) (01454) 325658
horseshoechippingsodbury.co.uk
7 changing beers (sourced nationally)
One of the oldest buildings in the town, this former stationery shop, then briefly a wine bar, was converted into a pub at the start of 2014. It serves seven beers, often unusual but mostly from the West Country, including dark or strong choices. The pub has three linked rooms with assorted furniture, a gin bar upstairs, a pleasant rear garden and a cellar. A selection of freshly made rolls is available at lunchtimes.

Churchdown

Old Elm

Church Road, GL3 2ER
12-11 (midnight Thu & Fri); 10-midnight Sat; 10-10.30 Sun
(01452) 530961 theoldelminn.co.uk
Sharp's Atlantic; 4 changing beers (sourced locally; often Gloucester, Hillside, Stroud)
Set in the heart of this village, the Old Elm has become popular since its refurbishment in 2015. It has gained a deserved reputation for its food, which includes good vegetarian options. Five quality beers are served, including LocAles and some cider. The pub hosts lively quiz and music nights, and food and drink tasting evenings; major sporting events are shown in the sports bar. Families are welcome and the garden has a children's play area. There are five letting rooms.
P

Cirencester

Drillman's Arms

34 Gloucester Road, GL7 2JY (on old A417, 200yds from A435 jct)
11-2.30, 5.30-11; 11-midnight Sat; 12-4, 7-10.30 Sun
(01285) 653892
Sharp's Doom Bar; 3 changing beers (sourced nationally)
A lively Georgian inn, perched beside a busy thoroughfare, comprising a convivial lounge with woodburner, a pub games-dominated public bar and a popular skittle alley. Graced by the same landlady for over 25 years, this cracking free house features low-beamed ceilings, horse brasses, fresh flowers and brewery pictures. Well-priced pub food is served at lunchtime. An annual beer festival swamps the small front car park over the August bank holiday weekend. May shut early some Sunday evenings.
P

Marlborough Arms

1 Sheep Street, GL7 1QW
12-midnight (01285) 651474
Box Steam Piston Broke; North Cotswold Windrush Ale; 6 changing beers (sourced nationally; often Corinium)
A real ale haven, this lively, wooden-floored pub lies opposite the old GWR station. It offers eight beers from regionals and microbreweries, plus a plethora of interesting boxed ciders and perries. Brewery memorabilia adorn the walls, with pews and a deep-set fireplace adding character. The ceiling is disappearing behind an encroaching pumpclip collection. The rear patio is used for barbecues during beer and cider festivals. Local CAMRA Pub and Cider Pub of the Year once again.

Coaley

Old Fox

The Street, GL11 5EG
12 (5 Mon-Wed)-11 (01453) 890905
oldfoxatcoaley.co.uk
Otter Bitter; Uley Pig's Ear Strong Beer; 4 changing beers
This attractive 300-year-old stone-built local in the centre of the village on the Cotswold Way was refurbished in 2018. It is now a free house with a single room, featuring a large oak bar with seating on benches and at tables. There are six real ale handpumps and three for cider. A wood-burning stove provides a focal point. A traditional pub menu is served and there are outdoor seating areas to the front and side.
Q P

Coates

Tunnel House Inn

Tarlton Road, GL7 6PW
11-11; 11-10.30 Sun (01285) 770702
tunnelhouse.com
Bristol Beer Factory Notorious; Ramsbury Pale Ale; Timothy Taylor Landlord; Uley Bitter; 1 changing beer
A popular pub with masses of character, originally built for the diggers of the Sapperton canal tunnel and subsequently the leggers; it continues to offer sustenance to all. Follow the brown signs from the Cirencester to Tetbury or Stroud roads to an unmetalled track, and you will be rewarded with a warm welcome, good ales and food. The pub also has log fires, interesting artefacts and a huge garden with great views. The source of the Thames is a pleasant and interesting walk along the redundant Thames-Severn canal.
P

Cold Aston

Plough Inn

GL54 3BN (in centre of village)
10-11 (01451) 822602 coldastonplough.com
Butcombe Original; 2 changing beers (sourced regionally)

A transformed stone-flagged country pub high in the Cotswolds. The attractive village went by the name of Aston Blank in the Domesday Book. The Plough was reopened in 2013 by young owners and their team, with an emphasis on real ale and good, interesting food. Look out for three changing beers from award-winning brewers, two served directly from the barrel. With an innovative internal extension of the 17th-century cottage, three luxury bedrooms are available. A former local CAMRA Pub of the Year finalist. Q♣🕮🌟🚲◑&▲♣P🖪☀

Coleford

Dog House Micro Pub
13-15 St John Street, GL16 8AP
🕸 closed Mon & Tue; 5-10 Wed & Thu; 4-10 Fri; 12-10 Sat; 12-3, 7-10 Sun ☎ 07442 787015
4 changing beers (sourced locally) Ⓗ/Ⓖ
A friendly micropub in an attractively fronted old chemist's shop. It serves two changing ales on handpump plus up to four more from the barrel, a couple of them usually LocAle. A fridge offers eight varying ciders plus a few Belgian beers. The pub's Facebook page highlights special events and music nights, which are invariably wonderful social occasions. Seating is limited, so arriving early is recommended. Q♣🐕🖳☀

Dursley

New Inn Ⓛ
82-84 Woodmancote, GL11 4AJ (on A4135 Tetbury Road)
🕸 closed Mon-Wed; 2.30 (5 Thu)-11 ☎ (01453) 519288
4 changing beers (sourced regionally; often Hal's Ales) Ⓗ
A dog-friendly establishment where the resident labrador often helps provide a welcome, this comfortable pub features a large, L-shaped public bar with tiled floor, plus a smaller lounge. An eclectic selection of regularly changing guest beers comes mostly from smaller local breweries, with many requested by regulars. The spacious suntrap garden at the rear is popular on fine days. Freshly made rolls are sometimes available. 🐕🌟♣🖳☀

Old Spot Inn Ⓛ
2 Hill Road, GL11 4JQ (by bus station and free car park)
🕸 12-11 ☎ (01453) 542870 ⊕ oldspotinn.co.uk
Uley Old Ric; 7 changing beers (sourced nationally) Ⓗ
Excellent free house dating from 1776, serving great ales, ciders and perries. Named after the Gloucestershire Old Spot pig, it has a porcine theme. Extensive brewery memorabilia, low ceilings, a wood-burning stove and welcoming staff add to the convivial atmosphere. There is an attractive garden and a heated, covered area. Freshly prepared food is served at lunchtime. The pub is on the Cotswold Way and is popular with walkers. It hosts regular events in the evenings. Q♣🐕◑&♣🖳☀🛜

Dymock

Beauchamp Arms
GL18 2AQ (on B4216)
🕸 7-11 Mon; 11-2.30, 6-11; 12-3, 7-11 Sun
☎ (01531) 890266 ⊕ beauchamparmsdymock.co.uk
2 changing beers (often Wye Valley) Ⓗ

This hostelry is found on the Gloucestershire/Herefordshire border - one of the few parish-owned pubs in the country. It is a focal point of the parish, and a genuine village pub that warmly welcomes families and the visitors who come to enjoy the fine beers, good food and friendly company that are to be found here. It has three rooms, a log fire and is dog-friendly. Q♣🌟◑🕯▲♣P

Eastington

Old Badger Inn Ⓛ ✅
Alkerton Road, GL10 3AT (on Spring Hill)
🕸 12-11; 12-10.30 Sun ☎ (01453) 822892
⊕ oldbadgerinn.co.uk
Uley Old Ric; Wickwar Cotswold Way; 3 changing beers (sourced regionally; often Otter, Prescott, Stroud) Ⓗ
Formerly The Victoria - closed by Punch in 2010 - the pub was reopened as a free house after being sympathetically renovated, modernised and extended. It was acquired by Wickwar in 2018. The large single bar features a wood-burning stove, with smaller rooms on either side plus a restaurant area - the pub has a formidable reputation for food. The walls are covered with breweriana and other memorabilia. Outside are a covered, heated patio and a large garden. Dogs are welcome. Q♣🌟◑&♣🖳(61,401)☀🛜

Ebrington

Ebrington Arms Ⓛ
GL55 6NH (off B4035; centre of village by green)
🕸 12-11 ☎ (01386) 593223 ⊕ theebringtonarms.co.uk
North Cotswold Moreton Mild; 3 changing beers (sourced regionally) Ⓗ
A 17th-century Cotswold stone-built pub in a beautiful village with excellent walks. This is a class-leading, family-run place with enthusiastic staff. The cosy bar has a lovely open fireplace. There are five handpumps, three dispensing the pub's own Yubby ales and two for changing guests. An excellent range of food is sourced from local suppliers. Open seven days a week, accommodation is available in five en-suite rooms, one with a four-poster. A regular Guide entry, it shares its owner with the Killingworth Castle in Wotton, Oxfordshire. 🐕🌟🕮◑&▲♣P

Forthampton

Lower Lode Inn Ⓛ
GL19 4RE (follow sign to Forthampton from A438 Tewkesbury to Ledbury road) SO8788231809
🕸 12-midnight (2am Fri & Sat) ☎ (01684) 293224
⊕ lowerlodeinn.co.uk
Sharp's Doom Bar; 4 changing beers (often Bespoke, Brains, Malvern Hills) Ⓗ
Blessed with views across the River Severn to Tewkesbury Abbey, this attractive 15th-century brick-built venue, with its three acres of lawns, is a popular stopover for boats and a Camping and Caravan Club site. Food is advertised as simple and wholesome and is excellent quality and value for money. A beer festival is held in September. A small ferry operates from the Tewkesbury side from Easter to mid-September. Day fishing is available, plus en-suite accommodation. Opening times are reduced in winter so check the website. Q♣🐕🌟🕮◑▲♣🖳☀

Fossebridge

Inn at Fossebridge ✔

GL54 3JS (on A429)
12-11 ☎ (01285) 720721 innatfossebridge.co.uk
Butcombe Original; North Cotswold Windrush Ale; Wadworth 6X; 2 changing beers (sourced locally) H
This hostelry is in a pretty hamlet where the Fosse Way drops into the Cotswolds valley of the River Coln, an Area of Outstanding Natural Beauty. An attractive one-bar inn, it has old timbers, a fine flagstone floor and open fires. The premises also benefit from a lovely four-acre garden with a lake and river. A selection of Wadworth ales and guests from local breweries are available in cosy surroundings. Local CAMRA Pub of the Year runner-up 2017. Q P

Frampton Cotterell

Globe Inn

366 Church Road, BS36 2AB
12-11; 12-10.30 Sun ☎ (01454) 778286
theglobeframptoncotterell.co.uk
Butcombe Original; Fuller's London Pride; St Austell Tribute, Proper Job; 1 changing beer (often Otter) H
Independent free house opposite the parish church and on the Frome Valley Walkway, which links the Cotswold Way with Bristol. The pub is open plan with an L-shaped bar, low ceilings and carpets that give a comfortable feel. At the far end of the bar is a large function room. Home-made, freshly cooked food is a speciality. The large enclosed lawned garden features a children's play area and is popular in summer. P

Rising Sun

43 Ryecroft Road, BS36 2HN
11.30-11.30; 12-11 Sun ☎ (01454) 772330
gwbrewery.co.uk/rising-sun
Great Western HPA, Maiden Voyage, Moose River; 3 changing beers (often Great Western) H
Village local and brewery tap for the Great Western Brewing Company in nearby Hambrook. There is a room as you enter with a log-burning stove, then three archways past slate pillars to the bar, additional seating up the stairs to the left and a restaurant in the warm conservatory. Lunchtime snacks and more substantial evening meals are served from an extensive menu, with all food made in-house. The skittle alley can also be used for private functions. Q P (Y4,Y6)

Frampton Mansell

Crown Inn L

GL6 8JG (off A419 Cirencester to Stroud road opp Jolly Nice café & farm shop in former filling station)
12-11 ☎ (01285) 760601 thecrowninn-cotswolds.co.uk
Butcombe Original; Stroud Organic Pale Ale; Uley Laurie Lee's Bitter; 2 changing beers (often Sharp's) H
A thriving village local dating back to 1633, when it was a cider house with a slaughterhouse next door. The three rooms feature exposed stone walls and wooden beams, with an open fire in each; lit candles replace the fires in summer. Good food is served. The suntrap front garden offers fine views over the Golden Valley. Children are welcome and books are provided for them. There is a modern 12-bedroom hotel annexe alongside with ample car parking. P

Frampton-on-Severn

Three Horseshoes L

The Green, GL2 7DY (off B4071)
11.30-2, 5.30-11 (1am Fri); 11.30-1am Sat; 11.30-10 Sun
☎ (01452) 742100 threehorseshoespub.co.uk
Sharp's Doom Bar; Timothy Taylor Landlord; Uley Bitter H
A 19th-century two-bar community pub originally built by a farrier at the south end of England's longest village green. Food is home-cooked, notably the unique 3-Shu pie, which is freshly baked to order. Both bars have coal fires. Evening jam sessions, largely biased towards folk music, are popular; as are pasty baking competitions, conker contests and veggie Olympics. A double boules court hosts annual championships. Dogs are welcome in the flagstoned public bar.
Q

Gloucester

Angie's ✔

Bull Lane, GL1 2HG
12-9; 12-6 Sun ☎ 07725 754852 angiesbar.co.uk
2 changing beers
Gloucester's smallest bar is a friendly and welcoming venue. Ask in the pub about how it got its name. You can choose to join in the conversation in the bar or tuck yourself away upstairs to play board games, quietly while away the time or work out how they got the pianola up here. Two regularly changing ales are served. The pub hosts a range of events, from bands to an occasional Sunday dinner and dance. Upstairs is also suitable for small functions.

Brewhouse & Kitchen

Unit R1, St Anne Walk, Gloucester Quay, GL1 5SH
11-11 (midnight Fri & Sat); 11-10.30 Sun
☎ (01452) 222965
Brewhouse & Kitchen Stevedore, Shed Head, Down a Pegg, SSB H
Based in the bustling Gloucester Quays development, this smart bar and restaurant is part of the growing Brewhouse & Kitchen chain, brewing its own range of ales on-site. Customers can sit in comfort and enjoy a quality beer, while watching the brewing process. Four cask ales are available, with seasonal specials on keg. On a fine day you can relax by the side of the Gloucester-Sharpness canal in the outdoor seating area.

Fountain Inn L ✔

53 Westgate Street, GL1 2NW
11-11; 12-11 Sun ☎ (01452) 522562
thefountaininngloucester.com
Bristol Beer Factory Independence; Dartmoor Jail Ale; St Austell Tribute; 4 changing beers H
An interesting 17th-century inn on the site of an alehouse known to have existed in 1216. A passage leads from Westgate Street into an attractive courtyard where there is a plaque to commemorate King William III riding his horse up the stairs. The Cathedral Bar has a panelled ceiling and carved stone fireplace. The Orange Room serves as a restaurant or as a venue for private functions.

Pelican Inn L ✔

4 St Marys Street, GL1 2QR
11-11.30 ☎ (01452) 582966

Wye Valley Bitter, The Hopfather, HPA, Butty Bach Ⓗ, Wholesome Stout Ⓗ/Ⓖ; house beer (by Wye Valley); 4 changing beers (sourced regionally; often Wye Valley) Ⓗ
The Pelican was licensed as an alehouse in the 17th century. Some of its beams are thought to be from Drake's Golden Hind, which began life as the Pelican. After a chequered history, Wye Valley Brewery refurbished the pub in 2012, since when its popularity has grown steadily. It has a main bar area, a side room and an attractive outdoor drinking area. The growing range of ciders and perries increases during the summer to complement the 10 ales, which include a guest beer. **Q**

Tank ✔
12-14 Llanthony Road, GL1 2EH
12-11 ☎ (01452) 690541 tankgloucester.com
Gloucester Cascade, Dockside Dark, American Pale; 3 changing beers (sourced nationally) Ⓗ
This brewery tap is a welcoming, urban warehouse-style bar with a contemporary feel, in the heart of the Gloucester Docks redevelopment. The decor utilises the building's strengths, and is well worth a look. Though primarily selling Gloucester beers, the Tank also offers a wide range of guest and craft brews, plus bottled beers and ciders. Food comes in the shape of local meats and cheeses served on platters, along with a selection of hand-made pizzas. (10)

Turk's Head
Southgate Street, GL1 2DX
12-9 (11 Fri & Sat); closed Sun ☎ 07869 711529
6 changing beers Ⓖ
Gloucester's first micropub, serving up to six beers on gravity. It also offers a wide selection of ciders and has been named CAMRA branch Cider Pub of the Year. Snack food is available. The cosy bar has various seating areas and conversation flourishes as mobile phones are discouraged and there is no Wi-Fi. No children either, but you can find sheep – meet Daisy, who sits in the window! **Q**(10)

Ham

Salutation Inn
Ham Green, GL13 9QH (from Berkeley take road signposted to Jenner Museum)
5-11; 12-2.30, 5-11 Fri; 12-11 Sat; 12-10.30 Sun
☎ (01453) 810284 the-sally-at-ham.com
Butcombe Original; 5 changing beers (sourced nationally; often Tiley's) Ⓗ
Multi award-winning rural free house, popular with locals and visitors alike, offering up to seven real ales and nine real ciders and perries plus an extensive bottled beer menu. The on-site microbreweries (Tiley's and Mills) produce hop-forward pale ales, traditional ales and lambic beers. There are three bars (two cosy ones share a central woodburner) and a skittles alley/function room. Food is served at lunchtime and on occasional evenings only; there are also folk nights and singalongs. **QP**

Hawkesbury Upton

Beaufort Arms
High Street, GL9 1AU (off A46, 6 miles N of M4 jct 18)
12-11; 12-10.30 Sun ☎ (01454) 238217
beaufortarms.com
Bristol Beer Factory Independence; Butcombe Original; 3 changing beers (sourced regionally) Ⓗ
A wonderful Grade II-listed Cotswold-stone free house, built in 1602, close to the historic Somerset Monument. It features separate public and lounge bars, a dining room and skittle alley/function room, which are required to house a veritable plethora of ancient brewery and local memorabilia. The pub serves up to five ales and a traditional cider on handpump. It has an attractive garden with a barbecue used for local community activities. A great bunch of regulars assures a warm welcome. **QP**

Hillesley

Fleece Inn
Chapel Lane, GL12 7RD (between Wotton-under-Edge and Hawkesbury Upton)
4.30-10 Mon-Wed; 12-11 Thu; 12-11.30 Fri & Sat; 12-10 Sun ☎ (01453) 520003 thefleeceinnhillesley.com
Sharp's Atlantic; Wye Valley Butty Bach; 4 changing beers (often Arbor, Oakham, Tiny Rebel) Ⓗ
An attractive 17th-century village pub set in the heart of Hillesley. It has a single bar with a wood-burning stove, a separate lounge/dining room and a snug area. The pub serves up to six real ales and also offers guest craft keg and draught cider. Food is available at lunchtime and in the evening up to 9pm. There is a large, attractive lawned garden with a safe play area for children, and a private car park. Dogs are welcome. **QP**

Leighterton

Royal Oak
The Street, GL8 8UN (signpost to Leighterton off A46)
closed Mon; 12-3, 6-11; 12-5 Sun ☎ (01666) 890250
royaloakleighterton.co.uk
TAP Old Dairy Gold; Uley Bitter; Wye Valley Bitter; 1 changing beer (often Clavell & Hind) Ⓗ
Sympathetically refurbished Grade II-listed Cotswold-stone pub in a small village setting. Split into a number of cosy areas for drinking and dining, it features an open fire, low ceilings, panelled rooms and exposed stone walls. Knowledgeable owners serve four real ales and two ciders or perries at a single bar. Delicious home-made bar snacks complement a popular food menu. There is a large car park to the front. **P**

Lydbrook

Royal Spring Inn
Vention Lane, GL17 9RL (off B4228 to W of village)
12-3, 7-11 ☎ (01594) 860492
Brains Rev James; Fuller's London Pride; 1 changing beer (sourced regionally; often Wye Valley) Ⓗ
Traditional whitewashed community free house, in an attractive position up a narrow lane above the Wye. The carpeted floors in the wooden bar areas vary in depth and help separate the pub games from diners enjoying their much-appreciated home-cooked food. A stream flows through the sloping, fenced rear garden, which houses a menagerie. The garden also has a playground and drinking area and provides some cracking views. The adjacent cottage is available to rent.
P

Marshfield

Catherine Wheel

39 High Street, SN14 8LR (if using postcode in sat nav check address is not showing Colerne)

12-11 ☎ (01225) 892220 thecatherinewheel.co.uk

Butcombe Original; Fuller's London Pride; 1 changing beer (sourced locally; often Bath Ales)

In a conservation area of buildings ranging from medieval to Georgian, the pub is an impressive late 17th-century building. Its interior has the feel of a traditional and cosy country inn, with panelled rooms, exposed stone walls and a large open fireplace – some rooms being a much earlier age than the frontage. This pub is well sited, just a short drive from Bath and the Cotswolds. Well worth visiting and staying overnight in one of the letting rooms. **QP**

Moreton-in-Marsh

Bell Inn

High Street, GL56 0AF (on A429)

11-11 ☎ (01608) 651688 thebellinnmoreton.co.uk

Prescott Hill Climb; Purity Pure UBU; Timothy Taylor Landlord; 2 changing beers (sourced locally; often Hook Norton, North Cotswold)

Old High Street coaching inn dating from the 18th century that has been pleasantly refurbished. The interior is mainly open-plan area but has been sympathetically divided into more intimate snug sections with a real fire. The pub serves good food. A large courtyard area is found through the old arched entrance with an enclosed garden at the rear. The Bell is famed for its links with JRR Tolkien, Lord of the Rings author; a map of Middle Earth adorns the walls. Local and national ales are stocked. **QP**

Moseley Green

Rising Sun

GL15 4HN (off A48 at Blakeney toward Parkend and first left)

12-11 (midnight Fri & Sat) ☎ (01594) 562008

Wickwar BOB; 3 changing beers (sourced nationally)

Enjoying panoramic views from its isolated position amid defunct coal mines, this extended pub was built for miners in the early 1800s. Popular with cyclists, hikers, cavers and families, it offers several patios, large gardens and a pond. It is hard to believe that trams and trains ran only yards from the pub doors. Attractions include a bar on both floors when busy, a games room and a special kids' menu in the dining areas. A local music ensemble rehearses here. **P**

Newent

King's Arms

Ross Road, GL18 1BD (on B4221)

11-11.30 (12.30am Fri & Sat); 12-10.30 Sun

☎ (01531) 820035

3 changing beers (often Bespoke, Shepherd Neame, Titanic)

Following major improvements that took place in 2017, this pub features a comfortable refitted bar area with open fires, a function room and skittle alley, a large lower bar and a dining room. There is also a large, outdoor decked courtyard. It has a good reputation for home-cooked food, including a speciality pizza menu. A big car park allows motorhomes to stay for free as the pub is a member of Brit Stop. **QP**

Parkend

Fountain Inn

Fountain Way, GL15 4JD (off B4234)

12-2.30, 6.30-11; 12-4, 6-11 Fri; 12-11 Sat; 12-4, 6.30-11 Sun ☎ (01594) 562189

Wye Valley Butty Bach; 2 changing beers (often Hillside, Wye Valley)

Popular village inn, situated close to cycle trails, a preservation railway, RSPB reserve and other major attractions. Built more than 200 years ago, it was extended when the Severn and Wye Railway reached the village in 1875. Many items of local historical interest are on display in the pub. A wide selection of local beers and ciders and an extensive menu of good quality food are on offer. On Sunday lunchtimes the pub also offers a popular carvery. Four star accommodation (including one room with disabled facilities) is available in the inn itself, while an adjoining bunkhouse caters for groups of 9-32. There are also two spaces, with electric hook-up points, allocated for motorhome stop-overs. **QP**

Quenington

Keeper's Arms

Church Road, GL7 5BL (from Fairford turn right at village green)

6-10.30 Mon & Tue; 12-3, 6-11; 12-4, 7-10.30 Sun

☎ (01285) 750349 thekeepersarms.co.uk

4 changing beers (sourced nationally; often Butcombe, Otter, St Austell)

A former CAMRA Pub of the Year, this wonderful community local has been transformed into a cracking modern hostelry by the delightfully enthusiastic owner. Dogs, children, cricketers, cyclists, art lovers and ramblers are welcome in both the refurbished oak bar and the petite front garden. The unpretentious menus help fill both dining areas (no food Mon or Tue), with regular theme nights and quizzes proving popular. Two fireplaces give a pleasant glow in winter. Good accommodation is offered in four swish en-suite rooms. **P**

Sheepscombe

Butchers Arms

GL6 7RH (signed off A46 N of Painswick and B4070 N of Slad) SO8911610434

11.30-3, 6.30 (6 Fri)-11; 11.30-11 Sat; 12-10.30 Sun

☎ (01452) 812113 butchers-arms.co.uk

Prescott Hill Climb; 3 changing beers (sourced regionally; often Butcombe, Derby, Mobberley)

Handsome 17th-century Cotswold stone pub overlooking a wooded valley. Its inn sign, a painted three-dimensional carving of a butcher quaffing ale while tethered to a pig, is world famous. An adventurous range of ales from across the country is served on the guest pump. In 2014 the outdoor toilets metamorphosed into a new bar, seamlessly executed in reclaimed stone and Welsh oak. This complements a quality pre-WWII refurbishment that added the generous bay windows and porch. A wood-burning stove offers warmth in winter; the forecourt tables and sloping side garden are suntraps in summer. **QP**

Slad

Woolpack

GL6 7QA (on B4070)

12-midnight (01452) 813429 thewoolpackslad.com

Stroud Budding; Uley Bitter, Old Spot Prize Strong Ale, Pig's Ear Strong Beer; 1 changing beer (sourced regionally)

Popular 17th-century inn clinging to the side of the Slad valley with superb views. It achieved fame through Cider with Rosie – author Laurie Lee was a regular and instrumental in saving the pub from closure. The pub has been thoughtfully restored, with built-in dark-wooden settles in the end rooms. Outside there is a decked patio area down steps to the side. Monday is the night for pizza, prepared on the hob in the revolutionary oven designed by the pub's owner, Daniel Chadwick. Q

Staple Hill

Wooden Walls

30 Broad Street, BS16 5NU

5-9.45 Mon & Tue; 3-10.30 Wed-Fri; 12-10.45 Sat; 12-10.15 Sun 07448 936034

the-wooden-walls-micropub.business.site

5 changing beers

Micropub opened in May 2018 in a former carpet shop on the main shopping street in Staple Hill. The single room has wooden walls and is pleasantly furnished. Conversation is king, with mobile phones tolerated if set to silent. Drinks are displayed on a large blackboard that surrounds the serving hatch. Several real ciders, gins and wines are sold alongside between four and 10 real ales, but no lager. There are a few steps up to the toilets and rear garden. Q

Stroud

Ale House

9 John Street, GL5 2HA (opp Cornhill farmers' market)

12-3, 5-11; 12-midnight Fri; 11-midnight Sat; 12-11 Sun (01453) 755447

Burning Sky Plateau; Tiley's Special Pale; 6 changing beers (sourced nationally; often Salopian, Siren, Vibrant Forest)

Built in 1837 for the Poor Law Guardians, this Grade II-listed building is a mecca for ale lovers. The bar occupies the double-height top-lit former boardroom, where an all-year-round beer festival showcases ales from Artisan, Electric Bear and many others, plus a cider and perry. Opposite is a blazing log fire and adjoining are two smaller rooms. Live music is played Friday or Saturday, and jazz once a month on Thursday. A fiendishly difficult quiz on Sunday is set by the landlord – who also prepares the speciality home-made curries, chilli and other dishes. Local CAMRA Pub of the Year 2019. Q

Bowbridge Arms

London Road, Bowbridge, GL5 2AY (on A419)

11-11; 11-5 Sun (01453) 298914

thebowbridgearms.co.uk

Bath Ales Gem; St Austell Proper Job; 1 changing beer (often Bath Ales, Butcombe, Stroud)

Friendly and traditional Cotswold-stone pub at the eastern edge of Stroud, close to the Bowbridge Lock on the Thames & Severn Canal, a 15-minute walk from the town centre and railway station. Its comfortable, modern interior is dominated by a stonking Clearview stove. A separate pool room leads to a small VIP lounge available for private hire or for watching sports on a large flat-screen TV. There is a large, south-facing, suntrap outdoor seating area, including a children's play space, with views across the valley to Rodborough Common. Good-value home-cooked food includes typical pub grub, with pies from Plenty Pies in Nailsworth. Pizzas are a speciality. Q P

Crown & Sceptre

98 Horns Road, GL5 1EG

3-11; 12-11 Fri & Sat; 12-10.30 Sun (01453) 762588

crownandsceptrestroud.com

Stroud Budding; Uley Bitter, Pig's Ear Strong Beer; 1 changing beer (sourced regionally; often Blue Anchor, Clavell & Hind)

Lively back-street local that is at the heart of its community. The walls display an eclectic mix of framed prints, posters and clocks. Local groups meet round a large oak table in a side room – including Knit and Natter on Tuesday. The pub also has its own motorcycle society. Highly regarded food includes a Sunday roast and a good-value Up the Workers set meal on Wednesday. Sport is screened in the back bar. A terrace to the rear offers panoramic views across the valley to Rodborough Common. P (8,227)

Prince Albert

Rodborough Hill, GL5 3SS (corner of Walkley Hill)

4-11.30 (12.30am Fri); 12-12.30am Sat; 12-10.30 Sun (01453) 755600 theprincealbertstroud.co.uk

Otter Ale; Stroud Alederflower; Timothy Taylor Landlord; 4 changing beers (sourced nationally; often Bristol Beer Factory, Gloucester, Sharp's)

Cosmopolitan Cotswold-stone pub below Rodborough Common that is bohemian, homely and welcoming and has a big reputation for live music. Its L-shaped bar boasts a log fire and an eclectic mix of furniture, fittings and memorabilia – the walls are covered with film and music posters. The pub hosts a May beer festival, exhibitions and open mic nights. Some events are ticketed; phone or check the website. Jamaica Inn Caribbean food is a feature Friday evening and Sunday lunchtime. Alternatively bring your own food or phone for a takeaway.

Tetbury

Royal Oak

1 Cirencester Road, GL8 8EY (on B4067)

11-11 (11.30 Fri & Sat); 12-11 Sun (01666) 500021

theroyaloaktetbury.co.uk

Butcombe Haka; Moor Beer So'Hop; Stroud Tom Long; 2 changing beers (sourced regionally)

This wonderful, award-winning pub utilises clever design to marry a traditional feel to a modern layout. The swathe of wooden surfaces provides a welcoming feel, with a small fireplace adding warmth. The choice from six handpumps includes Severn Cider and a vegan ale from Moor, matching the vegan menu offering. The one-pot option is often selected, especially on quiz nights. Upstairs dining rooms and the six letting rooms are popular, as are the pub's lively music and beer festivals. P

Tewkesbury

Berkeley Arms 🏆

8 Church Street, GL20 5PA (between Tewkesbury Cross and abbey on old A38)
⏲ 10-11 ☎ (01684) 290555 🌐 berkeleyarms.pub
Wadworth IPA, 6X, Swordfish; 2 changing beers (often Titanic, Wadworth) Ⓗ
A half-timbered, Grade II-listed pub dating from the 15th century, just off Tewkesbury Cross. A barn at the rear, believed to be the oldest non-ecclesiastical building in this historic town, is used for dining and also serves as a meeting room. Good-value home-cooked food is served daily in this two-bar establishment, with the landlord's home-baked pies of particular note. Live music is performed on Friday and Saturday evenings. Buses to Cheltenham and Gloucester stop close by. Best Wadworth pub 2018. **Q**♘✿◐◑♿⛺♣●🚌(41)🐾📶

Royal British Legion Club

50 Church Street, GL20 5SN
⏲ 8-11 Mon, Wed & Thu; closed Tue; 7-11.30 Fri; 12-3, 7.30-11.30 Sat; 12-3, 7.30-11 Sun ☎ (01684) 293798
🌐 branches.britishlegion.org.uk/branches/tewkesbury
2 changing beers (often Exmoor, Froth Blowers, Ludlow) Ⓗ
Services club near the abbey in a timber-framed building that used to be two pubs. The main lounge area is open to non-members. The venue has a great community feel; several clubs hold their meetings here and there is a team in the local crib league. Live music is performed on Saturday night. Local CAMRA branch Club of the Year 2017-2019.
Q✿⛺⇌♣🚌(41)🐾

Royal Hop Pole Hotel 𝕃 ✔

94 Church Street, GL20 5RS (centre of town between abbey and cross)
⏲ 7am-11 ☎ (01684) 278670
Great Western Old Higby; Greene King IPA; Hook Norton Old Hooky; Ruddles County; 4 changing beers (sourced locally; often Battledown, Exmoor, Prescott) Ⓗ
This well-known landmark is an amalgamation of historic buildings from the 15th and 18th centuries. It has been known as the Royal Hop Pole since being visited in September 1891 by Princess Mary of Teck (Queen Mary, Royal Consort of George V). The pub is mentioned in Dickens' Pickwick Papers. Purchased by JD Wetherspoon, it reopened in 2008. There is wood panelling on almost every wall of the spacious, multi-roomed drinking establishment, which has a large patio and garden area at the rear. **Q**♘✿🛏◐◑♿⛺**P**🚌📶

White Bear 𝕃

Bredon Road, GL20 5BU (off N end of High St)
⏲ 10-midnight ☎ (01684) 296614
🌐 famouswhitebear.co.uk
Salopian Oracle; Uley Old Spot Prize Strong Ale; 7 changing beers (sourced nationally; often Bristol Beer Factory, Sadler's, Uley) Ⓗ
On the north-western edge of the town, this good-value, friendly pub attracts ale and cider drinkers from far and wide. The open-plan L-shaped bar offers room to play pool and darts; there is also a skittle alley. Live music features every Sunday afternoon. The seven ales change frequently and include offerings from local and national award-winning breweries. At least five traditional ciders and perries are always on sale.
♘✿♿⛺♣●**P**🍺🚌🐾📶

Thornbury

Butcher's Hook 𝕃

8 High Street, BS35 2AQ
⏲ closed Mon; 4-10; 4-11 Fri; 12-11 Sat; 12-10 Sun
☎ (01454) 501800
8 changing beers (often Hop Back, Moor Beer, Tiley's)
A Grade II-listed building that was for 200 years a butcher's shop. It has some superb period features such as fireplaces, alcoves and ceiling beams in its three rooms, and a huge ancient front door. The pub offers up to eight cask beers on handpump, including at least two from Tiley's, brewed at the Salutation at Ham, and six real ciders. The food offering consists of locally produced cheese and pork pies. **Q**♣●🚌🐾📶

Upper Soudley

White Horse Inn

Church Road, GL14 2UA (b4227)
⏲ 7-11 (midnight Fri); 3-midnight Sat; 12-6 Sun
☎ (01594) 825968
2 changing beers (sourced nationally) Ⓗ
This inn was built as a railway hotel, next to the now defunct Soudley Halt, and provides great views across the valley from the garden. It is an interesting venue for geologists and walkers, with the Blue Rock Trail and Soudley Ponds. Run by an enthusiastic couple, this lovely old pub has a small main bar with a welcoming fireplace and two regularly changing guest ales. The old dining room down the passageway is used for functions, and leads through to a much-loved skittle alley.
♘✿♿♣●**P**🚌(717)🐾

Wanswell

Salmon Inn

Station Road, GL13 9SE (centre of village)
⏲ 11-11 ☎ (01453) 811306 🌐 the-salmon.co.uk
3 changing beers (sourced regionally; often Timothy Taylor) Ⓗ
This attractive 16th-century inn was originally a cider house. The bar, which has plenty of seating and standing space, features three draught ales, two of which are usually local. The extensive dining area behind the rustic bar provides fresh food from a varied and locally sourced menu. The large garden includes a play area for children, and there is outdoor seating to the front. Car parking is within the grounds of the pub. **Q**♘✿◐◑♿♣**P**

Westbury-on-Severn

Lyon Inn

The Village, GL14 1PA (on A48)
⏲ closed Mon; 12-3, 6-11; 11-11 Sat; 11-3, 7-11 Sun
☎ (01452) 760221 🌐 thelyoninn.com
2 changing beers Ⓗ
Formerly the Red Lion, the pub has been revived by its new owners. Areas have been opened up, creating a good-sized restaurant and separate bar area. Two or three real ales are served, with a local option when possible. A nice enclosed garden sits to the rear of the pub. Next door is the National Trust's Westbury Court Garden, which is worth a visit. **Q**♘✿🛏◐◑♣**P**🍺

Winchcombe

Lion Inn ✓

37 North Street, GL54 5PS

11-11 ☎ (01242) 603300 thelionwinchcombe.co.uk

Marston's EPA; Wye Valley Butty Bach; 4 changing beers (sourced locally; often North Cotswold, Prescott) H

A comfortable 15th-century coaching inn, renovated in 2011, that retains its traditional appearance with exposed oak timbers and stone fireplaces. It is a popular venue with locals and visitors alike, offering regularly changing locally sourced real ales on its four handpumps. Features include accommodation and an attractive restaurant, plus a secluded lawn and patio area at the rear of the premises. A recent award-winner of the local CAMRA Seasonal Pub of the Year.

P

Woolaston Common

Rising Sun

The Common, GL15 6NU SO5901500924

12-2.30, 6.30-11; 12-3, 6.30-midnight Sat; 12-3, 6.30-11 Sun ☎ (01594) 529282

Butcombe Adam Henson's Rare Breed; Wye Valley Bitter; 1 changing beer (sourced regionally) H

Off the beaten track, this comfortable 350-year-old stone-built pub enjoys gorgeous views over the Forest of Dean. There is a welcoming main bar with an open fire and a small snug, both of which display part of the landlord's large collection of framed banknotes. The Rising Sun is featured in the circular pub walks of the Forest, and its varied menu of good home-cooked food is popular with ramblers (no food Mon & Tue lunchtime). Friendly locals help make for a convivial atmosphere.

Q♣P

Royal Hop Pole, Tewkesbury (Photo: Dave_S./Flickr CC BY 2.0)

LocAle

LocAle
We are proud to serve locally-brewed real ale
CAMRA accredited 2019/20

Many entries in the Guide refer to pubs' support for CAMRA's LocAle scheme. The L symbol is used where a pub has LocAle accreditation. The aim of the scheme is to get publicans to stock at least one cask beer that comes from a local brewery, usually no more than 30 miles away.

The aim is a simple one: to cut down on 'beer miles'. Research by CAMRA shows that food and drink transport accounts for 25 per cent of all HGV vehicle miles in Britain. Taking into account the miles that ingredients have travelled on top of distribution journeys, an imported lager produced by a multi-national brewery could have notched up more than 24,000 'beer miles' by the time it reaches a pub.

Supporters of LocAle point out that £10 spent on locally-supplied goods generates £25 for the local economy. Keeping trade local helps enterprises, creates more economic activity and jobs, and makes other services more viable. The scheme also generates consumer support for local breweries.

Support for LocAle has grown at a rapid pace since it was created in 2007. It's been embraced by pubs and CAMRA branches throughout England and has now crossed the borders into Scotland and Wales.

For more information, see camra.org.uk/locale

What is CAMRA LocAle?

- An initiative that promotes pubs which sell locally-brewed real ale
- The scheme builds on a growing consumer demand for quality local produce and an increased awareness of 'green' issues.

Everyone benefits from local pubs stocking locally brewed real ale...

- Public houses, as stocking local real ales can increase pub visits
- Consumers, who enjoy greater beer choice and locally brewed beer
- Local brewers, who gain from increased sales and get better feedback from consumers
- The local economy, because more money is spent and retained in the local economy
- The environment, due to fewer 'beer miles' resulting in less road congestion and pollution
- Tourism, due to an increased sense of local identity and pride – let's celebrate what makes our locality different.

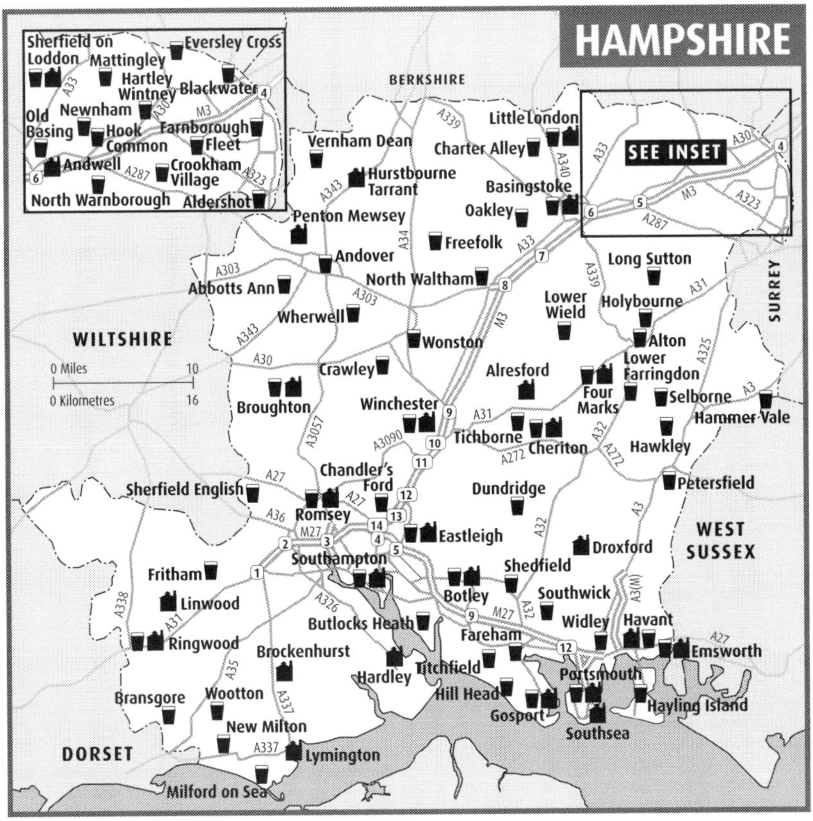

Please note: Ringwood Brewery renamed Best Bitter to Razorback but it is still available in some outlets as Best Bitter

Abbotts Ann

Eagle Inn L

Duck Street, SP11 7BG

11.30-11; 12-10.30 Sun ☎ (01264) 710339

theeagleinn.wordpress.com

Bowman Wallops Wood; 2 changing beers (sourced locally) H

In a picturesque village just two miles south-west of Andover, this pub is at the heart of the community. Friendly conversation rules the house. The three beers are often all locally produced and a real cider made in the village is also available. A beer and cider festival is held over the second weekend of June. The public bar has pool and there is a skittle alley at the rear. Locally sourced food features. No food Sunday and Tuesday evenings. ❀◑♣●P🚌(87)🐾📶

Aldershot

Garden Gate L ✔

2 Church Lane East, GU11 3BT

5-11 (midnight Thu; 1am Fri); 12-1am Sat; 12-10.30 Sun ☎ (01252) 219717

Surrey Hills Ranmore; 2 changing beers (sourced nationally; often St Austell, Surrey Hills, Twickenham) H

A focal point of the local community, where conversation and low-level background music reign, with occasional live music. The bar is two rooms knocked into one, now tastefully refurbished, freshly painted and given new pictures. There is a back room and an external covered patio. The Thursday night quiz is popular, and a music quiz is held monthly on Sunday. The pub is as popular with dogs as it is with humans. The beer range may vary, with Surrey Hills Ranmore as LocAle. ❀⇌P🚌🐾📶

White Lion L

20 Lower Farnham Road, GU12 4EA

1-10.30 Mon; 1-11 Tue & Wed; 1-11.30 Thu; 1-midnight Fri; 12-midnight Sat; 12-10.30 Sun ☎ (01252) 323832

Triple fff Alton's Pride, Pressed Rat & Warthog, Moondance; 1 changing beer (sourced nationally) H

A traditional two-room pub, established as a beer house around 1857. It remains a proper locals' pub, with plenty of '60s atmosphere and scooter memorabilia. The back room is usually the quieter, while the main bar is more basic, with church pews, piano and a real fire. It is always welcoming to visitors, including away fans when Aldershot Town are playing at home, while Millie the pub dog welcomes other pooches. A quiz and music bingo run on alternate Thursdays. ❀♣●🚌(3)🐾📶

Alton

Eight Bells L

33 Church Street, GU34 2DA (opp St Lawrence church)

11.30-11; 12-10.30 Sun ☎ (01420) 82417

Sharp's Doom Bar; 4 changing beers (sourced regionally; often Flowerpots, Longdog, Red Cat) Ⓗ
This genuine free house, which has been a pub since at least the 1840s, celebrates 20 continuous years in the Guide in 2020. The guest beer range changes frequently and always includes local breweries. The main bar is a haven for good beer and conversation while the rear drinking area has a TV for major sporting events. The open fire is welcoming in the winter months and, outside, the pleasant paved patio has a covered smoking refuge and an old well. Q❀⇌🚌(13)🐾📶

George ✔

Butts Road, GU34 1LH
🕘 11-11 (midnight Thu-Sat); 11-10.30 Sun ☎ (01420) 82331
🌐 thegeorgealton.co.uk
Sharp's Sea Fury; 4 changing beers (sourced nationally) Ⓗ
Celebrating 10 years as mine hosts, Susannah and Jason have turned a dreary pub previously called the Duke's Head into this friendly local serving up to five real ales. A dark beer is frequently included in the selection. Excellent food, cooked to order, is also available, from snacks to full meals. Quiz night is the first Tuesday each month. There is live music on other days and an annual beer festival, usually in July (details on website). ❀◑P🚌(64)🐾📶

King's Head 𝕃

28 Market Street, GU34 1HA (opp market square)
🕘 10.30-1am ☎ (01420) 82313 🌐 kingsheadalton.com
Courage Best Bitter; 1 changing beer (sourced locally; often Andwell, Itchen Valley) Ⓗ
This Grade II-listed two-bar traditional local combines a consistently high standard in beer quality with a discerning choice of guest ale, usually a local Hampshire brew. Happy Hour is 4.30-7pm Monday to Thursday and all weekend. The pleasant terraced garden at the rear, sometimes the venue for summer live music, backs on to the paying community centre car park and gives a peaceful contrast to this bustling town-centre pub. Poker night is Tuesday, with a quiz night on the first Wednesday of the month.
❀♣P🚌🐾📶

Andover

Angel Inn ✔

95 High Street, SP10 1ND
🕘 9am-11 (midnight Fri & Sat); 11-7 Sun ☎ (01264) 351646
Morland Old Speckled Hen; 2 changing beers (sourced nationally) Ⓗ
The oldest building in Andover, saved when the town centre was redeveloped, and one of Hampshire's oldest inns. A timber-framed courtyard inn, built by Winchester College 1445-55, it remains remarkably intact, hence its Grade II* listing. Note the coaching light window. There are two bars; the upper bar was once used as a court. A pleasant small patio is at the rear and there is a sheltered and decorated courtyard at the front. Live music and karaoke feature and pool and darts are played. Breakfasts are good value. ❀◑🚌🐾

Redbridge ✔

5 Bridge Street, SP10 1BE
🕘 8am-11 (1am Fri & Sat); 11-11 Sun ☎ (01264) 353908
Courage Best Bitter; Sharp's Doom Bar; 3 changing beers Ⓗ
In the town centre near the Market Place and River Anton, this lively pub has low lighting and a long bar. The food and beer are good-value and it is popular for breakfast and sports TV. Families are catered for and it is dog-friendly. The three changing guests are varied and often include a local ale. A loyalty card is on offer for real ale drinkers. ◑🚌🐾📶

Town Mills

20 Bridge Street, SP10 1BL
🕘 11-11 (midnight Fri, 12.30am Sat); 12-10.30 Sun
☎ (01264) 332540 🌐 thetownmills.co.uk
Wadworth IPA, 6X; 2 changing beers (sourced regionally; often Wadworth) Ⓗ
Just off the town centre in a historic mill with a working water wheel, and with the River Anton passing through. There are several separate areas for dining and drinking, including a comfy lounge upstairs. Pub games are also played upstairs and a well-supported quiz is held on Wednesday evenings. The riverside garden is popular in summer months. Usually three to four beers are available from the Wadworth range.
❀◑♿♣P🚌🐾📶

White Hart

Bridge Street, SP10 1BH
🕘 11-11 ☎ (01264) 352266
Marston's Pedigree; Ringwood Boondoggle; 2 changing beers Ⓗ
A 17th-century coaching inn with a traditional decor befitting the historic building. The downstairs area has a bar to the rear and there are separate seating areas and a restaurant. Functions including conferences and weddings can be catered for.

REAL ALE BREWERIES

Alfred's Winchester
Andwell Andwell
Betteridge's Hurstbourne Tarrant
Botley Botley
Bowman Droxford
Brewhouse & Kitchen 🛢 Portsmouth
Brewhouse & Kitchen 🛢 Southampton
Brewhouse & Kitchen 🛢 Southsea (NEW)
Brockenhurst Brockenhurst
CrackleRock Botley
Dancing Cows Lymington
Dancing Man 🛢 Southampton
Emsworth Emsworth
Emsworth Brewhouse Havant
Fallen Acorn Gosport
Flack Manor Romsey
Flowerpots Cheriton
Irving Portsmouth
Itchen Valley Alresford
Little London Little London
London Road Brew House 🛢 Southampton
Longdog Basingstoke
Newtown Gosport
Penton Park Penton Mewsey (NEW)
Queen Inn 🛢 Winchester
Red Cat Winchester
Red Shoot 🛢 Linwood
Ringwood Ringwood
Sherfield Village Sherfield on Loddon
Southsea Portsmouth
Steam Town Eastleigh
Tap It Southampton
Test Broughton
Triple fff Four Marks
Urban Island Portsmouth
Vibrant Forest Hardley

Although hard to believe, the building is much smaller than many years ago; in the 1800s it stretched right along Bridge Street to the river and had stabling for 75 horses. Q🐎🛏◖◗P🚌📶

Basingstoke

Angel 🄻 ✔

Unit R6, Lower Ground, Festival Place, RG21 7BB
⏲ 8am-12.30am (2am Fri & Sat) ☎ (01256) 854800
Greene King IPA, Abbot; Sharp's Doom Bar; 7 changing beers (often Andwell, Longdog) 🄷
Formerly a Lloyds No.1 Bar, this modern, spacious one-bar pub is at the edge of the restaurant quarter in the town's Festival Place shopping centre, handy for the nearby bus station and five minutes' walk from the rail station. Popular with younger people, the pub can get very busy and often noisy in the evenings, especially at weekends. Lunchtimes attract a wider age range and tend to be quieter. The walls are adorned with TVs, all in silent mode.
🐎❀◖◗♿≋🍎🚌📶

Basingstoke Sports & Social Club ✔

Fairfields Road, RG21 3DR
⏲ 11-3, 5-11; 12-11 Fri & Sat; 12-10.30 Sun
☎ (01256) 473646 🌐 basingstoke-sports-club.co.uk
Dark Star Hophead; Fuller's London Pride; Gale's Seafarers Ale; 2 changing beers (sourced nationally; often Andwell, Little London, Longdog) 🄷
This thriving sports-based members' club has a bar open to all. Founded in 1865, the site is home to a range of sports. It has seven handpumps with five beers available, including local guests. Widescreen TVs cover major sports events. An annual programme of social activities is held and sports and function room facilities can be hired. Opening hours and meal times are flexible depending on the season and sporting fixtures. Winner of CAMRA Branch Club of the Year 2018 and 2019.
🐎◖◗♣P🚌🐾📶

Maidenhead Inn 🄻 ✔

17 Winchester Street, RG21 7ED
⏲ 8am-midnight (1am Fri & Sat) ☎ (01256) 316030
Greene King Abbot; Ruddles Best Bitter; Sharp's Doom Bar; 4 changing beers (sourced nationally; often Andwell, Loddon, Longdog) 🄷
Formerly home to a building society and on the site of an inn of the same name, this Wetherspoon's pub is in the sometimes lively Top of Town area. The two banks of pumps have up to seven beers and good local representation. A dining area at the front leads to the compact bar, with further seating to the rear over two levels, complemented by a courtyard beer garden to the rear.
🐎❀◖◗♿≋🍎🚌📶

Wheatsheaf

Winton Square, RG21 8EU
⏲ 11.30-midnight (1am Fri & Sat); 12-midnight Sun
☎ (01256) 479601
Butcombe Original; Otter Ale; Sharp's Doom Bar, Atlantic 🄷
A lively local with the atmosphere you would expect from a popular town-centre pub, serving a wide choice of well-kept cask beers at prices good for the area. At weekends and some evenings there are large-screen televised sports fixtures. No frills, but a warm welcome. No food on Sunday.
◖◗≋🚌

Blackwater

Mr Bumble 🄻

19 London Road, GU17 9AP
⏲ 12-11 (midnight Thu-Sat); 12-10.30 Sun ☎ (01276) 32691
Fuller's London Pride; 3 changing beers (sourced regionally; often Dark Star, Triple fff, Windsor & Eton) 🄷
This large pub is ideally located in the centre of Blackwater's shopping area, and near the station and bus stops. With a large lower bar area for meeting and chatting, and an upper bar with darts and three pool tables, plus sports TVs, this is very much a community pub. Live music plays on Thursday and Saturday, and sometimes on Friday. The regular beer is supplemented by three guest beers, generally including LocAles.
🐎≋♣P🚌(3,2)🐾📶

Botley

CrackleRock Tap Room 🄻

30A High Street, SO30 2EA (down alley between Clarke Mews and Max Plumbing) SU5130213037
⏲ closed Mon; 6-11 Tue-Thu; 4-11 Fri; 12-11 Sat; 12-6 Sun
☎ 07733 232806 🌐 cracklerock.co.uk
CrackleRock Crackerjack, Fire Cracker, Gold Rush, Crafty Shag, Dark Destroyer, Crackatoa IPA; 3 changing beers (sourced locally; often Bowman) 🄷
Located in the heart of the old village of Botley, this ale and spirit house has nine traditional cask pumps, five keg lines, exciting nibbles and a huge selection of wines and spirits. CrackleRock has a unique ambience and is known for its friendly service and quality ales. On handpump is the core range of CrackleRock beer, seasonal brews and guest beers from local breweries. Multiple third-pint tasting flights are available for the ales, with an equivalent wine sampler. ⛺🍎🚌(3,X9)🐾

Bransgore

Three Tuns ✔

Ringwood Road, BH23 8JH
⏲ 11-11; 11.30-11 Sat; 12-10.30 Sun ☎ (01425) 672232
🌐 threetunsinn.com
Otter Amber; Ringwood Fortyniner; house beer (by Red Rock); 6 changing beers (sourced nationally) 🄷
A 17th-century thatched pub with a proper public bar and a lounge with plenty of room for drinkers, merging into the restaurant area. Food is high quality, with AA and Egon Ronay recognition. Five handpumps in each bar serve four regular and six changing beers, though one may sometimes be replaced with a cider. A large terrace and superb gardens provide plenty of outdoor space. A beer festival is staged at the end of September.
Q🐎❀◖◗♿⛺♣P🚌(125)🐾📶

Broughton

Tally Ho!

High Street, SO20 8AA
⏲ 12-11 (midnight Fri & Sat); 12-10.30 Sun
☎ (01794) 301280 🌐 thetallyhobroughton.co.uk
Ringwood Best Bitter; house beer (by Test); 2 changing beers (sourced nationally) 🄷
Although quite spacious, the interconnected rooms and eclectic furnishing give the pub a domestic, cottagey feel. The Tally Ho! house beer is from the village's own four-barrel brewery a few doors away; Ringwood's Razorback is badged as Best

Bitter. Changing beers usually include another from the Wessex area. In summer a cider is added. Award-winning, good-quality food is served, with takeaway options available. For walkers, the pub is ideally placed midway along the Salisbury to Winchester Clarendon Way. Dogs are very welcome. (16)

Butlocks Heath

Roll Call

Woolston Road, SO31 5FJ

12 (3 Mon & Tue)-11 (023) 8045 2358

therollcall.co.uk

Courage Best Bitter; Flowerpots Bitter H; 2 changing beers (sourced locally) G

The pub has two medium-sized bars decorated with numerous tankards hanging from the ceilings. The characteristic lounge bar has three handpumps and, at weekends, a guest local beer is also served from the cask. From Thursday to Sunday the lounge serves home-made pub food including a range of curries. Outside there is a patio and garden with a children's assault course. Note that the pub does not open until 3pm on Monday and Tuesday.
P (6,X15)

Chandler's Ford

Steel Tank Alehouse

1 The Central Precinct, Winchester Road, SO53 2GA

closed Mon & Tue; 3-10; 12-6 Sun 07379 553025

6 changing beers (sourced regionally; often Drop The Anchor, Siren, Vibrant Forest) H

CAMRA local Pub of the Year 2019, this friendly micropub serves a changing selection of beers, often from nearby brewers. Popular with locals and visitors from further afield, it is well served by public transport. A converted unit, previously a bank (hence the name), in a '60s/'70s shopping precinct, it is a great place to spend time chatting with friends or the knowledgeable staff. The decor includes beer and football-themed walls and wooden furniture. An oasis in a fine beer desert.
Q P (1,X7)

Charter Alley

White Hart

White Hart Lane, RG26 5QA (1 mile W of A340, opp turning for Little London)

closed Mon; 7-10 Tue & Wed; 12-2.30, 7-10 Thu; 12-2.30, 5.30-11 Fri; 12-2.30, 7-11 Sat; 12-3 Sun (01256) 850048

whitehartcharteralley.com

6 changing beers (sourced locally; often Hop Back, Langham, Loddon) H

Built in 1819, this cosy inn is at the epicentre of the village, where all comers are assured of a friendly greeting. Welcoming features include log fires, oak beams and a capacious dining area, serving a variety of quality food and home-made pies. The breweriana-decorated main bar dispenses an array of frequently changing ales. This stalwart Guide entry for the past 27 years recently started brewing a range of ales as the Secret Brewing Company. Its website shows the beers that are on and in the cellar. Q P

Cheriton

Flower Pots Inn

Brandy Mount, SO24 0QQ (¾ mile N of A272 Cheriton/Beauworth crossroads) SU581283

12-2.30, 6-11; 12-3, 7-10.30 Sun (01962) 771318

flowerpotscheriton.co.uk

Flowerpots Perridge Pale, Bitter, Goodens Gold; 1 changing beer (often Flowerpots) G

Home to Hampshire's oldest independent brewery, set in outbuildings to the right of the red-brick Georgian pub. The full range of Flower Pots beers, normally three regulars and several seasonal and special brews, are dispensed directly by gravity in the two bars. Draught ciders are also offered. Good-quality home-cooked food is served lunchtimes and evenings (no food Sun eve and all day Mon). Wednesday evening features real Punjabi curries. The garden has tables and a marquee for bad weather or overflow.
Q P (67)

Crawley

Fox

Main Road, SO21 2PR (150yds W of duck pond)

11-11 (10.30 Sun) (01962) 461302 the-fox.pub

Alfred's Saxon Bronze; Bowman Swift One, Wallops Wood; 1 changing beer (sourced locally; often Alfred's, Flowerpots) H

An upmarket country pub in this beautiful village, in the hills to the north-west of Winchester. The real ales are from top local breweries. The food is excellent quality, Hampshire-sourced and cooked fresh on-site. The bar area is complemented by a contemporary restaurant, and the dining room has viewing windows to the kitchen. The pub reopened in late 2018 after a significant extension and refurbishment. Accommodation is offered in five high-end en-suite rooms.
P (7,16)

Crookham Village

Spice Merchant

The Street, GU51 5SJ

12-11 (01252) 621126

Timothy Taylor Boltmaker; 1 changing beer (sourced nationally; often Hogs Back, Otter, Twickenham) H

A village pub, formerly the Black Horse, that reopened as the Spice Merchant in 2018. Redecorated in a light, airy style, it specialises in Thai and other south-east Asian food. The front area is laid out more as a pub and welcomes drinkers, especially by the bar. There are two real ales available, with a rotating beer from a choice of four from the Enterprise Inns list. The pub was successfully registered as an Asset of Community Value in April 2017. P (10)

Dundridge

Hampshire Bowman

Dundridge Lane, SO32 1GD (turn E off B3035 ½ mile N of Bishops Waltham, then 1½ miles further on) SU578184

12-11 (midnight Fri); 12-10.30 Sun (01489) 892940

hampshirebowman.com

Bowman Swift One; West Berkshire Good Old Boy; 4 changing beers (sourced regionally; often Andwell, Flack Manor, Longdog) G

This pub, set in the beautiful Hampshire countryside, began life as a coaching inn in around

1700. There is a large garden where children and dogs are welcome, with a play area. The inside is cosy and warm with an open fire. A great selection of beers is on tap, many local, poured straight from the cask. An even larger selection of real ciders is also on offer. Home-cooked, locally sourced food is served at reasonable prices lunchtimes and evenings. Q🐎❀◑♿♣🍎P🐾📶

Eastleigh

Steam Town Brew Co 🄻

1 Bishopstoke Road, SO50 6AD (on B3037)

⏲ 11-11 ☎ (023) 8235 9139 🌐 steamtownbrewco.co.uk

7 changing beers (sourced locally; often Steam Town) 🄷

Once a café, this is now an excellent pub with an integral, visible, five-barrel brewery. Eight handpumps serve house beers, one or more ciders, plus, usually, guest beers. Meanwhile 16 fonts on a tiled back wall supply small producers' craft ales, ciders and lagers. The dining area for lunch and evening meals is furnished with repurposed first-class train seating. The general decor is a funky industrial pastiche. Frequent live music, monthly beer tastings and other events ensure a lively ambience. 🐎❀◑♿🚆🍎🚌(2,3)🐾📶

Emsworth

Blue Bell ✔

29 South Street, PO10 7EG

⏲ 9am-11 (midnight Fri & Sat) ☎ (01243) 373394

🌐 bluebellinnemsworth.co.uk

Sharp's Doom Bar; 2 changing beers (sourced nationally; often Emsworth Brewhouse, Irving) 🄷

A modern-looking pub a short walk from Emsworth harbour. The pub was originally further along the road but was rebuilt in its current location in about 1960 as it blocked the access to buildings behind it. Inside, the single bar has the look and feel of a much older pub and is decorated with military and naval memorabilia. A large collection of banknotes from many countries is above the bar. Two walls are adorned with watercolours painted by local artists. ❀◑🚆🚌(700)📶

Coal Exchange ✔

21 South Street, PO10 7EG

⏲ 10.30-3, 5.30-11; 10.30-midnight Fri & Sat; 12-11 Sun

☎ (01243) 375866 🌐 thecoalexchange.co.uk

Dark Star Hophead; Fuller's London Pride; Gale's HSB, Seafarers Ale; 2 changing beers (sourced nationally; often Butcombe, Fuller's) 🄷

A compact pub near the harbour. The single bar has wooden tables with benches, traditional seats and stools. Open fireplaces contribute to a cosy atmosphere on cold winter days. To the rear is a walled garden, a real suntrap in summer. A good range of home-cooked food is available lunchtimes, and speciality dishes are on offer some evenings. The name derives from when the pub was used by local farmers as a place to trade with merchants delivering coal by sea.

🐎❀◑🚆🚌(700)🐾

Eversley Cross

Frog & Wicket

The Green, RG27 0NS

⏲ 11-11; 12-10 Sun ☎ (0118) 973 1126

Dark Star Hophead; Fuller's Oliver's Island, London Pride; Gale's HSB; Hogs Back TEA; 3 changing beers (often Fuller's) 🄷

A spacious double-fronted pub, in a great location directly opposite the cricket green, it was taken over by Fuller's in 2013, with a major refurbishment. As the pub's name suggests, the interior displays an array of both froggy and sporting memorabilia. There is a wood stove in the separate dining room area. An adjacent skittle alley can be booked for private functions. There is a large garden at the rear with a well-equipped playground for children. Quiz night is Tuesday.

🐎❀◑♿♣P🐾📶

Fareham

Delme Arms 🄻

1 Cams Hill, PO16 8QY

⏲ 12-11 (1am Fri); 11-1am Sat; 12-10 Sun

☎ (01329) 232638 🌐 delmearms.co.uk

Sharp's Doom Bar; 4 changing beers (sourced regionally) 🄶

Although on the outskirts of Fareham, it is well served by buses. The lower bar includes a games and TV area, with a quieter atmosphere in the upper bar, sometimes used for parties and other functions. Up to four guest beers are sold, often from local breweries. Ciders include Westons Old Rosie on handpump, and normally six others in boxes from various suppliers. A beer and cider festival is held at the end of May.

🐎❀🛏◑♣🍎P🚌(3,X4)🐾📶

Lord Arthur Lee ✔

100-108 West Street, PO16 0EP

⏲ 8am-11 (midnight Fri & Sat) ☎ (01329) 280447

Greene King Abbot; Ruddles Best Bitter; Sharp's Doom Bar; 4 changing beers (sourced nationally; often Ringwood) 🄷

Spacious Wetherspoon pub within walking distance of the bus and train stations. The walls are lined with photos of the pub's namesake and other famous local people. There is one large bar, with a smaller area set aside for families. Three guest beers are usually available from the Wetherspoon's list, including some local beers and up to three real ciders, with extra beers during the spring and autumn festivals. The usual range of food is served until 10pm. 🐎❀◑♿🚆🍎🚌📶

Farnborough

Prince of Wales 🄻 ✔

184 Rectory Road, GU14 8AL

⏲ 11.30-2.30, 5.30-11; 11.30-11.30 Fri & Sat; 12-11 Sun

☎ (01252) 545578 🌐 theprinceinfarnborough.co.uk

Andwell Gold Muddler; Dark Star Hophead; Fuller's London Pride; Hop Back Summer Lightning; Ringwood Fortyniner; 5 changing beers (sourced nationally) 🄷

This cosy free house has featured in the Guide for over 30 years, offering five regular beers, five guests, and a real cider. Farnborough North station is a short walk away and there is a popular beer festival every October. Good pub lunches are served throughout the week, and in the evenings there is curry on Monday, fish on Friday and diner night on Saturday. Quiz night is the first Sunday, and live music the third Sunday of each month.

❀◑🚆(N)🍎P🚌(41)🐾📶

Swan 🄻

91 Farnborough Road, GU14 6TL

11-11 (midnight Fri & Sat); 11-10.30 Sun

☎ (01252) 510920 🌐 swanfarnborough.com

4 changing beers (sourced regionally; often Andwell, Hogs Back, Triple fff) 🄷

A large, imposing building half a mile south of the town centre on the A325, overlooking the Farnborough Airport runway. Inside, clever use of partitions divides the large open-plan space into three distinct areas. It caters equally for diners and drinkers, with excellent food and a changing selection of four ales from small independents across southern England, including at least one LocAle. There are monthly live music and quiz nights and quarterly open mic nights. ❀◐◑♿P🚌(1,42)🐾📶

Tilly Shilling 🄻 ✔

Unit 2 to 5, Victoria Road, GU14 7PG

8am-midnight (1am Fri & Sat) ☎ (01252) 893560

Greene King Abbot; Ruddles Best Bitter; Sharp's Doom Bar; 4 changing beers (sourced nationally; often Ascot, Binghams, Hogs Back) 🄷

Modern town-centre Wetherspoon pub named after a celebrated engineer at the nearby former Royal Aircraft Establishment. Its aviation theme includes a row of airline seats and various Spitfire memorabilia. The large rectangular open-plan lounge features a glass frontage that opens in good weather, extending the pub onto the pavement. Ten handpumps serve three regular and four changing guest beers. Real cider is dispensed from polypins in fridges at the end of the bar. Alcohol is on sale from 9am. ◐◑♿≋🍎🚌📶

Fleet

Prince Arthur 🄻 ✔

238 Fleet Road, GU51 4BX

8am-midnight (1am Fri & Sat) ☎ (01252) 622660

Greene King Abbot; Ruddles Best Bitter; Sharp's Doom Bar; 4 changing beers (sourced nationally; often Twickenham, West Berkshire, Windsor & Eton) 🄷

A smaller Wetherspoon in a former shop building over 100 years old, with alcoves, wood surrounds and a traditional pub feel. It is named after Prince Arthur, son of Queen Victoria, who lived in Fleet in the 1890s while he was commander of Aldershot Garrison. It has celebrated 20 years since opening in July 2018. Seven different cask ales are on the bar, including local ales from breweries in Hampshire, Berkshire and Surrey. It hosts occasional tap takeovers and mini beer festivals. Q❀◐◑♿🍎🚌(7,10)📶

Four Marks

Offf the Rails 🄻

Unit 3, Magpie Works, Station Approach, GU34 5HN

closed Mon & Tue; 5-10 Wed & Thu; 5-10.30 Fri; 12-10.30 Sat; 12-6 Sun ☎ (01420) 561422

Triple fff Alton's Pride, Moondance; house beer (by Triple fff); 2 changing beers (sourced locally; often Triple fff) 🄷/🄶

Offf the Rails is an industrially styled yet cosy bar that serves three regular and three seasonal ales from the adjoining Triple fff Brewery. Mr Whitehead's and Meon Valley bottled ciders are available plus three craft beers from around the country, as well as locally produced gin. It adjoins the Triple fff off-licence, featuring bottled ales from microbreweries from far and wide, open 9-5 Mon, 9-7 Tue-Fri, 10-5 Sat (off-licence closed Sun and bank holidays). It holds a brewery open day in August. ♿≋P🚌(64)🐾📶

Freefolk

Watership Down Inn 🄻

Freefolk Priors, RG28 7NJ (just off B3400)

12-3, 6-11; 12-11.30 Fri & Sat; 12-9.30 Sun

☎ (01256) 892254 🌐 watershipdowninn.com

5 changing beers (sourced locally) 🄷

Built in 1840, in the Upper Test Valley, and still affectionately known locally as the Jerry, the pub is named in honour of local author Richard Adams' book Watership Down, set in the downland north of the pub. Outside there is an extensive garden, patio and family area. The pub is popular with walkers and cyclists in the Test Valley. Each May a beer festival is held and occasional live music evenings arranged. All beers are from local breweries. Q❀🛏◐◑P🚌(76)🐾📶

Fritham

Royal Oak 🄻 ✔

SO43 7HJ (W end of village)

11-3, 5.30-11; 11-11 Sat; 12-10.30 Sun

☎ (023) 8081 2606 🌐 royaloakfritham.co.uk

Flack Manor Flack's Double Drop; Ringwood Best Bitter; house beer (by Bowman); 4 changing beers (sourced locally; often Hop Back, Stonehenge, Three Daggers) 🄶

An unexpected thatched gem near the end of a narrow no through road. It has featured for over four decades in this Guide, with numerous awards. Inside meets expectation – colourwashed, wainscoted walls, log fires and head-cracking beams. Seven, mostly local, gravity dispensed cask ales await, discreetly, under black cooling jackets, and Razorback here retains the name Best Bitter. The garden houses accommodation in three high-spec shepherd's bothies. There is no food in the evening, although takeaway vans visit Thursdays (pizza) and alternate Fridays (fish and chips). Q❀🛏◐♿🐾

Gosport

Junction Tavern

1 Leesland Road, Camden Town, PO12 3ND

11-12.30am (11.30 Tue & Wed); 12-10.30 Sun

☎ (023) 9258 5140

3 changing beers (sourced regionally; often Cotleigh, XT) 🄷

The pub gets its name from being on the site of Lees Lane Junction station on the railway to Gosport, which closed in 1953. There are three regularly changing beers from independents and small breweries, and the walls above the bar are covered with pumpclips of beers previously stocked. Up to four real ciders and a perry from various suppliers are sold. A beer festival takes place over the Easter weekend. ❀♣🍎🚌(E1)🐾📶

Queen's Hotel 🄻

143 Queens Road, Forton, PO12 1LG

4.30-11; 11.30-2.30, 4.30-11.30 Fri; 11.30-11.30 Sat; 11.30-3, 7-11 Sun ☎ 07974 031671

🌐 queenshotelgosport.co.uk

Fallen Acorn Expedition IPA; Ringwood Fortyniner; Young's Bitter; 2 changing beers (sourced nationally; often Newtown, Titanic) H
Back-street locals' pub under the same management for over 35 years and in this Guide since 1984. The clientele includes both locals and visitors from all over the country. There are two frequently changing guest beers, one usually a dark beer, as well as up to two real ciders. A regular beer festival takes place in October. Snacks are served on Friday lunchtime. The pub can get crowded on major sporting occasions.

Hammer Vale

Prince of Wales

Hammer Lane, GU27 1QH
11-11; 12-10.30 Sun ☎ (01428) 652600
Dark Star Hophead; Fuller's London Pride; Gale's HSB; 2 changing beers (sourced nationally; often Fuller's) H
A recent refurbishment revealed previously unknown doorways dating from the 1924 construction. This pub is well worth visiting in order to sample the Pride, HSB and Fuller's and Dark Star guests. It has a large outside seating area and car park and is well sited for walkers and campers. Mine hosts Nick and Beccy do excellent meals and bar snacks (no food Mon). Stories abound as to how a large roadhouse was sited away from the main road. It has interesting stained-glass windows, one for Amey's of Petersfield.
QP

Hartley Wintney

Waggon & Horses

High Street, RG27 8NY
11-11 (midnight Fri & Sat); 12-11 Sun ☎ (01252) 842119
Courage Best Bitter; Gale's HSB; 3 changing beers (sourced locally) H
An old, traditional and award-winning picturesque High Street local on the old A30. The lively public bar contrasts with a quieter lounge, while tables outside on the pavement enable guests to enjoy the atmosphere of the village, renowned for its unique shops. At the rear is a large, pleasant courtyard garden and a heated, covered smokers' area. The changing guest beers are often selected from microbreweries. Food is served lunchtimes only, but not Sunday. Q(7)

Havant

Wheelwright's Arms

27 Emsworth Road, PO9 2SN
11-11; 9am-11 Sat; 12-10 Sun ☎ (023) 9247 6502
wheelwrightshavant.co.uk
4 changing beers (sourced locally; often Fallen Acorn, Irving, Langham) H
This imposing Edwardian pub on the edge of town is well regarded for its quality food and drink. Up to five cask beers are served, generally from local micros, with a handpulled cider also offered. A range of bottled beers is sold, plus a good selection of quality wines and spirits. The front terrace and courtyard garden are popular in warm weather. Live music and quizzes are hosted and rugby union matches are shown on TV.
QP(27,700)

Hawkley

Hawkley Inn

Pococks Lane, GU33 6NE
12-3, 5.30-11; 12-11 Sat; 12-7 Sun ☎ (01730) 827205
hawkleyinn.co.uk
Flowerpots Perridge Pale; Palmers Dorset Gold; house beer (by Greyhound); 4 changing beers (sourced regionally; often Flowerpots, Red Cat, Triple fff) H
A genuine free house, popular with locals and visitors, including cyclists, horse riders and walkers seeking outstanding views of the South Downs National Park. The pub offers a warm, welcoming ambience that proves difficult to leave. The real ales are from numerous microbreweries based in Hampshire and West Sussex, and the pub has a reputation for quality, locally sourced fresh food. A beer festival is held in May every year. B&B accommodation is available.

Hayling Island

Maypole

9 Havant Road, PO11 0PS
11.30-3, 6-10 (11.15 Thu-Sat); 12-5 Sun
☎ (023) 9246 3670 themaypolehaylingisland.co.uk
Fuller's London Pride; Gale's HSB, Seafarers Ale; 1 changing beer (sourced nationally; often Fuller's) H
A traditional family-run pub based in a semi-rural location offering cask ales, fine wines and home-made food sourced from local suppliers where possible, including beer-battered fish and chips, steaks and Sunday roasts. There is a large beer garden overlooking local farmland and a children's play area. An annual charity clay pigeon shoot provides funds for local First Responders, and there is a Public Access Defibrillator next to the front door. P(30,31)

Hill Head

Crofton

48 Crofton Lane, PO14 3QF
11-11; 12-10.30 Sun ☎ (01329) 314222
thecrofton.co.uk
St Austell Proper Job; Sharp's Doom Bar; 4 changing beers (sourced nationally) H
Estate pub in a quiet residential area, which celebrates its 15th year in this Guide. There are two bars: a public bar and a large lounge area which is set up for dining. The guest beer range normally includes two SIBA beers. The function room and skittle alley gets booked up well in advance, and is used for a beer festival in November. Home-cooked food is served all day every day.
P(21,21A)

Holybourne

Queen's Head

20 London Road, GU34 4EG
12-11.30 (12.30am Fri & Sat); 12-11 Sun
☎ (01420) 768213 queensheadalton.co.uk
Hardys & Hansons Olde Trip; 2 changing beers (sourced nationally; often Hogs Back, Triple fff) H
Traditional pub serving well-kept ales in a convivial atmosphere. Regularly changing beers are usually from local breweries or from the Greene King range. There is a separate restaurant area serving home-made food, with pub games in the bar area, a jukebox and a separate games room. The extensive garden is well appointed for the summer

months. There is also a seating area at the front. Live music events are held throughout the year. Happy hour is 4.30-6pm Monday to Friday. Q☆✿◑♣P⊟(65)☻☂

Hook Common

Crooked Billet
London Road, RG27 9EH
✿ 11.30-3, 6-11; 11.30-midnight Sat; 12-10 Sun
☎ (01256) 762118 ⊕ thecrookedbilletpub.co.uk
Courage Best Bitter; Sharp's Doom Bar; 2 changing beers (often Timothy Taylor) Ⓗ
On the London Road just outside Hook, this pub has been a free house under the safe ownership of Richard and Sally for 32 years. Enjoy the pleasant riverside garden or air-conditioned bars, restaurant or snug; in winter, warm up around a traditional log fire. A fine selection of good food and real ales is always available. A beer and music festival is held over the August bank holiday. Food is served until 8pm on Sunday and quiz night is the first Monday of the month. Q☆✿◑⑂P☻☂

Little London

Plough Inn
Silchester Road, RG26 5EP
✿ 12-3, 5.30 (6 Sat)-11; 12-3, 7-10.30 Sun
☎ (01256) 850628
Otter Amber; Ringwood Razorback Ⓗ; 2 changing beers (sourced regionally; often Branscombe Vale, Church End, Little London) Ⓖ
Excellent traditional village pub and recent CAMRA Regional Pub of the Year. Enjoy beer gravity fed from casks behind the bar and sit in front of a log fire or in the peaceful garden. A good range of baguettes is available (not Sun eve). It is popular with locals and also visitors to Pamper Forest and the nearby Roman remains in Silchester. Q☆✿♣🍴P⊟(14)☻

Long Sutton

Four Horseshoes
The Street, RG29 1TA (follow brown signs from B3349 Odiham to Alton Rd) SU748470
✿ 12-3 (not Mon), 6.30-11; 12-3 Sun ☎ (01256) 862488
⊕ fourhorseshoes.com
2 changing beers (sourced nationally; often Andwell, Palmers, Slater's) Ⓗ
A truly rural pub, situated to the east of Long Sutton in a well-known walking area. Formerly a Gale's tied house but now a free house, it normally offers two low-strength guest beers. There are twice-monthly quiz and jazz nights in the spacious but cosy bar, which has two real fires. The pub serves simple English dishes, with a popular roast on Sunday. It may not open at lunchtime so check in advance. Q☆✿◑ⱭP☻☂

Lower Farringdon

Golden Pheasant ♥ Ⓛ ✓
Gosport Road, GU34 3DJ
✿ 12-11; 12-10.30 Sun ☎ (01420) 588255
Courage Best Bitter; Sharp's Doom Bar, Atlantic; Triple fff Moondance; 3 changing beers (sourced regionally; often Bowman, Dark Star, Flowerpots) Ⓗ
The owners have run pubs in the area for over 10 years, and eight years ago brought their expertise to this delightful privately owned free house. The

beers are well kept, with seven handpumps serving four permanent and three guest beers. The food is freshly cooked, with vegetarian options; the fish and chips warrants special mention due to the secret batter recipe used. It opens at 8.30am for tea and coffee. Local CAMRA Pub of the Year 2019, this is a pub not to be missed. Q☆✿◑♣P☻☂

Lower Wield

Yew Tree Ⓛ
Alresford, SO24 9RX SU636398
✿ closed Mon; 12-3, 6-11; 12-10.30 Sun ☎ (01256) 389224
⊕ the-yewtree.org.uk
House beer (by Bowman); 1 changing beer (sourced locally; often Itchen Valley, Stonehenge, Triple fff) Ⓗ
Out-of-the-way rural local set in picturesque rolling Hampshire countryside, with an old yew tree growing outside (hence the name), on a quiet lane opposite the local cricket pitch. The house beer is Bowman Meon Bitter and the guest normally comes from a local brewery. All real ales are sold at attractive prices. The pub has a separate dining area where locally renowned, reasonably priced food is served. Cyclists, ramblers and dog walkers all welcome. Q☆✿◑P☻☂

Mattingley

Leather Bottle Ⓛ
Reading Road, Hook, RG27 8JU
✿ 11-11; 11-10.30 Sun ☎ (0118) 932 6371
Brunning & Price Original; 4 changing beers (sourced locally) Ⓗ
A classic old village inn, its beautiful tiled roof sheltering mellow Hampshire brick, and with a pleasant garden area in summer. Inside are comfortable, relaxed surroundings and a warm, friendly atmosphere – a great place to meet for a pint or two, a lunchtime bite, or a lingering dinner. The cask ale selection is displayed showing mileage to each brewery. Enjoy dog walks every third Saturday morning and live acoustic music monthly. Popular for Sunday lunch; early booking advised. Q☆✿◑⑂P☻☂

Milford on Sea

Wash House
27 High Street, SO41 0QF
✿ 11.30-11; 12-11 Sun ☎ (01590) 644665
⊕ thewashhousebar.co.uk
4 changing beers (sourced locally; often Andwell, Vibrant Forest) Ⓗ
Cosy one-roomed micropub, once a launderette (hence the name), serving four varying, local real ales, plus up to seven real ciders – a little gem! Furniture is a mismatched selection of tables and chairs, including repurposed casks. Customers wanting food can order from a varied menu, but with a twist: place your order with any of the friendly, local bar staff, and your food will be delivered to your table from the café two doors down. Q☆⑂🍴⊟(X1)☻

New Milton

Hourglass
8 Station Road, BH25 6JU
✿ 5-11; 3-11 Fri; 12-11 Sat; 12-10 Sun ☎ (01425) 616074
⊕ hourglassmicropub.co.uk
4 changing beers (sourced nationally) Ⓖ

New Milton's first micropub is a family-run free house focusing on a constantly changing selection of four cask and four keg beers, plus up to eight ciders, alongside wines and spirits. It has a quiet, friendly atmosphere, hosting a music jam the first Sunday of every month, a pub quiz every other Thursday, and offering an extensive collection of board games and puzzles. Tap takeovers and Meet the Brewer events also feature regularly. Takeaway food may be brought in. Q

Newnham

Old House at Home

Newnham Green, RG27 9AH

closed Mon; 12-3, 5.30-11; 12-11 Sat; 12-8 Sun

(01256) 761896 oldhousenewnham.uk

Dark Star Hophead; Sharp's Doom Bar; 1 changing beer (sourced locally; often Andwell)

Relaxed village pub with dining, dedicated to sourcing fresh, local and seasonal ingredients to devise creative menus, offering traditional pub classics alongside new, inventive dishes. Every Wednesday is steak night; you need to book as it is very popular (see the website for menus). Staying with the local produce theme, the pub only stocks gins and vodkas produced in Hampshire. Q P

North Waltham

Fox

Popham Lane, RG25 2BE (between village and A30)

11-11 (midnight Fri & Sat); 12-10.30 Sun

(01256) 397288 thefox.org

Courage Best Bitter; West Berkshire Good Old Boy; 2 changing beers (sourced locally; often Ringwood)

Lovely traditional country pub on the edge of the village and overlooking extensive farmland. The venue is divided into two – a popular restaurant, and a public bar where food is also served (booking advisable). Local seasonal produce is featured where possible. Outside, there is an extensive beer garden and a children's adventure play area. The Ushers signage remains on the rear of the pub. The bus service is minimal. Q P (16)

North Warnborough

Mill House

Hook Road, RG29 1ET (M3 jct 5; head towards Odiham)

11-11 (01256) 702953

Hogs Back TEA; house beer (by Brunning & Price); 4 changing beers (sourced regionally; often Andwell, Longdog, Triple fff)

Listed as one of eight mills of Odiham in the Domesday Book, current sections are 17th-century additions, and it was last used as a corn mill in 1895. Most recently a restaurant, it is now under Brunning & Price ownership. It has a pleasant central bar area, separate dining areas, and a lower-level view of the waterwheel and restaurant. The area surrounding the mill pond fed from the Whitewater provides a pleasant outdoor seating area linking the function barn and parking. Q P (13)

Oakley

Barley Mow

19 Oakley Lane, RG23 7JZ

12-11.30 (01256) 782591 barleymowatoakley.com

Flowerpots Goodens Gold; Sharp's Doom Bar; 2 changing beers (sourced locally)

An old-fashioned non-chain local pub in the heart of this picturesque village. It serves well-kept traditional ales and recently became free of tie as a market rent only (MRO) pub, which allows a greater variety of changing beers. On Monday evenings a fish and chips van visits, and you can eat in the pub or have a beer while waiting. A warm, family-oriented and dog-friendly pub, often used as a refreshment and meeting point for ramblers. Q P (11)

Old Basing

Barton's Mill

Bartons Lane, RG24 8AE (follow signs to Basing House)

11-11; 10-11 Sat; 10-10.30 Sun (01256) 331153

bartonsmillpubanddining.co.uk

Wadworth IPA, Horizon, 6X, Swordfish; 1 changing beer (often Black Sheep)

An attractively sited Wadworth house, once part of a still-existing water mill that overlooks the River Loddon and a water meadow. The pub is a short walk from the historic and picturesque ruins of Basing House and a large medieval tithe barn. It features traditional pub food, six Wadworth cask ales plus one rotating guest, served seven days a week by friendly staff. Children are welcome, as is the occasional duck from the river. Conference facilities are available, as well as 12 B&B rooms in the Barn. P (10)

Petersfield

Townhouse

28 High Street, GU32 3JL

9am-11 (midnight Fri & Sat) (01730) 265630

petersfieldtownhouse.com

3 changing beers (sourced regionally; often Downlands, Langham, Red Cat)

This is a popular bistro-style pub offering food (breakfast, lunch and dinner), local ales and ciders, at the eastern end of the High Street. There is a separate function room upstairs with its own bar, known as the Gin Bar. A bottle shop supplies regional beers. Outside at the rear of the premises is a patio garden. Children and dogs are welcome. P (67)

Portsmouth

Apsley House

Auckland Road West, Southsea, PO5 3NY

3-11 (1am Fri); 12-1am Sat; 12-11 Sun (023) 9282 1294

Hop Back Summer Lightning; Sharp's Doom Bar; Timothy Taylor Landlord

Named in honour of Arthur Wellesley, 1st Duke of Wellington, a painting of his London residence is above the door. Inside, the U-shaped bar has bare floorboards and a raised area to the right. The pub is a short walk from Southsea shopping centre and Southsea Common. There is a small patio drinking area at the front. A meat raffle is held on Sunday afternoons and a quiz on Monday evenings.

Artillery Arms

Hester Road, Milton, PO4 8HB

12-11.30 (midnight Fri & Sat) (023) 9273 3610

Triple fff Alton's Pride, Moondance; 4 changing beers (sourced locally; often Fallen Acorn, Langham, Urban Island) Ⓗ
Traditional two-bar pub operated by Triple fff but featuring many other independent brewers. It is one of the last surviving pubs on the course of the Portsmouth & Arundel Canal. It gets busy on match days as it is only five minutes' walk from Fratton Park, but is welcoming both to home and away supporters. The large enclosed garden is a suntrap in summer, with events most weekends.
P (1,2)

Barley Mow

39 Castle Road, Southsea, PO5 3DE
12-11; 11-11 Sat ☎ (023) 9282 3492
barleymowsouthsea.com
Fuller's London Pride; Gale's HSB; 6 changing beers (sourced nationally) Ⓗ
A true community pub that supports many events including a quiz, meat raffle, chess league, pool, darts and golf teams and monthly druid moots. The wood-panelled lounge bar has bar billiards and shove-ha'penny tables and once had a painting of the Battle of Southsea on the ceiling (which is now in the city museum). To the rear is an award-winning patio garden, a real suntrap on summer days. A mild, stout or porter is always available.
(3)

Brewhouse & Kitchen

26 Guildhall Walk, Landport, PO1 2DD
11-11 (midnight Fri & Sat); 11-10.30 Sun
☎ (023) 9289 1340
Brewhouse & Kitchen Sexton, Mucky Duck, Black Swan, Mary Rose; 1 changing beer (sourced locally; often Brewhouse & Kitchen - Portsmouth) Ⓗ
The first, and still one of the best, of the Brewhouse & Kitchen chain, with the brewing equipment on display, and often in use on your right as you enter the pub. There are also five or six KeyKeg beers, also brewed on the premises. Good food is served all day from an open kitchen, with some interesting choices. There is a lovely hidden roof garden accessed from the rear of the pub.

Eastney Tavern

100 Cromwell Road, Eastney, PO4 9PN
12-11 (midnight Fri & Sat); 12-10.30 Sun
☎ (023) 9282 6246 eastneytavern.co.uk
Sharp's Doom Bar; 3 changing beers (sourced locally; often Fallen Acorn, Irving) Ⓗ
Excellent community local, just two minutes from Eastney beach. As one of the few pubs at this end of town to offer food, which is of a good standard and popular, booking is recommended. The pub has one large bar divided into several areas. It has many TVs but the sound is muted apart from when there are important sporting events on. There is a suntrap patio which is popular in summer. May close early on Sundays. (16)

Hole in the Wall

36 Great Southsea Street, Southsea, PO5 3BY
4-11; 12-midnight Fri; 2-midnight Sat; 2-11 Sun
☎ (023) 9229 8085 theholeinthewallpub.co.uk
Flowerpots Goodens Gold Ⓖ; 5 changing beers (sourced nationally) Ⓗ
The Hole is one of the smaller pubs in Portsmouth but, being a genuine free house, it offers a wide range of beers from a changing selection of local and national breweries. (Check website for the current beer range.) Real ciders are usually available. It opens on Saturdays from noon for Pompey home games. No admittance after 11pm. Dogs must be on leads. (3)

Lawrence Arms

63 Lawrence Road, Southsea, PO5 1NU
12-11.30 Mon; 2-11 Tue-Thu; 2-12.30am Fri; 11-12.30am Sat; 11-11 Sun ☎ (023) 9282 1280
lawrence-arms-portsmouth.co.uk
Harvey's Sussex Best Bitter; 5 changing beers (sourced nationally; often Flowerpots, Irving, Langham) Ⓗ
Dating back to 1887, this street-corner pub's exterior retains some traditional tiles and lanterns. Very much a friendly community pub, there are darts and pool teams, weekly meat raffles, quizzes and themed days. The L-shaped bar faces a lounge area and offers a rotating selection of five local ales, one from further afield, plus a bottle shop. There is a good cider selection, sourced nationally. Food includes tasty gourmet toasties. Local CAMRA Pub of the Year 2018 and 2019. (18)

Lord Palmerston

84-90 Palmerston Road, Southsea, PO5 3PT
8am-midnight (1.30am Fri & Sat) ☎ (023) 9272 8000
Greene King Abbot, IPA; 8 changing beers (sourced nationally; often Irving, Langham, Weltons) Ⓗ
Named after the 3rd Viscount Palmerston, this Wetherspoon pub has a very traditional feel. The front part has a high ceiling with several chandeliers. To the rear, the walls are wood-panelled and adorned with old photographs. Palmerston himself was known for the fortifications built to protect the dockyard from French invasion. Two varying ciders are available from boxes in the fridge. On Friday and Saturday evening a DJ plays and ID is required to gain admission. (3,23)

Meat & Barrel

110-114 Palmerston Road, Southsea, PO5 3PT
11.30-11 (midnight Fri & Sat); 8am-11 Sun
☎ (023) 9217 6291 meatandbarrel.co.uk
2 changing beers (sourced nationally; often Irving) Ⓗ
A large, modern pub with a single bar divided into two areas. One has deep, comfortable sofas and the other a mix of high and standard tables. The walls are mostly bare brick and the front has large glazed wooden panels. The pub is handy for Southsea shopping centre and is a short walk from Southsea Castle and the D-Day Museum. As home of the Southsea Burger Club, it is not surprising that burgers feature heavily on the menu.

Merchant House

9-11 Highland Road, Eastney, PO4 9DA
3-11; 3-11.30 Thu; 1-midnight Fri; 12-midnight Sat; 12-10.30 Sun
4 changing beers (sourced nationally) Ⓗ
A fully independent free house specialising in beers from small breweries throughout the country. The bar is divided into two areas, one of which is slightly raised and gives access to a separate downstairs room. The style is modern, with bare walls and floor. The menu includes burgers, hot beef and pork rolls, and loaded fries, as well as a range of vegan options. Traditional roasts are served on Sunday. (1,2)

Northcote Hotel 𝕃

35 Francis Avenue, Southsea, PO4 0HL

12-midnight (1am Fri); 11-1am Sat ☎ (023) 9278 9888

Irving Invincible; Long Man American Pale Ale; Timothy Taylor Landlord; house beer (by Wadworth); 1 changing beer (sourced locally; often Irving, Langham) Ⓗ

A large, traditional pub a few minutes' walk from Albert Road. The public bar has pool and darts, the latter on a small raised area. The smaller lounge has seating round most of the walls and is decorated with memorabilia of comedians from the early days of cinema including Laurel and Hardy, Charlie Chaplin and the Marx Brothers, and fictional detective Sherlock Holmes. To one side of the building is a substantial patio garden. ❀♣●▣(2)

Pembroke

20 Pembroke Road, Old Portsmouth, PO1 2NR

11-11; 12-5, 7-10.30 Sun ☎ (023) 9282 3961

Draught Bass; Fuller's London Pride; Greene King Abbot Ⓗ

A typical street-corner pub with a single L-shaped bar decorated with naval memorabilia. Dating from 1711, under its former name of the Little Blue Line it featured in novels by Captain Marryat. Opposite the pub is the Royal Garrison Church built circa 1212 by the Bishop of Winchester but badly damaged in 1941. The pub is also probably the last one seen by Lord Nelson on his way to join HMS Victory to sail to Trafalgar.

Phoenix

13 Duncan Road, Southsea, PO5 2QU

10-midnight (1am Fri & Sat); 12-midnight Sun ☎ (023) 9278 1055

Ringwood Fortyniner; 2 changing beers (sourced nationally; often Irving, Red Cat, Urban Island) Ⓗ

A proper community local a few minutes from Albert Road. The public bar has bare floorboards and is decorated with photos connected to Portsmouth FC. The smaller lounge has comfortable seats and the walls are adorned with pictures of people who have performed at the nearby Kings Theatre. It has a number of tabletop games, including Space Invaders. Next to the lounge is a quirky patio garden, which separates the games room from the rest of the pub. ❀♣●▣(2)

Porters

31-35 Albert Road, Southsea, PO5 2SE

12-11 (1am Fri & Sat); 10.30 Sun ☎ (023) 9229 3474

Otter Ale; Sharp's Doom Bar; 3 changing beers (sourced nationally; often Irving) Ⓗ

A large pub with a single bar divided into several drinking areas. It is basically decorated with a tiled and flagstoned floor and wooden tables and chairs. There are also a few comfortable sofas to relax in. To the rear of the bar area is a small raised seating section. Good-value food is available every day; it specialises in Mexican dishes, with vegetarian options. The beer range usually includes an offering from one of the local breweries. ●▣(2)

Rose in June 𝕃 ✔

102 Milton Road, Milton, PO3 6AR

12-midnight (1am Fri & Sat) ☎ (023) 9282 4191

theroseinjune.co.uk

Fallen Acorn Twisted Oak; Gale's HSB; Irving Frigate; Purity Pure UBU; 3 changing beers (often Langham, Purity) Ⓗ

This two-bar pub is a hub of the community, popular with football fans, being a 10-minute walk from Fratton Park. It hosts regular events such as quizzes, pool and darts games, comedy nights and curry nights. The extensive garden has a play area and is used for barbecues and a popular summer beer festival. A winter beer festival is held in February. There are eight real ciders (see board) and a bottle shop. Q❀●P▣

Still & West Country House

Bath Square, Old Portsmouth, PO1 2JL

9.30am-11 (10.30 Sun) ☎ (023) 9282 1567

stillandwest.co.uk

Fuller's London Pride; Gale's HSB, Seafarers Ale; 1 changing beer (sourced nationally; often Fuller's) Ⓗ

By the entrance to Portsmouth Harbour, this pub offers a panoramic view of ships entering and leaving the port and naval base. Not surprisingly, the decor has a nautical theme, with artefacts including an old ship's telegraph. The single L-shaped bar on the ground floor has a ceiling decorated with paintings, including the history of the Mary Rose. The first floor is now a sizeable restaurant. ❀▣(16)

Wave Maiden

36 Osborne Road, Southsea, PO5 3LT

6-11; 12-midnight Fri & Sat; 12-10 Sun ☎ (023) 9217 8878

thewavemaiden.co.uk

2 changing beers (sourced nationally; often Franklins, Gun) Ⓖ

An individual pub which specialises in beer from small independent breweries, it is named after the nine daughters of Aegir from Norse mythology. On one wall is an apt quote from Dylan Thomas. In addition to the cask beers served on gravity there is a good range of bottled beers from various countries. Cheese features heavily on the menu, plus vegan versions of all the main dishes. The pub hosts events such as film, comedy and music nights, and painting evenings – check the Facebook page as some require booking. Q●▣(6,23)

Winchester Arms

99 Winchester Road, Buckland, PO2 7PS

4-11; 3-midnight Fri; 12-11 Sat & Sun ☎ (023) 9266 2443

Wychwood Hobgoblin Gold; 3 changing beers (sourced regionally) Ⓗ

The Winch is a proper back-street local, offering one regular beer and two or three varying guests. Ciders are available during the summer. Every third Sunday evening of the month is open-mic night with music and comedy, and there is live music on the other Sundays. A beer festival is held over the spring bank holiday weekend. The garden has a covered smoking shelter. It may stay open until midnight on Fridays and Saturdays if busy. ❀●▣

Ringwood

Railway 𝕃

35 Hightown Road, BH24 1NQ

12-11 (10 Sun) ☎ (01425) 473701 therailway.co

Ringwood Best Bitter; 4 changing beers (sourced nationally) Ⓗ

A traditional two-bar community pub whose name recalls the days when Ringwood station was opposite. The kitchen is always busy, with lots of choice for vegans and vegetarians, and a great reputation for Sunday lunches. Railway memorabilia including old photos, pictures and maps adorn the walls of the public bar. Four varied cask ales including one local ale, and a variety of keg beers are on offer, together with bag-in-box cider. Dogs are welcome. Q♉✿◐◑⛺♣●P🚌🐾📶

Romsey

Old House at Home

62 Love Lane, SO51 8DE (off Waitrose car park)
⏲ 11-11 (11.30 Fri & Sat); 12-8 Sun ☎ (01794) 513175
🌐 theoldhouseathomeromsey.co.uk
Fuller's London Pride; Gale's Seafarers Ale, HSB; 2 changing beers (often Fuller's) [H]
This warm, welcoming pub stands halfway between Romsey's rail and bus stations, and adjacent to a public car park. There is a beamed bar with booths, a raised area with banquettes, an elegant little restaurant, a garden, and a heated patio. Service is friendly and efficient; food is high quality and mainly locally sourced. Acoustic folk music plays on Monday evening, and major sporting events are shown on TV (terrestrial only). Under-18s are not permitted in the pub after 9pm. ✿◐◑⇌P🚌🐾📶

Three Tuns 🄻 ✔

58 Middlebridge Street, SO51 8HL
⏲ 11-11; 12-10.30 Sun ☎ (01794) 512639
🌐 the3tunsromsey.co.uk
Flack Manor Flack's Double Drop; 6 changing beers (sourced regionally) [H]
Smart, small building in a street of equally attractive modest houses. It has two rooms: an agreeable bar and a more formal dining room. A short menu of good-quality food, covering pub classics, snacks and unusual dishes, plus specials, comes Michelin-recommended. Seven handpumps serve a wide variety of real ales and there is an appealing four-thirds offer. Outside is a large patio, and beyond a car park accessible from the busy A27. ♉◐◑♣●P🚌🐾📶

Selborne

Selborne Arms 🄻

High Street, GU34 3JR
⏲ 11-3, 6-11; 11-11 Sat; 12-11 Sun ☎ (01420) 511247
🌐 selbornearms.co.uk
Bowman Swift One; Ringwood Fortyniner; 3 changing beers (sourced regionally; often Fallen Acorn, Hogs Back, Langham) [H]
A traditional two-bar but greatly extended village pub with real fires and a friendly atmosphere. Up to three guest beers come mainly from local breweries. Beer bats offering three thirds of cask beers for the price of a pint are available. Extensive menus showcase local and home-made produce, with vegetarian and gluten-free options. The safe play area in the garden is popular with children. All day opening runs from Easter to the Zig Zag festival in early October. Q♉✿◐◑P🚌(38)📶

Shedfield

Wheatsheaf Inn 🄻

Botley Road, SO32 2JG (on A334)
⏲ 12-11; 12-10.30 Sun ☎ (01329) 833024
Flowerpots Perridge Pale, Bitter, Goodens Gold; 3 changing beers (sourced locally; often Palmers, Steam Town, Stonehenge) [G]
Friendly, award-winning inn serving local beers direct from their casks, plus ciders from Westons. The two-room interior is warmed by a double-sided wood-burning stove. A side room provides more seating, with access to the delightful garden with its floral displays. Home-cooked food is served lunchtimes and on Tuesday and Wednesday evenings. Live music is hosted most Saturday evenings and the annual beer festival is on spring bank holiday weekend. Parking is across the busy road. Q✿◐◑♿♣●P🚌(69)🐾📶

Sherfield English

Hatchet Inn ✔

Salisbury Road, SO51 6FP (on A27)
⏲ 12-3, 5-11.30; 12-11.30 Fri-Sun ☎ (01794) 322487
🌐 hatchetinn.com
St Austell Tribute; Sharp's Doom Bar; Timothy Taylor Landlord; 1 changing beer (sourced nationally) [H]
In the same family for three generations, this friendly, unchanging pub is at the very edge of Hampshire. On the right as you enter is a square public bar, and on the left a long saloon bar, partly set for dining. Two ladies have shared the role of landlady for eight years, one of them chef for even longer. A large menu, very often home made, served in generous portions, and with special offers, makes this a popular place for quality-conscious diners. Q♉✿◐◑⛺♣P🚌(X7R)🐾📶

Sherfield on Loddon

Four Horseshoes ✔

Reading Road, RG27 0EX
⏲ 12 (4.30 Mon)-11; 12-6 Sun ☎ (01256) 882296
🌐 the4horseshoes.co.uk
Sharp's Doom Bar; 2 changing beers (often Sherfield Village) [H]
A 16th-century pub between Reading and Basingstoke in the heart of this Hampshire village. The venue has low-beamed ceilings and woodburners, and features a saloon and public bar, restaurant area, function room/skittle alley, a beer garden, a sunny outside seating area and a car park. No fee for the skittles for charity events. ♉✿◐◑♣P🚌(14)🐾

Southampton

Belgium & Blues

180 Above Bar Street, SO14 7DW
⏲ 12-11 (midnight Fri & Sat); 12-10.30 Sun
☎ (023) 8022 5411 🌐 belgiumandblues.co.uk
4 changing beers (sourced regionally; often Broken Bridge, Vibrant Forest) [H]
Located in Southampton's Cultural Quarter. Upstairs at street level is the Gin Bar. Down the stairs is the main Cellar Bar, serving four real ales and three real ciders, plus a selection of keg and bottled Belgian and other European beers. Seating includes a number of enclosed booths. The food menu features the expected Belgian specialities plus many other choices, including the renowned Sunday Cellar Roast. The Cellar Bar hosts local brewery tap takeovers plus regular music nights, often blues. Q◐◑⇌●🚌🐾📶

Bitter Virtue 🄻

70 Cambridge Road, SO14 6US (jct with Alma Rd)
⏲ closed Mon; 12-7; 10.30-8.30 Fri & Sat; 10.30-2 Sun
☎ (023) 8055 4881 🌐 bittervirtue.co.uk
2 changing beers (sourced regionally; often Bowman, Siren, Steam Town) [G]

A gem for beer enthusiasts, this off-licence has over 1,000 bottled and canned beers, two casks, and a good selection of bottled cider and mead. Sourced from breweries and producers from across the UK, Belgium, Germany, Scandinavia and America, there is something for everyone, from local favourites, rare and hard-to-get-hold-of beers, to one-off brews and brewery merchandise. Run by a knowledgeable team, Bitter Virtue has been in the Guide since 1997. Q

Bookshop Alehouse

21 Portswood Road, SO17 2ES

12-11

4 changing beers (sourced locally; often Eight Arch, Vibrant Forest) H

Located in a former bookshop with an Edwardian-style frontage, this friendly micropub features a varied selection of beers from local and national breweries on four handpumps and four keg taps, plus a range of bottled beers and bag-in-box ciders. The enthusiastic, knowledgeable team are keen to help customers choose drinks to their liking. Retaining original features, information of local events and good wheelchair access, the Bookshop has a strong community feel. Food may be brought in. Q(St Denys)

Butcher's Hook

7 Manor Farm Road, SO18 1NN

closed Mon & Tue; 6-11; 4-11 Fri; 1-11 Sat; 2-10 Sun

(023) 8178 2280 butchershookpub.com

4 changing beers (sourced nationally) G

Opened in 2014, the first of a new wave of micropubs opening in Southampton, the Butcher's Hook is always showcasing new and exciting beers from interesting breweries. As you enter the compact pub you will see the wall is dominated by a vast blackboard informing you of the cask, keg, bottles and cans on offer. Although no food is sold, it can be purchased from numerous local takeaways and consumed in the pub. Can be standing-room only. Q(Bitterne)(7)

Caskaway L

47 Oxford Street, SO14 3DP

closed Mon & Tue; 4-10 (11 Fri); 12-11 Sat; 4-8 Sun

caskaway.pub

4 changing beers (sourced regionally; often Broken Bridge, Drop the Anchor, Longdog) G

Sitting on Southampton's pedestrianised Oxford Street, Caskaway Tasting Rooms is a friendly, welcoming micropub. Inside, it is decked out in a nautical theme with benches and stools, leading through to the rear stillage and servery. Up to six cask ales, many craft keg beers and, notably, up to 10 ciders and perries, are all on offer. There is no bar counter so table service is provided, unless very busy. Simple bar snacks are available, including pies (not Jan). In winter it is cosy and homely; in summer the streetside seating and rear terrace can be enjoyed. Q

Crammed Inn

48 High Street, SO14 2NS

closed Mon; 4-midnight; 12-midnight Fri & Sat; 12-6 Sun

(023) 8057 6252

3 changing beers (sourced regionally; often Flowerpots, Longdog, Urban Island) H

Opened in October 2018, this modern-style micropub is in the old town part of Southampton, close to the waterfront and the Isle of Wight and Hythe ferries. It has a long, narrow single room with seating at the front and rear, separated by the bar and a long shelf for vertical drinkers. Three handpumps serve fined beers from Hampshire and Sussex, often including a stout or porter. The walls are adorned with maps of old Southampton and modern artwork.

Dancing Man L

Wool House, Town Quay, SO14 2AR

12-11 (midnight Thu-Sat) (023) 8083 6666

dancingmanbrewery.co.uk

6 changing beers (sourced nationally; often Dancing Man) H

A Grade I-listed, 14th-century, former merchants' wool store. It is now a remarkable brewpub, popular with both locals and tourists. It serves a selection of house-brewed cask ales plus some guest beers. Proximity to the registry office makes it sought after by wedding groups. Upstairs is a restaurant, though the varied menu is served throughout the pub. Sunday's food choice is chiefly roasts. Doors open at 11am Monday to Saturday for coffee, the bar at noon.

Freemantle Arms L

31 Albany Road, SO15 3EF

12-11 (8 Mon; 11.30 Fri); 12-10 Sun (023) 8077 2536

thefreemantlearms.co.uk

Sharp's Doom Bar; 4 changing beers (sourced regionally; often Fallen Acorn, Goddards, Red Cat) H

A hidden oasis in a quiet, no through road in the heart of Freemantle. It has a single bar with comfortable seating, tastefully decorated with pictures of old Southampton, and displaying interesting old tools. Five real ales are sold, four of which change regularly due to demand. A beautiful enclosed summer garden with picnic benches and an awning-covered area hosts the summer beer festival. Friendly staff and locals will always make you feel welcome. It also stages a quiz night, darts, two cribbage teams, and other occasional events. (Millbrook)

Giddy Bridge L

12-18 London Road, SO15 2AF

8am-11.30 (023) 8033 6346

Greene King Abbot; Ringwood Fortyniner; Ruddles Best Bitter; Sharp's Doom Bar; 6 changing beers (sourced nationally) H

A Wetherspoon pub on the busy London Road. Walls and pillars nicely divide the ground floor into separate areas, with plenty of glass frontage overlooking the wide pavement drinking area. A central staircase leads to more seating and the roof garden – ideal for alfresco summer drinks. The curious name comes from the time when the land the pub is on was a field known as Giddy Bridge. Open for breakfast from 8am, alcohol served from 9am. Q

Guide Dog L

38 Earl's Road, SO14 6SF (corner of Ancasta Rd)

12-11 (10.30 Sun) (023) 8063 8947

Dark Star Hophead, American Pale Ale; Flowerpots Goodens Gold; 8 changing beers (sourced nationally; often Binghams, Red Cat, Steam Town) H

Classic back-street establishment with 11 handpumps, regularly voted local CAMRA Pub of the Year. The pub is popular on match days with home and away fans as it is within walking distance of St Mary's Stadium. The front-room bar has newspapers and blackboards listing the beers. The Dog House at the back is regularly used for musical evenings. Weekly events include Thursday evening's Thai dishes (which sell out quickly) and Friday's meat draw. Q🚌(7,U6)🐾📶

Hop Inn 🄻

199 Woodmill Lane, SO18 2PH

12-11; 11-11.30 Fri & Sat; 12-10.30 Sun

☎ (023) 8055 7723

Bowman Swift One; Gale's HSB; Sharp's Doom Bar; 2 changing beers 🄷

Now in its 11th year in the Guide, this traditional corner community local goes from strength to strength. A 1930s pub, it has two bars; the homely lounge is divided by a central fireplace with the modern public bar having bar games and a jukebox. In summer the pub is adorned with flowers, winning numerous gold medals in Southampton in Bloom. Five cask ales are offered, with two changing. Bar meals are served Tuesday to Saturday, with a curry night on Wednesday. Dogs are welcome. The monthly quiz is every first Sunday. Q♿♣P🚌(16,7)🐾📶

Olaf's Tun

8 Portsmouth Road, SO19 9AA

closed Mon & Tue; 6-10 (11 Fri); 1-10 Sat; 1-6 Sun

☎ (023) 8044 7887 🌐 olafstun.co.uk

4 changing beers (sourced nationally) 🄶

Friendly, welcoming micropub serving four continuously changing real ales on gravity, usually including one dark beer, plus four keg craft beers and two real ciders. On one wall is a large painting of a Viking with his ship, beside which is an explanation of how Olaf's Tun was the original name for Woolston. If hungry, you can order pizza at the bar, which will then be delivered from the takeaway across the road; other brought-in food is also permitted. Q♿⇌(Woolston)🍎🚌🐾📶

Park Inn

37 Carlisle Road, SO16 4FN

3-11; 12-11 Fri & Sat; 12-10.30 Sun ☎ (023) 8078 7835

🌐 theparkinn.co.uk

Wadworth IPA, 6X, Bishops Tipple; 3 changing beers (sourced nationally) 🄷

Small street-corner pub, welcoming to locals and visitors alike. It has a two-bar feel although the bars are linked by a small gap where there used to be a door. There are two or three guest beers from national breweries and usually one real cider. On Fridays and Saturdays the landlady's different-flavoured Scotch eggs, sausage rolls and, sometimes, pies, are popular. The pub is also close to the local shops and bus stops. ❀♣🍎🚌🐾📶

Platform Tavern 🄻 ✔

Town Quay, SO14 2NY

12-11 (midnight Thu); 11.30-midnight Fri; 12-midnight Sat

☎ (023) 8033 7232 🌐 platformtavern.com

Fuller's London Pride; Gale's Seafarers Ale; 3 changing beers (sourced locally) 🄷

A popular pub close to Southampton's ferry terminals, serving five cask ales. In addition to the tables and chairs, comfy armchairs and a sofa encourage cosy drinking. Through an arch next to the bar is a more formally furnished dining area. Food is freshly prepared from a varied menu. The pub is built into the city's medieval wall, with part of it on display. This pub boasts an extremely good reputation for live music. Three annual beer festivals are held. ♣🍎🚌🐾📶

South Western Arms

38-40 Adelaide Road, SO17 2HW

12-11.30 (midnight Fri & Sat); 12-10.30 Sun

☎ (023) 8122 0817

Bowman Swift One; 7 changing beers (sourced nationally) 🄷

Refurbished in 2018, this two-floor Victorian pub retains some of its original features. Popular with Southampton's beer drinkers, it features up to nine changing real ales from local and national breweries. A paved back garden has a large partially covered smoking area, while the front has a popular pizza van Wednesday to Saturday. The football table, pool table and darts are located on the first floor, with regular music on the ground floor. ❀⇌(St Denys)♣🍎P🚌(7)🐾📶

Waterloo Arms 🄻

101 Waterloo Road, SO15 3BS

12-11 (midnight Fri & Sat) ☎ (023) 8022 0022

Downton New Forest Ale; Hop Back GFB, Crop Circle, Entire Stout, Summer Lightning; 2 changing beers (sourced locally; often Downton, Hop Back) 🄷

A popular locals' pub, a short bus ride from the city centre and central station and a 10-minute walk from Millbrook station. It has an L-shaped bar, a large conservatory and a paved garden area at the rear; the conservatory can be booked for private functions. There are two guest beers, usually from the Downton brewery, and also seasonal Hop Back beers. Filled rolls are usually available. Darts is popular and the conservatory hosts frequent bingo sessions. ❀⇌(Millbrook)♣🚌🐾📶

Witch's Brew 🄻

220 Shirley Road, SO15 3FL

closed Mon & Tue; 5-11 Wed-Fri; 4-11 Sat; 4-10 Sun

☎ 07403 871757 🌐 thewitchsbrewsouthampton.com

5 changing beers (sourced regionally; often Downlands, Drop the Anchor, Flowerpots) 🄶

Charming micropub with a witch-themed decor in Southampton's Freemantle suburb, on the busy Shirley Road. Ales are dispensed by gravity from their casks, and found at the rear through multiple connected rooms. The beer range changes constantly. Bottled and canned beers are sold in addition to multiple real ciders. Bespoke seating and tables give the pub character. The friendly pub dog roams and often greets arriving visitors. Finalist in the local CAMRA Pub of the Year 2019 competition. Q❀♣🍎🚌🐾

Southwick

Golden Lion 🄻

High Street, PO17 6EB

12-3, 5.30-11; 12-midnight Sat; 12-7 Sun

☎ (023) 9221 0437 🌐 goldenlionsouthwick.co.uk

Suthwyk Old Dick, Skew Sunshine Ale; 4 changing beers (sourced locally; often Langham, Palmers, Urban Island) 🄷

Historic free house set in an unchanging privately owned village, once a homebrew pub, with the Old Dick honouring the last brewer. Superb high-quality food is served, but this is a proper country pub, not just a restaurant. It has a charming enclosed garden for warmer weather and the historic brewhouse museum in the rear car park. Southwick village is transformed for D-Day weekend to commemorate the fact that D-Day was partly planned in the back bar.

Q❀♿♣🍎P🐾

Tichborne

Tichborne Arms

SO24 0NA (1¼ miles S from B3047 Alresford Rd jct) SU571304
closed Mon; 11.45-3, 6-10.30 Tue & Wed; 11.45-3, 6-11 Thu-Sat; 12-7.30 Sun ☎ (01962) 733760
tichbornearms.co.uk
Bowman Swift One; Flowerpots Bitter; Langham Arapaho; Palmers Copper Ale; 2 changing beers (sourced locally; often Bath Ales, Bowman) G
Lovely old-fashioned thatched pub with two cosy bars, the larger one with a logburner. There are a number of real ales poured from the cask; the varied beer selection includes at least two guest beers from local breweries, rotating regularly. The pub's changing menu features a variety of locally sourced home-made food. The large garden hosts an annual August bank holiday beer festival. The pub is dog-friendly. Q P

Titchfield

Wheatsheaf L

1 East Street, PO14 4AD
12-11 (midnight Fri & Sat) ☎ (01329) 842965
wheatsheaftitchfield.co.uk
Flowerpots Bitter; 4 changing beers (sourced regionally; often Fallen Acorn) H
This 17th-century building is in a conservation area and has been owned by the licensee since 2017. The premises comprise a main bar, a cosy snug and a gastro restaurant. Separate bar and restaurant menus are available. The four guest beers normally include a Fallen Acorn beer, and a real cider is usually on the bar. Beer and cider festivals are held at the end of January and July each year. Q P (X4)

Vernham Dean

George Inn

Back Lane, SP11 0JY
12-11; 12-6 Sun ☎ (01264) 737279
thegeorgeatvernhamdean.co.uk
Flack Manor Flack's Double Drop; Greene King Abbot; Hop Back Crop Circle; 1 changing beer H
Beautiful old-fashioned village pub dating back to the 17th century, with eyebrow windows. Situated in the upper reaches of the Bourne Valley, there are numerous footpaths and cycling routes, including to nearby Fosbury hillfort. Outside you will find an enclosed beer garden and seating to the front. Inside there are oak beams and fireplaces. Fresh cooked food is available most of the day, themed nights are regularly held, and there is a beer festival in August with camping arranged. Q P

Wherwell

White Lion

Winchester Road, SP11 7JF
closed Mon; 11-9.30 (11 Fri & Sat); 11-9 Sun ☎ (01264) 860317 thewhitelionwherwell.co.uk
Sharp's Doom Bar; Timothy Taylor Landlord; 1 changing beer H
A former coaching inn, dating from 1611, in the centre of this picturesque village near the River Test. A Civil War cannonball which hit the inn hangs by the bar. The pub is food-led, and popular with villagers and users of the nearby River Test Way. A range of ciders is available alongside the beers. There is a function room, separate dining area and three rooms for letting. Dogs and families are welcome, with an attractive courtyard garden at the rear. Q P (15)

Widley

George Inn

Portsdown Hill Road, PO6 1BE
11-11; 12-11 Sun ☎ (023) 9222 1097
the-george-inn.co.uk
Flowerpots Goodens Gold; Fuller's London Pride; Greene King Abbot; Sharp's Doom Bar; Timothy Taylor Boltmaker; 2 changing beers (sourced nationally; often Goddards, Irving, Langham) H
A Grade II-listed 18th-century hostelry offering commanding views across Langstone harbour and Portsea Island from atop Portsdown Hill. Unchanged for decades, the interior is divided into three distinct, comfortable areas, with seven well-kept beers always on the bar. A weekly quiz night is hosted, plus regular live music, including a popular Irish folk session on the last Sunday of each month. The walls are adorned with local brewery memorabilia. The outside patio proves popular in warm weather. P (7,8)

Winchester

Albion L

2 Stockbridge Road, SO23 7BZ
12-11 (11.30 Fri & Sat); 12-10.30 Sun ☎ (01962) 867991
Flowerpots Perridge Pale, Bitter, Goodens Gold; 1 changing beer (sourced locally) H
Small, acutely angled street-corner local at the bottom of the Station Hill approach, distinguished by an unusual battleship-grey paint scheme. It is the third pub in the ownership of the Flower Pots Brewery at Cheriton; three pumps feature the core beers and a fourth either a seasonal or a beer from another small local brewery. It is too small to provide a food service but pies and Scotch eggs are on offer. Trains are nearby and most city buses use the City Road stops just yards away. Q

Black Boy L

1 Wharf Hill, SO23 9NQ (just off Chesil St)
12-11 (midnight Fri & Sat); 12-10.30 Sun
☎ (01962) 861754 theblackboypub.com
Alfred's Saxon Bronze; Flowerpots Bitter; 3 changing beers (sourced locally; often Bowman, Hop Back, Itchen Valley) H
A unique pub that is well worth the walk from the city centre along the beautiful River Itchen. The multi-level interior of cosy interlinked rooms is adorned with an eccentric mixture of continuously changing curios ranging from taxidermy to a fire bucket collection. A central bar serves five local real ales, five ciders (three local) and five unusual lagers. Outside is a large terrace area with plenty of covered seating. Food consists of four varying pub classics plus sandwiches. Q (4)

Fulflood Arms L

28 Cheriton Road, SO22 5EF
12-2.30, 4.30-11; 12-midnight Fri & Sat; 12-11 Sun
☎ (01962) 842996 thefulfloodarms.co.uk
Greene King IPA; Morland Old Speckled Hen; Red Cat Prowler Pale; 6 changing beers (sourced locally; often Flack Manor, Flowerpots, Red Cat) H

A classic back-street local, the original dark-green tiled façade and etched windows remaining as evidence of this 19th-century pub's former Winchester Brewery ownership. Inside, a makeover has produced a smart and pleasant capacious single bar with a wood-burning stove, comfy chairs and a library which includes newspapers. Sports events are shown on TV and attract an enthusiastic local following. There are patios outside for alfresco drinkers. No food is served, but customers may order takeaways. Q❀⇌♣●🚌(4)🐾

Hyde Tavern

57 Hyde Street, SO23 7DY

5-11 Mon-Wed; 12.30-2, 5-11 Thu; 5-midnight Fri; 12.30-midnight Sat; 12-11 Sun ☎ (01962) 862592

hydetavern.co.uk

Flowerpots Bitter; Harvey's Sussex Best Bitter [H]; 4 changing beers (sourced locally; often Flowerpots, Red Cat, West Berkshire) [G]

An ancient, cosy pub with wooden floors, low-beamed ceilings and modern art paintings (for sale) on the walls. The bar serves six mostly local real ales including one dark, with two on gravity, plus two ciders in boxes. Narrow stairs lead to a hidden cellar room and small garden with rustic bench tables. The pub hosts regular folk and other live music upstairs and in the cellar. Takeaway food can be brought in, with a small charge for plates and cutlery. Q❀⇌♣●🚌🐾

Old Vine

8 Great Minster Street, SO23 9HA

11-11 (10.30 Sun) ☎ (01962) 854616

oldvinewinchester.com

Timothy Taylor Landlord; Ringwood Razorback; 2 changing beers (sourced regionally) [H]

A Grade II-listed Georgian inn with entrances in both Little and Great Minster Streets, overlooking the Square, city museum and the cathedral green. The friendly, welcoming bar has a sizeable restaurant attached, serving high-quality meals with much local produce. Four handpumps deliver probably the only Taylor's on offer in Winchester plus at least one local brew. For nice days, there is a small rear patio (no-smoking). The hotel provides six double rooms, including a top-floor suite. Q❀🛏◐◑♣🚌(1,69)🐾

Queen Inn

28 Kingsgate Road, SO23 9PG

11-midnight ☎ (01962) 853898

thequeeninnwinchester.co.uk

Greene King IPA; Morland Old Speckled Hen [H]; 8 changing beers (sourced locally; often Red Cat, Steam Town, Vibrant Forest) [H]/[G]

Close to Winchester College, the Queen Inn is relaxed and affable, appealing to many. Somewhat surprisingly, up to 10 beers are available, with half from local breweries, possibly one brewed at the pub. Up to four of the beers are served on gravity. The menu shows some enterprising twists on pub favourites, extended on Sundays to include roasts; and between mealtimes home-made snacks are available. Because of its location, this is a good pub to walk to (and from). Q❀◐◑P🚌(1,69)🐾

Westgate

2 Romsey Road, SO23 8TP

11-11 (midnight Fri & Sat) ☎ (01962) 820222

westgatewinchester.com

Flack Manor Flack Catcher; Flowerpots Goodens Gold; Red Cat Prowler Pale; 5 changing beers (sourced locally) [H]

Prominent Grade II-listed pub in a commanding position atop the High Street, close to the city centre. Dating from 1877, it became the Westgate Hotel in 1894, operated by Dorset brewers Eldridge Pope. A 2016 renovation retained the fine etched windows and provided a spacious, well-decorated bar area. A separate raised area doubles as a breakfast room for hotel guests and morning visitors from 8am daily. Up to five local or regional beers are normally available, mainly from the breweries listed. ❀🛏◐◑⇌♣●🚌🐾

Wykeham Arms

75 Kingsgate Street, SO23 9PE

11-11 (10.30 Sun) ☎ (01962) 853834

wykehamarmswinchester.co.uk

Flowerpots Goodens Gold; Fuller's London Pride; Gale's Seafarers Ale, HSB; 1 changing beer [H]

Grade II-listed Georgian (1755) building facing the historic Kingsgate, just yards from the college gates. Inside this most civilised pub, astonishing amounts of memorabilia, much Nelsonian, fill every crevice of several interconnected rooms. The bar seating reuses old school desks. A double-backed log fire provides warmth on cold days. Five cask ales usually include one from Hampshire's Flower Pots Brewery. The tearooms opposite (in common ownership) will serve beers. Acclaimed food and accommodation ensure the Wykeham features in many guides. Q❀🛏◐◑🚌(1,69)🐾

Wonston

Wonston Arms 🏆

Stoke Charity Road, SO21 3LS

closed Mon; 5-10; 12-10 Sat; 12-8 Sun ☎ 07909 993388

thewonston.co.uk

4 changing beers (sourced locally; often Bowman, Flowerpots, Red Cat) [H]

In the heart of the village, this true community pub is just a 15-minute walk from Sutton Scotney. Four real ales are served from local breweries plus 150 gins. A fish and chips van visits on Tuesday evening, a fishmonger on Thursday afternoon, and curries are delivered on Friday. There is folk music on the second and fourth Wednesday. A pop-up café, Jazz sessions, quizzes and a photography club also feature. CAMRA National Pub of the Year 2018 and local Pub of the Year 2019. Q❀♣●P🐾

Wootton

Rising Sun

Bashley Common Road, BH25 5SF

10-11 (10.30 Sun) ☎ (01425) 610360

therisingsunbashley.co.uk

Flack Manor Flack's Double Drop; Morland Old Speckled Hen; 1 changing beer (sourced nationally; often Andwell, Hop Back, Otter) [H]

In the south-west of the New Forest, this is an excellent place to meet with family and friends. The front bar faces open forest, while to the side is a large car park. The rear dining area has views of the large terrace, pleasant garden and excellent children's play facilities. Up to five cask ales are complemented by draught cider in summer. Quality food is served, with locally sourced meats and other produce where possible. Dogs are welcome in some areas.
❀◐◑♿P🚌(C32,C33)🐾

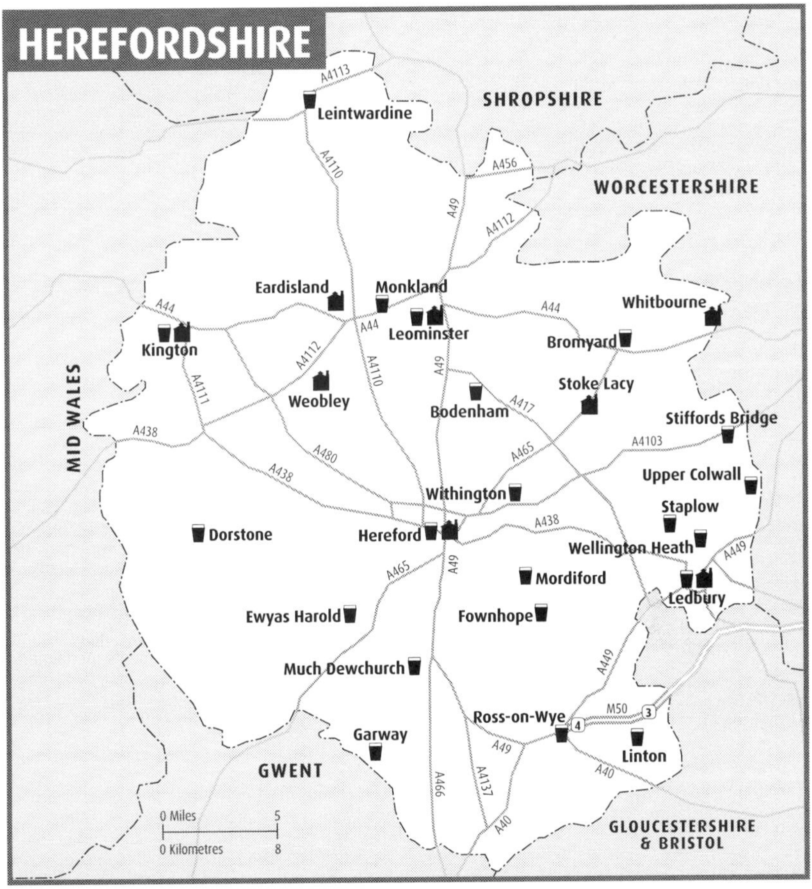

Bodenham

England's Gate Inn

HR1 3HU (just off A417, in village)
12-11; 12-10 Sun ☎ (01568) 797286
englandsgate.co.uk
Wye Valley HPA, Butty Bach; 1 changing beer (sourced locally; often Hobsons, Ludlow, Swan Brewery) H

A 16th-century black and white inn that has been opened out internally and extensively modernised, but that still retains fine original timbers and a flagstone floor. The single, large bar contrasts with a number of more intimate nooks and crannies. The guest beer is usually from a local brewery. It enjoys a loyal following for its excellent and affordable food (served daily), with traditional roasts on Sundays. Letting rooms are in the newly converted coach house. A beer, cider and food festival is held each July. P (426)

Bromyard

Rose & Lion

5 New Road, HR7 4AJ
11-11 ☎ (01885) 482381
Wye Valley Bitter, HPA, Butty Bach H

The Rosie is very much a traditional town pub, with a loyal following by locals. Two small original rooms are complemented by a further bar to the rear, plus a more contemporary annexe with accessible toilets, and a pleasant garden. Furnished throughout in a modern but appropriate style, there is always a real buzz about the place. No food is served. There is free on-street parking nearby. Q P (420)

Dorstone

Pandy Inn

HR3 6AN (signed off B4348)
5-10; 12-11 Fri & Sat; 12-6 Sun ☎ (01981) 550273
thepandyinn.co.uk
Sharp's Atlantic; Wye Valley Butty Bach; house beer (by Grey Trees); 1 changing beer H

Opposite the small village green, the Pandy has a history dating back to the 12th century. Although

REAL ALE BREWERIES

Arrow Kington
Bullen Ledbury (NEW)
Hereford Hereford
Ledbury Ledbury
Odyssey Whitbourne
Simpsons Eardisland
Swan Leominster
Weobley Weobley (NEW)
Wobbly Hereford
Wye Valley Stoke Lacy

opened out, discrete areas give a welcoming feel, with timber framing, exposed stone walls and a huge fireplace. The pub caters equally for drinkers and diners, with an interesting range of dishes, including vegetarian. It will open on weekday lunchtimes for large groups by prior arrangement. Gwatkins cider is on handpump. A monthly quiz and curry night is hosted (booking advisable).
Q❀◑♣●P🚌🐾📶

Ewyas Harold

Temple Bar 🄻

HR2 0EU (just off B4347, in village)
⏲ 11-3, 5-11.30; 11-1.30am Sat; 11-midnight Sun
☎ (01981) 240423 🌐 thetemplebarinn.co.uk
Ludlow Gold; Wye Valley Butty Bach; 2 changing beers (often Harviestoun, Hobsons) Ⓗ
First licensed in the 1850s, it has also been a courthouse, corn exchange and stable. It was extensively refurbished in 2011 with a bar, games room, restaurant, outside seating area, function room and three en-suite rooms. Meals are served lunchtimes daily and early evenings Wednesday to Saturday, and in the restaurant from 7pm and on Sunday lunchtimes.
Q❀🛏◑♿♣●P🚌(440)🐾📶

Fownhope

New Inn 🄻

HR1 4PE (on B4224, in village)
⏲ 12-3, 6-midnight; 12-midnight Sat & Sun
☎ (01432) 860350 🌐 thenewinnfownhope.co.uk
Hobsons Best; house beer (by Wye Valley); 1 changing beer (often Hobsons, Swan, Wood) Ⓗ
A true locals' pub at the heart of a thriving village community. The single room with exposed beams and light decor is divided into more discrete spaces by a central, bare-brick fireplace. Outside is a large, lawned garden. Typical pub food is served lunchtimes and Thursday to Saturday evenings, with a roast on Sunday. There are food events plus jam sessions and quiz evenings. Fownhope football team use the pub as a base.
❀◑♿▲♣P🚌(454)🐾📶

Garway

Garway Moon 🄻

Garway Common, HR2 8RQ SO465227
⏲ 5-10.30 (10 Mon; 11 Fri); 12-11 Sat; 12-9 Sun
☎ (01600) 750270 🌐 garwaymooninn.co.uk
Wye Valley HPA, Butty Bach; 1 changing beer (sourced regionally; often Butcombe, Kingstone) Ⓗ
A remote, welcoming pub overlooking the village green and cricket pitch, with a lounge, public bar, separate snug/family room and garden with play area. The British pub food and grill menu features specials inspired by local growers and farmers. Food events include curry on Tuesday, pizza on Wednesday and roasts on Sunday. The last Sunday of the month is quiz night. Opens lunchtimes Tuesday to Friday in summer.
❀🛏◑▲♣●P🚌(412)🐾📶

Hereford

Barrels 🄻 ✔

69 St Owen Street, HR1 2JQ
⏲ 11-11.30 (midnight Fri & Sat); 12-11.30 Sun
☎ (01432) 274968
Wye Valley Bitter, The Hopfather, HPA, Golden Ale, Butty Bach, Wholesome Stout; 1 changing beer (sourced locally; often Wye Valley) Ⓗ
The Barrels has been CAMRA Herefordshire Pub of the Year seven times, most recently in 2017, and is proud to be a community inn. No food, no gimmicks, but full of character across five bars, this is a pub where conversation and good times always hold sway. It has a cobbled courtyard to the rear which hosts a charity beer and music festival on the August bank holiday weekend.
❀≹♣●🚌🐾📶

Beer in Hand

136 Eign Street, HR4 0AP
⏲ 5-11 (10 Mon); 12-11 Fri & Sat; 3-9 Sun ☎ 07543 327548
5 changing beers (often Bristol Beer Factory, Odyssey) Ⓖ
Herefordshire's first micropub, this minimalist, single-bar establishment was converted from a launderette in 2013. In 2014 it was named CAMRA Herefordshire Pub of the Year and in 2015 Cider Pub of the Year. With an impressive chilled racking system, it typically sells up to six ales on cask, seven keg beers (including several from Odyssey Brewing Co), and eight mainly local ciders and perries. Meals are served Thursday and Friday evenings. Quiz night is the first Wednesday and folk night the third Thursday of the month.
Q❀◑♿♣●🚌🐾

Firefly

16 King Street, HR4 9BX
⏲ 4-11; 12-1am Fri & Sat; 12-11 Sun ☎ (01432) 358252
4 changing beers Ⓗ
Dating from the 17th century, this small, much-altered single-bar pub reopened in 2016 after a spell as a restaurant. At the trendier end of the spectrum, but with much original woodwork and floors, it is the younger sibling of its namesake in Worcester. It offers craft keg beers, an imaginative draught ale selection and real ciders, often local. Lunchtime and evening food menus are entirely vegan, with one of the beers normally vegan too. Live bands or a DJ play on Friday and Saturday.
❀◑●🚌🐾📶

Kington

Oxford Arms Hotel 🄻

Duke Street, HR5 3DR
⏲ closed Mon; 5-11 Tue & Wed; 4-11 Thu; 3-1am Fri; 12-1am Sat & Sun ☎ (01544) 230322 🌐 the-oxford-arms.co.uk
Hobsons Town Crier; 2 changing beers Ⓗ
The 17th-century timber construction of this building is now hidden behind a Victorian frontage. The public bar is popular with locals and attracts a younger clientele with pool, darts and quoits. The large dining lounge doubles as a function room, staging occasional live music. Good locally sourced home-prepared food is served. The range of regularly changing local beers is added to during annual beer festivals and the August sheep shearing event. Q❀🛏◑♿▲♣●P🚌🐾📶

Ledbury

Lion 🄻

38 Bye Street, HR8 2AA
⏲ closed Mon; 4-9.30 (10.30 Fri; 10 Sat); 1-5 Sun
☎ 07870 606270

3 changing beers (sourced locally; often Bullen, Ledbury, Wye Valley) [G]
Opened in July 2016, this two-room micropub has a bar at the front and a room with tables and chairs to the rear. The two beers, served direct from the cask, are expected to be mainly from the three counties of Gloucestershire, Worcestershire and Herefordshire. A darts team has now been established.

Prince of Wales ✓
Church Lane, HR8 1DL
11-11; 11-10.30 Sun (01531) 632250
powledbury.com
Eagle IPA; Ledbury Dark; Ringwood Razorback; Wye Valley HPA, Butty Bach; 2 changing beers [H]
Hidden away in a picturesque cobbled alley leading up to the church, this 16th-century timber-framed pub boasts two bars, plus a discrete alcove where a folk jam session is held each Wednesday evening. Orchard Pig draught cider is served, together with an extensive range of foreign beers. The bar meals are excellent value (booking advisable for the Sunday roasts). A former Herefordshire CAMRA Town Pub of the Year.

Talbot Hotel
14 New Street, HR8 2DX
11-11 (01531) 632963 talbotledbury.co.uk
Wadworth IPA, 6X; Wye Valley Butty Bach; 1 changing beer (often Wadworth) [H]
An outstanding, black-and-white, half-timbered hotel and bar dating back to the 1590s, with direct links to the Civil War. Various comfortably furnished seating areas, with discreet nooks and corners, surround a central bar-servery facing a splendid fireplace. The restaurant, with its superb wood-panelling, offers affordable fine cuisine using locally sourced ingredients, while snacks are available in the bar. Guest beers include those from Wadworth's seasonal range or Red Shoot subsidiary.

Leintwardine

Sun Inn ★
Rosemary Lane, SY7 0LP (off A4113, in village)
11-11 (10.30 Sun) (01547) 540705
suninnleintwardine.co.uk
Hobsons Mild, Best; Ludlow Stairway; 1 changing beer (sourced locally; often Ludlow, Three Tuns) [H]
A national treasure and one of the last parlour pubs, the Sun was saved in 2009 following a CAMRA-led campaign. The red-brick public bar features bench furniture and a simple fireplace. To the rear a modern pavilion-style extension overlooks the garden, which hosts the August bank holiday Sunday beer festival. Light lunches are served daily or you can bring in fish and chips from next door. Q

Leominster

Chequers ✓
63 Etnam Street, HR6 8AE
11-11 (midnight Fri & Sat); 12-10.30 Sun
(01568) 612473
Wye Valley Bitter, HPA, Golden Ale, Butty Bach, Wholesome Stout; 1 changing beer (often Wye Valley) [H]
Probably the oldest pub in the town, with a fine timber-framed façade and interesting protruding gables. A wonderful unspoilt front bar was at one time two bars, but still has much charm, with a fine tiled floor, original fireplace, timbers and cosy window alcoves. To the rear is a more conventional lounge bar and dining area serving good-value meals (no food Sun) and a games room. A quiz is held on alternate Wednesdays.
Q P

Grape Vaults
2-4 Broad Street, HR6 8BS
11-11 (midnight Fri & Sat) (01568) 611404
Ludlow Best, Blonde, Gold; Salopian Oracle, Darwins Origin; Swan Ruffled Feathers [H]
This is a real gem of a pub, with a welcoming fireplace, bench seating and much original woodwork. A small snug is tucked away behind a part-glazed screen. The Gents is probably the smallest in the country. A pull-down TV screen is used for sports fixtures. Typical pub food is served at reasonable prices (no food Sun eve). Live music features on Sunday afternoons. Q

Linton

Alma Inn
HR9 7RY (off B4221, W of M50 jct 3) SO659255
12-3 (not Mon), 6-11; 12-3, 7-10.30 Sun
(01989) 720355 almainnlinton.co.uk
Butcombe Original; Ludlow Gold; Malvern Hills Black Pear; Oakham JHB; 1 changing beer (often Bristol Beer Factory, Hop Shed, Swan) [H]
Behind a plain façade is an award-winning pub of true pedigree, with a warm welcome for drinkers and diners. The convivial front bar with real fire contrasts with the rear pool room and a separate wood-panelled dining room. Hearty freshly prepared pub classics are offered, with seasonal specials, light bites and bar snacks. Events include the nationally renowned Linton Music Festival in June and Summer Acoustic Sessions in August. A quiz is hosted on the last Sunday of the month. Local CAMRA Pub of the Year 2018. Q P

Monkland

Monkland Arms
HR6 9DE (on A44, W end of village)
12-2, 5.30-11; 12-3, 7-10.30 Sun (01568) 720510
themonklandarms.co.uk
Hobsons Best; Ludlow Blonde; Wye Valley Butty Bach; 2 changing beers (sourced locally; often Ludlow, Swan) [H]
A single bar serves the drinking area, with dining areas to the side and rear. The beer garden has covered seating, with views across open country. Home-cooked, locally sourced food is served every evening, as well as traditional Sunday lunches. Up to seven local draught ciders are available and a range of five real ales. Quiz night is the last Wednesday of the month and live music is hosted on some Saturdays and Sundays.
P (502)

Mordiford

Moon Inn ✓
HR1 4LW (on B4224, in village)
12 (10 Mon)-11; 12-midnight Sat & Sun
(01432) 873067 mooninnmordiford.co.uk
Bombardier; Otter Amber; St Austell Proper Job; Timothy Taylor Landlord; 1 changing beer [H]

This half-timbered and much-altered two-bar roadside village inn started life as a farmhouse over 400 years ago. Popular with locals and with families tripping out from Hereford, it benefits from its proximity to the Mordiford Loop – a well-known local walk – as well as the Rivers Lugg and Wye. Traditional locally sourced pub food is served, with a pie night on Wednesday. Quiz night is alternate Tuesdays. There is a children's play area in the garden, plus a camping and caravan site to the rear. P (453)

Much Dewchurch

Black Swan

HR2 8DJ (on B4348, in village)
12 (11.30 Sat)-3, 5.30-11; 12-4, 6.30-11 Sun
(01981) 540295
Timothy Taylor Landlord; 2 changing beers (often Butcombe, Hobsons, Slater's)
Possibly the oldest pub in Herefordshire. A small lounge leads to a dining room with an open fire. The separate public bar with flagstone floors is next to a pool and darts room. Home-prepared, mainly locally sourced food is available every session. The guest beers are typically from regional breweries. Draught Westons perry is available, plus local Cockyard cider. Thursday is folk night.
P

Ross-on-Wye

Tap House

1 Millpond Street, HR9 7BZ
12-2.30, 4.30-10.30 (11 Thu); 12-11 Fri & Sat; 12-10 Sun
6 changing beers (sourced nationally; often Hop Shed)
Opened in September 2018, this single-room, simply furnished micropub occupies what was, until 1965, the tap for Alton Court Brewery, situated just outside the town centre. Serving six real ales from smaller breweries far and wide, plus a local cider, it has transformed the choice of real ale in Ross, with beers from over 60 different breweries featuring in the first six months. The Tap does not serve meals, but cobs are available Friday to Sunday. Q

Staplow

Oak Inn

HR8 1NP (on B4214)
12-11 (10.30 Sun) (01531) 640954
oakinnstaplow.co.uk
Bathams Best Bitter; Ledbury Gold; Wye Valley Bitter; 1 changing beer
A stylishly renovated and well-run roadside country inn offering exceptional food, good beer and quality accommodation overlooking nearby hop yards. A contemporary public area neatly divides into three – a reception bar area with modern sofas and low tables, a snug and a main dining area featuring an open kitchen. At the rear is a further room with scrubbed tables. Such is the reputation of the Oak that booking is essential for food and accommodation. Q P (417)

Stiffords Bridge

Red Lion Inn

WR13 5NN (on A4103)
closed Mon; 12-11 (10.30 Sun) (01886) 880318
Pitchfork; Wye Valley Butty Bach; 4 changing beers (often Malvern Hills, Purity, Salopian)
A survivor of multiple floods, this place is characterised by modern flagstone floors, wood panelling, bare brick walls, cosy window alcoves and a large fireplace with a woodburner. There are pleasant and extensive gardens to the rear where events are hosted. Traditional locally sourced food dominates the menu. The guest beers are from breweries far and near, many unusual for the area, supplemented by a craft keg beer and two real ciders. P

Upper Colwall

Chase Inn

Chase Road, WR13 6DJ (off B4218, turning at upper hairpin bend signed British Camp) SO766431
12-3, 5-11; 12-11 Sat; 12-10.30 Sun (01684) 540276
thechaseinnmalvern.co.uk
Bathams Best Bitter; Courage Directors; 2 changing beers (often Cotleigh, Hobsons, Malvern Hills)
Two-bar free house hidden away in a quiet wooded backwater on the western slopes of the Malvern Hills. With a genteel atmosphere, it is popular with walkers. It comprises a small lounge for dining (booking advisable at weekends) and a long, narrow public bar. A delightful manicured rear beer garden commands panoramic views across Herefordshire to the Welsh Hills. A quiz is held on the first Monday of the month.
Q P (675)

Wellington Heath

Farmers Arms

Horse Road, HR8 1LS (in village, E of B4214)
closed Mon; 5.30-11 Tue; 12-3, 5.30-11 Wed-Fri; 12-11 Sat; 12-10 Sun (01531) 634776
farmersarmswellingtonheath.co.uk
Wye Valley HPA, Butty Bach; 2 changing beers (often Ledbury, Salopian, Tiny Rebel)
Follow the signs carefully to find this pub in its dispersed rural community. The bar and main dining area are in the original 18th-century building, and on either side are more modern extensions housing a games room with pool table and a restaurant. The food ranges from burgers and pub classics to steaks and speciality dishes. Eight local draught ciders are available. A popular Beer & Beast festival is held in July. Open on bank holiday Mondays. P (675)

Withington

Cross Keys

HR1 3NN (on A465 in Withington Marsh)
5-11; 12-11 Sat; 12-10.30 Sun (01432) 820616
Otter Ale; Wye Valley Butty Bach; house beer (by Wye Valley); 1 changing beer
Run by the same landlord for over 45 years, this is drinking in the slow lane, Herefordshire style. A long single bar divides a central servery into two drinking areas, with original beams, exposed stonework and comfortable bench seating along each wall, book-ended by woodburners. A folk jam session is held on the last Thursday of each month. Filled rolls are available on Saturday.
Q P (420)

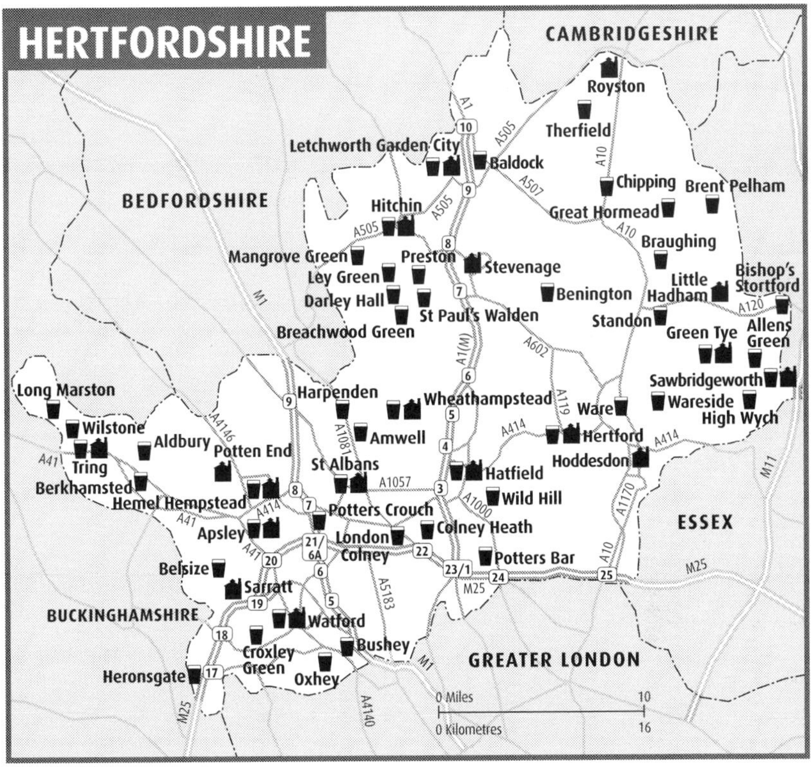

Aldbury

Valiant Trooper

Trooper Road, HP23 5RW

11-11; 10-11 Sat; 10-10.30 Sun (01442) 851203
valianttrooper.co.uk

Chiltern Beechwood Bitter; Tring Side Pocket for a Toad; 3 changing beers (sourced locally; often Leighton Buzzard, Tring, Vale) H

Situated in the heart of the Chiltern Hills, the Valiant Trooper is a classic 17th-century pub. It retains a lovely classic style and charm, with a beer garden for summer and roaring log fires for winter. The pub offers an outstanding selection of beers in excellent condition, from local breweries and further afield, and has a separate restaurant serving an array of classic British pub fare.
Q P (387,389)

Allens Green

Queen's Head

CM21 0LS TL455170

12-2.30 (not Mon), 5-11; 12-11 Sat; 12-10.30 Sun
(01279) 723393

Fuller's London Pride; Mighty Oak Maldon Gold H**; 2 changing beers (sourced locally)** H/G

This village inn was once closed, but was reopened by the efforts of a group of local people. Three local ales are usually served. Hot snacks are available unless the pub is busy. The pub boasts a large garden and is popular with walkers and cyclists as well as locals. A frequent winner of local CAMRA Pub of the Year over the past decade and current Hertfordshire Cider & Perry Pub of the Year.
Q P

Amwell

Elephant & Castle

Amwell Lane, AL4 8EA TL167131

12-11 (01582) 832175 elephantcastle.co.uk

Greene King IPA, Abbot; 3 changing beers (sourced nationally) H

Hidden away in a peaceful setting, this rural community pub is popular with cyclists and walkers. Five handpumps serve a choice of beers, usually including a local ale. The front bar features terracotta tiles and a fireplace, and the rear bar has a 100-foot well. There are two gardens – one where children are welcome, the other adults only. Lunches are served daily and evening meals Tuesday to Saturday. The pub has a strong community focus. Q P

Apsley

Paper Mill

Stationers Place, Apsley Lock, HP3 9RH (between retail park and station)

10-11 (midnight Fri & Sat); 10-10.30 Sun
(01442) 288800 papermillapsley.co.uk

Fuller's London Pride, ESB; 2 changing beers (sourced regionally; often Dark Star, Gale's) H

A canalside pub built on the site of Dickinsons Paper Works. The spacious two-storey building has a comfortable interior with an open fire creating a cosy feel on the ground level, and a restaurant upstairs. An expansive beer garden allows drinkers to enjoy the Apsley marina. Fuller's beers are joined by two guests on regular rotation. The pub hosts a quiz night on Thursday and regular live music. P (500,501)

Baldock

Orange Tree L ✓
Norton Road, SG7 5AW
✪ 12-2.30, 4.30-11; 12-midnight Thu-Sat; 12-10.30 Sun
☎ (01462) 892341 ⊕ theorangetreebaldock.com
**Greene King XX Mild, IPA, Abbot; 9 changing beers
(sourced nationally)** Ⓗ
Three-hundred-year-old, multi-roomed pub, home
to more than 10 local clubs and societies. Guest
ales always include two from the local Buntingford
Brewery, and five local real ciders are stocked. A
huge malt whisky collection is also kept, and a
large vintage beer bottle collection is on display.
Good home-cooked food is served, with meats and
sausages from the local, award-winning
Chapman's Butchers. Quiz night is Tuesday. Major
rugby matches are screened in all rooms and the
pub can get crowded.
ॐ⊛◑&≉♣●P🖪(91,98)☀♠

White Lion L ✓
46 High Street, SG7 6BJ
✪ 12-midnight (11 Sun) ☎ (01462) 893134
⊕ thewhitelionbaldock.co.uk
**Greene King IPA; 7 changing beers (sourced
nationally)** Ⓗ
This characterful 17th-century pub, sitting in the
middle of the High Street, has oak beams and a
large fireplace. The pub prides itself on selling local
ales, cider and food. A large, fully enclosed garden
provides an ideal setting for relaxation on a
summer afternoon. ॐ⊛◑≉●🖪(91,98)☀♠

Belsize

Plough
Dunny Lane, WD3 4NP
✪ 12-11 (10.30 Mon); 12-10.30 Sun ☎ (01923) 262261
⊕ theploughatbelsize.co.uk
**Greene King IPA; St Austell Tribute; 1 changing beer
(sourced nationally)**
This free house was purpose-built for the Kings
Langley Brewery in the 1840s. In a hamlet
between Chipperfield and Sarratt, it has a bar area
with open log fires and comfy settees, a separate
restaurant, a pleasant garden and a large car park.
Food is served Wednesday to Sunday lunchtimes
and Wednesday to Saturday evenings. Dogs are not
allowed in the restaurant area. Please ask for
assistance with wheelchair access.
Q ॐ⊛◑&♣P🖪(352)☀♠

Benington

Lordship Arms
42 Whempstead Road, SG2 7BX
✪ closed Mon; 12-3, 6-11; 12-3 Sun ☎ (01438) 869465
⊕ lordshiparms.com
**Black Sheep Best Bitter; Crouch Vale Brewers Gold;
Timothy Taylor Landlord; 6 changing beers (sourced
nationally)** Ⓗ
Under the same ownership for 25 years, this pub is
a repeat winner of local and county CAMRA awards.
The single bar is decorated with telephone
memorabilia - some of the handpumps are
modelled on telephones. The garden features floral
displays to be enjoyed in the summer. Wednesday
evening curries are popular and lunchtime snacks
are served (12-2pm Mon-Sat). There is a classic car
gathering on the third Tuesday of each month (Apr-
Sep). Winter Sunday hours can vary; call to check.
Q⊛◑●P🖪☀♠

Berkhamsted

Rising Sun L
1 Canal Side, George Street, HP4 2EG (at lock 55 on
Grand Union Canal)
✪ 12-11 (midnight Thu-Sat); 12-10.30 Sun
☎ (01442) 864913 ⊕ theriserberko.net
**Tring Drop Bar Pale Ale; house beer (by Tring); 3
changing beers (sourced nationally)** Ⓗ
The Riser is a thriving canalside pub with plenty of
outdoor space - a firm favourite of local hikers, dog
walkers and cyclists. The recipient of many well-
deserved CAMRA awards, it serves five well-kept
real ales and 15-20 real ciders. It hosts many
popular events including quiz nights, folk music
afternoons, a cheese club and quarterly beer and
cider festivals. A range of bar snacks is offered such
as pork pies and nachos, as well as the renowned
ploughman's. ॐ⊛◑≉♣●🖪(500,501)☀♠

Bishop's Stortford

Bishop's Stortford Sports Trust L
Cricketfield Lane, CM23 2TD
✪ 5-11; 12-11 Sat & Sun ☎ (01279) 654463
**Hadham Gold; 3 changing beers (sourced locally;
often Mauldons)** Ⓗ
Everyone is welcome at this pub within a club - no
membership required. Set in a large club house,
shared by the local cricket, hockey and squash
clubs. Conversation flourishes in the comfortable
seating area as the satellite sports screens usually
have the sound off. Local breweries always feature
within the varied selection of ales on its four
handpumps. Outside drinking in summer comes
with an attractive view. Easily reached from town
via Chantry Road; turn left at the end to see the
grounds on the right. ॐ⊛&P

Star L ✓
7 Bridge Street, CM23 2JU
✪ 11-midnight (2am Fri); 12-2am Sat; 12-10.30 Sun
☎ (01279) 654211 ⊕ thestar-bishopsstortford.co.uk
5 changing beers (sourced regionally) Ⓗ
A 17th-century town-centre pub catering for all
ages. It is busy on Friday and Saturday evenings
with a young crowd, and at other times attracts a
mixed clientele. Tuesday is quiz night. A quiet pint
can be enjoyed on other evenings and at

REAL ALE BREWERIES
3 Brewers of St Albans Hatfield
Ash Valley 🍺 Green Tye (brewing suspended)
Bog Brew 🍺 Stevenage
Buntingford Royston
Farr Brew Wheathampstead
Foragers 🍺 St Albans
Garden City 🍺 Letchworth Garden City
Hadham Little Hadham
Hitchin Hitchin (NEW)
Mad Squirrel Potten End
McMullen Hertford
Mix Hemel Hempstead
New River Hoddesdon
Old Cross 🍺 Hertford
Paradigm Sarratt
Pope's Yard Apsley
Sawbridgeworth 🍺 Sawbridgeworth
Tring Tring
Watling Street Watford
White Hart Tap 🍺 St Albans

lunchtimes. Reasonably priced traditional pub food is freshly prepared throughout the day. Beers from regional and local breweries are offered on an ever-changing basis. ❀◐≹⊟ᯤ

Braughing

Brown Bear
14 The Street, SG11 2QF
✪ 3-6 Mon; 3-11 Tue; 12-11.30; 12-6 Sun ☎ (01920) 822157
🌐 brownbearbraughing.co.uk
3 changing beers (sourced nationally) Ⓗ
A pub since at least 1740, the Brown Bear has a public bar and a restaurant, both with impressive fireplaces – have a go at identifying the implements. The Thursday pub quiz, darts and pétanque teams, a large garden with a pizza oven, occasional outside bars and monthly live music mean there is something for everyone. A widely varying choice of three real ales is usually available. ❀◐♣P⊟(331)🐾ᯤ

Breachwood Green

Red Lion ✔
16 Chapel Road, SG4 8NU
✪ 12-11 (midnight Sat) ☎ (01438) 833123
🌐 redlionbreachwoodgreen.co.uk
Adnams Broadside; Greene King IPA; St Austell Tribute; 1 changing beer (sourced nationally) Ⓗ
Being the only pub in the village, it attracts many locals and some from further afield. There is a TV showing main sporting events as well as a quiet dining area. It has darts, dominoes, association football and cricket teams. The garden provides great views of the countryside and a good vantage point to view the aircraft approaching Luton airport. It serves good home-made food and the guest beers are unusual for this area.
❀◐♣●P⊟🐾ᯤ

Brent Pelham

Black Horse
SG9 0AP (down lane to right of church)
✪ closed Mon; 5.30-11 Tue; 11.30-2.30, 5.30-11 Wed-Fri; 11.30-11 Sat; 11.30-7 Sun ☎ (01279) 778925
🌐 blackhorsebrentpelham.co.uk
Adnams Southwold Bitter; 2 changing beers (sourced nationally) Ⓗ
Much-extended country pub with separate drinking and dining areas on many different levels. The focus is on food but drinkers are welcome too. An old pub with records dating back to 1866, once frequented by farm workers, it now attracts walkers and cyclists. It has a huge garden for the summer, with a barbecue. Take a walk down to the church to see the ancient stocks outside.
❀◐P🐾ᯤ

Bushey

Swan
25 Park Road, WD23 3EE
✪ 11-11; 12-10.30 Sun ☎ (020) 8950 2256
🌐 swanpubbushey.co.uk
Black Sheep Best Bitter; Greene King Abbot; Timothy Taylor Landlord; Young's Bitter Ⓗ
Traditional Victorian pub just off the main high street with a single bar, two coal fires and four regular beers. A real gem, it has old photos and sporting mementos adorning the walls. The original jug-and-bottle window has been retained. Hot snacks are available at all times including toasties and pies. Pub games include darts, shut the box and board games, and the pub hosts a book club. The Ladies is accessed via the garden.
❀♣⊟(142,258)🐾ᯤ

Chipping

Countryman
Ermine Street, SG9 0PG TL356319
✪ closed Mon-Thu; 12-11 Fri & Sat; 12-10.30 Sun
☎ (01763) 272721
3 changing beers (sourced nationally) Ⓗ
Built in 1663 and a pub since 1760, the Countryman has a one-bar split-level interior with an impressive fireplace. The bar front features some well-executed carvings dating from the 1970s, and obscure agricultural implements decorate the walls. The beer range varies, with three real ales (and a cider in summer) usually available. There are chickens in the garden. This is a pub where conversation flourishes. Note the limited opening hours. Q❀●P⊟(331)🐾

Colney Heath

Crooked Billet 𝕃
88 High Street, AL4 0NP
✪ 11-2.30, 4.30-11 Mon & Tue; 11-11 Wed-Fri; 12-11 Sat; 12-10.30 Sun ☎ (01727) 822128 🌐 thecrookedbilletpub.com
Sharp's Doom Bar; Tring Side Pocket for a Toad; Young's Special Ⓗ
Popular and friendly cottage-style village pub dating back over 200 years. A genuine free house, it stocks three beers from national, regional and micro breweries. A wide selection of good-value, home-made food is served lunchtimes and Friday and Saturday evenings. Summer barbecues and Saturday events are held occasionally. This is a favourite stop-off for walkers on the many local footpaths. Families are welcome in the bar until 9pm and in the large garden, where there is play equipment. ❀◐♣P⊟(304)🐾

Croxley Green

Sportsman 𝕃
2 Scots Hill, WD3 3AD (at A412 jct with the Green)
✪ 2-11; 12-11 Fri & Sat; 12-10.30 Sun ☎ (01923) 443360
Oakham JHB; Sharp's Doom Bar; 5 changing beers (sourced nationally) Ⓗ
A family-run community pub with friendly, welcoming service. Up to seven real ales are on handpump, often from more obscure microbreweries as well as the regular favourites. Recently redecorated throughout, the popular dartboard and pool table have been retained. Quiz night is Wednesday, live music features every other Sunday afternoon, and a music jam on the last Sunday of the month. Comfortable outdoor seating is provided on the front decking and on the enclosed patio to the rear. Croxley tube station is a 12-minute walk. ❀♣●P⊖⊟

Darley Hall

Fox
Darley Road, LU2 8PP
✪ closed Mon; 12-3, 5-10 Tue-Thu; 12-11 Fri & Sat; 12-10 Sun
☎ (01582) 731366 🌐 thefoxdarleyhall.co.uk
4 changing beers (sourced locally) Ⓗ

Late 19th-century double-fronted pub in a small hamlet close to Luton Airport. It is first recorded as having a landlord in the 1891 census. The interior comprises a single bar with an adjoining dining area, with a warm welcome for all. Outside is a walled family-friendly garden and a large mezzanine decking area linked to the excellent restaurant overlooking the Hertfordshire countryside. Local CAMRA Most Improved Pub 2017. P

Great Hormead

Three Tuns

Pelham Road, SG9 0NT (b1038)
closed Mon; 12-3, 6-11; 12-7 Sun ☎ (01763) 289405
Adnams Southwold Bitter; 2 changing beers (sourced nationally) [H]
A 16th-century thatched pub with a new restaurant area added at the rear after a fire in 1996. The main bar has a lovely fireplace. Monthly quiz nights are popular. The food has a good reputation and Thursday night fish and chips often sells out. Adnams Bitter is a regular, with guest beers from local breweries Buntingford and New River.
P

Green Tye

Prince of Wales

SG10 6JP TL444184
12-3, 5.30-11; 12-11 Sat; 12-9.30 Sun ☎ (01279) 842139
thepow.co.uk
Abbeydale Moonshine; Wadworth IPA; 2 changing beers (sourced regionally) [H]
A traditional and friendly village local, whether you are a walker, cyclist, dog owner or just plain thirsty. Food includes sandwiches and great-value traditional pub grub. There is a small garden for fine weather. Beer festivals with a barbecue and entertainment in May and September are now well established. Q P

Harpenden

Cross Keys [L] ✓

39 High Street, AL5 2SD
11.30-11; 12-10.30 Sun ☎ (01582) 763989
Rebellion IPA; Timothy Taylor Landlord; Tring Side Pocket for a Toad [H]
A regular entry in the Guide, located on the lower High Street, this two-bar pub has retained its traditional charm with a rare fine pewter bar top and flagstone floors. The original oak-beamed ceiling has tankards from past and present customers. In spring and summer, enjoy your pint in the secluded, attractive rear garden, and in autumn or winter savour your beer in front of the saloon bar's fire. Traditional home-cooked lunches are served Monday to Saturday.
Q

Mad Squirrel Tap & Bottleshop [L]

72 High Street, AL5 2SP
12-10 (10.30 Thu; 11 Fri & Sat); 12-9.30 Sun
☎ (01582) 807848 madsquirrel.uk/venues/harpenden
Mad Squirrel Mister Squirrel, London Porter [H]**; 1 changing beer (sourced locally)** [H]/[A]
A modern, high-street bar with comfortable bench seating at tables and a covered patio area outside. This Mad Squirrel Brewery outlet offers up to three real ales alongside a selection of craft beers. Draught beer is also available to take away, as well as an extensive range of canned and bottled beers displayed in two large fridges. Sliders and chilli are on the food menu, with vegetarian options. Terrestrial TV sports are shown on a large screen and live bands occasionally play.

Hatfield

Harpsfield Hall ✓

13A Parkhouse Court, AL10 9RQ
8am-midnight (1am Thu-Sat) ☎ (01707) 265840
Greene King Abbot; Ruddles Best Bitter; 8 changing beers (sourced nationally) [H]
A new-build Wetherspoon pub opposite the Galleria shopping centre and close to Hertfordshire University. Harpsfield Hall was demolished in the 1930s to make way for Hatfield aerodrome, with its notable links to De Havilland aeroplanes including the Comet. The pub incorporates design features reflecting the town's former aviation history and offers a selection of beers from outside the standard company core range.
P (300/301,602)

Horse & Groom

21 Park Street, AL9 5AT
11.30-11 (midnight Fri & Sat); 12-10.30 Sun
☎ (01707) 264765 horseandgroom-oldhatfield.com
Greene King Abbot; Oakham JHB; Otter Bitter; 3 changing beers (sourced nationally) [H]
In the heart of Old Hatfield, this allegedly haunted, 16th-century, Grade II-listed building is thought to house a priest hole. The pub serves up to six real ales, and hosts beer festivals during the year. Tuesday is bangers and mash night and Saturday is chilli and rice night – purchase an ale for a free portion. Enjoy Thai food on Friday evenings. Hatfield railway and bus stations are nearby using 'blood and guts alley'.
Q (300/301,724)

Hemel Hempstead

Olde King's Arms ✓

41 High Street, HP1 3AF
12-11 (midnight Fri & Sat) ☎ (01442) 255348
theoldekingsarms.co.uk
Eagle IPA; 1 changing beer (sourced regionally; often Eagle) [H]
A 16th-century inn and listed building with character, centrally located in Hemel Old Town, adjacent to Gadebridge Park. You will find well-kept ales from the Eagle Brewery (formerly Charles Wells) and tasty meals, including stone-baked pizzas. The beer garden has its own dedicated bar. There are regular quiz nights and occasional beer festivals. The pub is a reasonably priced option for an overnight stay, with nine rooms to choose from.
P

Heronsgate

Land of Liberty, Peace & Plenty 🏆 [L]

Long Lane, WD3 5BS TQ023949
12-11 (midnight Fri & Sat); 12-10.30 Sun
☎ (01923) 282226 landoflibertypub.com
8 changing beers (sourced nationally) [H]
Welcoming, award-winning pub just off the motorway, popular with walkers, cyclists, locals and real ale enthusiasts. Up to eight microbrewery beers are offered in a range of styles and strengths.

Real cider, perry and a wide range of whiskies are also available, as are gins and bottled beers. Beer festivals, tastings and other events are held throughout the year. Bar snacks are served all day. There is a large outside pavilion and garden for families. ❀♣●P🚂(R2)🐾

Hertford

Black Horse 🄻

29-31 West Street, SG13 8EZ

12-11 (midnight Fri & Sat); 12-10.30 Sun

☎ (01992) 583630 🌐 theblackhorse.biz

6 changing beers (sourced nationally) 🄷

A community-focused, timbered free house, dating from 1642 and situated in one of Hertford's most attractive streets, near the start of the Cole Green Way. Six real ales from around Britain are on offer, including one from Hertfordshire. An interesting food menu features game and daily specials, and the pub has its own bakery producing pastries. The well-kept garden includes a separate and safe children's area. Handy for Hertford Town FC supporters, the pub also has a rugby team affiliated to the RFU. ❀◐≉♣●🐾

Great Eastern Tavern

29 Railway Place, SG13 7BS

12-11 ☎ (01992) 582048

McMullen AK, Cask Ale; 1 changing beer (sourced nationally) 🄷

Popular, buoyant and traditional back-street McMullen local with two contrasting bars bedecked with pictures and artefacts. There is live TV sport and interesting rock and blues piped music. A folk club is hosted on the first Thursday of the month and a quiz on the first Sunday. Sandwiches are available at lunchtimes. A chilli challenge is held every February. Outside are two small gardens – the largest, to the rear, is paved and adorned with beautiful pots and wall-planters.
❀≉♣P(395,310)🐾

Hertford Club

Lombard House, Bull Plain, SG14 1DT

12-11; 11-11 Sat; 12-10 Sun ☎ (01992) 421422

🌐 hertford.club

4 changing beers (sourced nationally) 🄷

Dating from the 15th century with later additions, Lombard House, on the River Lea, was built as an English hall house and is one of the oldest buildings in Hertford. It has been the home of this private members' club since 1897. CAMRA members are welcome and may be signed in on production of a membership card. You will find three or four changing beers and real cider, which in summer can be enjoyed in the delightful walled garden and riverside terrace. ❀◐≉♣●

Old Barge ✔

2 The Folly, SG14 1QD

11-11 (midnight Fri & Sat); 12-11 Sun ☎ (01992) 581871

🌐 theoldbarge.com

Marston's 61 Deep; 3 changing beers (sourced nationally) 🄷

A free house on Folly Island, pleasantly situated canalside on the River Lea, offering a good selection of ales – often including a dark brew – and a range of ciders and perries. Locally sourced home-cooked food is served all day, with roasts on Sunday. There is a popular Sunday night quiz and a music quiz on the last Thursday of the month. The Spring Fling music festival takes place on the second May bank holiday Monday. Look out for the annual duck race and the children's crayfish festival held on the August bank holiday.
❀◐≉♣●

Old Cross Tavern 🄻

8 St Andrew Street, SG14 1JA

4.30-11; 4-midnight Fri; 12-midnight Sat; 12-10.30 Sun

☎ (01992) 583133 🌐 oldcrosstavern.com

Timothy Taylor Landlord; 5 changing beers (sourced nationally) 🄷

Superb town free house offering a friendly welcome. Up to six real ales, usually including a dark beer of some distinction, come from brewers large and small, including the pub's own microbrewery, and there is a fine choice of Belgian bottle-conditioned beers. Two beer festivals are held each year – one over a spring bank holiday weekend, the other in October. No TV or music here, just good old-fashioned conversation. Home-made pork pies are available. **Q**≉♣(395)🐾

High Wych

Rising Sun

High Wych Road, CM21 0HZ

12-2.30 (not Tue & Thu), 5.30-11; 12-3, 6-11 Sat; 12-3, 7-10.30 Sun ☎ (01279) 724099

🌐 therisingsunhighwych.com

4 changing beers (often Oakham, Woodforde's) 🄶

This friendly village local has never used handpumps – a range of four or five beers is served on gravity, often featuring East Anglian breweries. Although refurbished, the original character has been preserved by means of a stone floor, attractive fireplace and wood panelling. A separate restaurant has opened upstairs. Parking is in the village hall car park opposite. Popular with locals and walkers. **Q**❀♣P(347)🐾

Hitchin

Half Moon 🄻

57 Queen Street, SG4 9TZ

12-midnight (1am Fri & Sat); 12-11 Sun ☎ (01462) 453010

Adnams Southwold Bitter; Young's Bitter; 8 changing beers (sourced nationally) 🄷

This welcoming one-bar pub dates from the 18th century. The two house ales and eight different guest ales ensure a variety of beer styles is always on offer from a range of breweries near and far, alongside a choice of traditional ciders. Home-cooked food is served every day except Monday, with bar snacks always available. Twice-yearly beer festivals, regular quizzes and music nights are popular in this friendly community pub. A former CAMRA Hertfordshire Pub of the Year.
❀◐≉♣●P🐾

Victoria ✔

1 Ickleford Road, SG5 1TJ (off A505)

12-11 (midnight Fri); 11-midnight Sat ☎ (01462) 432682

🌐 thevictoriahitchin.com

Greene King IPA, Abbot; 3 changing beers (sourced nationally) 🄷

This popular and busy community pub dating from 1865 hosts a range of events from quiz nights and live music to comedy and cabaret, as well as an annual beer and cider festival and the Vic Fest music festival. Two regular Greene King beers are complemented by two guests. Good-value home-made modern British food is served every day, plus roasts on Sunday. Pie nights feature regularly. The historic barn is available for community use and live events.

Letchworth Garden City

Garden City Brewery & Bar

22 The Wynd, SG6 3EN
closed Mon-Wed; 12-10 Thu; 12-11 Fri & Sat; 12-10 Sun
07932 739558 gardencitybrewery.co.uk
8 changing beers (sourced nationally) [G]
Award-winning family-run brew-bar opened in 2016 in a former café on a pedestrianised street. All ales are on gravity, usually four of the brewery's own, only available here, and four guests. A large selection of local and UK-wide ciders is also on offer, and locally produced bar snacks. The paved beer garden has hay bale seating and an awning. There is a regular events programme and the TV shows tennis and rugby. The bar is two minutes' walk from the town centre, five minutes from the station, with adjacent parking. CAMRA Hertfordshire Cider & Perry Pub of the Year 2018.
Q P (91,97/98)

Ley Green

Plough

Plough Lane, SG4 8LA (follow brown pub signs)
TL162243
4-11 Mon & Tue; 12-11 Wed (midnight Thu-Sat); 12-10.30 Sun (01438) 871394
Greene King IPA, Abbot; 1 changing beer (sourced nationally) [H]
This has been an ale house as far back as 1846 when it was called Godlets Hall. A warm and friendly traditional pub hidden deep in the countryside, the rear garden has a large patio with gorgeous views. There is an open invitation to join in the acoustic music session on a Tuesday evening. Hot and cold snacks are served throughout the week. On-site camping is available for campervans and tents (please ring to confirm availability). P

London Colney

Bull

Barnet Road, AL2 1QU
12-11 (midnight Fri); 10-midnight Sat (01727) 823160
Farr Brew Chief Jester; Mad Squirrel Mister Squirrel; Timothy Taylor Landlord; 2 changing beers (sourced nationally) [H]
A lovely 17th-century timbered building near the River Colne, offering a range of real ales. It has a cosy lounge featuring an original fireplace and a large public bar with a dartboard and TV. Evening events include live music sessions on Saturdays. Good-value home-made meals are served Monday to Saturday lunchtimes and evenings, with roasts on Sunday. Outside there is a children's play area.
P

Long Marston

Queen's Head

38 Tring Road, HP23 4QL
5-11 (10 Mon); 4-midnight Fri; 12-midnight Sat; 12-10 Sun
(01296) 668368
Tring Side Pocket for a Toad [H]/[G]; 2 changing beers (sourced nationally) [H]
The only pub in the village, this is now a true free house after it was bought by locals in 2017. The building is over 500 years old, with beamed ceilings and an open fire creating the impression you have stepped back in time. There is a pleasant patio with children's play equipment. Quiz night on Tuesday and the fish and chip van on Wednesday are popular with the regulars. There are monthly music evenings and an open mic night on Sunday.
Q P (164)

Mangrove Green

King William IV

LU2 8QE (follow directions to Cockenhoe on Luton Rd, then straight on to Mangrove Green via no through road)
TL124239
11-11 (midnight Fri & Sat); 12-midnight Sun
(01582) 728086 kingwilliamhotel.com
Sharp's Doom Bar; 3 changing beers (sourced nationally) [H]
The King William IV is thought to date back to the 17th century. Following renovation, it is now a country inn and restaurant, positioned in a quiet location facing the large village green. Blessed with views over open fields to the back, the Hertfordshire countryside is only a step away.
P (88)

Oxhey

Railway Arms

1 Aldenham Road, WD19 4AB
12-midnight (1am Fri & Sat); 12-10.30 Sun
07976 647569
Greene King IPA, Abbot; 2 changing beers (sourced nationally) [H]
Friendly and welcoming two-bar pub opposite Bushey station. All satellite TV sport is shown on screens throughout the pub. There is a jukebox and pool table in one bar and a selection of newspapers. As you would expect given the name, it also has some railway paraphernalia. Note the Masons Coat of Arms on the Pinner Road side of the building.
(Bushey) P (142,258)

Villiers Arms

108 Villiers Road, WD19 4AJ
4-11 (12.30am Fri); 1-12.30am Sat; 1-11 Sun
(01923) 448848
Timothy Taylor Landlord; 2 changing beers (sourced locally; often Tring, St Austell) [H]
Traditional family-run village pub with a roaring fire in winter and a large, sunny garden in summer, making it a year-round favourite. There are up to three ales on handpump including Timothy Taylor Landlord (at the request of the regulars), and a number of draught lagers and ciders. There is also the choice of many more bottled drinks and a seasonally changing wine menu. Although no meals are served, the landlord has been known to offer complimentary roast potatoes on a Sunday.
(Bushey)

Potters Bar

Admiral Byng

186-192 Darkes Lane, EN6 1AF
8am-midnight (12.30am Thu-Sat) (01707) 645484
Greene King IPA, Abbot; Sharp's Doom Bar; 10 changing beers (sourced nationally) [H]

A friendly community Wetherspoon pub with a display of two model sailing ships and other memorabilia celebrating the exploits and death of Admiral Byng, who was executed for 'failing to do his utmost' to save Minorca from falling to the French in 1756 (the family estate is nearby). In summer the frontage of the pub is opened onto the street, with additional seating provided. There is a good choice of real cider. ☺⊛◑&≠♣⊞🖩(84,610)🛜

Potters Crouch

Holly Bush
Bedmond Lane, AL2 3NN (off B5183 at jct of Potters Crouch Lane and Ragged Hall Lane) TL116052
🕑 12-2.30, 6-11; 12-3, 7-10.30 Sun ☎ (01727) 851792
⊕ thehollybushpub.co.uk
Fuller's London Pride, ESB; Gale's Seafarers Ale ⊞
This charming wisteria-covered early 17th-century pub sits in rural surroundings. Attractively furnished throughout, it has large oak tables and period chairs. With a convivial, conversational atmosphere, there are no jukeboxes, slot machines or TVs to disturb guests in any of the three pleasant bar areas. The food menu is not extensive but is of high quality. Well-behaved children are welcome. The garden is ideal in summer. Q☺⊛◑&P🖩

Preston

Red Lion 🏆 🅛
The Green, SG4 7UD (on green at crossroads)
🕑 12-2.30 (3.30 Sat), 5.30-11; 12-3.30, 7-10.30 Sun
☎ (01462) 459585 ⊕ theredlionpreston.co.uk
Fuller's London Pride; Young's Bitter; 3 changing beers (sourced nationally) ⊞
This attractive free house stands on the village green and was the first community-owned pub in Great Britain. It offers a variety of beers, many from small breweries. Fresh home-made food is served, often featuring locally sourced ingredients (no food Sun eve and Mon). The pub hosts the village cricket teams and fundraises for charity. CAMRA branch Pub of the Year 2018. Q☺⊛◑♣⊕P🖩🐾🛜

St Albans

Garibaldi ✅
61 Albert Street, AL1 1RT
🕑 2.30-11 Mon; 1-11 Tue & Wed; 1-11.30 Thu; 12-midnight Fri & Sat; 12-10 Sun ☎ (01727) 894745
⊕ garibaldistalbans.co.uk
Fuller's London Pride, ESB; Gale's Seafarers Ale, HSB; 2 changing beers (sourced nationally) ⊞
A community back-street local, in the heart of Sopwell near the cathedral. Serving an extensive range of Fuller's ales, the licensees received both the Fuller's Master Cellarman and Pride and Passion awards in 2017. The pub hosts regular live music on Saturday nights, occasional quiz nights, food nights and charity events throughout the year. A former CAMRA branch Most Improved Pub. ☺⊛◑≠♣🖩🐾🛜

Great Northern ✅
172 London Road, AL1 1PQ
🕑 11.30-11; 12-12.30am Fri & Sat; 12-11 Sun
☎ (01727) 730867 ⊕ greatnorthernpub.co.uk
Black Sheep Best Bitter; 3 changing beers (sourced nationally) ⊞

Originally called The Alma, the pub changed its name due to the nearby preserved railway station – alas, there are no longer any trains. Next door to the Odyssey Cinema, this is an independent Grade II-listed pub. It has a pleasant contemporary feel and offers a food menu of British classic dishes and Sunday roasts. There is a quiz every Tuesday night and a beer festival is held in July. ☺⊛◑&≠♣🖩🛜

Lower Red Lion 🅛
34-36 Fishpool Street, AL3 4RX
🕑 12-11 (10 Sun) ☎ (01727) 855669
⊕ thelowerredlion.co.uk
Tring Side Pocket for a Toad; 6 changing beers (sourced nationally) ⊞
Classic Grade II-listed pub located in a conservation area between the city centre and the site of Roman Verulamium – the pub stands in one of St Albans' most picturesque streets. The Lower Red was an early champion of CAMRA's values in the real ale revival movement and continues to stock quality real ales, ciders and perries. Home-cooked food is served lunchtimes and weekday evenings. Wednesday is curry night. B&B is available. Q⊛🛏◑♣⊕P🖩🐾🛜

Mermaid
98 Hatfield Road, AL1 3RL
🕑 12-midnight (11 Mon & Tue); 12-10.30 Sun
☎ (01727) 845700
Oakham Citra; 5 changing beers (sourced nationally) ⊞
Friendly, welcoming community local catering both for regulars and the after-work crowd. Oakham Citra and five regularly changing guests are always available, including a stout or porter, plus 15 real ciders and perries, as well as a selection of bottled foreign beers. Wednesday is live music night. Two beer festivals are hosted during the year and a 50-plus cider and perry festival at the end of May. A regular winner of the CAMRA branch Cider & Perry Pub of the Year competition. ⊛◑≠♣⊕P🖩(601/602,655)🐾🛜

Olde Fighting Cocks 🅛 ✅
16 Abbey Mill Lane, AL3 4HE
🕑 12-11 (midnight Fri & Sat); 12-10.30 Sun
☎ (01727) 869152 ⊕ yeoldefightingcocks.co.uk
Farr Brew Our Greatest Golden, Black Listed IBA; Purity Pure UBU; 6 changing beers (sourced nationally) ⊞
The Fighters claims to be the oldest pub in England, dating from the late 8th century, though the current building was completed in 1485. Some original features remain including the low ceilings, a bread oven next to one of the open fireplaces and of course the cockpit. Up to 16 real ales are available in the summer months. Not to be missed following a visit to the Abbey and nearby Roman remains in Verulamium Park. Parking nearby can be difficult. ☺⊛◑&♣⊕🖩🐾🛜

Robin Hood ✅
126 Victoria Street, AL1 3TG
🕑 12-11 (11.30 Fri & Sat); 12-10.30 Sun ☎ (01727) 856459
⊕ robin-hood-st-albans.co.uk
Harvey's Sussex Best Bitter; 2 changing beers (sourced nationally) ⊞
A warm and friendly single-bar community pub handy for St Albans City station and popular with homeward-bound commuters of an evening. Real cider or perry is always available to complement

the rotating beer range, as is the widest selection of pickled eggs you are likely to find. A secluded garden to the rear offers summer enjoyment, while traditional table skittles provides entertainment all year round. Toasted sandwiches are available lunchtimes (Mon-Fri).
👪❀☀☕♣🍴🖵🐾🐾🛜

Six Bells 🅛 ✅
16-18 St Michael's Street, AL3 4SH
🕐 11.30-11 (midnight Fri-Sun) ☎ (01727) 856945
🌐 the-six-bells.com
Oakham JHB; Timothy Taylor Landlord; Tring Ridgeway; 3 changing beers (sourced nationally) Ⓗ
Within the heart of Roman Verulamium and the attractive St Michael's village, this characterful 16th-century timbered pub is a short walk from the city centre and Abbey, and close to Verulamium Museum. It offers three regular beers and three changing guests – one always from a Hertfordshire brewer – plus real cider in the summer months. Good-quality home-cooked food is served lunchtimes and evenings (no food Sun eve). Outside there is a pleasant patio area.
👪❀☕◑♣🍴🖵(300/301)🐾🛜

White Hart Tap 🅛
4 Keyfield Terrace, AL1 1QJ
🕐 11-11; 12-11 Sun ☎ (01727) 860974
🌐 whitehearttap.co.uk
Castle Rock Harvest Pale; Timothy Taylor Landlord; Brakspear Bitter; Sharp's Doom Bar; 3 changing beers (sourced nationally) Ⓗ
Welcoming, one-bar, back-street local featuring three beers three free of tie. It also brews occasional beers on the premises in various styles. Good-value, home-cooked food is served lunchtimes and Monday to Saturday evenings, with roasts on Sunday and monthly themed food nights. Quiz night is Wednesday. There is a public car park opposite the pub and a heated, covered smoking area outside. Barbecues are held in the summer and several beer festivals hosted throughout the year. 👪❀☕◑♣♣🍴🖵🐾🛜

White Lion ✅
91 Sopwell Lane, AL1 1RN
🕐 12-11 ☎ (01727) 850540 🌐 whitelionstalbans.co.uk
Dark Star Hophead; Oakham Citra; St Austell Tribute; 3 changing beers (sourced nationally) Ⓗ
Recently refurbished, this 16th-century pub balances the traditional and contemporary. An intimate front bar is dominated by seven handpumps with four guest beers, while a larger main bar provides comfort for drinkers and diners, as well as newspapers and games. The large rear garden is a sunny summer haven and offers quick access to the locally revered 'golden triangle' of fine pubs, of which the White Lion is a part. Excellent home-cooked food is served lunchtimes and evenings. Live music plays on Tuesday.
👪❀☕◑☀♣🖵🐾🛜

St Pauls Walden

Strathmore Arms 🅛
London Road, SG4 8BT TL193222
🕐 6-11 Mon; 12-2.30, 5-11 Tue-Thu; 12-11 Fri & Sat; 12-10.30 Sun ☎ (01438) 871654 🌐 thestrathmorearms.co.uk
Tring Side Pocket for a Toad; 4 changing beers (sourced nationally) Ⓗ
On the Bowes-Lyon estate, this pub has been serving drinkers since 1882, offering a constantly

changing list of guest beers from obscure breweries. Unusual bottled beers are also available along with real ciders and perries. A regular in the Guide since 1981, the pub displays a full collection of the Guide going back to 1976. It has a separate snug. Pizza and pasta evening is Wednesday and gourmet food nights are held on occasion (booking essential). Well known for fundraising locally.
Q👪❀☕◑▲♣🍴🖵🐾🛜

Sawbridgeworth

Old Bell
38 Bell Street, CM21 9AN
🕐 11-11 (midnight Thu & Sat); 11-1am Fri; 12-11 Sun
☎ (01279) 725052
Adnams Broadside; Woodforde's Wherry; 1 changing beer (sourced nationally) Ⓗ
This 16th-century timber-framed pub among Bell Street's traditional village shops is cosy and friendly. There is a side bar where food is served and a popular courtyard and sunny garden with a children's play area for the summer. A quiz is held on Sunday evening and a ukulele jam session on Tuesday evening. Real cider and perry are always available. 👪❀☕◑♣🍴🖵🐾🛜

Standon

Star ✅
62 High Street, SG11 1LB
🕐 12-3, 5-11; 12-11.30 Fri & Sat; 12-11 Sun
☎ (01920) 823725 🌐 star-standon.co.uk
Greene King IPA, Abbot; 2 changing beers Ⓗ
Traditional 17th-century pub with exposed wooden beams. It has a separate sports-themed public bar and a quiet and comfortable saloon/restaurant. Food is classic pub grub with roasts on Sunday. Two guest beers are offered, at least one sourced independently of Greene King – usually from a small independent local brewer.
👪❀☕◑♣🖵(331,386)🐾🛜

Therfield

Fox & Duck
Village Green, SG8 9PN
🕐 closed Mon; 12-3, 5.30-midnight; 12-midnight Sat; 12-10 Sun ☎ (01763) 287246 🌐 thefoxandduck.co.uk
Greene King IPA, Abbot; 2 changing beers (sourced nationally) Ⓗ
Charming country pub-restaurant rebuilt in the 19th century, next to the Hertfordshire Way and Icknield Way long-distance footpaths. Food is available from à la carte, bar or children's menus. Quiz night is on the first Sunday of the month, with live music, a barbecue and bouncy castle on bank holiday Sundays. There is children's play equipment in the garden and there are tables on the village green. The pub is a multiple winner in the Hertfordshire Food and Drink awards.
👪❀☕◑♣🖵(23,24)🐾🛜

Tring

King's Arms 🅛
King Street, HP23 6BE (corner of Queen St and King St in middle of Tring Triangle) SP921111
🕐 12-2.30, 5.30 (5 Fri)-11.30; 12-11.30 Sat & Sun
☎ (01442) 823318 🌐 kingsarmstring.co.uk
Tring Moongazing; 4 changing beers (sourced nationally; often Chiltern) Ⓗ

This is a light, open and airy pub in the centre of Tring, popular with all ages. The atmosphere is bustling, with a friendly welcome assured. There is always an excellent choice of well-kept real ales and one real cider. A fantastic range of classic pub food is served, along with some international favourites, lunchtimes and evenings. There is no music or TV. An annual beer festival is held on the August bank holiday.
Q (64,500/501)

Robin Hood

1 Brook Street, HP23 5ED (at 4635/B486 jct)
11.30-11 (11.30 Fri); 12-11.30 Sat; 12-11 Sun
(01442) 824912 therobinhoodtring.co.uk
Fuller's Oliver's Island, London Pride, ESB; Gale's Seafarers Ale; 1 changing beer (sourced nationally; often Fuller's)
The Robin Hood is a classic Fuller's pub dating back to the 17th century on the edge of Tring town. The pub has a courtyard beer garden for summer evenings. There is a friendly welcome and a cosy, country-pub ambience. It offers a well-kept selection of Fuller's beers, with one changing ale. Classic pub food is served, with a Thai food night every Sunday. Q

Ware

Waterside Inn

Bridgefoot, SG12 9DW
10-11 (midnight Thu-Sat); 10-10.30 Sun
(01920) 468628
Adnams Ghost Ship; St Austell Tribute, Proper Job; 5 changing beers (sourced nationally)
Popular, large, town-centre pub beside the River Lea. The award-winning garden/patio is a summer suntrap where beers can be enjoyed against the backdrop of passing narrowboats and rivercraft. A fine bank of eight handpumps dispenses three regular and five guest ales, including some local beers from Hertfordshire's New River, Farr and Tring breweries. Good-value food is served all day and the pub hosts a well-attended quiz on Wednesday evening.
P (331,395)

Wareside

Chequers

Ware Road, SG12 7QY
12-3, 6-11; 12-4, 6.30-10.30 Sun (01920) 467010
Adnams Southwold Bitter; house beer (by Hadham); 1 changing beer (sourced regionally)
A rural free house dating from the 15th century, the Chequers was originally a coaching inn and has three distinct bars plus a restaurant. All the food is home made and reasonably priced, with plenty of vegetarian options. Walkers and cyclists are welcome, making this a good base for a ramble. No machines, no music, and a ban on swearing!
Q P (M3,M4)

Watford

Wellington Arms

2 Woodford Road, WD17 1PA
11-11 (11.30 Fri & Sat); 12-10.30 Sun (01923) 220739
wellingtonarmshotel.co.uk
Fuller's London Pride; 2 changing beers (sourced locally; often Tring)
Run by the same family for 29 years, this modernised free house has a focus on live sport, with major events displayed on various screens around the pub. The Wellington is conveniently located on a street corner between Watford Junction station and the town centre. Food is available until 9pm Monday to Thursday, 5pm Friday, and occasionally at weekends before Watford home games. There are 12 letting rooms.
(Junction) P

Wheathampstead

Reading Rooms

36 The High Street, AL4 8AA
12-9.30 (01582) 833000
3 changing beers (sourced locally; often Farr Brew)
The first brewery-owned micropub and bottle shop in south Hertfordshire, opened in June 2018. It is run by Farr Brew who are based on Samuels Farm two miles away, where there has been a taproom open on Saturday for several years. A former florists', the building has been transformed, with three distinct rooms including the whole of the upper floor. Two beers from Farr Brew feature, along with one guest and a real cider. Spirits from the local Black Bridge Distillery are also stocked.
Q (610,657)

Wild Hill

Woodman

45 Wildhill Road, AL9 6EA (between A1000 and B158)
TL264068
11.30-2.30, 5.30-11; 12-3.30, 7-10.30 Sun
(01707) 642618
Greene King IPA, Abbot; 4 changing beers (sourced nationally)
This superb inn is an unpretentious, friendly, rural community local. Ninety per cent wet-led, it thrives on and is a staunch supporter of real ale, with six beers including four guests. Lined oversized glasses are available on request. The large garden is ideal in summer. Good pub grub is served lunchtimes (no food Sun). Look for God's Waiting Room. Twelve-times winner of local CAMRA Pub of the Year and three times Hertfordshire CAMRA Pub of the Year. P

Wilstone

Half Moon

60 Tring Road, HP23 4PD
12-11 (01442) 826410
Sharp's Doom Bar; Tring Side Pocket for a Toad; 1 changing beer (sourced locally; often Malt, Tring, XT)
This is a lovely unspoilt pub in an attractive village with the canal nearby. Three beers are on handpump and good home-cooked food is served. Very popular with the locals and dog walkers, there are gardens front and back. Accommodation is in a self-catering cottage. Q P (164)

What care I how time advances: I am drinking ale today. **Edgar Allan Poe**

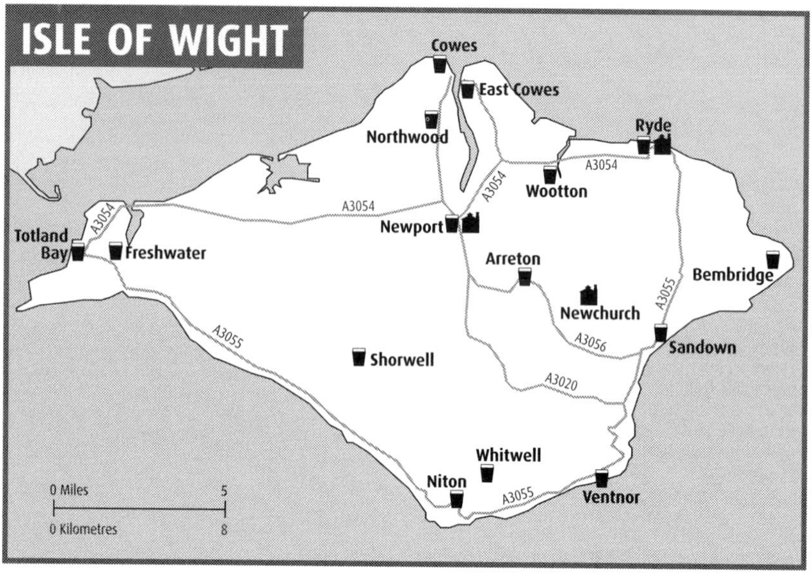

Arreton

Dairyman's Daughter

Main Road, PO30 3AA (on main road to Arreton from Newport) SZ53258680

10-11; 10-10.30 Sun (01983) 539361

thedairymansdaughter.com

Ringwood Razorback, Fortyniner; 4 changing beers (sourced nationally; often Lancaster Bomber)

Arreton Barns Craft Village includes the Dairyman's, Shipwreck Centre and Maritime Museum and IW Studio Glass, all worth visiting, plus the 11th-century church of St George and the grave of the original Dairyman's Daughter. The pub provides up to six beers including local ales, plus a large selection of bottled beers, in the old on-site brewery. Breakfast, lunch and evening meals can be enjoyed indoors or in the garden. Tuesday is folk night and live music plays on Friday, Saturday and Sunday. P(8)

Bembridge

Old Village Inn

61 High Street, PO35 5SF

12-11 (midnight Fri & Sat); 12-10.30 Sun

(01983) 872616 yeoldevillageinn.co.uk

4 changing beers (sourced nationally; often Brains, Joseph Holt, Marston's)

The Old Village is a welcome addition to the Bembridge scene, specialising in local meat and fish dishes. A fine choice of real ales and wines is served in a refined and relaxed atmosphere. Food is served 12-3pm and 5-9pm. Live music plays on Friday and Saturday, and a popular quiz is held on Monday. There is a patio area to the rear and a pétanque terrain. The pizza oven and outdoor covered area are recent additions.
Q P(8)

Cowes

Anchor Inn

1 High Street, PO31 7SA (opp Sainsbury's supermarket)

11-11 (midnight Fri & Sat); 12-10.30 Sun

(01983) 292823 theanchorcowes.co.uk

Fuller's London Pride; Goddards Fuggle-Dee-Dum; 2 changing beers (sourced nationally; often Fuller's)

This High Street pub, originally the Three Trumpeters back in 1704, is close to the marina, tempting visiting yachtsmen for their first pint ashore. A good selection of beer is on offer, with one Island ale and two guests always available. The varied food menu is served in prodigious quantities. Live entertainment is a regular feature. For the summer there is a pleasant courtyard beer garden. Accommodation is in seven comfortable rooms. (1)

East Cowes

Lifeboat

Britannia Way, PO32 6UB

10-11 (10.30 Sun) (01983) 292711

thelifeboatcowes.co.uk

Fuller's London Pride; Goddards Fuggle-Dee-Dum; 1 changing beer (sourced nationally)

Large, comfortable, waterfront bar and restaurant, in the heart of East Cowes marina. The modern interior is tastefully decorated with much wood and bare brick. The decked patio has a superb view over the river and marina activities, and is surrounded by stylish contemporary buildings. The focus here is on food but a good range of well-kept beers is available. The bar closes at 10.30pm in winter. Q P(4,5)

Ship & Castle

21 Castle Street, PO32 6RB

12-11 (midnight Sun) (01983) 716230

Fuller's London Pride; 2 changing beers (sourced regionally; often Goddards, Island)

Handy for the ferry terminal and near the floating bridge to Cowes, the pub has retained its character as a town-centre drinking establishment. Not overly large, you are assured of a warm welcome. After several years of being mishandled by a pubco, it is now a free house with three well-kept real ales on offer, even in winter. Prices are

reasonable, especially during happy hour. Frequent and very lively music sessions are hosted.
Q🐴⛺🚌(4,5)🐾📶

Freshwater

Red Lion Ⓛ

Church Place, PO40 9BP (leaving Freshwater, follow Hook Hill towards the Causeway) SZ34508738
🕘 11-11 (10.30 Sun) ☎ (01983) 754925
🌐 redlion-freshwater.co.uk
St Austell Proper Job; 3 changing beers (sourced nationally; often Adnams, Long Man, West Berkshire) Ⓗ
Former three-bar coaching inn dating back to the 11th century, now converted to one large bar but still retaining much of its character. It is situated in the most picture-postcard area of Freshwater in the church square and by the Causeway, and enjoys splendid views of the River Yar towards Yarmouth. The pub is noted for its fine food (diners are advised to book ahead). May close earlier during the winter. Q❀◐◑P🚌(7,12)🐾📶

Newport

Bargeman's Rest Ⓛ

Little London Quay, PO30 5BS
🕘 10.30-11 (10.30 Sun) ☎ (01983) 525828
🌐 bargemansrest.com
Goddards Fuggle-Dee-Dum; Ringwood Razorback; 4 changing beers (often Marston's, Wychwood) Ⓗ
This massive locally owned pub has previously been an animal feed store and a sail and rigging loft for the barge fleet that once used the river. The huge bar room provides intimate drinking areas, and the nautical memorabilia, decor and ambience are what you would expect from a traditional, well-seasoned pub. The outdoor drinking area is only a few feet from the bustling River Medina. Beer and food are consistently good and the range is varied. Live entertainment features most nights.
🐴❀◐◑♿P🚌🐾📶

Man in the Moon Ⓛ ✔

16-17 St James' Street, PO30 5HB
🕘 8am-midnight (1am Fri & Sat) ☎ (01983) 530126
Greene King Abbot; Sharp's Doom Bar; 7 changing beers (often Goddards, Island) Ⓗ
Opened in 2014, this impressive Wetherspoon conversion of the former Congregational Church maintains the character of the original while adding sympathetic extensions. The drinking and dining areas include an upstairs gallery and an outdoor area where dogs and children are welcome. Although a food-led pub, the beers are well kept, with a good selection of local brews among the large rotating selection of ales. You may find the excellent Island Brewery RDA here and often a cider on handpump. 🐴❀◐◑♿🍎🚌📶

Newport Ale House Ⓛ

24A Holyrood Street, PO30 5AZ
🕘 12-11; 11-midnight Fri & Sat; 12-10.30 Sun
☎ (01983) 559376 🌐 newportalehouse.co.uk
3 changing beers (sourced nationally) Ⓖ
Situated in a Grade II-listed building that has previously traded as a hairdresser's, undertakers and posting house and stables. It is the Island's smallest pub, recalling the days when there were many such establishments in Newport. This is a hugely popular venue with all generations, where conversation comes easy – it can get crowded and noisy. Live music is hosted, often on a Sunday afternoon. The beer choice is always interesting and varied. No meals, but snacks are high-quality locally sourced pies, rolls and sandwiches.
Q🐴🍎🚌🐾

Niton

Joe's Bar Ⓛ ✔

High Street, PO38 2AZ (centre of village)
🕘 11-11; 12-10 Sun ☎ (01983) 730280
Dartmoor Jail Ale; 2 changing beers (often Blue Monkey, Charnwood, Yates') Ⓗ
Joe's opened when the village inn closed for a short time and has since become the hub of village life, also serving as a post office, tea room, confectioner and newsagent. This thriving pub now serves food seven days a week, with a full-time chef and a wood-fired pizza oven. Ruby Mild and Plum Porter are regular visitors. A unique pub with an excellent garden and patio. Q🐴❀◐◑🚌(6)

Northwood

Travellers Joy Ⓛ ✔

85 Pallance Road, PO31 8LS SZ48009360
🕘 12-midnight ☎ (01983) 298024
🌐 travellersjoycowes.co.uk
Island Wight Gold; Theakston Old Peculier; 3 changing beers (sourced nationally; often Brains) Ⓗ
This long-standing country inn was the Island's first beer exhibition house and offers up to five ales including local favourite Island Brewery Wight Gold. Real cider is usually available. A good range of home-cooked food is served. With a well-cared-for garden and play area, and camping nearby, the pub is a good base for visitors as well as a thriving local community centre. Popular events are Derek's Sunday quiz and bingo night on Monday.
Q🐴❀◐◑⛺♣🍎P🚌(1)🐾📶

Ryde

Castle Inn

164 High Street, PO33 2HT
🕘 10-11.30; 11-11.30 Sun ☎ (01983) 613684
🌐 castleinnisleofwight.co.uk
Fuller's London Pride; Gale's HSB; 1 changing beer (often Fuller's) Ⓗ
The year 1850 saw the opening of this large public house by Thomas Vanner, who operated the Ryde to Newport stagecoach. A fine building that stands proud at the junction with the High Street, it is Grade II-listed owing to its impressive etched windows, which may have saved it from demolition or conversion in the mid '80s. It has enjoyed a long-standing reputation for its ales; HSB is a best-seller and is always in wonderful condition. Snacks are available. 🐴❀⇌♣🚌🐾📶

Railway 🏆 Ⓛ

68 St Johns Road, PO33 2RT (by St Johns Station)
🕘 3-11; 12-midnight Sat & Sun ☎ (01983) 611500
6 changing beers (often Heritage, Island) Ⓗ/Ⓖ

REAL ALE BREWERIES

Goddards Ryde
Island Newport
Yates' Newchurch

Refurbished to a high standard by the previous owner, the pub has retained the flagstone floors, beams and plenty of wood. For the horticulturally minded, note the ginkgo biloba tree in the garden, a species whose ancestry can be traced back over 200 million years. The handy train station is just yards away, bringing visitors from Portsmouth to enjoy the competitively priced, quality real ales. Six handpumps feature one regular and many changing beers. Live music is hosted on Friday. (St Johns) (2,8)

S Fowler & Co

41-43 Union Street, PO33 2LF (top of Union St)
7am-midnight (1am Fri & Sat); 8am-midnight Sun
(01983) 812112
10 changing beers (sourced nationally)
Although not the most charismatic pub in the Wetherspoon chain, this converted drapery store offers a varied range of well-kept beers. The pub is in the centre of town, with a bus stop conveniently outside. The pub name was at the suggestion of the local CAMRA branch – not only is Fowler the name of the former store, but also that of the first local CAMRA chairman and revered early campaigner. The family-friendly food area is upstairs. **Q**

Sandown

Castle Inn

12-14 Fitzroy Street, PO36 8HY (off High St)
11-11 (midnight Fri); 10.30-midnight Sat & Sun
(01983) 403169 sandowncastle.co.uk
Goddards Fuggle-Dee-Dum; Shepherd Neame Spitfire; Wadworth IPA; Wychwood Hobgoblin Gold; 2 changing beers (sourced regionally)
The Castle is an excellent town free house and locals' pub with crib and two darts teams. Six real ales are on offer including the best from local breweries. There is a children's room at the back and a patio for warm weather. The TV is only turned on for special occasions. Happy hour (5-7pm nightly) is popular, as is the Sunday quiz. Beer festivals are held twice a year, usually featuring local ales and cider. **Q** (3,8)

Shorwell

Crown Inn

Walkers Lane, PO30 3JZ
12-3, 5-10 Mon, Wed & Thu; 12-10 Tue; 12-10.30 Fri & Sat; 12-5 Sun (01983) 740293 thecrowninnshorwell.co.uk
Gale's HSB; Timothy Taylor Landlord; house beer (by Yates', IOW); 1 changing beer (sourced locally; often Goddards)
This 300-year-old hostelry in a picturesque village offers a range of four ales and a good home-cooked pub menu. The pub has a trout stream running through the garden, ducks in abundance, and plenty of car parking. There is a children's play area and free goody bags with kids' meals. The perfect stop-off point for walkers, cyclists and nature lovers, you will not be disappointed.
Q **P** (12)

Totland Bay

Highdown Inn

Highdown Lane, PO39 0HY (W of Alum Bay)
SZ32348596
11.30-11; 12.30-11 Sat (01983) 752450
highdowninn.com
3 changing beers (sourced regionally; often Goddards, Prescott)
Situated close to Farringford House, once home to Alfred Lord Tennyson, this hospitable pub is an ideal base for walkers and cyclists alike. An interesting range of home-cooked food includes a seasonal variety of fresh local game, fish and vegetables, served in generous portions, and a children's menu. B&B accommodation is in three comfortable rooms, and there is a campsite close by. Unfortunately, no buses serve the pub in winter. **Q** **P**

Waterfront

The Beach, PO39 0BQ
11-10 (11 Fri & Sat); 11-7 Sun (01983) 756969
thewaterfront-iow.co.uk
Sharp's Doom Bar; 3 changing beers (sourced regionally; often Andwell, Dorset, Island)
Pleasant and popular pub/restaurant beside the sea, enjoying excellent Solent views to Portland and beyond. Beers are reasonably priced and the range has increased in recent years, with up to 12 continually changing ales in the cellar, including stouts and milds. During the summer months there is a tented area outside, and the pub is accessible from the cliff path. Food includes a Sunday roast.
Q **P** (7,12)

Ventnor

Spyglass Inn

The Esplanade, PO38 1JX
10-11 (01983) 855338 thespyglass.co.uk
Ringwood Razorback, Fortyniner; 3 changing beers (sourced locally; often Goddards, Marston's, Yates')
Nineteenth-century ex-guesthouse at the western end of Ventnor Esplanade in a superb position overlooking the English Channel. The temptation has been avoided to knock all the rooms into one; instead they have been incorporated into the overall layout. The inn has considerable character and boasts a large collection of seafaring memorabilia. Local seafood is a speciality. There are usually five ales in summer and four in winter. Entertainment features most evenings and Sunday lunchtime, and families are welcome.
P

Volunteer

30 Victoria Street, PO38 1ES
closed Tue; 4-11; 4-12 Sat; 12-11 Sun (01983) 852537
5 changing beers (sourced regionally; often Adnams, Goddards, Marston's)
Built in 1866, this gem is one of the smallest pubs on the Island. No chips, no children, no fruit machines, no video games – just a pure adult drinking house and one of the few places where you can still play rings and enjoy a traditional games night. Run by Graham and Sue Perks, up to

five beers are available including a local brew. A former winner of local CAMRA Pub of the Year, this is a wonderful traditional establishment.
Q♣🍎🚌(3,6)🐾

Whitwell

White Horse Inn L

High Street, PO38 2PY SZ52007800
⏲ 10-11 (10 Sun) ☎ (01983) 730375
🌐 whitehorseiow.co.uk
4 changing beers (sourced nationally; often Bombardier, Goddards, Rudgate) H
Built in 1454, this stone building is considered to be the oldest established inn on the Isle of Wight. Fire destroyed the original thatch roof, which has now been replaced with more traditional slate. An extension to the side adds a family area and additional dining space. The remainder of the building is traditional, with intimate areas to the rear. Four handpumps serve a changing range of beers and the excellent food menu is extensive. A large garden is fine for children on warmer days. Breakfast is served 10am-midday.
Q🐴❀◐◑♿P🚌(6)🐾📶

Wootton

Cedars

2 Station Road, PO33 4QU
⏲ 11-11; 12-10.30 Sun ☎ (01983) 882593
🌐 cedarsisleofwight.co.uk
Fuller's London Pride; Gale's Seafarers Ale, HSB H
In a prominent position, this late Victorian two-bar village local is a large pub though, curiously, it has one of the smallest front doors on the Island. There is a children's room and a large garden with a play area. Smokers are spoilt as the outdoor smoking area is adapted from a beautiful Victorian outbuilding. An extensive food menu is offered, and the friendly bar staff ensure a welcoming atmosphere. **Q🐴❀◐◑♿⇌♣P🚌**(4,9)🐾📶

Red Lion, Freshwater (Photo: Charles Hutchins/Flickr CC BY 2.0)

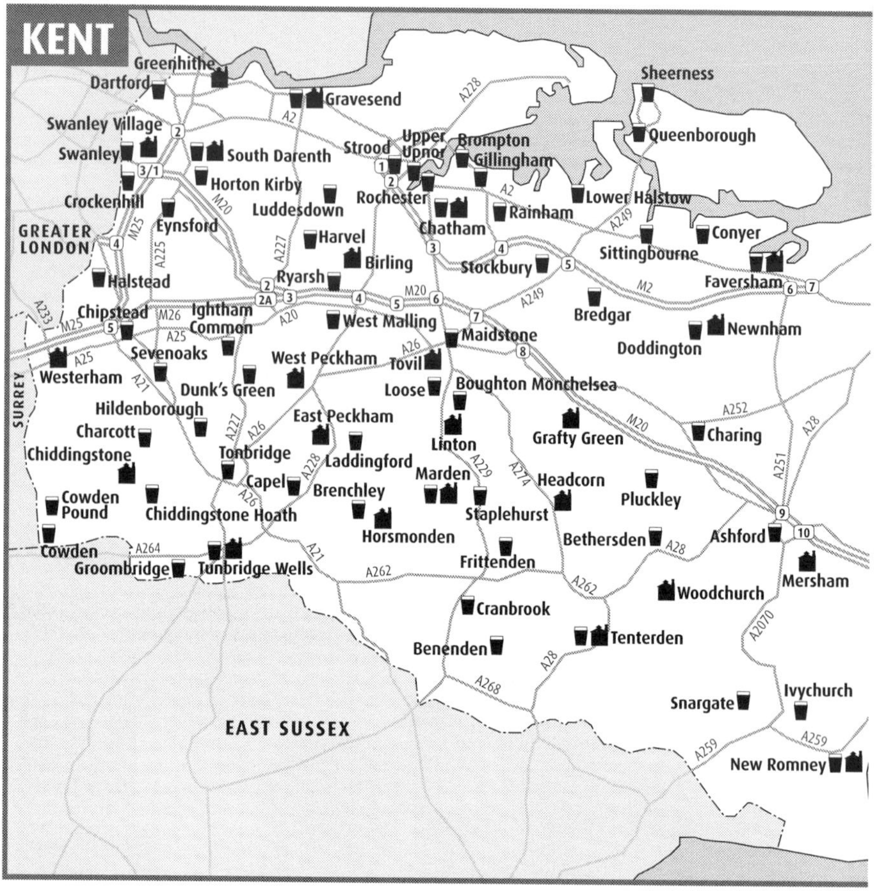

Ashford

County Hotel ✅
10 High Street, TN24 8TD (at lower end of High St)
🕐 8am-midnight (1am Fri & Sat); 8am-11 Sun
☎ (01233) 646891
Greene King Abbot; Ruddles Best Bitter; Sharp's Doom Bar; 4 changing beers (sourced nationally) Ⓗ
A spacious Wetherspoon pub in an 18th-century building in the centre of Ashford, with one bar and three separate seating areas. Originally red brick, the top floor and the parapet are now tile hung. Up to two real ciders are dispensed from polypins in the fridge. Food is available every day from 8am-11pm, and children are allowed in the dining area until 9pm. It stages summer and autumn national and international beer festivals and a summer cider festival. Q ➲ ❀ ◑ ᶀ ⇌ ● P 🚪 ☎

Beltinge

Copper Pottle Ⓛ
84 Reculver Road, CT6 6ND
🕐 closed Mon; 12-2, 6-9 Tue-Sat; 12-3 Sun ☎ 07710 001261
⊕ copperpottle.co.uk
Kent Session Pale; Ramsgate Gadds' No.5 Best Bitter Ale; 2 changing beers (sourced locally) Ⓖ
Originally a pet food shop, this friendly micropub has an attractive blue-tiled frontage. Drinks are

dispensed via a small bar counter and conversation is encouraged by the layout of high and low narrow tables. The walls are decorated with amusing posters and postcards. Every six weeks there is a charity fundraising event which might be a quiz or food evening or barbecue. The south-facing garden is a good place to enjoy the beers, ciders and wines. Open bank holiday Mondays. Q ➲ ❀ ♣ ● 🚪 (7,36) ❀

Benenden

Bull Ⓛ
The Street, TN17 4DE
🕐 12-midnight (11 Sun) ☎ (01580) 240054
⊕ thebullatbenenden.co.uk
Dark Star Hophead; Harvey's Sussex Best Bitter; Larkins Traditional Ale; 1 changing beer (sourced locally) Ⓗ
Imposing free house dating back to 1608 overlooking a picturesque village green. The public bar is dominated by a large inglenook fireplace and the interior features wooden floors and exposed oak beams throughout. Meals featuring locally grown produce can be taken in the public bar and the separate restaurant/function room (no food Sun eve). Booking is advisable for the Sunday lunchtime carvery. Acoustic music sessions are held monthly on Sunday (see website for details). Q ➲ ❀ ⌂ ◑ ♣ ● P 🚪 (297) ❀ ☎

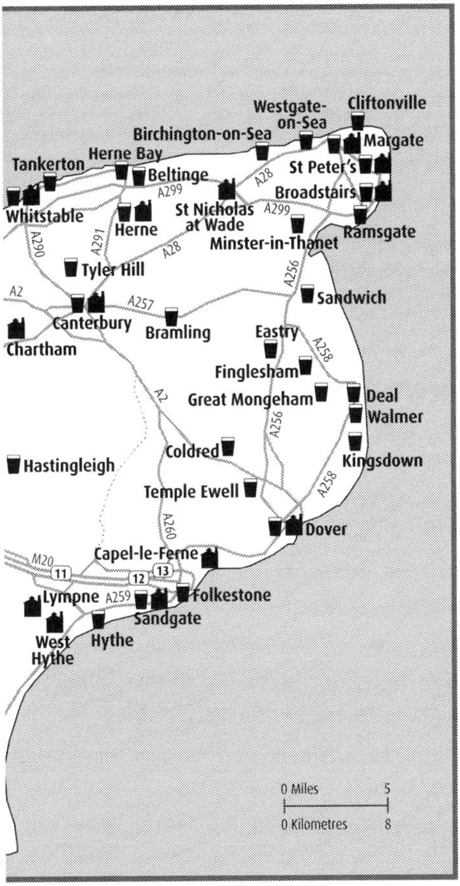

Bethersden

George 𝕃

The Street, TN26 3AG (off A28 between Ashford and Tenterden in centre of village)

12-11 ☎ (01233) 820235

Harvey's Sussex Best Bitter; St Austell Cornish Best Bitter; 2 changing beers (sourced nationally) 🄷

A two-bar free house in a picturesque Kentish village decorated with pictures of local life. The public bar is a survivor of what proper village inns used to be like: wood panelling, hops over the bar, a wood-burning stove, pub games, a jukebox, and good conversation. Food is served, except Monday lunchtime and Sunday evening, with carveries on Wednesday evening and roast lunches Sunday. A beer festival is held around St George's Day. Buses from Ashford and Tenterden stop outside.

❀♣P🚌(2)🐾

Birchington-on-Sea

Old Bay Alehouse

137 Minnis Road, CT7 9NS

closed Mon; 12.30-2, 5.30-9.30 (10.30 Fri & Sat); 12.30-4 Sun 🌐 oldbayalehouse.co.uk

3 changing beers 🄶

A fine micropub, an easy five-minute stroll from the beach at Minnis Bay, near Birchington. The bar counter serves real ales and ciders on gravity dispense from a temperature-controlled cool room behind. Seating is mostly at wall-mounted benches with high tables, but there are also some low tables and chairs and comfy armchairs in the front window. The real ale selection always includes at least one local beer. Bar snacks are available and there are occasional pop-up food events.

Q≈♣🍎🚌(34)🐾

Boughton Monchelsea

Cock Inn 𝕃 ✔

Heath Road, ME17 4JD TQ776512

11-11; 12-9 Sun ☎ (01622) 743166

🌐 cockinnmaidstone.co.uk

Shepherd Neame Master Brew, Spitfire Gold; 2 changing beers (sourced nationally; often Shepherd Neame) 🄷

A 16th-century coaching inn built to provide lodgings for Canterbury pilgrims, full of character, with oak beams and an inglenook fireplace. A large and varied menu complemented by real ales is served in both the bar and restaurant (no food Sun eve). There is a large patio area. Various board

REAL ALE BREWERIES

Alpha State Horsmonden (NEW)
Amazing 🛢 Sandgate
Angels and Demons Capel-le-Ferne
Boutilliers Faversham
Breakwater Dover
Brew Buddies Swanley Village
Brumaison Marden
By The Mile Broadstairs (brewing suspended)
Canterbury Ales Chartham
Canterbury Brewers 🛢 Canterbury
Dartford Wobbler South Darenth
Farriers Arms 🛢 Mersham
Fonthill 🛢 Tunbridge Wells (NEW)
Four Candles 🛢 St Peters
Goacher's Tovil
Goody Herne
Headcorn Hop Headcorn (NEW)
Hop Fuzz West Hythe
Hopdaemon Newnham
Iron Pier Gravesend
Isla Vale Margate
Kent Birling
Larkins Chiddingstone
Mad Cat Faversham
Musket Linton
NauticAles Broadstairs
Nelson Chatham
No Frills Joe Greenhithe
Northdown Margate
Old Dairy Tenterden
Pig & Porter Tunbridge Wells
Ramsgate (Gadds') Broadstairs
Range Lympne
Romney Marsh New Romney
Running Man Chatham (NEW)
Shepherd Neame Faversham
Stag Woodchurch
Swan on the Green 🛢 West Peckham
Tír Dhá Ghlas 🛢 Dover
Tonbridge East Peckham
Turnstone Whitstable
Wantsum St Nicholas at Wade
Westerham Westerham
Whitstable Grafty Green

games are available. Situated near the Greensand Way, dogs and walkers are welcome.
Q ⌂ ★ ◑ P ☒ (59) 🐾 ☏

Bramling

Haywain ⓛ
Canterbury Road, CT3 1NB
🕓 7.30-11 Mon; 12-3, 6-11 Tue-Sat; 12-4 Sun
☎ (01227) 720676 ⊕ thehaywainbramling.co.uk
Bombardier; Fuller's London Pride; 2 changing beers (sourced regionally; often Goacher's, Ramsgate, Whitstable) Ⓗ
Classic friendly country pub featuring hop bines and a cosy snug. Traditional games include darts and bat and trap. They have a Monday quiz night, a Wednesday crib night, a cheese club on the last Sunday of the month, and jazz on the last Tuesday. Guest beers are usually from Kent breweries and an annual beer festival is hosted over the late spring bank holiday weekend in a marquee in the attractive garden. Excellent home-cooked food, using local produce, is served.
⌂ ★ ◑ ♣ P ☒ (43) 🐾

Bredgar

Sun Inn
The Street, ME9 8EY
🕓 12-11 ☎ (01622) 884221 ⊕ thesuninn.co.uk
Sharp's Sea Fury; Shepherd Neame Master Brew; 1 changing beer (often Adnams) Ⓗ
Near to Sittingbourne and a village inn since the early 1700s, the pub, recently refurbished, has a sizeable front bar room with a long bar separating it from the large Old Barn restaurant to the rear. The front bar is warmed by a real fire. The clientele is a mixture of locals plus passing trade. Tastefully in keeping with its surroundings, the pub is food-led but does offer a fair choice of cask beers. A pub quiz is on the first Wednesday of the month and music nights are planned monthly. ⌂ ★ ◑ ₺ P ☒ 🐾

Brenchley

Halfway House ⓛ ✪
Horsmonden Road, TN12 7AX (½ mile SE of village)
🕓 12-11 (10.30 Sun) ☎ (01892) 722526
⊕ halfwayhousebrenchley.co.uk
Dark Star Hophead; Goacher's Fine Light Ale; Kent Session Pale; Skinner's Betty Stogs; Westerham 1965 Special Bitter Ale; Young's Special; 3 changing beers (sourced locally; often Cellar Head, Musket, Tonbridge) Ⓖ
Former coaching inn on the road to Horsmonden. It is a renowned free house and longstanding Guide entry, serving seven permanent and two or three guest beers direct from cooled casks, along with Chiddingstone and Turners ciders. Hops hang from wooden beams in rooms arranged over many levels; farming and brewery memorabilia and open fires combine to provide a cosy, rustic ambience. Beer festivals over Whitsun and August bank holidays are held in the garden, which includes its own bar and separate family area.
Q ⌂ ★ ◑ ♣ ₺ P ☒ (297) 🐾 ☏

Broadstairs

Mind the Gap
156 High Street, CT10 1JB
✪ closed Mon; 12-10.30 ☎ 07790 730205
3 changing beers Ⓖ
This micropub opened July 2016 in a former retail premises close to the town's railway station, hence its name. The pub is on two levels, with a seating area on the ground floor and a bar counter and cold room on the upper one. Usual micropub fare is on offer including real cider/perry and wine. It is railway themed, including a length of mainline rail used as a footrest in the upstairs bar. ⇌ ♣ ◑ ☒ 🐾

Brompton

King George V ⓛ
1 Prospect Row, ME7 5AL
🕓 12-11 (10.30 Sun) ☎ (01634) 842418
Tonbridge Coppernob; 2 changing beers (sourced locally; often Iron Pier, Mad Cat) Ⓗ
Picturesque and historic pub decorated throughout with military memorabilia. Three cask beers are available on handpump and four craft ales including a stout, all from Kentish breweries. A variety of Belgian bottled beers and, for spirit lovers, a range of gins, rums and whiskies are sold. Food is served every day, with roasts on Sundays, when booking is required. The pub also offers three en-suite rooms for guests. It has an outside covered area for smokers.
⌂ ★ ◑ ♣ ₺ ☒ (101,182) ☏

Canterbury

Dolphin
17 St Radigund's Street, CT1 2AA
🕓 12-11 (midnight Thu-Sat) ☎ (01227) 455963
⊕ thedolphincanterbury.co.uk
Sharp's Doom Bar; Timothy Taylor Landlord; 1 changing beer (sourced locally; often Ramsgate) Ⓗ
Friendly local decorated with 1950-1970 memorabilia, free of TV screens but with a comprehensive collection of board games. Pub food in generous portions is served, with roasts on Sundays. The attractive veranda is popular with diners, and there is a large suntrap garden, in which Henri the H van sells rotisserie food. One handpump serves cider, and there is a changing range of beers on other pumps. Opening hours vary from month to month (see website).
⌂ ★ ◑ ⇌ ♣ ☒ 🐾 ☏

Eight Bells ✪
34 London Road, CT2 8LN
🕓 3-11; 12-midnight Fri & Sat; 12-10.30 Sun
☎ (01227) 454794
Young's Bitter, Special Ⓗ
Small, traditional local dating from 1708 and rebuilt in 1902, retaining original embossed windows and decorated with memorabilia. It hosts live music fortnightly on Fridays and a quiz, usually on the last Wednesday of the month. Five darts teams play every week and their trophies are on display. Food is served Sunday lunchtime only. The pub has a small, attractive walled garden and a comfortable heated smoking area. ⌂ ★ ◑ ⇌ ♣ ☒ 🐾 ☏

Foundry Brew Pub ⓛ
77 Stour Street, CT1 2NR (just off High St)
☼ 12-midnight; 12-10 Sun ☎ (01227) 455899
⊕ thefoundrycanterbury.co.uk
Canterbury Foundryman's Gold, Foundry Torpedo, Streetlight Porter; 3 changing beers (often Canterbury) Ⓗ
The new home of Canterbury Brewers & Distillers, with a large bar area from which double doors open into the attractive brewery and restaurant area. Six ales are usually on tap, all brewed on the premises. They also produce their own cider, vodka, rum and gin. Good-value pub food is available till 8pm (6pm Sun and Mon, 9pm Fri and Sat). There is a small seating area outside.
≿✸⓪Åᖱ≋●ᕱ🕏

New Inn
19 Havelock Street, CT1 1NP (off ring road near St Augustine's Abbey)
☼ 12-3, 5.30-11.30; 12-midnight Fri & Sat; 12-11.30 Sun
☎ (01227) 464584 ⊕ newinncanterbury.co.uk
7 changing beers (often Oakham, Ramsgate, Thornbridge) Ⓗ
Victorian back-street terraced house a few minutes' walk from the Cathedral, St Augustine's Abbey and bus station. The main bar has a cosy woodburner and a jukebox. At the back is a long, bright conservatory with newspapers and a range of board games. Beer festivals are held over the Whitsun and August bank holiday weekends in the pub and the attractive garden. A large whisky and gin selection is available alongside the changing range of seven cask beers. ≿✸♣●ᕱ🕏

Thomas Tallis Alehouse ⓛ
48 Northgate, CT1 1BE
☼ 5-9.30 Mon; 2-11 Tue-Thu; 12-11 Fri & Sat; 12-10 Sun
⊕ thethomastallisalehouse.co.uk
3 changing beers (sourced locally; often Kent, Old Dairy, Ramsgate) Ⓖ
Canterbury's first micropub-style alehouse, in a lovely 15th-century half-timbered building, part of the historic Hospital of St John. Three different Kent cask beers and many national and international beers in KeyKeg, bottle and can are stocked, as well as five to six Kentish ciders. One of the two front rooms has a log-burning stove, the rear snug has armchairs and a sofa. Generally, a seat/table service applies. Outside seating is available on the street. Q≿✸≋♣●ᕱ🕏

Unicorn ⓛ ✓
61 St Dunstan's Street, CT2 8BS
☼ 11.30-11 (midnight Fri & Sat) ☎ (01227) 463187
⊕ unicorninn.com
4 changing beers (often Hopdaemon, Long Man, Shepherd Neame) Ⓗ
Comfortable 1604 pub near the historic Westgate, with an attractive suntrap garden. Bar billiards is played and a quiz, set by regular customers, is held every Sunday evening. One guest beer is often from one of several Kent microbreweries, and beer updates are posted on Facebook and Twitter. It also has a good range of bottled beers. Food is good value, with a two-meals-for-£12 special offer on selected meals. Sporting events (not Sky) are televised unobtrusively. Q≿✸⓪≋♣●ᕱ🕏

Capel

Dovecote Inn
Alders Road, TN12 6SU (½ mile W of A228 towards Tudeley)
☼ 5.30-10.30 Mon; 12-3, 5.30-11.30; 12-10.30 Sun
☎ (01892) 835966 ⊕ dovecote-capel.co.uk
Gale's HSB; Harvey's Sussex Best Bitter; 3 changing beers (sourced nationally; often Hook Norton, Long Man, Wye Valley) Ⓖ
Surrounded by orchards and hop fields, the pub is a popular destination for walkers attracted by the choice of five ales served direct from the cask alongside Westons Old Rosie cider. Substantial dishes of locally sourced, home-cooked food, including pies and puddings, are served in the restaurant, snug and bar, or alfresco in the rear shaded patio. The hop-strewn interior is especially cosy in winter when log fires burn. There is a children's play area and garden where bat and trap is played during summer months.
Q≿✸⓪Åᖱ♣●Pᕱ🕏

Charcott

Greyhound ⓛ
off Camp Hill, TN11 8LG (½ mile N of B2027 at Chiddingstone Causeway)
☼ closed Mon; 12-11; 12-8 Sun ☎ (01892) 870275
⊕ thegreyhoundcharcott.co.uk
Larkins Traditional Ale; 3 changing beers (sourced locally; often Cellar Head, Kent, Old Dairy) Ⓗ
New, young and enthusiastic owners have worked hard to revitalise this free house and transform it into the heart of the community, serving the hamlet and surrounding villages. Beers and ciders come from within a 30-mile radius, with much attention given to supporting local producers when creating the menus. Seemingly remote, the Greyhound is easily accessible from Penshurst railway station via a surfaced footpath across fields. The pub's engaging website gives information on current and forthcoming developments and special events. Q≿✸⓪≋●ᕱ(210)ᕱ

Charing

Bowl Inn
Egg Hill Road, TN27 0HG (signposted from A20 and A251)
☼ 12-11 (midnight Fri & Sat) ☎ (01233) 712256
⊕ bowlinncharing.com
Sharp's Doom Bar; 3 changing beers (sourced locally; often Hopdaemon, Wantsum, Whitstable) Ⓗ
A 16th-century free house on the top of the North Downs in an Area of Outstanding Natural Beauty. A large inglenook fire warms the bar and there is an extensive rural garden with a heated patio area. A good choice of home-cooked food includes traditional classics and ever-changing specials. The pub is a popular stop-off point for walkers and cyclists and offers five rooms. Camping is also available. An annual beer festival is held.
≿✸⇆⓪ÅPᕱ

Chatham

Prince of Wales ⓛ ✓
1-3 Railway Street, ME4 4HU

🕭 8am-11 (1.30am Fri & Sat); 12-10.30 Sun
☎ (01634) 829190 🌐 greatukpubs.co.uk/
princeofwaleschatham
**Greene King IPA; Sharp's Doom Bar; 4 changing beers
(sourced nationally; often Fuller's, Marston's,
Wantsum)** Ⓗ
In the pedestrianised area of Chatham town centre
and only a five-minute walk from the railway and
bus stations. On Tuesdays all ales are only £1.75 a
pint and it also has a loyalty card scheme. Great-
value food is served and drinkers can sit in comfort
and watch televised sports events on any of the 10
screens, located on the two floors. A large function
room is also available. The pub hosts DJ nights on
Fridays and Saturdays as well as a weekly quiz
night. ⭸❀◗❀&⬆🖵🛜

Thomas Waghorn Ⓛ ✅
14 Railway Street, ME4 4JL
🕭 9am-midnight (1am Thu-Sat) ☎ (01634) 831893
**Greene King IPA, Abbot; Sharp's Doom Bar; house
beer (by Rockin' Robin); 4 changing beers (sourced
nationally; often Wantsum)** Ⓗ
Just a short walk from the railway station and the
bus terminus, Wetherspoon has converted the
former post office into a pub on two levels, both
with outside seating. Inside there are discrete
drinking and dining areas as well as open space to
enjoy a wide range of well-kept real ales, cider and
wholesome food. A welcome outlet in the centre
of the town. ⭸❀◗&⬆♥🖵🛜

Chiddingstone Hoath

Rock Ⓛ
Hoath Corner, Rywell Road, TN8 7BS (1½ miles S of
Chiddingstone)
🕭 closed Mon; 11-11; 12-8 Sun ☎ (01892) 870296
🌐 therockpub.co.uk
**Larkins Traditional Ale; 2 changing beers (sourced
locally; often Dark Star, Long Man)** Ⓗ
Celebrating 500 years as a pub in 2020, this cosy
and characterful, two-roomed hostelry provides
hearty meals and well-kept local beer. Retaining
many original features it is extensively beamed
with a brick floor and wood-burning stove. Larkins
Brewery is less than two miles away, with its
renowned Porter available in winter. Service is
delivered with a smile. Visitors might pick up a
brace of pheasant if the shoot has been out that
day. An extensive programme of events caters for
a community dedicated to rural pursuits, with
much appreciation shown for the landlords who
have created a gem of a pub. Q⭸❀◗♣♥🐾🛜

Chipstead

Bricklayers Arms ✅
39-41 Chevening Road, TN13 2RZ (by entrance to
sailing club)
🕭 11-11.30 (midnight Fri & Sat); 11-10.30 Sun
☎ (01732) 743424 🌐 the-bricklayers-arms.co.uk
**Harvey's Sussex Best Bitter Ⓖ; 2 changing beers
(sourced locally; often Harvey's)** Ⓗ
This is a vibrant Harvey's Brewery-owned
community pub, its sign featuring Sir Winston
Churchill, who lived nearby. Sussex Best is served
direct from casks behind the bar, with Harvey's
monthly seasonal brews dispensed by handpump.
An excellent choice of home-cooked meals,
supplemented by many themed food nights, is

enjoyed in the side cottage-style restaurant or
throughout the rest of the pub. Walkers and dogs
are welcome in the flagstone-floored bar complete
with log fire. Q⭸❀◗P🖵(401)🐾🛜

Cliftonville

Banks Ale & Wine House
244 Northdown Road, CT9 2PX
🕭 2-10.45 (7 Mon); 12-10.45 Fri & Sat; 12-7 Sun
☎ (01843) 221251
3 changing beers Ⓗ
In former bank premises, this bar is tastefully
decorated with low tables and chairs and has a
collection of old keg beer fonts displayed on
shelves and window ledges. The front bar counter
has four handpumps which are purely decorative.
Real ales are dispensed either through two
handpumps or on gravity through wall taps
connected to casks in the cellar room behind the
wall. Q⭸♥🖵

Coldred

Carpenters Arms Ⓛ
The Green, CT15 5AJ
🕭 5-9 (11 Fri & Sat); 7-11 Sun ☎ (01304) 830190
**2 changing beers (often Ramsgate, Romney
Marsh)** Ⓗ
An 18th-century two-roomed pub overlooking the
village green and duck pond; a real gem and well
worth seeking out. It has been in the Fagg family
for over a century and has stayed largely
unchanged in the last 50 years. It is the centre of
the community where conversation is king. At least
two real ales are always served alongside three
real ciders, from Kentish Pip. Regular community
events are held including quizzes and vegetable
competitions. A beer festival is staged in June.
Q⭸❀♣♥🐾🛜

Conyer

Ship ✅
Conyer Quay, ME9 9HR (20-minute walk from Teynham
train station)
🕭 12-10 (11 Wed & Thu; midnight Fri); 11-11.30 Sat; 11-9.30
Sun ☎ (01795) 520881 🌐 shipinnconyer.co.uk
**3 changing beers (sourced regionally; often Adnams,
Old Dairy)** Ⓗ
An 18th-century creekside pub with a nautically
themed interior. Bare floorboards and scrubbed
pine tables add rustic charm and a real fire adds
character. Popular with the boating fraternity,
walkers and cyclists, it is located on the Saxon
Shore Way. Food, with an emphasis on local
produce, is served from noon daily. The pub has a
small courtyard garden overlooking the creek.
Q⭸❀◗♣P🖵(8,344)🐾🛜

Cowden

Fountain ✅
30 High Street, TN8 7JG (1 mile N of A264)
🕭 6-11 Mon; 12-3, 6-midnight (11 Tue); 12-11 Sun
☎ (01342) 850528 🌐 fountaincowden.com
**Harvey's IPA, Sussex Best Bitter; 1 changing beer
(sourced locally; often Harvey's)** Ⓗ

Friendly Harvey's village pub attracting locals, families, and walkers who may begin their journey from Cowden railway station, one mile away. The original bar has been expanded to incorporate a bright conservatory restaurant in which to enjoy generous helpings of fresh home-made fare, without losing any of the features or traditional atmosphere that is its hallmark. A pub for all seasons, it provides a warming log fire in winter and a lovely rear suntrap garden, complete with village mural, for summer use.
Q ❀⊛◑ ♣P☒ (234) ❀ ☎

Cowden Pound

Queen's Arms ★ 🄻
Hartfield Road, TN8 5NP (on B2026 halfway between Edenbridge and A264)
🕓 4-7.30; 5-10.30 Fri & Sat; 12-5 Sun
Larkins Traditional Ale Ⓗ
A unique gem built shortly after Queen Victoria ascended the throne and largely unchanged for more than a century, retaining a saloon and public bar complete with darts, shove-ha'penny and log fires. Local Larkins Trad and Chiddingstone cider may be accompanied by a seasonal beer and it is well worth seeking out the rare Porter served direct from the cask in winter. Lager and children are absent; friendly locals and dogs are plentiful. Customers may bring snacks to share on the bar.
Q ❀♣●P❀

Cranbrook

Larkins' Alehouse 🍸 🄻
7 High Street, TN17 3EB
🕓 2-9; 12-10 Thu & Fri; 12-10.30 Sat; 12-6 Sun
☎ 07786 707476 🌐 larkins-alehouse.co.uk
4 changing beers (sourced locally; often Cellar Head, Goacher's, Larkins) Ⓖ
Opened in 2017, this community-focused micropub is putting the heart back into the town. It comprises a single room with a small bar, simply furnished, plus a courtyard beer garden. Welcoming staff will guide you to the chalkboard displaying current beers and Kentish ciders (Biddenden, Turners), plus wines, spirits and soft drinks. Home-made pork pies, rolls and chutneys are for sale; alternatively, bring your own food or takeaways. On Sunday lunchtimes home-made food is provided by the pub and customers. Voted CAMRA branch Pub of the Year in 2019.
Q ❀⊛♣●☒ (5,297) ❀ ☎

Crockenhill

Chequers ✅
Cray Road, BR8 8LP
🕓 11-11; 12-9 Sun ☎ (01322) 662132
🌐 chequerscrockenhill.co.uk
Courage Best Bitter; 3 changing beers (sourced regionally; often Black Sheep, Fuller's, Wychwood) Ⓗ
Friendly village local. Lunches and evening meals are served, with discounts for over-55s at the beginning of the week. It holds a quiz on Monday evenings and various other events on regular occasions. Several pictures of old Crockenhill indicate that the pub has been a hub of village life for many years. ❀⊛◑♣☒ (477) ❀ ☎

Dartford

Dartford Jug 🄻
8 Market Street, DA1 1ET
🕓 1-9.30 Mon & Wed; closed Tue; 1-11.30 Thu; 12-11.30 Fri & Sat; 12-9 Sun ☎ (01322) 276600 🌐 dartford-jug.business.site
Kent Session Pale; 11 changing beers Ⓖ
Dartford's first micropub, with seating on modified beer casks at the front, leading to fixed tables and stools and a serving counter at the rear. The bar is decorated with a map and pictures of old Dartford. Beers and ciders (from Turners) are dispensed from a cold room, the current offerings being listed on a screen at the bar. Snacks such as crisps, peanuts, Scotch eggs and a cheeseboard are available. Newspapers are in a rack for customers' use.
Q ❀⊛≉●🛈☒

Dartford Working Men's Club ✅
Essex Road, DA1 2AU
🕓 11-11; 12-10.30 Sun ☎ (01322) 223646
🌐 dartfordwm.club
Courage Best Bitter Ⓗ; **14 changing beers (sourced regionally; often Oakham, Rooster's, Thornbridge)** Ⓗ/Ⓖ
Former CAMRA National Club of the Year winner, this modern CIU club serves 15 ales on handpump plus ciders on gravity. The club hosts the BBC award-winning Dartford Folk Club on Tuesday nights and has live music every Thursday, Saturday and Sunday night. A DJ plays northern soul on the third Sunday afternoon each month. A well-attended quiz takes place on the first Wednesday of the month. CAMRA members are welcome as guests. ❀◑≉♣●☒ ☎

Foresters
15/16 Great Queen Street, DA1 1TJ
🕓 1-11.30; 12-midnight Fri & Sat; 12-11 Sun
☎ (01322) 223087
Adnams Ghost Ship; Harvey's Sussex Best Bitter; 1 changing beer (sourced nationally; often Skinner's) Ⓗ
A traditional local five minutes' walk downhill to the town centre. Quiet at lunchtime, it is busy in the evenings with darts, pool and crib teams. There is an open log-burning fire at one end of the U-shaped single bar. The graveyard opposite contains the unmarked pauper's grave of famed steam pioneer Richard Trevithick, its approximate location being indicated by a plaque on the north wall.
❀⊛≉♣P☒ ❀ ☎

Malt Shovel
3 Darenth Road, DA1 1LP
🕓 3 (12 Thu)-11; 12-midnight Fri; 12-11 Sat; 12-10.30 Sun
☎ (01322) 224381 🌐 maltshovelda1.co.uk
St Austell Tribute; Young's Bitter, Special; 2 changing beers (sourced nationally) Ⓗ
Country-style pub in the town, dating from 1673, five minutes' walk from the High Street. It has two separate bars, a small taproom with a low ceiling featuring an 1880s Dartford Brewery mirror, and a larger saloon bar leading to a conservatory where meals are served Thursday to Sunday lunchtimes and Friday and Saturday evenings. The large beer garden is accessed from the conservatory. The pub holds a popular quiz night on Monday and crib night on Tuesday. A small car park is next to the pub. Q ❀⊛◑≉●P☒

Deal

Just Reproach

14 King Street, CT14 6HX

12-3, 5-8 Mon; 12-2, 5-9 Tue-Thu; 12-2, 5-11 Fri; 12-11 Sat; 12-4 Sun

4 changing beers G

Town-centre micropub with a welcoming ambience; high benches and table service make for a friendly, convivial atmosphere. Ales and ciders are gravity dispensed from a temperature-controlled room. Up to five real ales are served, at least one from a Kent brewery. Ciders are typically from Kent Cider Company but may be from further afield, with the wines from local Barnsole vineyard and Australia. Gins and quality soft drinks are also sold. Snacks include pork pies and local cheese. Q

Ship Inn

141 Middle Street, CT14 6JZ

11-midnight; 12-midnight Sun ☎ (01304) 372222

Dark Star Hophead; Ramsgate Gadds' No.7 Bitter Ale, Gadds' No.5 Best Bitter Ale; Timothy Taylor Landlord; 1 changing beer (often Dark Star, Ramsgate) H

Only 10 minutes' walk from the town centre, this is an unspoilt traditional pub located in Deal's historic conservation area. Dark-wood floors and subdued lighting give a warm and comfortable atmosphere, complemented by the nautical theme. A wide mix of drinkers enjoy the good range of beers dispensed from five handpumps. The pub has a small, cosy rear bar overlooking a large patio garden, accessed by a staircase, with a covered smoking area.

Doddington

Chequers

The Street, ME9 0BG (six miles W of Faversham)

closed Mon; 12-11 Tue; 12-3, 6-11 Wed & Thu; 12-midnight Fri; 9.30am-midnight Sat; 9.30am-8 Sun ☎ (01795) 886366

chequersinndoddington.co.uk

Shepherd Neame Master Brew; 1 changing beer (sourced regionally; often Shepherd Neame) H

Grade II-listed coaching inn with oak timbers, mullion windows and an inglenook fireplace. It is also reported to have two resident ghosts – a Cavalier from the Civil War and a ghoul with a passion for the piano. This centre of village life provides a full post office service every Tuesday 1-3pm. It also hosts regular live music. Frequent events are held, and up to three ales are available during the summer. P (345)

Dover

Breakwater Brewery Taproom

St Martin's Yard, Lorne Road, CT16 2AA

closed Mon & Tue; 5-10.30 Wed & Thu; 4-10.30 Fri; 12-10.30 Sat; 2-10 Sun ☎ (01304) 700043

breakwater.beer

Breakwater Dover Pale Ale, Hellfire Corner, Cowjuice Milk Stout; 5 changing beers (sourced locally; often Breakwater) G

Opened December 2016, this brewery tap is on the site of the Harding's Wellington Brewery which closed in 1890. It is a modern bar, well lit and furnished with chunky, wooden furniture. The bar counter resembles a stone breakwater. Cask ales from the brewery are served on gravity along with their own house ciders. No food is available; however, customers are welcome to bring their own food or takeaways. Tours of the brewery are possible by prior arrangement.

Eight Bells

19 Cannon Street, CT16 1BZ

8am-midnight (1am Fri & Sat) ☎ (01304) 205030

Greene King Abbot; Ruddles Best Bitter; Sharp's Doom Bar; 8 changing beers (often Old Dairy, Wantsum, Weltons) H

The name of this popular and bustling Wetherspoon pub, situated on the precinct, is linked to the church opposite. Inside is a large open-plan room with a long bar and raised restaurant area. At the front an enclosed seating area looks out onto the precinct. Twelve handpumps dispense a range of regular and guest ales, at least two from Kent microbreweries. There are real ale offers on Mondays. Q

Lanes

15 Worthington Street, CT17 9AQ

12-11 (6 Mon); closed Sun ☎ (01304) 213474

5 changing beers (sourced locally) G

Award-winning, friendly micropub, comfortably furnished and carpeted. Real ales, ciders, wines, a mead and soft drinks from Kent producers are sold. Five real ales from microbreweries, predominantly from Kent, and over 10 ciders, are served on gravity dispense from the temperature-controlled cellar room. There is no keg beer, lager or piped music. Snacks can be brought in from the local deli. A feasting board is available with 48 hours' notice. Dogs on a lead are allowed, but no children. Q

Louis Armstrong

58 Maison Dieu Road, CT16 1RA

3-11; 7-11 Sun ☎ (01304) 204759

3 changing beers (sourced locally; often Old Dairy, Ramsgate, Westerham) H

This down-to-earth pub and music venue has featured live music for over 50 years, with a spacious L-shaped bar and stage surrounded by music posters, a large mirror and long bench seating. Up to four real ales are sold, principally from Kent microbreweries, and occasionally real cider. On Wednesday evening good-value food is served and real ales from £3. Outside is a pleasant beer garden. The pub is easily accessible by bus and has car parking nearby. May open earlier by prior arrangement.

Mash Tun

3 Bench Street, CT16 1JH

closed Mon & Tue; 5-9 Wed; 12-10 Thu-Sat; 12-4 Sun summer; closed Mon-Wed; 5-9 Thu & Fri; 12-10 Sat; 12-4 Sun winter ☎ 07867 982141

4 changing beers (sourced locally)

Comfortable micropub on the edge of the shopping precinct. Soft armchairs, a sofa, tables and chairs give a homely feel. The bar is a 200-year-old church pulpit. It sells a varying list of ales, including a gluten-free, unrefined pilsner-style ale from Westerham, and a good range of ciders from rare and smaller cider makers, including Kent. There is no food but customers are welcome to bring their own or order a takeaway. May open Monday by arrangement. (62,68)

White Horse ✔

St James Street, CT16 1QF
12-11 (10 Sun) ☎ (01304) 213066
Harvey's Sussex Best Bitter; Timothy Taylor Landlord; 3 changing beers (sourced nationally; often Fuller's, Gale's) Ⓗ
This Grade II-listed building can trace its history back to 1365. In 1574 it is said to have taken its first recorded steps as an 'ale tasting house'. Today it is a hive of activity with an eclectic mix of tourists and locals enjoying the cosy surroundings. Up to three real ales are served from national breweries alongside real cider. Traditional home-cooked food is available. The hidden terrace at the rear is a treat during the summer months.

Dunk's Green

Kentish Rifleman

Roughway Lane, TN11 9RU (jct with Dunks Green Rd, 4 miles N of Tonbridge, off A227)
11.30-3, 6-11; 11.30-11 Fri-Sun ☎ (01732) 810727
thekentishrifleman.co.uk
Harvey's Sussex Best Bitter; 3 changing beers (sourced locally; often Tonbridge, Westerham, Whitstable) Ⓗ
Set in a hamlet surrounded by beautiful countryside, this fine old pub has been serving ale since the middle of the 16th century. Customers are drawn by the quality of the food where an emphasis is placed on fresh, locally-sourced ingredients (not served Sun or Mon evenings). An attractive destination all year round, it provides an open fire in the winter and a pretty beer garden appreciated by walkers in summer. The front wooden-beamed bar is decorated with historic rifles. QP

Eastry

Five Bells

The Cross, CT13 0HX
11-11.30 (1am Fri & Sat); winter 11-11; 11-10.30 Sun
☎ (01304) 611188 thefivebellseastry.com
Greene King IPA; 2 changing beers Ⓗ
Traditional community pub in the heart of the village with a comfortable lounge bar and dining room. Two ales are served, with an occasional mild from Wantsum Brewery. The old fire station, with historic memorabilia, serves as a sports bar and function room. The busy calendar features live music, quiz nights and an Easter beer festival. Home-made food is served all day, including a good-value two-course lunchtime menu Monday-Saturday. The suntrap patio has a children's play area and pétanque pitch. It may stay open later on Fridays and Saturdays. P (81)

Eynsford

Five Bells

High Street, DA4 0AB
3-11; 12-11 Sat; 12-10.30 Sun ☎ (01322) 863135
Harvey's Sussex Best Bitter; Sharp's Doom Bar; 2 changing beers (sourced regionally; often Skinner's) Ⓗ
Traditional community pub in the heart of an attractive village. The public bar retains a homely atmosphere, with wooden tables and a wood-burning fire in winter. It has a comfortable separate saloon bar. Quiz night is the third Thursday of each month. There is a pleasant garden to the rear and a small car park. Dogs are welcome in the public bar. Food is not served here but try its larger sister pub, the Malt Shovel, nearby. QP (421)

Faversham

Bear Inn

3 Market Place, ME13 7AG
10.30-11; 11.30-10.30 Sun ☎ (01795) 532668
bearinnfaversham.co.uk
Shepherd Neame Master Brew; 1 changing beer (sourced locally; often Shepherd Neame) Ⓗ
A 16th-century pub in the historic market square. It has a regionally important historic wood-panelled interior, with three separate bar areas off the corridor running the length of the building. The lunchtime menu is popular. The ale range often includes a seasonal Shepherd Neame or a guest beer. A general knowledge quiz is held on the last Monday of the month. The pub is equally frequented by visitors to Faversham and locals alike. A small number of tables outside at the front are popular in summer. Q

Corner Tap

37 Preston Street, ME13 8PE
2-10.30; 12-10.30 Fri-Sun ☎ 07718 649995
Whitstable Native Bitter, East India Pale Ale, Kentish Reserve; 3 changing beers (sourced nationally; often Blue Monkey, Oakham, Rudgate) Ⓖ
An increasingly popular and comfortable addition to the local drinking scene, which opened in late 2016. Following the micropub concept, it was converted from a former glazing shop. It has two rooms, with some solid and comfortable furniture: a lounge-type area with a Chesterfield, and armchairs in the room at the rear, and has air conditioning within. Cask beers and a range of keg products are dispensed from taps on the wall behind the bar in the front room, and it stocks a selection of ciders, wines and gins.
Q

Elephant ✔

31 The Mall, ME13 8JN
closed Mon; 3-11; 12-11 Sat; 12-7 Sun ☎ (01795) 590157
5 changing beers (sourced regionally; often Dark Star, Mighty Oak, Rother Valley) Ⓗ
A two-roomed traditional pub with a tastefully refurbished and extended function room at the back. The landlord, a former member of the Senior Service, hence the nautical pictures, prides himself on serving good real ale, occasionally including a beer matured in the cellar. The Elephant has won numerous CAMRA awards, and is host to local clubs and regular live music. A walled garden at the back and a log fire mean this is a good pub to visit at any time of the year.

Furlongs Ale House

6A Preston Street, ME13 8NS
4-10; 3-11 Fri; 12-11 Sat; 12-9 Sun ☎ 07747 776200
5 changing beers (sourced locally; often Canterbury Ales, Kent, Ramsgate) Ⓗ
Faversham's first micropub, opened in late 2014 and still proving popular. It has wooden bench-style seating and solid tables, together with a raised floor area against the wall to assist the older generation. Beers are drawn by handpump from the cellar to a small bar, many from Kent

microbreweries, although others from across the UK also feature. Kent gin, wines and ciders are also served. Q

Leading Light

20/22 Preston Street, ME13 8NZ

8am-11 (01795) 535075

Greene King Abbot; Ruddles Best Bitter; Sharp's Doom Bar; 2 changing beers H

The name of this Wetherspoon pub recalls Henry Wreight (pronounced rate), a leading light in the development of Faversham in the 19th century. It is a fairly typical example of this popular chain, with their normal range of beer and food; however, Kent beers are frequently available. The pub has a pleasant enclosed courtyard garden. It can be busy weekend evenings.

Shipwrights Arms L

Hollowshore, ME13 7TU (over a mile N of Faversham at the confluence of Faversham and Oare creeks) TR017636

closed Mon; 11-3, 6-10; 11-11 Sat; 12-10 Sun

(01795) 590088 theshipwrightsathollowshore.co.uk

Goacher's Real Mild Ale; Kent Prohibition; house beer (by Goacher's); 3 changing beers (sourced locally; often Harvey's) G

Remote 300-year-old family-run free house with jolly, welcoming old-style hosts, in young and old versions. Relax here after a 45-minute walk across the marshes from Faversham. The wooden-clad building's interior reflects its nautical heritage, with many associated ornaments and pictures on display or tucked into nooks and crannies. Comfortable seating options have recently been increased. The large garden at the rear is open spring to autumn, with outside seating at the front in all seasons. It has extended opening hours in summer. In severe winter weather telephone to check opening times. Q P

Finglesham

Crown Inn L

The Street, CT14 0NA

12-11 (10 Sun) (01304) 612555

thecrowninnfinglesham.co.uk

Dark Star Hophead; 2 changing beers H

Traditional village pub with a warm welcome and a friendly atmosphere. Three to four real ales are dispensed, one usually from a local microbrewery. Quality home-made food is served lunchtimes and evenings, including a roast on Sunday. Eat in the bar or restaurant, which opens onto the pleasant garden. Occasional live music events take place, bat and trap is played in summer, and there is a children's play area. The magnificent Kentish barn is available for functions and weddings. May stay open later in summer. P (81)

Folkestone

East Cliff Tavern

13-15 East Cliff, CT19 6BU

5-11; 12-11 Sat & Sun (01303) 251132

2 changing beers (sourced regionally) H

Friendly terraced back-street pub since 1862, in the same family since 1967, near a footpath across the disused railway line, a short walk from the harbour. The main bar is to the right and there are usually two beers, often from local breweries, with Biddenden or Kingswood cider on gravity behind the bar. Old photographs of Folkestone decorate the walls. Community events include weekly raffles. Opening hours may vary; check if making a special visit. Q

Firkin Alehouse

20 Cheriton Place, CT20 2AZ

12-9 (10 Fri & Sat); 12-6 Sun 07894 068432

firkinalehouse.co.uk

4 changing beers (sourced regionally) G

Folkestone's first micropub. Up to four cask beers, often including one from a Kent microbrewery, and up to six ciders are served on gravity from a temperature-controlled cellar room. The display fridge offers a selection of bottled/canned foreign and British beers; a limited wine selection is also stocked. Bar snacks include pickled eggs, onions and other basic fare. No music here, just good company, conversation and pub games, making the Firkin a place to relax and enjoy a good drink. Q

Kipps' Alehouse

11-15 Old High Street, CT20 1RL

12-10 (11 Fri & Sat) (01303) 246766

3 changing beers (sourced regionally; often Mad Cat) G

An alehouse following the general principles of a micropub, serving real ale directly from the cask, usually including a Kentish ale, an award winner, and another unusual beer from around the country, sourced from independent microbreweries. Several ciders are on sale from boxes and a variety of bottled craft beers and draught international lagers. A range of international vegetarian food is available. Music plays some Sunday afternoons.

Mariner L

16 The Stade, CT19 6AB

11-11; 10-10 Sun

Harvey's Sussex Best Bitter; Sharp's Doom Bar; 3 changing beers (sourced regionally) H

Formerly the Jubilee in Mackeson's days, this welcoming pub has an outstanding location overlooking the old fishing harbour and the revived harbour arm. It is just 50 yards from Sunny Sands, one of Kent's best bathing beaches. Approached through mid 19th-century railway arches, the Stade was rebuilt in the 1930s. All major sporting events are shown and there is even a handy post box for those holiday postcards. It allegedly has a ghost of uncertain gender in the cellar. (91,102)

Samuel Peto

23 Rendezvous Street, Baptist Galleries, CT20 1EY

9am-midnight (1am Fri & Sat) (01303) 251154

Greene King Abbot; Ruddles Best Bitter; 3 changing beers H

Unique Wetherspoon pub named after Samuel Morton Peto, great railway engineer and builder of Nelson's column, who funded this building as a Baptist church in 1874. The pub also features original stained-glass windows, a façade of the organ pipes, two pulpits upstairs, original memorial plaques of local dignitaries and a hand-painted ceiling of fluffy clouds across a blue sky. Cosily inviting booths wrap around both floors.

Q

Frittenden

Bell & Jorrocks

Biddenden Road, TN17 2EJ TQ815412
12 (3 Mon & Tue)-11; 12-10.30 Sun (01580) 852415
thebellandjorrocks.co.uk
Black Sheep Best Bitter; Harvey's Sussex Best Bitter; 2 changing beers (sourced nationally; often Dark Star, Fuller's, Rother Valley)
An archetypal village pub, the social centre of the local community. Previously called the Bell, it gained its current name when the pub opposite, the John Jorrocks, closed in 1969. Excellent food is available. Originally a coaching inn dating from the early 18th century, its stables are used for a mid-April beer festival with about 25 different beers. It is a good base for walks in the picturesque Low Weald countryside surrounding the village, and for nearby Sissinghurst Castle.

Knoxbridge

Cranbrook Road, TN17 2BT TQ788406
closed Mon; 12-9 Tue-Thu; 11-10 Fri & Sat; 12-6 Sun
(01580) 895374 theknoxbridge.co.uk
3 changing beers (sourced regionally; often Brumaison, Harvey's, Musket)
Relaxed family-friendly pub serving great food, cooked by a French chef, complemented by ales from local breweries, as well as the occasional distant one. Beers may not always be familiar, so may be purchased in three third-pint glasses in a wooden tray. The landlord stocks a large selection of gins and holds a gin festival in September. A beer festival is held on the weekend of St George's Day, featuring a large number of military vehicles.
P (5)

Gillingham

Frog & Toad

38 Burnt Oak Terrace, ME7 1DR
2-11; 12-11 Fri & Sat; 12-8 Sun (01634) 852231
3 changing beers (sourced nationally; often Cotleigh, Exmoor, Wadworth)
A three-times winner of local CAMRA Pub of the Year, this back-street corner, one-bar pub is only 10 minutes' walk from the railway station. In keeping with the frog theme, there is a treat to be found on the over-bar glass rack for the musically minded. A large patio garden at the rear has covered wooden bench tables and seating and a permanent outdoor stillage from which real ale and cider can be purchased during the regular festivals. Sunday lunches are served (booking required).
Q

Past & Present

2 Skinner Street, ME7 1HD
12-6 (11 Fri & Sat); 12-4 Sun 07725 072293
3 changing beers (sourced regionally; often Goacher's, Titanic, Wantsum)
Medway's first micropub, local CAMRA Pub and Cider Pub of the Year for the third consecutive year. At least three ales and up to eight ciders are dispensed by gravity from a temperature-controlled room. It has an interesting display of closed Gillingham pubs (Past) and Kent micropubs (Present). It holds ale and cider festivals throughout the year. No admittance after 10pm on Friday and Saturday. Q

Will Adams

73 Saxton Street, ME7 5EG
7-11; 12.30-4, 7-11 Sat; 12.30-4 Sun (01634) 575902
3 changing beers (sourced nationally; often Adnams, Oakham, St Austell)
A cosy back-street pub close to the town centre with a warm and friendly environment. Run by Peter and Julie for 26 years, it is noted for outstanding ale and service, proven by 25 consecutive entries in this Guide. Up to three ales and three to five ciders are available. On Gillingham FC match days it opens early, offering a varied food menu including a three-quarter-pound burger! The pub is a member of the Oakademy of Excellence, which grants access to limited and special brews.

Gravesend

Compass Alehouse

7 Manor Road, DA12 1AA
closed Mon; 12-2 (not Tue & Wed), 5-10; 12-10 Sat; 1-6 Sun 07951 550949
4 changing beers
Enterprising micropub opened in 2014 in a former estate agents. It has a small front room with high bench seats and a smaller snug off a little courtyard to the rear. Four different real ales are on sale and at least three ciders, often from Kent producers. There is a convivial atmosphere where conversation is paramount, but talking on mobile phones is discouraged and incurs a fine for charity. A water bowl is provided for dogs.
Q

Jolly Drayman

1 Love Lane, Wellington Street, DA12 1JA (off Milton Rd, E of town centre)
12-11.30 (midnight Fri; 1am Sat); 12-midnight Sun
(01474) 352355 jollydrayman.com
Dark Star Hophead; St Austell Proper Job; 2 changing beers (sourced nationally; often Skinner's)
A cosy pub in part of the former Walker's Wellington Brewery with an interior featuring quirky low ceilings and a relaxed atmosphere. Daddlums (Kentish skittles) is played most Sunday evenings and men's and women's darts teams are hosted. Lunches are served every day 12-3pm and on Sunday 12-5pm. Live music plays on the first Saturday of the month and themed food nights are on the last Saturday. Quiz night is Tuesday.
P

Three Daws

7 Town Pier, DA11 0BJ
11-11 (1am Fri & Sat); 12-11 Sun (01474) 566869
threedaws.co.uk
6 changing beers (sourced locally; often Dartford Wobbler, Iron Pier)
Historic riverside inn with stories of ghosts, press gangs, smugglers, secret tunnels and more, offering views of the Thames and passing river traffic. The bar is upstairs with a large function room below. Inside is divided into small rooms with photos and pictures of local or marine interest and very few right angles. Meals are served until 9pm every day using local ingredients. Live music features on Fridays, quizzes on Sundays and a beer festival in August.

Three Pillars

25 Wrotham Road, DA11 0PA (on A227 opp civic centre)

closed Mon; 2-10 Tue-Thu; 12-10 Fri & Sat; 12-4 Sun

07794 348529 threepillarsgravesend.co.uk

5 changing beers (sourced nationally) H

A small cellar bar underneath the Masonic Hall, reached by steep steps to the right of the hall. Two carpeted front rooms lead to the brick-floored bar area. Ceilings are low throughout and there are photos of Gravesend pubs past and present. Real ales and at least 10 ciders are served from a temperature-controlled room. A quiz is on the third Thursday of each month. The Masonic Hall car park must not be used by patrons. **Q**

Great Mongeham

Leather Bottle

103 Mongeham Road, CT14 9PE

5 (6.30 Tue)-11; 6.30-10 Thu; 6-11 Fri; 12.30-9 Sun

2 changing beers (sourced regionally; often Romney Marsh) H

Street-corner free house on the outskirts of Deal. Recent renovations give the large bar room a relaxed, smart, modern feel. It is a locals' pub with no frills, but top ales and good company. Large-screen sports TVs and quality ale do not always agree, but they do here. Darts and pool teams, occasional live music, karaoke and quiz nights all take place. Euchre night is Friday. Outside is a large garden and a small covered patio for smokers. **P**(82)

Groombridge

Crown Inn

Groombridge Hill, TN3 9QH (on village green)

12-3, 5.30-11; 12-11 Sat; 12-9 Sun (01892) 864742

thecrowngroombridge.com

Brumaison BB Traditional Ale; Harvey's Sussex Best Bitter; Larkins Traditional Ale H

Dating from the 16th century, with low beams and an inglenook fireplace, the Crown sits above the village green in an area popular with walkers and rock climbers. Local ales are complemented by food from an extensive menu, enjoyed in the bar area, snug, adjacent restaurant or on the rear patio. A gluten-free menu, curry specials on Tuesday and steak nights on Friday add to the culinary range. This is a family-run free house that shows rural England at its best.
Q(Spa Valley Railway)**P**(291)

Halstead

Rose & Crown

Otford Lane, TN14 7EA

12-11.30; 12-10.30 Sun (01959) 533120

Larkins Traditional Ale; 5 changing beers (sourced nationally; often Rudgate, St Austell, Tonbridge) H

Grade II-listed flint-built pub close to the North Downs Way in good walking and cycling country, accessible by bus from Orpington to the north and Sevenoaks to the south. The Larkins is always accompanied by an interesting choice of guest beers. A lively front bar hosts darts and has a TV showing sports events, while the side bar with log fire provides dining space, with value home-cooked food served lunchtimes every day. A separate restaurant or function room is also available. **P**(431,R5)

Harvel

Amazon & Tiger

Harvel Street, DA13 0DE

closed Mon; 4-11 Tue-Thu; 12-midnight Fri & Sat; 12-9.30 Sun (01474) 814705

3 changing beers (sourced locally; often Kent, Tonbridge, Westerham) H

Close to the North Downs Way and Pilgrims Way, this is a popular stop-off for walkers. Built in 1914, opposite the site of the original pub, it was designed to blend in with village houses. Inside, it has two distinct bar areas where modern furnishings combine with flagstones and wood floors. A large garden overlooks the village cricket ground. Real ales come mainly from west Kent and East Sussex. Fresh fish night is Thursday. One newly furnished holiday let is available, and there is an annual beer festival in August.
Q **P**

Hastingleigh

Bowl Inn

The Street, TN25 5HU TR095449

closed Mon & Tue; 5-9 Wed; 5-10 Thu; 5-11 Fri; 12-10 Sat; 12-9 Sun (01233) 750354 thebowlonline.co.uk

3 changing beers (sourced locally) H

This lovingly restored Grade II-listed village pub with vintage advertising material retains many period features. The main bar welcomes families but the snug room is child-free and used for village meetings. A beer festival is held on the August bank holiday Monday. Excellent sandwiches and baguettes are available weekends. The pub will stay open if custom warrants it, or you phone ahead. Local CAMRA Pub of the Year in 2017, 2018 and 2019. **Q**

Herne

Butcher's Arms

29A Herne Street, CT6 7HL (opp church)

closed Mon; 12-1.30, 6-9 Tue-Sat; 1-3 Sun

07908 370685 micropub.co.uk

Adnams Broadside; Oakham Citra; Old Dairy Copper Top; 2 changing beers (sourced locally; often Adnams, Old Dairy) G

Britain's first micropub, opened in 2005, a real ale gem and the inspiration for other micropubs. Once a butcher's shop, it still has the original chopping tables. With seating for 12 customers and standing room for 20, the compact drinking area ensures lively banter. The range of beers changes frequently. Customers may also buy beer to drink at home. The pub has won many CAMRA awards and the landlord was voted one of CAMRA's top 40 campaigners. **Q**(6)

Herne Bay

Parkerville

219 High Street, CT6 5AD

12-9; 1-4 Sun 07939 106172

House beer (by Four Candles); 3 changing beers (sourced locally) Ⓖ
A lively micropub in a former music store. The spacious front seating area has a corner bar and a small stage with a piano in the front window. The back bar has a TV screen for big events only. Beers are usually from local microbreweries, and an excellent range of artisan gins, plus other wines and spirits, is sold. Live music is staged once a month, and the pub celebrates its birthday every July the 24th with music and food. Q🕿🕾●🖵🗯❀

Hildenborough

Plough Ⓛ ✅
Leigh Road, TN11 9AJ (½ mile S of Hildenborough at Powdermills)
✪ closed Mon & Tue; 12-11; 12-9 Sun ☎ (01732) 832149
🌐 theploughatleigh.com
Tonbridge Coppernob; 2 changing beers (sourced locally; often Kent, Old Dairy, Westerham) Ⓗ
Real country gem found down a narrow lane away from nearby conurbations. It has everything you would wish for in a 16th-century inn: low-beamed ceilings festooned with hops, an impressive double-sided fireplace, rustic-style furniture and a large streamside garden. Gastro-pub food complements the drinks list, with an emphasis on local beers. The adjacent Great Barn is popular for functions, which may impact pub opening times; updates on its website and social media give information on these. Q🕿🕾●🕪♣P🖵(210)❀🛜

Horton Kirby

Bull Ⓛ
Lombard Street, DA4 9DF
✪ 12-11; 12-10.30 Sun ☎ (01322) 860341
🌐 thebullhortonkirby.com
Dark Star Hophead; 4 changing beers (often Kent, Oakham, Tonbridge) Ⓗ
Pleasant and friendly one-bar village local with a large garden affording views across the Darent Valley, within walking distance of Farningham Road railway station and close to the daytime 414 bus route. Real cider is served in summer. Open mic night is on the first Friday night of each month, and it has regular beer festivals in the garden normally over the Whitsun and August bank holidays. 🕾●🕪♣●🖵(414)❀🛜

Hythe

Potting Shed Ⓛ
160A High Street, CT21 5JR
✪ closed Mon; 12-6 Tue; 12-7 Wed & Thu; 12-9 Fri & Sat; 12-4 Sun ☎ 07780 877226
4 changing beers (sourced regionally) Ⓖ
Former café converted into a micro-alehouse at the Folkestone end of Hythe High Street serving an interesting range of ales from around the country. Normally they are on gravity dispense, although one ale may sometimes be on handpump. One local Kentish beer and three chilled ciders from boxes are usually available. Limited bar snacks are served. A good place to enjoy a drink and interesting conversation after visiting the High Street. 🕾●🖵❀🛜

Three Mariners Ⓛ
37 Windmill Street, CT21 6BH
✪ 4-10 Mon; 12-11 ☎ (01303) 260406
Young's Bitter; 4 changing beers (sourced regionally) Ⓗ
Hidden away in a side street not far from the Royal Military Canal, this traditional corner pub is well worth visiting and an ideal destination when visiting Hythe. You will find friendly staff and local customers happy to have a chat while you enjoy a pint of local or regional beer. No food is served, but the pub attracts customers for the excellent quality and selection of real ales and cider, enjoyed either in the bars or the outside, partly heated area. 🕾🕿♣●🖵❀

Ightham Common

Old House Ⓨ ★ Ⓛ
Redwell Lane, Redwell, TN15 9EE (½ mile SW of village, between A25 and A227) TQ590558
✪ 7-11 (9 Mon & Tue); 12-3, 7-11 Sat & Sun
☎ (01732) 886077 🌐 oldhouse.pub
6 changing beers (sourced locally; often Hopdaemon, Larkins, Long Man) Ⓖ
A Kentish red-brick, tile-hung cottage in a narrow, isolated country lane. The main bar features a Victorian wood-panelled counter, parquet flooring and an imposing inglenook fireplace. It is on CAMRA's National Inventory of Historic Pub Interiors. Beers are dispensed by gravity, often from wooden casks, including at least one bitter, a golden ale and a dark beer. Several Kentish ciders are also available. Local CAMRA branch Pub of the Year 2018 and 2019. May close earlier in the evening if not busy. Q🕾⚐♣●P❀🛜

Ivychurch

Bell Inn ✅
Ashford Road, TN29 0AL (signposted from A2070 between Brenzett and Hamstreet, 2 miles from A259/A2070 roundabout at Brenzett) TR028275
✪ 12-11 (10.30 Sun) ☎ (01797) 344355
🌐 thebellinnromneymarsh.co.uk
St Austell Trelawny; Sharp's Doom Bar, Atlantic; 2 changing beers (sourced regionally) Ⓗ
Pretty, medieval, 16th-century free house next to St George's church. A warm welcome awaits everyone who visits. The quality of the real beers has ensured many awards. During the colder months, a wood-burning stove adds to the comfortable atmosphere. The Bell is well worth finding and is steeped in marshland history; it was once the centre of the Romney Marsh Owlers (smugglers). 🕾🕿🕪♣●P🖵(11B)❀🛜

Kingsdown

King's Head Ⓛ
Upper Street, CT14 8BJ
✪ 5-11; 12-3, 6-11 Sat; 12-10.30 Sun ☎ (01304) 373915
🌐 kingsheadkingsdown.co.uk
Goacher's Special/House Ale; 2 changing beers (often Goacher's, Ramsgate) Ⓗ
Traditional 18th-century village pub with three beamed rooms surrounding the central bar. It has a dining/family room, a rear courtyard, skittle alley and smoking area. Local historical photos adorn the walls. In winter a log fire blazes in the public bar.

Three real ales feature and cider is available in summer. Home-made food is served in the evenings, and lunchtimes too on Saturday and Sunday. Events include quiz nights and a guitar club. ❀◐◑▲♣● (82)

Laddingford

Chequers ✔

The Street, ME18 6BP TQ689481

12-3, 5-11; 12-11 Sat; 12-10.30 Sun ☎ (01622) 871266

chequersladdingford.co.uk

Adnams Southwold Bitter; 3 changing beers (sourced nationally) H

Attractive oak-beamed pub dating from the 15th century. It is the heart of village life, with a variety of events held, including a beer festival at the end of April. A roaring log fire keeps customers warm in winter, and the pub frontage is a sea of flowers in summer. Good food is served and, on Thursdays, a wide selection of sausage dishes is available. The large garden has children's play equipment. Buses stop outside. Q❀◐◑♣P (23,25)

Loose

Chequers Inn L

Old Loose Hill, ME15 0BL

12-11; 12-10 Sun ☎ (01622) 743125

theloosechequers.com

Harvey's Sussex Best Bitter; Rockin' Robin Reliant Robin; Sharp's Doom Bar H

This former 17th-century coaching inn on the old road to Hastings has been tastefully decorated to emphasise original oak beams. It lies in Loose Valley by the side of a trout stream in the shadow of a Thomas Telford viaduct. Traditional home-cooked food is served including vegetarian options. Quiz night is Monday and there is regular live music. An annual duck race takes place on the river on spring bank holiday, and morris dancers feature every Boxing Day. ❀◐◑♿P (5,89)

Lower Halstow

Three Tuns L

The Street, ME9 7DY

12-11 (midnight Fri & Sat); 12-10.30 Sun

☎ (01795) 842840 thethreetunsrestaurant.co.uk

Goacher's Real Mild Ale; 3 changing beers (sourced locally; often Hop Fuzz, Romney Marsh, Wantsum) H

True family village pub with a friendly, bustling, cheerful atmosphere and lively chatter. The owners actively support real ale, offering mainly Kentish ales – third-pint flights are available if indecisive – and several local ciders are sold, including Dudda's Tun. The pub has a good reputation for high-quality locally sourced food and has won many awards. A beer festival is held during the summer bank holiday and there are monthly quizzes. A log fire, sofa seating, brick walls and beams add character. Outside is a large, now improved, stream-side garden. ❀◐◑♿♣●P (327)

Luddesdown

Cock Inn L ✔

Henley Street, DA13 0XB (1 mile SE of Sole Street station) TQ664672

4-11; 12-11 Fri & Sat; 12-10.30 Sun ☎ (01474) 814208

cockluddesdowne.com

Adnams Lighthouse, Southwold Bitter, Broadside; Goacher's Real Mild Ale; Harvey's Sussex Best Bitter; St Austell Trelawny H

Traditional rural free house dating from 1713, under the same ownership since 1984, with two distinct bars, a large conservatory, a separate function room and a comfortable, heated smoking area. Eight real ales are on handpump. The pub is a meeting place for many local clubs and societies, and traditional pub games are played, including pétanque and bar billiards. The free quiz on Tuesday evening is devised and hosted by the landlord. Children are not allowed in the bars or garden. Snacks including pies and pasties are available at all times. Q❀♣P

Maidstone

Cellars Alehouse L

The Old Brewery, Buckland Road, ME16 0DZ (if front gates are closed use rear via alley alongside railway)

closed Mon; 5-9 Tue & Wed; 5-11 Thu; 12-11 Fri & Sat; 12-6 Sun ☎ (01622) 761045 thecellarsalehouse.co.uk

5 changing beers (sourced nationally; often Bristol Beer Factory, Cellar Head, Gun) G

In a former barley wine cellar of the old Style & Winch brewery, with access down a flight of steps, this micropub has a surprisingly spacious interior, with high wooden seats and tables and a stone-flagged floor. The barrel-vaulted ceiling is adorned with pumpclips and hops. Real ales are served by gravity from the capacious cool room. At least 10 real ciders, a few craft keg beers and gins are also stocked. Regular evening events include quizzes, folk music, comedy and Meet the Brewer.

Q≥♣●

Flower Pot L

96 Sandling Road, ME14 2RJ

12-11 (1am Fri); 11-1am Sat; 12-10.30 Sun

☎ (01622) 757705 flowerpotpub.com

Goacher's Gold Star Strong Ale; 8 changing beers (sourced nationally; often Dark Star, Oakham) H

Street-corner alehouse, a must-visit when in Maidstone. The upper bar has nine handpumps, with the ales mainly from microbreweries. Up to four ciders and perries are served directly from the container and there is a small selection of KeyKeg beers. Beers and ciders are displayed on video screens. Simple pub-style food is served (Tue-Sat). Maidstone United football ground is nearby. There are music nights on some Saturdays, jam nights on Tuesdays and monthly vinyl nights on Fridays. It stages an annual beer festival, and was voted Kent CAMRA Pub of the Year 2017.

❀◐◑≥♣● (101,155)

Olde Thirsty Pig L ✔

4a Knightrider Street, ME15 6LP

12-1am (2am Fri; 3am Sat) ☎ (01622) 299283

thethirstypig.co.uk

4 changing beers (sourced locally; often Musket, Range Ales, Tonbridge) H

Reputedly the third-oldest building in the town, it dates from around 1430 with a wealth of massive timber beams, sloping floors and curious nooks and crannies on two storeys. It was originally a farmhouse within the estate of the Archbishop's palace. There is a heated and covered courtyard area. The beers are mainly from Kent microbreweries, draught cider is available, and many bottled beers are stocked, including several foreign ones. ❀♣●🚌🐾📶

Rifle Volunteers 🄻

28 Wyatt Street, ME14 1EU

12-3 (not Mon), 6-11; 12-11 Sat; 12-6 Sun ☎ (01622) 758891 🌐 theriflevolunteers.co.uk

Goacher's Real Mild Ale, Fine Light Ale, Crown Imperial Stout, Gold Star Strong Ale; 1 changing beer (sourced locally; often Goacher's) 🄷

One of only two Goacher's tied houses. A short walk away from the town centre, this Victorian stone-built single-bar pub has been recognised by CAMRA for its unspoilt interior. The absence of noisy machines ensures that it is a place for conversation or quiet drinking. A popular fun quiz, open to all, is held on alternate Tuesdays, with a local winter quiz league operating other weeks. Snacks can be made to order. Q❀⇌♣●🚌🐾📶

Society Rooms ✔

Brenchley House, Week Street, ME14 1RF

7am-midnight (1am Fri & Sat) ☎ (01622) 350910

Greene King Abbot; Ruddles Best Bitter; Sharp's Doom Bar; 7 changing beers (sourced nationally; often Old Dairy, Wantsum) 🄷

Spacious venue on the ground floor of a five-storey block that was once the site of a local newspaper works. The mainly glass external walls allow panoramic views of the pedestrian shopping street alongside. A large outside space is split into smoking and non-smoking areas. The name of the pub is taken from William Shipley, founder of the Royal Society of Arts and the Maidstone Society for Promoting Useful Knowledge, who is buried nearby. Live news is shown on TVs, with no sound. Beer is served from 9am.
Q❀◑♿⇌🚌(101,155)📶

Marden

Marden Village Club 🄻

Albion Road, TN12 9DT

6-11; 12-3, 5-11 Fri; 12-3, 5.30-11 Sat; 12-4, 6.30-10.30 Sun ☎ (01622) 831427 🌐 mardenvillageclub.co.uk

Shepherd Neame Master Brew; 5 changing beers (sourced locally; often Goacher's, Kent, Ramsgate) 🄷

Six real ales are now offered at this Grade II-listed community hub; five change regularly and are generally from Kent microbreweries. Many members are followers of football and rugby on the TV and are also involved in the club's snooker and darts teams; others simply enjoy the friendly ambience. Regularly voted CAMRA branch Club of the Year. Card-carrying CAMRA members are welcome but regular visitors will be required to join. ♿⇌♣●🚌(23)🐾📶

Margate

Fez

40 High Street, CT9 1DS

12-11 (11.30 Fri & Sat); 12-10 Sun summer; 3-11; 12-11.30 Fri & Sat; 12-10 Sun winter

4 changing beers 🄶

This eclectically furnished micropub which opened in 2015 has a mixture of high and low tables along with some raised bench seating. Brewery and fairground memorabilia adorn the walls while musical instruments are fixed on the ceiling. There is a small bar counter at the rear by a temperature-controlled cellar room in which cask ales and ciders are kept. A limited wine range is also sold, along with a selection of soft drinks.
⇌♣●🚌(56,33)🐾📶

Two Halves

2 Marine Drive, CT9 1DH

5-10.30; 12-10.30 Sat & Sun ☎ 07538 771904

3 changing beers 🄶

Friendly, welcoming micropub in an incredible location on Margate's seafront. Beers are served from all regions of the country and change regularly – the landlord knows his ale. No matter what the weather, this micropub has a great aspect, where you can enjoy spectacular sunsets out of the window or just watch the world go by. The beer and cider are kept in immaculate condition in a large stillage room. Look for the old-fashioned postcards in the loo. Local CAMRA Pub of the Year 2018. Q⇌●🚌(56)🐾

Minster-in-Thanet

Hair of the Dog

73 High Street, CT12 4AB

12-10 (11 Fri & Sat); 12-3 Sun ☎ 07885 362326 🌐 hairofthedogpub.co.uk

3 changing beers 🄶

Previously a dog groomer's premises, this micropub offers a warm welcome on the village high street. Real ales, and at least three ciders, are served from the cask in a cool room directly off the bar. Furniture is rustic with a combination of high and low seating and tables, where customers can play a mix of old games such as shove-ha'penny or try and crack some of the puzzles left out. Dogs remain welcome. Q⇌♣●🚌(9,11)🐾

New Romney

Smugglers' Alehouse 🄻

10 St Lawrence Court, High Street, TN28 8BU

12-9 (10 Fri & Sat); 12-8 Sun ☎ 07581 230397 🌐 smugglersalehouse.co.uk

3 changing beers (sourced regionally) 🄷

Welcoming micropub at the west end of the High Street, awarded runner-up CAMRA branch Pub of the Year 2017. You can relax, read the newspapers or join in with the varied conversations between customers and friendly staff. Well-behaved dogs on leads are welcome. In addition to the varied real ales and ciders on offer, there is a selection of wines, spirits, tea, coffee and snacks (including pickled eggs). Q⛺●P🚌🐾

Pluckley

Rose & Crown ✔

Mundy Bois Road, Mundy Bois, TN27 0ST (off the beaten track between Pluckley, Egerton and Smarden) TQ908455

12-11; 12-10.30 Sun ☎ (01233) 840048 🌐 theroseandcrownpluckley.co.uk

Harvey's Sussex Best Bitter; Whitstable Native Bitter; 1 changing beer (sourced nationally) 🄷

Tile-hung 17th-century pub combining the warmth of a traditional Kentish country free house with a first-class restaurant. It sits amid farmland in the heart of the Weald of Kent, with many good walks to be enjoyed nearby. The Village Bar is hop-entwined and has a welcoming fire; the saloon also features a logburner. The 1989 Guinness World Records named Pluckley the most haunted village in England, with 12 ghosts. P

Queenborough

Admiral's Arm

West Street, ME11 5AD (in Trafalgar Court, 30yds left from crossroads of High St and Park Rd)

4.30-9; 12-11 Fri & Sat; 12-9 Sun (01795) 668598

admiralsarm.co.uk

4 changing beers (sourced locally; often Oakham, Pig & Porter, Ramsgate) H/G

Located in the historic heart of Queenborough, with a nautical theme including local shipping maps. The welcoming owners happily serve a good range of beers direct from the cask or via handpump, plus some KeyKeg beers, ciders and many gin offerings. The pub is frequented by locals and visitors alike. It holds regular quiz nights and cheese Sundays, and serves excellent pizzas at weekends from the pizza oven. Mobile calls must be taken outside. Local CAMRA branch Pub of the Year 2018 and 2019. Q♣(360,362)

Rainham

Prince of Ales

121 High Street, ME8 8AN

closed Mon; 5.30-9.30 Tue-Thu; 12-10 Fri & Sat; 12-3 Sun

07982 756412 princeofales.co.uk

4 changing beers (sourced nationally; often Kent, Oakham, Tonbridge) G

On the outskirts of the town centre, this micropub is an ideal haven for those seeking good quality beer and conversation. The wooden benched bar area is divided into an open space to encourage discussion, while there are a number of booths if privacy is required. Beer and cider are dispensed from a temperature-controlled room. Cushions are available for your comfort in exchange for a charity donation. The garden is a suntrap during warmer months. Q♣(132)

Ramsgate

Conqueror Alehouse

4c Grange Road, CT11 9LR (on corner of St Mildred's Rd)

closed Mon; 11.30-2.30, 5.30-9 (9.30 Fri & Sat); 12-3 Sun

07890 203282 conqueror-alehouse.co.uk

3 changing beers G

Multi award-winning micropub, Thanet's first, a cosy place for gravity-dispensed ales, ciders and bottled beers. A former CAMRA national Pub of the Year finalist, it has been an entry in this Guide ever since opening in 2010. Although it underwent a major refurbishment in 2017, you can still find images of the paddle steamer it is named after, as well as memorabilia of local brewing history. Q♣

Hovelling Boat Inn

12 York Street, CT11 9DS

11.30-9 (10 Fri & Sat); 12-4 Sun summer; 11.30-7 (9 Wed & Thu; 10 Fri & Sat); 12-4 Sun winter 07974 613030

hovellingboatinn.co.uk

4 changing beers G

Sympathetic shop conversion micropub in a handy town-centre location. The name was chosen upon learning it had originally been the Hovelling Boat public house, which ceased trading in 1909. The interior has exposed brickwork displaying breweriana. The four constantly changing beers from Kent and beyond are served at table by friendly staff. Local cider along with wine, cold snacks, tea and coffee are also available. Q

Montefiore Arms

1 Trinity Place, CT11 7HJ

12-2.30, 5.30-11; 12-11 Sat; 12-3, 7-10.30 Sun

(01843) 593265

Ramsgate Gadds' No.7 Bitter Ale; 4 changing beers H

Award-winning traditional back-street local enjoying a good reputation among real ale drinkers in the Thanet area. The pub's name and sign are unique, honouring the great Jewish financier and philanthropist Sir Moses Montefiore, who lived locally for many years. Now under the personal control of Eddie Gadd of nearby Ramsgate Brewery (Gadds'), the pub showcases its beers alongside some interesting changing guest ales and Biddenden cider. ♣

Rochester

Coopers Arms

10 St Margarets Street, ME1 1TL

12-11 (midnight Fri & Sat) (01634) 404298

thecoopersarms.co.uk

Courage Best Bitter; Young's Special; house beer (by Tonbridge); 4 changing beers (sourced regionally; often Canterbury Ales, Tonbridge, Westerham) H

A short walk from Rochester Cathedral leads you to this historic and charming two-bar inn, built during the reign of Richard I (1189-1199). Originally the home of monks, it did not become an inn until 1543. Despite changes over the years, the original charm and character still remain. Local and regional ales are offered. Regular quiz nights are held and local artists perform a variety of music every Sunday evening. P

Flippin' Frog

318 High Street, ME1 1BT

closed Mon-Thu; 12.30-11 Fri & Sat; 12.30-9 Sun

07889 214000

6 changing beers (sourced locally; often Goody Ales, Kent, Old Dairy) G

Welcoming micropub with rustic wooden seating and tables. The ales, visible on stillage, are cooled by jackets, and there is a good range of real ciders and wines. The food is prepared in an open kitchen. Mussels are served on a Friday. Sunday roasts are good value, served 1-4pm. The priority is selling good-quality ale. Well-behaved children are welcome until 7pm. Q♣

Man of Kent Ale House

6-8 John Street, ME1 1YN (200yds off A2 from bottom of Star Hill)

2 (3 Mon)-11; 12.30-midnight Sat; 12.30-11 Sun

07772 214315

9 changing beers (sourced locally; often Bexley, Ramsgate, Tonbridge) H

Away from the Charles Dickens-themed Rochester High Street stands this alehouse showcasing the name of the defunct Style & Winch, an old Kent brewery. Upon entering you are faced with an L-shaped bar showing a good range of Belgian and German products. Turn the corner and the 10 handpumps proudly display real ales from the vast array of Kentish breweries. Regular music and quiz nights are held. ❀⇌♣●▯▭

Who'd Ha' Thought It

9 Baker Street, ME1 3DN

⏲ 12-midnight ☎ (01634) 843285 ⊕ whodha.co.uk

3 changing beers (sourced nationally; often Harvey's, Skinner's, Titanic) Ⓗ

Tucked away off the Rochester to Maidstone road is this sociable, wood-panelled pub. A snug bar to the rear leads to a pleasant garden, which is also used to house beer festivals. Main sports events are televised. There is a monthly quiz, and Murder Mystery nights are held. Children allowed up to 8pm. ❀♣P▭(155)🐾

Ryarsh

Duke of Wellington L ✔

Birling Road, ME19 5LS

⏲ 11-11; 12-10.30 Sun ☎ (01732) 842318

⊕ dukeofwellingtonryarsh.com

Harvey's Sussex Best Bitter; Kent Pale; 2 changing beers (sourced nationally; often Musket, St Austell) Ⓗ

A 16th-century pub with two bars, both with inglenook fireplaces; the main bar to the left includes a snug and the restaurant to the right has part of an original wall displayed behind glass. A covered and heated patio opens onto the garden, with additional tables outside the front of the pub. It serves a varied menu, including Sunday roasts. A popular jazz music evening is held monthly, and every other Sunday evening is quiz night. Ramblers welcome. **Q**❀P▭(58)🐾

St Peter's

Four Candles Alehouse

1 Sowell Street, CT10 2AT

⏲ 5-11.30; 12-11.30 Sat & Sun ☎ 07947 062063

⊕ thefourcandles.co.uk

3 changing beers Ⓖ

A former shop, now firmly established on the local micropub scene and renowned for its friendly atmosphere. Seating is provided at high bench tables, while the beer is served from a cooled cabinet in an adjacent room. The microbrewery in the cellar supplies excellent one-off beers to complement the offerings from other brewers. In warmer weather benches outside make the most of the sunshine. **Q**⇌●▭(56)🐾

Sandgate

Earl of Clarendon

Brewers Hill, CT20 3DH (25yds up footpath off A259 from seafront between Seabrook and Sandgate next to public phone box)

⏲ 12-11 (midnight Fri & Sat) ☎ (01303) 248684

4 changing beers Ⓗ

This ex-Mackeson and Shepherd Neame pub became a free house in 2009. Originally built as a hotel, it provided refreshment to troops on the path between Shorncliffe Camp and the sea. Three or four changing beers from all over Britain are served, usually including at least one local offering. Live music features occasionally during the summer; tasty home-made pub grub every day. Bar billiards and third-pint glasses are available, plus football, cricket and snooker on satellite TV. ♣▭🐾

Sandwich

Red Cow L

12 Moat Sole, CT13 9AU

⏲ 11-11 ☎ (01304) 613399

6 changing beers Ⓗ

You cannot miss the large red cow on the front of this timber-framed building used by market traders in years gone by. Tiled floors and exposed beams give a comfortable and traditional country pub ambience. Up to six ales are sold, usually including one from Ramsgate Brewery, and cider from Broomfield. There are areas for drinkers, diners and bar billiards players, and the pub has a pleasant suntrap garden. There is a quiz night every Sunday and a TV for major sporting events. ❀Ѧ♣●P▭🐾

Sevenoaks

Anchor L

32 London Road, TN13 1AS

⏲ 11-3, 6-11; 10.30-midnight Fri; 12-4, 7-10.30 Sun

☎ (01732) 454898 ⊕ anchorsevenoaks.co.uk

House beer (by Wantsum); 2 changing beers (sourced nationally; often Franklins, Sambrook's) Ⓗ

The Anchor continues its success based on the three pillars of home-cooked food, consistent real ale and musical entertainment, under the guidance of landlord Barry, who has served the community here for 40 years. A traditional, friendly locals' pub with a pool table and darts teams, where visitors are drawn by live blues bands on the first and third Wednesday of the month and alternate jazz and open mic nights, as well as Texas Hold 'em Poker on Monday nights. ♣▭🐾

Sheerness

Flying Sheep Micropub

193 High Street, ME12 1UJ

⏲ 4 (2 Thu)-9; 12-11 Fri & Sat; 12-9 Sun ☎ 07958 134282

4 changing beers (sourced regionally) Ⓗ

Micropub opened in 2018, with an aviation and local sheep theme reflecting Sheppey's past involvement in aircraft manufacture and sheep farming. Seating is mainly high tables and high stools but there are several comfortable airline seats. The bar counter offers an interesting and changing range of beers from near and far, with ciders on gravity dispense. There are themed nights on Wednesdays. The pub may occasionally close for private functions – check its Facebook page for advance notice. ⇌♣●▯▭🐾

Sittingbourne

Donna's Ale House

20 West Street, ME10 1AB

⏲ closed Mon; 12-11 (8 Tue & Wed); 12-4 Sun

5 changing beers (sourced locally; often Goody Ales, Mad Cat, Wantsum) Ⓗ

This micropub, opened in 2017, has a contemporary decor with seating at high benches, tables and stools. Handpumps dispense ales with an emphasis on Kentish makers, and occasionally out of county. A blackboard gives a description of the beers on offer. Gins are also available. A selection of snacks is served, currently ranging from cheeseboards to pie and mash until 6pm, and chilli with nachos thereafter. A welcome town centre addition to the local real ale scene. ≥●🚌

Paper Mill 🄻

2 Charlotte Street, ME10 2JN (N of Sittingbourne station, almost in Milton Regis at corner of Church St and Charlotte St)

❂ 5-9; 12-2, 5-9 Fri; 12-9 Sat; 12-6 Sun ☎ 07927 073584

🌐 thepapermillmicropub.co.uk

3 changing beers (sourced regionally; often Dark Revolution, Goacher's, Salopian) 🄶

Popular micropub close to Sittingbourne town centre and railway station. It is a one-room pub with bench seating around four large wood tables. Local beers feature alongside national ales from the likes of Blue Monkey and Redwillow, and a range of Dudda's Tun ciders is also served. Beers are listed on a blackboard including a couple of KeyKeg offerings. Occasional events such as Meet the Brewer and pub quizzes take place. Opening hours are flexible with advance notice.
Q♿≥♣●🚌(334,347)🐾

Snargate

Red Lion ★ 🄻

TN29 9UQ (on B2080, 1 mile NW of Brenzett) TQ990285

❂ closed Mon; 12-3, 7-10 (11 Fri & Sat); 12-4, 7-10.30 Sun ☎ (01797) 344648

Goacher's Real Mild Ale; 3 changing beers (often Goacher's) 🄶

Unspoilt, multi-room 16th-century smugglers' pub which has been in the same family for over 100 years. The pub passed to the current generation in 2016 but is still universally known as Doris's. Decorated with posters from the 1940s and the Women's Land Army, it has a nationally important historic pub interior and is well worth a visit. A beer festival is held in June near to the summer solstice, with a mini festival in October.
Q❀♣●P🚌(11B)🐾

South Darenth

Queen 🄻

58-62 New Road, DA4 9AR

❂ 2-11; 12-11.30 Sat; 12-10.30 Sun ☎ (01322) 862430

Fuller's London Pride; Greene King Abbot; Kent Session Pale, Brewers Reserve 🄷

Community back-street terraced local within walking distance of Farningham Road railway station, extended in 1998 to incorporate a former shop. It has two separate bars, one with a sports theme adorned with memorabilia of London football teams, the other a quieter saloon bar. A genuine free house, it promotes beers from Kent Brewery. The pub has a garden/patio area and free bar food is available Sunday lunchtimes. Children are welcome until 8.30pm.
❀◑≥♣●🚌(414)🐾

Staplehurst

Lord Raglan 🄻

Chart Hill Road, TN12 0DE (½ mile N of A229 at Cross-at-Hand) TQ786472

❂ 12-3, 6.30-11; closed Sun ☎ (01622) 843747

Goacher's Fine Light Ale; Harvey's Sussex Best Bitter; 1 changing beer (sourced locally) 🄷

A longstanding entry, this popular and unspoilt free house retains the atmosphere of a country pub from bygone days. The bar is hung with hops and warmed by two log fires and a stove. The large orchard garden catches the evening sun. Excellent snacks and full meals are always available, and the guest beer changes regularly. Westons perry and local Double Vision cider are stocked. Well-behaved children and dogs are welcome. It is a short walk from the Cross-at-Hand (No.5) bus stop on the A229. Q❀◑●P🐾

Stockbury

Harrow

The Street, ME9 7UH (close to jct 5 of M2)

❂ closed Mon; 12-11; 12-8 Sun ☎ (01795) 843222

🌐 theharrowstockbury.co.uk

House beer (by Tonbridge); 2 changing beers (often Canterbury Ales, Weltons) 🄷

A 200-year-old former Shepherd Neame pub in the heart of rural Stockbury, with a triangular village green in front. Owned by the local community after a major refurbishment, it is now the community hub. The manager is also a trained chef, and the venue serves good-quality, locally sourced food. The house ale is from Tonbridge. CAMRA's prestigious Pub Saving Award 2017 was awarded in 2018. The judges were impressed by how the residents came together to keep the pub in the village. ❀◑P

Strood

10:50 From Victoria 🏆 🄻

Rear of 37 North Street, ME2 4SJ (in railway arch opp Asda car park)

❂ 4-9; 12-10.30 Fri & Sat; closed Sun ☎ 07941 449137

🌐 1050fromvictoria.co.uk

Grainstore Ten Fifty 🄶**; 5 changing beers (sourced nationally)** 🄷/🄶

A justly popular micropub opened in 2015 and run by three real ale enthusiasts. The name relates to the Network Rail arch number, not a train time. The pub is full of railway memorabilia and bric-a-brac, and has internal bench seating. A logburner keeps everyone warm in the winter months and there is a large decked area outside, pleasant on a warm summer's day. Six real ciders are also sold. No children allowed. CAMRA branch Pub of the Year 2019. Q❀♿≥♣●P🚌(191)🐾

Swanley

Cotton Mill

10 Station Road, BR8 8ET

❂ 12-10 ☎ (01322) 669619 🌐 thecottonmillpub.com

4 changing beers (often Iron Pier, RedWillow, Tiny Rebel) 🄷

A micropub that opened 2018, serving four changing real ales on handpump, eight real ciders

in boxes, and four 'draught and craft' beers. It has an interesting tiled floor with bottle tops inlaid in mosaic patterns. The renovated building, with comfortable seating, is shared with a taxi office in former public toilets. It has a pleasant outside drinking area with plans for expansion and hosting beer festivals. Quiz night is Thursday evening. Winter weekday opening times are 4-10pm.
🐴❀⇌♣●P🚌🐾📶

Tankerton

Tankerton Arms Ⓛ

135 Tankerton Road, CT5 2AW

⏲ closed Mon; 12-9.30 (11 Fri & Sat) ☎ 07897 741811

🌐 thetankertonarms.co.uk

4 changing beers (sourced locally; often Mad Cat, Old Dairy, Turnstone) Ⓖ

A friendly micropub, with a firm policy of supporting Kent microbreweries, set among Tankerton's small shops. It does occasional beer swaps with regional breweries. The room is pleasant and airy, lined with high wooden tables and stools encouraging good conversation among customers, and there is a patio in front of the pub for outdoor drinking. It is adorned inside with bunting and pictures featuring Thames sailing barges and the sea forts. Italian antipasti evenings take place every few weeks. Q🐴❀♣●🚌🐾📶

Temple Ewell

Fox

14 High Street, CT16 3DU

⏲ 11.30-3.30, 6-11.30; 12-4, 7-11 Sun ☎ (01304) 823598

Exmoor Fox; 2 changing beers Ⓗ

Traditional village pub offering a warm welcome to locals and visitors. Enjoy a good range of styles and strengths of real ales in the main bar or one of the smaller rooms. A variety of events, quiz nights, curry nights and occasional music evenings keep the pub busy. In June a charity beer festival is organised by the local Rotary Club. There is an attractive streamside garden with skittle alley, and it is close to Kearnsey Abbey gardens and public transport. 🐴❀◐◑⇌♣P🚌(15,68)🐾📶

Tenterden

This Ancient Boro'

3 East Cross, TN30 6AD

⏲ 12-11; 12-10.30 Sun ☎ (01580) 388815

🌐 thisancientboro.com

9 changing beers (sourced nationally) Ⓖ

Reopened in July 2018 as an alehouse and tapas bar, the pub was previously known as the Honeymoon Chinese Restaurant. Until 1968 the site had, for many years, been a Whitbread house, This Ancient Boro'. The pub is a hybrid of this original incarnation and a micropub, with no live music or gaming machines. A variety of ales is dispensed by gravity from cooled casks on stillage in the bar area, while various ciders are served from a fridge.
Q🐴◐◑⇌♣●🚌🐾📶

Tonbridge

Foresters Arms

52 Quarry Hill Road, TN9 2RT

⏲ 12 (3 Mon)-11; 12-1am Fri & Sat ☎ (01732) 361927

🌐 forestersarmstonbridge.co.uk

Shepherd Neame Whitstable Bay Pale Ale, Spitfire; 1 changing beer (sourced nationally; often Black Sheep, Shepherd Neame) Ⓗ

A friendly, convivial and relaxed atmosphere has been created in a revitalised Shepherd Neame house with comfy seating and wooden tables with candles. It is decorated with imagery and artwork from around the world, with background music enhancing the bohemian feel. Part of the bar is devoted to playing pool, darts and bar billiards; customers can also search for board games to play, kept inside old school desks. A selection of pizzas is served until late. ❀◐◑♿⇌♣🚌🐾📶

Fuggles Beer Café ✔

165 High Street, TN9 1BX (N end of Tonbridge High St near parish church)

⏲ 12-11 (10.30 Sun) ☎ (01732) 666071

🌐 fugglesbeercafe.co.uk/tonbridge

Tonbridge Coppernob; 3 changing beers (sourced nationally; often Burning Sky, Downlands, Siren) Ⓗ

A welcome facility for the town since opening in 2017 in a former shop. Bright and airy, the café/bar offers a relaxed environment in which to study the choice of cask ales, 18 draught lines and two ciders displayed on a board behind the bar. The menu details a prodigious range of speciality bottled beers and spirits, along with food; sandwiches, cheeses and charcuterie. Regular Meet the Brewer and promotion events are advertised.
🐴◐◑♿♣●🚌🐾📶

Humphrey Bean ✔

94 High Street, TN9 1AP (near castle and river)

⏲ 7am-midnight (1am Fri & Sat); 8am-midnight Sun

☎ (01732) 773850

Greene King Abbot; Ruddles Best Bitter; Sharp's Doom Bar; 6 changing beers (sourced nationally; often Oakham, Old Dairy, Tonbridge) Ⓗ

Enjoying its 10th consecutive year in the Guide, this Wetherspoon house continues to promote interest and variety in real ale by hosting regular brewery and Meet the Brewer events, in addition to six-monthly festivals and a permanent choice of six guest beers. Westons Old Rosie cider and others such as Marcle Hill and Black Dragon are advertised behind the bar. The spacious garden, adorned with hanging baskets in summer, overlooks Tonbridge Castle. A quiz is held on Wednesday evenings.
Q🐴❀◐◑♿⇌●P🚌📶

Nelson Arms

19 Cromer Street, TN9 1UP

⏲ 4-11 (10 Mon; 11.30 Fri); 12-11.30 Sat; 12-10 Sun

☎ (01732) 358284 🌐 thenelsonarms.com

Young's Bitter; 5 changing beers (sourced nationally; often Goacher's, Kent, Tonbridge) Ⓗ

Beautifully refurbished local, a few minutes' walk from the railway station, featuring an interesting selection of cask ales and Chiddingstone and Double Vision cider. The interior has a nautical theme comprising the Nelson Saloon, Trafalgar Snug, Hardy's Public Bar and Victory Sports Bar. A drop-down screen is used for bigger sporting occasions. Meals are served from opening time until late, with main meal promotions on Mondays and Thursdays; Sunday roasts are served until 4pm. Live music, usually in the form of duos, is performed Friday evenings. Q❀◐◑⇌♣●🚌🐾📶

Tunbridge Wells

Fuggles Beer Café ✔

28 Grosvenor Road, TN1 2AP (opp Tesco bus stop)
⏲ 11.30-11; 12-10.30 Sun ☎ (01892) 457739
🌐 fugglesbeercafe.co.uk
Burning Sky Plateau; Tonbridge Coppernob; 2 changing beers (sourced nationally; often Bristol Beer Factory, Siren) 🄷
The café/bar that brought a hint of Bruges to the local scene. Cask ales are backed up by a wide range of British and Belgian offerings and a broad selection of bottled beers. Regular takeovers and Meet the Brewer events cater for drinkers who value good beer served by knowledgeable staff in relaxed surroundings. Gin, wine, whisky and two real ciders add to the mix, while charcuterie, cheeses, sandwiches and salads contribute to the continental ambience. A haven at any time.
☋◑⇌♣●🚌🐾ᯤ

George 🏆 ✔

29 Mount Ephraim, TN4 8AA
⏲ 12-11 (midnight Thu; 1am Fri); 10-1am Sat; 10-11 Sun
☎ (01892) 539492 🌐 thegeorgepubtunbridgewells.co.uk
Long Man Best Bitter; house beer (by Fonthill); 4 changing beers (sourced locally; often Burning Sky, Gun, Pig & Porter) 🄷
An old Georgian coaching inn that has been developed into a smart, friendly free house with an on-site microbrewery producing a range of Fonthill beers exclusive to the pub. Seacider and Turners cider are always available; the beer choice mainly supports Kent and Sussex brewers. Light bites supplement the main menu and are served every day beyond lunchtime. The attractive courtyard garden is pleasant in fine weather. CAMRA branch Pub of the Year 2018 and 2019.
☋✿◑⇌●🚌🐾ᯤ

Grove Tavern Ⓛ ✔

19 Berkeley Road, TN1 1YR
⏲ 11-midnight ☎ (01892) 526549 🌐 grovetavern.co.uk
Harvey's Sussex Best Bitter; Timothy Taylor Landlord; 2 changing beers (sourced nationally; often Marston's, Otter) 🄷
Five minutes' walk from the station, tucked away in backstreets of the old village, this narrow, single-bar pub, with a dartboard and pool table at either end, dispenses well-kept beers for thirsty customers. Friendly conversation and dogs attracted by the biscuits provided are a constant reminder that this is a neighbourhood tavern where the emphasis is on social interaction. It is a proper, traditional pub, the likes of which are becoming increasingly rare. A long term Guide entry. Q☋⇌♣🚌🐾ᯤ

Mount Edgcumbe

The Common, TN4 8BX
⏲ 11-11 (11.30 Thu-Sat); 12-10.30 Sun ☎ (01892) 618854
🌐 themountedgcumbe.com
Harvey's Sussex Best Bitter; 3 changing beers (sourced regionally; often Dark Star, Old Dairy, Pig & Porter) 🄷
Within walking distance of the town centre and railway station, this pub, restaurant and hotel occupies a large Georgian house on the common, surrounded by woods. Walkers and dogs are welcome in the garden, bar and the adjacent internal 6th-century cave complete with comfy sofas and chairs. The extensive patio beer garden includes a play area overlooking sandstone rock formations, popular in the warmer months. Quiz nights take place on the second and fourth Sunday of each month. ☋✿🛏◑⇌♣P🚌🐾ᯤ

Opera House ✔

88 Mount Pleasant Road, TN1 1RT
⏲ 8am-midnight (1am Fri & Sat) ☎ (01892) 511770
Greene King IPA, Abbot; Sharp's Doom Bar; 6 changing beers (sourced nationally; often Kent, Marston's, Old Dairy) 🄷
Wetherspoon has tastefully restored the old opera house to its former glory, featuring the theatre circle, boxes and a huge central chandelier. In the centre of town, close to the Victoria shopping centre, this is a convenient place to take refuge from the shopping crowds. A wide range of guest ales is always stocked, sourced locally and nationally. The stage bar provides the opportunity to eat and drink in splendid surroundings.
Q☋◑♿⇌🚌ᯤ

Royal Oak Ⓛ

92 Prospect Road, TN2 4SY
⏲ 12 (3 Mon)-11; 12-9 Sun ☎ (01892) 542546
Harvey's Sussex Best Bitter; 4 changing beers (sourced locally; often Cellar Head, Iron Pier, Ramsgate) 🄷
A strong community-focused pub, a rewarding few minutes' walk from the town centre. It has a prominent selection of Kent and Sussex beers, although customers are often pleasantly surprised by the appearance of unusual guest ales from afar; the owner is always seeking out something new and fresh. Cider enthusiasts may choose from Biddenden, Dudda's Tun or Turners. Menu choices range from pub classics, sandwiches, burgers and nachos through to Sunday roasts. The Royal Oak Stage hosts live music every Saturday night.
☋✿◑⇌♣●P🚌(6,285)🐾ᯤ

Tyler Hill

Tyler's Kiln 🏆

27 Hackington Road, CT2 9NE
⏲ 11-11.30 (12.30am Fri & Sat); 11.45-11 Sun
☎ (01227) 471912 🌐 tylerskiln.co.uk
Harvey's Sussex Best Bitter; Shepherd Neame Master Brew; 2 changing beers (sourced locally; often Harvey's) 🄷
Community-focused village pub, refurbished to a high standard with innovative touches, cosy armchairs, an open fire and a loyalty scheme. Check the website for the excellent £2 offer for the first drink. Tiles from the ancient nearby kiln are on display. The separate snug with its soft furnishings is a good place for families. The well-designed garden has a fountain and high-tech heating. Events include coffee mornings, live music and quizzes. A small range of groceries is sold. CAMRA branch Pub of the Year 2019.
Q☋✿◑♿P🚌(5)🐾ᯤ

Upper Upnor

King's Arms

2 High Street, ME2 4XG
⏲ 11.30am-midnight; 12-10.30 Sun ☎ (01634) 717490
🌐 kingsarmsupnor.co.uk
5 changing beers (sourced regionally) 🄷

Close to the free village car park, you will find a good choice of five guest real ales here, including a mild and a selection of ciders, perries and European bottled beers. The large garden often hosts beer festivals. The pub has a reputation for quality food, and offers restaurant and bar menus. Upnor Castle sits at the other end of the High Street.
Q☺♿◑▮●P🚃(197)☸

Tudor Rose ✅
29 High Street, ME2 4XG
🕐 12-11; 12-8 Sun ☎ (01634) 714175
🌐 tudorroseupnor.co.uk
Shepherd Neame Master Brew, Whitstable Bay Pale Ale; 2 changing beers (sourced nationally) ⓗ
A pub with character found in this quaint village on the River Medway. It is on a narrow cobbled street and dates from the 17th century. There is a large walled garden at the rear, and many rooms linked to its U-shaped bar. It has a good reputation for quality food. Customers can use the free car park at the far end of the High Street.
Q☺♿◑▮♣●P🚃(197)☸🛜

Walmer

Berry ♟ 🅛
23 Canada Road, CT14 7EQ
🕐 11 (3 Tue)-11; 12-11 Thu; 11-11.30 Fri & Sat; 11.30-11 Sun
☎ (01304) 362411 🌐 theberrywalmer.co.uk
Dark Star American Pale Ale; Harvey's Sussex Best Bitter; Oakham Citra; 8 changing beers (often Ramsgate, Time & Tide) ⓗ
Multi award-winning alehouse located off Walmer's seafront. The bar has a light and airy feel, and at the back is a pleasant patio. The welcome, service and quality of the ales and ciders over the years are evidence of the landlord's enthusiasm. There is plenty of choice, with up to 11 interesting cask ales at weekends, seven KeyKeg ales (many from Time & Tide), and more than 10 ciders. Three beer festivals are hosted annually. Entertainment includes darts, pool, a monthly quiz and live music.
❀♣●🚃☸

Freed Man 🅛
329 Dover Road, CT14 7NX
🕐 12-9 (10 Tue; 11 Fri & Sat); 12-8 Sun ☎ (01304) 364457
🌐 thefreed-man.co.uk
4 changing beers ⓗ
Here is everything for the discerning drinker in a micropub atmosphere. The decor is cosy and warm, with nautical memorabilia covering the reclaimed wood walls. Real ales come predominantly from local breweries, dispensed from the Victorian beer engine. Real ciders, wines, selected spirits and authentic draught and bottled European lagers are also stocked. Food can be brought in and plates and cutlery will be provided. Regular events include a Thursday ladies' night and a monthly quiz night. Q☺♿≉♣●🚃☸🛜

West Malling

Bull Inn 🅛
1 High Street, ME19 6QH
🕐 12-2.30, 4-11 Mon & Tue; 12-11; 12-10.30 Sun
☎ (01732) 842753 🌐 thebullinnwestmalling.com
Goacher's Gold Star Strong Ale; Timothy Taylor Landlord; Young's Bitter; 4 changing beers (sourced nationally; often Musket, Old Dairy, Tonbridge) ⓗ

At the north end of the village, near the railway bridge, you will come across this friendly free house, with wood panelling and a real fire. The focus is on local beers and ciders, with one cider on handpump. The terrace at the rear allows for outdoor drinking. A quiz is held on Monday evenings and live music some Saturdays. Good food using locally sourced ingredients is offered daily except Mondays. West Malling station is about 10 minutes' walk away.
Q☺♿◑♣●🚃(72,151)☸🛜

Malling Jug
52 High Street, ME19 6LU (in narrow alley opp Swan St between funeral directors and hospice shop)
🕐 12-9; closed Tue; 12-10 Fri & Sat ☎ (01732) 667832
🌐 themallingjug.co.uk
Kent Session Pale; 7 changing beers (sourced nationally; often Kent) ⓖ
A small, stylish, modern pub. Current and forthcoming beers are on a board near the bar and on clipboards dotted around, which also list various bottled and canned beers, mainly from the UK and Belgium, at relatively sensible prices. A periodic table of beer styles helps you to choose. There is no music, and food is limited to snacks. Table service is available at busy times. ❀♿≉●🍺🚃(72,151)☸

Westgate-on-Sea

Bake & Alehouse ♟
21 St Mildred's Road, CT8 8RE (down alleyway between Carlton cinema and bookmakers)
🕐 12-2, 5-8 Mon; 12-2, 5.30-9 Tue-Sat; 12-2 Sun
☎ 07913 368787 🌐 bakeandalehouse.com
5 changing beers ⓖ
A welcoming micropub and an oasis for the local real ale drinker. Around five different beers, mainly from Kentish breweries, are served from barrels kept in a temperature-controlled room, alongside a selection of Kentish ciders. Seating about 20 people, the small interior has been managed well, creating a friendly atmosphere. Locally produced cheese and pork pies are available. Winner of the local CAMRA branch Pub of the Year 2019.
Q≉♣●🚃☸

Whitstable

Black Dog 🅛
66 High Street, CT5 1BB
🕐 12-11.30 (midnight Thu-Sat)
Kent Session Pale; 4 changing beers (sourced regionally; often Kent, Angels & Demons, Four Candles) ⓖ
This attractive town-centre micropub has lush Victorian decor with a twist, consisting of a long, narrow room lined with high bench seating. The five changing real ales, displayed on handpumps on the bar counter, are actually gravity dispensed from the cooled cellar room. Up to 25 ciders and perries, mostly from Kent, are also stocked. The menu includes hot and cold food. A quiz is held on the first Wednesday of each month. ◑≉●🚃☸

Handsome Sam 🅛
3 Canterbury Road, CT5 4HJ
🕐 6-9 Mon; 12-2, 6-10.30 Tue-Thu; 12-4, 5-11 Fri; 12-11 Sat; 12-4, 6-9 Sun ☎ 07931 662081

House beer (by Four Candles); 4 changing beers (sourced regionally; often Dark Star, Mighty Oak, Ramsgate) Ⓖ
Popular micropub just outside the town centre, named after the owner's late pet cat. The high-ceilinged pub has original exposed beams, high tables and benches provide seating, and hops adorn the bay windows. Three or more ales always include one pale, one copper and a stronger one; the house beer is Old Hector. The pub also serves 10 ciders, wines, champagne, spirits, tea, coffee and snacks. **Q**

Ship Centurion

111 High Street, CT5 1AY
11-11 (11.30 Fri & Sat); 12-7 Sun ☎ (01227) 264740
Adnams Southwold Bitter; 4 changing beers (often Canterbury Ales, Old Dairy, Pig & Porter) Ⓗ
Friendly and traditional town-centre pub where a Kentish beer is always served. Colourful hanging baskets add to its charm in summer, while pictures of Whitstable adorn the bar. Home-cooked bar food often includes German dishes, and there is schnitzel on Saturdays (no food Sun). Live music is played Thursday evenings (except in January). The pub is a good place to watch sport on Sky.

Twelve Taps

102 High Street, CT5 1AZ
closed Mon; 5-11 Tue-Thu; 1-midnight Fri & Sat; 1-9 Sun
☎ (01227) 770777 thetwelvetaps.co.uk
House beer (by Time & Tide); 11 changing beers (sourced regionally; often Buxton, Pig & Porter, Wild Beer)
A craft beer bar decorated in warm colours, with wooden floors and a pleasant suntrap courtyard, serving KeyKeg beers conforming with CAMRA's definition of real ale. Try a sample paddle of three beers to find your favourites. The pub stocks many artisan gins (free tonic on Tuesdays), plus organic wines, bottled ciders and interesting soft drinks. It is open on bank holiday Mondays. There is a quiz on the last Wednesday of each month. Check Twitter for the winner of the Dog of the Day award.

Carpenters Arms, Coldred (Photo: Barry Marsh/Flickr)

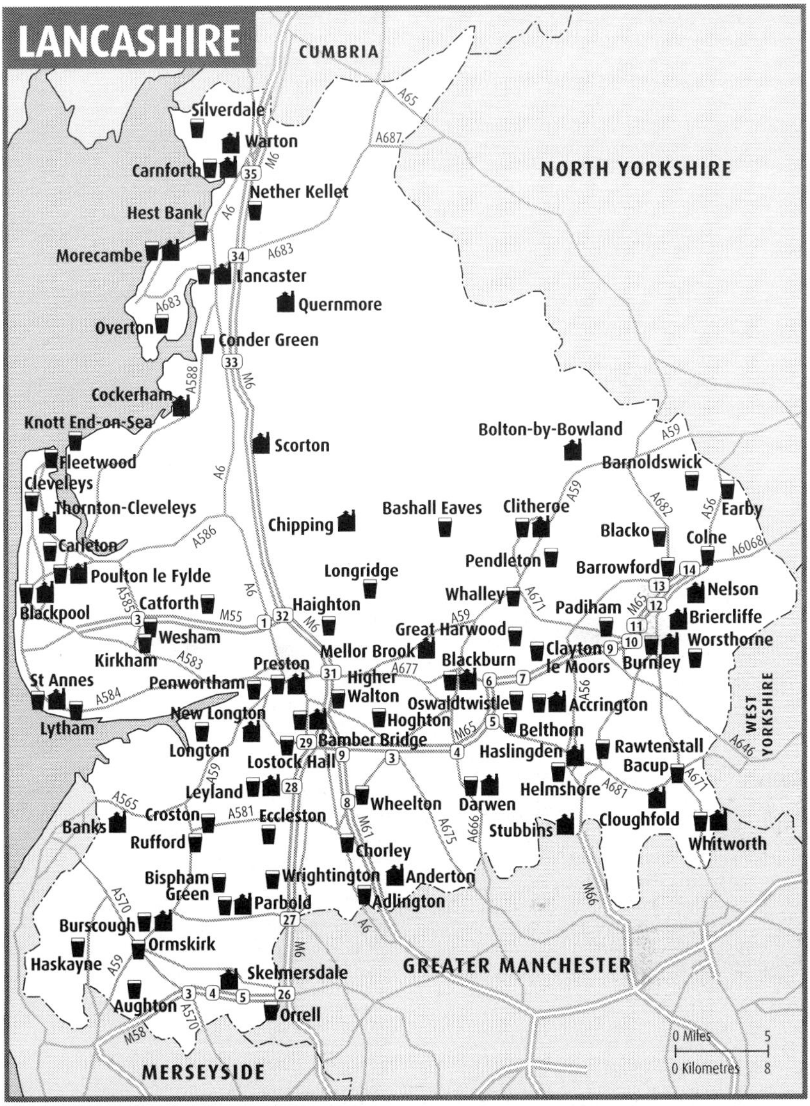

Accrington

Canine Club 𝕃

45-47 Abbey Street, BB5 1EN

11-11 ☎ (01254) 233999

Tetley Bitter; 3 changing beers (sourced nationally; often Old School, Reedley Hallows, Worsthorne) Ⓗ

A large, traditional street-corner social club on a busy street, in an area of the town centre known for its many independent retailers. The central bar serves a comfortable lounge to the front and a large games room to the rear, where snooker, pool and darts are played. A sizeable function room is available upstairs. This popular club is welcoming to all and hosts live entertainment most weekends. The changing range of beers usually features a couple of local East Lancashire breweries plus a guest ale from further afield. A finalist in CAMRA's National Club of the Year competition in 2019. ⇌♣🚌(464,X41)

Peel Park Hotel 𝕃

Turkey Street, BB5 6EW

12-11.30 ☎ (01254) 235830

Tetley Bitter; 5 changing beers (sourced nationally) Ⓗ

A true free house at the foot of the Coppice, opposite the site of the old Accrington Stanley football ground, still used by Peel Park FC. Six beers are sold, mainly from smaller regional breweries. The welcoming main bar is divided into split-level front, side and rear areas. There is a separate small pool room, and a smart rear room used for functions. To the side of the pub is a pleasant garden area. ❀♣P🚌(M3)🐾

Adlington

Spinners Arms 𝕃

23 Church Street, PR7 4EX

12-midnight (1am Fri & Sat) ☎ (01257) 483331

Moorhouse's Pride of Pendle; Southport Dark Night; 5 changing beers (sourced regionally; often Abbeydale, George Wright, Oakham) Ⓗ
The pub is known as the Bottom Spinners to differentiate it from the other Spinners Arms in the village. Built in 1838, the pub is welcoming and friendly; a single bar serves three seating areas. There is a pleasant outdoor drinking area to the front. It has no pool table or gaming machine, just an open log fire. The bar menu offers home-cooked food with Sunday specials. Five alternating guest beers are served, often from local breweries. Small functions are catered for. ❀◐≋♣P🚌(8A)🐾📶

Aughton

Derby Arms Ⓛ ✔
Prescot Road, L39 6TA (on B5197 at Bowkers Green between Ormskirk and Kirby)
✪ 12-midnight (1am Fri & Sat); 12-11 Sun ☎ (01695) 422237
Tetley Bitter; 4 changing beers (often Lytham, Rudgate) Ⓗ
Friendly country pub with a long CAMRA award-winning heritage. The interior is intimate, with many small nooks and crannies, and the pub serves a changing choice of beers from the three guest handpumps, from local and national breweries. It holds quiz nights on Tuesdays and Thursdays and regular charity events. Excellent-value food is available, with breakfast served on Saturdays from 9am. Q❀◐◑P🐾

Stanley Arms
24 St Michael Road, L39 6SA (off A59 at Aughton Springs) SD391055
✪ 12-11 (11.30 Tue & Thu; midnight Fri & Sat)
☎ (01695) 423241
Marston's Pedigree; Tetley Mild, Bitter; Timothy Taylor Landlord; 2 changing beers Ⓗ
Situated beside a historic Norman church, the Stanley has distinctive 18th-century architecture and was originally a coaching stop for postal deliveries. It is decorated throughout with Tudor-style woodwork. Several side rooms, decorated with brewing memorabilia, are served by the centrally placed bar, which dispenses from five handpumps. Immaculately kept both inside and out, the pub is exceptionally popular for its excellent home-cooked and locally sourced food.
❀◐◑♿♣P🚌📶

Bacup

Crown Inn Ⓛ
19 Greave Road, OL13 9HQ
✪ 5-11; 3-midnight Fri; 12-midnight Sat & Sun
☎ (01706) 873982
Pictish Brewers Gold; 3 changing beers Ⓗ
Cosy, traditional country pub with a large L-shaped bar and stone-flagged floors throughout. It was built in 1865 and once owned by Baxter's of Glentop Brewery. A welcoming coal fire adds warmth in the cooler months. There are always three beers available, usually sourced locally. Food is served most evenings. Quiz nights are held on Wednesday and Sunday. On the second floor is a function room accommodating up to 35 guests. There is a patio beer garden to the front of the pub. Beer festivals are held in July and October.
❀◑♿♣P🚌(465,464)🐾

Bamber Bridge

Brig 'n' Barrel Ⓛ
188 Station Road, PR5 6TP
✪ closed Mon; 4-9.30 Tue-Thu; 2-11 Fri & Sat; 2-9 Sun
☎ 07728 794755
6 changing beers (sourced locally) Ⓗ
This was Bamber Bridge's first micropub, opening in June 2018 in a former electrical shop premises. It specialises in quality cask and craft beers and gins. The six handpumps serve a changing selection of ales, mostly from small local breweries. There is just one room in this cosy rustic bar, with a small amount of outside seating available.
Q≋●🚌(125)🐾

Barnoldswick

Barlick Tap Ale House Ⓛ
8 Newtown, BB18 5UQ
✪ closed Mon & Tue; 4-9 Wed & Thu; 2-10 Fri & Sat; 2-8 Sun
☎ 07739 088846
5 changing beers (sourced nationally) Ⓗ

REAL ALE BREWERIES

3 Piers Poulton-le-Fylde
4 Mice ■ Bolton-by-Bowland (NEW)
Accidental ■ Lancaster (NEW)
Avid Quernmore
Beer Brothers Bamber Bridge
Big Clock ■ Accrington
Bloomfield ■ Blackpool
Bluestone Whitworth
Bowland Clitheroe
Brewsmith Stubbins
Chain House New Longton
Chapel Street ■ Poulton-le-Fylde
Clay Brow Skelmersdale (NEW)
Crankshaft Leyland
Cross Bay Morecambe
Darkwave Preston
Doghouse Darwen
Farm Yard Cockerham
Fuzzy Duck Poulton-le-Fylde
Hop Vine ■ Burscough
Hopstar Darwen
Horner Bros Lancaster (NEW)
Lancaster Lancaster
Lytham St Annes
Mighty Medicine Whitworth
Moonstone ■ Burnley
Moorhouse's Burnley
Northern Whisper Cloughfold
Old School Warton
Oscars Nelson
Parker Banks
Partridge Chipping (brewing suspended)
Priest Town Preston
Problem Child ■ Parbold
Providence Bamber Bridge
Q Brew Carnforth (NEW)
Reedley Hallows Burnley
Rivington Anderton
Rock Solid Blackpool
Rossendale ■ Haslingden
Skippool Creek Thornton-Cleveleys
Snowhill Scorton
Three B's ■ Blackburn
Thwaites Mellor Brook
West Coast Rock ■ Blackpool
Withnell's Bamber Bridge
Worsthorne Briercliffe

You will always get a warm welcome from Hazel and Steve at this friendly micropub just off the town square, two minutes from the main bus stop. It has a choice of five varying cask beers; one of them will be a dark beer. A selection of American and European bottled beers and lagers, bottled ciders and wines is also available. A place to meet and chat over a glass or two without the intrusion of loud music. Q (M1)

Barrowford

Bankers Draft

143 Gisburn Road, BB9 6HQ

closed Mon & Tue; 4-9 Wed & Thu; 4-10.30 Fri; 2-10.30 Sat; 2-9 Sun ☎ 07739 870880

5 changing beers (sourced nationally) H

An imposing detached former bank, this is now a small and friendly micropub specialising in real ale and conversation, with no loud music or TV. The five handpumps dispense rotating cask ales from small national brewers, offering a great variety of beer styles, from hoppy blondes and traditional bitters to dark beers. There is also a good selection of wines, bottled craft lagers and wheat beers, with at least one real cider normally on draught. Q P (2)

Bashall Eaves

Red Pump Inn

Bashall Eaves, BB7 3DA

closed Mon & Tue; 12-11 ☎ (01254) 826227

theredpumpinn.co.uk

3 changing beers (sourced regionally; often Bowland, Salamander, Wily Fox) H

This picturesque country inn located in the Forest of Bowland AONB offers stunning views across the Ribble Valley to Pendle Hill. The snug bar features a flagstone floor and an open fireplace. Good-quality food is served and the restored dining areas feature numerous settles and rustic furniture. There is lots of hunting and sporting memorabilia throughout. Browsholme Hall is close by. Accommodation is available in eight boutique bedrooms and outside in yurts (summer only). P

Belthorn

Dog Inn

61 Belthorn Road, BB1 2NN

5-11 (midnight Thu); 1-midnight Fri; 12-midnight Sat; 12-11 Sun ☎ (01254) 433188

Three B's Bobbin's Bitter, Doff Cocker H

This is the first community-owned pub in east Lancashire and is run as a community benefit society. It has flagged floors on several levels and a real fire. Situated in hill country, with great views across the moors and out to the coast, it is a place where dogs and walkers are welcome. Full meals are available lunchtime and evenings, with a coffee shop menu in between. Beers are mainly from the local Three B's and Blackedge breweries. P

Bispham Green

Eagle & Child

Malt Kiln Lane, L40 3SG

12-11; 12-10.30 Sun ☎ (01257) 462297

eagleandchildbispham.co.uk

Southport Golden Sands; Thwaites Original; Wainwright; 5 changing beers H

An 18th-century pub with eight handpumps showcasing local ales. Southport Golden Sands is always available alongside a variety of guest ales including Prospect, Wigan Brewhouse and Moorhouse's. This busy country pub has been Lancashire Dining Pub of the Year and is noted for its food. The huge beer garden, with its wildlife area and great views, hosts a beer festival on the first May bank holiday. Quiz night is every Monday. P

Blackburn

Black Bull

Brokenstone Road, BB3 0LL (corner of Brokenstone Rd and Heys Lane) SD666247

closed Mon & Tue; 4-11 Wed-Fri; 12-11 Sat; 12-10.30 Sun ☎ (01254) 581381 threebsbrewery.co.uk

Three B's Stoker's Slake, Bobbin's Bitter, Oatmeal Stout, Black Bull, Weavers Brew, Knocker Up H

In the heart of rural Lancashire, this is an independent award-winning family-run pub with a brewery attached. Eight handpumps serve a fine selection of Three B's real ales including the exclusive Black Bull Bitter. Try the three-beer sampler wedges, which are popular. Built as a farmhouse in the 18th century, more recently it was purchased by Robert Bell from Thwaites and transformed into a place for those who appreciate fine beer and friendly conversation. It has no jukebox or fruit machines, and no food is served; it just offers a friendly, relaxing atmosphere. Q P

Drummers Arms

65 King William Street, BB1 7DT

12-8 (11 Fri & Sat) ☎ 07341 565657

Three B's Stoker's Slake; 4 changing beers (sourced locally; often Big Clock, Cross Bay, Hopstar) H

A single-roomed bar on the pedestrianised area opposite the town hall. It is handy for the library and King George's Hall, and provides a refuge from the hordes of shoppers in the nearby mall. The walls are adorned with breweriana and old pub signs. The biweekly Sunday free-and-easy music sessions are legendary. At other times expect a range of classic tracks from the eclectic jukebox. A strong supporter of LocAle, the pub serves beer mainly from Lancashire breweries, though a visitor from afar sometimes makes an appearance. There is a pleasant seating area at the front.

Hare & Hounds

78 Lammack Road, BB1 8LA

4-11.30; 12.30-12.30am Sat; 12.30-11.30 Sun ☎ (01254) 676724

4 changing beers (sourced regionally; often Bowland, Reedley Hallows, Worsthorne) H

Former Whitbread estate pub rescued by the current landlord and backed by a passionate local community. It sits adjacent to Old Blackburnians FC, and to Pleckgate and Lammack playing fields. Local breweries such as Three B's, Bowland, Reedley Hallows, Moorhouse's and Worsthorne feature regularly. The large, comfortable open-plan lounge is served from a bar with five handpumps. There is high-quality live entertainment at weekends, when the pub can get busy. P (25,10)

Blacko

Rising Sun Ⓛ ✔

330 Gisburn Road, BB9 6LS

⏲ 3-midnight; 12-midnight Fri-Sun ☎ 07949 385462

Bank Top Flat Cap; Moorhouse's Premier Bitter, Pride of Pendle; 2 changing beers (sourced regionally) [H]

This former Moorhouse's pub is now a free house, a family-friendly three-room establishment in the award-winning village of Blacko. You will feel right at home in this traditional former weavers' cottage, complete with open fires in each of the cosy rooms. The elevated front terrace offers splendid views of the sunsets over the dramatic local landmark of Pendle Hill. 🐴❀◐◑🚌

Blackpool

1887 The Brew Room

139-141 Church Street, FY1 3NU

⏲ 12-11 (midnight Fri); 11-midnight Sat ☎ (01253) 319165 🌐 thebrewroom1887.co.uk

West Coast Rock Blackpool Blonde, Golden Mile, Oyston Stout, Tangerine Dream, Wonky Donkey; 5 changing beers (sourced nationally; often Cross Bay) [H]

Imposing Victorian brewpub on the edge of Blackpool town centre, approximately 150 yards inland from the main entrance to the Winter Gardens complex. A range of 10 cask ales is served, normally consisting of five from the on-site West Coast Rock Brewery, which can be viewed at the rear of the pub, and five guest ales. Cider, authentic German lagers and a range of craft keg beers is also sold. Smoked snacks and highly calorific milkshakes also feature. Live music is performed most weekends and a quiz most Mondays. 🐴⇌🚊♣🍎🚌🐾📶

Albert's Ale Micropub

117 Albert Road, FY1 4PW

⏲ closed Mon-Wed; 4-10.30 Thu & Fri; 2-10.30 Sat; 2-9 Sun ☎ (01253) 292827 🌐 m.blackpoolmicropub.co.uk

3 changing beers (sourced locally) [H]/[G]

Quirky hotel cellar bar behind the Winter Gardens in the heart of Blackpool's hotel quarter, 10 minutes' walk from the promenade and tower. It stocks three changing ales, supporting local brewers and normally including a dark beer, as well as a wide range of Belgian bottled beers. Local pork pies are available. Knowledgeable staff are welcoming to locals and visitors alike. Regular Meet the Brewers nights are held. The hotel has 11 comfortable bedrooms. ❀🛏⇌🚊🍎▯🚌🐾📶

Blackpool Cricket Club

Barlow Crescent, West Park Drive, FY3 9EQ (follow signs to Stanley Park)

⏲ 4-11; 12-midnight Sat; 12-11 Sun ☎ (01253) 393347 🌐 blackpoolcricket.co.uk

Wainwright; 4 changing beers (sourced regionally; often Bowland, Lancaster, Moorhouse's) [H]

On the western edge of Stanley Park, this club hosts many sports teams. Several TVs show major sports fixtures, and an upstairs lounge is available for social events. The club has its own squash courts and holds quiz and entertainment nights plus an annual beer festival. A ladies' cricket team is now established. Entry to the club and all cricket games – except Lancashire's – is free. A frequent local CAMRA branch Club of the Year. 🐴❀◐◑♿🍎P🚌🐾📶

Layton Rakes ✔

17-25 Market Street, FY1 1ET

⏲ 8am-midnight (1am Fri & Sat) ☎ (01253) 743710

Greene King Abbot; Ruddles Best Bitter; Sharp's Doom Bar; 5 changing beers (sourced regionally; often Acorn, Moorhouse's, Phoenix) [H]

Near to North Pier, this multi-floored Wetherspoon's is popular with locals and tourists alike. It features a bar on each floor, and lift access between all floors. A range of three regular and at least five changing guest beers is served. The pub, especially the ground floor, can get busy at weekends, particularly during the holiday season. There is outdoor seating to the front and side and on the roof terrace. The Layton Rakes has been a fixture in this Guide since 2014. 🐴❀◐◑♿⇌🚊🍎🚌📶

Saddle Inn ✔

286 Whitegate Drive, FY3 9PH

⏲ 10.30-11 (midnight Fri & Sat); 11-midnight Sun ☎ (01253) 767827 🌐 thesaddleblackpool.co.uk

Draught Bass; 5 changing beers (sourced nationally) [H]

A Blackpool institution, the building dates from about 1776 when it was owned by a saddler. Real fires are found in each of the two rooms adjacent to the main bar. The walls feature sporting prints. Six beers are available, and in summer a couple of ciders. Food is normally served until 9pm daily. Outdoor drinking is on a large terraced area with benches to the side of the pub. A beer festival is held yearly, with a marquee set up in the car park. 🐴❀◐◑♿🍎P🚌📶

Burnley

Bridge Bier Huis Ⓛ

2 Bank Parade, BB11 1UH

⏲ closed Mon & Tue; 12-midnight Wed & Thu; 12-1am Fri & Sat; 12-11 Sun ☎ (01282) 411304 🌐 thebridgebierhuis.co.uk

Moorhouse's Premier Bitter; 4 changing beers (sourced regionally) [H]

An award-winning true free house with a large open-plan bar that has a logburner and a small snug to one side. It offers mainly microbrewery beers alongside a changing real cider. More than 60 foreign bottled beers are sold plus seven foreign beers on tap, including rare German brews. Wednesday is quiz night and live music is hosted on occasional weekends. This welcoming pub opens 5pm Monday or Tuesday if Burnley FC are at home. 🐴❀◐⇌🍎P🚌🐾

New Brew-m Ⓛ

11 St James Row, BB11 1DR

⏲ 12-7 Mon; closed Tue; 12-8 Wed; 12-10 Thu-Sat; 2-6 Sun ☎ 07902 961426

Reedley Hallows Pendleside; 5 changing beers (sourced nationally) [H]

This smart micropub in the centre of town is run as the Reedley Hallows Brewery tap. At least one of its own beers always sits on the bar alongside five others sourced nationwide, using the head brewer's contacts from years in the trade. A good range of foreign bottled beers and bottled ciders is available. The fully glazed frontage makes the bar feel light and airy. There is a small room upstairs providing extra seating. Opens on Tuesday night if Burnley FC are at home. **Q**⇌🚌🐾

Rifle Volunteer 🄻

1 Smalley Street, BB11 3HH
2-11 (10.30 Tue); 12-11 Sat; 12-10.30 Sun
☎ (01282) 453839
Draught Bass; 2 changing beers (sourced locally; often Reedley Hallows) Ⓗ
The Vols is an award-winning pub and a rare outlet in this area for the iconic Draught Bass. This friendly free house is a supreme example of a street-corner local. There is no jukebox to disturb the quiet ambience; the emphasis is on good beer and conversation. Check out the Gents for a rare example of Burnley-manufactured Duckett's urinals. **Q♣P**🚌(483)🐾

Burscough

Hop Vine

Liverpool Road North, L40 4BY (village centre on A59)
10.30-midnight (12.30am Fri & Sat); 10.30-11 Sun
☎ (01704) 893799 🌐 thehopvinepub.co.uk
Timothy Taylor Landlord; 4 changing beers (sourced regionally; often Salopian) Ⓗ
Formerly a spacious coaching house, this is now a thriving community brewpub, renowned for its friendly atmosphere and popular for its exceptional ale and food. The classic country-pub interior has wood panelling and characterful wood flooring throughout and is decorated with historic local maps, photographs and vintage bottled ales. The Hop Vine Brewery operates from the attractive floral courtyard at the rear. Catering for all age groups, the pub offers great-value meals, live music and twice-yearly beer festivals.
♿**P**🚌

Old Packet House 🄻 ✔

29 Liverpool Road North, L40 5TN
12-11 (midnight Fri & Sat); 12-10.30 Sun
☎ (01704) 807330 🌐 theoldpackethouse.com
Coach House Blonde; 3 changing beers (often Bank Top, George Wright, Prospect) Ⓗ
A typical canalside village hostelry in the centre of Burscough with a new licensee. The focus is on serving real ale but food is available afternoon and evening. You can watch the canal boats go past from the garden or the canalside viewing area. The pub is just over the road from the Burscough Wharf complex, and is ideal for a ramble along the canal with its many pubs serving real ale in the vicinity. There is a series of old prints of Burscough on the walls inside. ♿🚌🐾

Carleton

Castle Gardens ✔

Poulton Road, FY6 7NH
10-11 (midnight Fri & Sat) ☎ (01253) 890015
Moorhouse's White Witch; Wainwright; house beer (by Black Sheep); 6 changing beers (sourced nationally) Ⓗ
There has been an inn on this site since about 1750. This popular establishment is both a food-led destination and a local community pub. A range of nine ales including six changing guests is available. A weekly quiz is held every Tuesday and live music is performed regularly at weekends. There is a large outdoor drinking area to the side of the building. ♿**P**🚌(14)🐾

Carnforth

Snug

Unit 6, Carnforth Gateway Building, LA5 9TR (at N end of former mainline up platform)
12-2 (not Mon & Tue), 5-9; 12-9 Sat; 1-4.30 Sun
☎ 07927 396861 🌐 thesnugmicropub.blogspot.co.uk
5 changing beers Ⓗ
The area's first micropub, where the only drinks are ale, cider, wine, a few soft drinks and at least 10 good-quality gins; the only food a few light snacks; and the only sounds conversation and the roar of passing trains. The decor is similarly stripped back to painted walls, bare floorboards and tall, chunky tables. The eye is naturally drawn to a beautiful glazed wooden cabinet, where all the drinks are stored. Parking is in the station car park (a charge applies). **Q**♿♣🚌🐾

Catforth

Running Pump

Catforth Road, PR4 0HH
closed Mon; 4.30-10 Tue-Thu; 4-midnight Fri; 12-midnight Sat; 12-10 Sun ☎ (01772) 690265 🌐 therunningpump.com
3 changing beers (sourced nationally) Ⓗ
An idyllic country pub surrounded by the rural Fylde countryside, its location affording super views of the distant Pennine fells. Over 400 years old, this building has had a recent extension but its authentic character is retained with antique furnishings, original woodwork, tiled floors and woodburners. There is a beer garden to the rear and seating to the front where an old watering trough remains. A delightful pub in a wonderful location, well worth a visit.
Q♿♣**P**🚌(77,77A)🐾

Chorley

Ale Station 🄻 ✔

60 Chapel Street, PR7 1BS
closed Mon; 4-11 Tue-Thu; 3-midnight Fri; 2-midnight Sat; 3-11 Sun ☎ (01257) 368003
6 changing beers (sourced locally; often Hawkshead, Rock the Boat) Ⓗ
Micropub conveniently near to both the bus and train stations. A modern-looking venue with a wine-bar feel, this inviting hostelry offers a full range of drinks. Five changing real ales are served, increasing to six at weekends. Most are from north-western microbreweries. There are also two changing real ciders. A digital display board provides price information and real ale details in addition to updated train times for the railway traveller. **Q**♿🚌🐾

Bob Inn

24 Market Place, PR7 1DA
10-6; closed Wed & Sun ☎ 07767 238410
3 changing beers (sourced nationally) Ⓗ
A tiny bar housed in a market stall, with an adjacent unit now used as a lounge area; this is the smallest pub in the branch region. Outside seating is available during summer and drinkers often spill out into the market area. There is something for every taste, with three changing cask beers from smaller breweries nationally, at least two real ciders and a good selection of bottled beers. No food is served, but you are welcome to bring your own. **Q**🚌🐾

Malt 'n' Hops 🅛

50-52 Friday Street, PR6 0AA

✪ 12 (1 Mon)-11; 12-midnight Sat & Sun ☎ (01257) 260074

Bank Top Dark Mild; Irwell Works Marshmallow Unicorn; 7 changing beers (sourced nationally; often Fernandes, Moorhouse's, Rat) 🅗

Converted from an old shop, this pub is handily situated for both the railway and bus stations. It has a single L-shaped bar on two levels with a bright yet traditional feel. This is a genuine free house, offering up to seven guest ales, usually from Lancashire and Yorkshire micros, with Rat, Ossett, Elland, Lancaster and Blackedge often featuring. Two regular dark beers are commonly served, and filled rolls and pork pies are normally available. Local CAMRA Pub of the Year 2017.

🌣☆✿♿⇆●🖳❀🛜

Masons Arms 🅛

98 Harpers Lane, PR6 0HU

✪ 3-11; 12-midnight Fri & Sat; 12-11 Sun ☎ 07464 841589

6 changing beers (sourced locally; often Blackedge, Hawkshead, Marble) 🅗

Tastefully modernised multi-room pub a short walk from the town centre; a recent convert to real ale. Six changing ales are on at any one time, usually including a dark beer. Most come from north-west micros but ales from further afield are also available from time to time. A separate taproom and two distinct lounges complete with wood-burning stoves give distinctly different drinking areas. Light and airy, this is a cosy pub with a growing reputation for good beer. Local CAMRA Most Improved Pub of the Year 2018.

🌣☆✿🖳(24,125)❀🛜

Shepherds' Hall Ale House 🅛

67 Chapel Street, PR7 1BS

✪ closed Mon; 12-10 (11.30 Fri & Sat); 12-10.30 Sun

🌐 shepherdshallalehouse.wordpress.com

5 changing beers (sourced nationally) 🅗

A friendly and welcoming bar next door to the bus station, this was the first micropub in Chorley. Now under new ownership, it serves up to five beers from microbreweries all over the country. You should find a wide range of beer styles, always including a dark ale. Third-of-a-pint beer paddles are available. There are two real ciders, one on handpump and one from a box behind the bar. Local CAMRA Cider Pub of the Year 2017.

Q⇆●🖳❀

Sir Henry Tate 🅛 ✪

New Market Street, PR7 1DB

✪ 8am-midnight (1am Fri; 2am Sat) ☎ (01257) 248470

Bank Top Dark Mild; Greene King Abbot; Ruddles Best Bitter; Sharp's Doom Bar; house beer (by Moorhouse's); 10 changing beers (sourced nationally) 🅗

A purpose-built pub trading under the Lloyd's banner, next to Booth's supermarket. This Wetherspoon establishment is on two levels and has an outside drinking area to the front. The main bar downstairs features five regular beers plus five guests, often including ales from Moorhouse's and Phoenix. Two changing real ciders are served from boxes behind the bar. To reflect local tastes, the beers tend to be of lower gravity than is often found in Wetherspoon pubs. 🌣🕪♿⇆●🖳🛜

Clayton le Moors

Forts Arms 🅛

1 Lower Barnes Street, BB5 5TA

✪ 4-midnight; 2-2am Fri & Sat; 2-11 Sun ☎ (01254) 433713

4 changing beers (sourced regionally; often Bowland, Snaggletooth, Wishbone) 🅗

Partially opened out in a modern style, yet still retaining a separate lounge, this corner pub boasts a large rear beer garden which is popular with families in warmer weather. There is a smart two-floor function suite to the side. Beers are mainly from the plethora of breweries in east Lancashire and Greater Manchester. Folk music sessions take place weekly and music, art and beer festivals are held twice a year. The pub sits across from Mercer Park and is a short walk downhill from the Leeds & Liverpool Canal. Q🌣☆✿♣P🖳❀

Cleveleys

Jolly Tars ✪

154-158 Victoria Road, FY5 3NE

✪ 8am-midnight (12.30am Fri & Sat) ☎ (01253) 856042

Greene King Abbot; Ruddles Best Bitter; Sharp's Doom Bar; 7 changing beers (sourced nationally; often Bank Top, Coach House, Lancaster) 🅗

Opened in 2011, this Wetherspoon's pub, a conversion from a former Kwik Save supermarket, is named after a highly popular nine-strong family team who entertained large crowds locally during the 1940s. It is a pleasant and welcoming environment in which to enjoy a quiet drink, with several secluded booths. The range of 10 beers comes from near and far, and real cider is also sold. The pub opens out onto a pleasant open-air drinking area at the front. 🌣☆🕪♿⇆●🖳🛜

Clitheroe

Ale House

12-14 Market Place, BB7 2DA

✪ 12-10 (midnight Fri & Sat) ☎ 07530 045365

🌐 thealehouseclitheroe.co.uk

5 changing beers (sourced nationally; often Oakham, Ossett) 🅗

Now a firm favourite on Clitheroe's vibrant beer scene, the Ale House has a kind of rustic charm. The beer choice changes regularly and is always interesting. Alongside the cask ales there is a good selection of bottles and cans from the UK and further afield. The pub hosts regular gigs and events including an open mic night. Situated in the town centre, it is on the circuit for the town's annual music festival. ⚲⇆🖳

Bowland Beer Hall ✪

Greenacre Street, BB7 1EB

✪ 11-11 (midnight Fri & Sat); 11-9 Sun ☎ (01200) 401035

🌐 holmesmill.co.uk/beer-hall

Bowland Pheasant Plucker, Gold, AONB, Boxer Blonde, Hen Harrier, Buster IPA; changing beers (sourced nationally) 🅗

The Beer Hall opened in 2016 in a converted mill and has been incredibly popular ever since. Its central bar has up to 24 guest ales on handpull, in addition to Bowland's own beers. There are regular Meet the Brewer nights, showcasing the likes of Saltaire, Farmyard and Tiny Rebel breweries. The beer list changes every Thursday, with discounted prices on Mondays and Tuesdays for some ales. Winner of a CAMRA architectural award for the conversion in 2018. 🌣☆🕪♿⇆●P🖳❀

New Inn

20 Parson Lane, BB7 2JN

11-11; 12-11 Sun ☎ (01200) 423312

Coach House Gunpowder Mild, Farrier's Best Bitter; Moorhouse's Premier Bitter, White Witch, Pride of Pendle, Blonde Witch; 5 changing beers (sourced regionally; often Goose Eye, Prospect, Worsthorne) H

This cracking pub is a must-visit if you are in the east Lancs area. There are always at least 10 beers on, so you will be spoilt for choice. Four rooms are arranged round the central bar area and are all regularly used for meetings, gigs and performances. This is a pub designed for conversation, with no jukebox and a TV in only one room. Clitheroe Castle is just across the road. Q

Colne

Boyce's Barrel

7 New Market Street, BB8 9BJ

closed Mon; 4 (1 Sat)-9 ☎ 07736 900111

5 changing beers (sourced nationally) H

The first micropub in Colne, a member of the Micropub Association, offering five real ales, no music, no lager, just a great atmosphere and plenty of banter. Tastefully styled with tall polished wooden sleeper tables, it is reminiscent of a rail staging post. Ales are rotated often, with new beers put on the bar almost as soon as a barrel runs dry. All ales are from non-local breweries. One mild and one porter or stout are always included. Q

Wallace Hartley

35-37 Church Street, BB8 0EB

8am-11 (midnight Thu; 1am Fri & Sat); 8am-11.30 Sun ☎ (01282) 857990

Greene King Abbot; Ruddles Best Bitter; 8 changing beers (sourced nationally; often Moorhouse's, Titanic, Worsthorne) H

Named after the bandmaster of the ill-fated Titanic who was born in Colne, the building was originally a pub in the 1920s, later becoming a Greek restaurant, then opening in 2008 as a Wetherspoon. The wood-panelled interior is split into a number of seating areas and has a relaxed, friendly atmosphere. Ten ales are usually available including, of course, Titanic. The history of Wallace Hartley and pictures of old Colne decorate the walls. Close to the bus station and a pleasant uphill walk from the railway station. Q

Conder Green

Stork

Corricks Lane, LA2 0AN

12-11 (midnight Fri & Sat) ☎ (01524) 751234 thestorkinn.com

Black Sheep Best Bitter; Jennings Cumberland Ale; Lancaster Blonde; Timothy Taylor Golden Best, Landlord H

Delightful, hospitable country inn close to the estuaries of the Lune and Conder. There is a main wood-panelled bar, a restaurant and several small rooms, including a pleasant snug and a playroom for children. The hilly garden has a play area and a well, and hosts barbecues in summer. There are cycle racks outside as the pub is handy for the Lune estuary cycle path. The earliest record of this pub is 1660, and some of the existing buildings may date back that far. AP(89)

Croston

Wheatsheaf

Town Road, PR26 9RA

12-11 (midnight Fri); 10-midnight Sat; 10-11 Sun ☎ (01772) 600370 wheatsheaf-croston.com

Hawkshead Windermere Pale; Hop Back Summer Lightning; Robinsons Dizzy Blonde; 2 changing beers (sourced nationally) H

Overlooking the village green, this recently refurbished pub has a contemporary feel. It has a distinct section for dining as well as a comfortable drinking area with sofas and chairs. The large patio to the front is used for an annual beer festival in October. Three regular ales and two changing ales are served. Children are welcome. Food is served lunchtimes and evenings during the week and all day at weekends, including breakfast from 10am. P

Darwen

Number 39

39-41 Bridge Street, BB3 2AA

12-midnight ☎ 07531 425352

Hopstar Dizzy Danny Ale, Dark Knight, Smokey Joe's Black Beer, JC, Lancashire Gold H

The Hopstar Brewery tap is a classic single-roomed continental-style bar with an eclectic range of background music and serving a variety of Hopstar beers. It is a strong supporter of real cider and two or more ciders or perries are available. Bottled continental and world beers and draught Timmermans are also on offer. Thursday night usually features quality live music concerts, Friday is tapas day and Sunday afternoon is the legendary apple, cheese and perry session. Frequent buses between Blackburn and Bolton pass close by. (1)

Earby

Red Lion

72 Red Lion Street, BB18 6RD

closed Mon & Tue; 5-11 Wed & Thu; 4-11 Fri; 1-midnight Sat; 2-10.30 Sun ☎ (01282) 843395

Naylor's Gold, Pinnacle Blonde; 4 changing beers (sourced locally; often Settle) H

A warm and friendly welcome awaits you here from host and locals. This is a traditional country local, owned by local people. Both rooms have been renovated with taste, the lounge being heated with a woodburner. An extensive menu is served in the lounge lunchtimes and evenings. The pub is close to the youth hostel and is a drinkers' delight. Q

Eccleston

Greenhaus

276B The Green, PR7 5TF

4-11 (midnight Fri); 2-midnight Sat; 2-11 Sun ☎ 07835 207762

5 changing beers (sourced nationally) H

Eccleston's only micropub and gin bar is housed in what used to be the Grocer's on the Green store. It originally opened in 2015 as the Cock T'Alehouse but changed ownership and name in 2017. The pub has a modern, light and airy feel. Up to five changing cask ales are available, including at least one that is locally sourced. Parking can be difficult.

Fleetwood

Royal Oak Hotel

171 Lord Street, FY7 6SR

12-midnight (1am Fri & Sat) ☎ (01253) 873486

Banks's Sunbeam; house beer (by Reedley Hallows); 5 changing beers (sourced locally; often Blackedge, Cross Bay, Lancaster) H

Known to locals as Dead 'Uns, this pub still retains many original features. Up to seven beers are sold along with Westons Old Rosie cider. The beers are usually from within a 50-mile radius. An upstairs function room is available for hire. Live music features occasionally on Friday and Saturday nights, and dogs are allowed in the vaults. Away fans are welcome when playing Fleetwood FC. There is a small outside drinking area at the rear of the pub. It also has a book lending service.

Steamer

Queens Terrace, FY7 6BT

11-10.30 Mon; 11-midnight Tue & Thu; 12-midnight Wed; 11-2am Fri & Sat; 11-midnight Sun ☎ (01253) 681001

Bombardier; Reedley Hallows Pendleside; 4 changing beers (sourced nationally; often Bowness Bay, Cross Bay, Lancaster) H

One of Fleetwood's oldest survinving pubs and opposite Fleetwood Market and the nearby museum, this old coaching inn has a former blacksmith's forge at the rear. It is convenient for the bus, trams and Knott End ferry. Up to six changing beers are stocked. Live music features on Friday and Saturday nights and there is a singer every Tuesday afternoon. Pool, darts and dominoes can be played. If you are lucky, you might be served by TV legend Syd Little. Food is available daily with curry night on Wednesday. A varying real cider is available on draught.

Great Harwood

1B Tap

1B Glebe Street, BB6 7AA

closed Mon; 4-10 Tue-Thu; 2-midnight Fri & Sat; 2-10 Sun

4 changing beers (sourced nationally)

Comfortable two-roomed bar opened in former office premises by three real ale enthusiasts. It is close to Towngate square and preservation area, on a side street opposite the post office. The main room, featuring plenty of beer and brewery-related items, sells a changing and skilfully selected range of cask beers which usually includes a strong stout or porter. A side room housing a separate bar specialising in gin and world beers offers additional seating. Note the collection of beer festival glasses on display in the bar. P

Haighton

Haighton Manor

Haighton Green Lane, PR2 5SQ

11-11; 11-10.30 Sun ☎ (01772) 706350

House beer (by Phoenix); 6 changing beers (often Hawkshead, Moorhouse's, Worsthorne) H

Refurbished and extended in 2016, this former country house hotel is now a bustling pub and dining venue. Seven handpumps offer a varied range of real ales, including the house offering from Brunning & Price. Beers usually include a dark mild or stout. Quality locally sourced food is served as well as a selection of beer tapas. Stone walls, flagged and wooden floors, low-beamed ceilings and open fires add to the country-house feel. Local CAMRA Cider Pub of the Year 2018, with up to 12 real ciders available. P

Haskayne

King's Arms Hotel

1 Delph Lane, L39 7JJ (near bridge where Leeds & Liverpool Canal crosses A5147)

2-midnight; 12-midnight Sat & Sun ☎ (01704) 840033

Salopian Oracle; 4 changing beers (sourced regionally; often Martland Mill, Rock the Boat, Windmill) H

The King's Arms is on the busy A5147 between Maghull and Scarisbrick, a real community pub with two rooms and many attractive original features. It hosts a small beer festival over the August bank holiday weekend which includes a family fun day featuring many quirky rural competitions. The pub organises occasional coach trips to local breweries and other places of interest. P

Helmshore

Robin Hood Inn

280 Holcombe Road, BB4 4NP

4-11; 12-11 Fri-Sun ☎ (01706) 404200

Hydes Original; 4 changing beers H

Traditional stone-built village pub which, although opened up, still retains the impression of having three separate rooms, with two open fires. The original Glen Top Brewery windows are a feature. Beers from the seasonal ranges of Hydes and Beer Studio dominate the guest ales. A quiz is held on a Thursday night. The small beer garden overlooking Helmshore Textile Museum and lodge can be reached by steps to the side of the pub.

Q (11)

Hest Bank

Crossing

6 Coastal Road, LA2 6HN

12-9 (10 Sat); 12-8 Sun ☎ 07584 660075

House beer (by Lancaster); 4 changing beers H

Former café opened as a micropub in 2018. It is a stone building, possibly Victorian, with a timber extension and a plate-glass window from café days. The bar has a U-shaped layout, with the bar counter near the entrance in one arm, a wood-burning stove in the middle, and a back room holding the games, bound copies of Railway magazine and photos of Hest Bank station (which closed in 1969). The name refers to the fact that the pub is close to both one of the last level crossings on the West Coast Main Line and the ancient route over the sands. Q

Higher Walton

Cann Bridge Ale House

47 Cann Bridge Street, PR5 4DJ

closed Mon & Tue; 4-10 Wed; 4-10.30 Thu; 12-11 Fri & Sat; 2-9.30 Sun

4 changing beers (sourced locally; often Crankshaft) H

A micropub that opened in 2018 in a former hardware store, and more recently a café. This is a sympathetic conversion, with comfortable seating and Art Deco lighting. The four handpumps showcase at least one beer from Crankshaft

Brewery, with changing ales from other local microbreweries. Two continental lagers and three craft beers along with a full range of drinks provide something for everyone. Q🐴🍎P🚌 (152)🐾

Hoghton

Royal Oak 🄻

Blackburn Old Road, Riley Green, PR5 0SL

🕒 11.30-11; 12-10.30 Sun ☎ (01254) 201445

🌐 royaloak-rileygreen.co.uk/index.htm

Thwaites Mild, Original, Gold; 2 changing beers (sourced regionally) 🄷

An attractive stone-built pub on the old road between Preston and Blackburn, near Riley Green basin on the Leeds & Liverpool Canal, popular with drinkers and diners alike. Four distinct rooms including the dining area are served from the long bar, while low-beamed ceilings, bare walls and horse brasses give the pub a rustic feel. A pleasant beer garden has views of nearby Hoghton Tower. The guest beers are normally from either the Thwaites or Marston's range.
Q🐴❀◖◗🍎P🚌 (152)🐾📶

Kirkham

Stable Bar

48 Preston Street, PR4 2ZA

🕒 12-12.30am; 12-midnight Sun ☎ (01772) 490689

🌐 stablebarkirkham.co.uk

Moorhouse's Blonde Witch, Pendle Witches Brew; 3 changing beers (sourced locally; often Bowland, Phoenix) 🄷

Converted stables with many pleasing features, on the main road just out of the town centre. It is now a large one-room open-plan pub which is cosy at the front and where games and sports TV dominate the rear. Darts and pool are popular, with live music or a DJ at weekends. A multi-level garden is out at the back of the pub. Two Moorhouse's beers are always on, with up to three changing guests.
🐴❀♣P🚌📶

Tap & Vent Brewhouse

26 Poulton Street, PR4 2AB

🕒 closed Mon; 12 (4 Tue & Wed)-11 ☎ (01253) 725440

8 changing beers (sourced regionally; often Lytham) 🄷

A traditional-looking pub from the outside with a modern take inside, this is Lytham Brewery's new venture in the centre of Kirkham, just up from the Market Square. The brewery's beers feature on the bar but do not dominate, with a good range of guest ales and continental lagers and bottled beers stocked as well. There are plans for an in-house brewery, which should open at some stage in 2019. Q🐴❀♿♣🍎🚌🐾📶

Knott End-on-Sea

Knott End Working Men's Club

Salisbury Avenue, FY6 0BP

🕒 11-11 (midnight Fri & Sat) ☎ (01253) 812226

🌐 knottendwmc.co.uk

Thwaites Original; 2 changing beers (often Bank Top, Cross Bay) 🄷

Friendly private members' club which allows CAMRA members free entry on production of a membership card or this Guide; otherwise entry is £1. There are three main rooms, with one bar central to all three. Three cask beers and two changing guest beers are served, mostly from fairly local breweries. There is a comfortable lounge to the right on entry. A large games room including snooker and pool tables is to the rear. A function room is available for private parties, live music and other club events. 🐴❀◖♿♣P🚌 (2C,89)📶

Lancaster

Bobbin ✔

36 Cable Street, LA1 1HH

🕒 11-midnight (1am Thu-Sat) ☎ (01524) 32606

5 changing beers (often Anarchy, Dark Star, Tiny Rebel) 🄷

A large pub, mainly Victorian but part 18th century, which is entirely open plan but divided up by raised areas and pillars. It is handy for the bus station. The pub is frequented by a goth/metal crowd, but they are by no means the only customers. It features '70s-style flock wallpaper and a laminate floor and there is an extremely eclectic jukebox. Live music features Friday and Saturday, with pool night on Wednesday. ❀♿⇌♣🍎🚌🐾📶

Merchant's ✔

29 Castle Hill, LA1 1YN

🕒 11.30-11 (12.30am Fri); 11-12.30am Sat ☎ (01524) 66466

🌐 merchants1688.co.uk

House beer (by Old School); 7 changing beers (sourced regionally; often Allendale, Kirkby Lonsdale, Tirril) 🄷

Converted wine-merchants' cellars built in 1688, with an extensive outdoor drinking area, creating a peaceful haven from the hubbub of the city centre. The main drinking areas are in three separate tunnels, with a fourth forming the entrance and bar area. One tunnel is now a restaurant, another used for functions as required. Quiz nights are on Sundays. Look out for the stoneware bottles used in the construction of the cellar walls. A house beer, Castle Blonde, is brewed by Old School. Many board games are available, and there is live music late every Saturday evening. ❀◖◗⇌🚌📶

Sir Richard Owen ✔

4 Spring Garden Street, LA1 1RQ

🕒 8am-midnight (11 Mon; 1am Fri & Sat); 8am-11 Sun ☎ (01524) 514500

Greene King Abbot; Ruddles Best Bitter; Sharp's Doom Bar; 4 changing beers 🄷

Dating from 2001, this is a typical Wetherspoon pub of that era with wide open frill-free spaces. Behind the old warehouse façade is a split-level design. The bar is on the upper level at the front; the lower level resembles the second-class dining saloon on an ocean liner. When no sport is showing, 24-hour news plays without sound on the many screens. Wheelchair access is via the rear (Russell Street). Q❀◖◗♿⇌🍎🚌📶

Sun ✔

63 Church Street, LA1 1ET

🕒 11-midnight; 11.30-1am Fri; 11-1am Sat; 11-11.30 Sun ☎ (01524) 66006 🌐 thesunhotelandbar.co.uk

Lancaster Amber, Blonde, Black, Red; Wainwright; 5 changing beers (often Lancaster, Marston's, Robinsons) 🄷

The decor here combines a mixture of exposed stonework, wood panelling and solid furniture, with ambient candlelight in the evenings. The original pub has open space for vertical drinking; the extension is mostly furnished with old dining tables. Some original features remain, including stone fireplaces (one with a wood-burning stove) and a well. The pub is the primary outlet for Lancaster Brewery in the city. Outside is a peaceful courtyard with a heated and covered smoking area. 🐴❀🛏◐◑♿⇌🚌📶

Three Mariners 🏆 ✔

Bridge Lane, LA1 1EE (near Parksafe car park entrance)
⏲ 12-midnight (1am Fri & Sat) ☎ (01524) 388957
Oakham Citra; Robinsons Wizard, Dizzy Blonde; 7 changing beers Ⓗ
Commonly claimed to be the oldest pub in Lancaster, it certainly looks that way inside as well as outside, but it is a popular watering hole with a thriving local clientele. Home-cooked, reasonably priced food is available. Irish folk takes place on a Tuesday, folk on the first Friday of the month, and blue-grass on the third Friday of the month. Parking is limited. Q❀◐◑♿⇌♣🍎🚌🐾📶

White Cross Ⓛ ✔

Quarry Road, LA1 4XT (behind town hall, on canal towpath)
⏲ 11.30-11 (12.30am Fri & Sat); 12-11 Sun ☎ (01524) 33999
🌐 thewhitecross.co.uk
Hawkshead Bitter; Timothy Taylor Landlord; 8 changing beers (sourced regionally; often Allendale, Settle, Tirril) Ⓗ
A canalside former warehouse with an open-plan interior and a light, airy feel. French windows open onto extensive canalside seating. There is a Tuesday quiz, and a beer and pie festival each April. The pub stands in the corner of an extensive complex of Victorian textile mills, now converted to other uses. The wide open spaces and general style makes it look like a circuit pub, but in fact much of the custom comes either from the residential areas up the hill or from nearby workplaces.
❀◐◑♿♣🍎P🚌📶

Leyland

Golden Tap Ale House Ⓛ

1 Chapel Brow, PR25 3NH
⏲ closed Mon; 3-10 Tue-Thu; 2-11.30 Fri & Sat; 2-10 Sun
☎ (01772) 431859
6 changing beers Ⓗ
Located in a former shop, the Golden Tap opened in 2016 and is a cosy one-roomed micropub, one of two in Leyland. Six changing cask ales are served from microbreweries far and wide, usually including two dark beers and at least one from the local region. No food is available other than a few snacks, but the pub is right in the heart of the town's fast food and takeaway area.
Q🐴⇌♣🍎🚌(109,111)🐾📶

Leyland Lion Ⓛ ✔

60 Hough Lane, PR25 2SA
⏲ 8am-11.30 (1am Fri & Sat) ☎ (01772) 643990
Greene King Abbot; Hawkshead Windermere Pale; Ruddles Best Bitter; Sharp's Doom Bar; house beer (by Moorhouse's); 6 changing beers Ⓗ
Opened in 2011, this conversion of a town-centre post office has recently been extended due to its popularity. The pub's name commemorates the buses that made this town famous, which were built only a few yards up the road. Up to eight guest beers are usually on the bar, often sourced from local breweries, plus a real cider. The house beer, Leyland Lion, is brewed by Moorhouse's. Handy for the Commercial Vehicle Museum.
🐴❀◐◑♿⇌🍎🚌📶

Market Ale House Ⓛ

33 Hough Lane, PR25 2SB
⏲ 2-10 (11 Thu); 12-11 Fri & Sat; 1-10 Sun
☎ (01772) 623363
6 changing beers (sourced locally) Ⓗ
Opened in 2013 in a former shop premises, this was the area's first micropub and is at the entrance to the former Leyland Motors North Works, which now serves as the town's market hall. Six changing real ales come from local and national breweries. A variety of ciders, wines and a few spirits is also served. Food is limited to Lancashire cheeses. There is no TV but there is live acoustic music on Sunday. In summer, tables are placed on the wide pavement to create an outside drinking area.
Q⇌♣🍎🚌🐾📶

Longridge

Hoppy Days Ⓛ

36A Derby Road, PR3 3JT
⏲ 4-8 Mon; closed Tue; 4-9 Wed & Thu; 4-10 Fri; 2-10 Sat; 2-8 Sun ☎ 07772 901515
5 changing beers Ⓗ
A warm and friendly welcome awaits at this pleasant single-room micropub. Five handpumps showcase changing beers, many from small local microbreweries. There is normally a range of strengths and styles, and always a dark beer. This is a true micropub serving quality real ale, real cider, Belgian bottled beers and wine in a relaxed, convivial atmosphere. 🐴🍎🚌(1)🐾📶

Tap & Vent ✔

4 Towneley Parade, PR3 3HU
⏲ 3-9 (8 Mon; 10 Fri); 2-10 Sat; 2-8 Sun ☎ (01772) 875781
4 changing beers Ⓗ
Opened in 2016, the Tap & Vent was the first micropub in Longridge. Situated in a row of shops, it has a welcoming, friendly ambience. Five handpumps serve a selection of cask ales, typically from microbreweries, with the fifth devoted to real cider. Craft, bottled and keg beers plus fine wines and prosecco are also available, and a large range of gins. ♿🍎🚌(1)🐾📶

Longton

Dolphin

Marsh Lane, PR4 5JY
⏲ 12-11; 11.30-11 Sun ☎ (01772) 612032
🌐 greencrabpubs.co.uk/details3
4 changing beers (sourced locally) Ⓗ
An isolated country pub, also known locally as the Flying Fish, at the end of a lane on Longton Marsh, close to the Ribble Way. The cask ales can be found in the wood-floored public bar to the right of the main entrance. Up to four handpulled real ales and a cider are available, in a changing selection with an emphasis on local microbreweries. The restaurant in the rear conservatory has a large and varied menu. Evening closing time is flexible dependent on trade. 🐴❀◐◑♿⛺🍎P🐾

Lostock Hall

Anchor ✔

Croston Road, PR5 5LA (300yds from B5254 alongside Preston-Blackburn railway line)
⏲ 4.30-11.30; 4-midnight Fri; 12-midnight Sat; 1-11.30 Sun
☎ (01772) 335637
5 changing beers (sourced nationally) Ⓗ

Just a short distance from the Tardy Gate shopping area, this friendly community pub offers five changing cask ales from across the country, but with LocAle beers often available. It has hosted outdoor beer festivals regularly over the years, with marquees erected on a large grassy area adjacent to the pub. This year the Anchor will be celebrating its 10th consecutive appearance in the Guide. A traditional roast is available on Sundays only 3-5pm. **Q**🪑❀♿⇌♣**P**🚌ᯤ

Lytham

Craft House Beer Café 🏆

5 Clifton Street, FY8 5EP

⌚ closed Mon; 4-11 Tue; 2-11 Wed & Thu; 2-11.30 Fri; 1-11.30 Sat; 1-8 Sun ☎ (01253) 730512

4 changing beers (sourced regionally) Ⓗ

Opened in 2016, this micropub guarantees a warm and friendly welcome. It has fast developed into a popular destination for real ale drinkers and was crowned local CAMRA Pub of the Year 2019. Four different beers are served, sourced from far and wide, nearly always including a dark, supplemented by a wide selection of world and British bottled beers. The pub is dog-friendly and offers pavement seating, weather permitting. Food is served daily until 4.30pm. **Q**🪑❀◐⇌●🚌🐾ᯤ

Railway Hotel ✔

Station Road, FY8 5DH (next to fire station on B5259)

⌚ 8am-midnight ☎ (01253) 797250

Greene King Abbot; Moorhouse's White Witch, Blonde Witch, Pendle Witches Brew; Ruddles Best Bitter; Sharp's Doom Bar; 4 changing beers (sourced nationally; often Bank Top, Phoenix) Ⓗ

A Wetherspoon conversion of a former Bass pub, the Hansom Cab, in 2012, reviving the original name from Victorian times, with memorabilia depicting this era. The bright new-look interior is on different levels. Distinct themed areas include golf, railways and Lytham's halcyon days. A pleasant, outdoor drinking area with wheelchair access is at the rear. The 10 handpumps include six for permanent beers. Families are welcome.
🪑❀◐◑♿⇌●🚌ᯤ

Taps ✔

12 Henry Street, FY8 5LE

⌚ 11-11 (midnight Fri & Sat) ☎ (01253) 736226

Greene King IPA; Moorhouse's Pendle Witches Brew; Morland Old Speckled Hen; Robinsons Dizzy Blonde; 6 changing beers (sourced nationally) Ⓗ

A multi award-winning longstanding Guide entry, the Taps continues to shine. A recent refurbishment has given it a more open aspect and broadened its appeal, lending a relaxed atmosphere with more seating. There is a TV for major sporting events only and a popular quiz on Monday evening. Food is home cooked from locally sourced ingredients. Children are welcome until 7.30pm, and dogs allowed in the outdoor covered area.
❀◐♿⇌♣●🚌ᯤ

Morecambe

Eric Bartholomew ✔

10 Euston Road, LA4 5DD

⌚ 8am-11 (midnight Fri & Sat) ☎ (01524) 405860

Greene King Abbot; Ruddles Best Bitter; Sharp's Doom Bar; 3 changing beers (often Cross Bay) Ⓗ

This Wetherspoon pub near the seafront is dedicated to Eric Morecambe (born Eric Bartholomew). It functions on two levels, with an upstairs lounge and dining area. The long bar services an open-plan pub with pictures of 19th-century Morecambe and some artwork with a Morecambe and Wise theme. There is outside seating at the front for smokers but drinking is not permitted there. **Q**❀◐◑♿⇌●🚌ᯤ

Little Bare

23 Princes Crescent, LA4 6BY

⌚ closed Mon; 5-9 Tue-Thu; 3-9 Fri; 1-9 Sat; 1-6 Sun

☎ 07490 690179

5 changing beers Ⓗ

A micropub opened in 2017 in a former off-licence and retaining the shop window, with grey paint, bare floorboards and candles after dark. It follows the micropub formula: no food, no music, no machines. There is a second room down a corridor with extra seating and board games. A microgarden is planned which may be open when you read this. ⇌(Bare Lane)♣●🚌🐾

Morecambe

25 Lord Street, LA4 5HX

⌚ 12-11 ☎ (01524) 415239 🌐 themorecambehotel.co.uk

Cross Bay Halo; 4 changing beers Ⓗ

The place to come to if you want a choice of Cross Bay beers. Reopened in 2015 after renovation in a contemporary style, it is light and airy, with flagged floors and a variety of seating and tables. There are four rooms around a bar and a surprisingly spacious garden. Screens show videos of 20th-century Morecambe. Most of the day, food dominates. The name is not hubris; this was a coaching inn built long before there was a town called Morecambe.
❀🛏◐◑♿⇌🚌🐾ᯤ

Owl's Nest

Bare Lane, LA4 6DD

⌚ 12-11; 11-midnight Sat ☎ (01524) 415039

Hawkshead Bitter; 4 changing beers (sourced regionally) Ⓗ

In a village location, close both to shops and the seafront, this rural single-storey mock-Georgian pub is a former lodge house. There is a games room at one end of the main bar, which has bare stone walls and many cosy corners. A covered smoking area is available outdoors. The pub hosts a quiz night on Thursday and live music on Friday and Saturday. The only food is pies.
❀⇌(Bare Lane)♣**P**🚌🐾ᯤ

Nether Kellet

Limeburner's Arms

32 Main Road, LA6 1EP

⌚ closed Mon; 7.45-11; 4-11 Sun

1 changing beer Ⓗ

Once – within living memory – most country pubs were like this: no food, no jukebox, plain and simply furnished. The building dates from the early 19th century, and minor improvements have not changed the character of the place. Unsurprisingly, most of the customers are locals; the landlord himself is a local farmer, and his family have run the pub for 80 years. The old photos in the bar are a rewarding study. **Q**❀⛺♣**P**🚌(51)🐾

Ormskirk

Court Leet
4 Wheatsheaf Walk, L39 2XA
8am-12.30am (1am Thu-Sat) (01695) 579803
Greene King Abbot; Ruddles Best Bitter; 10 changing beers (often Cross Bay, Moorhouse's, Weetwood)
This Wetherspoon pub, opened in 2014, is in the centre of Ormskirk in a small courtyard area off Burscough Street. It has a large open-plan main bar area fitted out in contemporary style. Virtually the entire upper floor is taken up by a fully exposed terrace which includes a non-smoking section. It is thought the pub site was a meeting place of the Court Leet, which was responsible for running the town's affairs until 1876.

Cricketers
24 Chapel Street, L39 4QF
12-midnight; 12-11 Sun (01695) 571123
thecricketers-ormskirk.co.uk
Thwaites Nutty Black; Wainwright; 4 changing beers (sourced regionally; often Blackedge, Mobberley, Old School)
Close to Ormskirk town centre, the pub prides itself on both quality food and cask ales, featuring six beers from local and regional breweries. The extensive food menu is served all day in the restaurant and bar area. Cricket memorabilia around the walls reflect a close relationship with Ormskirk cricket club, as does the successful Ormskirk Food and Drink Festival that is run each September and features over 60 cask ales.
P (375,385)

Tap Room No.12
12 Burscough Street, L39 2ER
closed Mon; 11-11; 12-8 Sun (01695) 575907
Hawkshead Windermere Pale; 3 changing beers (sourced regionally; often Windmill)
This former shop has been converted into a Belgian style single-room bar. It features four changing cask ales sourced regionally and an extensive range of foreign bottled beers and authentic foreign lagers on draught. There is a quiz every Wednesday and live music Friday and Saturday, with background music during the rest of the week. One of the cask ales is generally from Burscough, the house brewery.

Orrell

Delph Tavern
Tontine Road, WN5 8UJ
11.30-11.30 (12.30am Fri & Sat) (01695) 622239
5 changing beers
Free house popular with locals and visitors, stocking five changing ales with an emphasis on local breweries. Food is served every day and offers a balance of traditional pub classics alongside innovative street food. Live sports are shown on a number of unobtrusive screens while a vault area has pool and darts. The outside space includes a small play area as well as tables to enjoy food and drinks. Weekly quiz nights are popular.
P

Oswaldtwistle

Vault
343 Union Road, BB5 3HS
3-9.30 (closed Tue); 1-10.30 Fri & Sat; 1-9.30 Sun
(01254) 872279
JW Lees Bitter; 4 changing beers (sourced regionally)
This single-roomed bar with separate seating areas is on the busy main road through Oswaldtwistle. It is easy to reach by public transport as buses from Accrington and Blackburn pass the door every few minutes. There is high bench seating around the walls and a standing area at the bar. The six handpumps dispense four changing beers and two ciders. Q

Overton

Ship
9 Main Street, LA3 3HD
closed Mon & Tue; 5-10 Wed & Thu; 5-11 Fri; 4-11 Sat; 3-10 Sun 07979 030196
4 changing beers
Restored in 2016 to Victorian basics: bar and fittings, decorative floor tiles. Traces of 20th-century alterations have almost vanished and there remain four quite distinct public rooms, one a games room. A hole between two of them is occupied by a wood-burning stove. Upholstered bench seating is around the walls and café-style tables in the middle. The white or beige walls carry paintings for sale. Food is only available on occasion (booking required). Upstairs are two function rooms, one with the famous display of birds eggs. Q P (5)

Padiham

Free Gardeners
2 St Giles Street, BB12 8HL
5-midnight; 4-2am Fri; 1-2am Sat; 12-midnight Sun
(01282) 770965
4 changing beers (sourced nationally)
A street-corner local with four changing beers from near and far – often Lancaster, Deeply Vale and Heritage. Partially open plan, it features a pool table and a snug with a logburner. Hidden behind the optics are some of the original pub windows with the monogram WA; the pub was once part of the estate of William Astley, brewers of Nelson, who were taken over by Massey's of Burnley in 1924. There is a small display of Massey artefacts on the column by the middle of the bar.

Parbold

Railway Hotel
1 Station Road, WN8 7NU
5-11; 12-11.30 Fri & Sat; 12-10.30 Sun (01257) 462917
Tetley Bitter; 6 changing beers (sourced locally; often Hophurst, Problem Child, Prospect)
A former Marston's inn now privately owned, this non-food pub is frequented by locals, and puts its emphasis on excellent beer and hospitality. There is a central drinking area and two small rooms to either side. A coal fire adds to the ambience in winter together with comfy seats and sofas. There is a large-screen TV and pool table set back. The pub sells one regular beer, Tetley Bitter, and six changing locally sourced ales. Quiz night is Tuesday. Q P

Wayfarer Inn
1-3 Alder Lane, WN8 7NL
12-2, 5-10; 12-10 Sat & Sun (01257) 464600
wayfarerparbold.co.uk
Problem Child Good Spankin'; 5 changing beers

A country pub with a focus on dining. It has six handpulls, one of them for cider, and a range of craft keg beers. Landlord and brewer Jonny Birkett is happy to show you around his on-site microbrewery, Problem Child Brewing. The pub has low-beamed ceilings with cosy nooks and crannies. It is popular with walkers, being close to the Leeds & Liverpool Canal and Parbold Hill; suitable walks are shown on the website. The countryside beer garden offers pleasant views.
Q ❀ ◐ ♿ ⇌ ● P ☐ ▭ ❖ ᯤ

Pendleton

Swan With Two Necks 🏆 L

Main Street, BB7 1PT
12-2.30 (not Mon), 6-11; 12-11 Sat; 12-8 Sun
☎ (01200) 423112 🌐 swanwithtwonecks.co.uk
5 changing beers (sourced regionally; often Goose Eye, Phoenix, Tiny Rebel)
This multi award-winning pub is central to village life and continues to be a real delight. It has been run by the same owners, both CAMRA members, for over 30 years. The five handpulls offer a varied choice, with either a dark mild or stout always among the range. Food is high quality and reasonably priced. There are real fires during the winter months. A former CAMRA National Pub of the Year. Q ❀ ◐ ♣ ● P ❖

Penwortham

Black Bull Inn L ✔

83 Pope Lane, PR1 9BA
12-11 (midnight Fri); 11-11.30 Sat ☎ (01772) 752953
🌐 blackbull-penwortham.co.uk/ales
Robinsons Dizzy Blonde; Theakston Best Bitter; 3 changing beers (sourced nationally) H
Attractive cottage-style inn dating back to the early 1800s, with a village pub atmosphere despite its location in a well populated area. On entering, a narrow passageway leads through to a central bar serving several drinking areas including a separate public bar. One of the guest ales will come from a local brewery. The venue actively supports local charities and was the local CAMRA Community Pub of the Year in 2018. Q ❀ ♣ P ▭ ❖ ᯤ

Tap & Vine

69 Liverpool Road, PR1 9XD
11 (4 Mon & Tue)-11; 11-midnight Sat; 12-10.30 Sun
☎ (01772) 751116 🌐 tapandvine.co.uk
4 changing beers (sourced locally)
Penwortham's first micropub, this is an upmarket wine bar-type establishment housed in a former arts and crafts shop. It has limited seating and can get quite busy at times, although to the rear there is a small secluded room with a wood-burning stove, and there is also outside seating in the summer months. There are four changing beers always on, often including some from lesser-known microbreweries. Food, snacks and serving platters are offered. Q ♣ ● ▭ ❖ ᯤ

Poulton le Fylde

Old Town Hall ✔

5 Church Street, FY6 7AP
11-midnight (1am Fri & Sat); 12-11.30 Sun
☎ (01253) 892257
6 changing beers (sourced locally; often Kirkby Lonsdale, Moorhouse's, Rooster's) H
Used as council offices until 1987, this was originally a pub called the Bay Horse. Horse racing dominates the TV screens during the day. The pub gets busy with football fans whenever there is a match on. The rear portion has painted panels on the upper walls, a ceiling featuring the most revered Blackpool players, and a small stage area where bands play each Saturday. ♿ ⇌ ♣ ▭ ❖ ᯤ

Poulton Elk ✔

22 Hardhorn Road, FY6 7SR
8am-midnight (1am Fri & Sat) ☎ (01253) 895265
Greene King Abbot; Ruddles Best Bitter; Sharp's Doom Bar; 7 changing beers (sourced nationally; often Cross Bay, Moorhouse's, Phoenix) H
Formerly a series of short-lived night clubs, this busy Wetherspoon pub was built on the site of a telephone exchange. There is a terrace at the front and a suntrap beer garden overlooking a large public car park at the rear. A 13,000-year-old elk skeleton accompanied by two spear points was found locally, the earliest evidence of people living in north-west England, hence the pub's name.
❀ ◐ ♿ ⇌ ● ▭ ᯤ

Thatched House ✔

30 Ball Street, FY6 7BG
11.30-11 (midnight Fri & Sat); 12-11 Sun
☎ (01253) 891063
Chapel Street Brewhouse Blonde, Cream Stout, Double Hopped; 7 changing beers (sourced regionally; often Bradfield, Rooster's, Saltaire) H
Ten cask beers are on the bar here, three from the Chapel Street Brewhouse housed in the former stables at the back of the pub, seven from a changing range. The building is newly refurbished, with a tiled wall in the front room, booth-style seating in the side room, and a new terraced area above the brewery, while retaining some original wood-panelling. Often noisy with chatter, the pub is warmed in winter by log-burning stoves and a log fire. Q ❀ ⇌ ♣ ▭ ❖ ᯤ

Preston

Black Horse ★ ✔

166 Friargate, PR1 2EJ
11-11 (midnight Fri); 10.30-midnight Sat; 12-11 Sun
☎ (01772) 204855
Robinsons Dizzy Blonde, Unicorn, Trooper, Old Tom; 4 changing beers (sourced nationally) H
Victorian Grade II-listed pub close to the historic open market. With its tiled bar and walls, and mosaic floor, it has been identified by CAMRA as having a nationally important historic pub interior. The two front rooms are adorned with Robinsons memorabilia and photos of old Preston. The famous hall of mirrors seating area is to the rear. Real cider and a selection of pork pies are always available. Four Robinsons beers are served, with four changing guest beers coming from far and wide, sourced through Titanic. ⇌ ♣ ● ▭ ❖ ᯤ

Continental

South Meadow Lane, PR1 8JP
12-11 (12.30am Fri & Sat) ☎ (01772) 499425
🌐 newcontinental.net
House beer (by Fernandes); 6 changing beers (sourced nationally) H
Beside the River Ribble, railway line and Miller Park, the pub has a main bar area plus a lounge with a real fire in winter and a conservatory overlooking the garden. Live music and theatre

regularly feature in a separate events space which is also used to house beer festivals. Seven handpumps offer a cider and up to six microbrewery beers, including the house ale from Fernandes and a dark beer. Freshly cooked meals are served daily except Monday. A two-time local CAMRA Pub of the Year. Q♘❀◐♿⇌●P🐾ᯤ

Guild Ale House

56 Lancaster Road, PR1 1DD

❂ 12-11 (9.30 Mon); 12-10 Sun ☎ 07932 517444

7 changing beers (sourced regionally; often Bank Top, Elland, Pomona Island) 🄷

Preston's first micropub, it opened in 2016 just a few doors away from the town's Guild Hall complex. The main room has high- and low-level seating and the tall ceilings give a light and airy feel. A small lounge is tucked away to the rear and there is a comfortable lounge upstairs. Seven changing beers are served, mainly local or from Yorkshire, and at least one dark ale. There is also a range of continental beers in keg and bottle. There is no jukebox, music, TV, or food, but live acoustic music on Sunday afternoons. Local CAMRA Pub of the Year 2018. Q♘❀♿⇌♣●🚌🐾ᯤ

Market Tap ✔

33-35 Market Street, PR1 2ES

❂ 11-midnight ☎ (01772) 822455

John Smith's Bitter; 5 changing beers (sourced nationally) 🄷

Originally the Market Tavern, this is a traditional one-room pub dating back to the mid-1800s, with comfortable seating and a couple of intimate booths. Situated facing the historic Victorian market, there is outdoor seating to the front. John Smith's is the regular cask ale and there are five interesting changing guest beers served from all over the country, making this a popular real ale venue. Six traditional ciders are also on sale. Local CAMRA Cider Pub of the Year 2019. Q♘◐♿⇌♣●🚌🐾ᯤ

Moorbrook 🏆

370 North Road, PR1 1RU

❂ 12-midnight ☎ (01772) 823302

House beer (by Blackjack); 8 changing beers (sourced nationally) 🄷

Now privately owned, this pub is where the West Lancs CAMRA branch was formed in 1973. It has a traditional wood-panelled bar with two rooms off the main bar area. Eight guest beers are from all over the country plus a house beer, Moorbrook Pale Ale, which is brewed specifically for the pub by Blackjack of Manchester. Authentic wood-fired pizzas are a speciality. The beer garden to the rear is a suntrap. The pub gets busy on Preston North End match days. Local CAMRA Pub of the Year 2019. ♘❀◐♿♣🚌🐾ᯤ

Old Vic 🄻 ✔

79 Fishergate, PR1 2UH

❂ 10-11 (midnight Fri); 11-midnight Sat; 12-11.30 Sun ☎ (01772) 828519

Bombardier; 6 changing beers 🄷

Opposite the railway station and on bus routes into the city, this popular pub can get busy at weekends. A number of TVs show sports events and this is a rare city-centre hostelry for darts enthusiasts. To the rear is an outdoor decked smoking area. Seven handpumps serve a good range of beers from the area, with local microbreweries usually represented. Third-of-a-pint real ale taster paddles are on offer, as are carryouts. The car park is only available on a Sunday and in the evenings. ♘❀◐⇌♣P🚌ᯤ

Orchard

Earl Street, PR1 2JA

❂ 12-10 (11 Thu-Sat) ☎ 07756 583621

2 changing beers (often Farm Yard, Nightjar, Wily Fox) 🄷

This sister pub to the Guild Ale House opened in March 2018, located within the Grade II-listed covered market. Its framework and decor feature wood recycled from the old market trestle boards, plus lots of modern glass. No food is served but there is plenty in the neighbouring market, which can be ordered and taken in. Two cask ales and 10 craft ales are always available alongside real cider. Q❀⇌♣●🚌

Plug & Taps

32 Lune Street, PR1 2NN

❂ closed Mon; 1-10 (12.30am Fri & Sat); 1-8 Sun

4 changing beers 🄷

This real ale and craft beer bar opened in 2018, just 300 yards from the railway station, in a former hairdresser's shop opposite the Corn Exchange. It offers four handpumps and 10 keg lines, as well as a large can and bottle fridge with occasional real cider boxes. Changing beers from anywhere in the country are served with a commitment to having at least three beers from Outstanding Brewery; these can be cask or keg. Occasional tap takeovers are hosted, featuring various breweries. There is a large function room upstairs. ♘⇌♣🚌🐾ᯤ

Princess Alice 🄻 ✔

29-31 Cambridge Walk, PR1 7SL

❂ 4.30-11.30 (12.30am Fri); 12-12.30am Sat; 12-11.30 Sun ☎ (01772) 823737

Lancaster Blonde; 3 changing beers (sourced regionally; often Bowland, Lancaster, Worsthorne) 🄷

Warm and friendly Victorian street-corner local in a redeveloped residential area. The ornate tilework reflects the former Matthew Brown Brewery ownership. The interior has been modernised and opened out. There are a large number of TV screens showing multiple (often sports) channels. The pub is only 15 minutes' walk from Deepdale Stadium and popular on match days. The regular beer is Lancaster Blonde and changing beers are normally from small Lancashire breweries, often Bowland, Lancaster and Worsthorne. ❀♣P🚌(23)ᯤ

Vinyl Tap

28 Adelphi Street, PR1 7BE

❂ 11.30-11 (1am Fri & Sat) ☎ (01772) 561871

6 changing beers (sourced nationally) 🄷

A single-room bar, adjacent to the university, which opened in 2018. Food is served throughout the day, breathing new life into the old pub. There are six real ale pumps serving a wide range of microbrewery beers, often from unusual breweries for the area. Vinyl-themed events and a jukebox are attractions Sunday to Thursday; customers can pick and choose from an ever-growing collection or bring their own to play while enjoying a drink and a bite to eat. Friday and Saturday vary between live music and guest vinyl DJ slots with music spanning most genres. ◐⇌🚌ᯤ

Rawtenstall

Buffer Stops

Bury Road, BB4 6AG
12-11 (midnight Fri); 11-midnight Sat; 11-10 Sun
(0161) 764 7790 eastlancsrailway.org.uk
Northern Whisper Beltie; Outstanding Piston Broke; 3 changing beers
On the platform at the northern terminus of the East Lancs Railway, this unique one-roomed bar was once the station café. It is small, but further seating is available in the ticket hall and waiting room and on benches and at tables on the platform. The bar is busy both with railway visitors and locals. Snacks are available. Close to Ski Rossendale, Whitaker Park and museum and the Weavers' cottage. QP

Casked

16 Bury Road, BB4 6AA
closed Mon & Tue; 12-10 (11 Fri & Sat); 12-8 Sun
07764 695261
5 changing beers (sourced locally)
This cosy single-roomed micropub with its varied seating and imaginative lighting is on the edge of Rawtenstall town centre. It lies a short walk away from the northern terminus of the East Lancs Heritage Railway and just along from Fitzpatrick's famous temperance bar. Up to six mainly local cask beers are available on handpump, many from breweries around the Rossendale valley.
(464,x43)

Hop Micro Pub

70 Bank Street, BB4 8EG
10-9 Mon; 10-10 Tue & Wed; 10-midnight Thu-Sat; 11-9 Sun 07753 775150 hopmicropubs.com
Deeply Vale Hop; 5 changing beers
A micropub with a big heart. Situated on Rawtenstall's cobbled Bank Street, Hop is a pleasant and congenial venue more reminiscent of a traditional local pub. It is spread across three levels, with a heated outside drinking area. With six handpulled cask ales, including the permanent Hop from Deeply Vale, as well as keg craft beers and ciders, there is always a fantastic choice. Close to the northern terminus of East Lancs Heritage Railway.

Shepherds Inn

225 Haslingden Road, BB4 6RE (on A681)
5-midnight (1am Fri); 1-1am Sat; 1-11 Sun
(01706) 213025
Copper Dragon Golden Pippin; JW Lees Bitter
This stone-built free house is in the middle of a row of terraced houses and has been recently refurbished. There is an open-plan bar area with two handpumps, a smaller side room with pool table, and a small outdoor area to the rear. This is a community-oriented pub with a pool team, mixed darts, quiz nights and regular country music on Sunday evenings. (464,244)

Rufford

Hesketh Arms

81 Liverpool Road, L40 1SB (on A59 at jct with B5246)
12-11 (midnight Fri & Sat) (01704) 821002
Moorhouse's White Witch, Pride of Pendle; 7 changing beers (sourced regionally; often Cross Bay, Phoenix, Reedley Hallows)
A spacious former Greenall's inn, the Hesketh is now a free house serving up to six ales, mostly from local breweries. Set in a charming village, it is near to the National Trust property of Rufford Old Hall and the delightful St Mary's marina. A large split-level establishment with several dining areas, it serves good-quality food throughout the day. Monthly live entertainment and a Tuesday quiz attract a mixed clientele.
QP(2A,347)

St Annes

Fifteens at St Annes

42 St Annes Road West, FY8 1RF
11-11 (2am Fri & Sat); 12-11 Sun (01253) 725852
fifteensstannes.com
House beer (by Farm Yard); 4 changing beers (sourced nationally)
Set in a former Lloyds bank, this eccentric pub is far larger than it appears at first sight. Eclectically decorated, it incorporates many of the bank's original features, including the vault, which is both comfortable and peaceful. There is a quiet mezzanine towards the front. Live music plays at weekends and two beer festivals are hosted a year. Beers are mostly from local and regional brewers, and at least two ciders are generally on sale.

No.10 Ale House

10 Park Road, FY8 1QX
12-11 (midnight Fri & Sat) 07809 368682
5 changing beers (sourced locally; often Bank Top, Moorhouse's, Reedley Hallows)
Handy for the railway station, this quirky and friendly bar is larger than it looks and close to the shops in St Anne's Square, the buses and railway station. The bar usually has beers from local and regional brewers, and cider is always available. Decorated with retro Blackpool tourism posters, this bar is a real ale heaven. Well-behaved dogs are most welcome. Q

Trawl Boat

36-38 Wood Street, FY8 1QR
8am-midnight (1am Fri & Sat) (01253) 783080
Greene King Abbot; Moorhouse's Blonde Witch; Ruddles Best Bitter; Sharp's Doom Bar; 6 changing beers (sourced regionally; often Bank Top, Phoenix)
An imposing hostelry where all visitors are assured a warm and friendly welcome. Converted to a pub from a former solicitors' office, it is handy for the shops, railway station, buses and seafront attractions. Ten handpumps dispense four regular beers and a good selection of six changing ones. A well-maintained large front drinking area is ideal in summer months. Wheelchair access is via the side. The family area at the rear can get busy at weekends.

Silverdale

Woodlands

Woodlands Drive, LA5 0RU
5-11.30; 12-midnight Sat; 12-11.30 Sun
(01524) 701655
4 changing beers
A large country house on an elevated site dating from about 1878, converted to a pub with only minimal alterations. Most of the trade is provided by locals. The bar has a large fireplace as big as the counter and great views across Morecambe Bay.

Beer pumps are in another room, with a list of the four available ales on the wall facing the bar. Home-made sandwiches are served at weekends. The smoking area is covered and sheltered. There is a quiz on the last Sunday of the month, and a beer festival of 30 ales takes place in October. To telephone the pub you need to ring twice. Q🐎❀♣🍎P🚌🐾

Wesham

Stanley Arms

8 Garstang Road South, PR4 3BL
3-midnight; 12-midnight Thu & Fri; 11-midnight Sat; 10-midnight Sun ☎ (01772) 469495
stanleyarmswesham.co.uk
4 changing beers (sourced nationally; often Butcombe) Ⓗ
A street-corner establishment, formerly two terraced houses, this welcoming pub is just a three-minute walk from the railway station and bus stops, and a half-mile walk from AFC Fylde's football stadium. Photos of old Preston and Blackpool landmarks and a trophy display case are on show in this comfortable community venue. Opening hours and mealtimes may vary depending on the season. 🐎❀◐♿⇌♣🚌(61,78)🐾📶

Whalley

Dog Inn Ⓛ

55 King Street, BB7 9SP
11-11 (midnight Fri & Sat); 12-11 Sun ☎ (01254) 823009
dog-innwhalley.co.uk
6 changing beers (sourced regionally; often Peerless, Wishbone) Ⓗ
This popular pub lies close to the historic church and abbey in the centre of Whalley. It has featured in several earlier editions of the Guide. The central bar has six handpulls offering a varying list of beers, which often includes one of the more powerful brews (6% ABV or more). Beers are from a mixture of micros and local breweries, but regularly come from further afield. Food is only served at lunchtimes. Lots of hunting and sporting memorabilia are dotted around the pub.
🐎❀◐⇌🚌🐾📶

Wheelton

Dressers Arms Ⓛ ✔

9 Briers Brow, PR6 8HD (near jct with A674)
11-11 ☎ (01254) 830041 dressersarms.co.uk
Black Sheep Best Bitter; Copper Dragon Golden Pippin; Hawkshead Windermere Pale; 4 changing beers (sourced nationally; often Northern Monkey, Prospect) Ⓗ
A stone-built country pub with a surprisingly modern interior. A mixture of flagged and wooden floors, painted walls and open stonework gives the pub a bright and airy feel. Popular for food, with an extensive menu, it also offers up to seven cask ales, often including a dark beer and usually featuring beers from local microbreweries. The pleasant west-facing beer garden has views over the local countryside. Q🐎❀◐P🚌(24)🐾📶

Red Lion

Blackburn Road, PR6 8EU (in centre of village opp clock tower)
11-11 (11.30 Wed & Thu; 12.30am Fri & Sat)
☎ (01254) 659890 theredlionatwheelton.co.uk
Hawkshead Lakeland Gold; Timothy Taylor Landlord; 7 changing beers (sourced nationally; often Durham, Oakham, Salopian) Ⓗ
Built around 1826, this village pub reflects the former mill village it used to serve. It is a former Matthew Brown house, with a bar that retains Lion Ales windows and a large stone lion at roof level above the door. There is a comfortable lounge with an open fire and a second room up a few steps. Nine handpumps showcase two regular beers and seven varying ales from larger independent breweries. Food is served seven days a week. Close to the West Pennine Moors, the pub is convenient for many local walks. Q🐎❀◐P⛽🚌(24)📶

Whitworth

Whitworth Vale & Healey Brass Band Club

498 Market Street, OL12 8DP
7-midnight (1am Sat); 12-midnight Sun
☎ (01706) 852484
Thwaites Original; 3 changing beers (sourced nationally) Ⓗ
A popular local club, noticeable for being the home of the local brass band of the same name. The club is part of a terrace by the main road through the town, with the regular 464 bus service passing by the door. Quite spacious, despite the low ceiling, it also has an outside seating area. Up to four beers are on offer, with Thwaites Original as a regular. Local CAMRA Club of the Year. 🚌(464)

Worsthorne

Crooked Billet Ⓛ ✔

1-3 Smith Street, BB10 3NQ
7-midnight Mon & Wed; 6-midnight Tue; 5.30-midnight Thu; 4-1am Fri; 12-1am Sat; 12-12.30am Sun
☎ 07766 230175 crookedbilletworsthorne.co.uk
Tetley Bitter; Timothy Taylor Landlord; Worsthorne Packhorse, Some Like It Blond; 2 changing beers (sourced regionally; often Howard Town, Lancaster) Ⓗ
An award-winning true free house, this well-presented village pub has a beautiful wood and glass horseshoe bar serving both the main lounge area and snug. It serves as the Worsthorne Brewery tap. Quiz nights are popular, as are Thai nights and soul nights. Its position in the hills close to Burnley makes it popular with walkers and cyclists. It is dog-friendly and has a large covered outdoor drinking area where you can enjoy the flower-bedecked exterior. Q🐎❀◐♿♣P🚌(2)🐾📶

Wrightington

White Lion ✔

117 Mossy Lea Road, WN6 9RE
10-11 ☎ (01257) 425977 thewhitelionlancs.co.uk
Banks's Amber Ale; Jennings Cumberland Ale; 6 changing beers Ⓗ
A popular country pub with a good range of food and beers – with eight handpumps – for diners and drinkers. The pub hosts a Monday Club with drinks offers, a quiz on Tuesday, a poker league on Thursday, a monthly cocktail night and live music every Saturday. It is community-oriented, running the village scarecrow festival and themed evenings throughout the year. Families are welcome, with board games in the pub and a large beach hut-themed garden area. Q🐎❀◐♿P🚌(113)

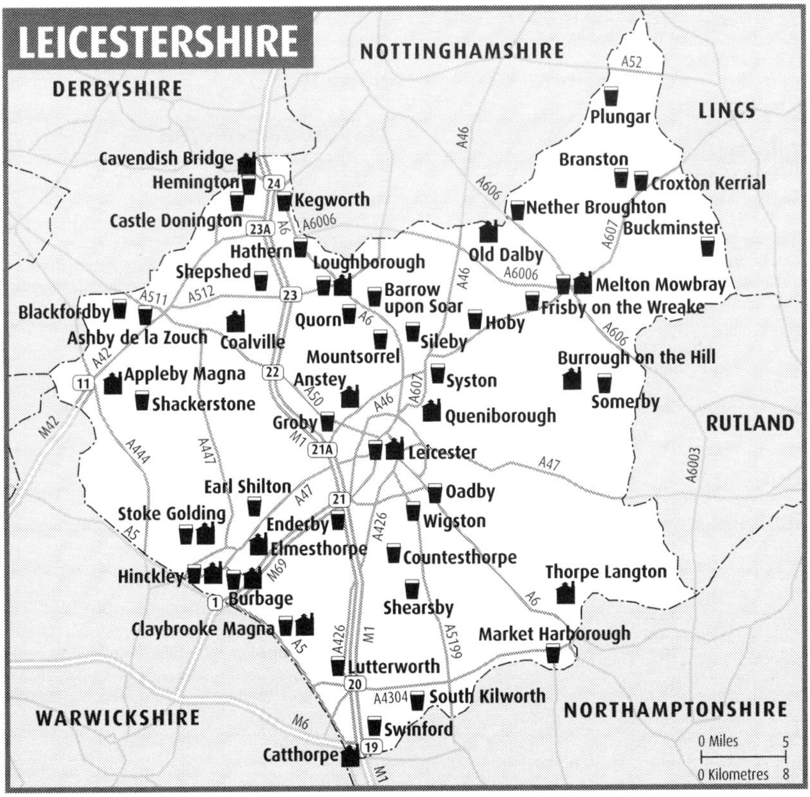

Ashby de la Zouch

Tap at No.76

76 Market Street, LE65 1AP

closed Mon; 4-11 Tue-Thu; 3-midnight Fri & Sat; 12-10 Sun

thetapatno76.co.uk

Tollgate Ashby Pale; 6 changing beers H

This Ashby micropub, on the high street, is a relatively recent addition to the Ashby scene. It is a traditional establishment for enjoying conversation. A Tollgate Brewery pub, it offers seven real ales, four on handpump, three on gravity. Third-pint tasting trays are available for those wishing to try the full range of beers. Pork pies are served.

Barrow upon Soar

Soar Bridge Inn

29 Bridge Street, LE12 8PN

12 (4 Mon)-11; 12-10.30 Sun ☎ (01509) 412686

Everards Tiger, Old Original; 4 changing beers (often Everards) H

Situated next to the bridge that gave it its name, this pub is popular with walkers, boaters and drinkers. The large single-room interior divides into distinct areas, with a separate restaurant, function room and skittle alley. Outside there is a floodlit pétanque court, beer terrace and garden. Well-behaved dogs and children are welcome. Home-made food is available Tuesday to Sunday, with a different theme each evening.

Q P (K2,CB27)

Blackfordby

Black Lion

3 Main Street, DE11 8AB

4-11 (1am Fri); 12-1am Sat; 12-11 Sun ☎ (01283) 337551

theblacklionblackfordby.com

Draught Bass; 5 changing beers (sourced locally; often Blue Monkey, Derby) H

Popular local in a quiet village in north-west Leicestershire, bought from Enterprise Inns and reopened in 2013 as a free house following a substantial refurbishment. Grade II-listed, with old beams and open fires, it has a lovely courtyard and covered smoking area. Guest beers are often sourced from small local breweries, and up to four ciders are on draught. Cheeseboards and ham and cheese cobs are available. Quiz night is the first Sunday of each month, jam night the last Wednesday. **Q P**

Branston

Wheel Inn L

Main Street, NG32 1RU

closed Mon; 12-11; 12-8 Sun ☎ (01476) 870376

thewheelinnbranston.co.uk

Black Sheep Best Bitter; 2 changing beers H

This attractive stone-built 18th-century village pub houses a cosy bar with seating plus a larger restaurant with rustic tables and a real fire. The outdoor area is quiet and relaxing in the summer months, with traditional outbuildings used for beer festivals and live music. The Wheel boasts an extensive food menu using locally sourced ingredients where possible, including produce from

the Belvoir Estate. Cask cider is usually available on the bar. A repeat local CAMRA Pub of the Year.
Q ♣ P

Buckminster

Tollemache Arms

48 Main Street, NG33 5SA
closed Mon; 11-3, 6-11; 11-11 Sat; 12-5 Sun
☎ (01476) 860477 tollemache-arms.co.uk
Oakham JHB; 2 changing beers [H]
This beautiful building is at the heart of what was the Tollemache family estate, with rows of stone buildings featuring heavily in the picturesque village. The pub was the first in the area to offer cask beer in third-pints, with three ales available, including local offerings. Food is served lunchtimes and evenings. Popular with locals and tourists alike, families and dogs are all welcome here.
P

Burbage

Burbage & District Constitutional Club [L]

Church Street, LE10 2DE
11-2, 6-11; 11-11.30 Fri; 11-11.45 Sat; 12-3, 7-11 Sun
☎ (01455) 615142 burbageconclub1911.com
Greene King Abbot; Marston's Saddle Tank; 3 changing beers (often Church End, Grainstore) [H]
Formerly the home of Prime Minister George Canning, the club was founded in 1911. This Grade II-listed building, in the heart of the village, features a comfortable lounge with open fire, wheelchair access, garden, function room equipped with skittle alley, snooker and pool tables, darts, dominoes, crib, chess and table tennis. Live music plays every Saturday night. Sandwiches and cobs are available. A regular CAMRA branch Club of the Year and East Midlands Club of the Year 2016-18. ♣

Lime Kilns Brew Pub [L] ✓

Watling Street, LE10 3ED
12-3, 5.30-11; 12-11 Sat; 12-10.30 Sun ☎ (01455) 631158
limekilnsinn.co.uk
Buswells Single Barrel; Langton Inclined Plane Bitter; Marston's Pedigree; 3 changing beers (sourced locally; often Timothy Taylor) [H]
Situated alongside the Ashby Canal and the A5, the pub was originally an 18th-century coaching inn. It offers free gardenside moorings and a large canalside beer garden with a marquee for functions. The first-floor lounge has canal views and an open fire. A ground floor canalside stable bar, with woodburner, opens to the beer garden. Traditional food is served all week, with special deals Monday to Thursday evenings. Buswells microbrewery is on site. A former CAMRA branch Pub of the Year. Q ♣ P

Castle Donington

Chequered Flag

32 Borough Street, DE74 2LA
4-10.30 (11 Fri & Sat); 12-5 Sun ☎ 07841 374441
House beer (by Dancing Duck) [G]**; 6 changing beers** [H]
A thriving micropub in the heart of a busy street. It serves real ale straight from the cask, visible from a temperature-controlled cool-room cellar. A range of eight ciders and quality wines is also kept. Award-winning local pork pies and pickles can be enjoyed with your beer, subject to availability. Skylink bus services make it accessible from Derby, Nottingham, Loughborough and Leicester until late.
Q

Claybrooke Magna

Pig in Muck [L]

Manor Road, LE17 5AY
12-2.30 (not Mon), 5-11; 12-11 Fri & Sat; 12-10 Sun
☎ (01455) 202859
Pig Pub Chinook Pale Ale, Pigs Best Bitter; Sharp's Doom Bar; 1 changing beer (sourced regionally) [H]
The only pub in the village, popular after a change of ownership in 2012. The licensee brews his Pig Pub beers in a small building behind the pub and there is a loyalty scheme on the in-house beers. A choice of craft keg beers is also offered, including one from the brewery. The increasingly popular traditional pub food is home cooked. Hinckley bus service 8 runs hourly between Hinckley and Lutterworth, Monday to Saturday daytimes.
♣ P (8)

Countesthorpe

Railway ✓

128 Station Road, LE8 5TD
5-11.15 (midnight Fri); 12-midnight Sat & Sun
☎ (0116) 277 3551
Draught Bass; Marston's Pedigree; 1 changing beer (sourced nationally; often Black Sheep) [H]
Close to the site of Countesthorpe railway station which fell under the Beeching axe on New Year's Day 1962. A cul-de-sac near the pub is aptly named Beeching's Close and the gardens of nearby houses meet with the boundary of the old line. The interior was refurbished in 2017 and comprises a front lounge bar, which appears to be two rooms knocked into one stretching the full width of the front elevation, and a similar-sized back public bar with skittles table and darts. ♣ P (85)

Croxton Kerrial

Geese & Fountain 🏆 [L]

1 School Lane, NG32 1QR
11-11; 12-10.30 Sun ☎ (01476) 870350
thegeeseandfountain.co.uk
5 changing beers [H]

REAL ALE BREWERIES

Anstey Ale Anstey
Belvoir Old Dalby
Buswells Burbage (NEW)
Charnwood Loughborough
Dow Bridge Catthorpe
Elliswood Hinckley
Elmesthorpe Elmesthorpe
Framework Leicester
Golden Duck Appleby Magna
Great Central Leicester (NEW)
Langton Thorpe Langton
Market Bosworth Stoke Golding
Mount St Bernard Coalville
Parish Burrough on the Hill
Pig Pub Claybrooke Magna
Q Brewery Queniborough
Round Corner Melton Mowbray (NEW)
Shardlow Cavendish Bridge
West End Leicester

This village inn reopened in 2016 after a long period of closure. With wood fires, a flagstone floor and rustic seating, it has a quiet, relaxed atmosphere. Dogs, children, cyclists and walkers are all welcome. Local breweries always feature on the five handpumps, with guest beers from other local microbreweries, plus lagers and three real ciders. B&B rooms are available, and food is served every day. Occasional mini beer and cider festivals feature throughout the year, and regular live music nights. Local CAMRA Pub of the Year 2018 and 2019. Q❀🛏◑♿♣●P🚌🐾📶

Earl Shilton

Constitutional Club

Station Road, LE9 7GE

3.30-11.30; 11.30-midnight Thu-Sat; 12-11.30 Sun

☎ (01455) 843837

Adnams Southwold Bitter; Camerons Strongarm; 2 changing beers (often Castle Rock, Church End, Greene King) H

A substantial building, dating from 1926, known locally as the Conny Club and popular for TV sports and pub games including snooker. The interior decoration is smart and modern. Local, regional and national beers are available on a rotational basis. Although a members' club, CAMRA members are welcome but must sign in. ❀♣P🚌🐾📶

Enderby

Mill Hill Cask & Coffee

12-14 Mill Hill, LE19 4AL

closed Mon; 4-10 Tue & Wed; 12-10 Thu & Fri; 1-10 Sat; 1-5 Sun

4 changing beers (sourced nationally) H

This micropub/coffee house, opened in 2018, has been sympathetically renovated and decorated in a modern, relaxed style and has a growing clientele of locals and passing trade. The owners have built up a reputation for selling well-conditioned ales from top breweries in the UK, with up to four cask ales and up to five KeyKegs to choose from. Food includes home-made sandwiches, cakes, locally sourced pies and Scotch eggs.
Q❀◑♿≈●P🚌(50)🐾📶

Frisby on the Wreake

Bell Inn L

2 Main Street, LE14 2NJ

closed Mon; 5-11; 12-11 Sat; 12-5 Sun ☎ (01664) 434736

thebellinnfrisby.co.uk

Charnwood Vixen; Hancock's HB; 1 changing beer (sourced nationally) H

A change of licensee saw the Bell reopen in 2017 after several periods of closure, and it has since regained popularity within the local community. The interior is clean and bright with simple decor. It has three rooms – a traditional wood-beamed front bar room, a dining area to the right of the entrance and a further room behind the bar. The pub prides itself on using fresh, local produce on the menu.
Q❀♣P🚌🐾

Groby

Stamford Arms L

2 Leicester Road, LE6 0DJ

10-11 (11.30 Fri & Sat) ☎ (0116) 287 5616

stamfordarms.co.uk

Everards Beacon Hill, Tiger; 6 changing beers (sourced nationally; often Everards) H

A popular local which has been modernised in a traditional style. Good food is available throughout the day at a fair price. Gins, craft beers and rough ciders are available. The location is ideal as a base for visits to Martinshaw Wood, Groby Pool, Bradgate Park, Charnwood Forest Regional Park and the rest of the National Forest. The pub now owns the neighbouring Blacksmiths Cottage which is available as a holiday let or for overnight stays. This was the home of Everards founder William Everard until 1921. ❀🛏◑♿♣●P🚌🐾📶

Hathern

Dew Drop ✔

49 Loughborough Road, LE12 5HY

12-3, 6-midnight; 12-3, 7-1am Fri-Sun ☎ (01509) 842438

Greene King XX Mild, Abbot; 1 changing beer H

A traditional two-roomed local with a long-serving landlord, in the centre of Hathern. It has a large bar and a small, well-upholstered, comfortable lounge with real fires. Do not miss a visit to the architecturally unspoilt toilets with their tiled walls and original features. A large range of malt whiskies is stocked and cobs are available at lunchtime. ♿●🚌

Hemington

Jolly Sailor

21 Main Street, DE74 2RB

4-midnight; 12-midnight Fri-Sun ☎ (01332) 812665

Black Iris Snake Eyes; Marston's Pedigree; Oakham Bishops Farewell; 3 changing beers H

This 17th-century building is thought to have originally been a weaver's cottage. A pub since the 19th century, it retains many original features including old timbers, open fires and a beamed ceiling – convenient for hanging a collection of blowlamps and beer mugs. Recently sold to private owners by Greene King, we hope to see a return to the form it was in when it won CAMRA branch Pub of the Year some years back. Well-filled rolls are available and a free cheeseboard is on the bar.
❀◑P🐾📶

Hinckley

Elbow Room Ale & Cider House L

26 Station Road, LE10 1AW (below Cineworld at The Crescent)

closed Mon; 2-11 Tue-Thu; 12-11.30 Fri & Sat; 12-7 Sun

☎ 07900 191388 elbowroomalehouse.co.uk

6 changing beers G

Family-run micropub decorated in an industrial style, offering a warm welcome and a great atmosphere. The ales and ciders are served by gravity directly from the cellar behind sliding glass doors. High-quality wines, gins, whiskies, vodkas, world craft beers and lagers plus a range of soft drinks are available. Pork pies and Scotch eggs complement the drinks. There is no TV, jukebox or gaming machine as conversation is king. Children are welcome until 8pm. Local CAMRA Pub of the Year 2018. Q❀◑♿≈♣●🚌(3,7)🐾📶

Pestle & Mortar 🏆 L

81 Castle Street, LE10 1DA

2-11; 12-11 Fri & Sat; 12-10 Sun ☎ 07715 106876

thepestlehinckley.co.uk

Draught Bass; 8 changing beers (sourced locally) H
Since opening in 2015, Hinckley's first micropub has been awarded CAMRA branch Cider Pub of the Year 2016-18. Up to 22 changing real ciders are available, with Westons Old Rosie Rhubarb and Gwynt y Ddraig Farmhouse Scrumpy permanently on offer. Handpumps deliver up to eight changing real ales from casks behind the bar. Cobs and pork pies are available. This comfortable, pleasantly quirky bar satisfies a wide range of drinking tastes, with a friendly atmosphere. Q

Queen's Head
Upper Bond Street, LE10 1RJ
5-11; 4.30-midnight Fri; 12-midnight Sat; 12-4 Sun
07887 770038
4 changing beers H
A warm welcome awaits at this multi award-winning Victorian free house serving four ever-changing real ales. It has been sympathetically refurbished and features open fires and a Victorian range, helping to enhance a cosy atmosphere. A regular local CAMRA Pub of the Year and three times one of CAMRA's top 200 pubs, it has featured in the Guide since 2013. Sorry, no children and no pets.

Hoby

Blue Bell L
36 Main Street, LE14 3DT
12-11 (01664) 434247 bluebell-hoby.co.uk
Everards Beacon Hill, Tiger; 4 changing beers (sourced nationally; often Everards) H
A picturesque thatched village pub with a beer garden providing fine views across the Wreake Valley. Exposed wooden beams and tiled floors with rug coverings give it a cosy and pleasant feel. The pub is often busy – it is an ideal stopping off point for those seeking refreshment while walking the Leicestershire Round footpath. There is always a good range of Everards beers available, and usually a guest ale or two. CAMRA branch Pub of the Year 2018. P

Kegworth

Red Lion
24 High Street, DE74 2DA
11.30-11; 12-10.30 Sun (01509) 672466
redlionkegworth.co.uk
Adnams Southwold Bitter; Castle Rock Harvest Pale; Charnwood Vixen; Draught Bass; Gale's HSB; 4 changing beers (sourced locally; often Milestone) H
Georgian building standing on the 19th-century route of the A6, with four rooms served from one bar. There are bench seats and original features including coal fires. Eight cask ales, including Nutbrook The Mild Side, and real cider, are on offer, plus a good selection of malt whiskies. Food is served every lunchtime and weekday evenings. Outside is a large car park and garden plus a pétanque court and children's play area. En-suite accommodation is available. A frequent winner of local CAMRA awards. Q P

Leicester

Ale Stone
660 Aylestone Road, LE2 8PR
11-11 (0116) 319 2320
House beer (by Leatherbritches); 4 changing beers H
A sister pub to the Blue Boar, this micropub opened in a converted shop unit in 2017. The nicely furnished interior has wooden benches and dados all round. Up to five real ales, plus four ciders and perries, are stillaged in a temperature-controlled glass-fronted cellar. Ham and cheese cobs and coffee are available. This and the Blue Boar are the only pubs in the city using oversize glasses to guarantee a full pint. Regular tap takeovers and beer bus trips are arranged with the Blue Boar. Q

Ale Wagon
27 Rutland Street, LE1 1RE
11 (4 Mon)-11; 7.30-10.30 Sun (0116) 262 3330
alewagon.co.uk
Hoskins Hob Bitter, IPA H**; house beer (by Hoskins)** P**; 4 changing beers (sourced regionally; often Hoskins)** H
Run by the Hoskins family, this city-centre pub with a 1930s interior, including an original oak staircase, has two rooms with tiled and parquet floors and a central bar. The interior features photos of the former Queens Hotel which was across the road from the pub in the 1930s, and the former Hoskins Brewery. A function room is available to hire. Handy for the nearby Curve Theatre. Plans are underway to brew on the premises.

Black Horse
65 Narrow Lane, LE2 8NA
11-11 (midnight Fri & Sat) (0116) 283 7225
Everards Beacon Hill, Tiger; 4 changing beers (sourced nationally; often Brunswick, Everards, Titanic) H
Welcoming, traditional Victorian pub with a distinctive bar servery, set in a village conservation area on the city's edge. It was sympathetically refurbished in 2018. Up to eight real ales are offered alongside home-cooked food. Quiz night is Sunday and comedy features regularly. There is a large beer garden, and a skittle alley and function room available to hire. Beer festivals and community events are regularly hosted. Coaches are welcome by prior arrangement. The pub has a customer loyalty scheme. Q

Black Horse
1 Foxon Street, LE3 5LT
12-midnight (11 Sun) (0116) 254 0446
Everards Beacon Hill, Sunchaser, Tiger, Old Original; 2 changing beers (sourced nationally) H
The only remaining traditional community pub in a street of youth-oriented bars. It has two rooms separated by a central bar, with wood-panelled walls and practical furniture providing a comfortable setting. There is live music four nights a week and a quiz night on Wednesday. The guest beers are sourced through Everards and the cider is Westons Old Rosie. A large roof terrace is popular for open-air drinking.

Blue Boar L
16 Millstone Lane, LE1 5JN
11-11 (0116) 319 6230 blueboarleicester.co.uk
Beowulf Finn's Hall Porter; house beer (by Leatherbritches); 6 changing beers H
Light, airy single-room micropub, opened in 2016. It is named after the Blue Boar Inn where Richard III stayed before the Battle of Bosworth Field. The cellar is visible through a glass partition behind the bar. The house beer is brewed by Leatherbritches, and guest beers come from microbreweries around the country. This and sister pub the Ale Stone are

the only pubs in the city using lined glasses to ensure customers get a full pint. Local CAMRA Pub of the Year 2018. Q

Globe

43 Silver Street, LE1 5EU
11-11 (1am Fri & Sat) (0116) 253 9492
eversosensible.com/globe
Everards Beacon Hill, Sunchaser, Tiger, Old Original; 3 changing beers (often Everards) H
Dating back to 1720, the pub was sympathetically remodelled in 2001, and has an island servery with small rooms around, while retaining some original features, the most interesting of which is the snug near the entrance. Upstairs is a function room with its own servery. There is a pleasing collection of local photos and bric-a-brac throughout, and restored gas lights are used on special occasions. It now serves a range of beers and ciders alongside good food.

Marquis Wellington

139 London Road, LE2 1EF
12-11.30 (1am Fri & Sat) (0116) 254 0542
eversosensible.com/marquis
Everards Beacon Hill, Sunchaser, Tiger, Old Original; 3 changing beers H
This historic pub with a richly decorated façade stands out on the London Road thoroughfare. It is popular with local workers, shoppers and students. A good range of real ales, ciders and quality food, including a vegan menu, is available. It hosts live music nights and a weekly quiz night on a Monday, raising money for charity. The garden has heated beach huts for cooler nights and shelter from the sun.

Old Horse

198 London Road, LE2 1NE
11-11.30 (12.30am Fri; 11-midnight Sat); 11-11 Sun
(0116) 254 8384 oldhorseleicester.co.uk
Everards Beacon Hill, Tiger; 4 changing beers (sourced nationally; often Everards) H
Recently refurbished 19th-century traditional coaching inn, handy for dog walkers, students and sports supporters. The four guest beers change monthly and can be from local microbreweries. The addition of a cider bar serving eight handpulled ciders earned the pub local CAMRA Cider Pub of the Year in 2017 and 2018. Tasty, good-value food is served, including a Sunday carvery. Behind the building is the largest pub garden in Leicester, complete with children's play equipment. Regular quiz nights, karaoke and special events take place. P

Parcel Yard

48A London Road, LE2 0QB
10-11 (midnight Fri & Sat); 12-9 Sun (0116) 261 9301
Steamin' Billy Bitter, Skydiver; 4 changing beers (sourced nationally; often Charnwood) H
The entrance to this pub is a shop front on London Road, with stairs taking you down to the spacious former sorting office and parcel yard for the adjacent railway station. This is a modern bar with a strong focus on beer – with six handpumps and craft keg taps – alongside a decent range of cocktails and wine. At one end of the bar is a restaurant area where the menu includes tapas, pizzas and burgers. Level access is available from Station Street.

Real Ale Classroom L

22 Allandale Road, LE2 2DA
closed Mon; 4-10 Tue-Thu (11 Fri); 12-11 Sat; 1-4 Sun
(0116) 319 6998 therealaleclassroom.com
5 changing beers (sourced regionally; often Grainstore, Oakham) G
A classroom-themed micropub run by career-change teachers in a converted shop. The furniture includes reclaimed desks with original graffiti, and the beers are written up on a blackboard. Cask ales and ciders are served from a home-made chiller cabinet behind the high bar. Takeaway cans are also available. A logburner warms the rear room. In both rooms seating around large tables encourages conversation between regulars and visitors. Bar snacks include local pork pies, a cheeseboard and charcuterie. Q

Rutland & Derby L

21 Millstone Lane, LE1 5JN
12-11 (1am Fri & Sat); closed Sun (0116) 262 3299
therutlandandderby.co.uk
Everards Sunchaser, Tiger; 2 changing beers H
Following refurbishment in around 2010, this pub has an open-plan interior with a contemporary ambience. The long servery bar is directly facing the front entrance, while off to the left is a lounge-style bar which in turn leads to a restaurant area on a raised level. Out back is a block-paved courtyard with a metallic spiral staircase leading up to a rooftop terrace. Good food features uncomplicated, ethically sourced ingredients. Ales are often local.

Salmon

19 Butt Close Lane, LE1 4QA (from clock tower walk down Churchgate; Butt Close Lane is second left)
11-11 (midnight Fri & Sat) (0116) 253 2301
Black Country Bradley's Finest Golden, Pig on the Wall, Fireside; 7 changing beers (sourced nationally) H
A small corner local with a U-shaped single-room interior, refurbished in 1992 in a bright, traditional style. It has a friendly, welcoming atmosphere, and a strong sports following. A Black Country Ales pub since 2016, 12 handpumps dispense the brewery's ales, guest beers, and two real ciders. Cobs, pork pies and Scotch eggs are available throughout the day, and a carvery on Sunday. Bus stations are nearby. Q

Sir Robert Peel

50 Jarrom Street, LE2 7DD
10-11; 11-11 Sat; 12-6 Sun (0116) 255 9419
Everards Beacon Hill, Tiger; house beer (by Everards); 3 changing beers H
Run by a friendly, knowledgeable couple, this is one of the few original pubs left in the city. It was given a refurbishment in traditional style by Everards in 2013. Well-kept Everards beers are served alongside a range of guests, plus a real cider. The recent addition of a large beer garden provides a relaxing space for dining and drinking. Traditional pub food is popular, and the pub gets busy on football and rugby match days.

Two-Tailed Lion

22 Millstone Lane, LE1 5JN
closed Mon & Tue; 12-11 Wed & Thu (midnight Fri & Sat); 12-5 Sun (0116) 224 4769 thetwotailedlion.com
4 changing beers (sourced nationally; often Framework) H

This cosy two-storey free house and bottle shop opened in 2018. It specialises in a changing selection of six kegs lines and three cask lines, local and national, with a range of bottles and cans alongside, as well as real cider. Locally sourced bar snacks are served every day. It is beautifully furnished, with plenty of seating downstairs, and two extra rooms upstairs available to hire free of charge. ◑▸🖥

West End Brewery
68-70 Braunstone Gate, LE3 5LG
✪ 5-11; 2-midnight Fri; 12-midnight Sat; 2-11 Sun
☎ 07875 745302 ⊕ thewestendbrewery.co.uk
West End Project Pale, Stout, Copper, West Coast IPA; 2 changing beers (sourced nationally) Ⓗ
Leicester's original brewpub, opened in 2016. The owner/brewer aims to produce innovative beers, and plans to extend the range over time – capacity increased to a five-barrel plant in 2019. He likes to experiment with his recipes and takes on board customers' feedback. The brewery is behind the pub and is open to visitors. Four house beers are available plus at least two guests or farmhouse ciders from quality local microbreweries or from further afield. Live music nights are hosted twice a month. ☎◑♣●🖥🐾📶

Wygston's House
12 Applegate, LE1 5LD
✪ 11-midnight (10.30 Sun) ☎ (0116) 296 4301
⊕ wygstonshouse.co.uk
Charnwood Vixen; 2 changing beers (sourced locally) Ⓗ
The best-preserved medieval house in Leicester, Wygston's opened as a bar and restaurant in 2017. The central entrance leads into a stone-flagged passage, with small, elegant rooms on either side. The corridor opens out at the back into the medieval part of the house, a bar area with a wood-beamed ceiling. Upstairs is a light, airy room with an old beamed ceiling and good views over historic Leicester. There is an extensive and attractive patio area outside. ☎🛏🏵◑👶🖥🐾📶

Loughborough
Blacksmiths
47 Wards End, LE11 3HB
✪ 12-11 (midnight Fri & Sat); 12-10.30 Sun
4 changing beers (often Robinsons) Ⓗ
The Blacksmiths is a large, recently refurbished, single-room pub on the west side of town, with four handpulled beers and a good selection of wines and spirits. The well-known and much-loved landlord is now back in town. There is a private function room at the rear. Breakfasts are available. Parking is close by in Bedford Square.
Q🛏🏵◑♣🖥

Needle & Pin
15 The Rushes, LE11 5BE
✪ closed Mon; 5-11 Tue-Thu; 3.30-11 Fri; 12-11 Sat; 12-10 Sun ☎ 07973 754236
4 changing beers Ⓗ
A micropub in what was the old H&R Electronics shop. Beer is served downstairs in a continental-style bar with high stools. The upstairs room has a record player, board games and music. More than 50 continental and craft beers are stocked. A CAMRA branch Cider Pub of the Year. 🛏●🐾

Organ Grinder 🏆
4 Woodgate, LE11 2TY
✪ 12-11 (midnight Fri & Sat); 12-10.30 Sun
☎ (01509) 264008
Blue Monkey BG Sips, 99 Red Baboons, Infinity, Guerrilla; 4 changing beers (sourced locally; often Blue Monkey) Ⓗ
Previously known as the Pack Horse, and bought by Blue Monkey in 2012, the building has received a top-to-bottom renovation, uncovering lots of interesting original features. The new stable bar at the back reflects the pub's past life as a coaching inn. Eight cask ales are always available alongside a choice of four real ciders, sometimes a perry, and Belgian bottled beers. Bar snacks include an interesting range of pork pies. A former local CAMRA Pub of the Year. 🛏🏵●◑🖥🐾📶

Swan in the Rushes
21 The Rushes, LE11 5BE
✪ 11-11 (midnight Fri & Sat); 12-11 Sun ☎ (01509) 217014
Castle Rock Sheriff's Tipple, Harvest Pale, Elsie Mo; 6 changing beers (often Castle Rock, Charnwood) Ⓗ
Traditional three-room Castle Rock pub comprising a quiet, traditionally styled lounge, a contemporary dining room and a lively bar with a jukebox. A constantly changing range of up to seven guest beers always includes a mild. Real cider, perry, a wide variety of continental bottled and draught beers and a good choice of malt whiskies and country wines are also available. Upstairs is the Hop Loft function room and first-floor outside terrace. Q🛏🏵◑👶🅿🖥🐾📶

Wheeltapper
60 Woodgate, LE11 2TZ
✪ 12-midnight (1am Fri & Sat) ☎ (01509) 230829
⊕ wheeltapper.co.uk
Shiny Affinity; 5 changing beers Ⓖ
A modern industrial-style bar in the centre of town, the Wheeltapper is the tap house for Leicester's Great Central Brewery. Two real ales are on the bar alongside regularly changing craft beers and real ciders, as well as a selection of German pilsners. Wines, cocktails and nitro cold brew coffee are all on draught. Wheelchair access is excellent. 🏵◑🖥🐾

White Hart
27 Churchgate, LE11 1UD
✪ 11-midnight; 12-11 Sun ☎ (01509) 236976
Draught Bass; Timothy Taylor Landlord; 3 changing beers (sourced locally; often Charnwood, Leatherbritches, Sarah Hughes) Ⓗ
Reopened in 2013 as a free house after an extensive refurbishment, the pub has a secluded patio and beer garden to the rear. Changing guest beers are sourced from local breweries such as Leatherbritches and Charnwood. Sarah Hughes Dark Ruby is also a regular. Bar snacks and tapas are available until early evening. Live music plays on Friday evening and Sunday afternoon. A former local CAMRA Pub of the Year. 🏵◑♣●🖥🐾

Lutterworth
Fox
34 Rugby Road, LE17 4BN (400yds from Whittle roundabout)
✪ 12 (5 Mon)-1am; 12-midnight Sun ☎ (01455) 550935
⊕ fox-lutterworth.co.uk

Draught Bass; Sharp's Doom Bar; 2 changing beers (sourced nationally; often Timothy Taylor, Wadworth) Ⓗ
Described as the village pub in Lutterworth, The Fox is situated south of the town not far off the M1. It has a friendly atmosphere and a warm welcome for all. The open-plan interior is warmed by two real fires, which add to the ambience in cooler months. Thai food is served in the evening in the separate Sawasdee restaurant. Outside there is a lovely landscaped garden. Quiz night is Tuesday. ❀◗●P🚌(58,X44)🐾📶

Real Ale Classroom 🏆
4 Station Road, LE17 4AP
⏲ closed Mon; 4-10 Tue-Thu; 3-11 Fri; 12-11 Sat; 3-8 (closed winter) Sun ☎ (0116) 319 6998 🌐 therealaleclassroom.com
10 changing beers (sourced nationally) Ⓖ
A spacious micropub with a schoolroom theme, owned by former teachers. It offers a constantly changing line-up of four cask, four craft keg, and five ciders from renowned brewers nationally. The bar has a logburner for the winter and a fantastic beer garden to enjoy in the summer months. Friendly staff are knowledgeable about the drinks on offer, including excellent gins and spirits from local distillers. Snacks are from local suppliers. Winner of Leicestershire Tourism Board Best Pub Experience. Q❀♿♣●🚌(X84,58)🐾📶

Unicorn ✔
29 Church Street, LE17 4AE (near church)
⏲ 10.30-11 (midnight Fri & Sat); 12-11 Sun
☎ (01455) 552486 🌐 unicornlutterworth.co.uk
Adnams Southwold Bitter; Draught Bass; Sharp's Sea Fury; 1 changing beer (sourced nationally; often Brains, Hobsons) Ⓗ
Traditional street-corner local built in the early 1900s, situated in the town centre. The main bar has an open fire, skittles table and dartboard used by teams in local leagues. Sport is shown on TV. A smaller lounge doubles as a family room, with another room used for dining. Home-cooked meals including vegetarian options and children's dishes are available at reasonable prices. Local photographs adorn the walls to peruse while enjoying your ale. ◖♣P🚌(8,X44)🐾📶

Market Harborough

Beerhouse
76 St Mary's Road, LE16 7DX
⏲ closed Tue; 6-11 Mon & Wed; 12-11 Thu-Sat; 12-10 Sun
☎ (01858) 465317
8 changing beers (sourced nationally; often Hart Family) Ⓟ
Market Harborough's first micropub, set in a converted furniture shop behind the chip shop on St Mary's Road. The focus is very much on beer – no food, gaming machines or loud music. There are 20 taps for draught products – the first eight are used for cask ales, the rest for KeyKegs and ciders. Monday is quiz night and occasional comedy nights, vinyl nights, live music and a book club are hosted. ♿⇌●P🚌🐾📶

Melton Mowbray

BeerHeadZ
7 King Street, LE13 1XA
⏲ closed Mon; 12-10 ☎ (01664) 561958 🌐 beerheadz.biz
6 changing beers (sourced nationally) Ⓗ
Opened in 2018, this is one of the newest micropubs from the BeerHeadZ company, offering a wide range of beer styles, many from innovative and new breweries. It is set in a manor house dating from the 14th century and one of Melton Mowbray's oldest buildings, with a timber frame going back to 1301. In the 1500s it was the manor of John Mowbray, and more recently it served as a toy shop. Real cider and a good range of craft beers are also available. Q❀⇌●🚌(5,19)🐾

Kettleby Cross Ⓛ ✔
Wilton Road, LE13 0UJ
⏲ 7am-11.30 ☎ (01664) 485310
Greene King IPA, Abbot; Sharp's Doom Bar; 6 changing beers (sourced nationally) Ⓗ
The Kettleby Cross is a Wetherspoon new-build opened in 2007 as a flagship eco pub, complete with a prominent wind turbine on the roof. It stands close to the bridge over the nearby River Eye and is named after the cross that once directed travellers in the direction of Ab Kettleby. A large single room on two levels, as with most Wetherspoons, it is usually busy with a good atmosphere. Q◖◗♿⇌●P🚌📶

Noels Arms Ⓛ
31 Burton Street, LE13 1AE
⏲ 11-11 (1am Fri); 12-1am Sat; 12-9 Sun ☎ (01664) 563694
Belvoir Dark Horse; 4 changing beers (sourced locally) Ⓗ
The Noels is a popular single-roomed town pub. It became a free house in 2013 and shows a commendable commitment to locally sourced ales. Live music features prominently and consequently the pub is often busy on a Friday and Saturday evening, with quieter sessions on Sunday afternoons, and an extensive local cheese and bread board available between sets. There always seems to be something going on at the Noels, with darts, pool and cribbage also played.
❀⇌♣●🚌🐾📶

Mountsorrel

Swan
10 Loughborough Road, LE12 7AT
⏲ 12-2.30, 5.30-11; 12-11 Sat; 12-10.30 Sun
☎ (0116) 230 2340
Black Sheep Best Bitter; Castle Rock Harvest Pale; 2 changing beers (often Dancing Duck, Greene King) Ⓗ
Seventeenth-century, Grade II-listed coaching inn on the banks of the River Soar, entered via a narrow arch into a courtyard. The split-level interior has open fires, stone floors and low ceilings, and includes a small dining area with a polished wood floor. Good-quality, interesting food is cooked to order, with the menu changing weekly with regular themed offerings. Outside is a long secluded riverside garden with moorings. A beer festival is held annually. Q❀◖◗P🚌🐾

Nether Broughton

Anchor
Main Road, LE14 3HB
⏲ 12-midnight ☎ (01664) 822461
Ringwood Razorback; 1 changing beer Ⓗ
A cosy village pub on the A606 which reopened in 2015. The main bar has a real fire and a dartboard, and there is a separate dining area offering a quieter space. Traditional pub food is served

regularly, with occasional themed nights. The pub hosts regular charity events, and welcomes families and dogs.

Oadby

Cow & Plough
Gartree Road, LE2 2FB
11-11 (0116) 272 0852
Fuller's London Pride; Steamin' Billy Bitter, Skydiver; 4 changing beers (sourced regionally; often Abbeydale, Belvoir, Charnwood)
Situated in a former farm building with a conservatory, the pub is decked out with breweriana. It is home to Steamin' Billy beers, named after the owner's now departed Jack Russell who features on the logo and pumpclips. A mild is always available and a real cider in the summer months. An annual beer festival is held. The renowned restaurant is in former dairy buildings.
Q P

Oadby Royal British Legion Club
4A Wigston Road, LE2 5QA
11-11 (11.30 Thu & Fri); 11-12.30am Sat; 12-11 Sun
(0116) 271 4415
2 changing beers
The club is open to CAMRA members, their guests and members of RBL/CIU. It was founded in a former 19th-century private dwelling situated in the shadow of St Peter's Church. At the front is a lounge bar and a chapel of remembrance. To the rear is a large concert room. On the first floor is a games room with darts and a skittles table. Adjacent to the car park to the side of the club is a small lawn with garden furniture.
P

Plungar

Anchor
Granby Lane, NG13 0JJ
5-11 Mon-Thu; 12-3, 5-11 Fri; 12-11 Sat; 12-10.30 Sun
(01949) 860589
3 changing beers
This brick building in the heart of a small Leicestershire village dates from 1774, having previously served as the local courtroom. The pub has a large bar, lounge area and separate restaurant, plus an annexe housing the pool table, and an attractive beer garden. Up to three beers, including at least one local brew, are available in a range of styles. The pub is popular with locals and visitors, cycling groups, horse riders and anglers using the nearby fishing lakes.
Q P (24)

Quorn

Royal Oak
2 High Street, LE12 8DT
5-11 Mon; 11-11 (11.30 Fri); 3-11.30 Sat; 12-10 Sun
(01509) 415816 theroyaloakquorn.co.uk
Black Sheep Best Bitter; Charnwood Vixen; Timothy Taylor Landlord; 1 changing beer
Traditional pub situated in the centre of the village, which has recently changed hands. An inn for around 160 years, the building was originally three terraced cottages. The internal walls have been removed to open up the interior, while retaining many original features including beamed ceilings, tiled floors and an open log fire. Light lunches are served (Tue-Fri). A sheltered, covered courtyard is to the side. Draught cider is available occasionally.
Q

Shackerstone

Rising Sun
Church Road, CV13 6NN
12-3 (not Mon), 5-11.30; 11.30-11.30 Fri-Sun
(01827) 880215 risingsunpub.com
Draught Bass; Marston's Pedigree; Timothy Taylor Landlord; 1 changing beer
A traditional family-owned free house in the heart of Shackerstone near the Ashby Canal and the preserved Battlefield Railway. It has a wood-panelled bar serving traditional ales, a restaurant, pool room with Sky Sports, family-friendly conservatory and an attractive garden. The pub, popular with locals and visitors alike, is renowned for the quality and variety of its ales and serves good food – the ideal hub for visiting this rural part of Leicestershire. P

Shearsby

Chandlers Arms
Fenny Lane, LE17 6PL
closed Mon; 6-11 Tue-Thu; 12-3, 6-11 Fri & Sat; 12-7 Sun
(0116) 247 8384 thechandlersinshearsby.co.uk
Belvoir Beaver Bitter; Dow Bridge Acris; 4 changing beers (sourced regionally)
Quintessential local inn with a big reputation – the pub is a community hub for the village and welcoming to visitors. Its name derives from the building's original use as a tallow candlemaker's premises. The beer garden overlooks the village green from a high vantage point. Microbrewery beers are always on the bar, often locally sourced, including a stout or porter. Good food is available, but the owners see it as primarily a drinkers' pub.

Shepshed

Black Swan
21 Loughborough Road, LE12 9DL
5-midnight Mon & Wed; 5-11.30 Tue; 12-midnight Thu-Sun
(01509) 506222
Charnwood Vixen; Draught Bass; Greene King Abbot; Timothy Taylor Landlord
Multi-roomed pub in a prominent position close to the town centre, offering two guest beers alongside the regulars. An extremely good range of whiskies is also kept. The main room has two drinking areas, both with comfortable seating. A further small room can be used by families and is available to hire for functions. Wednesday is quiz night. Local events include the ukulele orchestra. Shepshed Dynamo football ground is nearby.
P

Horse
196 Ashby Road West, LE12 9EF
12 (4 Mon)-11 (01509) 507006
thehorseshepshed.co.uk
Charnwood Vixen; Greene King Abbot; Marston's Pedigree; 1 changing beer
The Horse, one of the oldest free houses in the town, is traditionally built, with a restaurant and bar. In 2015 major extension work almost doubled the size of the premises, enabling a much greater emphasis on food. It has a feature fireplace with a

wood-burning stove, and outside an alfresco dining area with a wood-fired pizza oven. A good range of beers is available and the pub takes pride in serving freshly prepared food made on the premises, where possible using produce sourced within a five-mile radius of Shepshed. ᐅ❀◑▶P🚌

Sileby

Horse & Trumpet

4 Barrow Road, LE12 7LP

12-midnight (11 Sun) ☎ (01509) 812549

Belvoir Dark Horse; Charnwood Vixen; Steamin' Billy Tipsy Fisherman, Bitter, Skydiver; 2 changing beers Ⓗ

This multi-room inn with open fires has undergone a huge transformation since becoming part of the Steamin' Billy chain. Two guest beers plus a real cider and perry are on offer. No hot food is served but cobs are available. There is a monthly curry club. The pub hosts weekly open mic nights and monthly jazz nights, and has a function room. Well-behaved dogs are welcome in the bar and outside seating area. Q❀≥♣●P🚌(KB2)

Somerby

Stilton Cheese 🏆 Ⓛ

High Street, LE14 2QB

12-3, 6-11; 12-3, 7-11 Sun ☎ (01664) 454394

stiltoncheeseinn.co.uk

Marston's Saddle Tank; Grainstore Ten Fifty; 3 changing beers (sourced nationally) Ⓗ

Late 16th-century pub built in local ironstone, ideally located on the Leicestershire Round to provide refreshment and a warm welcome to walkers. The cosy bar and adjoining room are decorated with a large collection of objects including a stuffed pike and a badger, adding to the welcoming atmosphere. Tall customers beware the large number of pumpclips on the low beam above the bar. A repeat local CAMRA Pub of the Year including 2019. Qᐅ❀🛏◑▶♣●P🚌

South Kilworth

White Hart Ⓛ

Rugby Road, LE17 6DN

12-2.30, 5-11; 12-11 Sat & Sun ☎ (01858) 575416

thewhitehartsk.co.uk

3 changing beers (sourced nationally; often Langton, Marston's) Ⓗ

Newly refurbished village pub with low ceilings and a large fireplace with a wood-burning stove. Home-cooked food is available evenings in the small restaurant, including the house speciality, chargrilled steak. Traditional games include darts, skittles and pool, and a quiz is held on the second Sunday of the month. The annual beer festival is held in May. An exclusive range of gins is available. There is a large grassed drinking area outside ideal for summer. Nearby attractions include Stanford Reservoir and Stanford Hall. ᐅ❀▶♣P🚌(58)🐾

Stoke Golding

George & Dragon Ⓛ

Station Road, CV13 6EZ

closed Mon; 12-3, 6-11 Tue-Thu; 12-11 Fri & Sat; 12-10.30 Sun ☎ (01455) 213268 churchendbrewery.co.uk/pubs

Church End Goat's Milk, Gravediggers Ale, What the Fox's Hat, Stout Coffin, Fallen Angel; 3 changing beers (sourced locally; often Church End) Ⓗ

Renowned village local serving eight real ales from the Church End range and a real cider. Good home-cooked lunches feature local produce, and bar snacks, made on the premises, are always available. Each month, the second Tuesday is steak night, and lunch is served on the last Sunday. Close to the historic Bosworth battlefield, the pub supports a number of clubs and societies, and is popular with walkers, cyclists and boaters from the nearby Ashby Canal. Qᐅ❀◑Ⓐ♣●P🚌🐾

Swinford

Chequers ✔

High Street, LE17 6BL (near church)

7-midnight Mon; 5-midnight Tue; 12-2.30, 5-midnight Wed & Thu; 12-midnight Fri & Sat; 12-11 Sun ☎ (01788) 860318

chequersswinford.co.uk

Adnams Southwold Bitter; 2 changing beers (sourced nationally; often St Austell, Timothy Taylor) Ⓗ

In January 2019, the landlord celebrated 32 years at this family-run community local, where a warm welcome is assured. The food menu caters for all and includes vegetarian and children's options. The large garden and play area are popular with families in good weather. A marquee provides the venue for the annual beer festival and is available for private hire. Pub games include table skittles. Within a mile is the 18th-century Stanford Hall, with a caravan park and museum.
ᐅ❀◑▶Ⓐ♣P🐾

Syston

Queen Victoria

76 High Street, LE7 1GQ

4-11; 12-midnight Fri & Sat; 12-10.30 Sun
☎ (0116) 260 5750

Everards Beacon Hill, Sunchaser, Tiger, Old Original; 2 changing beers (sourced nationally) Ⓗ

A former coach house, the building is 200 years old. Everards has traded here since 1922. Three rooms have been knocked together to form the bar at the front, and there is a small room to the rear. At the back is a carvery restaurant, a courtyard drinking area and a large garden with a pétanque court. There is regular entertainment. Beer and cider festivals are held throughout the year. Guest beers are sourced through Everards and can include regional and microbrewery beers.
ᐅ❀◑▶≥♣P🚌🐾

Wigston

Tap & Barrel

58 Leicester Road, LE18 1DR

5-10 Mon, Tue & Thu; closed Wed; 2.30-11 Fri; 12-11 Sat; 3-8 Sun ☎ (0116) 319 0123 tapandbarrelwigston.co.uk

8 changing beers Ⓖ

This micropub has an unpretentious ambience enhanced by a rustic timber bar, bare wood floorboards, exposed ceiling joists braced with traditional herringbone strutting, a free-standing log-burning stove, and a wooden staircase that leads to an extra seating area. Behind the bar, beers are dispensed straight from casks kept in a cooler cabinet. ᐅ♿♣●P🚌🐾

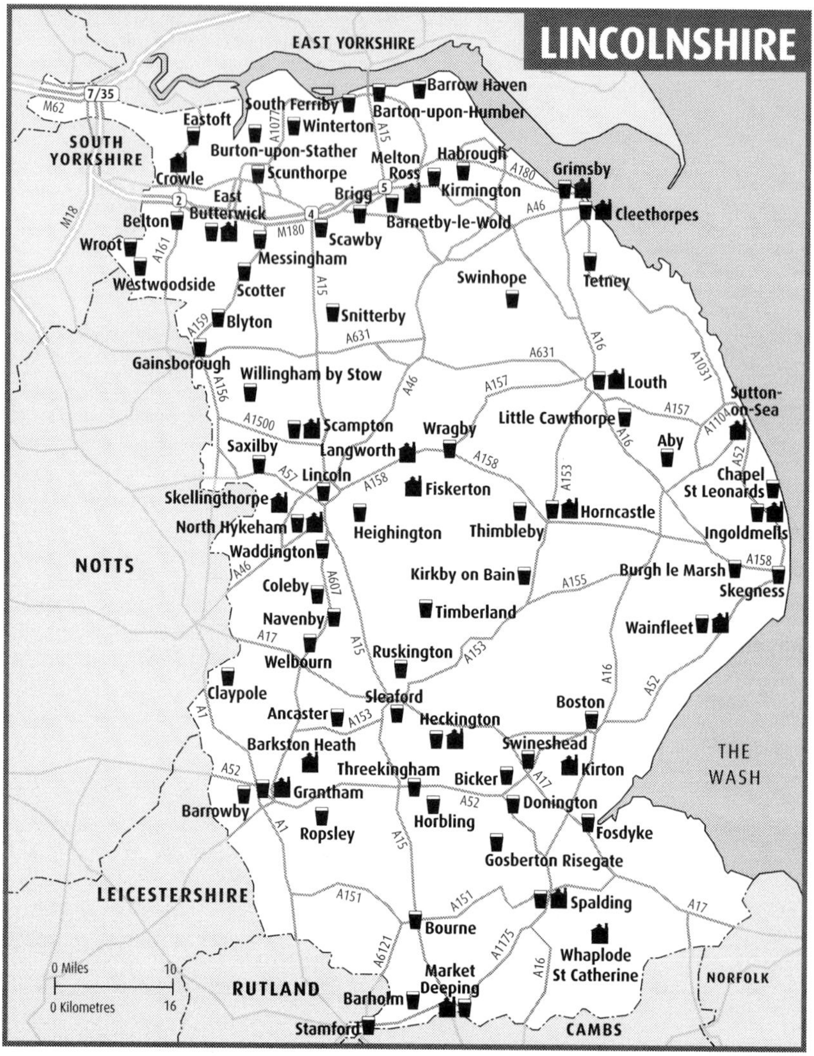

Aby

Railway Tavern

Main Road, Alford, LN13 0DR (off A16 via South Thoresby)

12-11.30 ☎ (01507) 480676 railwaytavern-aby.co.uk

2 changing beers (sourced nationally) Ⓗ

A rural inn that was closed down when the licensees took it on over 15 years ago; since then it has grown it to the venue it is now, serving the community and raising money for charity. The pub has won numerous awards including local CAMRA Country Pub of the Year four times (most recently in 2018). It serves a variety of real ales and has a menu based on local produce. Two holiday cottages have recently been built and are available for short breaks or week-long bookings.

Q❀♿♣P

Ancaster

Ancaster Social Club

Ermine Street, NG32 3PW

7-11; 4-1am Fri; 12-midnight Sat; 12-10.30 Sun

☎ (01400) 230896

Timothy Taylor Boltmaker; 2 changing beers (often Brewsters, Wood) Ⓗ

Located in the heart of the village, this club hosts various sporting events on its playing fields, including football, cricket and rounders. Inside, darts, pool and live sports are available. The venue has an airy conservatory and outside seating overlooking the sports field. ❀♿♣P

Barholm

Five Horseshoes Ⓛ

PE9 4RA

4-11; 1-11 Sat; 12-10.30 Sun ☎ (01778) 560238

Adnams Southwold Bitter; Draught Bass; Oakham JHB; 3 changing beers (often Grainstore, Hopshackle) Ⓗ

A classic 18th-century stone-built country pub, well known for supporting many charities. It comprises two bars, two cosy side rooms and a pool room. A wood fire burns throughout the winter. A real cider is served along with three permanent and three changing ales. Pizzas are available on Friday and Saturday evenings, while barbecues and live music events in the large garden are a feature of the summer months. Q ♿ P

Barnetby-le-Wold

Whistle & Flute

Railway Street, DN38 6DG

12-11 (midnight Fri & Sat) ☎ (01652) 688238

whistleandflute.net

Sharp's Doom Bar; Timothy Taylor Landlord; 1 changing beer (sourced nationally)

A local village pub that is also welcoming to passing travellers and overnight guests. A free house that caters for the tastes of its regulars, the Whistle & Flute offers standard national ales kept in excellent condition. The restaurant prepares home-made food sourced from local produce. On the station doorstep, convenient for Humberside airport and with the long-distance trail the Viking Way passing through the village, the pub offers welcome refreshment before, during or after a journey. Q ♿ ♣ P

Barrow Haven

Haven Inn

Ferry Road, DN19 7EX (approx 1½ miles E of Barrow-upon-Humber)

12-11 ☎ (01469) 530247 thehaveninn.co.uk

Theakston Old Peculier; Timothy Taylor Landlord; 2 changing beers (sourced locally; often Axholme, Lincolnshire Craft Beers)

Built in 1730 as a coaching inn in the quiet north Lincolnshire countryside for travellers using the former ferry, the Haven has been renowned for hospitality, good food and drink, and comfortable lodgings ever since. Full of character, a warm welcome awaits, with a bar, lounge and large comfortable conservatory, perfect for walkers from along the Humber bank to call in for a well-kept pint. The restaurant offers a blend of traditional dishes alongside nightly specials and a generous Sunday carvery. ♿ P

Barrowby

White Swan

Main Street, NG32 1BH

12-midnight (1am Fri & Sat) ☎ (01476) 562375

Castle Rock Harvest Pale; Sharp's Doom Bar; 2 changing beers

Popular village inn run by the same landlord for 26 years, an enthusiastic CAMRA member. There is a comfortable lounge, separate bar area and a further area where the local darts, cribbage and pool teams play. Offering two regular and two changing guest ales, the pub also provides locally sourced traditional home-made food Wednesday to Saturday. Outside there is a heated smoking area and a secluded garden. The first Sunday of the month is quiz night. Q ♿ ♣ P

Barton-upon-Humber

Wheatsheaf

3 Holydyke, DN18 5PS

12-11.30 (12.30am Fri & Sat); 12-11 Sun ☎ (01652) 633292

Moorhouse's White Witch; Theakston Best Bitter; Timothy Taylor Boltmaker; 1 changing beer (sourced nationally)

Serving four real ales and a real cider, and occupying a prominent place on the main road through the town, this friendly local pub from Enterprise Inns dates back to the 18th century. It has an unspoilt, traditional atmosphere with a front bar, a small snug at the rear and a seating area for drinkers and diners. A large beer garden to the rear of the pub makes for pleasant outdoor drinking. Q ♣ P

White Swan

66 Fleetgate, DN18 5QD (follow signs for railway station)

closed Mon; 11-midnight Tue-Thu; 11-1am Fri & Sat; 10-11 Sun ☎ (01652) 661222

3 changing beers (sourced regionally; often Crafty Little, Great Newsome)

Local CAMRA Pub of the The Year 2017 and 2018, this renovated 17th-century coaching inn opposite the bus/train interchange offers a warm welcome to all. Three changing cask ales from near and far are complemented by a rotating craft keg beer and changing real ciders, plus a perry in summer. Diverse community groups meet here, some using the charming converted farrier shed in the rear courtyard. Quiz night is on Sunday, with a monthly vinyl night plus a curiosity shop. Q ♿ ♣ P

Belton

Crown Inn

Church Lane, DN9 1PA (turn off A161 at All Saints church and follow road behind)

1-midnight; 12-midnight Sat & Sun ☎ (01427) 872834

Bradfield Farmers Blonde; Brakspear Bitter; Jennings Cocker Hoop; Oakham Citra; 2 changing beers (sourced regionally; often Abbeydale, Lacons)

Difficult to find but well worth the effort, this pub has long been a haven for the discerning drinker. Six cask ales are always on the bar, one of which is usually from the Cuckoo Brewery which is part-

REAL ALE BREWERIES

8 Sail Heckington
Austendyke Spalding
Axholme Crowle/Grimsby
Bacchus ■ Sutton-on-Sea
Batemans Wainfleet
Blue Bell ■ Whaplode St Catherine
Brewsters Grantham
Cheeky Imp Skellingthorpe
Consortium Louth
Dark Tribe ■ East Butterwick
Ferry Fiskerton
Firehouse Louth
Fuddy Duck Kirton
Greg's ■ Scampton
Hopshackle Market Deeping
Horncastle ■ Horncastle
Leila Cottage ■ Ingoldmells
Lincolnshire Langworth
Lincolnshire Craft Melton Ross
Newby Wyke Grantham
Oldershaw Barkston Heath
Poachers North Hykeham
Welland Spalding (NEW)
Willy's ■ Cleethorpes

owned by the licensees. The multi-roomed Crown is active in the community, hosting quizzes, beer festivals and live entertainment. A winner of several local CAMRA awards including District Pub of the Year. (399)

Bicker

Red Lion

Donington Road, PE20 3EF

closed Mon & Tue; 12-11; 12-7 Sun ☎ (01775) 821200
redlionbicker.co.uk

Adnams Southwold Bitter; Courage Directors; 1 changing beer (often Austendyke Ales, Black Sheep)

A typical country inn with low beams and tiled floor and in a pleasant setting. It was extensively and tastefully redecorated in 2015 and reopened after two years' closure. The welcoming multi-roomed pub has a small bar, and is popular for dining, with a varied, extensive menu. The pub is known to date from at least 1665.
P (59)

Blyton

Black Horse

93 High Street, DN21 3JX

11.45-10.30 ☎ (01427) 628277 blackhorseblyton.co.uk

3 changing beers (sourced regionally; often Batemans)

The Black Horse is one of two pubs in the village, sited at the northern end. The interior is divided into five distinct areas, two for dining, two for drinking and the fifth for pool and darts. There is usually a beer from Batemans and two changing ales, sometimes from local breweries. Self-contained accommodation is available and there is generous parking and outside drinking space.
P (100)

Boston

Church Keys Wine Bar & Restaurant

28-30 Church Street, PE21 6NW

9am-11.30 (1.30am Fri & Sat); 10-11.30 Sun
☎ (01205) 837030 churchkeys.co.uk

2 changing beers (sourced nationally; often Adnams, St Austell)

In the shadow of the Boston Stump, this building dates from about 1520 and has had many uses, from a Thai restaurant to a photography studio and antiques shop. The pub has many small, cosy areas, with armchair seating, and an upstairs restaurant room said to be haunted by former resident Sarah Preston. An outside patio area overlooks the river. The name is believed to originate from a time when the keys to the Stump were held here.

Coach & Horses

86 Main Ridge, PE21 6SY

4-11.30; 12-11.30 Sat; 2-11.30 Sun ☎ (01205) 612649

Batemans XB, XXXB; 1 changing beer (sourced locally; often Batemans)

Close to the Boston United football ground, the open-plan lounge here has a polished wooden bar frontage and wood-panelled ceiling. Wooden cabinets showcase a large collection of miniature bottles. Other items, such as a deer's antlers, a large clock and photographs of musicians, adorn the walls. The pub hosts pool, darts, poker and quiz teams, and is popular with football supporters. There is regular entertainment at weekends.

Eagle

144 West Street, PE21 8RE

11-midnight ☎ (01205) 361116

Castle Rock Black Gold, Harvest Pale, Preservation Fine Ale, Screech Owl; 7 changing beers

Part of the Castle Rock chain, the Eagle is known as the real ale pub of Boston. This friendly two-roomed hostelry has an L-shaped bar with a large TV screen for big sports events. The small cosy lounge has an open fire. The pub stocks a wide range of guest ales, and at least one cider. A function room upstairs is home to Boston folk club. Thursday is quiz night – allegedly the hardest in town. Q

Moon Under Water

6 High Street, PE21 8SH

9am-midnight (2am Fri & Sat) ☎ (01205) 311911

Greene King Abbot; Ruddles Best Bitter; Sharp's Doom Bar; 4 changing beers (often Elgood's, Milestone)

A large, lively Wetherspoon pub near the tidal section of the River Witham. Formerly a government building, an imposing staircase leads from the lounge up to the toilets. A conservatory dining area is supplemented by a second child-friendly dining room adjacent to the lounge. The pub offers a good number of guest ales and a large range of continental bottled beers. Photographs and information boards highlight important people associated with Boston.

Bourne

Anchor

44 Eastgate, PE10 9JY

3-11 (midnight Fri); 12-11.30 Sat & Sun ☎ (01778) 422347

House beer (by Dancing Duck); 4 changing beers (sourced regionally; often Nene Valley, St Austell, Thornbridge)

Traditional two-roomed locals' pub with a patio, by the banks of a tributary of the River Glen. It is strong on sports, with pool and darts played, Sky Sports on the TV and several sporting trophies on display, and raises funds for the local air ambulance service. The house beer, Bourne Particular, is supplied by Dancing Duck, as is Roundheart, brewed for the sister pub, the Hand & Heart in Nottingham. Presented with a local CAMRA Gold Award in July 2017. The car park is small. P

Smith's

25 North Street, PE10 9AE

10-11 (midnight Fri); 8.30am-midnight Sat; 8.30am-11 Sun
☎ (01778) 426819

Fuller's London Pride; Oakham JHB; 4 changing beers (often Hopshackle)

A successful conversion of an old grocery store into an atmospheric pub with exposed red-brick walls throughout. The building is a warren of interconnecting rooms spanning three floors, with drinking areas downstairs and restaurant rooms above. The main bar usually serves six beers, mostly from independent brewers. Outside there is a large patio and beer garden with a children's play area. There is an annual beer festival in summer as well as an annual cider and sausage festival in August. Q

Brigg

Yarborough Hunt

49 Bridge Street, DN20 8NS (across bridge from marketplace)

11-11 (11.30 Thu; midnight Fri); 10-midnight Sat; 11-10.30 Sun ☎ (01652) 658333

Lincolnshire Craft Beers Best Bitter, Lincoln Gold, Bomber County; 4 changing beers (sourced nationally; often Greene King, Jennings, Kelham Island)

The former Sergeants Brewery tap, the building has retained original rustic features. Several small rooms are linked to a central bar area, simply furnished and some with real fires. Eight handpumps dispense three real ales from Lincolnshire Craft Beers, four changing guest beers and a real cider. Fourteen keg taps offer a variety of craft beers and continental lagers. No food is served, but customers can bring in their own snacks. An enclosed beer garden is at the rear. Q (4,X4)

Burgh le Marsh

Bell Hotel

45 High Street, PE24 5JP

12-midnight ☎ (01754) 810318 bellhotelburgh.co.uk

Batemans XB, XXXB; 1 changing beer (sourced locally; often Batemans)

The pub lives up to its name, with a large bell above the entrance. Inside is an L-shaped bar room with a substantial bar area, which is popular with local groups. In addition to the hotel rooms there are three self-catering cottages in the hotel grounds. Regular live music evenings are held and, for those wanting something different, there is a fishing lake nearby. P

Burton-upon-Stather

Ferry House Inn

Stather Road, DN15 9DJ (follow campsite signs through village; down hill at church)

6-11; 11-midnight Sat; 12-11 Sun ☎ (01724) 721783

ferryhousepub.co.uk

3 changing beers (sourced locally; often Axholme, Lincolnshire Craft Beers)

Friendly village pub on the banks of the River Trent, which has been in the same family for 57 years. The pub has its own microbrewery, but check for availability; real cider is also sold. An annual beer festival is held on the first weekend of September. There is a large outdoor play area for children, and it hosts live music events and regular quizzes. Food is served Friday evening, Saturday lunchtime and evening and Sunday lunchtime. It is a popular meeting place for local heritage groups. Dogs are welcome. Q P (60)

Chapel St Leonards

Admiral Benbow

The Promenade, PE24 5BQ

10-7 (10.30 Fri & Sat); 10-8 Sun ☎ (01754) 871847

admiralbenbowbeachbar.co.uk

Black Sheep Best Bitter; 2 changing beers

A beach bar on the promenade, where opening times and facilities are dependent on the weather and are limited in winter. (Please see the website for current times.) Bar snacks and hot food are available. It has an outside seating area on the boat deck (Hispaniola). Picnic trays for the beach and plastic glasses are provided to take out your favourite ale onto the beach. Dogs are welcome on leads, with blankets and dog treats available. If the flag is flying the bar is open.

Claypole

Five Bells

95 Main Street, NG23 5BJ

11 (4 Mon & Tue)-11; 12-10.30 Sun ☎ (01636) 626261

thefivebellsclaypole.co.uk

4 changing beers (sourced nationally; often Tetley)

Traditional village pub where four beers and two ciders are always available at the bar. The guest ales are predominantly from local microbreweries, with small jars displaying the colour of the beers available. There is a large public bar, a small lounge and a restaurant serving home-cooked food. Outside is a spacious beer garden and children's play area. Accommodation is available in four en-suite rooms. Q P

Cleethorpes

Crow's Nest

Balmoral Road, DN35 9ND

11-11 ☎ (01472) 698867

Samuel Smith Old Brewery Bitter

A wonderful example of an old estate hostelry, this is a Sam Smith's pub in the best of traditions. It holds its neighbours and community near, at the same time giving occasional drinkers the same welcome as long-established regulars. A family pub, it has a large garden and some outside seating. Situated not far from the bus route, accommodation can be booked. Recently refurbished to a high standard. Q P (7,4)

Message in a Bottle

91-97 Cambridge Street, DN35 8HD

closed Mon-Fri; 12-8 Sat; 12-4 Sun ☎ (01472) 453131

miabcleethorpes.net

1 changing beer (often Axholme)

The pub is open only of a weekend but the bottle shop it belongs to is open most days. One to two cask ales are offered each weekend, and it seems to attract a mixed crowd of those seeking something different. The pub is outdoors so wear a jumper and coat in cold weather. It does not show any sports or even have a TV, but it does stage events such as Indian weekends where food and beer are paired. (4)

No.1 Pub

Railway Station, DN35 8AX

12-7.30 Mon; 1-midnight; 12-midnight Sat & Sun ☎ (01472) 696221

Batemans XXXB; Draught Bass; 6 changing beers (sourced regionally; often Axholme, Horncastle Ales)

Large railway bar on Cleethorpes station. This popular local has a main bar with a smaller one off it overlooking the platform. It is themed towards railway memorabilia and real ales, and there is a fair-sized seating area outside at the front. From the bar, customers can order quality real ales and home-cooked locally sourced food. Check the Facebook page for daily specials. P

No.2 Refreshment Room 🏆

Station Approach, DN35 8AX

8am-midnight (12.30am Fri & Sat); 9am-midnight Sun
☎ 07905 375587

Hancocks HB; Rudgate Ruby Mild; Sharp's Atlantic, Sea Fury; 2 changing beers (sourced nationally) Ⓗ

This small, friendly pub offers a warm welcome to all. It is known locally as Under The Clock because it is located under the recently restored Victorian wooden railway clock tower. Serving four regular beers and two guest ales, it has won numerous local CAMRA awards. It is a perfect place for a drink before or after a railway journey. Quiz night is on a Thursday. There is a covered outside area on the station concourse.

Signal Box Inn

Lakeside Station, King's Road, DN35 0AG

11-11 ☎ (01472) 604657 cclr.co.uk/signalboxinn

4 changing beers (sourced nationally) Ⓗ

This is an original signal box, just 8ft by 8ft, and proudly claims to be the smallest pub on the planet. Seating can be found in abundance outside, but the signal box can only hold a few people. The family-friendly venue runs events such as the Real Ale and Blues and the Folk and Cider festivals. It tends to be open only at weekends from October, closes a week before Christmas, and reopens a week before Easter. Q

Willy's

17 High Cliff, DN35 8RQ

11-11 (midnight Wed & Thu; 2am Fri & Sat); 11-1am Sun
☎ (01472) 602145

Draught Bass; Willy's Original; 2 changing beers (sourced nationally) Ⓗ

Willy's is a seafront bar with views over the Humber Estuary to the Yorkshire coast. Willy's Original Bitter is brewed in the on-site microbrewery. The pub mainly operates from a downstairs bar; an upstairs bar is used for functions. Limited outdoor seating is available. Good-quality locally sourced home-made food is served. A mix of ages sees a gentler, quieter crowd of an afternoon, with DJs at weekends.

Coleby

Tempest Arms

Hill Rise, LN5 0AG

closed Mon; 12-11 (midnight Fri & Sat); 12-8 Sun
☎ (01522) 810258 thetempestcoleby.co.uk

Brains Rev James; Timothy Taylor Landlord; 4 changing beers (sourced nationally; often Castle Rock, Fuller's, Purity) Ⓗ

A clifftop inn owned by a group of villagers – their photo hangs proudly above the pub's fireplace. Look out for the soapbox race that whizzes by in June. Quiz night features on the last Thursday of the month and an open mic night the second Tuesday. Views from the beer garden are to die for. Q P (1)

Donington

Black Bull

7 Market Place, PE11 4ST

11.30-11.30 ☎ (01775) 822228
theblackbulldonington.co.uk

Batemans XB; Sharp's Doom Bar; 2 changing beers (often Brains) Ⓗ

Busy local just off the A52. Five handpumps feature two regular beers and occasionally varying guest beers from small brewers as well as large regionals. The comfortable bar has low beamed ceilings, wooden settles and a cosy fire in winter. The restaurant offers a good choice of reasonably priced evening meals; lunches are served in the bar. Tables by the car park are used for outdoor drinking. Buses run from Boston and Spalding (not Sun). P

East Butterwick

Dog & Gun

High Street, DN17 3AJ (off A18 at Keadby Bridge, E bank)

4-9 (11 Thu & Fri); 12-11 Sat & Sun ☎ (01724) 782324
doggunpub.com

3 changing beers (sourced locally; often Dark Tribe) Ⓗ

Village pub popular with locals, walkers and cyclists, on the banks of the River Trent. It comprises three rooms of rustic decor including wooden tables and chairs throughout, and has real fires in cold weather. Its own DarkTribe microbrewery is at the back of the pub. Outside seating areas are at the front and side of the building and across the road on the river bank. Meals can be eaten here as well as in the pub itself. Q P (12)

Eastoft

River Don Tavern

Sampson Street, DN17 4PQ (on A161 Goole-Gainsborough road)

3.30-11; 12-11 Sun ☎ (01724) 798040
theriverdoneastoft.co.u

2 changing beers (sourced regionally; often Bradfield, Rooster's) Ⓗ

A welcoming local on the main road through the village. Open plan in design, it has two distinct drinking areas, one of which is also used for dining. A separate restaurant is available for the Sunday carvery. It is traditionally styled, with wooden ceiling beams, rustic furniture and vintage photographs. Two rotating real ales are served (three at weekends) plus a real cider. A large orchard at the rear is used for outdoor drinking during warmer months. B&B accommodation is in outdoor lodges and rooms in the pub. P (361)

Fosdyke

Ship Inn

Moulton Washway, PE12 6LH

11.30-10 (11 Fri & Sat) ☎ (01205) 260764
shipinnfosdyke.com

Adnams Southwold Bitter; Batemans XB; 1 changing beer Ⓗ

This former Batemans pub, just outside Fosdyke when travelling from Boston on the A17 and next to the bridge, is, as its name suggests, dedicated to all things maritime: maps, photographs, charts, model ships and artefacts of every description are in plentiful supply. The week's tidetable is also detailed on a blackboard. It is near to the busy Fosdyke marina, and boaters and landlubbers are well catered for, with excellent home-cooked food, good beer and a warm welcome. Q P

Gainsborough

Blues Club

Northolme, North Street, DN21 2QW

✪ 7-11.30 Mon, Wed & Thu; closed Tue; 5-midnight Fri; 11.30-midnight Sat; 12-11.30 Sun ☎ (01427) 613688

3 changing beers (often Horncastle Ales) Ⓗ

The club has a bar area with several TVs showing sport, a quieter lounge, and a large function room which hosts regular live entertainment (admission charges may apply). Two or three changing real ales are usually on tap and details of forthcoming beers can be emailed to customers on request. CAMRA guests are always welcome on production of a membership card. ⚓≉♣☐☎

Eight Jolly Brewers Ⓛ

Ship Court, DN21 2DW

✪ 11-midnight; 12-midnight Sun

Dukeries A Ray of Sunshine; Full Mash Apparition; changing beers Ⓗ

The branch's flagship real ale haven, in the Guide for 25 consecutive years since 1995, based in a 300-year-old Grade II-listed building. Six changing beers are always on sale, many from northern micros, but new breweries from all areas feature. Real cider and continental bottled beers are also stocked. There are fortnightly Wednesday quiz nights. Customers bring in food to share on Sunday lunchtimes. Q&≉♣☐☎(200)

Sweyn Forkbeard ▼ ✓

22-24 Silver Street, DN21 2DP

✪ 8am-11 (midnight Fri & Sat) ☎ (01427) 675000

Greene King Abbot; Ruddles Best Bitter; Sharp's Doom Bar; 3 changing beers Ⓗ

This town-centre Wetherspoon's establishment is making itself one of the must-do pubs in the city. Three rotating guest beers often include some oddities for this part of the country; customers can ask for their favourite beer and it often appears. The pub is named after the Danish King of England in 1013, whose son Canute is rumoured to have attempted to stop the aegir (the tidal bore on the River Trent). Really cheap good food is available until 10pm. ⚓◑&≉(Central)♠☐☎

Gosberton Risegate

Duke of York Ⓛ

106 Risegate Road, PE11 4EY

✪ 12 (6.30 Mon)-11; 11-3, 7-10.30 Sun ☎ (01775) 840193

Batemans XB; St Austell Tribute; 1 changing beer (sourced regionally) Ⓗ

A friendly pub and a longstanding entry in the Guide, with a deserved reputation for value-for-money beers and food. As well as the regular ales, guests come from a range of independent brewers. A wide choice of cooked food is available, with portions to suit the largest appetite. Local community life is supported through charities, sports teams and other social events. Q⚓❀◑♣P

Grantham

BeerHeadZ

27 Watergate, NG31 6NS

✪ 12-11 (midnight Fri & Sat); 12-10 Sun ☎ (01476) 330274

⊕ beerheadz.biz

5 changing beers (sourced nationally) Ⓗ

The sign 'Fancy a pint of the unusual?' greets the customer outside this pub in the area of town dominated by St Wulfram's church spire.

Grantham's long-awaited first micropub opened Easter 2016. Since then it has sold over 1,200 different cask ales and been voted CAMRA Town Pub of the Year for 2017 and 2018. Continental and craft beers are also available. There is a free function room and customers are welcome to bring in their own food. Q❀♣♠☐☐☎☎

Castlegate

69 Casltegate, NG31 6SJ

✪ 3-11; 2-midnight Fri & Sat ☎ (01476) 404646

1 changing beer Ⓗ

This large open-plan pub is popular with local bands. There are two raised areas – the one on the right is the darts oche and the one on the left is a viewing point for the large TV screen. A single handpump offers a continuously changing cask ale, usually from an East Midlands brewery. Bar snacks including filled sandwiches are served most days. ⚓&♣☎☎

Chequers Ⓛ

25 Market Place, NG31 6LR

✪ 12-midnight (2am Fri & Sat) ☎ (01476) 570149

3 changing beers (sourced nationally; often Brewsters, Oldershaw) Ⓗ

A cosmopolitan and contemporary bar that features beers from local breweries Brewsters and Oldershaw; other regulars include Bakers Dozen and Framework, and these are supplemented further with changing guest beers. On a paved side street off the High Street, known locally as Butchers Row, it has a relaxing atmosphere during the day and comes alive in the evenings and at weekends. Q❀&≉☐☎☎

Grantham Railway Club Ⓛ

Huntingtower Road, NG31 7AU

✪ 7-11; 11-3, 7-11 Sat; 12-2, 7-11 Sun ☎ (01476) 564860

2 changing beers Ⓗ

A community-run club which supports Grantham's three local brewers. This former British Rail Staff Association club plays host to numerous cribbage, darts and dominoes teams as well as supporting various social and community organisations. There is live music every Saturday night, with a spacious back room available to hire (previously used for the Grantham Beer Festival). Card-carrying CAMRA members welcome. ⚓❀&≉P☎☎

Lord Harrowby Ⓛ

65 Dudley Road, NG31 9AB

✪ 3-11; 1-11 Sat & Sun ☎ (01476) 563515

Oldershaw Heavenly Blonde; 4 changing beers Ⓗ

A friendly back-street community pub, one of the few remaining in Grantham. It has a bar and lounge with a real fire and is how pubs used to be, with a dartboard in the corner, and crib and dominoes played in leagues. There is a great enclosed area at the back where at least two beer festivals with live music are held. The landlord, a CAMRA member and real ale enthusiast, sources four changing guest beers. Q❀≉♣♠☎

Nobody Inn ▼ Ⓛ

9 North Street, NG31 6NU (opp Asda car park)

✪ 12-11; 12-10.30 Sun ☎ (01476) 565288

⊕ nobody-inn.business.site

6 changing beers (often Black Sheep, Newby Wyke) Ⓗ

The Nobody is famous for its hidden toilet door behind the bookcase. The pub sells beer from the award-winning Newby Wyke brewery in

Grantham. It gets lively at the weekends and when a big sporting event is taking place, but it is also a nice place for a quiet drink with good bar staff. Live music is staged during the year. Watch out for the giant spider! ♣

Grimsby

Spider's Web

180 Carr Lane, DN32 8LN

12-11 (midnight Fri & Sat) ☎ (01472) 692065

John Smith's Bitter; 3 changing beers (sourced nationally; often Leeds, Wainwright) H

A friendly family-run community pub with a lively bar, quiet lounge and a function room that holds frequent live music events from artists of many genres. In the bar, games such as poker, darts and pool are played. There is also a weekly quiz night. Outside is a large garden area which is a suntrap and includes a smoking area. Q♣P(4)

Yarborough Hotel

Bethlehem Street, DN31 1JN

7am-midnight (1am Fri & Sat); 7am-11 Sun

☎ (01472) 268283

Greene King Abbot; Kelham Island Easy Rider; Ruddles Best Bitter; 12 changing beers (sourced regionally) H

Large open-plan pub serving 15 real ales from national brands through to more local ales from the Lincolnshire area. Like many in the Wetherspoon chain, it can be popular for the Tuesday steak night and again on the Thursday curry night. The Yarborough is a Grade II-listed building next door to Grimsby Town railway station which has been restored following a troubled past where it was under threat of demolition, and is now a thriving hotel again. Q

Habrough

Station Inn

Station Road, DN40 3AP

11-11 ☎ (01469) 572896

3 changing beers (sourced regionally; often Caledonian) H

Originally a hotel built in 1848 for the Great Grimsby and Sheffield Junction Railway, this community pub has tastefully decorated walls adorned with memorabilia from the days of steam. Live bands play once a month on Saturday and this, together with karaoke, theme nights and traditional pub games, makes for a lively environment. Three handpumps feature changing beers from regional brewers. Dogs are welcome and an open fire adds warmth in the cold weather. ♣P

Heckington

8 Sail Brewery Bar

Heckington Mill, Hale Road, NG34 9JW

closed Mon-Thu; 12-8 Fri; 12-4 Sat & Sun

☎ (01529) 469308 8sailbrewery.co.uk

3 changing beers (sourced locally) H

In part of the Heckington Windmill complex, this is a single-room brewery bar featuring a restored Victorian bar and church pew and Britannia bar seating. Usually three changing 8 Sail Brewery beers and occasional guest beers are served. A selection of German bottled beer and local cider is also available. Beer festivals are held in mid-July over the Heckington Show weekend. On winter Saturdays and Sundays it tends to close at 3pm (see Facebook page for details). Q

Heighington

Butcher & Beast

High Street, LN4 1JS

12-11; 12-10.30 Sun ☎ (01522) 790386

butcherandbeast.co.uk

Batemans XB, XXXB; Timothy Taylor Landlord; 3 changing beers (sourced nationally; often Castle Rock, Oakham) H

A welcoming old stone Batemans pub with a splendid array of exterior floral decor. It has distinct drinking areas, a real fire and old photographs adorning the walls. The restaurant at the rear serves quality food and has a steak night Monday, fish Tuesday and a roast on Sunday. Beer festivals, quizzes and charity events are popular, along with a fine selection of gins. There is at least one real cider. The garden boasts a beautiful patio area. Local buses run until early evening.

Q♣P(2,10)

Horbling

Plough Inn

4 Spring Lane, NG34 0PF

11.30-2.30 (not Mon), 5.30-11; 11.30-midnight Fri & Sat; 12-10.30 Sun ☎ (01529) 240263 ploughinnhorbling.co.uk

Batemans XXXB; 1 changing beer H

A community pub owned by the parish of Horbling, built in 1832 and set just off the main road. In addition to the lounge/bar, its snug is surely one of the smallest and most intimate of its kind. Guest beers come from a wide range of breweries, often micros, and change frequently. Good-quality meals are served throughout the pub and in a separate restaurant. The Spring Wells, a feature worth seeing, are just a few yards down the lane.

♣P

Horncastle

King's Head

16 Bull Ring, LN9 5HU

12-11 ☎ (01507) 523360

Batemans XB, XXXB; 2 changing beers (sourced locally; often Batemans) H

A comfortable, cosy and friendly pub. Unusually for this locality, the building has a thatched roof, hence its local name, the Thatch. Three beers from Batemans are generally on tap plus a guest. Reputedly the pub inspired an 00 gauge Hornby model, an example of which is displayed behind the bar. Summertime sees the exterior resplendent with hanging baskets and it has been the winner of Batemans' Floral Display competition. Try spotting the pub cat, Rufus.

Old Nick's Tavern

8 North Street, LN9 5DX

closed Mon; 5-midnight (1am Fri); 2-1am Sat; 2-midnight Sun ☎ (01507) 526862 oldnickstavern.co.uk

4 changing beers (sourced locally; often Horncastle Ales) H

Built in 1752 as a coaching inn, this original venue is now a town-centre pub with its own microbrewery, the home of Horncastle Ales. The comfortable furnished interior has been refurbished and incorporates the old pub sign and

old photos of the pub. It hosts regular live bands. There are five handpumps, four of which are usually for the Horncastle Brewery. The head brewster is the the landlord's daughter.
🐴❀♣●🚌🐾📶

Ingoldmells

Countryman L

Chapel Road, PE25 1ND
⏲ 12-midnight summer; 12-3, 7-midnight winter
☎ (01754) 872268
Leila Cottage Leila's Lazy Days, Ace Ale, Lincolnshire Life, Leila's One Off H
The privately-owned Countryman appears to be a modern building but it incorporates the early 19th-century Leila Cottage, which gives its name to the brewery behind the pub. A notorious smuggler, James Waite, used to reside here when Ingoldmells was a wild and lonely place, but he certainly would not recognise the current holiday coast, with Skegness, Butlin's and Fantasy Island nearby. Information boards give brewery, pub and beer information for visitors. The pub is on northern bus routes from Skegness. 🐴❀◑♿⛺♣P🚆🚌

Kirkby on Bain

Ebrington Arms 🏆

Main Street, LN10 6YT
⏲ 12-2 (not Mon), 6-11 ☎ (01526) 354560
🌐 ebringtonarms.com
Adnams Broadside; Batemans XB; Black Sheep Ale; Sharp's Doom Bar; Timothy Taylor Landlord; 1 changing beer (often Adnams) H
Attractive country pub close to the River Bain and dating from 1610. World War II airmen used to slot coins into the ceiling beams to pay for beer when they returned from missions over Germany. Sadly, many of these coins are still in situ and make a unique memorial to the dead. The popular restaurant offers good food made with local produce (booking advised). One guest beer is on in winter, and often two in summer.
Q🐴❀◑♿⛺♣P🚌(65)🐾📶

Kirmington

Marrowbone & Cleaver

High Street, DN39 6YZ
⏲ 11.30-11 ☎ (01652) 688335
🌐 marrowboneandcleaver.com
Sharp's Doom Bar; house beer (by Batemans); 1 changing beer H
After a period of closure, this village pub was refurbished and reopened by motorbike racer Guy Martin. It is adorned inside with racing memorabilia and also items from the 166 Squadron. It is a family-run venue with Guy's sister, Sally, managing it. Although it is mainly food-oriented, it has three handpumps. Drinkers are given a warm welcome as well as diners. The house beer was developed as a collaboration between Guy Martin and Batemans Brewery.
Q🐴❀◑♿♣P🐾

Lincoln

Adam & Eve

25 Lindum Road, LN2 1NT
⏲ 12-11 (midnight Fri & Sat) ☎ (01522) 537108
🌐 adamandevelincoln.co.uk
Castle Rock Harvest Pale; Morland Old Speckled Hen; 2 changing beers (sourced nationally) H
Reported to be the oldest tavern in Lincoln, sitting opposite the medieval Pottergate arch and a stone's throw from the cathedral, this place has a number of areas, one housing a dartboard, and a pool table to the rear. A separate room at the front leads to a secluded beer garden. There are live music acts weekly and a popular quiz night. Sporting events are shown over two screens.
🐴❀◑P🚌🐾📶

BeerHeadZ

4 Eastgate, LN2 1QA
⏲ 12-11 (10 Mon; midnight Fri & Sat); 12-10 Sun
☎ (01522) 255430 🌐 beerheadz.biz
6 changing beers (sourced nationally) H
This bright pub is situated in uphill Lincoln. Part of a small chain of new generation indie pubs, it has an industrial feel. It serves up to six different cask ales, craft beers, two ciders and a range of bottled beers and cans in oversized glasses. Customers are welcome to bring in their own food. Regular events include quizzes, live music and tap takeovers. ●🚌(7,8)🐾

Cardinal's Hat

268 High Street, LN2 1HW
⏲ 12-11 (12.30am Fri & Sat) ☎ (01522) 527084
🌐 cardinalshatlincoln.co.uk
Adnams Mosaic; Lincolnshire Craft Beers Lincoln Gold; Rat White Rat; house beer (by Lincolnshire Craft Beers); 5 changing beers (sourced nationally) H
A Grade II-listed, timber-framed building that was an inn from the 15th to the 19th century. Restored in 1952, it became home to St John's Ambulance. During the refurbishment of the semi-derelict building a number of historical features were revealed. The pub has many rooms ideal for social gatherings, plus a selection of quiet snugs. Eight ales, four ciders and other drinks can be enjoyed alongside a food menu of charcuterie and cheese platters. Q🐴❀◑♿⇌♣●📶

Golden Eagle

21 High Street, LN5 8BD
⏲ 11-11 (11.30 Fri & Sat); 12-11 Sun ☎ (01522) 521058
Castle Rock Harvest Pale; Sharp's Doom Bar; 7 changing beers (sourced nationally; often Oakham, Pheasantry, Welbeck Abbey) H
A traditional two-roomed coaching inn with up to nine real ales and at least one real cider. The bar is welcoming but can get busy on home football match days. The lounge is quiet, relaxed and cosy. Outside is a large premier beer garden, including sheltered seating, lights and heaters. Social events include two summer beer festivals, occasional live music, speciality tasting events and brewery nights. A small function room is available for hire.
Q🐴❀♣●P🚌🐾📶

Joiners Arms

4 Victoria Street, LN1 1HU
⏲ 4-11; 3-11.30 Fri; 12-11.30 Sat; 4-10.30 Sun
☎ 07871 887459
5 changing beers (sourced nationally) H
Just off the city centre, the pub's deceptive '60s-style exterior leads into a traditional interior. There are two steps up to the bar, which features up to five changing ales. The main lounge has an open fireplace and is home to Lincoln's only bar billiards table. At the rear of the pub you will find a pool and darts area. This leads through to the newly

refurbished beer garden. Quiz night is every Tuesday and open mic night every Friday.
♘❀♣🐾

Jolly Brewer 𝕃
27 Broadgate, LN2 5AQ
closed Mon; 12-11 (midnight Fri & Sat); 12-10 Sun
☎ (01522) 528583 🌐 jollybrewer.org
Welbeck Abbey Henrietta, Portland Black; 4 changing beers (sourced nationally) Ⓗ
A characterful, city-centre pub that attracts a diverse clientele. The decoration is Art Deco in style and a side room has reclaimed cinema seating. Live music is a major feature, with a weekly open mic session and bands at weekends. The jukebox is usually playing at other times. The large courtyard has a covered area where bands perform in summer. There is a dartboard and table football. Good-value, home-cooked meals are served.
❀◑⇌♣●P📶

Ritz 𝕃 ✔
143-147 High Street, LN5 7PJ
8am-midnight (1am Fri & Sat) ☎ (01522) 512103
Greene King Abbot; Ruddles Best Bitter; Sharp's Doom Bar; 6 changing beers (sourced nationally) Ⓗ
Part of the JD Wetherspoon chain, this former cinema and entertainments venue is a split-level building with a family area on the ground floor and the bar with seating above. Its past use is reflected in both the interior and exterior decor. A Meet the Brewer event is held on the last Thursday of each month, and charity fundraisers take place regularly. Close to the city's railway station and bus station.
Q♘❀◑♿⇌●🚌📶

Strugglers Inn 🏆 𝕃
83 Westgate, LN1 3BG
12-1am (11 Mon; midnight Tue & Wed); 12-11 Sun
☎ (01522) 535023
Greene King Abbot; St Austell Tribute; Timothy Taylor Landlord; 7 changing beers (sourced nationally; often Dukeries, Pheasantry, Welbeck Abbey) Ⓗ
Full of character, the pub looks like it could be on a biscuit tin, with a real fire in both the main bar and the snug. The ceiling is adorned with pumpclips of beers that have previously featured. It is the winner of many CAMRA awards. Cold bar snacks are available, such as filled rolls, sausage rolls and pork pies. A must-visit destination while visiting uphill Lincoln. Q❀♣🚌🐾📶

Victoria
6 Union Road, LN1 3BJ
11-midnight (1am Fri & Sat); 12-midnight Sun
☎ (01522) 541000
Batemans XB; Castle Rock Harvest Pale; Timothy Taylor Landlord; 3 changing beers (sourced nationally) Ⓗ
The battlements of Lincoln Castle tower above this simple, traditional, two-roomed pub in one of the most historic parts of the city. Next to the formidable West Gate, the Victoria is a popular live music venue, and can be busy when there are special events in the Cathedral Quarter. The outdoor seating area is a summer suntrap, perfect for watching the world go by over a lazy alfresco lunch or a pint at any time of day. Q❀◑●🚌🐾📶

Little Cawthorpe

Royal Oak Inn (Splash)
Watery lane, LN11 8LZ (off A157 onto Pinfold Lane, then Buston Lane and through ford)
11-midnight ☎ (01507) 600750 🌐 royaloaksplash.co.uk
Black Sheep Best Bitter; Greene King IPA; 2 changing beers Ⓗ
Known locally as the Splash because of the picturesque ford nearby, this 400-year-old inn sits in its own large lawned gardens on the edge of the Lincolnshire Wolds near Louth. Four beers are regularly on tap, plus often a guest ale from a local brewery. Three restaurants cover most culinary requirements, and themed evenings are popular. The en-suite rooms are frequently used by visitors to Cadwell Park or by explorers of the Wolds.
♘❀🛏◑♿⛺♣P

Louth

Brown Cow ✔
133 Newmarket, LN11 9EG (top of Newmarket on jct of Church St)
5-midnight (11 Mon); 12-midnight Fri & Sat; 10-11 Sun
☎ (01507) 605146
Black Sheep Best Bitter; Castle Rock Harvest Pale; Fuller's London Pride; 1 changing beer Ⓗ
The owners are celebrating 10 years behind the bar of this friendly free house. With a great atmosphere and, most importantly, great beer, it is a must when visiting Louth. A free quiz is held every first Sunday of the month. The kitchen serves traditional, home-cooked food, made with locally sourced products. The pub is a popular community meeting place. ♘❀◑♿⛺🚌🐾📶

Cobbles Bar
New Street, LN11 9PU (off Cornmarket)
10-midnight
Black Sheep Ale; Marston's Pedigree; 1 changing beer Ⓗ
Traditional pub-style bar based in the centre of town, with friendly staff at all times. This small but accommodating venue has multiple personalities, from a bustling coffee shop serving light lunches to a busy pre-club local with a DJ and live music at weekends. It has a good beer trade, with two contrasting cask ales, as well as a huge selection of exotic spirits. Wheelchair access is right through the front doors. ◑♿🚌

Consortium Micropub 🏆 𝕃
13C, D&E Cornmarket, LN11 9PY
closed Mon & Tue; 12-7 Wed; 5-9 Thu; 12-midnight Fri & Sat; 12-5 Sun ☎ (01507) 600754
🌐 theconsortiumlouth.co.uk
5 changing beers (often Consortium Brewing Co)
A micropub in a small courtyard 100 yards from the marketplace, opened in 2017 to give a wider selection of ales from Lincolnshire, Leicestershire, Nottinghamshire and Derbyshire, as well as other counties. Six real ales and one real cider are always on, changing every week. The pub has its own microbrewery upstairs producing, usually, three of the six ales on the bar. Q♘♿⛺●P🚆🚌(51)🐾📶

Olde Whyte Swanne ✔
45 Eastgate, LN11 9NP
11 (10 Wed)-11; 11-midnight Fri & Sat; 12-11 Sun
☎ (01507) 824141 🌐 whyteswannelouth.co.uk
Rudgate Ruby Mild; 3 changing beers Ⓗ

The oldest pub in a pretty market town. Established in the early 1600s, upon entering this Grade II-listed building you are met by traditional low-beamed ceilings and a real fire. Beyond this is another modern room which is used for dining. The bar offers a variety of beers and ciders on handpump. Q

Wheatsheaf

62 Westgate, LN11 9YD
11-11 (01507) 606262
Batemans XB; Black Sheep Ale; Brains Bitter; Thornbridge Jaipur IPA; 1 changing beer H
This picturesque pub lies close to Louth's historic St James's church, which boasts the tallest single spire of any medieval parish church in the country and is visible for miles around. The Wheatsheaf offers a good selection of real ales and a tasty home-made food menu. It has a lovely beer garden and is a popular meeting place for walkers and ramblers. P

Woolpack

Riverhead Road, LN11 0DA (on outskirts of town)
11-11 (01507) 606568 woolpacklouth.com
Batemans XB, Gold, XXXB; 1 changing beer H
The Grade II-listed Woolpack is located next to the canal and close to the town's theatre. It is popular with drinkers and diners alike. Four or five real ales are usually on handpump. Good, traditional food is served, made with local produce. There is disabled access and baby changing facilities. Outside is a beer garden and ample parking. P

Market Deeping

Vine Inn

19 Church Street, PE6 8AN
4-11; 12-11 Fri-Sun (01778) 348741
Sharp's Doom Bar; house beer (by Hancock's); 3 changing beers (often Courage, Hopshackle, Lacons) H
Formerly a Charles Wells pub, now a free house, this small, friendly venue features oak beams and stone floors, with many 20th-century prints on the walls. There is a large patio at the rear. Five handpumps dispense Sharp's Doom Bar and Vine Ale (Hancock's HB) plus a changing range of guests. Boxed real cider is sold. Free nibbles are provided on Sunday lunchtime and early evenings during the week. The TV is only used for major sporting events. P(101)

Messingham

Pooleys

46 High Street, DN17 3NT
closed Mon; 6-11; 7-11 Sun (01724) 764016
5 changing beers (sourced regionally; often Batemans, Ossett, Rat) H
Cosy, traditionally styled village local, only open in the evenings. It has three distinct drinking areas characterised by bare-brick walls, rustic furniture, wooden and flagstone floors and real fires. The walls are attractively adorned with vintage posters and signs. The bar offers five changing real ales, often from Batemans, Ossett, Rat, Adnams and Everards, plus a large selection of malt whiskies, gins and wines. Always a pleasure to drink here.
Q(100,103)

Navenby

Lion & Royal

57 High Street, LN5 0DZ
12-11 (midnight Fri & Sat); 12-10.30 Sun
(01522) 810368
Greene King Abbot, IPA; 3 changing beers (sourced nationally; often Adnams, Castle Rock) H
A traditional pub serving food, in the centre of the village conveniently next to the Lincoln-Grantham bus stop. A warm welcome awaits in the imposing brick and stone building. The bar has a flagged floor and impressive fireplace. There is a separate area for pool. To the rear is a large beer garden and ample car park. Live music and a quiz are regular features of this popular village pub.
P(1)

North Hykeham

Centurion

Newark Road, LN6 8LB
11-11 (midnight Thu & Fri); 10-midnight Sat; 10-11 Sun
(01522) 509814
Black Sheep Ale; Bombardier Pale Ale; Sharp's Doom Bar; house beer (by Black Sheep); 2 changing beers (sourced nationally; often Timothy Taylor) H
Built in 1969, the aptly-named Centurion is right on the old Roman Fosse Way, just south of Lincoln. Although family friendly and popular with diners, it is a proper pub which serves food, not a mere restaurant with a bar. There is a changing line up of guest ales taken from Ember's Cask Club selection. Local regulars and visitors enjoy weekly quizzes. There is a convenient bus service and ample parking. P

Ropsley

Green Man

24 High Street, NG33 4BE
closed Mon; 11-11 (10.30 Sun) (01476) 585897
the-green-man-ropsley.co.uk
Wainwright; 3 changing beers (sourced nationally; often Caledonian, Grainstore, Theakston) H
Newly crowned CAMRA Pub of the Year 2017 and Country Pub of the Year 2019, this 17th-century village inn has a growing reputation for innovative food, including exotic meats, locally sourced game and seafood, and it is also renowned for an extensive bottled beer range. Its relaxed tearoom area is frequented by walkers and cyclists, and it also has a pleasant, tranquil beer garden. Themed food and drink matching evenings are held regularly. P

Ruskington

Shoulder of Mutton

11 Church Street, NG34 9DU
12-midnight (01526) 832220
Bombardier; John Smith's Bitter; 2 changing beers (sourced regionally; often Sharp's) H
A popular and thriving pub in the heart of the village, attracting customers of all ages. It is one of the oldest buildings here and was once a butcher's shop, hence the name. A few old meat hooks can still be seen in the wooden ceiling in the bar. Changes have been made in recent years but have not spoilt the essential character. Standing guard outside is Knight and Day, a sculpture from Lincoln's 2017 Knight's Trail. P(31)

Saxilby

Anglers ✓
65 High Street, LN1 2HA

🕑 11.30-11.30 (12.30am Fri & Sat); 12-11.30 Sun
☎ (01522) 702200 ● anglerspublichouse.com

Theakston Best Bitter; 3 changing beers (sourced nationally) Ⓗ

In the same hands for over 25 years, this lively village local is home to various pub sports teams, two golf societies and a football team. Poker is played on Tuesday and there is a boules court outside. The quieter lounge has old village photographs. The pub's name refers to fishermen using the nearby Fossdyke, the country's oldest canal, where there are visitor moorings.
Q✿≹♣P🖵❀🛜

Scampton

Dambusters Inn Ⓛ
23 High Street, LN1 2SD

🕑 closed Mon; 12-11 (9.30 Tue); 12-7.30 Sun
☎ (01522) 731333 ● dambustersinn.co.uk

Greg's Dambusters Ale, Scampton Ale; 5 changing beers (sourced nationally; often Oakham, Pheasantry, Shepherd Neame) Ⓗ

Award-winning village pub named after the RAF 617 squadron. The walls are adorned with RAF memorabilia, and the toilets are a must-see. An annual beer festival is held in May around the anniversary of the Dambusters raid. Two beers brewed by the landlord are always on the bar. The pleasant beer garden is adjacent to the runway at RAF Scampton – perfect for plane spotting.
Q✿◑●P🖵(103)❀🛜

Scawby

Sutton Arms
10 West Street, DN20 9AN (on main road through village)

🕑 11.30-midnight (11 Sun) ☎ (01652) 652430
● suttonarmsscawby.co.uk

Sharp's Doom Bar; Theakston Best Bitter; 2 changing beers (sourced regionally; often Horncastle, Milestone) Ⓗ

Comfortable, well-appointed, traditional village local. A central bar serves an open-plan dining area and a separate dining room, plus a narrow snug bar to one side used mainly for drinking. Good home-made food is available lunchtimes and evenings, and all day Sunday to 7pm. Sharp's Doom Bar and Theakston Best Bitter are the regular beers, supplemented by two rotating guest ales. Quiz night is Sunday. Dogs are allowed in the snug bar only. ➷✿◑♣P❀🛜

Scotter

Sun & Anchor
54 High Street, DN21 3RX

🕑 3-11; 12-11 Sat; 12-10.30 Sun ☎ (01724) 763444

Bradfield Farmers Blonde; John Smith's Bitter; Ossett Yorkshire Blonde; 1 changing beer Ⓗ

The main pub in the village, with one regular and two guest ales, also serving food. (The other two establishments are primarily eateries.) All the latest sporting matches and events are shown. There is a darts and pool area and a large private beer garden with a children's play area. Local CAMRA Pub of the Year 2017. ➷✿◑&♣P🖵❀🛜

White Swan
9 The Green, DN21 3UD

🕑 12-midnight; 11.30-midnight Fri-Sun ☎ (01724) 763061
● whiteswanscotter.com

Black Sheep Best Bitter; Sharp's Doom Bar; Thwaites Original; 2 changing beers Ⓗ

In a village between Gainsborough and Scunthorpe, this is a privately run hotel, restaurant and bar which also caters for weddings and conferences. The Mucky Duck Bar has tables by the fire and still has the traditional untouched ceiling beams, which give the feel of the coaching inn's history. There is a pleasant outdoor seating area.
Q➷✿🛏◑P🖵🛜

Scunthorpe

Blue Bell ✓
1-7 Oswald Road, DN15 7PU (at town-centre crossroads)

🕑 8am-midnight (1am Fri & Sat) ☎ (01724) 863921

Greene King IPA, Abbot; Ruddles Best Bitter; 5 changing beers (sourced regionally; often Bradfield, Hop Studio, Kelham Island) Ⓗ

A popular Wetherspoon town-centre pub, due for extensive refurbishment and expansion, currently open plan on two levels, with a small beer garden with heaters, which can be used by smokers. It hosts regular beer festivals and cider festivals as well as seasonal events such as Burns Night and Valentine's Day. There is a muted TV screen showing sports and news. Food is served daily to 11pm. A themed quiz is run every first Monday night of the month. ➷✿◑&●🖵🛜

Honest Lawyer
70 Oswald Road, DN15 7PG

🕑 12-11 (midnight Fri & Sat) ☎ (01724) 276652
● honestlawyerbar.co.uk

Sharp's Atlantic, Sea Fury; 1 changing beer (sourced locally) Ⓗ

Small pub on the edge of the town centre on two floors, with an upstairs dining area. The ground-floor bar runs half the length of the room and has several small counters to sit or stand at. There are low tables, chairs and sofas at the far end with sports TV. The menu features gourmet burgers and similar. Two regular real ales are supplemented by a rotating guest beer and real ciders. The pub has a small heated area with seating outside at the front. ✿◑&●🖵

Malt Shovel
219 Ashby High Street, DN16 2JP (in Ashby Broadway shopping area)

🕑 10-11 (midnight Fri & Sat) ☎ (01724) 843318

Exmoor Gold; 4 changing beers (sourced regionally; often Elland, Great Heck, Oakham) Ⓗ

A distinctive high-street pub, with a front beer garden overlooking the shopping area. The interior has a country-style, comfortably furnished, open-plan lounge, with a conservatory leading off to the beer garden. Often busy at mealtimes, booking is advisable. Accompanied children are allowed only if dining. Quiz night is Thursday, with live music every other Saturday night. It has an attached members-only social and snooker club. Four permanently rotating guest beers from regional breweries are stocked. Real ciders and perries are served from the cellar. ➷✿◑♣●🖵

Skegness

Seathorne Arms

Seathorne Crescent, PE25 1RP
⏲ 11-midnight ☎ (01754) 767797
2 changing beers (often Greene King, Morland) [H]
Set back from Roman Bank and a 15-minute walk from Butlin's, the pub has a large outside seating area and a spacious interior. The inside has partitioned areas for eating, pub games, drinking and TV watching. It enjoys a seasonal trade linked to local caravan sites, and the pub is shut in January, while closing times in February/March may vary. The landlord operates a constantly rotating two-beer selection. An extensive food menu includes locally sourced meat.
❀◑♿♣🚌🐾📶

Vine Hotel

Vine Road, PE25 3DB (off Drummond Rd)
⏲ 11-11 ☎ (01754) 763018
Batemans XB, XXXB; 1 changing beer (often Batemans) [H]
A delightful building, one of the oldest in Skegness, dating from the 18th century and set in two acres of pleasant grounds. Inside are comfortable wood-panelled bars in which to enjoy a quiet pint or two after experiencing some of the noisier attractions and bustle of Skegness. Within striking distance of the Gibraltar Point National Nature Reserve, walking trails, beach and golf links, the inn has reputed Tennyson connections.
❀🛏◑♿P🚌🐾📶

Sleaford

Carre Arms Hotel

Mareham Lane, NG34 7JP
⏲ 11-11 ☎ (01529) 303156 🌐 carrearmshotel.co.uk
3 changing beers (often Marston's, Oldershaw, Springhead) [H]
A privately run hotel previously owned by Bass, adjacent to the Bass Sleaford maltings complex which is now awaiting a regeneration scheme. It has a comfortable bar area with two rooms, offering three real ales which regularly change, featuring both larger regional and local breweries. A cider is often on handpump. An extensive food menu is offered, served in the bar area or restaurant. There is a pleasant covered courtyard, ideal on inclement days. ❀🛏◑♿⇌●P🚌

White Horse

Boston Road, NG34 7HD
⏲ 12 (11 Thu)-11.30; 11-midnight Fri & Sat; 12-11 Sun
☎ (01529) 968003
Bombardier; 2 changing beers (often Batemans, Horncastle Ales) [H]
On the junction of Carre Street and Boston Road, the pub serves the housing area along the Boston Road. It is one of the few remaining traditional locals' pubs in Sleaford, with wet sales only. The interior has been opened out into a single L-shaped room, but still retains a cosy feel. Sports predominate, with both darts and pool teams.
❀⇌♣P🐾📶

Snitterby

Royal Oak

High Street, DN21 4TP (1½ miles from A15)
⏲ 5-midnight; 12-midnight Sat; 12-9 Sun ☎ (01673) 818273
🌐 royaloaksnitterby.co.uk
Greene King XX Mild; JW Lees Bitter; Rooster's Buckeye; Sharp's Doom Bar [H]**; 4 changing beers (sourced regionally; often Pheasantry, Theakston)** [H]/[G]
A wet-led community pub. Here, beer is a backdrop to conversation, encouraging you to linger longer. Up to eight handpulled ales, three ciders and a bottled low ABV beer cater for all tastes. The pub has open fires and bare floorboards, plus two comfortable lounges and a snug with TV showing sports. On three Fridays per month there are themed food nights. Outside, there is bench seating overlooking a stream with a ford, and an ancient weeping ash tree. Q❀◗♿♣●P🐾

South Ferriby

Hope & Anchor L

Sluice Road, DN18 6JQ
⏲ closed Mon; 12-11 ☎ (01652) 635334
🌐 thehopeandanchorpub.co.uk
3 changing beers (sourced nationally; often Crafty Little, Lincolnshire Craft Beers, Theakston) [H]
A 19th-century pub standing at the confluence of the River Humber and River Ancholme next to the 150-year-old lock. Opening 18 months after the 2013 tidal surge and with subsequent refurbishment, it is now Michelin Bib Gourmand-listed. Extensive estuary views can be enjoyed from both the large rear dining room and the outside seating area. A cosier front bar with three separate areas houses three handpumps, one offering beer produced by one of several local breweries. ❀🛏◑♿P🚌🐾📶

Spalding

Ivy Wall ✔

18-19 New Road, PE11 1DQ
⏲ 8am-midnight (1am Fri & Sat) ☎ (01775) 719770
Greene King Abbot; Morland Old Speckled Hen; Ruddles Best Bitter; Sharp's Doom Bar; Wychwood Hobgoblin; 2 changing beers (sourced nationally) [H]
The town-centre site on which this spacious modern pub now stands has had a variety of uses over the years, and was once on the bank of the Westlode River. Excavations during the rebuild in 2005 discovered an undercroft and cellar from the late medieval period, on view beneath toughened glass at the front of the bar. Guest ciders are also sold, and food is available all day. Photographs and archeological finds are displayed on the walls.
❀◑♿⇌●🚌📶

Olde White Horse

Churchgate, PE11 2RA
⏲ 11.30-11; 12-10.30 Sun ☎ (01775) 766740
Samuel Smith Old Brewery Bitter [H]
An attractive white-painted early 17th-century building with a steep thatched roof, on the east river bank. The interior consists of several interconnected rooms with wood-panelled walls, with a flagstone floor in the bar. A number of pictures and artefacts add interest. Overall there is a convivial feel made even more cosy when the large open fire is burning hot and cheerfully in the stone fireplace. Q❀◑♿⇌♣P🐾

Prior's Oven L

1 Sheep Market, PE11 1BH
⏲ closed Mon; 12-8 (9 Thu; midnight Fri & Sat)
6 changing beers (sourced locally) [G]

The first micropub to be opened in Lincolnshire. The building was part of the Priory of Spalding and is believed to be almost 800 years old. Because of its shape it has always been known as The Oven or The Prior's Oven, and has been used as Spalding Monastic Prison. Its more recent use was as a bakery and it became a pub in 2013. As well as the ground-floor bar with its vaulted ceiling, a stone spiral staircase leads up to a gin bar. Beer is also served in third-pint measures. Q⇌●⊟

Red Lion Hotel ✔

Market Place, PE11 1SU

⌚ 10-midnight ☎ (01775) 722869

🌐 redlionhotel-spalding.co.uk

Bombardier; Draught Bass; Greene King Abbot [H]

The Red Lion is a carefully refurbished 18th-century family-run hotel. The cosy, comfortable and welcoming bar overlooks the marketplace. It is popular owing to its consistently well-kept range of cask ales, which the bar staff take great pride in serving in top condition. It is a rare outlet for Bass in the locality. On fine sunny days the experience is enhanced with tables and chairs outside beneath attractive floral displays. ♘⌂♿⇌P⊟🐾📶

Stamford

Jolly Brewer [L]

1 Foundry Road, PE9 2PP

⌚ 11-midnight; 12-11.30 Sun ☎ (01780) 755141

🌐 thejollybrewer.com

Brewsters Marquis; Oakham JHB; 4 changing beers (sourced locally; often Bakers Dozen) [H]

A locals' pub dating back to 1830 and twice local CAMRA Pub of the Year, the Brewer boasts a roomy split-level drinking area with open fires in the winter and a separate dining room. Six handpumps dispense LocAles, national ales and the pub's own Baker's Dozen beers. The real cider is usually Old Rosie. The car park and large patio host a beer festival in the autumn, while pub games, including the World Pushpenny Championships, are a feature. Q❀◐⇌♣●P⊟(9,202)🐾📶

King's Head

19 Maiden Lane, PE9 2AZ

⌚ closed Mon; 12-11; 12-5 Sun ☎ (01780) 753510

🌐 kingsheadstamford.com

5 changing beers [H]

A compact 19th-century pub just off the High Street and built of local stone. This is a one-roomed but split-level house, featuring a wood-burning stove and wooden-beamed ceiling, as well as a pleasant patio area to the rear. The pub operates a one-barrel policy, with five constantly changing ales from the length and breadth of the country. Over 400 beers were promoted in the first two years of the scheme. Popular with diners at lunchtime. Q❀◐⇌⊟

Tobie Norris

12 Saint Pauls Street, PE9 2BE

⌚ 10-11 (midnight Fri & Sat); 12-10.30 Sun

☎ (01780) 753800

Fuller's London Pride; Oakham JHB [H]**; 3 changing beers (sourced regionally; often Adnams)** [H]/[G]

The building, parts of which date back to 1280, was bought by Tobie Norris in 1617 and used as a bell foundry. Formerly a RAFA club, a major refurbishment gained it a CAMRA Conversion to Pub Use Award. It now has many small rooms with real fires, stone floors and low beams. Five handpumps serve beers from local and country-wide breweries. A former local CAMRA Pub of the Year. Q♘❀◐⇌♣⊟(202,203)🐾

Swineshead

Green Dragon

Market Place, PE20 3LJ

⌚ 5-11; 12-midnight Fri & Sat; 12-11 Sun ☎ (01205) 821381

Batemans XB, Gold; Theakston Best Bitter; 2 changing beers (sourced regionally) [H]

First called the Green Dragon years ago, the pub's fortunes gradually declined; it became run-down and, despite a change of name, it eventually closed. New owners brought it back to life as a vibrant and thriving village local, successfully blending old and new to recreate a genuine community pub with an emphasis on beer and traditional pub games. Another change of ownership has now seen the pub revert to its original name. ♘❀◑♣P⊟(K59)🐾

Swinhope

Clickem Inn

Binbrook Road, LN8 6BS (2 miles N of Binbrook on B1203)

⌚ 5-11 Mon-Wed; 12-3, 5-11 Thu; 12-11.30 Fri & Sat; 12-10.30 Sun ☎ (01472) 398253 🌐 clickem-inn.co.uk

Batemans XXXB; Timothy Taylor Landlord; house beer (by Pheasantry); 3 changing beers (sourced regionally; often Horncastle Ales, Rudgate, Springhead) [H]

Set in the picturesque Lincolnshire Wolds and a popular stopping place for walkers and cyclists, the pub's name originates from the counting of sheep passing through a nearby clicking gate. Renowned for its home-cooked food served in the bar and conservatory, it offers a choice of drinks, including six real ales and a traditional cider. The house beer is Terry's Tipple. There is pool, darts and a jukebox. Monday is quiz night. A covered, unheated area is provided for smokers. Q❀◐♣●P🐾📶

Tetney

Plough

Market Place, DN36 5NN

⌚ 3-midnight; 12-midnight Fri-Sun ☎ (01472) 812186

Batemans XXXB; Sharp's Doom Bar [H]

A well turned out sole village pub, situated facing an attractive spreading chestnut tree. To the left is a small lounge, while to the right is an equally small bar area. The other side of the servery caters for a larger seating area with plain furnishing, from where there is access to a decked area where smokers can sit, and also a TV room/play area for families. ♘◑♣P🐾

Thimbleby

Durham Ox

Main Road, LN9 5RB

⌚ 12-3, 6-11; closed Tue ☎ (01507) 527152

🌐 durhamoxpubthimbleby.co.uk

Batemans XB; Ferry Ales Spirit of Jane; 1 changing beer (often Charnwood) [H]

Fine country inn over 200 years old and reopened in November 2013. This welcoming pub, with its beamed ceilings, cowshed bar and RAF corner, also has a large field at the rear for caravans and camper vans. There is an extensive menu serving local produce. The pub is named after a huge 18th-century ox which toured the country; at its largest it weighed 270 stone. ⌂❄◐▲♠P🖵

Threekingham
Three Kings Inn
Saltersway, NG34 0AU
✪ closed Mon; 12-3, 6-11 (10.30 Sun) ☎ (01529) 240249
🌐 thethreekingsinn.com
Draught Bass; Morland Old Speckled Hen; Timothy Taylor Landlord; 1 changing beer (sourced regionally) Ⓗ
A classic country inn with charm and character. Its bright and comfortable lounge bar, with attractive rural prints, and panelled dining room serving locally sourced food, are deservedly popular with locals and visitors. Guest beers are usually from independent brewers. There is a pleasant beer terrace and garden for summer months and a large function room. The pub's name refers to the slaying, by the Saxons, of three Danish chieftains in battle in 870 at nearby Stow; look for the effigies above the entrance. Q⌂❄◐▲P♠

Timberland
Penny Farthing
4 Station Road, LN4 3SA
✪ closed Mon; 12-11 (midnight Fri & Sat); 12-9 Sun
☎ (01526) 378881 🌐 thepennyfarthinginn.co.uk
4 changing beers (sourced nationally; often Dukeries, Milestone, Pheasantry) Ⓗ
A country pub in the heart of the village which reopened in 2017, now serving four changing beers, many from local breweries. The pub features a large open-plan layout, with various spaces for dining and a comfortable seating area. Families and dogs are welcome. Locally sourced food is available to eat in or take out, and specials are on offer Tuesday-Friday. A regular quiz is on Tuesday which, for £1, includes supper. Accommodation comprises five en-suite rooms. Q⌂❄🛏◐♿♠P♠🛜

Waddington
Three Horseshoes Ⓛ
High Street, LN5 9RF
✪ 3-11; 2-midnight Fri; 11-midnight Sat; 12-11 Sun
☎ (01522) 720448
John Smith's Bitter; 5 changing beers (sourced nationally; often Milestone, Newby Wyke, Pheasantry) Ⓗ
Next to the church in the heart of the village, with easy access to the local bus routes, lies this real community pub, with log fires in both bars. Five real ale handpumps dispense local beers, with often a surprise from further afield. Large TVs cover live sport, and a selection of pub games is available. ⌂❄♠🖵(1,13)♠🛜

Wainfleet
Batemans Brewery Visitor Centre Ⓛ
Salem Bridge Brewery, Mill Lane, PE24 4JE
✪ 10-5 (9 Thu-Sat summer); closed Mon & Tue winter
☎ (01754) 882017 🌐 bateman.co.uk
Batemans XB, Gold, Salem Porter, XXXB; 1 changing beer (sourced locally; often Batemans) Ⓗ
Visiting this brewery provides the chance to experience the blend of Batemans' proud 140-plus

years of craft brewing tradition with its forward-looking attitude. Mr George's Bar, within the attractive windmill, is the ideal venue to sample a range of the beers. Further entertainment is to be found with brewery tours, featuring the Theatre of Beers, and in the pleasant beer garden with its games. Opening days and times vary throughout the year (see the website for details). Usually closed in January. ⌂❄◐♿▲⇄♠P🖵(7)🛜

Welbourn
Joiners Arms
21 High Street, LN5 0NH
✪ 4.30-11; 12.30-2, 4.30-midnight Fri; 12.30-midnight Sat; 12.30-11 Sun ☎ (01400) 279356
Draught Bass; Sharp's Doom Bar; 1 changing beer (sourced nationally) Ⓗ
Now the only pub in the village, the brick-built free house is cosy and welcoming. Inside is a single, long bar area with a small alcove at one end and a variety of seating. Good homely food is served Friday to Sunday, with special feature nights. There are occasional quiz, music and other social events. Two en-suite letting rooms are available. ⌂❄🛏◐♠🖵(1)♠🛜

Westwoodside
Carpenter's Arms
Newbigg, DN9 2AT (follow B1396 to centre of village)
✪ 4-midnight; 12-midnight Sat & Sun ☎ (01427) 752416
Black Sheep Best Bitter; Bradfield Farmers Blonde; 2 changing beers (sourced nationally; often Bradfield, Greene King) Ⓗ
A regular in the Guide for many years, this friendly village local takes an active part in community events, and has raised significant sums for local charities. A recent change of ownership has not altered the pub's long-held reputation for beer quality. Four cask ales are available, two of which change regularly. A past winner of several CAMRA awards and currently holder of the local Haxey Hood trophy. ⌂❄◐♠🖵(399)♠🛜

Willingham by Stow
Half Moon Ⓛ
23 High Street, DN21 5JZ
✪ 5-9 Mon; 5-11 Tue; 12-3, 5-11 Wed-Fri; 12-11 Sat; 12-10.30 Sun ☎ (01427) 788340
Sharp's Doom Bar; 3 changing beers (often Dark Tribe) Ⓗ
This establishment has grown out of the ashes of the former showcase for Grafters beers. The present owners have been here over 18 months and are turning it around. Four beers are available, with three changing. Tasty food is served from Thursday to Sunday – the fish and chips are legendary. A recent comedy evening went down well with customers, and more such evenings are planned. Q⌂❄◐♿♠♥🖵♠

Winterton
George Hogg Ⓛ ✔
25 Market Street, DN15 9PT
✪ 2-11; 11-midnight Sat; 12-11 Sun ☎ (01724) 732270
🌐 thegeorgehogg.co.uk
Draught Bass; 3 changing beers (sourced regionally; often Lincolnshire Craft Beers, York) Ⓗ

A Grade II-listed building in the marketplace, this popular pub has a large lounge and a public bar, both with real fires in cooler months. There is also an outdoor seating area. Good-value, locally sourced Sunday lunches are served (booking is recommended). A local CAMRA award winner, guest beers change regularly and many are from local breweries. The pub holds an annual beer festival, and is the local meeting place for football teams and the Scunthorpe United supporters' club. The 350 Fast Cat bus service stops outside.
Q ❀ ♣ P (350)

Wragby

Ivy

Market Place, LN8 5QU
12-11 (midnight Fri & Sat) ☎ (01673) 858768
theivywragby.co.uk
Draught Bass; Black Sheep Best Bitter; Castle Rock Harvest Pale; 2 changing beers (sourced nationally; often Dark Star, Ferry Ales) H
With its origins in the 17th century, the Ivy is in the centre of Wragby. It has three separate areas – a restaurant, lounge and bar. A wood-burning stove gives a homely feeling in winter. There is a varied selection of real ales, and tasty home-cooked food is served, with gluten-free options. Sport is screened in the main bar. Parking is available in the free car park opposite, and a bus stop is nearby.
Q (50,56)

Wroot

Cross Keys

High Street, DN9 2BT (in centre of village)
5-midnight (1am Fri); 4-midnight Sat; 12-11 Sun
☎ (01302) 770231
Theakston Best Bitter; 3 changing beers (sourced regionally; often Acorn, Pheasantry, Welbeck Abbey) H
A highly successful community pub serving a remote village of fewer than 500 inhabitants. This multi-roomed pub takes part in a whole range of local events and always has a friendly, welcoming atmosphere. It has four cask ales on the go, with the three guests usually coming from nearby breweries. Evening meals are available on Thursday and also at weekends.
Q ❀ ♣ P

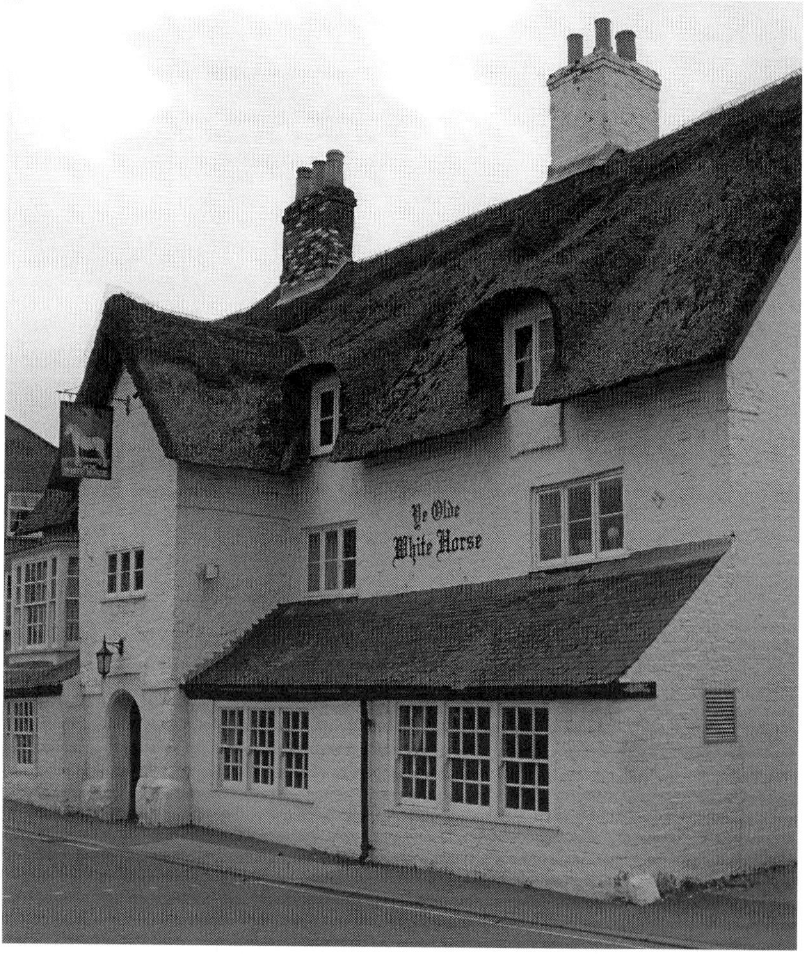

Olde White Horse, Spalding (Photo: Jim Linwood/Flickr CC BY 2.0)

London index

***Shown on Inner London map**

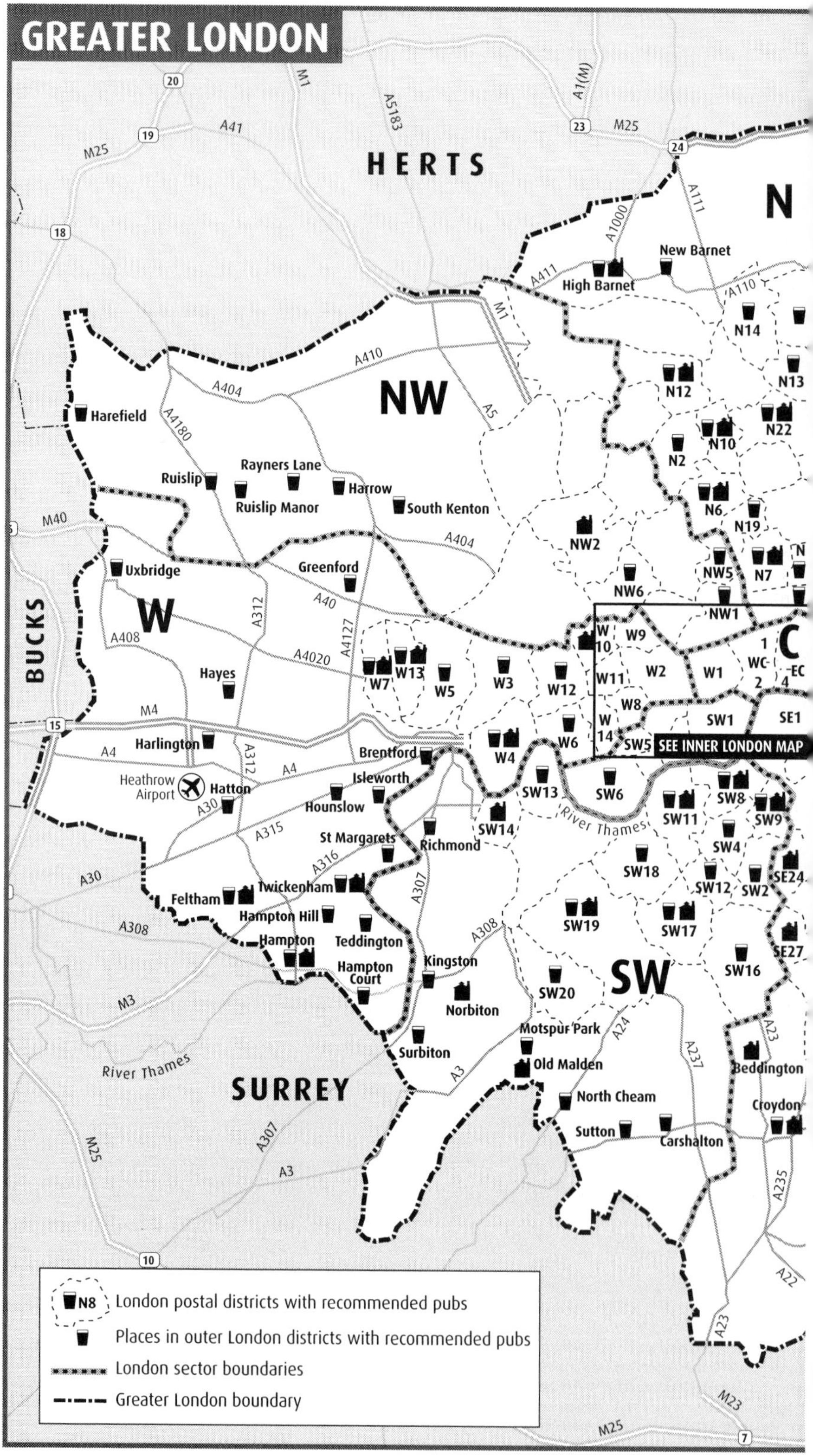
GREATER LONDON
HERTS
BUCKS
SURREY
NW
W
SW
N
C
Harefield
Ruislip
Rayners Lane
Ruislip Manor
Harrow
South Kenton
Uxbridge
Greenford
Hayes
Harlington
Heathrow Airport
Hatton
Brentford
Isleworth
Hounslow
St Margarets
Richmond
Twickenham
Feltham
Hampton Hill
Hampton
Teddington
Hampton Court
Kingston
Norbiton
Surbiton
Motspur Park
Old Malden
North Cheam
Sutton
Carshalton
Beddington
Croydon
New Barnet
High Barnet
SEE INNER LONDON MAP
River Thames
London postal districts with recommended pubs
Places in outer London districts with recommended pubs
London sector boundaries
Greater London boundary

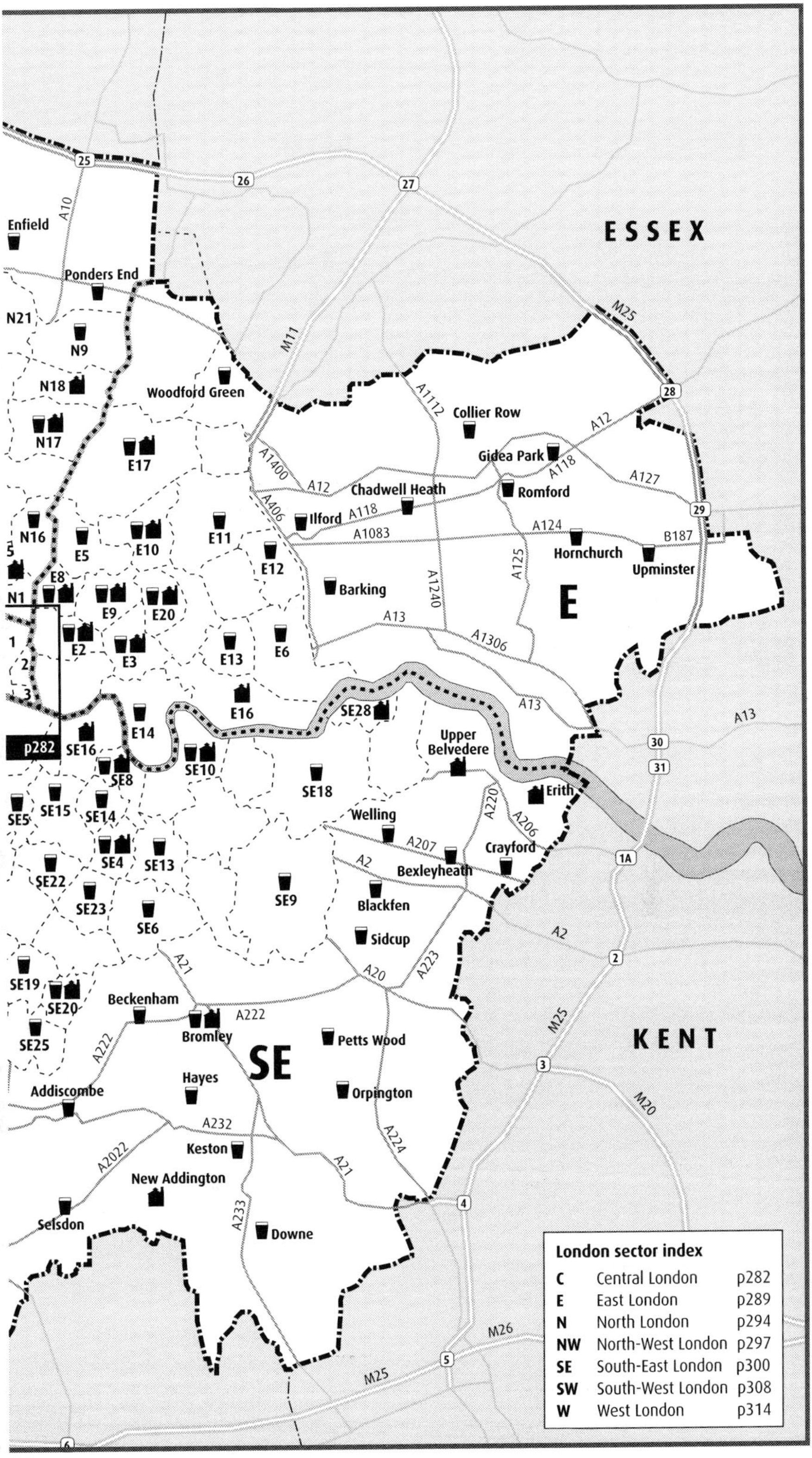
ESSEX
KENT
E
SE
Enfield
Ponders End
N21
N9
N18
N17
N16
N1
Woodford Green
E17
E5
E8
E10
E11
E12
E9
E20
E2
E3
E13
E6
E16
E14
SE16
SE28
SE10
SE8
SE18
SE15
SE14
SE5
SE4
SE13
SE22
SE23
SE9
SE6
SE19
SE20
SE25
Collier Row
Gidea Park
Chadwell Heath
Romford
Ilford
Hornchurch
Upminster
Barking
Upper Belvedere
Erith
Welling
Crayford
Bexleyheath
Blackfen
Sidcup
Beckenham
Bromley
Petts Wood
Hayes
Orpington
Addiscombe
Keston
New Addington
Selsdon
Downe
p282
A10
M11
M25
M26
M20
A12
A118
A127
A1112
A1400
A406
A1083
A124
B187
A125
A1240
A13
A1306
A220
A206
A207
A2
A20
A223
A21
A222
A232
A2022
A224
A233
London sector index
C Central London p282
E East London p289
N North London p294
NW North-West London p297
SE South-East London p300
SW South-West London p308
W West London p314

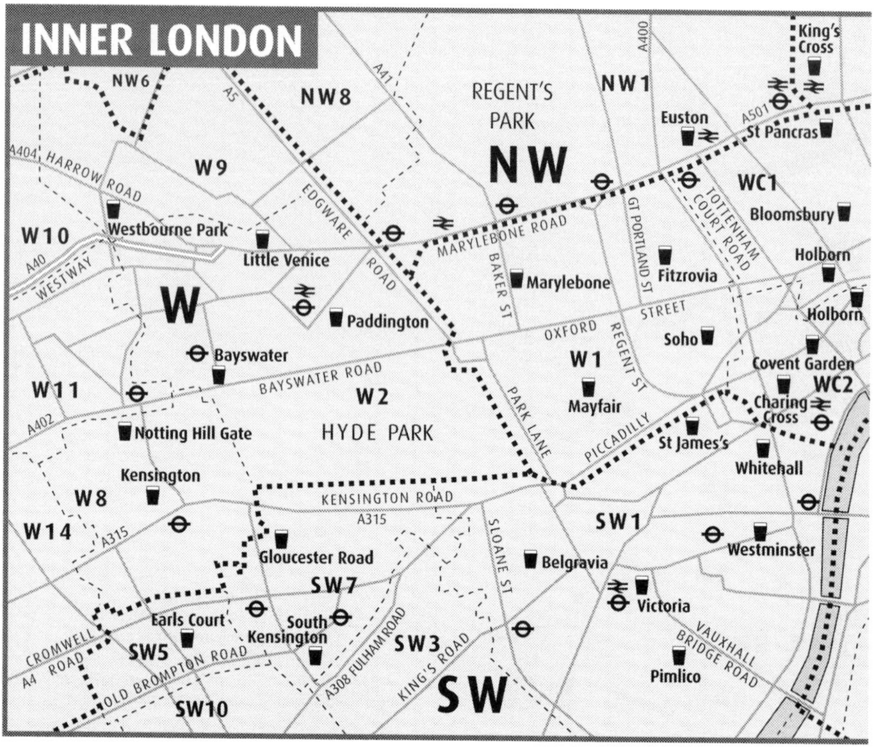

How to find London pubs

Greater London is divided into seven sectors: Central, East, North, North-West, South-East, South-West and West, reflecting postal boundaries. The Central sector includes the City (EC1 to EC4) and Holborn, Covent Garden and the Strand (WC1/2) plus W1, where pubs are listed in postal district order. In each of the other six sectors the pubs with London postcodes are listed first in postal district order (E1, E2 etc), followed by those in outer London districts, which are listed in alphabetical order (Barking, Chadwell Heath, etc) – see Greater London map. Postal district numbers can be found on every street name plate in the London postcode area.

CENTRAL LONDON

EC1: Clerkenwell

Exmouth Arms

23 Exmouth Market, EC1R 4QL

11-midnight (1.30am Fri & Sat); 11-11.30 Sun
(020) 3551 4772 exmoutharms.com

4 changing beers (often Dark Star, Revolutions) H

A former Courage pub, with traditional nameplate and green tiling, at the corner of Exmouth Market and Spafield Street. Rebuilt in the early 20th century, it is named after Viscount Exmouth, a decorated naval officer from the French and American wars. Operated by Barworks, it usually serves local ales, besides offering a dozen keg lines and a wide range of bottles. A choice of food is served daily until 10pm (9pm Sun).
(Farringdon) (Angel/Farringdon)

EC1: Farringdon

Jerusalem Tavern

55 Britton Street, EC1M 5UQ

12-11; closed Sat & Sun (020) 7490 4281

6 changing beers (often St Peter's) A

This is St Peter's Brewery's only pub in London. Although opened in 1996, it seems much older as it is an authentic re-creation of an 18th-century tavern, with bare wooden floors and a mixture of wooden tables and chairs. A changing selection of six St Peter's casks is served by air pressure from fake cask ends behind the bar. There is also a wide selection of bottled beers. A basic food menu is available. Q

EC1: Hatton Garden

Craft Beer Co

82 Leather Lane, EC1N 7TR

12-11; closed Sun (020) 7404 7049

House beer (by Kent); changing beers (sourced nationally) H

With an extensive beer offering of up to 14 cask ales, 20 keg lines, many bottles and two ciders, this pub can get busy. Downstairs it has stools and tables around the walls and plenty of standing room. There is more seating upstairs and a small standing area outside. Food is pies and Scotch

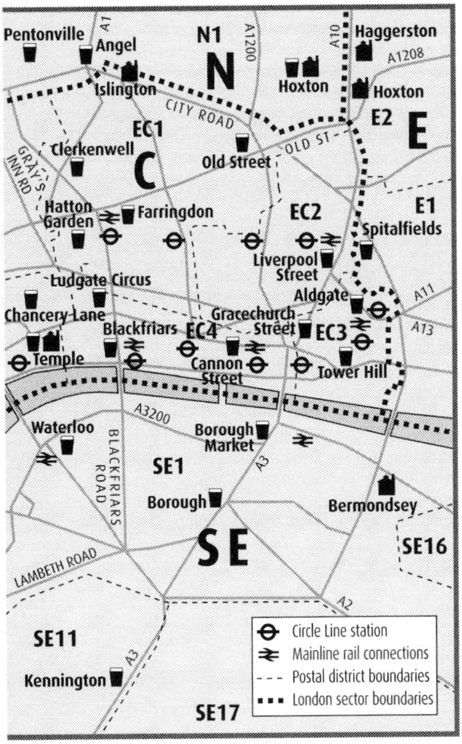

eggs, though you can order pizzas from next door. Interesting features include a glass ceiling and a large Bass mirror.
🐴❀⇌(Farringdon)⊖(Chancery Lane/Farringdon)
🍎🚌🐾📶

Olde Mitre ★ 🄻 ✔

1 Ely Court, Ely Place, EC1N 6SJ
✪ 11-11; closed Sat & Sun ☎ (020) 7405 4751
🌐 yeoldemitreholborn.co.uk
Fuller's Oliver's Island, London Pride; Gale's Seafarers Ale; 3 changing beers (often Clarkshaws, Sambrook's, Windsor & Eton) 🄷
Hidden in an alley between Hatton Garden and Ely Place, there has been a pub on this site since 1546. Mainly dating from the 18th century, the current pub has two bars and an upstairs function room, reached by a narrow staircase. All are wood panelled, giving a traditional feel, and it has been identified by CAMRA as having a nationally important historic interior. Bar snacks include a range of toasties.
Q❀◑⇌(City Thameslink)⊖(Chancery Lane/Farringdon)🍎🚌📶

EC1: Old Street

Old Fountain 🄻

3 Baldwin Street, EC1V 9NU
✪ 11-11; 12-11 Sat; 12-10.30 Sun ☎ (020) 7253 2970
Fuller's London Pride; Oakham Citra; house beer (by Signature Brew); 5 changing beers (sourced regionally) 🄷
This pub on the edge of the City has a single bar divided into two areas by a step. It is a family-owned free house with a classic pub food menu and its own roof terrace, which has heaters for winter. The guest ales are mainly from small breweries with new brews quite common. Tasting paddles of three thirds can be purchased. The large fish tank on the upper level is relaxing to look at.
🐴❀◑⇌⊖♣🍎🚌🐾📶

EC2: Liverpool Street

Magpie ✔

12 New Street, EC2M 4TP
✪ 11-midnight (11 Mon & Tue); 12-11 Sat; closed Sun
☎ (020) 7929 3889
Fuller's London Pride; St Austell Nicholson's Pale Ale; Sharp's Doom Bar; Truman's Runner; 4 changing beers (sourced nationally) 🄷
Close to Liverpool Street station, this pub can be busy in the evening with customers overflowing onto the pavement outside. The upstairs room can be reserved and food is available until 9pm. The building was an ambulance station at the beginning of the last century. Details of this and pictures of the local area adorn the walls. Children are admitted on Saturdays only. 🐴◑⇌⊖🚌📶

EC3: Aldgate

Craft Beer Co

29-31 Mitre Street, EC3A 5BU
✪ 12-11; closed Sat & Sun ☎ (020) 7929 5112
House beer (by Kent); 5 changing beers 🄷
Opened in 2015, this pub has bare brick walls with brewery mirrors, wooden floorboards and high tables with stools. As well as the house beer and guest ales, there are 18 keg lines and a boxed cider. Pies, Scotch eggs and sandwiches comprise the food offering. The toilets, and a separate drinking area, are downstairs. Smokers may use the pavement outside. Music is played.
🐴◑⇌(Fenchurch St)⊖(Aldgate/Aldgate E)
🍎🚌🐾📶

Hoop & Grapes ✔

47 Aldgate High Street, EC3N 1AL
✪ 12-11; 11-11 Sun ☎ (020) 7481 4583
Fuller's London Pride; St Austell Nicholson's Pale Ale; Sharp's Doom Bar; 5 changing beers (sourced nationally) 🄷
A Nicholson's pub that is a quirky Grade II*-listed building dating from before the Great Fire of London, famous for its lack of right angles. It is also one of only a handful of timbered buildings still left in London. The front of the building leans outwards and was saved by extensive renovation. A large food menu is available until 9.30pm Monday to Saturday and 9pm on Sunday.
🐴◑⇌(Fenchurch St)⊖(Aldgate/Aldgate E)
♣🚌📶

EC3: Gracechurch Street

Crosse Keys ✔

7-12 Gracechurch Street, EC3V 0DR
✪ 8am-11 (midnight Fri); 9am-11 Sat; 9.30am-9 Sun
☎ (020) 7623 4824
Fuller's London Pride; Greene King IPA, Abbot; Sharp's Doom Bar; changing beers 🄷
Housed in a grandiose building that used to be the headquarters of a banking corporation, this pub is named after a coaching inn that was once nearby. Twenty four handpumps dispense four regular Wetherspoon's ales and a range of rotating guests, listed on the screens above the bar and ordered by

pump number. Food is available all day and there are three function rooms for hire. Popular with city workers, it can be busy here at times.
Q☕◐♿⇌(Cannon St/Fenchurch St)⊖(Bank/Monument)🍎🚌📶

Ship ✔

11 Talbot Court, EC3V 0BP
🕐 11-11; 12-6 Sat; closed Sun ☎ (020) 7929 3902
Fuller's London Pride; St Austell Nicholson's Pale Ale; Sharp's Doom Bar; 6 changing beers (sourced nationally) Ⓗ
The original pub on this site, the Talbot, was destroyed in the Great Fire of London. The current pub, run by M&B Nicholson's has a single bar with two sets of handpumps and fonts dispensing the ales. Food is available throughout the day. It has the feel of a gin palace from a bygone age, with glass panels above the bar and mirrored panels on the walls. There is an upstairs restaurant.
◐⇌(Cannon St/Fenchurch St)⊖(Bank/Monument)🚌📶

EC3: Tower Hill

Liberty Bounds ✔

15 Trinity Square, EC3N 4AA
🕐 8am-midnight ☎ (020) 7481 0513
Adnams Ghost Ship, Broadside; Fuller's London Pride; Greene King IPA, Abbot; Sharp's Doom Bar; 6 changing beers (sourced nationally) Ⓗ
Close to the Tower, this grand building used to be the headquarters of the General Steam Navigation Company. Now it hosts a Wetherspoon pub on two levels, with ornate staircases between the floors. Each floor has a bar with 12 handpumps serving the same ales. Food is served till 11pm every day and is well priced for the area. Wheelchair access is at the rear entrance in Muscovy Street.
Q☕◐♿⇌(Fenchurch St)⊖(Tower Gateway/Tower Hill)🍎🚌📶

EC4: Blackfriars

Black Friar ★ ✔

174 Queen Victoria Street, EC4V 4EG
🕐 10-11; 9am-11 Sat; 12-10.30 Sun ☎ (020) 7236 5474
Fuller's London Pride; St Austell Nicholson's Pale Ale; Sharp's Doom Bar; 7 changing beers Ⓗ
Just opposite Blackfriars station, this M&B Nicholson's pub is popular with city workers and tourists alike. Saved from demolition by a campaign led by John Betjeman, it has an astonishing 1905 Art Nouveau interior complete with cavorting Dominican friars by Henry Poole RA, identified by CAMRA as of national importance. The grotto-like dining area is clad with Italian marble and has a vaulted gold mosaic ceiling. An extensive menu of meals and snacks is available until 10pm.
☕❀◐⇌⊖🚌🐾📶

EC4: Cannon Street

Pelt Trader

Arch 3, Dowgate Hill, EC4N 6AP
🕐 12-11; closed Sat & Sun ☎ (020) 7160 0253
🌐 pelttrader.com
6 changing beers (sourced nationally) Ⓐ

REAL ALE BREWERIES

40FT E8: Dalston
Anomaly Old Malden (NEW)
Anspach & Hobday SE1: Bermondsey
Barnet ▮ High Barnet
Battersea SW11: Nine Elms (NEW)
Beerblefish N18: Upper Edmonton
Bexley Erith
Block ▮ N1: Hoxton
Brewhouse & Kitchen ▮ E2: Hoxton (NEW)
Brewhouse & Kitchen ▮ EC1: Islington
Brewhouse & Kitchen ▮ N5: Highbury
Brick SE8: Deptford
Brixton SW9: Brixton
Brockley SE4: Brockley
Broken Drum Upper Belvedere (NEW)
Bullfinch SE24: Herne Hill
By The Horns SW17: Summerstown
Canopy SE24: Herne Hill
Clarkshaws SW9: Loughborough Junction
Craft Academy ▮ SE24: Herne Hill
Crate E9: Hackney Wick
Cronx New Addington
East London E10: Leyton
Enfield N18: Upper Edmonton
Essex Street ▮ WC2: Temple
Five Points E8: Hackney Downs
Fuller's W4: Chiswick
Gipsy Hill SE27: West Norwood
Gorgeous ▮ N6: Highgate
Greenwich ▮ SE10: Greenwich (NEW)
Hackney E2: Haggerston
Hammerton N7: Barnsbury
Hiver SE1: Bermondsey (NEW)
Hop Stuff SE28: Thamesmead (brewing suspended)
House ▮ N22: Wood Green (brewing suspended)
Howling Hops ▮ E9: Hackney Wick
Husk E16: West Silvertown
Kew SW14: East Sheen
Laine ▮ E9: South Hackney
Laine ▮ SW11: Battersea
London Beer Factory SE27: West Norwood
London Beer Lab SW9: Brixton
London Brewing ▮ N12: North Finchley
Magic Spells E10: Leyton
Maregade E9: Homerton (brewing suspended)
Marko Paulo ▮ W13: Northfields
Moncada NW2: Dollis Hill
Mondo SW8: South Lambeth
Muswell Hillbilly N10: Muswell Hill
Mutineers Bromley (NEW)
Oddly N17: Tottenham
One Mile End N17: Tottenham
Park Norbiton
Portobello W10: North Kensington
Redemption N17: Tottenham
Reunion Feltham
Sambrook's SW11: Battersea
Signal Beddington
Signature E10: Leyton
Southey SE20: Penge
Southwark SE1: Bermondsey
Spartan SE16: South Bermondsey
Tap East ▮ E20: Stratford
Three Sods ▮ E2: Bethnal Green
Tiny Vessel Hampton
Truman's E3: Hackney Wick
Twickenham Twickenham
Volden Croydon
Weird Beard W7: Hanwell
Wild Card E17: Higham Hill
Wimbledon SW19: Colliers Wood

Vibrant gem nestling in a railway arch under Cannon Street station. A free house, it serves up to six cask ales and one cider from wall-mounted taps. Local ales are usually on tap as well as the occasional special from further afield. Enjoy one of the pub's home-cooked pizzas while admiring the various Pelt Trader mirrors and the overhead canoe. Drinking on the pavement outside is allowed up until 9pm. The pub is available for private hire at weekends. ⏟❀◑◗≉⊖●🛢🚆❀☂

Sir John Hawkshaw ✅
Cannon Street Station, EC4N 6AP
☼ 7am-11.30 (midnight Thu-Sat); 8am-7 Sun
☎ (020) 3206 1004
Fuller's London Pride; Greene King IPA; Sharp's Doom Bar; 3 changing beers (sourced nationally) Ⓗ
A Wetherspoon bar next to Platform 1 on Cannon Street station. You navigate to the well-lit interior via an external seating area. A departure and arrival screen hangs by the bar. You can see the cellar section through the windows of the right-hand room. Seating comprises a mix of high stools and comfortable leather bench seats. As it is within the station, no smoking is allowed. The free toilets are by Platform 7. Q⏟◑◗≉⊖🛢☂

EC4: Ludgate Circus

Hoop & Grapes ✅
80 Farringdon Street, EC4A 4BL
☼ 12.30-11 (midnight Fri); 4-11 Sat & Sun
☎ (020) 7353 8808 ⊕ hoopandgrapes.co.uk
Shepherd Neame Whitstable Bay Pale Ale, Spitfire Gold, Spitfire; 1 changing beer (often Shepherd Neame) Ⓗ
A narrow pub that has been owned by Shepherd Neame for the last 15 years, with two handpumps upstairs and five on the ground floor. The pub usually closes at 11pm but has a licence to 2am if required. The upstairs bar can be hired for private parties at no cost and has a patio. To the rear is a large garden. Food is served to 9pm on weekdays. Check with the pub for availability at weekends. ⏟❀◑≉(City Thameslink)⊖(Blackfriars/ Chancery Lane)🛢❀

WC1: Bloomsbury

Calthorpe Arms
252 Grays Inn Road, WC1X 8JR
☼ 12 (11 Wed & Thu)-11.30; 11-midnight Fri; 11-11 Sat; 12-10.30 Sun ☎ (020) 7278 4732 ⊕ calthorpearmswc1.co.uk
Young's Bitter, Special; 3 changing beers (often Young's) Ⓗ
Unusual double doors lead into this single-bar corner local. With no music it is easy either to strike up a conversation sitting at the bar or to take one of the tables along the sides for more privacy. The upstairs dining room opens for lunch (12-2.30pm) but can be booked at other times. Evening meals are served 5.45-9.30pm Monday-Saturday. Young's bottle-conditioned beers are stocked plus a Young's seasonal and/or two guest beers (often from London). There is pavement seating outside. ❀◑⊖(Russell Sq)●🛢❀

Marlborough Arms Ⓛ ✅
36 Torrington Place, WC1E 7LY
☼ 12-11; 12-10.30 Sun ☎ (020) 7636 0120
Greene King IPA, Abbot; 6 changing beers (often Hammerton, Redemption, Sambrook's) Ⓗ

Traditional, welcoming inn, named after the coat of arms first worn by the third Duke of Marlborough, John Churchill. The pub attracts students, business people, tourists and locals from a surprisingly residential neighbourhood. A large open area is surrounded by oak panelling and some fine features, with the bar to one side, and plenty of tables and seating available, with a nod to informality and comfort in the small area beyond the bar. It has friendly, knowledgeable staff. ⏟❀◑◗≉⊖(Goodge St)🛢❀☂

Swan Ⓛ ✅
7 Cosmo Place, WC1N 3AP
☼ 11-11 (midnight Fri); 12-10.30 Sun ☎ (020) 7837 6223
Greene King IPA, Abbot; Hammerton N1; 4 changing beers (often Greene King) Ⓗ
Popular family-oriented pub among the tourist hotels on Southampton Row, close to Great Ormond Street Children's Hospital. There is a single long room, and tables in front on a pedestrian passage. Eight handpumps serve three regular real ales and four guests, mainly from London breweries, together with a real cider. Pub grub and snacks are served until 10pm (9.30pm Sun). A large-screen TV shows live sports events. Q⏟❀◑◗⊖(Russell Sq)●🛢❀☂

WC1: Holborn

Craft Beer Co
168 High Holborn, WC1V 7AA
☼ 12-midnight (1am Thu-Sat) ☎ (020) 7240 0431
15 changing beers (sourced nationally) Ⓗ
Although it is in the ancient parish of St Giles, whose church featured in several of Hogarth's etchings, including Gin Lane, its location on the north-eastern edge of Covent Garden will probably have a more modern resonance. On two levels, this, the sixth Craft Beer Co outlet, would be more at home in Beer Street, with its 15 pumps dispensing a changing range of beers from across the UK. There are frequent tap takeovers and Meet the Brewer events. ◑◗⊖(Covent Garden/Holborn)🛢

Holborn Whippet
25-29 Sicilian Avenue, WC1A 2QH
☼ 12-11; closed Sun ☎ (020) 3137 9937
⊕ holbornwhippet.com
5 changing beers (sourced nationally) Ⓟ
Here, a flow-jet is used to pump the beer to the taps; a blackboard above shows what is on sale. Real ales come from the likes of Adnams, Five Points, Mighty Oak, Moor, Oakham, Redemption and other London breweries; many other draught beers are sold. It has a simple menu: pizza, bratwurst, barbecue wings – all nicely done. The decor is basic, with bare wooden floors, brown tiles and cream-painted walls; there is outside seating on the attractive Sicilian Avenue. ❀◑⊖●🛢

WC1: St Pancras

Queen's Head Ⓛ
66 Acton Street, WC1X 9NB
☼ 12-midnight (11 Mon); 12-11 Sun ☎ (020) 7713 5772
⊕ queensheadlondon.com
Redemption Trinity; 2 changing beers (sourced regionally) Ⓗ
Narrow, late-Georgian premises off Gray's Inn Road, with a single bar, a smoking patio at the rear

and benches in front. The piano is used for jazz and blues on Thursdays and late Sunday afternoons. Guest beers from microbreweries usually include a dark one. One handpump serves cider, and there are three more real ciders and a range of other draught and bottled beers. Sharing snack platters are on offer at this comfortable pub frequented by locals and the occasional tourist.
❀◑⇌⊖(King's Cross St Pancras)●⊟ᯤ

Skinners Arms

114 Judd Street, WC1H 9NT
✪ 12-11; closed Sun ☎ (020) 7837 6521
🌐 skinnersarmslondon.com
Greene King IPA, Abbot; 4 changing beers (often Siren) [H]
Named after the City livery company and standing on a street named after a past master of the company, this traditional corner pub has essentially been converted to one bar, despite the signs on the doors and in the stained glass. A raised seating area is on the left as you enter, and the previously separate room at the back is now a large alcove with more seating. The decor is traditional, and there is a quiet ambience.
❀◑⇌⊖(King's Cross St Pancras)⊟

WC2: Chancery Lane

Knights Templar ✔

95 Chancery Lane, WC2A 1DT
✪ 8am-11 (11.30 Thu & Fri); 11-6.30 Sat; closed Sun
☎ (020) 7831 2660
Fuller's London Pride; Greene King IPA; Sharp's Doom Bar; 8 changing beers (sourced nationally) [H]
Named after its original landowners, this is an imposing conversion of a Grade II-listed bank retaining magnificent slender scroll-topped columns and a high, ochre-painted ceiling with illustrated panels and large chandeliers. The long curved wooden bar counter is overseen by a sculpted knight as the centrepiece of the ornate bar-back. Three mezzanine rooms may be reserved, two of them panelled libraries with balconies overlooking the bar. The whole pub can be hired at the weekend; check before visiting on a Saturday.
Q◑♿⊖(Chancery Lane/Temple)⊟ᯤ

WC2: Charing Cross

Harp 🄻 ✔

47 Chandos Place, WC2N 4HS
✪ 10.30-11.30 (midnight Fri & Sat); 12-10.30 Sun
☎ (020) 7836 0291
Dark Star Hophead, American Pale Ale; Fuller's London Pride; Harvey's Sussex Best Bitter; 5 changing beers (sourced nationally) [H]
Small and friendly Fuller's pub that became a haven for beer choice as a free house under the management of the late, legendary, Binnie Walsh. Ciders and perries complement the fine range of real ales. The narrow bar is adorned with mirrors and portraits. There is no intrusive music or TV, and a cosy upstairs room provides a refuge from the busy throng – this pub is deservedly popular. A former CAMRA National Pub of the Year winner among numerous other awards including Evening Standard's London Pub of the Year 2019.
Q◑⇌⊖●⊟ᯤ

Lemon Tree ✔

4 Bedfordbury, WC2N 4BP
✪ 12-11; 12-10.30 Sun ☎ (020) 7831 1391
🌐 lemontreecoventgarden.com
Harvey's Sussex Best Bitter; St Austell Tribute; 3 changing beers (often Adnams, Truman's) [H]
A small, one-bar pub next to the stage door of the Coliseum that is a favourite among locals, musicians and theatregoers. The Thai restaurant upstairs doubles as a function room. Look out for the pub entrance, slightly set back. In the choice of guest beers there is an emphasis on London brews, by popular demand. It is operated by All Our Bars, a small pub and bar management chain based in Edenbridge. ◑⇌⊖⊟ᯤ

WC2: Covent Garden

Coach & Horses

42 Wellington Street, WC2E 7BD
✪ 11-11; 12-10.30 Sun ☎ (020) 7240 0553
Fuller's London Pride; St Austell Tribute [H]
Much loved by the locals, this is a small, traditional, independent pub with a strong Irish influence, run by the same family for around 40 years. Visitors also make a beeline here, along with theatre- and opera-goers. It has a fantastic collection of approximately 70 Irish whiskeys and gins, and Scottish whiskies. There are photographs of Gaelic football teams, and the sport of hurling also features, plus theatre posters. Note the beautiful engraved front windows. Q◑♿⊖⊟🐾

Cross Keys

31 Endell Street, WC2H 9BA
✪ 11-11; 12-10.30 Sun ☎ (020) 7836 5185
🌐 crosskeyscoventgarden.com
Brodie's Bethnal Green Bitter, Piccadilly Pale Ale; Greene King IPA; Hardys & Hansons Olde Trip; 1 changing beer (sourced nationally) [H]
Built in the mid-1840s when Endell (formerly Belton) Street was widened as part of clearing the St Giles's rookery (slum), an ornate façade reveals a long, welcoming bar, subdued lighting, comfortable banquette seating and tables and chairs. Copper kettles, pans, street signs, stuffed fish, framed pictures and photos, Beatles memorabilia and a fine Truman, Hanbury, Buxton & Co mirror cover the walls. Families are welcome (over-12s only) until 7pm unless it is busy, but no dogs. ◑⊖⊟

Lamb & Flag

33 Rose Street, WC2E 9EB
✪ 11-11; 12-10.30 Sun ☎ (020) 7497 9504
Fuller's London Pride, ESB; Gale's Seafarers Ale; 3 changing beers (often Dark Star, Fuller's, Windsor & Eton) [H]
Tucked away up Rose Street from Garrick Street, this Grade II-listed pub owned by Fuller's since 2013 remains a pleasant traditional retreat without muzak or games machines. Two dark wood-panelled rooms, the rear one with an attractive fireplace, and a connecting passage, form the main bar on the ground floor. The upstairs bar and restaurant, where the main food service is provided is, please note, table service only. Charles Dickens and Karl Marx were both regulars.
◑⇌(Charing Cross)⊖(Covent Garden/Leicester Sq)⊟🐾ᯤ

White Swan

14 New Row, WC2N 4LF

11-11 (11.30 Fri); 10-11.30 Sat; 12-10.30 Sun

(020) 3077 1129

Fuller's London Pride; St Austell Nicholson's Pale Ale; 5 changing beers (sourced nationally)

Grade II-listed, once owned by the London banking firm of Hoare & Co, this M&B Nicholson's pub is popular with Covent Garden tourists. It may appear crowded at first glance, but it is longer than it looks and there are more seats at the back. The first-floor dining room can be booked for functions; note its contrasting fireplaces. A rare outlet for real cider in WC2.

(Charing Cross) (Leicester Sq)

WC2: Holborn

Shakespeare's Head

Africa House, 64-68 Kingsway, WC2B 6BG

7am-midnight (1am Fri); 8am-1am Sat; 8am-midnight Sun

(020) 7404 8846

Fuller's London Pride; Greene King IPA, Abbot; Sharp's Doom Bar; house beer (by Windsor & Eton); 5 changing beers (sourced nationally)

Large Wetherspoon bank conversion from 1998, named after a famous pub in the locality until the demolition of Wych Street over 100 years ago. It is usually busy with shoppers, tourists, local office workers and, during term time, students from the nearby London School of Economics. A convenient place for a couple of pints after your cultural sojourn at the British Museum.

Q

WC2: Temple

Edgar Wallace

40 Essex Street, WC2R 3JF

11-11; closed Sat & Sun (020) 7353 3120

theedgarwallace.co.uk

Crouch Vale Brewers Gold; 7 changing beers (often Dark Star, East London Brewing, Timothy Taylor)

Just off Fleet Street near the Royal Courts of Justice, this is a real gem of a one-room pub, with additional seating upstairs. The comfortable downstairs room, its walls and ceiling covered with beer mats and old advertising signs, has a fine wooden bar offering a wide range of rotating ales. This quiet pub allows no music, laptops, mobiles and so on. Good-value food is served all day (until 3pm Fri). Q

Temple Brew House

46 Essex Street, WC2R 3JF

12-11 (11.30 Thu; midnight Fri & Sat); 12-10.30 Sun

(020) 7936 2536 templebrewhouse.com

House beer (by Essex Street); 5 changing beers (often Essex Street)

This basement bar, just off the Strand and Fleet Street, is run by the City Pub Group and continues its development of microbrewpubs, joining the Guide-listed Bath Brew House and the Cambridge Brew House. The five-barrel plant is visible from the bar, which is a single room with minimal decor, novel lighting and schoolroom-style furnishings, with some tables set aside for dining. It is generally quiet during the day though it does get noisy of an evening. Q

W1: Fitzrovia

Queen Charlotte

43 Goodge Street, W1T 1TA

12-11 (midnight Fri & Sat); 12-10.30 Sun

(020) 7323 9361

BrewDog Dead Pony Club; 2 changing beers

A big welcome awaits you in this small, single-bar corner pub with bare wooden floors and simple furnishings. Changing offerings from Sambrook's and other smaller breweries are sold in one-third and two-third pint measures, as well as the usual halves and pints. Plenty of other interesting draught and bottled beers are also stocked. Meals, including speciality burgers, are served lunchtimes only during the week and until 9pm on Saturdays; bar snacks, such as giant pork scratchings, are otherwise available. (Goodge St)

Stag's Head

102 New Cavendish Street, W1W 6XW

11-11; 12-11 Sat; 12-10 Sun (020) 7580 8313

Fuller's London Pride; Tring Side Pocket for a Toad; 1 changing beer (often Tring)

A smart, oak-panelled pub with a historic interior of regional importance, offering a friendly welcome to regulars and visitors alike. Rebuilt in the late 1930s by brewers William Younger, it has a marvellous Art Deco exterior, sporting a curved corner profile. Vertical drinking is assisted by unusual peninsular shelf projections to the bar and elsewhere. Sun lovers and smokers can relax on shaded benches outside. Traditional pub food is served lunchtimes only.

(Great Portland St)

W1: Marylebone

Carpenters Arms

12 Seymour Place, W1H 7NE

11-11; 12-10.30 Sun (020) 7723 1050

Harvey's Sussex Best Bitter; 5 changing beers (sourced nationally)

A sister pub to Southwark's Market Porter, but with fewer beers, and a welcoming haven for escapees from the bustle of Oxford Street. TV sports and a dartboard add to the appeal for the regulars. A sensitive refurbishment has preserved the wall tiling and floor mosaics at the main entrance. Elsewhere is a display of woodworking tools. Pies are the main snacks.

(Marble Arch)

Golden Eagle

59 Marylebone Lane, W1U 2NY

12-11 (midnight Fri & Sat); closed Sun (020) 7935 3228

Fuller's London Pride; St Austell Tribute; 2 changing beers (often Adnams, Twickenham)

First licensed in 1842 and rebuilt in 1890, this single-bar pub is traditional in every way: small and cosy, with smart decor, a fine etched bar-back mirror and leaded windows. The historic interior is of regional importance. Landlady Gina Vernon and her family celebrated 25 years here in 2016. Piano singalongs on Tuesday, Thursday and Friday evenings maintain the timeless atmosphere. Real ales are quality, not quantity! Q (Bond St)

Thornbury Castle

29A Enford Street, W1H 1DN

12-11; closed Sat & Sun (020) 7402 2189

6 changing beers (sourced regionally)

A small, family-run pub in a side street near Marylebone station, with wood panelling throughout and a raised seating area at the back. There is a strong Rugby Union connection (Wasps) and the pub may open at weekends for big games on TV. Discerning drinkers will find it a worthwhile alternative to the more mainstream pubs in the area. Thai food is served. Q✪➔⊖♣🖨♿🐾🛜

W1: Mayfair

Clarence ✓
4 Dover Street, W1S 4LB
✪ 10-11 (midnight Fri & Sat) ☎ (020) 7491 3607
Fuller's London Pride; St Austell Nicholson's Pale Ale; Sharp's Doom Bar; 5 changing beers (sourced nationally) ℍ
Licensed in 1724 as the Coach & Horses, later named after the Duke of Clarence, who became King William IV in 1830. A smallish frontage belies a much larger area extending back, which incorporates a beer library. The atmosphere is convivial, especially since M&B Nicholson's refurbishment in 2012; it has a pleasant, quieter upstairs bar and a literary theme to the prints and inscriptions. It is close to the Ritz hotel in Piccadilly. ✪➔⊖(Green Park)🖨🛜

W1: Soho

Argyll Arms ★
18 Argyll Street, W1F 7TP
✪ 10-11 (midnight Fri & Sat); 10-10.30 Sun
☎ (020) 7734 6117
Fuller's London Pride; St Austell Nicholson's Pale Ale; 6 changing beers (sourced nationally) ℍ
A Victorian Grade II*-listed Nicholson's house with a nationally important historic pub interior. Three snugs are separated by etched-glass partitions; note the remarkable Bass mirror. The bar-back is impressive and adjacent is a rare survivor, a manager's office with more etched glazing. The magnificent saloon is decorated with ornate mirrors. Enjoy a reliable range of regular and guest ales on eight or more handpumps. ✪➔♿⊖(Oxford Circus)🖨🛜

Crown ✓
64 Brewer Street, W1F 9TP
✪ 11.30-11; 12-11.30 Sat & Sun ☎ (020) 7287 8420
Fuller's London Pride; St Austell Nicholson's Pale Ale; Sharp's Doom Bar; 2 changing beers ℍ
A popular Nicholson's pub on the site of the Hickford Rooms, London's main concert venue in the 1740s and '50s; a notice displays the history of the pub. The main bar, with its banquettes, is a welcome retreat from the bustling street. Accompanied children are welcome in the upstairs dining room. Starting with breakfast, food is served daily until 10pm. The guest beers are often unusual for the area. Q✪➔⊖(Piccadilly Circus)🖨🛜

Dog & Duck ★ ✓
18 Bateman Street, W1D 3AJ
✪ 11-11 (11.30 Fri & Sat); 12-10.30 Sun ☎ (020) 7494 0697
St Austell Nicholson's Pale Ale; Sharp's Doom Bar; 5 changing beers (sourced nationally; often St Austell, Sharp's) ℍ
In the heart of Soho, this Grade II-listed Nicholson's outlet, built in 1897, has a nationally important historic pub interior. An elaborate mosaic depicts dogs and ducks, and wonderful advertising mirrors

adorn the walls. The upstairs Orwell Bar can be hired for functions. The pub is small and so popular, especially with media people, that it is not just smokers who have to stand outside. The bar extends towards the Frith Street door. ✪➔⊖(Tottenham Court Rd)🖨🛜

Lyric ⎵
37 Great Windmill Street, W1D 7LT
✪ 11-11.30 (midnight Fri & Sat); 12-10.30 Sun
☎ (020) 7434 0604 🌐 lyricsoho.co.uk
9 changing beers ℍ
A small, independently owned bar just off Shaftesbury Avenue, bay-fronted with a tiled, panelled interior, popular with local trade. Once two adjacent taverns, the Windmill and the Ham, it merged in the mid-18th century to form the Windmill & Ham, renamed in 1890 and rebuilt 16 years later. As well as draught beers including London specialities, cask ales may come from Big Smoke, Brodie's, Dark Star, Magic Rock, Marble, RedWillow, Redemption, Tiny Rebel or Thornbridge. ✪➔⊖(Piccadilly Circus)🖨🛜

Old Coffee House
49 Beak Street, W1F 9SF
✪ 11-11; 12-10.30 Sun ☎ (020) 7437 2197
Brodie's Mild, Kiwi IPA; 4 changing beers (often Brodie's) ℍ
A large but cosy pub, close to the buzz of Carnaby Street, with six handpumps offering a range of ales from Brodie's. First licensed as the Silver Street Coffee House, it was rebuilt in 1894 and is now Grade II listed. The long bar and dark panelling are adorned with Watneys Red Barrel signage, brewery mirrors and sundry prints, posters, pictures and brassware. At lunchtimes you will find good sized portions of pub grub, reasonably priced. 🛏♿✪➔⊖(Piccadilly Circus)🖨🐾

Queen's Head ⎵ ✓
15 Denman Street, W1D 7HN
✪ 11-11.30 (midnight Fri & Sat); 12-10.30 Sun
☎ (020) 7437 1540 🌐 queensheadpiccadilly.com
Fuller's London Pride; Sambrook's Wandle Ale; 3 changing beers (sourced regionally; often Dark Star, Gun, Sambrook's) ℍ
A rare West End free house with plenty of vertical drinking space below and a restaurant upstairs. The traditional feel is enhanced by an attractive bar-back and wall mirroring downstairs and an unusual leather-fronted bar in the restaurant. With its real ales, good-value pies and other pub food, including snacks and cheeseboards at the bar, this is a popular pub both before and after theatre visits. 🛏✪➔⊖(Piccadilly Circus)🖨🐾🛜

Star & Garter
62 Poland Street, W1F 7NX
✪ 11-11; 12-11 Sat; closed Sun ☎ (020) 7437 9278
Fuller's London Pride; Greene King IPA; 1 changing beer (often St Austell) ℍ
A few minutes' walk from Oxford Circus, here is a proper unreconstructed beer house to gladden the hearts of aficionados; no fripperies like meals or Wi-Fi. Formerly a Courage house, as the painted windows attest, it has a small, cosy, wood-panelled bar with a matchboard ceiling. An additional bar upstairs is usually open on Thursday and Friday nights to cope with the throng. ➔(Oxford Circus/Piccadilly Circus)🖨🐾

EAST LONDON

E1: Spitalfields

Commercial Tavern

142 Commercial Street, E1 6NU
12-11; 12-10.30 Sun (020) 3137 9563
commercial-tavern.com
4 changing beers (often Burning Sky, Salopian, Siren) H
A Grade II-listed Shoreditch pub, built in 1865 and with a unique, wacky decor including chandeliers, lampshades, magazine covers and different wallpapers. It is quite small, but there is more room upstairs and tables outside on the pavement. Sometimes there will be a real cider on in the summer. Pizzas are served all day. There are no TVs or fruit machines, so just relax.
(Liverpool St)(Liverpool St/Shoreditch High St)

Pride of Spitalfields

3 Heneage Street, E1 5LJ
11-midnight (1am Fri & Sat) (020) 7247 8933
Crouch Vale Brewers Gold; Fuller's London Pride, ESB; Sharp's Doom Bar; 1 changing beer (often Truman's) H
Close to the curry houses on Brick Lane, this busy pub offers a friendly welcome and a warm atmosphere. Originally named the Romford Arms, being tied to the Star Brewery in Romford, it was given its present name in the mid-1980s. Persons suspected to be Jack the Ripper are reported to have frequented this venue. The small single bar is opposite the fireplace and piano. Many local pictures adorn the walls. A good selection of food is available weekday lunchtimes.
(Aldgate East/Shoreditch High St)

Williams Ale & Cider House

22-24 Artillery Lane, E1 7LS
11-11 (midnight Thu-Sat); 12-10 Sun (020) 7247 5163
williamsspitalfields.com
Greene King IPA, Yardbird; 5 changing beers (often Crouch Vale, Hackney, Truman's) H
This pub is on the edge of the City in a lane off bustling Bishopsgate. It is cosy, with a wide selection of cask beer and also seven handpumps for cider; it is the local CAMRA Cider Pub of the Year. Three third-pint paddles are available for the price of a pint. Meals are served all day; for snacks the home-made Scotch eggs and sausage rolls are recommended. Rugby is often shown at weekends.
(Liverpool St)

E2: Bethnal Green

Camel

277 Globe Road, E2 0JD
12-11; 12-10.30 Sun (020) 3620 2333
thecamele2.co.uk
Sambrook's Wandle Ale; 4 changing beers (often Adnams, Oakham, St Austell) H
A small refurbished Victorian pub with a single bar and a traditional feel. One of the guest beers usually comes from Five Points brewery in Hackney. There is food throughout the day, with a range of pies and mash, toasties and puddings. The distinctive exterior tiling gives a clue to the original brewery; the last one with a tie was Ind Coope. The pub is convenient for the Museum of Childhood and York Hall.

King's Arms

11A Buckfast Street, E2 6EY
12-11.30 (midnight Fri & Sat) (020) 7729 2627
thekingsarmspub.com
3 changing beers (often Five Points, Howling Hops, Siren) H
A back-street pub refurbished six years ago, with a central bar and benches on the pavement outside. Note that the pump handles do not have clips on them; customers need to check the bar menu on the wall. Alongside the changing cask beers are several keg taps. Two real ciders are available from boxes. Snacks such as cheese, meat and Scotch eggs are popular.
(Bethnal Green/Shoreditch High St)

E3: Bow

Eleanor Arms

460 Old Ford Road, E3 5JP
4-11; 12-11 Fri-Sun (020) 8980 6992
eleanorarms.co.uk
Shepherd Neame Master Brew, Whitstable Bay Pale Ale, Spitfire Gold; 2 changing beers (often Shepherd Neame) H
Near Victoria Park, this CAMRA award-winning pub has been run by the same three-person team for over 10 years, with occasional help from the customers. It is traditionally furnished, with wood panelling and an eclectic mix of pictures adorning the walls. At the back is a small beer garden. The pub becomes the Old Ford Jazz Club every Sunday. There are traditional games, including shove-ha'penny, skittles and dominoes, and a quiz on the first Thursday of the month. (8)

E5: Clapton

Anchor & Hope

15 High Hill Ferry, E5 9HG (800yds N of Lea Bridge Rd, along river path)
1-11; 12-11 Sat; 12-10.30 Sun (020) 8806 1730
Fuller's London Pride, ESB; 1 changing beer (often Fuller's) H
Dating from around 1850, this Fuller's tenancy is right next to the bank of the Lee Canal, with outside tables overlooking the water and Walthamstow Marshes. Very small, it has not changed much over the years, giving it a traditional charm. It has a strong local following and is also popular with passing walkers and cyclists. Boats can tie up outside. Hot pies are available all day. There is a roaring log fire in the winter.
(393)

Crooked Billet

84 Upper Clapton Road, E5 9JP
4-11; 12-midnight Fri & Sat; 12-11 Sun (020) 3058 1166
e5crookedbillet.co.uk
5 changing beers (often Hammerton, Siren, Truman's) H
Rebuilt in 1950, this pub has a central bar with three sides. It is owned by a local pub group and sells mainly local beer from breweries including ELB, Five Points and Redemption, as well as those listed. Popular for Sunday roasts, it has a large garden to the rear for smokers and a table tennis table. The horseshoe seating can be reserved for groups. Monday is quiz night.

E6: East Ham

Miller's Well

419-421 Barking Road, E6 2JX
8am-midnight (1am Fri & Sat); 8am-11 Sun
(020) 8471 8404
Greene King Abbot; Ruddles Best Bitter; Sharp's Doom Bar; 3 changing beers (sourced nationally) H
Converted from three adjacent shops in 1993, this Wetherspoon pub directly opposite East Ham town hall is popular with a mix of local customers. The interior has the usual displays of historic photographs and pictures of local sites, information about local celebrities (here including Lord Lister of medical fame, the original boy who stood on the burning deck, and MP Keir Hardie), and local industries. As well as Wetherspoon's festivals, the pub hosts Meet the Brewer events.
Q

E8: Hackney

Cock Tavern

315 Mare Street, E8 1EJ
12-11 (1am Fri & Sat); 12-10.30 Sun
thecocktavern.co.uk
8 changing beers (often Hackney, Maregade, Howling Hops) H
A friendly single-room town-centre establishment built in the 1930s, with exposed floorboards. In effect, it is now the Howling Hops Brewery cask taproom; the cellar currently houses Short Stack Brewery, which makes small batch brews. Alongside the beers, another eight handpumps offer an excellent choice of real ciders. Bar snacks include a selection of pickled eggs and you can bring outside food in.
(Downs) (Central/Downs)

Pembury Tavern

90 Amhurst Road, E8 1JH
4-midnight; 12-midnight Sat; 12-11 Sun
(020) 8986 8597 pemburytavern.co.uk
Five Points Pale; 5 changing beers (often Five Points, Milton) H
Acquired by Five Points Brewery as its taproom, the pub was stylishly refurbished in September 2018 retaining the spacious interior, hardwood floors and the bar billiards table. It has a buzzing atmosphere. The beer range includes two rotating guests, usually a classic and a modern craft ale, and 16 keg lines. New York-style pizzas are available Monday to Saturday and roasts on Sunday, including vegetarian and vegan options.
(Downs) (Central/Downs)

E9: Homerton

Adam & Eve

155 Homerton High Street, E9 6AS
4-11 (midnight Thu); 12-1am Fri & Sat; 12-11 Sun
(020) 8985 1494 adamandevepub.com
East London Brewing Pale Ale; Five Points Railway Porter; 4 changing beers (often Hackney, Siren) H
A pub dating back to the mid 18th-century, with impressive frontage added early in the 20th. Two doors lead into the large main drinking area extending both sides of the long circular bar. Facilities include an unusual L-shaped pool table and a dartboard. There is a garden at the rear. An interesting selection of food is available Monday-Thursday from 4pm and Friday-Sunday from 12pm.

Chesham Arms

15 Mehetabel Road, E9 6DU
4-11; 12-11 Fri & Sat; 12-10.30 Sun (020) 8986 6717
cheshamarms.com
4 changing beers (sourced nationally) H
A charming, popular back-street pub rescued from development by a successful local campaign and reopened in 2015. Tasteful renovation boasts traditional furnishings including wooden floorboards. The single bar serves two rooms and a rear terrace leading down to a leafy garden. Real cider is available, with occasional festivals; it was the local CAMRA Cider Pub of the Year for 2018. Bar snacks can be supplemented with food brought in or ordered for delivery.
(Hackney Central)

E10: Leyton

Coach & Horses

391 High Road, E10 5NA
12-11 (11.30 Thu; midnight Fri); 10-midnight Sat
(020) 8281 3398 thecoachleyton.com
Sharp's Doom Bar; 2 changing beers (often East London Brewing) H
A new entry to the Guide, this large corner pub was refurbished during 2018. It comprises a main bar at the front, a small bar at the back and an outside courtyard with tables. Handpumps dispense two or three local guest ales; there are also 14 keg lines. Near to the Leyton Orient ground; please note that on match days the pub is restricted to home fans only. There is live music on Friday and Saturday evenings.

Leyton Orient Supporters Club

Breyer Group Stadium, Oliver Road, E10 5NF
5-7.30, 9.30-11 Tue; 12-2.30, 5-8 Sat (020) 8988 8288
orientsupporters.org
Mighty Oak Oscar Wilde G**; 9 changing beers** H
Next to the medical centre, the club normally opens match days, ale nights and for some televised England football matches only. Show a CAMRA membership card for admission. At a long single bar at the back of the room, the volunteer staff serve a truly wonderful choice of ales, occasionally with a cask on the bar as well as the handpumps. The bar is often packed but service is prompt. Local CAMRA Club of the Year 2019.

Leyton Technical

265B High Road, E10 5QN
4-11 (midnight Thu); 12-1am Fri; 11-1am Sat; 12-11 Sun
(020) 8558 4759 leytontechnical.com
Volden Session Ale; 7 changing beers (often Crate, Five Points, Volden) H
Originally built as a Technical College (hence the name) in 1896, and later repurposed as a town hall, this pub retains many original features, such as chandeliers and marble mosaic flooring. There are numerous rooms furnished in typical Antic shabby-chic, and it is generally possible to find a quiet place. Regular events such as quizzes and music take place. Good food includes vegetarian options.

E11: Leytonstone

North Star

24 Browning Road, E11 3AR

🌣 4-11 (9 Mon); 12-11 Sat; 12-10.30 Sun ☎ 07747 010013
🌐 thenorthstarpub.com

East London Brewing Foundation Bitter; Oakham JHB; 4 changing beers (sourced nationally) 🅗

A real find! This friendly, comfortable local nestles in the quiet Browning Road conservation area behind the busy Leytonstone High Road. The bar serves the second room via a hatch. Thai food is available evenings (not Mon) and weekends. The covered garden sports a wood-fired pizza oven in use at weekends. There are occasional live music events and a Sunday quiz. Local CAMRA Pub of the Year 2019. 🌣🏠🍴🕭➰🛒🐾🛜

Northcote Arms

110 Grove Green Road, E11 4EL

🌣 2-11 (11.30 Tue); 12.30-12.30am Fri; 12-1am Sat; 12-midnight Sun ☎ (020) 8518 7516
🌐 thenorthcotee11.com

4 changing beers (often Crate, East London Brewing, Signature Brew) 🅗

A real East End pub with entertainment most evenings and weekends. Warm and friendly service ensures that many of the local community visit. Two doors lead into separate rooms with a circular bar. The bar on the left serves four beers from nearby breweries; the other door leads to a small snug and the garden, where there is a whisky bar. Local CAMRA Community Pub of the Year 2019. 🌣🏠➰(Leyton)➰🛒🐾🛜

Red Lion 🅛 ✅

640 High Road, E11 3AA

🌣 12-11 (midnight Thu; 2am Fri & Sat) ☎ (020) 8988 2929
🌐 theredlionleytonstone.com

Sharp's Atlantic; Volden Session Ale, Pale Ale; 7 changing beers (sourced nationally; often Volden) 🅗

A large Victorian pub with the shabby-chic decor associated with Antic interiors and an enclosed beer garden to the rear. Family-friendly until 9pm, it offers reasonably priced food including a late-night menu on Friday and Saturday (9.30pm-midnight) and Sunday roasts. DJs and live music also feature; the pub has a ballroom upstairs. 🌣🏠🍴🕭➰➰🛒🐾🛜

E11: Wanstead

George 🅛 ✅

159 High Street, E11 2RL

🌣 8am-midnight (12.30am Fri & Sat) ☎ (020) 8989 2921

Fuller's London Pride; Greene King IPA, Abbot; Sharp's Doom Bar; 8 changing beers (sourced nationally) 🅗

Taken over by Wetherspoon in 1992, the pub has two bars but upstairs there is no real ale. Twelve handpumps downstairs dispense the regular Wetherspoon's ales and eight guests, which sell quickly at the weekends. Food is served until 11pm and there are three beer festivals during the year. Photographs of famous Georges adorn the upper walls. There is a smoking area and car park at the back. Q🌣🏠🍴➰🛒🛜

E12: Manor Park

Golden Fleece ✅

166 Capel Road, E12 5DB

🌣 11-11 (midnight Fri & Sat) ☎ (020) 8478 0024

Greene King IPA, Abbot; 3 changing beers (often Castle Rock, Greene King) 🅗

This multi-room family pub has a comfortable interior with many photographs of old Manor Park on view. Two rotating guest beers come from national suppliers and an extensive food menu is always available. The large room at the back can be reserved for private functions. A large garden area has numerous canopied tables and picnic-style benches. There is a quiz on Wednesday evenings and an outside DJ the last Sunday of summer months. 🌣🏠🍴🕭➰🛒➰🛒🐾🛜

E13: Plaistow

Black Lion ✅

59-61 High Street, E13 0AD

🌣 11-11; 12-10.30 Sun ☎ (020) 8472 2351
🌐 blacklionplaistow.co.uk

Mighty Oak Captain Bob; 3 changing beers (sourced nationally) 🅗

An 18th-century wood-beamed coaching inn with two bars, an original cobbled courtyard, a function room in a converted outbuilding, and a garden. The narrow main bar is where four ales are on offer. There is a smaller back bar accessible by a separate door or through the main bar. Sports TVs can be viewed from all points. Home-cooked food and sandwiches are served weekday lunchtimes and evenings and also before West Ham home games. 🌣🏠🍴➰➰P🛒🛜

E14: Canary Wharf

Ledger Building ✅

4 Hertsmere Road, E14 4AL

🌣 9am-midnight; 9am-11 Sun ☎ (020) 7536 7770

Fuller's London Pride; Greene King IPA, Abbot; Sharp's Doom Bar; 5 changing beers (often Truman's, Twickenham) 🅗

In a building dating from 1800, this pub stands on the north-west corner of the former Import Dock and takes its name from the original use: to hold the ledgers. Pictures of the area's history adorn the walls. A large single bar serves the regular Wetherspoon's range along with five rotating guest ales, mostly from London breweries. Three further rooms give plenty of space. The main toilets are downstairs and the smoking area is at the front. Q🌣🏠🍴➰➰(West India Quay)🛒🛜

E14: Crossharbour

Pepper Saint Ontiod ✅

21 Pepper Street, E14 9RP

🌣 12-11 (midnight Fri); 12-10.30 Sun ☎ (020) 7987 5205
🌐 peppersaintontiod.com

3 changing beers (often East London Brewing, Truman's, Volden) 🅗

A Docklands pub taken over by Antic in 2009 with a spacious ground floor bar decorated in a modern style. There is a second bar upstairs but with no handpumps. Food is available lunchtimes and evenings weekdays and until 9pm Saturday and 6pm Sunday. Benches outside provide a view of the dock. Sports TV is shown and music is played. 🌣🏠🍴➰➰🛒➰🛜

E14: Limehouse

Craft Beer Co

576 Commercial Road, E14 7JD

🌣 3.30-11 (midnight Thu & Fri); 12-midnight Sat; 12-10.30 Sun ☎ (020) 7790 2726

House beer (by Kent); 5 changing beers (sourced nationally) Ⓗ
The steadily expanding Craft Beer Co acquired this former Charrington's house on the bustling Commercial Road in 2016. Six cask ales are complemented by 20 keg lines and a large range of bottles. The decor is neutral with original mirrors from Bass, Charrington and Worthington breweries adorning a stripped-back bare wall. Some original iron columns remain along with an uncovered mosaic bearing the legend Railway Tavern, the pub's previous name. ❀◑≹⊖▭🐾ᯤ

E17: Walthamstow

Bell 𝕃 ✔
617 Forest Road, E17 4NE
☉ 12-midnight (11 Mon; 1am Fri & Sat); 12-11 Sun
☎ (020) 8523 2277 ⊕ belle17.com
Sharp's Doom Bar; Timothy Taylor Landlord; 6 changing beers Ⓗ
This tall Victorian pub is at the crossroads of the two main streets of Walthamstow and is well-served by buses. The interior is open plan but has two distinct areas. With comfortable furnishings, the real open fire is a bonus. There is live music at least once a week. The pub has become trendy and is frequented by many young families, with children allowed until 8pm. It has a large smoking area to the rear. ❀◑♣▭🐾ᯤ

Coppermill
205 Coppermill Lane, E17 7HF
☉ 11-11 (12.30am Fri & Sat) ☎ (020) 8520 3709
⊕ coppermillpub.co.uk
Fuller's London Pride; Sharp's Doom Bar; 2 changing beers (sourced nationally) Ⓗ
An off-licence up until 1985, this is now a small, friendly corner pub with a cosy atmosphere. A fascinating collection of unusual objects decorates the interior, with old photographs of the area on the walls. There is live music on Friday and Saturday evenings, a quiz on Sunday and an open mic night on Monday. Live sport is shown. The bus service is twice an hour from outside the pub and there is easy access to the Walthamstow Wetlands. ❀⊖(St James St)♣▭(W12)ᯤ

Mirth, Marvel & Maud 𝕃
186 Hoe Street, E17 4QH
☉ 4-11 (midnight Thu; 2am Fri); 12-2am Sat; 12-11 Sun
☎ (020) 8520 8636 ⊕ mirthmarvelandmaud.com
6 changing beers (often East London Brewing, Volden) Ⓗ
A Grade II-listed building which has previously served as a church, the Granada cinema and a concert theatre. A rising Wurlitzer organ still exists, and many big names played here, including the Beatles. In the foyer the ex-ticket office bar has over a dozen cocktails on offer and at the back downstairs another bar serves the changing ales. Upstairs is a restaurant. There is a plan to reopen the cinema area as a 1,000-seat venue. ◗⊖(Central)▭🐾ᯤ

Nag's Head 𝕃
9 Orford Road, E17 9LP
☉ 4-11; 12-11 Sat; 12-10.30 Sun ☎ (020) 8520 9709
⊕ thenagsheade17.com
Timothy Taylor Landlord; 3 changing beers (sourced locally) Ⓗ
A cat-friendly pub with a pleasant, relaxed atmosphere, in the heart of Walthamstow Village conservation area. It has a courtyard garden at the rear and outside seating at the front. Food consists of pizzas and burgers during the week and a roast on Sundays. Bottled beers include gluten-free options. There is live jazz on Sundays. Children are allowed in the garden until 7.30pm and there are bike racks by the side entrance. ❀◑⊖(Central)▭(W12)ᯤ

Olde Rose & Crown 𝕃 ✔
53-55 Hoe Street, E17 4SA
☉ 10-11 (1am Fri & Sat); 12-11 Sun ☎ (020) 8509 3880
⊕ yeolderoseandcrowntheatrepub.co.uk
6 changing beers (sourced nationally) Ⓗ
A large, welcoming community pub offering a variety of beers from SIBA and local breweries, as well as up to two ciders, one on handpump. Roasts are served on Sunday lunchtime only, and there is a pop-up food stall outside on some nights. Many events are held here, with a theatre upstairs where a folk club and comedy club host regular nights. There is often live music in the bar. Alcohol is served from noon. ❀⊖(Central)♣●▭🐾ᯤ

E20: Westfield Stratford City

Tap East 𝕃
7 International Square, Montfichet Road, E20 1EE
☉ 11-11; 12-10 Sun ☎ (020) 8555 4467 ⊕ tapeast.co.uk
6 changing beers (sourced nationally; often Tap East) Ⓗ
Owing to the proximity of the West Ham football ground, it can be busy here on match days but at other times this brewpub, complete with comfortable sofas, has a relaxed atmosphere. The brewery is visible behind a glass door and windows. Three house beers are served, along with three guest beers, and there is the enticement of over 100 international bottled beers. See the screen behind the bar for the current beer selection. Bar snacks are available. ♿≹⊖(Stratford/Stratford Int)●▭ᯤ

Barking

Barking Dog ✔
61 Station Parade, IG11 8TU
☉ 8am-midnight ☎ (020) 8507 9109
Adnams Broadside; Greene King Abbot; Ruddles Best Bitter; Sharp's Doom Bar; 6 changing beers (sourced nationally) Ⓗ
Busy town-centre Wetherspoon pub, close to Barking station and many bus routes, popular with locals and passing commuters alike. There can be up to five regulars and six changing beers. The real ciders are bag-in-box, including Old Rosie and Black Dragon. Food is served all day from opening time until 11pm, alcoholic drinks from 9am. Muted TV screens show rolling news and occasional sport. ◑♿≹⊖●▭ᯤ

Chadwell Heath

Eva Hart ✔
1128 High Road, RM6 4AH (on A118)
☉ 8am-12.30am (1am Fri & Sat) ☎ (020) 8597 1069
Adnams Broadside; Fuller's London Pride; Greene King Abbot; Ruddles Best Bitter; Sharp's Doom Bar; Truman's Runner; 6 changing beers (often Fuller's, Nethergate, Otter) Ⓗ
Large and comfortable, split-level Wetherspoon pub, divided into several distinct drinking areas.

The building dates from 1892 and used to be the local police station. It is named after a local musical personality who was one of the longest-living survivors of the 1912 Titanic disaster; photographs and memorabilia are on display around the pub. Alcoholic drinks are served from 9am, food until 10pm. Toilets (except accessible) are upstairs. Muted TVs show subtitles. Q

Collier Row

Colley Rowe Inn

54-56 Collier Row Road, RM5 3PA (on B174)
8am-midnight ☎ (01708) 760633
Greene King Abbot; Ruddles Best Bitter; Sharp's Doom Bar; 4 changing beers (sourced nationally) H
Converted from two shops, the pub is close to six bus routes, giving easy access to and from Romford. As well as the ales there are two ciders on gravity dispense (usually Westons Old Rosie and Gwynt y Ddraig Black Dragon). It is often lively around the bar, but there are quieter alcoves at the rear. Alcoholic drinks are served from 9am, food all day, every day, with Steak Night particularly popular. (247,252)

Gidea Park

Gidea Park Micropub

236 Main Road, RM2 5HA (on A118)
4-11 Mon-Wed; 12-11 Thu-Sun ☎ (01708) 397290
realalefinder.com/beerboard/?gidea-park-micropub-romford
6 changing beers (sourced nationally) G
Havering Borough and East London's second micropub, opened at the end of 2017 after winning a planning appeal for change of use, is local CAMRA Pub of the Year 2019. Four to eight real ales from microbreweries are served in all legal measures from casks in the ground floor cellar, as well as real ciders, wines and gins. There are high and low tables and chairs, unusual spider lighting, and a growing display of pumpclips. Mobile phones must be silent. Card payments are welcome.
Q (174,498)

Ship

93 Main Road, RM2 5EL (on A118)
12-11 (midnight Thu-Sat) ☎ (01708) 741571
theshipgideapark.co.uk
Greene King IPA; Sharp's Doom Bar; Timothy Taylor Landlord; 1 changing beer (sourced nationally) H
More than 250 years old, this Grade II-listed split-level pub has extensive dark-wood panelling, timber beams and huge fireplaces. The building is largely unchanged and has low ceilings in places – so duck or grouse! It is a family-run business. Quiz nights are held on Thursdays and there is live music on Saturdays. Q (174,498)

Hornchurch

JJ Moon's

48-52 High Street, RM12 4UN (on A124)
8am-11.30 (midnight Thu; 1am Fri & Sat)
☎ (01708) 478410
Greene King Abbot; Ruddles Best Bitter; Sharp's Doom Bar; 8 changing beers (sourced nationally) H
A busy Wetherspoon pub, opened in 1993 and popular with all age groups, featuring a good variety of ales with an emphasis on breweries from London and the South-East. Watercolour paintings of local scenes provide the main decoration, with the usual local interest panels to the rear. Families are welcome until 6pm, and alcoholic drinks are served from 9am.
Q (Emerson Park/Hornchurch)

Ilford

Jono's

37 Cranbrook Road, IG1 4PA (on A123)
11-11 (midnight Thu; 1am Fri & Sat); 12-10.30 Sun
☎ (020) 8514 6676
Castle Rock Harvest Pale; St Austell Tribute H
A couple of minutes' walk from the station, Jono's is a converted shop with the front of the bar in dark wood and the rear half-timbered with a patch of thatch over the seating. Large-screen TVs show sports fixtures; it can be noisy at times. Friendly and efficient bar staff serve well-kept ales; Castle Rock beer is rare in East London. The pub hosts Thursday quizzes and live music on Friday and Saturday evenings.

Romford

Moon & Stars

99-103 South Street, RM1 1NX
8am-11.30 (1am Fri & Sat) ☎ (01708) 730117
Greene King Abbot; Ruddles Best Bitter; Sharp's Doom Bar; 5 changing beers (sourced nationally) H
A Wetherspoon pub close to Romford railway station and buses. Alongside the ales are real ciders on gravity dispense from glass containers in a cool cabinet behind the bar. There are local history displays on the walls and assorted books on the shelves. Children are allowed in the raised area at the rear until 6pm Friday and Saturday, later on other days. It gets quite busy on Thursday and Friday evenings. Toilets (except accessible) are upstairs. Alcohol is served from 9am.
Q

Upminster

Upminster TapRoom

1B Sunnyside Gardens, RM14 3DT (off B187, St Mary's Lane)
closed Mon; 4-11 Tue-Fri; 12-11 Sat; 12-10 Sun
☎ 07841 676225
Dark Star Hophead; house beer (by Mighty Oak); 5 changing beers (sourced locally) G
Upminster and East London's first micropub opened in a converted office in November 2015, initially as a real ale snack bar, before being granted change of use on appeal. There are high tables and chairs, with garlands of hops adorning the walls. Real ales come from the cool cellar visible from the bar; table service is optional. Set mobile phones to silent or pay a fee for charity. Local CAMRA Pub of the Year 2017 and 2018.
Q (346,347)

Woodford Green

Travellers Friend

496-498 High Road, Woodford Wells, IG8 0PN (on slip road off A104)
12-11 (midnight Wed-Sat) ☎ (020) 8504 2435
thetravellersfriendwoodford.co.uk
Bombardier; St Austell Tribute; Timothy Taylor Landlord; Young's Bitter; 2 changing beers H

After five years under the ownership of two local families, this friendly, comfortable local was completely refurbished in 2017 and extended above and to the back. The rare snob screens from the bar counter were relocated above the bar-back. The original oak panelling was removed, restored and reinstated, but some had to be replaced. There are picnic tables at the front and in the side beer garden. At the rear is a small car park.
Q P (20,179)

NORTH LONDON

N1: Angel

Angel

3-5 Islington High Street, N1 9LQ
8am-midnight (020) 7837 2218
Greene King IPA; Sharp's Doom Bar; 6 changing beers (often Truman's, Twickenham, Windsor & Eton)
A large, modern, open-plan Wetherspoon conversion with some booths towards the back giving slightly more privacy. The adjacent tower was a part of the Angel (one of the first talkie cinemas) that was sadly mostly demolished. With the long-gone Philharmonic Hall (subsequently Grand Theatre), this was always a centre of popular entertainment. Its classic columns and caryatids can apparently be seen in the Museum of London.

N1: Hoxton

Wenlock Arms

26 Wenlock Road, N1 7TA
3-11 Mon; 12-11 (midnight Thu; 1am Fri & Sat)
(020) 7608 3406 wenlockarms.com
Dark Star Hophead, American Pale Ale; Mighty Oak Oscar Wilde; 7 changing beers (sourced nationally)
Local CAMRA Pub of the Year 2017, this free house was saved from closure by a vigorous local campaign. It features beers from small and medium-sized breweries across the UK, usually including a mild, and subject to regular change. With up to seven ciders and perries and a small snacks menu of toasties, Scotch eggs, sausage rolls and pickled eggs, this is a truly welcoming street-corner local with an international reputation. Jazz is played in the bar on Thursday night.
(Old St)

N1: King's Cross

Parcel Yard

West Side, King's Cross Station, N1C 4AP
7.30am-11; 9am-10.30 Sun (020) 7713 7258
Dark Star Hophead; Fuller's Oliver's Island, London Pride, ESB; Gale's Seafarers Ale, HSB; 5 changing beers (sourced nationally; often Adnams, Dark Star, Fuller's)
A large pub approached by stairs at the rear of the concourse, converted from the former station parcel office. It is used by local workers, commuters and for meetings; as well as bars on two levels there are semi-private rooms converted from offices (bookable) and an indoor balcony. It has no music; the decor is minimal and features rescued furniture. Food, starting with breakfast, is served until 10pm (9.30pm Sun). Wheelchair access is by lift and there are no smoking facilities.
(King's Cross St Pancras)

N1: Pentonville

Craft Beer Co

55 White Lion Street, N1 9PP
4-11; 12-1am Fri & Sat; 12-10.30 Sun (020) 7278 0318
Kent Pale; 9 changing beers (sourced nationally)
Multi-room pub with a wooden bar displaying 10 handpumps, all serving beers from independent brewers. Green curtains and red carpet give some warmth to the main bar, which has two Victorian pillars, a wooden floor and raised tables and stools, all overseen by Winston Churchill. A cosy room, with settees and subtle lighting, is to the right as you enter, and there is a smaller room at the back. To the side is a small garden. (Angel)

King Charles I

55-57 Northdown Street, N1 9BL
12-11 (1am Fri); 3-10 Sun (020) 7837 7758
4 changing beers (sourced nationally)
The historic 1930s interior of this Georgian building is small and cosy, containing knick-knacks and homely artefacts, warmed by real fires in the winter. Food can be ordered in at the bar or from the Blue River café opposite during daytime. Live blues, folk and indie music can be impromptu or planned. Since 2015 the pub has been community-owned, with a 20-year lease shared by local residents and regulars.
(King's Cross St Pancras)

N2: East Finchley

Bald Faced Stag

69 High Road, N2 8AB
12-11 (midnight Fri & Sat) (020) 8442 1201
thebaldfacedstagn2.co.uk
Greene King IPA, Yardbird; 2 changing beers (often Old Dairy, Sambrook's, Truman's)
A short walk from the underground station – look for the iconic rooftop stag emblem overlooking the High Road. The two guest ales come from a range of local and regional breweries. The pub is popular with patrons from the local Phoenix cinema and has a large dining area with a smaller second area, both available for private functions. There is also a decked garden, built around an historic sycamore tree. A selection of board games can be played.
P

N5: Canonbury

Snooty Fox

75 Grosvenor Avenue, N5 2NN
4-11; 12-1am Fri & Sat; 12-10.30 Sun (020) 7354 9532
snootyfoxlondon.co.uk
Otter Ale; 3 changing beers (sourced nationally)
A vibrant community pub with 1960s icons depicted throughout, serving up to four real ales and a real cider. The airy bar features a 45rpm jukebox. Outside, there is a pleasant patio with seating. A function room accommodates local groups and private dining. The pub is well known for its ale and cider festivals, which attract people from far and wide. The kitchen serves quality modern British food and an excellent Sunday roast. Local CAMRA Pub of the Year 2019.

N6: Highgate

Duke's Head

16 Highgate High Street, N6 5JG

⌚ 12-midnight (1am Thu-Sat); 12-11.30 Sun
☎ (020) 8341 1310 🌐 thedukesheadhighgate.co.uk
8 changing beers (sourced nationally) Ⓗ
Former coaching inn with a courtyard, reopened as a specialist beer house offering a large range of real ale and cider. Local brewer Hammerton is a fairly permanent presence but expect to find beers from around the country, such as Burning Sky, Magic Rock, Moor and Siren. Usually at least a mild, a porter or stout, a pale and a best bitter are listed on a board behind the bar. Look for monthly pop-up kitchen rotations and tap takeovers.
(210,271)

N7: Holloway

Coronet

338-346 Holloway Road, N7 6NJ
⌚ 8am-midnight ☎ (020) 7609 5014
Fuller's London Pride; Greene King IPA, Abbot; Ruddles Best Bitter; Sharp's Doom Bar; 6 changing beers (sourced nationally) Ⓗ
Impressive Wetherspoon conversion of a cinema, the Savoy, designed by William Glen, that showed its last film in 1983 and now displays large prints of movie stars and former local entertainers, with an old projector the centrepiece of a raised dais towards the rear. Sometimes there are single brewery festivals. Expect plastic glasses and higher prices when Arsenal are playing at home. Tables (some under cover) are on the pavement.
Q(Holloway Rd)

N9: Lower Edmonton

Beehive

24 Little Bury Street, N9 9JZ
⌚ 12-11.30 (1am Fri); 9am-1am Sat; 12-11 Sun
☎ (020) 8360 4358 🌐 thebeehivebhp.co.uk
Greene King IPA, Abbot; St Austell Tribute; house beer (by Greene King); 1 changing beer (often Adnams, New River) Ⓗ
Tucked away in semi-detached suburbia, this imposing pub, rebuilt in 1929, has a through bar offering pool and darts at one end and a dining area at the other, with plenty of room in between to enjoy the ales. The garden houses an interesting selection of animals including goats, ducks, a pony, donkeys (Light and Bitter) and sheep. Home-made food is served daily, including Saturday breakfasts. Weekly quiz night is Tuesday, a music quiz is on the first Thursday monthly.
P(329,W8)

N10: Muswell Hill

Mossy Well

258 Muswell Hill Broadway, N10 3SH
⌚ 8am-1am (11.30 Mon; midnight Tue & Wed); 8am-11.30 Sun ☎ (020) 8444 2914
Fuller's London Pride; Greene King IPA, Abbot; Sharp's Doom Bar; 8 changing beers (often Redemption, Truman's) Ⓗ
A former Express Dairies tearoom and milk depot, but a pub since 1984, reopened by Wetherspoon in October 2015, its name derived from the etymology of Muswell. Many internal features reflect its milky history. It is spacious inside, with a mezzanine floor and outdoor drinking areas at both front and back (closing at 9pm). Despite the size it can be packed. A Westons cider is served from the fridge. Q

N12: North Finchley

Bohemia

762-764 High Road, N12 9QH
⌚ 12-11 (midnight Thu; 1am Fri & Sat); 12-10.30 Sun
☎ (020) 8446 0294 🌐 thebohemia.co.uk
London Brewing Company Beer Street, 100 Oysters Stout, Skyline; 2 changing beers (often London Brewing Company, Rooster's, Windsor & Eton) Ⓗ
A lively brewpub, home to London Brewing Company. Often all the ales are their own, including not only the award-winning 100 Oysters Stout but also London Lush, a new, refreshing 3.8% ABV pale ale. The pub also offers a wide range of other draught and bottled beers. Five more handpumps dispense cider. Games include table tennis and table football. Good food is served all day. No admission after 11.30pm on Friday and Saturday boogie nights.
(Woodside Park)(125,263)

Elephant Inn

283 Ballards Lane, N12 8NR
⌚ 11-11 (midnight Fri & Sat); 12-10.30 Sun
☎ (020) 8343 6110 🌐 elephantinnfinchley.co.uk
Fuller's London Pride, ESB; 2 changing beers (often Adnams, Dark Star, Fuller's) Ⓗ
Popular corner pub with wood pannelling and three distinct drinking areas in a U-shaped bar. A Dark Star or Fuller's seasonal ale is sometimes complemented by a true guest ale. The right-hand bar has sports TVs and the left bar is TV-free for a more relaxed atmosphere. The middle bar has raised tables, stools and newspapers. Thai food from the restaurant upstairs can be eaten in the pub. At the front is a large patio with wooden seating and huge umbrellas.
(West Finchley)

N13: Palmers Green

Alfred Herring

316-322 Green Lanes, N13 5TT
⌚ 8am-11 (midnight Thu-Sat) ☎ (020) 3232 1083
Greene King Abbot; Ruddles Best Bitter; Sharp's Doom Bar; 7 changing beers (often East London Brewing, Redemption, Sambrook's) Ⓗ
A busy Wetherspoon shop conversion opened in 2006 in the heart of the Green Lanes shops, comprising a large open drinking and dining area with side booths. Seven of the 10 handpumps offer a varying range, with the manager regularly obtaining beers from the wide list of London breweries. The pub is named after a local First World War soldier who was awarded the Victoria Cross for his heroic action in France in 1918.
Q

N14: Southgate

New Crown

80-84 Chase Side, N14 5PH
⌚ 8am-11.30 (12.30am Fri & Sat) ☎ (020) 8882 8758
Greene King IPA, Abbot; Ruddles Best Bitter; Sharp's Doom Bar; 5 changing beers (sourced nationally; often Enfield, New River, Tring) Ⓗ
There was an Old Crown on Chase Side until its demolition in the 1960s, hence the name. Once a Sainbury's, this large open-plan Wetherspoon pub, handy for the underground and bus stations, is well run by enthusiastic staff. Up to 10 real ales are available, with five guests from small and large breweries across the country, but with emphasis on

London brews whenever possible. The walls are adorned with pictures of Southgate from days gone by. Q♣

N16: Stoke Newington

Jolly Butchers

204 Stoke Newington High Street, N16 7HU

4-midnight (1am Fri); 12-1am Sat; 12-11 Sun

(020) 7249 9471 jollybutchers.co.uk

6 changing beers (sourced nationally)

A classic Art Deco-style bar boasting elaborate ironwork and glass, with a lively modern feel and the enviable status of being a true free house. Nine handpumps offer six different real ales, usually from microbreweries, and three ciders or perries. The beers are always changing but the website provides up-to-date pouring information. The beer is complemented by great food, served evenings only on weekdays, and lunchtime and evenings at weekends. Payment is now by card only.

N17: Tottenham

Antwerp Arms

168-170 Church Road, N17 8AS

4-11; 3-11 Fri; 12-11 Sat; 12-10.30 Sun

(020) 8216 9289 antwerparms.co.uk

Redemption Pale Ale, Hopspur; 2 changing beers (sourced locally; often Redemption)

Tucked away in the historic and atmospheric Bruce Castle Park area, this is Tottenham's longest-established working pub. Serving local people since 1822, this Georgian building with beer garden faced demolition in 2013. It was saved from developers by the local community and CAMRA campaigners, and is now run as a community collective-owned pub, and is in effect a permanent outlet for Redemption Brewery beers. Food is served Thursday-Sunday but do check the website for any changes.
(White Hart Lane)♣P

N19: Upper Holloway

Landseer Arms

37 Landseer Road, N19 4JU

12-11; 12-10.30 Sun (020) 7281 2569

landseerarms.com

Hammerton N1; 4 changing beers (often One Mile End, Reunion, Twickenham)

A Victorian pub, so different from most of the places on nearby Holloway Road, and one that has been through many incarnations, eventually being renamed after the Victorian artist whose works included the Trafalgar Square lions and the painting, Monarch of the Glen. The spacious interior includes a conservatory-style area (sometimes used for dining) on the other side of the bar. There is plenty of pavement seating, with retractable awnings and heaters. Food is available in one form or another all day. ♣

Shaftesbury Tavern

534 Hornsey Road, N19 3QN

5-11 Mon; 12-11 (12.30am Fri & Sat); 12-10.30 Sun

(020) 7272 7950 theshaftesburytavern.co.uk

Hammerton N1; 3 changing beers (sourced nationally; often Fuller's, Sambrook's)

A nice old venue, now operated by Remarkable Pubs and comprehensively restored following a 2014 refurbishment, with the former pool room turned into the restaurant area under a fine skylight. The historic interior is identified by CAMRA as of regional importance. Outside at the front there is seating on the terrace. Food comes from a predominantly Thai menu, with some pub classics such as fish and chips and sausage and mash. Quiz night is Tuesday. (Crouch Hill)

St John's Tavern

91 Junction Road, N19 5QU

5-11 Mon; 12-11 (midnight Fri & Sat); 12-10.30 Sun

(020) 7272 1587 stjohnstavern.com

Fuller's London Pride; 4 changing beers (often Crate, Hammerton, Howling Hops)

Another example of the real ale renaissance taking place in this part of London. Although the emphasis here is undeniably on food (hams hanging in the food preparation area are visible from the bar), this gastro-pub has up to five real ales on at any one time and is big enough for those who just want a drink to enjoy one without feeling uncomfortable. The whole impression is one of space, helped by a large bar area and high ceilings.
(Archway)♣

N21: Winchmore Hill

Dog & Duck

74 Hoppers Road, N21 3LH

12-11.30 (12.30am Fri & Sat) (020) 8886 1987

dogandduckn21.co.uk

Greene King IPA; Timothy Taylor Landlord; Young's Bitter; 1 changing beer (often Adnams, Fuller's, Sharp's)

Friendly one-bar pub, popular with locals and welcoming to visitors. Sporting events are shown on a large-screen TV, local football teams meet here and it hosts a golf society. The fortnightly quiz night is on Monday with complimentary pizza. Music nights are every other Sunday. There is a pretty walled patio garden at the rear. Dogs are welcome at quiet times. The pub has now featured in this Guide for 16 consecutive years, 29 in total.
♣(W9)

Little Green Dragon

928 Green Lanes, N21 2AD

closed Mon; 4-10 Tue-Thu; 12-10 Fri & Sat; 12-7 Sun

(020) 8351 3530 littlegreendragonenfield.com

4 changing beers (often Dark Star, Five Points, New River)

A shop conversion, this micropub was voted Greater London Pub of the Year in 2018 and is the local CAMRA winner again for 2019. The real ales from the temperature-controlled cellar room behind the bar, along with seven real ciders and perries, delight regulars and newcomers alike. KeyKeg beers, various bottled beers, gins and wines are also sold. An eclectic range of seating including a church pew, bus seats and padded kegs, contributes to the friendly community atmosphere. Q♣(125,329)

Orange Tree

18 Highfield Road, N21 3HA

12 (2.30 Tue & Wed)-midnight (020) 8360 4853

Greene King IPA; 3 changing beers (often Hook Norton, New River, Redemption)

A traditional back-street local, yards from the New River walk, with many original features including the Taylor Walker sign outside. It has been in this Guide since 1995 under the same welcoming landlord. Toby jugs, porcelain, pumpclips and sporting posters are displayed around the pub. There is a quiz night every other Thursday and darts on Wednesdays, a pool table, dartboard and TVs showing live sport. Enjoy a summer barbecue in the well-kept garden or a hearty Sunday lunch. 🐴❀◑⇌♣P🚌(329)📶

N22: Wood Green

Prince

1 Finsbury Road, N22 8PA

⏲ 12-11 (midnight Thu; 1am Fri & Sat); 12-10.30 Sun

☎ (020) 8888 6698 🌐 theprincen22.co.uk

Uley Bitter; 5 changing beers (often Almasty, Five Points) Ⓗ

A handsome two-roomed pub occupying a prominent corner site, brought back to life in 2016 with up to six regularly changing cask ales, nine keg beers and a range of ciders. The beers come from small breweries across the UK and are listed on the pub's website as they change. Hot food comes from changing pop-ups.
◑⇌(Alexandra Palace)⊖🍎

Enfield

Moon Under Water Ⓛ ✔

115-117 Chase Side, EN2 6NN

⏲ 8am-11; 8am-10.30 Sun ☎ (020) 8366 9855

Greene King IPA, Abbot; Morland Old Speckled Hen; Ruddles Best Bitter; Sharp's Doom Bar; 5 changing beers (often East London, Redemption, Twickenham) Ⓗ

Well-established Wetherspoon pub that used to be a dairy, within easy reach of both Enfield Chase and Gordon Hill stations. The L-shaped bar sports 10 handpumps, with real cider served from polypins. Look up while drinking and you will see exposed roof trusses, stained-glass windows and a mock balcony complete with library. The conservatory at the back adds to the light and airy ambience. The pub attracts all age groups; accompanied well-behaved children are welcome until 8.30pm.
🐴❀◑♿⇌(Chase)🍎P🚌(191,W9)📶

High Barnet

Olde Mitre Inne ✔

58 High Street, EN5 5SJ

⏲ 12-midnight (1am Fri & Sat) ☎ (020) 8449 5701

Adnams Southwold Bitter; Greene King Abbot; Timothy Taylor Landlord; Tring Side Pocket for a Toad; 4 changing beers (often Five Points, Redemption, Tiny Rebel) Ⓗ

The oldest coaching inn in Barnet, now free of tie, with eight beers from around the country served by efficient and well-trained staff. Awarded membership of Timothy Taylor's Champion Club for dedication to excellent cellarmanship, the pub oozes character and charm, enhanced by sensitive and barely perceptible internal alteration. Family-friendly (customers are requested to refrain from bad language), it has a large courtyard outside, heated and covered in winter months. There is live music every Sunday evening. 🐴❀◑⊖♣🍎🚌🐾📶

Olde Monken Holt ✔

193 High Street, EN5 5SU

⏲ 12-midnight (11 Mon; 1.30am Fri & Sat)

☎ (020) 8449 4280

Greene King IPA, Abbot; St Austell Tribute; Timothy Taylor Landlord Ⓗ

An historic inn with wood panelling, exposed brickwork and a real fire, at the north end of the High Street near the site of the 15th-century Battle of Barnet. The enclosed patio garden is popular with families. An Asset of Community Value since 2017, the pub attracts locals and newcomers alike. Regular entertainment includes a Thursday quiz, Friday DJ, Saturday live music, Sunday acoustic music and occasional Irish traditional music. Widescreen TVs at the rear show many sports events. 🐴❀♿♣🚌(84,399)🐾📶

New Barnet

Railway Bell ✔

13 East Barnet Road, EN4 8RR

⏲ 8am-midnight (1am Fri & Sat) ☎ (020) 8449 1369

Courage Directors; Greene King IPA, Abbot; Sharp's Doom Bar; 6 changing beers (often Adnams, Sambrook's, Truman's) Ⓗ

Built in the late 1800s following the arrival of the railway, this former Ind Coope house is one of the area's earliest Wetherspoon pubs. Extended a few years ago, it has a large conservatory giving it a bright, comfortable feel; families are welcome till 9pm. Up to 10 real ales are on offer, with some from London breweries. It is popular and always busy. The large patio to the side and at the back helpfully has a no-smoking section.
🐴❀◑♿⇌🍎🚌📶

Ponders End

Picture Palace Ⓛ ✔

Howard Hall, Lincoln Road, EN3 4AQ

⏲ 9am-11 (midnight Fri & Sat) ☎ (020) 8344 9690

Greene King Abbot; Sharp's Doom Bar; 4 changing beers (often 3 Brewers of St Albans, New River, Redemption) Ⓗ

Converted from a cinema with some architectural features still visible, this pub is adorned with murals of film stars from the 1920s. A large former Wetherspoon's, it is still a community- and family-focused pub in a beer desert, offering drink and meal promotions throughout the year. It aims to have at least one London cask ale available, along with brews from Hertfordshire. News and sport TV is shown without sound. Music night is the last Saturday of the month.
🐴❀◑♿⊖(Southbury)P🚌📶

NORTH-WEST LONDON

NW1: Camden Town

Camden Road Draft House

102-104 Camden Road, NW1 9EA

⏲ 12-11 (midnight Thu; 1am Fri & Sat); 12-10.30 Sun

☎ (020) 7485 4530

2 changing beers (sourced nationally; often Siren) Ⓗ

Previously the Eagle, Rosie O'Grady's, Mac Bar and Grand Union, this huge pub was massively improved by Draft House group in 2017 and in turn by BrewDog in 2018. It has a horseshoe-shaped bar, eclectic lighting and music memorabilia; a large mural reflects Camden's musical history. A board lists the various beers available. Food includes Sunday roasts. A function area to the side can be reserved. There is a quiz on Tuesdays and a DJ on Fridays.
🐴❀◑♿⊖(Camden Rd/Town)🍎🚌🐾📶

Constitution

42 St Pancras Way, NW1 0QT
11-midnight; 12-10.30 Sun ☎ (020) 7380 0767
coninca mden.co.uk
Dark Star Hophead; Sambrook's Junction Ale; 2 changing beers (sourced nationally) H
Founded in 1858, this community pub is a haven within bustling Camden and its vibrant market area. Dogs and families are welcome. Its award-winning terraced patio garden (four times Camden in Bloom finalist) has a pleasant south-facing outlook over the Regent's Canal. The downstairs cellar bar is host to live music and comedy events. Pool and darts are played and it has a large-screen TV. Weather permitting, there is occasional home-made street food outside.
(Camden Rd/Town)

Prince Albert

163 Royal College Street, NW1 0SG
12-11 (1am Fri & Sat); 12-10.30 Sun ☎ (020) 7485 0270
princealbert.pub
3 changing beers (sourced nationally) H
Following sensitive, tasteful refurbishment of a traditional Charrington tavern that dates back to 1843, this comfortable, welcoming and charming pub retains many original period features including the horseshoe bar, wood panelling, leaded windows, stunning outdoor tiling and a pleasant garden. The first-floor restaurant area or the whole pub can be booked for functions; check in advance if visiting on a Saturday. There is a Tuesday quiz, acoustic music on Sunday and twice-yearly beer festivals. Happy hour applies 3-7pm weekdays and all day Saturdays.
(Camden Rd/Town)

Tapping the Admiral

77 Castle Road, NW1 8SU
12-11 (midnight Wed-Sat) ☎ (020) 7267 6118
tappingtheadmiral.co.uk
House beer (by Brakspear); 7 changing beers (sourced regionally) H
Local CAMRA Pub of the Year 2018, this is a popular and enjoyable community pub where friendly, knowledgeable staff offer a warm welcome. Guest ales come mainly from local breweries. Great British food includes speciality home-made pies. Behind is a well-designed, heated and covered beer garden. There is a popular Wednesday quiz and live traditional music on Thursday evenings. Look out for monthly tap takeovers and pop-up events, and also for the pub's cat, Nelson.
Q(Kentish Town West)

NW1: Euston

Doric Arch

Euston Station Colonnade, 1 Eversholt Street, NW1 2DN
10-11 (10.30 Sun) ☎ (020) 7383 3359
Dark Star Hophead, American Pale Ale; Fuller's Oliver's Island, London Pride, ESB; 3 changing beers (often Adnams, Dark Star, Fuller's) H
Up a flight of stairs, the pub's large picture windows afford a bird's eye view of the busy urban world below. Right next to Euston station, it is used extensively by commuters, aided by the train times screen. The excellent staff are helpful and informative about the ales, including guest beers, increasingly from Dark Star. Brewery and railway memorabilia adorn the walls. Alcoholic drinks are served from 10am, food all day. Toilets are at basement level.
(Euston/Euston Sq)

Euston Tap

West & East Lodges, 190 Euston Road, NW1 2EF
11-11 (11.30 Fri & Sat); 11-10 Sun ☎ (020) 3137 8837
eustontap.com
10 changing beers (sourced nationally) P
Fronting the main station building, these impressive Grade II-listed Portland stone lodges, separated by a bus lane, are relics from the original 1830s station. Up to 10 changing beers are served, mostly from smaller breweries, and are pumped up to taps behind the bar. Small ground floor spaces are augmented by seating (and toilets) up the wrought-iron spiral staircases and large heated drinking areas outside. The East Lodge opens later in the afternoon and offers traditional cider.
(Euston/Euston Sq)

Exmouth Arms

1 Starcross Street, NW1 2HR
9am-11 (midnight Fri & Sat) ☎ (020) 7387 5440
Titanic Plum Porter; 4 changing beers (often Sambrook's, Signature Brew, Southwark) H
Adjacent to the HS2 works, this is a lively venue with a boutique hostel on the upper floors and an open-plan kitchen offering burgers and tapas from Burger Craft. The interior has large picture windows and comfortable seating – booths by the windows, high tables and benches – around a large L-shaped bar fronted by mosaic tiles. Local cask beers appear regularly; 32 bottled and canned beers are displayed on the Wall of Beer. Breakfasts are served. Outside is plentiful bench seating.
(Euston/Euston Sq)

NW5: Kentish Town

Grafton

20 Prince of Wales Road, NW5 3LG
12-11 (midnight Fri); 11-midnight Sat; 12-10.30 Sun
☎ (020) 7482 4466 thegraftonnw5.co.uk
3 changing beers (sourced nationally) H
Popular award-winning pub with beautiful Victorian features, combining a traditional feel with many contemporary touches and specialising in local cask beers. The spacious ground-floor horseshoe bar is partly tiled, with ample seating. An upstairs bar/function room is also available (no real ale) and an elegant, covered roof garden. Knowledgeable and friendly bar staff are happy to advise you. Quiz night is Tuesday and there is comedy on Wednesday, as well as the piano and board games.
(Kentish Town/Kentish Town West)

Lion & Unicorn

42 Gaisford Street, NW5 2ED
10-11; 12-10.30 Sun ☎ (020) 7267 2304
thelionandunicornnw5.co.uk
Young's Bitter; 3 changing beers (often Redemption, Southwark, Twickenham) H
This popular community venue is a great favourite, with its genuine homely feel, open fire and comfortable seating. Run by friendly management and staff as a Geronimo-branded gastro-pub, it offers a good-quality cask ale range featuring several local breweries. Both front and back gardens have won local and regional awards. A quiz is on Sunday. It occasionally hosts comedy

nights. Above the pub is the Proforca theatre; details of productions are available on the Proforca website.

Pineapple

51 Leverton Street, NW5 2NX
12-11 (midnight Fri & Sat); 12-10.30 Sun
(020) 7284 4631
Marston's Pedigree; 4 changing beers (sourced nationally)
An authentic and friendly community pub, saved from closure by the locals, Grade II-listed and with a regionally important historic interior, notable for its mirrors and splendid bar-back. The front bar, with comfortable seating around tables, leads through to an informal conservatory overlooking the patio garden. The food menu is Thai kitchen cuisine. Local beers can come from across London and, the pub being free of tie, the range changes regularly. Q

Southampton Arms

139 Highgate Road, NW5 1LE
12-11 (midnight Fri & Sat); 12-10.30 Sun
thesouthamptonarms.co.uk
8 changing beers (sourced nationally)
This pub does what it says on the sign outside: Ale, Cider, Meat. The multiple CAMRA award-winning venue has 14 handpumps on and behind the bar, serving almost equal amounts of cider and different beers from microbreweries across the UK. Snacks include pork pies, roast pork in baps, cheese and meat baps plus veggie options. Music is played on vinyl only and the piano is in regular use. At the back is a secluded patio.
(Gospel Oak/Kentish Town)

NW6: Kilburn

Sir Colin Campbell

264-266 Kilburn High Road, NW6 2BY
4-midnight; 1-1am Fri; 12-1am Sat; 12-12.30am Sun
(020) 7693 5443 thesircolincampbell.co.uk
3 changing beers (sourced nationally)
This pub was acquired and restored to its original beauty in early 2017 by three local people. Cask beer returned, plus a good selection of bottled/canned beers and extras such as live traditional Irish music every Friday, Saturday and Sunday night. The lovely wood cladding was cleaned up and the two separate rooms around a central bar give a real feel of how traditional pubs used to be. Rotating pop-up kitchen opening times vary with the supplier; check the website for current information. (Brondesbury)

Harefield

Old Orchard

Jacks Lane, off Park Lane, UB9 6HJ TQ0463190411
11.30-11; 12-10.30 Sun (01895) 822631
Tring Side Pocket for a Toad; house beer (by Brunning & Price); 4 changing beers (often Oakham, Redemption, Tring)
A Brunning & Price establishment that was once a country house before becoming a restaurant. Refurbished in 2010, the pub is lined with bookcases and pictures and has an unfussy array of mismatched tables and chairs, and three welcoming real fires in the colder months. The Original is brewed by Phoenix, and the cider is Westons Old Rosie, with an occasional guest. There are commanding views of the Colne Valley from the terrace and beer garden.
QP(U9)

Harrow

Castle ★

30 West Street, HA1 3EF
12-11 (midnight Fri); 10-midnight Sat (020) 8422 3155
Fuller's London Pride, ESB; Gale's Seafarers Ale, HSB; 1 changing beer (sourced nationally; often Butcombe, Dark Star, Fuller's)
A lively and friendly Fuller's house in the heart of historic Harrow-on-the-Hill. Built in 1901 and Grade II listed, it has a nationally important historic interior. Food is served until 9.30pm (8pm Sun); reservations are recommended for Sunday lunchtimes. Three real coal fires help to keep the pub warm and cosy in the colder months, and a secluded beer garden is popular during the summer. Local CAMRA Harrow Pub of the Year 2019. Q(258,H17)

Rayners Lane

Village Inn

402-408 Rayners Lane, HA5 5DY
8am-11 (12.30am Thu; 1am Fri & Sat) (020) 8868 8551
Greene King IPA, Abbot; Sharp's Doom Bar; Twickenham Naked Ladies; 4 changing beers
A split-level, double-fronted shop conversion. The rear of the pub, accessed down a few steps, sports the traditional Wetherspoon booths, with a row of tables down the centre. A terraced area behind has a variety of large potted plants among the picnic tables. The front pavement has a few tables and chairs for that alfresco moment. There is a good cross-section of customers who mingle quite happily together. Alcoholic drinks are served from 9am. Q

Ruislip

Hop & Vine

18 High Street, HA4 7AN
closed Mon; 5-10 Tue-Thu; 12-11 Fri & Sat; 12-6 Sun
5 changing beers (sourced nationally)
Converted from a former café, with seating at low tables with loose chairs and benches. The small bar counter in the right-hand corner dispenses real ales, keg beers and ciders from a temperature-controlled cellar room behind it. Bottled and canned beers, wines and spirits are also sold. Snacks are enhanced by cheeseboard and charcuterie board options. The real ale choice increases to six or seven at weekends, and table service often applies. Q

Ruislip Manor

JJ Moons

12 Victoria Road, HA4 0AA
8am-midnight (1am Fri & Sat); 8am-11 Sun
(01895) 622373
Courage Directors; Greene King IPA, Abbot; Sharp's Doom Bar; Vale Gravitas; 6 changing beers (often Twickenham)
A large Wetherspoon conversion conveniently located opposite the tube station. It is popular and often busy in the evening and at weekends. Food and beer alike are of good value, with the usual promotions. At the rear is an elevated section for

dining, leading to a small garden patio, while the front has a partitioned-off smoking area on the street. Q

South Kenton

Windermere ★

Windermere Avenue, HA9 8QT
2-11.30; 1-12.30am Fri & Sat; 11-11 Sun
(020) 3632 0020 windermerepub.com
Gale's Seafarers Ale; Young's Special H
Built in 1939 and next to South Kenton station, the Windermere has a nationally important historic interior. It is a genuine community pub with three bars, although the public bar is now used only for functions. The saloon and lounge retain many original features, including the large inner porches, bar counters, back fittings, wall panelling and fireplaces. A quiz is held on alternate Thursdays and there is sometimes live entertainment. P(223)

SOUTH-EAST LONDON

SE1: Borough

King's Arms

65 Newcomen Street, SE1 1YT
12-11; closed Sun (020) 7407 1132
kingsarmsborough.co.uk
Harvey's Sussex Best Bitter; Purity Mad Goose; Timothy Taylor Landlord; Truman's Swift; 1 changing beer (often Five Points) H
A Grade II-listed one-bar pub just off the busy Borough High Street, with a traditional and comfortable historic interior, of regional importance. The striking exterior plaque above the entrance originally adorned the old London Bridge before being installed here. Five cask beers are usually on tap, and traditional, mainly British, meals are served lunchtimes and evenings. This pub does not open on Sundays. (London Bridge)

Libertine

125 Great Suffolk Street, SE1 1PQ
12-11; closed Sun (020) 7378 7877
thelibertine.co.uk
Sharp's Doom Bar; 2 changing beers (often Signature Brew, Twickenham) H
Originally a Whitbread house, this is a lively and spacious pub popular with a mix of workers, locals and students. The food offering specialises in pizzas and there is a discount for students on Mondays and Wednesdays. It hosts live music or a DJ Thursday-Sunday evenings and a quiz on Tuesdays. Major sporting events are also shown and there is a dartboard.

Lord Clyde

27 Clennam Street, SE1 1ER
11-11; 12-11 Sat; 12-6 Sun (020) 7407 3397
lordclyde.com
Adnams Southwold Bitter; Hogs Back TEA; Sharp's Doom Bar; Young's Bitter; 1 changing beer (often Moorhouse's) H
A gem of a street-corner pub that has changed little since being rebuilt in 1913. It has been identified by CAMRA as having a regionally important historic pub interior, and it has traditional decor, comfortable seating and curtains over the doors. The exterior retains its beautiful Truman's Brewery tilework. There is one main bar and also a side room with its own serving hatch. The pub has been run by the same family for over 50 years.

Royal Oak

44 Tabard Street, SE1 4JU
11-11; 12-9 Sun (020) 7357 7173
Harvey's Sussex XX Mild Ale, IPA, Sussex Best Bitter, Armada Ale; 2 changing beers (often Fuller's, Gale's, Harvey's) H
A charming back-to-basics drinkers' pub separated into two sections by the bar counter and an off-sales hatch. This is Sussex-based Harvey's Brewery's first London tied house and is renowned for friendly and attentive service. The wide range of beers includes seasonal brews and, unusually for London, a mild, plus a changing guest Fuller's beer. Regulars come from miles around to spend time here. Q(London Bridge)

SE1: Borough Market

Market Porter

9 Stoney Street, SE1 9AA
11-11; 12-11 Sat; 12-10.30 Sun (020) 7407 2495
themarketporter.co.uk
Harvey's Sussex Best Bitter H**; 10 changing beers (sourced nationally)** H/A
This classic, rustic market pub next to the famous Borough Market still also retains its traditional 6am-8.30am weekday opening hours. It is a Guide regular, with up to 10 changing real ales plus four ciders, usually including a Westons. Adorning the walls is a vast array of pumpclips reflecting the huge range of beers offered over the years. Popular with locals and visitors alike, it can get busy, with drinkers spilling out onto the street. An upstairs restaurant serves lunches. (London Bridge)

Old King's Head

King's Head Yard, 45-49 Borough High Street, SE1 1NA
11-midnight (1am Fri & Sat); 12-midnight Sun
(020) 7407 1550 theoldkingshead.uk.com
Harvey's Sussex Best Bitter; St Austell Tribute, Proper Job; Sharp's Doom Bar; 2 changing beers (often Harvey's) H
A traditional pub down a narrow, cobbled lane off Borough High Street. Stained-glass windows hint at a bygone era and the pictures adorning the walls tell the story of a pub, and an area, that has a rich history. The layout inside is simple, with an L-shaped bar in one corner usually offering six real ales on handpump. The clientele is a mix of tourists, office workers and visitors to the nearby Borough Market. (London Bridge)

Rake

14 Winchester Walk, SE1 9AG
12-11; 11-11 Fri; 10-11 Sat; 12-8 Sun (020) 7407 0557
4 changing beers (sourced nationally) H
On the edge of Borough Market, this small pub prides itself on offering a high-quality, varied beer selection, and over the years has become a real global destination for beer aficionados and brewers. Four handpumps are complemented by a comprehensive range of bottled beers, mainly from North America and Europe, plus a small range of wines and spirits. It holds periodic beer festivals, brewery tap takeovers and other themed beer selections. Q(London Bridge)

SE1: Waterloo

Hole in the Wall

5 Mepham Street, SE1 8SQ

⏲ 11-11 (11.30 Fri & Sat); 12-10.30 Sun ☎ (020) 7928 6196

Hogs Back TEA; Sharp's Doom Bar; Young's Bitter; 4 changing beers (often Sambrook's, Southwark, Truman's) Ⓗ

A short hop across the road from Waterloo railway station, this unusual free house enjoys the comforting rumble of trains overhead. A long-time real ale outlet from when this was rare in the area, it has a small, cosy front bar and a larger bar to the rear showing sport on TV. Good food is served all day. The clientele is mixed and the pub gets busy when there is a rugby game at Twickenham.
♞❀◐◑⇌⊖●▯🚌🐾📶

King's Arms Ⓛ

25 Roupell Street, SE1 8TB

⏲ 11-11; 12-10.30 Sun ☎ (020) 7207 0784

🌐 thekingsarmslondon.co.uk

Adnams Southwold Bitter; house beer (by Sharp's); 7 changing beers (sourced nationally) Ⓗ

Tucked away in a back street, this pub is worth seeking out although it gets busy in the early evenings. It has been identified by CAMRA as having a regionally important historic pub interior. The two small rooms are separated by a central bar and drinking is also allowed outside the front of the pub. Nine real ales usually include two or more from London breweries and at least one dark beer. To the rear is a Thai restaurant.
♞◐◑⇌(Waterloo/Waterloo East)⊖🚌🐾📶

Waterloo Tap

Arch 147, Sutton Walk, SE1 7ES

⏲ 12-11 (11.30 Thu & Fri); 11-11.30 Sat; 12-10 Sun

☎ (020) 3455 7436 🌐 waterlootap.com

5 changing beers (often Gun, Siren, Titanic) Ⓐ

This fairly compact, modern sister pub to the Euston Tap is in a railway arch close to Waterloo station and a short stroll from the South Bank, making it handy for visitors to the BFI IMAX and Royal Festival Hall complex. The cask beers are all dispensed from taps mounted on the copper bar-back. Details of the selection available are listed on a blackboard above the bar. ♞❀♿⇌⊖●🚌🐾📶

SE4: Brockley

Brockley Barge ✔

184 Brockley Road, SE4 2RR

⏲ 8am-midnight (1am Fri & Sat) ☎ (020) 8694 7690

Greene King Abbot; Ruddles Best Bitter; Sharp's Doom Bar; 5 changing beers (often Exmoor, Rooster's, Tring) Ⓗ

A former Courage public house, now part of the Wetherspoon chain, a stone's throw from the railway station. It is a popular, thriving hub with a clientele reflecting the vibrant area. The pub's name derives from the former Croydon Canal which was where the railway line now runs. The interior is laid out in a semi-horseshoe shape with a variety of seating areas, and outside is a small courtyard area to the south side that is well used in the summer. Q♞❀◐◑♿⇌⊖●🚌📶

Talbot Ⓛ

2-4 Tyrwhitt Road, SE4 1QG

⏲ 4-11; 12-midnight Fri & Sat; 12-10.30 Sun

☎ (020) 8692 2665 🌐 talbotpublichouse.com

Harvey's Sussex Best Bitter; 3 changing beers (often Brockley, Fuller's, Mallinsons) Ⓗ

A fine Victorian suburban local on two floors, popular with all ages, families and dog owners. Tastefully redecorated inside and out, with large windows making the interior light and airy, it has a series of murals, highlighted with gilt, depicting Talbot dogs. An extensive, upmarket food menu also caters for vegetarians and vegans, with specials and meal deals on different days of the week. The pub hosts a quiz on Tuesday, live music, and other seasonal events.
♞❀◐◑♿⇌(St Johns)⊖(Elverson Rd)🚌🐾📶

SE4: Crofton Park

London Beer Dispensary

389 Brockley Road, SE4 2PH

⏲ 12-11 (midnight Fri & Sat); 12-10.30 Sun

☎ (020) 8694 6962

4 changing beers (often Siren, Southey) Ⓗ

This former wine bar was converted into a pub in 2014 and is now owned by the local Southey Brewery. There is no bar, with the handpumps instead fixed to a narrow shelf. Wood panelling, functional furniture and muted lighting lend a homely air to the interior. The beer range usually includes a guest from a microbrewery. In addition, up to three real ciders are served by gravity. The food menu is based around burger meals.
♞❀◐◑⇌●🚌🐾📶

SE5: Camberwell

Hermits Cave

28 Camberwell Church Street, SE5 8QU

⏲ 12-midnight (2am Fri & Sat) ☎ (020) 7703 3188

Dark Star Hophead; 4 changing beers (often Five Points) Ⓗ

An imposing corner pub run by the same family for 25 years and popular with a cross-section of local residents and art college students. The premises have remained essentially unchanged, with etched windows and wooden floors adding to the traditional feel. A corner TV provides the only distraction to convivial conversation. Guest beers come from independent breweries. Three real ciders on handpump increase to five during summer months. An impressive range of whiskies includes examples from Wales and Japan.
♿⇌⊖(Denmark Hill)●🚌🐾

Stormbird

25 Camberwell Church Street, SE5 8TR

⏲ 4-midnight (11 Mon; 1am Fri); 12-1am Sat; 12-midnight Sun ☎ (020) 7708 4460

4 changing beers (often Bristol Beer Factory, Dark Star, Five Points) Ⓗ

The sister pub to the Hermit's Cave across the road, offering a slightly more contemporary feel and attracting a mixed but generally younger crowd. There is a huge array of beers of all types on the bar, including an extensive bottled beer selection. The choice encompasses brews from the UK, continental Europe and the US. Draught beers are available in third-pint measures.
◐◑⇌⊖(Denmark Hill)●🚌📶

SE6: Catford

Catford Bridge Tavern

Station Approach, Catford Bridge, SE6 4RE

⊙ 4-11 (midnight Thu); 12-midnight Fri; 12-11 Sat & Sun ☎ (020) 8690 6759 🌐 catfordtavern.com
4 changing beers (often Southwark, Truman's) Ⓗ
A Tudor-style pub, originally named the Railway Tavern, dating from the mid 19th-century. It survived a supermarket redevelopment threat and then a catastrophic fire in 2015. Reopened in 2017, the interior has a long service bar plus a dining area to the rear with open kitchen. Sports and other local memorabilia add to the decor. A partially covered roof terrace overlooks the railway station. The ales are generally from independent London breweries. Varying daily meal deals are served.
(Catford/Catford Bridge)

Catford Constitutional Club

Catford Broadway, SE6 4SP
⊙ 4-midnight (11 Mon; 1am Fri); 12-midnight Sat; 12-11 Sun ☎ (020) 8613 7188 🌐 catfordconstitutionalclub.com
Volden Session Ale; 5 changing beers (often Brockley, East London Brewing, Volden) Ⓗ
Tucked away down a short, well-lit alley opposite Canadian Avenue, this multi-roomed Antic pub occupies a former Conservative Club in a delightfully distressed way. The bar and restaurant area features a large chandelier hanging from bare rafters. A quirky assortment of old furniture, pictures, mirrors and Private Eye covers creates a shabby-chic atmosphere. A mix of light and dark beers is available from the handpumps. The pub hosts weekly quizzes, monthly comedy and occasional film nights.
(Catford/Catford Bridge)

SE8: Deptford

Dog & Bell

116 Prince Street, SE8 3JD
⊙ 12-11 (11.30 Fri-Sun) ☎ (020) 8692 5664
Fuller's London Pride; 5 changing beers (often Clarkshaws, Dent, Old Dairy) Ⓗ
Traditional and welcoming pub down a side street, a short stroll from the centre of Deptford. A Guide stalwart for over 30 years, it offers six real ales plus a selection of Belgian bottled beers, malt whiskies and simple, tasty meals. A lively bar and a real fire in winter greet a good mix of customers including locals, cyclists and those strolling along the nearby Thames Path. Regular beer festivals are now held, often themed around the UK patron saints' days.
Q

SE9: Eltham

Long Pond

110 Westmount Road, SE9 1UT
⊙ 5-10 Mon; 11.30-2.30, 5-10 (11 Thu & Fri); 11-3, 6.30-11 Sat; 12-2.30 Sun ☎ (020) 8331 6767
House beer (by Tonbridge); 5 changing beers (often Goacher's, Kent, Pig & Porter) Ⓖ
Micropub in a former plumbers' merchants and named after the pond in nearby Eltham Park North. Mainly Kentish ales are served from a chilled stillage room at the back, as well as Dudda's Tun real cider/perry. In true micropub tradition, no lager or spirits are available, but there is wine, plus bar snacks. Seating is mainly high benches and tables, though the rear snug features low tables and chairs. Winner of several local CAMRA awards. No dogs are permitted. Q (B16)

Park Tavern

45 Passey Place, SE9 5DA
⊙ 12-11 ☎ (020) 8850 3216
8 changing beers (often Otter, Sambrook's, Shepherd Neame) Ⓗ
Attractive traditional Victorian pub with the original Truman's Brewery tiled frontage and signage. The compact interior has an L-shaped bar with stylish bar lamps and chandeliers. The etched windows have elegant drapes, and decorative plates and pictures line the walls. Jazz and light classical background music is played. There is a well-kept, heated rear garden and further seating to the front and side. As well as the range of real ales, an impressive selection of whiskies and wine is available.

Rusty Bucket

11 Court Yard, SE9 5PR
⊙ 4-10 (11 Wed & Thu); 2-midnight Fri; 12-midnight Sat; 12-10 Sun ☎ 07776 145990 🌐 therustybucket.pub
4 changing beers (often Oakham, Ramsgate, Siren) Ⓖ
A hostelry that reopened in April 2018 following the redevelopment of the former Crown pub, retaining the original ground floor frontage. Inside, the walls are half-panelled and brightly painted. Seating is at trestle style tables with low chairs. The venue is run along micropub lines by a couple of friends who are enthusiastic and knowledgeable about all beers. The cask ales and some real ciders are dispensed from a walk-in cellar cupboard. A host of other draught, bottled and canned beers are on offer. Live music sessions are held on Sundays.

SE10: East Greenwich

River Ale House

131 Woolwich Road, SE10 0RJ
⊙ 4-11; 12-11 Fri & Sat; 1-11 Sun ☎ 07963 127595
7 changing beers (often Burton Bridge, East London Brewing, Truman's) Ⓖ
Micropub opened in September 2017 in the classic style, in a converted shop unit, comprising two rooms with a rustic feel and a small step between them. Real ales and ciders are sold from a temperature-controlled cellar room behind the bar counter. A friendly, family-run house where conversations with strangers are inevitable and fulfilling, the pub has quickly become a part of the local community and developed a wider following too. Local CAMRA Pub of the Year 2019.
Q(Westcombe Park)

SE10: Greenwich

Morden Arms

1 Brand Street, SE10 8SP
⊙ 12-11; 12-10.30 Sun ☎ (020) 8858 2189
4 changing beers (often Truman's) Ⓗ
An ex-Courage corner house, now an independent pub with a strong orientation towards live music. Unpretentious, with no external pub sign or name even, this is one of a dying breed of back-street boozers in the area. Its clientele is a mix of locals and music lovers. A free cheeseboard is available on Sunday and cribbage night is Monday. The beer range is mainly from Truman's, with other local guest beers appearing occasionally.

ENGLAND

Plume of Feathers ✓

19 Park Vista, SE10 9LZ

12-11; 11-midnight Fri & Sat ☎ (020) 8858 1661
plumeoffeathers-greenwich.co.uk

Adnams Southwold Bitter; Harvey's Sussex Best Bitter; 2 changing beers (often Bexley, Dartford Wobbler) H

With parts dating from 1691, this cosy and quiet historic pub is near the northern entrance to Greenwich Park, close to the National Maritime Museum. The maritime theme is reflected inside the bar with much memorabilia on display and interesting historical paintings. As well as offering bar meals, there is a separate restaurant to the rear, and also a pleasant garden area. The pub is home to a football team, the Plume Rockets, and a golf society.
⇌(Maze Hill)⊖(Cutty Sark)

SE11: Kennington

Mansion House ✓

48 Kennington Park Road, SE11 4RS

12-midnight (1am Fri & Sat) ☎ (020) 7582 5599
oakalondon.com

Oakham JHB, Inferno, Citra, Bishops Farewell; 1 changing beer (often Gale's, Oakham) H

Oakham Ales' only tied outlet in London, in a former cocktail lounge and piano bar. The contemporary design includes a stylish juxtaposition of materials and textures. During the summer, the glass frontage can be opened onto the outside seating area. One guest or seasonal Oakham beer complements the permanent range. Attentive staff also serve in the attached pan-Asian Oaka restaurant. Discounted cask beers are on the bar 5-7pm every evening.
♿⇌(Elephant & Castle)⊖

Old Red Lion ✓

42 Kennington Park Road, SE11 4RS

4-11 (1am Fri); 12-1am Sat; 12-11 Sun
☎ (020) 7735 4312 theoldredlion.com

4 changing beers (sourced regionally; often Volden) H

Grade II-listed twin-bar Antic pub with plenty of character and a fine example of the Brewers' Tudor style, as rebuilt by Hoare & Co in 1933. Identified by CAMRA as having a regionally important historic interior, it has many original features including exposed wooden beams, fireplaces and low doors connecting the bars. There are usually two varying real ciders. Monthly quiz and folk music nights are held; often there is background music.
⇌(Elephant & Castle)⊖

SE13: Lewisham

Suttons Radio

139-141 Lewisham High Street, SE13 6AA

4-11 (midnight Fri); 12-midnight Sat; 12-10.30 Sun
☎ (020) 8463 0725 suttonsradio.com

Volden Session Ale; 3 changing beers (often Brew York, East London Brewing, Volden) H

The name of this Antic pub in the heart of Lewisham, opposite the busy, daily street market, was taken from an old shop sign belonging to a previous business and discovered during renovation works. Hence the various quirky displays of period radiograms, music centres and radios. Also note the large illuminated map extracted from Charles Booth's late-Victorian research into London's areas of poverty. Tables can be booked in advance for the quiz night every Sunday. ♿⇌⊖

SE14: New Cross

Royal Albert ✓

460 New Cross Road, SE14 6TJ

4-midnight (1am Fri); 12-1am Sat; 12-midnight Sun
☎ (020) 8692 3737 royalalbertpub.com

Volden Session Ale; 6 changing beers (often Burning Sky, Reunion, Siren) H

This Grade II-listed Victorian pub, retaining the original etched-glass windows and bar-back, has a convivial atmosphere and offers up to seven real ales and one real cider on handpump. The cask beer range always includes one of Antic's Volden brews. Furnishings and decor are an eclectic mix, and the food is distinctive and enticing. There is a quiz on Monday evening, a DJ on Friday and live music on Sunday. The pub is popular with local academia. ⇌⊖

SE15: Nunhead

Beer Shop London

40 Nunhead Green, SE15 3QF

closed Mon; 4-11 (11.30 Fri); 12-11.30 Sat; 12-8 Sun
☎ (020) 7732 5555 thebeershoplondon.co.uk

3 changing beers (often Moor Beer, Weird Beard) G

A former corner shop, haberdashery, and latterly a recording studio. The knowledgeable staff serve a varied selection of three real ales direct from the cask, along with an extensive range of bottled beers, plus wine, spirits and soft drinks. Boxed cider, from various producers, is also available, as are pub snacks. It hosts occasional events such as Meet the Brewer evenings. Note that January opening hours may vary.
♿⇌(78,P12)

Ivy House

40 Stuart Road, SE15 3BE

12-11 (midnight Fri & Sat); 12-10.30 Sun
☎ (020) 7277 8233 ivyhousenunhead.com

Brockley Pale Ale; Dark Star Hophead; Truman's Swift; 2 changing beers (often Brick, Buxton, Tiny Rebel) H

Large 1930s former Truman's pub with an original wood-panelled historic interior of regional importance. The building was saved in the nick of time from conversion to flats by being Grade II listed and is now community owned. There are three bars, the largest of which features a stage hosting regular live music, continuing the venue's proud history of live entertainment. One ale, often Truman's Runner, is sold at a discounted price.
Q(343,484)

SE15: Peckham

Beer Rebellion

129 Queens Road, SE15 2ND

12-11 (12.30am Fri & Sat) ☎ (020) 7732 7552

Dark Star Hophead; 3 changing beers (often East London Brewing, Siren) H

Close to Queens Road station, this bar is in the style of a micropub, situated in former shop premises. The concrete walls and floor give a post-industrial feel. Lamps fashioned from jars, along with high tables and stools, add to the utilitarian ambience. Details of the range of varying real ales and cider are listed on a large chalkboard. There is limited outdoor seating on the pavement at the front. ❀♿⇌⊖(Queens Rd)●🚌🐾📶

SE18: Shooters Hill

Bull

151 Shooters Hill, SE18 3HP

1-11; 12.30-11.30 Fri; 1-11.30 Sat; 12.30-10.30 Sun
☎ (020) 8856 0691

5 changing beers (often Castle Rock, Long Man, Moorhouse's) Ⓗ

On the brow of a hill, this reputedly haunted Grade II-listed pub was rebuilt in 1881. It retains separate public and saloon bars with individual street entrance doors and a central circular bar counter serving both rooms. The saloon bar is well appointed, whereas the public bar has a more basic appearance. There is a pool table and occasional live music events are held. The licensee makes good use of his landlord's beer range.
❀♣🚌🐾📶

SE19: Crystal Palace

Westow House

79 Westow Hill, SE19 1TX

12-midnight (2am Fri & Sat) ☎ (020) 8670 0654
westowhouse.com

Adnams Ghost Ship; Volden Session Ale; 5 changing beers (often Arbor, Marble, Volden) Ⓗ

Large Victorian corner pub bordering the edge of the Crystal Palace triangle, with a varied clientele. Antic's style of vintage shabby-chic provides a warm ambience and there is a spacious, partly covered, outdoor seating area at the front. Up to seven cask ales are complemented by changing ciders. It hosts regular live music, particularly on Fridays, and a quiz on Tuesday evenings. The rarely seen pinball machine and table football are both enthusiastically used. ❀◑⇌⊖♣●🚌🐾📶

SE20: Penge

Moon & Stars Ⓛ ✔

164-166 High Street, SE20 7QS

8am-11 ☎ (020) 8776 5680

Dark Star Hophead; Greene King Abbot; Kelham Island Pale Rider; Ruddles Best Bitter; 12 changing beers (sourced nationally) Ⓗ

Popular high-street Wetherspoon pub offering the widest choice of real ale in the area, in a variety of styles and usually including beers from local microbreweries. Customer suggestions for specific real ales are welcomed. The large L-shaped bar has a Wizard of Oz theme, with a huge sculpture of a lion. The pub hosts regular mini beer festivals and other beer-related events, including Meet the Brewer evenings.
❀◑♿⇌(Kent House)🚊(Beckenham Rd) ●P🚌📶

SE22: East Dulwich

East Dulwich Tavern ✔

1 Lordship Lane, SE22 8EW

12-midnight (1am Fri & Sat) ☎ (020) 8693 1316
eastdulwichtavern.com

Dark Star Hophead; Volden Session Ale; 4 changing beers (often Brick, Truman's, Twickenham) Ⓗ

Imposing pub in a prominent corner position and the home of the Antic pub company. The interior is classic boozer, but in tune with the times and alive with customers. Previously a hotel, the upper storeys are now offices, although the first-floor masonic hall with its own bar opens occasionally for music and events, including a monthly film club. There is usually real cider during summer months, and good-quality food is on offer.
❀◑♿⇌♣●🚌🐾📶

SE23: Forest Hill

Blythe Hill Tavern ★

319 Stanstead Road, SE23 1JB

11-11 (midnight Thu-Sat); 12-11 Sun ☎ (020) 8690 5176
blythehilltavern.org.uk

Courage Best Bitter; Dark Star Hophead; Harvey's Sussex Best Bitter; 2 changing beers (often Brockley, Dark Star, Ringwood) Ⓗ

A regular recipient of awards for beer and cider, this friendly Victorian local has an unusual three-bar layout which CAMRA has identified as a nationally important historic pub interior. Usually six cask beers and up to 13 real ciders are on the bar. In two of the bars TV screens show sporting events, especially horse racing. Listen to live, traditional Irish music on Thursday evenings. There are also regular poetry evenings. The pretty rear garden includes a children's play area.
Q❀⇌(Catford/Catford Bridge)●🚌🐾📶

Capitol Ⓛ ✔

11-21 London Road, SE23 3TW

8am-midnight (1am Fri & Sat) ☎ (020) 8291 8920

Greene King Abbot; Ruddles Best Bitter; 6 changing beers (sourced nationally) Ⓗ

This 1920s Grade II-listed former cinema, now a Wetherspoon outlet, retains its grandeur, with an imposing Art Deco frontage. Inside is a spacious open-plan drinking area and along the rear wall, where the screen was previously located, is a long, impressive bar. While at the bar, visitors should be sure to turn around and look up at the old seating circle – tours of non-public areas are occasionally run. There is also an outside area with picnic benches. ❀◑♿⇌⊖♣●🚌📶

SE25: South Norwood

Portland Arms

152 Portland Road, SE25 4PT

12-11 (midnight Fri & Sat) ☎ (020) 8655 0098
portlandarmspub.co.uk

House beer (by Sambrook's); 3 changing beers (often Bexley, Truman's) Ⓗ

Tagged as a Pub & Kitchen, and with a modern feel, this is a traditional building that reopened in 2016. The bar is light and airy with a mixture of seating. Real ales selected from London breweries complement a range of other draught beers. A loyalty membership scheme is available. Food includes burgers, pub classics and Sunday roasts. There is an outside drinking area at the rear.
❀◑♿⇌🚊(Woodside)⊖(Norwood Jct)🚌🐾📶

Shelverdine Goathouse Ⓛ ✔

7-9 High Street, SE25 6EP

4-11 (midnight Fri); 12-midnight Sat; 12-11 Sun
☎ (020) 8916 1001 shelverdinegoathouse.com

Volden Session Ale; 5 changing beers (sourced nationally) Ⓗ

Modern Antic pub with three distinct areas, all with large windows overlooking the High Street. These

are decorated in different styles: kitchen equipment, clocks (not accurate) and pictures. Guest beers are selected from around the country but often come from London breweries. A home fan-only policy operates when Crystal Palace are playing. Check social media for regular real ale club, quiz night and live music events.
◑♿⇌⊖(Norwood Jct)♣🚌📶

Addiscombe

Claret & Ale

5 Bingham Corner, Lower Addiscombe Road, CR0 7AA
11.30-11 (11.30 Thu; midnight Fri & Sat); 12-11 Sun
☎ (020) 8656 7452
Palmers IPA; 5 changing beers (sourced nationally) Ⓗ
Small, privately owned and friendly free house around the corner from Addiscombe tram stop, boasting 31 years in this Guide. A community pub where conversation is king, it received a sympathetic makeover in 2016. The changing beers come from all over the UK, mainly from microbreweries; see the board opposite the bar for beers on and coming next. Two draught ciders are also available, served from the cellar.
♿🚊🍎🚌🐾📶

Beckenham

Bricklayers Arms

237 High Street, BR3 1BN
12 (11 Thu-Sat)-11; 12-10 Sun ☎ (020) 8402 0007
bricklayersarms.co
St Austell Tribute, Proper Job; Young's Special; 1 changing beer (sourced nationally) Ⓗ
Traditional local high-street pub providing a friendly welcome to a clientele of all ages. There is an open log fire in winter and a covered outdoor seating area with heaters and even a TV screen. The changing guest ales often reflect recommendations by customers. The pub holds occasional beer festivals and in 2016 was the local CAMRA Community Pub of the Year. Sunday hours apply on most bank holidays. Sit under the super-lifesize Spider Man if you dare!
❀⇌(Junction/Clock House)🚊(Junction)
♣🍎🚌🐾📶

Bexleyheath

Furze Wren ✔

6 Market Place, Broadway Square, DA6 7DY
8am-midnight ☎ (020) 8298 2590
Greene King Abbot; Ruddles Best Bitter; Sharp's Doom Bar; 7 changing beers (often Rockin' Robin, Westerham) Ⓗ
Spacious Wetherspoon pub named after a local bird, better known as the Dartford Warbler. It is at the heart of the shopping area, with buses serving every route through town. Plenty of seating and large windows make it a great place to eat, drink and people-watch. It attracts a full mix of clientele. Local history panels are displayed around the pub. Alcoholic drinks are served from 9am.
Q❀◑♿♣🚌📶

Robin Hood & Little John 𝕃

78 Lion Road, DA6 8PF
11-3, 5.30-11; 11-3, 7-11 Sat; 12-4, 7-10.30 Sun
☎ (020) 8303 1128 robinhoodbexleyheath.co.uk
Adnams Southwold Bitter, Ghost Ship; Bexley Bexley's Own Beer; Fuller's London Pride; Harvey's Sussex Best Bitter; Sharp's Doom Bar; 1 changing beer (often Bexley, Shepherd Neame, Westerham) Ⓗ
A back-street local dating from the 1830s, when it was surrounded by fields. Eight real ales are on offer, mostly from independent breweries including the Bexley Brewery. It has a good reputation for its home-cooked food at lunchtimes (no food Sun) with Italian specials, which can be eaten at tables made from old Singer sewing machines. Frequent local CAMRA Pub of the Year and regional winner three times. Over-21s only.
Q❀◑🚌(B13)

Wrong 'Un 𝕃 ✔

234-236 Broadway, DA6 8AS
8am-midnight ☎ (020) 8298 0439
Greene King Abbot; Ruddles Best Bitter; Sharp's Doom Bar; 5 changing beers (often Shepherd Neame) Ⓗ
Bexleyheath's first Wetherspoon pub, opened in 1994 in a single-storey former furniture store. There are records of cricket being played locally since 1746 and the unusual pub name is an alternative expression for a googly. Westons Old Rosie cider is stocked. There are comfortable booths to sit in as well as an open-plan area. Alcoholic drinks are served from 9am and food until 11pm daily; pizza is served from a pizza oven.
Q◑♿⇌♣🚌📶

Blackfen

Broken Drum 𝕃

308 Westwood Lane, DA15 9PT
3-10; 12-10 Sat; 1-4 Sun ☎ 07803 131678
thebrokendrum.co.uk
3 changing beers (sourced nationally) Ⓖ
A micropub named after an inn in a Terry Pratchett novel – you can't beat it! Seating is a settee in each of the bay windows and a variety of tables and chairs, plus pavement tables and chairs for fair-weather drinking (up to 8pm). SPBW London Pub of the Year 2018 and local CAMRA Pub of the Year 2018. It holds Cheesy (the first) Thursday and Whisky (the third) Wednesday of the month. Occasional quizzes and excursions are arranged. A real community pub. Q♣🍎P🚌(51,132)🐾

George Staples ✔

273 Blackfen Road, DA15 8PR
11-11 (midnight Thu-Sat); 12-11 Sun ☎ (020) 8850 3181
Fuller's London Pride; Sharp's Doom Bar; 4 changing beers (sourced nationally) Ⓗ
Originally the Woodman, dating from 1845 and one of the first buildings in Blackfen. It was then demolished and rebuilt in 1931 when large-scale building began in the area. Refurbished in 2007 and renamed after the original landlord, and refurbished again in 2018, it is now a large and comfortable single-roomed pub/sports bar. There is a buy-five, get-one-free loyalty scheme. Plenty of outdoor seating is available.
❀◑♿P🚌(51,132)🐾📶

Bromley

Partridge

194 High Street, BR1 1HE
11-11 (midnight Fri & Sat); 11-10.30 Sun
☎ (020) 8464 7656 partridgebromley.co.uk
Dark Star Hophead; Fuller's London Pride, ESB; Gale's HSB; 2 changing beers (often Butcombe, Fuller's) Ⓗ

Grade II-listed former NatWest bank, now a Fuller's Ale & Pie house, retaining many original features including the high ceilings and chandeliers. There are two small snug rooms off the main bar. The upmarket food menu includes vegetarian choices. Located by the Market Square, the pub is popular with shoppers and for live music on Saturday nights. A refurbishment is planned for late 2019, with the real ale range going up from six to eight choices. Q♨❀◐♿⇌(North/South)🚌🐾📶

Red Lion ✔

10 North Road, BR1 3LG

⏲ 11-11; 12-11 Sun ☎ (020) 8460 2691

🌐 redlionbromley.co.uk

Greene King IPA, Abbot; Harvey's Sussex Best Bitter; 2 changing beers (often Black Sheep, Jennings, Oakham) [H]

A traditional, well-kept pub in the quiet back streets just north of Bromley town centre. The only pub in the borough to have featured in every edition of this Guide since the local branch was formed in 2011, it is well worth seeking out. It retains many original features, including tiling. An extensive library of books dominates one wall, a range of good-value meals is served and a real fire keeps you warm in winter. Q❀◐⇌(North)♣🚌

Star & Garter 🏆

227 High Street, BR1 1NZ

⏲ 4-11 (midnight Fri); 12.30-midnight Sat; 12.30-9 Sun

☎ (020) 3730 9458

7 changing beers (often Bristol Beer Factory, Fyne Ales, Siren) [H]

This late 19th-century Grade II-listed pub reopened in 2016 after more than two years' closure, and having not previously served real ale. The building has been completely refurbished and now boasts eight handpumps, one of which often dispenses real cider. Real ales are usually non-mainstream, with local and regional microbreweries well represented. Customers may order in food from local takeaways. Local CAMRA Pub of the Year for 2018 and 2019. Q♨♿⇌(North/South)🍎🚌🐾📶

Crayford

Penny Farthing 🏆 Ⓛ

3 Waterside, DA1 4JJ

⏲ closed Mon; 12-3, 5-9.30 Tue-Thu; 12-10.30 Fri & Sat; 12-3 Sun ☎ 07772 866645 🌐 pennyfarthingcrayford.co.uk

4 changing beers (often Old Dairy, Wantsum, Whitstable) [G]

Bexley's second micropub, opened in 2014. Ale and cider are served from a cold room with a viewing window. Kentish brewers feature mostly, with an increasing cider range supplementing Dudda's Tun and Westons. Pavement seating in summer overlooks a small riverside park. Usually open bank holidays, it is a good venue to watch local public events. A charity fine is levied should your mobile phone ring. Local CAMRA Pub of the Year and London regional runner-up 2018. Q♨⇌♣🍎▯🚌🐾

Croydon

Builders Arms

65 Leslie Park Road, CR0 6TP

⏲ 12-11 (midnight Fri & Sat) ☎ (020) 8654 1803

🌐 buildersarmscroydon.co.uk

Fuller's Oliver's Island, London Pride, ESB; 1 changing beer [H]

A back-street community local opened in the 19th century, serving beers from the Fuller's range. The two bars each have their own character. The smaller public-style bar has a dartboard and a large screen TV showing sport. The larger saloon bar with comfortable seating leads to a pleasant garden, with outdoor games available during the warmer months. Events include quiz night on a Tuesday. Q♨❀◐♿⇌(East)🚊(Lebanon Rd)♣🚌🐾📶

Cronx Ⓛ

Units 3 & 4, Boxpark Croydon, 99 George Street, CR0 1LD

⏲ 12-11; 12-10 Sun ☎ (020) 8688 4912 🌐 thecronx.com

Cronx Standard, Kotchin, Nektar, Pop Up!, Entire; 1 changing beer (sourced locally) [H]

A modern micropub-sized bar in Croydon's Boxpark development beside East Croydon station accessed via Dingwall Road by the bus stop. Six handpumps serve a range of Cronx beers and normally one varying guest, and a real cider. The decor is simple but stylish, employing scaffolding and adapted beer casks and fonts. Beer is served in plastic glasses to customers taking their drinks out of the bar into the Boxpark complex, where food is available. ♿⇌🚊(East)🍎🚌📶

Dog & Bull ✔

24 Surrey Street, CR0 1RG

⏲ 12-11 (11.30 Fri & Sat); 12-10.30 Sun ☎ (020) 8667 9718

🌐 dogandbullcroydon.co.uk

Young's Bitter, Special; 2 changing beers (sourced nationally) [H]

An ancient Grade II-listed marketplace pub with an island bar and stained-glass windows. The garden is unexpected and attractive; it is the largest in central Croydon, with a collection of booths with TVs and an outdoor bar and barbecue in the summer. The pub is a favourite with local traders and visitors to the Surrey Street market. A small upstairs function room can be hired. ♨❀◐⇌(East/West)🚊(George St/Reeves Corner) ⊖(West)🚌🐾📶

George Ⓛ ✔

17-21 George Street, CR0 1LA

⏲ 8am-midnight (1am Fri & Sat) ☎ (020) 8649 9077

Burning Sky Plateau, Aurora; Greene King IPA, Abbot; Sharp's Doom Bar; Thornbridge Jaipur IPA; 9 changing beers (often Surrey Hills, Tillingbourne) [H]

A converted shop, this town-centre pub is named after a former Croydon coaching inn. It has two bars, the rear one being slightly raised (a ramp allows access), with six handpumps often showcasing beers from breweries such as Dark Star, Oakham, Saltaire and Thornbridge. The front bar has a wider mix of beers, including real ales from local breweries and the Wetherspoon national range. A quiz is held on Sunday nights. ♨◐♿⇌(East/West)🚊(George St/Reeves Corner) ⊖(West)🍎🚌📶

Green Dragon Ⓛ ✔

58 High Street, CR0 1NA

⏲ 11-11 (midnight Thu; 1am Fri & Sat); 12-10.30 Sun

☎ (020) 8667 0684

8 changing beers [H]

A converted bank with a modern twist, the pub boasts a vast range of ales and other draught beers, both from local and national breweries, and also ciders. Located between the historic Surrey

Street market and the south Croydon restaurant quarter, it attracts all types of clientele. The upstairs function room hosts weekly events such as quizzes, poker and open mic nights.
🐴◐♿⇌(East/West)🚊(George St/Reeves Corner)
⊖(West)♣🍎🚌📶

Skylark ✔

34-36 South End, CR0 1DP
⏲ 8am-midnight (1am Fri & Sat) ☎ (020) 8649 9909
Fuller's London Pride; Greene King Abbot; Ruddles Best Bitter; Sharp's Doom Bar; 6 changing beers Ⓗ
Spacious Wetherspoon pub in the restaurant quarter south of the town centre. The main bar is wood panelled, with a raised library area to the rear. The decor includes pictures of nearby former Croydon airport, London's first civil airport. A grand staircase at the rear leads to an upstairs bar, not always in use and offering a reduced range of beers. Changing ales are mainly from microbreweries, often local ones.
🐴❀◐♿⇌(South)🍎🚌📶

Downe

Queen's Head Ⓛ

25 High Street, BR6 7US TQ432616
⏲ 12-11 (11.30 Fri & Sat); 12-10.30 Sun ☎ (01689) 852145
🌐 queensheaddowne.com
Fuller's London Pride; 3 changing beers (often Adnams, Westerham) Ⓗ
Attractive and traditional pub with open fireplaces, dating from 1565, and named following a visit by Queen Elizabeth I. Though situated in the centre of a historic country village, it is less than 20 minutes by bus from Bromley or Orpington. Charles Darwin, a regular patron, lived at nearby Down House. There are several dining areas offering a daily menu including home-made pies. The pub is popular with walkers and locals all year round.
🐴❀◐♣🍎P🚌(146,R8)🐾📶

Hayes

Real Ale Way Ⓛ

55 Station Approach, BR2 7EB
⏲ 2-10 (11 Fri & Sat); 2-8 Sun ☎ 07446 897885
🌐 therealaleway.com
House beer (by Tonbridge); 9 changing beers (often Larkins, Mad Cat, Whitstable) Ⓖ
Opened in July 2018, this family-owned micropub offers a welcome new choice for local drinkers and rail commuters alike. It overlooks the entrance to Hayes station, and numerous bus routes stop outside. Up to nine Kentish real ales are served from a cold room. The affiliation with all things Kent extends to the wines and spirits, and also to the bar snacks. The premises, once a bank and more recently an accountancy office, are quite large by micropub standards. Q⇌🍎🚌🐾

Keston

Greyhound ✔

Commonside, BR2 6BP TQ413646
⏲ 11-11; 9am-11 Sat; 10-10.30 Sun ☎ (01689) 856338
🌐 greyhoundkeston.co.uk
Sharp's Doom Bar; Timothy Taylor Landlord; 4 changing beers (sourced nationally) Ⓗ
A popular local with an enthusiastic and welcoming landlord. It overlooks the common and is on walking routes including the London Outer Orbital Path, but is also easily accessed by bus from Bromley. The pub is at the heart of village life, with a crowded calendar of local events, detailed in the newsletter. A beer festival is held during the Easter weekend, when up to 15 non-mainstream beers are available. Local CAMRA Pub of the Year for 2017. Q🐴❀◐♣🍎P🚌(146,246)🐾📶

Orpington

Orpington Liberal Club Ⓛ

7 Station Road, BR6 0RZ
⏲ 8 (7 Wed; 6 Fri)-11; 12-3, 7-11 Sat; 12-3, 8-10.30 Sun
☎ (01689) 820882 🌐 orpingtonliberalclub.co.uk
4 changing beers Ⓗ
Friendly club serving a changing selection of beers mainly from smaller and local breweries. Real cider and a variety of bottled low ABV and gluten-free beers are also available. Two real ale festivals are held each year. The club hosts live music, board game afternoons, local churches and bridge evenings in its hall, and enthusiastically supports local charities. Winner of many CAMRA awards including local Club of the Year 2019. CAMRA or NULC card required for entry.
Q🐴❀⇌♣🍎P🚌🐾📶

Petts Wood

One Inn the Wood Ⓛ

209 Petts Wood Road, BR5 1LA TQ445677
⏲ closed Mon; 12-2.30, 5-9.30 (11 Fri); 11.30-11 Sat; 12-8 Sun ☎ 07799 535982 🌐 oneinnthewood.co.uk
House beer (by Tonbridge); 4 changing beers (often Kent, Rockin' Robin, Wantsum) Ⓖ
The first micropub in the local area, opened in 2014 and winner of several CAMRA awards. Situated in a former wine bar, there is bench seating and a large woodland backdrop dominating the left-hand wall. Beer is served from a glass-fronted cool room. Wine, gin and soft drinks are also available, together with a range of mainly locally produced snacks. Families and dogs are welcome.
Q🐴⇌🍎🚌🐾

Selsdon

Sir Julian Huxley ✔

152-154 Addington Road, CR2 8LB
⏲ 9am-11; 9am-10.30 Sun ☎ (020) 8657 9457
Greene King IPA, Abbot; Sharp's Doom Bar; 5 changing beers Ⓗ
A mid-sized Wetherspoon pub which is named after a former local resident, one of the famous Huxley family, who became the first Director General of UNESCO. The interior is airy and well lit, and there is a conservatory and a small patio garden. The cask ales on offer are varied and the selection changes frequently. At least one real cider is usually on the bar. Q🐴❀◐♿🍎🚌📶

Sidcup

Hackney Carriage Ⓛ

165 Station Road, DA15 7AA
⏲ 3-10; 12-10.30 Fri & Sat; 12-8 Sun ☎ 07715 680727
🌐 thehackneycarriagemicropub.com
5 changing beers (sourced nationally) Ⓖ
A welcome addition to the micropub scene. Emphasis on local beers and ciders, together with strong-beer Thursday, give it a different feel from the other micropubs in the area. Ales and ciders are

dispensed from a cool room behind the bar, as well as local wines and a special brand of Kentish gin. Seating is at wall-mounted high benches at high tables.

Welling

Door Hinge

11 Welling High Street, DA16 1TR

closed Mon; 3-9 (10 Fri); 12-10 Sat; 12-3.30 Sun
(07956 845509 thedoorhinge.co.uk

3 changing beers (often Mighty Oak, Old Dairy, Rockin' Robin) G

A breath of fresh air on the local pub scene and handy for Welling United football ground, London's first permanent micropub opened in 2013 in part of a former electrical wholesaler's. There are usually at least three beers dispensed from a glass-fronted cold room. The cosy bar encourages conversation among previous strangers. Cider comes from various sources. Q

SOUTH-WEST LONDON

SW1: Belgravia

Antelope

22-24 Eaton Terrace, SW1W 8EZ

12-11 (11.30 Fri); 12-10 Sun (020) 7824 8512

Fuller's London Pride, ESB; Gale's Seafarers Ale; 2 changing beers (sourced nationally) H

Dating back to 1827, this Fuller's venue spent several years as a Nicholson's pub until 2005. Original preserved features include etched-glass windows, a side room used as a snug, and the central bar. This is an upmarket house and the clientele consists mainly of local professionals. The pub plays cricket matches against the Churchill Arms (Notting Hill). The upstairs bar and side room can be hired for functions.
Q(Sloane Sq)

Star Tavern

6 Belgrave Mews West, SW1X 8HT

11-11; 10.30-11 Sat; 12-10.30 Sun (020) 7235 3019

Fuller's London Pride, ESB; house beer (by Fuller's); 2 changing beers (sourced regionally; often Fuller's) H

Down a mews, near embassies and rich in the history of the powerful and famous, it is rumoured that the Great Train Robbery was planned here. Now it is a popular Fuller's pub where local residents, business people and embassy staff rub shoulders with casual visitors. Sometimes a special Fuller's beer can be found. Upstairs is a dining room, also bookable for functions. The pub has featured in all 47 editions of this Guide.
Q(Hyde Park Corner/Knightsbridge)

SW1: Pimlico

Cask Pub & Kitchen

6 Charlwood Street, SW1V 2EE

11-11; 12-10.30 Sun (020) 7630 7225
caskpubandkitchen.com

10 changing beers H

Formerly the Pimlico Tram, it was converted to a beer destination by owners who have since acquired and modernised several more pubs in the South-East. Ten handpumps serve real ales from many microbreweries such as Arbor Ales and Dark Star, and a vast range of bottled beers from the UK and around the world complements some unusual draught choices. Burgers feature on the weekday menu, with roasts on Sundays until late afternoon. Local CAMRA Pub of the Year 2019.
Q(Victoria)

SW1: St James's

Red Lion ★

2 Duke of York Street, SW1Y 6JP

11.30-11; closed Sun (020) 7321 0782

Fuller's Oliver's Island, London Pride, ESB; Gale's Seafarers Ale; 2 changing beers (often Fuller's) H

Close to the upmarket shops in Jermyn Street, this is a deservedly celebrated little gem, worth visiting just for its nationally important historic pub interior and, in particular, its spectacular Victorian etched and cut mirrors and glass. This Grade II-listed building dates from 1821 and was given a new frontage in 1871. With little space inside, visitors often spill out onto the pavement. Beware of the precipitous steps down to the toilets. Food is served 11.30-4pm (5pm Sat).
Q(Green Park/Piccadilly Circus)

SW1: Victoria

Willow Walk

25 Wilton Road, SW1V 1LW

7am-midnight; 8am-midnight Sat; 8am-11 Sun
(020) 7828 2953

Fuller's London Pride; Greene King IPA, Abbot; 9 changing beers H

Ground-floor Wetherspoon's pub converted from a Woolworth's in 1999, extending from just opposite the eastern side entrance to Victoria Station back to Vauxhall Bridge Road and with entrances on both. Some wood panelling, quite a low ceiling and subdued lighting create a warm atmosphere. One TV is usually switched off, the other silent. Friendly and attentive staff look after a mixed clientele including families. Local guest beers often come from Twickenham. Alcoholic drinks are served from 9am.

SW1: Westminster

Buckingham Arms

62 Petty France, SW1H 9EU

11-11 (9 Sat); 12-5 Sun (020) 7222 3386
buckinghamarms.com

Young's Bitter, London Gold, Special; 3 changing beers (often Young's) H

Said to have once been a hat shop, the Bell opened here in the 1720s and was renamed the Black Horse in the 1740s. Rebuilt in 1898, renamed again in 1901 and substantially renovated in recent years, it is another pub that has appeared in all 47 editions of this Guide, attracting civil servants, visitors and the occasional MP. It offers a mix of modern and traditional seats and tables, high and low. Open Sundays from the end of March through the summer. (St James's Park)

SW1: Whitehall

Lord Moon of the Mall

18 Whitehall, SW1A 2DY

8am-11.30 (midnight Fri & Sat); 8am-11 Sun
(020) 7839 7701

Fuller's London Pride; Greene King IPA, Abbot; Sharp's Doom Bar; 7 changing beers H

A 1995 Wetherspoon conversion of a bank built in the early 1870s. The pale pink sandstone, dark-wood panelling, high ceilings and arched windows would still be recognisable to the Victorian clerks. Even the portrait of a youthful Tim Martin, the chain's founder, on the pub sign seems in keeping! The pub is open plan, with a family dining area to the rear where children are welcome until 9.30pm. Alcoholic drinks are sold from 9am and meals all day, starting with breakfast.
Q🕏🍴🔥⊖(Charing Cross)●🚊🐾🛜

SW2: Brixton

Elm Park Tavern
76 Elm Park, SW2 2UB
🕐 5-11; 4-midnight Fri; 12-midnight Sat; 12-10.30 Sun
☎ (020) 8671 9823 ⊕ elmparktavern.co.uk
Sharp's Doom Bar; 4 changing beers (often Bullfinch, Gipsy Hill, London Beer Lab) Ⓗ
A sister pub to King & Co in Clapham, with a single bar serving separate front and back rooms, each with a cosy atmosphere. Cask beers often include Little Hopster brewed for both pubs at London Beer Lab. Alongside the handpumps are another 16 draught beers on tap. Tuesday evening ale club sees lower prices for all cask beers. A popular quiz night is held on Monday. Note the unique portrait of 18th-century stage mimic Samuel Foote.
🕏🍴●🚊🐾🛜

SW4: Clapham

King & Co
100 Clapham Park Road, SW4 7BZ
🕐 4-11 (midnight Thu); 2-1am Fri; 12-1am Sat; 12-11 Sun
☎ (020) 7498 1971 ⊕ thekingandco.uk
London Beer Lab Little Hopster; 4 changing beers (sourced nationally) Ⓗ
An innovative pub offering an enterprising and changing range of beers from microbreweries throughout the UK, plus real ciders from smaller producers. The Little Hopster is brewed locally by a member of staff. On Tuesday there is a £1 discount on a pint of real ale. The single bar is basically furnished, with current beer offerings displayed on a large board. The kitchen is periodically taken over by street-food specialists, and the Sunday roasts are popular. 🕏🍴⊖(Common)●🚊🐾🛜

SW5: Earls Court

King's Head
17 Hogarth Place, SW5 0QT
🕐 8am-11; 9am-11 Sat; 9am-10.30 Sun ☎ (020) 7373 5239
Fuller's Oliver's Island, London Pride; 2 changing beers (often Fuller's) Ⓗ
A comfortable, friendly corner pub with a modernised interior, hidden away off the busy Earls Court Road; the building is a 1937 rebuild of the oldest (circa 17th century) licensed premises in the area. Seating is a mixture of high stools around tall tables, dining tables and settees with low tables. Three Fuller's cask ales are supplemented by a guest, usually from another local brewery. Alcoholic drinks are served from 11am. On Monday there is a quiz at 8pm.
🕏🍴⊖⇌(West Brompton)⊖🚊🐾🛜

SW6: Fulham

Durell Arms Ⓛ ✅
704 Fulham Road, SW6 5SB
🕐 12-11 (1am Fri & Sat) ☎ (020) 7736 3014
⊕ durellarmsfulham.com
Greene King IPA; 3 changing beers (often Sambrook's, Sharp's, Wychwood) Ⓗ
A spacious Greene King Metropolitan corner pub with an L-shaped drinking area. The large rear room, with mouldings and mirrors giving an air of Victorian decadence, can be hired for functions. There is a big screen for sporting events. Attractive local ales complement Greene King and national guests, and it is busy on Sundays for the excellent roast. 🕏🍴🍴🔥⊖(Parsons Green)●🚊🐾🛜

King's Arms
425 New Kings Road, SW6 4RN
🕐 11-11; 12-10.30 Sun ☎ (020) 7371 9585
⊕ kingsarms-fulham.co.uk/home
Wadworth IPA, Horizon, 6X, Bishops Tipple, Swordfish; 1 changing beer (often Wadworth) Ⓗ
After a £300,000 refurbishment, this pub reopened as Wadworth's first in the capital. The large corner building at the north end of Putney Bridge has been divided into areas and comfortably and tastefully furnished with fabric-upholstered banquettes and chairs. A wide range of Wadworth's beers is on the bar. Food includes stone baked pizzas and Match Day menus; the restaurant is on the first floor. A patio smoking area is to one side. 🕏🍴🍴🔥⊖(Putney Bridge)🚊🐾🛜

SW6: Parsons Green

White Horse Ⓛ ✅
1-3 Parsons Green, SW6 4UL
🕐 9.30am-11.30 (midnight Thu-Sat) ☎ (020) 7736 2115
⊕ whitehorsesw6.com
Harvey's Sussex Best Bitter; Oakham JHB; 6 changing beers Ⓗ
A destination Mitchells & Butlers pub that normally boasts five guest beers on handpump and an international selection of bottled beers. Regular beer and food matching events take place as well as beer festivals; the Old Ale Festival in late November has run for 36 years, with a stillage in the Coach House, normally reserved for dining. The pub can get busy when Chelsea FC are playing at home, but upstairs there is room to escape the crowds. Q🕏🍴🍴🔥⊖●🚊(22,424)🐾🛜

SW7: Gloucester Road

Queen's Arms
30 Queen's Gate Mews, SW7 5QL
🕐 12-11; 12-10.30 Sun ☎ (020) 7823 9293
⊕ thequeensarmskensington.co.uk
Sharp's Doom Bar; Timothy Taylor Landlord; St Austell Proper Job; 5 changing beers (sourced nationally) Ⓗ
Lovely corner mews pub, discreetly tucked away off Queen's Gate, well worth seeking out for its real ales and its large range of interesting draught and bottled beers, malt whiskies and other spirits. Note the unusual curved doors. The L-shaped room has wooden floors and panelling. The clientele reflects the location: opulent locals, students from Imperial College and musicians from, and visitors to, the nearby Royal Albert Hall – all of whom, if wise, reserve tables. 🍴🔥⊖🐾🛜

SW7: South Kensington

Anglesea Arms

15 Selwood Terrace, SW7 3QG
11-11; 12-10.30 Sun (020) 7373 7960
angleseaarms.com
Greene King IPA; 5 changing beers (often Sambrook's, Triple fff, Wimbledon)
A real ale stalwart from CAMRA's early years, it has appeared in many editions of the Guide. Built in 1827, it was a Meux tied house for more than a century. Now a Grade II-listed Greene King Metropolitan pub, it has the air of a country inn, with outside seating and an interior featuring a diverse collection of mirrors, prints, photographs and paintings. Apart from the range of real ales, the menu offers a variety of food at reasonable prices for the area. Q

SW8: South Lambeth

Priory Arms

83 Lansdowne Way, SW8 2PB
5-11; 3-11 Sat; 3-10.30 Sun (020) 7622 1884
theprioryarms.com
5 changing beers (often Ilkley, Kent, Tiny Rebel)
Long-established free house with a modernised, split-level interior, attracting a youngish clientele. Microbreweries are well supported here, and there is a good choice of foreign beers. The pub hosts around four beer festivals annually, including on the May and August bank holiday weekends, and another, usually German-themed, in the autumn. The menu features Mexican dishes and burgers. Board games are available, while at the front is a small patio for smoking and outdoor drinking. Children are allowed before 7pm.
(Stockwell)

Surprise

16 Southville, SW8 2PP
12-midnight (1am Fri & Sat); 12-11 Sun
(020) 7622 4623
Young's Bitter, Special; 1 changing beer (often Young's)
Tucked away next to Larkhall Park, this small, down-to-earth, L-shaped local was refurbished in late 2018 and now includes a conservatory extension. It is the only building remaining from streets that were replaced by the park after WWII bomb damage. The back room walls display caricatures of regular customers, while the middle section has black and white photographs of Battersea power station. Outside there is a patio and boules (pétanque) pitch. A third real ale is only sometimes available.
(Stockwell/Wandsworth Rd)

SW9: Brixton

Craft Beer Co

11-13 Brixton Station Road, SW9 8PA
4.30-11 (midnight Thu; 2am Fri); 12-2am Sat; 12-10.30 Sun
(020) 7274 8383
House beer (by Kent); changing beers
Close to Brixton market, this modern pub has a retro feel with hints of American diner. Downstairs has red high stools and an industrial vibe while upstairs are bright blue bench seats, a tumbling blocks parquet floor, neon signs and enamel brewery advertisements from Belgium and France. London microbreweries feature heavily among the draught and bottled beers, as do Belgian Trappists and Lambic. Live music is played on Thursdays. The pub gets busy when concerts are on at the nearby O2 Academy.

Crown & Anchor

246 Brixton Road, SW9 6AQ
4.30-midnight (1am Fri); 12-1am Sat; 12-11 Sun
(020) 7737 0060 crownandanchorbrixton.co.uk
Oakham Citra; 7 changing beers (often Siren, Tiny Rebel, Titanic)
This modernised pub, with delicious food, in what had been rather a beer desert, serves real ale from microbreweries all over the country. There are three ciders from Seacider and others. A wide range of other draught and bottled beers, the latter including many from the US and Belgium, extend the drinker's choice. Meals are available every evening and weekend lunchtimes. There are tables outside with heating and coverings for smokers.

SW11: Battersea

Sambrook's Brewery Tap Room

Unit 1 & 2 Yelverton Road, SW11 3QG
closed Sun-Wed; 5-10.30 Thu & Fri; 12-10 Sat
(020) 7228 0598 sambrooksbrewery.co.uk
Sambrook's Wandle Ale, Pumphouse Pale Ale, Junction Ale, Powerhouse Porter; 1 changing beer
On the first floor with a view over the brewery plant, this taproom has an industrial feel, with a metallic bar counter, breeze block wall and lights hanging from cords. The coarse chipboard floor is rather pleasing. The furniture is mainly utilitarian but there is a leather sofa at one end for those who wish for comfort. There is covered and heated outside seating at ground-floor level, and on open days more seating is provided outside the brewery.
(Clapham Jct) (44)

SW11: Clapham Junction

Beehive

197 St Johns Hill, SW11 1TH
3 (12.30 Thu)-midnight; 12.30-1am Fri & Sat; 12-midnight Sun (020) 7450 1756
Fuller's London Pride, ESB; 2 changing beers (often Fuller's)
Tasteful and elegant refurbishment and enthusiastic management have revitalised this classic local, a former Fuller's Town Pub of the Year. A roll-up TV screen shows major sporting events. The rear area is available for functions and there is now a sheltered garden. The food menu, although limited, is excellent. Blankets are thoughtfully supplied for guests wishing to sit outside. Look out for the wonderful 1898 housing survey map of SW London; since then the Luftwaffe and town planners have altered things somewhat!

Draft House Northcote

94 Northcote Road, SW11 6QW
4-11; 3-midnight Fri; 11-midnight Sat; 11-10.30 Sun
(020) 7924 1814
Sambrook's Wandle Ale; 2 changing beers (often Sambrook's, Tiny Rebel)
This branch of the innovative Draft House chain, now owned by BrewDog, is a former shop that has two distinct areas. At the front there are high stools around the bar and high bench seating overlooking the street. At the rear is a dining area decorated

with old album covers and modern art posters. Outdoor pavement seating is at the front and side. The three cask ales are complemented by a wide range of beers in other formats, mostly from UK microbreweries. ♘❀◐⇌🚌(319,G1)🐾📶

Eagle Ale House Ⓛ

104 Chatham Road, SW11 6HG

⏲ 4-11; 3-11 Fri; 12-11 Sat; 12-10.30 Sun ☎ (020) 7228 2328

Surrey Hills Shere Drop; changing beers (often Downton, Hackney, Pilgrim) Ⓗ

Homely, traditional pub, a short uphill walk from Northcote Road, with a friendly welcome for all, regulars and visitors alike (and their canine companions). In recent years it has been at the heart of the Fair Deal For Your Local campaign. Major sporting events are shown on four TV screens, including in the heated marquee in the garden. The Eagle has been South-West London CAMRA Pub of the Year more than once, and several times the runner-up. ♘❀🚌(319,G1)🐾📶

Four Thieves

51 Lavender Gardens, SW11 1DJ

⏲ 12-midnight (2am Fri & Sat); 12-10.30 Sun

☎ (020) 7223 6927 🌐 fourthieves.pub

Laine@Four Thieves IPA; 8 changing beers (often Dark Star, Laine@Four Thieves) Ⓗ

This pub has the wow factor. The spacious downstairs bar extends over two levels. The theatre to the right hosts swing classes, comedy and live jazz. To the left, behind the brewery, the Gin Yard has heated and covered areas. The vast Arcade upstairs has table football, mini-golf, motor racing and all sorts of electronic wizardry, as well as a separate bar. Thieves' beers, other Laine's ales and guests from local breweries provide a welcoming range of styles. ♘❀◐⇌⊖🚌📶

SW12: Balham

Balham Bowls Club ✔

7-9 Ramsden Road, SW12 8QX

⏲ 4-11 (midnight Thu; 1am Fri); 12-1am Sat; 12-11 Sun

☎ (020) 8673 4700 🌐 balhambowlsclub.com

Volden Session Ale Ⓖ**; 3 changing beers (often By the Horns, Sambrook's, Twickenham)** Ⓗ

Converted to a pub by Antic in 2006, this former club just off Balham High Road retains a traditional feel but is now more popular with young people. The multi-roomed historic interior, which is of regional importance, features wood panelling, decorated with emblematic military shields and sporting paraphernalia. Guest beers may be from Volden but are typically from other London microbreweries. Live music entertains on Friday evenings. ♘❀◐⇌⊖🚌🐾📶

Hagen & Hyde ✔

157 Balham High Road, SW12 9AU

⏲ 3-11 Wed; 12-2am (11 Mon & Tue); 12-11 Sun

☎ (020) 8772 0016 🌐 hagenandhyde.com

3 changing beers (often Thornbridge, Volden) Ⓗ

A locally popular, eclectically decorated Antic pub over five floors and mezzanine levels. A large pair of windows dominates the façade, broken into smaller parts with wooden details that echo some of the sideboards within. Inside, umbrellas mounted in the ceiling provide an interesting talking point and help reduce noise from the bare-brick walls. The seating is functional and almost comfortable, with some nice benches.
❀◐♿⇌⊖🍎🚌🐾📶

Nightingale Ⓛ

97 Nightingale Lane, SW12 8NX

⏲ 12 (11 Sat)-midnight; 11-11 Sun ☎ (020) 8673 1637

🌐 thenightingalebalham.co.uk

Young's Bitter, Special; 3 changing beers (often By the Horns, St Austell, Sambrook's) Ⓗ

A country pub in town, this characterful local dates from the mid-19th century and features some fine etched-glass windows. It is renowned for its annual charity walk each June, which reached its 40th anniversary in 2019. There is a traditional public bar area at the front, while the larger but cosy saloon bar leads through to a rear extension and sheltered terrace garden.
♘❀◐♿⇌(Wandsworth Common)⊖(Clapham South)♣🚌(G1)🐾📶

SW13: Barnes

Red Lion

2 Castelnau, SW13 9RU

⏲ 11-11; 12-10.30 Sun ☎ (020) 8748 2984

🌐 red-lion-barnes.co.uk

Fuller's Oliver's Island, London Pride, ESB; 2 changing beers (often Dark Star, Fuller's) Ⓗ

Large Victorian landmark pub at the entrance to the Wetland Centre. Built in the 1830s and extensively refurbished in 2017, it has a spacious wood-panelled rear room that features a large coloured mosaic, central domed ceiling light and a fireplace. Outside is a covered patio and beyond that a large astroturfed garden with plenty of seating and a children's fenced play area. A garden bar has recently been opened for the summer months or as demand requires. Q♘❀◐♿P🚌🐾📶

SW16: Streatham

Earl Ferrers Ⓛ ✔

22 Ellora Road, SW16 6JF

⏲ closed Mon; 5-11 (midnight Thu & Fri); 1-midnight Sat; 1-11 Sun ☎ (020) 8835 8333 🌐 earlferrers.co.uk

Sambrook's Wandle Ale; 4 changing beers (often By the Horns, Twickenham) Ⓗ

Behind Streatham Leisure Centre, this Victorian single-room corner pub has been much improved over recent years. The airy main drinking and dining area is along the bar to the left as you enter. The changing beers are usually from local breweries, with the occasional beer from further afield. A draught cider is normally available. Outside tables and an enclosed back patio are suitable for smokers. Food is served all day at weekends. There is regular live music.
♘❀◐♿⇌(Streatham/Common)♣🍎📶

Railway Ⓛ ✔

2 Greyhound Lane, SW16 5SD

⏲ 12-11 (midnight Thu; 1am Fri & Sat) ☎ (020) 8769 9448

🌐 therailwaysw16.co.uk

Sambrook's Wandle Ale; 4 changing beers (often By the Horns, Redemption, Twickenham) Ⓗ

Close to Streatham Common station, this busy two-bar community pub showcases beers exclusively from London microbreweries, both cask and bottled. The back bar, which is available for hire, is open from 10am as a tearoom. There is seating outside and in the backyard. Regularly highly placed in the local CAMRA Pub of the Year ballot, it hosts a quiz on Tuesday, music nights and a popular comedy night on the last Sunday of the month. ♘❀◐♿⇌(Common)🚌(60,118)🐾📶

SW17: Summerstown

By the Horns Brewery Tap

25 Summerstown, SW17 0BQ

✪ closed Mon; 4-10.30 (11 Fri); 12-11 Sat; 2-10.30 Sun
☎ (020) 3417 7338 🌐 bythehorns.co.uk

3 changing beers (sourced locally) Ⓗ

A welcoming brewery taproom open Tuesday to Sunday. Three cask beers are usually on, with other draught and canned choices and occasional guests from small breweries. There is plenty of space in the bar and the enclosed area outside. Major sporting events are usually shown on two large projection TVs and are popular (it is often advisable to reserve your place in advance). Pizzas are available Thursday to Saturday evenings. Brewery tours and private event hire are also offered.
🐴❀P🚌🐾

SW17: Tooting

Antelope ✔

76 Mitcham Road, SW17 9NG

✪ 4-11 (midnight Thu; 1am Fri); 12-1am Sat; 12-11 Sun
☎ (020) 8672 3888 🌐 theantelopepub.com

Thornbridge Jaipur IPA; Volden Pale Ale; 4 changing beers (often Adnams) Ⓗ

A cavernous Victorian pub restored by Antic in 2009, featuring a panelled island bar and green-painted walls decorated with taxidermy and china plates. Friendly staff pour a variety of ales from different national breweries. At the back is a dining area, and a huge separate room known as the Anchor Bar open at weekends. The pub has real fires and serves popular Sunday roasts. There is a quiz on Monday, live music on Thursday and Sunday and various classes are held in the function room upstairs. 🐴❀◑♿⇌⊖(Broadway)🍎🚌🐾📶

SW18: Earlsfield

Jolly Gardeners ✔

214 Garratt Lane, SW18 4EA

✪ 12-11 (midnight Fri); 12-8 Sun ☎ (020) 8870 8417
🌐 thejollygardeners.com

Sambrook's Wandle Ale; 1 changing beer (sourced locally; often By the Horns) Ⓗ

A revived pub with a traditional feel, the U-shaped front bar featuring bare floorboards, old photographs of the area including a large one of the pub, and retro neon signs (some in the windows). There is a more spacious restaurant to the rear; a destination for dining out, especially for the Sunday lunches. 🐴❀◑⇌🚌🐾📶

SW18: Wandsworth

Cat's Back ✔

86-88 Point Pleasant, SW18 1NN

✪ 12-midnight (10 Mon); 12-10 Sun ☎ (020) 8617 3448
🌐 thecatsback.com

Harvey's IPA, Sussex Best Bitter, Old Ale; 1 changing beer Ⓗ

Harveys' first south-west London pub is an elegant, restrained refurbishment of a wonderful back-street local and a welcome survivor among the mass development of luxury riverside apartments that surrounds it. Four Harvey's cask beers are usually available: three regulars and one seasonal. The pub stages numerous events, including live music, a quiz night, impromptu comedy, a poker night, and life drawing classes, and it is the host of the annual Wandsworth fringe theatre. The food offering is excellent, especially Sunday lunch.
🐴❀◑♿♣🚌🐾📶

SW19: South Wimbledon

Trafalgar Ⓛ

23 High Path, SW19 2JY

✪ 12-11 (midnight Fri & Sat) ☎ (020) 8542 5342
🌐 trafalgarfreehouse.co.uk

Downton Quadhop; Surrey Hills Shere Drop; 4 changing beers (often Binghams, Great Heck, XT) Ⓗ

A narrow, one-bar, street-corner house dating from the 1860s with a 1906 extension. Refurbished in 2014, it is mostly carpeted, and furnished with farmhouse chairs and tables and Nelson memorabilia. Alongside the cask choice is an interesting range of bottled beers, canned beers and beers on tap, including KeyKeg varieties, and Lilley's Crazy Goat and guest ciders. Cold and hot snacks (pot meals) are available until 10pm. There is live music on Thursday evening and at other times. ❀🚊(Morden Rd)⊖♣🍎🚌🐾📶

SW19: Wimbledon

Hand in Hand Ⓛ

7 Crooked Billet, SW19 4RQ

✪ 11-11 (midnight Fri & Sat); 12-11 Sun ☎ (020) 8946 5720
🌐 thehandinhandwimbledon.co.uk

Courage Directors; Young's Bitter, Special; 5 changing beers (often Adnams, Young's) Ⓗ

Newly refurbished ale house on the edge of Wimbledon Common with separate drinking areas and a variety of seating. At least three guest beers are usually sold, increasingly from local breweries. Children are welcome in the garden room. This is a fine place to eat, inside or on the front patio, with beer included in several recipes. There is a monthly book club and occasional beer tastings and cellar tours. Four-legged friends are positively encouraged! Q🐴❀◑♿♣🚌(200)🐾

SW20: Raynes Park

Edward Rayne Ⓛ ✔

8-12 Coombe Lane, SW20 8ND

✪ 8am-11.30 ☎ (020) 8971 0420

Greene King IPA, Abbot; Sharp's Doom Bar; 6 changing beers (often Oakham, Thornbridge, Wimbledon) Ⓗ

A popular, comfortable and spacious Wetherspoon pub built in 2006, displacing a supermarket. The name commemorates the 19th-century landowner whose estate was sold for development of the railway and modern suburb. The half-panelled interior features mirrored pillars. A separate area at the rear is used mainly for dining, with accompanied children welcome until 9pm. Ciders are kept in a fridge behind the bar. Smokers can use the front veranda seating. Alcoholic drinks are served from 9am. Q🐴◑♿⇌🍎🚌📶

Carshalton

Hope 🏆 Ⓛ

48 West Street, SM5 2PR

✪ 12-11; 12-10.30 Sun ☎ (020) 8240 1255
🌐 hopecarshalton.co.uk

Downton New Forest Ale; Windsor & Eton Knight of the Garter; 5 changing beers Ⓗ

Traditional multi award-winning free house owned by a group of its regulars. Seven handpumps dispense a remarkable range of the country's finest beers, served in measures from third-pint upwards. The well-trained and knowledgeable staff can advise you about the latest offerings. In addition there is a good range of KeyKeg and bottled beers. Good value no-nonsense lunches are served until 3pm and pot meals until 10pm. Several times CAMRA Greater London Pub of the Year.
Q❀◐◑♿⇌♣🍎P🚆🚌🐾📶

Sun

4 North Street, SM5 2HU
⏲ 11-11 (10.30 Mon, midnight Fri & Sat); 12-10.30 Sun
☎ (020) 8773 4549 🌐 thesuncarshalton.com
6 changing beers (sourced nationally) [H]
This handsome and imposing Victorian pub was given a tasteful makeover several years ago and has not looked back since. Several distinct areas accommodate diners, with excellent food, and discerning drinkers, with a wide beer choice on six handpumps. In summer the large courtyard garden with its continental-style veranda is popular. The huge upstairs function room, available for hire, receives sunlight almost all day, hence the pub's name. Q🐴❀◐◑⇌♣🚌🐾📶

Kingston

Albion 🏆 L ✔

45 Fairfield Road, KT1 2PY
⏲ 12-11 (11.30 Fri & Sat); 12-10.30 Sun ☎ (020) 8541 1691
🌐 thealbionkingston.com
Big Smoke Solaris Session Pale Ale; 9 changing beers (often Big Smoke) [H]
One of a small chain that includes the Big Smoke Brewery, sharing a loyalty card scheme. Ales come from small breweries nationwide and there are up to five changing ciders. Varnished wooden floors and comfortable wood-panelled seating areas extend back to a rear patio garden with heaters. Music is from an extensive collection of vinyl LPs. Home-cooked food is served except on weekday afternoons. Local CAMRA Pub of the Year 2019.
🐴❀◐◑♿⇌🍎🚌🐾📶

Druid's Head ✔

3 Market Place, KT1 1JT
⏲ 11-11 (midnight Fri & Sat) ☎ (020) 8546 0723
Greene King IPA, Abbot; Timothy Taylor Landlord; 4 changing beers (often Park, Twickenham, Wimbledon) [H]
Kingston's oldest pub, originally a 17th-century coaching house. The old snug bar has been knocked through to become part of the split-level main bar, but the fireplace has been retained. Note the mews and interesting glasswork. There is a large, enclosed beer garden. Food is served every day until 10pm and includes traditional Sunday roasts. Upstairs rooms are available for hire. Live sports are shown. A Grade II*-listed building, the internal staircase and high rose ceiling can be viewed on request. Q🐴❀◐◑♿⇌🚌🐾📶

King's Tun L ✔

153-157 Clarence Street, KT1 1QT
⏲ 8am-midnight (1am Fri & Sat) ☎ (020) 8547 3827
Greene King IPA, Abbot; Oakham Citra; Sharp's Doom Bar; 8 changing beers (sourced locally) [H]
A Wetherspoon pub since 1997, in the former Empire theatre dating from 1910, and latterly a cinema, supermarket and Reject Shop. Two large bars on separate floors attract allcomers during the day, with a younger crowd in the often-busy evenings, with discos on Friday and Saturday nights from 9pm. Some guest beers come from local microbreweries; ciders include Westons Old Rosie and Gwynt y Ddraig Black Dragon. Alcoholic drinks are served from 9am. Children are welcome until 9pm. 🐴◐◑♿⇌🍎🚌📶

Willoughby Arms L

47 Willoughby Road, KT2 6LN
⏲ 10.30-midnight; 12-midnight Sun ☎ (020) 8546 4236
🌐 thewilloughbyarms.com
Hobsons Best; Twickenham Grandstand Bitter; Weltons Horsham Pale; 5 changing beers (often Long Man, Twickenham) [H]
Friendly Victorian back-street local, divided into a sports bar with games and large-screen TV, and a quieter lounge area. Now free of tie, it gets in beers from smaller breweries nationally. Upstairs is a soundproofed function room. Pizzas and pies are cooked to order. The spacious garden includes a covered, heated and lit smoking area with another large screen. Quiz night is Sunday. A loyalty card operates from 6pm on Sunday until Thursday. One or two beer festivals are held annually.
Q🐴❀♿♣🍎🚌(371,K5)🐾📶

Motspur Park

Earl Beatty ✔

365 West Barnes Lane, KT3 6JF
⏲ 12-11 (midnight Thu-Sat) ☎ (020) 8942 0263
Greene King IPA, London Glory, Abbot; house beer (by Greene King); 2 changing beers (often Twickenham, Wimbledon) [H]
Built in 1936 and named after the late Admiral of the Fleet. The front area on the corner was the public bar; this leads to the lounge area with a large TV above the fireplace, and then to the end saloon with the cask beers, usually from local breweries. Decor is modern in style, with abundant gastro-grey, the floor bare-boarded or tiled. Popular pub grub is reasonably priced. There is monthly live music and the back area of the saloon is available for hire. 🐴❀◐◑♿⇌P🚌(K5)📶

North Cheam

Nonsuch Inn ✔

552-556 London Road, SM3 9AA
⏲ 8am-midnight (1am Fri & Sat) ☎ (020) 8644 1808
Fuller's London Pride; Greene King Abbot; Ringwood Fortyniner; Ruddles Best Bitter; Sharp's Doom Bar; 5 changing beers [H]
This compact Wetherspoon pub opened in 1995 and stands on the site of the Granada cinema. It hosts occasional Meet the Brewer sessions that feature local breweries. The pub is named after what was probably the greatest of Henry VIII's palaces, which stood on the west side of today's Nonsuch Park. Its history is featured in texts and illustrations on the walls, along with a three-quarter-size statue of Henry VIII. Q🐴◐◑♿🍎🚌📶

Richmond

Mitre

20 St Mary's Grove, TW9 1UY
⏲ 3-11; 12-11 Sat; 12-9 Sun ☎ (020) 8940 1336
🌐 themitretw9.co.uk

Timothy Taylor Landlord; 6 changing beers (often Bristol Beer Factory, Tempest, Thornbridge) Ⓗ
A traditional pub tucked away off Sheen Road, simply furnished, with a decked area at the front and patio garden at the back. Leaded stained-glass windows feature different colourful church mitres. Six cask beers are on constant rotation from independent brewers outside the M25, with three handpumps dispensing cider or perry. A bar billiards table was recently acquired. Food can be delivered from Basilico Pizza. Rudi lives here, officially the cutest pub dog in Britain in a 2017 book.

Roebuck

130 Richmond Hill, TW10 6RN
12-11 (midnight Fri); 11-midnight Sat; 12-10.30 Sun
(020) 8948 2329
Greene King IPA, Abbot; 5 changing beers (often Purity, Surrey Hills, Thames Side) Ⓗ
Close to Richmond Park Gate, this 200-year-old pub overlooks the outstanding view of Petersham Meadows and the River Thames and has featured in a Sherlock Holmes movie. There are a number of comfortable secluded areas inside. The first floor has a function room and bar. Guest beers are on constant rotation and Old Rosie is now a regularly available cider. The outside terrace across the road can also be used by patrons. Local CAMRA Pub of the Year 2017. (371)

Tap Tavern

Princes Street, TW9 1ED
12-11.30 (1am Thu; 1.30am Fri & Sat); 12-10.45 Sun
(020) 8940 2118 taptavern.co.uk
3 changing beers (often Kew, Twickenham, Wimbledon) Ⓗ
Centrally located yet somewhat hidden away behind the main shopping street, the Tap (formerly the Richmond Arms) resembles a cross between a city pub and a craft beer bar. Mellow wood and pastel colours contrast with a zinc bar top and exposed brick, all with a watch-the-world-go-by ambience. The three – usually local – real ales are complemented by a daily listing of what is on the 17 keg taps. There is also an extensive bottle list and a modest food selection.

Surbiton

Antelope

87 Maple Road, KT6 4AW
12-11 (11.30 Fri & Sat); 12-10.30 Sun (020) 8399 5565
theantelope.co.uk
10 changing beers (sourced nationally; often Big Smoke) Ⓗ
The original home of the Big Smoke Brewery, from which two or three beers are usually available. The spacious split-level interior has a real fire in winter and a covered, heated and lit courtyard behind. Six changing ciders are usually sold. Home-cooked food includes Sunday roasts. Two beer festivals are held annually. Popular with locals and commuters, it can be particularly busy evenings and weekends. Local CAMRA Pub of the Year 2017 and 2018.

Black Lion

58 Brighton Road, KT6 5PL (on A243)
12-midnight; 12-11 Sun (020) 8399 8856
Surrey Hills Ranmore; Timothy Taylor Landlord; Young's Bitter, Special; 1 changing beer (often Harvey's) Ⓗ
Traditional, lively corner pub owned by Young's since 1840, when the coach to Brighton stopped outside. A dark-wood bar serves two areas, as well as some raised seating to the side. The lounge end is carpeted and has upholstered benches around the leaded windows, while the public end has a slate floor. Live sport is shown on TV. Quiz night is Tuesday, with bands playing twice a month on Thursday or Saturday. Seven letting rooms are available.

Coronation Hall

St Marks Hill, KT6 4LQ (on B3370)
8am-midnight (1am Fri & Sat) (020) 8390 6164
Greene King IPA, Abbot; Sharp's Doom Bar; 9 changing beers (sourced nationally) Ⓗ
Across the road from Surbiton Station, this Wetherspoon pub is in a 1911 building that has had a variety of former uses including music hall, cinema, bingo hall and nudist club. The decor is a mix of movie stars, film artefacts, the coronation of George V and the planets. Guest beers change regularly, many from local microbreweries. Occasionally the pub hosts local beer festivals. Westons Old Rosie and Orchard Pig Hogfather ciders are served. Children are welcome until 9pm.

Lamb

73 Brighton Road, KT6 5NF (on A243)
12-11.30 (12.30am Thu-Sat) (020) 8390 9229
lambsurbiton.co.uk
Black Sheep Best Bitter; Hop Back Summer Lightning; Surrey Hills Ranmore; 1 changing beer (sourced regionally) Ⓗ
Small, family-run free house, involved with the local community, especially in encouraging creative activities. Built in 1850 and formerly four separate rooms, it retains the original horseshoe-shaped bar. The pub had a small brewery in Victorian times. The changing beer is from a micro, sometimes local, or a family brewery. Specialist cheeses are always available, with cheeseboards on offer all day. Live music and other events are held regularly, including pop-up street food stalls in the garden.

Sutton

Shinner & Sudtone

67 High Street, SM1 1DT
4-midnight (11 Mon); 12-2am Fri & Sat; 12-11 Sun
(020) 8643 8395 shinnerandsudtone.com
3 changing beers (sourced nationally) Ⓗ
In the shopping area of Sutton, this is a pub acquired by Antic and decorated in its familiar shabby-chic style. Its name combines that of a former department store nearby and an old name for Sutton. The long bar has tables and chairs either side of a central walkway, leading to a small raised area at the rear. A Volden beer is usually available, and a board indicates guest beers waiting in the cellar. Quiz night is Tuesday.

WEST LONDON

W2: Bayswater

Champion

1 Wellington Terrace, W2 4LW
12-11 (midnight Fri & Sat); 12-10.30 Sun
(020) 7792 4527 thechampionpub.co.uk

Adnams Ghost Ship; 4 changing beers (often Purity, St Austell, Thornbridge) Ⓗ
The nearest pub to Kensington Palace, opposite the security-protected road on the northern side of Kensington Gardens. Built in 1838 and Grade II listed, it was refurbished in 2004 and spruced up more recently by owners Mitchells & Butlers. In warm weather the front windows are often opened into the bar with its tables and chairs and standing space. A plush basement area leads onto a sunken beer garden.
(Notting Hill Gate/Queensway)

Leinster Arms

17 Leinster Terrace, W2 3EU
12-11 (midnight Fri & Sat); 12-10.30 Sun
(020) 7402 4670
Fuller's London Pride; 3 changing beers (sourced nationally) Ⓗ
A Grade II-listed pub built in 1856 as the Scotch Stores and renamed 18 years later. The façade is impressive, the name extending across the arch to the adjacent mews. Inside are fascinating prints, portraits and paintings and a notable brewery mirror in the rear area. Beer mats and pumpclips on display attest to previous guest beers. Popular with tourists, it offers a loyalty card for regulars and locals. Quiz night is the first Monday of the month.
(Paddington) (Queensway)

W2: Little Venice

Bridge House ✔

13 Westbourne Terrace Road, W2 6NG
12-11 (11.30 Thu; midnight Fri & Sat); 12-10.30 Sun
(020) 7266 4326 thebridgehouselittlevenice.co.uk
Sharp's Doom Bar; Timothy Taylor Landlord; 2 changing beers (often St Austell, Thornbridge) Ⓗ
Dating from 1848, this pub beside the canal is now a lounge-styled bar, ideal for a quiet afternoon drink. There is a good solid bar counter, wooden floor and panelling, with old mirrors (Bass and HD Rawlings' High Class Mineral Waters) above the fireplace. A chandelier, pastel-painted walls, high and standard tables and chairs, and low easy chairs complete the setting. There is an extensive menu for lunch and dinner.
Q (Paddington) (Warwick Ave)

W2: Paddington

Mad Bishop & Bear

Upper Level, The Lawn, Paddington Station Concourse, W2 1HB
8am-11; 10-10.30 Sun (020) 7402 2441
Fuller's Oliver's Island, London Pride, ESB; 5 changing beers (often Dark Star, Fuller's) Ⓗ
Above the shopping complex just behind the station concourse, the modern pub interior features one long bar, railway memorabilia and train information screens. The raised areas can be hired for events and there are café-style seats outside. It may not be crowded even in the rush hour, but the bar may close early if football crowds are passing through.

Victoria ★

10A Strathearn Place, W2 2NH
11-11; 12-10.30 Sun (020) 7724 1191
Fuller's Oliver's Island Ⓗ/Ⓟ, London Pride, ESB; 3 changing beers (often Adnams, Fuller's) Ⓗ
There is plenty to admire in this Grade II-listed mid-Victorian inn, popular with tourists and locals alike. The nationally important historic interior includes ornately gilded mirrors above a crescent-shaped bar, painted tiles in wall niches and numerous portraits of Queen Victoria. The walls display cartoons, paperweights and a Silver Jubilee plate. Upstairs, via a spiral staircase, the Library and Theatre Bar provide extra space. Tuesday is quiz night. Paddington Station is a few minutes' walk away.
Q (Lancaster Gate/Paddington)

W3: Acton

George & Dragon

183 High Street, W3 9DJ
4-10 Mon; 4-11 Tue & Wed; 4-midnight Thu; 4-1am Fri; 12-1am Sat; 12-10.30 Sun (020) 8992 3712
georgeanddragonacton.co.uk
2 changing beers (often Clouded Minds) Ⓗ
At the heart of the historic Acton town centre, this Grade II-listed pub has three bars of real character. An atmospheric front bar, with a list of landlords dating back to 1759, leads through to a heritage bar with exposed original features, on to a cavernous and stylish back room. Two changing guest cask beers are served, and usually two real ciders. (Central)

Red Lion & Pineapple ✔

281 High Street, W3 9BP
8am-midnight (1am Fri & Sat) (020) 8896 2248
Greene King IPA, Abbot; Sharp's Doom Bar; 6 changing beers (often Binghams, Twickenham, Windsor & Eton) Ⓗ
A Wetherspoon pub formerly owned by Fuller's, originally two pubs which then combined. The larger room is home to the circular bar, surrounded by red and black tiles. The windows are large, with etched and stained tops, and the walls are decorated with photographs of old Acton. The smaller room is mainly for diners and families. Alcohol is served from 9am.
(Town)

West London Trades Union Club

33-35 High Street, W3 6ND
7pm-midnight (020) 8992 4557 wltuc.com
2 changing beers (often Nelson) Ⓗ
Small, friendly club, run as a co-operative, which combines excellent beer with a busy cultural and social life. Two real ales are served from a variety of independent breweries. The Acton Community Theatre is upstairs, and the club hosts summer barbecues in the courtyard. The local CAMRA branch is an associate member; show a CAMRA membership card or this Guide for entry.
Q (Central)

W3: North Acton

Castle

140 Victoria Road, W3 6UL
11-11 (midnight Fri) (020) 8992 2027
Fuller's London Pride; 2 changing beers (often Fuller's) Ⓗ
A 1938 Fuller's pub built for industrial North Acton and Park Royal, but now among new housing, hotels and student accommodation. BBC rehearsal rooms were next door and are reflected in historic photos in the bar. Usually busy with local workers

on weekday evenings, the pub is quieter during the day and at weekends. Seating areas surround the island bar, and there is a family room and a paved garden. ⛴🍴🍷🕹♿⊖P🚌♣🐾🛜

W4: Turnham Green

George IV
185 Chiswick High Road, W4 2DR
🕚 12-11 (1am Fri & Sat) ☎ (020) 8994 4624
Fuller's Oliver's Island, London Pride, ESB; 2 changing beers (often Anspach & Hobday, Fuller's, Windsor & Eton) Ⓗ
There has been an inn here in the heart of Chiswick since 1777, and the present inter-war pub is still reputed to have its own ghost, George. Inside, the different areas include the board game-themed mezzanine, while the Boston Room across the rear courtyard hosts events including a comedy club, and is available for private hire. Among the beers on offer are Fuller's small-batch brews. The pub normally has two staff with Fuller's Master Cellarman status. ⛴🍴🍷🕹♿⊖♣🚌🐾🛜

Tabard Ⓛ ✅
2 Bath Road, W4 1LW
🕚 12-11 (midnight Thu-Sat) ☎ (020) 8994 3492
Greene King IPA, Abbot; 7 changing beers (often Morland, Titanic, Truman's) Ⓗ
Built in 1880 as part of the Bedford Park estate, the first London garden suburb, this Grade II*-listed pub has a regionally important historic pub interior. Features include the replica swing sign (the original was painted by TM Rooke), interior tiling by William de Morgan and Walter Crane, and Arts and Crafts mirrors and pictures. Live music on Saturday evening and a quiz on Wednesday are usually held in the dining area. Upstairs is an intimate fringe theatre. ⛴🍴🍷🕹♿⊖♣🚌🐾🛜

W5: Ealing

Questors Grapevine Bar Ⓛ ✅
12 Mattock Lane, W5 5BQ
🕚 7-10.30 (11 Thu-Sat); 12-2.30, 7-10.30 Sun
☎ (020) 8567 0011 ⊕ questors.org.uk/grapevine
Fuller's London Pride; 2 changing beers Ⓗ
A friendly theatre club bar near the centre of Ealing and Walpole Park, run by enthusiastic volunteers. CAMRA members and Questors theatre ticket holders are also welcome. Guest beers include some from local breweries, beer festivals are held twice-yearly and there are malt whisky tastings. Some books and the odd board game are available. Local CAMRA Club of the Year 2019, and a former winner of the CAMRA national award.
Q⛴🍴🏵♿🚲⊖(Broadway)♣P🚌🐾🛜

Sir Michael Balcon ✅
46-47 The Mall, W5 3TJ
🕚 8-11.30 (midnight Fri & Sat) ☎ (020) 8799 2850
Greene King IPA, Abbot; Sharp's Doom Bar; 4 changing beers (often Adnams, Hogs Back, Sambrook's) Ⓗ
Located on the busy Uxbridge Road east of Ealing town centre, this became a Wetherspoon pub in 2008, named after the legendary film producer whose life and films form the basis of many of the wall displays. It is split level, with a raised area at the rear and a glass-covered area at the front for smokers. Q⛴🍴🍷🕹♿🚲⊖(Broadway)♥🚌🛜

W5: North Ealing

Greystoke Ⓛ ✅
7 Queens Parade, W5 3HU
🕚 11-11 (midnight Fri & Sat) ☎ (020) 8997 6388
Greene King IPA, Abbot; 5 changing beers (often Twickenham, Wimbledon) Ⓗ
A spacious family dining pub opposite North Ealing station, built in typical 1930s style, with affordable hot food and a changing selection of mostly local real ales. The single open-plan bar is comfortably furnished. All major sporting events from around the world (including NFL) are shown. The name derives from the Greystoke estate which owned Hanger Hill for many years.
⛴🍴🍷🕹♿⊖♣P🚌(112,483)🐾🛜

W6: Hammersmith

Andover Arms ✅
57 Aldensley Road, W6 0DL
🕚 12-11 ☎ (020) 8748 2155 ⊕ theandoverarms.com
Fuller's London Pride; Gale's Seafarers Ale; 1 changing beer (often Fuller's) Ⓗ
Hidden away in the back streets of Hammersmith, this popular and welcoming local is an enduring real ale champion with a rural feel about it. The attractive panelled bar counter, with its elaborate bar-back, separates two areas furnished with an assortment of dining tables and chairs. The kitchen offers a wide range of dishes lunchtimes and evenings. Quiz night is Sunday at 9pm.
⛴🍴🍷🕹⊖(Ravenscourt Park)♣🚌🐾🛜

Dove
19 Upper Mall, W6 9TA
🕚 11-11; 12-10.30 Sun ☎ (020) 8748 9474
Fuller's Oliver's Island, London Pride, ESB; 1 changing beer (often Fuller's, Gale's) Ⓗ
A Grade II-listed pub dating from the 1740s, with a regionally important historic interior, overlooking the Thames and hence often crowded in summer. The likes of Dylan Thomas, Ernest Hemingway and Alec Guinness have enjoyed a pint or two here. Down off the main bar area, a tiny public bar holds the Guinness world record for the smallest bar area. The food service can be slow at busy times but is worth the wait.
⛴🍴🍷🕹⊖(Ravenscourt Park)♥🚌🐾🛜

Plough & Harrow Ⓛ ✅
120-124 King Street, W6 0QU
🕚 8am-11.30 ☎ (020) 8735 6020
Fuller's London Pride; Greene King IPA, Abbot; Sharp's Doom Bar; 6 changing beers Ⓗ
On the site of an inn established in 1419, and more recently a Rolls-Royce showroom, this light and airy Wetherspoon pub dates from 2002. It has a mixture of stone and carpeted floors and a long metal-topped bar. Many of the guest beers come from microbreweries. There are several no-smoking tables outside. Alcoholic drinks are served from 9am.
Q⛴🍴🕹♿⊖(Hammersmith/Ravenscourt Park)🚌🛜

W7: Hanwell

Dodo Micropub Ⓛ
52 Boston Road, W7 3TR
🕚 closed Mon; 5-10 Tue; 12-2, 5-10 Wed & Thu; 12-10.30 Fri & Sat; 12-5 Sun ☎ (020) 8567 5959 ⊕ thedodomicropub.com
5 changing beers (sourced locally) Ⓖ

A classic micropub-style shop conversion that landed in Hanwell in early 2017. Up to five cask beers are served from a temperature-controlled cellar room at the rear, along with cider and wine. The beer range almost always includes some from local breweries. There is a small bar counter by the front door but table service is the order of the day here. Q ➤ ⇌ ● 🖪 🚍 ❄ 🛜

W8: Kensington

Elephant & Castle ✔
40 Holland Street, W8 4LT
🕐 11-11; 12-10.30 Sun ☎ (020) 7937 6382
Fuller's London Pride; Sharp's Doom Bar; St Austell Nicholson's Pale Ale; 3 changing beers (sourced nationally) Ⓗ
First licensed in 1865 as a beer house in what were two adjacent houses, and tucked away north-east of Kensington Town Hall, this busy, cosy, wood-panelled Nicholson's pub with its rural feel is a welcome refuge from the hurly-burly of Kensington High Street. Guest beers come from a wide range of breweries. Food, especially pies and sausages, is available all day except 4-5pm. Note the fine Charrington's bar-back. ➤ ❀ ◑ ⊖ (High St Kensington) 🚍 ❄ 🛜

W8: Notting Hill Gate

Churchill Arms
119 Kensington Church Street, W8 7LN
🕐 11-11 (midnight Thu-Sat); 12-10.30 Sun
☎ (020) 7727 4242
Fuller's Oliver's Island, London Pride, ESB; 2 changing beers (often Fuller's) Ⓗ
A multi award-winning, deservedly popular pub with a regionally important historic interior including snob screens, now rare. Churchillian and Irish memorabilia are among the bric-a-brac suspended from the panelled ceiling. The Thai restaurant in the conservatory was one of the first such in a London pub. Outside, at busy times, drinkers stand on the pavement below the numerous hanging flower baskets; at Christmas, the tree decorations are quite something to behold. Q ➤ ◑ ● ⊖ 🚍 ❄ 🛜

Windsor Castle ★ ✔
114 Campden Hill Road, W8 7AR
🕐 12-11; 12-10.30 Sun ☎ (020) 7243 8797
🌐 thewindsorcastlekensington.co.uk
Marston's Pedigree; Timothy Taylor Landlord; 4 changing beers Ⓗ
A back-street Grade II-listed pub built in 1830. Sited on a corner, it contrasts an old-world rural feel with a modern upmarket service and menu style. The bar room is divided into four drinking areas but, surprisingly, the partitions and other wood-panelling of the nationally important historic interior are not original but date from a 1933 refurbishment. Four of the real ales on offer rotate through some interesting brews. The beer garden to the rear boasts its own bar. Q ➤ ❀ ◑ ● ⊖ 🚍 ❄ 🛜

W9: Westbourne Park

Union Tavern 🄻
45 Woodfield Road, W9 2BA
🕐 12-11 (midnight Fri & Sat); 12-10.30 Sun
☎ (020) 7286 1886

Five Points Pale; Fuller's London Pride; 3 changing beers (often Windsor & Eton) Ⓗ
In a radical departure by Fuller's, this unbranded beer house offers cask ales from within 30 miles and, with only one exception, from London. A mainly young crowd enjoys reduced beer prices on Monday, various music nights and a Meet the Brewer event on the first Tuesday of the month. Good-value food is another attraction, with traditional Sunday lunches. The canalside terrace comes into its own on a warm, sunny day. ➤ ❀ ◑ ● 🚍 ❄ 🛜

W12: Shepherds Bush

Defector's Weld 🄻
170 Uxbridge Road, W12 8AA
🕐 12-midnight (2am Fri & Sat); 12-11 Sun
☎ (020) 8749 0008 🌐 defectors-weld.co.uk
Young's Bitter, Special; 3 changing beers (often Redemption, Truman's, Twickenham) Ⓗ
Since Young's took over this pub, it has continued to rotate local guest beers. The large horseshoe-shaped main bar has a welcoming mix of sofas, tables and chairs. An upstairs bar is available for hire. DJs play music Thursday to Sunday evenings (no admission after midnight Fri & Sat). Home fans only are admitted on Queen's Park Rangers match days, but card-carrying CAMRA members not wearing team colours are welcome. Q ❀ ◑ ♿ ⊖ (Shepherd's Bush/Market) 🚍 ❄ 🛜

W13: West Ealing

Drayton Court Hotel
2 The Avenue, W13 8PH
🕐 7am-11 (midnight Wed-Fri); 8am-midnight Sat; 8am-10 Sun ☎ (020) 8997 1019
Dark Star Hophead; Fuller's London Pride; 2 changing beers (often Fuller's, Gale's) Ⓗ
Known locally as Dracula's Castle owing to its neo-Gothic and towered brick construction, this large pub was fairly recently reconverted to a hotel. Ho Chi Minh is believed to have worked as a chef here. The downstairs function room has been completely refurbished and has its own bar. Regular music nights are held, particularly jazz. Quiz evenings, chess tournaments and an annual beer festival also feature. It has one of the largest pub gardens in West London. ➤ ❀ 🛏 ◑ ♿ ⇌ ♣ ● P 🚍 ❄ 🛜

Forester ★ ✔
2 Leighton Road, W13 9EP
🕐 11-11.30 (midnight Thu; 1am Fri & Sat); 11-11 Sun
☎ (020) 8567 1654 🌐 theforesterealing.com
Dark Star Hophead; Fuller's London Pride, ESB; 3 changing beers (often Adnams, Butcombe, Fuller's) Ⓗ
Built in 1909 from designs by Nowell Parr for the Royal Brewery of Brentford and bought by Fuller's in 2012, this pub has a nationally important historic interior. Thai and English food are available daily, except Sundays when the traditional carvery is served until 6pm. Wednesdays are quiz nights and on Thursdays there are poker tournaments. Two guest beers are supplemented by two additional beers from Fuller's (often Gale's HSB) and two beer festivals are held annually.
➤ ❀ ◑ ♿ ⊖ (Northfields) ♣ ● 🚍 (E2,E3) ❄ 🛜

Owl & the Pussycat 🏆 🄻
106 Northfield Avenue, W13 9RT
🕐 4-10; 1-10.30 Fri & Sat; closed Sun 🌐 markopaulo.co.uk

6 changing beers (sourced locally; often Marko Paulo) [H]
Unique to West London, this combination of microbrewery and pub retains the ambience of the bookshop it once was. Drinkers can view the brewing process while readers can browse the beer-related books and magazines. All the beers are currently brewed on the premises. The ciders, if not home-produced, are often from Oliver's. In this small, friendly environment, conversation is all-important. Local CAMRA Pub of the Year and Cider Pub of the Year for 2019. Q⊖♣🍎🚌(E2,E3)📶

Brentford

Black Dog Beer House

17 Albany Road, TW8 0NF
⏲ 12-11 (11.30 Fri & Sat); 12-10.30 Sun ☎ (020) 8568 5688
🌐 blackdogbeerhouse.co.uk
7 changing beers (often East London Brewing, Manchester Brewing, Tiny Rebel) [H]
Swiftly becoming a local favourite after reopening in 2018, this landmark building is a former Royal Brewery (Brentford) pub dating back to at least 1861. The light and open L-shaped room has plenty of seating, no TVs, music from classic vinyl LPs and an eclectic food menu. As well as seven real ales and five ciders, 14 more beers and ciders on keg taps are listed on two chalkboards. Dogs are welcome, though sadly the eponymous hound lives elsewhere. ❀◑⇄♣🍎🚌🐾📶

Express Tavern

56 Kew Bridge Road, TW8 0EW
⏲ 11-11 (midnight Fri & Sat) ☎ (020) 8560 8484
🌐 expresstavern.co.uk
Big Smoke Solaris Session Pale Ale; Draught Bass; Harvey's Sussex Best Bitter; 7 changing beers (sourced nationally) [H]
A local landmark since the 1800s, still featuring its illuminated external Bass signage, with Draught Bass remaining a fixture on the bar. It has a regionally important historic pub interior. The Chiswick Bar dispenses the ales and has an upright piano and music on vinyl LPs, while the Saloon and Lounge Bar handpumps serve five ciders and perries. At the rear is a beer garden with a covered and heated terrace.
❀◑♿⇄⊖(Kew Bridge)♣🍎🚌🐾📶

Feltham

Moon on the Square ✔

30 The Centre, High Street, TW13 4AU
⏲ 8am-midnight; 8am-10.30 Sun ☎ (020) 8893 1293
Bombardier; Courage Best Bitter; Greene King Abbot; Ruddles Best Bitter; changing beers (often Reunion, Thames Side, Twickenham) [H]
This real ale oasis continues to flourish. The spacious interior is early Wetherspoon, featuring split-level floors with a central square spiral staircase and glass-partitioned booths. The real ale range includes continually varying guests, often local brews, with a bar-top gravity cask during beer festival events in April and October. Westons cider is available. Alcoholic drinks are served from 9am, and food all day, starting with breakfast. Families with children are welcome until 6pm.
🐴◑♿⇄🍎🚌📶

Greenford

Black Horse

425 Oldfield Lane North, UB6 0AS
⏲ 11.30-11 (midnight Thu; 1am Fri); 9am-1am Sat; 9am-10.30 Sun ☎ (020) 8578 1384
Fuller's London Pride, ESB; 1 changing beer (often Dark Star, Fuller's, Gale's) [H]
Tastefully extended canalside pub close to mainline rail, tube and bus routes, with a landscaped garden. Bargees, cyclists and walkers are frequent visitors. Good food includes traditional Sunday roasts and is available 12-3, 6-9pm Monday to Thursday, 12-9pm Friday to Sunday. There is TV, a quiz on Thursday and live music on Friday and Saturday.
Q🐴❀◑♿⇄⊖♣P🚌(92,395)🐾📶

Hampton

Jolly Coopers

16 High Street, TW12 2SJ
⏲ 11-11 (midnight Fri & Sat); 12-10.30 Sun
☎ (020) 8979 3384 🌐 squiffysrestaurant.co.uk
Courage Best Bitter; Hop Back Summer Lightning; 2 changing beers (often Ascot, Reunion) [H]
A popular, traditional community pub, proud of its heritage; a wooden wall panel lists landlords from 1727 to the present owners, who took over in 1986. The small horseshoe bar features guest beers mainly from local breweries. Walls are adorned with water jugs and local memorabilia, including some coopers' tools. Extensive tapas and traditional food, including Sunday lunches (booking essential), are served in Squiffy's restaurant and, weather permitting, on the sun patio outside.
🐴❀◑⇄♣🚌🐾📶

Hampton Court

Mute Swan

3 Palace Gate, KT8 9BN
⏲ 11-11 (midnight Fri & Sat); 11-10.30 Sun
☎ (020) 8941 5959 🌐 muteswan.co.uk
House beer (by St Austell); 5 changing beers (often Crafty Beers, Red Cat, Wimbledon) [H]
A friendly pub and dining room opposite the palace gates. A good selection of food can be consumed either upstairs or in the main bar. Bar bites are also listed on a chalkboard. The cask beers change frequently, with a cider on handpump often available. Seating and tables are provided outside. There are no TV screens to spoil the atmosphere of this popular pub, which draws locals and tourists alike. No prams are allowed inside.
◑⇄♣🍎🚌🐾📶

Hampton Hill

Roebuck

72 Hampton Road, TW12 1JN
⏲ 11-11 (11.30 Fri & Sat); 12-4, 7-10.30 Sun
☎ (020) 8255 8133 🌐 roebuck-hamptonhill.co.uk
St Austell Tribute; Sambrook's Junction Ale; Young's Bitter; 2 changing beers (often Hammerpot, Triple fff, Windsor & Eton) [H]
Comfortable Victorian street-corner pub with screens dividing the single bar into various seating areas. An amazing array of bric-a-brac and other displays (framed banknotes, military memorabilia, model seaplanes, cigar-store Indian and the wickerwork Harley-Davidson) keeps growing, but

does not detract from the comfort of the pub. The real fire never goes out in winter. Outside, the small garden has a gazebo for smokers and there is a room (available for hire) for cooler evenings. ❀⇌(Fulwell)

Harlington

White Hart

158 High Street, UB3 5DP

11-11 (11.30 Thu; midnight Fri & Sat); 12-11 Sun ☎ (020) 8759 9608

Fuller's London Pride, ESB; 1 changing beer (sourced locally; often Dark Star, Fuller's, Gale's) Ⓗ

Large, Grade II-listed Fuller's pub standing proud at the north end of the village. The bar provides access to an open-plan area with soft seating, leading to an area favoured by diners. It was refurbished in 2009 to improve facilities and create the open feel it has now. Local history is the theme of the wall displays, enjoyed by regulars and visitors from the nearby Heathrow Airport. Quiz night is Thursday. Fuller's or Gale's seasonal ales are sometimes on the bar. ❀♿P

Hatton

Green Man ✔

Green Man Lane, TW14 0PZ

12-11 (midnight Fri & Sat) ☎ (020) 8890 2681

Greene King IPA, London Glory; Morland Old Speckled Hen Ⓗ

A surprisingly rural-looking pub for the area, dating from 1640. Recently it was sympathetically refurbished with several seating areas and varying floor levels; look out for low beams (though they are padded). The area at the front and large garden to the side provide good views of aircraft passing directly overhead on their way into Heathrow Airport – they can also be clearly heard. ❀⊖(Hatton Cross)♣

Hayes

Botwell Inn ✔

25-29 Coldharbour Lane, UB3 3EB

9am-midnight ☎ (020) 8848 3112

Greene King Abbot; Ruddles Best Bitter; Sharp's Doom Bar; 3 changing beers (often Adnams, Hogs Back, Windsor & Eton) Ⓗ

A large Wetherspoon pub opened in 2000 following a shop conversion from furnishers S Moore and Son, with several areas for dining and drinking. There is a fenced paved area to the front and a patio at the rear with large parasols with heaters. At least one Westons cider is stocked. Several beer festivals are held annually. Q❀♿⇌⊖(Hayes & Harlington)

Hounslow

Moon Under Water ✔

84-88 Staines Road, TW3 3LF

8am-midnight ☎ (020) 8572 7506

Greene King Abbot; Ruddles Best Bitter; Sharp's Doom Bar; 5 changing beers (sourced nationally) Ⓗ

Opening at 8am but licensed from 9am, this is a 1991 Wetherspoon shop conversion in original style, still displaying many local history panels and photographs. It is a regular venue for the town's beer lovers, also attracting others from surrounding areas. Up to five guest ales are offered, both national and local, with more at festival times, when 10 handpumps are put to work. The cider is usually Westons Old Rosie. Families are welcome until 7pm. Q❀♿⊖(Central)

Isleworth

London Apprentice ✔

62 Church Street, TW7 6BG

11-11 ☎ (020) 8560 1915

Greene King IPA, Abbot; 3 changing beers (often Oakham) Ⓗ

Famous Grade II-listed former Isleworth Brewery riverside pub in old Isleworth. In Tudor times it stayed open all night for the benefit of Thames travellers. Rebuilt in the early 1700s, the interior is classic traditional, although opened out, with an upstairs Riverview Room. One real cider is available (summer only). The large patio has many tables, with more on the riverbank. With good food, a Thursday poker night, varied music most Friday evenings and a Sunday quiz, it is well worth a visit. ❀♿P

St Margarets

Crown

174 Richmond Road, Twickenham, TW1 2NH

11-11 (11.30 Fri & Sat); 11-10.30 Sun ☎ (020) 8892 5896

crowntwickenham.co.uk

Harvey's Sussex Best Bitter; Oakham Citra; Surrey Hills Shere Drop; 1 changing beer (often Big Smoke, Twickenham) Ⓗ

A spacious pub from about 1730 and Grade II listed, with a substantial refurbishment enhancing the Georgian heritage of the original building. The Victorian hall at the back has been opened up for dining and the courtyard garden attractively remodelled. Inside are various seating areas and three fireplaces, one with a real fire. Several windows and doors are original and listed. Food is served 12-9.30pm (10pm Fri & Sat). ❀♿⇌P

Teddington

Masons Arms 🏆

41 Walpole Road, TW11 8PJ

12-11 (11.30 Fri & Sat); 12-10.30 Sun ☎ (020) 8977 6521

the-masons-arms.co.uk

Sambrook's Junction Ale; Wimbledon SW19; 2 changing beers (often Andwell, Coastal, Kissingate) Ⓗ

Small, friendly back-street community free house and a beer drinkers' haven, as reflected in the bottles, pictures and pub memorabilia on display (including an infamous Watney's Party Seven). Carpeting and comfortable seating create a cosy atmosphere. There is a log-burning stove, a dartboard and a small secluded rear patio. Guest beers come from a wide range of UK independent brewers, and the cider changes frequently. Bring-your-own vinyl nights are once a month. Local CAMRA Pub of the Year for 2018. ❀♿⇌♣

Twickenham

Sussex Arms

15 Staines Road, TW2 5BG

12-11 (11.30 Fri & Sat); 12-10.30 Sun ☎ (020) 8894 7468

thesussexarmstwickenham.co.uk

Big Smoke Solaris Session Pale Ale, Underworld Milk Stout; Harvey's Sussex Best Bitter; changing beers (sourced nationally) Ⓗ
A traditional pub with a real fire, now a firm favourite with beer lovers. Fifteen handpumps showcase independent UK breweries alongside six ciders and perries. Acoustic music features regularly, and music is also played on vinyl LPs. Food includes Anthea's famous pies and much more. Quiz night is Wednesday. Every 10th pint of ale is free with the chain's loyalty card. Twice CAMRA Greater London Cider Pub of the Year and local CAMRA Pub of the Year.
❀◐⇌(Strawberry Hill)♣🍎🚌🐾📶

White Swan

Riverside, TW1 3DN
☉ 11-11 (10.30 Mon); 11-10.30 Sun ☎ (020) 8744 2951
🌐 whiteswantwickenham.co.uk
Twickenham Naked Ladies; 4 changing beers (often Otter, Reunion, West Berkshire) Ⓗ
A Grade II-listed building and award-winning traditional pub, built around 1690. Entry is via steps up to the first floor, where the rooms have real fires and walls covered with rugby and other memorabilia. A small veranda/balcony and a triclinium (three-sided room with window seats) afford views of the river and Eel Pie Island. Directly opposite is a larger beer garden (tides permitting), right on the water's edge. A summer beer festival and an annual raft race are held.
Q🐴❀◐⇌🚌🐾📶

Uxbridge

Queen's Head Ⓛ ✔

54 Windsor Street, UB8 1AB
☉ 11-11 (midnight Thu; 1am Fri & Sat); 12-10.30 Sun
☎ (01895) 258750
Greene King IPA, Abbot; 5 changing beers (often Rebellion, Twickenham) Ⓗ
A Grade II-listed mid 19th-century pub that still retains its old feel, opposite the church and a few yards down from the tube station. The decorations and furnishings are in keeping with its age. It has bay windows, wooden floorboards, low ceilings and walls largely of exposed brick, and an irregularly shaped bar. Local CAMRA 2019 Pub of the Year in the Hillingdon area. 🐴◐⊖🚌🐾📶

Black Friar, EC4: Blackfriars (Photo: Emma Haines)

CAMRA's
Peak District Pub Walks

Bob Steel

Bob Steel's classic *Peak District Pub Walks* has been tempting people into the magnificent hills, dales and inns of the national park for over a decade.

Now fully revised, this third edition introduces many completely new routes, whilst favourite walks from previous editions have been altered and updated to reflect the changing Peakland pub scene. These walks not only reveal the wonderful diversity of the Peak landscape, from atmospheric gritstone moorland to deep limestone gorges, but are also an exploration and celebration of the area's abundant industrial and transport heritage.

For the outdoor enthusiast and real-ale lover alike, this book is an indispensable guide to the scenic highlights and some of the best pubs of the region.

RRP: £12.99 **ISBN:** 978-1-85249-353-0 **176 pages**

For this and other books on beer and pubs visit CAMRA's online bookshop at **shop.camra.org.uk** or call **01727 867201**

Discounts are available for CAMRA members.

GREATER MANCHESTER

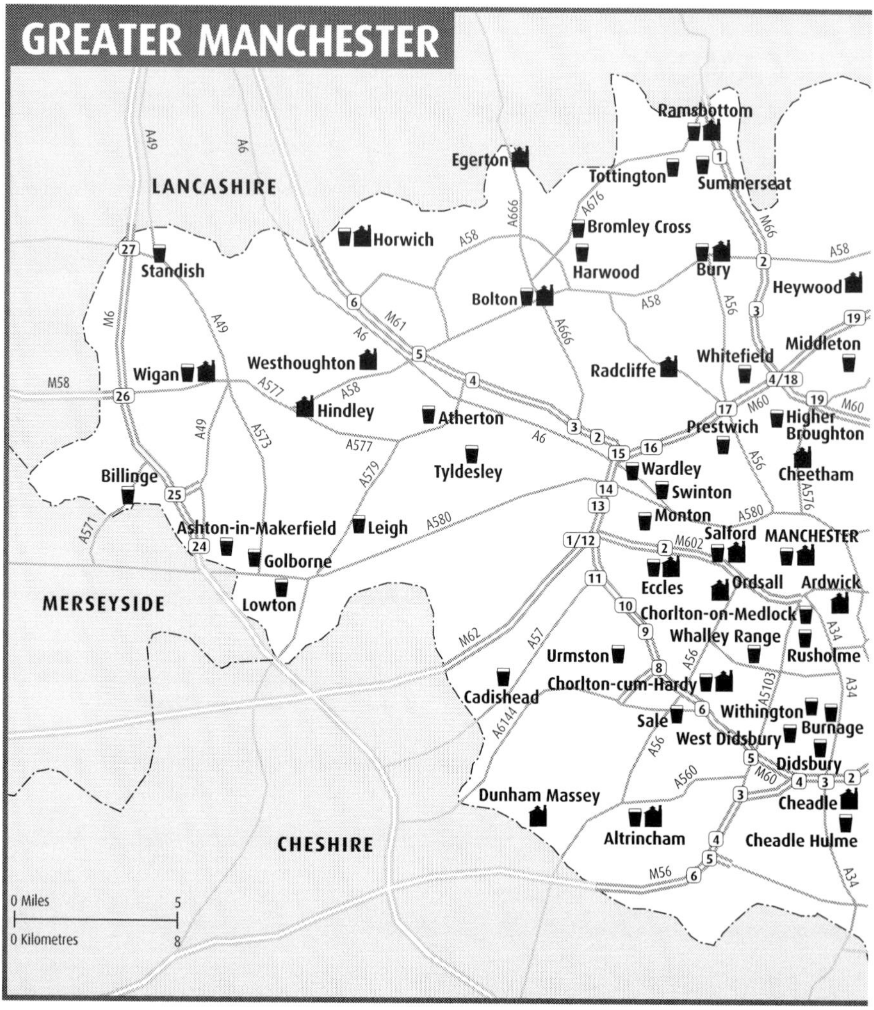

Altrincham

Costello's Bar

18 Goose Green, WA14 1DW (alleyway from Stamford New Rd)

12-11 (midnight Thu; 1am Fri & Sat) ☎ (0161) 929 0903

costellosbar.co.uk

Dunham Massey Big Tree Bitter, Dunham Dark; 5 changing beers (sourced locally; often Dunham Massey) H

This small bar is situated in Altrincham's attractive and popular Goose Green, behind the new hospital. The tap house for Dunham Massey Brewery, it has a modern feel and is a favourite with both locals and visitors. On the bar there are seven handpumps which feature a continually changing selection of beers from the brewery's 25 recipes. There are a large number of award certificates adorning the walls, reflecting the high regard the bar is held in.

Jack in the Box

Market Hall, Market Street, WA14 1SA

closed Mon; 12-10; 12-6 Sun ☎ 07917 792060

blackjack-beers.com

Blackjack JITB House Pale; 4 changing beers (sourced nationally) H

Inside the popular Altrincham Market House, part of the town's historic market, this is one of the Blackjack Brewery's bars. Six handpumps on the bar sit alongside eight keg fonts. Blackjack beers are always available as well as a changing cider. The guest beers are from local breweries including Track, Squawk and Stubborn Mule, plus others further afield. The casks are housed in a chilled cellar behind the bar.

Old Packet House

1 Navigation Road, WA14 1LW

12-11 (midnight Fri); 11-midnight Sat; 12-10.30 Sun

☎ (0161) 929 1331

Dunham Massey Little Bollington Bitter; Timothy Taylor Golden Best, Landlord H

Dating back to the 18th century, this was once the second inn on the journey from Manchester along the Bridgewater Canal, which runs just behind the pub. Leaded and stained glass feature in the back bar and partitions around the pub. The main bar area is divided by an impressive central chimney, warmed by a real fire in winter. Home-cooked food

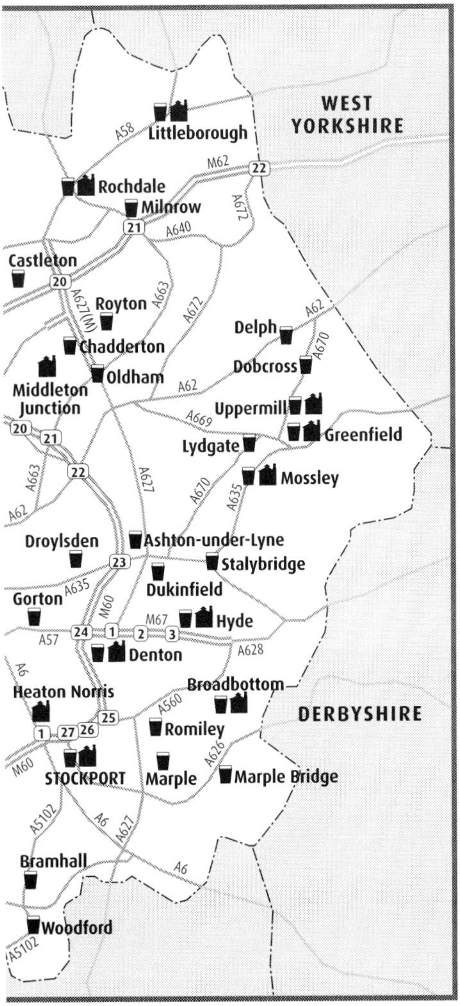

is popular with local office workers at lunchtime. Attractions include quiz night on Monday and karaoke on Friday. A spacious beer garden at the rear is perfect for sunny days. (Navigation Road) P

Pi L

18 Shaws Road, WA14 1QU

11-11 (midnight Fri & Sat) (0161) 929 9098

abarcalledpi.com

Tatton Blonde; 2 changing beers (sourced nationally; often RedWillow, Saltaire, First Chop Brewing Arm) H

Next door to the bustling Market Hall eatery, the smaller Pi is quieter but still popular. The bar is on the ground floor; upstairs is a larger room with more tables and seating. As well as a beer garden to the rear there are pavement tables with blankets for cooler weather. Pi serves one regular beer from Tatton Brewery, plus two guests from micros or more established, but still small, breweries. Pieminister pies and mash are served until 10pm daily. The bar is a sibling to Pi (Chorlton).

Ashton-in-Makerfield

Caledonian Hotel

154 Bolton Road, WN4 8PF

5-11.30; 3-midnight Fri; 12-1am Sat; 12.30-11.30 Sun

(01942) 727875

2 changing beers (sourced regionally) H

A large former Walkers free house, built in 1897, featuring an open-plan lounge, games room with large-screen TV and an upstairs function room. Two guest beers are served. Attractions include popular Thursday quiz nights and pool teams based at the pub. Open mic sessions are held on Tuesday; artists perform in the lounge most Saturday evenings. Prints of old Ashton are of interest. The pub holds occasional mini beer festivals. P

Hingemakers Arms

34 Heath Road, WN4 9DY

1.30-11 (11.30 Fri); 11.30-11.30 Sat; 11.30-11 Sun

(01942) 729317 thehingemakersarms.co.uk

1 changing beer H

An old pub located just off the main road into Ashton, the Hingemakers Arms is the only one in the world known to carry that name. It was run by the Corless family for decades until Walter Corless's retirement in 2006. The Hinge, as it is known by its clientele, is a true community pub – owned and run by locals, used by locals and appreciated by visitors as being a cut above the usual chain alternatives. P

Twisted Vine Ale House

15 Wigan Road, WN4 9AR

closed Mon & Tue; 4-10 Wed (11 Thu); 12-11 Fri & Sat; 1-10 Sun

7 changing beers (sourced regionally) H

A microbar from Hophurst Brewery, it opened in February 2018 offering seven cask handpumps, six keg taps, three real ciders and a selection of gins, spirits and wines. The pub has a quiz night and beer club, and hosts live music on Sundays and the first Thursday of the month. Dog-friendly, it is open to over-18s only. Local CAMRA Best New Cask Outlet 2018.

Ashton-under-Lyne

Ash Tree

9-11 Wellington Road, OL6 6DA

8am-midnight (0161) 339 9670

Greene King Abbot; Moorhouse's Blond Witch; Ruddles Best Bitter H; Sharp's Doom Bar; 4 changing beers (sourced regionally) H/G

Directly facing the Victorian market hall, this pub was extended into the former snooker hall next door in early 2019. Its new upper-floor veranda overlooks a beer garden that stretches the depth of the building, creating a space that is particularly attractive in fine weather. The pub's 11 handpumps serve Wetherspoon's regular beers plus others sourced locally and nationwide.

Ashton Tap House L

Unit 16, Ashton Market Hall, Market Street, OL6 7JU

10.30-5; closed Sun 07779 417117

3 changing beers (sourced locally; often Donkeystone, Fool Hardy Ales) H

Ashton's historic outdoor market is one of the largest in north-west England, but this bar in the market hall is one of the smallest to be found anywhere. Four tables are crammed into a stall, creating a cosy place to enjoy a pint while watching the market's business take place. No food is served but you are welcome to purchase pies from nearby stalls and eat them while enjoying your beer. Q

Dog & Pheasant

528 Oldham Road, OL7 9PQ

12-11; 12-11.30 Fri & Sat ☎ (0161) 330 4894

Marston's Saddle Tank, Pedigree H; 3 changing beers H/G

This popular, friendly local near the Medlock Valley Country Park has been a regular in this Guide since 1992. The large U-shaped large bar serves three areas, plus another room at the front. The beer range is supplemented by three guest beers from the Marston's portfolio. A menu of good-value food includes vegetarian options. Quiz nights are on Thursday evenings and open mic evenings take place on Monday. P (409,419)

Atherton

Pendle Witch

2-4 Warburton Place, M46 0EQ

3-11 Mon-Wed; 12-11.30 ☎ (01942) 884537

Moorhouse's Black Cat, Premier Bitter, Pride of Pendle, Blond Witch, Pendle Witches Brew; 2 changing beers H

A real gem hidden down a narrow alley. The entrance, part of a conservatory, leads to an open-plan bar that serves the full range of Moorhouse's beers plus guests. A large selection of Belgian bottled beers is also kept. The games area has a pool table and large-screen TV. Regular rock nights are hosted and food is served during the day, with a quiz night on Thursday. There is a well-kept patio at the rear, popular in summer. Parking is close by in the town centre. P (V2)

Wheatsheaf

48 Market Street, M46 0DG

12-midnight ☎ (01942) 895229

3 changing beers (sourced locally) H

The Wheatsheaf was comprehensively refurbished a few years ago, regaining its old name and retaining its best original features. It has kept the separate snug and games room for pool and darts, and has a large outdoor drinking area to the rear. Beers usually include a selection of three competitively priced offerings from local breweries. Live sport is shown on screens around the pub. Open to over-18s only. P (V2,582)

Billinge

Masons Arms

99 Carr Mill Road, WN5 7TY

2-11 (midnight Wed & Fri; 11.30 Thu); 12-midnight Sat; 12-11 Sun ☎ (01744) 603572 masonsarmsbillinge.co.uk

5 changing beers (sourced regionally)

Built in 1779 and run by the same family for over 200 years, the pub is well placed for walking or cycling in the local area. Five handpumps offer regularly changing guest beers alongside up to four real ciders. There is a smoking shelter with a logburner and a beer garden overlooking fields at the back. Dogs and children are welcome. Sky Sports is screened. Quiz night is Wednesday. Locally baked Burchall's pork pies are available Fridays only – be quick, they sell fast. P

Bolton

Bank Top Brewery Tap

68-70 Belmont Road, Astley Bridge, BL1 7AN

12-11 (11.30 Fri & Sat) ☎ (01204) 302837

banktopbrewery.com

REAL ALE BREWERIES

Alphabet Manchester
Bank Top Bolton
Beatnikz Republic Manchester
Beer Nouveau Manchester: Ardwick
Blackedge Horwich
Blackjack Manchester
Bootleg Chorlton-cum-Hardy
Brightside Radcliffe
Cheadle Cheadle (NEW)
Chorlton Manchester: Ardwick
Cloudwater Manchester
Deeply Vale Bury
Donkeystone Greenfield
Dunham Massey Dunham Massey
Federation Altrincham
First Chop Eccles
Fool Hardy Stockport: Heaton Norris
Four Kings Hyde
Gasworks Manchester
Green Mill Broadbottom
Greenfield Greenfield
Hay Rake Littleborough
Holy Well Egerton
Hophurst Hindley
Howfen Westhoughton (NEW)
Hydes Salford
Irwell Works Ramsbottom
Joseph Holt Cheetham
JW Lees Middleton Junction
Made of Stone Stockport (NEW)
Manchester Manchester
Manchester Union Manchester (NEW)
Marble Salford
Martland Mill Wigan
Mayflower Hindley
Millstone Mossley
Northern Monkey Bolton
Origami Manchester: Ardwick
Outstanding Manchester: Ordsall
Phoenix Heywood
Pictish Rochdale
Pomona Island Salford
Prospect Wigan
Remedy Stockport
Rising Sun Mossley
Robinsons Stockport
Runaway Manchester
Saddleworth Uppermill
Serious Rochdale
Seven Bro7hers Salford
Silver Street Bury
Squawk Manchester: Ardwick
Stockport Stockport
Stubborn Mule Altrincham
Thirst Class Stockport
Track Manchester
Tweed Denton
Wander Beyond Manchester
Watts Brewing? Stockport
Wigan Wigan
Wily Fox Wigan

Bank Top Dark Mild, Flat Cap, Pavilion Pale Ale; 5 changing beers (sourced locally; often Bank Top) ⊞
The original tap house for the multi award-winning Bank Top Brewery, based less than a mile away. This street-corner community local comprises two rooms plus a large outdoor area with smoking shelter. There are eight handpumps showcasing the brewery's ales – including regulars Flat Cap, Pavilion Pale and Dark Mild plus the current seasonal – and a guest beer. Up to six cellar-cool bag-in-box real ciders are also on offer.
🏠🕸️&♣️●🚐🐌🛜

Barristers Bar

7 Bradshawgate, BL1 1EL (entrance in passageway at rear of Swan Hotel)
🕐 10-2am (4am Thu; 6am Fri & Sat); 10-4am Sun
☎ (01204) 365174
6 changing beers (sourced locally; often Bank Top, Blackedge, Moorhouse's) ⊞
Barristers is a separate bar behind the Swan Hotel, a Grade II-listed building dating from 1845. The wood-panelled interior has been retained to recreate a traditional pub atmosphere, though the bar gets lively with karaoke, especially when open until the small hours on weekend evenings. The range of quality cask beers varies, but typically includes ales from Bank Top, Moorhouse's and Blackedge. 🕸️&🚅●🚐🐌🛜

Bolton Ukrainian Social Club L

99 Castle Street, BL2 1JP
🕐 3.30-11; 12-11 Sat & Sun ☎ (01204) 526038
3 changing beers (sourced locally; often Bank Top, Blackedge) ⊞
Welcoming club, home to several societies including brass band, choir, chess and Scottish pipers. The comfortable two-room bar has three handpumps serving mostly local beers from breweries including Bank Top and Blackedge, alongside guests from further afield. A selection of Ukrainian beers is often available in bottled or keg format. To gain entry press the intercom button and have your CAMRA membership card or Guide ready. Local CAMRA Club of the Year 2011-2019.
Q🏠🕸️🚅♣️P🚐🛜

Bunbury's

397 Chorley Old Road, BL1 6AH
🕐 1 (5 Mon & Tue)-10; 1-11 Fri & Sat ☎ 07952 344838
⊕ bunburys.co.uk
3 changing beers (sourced locally; often Brass Castle, Magic Rock, Rivington) ⊞
One of a growing number of micropubs based in former retail outlets, this cosy bottle shop with a bar serves a range of the more unusual beers and beer styles. The three changing ales on handpump are from local breweries such as Rivington, Holy Well and Northern Monkey plus similar-sized breweries further afield. Bunbury's also stocks many bottled beers from around the world, some rare, and a choice of interesting modern keg beers. Q🏠♣️●🚐(125)🐌🛜

Great Ale at the Vaults L

Vaults Below Market Place, BL1 2AL
🕐 11-11 ☎ (01204) 773458 ⊕ greataleathevaults.co.uk
4 changing beers (sourced locally) ⊞
Atmospheric bar situated in the centre of the refurbished vaults of the former Market Hall, whose upper floors contain shops and a cinema. Four handpumps dispense Vaults Bitter, specially brewed by Outstanding Brewery, and guest beers

from near and far. Tasting paddles of cask ale are available, plus usually one real cider. Cold bar food is offered. Adjoining the bar are numerous food opportunities plus a children's play area.
Q🏠🕀&🚅●P🚐🛜

Hen & Chickens ✪

143 Deansgate, BL1 1EX
🕐 11-midnight; 12-midnight Sun ☎ 07850 026681
5 changing beers (sourced locally; often Lancaster, Northern Monkey, Three B's) ⊞
The Hen & Chickens has long been one of the most pleasant and popular of town-centre pubs. The smart exterior and colourful floral displays brighten up this end of Deansgate. Inside there is a central horseshoe bar serving both sides of the pub. Although now open plan, the entrance doors lead on the left to the smaller vault with a comfortable raised seating area and on the right to the lounge where food is available. 🕸️🕀🚅♣️🚐

Olde Man & Scythe L ✪

6-8 Churchgate, BL1 1HL
🕐 11-11 (12.30am Fri & Sat); 12-11 Sun ☎ (01204) 559060
Bank Top Flat Cap; Hop Back Summer Lightning; 2 changing beers (sourced locally) ⊞
This Grade II-listed pub is reputedly the fourth oldest in the country and sits near the parish church on historic Churchgate, site of a famous Civil War execution. Rebuilt in 1636 and modified more recently, the pub retains some traditional features such as wooden beams, leaded windows and stone floors. There is a lively bar, a cosy snug and a separate room that is often used for jamming and open mic nights. Normally only the Stan's Traditional Cider is real. 🕸️🚅♣️●🚐🐌

One for the Road

Stalls F14-F15 Ashburner Street Lifestyle Hall, BL1 1TJ
🕐 9am-5.30; closed Sun, Mon & Wed ☎ 07725 338773
3 changing beers (sourced locally) ⊞
This microbar is in Bolton's award-winning indoor market. It serves three beers from a wide range of smaller breweries, plus a selection of nearly 80 bottled and canned beers from many countries. A large seating area at the front of the bar is home to takeaway food vendors, with dishes from Malaysia and Cameroon alongside more standard sandwiches and pasties. A former CAMRA local Pub of the Year. Q🏠&🚅●P🚐🛜

Bramhall

Mounting Stone

8 Woodford Road, SK7 1JJ (jct of Bramhall Lane South)
🕐 4 (2 Wed & Thu)-10.30; 12-11 Fri & Sat; 12-10.30 Sun
☎ (0161) 439 7563 ⊕ themountingstone.co.uk
Bollington Best, Long Hop; 4 changing beers (sourced locally) ⊞
The sister pub to Cheadle Hulme's Chiverton Tap, this is a cosy, friendly micropub right in the village centre. The former blacksmith's operates over two floors – ground and basement – with a small beer garden to the rear. The name derives from a local large stone that allowed riders to mount their horses. Alongside the Bollington beers are four from microbrewers, one usually a dark beer. The pub opened an on-site, one-barrel brewery named Made of Stone in 2018. Q🏠🕀&🕸️🚅●🚐🐌🛜

Broadbottom

Harewood Arms

2 Market Street, SK14 6AX
3-11 (midnight Fri); 2-midnight Sat; 2-11 Sun
(01457) 762500
Green Mill Chief, Old Git; 4 changing beers (sourced regionally)
A large pub for all the community in this quiet village on the edge of the Peak District. Home to the Green Mill Brewery, it serves five regular Green Mill ales plus seasonals, guests and a rotating real cider. Partially open plan, with various seating areas and two real fires, the pub also has a beer garden to the rear. Approximately five minutes' walk from Broadbottom railway station and on local bus routes.

Bromley Cross

Nook & Cranny

211/213 Darwen Road, BL7 9BS
closed Mon; 12-11 (10 Sun)
3 changing beers (sourced locally; often Northern Monkey, Northern Whisper)
This friendly micropub opened in a former shop in March 2018 and extended into the adjacent shop a year later to provide additional seating. Large bench tables help spark a convivial atmosphere that is popular with locals and visitors alike. Three handpumps dispense ales, most from local breweries and some from further afield. There is also a good range of real ciders and modern keg beers. Beer prices are reduced on weekdays before 3pm. There are plans for a microbrewery.
P

Burnage

Reasons to be Cheerful

228 Fog Lane, M20 6EL (jct of Elmsmere Rd)
closed Mon; 4.30-10 Tue; 3.30-11 Wed & Thu; 1.30-midnight Fri & Sat; 1.30-11 Sun (0161) 425 9678
3 changing beers (sourced locally)
Opened in 2017, this friendly, modern beer café occupies former shop premises on a shopping parade near Burnage railway station. Its small inconspicuous frontage hides a long but welcoming interior, including an alcove providing seating and a view of the street. The L-shaped bar is fitted with three handpulls; eight craft beer taps are mounted on the back bar. A secluded rear room can accommodate up to 20 people. Outside at the front is a small drinking area.
Q(Didsbury Village)

Bury

Clarence

2 Silver Street, BL9 0EX
closed Mon; 11-11; 12-11 Sun (0161) 464 7404
theclarence.co.uk
Silver Street Session, One, Ruby, Ruby, Ruby, Ruby; 3 changing beers (often Deeply Vale, Saltaire, Silver Street)
A gastropub with fine dining and excellent real ale, the Clarence has been lovingly and stylishly restored, recreating the pub as it was. Changing guest ales are served alongside beers from the firm's brewery at Britannia Mill. The ground floor contains the main bar, back to its former position, complete with original black and white floor tiles. The restaurant is on the first floor. The second-floor gin bar is invitation only after 11pm.
Q(Bolton Street ELR)

Lamb

533 Tottington Road, Woolfold, BL8 1UB (on B6213 from Bury)
4.30-11; 4-midnight Fri; 1-midnight Sat; 1-10.30 Sun
(0161) 764 2714
Sharp's Doom Bar; 1 changing beer (sourced locally; often Deeply Vale, Silver Street)
A well-run local with a reputation for being a friendly pub where all are welcome. The warm atmosphere is enhanced by an open fire in winter. The Lamb, originally a coaching house, was built in 1831. The landlord is keen on real ale with two pumps always in use, one permanent and one changing. Local microbreweries are promoted, mainly Deeply Vale and Silver Street. A real cider is always available. P(469)

Robert Peel

10 Market Place, BL9 0LD
8am-midnight (1am Fri & Sat) (0161) 764 7287
Greene King Abbot; Ruddles Best Bitter; Sharp's Doom Bar; 6 changing beers (often Brightside)
The Robert Peel is a well-established and popular pub in Bury's cultural quarter, named after the local mill owner and MP whose son became Prime Minister and founded the modern police force. The pub has the largest open public area in Bury. The decor celebrates other local worthies including Richmal Crompton, the author of the Just William books. Six handpumps include three dedicated to the regular brews, the others dispensing varying ales. Real cider is on three handpumps – two ever-changing guests and the house cider.
(Bolton Street ELR)

Thirsty Fish

Unit 1A Princess Parade, Millgate Shopping Centre, BL9 0QL
11-9
8 changing beers (often Beartown, Moorhouse's)
A true microbar that opened in June 2018 in a former unit that is part of this shopping centre. The Thirsty Fish is adjacent to the famous Bury Market and close to the Bury Interchange transport hub, handy for the bus and Metrolink. The bar sells eight constantly changing real ales. It also has a good selection of continental lagers and up to six real ciders. Children are not permitted.
(Bolton Street ELR)

Trackside Bar

Bolton Street Station, BL9 0EY (platform 2 East Lancs Railway)
12-11 Mon & Tue; 10.30am-11 Wed & Thu (midnight Fri); 9.30am-midnight Sat; 9.30am-11 Sun (0161) 764 6461
Northern Whisper ELR Pale; Brightside Odin; 10 changing beers
The Trackside combines some excellent ales and cider with the nostalgia of the East Lancashire Railway. At the bar, house beers from Northern Whisper and Brightside are joined by 10 varying guest ales alongside craft keg. It is a former local CAMRA branch Cider Pub of the Year and sells up to 10 real ciders or perries. The station platform just outside has seating under a roof canopy, creating a lovely suntrap, with wall heaters for cooler weather, for those wanting a closer railway experience. Winter hours are reduced.
(Bolton Street ELR)P

Cadishead

Grocers
152A Liverpool Road, M44 5DD

☻ closed Mon; 5-10 (10.30 Fri); 3-10 Sat; 3-9 Sun
☎ 07950 522468

3 changing beers (sourced nationally; often Cheshire Brewhouse, Pomona Island, Wishbone) Ⓗ/Ⓖ

Since opening in 2015, this micropub in what was a grocer's shop has gone from strength to strength. A former CAMRA branch Pub of the Year and Cider Pub of the Year, it has earned a reputation for serving the best beer and cider in the district. There is no music or TV, just friendly conversation, and no bar either. Drinks are brought to you at your table by the proprietor. Three ciders and perries are available. Q ☎ ⊛ ♿ ♠ ☐ (67,100) ☙

Castleton

Old Post Office Ale House Ⓛ
858 Manchester Road, OL11 2SP

☻ 2-11; 12-1am Fri & Sat; 12-11 Sun ☎ (01706) 645464

House beer (by Pictish); 4 changing beers (sourced locally; often Beartown, Outstanding) Ⓗ

Opened in 2016, this microbar is well served by public transport. The railway station is a two-minute walk; the 17 bus to Rochdale stops outside the front door. The bar serves five quality beers plus a good selection of ciders, wines and gins. Food is not sold but you can bring your own. The bar is dog-friendly and there is a well laid-out beer garden at the rear. Q ⊛ ≠ ♠ ☐ (17) ☙ 🖇

Chadderton

Rose of Lancaster ⊘
7 Haigh Lane, OL1 2TQ

☻ 11.30-11 (11.30 Fri & Sat); 12-11 Sun ☎ (0161) 624 3031
⊕ roseoflancaster.co.uk

JW Lees Manchester Pale Ale, Bitter; 3 changing beers (sourced locally; often JW Lees) Ⓗ

A lounge bar, conservatory restaurant and separate vault where sporting events are screened provide plenty of choice for the Rose of Lancaster's varied clientele. Beers from JW Lees' seasonal and Boilerhouse ranges are always available. A covered patio with views of the Rochdale Canal is popular in fine weather. Nearby bus and train links facilitate travel to this well-run and popular pub.
⊛ Ⓓ ♿ ≠ (Mills Hill) ♣ P ☐ 🖇

Cheadle Hulme

Chiverton Tap
8 Mellor Road, SK8 5AU (off Station Rd)

☻ 4-10.30; 12-11 Fri & Sat; 12-10.30 Sun ☎ (0161) 485 4149

Bollington Best, Long Hop; 4 changing beers (sourced locally) Ⓗ

A friendly micropub that opened in 2015 in what was once Arthur Chiverton's draper's shop. Note the mosaic in the doorway and framed displays of drapery tools on the wall and bar. Six handpumps dispense two regular beers plus four varying ales from small breweries both local and further afield. Beer tapas (a selection of three third-pints) is available. An ever-changing real cider is served straight from the box. Voted regional CAMRA Pub of the Year runner-up in 2018. Q ☎ ♿ ≠ ♠ ☐ ☙ 🖇

Chorlton-cum-Hardy

Beer House Ⓛ
57 Manchester Road, M21 9PW

☻ 12-11 (12.30am Wed & Thu; 1.30am Fri & Sat)
☎ (0161) 881 9206

Marble Manchester Bitter, Pint; 5 changing beers (sourced locally; often Marble, RedWillow, Pomona Island) Ⓗ

This much-loved Chorlton institution for over 20 years has been rejuvenated under new ownership. The name says it all – the focus of this precursor to the modern micropub is on excellent-quality beer with welcoming friendly service. Five guest cask ales from top local and national micros join two beers from former owners Marble Beers and a wide selection of quality keg ales. It has a patio to the front and a book swap library.
☎ ⊛ ✿ ♣ ♠ ☐ (86) ☙ 🖇

Chorlton Tap Ⓛ
533 Wilbraham Road, M21 0UE

☻ 4-11.30 (midnight Thu); 12-1am Fri & Sat; 12-11.30 Sun
☎ (0161) 861 7576

Wander Beyond Peak, Great Rift; 6 changing beers (sourced regionally; often Magic Rock, Pictish, Wander Beyond) Ⓗ

A beer specialist for 25 years as The Bar, the pub now operates as taproom for the group's Wander Beyond brewery. Two handpumps and up to six keg lines dispense the brewery's beers, including Peak pale ale which is exclusive to the group's pubs. Food is served Thursday-Sunday (roasts on the latter include a vegan option). Many beers are vegan, identified on pumpclips and boards. Quiz night is Monday. Outside there is an extensive street-facing patio and a sheltered beer garden to the rear. ☎ ⊛ Ⓓ Ⓠ ♣ ♠ ♠ ☙ 🖇

Dulcimer Ⓛ
567 Wilbraham Road, M21 0AE

☻ 4-12.30am (1.30am Fri); 12-1.30am Sat; 12-11.30 Sun
☎ (0161) 860 6444 ⊕ dulcimer-bar.co.uk

Wainwright; 4 changing beers (sourced nationally; often Magic Rock, Pomona Island, Squawk) Ⓗ

Now open for more than 11 years, this friendly bar in the heart of Chorlton continues to serve an impressive range of beers, with Wainwright backed up by ales from breweries such as Magic Rock and Pomona Island. A fine selection of draught, canned and bottled beers supplements the well-kept cask ales. Real cider is usually on handpump. Live acts perform on Tuesday and Wednesday, and DJs play an eclectic mix of music on Thursday, Friday and Saturday. Quiz night is Monday.
☎ ⊛ Ⓓ ♿ Ⓠ ♣ ♠ ♠ 🖇

Font Ⓛ
115-117 Manchester Road, M21 9PG

☻ 11-12.30am (1am Fri & Sat) ☎ (0161) 871 2022
⊕ thefontbar.wordpress.com

8 changing beers (sourced nationally; often RedWillow, Mallinsons, Track Brewing Co) Ⓗ

This real ale, cider and craft keg haven is sister to the Font bar in Manchester. Eight different real ales usually include one from RedWillow plus beers from breweries near and far including Track, Blackjack, Squawk, Thirst Class and Pomona Island. The bar also features 16 keg lines of which roughly half are regularly changing guests, and between four and 10 traditional ciders, varying seasonally. Local CAMRA Cider Pub of the Year five times in the last six years. ☎ ⊛ Ⓓ Ⓠ ♠ ☐ (86) ☙ 🖇

Pi

99 Manchester Road, M21 9GA
11-11 (12.30am Fri & Sat) ☎ (0161) 882 0000
abarcalledpi.com
Tatton Blonde; 3 changing beers (sourced regionally; often Blackjack, Runaway, Stubborn Mule) Ⓗ
Situated on the increasingly crowded northern part of Manchester Road, this popular bar celebrated its 10th anniversary in 2017 and is a long-standing Guide entry. Four real ales and a guest cider are dispensed by handpump, alongside a selection of world beers on draught plus an impressive menu of bottled beers. The main food offering is Pieminister's gourmet pies, which include a vegetarian option and are served with mashed potatoes and peas. Tea, coffee and cake are also available, and every drink purchase includes free peanuts. (86)

Chorlton-on-Medlock

Sandbar

120-122 Grosvenor Street, M1 7HL (off Oxford Rd A34/B5117 jct)
12-midnight (1am Thu; 2am Fri & Sat)
sandbarmanchester.co.uk
Beartown Polar Eclipse; Facer's Clwyd Gold; Phoenix Arizona; 4 changing beers (sourced regionally) Ⓗ
Originally two 18th-century town houses, this is now one of the longest-established bars on the university area beer scene. Quirky and bohemian, it is popular with students and university staff alike. There are regular exhibitions of photographs and paintings, and displays of old curios. The cask beers are usually local and are accompanied by modern British and European bottled, canned and kegged beers and a changing guest cider. Home-made pizzas are available at weekends. Payment is only by card or Bitcoin.
(Oxford Rd)(St Peters Sq)

Delph

Royal Oak (Th' Heights)

Broad Lane, OL3 5TX (via Thame Lane, off main Delph-Denshaw road)
closed Mon & Tue; 7-11 Wed & Sat; 5-11 Thu & Fri; 12-6.30 Sun ☎ (01457) 874460
House beer (by Coach House); 3 changing beers (often Millstone, Moorhouse's) Ⓗ
This stone-built pub, dating from 1767, has been in the Guide for 28 years consecutively. Situated on a pack horse route, it overlooks the Tame Valley in a popular walking area next to the Heights Chapel. The building comprises a cosy bar area and three rooms each with an open fire, with exposed wooden beams and a hand-carved stone fireplace. Local photographs of the inn decorate the walls. The house beer is from Coach House, supplemented by a Millstone beer and two other changing ales. QP

Denton

Carters Arms

Stockport Road, M34 6AQ
4-11; 12-11 Sat & Sun ☎ (0161) 320 3752
Black Sheep Best Bitter; Wainwright; 2 changing beers (sourced regionally) Ⓗ
Friendly local with two large open-plan rooms. The lounge-style room to the left is regularly hired out for functions for up to 70 people; the traditional bar/games room on the right features wood panelling and dark leather seating. The pool team plays on Wednesday, live music features on Friday, karaoke and disco night is Saturday. Accompanied children are welcome until 8pm. There is wheelchair access to the rear. The pub is accessible by bus from Manchester and Stockport.
Q♣P

Crown Point Tavern

16 Market Street, M34 2XW (in Civic Square)
11-10 (11 Fri & Sat) ☎ (0161) 337 9615
thecrownpointtavern.co.uk
House beer (by Tweed); 5 changing beers (sourced locally) Ⓗ
A micropub near the old post office and library, with outside seating at the front. Six real ales are served, typically sourced from Greater Manchester. These are complemented by an extensive selection of bottled local craft beers plus at least one real cider, typically Bootlegger Moonshine. Flights of three third-pints of ale are available. The pub hosts live acoustic music on Friday and a quiz on Sunday.
Q♣

Lowes Arms

301 Hyde Road, M34 3FF
12-midnight; 10.30-midnight Sat & Sun
☎ (0161) 336 3064 lowesarms.co.uk
4 changing beers (sourced locally; often Conwy, Cross Bay) Ⓗ
Built in 1824, this thriving local has a reputation for quality beers and good-value food. Ales from Cross Bay and Conwy breweries feature regularly on the frequently changing list of guest beers. The comfortable lounge is also the main food area. The vault has a pool table and can be used as a function room. The pub hosts local league darts and dominoes teams, and holds beer festivals in May, August and October.
Q♣P(150,201)

Didsbury

Gateway

882 Wilmslow Road, M20 5PG (jct Kingsway and Manchester Rd)
8am-11.30 (midnight Fri & Sat) ☎ (0161) 438 1700
Greene King Abbot; Ruddles Best Bitter; house beer (by Brightside); 5 changing beers (sourced nationally) Ⓗ
This comfortable and popular late-1930s roadhouse, conveniently located opposite the Parrs Wood leisure complex and public transport interchange, stands out due to its welcoming atmosphere, enthusiastic staff and excellent beer. The large Wetherspoon pub's central island bar is surrounded by distinct seating areas, ensuring that you can always have a quiet drink somewhere. An upstairs function room plays host to local social activities and groups.
Q(E Didsbury)P

Dobcross

Dobcross Band Social Club

Platt Lane, OL3 5AD
7.30-11; 7-11 Sat; 1-5, 7-11 Sun ☎ (01457) 873741
Millstone Tiger Rut; 2 changing beers (sourced locally; often Bradfield, JW Lees) Ⓗ
A free house with views of the hills of Saddleworth Moor, the Dobcross Band Social Club is famous for

its weekly Sunday night brass band concerts, featuring local and national players. The Band Club, which was established in 1967, also opens for bowls matches on Saturday afternoons in summer. Local CAMRA branch Club of the Year 2018.
♣P

Navigation Inn

21-23 Wool Road, OL3 5NS

12-3, 5-11 (9.30 Tue; 10 Wed); 12-3, 5-midnight Fri; 12-11 Sat; 12-8 Sun ☎ (01457) 872418

thenavigationdobcross.co.uk

Greene King Abbot; Millstone Tiger Rut; Timothy Taylor Landlord; 1 changing beer H

Nestling in the idyllic rolling countryside of Saddleworth and close to the Huddersfield Narrow Canal, the Navigation was built in 1806 to slake the thirst of navvies cutting the Standedge Tunnel. A traditional family-run pub with an open-plan bar and an L-shaped interior, it serves several real ales alongside a varied choice of freshly prepared food. It is a venue for the popular Rushcart Festival in August. Q P (184,354)

Droylsden

Silly Country Bar & Bottle Shop

121 Market Street, M43 7AR

12-10.30 (11 Fri & Sat); 12-10 Sun

5 changing beers (sourced locally) H

Modern open-plan bar and bottle shop on the corner of Droylsden Shopping Centre. Opened in May 2018 by a small group of local real ale enthusiasts, it has provided a much-needed boost to the real ale scene in the area. Five handpumped beers are available, mostly from local breweries, complemented by three ciders and an extensive range of bottled beers and ciders. Droylsden tram stop is across the road from the bar.
Q ♣ P

Dukinfield

Angel

197 King Street, SK16 4TH

4-11.30 (midnight Thu); 2-midnight Fri; 12-midnight Sat; 12-11.30 Sun ☎ (0161) 830 0223

4 changing beers (sourced nationally) H

A large red-brick pub on the main road close to the centre of Dukinfield, the Angel is something of an oasis for real ale in the area. The pub features four regularly changing beers, nearly always from national microbreweries. There is a large, comfortable lounge, a good taproom and a function room available to hire. This is a pub to suit all tastes and age ranges. It can get busy when one of the local Premier League football sides is on TV.
♣P (330)

Eccles

Lamb Hotel ★

33 Regent Street, M30 0BP (opp Metrolink)

11.30-11 (11.30 Fri & Sat); 12-11 Sun ☎ 07827 850252

Joseph Holt Mild, Bitter; 1 changing beer (sourced nationally) H

A Holt's house since 1865, then rebuilt in 1906, this imposing red brick hotel has a balustered parapet, lofty chimneys and a round corner tower with a copper cupola. Inside, the four rooms and bar are equally impressive. Curved etched glass, polished mahogany, Art Nouveau tiling and ornately carved fire surrounds feature in every room. A full-sized table occupies the purpose-built billiards room. There is karaoke on Friday night and Sunday afternoon. The car park on the left has a charge, refundable at the bar. Q ♣P

Golborne

Queen Anne

14 Bridge Street, WA3 3PZ

12-11 (10.30 Sun) ☎ (01942) 726922

queenanne-golborne.co.uk

2 changing beers (sourced regionally) H

Tucked away on Bridge Street just off the East Lancs Road, the Queen Anne is handy for Haydock Park Racecourse and caters for pre-race parties. Home-cooked food is served in the bar and separate dining area, with early-bird specials on weekdays 3.30-7pm plus Sunday roasts. The beer garden is a real suntrap in the summer. Q P (10)

Gorton

Vale Cottage

Kirk Street, M18 8UE (off Hyde Rd A57, E of jct Chapman St)

12-4, 7-11; 12-11.30 Fri & Sat; 12-11 Sun

☎ (0161) 223 4568 thevalecottage.co.uk

Timothy Taylor Landlord; 2 changing beers (sourced nationally) H

Well hidden in the Gore Brook conservation area, the Vale Cottage has the feel of a country pub. Parts date from the 17th century, hence the low-beamed ceilings, multiple drinking areas and reputed ghost. A relaxed, friendly atmosphere, where conversation predominates, is disturbed only by the lively, ever-popular quizzes (Tuesday general knowledge, Thursday music). Indulge in an excellent home-cooked meal in the garden to round off a visit or even partake in steak night on the last Thursday of the month.
Q (Ryder Brow/Belle Vue/Gorton)
♣P

Greenfield

Donkeystone Brewing Co

Unit 17-18, Boarshurst Business Park, OL3 7ER

closed Mon-Thu; 6-10 Fri; 12-10 Sat; 12-8 Sun

☎ (01457) 238710 donkeystonebrewing.co.uk

Donkeystone Hoppinsesh, Bad Ass Blonde, Bray, Cotton Clouds, DPA, Javanilla; 1 changing beer (sourced locally; often Donkeystone) H

Donkeystone is a 10-barrel brewery based in Saddleworth. From Friday evening to Sunday the brewery opens a tap where you can sample the ales. Ten or more of its hand-crafted beers are on offer, served by handpull, including two keg lines. Brewery tours are available by arrangement for groups of six or more. Dog walkers, children and mountain bikers are welcome at the tap, which is heated by log fire in the colder months.
♣P (180,350)

King William IV

134 Chew Valley Road, OL3 7DD

12-midnight (1am Fri & Sat) ☎ (01457) 873933

Black Sheep Best Bitter; Millstone Tiger Rut; Pictish Brewers Gold; Sharp's Atlantic; Tetley Bitter; 1 changing beer (sourced locally; often Donkeystone, Three B's) H

The King Bill, as it is known, is a stone-built pub offering six real ales, with food available from Wednesday to Sunday. It features a central bar and two rooms, one of which has a wood-burning stove. The cobbled patio is a pleasant area with heaters and a retractable awning. The Saddleworth Rushcart festival and Whit Friday Band Contest feature heavily in the summer. Children, dogs and walkers are welcome. Public transport links are good. (180,350)

Wellington Inn

29 Chew Valley Road, OL3 7AF (near Tesco)

3-9 Mon (11 Tue); 12-11 Wed-Sat; 12-9 Sun

Coach House Gunpowder Mild; Mansfield Cask Ale; Millstone Tiger Rut; Phoenix Arizona; Salopian Lemon Dream; Wainwright; 1 changing beer (sourced locally; often Donkeystone)

The Wellington is a family-owned village end-of-terrace free house with a friendly welcome. The building comprises a small bar area featuring seven handpulled cask ales, an attached main room popular with diners, and a side room with a dartboard, cribbage and dominoes. There is outdoor seating. A varied menu of good-value home-made food including daily specials is available on Wednesday, Friday and Sunday. Pies, puddings and real chips are particularly popular, and fish on a Friday. (180,350)

Harwood

House Without a Name

75 Lea Gate, BL2 3ET

12-midnight (1.30am Fri & Sat) (01204) 433568

housewithoutaname.co.uk

Joseph Holt Bitter; Sharp's Doom Bar; 4 changing beers (sourced locally; often Moorhouse's, Northern Monkey, Titanic)

Locally known as the No Name, this cosy terraced venue was originally two cottages built in the 1830s, now sensitively modernised and refurbished retaining the flag floors and wooden beams. The main lounge has a bar servery with a blackboard beer listing, a large-screen TV and a real fire, and there is a small bar to the left. Simple bar food is served during opening hours. All premium TV sports channels are screened.
(480,507)

Higher Broughton

Duke of York

97 Marlborough Road, Hightown, M7 4SP (opp Inghamwood Close)

11-11 (midnight Fri & Sat); 12-11 Sun 07827 850214

Joseph Holt Bitter, Two Hoots

An imposing red-brick late Victorian Holt's establishment dating back to 1899. A central drinking lobby and horseshoe bar lead to four separate rooms in which can be found some exquisitely etched glass panes. The pub is a rare survivor of the Hightown clearances of the early '70s. A warm welcome is always guaranteed in this most traditional of community pubs.
(42,135)

Horwich

Bank Top Brewery Ale House

36 Church Street, BL6 6AD

12-11 (11.30 Fri & Sat) (01204) 693793

banktopbrewery.com

Bank Top Bad to the Bone, Dark Mild, Flat Cap, Pavilion Pale Ale; 4 changing beers (sourced locally; often Bank Top)

The second award-winning Bank Top Brewery pub sits in a conservation area opposite Horwich parish church and alongside 18th- and 19th-century cottages associated with the area's history of textiles and bleaching. It is an immaculate pub showcasing eight beers from Bank Top, always including Dark Mild, former Champion Mild of Britain, plus one changing guest ale. Alongside this are up to six real ciders and perries, most kept cellar cool. A small but comfortable beer garden and smoking area is to be found at the rear. Walkers and their dogs are welcome.
Q (125)

Brewery Bar

Moreton Mill, Hampson Street, BL6 7JH (just behind the Old Original Bay Horse)

closed Mon & Tue; 4.30-10.30 Wed & Thu; 4-11.30 Fri; 12-11.30 Sat; 2-8.30 Sun (01204) 692976

thebrewerybar.co.uk

Blackedge HoP, Black, Pike; 4 changing beers (sourced locally; often Blackedge)

A friendly and popular upstairs bar above the award-winning Blackedge Brewery with seven handpumps showcasing the firm's beers plus a range of real ciders. Converted from a former industrial premises and retaining some original features, it has comfortable settees and barrel tables with stools spread throughout a spacious drinking area. Locally made pork and Blackedge ale pies are normally available. The brewery is visible downstairs through large glass windows as you enter the bar. The toilets are on the ground floor and there is no lift. P

Crown

1 Chorley New Road, BL6 7QJ (on B6226, 200yds from A673)

11-11 (midnight Fri & Sat); 12-11.30 Sun 07827 850221

Joseph Holt Mild, IPA, Bitter, Two Hoots; 4 changing beers (sourced locally; often Bank Top, Blackedge, Bootleg)

A spacious, comfortable and popular landmark pub whose multi-room layout provides a home to many community activities. The separate pool and games room with its own bar hosts darts, dominoes and pool teams. Elsewhere are quiet drinking areas and a large sports TV. There is live entertainment on Saturday or Sunday evenings and home-cooked food is served every day. The Crown's location attracts outdoor enthusiasts stopping for a pint after enjoying the beautiful countryside of the neighbouring West Pennine Moors. Q P (125,575)

Hyde

Cheshire Ring Hotel

72-74 Manchester Road, SK14 2BJ

4-11; 12-11 Sat; 12-10.30 Sun 07917 055629

6 changing beers

One of the oldest pubs in Hyde, the Cheshire Ring was comprehensively overhauled by Beartown Brewery several years ago. Seven handpumps offer a range of ales from Beartown plus micros from near and far, in addition to ciders, perries and continental beers. A selection of Belgian and German bottled beers is also stocked. Home-made curries are available on Thursday evening, Sunday is quiz night. Opening hours vary with the season and closing time may be earlier on Monday and Tuesday. P (201)

Tweed Tap

3 Hamnett Street, SK14 2EX

12-10.15; closed Tue 07889 750492

Tweed Hopster, Orange County IPA; 2 changing beers (sourced locally; often Tweed) H

A welcome addition to the Hyde real ale scene. Four handpumped beers are available, three from Tweed brewery and one guest. Cider is from the Broadoak range. The bar is situated in a side street just off the market square. It occupies former retail premises and is suprisingly spacious, decked out in old dark wood which gives an almost rustic feel. It is a two-minute walk from Hyde bus station and 10 minutes from Hyde Central station.

Q

Leigh

Bobbin

38A Leigh Road, WN7 1QR

closed Mon; 5-11 Tue & Wed; 2-11 Thu (midnight Fri & Sat); 2-11 Sun (01942) 581242

4 changing beers (sourced locally) H

The Bobbin takes its name from the nearby sewing shop where it was established before moving to the current premises in Leigh Road, on the edge of the town centre. There is one room with a central bar and comfortable seating. Prices are very competitive and a real cider is available. The beers are usually sourced from regional micros and shown on the pub's Facebook page. Q

Bowling Green Inn

110 Manchester Road, WN7 2LD

11-midnight; 12-11 Sun (01942) 673964

Joseph Holt Bitter; 1 changing beer H

Situated on a busy junction, this popular pub caters for a wide clientele and has a good reputation for food. With its two separate rooms it welcomes both families and adults who wish to drink and watch sport. A weekly changing guest beer is offered, usually from a local brewery. There are two quizzes every week and family events are held regularly, especially on bank holidays using the beer garden. P (9,34)

Littleborough

White House

Blackstone Edge, Halifax Road, OL15 0LG

12-3, 6.30-midnight; 12-11 Sun (01706) 378456

thewhitehousepub.co.uk

Theakston Best Bitter; 3 changing beers (often Abbeydale, Newby Wyke) H

The White House is a classic moorland pub on the A58 between Rochdale and Halifax. Built in 1691 as the Coach & Horses, it enjoys commanding views over the Lancashire plain. Handpumps offer Theakston Best as a regular, plus three changing beers. The pub has a bar area and four separate rooms. The bar stretches into the rear room, with two handpumps on that side. Good food is served daily from an extensive menu. A family-run pub for over 30 years. Q P (X58)

Lowton

Travellers Rest

443 Newton Road, WA3 1NZ

12-11 (10.30 Mon); 12-midnight Fri & Sat; 12-10.30 Sun (01925) 293222 travellersrestlowton.com

Theakston Best Bitter; Wainwright; 2 changing beers H

Traditionally furnished pub/restaurant between Lowton and Newton-le-Willows. The Travellers Rest has a number of seating areas and a separate restaurant. There is also a bar area to the right as you enter for customers who just prefer to drink, with ales from Thwaites and Theakston. Outside there is a large garden and car park. A private room is available to hire for special occasions.

Q P (34)

Lydgate

White Hart Inn

51 Stockport Road, OL4 4JJ

12-midnight; 12-11 Sun (01457) 872566

thewhitehart.co.uk

JW Lees Bitter; Timothy Taylor Golden Best, Boltmaker; 3 changing beers (often Donkeystone, Ossett) H

Free house in a classic stone building dating from 1788 and sympathetically extended. It commands impressive views over the surrounding hills and Greater Manchester. The multi-room layout has log burning stoves in the bar area and brasserie, behind which is a restaurant, function rooms and guest accommodation. Quality food is served daily from an award-winning kitchen. Three regular beers are joined by guests from local and regional breweries. Hosts the Whit Friday brass band contest at Lydgate in the beer garden.

Q P (180,184)

Manchester

Angel

6 Angel Street, M4 4BQ (off Rochdale Rd)

12-midnight (0161) 833 4786

theangelmanchester.com

House beer (by Howard Town); 9 changing beers (sourced nationally; often Blackedge) H

On a busy junction on the outskirts of the Northern Quarter, the Angel is a hard place to reach at times but is worth making the effort. With a fine selection of beers on offer from its dozen handpumps, there is something to suit most palates. The house beer is a light pale ale from Howard Town, often balanced by a powerful dark beer from Blackedge.

(Victoria) (Shudehill) P

Brink

65 Bridge Street, M3 3BQ

4-11 Mon (midnight Tue); 12-midnight Wed & Thu (1am Fri & Sat); closed Sun (0161) 834 6346 brinkmcr.co.uk

5 changing beers (sourced locally) H

This cosy single-room basement bar is a welcome addition to the Manchester craft beer scene. The bar serves several changing cask and keg beers plus ciders, all brewed within a 25-mile radius of nearby St Ann's Church. The bar is also a local gin specialist. Locally produced snacks are available. A spectacular panoramic photo of the Manchester skyline occupies most of one wall.

(Salford Central) (St Peters Sq)

Cafe Beermoth

40A Spring Gardens, M2 1EN (entrance on Brown St)
☼ 12-11.30 (12.30am Fri & Sat); 12-11 Sun
☎ (0161) 835 2049 ⊕ beermoth.co.uk
7 changing beers (sourced nationally) Ⓗ
A modern bar situated in the heart of the city, just off the main shopping street. Hops overhang the bar, which boasts seven different cask beers and 10 keg fonts dispensing both British and international beers. Tap takeovers feature on occasion. A mezzanine floor provides extra space when busy below. There is an impressive display of bottles for sale, many using wild yeast, to the left of the glass-fronted cellar behind the bar area.
⬥♿ℛ(Market St)●❀🛜

Cask

29 Liverpool Road, M3 4NQ
☼ 12-11 (midnight Fri & Sat); 12-10.30 Sun
☎ (0161) 832 2633
4 changing beers (sourced regionally; often Elland, Pictish) Ⓗ
In the heart of Castlefield, this deceptively deep pub holds a few gems. With beer on four handpumps, it usually offers a good range of flavours, including a dark. The selection of international beers is particularly impressive, both on fonts and in bottles. Although no food is provided, customers are permitted to bring their own, including takeouts from the excellent chippy next door.
❀◑⇌(Deansgate)ℛ(Deansgate/Castlefield)
●🚌❀🛜

City Arms ✓

46-48 Kennedy Street, M2 4BQ (near town hall)
☼ 12-11 (midnight Fri & Sat); 12-8 Sun ☎ (0161) 236 4610
Brightside Odin Blonde; Titanic Plum Porter; 6 changing beers (sourced regionally) Ⓗ
A compact multi award-winning pub with two traditional rooms and many original features. The room facing the street contains the bar and is fairly basic with a dartboard. To the rear there is a smarter, cosier room to hang out in good company. Eight handpulls offer a full range of beer styles in excellent condition – another reason why the City Arms regularly features in this Guide. The pub is often full and filled with groups of people conversing. ❀◑⇌(Oxford Rd)ℛ(St Peters Sq)♣●🚌🛜

Crown & Kettle ♆

2 Oldham Road, M4 5FE (corner Great Ancoats St)
☼ 12-11 (midnight Fri & Sat); 12-10.30 Sun
☎ (0161) 236 2923
8 changing beers (sourced nationally) Ⓗ
This Grade II-listed street-corner building has a large drinking area in front of the bar along with a small vault and a snug at the rear. The high ornate ceiling in the main bar is well worth seeing. Beers from far and wide are served by handpump. Open mic sessions are on the first and third Thursday of the month; weekends occasionally feature live music. There are regular tap takeovers and occasional beer festivals. Hot pies are available. ❀♿⇌(Victoria)ℛ(Shudehill)●🚌❀🛜

Font

7-9 New Wakefield Street, M1 5NP (off Oxford Rd by railway viaduct)
☼ 11-1am (12.30am Sun) ☎ (0161) 236 0944
⊕ fontbar.com

4 changing beers (sourced nationally; often Brewsmith, Mallinsons) Ⓗ
Its location helps make the Font popular with students, local business workers and people heading to Oxford Road station. The pub offers an interesting range of cask beers from larger breweries and micros, plus craft keg and bottled beers from the UK, US and Belgium. Three traditional ciders are usually available. A wide range of freshly cooked food is served daily.
⬥◑♿⇌(Oxford Rd)ℛ(St Peters Sq)●🚌❀🛜

Gas Lamp

50A Bridge Street, M3 3BW
☼ 4-midnight Mon & Tue; 12-midnight Wed (1am Thu; 2am Fri & Sat); 12-midnight Sun ☎ (0161) 478 1224
⊕ thegaslamp.co.uk
4 changing beers (sourced nationally; often Pomona Island, Squawk, Track) Ⓗ
An interesting pub housed in the former Manchester and Salford Children's Mission. It has an impressive frontage but the small doorway that leads down to the subterranean bar can easily be missed. The main bar area has Victorian glazed-brick walls and wooden flooring. A narrow passageway leads to a cosy back room. Quiet conversation prevails. The pub now has its own brewery in nearby Salford, Pomona Island.
⬥⇌(Salford Central)ℛ(St Peters Sq)●🚌❀🛜

Grey Horse ✓

80 Portland Street, M1 4QX (jct Princess St)
☼ 11-midnight (1am Fri & Sat); 12-midnight Sun
☎ (0161) 228 2595
Hydes Old Indie, Hydes Original, Lowry; 2 changing beers (sourced nationally) Ⓗ
Entered by steps from the street, this is a traditional single-roomed wood-floored pub set in the city centre on the edge of Chinatown. The fine and friendly Grey Horse is popular with locals and visitors, many from across Europe. It can get busy on match days for both Manchester teams. As well as the regular beers there are usually two from Hydes Beer Studio and a guest ale. There is 50p off cask ale on Monday.
⇌(Oxford Rd)ℛ(St Peters Sq)🚌(1,3)❀🛜

Hare & Hounds ★

46 Shudehill, M4 4AA (opp Shudehill Bus Station)
☼ 11-11; 12-10 Sun ☎ (0161) 832 4737
Joseph Holt Bitter; Robinsons Dizzy Blonde; Sharp's Doom Bar Ⓗ
Fine beers and friendly staff help make the Hare & Hounds popular, especially with older customers. This Grade II-listed pub on CAMRA's National Inventory of Historic Pub Interiors dates back to about 1800 and was remodelled in 1925. The building's mottled tile frontage and an interior featuring lots of attractive tiling make it a rare survivor of the period, particularly given its city-centre location. The entrance corridor leads to a lobby in front of the bar. There is a vault at the front and a comfortable lounge at the rear.
⇌(Victoria)ℛ(Shudehill)🚌❀🛜

Jack in the Box

1 Eagle Street, M4 5BU
☼ closed Mon; 12-10 Tue-Thu (11 Fri & Sat); 12-8 Sun
8 changing beers (sourced nationally) Ⓗ
Next to the Smithfield Market Tavern, another Blackjack Brewery pub, this is a modern bar in the Grade II-listed Mackie Mayor, a spectacular refurbished former meat market that hosts street

food outlets alongside coffee and wine bars. A great space for individuals and large groups, the pub offers beer from eight handpumps and 10 keg taps, plus a selection of bottles and usually three bag-in-box ciders.
🐴♿⇌(Victoria)🚊(Shudehill)🍏🥛🐾📶

Marble Arch Inn ★

73 Rochdale Road, Collyhurst, M4 4HY
🕛 12-11 (midnight Fri); 11-midnight Sat; 11-10 Sun
☎ (0161) 832 5914
Marble Pint, Manchester Bitter; 7 changing beers (sourced nationally; often Marble) 🄷
Marble brewery's flagship establishment, this famous real ale pub is a 10-minute walk from the city centre. It serves Marble beers alongside a guest ale, plus craft keg and a real cider. This Grade II-listed pub has many interesting features, with a mosaic sloping floor leading you inexorably to the bar and glazed-tile walls adding to the splendour of the interior. There is a plainer back room, and a beer yard at the rear.
Q🐴❀◐⇌(Victoria)🚊(Shudehill)🍏🚌🐾📶

Paramount ✔

33-35 Oxford Street, M1 4BH (jct Portland St)
🕛 7am-midnight (1am Fri & Sat) ☎ (0161) 233 1820
Greene King Abbot; Robinsons Trooper; Thornbridge Jaipur IPA; Wainwright; 6 changing beers (sourced nationally; often Acorn, Elland, Robinsons) 🄷
Named after the Paramount theatre (later Odeon cinema) nearby, which was demolished in 2017 and is among former theatres and cinemas recalled in photos displayed inside. This large and popular Wetherspoon pub has a lively yet controlled atmosphere. What really sets it apart is the enthusiasm of the team for the wide and interesting range of cask beers on offer. Changing guest ales are on the left set of handpumps and longer-term ales on the right.
🐴◐♿⇌(Oxford Rd)🚊(St Peters Sq)🍏📶

Pilcrow

Sadler's Yard, M4 4AH
🕛 12-10.30 (11.30 Fri & Sat); 12-8 Sun ☎ (0161) 832 6543
🌐 thepilcrowpub.com
Track Sonoma; 2 changing beers 🄷
Opened in 2016, the Pilcrow sits on the site of Manchester's first steam mill and is notable for having all its interior's fixtures and fittings made by volunteers. It offers three cask ales, with Track Brewing's Sonoma pale ale a regular, and 14 beers served from taps on the back wall. The outside drinking area is part of Sadlers Yard, a public square and event space.
🐴❀◐♿⇌(Victoria)🚊(Victoria)♣🍏🚌📶

Port Street Beer House

39-41 Port Street, M1 2EQ (opp Brewer St)
🕛 12-midnight (1am Sat) ☎ (0161) 237 9949
🌐 portstreetbeerhouse.co.uk
7 changing beers (sourced nationally) 🄷
Seven cask beers are served here from some of Britain's finest breweries, alongside a good range of contrasting worldwide keg beers, bottles and cans. With knowledgeable staff and regular beer tastings and tap takeovers, this is one of the best beer emporiums in the city and a treat for beer novices and connoisseurs. Seating is also available in a larger room upstairs and on a small terrace at the rear.
🐴❀⇌(Piccadilly)🚊(Piccadilly Gardens)
♣🍏🚌🐾📶

Smithfield Market Tavern

37 Swan Street, M4 5JZ
🕛 2 (4 Mon)-11; 2-midnight Fri; 12-midnight Sat; 12-11 Sun
6 changing beers (sourced nationally) 🄷
One of the premier cask pubs in the Northern Quarter, the Smithfield is the flagship for Blackjack Brewery; a modern-day proper pub. Six cask ales, including usually two from Blackjack, and several ciders, are stocked. It is a formidable presence on the Manchester beer scene, winning several CAMRA awards including Cider Pub of the Year 2019. 🐴⇌(Victoria)🚊(Shudehill)♣🍏🥛🚌🐾📶

Waterhouse 🄻 ✔

67-71 Princess Street, M2 4EG (opp town hall)
🕛 8am-midnight (1am Fri & Sat) ☎ (0161) 200 5380
Greene King Abbot; Hawkshead Windermere Pale; Phoenix Wobbly Bob; Sharp's Doom Bar; 6 changing beers (sourced nationally) 🄷
Standing opposite the Town Hall and named after Alfred Waterhouse, the architect who designed it, this Wetherspoon outlet is unusual for the chain in having a split interior with several areas for drinking and dining. The four regular beers are complemented by six changing guest ales of varied styles, many from local micros. Meet the Brewer nights are occasionally held.
Q🐴❀◐♿⇌(Oxford Rd)🚊(St Peters Sq)🍏🚌📶

Marple

Beer Traders

113 Stockport Road, SK6 6AF
🕛 closed Mon; 4-11; 1-11 Sat; 1-10 Sun ☎ (0161) 427 0667
🌐 marplebeertraders.com
3 changing beers (sourced regionally) 🄷
An interesting innovation for the area in that the business combines a bottle shop with a micropub, based in a converted shop premises. Three handpulls serve changing beers, normally from local micros. The aim is to have one traditional bitter, one darker beer and something hoppy. Three bag-in-box ciders are also available. Live music often features on Saturday evening. Opening times can vary – it may be worth checking prior to a visit. ❀⇌🍏🚌🐾

Samuel Oldknow

22 Market Street, SK6 7AD
🕛 1-11; 11-11 Sat; 12-10 Sun ☎ 07766 301627
6 changing beers (sourced locally) 🄷
Named after a local mill owner who was responsible for much of the development of Marple and Mellor some 200 years ago, this is a somewhat quirky two-level bar in a converted shop. Six vintage-style handpulls dispense five changing real ales plus a real cider. The regular beers are from Brightside and Outstanding, complemented by guests from local micros. A range of bottled beers is also available to take away or to drink on the premises. Opening hours are subject to change. Q🐴❀⇌🍏🚌🐾📶

Marple Bridge

Norfolk Arms

2 Town Street, SK6 5DS
🕛 12-11 (10.30 Sun) ☎ (0161) 427 8090
🌐 thenorfolkarms.co.uk
4 changing beers (sourced regionally) 🄷
A recently refurbished stone-built pub in an attractive setting next to the Goyt river bridge.

Comfortably furnished, it attracts a wide-ranging clientele by catering for all tastes. With four real ales usually from micros, the beer range is a good addition to the choice in the area. The atmosphere is warm and friendly, with good-value food available. Live music plays on Thursday and occasional beer festivals are held in the summer. Well served by public transport.
Q❀P

Northumberland Arms

64 Compstall Road, SK6 5HD
3-11 (midnight Fri); 12-midnight Sat; 12-11.30 Sun
☎ (0161) 285 3755 thenorthumberlandarms.com
Robinsons Unicorn; 3 changing beers (sourced locally; often Bank Top, Track) H
An ex-Robinsons hostelry reopened as a local community-owned and operated pub in December 2017. Used by numerous groups for meetings and activities, the pub fulfils its role as a true local and a well-used hub of the district. Its small bar area serves three rooms, one of which is used for pub games. The traditional exterior is enhanced by a pleasant beer garden. Frequent buses pass the door. ❀♣P

Middleton

Lancashire Fold ✔

77 Kirkway, M24 1EP
12-11 ☎ (0161) 643 4198 lancashirefold.co.uk
JW Lees Manchester Pale Ale, Bitter; 1 changing beer (sourced locally; often JW Lees) H
Built by Lees in 1961, the Fold is popular and busy. It boasts a large lounge, a small function room, a public bar (not always open) and a comfortable outside drinking area. Seasonal ales and one beer from Lees' Boilerhouse range are usually offered. Live football on screen is a big attraction and there is live music once a month. Food is home-cooked and hearty, and parties can be catered for. Buses to Middleton and Oldham pass the pub for onward travel. P(415)

Ring o' Bells

St Leonards Square, M24 6DJ
5-midnight; 12-1am Fri & Sat; 12-11 Sun
☎ (0161) 654 9245
JW Lees Manchester Pale Ale, Bitter; 2 changing beers (sourced locally; often JW Lees) H
A pub since 1831, the Ringers enjoys a fine elevated location opposite the medieval parish church within the conservation area above Jubilee Park. Visitors can enjoy stunning views across to Oldham and beyond, especially at night. Lees' seasonal and Boilerhouse beers are served. Very much community focused, the pub hosts a unique Pace Egg play on Easter Monday and a Maypole event on the May bank holiday Monday. Weekly quizzes and occasional live music add to its appeal. There is an attractive beer garden to the rear.
❀♣P(17)

Tandle Hill Tavern

14 Thornham Lane, M24 2SD (1 mile on unmetalled road from either A664 or A627)
closed Mon & Tue; 5-10 Wed & Thu (11 Fri); 12-10.30 Sat & Sun ☎ (0161) 376 4492
JW Lees Bitter, Stout; house beer (by JW Lees); 1 changing beer (sourced locally; often JW Lees) H
A one-mile walk from either end of an unmade, potholed lane rewards the drinker with a neat little pub nestling among a number of farms. There is a main bar area and a separate quiet side room, while a walled rear beer garden and benches to the front and side provide outdoor seating. The house beer is dry-hopped Lees Bitter. Food is limited to toasties. In adverse weather, or in winter, phone ahead to check opening times.
Q❀

Milnrow

Waggon Inn

35 Butterworth Hall, OL16 3PE
12-11 (midnight Fri & Sat) ☎ (01706) 648313
waggoninnmilnrow.co.uk
Banks's Amber Ale; 2 changing beers (often Jennings, Marston's) H
Built in 1782, this pub, locally known as the Back Waggon, always offers a warm welcome. The building has been sympathetically refurbished, retaining many original features including mullioned windows, and has a traditional ambience. Three Marston's beers are offered, always including Banks's Amber. An excellent food menu features daily specials, tapas and a Sunday roast. Awarded Marston's National Pub of the Year in 2017, the Waggon is within easy walking distance of Milnrow's Metrolink stop and local bus services. ❀P

Monton

Malt Dog L

169 Monton Road, M30 9GS
closed Mon; 5-11 Tue-Thu; 3-11 Fri; 1-11 Sat; 1-10 Sun
☎ 07541 553646 maltdog.com
3 changing beers (sourced locally; often Brew York, Brightside, Rooster's) H
A small but friendly pub converted from an old shop. The ground floor is open plan and upstairs is a spacious lounge which hosts live music twice a week, mainly jazz. A range of mostly German and Belgian draught beers is available plus a good number of bottled beers. A popular and thriving part of the Monton village scene. Local CAMRA Pub of the Year in 2017. Q❀

Park

142 Monton Road, M30 9QD
10-11 (midnight Fri & Sat); 12-11 Sun ☎ (0161) 789 5021
Bootleg Chorlton Pale Ale; Joseph Holt Mild, Bitter; 2 changing beers (sourced locally) H
A busy Joseph Holt pub situated on the village high street, the Park was recently refurbished in café-bar style. Beers from Holt and Bootleg breweries are served, with occasional guest ales from elsewhere. The front of the building opens to a patio in fine weather to embrace the vibrant local bar scene. Sport is shown throughout on TV. Bar meals are served during the day and early evening. The pub is served by regular buses through the village. ❀♣P

Mossley

Church Inn L

82 Stockport Road, OL5 0RF
5 (4 Thu)-midnight; 4-1am Fri & Sat; 2-midnight Sun
☎ 07739 396818 meliaschurchinnmossley.simplesite.com
Sharp's Doom Bar; 4 changing beers (often Cross Bay, Donkeystone) H
This corner terrace pub on the A670 takes its name from the nearby St John's Church. Now a free

house, the traditional stone-built local has a comfortable lounge whose bar also serves the games room, where the pool table is popular. Three of the six handpumps serve local beers. The rear veranda provides a commanding view down the Tame Valley. Saturday is karaoke night; Tuesday is more sedate with live bluegrass often enjoyed. P (353)

Fleece

53 Stamford Street, OL5 0LN

12-midnight (1am Fri & Sat) (01457) 835487

Tatton Best; house beer (by Green Mill); 6 changing beers (sourced nationally; often Brewsmith, Silver Street, Titanic)

The Fleece is in Brookbottom, less than half a mile from the station, but much higher up. You will deserve a pint after the climb (or you could catch the bus). In 1890 the inn could accommodate three travellers, feed up to 50 and stable one horse. Today the visitor will find a tidy pub with a small vault area, an airy back room and a lounge. Cider or perry is always available. Dogs are welcome but horses perhaps less so.

Rising Sun

235 Stockport Road, OL5 0RQ

12-midnight (01457) 238236

risingsunmossley.co.uk

Millstone Tiger Rut, Stout; Thornbridge Jaipur IPA; 6 changing beers (often Joseph Holt, Millstone, Rising Sun)

A former Wilsons pub but a free house for many years, the present owner added a brewery in 2004. A range of regular and guest beers, cider and own brewed beers is available on 10 handpumps. Open-plan with log burning fires, both in and on the raised patio there is a fine view over the Tame valley to the Pennines beyond. Large TVs are a feature for watching Manchester City and United matches, with occasional live music some nights. It can get busy. P (353)

Oldham

Ashton Arms

28-30 Clegg Street, OL1 1PL (opp Odeon cinema complex)

11.30-11 (11.30 Fri & Sat); 11.30-8.30 Sun

(0161) 630 9709

6 changing beers (often Millstone, Pictish, Riverhead)

A popular town-centre free house near the Oldham Central Metrolink tram stop, this pub features an open-plan interior with the bar on a raised area to the rear. An excellent range of four to six rotating beers is served; most are LocAles and from local micros, some from further afield. Traditional cider or perry is permanently available. The fridges contain a wide variety of Belgian and German bottled beers. Good-value food is served weekdays, with pork pies and sandwiches at the weekend. (Central)

Carrion Crow

271 Huddersfield Road, OL4 2RJ

12-midnight (10.30 Sun) (0161) 633 4490

6 changing beers (often Banks's, Jennings, Marston's)

A thriving community local serving up to six cask ales from the Marston's extended family, this open-plan pub is a past winner of local CAMRA pub awards. Refurbished in 2017, it hosts crib, darts, dominoes, football and quiz teams. All cask ales are discounted on Monday evenings; quiz night is Thursday. Live music often features on Saturdays, with occasional beer festivals on bank holiday weekends. The pub is about 15 minutes' walk from Mumps Metrolink tram stop.

P (350)

Prestwich

Crooked Man

7 Fairfax Road, M25 1AS

closed Mon; 5-11 Tue-Thu; 1-midnight Fri & Sat; 1-10 Sun

07738 670522 thecrookedmanbar.com

3 changing beers

The Crooked Man is located in a renovated Victorian building. It offers three constantly changing cask ales and is set over two floors, with the bar on the ground floor. The upstairs area has two rooms with comfortable seating. The walls display local artists' and photographers' work. There are often live DJs in the evening, and the upstairs space is also used for live music, comedy nights and quizzes. Bar snacks are available.

Ramsbottom

Irwell Works Brewery Tap

Irwell Street, BL0 9YQ

closed Mon; 12-11 (11.30 Fri); 11-11.30 Sat; 11-11 Sun

(01706) 825019 irwellworksbrewery.co.uk

Irwell Works Tin Plate, Copper Plate, Costa Del Salford, Iron Plate; 4 changing beers (often Irwell Works)

This small local is situated on the first floor above the Irwell Works Brewery, with a balcony for outside drinking. A range of Irwell's beers is served. The brewery prides itself on the brewing and sale of traditional beers made with predominantly English hops and barley. Snack food is served Friday to Sunday 12-5.30pm. The bar is decorated with old photographs of the Ramsbottom area. The pub is a short walk from the East Lancashire Railway, the local preserved railway, and features on its ale trail.

(ELR) (472,474)

Ramsbottom Royal British Legion

Central Street, BL0 9AF

3.30 (2.30 Mon & Fri)-5.30, 8-11; 12-5.30, 7.30-11.30 Sat; 12-5.30, 7.30-10.30 Sun (01706) 822483

2 changing beers (sourced locally)

A one-room establishment in a back street in the centre of Ramsbottom. The members and steward are more than welcoming; membership is not required unless you become a regular. Two handpumps are in use all the time with different beers including many from local microbreweries. The club is a short walk from the East Lancs Railway. On-street parking is close by. There is a smoking area outside the entrance.

(ELR) (472,474)

Rochdale

Baum

35 Toad Lane, OL12 0NU

11.30-11 (midnight Fri & Sat); 11.30-10.30 Sun

(01706) 352186 thebaum.co.uk

7 changing beers

Situated in the Toad Lane conservation area, next to the Rochdale Pioneers Museum, the Baum is within easy reach of the tram and bus interchange. It is a former CAMRA National Pub of the Year, with a traditional frontage and interior, together with a conservatory and beer garden at the rear. Seven changing cask beers and a traditional cider are served, plus a wide selection of bottled beers and continental lagers. Good food matches the well-kept beers and is reasonably priced.

Flying Horse Hotel

37 Packer Street, OL16 1NJ

11.30-11 (1am Thu); 1.30-2am Fri; 10-2am Sat; 10-1am Sun (01706) 646412

10 changing beers (sourced locally; often Phoenix, Pictish, Serious)

An impressive Edwardian stone free house situated in the Town Hall Square. Built in 1691 and rebuilt in 1926, it retains many original features including log fires. There is also accommodation and a function room for hire. Ten cask ales are sold alongside four real ciders. Live music plays on Thursday, Friday and Saturday and live sport is screened. The home-made food menu features meat from the local butcher and pies made on the premises. Local CAMRA Pub of the Year in 2018. P

Medicine Tap

Ground Floor, The Esplanade, OL16 1AE

10-11 (1am Fri & Sat); 10-10 Sun (01706) 869828
themedicinetap.co.uk

8 changing beers (often Mallinsons)

Set opposite Rochdale Town Hall, this bar and restaurant occupies the iconic old Grade II-listed central post office, renovated to retain all its historic character and charm. Owned and run by Whitworth-based Mighty Medicine brewery, it serves its own beers plus a choice of local ale, cider and international beers. The Tap opens at 10am every day for beer and food; closing times depend on trade. Outside seating is provided in warmer weather. Dogs are not permitted inside. P

Oxford

662 Whitworth Road, OL12 0TB

12-10 Mon (11 Tue-Thu; midnight Fri & Sat); 12-10 Sun (01706) 345709 theoxfordpub.com

Wainwright; 2 changing beers (sourced regionally; often Black Sheep, Serious, Timothy Taylor)

The Oxford is a busy stone-built pub on the A671 Rochdale to Burnley road, with a fine reputation for beer and fresh food. The layout is open plan in two areas, for dining and drinking. Three real ales are on handpump; Wainwright is a permanent beer, with the other changing ales usually coming from small local or regional breweries. Good well-presented meals are available daily, cooked to order. The beer garden at the rear has an excellent view of the nearby moors. The pub recently hosted a mini beer festival. P (486)

Regal Moon

The Butts, OL16 1HB

9am-midnight (1am Fri & Sat) (01706) 657434

Elland 1872 Porter; Hawkshead Windermere Pale; Moorhouse's Blond Witch; Ossett Silver King; Ruddles Best Bitter; changing beers (often Phoenix, Pictish)

A large and imposing former cinema in the town centre, refurbished in 2016. Rochdale icons Gracie Fields and Lisa Stansfield feature among the memorabilia, with a mannequin organist above the bar continuing the music theme. This is regularly the top-selling real ale establishment in the Wetherspoon estate, dispensing a wide variety of ales from local and Yorkshire breweries. Five ciders are available, one from Westons, plus rotating guests. The open-plan interior splits into discrete drinking areas. Close to the tram and bus interchange.

Romiley

Jake's Ale House

27 Compstall Road, SK6 4BT

3-10 Mon-Wed; 1-10.30 Thu (11 Fri & Sat); 1-10 Sun 07927 076941

5 changing beers (sourced locally; often Poynton)

Romiley's first micropub, formerly a shop, has become well established over the last couple of years. Its small front-bar area has a relaxed atmosphere and there is a smaller room at the rear. The changing range of beers, often from local micros, is a welcome addition to the local scene. The pub is close to the railway station and good bus routes, and the Peak Forest Canal is a short walk away. Opening hours may vary. Q

Royton

Puckersley Inn

22 Narrowgate Brow, OL2 6YD (off A671 via Dogford Rd & Fir Lane)

12-midnight (1am Fri & Sat) (0161) 652 2834

JW Lees Supernova, Manchester Pale Ale, Bitter; 1 changing beer (sourced locally; often JW Lees)

This welcoming JW Lees local is a detached, stone-fronted pub situated on the edge of the green belt, with panoramic views over Royton, Shaw and Oldham. The building has a traditional vault, a comfortable lounge and a dining extension where children are welcome. Cosy corners provide plenty of space to chat and enjoy the four Lees beers on offer. An excellent range of meals is served lunchtimes and evenings. P (408)

Rusholme

Ford Madox Brown

Unit 1 Wilmslow Park, Wilmslow Road, M14 5FT (jct Hathersage Rd)

8am-midnight (0161) 256 6660

Greene King Abbot; Ruddles Best Bitter; Sharp's Doom Bar; house beer (by Hafod); 4 changing beers (sourced nationally)

Modern Wetherspoon pub paradoxically named after the eminent Victorian Pre-Raphaelite painter (he lived nearby in Victoria Park), and built on the site of the old Rusholme Hall. Handy for the curry mile and Whitworth Gallery and University, it is popular not just with students but with a real cross-section of people. Although an open-plan pub, it has a warmer feeling than you might expect, the community atmosphere enhanced by brewery visits and local events. Q

Sale

JP Joule

2A Northenden Road, M33 3BR

8am-midnight (1am Fri & Sat) (0161) 962 9889

Greene King Abbot; Ruddles Best Bitter; Sharp's Doom Bar; Wychwood Hobgoblin Gold; 5 changing

beers (sourced nationally; often Peerless, Titanic, Hawkshead) Ⓗ
Named after the famous physicist who was a resident of Sale for a time, this popular Wetherspoon pub is close to the tram station and on several bus routes. Set on two floors, with a bar on each, the pub offers a total of 14 handpumps featuring nine real ales (four are duplicated upstairs). Five beers are constantly changing and sourced regionally. Real ale and cider and perry festivals are held twice a year. Q🐴❀◑♿🚊●🚌📶

Salford

Eagle Inn

18 Collier Street, M3 7DW (opp Rolla St)
⏲ 3-11 (1am Fri); 1-1am Sat; 1-11 Sun ☎ (0161) 819 5002
🌐 eagleinn.info
Bootleg Urban Fox; Joseph Holt Bitter, Two Hoots; 2 changing beers (sourced locally) Ⓗ
This hidden gem of a traditional back-street boozer is known to locals as the Lamp Oil. A Grade II-listed building dating from 1902, it features a fine terracotta plaque of an eagle above the door – for years this was the only pub sign. There are three small rooms off a central corridor with a central bar. Handpull offerings include several ales plus Old Rosie cider. The attached cottage next door has been converted into a live music venue.
Q🐴❀⇌(Central)🚊(Victoria)♣●🚌🐾📶

New Oxford Ⓛ

11 Bexley Square, M3 6DB (corner of Browning St)
⏲ 12-midnight ☎ (0161) 832 7082 🌐 thenewoxford.com
17 changing beers (sourced regionally; often Empire, Moorhouse's, Phoenix) Ⓗ
A recently refurbished multi award-winning corner house dating from the 1830s, with two main rooms either side of a central bar. It has 20 handpumps – 17 for regionally sourced ales from both new and established breweries, always including at least two dark ales. The other three pumps are for cider and perry. There is also an extensive range of bottled Belgian beers. Good-value lunches are served Tuesday to Friday.
🐴❀◐♿⇌(Central)●🚌🐾📶

Salford Arms Hotel

146 Chapel Street, M3 6AF (corner Bloom St)
⏲ 12-11.30 (1.30am Fri & Sat); 12-11 Sun
☎ (0161) 288 8883
6 changing beers (sourced nationally) Ⓗ
On the main A6 route into Manchester, this is a very welcoming establishment with six handpumps dispensing a changing range of beers from regional and national brewers. Cider is also available in spring and summer. Food is served lunchtimes and evenings until 9pm. There is a smaller side room which provides extra space when the main bar is busy. Pub games and pool are played. The pub hosts a variety of activities and events including language exchange on Wednesday. Accommodation is in nine rooms.
🐴❀🛏◑⇌(Central)♣●🚌🐾📶

Stalybridge

Bridge Beers Ⓛ

55 Melbourne Street, SK15 2JJ
⏲ 12-7 (9 Thu; 10 Fri & Sat); closed Sun & Mon
☎ 07948 617145 🌐 bridgebeers.co.uk
4 changing beers (sourced locally) Ⓖ
A former hairdresser's, now a micropub and bottle shop on the main pedestrianised shopping street in Stalybridge. A small entrance area leads to the bar which sits in front of a row of stillaged casks, of which four are generally in use. The bottle display is opposite. Upstairs is a comfortable lounge. Beers are constantly changing and all locally sourced. Last entry is one hour before closing. Q🐴⇌♣●🚌🐾

Crafty Pint

41 Melbourne Street, SK15 2JJ
⏲ closed Mon & Tue; 4-11 Wed-Fri; 12-11 Sat; 12-6 Sun
☎ 07512 753554
4 changing beers Ⓗ
Situated next to the canal in the main pedestrianised shopping street, this microbar offers four changing real ales, mainly from local breweries but some from further afield. There is also a good selection of bottled beers, mostly from Germany. This a bar where conversation dominates rather than piped music and TV screens. Board games are available. Children and dogs are welcome. Q🐴⇌🚌🐾📶

Society Rooms ✔

49-51 Grosvenor Street, SK15 2JN
⏲ 8am-midnight (1am Fri & Sat) ☎ (0161) 338 9740
Greene King Abbot; Ruddles Best Bitter; Sharp's Doom Bar; changing beers (sourced nationally) Ⓗ
This Wetherspoon pub is named after the former Co-op store premises it occupies within the town centre. It has a large main area and two elevated sections either side of the entrance. Enthusiastic management and a strong focus on real ales (on 10 handpumps) have made this a favourite destination for local drinkers. Beer-oriented events such as Meet the Brewer nights and beer requests by customers have helped to boost the pub's reputation. Real cider is always available.
🐴❀◑♿⇌●🚌📶

Station Buffet Bar 🏆 ★

Platform 4, Stalybridge Railway Station, Rassbottom Street, SK15 1RF (access from station platform 4)
⏲ 12-11 Mon; 11-11 Tue-Fri (midnight Sat); 12-11 Sun
☎ (0161) 303 0007
Changing beers (sourced regionally) Ⓗ
One of the few Victorian station buffet bars remaining and well worth missing a train for. A sympathetic refurbishment has allowed expansion of the food menu which includes home-cooked meals. Nine handpumps dispense a variety of beers, most of which are locally sourced, plus at least one real cider or perry. A good range of bottled beers is also available. Events include live music and Meet the Brewer nights. Monday is quiz night. On the Transpennine Real Ale Trail.
Q◑♿⇌●P🚌

White House ✔

1 Water Street, SK15 2AG
⏲ 12-midnight (11 Sun) ☎ (0161) 303 2154
Hydes Original; 5 changing beers Ⓗ
A busy pub close to both bus and rail stations, semi open plan but retaining four distinct drinking areas. Up to five guest beers from micros and Hydes Beer Studio complement the regular Original. Three or so real ciders are also offered and pies are available. A popular live music venue, a folk night is held every Thursday and bands play most Fridays and Saturdays. ❀⇌♣●P🚌🐾

Standish

Albion Ale House ✔
12 High Street, WN6 0HL
⏲ 4-7 Mon; 3-10 Tue & Wed (11 Thu); 2-midnight Fri & Sat; 2-9 Sun ☎ (01257) 367897 🌐 albionalehouse.co.uk.
8 changing beers [H]
The first micropub in Standish, located in a former shop right on the High Street, now well established with a loyal clientele and voted local CAMRA Community Pub of the Year 2018/19. Five cask ales are normally on offer, sometimes more, always including one dark beer. Snacks are also usually available. There is occasional live music and beer festivals. Q🐴✿♿🚌(362,113)🐾

Hoot Standish
34A High Street, WN6 0HL
⏲ closed Mon & Tue; 11-11 Wed & Thu (midnight Fri & Sat); 11-10.30 Sun ☎ (01257) 806262
7 changing beers (sourced nationally) [H]
This modern café/bar has interesting accent lighting, a slate-tiled floor and modest silent TVs with subtitles. Novelty owls feature around the large one-room bar area, and it has a wood-burning stove. Varying local real ales and cider are served alongside speciality coffees and Prosecco, making this venue popular with all age groups. Light bites and sandwiches are also available.
Q🐴✿◐♿♣🍎P🚌🐾📶

Standish Unity Club 𝕃
Cross Street, WN6 0HQ
⏲ 7.30-11 (midnight Fri & Sat) ☎ (01257) 424007
🌐 standishunityclub.com
Sharp's Doom Bar; 4 changing beers [H]
In the centre of Standish but tucked away so a little tricky to find, this popular club offers five real ales including one dark beer, often Titanic Plum Porter. The club is divided in two – a large function room and a bar area including the games room plus a quieter drinking area. A frequent winner of local CAMRA Club of the Year and a previous runner-up Regional Club of the Year.
Q🐴♿♣P🚌(362,113)📶

Stockport

Arden Arms ★ ✔
23 Millgate, SK1 2LX (jct Corporation St)
⏲ 12-midnight ☎ (0161) 480 2185
Robinsons Unicorn, Double Hop [H]**, Old Tom** [G]**, Dizzy Blonde, Wizard, Trooper; 1 changing beer (often Robinsons)** [H]
Grade II-listed and on CAMRA's National Inventory of Historic Pub Interiors, this multi-room pub is just down the hill from Stockport's Market Place. Note the superb curved, glazed bar, the grandfather clock, and particularly the snug, which can only be accessed through the bar area itself (one of only four such in the UK). The building alone warrants a visit, while the food is also recommended. The large, attractive courtyard hosts live music on Saturday nights. A true gem.
🐴✿◐◑♿♣🚌(300,384)🐾📶

Armoury ✔
31 Shaw Heath, Edgeley, SK3 8BD (on B5465, jct Greek St)
⏲ 1-midnight; 11-1am Fri & Sat; 11.30-midnight Sun
☎ 07931 621220
Robinsons Unicorn, Trooper, Dizzy Blonde, Double Hop; 1 changing beer (often Robinsons) [H]
Comfortable, multi-roomed local with a military history and a strong community following. It caters for so many functions and groups it is almost always busy, welcoming darts players, sports watchers, the White Ensign Association, the Army Reserve, and many others. Much memorabilia is on display in the bar room. Outside is a fine, secluded beer garden, which can be quite a suntrap in good weather. Q🐴✿♿⇌♣🚌🐾📶

Bakers Vaults 🏆 ✔
Market Place, SK1 1ES (jct Vernon St)
⏲ 12-11.30 (1.30am Fri & Sat); 12-10.30 Sun
☎ (0161) 480 9448
Robinsons Unicorn, Dizzy Blonde, Trooper, Old Tom; Titanic Plum Porter; 4 changing beers (sourced nationally; often Robinsons) [H]
Excellent market pub with a unique atmosphere, being both cosy and relaxed as well as lively and vibrant. The Grade II-listed building was refurbished in mid-2014. The layout, with the bar towards the back of the building, creates a spaciousness it once lacked. The bohemian feel of the gin palace-style interior is enhanced by high ceilings and arch windows. It is one of the few Robinsons Brewery houses to serve guest beers from other brewers. 🐴✿◐◑⇌♣🍎🐾📶

Blossoms
2 Buxton Road, Heaviley, SK2 6NU (at A6/A5102 jct)
⏲ 12 (3 Mon & Tue)-midnight; 11-midnight Sat & Sun
☎ (0161) 222 4150
Robinsons Unicorn [H]**, Old Tom** [G]**, Dizzy Blonde, Trooper, Double Hop; 1 changing beer (often Robinsons)** [H]
Landmark building with a traditional layout of three rooms radiating from a central bar. This Robinsons Brewery house is one of its Ale Shrine pubs. The rear room tends to be busiest, while the bar area is always crowded with locals. On a historical note, look for the Smoke Room etched glass on the door to the rear room, as well as some lovely leaded glass in the windows. Outside drinking is catered for in the cobbled alleyway and what was previously a public toilet. Q✿◐◑⇌♣P🚌🐾📶

Boar's Head
2 Vernon Street, Market Place, SK1 1TY (jct Market Place)
⏲ 11-11; 12-6.30 Sun ☎ (0161) 480 3978
Samuel Smith Old Brewery Bitter [H]
If you want a drink with atmosphere in Stockport centre, the Boar's Head is a must-visit. Entering the multi-room pub, with real fires adding warmth and ambience, feels like stepping back 50 years. Owners Samuel Smith have spent a fair sum restoring the building to what it may have looked like in previous years, and it really works. The front room is divided into a sparsely furnished public lounge to the right, on the left is a more comfortably furnished room with cushioned pews, high-back chairs and stools. To the rear is a second lounge leading outside to a small decked drinking area. Q✿⇌🚌(300)🐾

Hope Inn
118 Wellington Road North, Heaton Norris, SK4 2LL (N of Belmont Way)
⏲ 12-11 (midnight Fri & Sat) ☎ (0161) 637 6191
🌐 thehopestockport.co.uk
Fool Hardy Ales Risky Blond; Outstanding 3.9; 9 changing beers (sourced nationally) [H]

Transformed in 2013 from a dead duck to a multi-beer free house. Home to the Fool Hardy Ales microbrewery, it comprises two large rooms – to the right is the cask ale side where 11 handpumps dispense a mix of house-brewed beers and changing guests, to the left is a room dedicated to foreign/keg beers and real ciders. Enjoy the pinball machine, pool table and a variety of board games.
Q❀♣●P🚌🐾

Magnet

51 Wellington Road North, Heaton Norris, SK4 1HJ (jct Duke St)
4-11; 12-11 Fri-Sun ☎ (0161) 429 6287
themagnetfreehouse.co.uk
Salopian Oracle; 13 changing beers (sourced nationally; often Tiny Rebel) Ⓗ
Family-run, award-winning pub focusing on quality and choice. It offers 14 handpumped beers alongside 12 craft keg beers, plus a large range of foreign bottles. The in-house microbrewery produces seasonal ales. Digital beer boards display all the available beers. On the left is a bustling vault leading to a lower pool room and a series of other rooms. Outside, there is a twin-storey beer terrace with seating. An upstairs room opens at weekends. A former local CAMRA Pub of the Year.
Q❀≹♣P🚌🐾

Olde Vic

1 Chatham Street, Edgeley, SK3 9ED (jct Shaw Heath)
5-11 yeoldevic.pub
6 changing beers (sourced nationally) Ⓗ
Now owned by its regulars, Ye Olde Vic continues to benefit from a programme of improvements although inside it remains enjoyably shambolic. Bric-a-brac abounds, with something to catch your eye at every turn. The six ever-changing guest beers come from small breweries around the UK and the pumpclips on the ceiling are a potted history of lost beers and brewers. Look for the sign over the bar describing the various forms of sparkler used in dispensing your beer.
Q❀≹♣●🚌🐾

Petersgate Tap

19A St Petersgate, SK1 1EB (jct Etchells St)
closed Mon; 12 (4 Tue; 2 Wed)-11; 1-8 Sun
☎ 07925 078426 petersgatetap.com
Hawkshead Windermere Pale; 5 changing beers (sourced regionally) Ⓗ
This family-run bar, opened in 2016 in former betting shop premises, is a continuing sign of the regeneration of the town's Market Place. Set over two floors, downstairs the style is fairly modern with a continental feel to the bar area. Recycled oak-topped tables and a mix of seating sit under interesting posters and breweriana on the walls. Monthly events in the upstairs room range from tutored beer or cider tastings to live music and poetry and prose evenings.
Q❀♿≹●🚌(300)🐾

Railway

1 Avenue Street, Portwood, SK1 2BZ (jct Gt Portwood St)
12-11 (10.30 Sun) ☎ (0161) 429 6062
Dunham Massey Dunham Porter; Outstanding Ultra Pale, Blond; Phoenix Arizona; Pictish Brewers Gold; Thornbridge Jaipur IPA; 3 changing beers (sourced nationally) Ⓗ
This street-corner local is a favourite with both its loyal crowd of regulars and also shoppers from the Peel Centre across the road. Eleven handpumps showcase a range of beer styles, including three changing guest beers (one of which is a rotating mild). These are supplemented by a changing guest cider and a range of Belgian, German and other bottled beers. The bar billiards table is well used while the outside drinking area is a summer suntrap. Q❀♣●🚌🐾

Remedy Bar & Brewhouse

10-11 Market Place, SK1 1EW (jct Mealhouse Brow)
closed Mon; 12-11.30 (10.30 Sun) ☎ (0161) 477 1842
remedybarandbrewhouse.co.uk
6 changing beers (sourced regionally) Ⓗ
One of a number of cask outlets on Stockport's burgeoning Market Place, this conversion of two shop units opened in 2015. Its modern steampunk-style open interior is divided into two separate drinking areas, while the one-barrel in-house brew kit can be seen behind the glazed wall near the bar. Note the mosaic of pennies set into the floor in front of the bar. Live music plays on Thursday evening and sometimes over the weekend. No lunchtime food on Tuesday and Wednesday.
♿≹●🚌(300)🐾

Swan with Two Necks ★

36 Princes Street, SK1 1RY (jct Hatton St)
11-11; 11.30-9 Sun ☎ (0161) 480 2341
Robinsons Unicorn, Old Tom; 1 changing beer (often Robinsons) Ⓗ
The pub was rebuilt in the 1920s and the interior remains mostly unchanged since then – of particular note are the classic panelled drinking lobby and the top-lit middle room with mock-Tudor fireplace. The rear outside area has been stylishly reworked and is a lovely spot to enjoy a pint in the warmer months. Home-cooked food, available 12-3pm Tuesday to Saturday, is recommended. The cider is from the Westons range.
Q❀≹♣●🚌(300,330)🐾

Summerseat

Footballers Inn

28 Higher Summerseat, BL0 9UG
2-midnight; 1-1.30am Fri; 12-1.30am Sat; 12-12.30am Sun
☎ (01204) 880008
Bowland Hen Harrier; Theakston Best Bitter; Wainwright; 3 changing beers (often Moorhouse's, Timothy Taylor) Ⓗ
Once the regular haunt of some of the stars of Coronation Street in the '60s and '70s, this stone-built two-roomed pub is in higher Summerseat. It has a central bar with TV and a main lounge featuring a log burner. An extra handpump has been installed to give three regular and three guest real ales. The pub is frequently in this Guide and a 15-minute walk from the East Lancashire heritage railway line station.
❀≹(ELR)♣P🚌(477)🐾

Swinton

Park Inn

135-137 Worsley Road, M27 5SP (corner Shaftesbury Rd)
2-11 Mon (11.30 Tue); 12-11 Wed (11.30 Thu; midnight Fri & Sat); 11-11 Sun ☎ (0161) 793 1568
Joseph Holt Bitter Ⓗ
A smart, popular pub, winner of local CAMRA branch Best Traditional Local in 2017, serving Holt

beers since 1878. A small extension to the front vault was added later and the two rooms on the right were combined to create a spacious lounge. There is a cosy, tiny snug behind the central bar. Monday is quiz night and a bikers' club meets on the first Wednesday of the month. Darts matches are held regularly and the lounge is sometimes used for functions. Q♿♣P🚌(2,73)🐾📶

White Swan

186 Worsley Road, M27 5SN (opp Lyon St)
⏲ 12-11 (11.30 Fri & Sat); 12-10.30 Sun ☎ 07827 850294
Joseph Holt Bitter; 1 changing beer (sourced nationally) 🄷
A White Swan has stood on the same site since the 1820s. The building was bought by Joseph Holt in 1868 and replaced by today's pub in 1928. The vault and a large oak-panelled lounge behind the bar remain. A function room is found at the rear. A quiz and disco are held on Saturday and a coach takes regulars to Swinton rugby league games on Sunday. Live music and ladies' nights feature occasionally. Q🐴❀♣P🚌🐾📶

Tottington

Dungeon Inn

9 Turton Road, BL8 4AW
⏲ 4-11 (midnight Fri); 12-midnight Sat; 12-10.30 Sun
Lancaster Bomber; Wainwright; house beer (by Thwaites); 3 changing beers 🄷
A traditional, family-friendly Thwaites pub. There is a quiet front lounge with a real open fire in cold winter periods and a separate pool room off the main bar room. To the rear at a lower level is a suntrap beer garden. Six handpumps serve regular and guest ales. Bar snacks are available. The Dungeon Inn is recognised by CAMRA as having a historic interior of regional importance. Dogs are welcome until 7.30pm and children until 8.30pm. Q🐴❀♣P🚏🚌(480,469)🐾📶

Tyldesley

Mort Arms

235-237 Elliott Street, M29 8DG
⏲ 12-11 (midnight Fri & Sat) ☎ 07584 341099
Joseph Holt Bitter; 1 changing beer (sourced locally; often Bootleg) 🄷
From the façade to the interior, this 1930s pub is recognisable as a Holt's hostelry. The entrance has two etched doors directing you into either the tap room or the lounge, with a central bar serving both. This is very much a community-based pub that supports and participates in the local darts and dominoes leagues. As well as the Bitter, there is often a guest beer from Holt or Bootleg.
❀♣🚌(V2)📶

Union Arms

83 Castle Street, M29 8EW
⏲ 12-11 (midnight Fri & Sat); 12-10.30 Sun
☎ (01942) 870645
3 changing beers (sourced locally) 🄷
This family-friendly pub is part of the local community with regular charity events and occasional theme nights including live music. The interior is divided into a number of separate connected areas. The left side is the vault and the right is a lounge used for dining. There are usually three to four real ales including Wainwright, with good-value fresh home-cooked food served until 8pm and traditional lunch on Sunday until 6pm. Most sporting events are shown on TV.
🐴❀◑♣🚌(V2)🐾

Uppermill

Albion Tap 🄻

72 High Sreet, OL3 6AW
⏲ 4-11 Mon-Wed; 2-midnight Thu; 12-midnight Fri & Sat; 12-11 Sun
Donkeystone Bad Ass Blonde, Cotton Clouds, DPA; 1 changing beer (often Track) 🄷
This stylish bar was formerly a book shop and a bottle shop. It has a stainless-steel bar, high wooden tables, exposed brickwork and a mural of an old Saddleworth snow scene. Bees adorn the ceiling. The bar is owned by the licensees of the adjacent Hare & Hounds pub. In addition to the cask ales there are eight keg fonts, with Track, Cloudwater and Thornbridge breweries often featured. A carefully curated choice of UK and foreign bottles and cans is also available. 🐴❀🚌🐾

Cross Keys Inn ✔

Running Hill Gate, OL3 6LW (off A670 up Church Rd)
⏲ 12-11 (11.30 Thu-Sat); 12-10.30 Sun ☎ (01457) 874626
🌐 crosskeysinn.co.uk
JW Lees Dark, Manchester Pale Ale, Bitter, Founder's; 1 changing beer (sourced locally) 🄷
Overlooking St Chad church and Saddleworth, this attractive 18th-century stone building is Grade II-listed. It has exposed beams throughout and was sympathetically refurbished in 2017. The public bar has a stone-flagged floor and a Yorkshire range. Home-cooked food features daily specials. Outside, there is a small garden and children's play area to the rear, and an extended patio with smoking area to the front. Walkers and dogs are very welcome.
Q🐴❀◑♿P🐾📶

Urmston

Flixton Conservative Club ✔

Abbotsfield, 193 Flixton Road, M41 5DF
⏲ 12-3, 6-11; 12-11.30 Fri & Sat; 12-11 Sun
☎ (0161) 748 2846 🌐 flixtonconservativeclub.co.uk
6 changing beers (sourced nationally; often Elland, Pictish, Dunham Massey) 🄷
With six handpumps on the main bar, this national CAMRA award-winning club displays an ongoing commitment to quality real ales, offering a varied range of local, regional and national beers. A further five handpumps upstairs allow the club to run monthly brewery takeover nights with a small entry charge, pie and peas included. Various other events are held including regular quiz nights. The club is home to a wide range of sports teams, including snooker, bowls, darts, dominoes and chess. 🐴❀⇌(Chassen Rd)♣P🚌(255)📶

Lord Nelson

49 Stretford Road, M41 9LG
⏲ 11-11 (11.30 Fri; midnight Sat); 12-11 Sun
☎ 07827 850255
Bootleg Chorlton Pale Ale; Joseph Holt Mild, Bitter, IPA 🄷
The Nellie is your classic Holt's suburban pub, catering for the basic essentials in life – a drink, a chat and sport on the many TV screens. The building, which dates back to around 1805, has recently been refurbished but still retains its original character and is very much part of the local

community, raising astonishing sums of money for local charities. Food is limited to the usual pub fare of nuts, crisps and suchlike. Children are not allowed at any time. ❀⇌♣P🚌🐾📶

Prairie Schooner Taphouse 🄻

33 Flixton Road, M41 5AW

⏲ 1-11 (10 Mon); 12-midnight Fri & Sat; 12-10 Sun

🌐 prairie-schooner-taphouse.co.uk

4 changing beers (sourced locally; often Brightside, Dunham Massey, Outstanding) Ⓗ

A converted golf equipment shop, since its opening in 2014 the Schooner has been a great addition to the Urmston real ale scene. It offers four handpumps serving usually local beers, eight keg fonts and a wide variety of bottles and cans from all over the world. Real cider is available in bag in box, and gins and whiskies are also stocked. No regular food is served, just nibbles, nuts and crisps, however there are monthly street food events. May close early if quiet. Q❀♿⇌♣🚌(255)🐾📶

Wardley

Morning Star

520 Manchester Road, M27 9QW (opp Bagot St)

⏲ 12-11 (11.30 Fri & Sat) ☎ (0161) 727 8373

Joseph Holt Mild, Bitter, Two Hoots; 1 changing beer (sourced locally) Ⓗ

Built in 1890, this imposing red-brick building is a good example of a community establishment. A smart and tidy pub, to the left is the traditional vault with darts, dominoes and TV. To the right is a small front room leading to a much larger lounge/dining room. A central bar serves all rooms. Good pub food is available until 7.30pm. The pub hosts a Wednesday quiz night and Friday evening entertainment. A covered outside area is a real asset in summer. ❀◑⇌♣P🚌📶

West Didsbury

Wine & Wallop

97 Lapwing Lane, M20 6UR (jct Palatine Rd)

⏲ 11-11 (midnight Fri & Sat); 11-10.30 Sun

☎ (0161) 446 2464

Brightside Maverick IPA; First Chop HOP; Howard Town Super Fortress; 5 changing beers (sourced nationally) Ⓗ

This comfortable bar, previously a video shop and grocer's (you can still see tiling from its grocery days), is set over two floors. Upstairs you can sit on sofas gazing down on your fellow drinkers from the internal balcony. Downstairs, bare-boarded floors and part-plastered, wainscoted or bare-brick walls are adorned with occasional large mirrors. Feature chandeliers add a touch of class to the decor. Guest beers are mainly from local breweries.
❀◑♿🚌🐾📶

Whalley Range

Hillary Step 🄻 ✔

199 Upper Chorlton Road, M16 0BH

⏲ 4-11.30; 3-12.30am Fri; 12-12.30am Sat; 12-11.30 Sun

☎ (0161) 881 1978 🌐 thehillarystep.co.uk

5 changing beers (sourced nationally; often RedWillow, Squawk, Track) Ⓗ

Modern bar in a small strip of shops and bars a short walk north of Chorlton. Five handpumps feature mostly local and regional breweries, occasionally breweries from further south, and one dark beer over the winter. A range of draught and bottled continental beers is also kept, plus a large selection of whiskies. Light snacks are served such as pork pies and Scotch eggs. Live jazz features on Sunday evening and alternate Wednesdays. Quiz night is the first Tuesday of the month and games night Monday. No children are permitted.
❀◑♣🚌(86)🐾📶

Whitefield

Eagle & Child

Higher Lane, M45 7EY

⏲ 12-11 (midnight Fri & Sat) ☎ 07827 850229

Joseph Holt Mild, Bitter, Two Hoots; 1 changing beer (often Joseph Holt, Nethergate) Ⓗ

A half-timbered pub in the traditional style, with separate doors leading to the taproom and lounge, both served by a central bar. There is a dining area off the lounge. Food is served 12-8pm daily, including roasts on Sunday. Live music plays every Friday and alternate Wednesdays and Sky and BT Sports are shown on TVs. At the rear is a bowling green, available for hire during the summer months. Q❀◑♿♣P🚌(98,135)🐾📶

Wigan

Anvil

Dorning Street, WN1 1ND

⏲ 11-11; 12-10.30 Sun ☎ (01942) 239444

Banks's Mild; Brakspear Oxford Gold; Wainwright; 4 changing beers (sourced nationally) Ⓗ

Popular town-centre pub close to the bus station with seven handpumps offering various guest beers, two real ciders, six draught continental ales and a range of bottled beers. Several TV screens show sports action and the small snug contains the Wall of Fame displaying numerous award certificates. There is a garden at the rear. Over-18s only. ❀⇌(Wallgate/North Western)🍎🚌

Blundell's Café Bar 🄻

90 Wigan Lane, WN1 2LF

⏲ 6-11 Mon; closed Tue; 4-11 Wed & Thu; 2-11 Fri & Sat; 2-10 Sun ☎ 07810 396736

3 changing beers Ⓗ

Situated just off the main road with reasonable parking outside and in side streets, this is a quiet haven for a pint of local ale, a fine coffee and simple snacks. One wall has an impressive mural of a Venice canal, and other walls have a varied range of interesting posters and pictures. The bar is often candlelit in the evening. Family-sized functions are usually held Monday through to Wednesday.
Q◑P🚌🐾📶

Crooke Hall Inn

Crooke Road, WN6 8LR

⏲ 3-10 Mon-Wed; 12-11 ☎ (01942) 236088

6 changing beers Ⓗ

Multi-roomed canalside inn in a picturesque location in Crooke, three miles outside the centre of Wigan. Very popular with locals and visitors alike, dogs and children are welcome until 9pm. Home-made food features locally sourced ingredients where possible. It has a separate cellar bar ideal for functions and a large beer garden. The pub is very much the hub of the village community.
❀◑🍎P🐾📶

Doc's Symposium L

85 Mesnes Street, WN1 1QJ
closed Mon-Wed; 12-11 Thu-Sat; 1-10.30 Sun
☎ (01942) 567765
Weetwood Cheshire Cat; 4 changing beers H
A warm welcome awaits you from the well-respected landlords at Wigan's first micropub. Five cask ales, European beers, ciders and bottled beers are available. The deli counter offers a wide range of light snacks and nibbles made from fresh ingredients daily. Situated within walking distance of Wigan town centre, this bar has outdoor seating overlooking Mesnes Park. From March to the end of September it also opens Wednesday 4-7pm.
Q❀◗♿⇌P

John Bull Chophouse

2 Coopers Row, Market Place, WN1 1PQ
closed Mon; 4.30-11 Tue-Thu; 1-1am Fri; 12.30-1am Sat; 3-11 Sun ☎ (01942) 242862
johnbullchophousewigan.co.uk
House beer (by Thwaites); 10 changing beers H
A vibrant and lively inn in a town-centre building over 300 years old which has been cottages, stables and a slaughterhouse in the past. It has been run by the same family for over 40 years. This quirky pub is set over two floors, with six handpumps downstairs serving Thwaites beers and six further handpumps upstairs. The toilets are upstairs. There is seating outside. Closed Monday and Tuesday in winter.
❀⇌(Wallgate/North Western)

Raven Hotel ✔

5 Wallgate, WN1 1LD
11-11 (1am Fri & Sat) ☎ (01942) 239764
theravenwigan.com
Tetley Bitter; 4 changing beers H
An early 1900s commercial hotel, virtually derelict before a tasteful renovation in 2012 that retained and restored many original features including tiles, panelling and windows. The retro decor is typical of this small local pub chain, with cosy coal fires in winter and two unobtrusive TVs. It serves a varying range of real ales and cider on handpump, alongside good home-made pub food at reasonable prices. Loyalty cards are offered and a Wednesday cask critics night gives discounts on real ale.
❀◗♿⇌(Wallgate/North Western)

Tap 'n' Barrel L ✔

16 Jaxon's Court, WN1 1LR
12-10 Mon; closed Tue; 12-10 Wed & Thu (midnight Fri; 12.30am Sat); 1-10 Sun ☎ (01942) 386966
martlandmillbrewery.co.uk
Martland Mill Lancashire Loom; 6 changing beers (sourced regionally) H
Located adjacent to the bus station in a narrow shopping mews, this microbar is the brewery tap for Martland Mill. The main bar area is long and narrow, leading to a covered and heated, smoke-free garden, which hosts live music on Sunday afternoon. There is additional seating upstairs. Four real ciders are served from the fridge. Beer and cider are available in paddles of three third-pints. Occasional beer and sausage festivals are held.
Q⇌(Wallgate/North Western)

Wigan Central 🏆 L

Arch No.1 & 2, Queen Street, WN3 4DY
12-11 (midnight Fri); 11-midnight Sat; 12-10.30 Sun
☎ (01942) 246425 wigancentral.bar
House beer (by Prospect); 6 changing beers (sourced nationally) H
This award-winning two-roomed pub has a railway-themed interior with a live feed displaying arrival and departure times from both railway stations. The pub is owned by the nearby Prospect Brewery but sells real ales from all over, alongside continental bottled beers displayed in the 'library'. Live music plays on Sunday. Bar snacks are available. Local CAMRA Pub of the Year and Cider Pub of the Year 2018/19 and national CAMRA Pub of the Year runner-up 2017/18. Q♿⇌

Withington

Victoria ✔

438 Wilmslow Road, M20 3BW (on B5093, jct Davenport Av)
12-11 (midnight Thu-Sat) ☎ (0161) 434 2600
Hydes Original, 1863, Lowry; 5 changing beers (sourced nationally; often Hydes) H
This friendly late 19th-century community Hydes pub attracts a convivial cross-section of Withington life through its doors each day. Retaining a period exterior and etched windows, the interior has been opened out in recent refurbishments to create distinct drinking areas, each with their own atmosphere and intimacy. There is entertainment at weekends and sport on TV. ❀♣

Woodford

Davenport Arms (Thief's Neck)

550 Chester Road, SK7 1PS (on A5102, jct Church Lane)
11-11; 12-10.30 Sun ☎ (0161) 439 2435
davenportarms.co.uk
Robinsons Unicorn, Dizzy Blonde, Old Tom, Wizard; 1 changing beer (often Robinsons) H
Characterful red-brick farmhouse-style pub which received a smart refurbishment several years ago but retains a multi-roomed feel with real fires in winter. This is its 33rd consecutive year in the Guide, and the licence has now been in the same family for a mammoth 87 years. Excellent food is mostly home made, with some adventurous specials. Outside, the spacious forecourt and attractive garden, set well away from the road, are popular in summer, boasting impressive floral displays. ❀◗♣P(42B)

A quart a day keeps the doctor away

A judicious labourer would probably always have some ale in his house, and have small beer for the general drink. There is no reason why he should not keep Christmas as well as the farmer; and when he is mowing, reaping, or is at any other hard work, a quart, or three pints, of really good fat ale a-day is by no means too much.
William Cobbett, Cottage Economy, 1822

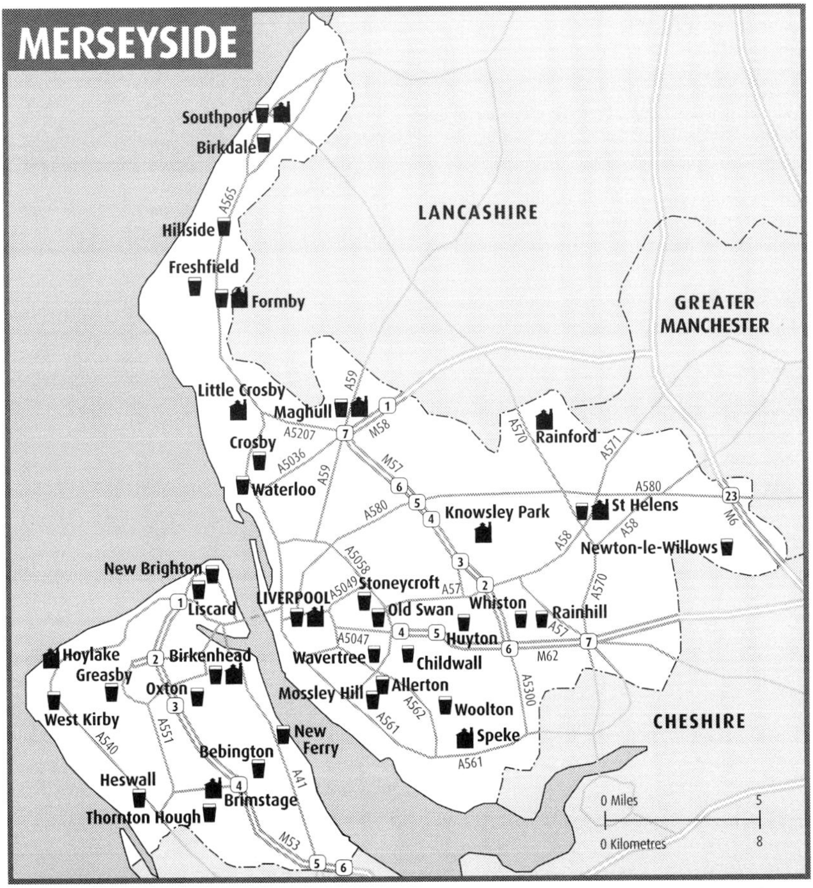

Bebington

Rose & Crown ✔

57 The Village, CH63 7PL

⏲ 12-midnight ☎ (0151) 644 5829

🌐 roseandcrownbebington.co.uk

Lancaster Bomber; Thwaites Original; house beer (by Thwaites); 5 changing beers (sourced nationally) [H]

A former coaching inn built in 1732, reopened in 2018, with traditional decor and old photos of the area adorning the walls. It is a thriving, vibrant and friendly community pub with a lounge, small bar and games room. In addition to the two permanent beers Thwaites brews the house beer, Rose Gold, and most of the changing beers. Nearby Port Sunlight Village was founded by William Hesketh Lever in 1888 to house his soap factory workers and is the home of the Lady Lever Art Gallery. Free car parking is available nearby. Q🐴≷♣🚌🐾📶

Birkenhead

Gallaghers Traditional Pub 🄻

20 Chester Street, CH41 5DQ

⏲ 12-11 Mon-Thu; 11.30-midnight Fri & Sat; 12-11 Sun ☎ (0151) 649 9095

Brimstage Trapper's Hat Bitter; 5 changing beers (sourced regionally; often Hawkshead, Rat, Salopian) [H]

Multiple award-winning genuine free house close to the Mersey ferries, rescued after closure and refurbished in 2010. It is decorated with a fascinating range of military memorabilia and a collection of shipping images. Several ciders are always on offer. Good-value meals are served until 9pm daily (no food Mon) with weekly themed food nights. Live music plays every Sunday, and poetry night is the fourth Monday of the month. Cheese night is the last Sunday – bring your own cheese. ❀◐≷(Hamilton Sq)♣🍎🚌🐾📶

Crosby

Corner Post 🄻

25 Bridge Road, L23 6SA

⏲ closed Mon; 4-9; 1-9 Sat; 1-7 Sun ☎ 07587 177453

4 changing beers (sourced locally; often Peerless, Rock the Boat) [H]

Crosby's second micropub, located in a former post office – hence the name – is easily spotted by the postbox outside. As well as the changing range of real ales, real cider, bottled continental beers and wine are available. Interesting pictures depicting the history of the building and local area adorn the walls. Close to the 53 bus route and a short walk from Blundellsands and Crosby railway station, it is also near the Iron Men attraction on Crosby beach. Well-behaved dogs are welcome.
Q≷♣🍎🚌(53)🐾

Liverpool Pigeon 🄻

14 Endbutt Lane, L23 0TR
🕓 closed Mon; 4-9; 2-9 Sat; 2-5 Sun ☎ 07766 480329
🌐 liverpoolpigeon.co.uk
5 changing beers (sourced locally; often Bristol Beer Factory, Salopian) Ⓗ
Merseyside's pioneering micropub is a fine example of the type, with real ales, ciders and bottled beers but no spirits, alcopops, keg beers or music. The cask beers will usually include a local brew and often a dark beer. Locally made pies are available at the bar. The Liverpool Pigeon is named after an extinct bird from Polynesia – long may this one live. A former local CAMRA Pub of the Year.
Q♿♣🍎🍺🚌 (47,X2)🐾

Formby

Sparrowhawk 🏆

Southport Old Road, L37 0AB (next to Formby bypass opp Woodvale Airfield)
🕓 10.30-11; 9am-11 Sat; 9am-10.30 Sun ☎ (01704) 882350
🌐 sparrowhawk-formby.co.uk
Salopian Oracle; Titanic Plum Porter; 3 changing beers (sourced regionally) Ⓗ
The Sparrowhawk is a Brunning & Price pub on the original road between Southport and Formby. It was built as the dower house to the nearby Formby Hall and is situated in five acres of woodlands and gardens. The pub is open plan with an emphasis on food but always offers up to six real ales in excellent condition. The bus stop at Woodpile traffic lights is less than five minutes' walk away.
Q🛋❀◐◑♿♣🍎P🚌 (47,49)🐾📶

Freshfield

Beer Station

3 Victoria Buildings, L37 7DB (opp railway station)
🕓 3-9; 12-10 Fri & Sat; 12-9 Sun ☎ (01704) 807450
3 changing beers (sourced locally; often Neptune, Red Star) Ⓗ
Freshfield's first micropub, with a focus on all things local. Beers are sourced to showcase local brewers, with the exception of one 'foreign' beer a month from out of the region. A fridge with bottled beers adds to the variety. The few spirits stocked also have their provenance checked. Food comes in the form of local pies and nuts. The walls are decorated with work by local artists. Dogs are welcome on a lead. Q🛋♿🚆♣🍎🚌🐾📶

Greasby

Coach & Horses 🄻 ✔

Greasby Road, CH49 3NG
🕓 12-midnight ☎ (0151) 677 4509
🌐 coachandhorsesgreasby.co.uk
Butcombe Original; Peerless Triple Blonde; 2 changing beers (sourced nationally; often Black Sheep, Marston's, Purity) Ⓗ
Charming whitewashed traditional street-corner local, dating back nearly 300 years. Formerly a farmhouse where ale was brewed and sold from 1725, it became a pub in the 1820s. Four small cosy rooms with real warming fires for the winter surround a compact central bar, with the ambience of a small country local. There is a folk/acoustic jam session every Monday. The darts team plays on Thursday. On Tuesday there is 25p off the price of a pint of cask ale. Q🛋❀♣P🚌🐾📶

Irby Mill 🄻 ✔

Mill Lane, CH49 3NT (on roundabout between Greasby and Irby)
🕓 12-11 (midnight Fri & Sat); 12-10.30 Sun
☎ (0151) 604 0194 🌐 irbymill.co.uk
Brains Rev James; Greene King Abbot; 6 changing beers (sourced nationally) Ⓗ
Formerly a café, the pub was originally the house of the miller of the windmill on the site, and opened as a pub in 1982. With thick sandstone walls, low beams and a real fire, it comprises a small L-shaped, stone-floored bar and a lounge used mainly by diners. The pub has an excellent reputation for its locally sourced home-made food, with a menu to suit most tastes.
Q🛋❀◐◑P🚌 (82)🐾📶

Heswall

Beer Lab 🄻

53 Telegraph Road, CH60 0AD
🕓 closed Mon; 4-10 Tue-Thu (11 Fri); 2-11 Sat; 2-8 Sun
☎ (0151) 342 5475
Brimstage Trapper's Hat Bitter; 3 changing beers (sourced regionally; often Lister's, Purple Moose, RedWillow) Ⓗ
Heswall's first micropub opened in July 2018 in a former cycle shop, an easy five minutes' walk from the main shopping area and the bus station. The relaxed and minimalist single-room bar is bright and airy, making the most of the available space. Four real ciders are always on the bar together with Belgian bottled beers. Beer is served in pint, one-third and two-third measures only (no half-pints). Q♣🍎🚌🐾📶

Johnny Pye

5 Pye Road, CH60 0DB (next to bus station)
🕓 11-11 ☎ (0151) 342 8215 🌐 johnnypyepub.co.uk
Banks's Amber Ale; Wychwood Hobgoblin; 3 changing beers (sourced nationally) Ⓗ
On the site of an old bus depot and adjacent to the new bus station, this lively, modern, open-plan pub is named after a local entrepreneur who was responsible for starting the local bus service. Close to the main shopping area, the pub has a strong local focus and hosts regular live music events raising money for charities. The changing beers are from the Marston's range. 🛋❀◐◑♿P🚌📶

REAL ALE BREWERIES

Ad Hop Liverpool
Big Bog Speke
Black Lodge ■ Liverpool
Brimstage Brimstage
Brooks Hoylake
Connoisseur St Helens
Craft, The Southport
George Wright Rainford
Gibberish ■ Liverpool
Handyman ■ Liverpool
Higsons ■ Liverpool
Liverpool Brewing Liverpool (NEW)
Melwood Knowsley Park
Neptune Maghull
Peerless Birkenhead
Red Star Formby
Rock the Boat Little Crosby
Southport Southport
Stamps Liverpool

Jug & Bottle

13 Mount Avenue, CH60 4RH

12-11 (0151) 342 5535 the-jugandbottle.co.uk

Brains Rev James; Brimstage Trapper's Hat Bitter; 4 changing beers (sourced nationally)

Originally a private house built in the 1870s, hidden behind the village hall and library a short distance from the main shopping street. This smart pub reopened in 2016 after a refurbishment. Open fires and various cosy areas create a warm and friendly atmosphere while, outside, the decking gives views towards the River Dee and North Wales.

Huyton

Barkers Brewery

Archway Road, L36 9UJ

8am-11 (midnight Fri & Sat) (0151) 482 4500

Greene King Abbot; Ruddles Best Bitter; Sharp's Doom Bar; 4 changing beers

A large, airy Wetherspoon pub with a traditional feel, popular with workers and families in the early evening. A good selection of ales means at least one local and one dark beer is on handpump. The main dining area leads to a beer garden at the rear. The pub is on the site of the old Huyton Brewery, founded in 1825, and managed by the Barker family over four generations until 1925; the sculpture is of Richard Barker. Alcohol is served from 9am, children welcome until 9.30pm.

QP

Liscard

Lazy Landlord Ale House

56 Mill Lane, CH44 5UG

4-10.30 Mon, Wed & Thu; closed Tue; 2-10.30 Fri; 12-10.30 Sat & Sun 07583 135616

Oakham Citra; 4 changing beers (sourced nationally; often Brimstage, Joseph Holt, Rat)

Wirral's first micropub, opened in former shop premises in 2014, is run by the Henry brothers, who are cask ale enthusiasts. Two small cosy rooms, decorated with large amounts of breweriana, local artworks and a small library, are served from the front bar. Mostly frequented by a more mature, discerning local clientele, the pub is a venue for meetings of local societies. There are two ciders, usually one from SeaCider. Awarded local CAMRA Pub of the Year 2017-19.

Q (410,432)

Liverpool: Allerton

Three Piggies

77-79 Allerton Road, L18 2DA

11-midnight; 10-midnight Sat & Sun (0151) 722 6510

threepiggies.co.uk

House beer (by Marston's); 3 changing beers (sourced regionally; often Hawkshead, Ilkley, Titanic)

Open plan with trestle tables, this bright, lively alehouse and canteen opened in 2016. Unlike numerous other businesses in the area, the owner says it is not a restaurant. Food starts with brunch in the morning, after which there is an extensive, varied menu, from mains to light bites, plus coffee and cakes. A wide selection of craft beers is available. Last entry is 10.45pm, although the pub often stays open until midnight. (86)

Liverpool: Childwall

Childwall Fiveways

179 Queens Drive, L15 6XS

8am-midnight (0151) 738 2100

Greene King Abbot; Ruddles Best Bitter; 6 changing beers (sourced nationally; often Robinsons)

A former Higson's tied house, this large single-roomed pub opened as a Wetherspoon in 2010. Located in a leafy suburb, it has good motorway and public transport links. The refurbished interior is decorated with wood panelling, and outside there is a beer garden. A popular establishment, it can get busy, especially at weekends. The site was used for a water tank during WWII.

P (79,81)

Liverpool: City Centre

Augustus John

Peach Street, L3 5TX (off Brownlow Hill)

11.30-11 (9 Sat); closed Sun (0151) 794 5507

5 changing beers (sourced nationally; often Peerless, Rock the Boat)

Opened in 1968 and run by the University of Liverpool, the Augustus John is an open-plan pub popular with students, lecturers and locals. A large number of ciders are on offer – two on handpump and many more from the cellar. Pizza is served at all times, sport is shown and there is a jukebox. Closed over Christmas and New Year. A local and regional CAMRA Cider Pub of the Year.

(79)

Baltic Fleet

33A Wapping, L1 8DQ

12-11 (midnight Fri & Sat) (0151) 709 3116

balticfleetpubliverpool.com

Brimstage Trapper's Hat Bitter; Melwood Derby Stout; Robinsons Trooper; 3 changing beers (sourced locally; often Big Bog, Rock the Boat)

This Grade II-listed building is located near the Albert Dock. It has a distinctive flat-iron shape and the interior is decorated on a nautical theme. The existence of tunnels in the cellar has led to speculation that the pub's history may involve smuggling. It also originally had many doors to allow customers to escape the press gangs. It can get busy when events are on at the nearby M&S Bank Arena.

Crown Hotel ★

43 Lime Street, L1 1JQ

8am-11 (midnight Fri & Sat); 10-midnight Sun (0151) 707 6027 thecrownliverpool.co.uk

Greene King IPA; Timothy Taylor Landlord; 6 changing beers (sourced nationally; often Peerless)

Grade II listed with a nationally important historic interior and ornate plasterwork ceilings, the building is noticeable for its Walker's Ales Warrington stucco frieze. Many original features are retained in the two downstairs rooms, including some impressive wood panelling and push bells. There is an ornate glass dome above the staircase. Breakfast is served until noon, a wide menu of pub food until 10pm. Close to Lime Street Station and public transport links.

(Lime St)

Dispensary

87 Renshaw Street, L1 2SP

12-11 (midnight Fri & Sat) (0151) 709 2160

George Wright Mild; changing beers (often Fyne Ales, Ossett, Titanic) Ⓗ
This lively city pub, where the licensee's impeccable attention to beer quality is renowned, is a haven for real ale drinkers of all ages. Seven handpumps serve an ever-changing choice of interesting microbrewery beers in a good range of styles and strengths. A regular local beer, Mark's Mild, commemorates the much-missed barman who died in 2012. The attractive bar area has Victorian features, and there is a raised wood-panelled area to the rear. ≷(Central)🚌

Fly in the Loaf ✔

13 Hardman Street, L1 9AS
12-11 (midnight Fri & Sat) ☎ (0151) 708 0817
Okell's Bitter; 5 changing beers (sourced nationally; often Kirkstall, Okell's) Ⓗ
A former bakery, the name comes from the slogan 'no flies in the loaf'. Owned by Isle of Man brewer Okell's, it serves its beers alongside a changing range of guests from around the country, many from microbreweries, and a good selection of foreign beers. The spacious interior has a light, airy frontage with contrasting wood-panelled areas towards the rear, and plenty of rugby league memorabilia. There is an attractive small on-street drinking area at the front and a function room upstairs. ◐♿≷(Central)🚌(86)📶

Globe ✔

17 Cases Street, L1 1HW (opp Central Station)
11-11; 10-11 Sat; 12-10.30 Sun ☎ (0151) 707 0067
Marston's EPA; Sharp's Doom Bar; Timothy Taylor Landlord; Wainwright; 2 changing beers (sourced nationally) Ⓗ
This small, cosy pub is a former winner of the local CAMRA Best Community Pub award. People travel here from all over the city, and a buzz of lively conversation prevails. In the small back room, a brass plaque commemorates the inaugural meeting of CAMRA Merseyside, and 40th year celebrations were held here in 2014. Tastefully refurbished in 2012, it retains its traditional atmosphere and photographs and newspaper cuttings on the walls lend insights into the pub's history and local characters. The sloping floor in the bar area is legendary. ≷(Central)🚌

Grapes 🄻

60 Roscoe Street, L1 9DW
1-12.30am (1.30am Thu-Sat) ☎ (0151) 709 3977
thegrapesliverpool.co.uk
8 changing beers Ⓗ
This corner local dates back to 1804 and retains its original Mellors signage outside. There is a total of nine handpumps, with a large number of beers coming from local microbreweries such as Mad Hatter and Liverpool Craft. After a major refurbishment during the summer of 2016, stairs now lead to a partly sheltered patio area, atop the extension. Live jazz features every Sunday night from 9pm. ❀≷(Central)🍎🚌📶

Head of Steam

85-89 Hanover Street, L1 3DZ
11-midnight (12.30am Fri & Sat) ☎ (0151) 708 6096
Camerons Strongarm, A-Hop-Alypse Now; Leeds Best; 5 changing beers (sourced locally; often Leeds, Neptune, Rock the Boat) Ⓗ
Opened in Sept 2017, with no connection to the Head of Steam previously on Lime Street, this is a large venue with plenty of seating in various arrangements. It screens most live major sporting events so it can get very busy, especially in the evening. Many foreign bottled and keg beers are on offer alongside the real ales. A private function area is available. Handy for Liverpool One shops. ◐≷(Central)🍎🚌📶

Lime Kiln 🄻 ✔

Fleet Street, L1 4NR
9am-midnight (1am Thu; 2am Fri & Sat)
☎ (0151) 702 6810
Greene King Abbot; Ruddles Best Bitter; changing beers (often Peerless) Ⓗ
On first impression, the decor and layout may appear not to offer much for the real ale drinker, but looks can be deceiving. Thanks to continued commitment, real ale is well catered for, with at least one local beer usually available. Handpulls are in the downstairs bar only. Situated in the Concert Square area, the pub is a peaceful haven during the day. A Victorian warehouse occupied the site, which was home to manufacturing chemists, from the early 1900s to the 1950s.
◐♿≷(Central)🍎🚌📶

Lion Tavern ★ 🄻 ✔

67 Moorfields, L2 2BP
12-11 (11.30 Fri-Sun) ☎ (0151) 236 9768
theliontavernliverpool.co.uk
Moorhouse's Pride of Pendle; house beer (by Red Star); 6 changing beers (sourced nationally; often Red Star, Rock the Boat) Ⓗ
Named after the locomotive that worked the Liverpool to Manchester railway, the Lion features exquisite artwork plus intricately etched and stained glass which bears testimony to its Grade II-listed status and its entry on CAMRA's National Inventory of Historic Pub Interiors. It was refurbished in 2017. Up to eight beers are from the SIBA list, usually including ales from local micros. The cider is from Westons. Lunchtime food is served and speciality pork pies are available at all times. ◐≷(Moorfields)🍎🚌📶

Pen Factory 🄻

13 Hope Street, L1 9BQ
11-midnight; closed Sun & Mon ☎ (0151) 709 7887
pen-factory.co.uk
5 changing beers (sourced nationally; often Brimstage, Hawkshead, Titanic) Ⓗ
The Pen Factory opened in 2015, brought to you by the innovator of the original Everyman Bistro, entrepreneur Paddy Byrne. This large open-plan bistro-style establishment with a wood-burning stove and a small garden is a convivial place to drink and eat. Up to six handpumps include beers from smaller breweries such as Brimstage. The venue can be busy before or after productions at the nearby Everyman Theatre or Philharmonic Hall. Excellent food, not your average pub grub.
❀◐♿≷🍎🚌(86)🐾📶

Peter Kavanagh's 🏆 ★

2-6 Egerton Street, L8 7LY (off Catharine St)
12-midnight (1am Fri & Sat) ☎ (0151) 709 3443
Greene King Abbot; 4 changing beers (sourced nationally; often Castle Rock) Ⓗ
On CAMRA's National Inventory of Historic Pub Interiors and situated in the Georgian area. The snugs feature murals by Eric Robinson on the walls and there are fine stained-glass windows with wooden shutters. The benches have carved armrests thought to be caricatures of Peter

Kavanagh, the licensee for 53 years until 1950. These features were not adversely affected when the pub was expanded, firstly in 1964 into next door, then in 1977 into next door but one. Local CAMRA Pub of the Year 2019. Q🚆(86)🌼

Richard John Blackler 🅛 ✔
Units 1 & 2 Charlotte Row, L1 1HU
🕑 9am-midnight (1am Fri & Sat) ☎ (0151) 709 4802
Greene King Abbot; Ruddles Best Bitter; Sharp's Doom Bar; Wychwood Hobgoblin; 8 changing beers Ⓗ
This Wetherspoon pub is the ground floor of the former Blackler's department store which opened in 1908 and finally shut in 1988. The famous rocking horse from that store is in the corner. Close to the bus station, Saint John's shopping centre and Liverpool One, it is always busy – especially when Liverpool or Everton are playing at home – but it is a good place to take a break. The Beatles' George Harrison served his electrician's apprenticeship at Blackler's. 🚲🕪♿🚆(Lime St/Central)●🚆🛜

Roscoe Head
24 Roscoe Street, L1 2SX
🕑 11.30-11 Mon; 11.30-midnight; 12-midnight Sun
☎ (0151) 709 4365 🌐 roscoehead.co.uk
Tetley Bitter; Timothy Taylor Landlord; 4 changing beers (sourced regionally; often Rock the Boat) Ⓗ
One of the Magnificent Five pubs in every edition of the Guide. Conversation and the appreciation of real ale rule in this cosy four-roomed hostelry. Run by members of the same family for over 30 years, the name commemorates William Roscoe, a leading campaigner against the slave trade. Pies and sandwiches are available. Since its sale by Punch Taverns to New River Retail in 2015 there has been concern over the future of the pub, with an active Save the Roscoe Head campaign.
Q🕪🚆(Central)♣🚆🛜

Sanctuary 🅛
72 Lime Street, L1 1JN
🕑 closed Mon; 4-11 Tue-Thu; 2-1am Fri; 12-1am Sat; 2-11 Sun
☎ (0151) 703 0116 🌐 sanctuarybar.co.uk
Adnams Ghost Ship; Robinsons Trooper; Titanic Plum Porter; 3 changing beers (sourced locally) Ⓗ
Opened in 2017, this free-of-tie pub is located next to the Design 4 Life tattoo parlour and owned by the same couple. Themed as a run-down 1920s hotel, the pub has Art Deco lighting and long-abandoned suitcases high up on the well-stocked wooden beer cabinet. There is a comfortable seating area. Flight boards are available and over 50 bottled beers are stocked for consumption off the premises. ♿🚆♣●🚆🛜

Ship & Mitre 🅛 ✔
133 Dale Street, L2 2JH (by Birkenhead Tunnel)
🕑 10-11 (midnight Thu); 9am-midnight Fri & Sat
☎ (0151) 236 0859 🌐 theshipandmitre.com
Flagship Sublime, Lupa, Silhouette; 5 changing beers (sourced nationally; often Big Bog, Flagship) Ⓗ
The name derives from two previous incarnations, the Flagship and the Mitre. The 1930s Art Deco pub is partly hidden by the Queensway Tunnel entrance and the Churchill Way flyover. A changing array of 15 beers and real ciders is served by friendly and knowledgeable staff, always willing to make a recommendation. There is also an impressive range of world beers. The pub now brews its own Flagship beers using the plant at Stamps Brewery in Crosby. 🕪🚆(Moorfields)♣●🚆🛜🌼🛜

Thomas Rigby's ✔
23-25 Dale Street, L2 2EZ
🕑 11.30-11 ☎ (0151) 236 3269
Okell's Bitter, Dr Okell's IPA; 4 changing beers (often Kirkstall) Ⓗ
This multi-roomed, Grade II-listed building, bearing the name of wine and spirit dealer Thomas Rigby, now supplies an extensive world beer range on draught and in bottles. The regular beers on handpump come from the pub's owner, Okell's. Good-value food including specials is served until early evening, with one room offering a friendly and efficient table service. The old coaching inn courtyard for outdoor drinking is shared with sister pub Lady of Mann. 🌼🕪🚆(Moorfields)🚆🛜

Vernon Arms 🅛
69 Dale Street, L2 2HJ
🕑 12-11 (midnight Fri & Sat) ☎ (0151) 236 6132
🌐 vernonarms.net
Brains Rev James; house beer (by Stamps); 3 changing beers Ⓗ
Situated close to the business district, the Vernon retains the feel of a street-corner local. The single long-roomed bar serves three drinking areas including a back room with frosted glass windows advertising the Liverpool Brewing Company, which used to serve the pub. The main bar has wood panelling, several large columns and a small snug area. Real cider on handpull is unusual for the city centre. 🕪🚆(Moorfields)●🚆🛜

Ye Hole in ye Wall 🅛
4 Hackins Hey, L2 2AW (off Dale St)
🕑 12-11; 12-10.30 Sun ☎ (0151) 227 3809
🌐 yeholeinyewall.com
6 changing beers (sourced nationally; often Red Star) Ⓗ
A traditional side-street pub rumoured to be the oldest hostelry in the city, dating back to the start of Liverpool's maritime heyday in 1726. Wood panelling and stained glass abound. Built on the site of an old Quaker graveyard, there are tales of ghosts, and this old coaching house boasts at least two. Unusually, the beer cellar is on the first floor above the bar. Five guest beers are offered on rotation and may be from local and micro breweries. A hidden gem. 🕪🚆(Moorfields)🚆🛜

Liverpool: Mossley Hill

Pi
106 Rose Lane, L18 8AG
🕑 11-11 (11.30 Fri & Sat) ☎ (0151) 222 0443
Tatton Blonde; 3 changing beers (sourced regionally) Ⓗ
A café-style bar in what was previously a shop, near to Mossley Hill railway station. Expansion into the premises next door has provided more space. The guest beers are from smaller breweries in the region. A number of foreign beers are also on tap alongside dozens of bottled beers. A simple hot-food menu – comprising real pies with sides – is available all day. 🕪🚆🚆(61,80)🛜

Liverpool: Old Swan

Ale House
674/676 Prescot Road, L13 5XG
🕑 2-10 (11 Fri & Sat); 2-10.30 Sun ☎ 07944 565323
🌐 thealehouse.pub
5 changing beers (sourced nationally) Ⓗ

Bigger than other micropubs in the area, this new bar opened in 2016 in a building that was previously a job centre. It currently has six handpumps, one dispensing cider. Another cider or perry is served from the cool room. Beers are a mixture of better- or lesser-known brands supplied by agents, and local ales supplied directly, usually including a porter or stout. **Q♿♣🍏🚌**(10,10A)🐾

Liverpool: Stoneycroft

Cask 🄻

438 Queens Drive, L13 0AR (on ring rd near jct of Queens Drive and Derby Lane)

🕐 closed Mon; 4-9.30; 2-9.30 Sat & Sun ☎ 07747 034499

7 changing beers (sourced nationally; often Hawkshead) 🄷

Comfortable, immaculate, one-roomed micropub that opened in 2015. An interesting collection of breweriana includes some from Higsons. There are usually four beers on Tuesday and Wednesday, five on Thursday and up to seven from Friday. Cider and perry are dispensed direct from taps at the rear of the bar. Occasional special beers are kept in wooden pins, and bottled beers are stocked. Local CAMRA Pub of the Year 2016-2018. Some roadside parking is available. **Q♣🍏🚆🚌**(60,81)

Liverpool: Wavertree

Handyman Supermarket 🄻

461 Smithdown Road, L15 3JL

🕐 12 (3 Mon-Wed)-11.30 ☎ (0151) 222 7422

🌐 handymansupermarket.co.uk

Handyman Coffee & Cardamom Pale; 3 changing beers (sourced locally; often Handyman, Melwood, Red Star) 🄷

A new brewpub opened in 2017 in a former hardware shop, hence the name. It has a large open-plan bar plus an events/function room at the rear. The brew plant is on the mezzanine above the bar. Handpumps serve the brewery's own cask beers and there is a selection of bottled beers and craft keg on taps. Beers often brewed collaboratively at other breweries. The Handyman beers are unfined. **🍏🚌**(60,86)📶

Liverpool: Woolton

Gardeners Arms ✔

101 Vale Road, L25 7RW

🕐 12-midnight (11.30 Sun) ☎ (0151) 428 0775

Adnams Ghost Ship; Greene King IPA; Sharp's Doom Bar; 3 changing beers (sourced regionally; often Big Bog, Taylors) 🄷

Friendly community village pub situated over the hill from Woolton village and separated from Menlove Avenue by blocks of flats. Guest beers regularly include a local Big Bog beer and a Welsh beer from Purple Moose, Heavy Industry or Cwrw Lal. A quiz is held on Tuesday evening. Woolton is famous as the home of the Beatles – their original name was The Quarrymen after the local school – and Eleanor Rigby's gravestone can be found in St Peter's churchyard. **Q🔥🚌**(76)🐾📶

Maghull

Frank Hornby 🄻 ✔

38 Eastway, L31 6BR

🕐 8am-11.30 (1am Fri & Sat) ☎ (0151) 520 4010

5 changing beers (often Brightside, Elland, Saltaire) 🄷

This Wetherspoon establishment is named after local man Frank Hornby, famous inventor of the Hornby train set. Unsurprisingly, samples of his work are on display in the pub including Meccano and Dinky Toys. Situated in a surburban street, the bar is spacious and light inside with a decked area outside at the front. The selection of guest ales includes some from local microbreweries. Alcohol is served from 10am. No children after 10pm. **Q🔥❀◐◑♿P🚌**📶

Maghull Cask Café

43 Liverpool Road South, L31 7BN

🕐 closed Mon-Wed; 4-9 Thu-Sat; 12-9 Sun

☎ (0151) 526 3877

5 changing beers (sourced locally; often Neptune) 🄷

This new micropub is a hidden gem. Opened in 2018, it serves a good range of changing cask ales, continental bottles and gins. Beers are from regional brewers such as Oakham, Titanic and Salopian. Friendly, knowledgeable staff help to create a welcoming atmosphere where conversation prevails. The Liverpool to Leeds canal runs through Maghull and the pub makes a good base for a nice walk towards Burscough. **Q♿🍏🚆🚌**(300,310)🐾📶

New Brighton

Bow-Legged Beagle 🄻

88 Victoria Road, CH45 2JF

🕐 3-10; 1-11 Fri & Sat ☎ 07739 032624

🌐 thebowleggedbeagle.co.uk

5 changing beers (sourced locally; often Neptune) 🄷

Wirral's second micropub opened in 2017 in a former street-corner shop with a basic no-frills format and immediately proved popular with locals and visitors. It offers a friendly welcome and a regularly changing range of new and unusual local beers. There is seating outside on the pavement in summer. Close to the seafront and other local attractions. **Q❀⇌🚌**(410,411)🐾📶

Magazine Hotel 🄻 ✔

7 Magazine Brow, CH45 1HP (above Egremont Promenade)

🕐 12-11 (11.30 Thu; midnight Fri & Sat) ☎ (0151) 630 3169

🌐 the-magazine-hotel.co.uk

Brimstage Trapper's Hat Bitter; Draught Bass; 3 changing beers (sourced regionally; often Big Bog, Brimstage, Higsons) 🄷

This unspoilt multi-roomed, low-beamed pub with an attractive black-and-white frontage, dating from 1759, suffered a fire in 2010 but has been restored without losing its unique character. Three rooms lead off the main central bar area with an open fireplace. Traditionally renowned for its Draught Bass, other beers are usually from local microbreweries. One changing real cider is kept. Overlooking Egremont Promenade, the pub has fine views over the River Mersey to Liverpool. **Q🔥❀♣🍏P🚌**(106,107)🐾📶

New Ferry

Freddie's Club 🄻

36 Stanley Road, CH62 5AS

🕐 7-11; 5-11 Fri & Sat; 12-11 Sun

Brimstage Trapper's Hat Bitter; 1 changing beer (sourced locally; often Brimstage) 🄷

Comfortable two-roomed former club located in a quiet residential area near the end of a cul-de-sac a short walk from New Ferry shopping centre. Two ales from the local Brimstage Brewery are served from a single bar in the main room. The adjoining room features two full-size snooker tables and there are men's and women's darts teams. Monday is quiz night. Q♿⇌♣P🚌(1,41)

John Masefield ✔

70-72 New Chester Road, CH62 5AD

8am-midnight (1am Fri & Sat) ☎ (0151) 644 4250

Greene King Abbot; Ruddles Best Bitter; 6 changing beers (sourced nationally; often Peerless) H

Pleasant open-plan Wetherspoon venue in what was a bicycle shop in the main shopping area. Named after the former poet laureate, who spent time in New Ferry as a young man, controversy surrounded the opening of the pub when locals suggested that the portrait on the sign looked more like Adolf Hitler – judge for yourself. Wetherspoon's meal deals are available, and at least one cider. A quiz is held on the first Thursday of the month. ⛀❀◐◑♿⇌●🚌(1,41)📶

Newton-le-Willows

Firkin

65 High Street, WA12 9SL

closed Mon-Wed; 5.30-11 Thu; 1-11.30 Fri & Sat; 1-10.30 Sun ☎ (01925) 225700 🌐 thefirkin.co.uk

8 changing beers (sourced locally) H

Once a shop, this small, friendly establishment dispenses a selection of eight real ales, including at least one dark beer, all from micro or SIBA breweries. Two traditional ciders are also stocked. Small seating areas are to the front and rear, and pictures of Newton of old adorn the walls. Free of electronic noise, this is a place in which to engage in conversation with like-minded people and to make new friends. Note, restricted opening times and over-18s only. Q⇌●🚌(34,22)🐾📶

Oxton

Caernarvon Castle ✔

Bidston Road, CH43 2JZ

11-11 (midnight Fri & Sat) ☎ (0151) 652 2831

Greene King IPA, Abbot; Timothy Taylor Landlord; 5 changing beers (sourced nationally; often Big Bog) H

Pleasant, traditional 1950s pub on a busy road next to St Saviour's Church, built on the site of the original Caernarvon Castle pub which was destroyed by bombing in WWII. A Greene King pub, three permanent ales are complemented by five changing beers. The outside patio is ideal for eating and drinking in the summer months and is popular as it catches the sun for most of the day. Q❀◐◑♿P🚌(91,217)📶

Oxton Bar & Kitchen L

2 Claughton Firs, CH43 5TQ

12-midnight (11.30 Fri & Sat); 12-11 Sun & Mon ☎ (0151) 651 2535 🌐 oxtonbar.co.uk

3 changing beers (sourced locally; often Brimstage, Higsons, Peerless) H

Situated in the centre of the attractive Oxton village among shops, bars and restaurants, this former John Smith's pub built in 1969 has been tastefully converted into a smart, comfortable, single-room lounge bar with an attractive outside seating area. There is a strong emphasis on quality food, ranging from sandwiches and snacks to full meals. Beers are usually from local microbreweries. ⛀❀◐◑P🚌(492,495)📶

Rainhill

Skew Bridge Alehouse L

5 Dane Court, L35 4LU

4-11; 2.30-11 Sat; 2.30-10.30 Sun ☎ (0151) 792 7906 🌐 skewbridge.co.uk

Outstanding 3.9; 5 changing beers (sourced locally; often Big Bog, Melwood, North Riding) H

Situated in Rainhill village, the pub offers a selection of cask ales, real ciders and craft lagers. Locally sourced ales are complemented by beers from all over. A range of gins and single malt whiskies is also stocked. With no TV or music to distract customers, conversation is very much encouraged. A selection of board games is available. Q⛀❀♿⇌♣●P🚌(61)📶

St Helens

Connoisseur Brewery & Tasting Rooms L

Church Street, WA9 1JS (1 min walk from Central train station)

12-10 first Sat of month ☎ 07921 838831 🌐 connoisseurales.com

6 changing beers (often Connoisseur Ales)

Only open on the first Saturday of the month, the cosy bar at the Connoisseur brewery serves beers brewed on site. There is always a dark beer and all new and test brews appear here first. Bottle-conditioned beers are also available as well as fruit wines and mead. Tours of the brewery are conducted between 12-6pm. Q⛀♿⇌●P🚏🚌🐾

Cowley Vaults ✔

50 Cooper Street, WA10 2BH

12-11 ☎ (01744) 750849

6 changing beers H

Set back on the north side of the town centre, this was a convert to real ale early in 2018. It now offers up to six rotating guest beers. Food is served Thursday-Friday 5-9, and Saturday-Sunday 12-7. ♣●🚌

Cricketers Arms 🏆 L ✔

64 Peter Street, WA10 2EB

12-11 (1am Fri & Sat) ☎ (01744) 361846

Fyne Ales Jarl; Listers Best Bitter; Oakham Citra; RAT White Rat; Rudgate Ruby Mild; 7 changing beers (sourced locally) H

CAMRA National Pub of the Year 2017, this family-run pub has 13 handpulls always offering at least one dark beer, plus 10 ciders, and a range of spirits including over 100 gins. The traditional community pub has beer gardens, darts and pool leagues, quiz nights and fundraising events. An outside bar is used for beer festivals and private events. The on-site brewery, Howzat, should now be up and running. ⛀❀♣●P🚌🐾📶

News Room L

89 Duke Street, WA10 2JG

5-11; 4-midnight Fri; 1-midnight Sat; 1-11 Sun ☎ (01744) 322129

2 changing beers (sourced nationally; often Salopian) H

The music-themed News Room offers three handpulls, craft beers and a range of foreign bottled beers as well as gins, rums and malt whiskies. Set in stylish surroundings where conversation is encouraged, it has a warm, friendly, laid-back atmosphere, with music from the '60s, '70s and '80s playing on large screens. Themed music nights are hosted every six to eight weeks.

Talbot Ale House

97 Duke Street, WA10 2JG

12-1am (2am Fri & Sat) (01744) 322185

11 changing beers (sourced nationally) H

A true community pub with a traditional bar, multi-function lounge and quiet room. The well-appointed beer garden adds extra drinking space. There are ales on 10 handpumps plus nine ciders, as well as a wide range of gins and malt whiskies. The pub hosts many games and quiz leagues, and karaoke on a Saturday night. A loyalty card is available for regular customers.

Q P

Turk's Head

49 Morley Street, WA10 2DQ

2-11; 12-12.30am Sat & Sun (01744) 751289

Changing beers H

This long-established pub is a must for real ale lovers. It offers a wide range of beers and ciders from around the country plus a large selection of gins and malt whiskies. Home-made food is served Thursday-Friday 5-9 and Saturday-Sunday 12-7. The quiet lounge is separated from the traditional bar with real fire by a pool room. Tuesday is quiz night and Wednesday is cheese night. Pets are welcome in the beer garden. Q (32,152)

Southport

Barons Bar

239 Lord Street, PR8 1NZ (on A565 opp Eastbank St)

12-11 (midnight Fri & Sat) (01704) 534000

Moorhouse's Pride of Pendle; Tetley Bitter; house beer (by Moorhouse's); 6 changing beers (sourced regionally; often Lancaster, Moorhouse's, Southport) H

An ornate baronial-style bar within the Scarisbrick Hotel complex, with a front lounge with chairs, tables and comfy settees overlooking the town's famous Lord Street. The bar has been a champion of real ale in Southport now for many years and has a varied selection of beers both local and national. One real cider is also available.

Q

Guest House

16 Union Street, PR9 0QE

11.30-11 (midnight Fri & Sat); 12-10.30 Sun

(01704) 537660 guesthouse-southport.blogspot.com

Butcombe Original; Ruddles Best Bitter; Theakston Best Bitter; house beer (by Caledonian); 4 changing beers (often Phoenix, Salopian, Southport) H

Close to the station and Lord Street, this Grade II-listed building has an impressive frontage and interior with three separate wood-panelled rooms. There is seating outside at the front and a courtyard area to the rear. The bar has 11 handpumps, one serving a local microbrewery beer, and a wide range of malt whiskies. A quiet, traditional pub, it attracts a mixed clientele, with a quiz night on Thursday and acoustic folk club on the first and third Mondays of the month. Q

Phoenix

4-6 Coronation Walk, PR8 1RF

10-midnight (1am Sat) (01704) 513233

phoenixpub.net

Sharp's Doom Bar; 2 changing beers (sourced regionally) H

A popular sports pub at the top end of Lord Street, serving good food at reasonable prices. Family-run and free of tie, it is a favourite with real ale drinkers. The pub has plenty of traditional games and hosts a poker night on Monday and Wednesday, darts on Tuesday, and live music on Friday. Football is shown on plasma TV screens scattered about the bar, with major fixtures shown on a large screen. A great family pub.

Tap & Bottles

19A Cambridge Walk, PR8 1EN

12-11 (midnight Fri & Sat); 12-10.30 Sun

(01704) 544322

4 changing beers (sourced nationally) H

A micropub in the arcade between Chapel Street and Lord Street next to the Atkinson Centre. Four real ales may come from virtually anywhere, with a preference for north-west England breweries. A huge range of bottles is also offered, but not all are real ale in a bottle. A small beer tapas menu is served all day. Q

Southport: Birkdale

Barrel House

42 Liverpool Road, PR8 4AY

10-10.30 (01704) 566601

2 changing beers (often Parker, Salopian, Southport) H

A micropub opened in 2014. A former newsagents', it still sells the daily paper. When a Sainsbury's supermarket opened over the road it changed business and became a beer shop. It is now an Aladdin's cave of wonderful bottled beers, wines, loose-leaf teas and speciality coffees. It also offers two real ales on handpump, usually from local breweries such as Southport and Parker.

Q (49,X2)

Up Steps

20 Upper Aughton Road, PR8 5ND

3-11; 12-midnight Sat & Sun (01704) 562943

Wainwright; 1 changing beer H

Formerly a residence named Bankfield House, a new sign outside the pub depicts the old name. A traditional street-corner hostelry, the Up Steps has recently been revitalised after two long periods of closure, with the new licensees showing a commitment to real ale. The building has been tastefully refurbished while retaining its original features including the old Matthew Brown Lion Ales windows. Q P

Southport: Hillside

Grasshopper

70 Sandon Road, PR8 4QD

5-10.30; 2-10.30 Sat & Sun (01704) 569794

8 changing beers (sourced regionally; often Bank Top, Salopian) H

A micropub opened in 2016 in what was once a Martins Bank branch – the logo of Martins was a grasshopper – situated in a row of shops close to Hillside train station. There is outdoor seating at the front and a secluded beer garden to the rear. Eight changing real ales and six real ciders are served, with oversized pint glasses available on request. Local CAMRA Pub of the Year and Cider Pub of the Year 2018.

Pines

3 Hillside Road, PR8 4QB

4-11; 3-11 Fri; 12-11 Sat; 12-10.30 Sun 07454 453090

2 changing beers (sourced regionally)

An attractively decorated former hairdresser's in an area that previously had no drinking establishments but now has two award-winning bars. Two handpumps offer a varied choice of beers, and a selection of bottled beers is also kept. Fresh sandwiches are available. An outside seating area at the front is popular in the warmer months. At times the bar can be noisy and at others it can be quiet and relaxing depending on custom. (47)

Thornton Hough

Red Fox

Neston Road, CH64 7TL

10-11 (10.30 Sun) (0151) 353 2920

House beer (by Phoenix); 7 changing beers (sourced locally; often Conwy, Neptune, Ticketybrew)

An impressive sandstone building dating from the 1860s, set in extensive grounds. Refurbished in 2014, it is now a smart gastro-pub. The front bar retains a pub feel, with the restaurant areas to either side. Offering up to 10 ciders, it was local CAMRA Cider Pub of the Year in 2018. A smaller bar area at the back serves seating on the terrace and in the garden. House beers are Facer's 4% ABV Sunlight Blonde and Phoenix 3.8% ABV Brunning & Price Original Bitter. Q P (487)

Waterloo

Four Ashes

23 Crosby Road North, L22 0LD

closed Mon; 5-10.30 Tue-Thu; 4-10.30 Fri & Sat; 2.30-9.30 Sun

6 changing beers (often Neptune, Rock the Boat, Wily Fox)

A family-run micropub owned by the Ashe family, hence the name. On the site of a former restaurant, it is a great addition to the vibrant real-ale scene in and around Waterloo station. Beers are ordered direct from local microbreweries or through a wholesaler, resulting in a varied and interesting selection, always including at least one dark beer. Beers conditioning in the cellar are displayed on the wall. Q (47,X2)

Volunteer Canteen ★

45 East Street, L22 8QR

2-11; 12-midnight Fri & Sat; 12-10.30 Sun

07891 407464

4 changing beers (sourced nationally)

A cosy, traditional pub in a Grade II-listed terraced building, the Volly, as it is locally known, still provides table service. Nestling in the back streets of Waterloo, the pub dates from 1871 and, until the 1980s, was owned by Higsons, evidence of which can be seen etched into its windows. Small breweries around Merseyside and north Wales often supply guest ales. Pies, pâté, olives and nuts are served at all times.

Q (Waterloo) (53)

Waterpudlian

99 South Road, L22 0LR (opp Waterloo Station)

12-11 (midnight Thu-Sat) (0151) 280 0035

5 changing beers (sourced locally; often Brimstage, Oakham, Salopian)

Previously Stamps Too, this is a former local CAMRA branch Pub of the Year and its original accredited LocAle pub. The friendly open-plan bar, where lively banter often prevails, is the haunt both of real ale enthusiasts and live music fans. Five handpumps serve mainly local beers, from Liverpool, Brimstage and Southport in particular, with occasional ales from further afield. A sixth handpump dispenses real cider. Bands and local musicians feature Thursday to Sunday.

(53,133)

West Kirby

West Kirby Tap

Grange Road, CH48 4DY

12-11 (11.30 Fri & Sat) (0151) 625 0350

westkirbytap.co.uk

Spitting Feathers Thirstquencher; 6 changing beers (sourced nationally; often Chapter, Neptune, Spitting Feathers)

A smart, modern, open-plan bar with plain wooden panelling, bare brick walls and a log-burning stove. The pub serves a wide range of beers, mainly from microbreweries, and one real cider. Food includes impressive platters of cheese, fish, cold meats and vegan snacks. Live music plays on Saturday night and the pub can get busy. Close to the West Kirby shops and a short walk to the beach for those trekking to Hilbre Island.

White Lion

51 Grange Road, CH48 4EE

12-11 (10.30 Sun) (0151) 625 9037

Black Sheep Best Bitter; Brains Rev James; 3 changing beers (sourced nationally)

A traditional inn in a 200-year-old sandstone building close to the centre of West Kirby. The pub is a little quirky and laid out on several different levels, with lots of cosy nooks to sit in, along with a real fire to keep you warm in winter. In warmer months you can enjoy the lovely beer garden at the rear. Quiz night is Monday.

Whiston

Beer EnGin

9 Greenes Road, L35 3RE

closed Mon; 4-9.30 Tue-Thu; 4-10 Fri & Sat; 4-9 Sun

07496 616132

5 changing beers

Set in a row of shops, this cosy single-room microbar is a delight from the moment you walk in. It serves five real ales from local breweries plus craft beers, wines and a variety of unusual gins. A selection of board games is available. Bank holiday hours may vary. A warm welcome is assured for all, including dogs. Q P (61)

> A fine beer may be judged with only a sip, but it's better to be thoroughly sure.
> **Czech proverb**

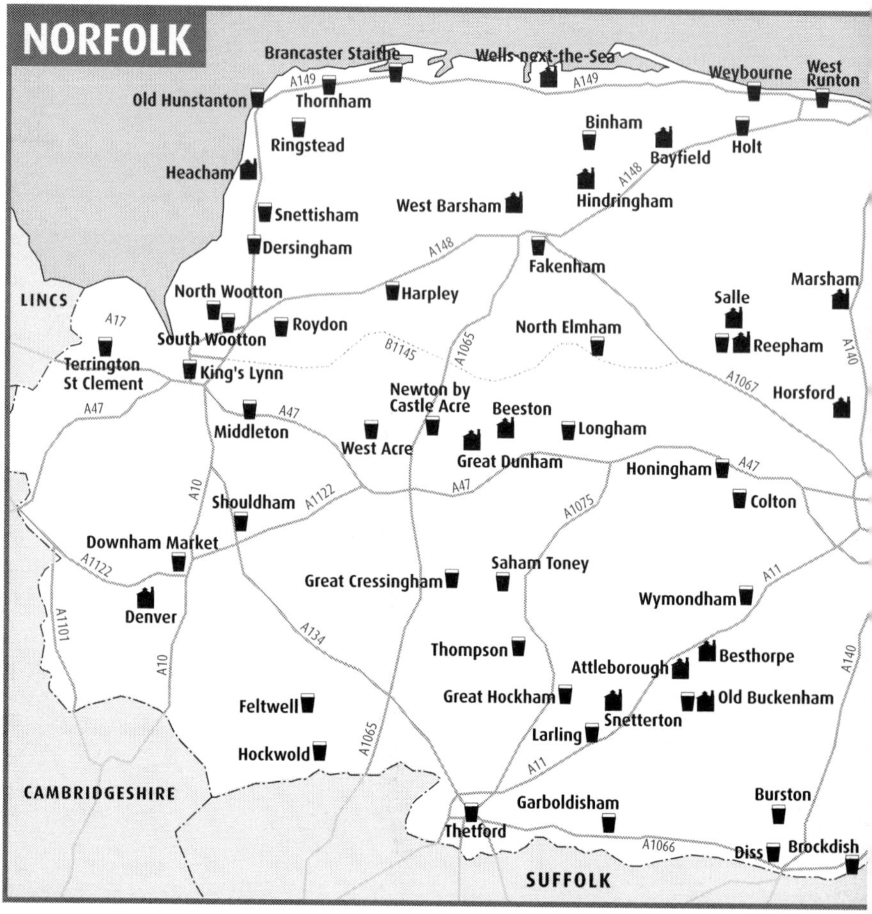

Banningham

Crown Inn

Colby Road, NR11 7DY (N of B1145, 1 mile E of A140)
12-11 (12.30am Fri & Sat) (01263) 733534
banninghamcrown.co.uk
5 changing beers H

Traditional 17th-century free house overlooking the village green. The warm atmosphere of the original beamed bar interior is further enhanced by the winter log fire. Seven handpumps feature four guest beers from regional and microbreweries, and one an artisan cider from local producers. The Crown is popular for fine cuisine using local produce; its restaurant features an open kitchen. The patio, garden and barbecue areas are ideal for summer alfresco dining. See the pub's website for regular events, the annual music festival and winter opening. Q❀◐◑♿⛺♣P🐾

Binham

Chequers Inn

Front Street, NR21 0AL
12-3, 6-11; 12-11 Fri & Sat; 12-10.30 Sun
(01328) 830297 binhamchequers.co.uk
Adnams Southwold Bitter; Norfolk Brewhouse Moon Gazer Golden Ale; 3 changing beers H

A traditional brick-and-flint village pub, the Chequers is a tremendously popular place both with locals and visitors, and a friendly local with strong support from the surrounding community. The menu comprises a range of good wholesome fare (including vegetarian) at reasonable prices. There is an additional specials menu and regular themed evenings. One of the guest beers is from Norfolk Brewhouse, and others are regional, but often from Norfolk. In addition to the bar area, there are benches and tables both inside and outside, and a large garden to the rear.
❀◐◑♣P🐾

Brancaster Staithe

Jolly Sailors

Main Road, PE31 8BJ
12-11; 12-10.30 Sun (01485) 210314
jollysailorsbrancaster.co.uk
Adnams Broadside; Woodforde's Wherry; 2 changing beers H

A cosy inn with several small drinking areas and two dining rooms, convenient for the Norfolk coast path and Brancaster Staithe harbour. It has a garden and play area, welcomes families and dogs, and has an ice cream hut. Brancaster beers are produced by a local brewery to the pub's recipes and at least one is always available. Food offerings

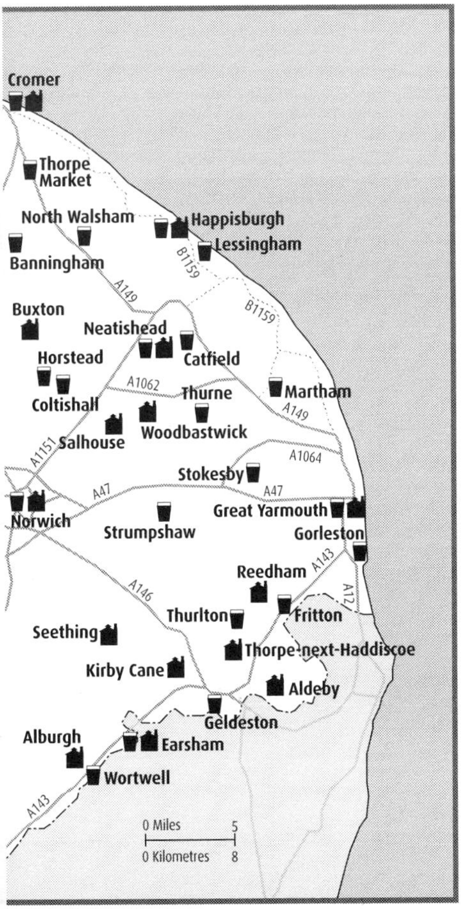

include local seafood and stone-baked pizza, with the oven visible from the bar. There is a beer and music festival every June. Coasthopper buses stop outside. Q🐎❀◑♿⛺♣P🚌🐾📶

Brockdish

Old King's Head 🏆

50 The Street, IP21 4JY

⏲ closed Mon; 10-10 (11 Fri & Sat); 10-9 Sun
☎ (01379) 668843 🌐 kingsheadbrockdish.co.uk

Adnams Southwold Bitter; Boudicca Queen of Hops; Humpty Dumpty Little Sharpie; Norfolk Brewhouse Moon Gazer Pacific Pale Ale, Golden Ale; 2 changing beers (often Grain, Lacons, Wolf) Ⓗ

A 16th-century beamed community inn with a friendly atmosphere. The pub reopened in 2015 with the addition of a coffee shop serving delicious home-made cakes and bread at weekends. It has a family-friendly bar, and a standing bar with a woodburner, both serving imaginative Italian food from noon. Locally sourced meats and ingredients are used where possible. Gluten-free meals and cakes are also available. Regular music events take place, usually on a Thursday. A gin club adds to the mix, with 150 gins available. Local artists display work in the bars and gallery. Local CAMRA Norfolk Pub of the Year 2018. 🐎❀◑♿♣P🚌🐾

Burston

Crown Inn

Mill Road, IP22 5TW (by crossroads in middle of village, on green)

⏲ 12-11; 12-10.30 Sun ☎ (01379) 741257
🌐 burstoncrown.com

Adnams Southwold Bitter Ⓗ/Ⓖ**; Greene King Abbot; 4 changing beers (often Adnams)** Ⓗ

An attractive 16th-century Grade II-listed pub featuring exposed beams, deep sofas, newspapers and a log fire blazing in the inglenook fireplace. There are two bars, one with a pool table and darts. Boules is played in the garden in summer. A small restaurant serves a mixed cuisine of locally sourced freshly cooked food – booking advisable (no food Sun eve or Mon). There is regular live music on Thursday evening and music and other entertainments regularly throughout the year, including a beer festival. The village is famous for the Burston School Strike that ran from 1914 to 1939. Q🐎❀◑♣P🐾📶

Catfield

Crown Inn Ⓛ ✔

The Street, NR29 5AA (in centre of village, S of A149, E of Stalham)

REAL ALE BREWERIES

All Day Salle
Ampersand Earsham
Barsham West Barsham
Beeston Beeston
Blimey! Norwich
Boudicca West Barsham
Bull of the Woods Kirby Cane
Chalk Hill 🛢 Norwich
Dancing Men 🛢 Happisburgh
Elmtree Snetterton
Fat Cat 🛢 Norwich
Fengate Marsham (NEW)
Fox 🛢 Heacham
Golden Triangle Norwich
Grain Alburgh
Humpty Dumpty Reedham
Lacons Great Yarmouth
Malt Coast Wells-next-the-Sea
Moon Gazer Hindringham
Neatishead 🛢 Neatishead
Opa Hay's Aldeby
Panther Reepham
People's Thorpe-next-Haddiscoe
Poppyland Cromer
Redwell Norwich
S&P Horsford
St Andrews 🛢 Norwich
Stumptail Great Dunham
Taylors 🛢 Attleborough
Tindall Seething
Tipples Salhouse
Tombstone 🛢 Great Yarmouth
Two Rivers Denver
Wagtail Old Buckenham
Waveney 🛢 Earsham
Why Not Norwich
Wildcraft Buxton
Winter's Norwich
Wolf Besthorpe
Woodforde's Woodbastwick
Yetman's Bayfield

⏲ 12-2.30, 6 (7 Mon)-11; 12-2.30, 5-11 Fri; 12-3, 6-midnight Sat; 12-10.30 Sun ☎ (01692) 580128 🌐 catfieldcrown.co.uk
Greene King IPA; 3 changing beers [H]
This 300-year-old village inn, with its real fire, is a genuine focus for village life. Ales are usually from local breweries. The food menu features home-cooked traditional pub meals, made with local ingredients where possible. There is a separate function/dining room and a secluded rear garden for the summer. An annual beer festival is held in the summer, usually in July. Accommodation is available in two holiday cottages.
Q❀🛏◐♣P🚌🐾📶

Coltishall

Red Lion [L]
77 Church Street, NR12 7DW
⏲ 12 (4 Mon)-11 ☎ (01603) 736644
🌐 redlion-coltishall.co.uk
Sharp's Doom Bar; 2 changing beers [H]
Intricate two-level pub with a separate dining area, complemented by a café. It is warm, friendly and comfortable, and dates from the 16th century. In the cosy lower bar with logburner up to five real ales can be found, sourced from local or regional microbreweries. The varied menu features specials and theme nights. Beer festivals are held at Easter and in late summer, and the pub even has its own taxi. Q❀◐♣🍎P🚌🐾📶

Colton

Norfolk Lurcher [L]
High House Farm Lane, NR9 5DG (2 miles from A47 Norwich Southern bypass)
⏲ 12-2.30 (not Mon & Tue), 6-11; 12-2.30, 6-9 Sun
☎ (01603) 880794 🌐 the-norfolklurcher.com
Beeston Worth the Wait; 3 changing beers [H]
A welcoming, family-owned and run country pub, in the heart of the Norfolk countryside yet only a short drive from Norwich. The landlord keeps his beers well, and always has four handpumps serving the best of local breweries. Alternatively, try one of the 60 single malts. Large, comfortable bar areas are complemented by the excellent Ugly Bug Restaurant serving locally produced food. There is an extensive beer garden for warmer days. The pub hosts monthly jazz evenings plus regular food and music nights. Eight en-suite bedrooms are available. Q🐴❀🛏◐♿⛺♣P🚌🐾📶

Cromer

Red Lion Hotel [L]
Brook Street, NR27 9HD (S of church on clifftop)
⏲ 11-11 ☎ (01263) 514964 🌐 redlion-cromer.co.uk
12 changing beers [H]
Splendidly situated with views of Cromer pier and the sea, the 19th-century Red Lion has retained many of its original features including panelling, a Victorian tiled floor and open wood fires. The work of local artists decorates the walls of the two bar areas. Up to 12 guest ales are usually on handpump, often from local breweries such as Winters and Green Jack. Beer festivals are held in the summer. The restaurant offers an extensive menu, including breakfast 7-10.30am. Accommodation is available.
Q🐴🛏◐♿⇌🍎🚌🐾📶

Wellington
Garden Street, NR27 9HN
⏲ 11-11 (midnight Fri & Sat); 12-10.30 Sun
☎ (01263) 511075 🌐 thewellycromer.co.uk
Adnams Lighthouse; 2 changing beers [H]
A stone's throw from the beach, the Welly is an interesting building with one long bar. There is a good selection of pub games and a widescreen TV for live sports, four en-suite rooms, and the Courtyard restaurant serving locally sourced food at good prices in a converted stable block. The house beer is from Wolf Brewery, with changing beers on handpump from Adnams and Woodforde's. Owned by the same family for over 20 years.
🐴❀🛏◐⇌♣🚌🐾📶

Dersingham

Coach & Horses ✓
77 Manor Road, PE31 6LN
⏲ 12-11 ☎ (01485) 540391 🌐 thecoachpub.com
Woodforde's Wherry; 3 changing beers [H]
A 19th-century carrstone pub near Sandringham offering three changing guest ales and one constant, plus a draught real cider, at reasonable prices. It is popular for home-made traditional meals. Entertainment includes quiz nights, piano, a pool table and live music Friday nights and some Sundays. The large garden includes a children's play area. There are three en-suite B&B rooms. An October beer festival offers around 20 real ales plus five real ciders. Dogs welcome.
Q🐴❀🛏◐⛺🍎P🚌🐾📶

Diss

Cock Inn ✓
63 Lower Denmark Street, IP22 4BE (to W of town off A1066)
⏲ 12-11 (midnight Fri & Sat); 12-10.30 Sun
☎ (01379) 643633 🌐 cockinndiss.co.uk
Adnams Southwold Bitter [G]**; 2 changing beers (often Earl Soham, Greene King)** [H]
Grade II-listed pub dating from 1520 which faces a large green on the outskirts of this market town. The bar serves four distinct drinking areas furnished with a range of sofas plus wooden tables and chairs. On cold nights a large log fire welcomes customers. The Cock normally offers three ales direct from barrels kept in the air-conditioned cask room behind the bar. Q🐴❀◐♿♣P🚌🐾📶

Downham Market

Crown Hotel
12 Bridge Street, PE38 9DH
⏲ 9.30am-11 ☎ (01366) 382322 🌐 crowncoachinginn.com
Adnams Southwold Bitter; Greene King IPA, Abbot; 2 changing beers [H]
An unspoilt 17th-century coaching inn at the heart of the town. Entering through a room with a lovely staircase reveals a bar with a beamed ceiling and large fireplace. A good selection of ales is served. There is a restaurant serving snacks, mains and specials, and plenty of outside seating, plus a separate function room that caters for parties and weddings. Accommodation is provided in 18 rooms, including family suites. Q❀🛏◐⇌P🚌📶

Earsham

Queen's Head 🄻
Station Road, NR35 2TS (just W of Bungay)
✪ 12-11; 12-10.30 Sun ☎ (01986) 892623
Waveney East Coast Mild, Lightweight; 2 changing beers 🄷
On the Norfolk-Suffolk border near Bungay, this busy 17th-century locals' brewpub has a large front garden overlooking the village green. The main bar has a flagstone floor, wooden beams and a large fireplace with a roaring fire in winter. The pub is home to the Waveney Brewing Company. Four ales and at least one real cider are usually on the go. There is a separate dining area serving food at lunchtimes (not Mon and Tue). The landlord has owned the pub since 1998. A previous local CAMRA Pub of the Year. **Q🐴✿◐♿♣🍎P🚌**(580)**🐾📶**

Fakenham

Limes 🄻 ✔
30 Bridge Street, NR21 9AZ
✪ 8am-midnight ☎ (01328) 850050
Adnams Ghost Ship; Greene King Abbot; Ruddles Best Bitter; Sharp's Doom Bar; 5 changing beers 🄷
Transformed into its present format in 2013, this popular Wetherspoon pub in the town centre has three interconnecting bar areas and front and rear patios. Up to nine real ales are on the bar together with a range of real ciders, and food is served all day. Several public car parks are in close proximity. The pub is within walking distance of Fakenham Racecourse and Fakenham Museum of Gas and Local History. **Q🐴✿◐◑♿⛺🍎🚌📶**

Feltwell

Wellington 🄻
27-29 High Street, IP26 4AF
✪ 12-11 (midnight Fri & Sat); 12-10.30 Sun
☎ (01842) 828224 🌐 feltwellington.co.uk
3 changing beers 🄷
A 17th century former general stores, the Wellington reopened after extensive refurbishment in 2014. Landlords Chris and Chris run a mainly wet-led pub while serving award-winning food. There is a cosy lounge bar with a separate games room featuring pool and darts, plus a restaurant to the rear. One real cider is always on handpump. There are lots of items of interesting memorabilia relating to the pub's namesake Wellington bomber. **🐴✿◐◑♿♣🍎P📶**

Fritton

Decoy Tavern
Beccles Road, NR31 9AB
✪ 11-11 ☎ (01493) 488277
2 changing beers 🄷
Traditional country free house, with a large car park, set back from the road between Beccles and Great Yarmouth, close to Fritton Lake and about a mile from Broads moorings on the River Waveney at St Olaves. There is a grassed beer garden with seating to the side of the pub. A wide range of home-cooked meals is available in the separate dining area. The beer selection varies but tends to be a choice of locally sourced real ales.
🐴✿◐◑♣P🚌(580)**🐾📶**

Garboldisham

Fox Inn 🄻
The Street, IP22 2RZ
✪ closed Mon-Thu; 5-10 Fri; 12-10 Sat; 12-5 Sun
☎ (01953) 688538
Lacons Encore; Norfolk Brewhouse Moon Gazer Norfolk Pale Ale; Old Chimneys Great Raft Bitter; Star Wing Spire Light; 3 changing beers (often Boudicca, Cliff Quay, Elmtree) 🄷
A 17th-century coaching inn with a welcoming feel, near Bressingham Gardens and Banham Zoo. After it was bought by locals to operate as a community pub it reopened in late 2016, although renovation continues. The pub serves ales from breweries such as Old Chimneys, Blimey, Norfolk Brewhouse and Wolf, as well as Adnams. A collection of old jugs belonging to a lady who lived in the Fox several years ago is on display. Rumour has it that one of the pub ghosts is a black labrador. Local ice cream is sold in tubs. Local CAMRA Cider Pub of the Year 2019. **Q🐴✿♣🍎P🐾**

Geldeston

Wherry 🄻
7 The Street, NR34 0LB
✪ 12-11 ☎ (01508) 518371 🌐 wherryinn.co.uk
Adnams Ghost Ship, Southwold Bitter; 1 changing beer 🄷
This old classic village pub sits on the roadside 200 yards from the Geldeston Dyke moorings. The main public bar and snug bar both boast a logburner in an open fireplace, along with seating for meals or socialising. There is a pleasant garden next to the car park area. Two, sometimes three, well-kept Adnams ales are stocked, with a varying guest ale. Good-quality home-cooked meals are served daily.
Q🐴✿◐◑♿⛺♣P🐾📶

Gorleston

Dock Tavern 🄻
Dock Tavern Lane, NR31 6PY (opp N side of Morrisons)
✪ 11-11; 12-11 Sun ☎ (01493) 442255
🌐 thedocktavern.com
Adnams Broadside; 3 changing beers 🄷
As its name suggests, the Dock Tavern is close to the river, and not far from the main shopping area. It has suffered flood damage many times; the various flood levels can be seen by the front door. The outside drinking area at the front has views of the river and docks. There is live music most weekends, and curry and quiz nights monthly, plus an annual charity music day. A warm, welcoming pub with a friendly atmosphere. **🐴✿◐♣🍎🚌🐾📶**

New Entertainer 🄻
80 Pier Plain, NR31 6PG
✪ 12-midnight ☎ (01493) 300022
Greene King IPA; 11 changing beers 🄷
This traditional and unusual pub with a curved frontage has an interesting design and layout. There is a varied choice of beers on offer, including up to 10 guest real ales, many of which are locally brewed, as well as up to nine traditional ciders. The customers are as widely varied as the beers, with pool and darts available along with a monthly quiz. This free house is well worth seeking out. Note that the main entrance is on Back Pier Plain.
✿⇄♣🍎🚌🐾📶

Oddfellows Arms 🄻

43 Cliff Hill, NR31 6DG
⏲ 4-10.30 (11 Fri); 2-11 Sat & Sun ☎ 07876 545982
🌐 oddiesgy.co.uk
Lacons Encore, Legacy; St Austell Tribute; 1 changing beer [H]
Cosy local pub with two bars, on Cliff Hill, a short distance from the harbour. Music and jam sessions are held on many Fridays, especially in summer. There are at least four beers on offer, mainly from the multi award-winning Lacons Brewery in Great Yarmouth; the pub could almost be considered its brewery tap. Various bottled and canned craft ales from around the world are also stocked. There is a west-facing outdoor seating area, and limited parking at the rear. 🐴✿♿♣P🐾ᯤ

Pub on the Shrubs

Hawthorn Road, NR31 8ET
⏲ 10-midnight (1am Fri & Sat); 10-11 Sun
☎ (01493) 603780 🌐 pubontheshrubs.co.uk
Adnams Broadside, Ghost Ship, Lighthouse; 1 changing beer [H]
Social club on the Shrublands estate which converted to a pub in 2014. This multi-roomed venue, with a large separate function room with a stage, supports local football teams and a wide variety of local clubs. It hosts live folk music on Tuesday and the East Coast Rock & Roll Club, and shows sporting events including Celtic football games on the numerous large-screen TVs dotted around the place. There is an outside smoking area and a large car park. 🐴✿♣Pᯤ

William Adams ✔

176-177 High Street, NR31 6RG
⏲ 8am-midnight ☎ (01493) 600295
Greene King Abbot; Ruddles Best Bitter; Sharp's Doom Bar; 6 changing beers (sourced nationally) [H]
A new-build Wetherspoon pub on Gorleston High Street, named after a famous Gorleston swimming instructor and lifesaver. It has one large open room with all the usual JDW facilities, plus a pleasant enclosed seating area outside with a designated smoking section (open until 9pm). The decor depicts the famous local fishing industry and seaside themes. Six real ales are served, with the chance of some real bag-in-box ciders.
🐴✿◐♿🍎🚌ᯤ

Great Cressingham

Olde Windmill Inn

Water End, IP25 6NN (off A1065 S of Swaffham)
⏲ 11-11 ☎ (01760) 756232 🌐 oldewindmillinn.co.uk
Adnams Southwold Bitter, Broadside; Greene King IPA; 2 changing beers [H]
The Windmill is a large rural pub and hotel, family-run for three generations, feeling cosy despite its size. It offers a rolling range of ales including house beers called Windy Miller, which are mostly supplied by Purity. Real cider is also sold. The popular food menu covers all tastes. Dining areas vary in size from a large conservatory to smaller, more intimate rooms. Modern hotel accommodation is located in separate buildings behind the pub. Q🐴✿🛏◐♿⛺♣🍎P🐾

Great Hockham

Eagle 🄻 ✔

Harling Road, IP24 1NP
⏲ 12-2.30, 6-11; 12-midnight Fri & Sat; 12-10.30 Sun
☎ (01953) 498893 🌐 hockhameagle.com
Adnams Southwold Bitter, Ghost Ship; Morland Old Speckled Hen; Woodforde's Wherry; 1 changing beer [H]
The year 2019 saw Aaron mark the 10th anniversary as landlord of this large family- and dog-friendly pub. The Eagle is set in a picturesque village close to Thetford Forest. Two bars divided by an open fire serve five real ales on handpump. Outdoor seating is provided at the front and in an enclosed brick-weave courtyard at the rear. The pub hosts three pool teams and a darts team in addition to having a fortnightly quiz and other regular events. 🐴✿◐♿♣P🐾ᯤ

Great Yarmouth

Mariners 🄻

69 Howard Street South, NR30 1LN (between Palmers and the Star Hotel)
⏲ 12-midnight ☎ (01493) 331164
Greene King Abbot; 10 changing beers [H]
Traditional two-bar flint-walled pub in the town centre which stocks up to 10 ales and several ciders or perries from all over the country. The pub has a maritime theme and displays photos of numerous ships on the walls. In the winter customers can enjoy their drinks next to a lovely open fire. Knowledgeable staff and a great choice of varying real ales make the Mariners well worth a visit.
🐴✿⇌♣🍎P🥃🚌🐾ᯤ

Red Herring 🄻

24-25 Havelock Road, NR30 3HQ (Havelock Rd is off St Peters St and at back of Time and Tide museum)
⏲ 12-3, 7-midnight; 12-midnight Sat & Sun ☎ 07876 644742
4 changing beers (sourced nationally) [H]
The Red Herring gets its name from the fish that were smoked in the nearby but now-closed smokehouses. It offers four changing beers alongside two ciders on the handpumps. The Herring is home to a darts team and a pool team. The pub is close to the impressive medieval walls and the award-winning Time and Tide museum. There is always a relaxed and friendly atmosphere here along with a good regular following.
Q✿♣🍎🥃🚌

Tombstone Saloon 🄻

6 George Street, NR30 1HR (on NE corner of Hall Quay)
⏲ closed Mon-Wed; 12-11 Thu-Sat; 12-8 Sun
☎ 07584 504444 🌐 tombstonebrewery.co.uk
10 changing beers (sourced nationally) [G]
Western-style bar specialising in real ale and cider, operated by the local Tombstone Brewery sited at the rear of the premises. Staff are friendly and knowledgeable about beer, and there are usually up to six Tombstone real ales plus four others from various breweries. The bar also has a stock of rare spirits from around the world as well as wines and a European bottle beer selection. Local CAMRA Pub of the Year 2018. Q⇌♣🍎🥃🚌🐾

Happisburgh

Hill House 🄻

The Hill, NR12 0PW (off B1159, behind church)
⏲ 12-11 ☎ (01692) 650004
6 changing beers [H]
A Grade II-listed, 16th-century former coaching inn in an attractive coastal village which was a haunt

of Sir Arthur Conan Doyle; the in-house brewery is named after his story The Adventure of the Dancing Men. The pub usually offers a range of up to six real ales and one cider, all from this brewery. Hot meals are served lunchtimes and evenings. The pub hosts a noteworthy beer festival each June that offers over 120 real ales and ciders.
Q🐴❀🛏◐◑▲♣●P🐾📶

Harpley

Rose & Crown 🏆

Nethergate Street, PE31 6TW
⏲ 12-11; 12-10.30 Sun ☎ (01485) 521807
Woodforde's Wherry; 4 changing beers [H]
Local CAMRA's Pub of the Year 2019 is just off the A148 King's Lynn to Fakenham road, an attractive 17th-century pub offering guest ales from local breweries. It features open bar areas with a stylish and comfortable feel and has log fires in winter, while outside is an enclosed beer garden for summer drinking. There is an extensive menu serving excellent food, including one of the best Sunday roasts in the area. The unspoilt village provides pleasant walks and is close to Houghton Hall. **Q🐴❀◐◑P🚌**(X29)**🐾📶**

Hockwold

Red Lion

114 Main Street, IP26 4NB
⏲ 11.30-3, 6 (5 Sat)-11.30; 12-10.30 Sun ☎ (01842) 829728
🌐 redlionhockwold.com
3 changing beers [H]
Traditional, friendly village pub set on a green. The Red Lion was refurbished and reopened as a free house in 2012. It has a smart but comfortable interior; see how many toby jugs you can spot! A good selection of home-made food is served all week, with a carvery on Sunday and Tuesday lunchtimes; Thursday is steak night. There are regular, well-supported quizzes and darts matches. Outside is a spacious garden with plenty of seating and a children's play area. **🐴❀◐◑♣P🐾**

Holt

King's Head

19 High Street, NR25 6BN
⏲ 11.30-11; 11.30-10.30 Sun ☎ (01263) 712543
🌐 kingsheadholt.org.uk
Norfolk Brewhouse Moon Gazer Golden Ale; Woodforde's Wherry [H]**; 4 changing beers** [G]
A Grade II-listed building in the centre of this delightful Georgian market town. The pub features two bars, one with a pool table, and hosts a free pool night on Sunday. There is also a snug, a conservatory which is home to the restaurant, and a large outside drinking area. A live band plays on the first Saturday of each month. There are three bedrooms, two with self-catering kitchens.
Q🐴❀🛏◐◑▲♣🚌🐾📶

Honingham

Buck L

29 The Street, NR9 5BL (centre of village)
⏲ 11.30-11; 11.30-10 Sun ☎ (01603) 880393
🌐 thehoninghambuck.co.uk
Lacons Encore, Charter, Legacy; 1 changing beer [H]
Dating back to 1789, this traditional one-bar village pub has a separate restaurant area with an emphasis on home-cooked food. The Buck has served Lacons real ales since the brewery bought it in 2015. Slate floors, oak beams, a large fireplace and period furniture enhance the image of a country pub. An excellent menu of unusual dishes is freshly cooked to order, making this a great venue for eating, and there is a large garden with plenty of seating. **Q🐴❀🛏◐◑♿P🚌🐾📶**

Horstead

Recruiting Sergeant

Norwich Road, NR12 7EE
⏲ 11-11; 12-11 Sun ☎ (01603) 737077
🌐 recruitingsergeant.co.uk
Adnams Southwold Bitter; Greene King Abbot; Timothy Taylor Landlord; 3 changing beers [H]
Popular pub/restaurant mostly given over to dining, but with a welcoming and accommodating bar area. Six real ales are dispensed on handpump (three regular, three changing), mostly sourced regionally. A comprehensive menu, with a good selection of fish and steak dishes, is served in two separate dining areas in addition to the bar. There is a good-sized car park and pleasant patio garden. Accommodation is available in five double rooms above the pub. **Q🐴❀🛏◐◑♿P🐾📶**

King's Lynn

Live & Let Live L

18 Windsor Road, PE30 5PL (off London Rd near Catholic church)
⏲ 11-10.30; 11-11 Fri & Sat ☎ (01553) 764990
5 changing beers [H]
A back-street locals' pub with two bars, a small cosy lounge and a larger public bar with a TV. Five beers are offered, from a variety of breweries both local and further afield. This is one of the few pubs in the area to regularly sell a mild. Cider drinkers are also catered for, with ciders from Westons and local producers. Live music is sometimes played in the public bar. **●🐾**

Stuart House Hotel

35 Goodwins Road, PE30 5QX (up gravel drive off Goodwins Rd)
⏲ 6-11 ☎ (01553) 772169 🌐 stuart-house-hotel.co.uk
3 changing beers [H]
The Stuart House has a public bar that has been a regular entry in the Guide for over 20 years. It is located up a secluded drive but within easy walking distance of the station and town centre. There are two or three changing beers on offer, usually from the larger regional breweries. The last week of July sees a beer festival staged in the garden. Note that the hours are evening only, but lunchtime opening may be possible by arrangement. Check out the website for special offers. **❀🛏◑⇌P🐾📶**

Larling

Angel

NR16 2QU (1 mile SW from Snetterton racetrack, just off A11)
⏲ 10.30-11 ☎ (01953) 717963 🌐 angel-larling.co.uk
Adnams Southwold Bitter; 4 changing beers [H]
Five real ales plus a real cider are on handpump here, always including a mild. Over 100 whiskies are stocked, as well as 50 gins on the gin menu. One whisky is featured each week. The lounge and

bar have real open fires. There is a dining room which boasts home-made fare in generous portions. A friendly atmosphere is enjoyed by locals, visitors, campers and rallyists who use the Angel's campsite. A popular long-running beer festival with live music in August showcases over 80 real ales. Q P

Lessingham

Star Inn

Star Hill, NR12 0DN (just off main B1159, corner of High Rd and Star Hill)

closed Mon; 12-3, 6-11; 12-11 Sun (01692) 580510

thestarlessingham.co.uk

Fat Cat Norwich Bitter; Lacons Encore; Woodforde's Once Bittern; 1 changing beer [G]

A traditional pub with a friendly atmosphere and a log fire in winter. Four ales, including one guest, are served from the cask, as are three ciders. The Star is popular for high-quality meals with carefully sourced ingredients served in decent portions. Meals may be enjoyed in the bar, a separate restaurant or the spacious beer garden. Two en-suite double B&B rooms make this the perfect base to explore the nearby coast and the Broads. May close early on Sunday winter evenings. A rural gem. Q P (34)

Longham

White Horse

Wendling Road, NR19 2RD

11.30-2.30, 5-11; 11.30-midnight Sat; 11-10.30 Sun (01362) 687464 longhamwhitehorse.co.uk

Greene King Yardbird; 3 changing beers [H]

An attractive and traditional village local with a cosy feel and a high standard of decor. It has a main bar area with separate dining rooms off to the left and right, plus a large conservatory that is also used for dining at the rear, overlooking the garden. The real ale is generally from local regional breweries, with one traditional cider also usually available. The extensive menu caters for all tastes and requirements, with ingredients sourced locally. B&B is also available. Q P

Martham

King's Arms

15 The Green, NR29 4PL

closed Mon; 12-11 (01493) 749156

5 changing beers [H]

Previously owned by Adnams, and before that Lacons, the King's Arms, situated in the centre of the village by the pond, became a free house in 2014. The pub serves four or five ales from local and less-local breweries, along with an extensive range of ciders. It has a nice garden out the back with a large car park, and food is available daily until 9pm. A sloe gin competition is held annually. Closed Monday, except bank holidays.
P

Middleton

Gate

Hill Road, Fair Green, PE32 1RW (N of A47; follow Fair Green signs)

closed Mon; 12-10 (11 Fri & Sat) (01553) 840518

thegatefairgreen.co.uk

Greene King IPA, Abbot; 2 changing beers [H]

It is worth the short detour off the A47, east of King's Lynn, to find what is at heart still a village local. The bar has a log fire in winter and welcomes dogs. It caters for drinkers and those who want to enjoy the good-value pub food, while those who prefer more formal dining can choose the smart restaurant area. Note that the pub is closed on Mondays except for bank holidays.
Q P

Neatishead

White Horse

The Street, NR12 8AD

11-11 (10.30 Sun) (01692) 630828

thewhitehorseinnneatishead.com

Woodforde's Wherry; 6 changing beers [H]

Traditional Broadland village pub tastefully modernised to retain many original features including log fires. There are three drinking areas. Of the seven real ales, six change frequently and are mainly from microbreweries across the UK, including the in-house brewery. Excellent, reasonably priced meals are home-prepared with local produce. There is a comfortable split-level restaurant. Beer festivals are held in spring and autumn. Just a short walk from the moorings.
Q P

Newton by Castle Acre

George & Dragon

Swaffham Road, PE32 2BX (on A1065)

8am-11 (10.30 Sun) (01760) 755623

newtongeorgepub.com

Adnams Ghost Ship; Woodforde's Wherry; 2 changing beers [H]

The pub reopened in 2018 after a major refurbishment. With a wooden floor, exposed beams, comfortable seats and walls lined with old books, it has something of the air of a gentlemen's club. The menu looks interesting, with items such as a meat platter featuring potted rabbit and venison alongside vegan 'steak'. Coffee, tea and cake cater for those who prefer an alternative. There is a play area for children at the rear and the Pig Shed motel at the back for those who wish to stay overnight. P

North Elmham

Railway Arms

40 Station Road, NR20 5HH

12-11.30 (01362) 668300 therailwayarms.co.uk

4 changing beers [H]

Situated in central Norfolk near the ancient remains of the Anglo-Saxon North Elmham cathedral and bishop's palace, this is both a rural gem and a fine community pub. It has an L-shaped open bar, with two real fires, together with a separate dining room off the main bar. The beers, all on handpull, usually come from microbreweries in Norfolk and Suffolk. Home-cooked meals using mainly locally sourced ingredients are served at lunchtime and in the evening.
Q P

North Walsham

Hop In

2 Market Street, NR28 9BZ

❂ closed Mon; 12-10.30 (11 Fri & Sat); 12-10 Sun
☎ 07426 139417 🌐 thehopin.co.uk
6 changing beers Ⓖ
Owned and run by keen CAMRA members, this is Norfolk's only (known) micropub, situated in a former taxi office just around the corner from the marketplace. Six changing ales are served on gravity dispense plus real cider and wine. There is usually one dark beer available. In keeping with the micropub philosophy, there is no Wi-Fi, music or machines, just good conversation. It has seating for about a dozen downstairs and around 20 more upstairs, plus a small patio area outside.
Q❀⇌●▯⊟

Orchard Gardens 𝕃 ✔
Mundesley Road, NR28 0DB
❂ 3-midnight; 1-midnight Fri; 12-midnight Sat & Sun
☎ (01692) 405152 🌐 theorchardgardens.co.uk
Adnams Ghost Ship; Lacons Encore; 3 changing beers Ⓗ
Town pub combining local beers, from breweries like Adnams and Lacons, with friendly service. A games area and conservatory are a feature in this Victorian building with a large garden. Pool and darts teams are supported, and there is live sport on the large-screen TV, a weekly quiz and live music every Saturday. ♨❀⛺♣●P⊟(5)🐾📶

North Wootton

Red Cat Hotel
Station Road, PE30 3QH (road is opp church of All Saints, at jct of N end of Nursery Rd and W end of Manor Rd)
❂ 5-11; 12-2, 7-11 Sun ☎ (01553) 631244
🌐 redcathotel.co.uk
Adnams Southwold Bitter; 1 changing beer Ⓗ
A village local with a reputation for well-kept beer, albeit of limited range. It is a nicely decorated bar in a quiet location. Ask about the history of the namesake red cat – if you can believe it. There are attractive gardens for summer drinks. The pub is near National Cycle Route 1, the Sandringham Estate and the west Norfolk coast.
Q♨❀P⊟(3)🐾📶

Norwich

Alexandra Tavern
16 Stafford Street, NR2 3BB (on corner of Stafford St and Gladstone St, off Dereham Rd)
❂ 12-11 (midnight Thu-Sat) ☎ (01603) 627772
🌐 alexandratavern.co.uk
Chalk Hill CHB, Tap Bitter; 3 changing beers Ⓗ
Popular, bustling and friendly, this pub is a real gem found just outside the city centre. The interior is brightly decorated, with the walls featuring pictures and articles of a nautical nature. The bar regularly serves three Chalk Hill Brewery beers as well as guest ales from breweries not often seen in the city. Food is served daily until 7pm, with a good variety including a soup menu. There is a dartboard and lots of board games to choose from, with children also welcome until 7pm.
Q♨❀◐◑♿♣⊟🐾📶

Angel Gardens 𝕃
96 Angel Road, NR3 3HT
❂ 11-midnight (1am Sat); 12-11 Sun ☎ (01603) 427490
Elgood's Black Dog; Oakham JHB; Sharp's Doom Bar; 6 changing beers Ⓗ
Friendly locals' pub with a good selection of four permanent and five changing local and national real ales. Up to six real ciders on gravity are stocked, depending on the season. The pub offers live entertainment on Saturday evening, a pool table, and runs darts and crib teams. It has a covered heated drinking area at the front and a garden with play equipment at the rear. There is a small function room with a bar available.
♨❀◐◑●P🐾📶

Beehive 𝕃
30 Leopold Road, NR4 7PJ (between Unthank and Newmarket roads)
❂ 12-11 (midnight Fri & Sat) ☎ (01603) 451628
🌐 beehivepubnorwich.co.uk
Green Jack Golden Best; 5 changing beers Ⓗ
A two-bar traditional friendly local with knowledgeable staff, featuring a comfortable lounge bar with sofas. A popular beer garden is used all year round and for charity barbecues during the summer months. The pub hosts a beer festival with around 25 ales and ciders in late June. There is a hireable function room upstairs with a pool table. The pub has hockey, korfball, golf, darts and pool teams, plus a regular Wednesday night quiz, folk music nights and themed food evenings.
Q❀◐♣●P⊟🐾📶

Coach & Horses
82 Thorpe Road, NR1 1BA
❂ 11-11 (1am Fri & Sat) ☎ (01603) 477077
🌐 thecoachthorperoad.co.uk
Chalk Hill CHB, Dreadnought, Gold, Tap Bitter; 3 changing beers Ⓗ
Close to the station, this coaching inn, with its iconic balcony, is the home of the Chalk Hill Brewery, and serves its full range of beers, along with Burnard's Cider. A tour of the brewery is available by appointment. Excellent-value food is available. Sport, especially rugby, is shown on big screens, and the large fire is welcome in winter. Located near the football ground, the pub gets busy before matches. ❀◐◑♿⇌●P⊟🐾📶

Coach & Horses
51 Bethel Street, NR2 1NR
❂ 12-midnight ☎ (01603) 618522
🌐 thecoachandhorsesbethelstreet.co.uk
6 changing beers Ⓗ
Historic city-centre local near the Theatre Royal, the Forum and City Hall. It is a bright, welcoming bar with several separate seating areas including cosy alcove-style seating. A Greene King house, it also stocks local ales from the likes of Moon Gazer, Humpty Dumpty and others. Food is based on an English tapas theme, which works well. Try some celeb spotting too, or a game of bar billiards. There is a large outdoor 'urban' seating area.
Q♨❀◐◑♣●⊟🐾📶

Coachmakers Arms
9 St Stephens Road, NR1 3SP
❂ 11-11; 12-10.30 Sun ☎ (01603) 662080
Greene King Abbot; Wolf Golden Jackal; Woodforde's Mardler's, Wherry, Reedlighter, Nelsons Revenge Ⓖ**; 4 changing beers** Ⓗ
Free house with a range of ales on gravity. Dating from the 17th century, this allegedly haunted former coaching inn stands on the site of an old asylum. A spacious courtyard converted into a large sports bar/function room complements a garden patio. Inside, it has one large L-shaped beamed bar

room. Unobtrusive Sky TV combines well with darts and it all adds up to a popular city-centre venue.

Duke of Wellington

91-93 Waterloo Road, NR3 1EG
12-11 (midnight Fri & Sat); 12-10.30 Sun
(01603) 441182 dukeofwellingtonnorwich.co.uk
Fuller's London Pride (H); Oakham JHB, Bishops Farewell (G); Wolf Golden Jackal (H), Wolf in Sheep's Clothing; 15 changing beers (G)
Friendly pub with a changing range of guest ales to complement the permanent beers, the majority of which are served on gravity from a taproom behind the bar. A beer of the month from Wolf Brewery is available at a discount. The attractive award-winning enclosed rear garden/patio area accommodates a beer festival in late August plus regular barbecues at weekends in summer. Events include monthly quiz evenings. Customers can bring their own food in or sample the filling and inexpensive pies and sausage rolls.
P

Fat Cat

49 West End Street, NR2 4NA
11-11 (midnight Fri & Sat) (01603) 624364
fatcatpub.co.uk
Crouch Vale Yakima Gold (H); Fat Cat Marmalade Cat (G), Norwich Bitter; Fuller's ESB (H); Greene King Abbot; Oakham Bishops Farewell; 20 changing beers (G)
The Fat Cat has been voted CAMRA National Pub of the Year twice. An amazing range of brewery memorabilia is displayed around the walls and alcoves of this traditional-style pub. It is a beer lover's paradise that no visitor to Norwich should miss out on. Ales are from the Fat Cat range, plus about 10 regular and 20 guest beers from all over the UK, real ciders, and several quality keg beers. Food is limited to good-value rolls and pies. An outstanding example of what a real ale pub should be, with excellent friendly service. Q

Fat Cat & Canary

101 Thorpe Road, NR1 1TR
12-11 (midnight Fri); 11-midnight Sat (01603) 432393
fatcatcanary.co.uk
Fat Cat Norwich Bitter, Hell Cat, Honey Ale, Marmalade Cat, Wild Cat; 7 changing beers (sourced nationally) (H)
The third member of the Norwich-based Fat Cat mini-chain, about a mile and a half from the centre of the city. It serves most of the Fat Cat Brewery's ales, and various guests from around the UK, together with continental beers and real ciders. There is a small TV to the rear of the main bar, a large car park and terraces to the front and rear, the latter being heated. Home-made rolls are available. Busy on Norwich City match days.
P

Fat Cat Brewery Tap

98-100 Lawson Road, NR3 4LF
12-11 (midnight Fri); 11-midnight Sat; 11-10.30 Sun
(01603) 413153 fatcattap.co.uk
Fat Cat Norwich Bitter, Marmalade Cat, Honey Ale (H); Fyne Ales Jarl; Oakham Bishops Farewell; 20 changing beers (G)
Home of the Fat Cat Brewery, it serves the Fat Cat range plus a huge selection of real ales, ciders and quality keg beers from across the country. A distinctive collection of breweriana adorns the ceiling beams and walls. Live music on Friday and Sunday complements a variety of events held at the pub including tap takeovers, themed beer evenings, a monthly cycling club, plus a fortnightly quiz. Motherchips (loaded chips) and cheeseboards are available. Norfolk CAMRA Pub of the Year 2018.
QP(11,11A)

Golden Star

57 Colegate, NR3 1DD
12-11 (midnight Fri & Sat) (01603) 632447
goldenstarnorwich.co.uk
Greene King IPA, Abbot; 3 changing beers (H)
A welcoming and relaxing pub with a main bar area and a second room to the left of the bar, hosting bar billiards and live music sessions. A quiz is held on Sunday evenings. An excellent specials menu is served daily, including locally sourced organic meat. A wide selection of music is played, but unobtrusively. Handy for Norwich Playhouse and Norwich University of the Arts. There is a small patio at the rear, and tables outside the front in summer.

Jubilee

26 St Leonards Road, NR1 4BL
12-11 (midnight Fri & Sat) (01603) 618734
Hop Back Summer Lightning; Woodforde's Reedlighter, Wherry; 5 changing beers (H)
An attractive Victorian corner pub with a warm welcome. There are two bars, a comfortable conservatory and an enclosed patio garden. Many of the well-kept ales and craft beers are local. This popular pub, within easy reach of the city centre, is at the heart of the community and caters for all tastes, from sports fans to those who enjoy local history talks. Customers are welcome to bring in takeaway food, and there are regular Sunday roasts and occasional pop-up street food fairs.
Q

King's Arms

22 Hall Road, NR1 3HQ
11-11 (11.30 Fri & Sat); 12-11 Sun (01603) 477888
kingsarmsnorwich.co.uk
Batemans Gold; 10 changing beers (H)
A friendly Batemans house to the south of the city, which serves an extensive and varied range of guest ales to complement the Batemans beers, usually including a stout or porter and a mild. Between three (in winter) and six (in summer) real ciders are also stocked. Customers can bring their own food from various nearby takeaways (plates and condiments provided). Monthly quiz nights, poker evenings and live music take place. Busy on match days! (39)

King's Head

42 Magdalen Street, NR3 1JE
12-midnight (11 Sun) (01603) 620468
kingsheadnorwich.com
13 changing beers (H)
Friendly and welcoming traditional-style two-bar pub which offers no keg beer, but up to 14 quality real ales, mostly local but with a few from around the country, plus one cider. The house beer, KHB, is brewed by Winter's. Local fresh eggs and honey are often available. No food is served except snacks, pork pies and pickled eggs but customers can bring or order in their own, with plates and cutlery supplied. Bar billiards is well supported, with two teams in the local league.
Q

Leopard 🏆 L

98-100 Bull Close Road, NR3 1NQ

12-11 (midnight Fri & Sat) ☎ (01603) 631111

5 changing beers H

A welcoming traditional single-bar corner local with a variety of changing ales from the smaller breweries, usually including at least one from Lacons. The pub has a clean and bright bar area which gives a spacious feel, plus a pleasant and quiet enclosed courtyard garden area at the rear. A guest KeyKeg real ale is dispensed via a Watney's Red Barrel tap. Open mic events are held on the first Wednesday of the month. Food can be brought in. Q (50a)

Lollards Pit L

69-71 Riverside Road, NR1 1SR

12-11 (midnight Fri); 12-1 Sat ☎ (01603) 624675

lollardspit.com

Woodforde's Nelsons Revenge, Wherry; 3 changing beers H

An attractive 17th-century pub, one of the first built outside the city walls, on the site of Lollard's Pit – a place of execution for heretics for over 200 years. The pub retains various historic features including a well in the patio area, and is close to the river and yacht station moorings. Guest ales are from interesting local and national breweries. Snacks include pork pies and sausage rolls. A venue for local community groups and weekly quiz, bingo and weekend parties.

Lord Rosebery L

94 Rosebery Road, NR3 3AB

3-11 (midnight Fri); 12-midnight Sat; 12-10.30 Sun

☎ (01603) 414284 theroseberynorwich.co.uk

4 changing beers H

A large Victorian pub, between Angel Road and St Clement's Hill, tastefully fitted out in a modern style with high ceilings and decorative lighting. It has up to four real ales from around the country, some local, some craft beers and a good range of spirits, especially gins, one the pub's own infusion. There is a regular pub quiz on Tuesday (snacks available), occasional music events, excellent Sunday roasts and evening meals from a varied menu. Bring your own food on Monday and after 9pm during the week. B&B-style accommodation is available upstairs. P

Louis Marchesi L

17 Tombland, NR3 1HF

11-11 (midnight Fri); closed Sun ☎ (01603) 763099

5 changing beers (sourced nationally) H/G

Four real ales from Norfolk and Suffolk breweries are always on sale in this Grade II-listed building, which dates in parts from the 15th century and is situated opposite the 11th-century Cathedral in the oldest part of the city. Quality home-cooked food, sourced locally, is available lunchtime and evening plus all day Saturday. The pub hosts regular live music and has a large function room upstairs. A cellar bar downstairs features vaulted ceilings and can be hired.

Murderers L

2-8 Timber Hill, NR1 3LB

10-11.30; 12-10.30 Sun ☎ (01603) 621447

themurderers.co.uk

Adnams Ghost Ship; Sharp's Doom Bar; Woodforde's Wherry; 6 changing beers H

A Grade II-listed 17th-century city-centre inn. On several levels, with lots of little alcoves, the pub has been family-owned for 30 years. Ten real ales come from local micros and around the country. The pub is popular with shoppers, office workers and the evening going-out scene alike. Its real name is The Gardener's Arms, but it has not been known as such since a 19th-century landlord convicted of murdering his wife gave the pub its alternative name. Tuesday is a regular blues night.

Plasterers Arms L

43 Cowgate, NR3 1SZ

12-midnight (1am Fri & Sat) ☎ (01603) 387525

theplasterersarms.co.uk

10 changing beers H

A friendly corner local with an ever-changing, wide range of beers from around the country, specialising in new and exciting breweries. A variety of craft keg beers is served alongside a great range of bottled and canned beers. Attractions include regular tap takeovers, sport (with a big screen for important events), music from DJs on Sundays, pizza every weekday and breakfast from 10am till 2pm at weekends. The pub also hosts one of the annual Fem.ale Festivals celebrating great women in the brewing industry. Q

Playhouse Bar

42-58 St George Street, NR3 1AB

10-midnight; 12-midnight Sun ☎ (01603) 612580

norwichplayhouse.co.uk/bar

4 changing beers H

The bar for the Norwich Playhouse theatre, so it can be crowded before performances and at the interval. It serves three or four ales including a couple of local brews and an eclectic selection of guests. The bar features a 3D cityscape on the ceiling, an unusual collection of objets d'art and comfortable seating. There is also a good-sized lounge across the foyer and a large tree-shaded patio by the river. Regular DJ sessions are popular at weekends.

Plough

58 St Benedict Street, NR2 4AR

12-11 (midnight Fri & Sat); 12-10.30 Sun

☎ (01603) 661384 theploughnorwich.co.uk

6 changing beers H

Popular pub in one of the city's oldest and trendiest areas near the Norwich Arts Centre. One of four Grain Brewery-owned pubs, it serves six ales, usually all from the brewery. The two-bar, split-level interior is fairly small, with wooden chairs and tables, and an open fire in winter. The large Mediterranean-style courtyard garden is a fine place to spend a summer's evening. Grain lager and craft beers are also stocked, along with Vic's special sausage pie. Barbecues feature in the summer.

Red Lion L

79 Bishopgate, NR1 4AA

11-11 ☎ (01603) 620154 redlionnorwich.com

6 changing beers H

A short walk from the rail station, and by the river, the pub offers an excellent range of up to six quality ales, mostly local. Great food is available, including pizza from a wood-fired oven, and a carvery on Sunday. The pub is family-friendly, and provides a fine view over the river. Tables on the patio area make for a great summer afternoon visit, with boat launch/mooring and canoe hire also available. Lunches are served Wednesday to Sunday and evening meals Tuesday to Saturday. ❀◑◗⇌♣P🚌(23,24)🐾ᯤ

Ribs of Beef L ✔

24 Wensum Street, NR3 1HY

11-11 (midnight Fri & Sat); 11-10.30 Sun
☎ (01603) 619517 🌐 ribsofbeef.co.uk

Adnams Ghost Ship; Oakham JHB; Woodforde's Wherry; Wolf Golden Jackal; 5 changing beers H

Traditional and well-decorated pub overlooking the River Wensum. A welcoming row of nine handpumps dispenses four regular ales and a selection from local and other micros, with several craft KeyKeg ales, foreign beers and real cider also on the bar. The pub is popular with visitors and the kitchen offers a great selection of meals made with locally sourced ingredients. The atmosphere is relaxed and friendly, with a room downstairs, a tiny veranda over the river, and several outdoor tables at the rear. ❀◑◗♿♣🍎🚌🐾ᯤ

Rose

235 Queens Road, NR1 3AE

closed Mon; 4-11 (midnight Fri); 12-midnight Sat
☎ (01603) 623942 🌐 theroseinnnorwich.co.uk

6 changing beers H

Popular pub close to Carrow Road, the home of Norwich City FC. The owner's passion for beer shows in the six or more regularly changing real ales and a similar number of craft beers from breweries around the country, plus several real ciders. Regular beer, cider and gin festivals and frequent tap takeovers are staged. The pub has an excellent food offering, with in-house burgers as well as fantastic Aussie pies from Flaming Galah and curries from Roti Indian Restaurant delivered to your table. ❀🛏◗♿⛺🍎🚌🐾ᯤ

St Andrew's Brewhouse ✔

41 St Andrews Street, NR2 4TP

11-11 Mon & Sun; 11-midnight Tue-Thu; 11-1am Fri & Sat
☎ (01603) 305995 🌐 standrewsbrewhouse.com

5 changing beers H

Grade II*-listed building refurbished during 2015 in distressed industrial style, now a brewhouse and smokehouse restaurant with an eclectic food menu. The bar and microbrewery face St Andrews Street, while the restaurant has views of the ancient St Andrews Hall, home of the Norwich Beer Festival. Six handpumps dispense mostly house beers. Wensum Ale (gluten-free) is served, with a couple of local guests or seasonal specials and sometimes a cider/perry, supplemented by a good range of craft beers. Upstairs rooms feature board games and views of the brewery fermentation tanks. Q❀◑◗♿♣🍎🚌🐾ᯤ

Trafford Arms L ✔

61 Grove Road, NR1 3RL

11-11 (11.30 Fri & Sat); 10-11 Sun ☎ (01603) 628466
🌐 traffordarms.co.uk

Adnams Southwold Bitter, Ghost Ship; 7 changing beers H

This pub stands at the junction of Trafford Road and Grove Road, near the city centre, and continues to be a flagship for real ale in Norwich. The cask beer offering includes both regular and guest ales, often including a dark brew. High-quality pub food is available and there are special themed food evenings. The Valentine's beer festival continues to be a major attraction, as is the regular pub quiz on the last Sunday of every month. ❀◑◗P🚌(38)ᯤ

Vine L

7 Dove Street, NR2 1DE

11-11; closed Sun ☎ (01603) 627362 🌐 vinethai.co.uk

Oakham JHB; 2 changing beers H

Norwich's smallest pub, just off the marketplace, serving up to four quality ales, mostly from local breweries, plus traditional Thai cuisine in an award-winning combination. Beer festivals are held in January and City of Ale week. The restaurant is upstairs, although customers often eat downstairs in the bar area, and functions are catered for outside normal opening hours on demand. Extra tables and chairs are set outside in the pedestrianised street. Occasionally open Sunday, the pub has been in the same hands for over 10 years. Q❀◑◗♣🍎🚌

Whalebone

144 Magdalen Road, NR3 4BA

12-11 (midnight Fri & Sat) ☎ (01603) 425482
🌐 whalebonefreehouse.co.uk

Adnams Southwold Bitter; Fuller's London Pride; Humpty Dumpty Little Sharpie; Oakham JHB, Citra; Wolf Golden Jackal; 2 changing beers H

A community local with eight real ales, conveniently situated just to the south of Sewell Park. The interior has three separate areas: the original front and rear bars plus a newly-refurbished area leading to a covered and heated terraced patio which is popular, with wood-fired pizzas Friday and Saturday and summer barbecues. A beer festival is held every July and the pub supports three cricket teams, a rugby team and a golf society. Bar snacks including locally sourced pork pies, Scotch eggs and sausage rolls are available daily, plus freshly made coffee and hot chocolate. ❀♣P🚌(10,18)🐾ᯤ

White Lion

73 Oak Street, NR3 3AQ

12-11 (11.30 Fri & Sat); 12-10.30 Sun ☎ (01603) 632333

6 changing beers H

A great cider pub serving up to 10 ciders and perries from across the UK. Several changing real ales are also available, from local and non-local breweries. The bar staff are helpful and knowledgeable. The traditional interior is split into three rooms, with a front and back bar plus a games room to the side. Food is varied and excellent value, using traditional local produce – check the daily specials menu. An annual beer festival is held in October, and bar billiards, board games and darts are played. Q❀◑◗♣🍎🚌🐾ᯤ

Wig & Pen L

6 St Martin at Palace Plain, NR3 1RN

11.30-11 (midnight Fri & Sat); 11.30-6.30 Sun
☎ (01603) 625891 🌐 thewigandpen.com

Adnams Southwold Bitter; 5 changing beers H

Pretty beamed 17th-century free house with a spacious patio, immediately opposite the Bishop's Palace, and with an impressive view of Norwich Cathedral spire. Six ales are always on, usually including two local beers. The small back room can be used for meetings. Good-quality food is served lunchtimes and evenings. The pub is a short walk from Tombland, where there are stands for several bus routes, and is an ideal starting or stopping place for a walk along the river. Q❀🛏◑◗♿🚌ᯤ

Old Buckenham

Ox & Plough

The Green, NR17 1RN (in centre of village overlooking green)

11-midnight; 12-midnight Sun ☎ 07887 691722

Adnams Southwold Bitter; Sharp's Doom Bar; 3 changing beers (often Hop Back, Oakham) H

Family-friendly community pub on one of the largest village greens in England and at the centre of village life. It has two open-plan drinking areas, one being quiet, without TV or electronic game machines. The garden at the front overlooks the village green. Real ale is dispensed from three to five handpumps. As a member of the Oakham Oakademy of Excellence it serves various changing Oakham ales. Oakham Green Devil is a regular keg. Bar snacks are the only food.

Old Hunstanton

Ancient Mariner ✔

6 Golf Course Road, PE36 6JJ (within Le Strange Arms hotel complex)

11-11 ☎ (01485) 534411 traditionalinns.co.uk/the-ancient-mariner-inn

Adnams Southwold Bitter, Broadside; 3 changing beers H

Adjoining the Le Strange Arms hotel, this popular pub dating back to the 1600s was originally the old barns and stables of the main house, and has a family room and restaurants. At least four ales are stocked. A large beer garden provides direct access to the beach, and as the Ancient Mariner is on the east coast facing west its rear decking offers superb views of sunsets over the sea.

Q P

Reepham

King's Arms L

Market Place, NR10 4JJ

11.30-3, 5.30-11; 11.30-11 Sat; 12-10.30 Sun

☎ (01603) 870345 kingsarmsreepham.com

Adnams Southwold Bitter, Ghost Ship; Greene King Abbot; Panther Golden Panther; Woodforde's Wherry; 1 changing beer (sourced nationally) H

A former coaching inn dating back to 1667, in the picturesque square of this small market town, with original beams, Norfolk brickwork and open fires. There are several comfortable drinking and dining areas, and tables in front with views across the square. Five permanent real ales are served, including at least one from the local Panther Brewery, plus a guest. The comprehensive menu is mostly sourced from nearby suppliers. Jazz bands play in the rear courtyard on summer Sundays. Dogs are welcome. Q

Ringstead

Gin Trap Inn

6 High Street, PE36 5JU

11-11 ☎ (01485) 525264 thegintrapinn.co.uk

Adnams Southwold Bitter, Ghost Ship; Greene King IPA; Woodforde's Wherry; 1 changing beer H

This attractive whitewashed village pub has an outside seating area at the front and an enclosed garden to the rear. There is a split-level bar area and a separate restaurant; food is available throughout. In addition to the main menu, there are regular themed food evenings as well as live music nights. The main bar area has a log-burning stove. The bar features a range of some 100 different gins including the pub's own Gin Trap gin.

P

Roydon

Union Jack

30 Station Road, PE32 1AW (off A148)

4 (2 Mon)-midnight; 1.30-midnight Fri; 12-midnight Sat & Sun ☎ 07771 660439

Adnams Broadside; 3 changing beers H

Popular with locals, this traditional village pub has twice been local CAMRA Pub of the Year. Four handpumps dispense one regular and three different ales, with beer festivals held over the Easter and August bank holidays usually featuring local breweries. There are occasional food nights, live music each month, regular bingo and quizzes, and weekly support for darts, crib and dominoes. Outdoor seating is at the front of the pub. Dogs are welcome. Q P (48)

Saham Toney

Old Bell ✔

1 Bell Lane, IP25 7HD

11-11; 11-10.30 Sun ☎ (01953) 884934

Woodforde's Wherry; 3 changing beers H

Next to a Breckland mere and near a medieval church, the Bell is a lovely old building with a long bar room and restaurant heated by open fires. The pub offers a friendly atmosphere and guest beers of good quality. There are events such as an annual Oktoberfest, live music most weekends, and a quiz every Wednesday. The food offering is wide-ranging: steak night on Thursday, fish day on Friday, Sunday carvery, and wood-fired pizza from May to October. P

Shouldham

King's Arms L

The Green, PE33 0BY

5-10.30 Mon; 12-11; 12-10.30 Sun ☎ (01366) 347410

kingsarmsshouldham.co.uk

2 changing beers G

Named the local CAMRA branch Pub of the Year again in 2018, completing a hat trick of successes, this is a community-owned business which also includes a café open from 9.30am. The beer is served straight from the cask and two or three choices are usually available. Lined glasses are used and cider is often also on tap. Lots of community activities take place, from poetry evenings and live music to quiz nights.

P

Snettisham

Rose & Crown

Old Church Road, PE31 7LX (off B1440)

11-11; 11-10.30 Sun ☎ (01485) 541382

roseandcrownsnettisham.co.uk

Adnams Broadside; Banks's Amber Ale; Marston's Pedigree; Woodforde's Wherry; 2 changing beers H

A popular traditional village inn with cosy bars, exposed beams, a real fire and a dining room. Head through the narrow passage to find a larger bar and dining areas with a contemporary feel. It is well known for quality traditional and exciting seasonal fare; the bars also remain popular with local drinkers. The garden and play area are appealing to families. Accommodation is available for those who wish to remain longer in this beautiful area. QP

South Wootton

Swan Inn

Nursery Lane, PE30 3NG
11.30-11 (midnight Friday) (01553) 672084
Adnams Southwold Bitter; Greene King Abbot; 2 changing beers (sourced nationally) H
Attractive carrstone two-bar pub with a conservatory dining area overlooking the village green. The large illuminated pub garden has numerous benches for those warm summer evenings. A large-screen TV caters for the many sports teams. There is a selection of four real ales, two of which change regularly. A beer festival is staged in the summer in a marquee, with numerous beers and ciders. Speciality evenings are held every week. This pub is the hub of the local village business area. QP

Stokesby

Ferry Inn

The Green, NR29 3EX (beside River Bure)
9am-11 (01493) 751096
Adnams Ghost Ship; 2 changing beers H
River-fronted country pub off the beaten track by car but on the equivalent of a motorway by water, with moorings, and popular with boaters – with good reason. It has splendid south-facing views, a pleasant riverside garden with protective walls, and a large games room. It is owned by Adnams. Food is served all day from 9am in the summer, when the selection of beers is also increased. P

Strumpshaw

Shoulder of Mutton

9 Norwich Road, NR13 4NT (on Brundall-Lingwood road)
11-11; 11-9.30 Sun (01603) 926530
Adnams Ghost Ship; Sharp's Doom Bar; Timothy Taylor Landlord; 3 changing beers H
Traditional village pub with a friendly welcome. A tasteful renovation has improved comfort and decor throughout. The two main bar areas share the logburner and there is a separate dining room. Beers are from a variety of regional and microbreweries, complemented by one local cider. Meals are freshly prepared from local produce, with seafood and home-made pies prominent. The rear patio overlooks the courtyard where pétanque is played. See the website for music and events. Close to the Broads and a nationally important RSPB site. P (15A)

Terrington St Clement

Wildfowler

28 Sutton Road, PE34 4PQ
11 (3 Mon; 12 Tue)-11; 11-midnight Fri & Sat
(01553) 829107 the-wildfowler.com
Greene King IPA, Abbot; 1 changing beer (sourced regionally) H
This village pub has an L-shaped bar which is pine-panelled at one end. It also boasts a large restaurant serving a variety of freshly cooked food, including a special children's menu and a carvery on Sunday. There are regular live music events and a monthly quiz. The guest ale is often from Adnams, Lacons, Woodforde's or Green Dragon, and changes each week. P

Thetford

Albion

93-95 Castle Street, IP24 2DN (opp Castle Park and Hill)
12-11.30 (1.30am Fri & Sat) (01842) 338208
Greene King IPA; Woodforde's Wherry; 1 changing beer H
A classic Norfolk flint town pub. The management team at the Albion revitalised the place a few years ago. Its Greene King-refurbished interior has been adapted with wherry-themed tables, giving a comfortable space to drink. The six handpumps offer a range of standards and more interesting choices. There is seating outside with a view of the Norman castle mound and its surrounding Iceni hill fort. Although food is not available you are welcome to order in from one of the food outlets in the town. P

Black Horse

64 Magdalen Street, IP24 2BP
11-11; 12-11 Sun (01842) 762717
Adnams Southwold Bitter; Greene King IPA; Woodforde's Wherry; 2 changing beers H
A good no-nonsense town pub that offers five handpumps with a varying range. It also stages a popular annual St George's Day beer festival. The food is home-made and good both in quality and value – desserts are a feature – served in a small but pleasant eating area. One feature of the Black Horse you should see are the changing murals on the end wall. P

Red Lion

Market Place, IP24 2AL
8am-11 (1am Fri & Sat) (01842) 757210
Adnams Broadside; Greene King IPA, Abbot; 3 changing beers H
On the market square, the Red Lion has had a varied history. It was opened by Lacons (the wall outside retains its plaque), then a Portuguese restaurant, before becoming a Wetherspoon seven years ago. The decor features much information about local history and attractions. The beer range is the usual fare, but well kept. The pub contains a variety of eating and drinking areas plus an outdoor spot for sunny days.

Thompson

Chequers Inn

Griston Road, IP24 1PX
12-3, 6.30-11; 11.30-11 Sun (01953) 483360
thompsonchequers.co.uk
Greene King IPA; Woodforde's Wherry; 1 changing beer H
A 16th-century gem in this pretty village near Watton, featuring a steep thatched roof and timber-framed construction. Stooping to Tudor height will keep your head from the beams. It has an excellent reputation for food; there are two rooms for dining, and a small area and another small room for drinking. It is better to drink outside in the summer. Guest beers are mostly from Woodforde's. P

Thornham

Lifeboat Inn

Ship Lane, PE36 6LT (signed from A149 Coast Road)
11-11; 12-10.30 Sun ☎ (01485) 512236
lifeboatinnthornham.com
5 changing beers H
Busy pub just off the North Norfolk Coastal Path on the edge of the salt marshes, with a wide range of drinking areas, from the dark and cosy bar to the light and airy conservatory. There is an enclosed garden area at the rear. The pub has been tastefully renovated while retaining the atmosphere of the smugglers' inn it undoubtedly once was. Food is available throughout and there is a separate large restaurant. Accommodation is offered in 12 rooms. Whatever the season and whatever the weather, this is a comforting place to enjoy a pint. **QP**

Thorpe Market

Gunton Arms

Cromer Road, NR11 8TZ (on W of A149 Cromer to North Walsham road SE of Thorpe Market; look for hanging sign, lit at night)
12-11; 12-10.30 Sun ☎ (01263) 832010
theguntonarms.co.uk
Adnams Broadside; Lacons Legacy; Woodforde's Wherry; 1 changing beer H
A fine country inn with magical vistas of Gunton Park and its deer herd. The tasteful interior features comfortable furnishings and a log fire in winter. East Anglian ales predominate, with regular guests. First-class cuisine is served in three restaurant areas; several dishes are cooked on an open range in the vaulted Elk Room. The beer garden offers alfresco dining. A food and music festival is held in summer. There are 16 luxurious rooms and suites, some with parkland views.
QP(4)

Thurlton

Queen's Head

Beccles Road, NR14 6RJ
12 (9am Wed)-3, 5-11; 12-midnight Sat; 12-10 Sun
☎ (01508) 548667 queensheadthurlton.co.uk
4 changing beers (often People's) H
Recently refurbished community-owned pub with four real ales, including exclusive beers from the award-winning People's Brewery. Other local and national ales are regularly available. The pub welcomes families and dogs – the village play area is to the rear, next to the car park. Excellent locally sourced food, often with themed menus, is served, and the pub opens for breakfast on Wednesday. It has a cosy log fire in winter and hosts two yearly real ale festivals supported by local breweries Lacons and Green Jack.
P(577)

Thurne

Lion Inn

The Street, NR29 3AP (at end of Thurne dyke)
12-11 ☎ (01692) 671806 thelionatthurne.com
6 changing beers H
Large country pub in a remote village near the River Ant. Plenty of moorings are available nearby for passing Broads cruisers. There is an amusement arcade in the side building for children and a large garden area. Meals made from locally sourced produce are served in the large restaurant or bar area. There are six changing real ales on handpump, plus a choice of up to six real ciders and 16 keg taps for craft offerings. **QP**

West Acre

Stag

Low Road, PE32 1TR
closed Mon; 12-3, 6.30 (5 Fri)-11 ☎ (01760) 755395
westacrestag.co.uk
3 changing beers H
This cosy pub is well worth finding at the east end of picturesque West Acre, and is popular with locals, walkers, cyclists and riders. It is a strong supporter of local ales, maintaining a high standard of three varying beers and hosting excellent beer festivals. There is a popular monthly quiz on Sunday night. The restaurant serves a variety of great-value freshly prepared meals using locally sourced ingredients. **QP**

West Runton

Village Inn

Water Lane, NR27 9QP
11-11; 12-11 Sun ☎ (01263) 838000
villageinnwestrunton.co.uk
Adnams Ghost Ship; 3 changing beers H
A large pub a short distance from the station and the beach, set in pleasant gardens in the centre of this quiet coastal village. Up to four well-kept and mostly local ales are stocked and rotated. Excellent home-cooked meals can be enjoyed in the dining areas or outside, with plenty of seating in the flint-walled garden. In the 1970s major rock bands such as Deep Purple played secret gigs at the Pavilion which was at the rear of the pub (sadly now demolished). **QP**

Weybourne

Ship Inn

The Street, NR25 7SZ
12-11 (midnight Fri & Sat) ☎ (01263) 588721
theshipinnweybourne.com
4 changing beers H
In the heart of this attractive north Norfolk coastal village, the Ship has up to four cask ales and only sells local beers including Woodforde's, Humpty Dumpty, Beeston, Norfolk Brewhouse, Wolf, Grain and Panther, plus a range of bottled craft beers. Home-cooked food is available lunchtimes and evenings. The enclosed garden is pleasant in summer. There is a monthly quiz night. The North Norfolk Railway and Muckleburgh Collection of military vehicles are close by and the Coasthopper bus stops outside. **QP**

Wortwell

Bell

52 Low Road, IP20 0HH
12-10 Mon; 5-10 Tue; 12-10 Wed; 12-11 Thu-Sat; 12-9 Sun
☎ (01986) 788025 wortwellbell.pub
Otter Bitter; Purity Pure UBU; house beer (by Woodforde's); 3 changing beers H
A 17th-century coaching inn with two bars and an open fire. A fishing lake and caravan park are nearby. The enthusiastic hosts, whose family were historically linked to the licensed trade, reopened

the pub in 2015. They have rejuvenated this community local to its former glory with regular village events, and have now added to the community feel with a village shop and a small borrowing library based at the pub and open during pub hours. A regular beer festival is held. ☺❀◐▲♣●P🚌(580)🐾📶

Wymondham

Feathers

13 Town Green, NR18 0PN

11-2.30, 7-11.30; 11-2.30, 6-midnight Fri; 11-2.30, 7-midnight Sat; 12-2.30, 7-10.30 Sun ☎ (01953) 605675

Adnams Southwold Bitter, Ghost Ship; Fuller's London Pride; 2 changing beers H

The Feathers dates from the 18th century. The interior consists of two main drinking areas with alcove areas served by one bar. The alcoves and walls are adorned with postcard collections, enamel signs and farming and rural memorabilia, including an old bike. There is a large, well-furnished patio garden at the rear, and good-value food is available lunchtime and evening. A folk evening takes place on the last Sunday of each month. Feathers Tickler is the popular house beer, brewed by Nethergate. Q☺❀◐⇌🚌📶

Green Dragon L ✔

6 Church Street, NR18 0PH (between Market St and Wymondham Abbey)

12-11 (midnight Fri & Sat); 12-10.30 Sun

☎ (01953) 607907 🌐 greendragonnorfolk.co.uk

5 changing beers H

A haunted half-timbered inn recognised by CAMRA as having a historic interior of regional importance with an attractive beer garden. On the road to Wymondham's beautiful Abbey, this inn dates back to 1371. One bar serves the downstairs bar, a snug and restaurant area. Excellent home-cooked food is made with locally sourced ingredients where possible. The interior has beamed timbers and carved stone, and evidence of medieval construction methods. The rotating real ales are mostly from local or East Anglian breweries. Beer festivals are held in May and August, with live music. Q☺❀◐⇌🚌🐾📶

Green Dragon, Wymondham (Photo: Roger Blackwell/Flickr CC BY 2.0)

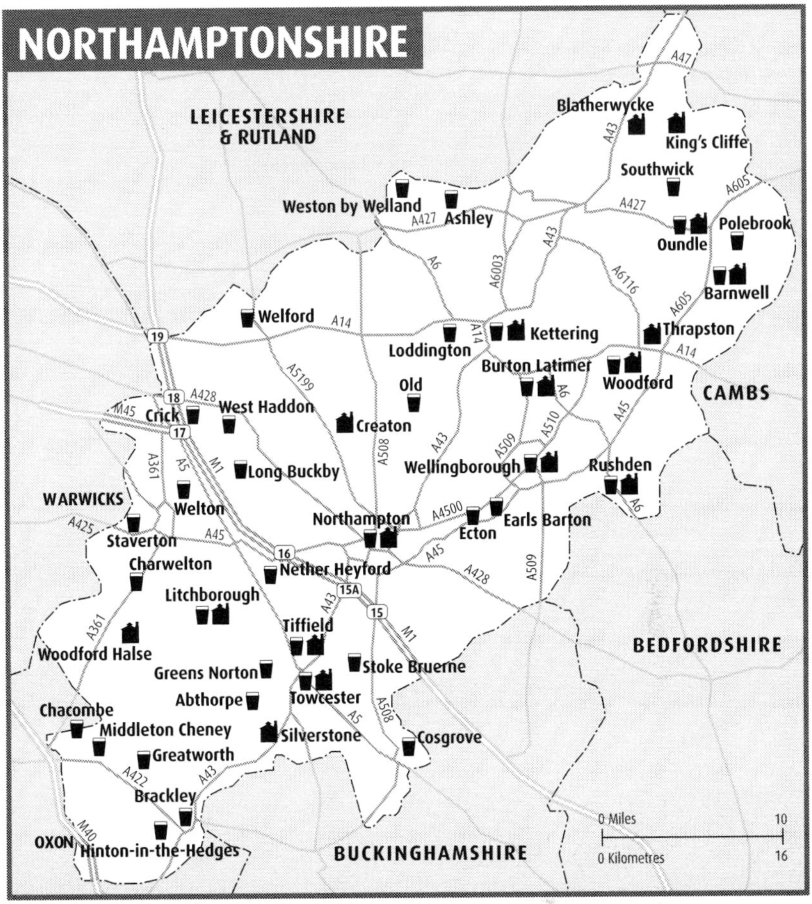

Abthorpe

New Inn

Silver Street, NN12 8QR (off Main St, left at church)
12-3 (not Mon & Tue), 5-11.30; 12-11.30 Fri & Sat; 12-11 Sun (01327) 857306 newinnabthorpe.co.uk
Hook Norton Hooky, Hooky Gold, Old Hooky; 1 changing beer (often Hook Norton)
A quintessentially English village pub built of local mellow sandstone complete with an inglenook fireplace with seating and low ceilings. Hidden up a cul-de-sac off the corner of the village green it is welcoming to visitors and locals alike. It serves good food including meats from the owner's farm, plus ales that are still brewed in the traditional way by Hook Norton – its seasonal beers feature as guests. Traditional pub games including darts and Northamptonshire skittles are played.

Ashley

George

21 Main Street, LE16 8HF (off B664)
closed Mon; 6-11 Tue-Thu; 12-2, 6-11 Fri & Sat; 12-6 Sun (01858) 565411 thegeorgeatashley.co.uk
3 changing beers (sourced locally; often Langton, Nobby's, Phipps NBC)
Following a campaign by residents, this traditional 17th-century ironstone village pub has been saved from being converted into houses. Re-opened since 2016, it stands proud behind a patch of grass at the roadside. Its interior has been opened out but still contains separate areas for dining and drinking. The pub serves three changing local ales, most from local microbreweries. Events include gourmet evenings, cheese and wine pairings and quizzes. Its redecorated Coach House to the rear offers accommodation with six individual rooms.

Barnwell

Montagu Arms

PE8 5PH
12-3, 6-11 Mon-Wed; 5-11 Thu & Fri; 12-11 Sat; 12-10.30 Sun (01832) 273726
Adnams Ghost Ship; Digfield Fools Nook, Barnwell Bitter; Sharp's Doom Bar
Overlooking the river and stone bridge, this 16th-century stone-built inn has a public bar at the front and a large restaurant to the rear. The car park is behind the inn and accessed via the village hall entrance. Also at the rear is a large play and camping area. There is wheelchair access from the rear to the restaurant only. The traditionally decorated bar area, enlarged by recent alterations, features original exposed wood beams on the ceiling and walls.

Brackley

Greyhound ✔

131 High Street, NN13 7BW
11-11 (midnight Fri & Sat) ☎ (01280) 840608
thegreyhoundinnbrackley.co.uk
Greene King IPA, Abbot; 1 changing beer (sourced nationally) H
Dating back to the 1600s, this whitewashed pub is a building of character, with low-beamed ceilings and an inglenook fireplace, making it a very cosy place. Outside there is a beautiful courtyard. It plays host to Brackley's folk club on Sunday evening. (8,500)

Burton Latimer

Duke's Arms ✔

123 High Street, NN15 5RL (off A14 jct 10)
4-11; 2-11 Sat; 12-11 Sun ☎ (01536) 390874
3 changing beers (sourced nationally)
For many years keg only, this revitalised pub now features three handpumps serving real ale and is the local outlet for Three Hills brewery. A central U-shaped bar serves the opened-out rooms, with comfortable leather seating and more traditional seating in the small bay windows. The walls are adorned with vinyl LPs and a collection of books is available for customers to read. There is no parking but a free car park is just across the road.

Chacombe

George & Dragon

1 Silver Street, OX17 2JR (1 mile from M40 jct 11)
12-11.30 (10 Sun) ☎ (01295) 711500
georgeanddragonchacombe.co.uk
Everards Beacon Hill, Tiger; 2 changing beers (sourced regionally) H
A traditional and welcoming stone-built pub situated in front of the village green. It has one room for drinkers and three for diners, with impressive fireplaces. The bars feature stone-flagged floors and wooden beams; the bar counter contains a well with a glass top. Outside is a patio area and a garden where the fairground game Aunt Sally is played. The pub also hosts band concerts and the village beer festival.
P (500)

Charwelton

Fox & Hounds L

Banbury Road, NN11 3YY (on A421)
11-11 (midnight Fri & Sat); 12-6 Sun ☎ (01327) 260611
foxandhoundscharwelton.co.uk
North Cotswold Shagweaver; house beer (by Gun Dog Ales); 1 changing beer (sourced locally) H
A newcomer to the Guide, this is an attractive stone-built pub, parts of which date from the 15th century. It was purchased by the local community following its closure in 2012, thus safeguarding its future. Comfortably furnished, it is a cosy place to enjoy the three beers on offer from local microbreweries. A house beer is supplied by Gun Dog Ales from nearby Woodford Halse. Food is available all week. A ceramic plaque by the entrance recalls Hunt Edmunds, the former Banbury brewery that once owned the pub.
P

Cosgrove

Barley Mow ✔

7 The Stocks, MK19 7JD
12-11 (10.30 Sun) ☎ (01908) 562957
thebarleymowcosgrove.co.uk
Everards Sunchaser, Tiger, Old Original; 1 changing beer (sourced regionally; often Titanic) H
An attractive countryside pub backing onto the Grand Union Canal. The 17th-century building's main bar and adjoining segregated areas provide a charming environment, especially when the log fire is ablaze. Outside is a patio leading onto a lovely garden. The home-cooked food caters for all dietary requirements. Events are staged throughout the year, including murder mystery evenings and a monthly quiz.
Q ΔP

Crick

Wheatsheaf L ✔

15 Main Road, NN6 7TU (on main road through village)
12-11 (midnight Fri & Sat); 12-10.30 Sun
☎ (01788) 823824 wheatsheafcrick.com
Bombardier; house beer (by Banks's); 3 changing beers (sourced regionally; often Marston's, Phipps NBC, Potbelly) H
An ironstone village local featuring a front bar area with tables and settees. To the rear is a large restaurant and function room providing well-priced meals. The pub hosts frequent theme nights in the restaurant, with booking essential. Other attractions include occasional live music plus a quiz night on Tuesday. Good-value accommodation is available in a recent extension.
Q P (96)

Earls Barton

Saxon Tavern L ✔

25B The Square, NN6 0NA
closed Mon; 7-11 Tue; 5-11 Wed & Thu; 3-11 Fri; 12-11 Sat & Sun ☎ 07956 462352
6 changing beers (often Nene Valley, Potbelly, Towcester Mill)

REAL ALE BREWERIES

Boot Town Burton Latimer
Cotton End Northampton
Creaton Grange Creaton
Digfield Barnwell
Great Oakley Tiffield
Gun Dog Woodford Halse
Hart Family Wellingborough
Holcot Hop-Craft Holcot (NEW)
Hoppy Family Kettering
King's Cliffe King's Cliffe
Litchborough Artisan Litchborough (NEW)
Maule Northampton
Nene Valley (NVB) Oundle
Nobby's Thrapston
Phipps Northampton
Potbelly Kettering
Purple Cow Kettering
Rockingham Blatherwycke
Silverstone Silverstone
Three Hills Woodford
Towcester Mill Towcester
Weldon Rushden

The county's fourth micropub is a large, comfortable and relaxed drinking environment, enhanced by welcoming hosts. The single-room pub is in the centre of the village between the famous Barker Shoes and the historic Saxon tower. Ale is served from six casks behind the bar. A wide selection of gins is offered, along with bottled beers and box ciders from the fridge.
Q❀♣●P🚌🐾

Ecton

Three Horseshoes L

23 High Street, NN6 0QA (off A4500)
⌚ 7-midnight; 5.30-midnight Fri; 12-midnight Sat & Sun
☎ (01604) 407446
St Austell Tribute, Proper Job; 2 changing beers (sourced regionally; often Oakham) H
A whitewashed stone pub extended over many years, although the original pub is said to date from 1757. The name is taken from the forge that was originally on the site and where Benjamin Franklin's Uncle Thomas was the last of the family to work the family business. The traditional multi-room layout has been retained, with a separate bar and games area featuring Northants skittles and darts. Happy hour is 5.30-7.30pm Friday.
❀♣P🚌🐾 wifi

Greatworth

Greatworth Inn L

Chapel Road, OX17 2DT (off B4525)
⌚ 12-11 (10.30 Sun) ☎ (01295) 521426
🌐 thegreatworthinn.co.uk
Fuller's London Pride; 3 changing beers (sourced locally; often Gun Dog Ales) H
A stone-built free house, dating from the 16th century and located in the centre of this attractive village. It was restored to its former glory by the current owners, who introduced numerous improvements while retaining a cosy and traditional pub atmosphere. The bar area features an inglenook fireplace with a log-burning stove; there is also a dining area. A annual soap box derby is held in June. Q❀◗♿♣P🐾 wifi

Greens Norton

Butchers Arms L

10 High Street, NN12 8BA
⌚ 12 (5 Mon)-11; 12-10 Sun ☎ (01327) 358848
🌐 thebutchersarms.pub
St Austell Tribute; 3 changing beers (sourced regionally; often Gun Dog Ales) H
Lively community gem that was recently rescued, refurbished and expanded by enthusiastic locals who had been mourning the loss of the village's only pub. Now managed by the Proper Pub Company, it has an interior comprising two rooms with wooden flooring and panelling, complemented by bay-window seating and a wood-burning fire. Rotating real ales include many from local breweries. Entertainment ranges from live bands and wine tastings to skittles and quiz nights. Q❀◖◗♿♣●P🚌(86,87)🐾 wifi

Hinton-in-the-Hedges

Crewe Arms L

Sparrow Corner, NN13 5NF
⌚ 4-11; 12-midnight Fri & Sat; 12-10.30 Sun
☎ (01280) 705801 🌐 crewearmshinton.co.uk
Hook Norton Hooky; Timothy Taylor Boltmaker; 1 changing beer (sourced nationally; often Vale) H
Stone-built and in a gully in the village, the Crewe Arms can be hard to find. The entrance is through the rear gravel car park. Four comfortably furnished rooms provide a relaxed environment. The pub's cellar, located in the main dining area, may have been part of a tunnel between the village manor and the local church. The pub has a choice of three real ales at weekends. Happy hour is 6-8pm Friday-Sunday. Q❀🛏◖◗♿P🚌 wifi

Kettering

Piper L ✔

Windmill Avenue, NN15 6PS (near Wicksteed Park)
⌚ 11-3, 5-11; 11-11 Fri & Sat; 12-10.30 Sun
☎ (01536) 513870 🌐 thepiper.net
Castle Rock Harvest Pale; Fuller's London Pride; 4 changing beers (sourced nationally; often Nobby's, Potbelly) H
Popular 1950s two-roomed pub which has been run by a CAMRA member for 29 years. There is a quiet lounge to the left, while to the right is a more lively bar/games room where a quiz is held on Sunday night. A beer festival is held on the third weekend of August. Nearby Wicksteed Park was one of Britain's first theme parks. An outdoor seating area is across the road from the pub.
Q❀◖◗♿⛺♣●P🚌🐾 wifi

Three Cocks L

48 Lower Street, NN16 8DJ (opp Morrisons)
⌚ 2 (12 Thu-Sat)-11.30; 12-11 Sun ☎ 07909 698798
Grainstore Ten Fifty; Mighty Oak Maldon Gold; 5 changing beers (sourced regionally; often Church End, Full Mash, Oakham) H
A popular locals' town-centre pub comprising an L-shaped servery at the centre looking after the two main bar areas, furnished with comfortable armchairs and high-backed stools. On an upper level is a games area featuring Northants skittles and darts. A variety of CAMRA branch magazines is available to read while sampling the well-kept ales. Attractions include two skittles teams, plus board games and monthly quiz evenings.
Q♿♣●🚌🐾

Litchborough

Old Red Lion L

4 Banbury Road, NN12 8JF (opp church)
⌚ 4-8 Mon; 2.30-11.30; 12-11.30 Sat; 12-9 Sun
☎ (01327) 830064 🌐 oldredlionlitchborough.co.uk
Great Oakley Wagtail; house beer (by Grainstore); 1 changing beer (sourced regionally) H
A traditional four-roomed stone-built village pub well worth seeking out, popular with walkers and cyclists on the Knightly Way. The bar has flagstone flooring and seats inside a large inviting inglenook. The snug to the rear of the bar is a comfy, casual room with double doors leading to a courtyard. The extension houses a restaurant and shop that sells local farm produce. Q❀◖◗♿P🚌🐾 wifi

Loddington

Hare at Loddington L

5 Main Street, NN14 1LA (on village loop)

closed Mon; 12-3, 5.30-11 Tue-Thu (11.30 Fri); 12-midnight Sat; 12-11 Sun ☎ (01536) 710337
thehareatloddington.com
Morland Old Speckled Hen; Sharp's Doom Bar; 2 changing beers (sourced regionally; often Gun Dog Ales, Nobby's) [H]
The Hare is situated in a picturesque village built from local ironstone, which is a conservation area. It stands back in the middle of Main Street and has a pleasant front garden. Now more open, it comprises four areas – two are spread around the central bar and two are for dining, with good home-cooked food sourced from local producers. The guest beers are often from established or county microbreweries. Q♿P(35)

Long Buckby

Badgers Arms
2 High Street, NN6 7RD
closed Mon; 4-10 Tue-Fri; 2-10 Sat; closed Sun
☎ (01327) 843003
4 changing beers (sourced regionally; often Potbelly) [G]
Opened in 2017, this micropub rapidly gained a reputation for quality local beers and ciders plus a pleasant ambience and welcome. Converted from a former Indian restaurant, the bar is unusually upstairs and features two distinct drinking areas. There is also a downstairs room and an outdoor patio area. Drinks can be served downstairs to customers unable to manage the stairs. Food can be brought in to eat on the premises for a small charitable donation. Q

Middleton Cheney

New Inn
45 Main Road, OX17 2ND
12-11 (10 Sun) ☎ (01295) 710978
newinnmiddletoncheney.co.uk
St Austell Tribute; Sharp's Doom Bar; 2 changing beers (sourced nationally) [H]
This ironstone pub, internally opened out over the years, features a long servery with flagstone flooring, dark beams and an inglenook with logburner. On the left is a separate cosy, wooden-floored dining area. There is a function room in a barn adjoining the rear patio. The pub runs darts and Aunt Sally teams, holds a quiz on the first Sunday of the month and hosts live music on the last Friday of the month.
♿♣P(500)

Nether Heyford

Foresters Arms
22 The Green, NN7 3LE
5-11; 12-midnight Fri & Sat; 12-10.30 Sun
☎ (01327) 340622
2 changing beers (sourced regionally) [H]
This double bay-fronted ironstone pub opposite the village green is the hub of village life. The current owner took over in 2012 and has made many improvements, notably his enlightened choice of rotating beers, one of which is always sourced locally. Two ciders are dispensed on gravity at the back of the bar. Simple bar meals are often available from the refurbished kitchen. A mobile pizza van sets up in the pub forecourt on Thursday and Friday evenings. ♣P(D3)

Northampton

Albion Brewery Bar
54 Kingswell Street, NN1 1PR
5-10.30 Mon; 12-3, 5-11 Tue-Thu; 12-12.30am Fri & Sat; 12-3.30 Sun ☎ (01604) 946606 phipps-nbc.co.uk
Phipps NBC Cobbler's Ale, India Pale Ale, Ratliffe's Celebrated Stout, Becket's Ale, Black Star, Gold Star; 1 changing beer (sourced nationally) [H]
Phipps NBC returned to its roots in a Victorian brewery in the heart of Northampton in 2014, 40 years after Phipps' Bridge Street brewery closed. The brewery bar subsequently opened, situated at the front of the 1884 Ratliffe & Jeffreys' Albion Brewery, with an oak and glass partition between the bar and brewery enabling the brewing process to be viewed. Eight handpumps serve six ales from the brewery including a Hoggleys beer plus a rotating guest, with the final pump reserved for a Northamptonshire cider. The bar also stocks Phipps Kingswell gin, which is distilled on the premises.
Q♿♣

Kingsley Park Working Men's Club
120 Kingsley Park Terrace, NN2 7HJ
12-11 (11.30 Tue); 12-11.30 Fri; 11-11.30 Sat; 11-11 Sun
☎ (01604) 715514 kpwmc.co.uk
Fuller's London Pride, ESB; Greene King IPA; Sharp's Doom Bar; Tetley Bitter; 3 changing beers (sourced nationally; often Great Oakley, Nobby's, Phipps NBC) [H]
Long-established club founded nearby in 1892. There are eight handpumps serving five regular and three changing beers, overseen by an award-winning steward. Live music is hosted three nights a week and trips out are organised for members. A former local CAMRA Club of the Year. ♿

Lamplighter
66 Overstone Road, NN1 3JS
12-midnight (1am Fri & Sat); 12-11 Sun
☎ (01604) 631125 thelamplighter.co.uk
Nobby's Plum Porter; Oakham JHB; Phipps NBC India Pale Ale; Vale Gravitas; 4 changing beers (sourced regionally) [H]
A deservedly popular, traditional, street-corner pub just off the town centre attracting young and old alike. There is a roaring fire in the bar, a lovely snug and a heated courtyard. Four local and four guest beers are from established micros, along with a selection of bottled beers. Home-cooked food is served and children are welcome during mealtimes. The pub hosts open mic, discos, live music and quiz nights each week, and beer festivals throughout the year. ♿♣

Malt Shovel Tavern
121 Bridge Street, NN1 1QF
11.30-11; 12-10.30 Sun ☎ (01604) 234212
maltshoveltavern.com
Fuller's London Pride; Hook Norton Old Hooky; Oakham Bishops Farewell; Phipps NBC India Pale Ale; 10 changing beers (sourced nationally) [H]
Close to the town centre and opposite the Carlsberg brewery, this popular pub has won many awards over the past 20 or more years. Breweriana features everywhere, with real cider, LocAle, Belgian draught and bottled beers available. Two beer festivals with live bands are held each year on bank holidays. Home-made lunches are served all week. Blues bands play on Wednesday nights. The pub has a strong rugby following. ♿♣

Olde England

199 Kettering Road, NN1 4BP (near racecourse)
5-11 Mon (midnight Tue-Thu); 12-midnight Fri & Sat; 12-11 Sun (01604) 603799
Digfield Chiffchaff; Jennings Cumberland Ale; Marston's Old Empire; Potbelly Beijing Black; Ringwood Fortyniner; Vale Gravitas H; changing beers (sourced regionally; often Nobby's, Phipps NBC) H/G
Converted end-of-terrace Victorian building on three floors with bars on two floors. The ground and first floors have a medieval theme with solid fuel burners. The cellar bar has a contemporary style and is more intimate. Up to 15 beers from local micros and regional breweries are served by gravity and handpump alongside 15 ciders. Various board games, cards and dominoes are provided. Live folk music plays on Thursday. A former local CAMRA Cider Pub of the Year and Northants Town Community Pub. Q

Pomfret Arms

10 Cotton End, NN4 8BS
12-11 (midnight Fri & Sat) (01604) 555119
pomfretarms.co.uk
Cotton End Aramis, Coffee Porter; Great Oakley Wot's Occurring; 3 changing beers (sourced locally) H
With its own microbrewery, this town pub is situated on the south-west side of the River Nene in Cotton End. Its small central bar has six handpumps serving both the front opened-out room and rear bar. Alongside three own-brewed ales are others from breweries including Great Oakley. The brewery and a function room are in a separate building in the lovely beer garden. Check Facebook for seasonal opening variations.

Road to Morocco

Bridgwater Drive, NN3 3AG
12-11 (midnight Fri & Sat); closed Sun (01604) 632899
Greene King IPA, Abbot; Theakston Old Peculier; 4 changing beers (sourced nationally) H
Run by a CAMRA member, this popular 1960s brick-built estate pub has a Moorish theme in some of the decor, reflecting its name. It has two connected but distinctly different rooms. The busy bar area, where darts and pool are played, can get especially lively when sport is on TV. The homely lounge is generally the quieter area for a drink. Quiz night is Tuesday. P (5)

St Giles Ale House

45 St Giles Street, NN1 1JF
closed Mon; 12-8 Tue & Wed (10 Thu; 11 Fri & Sat); 12-7 Sun (01604) 636332
6 changing beers (sourced nationally; often Framework, Grainstore) H
Northampton's first and only micropub, opened in 2016 following conversion from retail premises. It specialises in real ale, real cider and a small number of craft/continental bottled beers. Ales are from around the country and tend to be new releases or from more obscure breweries. With no music, fruit machines or Wi-Fi, this is an ideal place for drinking and conversation. Q (5)

Old

White Horse

Walgrave Road, NN6 9QX
closed Mon; 12-3, 5-11 Tue-Thu; 12-11 Fri & Sat; 12-7 Sun (01604) 781297 whitehorseold.co.uk
3 changing beers (sourced locally; often Nobby's, Potbelly) H
A rustic country pub comprising two opened-out rooms with polished wooden floors and a real fire, and a small snug towards the rear. Upstairs is the Millstone room which can be used for functions and leads to the south-facing garden overlooking the church. The menu is relatively small, offering interesting, home-cooked seasonal lunches and evening meals including pub classics and specials. Attractions are monthly live music and quiz nights and a weekly Tuesday pie night.
Q P

Orlingbury

Queen's Arms

Isham Road, NN14 1JD
3-9 Mon (11 Tue); 12-11 Wed & Thu (midnight Fri & Sat); 12-9 Sun (01933) 679110 queensarmsorlingbury.co.uk
Oakham JHB; Theakston XB; 2 changing beers (sourced locally; often King's Cliffe) H
A re-entry to the Guide after many years' absence for this large free house, whose solid front door leads to a main bar and a skittles room. The pub dates back to the early 19th century and was the King's Arms until its name was changed in 1852. Its main bar and lounge is on two levels and incorporates the former snug, which has been opened out but retains some privacy. Monthly brewery tap takeovers are an attraction.
P (38,39)

Oundle

Ship Inn

18 West Street, PE8 4EF
11-11.45 (midnight Fri & Sat); 12-11 Sun (01832) 273918 theshipinnoundle.co.uk
Brewsters Hophead; Fuller's London Pride; 2 changing beers H
This Grade II-listed pub is full of character with original beamed ceilings and the ghost of a former landlord. It has three bars with many small rooms adjoining, and a large function room available to hire for birthday celebrations and small weddings. Good food is served in all rooms. Accommodation is in two stone annexes and a small cottage to the rear. The rear car park is accessed through an archway off West Street.
Q P (X4)

Tap & Kitchen

Oundle Wharf, Station Road, PE8 4DE
10-11; 12-6 Sun (01832) 275069 tapandkitchen.com
6 changing beers (sourced locally) H
The main outlet for the Nene Valley Brewery, this pub has spacious eating and drinking areas. It is located in a revamped wharfside warehouse where chrome, wood, cogs and rails generate an industrial revolution ambience. At least six real ales from Nene Valley are served, plus a selection of craft beers and ciders. The extensive menu features home-cooked and locally sourced food. Attractions include live music and a new outdoor seating area.
P

Polebrook

King's Arms 🄻
Kings Arms Lane, PE8 5LW
⏲ 12-3, 6-11; 12-11 Sat & Sun ☎ (01832) 272363
🌐 kingsarmspolebrook.co.uk
Adnams Southwold Bitter; Digfield Fools Nook; 2 changing beers 🄷
Traditional stone-built thatched inn that can be accessed from doors at the front and rear off the car park. The pub is open plan with a main bar, three areas for diners and a small garden that incorporates a children's play area. Four beers are dispensed via handpump, some from the nearby Digfield Ales. Food is offered from an extensive menu and specials board. Third-pint glasses are available, giving the opportunity to taste a wider variety of beer. Happy hour is 6-7pm Monday.
Q❀◐◑♿♣P🚌🐾📶

Rushden

Rushden Historical Transport Society 🄻
Station Approach, NN10 0AW (on ring road)
⏲ 7.30-11 Mon & Tue; 6-11 Wed & Thu; 4.30-11 Fri; 12-11 Sat & Sun ☎ (01933) 318988 🌐 rhts.co.uk
Phipps NBC India Pale Ale; 6 changing beers (sourced regionally; often Marston's, Woodforde's) 🄷
This award-winning club occupies the former Midland Railway Station. The ladies' waiting room is now the bar, with gas lighting and walls adorned with enamel advertising panels, railway photos and many CAMRA awards. On the platform, carriages provide a meeting room, Northants skittles, and a buffet for the numerous open days held during the year when steam and diesel train rides are provided. A beer festival is held in September. Show a copy of the Guide for entry.
Q🐴❀♿♣🍎🚌🐾

Southwick

Shuckburgh Arms 🄻
Main Street, PE8 5BL
⏲ 6-10 Mon (11 Tue); 12-11 Wed-Sat; 12-10 Sun
☎ (01832) 272044 🌐 shuckburghpub.co.uk
Brewsters Hophead; Digfield Barnwell Bitter; 3 changing beers (sourced locally; often Fuller's, Grainstore, Greene King) 🄷
Thatched stone-built pub in the village centre, serving five real ales. The bar area doubles as a restaurant and there is a small side room. To the rear is a covered outdoor area, car park, large garden and the village cricket pitch. The pub is run by the local community with shareholders and a small committee. It hosts the annual World Conker Championship in October. Popular well-priced food is available, including breakfast by arrangement.
Q❀◐◑⛺♣P🚌🐾📶

Staverton

Countryman 🄻
Daventry Road, NN11 6JH (on A425)
⏲ 12-3, 6-11; 12-10 Sun ☎ (01327) 311815
🌐 thecountrymanstaverton.co.uk
Bombardier; 2 changing beers (sourced locally; often Church End, Phipps NBC) 🄷
A popular 17th-century ironstone coaching inn that is the sole survivor of the three pubs that once graced this lovely village close to Daventry. The long wooden-beamed bar serves four areas, and an open hearth fire between the rooms provides some seclusion. The enthusiastic landlord offers a good choice of ales, always including one local brew. There is also a wide choice of reasonably priced food, sourced locally whenever possible.
Q🐴❀◐◑♿P🚌(66)🐾📶

Stoke Bruerne

Boat Inn ✔
Shutlanger Road, NN12 7SB
⏲ 9am-11 ☎ (01604) 862428 🌐 boatinn.co.uk
Banks's Amber Ale; Jennings Cumberland Ale; Marston's Old Empire; Ringwood Boondoggle; Wychwood Hobgoblin; house beer (by Marston's); 1 changing beer (sourced nationally) 🄷
In a picturesque setting alongside the Grand Union Canal and opposite the National Canal Museum, the Boat Inn has been owned by the same family since 1877. The long, narrow stone building has a thatched roof and a wonderful tap bar with interconnecting rooms with canal views, open fires, original stone floors and window seats. An adjoining room has Northants skittles. A canal boat is available to hire. A loyalty card scheme rewards regulars. Breakfast is served until 11am.
Q🐴❀◐◑♿♣P🚌(86)🐾📶

Tiffield

George at Tiffield 🄻 ✔
21 High Street North, NN12 8AD (in centre of village)
⏲ 12-3, 6-11 Mon; 7-11 Tue; 12-3, 6-11 Wed & Thu; 12-midnight Fri; 12-11 Sat; 12-7 Sun ☎ (01327) 350587
🌐 thegeorgeattiffield.co.uk
Timothy Taylor Landlord; 3 changing beers (sourced regionally) 🄷
A true community inn central to many village activities – the building dates from the 16th century, with Victorian additions when it became a public house. It has a cosy bar, games room with Northants skittles and a back room restaurant which can be booked for small functions. It is the tap for Great Oakley Brewery, just outside the village. A beer festival is held in October. A former local CAMRA Rural Pub of the Year.
🐴❀◐◑♿⛺♣🍎P🚌🐾

Towcester

Towcester Mill Brewery Tap 🄻
Chantry Lane, NN12 6AD
⏲ 5-8 Mon (10.30 Tue-Thu); 3-11 Fri; 12-11 Sat; 12-8 Sun
☎ (01327) 437060 🌐 towcestermillbrewery.co.uk
Towcester Mill Mill Race, Amarillo, Bell Ringer, Black Fire; 4 changing beers (sourced locally; often Towcester Mill) 🄷
Popular and welcoming brewery tap in a historic Grade II-listed mill dating from 1794, straddling the old mill race and adjacent to Bury Mount on which the town's fort once stood. Two guest ales from other local breweries and six ciders are available. The bar retains many original features including beams, stonework and a wooden floor, with a second room to cope with demand. Outside is a large garden alongside the mill. A former local CAMRA Pub of the Year. Q🐴❀♿🍎P🚌🐾📶

Welford

Wharf Inn

NN6 6JQ (on A5199 by canal basin)
12-11 ☎ (01858) 575075 🌐 wharfinnwelford.co.uk
Grainstore Ten Fifty; Marston's Pedigree; Oakham Bishops Farewell; 3 changing beers (sourced locally) [H]
This original ironstone building dates from 1814 and is situated at the end of the Welford cut on the Grand Union Canal, a few yards from the border with Leicestershire. The main room is divided by an open fireplace. A smaller snug and back bar are occasionally used. Guest beers are mostly sourced locally or regionally; good-value food is served all week. Several walks can be started from here – a handy leaflet behind the bar provides details. Local CAMRA Rural Pub of the Year 2017.
Q ♿ P (60)

Wellingborough

Coach & Horses

17 Oxford Street, NN8 4HY (800yds from Market Square)
12-11 (9 Mon); 12-6 Sun ☎ (01933) 441848
🌐 thecoachandhorseswellingborough.co.uk
12 changing beers (sourced nationally; often Castle Rock, Elland, Salopian) [H]
A long-standing Guide entry, this popular town-centre local offers a constantly changing choice of 12 real ales and 15 ciders, including local ales. The central bar serves three drinking areas, all adorned with breweriana. Traditional home-cooked food is available (no food Sun eve, Mon & Tue), with 15 different pies on the menu. A quiz is held on alternate Wednesdays, and a beer festival in August. Q ♿ ♣

Little Ale House

14A High Street, NN8 4JU
closed Mon; 5-9 Tue; 12-9 Wed & Thu (11 Fri & Sat); 12-5 Sun ☎ 07870 392011
7 changing beers (sourced locally; often Castle Rock, Digfield, Oakham) [H]/[G]
A wonderfully friendly one-roomed micropub whose small size encourages interaction between guests and the landlady. Up to seven rotating real ales are served on handpump and gravity, including a porter or stout. In addition, up to seven draught ciders and a good selection of gins, single malt whiskies, wines and soft drinks are also stocked. A quiz is held on the first Tuesday of the month. Close to Jackson's Lane car park.
Q ♣ P

Old House

29-31 Sheep Street, NN8 1BS
closed Mon; 12-10 (11 Fri & Sat); 12-8 Sun
☎ (01933) 225932
Hart Family Brewers House Beer, Harts No.1, Harts No.3; 3 changing beers (sourced regionally; often Dark Star, Wild Beer) [H]
A two-floored pub set in a Grade II-listed, thatched and timber-framed building that was refurbished to a high standard in 2017. Much of the ground floor is medieval and the foundations are thought to date back to the year 948, with later Tudor additions. The pub is now home to Hart Family Brewers, whose beers feature strongly along with real ciders. Doorstop sandwiches are served at lunchtime. Attractions include regular quizzes and a monthly film night. Q ♿ ♣

Welton

White Horse

High Street, NN11 2JP (off A361 between Rugby and Daventry)
12-2 (not Mon & Tue), 5-11; 12-midnight Fri & Sat; 12-11 Sun ☎ (01327) 702820 🌐 thewhitehorsewelton.co.uk
Adnams Southwold Bitter; Oakham Bishops Farewell; Purity Pure Gold; 1 changing beer (sourced nationally) [H]
17th-century village pub with a bar with games, a small snug area and a lounge/dining room. Beers are looked after well and always in good condition. A cider from Vale of Welton is also available. Good-value meals are served lunchtime and evening. A logburner in one bar and a coalburner in the other give it a cosy feel on a winter's night. Outside is a covered patio area leading to a lawned garden with tables. ♣ P

West Haddon

Crown Inn

3 High Street, NN6 7AP (on A428)
4-11; 12-midnight Sat; 12-11 Sun ☎ (01788) 510381
🌐 thecrownwesthaddon.co.uk
Marston's Pedigree; 3 changing beers (sourced locally; often Phipps NBC, Potbelly, Towcester Mill) [H]
A welcome new entry to the Guide, this 18th-century, three-storey inn sits at the heart of the village on the old main road from Northampton to Rugby. The family-owned pub offers a terrific range of three rotating local beers alongside one regular from Marston's. A former Phipps pub, it also regularly sells the revived brewery's beers. Good-value food is served Monday to Thursday evenings.
(96)

Weston by Welland

Wheel & Compass

Valley Road, LE16 8HZ (off B664)
12-11 (10 Sun) ☎ (01858) 565864
🌐 thewheelandcompass.co.uk
Banks's Amber Ale; Greene King Abbot; Marston's Pedigree; 2 changing beers (sourced nationally) [H]
A rural pub in the picturesque Welland Valley, which has been refurbished, opening up the entrance lobby and incorporating part of the former dining area, with flagstone floors, a woodburner and sofas. The outside drinking area offers good views across the valley and is an ideal playground for children. This is a popular stopping-off place for walkers on the Jurassic Way. ♿ P

Woodford

Duke's

83 High Street, NN14 4HE (off A510)
12-11 ☎ (01832) 732224
Greene King Abbot; 7 changing beers (sourced nationally; often Oakham, Phipps NBC, Digfield) [H]
Overlooking the village green, this community-focused pub was a 17th-century manor. It is named in honour of the Duke of Wellington, who was a frequent visitor to Woodford. The interior includes a split main bar, lounge restaurant, rear room and an upstairs games room. The pub holds a May bank holiday beer festival and an August bank holiday music festival, plus regular open mic, disco, karaoke and acoustic music nights.
Q ♣ P (16X)

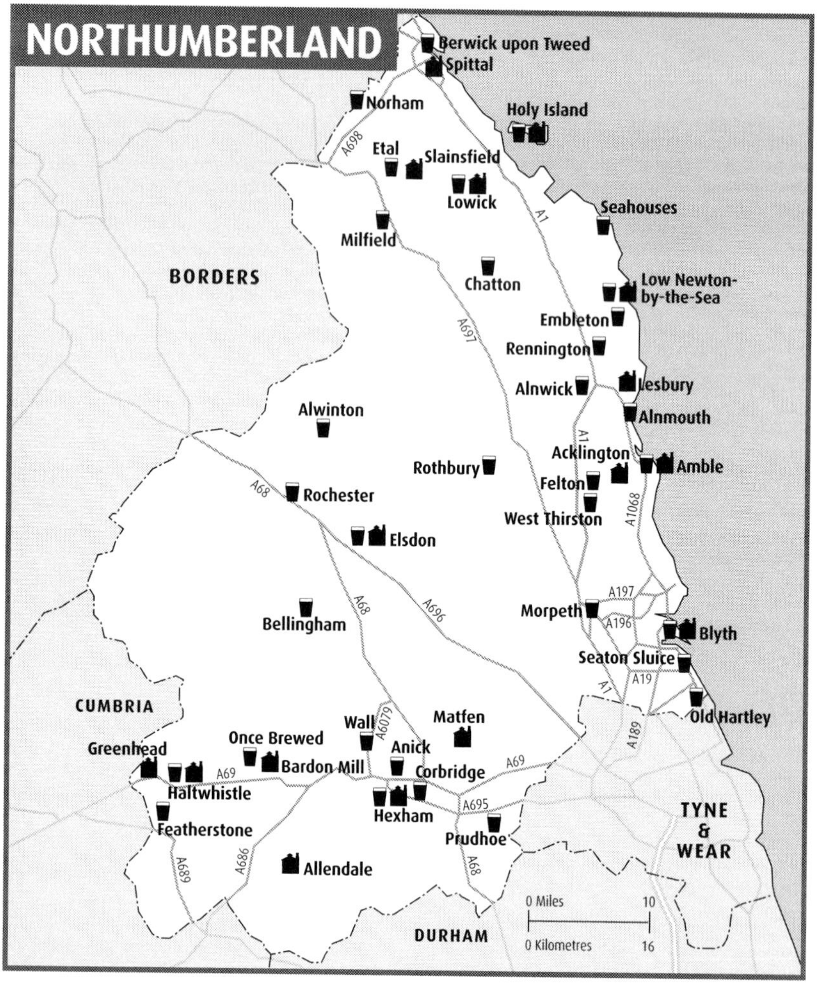

Alnmouth

Red Lion Inn L ✔

22 Northumberland Street, NE66 2RJ

⏲ 11-midnight ☎ (01665) 830584 🌐 redlionalnmouth.com

4 changing beers (sourced nationally) Ⓗ

Charming, family-run, 18th-century coaching inn with a cosy lounge bar with attractive woodwork. The decked area at the bottom of the garden enjoys panoramic views across the Aln Estuary. Guest beers usually include one local and two interesting brews from further afield. The pub welcomes dogs, and is popular with tourists and locals. Occasional live music plays – in the open air in summer. An annual beer festival is held in October. Open for breakfast from 9am.

Q🛝❀🛏◑🍏P🚌(X18)🐾📶

Alnwick

John Bull Inn L

12 Howick Street, NE66 1UY

⏲ 5-11; 12-3, 7-11 Sat; 12-3, 7-10.30 Sun ☎ (01665) 602055
🌐 john-bull-inn.co.uk

5 changing beers (sourced nationally; often Hadrian Border) Ⓗ

Many times local CAMRA Pub of the Year and a former Regional Pub of the Year, this 180-year-old inn thrives on its reputation as a back-street boozer. The landlord offers a wide selection of cask-conditioned ales including at least one Hadrian Border beer, real cider, the widest range of

REAL ALE BREWERIES

Allendale Allendale
Beacon Brauhaus Holy Island
Bear Claw Spittal
Chasing Everest Blyth (NEW)
Cheviot Slainsfield (NEW)
Credence Amble
First & Last 🛢 Elsdon
Grounding Angels Hexham (NEW)
Hawk Wing Lesbury
Hetton Law Lowick
Hexhamshire Hexham
High House Farm Matfen
Muckle Haltwhistle
Rigg & Furrow Acklington
Ship Inn 🛢 Low Newton-by-the-Sea
Twice Brewed 🛢 Bardon Mill
Wrytree Greenhead

bottled Belgian beers in the county and over 120 single malt whiskies. The pub upholds the North-East tradition of an annual leek show. Opening hours may be extended in summer. Q❀♣●🚌🐾

Tanners Arms Ⓛ

2-4 Hotspur Place, NE66 1QF

⏲ 5-11 (midnight Fri); 12-midnight Sat; 12-11 Sun
☎ (01665) 602553

5 changing beers (sourced nationally) Ⓗ

Ivy-covered stone-built pub just off Bondgate Without and a short distance from Alnwick Garden. The rustic single room has a flagstone floor and tree beer shelf. A large fireplace provides added warmth in winter. The ever-changing real ales frequently come from North-East and Scottish Borders microbreweries. Acoustic music nights feature regularly with open mic on the last Friday of the month. 🐴♿♣●🚌🐾📶

Alwinton

Rose & Thistle Ⓛ

NE65 7BQ

⏲ 7-midnight Mon; 12-5, 6-midnight Tue-Thu; 12-midnight Fri-Sun ☎ (01669) 650226 🌐 roseandthistlealwinton.com

Hadrian Border Grainger Ale; 1 changing beer (sourced nationally; often Timothy Taylor) Ⓗ

Welcoming historic former coaching inn, popular with walkers and cyclists, in the heart of the Northumberland National Park. An old-fashioned pub with two handpulls, it offers a very well-kept LocAle, complemented by good home cooking and excellent views. The roomy interior is matched by a large outside area. B&B and self-catering holiday accommodation are available. Q🐴❀🛏◑P🐾

Amble

Masons Arms Ⓛ

Woodbine Street, NE65 0NH

⏲ 4-11.30; 3-12.30am Fri; 12-11.30 Sat & Sun
☎ (01665) 799275 🌐 masonsarmsamble.co.uk

5 changing beers (sourced nationally; often Credence) Ⓗ

This large, multi-roomed pub is on a corner at the south edge of this coastal village. Five handpumps adorn the bar and dispense a range of local brewery beers, including ales from the Credence Brewery based in the village. Regular quizzes are held and a function room is available. Boat trips to Coquet Island depart from the nearby harbour. 🛏◐♣🚌🐾

Anick

Rat Inn

NE46 4LN (follow signpost at Hexham A69 roundabout)

⏲ 12-11 (10 Sun) ☎ (01434) 602814 🌐 theratinn.com

Timothy Taylor Landlord; 4 changing beers (sourced locally) Ⓗ

Superb 1750 country inn with spectacular views across the Tyne Valley. The pub has a welcoming and friendly ambience, with an open log fire surrounded by chamber pots hanging from the ceiling. It has an excellent reputation for good food prepared with locally sourced ingredients and appears in several food guides. Bottled beers are stocked. The first Thursday of the month is singers/poetry night. Well worth the short taxi ride from Hexham rail station. Q🐴❀◑♣●P🚌(74)

Bellingham

Cheviot Hotel ✔

Main Street, NE48 2AU

⏲ 10-midnight (1am Fri & Sat) ☎ (01434) 220696
🌐 thecheviothotel.co.uk

4 changing beers (sourced nationally) Ⓗ

Friendly hotel opposite the bus stop. A log-burning stove warms the bar area. Cask beer is available all year round including one ale supplied by Hadrian Border Brewery. There is plenty of outside seating at the front. Regular theme nights are hosted. Stay up to date with the monthly newsletter, The Sheep Dip. 🐴❀🛏◑♿⛺♣●P🚌(680)🐾📶

Berwick upon Tweed

Barrels Ale House Ⓛ

59-61 Bridge Street, TD15 1ES

⏲ 12-midnight (11.30 Sun) ☎ (01289) 308013

5 changing beers (sourced nationally) Ⓗ

There is an Old Curiosity Shop-ambience to this pub, located in the old part of Berwick next to the original road bridge over the Tweed. The excellent real ale no doubt helps customers brave the 'dentist's chair' at the side of the bar. A downstairs bar is used by DJs and bands at weekends. Outside is a unique open drinking area surrounded by high walls. A former CAMRA award winner. ❀🐾

Curfew Ⓛ

46A Bridge Street, TD15 1AQ

⏲ 12-9 (10 Fri-Sun) ☎ 07842 912268

4 changing beers (sourced nationally) Ⓗ

Berwick's first micropub is located up a small lane which opens out into a large courtyard off Bridge Street. It has a small bar area with a bottle fridge to one side. The courtyard makes a pleasant outdoor drinking area in summer. The cellar is in the shed at the top of the yard. Excellent pork pies are available. CAMRA Northumberland Pub of the Year in 2018. Q🐴❀≹♣●🐾

Pilot Ⓛ

31 Low Greens, TD15 1LZ (from station take road opp Castle Hotel towards coast)

⏲ 12-midnight; 11-midnight Sat; 11.30-11 Sun
☎ (01289) 304214

Caledonian Deuchars IPA; 2 changing beers (sourced nationally) Ⓗ

This popular pub with friendly bar staff is well patronised by locals and sought out by train trippers who have heard about this gem. The stone-built end-of-terrace hostelry dates from the 19th century and has a regionally important historic interior. It retains the original small room layout and boasts several nautical artefacts over 100 years old. It is home to a darts team and hosts music nights. 🐴❀🛏◐♿≹♣●🐾

Blyth

Wallaw Ⓛ ✔

14 Union Street, NE24 2DX

⏲ 8am-midnight (1am Fri & Sat) ☎ (01670) 356830

Greene King Abbot; Ruddles Best Bitter; Sharp's Doom Bar; 2 changing beers (sourced nationally) Ⓗ

Recently opened Wetherspoon free house, a former picture house whose name and Art Deco theme have been retained. Period features include the original projector in the entrance, and original seating and layout on the balcony, which is not open to the public. The staff aim to serve top-quality real ale from the 10 handpumps and are open to suggestions for guest ales. Alcohol is served from 9am. Q

Chatton

Percy Arms Hotel

Main Road, NE66 5PS
11-11 (01668) 215244 percyarmschatton.co.uk
6 changing beers (sourced nationally) H
Once the Duke of Northumberland's 19th-century hunting lodge, the Percy Arms was licensed for alcohol sales in 1879. It is now frequented by walkers, cyclists and holidaymakers due to the proximity of Chillingham Castle. A recent high-quality refurbishment has modernised the look and feel of the pub and its oak-panelled restaurant while retaining many original features.

Corbridge

Angel of Corbridge

Main Street, NE45 5LA
11-11; 12-11 Sun (01434) 632119
theangelofcorbridge.com
Great Corby Corby Ale; Hadrian Border Tyneside Blonde; Mordue Workie Ticket; Wylam Galatia; 2 changing beers (sourced locally) H
Superb former coaching inn dating from 1726 located on the main road with good transport links. Seven handpulls adorn the bar and a wonderful selection of malt whiskies is also kept. Family-friendly and with a reputation for good food, the pub is popular with tourists, ramblers and locals. A separate lounge area has comfy leather seating and outside is a relaxed seating area. The town has strong links with the Romans and Hadrian's Wall is nearby. QP

Elsdon

Bird in Bush

Village Green, NE19 1AA
closed Mon-Thu; 2-midnight Fri & Sat; 3-10.30 Sun
(01830) 520804
4 changing beers (sourced nationally) H
Vibrant community hostelry situated in a corner of the green in the quiet village of Elsdon. The only survivor of a number of pubs in the village, the Bird in Bush has been fully restored. It offers beers from a wide range of sources including the on-site brewery, so look out for First and Last ale at the bar. Food and accommodation are available.
P

Embleton

Greys Inn

Stanley Terrace, NE66 3UZ
12-11 (10.30 Sun) (01665) 576983
5 changing beers (sourced locally) H
Pleasant, traditional inn in a lovely seaside hamlet, just a short walk to a wonderful beach. It has three open fires and a framed 1904 grocery list hangs on the wall. The pub is an excellent venue to enjoy a bite to eat washed down with a locally sourced real ale, sitting outside on the superb patio in good weather. It is home to a ladies' darts team, clay pigeon club and golf club. (418,X18)

Etal

Black Bull

TD12 4TL
11-11 (01890) 820200 theblackbulletal.co.uk
3 changing beers (sourced locally) H
Northumberland's only thatched pub was fully renovated during a prolonged closure before reopening in 2018, and now has an attractive, modern interior with an exposed roof structure adding to the charm. Comfortable furniture features throughout the large, open-plan pub. Three handpumps serving locally produced beers adorn the pale wooden bar. There is also a function room and large outdoor seating area. (No food Mon; evening meals only Tue.) (267)

Featherstone

Wallace Arms

Rowfoot, NE49 0JF
5-10.30; 3-11.30 Fri; 12-11.30 Sat & Sun
(01434) 298921
Allendale Pennine Pale; Great North Eastern Rivet Catcher; 2 changing beers (sourced nationally) H
Cosy country pub warmed by real fires, with no jukebox or fruit machines to disturb the peace. Split over two levels and three rooms, it has a traditional bar area and various spaces. The welcoming landlady is always prepared to open early for groups of walkers, preferably if arranged in advance. Opening hours are reduced in winter – check ahead. QP

Felton

Foxes Den

Cellar 2, 4 Riverside, NE65 9EA
7-10.30 Mon; closed Tue; 6-10.30 Wed & Thu; 5-10.30 Fri & Sat 07957 721066
4 changing beers (sourced regionally) H
This micropub is a welcome addition to the mid-Northumberland pub scene. Situated in the basement below the Running Fox bakery and café, it has its own door on the main street. It is the sister pub to the Office in Morpeth. Four handpumps serve varied, mostly local, ales. Dogs are welcome and fussed over. QP(X15)

Haltwhistle

Milecastle Inn

North Road, NE49 9NN (on Military Rd)
12-11 (01434) 321372 milecastle-inn.co.uk
Big Lamp Bitter, Prince Bishop Ale; 1 changing beer (sourced nationally) H
This 1600s pub adjacent to Hadrian's Wall sells ale mainly from Newburn-based Big Lamp Brewery. Located a mile and a half north of Haltwhistle, the rural hostelry has a homely feel and is popular with ramblers and tourists. Food is home-made and locally sourced. There are also two comfy holiday cottages. The Hadrian's Wall bus stops outside April to September. Check ahead for winter opening hours. QP

Hexham

Dipton Mill Inn

Dipton Mill Road, NE46 1YA
12-2.30, 6-11; 12-3 Sun (01434) 606577
diptonmill.co.uk

Hexhamshire Blackhall English Stout, Devil's Elbow, Devil's Water, Old Humbug, Shire Bitter, Whapweasel H
The tap for Hexhamshire Brewery, now relocated to the beer garden, this small inn is run by real ale enthusiasts who brew their own excellent beers. Blackhall English Stout has proved so popular with drinkers that it has ousted Guinness. To complement the ales there is great home-cooked food – Saturday is curry night. A cosy atmosphere and warm welcome make this pub well worth seeking out. The large garden has a stream running through it and there is plenty of countryside to explore. Q P

Heart of Northumberland L

5 Market Street, NE46 3NS
11-11.30 (11 Mon); 11-11 Sun ☎ (01434) 608013
theheartexham.com
Timothy Taylor Landlord; 4 changing beers (sourced locally) H
Five handpumps, four selling local ales, adorn the bar in this recently refurbished and reopened, food-led pub. The single large room is divided almost in two near the end of the bar, with wooden floors throughout. A large open fire warms things nicely in the back room and another smaller fire keeps the front room cosy, too. Excellent food is served.

Holy Island

Crown & Anchor Hotel

Market Place, TD15 2RX (check tidetable for causeway crossing times)
11-11 ☎ (01289) 389215 holyislandcrown.co.uk
Hadrian Border Secret Kingdom, Tyneside Blonde; 1 changing beer (sourced locally) H
Cosy free house that serves three Northumbrian ales plus a wide selection of whiskies and gins. The bar features exposed floorboards and wooden tables and benches; note the Gothic carving of a local monk in the corner. There is a comfortable sitting room to the rear. The large beer garden provides scenic views to Lindisfarne Castle and the 12th-century ruined priory. (477)

Manor House Hotel

TD15 2RX (check tidetable for causeway crossing times)
11-11 ☎ (01289) 389207 manorhouseholyisland.com
3 changing beers (sourced locally; often Born in the Borders) H
The Manor House Hotel is located at the heart of the island, next to Lindisfarne Priory, and has magnificent views of the castle and harbour area. The bar area is light and airy with pale wood in abundance. The restaurant features seasonal and local produce. A large beer garden to the front is pleasant in summer. Opening times may vary with the tides. P (477)

Low Newton-by-the-Sea

Ship Inn L

Newton Square, NE66 3EL
11-11; 12-11 Sun ☎ (01665) 576262
shipinnnewton.co.uk
Ship Inn Sea Coal, Sea Wheat; 4 changing beers (sourced nationally) H
Nestling in the corner of three sides of a square of former fishermen's cottages a few yards from the beach, this small pub attracts a varied clientele. Drinkers seek ales from the in-house microbrewery; diners enjoy an excellent menu featuring fresh local ingredients; walkers appreciate the local scenery. A public car park is close by at the top of the hill. Opening times may vary in winter; phone ahead if travelling.
Q

Lowick

Black Bull L

Main Street, TD15 2UA
10-11 (midnight Sat) ☎ (01289) 388375
blackbulllowick.co.uk
4 changing beers (sourced locally) H
First licensed as a public house in 1817, it is believed that some of the building dates back to the mid-1600s, when it was part of a farm. The pub closed in 2014 after several years of brewery ownership and was declared an asset of community value after campaigning by the locals. In the same year a family business created to support rural and community development in Northumberland acquired the freehold. The pub was totally refurbished and reopened as a country inn in 2017. P (464)

Milfield

Red Lion Inn L

Main Road, NE71 6JD
11-2, 5-11; 11-11 Sat & Sun ☎ (01668) 216224
redlionmilfield.co.uk
Black Sheep Best Bitter; 2 changing beers (sourced nationally) H
A true local pub at the heart of the village, just eight miles inside the border, dating back to the mid-1700s. Rescued by the current licensee from the tight grip of Scottish & Newcastle, the Red Lion is a proper free house, with many varied guest beers served through the third handpump. Freshly prepared food is available, with blackboards proudly displaying where the local produce is sourced. Home to the local leek-growing club.
Q P (267)

Morpeth

Office L

The Toll House, Castle Square, NE61 1YL
5-10.30; 2-10.30 Sat; 12-10.30 Sun ☎ 07957 721066
8 changing beers (sourced locally) H
Formerly the brewery tap for Acton Ales, the Office is a micropub with no music or games machines. It features five handpulls and three craft keg beers, all of local origin, and three real ciders served on gravity from the glass-fronted fridge opposite the bar. No food is available. Northumberland CAMRA Pub of the Year 2019. Q

Tap & Spile L

23 Manchester Street, NE61 1BH
12-2.30, 4.30-11; 12-11 Fri & Sat; 12-10.30 Sun
☎ (01670) 513894
Everards Tiger; Greene King Abbot; Timothy Taylor Landlord; 5 changing beers (sourced nationally) H
The pub is popular with locals, though all are welcome here. It has eight handpulls offering a good choice of beers, with local ales from Northumbrian breweries often available, alongside Westons Old Rosie cider. The bar area at the front of the building is usually busy, though there is a

quieter, cosy lounge to the rear accessible from either side of the room. A traditional folk group plays on Sunday lunchtime. Close to the town's bus station.

Norham

Masons Arms

17 West Street, TD15 2LB
12-11 (01289) 382326
themasonsarmsnorham.co.uk
Allendale Wagtail Best Bitter; 3 changing beers (sourced nationally) H
The cosy wood-panelled public bar, with a real fire at its heart, is the hub of this pub. Photos of bygone Norham adorn the walls, along with collections of fishing gear and joinery tools, and an old Younger's brewery mirror. The area is popular with tourists – nearby are a ruined castle and the railway station museum. Close to the Tweed Cycle Way and bus stop. (67)

Old Hartley

Delaval Arms L

NE26 4RL (jct of A193/B1325 S of Seaton Sluice)
12-11 summer; 12-2.30, 4.30-10.30 Mon-Thu; 12-11 Fri-Sun winter (0191) 237 0489
thedelavalarms.wordpress.com
4 changing beers (sourced nationally) H
Multi-roomed Grade II-listed building dating from 1748, with a Grade II*-listed WWI water storage tower (part of Roberts Battery) behind the beer garden. It is the first pub in Northumberland for those following the coastal route. Good-quality, affordable meals complement the beer, with guest ales coming from local micros. To the left as you enter there is a room served through a hatch from the bar and to the right a room where children are welcome. Q P (308,309)

Once Brewed

Twice Brewed Inn L

Miltary Road, Bardon Mill, NE47 7AN (on B6318 Military Rd)
11-11 (01434) 344534 twicebrewedinn.co.uk
6 changing beers (sourced nationally; often Twice Brewed) H
A excellent remote inn on the Military Road, with Hadrian's Wall, Steel Rigg and Vindolanda nearby, attracting walkers and tourists. It has a totally refurbished bar area and offers a wide range of bottled beers from around the world. It has full disabled access and is now dog-friendly. B&B is offered in 18 en-suite bedrooms. The Twice Brewed Brew House started producing its own beers in 2017. Q P

Prudhoe

Wor Local L

Front Street, NE42 5HJ
4-10.30 Mon-Wed; 3-10.30 Thu & Fri; 2-10.30 Sat & Sun
(01661) 598150 worlocalmicropub.com
4 changing beers (sourced nationally) H
Wor Local (or Our Local if you are not a Geordie) is a micropub with room for around 40 customers. The layout of the bar, with its comfy seating, encourages conversation. There are lots of traditional pub and board games available. Four local beers in a variety of styles are offered, one always at a lower price. Real ciders are also available. Pork pies and cheese are on sale along with crisps and nuts. A welcome addition to the area.

Rennington

Horseshoes Inn L

6 Rennington Village, NE66 3RS (turn off at Alnwick for B1340 and via Denwick for 3 miles)
closed Mon; 12-3, 6.30-11 (01665) 577665
thehorseshoesrennington.co.uk
Hadrian Border Farne Island Pale Ale; 1 changing beer (sourced nationally) H
Superb traditional family-run village pub dating from 1841, with its history detailed on the chimney breast. The bar is warm and friendly without TV or jukebox, with dry hops hanging over the serving area and a cosy log fire. The restaurant seats 50 and has an excellent reputation. A pleasant beer garden is at the front. The pub hosts a scarecrow competition every August bank holiday Saturday and is home to two darts teams. Q P

Rochester

Redesdale Arms L

NE19 1TA
11.30-11; 12.30-10.30 Sun (01830) 520668
redesdale-arms.co.uk
2 changing beers (sourced locally) H
A 16th-century coaching inn, known as the First and Last due to its location near the Scottish border. The oldest part of the building dates back over 600 years and is a former bastle house, a fortified dwelling from the middle ages. The restaurant serves home-cooked food using local ingredients. Accommodation is available in 10 rooms. Situated in the Northumberland International Dark Sky Park, the pub provides telescopes and star maps to aid viewing on a clear night. Q P

Rothbury

Narrow Nick L

High Street, NE65 7TB
5-10.30; 12-10.30 Sat & Sun 07707 703182
6 changing beers (sourced locally) H
In a Northumberland market town, this micropub opened in 2016 in a former clothes shop. The single room has the bar at one side, with a more recent wooden bar-back. Six handpumps sell a selection of local brewery beers, and a large range of gins is stocked. The front windows feature Art Deco-style stained glass. Q

Seahouses

Black Swan Inn L

2 Union Street, NE68 7RT
1-11 (midnight Fri); 12-midnight Sat; 12-11 Sun
(01665) 720227
3 changing beers (sourced regionally) H
A cosy two-room pub, popular with locals and tourists alike. Situated on a hill close to the harbour, it offers sea views from the front window. The main bar features exposed beams and an open fire; there is also a dining room and courtyard beer garden. Attractions include a dartboard, jukebox and weekly quiz. Two TVs mainly show sport. (418,X18)

Olde Ship Inn

7-9 Main Street, NE68 7RD

11-11; 12-11 Sun (01665) 720200 seahouses.co.uk

Black Sheep Best Bitter; Courage Directors; Hadrian Border Farne Island Pale Ale; Morland Old Speckled Hen; Theakston Best Bitter; Ruddles County; 4 changing beers (sourced nationally)

This farmhouse, built in 1745, was converted to the licensed trade in 1812 and has a regionally important historic pub interior. Family owned since 1910, the pub has three quality bars adorned with a veritable treasure trove of 19th- and 20th-century maritime memorabilia. Fully residential, it offers an interesting menu of fish, fresh crab meals and snacks. Q P (418,X18)

Seaton Sluice

Melton Constable

Beresford Road, NE26 4QL

12-11 (10.30 Sun) (0191) 237 7741

themeltonconstable.co.uk

Adnams Southwold Bitter, Broadside; Ossett Yorkshire Blonde; 2 changing beers (sourced nationally)

Large roadside pub a few minutes' walk from the beach and local history sights. It is named after the southern seat of Lord Hastings, a member of the Delaval family – Delaval Hall is close by. Tuesday is steak night, Wednesday is quiz night, Sunday evening features live music. A fishing club meets here and the BSA owners' club meets on the first and third Thursdays of the month.
P

Wall

Hadrian Hotel

NE46 4EE

11-11 (01434) 681232 hadrianhotel.co.uk

House beer (by Twice Brewed); 3 changing beers (sourced locally; often Twice Brewed)

A pleasant hotel located on the main road at Wall. The Hadrian has a friendly local customer base and is popular with tourists all year round. Its bar is open to the public and meals are served all day until 8.30pm. Three log fires enhance the comfortable atmosphere. A PlusBus travelcard facilitates travel from Hexham railway station.
P

West Thirston

Northumberland Arms

The Peth, NE65 9EE

11.30-11 (10.30 Sun) (01670) 787370

northumberlandarms-felton.co.uk

3 changing beers (sourced nationally; often Allendale)

This fine stone inn was built in the 1820s by Hugh Percy, 3rd Duke of Northumberland, as a coaching inn. The building has been lovingly renovated in an eclectic style while remaining warm, comfortable and welcoming. Bare stone walls and real fires add to the ambience. A large function room caters for groups of up to 30. The beer range is predominantly from local breweries.
P (X15)

Barrels Ale House, Berwick upon Tweed (Photo: Chris/Flickr CC BY-SA 2.0)

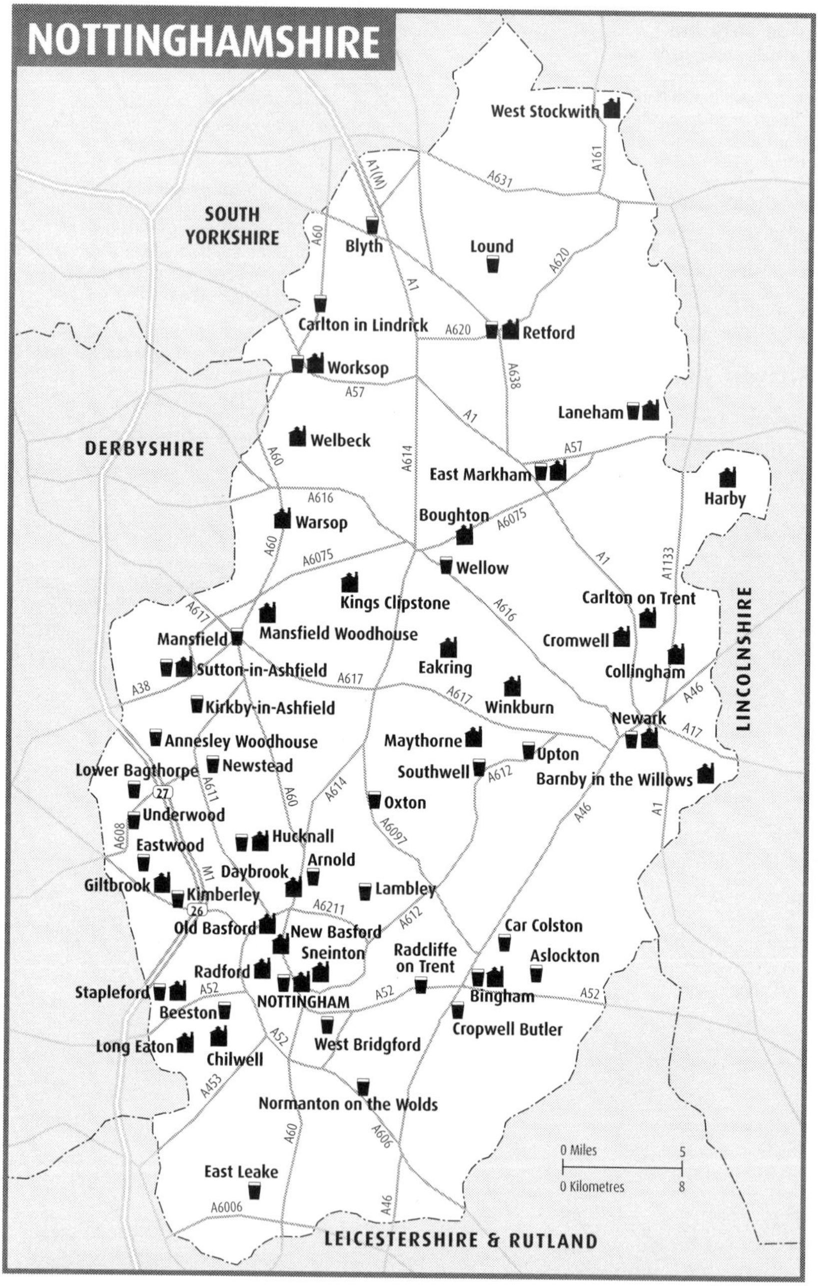

Annesley Woodhouse

Squire Musters

158 Forest Road, NG17 9HW

4-9 (10 Wed & Thu); 2-10 Fri; 1-10 Sat; 12-10 Sun

07742 553564

4 changing beers (often Flipside, Grasshopper)

Micropub offering four changing beers on handpump and up to five ciders on tap, plus a large range of spirits (mainly gins) and snacks. On the third Sunday of the month it hosts a walking club, starting or finishing here, with its sister pub, the Byron's Rest in nearby Hucknall. Quiz night is every Thursday. There is no off-road parking but a bus runs nearby. Q

Arnold

Abdication

89 Mansfield Road, Daybrook, NG5 6BH

closed Mon & Tue; 4-9.30; 2-6 Sun theabdication.co.uk

4 changing beers

Built in 1936/37, this modern micropub is part of the Home Brewery Coronation Buildings, opposite the gates of the former brewery, and was for many years a shop. The four ever-changing cask ales, two KeyKeg beers and three ciders are from microbreweries, small producers or the on-site nanobrewery, and come in a mix of styles. An archway divides the single room, giving an appearance of a much larger area. Participants in the monthly quiz are grouped into teams by a raffle. Q♿♣🍏🚌🐾

Robin Hood & Little John

1 Church Street, NG5 8FD (on corner of Cross St)
12-11 (midnight Fri & Sat); 12-10.30 Sun
☎ (0115) 920 1054 🌐 therobinhoodandlittlejohn.co.uk
Everards Tiger; Lincoln Green Marion, Archer, Hood, Tuck; 10 changing beers Ⓗ
Two-room Project William refurbishment between Lincoln Green and Everards breweries. The bar features Home Ales memorabilia, while the lounge has details of the pub's history and the local area. The rear courtyard has outdoor seating and a covered skittles alley. Along with 10 real ale pumps in each bar offering microbrewery beers, the real cider wall has eight taps dispensing ciders from small local producers and further afield. A former National CAMRA Cider Pub of the Year.
♿♣🍏🚌🐾

Aslockton

Cranmer Arms

Main Street, NG13 9AL
11.30-11.30 ☎ (01949) 859060
4 changing beers Ⓗ
A fine example of a traditional local pub, set in the heart of the village. It has a large beer garden and play area, plus a skittle alley. Basic bar meals are served, with Friday night fish and chips always popular. The cosy bar has up to four well-kept cask ales that keep the regulars coming back for more.
♿♣P🚌🐾

Beeston

Crown Inn ★

Church Street, NG9 1FY
12-11.30 (11 Sun) ☎ (0115) 967 8623
Blue Monkey Infinity; Brewsters Hophead; Dancing Duck Nice Weather; Nottingham Rock Ale Mild Beer; 9 changing beers (often Everards) Ⓗ
Nineteenth-century, Grade II-listed alehouse, acquired and sympathetically refurbished by Everards. Listed on CAMRA's National Inventory of Historic Pub Interiors, up to 14 ales and several real ciders and perries are served at this former East Midlands CAMRA Pub of the Year. An outside bar opens during the summer, extending the range to 22 beers. Inside, there are five distinct drinking areas including a snug and three-seat 'confessional', once used as a hideaway by the local vicar. Although busy, the pub retains a community feel, with a cosy atmosphere throughout. Substantial snacks are available.
Q♿♣🍏P🚌🐾

Star Inn

22 Middle Street, NG9 1FX
12-11 (midnight Thu-Sat) ☎ (0115) 854 5320
🌐 starbeeston.co.uk
House beer (by Totally Brewed); 9 changing beers Ⓗ
Former Shipstone's pub still with branded windows, restored beyond its former glory. The decor is tasteful and minimal with three separate rooms, complemented by a permanent marquee, sports/games room, spacious garden and patio outside. Visitors may recognise the bar, which featured in Boon and Auf Wiedersehen, Pet. Ten cask ales are on offer alongside a wide selection of whiskies, gins, rums and wines. Meals are served as well as a popular and extensive range of bar snacks. Families are welcome during the day.
♿♣🍏P🚌🐾

Victoria Hotel

85 Dovecote Lane, NG9 1JG
10.30-11 (midnight Fri & Sat); 12-11 Sun
☎ (0115) 925 4049 🌐 victoriabeeston.co.uk
Castle Rock Harvest Pale; Fuller's London Pride; 12 changing beers Ⓗ
Located alongside the platform of Beeston railway station, this restored Victorian masterpiece has mass appeal. Sixteen real ales are joined by real ciders and perries, an extensive whisky and wine list, and a renowned food menu. Taster trays of three third-pints are offered. Two distinct bars are complemented by a dining room and a covered, smoke-free seating area outside. VicFest is hosted

REAL ALE BREWERIES

Angel 🛢 Nottingham
Bang the Elephant Long Eaton
Beermats Winkburn
Beeston Hop Nottingham: Sneinton
Black Iris Nottingham: New Basford
Black Market 🛢 Warsop
Blue Monkey Giltbrook
Brewhouse & Kitchen 🛢 Nottingham
Castle Rock Nottingham
Cat Asylum Collingham
Dukeries 🛢 Worksop
FireRock Sutton-in-Ashfield (NEW)
Full Mash Stapleford
Good Stuff 🛢 Nottingham: Daybrook
Grafton Worksop
Handley's 🛢 Barnby in the Willows
Harby 🛢 Harby
Harrison's Retford (NEW)
Headstocks Boughton (NEW)
Idle 🛢 West Stockwith
Kings Clipstone Kings Clipstone
Lazy Bay Nottingham (NEW)
Lenton Lane Nottingham
Lincoln Green Hucknall
Linear Bingham
Liquid Light Nottingham (NEW)
Lord Randall's Newark (NEW)
Magpie Nottingham
Mallard Maythorne
Maypole Eakring
Milestone Cromwell
Navigation 🛢 Nottingham
Neon Raptor Nottingham
Newark Newark
Nottingham 🛢 Nottingham: Radford
Pheasantry East Markham
Prior's Well Mansfield Woodhouse
Reality Nottingham: Chilwell
Scribbler's Stapleford
Scruffy Dog 🛢 Sutton-In-Ashfield (NEW)
Shipstone's Nottingham: Old Basford
Springhead Laneham
Tom Herrick's Carlton on Trent
Totally Brewed Nottingham
Welbeck Abbey Welbeck

in July in addition to beer festivals throughout the year. NUS discounts are available Sunday to Thursday. Q❀◑♿⇌🍎P🚌🐾📶

Bingham

Horse & Plough 🏆 L

Long Acre, NG13 8AF

⏲ 11-11 (midnight Fri & Sat) ☎ (01949) 839313

Castle Rock Harvest Pale, Preservation Fine Ale; 7 changing beers Ⓗ

In the heart of a busy market town, this small pub is a former Methodist chapel with a traditional interior and flagstone floor. Up to nine cask ales and three ciders are available. A varied seasonal food menu is served in the bar and upstairs restaurant. Four times local CAMRA Pub of the Year, the pub always offers a wide range of styles and strengths of real ale and cider, showcasing smaller producers alongside established favourites.
◑♿⇌🍎🚌🐾📶

White Lion ✔

Nottingham Road, NG13 8AT

⏲ 10-11 ☎ (01949) 875541

House beer (by Theakston); 3 changing beers Ⓗ

Refurbished following a change of tenancy in August 2017, the White Lion has elements of a gastro-pub combined with features that make it a popular local. Four cask ales are regularly on tap, a mix of local ales in addition to well-known names from further afield. The pub screens televised sport and has a pool table in a covered area outside on the decking. ❀◑♿⇌♣P🚌

Blyth

Red Hart L

Bawtry Road, S81 8HG (opp church)

⏲ 12 (3 Mon)-11 ☎ (01909) 591221 🌐 redhart.co.uk

3 changing beers (sourced regionally) Ⓗ

An attractive village pub in the centre of Blyth with a lounge, traditional taproom – with a pool table, darts and sports TV – dining room and spacious seating area outside. The walls in the lounge are decorated with photographs and paintings from nearby locations. Food is served daily and it does three changing guest beers. The Red Hart is a previous winner of local CAMRA Pub of the Season.
Q❀🛏◑♿♣P🚌(25,29)🐾📶

Car Colston

Royal Oak ✔

The Green, NG13 8JE

⏲ 11.30-11 ☎ (01949) 20247 🌐 royaloakcarcolston.co.uk

4 changing beers Ⓗ

This country inn – a former hosiery factory – is on one of England's largest village greens. The pub has a cosy bar with comfortable seating and a real fire, a separate, generously sized restaurant and a function room. Four beers, all from the Marston's range but often less-heralded brews, are available in the bar. Food is served lunchtimes and evenings. There is a skittle alley to the rear, a beer garden and camping facilities. ❀◑♿⛺♣P🐾📶

Carlton in Lindrick

Grey Horses Inn L

The Cross, S81 9EW

⏲ 12-11 ☎ (01909) 730252

Welbeck Abbey Henrietta, Portland Black; house beer (by Welbeck Abbey); 3 changing beers (sourced regionally) Ⓗ

The Grey Horses is in the centre of the village within the conservation area, and has a front bar accessible from the street, a spacious lounge bar where excellent food is served and a large beer garden. The pub is the tap for Welbeck Abbey Brewery, serving three or four of its beers plus two or three guests. It hosts an annual beer festival, usually in June. A warm welcome is assured at this recent local CAMRA award-winning hostelry.
Q❀◑♿♣🍎P🚌(21,22)🐾📶

Cropwell Butler

Plough L ✔

Main Street, NG12 3AB

⏲ 12-3 (not Mon), 5-11; 12-midnight Fri & Sat; 12-10.30 Sun
☎ (0115) 933 3124 🌐 theplough-cropwellbutler.co.uk

Bradfield Farmers Blonde; 2 changing beers Ⓗ

Set in the heart of the village, this pub has a welcoming interior with real fires in both the bar and larger restaurant, and a spacious, picturesque beer garden. Three cask ales are available including one LocAle. A full lunchtime and evening food service is provided. Regular quiz nights take place, often combined with themed food menus.
❀◑♿♣P🚌(100)📶

East Leake

Round RobINN L

54 Main Street, LE12 6PG

⏲ closed Mon; 5-11 Tue-Thu; 4-11 Fri; 12-11 Sat & Sun
☎ (0115) 778 8168

6 changing beers (sourced locally) Ⓖ

Micropub opened in 2015, serving six local beers on gravity. The single room accommodates up to 45 patrons – seating is a mixture of chairs, cushioned benches and high stools. A small outdoor area to the front offers alfresco drinking. Light bar snacks are served. A range of ciders and continental bottled beers is available.
Q♿♣🍎🚌(1)🐾

East Markham

Queen's Hotel

High Street, NG22 0RE (turn left as you enter village from A57 and travel 200yds down road)

⏲ 12-11 ☎ (01777) 870288

Adnams Southwold Bitter; Everards Beacon Hill, Tiger; 2 changing beers (sourced regionally) Ⓗ

Situated on the main street, this cosy pub has a friendly atmosphere enhanced by an open fire in winter. A single bar with five handpumps serves the lounge and dining areas. Food ranges from hot and cold snacks to full home-cooked meals. There is a large garden area at the rear of the car park. The Queen's has received several local CAMRA awards. Q❀◑♿P🚌(36,37)🐾

Eastwood

Tap & Growler

209 Nottingham Road, Hill Top, NG16 3GS

⏲ 4-9 Mon-Wed; 12-11 Thu (11.30 Fri & Sat); 12-10 Sun
🌐 tapandgrowler.co.uk

8 changing beers (sourced locally) Ⓗ/Ⓖ

In a row of shops, this micropub sells a range of mostly local real ales, five on handpump and up to

NOTTINGHAMSHIRE

ENGLAND

five more on gravity. The pub gets its name from
the growler beer jug – when the building was
renovated a ceramic lion was found and he is now
proudly on display as 'The Growler'. A pub quiz is
held on Monday. Winner of local CAMRA LocAle
Pub of the Year in 2018. Q✿⑤&♣●🖵❀🛜

Hucknall

Byron's Rest 🅛
8 Baker Street, NG15 7AS
✿ 4-10; 2-10.30 Fri; 12-10.30 Sat; 12-10 Sun
**Titanic Plum Porter; 5 changing beers (often
Magpie)** 🅗
Formerly a sewing shop, converted into a micropub
and opened in 2017. The name is an allusion to the
local poet Lord Byron being buried in the nearby
Church of St Mary Magdalene. While narrow in
width, the bar extends considerably, creating the
illusion of separate drinking areas. A snug was
added in 2018 just off the entrance and a secret
garden created at the rear – a tranquil oasis in the
heart of Hucknall. Up to six real ales are served.
Q✿≢Ω●🖵❀

Station Hotel 🅛
Station Terrace, NG15 7TQ
✿ 12-11 (midnight Fri & Sat) ☎ (0115) 963 2588
⊕ thestationhotelhucknall.co.uk
**Lincoln Green Marion, Archer, Hood, Tuck; Wychwood
Hobgoblin; 15 changing beers** 🅗
An archetypal Victorian railway hostelry, originally
completed for GNR in 1893 and subsequently
owned by Nottingham's Home Brewery. Following
refurbishment in 2017, it is now the tap for Lincoln
Green Brewery. The walls feature much railway
memorabilia. Traditional pub games are played in a
separate room. Nineteen handpumps dispense a
range of cask beers both from Lincoln Green and
further afield, with one pump for real cider. B&B
accommodation is available. Local CAMRA Pub of
the Year in 2018.
✿❀🛏◐&≢Ω♣●P🖵(141)❀🛜

Kimberley

Cricketers Rest 🅛
4 Chapel Street, NG16 2NP
✿ 12-11.30 (12.30am Fri & Sat); 12-11 Sun
☎ (0115) 938 3105
**Castle Rock Harvest Pale; Sharp's Doom Bar; 4
changing beers (often Castle Rock)** 🅗
In Kimberley conservation area, this single-roomed
pub with a small snug is close to the centre of
town. Refurbished in 2016 after being sold by
Greene King, it is now operated by Castle Rock.
Handpumps dispense six cask ales, usually
including at least two Castle Rock beers. The range
of guest beers is mainly from local microbreweries.
Unsurprisingly, cricket memorabilia is much in
evidence. ✿❀●❀🛜

Roots Emporium
17 Nottingham Road, NG16 2NB
✿ closed Mon & Tue; 5-10 Wed; 4-11 Thu; 3-11 Fri; 12-11 Sat;
12-10.30 Sun ☎ 07864 572037 ⊕ rootsemporium.co.uk
6 changing beers 🅗
Converted from a furniture and gift shop, much of
this micropub's fixtures and fittings are made from
the stock of the former business. The open-plan
interior is small but reasonably spacious, with a
patio at the front extending the drinking area

further. Walls are adorned with interesting
memorabilia including items relating to the former
Kimberley Brewery. Beers are generally from
microbreweries, always including at least one local
brew. Q✿❀&♣●🖵❀

Kirkby-in-Ashfield

Dandy Cock Ale House ✔
184A Victoria Road, NG17 8AT
✿ closed Mon & Tue; 5-10 Wed & Thu; 2-10.30 Fri; 1-10.30
Sat; 1-9.30 Sun ☎ 07854 054060 ⊕ thedandycock.co.uk
**4 changing beers (sourced locally; often Dancing
Duck, Little Critters)** 🅗
CAMRA award-winning micropub offering four real
ales on handpull and up to six real ciders on tap. It
has two small rooms with views onto the cellar
behind the bar. A range of wines and spirits is
available including over 200 gins. Live acoustic
music nights are hosted. Dogs are always
welcome. There is on-street parking and a bus stop
directly outside the front door. Q✿⑤&●🖵❀

Lambley

Woodlark Inn 🅛
Church Street, NG4 4QB
✿ 12-11.30 (10.30 Sun) ☎ (0115) 931 2535
⊕ woodlarkinn.co.uk
**Theakston Best Bitter; Timothy Taylor Landlord; 3
changing beers (often Fish Key)** 🅗
The new home of the relocated Fish Key
microbrewery, this traditional pub dating back to
the 19th century is in the quaint-sounding Dumbles
area of the village. It has two rooms – a bare red-
brick bar with exposed beams and a lounge/
restaurant serving excellent home-cooked food. A
music-free environment enables customers and
staff to enjoy the art of conversation. The pub is
popular with both locals and visitors from afar.
Q✿❀◐♣●P🖵(46,47)❀🛜

Laneham

Bees Knees 🅛
Springhead Brewery, Robin Hood Site, Main Street,
DN22 0NA (centre of village)
✿ 4-midnight; 3-midnight Fri; 12-midnight Sat & Sun
☎ (01777) 228090 ⊕ springhead.co.uk
**Oakham Citra; Springhead Outlawed, Drop of the
Black Stuff, Roaring Meg; 5 changing beers** 🅗
A popular country pub with three small rooms
converted from a former shop on the Springhead
Fine Ales brewery site and well supported by
locals. It offers three or four Springhead beers
along with Oakham Citra and up to five rotating
guests. Over 100 gins are also available. Excellent
food is served (booking recommended). Quiz night
is Wednesday and live jazz plays on the first
Sunday of the month. There is an adequate outside
seating area. Q✿⑤◐&▲●P🖵❀🛜

Lound

Bluebell Inn
Town Street, DN22 8RN (on main road through village)
✿ 5-11; 12-11 Sat; 12-10.30 Sun ☎ (01777) 818457
⊕ bluebellinnretford.co.uk
**Abbeydale Moonshine; Lincolnshire Craft Beers
Lincoln Gold; Welbeck Abbey Harley** 🅗
A traditional village inn with a lounge bar where
food is served and a taproom with a pool table. The

pub is gaining a growing reputation for the quality of its food and its three beers which rotate on demand. There is a large car park and a fenced seating area outside. French boules is played in the summer on Wednesday and Sunday. Wednesday is quiz night. QP

Lower Bagthorpe

Dixies Arms

Church Lane Junction, NG16 5HF
12-11 (midnight Fri & Sat) (01773) 810505
dixiesarms.com
Greene King Abbot; Timothy Taylor Landlord; 1 changing beer (often Kelham Island) H
Vicky and Tony have run this pub since 2003, serving three real ales and usually a real cider. With a front terrace and garden with a playground for younger visitors, it is popular in the summer, and in winter two log fires add warmth to the cosy rooms. Live music plays every Saturday and occasional Sunday afternoons in winter. A true rustic inn with plenty of character. QP

Mansfield

Bold Forester

Botany Avenue, NG18 5NF
11-11 (midnight Fri); 10-midnight Sat; 10-11.30 Sun
(01623) 623970
Greene King IPA, Abbot; Hardys & Hansons Olde Trip; Morland Old Speckled Hen; 8 changing beers (often Little Critters, Pheasantry, Prior's Well) H
Hungry Horse-branded pub and restaurant offering up to 12 real ales, usually four from the Greene King range and up to eight guests. Food is served daily until 9pm. The spacious open-plan interior has large-screen TVs showing all major live sport. There is a covered smoking area outside with a TV. The enclosed beer garden is popular with families in the summer. Situated on the main road into Mansfield, it has a large car park and is well serviced by public transport.
P

Brown Cow

31 Ratcliffe Gate, NG18 2JA
12-11 (midnight Fri & Sat) (01623) 645854
browncow-mansfield.co.uk
Everards Tiger; 9 changing beers (often Silver Brewhouse) H
Owned by Everards and Silver Brewhouse (formerly Raw Brewery), a range of up to 12 real ales and ciders is offered alongside a selection of world bottled beers. There are two separate bar areas and a function room upstairs. Folk music features on a Tuesday night and a quiz on Wednesday. Regular beer festivals are hosted. The pub is a short walk from Mansfield town centre bus and railway stations and has ample car parking. Local CAMRA Pub of the Year in 2017. QP

Garrison

Leeming Street, NG18 1NA
closed Mon & Tue; 5-10 Wed; 12-11 Thu-Sat; 12-9 Sun
07702 253235
Moody Fox Cub, Pale Tale; 4 changing beers (often Falstaff, Sadler's, Theakston) H
This medium-sized bar is the brewery tap for the Moody Fox Brewing Co based nearby in Hilcote. It is inspired by TV show Peaky Blinders, with some beer names reflecting the theme. Six real ales and a range of ciders are available. Located in the pedestrianised area of Mansfield town centre, it is a five-minute walk from a public car park.
Q

Nell Gwyn

117 Sutton Road, NG18 5EX
5 (3.30 Mon)-midnight; 12-2am Fri & Sat; 12-midnight Sun
(01623) 659850
2 changing beers (often 3D Beers, Falstaff) H
Although located on a main road, this busy local pub is easy to miss. The Nell Gwyn describes itself as 'a little pub, not a club', and relaxing in front of the real fire here has the feel of being in a homely living room. A couple of real ales from a local brewer are usually available, with a customer loyalty scheme in operation. Traditional pub games can be played. There is very limited parking but buses stop directly outside and opposite.
QP

Railway Inn

9 Station Street, NG18 1EF
11-11 (01623) 623086
4 changing beers (often Dukeries, Kings Clipstone) H
A stone's throw from the railway and bus stations, this community pub serves home-cooked food and has two separate rooms for diners or those desiring a little privacy. Up to four real ales are available, at least one a local offering, and one or more real cider. A music night is held once a month. Outside there is a walled garden and smoking area. A former local CAMRA Pub of the Year.
Q

Widow Frost

41 Leeming Street, NG18 1NB
8am-midnight (1am Fri & Sat) (01623) 666790
Greene King Abbot; Ruddles Best Bitter; 4 changing beers H
A spacious open-plan pub not far from the town centre. It can get busy, especially at weekends, but families are welcome and there is usually a quiet corner to be found. The full range of Wetherspoon meals is served all day every day. Up to six real ales are available, plus real ciders, and Meet the Brewer events are held. Popular with visitors to the theatre just over the road. Q

Newark

Fox & Crown

4-6 Appletongate, NG24 1JY
10.30-11 (midnight Fri & Sat) (01636) 605820
Castle Rock Harvest Pale, Preservation Fine Ale, Elsie Mo, Screech Owl; 6 changing beers (sourced nationally) H
Popular, friendly, town-centre local with an open-plan layout featuring a central bar and three side rooms. The decor includes brewery pictures, posters, mirrors and old photos of Newark. It offers up to 10 real ales, four craft beers and over 100 bottled beers to drink in or take away (at a discount). Up to 20 traditional ciders and perries are also available on draught. Live music plays on Friday night. Local CAMRA Pub of the Year and Cider Pub of the Year 2019. Q(1,2)

Just Beer Micropub

32A Castle Gate, NG24 1BG (in Swan & Salmon Yard off Castle Gate)
1-11; 12-midnight Fri & Sat; 12-10 Sun (01636) 312047
justbeermicropub.biz

4 changing beers (sourced nationally) Ⓗ
Micropub concentrating on cask ales, cider and perries. Craft beers were added in 2019, and world and unusual UK craft ales are available from the fridge. Snacks include locally sourced pork pies, cheeseboards and pork scratchings. Traditional pub games are played, including an annual cribbage tournament. Three beer festivals are held each year. A repeat CAMRA award winner.
Q♿⛺⇌♣🍎🍺🚌🐾📶

Oscar's Inn

105 Balderton Gate, NG24 1RY
⏲ 12-11 (midnight Fri & Sat) ☎ (01636) 918130
🌐 oscarsinn.co.uk
Thornbridge Jaipur IPA; 5 changing beers (sourced nationally) Ⓗ
Refurbished two-roomed pub named after the owner's dog, situated a few minutes' walk from the town centre. The Oscar Wilde room is open at all times, displaying quotes from the great man, the Oscar Peterson room is open at busier times and for live music at the weekend. Six handpumps offer a great selection of local and national beers. A varied menu is available – pizza is a speciality in generous portions. 🔥❀◐◑🍎P🚌(3)🐾📶

Prince Rupert Ⓛ

46 Stodman Street, NG24 1AW
⏲ 11-11 (1am Fri & Sat); 12-11 Sun ☎ (01636) 918121
🌐 kneadpubs.co.uk
Brains Rev James; Oakham JHB; 6 changing beers (sourced nationally) Ⓗ
Reopened in 2010, this historic pub dates back to 1452. Multi-roomed on two separate levels, exposed beams are evident and various interesting artefacts and brewery memorabilia decorate the walls and ceilings. The Nelson room has an open fire. An extensive lunchtime and evening food menu featuring fresh local produce is available, with stone-baked pizzas a speciality. A former local CAMRA Pub of the Year, it has featured in the Guide for nine consecutive years. Q🔥❀◐◑⇌🍎🚌🐾📶

Newstead

Pit

Tilford Road, NG15 0BU
⏲ closed Mon; 7-10 Tue; 4-10 Wed & Thu; 12-10 Fri; 11.30-10 Sat & Sun ☎ 07794 875884 🌐 thepitmicropub.co.uk
4 changing beers (often Magpie, Milestone, Old Sawley) Ⓗ
The only pub in the village, this micropub is housed in the cricket pavilion. Situated right next to the pitch, you can watch football or cricket depending on the season most weekends. Live music plays on Friday, quiz night is Sunday. Four real ales are on handpull and a regular beer festival is held in March. Dogs are welcome and the pub is a popular stop-off for walkers. The train station is next door.
Q❀♿⇌♣P🍺🚌(3A)🐾

Normanton on the Wolds

Plough Inn Ⓛ

Old Melton Road, NG12 5NN (off A606 Melton Rd)
⏲ 11-11 (midnight Fri & Sat); 12-11 Sun ☎ (0115) 937 2401
🌐 theploughatnormanton.co.uk
Black Sheep Best Bitter; Bombardier; Castle Rock Harvest Pale; Timothy Taylor Landlord; 1 changing beer Ⓗ
Traditional country pub in an ivy-clad brick building, situated on the main street of this well-heeled sleepy village. Inside, to the right is a comfortable lounge bar area with a real fire, and to the left is a smaller bar linked to the restaurant through an archway. Outside, the huge garden hosts many events in the summer including a beer festival.
Q🔥❀◐◑♣P🚌🐾📶

Nottingham: Central

BeerHeadZ

Cabman's Shelter, 1A Queens Road, NG2 3AS
(adjoining Nottingham Station)
⏲ 12-10 (11 Fri & Sat) ☎ 07914 136055 🌐 beerheadz.biz
4 changing beers Ⓗ
Small but sympathetically restored Edwardian cabman's shelter, adjacent to the main railway station entrance. It is run by BeerHeadZ, who operate similar outlets across the East Midlands. The single room has a central bar and retains period features including bench chests, wooden panelling, windows and coat hooks. Beer barrels with wooden tops act as seats. The four real ales change regularly, and are seldom repeated. A large choice of bottles and cans is also available to enjoy in or take out. Q❀⇌🚊♣🍎🍺🚌🐾

Crafty Crow Ⓛ

102 Friar Lane, NG1 6EB
⏲ 12-11; 11-midnight Fri & Sat; 11-10 Sun
☎ (0115) 837 1992 🌐 craftycrownotts.co.uk
8 changing beers (often Magpie) Ⓗ
Magpie Brewery's first pub, with eight handpulls serving microbrewery beers and a further two offering real ciders. Maintaining a green ethos throughout, the majority of fittings are recycled or home-made – the sinks are made from beer casks with ex-keg fonts as taps. Snacks and light meals are served until 9pm, made from locally sourced produce. Situated on two levels, the side entrance leads directly to all facilities. Corvid birds feature strongly. 🔥◐◑♿⇌🚊🍎🚌🐾📶

Fox & Grapes Ⓛ

21 Southwell Road, NG1 1DL
⏲ 12-11 (midnight Fri & Sat) ☎ (0115) 841 8970
Castle Rock Harvest Pale, Preservation Fine Ale, Elsie Mo; 5 changing beers Ⓗ
An impressive renovation of an Edwardian-fronted Victorian pub by Castle Rock Brewery. Sadly the fancy Edwardian window frames were lost in an earlier refit. The former two-room layout has been opened up into a single L-shaped room with raised areas on either side of the front door. A high ceiling and large windows give a light, airy feel. Expect to find eight real ales, ciders, eight keg beers, locally produced coffee, gin and artisan food.
🔥❀◐◑♿🚊🍎🚌🐾📶

Kean's Head Ⓛ

46 St Mary's Gate, Lace Market, NG1 1QA
⏲ 11-11 (midnight Fri & Sat); 12-10.30 Sun
☎ (0115) 947 4052
Castle Rock Harvest Pale; 5 changing beers Ⓗ
Owned by Castle Rock, this cosy one-room pub is opposite the imposing medieval St Mary's Church in Nottingham's historic Lace Market district. Named after the 19th-century actor Edmund Kean, it is popular with a diverse clientele and serves inventive, freshly prepared food from a varied English and European menu. The guest beers always provide a broad choice of styles. There is

also a wide selection of craft beers, along with three handpumps dispensing real cider.

King William IV

6 Eyre Street, Sneinton, NG2 4PB

2-11 Mon; 12-11 Tue & Wed (11.30 Thu); 11-midnight Fri & Sat (0115) 958 9864

Oakham Citra, Bishops Farewell; house beer (by Black Iris); 6 changing beers

Known widely as the King Billy, this Victorian gem on the edge of the city centre is close to the Motorpoint Arena. A family-run free house that oozes charm and character, it is a haven for real ale drinkers, with a choice of up to eight microbrewery ales from near and far, as well as real cider. Folk music is popular on Thursday night. A selection of rolls is always available. Take a look at the award-winning pub sign. Q (43,44)

Lincolnshire Poacher

161-163 Mansfield Road, NG1 3FR

11-11 (midnight Thu & Fri); 10.30-midnight Sat; 12-11 Sun (0115) 941 1584

Castle Rock Harvest Pale, Sherwood Reserve, Elsie Mo, Screech Owl; Fuller's 1845; 8 changing beers

Thirteen handpumps offer a wide selection of guest ales. A mild, stout or porter is always available alongside real ciders and perries, continental bottled beers and a good selection of whiskies. The food menu features locally sourced ingredients. Walls display artwork celebrating the pub's twinning with In de Wildeman bar in Amsterdam, and various memorabilia of local and international interest. Live music plays on Sunday and Wednesday. Q

Newshouse

123 Canal Street, NG1 7HB

12-11 (0115) 952 3061

Castle Rock Harvest Pale; Totally Brewed Slap in the Face; 3 changing beers (sourced locally)

In times past, newspapers would be read out here to inform the illiterate of elections at home and military victories overseas, hence the name. The walls are covered with framed front pages of local newspapers showing headlines going back over many years. The public bar has a large TV screen, dartboard, bar billiards and table skittles. The lounge has more comfortable seating. Light lunches are served and snacks at all times. Beers from the local Totally Brewed Brewery should be available.

Organ Grinder

21 Alfreton Road, Canning Circus, NG7 3JE

12-11 (11.30 Thu; midnight Fri & Sat) (0115) 970 0630

Blue Monkey BG Sips, Infinity, Guerrilla; 6 changing beers (sourced regionally)

Previously the Red Lion, this inn was bought and refurbished by Blue Monkey Brewery. The single-roomed, multi-level pub boasts a wood-burning fire. To the rear is a small courtyard leading to a raised decked area and the first floor function room (where a TV is in occasional use). The full Blue Monkey range of beers is offered, as well as a guest and three real ciders or perries. No meals, but bar snacks such as Scotch eggs and pork pies are sold.

OverDraught

11-15 Alfreton Road, Canning Circus, NG7 3JE

3-11 Mon-Wed; 12-11 Thu & Sun; 12-11.30 Fri & Sat

7 changing beers (often Totally Brewed)

Opened in February 2018, the OverDraught is a former bank in a curving mid-20th century building. The bar frontage is adorned with 2p pieces, commemorating the building's former use. High ceilings and large windows with views of the busy Canning Circus junctions give the interior an airy feel, overlooked by a balcony room. The brewery tap for Totally Brewed, seven handpumps and 14 craft taps supply the beer. Snacks such as olives, cheeses and bread are available.

Vat & Fiddle

Queens Bridge Road, NG2 1NB

11-11 (midnight Fri & Sat) (0115) 985 0611

Castle Rock Sheriff's Tipple, Black Gold, Harvest Pale, Preservation Fine Ale, Elsie Mo, Screech Owl; 7 changing beers

The tap for the adjoining Castle Rock Brewery, this 1937 Art Deco gem two minutes from Nottingham rail station has 13 handpumps which serve at least seven from the Castle Rock range. There are also guest beers from near and far, as well as a range of real ciders. Tasting trays of six third-pints are available. Hot food is served all week. The outside area to the rear features an impressive mural depicting Nottingham events.

Nottingham: East

Bread & Bitter

153-155 Woodthorpe Drive, Mapperley, NG3 5JL

10-11.30 Mon (11 Tue & Wed; midnight Thu-Sat); 11-11 Sun (0115) 960 7541

Castle Rock Black Gold, Harvest Pale, Preservation Fine Ale, Elsie Mo, Screech Owl; Fuller's London Pride; 5 changing beers

Castle Rock pub converted in 2007 from the premises of an old bakery on Mapperley Top. The original baker's oven fronts are still embedded in an inside wall, giving the place a warm and welcoming feel. The pub started a revival of real ale outlets in Mapperley. Twelve handpumps serve Castle Rock beers, a mild, rotating guests and cider alongside an extensive foreign bottled beer list. Food is all home cooked and varies frequently – look for the specials board. Q

Old Volunteer

35 Burton Road, Carlton, NG4 3DQ

12-11 (midnight Fri & Sat) (0115) 987 2299

10 changing beers (often Flipside)

Refurbished by Flipside Brewing in 2014, the pub showcases five of the brewery's beers alongside several guests and a real cider. The interior is separated into distinct areas using wooden dividing beams and different types of flooring. Outside is a decked patio area with parasols. Food choices include speciality burgers, and snacks are always available. Beer festivals are held in a marquee in the car park. P

Willowbrook

13 Main Road, Gedling, NG4 3HQ

10-11 (midnight Fri); 9am-midnight Sat; 9am-11 Sun (0115) 987 8596

Castle Rock Harvest Pale, Preservation Fine Ale, Elsie Mo; Morland Old Speckled Hen; house beer (by Castle Rock); 4 changing beers

Formerly a club, this pub was refurbished in late 2013, and again in 2015 following to a fire. The 14 handpumps frequently offer a mild, stout or porter, as well as a selection of three real ciders or perries. A small side room and entrance lounge lead to the bar, which opens to a rear room, while patio doors lead to a paved, secluded, no-smoking outdoor area. A good food menu is complemented by daily specials.

Nottingham: North

Doctor's Orders

351 Mansfield Road, Carrington, NG5 2DA
12 (4 Mon-Wed)-10.30 (0115) 960 7985
doctorsordersmicropub.co.uk
5 changing beers (sourced locally)
Compact beer emporium with two distinct areas, refurbished in 2015. A small square lounge leads to a corridor flanked on one side by a narrow raised seating area with benches, with a small bar and serving area at the rear. Beer and cider are served at your table from handpumps at the rear of the pub. While now owned by Magpie Brewery, the pub continues with its original ethos of providing a range of microbrewery beers in an intimate atmosphere. Q

Nottingham: South

Embankment

282-284 Arkwright Street, The Meadows, NG2 2GR
11-11 (midnight Fri); 10-midnight Sat; 10-11 Sun
(0115) 986 4502
Castle Rock Harvest Pale, Elsie Mo; Fuller's London Pride; 6 changing beers (often Castle Rock)
Originally one of the largest shops belonging to Boots the Chemist, where Jesse Boot had his office, this was home to the Boots Members' Social Club. The white mock-Tudor building has been restored, retaining the original oak-panelled walls and stained-glass leaded windows. It is near Trent Bridge, close to three of Nottingham's well-known sports venues. A large range of real ales and ciders is available, both from the Castle Rock range and guest microbreweries, as well as a selection of craft beers. Q P

Nottingham: West

Plough Inn

17 St Peter's Street, Radford, NG7 3EN
12-11 (midnight Wed & Thu); 12-10.30 Sun
07972 094425
Nottingham Rock Ale Bitter Beer, Rock Ale Mild Beer, Legend, Extra Pale Ale; 4 changing beers
This is the brewery tap for the adjoining Nottingham Brewery. The present building dates from 1932 and the two-roomed establishment with its central servery is largely unchanged from that date. It offers the full range of the brewery's beers alongside guests and a couple of ciders. This popular local boasts two log-burning stoves and an outside skittle alley. The regular quiz night is well attended. Winner of local CAMRA Mild Trail Best Pint, four years running. Q P

Oxton

Old Green Dragon

Blind Lane, NG25 0SS
5-10 Mon (11 Tue-Thu); 4-11 Fri; 12-11 Sat; 12-10 Sun
(0115) 965 2243
6 changing beers
A tasteful refurbishment of the pub took place in 2013, creating a traditional village pub alongside a contemporary dining venue. It offers an ever-changing selection of six real ales from both local and national breweries as well as at least two real ciders. Outside is a patio area and an enclosed garden at the rear. The pub has three electric car-charging points. P

Radcliffe on Trent

Yard of Ale

1 Walkers Yard, NG12 2FF (off Main Rd, between Costa and public car park)
5-11 Wed-Sat; closed Sun, Mon & Tue (0115) 933 4888
yard-of-ale.business.site
6 changing beers
This small, friendly micropub opened in 2016 in a former café and chocolate shop in the centre of the village. The premises are narrow, with access from the side. Up to seven different guest ales always include at least one local brew and a dark ale. The pub has a separate gin bar known as Gin Within.
Q P

Retford

BeerHeadZ

3 Town Hall Yard, DN22 6DU (off Market Square, through arch to rear of 10 Green Bottles)
1-11; 12-1am Fri & Sat; 12-10 Sun (01777) 949631
beerheadz.biz
5 changing beers (sourced regionally)
A small, friendly pub serving five rotating guest beers, three ciders and a range of over 100 bottled beers. The beers, often one-offs from near or far, are always in excellent condition and served in oversized glasses so you can be sure of a full pint. There are also a limited number of wines and spirits. BeerHeadZ has won several CAMRA awards including Nottinghamshire Pub of the Year.
Q

Brew Shed

104-106 Carolgate, DN22 6AS (on Carolgate bridge opp Masonic Hall)
4-11 Mon-Wed; 2-11 Thu; 12-11 Fri-Sun
Harrison's Vacant Gesture, Best Bitter, Coconut Shy PA, Stout; 4 changing beers (sourced regionally)
The Brew Shed is the tap for Harrison's Brewery. It has an open-plan room at street level and a smaller downstairs room leading onto the large canal-side patio. Four Harrison's beers and four rotating guests, a variety of kegs, real cider and a good selection of gins, spirits and wines are on offer. Local CAMRA Pub of the Year 2019.
Q P

Idle Valley Tap

Carolgate, DN22 6EF
12-10.30 (11 Fri & Sat) (01777) 948586
4 changing beers (sourced regionally)
Originally the tap for Idle Valley, following the brewery's closure beers are now from elsewhere. There is usually a choice of four rotating guest ales, maybe up to seven, along with gins, wines and spirits. The one-room pub has a pool table and dartboard away from the bar. The outside space has been put to good use, with plenty of seating attracting large numbers in fine weather.
P

Ship Inn

Wharf Road, DN22 6EN (opp Little Theatre near Asda)
11-11; 10-1am Fri & Sat ☎ (01777) 704412
theshipinnretford.com
Batemans XB, Gold, Salem Porter, XXXB; 3 changing beers (sourced nationally) H
The pub has reverted to its original name, and has undergone an extensive upgrade. There are two rooms – the main one is on different levels and has space for drinking and playing pool, the other is the dining area. A large covered seating area outside has TVs and a stage for bands. Four Batemans beers and three guests are available. Q

Southwell

Final Whistle

Station Road, NG25 0ET
12-11.30 (11 Sun) ☎ (01636) 814953
Everards Tiger; house beer (by Salopian); 8 changing beers (sourced nationally; often Oakham) H
Located at the end of the Southwell Trail, a disused railway line, this comfortable multi-roomed pub has a railway theme and is teeming with memorabilia. The courtyard garden has been laid out like a mock station and has a separate bar and function room called The Locomotion. The main bar has 10 handpumps which always offer Bass and a stout or porter. Quiz nights are Sunday and Tuesday, folk club is on a Thursday. Various quality bar snacks are available.
QP (28,100)

Old Coach House

69 Easthorpe, NG25 0HY
12 (5 Mon & Tue)-11; 12-midnight Fri & Sat
☎ (01636) 813289
Fuller's London Pride; Sharp's Doom Bar; house beer (by Oakham); 3 changing beers (sourced regionally; often Newby Wyke, Pheasantry, Timothy Taylor) H
Traditional open-plan pub with five different drinking areas, oak beams and a large range fire. Five changing real ales are on handpump from all over the country. An open mic session is held on the last Sunday of the month, a New Orleans pianist plays on the first Sunday, and live bands also play monthly on a Saturday. Outside to the rear is a well-kept patio garden.
Q

Stapleford

Horse & Jockey

20 Nottingham Road, NG9 8AA
12-11 (midnight Fri & Sat) ☎ (0115) 875 9655
horseandjockeystapleford.co.uk
Full Mash Horse & Jockey; 13 changing beers H
A good mix of locals and travellers from afar frequent the Jockey, attracted by the offering of 13 cask ales, of which five are usually LocAle, alongside a choice of six ciders. There are two rooms on split levels, the higher level serving as a function room when required. A mainly quiet pub, the screen only shows major sporting events. Food is limited to filled rolls, pork pies and sausage rolls.
QP

Sutton-in-Ashfield

Duke of Sussex

Alfreton Road, NG17 1JN
12-11 ☎ (01623) 511469 duke-of-sussex.co.uk
Pentrich Soma; 5 changing beers (often Oakham, Pentrich, Welbeck Abbey) H
Large open-plan pub with up to six real ales. Owned by Pub People Company of South Normanton, who have links with Pentrich Brewing Co, its beers feature regularly. Sunday dinner and Thursday steak club are always popular. A jazz night is held on the first Thursday of the month and a quiz every Sunday. Most popular pub on CAMRA's Winter Ale Trail in 2019. QP (9.1)

Picture House

Forest Street, NG17 1DA
8am-midnight (12.30am Sat & Sun) ☎ (01623) 554627
Greene King Abbot; Ruddles Best Bitter; 6 changing beers H
A popular Wetherspoon pub near the bus station, open plan and Art Deco in style with a high ceiling. Originally built as the King's Cinema in 1932, it closed and reopened in 1967 as the Star Bingo and Social Club. The bingo hall survived into the 1990s, until becoming the Picture House Night Club. Sky Sports and BT Sports are shown on several TVs behind the bar, but the main feature is a huge screen projected onto the wall above the front door.

Scruffy Dog

Station Road, NG17 5HF
closed Mon & Tue; 4-11 Wed-Fri; 12-11 Sat; 12-10.30 Sun
☎ (01623) 550826 thescruffydog.co.uk
8 changing beers (often Abbeydale, Beartown, Thornbridge) H
Comfy sofas and a real fire on colder days welcome visitors to this dog-friendly pub. Superbly refurbished by the current owners, it has a small L-shaped bar and a large open-plan bar area, and its own small on-site brewery. Eight beers are usually available, with rotating beers from Scruffy Dog Brewery alongside the likes of Abbeydale and Thornbridge. The pub is closed on Monday and Tuesday except bank holidays. Local CAMRA Pub of the Year 2019. QP

Underwood

Ginger Giraffe Micropub & Gin Bar

14 Alfreton Road, NG16 5GB
4-10; 12-11 Fri-Sun ☎ (01773) 533090
gingergiraffebar.co.uk
5 changing beers (often Castle Rock, Thornbridge, Titanic) H
This micropub has five beers, six ciders, plus a range of spirits and gins. Located in an old factory unit, it has undergone a stylish makeover. It has a main bar and separate games room with a pool table and sports TV. Dogs and children are welcome. Regular live acts play here – check the website for details. QP

Upton

Cross Keys

43 Main Street, NG23 5SY
closed Mon; 5-11 Tue; 12-3, 5-11 Wed & Thu; 12-11 Fri-Sun
☎ (01636) 813269
Mallard Duck 'n' Dive; 2 changing beers (sourced regionally) H
Popular and busy split-level pub dating from the 16th century. It is the tap for Mallard Brewery located in Maythorne near Southwell. Two Mallard beers are usually available alongside two changing

guests. Excellent food is prepared by a French chef, served Wednesday to Saturday lunchtimes and evenings and Sunday lunchtime. Fish is a particular speciality. Locals enjoy the book club, dominoes and darts. The National Trust-owned Southwell Workhouse is within two miles.
Q P (28,29)

Wellow

Olde Red Lion

Eakring Road, NG22 0EG
12-11 (10.30 Sun) (01623) 861000 wellow.me/lion.htm
Bombardier; house beer (by Maypole); 2 changing beers (sourced locally) H
This 400-year-old village pub is situated on the village green with its maypole, and participates in a large event on May Day. The traditional wood-beamed interior includes a restaurant, lounge and bar areas, with photographs and maps depicting the history of the village on the walls. Good food is available to complement the Bombardier, Olde Lion Ale and two rotating guests, usually LocAle. An annual beer festival is hosted. Close to Rufford Park, Sherwood Forest and Clumber Park.
Q P

West Bridgford

Poppy & Pint

Pierrepont Road, NG2 5DX
9.30am-11; 10-11 Sun (0115) 981 9995
Castle Rock Sheriff's Tipple, Harvest Pale, Preservation Fine Ale, Screech Owl; 8 changing beers H
Former British Legion Club converted in 2011 to become a Castle Rock pub. It has a large main bar with a raised area and a family space with a café bar (children welcome until 9pm). A large upstairs function room features a folk club and the beer garden overlooks a bowling green. Twelve handpumps dispense Castle Rock beers plus guests, often from new breweries. There are usually two real ciders and excellent food. P

Stratford Haven

2 Stratford Road, NG2 6BA
11-11 (midnight Thu & Fri); 10-midnight Sat; 10-11 Sun (0115) 982 5981
Adnams Broadside; Batemans XB; Castle Rock Harvest Pale, Elsie Mo, Screech Owl; Everards Tiger; 6 changing beers H
A former pet shop, The Strat has a single central bar with extended seating at the back and a secluded snug to the right. Up to 12 cask ales plus a cider are available on handpump at any one time, including at least six from owner Castle Rock's portfolio. Guest ales are predominantly from microbreweries near and far. Themed food nights feature Monday to Thursday. Sunday is silent quiz night and 'new brew day' the first Thursday of the month.
Q

Worksop

Fuggle's Chapter One

20 Park Street, S80 1HB
closed Mon-Wed; 12 (4 Thu)-11 07813 763347
Fuggle Bunny Chapter 5 Oh Crumbs, Chapter 2 Cotton Tail, Chapter 8 Jammy Dodger, Chapter 1 New Beginnings, Chapter 4 24 Carrot H
Opened in 2017 following a modern refurbishment, this L-shaped single-roomed little alehouse is now firmly established, attracting a cosmopolitan clientele. It serves quality real ales alongside specialised gins, spirits and wine. The real ales rotate but are all from the award-winning Fuggle Bunny Brew House at Halfway near Sheffield. Q

Mallard

Station Approach, S81 7AG (on station platform; entrance from main car park)
4.30-11; 11.30-11 Fri; 11-11 Sat; 12-10.30 Sun
07973 521824
4 changing beers H
Formerly the station buffet, this small, cosy pub offers a warm welcome. Four changing real ales are available – usually a dark beer, one from Double Top Brewery and two guests – plus two ciders, a selection of foreign bottled beers, country fruit wines and specialist gins. There is a room downstairs used on special occasions. Four beer festivals are held each year. The recipient of many local CAMRA awards. Q P

Shireoaks Inn

Westgate, S80 1LT
11.30-11.30; 12-11 Sun (01909) 472118
shireoaksinn.co.uk
3 changing beers (sourced regionally) H
Warm, friendly pub converted from cottages, run by the family who own the Station Hotel. The public bar houses a pool table and large-screen TV, and the comfortable lounge bar has a separate dining area. Home-cooked food is good value for money. Three handpulls dispense regularly changing guest ales. For the summer there is a small outside area with tables. P

Station Hotel

Carlton Road, S80 1PS (opp railway station car park entrance)
3-11; 11.30-11 Sat; 12-11 Sun (01909) 474108
thestationhotelworksop.co.uk
5 changing beers (sourced regionally) H
Situated opposite Worksop railway station on the edge of the town centre, there is always a welcome in this pub. Four or five regularly changing real ales are available, with a discount scheme for regulars. The long bar serves a lounge drinking area with a separate dining room attached, and there is a further small room suitable for meetings. A spacious and well-maintained garden with seating is to the rear. Food is served lunchtimes and evenings and accommodation is offered. Q P (5)

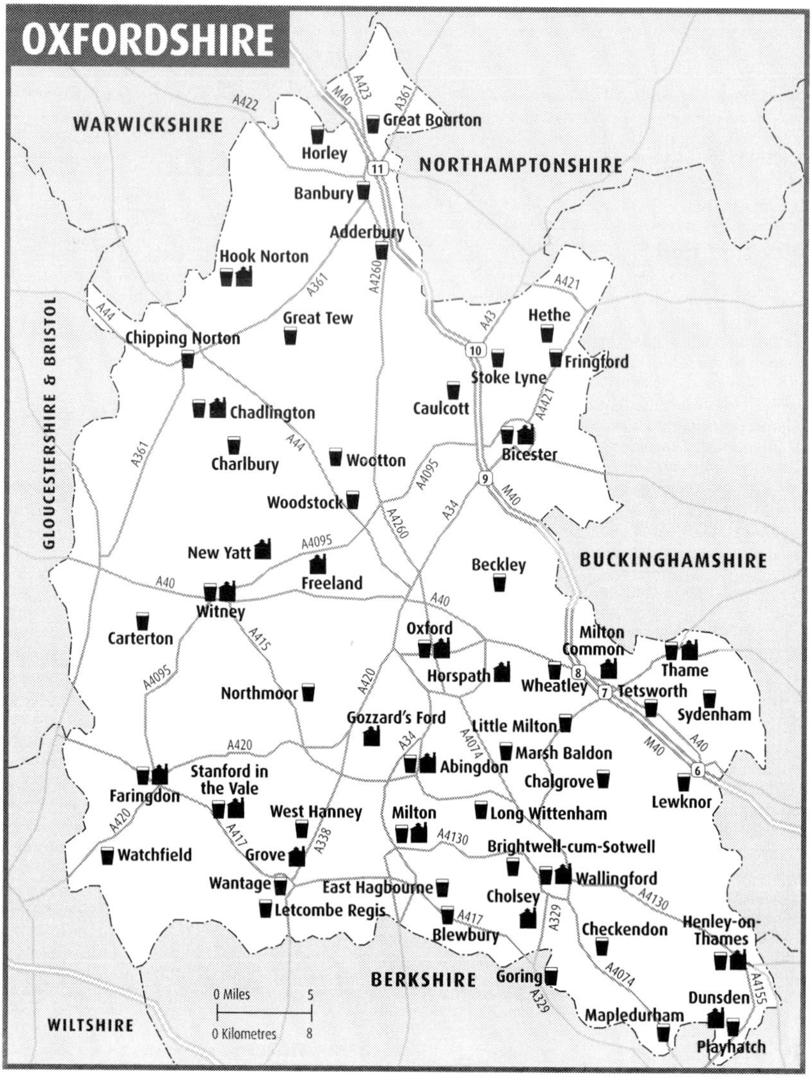

Abingdon

Brewery Tap

40-42 Ock Street, OX14 5BZ

11-11.30 (1am Fri & Sat); 12-11 Sun ☎ (01235) 521655

thebrewerytap.net

Loose Cannon Abingdon Bridge; 5 changing beers (sourced locally; often West Berkshire, XT)

Morland created a tap for its brewery in 1993 from three Grade II-listed town houses. The brewery is no more but the pub, run by the same family since it opened, has thrived. It offers a diverse range of six real ales all sourced from local breweries, and hosts three beer festivals each year with beers from further afield. The pub has three rooms, two of them away from the bar, and a courtyard outside. Food is available daily and includes theme nights. Quiz night is Tuesday. Local CAMRA Town and Village Pub of the Year 2019.

Broad Face

30-32 Bridge Street, OX14 3HR

11.30-midnight (1am Thu-Sat) ☎ (01235) 538612

broadfaceabingdon.co.uk

West Berkshire Good Old Boy; house beer (by Belhaven); 5 changing beers (sourced nationally; often Loddon, Loose Cannon, Morland)

Deceptively large, two-roomed, Grade II-listed pub near the river with a small outside seating area on Thames Street. The building was erected in 1840 but there are records of a pub on the site as far back as 1734. Following several recent changes of management it now has an emphasis on real ale. The interior is nicely decorated, bright and welcoming. Mystery surrounds the stories behind the unique pub name, which are written on the outside wall, but omit the most likely explanation – that it was previously called the Saracen's Head and the sign was over-painted.

Nag's Head on the Thames 🅛 ✅

The Bridge, OX14 3HX

🔵 11-11 (midnight Fri & Sat); 12-10 Sun ☎ (01235) 524516
🌐 thenagsheadonthethames.co.uk

Adnams Ghost Ship; Loddon Ferryman's Gold; White Horse Black Beauty; house beer (by Caledonian); 3 changing beers (sourced regionally) 🅷

Set on an island in the Thames, this Grade II-listed pub is split over two levels, with a large garden area next to the river and lovely views of the countryside and the town's historic buildings. A free house, it offers seven regularly changing beers, always including something local. Live music plays at weekends and some weekdays. Salter's Steamer cruises from Oxford stop nearby in summer. A three-times local CAMRA branch Town and Village Pub of the Year. ➰🏵️🍴🕭🛆🐾P🚪🐾🛜

Narrows 🅛 ✅

25 High Street, OX14 5AA

🔵 8am-midnight (1am Thu-Sat) ☎ (01235) 467680

Greene King Abbot; Ruddles Best Bitter; Sharp's Doom Bar; 4 changing beers (sourced nationally) 🅷

Wetherspoon converted the former post office in 2013. The pub is named after this part of the High Street which during the 19th century was called The Narrow. The area at the front of the pub has a long bar with 10 handpumps offering an impressive range of real ales, some from local breweries. To the rear, the former sorting office and telephone exchange provides more space for drinkers and diners. Abingdon's was the last manual telephone exchange in England when it closed in 1975. ➰🏵️🍴🛆🚪🛜

Adderbury

Bell Inn 🅛 ✅

High Street, OX17 3LS (off A4260 in centre of village)

🔵 12-3, 6-11; 12-midnight Fri & Sat; 12-10.30 Sun
☎ (01295) 810338 🌐 thebelladderbury.co.uk

Hook Norton Hooky, Hooky Gold, Old Hooky; house beer (by Hook Norton); 2 changing beers (sourced locally; often Hook Norton) 🅷

Back to its community-oriented best under the current stewardship, this gem at the heart of the village was justly awarded Hook Norton Brewery Pub of the Year in 2017, and six handpumps dispense ales from their portfolio. The spiritual home of the three village morris teams, it has a morris room with murals. A folk music session is held on Monday. The locally sourced bar menu and two bedrooms make it an ideal base for exploring the surrounding area. Q➰🏵️🛌🍴🕭🛆🅰️♣️🐾🚪(S4)🐾🛜

Banbury

Bailiff's Tap

4 Southam Road, OX16 2ED

🔵 closed Mon; 12-10 (8 Tue & Wed); 12-4 Sun

4 changing beers (sourced locally) 🅖

Banbury's first micropub opened in 2017. It is based in a former bailiff's office and serves a variety of beers, mostly from independent breweries, usually also with three ciders. In its first year it offered 232 different beers, all served direct from barrels on stillages in the bar. A traditional snack selection includes pork pies and crisps. The lively front bar buzzes with conversation. Q♣️🐾🚪🐾

Exchange 🅛 ✅

49-50 High Street, OX16 5LA

🔵 8am-midnight (1am Fri & Sat) ☎ (01295) 259035

Greene King Abbot; Ruddles Best Bitter; Sharp's Doom Bar; 9 changing beers (sourced nationally) 🅷

Now the only Wetherspoon bar in Banbury, the Exchange occupies an imposing split-level site in the former main post office and telephone exchange close to Banbury Cross. The walls abound with old photos and pictures of the building and surrounding area. It follows the usual Wetherspoon formula with several banks of handpumps offering a changing range of beers, normally including at least one local ale, in addition to the two regulars, real cider and a good-value food offering. ➰🕭🛆🍴🐾🚪🛜

Olde Reinedeer Inn ✅

47 Parsons Street, OX16 5NA

🔵 11-11 (midnight Fri & Sat); 12-10.30 Sun
☎ (01295) 270972 🌐 ye-olde-reinedeer-inn-banbury.co.uk

Hook Norton Hooky Mild, Hooky, Hooky Gold, Old Hooky; 3 changing beers (sourced locally; often Hook Norton) 🅷

Traditional pub which first became an inn in 1570, featuring original wood panelling dating from the Civil War. It is reported to be the location where Cromwell's men met to plan the Battle of Edgehill and siege of Banbury Castle. Identified by CAMRA as having a historic interior of regional importance, it features many items of interest including a large selection of pub jugs and other brewery artefacts. Good-value food is served; see the blackboard for details. Outside seating is available. Q🏵️🕭🍴♣️🐾P🚪🐾

White Horse 🅛

50-52 North Bar Street, OX16 0TH

🔵 2-10 Mon; 12-11 Tue-Thu; 12-midnight Fri & Sat; 12-10 Sun
☎ (01295) 277484 🌐 whitehorsebanbury.com

Everards Tiger; Turpin Golden Citrus; 8 changing beers (sourced nationally; often Titanic) 🅷

A warm and welcoming alehouse in an imposing building in the heart of Banbury. The White Horse serves an extensive range of up to 10 ales and a couple of ciders from its large L-shaped bar. A

REAL ALE BREWERIES

Amwell Springs Cholsey
Barn Owl Gozzard's Ford
Bell Street 🍺 Henley-on-Thames
Bellinger's Grove
Bicester 🍺 Bicester
Brakspear Witney
Brewery58 Wallingford (NEW)
Chadlington Chadlington
Church Hanbrewery New Yatt
Faringdon 🍺 Faringdon
Hook Norton Hook Norton
Little Ox Freeland
Loddon Dunsden
Loose Cannon Abingdon
LoveBeer Milton
Oxbrew Freeland
Philsters Milton Common
Shotover Horspath
Tap Social Movement Oxford
Thame 🍺 Thame
Turpin Hook Norton
White Horse Stanford in the Vale
Wychwood Witney

selection of home-made dishes, based on locally sourced ingredients, is freshly cooked to order. Alfresco drinking and dining can be enjoyed in the courtyard area to the rear. Regular events such as live music on Friday and a monthly pub quiz are organised. Q🔥❀◐◑♿⇌♣🍎🚌🐾📶

Beckley

Abingdon Arms 🄻

High Street, OX3 9UU
✪ closed Mon; 12-11; 12-9 Sun ☎ (01865) 655667
🌐 theabingdonarms.co.uk
Shotover Prospect; XT Four; 2 changing beers (sourced regionally; often Loddon, Vale) 🄷
A lovely old pub with a fine garden affording great views across Otmoor. It has a small bar and separate dining area. The arms in question are of James Bertie (1653-1699) who was created 1st Earl of Abingdon in 1682. The Bertie family owned the village until 1919 when it was broken up and sold off in lots. The pub was put up for sale in 2016 and bought by a local group after a community share offer. Q🔥❀◐◑♣P🐾📶

Bicester

Bell ✔

84 Sheep Street, OX26 6LP
✪ 12-11 (midnight Thu; 1am Fri & Sat) ☎ (01869) 328893
🌐 thebellbicester.com
2 changing beers (sourced nationally; often Hook Norton, Vale, XT) 🄷
This traditional 18th-century pub in the pedestrianised heart of Bicester has two rooms. The smaller is mainly used as a games room; the larger houses three handpumps serving a changing selection of beers, many from local breweries. The interior features stone floors with wooden tables and chairs; outside is a beer garden. Local bands perform on Friday night and most Saturdays. Monday is quiz night. ❀♿⇌(North)♣🚌📶

Blewbury

Blueberry 🄻

London Road, OX11 9NU (on A417)
✪ 12 (5 Mon)-11; 12-9 Sun ☎ (01235) 850296
🌐 the-blueberry.co.uk
Loose Cannon Abingdon Bridge; St Austell Tribute; West Berkshire Good Old Boy; 1 changing beer (sourced locally) 🄷
A 1930s roadhouse that has been the Blueberry since the current owner, a small local pubco, purchased it in 2014. Recently refurbished, it has a single bar that extends to the rear. Four real ales are served, including a guest. Reasonably priced food is available including the pub speciality – pizza cooked in the wood-fired oven – plus a takeaway option. 🔥❀◐◑♣P🚌(94,94S)📶

Brightwell-cum-Sotwell

Red Lion 🄻

Brightwell Street, OX10 0RT (S off A4130)
✪ 12-3, 6-11; 12-11 Sat; 12-10.30 Sun ☎ (01491) 837373
🌐 redlionbrightwell.co.uk
Loddon Hoppit; West Berkshire Good Old Boy; 2 changing beers (sourced nationally) 🄷
A popular traditional thatched inn dating from the 16th century in a quiet village. It has a cosy bar featuring exposed beams and brickwork, leading to a restaurant area to one side. The rear courtyard garden is a summer suntrap. The beers and ciders are usually from local breweries, and good-quality pub food is served (no food Mon or Sun eve). Sunday is jazz evening; charity quiz nights are held regularly. 🔥❀◐◑♿♣🍎P🚌(X2)🐾📶

Carterton

Siege of Orleans

5 The Giles Centre, Alvescot Road, OX18 3DH (down passage next to cycle shop)
✪ 3-11; 12-midnight Fri & Sat; 12-11 Sun ☎ (01993) 845663
🌐 siegeoforleans.co.uk
4 changing beers (sourced regionally) 🄷
Not so much a pub as a self-styled micro-alehouse, opened in 2015 in a former record shop, so on the small side. It has four handpumps dispensing mainly local ales from relatively unknown breweries alongside a selection of bottled beers from around the world and a real cider. Regular retro games nights and competitions are hosted. ◑♿♣🍎P🚌📶

Caulcott

Horse & Groom 🏆

Lower Heyford Road, OX25 4ND
✪ closed Mon; 12-3, 6-11; 12-3 Sun ☎ (01869) 343257
🌐 horseandgroomcaulcott.co.uk
Black Sheep Best Bitter; Church End Goat's Milk; 3 changing beers (sourced nationally; often Church End, Goff's, Vale) 🄷
Lovely 16th-century coaching house with an open fire in winter and a warm welcome whatever the season. Three guest ales are served along with the two regulars. The French landlord/chef offers wonderful seasonal and locally sourced food, including Thursday steak night and Sunday lunch (booking advised), along with themed French evenings. A Bastille Day beer festival is held in July. Dogs are allowed in the beer garden (but not the bar). Local CAMRA Pub of the Year 2019. Q🔥❀◐◑P📶

Chadlington

Tite Inn

Mill End, OX7 3NY
✪ 12-11 (10 Sun) ☎ (01608) 676910 🌐 thetiteinn.co.uk
Sharp's Doom Bar; 2 changing beers (sourced nationally; often Chadlington, Cotswold Lion, Sharp's) 🄷
This welcoming country inn sits in the Evenlode Valley. One regular and two guest ales are served along with a Westons cider on handpump. There is a beautiful hillside beer garden where a peaceful pint can be enjoyed. Tite is old local dialect for spring – water runs under the pub and down the hill. Good reasonably priced food is available in the comfortable bar and restaurant. Walkers are welcome. Q🔥❀◐◑⛺🍎P🚌(S3,X9)🐾📶

Chalgrove

Red Lion 🄻

115 High Street, OX44 7SS
✪ 11-3, 6-midnight (1.30am Fri & Sat); 12-11 Sun
☎ (01865) 890625 🌐 redlionchalgrove.com
Butcombe Original; Fuller's London Pride; 3 changing beers (sourced nationally; often Rebellion, West Berkshire) 🄷

Church-owned, picturesque and friendly 16th-century village local. The pub is divided into several distinct areas and used by a wide cross-section of the community. It is popular for its menu of locally sourced and freshly made food. Up to three guest beers are often from small local breweries. You can drink outside in both front and large rear gardens, while a real fire awaits inside in the winter months. Real local Hitchcox bottled cider is usually available in summer. Games evenings take place on Mondays. Q P (T1)

Charlbury

Rose & Crown

Market Street, OX7 3PL

12-11 (1am Fri); 11-1am Sat (01608) 810103
roseandcrown.charlbury.com

Ramsbury Farmer's Best; 8 changing beers (sourced nationally; often Dark Star, Oakham, XT)

This traditional wet-sales-only pub is north Oxfordshire's longest-standing Guide entry at 33 years. Eight handpumps serve a permanent ale plus seven different guests along with six traditional ciders and perries – one of the best selections in the area. Dark Star, Oakham, Turpin, Vale and XT feature regularly. There is live music fortnightly and an annual beer festival in January. Local CAMRA Pub of the Year 2018.
(S3,X9)

Checkendon

Highwayman

Exlade Street, RG8 0UA

closed Mon; 12-3, 6-11 Tue-Thu; 12-11 Fri & Sat; 12-5 Sun
(01491) 682020 thehighwaymaninn-checkendon.co.uk

Fuller's London Pride; Loddon Hoppit; West Berkshire Good Old Boy

The original building dates from 1625 but the inn now has a contemporary ambience while retaining the feel of a traditional pub, with two rooms for dining and a separate bar and drinking area with woodburner, beams and exposed brickwork. There may be occasional seasonal beers from Loddon and West Berkshire breweries as alternatives to the main beers listed. Excellent home-cooked and reasonably priced food is served. A large enclosed garden where numerous breeds of chicken roam is popular with families. Q P

Chipping Norton

Chequers

Goddards Lane, OX7 5NP (next to theatre, on corner of Spring St)

11-11 (midnight Fri & Sat); 11.30-11 Sun
(01608) 644717

Fuller's ESB, 1845; Gale's Seafarers Ale, HSB; 3 changing beers (sourced regionally; often Dark Star, Fuller's, Gale's)

Traditional English pub with an emphasis on real ale and home-cooked food. It serves up to six ales plus a gravity-poured cider. The bar has four separate areas, with an airy restaurant and function room to the rear. A large fireplace warms the main bar area in winter, providing an excellent place to relax. The pub is popular with discerning drinkers and visitors to the adjacent theatre.
Q

Fox

Market Place, OX7 5DD

10-11 (midnight Fri & Sat); 12-10 Sun (01608) 638535
foxchippingnorton.co.uk

Hook Norton Hooky, Hooky Gold, Old Hooky; 1 changing beer (sourced locally; often Hook Norton)

Traditional 16th-century inn in Chipping Norton's central marketplace, adjacent to the taxi rank and bus stops for all routes. It has a contemporary light and open style, also featuring a separate restaurant, upstairs snug and meeting room. The welcoming bar's four handpumps dispense ales from the Hook Norton range. There are 10 individually themed letting rooms, plus a courtyard seating area outside. Q P

East Hagbourne

Fleur de Lys

30 Main Road, OX11 9LN

11.30-2.30, 6-11 (10 Mon); 11.30-11 Fri & Sat; 12-10 Sun
(01235) 813247 thefleurdelyspub.co.uk

Morland Original Bitter; 5 changing beers (sourced nationally)

The Fleur de Lys is a family-friendly 17th-century pub situated in the rural village of East Hagbourne. It offers one regular beer from Morland and up to five nationally sourced guests. The spacious bar and dining area are comfortable and cosy, warmed by an open fire. Live music evenings are hosted regularly, including a weekend music festival in the summer. Outside is an extensive decked area with a separate beer garden where Aunt Sally is played in fine weather. No food Monday or Sunday evenings. Local CAMRA Pub of the Year 2017 and 2019. P (94,94S)

Faringdon

Swan

1 Park Road, SN7 7BP

12-2, 5-11 (midnight Fri); 12-midnight Sat; 12-11 Sun
(01367) 241480 swanfaringdon.co.uk

4 changing beers (sourced nationally; often White Horse)

An attractive free house with its own Faringdon microbrewery. The large, friendly, multi-level single bar has a small roadside patio for sunny afternoons. A selection of four constantly changing guest beers is complemented by two ciders on handpump. Third-pint glasses are available for the unsure. There is a regular quiz night on Tuesday.
Q (66)

Fringford

Butchers Arms

Main Street, OX27 8EB

12-3, 6-11 Mon; 12-11 (01869) 277363
thebutchersarmsfringford.com

St Austell Tribute; Young's Bitter; 2 changing beers (sourced nationally; often Black Sheep, Ringwood)

A pretty 18th-century country pub adjacent to the cricket ground in a beautiful village setting. The well-decorated bar area serves three ales from handpump. The separate restaurant, seating up to 40, is available for parties. Excellent traditional food is served daily, with a generously portioned and well-priced roast on Sunday; reservations are advised on all days. A large, paved seating area to the front is popular in summer.
P (37,88)

Goring

Goring Social Club

1 High Street, RG8 9BA

⏲ 6.30-11; 4.30-11 Fri; 12-11 Sat; 12-10.30 Sun
☎ (01491) 873105 🌐 goringsocialclub.co.uk

Hook Norton Hooky; 2 changing beers (sourced nationally) Ⓗ

This welcoming social club on the village high street continues to impress with the excellence of its ales. Its popular middle handpump serves an ever-changing selection of beers from across the country, and is flanked by pumps offering a regular session ale and a seasonally changing guest. Function and TV rooms are available, and the club hosts regular quizzes, meat draws and other community events. Entry is £1 with a CAMRA membership card. Local CAMRA Club of the Year multiple times including 2019.
⇌(Goring & Streatley)♣P🚌

Great Bourton

Bell Inn Ⓛ ✔

Manor Road, OX17 1QP (just off A361 Banbury to Southam road)

⏲ closed Mon & Tue; 6-11 Wed-Fri; 12-11 Sat; 12-7 Sun
☎ (01295) 750862 🌐 thebellgreatbourton.co.uk

Hook Norton Hooky; 2 changing beers (sourced locally; often Hook Norton) Ⓗ

The current landlords have restored this Hook Norton brewery outlet to its former glory since taking over in 2018, gaining rave reviews with the help of a revamped interior and an interesting, changing food menu. Two Hook Norton beers are served midweek, with three at weekends and in summer. They are enjoyed by an eclectic mix of local drinkers and diners plus visitors from the nearby caravan park. Q❀◑Å♣●P🐾

Great Tew

Falkland Arms

19-21 The Green, OX7 4DB

⏲ 11.30-11; 12-10.30 Sun ☎ (01608) 683653
🌐 falklandarms.co.uk

Wadworth IPA, Horizon, 6X, Bishops Tipple, Swordfish; 2 changing beers (sourced nationally) Ⓗ

A quintessential 16th-century English country pub, featuring simple wooden furniture on flagstone and bare-board floors, and an array of jugs hanging from the ancient beams. The walls are adorned with brewing memorabilia; in winter a fire in the large inglenook adds warmth. Eight handpumps serve five regular ales plus two guests and a cider. Accommodation and locally sourced food are available. A beer garden overlooking the picturesque Great Tew Estate is ideal for a summer pint. Q❀◑●P🐾

Henley-on-Thames

Bird in Hand

61 Greys Road, RG9 1SB

⏲ 12-2, 5-11; 12-11 Sat; 12-10.30 Sun ☎ (01491) 575775

Brakspear Bitter; Fuller's London Pride; Harvey's Sussex XX Mild Ale; 2 changing beers (sourced nationally; often Loddon, Rebellion, West Berkshire) Ⓗ

Celebrating 25 consecutive years in the Guide, the Bird has flourished under the stewardship of the same family throughout. Two different guest beers complement three regulars. TVs show sporting events, the pub is home to darts and cribbage teams and hosts regular quiz nights. The family room leads to a delightful garden boasting a pond and aviary, and dogs on leads are welcome. Hot and cold snacks are available all day. A frequent winner of local CAMRA Pub of the Year.
Q❀Å⇌♣🚌(151,152)🐾

Hethe

Muddy Duck

Main Street, OX27 8ES

⏲ 11-11 ☎ (01869) 278099 🌐 themuddyduckpub.co.uk

Hook Norton Hooky; St Austell Tribute; Timothy Taylor Boltmaker, Landlord Ⓗ**; 2 changing beers (sourced nationally; often Harvey's, Hawkshead, Skinner's)** Ⓗ/Ⓖ

Saved from becoming a residential property in 2011, the pub was purchased and renovated by a local businessman. Retaining the previous landlord as its cellar expert, it serves quality real ale from several handpumps and at least one gravity-fed cask. The pub has a reputation for good food with seasonal menus, and offers an extensive wine list. There is a large garden area at the rear. An Aunt Sally team plays here in the summer season. Walkers are welcome. ❀◑♿♣P🐾

Hook Norton

Sun Inn ✔

High Street, OX15 5NH

⏲ 12-midnight; 10-midnight Sat; 10-10.30 Sun
☎ (01608) 737570 🌐 thesuninn-hooknorton.co.uk

Hook Norton Hooky, Lion, Old Hooky; 3 changing beers (sourced locally; often Hook Norton) Ⓗ

A country pub/restaurant in the heart of the village opposite the church. The interior features oak beams, flagstone floors and a wood-burning stove. Food is seasonally inspired and locally sourced. Outside is seating to the front and back. Six en-suite bedrooms provide an ideal base for exploring the surrounding countryside, with its picturesque Cotswold villages and historic stately homes plus a local Victorian gem – Hook Norton Brewery, a short walk through the village.
❀◑♿Å♣●P🚌(488)🐾

Horley

Red Lion Ⓛ

Hornton Lane, OX15 6BQ

⏲ closed Mon; 6-11; 12-6 Sun ☎ (01295) 730427

Hook Norton Hooky; Purity Pure UBU; Sharp's Doom Bar; Turpin Golden Citrus Ⓗ

This traditional village pub is the focal point of the community, offering a friendly welcome to visitors, including walkers and well-behaved dogs. The garden provides a tranquil area for a summer evening's tipple. Three handpumped ales are served (four on special occasions). The annual beer festival on St George's Day has become a must with locals and visitors alike. Darts and dominoes are played, and a TV shows live sporting events. A recent local CAMRA Pub of the Year. ❀♣P🐾

Letcombe Regis

Greyhound Inn Ⓛ

Main Street, OX12 9JL

10 (3.30 Mon)-11; 11-10.30 Sun (01235) 771969
thegreyhoundletcombe.co.uk
4 changing beers (sourced regionally; often North Cotswold, Ramsbury, Thornbridge)
Large, welcoming pub in the centre of the village, refurbished to a high standard. Inside is a single bar with dining areas and an inglenook fireplace. Locally sourced home-cooked food and four constantly changing handpumped beers are served. The garden allows outdoor dining during the summer months. There is parking at the side of the building, as well as provision for tethering horses. Within a couple of miles of the Ridgeway, the Greyhound is a welcome place of refreshment for wayfarers. It has eight boutique en-suite bedrooms. Q P

Lewknor

Leathern Bottle

1 High Street, OX49 5TW (N off B4009 near M40 jct 6)
11-2.30 (3 Sat), 5.30-11; 12-3, 7-10.30 Sun
(01844) 351482 theleathernbottle.co.uk
Brakspear Bitter; Marston's Pedigree; 1 changing beer (sourced nationally)
This traditional old country pub, run by two generations of the same family for over 40 years, has featured in all but one edition of the Guide. It serves good home-cooked pub food, and has a family-friendly garden. The guest beer comes from the Brakspear pubco approved list. The venue offers a warm welcome to all, including walkers from the nearby Ridgeway, with some of the best trails starting and finishing here. It is also a short walk from the Oxford Tube and the airline coach stop. Q P

Little Milton

Lamb

High Street, OX44 7PU (on A329)
12-3, 6.30-midnight; 12-10.30 Sun (01844) 279527
lambinnlittlemilton.co.uk
Brakspear Bitter; 2 changing beers (sourced nationally; often Courage)
Thatched 16th-century stone pub situated on the main road through the village. The attractive, welcoming split-level bar features original beams and has seating areas for those who just want a drink, as well as for diners enjoying the high-quality pub food. To the rear is a patio and a large, quiet, well-kept garden where a beer festival is held in July. Brakspear Bitter is the regular ale, alongside two changing guests. Quiz night is the first Thursday of the month. P

Long Wittenham

Plough

24 High Street, OX14 4QH
12-11 (01865) 407738 theploughinnlw.co.uk
Butcombe Original; 2 changing beers (sourced nationally; often Amwell Springs, Loose Cannon, West Berkshire)
A traditional Grade II-listed family-friendly pub built in the 17th century in this village in rural south Oxfordshire. Its large garden stretches down to the River Thames and has ample outdoor seating and a children's play space. There are two bar areas and a separate restaurant. One regular and two changing beers are available, from breweries and microbreweries mainly in the South-East. Each June, the pub hosts Wittfest, a music festival that raises money for charities. Other attractions include fun runs, theatre performances and church fêtes. P

Mapledurham

Packhorse

Woodcote Road, RG4 7UG (on A4074)
11.30-11 (10.30 Sun) (0118) 972 2140
packhorsepub.co.uk
House beer (by Brunning & Price); 4 changing beers (sourced nationally)
Originally a farm on the Mapledurham House estate dating from the 1600s, this Brunning & Price establishment is now a cosy pub and restaurant. The low-beamed bar has ample seating for drinkers and usually features local microbrewery beers. The larger restaurant area offers a wide-ranging good-value menu. A large, secluded garden at the rear has a shaded seating area overlooking fields. There is 60p off a pint 5-7pm weekdays. Occasional Meet the Brewer evenings are popular. Q P

Marsh Baldon

Seven Stars on the Green

The Green, OX44 9LP (15-min walk from Nuneham Courtenay)
10-10 (11 Wed & Thu; midnight Fri & Sat); 10-7 Sun
(01865) 343337 sevenstarsonthegreen.co.uk
Fuller's London Pride; 3 changing beers (sourced locally; often Loddon, White Horse, Loose Cannon)
This old coaching inn has been community-owned since 2013, offering a welcoming main bar alongside a restaurant/function room. It sits next to the village green, which is claimed to be the largest in Europe, and has a big garden for the summer. Three local ales are always available and good food is served including extensive gluten-free options. A former local CAMRA Town and Village Pub of the Year. Q P

Milton

Plum Pudding

44 High Street, OX14 4EJ
11.30-2.30, 5-11; 11.30-midnight Fri & Sat; 12-10.30 Sun
(01235) 834443 theplumpuddingmilton.co.uk
Loose Cannon Abingdon Bridge; LoveBeer OG; Young's Bitter; 1 changing beer (sourced nationally)
Plum Pudding refers to the Oxford Sandy and Black pig, one of the older and rarer British breeds, which features on the menu. The pub serves four real ales, plus up to four real ciders. Regular live music is hosted, and two beer festivals are held each year. Sitting in the pleasant walled garden, you would not know it, but you are only a couple of minutes from the busy A34. A Guide regular, the pub is a former local CAMRA Pub of the Year and Cider Pub of the Year in 2018 and 2019. P

Northmoor

Red Lion

Standlake Road, OX29 5SX
closed Mon; 12-3, 5.30-11; 11-11 Sat; 12-6 Sun
(01865) 300301 theredlionnorthmoor.com

Brakspear Bitter; Loose Cannon Abingdon Bridge; 2 changing beers (sourced locally; often Cotswold Lion, North Cotswold, Vale) ℍ
Traditional village inn with whitewashed stone walls, heavy oak beams, real fires and a large garden. Purchased by the local community from Greene King in 2014, the pub has gone from strength to strength ever since. The focus is on local produce, with a changing menu of home-cooked food, some of which is grown in the pub's kitchen garden. A selection of three or four local beers is available in the small bar alongside locally made soft drinks from Samuelsons of Witney.
Q🕭🕭🏵◑♣Pₐ(18)❀❖

Oxford

Bear Inn
6 Alfred Street, OX1 4EH
☼ 11-11 (midnight Fri & Sat); 11.30-10.30 Sun
☎ (01865) 728164 ⊕ bearoxford.co.uk
Fuller's London Pride, ESB; Gale's HSB; Shotover Scholar; 2 changing beers (sourced regionally; often Fuller's) ℍ
The Bear's precise age is open to debate but it's definitely old; the present building dates back to 1606 and is listed by CAMRA as having a regionally important historic pub interior. Tucked away behind the town hall, it is a tied house in more ways than one, renowned for its collection of tie remnants taken from customers. A small pub popular with students and visitors, it gets crowded at times but offers extra seating in a paved area to the rear. Q🕭🏵◑⇌♣🖵❖

Butcher's Arms
5 Wilberforce Street, Headington, OX3 7AN (from centre of Headington, past the shark, first left, first right)
☼ 12-2.30, 4.30-11; 12-midnight Fri & Sat; 12-11 Sun
☎ (01865) 742470 ⊕ butchersarmsoxford.co.uk
Fuller's London Pride, ESB; Gale's Seafarers Ale; 2 changing beers (sourced regionally; often Fuller's) ℍ
A friendly, back-street, late-Victorian, red-brick pub; a little hard to find but worth searching out. The long single room has the bar in the middle, and outside is a paved area. It offers a good range of Fuller's beers, traditional pub food and light lunch options. The inn sign, a parody of the arms of the Butchers' Company, and the motto, which means 'God gives us everything', are both of unknown origin. Q🕭🏵◑🕭♣♣🖵❀❖

Chequers 🄻 ✔
130A High Street, OX1 4DH (down narrow passageway off High St)
☼ 12-11 (11.30 Fri & Sat); 12-10.30 Sun ☎ (01865) 727463
St Austell Nicholson's Pale Ale; Thornbridge Jaipur IPA; 7 changing beers (sourced nationally; often Brakspear, Sharp's) ℍ
Worth searching out down a passageway off the High Street, much of this Grade II-listed pub dates back to the early 16th century when it was converted from a moneylender's tenement to a tavern, hence the name. Note the fine carvings, windows and the ceiling in the lower bar. There is an upstairs bar with three handpumps, and a cobbled courtyard provides alfresco drinking, dining and smoking space.
Q🕭🏵◑⇌♣♣🖵❀❖

Fir Tree 🄻 ✔
163 Iffley Road, OX4 1EJ
☼ 4-11 (2am Fri & Sat); 12-10.30 Sun ☎ (01865) 245290

5 changing beers (sourced nationally; often Greene King) ℍ
Multi-level pub with a quiet snug at the back and a small patio garden and smoking area to the rear. There are some pavement tables at the front. The house speciality is pizza and a pop-up diner serves a vegan roast dinner on Sunday afternoon. The interior of this quirky pub still bears the scars of its days as a Morrells alehouse, with a whole bank of handpumps and a mishmash of finishes and artefacts. 🕭🏵♣🖵❀❖

Gardener's Arms 🄻
39 Plantation Road, OX2 6JE
☼ 5-midnight Mon & Tue; 12-2.30, 5-midnight Wed-Fri; 12-midnight Sat; 12-11 Sun ☎ (01865) 559814
⊕ thegarden-oxford.co.uk
4 changing beers (sourced locally; often Little Ox, Loose Cannon, XT) ℍ
Cosy pub down a narrow street off Woodstock Road. The small bar opens up to a spacious dining area, once two rooms, serving some of the finest vegetarian and vegan food in the city. At the rear is a large and pleasant garden as well as the outside toilets. A popular and relaxing place to eat and drink. Hosts a popular quiz night on Sunday.
Q🕭🏵◑♣🖵❀❖

Lamb & Flag
12 St Giles, OX1 3JS
☼ 12-11 (10.30 Sun) ☎ (01865) 515787
Palmers IPA; Skinner's Betty Stogs; Theakston Old Peculier; house beer (by Palmers); 3 changing beers (sourced nationally; often XT) ℍ
Grade II-listed building owned by the adjacent St John's College. Some of the profits from the pub support student scholarships. This is a classic city pub with no music, Wi-Fi or other distractions from friendly conversation. Beers from the South-West feature – the house beer Lamb & Flag Gold (4.5% ABV) is brewed by Palmers of Bridport. It has many literary links but is not the pub of the same name in Thomas Hardy's novel Jude the Obscure; that was actually the Turf Tavern. Q🕭◑⇌♣🖵

Masons Arms 🄻 ✔
2 Quarry School Place, Headington Quarry, OX3 8LH
☼ 5 (7 Mon)-11; 12-11 Sat; 12-4, 7-10.30 Sun
☎ (01865) 764579 ⊕ themasonsarmshq.co.uk
Oakham JHB; Timothy Taylor Boltmaker; 3 changing beers (sourced nationally; often Marble, Rebellion, Wild Beer) ℍ
Family-run community pub hosting many games leagues, including bar billiards and Aunt Sally. The guest ales are varied and a wide range of bottled beers is stocked. The pub is home to the Headington beer festival in September. A heated decking area and garden lead to a function room, which hosts music and comedy nights. A regular CAMRA Pub of the Year winner and City Pub of the Year 2019. 🕭🏵♣🖵(H2)❀❖

Old Bookbinders ✔
17-18 Victor Street, Jericho, OX2 6BT
☼ 12-11 ☎ (01865) 553549 ⊕ oldbookbinders.co.uk
House beer (by Greene King); 5 changing beers (sourced nationally; often Greene King, Oakham, Robinsons) ℍ
This family-run pub near the Oxford canal mixes a Victorian tavern with a French bistro. The Bookbinders Arms became the Old Bookbinders Ale House when sold by Morrells. Two rooms are served by a single bar and furnished in typical style

with an eclectic mix of decor and bric-a-brac. Free monkey nuts are available from the barrel by the entrance. The outside of the pub featured on TV in the first episode of Inspector Morse as The Printer's Devil. Q (17)

Rose & Crown

14 North Parade Avenue, OX2 6LX (½ mile N of city centre, off Banbury Rd)

11-midnight (1am Fri & Sat) (01865) 510551

roseandcrownoxford.com

Adnams Southwold Bitter; Hook Norton Old Hooky; Shotover Scholar; 1 changing beer (sourced nationally)

Now a free house, this popular Victorian local on a vibrant north Oxford street is a time capsule with two small rooms and many original features. A friendly community pub, it has been run by the same landlords for over 30 years. No intrusive music or mobile phones are permitted. Its fame has even spread to Everest – see the photo on the wall. Identified by CAMRA as having a historic pub interior of some regional importance.

Q

Royal Blenheim

13 St Ebbes Street, OX1 1PT

12-11 (11.30 Wed & Thu; midnight Fri); 11.30-midnight Sat; 12-10.30 Sun (01865) 242355 royalblenheim.co.uk

Everards Tiger; Titanic Plum Porter; White Horse Bitter, Stable Genius, Village Idiot; 5 changing beers (sourced nationally)

Single-room Victorian pub with a bright, airy interior located on a street corner next to the Museum of Modern Art. The original Royal Blenheim was a stagecoach. The pub, which was built in 1889 on the site of two earlier inns, is owned by Everards and leased to the White Horse Brewery. Its 10 handpumps dispense a range of White Horse and Titanic beers, one from Everards, plus guests. Good food and bar snacks are offered, with vegetarian and gluten-free options.

Q

St Aldates Tavern

108 St Aldates, OX1 1BU

11.30-11 (midnight Thu & Fri); 11-midnight Sat; 11-11 Sun (01865) 241185 staldatestavernoxford.co.uk

House beer (by West Berkshire); 6 changing beers (sourced nationally; often Hook Norton, Shotover, XT)

Not the original St Aldates Tavern – that was at no. 61 – but there was an inn recorded at this site in the centre of town in 1397. The pub has been rebuilt at least once since then and was a coaching inn in the 18th century. It features up to seven well-kept real ales, with at least two often from local breweries. Good-quality, freshly cooked food is served all day using locally sourced ingredients where possible. Q

White Hart

12 St Andrew's Road, Headington, OX3 9DL (opp church in Old Headington village)

12-11 (midnight Fri & Sat) (01865) 761737

thewhitehartheadington.com

Everards Beacon Hill, Tiger; 3 changing beers (sourced nationally; often Everards)

Terraced stone-built pub offering a good selection of Everards ales. The interior is divided into three, with two small bars, and it has a large garden. Note the framed extract from a play, The Tragi-comedy of Joan of Hedington, by Dr William King of Christ Church, written in 1712 about the proprietor of a dishonourable ale house – thankfully the pub now has a much better reputation. The food is traditional and home made, with pies a speciality.

P

White Rabbit

21 Friars Entry, OX1 2BY (alley between Magdalen St and Gloucester Green)

12-midnight (01865) 241177

whiterabbitoxford.co.uk

5 changing beers (sourced locally; often Loose Cannon, Shotover, Siren)

This pub has been the White Rabbit since 2012, having previously been Oxford's premier rock pub as the Gloucester Arms. With a central bar surrounded by three areas, it feels reasonably bright and spacious despite not being particularly large. Five local changing real ales are usually on offer, with one sometimes swapped for cider. Hand-made pizzas are a speciality, with organic, gluten-free bases optional. The pub is recognised by CAMRA as having a historic interior of some regional importance.

Playhatch

Flowing Spring

Henley Road, RG4 9RB (on A4155)

closed Mon; 12-2.30, 5.30-11; 12-11 Sat & Sun

(0118) 969 9878 theflowingspringpub.co.uk

Palmers 200; Tring Ridgeway; 4 changing beers (sourced nationally)

Sociable 18th-century country pub on the edge of the Chilterns. Now a free house owned by the former tenants, it features two regular plus three or four varying beers. It serves home-made food with award-winning gluten-free, dairy-free, vegetarian and vegan options. Events include a monthly unplugged night, classic car and bike meets, murder mysteries, and annual beer and cider festivals. The pleasant covered balcony and large riverside garden are ideal for summer. Local CAMRA Pub of the Year 2018. P

Stanford in the Vale

Stanford Social Club

Sheards Lane, SN7 8LW

8-11; 12-6 Sun (01367) 710734

stanfordsocialclub.net

2 changing beers (sourced nationally)

Formerly known as The Working Men's Club, it was built in 1928 on donated land using volunteer labour, and later run by steward Fred 'Buster' Smith until his death in 1977, after which it was run by a group of 12 people as the Stanford Social Club. CAMRA members are welcome on production of a membership card and a contribution of 50p. Two constantly changing beers are served on handpump. Local CAMRA Club of the Year for the last three years. P

Stoke Lyne

Peyton Arms

School Lane, OX27 8SD

closed Mon & Tue; 5-11 Wed-Fri; 12-7 Sat & Sun

07546 066160

Hook Norton Hooky, Old Hooky; 1 changing beer (sourced locally; often Hook Norton)

Just two miles from junction 10 of the M40, enter here and step back in time. Up to three Hooky ales are served through a hatch, direct from casks. Simple filled rolls are usually available. Regular users of the pub include members of the local farming community looking to enjoy quality beers and great conversation. The bar area is for adults only; however, children are welcome in the garden. No dogs allowed. Weekday opening hours can vary. Identified by CAMRA as having a regionally important historic pub interior. Q❀P

Sydenham

Inn at Emmington 𝕃

Sydenham Road, OX39 4LD

4-11; 3-11 Fri; 12-11 Sat; 12-7 Sun ☎ (01844) 351367
theinnatemmington.co.uk

Chiltern Beechwood Bitter; Rebellion IPA; 1 changing beer (sourced locally; often Loose Cannon, XT) H

On the edge of this delightful village, this hostelry is known for its convivial atmosphere, excellent home cooking and cask ales – two regulars plus one changing guest. Its prime location, close to the Chiltern Hills and just off the M40, is also a big draw. Those looking to explore the area can stay in one of the inn's seven guest rooms, some of which boast views over the Oxfordshire countryside.
Q❀🛏◐♣●P🚌(40)🐾📶

Tetsworth

Old Red Lion 𝕃

40 High Street, OX9 7AS

11-10 (midnight Fri); 11-5 Sun ☎ (01844) 281274
theoldredliontetsworth.co.uk

XT Four; 1 changing beer (sourced locally) H

The pub has a warm and friendly atmosphere, with wood-burning stoves in the winter, and serves up to three well-kept real ales from local breweries. Traditional pub food is offered all day. The Old Red Lion is a member of Brit Stops and allows motorhomes free overnight parking. It also serves as the village shop and offers B&B accommodation. Truly an asset of community value.
Q❀🛏◐♿♣●P🚌(275)🐾📶

Thame

Cross Keys 𝕃 ✔

East Street, OX9 3JS

12-2, 5-11; 12-11 Sat; 12-10.30 Sun ☎ (01844) 218202

XT Four; 7 changing beers (sourced locally; often Thame) H

Once almost lost forever, the Cross Keys was saved by the current tenants, who have transformed it from a failing keg-only pub into a drinkers' local that serves a wide range of ales and ciders. The on-site Thame Brewery and other local breweries are often represented, along with others from further afield. At busy times it is not uncommon for several beers to change during the evening. Local CAMRA Cider Pub of the Year 2019. Q❀♣●🚌🐾📶

Wallingford

George Hotel 𝕃

25 High Street, OX10 0BS

11-11; 12-10.30 Sun ☎ (01491) 836665

Rebellion IPA; 2 changing beers (sourced locally; often Rebellion) H

A coaching inn dating from the 16th century and close to the town centre. This Peel Group hotel hosts various functions and is licensed for civil wedding ceremonies. Cask ales are available in the Tavern Bar, which has several separate areas, and can also be enjoyed in the spacious hotel courtyard, ideal for alfresco dining and drinking. Food ranges from bar snacks to fine dining from an à la carte menu in the bistro.
❀🛏◐♿⛺●P🚌📶

Wantage

King's Arms 𝕃

39 Wallingford Street, OX12 8AU

2-11; 12-midnight Fri & Sat; 12-10.30 Sun
☎ (01235) 765465 kingsarmswantage.co.uk

6 changing beers (sourced nationally)

This friendly, open-plan pub with polished wooden floors and panelling has been transformed by owners Oak Taverns, giving it a new lease of life. Six handpumps serve constantly changing beers, with six ciders also available. Outside, to the rear, is a large, grassy, sloping garden with tables for drinkers. There is a small on-site microbrewery, Wantage Brewery. Q❀♿♣●🚌🐾📶

Royal Oak 🏆 𝕃

Newbury Street, OX12 8DF (S of Market Square)

5.30-11; 12-2.30, 7-11 Sat; 12-2, 7-10.30 Sun
☎ (01235) 763129 royaloakwantage.co.uk

Wadworth 6X; West Berkshire Maggs' Magnificent Mild, Dr Hexter's Healer; 8 changing beers (sourced nationally; often West Berkshire) G

This multi award-winning street-corner pub is a mecca for the discerning drinker. The pub is the primary outlet for West Berkshire ales in the area – two carry the landlord Paul Hexter's name – together with 30 or more ciders and perries. All beers are served by gravity. Photographs of ships bearing the pub's name are displayed. The lounge features wrought-iron trelliswork covered in pumpclips. Many times a local CAMRA Pub of the Year and Cider Pub of the Year, including 2018 and 2019. Q♣●🚌🐾📶

Shoulder of Mutton 𝕃

38 Wallingford Street, OX12 8AX (E of Market Square)

12-11 (midnight Fri & Sat); 12-10.30 Sun
☎ (01235) 767158 theshoulder.pub

10 changing beers (sourced nationally) H

Popular Victorian corner pub close to the town centre with 10 constantly changing beers on handpump to suit all tastes. The sympathetically renovated interior comprises public and lounge bars, a cosy snug and a 'lay-by' leading to small courtyard and function room. A former CAMRA local, regional and county Pub of The Year, it has been identified by CAMRA as having a regionally important historic pub interior. Q🛏●🚌📶

Watchfield

Eagle

Eagle Lane, SN6 8TF

closed Mon; 2-1am (11 Tue & Wed); 1-11 Sun
☎ (01793) 784870

Sharp's Doom Bar; 2 changing beers (sourced nationally; often Black Sheep, Timothy Taylor) H

A friendly local in a picturesque village. Its single bar has seating at one end, and a pool table and TV showing sports at the other. Handpumps serve one regular and two changing beers. The pub now offers home-made food and is well-placed for lunchtime trade from the nearby business park and military academy. ☺❀◑♿♣●P🚌(S6)🐾📶

West Hanney

Plough 🄻 ✔

Church Street, OX12 0LN

⏲ closed Mon; 12-3, 6-11 Tue-Thu (midnight Fri); 12-midnight Sat; 12-9 Sun ☎ (01235) 868987

🌐 theploughatwesthanney.co.uk

4 changing beers (sourced regionally; often Loose Cannon, St Austell, Shotover) Ⓗ

Picturesque, friendly, 16th-century thatched pub, opposite the church. Sold in 2015 by Punch Taverns to a local community group, it has been refurbished and now offers four changing beers. The cosy beamed and alcoved split-level bar has an open fire, and the separate dining room serves traditional British food. The pub is the hub of the community and hosts many local clubs. In summer Aunt Sally is played. ☺❀◑♿▲♣P🐾📶

Wheatley

Cricketers Arms 🄻

38 Littleworth, OX33 1TR (walk W along Littleworth Rd from Wheatley)

⏲ 6-11; 5-11 Fri; 12-3, 6-11 Sat; 12-4, 7-10.30 Sun

☎ (01865) 872738 🌐 cricketers-arms.co.uk

Hook Norton Hooky; 2 changing beers (sourced locally) Ⓗ

A friendly, traditional free house that serves three cask ales from local breweries, often including darker beers. A range of local bottled beers is also available along with real cider. Regular beer festivals are held in spring and autumn. The pub welcomes children and dogs and is a popular stop-off for walkers. It benefits from a frequent bus service to Wheatley (a 15-minute walk away) and is on National Cycle Route 57. Q☺❀◑♣●P🐾📶

Witney

Angel Inn 🄻 ✔

42 Market Square, OX28 6AL

⏲ 9.30am-11 (midnight Fri & Sat); 11-11 Sun

☎ (01993) 703238

Brakspear Oxford Gold; Wychwood Hobgoblin Gold, Hobgoblin; house beer (by Marston's) Ⓗ

A Grade II-listed free house at one time owned by Joseph Early of the blanket manufacturing dynasty and a brewer. It has a fine front bar with low beams and a bay window with plenty of space for drinkers and diners beyond. Outside is a small paved and walled courtyard. The beer range is mostly from Marston's – its Wychwood Brewery is just around the corner. One of the regular beers may sometimes be replaced by a guest.

❀◑♣🚌(S1,S2)

Oxbrew Witney

8 Langdale Court, OX28 6FG (down passageway opp Blue Boar in town centre)

⏲ closed Mon & Tue; 12-10 Wed & Thu (11 Fri & Sat); 12-8 Sun ☎ (01608) 677717 🌐 oxbrewmicropub.co.uk

2 changing beers (sourced locally; often Church Hanbrewery, Little Ox, Oxbrew) Ⓗ

Witney's first micropub is a venture into running a pub by a father-and-son team, who in 2017 started Oxbrew, an eight-barrel brewery. The pub, a former charity shop, serves Oxbrew beers alongside others from nearby small breweries via two handpulls from casks plus six taps from kegs. All beers are kept in the air-conditioned cold room, visible behind the bar. Q❀P🚌(S1,S2)

Woodstock

Black Prince ✔

2 Manor Road, OX20 1XJ

⏲ 12-11 (7 Sun) ☎ (01993) 811530

🌐 theblackprincewoodstock.com

Loddon Hullabaloo; St Austell Tribute; 2 changing beers (sourced nationally; often Bath Ales, Vale) Ⓗ

Historic 16th-century pub beside the River Glyme, opposite Blenheim Palace. The garden and terrace offer a tranquil setting to enjoy a well-kept pint. You can choose from two regular ales and two changing guests, often from local breweries. Fresh well-cooked snacks and meals are available daily at reasonable prices. The open-plan interior boasts two ancient fireplaces and a French suit of armour. Aunt Sally is played, and families, walkers and well-behaved dogs are welcome.

Q☺❀◑♿♣P🚌🐾📶

Wootton

Killingworth Castle

Glympton Road, OX20 1EJ

⏲ 9am-11 ☎ (01993) 811401 🌐 thekillingworthcastle.com

4 changing beers (sourced locally; often Little Ox, North Cotswold) Ⓗ

This welcoming coaching inn on the ancient Worcester to London road dates from 1637. There is a small bar and dining area to the front with a wood-burning stove, and to the rear a larger restaurant serving award-winning food. Four handpumps offer two ales from sister brewery Yubberton and two guests from regionals and micros. Eight letting rooms provide a good base for a visit to nearby Blenheim Palace.

Q☺❀🛏◑♣P🐾📶

Choosing pubs

CAMRA members and branches choose the pubs listed in the Good Beer Guide. There is no payment for entry, and pubs are inspected on a regular basis by personal visits; publicans are not sent a questionnaire once a year, as is the case with some pub guides. CAMRA branches monitor all the pubs in their areas, and the choice of pubs for the guide is often the result of democratic vote at branch meetings. However, recommendations from readers are welcomed and will be passed on to the relevant branch: write to Good Beer Guide, CAMRA, 230 Hatfield Road, St Albans, Hertfordshire, AL1 4LW; or send an email to: **gbgeditor@camra.org.uk**

RUTLAND

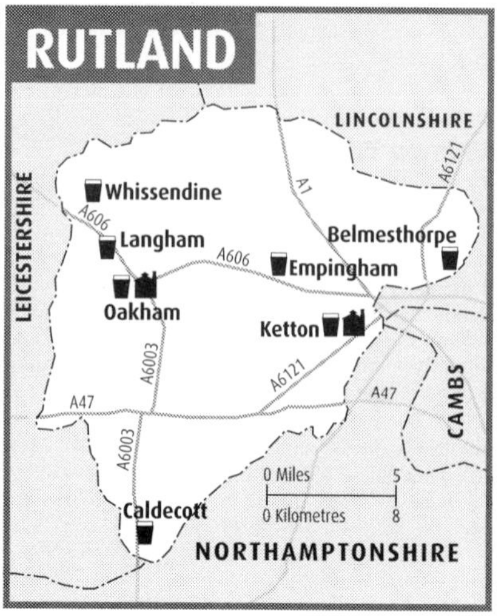

Belmesthorpe

Blue Bell L ✔

Shepherds Walk, PE9 4JG

⏲ 12-2.30 (not Mon), 6-11; 12-2.30, 5-11 Fri; 12-11 Sat & Sun ☎ (01780) 753081

Draught Bass; Grainstore Ten Fifty; Greene King IPA; Oakham Bishops Farewell; 1 changing beer (often Abbeydale) [H]

A historic village pub with low ceilings, a roaring fire and stone walls, all part of its charm. Six handpulls offer a wide range of well-kept guest beers, including at least one LocAle and a real cider. Dogs on leads are welcome in the bar area. Good honest home-made pub food is available Tuesday to Sunday lunchtimes (booking advisable). **Q🛋❀◑♿⛺♣🍎P🐾**

Caldecott

Plough Inn

16 Main Street, LE16 8RS

⏲ 6-11; 11-3.30, 6-11 Sat & Sun ☎ (01536) 770284

Grainstore Red Kite; Langton Angler; 2 changing beers [H]

Attractive sandstone pub on the village green with a traditional open-plan interior incorporating a bar area, restaurant and a relaxing snug. The restaurant is popular and booking is essential. Outside, there is a front terrace and a large garden to the rear. Beers are often from local breweries Grainstore in Rutland and Langton in nearby Leicestershire. **Q🛋❀◑♿⛺P🚌🐾**

Empingham

Empingham Cricket & Social Club

Exton Road, LE15 8QB

⏲ closed Mon, Tue, Thu & Sat; 8-11 Wed; 8.30am-midnight Fri; 1-3 Sun ☎ (01780) 460696 🌐 empinghamcsc.com

Magpie Best; 3 changing beers (often Great Heck, Greg's, Stockport) [H]

Recently refurbished, the Cricket & Social Club is noted for the quality and variety of the ales. It has limited hours, often extended by sporting and other functions – check the website for events. An annual beer festival is held to coincide with the final matches of the Six Nations rugby in March. **Q🛋❀♿P🚌🐾📶**

Ketton

Railway

Church Street, PE9 3TA

⏲ 5-11; 12-11.30 Sat; 12-11 Sun ☎ (01780) 721050

Grainstore Rutland Osprey, Ten Fifty; Oakham JHB [H]

A Grade II-listed building several hundred years old, with much character and more than a little charm. The traditional village local is set in the shadow of the impressive church. Good beer and wine are served in a welcoming and friendly atmosphere. A fourth beer can be added at busy times. There is no food but functions can be catered for. **Q🛋❀♣P🚌🐾**

Langham

Wheatsheaf

2 Burley Road, LE15 7HU

⏲ 5-11 Mon & Tue; 12-11 (midnight Fri & Sat); 12-11 Sun ☎ (01572) 869105 🌐 thewheatsheaf-langham.co.uk

Adnams Southwold Bitter; Draught Bass; Greene King Abbot [H]

The Wheatsheaf is an attractive village inn, just north of Oakham. A former Mann's pub, it is now free of tie and serves beers from many breweries, micro and otherwise. It has an excellent reputation for its food and can be extremely busy, particularly in the summer months. A children's menu is available. A frequent Rutland CAMRA award winner. **Q🛋❀◑♿P🚌🐾**

Oakham

Lord Nelson

Market Square, LE15 6DT

⏲ 11-11 (midnight Fri & Sat); 11-10.30 Sun ☎ (01572) 868340

Fuller's London Pride; Oakham JHB; 3 changing beers (often Bakers Dozen) [H]

A sympathetic refurbishment of Nick's Restaurant in the corner of the market place. Part of the Knead group of pubs, the Lord Nelson is a characterful venue in a traditional town. It serves good beer and has become a popular addition to the county's real ale circuit. High-quality home-cooked food is available daily. A regular quiz night is hosted. **Q◑♿🚆🚌📶**

Whissendine

White Lion Inn 🏆

Main Street, LE15 7ET

⏲ 12-3 (not Mon), 5-11; 12-11 Sat; 12-10.30 Sun ☎ (01664) 474233 🌐 whitelioninn.com

Everards Tiger, Old Original; changing beers (often Brunswick) [H]

Recently refurbished Everards pub next to the village brook with a restaurant and accommodation in eight rooms. There are 11 handpumps which are all put to use during special events, with one dedicated to real cider. The landlord is a member of The Magic Circle and regularly entertains customers with his close-up magic. **Q🛋❀🛏◑⛺♣🍎🚌📶**

REAL ALE BREWERIES

Bakers Dozen Ketton
Grainstore Oakham

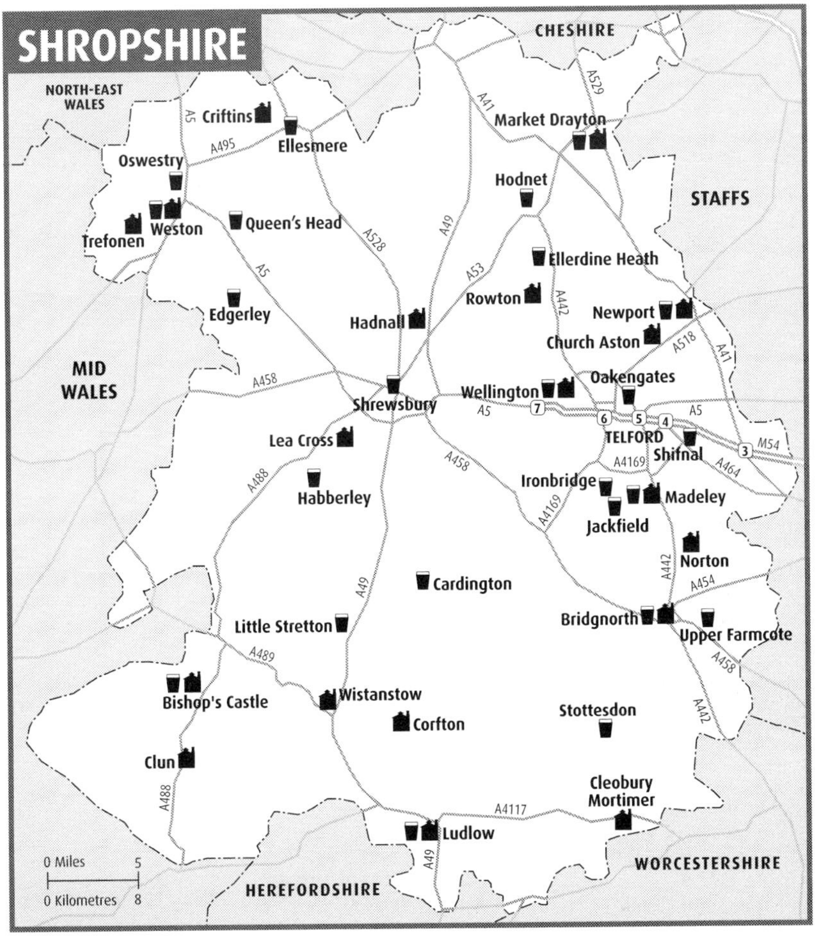

Bishop's Castle

Castle Hotel

The Square, SY9 5BN

11-11 (10.30 Sun) ☎ (01588) 638403

thecastlehotelbishopscastle.co.uk

Hobsons Best; Salopian Oracle; 1 changing beer (sourced locally; often Clun, Six Bells, Three Tuns) Ⓗ

The 18th-century, Grade II-listed Castle Hotel has a great deal going for it. Beautifully sited at the top of the town and with character-filled rooms, it boasts a wonderful beer garden with fine vistas, and fires in each of the three bars in winter. Traditional pub games are available. Three beers are on offer from local breweries plus the regional brew, Salopian's Oracle.

Q P (553)

Bridgnorth

Bell & Talbot L

2 Salop Street, High Town, WV16 4QU

4-11; 12-11 Sat; 12-10.30 Sun ☎ (01746) 763233

bellandtalbotbridgnorth.co.uk

Bathams Best Bitter; Wye Valley HPA; 3 changing beers (often Hobsons, Salopian) Ⓗ

A friendly two-roomed traditional locals' pub, formerly a 19th-century coaching inn. It is used by local groups and is popular with bikers, walkers, cyclists and bridge players. Beers on the five handpumps are always local ales. The conservatory leads to a small covered courtyard used as a smoking area. Filled cobs and traditional snacks are

REAL ALE BREWERIES

All Nations Madeley (NEW)
Chapel Criftins
Church Aston Church Aston (NEW)
Clun Clun
Corvedale Corfton
Finney's Wellington (NEW)
Hobsons Cleobury Mortimer
Hop & Stagger Norton
Joule's Market Drayton
Ludlow Ludlow
Offa's Dyke Trefonen
Plan B Newport
Rowton Rowton/Wellington
Salopian Hadnall
Severn Valley Bridgnorth (NEW)
St Annes Lea Cross
Stonehouse Weston
Three Tuns Bishop's Castle
Wood Wistanstow

available. Note the bar in the front snug room is partially made from railway sleepers.
❀⇌(SVR)♣▣❀ᯤ

Black Horse 🄻

4 Bridge Street, Low Town, WV15 6AF
☉ 12-midnight (11 Sun) ☎ (01746) 762415
🌐 theblackhorsebridgnorth.co.uk
Bathams Best Bitter; Hobsons Town Crier; Three Tuns XXX; Wye Valley HPA, Butty Bach; 3 changing beers (sourced regionally) Ⓗ
A popular free house close to the bridge over the River Severn serving five locally sourced beers plus up to three changing ales. The large front bar hosts regular live music, usually on Saturday evening. The wood-panelled side bar and conservatory are fitted with wide-screen TVs showing major sporting events. Filled rolls are often available but no meals. The smoking area leads to a long courtyard and car park accessed from Severn Street.
❀♿⇌(SVR)♣P▣❀ᯤ

Golden Lion 🄻

83 High Street, High Town, WV16 4DS
☉ 11.30-11; 12-10.30 Sun ☎ (01746) 762016
🌐 goldenlionbridgnorth.co.uk
Holden's Black Country Mild, Black Country Bitter, Golden Glow, Special; 1 changing beer (sourced locally) Ⓗ
This 17th-century coaching inn is a traditional town-centre pub with separate public and lounge bars. Purchased in 2017 by Holden's Brewery and extensively refurbished, pictures on the walls of the two comfortable lounge bars record the history of the building. At the rear there is an outdoor patio drinking area, a covered smoking area and a car park. Fresh cobs are served and B&B accommodation is available.
Q❀⇌(SVR)♣●P▣❀ᯤ

King's Head 🄻

3 Whitburn Street, High Town, WV16 4QN
☉ 11-11 (midnight Fri & Sat); 12-11 Sun ☎ (01746) 762141
🌐 thekingsheadbridgnorth.co.uk
Hobsons Twisted Spire, Town Crier; Wye Valley HPA; 2 changing beers (sourced nationally) Ⓗ
A busy Grade II-listed town-centre pub which features oak beams, leaded windows and three open fires in winter. Good food, sourced from local suppliers, is served daily (booking recommended). Three regular beers are served from nearby breweries plus seasonal and guest ales. The pub is popular with locals and visitors at all times of the year. Well-behaved dogs are welcome in the bar and lounge area. ❀◑♿⇌(SVR)▣❀ᯤ

Old Castle 🄻 ✔

10/11 West Castle Street, WV16 4AB (between SVR and town centre)
☉ 11.30-11 (10.30 Sun) ☎ (01746) 711420
🌐 oldcastlebridgnorth.co.uk
Hobsons Town Crier; Sharp's Doom Bar; Wye Valley HPA, Butty Bach Ⓗ
A popular pub dating from the 1600s, a short walk from the Severn Valley Railway. The bar in the middle has four handpumps serving local and regional ales. The dining area caters for meals served lunchtimes and evenings. Games are played in the conservatory at the rear, with a pool table and dartboard, and there is a small adjoining function room. Outside, the garden has lovely views, ideal for dining on a beautiful summer's day. ❀◑⇌(SVR)♣▣(436,890)❀ᯤ

Railwayman's Arms 🄻 ✔

Severn Valley Railway Station, Hollybush Road, WV16 5DT (follow signs for SVR, pub is on Platform 1)
☉ 11-11 (10.30 Sun) ☎ (01746) 760920 🌐 svr.co.uk
Bathams Best Bitter; Bewdley Worcestershire Way; Hobsons Mild, Best, Town Crier; 4 changing beers (sourced nationally) Ⓗ
Located on Platform 1, this unique and popular pub at Bridgnorth Station is owned by the Severn Valley Railway and gets busy at weekends and holidays. It has been licensed since 1861 and is full of railway memorabilia. There are 10 handpumps, nine serving real ales from near and far, and one for real cider. The platform drinking area is alongside the steam locomotives. There are plans for a major refurbishment.
Q❀⇌(SVR)●P▣(436,101)❀ᯤ

Cardington

Royal Oak

SY6 7JZ
☉ closed Mon; 12-2.30, 6-11 Tue-Fri; 12-midnight (11 winter) Sat; 12-9 (4 winter) Sun ☎ (01694) 771266
🌐 at-the-oak.com
Ludlow Best; Sharp's Doom Bar; 2 changing beers Ⓗ
The Royal Oak, dating back to the 15th century, is reputedly Shropshire's oldest continually licensed pub, and is the archetypal country inn. The single room is multi-functional with a bar, lounge and dining area, and has a relaxed ambience. It is low beamed and dominated by a large inglenook fireplace which provides a home for various interesting artefacts. A good choice of beers includes a mix of local and regional brews.
Q❀◑▲♣●P▣(540)❀ᯤ

Edgerley

Royal Hill Inn

SY10 8ES
☉ 12-3, 5-11; 12-11 Fri-Sun ☎ (01743) 741242
Salopian Shropshire Gold; Three Tuns XXX; 1 changing beer (often Wye Valley) Ⓗ
Set on a quiet road with its garden bordering the River Severn, this delightful pub dating from the 18th century looks out toward the Breidden Hills. The extended but well-preserved building comprises a number of cosy rooms and a tiny bar. Food is served lunchtime and evenings, but if travelling you may wish to phone in advance. Camping is available at the back of the pub grounds and caravans are welcome too.
❀◑▲P❀

Ellerdine Heath

Royal Oak 🄻 ✔

Hazles Road, TF6 6RL (midway between A442 and A53) SJ603226
☉ 12-11 ☎ (01939) 250300
Hobsons Best; Rowton Star Light; Wye Valley HPA; 3 changing beers (sourced locally; often Rowton, Salopian) Ⓗ
This long-standing Guide entry, also known as the Tiddly, is at the heart of the local rural community, used by young farmers, shooting parties and folk groups. Rallies are also hosted. Features include a pool table, dartboard, real fires in both main rooms, a smoking shed and a marquee Easter to October. Food is served in the dining room – lunchtimes weekends only and evenings

Wednesday to Sunday. A real gem, well worth the short detour from the main roads.
Q🐎❀◑♿⛺♣●P🐾📶

Ellesmere

Vault
Old Town Hall, High Street, SY12 0EP
⏲ closed Mon & Tue; 1-10 Wed; 1-11 Thu-Sun
☎ (01691) 587481
3 changing beers (often Chapel, Salopian, Stonehouse) Ⓗ
Located in the cellar of the old town hall, the Vault resembles a brick-built undercroft but, because of its size, there is no feeling of being closed-in. Opened in 2017, it has already proved popular with all ages by selling real ale, craft beer, speciality wines and cocktails. Up to three handpumps usually offer beers from local breweries such as Chapel, Stonehouse and Salopian. The food is basic but nutritious, including ploughman's, platters, pies and pasties. ◑🚌

White Hart Ⓛ
Birch Road, SY12 0ET
⏲ 3-midnight; 1-1am Sat & Sun ☎ (01691) 624653
Salopian Shropshire Gold; 3 changing beers Ⓗ
A Grade II-listed building of the early Jacobean period with a wealth of exposed timber, but with some later alterations. The interior comprises a public bar and a lounge. Outside, the drinking area to the rear has a tented gazebo. The pub was once owned by the Border Brewery of Wrexham. Three guest beers are often sourced from local breweries. Convenient for boating folk on the Llangollen Canal as the marina is close by. ❀P🚌🐾📶

Habberley

Mytton Arms Ⓛ
SY5 0TP
⏲ 4-11; 12-11 Fri-Sun ☎ (01743) 792490
Hobsons Best; Three Tuns XXX; 2 changing beers (often Hobsons, Joule's) Ⓗ
Situated in a small village on the edge of the south Shropshire Hills, somewhat off the beaten track, this popular pub is worth finding. There are four low-beamed rooms and a friendly rustic atmosphere where conversation predominates. Outside are seats to the front and a paved area with a vine-covered pergola to the side. A well-known local character and pub regular features on the inn sign. The South Shropshire Hills shuttle bus provides transport in summer. Q❀♣●P🚌🐾

Hodnet

Bear Ⓛ
Drayton Road, TF9 3NH
⏲ 12-11; 12-10 (7 winter) Sun ☎ (01630) 685214
🌐 bearathodnet.co.uk
4 changing beers (sourced nationally; often Black Sheep, Rowton, Three Tuns) Ⓗ
A welcoming 17th-century village pub opposite a historic church famed for its Holy Grail connections. There are four main public areas with cosy log-burning fires catering both for diners and drinkers. The original bear pit can be viewed through a glass panel in the floor of Wilfred's Retreat. Dogs are welcome in the snug. Four regularly changing real ales are from local and national breweries.
Q🐎❀🛏◑♿⛺♣P🚌(64)🐾📶

Little Stretton

Green Dragon
Ludlow Road, SY6 6RE
⏲ 11.30-11.30 ☎ (01694) 722925
Ludlow Gold; Wye Valley Bitter; 2 changing beers (often Hobsons, Wye Valley) Ⓗ
The pub is in a picturesque location in the Shropshire Hills Area of Outstanding Natural Beauty, with an abundance of walks in the district. The L-shaped bar has a comfortable and welcoming feel and the pleasant dining areas are well used. A collection of wonderfully shaped clay pipes on the bar wall may be of interest. The beers are mostly from local breweries, and the cider is local too.
🐎❀◑♣●P🚌(435)🐾📶

Ludlow

Blood Bay
13 High Street, SY8 1BS
⏲ 5-9; 12-9 Sat & Sun ☎ (01584) 872381
2 changing beers Ⓗ
This conserved Victorian property has a public bar, a tiny snug and a back bar, with original features exposed on the ground floor and much-earlier Georgian panelling on the first floor. Two beers are served: an IPA and a stout, brewed locally to an authentic recipe. Dogs on leads are welcome on ground floor only. Toilets are on the first floor. Under-16s, mobile phone use and smoking are prohibited. Q⇌🚌🐾

Church Inn
The Buttercross, SY8 1AW
⏲ 11-11; 12-midnight Fri & Sat; 12-10.30 Sun
☎ (01584) 874034 🌐 thechurchinn.com
Hobsons Best; Ludlow Gold, Black Knight, Boiling Well; Salopian Darwins Origin; 1 changing beer (sourced nationally) Ⓗ
Popular 14th-century town-centre pub, which has recently undergone a comprehensive refurbishment. The ground-floor drinking area has a contemporary feel with a range of seating types. There is also upstairs seating with spectacular views of the Church of St Laurence, from which the pub takes its name. Accommodation is available. Traditional, hearty pub grub is served.
🐎❀🛏◑⇌🚌🐾📶

Railway Shed Ⓛ
Station Drive, SY8 2PQ
⏲ 10-5 (6 Fri); 11-4 Sun ☎ (01584) 873291
🌐 theludlowbrewingcompany.co.uk
Ludlow Best, Blonde, Gold, Black Knight, Boiling Well, Stairway Ⓗ
The brewery tap and visitor centre for the Ludlow Brewing Company and, as the name suggests, once a transit depot for railway goods. An imaginative conversion, it is built on two levels, with two huge mash tuns on the upper level, and more comfortable seating and tables. On the ground floor there are hand-crafted timber tables and benches, together with a shop. Brewery visits are welcome and the centre is available for hire.
Q❀♿⇌●P🚌🐾📶

Rose & Crown
8 Church Street, SY8 1AP
⏲ 11-11 (midnight Fri & Sat); 11-10 Sun ☎ (01584) 875726
🌐 roseandcrowninnludlow.co.uk
Joule's Blonde, Pale Ale, Slumbering Monk, Old No.6; 2 changing beers (often Hobsons, Hop Back) Ⓗ

Hidden away in a courtyard, the Rose & Crown is probably Ludlow's oldest inn, possibly 12th century. Recent refurbishment has created a much larger pub with exposed beams and a fireplace. The Sun Room is open to the elements on one side and there is a garden area. A private room upstairs is available to small groups. Food is good honest pub grub such as bangers and mash or bubble and squeak. There is a carvery on Sunday.

Market Drayton

Clive & Coffyne

6 Shropshire Street, TF9 3BY

5-11 (midnight Thu; 2am Fri); 12-2am Sat; 12-midnight Sun
(01630) 657523

4 changing beers (sourced locally; often Hancocks, Hobsons) H

A town-centre Georgian house built in 1753 and named after Market Drayton's famous son, Sir Robert Clive (of India), and a mutton pie, a coffyne, once served to customers. The Clive offers four changing ales at the weekend with at least two on during the week, and is one of only three free houses in the town. With three open fires, it boasts a large outside decking area for the summer. The pub holds regular music and comic nights in the function room. P (64,164)

Red Lion

Great Hales Street, TF9 1JP

11-11 (midnight Fri & Sat) (01630) 652602

Joule's Blonde, Pale Ale, Slumbering Monk; 1 changing beer (sourced locally; often Joule's) H

A previous winner of the CAMRA/English Heritage Pub Design Award, this Joule's brewery tap was once a coaching inn, built in 1623. Its unique features include the Mouse Room – a Robert Thompson-inspired function room featuring carved mice – and an illuminated well in the main bar. Log fires and oak beams create a comfortable atmosphere where locally sourced food can be enjoyed from an extensive menu, with the Joule's range of beers brewed at the adjacent brewery.
Q P (64,164)

Salopian Star

21 Stafford Street, TF9 1HX

12-11; 9am-11 Fri-Sun (01630) 652530

Plan B New Alchemy, New Session IPA, Newport Pale Ale, Boscobel Bitter, Steam Stout H

With its larger-than-life landlord Harvey, this is a friendly, no-frills boozer – what you see is what you get. The pub serves three of the five ales produced by one of Shropshire's newest breweries, Plan B, or New Brew as it is more commonly known, based in Newport. Traditional pub games are popular here. Outside is an attractive and colourful seating area for warmer weather. A little gem.
(64,164)

Sandbrook Vaults

4 Shropshire Street, TF9 3BY

5-11; 12-midnight Fri & Sat; 11-11 Sun (01630) 478405

Joule's Blonde, Pale Ale, Slumbering Monk; 1 changing beer (sourced locally; often Joule's) H

You are guaranteed a warm welcome at this Joule's pub, originally built in 1653. It has a familiar easy-on-the-eye Joule's interior and well-kept ales from the brewery close by. Free hot food is available at the weekend (with an optional donation to charity). The pub hosts high-quality live acoustic music nights on Thursday and Sunday featuring regional bands.
Q (64,164)

William Chester

20 Shropshire Street, TF9 3BY

11-11 (01630) 652315

4 changing beers (sourced locally; often Beartown, Burton Bridge, Slater's) H

A small, comfortable bar in the centre of town offering three local beers on handpull, including a regular Slater's ale, as well as a cider. With a thoughtfully furnished interior, this pub is full of character and has a cosy atmosphere. Outside, there is a bright, terraced courtyard at the rear open until 10pm, which is a suntrap in the summer months. Q (64,164)

Newport

New Inn

2 Stafford Road, TF10 7LX

12-11.30 (01952) 812295 thenewinnnewport.co.uk

Joule's Blonde, Pale Ale, Slumbering Monk; 2 changing beers (sourced locally; often Joule's, Ludlow, Wood) H

Originally a coaching inn, the building was extended and refurbished by Joule's in 2016, retaining some old features and complementing them with wood panelling and tiled floors. A woodburner and open fireplace give a cosy feel to the drinking and dining areas. There is always a seasonal beer and a changing guest ale, plus two real ciders. Good home-cooked food includes vegetarian dishes. Live music plays on Sunday evening and a beer and cider festival is held in September. Q (5,519)

Oswestry

Bailey Head

Bailey Head, SY11 1PZ (opp Guildhall)

12 (3 Mon)-11.30; 12-12.30am Sat; 12-10.30 Sun
baileyhead.co.uk

6 changing beers (sourced nationally; often Oakham, Salopian) H

Located in the market near the old castle, this free house opened in 2016. Seven constantly changing real ales, three KeyKeg beers and draught cider are on offer. Beers are sourced locally, regionally and nationally, usually from microbreweries, and served in thirds on request. Locally produced, traditional food is available until 10pm. Events include Meet the Brewer and quiz nights. The market car park is close by.

Black Lion

Salop Road, SY11 2RJ (S of town centre on B4579)

6-11; 4.30-midnight Fri; 12-midnight Sat; 12-11 Sun
(01691) 652745

Salopian Oracle; 4 changing beers (sourced locally; often Hobsons, Salopian, Wood) H

Just inside the town's conservation area, this family-run establishment is a true community pub and has a warm and friendly atmosphere. It is home to sports teams and social groups, with plenty of TVs for sports fans and tasting boards for beer lovers. The central bar divides the pub into a comfortable lounge at the front and public bar at the rear. Well-kept ales from various local and regional brewers can be enjoyed.
Q P

Queen's Head

Queen's Head
West Felton, SY11 4EB
🌐 12-11 ☎ (01691) 610255
🌐 the-queens-head-oswestry.co.uk
Church End Fallen Angel; Stonehouse Station Bitter, Off the Rails Ⓗ
Located next to the Montgomery Canal, this is one of only two Shropshire pubs on the canal. Primarily a dining venue, it has an attractive conservatory and a pleasant bar area. Meals are served from noon until 9pm. All beers are locally sourced, and Sweeney Mountain real cider is served. The front patio has views over the canal.
Q🕸🚸◐◖&●P🚃(70)🌸🛜

Shifnal

Plough Inn ⓛ
26 Broadway, TF11 8AZ
🌐 12 (4 Mon)-11; 12-10.30 Sun ☎ (01952) 463118
🌐 theploughinnshifnal.co.uk
Hobsons Mild, Best; 6 changing beers (sourced regionally; often Bathams, Sarah Hughes, Six Bells) Ⓗ
Traditional, family-run free house dating back to the 17th century, with exposed beams and tiled floors. Ten handpulled ales including at least one strong and one dark beer are on offer, together with two ciders. Hearty home-cooked meals are served, including a popular roast on Sunday. The huge beer garden is a suntrap in the summer months, and a large function room is available to hire. The weekly Wednesday quiz night is a must. Opening hours can vary in the winter, so please call ahead. Q🕸🚸◐◖≠♣●🚃🌸🛜

White Hart 🏆 ⓛ ✅
High Street, TF11 8BH
🌐 12-11 ☎ (01952) 461161
Greene King Abbot; Salopian Shropshire Gold; Wye Valley HPA, Butty Bach; 5 changing beers (sourced regionally; often Enville) Ⓗ
This Grade II-listed, 17th-century free house has been a regular in the Guide for more than 24 years, with nine handpumps and real cider from the cellar. The timber-framed, two-room pub has a large car park, beer garden, and sunny walled patio area off the lounge. There are no noisy games machines; only good conversation, convivial company and a popular lunchtime food menu (no food Sun). Family run and community oriented, with knowledgeable staff, it has won local CAMRA branch Pub of the Year numerous times.
Q🕸🚸◐≠♣●P🚃🌸

Shrewsbury

Abbey ⓛ ✅
83 Monkmoor Road, Monkmoor, SY2 5AZ
🌐 12-11 (midnight Fri & Sat) ☎ (01743) 236788
🌐 theabbeyshrewsbury.co.uk
Bombardier; Sharp's Doom Bar; 6 changing beers Ⓗ
A large pub with several alcoves and multiple fireplaces. The publican is an ale enthusiast, running frequent Meet the Brewer sessions and several beer festivals a year. In between, he has expanded the range of guest ales and real ciders. Food is served until 10pm every night. There are regular community events including quizzes and occasional live music. 🚸🚸◐◖&●P🚃(1)🛜

Admiral Benbow ⓛ
24 Swan Hill, SY1 1NF (just off Main Square)
🌐 5-11; 12-11 Sat; 7-10.30 Sun ☎ (01743) 244423
Ludlow Gold; Slater's Top Totty; 4 changing beers (sourced locally; often Hobsons, Salopian, Wye Valley) Ⓗ
Spacious free house serving a range of Shropshire and Herefordshire beers plus a selection of ciders from Rosie's including Black Bart and Wicked Wasp. A good choice of Belgian, American and other foreign beers is also offered. A small room off the bar can be used for private functions, and there is a seating and smoking area outside at the rear. Children are not permitted. The Admiral was a notorious 17th-century naval officer born in Shrewsbury. Q🕸≈♣●🚃🛜

Coach & Horses ⓛ
23 Swan Hill, SY1 1NF
🌐 11.30-midnight (12.30am Fri & Sat); 12-11.30 Sun
☎ (01743) 365661
Salopian Shropshire Gold, Oracle; Stonehouse Station Bitter; 3 changing beers Ⓗ
Set in a quiet street off the main shopping area, the pub is a peaceful haven, with magnificent floral displays in summer. Victorian in style, it has a wood-panelled bar, a small side snug area and a large lounge where meals are served lunchtimes and evenings. Bar snacks are also available at lunchtimes. Cheddar Valley or Sweeney Mountain cider is dispensed on handpull.
Q◐◖&≈♣●🚃🌸🛜

Cross Foxes
27 Longden Coleham, SY3 7DE (close to River Severn)
🌐 11-midnight (11 Sun) ☎ (01743) 355050
Draught Bass; Salopian Shropshire Gold; Three Tuns XXX; Wood Shropshire Lad Ⓗ
The pub has been a free house since its purchase from Mitchells & Butlers in the late 1980s, and run by the same family since 1985. It has one large, L-shaped room, with the bar and major drinking area on the large stroke, the smaller stroke occupied by the darts and a smaller drinking area. The main area has an efficient woodburner and the walls are adorned with sports trophies and a fine Bass mirror. Q&♣🚃🛜

Loggerheads ★ ⓛ ✅
1 Church Street, SY1 1UG
🌐 11-11; 12-11 Sun ☎ (01743) 362398
Banks's Amber Ale; Eagle Firsty 15; Jennings Sneck Lifter; Marston's Pedigree; Young's London Gold; 4 changing beers (sourced nationally) Ⓗ
This 18th-century, Grade II-listed, town-centre pub has a nationally important historic interior, comprising a small bar, servery and three other rooms. The bar to the left is served from a hatch and was 'Gents Only' until 1975. The rear room served from the same hatch has portraits of Shropshire poets. The pub hosts regular folk and acoustic music events. Q≈🚃🌸

Montgomery's Tower ⓛ ✅
Lower Claremont Bank, SY1 1RT
🌐 8am-midnight (1am Wed & Thu; 2am Fri & Sat)
☎ (01743) 239080
Greene King IPA; Salopian Shropshire Gold; Wood Shropshire Lad; 4 changing beers (often Sadler's, Sharp's, Slater's) Ⓗ
Close to the Quarry Park and handy for Theatre Severn, this Lloyds No.1 offers a choice of two bars. To the left is a large open area rich in natural light,

with a smoking area to the rear. The bar to the right provides quieter surroundings and subdued lighting, except on Friday and Saturday when there is a DJ. The walls display prints illustrating local history and famous Salopians.

Nag's Head

22 Wyle Cop, SY1 1XB

11.30-midnight; 10.30-1am Fri; 12-midnight Sun (01743) 362455

Hobsons Best; Timothy Taylor Landlord; Wye Valley HPA; 2 changing beers (often Titanic) H

Situated on the historic Wyle Cop, the main features of this Grade II-listed, timber-framed building are best appreciated externally – in particular the upper-storey jettying and, to the rear, the timber remnants of a 14th-century hall house including a screened passage which provided protection from draughts (and now offers shelter for smokers). The old-style interior has remained unaltered for many years. The pub is said to be haunted and features on the Shrewsbury Ghost Trail.

Prince of Wales

30 Bynner Street, Belle Vue, SY3 7NZ

5-midnight; 12-midnight Fri-Sun (01743) 343301 theprince.pub

Hobsons Mild, Twisted Spire; St Austell Tribute; Salopian Golden Thread; Wainwright; 1 changing beer (sourced locally; often Rowton, Stonehouse, Wood) H

Welcoming two-roomed community pub with a heated smoking shelter and a large suntrap deck adjoining a bowling green. The green is overlooked by a 19th-century maltings. Darts, dominoes and bowls teams abound. Beer festivals take place each year in February and May. Shrewsbury Town FC memorabilia adorn the building both inside and out, with some of the seating from the old Gay Meadow ground skirting the bowling green. Westons Rosie's Pig is on handpull.

Q P

Salopian Bar

Smithfield Road, SY1 1PW

11-midnight (11 Tue); 11-11 Sun (01743) 351505

Hobsons Best; Oakham Citra; Salopian Oracle; 5 changing beers (often Oakham, Salopian) H

A single-room pub popular with all age groups. The bar's management strives to vary the beer, cider and perry range to satisfy public demand. Regular cider and perry are provided by Westons and Thatchers, and an increasing range of bottled beer, including gluten-free, is also available. Large-screen TVs show coverage of major sporting events. Live music features on Friday evening.

Three Fishes

4 Fish Street, SY1 1UR

11.30-3, 5-11; 11.30-11.30 Fri & Sat; 12-10.30 Sun (01743) 344793

Three Tuns Stout; 4 changing beers (often Oakham, Salopian, Stonehouse) H

Fifteenth-century building standing in the shadow of two churches, St Alkmund's and St Julian's, within the maze of streets and passageways in the town's medieval quarter. Freshly prepared food is available lunchtimes and early evenings Monday to Saturday. The pub offers a range of up to five local and national ales, usually including some dark beers, and a choice of real ciders and perries.

Q

Woodman

32 Coton Hill, SY1 2DZ

4-midnight; 12-midnight Sat & Sun (01743) 351007

Salopian Shropshire Gold; Wye Valley Butty Bach; 3 changing beers (sourced regionally; often Abbeydale, Ossett) H

Half-brick and half-timbered black and white corner pub, originally built in the 1800s, destroyed by fire in 1923, and rebuilt in 1925. The building is reputedly haunted by the ex-landlady who died in the fire. The wonderful oak-panelled lounge has two real log fires and traditional settles, and the separate bar has the original stone-tiled flooring, wooden seating, fire and leaded windows. The courtyard has a heated smoking area and seating. The bar specialises in pale, hoppy beers.

Q

Stottesdon

Fighting Cocks

1 High Street, DY14 8TZ

closed Mon; 12-2.30, 5-11.30; 12-midnight Sat; 12-11 Sun (01746) 718270 fightingcocks.co.uk

Hobsons Twisted Spire; Ludlow Blonde; Wye Valley HPA, Butty Bach H

Set in the heart of rural south Shropshire, this local CAMRA award-winning pub was first licensed in 1830. A traditional bar with log fire leads to two dining rooms where locally sourced food is served. Live music features most weekends. Outside is a patio area and lawned garden with a children's play area. Walkers and cyclists are welcome. A shop/cafe/function room is at the rear of the premises. P

Telford: Ironbridge

Coracle Micropub & Beer Shop

27 High Street, TF8 7AD

12-10 (01952) 432664

6 changing beers (sourced nationally; often Salopian, Tiny Rebel) H/G

Opened in May 2018 by two beer enthusiasts, this is a quiet bar where conversation is enjoyed between locals and visitors. It has one main room but a semi-dividing wall effectively creates two separate drinking areas, enhancing the intimate drinking ambience. The well-stocked fridge contains up to 80 bottled and canned beers from far and wide, and there are more bottled beers in the cellar. A good selection of bar snacks is available, including a gratis cheeseboard on Sunday. Children are welcome until 7pm.

Q

Telford: Jackfield

Black Swan

Lloyds Head, TF8 7LZ (on road through Jackfield village)

12-midnight (01952) 882471 theblackswanjackfield.com

Hobsons Old Prickly, Town Crier; Sharp's Doom Bar; Thwaites Original H

A traditional country free house, over 350 years old, situated next to the River Severn, within the Ironbridge Gorge World Heritage Site. The original rooms have been knocked through and are warmed by a woodburner in the winter. The walls are adorned with old photos and prints of the local area and its industrial heritage. In an idyllic spot, especially in summer, the garden overlooks the

River Severn. Home-cooked food is available every day including daily specials.
Q🛌❀◐▲P🚌(8,18)🐾📶

Telford: Madeley

All Nations 🄻

20 Coalport Road, TF7 5DP (signed off Legges Way, opp Blists Hill Museum)
12-midnight ☎ (01952) 585747
Hobsons Twisted Spire; 2 changing beers (sourced regionally; often Hobsons, Ludlow, Wye Valley) 🄷
A traditional 1832 brewhouse in a secluded setting in the Ironbridge Gorge World Heritage Site. The walls are decorated with local memorabilia and there is an outside courtyard with seating. Families and dogs are welcome. Newspapers are available and there is a book exchange. A quiz is hosted on Monday and live bands on Sunday from May to July. The refurbished brewhouse brews All Nations beers on Mondays, only available in the pub.
Q🛌❀🛏▲P🐾

Telford: Oakengates

Crown Inn 🄻 ✔

Market Street, TF2 6EA
12-11 ☎ (01952) 610888 🌐 crown.oakengates.net
Hobsons Twisted Spire, Best; 10 changing beers (sourced nationally; often Burton Bridge, Joule's, Rudgate) 🄷
Traditional town pub with three separate drinking areas. Beer festivals are held in May and October with up to 34 handpulls. A good range of continental bottled beers is also kept. The pub is home to Telford Acoustic Club, and features live music and quiz nights. Food includes pies and pasties, plus takeaways from the neighbouring Indian restaurant. At the rear is a suntrap courtyard; disabled access is also via the rear.
Q🛌❀♿🚂♣P🚌🐾📶

Station Hotel 🄻

42 Market Street, TF2 6DU
11-11; 12-11 Sun ☎ (01952) 612949
8 changing beers (sourced nationally; often Abbeydale, Pictish, Salopian) 🄷
This multi-roomed, traditional pub has been in the Guide for many years, attracting locals and visitors. It specialises in beers from northern breweries, as well as beers from the local area. The tiled front room has a warming real fire, bench seating surrounded by railway memorabilia and a blackboard listing current and forthcoming beers. Excellent home-made rolls, pies and cheese are also usually available to eat in or take home.
Q❀🚂♣🚌🐾

Telford: Wellington

Cock Hotel 🄻

148 Holyhead Road, TF1 2DL
4-11.30; 12-11 Fri-Sun ☎ (01952) 244954
🌐 cockhotel.co.uk
Joule's Blonde, Pale Ale, Slumbering Monk; 4 changing beers (sourced regionally; often Finneys, Hobsons, Joule's) 🄷
An award-winning 18th-century Grade II-listed coaching inn with eight handpulls dispensing mostly regional ales. Friendly and comfortable, this two-roomed pub has a large main room with the bar and a fire in winter, while the smaller front room provides more seating. A rear semi-covered courtyard is used by smokers. Award-winning pork pies are served from the bar. B&B accommodation and a meeting room are available. There is no music or TV, just interesting conversation and good ales. Q❀🛏♣P🚌🐾📶

Pheasant Inn 🄻

54 Market Street, TF1 1DT
11-11 (midnight Fri & Sat); 12-10.30 Sun
☎ (01952) 260683
Everards Tiger; Rowton Ironbridge Gold; 5 changing beers (sourced nationally; often Finneys, Rowton) 🄷
Family-run Rowton Brewery tap with nine handpulls, three devoted to Rowton's own ales, plus one dark beer and two ciders. Situated opposite the market, it has one large comfortable room with a logburner. The large suntrap beer garden next to the brewery has a covered smoking area. Home-made food is available Monday to Saturday 11am-4pm plus bar snacks at any time. A popular cheese night is held on the last Tuesday of the month, plus other community/charity events throughout the year. Q🛌❀◐♿🚂🍎P🚌🐾📶

Upper Farmcote

Lion o' Morfe 🄻

WV15 5PS (½ mile from A458 signposted Claverley) SO770919
12-11 ☎ (01746) 389935
Enville Ale; Hobsons Town Crier; Three Tuns XXX; Wye Valley HPA; 2 changing beers (sourced locally) 🄷
First licensed in the 1850s, this former Georgian farmhouse is situated in open countryside three miles east of Bridgnorth. A cosy bar and snug, both with open fires, are complemented by a smart lounge. Six handpumps dispense cask ales, mainly from local breweries, and cider from a nearby farm. Darts and other games are played, as well as boules on an outside piste. Popular with walkers and cyclists, a warm welcome awaits all visitors.
Q🛌❀◐▲♣🍎P🐾

Weston

Stonehouse Brewery 🄻

Stonehouse, Weston Road, SY10 9ES (just off A483 Oswestry bypass)
9am-5 (7 Thu & Fri); 10-7 Sat; closed Sun
☎ (01691) 676457 🌐 stonehousebrewery.co.uk
Stonehouse Sunlander, Station Bitter, Zaffir, Cambrian Gold, Off the Rails; 1 changing beer (often Stonehouse) 🄷
The family-run Stonehouse Brewery bar and shop is part of the brewery and is next to the preserved Cambrian Railway. The building has a pleasant rustic style and serves only Stonehouse products – at least four beers plus Sweeney Mountain Cider and Henstone spirits (whisky, gin, apple brandy, vodka) distilled on site. Bottles, gift packs and 'fill your own' are available. Brewery tours are by appointment. Q🛌❀♿♣🍎P🚌🐾📶

Not all chemicals are bad. Without chemicals such as hydrogen and oxygen, for example, there would be no way to make water, a vital ingredient in beer. **Dave Barry**

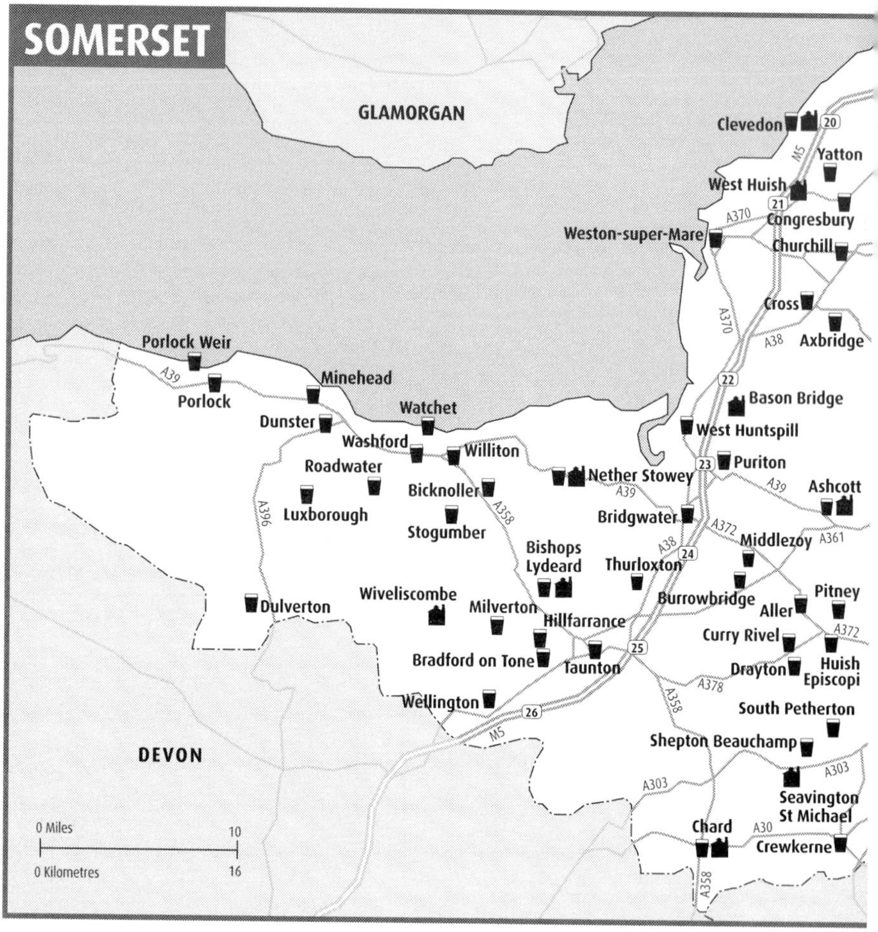

Aller

Old Pound Inn

1 High Street, TA10 0RA (centre of village)
11.30-11; 12-10.30 Sun ☎ (01458) 250469
oldpoundinn.com
Butcombe Original Ⓗ**; 1 changing beer (sourced regionally; often Exmoor, Otter, Teignworthy)** Ⓗ/Ⓖ
Formerly known as the White Lion, this pub was renamed in 1980 as it stands on the ground of the old village pound. It has a Dutch open fire in the centre of the bar, and offers a varying selection of regional beers on a sprung stillage. In addition to the main bar is a snug which is said to be haunted. Excellent food is served in the restaurant or bar area. Accommodation is available in the seven bedrooms. Q❀◑♿⛺♣P🚌(16)🐾📶

Ashcott

Ring o' Bells

16 High Street, TA7 9PZ (signposted off A39)
12-2.30, 7-11; 12-2.30, 7-10.30 Sun ☎ (01458) 210232
ringobells.com
2 changing beers (sourced regionally; often Bays, Cheddar Ales, Teignworthy) Ⓗ
An 18th-century free house which has been in the same family ownership for over 30 years. There are traditional beamed areas on split levels with a real fire and a separate restaurant. In contrast, there is a modern skittle alley/function room at the rear. Good home-cooked food is served, with meals and ales available to take away. Wilkins cider is on tap. Regular live music and a monthly pub quiz night are some of the attractions. Close to Ham Wall and Shapwick Heath nature reserves.
❀◑♿⛺♣P🚌(29,75)🐾📶

Axbridge

Lamb ✔

The Square, BS26 2AP
11.30-11 (midnight Fri & Sat); 12-11 Sun
☎ (01934) 732253
Butcombe Original; 2 changing beers (often Butcombe, Milestone) Ⓗ
Lovely Butcombe-owned Grade II-listed coaching house in the village square. Inside is a large low-beamed bar area with several smaller, quieter areas leading off it, where traditional pub games can be played. Outside drinking spaces are to the front, as well as to the rear via the courtyard. Real cider is sold and there is an interesting food menu, including bar snacks. Directly opposite is the National Trust's medieval King John's Hunting Lodge, where Hanging Judge Jeffreys held court.
Q❀◑♿♣🚌(26,126)🐾📶

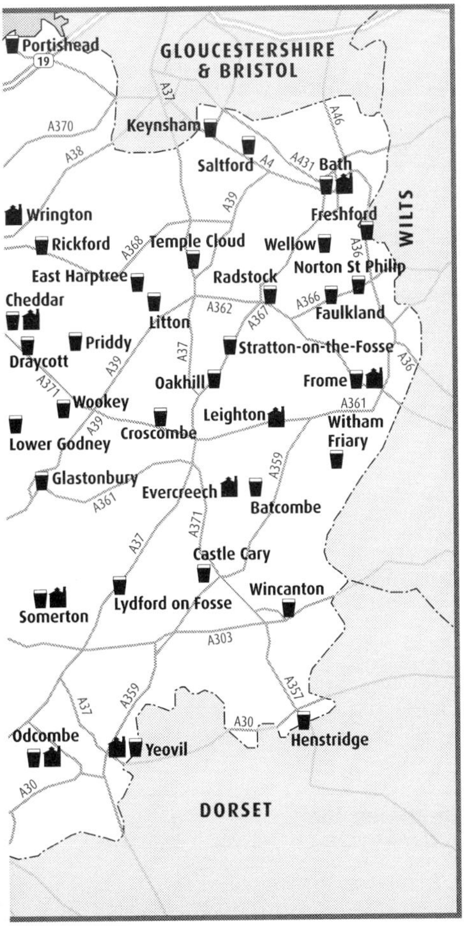

Batcombe

Three Horseshoes Inn

BA4 6HE (off Back Lane) ST69023908

11-3, 6-11; 11-11 Sat; 12-10.30 Sun ☎ (01749) 850359

thethreehorseshoesinn.co.uk

Butcombe Original; 3 changing beers H

A 400-year-old country pub which has a spacious bar with an inglenook fireplace and beamed ceiling, a stunning dining room with a vaulted ceiling, and a lawned garden overlooked by the church tower. Food is from local suppliers. Open to all, it welcomes drinkers, foodies, walkers, children (with colouring books and games, to keep them entertained) and dogs. Local cider is from Rich's.

Q❀◑P

Bath

Bath Brew House ✔

14 James Street West, BA1 2BX

12-midnight (1am Fri & Sat); 12-11 Sun

☎ (01225) 805609 thebathbrewhouse.com

Bath Brew House Gladiator, Emperor; 5 changing beers (sourced regionally; often Bristol Beer Factory, Flying Monk, Siren) H

Refurbishment in 2013 saw the former Midland Hotel transformed into a City Pub Company brewpub. The on-site brewery produces two regular beers, the refreshing and malty Gladiator (3.9% ABV) and the hoppy, citrussy Emperor (4.4% ABV), and rotating seasonal ales. Five guests, usually from nearby micros, are complemented by four craft beers. A large L-shaped bar gives out onto a dining area and a good-sized beer garden. The upstairs room hosts sports TV, quizzes, comedy and the like. ❀◑♿

Bell

103 Walcot Street, BA1 5BW

11.30-11 (midnight Fri & Sat); 12-10.30 Sun

☎ (01225) 460426 thebellinnbath.co.uk

Abbey Bellringer; Bath Ales Gem; Box Steam Golden Bolt; Butcombe Original; Hop Back Summer Lightning; Otter Ale; 3 changing beers (sourced regionally; often Arbor, Cotswold Lion, Keystone) H

Purchased by 518 of its regulars, fans and staff in a community buy-out in 2013, the Bell serves six regular ales plus three changing guests from local micros. Live music is a mainstay, with bands playing Monday and Wednesday evenings and Sunday lunchtime. In the separate back bar there are open mic nights on Thursday evenings. Features include bar billiards, board games and even a tiny launderette. At the rear is a walled garden with covered seating. ❀◑♣

Cross Keys ✔

Midford Road, Combe Down, BA2 5RZ

12-3, 5-11; 12-midnight Fri & Sat; 12-11 Sun

☎ (01225) 832002 crosskeysbath.co.uk

Butcombe Original; Sharp's Doom Bar; 2 changing beers (sourced locally) H

Historic inn dating from 1718 on the southern outskirts of the city, close to the beautiful Midford Valley and popular with walkers. Four ales are on the bar including guests, often from a local brewery of the month range of ales. Highly recommended, gastro standard, home-made food is served at all sessions. The main bar on the left still has many original features and an open fire. The restaurant is on the right and split across three levels. Parking is a bit restricted.

❀◑♿P(3,267)

REAL ALE BREWERIES

Abbey Bath
Bason Bridge Bason Bridge (NEW)
Bath Brewhouse Bath
Black Bear Wiveliscombe
Blindmans Leighton
Butcombe Wrington
Cheddar Cheddar
Cotleigh Wiveliscombe
Electric Bear Bath
Epic Beers (Pitchfork/3D Beer) West Huish
Exmoor Wiveliscombe
Fine Tuned Somerton
Frome Frome
Glastonbury Somerton
Glede Clevedon
Isle of Avalon Ashcott
Odcombe Odcombe
Quantock Bishops Lydeard
Ralph's Ruin Bath
Stowey Nether Stowey
Tapstone Chard
Twisted Oak Wrington
Wild Beer Evercreech
Windy Seavington St Michael
Yeovil Yeovil

Garrick's Head
7-8 St John's Place, Saw Close, BA1 1ET
🕔 12-11 (midnight Fri & Sat); 12-10.30 Sun
☎ (01225) 318368 ⊕ garricksheadpub.com
House beer (by Stonehenge); 4 changing beers (sourced locally; often Stonehenge) Ⓗ
A theatre pub for over 200 years, this was originally the town house of Richard 'Beau' Nash, Bath's 18th-century Master of Ceremonies. It is reputedly the most haunted pub in the city. Four guest ales are dispensed, mostly from regional micros and including some rarities. Traditional food sourced from local ingredients is served lunchtimes and evenings. Tables in the pedestrianised area outside are ideally placed for watching the world go by. ◑▶➡●🚊☺🛜

Old Green Tree ★
12 Green Street, BA1 2JZ
🕔 11-11; 12-6 Sun ☎ (01225) 448259
Butcombe Original; Pitchfork; house beer (by Blindmans); 3 changing beers (sourced locally) Ⓗ
A classic, unspoilt pub in a 300-year-old building. The three oak-panelled rooms include a superb northern-style drinking lobby. Although the pub can get crowded there is often space in the comfortable back bar. Guest beers are generally from local microbreweries, with a stout or porter usually on offer in the winter months. A local farmhouse cider is also sold, along with a range of fine wines and malt whiskies. Winter Sunday hours may be longer. Q◑➡●🚊

Pulteney Arms ✔
37 Daniel Street, BA2 6ND (on corner of Daniel St and Sutton St)
🕔 12-11 (midnight Thu-Sat); 12-10.30 Sun
☎ (01225) 463923 ⊕ thepulteneyarms.co.uk
Box Steam Piston Broke; Exmoor Ale; Otter Amber; Timothy Taylor Landlord; 2 changing beers (sourced nationally; often Black Sheep, Whitstable) Ⓗ
Tucked away near the end of Great Pulteney Street, this hostelry has been open since 1792. There are five gas light fittings, now sadly condemned, above the bar. The decor displays an emphasis on sport, particularly rugby. The cat symbol on the pub sign refers to the Pulteney coat of arms. The food menu is extensive and deservedly popular (not served Sun eve). The guest beers are usually from a national brewery. Note winter hours: pub is closed 3-5pm, Monday-Thursday. 🚲☺◑♣●🚊☺🛜

Raven
6-7 Queen Street, BA1 1HE
🕔 11.30-11 (midnight Fri & Sat); 12-10.30 Sun
☎ (01225) 425045 ⊕ theravenofbath.co.uk
House beer (by Blindmans); 4 changing beers (sourced regionally; often Gloucester, Moor Beer) Ⓗ
A busy 18th-century free house in the heart of Bath, voted the local CAMRA branch's Pub of the Year in 2018. The six ales include two brewed exclusively by Blindmans; guest beers come from far and wide. The main bar and quieter first-floor bar serve the same range of ales. Famous for its sausages and Pieminister pies, the Raven is one of the few pubs in Bath serving food on Sunday evening. It hosts several mini beer festivals each year. Q◑➡♣●◑🚊🛜

Royal Oak
Lower Bristol Road, Twerton, BA2 3BW (on A36 at intersection with road to Windsor Bridge)

🕔 4-midnight; 12-1am Fri & Sat; 12-midnight Sun
☎ (01225) 481409 ⊕ theroyaloakbath.co.uk
Downton IPA; Ralph's Ruin Sirius, Dark Side of the Ralph; 5 changing beers (often Butts, Downton, Stonehenge) Ⓗ
One regular from Downton, up to three from the pub's own brewery, Ralph's Ruin, and up to five guest ales from microbreweries near and far are served here alongside an interesting range of ciders, perries and bottled beers. Live music features on Wednesday evening and most weekends; Tuesday is quiz night. There is a small secluded garden and car park. Occasional beer festivals take place. Local CAMRA City Pub of the Year 2017. ⊛➡●P🚊☺

Star Inn ★ ✔
23 Vineyards, BA1 5NA
🕔 12-2.30, 5.30-midnight; 12-1am Fri & Sat; 12-midnight Sun
☎ (01225) 425072
Abbey Bellringer Ⓖ**; Draught Bass; 3 changing beers (sourced nationally; often Robinsons, Titanic)** Ⓗ
A main outlet for Abbey Ales, this classic town pub was fitted out by Gaskell and Chambers in 1928. Its four small rooms have benches around the walls, wood panelling and roaring fires. The smallest room has a single bench, called Death Row. The pub itself, which dates from around 1760, is coffin-shaped. Abbey Bellringer is served from the cask, and complimentary snuff is available. Cheese night is every Thursday and live music features on Fridays from 8.30pm. Q♣●🚊☺🛜

Bicknoller

Bicknoller Inn
32 Church Lane, TA4 4EL (off A358 SE of Williton)
🕔 11.30-3, 6-11; 11.30-11.30 Sat; 12-10 Sun
☎ (01984) 656234 ⊕ thebicknollerinn.co.uk
Palmers Copper Ale, Dorset Gold, 200, Tally Ho! Ⓗ
Set in the centre of a delightful village, this Palmers Brewery pub has small rooms off the main bar and a restaurant at the back. There is a large courtyard outside for a pleasant summer tipple. Charity and themed nights feature on the event calendar. The pub runs two boules teams and five skittles teams. Fish and chips night is popular on Tuesday. There is a TV for selected sports events such as Six Nations rugby.
Q🚲⊛◑♿♣●P🚊(28)☺🛜

Bishops Lydeard

Bird in Hand Ⓛ
34 Mount Street, TA4 3LH (signposted off A358 Taunton to Minehead road)
🕔 12-11 ☎ (01823) 432090
Sharp's Doom Bar; 4 changing beers (sourced regionally; often Exmoor, Otter, St Austell) Ⓗ
A free house that is very much a community pub at the centre of the village, and 10 minutes' walk from West Somerset Railway. Five ales are served, from local and South-West breweries. The slate-floored bar, warmed by an open fire in winter, leads to an eating area. Good locally produced and home-cooked food is served. The skittle alley accommodates functions. Families and dogs are welcome in the pub and large garden. Sport is shown on the TV in the bar.
Q🚲⊛◑♣P🚊(28)☺🛜

Quantock Brewery Tap

Westridge Way, Broadgauge Business Park, TA4 3RU (follow signs to West Somerset Railway and the shop can be found on the left just before the railway station)
10-5.30 (9 Thu; 11 Fri & Sat); closed Sun
(01823) 433812 quantockbrewery.co.uk
Quantock Ale, Ralehead, QPA, Wills Neck, Plastered Pheasant, Stag; 1 changing beer (sourced locally; often Quantock)
Brewery taproom with seven cask beers on handpump from the brewery. Two Quantock KeyKeg ales are always available, plus a monthly small-batch KeyKeg (subject to availability). Three guest KeyKeg beers are also served, typically from Northern Monk, Salopian, Thornbridge and Weird Beard. A brewery shop supplies takeaway bottles and other brewery gifts. An annual beer festival takes place in July and there are regular live band, comedy and quiz nights. Street food is available Friday and most Saturday evenings.
P (28)

Bradford on Tone

White Horse Inn

Regent Street, TA4 1HF (off A38 between Taunton and Wellington at Worlds's End jct)
12-3 (not Mon), 6.30-11; 12-3, 6-11.30 Fri & Sat; 11.30-5 Sun (01823) 461239
3 changing beers (sourced regionally; often Exeter, Otter, St Austell)
A friendly, well-established and well-run freehold pub, with real fires in winter warming both the bar and restaurant. Three different local and regional ales are sold. Good-standard home-cooked pub food is served at reasonable prices. The beautiful large garden hosts barbecues in summer. Regular events include music, skittle matches, quiz nights and gatherings of local interest groups. The pub closes at 5pm on Sunday from October till April.
P (22)

Bridgwater

Carnival Inn

37-39 St Mary Street, TA6 3LX
8am-midnight (1am Fri & Sat) (01278) 726180
Dartmoor Jail Ale; Greene King Abbot; Ruddles Best Bitter; Sharp's Doom Bar; 3 changing beers (sourced nationally; often Cotleigh, Exmoor, Quantock)
A town-centre Wetherspoon pub named after the famous illuminated carnival held in Bridgwater every November. There is a large bar area, with another room off to one side. At the rear is a family space, and outside is a courtyard garden with a smokers' area. A good range of changing Somerset and Devon ales is offered, complemented by an extensive food menu. Q

Burrowbridge

King Alfred Inn

Burrow Drove, TA7 0RB (on A361, 9 miles from Taunton)
12-11; 12-8 Sun (01823) 698379 king-alfred.co.uk
Bristol Beer Factory Fortitude; Butcombe Original; Otter Amber
A welcoming old-fashioned free house on the Somerset Levels north-east of Taunton, under the shadow of Burrow Mump, where allegedly King Alfred famously burnt the cakes. This pub is a perfect stopping-off point for walkers on the River Parrett Trail. Good locally sourced seasonal food is served, including excellent-value weekday hearty lunches and a Friday fish supper (no food Sun eve). Local ciders from Parsons are served alongside Somerset guests. Quiz night is the first Tuesday of the month. Coaches are welcome by arrangement.
P (29)

Castle Cary

George Hotel

Market Place, BA7 7AH
12-11; 12-10.30 Sun (01963) 350761
thegeorgehotelcastlecary.co.uk
Timothy Taylor Landlord; Wadworth 6X; 1 changing beer (sourced regionally)
A friendly thatched 15th-century hotel in the historic town centre. The main bar has an original inglenook fireplace with an elm beam said to date back to the 10th century; the rear bar provides a contemporary alternative. A separate restaurant and a snug add to the facilities. There is a small patio to the rear. Note that parking is for residents only. Q (667)

Chard

Cerdic

49-51 Fore Street, TA20 1PT (on A30 in centre of town)
7.30am-midnight (1am Fri & Sat) (01460) 260070
Greene King Abbot; Ruddles Best Bitter; Sharp's Doom Bar; 4 changing beers (sourced nationally; often Dorset, Exmoor, Otter)
A Wetherspoon pub that used to be a cinema of the same name before it closed in the 1960s. The well-kept guest beers are normally local and you may find a bigger selection at the weekend. In addition there are usually six real ciders. The pub has a bar area and a family eating area down some steps in a conservatory. A pleasant rear garden has been added and this closes at 9.30pm each evening.

Cheddar

White Hart

The Bays, BS27 3QN
10-midnight (1.30am Fri & Sat); 10-11.30 Sun
(01934) 741261 thewhitehartcheddar.co.uk
Butcombe Original; St Austell Tribute; 1 changing beer (often Cheddar Ales)
A traditional family-friendly country pub at the bottom of Cheddar Gorge, in a quiet street just off the main road through the Gorge. Good food, including vegan and gluten-free options, is served daily from 10am, with a popular carvery on Sunday. There is a large upstairs function room and a pleasant garden to the side. Folk music is played every other Thursday and there is a monthly quiz night on the third Wednesday of the month.
P

Churchill

Crown Inn

The Batch, Skinners Lane, BS25 5PP (off A38, 400yds S of A368 junction)
11-11 (midnight Fri); 12-11 Sun (01934) 852995
the-crown-inn.co.uk
Bath Ales Gem; Butcombe Original; Exmoor Ale; Palmers IPA; St Austell Tribute; house beer (by St Austell); 1 changing beer

Long-time Guide regular and winner of many CAMRA awards, the Crown is tucked away down a small lane close to the village centre. Several cosy rooms with stone-flagged floors are warmed by two log fires, and offer an assortment of seating. Excellent food is provided at lunchtimes using local ingredients. Up to eight beers, usually local, are served on gravity. Outside drinking areas are to the front and rear. Families are welcome away from the bar itself. A classic unchanged old pub; cash only, no cards. Q❀◐▲●P🚌(A2)🐾📶

Clevedon

Fallen Tree Micropub [L]

43 Hill Road, BS21 7PD
5.30 (4.30 Fri)-9.30; 12.30-9.30 Sat & Sun
☎ (01934) 310515 🌐 twistedoakbrewery.co.uk
Twisted Oak Fallen Tree, Spun Gold, Slippery Slope; 6 changing beers (sourced locally; often Twisted Oak) [G]
New micropub opened in February 2018 in a shopping area up a hill from the Grade I-listed Clevedon Pier. Between five and eight ales are served straight from casks located in the wooden stillage behind the bar. The pub is owned by Twisted Oak Brewery and guest beers are usually from local breweries such as Pitchfork, Bristol Beer Factory and Cheddar Ales. The filled rolls available at weekends come from Murrays deli on the same road. Q●🚌(X5,X6)🐾

Royal Oak ✔

35 Copse Road, BS21 7QN (behind ice cream parlour near pier)
12-11 (midnight Fri & Sat) ☎ (01275) 563879
🌐 theroyaloakclevedon.co.uk
Butcombe Original; St Austell Tribute; Sharp's Doom Bar, Atlantic; 1 changing beer [H]
Lively, friendly, mid-terrace pub close to the seafront and connected via an alley. It has a big front window and an unexpectedly large interior with many rooms. This community hub is home to cribbage and cricket teams, with a quiz on Monday and acoustic music on Wednesday. The winner of various awards, it hosts many events, including a street party every two years. The food is restricted to lunchtimes and includes daily specials and a range of salad options. Q◐♣●🚌(X5,X6)🐾📶

Congresbury

Plough [L]

High Street, BS49 5JA (off A370 at B3133 jct)
11.30-2.30, 4.30-11; 11.30-11 Sat; 12-2.30, 7-10.30 Sun
☎ (01934) 877402 🌐 the-plough-inn.net
Butcombe Original; St Austell Tribute [H]/[G]**; Twisted Oak Fallen Tree** [G]**; 4 changing beers (sourced locally)** [H]/[G]
Characterful village pub with flagstone floors and many original features, decorated with interesting local artefacts. Four guest beers, mainly from local breweries, are delivered from a row of old caskheads behind the bar. Up to 16 ciders are also stocked. The pub has a deserved reputation for the quality of its food, which is served lunchtimes and evenings, except Sunday evening, which is quiz night. The pub has real fires and a large garden. Mendip morris men meet here.
Q❀◐◑♿♣●P🚌(X1,353)🐾📶

Crewkerne

King William Inn

Barn Street, TA18 8BP (take A30 towards Chard and at fringe of town uphill Barn St will be found on left)
5-midnight; 3-midnight Fri; 12-midnight Sat; 12-6.30 Sun
☎ (01460) 279615
Butcombe Original; 2 changing beers (sourced nationally; often Bristol Beer Factory, Oakham, Tapstone) [H]
A short walk from the town centre towards Chard takes you to this well-hidden traditional pub. There are two changing ales and the array of pumpclips adorning the beams gives some indication of a huge range of beers that have been served. Twitter shows the ones that are being added. There is a happy hour every Monday and Wednesday 5-7pm. For music lovers there is an acoustic night the last Wednesday of each month. ❀♣●P🚌🐾

Croscombe

George Inn

Long Street, BA5 3QH (on A371 between Wells and Shepton Mallet)
7.30-11 (midnight Fri & Sat); 8-11 Sun ☎ (01749) 342306
🌐 thegeorgeinn.co.uk
House beer (by Blindmans); 3 changing beers (often Cotleigh, St Austell, Yeovil Ales) [H]
Attractive 17th-century inn refurbished by the owner, serving at least four guest ales from West Country independents and hosting two beer festivals a year. Blindmans King George, and George & Dragon, are brewed exclusively for the pub. Four real ciders are also stocked, with Hecks Kingston Black and Thatchers ciders as regulars. There is a large main bar, a snug with fireplace, a family room and a separate dining room. Food is home cooked using locally sourced ingredients in a modern theatre kitchen. A skittle alley/meeting room is to the rear. The large garden has a covered terrace.
Q❀◐◑♿♣●P🚌🐾📶

Cross

New Inn ✔

Old Coach Road, BS26 2EE (on A38/A361 jct)
12-11 (midnight Fri & Sat) ☎ (01934) 732455
🌐 newinncross.co.uk
Otter Bitter, Ale; 4 changing beers (often Box Steam, Bristol Beer Factory, Tiny Rebel) [H]
A 17th-century roadside inn on the A38, close to the historic medieval town of Axbridge. It is popular for its extensive food menu served all day until 9pm (8pm Sun) and its beer festival at Easter. Four guest beers, often rare for the area, are usually available. Families are welcome; dogs too. The large hillside garden with children's play facilities offers a fine view of the Mendip Hills and Somerset Levels. There is a small car park opposite.
❀◐◑♣P🚌(126)🐾📶

Curry Rivel

Firehouse

Church Street, TA10 0HE (Church St is off A378 Langport to Wrantage road)
12-11; 11-10 Sun ☎ (01458) 887447
🌐 thefirehousesomerset.co.uk
Butcombe Adam Henson's Rare Breed, Original; 2 changing beers (often Butcombe, Otter, Salcombe) [H]

This enticing hostelry has been beautifully restored with a modern twist and is also packed with traditional charm. On the left when entering is the house bar which serves up to five real ales with three changing choices. In addition there is real cider from local producers. Leading off from the bar are five further sitting/dining areas arranged over three floors, with wood-burning stoves in abundance. Well worth a visit in this delightful village. 🛏❀◑♿●P🚌(54)📶

Draycott

Cider Barn

Latches Lane Crossroads, Draycott Road, BS27 3RU
✪ 12-10 (11 Thu-Sat) ☎ (01934) 741837
2 changing beers (sourced locally; often Box Steam, Cheddar Ales) [G]
Quirky, relaxing bar, café and takeaway cider and ale barn on the main A371 near Cheddar. Here you can also buy coffee, tea and simple locally sourced home-cooked food and snacks, including pizzas. Up to 13 real ciders and two or three, usually local, real ales are served. There is live music every Sunday 5-8pm. The bar sometimes stays open until 11pm. Camping and electric hook-ups for caravans are available. Q🛏❀◑♿▲●P🚌(126)🐾📶

Drayton

Drayton Crown

Church Street, TA10 0JY (in centre of village near church)
✪ 11-11 ☎ (01458) 250712 🌐 thedraytoncrown.co.uk
Butcombe Original; Timothy Taylor Landlord; 2 changing beers (sourced nationally; often Butcombe, Otter, Tapstone) [H]
This pub has undergone a modern refurbishment but has retained character, with flagstone floors and beams. Three or four ales from regional and national breweries are normally served, alongside a cider. Food is provided from a modern kitchen and there is a skittle alley/function room. Happy hour is 5-7pm Tuesday to Sunday, with £1 off a pint. Outside there is lots of seating and a lawn area. There are four en-suite quality B&B rooms if you want to stay. 🛏❀🛌◑♿♣●P📶

Dulverton

Bridge Inn [L]

20 Bridge Street, TA22 9HJ
✪ 11-11 ☎ (01398) 324130 🌐 thebridgeinndulverton.com
Exmoor Ale; 3 changing beers (sourced regionally; often Burning Sky, Butcombe, Dark Star) [H]
A warm, welcoming pub dating from 1845. As the name implies, it is close to a bridge crossing the River Barle upstream from its confluence with the River Exe. Situated in this delightful small town, the pub has a cosy single-room bar with a wood-burning stove and an extended restaurant area. There is always an interesting selection of national cask ales, and bottled beers include a Belgian selection. Check on the website for restricted opening hours in winter. Q🛏❀◑▲♣●P🚌🐾📶

Dunster

Luttrell Arms Hotel

36 High Street, TA24 6SG
✪ 10-11.30 ☎ (01643) 821555 🌐 luttrellarms.co.uk
Exmoor Ale; Otter Amber; 2 changing beers (sourced locally; often Quantock) [H]
The hotel, with its 28 beautiful bedrooms, is on the site of three ancient houses dating back to 1443. The back bar has an open log fire and features some of the oldest glass windows in Somerset; there is also fine plasterwork on the lounge ceiling. You can dine in the à la carte restaurant or, if you prefer, order a bar snack. The view of Dunster Castle from the back garden is spectacular. Mini beer and cider festivals are held.
Q🛏❀🛌◑▲♣●🚌(28,198)🐾📶

East Harptree

Castle of Comfort

Old Bristol Road, BS40 6DD (on B3134 just N of jct with B3135)
✪ 12-3, 6-11 ☎ (01761) 221321 🌐 thecastleofcomfort.co.uk
Butcombe Original; Sharp's Doom Bar; 1 changing beer (often Cheddar Ales) [H]
Splendid, sprawling, isolated inn on the Mendip Hills, within reach by car of both Cheddar Gorge and Wookey Hole caves, and 1½ miles from a campsite. The name is believed to derive from the time when the pub housed condemned criminals on their last night. A hostelry since 1684, it is popular for locally sourced and generously portioned food. One guest beer features regularly from the South-West and sometimes further afield. The child-friendly garden is busy in summer.
Q🛏❀◑♣●P🐾

Faulkland

Tucker's Grave ★

BA3 5XF
✪ 12-3 (not Mon), 6-11; 12-11 Sat; 12-10 Sun
☎ (01373) 834230 🌐 tuckersgraveinn.co.uk
Butcombe Original [G]
A gem from a bygone age, with a nationally important historic pub interior, this pub was built in the mid-17th century and has changed little since. It was named after Tucker, who hanged himself close by and was buried at the crossroads outside. He featured in a song by the Stranglers. There is no bar - the beers and Thatchers cider are served from an alcove. Shove-ha'penny is played and there is a skittle alley. Camping is available. Q❀▲♣●P📶

Freshford

Inn at Freshford

The Hill, BA2 7WG
✪ 11-11; 10-10 Sun ☎ (01225) 722250
🌐 theinnatfreshford.com
Box Steam Ghost Train; 2 changing beers (sourced regionally) [H]
Recently reopened after an extensive refurbishment, this is a picturesque 16th-century village inn, owned by the same small pubco as the Cross Guns in Avoncliff. It is on the bank of the River Frome, in the Cotswolds Area of Outstanding Natural Beauty, and is popular with cyclists, joggers and walkers, being on the Two Valleys Walk. Ales will come from local breweries. The food is excellent and good value. 🛏❀◑⇌P🚌(94)🐾📶

Frome

Griffin

Milk Street, BA11 3DB

4-11; 12-11 Fri & Sat; 12-10 Sun ☎ (01373) 228283
griffinfrome.com
Frome Funky Monkey, Zig-Zag Stout, Beer; 3 changing beers (sourced nationally; often Frome) H
In the part of Frome known as Trinity, the Griffin was formerly the brewery tap for Milk Street (now Frome) Brewery. A wide range of Frome ales is featured along with seasonal beers and guests, as well as a range of craft brews. Recently refurbished and under new management, the single bar retains some original features including etched windows and a wooden floor. Food is regularly available, with supper club on Wednesday and Sunday lunch popular. P (184)

Just Ales
10 Stony Street, BA11 1BU
2-9 Mon & Tue; 12-11; 12-8.30 Sun ☎ (01373) 462493
justalespart2.com
4 changing beers (sourced nationally) H
Frome's first micropub opened in March 2018 serving four real ales on handpump as well as a large range of local ciders. Set in what was a small former café, in the heart of Frome's vibrant St Catherine's District, Just Ales has a welcoming atmosphere and is run by the same team as Just Ales in Wells, including the friendly hound. Biltong is sold as a quick and tasty snack. Q

Three Swans
16-17 King Street, BA11 1BH
5-midnight; 12-midnight Fri & Sat; 12-11 Sun
☎ (01373) 452009 threeswans.pub
Abbey Bellringer; Butcombe Original; 1 changing beer (sourced nationally; often Butcombe) H
A 17th-century Grade II-listed two-bar pub in the centre of Frome. Quirky and traditional, it was extensively refurbished in 2013, and has a comfortable and inviting feel. The interior is heated by traditional gas burners; paintings and various ornaments adorn the walls. The back door leads out to a beautiful secluded courtyard. There is also an upstairs function room. Home-made pies are served on Friday and at weekends, and Sunday lunch is available.

Glastonbury

Beckets Inn ✔
43 High Street, BA6 9DS (at top of High St in town centre)
12-11; 12-10.30 Sun ☎ (01458) 832928
becketsinnglastonbury.co.uk
Wadworth IPA, 6X; 1 changing beer (often Wadworth) H
A traditional pub named after Thomas Becket, with a pool room and three separate bar areas. There is no food, but customers are welcome to bring takeaways (plates and cutlery provided) to eat in or have as a picnic in the garden. The pub will even do the washing up. Children are welcome until 5pm but as there is a pub dog access can only be given to assistance dogs. Three well-kept Wadworth beers are on handpump.

George & Pilgrims
1 High Street, BA6 9DP (near Market Cross)
11-11 ☎ (01458) 831146 historicinnz.co.uk/glastonbury
Otter Bitter; St Austell Tribute; 3 changing beers (sourced nationally; often Bristol Beer Factory) H
This three-storeyed Grade I-listed stone-built gatehouse inn boasts a panelled, embattled frontage with mullion windows. Walking through the stout doorway there is a corridor leading to the rear patio and several tabled alcoves on the right. The Pilgrims Bar on the left oozes old-world charm, including medieval artefacts. There are five well-kept real ales and a choice of ciders. It is worthwhile reading about the history of the inn over a pint. Q

Hawthorns
8-12 Northload Street, BA6 9JJ (at bottom of Glastonbury High St turn into Northload St at Market Cross)
6-11 (11.30 Tue & Thu); 12-11.30 Fri & Sat; 12-11 Sun
☎ (01458) 831255
2 changing beers (often Fine Tuned, Glastonbury, Pitchfork) H
Quirky hotel and bar in the centre of this historic town within walking distance of Glastonbury Tor and Glastonbury Abbey. A well-known music venue, it puts on an open mic session on Tuesday, blues jam on Sunday, and regular music on Friday night. The pub is famous for serving authentic curries from around the world, and its Sunday carvery is also popular. In May there is a well-supported beer festival with 20 ales and six ciders. P

Henstridge

Bird in Hand
Ash Walk, BA8 0QD
11-2.30, 5.30-11; 11-11 Sat; 12-10.30 Sun
☎ (01963) 362255
Butcombe Original; 2 changing beers (often Sharp's) H
Old stone village pub with low ceilings, beams, a fireplace at each end of an attractive long bar, and a games room housing a TV. There is an adjoining skittle alley. Excellent-quality ales and good-value snacks make a visit to this friendly pub always worthwhile. At the heart of most village activities, this really is a true community pub. Thatchers cider is dispensed on handpump and there is more cider in boxes. Local CAMRA branch Pub of the Year 2017. Q P (58)

Hillfarrance

Anchor Inn L
TA4 1AW
12-2.30 (3.30 Sun), 6-11 ☎ (01823) 461334
theanchorinn.net
Exmoor Ale; Otter Ale; St Austell Cornish Best Bitter, Tribute H H H/G
Large 300-year-old family-run free house that caters for drinkers in a cosy bar, and for diners in the large restaurant. A two-sided logburner separates the bar from a smaller dining area. There is also a large function room. Food is locally produced and home-cooked, including a Sunday carvery. Outside is a large car park and garden with a children's play area. Accommodation is available in five en-suite rooms. Q P

Huish Episcopi

Rose & Crown ★ L
TA10 9QT (on A372 in village)
11.30-3, 5.15-10.30 (8 Mon); 11.30-11.30 Fri & Sat; 12-10.30 Sun ☎ (01458) 250494

Teignworthy Reel Ale; 2 changing beers (sourced regionally; often Fine Tuned, Hop Back, Otter) H
A 17th-century thatched inn known as Eli's after the former owner, Eli Scott, who took over the pub in 1920; it is still in the same family. The hub of the place is the rare counterless flagstoned taproom which leads out to four parlours. Good-value meals are served (no food Sun eve). Regular music features, and there is a meeting of the Elderflower Food Co-operative every Friday, with organic produce for sale. A Brit Stop pub for travellers.
Q❀◐▲♣P🐾

Keynsham

Old Bank

20 High Street, BS31 1DQ
10-11.30 (1.30am Fri & Sat) ☎ (0117) 904 6356
Severn Copper Ale; 3 changing beers H
This Grade II-listed building was originally a coaching inn, then a branch of Westminster Bank, before becoming a pub again. It is a free house with one large room for drinking, and a covered, heated outdoor area at the back. There is a small car park to the rear, reached through a narrow archway. The landlord tries to have at least one dark, often strong, beer on at all times. The pub has a large TV screen for sport and can get lively on late weekend openings. ❀♿♣P🐾

Litton

Litton

BA3 4PW
12-11; 12-10.30 Sun ☎ (01761) 241554 thelitton.co.uk
Bristol Beer Factory Notorious; Cheddar Ales Potholer; house beer (by Great Western); 3 changing beers (often Cheddar Ales, Great Western, Twisted Oak) H
Large 15th-century village pub where the emphasis is on comfort without ruining the character of a lovely building. The old part of the pub has been retained largely in its original format, with a separate whisky bar. At the right of the central bar is a restaurant area with a riverside terrace where you can take your drinks. Accessible parking is at the rear of the building, from where you can get to the pub and the upmarket accommodation. ❀◐♿▲P🐾

Lower Godney

Sheppey Inn

BA5 1RZ
12-3, 5.30-11; 12-midnight Sat; 12-11 Sun
☎ (01458) 831594 thesheppey.co.uk
4 changing beers (sourced nationally; often Bristol Beer Factory, Dawkins, Glastonbury) H
A many-roomed quirky pub with off-the-wall decoration, including graphic arts, taxidermy, and surreal ornaments, set in the wilds of the Somerset levels to the west of Wells. It has a good range of changing real ales, plus six or more craft beers from home and overseas, and up to 12 ciders on gravity. Outside the barn-like interior is a lovely terrace overlooking the River Sheppey, where otters have been spotted. The food is highly recommended. ❀◐♿▲♣P🐾

Luxborough

Royal Oak Inn L ✔

TA23 0SH (2½ miles from B3224 between Wheddon Cross and Raleghs Cross)
closed Mon; 12-11 ☎ (01984) 641498
theroyaloakinnluxborough.co.uk
Exmoor Ale; 3 changing beers (sourced nationally; often Butcombe, Cheddar Ales, Quantock) H
Set in the Brendon Hills, this ancient village pub has an original flagstone floor in the main bar and a large inglenook fireplace. A second bar has a pool table and a radiogram if you wish to play some vinyl. There is a children's room, and to the rear is the dining room where you can sample meals freshly cooked using seasonal produce. A courtyard is pleasant on sunny days. The pub is popular with ramblers and shooting parties.
Q❀◐♣P🐾

Lydford on Fosse

Cross Keys Inn L

TA11 7HA (next to A37 between Yeovil and Shepton Mallet at traffic lights in village)
11.30-11; 12-11 Sun ☎ (01963) 240473
crosskeysinn.info
House beer (by Downton); 4 changing beers (sourced regionally; often Bristol Beer Factory, Downton, Twisted Oak) G
An 18th-century traditional pub with flagstone floors, blue lias stonework and a wealth of beams. An open-plan bar area has two fireplaces at each end and a snug. Up to five gravity-poured ales are served, including the house beer. This is a community pub with many events organised including live music, a beer festival, comedy nights and charitable functions. There is camping on-site, with 29 pitches, a shower block and toilets.
Q❀◐♿▲♣P (667)🐾

Middlezoy

George Inn L

42 Main Road, TA7 0NN (off A372, 1 mile NW of Othery, 5 miles E of Bridgwater)
closed Mon; 6.30-midnight; 12-3, 6.30-midnight Sat; 2-7 Sun ☎ (01823) 698215 thegeorgeinnmiddlezoy.co.uk
House beer (by St Austell); 2 changing beers (sourced regionally; often Bath Ales, Cheddar Ales, Fine Tuned) H
This pub, which has been in the Guide for over 20 years, is a 17th-century free house with stone-flagged floors, exposed beams and log fires. Excellent locally sourced food is served Wednesday to Saturday evenings and Saturday lunchtime. A private dining room (seating 12) can be reserved. Samford Orchards and local guest ciders are sold. Live acoustic music takes place on the third Sunday of each month and there is a monthly bingo night. Accommodation is provided, in three bedrooms.
Q❀◐▲♣P (16)🐾

Milverton

Globe L

Fore Street, TA4 1JX (15 mins through country lanes from M5 jct 26 at Wellington)
closed Mon; 12-3, 6-11 (11.30 Fri & Sat); 12-3 Sun
☎ (01823) 400534 theglobemilverton.co.uk
Exmoor Ale; 3 changing beers (sourced regionally; often Exeter) H

A 15th-century former coaching inn in an interesting village founded on the cotton industry. This is an excellent family-run pub where a warm welcome is guaranteed. It offers a locally sourced, cooked-to-order and varied food menu, as well as themed food evenings. Real cider is on the bar in the summer months only. Parking is limited but there is a village car park 150 yards away. There are two double bedrooms should you wish to stop at the pub. Q✿☺🚪🍴◗🖐♿▲♣P🅿(25)🐾❄

Minehead

Kildare Lodge ✅
Townend Road, TA24 5RQ
☼ 11-3, 6.30-11; 12-5 Sun ☎ (01643) 702009
🌐 kildarelodge.co.uk
St Austell Tribute; 3 changing beers (sourced regionally) Ⓗ
This cracking locals' pub is close to Minehead town centre. The Grade II-listed building in the Arts & Crafts style has a bar, two lounges and a dining room. There are 12 en-suite rooms including a bridal suite with a four-poster bed. Two beer festivals are held every year with up to 20 beers to try. The pub is in the local boules and quiz leagues. It is a great base for exploring Exmoor National Park, Dunster and the coast.
Q✿🚪🍴◗🖐♿◀≉♣P🅿🐾

Nether Stowey

George Ⓛ
1 St Mary Street, TA5 1LJ
☼ 12-11; 12-10.30 Sun ☎ (01278) 732248
Exmoor Ale; 1 changing beer (often Bays, St Austell, Stowey) Ⓗ
The oldest pub in the village, the George can trace its history back to 1616; the original building dates back another century. It is a friendly multi-roomed place with a real fire, dark-wood interior, Tiffany lamps and historical photographs of the village adorning the walls. A function room is upstairs. The pub serves as an outlet for the nearby Stowey Brewery, and hosts occasional live music.
🚪✿🍴🖐♣❄🐾❄

Norton St Philip

Fleur de Lys
High Street, BA2 7LG
☼ 5-midnight; 3-midnight Fri; 11-midnight Sat; closed Sun
☎ (01373) 834333 🌐 fleurdelysnsp.co.uk
Wadworth 6X, Bishops Tipple; 1 changing beer (sourced nationally) Ⓗ
An inn since 1584, the Fleur is a warm, welcoming pub. Its three main drinking/dining areas are served by a single bar. Original beams, stone walls and a log fire impart a cosy feeling. Old hand-painted Wadworth's pub signs are displayed on the walls. At the rear of the pub is a much-used skittle alley where a number of local teams play regularly. The food offering is based mainly around pizzas but other dishes are available. 🚪◗♣P🅿🐾❄

Oakhill

Oakhill Inn
Fosse Road, BA3 5HU (on A367 between Radstock and Shepton Mallet)
☼ 12-2.30, 5-11 (midnight Fri); 12-midnight Sat; 12-11 Sun
☎ (01749) 840442 🌐 theoakhillinn.com

House beer (by Stonehenge); 3 changing beers (sourced regionally; often Cheddar Ales, Glastonbury, Otter) Ⓗ
Large village-centre pub that is both a popular local and a family-friendly gastro-pub, with a strong emphasis on organic and locally sourced food. The bar serves two areas with an open feel. Up to three changing guest ales, normally from local and regional micros, are on offer. Regular quiz nights are held. There is a garden at the rear and the car park is 20 yards up the road in the Shepton Mallet direction. Accommodation is in five 4-star rooms.
🚪✿🍴◗🖐♿♣P🅿🐾❄

Odcombe

Masons Arms
41 Lower Odcombe, BA22 8TX (off Yeovil to Montacute road)
☼ 8am-3.30, 6-midnight; 8am-midnight Sun
☎ (01935) 862591 🌐 masonsarmsodcombe.co.uk
Odcombe No.1; 2 changing beers (sourced locally; often Odcombe) Ⓗ
Drew and Paula have been running this picturesque thatched free house since 2005. With six en-suite bedrooms, glamping in a shepherd's hut, camping in the grounds, an on-site brewery and Poetic Paws dog-training school, this is not your average country pub. Food is served every day, alongside local draught cider and three cask ales from the brewery. Open mic nights and a monthly quiz are regular events. Families and dogs are welcome. Q🚪✿🍴◗🖐♿▲♣P🅿(81)🐾❄

Pitney

Halfway House Ⓛ
Pitney Hill, TA10 9AB (on B3153 between Langport and Somerton)
☼ 11.30-3, 4-11; 11.30-11 Sat & Sun ☎ (01458) 252513
🌐 thehalfwayhouse.co.uk
Hop Back Summer Lightning; Otter Bright; Teignworthy Reel Ale; 6 changing beers (sourced regionally; often Cheddar Ales, Plain, Quantock) Ⓖ
An outstanding pub serving eight to nine regional ales on gravity plus many bottled beers and real ciders. The inside is traditional, with flagstone flooring, old, solid wooden tables and benches and three real fires. This busy pub deserves its many accolades, including being in the Guide for over 25 years. Superb home-cooked food is offered; a sample menu can be found on the website.
Q✿◗🍴♣P🅿(54)🐾❄

Porlock

Ship Inn Ⓛ ✅
High Street, TA24 8QD
☼ 11-midnight; 12-midnight Sun ☎ (01643) 862507
🌐 shipinnporlock.co.uk
Exmoor Beast; Otter Bitter; 6 changing beers (sourced regionally; often Otter) Ⓗ
Known locally as the Top Ship, the bar is a gem, with its flagstone floor, open fire and settle seating. It has changed little since featuring in RD Blackmore's novel Lorna Doone. The pub dates from the 13th century and sits at the bottom of the notorious Porlock Hill that takes you up to Exmoor. Eight ales and a local cider are on tap. Good food can be enjoyed in the restaurant, and in the delightful three-tiered garden in summer.
Q🚪✿🍴◗🖐♿♣♣P🅿(10)🐾

Porlock Weir

Ship Inn [L]

TA24 8PB (take B3225 from Porlock)
11-11; 12-10.30 Sun ☎ (01643) 863288
shipinnporlockweir.co.uk
Exmoor Ale, Stag; St Austell Tribute, Proper Job; 2 changing beers (sourced regionally) [H]
The pub offers fantastic view of the Bristol Channel and the coastline of South Wales. It is next to the small harbour and pebbled beach where oyster beds have been installed. This 400-year-old inn, in Exmoor National Park, is on the South-West Coast Path and gets busy in the summer. It holds a beer festival in June with up to 50 ales to enjoy. There is a Pay & Display car park opposite.
Q P (10)

Portishead

Ship

310 Down Road, BS20 8JT
11.30-2.30, 5.30-11; 12-2.30, 7-10.30 Sun
☎ (01275) 848400
Draught Bass; Otter Bitter; 1 changing beer [H]
Large pub with traditional opening hours, on the coast road between Clevedon and Portishead with views over the Severn estuary. The landlord has been at the pub that he built since 1973, and is a fount of local knowledge. Meals are served lunchtime only, but you can get pasties in the evening. There is a small library of books on-site, with a particularly good selection on local history. Cash only, no cards. P

Siren's Calling [L]

315 Newfoundland Way, Portishead Marina, BS20 7QH
4-11; 12-11 Fri-Sun ☎ (01275) 268278
5 changing beers
This single-room, modern waterside bar opened in 2018 and serves up to six cask ales and nine craft keg beers in a variety of styles. Some are from breweries in the Bristol area, others from further afield. Still ciders are also available. The pub is simply furnished with large front windows overlooking the many boats moored in the marina. It has a selection of interesting beers in bottles from around the world. Food is always available but is limited to cheese platters and other bar snacks.

Priddy

Hunters Lodge

Hillgrove Road, BA5 3AR (on isolated crossroads 1 mile from A39 close to TV mast) ST549500
11.30-2.30, 6.30-11; 12-2, 7-11 Sun ☎ (01749) 672275
Butcombe Original; Cheddar Ales Potholer; 1 changing beer (often Butcombe) [G]
The landlord of this timeless classic roadside inn has been in charge for 49 years. At a crossroads near Priddy, the highest village in Somerset, the pub is popular with cavers and walkers. Three rooms include one with a flagged floor. All beer is served direct from casks behind the bar; local cider is also on offer. The simple home-cooked food is excellent and exceptional value. A folk musicians' drop-in session is held on Tuesday evening. The garden is pleasant and secluded. Mobile phones are not welcome but dogs are. Q P

Queen Victoria Inn

Pelting Drove, BA5 3BA
12-11; 12-10.30 Sun ☎ (01749) 676385
thequeenvicpriddy.co.uk
Butcombe Original; 2 changing beers (often Butcombe, Fuller's) [H]
Creeper-clad inn, a pub since 1851, with four rooms that feature low ceilings, flagged floors and three log fires. It is a wonderfully warm and relaxing haven on cold winter nights, and is particularly popular during the Priddy Folk Festival in July. Reasonably priced home-cooked food is a speciality. Children are welcome and there is a play area by the car park. Cheddar Valley and Ashton Still ciders are sold. May close briefly on some afternoons. Q P

Puriton

37 Club [L]

1 West Approach Road, Woolavington Road, TA7 8AD
(5 mins from jct 23 of M5 between Bridgwater and Wells)
4-11; 2-midnight Fri; 12-midnight Sat; 12-11 Sun
☎ (01278) 685190 37club.co.uk
Otter Amber, Ale; St Austell Tribute; 3 changing beers (often Bath Ales, Exmoor, Glastonbury) [H]
On the site of the former Royal Ordnance Factory, which was allocated the number 37, this is a large club offering a great many facilities to members and visitors. It has two bars and its multi-roomed layout incorporates a concert room, two skittle alleys, dining room, snooker room with five tables and, outside, a beer garden, fishing lake and football pitch. CAMRA members are welcome with a membership card. P (75)

Puriton Inn

Puriton Hill, TA7 8AF
11.30-11; 12-10.30 Sun ☎ (01278) 683464
thepuritoninn.co.uk
Exmoor Fox; Otter Bitter; 1 changing beer (sourced locally; often Quantock) [H]
A traditional family-run country pub close to junction 23 of the M5 and therefore ideal for a stop-off if heading to the West Country. It is a large multi-roomed pub which includes a pool room and skittle alley. Popular for home-cooked food, the pub has special food nights and provides a Sunday roast. Ales are from Somerset breweries. There is a September beer, cider and music festival.
P (75)

Radstock

Fromeway

Frome Road, BA3 3LG
closed Mon; 12-3, 6-11; 12-11 Sun ☎ (01761) 432116
fromeway.co.uk
Butcombe Original [H]**; 2 changing beers (sourced nationally; often Otter, Twisted)** [H]/[A]
This friendly free house is now run by the sixth generation of the same family. Emily and Andrew welcome you with a great selection of weekly changing ales. In the first year of their takeover they have served over 100 different beers from all over the country. There is an emphasis on food here, with traditional classics as well as more contemporary dishes. Outside is an award-winning garden. Regular charity events, quiz nights and walks take place throughout the year.
P (768,178)

Rickford

Plume of Feathers

Leg Lane, BS40 7AH (off A368, 2 miles from A38; approaching from Churchill, left U-turn into Leg Lane is extremely tricky)

✪ 12-11 ☎ (01761) 462682 ⊕ theplumeoffeathers.com

Butcombe Original; Cheddar Ales Potholer; 2 changing beers (often Butcombe, Cheddar Ales, Pitchfork) ⓗ

This 17th-century building has been a pub since the 1800s. The interior is divided into several areas including a restaurant with real fire. The pub provides a pleasant and convenient base from which to walk, fish or explore the Mendips. It has a garden at the rear and a stream running along the front, leading to a ford. A popular charity duck race occurs here in July. Car parking is limited.

Q ℥ ❀ ⇔ ◐ ▲ ♣ ● P ⊟ ⬚ (791) ❀ 🛜

Roadwater

Valiant Soldier 🅛 ✅

TA23 0QZ (off A39 at Washford)

✪ 11.30-2.30, 6-11; 12-3, 6-11 Sun ☎ (01984) 640223

⊕ thevaliantsoldier.co.uk

Exmoor Ale; Greene King IPA; 1 changing beer (sourced locally; often Red Rock) ⓗ

The inn dates back to 1720 and is ideal for country walks and exploring nearby Exmoor, the coast and Dunster. This vibrant locals' pub has quiz, pool, darts and skittles teams to see it through the winter months. It is by a small river where you can relax and watch the ducks and, if you are lucky, kingfishers. Food is of good quality and locally sourced. The pub has been run by the landlord, Mike, for over 30 years. ℥ ❀ ⇔ ◐ ♣ ● P 🛜

Saltford

Bird in Hand ✅

58 High Street, BS31 3EJ

✪ 11-11 ☎ (01225) 873335 ⊕ birdinhandsaltford.co.uk

Butcombe Original; Sharp's Doom Bar; 2 changing beers ⓗ

A convenient stopping-off point for cyclists on the Bristol to Bath Railway Path, this traditional 19th-century country inn is close to the River Avon and only 400 yards from the A4. There is a long L-shaped bar and a pleasant conservatory with fine views across the garden to the hills beyond. Quality food is served lunchtimes and evenings and all day at weekends, with gluten-free options. There is a pétanque piste in the garden.

℥ ❀ ◐ ▵ ♣ ● P ⊟ ❀ 🛜

Shepton Beauchamp

Duke of York

North Street, TA19 0LW

✪ 4.30-11 Mon; 3.30-11 Tue & Wed; 12-11 Thu; 12-midnight Fri & Sat; 12-10.30 Sun ☎ (01460) 240314

St Austell Tribute, Proper Job; Sharp's Doom Bar; 1 changing beer (sourced regionally; often Teignworthy) ⓗ

A typical south Somerset village, with the inn, school, shop and church dominating the centre. The Duke of York has a split-level interior; externally a high pavement with benches gives a village overview. To the rear is a pleasant garden and letting rooms. The pub, which has been in the Guide for over 15 years, also features a Sunday

carvery, a nightly food specials board, bingo nights and breakfast on the first Saturday of the month (9-11am). No food Monday. ℥ ❀ ⇔ ◐ ♣ P ❀ 🛜

Somerton

White Hart Inn

Market Place, TA11 7LX (centre of village)

✪ 9am-11; 9am-10.30 Sun ☎ (01458) 272273

⊕ whitehartsomerton.com

Bath Ales Gem; Cheddar Ales Potholer; 1 changing beer (sourced locally; often Otter) ⓗ

The White Hart has been trading as an inn in Somerton's delightful market square since the 16th century. You cannot miss it, as there is a large model of a white hart on the entrance porch. The pub is much larger inside than you might envisage, and has plenty of tables for dining or coffee and cakes. A courtyard allows alfresco eating and drinking. Numerous awards and newspaper reviews are featured on the website.

℥ ❀ ⇔ ◐ ⅄ ● ⊟ (54,77) ❀ 🛜

South Petherton

Brewers Arms 🅛 ✅

18-20 St James Street, TA13 5BW (½ mile off A303 in centre of village)

✪ 11.30-2.30, 6-11; 11.30-midnight Fri & Sat; 12-11 Sun ☎ (01460) 241887 ⊕ the-brewersarms.com

Butcombe Original; 3 changing beers (sourced nationally; often Butcombe, St Austell, Thornbridge) ⓗ

This pub has appeared in over 20 consecutive editions of the Guide. During this time around 3,000 different ales have been served and documented. The Brewers is a hub of village life, a true community pub that keenly supports local events and charities. Beer festivals are held over both spring and summer bank holiday weekends. Regular live music and quiz nights feature. The adjoining Old Bakehouse Restaurant was acquired and successfully incorporated into the business to provide the food. ℥ ❀ ⇔ ◐ ▲ ♣ ● ⊟ (81) ❀ 🛜

Stogumber

White Horse Inn

High Street, TA4 3TA (turn left off A358 at Crowcombe)

✪ 12-2.30, 4.30-11; 12-11 Sat & Sun ☎ (01984) 656277

⊕ whitehorsestogumber.co.uk

Otter Bitter; St Austell Proper Job; 2 changing beers (sourced regionally; often Otter, Quantock) ⓗ

In a picturesque village near the Brendon Hills and close to the WSR steam railway, this traditional free house is a Grade II-listed building. The bar has a friendly atmosphere and a cosy log fire, and dispenses ales from local and regional breweries. The separate restaurant, originally the Market Hall, serves Somerset-produced food. The skittle alley doubles as a function room and hosts a music festival in September. There is a courtyard garden. Accommodation is reached via an outside stairwell.

℥ ❀ ⇔ ◐ ♣ P ❀ 🛜

Stratton-on-the-Fosse

White Post Inn

BA3 4QA

✪ 12-2.30, 5.15-11; 10-3, 6-11 Sat; 12-10.30 Sun

☎ (01761) 413394

Abbey Bath Best; Butcombe Original; 1 changing beer (sourced regionally) ⓗ

A popular community-based pub serving good real ales and three ciders. It offers traditional home-cooked food daily, lunchtime and evening. Alongside the two regular beers is one guest, which could be local or national. In winter months there is a welcoming real fire. Outside is a large, well-kept garden with a children's play area. ⌂⊛❍➊♣●Ｐ☀

Taunton

Bank

Middle Street, TA1 1SJ

✪ 11-11 (midnight Sat); closed Sun ☎ (01823) 257788
⊕ thebanktaunton.co.uk

3 changing beers (sourced nationally; often Arbor, Moor Beer, Oakham) ⓗ

Close to Somerset cricket ground, the Bank features three different cask ales from small breweries. The pub has two floors: the ground is a cosy bar, and upstairs is reserved for diners, with doors opening onto a terrace. A popular choice of keg beers and cans is served in addition to the cask offering. The excellent food can be described as modern British with an international influence. Bar meals reflect the quality of the main menu. ⊛❍➊₰≠●₽☀

Coal Orchard ⓛ ✪

30-32 Bridge Street, TA1 1UD (near to River Tone bridge in town centre)

✪ 8am-midnight (1am Fri & Sat) ☎ (01823) 447330

Greene King Abbot; Ruddles Best Bitter; Sharp's Doom Bar; 4 changing beers (sourced regionally; often Dartmoor, Exmoor, Quantock) ⓗ

North Town Wharf once stood behind this Wetherspoon house, next to the River Tone. Facing it was the Coal Orchard, the site of an orchard which became the landing place for Welsh coal. Latterly the pub was converted from a former hardware store, becoming one of the chain's smaller premises. The frontage has Art Deco styling. Seating is arranged over a single open-plan level. There is a small garden with patio area at the rear. Ｑ⌂⊛❍➊₰≠●₽☀

Racehorse Inn ✪

East Reach, TA1 3HT

✪ 12-4, 6-11 Mon; 12-11.30 Tue-Thu; 12-1am Fri; 12-2.30am Sat; 12-11 Sun ☎ (01823) 327513

St Austell Trelawny, Tribute, Proper Job; 1 changing beer (sourced nationally; often Dartmoor, Fuller's, Marston's) ⓗ

A popular St Austell Brewery venue close to the town centre at the top of East Reach. This is a traditional community pub with front and rear bars and a small lounge with comfortable armchairs. Both skittles and darts are played regularly and there is weekly live music, which is well attended. A large walled garden at the rear is ideal for a relaxing drink on those warm summer days. No food is served. ⊛₰♣●₽☀

Ring of Bells ⓛ

16-17 St James Street, TA1 1JS

✪ 11-11 ☎ (01823) 259480 ⊕ theringofbellstaunton.com

5 changing beers (sourced nationally; often Dark Star, Oakham, Quantock) ⓗ

Situated close to Somerset cricket ground, this pub is much visited by fans of the sport. It has two wooden-floored bar areas with open fires, a downstairs dining area, upstairs restaurant and

outside, a large courtyard. The five cask beers are from local, regional and national breweries, and you may find some interesting keg beers if this is your preference. Excellent locally produced food is served; booking is recommended. Sporting events are shown on a TV in the bar area. ⌂⊛❍➊≠●☀🖡

Wyvern Social Club ⓛ

Mountfields Road, TA1 3BJ (off South Rd, approx 1 mile from town centre)

✪ 6-11; 2-11 Sat; 12-3, 7-10.30 Sun ☎ (01823) 284591
⊕ wyvernclub.co.uk

Exmoor Ale; 2 changing beers (sourced regionally; often Exmoor, Quantock, St Austell) ⓗ

For over 30 years this club has been a great venue to drink real ales and now real cider. It is a members-only club with a visitors' licence – show a CAMRA membership card to be signed in as a guest. The Wyvern is the hub for the rugby, cricket and squash clubs who use the attached playing fields. It holds an annual beer festival in October. Buses shown here only run on Saturday daytime. Local CAMRA Club of the Year 2018 and 2019. ⌂⊛❍➊₰♣●Ｐ₽(6,99)🖡

Temple Cloud

Temple ✪

Main Road, BS39 5DA

✪ 7am-11; 8am-11 Sat; 8am-10.30 Sun ☎ (01761) 451145
⊕ thetempleinn.com

Butcombe Original; 3 changing beers (often Bath Ales, Otter, Quantock) ⓗ

Friendly roadside pub, just off the A37, which reopened in December 2017 following a major internal refurbishment. The pub is a popular dining venue (it is advisable to book) but also welcomes drinkers, with a changing range of guest beers, often from local South-West breweries. There is a small car park, an outdoor drinking area and accommodation in 10 en-suite rooms. A quiz night is held every Tuesday. Ｑ⌂⊛❍➊₰●Ｐ₽☀🖡

Thurloxton

Maypole Inn ⓛ ✪

TA2 8RF (on A38 between Taunton and N Petherton)

✪ 11.30-3, 6-11; 12-10 Sun ☎ (01823) 412286
⊕ maypoleinn.co.uk

Sharp's Doom Bar; 1 changing beer (sourced regionally; often Exmoor, Otter, St Austell) ⓗ

Originally a cider house dating back to 1880, this large but cosy village hostelry is split into various areas, mainly for dining but with ample space for those who just want a drink. It is a family-friendly pub with an extensive menu plus specials, and caters for small appetites. The large garden includes a children's play area. There is a skittle alley and a large function room. Occasional live music and quizzes feature. ⊛❍➊♣●Ｐ₽(21)

Washford

White Horse Inn ⓛ

Abbey Road, TA23 0JZ (take road towards Cleeve Abbey off A39)

✪ 12-11 ☎ (01984) 640415 ⊕ exmoorpubs.co.uk

3 changing beers (sourced regionally; often St Austell, Sharp's) ⓗ

The inn dates from 1709 and is near to the ruins of Cleeve Abbey and to the Torre Cider Farm. This

riverside free house is an ideal base for visits to the coast, Exmoor National Park, Quantock Hills and the West Somerset Steam Railway. The inn has a fine skittle alley and is in the local quiz leagues. Various charity events are held including the famous bike pub run. B&B is available in the pub and in a separate lodge. Q❀🛏◐♿♣🍎P🚌 (28)🐾📶

Watchet

Esplanade Club

5 The Esplanade, TA23 0AJ (opp marina)
12-3 (not Tue), 7-midnight; 12-midnight Fri & Sat; 12-11 Sun ☎ (01984) 634518
House beer (by St Austell); 4 changing beers (sourced regionally; often Exmoor, Quantock, St Austell) H
Built in the 1860s as a sailmaking factory and now home to the Boat Owners Association, the club is an archive of local history and memorabilia with unique murals and even its own Tardis. There are great views over the marina and Bristol Channel. The club is a busy music venue with live acts every weekend, open mic on the first Tuesday of the month and folk every fourth Wednesday. Winner of local CAMRA Club of the Year five times.
❀♿▲≠♣🍎🚌 (28)🐾

Pebbles Tavern

24 Market Street, TA23 0AN (in the heart of Watchet, near museum)
11 (5 Wed)-11; 12-11 Sun ☎ (01984) 634737
pebblestavern.co.uk
Timothy Taylor Boltmaker, Landlord H**; 1 changing beer (sourced nationally)** H/G
This small, unique tavern has won numerous CAMRA awards for Cider Pub of the Year. As well as the ales there can be up to 30 ciders, 60 gins, 24 rums and 64 whiskies. You are allowed to bring in your fish and chips from the shop next door. Poetry night is the first Tuesday of the month and regular music nights include folk, sea shanty, acoustic and jazz. ▲≠♣🍎🚌 (28)🐾📶

Star Inn

Mill Lane, TA23 0BZ
12-3, 6.30-11; 12-11 Sun ☎ (01984) 631367
starinnwatchet.co.uk
House beer (by Exmoor); 3 changing beers (often Butcombe, Dartmoor, Exmoor) H
A 16th-century pub that has been in the Guide for over 15 years and was the local CAMRA branch Pub of the Year runner-up in 2019. It is renowned for friendly staff and its congenial atmosphere. The pub hosts darts, quiz and boules teams and holds music nights in the summer. It also has port and cheese nights and is home to the Sunday night Bad Boys club. Mick's beer tours have run over 90 trips from the pub. ❀◐♿▲≠♣🍎🐾📶

Wellington

Dolphin

37 Waterloo Road, TA21 8JQ
4-11; 12-11 Sat; 12-10 Sun ☎ (01823) 665889
thedolphinwellington.co.uk
Exmoor Ale; Otter Amber; 2 changing beers (often Exeter, Exmoor, Quantock) H
Traditional town-centre pub serving up to four local ales on weekends. Home-cooked food is available daily including pizzas to eat in or take away, with vegan and gluten-free varieties. Live music features twice a month, normally on Thursday or Saturday, to include an open mic session. The monthly quiz night is popular. The colourful pub frontage has an unusual mural featuring handpumps depicting local breweries and wine bottles. Q❀◐♿♣🍎🚌 (22a)🐾📶

Wellow

Fox & Badger

Railway Lane, BA2 8QG
11.30-3, 6-11; 11.30-11 Fri & Sat; 12-4 Sun
☎ (01225) 832293 thefoxandbadger.com
Butcombe Original; 2 changing beers (sourced regionally; often Electric Bear, Flying Monk, Otter) H
An unspoilt village local with a single central bar decorated with hops. Up to three ales are on, including two changing guests. Rustic furniture rests on flagstone and wooden floors, and there is a fine stone fireplace with a wood-burning stove. The pub is popular in the evenings for food, so book if you wish to eat. A great destination for walkers and cyclists (close to National Cycle Route 244). Car parking can be a problem.
◐♣🍎P🚌 (757)🐾📶

West Huntspill

Crossways Inn

Withy Road, TA9 3RA (on A38)
12-midnight (1am Fri & Sat); 12-11 Sun
☎ (01278) 783756 thecrosswaysinn.com
8 changing beers (sourced nationally; often 3D Beers, Exmoor, Pitchfork) H
This fabulous 17th-century inn has been a well-deserved winner of local CAMRA Pub of the Year for the last four years. It has several bar areas, a dining room, and two log fires during winter, with a fireplace outside for smokers. A skittle alley can also be used as a function room. Eight ales, normally from the South-West, are on tap, alongside real ciders from the cellar. A beer festival is held in July. ❀🛏◐♿▲♣🍎P🚌 (21)🐾📶

Weston-super-Mare

Bear

66 Walliscote Road, BS23 1ED
1-11.30; 12-midnight Fri & Sat; 12-11 Sun
☎ (01934) 641722 thebearinnweston.co.uk
4 changing beers (sourced regionally) H
Spacious and comfortable pub a few minutes' walk from the seafront. It was formerly called the Balmoral, but reopened in 2012 with a new name after a period of closure. Beers can be unusual for the area and come in a variety of styles. Live music is popular every Saturday evening. Attractions include a skittle alley, a refurbished function room at the back with a stage, and 23 en-suite rooms. Sport is occasionally shown on TV.
❀🛏♿≠♣🍎P🚌 (5,7)🐾📶

Black Cat

135 High Street, BS23 1HN
12-10 ☎ (01934) 283286
5 changing beers G
Micropub opened in November 2018 in a former clothes shop at the Playhouse Theatre end of the High Street. Five cask ales are served, chosen from local breweries and a few from further afield. Dogs are welcome, as are children until 8pm. The owners have gone out of their way to create separate Ladies and Gents facilities, which is not

always the case with micropubs. Access for those of limited mobility is reasonable. There is an impressive Black Cat mural inside. Q

Brit Bar

118 High Street, BS23 1HP

12-1am (01934) 632629 thebritbar.co.uk

5 changing beers (often Quantock)

Formerly the Britannia, this long-standing town-centre pub was bought by the current owners at auction after a period of closure, and has now been given a bright, modern makeover while retaining the important traditional elements. Five changing beers are served, always including some dark ales. Bag-in-box real cider is usually available too. Live music features at weekends. Families are welcome all hours in the covered courtyard, which is heated in cold weather.

Criterion

45 Upper Church Road, BS23 2DY

12-11 Mon; 12-11.45 Tue-Thu; 11-1am Fri & Sat; 12-11 Sun

07538 753350

Courage Directors; St Austell Tribute; 3 changing beers

Genuine free house and traditional community pub, just off the seafront in the Knightstone area. Believed to be one of the oldest pubs in town, it has interesting local photos on the walls. Pub games feature strongly, with darts and table skittles, plus a quiz on Tuesday. Bar snacks are served, with filled rolls at lunchtime. Between three and five guest ales are sold, with all beer styles and local breweries well supported.
(1,4)

Regency

22-24 Lower Church Road, BS23 2AG

10-11.30 (midnight Fri & Sat); 10.45-11.30 Sun

(01934) 633406

Butcombe Original; Courage Best Bitter; Draught Bass; 2 changing beers (sourced nationally)

Comfortable, friendly town-centre local, attracting a mixed clientele including students at lunchtime. The pub has pool, skittles and crib teams, but also offers a quiet refuge for conversation. The pool room with TV and jukebox is separate from the main bar area, and children are welcome here. Keenly priced home-cooked food is served lunchtimes, and there are also Wednesday curry and Thursday grill evenings. Pub outings feature, as well as occasional live bands. There are patios to the front and rear.

Williton

Masons Arms

2 North Road, TA4 4SN

11-11; 12-11 Sun (01984) 639200

themasonsarms.com

Exmoor Ale; St Austell Tribute; 1 changing beer (sourced regionally; often Dartmoor)

A beautiful thatched 16th-century inn with oak beams throughout, and a pleasant beer garden where locals and visitors alike sit and relax. The pub hosts quiz teams in the local league. It has a good reputation for its food and the quality of its ales, and Rich's cider is always available. Close to the Quantock Hills, West Somerset Railway and a short drive to Exmoor National Park. Accommodation is in five en-suite rooms in the adjoining annexe.
Q P (28)

Railway Inn

55 Long Street, TA4 4QY

11-midnight (01984) 632508

3 changing beers (sourced regionally; often Butcombe, Exmoor)

This old inn set beside the A39 has two bars, a small lounge and a games room. Internally, white walls are interspersed with black beams and stone fireplaces. The pub has teams in the local quiz, darts, skittles and pool leagues, and hosts its own quiz on a Monday night. There is an outside seating area by the skittle alley at the back. Close to the West Somerset Railway and the Quantock Hills.
P (28)

Wincanton

Nog Inn

South Street, BA9 9DL

10.30-11 (midnight Fri & Sat); 12-11 Sun

(01963) 32998 thenoginn.com

Otter Bitter; house beer (by Sharp's); 2 changing beers (sourced regionally; often Cotleigh, Otter, Sharp's)

An attractive Grade II-listed pub with a striking Georgian façade that fronts a long, narrow building with parts dating back to the 16th century. A secluded sunny garden with covered seating can be found to the rear. The guest ales are often seasonal and an extensive range of continental beers on tap is always available. The pub offers home-cooked classics using locally sourced and seasonal ingredients where possible.
P (58, 667)

Witham Friary

Seymour Arms

BA11 5HF

11-3, 6-midnight; 12-midnight Sun (01749) 850742

Cheddar Ales Potholer

A hidden rural gem, this pub has probably changed little over the last 50 or so years (apart from new loos!). Built in the 1860s as a hotel to serve the nearby Mid-Somerset GWR branch railway station, it was part of the Duke of Somerset's estate. Sadly, in the 1960s Mr Beeching closed the station, and the hotel became a quiet country pub. One locally sourced beer is served, alongside cider, from a glass-panelled hatch in the central hallway.
Q P

Wookey

Ring o' Bells

High Street, BA5 1JZ

11-11 (midnight Fri & Sat) (01749) 678079

ringobells2016.wixsite.com/ringer

Butcombe Original; Cheddar Ales Potholer; Hop Back Summer Lightning; 1 changing beer (sourced locally)

A vibrant, handsome old pub in the village centre, serving a good range of four beers and two ciders, with a pleasant terrace at the front and small courtyard garden to the rear. Formerly a Wadworth pub, it is now a free house under new ownership since 2016, and has a large single bar – with the bar itself made from old cider barrels – and a small dining room adjoining. There is a skittle alley which also acts as a function room. Food is sourced locally. Q (67)

Yatton

Butchers Arms L

31 High Street, BS49 4JD
12-10 Mon; 12-11 Tue, Wed & Sun; 12-11.30 Thu-Sat
(01934) 838754 thebutchersarms.info
Butcombe Original; Twisted Oak Fallen Tree; 1 changing beer (sourced locally; often Bristol Beer Factory, Glede) H
Reopened and refurbished after a period of closure, this traditional village pub is now free of tie. Mind your head as you go in – there are low ceilings throughout. The front bar has flagstones on the floor and a feature bay window with a settle beneath. Up a step is the rear lounge bar, and there is a beer garden beyond. The guest ale is normally from a local brewery such as Bristol Beer Factory, Glede or Twisted Oak. (W1)

Yeovil

Quicksilver Mail

168 Hendford Hill, BA20 2RG (at jct of A30 and A37)
11-11; 12-11 Sun (01935) 424721
quicksilvermail.com
Butcombe Original; 2 changing beers (sourced nationally; often Bath Ales, St Austell) H
Roadside pub with a unique name commemorating a high-speed mail coach. The pub has been run by the same landlord since 2002 and has been almost ever-present in the Guide. There is a large single bar and a separate dining area serving excellent food and an attractively priced range of wines. The pub is a well-known live music destination, with regular gigs held in the bar and function room.
P (40,96)

Beckets Inn, Glastonbury (Photo: Jim Linwood/Flickr CC BY 2.0)

STAFFORDSHIRE

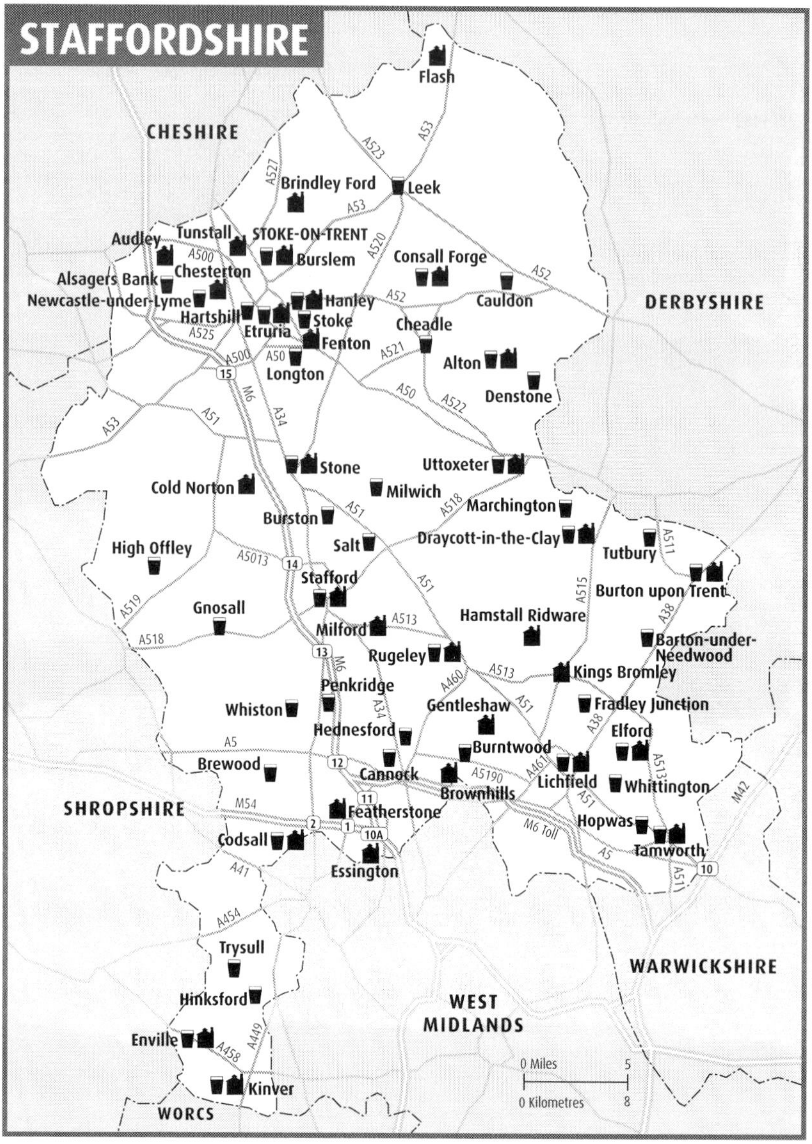

Alsagers Bank

Gresley Arms

High Street, ST7 8BQ (on B5367)

12 (3 Mon-Wed)-11 ☎ (01782) 722469

gresleyarms.co.uk

8 changing beers (often Abbeydale, Marston's, Townhouse)

Sitting on the top of Alsagers Bank for over 200 years, this real ale haven commands breathtaking views over nine counties. Eight real ales are served, including the house beer, Gresley Blonde. Six ciders and perries are also available. The pub's home-cooked, affordable meals are popular. The interior has three separate areas: a main bar with a real fire, a comfortable lounge and a dining room. There is also an outside seating area, ideal for a pint after a local walk.

P (1A)

Alton

Bull's Head

High Street, ST10 4AQ

5-11.30; 12-11.30 Fri-Sun ☎ (01538) 702307

thebullsheadalton.co.uk

Timothy Taylor Boltmaker, Landlord; 2 changing beers (often Ringwood, Vocation)

This pub has been tastefully redecorated while staying faithful to its origins as a 17th-century coaching inn. It comprises a two-room bar, cosy snug with vintage chesterfield sofas and a log burner and an updated restaurant area, with an outside patio and parking to the rear. A function room is available to hire. Guests can expect real and craft ales plus an extensive gin menu and gourmet coffee. Two permanent real ales and two changing ales provide excellent choice and quality.

Q P

Barton-under-Needwood

Royal Oak ✔

74 The Green, DE13 8JD (½ mile S of B5016 via Wales Lane)
12-11.30 (12.30am Fri & Sat); 12-11 Sun
☎ (01283) 713852
Marston's Pedigree; 2 changing beers (sourced nationally) H/G
Bustling community local on the southern edge of the village, home to many traditional pub games teams. While parts of the building date back to the 16th century, the pub has only existed since the mid-1800s. Public bar and lounge customers are served from a central sunken bar below the level of the rest of the ground floor. A separate conservatory offers access to the garden. Beers are on handpump or by gravity, direct from the cask, on request. **Q**P (811,812)

Shoulder of Mutton ✔

16 Main Street, DE13 8AA (on B5016, on jct with Dunstall Rd)
12-11 (12.30am Fri & Sat) ☎ (01283) 716716
shoulderofmuttonbarton.co.uk
Draught Bass; Marston's Pedigree; Timothy Taylor Landlord H
A 17th-century former coaching inn, with more recent additions, opposite the church in the centre of this historic village. Two front entrances directly access the simple public bar and large, comfortable lounge/dining area. The latter comprises several linked rooms and has retained low-beamed ceilings, wood panelling and an inglenook. A single Bass lantern survived a 2014 refurbishment and is located over an annexe entrance. A small landscaped patio garden adjoins the car park to the rear. P (811,812)

Brewood

Swan Hotel 🏆 L ✔

15 Market Place, ST19 9BS
11.45-midnight ☎ (01902) 850330
Courage Directors; Salopian Lemon Dream; Wye Valley HPA; 3 changing beers (sourced locally; often Burton Bridge, Three Tuns, Weetwood) H
Characterful old coaching inn with low-beamed ceilings and seasonal log fires. Its village-centre location makes it convenient for the Shropshire Union Canal and the Staffordshire Way. Cosy snugs displaying early prints of the district flank the central bar which, unusually for the area, stocks nearly 80 malt whiskies and 20 gins from around the world. There is a traditional skittle alley upstairs which doubles as a function room and hosts a fun quiz on Sunday evenings. Major Freeview sporting events are shown. **Q**P (877,878)

Burntwood

Sankey's Tap House

Unit 1, Lambourne House, Bridgcross Road, WS7 2BX
closed Mon; 12-10 (10.30 Fri & Sat) ☎ 07982 923744
4 changing beers H
Burntwood's first micropub is a friendly place with no loud music or television, just good conversation and great beer. Its four ales and six ciders change all the time and are from local and national breweries. Cobs, pork pies and the usual pub offerings are also available. Closed on Monday except for bank holidays.
QP (60,61)

Burston

Greyhound Inn

ST18 0DR (just off A51 N of Sandon and 3 miles S of Stone)
11.30-3, 6-11; 11.30-11 Sat; 12-11 Sun ☎ (01889) 508263
greyhoundinn.info
Lancaster Bomber; 2 changing beers H
A spacious and friendly family-owned pub located a 15-minute walk from the Trent & Mersey Canal's Bridge 86. Refurbished in 2017, the pub has a reputation for food and good beer, with a separate bar for those who just want a drink. The garden with farm animals helps make children welcome. A well-maintained camping field adjoins the car park.
P

Burton upon Trent

Coopers Tavern ★ ✔

43 Cross Street, DE14 1EG (off Station St)
5-10 Mon (closed Jan-Mar); 5-11.30 Tue & Wed; 2-11.30 Thu; 12-midnight Fri & Sat; 12-10 Sun; Jan-Mar closed Mon; 5-11.30 Tue & Wed; 2-11.30 Thu; 1-midnight Fri; 12-midnight Sat; 12-9.30 Sun ☎ (01283) 567246
Draught Bass G**; Joule's Pale Ale, Slumbering Monk** H**; 6 changing beers (sourced regionally)** H/G
Classic 19th-century alehouse, once the Bass Brewery tap but currently part of the Joule's estate. Following a sympathetic refurbishment and expansion in early 2017, the pub now features five linked rooms, but the intimate inner taproom has retained its barrel tables and bench seating, with

REAL ALE BREWERIES

Beowulf Brownhills
Blythe Hamstall Ridware
Brewhouse & Kitchen Lichfield
Burton Bridge Burton upon Trent
Burton Town Brewery Burton upon Trent
Consall Forge Consall Forge
Crown Brewhouse Elford
Dogbreath Kinver
Enville Enville
Firs Codsall
Flash Flash
Front Row Brindley Ford
Gates Burton Burton upon Trent
Gentlewood Gentleshaw (NEW)
Grey Friars Featherstone (brewing suspended)
Heritage Burton upon Trent
Inadequate Stoke-on-Trent: Etruria
Izaak Walton Cold Norton (NEW)
Kinver Kinver
Lymestone Stone
Marston's Burton upon Trent
Marts Stoke-on-Trent: Hanley
Morton Essington
Peakstones Rock Alton
Quartz Kings Bromley
RAN Stoke-on-Trent: Fenton
Roebuck Draycott-in-the-Clay
Shugborough Milford (brewing suspended)
Six Towns Tunstall
Slater's Stafford
Tamworth Tamworth
Titanic Stoke-on-Trent: Burslem
Tower Burton upon Trent
Townhouse Audley
Uttoxeter Uttoxeter
Vine Inn Rugeley
Weal Chesterton

beer served from a small counter by cask stillage. Up to six changing ciders/perries plus fruit wines are also available. Impromptu folk music may feature on Tuesday evenings and live music some Sunday afternoons. Opening hours vary January-March. Q

Derby Inn

17 Derby Road, DE14 1RU (on A5121, 350yds N of jct with A511)

5 (12 Thu-Sat)-11; 12-10 Sun ☎ 07736 953206

Draught Bass; Timothy Taylor Boltmaker; 2 changing beers (sourced nationally) H

Friendly Victorian two-roomed local, towards the northern edge of the town. Very much a community pub, it offers a step back in time to a more relaxed pace of life. It is popular with football supporters on match days as it is en route between the railway station and Burton Albion's Pirelli Stadium. Evening meals, with limited choice, are only available on Wednesdays, but fresh filled cobs can be ordered at all times. Cheesy quiz night is Tuesday. P (V1,X38)

Dog Inn

5 Lichfield Street, DE14 3QZ (opp Burton College, near jct with High St/New St)

12-11 (10 Tue; 11.30 Fri & Sat); 12-10 Sun

☎ (01283) 517060

Black Country Bradley's Finest Golden, Pig on the Wall, Fireside; Draught Bass; 7 changing beers (sourced regionally) H

Attractive half-timbered terrace pub near the town centre, dating back to the early 19th century. Purchased and refurbished by Black Country Ales in 2015, this radically revitalised pub offers an impressive selection of cask ales and ciders. Internally, a large, comfortable, square-shaped single room surrounds a central bar and features a wood-framed ceiling and wood panelling on the walls, plus three real fires and numerous framed old photographs of Burton. Available beers are listed on two boards on opposite sides of the room.

Elms Inn

36 Stapenhill Road, Stapenhill, DE15 9AE (on A444)

12-11.30 (midnight Fri & Sat); 12-10.30 Sun

☎ (01283) 535505 the-elms-burton.co.uk

Draught Bass; Marston's Pedigree; 2 changing beers (sourced nationally) H

Lively local on the opposite bank of the River Trent from the town centre. Built as a private house in the late 19th century, this is one of Burton's original parlour pubs. Sensitively renovated, the small public bar, snug and a side room at the front are largely unchanged. In contrast, the lounge to the rear has been extended and refurbished in a modern style. Meals are available to 7pm Wednesday-Saturday, 3pm Sunday. Occasional live entertainment features.

Last Heretic

95 Station Street, DE14 1BT (between Grant's Yard and Mosley St)

closed Mon; 4-10.30 (11 Fri); 12-11 Sat; 1-10 Sun

☎ 07715 097797 thelastheretic.co.uk

4 changing beers (sourced regionally) G

Smart micropub in a terrace of commercial properties close to the station, named after Edward Wightman, a resident of Burton, who in 1612 was the last person to be burned at the stake in England for heresy. The comfortable single room features a small bar counter towards the rear, with the stillage visible through a glass door and window. Up to six beers are available and up to seven ciders/perries from various sources, listed on boards near the bar. There is a narrow garden at the rear for outdoor drinking. Opening hours vary January and February. Q

National Brewery Centre (Brewery Tap)

Horninglow Street, DE14 1NG (on A511, near jct with Guild St)

11-11 (5 Mon & Tue); 11-5 Sun ☎ (01283) 532880

nationalbrewerycentre.co.uk

Heritage St Modwen Golden Ale, Charrington IPA, Masterpiece IPA; 3 changing beers (sourced locally) H

This tap for the National Brewery Centre (formerly Bass Museum and later Coors Visitor Centre) serves beers from Worthington Brewery which are marketed under the name Heritage Brewing Company. The comfortable single-room bar is bright and airy, furnished in a modern style with much brewery memorabilia. Food is served in the bar and adjacent restaurant; a conservatory overlooks the garden and children's play area. Numerous events including live music are hosted (details on the NBC website).

Q P (1)

Roebuck Inn

101 Station Street, DE14 1BT (on corner of jct with Mosley St)

12-11 ☎ (01283) 511213 roe-buck-inn.co.uk

Draught Bass; Greene King Abbot; Marston's Pedigree; Theakston Old Peculier; 2 changing beers (sourced regionally) H

Friendly Victorian corner-terrace pub near the railway station, once the Ind Coope Brewery tap, opposite the former brewery. The original classic Draught Burton Ale was launched here in 1976. Inside, there is a long, narrow, single room with dark-wood panelling and the bar counter down one side. A small patio at the rear can be used for outdoor drinking, as well as a few tables and chairs at the front in summer. Live music plays early Sunday evenings.

Cannock

Linford Arms

79 High Green, WS11 1BN

8am-midnight (1am Fri & Sat) ☎ (01543) 469360

Greene King Abbot; Ruddles Best Bitter; Sharp's Doom Bar; 5 changing beers (sourced nationally; often Backyard, Beowulf, Salopian) H

Established town-centre Wetherspoon pub serving eight real ales and ciders. Its name originates from the builders' merchants that formerly occupied the premises. It has a seating area on two floors, with quieter alcoves and a separate snug. Food is served daily 8am-11pm. Two ale festivals are held each year and local breweries feature regularly. It has often been a local CAMRA Pub of the Year finalist in recent years. With good bus and rail links, it is not to be missed if visiting Cannock.

Newhall Arms

81 High Green, WS11 1BN

12-10 (11 Wed & Thu; midnight Fri); 11-midnight Sat

☎ 07852 573042 thenewhallarms.co.uk

8 changing beers H

Cannock's first micropub, owned and run by Kev and his sons. This is a friendly place, with no loud music or TV, just good conversation and great beer. The pub is located in the centre of the town and the bar serves eight ales and two ciders. Fresh cobs are available as well as the usual snacks. The beers change all the time, sourced locally as well as nationally. A real gem, it is current CAMRA branch Pub of the Year. Q

Cauldon

Yew Tree Inn

ST10 3EJ (turn right at Ye Olde Crowne pub, Waterhouses; approx 1 mile from jct)
12-3, 6-midnight; 12-midnight Sat & Sun
(01538) 309876 yewtreeinncauldon.co.uk
Burton Bridge Bridge Bitter; Rudgate Ruby Mild; 1 changing beer (sourced nationally; often Blue Monkey, Dancing Duck, McMullen) H
On a quiet bend just outside Leek, this is possibly one of the most famous pubs in the country, and one of the few where even the local CAMRA committee would admit that the good real ale is the least of its attractions; the inside is stuffed to the brim with antiques, guns, pianos, penny farthings, a working pianola and so much more bric-a-brac that it is impossible to list it all here. The entrance is dominated by the eponymous yew tree. Q P (109)

Cheadle

Huntsman

The Green, ST10 1XS (at bottom of hill)
12-midnight (01538) 750502
thehuntsmancheadle.com
Marston's Pedigree; Sharp's Doom Bar; 4 changing beers (sourced regionally; often Joule's, Peakstones Rock, Sarah Hughes) H
Now a regular entry in this Guide, the Huntsman always provides a warm welcome. Recently refurbished with a rustic brickwork theme, it features two log fires. Friendly bar staff serve a good range of beers to the discerning real ale drinker. Traditional pub food is available, with excellent service. Annual beer and cider festivals are held in the beer garden to the rear. A great pub for families as well as those who enjoy a quiet pint. P

Codsall

Codsall Station

Chapel Lane, WV8 2EJ
11.30-11 (11.30 Fri & Sat); 12-10.30 Sun
(01902) 847061 holdenscodsallstation.co.uk
Holden's Black Country Bitter, Golden Glow, Special; 3 changing beers (sourced regionally; often Holden's, Salopian) H
Sensitively converted from the waiting room, offices and stationmaster's house, the Grade II-listed building comprises a bar, lounge, snug and conservatory, and displays worldwide railway memorabilia. Steps lead to a drinking area outside with tables and benches overlooking the working platforms. Bar meals are served except Sunday and Monday; cobs and locally made pork pies are available all week. Beer festivals are held over the May and August bank holiday weekends. Q P (5,10B)

Crown Joule's

1 Wood Road, WV8 1DB
10.30-11 (11.30 Fri & Sat) (01902) 844876
thecrownjoules.pub
Joule's Blonde, Pale Ale, Slumbering Monk; 5 changing beers (sourced regionally; often Joule's) H
The oldest pub in Codsall was bought by Joule's and reopened in 2016 after a major refurbishment which transformed it into a slightly grand Edwardian-style pub with a modern twist; it features open fires, stained-glass windows, old beams and reclaimed furniture. The former function room, which in the '60s and '70s hosted a renowned jazz club, has been fitted out in the style of a library. The pub opens early for breakfast. Canine cuisine, with optional gravy, is available for dogs. Q P (5,10B)

Firs Club

Station Road, WV8 1BX (entrance from shared Co-op car park off Station Rd)
7.30-11 (midnight Fri); 2-midnight Sat; 12-8 Sun
(01902) 844674 thefirscodsall.com
3 changing beers (sourced locally; often Hobsons, Ludlow, Wye Valley) H
A previous CAMRA regional Club of the Year runner-up, the club contains a bar area, quiet lounge and sports lounge with pool table, dartboard and card table. Snooker tables are upstairs. Up to three guest ales, mainly local, are served. The club has recently started brewing its own beer, and holds a beer festival in November. The large function room is available to hire. A pedestrian entrance in Wood Road is handy for the bus stop.
Q P (5,10B)

Consall Forge

Black Lion

ST9 0AJ (off A522 follow signs to Consall Gardens then Nature Reserve on hairpin bend; go straight on, ignore No Vehicular Access sign; at bottom of hill go left along track to car park)
12-11; 12-10.30 Sun (01782) 550294
blacklionpub.co.uk
Peakstones Rock Black Hole; 3 changing beers (sourced regionally; often Consall Forge, Falstaff) H
Walk, drive or travel by boat or train to visit this destination pub located in an Area of Outstanding Natural Beauty. It offers a changing selection of beer and cider and holds regular beer festivals, normally to coincide with a steam gala on the neighbouring Churnet Valley Railway. Typical pub food is served; arrive hungry as the portions are large! Though not easy to find by car, the pub has a large car park – it is well worth the effort. Seek it out! Q P

Denstone

Tavern

College Road, ST14 5HR
6-11 Mon; 12-2, 5.30-11 Tue-Thu; 12-midnight Fri-Sun
(01889) 590847 thetaverndenstone.co.uk
Marston's Pedigree; house beer (by Marston's); 2 changing beers (sourced nationally; often Courage, Lancaster Bomber) H
The Tavern is a newly refurbished 17th-century village inn offering fine food and good beers in comfortable surroundings. There is a bar area with darts, a cosy lounge area and a conservatory for dining. Quiz night is Monday when there is no food.

Fresh wood-fired stone-baked pizzas are served Friday and Saturday evenings, to eat in or take away. Booking ahead for food is advisable. Guest beers come from the Marston's range.
Q❀◐⛺♣P🚌(32A)🐾📶

Draycott-in-the-Clay

Roebuck ✔

Toby's Hill, DE6 5BT (at Toby's Hill/A515 jct, 600yds N of village)
5-10 Mon; 12-2, 5-11; 12-midnight Fri & Sat; 12-8 Sun
☎ (01283) 821135 🌐 theroebuckdraycott.co.uk
Roebuck Blonde, Hopzester, Bitter, IPA; 2 changing beers (sourced locally) Ⓗ
Dating back to at least the early 19th century, this friendly country pub is now a privately owned free house, offering a warm welcome and pleasant atmosphere. It has a comfortable single-room main bar and a separate smart restaurant beyond. The pub is gaining a good reputation for food (no meals Sun eve). Beers from the associated Roebuck Brewery alongside are served in the pub.
❀◐P🚌(402)🐾📶

Elford

Crown Inn

The Square, B79 9DB (600yds E of A513) SK189106
5-11; 12-midnight Fri-Sun ☎ (01827) 383602
Burton Bridge Sovereign Gold; Draught Bass; 2 changing beers (sourced locally; often Crown Brewhouse) Ⓗ
Welcoming, multi-room village pub featuring beamed ceilings and real fires that create a cosy glow. The upstairs rooms were used as a courthouse in the 18th century; the dining room once served as the cells. A changing ale from the in-house Crown Brewhouse is generally offered, with a guest ale that is often from Burton Bridge. Darts and pool are played in a modern room at the side. It is advisable to book in advance for the good-quality food. No evening or Sunday bus service. ◐♣P🚌🐾📶

Enville

Cat Inn

Bridgnorth Road, DY7 5HA (on A458)
12-2.30 (not Mon), 5-11; 12-11 Fri & Sat; 12-6 Sun
☎ (01384) 872209 🌐 thecatinn.com
Enville Ale, Ginger Beer; Olde Swan Original; 4 changing beers (sourced regionally; often Enville, Hobsons, Purity) Ⓗ
A quiet community inn with low oak-beamed ceilings, this is a fine place to enjoy a quality pint of real ale and a bite to eat. Each room has a real fire and, throughout summer, hanging baskets adorn the beer garden and courtyard. House beers are from Enville Ales and Olde Swan; changing beers are typically from regional breweries. A smaller selection of rotating real ciders is also kept. Local CAMRA Pub of the Year 2018. Q❀◐P🐾📶

Fradley Junction

Swan Inn

Alrewas, DE13 7DN (by Trent & Mersey Canal, about 1 mile W of Fradley village) SK140140
12-11; 12-10.30 Sun ☎ (01283) 790330
🌐 swanfradley.co.uk
Everards Beacon Hill, Sunchaser, Tiger, Old Original; 2 changing beers (sourced regionally) Ⓗ
Inevitably known locally as the Mucky Duck, this late 18th-century, Grade II-listed, mid-terrace pub overlooks the junction of the Trent & Mersey and Coventry canals. The cosy public bar, which retains an old-fashioned charm, and a smaller lounge, are on opposite sides of a central serving area. There is a cellar room, with vaulted brick ceiling, down steps beyond the lounge. Guest beers are usually from Midlands microbreweries. Folk night is Thursday, open mic nights the second and fourth Sundays of the month. Boaters and walkers welcome. Q❀◐♣P🐾📶

Gnosall

George & the Dragon

46 High Street, ST20 0EX
4-10.30; 2-10.30 Sat; 12-10.30 Sun ☎ 07779 327551
🌐 georgeandthedragongnosall.com
Holden's Golden Glow; Wood Shropshire Lad; 3 changing beers (sourced locally) Ⓗ
This lovely little pub opened in 2015 and soon received acclaim, winning the CAMRA branch Cider Pub of the Year and Pub of the Year the following year. The building dates from 1736, with a past life as a home, shop and off-licence. It has two rooms served by one bar. With no TV, no music and no bandits, it has a good old-fashioned appeal. Tasty home-made snacks are available at the bar but they do sell out fast. Q♣🚌(5)🐾

Hednesford

Bridge Inn

387 Cannock Road, WS11 5TD (on jct of Belt Rd and Cannock Rd)
12-11 (midnight Fri & Sat) ☎ (01543) 423651
Banks's Amber Ale; 6 changing beers (sourced nationally) Ⓗ
Located close to Cannock Chase, this real ale-based pub prides itself on a changing selection of beers as well as real cider. Food is served Thursday to Sunday, all produced on-site using only fresh local produce. The chips are triple-cooked and the burgers are from the pub's own special recipe. Theme nights and live music feature most Saturday nights, and pool and darts teams are also based at the pub. ❀◐♣P🚌🐾📶

Cross Keys Hotel

42 Hill Street, WS12 2DN
12-midnight ☎ (01543) 879534
Draught Bass; Holden's Golden Glow; Salopian Oracle; Wye Valley HPA; 5 changing beers (sourced nationally; often Beowulf, Ludlow, Three Tuns) Ⓗ
A former coaching inn dating back to 1746 and serving up to eight real ales including several guests. Hednesford Town football club was originally based behind the pub; the licensee is a former player and manager. Sporting and historic photographs decorate the walls. It is rumoured that the highwayman Dick Turpin stopped here on his famous ride to York. Local CAMRA Pub of the Year many times. ❀♣P🚌🐾📶

Ex-Serviceman's Club (Soldiers)

Anglesey Street, WS12 1AB
7-11; 12-3, 7-11 Sat & Sun ☎ (01543) 422407
2 changing beers (sourced nationally) Ⓗ

Also known as the Soldiers, the club hosts many sports teams including darts, dominoes, bowls, snooker and pool, as well as a pigeon flying club. Visitors can gain admission to sample its wide range of beers by showing a current CAMRA card. Attractions include live music, a monthly soul night and well-supported weekend bingo. A large room can be hired for private parties. Handy for local rail and bus stations. P

High Offley

Anchor Inn ★

Peggs Lane, Old Lea, ST20 0NG (by bridge 42 of the Shropshire Union Canal) SJ775256

12-2.30, 7-11; 12-3, 7-10 Sun ☎ (01785) 284569

Wadworth 6X H

An unspoilt example of a 19th-century canalside pub, built around 1830 on the Shropshire Union Canal, England's last narrow trunk canal. It has been run by the same family since 1870. The right-hand room has a quarry-tile floor, two high-back settles, a window bench and scrubbed tables, all of which create a timeless atmosphere. Winter opening hours are shorter so check before travelling. Q P

Hinksford

Hinksford Arms ✔

Swindon Road, DY6 0BA

12-11; 12-10 Sun ☎ (01384) 271272

hinksfordarms.co.uk

Enville Ale; Holden's Golden Glow; Wye Valley HPA, Butty Bach; 1 changing beer (sourced locally; often Ludlow, Sarah Hughes, Three Tuns) H

Previously named the Old Bush, this pub on the road between Wall Heath and Swindon has been extensively refurbished since a new landlord arrived in 2016. The tastefully decorated open-plan room serves four permanent real ales, one changing beer and one real cider. A former function room caters mainly for food, with an extensive menu featuring daily specials. Many family-friendly events are held in the warmer months. P (15)

Hopwas

Coton & Hopwas Social Club

School Lane, B78 3AD (turn into School Lane opp The Tame Otter; after 200yds bear left over the canal bridge)

5-11 (midnight Fri); 12-midnight Sat; 12-11 Sun

☎ (01827) 62684 cotonandhopwassocialclub.co.uk

Draught Bass; 2 changing beers (sourced regionally; often Backyard, Salopian) H

A small CIU affiliated members' club – non-members are always welcome. Situated at the end of School Lane, its grounds are bordered by the Coventry Canal and Hopwas Woods. There is a pleasant bar plus a room for private functions. A regular programme of activities includes ladies' darts, karate, zumba and bingo. Thursday is folk club night and Sunday is charity quiz night. A popular summer beer festival draws crowds. P

Kinver

Cross Inn 🏆 L

Church Hill, DY7 6HZ

12-11 (midnight Fri & Sat) ☎ (01384) 878481

Black Country Bradley's Finest Golden, Pig on the Wall, Fireside; 4 changing beers (sourced nationally; often Fixed Wheel, Oakham, Salopian) H

CAMRA branch South Staffordshire Pub of the Year 2019, the Cross is a 19th-century pub near to the Staffordshire & Worcestershire Canal. It originally brewed its own beers but today operates as part of the Black Country Ales chain. The pub has a large L-shaped room with a log-burning fire. Cobs and snacks are served at the bar while hot pork sandwiches and 'grey paes' are available on weekends and bank holidays. Stourbridge buses stop nearby, but there is no service after 6pm or on Sunday. P (228)

Kinver Constitutional Club L

119 High Street, DY7 6HL

12 (5 Mon & Tue)-11; 12-midnight Fri; 11.30-midnight Sat

☎ (01384) 872044 kinverconstitutionalclub.co.uk

Enville Ale; Hobsons Best; Holden's Golden Glow; Olde Swan Bumble Hole Bitter; Wye Valley HPA, Butty Bach; 6 changing beers (sourced locally; often Kinver, Mallinsons, Sarah Hughes) H

Popular club at the heart of Kinver High Street with a large snooker room at the rear and an open-plan bar area with separate tables for diners. Card-carrying CAMRA members are welcome but prices are higher. It is a festival of beer every day, with over a dozen to choose from. Buses from Stourbridge stop nearby, but there is no service after 6pm or on Sunday. CAMRA branch Club of the Year 2008-19. P (228)

Leek

Blue Mugge L

17 Osbourne Street, ST13 6LJ (off A53 Buxton Rd)

12-3, 6-11; 12-3, 5-11 Fri; 12-11 Sat & Sun

☎ (01538) 384450 thebluemugge.co.uk

Draught Bass; 4 changing beers (often Coach House, Slater's) H

A well-deserved new entry in the Guide, this deceptively spacious terraced street-corner pub has been owned and run by the same family since the 1970s. Several themed areas are served from a central island bar. Beer pumps located on the back bar are an unusual feature. Blackboards show which four guest beers complement the regular Bass; they usually include a local brewery's ale and a darker offering. This friendly local is home to several games teams and gets busy with meals at lunchtime.

Earl Grey Inn L

38 Ashbourne Road, ST13 5AT

3 (5 Mon)-11; 12-11.30 Sat; 12-10.30 Sun

☎ (01538) 372570

Whim Earl Grey Bitter; 4 changing beers (sourced nationally; often Blackjack, Great Heck, Marble) H

A multi award-winning little gem in this great pub town, the Earl Grey has become a regular Guide entry since reopening in 2014, specialising in unusual ales and keg craft beers. A former branch, county and regional Pub of the Year winner, this free house has a growing wall of certificates. House Earl Grey Bitter by local brewery Whim of Hartington is served plus four changing guests, always including a darker offering, plus a range of craft beers and real cider. Knowledgeable and passionate staff are always willing to advise on beer styles. Q

Fountain Inn 🏆 L

14 Fountain Street, ST13 6JR

12-midnight (1am Fri & Sat); 12-11 Sun ☎ (01538) 387205

Draught Bass; St Austell Tribute; 6 changing beers (sourced nationally; often Exmoor, Front Row, Wincle) H

A smart and well-appointed free house just outside the town centre, the Fountain offers a visual treat of 10 handpumps serving a good range of well-kept real ales and ciders. Attractive decor and real fires enhance the interior; outside is seating to the front and rear. An almost complete set of past Guides provides interesting reading over a pint in this multi award-winning former CAMRA regional Pub of the Year. Self-contained accommodation is available.

Wilkes Head L

15 St Edwards Street, ST13 5DS

12 (3 Mon)-midnight; 12-11 Sun ☎ 07976 592787

Whim Hartington Bitter, Hartington IPA, Flower Power; 2 changing beers (sourced nationally; often Broughton, Burton Bridge) H

The longest continuous Guide entry in Leek has an interesting history and a talented musician landlord. House beers from nearby Whim brewery are complemented by guests including a darker ale and a range of real cider. A collection of CAMRA awards hangs over the bar. Regular live outdoor music events, dubbed Wilkestonbury, attract increasing numbers of musicians and fans, both local and international. The pub also hosts anything-goes music jam sessions on Monday night. QP

Lichfield

Beerbohm

19 Tamworth Street, WS13 6JP

closed Sun & Mon; 11-11 ☎ (01543) 898252

beerbohm.co.uk

4 changing beers (sourced nationally) H

A Belgian-accented café-bar, featuring continental draught and bottled beers alongside the four real ales. A large but cosy upstairs room offers views of the busy pedestrian street below, while the downstairs bar room is decorated with beer enamels, gilded mirrors and globular chandeliers. The ales can be sampled with a three-thirds paddle. Customers are welcome to bring their own food. The unisex toilets are upstairs. Q

Bitter-Suite L

55 Upper St John Street, WS14 9DT

7-10 Mon; closed Tue; 5-10 Wed & Thu; 12-10 Fri & Sat; 2-9 Sun ☎ 07852 179340 bittersuite-micropub.co.uk

4 changing beers (sourced nationally) G

Convivial micropub occupying a building that was a pub 30 years ago. There are two comfortable rooms, and service is to your table – make your choices from the chalkboard. Four diverse ales, always changing, are complemented by four ciders. Gins, wines and bottled beers are available, plus simple snacks. Monday is quiz night, which includes a supper from the local chippy. There is a small beer terrace to the rear. Children are welcome until 5pm. Q

George & Dragon ✔

28 Beacon Street, WS13 7AJ

11-midnight (1am Fri & Sat); 12-11.30 Sun ☎ (01543) 254854

Banks's Amber Ale; Marston's 61 Deep, Pedigree; house beer (by Marston's); 2 changing beers H

Traditional local with the city's best beer garden, overlooking the cathedral and also the site of an artillery battery that bombarded the cathedral during the Civil War. Inside, the central serving area supplies a pub-games focused bar and a cosy lounge. Snacks include a tempting selection of cheeses. Two or three guest ales are usually available, generally from local breweries. The nearby historic home of Erasmus Darwin, Lunar Society founder and grandfather of Charles, is well worth visiting. P

Horse & Jockey L

8-10 Sandford Street, WS13 6QA

11.30-11; 11-11.30 Sat; 11-11 Sun ☎ (01543) 410033

Greene King Abbot; Holden's Golden Glow; Marston's Pedigree; Timothy Taylor Landlord; Wye Valley HPA; 3 changing beers H

This long-standing real ale bastion always proves popular with visitors and locals alike. The regular ales are joined by three guests, mainly from microbreweries. There is a cosy snug and a separate games room at the back of the large open-plan bar. A small suntrap beer terrace at the rear is pleasant in summer. Hot food is served 12-3pm Tuesday-Saturday, and a pork pie/cheeseboard selection is always available. Over-21s only. P

Whippet Inn

21 Tamworth Street, WS13 6JP

closed Mon & Tue; 4-10 Wed & Thu; 12-10 Fri & Sat; 12-6 Sun ☎ 07922 581468

4 changing beers H

First-rate micropub named after a cheeky boozer in a Carry On film. The four well-chosen, varying ales veer towards specialist. There are also two changing real ciders and a selection of craft keg beers. The pub has seating for around 25 and a maximum capacity of around 40, ensuring an unusual degree of conviviality. Food is simple snacks including cobs and pork pies. Q

Marchington

Dog & Partridge

Church Lane, ST14 8LJ (250yds along Church Lane from High St)

12-3, 6-11; 12-3, 5-midnight Fri; 12-midnight Sat; 12-11 Sun ☎ (01283) 820394

dogandpartridgemarchington.co.uk

Draught Bass; 3 changing beers (sourced locally; often Abbeydale, Gates Burton, Uttoxeter) H

A gem of a village inn with Bass always available, plus a selection of local guest ales on several handpumps. Formerly a restaurant, the pub is split into four main indoor areas with open fires. Food is served lunchtimes and evenings. A pleasant beer garden to the rear is popular in the summer months. The venue is renowned locally for its weekly live music sessions and regular beer festivals. Parking is available to the side. Children are welcome. Q ▲P (402)

Milwich

Green Man

Sandon Lane, ST18 0EG (on B5027 in centre of village)

5 (12 Thu-Sat)-11; 12-10.30 Sun ☎ (01889) 505310

greenmanmilwich.com

Draught Bass; 5 changing beers (sourced nationally) 🄷
A country pub well worth a visit, with 26 consecutive years in the Guide and multiple local CAMRA Pub of the Year awards. The hub of a vibrant village community, it is popular with walkers and cyclists. The licensee, in charge since 1990, drinks Bass and there is usually a dark beer available. A large garden to the rear hosts many events including an annual free music festival. Food is served Wednesday to Sunday.

Newcastle-under-Lyme

Bridge Street Ale House

31 Bridge Street, ST5 2RY
1-10; 12-11 Fri & Sat; 12-9 Sun ☎ (01782) 499394
5 changing beers (sourced nationally; often Coach House, Dorking, Rat) 🄷
The first micropub in the area, the Bridge is a special place for regulars and newcomers alike, in the capable hands of Grum, the charismatic owner, and his hospitable staff. The pub oozes charm and appeal, enhanced by the quirky decor. There are five changing guest beers on handpull from various breweries, with more usually available straight from the barrel. An array of ciders also features, several exceptional rums adding to the individuality of this fantastic pub. A Newcastle real ale institution. Q

Cask Bar

1-2 Andrew Place, ST5 1DL
12.30-9 (10.30 Fri); 1-10.30 Sat; 1-9 Sun
☎ (01782) 870560
Sarah Hughes Dark Ruby Mild; 4 changing beers (sourced nationally; often Kelham Island, Ossett, Rudgate) 🄷
Cask Bar opened in July 2017 and immediately became a firm favourite on the Newcastle scene. This bright and welcoming one-room community pub serves four varying real ales across all beer styles, plus Sarah Hughes' Dark Ruby Mild, the sole permanent beer. Two real ciders are also available plus a wide range of gins. Excellent home-cooked food includes curry on Monday and pies on Thursday. A well-maintained, covered beer patio allows alfresco drinking. Q

Hopinn

102 Albert Street, ST5 1JR
4-midnight; 12-midnight Sat; 12-11 Sun
☎ (01782) 711121
Black Sheep Best Bitter; Draught Bass; Oakham Citra; 11 changing beers (sourced nationally; often Mallinsons, Northern Monk, Oakham) 🄷
This glorious three-roomed, family-owned free house has excelled since opening in 2014, twice winning local CAMRA Pub of the Year. Its main focus is the nine perfectly kept real ales, sourced from an array of changing breweries as well as a few regulars. KeyKeg ales are also well represented, with five lines dispensing an abundance of quality flavours. Go in – you are guaranteed a warm welcome and a wonderful tipple.

Hopwater Cellar

2 Bridge Street, ST5 2RY
12-8 (9 Fri & Sat); 12-4 Sun ☎ (01782) 713311
8 changing beers (sourced nationally; often Front Row, Twisted Barrel, Weal Ales)
A small cellar bar that opened in 2015, the Hopwater has three drinking areas, including seating areas to the left and right of the main bar. The bar offers over 500 bottles from around the world, in addition to the two handpulls and six KeyKegs serving beers of different styles from Britain. Regular tap takeovers are popular and the Hopwater co-hosts meetings of the local home-brew club. Q

Lymestone Vaults

Pepper Street, ST5 1PR
11-11 (midnight Fri & Sat); 12-10.30 Sun
☎ (01782) 615801
Lymestone Stone Cutter, Stone Faced, Foundation Stone, Ein Stein, Stone the Crows; 3 changing beers (sourced regionally; often Derventio, Lymestone, Springhead) 🄷
Located off the high street in the town centre, this Lymestone Brewery taphouse offers a comfortable and relaxed environment in which to sample the range of Lymestone beers and guest ales from around the country. Real ciders and bottled beers are also always available. A log-burning stove helps give a cosy atmosphere; good home-cooked food is served in the afternoon. The friendly staff are welcoming to all, dogs very much included.

Wellers

3 Pepper Street, ST5 1PR
4-10 Mon & Tue; 3-10.30 Wed & Thu; 12-11 Fri & Sat; 1-7 Sun ☎ (01782) 698080
Weal Ales Weller Weal, Centwealial Milk Stout; 4 changing beers (often Derby, Slater's, Weal Ales) 🄷
Having found success with its nearby brewery, Weal Ales opened Wellers to showcase its beers, which stand alongside rotating guests from across the country. A mix of six light and dark ales is always on offer, along with two real ciders plus gins and vodkas. Tucked away on a quiet street just off the town centre, this is a perfect place for a quality beer. Bring your own food and eat in as long as you buy a drink. Thursday is quiz night.

Penkridge

Star Inn

Market Place, ST19 5DJ
12-11 (11.30 Thu; midnight Fri & Sat) ☎ (01785) 712513
thestarpenkridge.wixsite.com/home
Marston's Pedigree; Wainwright; 4 changing beers (sourced nationally) 🄷
A popular and friendly one-room Marston's pub with several distinct areas and a cosy and welcoming feel. The pub is in the old Market Place and first traded as an inn in 1830. After becoming a private house and a shop, it was restored as a pub in 1981. It has become an important part of the town and community life, offering an excellent choice of permanent and changing ales. There are patio and seating areas outside.
P

Rugeley

Rusty Barrel

103 Fernwood Drive, WS15 2GS
closed Mon; 4-11; 1-11 Sat & Sun therustybarrel.co.uk
4 changing beers (sourced locally; often Blythe, Titanic) 🄷

Rugeley's first micropub has a single room with a friendly atmosphere. The decor is simple painted brick with the ceiling adorned with pumpclips showing the vast array of beers that have been sold. There are four handpumps offering a varied selection of beers. At least five ciders are also available, plus a good choice of wines, gins and whiskies. Dogs are are welcome, as are children up to 7pm. Q P (22,825)

Vine Inn ✔

Sheep Fair Close, WS15 2AT
12-12.30am (2.30am Fri & Sat); 12-1.30am Sun
(01889) 574443
Vine Inn EPA, Vanilla Porter, Grapefruit IPA, Pecan Porter [H]
This old boozer on a quiet street is a locals' pub that now has its own brewery. The pub retains a traditional multi-room layout, with a spacious bar to the front, a small snug behind the bar, plus a room to the rear offering pool. The bar feels pleasantly dated, with quarry tiles and an open log fire. These is also a large function room upstairs and a small beer yard at the front, underneath the sign. The guest ale is generally Bass.
Q

Salt

Holly Bush Inn ✔

Salt Road, ST18 0BX (turn W off A518 opp Weston Hall) SJ959277
12-11 (01889) 508234 hollybushinn.co.uk
Adnams Southwold Bitter; Marston's Pedigree; 1 changing beer (sourced regionally) [H]
The pub claims to have origins as far back as 1190 and is reputed to be the second oldest inn to be granted a licence. The oldest part of the existing building retains a thatched roof and probably dates from the early 17th century. Alterations over the centuries mean there are now three distinct areas: a bar, dining room and snug. It has a stellar reputation for its food so there is limited standing room for drinkers. P

Stafford

Bod

57-59 Bodmin Avenue, ST17 0EF
12-11 (01785) 661506
Titanic Anchor Bitter, Plum Porter; 2 changing beers [H]
The first of Titanic Brewery's Bod chain of café bars opened in April 2018, named after its location on Bodmin Avenue and providing 'breakfast, brunch, lunch, dinner, snacks or even a well-deserved pint after a hard day's graft'. It opens for coffee and the like from 8am, for alcoholic drinks from noon. There are four Titanic beers on draught. Gluten-free and vegan options are available on the menu. The pub occupies a former Co-op shop; ironically, the new Co-op opposite occupies the site of a former pub. Q

Floodgate Ale House

147 Newport Road, ST16 2EZ
closed Mon; 5-10 Tue-Thu; 2-11 Fri & Sat; 2-10 Sun
07917 885821
5 changing beers (sourced nationally) [H]
Stafford's first micropub opened in 2015. The hours may vary and it is advisable to check the Facebook page for current opening times and beers. It was winner of the local CAMRA Urban Pub of the Year in 2017. The name derives from the council insisting on flood defences, and the owner has cheekily provided various emergency warnings and devices.
Q

Greyhound

12 County Road, ST16 2PU (off A34, opp jail)
11-11 (midnight Fri & Sat); 11-10 Sun (01785) 222432
greyhoundfreehousestafford.co.uk
Bradfield Farmers Blonde; 7 changing beers (sourced nationally) [H]
A short walk from the centre of Stafford, this two-room free house is well worth a visit. The Greyhound dates from 1831 and a newspaper article from the day it opened can be seen above the bar. Today it offers a changing range of eight ales, often from breweries in the north-east, especially Yorkshire. It also stocks a range of bottled ciders. The pub quiz is on a Tuesday and Sunday. A winner of a number of CAMRA awards, including local Pub of the Year. Q

King's Arms

11-12 Peel Terrace, ST16 3HD (off B5066, Sandon Rd)
12-11.30 (11 Mon-Wed) (01785) 246562
kings-arms-staffordshire.co.uk
Draught Bass; 4 changing beers (sourced nationally) [H]
Converted a long time ago from two terraced houses, it has been further opened up in more recent years but retains a separate bar and snug, and has a surprisingly large garden. Although this traditional pub does not offer any parking, it is only a 10-minute walk from the town centre. It serves a wide-ranging selection of guest beers from the Dorbiere range and up to six real ciders, and is a regular CAMRA branch Cider Pub of the Year.

Olde Rose & Crown

10 Market Street, ST16 2JZ
12-11 (midnight Fri & Sat); 12-10.30 Sun
(01785) 251343
Joule's Blonde, Pale Ale, Slumbering Monk; 1 changing beer (sourced locally) [H]
This comfortable Joule's house was extensively refurbished in 2011 and is right in the heart of Stafford; it is much larger than it looks from the outside. Four handpumps serve Joule's ales. Lunches are served Monday to Saturday, and bar snacks using locally sourced ingredients are available all day. Situated next to the Gatehouse Theatre, the pub is a favourite of theatregoers and is frequented by cast members enjoying an after-show pint. Over-18s only. Q

Slater's Bar

28 Gaolgate Street, ST16 2NT
11-11 (midnight Fri & Sat); 11-10 Sun 07977 982884
Slater's Top Totty, Premium, Haka; 2 changing beers [H]
A straightforward micropub with friendly staff selling real ale, craft lager, cider, speciality gins and spirits, wine, tea and coffee. A good conversion from a former shop, there is a pavement drinking area with tables and chairs to enjoy the sun – set in a pedestrianised area, there is little traffic. No food is served but you are welcome to bring your own lunch. Open mic night features every Tuesday.
Q

Star & Garter

87 Wolverhampton Road, ST17 4AW (on A449)
12-midnight ☎ (01785) 251717
the-star-and-garter.co.uk
Sharp's Doom Bar; 4 changing beers
Close to the town centre along the busy Wolverhampton Road, this establishment dates back to the 1820s. It was developed from a doctor's surgery and was the last pub in Stafford to admit women. Refurbished and reopened by the Dorbiere group in 2011, some of whose beers always feature, it is now a cheery local with two roaring fires on cold days. There is a pleasant beer garden to relax in on summer evenings.
P

Sun

7 Lichfield Road, ST17 4JX
12-11 (midnight Fri & Sat) ☎ (01785) 248361
Everards Tiger; Titanic Steerage, Anchor Bitter, Iceberg, White Star, Captain Smith's Strong Ale; 5 changing beers (sourced nationally)
One of Titanic Brewery's pubs, this is a multi-roomed, multi-level establishment with 12 handpumps. At least one cider is available, usually from Westons. Food is served throughout the day, using locally sourced ingredients; the Sunday menu includes a traditional roast. An outdoor drinking area with its own bar is great on warmer days. Beer festivals are held in spring and late summer in a large marquee at the rear of the building. Buses stop outside the front door.
Q P

Stoke-on-Trent: Burslem

Bull's Head

14 St John's Square, ST6 3AJ
3-11 (11.30 Wed & Thu); 12-midnight Fri & Sat; 12-11 Sun
☎ (01782) 834153
Titanic Steerage, Iceberg, White Star, Plum Porter; 6 changing beers (sourced nationally)
Titanic's brewery tap offers 10 real ales, 10 ciders and perries served from the cellar, and a selection of draught and bottled Belgian beers. The large central bar allows customers to choose between the snug or the bar where bar billiards, a skittles table and a jukebox can be found; a beer garden is to the rear. Close to Port Vale, the pub opens at 11am on home match days; all fans are welcome. The pub supports community events in the area.
Q

Duke William

2 St John's Square, ST6 3AJ
12-11 (midnight Fri & Sat) ☎ (01782) 814809
dukewilliamburslem.co.uk
Greene King Abbot; Oakham Citra; Sarah Hughes Dark Ruby Mild; 5 changing beers (sourced nationally; often Abbeydale, Acorn, Salopian)
An imposing mock-Tudor building in the heart of the Potteries mother town with a friendly and relaxed atmosphere. It has become a popular haunt for both diners and drinkers since reopening in 2010 after a sympathetic refurbishment. Original features abound, such as the horseshoe-shaped bar and its heated foot rail, bell pushes in the lounge, the serving hatch and leaded windows. The ground floor has a lounge and a snug, plus a large public bar. The splendid restaurant with its own bar is on the first floor.

Stoke-on-Trent: Etruria

Holy Inadequate

67 Etruria Old Road, ST1 5PE
4-11 (midnight Thu); 12-midnight Fri & Sat; 12-11 Sun
☎ 07771 358238
Joule's Pale Ale; 5 changing beers (sourced nationally; often Beartown, Burton Bridge, Hawkshead)
A welcoming free house occupying a corner plot on the outskirts of Hanley, comprising an L-shaped room and bar, and a room at the back. Both have logburners, making them cosy and warm in the winter. As well as the regular Joule's Pale Ale, there are beers from all over the country, with some from the onsite Inadequate Brewery, which is going from strength to strength. Three real ciders are also available. Regular beer festivals are staged. A true classic. P

Stoke-on-Trent: Hanley

BottleCraft

33 Piccadilly, ST1 1EN (next to Regent Theatre)
12-9 (11 Fri & Sat); 12-6 Sun ☎ (01782) 911819
bottlecraft.beer
12 changing beers (sourced nationally; often Brew by Numbers, Kernel, Partizan)
Modern, friendly craft beer bar in the heart of the city centre, with two cask beers, 10 craft beers and over 200 bottles and cans from around the world. If you are stuck for choice, the bar staff are always happy to help. The bar is found on two levels; there is a small bar area with a larger seating area upstairs, and an outdoor area at the front. Tasting nights are run regularly. Q

Victoria Lounge

5 Adventure Place, ST1 3AF (next to Hanley bus station)
10-11 ☎ (01782) 273530
6 changing beers (sourced nationally; often Blue Monkey, Brains, Cottage)
A family-run pub for 35 years, unassuming from the outside but a gem inside. You can enjoy one of six changing cask beers from around the country, while relaxing on a Chesterfield settee. Beer styles are clearly shown and the friendly staff are more than happy to help and advise. The ideal place for pre-theatre or interval drinks, meeting friends or while waiting for your bus; a warm welcome and good beer are guaranteed. Basic bar snacks can be eaten outside the usual food hours. Q

Stoke-on-Trent: Hartshill

Artisan Tap

552 Hartshill Road, ST4 6AF
4-10 (11 Wed & Thu); 1-11 Fri & Sat; 1-10 Sun
☎ (01782) 618378
4 changing beers (sourced nationally; often Abbeydale, Lymestone, Rudgate)
Popular bar housed in a converted workshop, opened in summer 2017. The main bar area includes a raised area that also hosts live music, while the rear room features comfortable seating and a fine collection of wall decorations. A large seating area at the front is also popular. Four changing handpumps serve beer from anywhere in the UK, usually of different styles, alongside three traditional ciders, craft keg, bottles, cans and a selection of gins. Q

Greyhound 🄻

67 George Street, ST5 1JT

⏲ 12-11 (11.30 Wed & Thu; midnight Fri); 11-midnight Sat; 11-11 Sun ☎ (01782) 635814

Titanic Steerage, Iceberg, White Star, Plum Porter; 5 changing beers (sourced nationally; often Nethergate, Rooster's, Wensleydale) 🄷

A warm welcome awaits at this dog-friendly pub on the outskirts of Newcastle. The second pub in the Titanic fleet, the Greyhound boasts nine handpumps showcasing Titanic ales as well as a fantastic varied range of ales from across the UK. A great selection of bottled beers as well as country wines and real cider make this an excellent choice for a quality drink. Tasty bar snacks are available. There is occasional live music from local groups and a regular pub quiz on Sunday nights. **Q♣🍎🚌🐾📶**

Sanctuary 🄻

493-495 Hartshill Road, ST4 6AA

⏲ closed Mon; 3-10 Tue-Thu; 3-11 Fri; 12-11 Sat; 3-8 Sun ☎ (01782) 437523

4 changing beers (sourced nationally; often Backyard, Cross Bay, Lymestone) 🄷

Opened in 2016 in an old converted café, four handpulls here dispense beer from around the country and of different styles. Four traditional ciders and perries are also always available. The layout is a single room with the bar on the right, while the rest of the space is occupied by an eclectic mixture of seating, including a couple of old car seats. Much bric-a-brac, brewery-related and otherwise, adorns the walls, making this a comfortable and welcoming place. **♣🍎🚌🐾📶**

Stoke-on-Trent: Longton

Congress Inn 🄻

14 Sutherland Road, ST3 1HJ (Seven-minute walk from Longton railway station)

⏲ 2-11; 12-midnight Fri-Sun ☎ (01782) 763667

🌐 congressinnlongton.co.uk

Adnams Broadside; Castle Rock Sheriff's Tipple; Townhouse Styrian Pale; 6 changing beers (sourced nationally; often Abbeydale, Castle Rock, Wincle) 🄷

A family-run community pub with friendly bar staff and regulars. It has two rooms off a quarry-tiled corridor, and a beer terrace outside. Nine real ales, four real ciders and a large selection of bottles are available, including Belgian and Samuel Smith beers. An extensive collection of beer memorabilia includes the original, now restored Joule's Brewery gates. Live entertainment features, as well as a jukebox, pub games and a beer festival every May. CAMRA awards include the Barry Underwood Memorial Award 2018. **⇌♣🍎🚌📶**

Stoke-on-Trent: Stoke

London Road Ale House 🄻

241 London Road, ST4 5AA

⏲ closed Mon; 3-10.30; 12-10.30 Sat; 12-9 Sun ☎ (01782) 698070

6 changing beers (sourced nationally; often Burton Bridge, Coach House, Snowdon Craft) 🄷

A short walk from Stoke town centre, this is a vibrant, convivial one-room pub where conversation is encouraged. The bar offers six varying high-quality real ales plus several rotating real ciders. Smaller breweries feature heavily and all beer styles are accounted for. These sit alongside an extensive bottled beer selection plus wines and spirits. Cheeses and pork pies are available or bring in your own food to accompany your beer. Occasional acoustic music nights are held. **Q♣🍎🚌**(21,21A)**🐾**

White Star 🄻

63 Kingsway, ST4 1JB (off Church St, close to King's Hall)

⏲ 11-midnight; 12-11 Sun ☎ (01782) 848734

Titanic Steerage, Anchor Bitter, Iceberg, White Star, Plum Porter; 5 changing beers (sourced nationally; often Everards, Titanic) 🄷

This popular, multi award-winning pub is one of the renowned Titanic Brewery fleet, with a well-established reputation for the quality of its beers. Internally, the pub has a large, comfortably furnished split-level bar, with photos and information about the Titanic adorning the walls, adding to the atmosphere. With 10 handpumps, five Titanic beers are supplemented by five changing guests. A menu of fresh home-cooked food is served lunchtimes and evenings; a function room is available. **Q🛋◐◑♿⇌♣🚌🐾📶**

Stone

Borehole 🍸

Unit 5 Mount Road Industrial Estate, Mount Road, ST15 8LL

⏲ 12-10 (11 Fri & Sat) ☎ (01785) 813581

Lymestone Stone Cutter, Stone Faced, Ein Stein, Stone the Crows; 2 changing beers (sourced regionally; often Lymestone) 🄷

A traditional pub and Lymestone Brewery tap on the site of the old Bent's Brewery well, hence the name. It is a bit of a Tardis inside, with rooms all centred around a logburner. A wide range of bottled beers and real ciders is available; the changing beers include a seasonal brew from Lymestone. Families and dogs are welcome. A light food menu is served, locally sourced where possible. There is a small, enclosed suntrap beer garden to the rear. **Q🛋❀⇌♣🍎P🐾**

Poste of Stone ✔

1 Granville Square, ST15 8AB (top of High St)

⏲ 9am-midnight ☎ (01785) 827920

Greene King Abbot; Ruddles County; Sharp's Doom Bar; house beer (by Lymestone); 3 changing beers 🄷

A large, open-plan Wetherspoon's pub, which was previously the town's post office. It is a short walk from the Trent and Mersey Canal and the station, and there is a bus stop outside. The pub stocks a wide range of regularly changing real ales including locally produced Lymestone, Slater's, Blythe and Salopian beers. This venue also has its own beer, Poste of Stone, brewed by Lymestone, which is only available here. **Q🛋❀◐◑⇌🍎🚌📶**

Royal Exchange

26 Radford Street, ST15 8DA (on corner of Northesk St and Radford St)

⏲ 12-11 (midnight Fri & Sat) ☎ (01785) 812685

Everards Tiger; Titanic Steerage, White Star, Plum Porter, Captain Smith's Strong Ale; 4 changing beers (sourced nationally; often Titanic) 🄷

A one-roomed pub, refurbished sympathetically to a high standard in 2015, with four distinct drinking areas and real fires at either end. Ten real ales and one real cider are always available including three varying guest ales, one of which is usually a Titanic seasonal beer. There are no TVs or piped music, just good conversation. Acoustic music and monthly quiz nights are held and many clubs meet here.

Lunches are served on Fridays and Saturdays, with totally locally sourced ingredients. There is a set evening meal on Mondays (except bank holidays). Q≋❀◐▶⇌♣●🚍🐾📶

Swan Inn

18 Stafford Street, ST15 8QW (on A520 near Trent & Mersey Canal)

12-1am (11 Mon; midnight Tue & Wed); 12-11 Sun ☎ (01785) 815570 🌐 swaninnstone.co.uk

House beer (by Coach House); 8 changing beers (sourced nationally) H

A thriving free house in a carefully renovated, Grade II-listed building close to the Trent & Mersey Canal. It has nine handpumps serving a variety of beers and four real ciders on draught, plus bottled versions. The pub comprises one long room, with coal fires at each end. It is a multiple CAMRA award winner, and its themed beer festival each July is a mecca for beer lovers. Live, free music plays on Thursday and Saturday; often rock and sometimes featuring national acts. Dogs are welcome. Strictly no under-18s. ❀♿●🚍(101)🐾

Tamworth

King's Ditch L

51 Lower Gungate, B79 7AS

5-7 Mon; 5-9 Tue & Wed; 5-10.30 Thu; 4-10.30 Fri; 12-10.30 Sat; 12-9 Sun ☎ 07989 805828 🌐 kingsditch.co.uk

Changing beers G

Tamworth's first micropub, opened in 2015 but quickly making its mark, having been a finalist in CAMRA's national Cider Pub of the Year competition for both 2016 and 2017. The single ground-floor room is simply decorated, with the novel feature of a TV screen showing the cellar. There is an additional small drinking area upstairs. Up to six ales and 30 real ciders are served, and simple snacks are available. Occasional beers festivals are held. Children are welcome until 7pm. Q≋⇌●🍷🚍🐾📶

Sir Robert Peel L

13-15 Lower Gungate, B79 7BA

2-11 (11.30 Fri); 12-11.30 Sat; 12-11 Sun ☎ (01827) 300910

House beer (by Church End); 4 changing beers (often Salopian) H

Sixteen consecutive appearances in the Guide are testament to the beer quality here. This popular town-centre free house is named after the town's historic statesman. Attentive staff dispense up to five changing ales, plus four real ciders and a large selection of foreign bottled beers. The pub can get lively, particularly at the weekend. Towards the rear is a large and peaceful beer garden with ancient stone walls, overlooked by the historic St Editha's Church. ❀⇌●🚍🐾📶

Tamworth Tap 🏆 L

29 Market Street, B79 7LR

closed Mon; 5-10.45 Tue-Thu; 4-10.45 Fri; 12-10.45 Sat; 12-9 Sun ☎ (01827) 319872 🌐 tamworthbrewing.co.uk

8 changing beers (often Beowulf, Blythe, Tamworth) H

Home to Tamworth Brewing Company, this former tourist information office is now an elegant and cosy pub. Exposed wall beams in the upstairs rooms reveal the Tudor heritage of the building, while the historic courtyard beer terrace to the rear offers unique views of Tamworth Castle. Eight handpulls usually feature two Tamworth beers, with the remainder chosen from near and far. An eclectic range of snacks is offered, plus a wide choice of gins and Belgian bottled beers. ❀⇌●🍷🚍🐾📶

> I never drink water. I'm afraid it will become habit-forming.
> **W C Fields**

Trysull

Bell Inn L

Bell Road, WV5 7JB

11.30-3, 5-11 (midnight Fri); 11.30-midnight Sat; 12-11 Sun ☎ (01902) 892871 🌐 holdensbellinntrysull.co.uk

Bathams Best Bitter; Holden's Black Country Bitter, Golden Glow; 1 changing beer (sourced nationally; often Hop Back, Ludlow, Monty's) H

Idyllic country pub serving an extensive food menu to the residents of Trysull, Seisdon, and visitors from further afield. There is a large patio area at the front of the pub which overlooks several picturesque residential properties. It is popular with walkers, and the Staffordshire & Worcestershire canal is a 15-minute walk away. The house beers experience high turnover and are typically accompanied by one changing pale beer. Q≋❀◐▶P🐾📶

Tutbury

Cask & Pottle

2 High Street, DE13 9LP (close to mini roundabout at centre of village)

12-2 (not Mon), 5-9; 12-2, 5-10 Fri; 1-10 Sat; 1-4 Sun ☎ 07595 423614 🌐 caskandpottle.co.uk

4 changing beers (sourced regionally) G

East Staffordshire's first micropub, opened in 2013 in a former sweet shop. The small, bright, single room on the ground floor of a Victorian terrace features pine benches and tables but no bar counter. One wall is decorated with an aphorism, a mural and a table of ale measures (a pottle is an archaic name for a half-gallon measure). A window at the rear offers a view of the stillage. Three ciders and a perry are usually available from various sources. Q≋♿●🚍🐾

Uttoxeter

Horse & Dove

21 Market Place, ST14 8HY

3.30-10 (11 Thu); 12.30-11 Fri & Sat; 12.30-10 Sun ☎ (01889) 735942 🌐 horsendove.co.uk

6 changing beers (sourced locally; often Heritage, Titanic, Uttoxeter) H

A warm welcome awaits visitors to the town's first micropub. Pleasant, traditional decor with plenty of hard and soft furnishings ensures a cosy but vibrant atmosphere. An excellent selection of up to six real ales with many offerings from local breweries, plus a lengthy real cider list and a selection of gins, mean all tastes are catered for. Limited snacks are served from the bar. Friendly staff and regulars ensure a pleasant and varied drinking experience. ⇌●🚍🐾📶

Whiston

Swan at Whiston

Whiston Road, ST19 5QH (in Penkridge turn W off A449 at roundabout by Hodsons onto Bungham Lane, cross Cuttlestone Bridge and follow signs to Whiston) SJ895144

12-3 (not Mon), 5-11; 12-11 Sat; 12-10.30 Sun

☎ (01785) 716200 swanwhiston.co.uk

Holden's Black Country Bitter, Golden Glow; 4 changing beers (sourced nationally) H

Although in a remote location, a warm ambience, well-kept ales and superb food make this a thriving establishment. Built in 1593, burnt down and rebuilt in 1711, the oldest part today is the bar housing an inglenook fireplace. The lounge has a central double-sided log fire. Six acres of grounds include a children's play area, an aviary and a beer garden. Q P (878,76)

Whittington

Dog Inn

2 Main Street, WS14 9JU

12-11; 10-midnight Sat; 10-11 Sun ☎ (01543) 432601

doginnwhittington.com

Holden's Golden Glow; Marston's Pedigree; St Austell Tribute H

Spacious village pub with a long frontage, recently refurbished. The interior is split into a number of areas, with an exuberant style of decor including a red piano and a number of elaborate and colourful chandeliers. The upmarket food menu, available every day, has a Mediterranean slant and includes themed events. Bus services dry up in the early evening, but note that reasonably priced accommodation is available in four rooms.

P (765)

Dog Inn, Burton upon Trent (Photo: Elliott Brown/Flickr CC BY-SA 2.0)

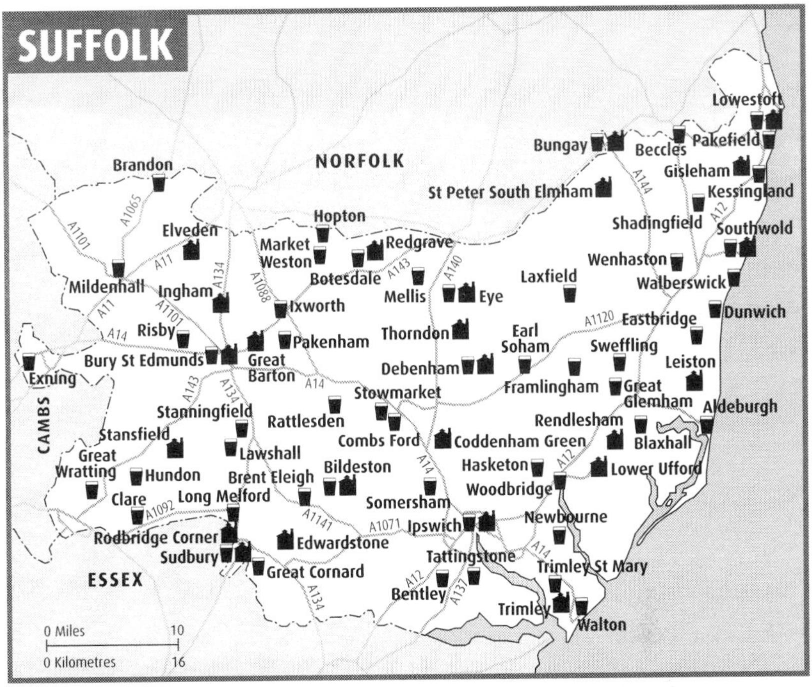

Aldeburgh

White Hart 🄻

222 High Street, IP15 5AJ

11.30-11; 12-10.30 Sun ☎ (01728) 453205

Adnams Southwold Bitter, Ghost Ship, Broadside; 3 changing beers (often Adnams) 🄷

Friendly single bar, formerly used as a public reading room, next door to the town's renowned fish and chip shop. Drinkers can buy fish and chips and eat them in the garden, when weather permits, together with a drink from the bar. Live music features on occasion. Families are welcome to use the garden in the summer months, with a covered barbecue and wood-fired pizza oven in use Easter to mid-September.

Beccles

Butchers Arms 🄻

51 London Road, NR34 9YT

4-midnight; 12-12.30am Fri & Sat; 12-midnight Sun ☎ (01502) 712243 mypub.org.uk

6 changing beers (sourced regionally; often Greene King, St Peter's, Woodforde's) 🄷

Situated opposite Beccles Cemetery, this popular pub serves up to six real ales. Live music, open mic evenings and charity events are hosted. The pub originally had separate lounge and public bars, both with bay windows, but is now open plan. The bar and real fire are in the original pub area, with more seating and pool tables in an extension. Customers are welcome to bring their own meals to eat on the premises. P

Caxton Club 🄻

Gaol Lane, NR34 9SJ

12-1.30 (not Tue), 7-11; 12-2, 6.30-11 Fri; 12-11 Sat; 12-10.30 Sun ☎ (01502) 712829

4 changing beers (sourced nationally; often Green Jack, Greene King, Woodforde's) 🄷

A large, comfortable club that welcomes CAMRA members and serves four real ales plus a wide choice of real ciders. One side of the central bar and seating area has a function room while the other has a pool table and leads to a room with additional seating, TV screen, dartboard and a further separate snooker room. Outside, the garden

REAL ALE BREWERIES

Adnams Southwold
Brewshed Ingham
Briarbank Ipswich
Calvors Coddenham Green
Cliff Quay Debenham
Deben Peninsular Rendlesham
Dove Street Ipswich
Earl Soham Debenham
Green Dragon Bungay
Green Jack Lowestoft
Greene King Bury St Edmunds
Iceni Elveden
Kings Head Bildeston
Krafty Braumeister Leiston (NEW)
Little Earth Project Edwardstone
Mauldons Sudbury
Mr Bees Trimley
Nethergate Rodbridge Corner
Old Cannon Bury St Edmunds
Shortts Thorndon
St Judes Ipswich
St Peter's St Peter South Elmham
Stansfield Stansfield (NEW)
Star Wing Redgrave
Station 119 Eye
Trinity Gisleham
Uffa Lower Ufford
Weird Sisters Great Barton (NEW)

has a children's play area and bowling green. Guide dogs only are allowed. A small charge is made to cover entertainment on Saturday evening.

Bentley

Case Is Altered

Capel Road, IP9 2DW

closed Mon & Tue; 12-2.30 (3 Sat), 6-11.30; 12-4, 7-10.30 Sun (01473) 805575 thecasepubbentley.co.uk

Adnams Southwold Bitter; 3 changing beers (sourced locally) [H]

Local community-owned and run pub with a single bar serving two drinking areas, a restaurant area with a wood-burning stove, and a pretty beer garden with plenty of seating. Various music evenings and themed food nights are hosted but there is no TV. Traditional pub games are available including darts, cards and dominoes. A quiz is held on the last Saturday of the month. Local artists' work is on display. Some of the produce used in the kitchen is now grown at home by the local community. P

Bildeston

King's Head

132 High Street, IP7 7ED

closed Mon & Tue; 6-11 Wed & Thu; 4-midnight Fri; 12-midnight Sat; 12-10.30 Sun (01449) 741434 bildestonkingshead.co.uk

King's Head Bildeston Best, Brettvale Gold; 1 changing beer (sourced locally; often Mauldons, Nethergate) [H]

Home of the King's Head Brewery since 1996, the building's carved timbers indicate its history as part of a larger complex dating from around 1530. Now a single bar with a large, cosy inglenook fireplace, a friendly drinking house atmosphere has evolved, with food available at weekends only. There is a fully enclosed rear garden with a covered patio area, lawns and play equipment. The late May bank holiday beer festival is long established and popular.

Blaxhall

Ship

School Road, IP12 2DY

12 (11 Mon)-11.30 (01728) 688316 blaxhallshipinn.co.uk

Adnams Southwold Bitter; Woodforde's Wherry; 3 changing beers [H]

A cosy two-roomed 16th-century pub with a long reputation for traditional singing in the main bar. The menu offers a wide choice of home-made dishes and daily specials using locally sourced ingredients (book for breakfast from 10.30am in the summer months). Live entertainment includes folk music, bands and story-telling, and the pub hosts a Folk East stage during the festival weekend. Letting chalets are available beside the pub and there is camping at the nearby village hall by arrangement. P

Botesdale

Greyhound

The Street, IP22 1BS

5-11 (midnight Fri & Sat); 12-10.30 Sun (01379) 898003 greyhoundbotesdale.co.uk

Woodforde's Wherry [H]**; 2 changing beers (often Elmtree, Nethergate, Star Wing)** [H]/[G]

Once a coaching inn on the London to Norwich road, this no-frills pub has a loyal following of regulars. Full of character, bare floorboards, old furniture, old photos and taxidermy exhibits add to the atmosphere. It has a busy bar, quieter lounge and a pool room. Home-made burger nights, curry nights and steak nights are popular. Sunday food is hog rolls and wedges only. Some beers may be served using CO2. Parking is very limited. P (304)

Brandon

Ram

High Street, IP27 0AX

11-1am; 12-1am Sun (01842) 810275

Greene King Abbot; 6 changing beers (often Woodforde's) [H]

Said to be one of the oldest surviving buildings in Brandon, this attractive Grade II-listed inn dates back 500 years in parts. A wonderful log fire greets you as you enter this friendly, family-owned and run free house. It is home to regular club nights for the Iceni Car Club, Classic Vehicle Club, Model Engineering Club, Brandon Speakers Club and the Champions Poker League. P

Brent Eleigh

Cock ★

Lavenham Road, CO10 9PB

12-3, 5-11; 12-11 Fri & Sat; 12-10.30 Sun (01787) 247371

Adnams Southwold Bitter; Greene King Abbot; 2 changing beers (sourced locally; often Bishop Nick, Mauldons) [H]

An unspoilt gem, well worthy of its place on CAMRA's National Inventory of Historic Pub Interiors. With just two small bars, conversation with the pub regulars is assured. The public bar has a 'pinch penny' cut into the settle beside the main table which has been deeply etched with shove ha'penny grooves. The snug bar is ideal for families. Home-cooked food is a new addition but does not intrude on the classic pub ambience. Q P (111)

Bungay

Green Dragon

29 Broad Street, NR35 1EE

11-midnight; 12-midnight Sat; 12-9 Sun (01986) 892681 greendragonbungay.co.uk

Green Dragon Chaucer Ale, Gold, Bridge Street Bitter [H]**, Strong Mild; 1 changing beer (sourced locally; often Green Dragon)** [G]

On the northern edge of town, this is Bungay's only brewpub and the home of the Green Dragon Brewery, with ales created in outbuildings adjacent to the car park at the rear. The pub is popular and a regular in the Guide. It has a public bar and a separate spacious lounge with a side room where families are welcome, leading to a small enclosed garden surrounded by a hop hedge. Seasonal ales are often available. P

Bury St Edmunds

Beerhouse

1 Tayfen Road, IP32 6BH

⌚ 5-11; 12-11 Sat; 12-10 Sun ☎ (01284) 766415
🌐 burybeerhouse.co.uk
Brewshed Best; 7 changing beers (sourced nationally) [H]
Traditional beer house in an unusual semicircular Victorian building (previously called the Ipswich Arms), handy for the railway station, and refurbished with a modern feel. Seven beer engines provide a changing selection of well-kept real ales. It also serves its own beers from the Brewshed Brewery, which is now located out of town and supplies the company's three other local pubs. Three real ciders are also available. Regular beer festivals and an annual cider festival are hosted. Major sporting events are shown on a big screen. 🐴❀≋●P🚌🐾📶

Dove [L]

68 Hospital Road, IP33 3JU
⌚ 5-11; 12-3, 6-11 Sat; 12-3, 6-10.30 Sun ☎ (01284) 702787
🌐 thedovepub.co.uk
Woodforde's Wherry [H]**; changing beers** [H]/[G]
Local Cider Pub of the Year and the first Suffolk pub to be voted East Anglia CAMRA Regional Pub of the Year twice, this back-street community free house has six handpumps and a good selection of real ciders. Locally made pies and snacks are sold. Just five minutes' walk from the town centre, the main bar is traditionally basic and there is a parlour area. The staff are knowledgeable about their beers. No lager, TVs, pool or gaming machines – the Dove is how pubs used to be. Q❀♣●P🚌🐾

Greene King Beer Café

Westgate Street, IP33 1QT
⌚ 10-6; closed Sun ☎ (01284) 714297
🌐 greenekingshop.co.uk/beer-cafe
Greene King IPA, Abbot; Morland Old Speckled Hen; 3 changing beers (often Greene King) [H]
The former visitor centre beside the historic Westgate Brewery has been converted into a modern café, shop and bar. It is now the closest public bar to the brewery complex. It offers a selection of draught Greene King ales and a full range of bottles and cans from the brewery. Food, snacks and brewery tours are available. ◐♿📶

Oakes Barn

St Andrews Street South, IP33 3PH (opp Waitrose car park)
⌚ 11-11.30; 12-5 Sun ☎ (01284) 761592 🌐 oakesbarn.co.uk
Oakham JHB; Woodforde's Wherry; 4 changing beers (sourced nationally) [H]
A real ale free house and social hub near the town centre with some period features and historic links to the medieval town. Six real ales are always on the bar, including one dark beer alongside craft cider. Home-made food comprises lunchtime specials and snacks served all day. There is a covered smoking area outside and an open courtyard with seating. Regular events are held in the bar. An upstairs function room can be hired. 🐴❀◐♿♣●🚌🐾📶

Rose & Crown 🏆 ✔

48 Whiting Street, IP33 1NP (on corner of Whiting St and Westgate)
⌚ 11.30-11.30; 11.30-3, 7-11.30 Sat; 12-2.30, 8-11.30 Sun
☎ (01284) 755934
Greene King XX Mild, IPA, Abbot; 3 changing beers (sourced nationally) [H]
In sight of Greene King's Westgate Brewery, this is a traditional inn with two bars, a serving hatch and a separate off-sales hatch. The tenants have run the pub for over 30 years and it has been in the same family for over 40 years. Good-value wholesome food is served lunchtimes Monday to Saturday. Regular darts and crib matches and pub quizzes are held. Children are not allowed in the bars but are welcome in the garden. The pub is a Grade II-listed building within the conservation area of Bury St Edmunds and has a regionally important historic pub interior. Local CAMRA Pub of the Year 2019. Q❀◐♣🚌📶

Clare

Globe

10 Callis Street, CO10 8PX
⌚ 5-11.30; 4-11.30 Fri; 11-11.30 Sat; 12-7 Sun
☎ (01787) 278122
Young's Bitter; 3 changing beers (sourced nationally) [H]
A phoenix risen from the ashes, the Globe reopened in 2013 after a two-year closure. Serving one well-kept regular beer and up to three changing guests, it is now a thriving local where beer and conversation dominate. Live music plays every other Saturday night and afternoon sessions every other Sunday. It has a separate pool room at the rear and a newly refurbished garden for summer drinking. No food is served.
Q🐴❀♣P🚌🐾📶

Combs Ford

Gladstone Arms [L]

2 Combs Road, IP14 2AP
⌚ 12-midnight (11 Sun) ☎ (01449) 771608
🌐 gladstonearms.co.uk
Adnams Southwold Bitter, Broadside; Crouch Vale Brewers Gold; Fuller's London Pride; Sharp's Doom Bar; Woodforde's Wherry [H]**; 4 changing beers** [H]/[G]
A large open-plan pub serving consistently good beer. The owners also run the Dove Street Inn in Ipswich. The two pubs share a similar beer range, with between 12 and 14 ales, including house beers brewed in Ipswich. Four or five ciders and a wide range of craft lagers, imported foreign beers and whiskies are also available. Good-value snacks and meals are served with vegetarian options. There are board games, sports TV and regular live music. A beer festival features over the Easter weekend. The garden at the rear is by the river.
Q🐴❀◐◑♿♣●P🚌🐾📶

Debenham

Woolpack

49 High Street, IP14 6QN
⌚ 11-11; 12-10.30 Sun ☎ (01728) 860516
Earl Soham Victoria Bitter [H]**, Sir Roger's Porter** [G]**; Fuller's London Pride; 1 changing beer (often Earl Soham)** [H]
Small one-bar wooden-floored pub with steps up from the road. Until recent years it was licensed as a beer house. Horse brasses, village photographs and miniature bottles decorate the bar area. Two TVs show terrestrial sport. Keenly priced home-cooked food is served. The pub is home to a darts team and hosts occasional live music, karaoke and quiz nights. There is a splendid view of the church from the patio – bell-ringers meet here after practice on Tuesday. 🐴❀◐◑♣🐾📶

Dunwich

Ship

St James Street, IP17 3DT
11-11 (01728) 648219 shipatdunwich.co.uk
Adnams Southwold Bitter; 3 changing beers [H]
Once a haunt of smugglers, this is now a great place to eat, drink, relax and get away from it all. Comfortable, traditionally furnished rooms have views across the sea or nearby salt marshes. The small public bar is simply furnished with wooden furniture and a woodburner. Beers are from local brewers and bottled local cider is available. There is an extensive food menu. The enormous garden has fruit trees including a 300-year-old fig. The beach is a short walk away. Beer festivals are held in March and September. P

Earl Soham

Victoria L

The Street, IP13 7RL
12-2.30, 6-11; 12-3, 7-10.30 Sun (01728) 685758
earlsohamvictoria.co.uk
Earl Soham Victoria Bitter; 2 changing beers (often Cliff Quay, Earl Soham) [H]
A popular, traditional pub that has changed little over the years and still has an outside toilet, with two small bars and a prominent fireplace with a woodburner. A varied food menu with daily specials is offered lunchtimes and evenings, all home-cooked. The pub gets very busy at weekends, especially on sunny days when even a seat in the garden can be hard to find. Dogs and children are welcome. The Earl Soham Brewery was originally behind the pub.
Q P

Eastbridge

Eel's Foot L

Leiston Road, IP16 4SN (close to Minsmere Nature Reserve)
12-3, 6-11; 12-11.30 Fri; 11.30-11.30 Sat; 11.30-10.30 Sun
(01728) 830154 theeelsfootinn.co.uk
Adnams Southwold Bitter, Ghost Ship, Broadside; 2 changing beers (often Adnams) [H]
Much-improved pub adjacent to the famous nature reserve where avocets and otters are local success stories. Popular with ramblers and birdwatchers, it has a good reputation for locally sourced home-cooked food, with a small refurbished restaurant area leading to new terraced seating for alfresco drinking and dining on summer days. There is an enlarged outdoor play area for children. Traditional music sessions feature on Thursday evenings and live bands monthly. En-suite accommodation is available. Q P

Exning

White Horse

23 Church Street, CB8 7EH
12-midnight (01638) 577323
whitehorseexning.co.uk
Changing beers [H]
Mentioned in the Domesday Book and a pub for 300 years, this fine free house has been run by the same family since 1935. Still retaining much original character, it comprises a public bar, cosy lounge and separate restaurant. At least 10 changing real ales are on offer each week, plus cider on draught, and a good choice of home-cooked food is served. A private room can be hired.
Q P

Eye

Queen's Head

7 Cross Street, IP23 7AB
11-11 (01379) 870153 queensheadeye.co.uk
Adnams Southwold Bitter, Broadside; 3 changing beers (often Batemans, Nethergate) [G]
Dating from 1590, this is now the only pub remaining in this delightful north Suffolk town with many buildings of character and historic significance. The main bar has a wood-burning stove, Cross Street bar is a former butcher's shop, and there is also a snug bar. Beers are dispensed direct from casks (with water-cooling jackets) in the main bar. Traditional pub food and daily specials are served, including breakfast 8.30-10.30am. A community pub where families are welcome. Local CAMRA Cider Pub of the Year 2018.
P

Framlingham

Station Hotel L

Station Road, IP13 9EE
12-2.30, 5-11; 12-11 Sat; 11-2.30, 7-10.30 Sun
(01728) 723455 thestationframlingham.com
Earl Soham Gannet Mild, Victoria Bitter, Brandeston Gold; 2 changing beers (often Earl Soham) [H]
Cosy two-bar pub set in a former station buffet (the branch line closed in 1963). Beers and a guest cider are dispensed from a set of Edwardian German silver handpumps. It enjoys a good reputation for food, made with locally sourced ingredients and prepared on the premises. An ever-changing menu is displayed on chalkboards. On Sundays, brunch and beers are available from 11am. The garden bar has a wood-fired pizza oven. A beer festival is held on the third weekend in July. Children and dogs welcome. Q P

Great Cornard

Five Bells

63 Bures Road, CO10 0HU
12-11 (01787) 379016
Adnams Broadside; Greene King XX Mild; 1 changing beer (sourced nationally) [H]
A friendly community free house near the church (home of the five bells) on the main Sudbury to Bures road. The main bar has a library and a piano. A separate small bar is home to a Tunisian restaurant. Pub games include bar billiards. An open mic session is hosted every third Thursday and karaoke every second Friday of the month. The home-made pies are legendary. Outside is a large beer garden behind the car park. A rare outlet for Greene King XX Mild. Q P

Great Glemham

Crown

The Street, IP17 2DA
12-3 (not Tue), 6-11; 12-4 Sun (01728) 663693
thecrowninnglemham.co.uk
6 changing beers (sourced locally) [H]
Refurbished to a high standard, this multi-roomed pub has woodburners, traditional tiled floors and many lovely seating areas. Up to six beers are on

offer during the busy summer months and at least four during quieter periods. Acoustic music sessions feature regularly. The pub hosts a local community lunch once a month and caters for private parties. All food is cooked on the premises, from bar snacks to an à la carte menu (no food Tue).

Great Wratting

Red Lion

School Road, CB9 7HA

11-2.30, 5-11; 11-1.30am Sat; 12-3, 7-10 Sun

(01440) 783237

Adnams Southwold Bitter, Broadside; 1 changing beer H

A whale's jawbones frame the doorway to this village local dating from the 17th or 18th century, making an unusual and amusing entrance. Now a free house, this ex-Adnams pub offers good beer, quality food and conversation as its mainstay. Locals love this hostelry and are passionate supporters of the activities overseen by an enthusiastic landlord of long experience. Quiz nights and a darts league thrive here.

Q

Hasketon

Turk's Head

Low Road, IP13 6JG

11-11 (midnight Fri & Sat); 11-8 Sun (01394) 610343

theturksheadhasketon.co.uk

Adnams Ghost Ship; Morland Old Speckled Hen; Woodforde's Wherry; 2 changing beers (sourced locally) H

The pub has been much refurbished and extended in recent years but retains a cosy two-room timber-framed bar. The main area has a large fireplace with a woodburner, and there is a spacious restaurant and kitchen to the rear. Good food includes renowned Sunday lunches. Three to five beers are on handpump and change regularly. An annual beer festival is held in the summer. Events include quiz nights and themed food nights. The beautiful two-acre garden has two pétanque pistes and a fireplace.

Hopton

Vine

High Street, IP22 2QX

3-11; 12-midnight Sat; 12-10.30 Sun (01953) 688581

Adnams Southwold Bitter, Broadside; Greene King IPA, IPA Gold; 5 changing beers (sourced locally; often Colchester, Lacons, Wolf) H

On the main road near the church, this village local has been revitalised since it was taken over by the current landlord in 2013. Nine ales including a selection of local and regional guests are offered at reasonable prices. A variety of ciders is also available. This welcoming pub, popular with locals and visitors, is a regular winner of local CAMRA branch Pub of the Year. P (100)

Hundon

Rose & Crown

20 North Street, CO10 8ED (centre of the village)

closed Mon; 6-10 Tue; 12-2, 6-10 Wed & Thu; 12-midnight Fri & Sat; 12-9 Sun (01440) 786261

hundon-village.co.uk/roseandcrown.html

Sharp's Doom Bar; 3 changing beers (sourced nationally; often Fuller's, Mauldons, St Austell) H

A traditional country pub comprising two bars with open fires. Home-cooked food is available Thursday to Sunday including popular Sunday lunchtime roasts. The deceptively large beer garden has a patio for alfresco dining leading to a lawned area with a stage. The outside bar is used for weddings, parties, an annual community music festival over the August bank holiday and other events. The morris men gathering on St George's Day is enjoyed by all. A proud previous winner of local CAMRA Community Pub of the Year.

Ipswich

Arcade Street Tavern

Arcade Street, IP1 1EX (located behind Corn Exchange)

10.30-3 Tue (11 Wed & Thu; midnight Fri; 1am Sat); closed Sun & Mon (01473) 805454 arcadetavern.co.uk

2 changing beers H

A stylish and highly popular multi-roomed café bar with a traditional wooden interior, with an emphasis on craft and imported beers. Two handpumps dispense a variety of beers, mainly from East Anglia. There is no food in-house but the bar regularly hosts street-food Friday in conjunction with other local traders. There are heated seating areas outside and two function rooms upstairs – one used for product launches and tasting evenings. Artisan coffee is available. Q

Briarbank L

70 Fore Street, IP4 1LB

4-11; 12-11 Fri-Sun (01473) 284000

Briarbank Perpendicular, Old Spiteful; 3 changing beers (sourced locally; often Briarbank) H

A smart and modern first-floor drinking bar above the Briarbank Brewery. The building was previously a bank. Many beers from the brewery are also available as craft keg. The bar frequently opens earlier, and for longer, in the summer months and provides seating outside if weather permits. Live music, often jazz, features twice monthly either in the bar or outside. Easter and summer beer festivals are hosted. The TVs are turned on for sport only. P

Dove Street Inn L

76 St Helen's Street, IP4 2LA

12-midnight (10.30 Sun) (01473) 211270

dovestreetinn.co.uk

Adnams Broadside; Crouch Vale Brewers Gold; Fuller's London Pride; Greene King Abbot H**; changing beers (often Dove Street)** H/G

Popular multi-roomed inn with a large selection of real ales including milds, plus ciders and continental beers. Some ales are from its own Dove Street Brewery opposite, where there is also a gin bar. Home-cooked food and bar snacks are served at all times. Sports TV is shown in the conservatory. A covered and heated seating area outside hosts various events including three beer festivals. Well-behaved dogs and children are welcome. A sister pub to The Gladstone Arms in Combs Ford. Last admission is 10.45pm. (66)

Fat Cat

288 Spring Road, IP4 5NL

12-11 (midnight Fri & Sat) (01473) 726524

fatcatipswich.co.uk

Adnams Southwold Bitter [H]**; Woodforde's Wherry; 14 changing beers** [G]
A small, multi-roomed drinking bar, free from background music and games machines. Up to 18 beers are dispensed from the taproom and up to five ciders. Bar snacks include Scotch eggs and pasties cooked on the premises. An airy conservatory behind the main bar leads to the pretty garden, providing extra space on sunny afternoons, with the occasional barbecue. A quiz is held monthly. Often voted the best pub in town by local CAMRA branch members. No under-16s.
Q❀◐🍎🚌🐾📶

Greyhound

9 Henley Road, IP1 3SE
⏲ 11.30-2.30, 5-11 Mon; 11.30-11 Tue-Thu (11.30 Fri & Sat); 10-10.30 Sun ☎ (01473) 252862
🌐 thegreyhoundipswich.co.uk
Adnams Southwold Bitter, Ghost Ship, Broadside; 3 changing beers (often Adnams) [H]
The Greyhound has a small, traditional public bar at the front and a larger, more modern drinking and dining room to the side and rear. The outside drinking space can be busy during the summer months and hosts occasional barbecues. A freshly prepared food menu and various specials are available daily, with vegetarian options. Quiz nights are twice a month on Sundays. The TVs are only turned on for sporting events. On Sunday, breakfast is also available 10-11.30am.
Q❀◐♿♣P🚌(116)📶

Spread Eagle [L]

1-3 Fore Street, IP4 1JW
⏲ closed Mon; 12-midnight; 12-10.30 Sun
☎ (01473) 421858
Grain Oak, Best Bitter, Redwood, Slate, Lignum Vitae; 1 changing beer (often Grain) [H]
This historic inn was restored to a high standard a few years ago by Grain. Up to six real ales are on handpump, all from Grain, plus a selection of craft beers and imported bottled beers. Some bar snacks are available and quality, locally roasted coffee. There is a secluded seating area outside. The pub is candlelit throughout on Tuesday evenings. The distinctive Grade II-listed building is the sole survivor of four pubs that once stood at this busy road junction. Q❀🚌🐾📶

Thomas Wolsey

9-13 St Peters Street, IP1 1XF (300yds from bus station)
⏲ 4.30-11.30 (1am Fri & Sat); closed Sun ☎ (01473) 210055
Adnams Ghost Ship; Crouch Vale Brewers Gold; Woodforde's Wherry; 1 changing beer [H]
Single-room lounge bar set in a historic Grade II-listed building. It has a patio area to the side and two nicely furnished function rooms upstairs, used for a wide variety of events including story-telling nights, charity quizzes and meetings. Craft ales are on draught plus over 25 bottled beers and 40 quality wines. Games are available including darts. Home supporters only on football match days.
❀⇌♣🚌📶

Ixworth

Greyhound ✔

49 High Street, IP31 2HJ
⏲ 11.30-2.30, 6 (5 Fri & Sat)-11; 12-3, 7-11 Sun
☎ (01359) 230887
Greene King XX Mild, IPA, Abbot; 2 changing beers (sourced nationally) [H]
Situated on the village's attractive high street, this welcoming traditional inn has three bars, one a lovely central snug. The heart of the building dates back to Tudor times. The pub is a rare outlet for Greene King XX Mild. Good-value lunches and early evening meals are served in the restaurant including a daily special. Dominoes, crib, darts and pool are played in leagues and for charity fundraising. Dogs and children are welcome.
Q❀◐⛺♣P🚌🐾

Kessingland

Sailors Home [L] ✔

302 Church Road, NR33 7SB
⏲ 12-11 ☎ (01502) 740245 🌐 sailorshome.co.uk
Adnams Southwold Bitter [H]**; 6 changing beers (sourced locally; often Green Jack, Lacons, Wolf)** [H]/[G]
Located within easy reach of the shingle beach and with views of the North Sea, the pub is popular all year round with locals, walkers and holidaymakers alike. The interior has a mock-Tudor design with four adjoining rooms – one for diners serving value-for-money food, a large central bar area with a TV screen, a games room and a side room. Four handpulled beers are available plus up to three on gravity, and a changing real cider.
❀◐⛺♣🍎P🚌(99)🐾📶

Lawshall

Swan

The Street, IP29 4QA
⏲ closed Tue; 12-3, 5 (6 Mon)-10; 12-10 Sat & Sun
☎ (01284) 828477 🌐 swaninnlawshall.com
5 changing beers (sourced nationally; often Adnams, Colchester, Woodforde's) [H]
A classic Suffolk country pub. The beautiful 18th-century thatched building with a low-beamed bar and an inglenook fireplace has been lovingly restored and is crammed full of period features. On the food menu you will find all the traditional pub classics and a few extra culinary delights. The large garden encourages children to play.
Q❀◐♣P🐾📶

Laxfield

King's Head ★

Gorams Mill Lane, IP13 8DW (walk through churchyard and exit via lower street gate; pub is on your right)
⏲ 12-3, 6-11; 12-11 Sat; 12-7 Sun ☎ (01986) 798395
🌐 lowhouselaxfield.com
Adnams Southwold Bitter; 3 changing beers (sourced locally) [G]
Also known as the Low House, bought from Adnams in 2018, this timeless thatched inn is a welcoming community hostelry. The classic building is always worth a visit, with a main room featuring high-back settles set around a small fireplace, and a small taproom to the rear where the beer is served on gravity. A separate dining room offers an interesting menu of locally sourced food, including roast lunch on Sunday. There is an enclosed garden and patio to the rear. Accommodation is available in an out-building.
Q❀🛏♣P🚌🐾

Long Melford

Crown Inn

Hall Street, CO10 9JL

11-11; 12-10.30 Sun (01787) 377666
thecrownhotelmelford.co.uk
Adnams Southwold Bitter, Ghost Ship; 2 changing beers (sourced nationally) H
A busy family-run free house and cosy hotel set in the popular antiques centre of Long Melford. Two regular ales and two changing guests, together with real cider, are on handpump. A high-quality home-cooked menu is served in the spacious bar and separate restaurant. There is a large attractive patio garden for summer dining and drinking. It has 11 comfortable bedrooms for those wishing to stay and explore this picturesque area.
Q P

Nethergate Brewery Tap

Rodbridge Corner, CO10 9HJ
9am-6 (8 Thu-Sat); 10-4 Sun (01787) 377087
nethergate.co.uk
8 changing beers (sourced locally; often Nethergate)
Nethergate Brewery was founded in 1986 and its new visitor centre and taproom opened in 2017. The taproom has a bar offering a range of Nethergate ales on draught, and a shop selling bottled beers, wines and spirits. There is a window to view the brewery and tours are available to book. Q P

Lowestoft

Norman Warrior

Fir Lane, NR32 2RB
11-11.30 (12.30am Fri & Sat); 12-11.30 Sun
(01502) 561982 thenormanwarrior.co.uk
Greene King IPA; 4 changing beers (sourced nationally; often Greene King, Sharp's, Wolf) H
Large 1930s estate pub on the northern side of town with ample parking, 20 minutes' walk from Oulton Broad North train station. The public bar has a pool table and dartboard, and leads to the terraced garden with a large, grassed area where an annual beer and cider festival with live music is held over the August bank holiday weekend. The comfortable lounge area with separate bar leads to a spacious restaurant serving home-cooked meals daily. Q P (102)

Stanford Arms

Stanford Street, NR32 2DD
closed Mon; 4-midnight Tue-Thu; 3-1am Fri; 12-midnight Sat; 12-10 Sun (01502) 587444
10 changing beers (sourced locally; often Star Wing, Three Blind Mice, Wolf) H
A quality free house a short walk from train and bus stations and close to Lowestoft football club. The spacious open-plan bar serves beers mainly from East Anglia and up to six ciders on gravity. A woodburner has been installed near the patio doors leading to a courtyard garden with an aviary and a wood-fired pizza oven (Friday is pizza night). Wednesday is speciality food night (booking required). Live music plays on Sunday afternoon. No under-14s.

Triangle Tavern

29 St Peters Street, NR32 1QA
11-11 (midnight Thu; 1am Fri & Sat); 12-10.30 Sun
(01502) 582711 green-jack.com
Green Jack Golden Best, Trawlerboys Best Bitter, Lurcher Stout, Gone Fishing ESB, Ripper Tripel H/G; 2 changing beers (sourced regionally; often Crouch Vale, Green Jack, Oakham) G
This lively town-centre tavern is the brewery tap for Green Jack Brewery. The parlour-style front bar is decorated with brewery memorabilia and CAMRA awards and is home to live music every Friday evening. A corridor leads to a back bar with a central pool table and a jukebox. Alongside the full Green Jack range are guest ales, real ciders and continental keg beers. Snacks are available and customers are welcome to bring in their own food.

Market Weston

Mill

Bury Road, IP22 2PD
12-3 (not Mon), 5-11; 12-3, 7-10.30 Sun
(01359) 221018
Adnams Southwold Bitter; Morland Old Speckled Hen; 1 changing beer (sourced nationally; often Greene King, Lacons, St Austell) H
Striking white brick and flint-faced inn standing at a crossroads on the main B1111. The landlady has been at the Mill for almost 25 years. It offers an excellent choice of beers, complemented by a good menu of home-cooked meals.
Q P

Mellis

Railway Tavern

Yaxley Road, IP23 8DU
closed Mon; 6-10.30 Tue-Thu; 4-11 Fri; 12.30-11.30 Sat; 12.30-10.30 Sun (01379) 783416
Adnams Southwold Bitter; Crouch Vale Brewers Gold; Greene King IPA; 1 changing beer H
Two-bar pub close to the mainline railway crossing point (the station is no longer in use) with two snug railway carriage booths and good views over the large village green. It has a covered and heated terrace outside and seating out on the common to the side of the pub. Well-supported music events are offered, plus Ruby Tuesday curry nights and fish and chips on Friday. Art exhibitions by Mellis Arts are regularly hosted. An annual beer festival with music is held on the last Saturday in July on the common. The bus service is limited.
P

Mildenhall

Mildenhall Town Football Club

Recreation Way, IP28 7HG
5-11; 1-midnight Fri & Sat; 12-9 Sun (01638) 713449
mildenhalltown.co.uk
Greene King IPA, Abbot; 3 changing beers (sourced nationally; often Lacons, Mighty Oak) H
The football club is open to visiting CAMRA members on production of a membership card. The licensee is a real ale enthusiast and there are up to five beers on draught. Beer festivals are held annually, and the club is renowned for its hospitality in the local leagues. The entrance is through the gate to the main stand.
P

Newbourne

Fox Inn

The Street, IP12 4NY
11-11; 12-10.30 Sun (01473) 736307
debeninns.co.uk/fox
Adnams Southwold Bitter; 3 changing beers H

Picturesque timber-framed, two-bar village local, popular with ramblers and cyclists. A wide range of home-cooked local food is served every day, with an à la carte menu, gluten-free options and daily specials. The spacious garden has a large pond and a shed which houses an old skittle alley – the only one in Suffolk. Q❀◐♿⛺♣P🚌(179)🐾📶

Pakefield

Oddfellows Ⓛ

6 Nightingale Road, NR33 7AU

11-11; 12-10.30 Sun ☎ (01502) 538415

Adnams Southwold Bitter; house beer (by Green Jack); 3 changing beers (sourced locally; often Green Jack, Lacons, Woodforde's) Ⓗ

Popular inn situated near Pakefield's cliffs and a stone's throw from the sea. The small, cosy interior has three open-plan areas with wooden flooring and panelling throughout, with one area reserved for diners (booking advised). The walls are festooned with pictures of old Pakefield. Up to five beers are available, usually including one or two from Green Jack Brewery. The pub hosts its main beer festival in the summer and a smaller one in winter showcasing dark beers. ❀◐🚌🐾📶

Pakenham

Fox

The Street, IP31 2JU

12-2.30 (not Mon & Tue), 5-11; 12-2.30, 5-11.30 Fri & Sat; 12-2.30, 6-11 Sun ☎ (01359) 230194 pakenhamfox.co.uk

Mighty Oak Kings; Woodforde's Wherry; 2 changing beers (sourced locally; often Elmtree, Old Chimneys, Shortts) Ⓗ

Traditional 18th-century pub in a picturesque village, recently beautifully restored with a hand-crafted central bar. A free house, the Fox serves four well-chosen ales from local breweries and two real ciders on draught. The chef prepares lunches Wednesday to Sunday and evening meals Wednesday, Thursday and Saturday using local ingredients. The spacious beer garden, smokers' shelter and pétanque pitch overlook a wildflower meadow. Friday is home-made pizza night and every second Tuesday is quiz night.
Q❀◐♿♣🍎P🚌🐾📶

Rattlesden

Five Bells

High Street, IP30 0RA

12-midnight (11 Sun) ☎ (01449) 737373

3 changing beers (sourced locally; often Earl Soham, Elgood's, Woodforde's) Ⓗ

Set on the high road through a picturesque village, this is a good old Suffolk drinking house – few of its kind still survive. Three excellent ales on the bar usually come direct from the breweries, and often include a mild. The cosy single-room interior has a games area on a lower level and there is occasional live music. Pub games include shut-the-box and shove-ha'penny plus pétanque in the garden in summer. Q❀♣🚌🐾

Risby

Crown & Castle

South Street, IP28 6QU

12-3, 5 (6.30 Sat)-11; 12-3, 7-10.30 Sun
☎ (01284) 810393 crownandcastle.com

Adnams Southwold Bitter; 2 changing beers (sourced nationally) Ⓗ

This attractive flint-faced building opened as an inn and shop in the late 1800s and was sold by Greene King in 2014. The current licensees have run the pub for 17 years. A 120ft unrecorded well was discovered during alterations in recent times and is now a feature beneath a grille in the entrance lobby. The pub has classic back and front bars, with food served in both. The back bar is the public, dominated by games and conversation, and well-behaved dogs are allowed in here.
Q❀◐♣P🚌🐾

Shadingfield

Fox Ⓛ

London Road, NR34 8DD

12-11.30 (10.30 Sun) ☎ (01502) 575100
shadingfieldfox.co.uk

8 changing beers (sourced locally; often Lacons, Nene Valley, Wolf) Ⓗ

Situated in a tiny village on the edge of Sotterley Park, this inn dates back to the 16th century. The interior comprises a bar with comfortable seating leading to a conservatory and a separate restaurant area. Outside, a patio and small garden are popular in the summer months. Beer festivals are held twice yearly, one over the Father's Day weekend and the other close to Guy Fawkes Night. Live music features every Friday evening. Suffolk CAMRA Pub of the Year 2018. Q❀◐P🐾📶

Somersham

Duke of Marlborough

Main Road, IP8 4QA

closed Mon & Tue; 12-11; 12-6 Sun ☎ (01473) 831283
thedukeofmarlborough.com

Earl Soham Victoria Bitter; 3 changing beers (often Adnams) Ⓖ

This 15th-century inn was saved by the local community and has been restored to a high standard. The timber-framed building offers several seating areas for drinking and eating. Freshly cooked food made with locally sourced ingredients is served, including stone-baked pizzas. Various events are organised including a quiz on the first Wednesday of the month. A beer festival is hosted over the August bank holiday weekend.
Q❀◐♣P🚌(111)🐾📶

Southwold

Lord Nelson Ⓛ ✔

42 East Street, IP18 6EJ

10.30-11; 12-10.30 Sun ☎ (01502) 722079
thelordnelsonsouthwold.co.uk

Adnams Southwold Bitter, Ghost Ship, Broadside; 2 changing beers (sourced locally; often Adnams) Ⓗ

Always busy and lively, the Lord Nelson is popular with locals and visitors enjoying coastal views from the nearby clifftop. It has a flagstone floor and an open fire in the winter months. The large central bar offers the full range of Adnams beers. Children are welcome in the side room and the partly covered and heated patio area to the rear. This timeless pub is decorated throughout with naval and seafaring memorabilia. ❀◐⛺🚌🐾📶

Stanningfield

Red House

Bury Road, IP29 4RR

12-11.30 (01284) 828330 theredhousesuffolk.co.uk

Greene King IPA; 2 changing beers H

Red brick in construction and displaying the red dress uniform of the Suffolk Regiment on its sign, the Red House is a family-run free house at the heart of the village. Good-value lunches and early evening meals are home cooked. The pub supports darts, cribbage and bar billiards teams and hosts regular evening entertainment. P

Stowmarket

Little Wellington

12 Stowupland Road, IP14 5AG

12-midnight (11 Sun) (01449) 614174

Greene King IPA; St Austell Tribute; 2 changing beers H

Good local community pub, convenient for the railway station, especially if travelling eastwards. It is accessed via a short flight of steps up from the street level. The pub has a central servery and a reputation for good-value Sunday lunches. Pizzas are cooked outside in the summer. The beer garden has a play area for children. Live music plays on Saturday evening. It hosts occasional events such horse-racing evenings and private parties. P

Royal William

53 Union Street East, IP14 1HP

11-11; 12-midnight Sat; 12-10.30 Sun (01449) 674553

Greene King IPA; 10 changing beers G

An end-of-terrace back-street bar, tucked away down a narrow side street, a short walk from the town centre and railway station, well supported by locals. Ales are served by gravity dispense from the cellar behind the bar, with up to 10 beers and five ciders. There is a games room, home to regular dominoes, darts and crib matches, and a smoking area in the garden to the rear. Sport is shown on TV and traditional music hosted monthly. Home-made bar snacks are available. A winner of many local CAMRA awards.

Sudbury

Bay Horse

61-65 Melford Road, CO10 1JS

4-11; 12-midnight Fri & Sat; 12-11 Sun (01787) 377450

bayhorsesudbury.co.uk

Woodforde's Wherry; 8 changing beers H

On the bar at this traditional family-run free house is an impressive array of nine handpumps. Outside, there is a heated patio and a large rear garden overlooking the water meadows and River Stour. Filled baguettes are available and free food for sport lovers on Sundays. There are regular music sessions, a beer festival and five en-suite letting bedrooms. The pub is a short walk from the town centre. P

Brewery Tap

21-23 East Street, CO10 2TP (200yds from market place)

11-11 (midnight Fri & Sat); 12-10.30 Sun

(01787) 370876 blackaddertap.co.uk

Mauldons Moletrap Bitter, Suffolk Pride, Black Adder H**; 7 changing beers (sourced nationally)** H/G

The Mauldons Brewery Tap is a haven for ale lovers. A good selection of the brewery's beers is always stocked, complemented by a range of national and locally sourced ales, up to 10 at any one time, on both handpump and gravity. Hearty snacks are served at lunchtime including pies and sandwiches. Beer festivals are held in April and October and quiz, music and comedy nights are regular attractions in a pub where conversation dominates. A former CAMRA branch Pub of the Year. Q

Sweffling

White Horse

Low Road, IP17 2BB

7-11 Mon, Fri & Sat; closed Tue-Thu; 12-3, 7-11 Sun

(01728) 664178 swefflingwhitehorse.co.uk

3 changing beers G

A cosy, traditional two-room pub, warmed by a woodburner and wood-fired range. The owners have refurbished the building in an environmentally friendly manner. Beers from local brewers are dispensed on gravity, served through a taproom door. Fair-trade, organic and locally produced bottled beers are also available, and cider too. Hot and cold bar snacks are sold. Pub games include bar billiards, darts, crib and board games, and live music features twice a month. Horse and trap rides are offered in summer. A former CAMRA East Anglian Pub of the Year.

Q P

Tattingstone

Wheatsheaf

Church Road, IP9 2LY

closed Mon; 6-11 Tue; 12-3, 6-11 Wed & Thu; 12-midnight Fri & Sat; 12-8 Sun (01473) 805470

wheatsheaftattingstone.com

3 changing beers (sourced locally) G

Comfortable open-plan single bar pub, fully refurbished by the current owners. It is located on the outskirts of a small village divided by the nearby Alton Water Park reservoir. Beers are usually from local brewers. Themed food evenings and Sunday roasts are popular. (Food served Wed eve, Thu-Sat lunch & eve, and Sun lunch.) Live music and quiz nights feature occasionally. The pub hosts local cribbage league matches and caters for parties and private events. There is a large garden to the side and plans for a conservatory and accommodation. P (94,96)

Trimley St Mary

Mariner's Freehouse

193 High Road, IP11 0TN

12-3, 5-11; 12-midnight Fri & Sat; 12-11 Sun

(01394) 670444 marinersfreehouse.co.uk

Adnams Southwold Bitter, Ghost Ship, Broadside; 3 changing beers H

The pub's name was changed from the New Inn to remember Thomas Cavendish, who was born in Trimley St Martin and who was the first man to command a ship that deliberately circumnavigated the world (previous circumnavigators had done so accidentally). The Grade II-listed building dates back to the 18th century. Various drinking areas surround a large servery. There are tables outside at the front and a pleasant beer garden.

Q P

Walberswick

Anchor (L) ✔

The Street, IP18 6UA

11-11; 12-11 Sun ☎ (01502) 722112

anchoratwalberswick.com

Adnams Southwold Bitter, Ghost Ship; 1 changing beer (often Adnams) [H]

Situated in an idyllic coastal village, this bar and hotel caters for holidaymakers and locals alike. It has two cosy alcove areas heated by a fire on both sides, and another room for families. A spacious restaurant to the rear serves high-quality local produce. As well as the ales from Adnams, a large selection of craft bottled beers is stocked. Accommodation is available in the main building and in chalets in the garden. Q ❀ 🛏 ◐ ▲ P 🐾 📶

Walton

Half Moon (L)

303 High Street, IP11 9QL

12-3 (not Mon), 5-11; 12-3, 5-midnight Fri; 12-11 Sat; 12-3, 7-11 Sun ☎ (01394) 285586

Adnams Lighthouse, Southwold Bitter, Broadside; 3 changing beers (often Adnams) [H]

An excellent, traditional, two-bar local community pub with wood panelling and an open fire in the public bar in winter. A meeting place for local groups, it has quiz nights, darts matches, cribbage and a selection of books to read. There are no gaming machines or music. The garden has a children's play area which has proved popular with families in the summer. Food is served lunchtimes only. Monthly folk nights are hosted as well as other live music on occasion. ❀ ◐ ♿ ♣ P 🚌 🐾 📶

Wenhaston

Star Inn (L)

Hall Road, IP19 9HF

12-3, 6-11; 12-11 Sun ☎ (01502) 478240

Adnams Southwold Bitter; Green Jack Golden Best; 4 changing beers (sourced locally; often Colchester, Green Jack, Wolf) [H]

Free house situated on the outskirts of the village, with fine views of the Blyth Valley. It has three small public rooms – the front bar is full of character with old enamel advertising signs and an open fire in winter. Good food is all home-cooked using local produce (no food Sun). Beer festivals are held over the late May and August bank holiday weekends. Camping is available by prior arrangement. Q ❀ ◐ ▲ ♣ P 🚌 (99A) 🐾 📶

Woodbridge

Angel (L)

2 Theatre Street, IP12 4NE

2-11 (midnight Fri & Sat); 12-10.30 Sun

☎ (01394) 382660 theangelwoodbridge.co.uk

Adnams Southwold Bitter; 5 changing beers [H]

A traditional two-bar drinking pub with beams and tiled floors. The regularly changing range of real ales is complemented by a selection of over 270 gins. There is seating outside and a former stables to the rear. No food is served but there is a wood-fired oven in the garden for pizza. Open mic is hosted on the second and fourth Wednesday of the month plus a DJ every Saturday evening and more live music. ❀ ⇌ ♣ P 🚌 🐾 📶

Cherry Tree

73 Cumberland Street, IP12 4AG

7.30am-11; 9am-11 Sun ☎ (01394) 384627

thecherrytreepub.co.uk

Adnams Southwold Bitter, Ghost Ship, Broadside; Elgood's Black Dog; 5 changing beers (often Adnams) [H]

Spacious family-friendly lounge bar/diner with a large central counter and several distinct seating areas. Up to nine beers are usually on offer and an annual summer beer festival is hosted. Food is locally sourced and home cooked, including some gluten-free options, and served all day every day, with breakfast until 11am. Board games and cards are available to play and a quiz is held on Thursday. The large garden has children's play equipment. Accommodation is in a converted barn. ❀ 🛏 ◐ ⇌ ♣ P 🐾 📶

Ye Olde Bell & Steelyard ✔

103 New Street, IP12 1DZ

12-3, 5-11.30; 11-12.30am Fri & Sat; 12-11 Sun

☎ (01394) 382933 yeoldebellandsteelyard.co.uk

Greene King IPA, Abbot; 2 changing beers (often Greene King) [H]

Large family-friendly pub with oak beams in two bars and a separate function room. The steelyard – a former cart weighbridge that still worked until hit by a lorry in 2018 – dates from 1650 and was on show at the Great Exhibition in 1851. Good home-cooked food is served. Traditional games include bar billiards, chess and bar skittles. Live rugby is shown on TVs in the side-bar area. To the rear of the building is a heated and covered patio area and wheelchair access. ❀ ◐ ♿ ⇌ ♣ 🚌 🐾 📶

A short history of the Good Beer Guide

The Good Beer Guide was first published in 1972 and was just 18 pages long. Rather than a printed and bound edition, it was just a collection of sheets of paper stapled together and posted out to CAMRA members. The first printed edition was published in 1974 and contained a comment on Watney's brewery that was considered libellous, causing the first print run to be pulped and the description for the brewery to be revised. There are a few copies of the first print run out there but they change hands for a fair amount of money.

There has been an edition of the Guide printed annually since 1974, meaning it is now in its 47th year. The longest serving editor was Roger Protz, who edited the Guide from 1978-1983 and 2000-2018. It has grown from 96 pages in 1974 to 1,060 pages in 2020 with 4,500 pubs listed and more than 1,800 breweries.

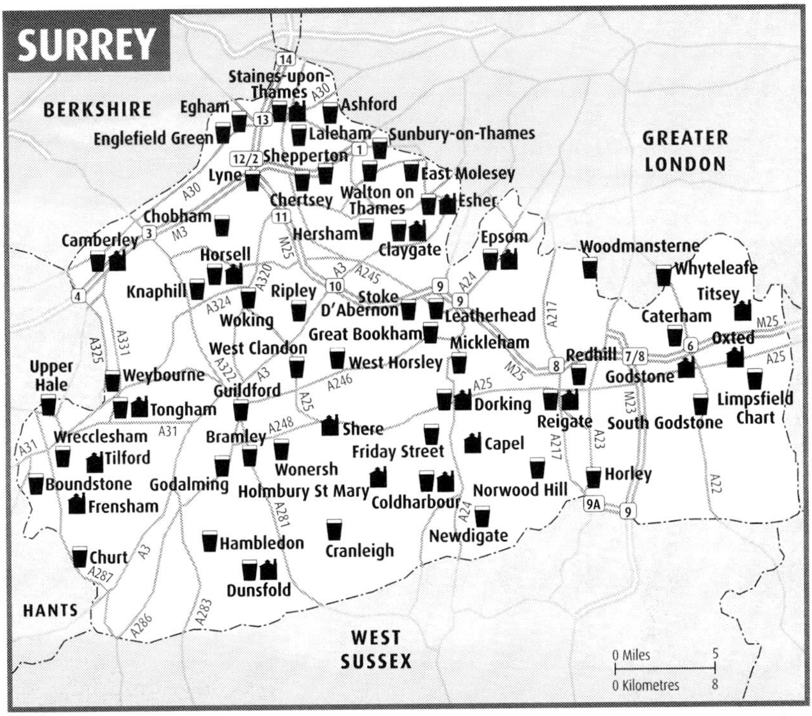

Ashford

King's Head

4 Feltham Road, TW15 2EB

11-11 (midnight Fri & Sat) (01784) 244631
kingsheadpubashford.co.uk

Marston's Saddle Tank, Pedigree; 2 changing beers (often Bombardier, Wychwood) H

Large Marston's dining house with several adjoining rooms. It retains a separate bar with seating on high stools and sports TV, and hosts poker, darts and quiz nights. Two regular and two guest ales are available from the Marston's portfolio. Good-value food from an extensive menu is available every day, with special offers such as Wednesday curry night and Thursday steak house. Outside is a patio garden with covered areas.
P

Boundstone

Bat & Ball

15 Bat & Ball Lane, GU10 4SA (off Sandrock Hill Rd via Upper Bourne Lane) SU833444

11-11; 12-10.30 Sun (01252) 792108
thebatandball.co.uk

Dark Star Hophead; Hogs Back TEA; Hop Back Summer Lightning; 3 changing beers (sourced locally) H

A traditional country free house dating back 150 years, set in the Bourne Valley near Farnham. It has been run by the same family for two generations. The pub has several different rooms, with an open log fire, panelled walls and oak beams. The attractive garden has a children's play area and is popular with families on warmer days. There is an annual beer festival, a weekly quiz on Tuesday and live music once a month. An afternoon menu is served at weekends. Q P (16,17)

Bramley

Jolly Farmer

High Street, GU5 0HB

11-11; 12-11 Sun (01483) 893355 jollyfarmer.co.uk

Greene King IPA; 7 changing beers (sourced nationally; often Crafty, Langham) H

A stagecoach inn that seems almost unchanged from yesteryear, with accommodation available. Dark wood beams hint of its long-ago upgrade from an entirely timber-framed construction. The decor is a celebration of the countryside and beer, featuring many historic beer mats and a large selection of pumpclips. The L-shaped bar offers a diverse range of up to eight real ales plus, in summer months, real ciders.
P (53,63)

Camberley

Claude du Vall

77-81 High Street, GU15 3RB

8am-midnight (12.30am Wed; 1am Fri & Sat)
(01276) 672910

Greene King Abbot; Ruddles Best Bitter; Sharp's Doom Bar; 4 changing beers (often Ascot, Tillingbourne, Windsor & Eton) H

The Claude du Vall is conveniently close to the station and bus stops, at the end of the High Street. The large, modern interior is divided into a number of different areas. The long bar offers three regular beers, four guests including at least one LocAle, and a real cider. Wetherspoon's reputation for good-value food and drinks attracts customers throughout the day, from breakfast onwards. Silent TVs generally show news programmes.

Caterham

King & Queen 𝕃

34 High Street, CR3 5UA (on B2030)
⏲ 11-11 (midnight Fri & Sat); 12-11 Sun ☎ (01883) 345438
🌐 kingandqueencaterham.co.uk
Fuller's London Pride, ESB; Gale's Seafarers Ale; 1 changing beer Ⓗ
You are assured of a friendly welcome at this popular community pub. Once three cottages, the 400-year-old building became an inn in the 1840s. It features a traditional public bar together with a beamed room with an inglenook fireplace. A side room has a dartboard and there is a rear patio outside which hosts occasional theatrical events. Portraits of King William and Queen Mary, after whom the pub is named, adorn the walls.
🐎❀◑♣P🚌🐾📶

Chertsey

Olde Swan 🏆

27 Windsor Street, KT16 8AY
⏲ 12-11 (midnight Fri & Sat) ☎ (01932) 562129
🌐 theoldeswanhotel.co.uk
Sharp's Doom Bar; Tring Side Pocket for a Toad; Wainwright; 1 changing beer (sourced nationally; often Fuller's) Ⓗ
Refurbished when acquired by Mclean Inns, without spoiling its charm, the Olde Swan's shabby-chic decor gives drinkers and diners a mellow experience. Four ales are usually on offer and the food menu features stone-baked pizza, home-made burgers and sizzling steaks, while Friday is Mexican night. Accommodation includes double, twin and family rooms. Chertsey is handy for the M3 and Thorpe Park.
🐎❀🛏◑⇌🍎P🚌(446,456)📶

Chobham

White Hart 𝕃

58 High Street, GU24 8AA
⏲ 11-11; 12-10.30 Sun ☎ (01276) 857580
House beer (by St Austell); 4 changing beers (sourced locally) Ⓗ
A lovely rambling building with interesting nooks and crannies, decorated with historic prints and early 20th-century photos and posters. Five ales are on handpump in a range of strengths and styles. Brunning & Price Traditional is St Austell Cornish Best Bitter rebadged – the others could come from any of the many local breweries, with the distance from the pub prominently displayed. There are two restaurant areas and a less formal area for drinkers as you enter the pub. Brunch is served from 9am at weekends.
Q🐎❀◑♿P🚌(73)🐾📶

Churt

Crossways Inn 𝕃

Churt Road, GU10 2JS
⏲ 11-3, 5-11; 11-11 Fri & Sat; 12-4, 7-10.30 Sun
☎ (01428) 714323 🌐 weydonian.net/crossways
Arundel Sussex IPA; Hop Back Crop Circle Ⓗ**; 4 changing beers** Ⓖ
Friendly two-bar pub with a homely ambience. At the centre of village life, it is popular with local groups as well as customers from further afield including ramblers and cyclists. Guest beers are fetched from their casks in the cellar, usually including local ales and a stout or porter. Good-value food is served lunchtimes, plus fish and chips on Wednesday night (no food Sun).
❀◑♣🍎P🚌(19)🐾

Claygate

Platform 3 𝕃

Claygate Station, The Parade, KT10 0PB
⏲ closed Mon-Wed; 3-9 Thu-Sun ☎ 07802 316389
🌐 brightwaterbrewery.co.uk
3 changing beers (sourced locally; often Brightwater) Ⓗ
The outlet for locally brewed Brightwater beers, housed in a former coal office at Claygate Station. A guest ale from another brewer is sometimes available. All seating is outside on the station forecourt under a gazebo, heated in winter. One of the smallest pubs in the UK, but well established as a focal point for the local community. Check before visiting as opening hours are weather-dependent and seasonal. Q🐎❀⇌♣🍎🚌(K3)🐾📶

Coldharbour

Plough Inn 𝕃

Coldharbour Lane, RH5 6HD
⏲ 12-11 (9 Sun) ☎ (01306) 711793 🌐 ploughinn.com
Leith Hill Crooked Furrow, Smiler's Happiness, Surrey Puma; Tillingbourne Falls Gold; 1 changing beer Ⓗ
Home to the Leith Hill Brewery, this smart 17th-century inn is set in lovely countryside down narrow lanes close to Leith Hill. High-quality food, made with local produce where possible and changing with the season, is served lunchtimes and evenings (not Sun eve). The pub is understandably popular with walkers and cyclists. The pub shop provides hot drinks and snacks alongside local produce (open 8.30am-6pm). Six en-suite letting rooms are available.
Q🐎❀🛏◑♿P🚌(50,433)🐾📶

Cranleigh

Three Horseshoes 𝕃

4 High Street, GU6 8AE (on B2128)
⏲ 12-11 ☎ (01483) 276978
🌐 threehorseshoescranleigh.co.uk
Crafty Loxhill Biscuit Ⓖ**; Harvey's Sussex Best Bitter; Timothy Taylor Boltmaker** Ⓗ**; 5 changing beers** Ⓗ/Ⓖ

REAL ALE BREWERIES

Ascot Camberley
Big Smoke Esher
Brightwater Claygate
Crafty Brewing Dunsfold
Dorking Capel
Feldày 🛢 Holmbury St. Mary
Frensham Frensham
Fuzzchat 🛢 Epsom
Godstone Godstone
Hogs Back Tongham
Leith Hill 🛢 Coldharbour
Oxted Oxted
Pilgrim Reigate
Surrey Hills Dorking
Thames Side Staines-upon-Thames
Thurstons Horsell
Tilford 🛢 Tilford
Tillingbourne Shere
Titsey Titsey

This two-bar 17th-century pub features an inglenook fireplace with a roaring wood fire in winter. The long gone Brufords Brewery used to stand behind the pub and some photos in the lounge bar show the building. Good home-made food is available each day (no food Sun eve). The garden has children's play equipment. Five constantly changing guest beers are available, frequently served straight from the cask – check to see what is available. ❀◑♿♣P🚌🐾

Dorking

Cobbett's L

23 West Street, RH4 1BY (on A25 one-way system eastbound)

12-8; 11-8.30 Fri; 10-8 Sat; 12-6 Sun ☎ (01306) 879877

cobbettsrealales.com

6 changing beers [H]/[G]

In an old part of town, this excellent real ale off-licence and micropub offers the largest choice of ale in Surrey. The beer range, served by knowledgeable staff, is constantly changing, with up to six cask ales alongside six KeyKeg (one always from De Molen) and over 200 bottles and cans from Britain and beyond. The tiny bar (open from noon) in a back room has its own garden, and is a great place to drink and chat.

Q❀⇌(West)🚌🐾

Cricketers L ✔

81 South Street, RH4 2JU (on A25 one-way system westbound)

12-11 (midnight Thu-Sat) ☎ (01306) 889938

cricketersdorking.co.uk

Dark Star Hophead; Fuller's London Pride, ESB; 2 changing beers [H]

This small and well-run pub has an L-shaped interior covered with old photographs and adverts. Rugby is popular here and when England play it is standing room only. The multi-level walled Georgian garden hosts the pub's May bank holiday and autumn beer festivals. An annual slot-car racing championship and an onion-growing competition are among the quirky events held here. On alternate Monday evenings a classic film is shown. Food is served weekday lunchtimes only.

❀◐♣🚌🐾

Red Bar & Lounge L

45 Dene Street, RH4 2DW (off A25 opp post office)

12-11 (midnight Fri & Sat); 12-10.30 Sun

☎ (01306) 882222

Surrey Hills Shere Drop; 3 changing beers [H]

A smart, modern lounge bar in a 1920s building set back from the road. The brightly lit interior features an eclectic mix of contemporary and traditional furnishings, with a variety of pub tables, comfy sofas and benches. Food is popular and locally sourced ingredients play a big part on the menu. The guest ales are from local brewers and sometimes include vegan beers. Outside, there is a seating area and a large patio garden.

❀◑♿P🚌🐾

Dunsfold

Sun Inn L ✔

The Common, GU8 4LE

11-midnight (1am Fri & Sat); 11-11.30 Sun

☎ (01483) 200242 suninndunsfold.co.uk

Sharp's Doom Bar; 3 changing beers (often Crafty, Firebird, Triple fff) [H]

Overlooking the village green, this quintessential country pub is the hub of local life. Full of character, it retains exposed wooden beams that date back 400 years to when it was a coach house. An open log fire adds to the cosy ambience in cold weather. Outside seating on the village green is popular on warmer days. Three different guest ales are served, with one always from a local brewery.

Q❀◑♿♣P🚌(42)🐾

East Molesey

Bell ✔

4 Bell Road, KT8 0SS (off B369)

12-11 (midnight Fri & Sat); 12-10 Sun ☎ (020) 8941 0400

Greene King IPA, Abbot; house beer (by Twickenham); 3 changing beers (often Andwell, Greene King, Wimbledon) [H]

Historic coaching inn known locally as the Crooked House. It dates from 1460 and was later East Molesey's first post office. The 18th-century highwayman Claude Duvalier hid from the Bow Street Runners here. The walls are decorated with old photos of the area. Full of nooks and crannies, it is ideal for romantic liaisons. The large garden has a children's play area. Various TV screens show sport, which can be avoided if preferred. Quiz night is Tuesday. ❀◑♣P🚌(411)🐾

Egham

Egham United Services Club L

111 Spring Rise, TW20 9PE (close to A30 Egham Hill)

12-11 (midnight Fri & Sat) ☎ (01784) 435120 eusc.club

Rebellion IPA; Surrey Hills Ranmore; 3 changing beers (sourced nationally; often Burning Sky, Thames Side, XT) [H]

Local CAMRA Club of the Year and National Club of the Year finalist. An extremely varied range of guest ales includes something dark, and a wide choice of ciders is available from the cellar. Three beer festivals a year showcase an eclectic range of ales, mostly from the newest micros around. Comfortably furnished with sports TV, the club hosts live music most Saturday evenings. Show a copy of this Guide or CAMRA membership card for entry. ❀♿⇌♣P🚌(8,441)

Englefield Green

Beehive L

34 Middle Hill, TW20 0JQ (200yds N of A30 Egham Hill)

12-11 (11.30 Fri); 9.30am-11.30 Sat; 12-9 Sun

☎ (01784) 431621 beehiveegham.co.uk

Fuller's London Pride; 2 changing beers (often Dark Star, Fuller's) [H]

This Fuller's local is open plan with a light and airy feel. On cooler days there is a real log fire, and on warmer days the sheltered patio garden is pleasant. As well as rotating guest ales, occasional beer festivals add to the range. Hot drinks are available including posh coffees, and an extensive daily food menu is served, with offers Monday to Wednesday and traditional roasts on Sunday.

❀◑P🚌(8,441)🐾

Happy Man L

12 Harvest Road, TW20 0QS (off A30)

12-11.30 (midnight Fri & Sat); 12-10.30 Sun

☎ (01784) 433265

Hop Back Summer Lightning; 3 changing beers (sourced nationally; often Crouch Vale, Purity, Reunion) H
In Victorian times two houses were converted to a pub serving workers building Royal Holloway College. Refurbished but virtually unchanged, this is now a popular haunt for students and locals. Three changing guest ales are sourced from local and national breweries. Regular beer festivals are held on the rear patio, which has a heated marquee. Darts and quiz nights are hosted and food is available every day. A former local CAMRA Pub of the Year. (8,441)

Epsom

Cricketers

1 Stamford Green Road, KT18 7SR (off B280)
10-11 (midnight Fri & Sat) (01372) 729384
thecricketersinnepsom.co.uk
4 changing beers (sourced regionally; often Ringwood, Surrey Hills, Wimbledon) H
Weatherboarded pub with a brick extension in an idyllic setting next to a pond with its waterfowl, opposite the cricket green. The building is 250 years old and was originally two cottages, becoming a pub in 1836. It is divided into two wood-floored bar areas with a mix of seating, while to the rear is a split-level area used for dining. Breakfast is served 10am-midday. The cider is from Lilley's. (E9,E10)

Jolly Coopers

84 Wheelers Lane, KT18 7SD (off B280 via Stamford Green Rd)
12-11 (10.30 Mon); 12-8 Sun (01372) 723222
jollycoopers.co.uk
Dark Star Hophead; 3 changing beers (sourced regionally; often Fuzzchat, Hop Back, Surrey Hills) H
On the edge of Epsom Common, this pub is more than 200 years old. The interior is divided into two – a carpeted bar area to the left and another larger area with polished parquet flooring to the right used more for dining, but not exclusively so. The decor is modern, with painted walls. There is a large paved garden at the rear. The pub can get busy at weekends but is quieter during the week. The Fuzzchat Brewery is in an outbuilding behind the pub. Varying cider is sold in the summer.
Q P (E9,E10)

Rifleman

5 East Street, KT17 1BB (on A24)
12-11 (midnight Fri & Sat); 12-10 Sun (01372) 721244
therifleman.co.uk
Greene King London Glory; house beer (by Hardys & Hansons); 3 changing beers (sourced regionally; often Hammerpot, Westerham) H
Small corner pub in the shadow of a bridge carrying the railway to and from London. It is decorated in a traditional style featuring two fireplaces and dark green wood panelling, but also has some modern features such as bare brickwork and high tables at the front. There is a pleasant garden to the rear, an oasis of calm close to central Epsom. The name comes from the Surrey Rifle Volunteers who trained nearby. A changing cider is available.

Esher

Wheatsheaf

40 The Green, KT10 8AG
11-11 (11.30 Fri & Sat); 11-10.30 Sun (01372) 464014
wheatsheafesher.co.uk
Harvey's Sussex Best Bitter; Surrey Hills Shere Drop; house beer (by Hardys & Hansons); 1 changing beer (sourced locally; often Big Smoke, Wimbledon) H
Imposing inn about 200 years old opposite Esher Green. This is a smart community pub where diners and drinkers alike are looked after with the same friendly service. Comfortably furnished throughout in a modern style, the original oak flooring in the main part has been retained and replicated in the extended areas. The bar area has an open fire. A bicycle rack is provided at the rear. Changing guest beers include local ales. A former local CAMRA Pub of the Year. P

Friday Street

Stephan Langton Inn

RH5 6JR TQ12804559
closed Mon; 11-11 (7 Sun) (01306) 730775
stephanlangton.pub
Tillingbourne Dormouse, Falls Gold, Hop Troll; 1 changing beer H
Nestling in a remote and well-wooded valley deep in the Surrey Hills, this is an award-winning pub and restaurant, named after a local man who became the Archbishop of Canterbury in 1207. Local foods are favoured on the excellent menu and all meals are freshly home-cooked. The pub is cosy and welcoming with wood-burning fires in winter. The guest beer is usually from Tillingbourne and over 40 gins are sold. Q P

Godalming

Star Inn

17 Church Street, GU7 1EL
12-11 Mon; 11.30-11 (12.30am Fri); 11-12.30am Sat; 12-11 Sun (01483) 417717 staringodalming.co.uk
Hardys & Hansons Olde Trip H**; 9 changing beers (sourced nationally; often Hardys & Hansons)** H/G
Dating from around 1830, the Star has a small public bar at the front and a main room to the side that leads to a patio garden and smoking area. There is a separate lounge with a bespoke cider bar, open Thursday to Sunday. Up to 10 real ales are stocked, some from the Greene King range. Beer festivals are held at Easter and Halloween. The pub is a regular winner of local and regional CAMRA cider awards.

Great Bookham

Anchor

161 Lower Road, KT23 4AH (off A246 via Eastwick Rd)
11.30-11.30; 12-10.30 Sun (01372) 452429
Brakspear Bitter; Sharp's Doom Bar; Young's Bitter; 1 changing beer (often Tillingbourne) H
Historic Grade II-listed inn dating from the 15th century. Low-beamed ceilings, wooden floors, exposed brickwork and an inglenook with a real fire in winter give the pub a traditional and homely feel. A charity quiz night is held every Tuesday (book ahead) and a meat raffle on Sunday. There is a patio garden with a pond, and a heated smoking area at the front. Children are not allowed in the bar. Q P (479)

Guildford

Drummond 🄻 ✔

55 Woodbridge Road, GU1 4RF
12-11 (11.30 Thu; midnight Fri & Sat) ☎ (01483) 579395
thedrummondguildford.co.uk
Hogs Back TEA; St Austell Tribute; Thornbridge Jaipur IPA; 1 changing beer (sourced regionally; often Ringwood) Ⓗ
A large open-plan pub with an eclectic range of furniture, several pieces of modern art and an impressive selection of chandeliers. Classic pub food and modern dishes are served all day. Burger night is Wednesday and booking is essential for the popular Sunday roasts. Hidden behind the pub is a large heated patio and garden. A quiz is held on Sunday and major rugby matches are shown.
❀◑⇌🚌🐾📶

King's Head

27 King's Road, GU1 4JW (on A320 Stoke Rd)
11-11 (11.30 Tue & Thu; midnight Fri & Sat); 12-10.30 Sun
☎ (01483) 568957 kingsheadguildford.co.uk
Fuller's Oliver's Island, London Pride, ESB; 1 changing beer (often Fuller's) Ⓗ
Built in 1860 as two cottages, which soon became a beer house, the interior is deceptively spacious after much enlargement. Service is from both sides of a central bar. The full range of Fuller's beers including seasonals is available, complemented by a draught cider. Acoustic music features on Tuesday, quiz night on Wednesday, and open mic on Thursday. TV sport is screened in most areas. The pub is noted for its attractive hanging baskets.
❀◑♿⇌(London Rd)●P🚌🐾📶

Rodboro Buildings 🄻 ✔

1-10 Bridge Street, GU1 4SB (opp Friary Centre)
8am-midnight (1am Mon; 1.45am Fri & Sat); 9am-10.30 Sun ☎ (01483) 306366
Greene King IPA, Abbot; Hogs Back TEA; Sharp's Doom Bar; 6 changing beers Ⓗ
This Wetherspoon pub is a Lloyds No.1 bar spread over three levels in a Grade II-listed former industrial building which was the original home of the Dennis car (later truck) company. It changes character in the evening, with door staff working after 9pm and the downstairs dance floor in use, often with live DJs at the weekend. A range of up to 10 real ales is available, frequently from local breweries. ◑♿⇌●🚌📶

Royal Oak

Trinity Churchyard, GU1 3RR (behind the church)
12-11 (midnight Thu, 12.30am Fri & Sat); 12-10.30 Sun
☎ (01483) 457144 royaloakguildford.co.uk
Fuller's Oliver's Island, London Pride; Gale's HSB; 2 changing beers (sourced nationally) Ⓗ
This pub has been serving real ale since 1870, currently mainly Fuller's beers. It was built as an extension to the next door rectory, with a hall upstairs and rooms at ground level. These rooms are now the bar area and show the building's heavily beamed structure. The ambience is one of a cosy village pub with a modern feel. A patio area is on one side, and a couple of tables overlooking Trinity churchyard are on the other.
❀◑♣🚌🐾📶

Hambledon

Merry Harriers 🄻 ✔

Hambledon Road, GU8 4DR SU967391
11.30 (5.30 Mon)-11; 12-8 Sun ☎ (01428) 682883
merryharriers.com
Surrey Hills Shere Drop; 3 changing beers (sourced locally; often Crafty, Dorking, Greyhound) Ⓗ
This impressive 16th-century country inn, popular with walkers and cyclists, takes you back in time. It is in the heart of this picturesque village, set against the backdrop of the Surrey Hills, surrounded by open fields, in a designated area of outstanding natural beauty. The free house is owned by local resident Peter de Savary. An open field at the rear of the pub is home to the pub's llamas. Q❀🛏◑●P🚌🐾📶

Hersham

Royal George

130 Hersham Road, KT12 5QJ (off A244)
11-11 (midnight Fri & Sat); 12-11 Sun ☎ (01932) 220910
Young's Bitter, Special; 1 changing beer (sourced regionally) Ⓗ
The pub was built in 1964 – the name refers to a 100-gun ship from the Napoleonic Wars. It has one L-shaped bar with tartan carpet and upholstered banquette seating. A real fire adds to the comfortable atmosphere. The food menu features excellent Thai food alongside more traditional British fare, with a roast on Sunday lunchtime. There are paved outdoor seating areas to the front and rear for the warmer months. Quiz night is every Tuesday. ❀◑♿P🚌(555)🐾📶

Horley

Farmhouse ✔

Ladbroke Road, Langshott, RH6 9LJ
12-11 ☎ (01293) 782146 thefarmhousehorley.co.uk
Harvey's Sussex Best Bitter; 3 changing beers Ⓗ
Originally Hewitt's Farm, a farmhouse dating from the 17th century, this Grade II-listed building became a pub in 1985. The bar area retains many original features. Guest beers change frequently and are mainly from national or regional brewers. Food is available until 9.30pm (8pm Sun). The large garden has plenty of seating alongside play facilities for children. ❀◑♿P🚌(20)🐾📶

Jack Fairman ✔

30 Victoria Road, RH6 7PZ
8am-midnight (1am Fri & Sat) ☎ (01293) 827910
Greene King Abbot; Ruddles Best Bitter; Sharp's Doom Bar; 4 changing beers (sourced nationally) Ⓗ
Conveniently close to the station and the town centre, this Wetherspoon pub occupies a former Kwik Fit tyre centre built in the 1930s as Fairman's Garage. Jack Fairman himself was a motor racing driver in the '50s and his history and posters are displayed inside. The bar has an industrial look with large pipes coming from the ceiling. Three big screens show televised sport. Food is available all day. Q❀◑♿⇌🚌📶

Horsell

Crown 🏆 🄻

104 High Street, GU21 4ST
12-11 (11.30 Fri & Sat) ☎ (01483) 771719
6 changing beers (sourced locally; often Surrey Hills, Thurstons) Ⓗ
Welcoming two-bar community local with six real ales in the saloon bar. Three beers are brewed by Thurstons, who started brewing in the Crown and

are now located next door. Other beers come from independent local or regional breweries. Behind the pub is a sturdy smokers' shelter and beyond that a large garden with two pétanque pistes. There is a weekly quiz on Wednesday, and an annual beer festival in late May. Local CAMRA Pub of the Year 2019. P (48)

Knaphill

Garibaldi

134 High Street, GU21 2QH

12-11 (midnight Fri & Sat); 12-10.30 Sun

(01483) 473374 thegaribaldi-knaphill.co.uk

2 changing beers (sourced regionally) H

Enterprising pub on the edge of Knaphill. Its compact interior has exposed beams and wooden floors. Two or three changing cask ales are served, with regional beers favoured. A real cider is available direct from the cellar. Monday is real ale club night, with beers sold at a reduced price. There is a quiz on Sunday evening, a Tuesday curry night and a Thursday steak night. Beer festivals are held in April and October. P (34,91)

Royal Oak

Anchor Hill, GU21 2JH

12-10.30 (midnight Fri & Sat) (01483) 473330

5 changing beers (often Exmoor, Ringwood, St Austell) H

An attractive 17th-century building at the bottom of the hill and set back from the road. The five beers include one of premium strength, and up to seven ciders are sold. Food is available Wednesday to Sunday, with roasts on Sunday. Behind the pub is a superb garden with a barbecue and children's play equipment. An outside bar opens at the weekend in the summer months. Two cider festivals and a beer festival are held. Live music is hosted twice monthly. P (48,91)

Laleham

Three Horseshoes

25 Shepperton Road, TW18 1SE

11-11 (11.30 Fri & Sat); 11-10.30 Sun (01784) 455014

threehorseshoeslaleham.co.uk

Fuller's London Pride; Gale's Seafarers Ale; 1 changing beer (sourced regionally; often Dark Star) H

New in the Guide this year, this rambling old inn has a number of separate bar and restaurant areas. Outside is an extensive partly paved garden at the rear and a small patio at the front. The smart, comfortable pub is food-led, with a menu featuring fresh seasonal ingredients. Well-behaved children are welcome in the bar until 7pm and 7.30pm in the restaurant. Dogs are permitted in the garden and bar areas. P (458)

Leatherhead

Running Horse

38 Bridge Street, KT22 8BZ (off B2122)

11.30-11; 12-10.30 Sun (01372) 372081

running-horse.co.uk

Shepherd Neame Master Brew, Spitfire; Surrey Hills Ranmore; 1 changing beer (sourced regionally; often Shepherd Neame) H

Overlooking the River Mole, this Grade II*-listed two-room pub, dating from 1403, features a real log fire, home-made food, a courtyard seating area plus a large back garden. Elizabeth I apparently spent the night here. The public bar has TV, pool table and dartboard, and the cosy lounge bar features low ceilings and exposed beams. Quiz night is Tuesday. Live jazz plays on Sunday lunchtime and live bands monthly, with a charity music event on May Day. Children are allowed until 9pm. Q P

Limpsfield Chart

Carpenters Arms

12 Tally Road, RH8 0TG (off B269)

10-11 (midnight Thu-Sat); 12-10.30 Sun

(01883) 722209 carpenterslimpsfield.co.uk

Westerham British Bulldog, 1965 – Special Bitter Ale, Summer Perle; 2 changing beers H

This Westerham Brewery tied house is located adjacent to the National Trust's Limpsfield Common and attracts both walkers and horse riders. The L-shaped bar has parquet flooring and the walls are adorned with an interesting collection of old photos and artwork. One side of the bar caters for diners enjoying the good food on offer. There is a quiz on the first Sunday of the month. P (594)

Lyne

Royal Marine

Lyne Lane, KT16 0AN

12-2.30, 5.30-11; closed Sat; 12-3 Sun (01932) 873900

royalmarinelyne.co.uk

Greene King IPA, London Glory; 1 changing beer (sourced nationally; often Cotleigh) H

The name of this rural pub commemorates Queen Victoria's review of her troops in 1853 on nearby Chobham Common. Royal Marine memorabilila, a collection of drinking jugs and other bric-a-brac are on display. Generous portions of home-cooked food are served Monday to Friday and Sunday lunchtime. Friday is bingo quiz night. Occasional beer festivals are held. Q P

Mickleham

King William IV

4 Byttom Hill, RH5 6EL

11-11.30; 12-10.30 Sun (01372) 372590

thekingwilliamiv.com

Hogs Back TEA; Surrey Hills Shere Drop; 1 changing beer (sourced regionally; often Crafty, Dorking, Hammerpot) H

A quaint, welcoming country pub nestled on a hillside. The main bar is homely with a log fire and there is a smaller bar to the front. An attractive outside terrace, with some tables under cover, enjoys stunning views over the Mole Valley. Good home-made food is served – book ahead for lunch, especially on summer weekends. Steep steps can make access difficult. A shared car park is on the A24 southbound. Q P (465)

Newdigate

Surrey Oaks

Parkgate Road, Parkgate, RH5 5DZ (between Newdigate and Leigh) TQ20524363

11.45-11; 9am-10.30 Sun (01306) 631200

thesurreyoaks.com

Surrey Hills Ranmore, Shere Drop; 4 changing beers H

This multi award-winning 16th-century inn is renowned for its commitment to good-quality real ale from microbreweries. Six cask beers including a dark ale, 12 KeyKeg beers, a dozen ciders and perries, plus a well-stocked fridge, provide great choice. The main bar features low beams, flagstones and an inglenook fireplace with a log-burning stove. Excellent food includes daily specials. The large garden has its own kitchen in summer and hosts the extremely popular late spring and August bank holiday beer festivals. Q (21,50)

Norwood Hill

Fox Revived

RH6 0ET

10.30-11 (10.30 Sun) (01293) 229270

foxrevived.co.uk

St Austell Cornish Best Bitter; Surrey Hills Shere Drop; house beer (by St Austell); 4 changing beers H

This deceptively spacious country inn serves a good range of food and beer. The guest ales change frequently and are mainly from local breweries. There is a large and comfortable bar area as you enter, with several big tables. The restaurant is popular for its wide-ranging menu, served all day from midday. Set on high ground, from the sizable garden there is a fine view to the north, with the North Downs and Box Hill ahead, rising towards Leith Hill in the west. P (22)

Redhill

Garibaldi

29 Mill Street, RH1 6PA

12-11; 4-midnight Fri; 12-midnight Sat; 12-10.30 Sun (01737) 773094 thegaribaldiredhill.co.uk

4 changing beers H

The Garibaldi has been a pub for over 150 years and after threatened closure for redevelopment is now run by a community group. One beer will usually be from Pilgrim. A single narrow room has TV screens at both ends showing sport at a discreet volume and a small side room has a dartboard. The ghost of Albert, a former coachman, is reputed to sometimes sit at one end of the bar. There are views across Redhill from the large pub garden. (Earlswood)

Hatch

44 Hatchlands Road, RH1 6AT (on A25 W of town)

5-10 Mon; 12-11 (01737) 423342 thehatch.pub

5 changing beers (often Godstone) H

A very comfortable pub dating from the 17th century and a former workhouse with a hayloft for horses. Good home-cooked food is served each day (no food Sun or Mon evenings). There is also a good selection of wine on offer, plus a choice of teas and coffees. The number of beers is reduced to three in winter and usually includes a house beer from Godstone. Q

Sun

17-21 London Road, RH1 1LY (on A25 in town centre)

8am-midnight (1am Fri & Sat) (01737) 766886

Greene King Abbot; Ruddles Best Bitter; Sharp's Doom Bar; 5 changing beers H

A large town-centre Wetherspoon pub within easy walking distance from the bus and train stations. The large bar room has a raised dining area, a few sofas and a corner allocated to families (children welcome until 6pm). An extensive menu of reasonably priced food is available all day. TVs show major sporting events but with the sound turned off. There is no garden, but there is a separate smoking area outside at the front. Q

Reigate

Bell Inn

21 Bell Street, RH2 7AD (on A217)

11-11 (midnight Thu-Sat); 12-10 Sun (01737) 244438

thebellreigate.co.uk

Greene King IPA, Abbot; 4 changing beers H

This long, narrow pub is one of the oldest in town, with low ceilings, wooden floors and tables, and a comfortable and welcoming feel. The guest beers change frequently and are often from local microbreweries. Food is served 12-2.30pm and 6-9pm daily – the menu includes over a dozen varieties of burger sourced from local butchers. Various board games are available. Note the old Ordnance Survey map on the ceiling.

Pilgrim Brewery Tap Room

11 West Street, RH2 9BL (off A25 towards Dorking)

4.30-9 Thu & Fri; 12.30-9 Sat; closed Sun-Wed

(01737) 222651 pilgrim.co.uk

Pilgrim Surrey, Progress, Quest; 3 changing beers (sourced locally; often Pilgrim) G

Surrey's oldest brewery is sited in an old bakery hidden in a yard off the main A25 – the entrance is marked by a hanging barrel sign. New owners took over in 2017 and have opened up a cosy taproom where the old ground-floor offices used to be. It sells around six cask beers including three guests from other breweries, and four keg beers. Dominoes and shove-ha'penny are played.

Q P

Ripley

Anchor

High Street, GU23 6AE

closed Mon; 12-11 (01483) 211866

ripleyanchor.co.uk

Exeter Avocet; 1 changing beer (sourced locally; often Crafty, Dorking, Tillingbourne) H

An ancient Grade II-listed public house with parts of the building dating back to the 1500s, so expect some low beams. It is surprisingly light and airy inside, with a feeling of the contemporary meeting the historic. This is essentially a dining pub but the friendly staff can serve you beer at the bar. Fresh and reasonably priced bar snacks are available, with a fuller menu in the dining area. Q P

Half Moon

High Street, GU23 6AN

11.30-2.30, 5.30-11; 11.30-3, 6-midnight Sat; 12-5 Sun

(01483) 224380 thehalfmoonripley.co.uk

Surrey Hills Shere Drop; 1 changing beer (often Exeter) H

The bar in this 18th-century building has the feel of a cross between a café and a pub, with a stripped wood floor and some bare brick walls contrasting nicely with white painted ones, decorated with historic photographs of the inn. The fare is diverse, with a traditional roast on Sunday. Outside is a tiny, well-maintained and oasis-like courtyard garden. B&B is available in eight rooms.

Shepperton

Barley Mow 🅛
67 Watersplash Road, TW17 0EE (off B376 in Shepperton Green)
🕐 12-11 (10.30 Sun) ☎ (01932) 225326 🌐 themow.co.uk
Hogs Back TEA; Hop Back Summer Lightning; 3 changing beers (sourced locally; often Thames Side, Twickenham) 🅷
Friendly community local in Shepperton Green to the west of the main village centre. Five handpumps serve two regular beers plus up to three – usually local – guest ales. Many pumpclips adorn the bar and beams. Entertainment includes jazz on Wednesday, a quiz night on Thursday, live rock or blues bands on Friday or Saturday night, and a traditional charity meat raffle on Sunday afternoon. Outside, there is a covered, heated patio area at the rear. 🏵🍺♿P🚐(400,458)🐾🛜

South Godstone

Fox & Hounds 🅛 ✅
Tilburstow Hill Road, RH9 8LY
🕐 closed Mon; 12-3, 5-11; 12-11 Sat; 12-10 Sun
☎ (01342) 893474 🌐 foxandhounds.org.uk
Greene King IPA, Abbot; 2 changing beers (sourced locally; often Dorking, Hogs Back, Weltons) 🅷
This attractive building, with parts dating back to 1368, became a pub in 1601. There are original beams throughout and a large inglenook in the restaurant. The bar area is low-ceilinged and very cosy with high-back settles and a fire. The pleasant garden at the rear has a children's play area. One or two guest beers are available, often from Hogs Back as well as local breweries such as Dorking and Weltons. Open bank holiday Mondays. 🐕🏵🕽P🐾

Staines-upon-Thames

Old Red Lion ✅
Leacroft, TW18 4PB
🕐 11-11 (midnight Fri & Sat); 12-10.30 Sun
☎ (01784) 453355
Bombardier Pale Ale; Courage Best Bitter; Fuller's London Pride; 1 changing beer (sourced nationally) 🅷
Cosy old local pub dating back to 1610 – look out for the low ceilings. It is set in a quiet location facing a green and woods, yet only a few minutes' walk from the railway station. Home-cooked food is available lunchtime and evenings (not Mon) with Sunday roasts and steak nights. Quiz nights and live music are hosted. There is decking at the front and a garden to the rear for alfresco drinking. 🏵🕽🚆P🚐(117,216)🐾

Wheatsheaf & Pigeon 🅛 ✅
Penton Road, TW18 2LL (corner of Wheatsheaf Lane and Penton Rd)
🕐 12-11 ☎ (01784) 452922
🌐 thewheatsheafandpigeon.co.uk
Bombardier; Fuller's London Pride; Otter Ale; 2 changing beers (sourced nationally; often Robinsons, Thames Side) 🅷
Welcoming community local between Staines and Laleham, a short signposted walk from the Thames Path. Ales often include local micro beers or guests from the West Country. Good-value, interesting food is served (no food Sun or Mon eves). There is outside seating front and back, plus a covered area. Quiz night is Sunday and occasional beer festivals are held. A local bus stops in Laleham Road. Staines Town FC is nearby. 🐕🏵🕽🚆♿P🚐(458,570)🐾🛜

Stoke D'Abernon

Old Plough
2 Station Road, KT11 3BN (off A245)
🕐 11-11 (11.30 Fri & Sat); 12-10.30 Sun ☎ (01932) 862244
🌐 oldploughcobham.co.uk
Fuller's London Pride; Surrey Hills Shere Drop; 1 changing beer (often Fuller's) 🅷
Dating from the late 16th century, this listed building was once a courthouse with the gallows outside, and the stables were used for hansom cab trade. The interior has been opened out but retains much of its original character, particularly at the front. An extension houses a dining area at the rear. The decor is a mix of bare brick, wood panelling and painted walls. There is a pleasant garden area to the side and rear. The pub has a good reputation for food, which makes it busy at times. Q🐕🏵🕽🚆♿🚆P🚐🐾🛜

Sunbury-on-Thames

White Horse ✅
69 Thames Street, TW16 5QF
🕐 11-11; 12-10 Sun ☎ (01932) 770999
🌐 whitehorsesunbury.co.uk
Black Sheep Best Bitter; Fuller's London Pride; Morland Old Speckled Hen; Sharp's Doom Bar 🅷
A warm welcome to the Guide for this two-bar corner local. First documented in 1729, the present building probably dates from a later period. The function room and dining area have been brought back into use, with an interesting menu including Sunday roasts. The pub has a golf society, occasional music nights and sports TV. Buses run from nearby Green Street, and Sunbury Walled Garden and the Thames towpath are a short walk away. 🐕🏵🕽🚐(216)🐾🛜

Tongham

White Hart 🅛
76 The Street, GU10 1DH
🕐 12-11 (10.30 Mon; midnight Fri & Sat); 12-10.30 Sun
☎ (01252) 782419 🌐 whitehearttongham.co.uk
Hogs Back TEA; 5 changing beers (sourced nationally; often Longdog, Surrey Hills, Triple fff) 🅷
Situated in the centre of the village, just down from the Hogs Back Brewery. The rear bar is a focal point for the darts and pool teams. The listed middle bar caters for diners and the front bar is ideal for a quiet drink. Up to seven beers of different styles and strengths, including at least one dark beer often from a local brewery, are usually available, as well as a real cider. The pub is renowned for good-value food (no food Mon). Q🐕🏵🕽♣🍺P🚐(520)🐾🛜

Upper Hale

Alfred Free House
9 Bishops Road, GU9 0JA
🕐 5.30-11 (11.30 Fri & Sat); 12-10.30 Sun ☎ (01252) 820385
🌐 thealfredfreehouse.co.uk
Bowman Wallops Wood 🅷; 4 changing beers (sourced nationally) 🅷/🅖
This friendly local pub, tucked away down a residential road, features a bar area and a restaurant/function room. The regular beer is supplemented by three or four guest ales, usually including a dark beer. Two beer festivals are held each year at Easter and October. Live music and

other events feature regularly. Fresh home-made food, using locally sourced ingredients, is available Wednesday to Saturday evenings and Sunday lunchtime. Q🛝❀◐♿♣P🚌(5)🐾📶

Walton-on-Thames

George Inn

24 Bridge Street, KT12 1AH
🕐 12-11 (midnight Fri & Sat); 12-10.30 Sun
☎ (01932) 223046 🌐 georgeinnwalton.co.uk
Shepherd Neame Whitstable Bay Pale Ale, Spitfire; 1 changing beer (often Shepherd Neame) Ⓗ
Friendly local pub with a single bar traditionally decorated with a wood and tiled floor and an open fireplace. A large plaque on the front shows its Lascelles, Tickner & Co heritage. There is a pleasant enclosed beer garden to the rear. The food menu offers hot meals and a good sandwich selection, all-day breakfasts and traditional Sunday roasts. Live music plays every second Saturday and sport is shown on TV. The changing beer can be from a brewery other than Shepherd Neame.
🛝❀◐♣🚌🐾📶

Walton Village

29-31 High Street, KT12 1DG
🕐 9.30am-11 (12.30am Fri & Sat); 10-10.30 Sun
☎ (01932) 254431 🌐 thewaltonvillage.com
Fuller's London Pride; 1 changing beer (sourced nationally) Ⓗ
Modern high-street pub with exposed brickwork and wood panels. The large front bar has a raised seating area and there is a room to the rear for private events. A wide range of food is served all day, prepared in an open-plan kitchen in the centre of the pub, including vegan and gluten-free choices. Poker night is Monday and quiz night Thursday. A table tennis table is available. Lilley's cider is on draught in the summer.
🛝❀◐♿♣🍎🚌🐾📶

West Clandon

Bull's Head Ⓛ

The Street, GU4 7ST
🕐 11.30-3, 5.30-11; 12-10.30 Sun ☎ (01483) 222444
🌐 bullsheadwestclandon.co.uk
Hogs Back TEA; Surrey Hills Shere Drop; Young's Bitter Ⓗ
Sixteenth-century village inn close to Clandon Park, in an area of outstanding natural beauty. The interior retains some original features with oak beams and low ceilings as well as a cosy log fire. Food is an important part of the pub's trade and the focus is very much on traditional British cooking at reasonable prices (no food Sun eve). To the rear is a hedged garden, where you can while away a couple of hours on a warm day with a good pint.
Q🛝❀◐P🚌(463)🐾📶

West Horsley

Barley Mow

181 The Street, KT24 6HR
🕐 11-11; 12-10 Sun ☎ (01483) 282693
🌐 barleymowhorsley.com
Fuller's London Pride; Surrey Hills Ranmore, Shere Drop; 1 changing beer Ⓗ
A friendly, traditional pub set in the heart of the Surrey Hills. The large building incorporates the Malting House to the rear, which is available for functions. Thai food is available lunchtime and evening, with traditional English cooking lunchtimes only (no food Sun eve). The substantial grassed garden is great for families and dogs, with seating dotted around. 🛝❀◐P🚌(478)🐾📶

Weybourne

Running Stream ✔

66 Weybourne Road, GU9 9HE
🕐 11-11 (10.30 Sun) ☎ (01252) 323750
Greene King XX Mild, IPA, Abbot; Morland Old Speckled Hen; Ruddles Best Bitter Ⓗ
A good old-fashioned friendly locals' pub. A horseshoe-shaped room surrounds a central bar, with tables around the outer perimeter and stools at the bar. The interior is simply decorated, with pictures of the old pub on the wall. Greene King beers, always in excellent condition, are served. Good-value home-cooked food, including a daily special Monday to Friday, is available at lunchtime. A quiz is hosted on Wednesday and Sunday plus occasional live music. ❀◐P🚌📶

Whyteleafe

Radius Arms

205 Godstone Road, CR3 0EL (on A22)
🕐 closed Mon; 4-9.30 Tue-Thu; 12-10.30 Fri & Sat; 12-5.30 Sun ☎ 07514 916172
4 changing beers (sourced nationally) Ⓗ/Ⓖ
This friendly and popular micropub opened in 2015. Some of the tables were recycled from the Olympic Park in London. The walls and ceiling are decorated with dried hops and hundreds of beer mats. A changing selection of cask-conditioned ales (up to six at weekends) from around Britain is sold alongside four KeyKeg beers and up to 13 ciders and perries. There is a book library and the pub hosts an annual pickled onion competition.
Q❀⇌(Whyeleafe/Upper Warlingham)🍎🚌🐾

Woking

Herbert Wells Ⓛ ✔

51-57 Chertsey Road, GU21 5AJ
🕐 8am-midnight (1am Fri & Sat) ☎ (01483) 722818
Courage Best Bitter; Greene King Abbot; Hogs Back TEA; Sharp's Doom Bar; 7 changing beers (sourced nationally) Ⓗ
A varied range of up to seven guest beers, plus eight ciders and perries, is available in this popular town-centre Wetherspoon, which is close to bus stops and the railway station. The large open-plan bar is decorated with HG Wells-inspired features including an invisible man sitting in the window and its own time machine. A wealth of information about local history covers the walls of both the main bar and the smaller side room.
Q◐♿⇌🍎🚌📶

Woking Railway Athletic Club

Goldsworth Road, GU21 6JT (behind offices at E end of Goldsworth Rd)
🕐 10.30-11; 11.30-10.30 Sun ☎ (01483) 598499
3 changing beers (sourced nationally) Ⓗ
Friendly and lively social club tucked away near Victoria Arch, serving three or four beers. One side of the bar is sports-oriented with darts, free-to-play pool and Sky Sports, while the other side is quieter. Children are welcome at all times and free Wi-Fi is available. Filled rolls are on sale on Saturday

afternoon. Show a CAMRA membership card or a copy of this Guide for entry. Local CAMRA Club of the Year 2019. ♞≈♣🚌📶

Wonersh

Grantley Arms

The Street, GU5 0PE

11-11 (11.30 Fri & Sat); 11-10.30 Sun ☎ (01483) 893351
thegrantleyarms.co.uk

Harvey's Sussex Best Bitter; Surrey Hills Shere Drop; 2 changing beers (sourced regionally; often Hogs Back, Tillingbourne) Ⓗ

Half-timbered village pub dating back to the late 16th or early 17th century, with later extensions. A recent refurbishment has exposed more of the frame of the building and created a bright and cheerful interior. The pub is food-led, offering a quality menu all day every day, but four real ales are stocked, with the changing beers predominantly local, and there is no pressure to have a meal. Buses stop outside, and there are evening and Sunday services from Cranleigh and Guildford. ♞❀◐♿P🚌(53,63)🐾📶

Woodmansterne

Woodman ✔

Woodmansterne Street, SM7 3NL (on B278)

11-11 (midnight Fri & Sat); 11-10.30 Sun
☎ (01737) 371841 thewoodmanbanstead.co.uk

Harvey's Sussex Best Bitter; Sharp's Doom Bar; 2 changing beers Ⓗ

One-bar pub with a woodburner, built in the early 1900s as an annexe to the local manor house. One or two guest beers are available, and occasionally a cider in the summer. Food is served all day. Events such as poker, quizzes, live music and barbecues are held, and there are two screens for sport. The large garden has a sandpit for children, and there is a heated smoking area. ♞❀◐♣P🚌(166)🐾📶

Wrecclesham

Sandrock

Sandrock Hill Road, GU10 4NS

12 (4 Mon)-11; 12-10.30 Sun ☎ (01252) 447289
sandrockwrecclesham.co.uk

Bowman Swift One; Fuller's London Pride; Hop Back Summer Lightning; Sharp's Cornish Coaster; Timothy Taylor Landlord; Triple fff Moondance; 1 changing beer (often Exmoor) Ⓗ

Following almost a year of closure, the Sandrock was refurbished and reopened as a traditional pub with a contemporary feel late in 2018. It has a Thai food restaurant and take-away service, as well as providing quality real ale. There is a patio garden and a small car park. The pub is dog- and family-friendly. Q♞❀◐♿♣P🚌(16,17)🐾📶

Wheatsheaf & Pigeon, Staines-upon-Thames (Photo: Steve Owen)

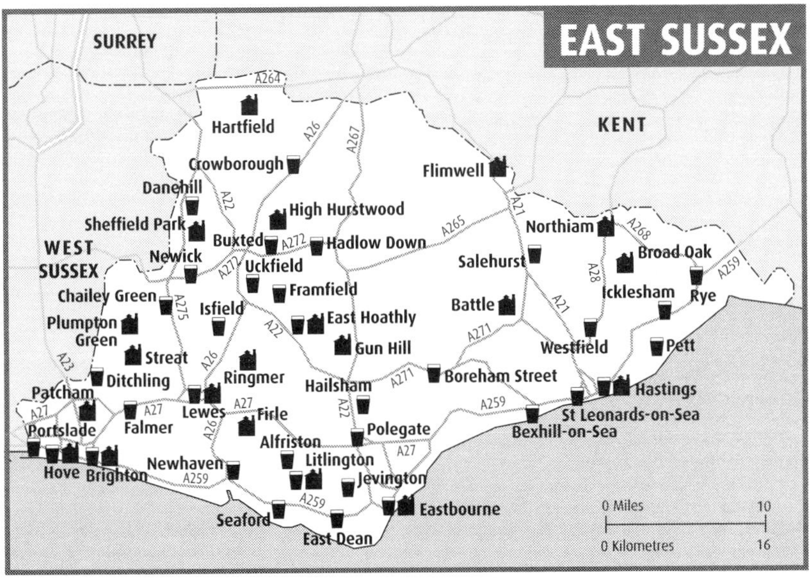

SUSSEX (EAST)

Alfriston

Olde Smugglers Inn L

Waterloo Square, BN26 5UE

12-11 (10 Sun winter) ☎ (01323) 870241

smugglersalfriston.co.uk

Harvey's Sussex Best Bitter; 4 changing beers (sourced locally; often Long Man) H

Historic, friendly pub that oozes charm and character with its impressive inglenook fireplace, oak beams and ancient brick floor in the main bar area. Parts date from 1358, and the pub is known to have been a meeting place for smuggling gangs. A series of small rooms at various levels lead through to a conservatory, large patio and tranquil walled garden. Good-quality locally sourced food is on offer. Traditional Sussex games such as toad in the hole can be played. **Q**

Bexhill on Sea

Albatross Club (RAFA) L

15 Marina Arcade, TN40 1JS (on seafront)

11-2.30, 7 (5 Thu)-11; 11-11 Fri; 12-5 Sun

☎ (01424) 212916 bexhillrafa.co.uk

5 changing beers (sourced locally) H

This most welcoming and friendly RAFA club consistently wins local and regional CAMRA awards, and won CAMRA National Club of the Year for 2016. Regular music and quiz nights are held, also meat raffles and popular public beer festivals. Food is available at lunchtimes Tuesday to Friday. Local beers feature strongly here alongside national beers on the five handpumps, with real cider also available. CAMRA members are always welcome to sample the range of quality ales on offer. **Q** (98,99)

Boreham Street

Bull's Head L

The Strait, BN27 4SG

11.30-11 (7 Sun) ☎ (01323) 831981

bullsheadborehamstreet.com

Harvey's Sussex Best Bitter; house beer (by Harvey's); 2 changing beers H

A welcoming village pub, this was the original Harvey's tied house, and continues its tie. Alongside Sussex Best Bitter can be found the exclusive house beer, Bull's Head Ale, and usually two others, one changing monthly and the other seasonally. Good-quality food is served, including a great selection of pies. The pub may close early Monday to Wednesday on winter evenings when it is quiet. It has a popular campsite to the rear of the garden. **Q** **P** (98)

Brighton

Basketmakers Arms L ✔

12 Gloucester Road, BN1 4AD

11-11 (midnight Fri & Sat); 12-11 Sun ☎ (01273) 689006

Dark Star Hophead; Fuller's London Pride, ESB; Gale's Seafarers Ale, HSB; 4 changing beers (sourced nationally; often Adnams) H

A much-loved Brighton institution, this busy two-room street-corner pub, popular with young and old alike, is on the edge of Brighton's famous bohemian North Laines. Eight handpumps serve a selection of the Fuller's range plus guests. Locally sourced home-made food is available every day including on Seafood Saturday and for the popular traditional Sunday roasts. The walls are adorned with old metal signs and tobacco tins. Live jazz music is performed on the first Sunday of every month. **Q**

Brighton Beer Dispensary

38 Dean Street, BN1 3EG

12-11 (midnight Fri & Sat) ☎ (01273) 710624

4 changing beers (sourced nationally; often Arbor, Brighton Bier, Southey) H

Formerly the Prince Arthur, this pub reopened in 2014 and is sandwiched between domestic terraced premises on a steep hill off the Western Road shopping area. Its bar usually offers four changing beers and three ciders. A blackboard shows beers available with prices and ABV. There is a conservatory with seating at the rear, and decking at the front with seating and a smoking area. A varied, locally sourced food menu features vegan options and Sunday roasts. Local CAMRA branch Pub of the Year 2017.

Brighton Bierhaus

161 Edward Street, BN2 0JB

12-midnight (01273) 686386 brightonbierhaus.pub

Brighton Bier West Pier; 4 changing beers (sourced locally; often Brighton Bier) H

This single-bar pub is the Brighton Bier Brewery tap and is centrally situated near the Royal Pavilion and Palace Pier. It serves up to five changing beers and two ciders on handpump, along with a number of keg and bottled beers. An extensive pizza range can be ordered from a nearby source to eat in the bar. There is a free cheeseboard on Sunday. The muted television shows BT Sport. Local CAMRA branch Pub of the Year 2019.

Craft Beer Co

22-23 Upper North Street, BN1 3FG (a short walk from Churchill Square shopping centre)

12 (4 Mon)-11; 12-1am Fri & Sat; 12-10.30 Sun

(01273) 723736

House beer (by Kent); 4 changing beers (sourced regionally; often Kent, Pig & Porter) H

Near the Grade II-listed St Nicholas Church, this award-winning pub boasts five beers on handpump, 22 craft beers on tap and up to 90 bottled beers from home and abroad. A discount is available on take-home bottles. The pub is comfortable and friendly, an ideal place to get away from the busy city centre. Tutored beer tastings are held; see website for details. Food is available except on Monday.

Evening Star L

55-56 Surrey Street, BN1 3PB (200yds S of station)

12-11 (midnight Fri & Sat) (01273) 328931

6 changing beers (sourced regionally; often Dark Star) H

A classic, compact Brighton pub five minutes from the station, majoring in good real ale and craft beers. Fairly basic in decor, with a few tables outside on the street, it is no longer tied to Dark Star Brewery as it was originally, with the brewery in the cellar. Dark Star beers may be on even so, together with several interesting brews from around the UK. Offering good beer, board games and window seats, and handy for transport, what is not to like?

Hanover L

242 Queens Park Road, Hanover, BN2 9ZB

3-11 (midnight Thu); 12-midnight Fri & Sat; 12-11 Sun

(01273) 679902 hanoverbrighton.co.uk

Sharp's Doom Bar; 4 changing beers (sourced locally) H

An estate pub dating from the late 1920s, now opened out but retaining its well-used function/meeting room. The pub is quite large and features discrete areas with seating and tables. Part of the Indigo chain, it dispenses a variety of Sussex ales plus a local cider on handpump. Food is available 12.30 to 10pm, with a feature of the bar area being its pizza oven. Sunday roasts are served midday to 9pm. Attractions include Tuesday quiz night and occasional live music. (21,23)

Haus on the Hill L

58 Southover Street, Hanover, BN2 9UF

12-midnight (1am Fri & Sat); 12-11 Sun

(01273) 601419 hausonthehill.pub

Brighton Bier West Pier; 3 changing beers (sourced locally; often Brighton Bier, Hand Brew Co) H

Previously the Southover, this venue is now operated by Brighton Bier. Situated at the top of a steep hill, it is probably best approached by bus. There are two upstairs function rooms and a covered patio for smokers. Conversation is the norm here and there is no TV or jukebox. A guest beer is always sold along with three from Brighton Bier, plus a cider. A number of bottled and keg beers, both British and foreign, are also on offer. (18,23)

Holler Brewery & Taproom L

19-23 Elder Place, BN1 4GF

12-11 (01273) 894563 hollerbrewery.com

Holler Extra Pale, Mr Best, Juicy Pale, West Coast IPA; 5 changing beers (sourced locally; often Holler) H

This newly opened brewery taproom is next to Preston Circus Brewery, just off London Road and less than 10 minutes' walk from Brighton mainline station. It gives customers the chance to visit the home of Holler beer and try the whole range, right where it is brewed. Brewery visits are available for pre-booking every day except Thursday and Friday. There are regular offerings of one-off beers from the brewery. Pizzas can be ordered in.

Lord Nelson Inn

36 Trafalgar Street, BN1 4ED

12-11 (11.30 Fri & Sat); 12-10 Sun (01273) 695872

lordnelsonbrighton.co.uk

Harvey's Sussex Best Bitter; 5 changing beers (often Harvey's) H

A flagship Harvey's pub just down Trafalgar Street from the station, the Lord Nelson recently took over the shop next door and was given a

REAL ALE BREWERIES

1648 East Hoathly
360° Sheffield Park
Bartlebys Brighton
Battle Battle
Bedlam Plumpton Green
Beer Me Eastbourne
Brewery at the Watchmaker's Arms Hove (NEW)
Brewing Brothers Hastings
Brick House Patcham (brewing suspended)
Brighton Bier Brighton
Burning Sky Firle
Cellar Head Flimwell
Engineer High Hurstwood
FILO Hastings
Franklins Ringmer
Gun Gun Hill
Hand Brighton
Harvey's Lewes
High Weald Hartfield
Holler Brighton
Laine Brighton
Long Man Litlington
Loud Shirt Brighton
Old Tree Brighton
Rectory Streat
Rother Valley Northiam
Three Legs Broad Oak

makeover. Still cosy and traditional, it serves food until 9pm (8pm Sun) and is the place to sample the Harvey's beer range including its craft ales. The pub is divided into separate drinking areas based on the original layout, with bare wood floors and the occasional rug. Located on a gently sloping road, it is on various levels. ❀◑⇌●🚌🐾📶

Mitre Tavern

13 Baker Street, BN1 4JN

10.30-11; 12-10.30 Sun ☎ (01273) 683173

mitretavern.co.uk

Harvey's Sussex XX Mild Ale, Sussex Best Bitter; 3 changing beers (sourced locally; often Harvey's) Ⓗ

Between the London Road shops and the Level park, this is a good old-fashioned side-street pub that has barely changed in decades. Subdued background music does not detract from the lively banter in this two-roomed Harvey's-run pub. The regular beers are Harvey's XX Mild and Sussex Best Bitter, with Old Ale served in winter and Olympia during the summer, when a cider is also available. A small rear patio caters for smokers.
❀⇌♣🚌🐾📶

Buxted

White Hart

Station Road, TN22 4DP

closed Mon; 12-3, 6-11; 12-11 Sat; 12-10 Sun

☎ (01825) 732068 thewhitehartbuxted.co.uk

Harvey's Sussex Best Bitter; 2 changing beers (often Long Man) Ⓗ

Open-plan but cosy 18th-century pub with separate, connected areas for casual seating and more formal dining, the latter with a feature inglenook fireplace. The pub also has a large conservatory restaurant/function room. At least one beer from local brewer Harvey's is always offered, alongside a rotating guest. Live music sessions are held once a month. The pub has ample parking and is a short walk from the mainline railway station. ❀◑♿⇌P🐾📶

Chailey Green

Five Bells

East Grinstead Road, BN8 4DA

11-11 ☎ (01825) 722259 thefivebellschailey.com

Harvey's Sussex Best Bitter; 3 changing beers (sourced locally; often Gun, Harvey's) Ⓗ

Country pub on the A275 between Lewes and East Grinstead, popular with car enthusiasts. It has three gardens, with a smoking area to the front of the pub. There is a timber-fronted bar with carved moulded pilasters separating the shelving areas on the gantry, and a mixture of tiled and timber floors. Look out for the brass wall lanterns and the picture supposedly signed by Picasso. There is no food on Mondays. Check closing times in winter.
Q❀◑P🚌

Crowborough

Cooper's Arms

Coopers Lane, TN6 1SN

12-2 (not Mon), 5-10; 12-8 Sun ☎ (01892) 654796

Harvey's Sussex Best Bitter; 3 changing beers (sourced nationally) Ⓗ

A Guide regular for 16 consecutive years, this friendly local offers changing ales from far and wide, many sourced locally and all in excellent condition. Selected keg beers are also stocked. Food is often available Sunday lunchtime but it is worth enquiring first. The regular beer festivals feature up to 12 handpumps in use and are highly recommended. There is a real fire in winter and, for warmer weather, a secluded garden with views over Ashdown Forest. Q❀◑P🚌🐾📶

Wheatsheaf

Mount Pleasant, TN6 2NF

12-11; 12-10.30 Sun ☎ (01892) 663756

wheatsheafcrowborough.co.uk

Harvey's Sussex XX Mild Ale, IPA, Sussex Best Bitter; 1 changing beer (often Harvey's) Ⓗ

The Wheatsheaf is a popular family- and dog-friendly local on the southern outskirts of Crowborough. Its welcoming atmosphere is complemented by the focus on serving nurtured Harvey's ales and good pub food. There is a sense of history within the pub, supported by the layout, stepped levels between previously separate bar areas, dated photographs and a unique, ex-maritime copper fireplace. A well-attended summer beer festival is held at the end of May.
Q❀◑⇌♣P🚌(228,229)🐾📶

Danehill

Coach & Horses

School Lane, RH17 7JF

12-3, 5.30-11; 12-11.30 Sat; 12-10.30 Sun

☎ (01825) 740369 coachandhorses.co

Harvey's Sussex Best Bitter; 3 changing beers (sourced locally; often Cellar Head, Dark Star, Franklins) Ⓗ

Dating from 1847, this traditional country pub retains many original features. Its public and saloon bars feature real fires and simple farmhouse-style furniture. Locally produced Black Pig cider is always on the bar. A separate restaurant area, converted from the former adjoining stables, serves locally sourced, high-quality food. The rear patio offers farmland views. The large garden includes a children's play area and is a delight in summer.
Q❀◑♣●P🚌(270)🐾📶

Ditchling

White Horse

16 West Street, BN6 8TS

11-10.30 (11 Fri & Sat) ☎ (01273) 842006

whitehorseditchling.com

Dark Star Hophead; Harvey's Sussex Best Bitter; 3 changing beers (sourced regionally) Ⓗ

This inn, which dates back to the 12th century, lies below the parish church in this picturesque and historic village. The accommodation at the White Horse can cater for weddings, birthday parties or act as a stopover while walking the South Downs Way. Log fires in winter, excellent food and guest beers of varying quality are certain to fortify the traveller. Q❀🛏◑P🚌(167,168)🐾📶

East Dean

Tiger Inn

The Green, BN20 0DA

11-10.30 (11 Fri & Sat); 10-10 Sun ☎ (01323) 423209

beachyhead.org.uk/the-tiger-inn

Harvey's Sussex Best Bitter; Long Man Long Blonde; St Austell Tribute; 3 changing beers (sourced locally) Ⓗ

Facing the village green, this idyllic, popular 15th-century inn, featuring wooden beams and stone flooring, is split into three areas. The bar, serving at least one real cider, is located within the central section and features a log fire. The lower area has access for wheelchairs with appropriate toilet facilities; the remainder is mainly laid out for dining. Good-quality food is served both inside and out. Several times winner of local CAMRA Country Pub of the Year. Q ⛅ 🕮 ⚟ ⏰ ◑ ᕕ ♣ ♠ P ☕ 🐾 ☂

East Hoathly

King's Head ♇ 🅛

1 High Street, BN8 6DR

⏰ 11-11; 12-11 Sun ☎ (01825) 840238 🌐 thekingshead.org

1648 Triple Champion, Signature; Harvey's Sussex Best Bitter; 1 changing beer (often 1648) 🅷

A long-established family-run free house which has been a pub for over 250 years. The 1648 Brewing Company was established in 2003 in the old stables next door; two of its beers are always on tap as well as a changing cider. An extensive range of home-cooked food is served every day. There is a walled garden to the rear of the pub and additional outside seating at the front. Local CAMRA Cider Pub of the Year 2018.
Q ⛅ 🕮 ⚟ ◑ Å ♠ P ⊟ (54) 🐾 ☂

Eastbourne

Crown 🅛 ✔

22 Crown Street, Old Town, BN21 1PB

⏰ 11-11 (midnight Fri & Sat); 12-11 Sun ☎ (01323) 724654

Dark Star Hophead; Harvey's Sussex Best Bitter; Shepherd Neame Spitfire 🅷**; Young's Special** 🅷**/**🅖**; 1 changing beer (sourced locally)** 🅖

Friendly two-bar local with a log fire and separate pool room. A small range of home-made bar snacks is offered. Sunday lunchtime features beer discounts, a cash draw and meat raffle. Events include occasional live music, three annual beer festivals and a popular monthly themed quiz night with complimentary hot buffet. Summer barbecues are held in the large enclosed rear garden, which has children's play equipment. Recent local CAMRA branch awards include Pub of the Year runner-up.
⚟ 🕮 ♣ ⊟ 🐾 ☂

Eagle 🅛

57 South Street, BN21 4UT

⏰ 11-11 (12.30am Fri & Sat) ☎ (01323) 417799

Harvey's Sussex Best Bitter; 3 changing beers (sourced regionally) 🅷

Popular town-centre pub, close to the Beacon shopping centre, railway station and main bus routes. It is a one-bar former Kemptown Brewery venue featuring some fine restored internal decorations. Attractions include a pool table, dartboard and six TVs showing sporting events, as well as a roof beer garden. Four reasonably priced real ales are on tap, plus two ciders. Food is served 12-9pm with an American diner-inspired menu. Live entertainment takes place at weekends.
⚟ 🕮 ◑ ⇌ ♣ ♠ ⊟ 🐾 ☂

Hurst Arms 🅛

76 Willingdon Road, Ocklynge, BN21 1TW

⏰ 12-2 (not Mon), 5-11.30; 12-midnight Fri & Sat; 12-11.30 Sun ☎ (01323) 419440 🌐 thehurstarms.pub

Harvey's Forward's Choice, Sussex Best Bitter; house beer (by Harvey's); 2 changing beers (sourced locally) 🅷

A Victorian building near the Old Town of Eastbourne. The pub has two bars: one public with pool table, darts and a jukebox; the other a comfortable, quieter lounge. This is a tied Harvey's house, offering three regular ales, generally complemented by two seasonals. Unusually for pubs in the area, it does not serve food. Music events are held fortnightly. There is a heated smoking area outside, but e-cigarette users may stay inside. 🕮 ♣ P ⊟ 🐾 ☂

Lamb Inn 🅛 ✔

36 High Street, Old Town, BN21 1HH

⏰ 11-11 (midnight Fri & Sat) ☎ (01323) 720545
🌐 thelambeastbourne.co.uk

Harvey's Sussex Best Bitter, Armada Ale; 1 changing beer 🅷

A Harvey's tied house that is one of the oldest houses of entertainment in the country, with cellars dating from 1180; tours can be arranged to view the crypt. The interior features two traditional bars and a wealth of period features. Food served all day includes vegetarian and vegan dishes using organic products. Beer-battered fish and chips are a speciality. Regular events include live music, theatrical productions and comedy nights. B&B can be booked through Stay in a Pub.
Q ⛅ ⚟ ◑ ᕕ ♣ P ⊟ 🐾 ☂

London & County 🅛 ✔

46 Terminus Road, BN21 3LX

⏰ 8am-midnight (1am Fri & Sat) ☎ (01323) 746310

Greene King Abbot; Ruddles Best Bitter; Sharp's Doom Bar; 3 changing beers (sourced nationally) 🅷

A Wetherspoon Lloyds No.1 bar occupying the former 1880s London & County Bank, arranged over two floors, each with a bar. It is in the town centre close to bus stops and the railway station. Varying guest beers are on offer, including at least one LocAle. Good-value food is served all day. Muted TV screens display news. Music is played each evening and a DJ performs on Friday and Saturday, when a smart-casual dress code applies.
⚟ ◑ ᕕ ⇌ ♠ ⊟ ☂

Victoria Hotel 🅛

27 Latimer Road, BN22 7BU (behind TAVR centre from seaside)

⏰ 12-11; 12-10.30 Sun ☎ (01323) 722673
🌐 thevictoriaeastbourne.co.uk

Harvey's Sussex Best Bitter, Armada Ale; 1 changing beer (sourced locally) 🅷

A London-style pub with a high ceiling, wooden bar with glasses shelf supported by turned wooden pillars and flock wall paper, but this pub is in a quiet back street near Eastbourne's sea front. The other difference, Eastbourne rather than London prices. Well kept Harvey's is always available with the seasonal ales on at the appropriate times and Weston's Old Rosie cider on draught. Home prepared and cooked meals are available Thursday to Sunday lunchtimes and Thursday to Saturday evenings. ⚟ 🕮 ⚟ ◑ ᕕ ♣ ♠ ⊟ 🐾 ☂

Falmer

Swan Inn 🅛 ✔

Middle Street, BN1 9PD (just off A27 in N of village)

⏰ closed Mon; 12-11; 12-10.30 Sun ☎ (01273) 681842
🌐 swanfalmer.co.uk

ENGLAND

Palmers Tally Ho!; 4 changing beers (sourced regionally; often Downlands, Long Man, Palmers) [H]
A family-run free house located near the universities. It has three bar areas and a barn available for functions. Good-value food is served at lunchtime plus Thursday and Friday evening. The pub gets busy when Brighton & Hove Albion play at home. It opens at varying times on match days and will also open for Monday evening games. There is a small courtyard area at the side of the pub.
Q P (28,29)

Framfield

Hare & Hounds L
The Street, TN22 5NJ
11-11; 12-10.30 Sun ☎ (01825) 890118
hareandhounds.net
Harvey's Sussex Best Bitter; 1 changing beer [H]
Traditional, family-friendly village pub that dates from 1428 and features beams and an inglenook fireplace in a snug area of the bar. The pub was refurbished by the current licensees when they took over in 2018, creating a formal restaurant on one side of the building. Live music is performed during the summer months, when the large beer garden is popular. No food on Monday.
Q P

Hadlow Down

New Inn ★ L
Main Road, TN22 4HJ
6 (1 Wed)-11; 12-11 Sat & Sun
Harvey's IPA, Sussex Best Bitter; 1 changing beer (often Harvey's) [H]
Call into this village pub and you will not be disappointed with the welcome you receive from locals. The New Inn was rebuilt in 1885 following a fire. It has earned its inclusion in the CAMRA National Inventory of Historic Pub Interiors, as the original back bar fittings, ceramic spirit casks and a panelled counter are still there. A quiz is held on the second Tuesday of the month, raising money for local charities and organisations. No food is available. Q P (248)

Hailsham

George Hotel L ✔
3 George Street, BN27 1AD
8am-1am (midnight Fri & Sat); 8am-11 Sun
☎ (01323) 445120
Greene King Abbot; Ruddles Best Bitter; Sharp's Doom Bar; 2 changing beers (sourced nationally) [H]
A well-run Wetherspoon's with inexpensive ales, ciders and food, served all day to a high standard. Up to 12 real ciders, poured at optimum temperature from a dedicated cool room, helped the George win CAMRA's branch Cider and Perry Pub of the Year award in 2017, 2018 and 2019. The range of real ales includes at least one LocAle. Outside seating is provided on a side terrace and a quieter enclosed patio at the rear.
Q

Hastings

Albion L
33 George Street, Old Town, TN34 3EA
12-11 (midnight Fri & Sat) ☎ (01424) 439156
albionhastings.com
Harvey's Sussex Best Bitter; Three Legs English IPA; 2 changing beers (often Bedlam) [H]
First licensed for drinks in 1730, this spacious and tastefully refurbished former hotel has a stage for live music, beautifully designed bar tops and stylish furniture. There is a bar which can act as a small function room, plus a separate larger bar. Four Sussex real ales are served along with up to six changing real ciders from Sussex and Kent. Excellent food includes a selection of pies with unusual fillings. Outside is a large paved seating area on Marine Parade. Q

Dolphin L ✔
11-12 Rock-A-Nore Road, Old Town, TN34 3DW
10-11 (midnight Fri); 9am-midnight Sat; 9am-11 Sun
☎ (01424) 434326
Dark Star Hophead; Harvey's Sussex Best Bitter; Young's Special; 3 changing beers (sourced nationally) [H]
An 18th-century traditional family-run pub in Hastings Old Town. It has long links to the local fishing community – witness the memorabilia and old photographs that adorn the walls. The south-facing outside area overlooks the famous fishermen's huts, and is popular with tourists and locals alike. Fish is often sourced locally and the menu now offers breakfast every day and a roast on Sunday. Local CAMRA Branch Community Pub of the Year 2018. Q

First In Last Out L
14-15 High Street, Old Town, TN34 3EY (near Stables Theatre)
12-11; 11-midnight Fri & Sat ☎ (01424) 425079
thefilo.co.uk
FILO Crofters, Churches Pale Ale, Old Town Tom, Gold; 1 changing beer (sourced regionally) [H]
A popular Old Town pub serving six cask beers, mainly from its own nearby brewery. In winter a central open fire gives a cosy warmth. Good food is served in the restaurant area at the back, Monday is tapas night and Thursday thali. Live music features on Tuesday and Thursday; Jazz Sunday is once a month – check the website for details. The council car park to the rear, entered from the Bourne, has pedestrian access to the pub via an alley. Q

John Logie Baird ✔
29-31 Havelock Road, TN34 1BE
8am-midnight (1am Fri & Sat); 8am-11 Sun
☎ (01424) 448110
Greene King Abbot; Ruddles Best Bitter; 6 changing beers [H]
A typical large and busy town-centre Wetherspoon's pub with real ales on the bar at all times from up to 10 handpumps. As many as four changing real ciders are usually stocked in one of the large refrigerated units behind the bar. The pub holds a cider festival as well as the regular Wetherspoon beer festivals.

White Rock Hotel L
White Rock, TN34 1JU (opp pier)
10-11; 12-11 Sun ☎ (01424) 422240
4 changing beers [H]
On the seafront, next-door to the White Rock Theatre and opposite the award-winning pier, the hotel welcomes non-residents as well as leisure and business guests. Its spacious contemporary ground-floor café bar offers up to four regularly changing beers from Sussex breweries, as well as

light snacks every day 7am-10pm; a dinner menu is served 5.30-9.30pm. There is a superb seafront terrace and a new downstairs bar open on Friday and Saturday. Q P

Hove

Blind Busker

75-77 Church Road, BN3 2BB
10-midnight (1am Fri & Sat); 11-11 Sun
(01273) 749110 blindbuskerhove.co.uk
Greene King Abbot; Ringwood Razorback; 4 changing beers (sourced regionally) H
Traditional pub with many rooms, on the eastern edge of the main shopping area. A new large secluded back garden with plenty of seating and a big screen was part of a major refurbishment, as was a wheelchair ramp and accessible toilets. The pavement area outside has plenty of seating. An extensive menu is now available, with a special lunchtime menu Monday to Friday. Beers are constantly changing, with reduced prices for all ales on Tuesday. Dogs are welcome.
♿

Foghorn

55 Boundary Road, BN3 4EF
closed Mon; 12-2, 5-9.30; 12-11 Fri & Sat; 12-5 Sun
(01273) 419362 thefoghornmicro.com
5 changing beers (sourced regionally; often Dark Star, Thornbridge) G
Situated on the busy corner of New Church Road and Boundary Road, the Foghorn is a quiet haven for drinkers. Opened in December 2018, this enterprise soon became a go-to venue with its wide-ranging selection of beers. The new owners are happy to help and advise. The cellar sits just behind the bar and can be viewed through a glass partition. Furniture and decor is best described as minimalist. Q ♿

Neptune Inn L

10 Victoria Terrace, BN3 2WB (on coast road E of King Alfred leisure complex)
12-1am (2am Fri & Sat); 12-midnight Sun
(01273) 736390 theneptunelivemusicbar.co.uk
Dark Star Hophead; Greene King Abbot; Harvey's Sussex Best Bitter; 2 changing beers (sourced regionally) H
No-frills single-bar Victorian pub close to the King Alfred centre and Hove seafront. A reclining figure of Neptune rests above the old Courage signage at the front. Five beers are sold including two changing guests. Children are welcome until 8pm. Live music features strongly, with blues or rock every Friday and jazz on Sunday; see website for details. Dog-friendly. (700)

Watchmaker's Arms

84 Goldstone Villas, BN3 3RU
closed Mon; 12-2, 5-9 (11 Fri); 12-11 Sat; 12-3 Sun
(01273) 776307 thewatchmakersarms.co.uk
5 changing beers (sourced regionally; often Brighton Bier, Downlands, Hammerpot) G
This micro is handy for Hove station. The clock theme is recognised, with old watches and timepieces on the wall – not always correct! A small on-site brewery is now in full swing and the output can be sampled here. Pizzas can be ordered from a local takeaway, for consumption at the tall tables and benches which line the walls. Otherwise, sausage rolls and scratchings are the fare. Q (7,21)

Icklesham

Queen's Head L

Parsonage Lane, TN36 4BL (opp village hall)
11-11; 12-10.30 Sun (01424) 814552
queenshead.com
Greene King Abbot; Harvey's Sussex Best Bitter; 4 changing beers (sourced locally; often Hardys & Hansons) H
A 17th-century free house set in beautiful Sussex countryside at the edge of a village halfway between Hastings and Rye. The large garden has sweeping views over the Brede Valley to Winchelsea and Rye and is a popular stop for those walking the 1066 footpath which runs nearby. Locally sourced food is a feature of the extensive and popular menu. There is a pétanque piste at the back of the pub. ♣ P (100)

Isfield

Laughing Fish L

Station Road, TN22 5XB (off A26 between Lewes and Uckfield)
11.30-10 (01825) 750349 laughingfishisfield.com
Dark Star Hophead; Greene King IPA; Hardys & Hansons Olde Trip; Long Man Best Bitter; 2 changing beers (sourced regionally; often Holler, Oakham) H
Formerly the Half Moon, then the Station Hotel, this 1860s pub is next to the preserved Lavender Line. WWII brought the custom of Canadian troops, not without incident. In the 1950s the pub was the headquarters of the local angling club, the probable origin of its current name. Beers from the Greene King portfolio are dispensed alongside guests from other Sussex breweries. Good pub food is served. Games including bar billiards are played, and a quiz is held on the first Sunday of the month.
♿ ♣ P (29,29B)

Jevington

Eight Bells L

High Street, BN26 5QB
11-10.30; 12-9 Sun (01323) 484442
theeightbellsjevington.co.uk
Dark Star Hophead; Hardys & Hansons Olde Trip; Harvey's Sussex Best Bitter; 1 changing beer H
This picturesque village pub is on the South Downs Way and popular with walkers. Its interior is traditionally decorated, and made cosy by a real fire. Traditional pub food is offered, with some good vegetarian options. The pub often holds live music events and has a separate function room for hire. The large, well-kept garden provides fantastic views of the surrounding countryside.
♿ ♣ P (41)

Lewes

Black Horse

55 Western Road, BN7 1RS
11-11; 12-10.30 Sun (01273) 473653
theblackhorselewes.co.uk
Burning Sky Plateau; Greene King Abbot; Morland Old Speckled Hen; house beer (by Greene King); 3 changing beers (sourced regionally; often Dark Star, Franklins, Old Dairy) H
A Greene King Local Hero pub that allows the licensee to source and stock Sussex ales and produce. This traditional community pub in the western end of the town has feature bay windows

and a large main bar with a real fire, plus a quieter back bar. Two TVs show major sporting events. Home-made food includes vegan options. The pub's teams play a wide variety of games including toad in the hole and crib.
(28,29)

Brewers Arms

91 High Street, BN7 1XN (near Lewes Castle)
10-11; 12-10.30 Sun (01273) 475524
brewersarmslewes.co.uk
Harvey's Sussex Best Bitter; 4 changing beers (sourced regionally; often Burning Sky, Gun, Holler)
This pub's two bars have distinct characteristics: the front one is quiet and food-oriented; the back bar hosts sports TV, darts and pool. Food, including traditional breakfasts, is served until 8pm. An annual beer festival is held. The pub has a dwyle flunking team and is also popular on match days with supporters of Lewes FC, Brighton & Hove Albion and away teams. Exterior features commemorate Page & Overton's Brewery, the former owner. (28,29)

Elephant & Castle

White Hill, BN7 2DJ (off Fisher St, near old police station)
11.30-11 (midnight Fri & Sat); 12-11 Sun
(01273) 473797
Harvey's Sussex Best Bitter; 3 changing beers (sourced nationally)
Spacious pub with three rooms, which allow it to show football, rugby and other sports in different areas. On Thursday a large selection of bottled and canned craft beer is offered at takeaway prices for consumption on the premises. The food is locally sourced. The pub is home to many clubs, including the Commercial Bonfire Society. A large upstairs function room is available for hire.
(127,132)

Gardener's Arms

46 Cliffe High Street, BN7 2AN
11-11; 12-10.30 Sun (01273) 474808
Harvey's Sussex Best Bitter; 5 changing beers (sourced regionally; often Harvey's)
Traditional single-roomed free house near Harvey's Brewery, featuring a wooden floor and central bar. Five changing guest ales are dispensed, generally from small breweries across the country; a real cider is always available. The pub is popular with Lewes and Brighton FC supporters on match days. Its food consists of locally made pies and pasties. A dark beer festival is held in March. Children are not allowed. Dogs are especially welcome.
(28,29)

Lansdown Arms

36 Lansdown Place, BN7 2JU
12-11 (midnight Fri); 11.30-midnight Sat
(01273) 470711
Harvey's Sussex Best Bitter; Timothy Taylor Landlord; 2 changing beers (sourced locally; often Gun, Long Man)
Close to the railway station at the foot of a steep hill, this smallish pub is popular with fans and visitors to both Lewes FC and Brighton & Hove Albion on match days. The dark and cosy pub was built in 1827, before the arrival of the railway in Lewes, and was at one time a Whitbread house. It regularly hosts popular live music, featuring local bands, and has a free jukebox. Local artists' work is displayed on the walls.

Lewes Arms

1 Mount Place, BN7 1YH
11.30-11 (midnight Fri); 11-midnight Sat; 12-11 Sun
(01273) 473152
Dark Star Hophead; Fuller's London Pride; Gale's Seafarers Ale, HSB; Harvey's Sussex Best Bitter; 2 changing beers (sourced regionally; often Adnams, Everards)
Corner pub featuring three small rooms plus a central lobby with a serving hatch. An upstairs function room contains a small theatre stage. Good food is served, including excellent Sunday lunches. The pub is home to the world pea throwing championship, dwyle flunking, spaniel racing and other unusual events. Toad in the hole is also played. An annual pantomime is hosted in March, and a three-day music festival in August.
Q (28,29)

Snowdrop Inn

119 South Street, BN7 2BU
12-midnight; 12-11 Sun (01273) 471018
thesnowdropinn.pub
Harvey's Sussex Best Bitter; 3 changing beers (sourced locally; often Burning Sky)
On the outer edge of the Cliffe area of this historic town, the Snowdrop is a popular and welcoming free house. It serves six cask ales and one cider, plus four often unusual beers on KeyKeg. There is a central bar, with additional seating upstairs and two outside drinking areas. The pub is family-friendly and serves good home-cooked food all day. Monday is jazz night, and music features on most Saturdays. A beer festival is held in October.
(28,29)

Litlington

Plough & Harrow

The Street, BN26 5RE
11.30-11; 12-10.30 Sun (01323) 870632
ploughandharrowlitlington.co.uk
Long Man Best Bitter; 4 changing beers (sourced locally)
Village local with six handpumps on the bar, in a building whose original parts date back to the 17th century. The pub generally offers a good range of beers from local brewers, including the Long Man Brewery which is just down the road. High-quality food is served daily and is enjoyed both by locals and walkers on the South Downs.
P

Newhaven

Hope Inn

West Pier, BN9 9DN (follow signs for Newhaven Fort; pub is 200yds further on)
11-10.30 (midnight Wed); 11-midnight Fri & Sat
(01273) 515389 hopeinnnewhaven.co.uk
Harvey's Sussex Best Bitter; 2 changing beers (sourced regionally)
A family-run pub at the far end of the western side of Newhaven harbour, from where there are scenic views along the coastline towards Seaford Head. The interior abounds with all things nautical, including many old pictures of the harbour. The bar has various areas leading off it, in which refreshment, liquid or otherwise, may be partaken. An annual beer festival is held in August. There is an interesting beer mat collection in the gents' toilet. P

Newick

Crown Inn

22 Church Road, BN8 4JX
12 (3 Mon & Tue)-11 ☎ (01825) 723293
thecrownatnewick.co.uk
Harvey's Sussex Best Bitter; 3 changing beers (sourced regionally)
Located at the southern end of the village, near the post office, this family-run free house has a central bar with two smaller rooms off to either side, and a pleasant garden to the rear. Good-value meals are served using local produce. The 121 bus stops just round the corner. Newick has two other pubs on its village green and is well worth a whole afternoon's stay, but do not miss the last bus!
P (31,121)

Pett

Two Sawyers

Pett Road, TN35 4HB
11-midnight ☎ (01424) 812255 twosawyers.co.uk
Harvey's Sussex Best Bitter; Ringwood Fortyniner; 3 changing beers
Situated in a typically picturesque Sussex village, this pub has a clientele consisting of friendly locals and visitors from around the world, many taking advantage of the superb country walks in the area. The pub, a warren of rooms, many with low half-timbered ceilings and log fires, is well known for its good, locally sourced food. Reservations for dining are recommended. There is a pétanque piste in the pub's extensive grounds. Real cider is available in the summer only. P (347)

Polegate

Dinkum

54 High Street, BN26 6AG
11-11; 12-6 Sun ☎ (01323) 482106
Harvey's Sussex Best Bitter; 2 changing beers
Lively and friendly Harvey's tied house in Polegate's centre, serving three of the brewery's ales. The pub has a loyal core of locals, many of whom gather for important sports events shown in one of the two bars. There is plenty of couch seating around tables; patrons often organise card games taking advantage of this layout. Pizzas and warm flatbreads are available along with typical pub snacks. P

Portslade

Stag's Head

35 High Street, Old Portslade, BN41 2LH
12-3, 4.30-11; 12-11.30 Fri & Sat; 12-10 Sun
☎ (01273) 416058
Harvey's Sussex Best Bitter; Long Man American Pale Ale; 3 changing beers (sourced nationally; often Brains, Goddards)
Originally named the Bull, this pub dates from the 16th century. It stands in the shadow of John Dudney's magnificent 1881 brewery, to which it was allegedly linked by a tunnel fitted with rails to allow the rolling of barrels. The brewery was closed in 1930. The pub was enlarged in 1959, with the adjacent cottage becoming the saloon bar. The interior shows little sign of the pub's age but some evidence of Watneyisation remains.
Q (1,1A)

Stanley Arms

47 Wolseley Road, BN41 1SS (on corner of Wolseley Rd and Stanley Rd)
4 (3 Thu & Fri; 12 Sat)-11; 12-10.30 Sun ☎ (01273) 973531
5 changing beers (sourced regionally; often Downlands, Long Man, Sharp's)
An excellent street-corner local, recently under new ownership but unchanged otherwise, tucked away in a residential area. It is a genuine free house with a changing range of beers and ciders, along with British and foreign bottled beers. A large TV shows football, rugby and other sports. The first Monday of the month is cellar night, featuring reduced-price beers and free nibbles. The pub hosts occasional live music plus weekly quiz and crib nights. Q (2,46)

Rye

Waterworks

Tower Street, TN31 7AT
2 (12 Sat & Sun)-11 summer; 2-10 (11 Fri); 12-11 Sat; 12-10 Sun winter ☎ (01797) 224110
8 changing beers (sourced locally)
In a building dating from 1718, this former pump house, soup kitchen, public toilet and antique shop opened in May 2018 as a micropub serving local ales, ciders and soft drinks, all sourced within a 22-mile radius of Rye. As the area's first micropub it has had a big impact on the local community. It currently stocks eight ales and 12 ciders. Food includes pork pies and Scotch eggs with chutney, all home-made. Q

Ypres Castle Inn

Gun Garden, TN31 7HH (can be accessed from A259 up a flight of steps; for fewer steps approach from Church Square)
12-11 (midnight Fri; 10.30 Sun) Apr-Oct; closed Mon; 12-11 (10.30 Sun) Nov-Mar ☎ (01797) 223248
yprescastleinn.co.uk
Old Dairy Uber Brew; Rother Valley Level Best; 2 changing beers (sourced locally)
The Wipers is an attractive weatherboarded pub dating from 1640. Its outside drinking areas include part of the top of the town ramparts, giving fantastic views across Romney Marsh down the river estuary. The large bar room has an open fire; an adjoining room is used for functions. Cider and perry comes from nearby Nightingale's. The food menu usually includes locally sourced seafood. Live music, mainly acoustic, is performed on Sunday afternoon. Closed on Monday in winter.

St Leonards on Sea

Tower

251 London Road, Bohemia, TN37 6NB
11-11.30 (12.30am Fri & Sat); 11-11 Sun
☎ (01424) 721773
Dark Star Hophead, American Pale Ale; 4 changing beers (sourced nationally)
Up to six reasonably priced ales and eight ciders are served in this popular, award-winning community pub. It has a convivial atmosphere, with a wood-burning stove, and shows all the main football, cricket and rugby matches on HD screens. There is also a pool table. An annual beer festival is held, usually in February, and occasional trips are arranged to breweries and sporting events.

Salehurst

Salehurst Halt L
Church Lane, TN32 5PH (by church)
🕙 closed Mon; 12-11 ☎ (01580) 880620
🌐 salehursthalt.co.uk
Harvey's Sussex Best Bitter; 2 changing beers (sourced locally) 🅗
Established in 1837, this charming, dog-friendly pub is the heart of the village. Three excellent real ales are served, normally alongside local ciders. A quirky menu of exceptional fresh, home-cooked food is available; booking is advisable. On summer Wednesday evenings fresh-baked pizza is served from the wood-fired oven outside. An upstairs function room, opened in 2019, can be used as a restaurant. The garden offers lovely views over the tranquil Rother Valley. Q🏡❀◐◑&♣●❀❅

Seaford

Old Boot Inn
16 South Street, BN25 1PE
🕙 10-11 (midnight Fri & Sat); 11-10.30 Sun
☎ (01323) 895454
Harvey's Sussex Best Bitter; 4 changing beers (sourced regionally; often Dark Star, Harvey's, Thornbridge) 🅗
This deceptively large pub, under the same ownership as the Gardener's Arms in Lewes, has entrances in both South Street and the High Street. Harvey's Best Bitter is always to be found on one of the six handpumps, along with Old Ale in season. Four different guests and six bag-in-box ciders complete the range. The pub has plenty of tables and serves food, including a wide range of roasts on Sunday. Wheelchair access is possible.
🏡❀◐◑&♣●❀❅

Steamworks L
Cafe Unit, Seaford Station, Station Approach, BN25 2AR
🕙 8am-11 (midnight Fri); 9.30am-11 Sat; 12-10 Sun
☎ 07541 858999
3 changing beers (sourced locally) 🅖
Right on the station platform, the Steamworks is a two-room buffet bar which is busy with coffee service to the early morning commuters and then becomes a micropub with three interesting beers, using an unusual gravity system. The decor and furniture is distressed industrial sanded-down woodwork, as if the Ragged-Trousered Philanthropists had only recently left! The toilet is down the platform, with the key hanging left of the door. Food is pasties. Q&≠●❀

Uckfield

Alma Arms L
65 Framfield Road, TN22 5AJ (on B2102)
🕙 11-11 (11.30 Fri & Sat); 12-10.30 Sun ☎ (01825) 762232
🌐 almaarmsuckfield.co.uk
Harvey's Sussex XX Mild Ale, Sussex Best Bitter; 2 changing beers (often Harvey's) 🅗
A Harvey's tied pub which dates from 1851, named after the Crimean Battle of the Alma in 1854. The town centre, bus and train stations are all within easy walking distance of this popular town pub. Westons Rosie's Pig is the regular draught cider. A weekly quiz is held on Thursday and there is a monthly acoustic session. No food is served on Monday or Tuesday.
Q🏡❀◐◑&≠♣●P🚃(31)❀❅

Westfield

New Inn L
Main Road, TN35 4QE
🕙 12-11 (11.30 Sat); 12-8 Sun ☎ (01424) 752800
🌐 newinnwestfield.com
4 changing beers (sourced locally) 🅗
Situated in the heart of the village, this friendly community-focused pub offers a warm welcome to all. Beers from New Inn House Brew and Rother Valley are usually on, together with other changing ales, often local, from the four handpumps. Following complete refurbishment in 2015, the pub has a modern light and airy feel, as has its conservatory which serves as a restaurant. Good home-cooked, locally sourced food is available at reasonable prices; booking is advisable to avoid disappointment. Q🏡❀◐◑&P🚃❀❅

SUSSEX (WEST)

Amberley

Bridge Inn L ✓
Houghton Bridge, BN18 9LR (on B2139 just W of railway bridge at Amberley station)
🕙 11-11; 12-9 Sun ☎ (01798) 831619
🌐 bridgeinnamberley.com
Harvey's Sussex Best Bitter; Long Man Long Blonde; 1 changing beer (sourced nationally; often Timothy Taylor) 🅗
Close to the South Downs Way and Amberley railway station, this Grade II-listed inn dispenses three real ales. Its interior has a single cosy bar and open log fires. A large dining area to the side serves mainly locally sourced home-cooked produce. There is a patio at the front and an attractive gated garden to the side.
Q🏡❀◐◑≠P🚃(73)❀❅

Balcombe

Half Moon
Haywards Heath Road, RH17 6PA
🕙 12-10 (midnight Fri & Sat); 12-9 Sun ☎ (01444) 811582
Harvey's Sussex Best Bitter; 3 changing beers (sourced locally; often Bedlam, Dark Star, Long Man) 🅗
A small, food-led pub with tables in the lower part as you enter, and the bar beyond up a couple of steps. This is north Sussex's first community-owned pub. Its four handpumps normally dispense Harvey's Sussex Best, a beer from High Weald and two rotating guests, which are mostly local. The pub also serves a varied range of locally sourced meals. 🏡◐◑≠●P❀❅

Billingshurst

King's Head L ✓
40 High Street, RH14 9NY
🕙 11-11 (midnight Fri & Sat); 12-11 Sun ☎ (01403) 782012
Hogs Back TEA; 7 changing beers (sourced locally; often Firebird, Kissingate, Weltons) 🅗
Formerly an Enterprise pub, this is now a free house and enjoying a resurgence after many years out of the Guide. It offers a wide range of real ales from its eight handpumps, many from local breweries. This is a large town-centre establishment dating from the 18th century, with plenty of space for drinkers and diners. It is a great place for watching sport. 🏡❀◐◑P🚃(100)❀❅

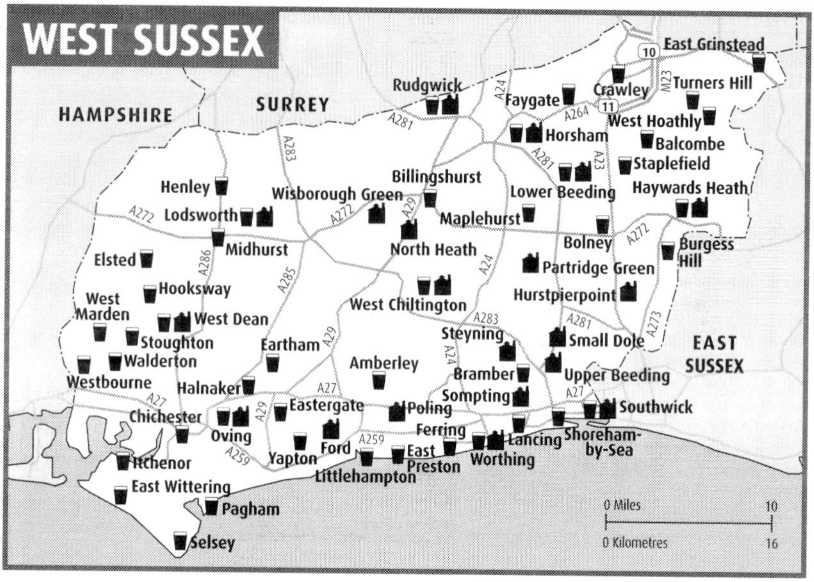

Bolney

Bolney Stage

London Road, RH17 5RL
11-11; 11-10.30 Sun (01444) 881200
6 changing beers
This place dates back to the 16th century, on the old A23 coaching route. It has a large bar area with three separate dining sections and a beer garden. The rooms feature huge inglenook fireplaces, ancient flagstones, open-timbered ceilings and crooked beams, together with comfy old furniture. A blackboard by the bar gives tasting notes on the four regularly changing beers, which are mostly from Sussex breweries. P (273)

Bramber

Castle Inn Hotel

The Street, BN44 3WE (just off A283, near S Steyning roundabout)
11-11; 11-10.30 Sun (01903) 812102
castleinnhotel.co.uk
Downlands Bramber; Harvey's Sussex Best Bitter; Sharp's Doom Bar; 1 changing beer (sourced locally; often Dark Star, Riverside)
Set in a rural Sussex village, this historic inn has been called the Castle Inn Hotel since Victorian times, and there has been a coaching house or inn on the site since the early 13th century. The oldest part of the current building dates back to the 17th century. This is a family-run pub and 3-star B&B with local ales and good food on offer. There is a picturesque garden at the rear with a stream flowing through it. Q P

Burgess Hill

Quench Bar & Kitchen

2-4 Church Road, RH15 9AE
9am-11 (12.30am Fri; 1am Sat); 10-10.30 Sun
(01444) 253332 quenchbar.co.uk
Harvey's Sussex Best Bitter; 2 changing beers (sourced locally; often Downlands, Franklins)
Within sight of the railway station, this bar occupies a location at the top end of the town's original shopping street. It comprises a bar area together with a comfortable lounge. Quality local beers prevail, together with a range of bottled ales, spirits, teas and espresso coffees. Occasional live music events and beer festivals are held. A limited number of tables and chairs are provided outside. All buses that serve Burgess Hill pass by the door.

Chichester

Chichester Inn

38 West Street, PO19 1RP (at Westgate roundabout)
12-11.30; 12-6 Sun (01243) 783185
chichesterinn.co.uk
Harvey's Sussex Best Bitter; Vibrant Forest Summerlands; 2 changing beers (sourced regionally; often Staggeringly Good, Vibrant Forest)
Pleasant two-bar pub with a real fire in the front bar surrounded by comfortable chairs, with a mix of seating and table types elsewhere. There is a strong emphasis on LocAles. Food includes Sunday lunches. The larger public bar to the rear features regular live music on Wednesday, Friday and Saturday evening. Outside is an attractive walled garden with a heated and covered smoking area. Four B&B rooms are available.
P

Eastgate

4 The Hornet, PO19 7JG (500yds E of Market Cross)
11-11; 10-1am Sat; 11-11.30 Sun (01243) 774877
Fuller's London Pride; Gale's Seafarers Ale, HSB; 2 changing beers (sourced nationally; often Adnams, Dark Star, Fuller's)
Welcoming town pub with an open-plan bar and tables for diners. Good-quality traditional pub meals are served daily. There is a heated patio garden to the rear, which is the venue for a beer festival in July. The pub attracts locals, holidaymakers and shoppers from the nearby market, with a warm welcome and traditional pub games such as darts, cribbage and pool. Music is

turned up on Friday and Saturday late evenings. Live bands perform once a month.
♣(51,700)

Hornet Alehouse

23 The Hornet, PO19 7JL (from market cross head due E)
12 (4 Mon & Tue)-9.30 ☎ (01243) 696387
thehornetalehouse.co.uk
5 changing beers (sourced nationally; often Downlands, Siren) G
Busy split-level micropub with plenty of standing room at the bar in addition to seating both downstairs and upstairs. The upstairs room has board games and hosts twice-monthly quiz nights and monthly Meet the Brewer events. Friendly, knowledgeable staff will make tasters available. Four ciders are always stocked alongside four craft keg taps. A wonderful addition to the city, the pub is a mecca with its changing range of cask ales, served from a temperature-controlled cool room. Sussex CAMRA Pub of the Year 2019.
Q♣(700)

Crawley

Brewery Shades

85 High Street, RH10 1BA
10-11.30 (1.30am Fri & Sat) ☎ (01293) 514255
Dark Star Revelation; Greene King Abbot; 8 changing beers H
Possibly the oldest building in Crawley High Street, dating back to the 1400s and complete with two active ghosts. The pub is wet-sales led. The licensee has a true passion for the trade, demonstrated by the inspired range of guest ales and ciders which are always in excellent condition. The haunted upstairs room is now available for meetings. Good food is served during the day and evening – check the specials board.

Eartham

George

PO18 0LT (turn N off A27 at Crockerhill or W of Fontwell and proceed 2 miles to centre of village)
closed Mon; 11.30-11; 12-6 Sun ☎ (01243) 814340
thegeorgeeartham.com
House beer (by Otter); 3 changing beers (sourced locally; often Downlands, Gun, Langham) H
A tastefully refurbished old village pub whose landlord's passion for the best of English, and especially Sussex, extends to the entire drinks and food menu. All changing beers are LocAle and always include one from Langham. Usually one is a hoppy golden brew while another is a porter, old ale or mild. The food menu has locally sourced ingredients. Popular with walkers and cyclists, the pub holds a beer festival in its garden each April featuring LocAles and live music.
Q♿▲P(99)

East Grinstead

Old Dunnings Mill

Dunnings Road, RH19 4AT
11-11 ☎ (01342) 821080 olddunningsmill.co.uk
Harvey's Sussex Best Bitter, Armada Ale; 2 changing beers (often Harvey's) H
Large, family- and pet-friendly pub on the edge of town, based on an old water mill. Separate bar and restaurant areas are on various levels; the main ones are accessible by wheelchair. A heated covered area to the rear has a working water wheel. Although this is basically a quiet pub, music is played on appropriate occasions. Two beer festivals a year are planned. Q♿P(84)

East Preston

Clockhouse Bar

103-105 Sea Road, BN16 1NX (beach end of village, opp green)
12-11 (11.30 Fri & Sat); 12-10 Sun ☎ (01903) 788367
theclockhousebarep.co.uk
St Austell Tribute; 2 changing beers (sourced locally; often Hammerpot) H
This former bank building, dating from 1929, has plenty of character and its own deli next door. The working clock above the pub is a retained war memorial; inside there are many different types of clock on the walls. The interior features cork-style tables and a raised level with comfy seating. The emphasis is on local ales, with Hammerpot brews a regular. Guest beers from other regions add to the variety. Q(700)

East Wittering

Shore

Shore Road, PO20 8DZ (50yds from sea)
11-11; 11-10.30 Sun ☎ (01243) 674454
theshorepub.co.uk
Castle Rock Elsie Mo; Dark Star Hophead; Hop Back Summer Lightning; Palmers Copper Ale, Dorset Gold; Sharp's Doom Bar; 1 changing beer (sourced regionally; often Dark Star) H
Friendly beachside pub popular with the locals, particularly dog owners, and the many summer visitors. Outside seating affords splendid sea views. There are two main bars, a children's area and a fair-sized space for outside drinking as well as smoking. The good-quality lunchtime menu can be enjoyed in either the bar or restaurant, with

REAL ALE BREWERIES

81 Artisan West Dean
Adur Steyning
Arundel Ford
Bestens Lower Beeding (NEW)
Brew Studio Sompting
Brewhouse & Kitchen Horsham (NEW)
Brolly Wisborough Green
Chapeau Brewing Horsham
Dark Star Partridge Green
Downlands Small Dole
Firebird Rudgwick
Goldmark Poling
Greyhound West Chiltington
Gribble Oving
Hammerpot Poling
Heathen Haywards Heath
Hepworth North Heath
Hurst Hurstpierpoint
Kissingate Lower Beeding
Langham Lodsworth
Lister's Ford
Pin-Up Southwick
Polarity Worthing
Ridgeway North Heath
Riverside Upper Beeding
Top-Notch Haywards Heath
Weltons Horsham

extremely inviting dishes on offer at fair prices. Live music plays occasionally – see website for details. QP(52,53)

Eastergate

Wilkes' Head

Church Lane, PO20 3UT (off A29 in old village, 350yds S of B2233 roundabout, 1¼ miles W of Barnham station) SU943053

12-11 ☎ (01243) 543380

Adnams Southwold Bitter; 5 changing beers (sourced nationally; often Bedlam, Downlands, Langham) H

Small Grade II-listed red-brick pub, built in 1803 and named after 18th-century radical John Wilkes. There is a cosy lounge left of the central bar and to the right a larger room with inglenook fireplace, flagstones and low beams, plus a separate restaurant. At the rear is a permanent marquee with seating plus a heated smokers' shelter and a large garden. Five well-chosen changing beers are served. Regular beer festivals are held. QP

Elsted

Three Horseshoes

GU29 0JY (at E end of village)

11-2.30, 6-11; 12-3, 7-10.30 Sun ☎ (01730) 825746

3hs.co.uk

Bowman Wallops Wood H/G**; Flowerpots Bitter; Young's Bitter; 2 changing beers (sourced locally; often Hop Back, Langham, Red Cat)** G

Old and cosy rural inn divided into small rooms, including one reserved for dining and one with a blazing wood-burning stove in winter. Five beers are offered in summer, mainly from local micros, and three in winter, all served by gravity from a stillage alongside the bar. Meals are substantial and of high quality. The large, pleasant garden enjoys superb views of the South Downs. This is a popular and homely pub that you will be reluctant to leave. QP

Faygate

Frog & Nightgown

Wimland Road, RH12 4SS

5-10 Mon; 10.30-11; 12-7 Sun ☎ (01293) 852764

thefrogandnightgown.co.uk

Fuller's London Pride; 3 changing beers (sourced regionally; often Dark Star, Harvey's) H

Coral and Ritchie bought the pub in December 2015 and spent several months refurbishing it. Now run by their son Lewis, it is known as the fastest pub in West Sussex due to its motorsport connections. Regular events include classic car meets, quiz nights, live music and open mic sessions. Street food is often available on a Friday night. QP

Ferring

Henty Arms

2 Ferring Lane, BN12 6QY (just N of level crossing)

11-11 (midnight Fri & Sat); 12-11 Sun ☎ (01903) 241254

hentyarms.co.uk

Fuller's London Pride; Harvey's Sussex Best Bitter; St Austell Tribute; Sharp's Doom Bar; 1 changing beer H

The pub was constructed on the present site in 1830, which predates the nearby railway line. It was then called the New Inn and renamed the Henty Arms in 1927. There are two separate bars. Pool and darts can be played in the public bar, where a large TV screen shows live sport. Outside are three beer gardens, which come in useful for the annual beer festival in July. A quiz is held on Sunday night. P

Halnaker

Anglesey Arms

Stane Street, PO18 0NQ (on A285)

11-3, 5.30-11; 11-11 Fri & Sat; 12-7 Sun

☎ (01243) 773474 angleseyarms.com

Harvey's Sussex Best Bitter; Young's Bitter; 2 changing beers (sourced locally; often Arundel, Hammerpot, Langham) H

Family-run, Grade II-listed Georgian pub close to the Goodwood Estate, which owns the freehold. There is a wood and flagstone-floored public bar with a log fire, plus a comfortable restaurant renowned for good food made with local produce (reservation essential). Two local SIBA guest beers are usually available. Dogs are welcome. The large rear garden with pétanque court is popular for wedding receptions and classic car meetings, as well as regular boules matches in summer. QP(55,99)

Haywards Heath

Lockhart Tavern

41 The Broadway, RH16 3AS

12-11; 11-11 Sat; 12-7 Sun ☎ (01444) 440696

6 changing beers (sourced nationally; often 360 Degree Brewing, Pig & Porter) H

Centrally located café-style pub, formerly tied to the local Dark Star Brewery, which is popular without being noisy. There is a bar area at the front with a wood-panelled eating area behind, and a few picnic tables outside on a patio. Good food is served for both lunch and dinner; the menu changes regularly. Usually, six handpumps dispense real ale and there is a choice of wine, keg beers, cans and bottles.

Henley

Duke of Cumberland

GU27 3HQ (off A286, 2 miles N of Midhurst) SU894258

11-11; 12-10.30 Sun ☎ (01428) 652280

dukeofcumberland.com

Harvey's Sussex Best Bitter; Langham Hip Hop; Timothy Taylor Landlord; 1 changing beer (sourced locally; often Langham) G

Stunning 15th-century inn nestling against the hillside in over three acres of terraced gardens with extensive views. The rustic front bar has scrubbed-top tables and benches, plus log fires at both ends, while to the rear is a dining extension that blends in perfectly with the original pub and offers much-needed additional space. Outside is a smokers' shelter with its own woodburner. A former local CAMRA Pub of the Year, this is a rural gem. May close winter Sunday evenings. QP(70)

Hooksway

Royal Oak

PO18 9JZ SU815163

closed Mon; 11.30-2.30 Tue-Thu; 11.30-2.30, 7-11 Fri & Sat; 12-3 Sun ☎ (01243) 535257 royaloakhooksway.co.uk

Langham Hip Hop; 3 changing beers (sourced nationally; often Arundel, Hammerpot) Ⓗ
An idyllic country pub, unspoilt and with great country walks, close to the South Downs Way. In winter two lovely log fires greet you. The extensive menu caters for all tastes, and includes a varied children's selection. Three permanent real ales and a regular guest are served, mainly from local breweries. There is a large garden with a play area for children. The pub is popular with hikers, horse riders and people with young families, and perfect for getting away from it all. Q❀◑◗P🐾

Horsham

Anchor Tap 🄻
16 East Street, RH12 1HL
closed Mon; 12-10.30; 12-11 Fri & Sat ☎ (01403) 274542
Dark Star Hophead, Partridge Best Bitter, American Pale Ale; 4 changing beers (sourced regionally) Ⓗ
Having been closed for 30 years, this pub was reopened in February 2016 by Dark Star Brewery and has been refurbished in an early 20th-century style. A much-welcome addition to the town's drinking establishments, it is popular with customers both local and from afar. The six handpumps offer Dark Star beers together with other ales from across the country, plus real cider. There is a back bar with 10 keg brews from Dark Star and other brewers. Bar snacks are served lunchtimes.

Black Jug
31 North Street, RH12 1RJ
11.30-11; 12-10.30 Sun ☎ (01403) 253526
blackjug-horsham.co.uk
Harvey's Sussex Best Bitter; Long Man Best Bitter; 3 changing beers (sourced nationally; often Marston's) Ⓗ
A large, bustling, town-centre pub, the Jug is something of a Horsham institution. Close to the railway station and arts complex, and with no intrusive music, it is a popular place to meet and chat. It has a welcoming interior with bookshelves, pictures, a fire and friendly, efficient staff. Two regular ales are available plus rotating guests and a cider. An extensive range of malt whiskies and gins is also kept. Excellent food is served all day.
Q

King's Arms 🄻
64 Bishopric, RH12 1QN
12-11 (midnight Fri & Sat) ☎ (01403) 451468
kingsarmshorsham.godaddysites.com
St Austell Tribute; 3 changing beers (sourced locally; often Chapeau Brewing, Hepworth, Weltons) Ⓗ
Situated in the Bishopric, near the town centre and close to the site of the former King & Barnes Brewery. A comfortable two-bar pub, it is an 18th-century coaching inn which has long been popular with locals. There are five handpulls with at least three rotating local ales, and a keg line which serves Brolly ale. Sport is shown on TV at the weekend. ❀◑◗

Malt Shovel 🄻
15 Springfield Road, RH12 2PG
11-11 Mon (midnight Tue-Thu; 1am Fri & Sat); 12-11 Sun
☎ (01403) 252302
6 changing beers Ⓗ
Located close to the town centre, the pub has six handpumps on year round, plus two ciders and a mix of bottled and canned ales. It has no regular beers, but instead features local brews and usually offers at least one dark ale. The pub hosts live music every Saturday night, as well as regular open mic and jam events. The landlord takes great pride in his real ale and his friendly staff have a similar approach. Good parking for a town-centre pub.
❀◑P🐾

Piries Bar 🄻
Piries Alley, The Carfax, RH12 1NY
11-midnight (1am Fri-Sun) ☎ (01403) 267846
Burning Sky Plateau; 2 changing beers (sourced locally; often Long Man) Ⓗ
In a building dating from the 15th century, with exposed original timber beams, this bar is well worth a visit. Tucked away down a narrow alley adjoining Horsham's Carfax, it comprises a small downstairs room, an upstairs lounge bar and a small, modern extension in character with the building. Two cask ales are always available. Regular charity events are organised. Evenings here can be lively, with karaoke on Sunday, quiz night on Tuesday and occasional live music.
◑🐾

Itchenor

Ship
The Street, PO20 7AH (on main street, 100yds from waterfront)
10-11 ☎ (01243) 512284 theshipinnitchenor.co.uk
Arundel Castle; Langham Hip Hop, Best; 1 changing beer (often Itchen Valley) Ⓗ
Popular pub in the main street of an attractive village on the shore of picturesque Chichester harbour. The cosy bar decorated with yachting memorabilia adds to the pub's character and is complemented by a pleasant patio that is a suntrap in summer. The separate restaurant area offers a wide range of meals, including local seafood. Accommodation is available in a two-bedroom apartment and a three-bedroom cottage.
Q❀◑◗P🐾

Lancing

Stanley Ale House 🄻
5 Queensway, BN15 9AY
12 (2 Mon)-10; 12-8 Sun ☎ (01903) 366820
thestanleyalehouse.com
Langham Arapaho; 3 changing beers (sourced regionally; often Downlands, Franklins) Ⓗ
This former launderette opened as a welcoming, family-oriented ale house in 2014. Located 200 yards north of the railway station, near local shops, it offers up to four changing ales plus ciders and craft beers. There is ample seating both inside and out. Bar snacks are available and you can bring in takeaways to eat. A variety of board games are played, and the pub hosts events including a weekly quiz and regular music nights.
Q◗🐾

Littlehampton

Arun View Inn
Wharf Road, BN17 5DD (turn right from station into Terminus Rd)
10.30-11 (midnight Fri & Sat); 12-10.30 Sun
☎ (01903) 722335 thearunview.co.uk
Fuller's London Pride; Long Man Long Blonde; 1 changing beer (often Arundel) Ⓗ

The inn is on the side of the River Arun, offering a relaxed venue for a quiet drink or meal. A selection of local and national ales are on the bar. Live music and events take place throughout the year. The relaxing and comfortable restaurant serves fresh, locally sourced food. There is a separate bridge bar offering live sport on large-screen TVs. The riverside patio is perfect for the summer.
🐴❀🛏◑⇌P🚌🐾

New Inn ✔

5 Norfolk Road, BN17 5PL (N from Sea Rd)
🕐 12-11 (midnight Fri & Sat); 12-10.30 Sun
☎ (01903) 713112 🌐 newinnla.co.uk
3 changing beers (sourced nationally) Ⓗ
A friendly community pub, offering three regularly changing ales, just a short walk from the beach. This traditional inn has two bar areas. The front one has ample seating, a real fire and hosts weekly pub quizzes and regular charity events; the rear one has a pool table and dartboard, and shows live sport. A free jukebox is a feature of Monday nights. There is a heated courtyard at the back. 🐴❀♣🚌🐾📶

Steam Packet 𝕃

54 River Road, BN17 5BZ
🕐 closed Mon; 5.30-11 Tue; 12-3, 5.30-11 Wed-Fri; 12-11 Sat; 12-10 Sun ☎ (01903) 715994
Fallen Acorn Pompey Royal; 3 changing beers (sourced locally; often Bedlam, Franklins, Vibrant Forest) Ⓗ
This pub has just the one pleasing, light and airy bar which makes good use of the available floor space. It overlooks the harbour and is near the river footbridge, a short distance from where a cross-channel steam packet ferry service operated from Littlehampton to Honfleur. All ales are from independent microbreweries, mainly locally sourced. Real ciders plus craft beer in cans are served. Fresh food is prepared on the premises, with vegetarian, vegan and allergies catered for.
❀🛏◑⇌🍎🚌(700)🐾

Lodsworth

Hollist Arms

The Street, GU28 9BZ (in village centre, 1 mile N of A272)
🕐 11-3.30, 5.30-11; 11-11 Sat ☎ (01798) 861310
🌐 thehollistarms.com
Dark Star Hophead; Timothy Taylor Landlord; 3 changing beers (often Langham) Ⓗ
Set in the village centre overlooking the green, the building was formed from two cottages in 1825. A small bar leads to a larger restaurant area serving home-cooked food all week. There is also a small snug with an inglenook fireplace. At the rear the raised beer garden has a barbecue area; in front there are seats on the green. The back car park houses the village's community shop.
Q❀◑♣P🐾📶

Lower Beeding

Kissingate Brewery

Pole Barn, Church Lane Farm Estate, Church Lane, RH13 6LU
🕐 11-6 (8 Fri; 3 Sat); closed Sun ☎ (01403) 891335
🌐 kissingate.co.uk
Kissingate Black Cherry Mild, Pernickety Pale, Chennai, Powder Blue; 2 changing beers (sourced locally) Ⓖ
This pub is the taproom for the renowned Kissingate Brewery. It offers a selection of beers from the Kissingate range served on gravity, plus cider and perry from Black Pig and JB. In addition to normal hours the tap is open until 9.30pm on the last Friday of the month. Various events including curry nights are held. There is a function area upstairs. ♿🍎P🗑

Maplehurst

White Horse 🏆 𝕃

Park Lane, RH13 6LL
🕐 6-11 Mon; 12-2.30, 6-11 (11.30 Fri & Sat); 12-3, 7-11 Sun
☎ (01403) 891208 🌐 whitehorsemaplehurst.co.uk
Weltons Pride 'n' Joy; 4 changing beers (often Harvey's, Hepworth, Kissingate) Ⓗ
Under the same ownership for 37 years, this splendid and welcoming country pub has featured in the Guide 34 times and remains popular with locals, cyclists and walkers. The cosy interior, with its unusually wide wooden bar, boasts real fires and many interesting artefacts and bric-a-brac. While good honest pub fare is provided, the emphasis is on beer and conversation. Many local brews feature, with a good selection of dark ales. Local JB cider is also served. Q🐴❀◑♣🍎P🐾📶

Midhurst

Swan 𝕃 ✔

Red Lion Street, GU29 9PB (opp church in Old Town)
🕐 12-midnight; 12-10 Sun ☎ (01730) 812853
🌐 theswaninn.pub
Harvey's Sussex Best Bitter; 1 changing beer (sourced locally) Ⓗ
This pub now has just one bar as the upstairs area has been given over exclusively to dining. During the week the only available beer may be Sussex Best but in spring, summer and at weekends there is also at least one changing ale, with all in great condition. The bar has a TV and silent quiz machines as well as a dartboard. Accommodation is in six en-suite rooms. There is limited public parking nearby. Q🐴❀🛏◑♣🚌(1,60)🐾📶

Oving

Gribble Inn 𝕃

Gribble Lane, PO20 2BP (at W end of village)
🕐 11-11; 12-11 Sun ☎ (01243) 786893 🌐 gribbleinn.co.uk
Gribble Sussex Quadhopper, Ale, Fuzzy Duck, Reg's Tipple, Lazy Buzzard, Pig's Ear Ⓗ
Once home to a Miss Gribble, this attractive thatched cottage has been a traditional village pub for over 30 years and shares the premises with the Gribble Brewery. The pub is cosy, with log fires in winter. The full range of Gribble regular beers is always available, complemented by seasonals. Home-made food is served in the bar/restaurant. In summer a large, attractive garden offers occasional weekend barbecues. The skittle alley is also available for functions.
Q🐴❀◑♿♣P🚌(85,85A)🐾📶

Pagham

Inglenook 𝕃

255 Pagham Road, PO21 3QB
🕐 11-11 (midnight Fri & Sat) ☎ (01243) 262495
🌐 the-inglenook.com

Fuller's London Pride; Young's Special; 4 changing beers (sourced nationally; often Brighton Bier, Dark Star, Staggeringly Good)

A 16th-century Grade II-listed hotel, restaurant and free house, owned and run by the Honour family for over 40 years. It always has a selection of excellent, well-hopped real ales from highly regarded microbreweries alongside local real ciders. The cosy bar areas have real fires. There is a large garden to the rear and a patio area at the front. Local CAMRA Pub of the Year 2017.
Q P (600)

Rudgwick

King's Head

Church Street, RH12 3EB
11.30-11; 11-11 Sun ☎ (01403) 822200
kingsheadrudgwick.co.uk
Crafty Brewing Crafty One; 2 changing beers (often Harvey's, Morland)

An 18th-century low-beamed pub at the northern end of the village. It is opposite the Norman church and in a conservation area. Food is freshly prepared and includes pizzas. The restaurant is at one end of the pub; the bar with its wood-burning stove and leather sofas at the other. The Downslink footpath passes nearby. Q P

Selsey

Crab Pot

145 High Street, PO20 0QB (opp Lloyds Bank)
closed Mon; 12 (4 Tue & Wed)-9.30; 12-5.30 Sun
☎ 07834 226751 crabpotmicropub.co.uk
3 changing beers (sourced locally; often Downlands, Vibrant Forest)

A micropub opened in July 2017. Beers and ciders are served by gravity from a glass-fronted temperature-controlled stillage in the single bar. High wooden tables with steel-framed chairs create a typically convivial micropub atmosphere. The walls have a selection of pictures featuring Selsey scenes. Beers and ciders change regularly and are usually from within a 45-mile radius. The rear garden area has seating for good weather. Regular live music features. Local CAMRA Pub of the Year 2018. Q (51)

Seal

6 Hillfield Road, PO20 0JX (on B2145, 600yds from sea)
10.30-midnight; 12-11 Sun ☎ (01243) 602461
the-seal.com
Dark Star Hophead; Young's Bitter; 3 changing beers (sourced nationally; often Dorking, Hammerpot, Hop Back)

A real community hub, family-run for over 45 years. It has a spacious public bar with a pool table at one end and a comfortable lounge with extended restaurant featuring quality home-cooked food, including locally caught fish (booking advised). The pub serves a good variety of guest beers, mostly from southern area micros. Acoustic live music often features on Sunday. The patio has seating and umbrellas to cater for smokers. Camping is available nearby at West Sands caravan park. The 13 en-suite B&B rooms are popular.
P (51)

Shoreham-by-Sea

Duke of Wellington

368 Brighton Road, BN43 6RE (on A259)
12-11 (12.30am Fri & Sat) ☎ (01273) 441297
dukeofwellingtonbrewhouse.co.uk/home
7 changing beers (sourced regionally)

A pub of contrasts: on some nights it is a quiet drinking emporium, on others it is packed to the gills with a ukulele band, the Wellington Wailers or a local group. What is consistent is the beer quality and range. The pub's features include original Kemp Town Brewery windows. Its past as a Dark Star establishment is reflected by a small shrine of certificates, displayed in a case with copies of all of the Guides. (2,700)

Southwick

Schooner Inn

146 Albion Street, BN42 4AU
12-11 (1am Fri & Sat) ☎ (01273) 592991
the-schooner.com
4 changing beers (often Franklins, Gun)

Family-run free house serving beers sourced entirely from local Sussex breweries. The main bar provides an excellent view of the shipping in Shoreham harbour and is close to the Lady Bee marina. Downstairs there is a large quiet room. Food, including vegan options, is available until 9.30pm Monday-Saturday and until 5.30pm on Sunday. Various seasonal functions are held.
Q P (46,700)

Staplefield

Jolly Tanners

Handcross Road, RH17 6EF
11-3, 5.30-11; 11-11 Fri & Sat; 12-10.30 Sun
☎ (01444) 400335
Fuller's London Pride; Harvey's Sussex Best Bitter; 4 changing beers (sourced locally)

On the north corner of the village green, this welcoming pub combines all the best elements of a local inn. The spacious bar is divided into two distinct areas, with two log fires adding to the cosy feel. There is an extensive range of guest beers, and real cider is also served. A mild is always on tap. A good range of tasty food is available at all sessions. This is a friendly place and definitely a locals' pub. Q P (271)

Stoughton

Hare & Hounds

PO18 9JQ (off B2146, through Walderton) SU803115
11-11; 12-10.30 Sun ☎ (023) 9263 1433
hareandhoundspub.co.uk
Dark Star Hophead; Long Man Best Bitter; Otter Amber; 1 changing beer (sourced locally)

Traditional country pub in a beautiful setting that makes it an ideal base for walking. The large dining room serves fresh local produce in comfortable surroundings, with an open fire in winter. A separate public bar has pictures of vintage racing cars and its own open fire, which attracts locals. The fires, stone-flagged floors and simple furniture create a wonderful atmosphere. Outside, the paved patio area complements a rear garden for outside dining and drinking. Two ciders are sold.
Q P

Turners Hill

Red Lion

Lion Lane, RH10 4NU
11-3, 5-11; 11.30-11 Sat; 12-10.30 Sun (01342) 715416
redlionturnershill.com
Harvey's Sussex XX Mild Ale, IPA, Sussex Best Bitter, Armada Ale; 2 changing beers (often Harvey's) H
An old favourite that is still very much a village local, offering a warm welcome to all who enter. It is a split-level pub with a large inglenook fireplace. Good-value and high-quality lunchtime food is served. The dining area has recently been tastefully extended. Children and dogs are welcome and there is a fortnightly quiz. Local CAMRA held its first meeting here in 1974, and a beer festival was held to celebrate its 40th anniversary in 2014.
Q P (84,272)

Walderton

Barley Mow

Breakneck Lane, PO18 9ED
11-3, 5.30-11; 11-11 Sat; 12-6 Sun (023) 9263 1321
thebarleymow.pub
Dark Star Hophead; Harvey's Sussex Best Bitter; Otter Amber; Ringwood Fortyniner; 1 changing beer (sourced locally; often Harvey's) H
An attractive free house in the centre of this picturesque village, popular with walkers and visitors to the South Downs National Park. Much of this cosy traditional pub caters for diners, but drinkers are most welcome in the large bar area. There are log fires in winter and the pretty garden alongside the River Ems is popular in summer. There are usually five handpumps in use, featuring two choices from Harvey's. The skittle alley can double as a function room.
Q P (54)

West Chiltington

Five Bells

Smock Alley, RH20 2QX (approx 1 mile S of old village centre) TQ092171
12-3, 6-11; 12-3, 7-10.30 Sun (01798) 812143
thefivebellsinn.com
5 changing beers (sourced nationally; often Harvey's, Jennings, Palmers) H
A friendly village free house that is a Guide regular. Dating from 1935, this former King & Barnes pub has been run by the same couple since 1983. Five handpumps are on what is probably Sussex's longest copper-top counter. Local and regional beers are served; one is usually a dark ale. There is a large copper-hooded open fire. Locally sourced home-cooked food is served in the bar and large conservatory (no food Sun eve). Local CAMRA branch Country Pub of the Year 2017 and 2018.
Q P (1,74)

West Hoathly

Cat

North Lane, RH19 4PP
12-11; 12-10 Sun (01342) 810369 catinn.co.uk
Firebird Parody; Harvey's Sussex Best Bitter; Larkins Traditional Ale; 3 changing beers (often Bedlam, Dark Star, Harvey's) H
Set in a picturesque hilltop village in the heart of the Sussex countryside, this 16th-century free house is within reach of several attractions. The pub retains oak beams and two inglenook fireplaces. There is an outside terrace, where food and drink can be enjoyed in the summer months. Five local ales are served, and good-quality food is cooked to order, using mostly local suppliers. This cosy pub has four letting rooms.
Q P (84)

West Marden

Victoria

PO18 9EN (just W of B2146 in village centre)
closed Mon; 12-2.30, 6-10 (11 Thu); 12-2.30, 5-11 Fri; 12-11 Sat; 12-9 Sun (023) 9263 1330
victoriainnwestmarden.co.uk
Harvey's Sussex Best Bitter; Langham Hip Hop; 2 changing beers (sourced locally; often Flowerpots, Goddards, Purity) H
Comfortable old rural inn at the heart of its tiny Downland community. Cricket and bar billiards teams plus a golf society help maintain the pub's local involvement, and many country pursuits are supported, including walking, riding and shooting. Inside there are several intimate spaces in which to drink and dine, with a log-burning stove for cold evenings. The front garden has splendid views of surrounding hills. Changing beers come from mainly local breweries; those at occasional festivals are sourced from further afield.
Q P (54)

Westbourne

Cricketers

Commonside, PO10 8TA (N from The Square, turn E at Chidham Garage)
12-3, 5-11; 12-11 Thu-Sat; 12-8 Sun (01243) 372647
Dark Star Hophead; Flack Manor Flack's Double Drop; Flowerpots Bitter; 2 changing beers (sourced locally; often Hop Back, Langham) H
This 300-year-old local is the only true free house in the village. Situated on the northern outskirts, it is hard to find but well worth the effort. Conversation abounds in the single L-shaped, half-panelled bar. There is a suntrap garden to the side, with a covered and heated smoking area. Up to two guest beers come from mainly Hampshire and Sussex micros. The ale range may occasionally vary from the beers listed above.
Q P (11,36)

Worthing

Anchored in Worthing

27 West Buildings, BN11 3BS (close to seafront)
closed Mon; 12-9.30; 12-5.30 Sun (01903) 529100
anchoredinworthing.co.uk
3 changing beers (sourced locally; often Goldmark, Gun, Long Man) G
Look for the Tardis-style entrance to Sussex's original micropub, where you can be assured of a warm welcome. High wooden tables are arranged so customers face each other and conversation quickly flows. All drinks are from award-winning artisan Sussex producers. The ceiling is adorned with pumpclips of the many ales sold since opening. The walls have maps showing breweries and micropubs, plus CAMRA and local event information. A cheeseboard is provided on Sundays. A multiple CAMRA award winner.
Q

Brooksteed Alehouse

38 South Farm Road, BN14 7AE (100yds N of South Farm Rd level crossing, 5 mins' walk from Central station)
12-9.30 (8 Mon); 12-5 Sun ☎ 07484 840103
brooksteedalehouse.co.uk
House beer (by Arundel); 5 changing beers (sourced nationally; often Goldmark, Gun, North Riding Brewpub) G
Worthing's second micropub opened in 2014, with a change of ownership in 2017. There are usually five changing cask ales, four KeyKeg and up to five ciders or perries from local and national brewers, plus a range of bottled beers, wines and gins. Locally sourced pub snacks are served, with a cheeseboard on Sunday. The pub has stylish and quirky decor, with comfortable areas and outdoor seating on the forecourt. Many regular events take place, often including other local businesses and the community. **Q** (16)

Corner House

80 High Street, BN11 1DJ (opp Waitrose)
12-11 (midnight Sat); 12-10.30 Sun ☎ (01903) 216463
cornerhouseworthing.co.uk
4 changing beers (sourced regionally; often Burning Sky, Goldmark, Shepherd Neame) H
The Corner House occupies a prominent position at the town centre's eastern edge. The original pub, the Anchor, dates back to 1805 and was one of Worthing's oldest. It had an interesting history, but was rebuilt in 1895. The pub reopened in late 2015 under new ownership, with a new name, and quickly took off. There is an emphasis on local suppliers for both food and drink. The large beer garden is popular all year round.

Egremont

32 Brighton Road, BN11 3ED (short walk from seafront and town centre)
12-11 ☎ (01903) 600064 theegremont.co.uk
Harvey's Sussex Best Bitter; house beer (by Goldmark); 3 changing beers (sourced regionally; often Burning Sky) H
Previously, when Worthing was its headquarters, the English Bowls Association nicknamed this pub the Bowlers' Arms. It was thoroughly refurbished in 2015 and now feels much lighter, brighter and more spacious, while retaining the lovely old doors and stained-glass Kemp Town Brewery windows. Several different seating areas allow space for regular mini beer festivals, quizzes and weekend live music. A house beer is served alongside up to four other ales, and an extensive range of over 50 gins.

Georgi Fin

54 Goring Road, BN12 4AD (on A259, N side, in Goring Rd shops)
closed Mon; 12-2, 5-10 Tue-Thu; 12-10 Fri & Sat; 12-5 Sun ☎ (01903) 240933 thegeorgifin.co.uk
4 changing beers (sourced regionally; often Franklins, Thornbridge) G
A popular micropub opened in June 2017. Named after the owners' children, it is in a busy shopping parade. The wooden tables and seats use scaffolding poles as legs. The drinks are served from a purpose-built cold room and include four ales from local and national brewers, three traditional ciders, wines, plus a selection of English, Belgian and German bottled beers. A cheeseboard is available on Sundays. Unusually for a micro, the pub has both ladies' and gents' toilets. **Q**

Green Man Ale & Cider House

17 South Street, BN14 7LG (40yds N of West Worthing railway crossing)
2 (12 Thu-Sat)-9; 12-4 Sun ☎ 07984 793877
5 changing beers (sourced regionally; often Goldmark, Gun, Wantsum) G
Worthing's third micropub opened in 2016 in a former café. The temperature-controlled cellar is visible from the bar, which is furnished with high-level tables, benches and stools arranged to encourage interaction and chat. Offering up to six gravity-dispensed ales, 10 ciders plus a good selection of gins, wine and soft drinks, the pub is known for its friendly atmosphere. CAMRA branch Pub of the Year 2018 and 2019. **Q**

Hare & Hounds

79-81 Portland Road, BN11 1QG
11-11 (11.30 Tue & Thu); 11-midnight Fri & Sat; 12-11 Sun ☎ (01903) 230085 hareandhoundsworthing.co.uk
Exmoor Ale; Fuller's London Pride; Harvey's Sussex Best Bitter; St Austell Proper Job; Timothy Taylor Landlord H
Located in the heart of Worthing, this 18th-century Grade II-listed flint building became a pub in 1814, extending into the adjoining property in the 1990s. The large wood-panelled, U-shaped bar leads to the rear conservatory and a heated and covered patio. Old prints featuring hunting hang from the walls. There are five handpumps, serving local and national ales. Tuesday evening hosts live jazz, Saturday evening has live bands, and Sunday is music quiz night. **Q**

Park View

Salvington Road, BN13 2JR (corner of Salvington Rd and Durrington Lane)
12-11; 12-10 Sun ☎ (01903) 521397
parkview-worthing.co.uk
Bath Ales Gem; Dark Star Hophead; 2 changing beers (sourced regionally; often Dartmoor, Greyhound) H
Formerly the Lamb, the Park View is a newly reopened community pub in the Durrington and Salvington area of Worthing. It consists of a sports bar showing live Sky Sports and BT Sport, an informal lounge bar and extensive garden. A changing selection of real ales is on offer from both local and national breweries, along with good food. Regular events include a weekly quiz on Thursday. (5,6)

Parsonage Bar & Restaurant

6-10 High Street, BN14 7NN (at S end of Tarring High St – not to be confused with High St Worthing)
12-10.30 (10 Mon); 12-11 Fri & Sat; 12-9 Sun ☎ (01903) 820140 theparsonage.co.uk
Burning Sky Plateau; Harvey's Sussex Best Bitter H**; 2 changing beers (sourced nationally; often Downlands, Hammerpot, Lister's)** H/G
This interesting Grade II-listed 15th-century building was originally three cottages. It has been a quality restaurant since 1987 and now has four handpumps on the bar offering a selection of well-kept local ales. Guest beers usually include a dark brew, and an old ale in winter. Customers are welcome to drink without having a meal but might be tempted by the good-value bar menu. The courtyard garden is great for the warmer weather. **Q** (6,16)

Selden Arms

41 Lyndhurst Road, BN11 2DB (about 5 mins from centre of town and 2 mins from Worthing Hospital on Lyndhurst Road, opp gasometer)
⏲ 11-11; 12-11 Sat & Sun ☎ (01903) 523361
🌐 seldenarms.co.uk
6 changing beers (sourced nationally; often Brighton Bier, Burning Sky, Gun) 🄷
A welcoming 19th-century free house that is a Guide regular. Six handpumps serve a changing selection of local and national beers, one of which is always a dark ale. There is also a selection of craft brews, both keg and in cans and bottles, plus an extensive range of around 80 bottled Belgian beers. A blackboard displays upcoming ales. Lunchtime food is served from Monday to Saturday, with curry on Friday and Saturday evenings. The pub holds an annual winter beer festival in January. ◑♣🍎🚌🐾📶

Yapton

Maypole 🄻

Maypole Lane, BN18 0DP (off B2132 ½ mile N of village, with pedestrian access across railway from Lake Lane, 1¼ miles E of Barnham station) SU978042
⏲ 12-11 (midnight Fri & Sat) ☎ (01243) 551417
Lister's Best Bitter; 4 changing beers (sourced nationally; often Bedlam, Fallen Acorn, Holler) 🄷
Small 18th-century flint-built free house of character hidden away from the village centre, down a narrow lane ending in a pedestrian crossing over the railway. The cosy, often lively, lounge boasts two open fires and a row of six handpumps dispensing beers from local micros. Real cider is served from the cellar. There is also a traditional public bar with pool and darts, plus a skittle alley/function room with bar billiards. Lunchtime food is served Monday to Friday. Dogs are welcome. **Q**🐴❀◑♿⛺♣🍎**P**🚌🐾📶

Brighton Bierhaus, Brighton, East Sussex (Photo: grassrootsgroundswell/Flickr CC BY 2.0)

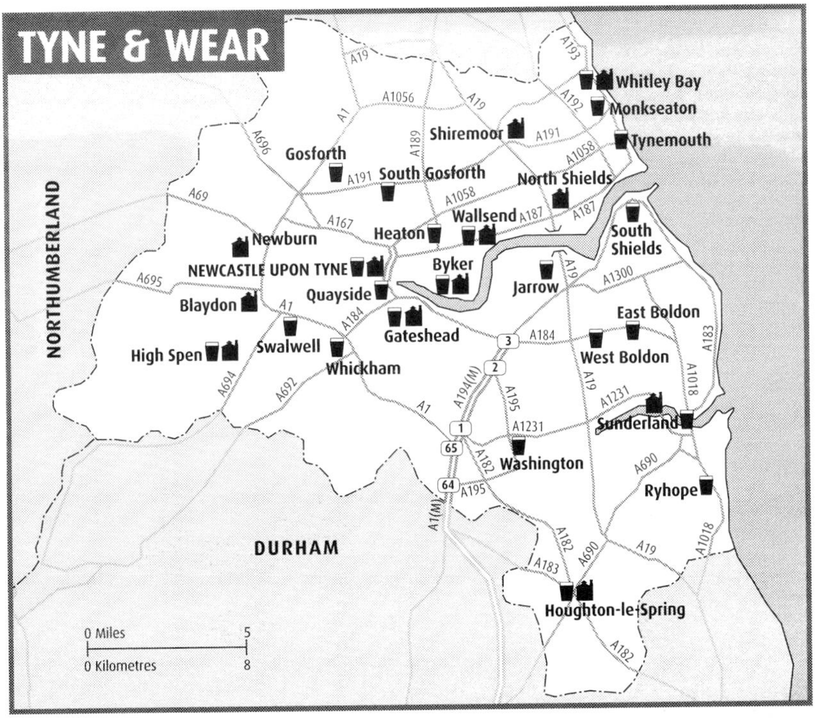

East Boldon

Grey Horse

Front Street, NE36 0SJ

11-11 (midnight Thu-Sat); 12-midnight Sun
(0191) 519 1796 classicinns.co.uk/greyhorseeastboldon

6 changing beers (sourced nationally) H

Distinctive mock-Tudor building with separate pleasant and comfortable lounge and bar areas and an upstairs function room. Up to six changing ales are available, from local and national breweries. Meals are served daily with themed nights during the week. There are large-screen TVs in the bar for football and other sports. Quiz night is every Wednesday and the Boldon History Society meets on the last Tuesday of the month.
Q P (9,30,558)

Gateshead

Old Fox

10-14 Carlisle Street, Felling, NE10 0HQ

4-11; 12-11 Fri; 12-midnight Sat & Sun (0191) 447 1980

5 changing beers (sourced nationally) H

This superb traditional community street pub is only a short walk from Felling Metro station, serving a changing range of real ale and craft beers. The open fire gives the bar a homely feel. Live bands and buskers' nights are a feature and Sunday lunches are a highlight. A friendly and welcoming pub with a beer garden at the rear.

Station East

Hills Street, NE8 2AS

12-11 (0191) 435 3389

Hadrian Border Farne Island Pale Ale, Grainger Ale, Tyneside Blonde; 3 changing beers (sourced nationally; often Hadrian Border) H

Occupying the site of the former Gateshead East Station and Railway Hotel, the building is now stripped back and enlarged with much structural work. Formerly a small pub, it is now open and spacious. There is a pleasant mezzanine floor above the main room and a further arched room to the rear below another railway bridge. A rear room is available for functions. Q

Wheat Sheaf

26 Carlisle Street, Felling, NE10 0HQ

5 (3 Thu; 12 Fri & Sat)-11; 12-10.30 Sun
(0191) 597 2981

Big Lamp Bitter, Prince Bishop Ale, Sunny Daze; 1 changing beer (sourced nationally) H

Welcoming street-corner pub owned by Big Lamp Brewery and patronised by a loyal band of regulars who often travel quite a distance to drink here. The pub features some original details, mismatched furniture and, when needed, real coal fires. The outdoor toilets have original Victorian urinals. There is a fortnightly Monday night quiz, traditional folk music featuring keen local musicians on Tuesday night and dominoes on Wednesday night. An original CAMRA clock keeps time behind the bar. Snacks are available.

High Spen

Wig's Place

49-51 Ramsay Street, NE39 2EJ

closed Mon-Wed; 3-9 (01207) 549333
wigsplace.co.uk

6 changing beers (sourced nationally; often Wylam, TOPS) H

A micropub spread over two rooms, named after the male half of the couple running it. A true community pub, families are welcome and local groups use the comfy lounge bar for meetings. Ales are from the North-East and North Yorkshire. A very local ale from the neighbouring TOPS nanobrewery is usually on offer. Around five real ciders in boxes are also served. To visit from Newcastle or Gateshead check local bus timetables carefully as links can be sparse, especially on Sunday. 🍎🚌(10A)

Houghton-le-Spring

Wild Boar ✔

Frederick Place, DH4 4BN
☉ 8am-midnight ☎ (0191) 512 8050
Greene King Abbot; Ruddles Best Bitter; 6 changing beers (sourced nationally) Ⓗ
Previously a club, the Wild Boar is named after the Black Sabre boar on the crest of the former rector of Houghton. This open-plan Wetherspoon pub offers well-priced ales and a good-value food menu. Its 10 handpulls serve a selection of national and local beers, as well as two real ciders. Popular brewery visits and day trips are organised, often during the spring and summer months.
Q🐎❀◐♿🍎P🚌📶

Jarrow

Jarrow's Gin & Ale House

Walter Street, NE32 3PQ (behind Town Hall)
☉ 2-11.30; 12-12.30 Fri & Sat; 12-11.30 Sun
☎ (0191) 489 7222
4 changing beers (sourced nationally) Ⓗ
A well-appointed conversion of the old Crusader, with an emphasis on wooden panelling, vintage photographs of the area and pub memorabilia. Note the ornate tiling on the outside of the building. The pub serves up to four ales and also promotes over a dozen gins. There is an ale of the day, offered at a discount. A quiz is held every Sunday night, and live music hosted three nights a week. 🚆P🚌

Monkseaton

Left Luggage Room Ⓛ

Unit 6, Monkseaton Train Station, Norham Road, NE26 3NR
☉ 12-10.30 (11 Fri & Sat) 🌐 leftluggageroom.co.uk
6 changing beers (sourced nationally) Ⓗ
Situated in the disused former left luggage room of Monkseaton Metro station, access is directly from the southbound platform. A single open-plan room has the bar at one end and a variety of rustic fixtures and fittings. The area between the building and the platform fence provides covered outdoor seating until mid-evening. Sunday lunch can sometimes be supplied by the nearby café.
Q🐎❀♿🚆🍎🚌🐾

Newcastle upon Tyne: Byker

Brinkburn Street Brewery Bar & Kitchen

Unit 1B, Ford Street, Ouseburn, NE6 1NW
☉ 11-11 ☎ 07933 336991 🌐 brinkburnbrewery.co.uk
8 changing beers (sourced locally) Ⓗ
Inspired by American craft breweries and taprooms, this bar offers a wide range of quality beers, most brewed on-site, alongside a couple of guest ales. Food is also a major feature, with a kitchen that uses locally sourced ingredients and serves traditional local dishes. Monday offers 'home comforts' (food from £5), Tuesday is 'beer and board games', and on Thursday evening there is a jam session. The quirky bar features a collection of armoury and objets d'art. ◐🚆♣

Cumberland Arms Ⓛ

James Place Street (off Byker Bank), NE6 1LD
☉ 3-11 (midnight Fri); 12-midnight Sat; 12-11 Sun
☎ (0191) 265 1725 🌐 thecumberlandarms.co.uk
6 changing beers (sourced nationally) Ⓗ
Three-storey venue rebuilt over 100 years ago and relatively little changed since. It stands in a prominent position overlooking the lower Ouseburn Valley and is the brewrey tap for the nearby Northern Alchemy brewery. The pub is home to traditional dance and music groups. A multiple winner of CAMRA regional Cider Pub of the Year awards, it generally offers up to 12 ciders and perries. Winter and summer beer festivals are held each year. Closing time may vary.
Q🐎❀🛏🚆♣🍎P🐾📶

Free Trade Inn Ⓛ

St Lawrence Road, NE6 1AP
☉ 11-11 (midnight Fri & Sat); 12-10.30 Sun
☎ (0191) 265 5764
7 changing beers (sourced nationally) Ⓗ
Unique former S&N pub with wonderful views of the Tyne bridges and Newcastle and Gateshead quaysides. Up to seven changing beers and five ciders are available on the bar. Interesting ales come from far and wide including an extensive range of foreign bottled beers. Service is with a smile, friendly and knowledgeable. The jukebox is classic and free. The beer garden is excellent. Winner of many annual local and regional Cider Pub of the Year and Pub of the Year awards.
Q🐎❀🚆♣🍎🚌(Q3)🐾📶

REAL ALE BREWERIES

Almasty Shiremoor
Anarchy Newcastle upon Tyne
Big Lamp Newburn
Box Social Newburn
Brinkburn Street Newcastle upon Tyne: Byker
Cullercoats Wallsend
Darwin Sunderland
Dog & Rabbit 🛢 Whitley Bay
Errant Newcastle upon Tyne
Firebrick Blaydon
Flash House North Shields
Great North Eastern Gateshead
Hadrian Border Newburn
Maxim Houghton-le-Spring
Newcastle Newcastle upon Tyne
Northern Alchemy Newcastle upon Tyne: Byker
Out There Newcastle upon Tyne
Redhouse 🛢 Newcastle upon Tyne
Stu Brew Newcastle upon Tyne
Tavernale 🛢 Newcastle upon Tyne
Three Kings North Shields
TOPS (The Olde Potting Shed) High Spen
Two by Two Wallsend
Tyne Bank Newcastle upon Tyne
Whitley Bay 🛢 Whitley Bay
Wylam Newcastle upon Tyne

Tyne Bank Tap Room L
375 Walker Road, NE6 2BS
closed Mon-Wed; 4-11 Thu; 12-midnight Fri & Sat; 12-8 Sun
☎ (0191) 265 2828
14 changing beers (sourced nationally; often Tyne Bank) H
Tyne Bank's brewery and taphouse has an industrial feel with open steel roof trusses on display. The bar is constructed from scaffolding planks and corrugated iron, continuing the theme. Downward-facing gas heaters provide interesting feature heating. The corner stage is used for live music and events. Eight real ales and a range of keg beers are served. The huge steel pipe keg fonts are unusual. (Q3)

Newcastle upon Tyne: City Centre

Bacchus L
42-48 High Bridge, NE1 6BX
11.30-midnight; 12-11 Sun ☎ (0191) 261 1008
6 changing beers (sourced nationally) H
Formerly local CAMRA Pub of the Year for four years running, this smart city-centre pub boasts nine handpumps offering a range of changing guest beers, with one pump dedicated to cider. A seasonal house beer is brewed by Yorkshire Dales, and a large range of draught and bottled foreign beers is available. Photographs and posters showing the industries in which this region used to lead the world cover the walls.
(Monument)

Beer Street L
Arch 10 Forth Street, NE1 3NZ
3-11; 12-midnight Fri & Sat
5 changing beers (sourced nationally) H
Sited in a railway arch, this micropub with seating for 50 people opened in 2018. There is a main bar area with five handpumps. Stairs at the rear give access to a mezzanine floor above, with pump badges from former beers adorning the staircase. Interesting artwork covers the walls, apparently inspired by the famous Hogarth paintings Beer Street and Gin Lane. (Central)

Bodega L
125 Westgate Road, NE1 4AG
12-11 (midnight Fri); 11-midnight Sat; 12-10.30 Sun
☎ (0191) 221 1552
Big Lamp Prince Bishop Ale; Fyne Ales Jarl; Oakham Citra; 5 changing beers (sourced nationally; often Almasty) H
Two fine stained-glass domes are the architectural highlights of the pub, which is popular with football and music fans. TVs show sporting events and the pub can be busy on match days. The interior offers a number of standing and seating areas with separate booths for more intimate drinking. A number of old brewery mirrors adorn the walls. Eight handpumps include beers from Oakham and Fyne Ales, alongside a good selection of foreign bottled beers. (Central)

Box Social L
Arch 11 Forth Street, NE1 3NZ
12-midnight boxsocial.pub
Box Social Gentleman's Nectar Pale Ale; 3 changing beers (sourced nationally; often Box Social) H
Welcoming micropub with a pleasant ambience, owned by Box Social Brewery, occupying the former site of the Split Chimp. A mezzanine floor gives extra seating to the rear. The bar is constructed from scaffolding planks with a wooden bar back. There are 10 keg beer taps on the wall behind the bar and a colourful tap board provides details of what is on the handpumps and wall taps.
Q(Central)

Bridge Hotel L
Castle Square, NE1 1RQ
11.30-11 (midnight Fri & Sat); 12-10.30 Sun
☎ (0191) 232 6400
Anarchy Blonde Star; Sharp's Doom Bar; 7 changing beers (sourced nationally) H
Large Fitzgerald pub situated next to Stephenson's spectacular High Level Bridge – the rear windows and patio have views of the city walls, River Tyne and Gateshead Quays. The main bar area, with many stained-glass windows, is divided into a number of seating areas, with a raised section at the rear. Guest beers come from far and wide. What claims to be the oldest folk club in the country is among live music events hosted in the upstairs function room. (Central)

Head of Steam
1 Neville Street, NE1 5EN
12-2am (3am Fri & Sat) ☎ (0191) 230 4236
6 changing beers (sourced nationally; often Camerons) H
Facing the central railway station, this is an unusual pub in that there is nothing on the ground floor. Upstairs is the main bar with six cask beers, three real ciders and a good selection of continental draught beers. Downstairs is one of the most popular music venues in the city centre (no draught beers served here although there is an extensive range of cans and bottles). (Central)

Lady Greys L
20 Shakespeare Street, NE1 6AQ
11-2am ☎ (0191) 232 3606 ladygreys.co.uk
Mordue Northumbrian Blonde; 7 changing beers (sourced nationally) H
Close to the historic Theatre Royal and busy shopping areas, this pub, formerly The Adelphi, is a welcome addition to the city-centre real ale scene. Beers are mainly from local brewers Mordue, Hadrian Border, Allendale and Wylam, with guests from all over the country. Refurbishment has added two more handpumps for beer and two for real cider. Food is served all day.
(Monument)

Mean-Eyed Cat
1 St Thomas Street, NE1 4LE
12-10 (10.30 Thu-Sat); 1-10 Sun ☎ (0191) 222 0952
Rat White Rat; 5 changing beers (sourced nationally) H
Situated in a former newsagent's in the street opposite Haymarket bus station, this one-room micropub opened in March 2018 with six handpumps. It serves beers from local, national and international suppliers, alongside a range of eight craft keg beers. A good selection of up to six ciders is also available – traditional still and served from the 'cellar'. (Haymarket)

Newcastle Tap
Ground Floor, Baron House, 4 Neville Street, NE1 5EN
12-11 (midnight Thu & Fri; 1am Sat) ☎ (0191) 261 6636
tapnewcastle.com
8 changing beers (sourced nationally) P

Opened in 2017 on the ground floor of a former office block next to Head of Steam and opposite Royal Station Hotel and Newcastle Central station. The open-plan single room has beer casks and kegs displayed behind glass on a mezzanine above the bar. Cask beers are dispensed through taps in the bar back rather than handpumps, there being no dispensers on the bar counter itself. Gravity dispense is assisted by Flojet pumps. A pizza menu is available all day. ◑⇌🚉(Central)🚌

Split Chimp L

Arch 7, Westgate Road, NE1 1SA

🕒 3-10; 12-11 Fri & Sat; 12-8 Sun 🌐 splitchimp.pub

5 changing beers (sourced nationally; often Errant) [H]

Newcastle's first micropub opened in 2015 in a refurbished railway arch behind Central station opposite the site of the former Federation Brewery. It relocated to a larger arch on Westgate Road in 2016. More spacious than some micropubs and split over two levels, six handpumps serve an ever-changing selection of real ales, with one dedicated to the house beer, Clever Chimp, from nearby Errant Brewery. Foreign bottled beers are also available. ✿⇌🚉(Central)♣🍎🐾

Town Mouse Ale House L

Basement, 11 St Mary's Place, NE1 7PG

🕒 2-10; 12-11 Fri & Sat; 12-8 Sun

🌐 townmousealehouse.co.uk

4 changing beers (sourced nationally) [H]

This well-designed micropub opened in 2017. The basement bar is located in a former coffee shop and has space for around 50 people. The bar area is to the front with another seating area to the rear. A large blackboard gives details of the four cask beers and larger range of keg and bottled beers. Local CAMRA Pub of the Year 2018.
✿🚉(Haymarket)♣🐾

Trent House L

1-2 Leazes Lane, NE1 4QT

🕒 11-11.30; 12-11.30 Sun ☎ (0191) 261 2154

9 changing beers (sourced nationally) [H]

Friendly and laid back, the Trent is popular with students. It is home to the best jukebox in town, featuring an eclectic mix of classic rock, jazz and electronica. There is an upstairs room with a pool table, and board games are available at the bar. The pub has a nightly happy hour 8-9pm, with cask ales at reduced prices. 🚉(Haymarket)♣🍎🚌📶

Tyneside Cinema Bar Café L

Pilgrim Street, NE1 6QG

🕒 8am-11 (midnight Fri & Sat); 10-11 Sun ☎ 0845 217 9909

🌐 tynesidecinema.co.uk/food-drink/tyneside-bar-cafe

4 changing beers (sourced nationally; often Wylam) [H]

Part of Tyneside Cinema, the Bar Café is a large open-plan bar with its own curtained-off cinema screen. The bar has three handpumps serving a range of locally brewed cask ales including the house beer, 35mm from Wylam Brewery. Beers can be taken into cinema screenings. A tasty selection of cakes and pastries is also available. The cellar is in the vault of a former bank.
◑♿⇌🚉(Monument)🍎📶

Newcastle upon Tyne: Gosforth

County L ✔

High Street, NE3 1HB

🕒 11-11; 12-10.30 Sun ☎ (0191) 285 6919

Draught Bass; Great North Eastern Rivet Catcher; Greene King Abbot, IPA; Hadrian Border Farne Island Pale Ale; Sharp's Doom Bar; 8 changing beers (sourced nationally) [H]

A large L-shaped bar with pleasant stained-glass windows on the main road frontage. It attracts a variety of visitors, from office workers to students, and can get busy, especially at weekends. A separate quiet room at the back offers respite from the hustle and bustle of the main bar, and also doubles as a small meeting or function room. Several guest beers are available. ✿🍎P🚌🐾📶

Gosforth Hotel L ✔

High Street, NE3 1HQ

🕒 10-11 (midnight Fri & Sat) ☎ (0191) 285 6617

🌐 gosforthhotelnewcastle.co.uk

Anarchy Blonde Star; Mordue Workie Ticket; 6 changing beers (sourced nationally) [H]

Located on the corner of a busy junction at the top of the High Street, this is a stalwart of the lively Gosforth pub scene. Popular with a wide clientele, from nearby office workers to locals and students, the pub often gets busy. The rear bar opens at 5pm Monday to Thursday and midday Friday to Sunday. A good range of local ales is always available.
◑♿🚉🚌📶

Newcastle upon Tyne: Heaton

Chillingham L

Chillingham Road, NE6 5XN

🕒 11-11 (midnight Fri & Sat); 12-11 Sun ☎ (0191) 265 3992

Anarchy Blonde Star; Sharp's Atlantic; 8 changing beers (sourced nationally) [H]

Close to Chillingham Road Metro station, this large two-roomed pub was extensively renovated, refurbished and reopened in 2016. It has a comfortable bar and lounge, with sport shown on TVs, appealing to the widest-possible clientele. The food menu is popular with locals and visitors alike. An excellent choice of local microbrewery beers is offered – and look out for the bottled beer, whisky and wine of the month. A function room upstairs hosts regular quiz nights. ◑🚉♣🍎P🚌(62,63)📶

Newcastle upon Tyne: Quayside

Bridge Tavern L

7 Akenside Hill, NE1 3UF

🕒 12-midnight (1am Fri & Sat); 12-11 Sun

☎ (0191) 261 9966 🌐 thebridgetavern.com

7 changing beers (sourced nationally) [H]

There has been an alehouse on this site for over 200 years – the original building was demolished in 1925 and a new premises built following the construction of the town's most famous landmark, the Tyne Bridge. This popular pub has its own microbrewery – the Bridge Tavern's one-barrel plant brews a range of beers under the Tavernale name. Food ranging from bar snacks to buffets and full meals is prepared and cooked by a professional chef. Children are welcome until 7pm.
🍺✿◑♿⇌🚉(Central)🍎🚌🐾📶

Crown Posada L

31 Side, NE1 3JE

🕒 12 (11 Thu)-11; 11-midnight Fri; 12-midnight Sat; 12-10.30 Sun ☎ (0191) 232 1269

Allendale Pennine Pale; Hadrian Border Tyneside Blonde; house beer (by Hadrian Border); 3 changing beers (sourced nationally) [H]

An architecturally fine pub, recognised by CAMRA as having a historic interior of regional importance. The narrow street frontage with its two impressive stained-glass windows leads to a small snug, bar counter and a longer seating area. There is an interesting coffered ceiling, as well as local photographs and cartoons of long-gone customers and staff on the walls. Local small brewers are enthusiastically supported, with three regular local ales. Q(Central)

Newcastle upon Tyne: South Gosforth

Brandling Villa

Haddricks Mill Road, NE3 1QL
12-11 (midnight Fri & Sat) (0191) 284 0490
brandlingvilla.co.uk
10 changing beers (sourced nationally) H
Large double-fronted establishment, keen to promote real ale, offering a constantly changing selection of 10 beers – also available in third-pint tasting glasses – plus two ciders on handpump. The manager organises various well-attended beer-related events, including brewery tap takeovers, local sausage and pie festivals, music, cinema and beer festivals. P

Ryhope

Guide Post

Ryhope Street South, SR2 0RN
12-midnight (0191) 523 5735
Maxim Double Maxim; 2 changing beers (sourced nationally) H
This friendly, popular, street-corner local has three handpulls – the guest beers will always include one light ale. With a cask ale club, sports TV, a pool table, a Wednesday quiz, entertainment every Friday and Saturday and dominoes and poker on Sunday, there is something for everyone here. Bar snacks are available. Outside at the back is a pleasant enclosed garden with a play space for children.

South Shields

Alum Ale House

Ferry Street, NE33 1JR
11-11 (midnight Sat) (0191) 427 7245
Brakspear Oxford Gold; Jennings Cocker Hoop, Cumberland Ale; Ringwood Boondoggle; Wychwood Hobgoblin, Hobgoblin Gold; 5 changing beers (sourced nationally) H
Traditional pub close to the Shields Ferry landing, River Tyne and Market Place. It is popular with local ale drinkers as a haven of good beer. There are 12 handpumps offering ales from the Marston's range plus a real cider. Note the large blackboard to the right of the bar with details of the beers. A lively Irish folk session is hosted on the first Sunday of each month. Bar snacks are available. Seating on the decking outside has views of the river.

Cask Lounge

Charlotte Terrace, NE33 1QQ
closed Mon & Tue; 5-11 Wed & Thu; 2-11 Fri & Sat; 12-5 Sun
07387 750551
4 changing beers (sourced nationally) H
This micropub was opened in 2018 in a former housing office opposite the Town Hall, sharing premises with a vinyl album store/coffee shop. The Cask Lounge is run by an experienced couple who value the principle of the micropub, encouraging conversation with no TVs or gambling machines. There are four handpulls dispensing changing real ales. The pub is light and airy and includes a comfortable sofa, soft carpeting and background music.

Marine

230 Ocean Road, NE33 2JQ
11-11 (midnight Fri & Sat); 12-10.30 Sun
(0191) 455 0280
4 changing beers (sourced nationally) H
Large 1840s pub opposite Marine Park, near the seafront. This family-run free house serves six changing real ales and two real ciders. To the left of the bar are raised areas with plenty of seating, and to the right is a games area. There is a function room upstairs. Unobtrusive background music plays. Pub food is served daily. Local CAMRA Cider Pub of the Year 2019. P(E1,516)

Steamboat

Mill Dam, NE33 1EQ (follow signs for Customs House)
12-11 (midnight Thu-Sat); 12-11.30 Sun
(0191) 454 0134
9 changing beers (sourced nationally) H
Under the same management for around 30 years, this multi award-winning pub has one of the largest selections of cask ales in South Shields. Ten handpumps dispense beers from local and national breweries, and a real cider. Meet the Brewer events, beer festivals and regular music nights take place throughout the year. The split-level bar and small lounge have a nautical decor. The pub is close to the Shields Ferry, Customs House and buses. Q

Wouldhave

16 Mile End Road, NE33 1TA
8am-midnight (0191) 427 6014
Greene King Abbot; Ruddles Best Bitter; 3 changing beers (sourced nationally) H
Named after local boat builder William Wouldhave, co-inventor of the self-righting lifeboat, this town-centre Wetherspoon pub offers a selection of real ales and ciders from six handpumps, with two regular beers and a rotation of guests. Well-priced bar meals are available all day. The downstairs bar has ample seating and tables while upstairs there is a family-friendly area. The pub hosts twice-yearly beer festivals. Five minutes from the public transport interchange. QP

Sunderland

Avenue

Zetland Street, Roker, SR6 0EQ (just off Roker Avenue)
12-11 (midnight Fri); 11-midnight Sat; 11-11 Sun
(0191) 567 7412 theavenue.pub
6 changing beers (sourced nationally) H
Fifteen minutes' walk from the Stadium of Light, this local pub offers six changing real ales on handpull and several real ciders. It hosts various themed nights including poker, bingo, pool, a popular Thursday night quiz and a Sunday dominoes handicap. A snooker table and dartboards can be found in the upstairs games room. A function room provides extra space during busier periods and is available to hire. Local CAMRA Cider Pub of the Year 2019. P(E1)

Chaplins
40 Stockton Road, SR1 3NR
⏲ 10-midnight ☎ (0191) 565 3964
6 changing beers (sourced nationally) Ⓗ
A city-centre pub with seven real ale handpulls and one for real cider. Good-value food is served every day. A quiz with free snacks is held on Thursday evening. There is plenty of seating either side of the main entrance, as well as outside. Some tabletops to the right of the main entrance depict scenes of Sunderland's industrial heritage. Handy for public transport, with Park Lane Interchange two minutes away. ❀◐♿⇌🚉🍎🚌📶

Chesters Ⓛ ✔
Chester Road, SR4 7DR
⏲ 10-11 (midnight Fri & Sat); 11-10.30 Sun
☎ (0191) 565 9952
6 changing beers (sourced nationally) Ⓗ
This popular pub just outside the city centre has a smart interior, with a large main bar and a more intimate area at the back. With six handpulls, there is always one beer from a local brewery as well as guest ales, alongside a real cider. Meals are served all day. Outside is a pay car park (you can claim the charge back at the bar) and a large beer garden. A function room with a private bar is available.
🐎❀◐♿🚉🍎P🚌📶

Dun Cow ★ Ⓛ
High Street West, SR1 3HA
⏲ 11-11 (midnight Fri & Sat) ☎ (0191) 567 2262
Anarchy Blonde Star; Sharp's Doom Bar; 5 changing beers (sourced nationally) Ⓗ
Owned by Pub Culture, this Grade II-listed building is an architectural gem and features on CAMRA's National Inventory of Historic Pub Interiors. It was a winner of two CAMRA/Historic England awards for restoration and conservation following a refurbishment in 2014. Real ale and cider feature on eight handpulls. The pub is next to the Empire Theatre and can get very busy around performance times. There is a Tuesday buskers' night and a Thursday quiz. Meals are served upstairs.
Q◐♿⇌🚉🍎🚌📶

Fitzgeralds Ⓛ
12-14 Green Terrace, SR1 3PZ
⏲ 11.30-11 (11.30 Fri & Sat) ☎ (0191) 567 0852
Titanic Plum Porter; 8 changing beers (sourced nationally) Ⓗ
This city-centre pub celebrated 25 years in the Guide in 2018. It serves two regular beers complemented by up to eight guests. The pub comprises a large main bar offering a number of different seating areas and the smaller, quieter, nautically themed Chart Room. Lunchtime meals are served daily. Live music features on Tuesday and Sunday nights, and a quiz is held every Thursday evening. 🐎❀◐⇌🚉🚌📶

Harbour View
Roker, SR6 0NU
⏲ 10.30-midnight ☎ (0191) 567 1402
6 changing beers Ⓗ
The Harbour View is a modern local pub with six handpulls offering regularly changing beers chosen by local CAMRA members. A board displays a tally of beers to date from 1 January – the aim is to offer in excess of 600 ales a year. A cask ale club is held every Wednesday evening. This is a relaxing pub for a drink, with additional seating outside to take in the sun. ❀🚌(E1,18)🐾📶

Ivy House
7A Worcester Terrace, SR2 7AW
⏲ 12-11 (midnight Fri & Sat) ☎ (0191) 567 3399
5 changing beers (sourced nationally) Ⓗ
Tucked away but close to the Park Lane bus and Metro interchange, the Ivy House is well worth seeking out. Five varying guest ales and a cider are on offer, as well as extensive range of bottled international beers. Home-made pizzas and burgers are prepared in an open kitchen. There is a weekday happy hour from 5pm, themed meal nights and a Wednesday night quiz. Live music features on the second Saturday and last Sunday of the month. ❀◐♿⇌🚉🍎P🚌🐾📶

Ship Isis 🏆 Ⓛ
26 Silksworth Row, SR1 3QJ
⏲ 12-11.30 (midnight Fri & Sat) ☎ (0191) 514 7684
9 changing beers (sourced nationally) Ⓗ
Restored to its original Victorian splendour by the Jarrow Brewery in 2011, this is now a Camerons Head of Steam pub. Twelve handpumps offer nine cask beers, two real ciders and a perry, complemented by an extensive selection of bottled beers and a range of craft gins, all served by knowledgable staff. There is live music on Sunday, a Monday quiz and Wednesday is buskers' night. Local CAMRA Pub of the Year 2019, the Ship Isis has something for everyone. ♿⇌🚉🍎🚌📶

William Jameson ✔
30-32 Fawcett Street, SR1 1RH
⏲ 8am-midnight (1am Fri & Sat) ☎ (0191) 514 5016
Greene King Abbot; Ruddles Best Bitter; 6 changing beers (sourced nationally) Ⓗ
Sunderland's first Wetherspoon is in a former department store opposite the Winter Gardens in the heart of the city centre. All the usual features associated with the chain can be found in this busy corner pub, including good-value meals served all day. Twelve handpumps offer up to six guest beers and a cider to complement the regular range. The pub is a keen supporter of local brewers and holds twice-yearly beer festivals. Q🐎◐♿⇌🚉🍎🚌📶

Swalwell

Owa the Road
Unit 1 Spencer House, Market Lane, NE16 3DS
⏲ 3-10; 2-10 Fri; 2-9 Sat & Sun
4 changing beers (sourced nationally) Ⓗ
Situated within the old Co-op building directly opposite the Sun Inn, this micropub has no music and no TV. It does have four changing beers on handpull though, two of which are generally beers from the wood. The owner is working with a number of breweries to bring beers to the pub that are not normally found in wooden casks. Alongside the real ale and real ciders (in boxes), there is a wide range of gins, plus wines, soft drinks and bar snacks. Q🍎P🚌🐾

Sun Inn ✔
Market Lane, NE16 3AL (just off roundabout at end of Front St)
⏲ 11-11; 12-11 Sun
6 changing beers (sourced nationally) Ⓗ
The Sun is situated in the heart of the historic village that spawned many internationally renowned engineers and industrialists, and of course the famous Swalwell cabbage. This truly no-nonsense community pub provides good company

for locals and strangers alike. Sword dancers, darts, dominoes handicaps, a monthly pie competition and buskers' nights all feature. Bar food and snacks are available, free on Sunday. There is a regular bus service from Newcastle.

Tynemouth

Platform 2 Craft Ale Bar

Station Terrace, NE30 4RE

3-10.30; 12-11 Fri & Sat; 12-10.30 Sun

platform2tynemouth.com

4 changing beers (sourced locally)

Set on Platform 2 of Tynemouth Metro Station in what was the waiting room, the bar room has some bench seating around the walls plus a mix of tables and chairs, with a limited drinking area out on the station concourse. Four handpumps offer beers from local breweries. There is a free vintage-style jukebox and board games are available. Drinkers are welcome to bring in their own food.

Tynemouth Lodge Hotel

Tynemouth Road, NE30 4AA

11-11; 12-10.30 Sun (0191) 257 7565

tynemouthlodgehotel.co.uk

Caledonian Deuchars IPA; Draught Bass; Marston's Pedigree; Mordue Northumbrian Blonde; 1 changing beer (sourced nationally)

This attractive externally tiled 1799 free house, next to a former house of correction, has featured in every issue of the Guide since 1983. The comfortable pub has a U-shaped lounge with the bar on one side and a serving hatch on the other, and is noted in the area for the quality of its Draught Bass. An ideal stopping-off point for those completing the Coast-to-Coast cycle route.

QP(1,1A)

Tynemouth Social Club

15/16 Front Street, NE30 4DX

12-11 (11.30 Fri); 11.30-11 Sun (0191) 257 7542

2 changing beers (sourced nationally)

Formerly a Co-op, this well-established social club is situated at the heart of Tynemouth. Visitors are welcome and no membership is required. After several attempts to sell real ale, the club now has a rotating guest beer policy which has stimulated demand. The ale is well kept by the bar/cellarman and the club is worth a regular visit. Local CAMRA branch Club of the Year 2019.

Wallsend

Ritz

87/93 High Street West, NE28 8JD

7am-11 (0191) 296 9600

Greene King Abbot; Ruddles Best Bitter; Sharp's Doom Bar; 4 changing beers (sourced nationally)

A welcome addition to Wallsend High Street, this place opened in May 2015. The building was originally the Ritz cinema and later a bingo hall before Wetherspoon took it over. Entering from the High Street, the original period decoration can be seen. Quiz night is Monday. There is a large car park at the rear.

Washington

Courtyard

Biddick Lane, NE38 8AB

11-11 (midnight Fri & Sat); 12-11 Sun (0191) 417 0445

8 changing beers (sourced nationally)

Located within the Washington Arts Centre, this light and airy café/bar offers a warm welcome to drinkers and food lovers alike. Eight changing handpulled beers, two real ciders and a perry are available. An extensive range of food is served at lunchtime and early evening, with specials nights Tuesday to Saturday. Quiz night is Thursday. There is outdoor seating within the spacious courtyard. Popular beer festivals are held over the Easter and August bank holidays. P

Sir William De Wessyngton

2-3 Victoria Road, NE37 2SY

7am-midnight (1am Fri & Sat); 8am-midnight Sun

(0191) 418 0100

Greene King Abbot; Ruddles Best Bitter; 6 changing beers (sourced nationally)

Large open-plan Wetherspoon pub that used to be a snooker hall and ice cream parlour. It is named after a Norman knight and lord of the manor whose descendants later emigrated to the United States. The pub offers value-for-money beer and the usual well-priced Wetherspoon menu. The regular ales are complemented by at least four guests and two real ciders. Twice-yearly beer festivals are held. A good selection of local and international bottled beers is available.

QP

Steps

47 Spout Lane, NE38 7HP

3.30-11; 12-11 Sat; 12-10.30 Sun (0191) 415 0733

5 changing beers (sourced nationally)

Opened in 1894 as the Spout Lane Inn, the pub was renamed the Steps in 1976. The small, comfortable and friendly single-room lounge bar is divided into two drinking areas with pictures of old Washington decorating the walls. Five varying beers are on offer, often selected by the regulars, with some from local microbreweries. Quizzes are held on Tuesday and Thursday nights, and live entertainment features on the last Saturday of the month. Opening hours vary. QP(84)

West Boldon

Black Horse

Rectory Bank, NE36 0QQ (off A184)

11 (5 Mon & Tue)-11; 12-10.30 Sun (0191) 536 1814

Jennings Cumberland Ale; 1 changing beer (sourced nationally)

An old-fashioned pub with one small L-shaped bar and two handpulls offering Cumberland ale and a guest beer. Every available wall and shelf is adorned with bric-a-brac, and photographic prints are on display. Note the assorted headgear hanging from the ceiling. With a popular restaurant serving high-quality food, the pub can get busy in the evenings and at weekends. P

Whickham

One-Eyed Stag

5 The Square, NE16 4JB

11.30-10.30 (11 Fri & Sat); 12-10 Sun 07811 261924

4 changing beers (sourced nationally)

A welcome addition to the Whickham pub scene, this micropub has a tile-topped bar with four handpumps serving beer from local microbreweries. Blackboards adorn the wall behind the bar giving details of the beers and other drinks available. There is an interesting light fitting covering most of the ceiling and a wood-burning stove in an alcove.

Whitley Bay

Dog & Rabbit

36 Park View, NE26 2TH

12-10; 3-10 Sun ☎ 07944 552716

dogandrabbitbrewery.co.uk

4 changing beers (sourced nationally) H

This new micropub, converted from a women's clothing shop, is a welcome addition to the pub scene in Whitley Bay. The corner bar has four handpumps serving mostly local beers. A microbrewery has now been installed in the pub by the owner brewing Dog & Rabbit beers for the pub. With no music, Wi-Fi or sports TV, conversation is encouraged among visitors. Local CAMRA Pub of the Year 2019. Q

Storm Cellar

10 York Road, NE26 1AB

12-10 (11 Thu-Sat) ☎ 07725 762102

blackstormbrewery.com

Black Storm IPA; house beer (by Black Storm); 1 changing beer (sourced nationally) H

This bottle shop and tasting room is nestled in the heart of Whitley Bay. Four cask ales and a range of bottled beers, keg beers and ciders are available. Comfy sofas alongside rustic benches and tables add to the relaxed ambience. Despite its diminutive size, the pub has a light and airy feel with large windows all down one side.

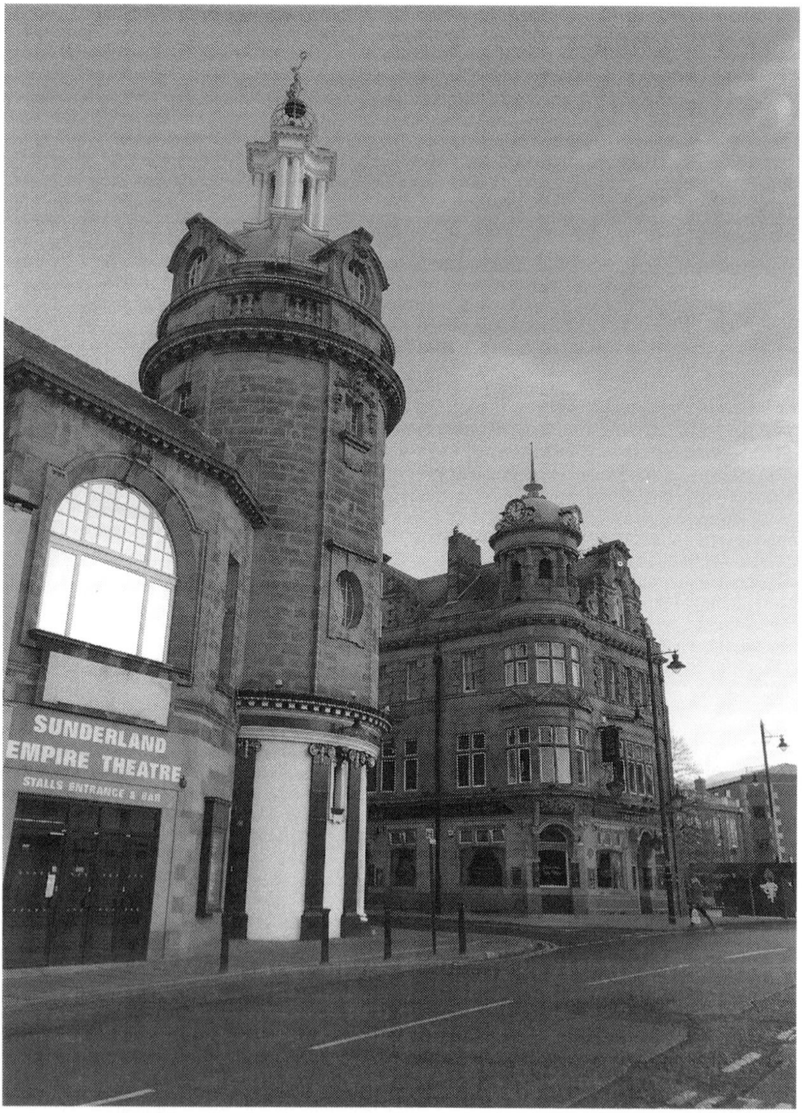

Dun Cow, Sunderland (Photo: John Lord/Flickr CC BY 2.0)

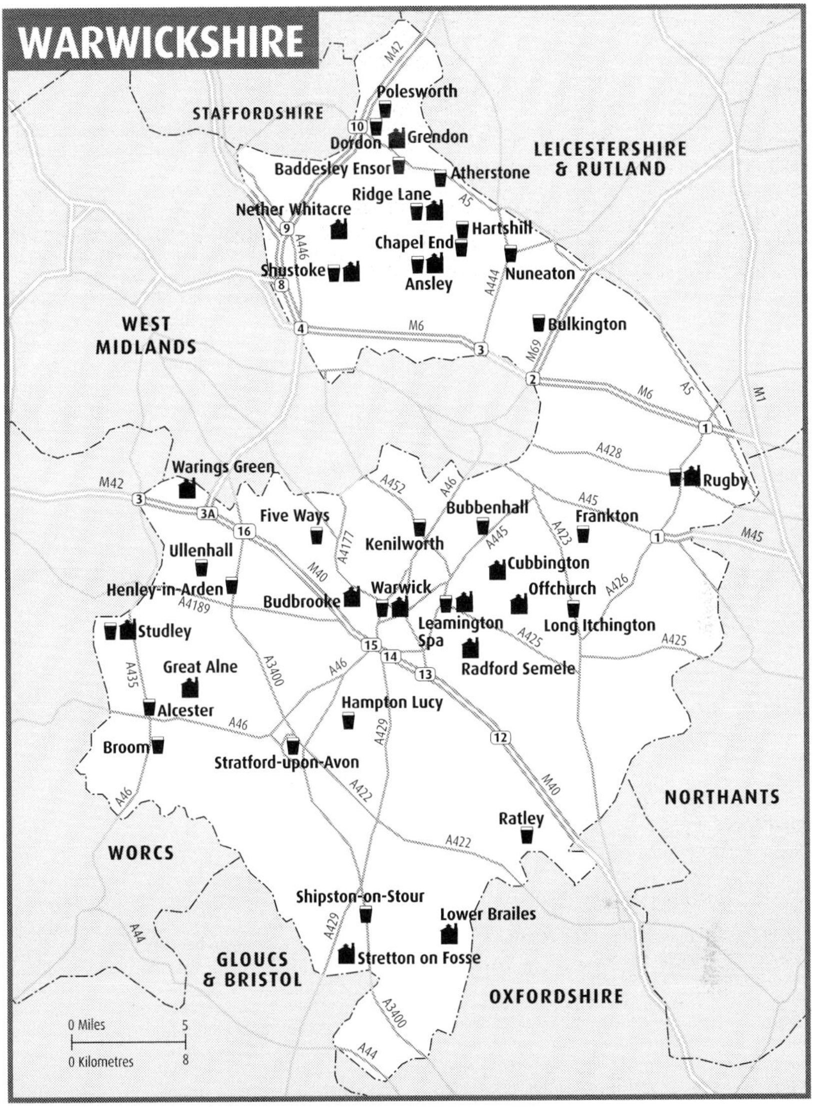

Alcester

Three Tuns

34 High Street, B49 5AB

1-midnight ☎ 07772 530119 thethreetunsalcester.com

Adnams Southwold Bitter; 5 changing beers (sourced regionally; often Bathams, Hobsons, Titanic) H

Nestled in the historic market town of Alcester, this welcoming single-bar pub retains the original beams, stone-flagged floors and sections of wattle and daub. No food, no loud music, but a relaxed atmosphere and a fantastic selection of real ales, fine wines and an array of ciders await you. There is also a varied range of malt whiskies and gins, plus prosecco from the bottle and tap. The pub hosts monthly bake-off nights and ale, cider and whisky tasting nights. Small parties can be catered for.

Turk's Head

4 High Street, B49 5AD

12-10 Mon (11 Tue-Fri); 10-11 Sat; 12-10.30 Sun

☎ (01789) 765948 theturkshead.net

Wye Valley HPA; 3 changing beers (sourced nationally; often Purity, Salopian, Skinner's) H

Central to the town, this busy pub is dedicated to real ale and is well worth a visit with its bare wood floors, exposed beams and roaring log fires. Beers served are from local breweries as well as Shropshire, Yorkshire and South Wales, and it offers three real ciders. Good food is a daily feature; there is a separate dining room as well as a quiet garden. The pub holds beer festivals and provides a bar during Alcester's popular food festivals. Local CAMRA Pub of the Year 2018 and 2019.

Q

Ansley

Lord Nelson Inn ▼ 🗍 ✅
Birmingham Road, CV10 9PQ
🕐 12-11 (10 Sun) ☎ (024) 7639 2305
🌐 thelordnelsoninnansley.co.uk
Sperrin Ansley Mild, Head Hunter, Band of Brothers, Third Party, Thick as Thieves; 3 changing beers Ⓗ
This nautically themed pub has been run by the Sperrin family since 1974 and has featured in the Guide for more than 20 consecutive years. Nine handpulls dispense the pub's own Sperrin brews, ales from other breweries and a real cider. There is an extensive food menu with meal nights and tribute nights hosted. The suntrap courtyard garden is a venue for beer festivals and barbecues.
🚲🕮🕽🕆🖪P🖳🐾🛜

Atherstone

Angel Ale House ▼ 🗍 ✅
24 Church Street, CV9 1HA
🕐 4-11 (midnight Fri); 12-midnight Sat; 12-10.30 Sun
☎ 07525 183056
Blythe Palmers Poison; Oakham Citra; 4 changing beers Ⓗ
This popular real ale flagship on the historic market square is a frequent local CAMRA Pub of the Year winner. It offers six real ales, often local and always including a dark beer, plus up to 10 real ciders. Wednesday is quiz night; music is via customer select-and-play from a large vinyl LP collection. There is a large free council car park to the rear. 🚲🕮🛱P🖳🐾

Baddesley Ensor

Red Lion
The Common, CV9 2BT (from Grendon roundabout on A5 go S up Boot Hill) SP273983
🕐 7 (4 Fri)-11; 12-3, 7-11 Sat; 12-3, 7-10.30 Sun
☎ (01827) 718186
Draught Bass; Greene King Abbot; Marston's Pedigree; 3 changing beers Ⓗ
Popular community local whose landlord has been at the helm for more than 20 years. Food does not feature, just ale and conversation. Comfy seating and the log fire are enhanced by a music-free environment. Three guest ales are served, often from major concerns such as Greene King and Everards, but sometimes from small local breweries. The sparkler is willingly removed on request. Off-road parking is available opposite the pub. Lunchtime opening is weekends only.
Q🕆🛱🐾

Broom

Broom Tavern 🗍
32 High Street, B50 4HL
🕐 12-11 ☎ (01789) 778199 🌐 broomtavern.co.uk
Purity Pure UBU; Wye Valley Bitter; 2 changing beers Ⓗ
A lovely brick and timber multi-room building which retains a great amount of character. It has been tastefully made over, while keeping the cosy snug and log fire in winter. Reopened by two experienced chefs with a good pedigree in the kitchen, it serves great food lunchtimes and evenings, made with local ingredients. Local beers are frequently found here along with at least one real cider. There is a choice of beer gardens. 🕮🕽🕆

Bubbenhall

Malt Shovel 🗍
Lower End, CV8 3BW
🕐 12-11 ☎ (024) 7630 1141
Black Sheep Best Bitter; Greene King Abbot; 2 changing beers (sourced nationally; often Church End) Ⓗ
Friendly village free house in a 17th-century Grade II-listed building, comprising a large L-shaped lounge bar at the front and a small public bar to the rear. Outside, there is a small patio to the front and a large walled garden and adjacent bowling green behind the spacious car park. The pub is popular for home-cooked food and holds regular fish, pie and tapas nights. Convenient for the nearby Ryton Pools Country Park. 🕮🕽🖪🖳(539)🐾

Bulkington

Weavers' Arms
12 Long Street, CV12 9JZ
🕐 4-midnight; 12-midnight Sat & Sun ☎ (024) 7631 4415
Draught Bass; 1 changing beer Ⓗ
Family-owned, two-roomed, traditional village pub converted from weavers' cottages. Well known for the quality of its Bass ale, it has a wood-panelled games room, log-burning fireplace and a slate floor. Outside, the extensive, well-kept beer garden hosts barbecues in the summer. Children are welcome and private functions can be catered for. The Pork Pie Club, Weavers Walkers and Hillbilly Golf Society hold regular meetings here.
🚲🕮🛱🖳(56)🐾

Chapel End

Salutation
Chancery Lane, CV10 0PB
🕐 1-11 (midnight Thu); 12-1am Fri & Sat; 12-10.30 Sun
☎ (024) 7704 7573
Draught Bass; 2 changing beers Ⓗ
Chapel End used to have five pubs but the only survivor is the Sally, a popular, award-winning community inn. Bass is served regularly, along with guest beers from a variety of breweries. The pub hosts quizzes and other events, and shows major football, rugby and boxing matches on TV. Live bands perform regularly, usually on Saturday night or Sunday late afternoon. 🚲🛱P🖳🐾🛜

REAL ALE BREWERIES
Atomic 🍺 Rugby
Blue Bell 🍺 Warings Green
Church End Ridge Lane
Church Farm Budbrooke
Clouded Minds Lower Brailes
Custom Head Grendon
Fizzy Moon 🍺 Leamington Spa
Fosse Way Offchurch (NEW)
Freestyle 🍺 Shustoke
North Cotswold Stretton-on-Fosse
Old Pie Factory Warwick
Purity Great Alne
Slaughterhouse Warwick
Sperrin 🍺 Ansley
Warwickshire Cubbington
Weatheroak Studley
Whitacre 🍺 Nether Whitacre
Windmill Hill Radford Semele

Dordon

Mini Miner

13 Browns Lane, B78 1TR

3-10.30 (11 Fri); 12-11 Sat; 12-10.30 Sun 07455 242415

3 changing beers (often Church End)

Since opening in 2018, this small single-roomed pub, in a parade of shops, has provided much-needed refreshment for Dordon drinkers following the closure of local pubs and clubs over the years. Its name pays homage to the former Merrie Miner in the village, later renamed the Cuckoo's Rest, and it incorporates the original bar frontage from the now closed pub. Up to three ales are served, usually including something local and something well known. P (65)

Five Ways

Case is Altered

Case Lane, CV35 7JD (off Five Ways Rd near A4141/A4177 jct) SP225701

12-2.30, 6-11; 12-7.30 Sun (01926) 484206

Wye Valley Butty Bach; house beer (by Old Pie Factory); 3 changing beers (sourced locally)

A classic unspoilt country pub with a bar and separate snug. The current landlady has been here for over 30 years, after taking over from her grandmother. The traditional bar billiards table still takes the old sixpences which have to be bought from the bar. Monday is cribbage night. Do not miss the Victorian print of a former Leamington brewer in the bar plus a clock from another old local brewer. There is even a propeller from a World War I fighter plane on the ceiling. Q P

Frankton

Friendly Inn

Main Street, CV23 9NY

12-3 (not Mon), 5.30-10.30; 12-10.30 Sat & Sun (01926) 632430

Greene King IPA; 2 changing beers (sourced nationally; often Draught Bass, Fuller's)

The original black and white timber-framed building, which is now the restaurant, dates from 1550 and was converted to a pub in the late 19th century. The bar, housed in an extension at the rear, continues the beamed theme. This traditional village pub is very popular with diners, especially for its lunchtime offer of two meals for £12. Vegetarian options are available. The pub stays open later when busy. The entrance is at the back from the car park. P (580)

Hampton Lucy

Boar's Head

Church Street, CV35 8BE

12-11 (midnight Fri & Sat); 12-9.30 Sun (01789) 840533 theboarsheadhamptonlucy.com

Ringwood Razorback; 4 changing beers (sourced locally; often Church End, North Cotswold, Slaughterhouse)

A friendly, popular village pub dating back to the 17th century. It was originally built as a cider house; the present kitchen was once a mortuary. On a Sustrans route and close to the River Avon, the pub is frequented by cyclists, walkers and visitors to nearby Charlecote Park. Five real ales are served including at least two LocAles. The menu offers fresh, home-made food. The walled rear garden is popular in good weather. An annual themed beer festival is held in summer. P

Hartshill

Royal Oak

Oldbury Road, CV10 0TD

4-11; 12-midnight Fri & Sat; 12-11 Sun (024) 7639 6442

theroyaloakhartshill.co.uk

Draught Bass; 2 changing beers

A free house close to Hartshill Hayes Country Park, the Royal Oak has been refurbished to give a good old-fashioned community feeling, with many pictures of old Hartshill on display. It offers a changing range of beers from breweries near and far, alongside a real cider. A garden at the rear accommodates live music and beer festivals during the summer months. The bar is sports oriented, showing all major events. Various functions are hosted throughout the year. (48)

Henley-in-Arden

Three Tuns

103 High Street, B95 5AT

12 (3.30 Mon & Tue)-11; 12-10.30 Sun (01564) 792723

Fuller's London Pride; Sharp's Doom Bar, Atlantic; Wye Valley Butty Bach; 1 changing beer

An unpretentious 16th-century two-roomed inn with a single bar serving both areas. Popular with locals, this traditional drinkers' pub is usually busy and the atmosphere is always friendly. Five real ales are served in consistently good condition from the bar. Pub snacks plus home-made cobs and sausage rolls are usually on sale. Parking is on the street outside the pub. Q (X20)

Kenilworth

Green Man

Warwick Road, CV8 1HS

10-11 (midnight Fri & Sat) (01296) 863061

Purity Mad Goose; house beer (by Black Sheep); 6 changing beers (sourced nationally)

Popular Ember Inn within walking distance of Kenilworth town centre. The central bar has two banks of five handpumps dispensing a range of permanent and changing beers. The house beer, Ember Ale, is brewed by Black Sheep. Good-quality food is served daily 11.30am-10pm. There is an assortment of distinct seating areas and a pleasant patio. Ample parking is available and public transport passes nearby.
P (11,X17)

Old Bakery

12 High Street, CV8 1LZ (near A429/A452 jct)

5.30-11.30; 5-11.30 Sat; 5-11 Sun (01926) 864111

theoldbakery.eu

Wye Valley HPA; house beer (by Byatt's); 2 changing beers (sourced regionally)

Located in the old part of Kenilworth near St Nicholas Church and Abbey Fields, this interesting two-roomed bar is set in an oak-beamed 400-year-old building. There are four ales served in a friendly atmosphere, without TV screens, music or noisy games machines. The house beer is from Byatt's, brewed locally. Wheelchair access is to the rear of the building. Accommodation is in 14 en-suite rooms. Local CAMRA Pub of the Year 2018.
Q P (11)

Virgins & Castle

7 High Street, CV8 1LY (A429/A452 jct)
11 (3 Mon)-11; 11-midnight Fri & Sat; 11-10.30 Sun
☎ (01926) 853737 🌐 virginsandcastle.co.uk
Everards Beacon Hill, Tiger; 3 changing beers (sourced regionally; often Everards)
Famous old pub which gets its unusual name from a visit by Elizabeth I to Kenilworth Castle. Situated in the quaint old town and dating from the 16th century, it is reputed to be Kenilworth's oldest pub. Its several small rooms give a cosy feel. Look out for the names etched into the internal glasswork, some of which are at least 100 years old. The pub holds periodic festivals and has a good reputation for its food. The Coventry & Warwickshire branch of CAMRA was formed here in 1974.
(11)

Leamington Spa

New Inn

197 Leam Terrace, CV31 1DW
12 (4 Mon)-midnight; 12-1am Fri & Sat; 12-11 Sun
☎ (01926) 422861 🌐 thenewinnleamington.co.uk
Eagle IPA; Greene King Abbot; Sharp's Doom Bar, Atlantic; 2 changing beers (often Byatt's)
A traditional pub in a wide Victorian terrace on the outskirts of Leamington Spa. The original pub has been extended into the next-door property. A central door opens directly on to the bar, with a seating area to the left and a games area to the right leading to an extension at the rear. Outside is a good-sized walled garden. Quality home-cooked food is served. A quiz is hosted fortnightly on a Wednesday. (63,64)

White Horse

4-6 Clarendon Avenue, CV32 5PZ
12-11 (midnight Thu; 1am Fri); 10-1am Sat; 11.30-11 Sun
☎ (01926) 426892 🌐 thewhitehorseleamingtonspa.co.uk
5 changing beers
This popular town pub dates back to the 1830s and has been extended and modified over the years. The extended section now holds the main bar, serving a large selection of cask, craft and continental beers, while the original bar area is reserved for private functions. An arched stable entrance featuring a full-sized white horse leads to a courtyard and beer garden with covered and heated seating.

Woodland Tavern

3 Regent Street, CV32 5HW
12-midnight (1am Fri & Sat); 12-11.30 Sun
☎ (01926) 425868
Sharp's Atlantic; Slaughterhouse Saddleback Best Bitter; 2 changing beers
Traditional Victorian street-corner pub situated close to the centre of Leamington Spa and enjoyed by locals and visitors alike. It has a public bar and a separate lounge, also used as a function room. The unique partially covered courtyard features murals depicting local references and jokes. On the side of the building is a large colourful mural showing a dray and horses delivering ale to the pub. Real cider is served from the Napton Cidery.

Long Itchington

Harvester

6 Church Road, CV47 9PE (off A423 at village pond, then first left)
12-2.30, 6-11; 12-3, 7-10.30 Sun ☎ (01926) 812698
🌐 theharvesterinn.co.uk
3 changing beers
This white-fronted pub is near the village pond, on the corner of the square. Inside is a main bar, a small drinking area and a restaurant specialising in good-value steaks. The beer range changes frequently, usually supporting smaller breweries. Real cider and a Belgian fruit beer are also on the bar. The pub hosts a beer festival each May bank holiday. A large walled courtyard garden to the rear has a wood-fired pizza oven. Gruntfuttocks Speciality Pickles can be purchased to take home.
(64)

Nuneaton

Black Swan in Hand

Bond Gate, CV11 4AE
10-11 (midnight Thu; 1am Fri & Sat); 10-midnight Sun
☎ (024) 7634 9548
4 changing beers
A town-centre pub, formerly known as the Granby, extensively refurbished by Amber Taverns in 2018. Its name acknowledges local pubs including the Black Swan, Heart in Hand, Black Horse and White Swan, all of which were demolished between 1959 and 1970. Four handpulls dispense changing ales from various breweries. The ground-floor bar offers open and booth seating. Sport is shown on TVs dotted around the bar and outside areas.
(Trent Valley)

Felix Holt

3 Stratford Street, CV11 5BS
8am-11 (midnight Fri & Sat) ☎ (024) 7634 7785
Byatt's Regal Blond; Greene King Abbot; Ruddles Best Bitter; Sharp's Doom Bar; changing beers
Large Wetherspoon outlet in the town centre. The pub takes its name from a novel by Nuneaton-born George Eliot and the literary theme is reflected in the décor of books and pictures of local history. Look out for the comical metal sculptures on the walls. A good range of guest beers includes local ales, with Byatt's and Oakham often represented. Food is served 8am-10pm. There are tables and chairs outside, and a heated area for smokers.
Q

Lord Hop

38 Queens Road, CV11 5JX
closed Mon; 12-9; 12-11 Fri & Sat ☎ (024) 7798 1869
4 changing beers
Town-centre micropub on two levels, the upper level boasting settees, books and board games. Four or more real ales from local and far-away breweries are served on handpull or straight from the cask, along with two ciders or perries on handpull and up to six more in the chiller. Wine, gin and soft drinks are also sold. Snacks are available, or bring your own takeaway. No under-18s, and assistance dogs only. A former local CAMRA Pub of the Year and Cider Pub of the Year. The pub has a collection of CAMRA magazines from various branches. **Q**

Polesworth

Bull's Head

Tamworth Road, B78 1JH (by canal bridge on B5000)
11-midnight (11.30 Sun) (01827) 898990
2 changing beers [H]
Solidly traditional community local next to the canal. The L-shaped bar is generally busy but the small lounge through the archway tends to be quieter. There is plenty going on here including darts and bowls clubs, quizzes, raffles and sports screenings. Up to three guest beers feature depending on the time of week. Aside from snacks on occasion, there is no food, but the independent Indian restaurant upstairs is happy to fetch ale for you from downstairs. P

Ratley

Rose & Crown

Chapel Lane, OX15 6DS
5-9 Mon; closed Tue; 12-3, 5-11 Wed-Thu; 12-11 Fri-Sun
(01295) 678148 roseandcrownratley.co.uk
St Austell Tribute; Wye Valley Bitter, Butty Bach; 2 changing beers (sourced locally; often Prescott, Purity) [H]
Tucked away at the bottom of an ancient village on the northern extremity of the Cotswolds escarpment, this 11th-century golden-stone pub has a wealth of detail, with cosy log fires in winter and a suntrap garden in summer. High-quality food is served. Walkers, dogs, locals and visitors are all welcome. This friendly local is reputedly haunted by the ghost of a Roundhead soldier.
Q

Ridge Lane

Church End Brewery Tap

CV10 0RD (2 miles SW of Atherstone)
closed Mon & Tue; 6-11 Wed & Thu; 12-11 Fri & Sat; 12-10.30 Sun (01827) 713080 churchendbrewery.co.uk
Church End Goat's Milk, Gravediggers Ale, What the Fox's Hat, Fallen Angel; 4 changing beers [H]
This brewery tap is hidden from the road, with access signposted by a board positioned at the entrance. Eight handpulls serve the bar and vestry – beers change regularly but always include one guest ale and a mild. The ever-changing ciders are dispensed direct from the barrel. There is a large meadow garden with ample seating. Under-18s are allowed in the vestry until 6pm.
Q P

Rugby

Bull Inn

33-35 Main Street, Clifton upon Dunsmore, CV23 0BH
12-3, 5-11 Mon-Wed; 12-11 Thu-Sat; 12-10 Sun
(01788) 552237 thebullinnclifton.co.uk
St Austell Tribute, Proper Job; 1 changing beer (sourced nationally) [H]
Situated on the main road, this is a family-oriented pub catering for the local villagers. There is a large main bar, separate pool room and dining area. The extensive, traditional home-cooked food includes a Sunday roast (no food Sun eve). The pub holds regular activities, including theme nights and quizzes. Guest ales are selected by the locals.
P

Crafty Banker

11a Bank Street, CV21 2QE
closed Mon; 4-11; 5-10 Sun 07398 715365
XT Hop Kitty; house beer (by XT); 4 changing beers (sourced nationally; often Driftwood, Electric Bear, Moor Beer) [H]
A friendly pub that serves quality ales in an atmosphere perfect for conversation. The pleasant, open-plan bar area has a retro feel. Its six handpumps dispense a wide range of real ales, complemented by four craft beers and a traditional cider. The Crafty Banker also stocks more than 70 gins plus a range of other spirits from independent producers. Q

Merchants Inn

5-6 Little Church Street, CV21 3AW
12-midnight (1am Fri & Sat); 12-11.30 Sun
(01788) 571119 merchantsinn.co.uk
Oakham Bishops Farewell; Purity Mad Goose; house beer (by Nethergate) [H]**; 6 changing beers (sourced nationally)** [H]/[G]
This popular town-centre pub attracts a varied clientele and is a living museum of brewery memorabilia. Flagstone floors and an open fire greet you on arrival. Food is available Monday to Saturday, and a traditional roast is served on Sunday until 5pm. A large-screen TV shows sport including rugby and cricket. Beer festivals, Belgian and German themed nights plus gin and cider weekends are hosted around the calendar.

Seven Stars

40 Albert Square, CV21 2SH
4-11 Mon; 12-11 Tue-Thu (midnight Fri & Sat); 12-10 Sun
(01788) 535478 sevenstarsrugby.co.uk
Everards Tiger; Oakham JHB; 9 changing beers (sourced nationally; often Grainstore) [H]
A traditional multi-roomed community pub that serves quality beers and ciders from its 14 handpumps. Everards Tiger is usually on as well as ales from Grainstore and Oakham, along with guests including a mild, stout and porter. Food includes home-made Scotch eggs, which sell out quickly, plus filled rolls and locally produced pork pies. Rugby is televised in the bar. Flowers brighten the rear courtyard garden of this recent local CAMRA Pub of the Year. Q

Squirrel Inn

33 Church Street, CV21 3PU
12-11; 4-10.30 Sun (01788) 578527
4 changing beers (sourced nationally; often Dow Bridge, Marston's, Pitchfork) [H]
There is always a warm welcome, and often a real fire, at Rugby's local jewel in the town. This historic free house has an abundance of character, with pictures of old Rugby contributing to its unique and intimate interior. Beers from Dow Bridge, Pitchfork, 3D and Merry Miner are regularly served alongside Marston's ales, plus four ciders. Live music is a big part of the pub's appeal: various genres feature on Saturday night, with open mic on Wednesday. Poetry night is the last Sunday of the month.

Town & County Club

12 Henry Street, CV21 2QA
7.30-11 Mon, Thu & Fri; 12-4, 7.30-11 Tue; 11.30-5, 7.30-11 Sat; 12-5, 7.30-10.30 Sun 07931 661840

Church End Gravediggers Ale; Greene King IPA; 2 changing beers (sourced nationally; often Donnington, Otter, Timothy Taylor) Ⓗ
This is a second consecutive appearance in the Guide for the Town & County, which has been trading since 1933. The small town-centre club is a local CAMRA award winner with four handpumps, two of which dispense changing guest ales. Regular events include Tuesday bingo, a monthly quiz, Sunday night rock DJ, occasional live music and coach trips. The club runs dominoes and skittles teams. CAMRA members are welcome and guests may be signed in. Q♣🚌🐾

Victoria Inn

1 Lower Hillmorton Road, CV21 3ST
12 (4 Mon-Wed)-midnight ☎ (01788) 544374
downthevic.com
Atomic Strike; Hook Norton Hooky; 5 changing beers (sourced nationally; often Abbeydale, Atomic, Titanic) Ⓗ
A beautiful Victorian pub, built in a wedge shape and situated just outside the town centre. The multi-roomed local features a traditional bar, a larger lounge and two relatively new snugs. Owned by the town's Atomic Brewery, it stocks two of the brewery's beers plus five other rotating guest ales. TV sport is regularly screened and quiz nights are held on Wednesday and Sunday evenings. A true gem of a pub, the last of its kind in Rugby. ❀♣🍎🚌🐾

Shipston-on-Stour

Black Horse Inn

Station Road, CV36 4BT
12-3 (not Mon), 6-11; 12-11 Thu-Sun ☎ (01608) 238489
blackhorseshipston.co.uk
Prescott Hill Climb; Wye Valley Butty Bach; 1 changing beer (sourced regionally; often North Cotswold, Vale, Young's) Ⓗ
This stone-built 15th-century inn is the oldest pub and only thatched building in Shipston, with a licence that dates back to 1540. A warm welcome from the landlord is assured. It has two rooms – the main bar is cosy with a large inglenook log fireplace, the second bar has a log fire. Thai food is available. There is live music in the garden in summer and several beer and cider festivals are staged. Q❀◐♣🍎P🚌🐾

Thirst Edition

46B Church Street, CV36 4AS
closed Mon; 4-9 Tue-Fri; 12-9 Sat; 4-7.30 Sun
☎ (01608) 664974 thirstedition.co.uk
Kelham Island Pale Rider; Skinner's Betty Stogs; Thornbridge Jaipur IPA; 3 changing beers (sourced regionally; often Byatt's, North Cotswold, Sadler's) Ⓗ
A micropub in a shop on the main road, the Thirst Edition offers a varied selection of real ales, ciders and gins. Since opening in March 2018 it has developed a good reputation for its well-kept beers and ciders. The pub has seating for 20; free from music, TV and food, conversation is encouraged. Outside is a stop for the number 50 bus from Stratford, which runs every two hours. Over-18s only. Q🍎🚌(50)🐾

Shustoke

Griffin Inn

Church Road, B46 2LB (on B4116 on sharp bend)
12-2.30, 7-11; 12-11 Fri-Sun ☎ (01675) 481205
Freestyle Griffin Dark; Oakham Citra; Theakston Old Peculier; Wye Valley Butty Bach; 6 changing beers (sourced nationally; often Freestyle, Oakham) Ⓗ
This rural Guide regular attracts customers from miles around. In winter the pub is gloriously cosy, its inglenook fireplaces featuring solid fuel stoves. The summer highlight is a large, busy beer festival. Freestyle ales from the adjacent brewery usually feature among the six guest beers. Up to 10 real ciders are offered, depending on the time of year. Children are welcome in the conservatory, beer terrace and meadow-style garden. Home-cooked lunches are served (no food Sun). Q❀◐⛺🍎P🐾

Plough

The Green, B46 2AN
12-11 (10.30 Sun) ☎ (01675) 481557
theploughinnshustoke.co.uk
Draught Bass; 4 changing beers Ⓗ
An attractive old pub on the village green, featuring four low-ceilinged rooms around the bar, a separate games room and a modern conservatory. The Plough is popular for a wide range of home-cooked food. It has is a tidy beer terrace with greenery at the front, and a pets' corner to entertain young children at the rear. The pleasant surrounding countryside attracts ramblers and cyclists; note the vintage Cyclists' Touring Club plaque on the front wall. ❀◐♿♣P🐾

Stratford-upon-Avon

Stratford Alehouse

12B Greenhill Street, CV37 6LF
2-11; 1-11 Fri & Sat; 2-8 Sun ☎ 07746 807966
thestratfordalehouse.com
4 changing beers (sourced nationally; often Byatt's, North Cotswold, Wye Valley) Ⓖ
A family-run, one-bar micropub serving the finest real ales, ciders and wines. There is no loud music (except on live music nights), noisy children or gaming machines to distract you here – just a friendly welcome in a relaxing environment for drinking, chatting, making new friends or reading the newspapers. Snacks are served. Since opening in 2013, more than 1,000 different beers have made an appearance. Home to Stratford Folk Club on a Wednesday, and live bands at the weekend plus Thursday and alternate Mondays. A recent local CAMRA Pub of the Year. Q♿🍎🚌🐾

Studley

Weatheroak Tap House

21A High Street, B80 7HN (up Studley High St next to chippy)
4-9 Mon; 12.30-10.30 Tue-Thu (11 Fri); 12-11 Sat; 12-9 Sun
☎ (01527) 854433 weatheroakbrewery.co.uk
Weatheroak Bees Knees, Victoria Works, Keystone Hops; house beer (by Weatheroak); 2 changing beers (sourced locally; often Beowulf, Church End, Weatheroak) Ⓗ
This micropub with two small, cosy rooms opened in 2016 and is an outlet for the nearby Weatheroak Brewery. Basic snacks are available and there is a chip shop next door – you are welcome to bring in food to the pub. Off-sales from Weatheroak are also available in various quantities.
Q♣🍎P🚌🐾

Ullenhall

Winged Spur ✔

Main Road, B95 5PA (in village) SP122674
12-11 (10.30 Sun) ☎ (01564) 797396
thewingedspurullenhall.co.uk
4 changing beers (sourced regionally) H
A quintessentially rural British pub in the heart of Ullenhall village, with an emphasis on food and drink for families. The pub is under new ownership and was fully refurbished and extended in 2018; its light and airy interior can seat more than 100 diners. The name derives from Robert Knight, a former local landowner, whose family crest was a spur – the medieval symbol of knighthood.
Q P

Warwick

Cape of Good Hope L

66 Lower Cape, CV34 5DP (off Cape Rd)
12-11; 11-1am Fri & Sat; 11-midnight Sun
☎ (01926) 498138 thecapeofgoodhopepub.com
Church Farm Harry's Heifer; Hook Norton Hooky; Wye Valley Butty Bach; 3 changing beers H
This historic 1798 alehouse on the Grand Union Canal welcomes canal users and locals alike. The original building on the waterside is now the front bar, with a modern extension to the rear. Internal decorations feature canal memorabilia, including interesting maps. Three permanent real ales are offered along with three locally sourced guest beers. The friendly staff are knowledgable and proud to serve local ales and food. There is outside seating alongside the water next to a sometimes-busy double lock. P (G1)

Fourpenny Pub

27/29 Crompton Street, CV34 6HJ (near racecourse, between A429 and A4189)
12-11 ☎ (01926) 491360 4pennyhotel.co.uk
6 changing beers H
The pub is located in a Georgian building dating from around 1800 and lies a short distance from the town centre, close to the racecourse and castle. Its name derives from the price of a cup of coffee and tot of rum that was charged to workers building the nearby Grand Union Canal in the early 1800s. The single, split-level room has a contemporary feel and a relaxed atmosphere, enhanced by the absence of machines or loud music. Q P

Old Post Office L

12 West Street, CV34 6AN
closed Mon; 12-9; 12-5 Sun ☎ 07765 896155
oldpostofficewarwick.com
Slaughterhouse Saddleback Best Bitter H**; 5 changing beers** H/G
Warwick's first alehouse offers a friendly, relaxed atmosphere and traditional beers served on handpump and straight from the cask. Popular with real ale enthusiasts and local residents, the small bar is housed in a former shop just below the West Gate and within easy walking distance of the castle. It is decorated with a large collection of pub memorabilia. A good selection of ciders is also available. No food is served but you are welcome to bring your own.

Punch Bowl

1 The Butts, CV34 4SS
closed Mon; 12-2.30, 5-11 Tue-Thu; 12-11 Fri & Sat; 12-10 Sun ☎ (01926) 403846 punchbowlwarwick.co.uk
5 changing beers H
The building is an old coaching inn and hostelry dating back to the early 19th century. It has a large, open bar area on different levels – a raised area serves as a stage for popular music events held every Thursday evening and on special occasions. Sports events are shown on a large screen. The pub promotes real ale, with five changing guest beers available at all times. A blackboard behind the bar keeps a tally of all the different ales sold.
P (X17)

Wild Boar L

27 Lakin Road, CV34 5BU
12-11.30 (12.30am Fri & Sat); 12-10 Sun
☎ (01926) 499968 thewildboarwarwick.co.uk
Slaughterhouse Saddleback Best Bitter; 9 changing beers (often Everards, Slaughterhouse) H
Award-winning Project William community pub, close to the railway station. An end-of-terrace Victorian building, it has a bar, snug and separate beer hall which was formerly a skittle alley. The pub is the taphouse for Slaughterhouse Brewery, and provides views of the on-site two-barrel microbrewery. Ten handpumps deliver Slaughterhouse, Everards and guest ales. Outside is an attractive patio hop garden – the hops are used for Slaughterhouse's annual brew, the Green Hopper. Q (X17)

Beers suitable for vegetarians and vegans

A number of cask and bottle-conditioned beers in the Good Beer Guide are listed as suitable for vegetarians and vegans. The main ingredients used in cask beer production are malted grain, hops, yeast and water, and these present no problems for drinkers who wish to avoid animal products. But many brewers of cask beer use isinglass as a clearing agent: isinglass is derived from the bladders of certain fish, including the sturgeon. Isinglass is added to a cask when it leaves the brewery and attracts yeast cells and protein, which fall to the bottom of the container. Other clearing agents – notably Irish moss, derived from seaweed – can be used in place of isinglass and the Guide feels that brewers should take a serious look at replacing isinglass with plant-derived finings, especially as the sturgeon is an endangered species.
Vegans avoid dairy products: lactose, a bi-product of cheese making, is used in milk stout, of which Mackeson is the best-known example.

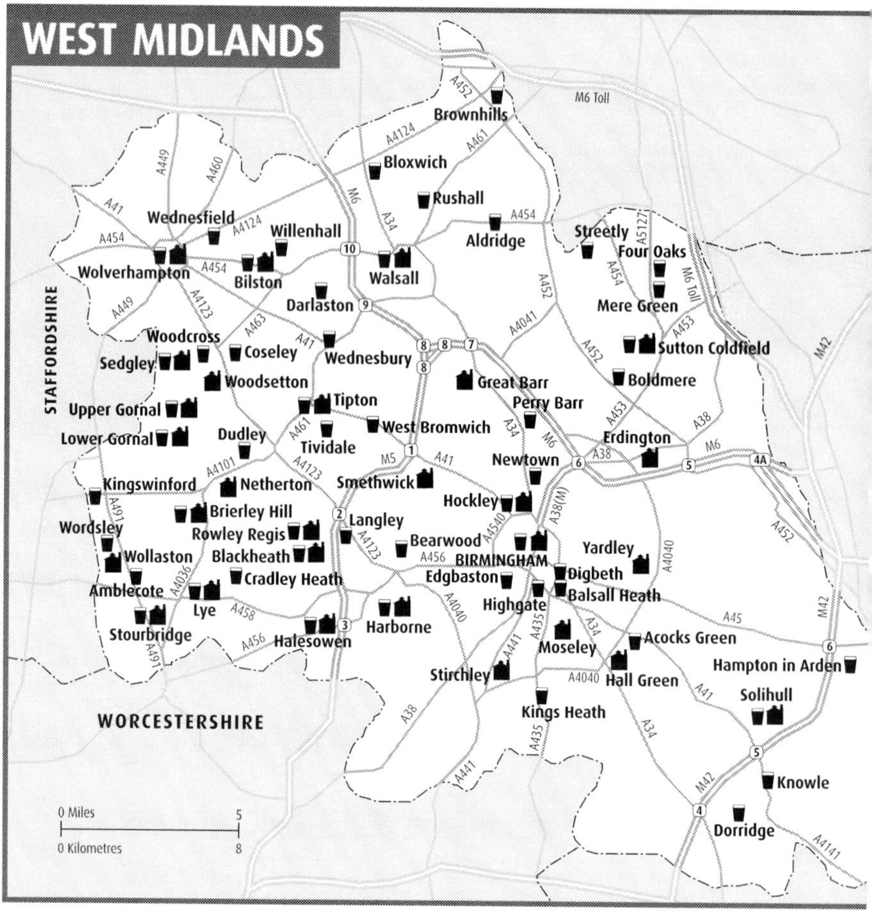

Aldridge

Turtle's Head

14 Croft Parade, WS9 8LY

closed Mon; 12-10 (10.30 Fri & Sat); 12-9 Sun

(01922) 325635 theturtleshead.co.uk

4 changing beers (sourced locally; often Backyard, Church End, Fixed Wheel)

Micropub with a warm welcome, opened in 2015 in the centre of Aldridge town. Four handpumps serve a range of ales from throughout the UK. No regular beers are sold, but the beer menu changes daily. Up to four real ciders are also offered, increasing to eight in the summer months. Various filled rolls and bar snacks are available, and a selection of complimentary cheeses and pates on Sunday (you can also bring your own food as long as you buy a drink). Dog and child friendly.

Amblecote

Robin Hood

196 Collis Street, DY8 4EQ (on A4102 one-way street off Brettell Lane A461)

12 (4 Mon & Tue)-11; 12-midnight Fri & Sat

07436 793462

Bathams Best Bitter; Enville Ginger Beer; Holden's Golden Glow; Kelham Island Pale Rider; St Austell Proper Job; Wye Valley HPA; 4 changing beers (often Titanic)

Great ales, quality food and a warm welcome – a fine traditional Black Country local. The Robin Hood celebrated 160 years as a licensed house in 2015. Its front rooms house a wonderful beer bottle collection including international and historic brews. The LocAle scheme is emphasised, with many local beers always available. The pub serves food at the weekend and hosts occasional themed culinary nights. Q P (6,16)

Bearwood

Bear Tavern

500 Bearwood Road, B66 4BX

9am-11 (midnight Fri; 1am Sat); 10-11 Sun

(0121) 429 1184

Greene King IPA; 5 changing beers (sourced nationally; often Fixed Wheel, Purity, Titanic)

Busy, open-plan, community pub dominated by a central bar. There are sports screens throughout as live matches are often shown. Attentive, CAMRA-friendly staff serve an interesting range of nationally sourced real ales, including five changing beers. There is a large function room upstairs with a wooden floor. Affordable pub food is served. The pub attracts a diverse clientele spanning all age groups.

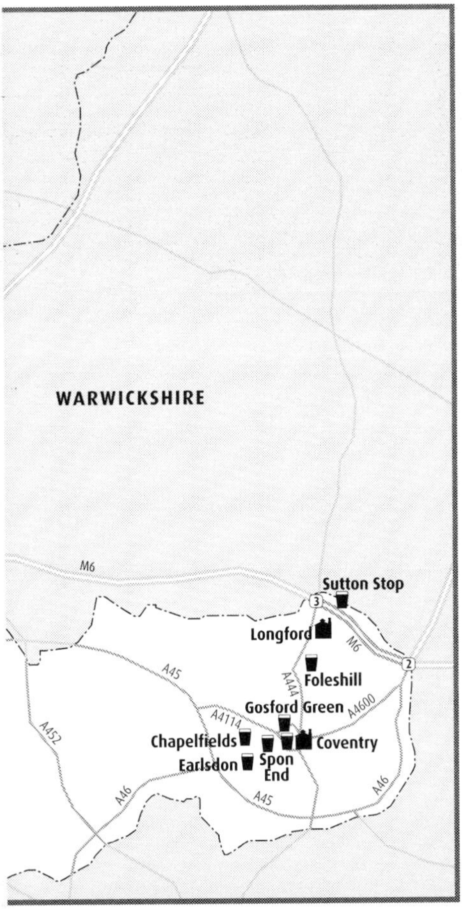

Midland

526-528 Bearwood Road, B66 4BE

10-11 (midnight Fri & Sat); 12-11 Sun ☎ (0121) 429 6958

Black Country Bradley's Finest Golden, Pig on the Wall, Fireside; changing beers (sourced nationally; often Downton, Fixed Wheel, Springhead) Ⓗ

A former Midland Bank, this is a single-room, open-plan pub serving up to 13 real ales and two traditional ciders. It has a beer cellar on the same floor which can be viewed through a glass inspection panel. A small selection of continental beers, fruit wines and freshly made cobs is available. There is a quiz on Wednesday. Q♿♣🍎🚌📶

Bilston

Cafe Metro Ⓛ

46 Church Street, WV14 0AH (opp St Leonards church, close to town hall)

10-2.30, 5-8 Mon; 9am-2.30, 5-10 Tue; closed Wed; 10-3, 5-10 Thu; 9am-3, 5-11 Fri & Sat; 4-8 Sun ☎ (01902) 498888

Thornbridge Jaipur IPA; Wye Valley Butty Bach; 4 changing beers (sourced nationally) Ⓗ

Friendly, busy high-street café/bar near both bus and Metro stations; it operates more as a café in the mornings and afternoons and as a bar in the evenings. The small, welcoming bar area at the front leads to a further room with seating. There is a large function room at the rear where regular beer festivals are held which is also available for hire. Q◐♿🍎P🚌📶

Birmingham: Acocks Green

Inn on the Green Ⓛ

2 Westley Road, B27 7UH

11-11 (midnight Fri); 10-midnight Sat & Sun

☎ (0121) 708 0108

6 changing beers (sourced nationally; often Wye Valley) Ⓗ

Run by a keen and passionate landlord who is an active CAMRA member, with friendly and knowledgeable staff. The pub hosts regular entertainment and live music at weekends, and screens live sport. Excellent beer festivals are held four times a year. Four handpulls are in use during the week and six at the weekend. The same beers are rarely on twice – this is a great place to find beers from new breweries. It is also notable for the Bottle Shed craft beer and bottle shop, accessible from the pub. Well worth a visit. ❀♿🍎P🚌📶

Birmingham: Balsall Heath

Old Moseley Arms Ⓛ

53 Tindal Street, B12 9QU (400yds off Moseley Rd)

REAL ALE BREWERIES

AJ's Walsall
Angel Halesowen
Attic Birmingham (NEW)
Backyard Walsall
Banks's Wolverhampton
Bathams Brierley Hill
Beat Lye
Birmingham Birmingham
Black Country ▮ Lower Gornal
Brewhouse & Kitchen ▮ Sutton Coldfield
Burning Soul Birmingham: Hockley
Byatt's Coventry
Craddock's ▮ Stourbridge
Davenports Smethwick
Dhillon's Longford
Dig Birmingham
Fixed Wheel Blackheath
Fownes Upper Gornal
Froth Blowers Erdington
Glasshouse Stirchley (NEW)
Green Duck Stourbridge
Halton Turner Birmingham: Hall Green (NEW)
Holden's Woodsetton
Indian Great Barr
Leviathan Sutton Coldfield (NEW)
Moseley Moseley
Newbridge Bilston
Olde Swan ▮ Netherton
Ostlers ▮ Harborne
Pig Iron Rowley Regis
Punchline Wolverhampton
Red Moon Yardley
Rock & Roll Birmingham: Hockley
Sadler's Lye
Sarah Hughes ▮ Sedgley
Silhill Solihull
Toll End ▮ Tipton
Triumph Coventry (NEW)
Twisted Barrel Coventry
Two Towers Birmingham
Websters ▮ Wollaston

12-11 (midnight Fri & Sat) (0121) 440 1954
oldmoseleyarms.co.uk
Church End Goat's Milk; Enville Ale; Wye Valley HPA, Butty Bach; 1 changing beer (sourced nationally)
A traditional 19th-century pub hidden away in a back street. The left bar has a large screen for sport, the right bar has the jukebox. Upstairs is used for functions and has a pool table; the covered garden/smoking area has comfy sofas. A superb tandoori menu is served in the evenings and all day Sunday. Regular beer festivals offer 16 ales and two ciders. There is live music featuring local talent upstairs or outside every Sunday evening.
(50)

Birmingham: City Centre

Cherry Reds

88-92 John Bright Street, B1 1BN
8.30am-11 (1am Fri); 10-1am Sat; 10-11 Sun
(0121) 643 5716 cherryreds.com
Backyard Blonde; 2 changing beers
Stylish independent pub open since 2010, near the Victoria, Brewdog, the Railway, Stable and BoneHead, and within walking distance of New Street station. Expect three good-quality ales alongside a range of bottled beers and keg products. Freshly cooked and interesting food is served every day, with a focus on local produce and vegan-friendly options. There is more seating upstairs. The bar is popular with local groups as a meeting place. Opens at 10am on bank holidays.
(Grand Central)

Craven Arms

47 Upper Gough Street, B1 1JG (in side street)
12-11 (0121) 643 2852
Black Country Bradley's Finest Golden, Pig on the Wall, Fireside; 8 changing beers (sourced nationally)
This early 19th-century former Holder's pub, recently restored by Black Country Ales, sports an attractive blue-tiled exterior and a cosy interior. In addition to three permanent Black Country beers, between six and eight different guest casks are available from breweries often new to Birmingham. Beer festivals are held regularly and customers are welcome to bring their own food.
P

Gunmakers Arms

93 Bath Street, B4 6HG
12-11 (midnight Fri & Sat); 3-11 Sun (0121) 236 8486
gunmakersarms.com
Two Towers Baskerville Bitter, Hockley Gold, Complete Muppetry, Chamberlain Pale Ale; 6 changing beers (sourced regionally; often Two Towers)
Small, pleasant, back-street pub just off the city's inner ring road, five minutes' walk from Snow Hill station. This Grade II-listed Regency period building, the Two Towers Brewery taphouse, was tastefully refurbished in 2017 and has 10 handpulls and a range of craft beers. There is a large bar in front, snug areas and a smaller room behind, then a rear courtyard accessing the brewery. Cobs are sold, plus pies Tuesday evenings.
(St Chads)

Head of Steam

Somerset House, 36 Temple Street, B2 5DP
12-midnight (1am Fri); 11-1am Sat; 12-11 Sun
(0121) 643 6824
10 changing beers (sourced regionally; often Birmingham, Camerons, Dig)
Recently opened addition to the Camerons Head of Steam chain. The pub features a large and spacious interior decorated in a steampunk style, with plenty of seating and booths for people to enjoy a wide variety of food and drinks. Ten handpulls showcase Camerons own beers and offerings from local breweries. Keg lines include international beers such as Delirium and La Chouffe. There is a strong emphasis on beer and food-matching, with the menu suggesting which beer to pair with your dinner. (Corporation St)

Pint Shop

38 Bennetts Hill, B3 2AA
12-11 (midnight Thu & Fri); 11-midnight Sat; 11-11 Sun
6 changing beers
The latest offering from the Pint Shop team, originally started in Cambridge. A stylish pub with a busy bar downstairs and restaurant upstairs, where six handpumps dispense a range of cask ales of various styles and strengths. There are also 20 keg lines and one keg cider line. There is an emphasis on food here but visitors are welcome to drink without eating. Sky Sports is shown, but not BT. Dogs welcome in the ground-floor bar.
(Grand Central)

Post Office Vaults

84 New Street, B2 4BA (entrances are on both New St and Pinfold St)
11-11 (midnight Fri & Sat); 12-11 Sun (0121) 643 7354
postofficevaults.co.uk
Hobsons Mild; house beer (by Kinver); 6 changing beers (sourced nationally)
Only a two-minute walk from the Stephenson Street entrance to New Street station and close to Victoria Square, this subterranean pub offers a range of eight traditional beers in excellent condition. It always has at least 350 different bottled beers from all over the world, one of the largest ranges in the country, and it also serves 14 ciders and perries. The extremely knowledgeable staff will make your visit a pleasure.
Q(Grand Central)

Pure Craft Bar & Kitchen

30 Waterloo Street, B2 5TJ (5 mins from New St and Snow Hill stations)
11-11 (midnight Fri & Sat); 12-10 Sun (0121) 237 5666
purecraftbars.com
Purity Bunny Hop, Pure Gold, Mad Goose; 4 changing beers (sourced nationally; often Kirkstall, Rooster's, Tiny Rebel)
This bar was the first in the chain to open, and is set in a traditional building with an industrial interior on Waterloo Street in the centre of the business district. The walls are adorned with modern art. There are six cask and 16 craft beer lines plus a selection of 60 bottled craft beers, along with gourmet food. All food is made with beer, and the menu has been matched to the beers available. Meals can be booked online. There is also a cellar bar. Popular with local office workers.

Shakespeare

31 Summer Row, B3 1JJ (200yds from city end of Broad St)
11.30-11 (midnight Fri & Sat); 12-10 Sun
(0121) 236 8702

St Austell Nicholson's Pale Ale; Sharp's Doom Bar; 4 changing beers (sourced nationally; often Purity) ⊞
A red-bricked Victorian city-centre local, part of the Nicholson's brand, with changing guest ales, near the Jewellery Quarter and the new Library of Birmingham. The traditional bar has a small hatch to serve the rear snug which is normally reserved for diners. There is a decorated patio garden to the rear and seating at the front. The pub has an excellent reputation for good food, with frequent offers such as beer and a burger, pie and a pint, and so on. Families are welcome during food service times (usually until 10pm). ❀◑♿⇌🚊🚌ᯤ

Victoria ✔

48 John Bright Street, B1 1BN (next to stage door of Alexandra Theatre)
12-midnight (2am Fri & Sat) ☎ (0121) 633 9439
thevictoriabirmingham.co.uk
8 changing beers ⊞
The locally based Bitters 'n' Twisted chain has resurrected this 19th-century theatre bar next to the stage door of the Alexandra Theatre, which gets busy before theatre performances and gigs at the nearby O2 Arena. One regular beer and three rotating guests are served alongside food with an American Deep South flavour and a twist on the classic British roast. Quiz night is Tuesday and music plays Thursday, Friday and Saturday. The pub is reportedly haunted. ⇌🚊🚌ᯤ

Wellington 𝕃

37 Bennetts Hill, B2 5SN
10-midnight ☎ (0121) 200 3115
thewellingtonrealale.co.uk
Black Country Bradley's Finest Golden, Pig on the Wall, Fireside; Oakham Citra; Purity Mad Goose; Wye Valley HPA; 10 changing beers (sourced nationally; often Froth Blowers, Titanic) ⊞
Recently refurbished and extended, with an additional upstairs bar and roof terrace beer garden, this multiple award-winner is a veritable beer festival every day. Sixteen ales and three traditional ciders are served on handpump, and a wide selection of bottled beers and whiskies is also available to the varied clientele from knowledgeable staff. Regular quizzes, cheese nights and darts competitions are held. No food is served but you are welcome to bring your own – plates, cutlery and condiments are provided. Q❀♿⇌🚊(Grand Central)♣🍎🚌ᯤ

Birmingham: Digbeth

Spotted Dog 𝕃

104 Warwick Street, B12 0NH
5-11; 3-1am Fri; 12-1am Sat; 12-midnight Sun
☎ (0121) 772 3822 spotteddog.co.uk
Castle Rock Harvest Pale; Holden's Black Country Mild; 2 changing beers (sourced nationally) ⊞
This is a traditional multi-roomed pub with an Irish feel. It is off the beaten track but well worth a trip. Excellent Holden's Mild is sold at a competitive price. There is a large covered garden/smoking area with heaters and a barbecue area. Live traditional Irish music plays on Monday, jazz on Tuesday, and blues on Thursday. There is a mixture of sports on the large screen, especially rugby. Excellent Scotch eggs, including vegetarian and gluten-free versions, are served. It can be busy when Birmingham City are at home.
🐴❀♿⇌♣🚌ᯤ

Woodman ★ 𝕃

New Canal Street, B5 5LG (opp old Curzon St by Millennium Point)
12-11 (midnight Fri & Sat); closed Sun ☎ (0121) 643 4960
thewoodmanbirmingham.co.uk
Castle Rock Black Gold, Harvest Pale; 3 changing beers (sourced nationally) ⊞
Recently given an environmentally friendly refurbishment, this pub is Grade II-listed and on CAMRA's National Inventory of Historic Pub Interiors. It has a red-brick tile and terracotta exterior, with an L-shaped bar tiled above a wooden dado. A tiled lobby on Albert Street leads to an attractive small drinking area, with a hatch to the servery, which also has a real fire. The third plain room on the left now makes for a pleasant dividing area, and there is an outside seating/dining area. Good food is served daily. Quiz night is Wednesday. ❀◑♿⇌🚊(Bull Street)♣🍎🚌🐾ᯤ

Birmingham: Edgbaston

Physician

Harborne Road, B15 3DH
10-11; 10-10.30 Sun ☎ (0121) 272 5900
Brunning & Price Original; Purity Mad Goose; Timothy Taylor Landlord; 3 changing beers (sourced regionally) ⊞
A large historic former BMI building used to house the vast Sampson Gamgee Library for the History of Medicine, recently converted into a pub. It is an upmarket establishment with several drinking and dining areas. A range of ales is available, often featuring a lot of local brews, alongside quality food, wine and spirits. ❀◑♿⇌P🐾

Birmingham: Harborne

Hop Garden

19 Metchley Lane, B17 0HT
closed Mon; 4-11 (midnight Fri); 12-midnight Sat; 2-11 Sun
☎ (0121) 427 7904 hopgardenpub.co.uk
5 changing beers (sourced nationally) ⊞
Formerly the Sportsman and recently reopened, the pub now serves five real ales from small and local breweries, seven craft beers and five craft ciders as well as real cider. There is also an interesting selection of bottled beers. The décor is original and eclectic. There are plans to grow hops in the large garden, hence the name. 🐴❀🚌🐾

White Horse 𝕃 ✔

2 York Street, B17 0HG
11 (12 Mon)-11.30; 11-12.30am Fri & Sat; 12-11.30 Sun
☎ (0121) 608 7641 whitehorseharborne.com
Greene King Abbot; Ostlers Terry's Gold; 9 changing beers (sourced regionally; often Bathams, Church End, Wye Valley) ⊞
A much-improved and extended free house just off the busy High Street. It has an island bar with a front snug and a rear heated area. There is a great emphasis on real ale, with an electronic beer board linked to the pub's website. Regular live music nights are held on Friday and Saturday, a monthly open mic night on the last Wednesday, and a quiz night every Tuesday. A basic food menu is available. The artwork on the walls is by local artists, including the landlord. Ostlers ales are brewed on the premises. ❀♿🍎🚌🐾ᯤ

Birmingham: Highgate

Lamp Tavern ▼ 🄻
157 Barford Street, B5 6AH
✪ 1-11 (9 Mon & Wed); 1-7 Sun ☎ (0121) 688 1220
Hobsons Mild; 4 changing beers (sourced nationally; often Stanway) 🄷
This hidden gem of a pub with a homely feel, close to Digbeth and the Arcadian areas, has two excellent permanent real ales – Hobson's Mild and one from the Stanway range. Three wonderful changing guests/LocAles are available too. The pub has been run by the same friendly landlord for 25 years. It hosts a folk club on Friday evening and a jazz club on some Tuesday evenings. There is road parking only, and good local bus routes. Closes early if no customers. Q&⛟

Birmingham: Hockley

1000 Trades
16 Frederick Street, B1 3HE
✪ 11-11 (midnight Thu & Fri); 12-midnight Sat; 12-11 Sun
☎ (0121) 233 6291 ⊕ 1000trades.org.uk
House beer (by Rock & Roll); 3 changing beers (sourced nationally; often Titanic) 🄷
This delightful addition to the Jewellery Quarter has bare boards and brickwork, with full-width doors opening onto the pavement, all of which give this independent craft beer bar a distinctive atmosphere. Four handpumps serve a changing range of beers, usually including at least one from a local micro. The cask offering is supported with five KeyKeg taps and an interesting range of bottled beers. The bar is a music venue showcasing independent labels. Kitchen residencies ensure that the food offering always varies. ▶&⇌⛟

Burning Soul Brewery 🄻
Unit 1 Mott Street Industrial Estate, B19 3HE
✪ closed Sun-Thu; 4-8 Fri; 1-8 Sat ☎ (0121) 439 7253
⊕ burningsoulbrewing.com
10 changing beers (sourced locally)
Tap for the Burning Soul Brewery; note the limited opening hours. There is a changing list of smaller experimental pilot brews so the brewers can capture at first-hand what people think of their beer; those liked most are brewed again and sold outside of the brewery. All ales are on KeyKeg and meets CAMRA's definition of real ale. Tours are available on request. There is a pool table. Card payments are preferred. ⇌⛟♣P⛟

Jewellers Arms
23 Hockley Street, B18 6BW
✪ 12-11 (midnight Fri & Sat) ☎ (0121) 236 4402
Black Country Bradley's Finest Golden, Pig on the Wall, Fireside; 7 changing beers 🄷
Refurbished and reopened by Black Country Ales in late 2017, this pub has 10 real ales and two ciders, and gets busy in the evenings. Food is limited to cobs. There is no separate bar as the pub is now all open plan, and there is just one fruit machine. A real fire is at one end of the pub, lit daily in winter, and there is a function room upstairs. Parking is available at the side of the pub. Q&⇌⛟♣⛟❀

Rock & Roll Brewhouse 🄻
Unit 2, 60 Regent Place, B3 1UG
✪ closed Sun-Thu; 5-9 Fri; 1-7 Sat ☎ 07969 759649
Rock & Roll Brew Springsteen, Thirst Aid Kit; 1 changing beer (often Rock & Roll) 🄷

A small and quirky brewery taproom bedecked with music memorabilia. There are usually three vegan-friendly ales available, always including a dark ale. The bar staff and their knowledge of beer is excellent; the other shared love in the bar is music and there is a playlist of what you are hearing on the wall. Hogan's cider is also available. Note the limited opening hours and check before visiting as the bar occasionally closes for music festivals. ⇌⛟

Birmingham: Kings Heath

King's Heath Cricket & Sports Club
Charlton House, 247 Alcester Road South, B14 6DT
✪ 12-midnight ☎ (0121) 444 1913
⊕ kingsheathsportsclub.com
Wye Valley HPA, Butty Bach; 2 changing beers (sourced nationally) 🄷
Welcoming sports club where CAMRA members are permitted entry on production of a membership card (maximum 10 visits per year). The club has two rooms: the comfortable lounge for relaxed drinking, and the large room for watching sporting events on big screens and also housing two full-size snooker tables. The beer range always includes two rotating guest ales. Varying social events are held throughout the year including live music. Q⛟❀⛟▶&♣⛟P⛟❀

Birmingham: Newtown

Bartons Arms ★ ✔
144 High Street, B6 4UP
✪ 12-11 (1am Sat); 12-10.30 Sun ☎ (0121) 333 5988
⊕ thebartonsarms.com
Oakham JHB, Inferno, Citra, Bishops Farewell; 2 changing beers (sourced nationally; often Oakham) 🄷
A stunning red-bricked pub run by Oakham Brewery from Peterborough. The 1901 interior is Grade II*-listed and on CAMRA's National Inventory of Historic Pub Interiors. The Bartons has ornate Minton tiles throughout, including a central tiled staircase, original stained-glass windows and snob screens on the bar. Superb Thai food is served in the lounge. A range of Oakham Ales is available, with usually one guest and a cider. Quiz nights are on Mondays and regular music and beer festivals are held. ⛟▶⛟P⛟❀

Birmingham: Perry Barr

Arthur Robertson ✔
51-53 One Stop Retail Park, Walsall Road, B42 1AA
✪ 8am-11 ☎ (0121) 332 5910
Greene King Abbot; Ruddles Best Bitter; 3 changing beers
A JD Wetherspoon outlet at the One Stop shopping centre in Perry Barr, named after Birchfield Harriers' very first Olympian and medal winner. The manager tries to keep three local guests on the go when possible and the venue serves the standard Wetherspoon's food menu. It can get busy when Aston Villa are playing at home. ⛟▶⇌⛟P⛟❀

Blackheath

Britannia ✔
124 Halesowen Street, B65 0ES
✪ 8am-midnight (1am Fri & Sat) ☎ (0121) 559 0010

Exmoor Gold; Greene King Abbot; Sharp's Doom Bar; 7 changing beers (sourced nationally; often Backyard, Kinver, Slater's) H
An L-shaped JD Wetherspoon outlet at the heart of Blackheath. The secure garden at the rear of the property provides a pleasant space away from the main A4099. The exposed brick façade is often decorated with hanging baskets in the warmer seasons. Seven changing beers (commonly from Backyard, Kinver and Slater's) are accompanied by three permanent beers. Pictures placed throughout the pub depict local monuments and historic characters. Food is served all day, every day.
♘❀◐◑♿⇌♣●P🚌≋

Bloxwich

Bloxwich Showman ✔
156 High Street, WS3 3JT
⏲ 8am-midnight (1am Fri & Sat); 8am-11 Sun
☎ (01922) 495366
Greene King Abbot; Ruddles Best Bitter; Sharp's Doom Bar; 3 changing beers (often AJ's Ales, Lymestone, Slater's) H
Busy high-street pub, a Wetherspoon conversion of a former cinema; the pub is themed around Pat Collins, well known in the early 1900s for his funfairs, and for being President of the Showman's Guild, local councillor, Mayor of Walsall and MP for the area. Easily accessible by public transport, the airy, split-level pub serves up to six real ales. The pub also serves real cider and craft ales, together with a large range of bottled beer.
♘◐◑♿⇌●🚌(32)≋

Boldmere

Bishop Vesey L
63 Boldmere Road, B73 5XA
⏲ 8am-11 (midnight Fri & Sat) ☎ (0121) 355 5077
Backyard Blonde; Greene King Abbot; Oakham Citra; Ruddles Best Bitter; Sharp's Doom Bar; 11 changing beers (sourced nationally; often Oakham) H
Busy, popular Wetherspoon named after the town's Tudor benefactor. With 19 consecutive years in the Guide, it is a frequent Pub of the Year for the local CAMRA branch. Up to 11 interesting guest beers are offered, many from local microbreweries, plus two changing real ciders. As well as extensive seating areas upstairs and down, there is a spacious rooftop garden, and a quieter beer garden downstairs. ♘❀◐◑♿⇌♣●🚌≋

Brierley Hill

Garrison
Waterfront E, DY5 1XL
⏲ 3-11; 12-11 Fri & Sat; 12-10.30 Sun
Enville Ale; Fixed Wheel Chain Reaction Pale Ale; Green Duck Blonde; Salopian Shropshire Gold; house beer (by Salopian); 3 changing beers (sourced nationally; often Salopian, Tiny Rebel, Titanic) H
This 1920s-themed saloon bar is a welcome addition to the Waterfront business park which was once a hotspot for drinkers. The seven real ales include Garrison Gold (Shropshire Gold), Garrison Pale (Chain Reaction) and three changing beers. There are also real ciders, keg and lager lines and a selection of top-shelf tipples. The decor includes a Peaky Blinders mural, and there is a jukebox and a small stage to accommodate live acts.
Q♘♿●P🚌🐾

Vine
10 Delph Road, DY5 2TN
⏲ 12-11; 12-10.30 Sun ☎ (01384) 78293
Bathams Mild Ale, Best Bitter H
An unspoilt brewery tap with an ornately decorated façade proclaiming the Shakespearian quotation 'Blessing of your heart, you brew good ale'. An elongated pub with a labyrinthine feel, the front bar is staunchly traditional, while the rear room has its own servery and dartboard. The lounge was partly converted from former brewery offices. Black Country lunches, such as faggots and pies, are served weekdays, with generously filled rolls and pork pies at other times.
Q♘❀◐♣P🚌(8)🐾≋

Brownhills

Jiggers Whistle L
5-7 Brownhills High Street, WS8 6ED
⏲ 3-10 Mon; closed Tue; 3-10.30 Wed & Thu; 12-11 Fri & Sat; 12-9 Sun ☎ 07854 356976
House beer (by Green Duck); 3 changing beers (sourced regionally; often AJ's Ales, Backyard, Green Duck) H
Micropub opened in 2017 offering a wide range of cask and craft keg ales, and eight real ciders; bar snacks are also available. This bar has grown hugely in popularity and now sponsors a darts team. The staff offer customers a warm welcome and are keen to support local events. There is a cheese night every Monday from 7pm. The pub now has its own beers produced locally by Backyard and Green Duck. Q♘♣●P🚌🐾≋

Coseley

Old Chainyard L
63 Castle Street, WV14 9DW
⏲ 12-11 (11.30 Fri & Sat)
2 changing beers (sourced regionally; often Olde Swan, Salopian) H
Lively single-roomed community pub serving two rotating cask beers, one always from Salopian Brewery. It is a five-minute walk from Coseley train station and a three-minute walk from the A4123, both of which offer direct links to Birmingham and Wolverhampton. The handpulls not in use will advertise beers currently resting in the cellar and coming soon. The manageress, Amanda, always sources beers that her regular customers approve of. There is a real fire and a car park.
♘❀⇌♣P🚌🐾≋

Coventry: Chapelfields

Hearsall Inn L
45 Craven Street, CV5 8DS (1 mile W of city centre, off Allesley Old Rd)
⏲ 12-11; 11-11 Sat ☎ (024) 7671 5729 🌐 hearsallinn.com
Church End Goat's Milk; Draught Bass; 2 changing beers (sourced locally; often Byatt's) H
Built in the 1850s to serve Chapelfields' historic watchmaking district, this popular family-run free house makes a welcome return to the Guide. It has separate bar and lounge areas and a paved patio to the front. The pub is home to darts and football teams and hosts traditional Irish music, including a tuition session on Tuesday evening. Four handpumps tend towards locally produced beers. A variety of freshly made batches is available throughout the day. ♘❀♣🚌🐾≋

Nursery Tavern

38-39 Lord Street, CV5 8DA (off Allesley Old Rd)

✪ 12-11.30 (midnight Fri & Sat); 12-11 Sun

☎ (024) 7667 4530

Fuller's London Pride; Otter Bitter; 4 changing beers (sourced nationally) Ⓗ

A venue that has been in the same hands for over 25 years and named after Thomas Weare's nearby nursery business when first licensed in 1852. This mid-terrace community pub in the historic watchmaking area remains a regular Guide entry. There are three rooms, with conversation dominating in the lounge and bar. The back room hosts local societies, charity events, Sunday lunches and regular live music. Mini beer festivals are held in the rear garden every June and December. Q ☎ ⊛ Ⓓ ♣ ♠ 🚃 ❀ 🛜

Coventry: City Centre

Earl of Mercia ✔

18 High Street, CV1 5RE

✪ 8am-midnight (1am Fri & Sat) ☎ (024) 7643 3990

Greene King Abbot; Ruddles Best Bitter; Sharp's Doom Bar; 5 changing beers (sourced nationally) Ⓗ

Originally built as a bank in the late Victorian era, this is an attractive Wetherspoon pub. It is named after Leofric, Earl of Mercia, who founded Coventry's first cathedral in 1043 with his wife Godiva. Offering a fine view of the Council House, it is handily situated for the city-centre shops, cathedrals and other attractions. Increasingly popular, the pub now stocks eight real ales. Additional seating is provided on a mezzanine floor and paved patio to the front. ☎ ⊛ Ⓓ & ♠ 🚃 (8,9) 🛜

Gatehouse Tavern Ⓛ

44-46 Hill Street, CV1 4AN (close to Belgrade Theatre)

✪ 11-11 (11.30 Fri & Sat); 12-10.30 Sun ☎ (024) 7663 0140

Draught Bass; Fuller's London Pride; 4 changing beers (sourced locally; often Byatt's, Church End, Purity) Ⓗ

The former Leigh Mills Weaving Company gatehouse, converted to a pub in 1995 by the current landlord. A long-standing entry in the Guide, it is sports-oriented, with all major events shown on several large screens and an interesting stained-glass window portraying the Six Nations rugby emblems. The pub has an attractive, well-tended beer garden and offers home-cooked lunchtime and evening meals Monday to Saturday lunchtime. One handpump is given over to real cider. ☎ ⊛ Ⓓ ♠ 🚃 🛜

Golden Cross Ⓛ ✔

8 Hay Lane, CV1 5RF (near old cathedral ruins)

✪ 11-11 (midnight Sat); 12-7 Sun ☎ (024) 7655 1855

⊕ thegoldencrosscoventry.co.uk

House beer (by Caledonian); 3 changing beers (sourced locally; often Adnams, Byatt's, Church End) Ⓗ

One of Coventry's finest medieval buildings and a lucky survivor of the Blitz. Although claiming to be the oldest pub in the city, the sympathetically refurbished interior does not reflect this. Much effort has gone into creating a comfortable lounge on the ground floor and an upstairs room, which often hosts live music. A convenient and welcoming stop for a pint and a bite after visiting the city's three cathedrals and its historic lanes. ⊛ Ⓓ ♠ 🚃 🛜

Old Windmill Ⓛ ✔

22-23 Spon Street, CV1 3BA (behind IKEA)

✪ 4-11 Mon; 12-11.30 (1am Fri & Sat) ☎ (024) 7625 1717

Morland Old Speckled Hen; Theakston Old Peculier; Timothy Taylor Landlord; 4 changing beers (sourced locally; often North Cotswold) Ⓗ

An ancient building in this historic medieval street, and one of two claimants to being the oldest pub in the city. It is still known locally as Ma Brown's in honour of an early 20th-century landlady. There are many small rooms, with one possessing an old range that warms the pub in winter and another housing an old brewhouse from Victorian times. Locally produced pork pies are highly recommended. ♣ ♠ 🚃 ❀ 🛜

Town Wall Tavern

Bond Street, CV1 4AH (behind Belgrade Theatre)

✪ 12 (4 Mon)-11; 12-midnight Fri & Sat; 12-10 Sun

☎ (024) 7622 0963

Adnams Southwold Bitter; Brains Rev James; Draught Bass; Theakston Old Peculier; Wye Valley HPA; 3 changing beers (sourced nationally; often Goff's, North Cotswold) Ⓗ

Convivial, traditional city-centre local amid high-rise buildings, sometimes busy with patrons before and after performances at the theatre. Open fires feature both in the cosy bar and attractive lounge, where discrete smaller areas add charm. The delightful Donkey Box snug has been fashioned out of the former off-sales counter. An internal window bears the long defunct Atkinsons Brewery crest. The pub holds a Sunday evening acoustic jam session, and afternoon tea on Tuesday. Excellent food is served Tuesday to Sunday lunchtime. No under-18s. ⊛ Ⓓ ♠ 🚃 ❀

Coventry: Earlsdon

City Arms Ⓛ ✔

1 Earlsdon Street, CV5 6EP (on roundabout)

✪ 8am-midnight (1am Fri & Sat) ☎ (024) 7671 8170

Greene King Abbot; Ruddles Best Bitter; Sharp's Doom Bar; 7 changing beers (sourced nationally; often Byatt's, Grainstore, Purity) Ⓗ

Named after the Coventry coat of arms, the pub is a large mock-Tudor building on a prominent site in the heart of Earlsdon with easy transport links to the city centre. It has a large-open plan main room with a quieter smaller room at the rear and additional seating outside. Part of the Wetherspoon chain, it is an enthusiastic supporter of real ale, allowing customers to assist in the selection of forthcoming ales. ☎ ⊛ Ⓓ & ♠ 🚃 (5,11) 🛜

Coventry: Foleshill

Byatt's Brewhouse Bar Ⓛ

Unit 7-8, Lythalls Lane Industrial Estate, Lythalls Lane, CV6 6FL

✪ closed Sun-Wed; 4-9 Thu & Fri; 12-9 Sat

☎ (024) 7663 7996 ⊕ byattsbrewery.co.uk

6 changing beers (sourced locally; often Byatt's) Ⓗ

Modern taproom in front of a Byatt's Brewery in a small industrial estate comprising a ground-floor bar area and mezzanine. Handpumps dispense up to six changing beers from the Byatt's range and three or four ciders are offered on gravity. Byatt's vegan-friendly bottle-conditioned beers are sold, along with carryout containers. Mini beer festivals are held and occasional quiz and music nights. Opening hours are limited but the taproom also

opens some Sundays prior to Wasps Rugby Club home fixtures at the nearby Ricoh Arena.
P

Coventry: Gosford Green

Twisted Barrel Brewery & Tap House

Fargo Village, Far Gosford Street, CV1 5ED
closed Mon & Tue; 2-10 Wed & Thu; 12-midnight Fri & Sat; 12-10 Sun ☎ (024) 7610 1701 twistedbarrelale.co.uk
Twisted Barrel Beast of a Midlands Mild, Detroit Sour City, God's Twisted Sister, Sine Qua Non, Naido; 18 changing beers (sourced nationally) H/P
Popular with a range of appreciative drinkers, the taphouse is in vibrant Fargo Village just outside of the city centre. A large seating area is adjacent to the brewery equipment, while the bar has over 20 beers available on KeyKeg. The core range of beers is supplemented with seasonal and pilot brews as well as guests from elsewhere. All products are suitable for vegans. It hosts a popular home-brew club plus many other events throughout the year.
P

Coventry: Spon End

Broomfield Tavern

14-16 Broomfield Place, CV5 6GY (adjacent to rugby ground but hidden from main road)
12 (4 Mon-Wed)-midnight ☎ (024) 7663 0969
11 changing beers (sourced locally; often Church End, Froth Blowers, Hobsons) H
Well worth the short walk from the city centre, this established entry in the Guide was local CAMRA Pub of the Year and West Midlands Regional Cider Pub of the Year 2018. Its small bar is virtually filled with handpumps, with up to 18 ciders and perries also available on gravity. The pub can get busy at weekends when live music is hosted, but the efficient and attentive staff will make sure that service is prompt. Q

Coventry: Sutton Stop

Greyhound Inn

Sutton Stop, Hawkesbury Junction, CV6 6DF (off Grange Rd at jct of Coventry & Oxford canals)
11-11; 12-10.30 Sun ☎ (024) 7636 3046
Draught Bass; Greene King Abbot; 3 changing beers (sourced nationally; often Brains, Holden's, Kelham Island) H
A canalside hostelry popular with locals and visitors alike. It is a four-times winner of the Godiva award for best pub in Coventry and Warwickshire, and has been local CAMRA Pub of the Year several times. The pub dates from the 1830s and the front terrace overlooks a bustling canal junction. An extensive menu of freshly cooked food is offered. Beer festivals are held twice yearly. The Whippet Bar in the garden is open at weekends in the summer.
Q P

Cradley Heath

Plough & Harrow

82 Corngreaves Road, B64 7BT
11-11 ☎ (01384) 638351
Banks's Mild; Ludlow Gold; Wye Valley HPA, Butty Bach; 2 changing beers (sourced nationally; often Abbeydale, Bristol Beer Factory, Kelham Island) H
Local CAMRA Pub of the Year 2019, this is a traditional community inn, tastefully modernised to provide a pleasant, comfortable hostelry in the heart of the Black Country. Children are allowed until 9pm, and dogs are welcome but must remain on a lead. Baguettes and cobs are available. Sports TV is a background feature and does not detract from an enjoyable drinking environment. The pub serves four regular beers and two changing pale and hoppy beers that are all keenly priced.
Q P (18)

Darlaston

Green Dragon

55 Church Street, WS10 8DY
12-11 (11.30 Sat); 11-9 Sun ☎ 07707 101276
3 changing beers (sourced locally; often AJ's Ales, Backyard, Salopian) H
This modified traditional two-roomed pub has an original lantern still hanging over the entrance. Pictures of old pubs adorn the walls. The front room has four handpulls offering at least one local ale. Pub games are played in both rooms, and outside is a paved garden area for the summer. Bar snacks are available. (34)

Dorridge

Knowle & Dorridge Cricket Club

Station Road, B93 8ET
5.30-10.30 (11 Fri); 12-11 Sat; 12-10.30 Sun ☎ (01564) 774338 knowleanddorridgecc.co.uk
3 changing beers (sourced nationally) H
An established cricket club set in an upmarket residential area. Visitors are welcome to try the varied range of up to three cask-conditioned ales, always in excellent condition and often from interesting breweries. There are no entry restrictions, but club members are able to purchase drinks at a reduced price. There is outside seating to watch top-class cricket in the Birmingham league. Bar snacks and filled rolls are usually available. CAMRA branch Club of the Year two years in succession. P (S2,S3)

Dudley

Lamp Tavern

116 High Street, DY1 1QT
12-11; 12-10.30 Sun ☎ (01384) 254129
Bathams Mild Ale, Best Bitter H
Classic Bathams pub with a large front bar containing traditional games and a cosy back room with a more relaxed feel. The old Queens Cross Brewery has been converted into a large function room available for hire and staging music nights. B&B accommodation is in the adjacent Lamp Cottage. An outside area for drinking overlooks the southern area of the Black Country to the Clent Hills. Bathams XXX is available for a limited window of time in winter. P

Malt Shovel

46 Tower Street, DY1 1NB (off Broadway, A459, opp Dudley College Evolve campus)
12-10.30 (midnight Fri & Sat) ☎ (01384) 252735
5 changing beers (sourced nationally; often Holden's, Oakham, Pictish) H
A former back-street Banks's pub which reopened in October 2017 following an extensive but sympathetic refurbishment. Now a free house, this

iconic town-centre boozer offers an eclectic range of both local and national cask and keg products in a stylish setting. The real ales come from a mixture of local breweries (such as Fixed Wheel and Enville) plus national breweries (such as Oakham and Abbeydale). Traditional Black Country pub snacks are served including cobs, pork pies and scratchings. Live music plays fortnightly.
P

Four Oaks

Butlers Arms

444 Lichfield Road, B74 4BL
12-11 (midnight Fri & Sat); 12-10.30 Sun
(0121) 308 0765 butlersarms.co.uk
4 changing beers H
Plushly comfortable suburban pub, with seating in many colourful and eccentric styles, plus lamps, mirrors and curiosities. Family-run, the pub is geared towards dining though drinkers are always made welcome. The four guest ales vary but will usually include at least one well-known beer such as Greene King Abbot. The varied food menu is strong on fish dishes. There is a small beer terrace to the front. Car parking is free but requires registration number entry at the bar.
Q P

Halesowen

Crafty Pint H'ales'owen

8 Wassell Road, B63 4JU
closed Mon; 4.30-10 Tue-Thu; 1-11 Fri & Sat; 1-8 Sun
07823 880240
Wye Valley Butty Bach; 5 changing beers (often Fixed Wheel, Oakham, Salopian) H
This micropub, now occupying the adjacent building as well, is run by a local resident. It offers traditional ale, cider, wines and beverages, plus pork pies, in a small pub environment. Coffee is generally available into the evening during the week, along with crusty cobs and sausage rolls. No children allowed after 7pm. On Sunday last orders are at 7.40pm. Q P (142,192)

Hawne Tavern

76 Attwood Street, B63 3UG (opp Tesco Express)
4.30-midnight; 12-midnight Sat & Sun (0121) 602 6743
Bathams Best Bitter; Oakham Citra; Wye Valley HPA; 6 changing beers H
A back-street locals' pub just off the main bus route. It has a large bar with pool table and TV showing sports (not Sky) with separate seating areas, plus a smaller cosy lounge. There are three regular, and up to six guest ales, many of which are from microbreweries, specialising in northern beers. Real cider is also sold. Baguettes are available in the evening, hot sandwiches and chips at weekends. The enclosed rear garden is ideal for smokers and sun-worshippers. Q

Swan

282 Long Lane, B62 9JY
12-midnight (0121) 559 5207
Black Country Bradley's Finest Golden, Pig on the Wall, Fireside; 8 changing beers H
Former CAMRA branch Pub of the Year, this popular, comfortable hostelry was saved from the bulldozers in 2014 by local campaigners and Black Country Ales. The central bar serves two main drinking areas. Eleven ales and six real ciders are available as well as a fine selection of gins. Regular beer festivals are held. A staircase leads to the toilets and gives access to the garden and smoking area to the rear. It has limited parking but there is adequate street parking nearby.
Q P (14,X8)

Waggon & Horses

21 Stourbridge Rd, B63 3TU (on main A458, ½ mile from bus station)
12-11 (11.30 Fri & Sat); 12-10.30 Sun (0121) 585 9699
Black Country Bradley's Finest Golden, Pig on the Wall, Fireside; 10 changing beers (sourced nationally) H
Former CAMRA branch Pub of the Year, the Waggon dates from the 1850s and was recently refurbished by Black Country Ales, retaining many of its historical features. One long bar serves three drinking areas. The main bar is narrow with a famous sloping floor. Eighteen handpulls serve three regular ales and 10 guests; five real ciders are also available, as well as cobs and snacks. There is no car park, but there is adequate street parking nearby. Q (9)

Hampton in Arden

White Lion

10 High Street, B92 0AA
12-11 (midnight Thu-Sat); 12-10.30 Sun
(01675) 442833 thewhitelioninn.com
Banks's Mild; Hobsons Best; Holden's Golden Glow; M&B Brew XI; Skinner's Betty Stogs; Wye Valley HPA H
Charming 17th-century, Grade II-listed, timber-framed building, the White Lion has been licensed since 1838. There is an L-shaped lounge and dining area with a separate public bar, with lovely real fires. Quality British pub food with a French accent is served lunchtime and evening. The quantity and quality of real ales is always of the highest level, with two beers rotated every five to six months. This is a traditional country pub well worth a visit.
Q P (82)

Kingswinford

Cottage

534 High Street, DY6 8AW
12-11 (midnight Fri & Sat); 12-10.30 Sun
(01384) 287133
Enville Ale; St Austell Tribute; 2 changing beers (sourced nationally; often Exmoor, Three Tuns, Wye Valley) H
A comfortable pub set on two levels. The frontage would not look out of place on a postcard and inside it is homely and inviting. The spacious layout is L-shaped and diners and drinkers intermingle throughout. A good food menu includes lunchtime specials, sandwiches and cobs, plus a carvery on Sunday. Guest beers are always pale and sessionable. A range of country wines is also available. Q P

Knowle

Ale Rooms

1592 High Street, B93 0LF
12-11 (01564) 400040 alerooms.co.uk
7 changing beers (sourced nationally; often Church End, Silhill) H

This micropub in a converted shop (formerly a funeral directors) on the High Street is a welcome addition to the Knowle pub scene. The pub stocks at least one real ale from the local Silhill Brewery, along with one from Church End, plus guests and real cider. Wines and spirits, including speciality gins, are also on offer. Pieminister pies are available up until 10pm. Local CAMRA Pub of the Year 2018 and County Champion Pub of the Year.
◑🍎🚌(S3)🐾📶

Langley

Old Dispensary

Causeway Green Road, B68 8LS
⏲ 4-10 Mon-Wed; 12-11 Thu-Sat; 2-10 Sun
Wye Valley Butty Bach; house beer (by Fownes); 3 changing beers (sourced nationally; often Arbor, Oakham, Salopian) Ⓗ
Formerly Oldbury Pharmacy, this one-time drugstore opened its doors in February 2017 and is now a thriving free house serving five real ales and several real ciders. Also available are a number of KeyKeg beers and a variety of gins. There are regular themed events including live comedy. Scotch eggs and pork pies are served. Opening hours may vary – check Facebook. CAMRA branch Cider Pub of the Year 2018.
Q🛋❀♿🍎🚌(49,126)🐾

Lower Gornal

Black Bear

86 Deepdale Lane, DY3 2AE
⏲ 6.30-11; 3-11 Sat & Sun ☎ (01384) 253333
House beer (by Kinver); 2 changing beers (sourced nationally; often Oakham, Salopian) Ⓗ
Named after a 19th-century print of a dancing bear in Sedgley Bull Ring, this former farmhouse has been a pub for over 180 years. The house beer, Black Bear from Kinver Brewery, is always on tap. There are also two changing beers from breweries such as Salopian and Oakham. Bus stops are close by or you could choose to walk uphill from Gornal Wood bus station or downhill from the No.1 bus route. ❀♣🚌(17,27)🐾

Fountain Inn

8 Temple Street, DY3 2PE (on B4157 5 mins from Gornal Wood bus station)
⏲ 12-11 (midnight Fri & Sat); 12-10.30 Sun
Greene King Yardbird, Abbot; Hobsons Town Crier; Wye Valley HPA, Butty Bach; 7 changing beers (sourced nationally; often Backyard, Bewdley, Malvern Hills) Ⓗ
A local CAMRA Pub of the Year title holder in a previous life, the Fountain reopened in October 2018 with a new management team. The already extensive offering of real ale was increased to 12 and a comprehensive food menu reinstated, served in the separate restaurant at the rear of the pub. There is a private garden accessed at the side of the pub with benches for those warmer days.
🛋❀♿♣🚌(17,27)🐾

Red Cow Ⓛ

84 Grosvenor Road, DY3 2PR
⏲ 4-11.30; 12-11.30 Sat & Sun ☎ 07943 189351
9 changing beers (sourced nationally; often Abbeydale, Holden's, Wye Valley) Ⓗ
An early 19th-century hostelry in a cul-de-sac which is part of Grosvenor Road. This thriving community inn supports several pub games teams. To the left is a large bar with a dartboard. The cosy lounge to the right is partly divided by a chimney with a wood-burning stove. A large garden is at the rear. The varied real ales are sourced both locally and nationally. The pub is a five-minute walk from the bus stop in Corncrake Road. 🛋❀♣P🚌(17)🐾

Lye

Shovel Ⓛ

81 Pedmore Road, DY9 7DZ (on A4036, just S of Lye Cross)
⏲ 6-11; 5-midnight Fri; 1-midnight Sat; 12-11 Sun
☎ (01384) 423998 🌐 theshovelinn.co.uk
Enville Ale, Ginger Beer; Holden's Golden Glow; Morland Old Golden Hen; house beer (by Enville); 7 changing beers (sourced nationally) Ⓗ
Extensive refurbishment has given this pub a smart feel. A central bar serves three separate areas: a bar area with sports TV, a plush lounge, and a rear seating area. The outside Mediterranean-style covered smoking area, heated by a real fire, has the real ale wall displaying over 1,000 pumpclips. Good food includes Mexican and Balti nights, and a traditional Sunday lunch (no food on Sat except fresh rolls). Opens some lunchtimes during the football season. ❀◑♿🍎🚌(9,7)

Wheelie Thirsty Ⓛ

11 High Street, DY9 8JT
⏲ closed Mon; 4-9 Tue; 4-10 Wed & Thu; 12-10 Fri & Sat; 12-8 Sun ☎ 07766 162794 🌐 fixedwheelbrewery.co.uk
4 changing beers (sourced nationally) Ⓗ
Situated in the small suburb of Lye between Halesowen and Stourbridge, this micropub is one of the Fixed Wheel Brewery flagship establishments. It features six beers on KeyKeg and four beers on cask, alongside two cider options, together with cans and bottles from Fixed Wheel and a range of rotating guest stock. Each first Wednesday of the month it holds a cheese night, and pizza and a pint every third Thursday. 🍎🚌(9)

Mere Green

Mare Pool 🏆 Ⓛ ✔

297 Lichfield Road, B74 2UG (behind shops on E side of Lichfield Rd)
⏲ 8am-midnight (1am Fri & Sat) ☎ (0121) 323 1070
Greene King IPA, Abbot; Sharp's Doom Bar; 5 changing beers Ⓗ
Busy Wetherspoon establishment which works hard to keep its ale choices interesting. Both local and national ales are stocked, with an emphasis on change. The pub name refers to one of the many pools that used to surround Sutton, and the theme continues inside with hundreds of hanging glass droplets. The comfortable interior is complemented by café-style seating to the front, plus a beer terrace to the side accessed from inside the pub.
Q🛋❀◑♿≹P🚌📶

Rowley Regis

Britannia Pub & Brewery

Rowley Village, B65 9AT
⏲ 12-11 (1am Fri & Sat) ☎ (0121) 559 3415
Fownes Elephant Riders; 8 changing beers (sourced nationally; often Britt, Three Tuns, Wye Valley) Ⓗ
Following a high-spec refurbishment, this multi-roomed pub reopened in September 2017 offering

a welcome combination of nine real ales, five real ciders and hearty food. The bay windows in the shabby-chic lounge offer natural lighting and there are multiple real fires. Dean Cartwright, from Pig Iron, is brewing under the pseudonym of Britt Brewery in a satellite unit at the rear. Live music takes place on Saturdays, advertised on the pub's Facebook page. Local CAMRA Cider Pub of the Year 2019. P (X8)

Rushall

Manor Arms ★

Park Road, off Daw End Lane, WS4 1LG (off B4154 at canal bridge)
12-11 (midnight Thu-Sat) ☎ (01922) 642333
Banks's Amber Ale, Sunbeam; house beer (by Marston's); 3 changing beers (sourced locally) H
A canalside pub built around 1105, thought to have held a licence for ale since 1248; it is one of the oldest pubs in the country. Original features including exposed beams and open fires remain in both bars. Beer pulls come straight out of the wall, resulting in the place being known locally as the pub with no bar. The building is next to a country park and nature reserve. Although a little off the beaten track, it is well worth a visit.
QP

Sedgley

Beacon Hotel ★

129 Bilston Street, DY3 1JE (on A463)
12-2.30 (3 Fri), 5.30-11; 12-3, 6-11 Sat; 12-3, 7-10.30 Sun
☎ (01902) 883380 sarahhughesbrewery.co.uk
Sarah Hughes Pale Amber, Sedgley Surprise, Dark Ruby Mild; 3 changing beers (often Bristol Beer Factory, Fixed Wheel, Shiny) H
This is the brewery tap for Sarah Hughes and the award-winning Dark Ruby Mild. While this is a destination pub for beers produced by the on-site brewery, there is also a large following for the changing beers, which are typically pale and hoppy in order to complement the sweeter house beers. Customers fill all four rooms and the foot of the stairway in the main corridor, too, all served from an efficiently staffed central bar. Local CAMRA Pub of the Year 2017. QP (229,224)

Mount Pleasant

144 High Street, DY3 1RH (on A459)
6.30 (7 Mon & Tue)-11; 12-3, 7-10.30 Sun
☎ 07950 195652
9 changing beers (sourced nationally; often Church End, Oakham, Wychwood) H
Known locally as the Stump, this popular free house serves a selection of nine beers. It possesses a mock-Tudor frontage and a Tardis-like interior. The front bar is the first room off a long corridor. The lounge areas have an intimate feel, with two rooms on different levels housing various nooks and crannies, both with a real coal stove. The pub is on the main No.1 bus route or a five-minute walk from the centre of Sedgley. QP (1)

Solihull

Fieldhouse

10 Knightcote Drive, Monkspath, B91 3JU
11.30-11.30 (midnight Fri); 10-midnight Sat & Sun
☎ (0121) 703 9209
Purity Pure UBU; St Austell Proper Job; house beer (by Black Sheep); 3 changing beers (sourced nationally; often Black Sheep) H
Part of the Ember Inns chain, this large, modern pub is tastefully decorated and comfortably furnished. It features three large fires (one real, two coal-effect) and pleasant patio areas. The pub normally serves six ales, with four guest ales from across the country, sometimes unusual ones, which change frequently. Often busy, it attracts a wide age range. Quiz nights are Sunday and Tuesday; on Monday cask ales are discounted. The pub holds monthly tribute acts and occasional Meet the Brewer events. P (S15,5)

Pup & Duckling

1 Hatchford Brook Road, Olton, B92 9AG
closed Mon & Tue; 5-10; 12-3 Sun ☎ (0121) 247 8358
pupandduckling.co.uk
6 changing beers (sourced nationally; often Fixed Wheel) H
Solihull's first micropub, opened in 2016 in a vacant shop. Family-run, it has added a garden area and another room to the initial two-room layout. Six rapidly changing real ales are on handpull, along with six ciders. The latest ales are listed on Facebook, but can sell out in an evening. Bar snacks are served and customers are welcome to bring in their own food from the nearby Chinese, Indian and fish and chips takeaways. CAMRA branch Pub of the Year 2017.
Q (73,957)

Stourbridge

Barbridge

Victoria Passage, DY8 1DP (at end of Victoria Passage on Talbot St)
10.30-11 (1.30am Fri & Sat) ☎ (01384) 379898
4 changing beers (sourced nationally; often Fixed Wheel) H/G
Opened in 2015 in an old retail unit at the end of Victoria Passage behind the Rye Market, this is a busy, bustling bar appealing to all age ranges. Four ales are stocked, usually one from Fixed Wheel, served from a chiller unit to the rear through handpulls at the end of the bar. Four KeyKegs, frequently at least one from Beavertown, and six real ciders, are also available. Cobs are sold.
P

Queen's Head

111 Enville Street, DY8 3TQ
12-11 ☎ (01384) 396283
Black Country Bradley's Finest Golden, Pig on the Wall, Fireside; 7 changing beers (sourced nationally) H
Recently purchased by Black Country Ales, this is a real ale-centric pub with 12 handpulls, bar snacks and open fires. At the rear, there is a comfortable heated smoking shelter and a separate function room with a newly renovated skittle alley, ideal for events and private functions. Regular live music and comedy events now feature. Just a short walk from Stourbridge town centre. (8,228)

Red House Boutique

21-26 Foster Place, DY8 1EL
11-11 (midnight Fri & Sat); 12-8 Sun ☎ (01384) 936430
Enville Ale; Holden's Golden Glow; Wye Valley HPA; 5 changing beers (sourced nationally; often Fixed Wheel, Three Tuns) H

Large, single-bar free house near Stourbridge Interchange. Originally part of the Hogshead chain, this refurbished pub has returned to being an alehouse. Beers from Enville, Fixed Wheel and Three Tuns will usually be stocked, but may change from those listed. A range of KeyKegs is also on sale. Gourmet snacks are served at all times including Scotch eggs and flavoured scratchings. Fridges behind the bar contain many bottles from around the world. ❀♿⇌●🚌🐾ᯤ

Waggon & Horses L

31 Worcester Street, DY8 1AT

12-11 (midnight Thu-Sat) ☎ (01384) 395398

Church End Goat's Milk; Enville Ale; Holden's Golden Glow; 4 changing beers H

Recent refurbishment has created a comfortable, welcoming alehouse. There is a small cask ale bar to the front with a narrow passageway leading to a larger rear bar. To the side is a cider bar with a small serving hatchway. Parking can be difficult in the narrow surrounding streets. Two or more real ciders are usually available.
❀♿⇌●🚌(7,125)🐾ᯤ

Streetly

Brew House L

49 Boundary Road, B74 2JR

closed Mon; 5-10.30 Tue-Thu; 3-10.30 Fri; 12-10.30 Sat; 12-9 Sun ☎ (0121) 679 8512

4 changing beers H

Rescued from a near-derelict shop unit, this cosy micropub opened in mid 2018. The four handpulls offer a changing range of ales; four real ciders are also on the bar. Eight keg beers are stocked, four changing and four German beers from Aktien. Simple bar snacks are served. Plenty of car parking is available at the front in an area shared a row of shops. ♉◑♿●P🚌🐾ᯤ

Sutton Coldfield

Brewhouse & Kitchen ✓

8 Birmingham Road, B72 1QD

11-11 (1am Fri & Sat) ☎ (0121) 796 6838

Brewhouse & Kitchen The Cup, Sutton Pale Ale, 004 Oaks, Marksman H

Spacious and prominent brewpub, part of a small national chain. The real ales are produced in the small brewery which is a showcase feature at the entrance. Premium prices are charged. The decor style is rustic wood and bare brick. A large beer garden to the rear features rustic cabins and wooden cask tables. There is also a streetside beer terrace; note its ironwork cup sign relating to a former name of the pub. ♉❀◑♿⇌●🚌🐾ᯤ

Station ✓

Station Street, B73 6AT (near Sutton station southbound platform)

12-11; 11-1am Fri & Sat; 12-10 Sun ☎ (0121) 362 4961

craft-pubs.co.uk/thestationsuttoncoldfield

Black Sheep Best Bitter; Holden's Golden Glow; Timothy Taylor Landlord; 5 changing beers H

Up to eight ales feature at this attractive rail-themed pub; with four handpulls in both front and back bars, it is best to check the chalkboard. Monthly Meet The Brewer sessions reflect the often local-ish ale choices. Wednesday is quiz night, Tuesday and Friday are live music nights, and the last Thursday in the month is comedy night. The multi-level beer terrace to the rear hosts DJs and live music in summertime. Children are welcome until 6pm. ♉❀◑♿⇌🚌🐾ᯤ

Tipton

Fountain ✓

51 Owen Street, DY4 8HE

11.30-11; 11-midnight Fri & Sat; 11-11 Sun

☎ (0121) 522 3606

Greene King Abbot; Wye Valley HPA; 4 changing beers (often Sharp's, Wadworth, Wye Valley) H

Canalside pub attracting gongoozlers, boaters, families and lovers of real ale. It became a Grade II-listed building in 1982. Changing beers include national brands, namely Sharp's and Wadworth, but also core-range beers from Salopian and Hobsons. Lunchtime meals, such as beef and onion pie, are served weekdays. Snacks are available all week including cobs and pork pies. A small car park can be accessed from Factory Road.
♉❀◑⇌♣P🚌🐾ᯤ

Tame Bridge

45 Tame Road, DY4 7JA (off A461)

12-11 ☎ (0121) 557 2496

Wye Valley HPA; 3 changing beers (sourced nationally; often Church End, Hop Back, Three Tuns) H

A reliable locals' pub with a trio of changing keenly priced real ales. The front bar has an open fire, above which there is a wall-mounted flat-screen TV showing live sport, teatime quiz shows and, occasionally, a music channel. The comfortable White Room at the rear is frequently occupied by families and has a smaller bar counter with a bell to catch the attention of the bartender. The 'coming soon' ale board is often shared on Facebook. ♉❀⇌🚌(74)🐾ᯤ

Tividale

Tivi Ale

45-47 Regent Road, B69 1TL

12-11 (midnight Fri & Sat)

Holden's Golden Glow; 2 changing beers (sourced nationally; often Kelham Island, Salopian, Thornbridge) H

Friendly microbar which opened in June 2018 in the premises of a former convenience store. There is an interesting range of real ales, keg lines and speciality gins. The managers, Del and Lynn, have refurbished the unit with the help of friends and family, and the end result is a comfortable and spacious bar. Various community events are held during the year. Fresh cakes are displayed in a cabinet near the bar. ♉❀♿🚌(14,126)ᯤ

Upper Gornal

Britannia ★ L

109 Kent Street, DY3 1UX (on A459)

12-11; 12-10.30 Sun ☎ (01902) 883253

Bathams Best Bitter H

Dating to the early 19th century, this inn has a nationally important historic pub interior in the taproom at the rear, including wall-mounted handpulls. Service can be obtained from the front bar, itself a comfortable place to be. There is also a family/games room with a TV. Large cobs and pork pies are served. Outside to the rear is the former brewhouse and the garden. ♉❀♣🚌(1)🐾ᯤ

Jolly Crispin

25 Clarence Street, DY3 1UL (on A459)
4-11; 12-11 Fri & Sat; 12-10.30 Sun ☎ (01902) 672 2209
thejollycrispin.co.uk
Fownes Crispin's Ommer; 8 changing beers (sourced nationally; often Fownes, Oakham, Salopian) H
A shoemaker's house in the 18th century, and a pub for 200 years. The building sits on the top of the Black Country ridge, with distant views from the rear. Inside, the fires glow and dogs are welcome. The house beer, Crispin's Ommer, comes from the onsite Fownes Brewing Company. Fownes ales regularly feature among the eight changing beers, and Oakham Bishop's Farewell and Citra are usually available at weekends. Real cider and cobs are also served. ❀♣🍎P🚌(1)🐾

Walsall

Black Country Arms

High Street, WS1 1QW (in market, opp Asda)
11-11 (midnight Fri); 12-midnight Sat; 12-11 Sun
☎ (01922) 640588 blackcountryarms.co.uk
Black Country Bradley's Finest Golden, Pig on the Wall, Fireside; 11 changing beers (sourced nationally; often Fixed Wheel, Mallinsons, Salopian) H
A large, imposing, multi award-winning pub on three levels, part of which was originally the Green Dragon Inn that dated back to the 18th century. The pub lay empty for 70 years until extensive refurbishment saw it reopen in 1987. The impressive bar boasts 16 handpumps serving up to 11 guest ales, mainly from microbreweries, with two real ciders always on. One changing craft beer is also served. Live music features frequently; check website for details. Booking is recommended for Sunday lunches. ❀♣🍎P🚌🐾

Butts Tavern

44 Butts Street, WS4 2BJ (200yds from Arboretum's Lichfield St entrance)
12-midnight; 11-midnight Sun ☎ (01922) 629332
buttstavern.co.uk
Holden's Golden Glow; Wye Valley Butty Bach; 2 changing beers (often Castle Rock, Church End, Enville) H
Community-based local with a spacious main bar including a small stage and sports TV, plus a smaller bar at the rear with a pool table and darts. A warm welcome is assured from the staff. Two guest beers are usually on the bar, including one at 5% ABV or above, to accompany the regular ales. Local dominoes and crib teams are based here, and entertainment is often held on Friday or Saturday nights. Outside is a patio area for smokers and summer drinking. ❀♿♣🚌

Fountain Inn

49 Lower Forster Street, WS1 1XB (off A4148 ring road)
12-2, 5-11; 12-midnight Fri & Sat; 12-11 Sun
☎ (01922) 633307
Backyard The Hoard, Blonde; 5 changing beers (sourced nationally; often Holden's, St Austell) H
A family-run pub with welcoming staff, this is the brewery tap for Backyard Brewhouse and up to eight real ales are available. It has two rooms, both with log fires, and a friendly atmosphere. Regular music events are held, including vinyl, indie, classic rock, reggae, funk and soul nights. There are also monthly film nights on Mondays and drawing classes. Bar snacks include cobs and pork pies. Q♣🚌

Lyndon House Hotel

9-10 Upper Rushall Street, WS1 2HA
11-11 (1am Fri & Sat); 12-11 Sun ☎ (01922) 612511
lyndonhousehotel.co.uk
Bathams Best Bitter; Burton Bridge XL Mild, Stairway to Heaven; Caledonian Deuchars IPA; Greene King Abbot; Holden's Golden Glow H
At the top of Walsall Market, the New Royal Exchange pub was incorporated into an adjoining Salvation Army hostel and leather factory in 1995. The premises is now the luxurious Lyndon House Hotel. It has a comfortable bar with an island counter and cosy corners in a traditional old brick and wood style, a function room, downstairs Sally Ann bar and outdoor terraces. Popular with business people, this is a slice of Walsall life. Live music takes place most Sunday afternoons, and tribute bands on Saturdays, in the separate function room. Q❀♿P🚌(7,51)

Pretty Bricks

5 John Street, WS2 8AF
12-midnight (1am Fri & Sat) ☎ (01922) 612553
Black Country Bradley's Finest Golden, Pig on the Wall, Fireside; 5 changing beers (sourced nationally; often Salopian) H
Small, friendly and cosy pub, dating from 1845. There is a front bar with a wood fire, a lounge, an upstairs function room and a small blue-brick courtyard with a couple of benches. Originally called the New Inn, its current name derives from the part-glazed frontage. Tasty cobs and pork pies provide sustenance alongside a great range of ales. Folk night is every second Thursday of the month. Q❀♣🍎🚌🐾

St Matthews Hall

Lichfield Street, WS1 1SX (adjacent to town hall)
8am-midnight (2am Fri & Sat) ☎ (01922) 700820
Greene King Abbot; Ruddles Best Bitter; Sharp's Doom Bar; 4 changing beers (sourced regionally; often AJ's Ales, Backyard, Salopian) H
A stunning Grade II-listed Lloyds No.1 Bar in the centre of town, easily accessible by public transport with plenty of parking nearby. Monthly beer festivals feature throughout the year. Live entertainment takes place every Friday and Saturday evening. A full food menu is served 8am-11pm each day. A selection of local and national guest ales supplements the three regular offerings. There is a large beer garden at the side with a no-smoking area. ❀♿🍎🚌

Victoria

23 Lower Rushall Street, WS1 2AA
12-11.30 (midnight Fri & Sat); 12-11 Sun
☎ (01922) 635866
Backyard Bitter; Church End Gravediggers Ale; Jennings Sneck Lifter; 3 changing beers (sourced regionally; often AJ's Ales, Salopian) H
Popular two-roomed pub, close to the town centre, dating from 1845. The former brewhouse is at the rear. It does excellent Sunday lunches, and great cobs are on offer on other days. One real cider is permanently available. Open mic and quiz nights are held regularly, plus Sunday evening live entertainment. Retro games nights take place on a monthly cycle. A pool table is located upstairs, and it has a pleasant garden and smoking facilities out back. There is a large Pay & Display car park behind the pub. ❀♣🐾

Walsall Cricket Club

Gorway Road, WS1 3BE (off A34, by university campus)
🌣 closed Mon & Thu; 8-10.30 Tue & Wed; 6-11 Fri; 4-10.30 Sat; 12-8 Sun ☎ (01922) 622094 ⊕ walsall.play-cricket.com

Wye Valley HPA; 1 changing beer (sourced regionally; often Backyard) ℍ

On a fine summer evening the click of bat on ball welcomes you to a green oasis in the heart of town. The club room has had a major renovation and now provides luxurious comfort, with a panoramic view of the field. It is decorated with local cricket memorabilia and has two large screens showing sport. There is occasional entertainment and the venue is popular for function hire. Non-members entry is by CAMRA membership card. Weekend hours are reduced in winter (5-11pm Sat; 12-8.30pm Sun). 🌣🕏&♣🖳(51)📶

Wednesbury

Bellwether ✅

3-4 Walsall Street, WS10 9BZ
🌣 7am-midnight (1am Fri & Sat) ☎ (0121) 502 6404

Greene King Abbot; Oakham JHB; Ruddles Best Bitter; 7 changing beers (sourced nationally) ℍ

Near the main shopping area and market, the pub attracts a wide ranging clientele. It has a large, L-shaped room on a split level, with open-plan tables and chairs in front of the bar. More intimate seating at the rear leads out to a tranquil garden area. The pub is decorated with historic events and characters associated with the town. Ten handpumps serve a large selection of guest ales.
Q🌣🕏🕭&♣🖳📶

Queen's Head ✅

100 Brunswick Park Road, WS10 9QR
🌣 12 (5 Mon)-11; 12-midnight Fri & Sat ☎ 07713 756570 ⊕ queensheadwednesbury.com

Wye Valley HPA; house beer (by Backyard); 1 changing beer (often Oakham) ℍ

Enthusiastically run, this brick-built twin-gabled pub provides a warm welcome to all. There are two rooms: the front bar has tables and booths and is popular with diners, while the side bar has a TV and dartboard. Home-made food, good beer and entertainment, including frequent live bands and DJs, ensure that the Queen's Head is well supported by the local community. Tennis, football and water polo teams all meet here. Summer barbecues and the occasional beer festival also feature. Q🌣🕏🕭&♣🖳🐾📶

Wednesfield

Vine ★ Ⓛ

35 Lichfield Road, WV11 1TN
🌣 12-11 (midnight Fri & Sat) ☎ (01902) 733529

Black Country Bradley's Finest Golden, Pig on the Wall, Fireside; 6 changing beers (sourced nationally) ℍ

Built in 1938, this Grade II-listed community local is a rare intact example of a simple inter-war working-class pub. It has been identified by CAMRA as having a nationally important historic pub interior for retaining its original bar, lounge and snug. Darts and dominoes are played and there are TVs showing sport. Cobs and pork pies are available at all times. Live music is a feature on alternate Saturdays and open mic on the third Tuesday of the month. 🌣🕏♣🖳(59,89)🐾📶

West Bromwich

Crown & Cushion ✅

2 Lloyd Street, B71 4AT
🌣 12-11 ☎ (0121) 553 4493

Castle Rock Harvest Pale; St Austell Tribute; 1 changing beer (sourced nationally; often Harviestoun) ℍ

Family-friendly hostelry, run by a pleasant and welcoming landlady, with a single L-shaped room. The pub is popular in summer with visitors to nearby Dartmouth Park. It is within easy walking distance of West Bromwich Albion's football ground and can therefore get busy on match days; away supporters are made welcome. A well-attended quiz night is held on Thursday.
🌣🕏♣🖳(46)📶

Royal Oak Ⓛ ✅

14 Newton Street, B71 3RQ (down side road off Hollyhedge Rd)
🌣 2-11; 12-midnight Fri & Sat; 12-11 Sun ☎ (0121) 588 5857

St Austell Proper Job; Wye Valley HPA; 2 changing beers (sourced nationally) ℍ

Traditional back-street local pub with two small rooms. The bar on the left is adorned with West Bromwich Albion football club pictures, and on the right is the quieter lounge. There is sports TV in both rooms, usually with the sound down low. Outside is a yard to the rear for smokers and two benches at the front for basking in the summer sunshine. Parking is difficult, but available on neighbouring streets. 🌣🕏♣🖳

Three Horseshoes Ⓛ

86 Witton Lane, B71 2AQ
🌣 12-11 (midnight Fri & Sat) ☎ (0121) 502 1693

Black Country Bradley's Finest Golden, Pig on the Wall, Fireside; 10 changing beers (sourced nationally) ℍ

This refurbished one-room pub was taken on by Black Country Ales in 2016, with 10 handpulls added. The spacious interior is furnished in a traditional style, with TVs showing sport. The warm welcome provided by the staff makes you feel right at home. There are bar snacks available and a beer garden for fine weather enjoyment.
🌣🕏&♣🖳(79)🐾📶

Vine

152 Roebuck Street, B70 6RD
🌣 11.30-2, 5-11; 11.30-11 Fri; 12-11 Sat; 12-10.30 Sun ☎ (0121) 553 2866 ⊕ thevine.co.uk

2 changing beers (sourced nationally; often Backyard, Holden's, Otter) ℍ

From the street it appears a traditional corner pub, but be prepared for a surprise. The 'traditional' part consists of three small rooms off the corridor. Continue further in and the building opens up into a large dining area, where an extensive range of Indian meals are available together with British and vegetarian options, which are all excellent value. Two guest ales are regularly on tap. This popular establishment gets busy, especially when West Bromwich Albion are at home.
🌣🕏🕭⇌🖳🖳(74,79)📶

Willenhall

Falcon

77 Gomer Street West, WV13 2NR (off B4464)
🌣 12-11; 12-10.30 Sun ☎ (01902) 633378

Hobsons Town Crier; 3 changing beers (sourced regionally; often Castle Rock) Ⓗ
A two-roomed pub with a lively public bar and a quieter lounge at the rear, just a short walk from the town centre. Dating back to 1936, the Falcon has been in the same family for over 30 years. Both rooms are adorned with old pub memorabilia. The beers are keenly priced. A beer garden is at the rear and there is plenty of on-street parking nearby. (529)

Robin Hood

54 The Crescent, WV13 2QR (200yds from A462/B4464 jct)
12-11 (midnight Fri & Sat) ☎ (01902) 635070
Black Country Bradley's Finest Golden, Pig on the Wall Ⓗ**, Fireside** Ⓗ/Ⓖ**; 6 changing beers (sourced nationally; often Backyard, Beowulf, Salopian)** Ⓗ
A Black Country Ales-owned pub, with an old-fashioned feel and welcoming, friendly staff. One central bar serves both drinking areas: a large bar at the front, with a more intimate lounge at the rear. The three permanent beers are supplemented by six changing guest beers from throughout the UK. Two real ciders are also sold. Bar snacks, including cobs and pork pies, are available throughout the day. A heated and covered smoking area is to the rear. A beer festival is held every July in the beer garden. P (529)

Wolverhampton

Chindit

113 Merridale Road, WV3 9SE
4-11 (midnight Fri); 12-midnight Sat; 2-11 Sun
☎ 07986 773487 thechindit.co.uk
Hop Back Summer Lightning; Wye Valley HPA; 3 changing beers (sourced regionally; often Ossett, Rat, Titanic) Ⓗ
Built in the 1950s as an off-licence, the first landlord here served in the Chindit Regiment in Burma in WWII and named it after his comrades. It is thought to be the only pub in the country honouring Major General Orde Wingate's WWII special forces; their history is displayed in the lounge. The two-roomed pub consists of a small lounge and a bar featuring an original Wurlitzer jukebox stocking '60s and '70s 45s. There is live music every Friday and open mic night is Sunday. P (3,4)

Combermere Arms

90 Chapel Ash, WV3 0TY (on A41 Tettenhall Rd)
12-3 (not Mon winter), 5-11; 12-midnight Fri & Sat; 12-11.30 (10.30 winter) Sun ☎ (01902) 421880
5 changing beers (sourced nationally; often Greene King) Ⓗ
A Grade II-listed building with original sash windows, situated a short walk or bus ride from the city centre. It has three charming rooms with cosy fireplaces replete with classic adverts. Pie, sausage and cheese-tasting festivals are held annually and there is occasional live entertainment. To the rear is a courtyard and beer garden. The renowned tree in the Gents is reduced to a trunk. One locally brewed beer, four from the Greene King portfolio, and a varying cider are available. Q P

Great Western

Sun Street, WV10 0DG (pedestrian access from city centre via Corn Hill)
11-11; 11-10.30 Sun ☎ (01902) 351090
Bathams Best Bitter; Holden's Black Country Mild, Black Country Bitter, Golden Glow, Special; 3 changing beers (sourced regionally) Ⓗ
A previous CAMRA National Pub of the Year, near to the former low-level railway station. It attracts a varied clientele, including a rock-climbing club and railway groups. Plenty of railway and Wolverhampton Wanderers memorabilia is on display, and cosy real fires blaze in the winter. Meals are served at lunchtime (not Sun) and hot pork baps, gray pays and bacon, beef and vegetable stew are all available every day until 10pm. A beer festival is held over November's Remembrance weekend.
Q P

Hail to the Ale

2 Pendeford Avenue, Claregate, WV6 9EF
closed Mon-Wed; 5-10 Thu & Fri; 12-10 Sat; 12-5 Sun
☎ 07846 562910 hailtothealemicropub.co.uk
4 changing beers (sourced locally; often Beowulf, Lymestone, Morton) Ⓗ
Welcoming one-room beer and conversation focused pub, the West Midlands' first micropub, opened in 2013 by Morton Brewery. Four handpulls serve at least one Morton beer, and guest ales usually come from local microbreweries. Also on handpull and from the cellar are four ciders or perries. Locally sourced pies, cheese, sausage rolls and Scotch eggs are available, along with fruit wines. A regular CAMRA branch award winner. Open 5-10pm on the last Wednesday of the month.
Q P (5,6)

Hogshead

186 Stafford Street, WV1 1NA
10-midnight (1am Fri); 10-2am Sat ☎ (01902) 717955
hogsheadwolverhampton.co.uk
10 changing beers (sourced nationally) Ⓗ
A large 19th-century city-centre pub with an attractive brick terracotta exterior and a stained-glass window above the entrance displaying the original name, the Vine. Its large single room is divided into separate areas, with TVs showing sport throughout. A range of 10 guest ales is available, with regular brewery tap takeovers, and a large number of ciders, mostly from Lilley's. The pub is popular with all age groups. It holds a quiz on Wednesday evening, games on Monday evening.

Keg & Comfort

474 Stafford Road, Oxley, WV10 6AN
closed Mon-Wed; 4-10 Thu & Fri; 12-10 Sat; 1-6 Sun
☎ 07952 631032 kegandcomfort.co.uk
4 changing beers (sourced locally)
The city's second micropub opened in June 2018 in a former bank. The main contemporary room has a striking bar, custom-built using various coloured bottles, seating for around 40 and old barrels as tables for people who prefer to stand. A small side room houses a large sofa and a games cupboard. Four changing cask ales, one dark, five ciders or perries, a selection of fruit wines, and bottled beers are all served. Live music plays on the first Wednesday of the month, 6.30-10pm.
Q P

Lych Gate Tavern

44 Queen Square, WV1 1TX (by St Peter's church)
11-11 (midnight Fri & Sat) ☎ (01902) 399516
lychgatetavern.co.uk

Black Country Bradley's Finest Golden, Pig on the Wall, Fireside; 6 changing beers (sourced nationally)

Friendly, traditional, city-centre pub housed in one of the oldest timber-framed buildings in Wolverhampton; the Georgian frontage dates from 1726, while the timber-framed rear dates from about 1500. The bar area is reached by a short flight of stairs down from street level and there is a function room available for hire upstairs. Cobs are served but customers may bring their own food; plates and cutlery are provided. All floors are accessible via a lift. Previous CAMRA branch Pub of the Year. Q

Posada

48 Lichfield Street, WV1 1DG

12-11 (1am Fri); 11.30-1am Sat; 12-6 Sun

Hobsons Town Crier; Sharp's Doom Bar; 3 changing beers (often AJ's Ales, Salopian, Wye Valley)

Little altered Victorian city-centre pub with a regionally important historic interior, having tiled walls and original bar fittings, including rare snob screens. It attracts a varied clientele and is quiet during the day but busy in the evenings and weekends, especially when Wolverhampton Wanderers are at home. There is a courtyard to the rear with a smoking area. Cobs are available and Westons Old Rosie is served on handpump.

Royal Oak ✔

70 Compton Road, WV3 9PH

11.30-11 (midnight Fri & Sat); 12-11 Sun

(01902) 422845 royaloakwolverhampton.co.uk

Banks's Mild, Amber Ale, Sunbeam; Wainwright; Wychwood Hobgoblin Gold; 3 changing beers (sourced nationally; often Jennings, Ringwood, Wychwood)

A friendly local, a short walk or bus ride from the city centre, which serves a wide range of real ales from Marston's portfolio. The bustling pub with good sports coverage hosts open mic evenings on Wednesdays and live bands on Fridays and Saturdays (also Sunday afternoons in summer). Part of the community, the pub raises money for local and national charities and is the headquarters of Old Wulfrunians hockey club. Pub and local history and maps are displayed on a wall. Cobs are available at the bar. P(10,9)

Starting Gate

134 Birches Barn Road, Penn Fields, WV3 7BG

6-10.30 Mon-Wed; 5.30-11 Thu & Fri; 2-11 Sat; 1-6 Sun

5 changing beers (sourced regionally; often Ludlow, Sarah Hughes, Wye Valley)

Opened in autumn 2018, this small pub occupies a former bank branch and retains the original bank counter and wings. The impressive rear door to the garden area also reflect its previous use. The small bar area leads to a cosy lounge, with another lounge upstairs reached by an open spiral staircase. Paintings, silks and other memorabilia reflect an interest in horse racing, hence the name of the pub. Cider is served in summer only.
Q(2)

Stile Inn ✔

3 Harrow Street, Whitmore Reans, WV1 4PB

11.30-11 (midnight Fri; 1am Sat) (01902) 425336

Banks's Mild, Amber Ale, Sunbeam; 1 changing beer (sourced nationally)

A typical late-Victorian street-corner pub built in 1900, featuring a public bar, smoke room and snug. It is a true community local with an emphasis on sports; darts and dominoes feature inside, Crown Green bowls on the unusual L-shaped green outside, and it gets busy with Wolverhampton Wanderers fans on match days. Excellent-value food, including Polish dishes, is served all day. Friday is disco night and Saturday is karaoke. Sky and BT Sports are shown in all rooms. Westons Old Rosie is stocked. (5,6)

Swan

Bridgnorth Road, Compton, WV6 8AE (at Compton island on A454)

12-11 (11.30 Thu; midnight Fri & Sat) (01902) 754736

swanpubwolverhampton.co.uk

Banks's Mild, Amber Ale, Sunbeam; Marston's Old Empire; Wainwright; 3 changing beers (sourced nationally; often Brakspear, Jennings, Wychwood)

Built around 1780, this Grade II-listed former coaching inn close to the Staffordshire & Worcestershire Canal and Smestow Valley Nature Reserve is popular with locals, boaters, ramblers and cyclists. It comprises a lively bar with local banter, a games room and a more sedate snug. It hosts charity dog shows, three beer festivals featuring ales from outside the Marston's range and the local Pigeon Flyers Club. A well-considered and sympathetic refurbishment was carried out mid 2016. QP

Woodcross

Horse & Jockey ✔

Robert Wynd, WV14 9SB

12-11 (11.30 Fri & Sat) (01902) 662268

horseandjockeywoodcross.pub

Hobsons Twisted Spire, Town Crier; 4 changing beers (sourced locally; often Backyard, Salopian, Three Tuns)

Run by two CAMRA members, this friendly and thriving community pub comprises a bar, a large contemporary lounge with seasonal open fire, a rear beer garden and a small smoking shelter at the front. Good-value, home-cooked food, including vegetarian options, is served daily until 8.30pm (6pm Sun). Tuesday evening is quiz night. Under-18s are allowed in the lounge area and garden until 8pm. QP

Wordsley

Bird in Hand

57 John Street, DY8 4AZ

12-11

Enville Ale; Hobsons Town Crier; Holden's Golden Glow; 3 changing beers (sourced nationally; often Fixed Wheel, Olde Swan, Tiny Rebel)

Local CAMRA Community Pub of the Year 2019, this place is homely and not far from the Red House Cone and old glassworks. The current manageress inherited a thriving wet-led locals' pub from the outgoing publican towards the end of 2017. The number of handpulls increased to accommodate three guest beers. Although local breweries such as Wye Valley and Olde Swan are particularly popular, the guest beers are also sourced nationally, including from Ossett group and Tiny Rebel.
Q(16,17)

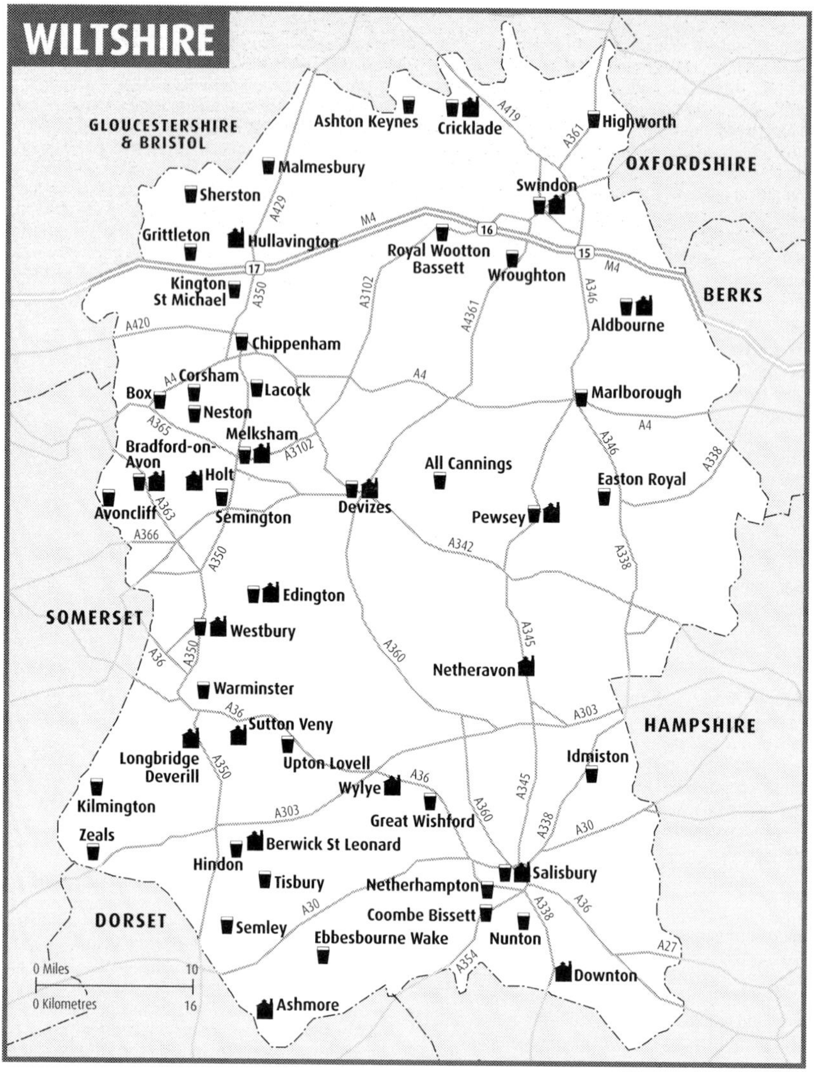

Aldbourne

Crown Inn ✔

The Square, SN8 2DU

✪ 12-11.30 (12.30am Sat); 12-11 Sun ☎ (01672) 540214

🌐 thecrownaldbourne.co.uk

Sharp's Doom Bar; Shepherd Neame Spitfire; Timothy Taylor Landlord; 1 changing beer (sourced nationally) 🄷

Situated in the middle of the village opposite the duck pond, the Crown has a relaxed and pleasant atmosphere despite the Dalek standing guard outside. The main bar is stylishly refurbished and has a welcoming fire during the colder seasons. A smaller bar shows films on Monday night. The restaurant serves freshly prepared food, cooked to order, until 9pm, with daily specials and a Sunday carvery. Tuesday is quiz night and there is a meat raffle on Saturday afternoon. Live music features every Saturday evening. Accommodation is available in four en-suite bedrooms.

❀🛏◑▲♣🚌(46,48)🐾📶

All Cannings

King's Arms Inn

The Street, SN10 3PA

✪ 12-3 (not Mon), 6-11; 12-11 Sat & Sun ☎ (01380) 860328

🌐 kingsarmsallcannings.co.uk

Wadworth IPA, 6X; 1 changing beer (sourced nationally) 🄷

A genuine traditional pub serving good home-made food, with menus changing all the time and a daily specials board. Drinks include first-class Wadworth ales, guest beers, ciders on draught and bottle, and wine by the glass or bottle. An annual charity rock concert is held in the pub's camping field every May, when the range of Wadworth beers is expanded to include a special concert ale.

❀◑▲♣🍏P

Ashton Keynes

White Hart ✔

High Road, SN6 6NX

⏲ 12-3 (not Mon), 6-11; 12-3, 5-midnight Fri; 12-midnight Sat; 11.30-10 Sun ☎ (01285) 861247
🌐 thewhitehartashtonkeynes.com
Ramsbury Gold; house beer (by Stroud); 2 changing beers (sourced regionally; often Exmoor, Ramsbury) [H]
Set in a pretty village, the pub has been owned by a group of local residents since 2011. Its interior is divided into three distinct areas: the main bar area, a smaller bar with games and TV, and a dining room. To the side of the pub is a pleasant garden; outside the front is one of the village's four ancient stone crosses. Four real ales are served, along with good food every day except Monday.
❀◑♣P🚌(51,93A)🐾📶

Avoncliff

Cross Guns

159-160 Avoncliff, BA15 2HB
⏲ 10-11 ☎ (01225) 862335 🌐 crossgunsavoncliff.com
4 changing beers (sourced nationally; often Cairngorm, Island, Pheasantry) [H]
A world away, yet only 12 minutes by rail from Bath, this 16th-century canalside inn is popular with walkers, cyclists and narrow-boaters. Overlooking the small village is the historic Avoncliff aqueduct where the Kennet & Avon Canal crosses the River Avon and the railway line. Features include an inglenook fireplace, priest hole, garden bar, weekend barbecues and a resident ghost. Live music plays every Tuesday. Beers can be from local breweries and from far and wide. Just 100 yards from Avoncliff station (a request stop). Q❀◑♿⛺≠♣●🐾📶

Box

Quarrymans Arms 🄻 ✔

Box Hill, SN13 8HN (signed from A4)
⏲ 10-11 (midnight Fri & Sat) ☎ (01225) 743569
🌐 quarrymans-arms.co.uk
Butcombe Adam Henson's Rare Breed, Original; 3 changing beers (sourced nationally; often Liberation, Oakham, VOG) [H]
Originally miners' dwellings dating back 300 years, supporting the local Bath stone mines. There are three comfortable areas to enjoy a drink and locally sourced food – the snug, bar and the restaurant area overlooking the stunning valley towards Colerne and Bath. The beams are adorned with old pumpclips celebrating the range of beers served here over the years. The garden terrace also enjoys fine views. Beer tapas is available.
Q❀🛏◑♿⛺♣●P📶

Bradford-on-Avon

Castle Inn

Mount Pleasant, BA15 1SJ
⏲ 8.30am-11; 10-10.30 Sun ☎ (01225) 865657
🌐 flatcappers.co.uk/the-castle-inn
Three Castles Barbury Castle, Vale Ale; 4 changing beers (often Arbor, Electric Bear, Great Western) [H]
A popular, comfortable pub commanding splendid views across the town towards Salisbury Plain. The recent refurbishment by Flatcappers won it joint Best Refurbishment in the CAMRA Design Awards. A wide range of handpulled real ales is complemented by excellent food, served all day until 10pm. The three guest beers are usually from microbreweries in Wiltshire and east Somerset. There is a good-sized garden at the front and children are welcome. Local CAMRA Pub of the Year 2017. ❀🛏◑♿⛺≠●P🚌(D1)🐾📶

Stumble Inn

Market Street, BA15 1LL
⏲ 7-11; 6-11 Thu; 5-11 Fri; 12-11 Sat; closed Sun & Mon
☎ (01225) 862115 🌐 thestumbleinnboa.com
4 changing beers (sourced locally; often Cheddar Ales, Kettlesmith, Twisted) [H]/[G]
A micropub that is now well established after opening in 2017. Set on the ground floor of what was previously a club in the centre of town, it has a main bar at the back with seating and a good-sized comfortable room at the front overlooking the main street. The pub serves a varying range of up to four beers, with two on handpump and two on gravity. Local brewers Kettlesmith sometimes have a tap takeover on Sunday. ≠♣●🚌(D1)🐾📶

Three Horseshoes

55 Frome Road, BA15 1LA
⏲ 11-11; 12-7 Sun ☎ (01225) 867856
3 changing beers (sourced regionally) [H]
The Horseshoes is a nice old coaching inn on the edge of the town centre next to the railway station. It comes complete with the old wooden door where the horses went through to the yard. At the bar there are usually three constantly changing beers, often local. Live bands play at weekends. Outside at the back is a small garden and terrace with seating. Parking is at the rear and is a bit limited. ❀≠P🚌(D1)🐾📶

Chippenham

Flying Monk Tavern 🄻

6 Market Place, SN15 3HD (by the buttercross)
⏲ 11-11; 12-6 Sun ☎ (01249) 460662
Flying Monk Elmers, Habit, Birdman; 4 changing beers (often Flying Monk) [H]
As its name suggests, this former Buttercross Inn is now a tied outlet for the Flying Monk brewery from nearby Hullavington. Although looking like an old historic pub, it was a sports shop until about 30

REAL ALE BREWERIES

Arkell's Swindon
Blonde Brothers Wylye (NEW)
Box Steam Holt
Brotherhood Westbury
Dark Revolution Salisbury
Downton Downton
Flying Monk Hullavington
Gritchie Ashmore
Hop Back Downton
Hop Kettle ▮ Cricklade/Swindon
Kettlesmith Bradford-on-Avon
Keystone Berwick St Leonard
Plain Sutton Veny
Ramsbury Aldbourne
Shed Pewsey
Stealth Melksham
Stonehenge Netheravon
Three Castles Pewsey
Three Daggers Edington
Twisted Westbury
Wadworth Devizes
Weighbridge ▮ Swindon
Wessex Longbridge Deverill
World's End ▮ Pewsey

years ago. There are seven handpumps serving the brewery's full range plus three more pumps for traditional cider. Across the marketplace behind the church is the house that opens out in the opening sequence of Antiques Roadshow.

Old Road Tavern

Old Road, SN15 1JA (over bridge from station)
11-11.30 (12.30am Fri & Sat); 12-11.30 Sun
(01249) 247080
Bath Ales Gem; Hop Back Summer Lightning; Otter Bitter; Wye Valley HPA; 2 changing beers (sourced nationally; often Adnams, Exmoor, Prescott)
The pub has been a traditional community local since 1842. It has a large garden with plenty of seating, well used in the summer. A diverse mix of regulars ensures lively and friendly conversation. Four regular ales are supplemented with two varying guest beers. The pub hosts regular live music and comedy sessions in its adjoining, recently refurbished hall, which is available for hire. Well-behaved dogs are welcome in the pub and garden.

Three Crowns

18 The Causeway, SN15 3DB (S of town centre)
5-11; 12-midnight Fri & Sat; 12-11 Sun (01249) 449029
threecrownschippenham.co.uk
7 changing beers (sourced nationally; often Arbor, Slater's, XT)
Friendly 18th-century two-roomed waggoners' pub. Popular with locals and visitors, it has a large log fire in the winter. Seven continually changing beers include at least two dark ales, as well as four ciders and a perry, usually from local producers. Four seasonal beer festivals are held each year. The pub supports a darts team, hosts the local ukulele club and welcomes dogs. A multiple CAMRA award winner. **Q P**

Coombe Bissett

Fox & Goose

Blandford Road, SP5 4LE
11-11; 12-10.30 Sun (01722) 718437
foxandgoose-coombebissett.co.uk
Sharp's Doom Bar; Sixpenny Best Bitter; 1 changing beer (sourced nationally)
An 18th-century coaching inn on the A354, three miles south of Salisbury. This popular community pub has a loyal village clientele and a welcoming atmosphere. Divided into a bar and restaurant, it offers an extensive food menu with ever-changing specials. There is a loyalty card scheme for regular diners. Outside, there are pleasant gardens to the rear. This year the licensee is celebrating 20 years in the pub. **Q P** (20,29)

Corsham

Flemish Weaver

63 High Street, SN13 0EZ (next to town hall)
11-11; 12-10.30 Sun (01249) 701929
flemishweaver.co.uk
House beer (by Wadworth); 4 changing beers (sourced nationally; often Marston's, Salopian, Wadworth)
Extensively refurbished in 2017, the Flemish Weaver is an intriguing pub and full of character with many nooks and crannies. The garden is a pleasant and unexpected surprise. There is a focus on quality service and real ale, with four handpumps offering a varied range. The building is in the oldest part of Corsham where you may notice locations from the TV series Poldark, some of which was filmed here.

Cricklade

Red Lion

74 High Street, SN6 6DD
12-11 (10.30 Sun) (01793) 750776
theredlioncricklade.co.uk
Hop Kettle Cricklade Ordinary Bitter, North Wall; Wadworth 6X; 7 changing beers (sourced nationally; often Hop Kettle)
Friendly, popular and comfortable inn, parts of which are quite ancient – the old Saxon town wall passes through the building. It is home to the Hop Kettle Brewing Co, which brews here and in Swindon. Ten real ales – three regular, four from Hop Kettle and three guests – are on handpump, plus real cider. A winter beer festival is held in February, a summer festival in June. Excellent food is served every day except Monday. There is a large garden at the back. **Q** (51,53)

Devizes

British Lion

9 Estcourt Street, SN10 1LQ (on A361 opp Kwik Fit)
11-11 (midnight Fri & Sat); 12-11 Sun (01380) 720665
britishliondevizes.co.uk
4 changing beers (sourced nationally; often Palmers, Plain, Stonehenge)
The British has been ever-present in the Guide for over 25 years. An unpretentious free house with wooden floors, cosy settles and an eclectic group of talkative regulars, it is an essential port of call in town. There are four handpumps and the beers change frequently throughout the week – time it right and you can savour eight different ales. The knowledgeable landlord is always pleased to offer his advice. **P**

Vaults

28A St John's Street, SN10 1BN (opp town hall)
5-9; 12-9 Fri-Sun (01380) 721443
thevaultsdevizes.com
5 changing beers (often Stealth)
The Vaults maintains its high standards, with five ale handpumps usually offering at least one beer from Stealth Brew Co, plus up to three still ciders. A vast selection of bottles and tins from around the world is also stocked. Paddles are available – three or five third-pint glasses allow you to sample several ales at a time. The pub has a long, galley-style bar and a huge cellar used for events. Conversation rules here – there is no music or fruit machines but a great atmosphere. Dogs are welcome. **Q P**

White Bear

33 Monday Market Street, SN10 1DN
closed Mon; 12-11; 12-3 Sun (01380) 727588
whitebeardevizes.co.uk
Wadworth IPA; 5 changing beers (often Wadworth)
Recently refurbished throughout, this old coaching inn dates from the 1500s and features original beams and wood-burning stoves. It has six pumps serving real ales, of which two are Wadworth – usually IPA and a seasonal or varying offering - plus four other guest ales. A dark beer is often among

the range, and a still cider. Food is served all week. There is no pub car park but there is plenty of on-street parking and nearby car parks. 🛏◑🍎🚌🐾📶

Easton Royal

Bruce Arms ★ ⓁL

Easton Road, SN9 5LR

⏲ 5-11; 12-11 Sat; 12-7 Sun ☎ (01672) 810216

🌐 thebrucearms.net

Sharp's Atlantic; Stonehenge Pigswill; Wadworth 6X; 2 changing beers (sourced regionally) Ⓗ

A 19th-century local with a nationally important historic pub interior. There is a small, cosy bar with furniture that probably dates back to the 1850s, and a small lounge with easy chairs and a piano. At the back is a larger dining and function room. The pub sits in splendid isolation, so its campsite with full facilities is an asset that makes it a good venue for meetings and rallies.
Q🐎❀⛺♣🍎P🚌(96,19)🐾📶

Ebbesbourne Wake

Horseshoe

The Cross, SP5 5JF

⏲ closed Mon; 12-3, 6.30-11; 12-4 Sun ☎ (01722) 780474

🌐 thehorseshoe-inn.co.uk

Bowman Swift One; Gritchie English Lore; Otter Bitter; 1 changing beer (sourced nationally) Ⓖ

Unspoilt 18th-century inn in a remote rural setting at the foot of an old ox drove. This friendly pub has two small bars displaying an impressive collection of old farm implements, tools and lamps, plus a restaurant, conservatory and pleasant garden. Good local food is available Tuesday to Sunday and four or five beers are served direct from casks stillaged behind the bar. The original serving hatch just inside the front door is still in use. Real cider is usually available, often from Wessex or Orchard Pig. Q🐎❀🛏◑⛺🍎P🚌(29)🐾

Edington

Three Daggers

Westbury Road, BA13 4PG

⏲ 10-11 (10.30 Sun) ☎ (01380) 830940

🌐 threedaggers.co.uk

Three Daggers Daggers Blonde, Daggers Ale, Daggers Edge; 1 changing beer (often Three Daggers) Ⓗ

This refurbished village pub is now the brewery tap for the eponymous brewery, situated in an adjacent farm shop. The pub has a main bar with three distinct drinking areas, leading into a seating area and a dining room. Two mirrors hide TV screens that are occasionally used for sporting events. At the rear is a lovely garden, and it offers accommodation. Regular seasonal beers are brewed, and carryouts and bottles are available in the shop. Q🐎❀🛏◑♿P🚌🐾📶

Great Wishford

Royal Oak

Langford Road, SP2 0PD

⏲ 12-midnight (10.30 Sun) ☎ (01722) 790613

🌐 royaloakgreatwishford.com

House beer (by Shepherd Neame); 7 changing beers (sourced nationally) Ⓗ

A traditional, ivy-clad village pub that dates from the 17th century and serves up to eight real ales, including rapidly changing local and national brews. The comfortable main bar area leads to a large rear restaurant serving good, freshly prepared food. The pub is popular with walkers on the Monarch's Way or visiting Grovely Wood, and cyclists using Route 24 of the National Cycle Network. It hosts regular quizzes and music events and is involved in village celebrations for Oak Apple Day on 29 May. Q🐎❀◑P🚌(2)🐾📶

Grittleton

Neeld Arms

The Street, SN14 6AP

⏲ 12-3, 5.30-11; 12-midnight Sat; 12-11 Sun

☎ (01249) 782 4709 🌐 neeldarms.co.uk

Flying Monk Elmers; St Austell Tribute; 1 changing beer (sourced locally; often Plain) Ⓗ

The motto 'Proud to be a Pub' sums up this welcoming 17th-century, Grade II-listed inn with its four handpumps, beamed ceiling, two stoves and bench tables in the bar. A reasonably priced lunch and evening menu includes an interesting specials board. An annexe can also be used for private functions. The owners of 18 years host an event each month. Ample roadside parking is available for guests of the six en-suite rooms.
Q🐎🛏◑P🐾📶

Highworth

Rose & Crown ⓁL

19 The Green, SN6 7DB

⏲ 9am-11 (midnight Fri & Sat); 12-10.30 Sun

☎ (01793) 764699 🌐 roseandcrownhighworth.co.uk

Sharp's Doom Bar, Sea Fury; 3 changing beers (sourced nationally; often Halfpenny, Old Forge) Ⓗ

A free house since 2014, following a major facelift, this is one of the oldest pubs in Highworth. Cheerful and friendly staff add to the pleasant atmosphere. It has five handpumps, three serving changing guest ales. The lunch menu is good quality and value. Open mic and folk sessions are held occasionally. The garden has a boules pitch.
Q🐎❀◐♣🍎P🚌(7)🐾📶

Hindon

Angel Inn

High Street, SP3 6DJ

⏲ 11-11 (10.30 Sun) ☎ (01747) 820696

🌐 the-angel-hotel.co.uk

Timothy Taylor Landlord; 1 changing beer (sourced nationally) Ⓗ

A beautifully restored 18th-century coaching inn near the spired church in this attractive village. Its many original features include wooden floors, beams and a huge stone fireplace. The pub was originally known as the Grosvenor Arms; before its construction in 1750 a medieval inn called the Angel existed on the site. Access to the bar is through an attractive, south-west facing walled garden and terrace. Q🐎❀🛏◑♿P🚌(25)🐾📶

Idmiston

Earl of Normanton

Tidworth Road, SP4 0AG

⏲ 12-2.45, 6-11; 12-7 Sun ☎ (01980) 610251

🌐 theearlofnormanton.co.uk

Exmoor Gold; Fuller's London Pride; Hop Back Summer Lightning; 3 changing beers (sourced locally; often Andwell, Cotleigh) Ⓗ

Popular roadside pub with a welcoming atmosphere enhanced by two real fires in winter. A recent extension has increased the dining area and added adjacent toilets with fully accessible facilities. Good-value, home-cooked food is served, with a traditional roast on Sunday. There is a small, pleasant garden on the terraced hill behind the pub with a fabulous view across the River Bourne to the countryside beyond. Occasional live music is hosted. A former local CAMRA Country Pub of the Year. Q P (66,67)

Kilmington

Red Lion Inn

BA12 6RP (B3092 between Mere and Frome)
11-2.30, 5-8 (9 Thu & Fri); 11-9 Sat; 12-6 Sun
(01985) 844263 theredlionkilmington.co.uk
Butcombe Original; Wessex Stourton Pale Ale; 1 changing beer H
A friendly, traditional free house with a low-beamed, flagstoned front bar featuring cushioned wall and window seats, curved high-backed settles and woodburners. The larger back bar has tables for diners to enjoy the home-cooked food supplied by high-quality local food producers (some from the village itself). Thatchers Heritage cider contributes to the excellent drinks range. Dogs are welcome to join their owners in the front bar or in the large, attractive garden which has fine views of White Sheet Hill. Q P

Kington St Michael

Jolly Huntsman

SN14 6JB (signed from A350)
11.30-2.30, 6-11 (midnight Fri & Sat); 12-3, 7-10.30 Sun
(01249) 750305 jollyhuntsman.com
Flying Monk Elmers; Moles Best; 2 changing beers (sourced locally; often Goff's, Ramsbury) H
A former brewery situated on the village high street, this free house offers a warm and friendly welcome, with a large open fire in the winter. It serves a selection of locally brewed real ales and a choice of ciders, usually from regional suppliers. An excellent food menu is available lunchtimes and evenings, featuring a range of traditional fare and chef's specials, plus occasional themed evenings. Accommodation is en-suite. Q P (99)

Lacock

Bell Inn

The Wharf, SN15 2PJ (over bridge to Bowden Hill)
11.30-2.30, 5-11; 11.30-11 Sat; 12-10.30 Sun
(01249) 730308 thebellatlacock.co.uk
House beer (by Great Western); 4 changing beers (sourced regionally; often Butts, Great Western, Plain) H
Renowned for its friendly welcome and superbly kept ales, this free house on the edge of the National Trust village of Lacock is popular with locals and visitors alike. Local CAMRA Pub of the Year on a number of occasions, it has an excellent reputation for the variety of ales served, quality food and all-round good value. Two beer festivals are held each year. The house beer, Beau Bell, celebrates the birth of the first child of the landlord and landlady. Q P

Malmesbury

Whole Hog

8 Market Cross, SN16 9AS
11-11; 12-midnight Fri & Sat; 12-11 Sun
(01666) 825845
Ramsbury Same Again; Stonehenge Pigswill; Wadworth 6X; 2 changing beers (sourced regionally; often Flying Monk, Hook Norton) H
Popular free house, central to the community and located between the 15th-century Market Cross and 12th-century Abbey at the top end of the town centre. It offers well-kept ales plus freshly prepared food, served in the separate dining room. The diverse range of seating areas goes from cosy nooks and crannies to a former shop window overlooking the Market Cross. Welcoming both to regulars and visitors looking for a respite from sightseeing. Q

Marlborough

Royal Oak

111 High Street, SN8 1LT
10-11 (midnight Fri & Sat) (01672) 512064
Greene King IPA, Abbot; 3 changing beers (sourced nationally; often Bath Ales, Great Western, Timothy Taylor) H
This busy pub is well located halfway along Marlborough High Street. Alongside two regular Greene King real ales, it adds welcome variety with three changing guests. Good-value pub food is available all day, every day. Major sports events are shown on TV and live music is hosted on Friday and Saturday. A large beer garden to the rear attracts customers preferring a quiet drink.
(X5)

Melksham

Bear

3 Bath Road, SN12 6LL
8am-midnight (1am Fri & Sat) (01225) 792690
Greene King Abbot; Ruddles Best Bitter; Sharp's Doom Bar; 2 changing beers (sourced nationally; often Prescott, Wadworth) H
A spacious Wetherspoon pub, close to the town centre, with interesting features including milk churn lights in the rear dining area and an open fire in the ladies' toilets. Two banks of mirrored handpumps usually serve five beers. There is plenty of seating inside and out, where guests can enjoy a good variety of meals at reasonable prices. The manager organises numerous charity events at the pub. The bus stops right outside.
Q P

Neston

Neston Country Inn

25 Pool Green, SN13 9SN (N of village)
12-2.30 (not Mon), 6-11; 12-11 Sat; 12-9 Sun
(01225) 811694 theneston.com
Stonehenge Pigswill; 1 changing beer (sourced locally) H
This classic, cosy and welcoming village pub with well-kept cask ales and real cider dates back to 1820. It has been in the safe hands of the current landlords for more than 10 years, and the pub is thriving in their care. Excellent, traditional food uses high-quality ingredients with interesting twists, and is popular. Visitors can enjoy monthly

quiz nights, darts and live music. The garden is a good size for families and leads to the local park.
Q❀⊨◐◑♣●P🚌(10)🐾📶

Netherhampton

Victoria & Albert

Netherhampton Road, SP2 8PU

11-3, 5.30 (5 Sat)-11; 12-5 Sun ☎ (01722) 743174

🌐 victoriaandalbert.org

3 changing beers (sourced regionally) Ⓗ

A genuine classic English country inn, dating back to 1540 and little changed over the years. The beautiful thatched building lies in the centre of the village opposite the church and is a focus of local life. Inside, it boasts flagstone floors, a log fire and original oak beams, while outside are a large covered patio and spacious garden. Snacks and full meals are available lunchtimes and evenings (excluding Sun eve). A long-established family business and winner of numerous awards including local CAMRA Pub of the Year 2018.
Q❀◐◑♣●P🐾📶

Nunton

Radnor Arms L ✔

SP5 4HS

12-11 (10 Sun) ☎ (01722) 329722 🌐 theradnor.com

Sharp's Doom Bar; Sixpenny Best Bitter; 3 changing beers (sourced nationally) Ⓗ

Built as a cottage in the mid-18th century, it became a pub in 1853 and is named after Lord Radnor whose descendants still own the nearby estate. The open-plan interior has low ceilings and various seating areas allowing for privacy. Two guest beers are available, one usually from Hop Back. Popular with diners, it offers an extensive family-friendly menu. The large open garden has a children's play area and leads down to the River Ebble. Q❀◐◑♿P🚌(44,X3)🐾📶

Pewsey

Coopers Arms L

37-39 Ball Road, SN9 5BL

5-11; 12-11 Sat; 12-10.30 Sun ☎ (01672) 562495

Wadworth 6X; 3 changing beers (sourced nationally; often Ramsbury, Skinner's, Three Castles) Ⓗ

Worth seeking out, this down-to-earth thatched pub on the eastern edge of Pewsey has a historic interior with an open-plan bar and two side rooms. A warming fire is an attraction in winter. Four real ales are served: two local regulars plus two guests, usually from the South-West region. The pub hosts live music on alternate Friday nights and a quiz on the first Sunday of the month. No food, but snacks are available. Q❀⊨♣●P🚌(X5)🐾📶

Crown Inn L

60 Wilcot Road, SN9 5EL

4-11 Mon & Tue; 12-11 Wed & Thu (11.30 Fri; midnight Sat); 12-6 Sun ☎ (01672) 562653

🌐 thecrowninnpewsey.com

5 changing beers (sourced locally; often Stonehenge, Three Castles, World's End) Ⓗ

The tap for World's End brewery, which is behind the pub. The building dates from the 1860s and has a small bar with an attractive stone and brick fireplace in its centre. Corridors on either side lead to another seating area. Food is served on Friday evening, Sunday lunchtime and theme nights only, except by prior arrangement. Beer festivals are held to mark summer and winter solstices. The pub hosts fortnightly live music plus chess and poetry nights. Q❀◐◑♿⇌♣●🚌(X5)🐾📶

Shed Alehouse L ✔

20 North Street, SN9 5EX

closed Mon & Tue; 5-9.30 Wed & Thu; 4-10 Fri; 2-10 Sat; 1-5 Sun ☎ 07769 812643 🌐 theshedalehouse.com

5 changing beers (sourced regionally) Ⓗ

A former shop converted to a cosy award-winning micropub, the interior reflecting its name with a basic wood-panelled decor complete with tools. This is a free house with five handpumps serving a changing range of beers from local and regional brewers, often including Shed Ales from Pewsey. The total number dispensed since 2015 exceeds 800. A craft pilsner and up to four real ciders are also offered. There is not much space inside, so you soon get to know your fellow drinkers. No dogs allowed. Q⇌♣●🚌(X5)

Royal Wootton Bassett

Five Bells L ✔

Wood Street, SN4 7BD

12-3, 5-11.30; 12-midnight Fri-Sun ☎ (01793) 849422

Black Sheep Best Bitter; Fuller's London Pride; 4 changing beers (sourced nationally; often Sharp's, Timothy Taylor) Ⓗ

Dating from before 1841, this is a busy and cosy traditional thatched local with a beamed ceiling and open fires. The bar, which has now been extended, has seven handpumps for two regular beers, four guests and a cider. Food is served lunchtimes and Wednesday and Thursday evenings (booking recommended). The pub has darts and crib teams. Special events are held throughout the year including a beer festival in the summer. Local CAMRA Pub of the Year 2018.
Q❀◐◑♣●P🚌(55)🐾📶

Salisbury

Deacons ✔

118 Fisherton Street, SP2 7QT

4-11 (midnight Fri); 12-midnight Sat; 12-11 Sun ☎ (01722) 322866 🌐 deaconssalisbury.com

Hop Back GFB, Summer Lightning; Sharp's Doom Bar; 1 changing beer (sourced regionally) Ⓗ

A friendly, independently owned free house a stone's throw from Salisbury railway station and a short walk from the cathedral. The landlord collaborates with local breweries to showcase quality real ale. Sport is shown on TV in one room; the front room has a digital jukebox. The pub hosts live music, quiz nights and beer festivals.
⊨⇌♣🚌🐾

Haunch of Venison ★ L

1 Minster Street, SP1 1TB

11-11 (midnight Fri & Sat); 11-10 Sun ☎ (01722) 411313

🌐 haunchpub.co.uk

Hop Back GFB, Summer Lightning; 1 changing beer (sourced nationally) Ⓗ

Known as one of Britain's finest old inns and identified by CAMRA as having a nationally important historic interior. The main bar, the Commons, is timber-panelled and has a rare zinc-topped bar. A tiny second bar features original spirit taps and floor tiles recovered long ago from a refurbishment of the cathedral. An upstairs seated area, the Lords, houses the mummified hand of a card cheat. Another flight of stairs leads to two unique dining rooms. A gem in the heart of this historic city.

Pheasant

19 Salt Lane, SP1 1DT

12-10.30 (11 Fri & Sat); 12-7 Sun (01722) 421841

thepheasantsalisbury.co.uk

St Austell Proper Job; Sharp's Doom Bar; 2 changing beers (sourced regionally)

A historic building, situated close to the city centre and opposite Salt Lane car park, that dates back to 1435 when it was known as the Crispin Inn. Steeped in history, it is a characterful, atmospheric and cosy, two-bar pub. Following sympathetic restoration, it has a stylish country feel with open brick walls, exposed beams and a logburner. Food takes centre stage but there is a large lounge area for those who just want a drink. A partially covered courtyard offers outdoor shelter in inclement weather. Proudly dog-friendly.

Rai d'Or

69 Brown Street, SP1 2AS

5-10 (11 Thu-Sat); closed Sun (01722) 327137

raidor.co.uk

2 changing beers (sourced locally)

Characterful 13th-century free house whose fascinating history is highlighted by a blue plaque recalling an early landlady. An inglenook fireplace and low ceilings make for an appealing ambience. Excellent, reasonably priced Thai food is complemented by two changing, usually local, beers. It can be busy at mealtimes but drinkers are always welcome. There is a discount on food before 6.30pm. Local CAMRA Town Pub of the Year 2018, with 15 years in the Guide.

Rugby Club

Castle Road, SP1 3SA

closed Mon; 7-11; 12-11 Sat; 8-11 Sun (01722) 325317

salisburyrfc.org

Hop Back GFB, Crop Circle, Summer Lightning; 1 changing beer (sourced locally)

Occupying a corner of the large club house, this cosy, refurbished lounge bar is open to the public. Retaining its sporting roots, the bar features rugby memorabilia. Two TVs generally show rugby or other sport. The function room bar is open at busy times such as match days. The three Hop Back ales are often joined by a Hop Back or Downton seasonal brew. Quiz night is Wednesday. Various events, including a beer festival, are held each year. There are camping facilities close by.

P

Village Freehouse

33 Wilton Road, SP2 7EF

4-11; 12-11 Fri-Sun (01722) 329707

Downton Quadhop; 4 changing beers (sourced nationally)

A lively pub, handy for those arriving by train. Microbrewery beers come from near and far, with customer requests welcomed. There is always at least one dark brew, either stout, porter or mild. Teams are fielded in the local crib, cricket and football leagues and a TV shows BT Sport, with the sound off much of the time. Filled rolls are available or you are welcome to bring your own food. Local CAMRA Pub of the Year three times.

Winchester Gate

113-117 Rampart Road, SP1 1JA

4-11; 2-11 Fri; 12-11 Sat & Sun (01722) 503362

5 changing beers (sourced regionally)

Characterful free house, an inn since the 17th century which once provided for travellers at the city's east tollgate. Five handpumps offer changing ales and real ciders from across the country. Beer and cider festivals are held on several occasions during the year. A small lawned garden offers a pleasant area to sit out, particularly during the summer. The pub is renowned for live music every Friday and Saturday and frequently on Thursday.

P

Wyndham Arms

27 Estcourt Road, SP1 3AS

4.30 (12 Thu)-11.30; 12-midnight Fri & Sat; 12-11.30 Sun (01722) 331026

Hop Back GFB, Citra, Crop Circle, Summer Lightning; 2 changing beers (sourced locally)

The birthplace of the Hop Back Brewery, now celebrating 33 consecutive years in the Guide. A traditional ale house, it has a single bar with six handpumps serving a selection of Hop Back ales – normally including Taiphoon in summer and Entire Stout in winter – alongside seasonal offerings and a fine selection of bottled beers and wines. Two small, quiet rooms off the main bar area provide more seating. This is a pub for conversation, good-natured banter and fine ales. Local CAMRA Pub of the Year 2019. (R2,R6)

Semington

Somerset Arms

High Street, BA14 6JR

9am-11 (10 Sun) (01380) 870067

somersetarmssemington.co.uk

4 changing beers (sourced regionally; often Box Steam, Plain, Twisted)

A coaching inn possibly dating back to the 16th century. It offers four changing beers from microbreweries within 50 miles, and between two and four ciders depending on the time of year. The food is cooked using local ingredients. The village is now a backwater following construction of the bypass a few years ago. Close to the Kennet & Avon Canal, the pub is popular with boaters, walkers and cyclists. Accommodation is available in three luxury en-suite bedrooms.

QP(234)

Semley

Benett Arms

Village Green, SP7 9AS (1 mile E of A350) ST891270

12-3, 5 (5.30 Sat)-11; 12-3, 5.30-10 Sun (01747) 830221 benettarms.co.uk

3 changing beers

A genuine free house sitting by the green and pond in a quiet village, with a single small bar and separate dining areas. The beer choice varies but there are usually three to choose from, either on handpump or direct from the cellar. Excellent home-cooked food is available at all sessions. A warm welcome is extended to all, including families and dogs, in an area popular with walkers. There are three letting rooms. Local CAMRA Pub of the Year 2018. QP(84,247)

Sherston

Rattlebone Inn L
Church Street, SN16 0LR
☼ 12-3, 5-11; 12-midnight Fri & Sat; 12-11 Sun
☎ (01666) 840871 ⊕ therattlebone.co.uk
Flying Monk Elmers; St Austell Tribute; 1 changing beer (sourced nationally; often Butcombe) Ⓗ
A classic, well-managed Cotswold village pub. Popular with locals and visitors alike, it offers a warm welcome, rambling rooms and perfectly conditioned ales. The building dates from the 17th century and its comfortable decor, with lots of cosy nooks, provides a relaxed ambience. The traditional pub food is locally sourced and much in demand. Attractions include a skittle alley and other pub games, plus a double garden and terrace featuring boules pitches. Q➲❀◑♣P🚍(37,41)❀🐾

Swindon

Beehive ✔
55 Prospect Hill, SN1 3JS
☼ 12-midnight (1am Thu-Sat) ☎ (01793) 523187
⊕ bee-hive.co.uk
Hardys & Hansons Olde Trip; house beer (by Hardys & Hansons); 4 changing beers (sourced regionally; often Greene King) Ⓗ
This multi-levelled, four-room pub dates from 1871 and has retained its quirky layout and charm. It serves six real ales including three changing guests, with a regional focus. A popular live music venue, it hosts performances on most Thursday and Friday nights and some Mondays. The walls are adorned with pictures and other art, often for sale. Locally sourced pies are available lunchtime until early evening. Complimentary crisps and snacks are provided from late afternoon. Poker night is Monday. ◑♣🚍(9,11)🐾🍺

Blunsdon Arms ✔
Lady Lane, SN25 2NA
☼ 10-midnight (12.30am Fri & Sat) ☎ (01793) 729801
St Austell Tribute; house beer (by Black Sheep); 6 changing beers (sourced nationally; often Bath Ales, Butcombe) Ⓗ
This Ember Inns pub opened in 2006 and has a large open-plan interior with lots of comfortable seating. The six guest ales rotate from a selection of 12 ales changing quarterly. There are also three real ciders. Food is served every day until 10pm. Quiz nights are Wednesday and Sunday, poker night every Monday. Live music features on the last Saturday of the month. A friendly welcome is assured from the pleasant staff.
➲❀◑&♣●🚍(11,15)🍺

Glue Pot
5 Emlyn Square, SN1 5BP
☼ 12 (4.30 Mon)-11; 11.30-11 Fri & Sat; 12-10.30 Sun
☎ (01793) 497420
Hop Back Citra, Fugglestone, Crop Circle, Entire Stout, Summer Lightning; 3 changing beers (sourced nationally; often Downton, Hop Back) Ⓗ
The Glue Pot is part of the historic Swindon Railway Village, built for workers in the 1840s. Its interior is basic with wooden bench seats. The pub serves seven Hop Back or Downton ales, plus one guest

> Beer: a high and mighty liquor.
> **Julius Caesar**

and 11 real ciders. A range of sandwiches, wraps and subs is always available. There is a pub quiz on Wednesday night and a beer festival over the Easter weekend. Local CAMRA Cider Pub of the Year three times in recent years. Q❀⭲●🚍(1,5)🐾

Hop Inn L
8 Devizes Road, SN1 4BJ
☼ 12-11 (10.30 Mon); 12-midnight Fri & Sat; 12-10.30 Sun
☎ (01793) 976833 ⊕ hopinnswindon.co.uk
House beer (by Ramsbury); 4 changing beers (sourced regionally) Ⓗ
Swindon's first micropub has been so successful it has moved two doors down the road to larger premises. No longer micro, but with exactly the same formula, it has three extra handpumps, giving eight real ales on tap. There are at least two changing real ciders. The interior is furnished in an eclectic style, including chairs and tables made from reclaimed wood. Food will be available (check website). Q➲◑&♣●🚍(12,15)🐾🍺

Savoy L ✔
38-40 Regent Street, SN1 1JL
☼ 8am-midnight (1am Fri & Sat) ☎ (01793) 533970
Greene King Abbot; Ruddles Best Bitter; Sharp's Doom Bar; 10 changing beers (sourced nationally) Ⓗ
This lively and friendly town-centre pub is the oldest Wetherspoon in Swindon, converted from the foyer and ground floors of a 1930s cinema. Cinema photos and information from the era decorate the walls. It has a spacious interior on different levels, divided into separate areas. There is a TV screen in one corner, mainly silent. A large selection of well-kept beers is available and food is served 8am-11pm. Handy for the theatre, cinema, restaurants and shopping.
Q➲❀◑&♣●🚍(1,1A)🍺

Wyvern Tavern
49-50 Bridge Street, SN1 1BL
☼ 10-11 (1am Fri & Sat); 11-10 Sun ☎ (01793) 484924
Bombardier; Wadworth 6X; Wychwood Hobgoblin; 3 changing beers (sourced nationally) Ⓗ
Large town-centre chain pub which unusually has a better-than-average interest in and sale of real ales and ciders. It can be very lively, especially at weekends. Essentially a sports bar, it has a number of TV screens showing various sports throughout the week. Refurbished in recent years, facilities are all on one level. ➲❀◑&⭲♣●🚍(1,8)🍺

Tisbury

Boot Inn L
High Street, SP3 6PS
☼ 12-2.30 (not Mon & Tue), 7-11; 12-3 Sun
☎ (01747) 870363
3 changing beers (sourced locally) Ⓖ
Fine village free house, licensed since 1768 and run by the same landlord since 1976. Its relaxed, friendly atmosphere ensures a cordial welcome for locals and visitors alike. Join in the conversation at the bar or find a quiet table at which to enjoy mainly local ales served from casks behind the bar. The beer range may increase at weekends and in summer. Excellent food is served and there is a spacious garden. The third Tuesday of the month is quiz night, attracting a full house.
Q❀◑⭲♣P🚍(25)

Upton Lovell

Prince Leopold Inn

54 Upton Lovell, BA12 0JP

closed Mon; 12-3, 6-11; 12-8 Sun (01985) 850460

princeleopold.co.uk

Butcombe Original; Fuller's London Pride

Hidden away in the beautiful Wylye Valley, the pub has returned to being a proper local as well as catering for visitors. The main bar is reserved for those wishing to enjoy a drink, and there is a small snug with an open fire, books, newspapers and board games. Several areas are dedicated to excellent food, including the large restaurant which overlooks the River Wylye. The lovely garden runs right down to the riverbank. **Q P**

Warminster

Fox & Hounds

6 Deverill Road, BA12 9QP

11-11 (01985) 216711

Wessex Warminster Warrior; house beer (by Wessex); 2 changing beers (sourced regionally; often Bath Ales, Flying Monk, Palmers)

A friendly two-bar local – the main bar with a pool table and sports TV is at the rear, and a quiet snug bar is to the right of the entrance. There is a large skittle alley and function room at the back. Guest real ales are usually from local and regional breweries. Regular ciders are from Thatchers and Rich's, plus up to five guests. Closing time may be later than 11pm. A local CAMRA multiple award-winning pub. **Q P**

Organ Inn

49 High Street, BA12 9AQ

4-midnight; 12-midnight Sat; 4-11 Sun (01985) 211777

3 changing beers (sourced regionally; often Branscombe Vale, Cheddar Ales, XT)

An inn until 1913, the Organ reopened as a pub in 2006. The welcoming interior comprises three rooms with a traditional feel, plus a snug, games room and skittle alley. The beer range constantly changes but will always include Organ Bitter (the brewery is a secret). The cider is mainly from Westons with guests. A beer festival is held in September. Bar snacks are interesting and there is an art gallery upstairs. Local CAMRA Rural Pub of the Year 2018. **Q**

Westbury

Hollies

55A Westbury Leigh, BA13 3SF

12-11 (midnight Fri & Sat); 12-10.30 Sun

(01373) 864493 theholliesinn.com

Twisted Gaucho; 2 changing beers (sourced locally; often Twisted)

A handsome old red-brick village pub in the Westbury Leigh area of town. Inside there is plenty of comfortable seating in multiple areas including a separate dining room. The pub is an outlet for the local Twisted Brewery, with at least two of its extensive range on offer, and usually a guest from elsewhere. The food is highly rated. (Dilton Marsh)**P**

Wroughton

Carters Rest

57 High Street, SN4 9JU

4-11 (midnight Fri); 12-midnight Sat; 12-10 Sun

07816 134966

Ramsbury Deerstalker; 6 changing beers (sourced regionally)

First mentioned in 1671, this popular real ale pub was extensively altered in 1912/13 to give its current Victorian appearance, and was refurbished with a smart new interior in 2017. There are 12 handpumps but the current beer range is seven, with eight at the weekend. Beers are mainly from small independent breweries within a 50-mile radius, occasionally from further afield. **Q P**(9,49)

Zeals

Bell & Crown

New Road, BA12 6NJ

closed Mon; 11-3, 5-11; 11-11 Fri & Sat; 12-3 Sun

(01747) 840404 bellandcrown.com

3 changing beers (often Bristol Beer Factory, Otter, Palmers)

A fine-dining pub with a traditional bar and real ales. Its interior features an open fire and flagstone floors, the layout allowing almost complete separation of the bar and dining areas. The beers on offer change regularly, with West Country breweries always well represented. The pub is equally popular with locals and visitors to the nearby National Trust property of Stourhead. **Q P**

Kitchen of an inn

In the evening we reached a village where I had determined to pass the night. As we drove into the great gateway of the inn, I saw on one side the light of a rousing kitchen fire beaming through a window. I entered, and admired for the hundredth time that picture of convenience, neatness, and broad honest enjoyment, the kitchen of an English inn. It was of spacious dimension, hung around by copper and tin vessels, highly polished, and decorated here and there with a Christmas green. Hams, tongues, and flitches of bacon were suspended from the ceiling; a smoke-jack made its ceaseless clanking behind the fireplace, and a clock ticked in one corner. A well-scoured deal table extended along one side of the kitchen, with a cold round of beef, and other hearty viands upon it, over which two foaming tankards of ale seemed mounting guard. Travellers of inferior order were preparing to attack this stout repast, while others sat smoking or gossiping over their ale, on two high-backed oaken settles beside the fire.

Washington Irving, Travelling at Christmas, 1884

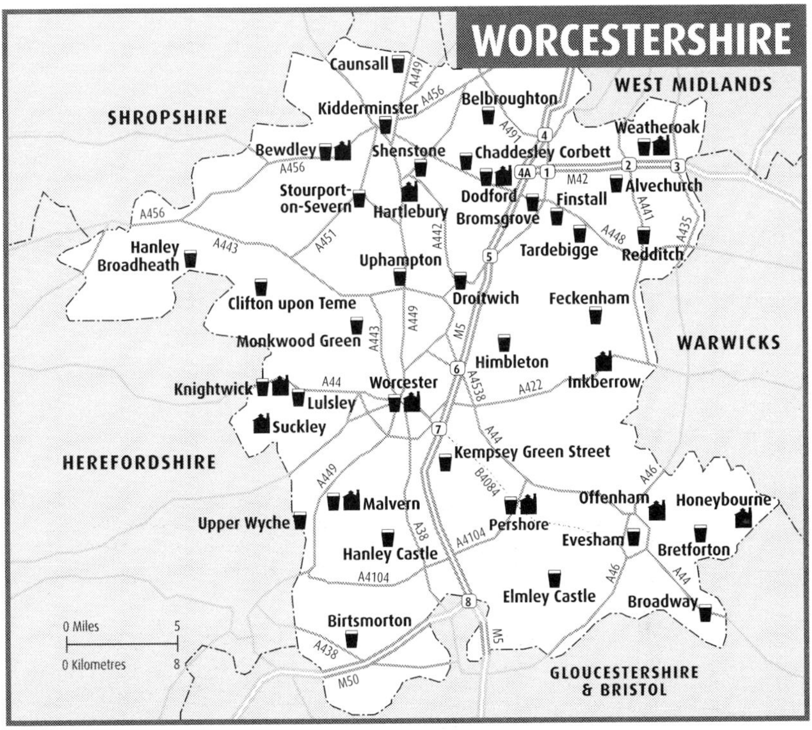

Alvechurch

Weighbridge ⓛ
Scarfield Wharf, Scarfield Hill, B48 7SQ (follow signs to marina from village) SP022721
☀ 12-3, 7-11 (10.30 Sun) ☎ (0121) 445 5111
∰ the-weighbridge.co.uk
6 changing beers (sourced locally; often Wye Valley) Ⓗ
Starting life as a private members club, the Weighbridge is now a cosy, three-roomed canalside pub that has received many CAMRA awards. It has two small lounges, a public bar and a pleasant garden. Good-value, home-cooked food is served lunchtimes and evenings, with excellent Sunday lunches (no food Tue and Wed). A covered area outside can be used for functions. There are changing beers from Kinver, Weatheroak and Wye Valley, plus three changing guests from other breweries, one of which is a mild, as well as a real cider. Spring and autumn beer festivals are held.
Q☆⊛◑⇥●P☂

Belbroughton

Holly Bush Inn
Stourbridge Road, DY9 9UG (on A491 Stourbridge Rd, not within village centre)
☀ 11.30-11; 11.30-3, 6-11 Sat; 12-3, 7-10.30 Sun
☎ (01562) 730207
Hobsons Mild, Twisted Spire, Old Prickly, Town Crier; 1 changing beer (sourced regionally) Ⓗ
This popular pub, set back from the A491 dual carriageway near the Clent Hills, was originally terraced cottages dating back to 1845. Excellent beers from the Hobsons range are served, along with Thatchers cider on handpump. The lively public bar hosts traditional games including cards

and dominoes, while two other areas, one with a real fire, are used for dining. Good food is served from a traditional menu. Dogs are welcome.
Q☆⊛◑&●P☲(318)❀

Bewdley

Bewdley Brewery Tap
Bewdley Craft Centre, Lax Lane, DY12 2DZ
☀ closed Mon-Wed; 4-9 Thu; 12-9 Fri & Sat; 12-3 Sun
☎ (01299) 405148 ∰ bewdleybrewery.co.uk
Bewdley Worcestershire Way, Sir Keith Park, Worcestershire Sway; 2 changing beers (sourced locally; often Bewdley) Ⓗ
Bewdley Brewery produces a range of six regular cask ales and a greater number of bottled beers, some for the Severn Valley Railway. The spacious taproom, behind an old school building, is adorned with railway and brewery memorabilia. Five of the brewery's cask ales are served through half-pint pulls, giving each pint a perfectly clear dispense, and the full range of bottled beers is available. Open on bank holidays; winter hours may vary.
&☲

Black Boy ⓛ
50 Wyre Hill, DY12 2UE (up Sandy Bank from Cleobury Rd at Welch Gate)
☀ 5 (12 Wed & Thu)-11; 12-midnight Fri & Sat; 12-10.30 Sun
☎ (01299) 400088
Bewdley Worcestershire Way; Hobsons Mild; Ludlow Gold; Wye Valley Butty Bach; 1 changing beer (sourced locally; often Hobsons, Hop & Stagger, Swan Brewery) Ⓗ
Up a hill from the town centre, this friendly, ancient inn is worth the climb. The attractive, half-timbered building is the oldest pub in Bewdley. An open fire warms its wood-beamed interior in

winter. Up to five beers are served. Cobs and pork pies are always on offer, with hot meals available on four lunchtimes and two evenings a week. This little gem's attractions include bar skittles, bagatelle and a selection of board games.
Q

Great Western

Kidderminster Road, DY12 1BY (near SVR station, walk past signal box and under viaduct)
11.30-11 ☎ (01299) 488828
Bewdley Worcestershire Way; Morland Old Golden Hen; house beer (by Bewdley); 2 changing beers (sourced regionally; often Belhaven, Enville, Ludlow)
This comfortable pub has a simple railway theme reminiscent of an earlier age. Overlooking the bar is an upper level from which to admire the decorative glazed wall tiles. Five real ales including regulars from Holden's and Bewdley are served, plus two Westons ciders. Snacks including cobs and pork pies complement the traditional pub atmosphere. Q(SVR)P

Mug House

12 Severnside North, DY12 2EE (150yds along Severnside North from river bridge)
12-11 (11.30 Fri & Sat) ☎ (01299) 402543
mughousebewdley.co.uk
Bewdley Worcestershire Way; Purity Mad Goose; Timothy Taylor Landlord; Wye Valley HPA; 1 changing beer (sourced locally; often Holden's, Salopian, Wye Valley)
A friendly pub that welcomes locals and visitors with comfortable settles and a log fire in the lounge bar. Outside is a sun terrace and glass-covered patio with grapevines and wisteria. The pub serves five well-kept beers from Bewdley, Purity, Wye Valley and Timothy Taylor, a changing guest and two ciders. The restaurant's evening à la carte menu is backed up by meals in the bar at lunchtime. Q(SVR)

Old Waggon & Horses

91 Kidderminster Road, DY12 1DG (on Bewdley to Kidderminster road at Catchem's End)
12-11; 11.30-11 Fri; 11.30-1am Sat ☎ (01299) 403170
waggonbewdley.co.uk
Banks's Mild; Bathams Best Bitter; Ludlow Gold; Wainwright; 2 changing beers (sourced locally; often Enville, Hobsons, Holden's)
Popular pub with a central bar serving three distinct areas. The small wooden-floored snug has a dartboard and the larger room a woodburner. There is a roll-down screen for major sporting events, but at most times conversation prevails. An old kitchen range adds to the cottagey feel. Guest ales come from local independents. Pub food is available, plus a pie night and a tapas night once a month, and a carvery on Sunday. The attractive terraced flower garden is on many levels.
(SVR)P

Real Ale Tavern

67 Load Street, DY12 2AW
11-11 ☎ (01299) 404972
Black Country Bradley's Finest Golden, Pig on the Wall, Fireside; 7 changing beers (sourced regionally; often Byatt's, Fixed Wheel, Salopian)
A traditionally styled pub, converted in 2017 from a former bank, specialising in real ale and cider. From the front space warmed by a cosy fire in winter, the pub's depths are revealed in a succession of areas. The bar's impressive array of 12 handpulls serves beers from Black Country Ales and local and regional breweries plus two ciders. Current beers are displayed on screens, making it easy to order at the bar. Cobs and tasty local Wyre pork pies are always available. (SVR)

Birtsmorton

Farmers Arms

Birts Street, WR13 6AP (off B4208) SO790363
11.30-3.30, 6 (5 Fri)-midnight; 11.30-midnight Sat; 12-midnight Sun ☎ (01684) 833308
farmersarmsbirtsmorton.co.uk
Hook Norton Hooky, Old Hooky; 2 changing beers (sourced locally)
Grade II-listed black-and-white village pub dating from 1480, found down a quiet country lane. The large bar area features a splendid inglenook fireplace while the cosy lounge has old settles and low beams. Good-value, home-made food is on offer daily (lunch until 2.30pm, eve meals until 9pm weekdays, 9pm Sun). A beer from a local independent brewer is often available, and a real cider. The spacious garden, complete with swings, provides fine views of the Malvern Hills. A caravan site is nearby. QP(577)

Bretforton

Fleece Inn ★

The Cross, WR11 7JE (near church)
11-11 ☎ (01386) 831173 thefleeceinn.co.uk
Purity Mad Goose; Uley Pig's Ear Strong Beer; Wye Valley Bitter; 4 changing beers (sourced regionally; often Bathams, Marston's, North Cotswold)
Originally a farmhouse in the 15th century, the Fleece was owned by the Taplin family until 1977 when the last Miss Taplin died in the bar, bequeathing the pub to the National Trust. The interior, which has low wooden beams and open fires, houses a famous pewter collection that was saved by locals from a fire in 2004. Now serving seven cask ales alongside local and home-made ciders, the pub is definitely worth a visit. Its medieval barn hosts events.
QP

Broadway

Broadway Hotel

The Green, WR12 7AA

REAL ALE BREWERIES

- **Ambridge** Inkberrow
- **Bewdley** Bewdley
- **Boat Lane** Offenham
- **Cannon Royall** Honeybourne
- **Friday Beer** Malvern
- **Hartlebury** Hartlebury (NEW)
- **Hop Shed** Suckley
- **Lakehouse** Malvern
- **Malvern Hills** Malvern
- **Pershore** Pershore
- **Sociable** Worcester
- **Teme Valley** Knightwick
- **Weatheroak Hill** Weatheroak
- **White Rabbit** Honeybourne (NEW)
- **Wintrip** Worcester
- **Woodcote Manor** Dodford
- **Worcester** Worcester

11-11; 12-10.30 Sun (01386) 852401
Goff's Jouster; Hook Norton Hooky; Wickwar BOB; 1 changing beer (sourced locally; often Hook Norton)
This opulent, refurbished 16th-century hotel, partly black and white, is a former coaching inn that once belonged to Pershore Abbey. A countryside ambience blends with cosy home furnishings and quirky decor, featuring comfy armchairs, a minstrels' gallery and a huge inglenook with log fire. Real ale and bar meals are served in the racing-themed Jockey Club Bar; seasonal food in the elegant attached brasserie.

Crown & Trumpet Inn

14 Church Street, WR12 7AE
11-10.30 (11.45 Fri & Sat) (01386) 853202
crownandtrumpet.co.uk/home
Prescott Chequered Flag; Stanway Broadway Artist's Ale; Stroud Tom Long; Timothy Taylor Landlord; 2 changing beers (sourced locally; often Bath Ales, North Cotswold)
Picturesque 17th-century Cotswold-stone inn, just off the village green, run by a landlord with 34 years' experience as a Guide licensee. This hostelry has oak beams, log fire and Flowers Brewery memorabilia. Good, honest, home-made local dishes are offered at reasonable prices alongside regular ales and guests plus ciders and perries. Entertainment includes midweek live jazz and blues nights. A former local CAMRA award winner.
Q P

Bromsgrove

Little Ale House

21 Worcester Road, B61 7DL (on corner of Station St)
2-10; 12-10 Fri & Sat; 12-8 Sun 07791 698641
6 changing beers (often Hobsons, Malvern Hills, Wye Valley)
Bromsgrove's first micropub has a friendly and cosy atmosphere. Six ales are served straight from the cask, normally from Hobsons, Malvern Hills and Wye Valley, with the house ale, Half Cut, brewed by Woodcote Manor. A range of ciders and perries is also stocked and takeaway containers are available. Snacks include fresh rolls. A council car park is nearby and the bus station is parallel with the high street. Q

Park Gate

Kidderminster Road, B61 9AJ
12-11 (1am Fri & Sat) (01527) 272665
parkgateinn.co.uk
4 changing beers
Situated just off the A448 and popular with walkers, the pub features a small bar and a lounge for functions and events. It serves a range of local ales on handpull along with boxed real cider. Four or five beers are offered at all times and there can be 10 or more in the summer festival season, including gravity-poured ales from stillages on the terrace. Attractions include darts, pool and a Wednesday folk night. The large, terraced garden provides attractive views, is dog friendly and incorporates a play area.
Q P (42,322)

Caunsall

Anchor Inn

DY11 5YL (off A449 Kidderminster to Wolverhampton road)
11-4, 7-11 (10.30 Sun) (01562) 850254
theanchorinncaunsall.co.uk
Hobsons Best, Town Crier; Wye Valley HPA, Butty Bach; 1 changing beer (sourced regionally; often Backyard, Sadler's, Three Tuns)
Friendly village inn renowned for its five real ales, traditional ciders and especially its well-filled cobs. A central doorway leads into the bar with its original 1920s furniture and horse-racing memorabilia. Outside, the garden is a suntrap in summer, and this popular pub can get busy, especially at lunchtimes and weekends. Easily reached from the nearby canal, this gem is well worth stopping off for. Local CAMRA Pub of the Year finalist 2016-2019. Q P

Chaddesley Corbett

Swan

High Street, DY10 4SD SO892737
11-11 (midnight Fri); 12-11 Sun (01562) 777302
theswanchaddesleycorbett.co.uk
Bathams Mild Ale, Best Bitter
Characterful village pub dating from 1606, featuring a traditional public bar, a cosy side room with a real fire, and an impressive lounge with a raised stage area for entertainment. Live jazz is hosted on Thursday evening and open mic on the first Friday of the month. There is a large garden at the rear overlooking the beautiful countryside. Guest real ciders are on handpull. The pub is popular with walkers and cyclists and is close to historic Harvington Hall. Q P

Clifton upon Teme

New Inn

Old Road, WR6 6DR (signposted 200yds off B4204) SO724609
5-11 (midnight Fri); 12-midnight Sat; 12-11 Sun
(01886) 812226 thenewinncliftonuponteme.com
Wye Valley HPA; 2 changing beers
On the old road on the hill and dating back several centuries, the New Inn has an imposing yew tree at its front and provides fine views over the Teme and Severn valleys. Its large bar area has fireside tables to one side, with darts and pool on the other. An adjoining dining room serves home-made meals using locally sourced produce. A secluded garden is to the rear. The pub hosts pheasant shoots and indoor rifle shooting, plus lawnmower racing in the summer.
Q P (308,310)

Dodford

Dodford Inn

Whinfield Road, B61 9BG SO939729
12-3, 6-11; 12-11 Sat; 12-7 Sun (01527) 835825
thedodfordinn.co.uk
Wye Valley Butty Bach; house beer (by Banks's); 2 changing beers (sourced regionally; often Purity, Sadler's)
The Dodford has recently been redeveloped and boasts a stylish restaurant alongside a cosy, comfortable lounge. It usually has four cask ales available from across the Midlands. Banks's Sunbeam is badged as Dodford Pale Ale. An outside patio provides beautiful views during the warmer months. Popular with ramblers, the pub is close to a 19th-century Chartist cottage, Rosedene, owned by the National Trust. P

Droitwich

Hop Pole

40 Friar Street, WR9 8ED (100yds from Norbury Theatre)
12-11 (10.30 Sun) (01905) 770155
Wye Valley HPA, Butty Bach, Wholesome Stout; 2 changing beers (often Ambridge)
Popular and unchanging 18th-century pub located at a dead end in the old part of Droitwich close to the Norbury Theatre. There is a separate pool room adjoining the bar and a heated patio area at the rear to accommodate smokers. Three locally sourced beers are usually available with an occasional guest. Good-value food is served at lunchtimes, and pub games and live music on some weekends ensure a convivial atmosphere.

Old Cock Inn

77 Friar Street, WR9 8EQ (opp Norbury Theatre)
12-11 (midnight Fri & Sat) (01905) 936771
Banks's Mild; Courage Directors; Marston's Pedigree, Old Empire
Droitwich's oldest licensed premises, first licensed in 1712. Its central bar serves four open-plan rooms decorated with interesting old artefacts and local photographs. Guest beers are all from the Marston's portfolio; Thatchers Heritage cider is served on handpump. There is a small function room and a patio garden. Live music is performed most Saturday evenings.
P (144)

Elmley Castle

Queen Elizabeth

Main Street, WR10 3HS
6-10 Mon; 10-11 Tue-Fri; 9am-11.30 Sat; 10-8 Sun
(01386) 710251 elmleycastle.com
Purity Mad Goose; Wye Valley Bitter; 2 changing beers (sourced regionally; often Goff's, North Cotswold)
An old pub with a fresh, modern feel inside, named after Elizabeth I's visit to the village in August 1575. This is a community pub, owned by a group of local residents who rescued it from closure. The bar has a flagstone floor, timber beams and a roaring fire and normally serves one locally sourced beer. There is a comfortable lounge and a separate dining room. Themed food evenings are held regularly and two annual beer festivals on the May and August bank holidays. The café serves snacks Tuesday to Friday and opens early for Saturday breakfast. Q P

Evesham

Red Lion

6 Market Place, WR11 4RE
11-11 (midnight Fri & Sat); 12-10.30 Sun
(01386) 761688
Cannon Royall Arrowhead Bitter; White Rabbit Elwood's Dark; house beer (by Cannon Royall); 2 changing beers (sourced locally; often Cannon Royall, White Rabbit)
This historic town-centre local overlooking Evesham's market, first recorded as a public house in 1729, reopened in 2014 after being closed for over 100 years. Its central bar serves all areas including a rear snug with an historic inglenook fireplace. Up to six real ales are offered. There is no TV or piped music but live music is performed; generally acoustic on Monday and Friday evening and Sunday afternoon. Food is not served but plates and cutlery are provided for customers who bring their own. Q

Feckenham

Rose & Crown

High Street, B96 6HS
11-3, 6-11; 12-11 Sat & Sun (01527) 892188
roseandcrownfeckenham.co.uk
Banks's Amber Ale; Brakspear Oxford Gold; 2 changing beers (often Ambridge, Marston's)
A welcoming family-run Grade II-listed village pub near the church. Its traditional bar offers up to four real ales, with an emphasis on local breweries, plus at least one real cider. Attentive staff serve food from a wide menu of pub classics in the cosy lounge. The large enclosed beer garden at the rear is suitable for children. An annual beer festival is held over the August bank holiday. Parking is limited but there is a free car park 200 yards away.
Q

Finstall

Cross Inn

34 Alcester Road, B60 1EW (on B4184 Finstall corner)
12-11 (midnight Fri & Sat) (01527) 577328
Black Country Bradley's Finest Golden, Pig on the Wall /, Fireside; 4 changing beers
The Cross Inn was taken over and refurbished by Black Country Ales in 2018. Its nine handpumps dispense three beers from the brewery's range plus four guests, including one dark ale, and two ciders, displayed on a screen above the bar. Cobs, pork pies and local Scotch eggs are available. Crib and dominoes are played and the pub hosts fêtes, mini beer festivals and charity events for the local Primrose Hospice. The garden incorporates a heated smokers' shelter.
P (43,42)

Hanley Broadheath

Fox Inn

WR15 8QS (on B4204 E of Tenbury Wells) SO671652
5-11; 3-12.30am Fri; 12-12.30am Sat; 12-10 Sun
(01886) 853189
Bathams Best Bitter; Brakspear Oxford Gold; 1 changing beer
The main bar of this 16th-century black-and-white timbered free house is decorated with hops and has a large fireplace with a wood-burning stove. The panelled dining area is separated from the bar by wood beams. The games room has a pool table, TV and darts. Home-made food, including Sunday lunch, is available, with bar snacks at any time.
Q P (309)

Hanley Castle

Three Kings ★

Church End, WR8 0BL (signed off B4211) SO838420
12-3, 7-11 (10.30 Sun) (01684) 592686
Butcombe Original; Hobsons Best; 3 changing beers (often Beowulf, Malvern Hills, Slater's)
On CAMRA's National Inventory of Historic Pub Interiors, this unspoilt 15th-century country pub on the village green near the church has been run by the Roberts family since 1911. The three-room interior comprises a small snug with large inglenook, serving hatch and settle wall, a small

side room, and Nell's Lounge with another inglenook, beams and its own entrance. Three guest ales are on offer, often from local breweries, plus Westons Old Rosie draught cider. Live music sessions feature regularly and a beer festival is held in November. Q🐴❀♣●P🚌(363)🐾

Himbleton

Galton Arms Ⓛ

Harrow Lane, WR9 7LQ (on edge of village)
⏲ 12-3 (not Mon), 4.30-11; 12-10.30 Sun ☎ (01905) 391672
🌐 thegaltonarms.co.uk
Banks's Amber Ale; Bathams Best Bitter; Prescott Hill Climb; Wye Valley HPA Ⓗ
Splendid rural pub situated on the edge of the village with a friendly welcome attracting locals and visitors alike. Its unspoilt interior is warmed by open fires and retains the original beams that divide up the space. The bar area shows sports TV. Good-value food is served in two separate dining areas. The beer garden is suitable for children. Q🐴❀◑♿P🚌(356)🐾

Kempsey Green Street

Huntsman Inn Ⓛ

Green Street, WR5 3QB (from A38 at Kempsey via Post Office Lane) SO868490
⏲ 5-11; 12-11 Sat & Sun ☎ (01905) 820336
Bathams Best Bitter; Greene King IPA; Morland Original Bitter Ⓗ
Cosy and friendly multi-roomed local created from a 300-year-old farmhouse with exposed beams. There is a small main bar with a real fire to the front and a larger bar down steps. A separate restaurant serves reasonably priced home-cooked food. There is also a skittle alley with its own bar, an attractive garden and a large car park. The pub is closed at lunchtimes during the week. Dogs are welcome in the bar and lounge. 🐴❀◑♣P🐾

Kidderminster

Beer Emporium & Cider House

Oxford Street, DY10 1AR (between railway station and town centre)
⏲ closed Mon & Tue; 4-10 Wed; 4-11 Thu & Fri; 12-11 Sat; 12-8 Sun ☎ 07803 357362
4 changing beers (sourced nationally) Ⓖ
Micropub open Wednesday to Sunday. There is plenty of conversation around the room and table service is the norm. A chalkboard shows four real ales from around the country, usually including a dark. Craft key cask ales, an interesting selection of foreign bottled beers, four ciders and two perries, plus wines and soft drinks ensure there is something for everyone. Local CAMRA Gold Cider Pub of the Year 2019. Q🐴♿⇌(SVR)●P🗑🚌🐾📶

King & Castle 🏆 Ⓛ ✔

Comberton Hill, DY10 1QX (next to main line station and part of SVR terminus)
⏲ 10-11 (11.30 Sat); 11-11 Sun ☎ (01562) 747505
Bathams Best Bitter; Bewdley Worcestershire Way; Hobsons Mild, Town Crier; Wye Valley Butty Bach; 3 changing beers (sourced regionally; often Enville, Exmoor, Malvern Hills) Ⓗ
Atmospheric recreation of a GWR terminus station bar and gateway to the Severn Valley Railway. Eight handpumps dispense beers from local, regional and national breweries, and it has three ciders. Breakfast is served until 11am, then pub meals, cobs and snacks from the bar until 10pm. Bottled beers from Bewdley are available on trains, and pubs along the line are an attraction for locals and visitors using the railway. Local CAMRA Gold Pub of the Year 2019.
Q🐴❀◑♿⇌(SVR)♣●P🚌🐾📶

Olde Seven Stars Ⓛ ✔

13-14 Coventry Street, DY10 2BG (upper end of High St facing Swan Centre)
⏲ 11-11 (11.30 Fri & Sat); 12-11 Sun ☎ (01562) 228641
5 changing beers Ⓗ
With five well-kept real ales and two draught ciders, this historic town-centre and family-friendly pub is well worth visiting. It serves cobs and pork pies, and customers can bring their own food (there are plenty of takeaways nearby), with tableware and condiments provided. Live music plays on the last Friday evening of the month. The quiet rear garden is popular in summer. The pub's friendly atmosphere and excellent ales won it local CAMRA Bronze Pub of the Year 2019.
🐴❀♣●🚌🐾📶

Station Inn Ⓛ ✔

7 Farfield, DY10 1UG
⏲ 12-11 ☎ (01562) 569621 🌐 stationkidderminster.co.uk
Enville Ale; Wye Valley HPA, Butty Bach; 2 changing beers (sourced locally; often Bewdley, Kinver) Ⓗ
A friendly pub a short walk from the railway station. Two rooms are served from a central bar and there is a large beer garden to the rear. Five handpulled beers are from Enville, Wye Valley and local breweries. Good-value, home-cooked food is served during the day, and traditional roast dinners on Sunday. The friendly welcome, community atmosphere and excellent ales have earned the pub CAMRA awards in recent years.
Q🐴❀◑⇌(SVR)♣P🚌🐾📶

Weavers Real Ale House Ⓛ

98 Comberton Hill, DY10 1QH (300yds down hill from railway station)
⏲ 12-11 (10.30 Sun) ☎ (01562) 229413
Three Tuns XXX; Wye Valley Butty Bach; 6 changing beers (sourced nationally; often Bewdley, Fixed Wheel, Fownes) Ⓗ
A light and airy micropub that is ideal for conversation and offers a warm welcome. Its walls display pictures of old Kidderminster alongside beer memorabilia. It serves eight excellent ales, four ciders and a perry on handpump, plus six craft beers. Cobs are always available. It is convenient for a pint and a chat on the way into town. Local CAMRA Pub of the Year 2018 and Silver Cider Pub of the Year 2019. Q🐴♿⇌(SVR)●🚌🐾📶

Knightwick

Talbot Ⓛ

WR6 5PH (on B4197, 400yds from A44 jct)
⏲ 8am-11 ☎ (01886) 821235 🌐 the-talbot.co.uk
Teme Valley T'Other, This, That Ⓗ**; changing beers (often Teme Valley)** Ⓖ
Originally a 14th-century coaching inn, this country pub has a large lounge bar divided into two by a fireplace and a separate taproom. The bar usually offers three or four beers from the Teme Valley Brewery behind the pub. The small wood-panelled restaurant serves an imaginative menu using local ingredients (6-9pm). There is a farmers' market outside on the second Sunday of the month. Beer

festivals are held in April, June and early October (for green hop beers). Dogs and walkers are welcome. Q (420)

Lulsley

Fox & Hounds

WR6 5QT

12 (5 Mon & Tue)-11 (01886) 821228

foxandhoundslulsley.com

Hop Shed Sebright Golden Ale; Wye Valley Butty Bach; 2 changing beers (often Ambridge, Ledbury) H

A purpose-built Victorian pub with two bars, a dining area and a conservatory that has been recently renovated to a high standard. The two guest beers are usually locally sourced, as is the food on a menu that features seasonal dishes. Behind the pub is an extensive garden and children's play area with the River Teme beyond. A beer festival is held over the spring bank holiday weekend. QP

Malvern

Great Malvern Hotel

Graham Road, WR14 2HN (by crossroads with Church St)

10-11; 11-10.30 Sun (01684) 563411

great-malvern-hotel.co.uk

Malvern Hills Black Pear; Wye Valley HPA, Butty Bach; 2 changing beers (often Draught Bass, Friday Beer, Lakehouse) H

Popular hotel public bar, a short walk from the Malvern Theatres complex, ideal for pre- and post-performance refreshment. Meals are served in the bar and the adjoining brasserie, including Sunday lunches. There is a comfortable lounge with lots of sofas. Live music sessions are hosted weekly. On-site parking is limited but there is plenty of public parking nearby. P

Morgan

52 Clarence Road, WR14 3EQ

12-3, 5-11; 12-11 Fri & Sat; 12-10.30 Sun

(01684) 578575

Wye Valley Bitter, HPA, Butty Bach; 2 changing beers (sourced locally) H

Named after the town's Morgan car factory, this Wye Valley Brewery-owned premises has an open-plan interior divided into a games area for darts, a drinking space and a slightly raised seating area with comfy settees. The landscaped patio has ample seating, a fish pond and 'Them Organ' gates. Activities include a monthly book club and weekly quizzes. The TV is only turned on for major sporting events. Up to two guest beers come from the Wye Valley range, often the stout and lager.

Nag's Head

19-21 Bank Street, WR14 2JG (off Graham Rd at Link Top common)

11-11.15 (11.30 Fri & Sat); 12-11 Sun (01684) 574373

nagsheadmalvern.co.uk

Banks's Amber Ale; Bathams Best Bitter; Wood Shropshire Lad; 5 changing beers (often Otter) H

A free house where the permanent beers are joined by guests from all over the county plus two draught ciders. Mismatched furniture, nooks and crannies, newspapers and foliage create a homely environment and draw visitors, making the pub busy throughout the week. Quality food is served in the bar and separate restaurant (open until 9pm Fri and Sat). Outside is a large covered and heated area to the front and a garden to the rear. A no-swearing rule is enforced. The small car park is backed up by ample street parking.

P (44)

Monkwood Green

Fox

WR2 6NX (S edge of Monkwood Nature Reserve) SO803601

5-11; 12-11 Sat; 12-10.30 Sun (01886) 889123

Malvern Hills Feelgood; Wye Valley HPA, Butty Bach H

A single-bar village local set on the common near the nature reserve, which is renowned for butterflies and moths. The pub has seating around a fireplace and hearth at one end, and games at the other. It is a rare outlet for Barkers cider and perry. Many events are hosted, including skittles and indoor air rifle shooting. Music nights are held on the last Friday of the month. Food is not generally sold but can be provided by arrangement for groups. This Fox is dog-friendly. It has a very limited bus service. QP (308)

Pershore

Pickled Plum

135 High Street, WR10 1EQ

12-11 (midnight Fri & Sat) (01386) 556645

pickledplum.co.uk

Brakspear Bitter; Wye Valley Butty Bach; 4 changing beers (often Purity, Salopian) H

A large, smart pub with a modern, airy interior, divided into several areas, with exposed beams and real fires adding a cosy old-world charm. The bar serves up to six real ales, always including something from Purity and Salopian, and alternating between Hobgoblin and Wye Valley HPA, plus six real ciders. A three third-pint tasting option is offered. Food is available lunchtimes and evenings. The pub hosts a regular Sunday night quiz and an acoustic jam on the first Monday of the month. P

Redditch

Black Tap

Church Green East, B98 8BP (near top of Church Green East, opp fountain)

closed Mon & Tue; 4-11 Wed & Thu; 12-11 Fri & Sat; 12-6 Sun (01527) 585969 blacktapredditch.co.uk

House beer (by Backyard); 3 changing beers (sourced locally; often Oakham) H

A converted office building and former brewpub. The main bar has a roaring fire, which adds to the friendly atmosphere among regulars. Conveniently located near the town centre, a good mix of beer styles is usually available along with cider. A small side room can also be booked and live music is usually featured at weekends.

P (57,58)

Shenstone

Plough

Shenstone Village, DY10 4DL (off A450/A448) SO865735

12.30-3.30, 6-11; 12-11 Fri-Sun (01562) 777340

bathams.co.uk

Bathams Mild Ale, Best Bitter H

A traditional rural village pub dating back to 1840. The long single bar serves both the lounge, complete with real fire, and public areas. A large enclosed courtyard/conservatory where families are welcome provides extra space. There is a small patio with seating to the front. Snacks include cobs and pork pies. The stronger Christmas brew, Bathams XXX, is served briefly during the winter months. The Elizabethan Harvington Hall is nearby. Q P

Stourport-on-Severn

Black Star

Mitton Street, DY13 8YP (just off top end of High St)
12-11 (midnight Fri & Sat); 12-10.30 Sun
(01299) 488838 theblackstar.co.uk
Wye Valley HPA, Golden Ale, Butty Bach, Wholesome Stout; 3 changing beers (sourced regionally; often Hobsons, Ludlow, Wye Valley)
Situated next to the canal, the pub has a historic feel. The main bar has a real fire, beamed ceilings and cosy corners. An attractive beer garden with a shelter, tables and raised flowerbeds overlooks the canal. Moorings are just through the bridge towards the basins. Five beers are from Wye Valley plus two guests and two ciders. The varied food menu includes vegan options, doorstep sandwiches, baguettes, rib-eye steaks and everything in-between. A runner-up local CAMRA Pub of the Year 2018.

Swan

56 High Street, DY13 8BX
12-midnight (11 Sun) (01299) 877832
Brains Rev James; Butcombe Gold; Hobsons Old Prickly; Wainwright; 2 changing beers (sourced nationally)
Former hotel with a large lounge bar decorated with vinyl LPs – this is a pub by day and a music venue by night. Six well-kept real ales grace the bar, along with a range of gins. At the back there is a tranquil, secluded garden. The integral Mimi's Bistro serves breakfast from 9am and Mediterranean specialities from a wood-fired oven during the day. Live music on most evenings has a loyal following. An interesting and unusual venue, well worth a visit.

Tardebigge

Alestones

Unit 23 Tardebigge Court, B97 6QW
closed Mon-Wed; 5-9 Thu; 3-9 Fri; 12-9 Sat; 12-3 Sun
(01527) 275254 alestones.co.uk
Woodcote Manor SSS; 3 changing beers
A well-maintained micropub, opened in 2016, which sits in a courtyard alongside several small independent shops and businesses. There are usually four beers, including a golden ale, a dark beer and a best bitter, plus real cider and perry. Although recently expanded, the pub retains its cosy, convivial atmosphere – but now there is room to stretch your legs. Local musicians play on Sunday and comedians perform once a month on a Thursday. Pub snacks are usually available. Q P (43,42)

Uphampton

Fruiterer's Arms

Uphampton Lane, WR9 0JW (off A449 by Oldfields of Ombersley, a mile N of Ombersley) SO838648
12 (1 Tue)-11; 12-11.30 Sat (01905) 622353
Wye Valley Bitter, HPA, Butty Bach; 3 changing beers (sourced locally; often Bewdley, Weatheroak, Wye Valley)
The Fruiterer's Arms has been in the same family since 1848. Its traditional bar and comfortable lounge with logburner serve reasonably priced drinks and seasonal guest ales along with local cider and perry. Filled rolls are available from Monday to Sunday, and the pub also offers local produce such as pickles. Children under 14 are welcome until 9pm. P

Upper Wyche

Wyche Inn

Wyche Road, WR14 4EQ (on B4218, follow signs from Malvern to Colwall)
12-11 (9 Mon); 11-11 Sat & Sun (01684) 575396
thewycheinn.co.uk
Wye Valley HPA; 3 changing beers (sourced regionally)
The highest pub in Worcestershire, this free house has panoramic views towards the Cotswolds. Ideally situated for hill walkers, it has two bars – one with pool and darts, the other dedicated to drinking and dining. The range of real ales from smaller breweries always includes some locals. Home-cooked food is served lunchtimes and evenings, featuring popular specials including curry on Thursday, cod and chips on Friday and steak on Tuesday and Saturday. B&B accommodation and a holiday cottage are AA 4-star rated.
Q P (675)

Weatheroak

Coach & Horses

Weatheroak Hill, B48 7EA (Alvechurch to Wythall road) SP057740
11.30-11; 12-10.30 Sun (01564) 823386
coachandhorsesinn.co.uk
Holden's Golden Glow; Hook Norton Old Hooky; Weatheroak Hill Gold, Icknield Pale Ale, Impossible IPA, Cofton Common; 4 changing beers (sourced nationally; often Hobsons, St Austell, Wood)
Award-winning country free house featuring a traditional bar with a real fire and quarry-tiled floor, a modern lounge bar and a restaurant. Outside, the large garden is popular in the summer. Formerly a coach house, the pub has been in the same family for 50 years. Ten real ales are stocked from national and regional breweries including the on-site Weatheroak Hill, which also provides beer to take out. Fresh rolls are always available. The pub is adjacent to Icknield Street Roman road.
P

Worcester

Cardinal's Hat

31 Friar Street, WR1 2NA
12 (4 Mon)-11; 12-11.30 Sat; 12-10.30 Sun
(01905) 724006 the-cardinals-hat.co.uk
Purity Mad Goose; 4 changing beers (sourced locally)

ENGLAND

Worcester's oldest pub is a period building set in the heart of the city centre. The main bar at the front has a scrubbed wooden floor, beams and leaded windows. A stone-flagged, panelled passageway leads to a patio at the rear. The atmospheric back room features wood panelling, a stone-flagged floor, serving hatch and impressive fireplace with woodburner and dribbly candles. A small snug has views of the bustling old street outside. Folk night is the first Tuesday of the month. ☺🏠🍴🍷◐≷🚃🚌🐾🛜

Dragon Inn ♟

51 The Tything, WR1 1JT (on A449, 300yds N of Foregate St Station)
🕑 4-11; 12-11 Fri & Sat; 12-10.30 Sun ☎ (01905) 25845
🌐 thedragoninnworcester.co.uk
Church End Goat's Milk, Gravediggers Ale, What the Fox's Hat, Fallen Angel; 4 changing beers (often Church End) Ⓗ
A Georgian building on the edge of the city centre run by Church End Brewery. The bar is towards the back while the front space offers the opportunity to watch the world go by. Behind the pub is a large, quiet patio area with a covered space in the old side passage. A changing variety of Church End beers is on the bar plus two guest ales from other small breweries. Pork pies and sausage rolls are always available. Q☺👶♿♣●🚃🚌🐾🛜

Firefly Ⓛ

54 Lowesmoor, WR1 2SE
🕑 3-midnight; 12-1am Fri (2am Sat); 12-11 Sun
☎ (01905) 616996
5 changing beers (often Oakham, Tiny Rebel) Ⓗ
Once the old vinegar works manager's Georgian residence, this is now a comfortable, stylish bar. It has five handpulls for beers and two for ciders – one usually from Snails Bank. The interior has soft furnishings, subtle lighting and an open fire. Downstairs is a cosy snug with bench sofas. The upstairs bar hosts live music including open mic on Tuesday. Food includes a burger deal on Wednesday. Outside is a paved, partially covered beer garden. ☺◐≷🚃🚌🐾🛜

Imperial Tavern Ⓛ

35 St Nicholas Street, WR1 1UW
🕑 12-11 ☎ (01905) 619472 🌐 blackcountryales.co.uk
Black Country Bradley's Finest Golden, Fireside; 5 changing beers Ⓗ
This smart city pub is run by the Black Country Brewery. It serves three real ales from the brewery alongside up to four from small breweries across the country and 10 real ciders, three on handpump. Three drinking areas are joined by the bar which runs from front to back. Pictures of old Worcester pubs and street scenes decorate the walls. Cobs are available at lunchtime. Q◐≷♣●🚃

King Charles II Ⓛ

29 New Street, WR1 2DP
🕑 11.30-11 (11.30 Fri & Sat) ☎ (01905) 726100
🌐 thekingcharleshouse.com
Craddock's Saxon Gold, Crazy Sheep, Troll; 3 changing beers (sourced locally) Ⓗ
A black-and-white Grade II*-listed building in the heart of the historic city. King Charles II escaped from here in 1651 after losing the Battle of Worcester. Be sure to check out the skeleton in the concealed dungeon, and the first floor where there is a piano for passing musicians. The bar serves beers from Bridgnorth, Craddock's and Two Thirsty

Brewers. Barbourne cider on the pumps is occasionally supplemented by its perry. Speciality pies feature on the menu. Tuesday is quiz night, Wednesday board games. Q☺🏠🍴🍷≷♣●🚃🚌🐾🛜

Lamb & Flag Ⓛ

30 The Tything, WR1 1JL
🕑 12-midnight ☎ (01905) 729415
🌐 twocraftybrewers.co.uk
Wye Valley HPA; 3 changing beers Ⓗ
A Worcester institution, this Two Crafty Brewers pub has a traditional feel but with a subtle urban twist. The popular community local is renowned for its niche activities such as backgammon, poetry reading and folk music. At the front is a no-frills saloon which caters for all tastes but can get rather noisy. The cosy lounge bar offers a bar menu. Upstairs is the SUGO Italian restaurant, serving proper Italian food freshly prepared by an Italian chef. The world conker championship is held here in early October. ☺◐≷♣🚃🚌

Oil Basin Brewhouse

7 Copenhagen Street, WR1 2HB (just off high street)
🕑 4-11 Mon-Wed; 12-midnight Thu (1am Fri & Sat); 12-10 Sun ☎ 07964 196194 🌐 wintripbrew.co
Wintrip Butchers Beastly Best, Lady Marmalade; 4 changing beers (often Salopian, Teme Valley, Tiny Rebel) Ⓗ
A small, cosy bar with comfy chairs, wood-beamed ceiling, bare boards and a small brewery out the back. It serves a variety of interesting real ales, mostly local, and craft keg. There is also a good selection of craft beers and ciders in the fridge. The pub is centrally located, just off the high street. Chad's Smashery on the floor above produces fine pizzas cooked in a wood-fired oven. Q◐≷♣●🚃🐾

Plough Ⓛ

23 Fish Street, WR1 2HN (on Deansway)
🕑 12-11 (11.30 Fri & Sat); 12-10.30 Sun ☎ (01905) 21381
Hobsons Best; Malvern Hills Black Pear; 4 changing beers (sourced regionally; often Beowulf, Mighty Oak, Salopian) Ⓗ
A Grade II-listed pub near the cathedral. There is a short flight of steps leading to a tiny bar with rooms to either side. The beers usually come from Worcestershire and surrounding counties but occasionally from small breweries further afield. Draught cider and perry are from Barbourne in the city. There is also an ever-changing range of whiskies. Outside is a small patio area. Rolls are available at weekends and when the cricket is on, with cooked meals Friday to Sunday lunchtime. ☺🏠◐≷♣●🚃🐾

Postal Order ✅

18 Foregate Street, WR1 1DN
🕑 8am-midnight (1am Fri & Sat) ☎ (01905) 22373
Greene King Abbot; Ruddles Best Bitter; 10 changing beers (sourced nationally; often Bespoke, Lakehouse, Pershore) Ⓗ
A classic Wetherspoon pub, formerly the old Worcester telephone exchange. It serves a wide range of ales of different styles and strengths, some from local breweries. Beer festivals throughout the year add even more variety. A cider from local producer Barbourne and Old Rosie from Westons are always available plus two others. Good-value food is served daily 8am-11pm (alcohol from 9am). The volume on the TV may be turned up for important games. Q☺🏠◐👶≷●🚃🐾🛜

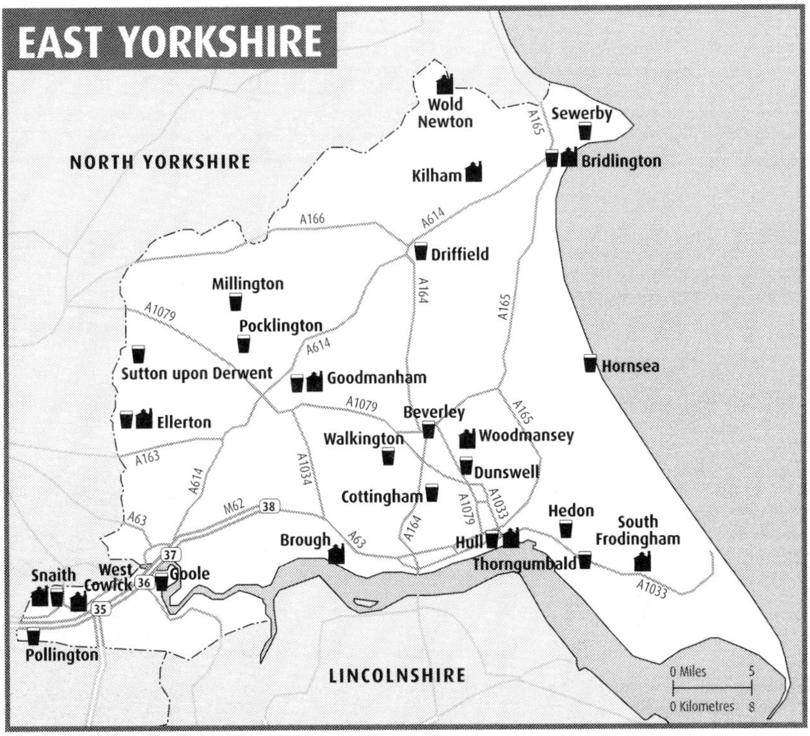

YORKSHIRE (EAST)

Beverley

Chequers Micropub

15 Swaby's Yard, Dyer Lane, HU17 9BZ (off Saturday Market)

12-10 (11 Thu-Sat) ☎ 07964 227906

5 changing beers (sourced regionally; often Brass Castle, North Riding)

Yorkshire's first micropub, in a former baker's shop near the bus station. Local breweries are well represented on the bar plus micros from throughout the UK. Several ciders/perries are sold and it has three KeyKeg lines. Typically for a micropub, no lager is served. There is no TV or loud music either, making Chequers a place for real conversation, like pubs used to be. A selection of board games is available for customers. The cellar is above the bar. Q

Dog & Duck

33 Ladygate, HU17 8BH (off Saturday Market)

11-4, 7-midnight; 11-midnight Fri & Sat; 11.30-3, 7-11 Sun ☎ (01482) 862419 bedandbreakfastbeverley.com

Ossett Excelsior; 3 changing beers (sourced nationally; often Timothy Taylor)

On a side street adjacent to Brown's department store, the pub was built in the 1930s and has been run by the same family for 45 years. It comprises three areas: a bar with a period brick fireplace and bentwood seating, a front lounge with an open fire, and a rear snug. The good-value, home-cooked lunches are popular. Guest accommodation is in six purpose-built self-contained rooms to the rear. It is dog-friendly after food service. Close to Beverley bus station.

Green Dragon

51 Saturday Market, HU17 8AA

9am-11 (midnight Fri & Sat) ☎ (01482) 889801

thegreendragonbeverley.co.uk

Black Sheep Best Bitter; Sharp's Doom Bar; Timothy Taylor Landlord; Wainwright; 5 changing beers (sourced nationally; often Adnams, Purity, Rudgate)

Narrow-fronted Tudor-style inn accessed down a side passageway, it was refurbished in 2018 and updated to increase its appeal to family diners. It opens for breakfast at 9am and serves other meals all day. Sports fans are catered for with several large-screen TVs. There is a wide range of beer styles from the nine or ten handpumps and further KeyKegs. Quizzes are held Tuesday and Thursday.

REAL ALE BREWERIES

All Hallows Goodmanham
Atom Hull
Bone Machine Hull (NEW)
Bricknell Hull
Bridlington Bridlington (brewing suspended)
Crafty Little Brough
East Yorkshire Woodmansey
Great Newsome South Frodingham
Half Moon Ellerton
Old Mill Snaith
Raven Hill Kilham (NEW)
Spotlight West Cowick
Vittles Hull (NEW)
Wold Top Wold Newton
Wooly Butt Hull (NEW)
Yorkshire Hull
Yorkshire Brewhouse Hull

Monks Walk
19 Highgate, HU17 0DN
12-11; 12-10.30 Sun (01482) 864972
monkswalkinn.co.uk
5 changing beers (sourced locally; often Atom, Brass Castle, Yorkshire) H/G
Dating back to the 13th century and built as a merchant's warehouse, records show there was a brewery attached in the 19th century. The pub was known as the George & Dragon until the 1980s. Access to the Minster Bar is by an open passageway, plus a dining room which features exposed roof beams and open fire. Conversation is encouraged at this genuine free house. The sheltered beer garden has splendid views of the Minster. Access to the car park is off Eastgate.
Q P

Sun Inn
1 Flemingate, HU17 0NP (adjacent to Beverley Minster)
4-11 (12.30am Fri); 12-12.30am Sat; 12-10.30 Sun
07541 456215 suninnbeverley.co.uk
Black Sheep Best Bitter; Morland Old Speckled Hen; Timothy Taylor Boltmaker; York Guzzler; 1 changing beer (sourced nationally; often Robinsons) H
The pub's medieval timber-framed building is set opposite the eastern front of Beverley's famous minster, and the view from the courtyard beer garden should not be missed. Formerly a Tap & Spile, the pub's stripped-back interior featuring bare brick walls reflects that style. It is a live music venue with blues and rock bands on a weekend and folk sessions on Saturday teatime. Among other events there is a popular quiz on Thursday. Sunday lunches served noon-3pm.

Bridlington

Board Inn
62 High Street, YO16 4QA
3-11; 12-11 Fri & Sun; 12-midnight Sat (01262) 672087
Adnams Ghost Ship; Fuller's ESB; St Austell Proper Job; Tetley Bitter; Titanic Plum Porter; 2 changing beers (sourced nationally) H
Located in Bridlington's old town, this lovingly restored historic inn dates back to the 18th century and has wood panelling, flagged and timber floors and four open fires, a multi-roomed interior with three comfortably furnished rooms, and a snug upstairs. It hosts music nights at weekends. To the rear, a new tap has been established selling 10 craft-brewed beers in converted stables, with further open fires. Recognised by CAMRA for the restoration undertaken, it is a real gem, not to be missed. Q P

Marine Bar
North Marine Drive, YO15 2LS (1 mile NE of centre)
12-11 (11.30 Sat) (01262) 675347
John Smith's Bitter; Timothy Taylor Landlord; Wold Top Bitter; 2 changing beers (sourced regionally; often Daleside, Rooster's) H
Large open-plan bar, part of the Expanse Hotel. Spectacular sea views are the perfect accompaniment to enjoying the home-cooked food served here daily. Attracting a good mix of regulars, a warm welcome awaits the influx of summer visitors. Two regional guest beers complement the three regular ales, and it also does real cider. Ample parking is available along the promenade, where a land train operates during the summer. P (512,513)

Pack Horse
7 Market Place, YO16 4QJ
closed Mon; 12-10 (11 Fri & Sat); 12-9 Sun
(01262) 603502
Abbeydale Moonshine; 4 changing beers (sourced regionally; often Acorn, Salamander, Wold Top) H
This pub was restored by its owners as a labour of love to create an open-plan yet intimate layout. There are three customer areas: one to the right of the bar, one to the left, and a third at the rear. Home-cooked food is served, with a carvery on Sunday (no food Mon). Outside, there is a paved area to the rear. The famous stocks remain in place in front of the pub. P (121,120)

Prior John
34-36 The Promenade, YO15 2QD
9am-midnight (01262) 674256
Greene King Abbot; Ruddles Best Bitter; 5 changing beers (sourced nationally) H
Large, busy Wetherspoon pub, close to the bus station, busier still during the summer months. The Prior has one large crescent-shaped room, with a first-floor gallery reached by a spiral staircase. It takes its name from John de Tweng, who was a prior of the medieval monastery in Bridlington which became a place of pilgrimage after his death, leading to the development of this well-known seaside town. Q

Telegraph
110 Quay Road, YO16 4JB
12-11 (1am Fri & Sat) (01262) 674592
Wold Top Anglers Reward; 3 changing beers (sourced regionally; often Brown Cow, Caledonian, Great Newsome) H
This welcoming, traditional, family-run free house is well used by locals and visitors. The one-room open-plan interior is warmed by logburners. Outside, a spacious walled beer garden encompassing a covered area with a chiminea expands the capacity of the pub as the weather allows. Live music, pool and darts teams, and a scooter club all add to a community feel. The range of real ales comes from breweries both local and across Yorkshire. P

Cottingham

Hallgate Tavern
125-127A Hallgate, HU16 4DA
12-11 (midnight Fri & Sat) (01482) 844448
Banks's Sunbeam; Wychwood Hobgoblin Gold; 1 changing beer (sourced nationally; often Jennings, Marston's) H
Converted from a former shop some years ago, with a deceptive street frontage, the pub itself is one large space but with a cosy feel; different areas cater for a diversity of tastes and ages. There are pool tables and various gaming machines, but these are out of sight at one end, and the other end has the feel of a lounge. Sports on large TVs and live music are also provided.

King William IV
152 Hallgate, HU16 4DB
11-11 (midnight Fri & Sat); 12-11 Sun (01482) 875996
Banks's Sunbeam; Jennings Cumberland Ale; Marston's Pedigree; Wainwright; Wychwood Hobgoblin; 2 changing beers (sourced nationally; often Brakspear, Ringwood, Wychwood) H

Village-centre pub with a traditional bar and quiet lounge. The pub hosts weekly quiz nights and is a venue during the village's annual music festival. At the rear a former brewery has been converted into a function room offering live music and special events. The beer garden and side courtyard have covered smoking areas. Excellent-value meals are served in large and small portions. Thatchers cider is on handpump. Local CAMRA Village Pub of the Year runner-up for last two years.
Q❀◐◑≹♣●🚌🐾📶

Driffield

Benjamin Fawcett

Middle Street North, YO25 6SW
8am-midnight (1am Fri & Sat) ☎ (01377) 249130
Greene King Abbot; Ruddles Best Bitter; changing beers H
Like most Wetherspoon outlets, this is now a spacious one-room pub, a conversion from former licensed premises on the site. It has quieter areas and other more lively spaces, and family diners are welcome. The name comes from a local printer who was one of the first to print in colour, and framed examples are on display. The interior is decorated with artefacts that pay tribute to members of the Armed Forces stationed in the area during World War II. ◐◑♿●📶

Butcher's Dog

24 Middle Street South, YO25 6PS
closed Mon; 12-11 (10 Tue & Wed); 12-10 Sun
☎ (01377) 252229 thebutchersdog.co.uk
5 changing beers (sourced locally; often Wold Top, Yorkshire, Yorkshire Heart) H
A one-room micropub but returning to traditional pub values with modern twists. Five real ales from local and regional breweries are served in oversized glasses (tasting paddles available), alongside a wide selection of real ciders, but no spirits. Customers are encouraged to rely on good conversation in the music- and WiFi-free environment. Simple bar snacks are available including a cheeseboard on Sunday afternoon, but customers may also bring their own food. Local CAMRA Town Pub of the Year 2018.
Q♿≹♣●🚌(121)🐾

Dunswell

Ship Inn

Beverley Road, HU6 0AJ
11.30-11 (11.30 Thu; midnight Fri & Sat); 12-11.30 Sun
☎ (01482) 859160 shipsquarters.co.uk
4 changing beers (sourced regionally; often Great Newsome) H
Fronting the old Hull-Beverley road, this inn once served traffic on the nearby River Hull, and is decorated with nautical memorabilia, including the bell from the shipwrecked Caroline. Log fires warm the convivial interior which is partly divided to create a separate dining area with church pew seating. Former outbuildings have been developed to create en-suite accommodation in the Ship's Quarters. The large garden has an outside bar and barbecue area for summer events. The pub maintains good links with the local primary school and church. ❀◐◑♿♣P🚌🐾📶

Ellerton

Boot & Shoe

Main Street, YO42 4PB
5.30-11; 4-midnight Fri & Sat; 12-11 Sun
☎ (01757) 288346
House beer (by Dark Horse); 2 changing beers (sourced nationally; often Dark Horse) H
A welcoming country village inn of character dating from the 17th century. The building wraps around a large tree and features low-beamed ceilings. There is a cosy bar area with exposed brick and an open fire, plus two separate intimate dining rooms. Three real ales are on offer in this free house, including two from Dark Horse. Food is served Friday and Saturday evenings and Sunday lunchtime (booking advisable). Q◐◑♣P🐾

Goodmanham

Goodmanham Arms

Main Street, YO43 3JA
11.30-midnight; 11.30-11 Sun ☎ (01430) 873849
goodmanhamarms.co.uk
All Hallows Peg Fyfe Dark Mild, No Notion Porter; Hambleton Stallion Amber; Theakston Best Bitter; 4 changing beers (sourced regionally; often All Hallows, Oakham, Wold Top) H
Unique village local with All Hallows Brewery attached, also close to the Wolds Way footpath. There are three log fires warming the bar, dining room and kitchen, and the place is candlelit during dark winter nights. Hearty meals are served including a gypsy pot in the winter. Folk nights are held every first Thursday and blues/jazz/country every third Thursday of the month, with further events on bank holidays. Local CAMRA Village Pub of the Year winner 2017 and 2018. Q❀◐◑●P

Goole

Tom Pudding

20 Pasture Road, DN14 6EZ (2 mins walk from Goole station)
4-11; 12-11 Fri & Sat; 2-11 Sun ☎ 07762 525114
4 changing beers (sourced regionally; often Exit 33, Isaac Poad, Wold Top) H
Once a newsagents', this micropub has interesting internal brickwork and an exposed wooden-beamed ceiling. It was opened in 2017 by two CAMRA members with an enthusiasm for real ale. There is always a gluten-free beer, as well as up to four real ciders, often from Henry Weston and Gwynt y Ddraig. The pub can accommodate up to 50 people, and is sought out by travelling football fans on their way to a match at Scunthorpe or Hull.
≹♣●🚌(155,X55)🐾

Hedon

Hed'On Inn

7 Watmaughs Arcade, St Augustine Gate, HU12 8EZ
1-11 (11.30 Fri & Sat) ☎ (01964) 601100
Black Sheep Best Bitter; Theakston Old Peculier; 4 changing beers (sourced nationally; often Great Newsome) H
A micropub adjacent to a car park at the end of a shopping arcade in the centre of this old market town, converted from a disused carpet shop office. The premises are tastefully decorated with recycled fittings. There are two regular and four changing beers covering the full spectrum of styles, together

with real ciders, bottled beers and a range of spirits and wines. Acoustic music sessions take place on Tuesday nights and Sunday afternoons, with quizzes and games on Wednesday nights.
Q♣🍎P🚌

Shakespeare Inn 🄻 ✔

9 Baxtergate, HU12 8JN
⏲ 12 (5 Mon)-11; 12-midnight Fri & Sat; 12-10.30 Sun
☎ (01482) 891892
Tetley Bitter; Timothy Taylor Landlord; 3 changing beers (sourced nationally; often Great Newsome) 🄷
This welcoming local has been serving the people of Hedon for generations and is around 300 years old. Set in the centre of the historic town, it has been largely unaltered for the past 50 years and is traditionally fitted out, featuring original Darley's wall sconces. Popular with all ages, a friendly atmosphere encourages conversation. The menu features freshly cooked local produce with a popular changing specials menu. Of the three guest beers, one is usually from a local brewery.
Q🐴❀◐♣P🐾ᯤ

Hornsea

Stackhouse Bar

8a Newbegin, HU18 1AG
⏲ 4-11; 2-11 Fri; 12-midnight Sat & Sun ☎ (01964) 534407
4 changing beers (sourced regionally) 🄷
A former shop converted to a micropub in 2014, with an interesting choice of regional ales and a large range of real ciders. Attracting a mixed clientele, customers are encouraged to engage in conversation. There is a separate function room. An autumn beer festival is held in the nearby Hornsea Museum gardens. Although no food is provided, customers are allowed to bring in their own.
🐴⛺♣🍎🚌(240,246)🐾ᯤ

Hull

Admiral of the Humber 🄻 ✔

5-7 Anlaby Road, HU1 2NT
⏲ 8am-midnight (1am Fri & Sat) ☎ (01482) 381850
Greene King Abbot; Ruddles Best Bitter; Sharp's Doom Bar; 6 changing beers (sourced nationally) 🄷
Following a £2.5m upgrade, the Admiral is now a Wetherlodge hotel. A former paint and wallpaper shop, the site was previously connected to Hull's seafaring past. Now a large single room, mostly on one level, the building is ideally suited to those finding steps or stairs a problem. There is a large rooftop garden (closes 10pm nightly). A designated area is set aside for diners during the day, and children are welcome until 6pm.
Q🐴❀🛏◐♿🚆🍎P🚌ᯤ

Chilli Devil's 🄻

Manor Street, HU1 1YP
⏲ 4-11; 12-11 Fri-Sun ☎ (01482) 961666
4 changing beers 🄷
A small one-room pub in the heart of the city, with an extensive collection of photographs of Hull in bygone times on show. Cask ales and real ciders are the main offering, although a varied selection of bottled beers meeting LocAle criteria is also available. Prior to becoming a licensee, the landlord was well known locally for his passion for all things related to chilli, which is reflected in the ever-changing chilli-based food menu.
Q◐🚆🍎🚌🐾

Furley & Co 🄻

18-20 Princes Dock Street, HU1 2LP (opp dockside entrance to Princes Quay shopping centre)
⏲ 11-10 (midnight Thu-Sat); 11-8 Sun ☎ (01482) 229649
Atom Blonde Ale; 4 changing beers (sourced nationally; often Atom, Half Moon, North Riding) 🄷
Popular family-friendly bar offering local and regional cask and craft beers, overlooking the waterfront of the former Princes Dock. Historically it was warehousing and offices for a local shipping company and the first bottled gas merchant in Hull. The decor is now neo-industrial, portraying music and film iconography on the walls. Varied events include occasional live music and monthly visits from the chess society. A room upstairs with additional seating can be used for functions.
🐴❀◐♿🚆♣🍎🚌🐾

George Hotel ✔

Land of Green Ginger, HU1 2EA
⏲ 12-midnight ☎ (01482) 226373
Abbeydale Moonshine; Theakston Old Peculier; 5 changing beers (sourced regionally; often Bradfield) 🄷
In the heart of the old town on Hull's most famous street, this one-roomed pub is of historic interest. The Georgian interior featuring beamed ceilings, wood-panelled walls and pictures of old Hull remains virtually unaltered. The fine glazed leaded windows have been retained, and of note is reputedly the smallest pub window in England, dating from its former coaching days. Local CAMRA branch City Pub of the Year 2017. 🐴♣🍎🚌🐾

Head of Steam 🄻

10 King Street, HU1 2JJ
⏲ 11-11 (midnight Thu-Sat); 11-10.30 Sun
☎ (01482) 217236
Atom Blonde Ale; Camerons A-Hop-Alypse Now; 4 changing beers (sourced regionally) 🄷
This is a single-roomed pub decorated with beer-related artefacts. Its large picture windows overlook Hull Minster and Trinity Square. An outdoor seating area to the front of the premises provides an ideal location to watch the world go by. The cask ales constantly vary, often promoting new breweries, and are complemented by an extensive selection of craft products reflecting the passion of the management team. Food is from a local independent street food vendor.
❀◐🚆🍎🚌🐾

Hop & Vine 🄻

24 Albion Street, HU1 3TG (250yds from Hull New Theatre and Central Library)
⏲ 11 (4 Tue)-11; closed Sun & Mon ☎ 07507 719259
3 changing beers (sourced nationally; often Great Newsome, Isaac Poad, Wold Top) 🄷
Atmospheric basement bar free house serving three changing guest beers largely from Yorkshire's independent breweries. Unusual still ciders and perries are also sold, and some continental bottled beers. The landlord is continuing to vary the choice of other drinks. Oversized lined glasses are used. A selection of freshly prepared food including home-baked bread is served until 9pm. It is a former CAMRA National Cider Pub of the Year and a four-times Yorkshire regional winner. Shove-ha'penny, cribbage and shut the box are played.
🐴◐⛺🚆♣🍎🚏🚌🐾

Larkin's L

48-52 Newland Avenue, HU5 3AE (near jct of De Grey St)
11-11 (11.30 Fri & Sat) (01482) 440991
larkinsbar.co.uk
3 changing beers (sourced regionally; often Great Newsome, Wold Top) H
One-roomed café-bar named after poet Philip Larkin. Formerly two shops, it can still be partitioned for small private functions. A good selection of home-cooked food is served every day. There is a paved area to the front and a family-oriented beer garden to the side and rear. Beer festivals with live music from local acts are usually held over bank holiday weekends in spring and summer, and there is occasional live music outdoors in the summer. Q

Minerva Hotel L

Nelson Street, HU1 1XE
11.30-11.30 (midnight Fri & Sat) (01482) 210025
minerva-hull.co.uk
Tetley Bitter; 5 changing beers (sourced regionally; often Atom, Revolutions, Yorkshire) H
Overlooking the Humber estuary and Victoria Pier, this famous pub, built in 1829, is a great place to watch the ships go by. Photos and memorabilia are a reminder of the area's maritime past. The central bar serves various rooms including a tiny three-seat snug. The former brewhouse was converted to provide an additional drinking area and is available for functions. Connected to The Deep visitor attraction by a footbridge at the mouth of the River Hull. (16)

Olde White Harte ★

25 Silver Street, HU1 1JG (in alley between Silver St and Bowlalley Lane)
11-midnight (01482) 326363
Caledonian Deuchars IPA; Theakston Best Bitter, Old Peculier; 3 changing beers (sourced nationally) H
Historic pub in a 17th-century merchant's house, with strong connections to the English Civil War, hidden down an alley near Hull's old town. The existing ground-floor interior dates back to a major refurbishment in 1881, which was an idealised re-creation of an old English inn, complete with massive inglenook fireplaces and stained-glass windows. The first floor features the Plotting Parlour which is available for meetings and functions. There is also a heated courtyard providing an all-weather outdoor drinking area.

Pave L

16-20 Princes Avenue, HU5 3QA
11-11 (11.30 Fri & Sat) (01482) 333181
pavebar.co.uk
Tetley Gold; Theakston Best Bitter; 3 changing beers (sourced regionally; often Great Yorkshire, Saltaire, Scarborough) H
The original pavement café in this popular area of the city, this continental-style bar attracts a diverse range of customers. As well as the regular ales there are three guest ales including one stout, usually regional, and a varied range of European draught and bottled beers. Home-cooked food including vegetarian and gluten-free options is served daily. Complimentary live music is provided on Tuesday evening and Sunday afternoon. A changing Westons cider is sold.
(Interchange)

St John's Hotel

10 Queens Road, HU5 2PY
12-11.30 Mon, Wed & Sun; 12-midnight Tue & Thu; 12-12.30am Fri & Sat (01482) 341013 stjohnshull.com
Marston's 61 Deep; Wainwright; 3 changing beers (sourced nationally) H
Grade II-listed classic street-corner local that boasts one of the least-altered interiors in the city, now identified by CAMRA as having a regionally important historic pub interior. The front corner public bar complements a quiet back room, with original bench seating. A basic larger room accommodates the pool table and is home to regular beer festivals. The pub is a community local with two darts teams, a football team and the Oddfellows cricket league, and hosts quiz nights in the winter. Open mic night is Tuesday.
Q P

Three John Scotts L

Lowgate, HU1 1AA
8am-midnight (1am Fri & Sat) (01482) 381910
Greene King Abbot; Ruddles Best Bitter; Sharp's Doom Bar; 7 changing beers (sourced regionally; often Great Newsome) H
Originally an Edwardian post office, this open-plan Wetherspoon features modern decor and works of art. The name derives from three successive 19th-century vicars of St Mary's church opposite. The pub has established a broad customer base appealing to all types of clientele. Up to 10 real ales and two real ciders are on the bar. Children are welcome up to 9pm. There is a large rear courtyard seating area which is a great suntrap in the summer.

Whalebone L

165 Wincolmlee, HU2 0PA
12-midnight (11 Tue & Wed); 12-11 Sun 07506 868461
Half Moon Old Forge Bitter; Rudgate Viking; 5 changing beers (sourced regionally; often Abbeydale, North Riding, Rat) H
A rare gem sited within the old Greenland whaling trading area. Licensed since 1791, the current building dates from 1890, and has been a free house since 2002. Photos celebrating the city's sporting heritage and bygone Hull pubs adorn the walls. Artefacts showcasing the whaling industry can be viewed in the quiet room, once the pub's brewery. Hung outside from a bygone year is a Moors' & Robson's brewery sign. Local CAMRA City Pub of the Year 2018, and many times previously.
Q

White Hart ★ L

109 Alfred Gelder Street, HU1 1EP
4-11; 2.30-midnight Fri; 12-midnight Sat; 12-8 Sun
07793 710160 whitehartthullpub.co.uk
7 changing beers (sourced regionally; often Crafty Little, Great Heck, Revolutions, Stod Fold) H
Reopened in 2018 after many years of closure, the White Hart is located on the edge of Hull's Old Town and features on CAMRA's National Inventory of Historic Pub Interiors, with a rare bar front and many other original features. It is largely the brewery tap for Crafty Little Brewery, with at least one of its beers usually available. It also showcases more progressive regional breweries and offers a number of craft and KeyKeg beers.
Q P

Millington

Gait

Main Street, YO42 1TX

closed Mon; 6.30-11 Tue-Thu; 12-3, 6.30-11 Fri; 12-4, 6-11 Sat; 12-3, 6-11 Sun (01759) 302045
gait-inn-millington.co.uk

Black Sheep Best Bitter; Tetley Bitter; Theakston Best Bitter; 2 changing beers (sourced locally; often Great Yorkshire, Half Moon, Wold Top) H

This delightful Yorkshire Wolds pub provides a warm welcome (enhanced in winter by means of a wood-burning stove) both to locals and the many walkers enjoying the attractions of Millington Wood and Pastures. It is an idiosyncratic bar filled with a range of ornaments and local pictures. Sit at kitchen-style tables to enjoy hearty, home-made food served from an extensive menu. The annual beer festival has up to 35 beers. Three regular beers are on handpump and at least one guest, often all from Yorkshire. P

Pocklington

Market Tap

11-13 Market Place, YO42 2AS

4.30-10.30 Mon; 12-10.30 (10 Thu; midnight Fri); 10.30-midnight Sat; 10.30-10.30 Sun (01759) 307783

Hop Studio Bitter, Mosaic, Porter, XS; 4 changing beers H

Overlooking the marketplace, this 19th-century building and former newsagents' has recently been refurbished, providing a light, spacious and modern feel over two floors. An extensive range of nine cask and nine keg beers is on offer, including five cask regulars from Hop Studio and four changing guests. It also does off-sales for wines, beers and ciders.

Pollington

King's Head

Main Street, DN14 0DN (on main road through village)

5-11 (midnight Fri); 12-midnight Sat; 12-11 Sun (01405) 861507 kingsheadpollington.co.uk

Isaac Poad No.86 Golden Ale; Old Mill Traditional Bitter; Tetley Bitter; 1 changing beer (sourced locally; often Black Sheep, Theakston, Timothy Taylor) H

A lively village pub comprising a U-shaped bar and a single-room lounge. Four real ales are served. The pub holds a beer festival on August bank holidays, and is also the location for a steam rally in September. The Trans Pennine Way is nearby, and walkers are always welcome. The pub supports a variety of local events, and has a reputation for good food and cask ale, served by friendly staff. Q P

Sewerby

Ship Inn

Cliff Road, YO15 1EW

11-11 (01262) 672374 shipinnsewerby.co.uk

Jennings Cumberland Ale; Mansfield Cask Ale; 3 changing beers (sourced nationally; often Banks's, Ringwood, Wychwood) H

This village-centre pub, featuring a wood-panelled bar with a beamed ceiling, serves both locals and holidaymakers; there is also a separate dining room and lounge. Dogs are welcome and it has a beer garden with a children's play area overlooking the sea. The restaurant serves main meals and booking is recommended for the Sunday carvery (no meals winter Mon). Nearby attractions include a model village and Sewerby Hall, along with clifftop walks. P

Snaith

Yorkshire Ales Beer Café Bar

Selby Road, DN14 9HT (on edge of marketplace)

4-midnight (10 Mon & Tue); 2-midnight Sat; 2-10 Sun (01405) 860603 yorkshireales.co.uk

Brown Cow White Dragon; 4 changing beers (sourced regionally; often Bad Seed, Brown Cow, Little Critters) H

Yorkshire Ales showcases beers brewed by small, independent Yorkshire microbreweries. The building dates back to 1750 and has seating for 80 over two floors, plus the beer garden. Food is snacks only, but artisan chefs and street food vendors are booked regularly. With no TVs and music at background volume, the art of conversation is promoted. Local cycling and photography clubs meet regularly, and the weekly general knowledge quiz is popular. Q (401)

Sutton upon Derwent

St Vincent Arms

Main Street, YO41 4BN

11.30-3, 6-11; 12-3, 6.30-10.30 Sun (01904) 608349
stvincentarms.co.uk

Fuller's London Pride; Greene King IPA; Theakston Old Peculier; Timothy Taylor Landlord; York Guzzler; 2 changing beers (sourced nationally) H

Former winner of many York CAMRA awards, this pretty white-painted village free house on a bend in the road has been family-owned and well run for many years. A long-time supporter of Fuller's beers, it has a consistent but large beer range. The bar, featuring a large Fuller, Smith & Turner mirror, is popular with locals. Another small bar with a serving hatch leads to the dining rooms. It also serves excellent food, catering for a variety of tastes. Q P

Thorngumbald

New Royal Mail

Sorting Room, Main Road, HU12 9LN (behind café)

4-11; 2-11 Sat & Sun

Brakspear Bitter; Theakston Best Bitter; Wainwright; 3 changing beers (often Great Newsome) H

This pub commemorates a previous one, now lost, with almost the same name – hence the New in the name. The building arose, like a phoenix from the ashes, on a neighbouring site to the lost pub, and many of the fixtures are made from materials taken from the previous Royal Mail when it was demolished. A small, intimate pub has been created, catering for a diverse range of customers. Promotional prices are offered on Tuesday. The window boxes are spectacular. Q P

Walkington

Barrel Inn

35 East End, HU17 8RX

4.30-midnight (1am Fri); 12-1am Sat; 12-midnight Sun
07550 078833

Lancaster Bomber; Wainwright; 1 changing beer (sourced regionally) H

Friendly drinkers' local in a quiet three-pub village, and one of only a handful of Thwaites pubs in East Yorkshire. The interior comprises a front bar with a log fire and beamed ceiling; a step leads to a connecting lounge, also with a log fire. To the rear is a secluded cottage-style garden. Families and dogs are welcome throughout. Although essentially a quiet pub, major Premier League football matches and other sporting events are shown. Thursday is quiz night. ☕❀♣🚌🐾

YORKSHIRE (NORTH)

Acaster Malbis

Ship

Moor End, YO23 2UH

12 (4 Mon & Tue)-11; 12-10.30 Sun ☎ (01904) 703888

shipinnacastermalbis.co.uk

Black Sheep Best Bitter; Camerons Strongarm; Timothy Taylor Golden Best; 3 changing beers (sourced regionally; often Ossett, Theakston) [H]

Located by the river and attractively refurbished after the December 2015 floods, this friendly country pub serves a good range of real ales and quality food in a pleasant and relaxing location. The welcoming real fire inside and a riverfront garden offer choices depending on the weather. The pub is popular in spring and summer, with four nearby camping/caravan sites, and quieter the rest of the year. The York waterbus in the summer makes an interesting trip. Quiz night is Wednesday. Q☕❀◐♿ÅP🚌(21)🐾

Appletreewick

Craven Arms 𝕃

BD23 6DA

12-11; 12-10.30 Sun ☎ (01756) 720270

craven-cruckbarn.co.uk

Dark Horse Craven Bitter, Hetton Pale Ale, Night Jar; Theakston Old Peculier; Wharfedale Blonde; 2 changing beers (sourced regionally) [H]

Dating from 1548, this multi-roomed free house has stone-flagged floors, oak beams and gas lighting. The bar features an original Yorkshire range while the cosy taproom has an open fire and ring the bull. A snug behind the bar leads to the cruck barn, added in 2006 using traditional techniques. This can be hired for functions and hosts occasional events including music and a beer festival in October. Two additional guest beers are on in summer. Accommodation is in three shepherds' huts. Q☕❀◐Å♣🍎P🚌(74A)🐾

Askrigg

King's Arms 𝕃

Main Street, DL8 3HQ

11-11 ☎ (01969) 650113

Black Sheep Best Bitter; Theakston Best Bitter; house beer (by Yorkshire Dales) [H]

This historic multi-roomed Dales free house of great character starred as The Drover's Arms in TV's All Creatures Great and Small. A huge open fireplace and painting of the local friendly society add character to the stone-flagged bar. There are separate dining rooms plus a vaulted games room to the rear and a small outdoor courtyard. Three house beers are from the Yorkshire Dales Brewery, a few hundred yards away. ☕❀◐🚌🐾

Austwick

Game Cock

LA2 8BB (on Horton road)

11.30 (3 Mon)-11; 12-11 Sun ☎ (015242) 51226

gamecockinn.co.uk

Thwaites Nutty Black, Original; Wainwright; 1 changing beer [H]

Multi-roomed pub with the emphasis on good food. The old-fashioned bar, used mainly for drinking, has a warming real fire and is decorated with cartoons and old photos. Popular with locals, hikers and cyclists, it can be quite intimate, with conversation involving the whole room. There are two cosy snugs behind the bar, and the dining rooms extend into the small south-facing conservatory. Food specials include French night Wednesday, steak night Thursday, fish & chips Friday and Sunday roasts. Q❀◐Å♣P🚌(581)🐾

Aysgarth

George & Dragon 𝕃

DL8 3AD (on main A684 between Hawes and Leyburn)

12-11 ☎ (01969) 663358

georgeanddragonaysgarth.co.uk

Black Sheep Best Bitter; Theakston Best Bitter; house beer (by Yorkshire Dales); 1 changing beer (sourced locally) [H]

One of the Yorkshire Dales' most famous natural features, the famous Aysgarth falls on the River Ure, lies less than a mile away from this attractive 17th-century coaching inn. Drinkers are welcome in the pub's cosy, wood-panelled bar which serves up locally brewed real ales, while for diners there is a separate restaurant. An outside drinking area has great views of the stunning surrounding Wensleydale countryside. En-suite accommodation is available. Q☕❀◐Å♣P🚌🐾

Beck Hole

Birch Hall Inn ★ 𝕃

YO22 5LE (approx 1 mile N of Goathland)

11-11 ☎ (01947) 896245 beckhole.info

Black Sheep Best Bitter; North Yorkshire Beckwatter; 1 changing beer [H]

Unspoilt, family-run rural gem, resting among a hamlet of cottages, run by the same licensee, an accomplished fine artist, for 39 years. A winner of multiple CAMRA awards, only beers from Yorkshire are served. It comprises the Big Bar and the Small Bar, which sandwich a sweet shop. Pleasant outdoor drinking facilities overlook the Murk Esk. The house beer, Beckwatter, is brewed organically by North Yorkshire. Sandwiches, pies, beer cake and traditional sweets are always available. Hours change during winter. Q☕❀♿♣🍎🐾

Beckwithshaw

Smith's Arms 𝕃 ✔

Church Row, HG3 1QW

11-11 (midnight Sat); 11.30-10.30 Sun ☎ (01423) 504871

Black Sheep Best Bitter; Greene King IPA, Abbot; 2 changing beers (often Saltaire) [H]

A Chef & Brewer food-led venue in an 18th-century inn that, as the name suggests, was formerly a blacksmith's forge. Situated in a quiet hamlet to the south-west of Harrogate, the pub comprises an L-shaped bar area and a separate restaurant. An

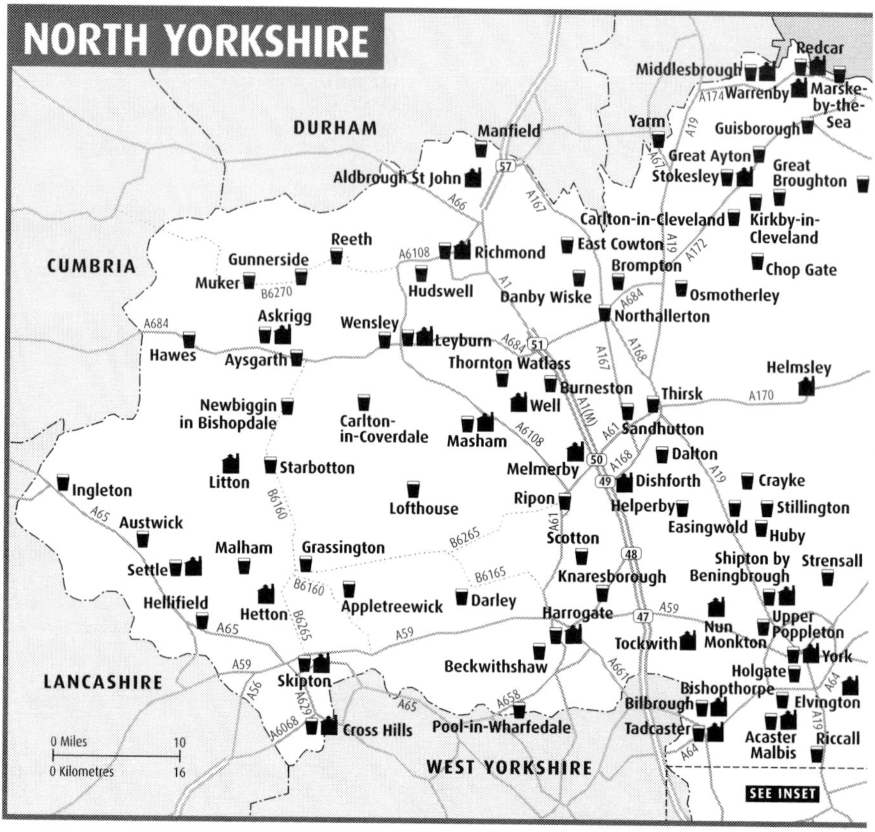

excellent menu with many seasonal dishes is available throughout the day in both the restaurant and bar. The five handpumps serve three permanent beers and widely sourced guest ales; flights of three thirds are available.
🐴❀◐♿P🐾📶

Bilbrough

Three Hares
Main Street, YO23 3PH
⏲ closed Mon; 12-2.30, 5.30-11; 12-11 Sat; 12-9 Sun
☎ (01937) 918005 🌐 thethreeharesinn.co.uk
Bilbrough Top Blond; Hambleton Stud Blonde; Timothy Taylor Landlord; 2 changing beers (sourced regionally; often Ossett, Theakston) Ⓗ
A comfortable and inviting village pub and the unofficial tap for the local Bilbrough Top Brewery. The three real ales are chosen in conjunction with the locals, and a gluten-free beer is available. A combination of traditional pub food and interesting specials, plus a regular quiz night and live music, make this a community hostelry that attracts locals and regulars from further afield. Q❀◐♿♣P🐾📶

Bishopthorpe

Ebor
46 Main Street, YO23 2RB
⏲ 11-midnight; 12-11.30 Sun ☎ (01904) 706190
Samuel Smith Old Brewery Bitter Ⓗ
Officially haunted, with 16th-century origins, this two-bar pub is uniquely the only tenanted Sam Smith's property. Landlord of 38 years Gordon Watkins provides a welcoming ambience, well-kept Old Brewery Bitter, and an extensive, home-cooked menu (Whitby fish a speciality and vegetarian and vegan options) lunchtime and evenings. The Ebor is at the heart of the local community, with a family atmosphere and a large beer garden. 🐴❀◐♿▲♣P🚌(11)🐾📶

Marcia Ⓛ ✔
29 Main Street, YO23 2RA
⏲ 11-midnight; 12-11 Sun ☎ (01904) 706185
Leeds Pale; Ossett Yorkshire Blonde; Rooster's Yankee; Timothy Taylor Landlord; 2 changing beers (sourced locally; often Half Moon, Treboom, York) Ⓗ
Welcoming and popular village local where the landlord is passionate about real ale, offering six handpumps serving mainly LocAle. There is an annual summer beer and cider festival in the large rear garden which has a children's play area. A good range of food is served every day in the bar and the large restaurant/conservatory, including award-winning fish and chips. The pub has a relaxed and friendly atmosphere, pub games and occasional live music. Quiz night is Wednesday.
Q🐴❀◐♿▲♣P🚌(11)🐾📶

Brompton

Green Tree
Stokesley Road, DL6 2UA
⏲ closed Mon; 5-11; 12-10 Sun ☎ (01609) 780251

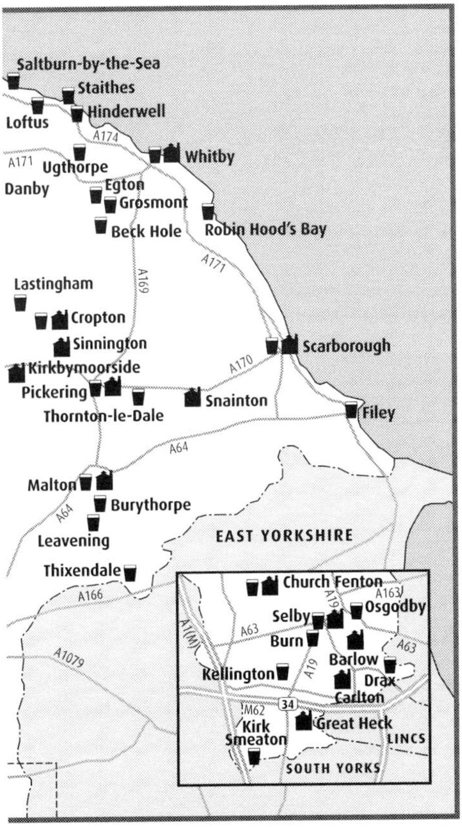

Beer Monkey Bitter Revival; Theakston Best Bitter; 3 changing beers (sourced locally) H

Situated on the edge of the village on the main A684 Northallerton-Osmotherley road, this traditional single-room free house retains the feel of a friendly community local. There are two distinct drinking areas either side of a central bar, with real fires at both ends of the room. To the rear, a sheltered beer garden includes a quoits pitch and is a suntrap on a good day. Guest beers are usually from Yorkshire microbreweries.
P

Burn

Wheatsheaf L

Main Road, YO8 8LJ
12-11 (midnight Fri & Sat) ☎ (01757) 270614
wheatsheafburn.co.uk
5 changing beers (often Brown Cow, Great Heck, Ossett) H

Traditional country pub serving a varied range of guest beers mainly from Yorkshire breweries. A narrow entrance leads to the bar, with a small room to the left and a spacious lounge with a huge open fire to the right. There is a collection of artefacts from bygone days and memorabilia of 578 and 431 Squadrons, stationed at Burn in WWII. Food is served every lunchtime and Wednesday to Saturday evenings. Regular beer festivals, a popular Sunday quiz night and occasional live entertainment take place.
Q P (476,405)

Burneston

Woodman Inn

Main Street, DL8 2HX
12-2.30, 5.30-11; 12-11 Sat & Sun ☎ (01677) 426123
thewoodmaninnburneston.co.uk
Theakston Best Bitter; 2 changing beers (sourced locally; often Pennine) H

A comfortable, family-run village pub catering for locals and visitors. It is now bypassed by the nearby A1(M) motorway but can be easily reached from the parallel service road for non-motorway traffic. A thriving community free house, it has a pleasant decor with an inviting bar and a separate dining area. There is usually something going on – Tuesday is steak night, Wednesday has an open mic session and there is a quiz each Thursday.
Q P

Burythorpe

Bay Horse

Main Street, YO17 9LH
11.30-11.30 ☎ (01653) 658302
thebayhorsealehouse.co.uk
Ossett Yorkshire Blonde; Theakston Best Bitter; 3 changing beers (sourced locally; often All Hallows, JW Lees, Wadworth) H

Nestled in the Yorkshire Wolds, the Bay Horse was reopened in 2016 following extensive renovation and has the homely feel of a family farmhouse, with open fireplaces, traditional furniture and a tiled floor. A wide range of beers is on offer including three from the All Hallows Brewery at Goodmanham. The menu is wide ranging and adventurous, using locally sourced ingredients and attractively priced, with a steak and pie night on Tuesday. Q P

Carlton-in-Cleveland

Blackwell Ox Inn

TS9 7DJ (800yds E of A172)
11.30-11 ☎ (01642) 712287 blackwellox.co.uk
4 changing beers H

Set in a beautiful area on the northern edge of the North York Moors, with the same licensee for over 30 years, this popular, multi-roomed village inn is as renowned for its fine beers as it is for its authentic Thai food. Look out for the lunchtime and early-doors food offers. But you do not have to eat; four handpumps provide an eclectic range of beers in various styles. The garden has an extensive well-designed children's play area. Q P (89)

Carlton-in-Coverdale

Foresters Arms L

DL8 4BB
closed Mon & Tue; 12-3, 6-11 Wed & Fri; 12-3, 5-11 Thu; 12-3, 6-midnight Sat; 12-4, 7-11 Sun ☎ (01969) 640272
forestersarms-carlton.co.uk
Theakston Best Bitter; Wensleydale Coverdale Gamekeeper; 3 changing beers (sourced locally; often Black Sheep, Yorkshire Dales) H

Worth seeking out, this 250-year-old free house is named after the Foresters Friendly Society, a mutual aid body for local people in this picturesque area. It is on the Dales cycle route and convenient for the Forbidden Corner fantasy maze (advance booking essential). In community ownership since 2011, the pub's low-beamed ceilings and open fire contribute to its character, with wooden settles fashioned from pews from the former village church. There is always a guest ale, almost always from a Yorkshire brewery. Q🐴🛏🍽♿♣P🐾📶

Chop Gate

Buck Inn 🄻

Chop Gate, TS9 7JL (on B1257, between Stokesley and Helmsley)

⏲ 12 (5 Mon-Wed)-9 ☎ (01642) 778334

🌐 the-buck-inn.co.uk

3 changing beers 🄷

Set amid a walkers' paradise, and close to the route of Wainwright's Coast-to-Coast walk, this picturesque family-run village pub offers a truly Yorkshire/Teutonic twist. Three locally sourced beers and seven specially imported draught lagers, brewed under the 504-year-old German Purity Laws, are served, together with real home-made food, again half-Yorkshire/half-German. There are six en-suite bedrooms, some designated dog-friendly, while free camping is offered to those campers who also choose to dine here. Check winter opening hours. Q🐴❀🛏🍽▲♣P🐾📶

Church Fenton

Fenton Flyer 🄻 ✔

Main Street, LS24 9RF

⏲ 4-midnight; 12-midnight Sat; 12-11.30 Sun

☎ (01937) 558137

Rat White Rat; 4 changing beers (sourced regionally; often Ilkley, Leeds, Ossett) 🄷

Friendly village pub with pictures of the nearby WWII airbase which is now a commercial airport. The beers are chosen from the SIBA list and are often LocAle. It has live music on the first Friday of each month, a monthly Saturday disco with karaoke, and a quiz night on Wednesday raising money for local charities. There is a Sky and BT Sports TV in the main bar and an adjacent games room with pool table and darts. Beer festivals are held in June and November.

🐴❀▲♣P🚌(492)🐾📶

Crayke

Durham Ox

Westway, YO61 4TE

⏲ 12-11; 11-10.30 Sun ☎ (01347) 821506

🌐 thedurhamox.com

Black Sheep Best Bitter; Timothy Taylor Boltmaker; York Guzzler; 1 changing beer 🄷

A fine-dining pub, winner of numerous food awards, but not exclusively so, with a separate bar for drinkers. Walkers and cyclists will feel at home here too. Live music plays on Thursday evenings, usually of the jazz/folk variety. Accommodation is available for those who wish to linger longer in the scenic Howardian Hills overlooking the Vale of York. Q🐴❀🛏🍽♿P🚌🐾📶

Cropton

New Inn 🄻

Cropton Lane, YO18 8HH (leave A170 at Wrelton and follow signs for Cropton)

⏲ 11-11 (midnight Fri & Sat) ☎ (01751) 417330

🌐 newinncropton.co.uk

Great Yorkshire Classic, Golden, Moors, Blackout, Monkmans Slaughter; 1 changing beer (sourced locally; often Great Yorkshire) 🄷

A family-run pub on the edge of the North Yorkshire Moors National Park, this is the tap for the Great Yorkshire Brewery (formerly Cropton Brewery). An attractive stone building, it is the perfect base for walking and cycling, offering good food in the bars, conservatory and restaurant, and both B&B and camping. With up to six of the well-regarded Great Yorkshire ales on offer, it does not get more LocAle than this. A legendary beer festival is held every November, plus a music festival in the summer.

Q🐴❀🛏🍽♿▲♣P🚆🚌🐾📶

Cross Hills

Gallagher's Ale House 🄻

1-3 East Keltus, BD20 8TD (in village centre)

⏲ closed Mon & Tue; 3-10 Wed & Thu; 1-11 Fri; 12-11 Sat; 12-8 Sun ☎ 07834 456134

REAL ALE BREWERIES

Ainsty Acaster Malbis
BAD Dishforth
Bad Seed Malton
Beer Monkey Skipton
Bilbrough Top Bilbrough
Black Sheep Masham
Brass Castle Malton
Brew York York
Brown Cow Barlow
Captain Cook Stokesley
Crooked Church Fenton
Daleside Harrogate
Dark Horse Hetton
Great British Breworks 🛢 Pickering
Great Heck Great Heck
Great Yorkshire 🛢 Cropton
Hambleton Melmerby
Harrogate Harrogate
Helmsley Helmsley
Hop Studio Elvington
Hops & Dots Middlesbrough (NEW)
Jolly Sailor 🛢 Selby
Lady Luck 🛢 Whitby
LAMB 🛢 Litton (NEW)
Little Black Dog Carlton
Mithril Aldbrough St John
Naylor's Cross Hills
North Riding (Brewery) Snainton
North Riding (Brewpub) 🛢 Scarborough
North Yorkshire Warrenby
Pennine Well
Redscar 🛢 Redcar
Richmond Richmond
Rooster's Harrogate
Rudgate Tockwith
Ryedale Sinnington
Samuel Smith Tadcaster
Scarborough Scarborough
Settle Settle
Taylor Illingworth Middlesbrough
Theakston Masham
Three Peaks Settle
Treboom Shipton-by-Beningbrough
Turning Point Kirkbymoorside
Wensleydale Leyburn
Whitby Whitby
Yorkshire Dales Askrigg
Yorkshire Heart Nun Monkton

5 changing beers (sourced nationally) Ⓗ
This popular micropub, established in 2015, is in what used to be Gallagher's bookmakers'. The five changing ales usually include a dark beer, a pale bitter and a strong or speciality beer. The cellar can be viewed through a window to the left of the bar. No electronic music or TV disturb the conversation. Parking is available adjacent to the Co-op store round the corner. The phone number is shared with the Beer Engine in Skipton. Q♣●🚌(M4,66)🐾📶

Dalton

Jolly Farmers Inn Ⓛ
Brookside, YO7 3HY
⏲ 4-11; 12-midnight Sat & Sun ☎ (01845) 578053
John Smith's Bitter; 1 changing beer Ⓗ
Large village local in the heart of a working village. The three rooms offer drinking, dining and pub games, with sports TV in the bar and the games room. Various pub games league teams are supported by the regulars. Accommodation is available across the courtyard from the main building in what were formerly outbuildings. The village is conveniently located close to the A1M and A19 near the foot of the North York Moors escarpment. A takeaway food service is available.
♣P🐾

Danby

Duke of Wellington Ⓛ
West Lane, YO21 2LY (300yds N of railway station)
⏲ 12-2.30 (not Mon), 7-11; 12-11 Fri-Sun ☎ (01287) 660351
🌐 dukeofwellingtondanby.co.uk
Daleside Bitter; Whitby Saltwick Nab; 1 changing beer Ⓗ
An 18th-century inn, and previous local CAMRA Pub of the Year, set in idyllic countryside, close to the Moors National Park Centre and equally popular traditional local bakery. The inn was used as a recruiting post during the Napoleonic Wars. A cast-iron plaque of the first Duke of Wellington, unearthed during restorations, hangs above the fireplace. All beers are from Yorkshire, with cider/perry served Easter to October. The kitchen offers traditional British home-cooked meals at their best, using local produce. Q≥♣●🚌🐾

Danby Wiske

White Swan Ⓛ
DL7 0NQ (approx 3 miles N of Northallerton off A167)
⏲ 12-11 ☎ (01609) 775131
🌐 thewhiteswandanbywiske.co.uk
Three Brothers The Ex Wife; 3 changing beers (sourced locally; often Three Brothers) Ⓗ
A much-appreciated inn on the 192-mile Coast-to-Coast route, this village green pub offers a warm welcome to walkers and locals alike. The opened-out interior features a stone floor and wood-burning stoves, and is home to the local sword dancers. A cider and a perry are usually available. Food is served April to October and geared to walkers' needs, with lunchtime snacks and hearty evening meals using much locally sourced produce – booking is advisable. Winter hours vary and are much more limited (closed Tue, evenings only weekdays, closed weekend afternoons).
Q⛺♣●P🐾📶

Darley

Wellington Inn Ⓛ
Main Street, HG3 2QQ (on B6451 W of village)
⏲ 12-10.30 (11.30 Fri & Sat); 12-10 Sun ☎ (01423) 780362
🌐 wellington-inn.co.uk
Black Sheep Best Bitter; Tetley Bitter; Timothy Taylor Boltmaker, Knowle Spring Ⓗ
Popular, much-extended, stone-built pub on the edge of Nidderdale. It is a food-led establishment, but with a range of well-kept ales from Yorkshire and further afield. The original pub houses a comfortable bar with pool table and dartboard, and the long extension provides more space, essentially for diners, in a baronial hall-styled room - the fireplace is especially magnificent. Behind is a dining room and separate conservatory with spectacular views across Nidderdale. There are bench tables outside at the front.
Q♣P🚌(24)🐾📶

Drax

Drax Sports & Social Club ✔
Main Road, YO8 8PJ
⏲ 8am-11 ☎ (01757) 618041 🌐 draxsandsclub.co.uk
2 changing beers (sourced regionally)
Nestled in the shadow of the giant Drax power station, this club is full of energy and enthusiasm. A lively bar area is supplemented by a huge function room which is often the venue for beer festivals and similar events. The club takes a little effort to get to, but there are some buses from nearby Selby. A well-deserved CAMRA branch Club of the Year in 2018.

Easingwold

George Hotel Ⓛ ✔
Market Place, YO61 3AD
⏲ 11-11 ☎ (01347) 821698
Black Sheep Best Bitter; Timothy Taylor Boltmaker; 1 changing beer (sourced regionally) Ⓗ
A smart country hotel in the centre of this attractive Georgian town just north of York. Step off the bus and cross the road to enjoy an unstuffy atmosphere at any time of day. High standards are maintained throughout and this extends to the beer. The guest is usually from a Yorkshire brewery and sometimes there will be more than one on offer. Shut the door when you go in – you may be there for a while.
Q♿P🚌📶

East Cowton

Beeswing
Main Road, DL7 0BD
⏲ 4-11; 12-11 Fri; 11.30-11 Sat & Sun ☎ (01325) 378349
🌐 thebeeswing.weebly.com
3 changing beers (sourced nationally) Ⓗ
Traditional country village pub with two bars, a pool room and a highly rated restaurant. Named after a locally bred champion racehorse, there are numerous racing references here. It serves up to three different beers from breweries countrywide, and one craft beer. Real fires create a relaxing atmosphere, and the staff are welcoming. It supports the local community with regular music and quizzes, and has a pool table.
Q♿♣P🐾📶

Egton

Wheatsheaf Inn ⃝

YO21 1TZ
✪ closed Mon; 11.30-2.45, 5.30-11; 11.30-11 Sat & Sun
☎ (01947) 895271 ⊕ wheatsheafegton.com
Black Sheep Best Bitter; Timothy Taylor Landlord; 2 changing beers Ⓗ
Winner of many industry awards, this Grade II-listed 19th-century pub serves four Yorkshire beers. It is now in its 20th year in the Guide, and remains under the stewardship of a licensee with over 30 years of continuous Guide recognition. Church pews, country collectables and a roaring range add to the ambience. The grassy area to the front and boules to the rear are ideal for summer drinking. The renowned first-class restaurant always features local meat, fish and game.
Q✿🏠◑🏃♿♣P🖵(95)🐾

Filey

Bonhomme's Bar

Royal Crescent Court, The Crescent, YO14 9JH
✪ 11-midnight (1am Fri & Sat) ☎ (01723) 515325
Isaac Poad Bonhommes Best; Rudgate Ruby Mild; 5 changing beers (sourced nationally; often S43, Scarborough) Ⓗ
Near the fine Victorian Royal Crescent Hotel complex, this bar's name celebrates John Paul Jones, father of the American Navy. His ship, the Bonhomme Richard, was involved in a battle off nearby Flamborough Head during the War of Independence. Five handpumps deliver rotating guest beers. A quiz is held on Thursday evening and Saturday afternoon each week. Live music features most Sundays from 4pm.
🏃🅰🚞♣●🖵(12,13)🐾🛜

Cobbler's Arms

2 Union Street, YO14 9DZ
✪ 4 (12 Sat & Sun)-11 summer; 4-9 Mon; 4-11 Tue & Fri; 4-10 Wed & Thu; 12-11 Sat; 12-9 Sun winter ☎ (01723) 512511
Wainwright; 4 changing beers (sourced regionally; often Great Newsome, Isaac Poad, Milestone) Ⓗ
Micropub in the centre of Filey which started out as a private residence before becoming the cobbler's shop from which it takes its name. The front bar area encourages conversation and there is a second smaller snug to the rear which is available for meetings, free of charge. The bar offers four changing guest ales and seven real ciders. Families are welcome. There is a regular quiz on a Tuesday night and live music occasionally.
Q🏃♿🚞●🖵(12,13)🐾🛜

Star Inn ⃝

23 Mitford Street, YO14 9DX
✪ 12-midnight (1am Fri & Sat) ☎ (01723) 512031
⊕ thestarfiley.co.uk
Black Sheep Ale; Bradfield Farmers Blonde; Theakston Best Bitter; 3 changing beers (sourced nationally) Ⓗ
An inn just off Filey town centre with a large main room and separate restaurant/function room. Three regular beers and three rotating guests are offered. Freshly cooked meals are served lunchtimes and evenings (no food Mon). Live entertainment features occasionally, and pub teams participate in a local pool league. Smokers are catered for both front and rear of the building, while parking is provided behind the pub.
🏃✿◑♿♣●P🖵(12,13)🛜

Grassington

Foresters Arms ⃝ ✓

20 Main Street, BD23 5AA
✪ 11-midnight (1am Fri & Sat) ☎ (01756) 752349
⊕ forestersarmsgrassington.co.uk
Black Sheep Best Bitter, Riggwelter; Tetley Bitter; Timothy Taylor Landlord; Wharfedale Blonde; 1 changing beer (sourced locally; often Tetley, Timothy Taylor) Ⓗ
Close to the cobbled town square, the Foresters is a lively inn, popular with locals and visitors alike, which has been run by the same family for decades. The main bar and pool/TV area are to the left and further seating to the right leads to a separate dining room. Accommodation is available in seven en-suite rooms, and fishing permits for the local River Wharfe can be bought at the pub. The quiz is on Mondays. Secure cycle storage is available for staying guests.
🏃✿🏠◑♣●🖵(72,72B)🐾🛜⟲

Great Ayton

Royal Oak Hotel ⃝ ✓

123 High Street, TS9 6BW (in centre of village opp High Green)
✪ 10-11 (midnight Fri & Sat); 11.30-11 Sun
☎ (01642) 722361 ⊕ royaloakgreatayton.co.uk
Theakston Old Peculier; Timothy Taylor Landlord; Wainwright; 1 changing beer Ⓗ
A warm welcome is extended at this 18th-century Grade II-listed building and former coaching inn, at the heart of village life. Always busy, the pub is as famed for its four beers as for its food – breakfast, lunch and dinner are served – with offers on food throughout the week. There is also a takeaway service. The premises include an enclosed courtyard to the rear, a function room and four en-suite bedrooms. Q🏃✿🏠◑●🖵(28,81)

Great Broughton

Bay Horse ⃝

88 High Street, TS9 7HA (at S end of village)
✪ 11.30-3, 5.30-11; 11.30-11 Sat; 12-11 Sun
☎ (01642) 712319 ⊕ thebayhorse-greatbroughton.co.uk
Camerons Strongarm; 3 changing beers Ⓗ
Visitors and locals alike enjoy the welcoming hospitality offered by the friendly bar staff at this spacious village country inn, situated beneath one of the northern entrances to the North York Moors. Always busy, with an emphasis on good-value, freshly prepared, home-cooked meals, the pub also caters well for drinkers. As well as the Strongarm, which the pub has served for many years, three changing guest beers from the Marston's stable are also available.
Q🏃✿◑P🖵(89)

Grosmont

Crossing Club

Co-operative Building, Front Street, YO22 5QE
✪ 8-11 ☎ 07766 197744
4 changing beers Ⓗ
Set amid beautiful scenery in the Esk Valley, this former local CAMRA Club of the Year is opposite the NYMR/Esk Valley railway stations in what was the village Co-op's delivery bay. Converted by dedicated villagers 21 years ago, a warm welcome always awaits CAMRA members. Up to four beers

are on offer, while over 1,250 different beers have been served during the club's history. For railway enthusiasts, both steam and diesel memorabilia adorn the walls. Hours vary in winter. Ring the doorbell for entry. Q≹♣▯🐾

Guisborough

Monk L ✔

27 Church Street, TS14 6HG (at E end of Westgate)
⏲ closed Mon; 5-11 Tue; 11.30-3, 5-11 Wed; 11.30-11.45 Thu-Sat; 12-11 Sun ☎ (01287) 205058
Timothy Taylor Landlord; 4 changing beers Ⓗ
This contemporary venue is an upmarket addition to the town's social life and attracts a discerning clientele. It is opposite Gisborough Priory, which was razed to the ground by King Henry VIII in 1540. The pub is aptly named as, legend has it, the 12th-century Black Monk made use of a tunnel, discovered during recent renovations, for his nefarious night-time activities. The tunnel's access steps are now on view. Five beers and a real cider are served. Good-value four-drink paddles are available. ♿🍎🚌(5,X93)🐾📶

Gunnerside

King's Head L

DL11 6LD
⏲ 12-11; 12-10.30 Sun ☎ (01748) 886261
🌐 kingsheadgunnerside.com
Black Sheep Best Bitter; 2 changing beers Ⓗ
An atmospheric inn occupying a village corner next to Gunnerside Beck. Settled by the Vikings, this was once a lead-mining centre, for which most of the cottages were built in the 18th century. It later gave its name to the commando raid made famous in the film The Heroes of Telemark. The single-room stone-flagged bar is dominated by a magnificent stone fireplace and offers a range of bar snacks and home-cooked meals. There is a happy hour 6-7pm on Fridays and a pub quiz on alternate Sundays. Q🔥◐▲♣🚌🐾

Harrogate

Blues Café Bar L

4 Montpellier Parade, HG1 2TJ
⏲ 12-1am; 12-11 Sun ☎ (01423) 566881 🌐 bluesbar.co.uk
4 changing beers (often Daleside, Ossett, Rooster's) Ⓗ
Small single-room bar in the town centre overlooking the lovely Montpellier gardens. Noted for live music seven days a week with three sessions on a Sunday, it is popular with music lovers and can get busy. Modelled on an Amsterdam café bar, it has been going for more than 30 years. Four handpumps dispense beers mostly from local breweries, usually including one dark beer. Food is served in the evenings Wednesday to Saturday. ◐≹🚌📶↺

Coach & Horses L

16 West Park, HG1 1BJ
⏲ 11-11; 12-10.30 Sun ☎ (01423) 561802
🌐 thecoachandhorses.net
Daleside Bitter, Blonde; Tetley Bitter; Timothy Taylor Landlord; 4 changing beers Ⓗ
A busy traditional pub popular with locals and visitors and overlooking Harrogate's famous Stray. A central bar is surrounded by snugs and alcoves, creating a cosy atmosphere. Tables are provided outside for customers in summer while window boxes create a spectacular display adding year-round colour. Eight handpumps dispense four regular and four changing beers. Excellent meals are served lunchtimes with frequent themed food evenings; these, together with a Sunday night quiz, have raised over £1 million for a local children's hospice. Q◐≹🚌📶↺

Harrogate Tap

Station Parade, HG1 1TE
⏲ 11-11 (midnight Fri); 10-midnight Sat ☎ (01423) 501644
11 changing beers (often Harrogate, Rooster's) Ⓗ
Overlooking Harrogate station, this is an impressive transformation of a neglected railway building into a fine pub of similar style to the Tapped Brew Company's other bars in York and Sheffield. Comprising a long bar room and a separate snug, the decor features dark-wood panelling, tiled floor and tasteful Victorian-style fittings. A diverse range of cask ales is available on 12 handpumps, with one devoted to cider. The cask ales are complemented by craft kegs and bottled world beers. Bar snacks are served. 🔥♿≹🍎🚌🐾📶

Little Ale House

7 Cheltenham Crescent, HG1 1DH
⏲ 2-9 (10 Thu & Fri); 12-10 Sat; 1-7 Sun ☎ (01423) 391996
🌐 alehouseharrogate.co.uk
5 changing beers Ⓗ
Harrogate's first micropub, comprising one room with the counter at the back and a downstairs cellar room. As in many other micropubs, the beers are kept cool in a glass cabinet to one side. Five handpumps dispense cask beers and there is always at least one real cider. KeyKeg and local artisan gins are also stocked. There is an outside seating area at the front as well as a pleasant yard with pub benches at the rear, with service at the window in summer. Q❀≹🍎🚌🐾📶

Major Tom's Social

The Ginnel, HG1 2RB
⏲ 12-11.30 (1am Fri & Sat) ☎ (01423) 566984
🌐 majortomssocial.co.uk
4 changing beers Ⓗ
Described on its website as a youth club for grown-ups, this café bar housed above a vintage shop provides real ale, craft keg, pizza, music and art all in one package. Simply furnished with wooden tables, bench seating and plastic chairs, it has some soft furnishings in one corner. The decor is in a mix of styles to suit its eclectic customers, including artwork for sale. Four handpumps dispense a variety of ales, usually from a range of smaller breweries. 🔥◐≹🚌🐾📶

Old Bell L ✔

6 Royal Parade, HG1 2SZ
⏲ 12-11; 12-10.30 Sun ☎ (01423) 507930
Theakston Best Bitter; Timothy Taylor Boltmaker; 6 changing beers (often Ilkley, Leeds, Rooster's) Ⓗ
A Market Town Taverns pub, the Old Bell opened in 1999 on the site of the Blue Bell Inn which closed in 1815 and was later demolished. In 2001 it expanded into the former Farrah's toffee shop where there is a collection of Farrah's memorabilia. The pub was refurbished in 2017 with leather armchairs and revised decoration. Eight handpumps serve a changing beer range, including two regular and six changing beers, usually a Rooster's and a dark beer. 🔥◐≹🚌🐾📶

Starling Independent Bar Café Kitchen

47 Oxford Street, HG1 1PW
9am-10 (11 Thu-Sat); 10-9 Sun (01423) 531310
murmurationbars.co.uk
Hawkshead Windermere Pale; 4 changing beers (often Harrogate, Rooster's)
A modern bar and coffee shop in a converted shop, also serving stone-baked pizzas. It has a contemporary look with whitewashed, stripped-back brickwork. One wall features a mural of a murmuration of starlings in homage to the owners. The pallet-fronted counter holds six pulls with a well chosen range of mainly Yorkshire beers, offering a good mix of styles and strengths. In addition to the regular Windy, there are often beers from the local Harrogate Brewing Co and Rooster's Brewery, and the sixth pump is devoted to real cider.

Hawes

Board Inn

Market Place, DL8 3RD
11-midnight (01969) 667223 theboardinn.co.uk
Black Sheep Best Bitter; Theakston Best Bitter; Timothy Taylor Landlord; 1 changing beer (sourced nationally)
A comfortable and traditional pub in the heart of this busy Dales centre, popular with walkers and other visitors. The main front bar has a warming coal fire in winter and there is also a pleasant dining room, plus an outdoor seating area at the front. Home-cooked food is served all day during the summer but not during winter afternoons. There are five en-suite letting rooms.

Fountain Hotel

Market Place, DL8 3RD
11-11 (01969) 667206 fountainhawes.co.uk
Black Sheep Best Bitter; 4 changing beers (sourced locally)
This thriving Dales community free house is located on the Pennine Way and is popular with walkers and other outdoor enthusiasts. In the same hands for more than 30 years, this 17th century inn old coaching inn has a spacious interior and offers good value food, served until 9pm in summer. There is TV sport and up to four guest ales are usually available, often from local breweries such as Wensleydale, Yorkshire Dales and Theakston's. Sunday food hours may vary. Accommodation is in 11 en-suite bedrooms. The Dales Countryside Museum is nearby. P

Hellifield

Black Horse Hotel

Main Road, BD23 4HT
12-11 (7 Sun) summer; 3-11; 12-11 Fri & Sat; 12-7 Sun winter (01729) 851402
3 changing beers
This large, rambling village pub is a popular venue for dining and drinking. The spacious main lounge has comfy settees and coffee tables surrounded by more conventional seating. Note the collection of musical instruments. There is also a taproom, accessed off the main A65, and a small dining room suitable for meetings and family gatherings. Paved areas either side of the building offer ample outdoor seating. Three changing real ales are on the bar (four in summer), often from local breweries. On Sunday there is a carvery.
P (580)

Helperby

Golden Lion

Main Street, YO61 2NT
5 (4 Sat)-11; 12-11 Sun (01423) 360601
Theakston Best Bitter; 2 changing beers (sourced nationally)
In the historic centre of the village, this is one of two pubs left of an original six. It supports village sports teams, has its own pool and darts teams, and also fundraises for local charities with regular events. The pub offers entertainment including live music, a quiz, sports TV and a jukebox. Although just one room, the sound is zoned so you can have a quiet drink or listen to the jukebox or TV as takes your fancy. Adnams Bitter makes a regular appearance among the beers.
P (29,31)

Hinderwell

Brown Cow

55 High Street, TS13 5ET (on A174)
11-midnight (1am Fri); 12-midnight Sun
(01947) 840694
2 changing beers
Pubs like this are hard to find! Set between the moors and the coast, and with an interior reminiscent of a 1960s front parlour, this longstanding family-run inn offers two interesting rotating guest beers. The pub supports darts teams, charity nights and domino drives, and has a quiz night on Sunday. Children and dogs are welcome, while smokers are well provided for. Bar snacks are available all day alongside more substantial lunchtime and evening meals. Accommodation is in four bedrooms. Q P (X4)

Holgate

Fox

168 Holgate Road, YO24 4DQ
12-11 (midnight Thu-Sat) (01904) 787722
Ossett Yorkshire Blonde, Silver King, Excelsior; Rat White Rat; Tetley Bitter; 4 changing beers (sourced regionally; often Fernandes, Rat, Riverhead)
Set in the Holgate district of York, the Fox is a pub whose history is linked to the golden age of rail. Sympathetically restored by Ossett Brewery in 2014, it is a blue plaque heritage inn, making it a must-visit for anyone seeking out the city's finest historic pubs. It offers a good range of Ossett beers plus real cider and interesting guest ales. The pub also has a large and popular beer garden.
P (1,5)

Huby

Mended Drum

Tollerton Road, YO61 1HT
5-11.30; 4-midnight Fri; 12-12.30am Sat; 12-11.30 Sun
(01347) 810264 themendeddrum.com
Tetley Bitter; 4 changing beers (sourced locally; often Brass Castle)
Large open-plan pub that is bigger than it looks. It is the lively centre of this rural community and is known for its interesting range of frequently changing local beers and knowledgeable staff. The

food is pretty popular, too. York CAMRA branch Pub of the Year 2019 and well worth seeking out. ⛄🕯🍴♿🅰♣●🅿🚻(X30)🐾🛜

Hudswell

George & Dragon 🍺 Ⓛ
DL11 6BL
🕐 11-3, 5-11; 11-11 Sat & Sun ☎ (01748) 518373
🌐 georgeanddragonhudswell.co.uk
Rudgate Ruby Mild; Wensleydale Falconer Session Bitter; 4 changing beers (sourced locally) Ⓗ
Rescued from closure by the local community in 2010, this homely, two-roomed village inn became CAMRA's National Pub of the Year just six years later. It now features its own library, shop, allotments and other local facilities as well as great food and Yorkshire-brewed beers, together with a selection of nearly 70 whiskies. A large beer terrace to the rear offers stunning panoramic views over the Swale valley and it is a pleasant hike from Richmond, so long as you do not mind the 300-plus steps! Open all day bank holidays.
Q⛄🕯🍴🅰♣●🅿🚻(32)🐾🛜

Ingleton

Masons
New Road, LA6 3HL
🕐 2-11; 12-11 Sat; 12-10 Sun ☎ (015242) 42040
🌐 masonsismoran.co.uk
Sharp's Doom Bar; 4 changing beers Ⓗ
Early-Victorian building on the busy main road away from the centre of this popular tourist village. Extensively refurbished in 2016, it is now a true family-run free house. A small bar counter serves a long drinking space of linked areas with light and airy decor. Live music takes place, but not yet regularly. There is a patio with a glazed roof.
🚪🕯🅰🅿🚻(80)🐾🛜

Kellington

Red Lion
1 Ings Lane, DN14 0NT (follow road from A19 into centre of village)
🕐 3 (2 Fri)-2am; 12-2am Sat & Sun ☎ (01977) 661008
🌐 redlionkellington.co.uk
Brown Cow White Dragon; 1 changing beer (sourced locally; often Batemans, Bradfield, Brown Cow) Ⓗ
A friendly family-run pub which plays an active part in the local community. A genuine free house, it always has two cask ales on, usually from the nearby Brown Cow Brewery. To cater for all tastes, the choice of cask ales normally includes one dark and one light beer. A recent local CAMRA award winner, the pub hosts quizzes, live entertainment and events in support of local charities. Happy hour is 5-6pm weekdays. Q⛄🕯🚪♿♣🅿🐾🛜

Kirk Smeaton

Shoulder of Mutton
Main Street, WF8 3JY (follow signs from A1)
🕐 12-midnight; 11.30-midnight Sun ☎ (01977) 620348
Black Sheep Best Bitter; 1 changing beer (sourced regionally; often Theakston) Ⓗ
Convenient for the Went Valley and Brockadale Nature Reserve, this welcoming, traditional village pub is popular with walkers and the local community. The beer comes direct from the brewery and the quality is superb. It is an award-

winning free house and comprises a large lounge with open fires and a cosy, dark-panelled snug. The spacious beer garden has a covered and heated shelter for smokers, and there is ample parking. Quiz night is Tuesday. Q⛄🕯♣🅿🚻(409)🐾🛜

Kirkby-in-Cleveland

Black Swan
Busby Lane, TS9 7AW (800yds W of B1257) NZ539060
🕐 12-midnight ☎ (01642) 712512
Bradfield Farmers Blonde; Sharp's Doom Bar; Timothy Taylor Landlord; Wainwright; 1 changing beer Ⓗ
Nestling at the foot of the Cleveland Hills, at the crossroads of this ancient village, this warm and cosy free house comprises a bar, an adjacent pool room, a lounge/restaurant, a pleasant conservatory and a patio seating area. A genuine welcome is always afforded from the friendly staff. Four regular beers, together with a changing guest beer, are stocked, while good-value meals are served every day from a comprehensive restaurant menu, including daily specials and bar meals.
⛄🕯🍴♿♣●🅿🚻(89)🐾🛜

Knaresborough

Blind Jack's Ⓛ
19 Market Place, HG5 8AL
🕐 5 (12 Wed)-11; 12-11 Fri & Sat; 12-10.30 Sun
☎ (01423) 860475
Black Sheep Best Bitter; 6 changing beers Ⓗ
A multi-roomed pub with bare-brick walls, wooden floorboards and panelling. This award-winning alehouse provides a focal point both for locals and the many visitors who appreciate the excellent selection of ales, cosy ambience and lively banter. The beer range usually includes some from smaller national and Yorkshire breweries, including at least one dark beer, and also a range of craft kegs. The pub has been listed in the Guide since 1993. Q🚶🚉🚻🐾🛜

Cross Keys ✓
17 Cheapside, HG5 8AX
🕐 4-11; 12-midnight Fri & Sat; 12-11 Sun ☎ (01423) 863562
Ossett Yorkshire Brunette, Yorkshire Blonde, Silver King; Rat White Rat; 3 changing beers (sourced regionally; often Fernandes, Riverhead) Ⓗ
A former Tetley's house, refurbished by Ossett Brewery in its trademark style of stone-flagged floors, bare-brick walls and stained glass. This traditional pub serves four regular beers, including three from Ossett, one from Rat Brewery and three changing guests, one of which is usually a dark beer from either a microbrewery or from one of the other breweries within the Ossett company. Thursday is quiz night and a live band plays on most Saturday nights. Lunches are served on Sundays. ⛄🕯🚉●🅿🚻🐾🛜♺

Half Moon Ⓛ
1 Abbey Road, HG5 8HY
🕐 5 (4 Fri)-11; 12-11 Sat; 12-10.30 Sun ☎ (01423) 313461
Rooster's Yorkshire Pale Ale; 3 changing beers (sourced locally) Ⓗ
A popular watering-hole down from the town by Low Bridge. This lovingly restored independent free house with bare-brick walls, a real fire and a wood-burning stove provides a welcoming atmosphere. Four handpumps dispense a varying range of beers, one from Rooster's and three

others often from Yorkshire breweries. The pub hosts a popular quiz every Tuesday, and a grazing menu of boards and light snacks is available every evening until 10pm. Dogs are welcome in the outdoor area. ▷⊛⊙◑≢⊟(22)☞

Mitre Hotel 🗓 ✅
4 Station Road, HG5 9AA (opp railway station)
🕐 12-11 ☎ (01423) 868948
Timothy Taylor Boltmaker; 5 changing beers (often Rooster's) H
Opposite Knaresborough's Grade II-listed railway station and signal box, this Market Town Taverns pub offers a modern split-level bar with wooden flooring throughout. There is a side room with additional seating, a function room in the basement and a south-facing paved terrace at the back with views of the local church. The six handpumps are on the lower bar and dispense a regular Timothy Taylor beer, a changing Rooster's beer and four others from Yorkshire and smaller national breweries. ▷⊛≢◑&≢⊟(1)⚘☞

Six Poor Folk 🗓 ✅
25 Castlegate, HG5 8AR
🕐 closed Mon; 3-11 Tue-Thu; 12-midnight Fri & Sat; 12-11 Sun
☎ (01423) 869918 ⊕ sixpoorfolk.com
4 changing beers (often Timothy Taylor) H
A former almshouse dating back to the 15th century, Six Poor Folk was converted from a restaurant to a bar in early 2018. It now serves four real ales from a range of national and Yorkshire breweries as well as craft kegs and a wide selection of cans and bottles. The pub hosts a themed quiz on Wednesday, a DJ playing soul and funk music on Friday, and an open mic night on Sunday. Roast dinners are served 12-3pm on Sunday. ⊛◑≢⊟⚘☞

Lastingham

Blacksmiths Arms
Anserdale Lane, YO62 6TN
🕐 11.30-11.30 ☎ (01751) 417247
⊕ blacksmithsarmslastingham.co.uk
Saltaire Blonde; Theakston Best Bitter; 1 changing beer (sourced regionally; often Daleside, Rudgate) H
Pretty stone inn in a conservation village opposite St Mary's church, famous for its 11th-century crypt. The interior comprises a cosy bar with a York range lit in winter, a snug, and two dining rooms. Excellent-quality food including local game dishes is served alongside interesting guest beers and a changing guest cider, often Thistly Cross. A secluded beer garden is to the rear, now with a pizza oven. This remote pub is popular with locals, walkers and shooting parties. Dogs are welcome outside only. Q▷≢◑◑●

Leavening

Jolly Farmers 🗓
Main Street, YO17 9SA
🕐 5.30-midnight; 12-midnight Sat & Sun ☎ (01653) 658276
Timothy Taylor Landlord; York Guzzler; 2 changing beers (sourced locally; often Great Newsome, Half Moon) H
Seventeenth-century pub on the edge of the Yorkshire Wolds between York and Malton. It has an intriguing series of rooms with low ceilings and tiled flagged floors, making it homely and welcoming, and serves locally sourced food and a

range of local and regional ales. The pub hosts annual beer and gin festivals. The outside drinking area boasts table football and a cask of drinking water for dogs, complete with handpump. A popular stopping off point for ramblers as well as locals. Q▷⊛◑&●P⊟⚘☞

Leyburn

Golden Lion 🗓
Market Place, DL8 5AS
🕐 11-11 ☎ (01969) 622161 ⊕ goldenlionleyburn.co.uk
John Smith's Bitter; Wensleydale Semerwater Summer Ale, Coverdale Gamekeeper; 1 changing beer (sourced locally) H
Facing the main square of this busy and attractive Dales centre, this traditional market-town pub is a short walk from the revived Wensleydale Railway, with steam trains in summer. The comfortable main bar area is opened out and largely wood-panelled, with a real fire at each end, and there is a separate dining room to the rear, particularly popular for the Sunday carvery. There are tables outside for eating and drinking in fine weather. ▷⊛≢◑&▲≢♣⊟⚘☞

Lofthouse

Crown Hotel 🗓
Thorpe Lane, HG3 5RZ
🕐 12-3, 7-11; 12-3, 7-10.30 Sun ☎ (01423) 755206
Black Sheep Best Bitter; Theakston Best Bitter H
A traditional Dales pub and hotel in the Nidderdale Area of Outstanding Natural Beauty, a short way uphill from the main part of the village on a road with spectacular views. There is an unusual panelled entrance corridor leading to a traditionally furnished comfortable bar decorated with local pictures, maps and brassware; a more formal dining room is reached through the bar. There is no cellphone coverage indoors. ⊛≢◑⚘

Loftus

Station Hotel 🗓
Station Road, TS13 4QB (100yds S of A174)
🕐 3-11; 12-11.30 Sat & Sun ☎ (01287) 640373
2 changing beers H
This once-bustling railway hotel is now a free house. The last passenger train left in 1953 – the nearby overgrown platform is still in-situ. The licensee, a keen musician, has served best/premium bitters for 28 years, with the range favouring beers over 4% ABV. The pub comprises a cosy bar, a lounge and a function room where live music plays on Thursday and Saturday. Fans of eccentric railway memorabilia are especially well catered for. ⊛&⊟⊟(X4,5)⚘

Malham

Lister Arms 🗓 ✅
Gordale Scar Road, BD23 4DB
🕐 8am-11 ☎ (01729) 830444 ⊕ listerarms.co.uk
Lancaster Bomber; Thwaites Nutty Black, Original; Wainwright; 3 changing beers (sourced locally; often Dark Horse, Settle, Thwaites) H
Substantial stone-built Grade II-listed inn dating from 1723 or earlier, overlooking the green. The tiled entrance hall opens to a stone-flagged main bar, with further areas to the left and right, and a dining room/restaurant beyond. The large,

secluded garden at the rear has ample comfortable seating. Food is served all day, with breakfast/brunch on offer before midday and the main menu available thereafter. Home-made cakes and cream teas are also sold. Malham can get busy weekends and school holidays.

Malton

Brass Castle Brewery Tap House

10 Yorkersgate, YO17 7AB

closed Mon; 4-9 Tue-Thu; 12-10 Fri & Sat; 12-8 Sun (01653) 698683 brasscastle.co.uk

2 changing beers (sourced locally; often Brass Castle)

Formerly a temperance hotel in the town centre, Malton's newest hostelry is a short walk from the railway station. The single-roomed bar is designed in a rustic style, with one wall partially adorned with barrel staves. Two regularly changing cask ales are offered together with six craft keg ales. An extensive range of bottled beers is also available. Snacks are on offer at the bar. There is a smoking/drinking area to the rear of the premises and an upstairs seating area. Q

Cross Keys

47 Wheelgate, YO17 7HT

closed Mon; 11.30-11 (11.30 Fri); 10am-11.30pm Sat; 10am-11pm Sun (01653) 228180

Timothy Taylor Boltmaker; house beer (by Castle Eden); 4 changing beers (sourced regionally; often Atom, Brass Castle)

The Grade II-listed Cross Keys is a traditional English pub, recently refurbished and modernised, with three separate drinking areas including a quiet snug bar. The present building was constructed in the 18th century but the cellars contain the original vaulted crypt of the Hospitium (a guest house for pilgrims travelling to the Gilbertine Priory at Old Malton some centuries earlier). To the rear is a drinking/smoking area. Food is served daily (except Mon), with breakfasts from 10am at weekends. Q

New Malton

4 Market Place, YO17 7LX

11.30-11; 12-10.30 Sun (01653) 693998

thenewmalton.co.uk

3 changing beers (sourced regionally)

Situated in the busy market place, this Grade II-listed building, formerly tea rooms, has been sensitively renovated. The large single-room interior is divided into three distinct drinking and dining areas. Three handpumps dispense varying beers, mainly originating from Yorkshire breweries. Meals are served from midday throughout the week, all using locally sourced ingredients and prepared on-site. There is a small area at the front for alfresco drinking. Children and dogs are welcome. Q

Manfield

Crown Inn

Vicars Lane, DL2 2RF (500yds from B6275)

4-11.30; 12-11.30 Sat & Sun (01325) 374243

Draught Bass; Village White Boar; 5 changing beers (sourced nationally)

Local CAMRA Country Pub of the Year 15 times, and previously Yorkshire Pub of the Year, this 18th-century hostelry is in a quiet village. It has two bars, with a real log fire in the main bar, and a games room. A mix of locals and visitors creates a friendly atmosphere. Up to six guest beers from microbreweries and five ciders or perry are served. Two seasonal beer festivals are held.

Q P (29)

Marske-by-the-Sea

Clarendon

88-90 High Street, TS11 7BA

11-11 (11.30 Fri-Sun) (01642) 490005

Beer Monkey Blond; Black Sheep Best Bitter; Camerons Strongarm; Theakston Old Peculier, Best Bitter; 1 changing beer

A CAMRA local award winner, the Middle House, as it is also known, is a popular one-room locals' pub, where little has changed since the 1960s. Six beers are served from the mahogany island bar, a rarity on Teesside. The walls are adorned with interesting photographs of yesteryear. There is no TV or jukebox, no pool table, no children or teenagers – just locals indulging in convivial conversation. There is no catering either, but tea and coffee are always available. It has a pleasant south-facing outdoor drinking area. Q P (X3,X4)

Masham

Bay Horse

5 Silver Street, HG4 4DX

12-11 (midnight Fri & Sat) (01765) 688297

bayhorseatmasham.co.uk

Black Sheep Best Bitter; Morland Old Speckled Hen; Theakston Best Bitter; 3 changing beers (sourced nationally; often Greene King)

Friendly pub welcoming tourists and locals alike with a range of ales unusual to Masham, although both the town's breweries are represented. As well as the front bar there is a dining area up a short flight of steps, and a rear garden, and there are five letting rooms. A wide variety of home-cooked food is served, with ingredients coming from local suppliers. Cask ends and pipework form a feature in the main front bar.

Bruce Arms

3 Little Market Place, HG4 4DY

9am-11 (01765) 689372

Black Sheep Best Bitter; Theakston Best Bitter, Lightfoot, Old Peculier; 2 changing beers (sourced locally)

A traditional pub tucked away in a side street off the marketplace. This is a whitewashed building with an interior of partly exposed stone, ceiling beams and wood, with bench seating throughout. Good pub food is served. It has a large TV and a dartboard, and there is also a pleasant rear garden. Two letting rooms are available.

White Bear

Wellgarth, HG4 4EN

7.30-midnight (01765) 689319

thewhitebearhotel.co.uk

Caledonian Deuchars IPA; Theakston Best Bitter, Black Bull Bitter, XB, Old Peculier; 1 changing beer

Theakston's only pub, an award-winning hostelry and a great favourite with the locals as well as directors and staff from the Theakston Brewery. A large dining area to the left and a cosy taproom to the right offer almost the full range of Theakston's beers. Oddly for the Yorkshire Dales, the pub was a

victim of wartime bombing, following which it was derelict for many years before being renovated to a high standard. It hosts a popular beer festival in June featuring over 30 beers.
❀♿♣P🚌🐾

Middlesbrough

Dr Phil's Real Ale House

10 Pilkington Buildings, Roman Road, Linthorpe, TS5 6DY (100yds N of The Crescent and Roman Road jct)
3-10 (11 Fri); 12.30-11 Sat; 12.30-8.30 Sun
☎ 07883 072389
3 changing beers H
The first micropub in the area is among a terrace of shops in the leafy suburbs of Linthorpe, a mile south of Middlesborough. Opened in 2013 by an enthusiastic CAMRA member, it soon became a local CAMRA multi award-winner. It is now in the safe hands of an experienced local brewer. The five-yards-square space accommodates an eclectic mix of drinkers, who have a choice of three changing beers. Often, a cask does not manage to last the day. Q♿♣🚌(11,17)🐾

Infant Hercules

84 Grange Road, TS1 2LS (just S of Cleveland Centre and N of university campus)
1-10 (11 Fri & Sat) ☎ 07980 321626
4 changing beers H
One of many micropubs in the town's original solicitors' quarter, all located in a series of parallel streets of Victorian terraced houses close to the law courts. The pub is named after Gladstone's description of the town in 1862, after he had witnessed the rapid expansion of the area's steel furnaces and shipbuilding industries. Three more interesting beers are served, and third-pint tasting bats are available. Teesside University's Real Ale Society (TURAS) continues to meet here on Thursdays. Q❀🚌🐾

Isaac Wilson

61 Wilson Street, TS1 1SF (at N end of town, close to railway station)
8.45am-11 (midnight Fri & Sat) ☎ (01642) 247708
Camerons Strongarm; Sharp's Atlantic; 3 changing beers H
Popular pub named after a 19th-century railway industry magnate and company director of the world's first railway, the Stockton and Darlington. The Isaac, a former Wetherspoon conversion of the law courts, gained new owners in 2017 but continues to follow, more or less, the chain's formula. Two regular beers, three local guests and real cider, together with good-value food, are served in a single room, where walls are adorned with photographs of old Middlesbrough. Third-pint glasses are available. ♿🚌

Muker

Farmers Arms

DL11 6QG
11.30-midnight (11 Mon); 11.30-11 Sun
☎ (01748) 886297 farmersarmsmuker.co.uk
Black Sheep Best Bitter; Theakston Best Bitter, Old Peculier; Yorkshire Dales Muker Silver; 1 changing beer (sourced locally) H
A traditional hostelry in the centre of a former lead-mining village, set in bleak but beautiful Swaledale countryside. Near both the Coast-to-Coast and Pennine Way routes, it attracts countless visitors. The stone-flagged bar with its open fire is popular both with locals and walkers, cyclists and others. As well as a range of local ales there is a guest beer in summer, and home-prepared food is served every day. Q❀♣P🚌🐾

Newbiggin in Bishopsdale

Street Head Inn

DL8 3TE
11-3 (not Mon & Tue), 6-midnight ☎ (01969) 663282
thestreetheadinn.co.uk
Black Sheep Best Bitter; John Smith's Bitter; Theakston Best Bitter; Wensleydale Semerwater Summer Ale; 1 changing beer (sourced locally) H
This modernised but homely 300-year-old inn lies in a remote but delightful location, and is popular with walkers and others exploring the local Dales countryside. It attracts much of its trade from the nearby caravan site and former YHA bunk barn, now owned by the pub. Home-cooked food is served both in the bar, with its impressive fireplace, or in the separate restaurant, and a carvery is offered on Sundays. The pub has its own en-suite accommodation and dogs and children are welcome. ❀♣P🐾

Northallerton

Stumble Inn

4 Garthway Arcade, DL7 8NS (in pedestrian arcade off High St next to Grovers shop)
closed Mon; 4.30-9.30 (11 Fri); 12-11 Sat; 1-8 Sun
☎ 07817 568042
5 changing beers (sourced locally) H
A friendly and cosy micropub hidden away in a shopping arcade off the town's high street and near the Applegarth car park. It serves a selection of local ales, craft beers and up to 20 real ciders, and staff are keen to offer tasting advice and guidance. With no music, gaming machines, Wi-Fi, children or sports TV, there is just good old-fashioned chat plus a quiz on the last Sunday each month. Beer and cider festivals are held seasonally.
Q🚌🐾

Tithe ✔

2A Friarage Street, DL6 1DP
10-11 (midnight Fri & Sat); 11-11 Sun ☎ (01609) 778482
Okell's Manx Pale Ale; Timothy Taylor Boltmaker; 4 changing beers (sourced regionally) H
Lying between the busy High Street and the Friarage hospital, this is a pleasant town-centre bar. There is a strong commitment to cask beer and it is part of the real ale-championing Market Town Taverns chain. A good range of continental and speciality beers is also stocked, plus a wide choice of gins. The decor is simple, with wooden floors throughout. Food is served in the bar and upstairs brasserie. Children are welcome during the daytime. ♿🚌🐾

Osgodby

Wadkin Arms ✔

Cliffe Road, YO8 5HU
12-11 (midnight Fri & Sat) ☎ (01757) 702391
wadkinarms.co.uk
Brown Cow White Dragon; Sharp's Doom Bar; Theakston Best Bitter; house beer (by Tetley); 1

changing beer (sourced nationally; often Marston's, Theakston) Ⓗ
A true community pub at the heart of the village, with five handpumps dispensing ales largely sourced from Yorkshire breweries. The Wadkin has a homely feel, with open fires and a friendly welcome, and is home to locals and visitors alike. The nearby Trans Pennine cycle trail sees cyclists and walkers visiting in the summer months, and a local bus service passes too. There is much evidence of CAMRA sympathies on display and the pub is a previous winner of local CAMRA awards. TV sport is screened. Bar meals are served throughout the week except Monday and Tuesday.
♘❀◖◗⛺♣P🚌(4)🐾📶

Osmotherley

Golden Lion 𝕃 ✔
6 West End, DL6 3AA (in village centre, 1 mile E of A19)
⏲ 12-3 (not Mon & Tue), 5-11; 12-midnight Sat; 12-11 Sun
☎ (01609) 883526 🌐 goldenlionosmotherley.co.uk
Timothy Taylor Landlord; 3 changing beers (sourced locally) Ⓗ
Set in the centre of a picturesque village on the edge of the North York Moors National Park and at the start of the long-distance Lyke Wake Walk, this old inn is popular with hikers, casual visitors and locals. Much of the focus is on high-quality locally sourced food, but drinkers are always made welcome. The view from the outdoor drinking area is an attraction on fine days. Regularly changing beers are from local breweries and there is a beer festival each November. Dogs are welcome.
Q❀🛏◖◗⛺🚌(80,89)🐾📶

Pickering

Sun Inn 🏆 𝕃
136 Westgate, YO18 8BB (on A170, 400yds W of traffic lights in town centre)
⏲ 4-11; 12-midnight Fri & Sat; 12-11 Sun ☎ (01751) 473661
🌐 thesuninn-pickering.co.uk
Helmsley Yorkshire Legend; Tetley Bitter; 4 changing beers (sourced regionally; often Daleside, Hadrian Border, Saltaire) Ⓗ
Friendly local CAMRA Rural Pub of the Year, close to the steam railway. Four ales are offered (three from Yorkshire micros) and several traditional ciders. A cosy bar with real fire leads to a separate room, ideal for families and special events, where local artists display their work. The large beer garden is used for the annual beer festival in September. Regular events include fortnightly acoustic music, charity quizzes and monthly vinyl nights. Dogs (on leads), children and walkers are welcome. ♘❀♿⇌♣🍎🚂🚌(128)🐾

Pool-in-Wharfedale

Hunters Inn 𝕃
Harrogate Road, LS21 2PS
⏲ 12 (2 Mon)-11; 12-10.30 Sun
Black Sheep Best Bitter; Morland Old Speckled Hen; 7 changing beers (often Abbeydale, Rat) Ⓗ
Located on the main Harrogate to Bradford road with views across lower Wharfedale, this is a single-storey building with a large open-plan interior incorporating a raised area at one end, warmed by a real fire during the colder months. Nine handpumps dispense a varying selection of ales mainly from Yorkshire breweries. There is a pool table at one end and a small games room with fruit and pinball machines. Children are welcome in the pub until 8pm. ♘❀◖♣P🚌🐾📶↺

Redcar

Rita's Pantry 𝕃
1 Esplanade, TS10 3AA (opp Beacon)
⏲ 4-10; 2-11 Fri; 12-11 Sat & Sun ☎ 07730 445483
4 changing beers Ⓗ
A former amusement arcade, this is the town's first micropub. It is on the seafront, with views of the petrified forest at low tide. A warm welcome is extended to CAMRA members, locals and visitors alike. Three interesting beers are served, as well as real cider, and third-pint glasses are available. The amiable licensee hosts various social events including a music quiz on Sunday, and occasional Belgian beer nights. ❀◖♿⛺⇌🍎🚌(X3,X4)🐾📶

Reeth

Buck Hotel 𝕃 ✔
DL11 6SW
⏲ 12-2.30, 5-11; 12-11 Fri-Sun ☎ (01748) 884210
🌐 buckhotel.co.uk
Black Sheep Best Bitter; Timothy Taylor Boltmaker, Knowle Spring, Landlord; house beer (by Wensleydale) Ⓗ
At the top of the green in the centre of an attractive Swaledale village, this 18th-century former coaching inn, known as the top house, retains its beamed ceilings, open fire and even an ice house. Home-cooked food is offered along with up to six real ciders (beer and cider choice is reduced in winter). Quoits is a popular summer activity, with three teams based here, along with two darts teams. A beer festival is held in early July. Open all day April-September, 12-midnight (11 Sun). ♘❀🛏◖◗♿⛺♣🍎🚌(30)🐾📶

Riccall

Greyhound 𝕃 ✔
82 Main Street, YO19 6TE
⏲ 12-midnight (11.30 Sun) summer; 3 (12 Sat)-midnight; 12-11.30 Sun winter ☎ (01757) 249101
🌐 thegreyhoundriccall.co.uk
Tetley Bitter; Theakston Best Bitter, Old Peculier; 4 changing beers (sourced regionally; often Ossett, Rooster's, Rudgate) Ⓗ
Four miles north of Selby you will find the Greyhound, a welcoming venue in the heart of a historic village. This family-run village pub dates back to the late 1800s and nowadays has up to seven cask beers on the bar. It is popular with locals and visitors alike, set in a location close to River Ouse walks and the Trans Pennine cycle trail. The large beer garden can get busy on warmer days. Food is served daily except Saturday. Check ahead for winter opening hours and meal times.
♘❀🛏◖◗⛺♣P🚌🐾📶

Richmond

Buck Inn ✔
29 Newbiggin, DL10 4DX
⏲ 11-11 (midnight Fri & Sat); 12-10.30 Sun
☎ (01748) 517300
Black Sheep Best Bitter; Timothy Taylor Golden Best, Landlord Ⓗ

This rambling old traditional pub is on a cobbled street just off Richmond's historic town centre. It features several drinking areas, ranging from the small snug at the front to the large main bar to the rear, with its sports TV and pool table. Beyond this, the beer garden offers glorious views over the River Swale and the historic Richmond castle. Good-value food is offered Thursday-Sunday.
Q

Holly Hill Inn

Sleegill, DL10 4RJ
11-11 (midnight Fri & Sat); 11-10.30 Sun
(01748) 822192 holly-hill-inn.co.uk
Black Sheep Best Bitter; Sharp's Doom Bar; Timothy Taylor Landlord; 1 changing beer H
A pleasant but strenuous walk half a mile south from the town centre, this popular pub lies beyond the castle, across the River Swale and high above it. The main bar is split into two levels separated by a stone chimney breast with a cast-iron stove, while a large extension in the style of a baronial hall with impressive fireplace is used as a restaurant and function room. Quiz nights are on Wednesdays. Q P (30)

Ripon

King William IV

10 Blossomgate, HG4 2AJ
4-11 (midnight Fri); 12.30-midnight Sat; 12.30-11 Sun
(01765) 640108
Theakston Best Bitter; Village White Boar; 2 changing beers (sourced locally; often Hambleton) H
Known locally as the King Billy, this is a community-led pub with a large sporting following; five screens show Sky and BT sports channels. The pub hosts many local sports teams and has regular quiz and music nights including the ever-popular GlastonBilly in August, when local musicians play for charity over a full day. The pub is Hambleton Ale's brewery tap but also serves beers from other breweries. There is a hidden beer garden for the summer and roaring fires in winter.

One-Eyed Rat

51 Allhallowgate, HG4 1LQ
5-11; 12-11 Fri & Sat; 12-10.30 Sun (01765) 607704
oneeyedrat.com
7 changing beers H
A family-run hostelry that is well known and highly regarded for the quality of its ales; it has been in this Guide for 30 years. The narrow frontage belies a long interior with traditional seating and an open fire, with a large garden at the rear. Seven changing ales are available, including a dark ale and a stronger beer, plus a real cider. Sarah Hughes Dark Ruby from the Black Country is sometimes stocked. The pub hosts regular live music.
Q

Robin Hood's Bay

Bay Hotel

The Dock, YO22 4SJ (at end of a steep road, down towards bay from top car park; less able-bodied guests can be dropped off by car)
11-11 (01947) 880278 bayhotel.info
Leeds Pale; Theakston Lightfoot, Best Bitter; Wainwright H
This magnificent Grade II-listed 1822 building is the finish line for Alfred Wainwright's Coast-to-Coast 192-mile walk. The pub's bottom bar, named in his honour, provides access to the Dock patio, situated at the seawater's edge with superb panoramic views. A friendly welcome awaits regulars, visitors, their children and their dogs. Four beers are on tap, while an extensive good-value home-cooked menu is also served. Access to this part of the village is not easy for the less mobile.
(X93)

Saltburn-by-the-Sea

Saltburn Cricket, Bowls & Tennis Club

Marske Mill Lane, TS12 1HJ (next to leisure centre)
7-midnight; 4-midnight Sat & Sun (01287) 622761
saltburn.play-cricket.com
3 changing beers H
Well supported by the local community, visitors are made most welcome at this local CAMRA multi award-winner, now celebrating 24 years of continuous Guide recognition. Three interesting beers are served. An enthusiastic steward hosts a variety of events, including both a jazz club and a blues club. A balcony overlooks the cricket field. On Saturday/Sunday match days, the club opens at noon. Check winter opening hours.
P (X3,X4)

Sandhutton

King's Arms

YO7 4RW
12-11.30 (01845) 587887
thekingsarmssandhutton.co.uk
Black Sheep Best Bitter; 2 changing beers (sourced locally) H
A well-appointed 200-year-old roadside inn in a small village. Although it retains a popular public bar, the focus is largely on food served to a high standard, featuring locally sourced ingredients and organic vegetables. Three beers are usually dispensed, often including brews from Rudgate, and the licensee is an enthusiastic supporter of LocAle. Outside, an honesty box vegetable shop sells local produce and also offers bicycle spares and storage, gels and free air. P

Scarborough

Cellars

35-37 Valley Road, YO11 2LY
12-midnight (11.30 Sun) summer; 4-11; 12-midnight Sat; 12-11.30 Sun winter (01723) 367158
scarborough-brialene.co.uk/cellars.htm
Bradfield Farmers Blonde; Camerons Strongarm; Daleside Monkey Wrench; 3 changing beers (sourced nationally; often Rooster's) H
Scarborough's most frequent Guide entry, this family-run pub was converted from the cellars of a Victorian town house. Six handpumps dispense guest beers from nationwide micros. Locally sourced, home-cooked food is served lunchtimes and evenings, with Sunday lunches always popular. Quiz night is Tuesday, open mic night is Wednesday, local acoustic acts play on Thursday, and Saturday is live music night. The patio fronting the pub is popular in summer. Children and dogs are welcome and accommodation is available.
P (64)

Indigo Alley

4 North Marine Road, YO12 7PD

12-2 (3 Sat & Sun), 7-1am ☎ (01723) 350599

3 changing beers (sourced nationally)

Recently upgraded into a welcoming open-plan establishment while retaining a rustic feel and sporting a logburner, this pub has come back on the real ale and traditional cider trail after a few years in the wilderness. It is a true free house, with bare floorboards and the advantage of pool, darts and dominoes. Locally brewed ales from Scarborough Brewery and assorted traditional-style ciders complement specialist lagers. Families are welcome and dogs too (but not in letting rooms). Entertainment of one sort or another features most evenings. (9,9A)

North Riding Brew Pub

161-163 North Marine Road, YO12 7HU

12-midnight (1am Fri & Sat) ☎ (01723) 370004

northridingbrewpub.com

6 changing beers (sourced nationally; often North Riding Brew Pub, North Riding Brewery)

Scarborough's only brewpub, serving at least six continually changing beers from local producers and microbreweries around the UK. One or more North Riding beer together with beers brewed at the pub are always on offer. These are complemented by three craft keg beers from around the world and an extensive range of craft bottled beers. The pub has a public bar and quiet lounge, both with real fires. Quiz night is Thursday. Local CAMRA Town Pub of the Year 2019.

Q (9,9A)

Scholars Bar

6 Somerset Terrace, YO11 2PA

4-midnight; 12-midnight Sat & Sun ☎ (01723) 372826

Hambleton Nightmare Porter; 5 changing beers (sourced regionally; often North Riding, Ossett)

A warm, friendly atmosphere prevails at this town-centre pub at the rear of the main shopping centre. The large front bar is dominated by TV screens showing major sporting events, with a smaller games area to the rear. Five rotating guest beers, usually from Yorkshire microbreweries, are offered plus numerous ciders and perries. The Thursday night quiz is popular with a first prize of 28 pints.

Stumble Inn

59 Westborough, YO11 1TS (approx 200yds SW of railway station)

12-11; 12-10.30 Sun ☎ 07779 456662

stumbleinnmicropub.weebly.com/home.html

6 changing beers (sourced nationally)

The first micropub in Scarborough, this was formerly a solicitors' office. A welcome addition to the local real ale scene, it quickly gained a positive reputation for its beer and cider. Six rotating guest ales are available, with local breweries always represented, alongside up to 26 ciders and perries. Situated a short walk from the railway station, the single-room establishment is ideal for a cosy chat and chill out. One of four finalists in CAMRA's 2017 National Cider Pub of the Year competition.

Valley Bar

51 Valley Road, YO11 2LX

12-midnight (1am Thu-Sat) ☎ (01723) 372593

valleybar.co.uk

Dark Star Hophead; 4 changing beers (sourced nationally; often Scarborough)

The pub, recently relocated upstairs from the original cellar bar, is a large room divided into several drinking areas. Of note is the remarkable décor utilising antique furniture. Four guest beers are offered, usually including one or more from Scarborough Brewery. Up to 10 real ciders and perries are served together with a selection of Belgian bottled beers. There is also a pool room and a separate function room. Accommodation is available. (64)

Wilson's

West Sandgate, YO11 1QL

12-11 ☎ 07544 775051

8 changing beers (sourced nationally)

The Grade II-listed Wilson's (formerly Leeds Hotel) is close to the seafront and provides a warm welcome to locals and visitors. This is a single-roomed pub with a horseshoe bar, adorned with numerous photographs relating to the local fishing industry. Up to eight cask ales are offered. Pub teams participate in a local darts league. Live music is a feature on Saturday evenings and Sunday afternoons. En-suite accommodation is available in five letting rooms.

Scotton

Guy Fawkes Arms

Main Street, HG5 9HU

12 (4 Mon & Tue)-11 ☎ (01423) 868400

guyfawkesarms.co.uk

Black Sheep Best Bitter; 3 changing beers

Popular village pub rescued from closure in 2013 by two local families. The L-shaped interior features a cosy lounge area, part-flagged, part-carpeted, with a mix of traditional and modern furniture and a real fire. A separate dining room occupies one end and a raised seating area is at the other with its own mini library. Guy Fawkes lived in the village and there are several related items displayed. Complementing the regular Black Sheep Bitter are three changing beers from Yorkshire breweries. P (22)

Selby

Giant Bellflower

47A Gowthorpe, YO8 4HF

8am-midnight (1am Fri & Sat) ☎ (01757) 293020

Greene King Abbot; Ruddles Best Bitter; 6 changing beers (sourced nationally; often Adnams, Rudgate, Sharp's)

Named after a flower associated with a local 17th-century botanist and converted from a furniture showroom, this modern and spacious pub is completely different from all the others in Selby. Artefacts and pictures from Selby's past complement the light and airy interior, and the pub is deceptively large given its small frontage, with an enormous stainless steel bar taking pride of place. Offering a typical Wetherspoon's range of keenly priced beers, real ciders and LocAles, it is an important addition to the town's pub scene.

Nelson Inn

134 Ousegate, YO8 8BL

12-11 (midnight Fri); 11-midnight Sat; 10-11 Sun ☎ (01757) 702187

John Smith's Bitter; 1 changing beer (sourced locally; often Brown Cow)
A popular watering hole on the south bank of the Ouse offering two regular cask beers and the occasional guest beer. The pub is a locals' haunt but visitors are always made to feel welcome. The bar to the right is rarely used, making the main room lively at any time, so expect to be drawn into conversation. Beer festivals are held twice a year, usually May and September.

Settle

Bar 13

13 Duke Street, BD24 9DU
3-11; 2-11 Fri-Sun ☎ (01729) 824356 bar13settle.co.uk
Goose Eye Chinook Blonde; 2 changing beers (sourced locally; often Kirkby Lonsdale, Wishbone, York)
On the main street between the square and the railway station, 13's narrow frontage hides a long, thin room with a well-stocked bar on the left-hand side. Created in 2005 from a small hardware store, its relaxed atmosphere and modern feel attract both locals and visitors to the town; you are as welcome in hiking boots as you are in high heels. Three LocAles are stocked, with the emphasis on pale, hoppier beers.

Talbot Arms

High Street, BD24 9EX
12-11 ☎ (01729) 823924 talbotsettle.co.uk
Settle Mainline; Theakston Best Bitter; 3 changing beers (sourced regionally; often Beer Monkey, Wishbone, Worsthorne)
Just off the square, this family-run free house, claiming to be the oldest pub in town, offers a welcoming and friendly atmosphere. In winter a stove glows in the large stone feature fireplace to the left, with a pool table and dartboard beyond providing a base for teams in local leagues. A pleasant, terraced beer garden is at the rear. The guest beers are usually from Cumbria, Lancashire or Yorkshire. Good-value food is served 12-8pm all week. Occasional live music features on a Friday.

Shipton by Beningbrough

Dawnay Arms

Main Street, YO30 1AB
closed Mon; 5.30-10.30 Tue; 12-2, 5.30-midnight Wed & Fri; 12-2, 5.30-10.30 Thu; 12-2, 6-10.30 Sat; 12-9.30 Sun
☎ (01904) 470334 thedawnayarms.co.uk
Tetley Bitter; 2 changing beers (sourced nationally; often Caledonian, Robinsons, Treboom)
A traditional country inn dating from 1730 in the village centre. It has three interconnecting rooms, with old pictures and items of local history on display. One of the handpumps always serves a LocAle. The wide ranging pub food menu includes gluten free/vegetarian options. Themed events include steak night Tuesday, quiz night Wednesday, fish lunch Friday, a monthly music quiz and a six-weekly supper club. Live music is also hosted on occasion. There is a decked seating area outside to the rear. Situated close to designated cycle routes, cyclists are very welcome.

Skipton

Beer Engine

1 Albert Street, BD23 1JD
12-8 Mon; closed Tue; 12-10 Wed, Thu & Sun; 12-11 Fri & Sat ☎ 07834 456134
5 changing beers (sourced nationally)
Well-established micropub in a tiny street between the town centre and the canal. Five handpumps dispense changing beers; there is always one blonde/pale ale and one dark beer, plus a character beer. A still cider and a fruit cider are also on tap, alongside a selection of bottled beers and wines. The beers are stored in refrigerated cabinets behind the bar. The ambience is friendly and welcoming, and closing time can be flexible. Well-behaved dogs welcome.

Boat House

19 Coach Street, BD23 1LH
12-10 ☎ (01756) 701660
5 changing beers (sourced regionally)
Tucked out of the way, access is through an arch from Coach Street or via the canalside path. The bar is light and airy, with picture windows looking onto the canal basin, and the decor is canal-themed. The cobbled outdoor drinking area offers the opportunity to enjoy a beer while watching the boats go by. An old-style stove keeps the bar warm in winter. One dark cask ale and keg craft beers are usually sold.

Early Doors

14 Newmarket Street, BD23 2HX
12-8 (9 Fri & Sat); 2-6 Sun ☎ 07517 334142
earlydoorspub.co.uk
Moorhouse's Blond Witch; 4 changing beers (sourced locally; often Daleside, Reedley Hallows, Settle)
A micropub, opened in 2016, with no frills, no music, no Wi-Fi and no food, just good beer and conversation. The bar in the long, narrow room has six handpumps and is without keg fonts and other clutter. Beers, usually including a dark brew, are from Yorkshire or Lancashire breweries and are priced the same regardless of strength. A choice of foreign bottled beers is also stocked. A small rear yard acts as both beer garden and smoking area.

Narrow Boat

36-38 Victoria Street, BD23 1JE (alleyway off Coach St near canal bridge)
12-11 ☎ (01756) 797922
Ilkley Mary Jane; Okell's Bitter; Timothy Taylor Landlord; 5 changing beers
Eight handpulls dispense an eclectic selection of cask ales; there should always be one to suit every taste. Bottled and keg continental and craft beers and up to three ciders or perries complement the ale range. Two separate rooms downstairs and an upstairs gallery and function room plus a drinking/smoking area at the front provide ample space for all. Note the unusual interpretation of the Leeds-Liverpool canal map on the wall. Children are welcome if eating. Skipton Folk Unplugged play on Monday.

Woolly Sheep

38 Sheep Street, BD23 1HY
10-11 (midnight Thu; 1am Fri & Sat); 12-11 Sun
☎ (01756) 700966 woollysheepinn.co.uk

Timothy Taylor Dark Mild, Golden Best, Boltmaker, Knowle Spring, Landlord, Ram Tam; 1 changing beer (sourced locally)
An 18th-century pub at the bottom of the High Street, handy for the bus station and town-centre shops. The cosy front lounge has a roaring fire in winter, the area around the main bar has stone flags, and the traditional cobbled courtyard has decking with comfortable seating, a canopy and infra-red heaters. The split-level restaurant serves food throughout the day. Accommodation is in 12 en-suite rooms upstairs. It serves all six regular Timothy Taylor beers plus one of its seasonals.

Staithes

Cod & Lobster Inn

High Street, TS13 5BH (at end of High St)
11-11 (01947) 840330 codandlobster.co.uk
4 changing beers
Superbly positioned at the seawater's edge in this picturesque, sleepy fishing village, the pub has a large open-plan interior. Three beers are provided alongside the house beer, Old Jack's Tipple, named after a character from a locally filmed children's TV show and brewed by North Yorkshire. Good-value traditional meals are served. On sunny days a pleasant patio, overlooking the chilly sea, becomes popular. During high tides, combined with easterly winds, you are advised to use the roadside door or risk getting wet.

Starbotton

Fox & Hounds

BD23 5HY
12-11; 12-10.30 Sun (01756) 760269
foxandhoundsstarbotton.co.uk
Black Sheep Best Bitter; Wharfedale Blonde; 2 changing beers (often Naylor's, Wensleydale, Yorkshire Dales)
A family-run, whitewashed 17th-century inn, divided into two cosy rooms, with flagstone floors and a large stone fireplace enhancing the atmosphere. In fine weather the sheltered patio at the front provides additional seating. A locally brewed golden ale and dark beer are sold alongside the regular beers. Lunch is available daily with evening meals served Wednesday to Sunday. A piano has been installed in the bar area which visitors are encouraged to play. The daytime community-run bus stops outside.
P (72B,874)

Stillington

White Bear

Main Street, YO61 1JU
12-3 (not Mon), 5.30-11; 12-11 Sat & Sun
(01347) 810338
Leeds Pale; house beer (by Rudgate); 3 changing beers (sourced regionally)
You are assured of a warm welcome at this traditional pub. To the right is a classic pub bar and to the left a gem of a restaurant for which you may need to book. The autovac system here is put to good use so the beer is always fresh and lively. Twice winner of York CAMRA branch Pub of the Season, this is a pub definitely worth making the effort to visit if you are not already a lucky regular.
P (40)

Stokesley

White Swan

1 West End, TS9 5BL (at W end of town, 150yds beyond shops)
11-midnight (12.30am Fri & Sat); 11-11.30 Sun
(01642) 714985 whiteswanstokesley.co.uk
Captain Cook Black Porter, Endeavour, IPA, Navigator, Skippy, Slipway, Sunset; 2 changing beers
Home of the Captain Cook Brewery, this friendly 18th-century pub set in a pretty market town is the winner of many local CAMRA awards. At least five beers from the Captain Cook portfolio of ten, two guest beers and two real ciders are served. Beer festivals are held at Easter and in October. Open mic night is Tuesday, quiz night is Wednesday, while music night is Thursday. The sheltered outdoor drinking area overlooks the brewery. Over-18s only, please. (81,89)

Strensall

Ship

23 The Village, YO32 5XS
12-11 (midnight Fri & Sat) (01904) 490302
theshipinn-strensall.co.uk
Timothy Taylor Landlord; 3 changing beers (sourced regionally)
Popular family-run village pub near the River Foss, offering four real ales and a real cider. Although renowned for its food, it has a dedicated area for visitors just wanting a quiet drink. Open all day and late at the weekend, it is popular with walkers, cyclists and caravanners in summer, with outside seating and a children's play area at the rear. Regular events include music, quizzes and an annual spring beer festival. P

Tadcaster

Angel & White Horse

23 Bridge Street, LS24 9AW
11-11; 12-10.30 Sun (01937) 835470
Samuel Smith Old Brewery Bitter
An old coaching inn in the centre of town and next to the Samuel Smith Brewery, making it the brewery tap. It has a large wood-panelled interior with two huge log fires in winter. A rear door leads to the courtyard, the brewery and the stables for the grey shire horses used for dray deliveries to local pubs. All cask beer is served from wooden casks. Q

Thirsk

Little 3

13-15 Finkle Street, YO7 1DA
11.30-10.30 (11.30 Thu; midnight Fri & Sat); 12-10 Sun
(01845) 523782 littlethree.co.uk
5 changing beers (sourced nationally; often Theakston)
Just off the Market Place, this old, low-beamed pub of character claims a history from 1214. It is a warren of nooks and crannies, all decorated in mock half-timbering, and there is an impressive fireplace in the main bar. Formerly the Old Three Tuns, it was renamed to avoid confusion with the nearby Three Tuns. Regularly changing guest beers are from local and national brewers and there is a happy hour 3-6pm daily except Saturdays. Food is served in the upstairs bistro and there is live music every Thursday. P

ENGLAND

Thixendale

Cross Keys
YO17 9TG
6-11; 12-3, 6-11 Fri & Sat; 12-3, 7-10.30 Sun
(01377) 288272
Tetley Bitter; 2 changing beers (sourced locally; often Great Newsome, Half Moon, Wold Top) H
This single-room hostelry appears on a map dated 1851. At the heart of five dry valleys, it is popular with walkers, including those on the Wolds Way and, though remote, is well worth seeking out. It has had the same landlord for over 30 years. The two guest beers come from independent breweries and are usually not more than 4% ABV. Children are welcome in the beer garden. Good-value, traditional home-cooked food is served. Accommodation is in the adjoining converted stable. Q

Thornton Watlass

Buck Inn
Village Green, HG4 4AH
12-11 (01677) 422461 buckwatlass.co.uk
Black Sheep Ale; Theakston Best Bitter; 2 changing beers H
Overlooking the village green, this traditional country inn features a cosy bar room with a real fire, a lounge/dining room and a large function room known as the Long Room. The new owners have redecorated, brightening the place up but retaining the village pub atmosphere. Local beers are a favourite here and excellent meals are served. The number and range of beers is likely to vary a little according to the season; the guest ales are usually from Yorkshire. P

Thornton-le-Dale

New Inn
The Square, YO18 7LF
12-11; 12-10.30 Sun (01751) 474226
the-new-inn.com
Theakston Best Bitter; 2 changing beers (sourced nationally) H
Family-owned Grade II-listed pub, restored to create the feel of yesteryear. Dating to around 1720, this former coaching inn overlooks the medieval village stocks and market cross. It is an ideal touring base for the North Yorkshire moors, Dalby Forest, Ryedale and the coast. The pub prides itself on freshly cooked food, with a wide range of specials. The large main room is separated into drinking and eating areas. A smoking/drinking space is located at the rear. En-suite accommodation is available. Dogs are welcome away from dining areas.
Q P (128,840)

Ugthorpe

Black Bull Inn
Postgate Way, YO21 2BQ
12-2 (not Mon & Tue), 6-11 (01947) 840286
blackbullwhitby.co.uk
Theakston Old Peculier; 1 changing beer H
A warm welcome is assured at this Grade II-listed pantiled country inn, where photographs of yesteryear adorn the walls. It is a comfortable, family-run establishment comprising a main bar, snug, restaurant and games room. The guest beers complement the Old Peculier and change weekly. Portions of home-cooked food are such that going home hungry is not an option. Diners travel from far and wide for the impressive Sunday lunchtime carvery, for which booking in advance is advised.
Q P

Upper Poppleton

Lord Collingwood
The Green, YO26 6DP
12-11 (midnight Fri & Sat); 12-10.30 Sun
(01904) 801750
Marston's 61 Deep; Ringwood Razorback; house beer (by Thwaites); 3 changing beers (sourced nationally; often Jennings, Marston's, Wychwood) H
A fine country pub on the village green set in a lovely 17th-century Grade II-listed building, with friendly, welcoming staff. Up to five ales from the Marston's list are on offer, including seasonals. The comfortable interior features a timber ceiling and pillars, real fires and a 19th-century carved oak bar. It has a beer garden with fairy lights, patio, children's play area and car park. Quiz night is Wednesday. Accessible from York by bus or rail.
P (10)

Wensley

Three Horseshoes
DL8 4HJ (on A684)
11.30-11; 11-10.30 Sun (01969) 622327
thethreehorseshoeswensley.co.uk
Theakston Best Bitter; Wainwright; Wensleydale Semerwater Summer Ale; 2 changing beers (sourced nationally) H
A traditional country pub on the A684 full of atmosphere, with its small bar and dining room both featuring low beams and real fires. Outside there is a terraced beer garden offering glorious views across Wensleydale, forming a real suntrap on fine days. Wholesome and reasonably priced lunchtime and evening meals are served daily (no food Mon). Guest beers in busier months are usually from the Marston's range.
Q P

Whitby

Arch & Abbey
2-4 Skinner Street, YO21 3AJ (at S end of Skinner St)
11-10.30
4 changing beers H
Recently opened micropub operated by enthusiastic licensees in keeping with the micropub ethos of no music, no TV, no global brands; just good beer and good conversation. This successful crowd-funded start-up is located in a truly old-fashioned ladies' dress shop that would not look out of place in a heritage museum. Four interesting beers, a couple of real ciders, and light bites and snacks are served. Check ahead for winter opening hours. Q (X93,840)

Black Horse
91 Church Street, YO22 4BH (on E side of swing bridge on way to Abbey steps, close to market place)
11-11; 12-10.30 Sun (01947) 602906
the-black-horse.com
5 changing beers H
A former CAMRA local award winner, this little multi-roomed gem, dating from the 1600s, offers a

warm welcome. The frontage, with its frosted glass, together with one of Europe's oldest public serving bars, was built in the 1880s and remains largely unchanged. Beer is served from five handpumps. Snuff, tapas, olives, Yorkshire cheeses and hot drinks are always on offer, while hot lunches are also served during the winter months. The cider is Westons Rosie's Pig. Accommodation is in four bedrooms.
Q (X93,840)

Endeavour

66 Church Street, YO22 4AS (on E side of swing bridge, close to an award-winning fish & chip shop)
12-11 (01947) 603557 endeavourpub.co.uk
4 changing beers
Cosy, friendly, one-room pub dating from 1935, named after the ship in which James Cook made his voyages to the Antipodes. The warming fire and pleasant conversation add to the welcome from an enthusiastic licensee, who serves 140 different beers annually. Four handpumps, Yorkshire tapas and permission to bring your own fish and chips into the pub all make for a relaxing visit. Folk/Irish music on Friday evenings and Sundays are well supported, and it gets manic during Goth weekends. Local CAMRA Town Pub of the Year 2018. Q (X93,840)

Little Angel

18 Flowergate, YO21 3BA (200yds W of swing bridge, 200yds N of railway and bus stations)
12-midnight (1am Fri & Sat) (01947) 820475
littleangelwhitby.co.uk
5 changing beers
Locals and visitors alike are afforded a genuine friendly welcome at this extremely popular pub where, it is rumoured, the remains of the castle form part of the structure. Large-screen sports TVs, live music, an outdoor beer terrace, and even a horse mount for those requiring this facility, complement the five beers and real cider served to three separate rooms from a central bar. Cask ale day is Wednesday. Local CAMRA branch Best Whitby Pub for three years running.
(X93,840)

Station Inn

New Quay Road, YO21 1DH
10-midnight; 10-11.30 Sun (01947) 603937
stationinnwhitby.co.uk
Black Sheep Best Bitter; Ossett Yorkshire Blonde, Silver King; Theakston Old Peculier; Timothy Taylor Boltmaker; Whitby Jet Black; 2 changing beers
Next to the harbour and marina, this popular multi-roomed pub offers a warm welcome. The enthusiastic licensees ensure that the eight beers, including two guests, always encompass an eclectic range of varying styles, while real cider and fruit wines mean there is something for everybody. Situated opposite the bus station and NYMR/Esk Valley Railway station, the pub has become the discerning travellers' waiting room. Live music features three evenings a week. There are three letting bedrooms.
(X93,840)

Waiting Room

2 Whitby Station, Langborne Road, YO21 1YN (by main entrance to NYMR/EVR station)
closed Mon & Tue; 4.30-9 Wed & Thu; 4-9 Fri; 12-9 Sat; 12-5 Sun (01947) 821640
5 changing beers
On the platform used by the NYMR steam trains, Whitby's first micropub strives to adhere to the original micropub values – no craft beer or lager, no spirits, no jukebox, no TV. Friendly owners and plenty of convivial conversation promote a pleasant atmosphere, together with five handpumps and a dozen or more ciders. The six-yards-square pub gets very busy at times. Local CAMRA 2019 Cider Pub of the Year.
Q (X93,840)

Yarm

Ketton Ox

98-100 High Street, TS15 9AU (at N end of High St)
10-11 (midnight Fri & Sat) (01642) 788311
craft-pubs.co.uk/kettonoxyarm
Draught Bass; Timothy Taylor Landlord; 4 changing beers
Historic 17th-century Grade II-listed inn, once renowned for its illegal cock fighting and its morgue. The pub is named after a famous shorthorn ox, Comet, born in nearby Ketton Hall in 1796, who established the standards by which the breed is defined. Recently refurbished, this contemporary outlet ticks all the boxes, including friendly staff, six handpulls and pub food served all day, every day. The large upstairs function room can be used for private parties. Third-pint glasses are available. (7,17)

York

Ackhorne

9 St Martins Lane, YO1 6LN
12-11 (midnight Fri & Sat) (01904) 671421
Caledonian Deuchars IPA; Rooster's Wild Mule; 3 changing beers
A historic city-centre inn, hidden off the beaten track down a narrow cobbled lane at the bottom of the famous Micklegate Run. Partially open plan, it has separate areas up a couple of steps or through an archway. There is also a small, pleasant beer garden on a raised area to the rear. A friendly pub, full of character and atmosphere, which appeals to a wide audience.

Blue Bell ★

53 Fossgate, YO1 9TF
11-11 (midnight Fri & Sat); 12-10.30 Sun
(01904) 654904
Bradfield Farmers Blonde; Kelham Island Best Bitter; Rudgate Ruby Mild; Timothy Taylor Landlord; 3 changing beers (sourced locally; often Half Moon, Ilkley, Rooster's)
This small Edwardian pub has a nationally important Grade II*-listed historic interior (1903), with a central bar supplying two small rooms and, in summer, the side corridor. It can get crowded so entry may be restricted at busy times and it has a no-groups policy. Permanent beers are complemented by great range of rotating guests on eight handpumps. Bar snacks and pork pies are served. A friendly and welcoming pub, well worth a visit. Q

Brew York Tap Room

Unit 6, Enterprise Complex, Walmgate, YO1 9TT
closed Mon & Tue; 6-11 Wed & Thu; 4-11 Fri; 12-11 Sat; 12-9 Sun (01904) 848448 brewyork.co.uk
Brew York Jarsa, Maris the Otter, Viking DNA; changing beers (sourced locally; often Brew York)

Brew York's Tap Room is inside the brewery and the Beer Hall in the adjacent old maltings. This multiple award-winning brewery offers a selection of over 50 regular, seasonal, experimental and collaboration real ales (including gluten free) through 10 handpulls and 50 KeyKeg pumps. There is plentiful seating inside by the brew tanks and outside in the beer garden by the River Foss. Innovative fresh food is available, with a good vegan choice.

Brigantes

114 Micklegate, YO1 6JX

12-11; 12-10 Sun ☎ (01904) 675355

Okell's Manx Pale Ale; 9 changing beers (sourced nationally; often Black Sheep, Brass Castle, Great Heck) H

A bright, roomy and welcoming real ale haven just inside the city walls. This Market Town Taverns pub has 10 handpumps that regularly feature ales from York, Leeds, Great Heck and Black Sheep breweries, and interesting guests from around the country, alongside a range of continental beers. At least one real cider is also on offer, plus and a Wall of Cider festival in October with 25+ ciders and perries. The ground floor bar area extends to a lounge area at the rear. High quality food is served in the bar and adjoining restaurant. Q

Gillygate

48 Gillygate, YO31 7EQ

12-midnight (1am Fri & Sat) ☎ (01904) 654103

thegillygate.com

4 changing beers H

Spacious pub with three pleasant, comfortable rooms, just outside the York city walls and near the Minster, which appeals to locals and tourists alike. The pub, refurbished in 2014, also benefits from a patio garden with a seating area. It currently offers four real ales, but plans to expand the range to eight in time. Bed & Breakfast accommodation is offered in nine rooms.

Golden Ball ★

2 Cromwell Road, YO1 6DU

5-11 (11.30 Thu); 4-11.30 Fri; 12-11.30 Sat; 12-11 Sun ☎ (01904) 849040 goldenballyork.co.uk

Half Moon Dark Masquarade; Timothy Taylor Golden Best; Treboom Yorkshire Sparkle; 4 changing beers (sourced regionally; often Salamander, Salopian, Whitby) H

In the residential Bishophill district, this is a fine, welcoming Victorian street-corner local. Identified by CAMRA as having a nationally important historic pub interior and Grade II-listed, it has an impressive glazed brick exterior and was extensively refurbished by John Smith's in 1929. Outside is a large south-facing beer garden. This is now a community pub, run by a co-operative, with seven handpumps serving three permanent ales plus four guests. Bread and fresh eggs from local suppliers are on sale in the bar. Q

Maltings

Tanners Moat, YO1 6HU

11-11; 12-10.30 Sun ☎ (01904) 655387 maltings.co.uk

Black Sheep Best Bitter; Treboom Yorkshire Sparkle; York Guzzler; 4 changing beers (sourced nationally; often Bad Seed, Hop Studio, Wilde Child) H

A popular pub close to the station. At any one time customers can choose from seven real ales and four traditional ciders. The three permanent beers are from Black Sheep, Treboom and York breweries. A brew from Rooster's is always among the range. Cask ales from microbreweries, sourced both locally and from further afield, change regularly. An extension has provided more seating and a small outside area, while maintaining the original character.

Phoenix

75 George Street, YO1 9PT

12-11 (11.30 Fri & Sat) ☎ (01904) 656401

phoenixinnyork.co.uk

Timothy Taylor Landlord; Wold Top Bitter; 3 changing beers (sourced regionally; often Beer Monkey, Black Sheep, Phoenix) H

An independently run pub with a regionally important historic pub interior, where a friendly welcome awaits. Relax in the traditional pub atmosphere without the noise of gaming machines, TVs or jukebox. You can enjoy your beer while reading a newspaper and listening to the muted conversation of fellow drinkers. In the winter months, warm yourself by the real log fire in the front room. The rear room boasts a bar billiards table. Q

Pivni

6 Patrick Pool, YO1 8BB

11.30 (12 Mon)-11.30; 12-11.30 Sun ☎ (01904) 635464

pivni.co.uk

5 changing beers (sourced nationally; often Tapped) H

The founding bar of the Pivovar UK group, in a beautiful three-storey timber-framed building dating back to 1190. It serves five regularly rotating cask ales sourced from across the UK, usually including one from its brewery, Tapped in Sheffield. There is also a changing range of seven craft keg beers mostly from Europe, the US and the UK, four real ciders and over 40 varied bottled beers. There are bar games available, fresh coffee and a jukebox. Bar snacks, including local pork pies, are on offer.

Rook & Gaskill

12 Lawrence Street, YO10 3WP

4-midnight; 3-1am Fri & Sat; 4-11 Sun ☎ (01904) 674067

rookandgaskillyork.co.uk

Castle Rock Harvest Pale; 22 changing beers (sourced nationally; often Bad Seed, Brass Castle, Brew York) H

Just outside Walmgate Bar, this pub focuses on good quality beer and cider at competitive prices, and is popular with locals, beer enthusiasts and the university community. A large range of carefully chosen cask ales is served through eight handpulls and several KeyKeg taps, complemented by rare lagers and real ciders. Home-made burgers and wood-fired pizzas are available. There is a quiz on Thursday. CAMRA branch Pub, and Cider Pub, of the Year 2018.

Slip Inn

Clementhorpe, YO23 1AN

4-11.30; 1-midnight Fri; 12-midnight Sat; 12-11 Sun ☎ (01904) 621793 theslipinnyork.co.uk

Leeds Pale; Rudgate Ruby Mild; Timothy Taylor Boltmaker; 2 changing beers (sourced regionally; often Great Heck, Revolutions, Ridgeside) H

This independent free house is a thriving community local with two bars, a snug and a sheltered courtyard beer garden. There are plans to double the beer range on the bar and create a dedicated outside festival bar. The Slip hosts regular beer festivals and events each year, including one jointly run with the Swan up the road. It supports traditional pub games including darts, dominoes and cribbage. (11)

Swan ★

16 Bishopgate Street, YO23 1JH

4-11 Mon-Wed; 3-11.30 Thu; 12-midnight Fri & Sat; 12-10.30 Sun (01904) 634968 theswanyork.co.uk

Tetley Bitter; Timothy Taylor Landlord; house beer (by Treboom); 3 changing beers (sourced regionally; often Half Moon, Revolutions, Salamander)

This thriving street-corner pub, within sight of the city walls, has been free of tie since 2017. Grade II listed, the traditional West Riding-style drinking lobby and two bars have a friendly and comfortable feel, and are of national historic importance. To the back is a heated and partially covered beer garden where an annual beer festival is held jointly with the nearby Slip Inn. (11)

Volunteer Arms

5 Watson Street, YO24 4BH

5-11 (midnight Fri); 12-midnight Sat; 12-11 Sun (01904) 541945 volunteerarmsyork.co.uk

Brown Cow Mrs Simpsons Thriller in Vanilla; Leeds Yorkshire Gold; Saltaire Pride; Timothy Taylor Landlord; Treboom Yorkshire Sparkle; 2 changing beers (sourced locally)

An independent free house just off Holgate Road, close to the centre of York. It has a real community feel, while welcoming to all. With five permanent beers and two changing guests, the beer range is excellent for a suburban pub. Loyalties are firmly with local breweries, emphasising the Volunteer's commitment to LocAle. Other attractions include live blues every Saturday night and a quiz every Sunday night. Q (1,10)

Waggon & Horses

19 Lawrence Street, YO10 3BP

3-11; 12-11.30 Fri & Sat; 12-10.30 Sun (01904) 637478 waggonandhorsesyork.com

Batemans XB, XXXB; Oakham Citra; 4 changing beers (sourced nationally; often Ossett, Rooster's, Titanic)

Run by a landlord who loves real ale, this Batemans-owned multi-roomed family-run pub has eight handpulls. The bar area and front room have TVs showing BT sports. Two other rooms at the back of the pub are quieter and used by local groups to hold meetings. There is a free bar billiards table and board games are available. Beers from the wood are occasionally on offer. CAMRA Pub of the Year 2017.

YORKSHIRE (SOUTH)

Armthorpe

Wheatsheaf

Church Street, DN3 3AG

5-11 Mon; 12-11.30 Tue-Sat; 12-5, 7-11 Sun (01302) 835868

Purity Pure UBU; Timothy Taylor Boltmaker

A roadside pub serving excellent beers and a variety of good-quality food. You are assured of a warm welcome here, and there is plenty of entertainment including darts, dominoes and pool. Food is served Tuesday to Saturday, lunchtimes and evenings, with a carvery on Sunday. There is a good-sized outside drinking area at the front. Sunday is quiz night. Q P (81,82)

Auckley

Eagle & Child

24 Main Street, DN9 3HS

11.30-11 (11.30 Fri & Sat); 12-10.30 Sun (01302) 770406 eagleandchildauckley.co.uk

Acorn Barnsley Bitter; Black Sheep Best Bitter; Timothy Taylor Landlord; 2 changing beers (sourced regionally; often Milestone, Welbeck Abbey)

A much-loved pub, on the main road in the village, and winner of numerous CAMRA awards. Dating from the early 19th century, it has real character. There are two bars, one with a TV, the other quieter, with tables for bar meals. The separate restaurant is decorated with photographs of local historic interest, and home-cooked meals have a deserved reputation. There is an outside seating area and a beer garden. Doncaster Sheffield Airport is just a mile away. Q P (57F)

Barnsley

Arcade Alehouse

31 The Arcade, S70 2QP

closed Mon-Wed; 12-10 Thu-Sat; 12-8 Sun 07843 930974

6 changing beers (sourced regionally; often Geeves, Nailmaker)

Barnsley's first micropub, a tiny one-up, one-down place belonging to the former owner of Two Roses Brewery. The bar serves up to six real ales and up to four real ciders, and most are either local or regional. The pub is in the lovely Victorian Arcade and was previously a cake shop. The staff are welcoming and knowledgeable about the cask ales on offer, and there is also a large choice of craft beers. Q

Old No.7

7 Market Hill, S70 2PX

11-midnight (11 Sun-Tue) (01226) 244735 oldno7barnsley.co.uk

Acorn Barnsley Bitter, Blonde; 6 changing beers (sourced nationally; often Acorn)

The Acorn Brewery Tap, it offers two bars; the main upstairs bar is open each day while the downstairs bar opens Friday and Saturday evenings. Regular live music is performed, and a couple of beer festivals take place each year in the downstairs bar. The two bars serve a range of up to eight real ales from Acorn Brewery and other microbreweries, a choice of real ciders and perry, and a wide range of craft and continental beers.

Silkstone Inn

64 Market Street, S70 1SN

8am-midnight (1am Fri & Sat) (01226) 320860

Greene King Abbot; Ruddles Best Bitter; Sharp's Doom Bar; 4 changing beers (sourced nationally)

This JD Wetherspoon pub offers a good turnover of excellent real ales, serving beers requested by customers. Outside is a seating forecourt with a no-smoking area. Inside, the dark-themed décor emphasises the coal seam on which Barnsley sits. The large one-roomed bar has plenty of snugs dotted around its central fireplace, creating a cosy feel. Q

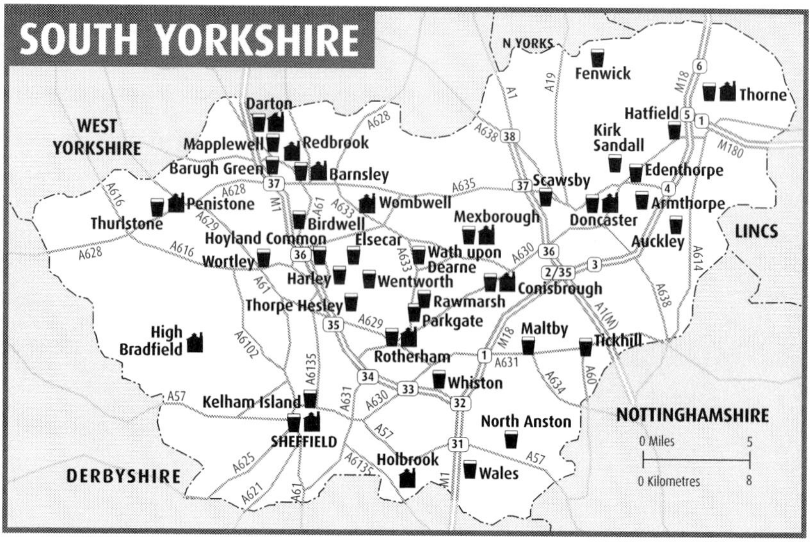

Barugh Green

Crown & Anchor

Barugh Lane, S75 1LL (on B6428)
11.30-11.30 (midnight Thu; 1am Fri & Sat)
(01226) 387200 thecrownandanchor.com
5 changing beers (sourced regionally; often Acorn, Bradfield, True North)

Known locally as The Whitehouse, this large pub is the Barnsley outpost of the True North portfolio. Seven handpulls (three always serving True North beers, the others ales from anywhere in the country) ensure there are styles to suit all drinkers, along with a good selection of bottled world beers and a lengthy list of gins. The food menu changes often but the good pies are a constant.
P

Birdwell

Cock Inn

Pilley Hill, off The Walk, S70 5UD (across road on corner of Chapel St and The Walk)
4-10 Mon; 12-11 Tue & Wed; 12-midnight Thu-Sat; 12-10.30 Sun (01226) 744227
Tetley Bitter; 3 changing beers (sourced nationally; often Chantry)

Stone-built pub a little out of the village but well worth finding. Inviting, with a large open fire, the bar area leads into another lounge area with plush seating. A separate room is available for small parties or meetings. The Cock is well known for its good food, so can get busy during mealtimes (booking for Sunday lunch is advised). One of the cask beers is free of tie, and there is a real cider. A large beer garden is to the rear.
Q P (67A)

Conisbrough

Hilltop

Sheffield Road, DN12 2AY (on main A630)
5-10 Mon; closed Tue; 12-10.30 Wed-Sun
(01709) 868811 thehilltophotel.co.uk
Hilltop Classic Bitter, Blonde, Stout, Porter

A traditional free house standing alone on the Rotherham side of Conisbrough, offering a relaxed and friendly atmosphere. Family run, it is split into a public bar and lounge area. A wall of old Conisbrough photos includes pictures of a trolleybus. Four real ales are served, all from the on-site brewery. Quiz night is on a Wednesday and includes supper. The Hilltop has won several local CAMRA branch awards and has been in the Guide since 2014. Q P (X78)

Darton

Darton Tap

70 Church Street, S75 5HQ
closed Mon; 5-10.30 Tue-Thu; 2.30-11 Fri; 12-11 Sat; 12-10 Sun
Rat White Rat; house beer (by Molson Coors Burton); 2 changing beers (sourced locally)

A newly opened micropub in the increasingly popular Darton and Mapplewell corridor. This stylish pub offers four cask lines, several draught lines and a large spirits selection. The wood-burning stove invites you in. Drinkers can enjoy a beer in a modern and comfortable environment, close to transport links. Strictly over-18s only.
P

Old Co-op Ale House

28 Church Street, S75 5HG
closed Mon; 5-10 Tue-Fri; 12-10 Sat & Sun
07718 974622
Timothy Taylor Landlord; house beer (by Nailmaker); 6 changing beers (sourced nationally)

This welcoming micropub in the heart of Darton, in a former Co-op building, has been tastefully refitted into a large open bar, exposing the building's stonework and including a wood-burning fire. It serves up six changing handpulled beers, including the house beer, Grumpy's Ale, alongside three real ciders and 10 lines of draught craft beers, plus a large spirits collection. Dogs are welcome.
Q

Doncaster

Doncaster Brewery Tap

7 Young Street, DN1 3EL
closed Mon; 5-11 Tue-Thu; 12-11 Fri & Sat; 12-5 Sun
(01302) 376436 doncasterbrewery.co.uk
Doncaster Sand House, Cheswold; 4 changing beers (sourced locally; often Doncaster) H
Convenient for the town centre but down a quiet side street, Doncaster Brewery Tap was opened in 2014. The brewery, originally launched in 2012, was relocated here, and provides up to six beers, all served from handpumps into lined glasses. Guest beers are often stocked, as are six traditional ciders and perries. This welcoming pub always has something different going on, from a quiz night every Tuesday and spoken word night on Thursday to ukulele singalong on Saturday.
Q

Draughtsman Alehouse

Station Court, DN1 1PE
10-9 (10 Fri); 9am-7 Sat; 11-7 Sun 07999 874660
thedraughtsmanalehouse.co.uk
3 changing beers (sourced regionally; often Abbeydale, Imperial, Northern Monk) H
On Platform 3B of Doncaster station and opened in 2017, this bar is the project of one man, Russell Thompson, who now runs it with assistance from his sons. The former Victorian buffet bar stood empty for 18 years before restoration. Be sure to inspect the Victorian tiles and mounted plan drawings of steam locomotives. Real ales on offer mainly come from regional brewers, with occasional collaborations and exclusives. Snacks include locally made pies. **Q**(21)

Hallcross

33-34 Hall Gate, DN1 3NL
12-midnight; 11-2am Sat; 12-11 Sun (01302) 328213
Tetley Bitter; house beer (by Welbeck Abbey); 2 changing beers (sourced nationally; often Little Critters, Robinsons, Saltaire) H
This pub has been recently refurbished, with real ale and cider reinstated after many years' absence. It has a front bar playing background music, and showing sports but with sound only for major events. There is a separate soundproofed function room for live music at weekends, and a patio area at the back. It is the home of the resurrected Stocks Beers (brewed at Welbeck Abbey) that were previously brewed on the premises 20 years ago.
(21,25)

Leopard

2 West Street, DN1 3AA (less than 5 mins walk from railway station)
10-10 (11 Mon & Fri; 11.30 Sat); 12-9 Sun
(01302) 739460 leopard-doncaster.co.uk
Sharp's Atlantic; 4 changing beers (sourced regionally; often Oakham, Ossett) H
A street-corner pub, close to the town centre and railway station, which has been a regular CAMRA award winner over the years. It has a superb tiled frontage, recalling its days as a Warwicks & Richardsons house. There are two rooms downstairs, and a large one upstairs that regularly hosts rock and pop gigs. Owned by Doncaster Culture and Leisure Trust, one of the five real ales on offer is from their own Ten Eighty Six brewery.
P(71,72)

Plough (Little Plough) ★

8 West Laith Gate, DN1 1SF (close to Frenchgate shopping centre)
11-11 (midnight Fri & Sat); 11-4, 7-11.30 Sun
(01302) 738310
Acorn Barnsley Bitter; 2 changing beers (sourced regionally; often Moorhouse's, Ossett, Shipstones) H
Known as the Little Plough by locals, this is a friendly, quiet haven to anyone wishing to escape the town-centre bustle, where three real ales are served from handpumps, mostly from regional breweries. The interior dates from 1934 and is mentioned in CAMRA's National Inventory of Historic Pub Interiors. It consists of a public bar at the front and a smaller, comfortable lounge to the rear. The pub is adorned with pictures of old agricultural scenes and has won many local CAMRA awards. **Q**

Queen Crafthouse & Kitchen

1 Sunny Bar, DN1 1LY (on corner of Sunny Bar and Market Place)
12-midnight (1am Thu-Sat) (01302) 562908
5 changing beers (sourced nationally; often Chantry, Imperial, Neepsend) H
Old established market place pub, recently renovated under new ownership. An interior created out of unusual boarding sets the scene, and the pub has drawn new customers to sample the real ales, atmosphere and live music at weekends. Close by the historic corn exchange and bustling market, this is a welcome addition to the town's real ale scene. Five changing real ales are

REAL ALE BREWERIES

1086 Doncaster (NEW)
Abbeydale Sheffield
Acorn Wombwell
Blue Bee Sheffield
Bradfield High Bradfield
Chantry Rotherham
Concertina Mexborough
Crosspool Alemakers Sheffield
Dead Parrot Sheffield
Don Valley Mexborough
Doncaster Doncaster
Exit 33 Sheffield
Fuggle Bunny Holbrook
Geeves Barnsley
Hilltop Conisbrough
Imperial Mexborough
Jolly Boys Redbrook
Kelham Island Sheffield
Little Critters Sheffield
Lost Industry Sheffield
Loxley Sheffield
Nailmaker Darton
Neepsend Sheffield
Old Vault Thorne (brewing suspended)
On the Edge Sheffield
Penistone Penistone
Regather Sheffield (brewing suspended)
Sheffield Sheffield
St Mars of the Desert Sheffield (NEW)
Stancill Sheffield
Tapped Sheffield
Toolmakers Sheffield
Triple Point Sheffield (NEW)
True North Sheffield
White Rose Mexborough
Whitefaced Penistone (NEW)

on the bar, usually from regional breweries, and two real ciders are also on offer.
Q♿⇌🍎🚌(15)🐾📶

Edenthorpe

Eden Arms ✔
Eden Field Road, DN3 2QR (adjacent to Tesco)
⏲ 11.30-11 (midnight Wed, Fri & Sat) ☎ (01302) 888682
Abbeydale Moonshine; house beer (by Black Sheep); 3 changing beers (sourced nationally; often Black Sheep, Marston's, Thornbridge) 🄷
A fine, busy, estate pub, built in the late '80s. Attractive and comfortable, it is one of the area's most CAMRA-friendly pubs. On Mondays all cask ales are generously discounted all day. On offer are usually five real ales, including Ember Inns Pale Ale, brewed by Black Sheep, with a display at the entrance informing customers about present and future cask beers. It has a large outside drinking area. Meet the Brewer evenings are popular. Notable for good-quality classic pub meals.
Q🐴❀◑◐♿P🚌(87,8)📶

Elsecar

Crown Inn 𝕃 ✔
22 Hill Street, S74 8EL
⏲ 12-midnight (1am Fri & Sat) ☎ (01226) 361488
3 changing beers (sourced regionally; often Abbeydale, Acorn, Bradfield) 🄷
A community pub in a picturesque village. A recent refurbishment has seen a new bar and the opening up of the main room. The TV usually shows football. The lounge to the rear leads to a large conservatory area which overlooks the garden and children's play area. Various local groups meet here. Close to the Elsecar Heritage Centre and train station.
🐴❀◑◐♿⇌♣P🚌(66)🐾📶

Maison du Biere 𝕃
Wath Road, S74 8HJ (Unit 15, Elsecar Heritage Centre)
⏲ closed Mon & Tue; 12-7 (9 Thu-Sat) ☎ (01226) 805255
🌐 maisondubiere.com
Changing beers (sourced nationally)
This beer shop and tap is in the heart of the historic Heritage Centre, serving up over 400 bottled and canned beers and ciders, 10 lines of craft/draught beers and real ales, and many real ciders. The knowledgeable staff can navigate you on a taste experience. The tap is popular with locals and visitors alike. Lots of monthly events take place in the Heritage Centre.
🐴❀♿⇌♣🍎P🚆🚌(66,227)🐾📶

Fenwick

Baxter Arms
Fenwick Lane, DN6 0HA (between Askern and Moss)
⏲ 11.30 (5.30 Mon)-11 ☎ (01302) 702671
Theakston Best Bitter; 2 changing beers (sourced regionally; often Bradfield, Ossett, York) 🄷
This award-winning free house is truly a rural gem, and well worth seeking out. The pub has been run by the same family for nearly 30 years, and you can be sure of a warm welcome. Three real ales from small independent breweries are always on handpump, and reasonably priced, locally sourced fresh food is served all day. Outside is a large garden with seating, and ample parking. Quiz night is Wednesday. Local CAMRA Pub of the Year 2017.
Q🐴❀◑◐⛺♣P🐾📶

Harley

Horseshoe 𝕃
9 Harley Road, S62 7UD (off A6135 on B6090, 1 mile from Wentworth)
⏲ 4-11 (10 Mon); 2-11 Sat; 12-10.30 Sun ☎ (01226) 742204
🌐 thehorseshoeharley.co.uk
Neepsend Blonde; 3 changing beers (often Greene King, Little Critters) 🄷
Cosy village local, in the same family for many years and the community hub for well over a century. Real ales change frequently and often come from local breweries. Food includes pizza on Monday evening and a bar menu Friday to Sunday evenings. Home to sports teams, the Horseshoe gets busy when the pool team are playing and when the village gala is held in July. There is some seating outside in front of the pub, and a small area to the rear. Handy for the nearby Wentworth estate, Needles Eye and Elsecar Heritage Centre.
❀◑◐♣P🚌(44)🐾

Hatfield

Jack Hawley at the Grange
Manor Road, DN7 6SB
⏲ 5-11; 12-11 Sat & Sun ☎ 07769 927603
Timothy Taylor Boltmaker; 4 changing beers (sourced regionally; often Neepsend, Thornbridge, Welbeck Abbey) 🄷
This micro is the project of a real ale enthusiast who was previously landlord of the Black Swan in Asselby. Access is via a staircase to the first floor. There is a long, narrow lounge, with mixed seating. Four guitars are mounted on one wall, and on another wall you can read the story of Jack Hawley, a local character from the 19th century, who was renowned for his hospitality. ❀🍎P🚌(84,87a)

Hoyland Common

Tap & Brew 𝕃
9 Hoyland Road, S74 0LT
⏲ 1-11 Mon-Wed; 8am-11 Thu-Sat; 12-11 Sun
☎ (01226) 824614
6 changing beers (sourced regionally) 🄷
Converted from a Victorian tea shop in 2017 but retaining its fine overmantel and fireplace, this micropub has quickly become popular, stocking a selection of bottled beers and a range of gins alongside regularly changing cask beers and cider. Snacks are served including sandwiches, jacket potatoes, cheeseboards and pie and peas. Afternoon teas are also available. Board games and local history books abound. Open mic night is the first Sunday of each month, with occasional live music. ❀◑♣🍎🚌🐾📶

Kirk Sandall

Glasshouse
1 Doncaster Road, DN3 1HP (opp station)
⏲ 11.30-11; 12-midnight Fri & Sat ☎ (01302) 884268
🌐 glassh.co.uk
Old Mill Blonde Bombshell; 3 changing beers (sourced nationally; often Old Mill, Robinsons, Wychwood) 🄷
Large, modern roadside pub whose name refers to the nearby Pilkington Glass factory. Extensively refurbished in recent years, the pub is spacious, has varied seating and a separate function suite. Large TV screens are found throughout. Three regularly changing cask ales are always available, with

locally brewed beers often featured. Beer prices are generally lower than the local average. 🐴❀◑♿⇌♣P🚌📶

Maltby

Queen's Hotel ✔

Tickhill Road, S66 7NQ

⏲ 8am-midnight (1am Fri & Sat) ☎ (01709) 797120

Greene King Abbot; Ruddles Best Bitter; 4 changing beers Ⓗ

A former residential hotel on a busy crossroads, completely refurbished and opened by Wetherspoon after a lengthy period of closure. Its reopening led to a much-needed raising of the profile of real ale in Maltby. Now firmly established, this spacious pub has an attractive family dining area offering typical Wetherspoon value-for-money food and drink. Regular Meet the Brewer nights are held. Next to Coronation Park and handy for Maltby Crags and Roche Abbey. 🐴❀◑♿🍎P🚌📶

Mapplewell

Old Bakery L

16 Blacker Road, S75 6BN

⏲ closed Mon & Tue; 6-9 Wed; 4-9 Thu; 4-11 Fri; 2-11 Sat; 2-10 Sun ☎ 07541 660287

5 changing beers (sourced regionally) Ⓗ

A micropub in the heart of the real ale corridor of Mapplewell. It is in a converted bakery (which still has the working ovens in the bar area) with changing local and regional beers on sale. There is an extensive beer garden at the rear. Weekly and monthly events, including quiz nights and vinyl music takeovers, make this a popular destination. Q❀♿🍎P🚌

Talbot Inn L ✔

Towngate, S75 6AS

⏲ 12-11 (11.30 Wed); 11.30-midnight Fri & Sat; 11.30-11 Sun ☎ (01226) 385629 🌐 thetalbotmapplewell.co.uk

4 changing beers (sourced locally; often Acorn, Magic Rock, Nailmaker) Ⓗ

This 17th-century coaching house, which is popular with diners, serves bar meals and has the 1776 restaurant upstairs. The bar has an extensive beer and wine list to complement food offerings, and four changing beers. The pub is accredited to a buy-local policy and has received numerous awards. It is the official tap of Nailmaker Brewing Co, and wider locals like Acorn and Magic Rock provide regular guest beers here. Q🐴❀◑♣P🚌🐾📶

Wentworth Arms L ✔

Greenside, S75 6AU

⏲ 4-10 (11 Wed & Thu); 12-midnight Fri; 10.30-midnight Sat; 10.30-10.30 Sun ☎ (01226) 390702 🌐 wentwortharms.co.uk

4 changing beers (sourced regionally; often Acorn, Nailmaker) Ⓗ

A large pub that has recently been extensively refurbished, exposing the stone brick both externally and internally, making it more in keeping with the rest of the village. There is a large beer garden to the side and rear of the building. The bar stocks local and regional beers from breweries such as Nailmaker and Acorn. It is the sister pub to the Talbot Inn. ❀◑♿P🚌🐾📶

Mexborough

Imperial Brewery Tap L

Cliff Street, S64 9HU (opp bus station)

⏲ closed Mon & Tue; 4.30-midnight Wed & Thu; 4.30-12.30am Fri; 12-12.30am Sat; 12-10 Sun ☎ (01709) 584000 🌐 impbreweryandbar.co.uk

Imperial Classical Bitter, Platinum Blonde, Bees Knees, Nah Then; 3 changing beers (sourced locally; often Chantry, Great Heck, Neepsend) Ⓗ

An amazing, friendly brewery tap with a multitude of offerings. It has a main bar where all the entertainment is held, a cosy lounge area, plus a games/function room. The eight handpumps dispense a range of quality ale, with two permanent and six rotating beers from its own Imperial brewery, plus a plethora of excellent ales from breweries around the country. Entertainment includes Wednesday karaoke, Thursday award-winning acoustic night, Friday/Saturday live music, and Sunday chillout music in the afternoon. 🐴❀♿⇌♣🚌(220,221)🐾📶

North Anston

Little Mester L ✔

Nursery Road, S25 4BZ

⏲ 11-11 (midnight Fri & Sat); 12-11 Sun ☎ (01909) 562484

Greene King IPA; 4 changing beers (sourced locally; often Stancill, Welbeck Abbey) Ⓗ

A modern estate pub, built in the 1960s, reopened following refurbishment in 2016 and now emphasising real ale. Beers may be from far and wide but local breweries feature strongly among the range of up to four guests. There is a cask ale club, with a free pint offered for every seven purchased. The pub gets lively at the weekend, when a DJ and live entertainment feature. It is handy for visiting the nearby Butterfly Farm and walks around Anston Stones. 🐴❀◑♿P🚌

Parkgate

Little Haven L

96 Broad Street, S62 6EN

⏲ 4-11.30; 12-midnight Fri & Sat; 12-10.30 Sun ☎ (01709) 710134

Chantry New York Pale; 3 changing beers (sourced locally; often Chantry, Double Top, Exit 33) Ⓗ

A compact and welcoming micropub opened in June 2018 in a former post office and hair salon. It has four handpumps plus four craft taps, with local breweries favoured, and it sells real cider. Nibbles are available plus pie and peas on Wednesday, burger and a pint on Thursday and breakfast on Sunday morning. It has board games, and musicians play on Tuesday and Saturday evenings. Outside seating is accessed via the pub. You will find it a welcome break from Parkgate Retail World, and it is a 10-15 minute walk from the tram and train stop there. Q❀◑♣🚌🐾📶

Rawmarsh

Something Brew Inn L

2 Stocks Lane, S62 6NL

⏲ closed Mon; 2-7 Tue; 10-11 Wed-Sun

Chantry New York Pale; Sharp's Doom Bar; 4 changing beers (often Abbeydale, Bradfield, Chantry) Ⓗ

This micropub and coffee house, in a former office building behind the Star pub, opened in May 2018 in an area not renowned for selling real ale. The four changing beers are often from Chantry and other local breweries. Craft keg and bottled beers are also sold. Tastefully decorated inside with a long bar, it has outside seating at the front and rear of the building, including deckchairs in the rear yard. A Sunday jam session and Wednesday night quiz are held. Q❀🚌🐾📶

Rotherham

Bluecoat L ✔

The Crofts, S60 2DJ (behind town hall, off Moorgate Rd, A618)

8am-midnight (1am Fri & Sat) ☎ (01709) 539500

Greene King IPA, Abbot; Welbeck Abbey Cavendish; 7 changing beers (sourced locally) H

A former charity school, opened in 1776 by the Feoffees of Rotherham, which became a pub named Feoffees in 1981 and a Wetherspoon in 2001. Up to 10 handpulled beers are served, listed on a screen behind the bar, with local microbreweries favoured. Three real ciders or perries are dispensed from boxes. Regular Meet the Brewer nights take place, and special beers are brewed for the pub four times a year. Wednesday night has a general knowledge quiz. This place is a Guide regular, and winner of numerous local CAMRA branch awards. ❀♿♣P🚌📶

Cutler's Arms L

29 Westgate, S60 1BQ

12-10 (11 Wed & Thu; 1am Fri & Sat); 2-10 Sun

☎ (01709) 382581 cutlersarms.co.uk

Chantry New York Pale, Iron and Steel Bitter, Diamond Black Stout; house beer (by Chantry); 2 changing beers (sourced locally; often Chantry) H

Rebuilt for Stones Brewery of Sheffield in 1907, with an impressive façade. It was saved from demolition in 2004, following statutory listing, and restored to Edwardian splendour by Chantry Brewery, reopening in 2014. It has a regionally important historic pub interior, having retained its original Art Nouveau windows, tiling and curved bar counter with dividing screen. The full range of Chantry beers, two real ciders and quality craft beers are served. Live music is played on Friday, Saturday and Sunday, and there are student nights on Thursday. No meals, but there are snacks. Q❀🚌🐾📶

Dragon's Tap L

477 Herringthorpe Valley Road, Broom, S65 3AD

12-11 ☎ 07864 680301

Chantry New York Pale; 5 changing beers (sourced locally; often Elland, Great Heck, Little Critters) H

Micropub on two floors opened in April 2018 in a former DIY shop, simply but tastefully decorated with modern art prints, and offering a contrast to the nearby Stag. The six changing beers are from local and national microbreweries. Four craft keg beers and real ciders are sold, plus bottled beers. No food is served, save for snacks, but you can bring in food from nearby takeaways. There are tables at the front of the pub. A general knowledge quiz takes place on Wednesday evening and live acoustic music on Thursday evening. Q❀♿P🚌🐾

New York Tavern L

84 Westgate, S60 1BD (jct of Coke Lane)

12-11 (midnight Fri & Sat) ☎ (01709) 375596

newyorktavern.co.uk

Chantry New York Pale, Iron and Steel Bitter, Diamond Black Stout; house beer (by Chantry); 2 changing beers (sourced locally; often Chantry) H

A wedge-shaped house that became a pub in 1856, reopened by Chantry Brewery in September 2013 as a real ale-led pub. Previously the Prince of Wales Feathers, it was renamed after a pub demolished when the nearby ring road was built. At least six Chantry beers and two real ciders or perries are sold at competitive prices, and it has a large selection of foreign bottled beers. Snuff and bar snacks are available. It is handy for the New York Stadium, and has Rotherham United memorabilia on display. Occasional live entertainment is put on. Local CAMRA Branch Town Pub of the Year 2017-2019. 🚌🐾

Stag L ✔

111 Wickersley Road, Broom, S60 4JN (on A6021)

11-11 (midnight Wed-Fri); 10-midnight Sat & Sun

☎ (01709) 838929

4 changing beers (often Bradfield, Exmoor) H

Former coaching inn on a busy roundabout east of town, refurbished in 2017, making one large room and a conservatory leading to extensive gardens on two levels. Up to four changing beers from local and national breweries are on handpump. Food is not generally available, but home-made sandwiches sometimes are; enquire at the bar. TV sport is popular, with several screens. It has karaoke and a music quiz on Wednesday evenings, and live music or a DJ most Friday or Saturday evenings. Voted the local CAMRA branch's Most Improved Pub in 2018. ❀♣P🚌(X1,X10)📶

Scawsby

Sun Inn

York Road, DN5 8RN

11-11 (midnight Fri & Sat) ☎ (01302) 784109

Wychwood Hobgoblin Gold, Hobgoblin; 2 changing beers (sourced nationally; often Jennings, Ringwood) H

Large pub at the junction of York and Barnsley roads. The Sun caters for a diverse clientele, with an extensive food menu and booths where children can play on interactive TVs. The beers are from the Marston's range and are invariably in good order. This place offers a welcoming atmosphere and is always worth a visit. ❀♿♣P🚌📶

Sheffield: Central

Bath Hotel ★ L ✔

66-68 Victoria Street, S3 7QL

12-11 (midnight Fri & Sat); closed Sun ☎ (0114) 249 5151

beerinthebath.co.uk

Thornbridge Jaipur IPA; 6 changing beers (sourced regionally; often Thornbridge) H

A careful restoration of the 1930s interior gave this two-roomed pub a CAMRA Conservation Pub Design Award and is recognised as having a nationally important historic interior. The bar lies between the tiled lounge, a small corridor drinking area, and the cosy well-upholstered snug. It usually has three Thornbridge beers and three guests to try. There is regular live music and a weekly quiz on Thursday. Light snacks are available. Q♣🚌🐾

Devonshire Cat L ✔
49 Wellington Street, S1 4HG
⏲ 12-2am ☎ (0114) 279 6700 🌐 devonshirecat.co.uk
Abbeydale Deception, Moonshine, Absolution; 9 changing beers (often Abbeydale) Ⓗ
With 12 handpumps adorning the bar and over 100 beers from around the world, the Dev Cat is a great place for the discerning drinker. Now operated by Abbeydale Brewery, there are usually up to six of its beers as well as a number of interesting guests. A recent refurbishment has created a central island bar with various seating areas around. The menu ranges from light snacks through to full meals served all day to 9pm (8pm Sun).
🐴◑♿🚊(West Street)🍎🚌🐾📶

Fagan's L
69 Broad Lane, S1 4BS
⏲ 12-11.30 (midnight Fri & Sat); 11-11 Sun
☎ (0114) 272 8430
Abbeydale Moonshine; Tetley Bitter Ⓗ
With no significant changes in over 60 years, this traditional local comprises a main bar area, a smaller room to the rear, and a tiny snug at the front. The walls are decorated with pictures of bombers in tribute to the former landlord Joe Fagan, after whom the pub is named, and who had previously served as a pilot in Bomber Command. The pub is noted for its folk music and the challenging Thursday night quiz.
🐴◑🚊(City Hall)♣🚌🐾

Head of Steam L
103-107 Norfolk Street, S1 2JE
⏲ 11-11.30 (12.30am Fri & Sat) ☎ (0114) 272 2128
Camerons Strongarm, A-Hop-Alypse Now; 6 changing beers (sourced regionally; often Abbeydale, Leeds) Ⓗ
A pub for some 20 years, this former bank was acquired by Camerons Brewery in 2015 and, after extensive refurbishment, reopened as part of the Head of Steam chain. Behind the imposing frontage, the large single room is served by a central island bar, with a separate seating area at the rear leading on to an outside drinking area in Tudor Square. In addition to the brewer's own beers, the handpumps usually dispense beers from independents in Yorkshire and the North-East.
❀◑♿⇌🚊(Cathedral)🍎P🚌🐾📶

Old Queen's Head L ✔
40 Pond Hill, S1 2BG
⏲ 10-11 ☎ (0114) 327 0704 🌐 theoldqueenshead.co.uk
Lancaster Bomber; Thwaites Nutty Black; Wainwright; 3 changing beers (sourced locally; often Abbeydale, Blue Bee, Little Critters) Ⓗ
Dating from Tudor times when it was originally the hunting lodge for nearby Sheffield castle, the pub is the oldest surviving domestic building in the city, but now adjoins the transport interchange. The central bar serves a U-shaped lounge and is adjacent to a superb beamed dining room in the oldest part of the building. It is the meeting place for history groups, and is included in ghost tours. There are themed food evenings, including a Czech night. 🐴❀◑♿⇌🚊(Fitzalan Sq)♣🍎🚌🐾📶

Red Deer L
18 Pitt Street, S1 4DD
⏲ 12-midnight (1am Fri & Sat); 12-11 Sun
☎ (0114) 272 2890 🌐 red-deer-sheffield.co.uk
Abbeydale Moonshine; Little Critters Little Hopper; Moorhouse's Pride of Pendle; 5 changing beers (sourced regionally) Ⓗ
A genuine, traditional local in the heart of the city. The small frontage of the original three-roomed pub hides an open-plan interior extended to the rear with a gallery seating area. As well as the impressive range of eight cask beers, including five guest ales, there is also a selection of continental bottled beers. Meals are served lunchtimes and evenings daily. The quiz is held Tuesday night, and an upstairs function room is available for bookings.
Q❀◑🚊(West St)🍎🚌🐾📶

Rutland Arms L
86 Brown Street, S1 2BS
⏲ 12-11 (midnight Fri & Sat) ☎ (0114) 272 9003
🌐 therutlandarmssheffield.co.uk
Blue Bee Reet Pale; 6 changing beers (sourced regionally; often Blue Bee) Ⓗ
Occupying a corner site in the Cultural Industries Quarter and near Sheffield's main railway station, the pub has operated as a free house since 2009. The comfortable interior provides ample seating either side of the central entrance, and the walls display photos of old Sheffield pubs. Most of the guest beers come from local and regional microbreweries, together with specials from Blue Bee. Food is served throughout the day to 9pm (6pm Sun). 🐴❀◑⇌🚊(Station)🍎🚌🐾📶

Sheffield Tap ★ L
Platform 1B, Sheffield Station, Sheaf Street, S1 2BP
⏲ 11-11; 10-midnight Fri & Sat ☎ (0114) 273 7558
🌐 sheffieldtap.com
Thornbridge Jaipur IPA; 9 changing beers (sourced nationally; often Tapped Sheffield) Ⓗ
Opened in 2009, this was originally the First Class refreshment room for Sheffield Midland Station, built in 1904. After years of neglect, the main bar area has been the subject of an award-winning restoration retaining many original features. Further seating has been provided in the entrance corridor and to the right of the bar. Usually, three beers are from the on-site Tapped Brewery, opened in 2013 in the impressive former dining room. The brewery can be viewed behind the glass screen. Q🐴❀♿⇌🚊(Station)🍎🚌🐾📶

Sheffield: Kelham Island

Bar Stewards
163 Gibraltar Street, S3 8UB
⏲ closed Mon; 4-10 Tue; 4-11 Wed & Thu; 2-11 Fri & Sat; 2-9 Sun ☎ (0114) 327 3580 🌐 thebarstewards.uk
4 changing beers (sourced nationally; often Abbeydale, Blue Bee, North Riding) Ⓗ
Opened in a shop unit in July 2017, the Bar Stewards is a modern-style bar and bottle shop, and is a welcome addition to the Kelham Island circuit. The four well-chosen cask beers often include a local ale, and there is also a good range of keg beers, bottles and cans from independent breweries. The venue is available for private hire, and offers a mobile bar service.
❀🚊(Shalesmoor)🚌🐾📶

Fat Cat L
23 Alma Street, S3 8SA
⏲ 12-11 (midnight Fri & Sat) ☎ (0114) 249 4801
🌐 thefatcat.co.uk
Kelham Island Best Bitter, Pale Rider; Timothy Taylor Landlord; 8 changing beers (sourced nationally; often Kelham Island) Ⓗ
Opened in 1981, this is the pub that started the real ale revolution in the area. Beers from around the

country are served alongside those from the adjacent Kelham Island Brewery. Vegetarian and gluten-free dishes feature on the menu (food is served 12-3, 6-8pm Mon-Thu; 12-3pm Fri; 12-4pm Sat; 12-5pm Sun). The walls are covered with many awards presented to the pub and brewery. An anniversary beer festival is held in August. Monday is curry and quiz night.
Q❄🐾🅳🦽&♿(Shalesmoor)◆P🚃🐾

Harlequin ㏇

108 Nursery Street, S3 8GG
☀ 12-11 (11.30 Thu & Fri; midnight Sat) ☎ 07794 156916
🌐 theharlequinpub.wordpress.com
Exit 33 Blonde, Northern Best; 8 changing beers (often Exit 33) Ⓗ
Operated by Exit 33 Brewing, the Harlequin takes its name from another former Ward's pub just round the corner, now demolished. The large open-plan interior features a central bar with seating on two levels. There are two regular and usually four other beers from Exit 33, as well as guests from far and wide, with the emphasis on microbreweries. A large range of real ciders is also available. Wednesday is quiz night and there is live music at weekends. ❄🅳🦽♿(Castle Sq)♣◆🍴🚃🐾

Kelham Island Tavern ㏇

62 Russell Street, S3 8RW
☀ 12-midnight ☎ (0114) 272 2482 🌐 kelhamtavern.co.uk
Acorn Barnsley Bitter; Blue Bee Triple Hop; Bradfield Farmers Blonde; Pictish Brewers Gold; 9 changing beers (sourced nationally; often Abbeydale, Blue Bee, North Riding) Ⓗ
Twice CAMRA National Pub of the Year and regular regional and local winner, this small gem was rescued from dereliction in 2002. Thirteen handpumps dispense an impressive range of beers, always including a mild, a porter and a stout. In the warmer months you can relax in the pub's multi award-winning beer garden. Folk music features on Sunday evening and quiz night is Monday. No meals Sunday. Q❄🐾🅳♿(Shalesmoor)♣◆🍴🚃🐾

Riverside ㏇

1 Mowbray Street, S3 8EN
☀ 11.30-11.30 (1am Fri & Sat) ☎ (0114) 272 4640
🌐 riversidesheffield.co.uk
True North Best Bitter, Pale Ale; 5 changing beers (sourced regionally; often Abbeydale, Blue Bee, True North) Ⓗ
On the banks of the River Don, this hostelry has a pleasant terrace overlooking the river. The interior is largely open plan but with a separate room to the right of the main entrance. Furnishings comprise a mix of comfortable sofas and armchairs together with canteen-style tables and chairs. The regular beers from owners True North are complemented by a changing selection of guest ales, mostly from local breweries. Live music is featured at weekends and there is a quiz on Monday. 🐾🅳🦽&♿(Shalesmoor)♣◆🍴🚃(7,8)🐾

Shakespeare's Ale & Cider House ㏇

146-148 Gibraltar Street, S3 8UB
☀ 12-midnight (1am Fri & Sat) ☎ (0114) 275 5959
🌐 shakespeares-sheffield.co.uk
Abbeydale Deception; Stancill Barnsley Bitter; 7 changing beers (sourced nationally; often Bad Seed, Blue Bee, North Riding Brewery) Ⓗ
Originally built in 1821, the pub reopened as a free house in 2011 following a refurbishment that included incorporation of the archway to the rear

yard. The central bar serves three rooms as well as the extension, and there is a further room across the corridor. The eight handpumps have featured in excess of 5,000 different beers over the last seven years, and over 100 whiskies are also stocked. There is regular live music and beer festivals twice a year. Q❄🐾♿(Shalesmoor)♣◆🍴🚃🐾📶

Wellington ㏇

1 Henry Street, S3 7EQ
☀ 3-11; 12-midnight Fri & Sat; 12-11 Sun ☎ (0114) 249 2295
Neepsend Blonde; 6 changing beers (sourced regionally; often Neepsend) Ⓗ
A traditional two-roomed local opened as a free house in 1993. Now part of the small Sheaf Inns group of pubs, it is the brewery tap for the nearby Neepsend Brewery. Sympathetically refurbished following the recent takeover, the rooms are comfortably furnished and welcoming. The seven handpumps feature at least three Neepsend beers and up to three changing guests mainly from micros, together with a real cider. An extensive range of malt whiskies is also on offer.
Q❄🐾♿(Shalesmoor)♣◆🍴🚃🐾

Sheffield: North

Blake Hotel ㏇

53 Blake Street, Upperthorpe, S6 3JQ
☀ 12-11.30 (midnight Fri & Sat) ☎ (0114) 233 9336
Neepsend Blonde; 5 changing beers (sourced regionally; often Blue Bee, Neepsend) Ⓗ
This community pub, at the top of a steep hill (pedestrian handrails provided), reopened in 2010 after being closed for seven years. Although it has been extensively restored, it retains many Victorian features, including etched windows and mirrors. There is also a large decked garden to the rear. The pub has probably the largest selection of whiskies in Sheffield and a growing range of rums and other spirits. No electronic games, TV or jukebox.
Q❄🐾♿(Langsett)♣◆🍴🚃

Gardeners Rest 🍻 ㏇ ✔

105 Neepsend Lane, Neepsend, S3 8AT
☀ 3-11; 12-midnight Fri & Sat; 12-11 Sun ☎ (0114) 272 4978
🌐 gardenerscomsoc.wordpress.com
Sheffield Crucible Best, Five Rivers, Blanco Blonde; 6 changing beers (sourced locally) Ⓗ
Taken over by the Gardeners Rest Community Society in 2017, this friendly pub acts as the brewery tap for the nearby Sheffield Brewery. There are also at least six guest beers sourced nationwide from independent breweries. To the rear is a conservatory leading to a beer garden overlooking the River Don. The cosy Dram Shop includes a restored bar billiards table. There is live music at weekends and regular beer festivals throughout the year. Cask Marque accredited.
Q❄🐾&♿(Infirmary Rd)♣◆🍴🚃🐾

Hillsborough Hotel ㏇

54-58 Langsett Road, Hillfoot, S6 2UB
☀ 4-10 Mon; 12-11 (midnight Fri) ☎ (0114) 232 2100
🌐 hillsborough-hotel.co.uk
Acorn Barnsley Bitter; Tapped Mojo; 5 changing beers (sourced nationally; often Abbeydale) Ⓗ
Privately owned 4-star hotel with six en-suite rooms, providing beer from a wide range of independent breweries. There are regular themed events, with a quiz on Tuesdays, live bands at weekends and folk music sessions on the second and fourth Sundays in the month. The conservatory

at the rear offers extensive views over the Don Valley, and a function room is also available. Q(Langsett)

New Barrack Tavern

601 Penistone Road, Hillsborough, S6 2GA
5 (11 Thu)-11; 11-midnight Fri & Sat; 12-11 Sun
(0114) 232 4225 newbarracktavern.com
Bradfield Farmers Bitter; Castle Rock Harvest Pale, Screech Owl; 6 changing beers (often Castle Rock)
Multi-roomed pub with an original 1936 floor plan, including a Gilmours-branded doorstep and distinctive colourful exterior tiles. The snug has a local sports theme. The lounge features live bands at weekends and a monthly comedy club on the first Sunday. In 2018 a new bottle room was converted from a kitchen. The function room has three handpumps. Outside is an award-winning heated and covered patio garden. Home-cooked food is served daily.
Q(Bamforth St)

Sheffield: South

Beer Engine

17 Cemetery Road, Highfield, S11 8FJ
4-11; 12-midnight Fri & Sat; 12-11 Sun (0114) 272 1356
beerenginesheffield.com
Neepsend Blonde; 5 changing beers (sourced nationally; often Bristol Beer Factory, Kirkstall, Manchester)
A traditional-style, multi-roomed pub, cosy with a great atmosphere. It reopened in 2015 as a free house following a sympathetic refurbishment. A generous choice of high-quality drinks is provided for its wide ranging clientele. The five changing handpulled beers come from an interesting mix of microbreweries in Sheffield and across the country. Excellent, mainly tapas-style, food is served each evening and Friday and Saturday lunchtimes, plus a traditional roast on Sunday lunchtime. The large beer garden has a heated, covered area.

Broadfield

452 Abbeydale Road, Nether Edge, S7 1FR
11.30-midnight (1am Fri & Sat); 11.30-11 Sun
(0114) 255 0200 thebroadfield.co.uk
Abbeydale Moonshine; True North Blonde; 6 changing beers (sourced nationally; often Abbeydale, Ilkley, True North)
Dating from 1896, the Broadfield has established a deserved reputation for quality food, served until 10pm daily, with an extensive menu including hearty meat pies and home-made sausages. There are nine cask ales including beers from owners True North, and large ranges of bottled beers and whiskies. The pub has a great atmosphere and, located in the City's Antiques Quarter, is now a leading player in the local social scene.
P

Brothers Arms

106 Well Road, Heeley, S8 9TZ
12-11 (midnight Fri & Sat) (0114) 258 3544
Bradfield Farmers Blonde; house beer (by Abbeydale); 6 changing beers (sourced nationally)
A classic, traditional local. Although the interior is open plan, it is designed so the various seating and games areas all feel individual and cosy. The pub's name reflects its association with the locally well-known parody ukulele band, The Everly Pregnant Brothers, and live music is hosted every Monday evening, supplemented by folk sessions on the third Sunday. The bar features eight real ales, with two regular beers and six changing guests, together with a real cider. P

Sheaf View

25 Gleadless Road, Heeley, S2 3AA
11.30-11.30 (12.30am Fri & Sat) (0114) 249 6455
Neepsend Blonde; 7 changing beers (sourced regionally; often Neepsend, Pictish, Saltaire)
A 19th-century pub near Heeley City Farm, the Sheaf experienced a chequered history before becoming a real ale oasis since reopening as a free house in 2000. The walls and shelves are adorned with assorted breweriana and provide an ideal background for good drinking and conversation. A wide range of international beers, together with malt whiskies and a real cider, complement the eight reasonably priced real ales. A busy pub, especially on Wednesday quiz night and Sheffield United match days. QP

White Lion

615 London Road, Heeley, S2 4HT
4-midnight (1am Fri); 12-1am Sat; 2-11 Sun
(0114) 255 1500 whitelionsheffield.co.uk
Abbeydale Moonshine; Tetley Bitter; Wychwood Hobgoblin; 9 changing beers (sourced nationally)
This Grade II-listed pub has been respectfully refurbished over the years. A tiled central corridor links a number of delightful small rooms and leads to the larger rear concert room. A wide selection of cask-conditioned beers always includes a vegan option, and the pub is also proud of its selection of whiskies. Many community events are hosted, and live music features every night except Wednesday, which is quiz night.

Sheffield: West

Ale Club

429 Ecclesall Road, Sharrow, S11 8PG
11.30-11.30 (0114) 453 6818
thebrewfoundation.co.uk/tap-house
5 changing beers (sourced regionally; often Bad Seed, Brew Foundation, Don Valley)
A busy micropub in the heart of the Ecclesall Road social scene, but only a stone's throw from the tranquil botanical gardens. Comfortably furnished, it has a cosy atmosphere in contrast to the usual spartan decor of most micropubs. It is owned by the Brew Foundation, and the brewer is often on hand to answer questions about the beers and advise on home brewing. In addition to the cask ales there is an extensive range of craft keg beers, bottles and cans from independent brewers.
Q

Beer House

623 Ecclesall Road, Sharrow, S11 8PT
12-11
6 changing beers (sourced nationally; often Abbeydale, Blue Bee, Exit 33)
Sheffield's first micropub opened in a small former shop unit in late 2014. The front of two rooms has level access from the street, and contains the bar with its bank of six handpumps displaying a varied range of beers, mainly from microbreweries, with local breweries well represented. The rear room has seating focused around the fireplace, and there is a quiz on Wednesday evening. Q

Hallamshire House

49 Commonside, S10 1GF
4-11.30; 2-12.30am Fri; 12-12.30am Sat; 12-11.30 Sun
☎ (0114) 263 1062
Thornbridge Brother Rabbit, Jaipur IPA; house beer (by Thornbridge); 5 changing beers (sourced locally; often Thornbridge) [H]
Operated by Thornbridge Brewery, and known locally as the Tardis, the pub has two small comfy rooms at the front, and leading from the bar area are a large lounge and a snooker room with full-sized table. There is a courtyard drinking area downstairs with ample seating and a covered space with soft furniture. Quiz night is on Monday, and some Saturdays there is live music or a DJ.
Q ♿ ♣ (95)

Itchy Pig Ale House

495 Glossop Road, Broomhill, S10 2QE
3-11; 12-11 Fri & Sat; 3-10.30 Sun ☎ (0114) 327 0780
theitchypig.co.uk
5 changing beers (sourced regionally; often Abbeydale, Exit 33) [H]
A cosy, friendly micropub with a relaxed atmosphere and continental feel. The whitewashed walls are decorated with porcine-themed artwork, hop sacks and dried hops. There is craftsman-standard carpentry here, including a bar made from Victorian-era doors with a glass-covered bar top formed from 2p coins set in resin. A wide range of pork scratchings is available.
Q ♣ (120)

Rising Sun

471 Fulwood Road, Nether Green, S10 3QA
12-11 (11.30 Fri & Sat) ☎ (0114) 230 3855
risingsunsheffield.co.uk
Abbeydale Deception, Moonshine; 10 changing beers (sourced regionally; often Abbeydale, Ulverston) [H]
This pub is a large suburban roadhouse operated by local brewer Abbeydale. There are two comfortably furnished rooms with a log-burning fire between the main bar and the glass-roofed extension, which also has glass panels in the end wall. A range of Abbeydale beers is always served, with up to six guests – mainly from micros – dispensed from the impressive bank of 13 handpumps. Quizzes are on Sunday and Wednesday evenings, and the Sunfest beer festival is in July.
Q ♿ ♣ P (120,83a)

University Arms

197 Brook Hill, Broomhall, S3 7HG
11-11 (midnight Fri); 12-11 Sat; closed Sun
☎ (0114) 222 8969
Kelham Island Pale Rider [H]**; Welbeck Abbey Red Feather** [H]/[G]**; house beer (by Acorn); 5 changing beers (sourced regionally)** [H]
Owned by the University of Sheffield, this former staff club has an open-plan lounge with a bar at one end adjacent to a small alcove seating area, and a conservatory leading to the large garden. There is additional seating upstairs with separate rooms for snooker and darts. The guest beers are mostly local and there are regular beer festivals. Entertainment includes a quiz on Tuesday and open mic night on Wednesday, during term time.
Q ♿ ♣ (51,52)

Thorne

Old Vault

Market Place, DN8 5DP (follow A614)
3-11 (midnight Fri); 12-midnight Sat; 12-11 Sun
☎ 07809 471355
4 changing beers (sourced locally; often Hilltop, White Rose) [H]
Popular micropub and brewery, conveniently situated in the town's market place. At least four different beers are on handpump, mainly from small independent breweries, and often including beers brewed on-site. Real cider is sometimes stocked. There are live music events most Saturdays, and occasional outdoor events. The last Thursday of every month is open mic and jam night, and quiz night is Sunday.
Q ♿ ♣ (87,88)

Windmill

19 Queen Street, DN8 5AA
2-11 (midnight Fri); 12-midnight Sat; 12-11 Sun
☎ (01405) 812866
Kelham Island Pale Rider; 3 changing beers (sourced regionally; often Abbeydale, Castle Rock) [H]
Friendly community pub close to the town centre on a street parallel with the main road. Four real ales from small independent breweries are sold, and good-natured conversation with staff and clientele is assured. The pub has a smart lounge with a conservatory at the side, which is linked by an archway to another room with a pool table. Outside is a large garden with play equipment and ample parking. Sunday is quiz night.
♣ P (87,88A)

Thorpe Hesley

Red Lion

1 Brook Hill, S61 2PY
3-11.30; 12-midnight Fri & Sat; 12-11 Sun
☎ (0114) 245 8208 redlionthorpehesley.co.uk
Bradfield Farmers Blonde; 2 changing beers (often Bradfield) [H]
Recently refurbished local in a prominent position at the heart of the village. Reopened by a community group, who reintroduced real ale, the lease was latterly taken over by an individual. The real ale range has increased to four, usually sourced from local breweries, with Bradfield often featured. One handpump is now dedicated to a real cider. The pub has become very much a community hub and can get very lively, especially on weekend evenings. The Wednesday night quiz is popular.
P (66)

Thurlstone

Huntsman

136 Manchester Road, S36 9QW (on main A628 towards Woodhead through village)
5-11; 3-midnight Fri; 12-midnight Sat; 12-10.30 Sun
☎ (01226) 764892 huntsmanthurlstone.co.uk
Black Sheep Best Bitter; Timothy Taylor Landlord; 4 changing beers (sourced nationally) [H]
The positioning of this village local on the main east-west Pennine route provides an interesting mixture of regular and passing trade customers. Genuine and friendly meeting, drinking and talking are this pub's lifeblood. Throw in old-fashioned pub games, LocAle, and a seriously dog-friendly attitude, and you have a venue that just should not be passed by. Food is served Tuesday evening

and Sunday lunch only. It has no jukebox or TVs, but Wednesday evening is live music night.
Q🐴❀◐♣●🚌🐾

Tickhill

Scarbrough Arms L
Sunderland Street, DN11 9QJ (on A631 near Buttercross)
⏲ 12-11; 12-10.30 Sun ☎ (01302) 742977
Greene King Abbot; John Smith's Bitter; Timothy Taylor Landlord; 2 changing beers (sourced locally; often Bradfield, Pheasantry, Welbeck Abbey) H
An entry in the Guide since 1990, this stone-built pub dates back to the 16th century. There is a taproom at the rear which features a dartboard and sports TV, while a spacious lounge can be found at the front. Between the two is the Barrel Room, a small snug with barrel-shaped furniture. There is a covered smoking area and a large, attractive beer garden. Quiz nights are Monday and Thursday.
Q🐴❀♣●P🚌(22,205)🐾 📶

Wales

Duke of Leeds L ✔
16 Church Street, S26 5LQ (off A618 into School Rd, opp parish church)
⏲ 12-11 ☎ (01909) 515490 🌐 thedukeofleeds.co.uk
Bradfield Farmers Blonde; 3 changing beers (sourced regionally; often Abbeydale, Box Steam) H
Extensively refurbished, the pub reopened in 2015 under new ownership. Three hundred years old, it is the former coaching inn of the Duke of Leeds. The bar area leads to three other areas where drinks and meals can be taken. Outdoor drinking areas afford views of the village, and the upstairs function room holds 60 people. Changing beers are both local and from further afield. Food is freshly cooked to order. The pub is popular with walkers and is on the Five Churches walk. Ample parking space is provided behind the pub and it is handy for the Kiveton Bridge railway station. Local CAMRA Rural Pub of the Year 2017. 🐴❀◐P🚌🐾

Wath upon Dearne

Church House L ✔
Montgomery Square, S63 7RZ
⏲ 8am-midnight ☎ (01709) 879518
Greene King Abbot; Ruddles Best Bitter; 4 changing beers (often Bradfield, Great Heck) H
Large pub with an impressive frontage set in a pedestrianised square in the town centre, with excellent access to local bus services (across the square). It was built in 1810 and consecrated by the nearby church in 1912. It became a pub in the 1980s and then a Wetherspoon's in 2000. A wide variety of beers is available from both national and local brewers. Real ciders and perries are also on handpull. Handy for exploring the RSPB Old Moor Wetlands Centre and for Manvers Commercial Park.
❀◐♿●P🚌📶

Wath Tap 🏆 L
49 High Street, S63 7QB
⏲ 12-11 ☎ (01709) 872150 🌐 wathtap.co.uk
6 changing beers (sourced locally; often Fernandes, Geeves, Ossett) H
Rotherham district's first micropub, opened in a former butcher's shop in March 2016, serving up six changing real ales, mostly from local breweries, and five real ciders. These are listed on chalkboards by the bar. Food may be brought in from the surrounding takeaways. What was the walk-in cold store is now the cellar. Seats at the front of the pub are protected from the rain by the original shop canopy. Jam sessions are sometimes held and board games are available. A warm welcome is guaranteed. Local CAMRA Pub of the Year 2017-2019. Q♿♣●🚌🐾📶

Wentworth

George & Dragon L
85 Main Street, S62 7TN (set back from road on B6090)
⏲ 11-11 (11.30 Thu; midnight Fri & Sat) ☎ (01226) 742440
🌐 georgeanddragonwentworth.com
Theakston Old Peculier; 7 changing beers (often Bradfield, Chantry, Geeves) H
A village free house, licensed since 1804, offering eight changing real ales from local and national brewers, with a front patio and a large garden and children's adventure playground at the rear. It also has a craft shop and function rooms for hire. Home-cooked food is served from an extensive menu, and a pop-up pie shop opens every Saturday and Sunday noon-4pm. Handy for historic Wentworth Woodhouse, Needle's Eye and Hoober Stand. The pub is a Guide regular and winner of numerous local CAMRA branch awards.
Q🐴❀◐P🚌(44,136)🐾📶

Whiston

Hind L ✔
285 East Bawtry Road, S60 4ET (on A631 link road between M1 and M18)
⏲ 11.30-midnight; 10-midnight Sat & Sun ☎ (01709) 532490
Abbeydale Moonshine; Tetley Bitter; house beer (by Black Sheep); 3 changing beers (sourced nationally; often Fyne, Kirkstall, St Austell) H
Originally built for Mappins Brewery of Rotherham in 1936, the interior has been opened out since its refurbishment, creating good wheelchair access. There are extensive gardens, a patio to the rear and a function room upstairs. Food is served daytime and evening and is also available to take away. Cask beers come from breweries large and small throughout the country and are cheaper on Mondays; there is also a cask club. General knowledge quizzes take place on Tuesday, Thursday and Sunday evenings. Q🐴❀◐♿P🚌📶

Wortley

Wortley Men's Club L ✔
Reading Room Lane, S35 7DB (in centre of village at back of Wortley Arms pub)
⏲ 2-11; 12-11 Sat & Sun ☎ (0114) 288 2066
🌐 wortleymensclub.co.uk
Timothy Taylor Landlord; 2 changing beers (sourced nationally) H
Winner of many CAMRA awards including national and local Club of the Year, set in a pretty rural village near to Wortley Hall and gardens. With an opulent exterior and interior, features include exposed timber frames, ornate ceilings, wooden panelling and a real fire. Guest ales are from local and national breweries, and a guest cider is stocked. The club runs an annual beer festival in July. Show your CAMRA membership card or a copy of this Guide on entry. Q❀♿♣●P🚌(23,23A)

YORKSHIRE (WEST)

Ackworth

Masons Arms

Bell Lane, WF7 7JD (turning off A628 by disused railway bridge)

4-midnight; 1.30-1am Fri; 12-1am Sat; 12-midnight Sun

07966 501827

Bradfield Farmers Blonde, Farmers Brown Cow; 2 changing beers (sourced regionally)

A Grade II-listed former coaching house dating from 1682, built of locally quarried stone, and one of seven real ale establishments in the village. A central bar serves the main room, pool room and smaller lounge. There are log-burning fireplaces in both the main rooms, that were discovered 15 years ago during a refurbishment. Live music plays on Saturday and Sunday, bingo night is Tuesday and quiz night is Thursday. P

Altofts

Robin Hood

10 Church Road, WF6 2NJ (from Normanton town centre take road over railway into Altofts, continue through Lee Brigg, then High Green Rd and left on to Church Rd)

12-11 (midnight Fri & Sat) (01924) 892911

robinhoodaltofts.co.uk

Acorn Barnsley Bitter; 5 changing beers (sourced locally; often Tarn 51)

Locally owned free house/brewpub at the top end of the village. This village pub has a new large patio area seating 70 people. Tarn 51 microbrewery will move into a new brewhouse adjacent to the pub in midsummer. The pub is within easy reach of the Pennine Trail and Aire & Calder Navigation, being only a mile from Stanley Ferry Marina. P

Alverthorpe

New Albion

2 Flanshaw Lane, WF2 9JH (accessible from A638, right at lights past Morrisons and follow bends of Flanshaw Lane)

12-11 (midnight Fri & Sat) (01924) 376946

5 changing beers (sourced regionally)

Traditional, multi-roomed free house including a raised area furnished with sofas and easy chairs. Outside is a large, award-winning decking and seating area which is a suntrap, enhanced with many attractive planters. BT Sports is available to armchair enthusiasts in two of the four rooms. Wednesday is quiz night. Five rotating guest beers and a traditional cider are served at all times.

P

Armitage Bridge

Armitage Bridge Monkey Club

Dean Brook Road, HD4 7PB

7-11 Mon, Wed & Thu; closed Tue; 5-midnight Fri; 4-11 Sat; 12-10 Sun (01484) 522370 monkeyclub.co.uk

Goose Eye Bitter; 2 changing beers (sourced nationally; often Empire)

Refurbished and air-conditioned, this thriving little club in the hamlet of Armitage Bridge serves two guest beers. The annual Monkeyfest held in early July is now into its 12th year and is ever popular. A regular local CAMRA Club of the Year, the venue is well worth seeking out. P

Baildon

Bull's Head Inn

6 Westgate, BD17 5ES

12-11.30 (midnight Fri & Sat) (01274) 976416

Goose Eye Chinook Blonde; Saltaire Blonde; Sharp's Doom Bar; Tetley Bitter; 1 changing beer (sourced nationally; often Nightjar)

A two-roomed traditional pub with log fires and a warming atmosphere. This village local is frequented by a wide age range of customers, where visitors and well-behaved dogs are always welcome. Local photos of Baildon adorn the walls. As well as the four regular ales, a varying guest beer, usually of a darker style, is also offered. Sunday and Tuesday evenings are quiz nights, and live music plays fortnightly on Saturday. The separate taproom houses darts and dominoes.

P

Junction

1 Baildon Road, BD17 6AB (on A6038/B6151 jct)

12-midnight (1am Fri & Sat) (01274) 582009

Fuller's ESB; Junction Blonde, Dark Thoughts; Tetley Bitter; 2 changing beers (sourced nationally; often Junction, Tetley)

Three-roomed traditional local comprising a lounge, public bar and a games area. Four regularly available beers, usually including two from the in-house Junction Brewery, are complemented by two guest ales. Bottled ciders and foreign beers are also sold. Sports events on TV are popular. Quiz nights are held on Tuesday and Thursday and there is a piano for those wanting to provide impromptu live music and singalongs. A regular beer festival features at the end of July.

Battyeford

Pear Tree

259 Huddersfield Road, WF14 9DL (on A644)

12-midnight (1am Fri & Sat) (01924) 491360

thepeartree-mirfield.co.uk

Sharp's Doom Bar; 3 changing beers

This is an inviting pub boasting a riverside beer garden with free overnight boat moorings. The relaxed atmosphere combined with good home-cooked food served lunchtimes and evenings is appealing to locals and visitors alike. The bar offers four ales, two being free of tie. Thursday is quiz night and on Sunday evening an acoustic jam session is held. P(262)

Bingley

Chip N Ern

73 Main Street, BD16 2JA

4-11 (midnight Fri); 12-midnight Sat; 1-10 Sun

(01274) 985501

7 changing beers (sourced locally; often Bingley, Bridgehouse, Goose Eye)

This traditionally-styled micropub is a popular destination on the local real ale scene. The wood-panelled ground-floor bar has a distinctive range of decorations. There is additional seating in the upstairs gin bar. The seven cask ales include a varying range from Bingley, Bridgehouse, Goose Eye and other guest breweries. A changing range of ciders is also offered. The pub is close to the railway station and handy for exploring the famous Five Rise Locks on the adjacent Leeds-Liverpool Canal.

Foundry Hill

Wellington Street, BD16 2NB

4-11 (1am Fri); 12-1am Sat; 2-11 Sun ☎ (01274) 566144

5 changing beers (sourced nationally)

Opposite the railway station, this modern basement pub comprises a small bar area and an adjacent larger room. There is a focus on selling a varying range of up to five good-quality real ales, sourced both regionally and nationally. The styles offered tend to comprise a pale, two golden, one bitter/amber and one dark. Closing times may vary depending upon the demand. Children are welcome until 7pm and dogs are also permitted.

Platform 1¾

1 Burrage Street, BD16 1GH (off Chapel Lane)

4-8; 2-11 Fri & Sat; 2-9 Sun ☎ 07561 195586

8 changing beers (sourced regionally; often Abbeydale, Empire, Old Spot)

A single-room pub in the town centre close to the railway station. The interior seating is zoned and includes some unusual recycling. Eight handpulls serve two regular house beers (a bitter and a blonde) and up to six varied guest beers, usually from the surrounding region. Lagers and an extensive range of ciders are also offered. Dogs are welcome, as are children until 8pm. Opening and closing times may vary depending upon the demand.

Birkby

Magic Rock Brewery Tap

Willow Park Business Centre, Willow Lane, HD1 5EB

closed Mon; 4-10 Tue-Thu; 1-11 Fri; 12-11 Sat; 12-9 Sun

magicrockbrewing.com

Magic Rock Hat Trick, Ringmaster, High Wire; 3 changing beers (sourced locally)

The Tap opened in 2015. It sells up to five cask beers from the brewery, with Ringmaster and Hat Trick doubling up on busy match days. Less than 10 minutes' walk from the town centre, the Tap itself is housed in a 1,700 square foot area to the far end of the brewery, with a view directly into it. Street-food outlets are laid on every weekend. Regular events include brewery tours, available on Saturday afternoons and week nights (book in advance), and exhibitions and festivals – all of which make the tap well worth a visit.

P

Birstall

Black Bull

5 Kirkgate, WF17 9HE (off A652 near jct of A643)

12-10.30 (midnight Fri & Sat) ☎ (01274) 973203

theblackbullinnbirstall.co.uk

Black Sheep Best Bitter; Saltaire Blonde; 1 changing beer (sourced nationally; often Exmoor, Hook Norton, York)

A stone-built 17th-century community pub. The upper room was a local magistrates' court in times gone by; still preserved, it is used for functions. On the ground floor is a snug, main bar area and a piano room. There is an open fire in the winter, while behind is a car park and a spacious beer garden. All visitors receive a warm welcome and can enjoy the comfortable surroundings. Games are available such as chess, draughts, dominoes plus Jenga. P

Horse & Jockey

97 Low Lane, WF17 9HB (on A643 near village centre)

12-11.30 Mon & Tue; 4-11.30 Wed; 12-midnight Thu; 12-1am Fri & Sat; 12-11.30 Sun ☎ (01924) 472559

Bradfield Farmers Blonde; Rat White Rat; Tetley Bitter; Timothy Taylor Boltmaker; 2 changing beers (sourced nationally; often Jennings, Rudgate, Timothy Taylor)

A country-style pub licensed from the 1750s. The open-plan bar is split into four areas, with half-panelled walls and beamed ceilings. Darts, dominoes and pool are played, and on Thursday there is a music and knowledge quiz. Guest beer comes mainly from independent breweries, local where possible. One of the seven pumps serves real cider. Outside, the patio has a beautiful, award-winning flower display. Last admission is 11pm. P

Bradford

Corn Dolly

110 Bolton Road, BD1 4DE

11.30-11; 12-10.30 Sun ☎ (01274) 720219

corndolly.pub

Everards Tiger; Moorhouse's White Witch; Timothy Taylor Boltmaker; 5 changing beers (sourced regionally; often Abbeydale, Pictish, Wishbone)

Award-winning traditional free house run by the same family for over 25 years, close to the city centre and Forster Square railway station. Previously called the Wharfe, due to its location near to the former Bradford canal, it first opened its doors in 1834. An open-plan layout incorporates a games area to one end. Good-value food is served weekday lunchtimes. It has a friendly atmosphere and is busy before Bradford City matches. A collection of pumpclips adorns the beams.

P (640,641)

Fighting Cock

21-23 Preston Street, BD7 1JE (close to Grattans, off Thornton Rd)

11.30-11; 12-10.30 Sun ☎ (01274) 726907

Ilkley Mary Jane; Theakston Old Peculier; Timothy Taylor Golden Best, Boltmaker, Landlord; 7 changing beers (often Bath Ales, Bingley, Salopian)

A drinkers' paradise in an industrial area, this multi award-winning traditionally-styled free house is 20 minutes' walk from the city centre and close to bus routes along Thornton Road and Legrams Lane. Twice-yearly beer festivals take place. Twelve real ales are usually on sale including at least one dark beer. A variety of real ciders is sold as well as foreign bottled beers. Good-value lunches are served Monday to Saturday. Awarded CAMRA branch Cider Pub of the Year 2019.

Jacobs Beer House

14 Kent Street, BD1 5RL (by Jacobs Well roundabout at end of Hall Ings)

4-10 (11 Thu); 12-11 Fri & Sat ☎ (01274) 395628

Abbeydale Deception; Half Moon Dark Masquarade; 7 changing beers (sourced regionally; often Salamander, Spotlight, Stancill)

Traditionally styled real ale and cider free house with a rustic feel, formerly known as Jacobs Well and dating from 1811. The layout is open plan but with a snug to the side of the bar. Nine handpulls offer a varying range of beers from local and regional independents, always featuring some darker ales. Numerous ciders are also available

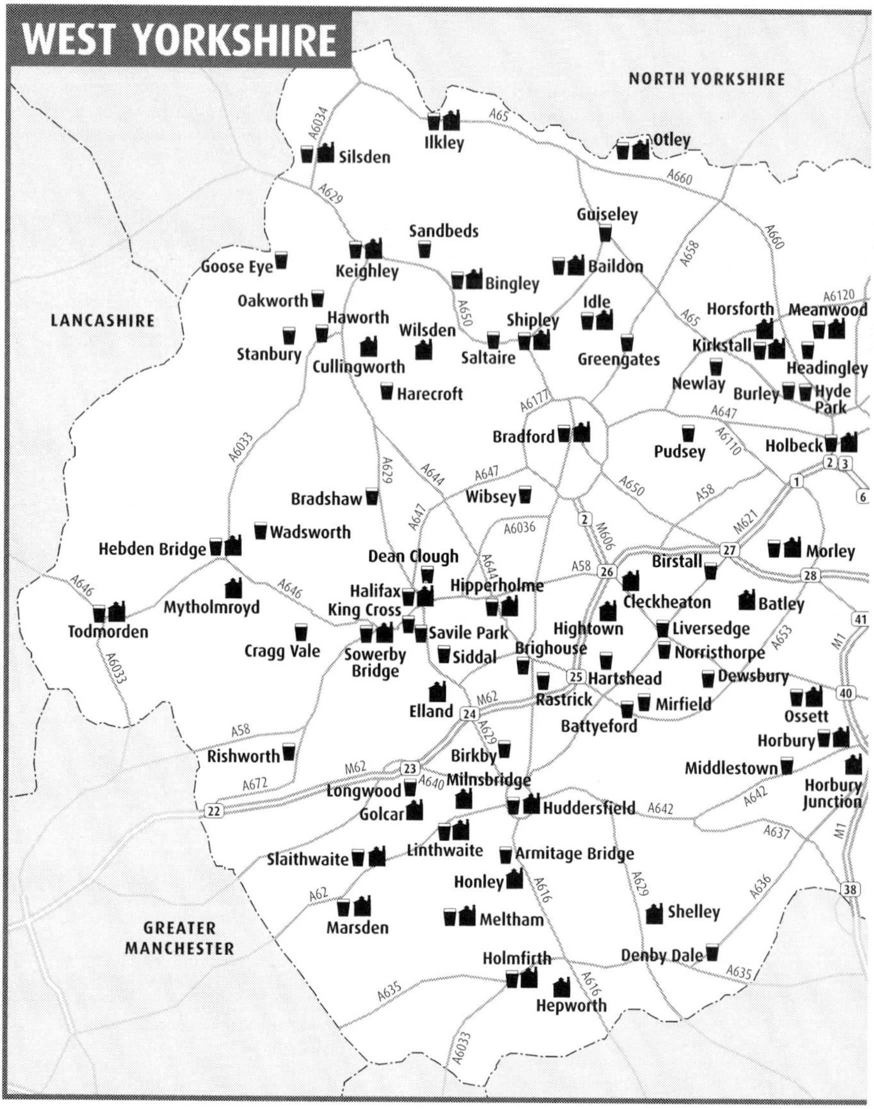

together with a good range of foreign bottled beers. Sit outside and watch the city bustle while supping good ale.

Old Bank

69 Market Street, BD1 1NE (near City Hall)
10-11 (01274) 738218 theoldbankbar.co.uk

6 changing beers (sourced nationally; often Coach House, Empire, Moorhouse's)
An impressive city-centre building that was formerly a bank. This traditionally style pub has a large ground-floor room with a semi-enclosed room to the rear, finished with oak woodwork and neutral colours. An additional seating area upstairs, primarily for dining, has an opulent classical style to it. Six handpulls serve a varying range of beers, often including one from Coach House Brewery. Good-value meals are offered throughout the day. Sections of the pub can be hired.

Peacock Bar

25 North Parade, BD1 3JL
2 (1 Wed)-10.30; 12-1am Fri & Sat; 12-10.30 Sun
07979 182599 peacockbar.co.uk

Bradfield Farmers Blonde; Thornbridge Jaipur IPA; 2 changing beers (sourced regionally; often Saltaire)
Opened in 2016, this Indian-themed bar offers real ale and Indian street food with a twist. Four handpumps serve real ale while a further two pumps serves cider. There are two permanent beers and varying regional guest ales, usually including one from Saltaire Brewery. Indian street food is prepared and sold on the ground floor. The upstairs room, with a large TV showing sports, is available for hire. Popular with football fans, especially when Bradford City are at home, and it can be busy on weekend evenings. Quiz night is the last Wednesday of the month and comedy acts perform on a Thursday every few months.

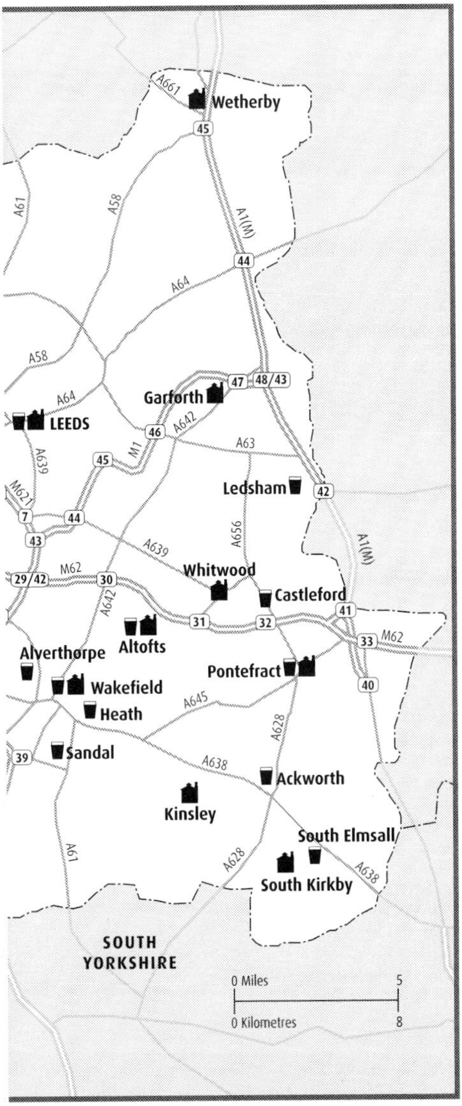

Record Café

45-47 North Parade, BD1 3JH
11-8 Mon; 11-11 Tue-Thu; 11-midnight Fri & Sat; 1-6 Sun
☎ (01274) 723143 therecordcafe.co.uk
4 changing beers (sourced regionally; often Brass Castle, North Riding Brewery, Wilde Child)
Modern café-style bar located in the city's independent quarter, selling ale, vinyl and ham. Four handpulls serve real ales sourced regionally in varying styles, usually including a dark beer. Real cider and perry are offered and there are seven craft keg beers from independent brewers on tap. Food comes in a charcuterie style, specialising in hams and cheeses from Spain. In the upstairs mezzanine area vinyl records are for sale. Local CAMRA Pub of the Year 2019.

Sparrow

32 North Parade, BD1 3HZ
12-11; 11-midnight Thu-Sat ☎ (01274) 270772
Kirkstall Pale Ale, Three Swords, Dissolution IPA; 3 changing beers (sourced nationally)
This simply furnished café-style pub was refurbished in May 2018 by its new owners, Kirkstall Brewery. The interior now has a more traditional feel, with painted walls decorated with pictures and mirrors, many having a breweriana theme, and dark-wood panelling behind the bar. There is additional seating in the basement. Three regular real ales from the brewery are complemented by an additional three guest ales. The pub can be busy when Bradford City FC are playing at home.

Bradshaw

Golden Fleece

1 Bradshaw Lane, HX2 9UZ
4-11 (midnight Fri); 12-midnight Sat; 12-10.30 Sun
☎ 07522 190990 goldenfleecebradshaw.co.uk
Saltaire Blonde; Tetley Bitter; 2 changing beers (sourced regionally; often Fuzzy Duck, Lytham)
Set in the heart of this picturesque village, the pub has a spacious, comfortable lounge and a separate room at the rear. A small snug leads out to a large beer garden with tables and chairs. Barbecues are held during the summer to take advantage of the scenic views. The pub supports local pool and dominoes teams, quiz night is on a Wednesday, and there is a disco every Saturday.

Brighouse

Market Tavern

2 Ship Street, HD6 1JX
closed Mon & Tue; 2-10 Wed & Thu; 12-10 Fri-Sun
☎ 07908 698360
6 changing beers (sourced regionally; often Abbeydale, Salopian, Squawk)
A single-storey former pork pie factory, next to the canalside open-air market, has been transformed into a micropub. There is seating in the bar, a small snug by the entrance, and a sheltered outside drinking area. At least one dark beer and a choice of real ciders, including Thistly Cross, are on the bar at all times. Snacks are available and treats for dogs. Open bank holiday Mondays.

Castleford

Griffin Inn

Lock lane, WF10 2LB (10 mins from town centre on A656)
11-midnight ☎ (01977) 731706
3 changing beers (sourced regionally)
Traditional, refurbished two-roomed free house with a separate lounge and bar. It is close to the town centre and Castleford Tigers rugby ground, and next to the Aire & Calder canal, where moorings are available. Families and dogs are welcome. Food is served on Wednesday evening and Saturday and Sunday lunchtimes. Local CAMRA branch Most Improved Pub of 2017.

Junction

Carlton Street, WF10 1EE (enter Castleford on A655; pub is on corner with Carlton St at top of town centre)
2-9 (11 Thu); 12-midnight Fri; 12-11.30 Sat; 12-9 Sun
☎ (01977) 277750 thejunctionpubcastleford.com
6 changing beers

A rejuvenated pub, handy for bus and train stations, specialising in beers in the landlord's own wooden casks. Up to six guest beers are served, sourced from enterprising local brewers. The large horseshoe-shaped bar is kept warm with open fires, and there is a stove-heated snug available for functions. Folk night is on the last Sunday of each month and a live band plays on Friday evening. The pub holds an annual Easter Woodfest beer festival.
Q☻≠♣●🚌🐾📶

Cragg Vale

Robin Hood 𝕃

Cragg Road, HX7 5SQ (on B6138 1½ miles south of Mytholmroyd)
⏲ 3-11; 12-midnight Fri & Sat; 12-11 Sun ☎ (01422) 885899
Timothy Taylor Boltmaker, Landlord; 3 changing beers (sourced regionally; often Goose Eye, Millstone, Oakham) Ⓗ
Welcoming, comfortable, traditional village pub. It is in the scenic Cragg Valley, ideal for countryside walkers and for those investigating the history of the Cragg Vale Coiners. The venue is compact and has two split-level rooms, with a cosy real fire in the winter. Food is served Friday to Sunday (telephone to check times). The pub is customer-led and guest ales can come from local breweries.
Q☻❀◑⛺🚌(900,901)🐾📶

Denby Dale

Dunkirk 🏆 𝕃

231 Barnsley Road, HD8 8TX
⏲ 12-11 (midnight Fri & Sat); 12-10 Sun ☎ (01484) 862912
🌐 thedunkirk.co.uk
Magic Rock Ringmaster; Small World Barncliffe Bitter; Timothy Taylor Landlord; 6 changing beers (sourced locally; often Abbeydale, Mallinsons, Saltaire) Ⓗ
When four local families found out their village pub was closing and in danger of being turned into housing, they decided not to let this community asset go without a fight. The Dunkirk is now a worthy entry in the Guide, stocking six ales, mainly from local microbreweries (Small World, Magic Rock), including a dark beer, and three real ciders, with at least one from the local Pure North. Good food is served in the bar and restaurant.
☻❀◑♿●P🚌(83)🐾📶↺

Dewsbury

West Riding Refreshment Rooms 🏆 𝕃

Dewsbury Railway Station, Wellington Road, WF13 1HF
⏲ 12-11 Mon; 11-11 Tue-Thu; 11-midnight Fri; 10-midnight Sat ☎ (01924) 459193

REAL ALE BREWERIES

Anthology Leeds
Beer Ink Huddersfield
BEEspoke 🛢 Shipley
Bingley Wilsden
Bone Idle Idle (NEW)
Bosun's Huddersfield
Bridgehouse Keighley
Briscoe's Otley
Burley Street 🛢 Leeds
Cap House Batley
Chin Chin South Kirkby
Cobbydale 🛢 Silsden
Cooper Hill Leeds (NEW)
Copper Dragon Keighley
Darkland Halifax (NEW)
Eagles Crag Todmorden
Elland Elland
Empire Slaithwaite
Eyes Bradford
Fernandes 🛢 Wakefield
Five Towns Wakefield
Frisky Bear 🛢 Leeds: Morley
Ghost Baildon
Golcar Golcar
Goose Eye Bingley
Halifax Steam 🛢 Hipperholme
Haworth Steam 🛢 Cleckheaton
Henry Smith 🛢 Pontefract (NEW)
Hogs Head 🛢 Sowerby Bridge
Horbury 🛢 Horbury
Horsforth Leeds: Horsforth
Hungry Bear Leeds
Ilkley Ilkley
Junction 🛢 Baildon
Kirkstall Leeds: Kirkstall
Lazy Turtle Hepworth (NEW)
Leeds Leeds: Holbeck
Legitimate Industries Leeds
Linfit 🛢 Linthwaite
Little Valley Hebden Bridge
Lord's Golcar
Luddite 🛢 Horbury Junction (NEW)
Magic Rock Huddersfield
Mallinsons Huddersfield
Malt Brewhouse 🛢 Leeds: Horsforth (NEW)
Meanwood Leeds: Meanwood
Mill Valley Hightown
Milltown Milnsbridge
Morton Collins Wakefield
Nightjar Mytholmroyd
Nomadic Leeds
Nook 🛢 Holmfirth
North Leeds
Northern Monk Leeds: Holbeck
Old Spot Cullingworth
Ossett Ossett
Outgang Kinsley
Quirky Leeds: Garforth
Rat 🛢 Huddersfield
Revolutions Whitwood
Ridgeside Leeds: Meanwood
Riverhead 🛢 Marsden
Salt Shipley (NEW)
Saltaire Shipley
Shadow Otley (NEW)
Small World Shelley
Stod Fold Halifax
Summer Wine Honley
Sunbeam Leeds
Tapped 🛢 Leeds
Tarn51 🛢 Altofts
Three Fiends Meltham
Three Valleys Todmorden
Tigertops Wakefield
Timothy Taylor Keighley
Truth Hurts Leeds: Morley
Vocation Hebden Bridge
Wetherby Wetherby
Wharfedale 🛢 Ilkley
Wilde Child Leeds
Wishbone Keighley

Black Sheep Best Bitter; Timothy Taylor Landlord; 7 changing beers (sourced nationally; often Brass Castle, Magic Rock, Vocation) H
Multi award-winning pub in a Grade II-listed station building. The eclectic range of nine real ales always features a variety of styles and strengths. Real cider and a choice of speciality cans and bottled beers are also sold. Live music plays outside in summer and occasional beer festivals are held. Good meals are served daily plus pizzas all day, pie night is Tuesday, and curries on Wednesday. The pub is a mainstay of the Transpennine Rail Ale Trail, hence Saturdays can be busy. There are monthly brewery tap takeovers.

Goose Eye

Turkey Inn

BD22 0PD (village centre) SE028406
12-11; 12-10 Sun (01535) 681339 theturkeyinn.com
Goose Eye Bitter, Chinook Blonde; Timothy Taylor Golden Best, Landlord; 6 changing beers (sourced nationally) H
Friendly, historic pub in a tiny hamlet approached by steep roads or a riverside footpath. It has three snugs, each with a real fire to keep out the winter chill, and is a good base for exploring the surrounding countryside. It has a pool table, holds a quiz night on Wednesday, and hosts occasional live music and special theme nights. Food is served every day. Up to six guest beers are usually on handpump.

Greengates

Cracker Barrel

832 Harrogate Road, BD10 0RA
1-10 (11 Fri); 12-11 Sat; 12-10 Sun
Tetley Bitter; 4 changing beers (sourced regionally; often Abbeydale, Great Newsome, Salamander) H
Opened in April 2017, this small, friendly, family-run micropub comprises a single room with the bar positioned to the rear. It has a cosy, homely feel. Tetley's Cask bitter is the regular real ale. The other four handpulls serve a varying range of real ales, often including a dark beer, from regional breweries. The pub welcomes families and dogs. Outside seating to the front is next to a busy main road.

Guiseley

Coopers

4-6 Otley Road, LS20 8AH
12-11 (midnight Fri & Sat) (01943) 878835
Okell's Bitter; Rooster's Yorkshire Pale Ale; Timothy Taylor Landlord; 5 changing beers (sourced regionally; often Anarchy, Tapped Sheffield, Thornbridge) H
A light, modern, airy bar/diner converted from a former Co-operative store. It has a bar with a separate dining area and an upstairs function room. Eight ales are served, generally from Yorkshire or northern micros, with a dedicated dark beer pump and a large selection of other beers on tap and in bottles and cans. A diverse range of meals is available. The large upstairs function room has regular music events and a monthly comedy club, and this area also serves as extra dining space.

Guiseley Factory Workers Club

6 Town Street, LS20 9DT
1-11 (midnight Fri); 11.30-midnight Sat; 11-11 Sun
(01943) 874793 guiseleyfactoryworkersclub.co.uk
Tetley Bitter; 3 changing beers (sourced locally; often Acorn, Salamander, Saltaire) H
Three-roomed club founded over 100 years ago by the Yeadon and Guiseley Factory Workers Union, and a multi award-winner. The bar serves both the lounge and the concert room and has changing guest ales from micros and independents. There is also a snooker room and a small outdoor drinking area. Varied musical acts perform occasionally on Friday and Saturday nights, and the venue hosts many other local clubs and organisations. CAMRA members are welcome with this Guide or a membership card.

Halifax: Dean Clough

Stod Fold Brewery Tap

HX3 5AH
12-11 (midnight Fri & Sat); 12-10 Sun (01422) 355600
stodfold.com
Stod Fold Gold, Best Yorkshire Bitter, The West American Pale, Yorkshire Blonde, Dark Porter; 3 changing beers (sourced nationally; often Stod Fold) H
A sympathetically restored industrial-chic bar tucked just inside Gate One of the architecturally significant Dean Clough Mills in central Halifax. Food is provided by street-food vendors and the pop-up food changes fortnightly. At the end of every month the pub hosts a comedy night introducing new comics. Live music plays every Sunday.

Halifax: King Cross

Wainhouse Tavern

Upper Washer Lane, Pye Nest, HX2 7DR (take Edwards Rd off Pye Nest Rd)
4-11; 12-midnight Fri & Sat; 12-10.30 Sun
(01422) 339998 wainhousetavern.co.uk
Stod Fold Gold; 5 changing beers (sourced regionally; often Elland, Mallinsons, Rudgate) H
Former home to industrialist JFE Wainhouse, most famous for his nearby tower, converted to a public house in the 1960s and saved from an uncertain future by the present owners. No two windows are alike in this Grade II-listed Gothic-fronted building. A small lounge at the front opens up to a much larger bar at the rear. Private functions, live music and game nights take place. Traditional home-cooked food is served in the evenings and at weekends. (579,560)

Halifax: Savile Park

Big Six

10 Horsfall Street, HX1 3HG (off A646 Skircoat Moor Rd at King Cross)
4-11; 3.30-11 Fri; 12-midnight Sat & Sun
(01422) 350169
Old Mill Traditional Bitter; 4 changing beers (sourced regionally) H
Characterful hidden gem in a row of terraces, comprising two houses knocked together, adjacent to the Free School Lane recreation ground. The emphasis in this friendly pub is on good beer and conversation. It has a regionally important historic pub interior with a through corridor separating the

bar and cosy snug from the games room and two lounges. A regular beer and four rotating guest beers from regional or microbreweries are served, and it stocks a large range of gins and malt whiskies. A quiz night is held on Monday.
Q❀♣🍎🚌(577)🐾↺

Halifax: Siddal

Cross Keys

3 Whitegate, HX3 9AE
⏲ 3-11; 12-11 Fri-Sun ☎ (01422) 300348
8 changing beers (sourced regionally; often Abbeydale, Half Moon, Salopian) Ⓗ
This 17th-century pub has a real traditional feel. There is a snug adjacent to the bar, with an inglenook fireplace dividing the remaining area and a taproom to the rear of the bar. The walls have various displays of beer mats from many now-closed breweries. Live music is featured on Sunday afternoon. There is a spacious, sheltered beer garden at the back of the pub. Walkers and cyclists are welcome and two letting rooms are available. Q🐴❀🛏♣🍎🚌(542,555)🐾📶

Halifax: Town Centre

Alexandra

17 Alexandra Street, HX1 1BS
⏲ 4-9 Mon; 4-10 Tue & Wed; 1-11 Thu; 2-11.30 Fri & Sat; 2-10 Sun ☎ 07535 617503
2 changing beers (sourced regionally; often Hawkshead, Ilkley, Nightjar) Ⓗ
A very micro micropub set on two levels. The downstairs has wall-to-wall bottles of beer, many bottle-conditioned, all for sale. Upstairs is called the snug. The friendly staff know how to keep their beer, and there are always two regionally sourced real ales, mainly from northern microbreweries.
Q⇌🚌🐾

Grayston Unity L

1-3 Wesley Court, HX1 1UH
⏲ closed Mon; 4-10 Tue & Wed; 4-11 Thu; 12-11.30 Fri & Sat; 1-10 Sun ☎ 07807 136520 🌐 thegraystonunity.co.uk
Goose Eye Chinook Blonde; 4 changing beers (sourced regionally; often Elland) Ⓗ
This bar is opposite Halifax's town hall in a Grade II-listed building. There is a café-style seating area in front of the bar, a side room with comfy chairs, and a vestibule leading to an outside seating area. It is officially the UK's smallest music venue and hosts music nights, quizzes and local history talks. On Sunday there is an ale of the day offer. Cutlery is provided if you bring your own food. Open 1-10pm on bank holiday Monday. 🐴❀⇌♣🚌🐾📶

Pump Room Micropub L

33 Northgate, HX1 1UR
⏲ 4 (2 Wed & Thu; 12 Fri & Sat)-11; 1-10 Sun ☎ 07808 147575
5 changing beers (sourced regionally; often Mallinsons, Salopian, Vocation) Ⓗ
Welcoming, quirky and atmospheric one-roomed micropub. There is extra seating downstairs which is ideal for private meetings. It takes its name from an old, recently demolished pub on New Road. Some of the artefacts have been incorporated into the new place. Behind the bar are glass panels with four shelves hosting casks of real ale. The bus station is less than a minute away.
Q🐴⇌🍎🚌🐾📶

Square Chapel Café & Bar L

10 Square Road, HX1 1QG
⏲ 12-11 ☎ (01422) 349422 🌐 squarechapel.co.uk
4 changing beers (sourced nationally) Ⓗ
An impressive modern structure between the original Grade II-listed Square Chapel and the historic Grade I-listed Piece Hall. It acts as the foyer for the arts centre, which hosts live music, films and other events. The centre won a RIBA Yorkshire 2018 award. The long bar sells four real ales and a real cider. Good-value, high-quality seasonal food is served lunchtimes, evenings and noon-8pm on Sunday. Hot drinks and cakes are available all day from 10am. 🐴❀◐♿⇌🍎🚌📶

Three Pigeons ★ L ✔

1 Sun Fold, HX1 2LX
⏲ 4-11.30; 12-11.30 Fri & Sat; 12-11 Sun ☎ (01422) 347001
Ossett Yorkshire Brunette, Yorkshire Blonde, Silver King; Rat White Rat; 4 changing beers (sourced nationally; often Fernandes, Jennings, Ossett) Ⓗ
A striking octagonal drinking lobby forms the hub from which five distinctive rooms radiate in this Art Deco pub, built in 1932 by Websters Brewery. Sensitively refurbished and maintained by Ossett Brewery, this venue attracts a variety of local groups and societies as well as football and rugby enthusiasts. Three changing guest beers plus one stout/porter come from regional and national microbreweries as well as from Ossett's own stable of pub-based microbreweries.
Q❀⇌♣🍎P🚌🐾📶↺

Victorian Craft Beer Café L

18-22 Powell Street, HX1 1LN
⏲ 11-11 (midnight Fri & Sat) 🌐 victorian.beer
10 changing beers (sourced nationally; often Squawk, Vocation) Ⓗ
An award-winning pub behind the Victoria Theatre, which opened in 2014 after a complete refurbishment of a once-popular Italian restaurant. On entry you will find the main seating area, with wooden floors and a tiled bar. To the left is a more secluded area and steps to an upper level with additional seating. As well as eight rotating real ales from microbreweries nationwide, it also offers 18 keg lines, a choice of world bottled beers, and two draught ciders. 🐴⇌🍎📶↺

Harecroft

Station Hotel L

122 Lane Side, BD15 0BP (on B6144)
⏲ 4-midnight; 12-midnight Sun ☎ (01535) 272430
Timothy Taylor Landlord; 2 changing beers (often Bingley, Naylor's) Ⓗ
In the heart of a small village between Bradford and Haworth, this traditional, homely community pub is named after a station on the long-gone Great Northern Railway. It comprises two linked rooms with real fires and a games room which is home to the local pool team. A jazz/swing band plays on Monday night. The local bus stops running early in the evening and does not run at all on Sunday. 🐴❀♣P🚌(K17)🐾

Hartshead

Hartshead L

86 Prospect Road, WF15 8AY
⏲ 5-11; 12-midnight Sat & Sun ☎ (01274) 873365
🌐 thehartshead.co.uk

Copper Dragon Scotts 1816; 2 changing beers (sourced regionally; often Abbeydale, Moorhouse's, Saltaire) 🄷
An attractive club in a rural location, founded in 1895. The layout is open plan, featuring a large horseshoe bar, comfortable seating, a full-size snooker table and a small stage regularly used for live music, including resident band Blondhart. Open mic sessions are hosted on Fridays plus quiz nights on Wednesdays. The friendly community club, popular with walkers and ramblers, also serves non-members. The guest beers are carefully chosen. There are good views from the small beer garden. ♞❀♣P🚌(229,259)🐾📶↺

Haworth

Fleece Inn Ⓛ ✔
67 Main Street, BD22 8DA
🕒 11-11 (11.30 Fri & Sat); 11-10.30 Sun ☎ (01535) 642172
🌐 fleeceinnhaworth.co.uk
Timothy Taylor Golden Best, Boltmaker, Knowle Spring, Landlord, Ram Tam; 1 changing beer (often Timothy Taylor) 🄷
Stone-built coaching inn on Haworth's famous cobbled Main Street, with spectacular views over the Worth Valley and close to the KWVR historic heritage railway. A room to the right and a lower-level dining area offer quiet alternatives to the busy bar. Locally sourced food and accommodation are to be enjoyed here. Open for breakfast 10am-noon for non-residents. The beer garden is three storeys up from the bar, on the roof. A Timothy Taylor tied house, popular with tourists and locals alike. ♞❀🛏◑♿⛺⇌♣🚌🐾📶

King's Arms Ⓛ
2 Church Street, BD22 8DR
🕒 11.30-10 (midnight Fri & Sat) ☎ (01535) 645197
House beer (by Bridgehouse); 2 changing beers (often Bridgehouse, Naylor's) 🄷
A 17th-century former manor house at the top of Haworth's famous Main Street. Bridgehouse beers are renamed after Bronte family members. The pub is on two levels, with an L-shaped bar and a quieter area to the rear, and is pleasantly decorated with pale panelling and exposed stonework. On cask ale club Monday, ales are served at a discount. Live music, open mic nights and themed food evenings are held regularly. Families and dogs are welcome. A beer garden is to the rear. ♞❀◑⛺⇌🚌(B1,B2)🐾📶

Heath

King's Arms ★ Ⓛ ✔
Heath Common, WF1 5SL (at edge of village, off A655 Wakefield-Normanton road)
🕒 12-11 (midnight Fri & Sat) ☎ (01924) 377527
🌐 thekingsarmsheath.co.uk
Ossett Yorkshire Brunette, Yorkshire Blonde, Silver King; Rat White Rat; 4 changing beers 🄷
Acquired by Clark's Brewery in 1989, this establishment is now leased to Ossett Brewery. Built in the early 1700s and converted into a public house in 1841, it has three oak-panelled rooms with gas lighting, plus a conservatory and gardens to the rear. In the summer months you can sit outside and relax peacefully amid the acres of common grassland surrounding the area. Quiz night is Tuesday. Time may be called early on quieter evenings. Q♞❀◑♿🍎P🚌(188)🐾📶

Hebden Bridge

Calan's Micropub Ⓛ
3 The Courtyard, Bridge Gate, HX7 8EX (from A646 turn into Bridge Gate; at start of pedestrian section turn into yard on right)
🕒 closed Mon & Tue; 12-10 ☎ 07421 768511
🌐 calansmicropub.co.uk
House beer (by Elland); 5 changing beers (sourced nationally; often Great Heck, Mallinsons) 🄷
Calderdale's first micropub, set in a suntrap courtyard just off the main pedestrianised shopping street, providing an intimate, friendly and welcoming experience. Five rotating ales, mainly from Northern microbreweries, are complemented by cider. No piped music or other distractions disturb the conversation, but there are books, cards and dominoes to while away the time. Dogs are welcome. Q♞❀⇌♣🍎🚌🐾📶

Fox & Goose 🏆 Ⓛ ✔
7 Heptonstall Road, HX7 6AZ (at traffic lights on jct of A646 and Heptonstall Rd)
🕒 2-11 Mon; 12-11 Tue-Thu; 12-1am Fri; 9.45am-1am Sat; 12-11 Sun ☎ (01422) 648052 🌐 foxandgoose.org
Pictish Brewers Gold; 5 changing beers (sourced nationally; often Eagles Crag, Hop Studio, Squawk) 🄷
West Yorkshire's first community co-operative pub has a single bar serving three flagstone-floored rooms. The main bar is warmed by a roaring coal fire in winter. The left-hand room is often used for live music, while the room to the right has a dartboard. Monday is quiz night. There is a welcoming, inclusive feel and a diverse clientele. At least one vegan beer and one dark ale are always stocked. Do not miss the upstairs hillside beer garden with great views.
Q❀♣🍎🥛🚌(590,592)🐾📶

Old Gate Bar & Restaurant Ⓛ
1-5 Old Gate, HX7 8JP
🕒 10-11.30 (midnight Fri & Sat); 10-11 Sun
☎ (01422) 843993 🌐 oldgatehebden.co.uk
Moorhouse's Pride of Pendle; Saltaire Cascade Pale Ale; Vocation Heart & Soul; 6 changing beers (sourced nationally; often Arbor, Marble, Thornbridge) 🄷
Smart, modern bar and restaurant on two floors with an impressive long copper bar top. Ten handpumps dispense the biggest selection of real ales in the town, plus one rotating cider. At least one dark beer is always on the bar. Quality food is served all day. Comfortable furnishings comprise a mix of tables with chairs or benches and cosy settles. The big picture windows are an ideal spot for people watching. Q♞❀◑⇌🍎🚌🐾📶↺

Hipperholme

Travellers Inn Ⓛ ✔
53 Tanhouse Hill, HX3 8HN (off A58)
🕒 12-11.30 (midnight Thu-Sat); 12-11 Sun
☎ (01422) 202434
Ossett Yorkshire Blonde, Silver King, Excelsior; Rat White Rat; 4 changing beers (sourced regionally; often Fernandes, Goose Eye, Rat) 🄷
Opposite the site of the former railway station, this 18th-century local has taken in adjoining cottages to create a series of distinct spaces. Well-behaved children and dogs on leads are welcome until 7pm. Thursday is quiz night. A heated and covered yard is provided for smokers. A dark beer is always among the guest ales. ♞❀♣🍎🚌🐾📶↺

Holmfirth

Nook (Rose & Crown) 🄻 ✔

7 Victoria Square, HD9 2DN (down alley behind Barclays bank)
⏲ 11.30-midnight ☎ (01484) 682373
🌐 thenookbrewhouse.co.uk
Nook Baby Blond, Best, Blond, Oat Stout; 3 changing beers (often Nook) 🄷
The Nook (properly, the Rose & Crown) dates from 1754, and is a well-known real ale pub in the village. It has been dispensing beers from its own adjacent brewhouse since 2009. There are occasional guest beers and Pure North ciders. Home-cooked food is served daily. It is a popular pub for all age groups. The log fire is particularly warming on cold winter nights. A folk evening is hosted every Sunday, and real ale festivals on the weekend before Easter and on the August bank holiday. Under the same management, the next door Tap House also has a restaurant.
🐴❀🛏◐◑♣🍎🚌🐾📶↺

Horbury

Boons Horbury 🄻 ✔

6 Queen Street, WF4 6LP (in town centre off B6128 Horbury-Ossett road, opp Co-Op)
⏲ 11-11; 12-10.30 Sun ☎ (01924) 280442
Timothy Taylor Landlord; 7 changing beers (sourced regionally) 🄷
Community pub in the centre of town just off the high street, attracting people of all ages. The interior is based on a traditional layout around a central bar, with rugby league memorabilia on the walls. It has a sizeable outdoor drinking area that is well used in summer. The cider is Westons Old Rosie. ❀♣🍎🚌📶

Cricketers Arms 🏆 🄻 ✔

22 Cluntergate, WF4 5AG (a right fork off High St at its lower end)
⏲ 4-11; 12-midnight Fri & Sat; 12-11 Sun ☎ (01924) 267032
8 changing beers (sourced regionally) 🄷
On the edge of the town centre, this former Tetley's venue is now a genuine free house, with a frequent bus service to Wakefield, Ossett and Dewsbury. Poker night is on Monday, quiz night on Wednesday and open mic night on the second Sunday of each month. Beer festivals are staged in late May (Yankee Fest) and mid-October (Oktoberfest). ❀♣P🚌🐾📶

Huddersfield

Corner 🄻

5 Market Walk, HD1 2QA
⏲ 11-11 (midnight Fri & Sat); 12-10 Sun
🌐 thecornerhudds.co.uk
Mallinsons Wappy Nick; 6 changing beers (sourced nationally; often Mallinsons, Outstanding) 🄷
With the brewing pedigree of Tara and Elaine at Mallinsons and the award-winning front of house persona of Sam Smith, something special was expected when this Mallinsons tap opened in September 2016. Those expectations have been fully realised. Seven cask ales are on offer – two Mallinsons and five rotating guests – always including a dark beer. Also sold are least five real ciders and food seven days a week. The light, modern bar is on the first floor, with a function room on the second floor. 🐴◐◑⇌♣🍎🚌🐾📶

Grove 🄻

2 Spring Grove Street, HD1 4BP
⏲ 2-11 (midnight Thu); 12-midnight Fri & Sat; 12-11 Sun
☎ (01484) 430113 🌐 thegrove.pub
Kirkstall Pale Ale; Oakham Citra; 17 changing beers (often Hawkshead, Mallinsons, Northern Monk) 🄷
The antithesis of all that is mass market, with artwork, a snack range and live music that are unusual to say the least. However, it is the array of 31 beers, lagers and a real cider that set this pub apart, including a confusion-inducing 19 handpulled ales. Ranging from table beers through IPAs to imperial stouts, there is something for all. In addition there is a superb menu of 200-plus bottled beers and a comprehensive spirits range. The area's must-visit pub. Q🐴❀⇌♣🍎🗍🚌🐾📶

King's Head

St George's Square, HD1 1JF (on left when exiting station)
⏲ 11.30-11; 12-11 Sun ☎ (01484) 511058
Bradfield Farmers Blonde; Magic Rock Ringmaster; Timothy Taylor Golden Best, Landlord; 6 changing beers (sourced regionally; often Abbeydale, Oakham, Pictish) 🄷
A friendly welcome awaits in this Huddersfield institution. In the Grade I-listed railway station and winner of a railway heritage award, the King's Head has been carefully restored, with features including a beautiful tiled floor, wood panelling and wood-burning stoves. Top-quality, competitively priced beers from breweries near and far are dispensed from 10 handpumps. A mild and a dark beer are always among the range, and there is also a real cider on handpump. Live music plays on Sunday afternoon. ◐⇌🍎🚌🐾↺

Rat & Ratchet 🄻 ✔

40 Chapel Hill, HD1 3EB (on A616, just off ring road)
⏲ 3-11 Mon; 3-midnight Tue-Thu; 12-midnight Fri & Sat; 12-11 Sun ☎ (01484) 542400
Ossett Yorkshire Blonde, Silver King; Rat White Rat, King Rat; 9 changing beers (sourced regionally; often Acorn, Fernandes, Riverhead) 🄷
Multi award-winning pub owned by Ossett, but with its own on-site Rat microbrewery. The 12 handpumps offer ales from a range of breweries, always including two dark beers, alongside a good selection of ciders and perries. The large open-plan main area still retains the feel of separate rooms. A further room at the back leads to an outside drinking area. The pub has a dartboard and pinball machine. Quiz night is Wednesday and live bands play on occasional Sundays. There is a car park at the rear. 🐴❀⇌♣🍎P🚌🐾📶↺

Sportsman ★ 🄻 ✔

1 St John's Road, HD1 5AY
⏲ 12-11; 11-midnight Fri & Sat ☎ (01484) 421929
Timothy Taylor Boltmaker; 7 changing beers (sourced regionally; often Mallinsons) 🄷
This 1930s pub, with a 1950s refit by Hammonds (note the windows), has won a CAMRA English Heritage Conservation Pub Design award. The superb curved bar has eight handpumps, including a dedicated Mallinsons pump. A dark beer is usually available, along with two ciders (one from Pure North). The central bar has a parquet floor and an interesting wooden entrance. The two rooms off are regularly used for clubs and meetings, such as poker, poetry and music. A Meet the Brewer night is held on the last Tuesday of the month.
🐴❀◐◑⇌🍎🚌🐾📶↺

Vulcan

32 St Peters Street, HD1 1RA

9am-1am (2am Fri; 2.30am Sat) (01484) 302040

Bradfield Farmers Blonde; Copper Dragon Best Bitter; 4 changing beers (sourced nationally; often Bradfield, Timothy Taylor) H

Run by the same landlord for over 25 years, this town-centre pub has a local feel and generous opening hours. Six handpumps include guest beers often from local brewers, with Mallinsons and Bosun's featuring regularly. Bargain-priced lunches, popular with shoppers, are served every day, and free food is available for customers on Friday teatimes. There are daily morning happy hours and the pub caters for enthusiasts of pool, karaoke and televised horse racing. Live bands feature every Sunday evening. It can be busy on match days.

Idle

Idle Draper

28 The Green, BD10 9PX

4-11; 1-11.30 Fri; 12-11.30 Sat; 1-10.30 Sun

07525 751574

3 changing beers (sourced regionally; often Bingley, Bone Idle, York) H

In the centre of Idle, this modern microbar is housed within the premises of the former Briggs draper's. It comprises a single room containing the bar on the ground floor and an additional lounge area above. The in-house Bone Idle Brewery is in a converted barn to the rear. Three handpulls offer a varying range of real ales. The upstairs room and barn can be hired for private functions. The Bone Idle Men's Club meets every Wednesday evening.

Ilkley

Crescent Inn

Brook Street, LS29 8DG (within the Crescent Hotel)

12-11 (midnight Fri & Sat) (01943) 811250

thecrescentinn.co.uk

Acorn Yorkshire Pride; Goose Eye Bitter; Ilkley Mary Jane; Saltaire Blonde; 4 changing beers (sourced regionally; often Copper Dragon, Saltaire) H

Traditional comfortably furnished town-centre pub with original plasterwork and decorations. Refurbished in 2011, it is on the ground floor of a building that has been a hotel since 1861. Eight real ales, comprising four regulars and four varying guests, are always available and usually come from local breweries. Bar meals are offered, with meal deals during the week. There are fully accessible facilities but the rear door provides best access. A quiz takes place on Monday night.

Flying Duck

16 Church Street, LS29 9DS (on A65)

12-11 (12.30am Thu-Sat) (01943) 609587

wharfedalebrewery.com/the-flying-duck

Dark Horse Hetton Pale Ale; Wharfedale Black, Blonde, Best; 4 changing beers (sourced regionally; often Ilkley, Rooster's) H

A beautifully refurbished Grade II-listed traditional-style pub close to the town centre. Originally constructed as a farmhouse in 1709, this is reputed to be Ilkley's oldest pub building. It retains many original features including York stone and oak flooring, beamed ceilings, internal stonework and mullioned windows. Up to eight real ales, including four regulars, and two real ciders are sold. Wharfedale Brewery is to the rear. Food is served Tuesday to Sunday and also on bank holiday Monday.

Keighley

Lord Rodney Bar & Kitchen

Church Street, BD21 5HT

11.30-11 (2am Fri & Sat); 12-10 Sun (01535) 603053

lordrodney.co.uk

Timothy Taylor Golden Best, Boltmaker, Knowle Spring, Landlord; 1 changing beer (often Timothy Taylor) H

On Church Green and the site of Keighley's oldest pub, the Olde Red Lion, the Lord Rodney offers a splendid view along North Street. A Timothy Taylor managed house, it is a bright and modern town-centre pub. Furniture from tall stools to comfy armchairs surrounds the bar in the long single room, warmed by a real fire. A separate eating area leads to a heated beer garden at the rear. Look out for the seasonal Taylor Made cask and bottle range.

Ledsham

Chequers Inn

Claypit Lane, LS25 5LP

11-11; 12-6 Sun (01977) 683135

thechequersinn.com

Leeds Best; Theakston Best Bitter; Timothy Taylor Landlord; house beer (by Brown Cow); 1 changing beer (sourced locally; often Brown Cow, Stod Fold) H

A classic 16th-century family-run inn near All Saints church (the oldest building in the county). Noted for good food and Yorkshire beers, it is walker- and dog-friendly, and situated close to the Fairburn Ings RSPB reserve. Various rooms lead off from the passageway, featuring low beams, alcoves, open fires, photographs, trinkets and unusual tabletops with interesting quotations. A marquee at the top of the garden is available for functions in the lighter months. Q P (175)

Leeds: Burley

Cardigan Arms ★

364 Kirkstall Road, LS4 2HQ

12-11 (10.30 Mon; midnight Fri & Sat); 12-10.30 Sun

(0113) 226 3154 cardiganarms.co.uk

Kirkstall Pale Ale, Three Swords, Dissolution IPA, Black Band Porter; 4 changing beers (sourced regionally; often Kirkstall, Track Brewing Co, Wylam) H

Built in 1896, this is a classic Grade II-listed Victorian inn with four rooms off an L-shaped bar area. Reopened in 2017 as a Kirkstall Brewery pub after a sensitive refurbishment, its fine woodwork, etched glass and ornamented ceilings are now displayed in their full glory. On the bar there are eight handpumps and a good range of keg and bottled beers. The pub is named after the Cardigan family who owned land locally. It has a first-floor function room. Q

Leeds: City Centre

Brewery Tap

18-24 New Station Street, LS1 5DL

12-11 (midnight Fri & Sat); 12-10.30 Sun
(0113) 243 4414 brewerytapleeds.co.uk
Leeds Pale, Best, Midnight Bell; 5 changing beers (sourced locally; often Camerons, Ilkley, Leeds)
Busy pub on the the approach road to the front of Leeds railway station. The downstairs bar area is a wide, narrow room with a variety of comfortable seating. Four beers from Leeds Brewery are served, with one of the guests regularly from Camerons and the other three often from Yorkshire breweries. There is also a wide range of additional beers available. Upstairs is a function room with a small bar and roof terrace with seating.

Brunswick

82 North Street, LS2 7PN
11-11.30; 10-11.30 Sat; 11-10 Sun (0113) 247 0546
thebrunswick.co.uk
5 changing beers (sourced locally; often Kirkstall, Saltaire)
Three-storey pub on the edge of the city centre with a bar area on the ground floor, additional seating on the first floor, and an art gallery and events space on the second. The bar area is wooden-floored with bench tables and stools by the window. From the wooden bar, five real ales are served along with two ciders on handpump and a good range of draught and bottled beers. One of the handpumps is dedicated to dark beers.

Duck & Drake

43 Kirkgate, LS2 7DR
10-11 (midnight Fri & Sat); 11-11 Sun (0113) 245 5432
duckndrake.co.uk
Brains Bitter; Rooster's Yankee; Saltaire Blonde; Theakston Old Peculier; Timothy Taylor Landlord; 10 changing beers (sourced locally; often Elland, Salamander, York)
A fine example of a two-roomed Victorian corner pub retaining some original features. Wood floored throughout, some of the floorboards have survived 200 years of trade. The central bar with 15 handpumps sits in between and serves both rooms. There is live music most nights from a small stage in the corner of the front room, which also features a mural on the back wall depicting many blues and rock legends and is decorated with various music memorabilia.

Foleys Tap House

159 The Headrow, LS1 5RG
12-11; 11-1am Fri & Sat; 12-10 Sun (0113) 242 9674
York Guzzler, Centurion's Ghost Ale; 10 changing beers (sourced locally; often Abbeydale, Black Sheep, York)
This busy city-centre pub usually offers four beers from York Brewery's range plus up to eight guest beers. It also stocks a choice of real ciders and perries along with draught and bottled beers from around the world. The building is an impressive edifice which was previously owned by the Pearl Assurance Company and is named after the company's founder. The interior is on several levels with a variety of seating. Pies, home-made cakes and beer tasting trays are available.

Head of Steam

13 Mill Hill, LS1 5DQ
11-midnight (1am Fri & Sat); 12-11 Sun
(0113) 243 6618
Camerons Strongarm; 8 changing beers (sourced locally; often Leeds, Northern Monk, Timothy Taylor)
Single-roomed pub with a high ceiling and a central island bar surrounded by various drinking areas with a variety of seating. The walls are decorated with breweriana. On the bar are nine handpumps, serving beers mainly from Yorkshire and the North-East. Complementing these are many international beers on draught, and in the fridges behind the bar is an extensive array of beers in bottles and cans, especially focusing on those from Belgium and the United States.

North Bar

24 New Briggate, LS1 6NU
11-2am (1am Mon & Tue); 12-midnight Sun
(0113) 242 4540
5 changing beers (sourced locally; often Kirkstall, Magic Rock, North)
North Bar has been a pioneer of the Leeds beer scene since 1997. The quality cask ales are supported by a wonderful range of draught and other ales from the UK and far beyond. Often a champion of new brewers, North is always moving forward. The staff here are friendly and knowledgeable. This is a narrow bar and seating area, with wood featuring heavily in the design. Two of the five cask ales are permanently from North and Kirkstall breweries.

Reliance

76-78 North Street, LS2 7PN
12-11 (midnight Fri & Sat); 11-10.30 Sun
(0113) 295 6060 the-reliance.co.uk
House beer (by Acorn); 3 changing beers (sourced locally; often Magic Rock, Rooster's, Sunbeam)
Glass-fronted high-ceilinged corner local with three areas; the rear raised section is usually for diners. The two main drinking areas are bare-boarded, furnished with mix and match furniture and linked by a mini slope. Alongside the four ales on handpump is a good range of other beers from around the world – on draught and in bottles and cans. Not just a modern pub but also a wine shop and charcuterie, food is served most of the time including a good range of bar snacks.

Scarbrough Hotel

Bishopgate Street, LS1 5DY
10-midnight (1am Fri & Sat); 10-10.30 Sun
(0113) 243 4590
St Austell Nicholson's Pale Ale; Tetley Bitter; 5 changing beers (sourced regionally; often Adnams, Great Heck, Vocation)
The Scarbrough is a busy ale house conveniently close to Leeds railway station. The building dates from 1765 and became a pub in 1826. It is named after Henry Scarbrough, the first owner of the pub, though it was then known as the King's Arms. At either end of the long bar are comfortable seating areas. The selection of guest ales is both from local breweries and a wide variety of breweries around the country.

Slocken

10-12 Call Lane, LS1 6DN
12-9 Mon; 12-11; 12-1am Fri & Sat; 12-9 Sun
(0113) 245 7101
3 changing beers (sourced locally; often Kirkstall, Nomadic, Northern Monk)

Slocken is a Yorkshire dialect word derived from Old Norse, which means to quench thirst or to drink greedily. The pub is on three levels, with a ground-floor bar, additional seating on the first floor, and a games room on the second floor with a dartboard, table football and pool tables. The bar area has wooden flooring and exposed brickwork, with brewery signs on the walls. On one end of the bar are four handpumps, and there are 10 keg taps behind the bar. ◑⇌♣🚌🐾📶

Tapped Leeds

51 Boar Lane, LS1 5EL

⏲ 11-11 (midnight Thu; 1am Fri & Sat) ☎ (0113) 244 1953

🌐 tappedleeds.co.uk

13 changing beers (sourced regionally; often Tapped Sheffield) Ⓗ

This modern one-room bar has a long bar to the right of the entrance and brewing equipment along the left-hand wall. Tapped Brewing Company real ales are usually brewed at Tapped's sister pub on Sheffield station. Signs above the bar give details of the beers available. There are no handpumps, but the lower set of taps on the back wall dispense the real ale. A wide range of other draught, bottled and canned beers is also available. ◑♿⇌🚌📶

Templar Ⓛ ✔

2 Templar Street, LS2 7NU

⏲ 11-11 (midnight Fri & Sat) ☎ (0113) 243 0318

Bradfield Farmers Blonde; Greene King IPA, Abbot; Kirkstall Three Swords; Tetley Bitter; 3 changing beers (sourced locally; often Acorn, Ilkley) Ⓗ

Traditional community local on the corner of Vicar Lane in the city centre. The pub has a fine cream and green faience exterior from a former Leeds brewery, Melbourne. The interior, dating from 1928, displays fine wood panelling and is of regional historic importance. A number of original features remain and the small rear lounge is particularly noteworthy. Large-screen TVs around the pub show a range of sporting events. Guest beers are sourced both locally and nationally. ⇌♣🚌📶

Town Hall Tavern Ⓛ ✔

17 Westgate, LS1 2RA

⏲ 11.45-11 (10 Mon); 12-11 Sat; 12-8 Sun

☎ (0113) 244 0765 🌐 townhalltavernleeds.co.uk

Timothy Taylor Dark Mild, Golden Best, Boltmaker, Knowle Spring, Landlord, Ram Tam Ⓗ

This Timothy Taylor Champions Club gastropub has a single-room interior with open alcoves to the left and right of the door. A semicircular bar is along the left-hand wall. The alcove on the left is perhaps best for drinking only, and is complete with circular copper-topped tables and old photographs of Leeds. Dining tends to be towards the rear. The pub may close early if quiet, especially on Monday. ◑⇌🍎🚌📶

Wapentake Ⓛ

92 Kirkgate, LS2 7DJ

⏲ 7.30am-11 (9 Mon); 10-11 Sat; 10-9 Sun

☎ (0113) 243 6248 🌐 wapentakeleeds.co.uk

Sharp's Atlantic; 3 changing beers (sourced locally; often Nomadic, Northern Monk, Sunbeam) Ⓗ

Its name referring to a parcel of land in northern England, this bakery, café and bar is 'a little piece of Yorkshire' and dedicated to local produce and the community. With many strings to its bow, it makes its own bread and cakes, serves meals using locally sourced ingredients, and of course offers a good range of real ales and other beers, predominantly from Leeds and Yorkshire. Wapentake is very welcoming, with a locally customised piano, a sports TV upstairs and friendly bartenders. ❀◑⇌🚌🐾📶

Whitelock's Ale House ★ Ⓛ

Turk's Head Yard, LS1 6HB (off Briggate)

⏲ 11-midnight (1am Fri & Sat); 11-11 Sun

☎ (0113) 245 3950 🌐 whitelocksleeds.com

Ilkley Mary Jane; Kirkstall Pale Ale; Theakston Best Bitter, Old Peculier; Timothy Taylor Landlord; 6 changing beers (sourced locally; often Acorn, Great Heck, Saltaire) Ⓗ

Described by John Betjeman as the very heart of Leeds, Whitelock's dates from 1715 and occupies a long narrow yard. The interior is unchanged from 1895 and is a feast of mirrors, woodwork, stained glass and a fine faience bar. A varied beer selection is offered from local and national breweries. Its sister bar, The Turk's Head, is in the same building just down the yard and offers two real ales on handpump and a number of other draught beers. ❀◑⇌🍎🚌🐾📶

Leeds: Headingley

Arcadia Ale House Ⓛ

34 Arndale Centre, Otley Road, LS6 2UE (corner of Alma Rd)

⏲ 12-11 ☎ (0113) 274 5599

Timothy Taylor Boltmaker; 7 changing beers (sourced regionally; often Elland, Ilkley, Okell's) Ⓗ

This cleverly converted former bank is now a well-established and multi award-winning pub. The bar has ground-floor rooms plus an upstairs mezzanine level. The modern décor features a chandelier formed of foreign beer crates and a mural of Headingley over the bar area. Eight real ales are offered along with a range of canned, bottled and draught beers. There is also a wide selection of gins, some locally produced. Children, large groups and fancy dress are not permitted. Q♿🍎🚌🐾📶

Leeds: Holbeck

Grove Inn Ⓛ

Back Row, LS11 5PL

⏲ 11-midnight ☎ (0113) 244 2085

🌐 thegroveinnleeds.co.uk

Daleside Blonde; 7 changing beers (sourced regionally; often Acorn, Moorhouse's, Settle) Ⓗ

Classic West Riding pub, which would have originally been at the end of a row of houses, but is now hidden away among modern offices. Eight real ales from local and regional breweries are available, with service both to the public bar and corridor. There are two small side rooms and the Concert Room to the rear, which hosts a variety of music six nights a week including, every Friday since 1962, reputedly the oldest folk club in the world. ❀◐⇌♣🍎🚌🐾📶

Leeds: Hyde Park

Brudenell Social Club Ⓛ

33 Queen's Road, LS6 1NY

⏲ 12-midnight (1am Fri & Sat) ☎ (0113) 275 2411

🌐 brudenellsocialclub.co.uk

Kirkstall Pale Ale, Three Swords; 2 changing beers (sourced locally; often Ossett, Partners) Ⓗ

A hidden gem, the Brudenell is much more than just a renowned music venue. The four handpumps have a huge turnover, ensuring a top pint, with a focus on local ales, alongside a range of other beers on handpump and real ciders available seasonally. As well as hosting live music, sport is shown in the bar room and a separate games room includes snooker and pool tables. Hearty pies are served and food trucks frequently set up in the car park. ❀◗♿⇌♣🍎P🚌(56)📶

Leeds: Kirkstall

Kirkstall Bridge Inn Ⓛ

12 Bridge Road, LS5 3BW

⏲ 12-11.30 (12.30am Fri & Sat) ☎ (0113) 278 4044
🌐 kirkstallbridge.co.uk

Kirkstall Pale Ale, Three Swords, Dissolution IPA, Black Band Porter; 4 changing beers (sourced regionally; often Sunbeam, Thornbridge, Wylam) Ⓗ

This multiple CAMRA Pub of the Year winner is a living museum of breweriana. Spread over two floors, with an extensive canalside beer garden, the pub offers a large range of Kirkstall Brewery ales and changing guests, plus a range of continental lagers and craft beer on draught. Food is available every day, with booking advised for dining at weekends, and there is a pie and pint deal every Monday. Events include the annual Kirkstapalooza music and beer festival and a popular bonfire night. ❀◗♣P🚌🐾📶

West End House

26 Abbey Road, LS5 3HS

⏲ 11-11; 11.30-11.30 Thu; 11.30-midnight Fri & Sat; 12-11 Sun ☎ (0113) 278 6332 🌐 thewestendhouse.co.uk

3 changing beers (sourced nationally; often Abbeydale, Marston's, Woodforde's) Ⓗ

A bustling local, this traditional 150-year-old pub is close to Kirkstall Abbey and museum. The bar room shows sports and a large lounge area does a roaring trade in quality, hearty food. The bar features four handpumps dispensing frequently changing real ales and real cider, along with foreign beers, lagers and a well-stocked fridge and wine rack. It has a small smoking area and drinking patio. Quizzes take place on Tuesday and Thursday evenings. ❀◗⇌🍎🚌🐾📶

Leeds: Meanwood

East of Arcadia Ⓛ ✔

607 Meanwood Road, LS6 4HQ

⏲ 11.30-11; 12-11 Sun ☎ (0113) 275 5488

Kirkstall Pale Ale; Timothy Taylor Boltmaker; 6 changing beers (sourced regionally; often Kirkstall, Okell's, Ridgeside) Ⓗ

This modern bar occupies a prominent corner position on the junction with Monk Bridge Road, in the heart of Meanwood. The open-plan design, which follows the sweep of tall windows curving around the pub, is on one level but with contrasting areas. Rotating real ales often come from Ridgeside and Ilkley breweries; bottled, canned and draught foreign and UK beers are also available. One real cider is normally stocked, and there is a summer cider festival. A quiz night is held on Wednesday. Q♘◗♿🍎🚌(51,52)🐾📶

Leeds: Newlay

Abbey Inn Ⓛ

99 Pollard Lane, LS13 1EQ (vehicle access from B6157 only)

⏲ 12-11 ☎ (0113) 258 1248 🌐 abbeyinn.org

Leeds Pale; Marston's 61 Deep; 6 changing beers (sourced locally; often Kirkstall, Ossett, Revolutions) Ⓗ

A historic ale house nestling between the River Aire and the canal towpath. A celebrated community pub, the Abbey showcases a selection of predominantly local ales, with pumps dedicated to dark ale and real cider. Ample seating outside attracts dog walkers and cyclists. Large annual events include beer and music festivals and bonfire night celebrations. The pub is accessible by road from Pollard Lane, Bramley and on foot over Pollard Bridge from Horsforth, or along the canal from the new Kirkstall Forge train station. ♘❀◖♿⇌(Kirkstall Forge)♣🍎P🐾📶

Linthwaite

Sair Ⓛ ✔

139 Lane Top, HD7 5SG (top of Hoyle Ing, off A62)

⏲ 3-11; 12-11 Fri & Sat; 12-10.30 Sun ☎ (01484) 842370

Linfit Bitter, Gold Medal, Special, Swift, Autumn Gold, Old Eli Ⓗ

A traditional multi-roomed stone building with a central bar and real fires. High on the edge of the Colne Valley, the Sair has been home to Linfit Brewery since 1982, and sells its own beers exclusively. Up to 10 beers are available including three dark brews, and real cider from Pure North. The pub is a popular community venue providing a welcome for all – locals, visitors, walkers and their dogs alike. Q❀♣🍎🚌🐾📶↺

Liversedge

Black Bull Ⓛ ✔

37 Halifax Road, WF15 6JR (on A649, close to A62)

⏲ 12-midnight (1am Fri & Sat) ☎ (01924) 403779

Ossett Yorkshire Brunette, Yorkshire Blonde, Silver King, Excelsior; 5 changing beers (sourced nationally) Ⓗ

This was Ossett Brewery's first pub. The five rooms each have a unique style, including one dubbed the Chapel, which has a high ceiling and reminders of local industrial heritage. Nine handpumps always include a dark ale plus guest beers from the group and a wide range of independents. A regular Guide entry, the Black Bull is a sociable community local with a warm welcome. Quiz night is Tuesday. Q♘❀♿♣P🚌(254,254A)🐾📶↺

Longwood

Dusty Miller Inn Ⓛ ✔

2 Gilead Road, HD3 4XH

⏲ 5-11; 4-midnight Fri; 12-midnight Sat; 12-11 Sun
☎ 07946 589645 🌐 dustymillerlongwood.com

Milltown Platinum Blonde, Black Jack Porter, Weaver's Bitter; Timothy Taylor Landlord; 3 changing beers (often Elland, Newby Wyke, Phoenix) Ⓗ

Here at the Milltown Brewery tap, the interior is open plan but with three distinct areas. Local historic photographs adorn the walls and stone floors dominate. Seven real ales are served, showcasing the Milltown brews – three changing guests and a dark beer are always on offer. The only food is locally made pies. From the pub's outside benches there are great views up the Colne Valley. Q ♣ (356) ↺

Marsden

Riverhead Brewery Tap

Peel Street, HD7 6BR

12-midnight ☎ (01484) 844324

theriverheadmarsden.co.uk

Ossett Yorkshire Blonde, Silver King; Riverhead Butterley Bitter, March Haigh, Redbrook Premium; 5 changing beers H

A brewpub since 1995, now owned by Ossett Brewery and welcoming to all. The brewery is visible from the bar. Ten beers are on the bar, four from the on-site brewery, two from Ossett, plus guests. A dark beer is almost always available and occasionally real cider. A popular stop on the Real Ale Trail, Saturdays are extremely busy. There is a riverside terrace for those summer days and an upstairs bar with comfy seating.
♿ P (185) ↺

Meltham

Wills o' Nats

Blackmoorfoot Road, HD9 5PS

12-3, 5-11; 11.30-midnight Sat; 11.30-11 Sun

☎ (01484) 850078 willsonats.com

Black Sheep Best Bitter; Bradfield Farmers Blonde; Timothy Taylor Landlord; 3 changing beers (sourced nationally) H

In 1852, William, son of Nathaniel, took over the Spotted Cow, which gradually became Wills o' Nats. Today it is renowned for locally sourced home-cooked food and six or more ales. Live music events are held on the first Saturday of each summer month, when you can camp behind the pub. The pub is close to the Peak District and the Pennines, with stunning views, and a welcome stop for families, walkers and their dogs.
P

Middlestown

Little Bull

72 New Road, WF4 4NR (on A642 at crossroads in centre of village)

12-11.30 (12.30am Thu-Sat) ☎ (01924) 726142

thelittlebull.co.uk

Abbeydale Deception; 2 changing beers (sourced locally) H

This pub has been established since 1814 and is free of tie. Beers come from local and regional breweries and it also sells a range of world bottled beers. All food is locally sourced and home-cooked. A single bar services a number of smaller rooms, with an open fire in colder weather. Meals are served lunchtimes every day and Wednesday and Thursday evenings. There is a beer festival on the last weekend in July. The National Coal Mining Museum is nearby. P (232,128)

Mirfield

Flowerpot

65 Calder Road, WF14 8NN (over river, 400yds S of railway station)

12-12.30am (1.30am Fri & Sat); 12-midnight Sun

☎ (01924) 496939

Ossett Yorkshire Brunette, Yorkshire Blonde, Silver King, Excelsior; Rat White Rat; 4 changing beers (often Acorn, Marston's, Riverhead) H

An 1807 pub with a typically sensitive, tasteful restoration by Ossett Brewery, having an impressive tiled flowerpot as the centrepiece. There are real fires in each of the four inviting rooms. Nine ales are offered from Ossett, Rat, Riverhead, Fernandes and independents, including a mild or stout, plus a rotating cider. The pub is on the Transpennine Rail Ale Trail and holds occasional beer festivals. Q ♿ ♣ P (262) ↺

Knowl Club

17 Knowl Road, WF14 8DQ

closed Mon; 7-11 Tue & Wed; 7-midnight Thu; 5-midnight Fri; 12-midnight Sat & Sun ☎ (01924) 493301

knowlclub.co.uk

Old Mill Traditional Bitter; Sharp's Atlantic; 2 changing beers (sourced nationally) H

Having celebrated its 125th anniversary in 2013, the former Mirfield Liberal Club is ideal for a quiet pint, open both to members and the public as it holds club and public house licences. A single bar occupies a long, well-furnished room and offers up to four beers. There is also a private function room downstairs and a snooker room upstairs. The small car park at the rear is accessed down an adjacent narrow alley. ♿ ♣ P ↺

Navigation Tavern

6 Station Road, WF14 8NL (next to Mirfield railway station)

11.30-11; 12-11 Sun ☎ (01924) 492476

John Smith's Bitter; Theakston Black Bull Bitter, Lightfoot, XB, Old Peculier; 3 changing beers (sourced nationally; often Small World) H

A canalside free house with the same host for 20 years, the pub is an ambassador for Theakston beers and has up to three guests, mainly at weekends, all at keen prices. It features on the Transpennine Rail Ale Trail and hosts occasional fundraising events plus Saturday night entertainment (often Motown) and active sports and pool teams. A large function room and en-suite B&B with stairlift are available, and winter comfort is aided by a large wood-burning fire.
♿ ♣ P

Old Colonial

Dunbottle Lane, WF14 9JJ (off A644 up Church Lane, 1 mile NE of station)

5-11 Mon-Wed; 12-2, 5-11 Thu & Fri; 12-midnight Sat; 12-11 Sun ☎ (01924) 496920

theoldcolonial.webplus.net/index.html

Copper Dragon Best Bitter; 5 changing beers (sourced regionally; often JW Lees) H

A former club with fascinating colonial memorabilia, offering a cosy retreat with sofas around the fire. There is a Royal British Legion memorial in the prize-winning garden and local charities are well supported. The spacious conservatory is popular for functions and meetings. Three to five guests, including a dark ale from such as Thwaites, Lees, Marston's and small brewers, are on the bar. Evening meals are served Thursday to Saturday and the excellent-value Sunday lunch is recommended. ♿ ♣ P (202,205) ↺

Morley

Oscar's Bar

2A Queen Street, LS27 9DG

⏲ 5-11; 2-11 Sat; 2-10.30 Sun
3 changing beers (sourced locally; often Nomadic) Ⓗ
Named after a previous owner's cat, this is a small, friendly bar which is also home to the Frisky Bear Brewery. Three handpumps supply beers both from local and regional brewers, often including one from its own brewery. There is also a range of quality keg beers, bottles, cans and an array of different gins. The wooden-floored single room has seating for around 20 people, with one high and two low tables, plus stools along the window.
♨⇌🍎🚌🐾📶

Norristhorpe

Rising Sun Ⓛ

254 Norristhorpe Lane, WF15 7AN (½ mile off A62)
⏲ 12-11 (midnight Sat) ☎ (01924) 400190
Abbeydale Moonshine; Acorn Barnsley Bitter; Saltaire Blonde; Timothy Taylor Landlord; 3 changing beers (sourced locally; often Bradfield, Copper Dragon, Hawkshead) Ⓗ
This village local, under family ownership, is tastefully decorated, featuring a light and spacious bar area and cosy lounge areas with exposed brickwork and real fires. The beer range is mainly from Yorkshire but with guests from local and national sources. Every Tuesday there is a popular quiz with prizes, as well as occasional live music (advertised on Facebook). Outside, the large, well-maintained beer garden has plenty of seating and extensive views over the valley towards Mirfield and Emley Moor. ♨❀♣P🚌(261)🐾📶↺

Oakworth

Oakworth Social Club Ⓛ

Chapel Lane, BD22 7HY
⏲ 12-11.30; 11-midnight Fri & Sat; 11-11.30 Sun
☎ (01535) 643931
Saltaire Blonde; Timothy Taylor Golden Best; 1 changing beer Ⓗ
Friendly and welcoming, this imposing Victorian building on the main thoroughfare was originally built as the Liberal Club in the late 19th century and has always been a club. Now a social club with a thriving membership, it has a comfortable front lounge and a back bar with traditional games and a TV. Upstairs, a third room caters for functions and meetings. Quiz night is Monday. Regular live music events are advertised on Facebook. Yorkshire CAMRA Club of the Year runner-up 2017 and 2018.
♨❀♿⛺⇌♣P🚌(K7,K10)🐾📶

Ossett

Bier Huis Ⓛ

17 Towngate, WF5 9BL (in shopping parade which backs onto bus station)
⏲ 9.30am-6.30 (8 Fri & Sat); 11-3 Sun ☎ (01924) 565121
🌐 bierhuis.co.uk
3 changing beers (sourced locally) Ⓗ
A beer shop selling bottled beers from many Yorkshire breweries as well as an extensive selection of foreign bottled beers. Two draught ales come mainly from Bradfield and Saltaire breweries, and can be drunk on the premises, and there is also a changing KeyKeg beer. On Thirsty Fridays there are more beers are on draught. Meet the Brewer evenings are held at regular intervals and brewery visits are popular. Q♨♿🍎P🛍🚌📶

Brewers Pride Ⓛ

Low Mill Road, Healey, WF5 8ND (in Healey Mills industrial area beside River Calder)
⏲ 12-11; 12-10.30 Sun ☎ (01924) 273865
🌐 brewers-pride.co.uk
Ossett Yorkshire Blonde; Rat White Rat; Rudgate Ruby Mild; 6 changing beers (often Ossett) Ⓗ
Set on the outskirts of the town in a regenerated industrial area close to the Calder & Hebble canal, this was one of the best free houses in the area for many years and was sold to Ossett Brewery in 2018. Under the guidance of Stephen (Chalky) Whyte, the pub is finding its feet again after the transition from free to tied house. Good-value meals are served. Q♨❀◑♣🍎🛍🚌(102,121)🐾📶

Otley

Junction Inn Ⓛ ✔

44 Bondgate, LS21 1AD
⏲ 11-11 (11.30 Thu; midnight Fri & Sat); 12-11 Sun
☎ (01943) 463233
Hambleton Stud Blonde; Robinsons Dizzy Blonde; Theakston Best Bitter, Old Peculier; Timothy Taylor Boltmaker, Landlord; 5 changing beers (sourced regionally; often Acorn, Adnams, Saltaire) Ⓗ
A solid-looking stone-built pub on a prominent street-corner site on the approach from Leeds. To the front, roadside tables allow for outdoor drinking. Eleven real ales are served, along with a real cider and a wide range of malt whiskies. There is a central fireplace, and comfortable fixed seating runs around the walls. A collection of farming implements hangs from the ceiling and on the walls are enamel brewery signs and pictures of old Otley. ♨❀♣🍎🚌🐾

Old Cock Ⓛ

11-13 Crossgate, LS21 1AA
⏲ 11-11 ☎ (01943) 464424 🌐 theoldcockotley.co.uk
Ilkley Mary Jane; Theakston Best Bitter; Timothy Taylor Landlord; 6 changing beers (sourced locally; often Bradfield, Briscoe's, Great Heck) Ⓗ
This genuine free house is a winner of multiple local CAMRA awards. It was painstakingly converted from a former café to create a pub that feels like it has been here for many years. There are two low-ceilinged rooms downstairs with stone-flagged floors, and a further room upstairs. The guest ales are mostly from local breweries. It also has at least two real ciders plus a range of foreign beers. Frequent beer festivals are held. No under-18s. Q♿🍎🚌🐾📶

Pontefract

Carleton Ⓛ ✔

Hardwick Road, WF8 3PQ (on A639 1 mile S of town centre)
⏲ 11-11 (midnight Fri) ☎ (01977) 703797
Greene King IPA; house beer (by Greene King); 7 changing beers Ⓗ
A popular estate pub which now offers 10 well-kept cask ales, not just from the Greene King stable. The house beer is brewed by Greene King to the landlady's recipe. Plenty of outdoor seating is available round the side and to the rear. It gets busy at weekends, with the locals enjoying sport from the many TV screens, and holds beer festivals and Meet the Brewer evenings. ♨❀◑♿P🚌📶

Robin Hood 🄻

4 Wakefield Road, WF8 4HN
12-midnight ☎ (01977) 702231
10 changing beers (sourced regionally; often Abbeydale, Ossett, Revolutions) Ⓗ
Recently bought and totally refurbished by a local landlord, the Robin has been a pub since 1791, when it was owned by the Duchy of Lancaster. It is the home of the Henry Smith Brewery, which is named after the grandfather and son of the present owner. There is a folk session on Sunday and live music on Thursday. The locals are invited to choose the guest beers. Q

Pudsey

Fleece

100 Fartown, LS28 8LU
12-11 ☎ (0113) 236 2748 fleecepudsey.co.uk
Tetley Bitter; Timothy Taylor Golden Best, Landlord; 2 changing beers (sourced locally; often Elland, Ossett, Pennine) Ⓗ
A multi award-winning local pub on the outskirts of Pudsey, this hostelry has built a reputation for exceptionally well-kept ales and a welcoming atmosphere. It is a comfortable, traditional, two-roomed venue with community at its heart, decorated with film and music memorabilia from a golden era. The outdoor area is well kept and ideal for hosting the annual summer beer festival. Of the two guest ales, one will be a pale beer while the other will vary in style. P

Manor Inn 🄻

Manor House Street, LS28 7BJ
2-11; 12-midnight Sat & Sun
Saltaire Blonde; 3 changing beers (sourced locally; often Brew York, North, Wishbone) Ⓗ
A fairly new single-room pub which has built a strong local following across a wide age demographic and has a welcoming atmosphere. The three changing guest beers are always from Yorkshire breweries, with a dark beer sometimes available. The landlord and landlady are keen to promote CAMRA and real ale. The tables by the large windows are actually wooden barrels. Live music features on Sunday evenings, with easy listening background music at other times.

Rastrick

Roundhill Inn 🄻

75 Clough Lane, HD6 3QL (400yds from A643/A6107 jct towards M62 motorway bridge)
4-11.30; 12-11.30 Sat & Sun ☎ (01484) 713418
roundhillinn.co.uk
Bradfield Farmers Blonde; Sharp's Doom Bar; Timothy Taylor Golden Best, Landlord; house beer (by Ashover); 2 changing beers (sourced nationally) Ⓗ
A two-roomed genuine free house and locals' pub lying on the edge of Rastrick, easily reached by bus from Brighouse or Huddersfield. In daytimes during the week the pub operates as a private function venue, often hosting wakes, as the crematorium in neighbouring Kirklees is less than half a mile away. The two-roomed layout has been maintained following a tasteful refurbishment, which included extending into an adjacent former barn.
QP(547,549)

Rishworth

Booth Wood Inn 🄻

Oldham Road, HX6 4QU (on A672 towards jct 22 of M62) SE034170
12-10 (11 Fri & Sat) ☎ (01422) 825600
boothwoodinn.co.uk
Bradfield Farmers Blonde; Joseph Holt Bitter; 3 changing beers (sourced locally; often Bradfield, Pennine, Salopian) Ⓗ
Characterful country pub and restaurant close to the scenic Yorkshire moors. It is open plan, with a large central bar and two restaurant areas featuring beams and stone-flagged floors. All food is freshly prepared each day. Alongside the main menu there are daily specials including classic and retro dishes. The pub hosts live music every Friday 6-8pm. P(560)

Saltaire

Cap & Collar 🄻

4 Queens Road, BD18 4SJ
closed Mon; 5-10 Tue-Thu; 4-11 Fri; 1-11 Sat; 1-6 Sun
4 changing beers (sourced nationally; often Northern Monk, Saltaire, Wishbone) Ⓗ
Popular, modern micropub with an open plan café-style layout accommodating up to 35 customers. A beer garden and smoking area are at the rear. Four handpulls serve a variety of real ales, many sourced regionally. Real cider is also on draught and there is a good selection of bottle-conditioned ales. Meet the Brewer and tap takeover events are held regularly, and a homebrew club also meets here. Pub snacks are available. Live music plays on Sunday afternoons and occasional evenings.
Q

Salt Cellar 🄻

192 Saltaire Road, BD18 3JF (on A657)
2-11; 12-midnight Fri & Sat; 12-10.30 Sun
☎ (01274) 955051
House beer (by Bingley); 5 changing beers (sourced regionally; often Bosun's, Copper Dragon, Stod Fold) Ⓗ
Traditional two-room pub on the edge of the World Heritage Site of Saltaire village, with a friendly feel. The interior has a Victorian character, with comfortable seating, stained-glass partitions and bookshelves. Numerous pictures of old Saltaire adorn the walls. Six handpulls offer a varying range of real ales from local and regional breweries, usually including two blondes, two ambers and two dark beers. Closing times on a Friday and Saturday may vary. P

Sandal

Star

Standbridge Lane, WF2 7DY (near Asda on A6186 which links A61 and A636)
12-midnight ☎ (01924) 255254
6 changing beers (sourced regionally; often Morton Collins) Ⓗ
A pub dating from 1821 with a streamside beer garden, recently leased from Enterprise Inns by the Morton Collins Brewery and serving one or two of its beers plus four or five guests mainly from local breweries. It is welcoming, with an open-plan layout and open fires in winter. The brewery has recently moved to the pub.
QP(110)

Sandbeds

Airedale Heifer

Bradford Road, BD20 5LY

12-11 (01274) 515870 theairedaleheifer.co.uk

Bridgehouse Blonde, Aired Ale, Porter, Holy Cow; 2 changing beers (often Bridgehouse)

An extensive roadside pub with a substantial food presence, many dishes featuring the brewery's beers. It is the tap for Bridgehouse Brewery situated in car park behind. The pub is named after the famous Airedale cow of the early 1800s, the heaviest in the UK (see the statue at the front). The open-plan layout has a single L-shaped bar, and outside is a sizeable, south-facing garden with patio heaters. Children are welcome until 8pm, later if dining. Brewery tours are available (see website for details). P (662)

Shipley

Fox

41 Briggate, BD17 7BP

10.30-11; 10-midnight Fri & Sat; 12-10.30 Sun
(01274) 594826 thefoxshipley.co.uk

BEEspoke Plan Bee, Shipley Stout; 4 changing beers (sourced regionally; often Great Heck, Small World)

Small, independent, single-roomed café-style bar which is friendly and welcoming, simply but smartly furnished featuring recycled church pews. Six handpulled ales include some from the in-house BEEspoke microbrewery. Real ciders, often including one from a local producer, are sold, as is a wide range of international bottled beers. The bar is handy when waiting for a train as the station is close by. Live music plays on Tuesday and Wednesday evenings and often on a Saturday night, when it can be busy.

Hullabaloo

37-41 Westgate, BD18 3QX

closed Mon & Tue; 4-11 Wed-Fri; 12-11 Sat; 12-10.30 Sun
07974 910838

4 changing beers (sourced regionally; often North Riding Brewery, Northern Monk, Wishbone)

Modern-style bar close to Shipley town centre and the bus interchange. Opened in October 2017, it is open plan but with three distinct areas in a variety of styles over split levels. Four handpumps serve a range of real ales, usually from regional brewers and often different to the other pubs in the area. A further handpump is dedicated to cider. Artisan craft beers are also available on six keg taps. Children are welcome.

Sir Norman Rae

Victoria House, Market Place, BD18 3QB

8-11 (01274) 535290

Elland 1872 Porter; Greene King Abbot; Ruddles Best Bitter; 7 changing beers (sourced nationally; often Goose Eye, Wychwood)

A typical conversion by Wetherspoon from a former Co-op department store, originally opened as a Lloyds No.1 but then converted to the standard format. Ten handpumps dispense real ale, offering three regulars and seven guests, often focusing on local breweries. Meet the Brewer nights are occasionally held. The good-value food is from the usual Wetherspoon menu. The pub is nicknamed the Waiting Room due to its proximity to Shipley bus interchange. The railway station is also nearby.

Silsden

Counting House

23 Kirkgate, BD20 0AJ

closed Mon & Tue; 3-10.30 Wed; 3-11 Thu; 11-11 Fri & Sat; 11-10.30 Sun (01274) 405644

Dark Horse Hetton Pale Ale; 3 changing beers (sourced regionally; often Ilkley, Saltaire)

A brightly decorated bar with a welcoming atmosphere, previously the branch of a bank, hence the name. It has exposed brickwork, feature light fittings and multiple clocks and mirrors. The L-shaped drinking/dining area has plenty of tables and small standing areas at the bar and by the door. The three guest beers change weekly. Food is only served Thursday evening, Sunday lunchtime and at special events, so booking is advisable. (62,903)

King's Arms

Bolton Road, BD20 0JY

12-midnight (11 Mon) (01535) 653216

Black Sheep Best Bitter; Saltaire Blonde; 5 changing beers (sourced nationally; often Rudgate, Wishbone)

Award-winning, bustling community pub, run by the same couple since 2003, with music nights on Tuesday and Thursday, quiz night on Wednesday, and a pool table, all combining to make it a great place to visit. Partitions divide the main bar into three distinct areas, each with its own feel. Westons cider and four to six guest beers from near and far, usually including a darker beer, provide something for all tastes. Regular buses between Keighley and Ilkley stop close by.
P (62,903)

Slaithwaite

Commercial

1 Carr Lane, HD7 5AN (village centre, off A62)

12-midnight (1am Fri & Sat) (01484) 846258

Empire Moonrakers Mild; house beer (by Empire); 5 changing beers

Since reopening in 2009, this village-centre free house has enjoyed deserved success. Nine handpumps provide ample variety, with the keenly priced house beers, Commerciale and Moonraker Mild, supplied by Empire Brewery, plus five rotating guests from far and wide, and a rotating guest cider. The pub is an essential stop for Transpennine Rail Ale trailers and welcomes ramblers and their dogs. Downstairs, the open-plan drinking area has the feel of separate spaces, and there is also an upstairs pool room. Sky Sports and Racing UK are screened in the bar.

South Elmsall

Barnsley Oak

Mill Lane, Minsthorpe, WF9 2DT (from S Elmsall centre go up hill by station then second major left turn)

12-11.30; 11.30-11.30 Fri-Sun (01977) 643427

Black Sheep Best Bitter; 1 changing beer

About a mile from the village centre, this is a thriving community pub run to high standards. Built in 1971, it has been smartly refurbished. Excellent value food is served daily, made with locally sourced produce and freshly prepared. There are good views of the Elms Valley from the conservatory. Quiz nights and TV sport are popular. Guest ales are usually from Yorkshire breweries.
P

Sowerby Bridge

Blind Pig

4 Tower Hill, HX6 2EQ

5-11.30 (12.30am Thu; 2am Fri); 2-2am Sat; 12-11.30 Sun
(01422) 833023 blindpig.pub

3 changing beers (sourced locally; often Nightjar, Vocation, Worsthorne) H

This stylish bar occupies a former bank building. Under present management since 2014, it specialises in real ales, cocktails, bottled world beers and ciders, and live music/DJ nights at weekends. The downstairs bar area has seating around the edge in boothed areas and at the bar. An area to the right has the DJ booth which is used on Saturdays. A spiral staircase on the left takes you to a bookable function room/bar which is used for live music events. Three changing beers are served, often from local breweries.

Hog's Head Brew House & Bar

1 Stanley Street, HX6 2AH

3-11 (midnight Fri); 12-midnight Sat; 12-11 Sun
(01422) 836585 hogsheadbrewhouse.co.uk

Hogs Head Maltings Ale, 6 to 8 Weeks, White Hog, Hoppy Valley, Old Schnozzler; 3 changing beers (sourced regionally; often Phoenix, Salopian, Vocation) H

Close to the centre of Sowerby Bridge, the venue was an 18th-century malthouse which has been extensively renovated. The brewery is at the back of the building and can be viewed from the bar area. Five core Hogs Head beers are stocked as well as guest ales. There is plenty of seating in the huge, sprawling bar area where snacks are also served. **Q**

Stanbury

Wuthering Heights Inn

Main Street, BD22 0HB (village centre)

12-11 (01535) 643332 thewutheringheights.co.uk

Moorhouse's White Witch; Theakston Best Bitter; 2 changing beers (sourced regionally; often Abbeydale, Bradfield) H

A friendly local dating from 1763, set in the tiny village of Stanbury on the Bronte moors with spectacular rural views. Warmed by logburners, the traditional main bar has photographs showing the history of the village. Hearty home-cooked food is served in the cosy dining room, which has a Bronte theme. A third room can be booked for parties and meetings. A quiz takes place every Thursday. The rear garden overlooks the Worth Valley, and has a separate camping area (no caravans). Well-behaved dogs and children are welcome.
P

Todmorden

Pub

3 Brook Street, OL14 5AJ

12-9 (11 Fri & Sat) (01706) 812145

6 changing beers (sourced nationally; often Eagles Crag) H

Todmorden's first micropub opened in 2017 in a former café close to the market. The décor - exposed stone walls, reclaimed wood bar - enhances the simple layout, making the most of the limited space. It has 20 seats downstairs, with a further 12 up a flight of steep stone steps also accessing the toilets. Six handpumps serve a changing range of beers, with a dark beer on the left-hand pump. Full tasting notes are on a chalkboard by the stairs. Up to 30 UK-distilled gins are stocked. **Q** (590,592)

Wadsworth

Hare & Hounds

Lane Ends Lane, HX7 8TN

6-11; 12-11.30 Sat; 12-10.30 Sun (01422) 842671
hareandhounds.me.uk

Timothy Taylor Dark Mild, Golden Best, Boltmaker, Landlord, Ram Tam H

Known locally as Lane Ends, this attractive stone-built pub opened in the 1840s, although the building is 400 years old. Located between Hebden Bridge and the moors, it offers good views of the surrounding countryside. The entrance leads directly into a lounge, with tables and chairs for diners, stone walls, an original stone fireplace, photos by local photographers and an old clocking-in machine. To the left is a seating area which contains yet more photos. The modern but appropriate bar faces a separate seating area, with a door leading onto the patio and its excellent views. **Q** **P** (595)

Wakefield

Black Rock

19 Cross Square, WF1 1PQ (between Bull Ring and top of Westgate)

11-11 (midnight Sat); 12-10.30 Sun (01924) 375550

Oakham Citra; Tetley Bitter; 4 changing beers (sourced regionally) H

An arched, tiled façade leads into this compact city-centre local, with a warm welcome and comfy interior including photographs of old Wakefield. The Rock stands as one of the few proper pubs left in the middle of the clubs and bars of Westgate, and is popular with drinkers of all ages looking for a real pint. Drinkers are encouraged to suggest beers to try, with four regularly changing guest ales on offer. There is a free function room for private use. **Q**

Fernandes Brewery Tap & Bier Keller

5 Avison Yard, Kirkgate, WF1 1UA (turn right approx 100yds S of George St/Kirkgate jct near Scartop Pine)

4-11 (11.30 Thu); 12-12.30am Fri & Sat; 12-11 Sun
(01924) 386348

Fernandes Ale to the Tsar, Black Voodoo; Ossett Yorkshire Brunette, Yorkshire Blonde; 4 changing beers (sourced regionally; often Fernandes) H

An Ossett Brewery tied house, with Fernandes Brewery operating in the cellar. With 10 handpulls, there are four Fernandes beers, two Ossett, and two guest beers, plus two draught ciders. The Bier Keller, open 6pm-midnight Friday and Saturday, has premier foreign beers on draught, plus an Ossett beer and a cider on handpump. A quiz takes place on Wednesday evening, and folk music on the first Sunday of each month. **Q**

Harry's Bar

107B Westgate, WF1 1EL (turn right from Westgate station, cross road at traffic lights; pub is at back of car park on right)

5-midnight; 4-1am Fri & Sat; 12-midnight Sun
(01924) 373773

House beer (by Five Towns); 7 changing beers (often North Riding) H

This small, one-roomed pub is set in an alleyway just off Westgate. A real fire and a bare-brick and wood interior plus vintage sporting pictures enhance the small venue. There is also a fantastic view of Wakefield's famous 99-arch viaduct; if only steam trains were still a regular feature. The bar has a selection of bottled Belgian beers to add to the temptation. Q❀♿⇌●P🚌ᯤ

Hop 🄻 ✔

19 Bank Street, WF1 1EH (a cobbled street off Westgate almost opp Theatre Royal)

4-11 (midnight Thu); 12-2.30am Fri & Sat; 12-10.30 Sun

☎ (01924) 367111 🌐 thehopwakefield.co.uk

Ossett Yorkshire Brunette, Yorkshire Blonde, Silver King, Excelsior; Rat White Rat; 4 changing beers Ⓗ

Converted into a venue for music and conversation, this Georgian building retains bare-brick walls, fireplaces and other original features, along with an extension which includes an open fire. The main bar has nine handpumps, one reserved for a dark beer, and serves a selection of bottled Belgian and American beers. There is a quiz on Tuesday, and live music Thursday, Friday and Saturday. Kebabs are served on Friday and Saturday nights. Rooms are available for hire (midweek only). ❀♿⇌●🚌

Wakefield Labour Club 🄻

18 Vicarage Street, WF1 1QX (at top of Kirkgate, round corner from Wakey Tavern)

7-11 (midnight Fri); 11-midnight Sat; 7-midnight Sun

☎ (01924) 215626 🌐 theredshed.org.uk

5 changing beers (sourced regionally) Ⓗ

The Red Shed, as the club building is known, is a secondhand army hut that has been extensively refurbished, and is home to many union, community and charity groups. It has three rooms, two of which can be hired for functions. Quiz night is Wednesday, and each month there is occasional live music on the second Saturday and an open mic folk music night on the last Saturday. There is an extensive collection of Union plates and badges over the bar as well as numerous CAMRA awards adorning the walls.

Q♿⇌(Kirkgate/Westgate)♣P🚌🐾

Wibsey

Hooper Micropub 🄻

209 High Street, BD6 1JU

closed Mon; 4.30-10 Tue & Wed; 4-11 Thu; 4-midnight Fri; 2-midnight Sat; 2-9 Sun 🌐 thehoopermicropub.co.uk

5 changing beers (sourced regionally; often Bingley, Kirkstall, Wishbone) Ⓗ

A friendly, split-level micropub that has quickly established itself with local people in this urban village. The bar is on the upper level and there is comfortable seating in the lower part. Five handpulls offer a varying selection of beers, primarily from the Yorkshire region but also occasionally from further afield. Photographs of old Wibsey provide interest in an otherwise minimalist décor. Closing time may vary depending upon demand. Q♣🚌🐾ᯤ

New York Tavern, Rotherham, South Yorkshire (Photo: Paige.../Flickr CC BY 2.0)

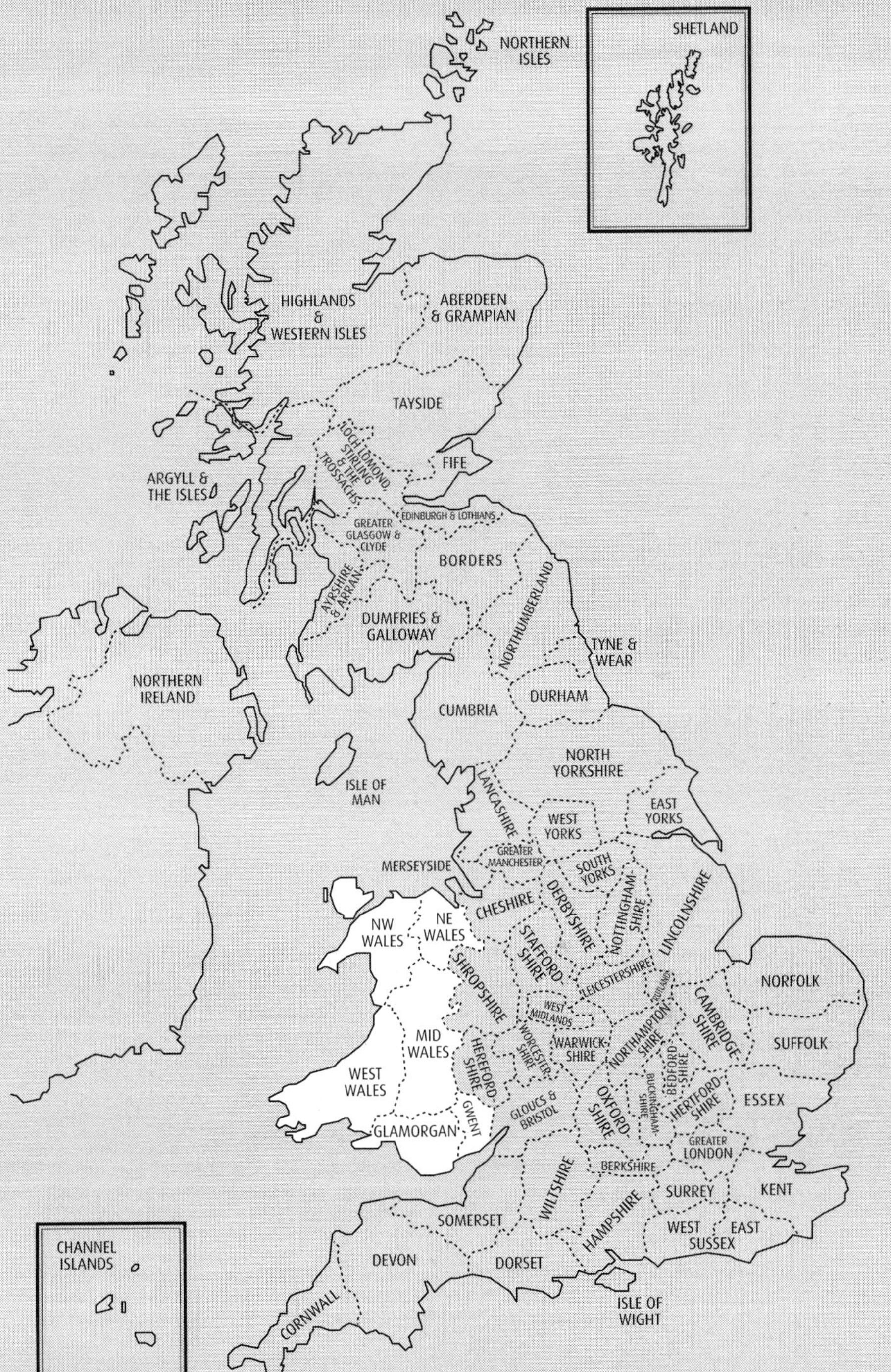
NORTHERN ISLES
SHETLAND
HIGHLANDS & WESTERN ISLES
ABERDEEN & GRAMPIAN
TAYSIDE
LOCH LOMOND, STIRLING & THE TROSSACHS
FIFE
ARGYLL & THE ISLES
EDINBURGH & LOTHIANS
GREATER GLASGOW & CLYDE
BORDERS
AYRSHIRE & ARRAN
DUMFRIES & GALLOWAY
NORTHUMBERLAND
TYNE & WEAR
NORTHERN IRELAND
DURHAM
CUMBRIA
NORTH YORKSHIRE
ISLE OF MAN
LANCASHIRE
WEST YORKS
EAST YORKS
GREATER MANCHESTER
MERSEYSIDE
SOUTH YORKS
CHESHIRE
DERBYSHIRE
NOTTINGHAM SHIRE
LINCOLNSHIRE
NW WALES
NE WALES
STAFFORD SHIRE
SHROPSHIRE
LEICESTERSHIRE
RUTLAND
NORFOLK
WEST MIDLANDS
CAMBRIDGE SHIRE
MID WALES
HEREFORD SHIRE
WORCESTER SHIRE
WARWICK SHIRE
NORTHAMPTON SHIRE
BEDFORD SHIRE
SUFFOLK
WEST WALES
BUCKINGHAM SHIRE
HERTFORD SHIRE
ESSEX
GWENT
GLOUCS & BRISTOL
OXFORD SHIRE
GLAMORGAN
GREATER LONDON
BERKSHIRE
WILTSHIRE
SURREY
KENT
HAMPSHIRE
SOMERSET
WEST SUSSEX
EAST SUSSEX
CHANNEL ISLANDS
DEVON
DORSET
ISLE OF WIGHT
CORNWALL

Wales

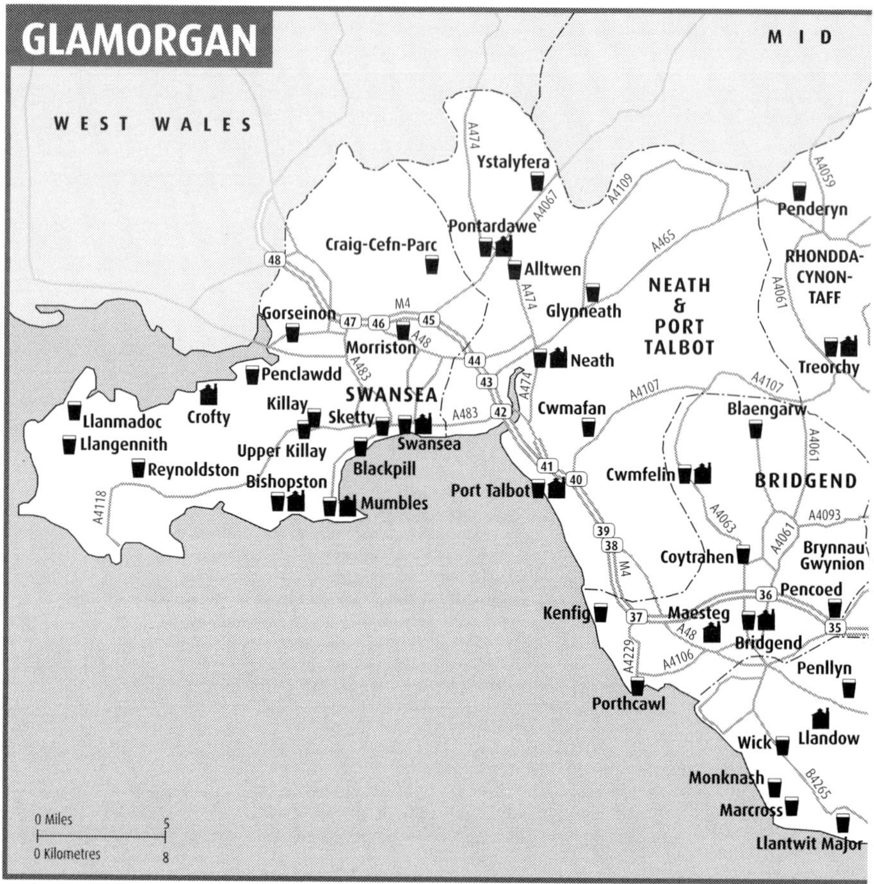

Authority areas covered: Bridgend UA, Caerphilly UA (part), Cardiff UA, Merthyr Tydfil UA, Neath & Port Talbot UA, Rhondda, Cynon & Taff UA, Swansea UA, Vale of Glamorgan UA

Aberdare

Ieuan ap Iago ✔

High Street, CF44 7AA

8am-midnight ☎ (01685) 880080

Greene King Abbot; Ruddles Best Bitter; Sharp's Doom Bar; 5 changing beers (sourced nationally; often Boss, Glamorgan) H

Popular Wetherspoon pub in the town centre, with regularly changing beers. Real cider is always available. The food service offers a varied choice and covers long hours. Well worth a visit, the pub is a modest stroll from Dare Valley Country Park and has good transport links. A public car park is opposite. ♿

Whitcombe Inn

Whitcombe Street, CF44 7DA

12-midnight (12.30am Sat); 12-11.30 Sun

☎ (01685) 875106

Felinfoel Double Dragon; Wye Valley Butty Bach; 1 changing beer (sourced nationally; often Pitchfork) H

Friendly street-corner local, close to the town centre. The single bar backs on to a pool room at the rear. Sport often plays on TV screens but is rarely obtrusive. Children are welcome until 9pm. A mobile ramp is available to assist wheelchair users entering from the street. The pub is approximately a mile from the picturesque Dare Valley Country Park, which accommodates campers and touring vans. ♿

Aberthin

Hare & Hounds

Aberthin Road, CF71 7LG

12 (3 Mon & Tue)-midnight; 12-1am Fri & Sat

☎ (01446) 774892 hareandhoundsaberthin.com

Hancocks HB; Wye Valley HPA; 2 changing beers (sourced regionally; often Glamorgan) H

A characterful village pub whose cosy public bar with its traditional stone walls, wooden beams and log fire is the focal point where the locals gather. The dining area serves high-quality nouvelle cuisine, with some ingredients grown by the chef. A full menu is also available in the bar. The guest ales are mainly sourced locally, the ciders are from Llanblethian Orchards and Apple County. Outside, the beer garden has its own bar and, occasionally, live music. There is limited parking.

Q ♿ P (321)

Alltwen

Gwyn Arms

Gwyn's Place, SA8 3AJ

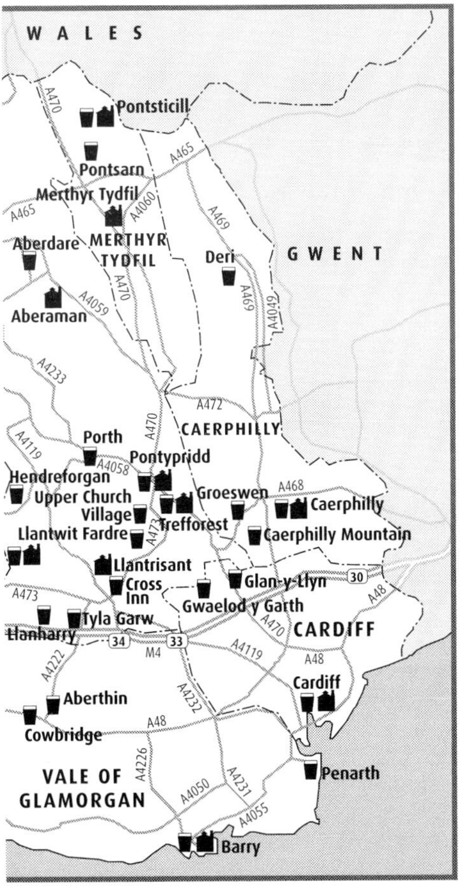

4-midnight; 12-midnight Sat & Sun ☎ 07754 716444

Wye Valley Butty Bach H

Traditional village local, high up on the side of the picturesque Swansea Valley. Although refurbished, it retains the old wooden fittings. Conversation is the norm in the absence of games machines, and the TV is always set at a low volume. Darts is popular and there is a separate games area for the pub's teams. Live music features at weekends and an open guitar jam session on Wednesday. There is plenty of scope for walkers and cyclists here - the National Cycle Path 43 is nearby. Q (256)

Barry

Barry West End Club L

54 St Nicholas Road, CF62 6QY

1-11.30; 12-midnight Sat & Sun ☎ (01446) 735739

barrywestendclub.webs.com

Wychwood Hobgoblin; Wye Valley HPA, Butty Bach; 2 changing beers H

Many times local CAMRA Club of the Year, this establishment is housed in a large multi-floored red-brick building overlooking the old harbour. Visitors are welcome and CAMRA members are treated as honorary club members. Home to cricket, football, snooker and skittles teams as well as chess, scuba diving and fishing clubs, among others, there is always something going on here. Two beer festivals a year, live music at the weekend and pub grub including the amazing sandwiches help make it a must-visit.

Q

Butterfly Collector

50A Holton Road, CF63 4HE

11-11 ☎ 07542 673794

8 changing beers (sourced nationally; often Brew Monster) G

Formerly a shop, this is a single room with no bar – customers are served at their tables with blackboards showing the offerings. As well as up to eight predominantly Welsh cask ales on gravity, there are two craft keg beers and more than a dozen real ciders. The enthusiastic licensee is a fan of The Jam and named the pub after one of their songs; memorabilia includes a series of tiles in the toilet. Ample free car parking is available nearby.

Q

Bishopston

Joiners Arms L

50 Bishopston Road, SA3 3EJ

11.30 (3 Mon & Tue)-11; 11.30-11.30 Fri; 12-11 Sun

☎ (01792) 232658 thejoiners.info

Marston's Pedigree; Swansea Bishopswood Bitter, Three Cliffs Gold, Original Wood; Theakston Best Bitter; 1 changing beer (sourced nationally) H

Situated in the heart of the village, this 1860s free house remains popular with locals and visitors. Home of the Swansea Brewing Company, the pub has two bars, with the six cask handpumps recently consolidated in the rear lounge. Good-value food is

REAL ALE BREWERIES

Arcadian Cardiff
Bang-On Bridgend
Borough Arms Neath
Boss Swansea
Brains Cardiff
Brewhouse & Kitchen Cardiff
Bullmastiff Cardiff
Cerddin Cwmfelin
Coach Bridgend (NEW)
Cold Black Label Bridgend
Crafty Devil Cardiff
Crafty Dragon Pontsticill
Cwm Rhondda Treorchy
Dog's Window Bridgend
Fairy Glen Maesteg (NEW)
Freetime Swansea
Glamorgan Llantrisant
Gower Crofty
Grey Trees Aberaman
Little Goat Pontardawe (NEW)
Mabby's Treforest
Mountain Hare Brynnau Gwynion
Mumbles Swansea
Neath Port Talbot
Pilot Mumbles
Pipes Cardiff
Swansea Bishopston
Tomos a Lilford Llandow
Tomos Watkin Swansea
Twin Taff Merthyr Tydfil
Twt Lol Pontypridd
VOG Barry
Well Drawn Caerphilly
Zepto Caerphilly
Zerodegrees Cardiff

WALES

served lunchtimes and evenings (except Mon and Sun eve) and there are occasional music events, usually around public holidays. The pub has won several local CAMRA awards over the years. There is a small car park. P (14)

Valley

41 Bishopston Road, SA3 3EJ (on main road in village)
11.30-11 (01792) 234820
valleyhotelbishopston.co.uk
Courage Best Bitter; 3 changing beers (sourced nationally; often Sharp's) H
Traditional family-run country pub set in the heart of this pleasant village. A large porch area (which doubles as a convenient bus shelter) leads to a split-level bar and dining area, with exposed beams, a hearth and an open fire. A wide variety of home-cooked meals using local ingredients is served daily and a Sunday lunch takeaway service is available. Live music plays on occasion.
P (14)

Blackpill

Woodman

120 Mumbles Road, SA3 5AS (opp Blackpill Lido)
12-11; 11.30-10.30 Sun (01792) 402700
Greene King IPA, Abbot; 3 changing beers (sourced nationally; often Greene King, Mumbles, Tomos Watkin) H
This historic pub and restaurant dating back to 1819 has been attractively refurbished. The deceptively spacious establishment, with its various nooks and alcoves, is situated on the main seafront road by the entrance to the beautiful Clyne Gardens. Popular with both families and diners, the pub also welcomes those seeking only liquid refreshment. A constantly changing range of ales is offered, including at least one from a local brewery. There are three outside seating areas and a small beer garden. P

Blaengarw

Blaengarw Hotel

The Strand, CF32 8AA
11.30-11; 11-midnight Fri & Sat; 11-10.30 Sun
(01656) 870287
1 changing beer (often Evan Evans, Glamorgan, Rhymney) H
An oasis in a real ale desert, this large street-corner local is at the heart of the community. Just one carefully chosen changing cask beer is on sale along with a cider. The public bar is popular for sports TV and hosts pool and darts league teams, and there is a fine jukebox. Meals are available in the lounge/dining room noon-8pm Tuesday and Thursday; Sunday lunches (until 3pm) are also popular. The famous Welsh hymn Calon Lan was written upstairs.

Bridgend

Coach

37 Cowbridge Road, CF31 3DH
11.30-11; 12-10.30 Sun
Wye Valley Butty Bach H**; 6 changing beers (often Grey Trees, Thornbridge, Tiny Rebel)** H/G
An incredible commitment to real ale, cider and independent producers has been the basis for the running of this pub since it was taken over by the current owners, who ventured into brewing in 2018. The brewery is visible from the pub, which is basically furnished but comfortable. Normally one Coach cask beer is on sale. An art wall allows local artists to display their work. The pub runs outings and events, including open mic nights and two beer festivals each year.
(303,X2)

Brynnau Gwynion

Mountain Hare

Brynna Road, CF35 6PG
4 (5 Mon)-11; 3-midnight Fri; 12-midnight Sat; 12-10.30 Sun (01656) 860453 mountainhare.co.uk
Mountain Hare Gold; Wickwar BOB; 2 changing beers (sourced nationally; often Glamorgan, Mountain Hare, St Austell) H
The Mountain Hare is a typical Welsh village pub and has featured in the Guide for more than 10 years. The licensee and brewer began brewing on-site in 2014 and one of his two beers is always available. The pub has been in the same family for over 40 years and boasts a traditional public bar, games room and a lovely old stone-walled lounge. Sport is often on TV in this rugby lovers' pub.
Q P (64,404)

Caerphilly

Malcolm Uphill

89-91 Cardiff Road, CF83 1FQ
8am-midnight (1am Fri & Sat) (029) 2076 0720
Greene King Abbot; Ruddles Best Bitter; Sharp's Doom Bar; 3 changing beers (sourced nationally; often Exmoor, Purity, Saltaire) H
Busy Wetherspoon pub, handy for the rail and bus interchange, named after the local motorcycle ace famed for being the first to lap the Isle of Man TT circuit at 100mph. At least one guest beer is usually on sale, rising to three at weekends. Up to two guest ciders are available, one often Gwynt y Ddraig Black Dragon. The pub can be crowded at weekends and hosts a popular quiz on quieter Sundays. A separate accessible entrance is available. Q

Caerphilly Mountain

Black Cock Inn

Waunwaelod Way, CF83 1BD (off A469, along Ffordd Waenwaelod.)
12-11 (9.30 Mon); 12-10.30 Sun (029) 2088 0534
Wye Valley Butty Bach; 3 changing beers (sourced regionally; often Grey Trees, St Austell, Wye Valley) H
A country inn popular with ramblers and dog walkers. Although rural it is easily accessed by car, but poorly served by public transport. Its two bars are either side of a wood-burning fireplace. The traditional bar is popular with dog walkers; the second bar is adjacent to the dining room. A pleasant beer garden overlooks country lanes. Boards list the ales available on pumps in the other bar. The pub is popular for lunch and evening meals; booking is recommended for Sunday and some evenings. Q P

Cardiff

Cambrian Tap

51 St Mary Street, CF10 1AD
12-11 (midnight Fri & Sat) (029) 2064 4952
6 changing beers (often Brains) H

Prominent 19th-century pub turned craft beer bar, situated on a street corner in the city centre. Its single bar sports eight handpumps, some of which serve beers from the Brains craft brewery. A mural depicts the craft beers that have been brewed, some in collaboration with other breweries. Guest beers are sourced from microbreweries across the UK. A good range of ciders and perries is served. The food offering includes pork pies. ❀◑≠●▭ᯤ

Chapter Arts Centre

Market Road, Canton, CF5 1QE (off Cowbridge Road E behind Iceland store)

10-11; 12-12.30am Fri; 12-midnight Sat; 10-10.30 Sun
☎ (029) 2030 4400 chapter.org

5 changing beers (sourced nationally) Ⓗ

Arts centre and cinema complex situated in a converted Victorian school, just off a busy main road. The open-plan bar has plenty of seating, and there is additional space in a covered area outside. The five guest beers come from across the UK, usually from small independent breweries, as well as a local ale. A number of fridges contain an impressive range of bottled beers from continental producers, with the accent on German beers. Occasional beer festivals are held.
❀◑♿Å≠P▭(16,17)ᯤ

City Arms Ⓛ ✔

10-12 Quay Street, CF10 1EA

12-midnight (1am Fri & Sat) ☎ (029) 2064 1913

Brains Dark, Bitter, SA, Rev James; 6 changing beers (sourced nationally) Ⓗ

This flagship Brains pub's wood-panelled bar helps give it the ambience of a traditional Amsterdam 'brown bar'. The pub is in the shadow of the Principality Stadium and gets busy on match days. Its three-sided bar serves the whole range of Brains beers plus up to seven guest ales, some rarely seen in the area and from anywhere in the UK. A range of ciders and perries is also available.
♿≠(Central)♣●▭ᯤ

Discovery Ⓛ

Celyn Avenue, Lakeside, CF23 6EH

12-11 Mon; 12-11.30 (12.30am Fri & Sat); 12-11 Sun
☎ (029) 2075 5015

Brains Bitter; Wye Valley HPA; 6 changing beers (often VOG) Ⓗ

Situated up the hill from Roath Park Lake, this pub is popular with locals and those coming to eat from further afield. Its lounge area has been transformed into a dining room that serves high-quality food all day from a changing blackboard menu. The public bar area boasts a dartboard and large TV. A door leads to the outdoor seating area.
❀◑♿♣P▭(54)ᯤ

Flute & Tankard

4 Windsor Place, CF10 3BX

12-midnight (11 Sun) ☎ 07870 289735
thefluteandtankard.com

3 changing beers (sourced nationally; often Brew Monster) Ⓗ

You will find this pub just off the eastern end of Queen Street, one of Cardiff's main shopping streets. Comfortable and quiet, it is just the ticket for anyone wanting a break from the hustle-bustle of city-centre activity. You can sample a choice of three real ales, sourced from across the UK. Enjoy the live jazz in the upstairs function room Tuesday and Wednesday evenings. Q❀≠(Queen St)●

Goat Major ✔

33 High Street, CF10 1PU

12-11 (midnight Fri & Sat); 12-6 Sun ☎ (029) 2033 7161

Brains Dark, Bitter, SA; 2 changing beers (sourced nationally) Ⓗ

Formerly named the Bluebell, this popular Brains pub has a traditional appearance and attracts a brisk trade from both locals and visitors. It is named after the mascot of the Royal Welsh Regiment, as proudly illustrated by many photographs adorning the interior. The occasional guest beer may come from anywhere. Traditional Welsh food is served into the early evening. A handy watering hole if visiting Cardiff Castle – which is directly opposite – and other local attractions.
Q◑♿≠(Central)▭ᯤ

Grange

134 Penarth Road, CF11 6NJ

12-11 (11.30 Fri & Sat); 12-10.30 Sun ☎ (029) 2025 0669

5 changing beers (sourced nationally) Ⓗ

A real community pub, this former Brains house has been brought back to life by the team that operates the award-winning Lansdowne pub. The Grange has rapidly gained popularity under its new management regime. A central serving area divides the two bars. There is a refurbished skittle alley. The decor is tidy, if on the functional side, but the accent on quality real ales, cider and food earned the pub the local CAMRA branch's Pub of the Year award for 2018.
Q◑≠(Grangetown)♣●▭

Halfway ✔

247 Cathedral Road, CF11 9PP

11.30-11.30 (midnight Fri & Sat); 11.30-11 Sun
☎ (029) 2066 7135

Brains Bitter, SA, Rev James; 4 changing beers (sourced nationally; often Hook Norton, Titanic) Ⓗ

Bustling Victorian-era pub with a varied clientele in the trendy urban village of Pontcanna. The large, open-plan interior has recently been refurbished and offers a number of comfortable areas for drinking and eating. Beers from the Brains craft brewery often feature, alongside a range of guest ales. Food is served all day. Sporting events are shown on multiple screens. The skittle alley is available to hire. ◑♿Å♣●▭ᯤ

Hopbunker

Northgate House, Kingsway, CF10 3FD

12-11; 11-midnight Fri & Sat; 11-11 Sun
☎ (029) 2039 8889 hopbunker.com

15 changing beers (sourced nationally; often Hopcraft) Ⓗ

Multi award-winning basement bar opposite Cardiff Castle offering the widest choice of real ales in the area – up to 15 are available at competitive prices. It is the tap for Hopcraft so expect to find a few examples of the brewery's beers on the bar. In addition, there is a bank of taps serving a range of keg beers, and a selection of up to 15 bag-in-box real ciders. Monday is quiz night, and you can also enjoy a selection of board games.
Q≠(Queen St/Central)●▭ᯤ

Lansdowne 🏆

71 Beda Road, CF5 1LX

12-11 (11.30 Fri & Sat); 12-10.30 Sun ☎ (029) 2022 1312

5 changing beers (often Grey Trees) Ⓗ

A ground-floor community pub with an open-plan layout, split into three distinct areas. Five handpumps serve one dark beer and one local ale.

The rest are dedicated to independent brewers, a rarity in the area. At least one keg beer from a local craft brewery is also offered, as is a traditional cider. Good-quality food includes award-winning Sunday lunches. The pub is popular with families and hosts quizzes and open mic nights, plus a beer festival in mid-June.

🛇🕏🕮&≷(Ninian Park)♣●🖫(96,X2)🐾🛜

Pen & Wig 🗕 ✔

1 Park Grove, CF10 3BJ

🕐 11.30-midnight; 11-1am Fri & Sat; 11.30-11.30 Sun

☎ (029) 2037 1217 ⊕ penandwigcardiff.co.uk

8 changing beers (sourced nationally; often Grey Trees) Ⓗ

Formerly a large Victorian terraced residence, just off the city centre and near the university and National Museum. The clientele is typically young professionals and office workers during the day, students in the evening. The beer range is from local, regional and national breweries, plus some craft keg offerings. Two ciders are also available. Regular Meet the Brewer events and brewery takeovers are held. The large garden includes a covered section and a smokers' area.

🕏🕮≷(Cathays/Queen St)●🖫🐾

Queens Vaults

29 Westgate Street, CF10 1EH

🕐 10-11 (midnight Fri & Sat); 11-11 Sun ☎ (029) 2022 7966

5 changing beers (sourced nationally) Ⓗ

A busy pub on Cardiff's Westgate Street strip offering good-value drinks and meals. There is a raised lounge/dining area at the front and pool tables and dartboards towards the rear. TVs show live sport and can be quite noisy, although frequently the volume is muted. Guest beers can be from anywhere but are often from microbreweries. Up to six ciders and perries are regularly available from a cooled stillage.

🕏🕮&Å≷(Central)♣●🖫🛜

St Canna's Ale House

42 Llandaff Road, CF11 9NJ

🕐 4-11; 12-11 Sat; 12-10 Sun ☎ 07890 106449

7 changing beers (often Grey Trees, Tiny Rebel, Untapped) Ⓗ

Micropub in a former corner shop, just off Cowbridge Road East in the centre of Canton, with two distinct rooms and an outdoor area. It serves up to six real ales on cooled gravity stillage, and four real ciders. The pub was founded to build community spirit and hosts regular activities such as tap takeovers, open mic nights and street food events. It is dog-friendly and has a piano and traditional board games to play. The yard, reached via a second room, has a covered smoking area.

Q🛇🕏&♣●🖫🐾

Tiny Rebel 🗕

26 Westgate Street, CF10 1DD

🕐 12-2 ☎ (029) 2039 9557

8 changing beers (sourced nationally; often Hawkshead, Thornbridge, Tiny Rebel) Ⓗ

This distinctive red-brick pub is in the city centre opposite the Principality Stadium. It has several rooms upstairs and downstairs, decorated in Tiny Rebel brewery's unique style, with some available for private hire. The pub hosts regular quizzes, bring your own vinyl and board game nights, and occasional brewery tap takeovers. Eight handpumps offer four changing Tiny Rebel ales plus a range of independent brewery beers from

across the UK. Four further handpumps serve ciders and perries. A former local CAMRA Pub of the Year. 🕏&≷(Central)♣●🖫🛜

Cowbridge

1 Town Hall Square

1 Town Hall Square, CF71 7DD

🕐 11.30-11 ⊕ 1townhallsquare.com

Wye Valley Butty Bach Ⓗ**; 3 changing beers (sourced nationally; often Grey Trees, Thornbridge)** Ⓗ/Ⓖ

A fairly recent addition to the local beer scene, this small pub is aimed squarely at the ale enthusiast. The bar has a seating area off it while upstairs are another two rooms. The decor is traditional with exposed stonework, tiled and wooden floors, and low beams. The entrance courtyard is a nice suntrap. No food is served but customers are welcome to bring their own. Butty Bach may be substituted by a beer from the Coach brewpub in Bridgend, which is under the same ownership.

🕏♣●🖫(X2,321)🐾🛜

Vale of Glamorgan Inn

51 High Street, CF71 7AE

🕐 11.30-11 (midnight Fri & Sat); 12-11 Sun

☎ (01446) 772252

Glamorgan Jemimas Pitchfork; Hancocks HB; Wye Valley Bitter, Butty Bach; 2 changing beers (sourced nationally; often Borough Arms, Grey Trees, VOG) Ⓗ

Popular town-centre pub where conversation is the usual entertainment. The single room's wooden-floored bar area has a warming range fire; to the rear is a flagstone-floored area with more seating around another stove. Outside is an attractive enclosed beer garden with a separate covered and heated smoking area. An annual beer festival coincides with the town's food and drink festival in May. Good-value home-made food is served 12-2.15pm (no food Sun). Q🛇🕏🕮🖫(X2,321)🐾≷

Coytrahen

Nicholls Arms

Nicholls Road, CF32 0ED

🕐 closed Mon; 12-11; 12-4 Sun ☎ (01656) 724680

⊕ nichollsarms.co.uk

Greene King Abbot; 1 changing beer (often Greene King) Ⓗ

Grade II-listed building on the Bridgend to Maesteg road with a truly stunning interior featuring wood-panelled and exposed stone walls, brass, paintings, a superb collection of Spode plates, and photos commemorating the area's mining history. Seating includes luxurious old leather armchairs and settees. There is no music, games or TV. A friendly group of locals regularly enjoys the quality meals served in the dining room.

Q🛇🕮ÅP🖫(70,71)🐾🛜

Craig-Cefn-Parc

Rock & Fountain

Rhyddwen Road, SA6 5RA

🕐 5-11; 4-11 Fri; 3-11 Sat & Sun ☎ (01792) 447800

⊕ therockandfountaininn.co.uk

Felinfoel Best Bitter; 2 changing beers (sourced nationally; often Evan Evans, Wye Valley) Ⓗ

Friendly local situated on the side of a steep hill close to the RSPB Cwm Clydach bird sanctuary. There is an outside patio area with seating where customers can enjoy the view across the valley.

The pub has a comfortable lounge featuring pictures of local interest and pub memorabilia, with a separate games bar for pool, darts, dominoes and sport on TV. ⮞😊♣P🖳(121)😊

Cross Inn

Cross Inn Hotel ✓
Main Road, CF72 8AZ
🍽 12-11 ☎ (01443) 223431
Hancocks HB; Sharp's Doom Bar; Wye Valley HPA; 1 changing beer (sourced nationally) Ⓗ
A welcoming, traditional pub that is immaculately maintained throughout, attracting locals and visitors alike. The large single room is divided into a bar area and a comfortable lounge in which home-prepared meals are served. Sunday lunches are popular; booking is strongly recommended. There is a large car park at the rear. Q😊◑&♣P🖳😊🛜

Cwmafan

Brit Pub ♟ Ⓛ
London Row, SA12 9AH
🍽 12-10 Mon; 11.30-10 Tue (11 Wed & Thu; midnight Fri & Sat); 11.30-10.30 Sun ☎ (01639) 680247 ⊕ thebrit.wales
3 changing beers (sourced regionally; often Glamorgan, Grey Trees, Mumbles) Ⓗ
Dating back to 1845, this pub offers a warm welcome to drinkers, diners, backpackers, locals and tourists. It serves up to three real ales and cider, mostly sourced locally. Attractions include a bunkhouse, real fireplace and award-winning food, not to mention a picturesque riverside beer garden. The pub hosts acoustic music evenings, and a beer and cider festival in summer. Tradition mixes with quirkiness at this community-focused gem in the beautiful Afan Valley. Local CAMRA Pub of the Year 2019. Q⮞😊◑&🖳(83)😊🛜

Cwmfelin

Cross Inn ♟
Masteg Road, CF34 9LB
🍽 11.45-midnight (1am Fri & Sat); 11-midnight Sun ☎ (01656) 732476
Cerddin Solar, Cascade; 3 changing beers (often Cerddin) Ⓗ
Home to the Cerddin Brewery, this is a must-visit pub. Alongside five cask beers it offers the brewery's bottle-conditioned range as well as eight real ciders. The traditional two-roomed Valleys pub has strong community links, friendly locals and knowledgeable staff. Its Tuesday night quiz raises money for the local food bank. A multiple local CAMRA Pub of the Year winner. Q😊🚲(Garth)♣🖳(71)😊🛜

Deri

Old Club
93 Bailey Street, CF81 9HX
🍽 5-2am; 3-2am Sat & Sun ☎ (01443) 839333
Grey Trees Ind Craft Brewers Diggers Gold; 2 changing beers (sourced locally; often Grey Trees Ind Craft Brewers) Ⓗ
Friendly village free house, the quirky name recalling its previous club status, a genuine community hub where locals come to relax. Two beers from award-winning Grey Trees Brewery are regularly on sale, with a third occasionally added at weekends. Sports TV tends only to be on when

there is interest. It is a short bus or taxi ride from Bargoed, or Sustrans cycle path route 469 offers a pleasant alternative. Cwm Darran Country Park is nearby in this pleasant semi-rural valley.
🏕♣🖳(1)😊🛜

Glan-y-Llyn

Fagins Ale & Chop House Ⓛ
9 Cardiff Road, CF15 7QD
🍽 12 (3 Mon)-11; 12-10.30 Sun ☎ (029) 2081 1800
3 changing beers (sourced nationally; often Dark Star, Grey Trees, Twt Lol) Ⓗ/Ⓖ
Situated just north of Taffs Well, this friendly free house offers a convivial and comfortable atmosphere. Handpulled beers vary occasionally, but always come from local breweries. The gravity-dispensed guest beers tend to be modern, well-hopped styles. Bottled ciders are from Gwynt y Ddraig. Good-value pub food is served (no food Mon). The logburner is most welcome on winter days. The pub is well served by buses and is a 15-minute walk from Taffs Well railway station.
Q⮞😊◑●🖳(26,132)😊🛜

Glynneath

Dinas Rock Hotel Ⓛ
High Street, SA11 5AP
🍽 5-11; 4-11 Fri; 1-midnight Sat; 12-11 Sun
☎ (01639) 722816
2 changing beers (sourced regionally; often Draught Bass, Glamorgan, Grey Trees) Ⓗ
Traditional local in the centre of the village, a welcome refuge in an area where real ale can be hard to find. Two wood-burning stoves and original stone walls make for a cosy atmosphere. Live rugby is popular on TV, especially Six Nations and Ospreys games. The real cider is hand-produced by one of the pub's regulars. Quiz night is Wednesday; live music is often performed at weekends.
Q⮞😊&♣●🖳(8,X7)😊🛜

Gorseinon

Mardy Inn ✓
117 High Street, SA4 4BR
🍽 8am-midnight (1am Fri & Sat) ☎ (01792) 890600
Greene King Abbot; Ruddles Best Bitter; Sharp's Doom Bar; 4 changing beers Ⓗ
This modern Wetherspoon establishment opened in 2013 following refurbishment of a former traditional high-street pub. It has a large single bar with several TVs for news and sport, and an adjoining airy extension overlooking the furnished patio area. Pictures of old Gorseinon adorn the walls, depicting the town and its inhabitants in years gone by. A good selection of local and national beers can be enjoyed in the beer garden.
⮞😊◑&●P🖳🛜

Groeswen

White Cross Inn
CF15 7UT (overlooking Groeswen Chapel)
🍽 4-midnight; 3-midnight Fri; 12-midnight Sat & Sun
☎ (029) 2085 1332
4 changing beers (sourced nationally) Ⓗ
A friendly old pub on the outskirts of Caerphilly that is well worth finding. Its six handpumps serve four changing beers alongside two ciders from local producer Williams Brothers. Four guest beers, one

always a dark, come in a diverse range of styles and strengths. Local and emerging breweries often feature, many new to the area. The pub hosts a popular monthly Beer Bellies gathering, featuring visiting brewers and beer-related talks. Beer festivals are held on most bank holidays. Road access is narrow. P

Gwaelod Y Garth

Gwaelod y Garth Inn

Main Road, CF15 9HH

10-11; 12-10.30 Sun (029) 2081 0408

gwaelodinn.co.uk

Wye Valley Bitter; 5 changing beers (sourced nationally; often Thornbridge) [H]

A stone-built, multi award-winning village local. On the extreme outskirts of Cardiff and on the lower slope of Garth Mountain, in the village centre, it is frequented by locals as well as cyclists and walkers. The pub offers a choice of real ales which could originate from anywhere across the UK. There is a games room downstairs and an upstairs restaurant which serves high-quality meals.
Q P (26B)

Hendreforgan

Griffin Inn

CF39 8YL (from Tonyrefail on A4093, turn down lane after Gilfach Goch village sign)

7-11; 6-11 Fri; 12-11 Sat & Sun (01443) 670379

Brains SA; 1 changing beer (sourced locally; often Glamorgan) [H]

A warm welcome is assured at the Griffin, known locally as the Bog, which has been in the same family for almost 60 years. Recognised by CAMRA as one of the Real Heritage Pubs of Wales, it has immaculate decor featuring oak furniture, gleaming brasses and a Victorian counter with an 1870 till. The pub is a little difficult to find but well worth the effort for its quirkiness and superbly kept beer. Q P (150,172)

Kenfig

Prince of Wales

CF33 4PR

12-11 (10 Mon); 12-10.30 Sun (01656) 740356

princeofwalesinn.co.uk

Draught Bass; Gower Gold; Worthington's; 1 changing beer (sourced regionally) [G]

A heritage award-winning inn dating from the 15th century and steeped in local history. Visitors can expect three quality ales on gravity, good locally sourced food and a warm welcome. Family-friendly and popular with dog walkers, the pub is comfortable and cosy. Outside there is a stunning view over Kenfig Nature Reserve. The Draught Bass is renowned throughout the local area and outsells all the pub's lagers combined. Guest beers and cider are occasionally available.
Q P (63B)

Killay

Village

5-6 Swan Court, The Precinct, SA2 7BA

10.15-11 (midnight Fri & Sat); 12-11.30 Sun

(01792) 203311

Sharp's Doom Bar; 3 changing beers [H]

Situated in a small shopping precinct in Killay, the Village has recently been refurbished, with a change of focus from traditional pub to café bar. It retains a single, split-level bar serving four real ales, one regular, complemented by three changing ales with one on gravity. There is a quiz on Tuesday and Sunday nights. On Monday the kitchen is closed but the pub offers cake, coffee and other drinks. P

Llangennith

King's Head

SA3 1HX

12-11 (01792) 386212 kingsheadgower.co.uk

Gower Brew 1, Gold; 3 changing beers (often Gower) [H]

Formerly three 17th-century stone-built cottages, the pub offers quality 4-star accommodation, with some rooms pet-friendly. It is situated at the western end of the Gower Peninsula, a short distance from the sandy stretches of Llangennith Beach. Ales from nearby Gower Brewery are available (up to six in summer) plus a cask cider. An impressive variety of home-made food is served, with dishes inspired by fresh local produce. An annual beer festival is held in October and a themed fancy dress event over the August bank holiday. P (116)

Llanharry

Fox & Hounds

Llanharan Road, CF72 9LL

12-11 (midnight Fri & Sat) (01443) 222124

foxandhoundsllanharry.co.uk

Courage Directors; 4 changing beers (sourced nationally; often Glamorgan, Oakham, Salopian) [H]

A traditional stone building, tastefully refurbished to provide a lounge with open fire and comfortable settees as well as more typical pub furniture. There is also a games room and separate restaurant area. Guest beers are often modern and progressive in style, and have developed a keen following. The pub has a growing reputation for serving good food. There is a large car park to the side.
P (64,404)

Llanmadoc

Britannia Inn

SA3 1DB

12-11 (01792) 386624 britanniainngower.co.uk

Gower Gold; Sharp's Doom Bar; Wye Valley HPA [H]

Timbers from ships wrecked on the nearby coast were used in the construction of this pretty and popular 17th-century pub in a quiet corner of Gower. A cosy bar at the entrance serves good food and beer; the back bar area has been converted into a fine restaurant. Beer gardens to the front and rear offer stunning views over the nearby estuary. An aviary and pet area is popular with children.
P (30)

Llantwit Fardre

Bush Inn

Main Road, CF38 2EP

4-midnight (1am Thu); 3-1am Fri; 12-1am Sat; 12-midnight Sun (01443) 203958

Hancocks HB; 2 changing beers (sourced regionally) [H]

Bustling village pub on the old course of the A473. The interior is semi open plan, featuring exposed stone walls and timber. At least one of the guest beers tends to be from a larger Welsh independent brewery. Quizzes are hosted on Tuesday and Wednesday, and a music jam on Thursday. A band often plays on Saturday, when the pub can get busy. (100,400)

Ship Inn

Crown Hill, CF38 1BH (100yds from A473, signposted Llantwit Fardre)

11-11 (01443) 202341

Greene King Abbot; Wickwar BOB H

Traditional one-bar pub in a semi-rural location, convenient for the local foot and cycle path. Outside is a large terrace with seating and a children's play area. The pub is popular for its classic pub food, served in the bar and separate restaurant (booking advisable). The menu includes healthy options and caters for vegetarians. P (90)

Llantwit Major

Llantwit Major Rugby Club

Old Market, Boverton Road, CF61 1XZ

4.30-11 (midnight Fri); 12-midnight Sat; 11-11 Sun (01446) 792276 llantwitmajor.rfc.wales

Sharp's Doom Bar; 2 changing beers (often Wadworth, Wye Valley) H

A friendly and vibrant community club where visitors are welcome – dogs too, in the players' bar. The big-selling regular beer and two changing guest ales are excellent value for money. There is a small patio area which is popular in summer and some covered seating at the side for smokers. The club has a cosy lounge bar and a function room. P (303,321)

Marcross

Horseshoe Inn

CF61 1ZG

12-2.30 (not Mon), 6-11; 12-11 Sat; 12-10.30 Sun (01656) 890568 theshoesmarcross.co.uk

Sharp's Atlantic; Wye Valley Butty Bach; 2 changing beers (often Gower, VOG) H

The Shoes is a beautiful 19th-century pub in the hamlet of Marcross. It usually has a range of three ales, one a Welsh brew. The bar is cosy on cold winter nights, with a large logburner; the beer garden is a delight in summer. An extensive food menu offers good pub fare. The pub and its friendly staff are popular with international students from the local college. It is convenient for spectacular coastal walks, taking in the nearby Nash Point lighthouse. Q P (303)

Monknash

Plough & Harrow

CF71 7QQ

12-11 (midnight Fri & Sat); 12-10.30 Sun (01656) 890209

Draught Bass G**; Hancocks HB; Wye Valley HPA** H**; 5 changing beers (often Grey Trees, Tudor)** H/G

Renowned 14th-century pub, originally a monastic farmhouse, with many original features and an eclectic farmhouse-style interior that surprises newcomers. Up to eight real ales are served, four on handpump and others gravity fed, with local breweries well supported. There is a large selection of ciders and perries from Gwynt y Ddraig. Food is home-cooked and a large beer garden hosts festivals and live music in summer. Local CAMRA Cider Pub of the Year. Q P (303)

Morriston

Red Lion Hotel

Sway Road, SA6 6JA

8am-midnight (1am Fri & Sat) (01792) 761870

Greene King Abbot; Ruddles Best Bitter; 6 changing beers (sourced nationally) H

This Wetherspoon pub features a large dining area with an open log fire at the front and high bar stools at the back. Numerous pictures on the walls depict the area's long-gone industrial past. A community board advertises trips to breweries and other local events. An outside patio area provides tables and chairs plus a smoking area. The pub offers good parking facilities and disabled access. P (4)

WALES

Mumbles

Beaufort Arms

1 Castle Road, Norton, SA3 5TF

4-11; 2-11 Sat; 12-10.30 Sun (01792) 514246

Brains Rev James; Draught Bass; Glamorgan Jemimas Pitchfork; Gower Gold H

Charming 18th-century local with a welcoming atmosphere. Previously closed by its owning pub group, it was bought privately in 2017 by a couple who have tastefully renovated it and delighted the locals by increasing the range of beers. The pub has a traditional main bar with TV and dartboard, and a small, comfortable lounge. Both rooms have real fires and there is a small beer garden at the rear. A quiz is held on Tuesday. Q (2A,3A)

Park Inn

23 Park Street, SA3 4DA

4-11; 2-11 Sat & Sun (01792) 366738

5 changing beers (sourced regionally; often Evan Evans, Mumbles, Tiny Rebel) H

The convivial atmosphere in this small establishment in a village side street attracts discerning drinkers of all ages. Five handpumps dispense an ever-changing range of beers, with particular emphasis on independent breweries from Wales and the west of England. Alongside a fine display of pumpclips are pictures of old Mumbles and its pioneering railway. A popular quiz is held on Thursday, with occasional music at weekends. Q (2,3)

Pilot Inn

726 Mumbles Road, SA3 4EL

12-11 (midnight Fri & Sat) 07897 895511 thepilotofmumbles.co.uk

Draught Bass; 6 changing beers (sourced nationally; often Pilot) H

Welcoming and friendly local on the seafront at Mumbles and home to the Pilot Brewery. Seven ales are always available, usually including up to three brewed on site. A wide range of bottled ciders is also kept and hot drinks are served. This historic pub, built in 1849, is next to the coastal path and popular with lifeboatmen, locals, walkers, cyclists and, of course, real ale fans. Local CAMRA Pub of the Year 2018. Q

Neath

Borough Arms Ⓛ

2 New Henry Street, SA11 1PH (off Briton Ferry road, near Stockhams Corner roundabout)
🕓 4.30-9 Mon (11 Tue & Wed); 4-11 Thu & Fri; 12-11 Sat; 12-3 Sun ☎ (01639) 644902
House beer (by Draught Bass); 4 changing beers (sourced nationally) Ⓗ
On entering, you are greeted by an unusually shaped one-room bar that is welcoming and cosy. The bar itself hosts one regular (Bass), and four well-kept ales from various sources. The new owner, a former brewer, has again returned to the venue to a brewpub by making use of the original brewery at the rear. Conversation is the main pastime in this terraced back-street pub.
Q❀⇌🚌📶

David Protheroe Ⓛ ✔

7 Windsor Road, SA11 1LS (opp railway station)
🕓 8am-midnight (1am Fri & Sat) ☎ (01639) 622130
Greene King Abbot; Ruddles Best Bitter; Sharp's Doom Bar; 5 changing beers (sourced nationally; often Brains, Glamorgan, Tomos Watkin) Ⓗ
Situated opposite Neath railway station and a short walk from the bus terminus, this popular town-centre venue is a typical Wetherspoon pub. The building is the former police station and is named after the town's first policeman. It has an airy, open-plan interior. Local beers are regularly served alongside real ciders. The varied food menu includes Welsh dishes and comes with friendly service. 🐴❀◐♿⇌🍎🚌📶

Penarth

Golden Lion Ⓛ

69 Glebe Street, CF64 1EF
🕓 10-11; 11-midnight Fri & Sat; 12-10.30 Sun
☎ (029) 2070 1574
4 changing beers (often Glamorgan, Grey Trees, VOG) Ⓗ
A genuine locals' pub with a reputation for serving some of the best-kept quality real ale in the area. Three or four beers from Welsh breweries are usually available, along with good-value food. The pub can sometimes be loud and lively with its popular jukebox and numerous sports TVs; football and darts teams are among the regular customers. The small beer garden is a delight in warmer weather, with artificial grass and wall paintings depicting Penarth. ❀◐♿⇌♣🚌🐾📶

Pilot

67 Queen's Road, CF64 1DJ
🕓 12-11 (midnight Fri & Sat) ☎ (029) 2071 0615
4 changing beers (often Dukeries, Milton, VOG) Ⓗ
The Pilot has established a reputation for high-quality beer, wine and food. Its ales are chosen from some of the best Welsh breweries and served alongside more unusual offerings from around the country. Five handpumps offer up to four quality cask ales plus a real cider. The front bar is dog-friendly, there is pleasant seating outside at the front for warm weather, and the rear restaurant area with its log-fired stove is comfortable in winter. Q🐴◐♿⇌🍎🚌🐾📶

Windsor Ⓛ ✔

95 Windsor Road, CF64 1JE
🕓 11-11.30 (10.30 Sun) ☎ (029) 2070 8675
Brains Bitter, Rev James Gold, Rev James; 3 changing beers (sourced nationally; often Oakham, St Austell) Ⓗ
The Windsor was recently refurbished to a high standard and has an emphasis on quality dining. It serves up to six real ales, several from the Brains portfolio alongside guest beers that are often from national breweries. The pub offers a relaxing environment, with a cosy front area with comfortable seating, a long dining/drinking space opposite the bar, and further tables to the rear. It is popular with families for Sunday lunch.
Q🐴◐♿⇌(Dingle Rd)🚌🐾📶

Penclawdd

Rake & Riddle Ⓛ

Penclawdd Road, SA4 3RB
🕓 11-11 (midnight Fri & Sat) ☎ (01792) 872886
🌐 therakeandriddle.com
Gower Gold, Power; 2 changing beers (sourced nationally; often Gower, Sharp's) Ⓗ
Located in a large two-storey building on the main north Gower road, this pub is popular for food. It has a restaurant and bar on the ground floor, with the main bar and another smaller dining room upstairs. Its decor is simple and modern. The pub serves ales from the nearby Gower Brewery, with which it has business links, including a range of takeaway options. The upstairs bar and a garden terrace can be accessed from the rear car park.
🐴❀◐♿P🚌(116)🐾

Pencoed

Britannia

7 Hendre Road, CF35 5NW
🕓 12-11 (1am Fri & Sat) ☎ (01656) 860077
1 changing beer (often Glamorgan, Wickwar) Ⓗ
Until early 2018 the Britannia did not sell real ale. Now it serves one changing beer, has a second handpump for future use, and has been voted local CAMRA Most Improved Pub for 2019. Its L-shaped interior is on split levels, with two pool tables on the raised area. The pub also has pool and football teams. Stained-glass windows on the main door commemorate the pub's past as the Railway, named after its location alongside Pencoed station.
🐴❀⇌♣P🚌🐾📶

Little Penybont Arms

11 Penybont Road, CF35 5PY
🕓 3-11; closed Tue; 12-11 Fri & Sat ☎ 07734 767937
2 changing beers (often Grey Trees, Mumbles, VOG) Ⓖ
A cosy micropub converted from a café, offering up to four changing beers on gravity, 20-plus ciders and 15-plus single malt whiskies. The Steak & Stamp restaurant two doors down is under the same ownership and serves the same range of drinks. In the pub, excellent bar snacks are available including pork pies, nuts and home-made pork scratchings. A quiz and pizza night is held on Wednesday. Since opening, the pub has built up a strong local following. Q🐴◐⇌♣🍎🚌🐾📶

Penderyn

Red Lion

Church Road, CF44 9JR
🕓 12-3 (not Mon), 6-11; 12-11 Sat; 12-10.30 Sun
☎ (01685) 811914 🌐 redlionpenderyn.com

Brains Rev James; Draught Bass; Fuller's ESB; Gower Gold; 3 changing beers (sourced nationally; often Marston's) G
An independent, 12th-century drovers' inn with wonderful views across the Brecon Beacons National Park. Run by the same family since 1978, it features flagstone floors and two log fires that create a wonderful atmosphere in winter. The pub dispenses six or seven beers by gravity; the favourite Fuller's ESB has been served for more than 40 years. Three real ciders and a perry are also available. The focus on food has increased of late, with a changing menu of traditional home-cooked dishes. Q

Penllyn

Red Fox

CF71 7RQ
12-11 (01446) 772352 redfoxinn.co.uk
Hancocks HB; 3 changing beers (sourced nationally; often Evan Evans, Goff's, Wye Valley) H
A warm welcome is guaranteed at this friendly, well-run village local, within whose thick stone walls phone signals fear to tread. The interior comprises a stone-floored main bar area, warmed by a log fire on colder days, and a separate restaurant. A neat patio at the front is popular in fine weather. To the rear is a large enclosed garden where children can play safely or climb the trees. QP

Pontardawe

Pontardawe Inn

123 Herbert Street, SA8 4ED
12-11.30 (midnight Fri & Sat) (01792) 447562
pontardaweinn.co.uk
Marston's Pedigree; Ringwood Fortyniner; 2 changing beers (sourced nationally; often Mumbles) H
Originally a drovers' pub, the Gwachel, as it is known locally, sits beside the picturesque River Tawe and is well worth the short walk from Pontardawe. This community-focused pub serves four ales from Marston's portfolio, often alongside Mumbles beers, and a range of real ciders. Good food is offered from a varied menu. Live music is prominent on Friday and Saturday evenings, and seasonal beer and music festivals are held. The landscaped rear garden is a welcome feature in summer. Local CAMRA Pub of the Year on numerous occasions. P

Pontsarn

Aberglais Inn

CF48 2TS (between Trefechan and Pontsticill) SO043098
10.30-11 (01685) 377344 aberglais.com
3 changing beers (sourced nationally; often Grey Trees, Sharp's, Wye Valley) H
Enjoying a new lease of life following renovation, the Aberglais is in a picturesque setting on the route to Pontsticill Reservoir and Morlais Castle. Its traditional exterior conceals a modern interior that displays photographs of the former railway viaduct and station. Holidaymakers, hikers and cyclists are welcomed, and the pub is equally popular with diners and those popping in for a pint. Guest beers change occasionally. Booking is essential for Saturday meals, and recommended at other times. The pub is midway along Sustrans Taff Trail Route 8 between Cefn Coed and Pontsticill. P

Pontsticill

Red Cow

CF48 2UN (middle of Village)
11.30-8.30 Mon (9.30 Tue; 11 Wed & Thu; midnight Fri & Sat); 11.30-10 Sun (01685) 387775
Grey Trees Afghan Pale; Wye Valley Bitter; 1 changing beer (sourced locally; often Twt Lol) H
Delightful and tranquil stone-built village pub at the southern edge of the Brecon Beacons National Park. Pontsticill Reservoir is nearby and the Brecon Mountain Railway is just across the valley. The pub is an ideal lunchtime stop when touring the Beacons, with scenic paths and trails nearby. A popular quiz is held on Wednesday evening. The local community bus runs in response to phone bookings. P

Pontypridd

Bunch of Grapes

Ynysangharad Road, CF37 4DA (off A4054)
11-1am (midnight Sun) (01443) 402934
bunchofgrapes.org.uk
10 changing beers (often Crouch Vale, Oakham, Salopian) H
A rustic pub just off the town centre, dating from the 19th century. The bar features a log fire and cosy sofas, and attracts a diverse clientele. Ten guest beers are offered, of which four are usually local. Two guest ciders or perries are also available. Beer and cider festivals, themed nights and the regular Tuesday quiz are popular. Good-quality food is served both in the bar and the highly acclaimed restaurant. Local CAMRA Pub of the Year 2019. QP

Llanover Arms

Bridge Street, CF37 4PE (opp N entrance to Ynysangharad Park, off A470)
11-11 (01443) 403215
3 changing beers (sourced nationally; often Salopian) H
Built around 1794 to serve thirsty boatmen working the newly opened Glamorganshire Canal, this historic free house has been in the same family for over a century. Passageways link its three rooms, each of which has a distinct character and atmosphere. Nearby is the famous old town bridge and Ynysangharad Park with its restored National Lido of Wales. The Taff Trail passes close by. QP

Patriot Bar

25B Taff Street, CF37 4UA
12-midnight (01443) 407915
Rhymney Best, Bevans Bitter, Export; 2 changing beers (often Rhymney) H
A Rhymney Brewery tied pub, near the bus station and a short stroll from the railway station. Its exceptionally well-kept beers include two guests from the Rhymney range. Trade is brisk, with beers turning over quickly, not least due to reasonable prices. Real cider is sometimes available. The pub is easy to find, located in a former shop in Taff Street. It is fondly known as the Wonky Bar, recalling its former twisted entrance.

Tumble Inn

Broadway, CF37 1BA
8am-midnight (1am Fri; 2am Sat) (01443) 484390

Greene King Abbot; Ruddles Best Bitter; Sharp's Doom Bar; 3 changing beers (sourced regionally; often Boss, Glamorgan, Rhymney) H
A long single bar serves this roomy pub, one of Wetherspoon's music-themed Lloyds No.1 Bar outlets. The former post office is near the town centre and railway station and on several main bus routes. Its open-plan space is mainly on one level. The food service offers a varied choice and covers long hours. An outdoor patio is divided into smoking and no-smoking areas. Monday is poker night, Wednesday is quiz night.

Port Talbot

Lord Caradoc

69-73 Station Road, SA13 1NW
8am-midnight (1am Fri & Sat) (01639) 896007
Greene King Abbot; Ruddles Best Bitter; Sharp's Doom Bar; 7 changing beers (sourced nationally; often Glamorgan, Mumbles, Rhymney) H
Named after a 12th-century Lord of Afan, this Wetherspoon pub has a relaxed atmosphere. Its walls display old photographs of Port Talbot and famous local people. The spacious, open-plan layout includes a family-friendly area. Choice of beers is open to suggestion from regular customers, with a wide range available. Situated on the main shopping street, the pub is easily accessible from Port Talbot Parkway railway station and the bus terminus. P

Porth

Rheola

Rheola Road, CF39 0LF
2-midnight; 1-1am Fri; 12-1am Sat; 12-midnight Sun
(01443) 682633
Rhymney Hobby Horse, Bitter, Export H
Another Rhymney Brewery tied house, with contrasting rooms. The bar features a jukebox, pool table and dartboard, and is often lively; the lounge has an over-25 rule and is more relaxed although it can get busy at weekends. Rhymney beers retail at keen prices and are excellent value. The pub is situated at the confluence of the two Rhondda rivers, and is well served by rail and bus. Activities include quiz night on Monday, a pool tournament on Tuesday and an emerging open mic session on Thursday. P (132)

Porthcawl

Lorelei Hotel

36-38 Esplanade Avenue, CF36 3YU
5-11 Mon; 12-1.30, 5-11 Tue; 12-11 Wed-Sat; 12-10.30 Sun
(01656) 788342 loreleihotel.co.uk
Draught Bass G**; Rhymney Export; 3 changing beers (often Boss, Grey Trees, VOG)** H
Near the seafront and the Grand Pavilion, this is the 21st year the Lorelei has been in this Guide. Good-quality and good-value food is served evenings (except Mon) and Sunday lunchtime. Four draught beers are available plus cider in summer. Beer festivals are held twice a year on Grand National and Halloween weekends. Built around the end of the 19th century, during World War I it was two separate buildings – one used as a hospice for injured soldiers. Q

Reynoldston

King Arthur Hotel

Higher Green, SA3 1AD (on village green)
10-11 (01792) 390775 kingarthurhotel.co.uk
Gower Gold; Sharp's Doom Bar; 2 changing beers (sourced nationally; often Glamorgan, Tenby, Tiny Rebel) H
Traditional family-owned hotel and acclaimed wedding venue, situated at the foot of Cefn Bryn in beautiful Gower, overlooking the village green. There is covered outdoor seating by the pub entrance and a large seating area on the green itself. The cosy, atmospheric main and rear bars are welcoming to drinkers and diners, serving home-cooked food made with local produce. Main meals and bar snacks are available all day, breakfasts for non-residents 8-11am. P

Sketty

Vivian Arms

106 Gower Road, SA2 9BT (Sketty Cross, jct of A4118 and A4216)
11.30-11 (midnight Fri & Sat); 12-11 Sun
(01792) 516194
Brains Bitter, Rev James Gold, SA, Rev James; 1 changing beer H
Situated on the main crossroads in Sketty, The Vivs attracts a wide range of customers young and old. The spacious pub has a mixture of seating areas, and plenty of TV screens throughout to show live sport. It is popular for family dining and serves a carvery on Sunday. Live music plays on Friday and occasionally Saturday. A general knowledge quiz is held on Sunday and a music quiz on Wednesday. A small meeting room provides extra seating. (20,21)

Swansea

Bank Statement

57/58 Wind Street, SA1 1EP
8am-midnight (1am Wed & Fri); 8am-2am Sat
(01792) 455477
Sharp's Doom Bar; 5 changing beers (sourced nationally; often Boss, Exmoor, Fuller's) H
A former Midland Bank, sympathetically transformed by Wetherspoon while retaining its original ornate interior. Trading as a Lloyds No.1, the pub is at the heart of the city's popular bar quarter and has a large ground floor with plenty of seating. Attracting all ages, it is busy throughout the week as well as at the weekend. Sport is shown on its many screens. The bottled beer selection includes real ales.

Brunswick Arms

3 Duke Street, SA1 4HS (between St Helens Rd and Walter Rd)
11.30-11; 12-10.30 Sun (01792) 465676
brunswickswansea.com
Caledonian Deuchars IPA; Courage Best Bitter, Directors; Wye Valley Butty Bach H**; 3 changing beers (sourced nationally; often Gower)** H/G
A side-street pub with the air of a country inn. Wooden beams and comfortable seating create a traditional, relaxing atmosphere and a local resident artist's work is displayed for sale. One of the changing beers is gravity dispensed, often from a local microbrewery. Home-made specialities are available on the food menu, including curry and a pie of the week. Attractions include a quiz on

Monday, live acoustic music on Thursday and an open mic session on the second Tuesday of each month. ◗♿🍎🚌(200)📶

No Sign Bar 🏆
56 Wind Street, SA1 1EG
11-11 (midnight Wed & Thu; 1am Fri & Sat); 12-11 Sun ☎ (01792) 465300 🌐 nosignwinebar.com
Gower Gold; 3 changing beers (sourced nationally; often Butcombe, Mumbles, Tiny Rebel) Ⓗ
Historic narrow bar established in 1690, formerly known as Mundays Wine Bar and reputedly a regular haunt of Dylan Thomas. Architectural clues from various periods of the pub's past remain, some dividing the interior into separate areas. Quality food and wine are available, and up to five real ciders. Live music features in the bar on Friday, Saturday and often Sunday evenings. Bands also play in the Vault basement later at night.
🐎❀◗⇌🍎🚌📶

Potters Wheel
85-86 The Kingsway, SA1 5JE
8am-midnight (1am Thu-Sat) ☎ (01792) 465113
Adnams Broadside; Fuller's London Pride; Ruddles Best Bitter; Sharp's Doom Bar; 6 changing beers (sourced nationally) Ⓗ
A city-centre Wetherspoon outlet with a long sprawling bar area offering various seating arrangements, attracting customers of all ages and backgrounds. An interesting selection of guest beers is kept, with a commitment to local breweries. Real cider is always available. Photographs on the walls feature local dignitaries associated with the area's industrial past, particularly the ceramics and pottery industries. Look for the CAMRA board and beer suggestion box. 🐎◗♿🍎🚌📶

Queen's Hotel
Gloucester Place, SA1 1TY (near Waterfront Museum)
11-11 (11.30 Sat); 12-11 Sun ☎ (01792) 521531
Theakston Best Bitter, Old Peculier; 2 changing beers (sourced nationally; often Fuller's, Glamorgan, Shepherd Neame) Ⓗ
This vibrant free house is near the Dylan Thomas Theatre, City Museum, National Waterfront Museum and marina. The walls display photographs depicting Swansea's rich maritime heritage. The pub enjoys strong local support and home-cooked lunches are popular. Evening entertainment includes a Sunday quiz, bingo on Wednesday and live music on Saturday. This is a rare local outlet for Theakston Old Peculier in addition to a seasonal guest beer often from a local microbrewery. Local CAMRA Pub of the Year 2017.
◗🚌📶

Uplands Tavern ✔
42 Uplands Crescent, Uplands, SA2 0PG
11-11 (midnight Fri & Sat) ☎ (01792) 458242
Greene King IPA, Abbot; 2 changing beers (sourced locally) Ⓗ
Although situated in the heart of Swansea's student quarter, the Tav continues to attract regulars from all walks of life. It is another former haunt of Dylan Thomas, commemorated in a separate snug area. The spacious single-room pub has a deserved reputation for the quality and variety of its live music at weekends, and hosts an open mic night on Monday. Tuesday is quiz night. There is a large heated outdoor drinking area at the front. ❀♿♣🚌📶

Trefforest

Otley Arms Ⓛ
Forest Road, CF37 1SY (on gyratory system)
12-11 (midnight Fri & Sat) ☎ (01443) 402033
🌐 theotley.co.uk
Mabby Blue, Red, Black, Green; 3 changing beers (sourced regionally; often Grey Trees, Salopian, Tiny Rebel) Ⓗ
Welcoming and informal pub, popular with students from the nearby university as well as a varied mix of locals. The open-plan main bar has a log fire and leather sofas. It offers a wide variety of guest and craft ales alongside Mabby beers brewed on-site. Traditional food is of a high standard, and the service and atmosphere are always friendly. Board games are available and a quiz is held on Monday. Particularly well served by public transport. 🐎❀◗⇌♣🍎🚌(90,100)🐾📶

Rickards Arms Ⓛ
61 Park Street, CF37 1SN
11-midnight; 12-11 Sun ☎ (01443) 402305
3 changing beers (sourced nationally; often Grey Trees) Ⓗ
Located 100 yards from Trefforest railway station, the pub backs on to the railway line and is popular with students at the nearby university. It is divided into four distinct areas, served by a central bar. Three guest beers are served, one usually local and two national. Food is of good value, especially the famous cooked breakfasts. The pub hosts regular quiz and music nights. ❀◗⇌♣🚌(90,100)🐾📶

Treorchy

Pencelli Hotel ✔
Pencae Terrace, CF42 6HL
closed Mon; 4-11 Tue & Wed; 2-midnight Thu & Fri; 12-12.30am Sat; 12-11 Sun ☎ (01443) 775181
5 changing beers (sourced nationally; often Glamorgan, Salopian, Tiny Rebel) Ⓗ
A welcoming community hostelry whose two large rooms are served by a central bar offering a range of beer styles. A log fire adds warmth in winter. The pub has a strong musical following and hosts live bands on Thursday, Saturday and bank holidays. It is easily reached by bus or train and has ample car parking opposite. A winner of many local CAMRA Pub of the Year awards, including both Highly Commended and Cider Pub of the Year in 2019. 🐎❀◗⇌♣🍎🚌

Tyla Garw

Boar's Head
Coedcae Lane, CF72 9EZ (600yds from A473 over level crossing)
4-10 Mon; 12-11 Tue-Sat; 12-10 Sun ☎ (01443) 225400
5 changing beers (sourced nationally; often Dark Star, Oakham, Salopian) Ⓗ
This award-winning pub, successfully promoted as a community hub, includes a bar, lounge, dining room and the Piglets lounge, which is a coffee bar during daytime. The central bar serves up to five real ales plus a selection of keg beers. A large beer garden has a marquee for special events. Booking is advised for Sunday lunch. Quiz night is popular on alternate Tuesdays. There is a quick walking route to Pontyclun railway station.
Q🐎❀◗♿⇌🍎P

WALES

Upper Church Village

Farmers Arms ✔

St Illtyd Road, CF38 1EB
✪ 3-11 Mon-Wed; 12-midnight Thu-Sat; 12-10.30 Sun
☎ (01443) 205766
Brains Rev James; 2 changing beers (sourced nationally) Ⓗ
Comfortable village local with one large bar, and a pleasant split-level beer garden and patio outside. The changing beers often include choices rarely found in the area. A popular quiz night is hosted on Tuesday, but beer and conversation are the main attractions. Traditional pub food and a logburner add to the appeal. ❀◑P🚌 (90)🐾

Upper Killay

Railway Inn ⓛ

553 Gower Road, SA2 7DS
✪ 12-11 (10.30 Sun) ☎ (01792) 203946
Swansea Deep Slade Dark, Bishopswood Bitter, Three Cliffs Gold, Original Wood; 1 changing beer Ⓗ
A locals' pub set in woodlands in the Clyne Valley. The adjacent former railway line forms part of Route 4 of the National Cycle Network. One of the two small front rooms is the main bar and snug. A larger rear lounge has a fire for welcome warmth in winter. Traditional cider and at least one guest ale are kept alongside the Swansea Brewing Company beers. An outside area hosts occasional barbecues and music events. Q❀♣●P🚌

Wick

Star Inn

Ewenny Road, CF71 7QA
✪ 12 (5 Mon)-11.30; 12-10.30 Sun ☎ (01656) 890080
🌐 thestarinnwick.co.uk
Glamorgan Welsh Pale Ale; 2 changing beers (often Glamorgan) Ⓗ
Originally three farm cottages, the pub now comprises a traditional bar with pew seating, a lounge/diner with flagstone flooring – both with log-burning fires – and an upstairs pool/function room. The landlady, her staff and locals make this a pleasant place to visit. Excellent food is available – the meat is supplied by an award-winning local farm butcher just a few hundred yards away. Dogs are welcome in the bar. Local CAMRA Pub of the Year 2019. Q⛵❀◑♣●P🚌 (303)🐾📶

Ystalyfera

Corner House Café Bar

70 Commercial Street, SA9 2HS (on main Top road through Ystalyfera)
✪ 4-11 Mon-Thu; 3-11 Fri; 1-midnight Sat; 12-10.30 Sun
☎ (01639) 849420
2 changing beers (sourced nationally) Ⓗ
Traditional village pub run by the same family for two generations. Its beers are mainly sourced nationally, although locally produced Grey Trees ales are often stocked. One real cider is always on offer. Sunday lunch is served. The ground floor is a large, open bar-lounge area; the basement is used for darts matches. Live music is occasionally performed at weekends. ◑♣●🚌 (X6)🐾

Wern Fawr ⓛ

47 Wern Road, SA9 2LX
✪ 2-5, 7 (6.30 Fri)-11; 12-3, 7-midnight Sat; 12-11 Sun
☎ (01639) 843625
9 Lives Amber, Dark, Gold; 1 changing beer (sourced nationally; often Adnams, Exmoor) Ⓗ
Small pub, run by the same family for three generations, with a cosy atmosphere in its separate bar and lounge. The bar displays a collection of bricks plus mining, industrial and domestic items from the locality. The pub previously had its own brewery but is now supplied by the nearby 9 Lives Brewing. Q🚌 (X6)🐾

Hops: the essential flavouring

Hops are famous for adding bitterness to beer. But this remarkable perennial climbing plant – a member of the hemp family, Cannabinaceae – also contains acids, oils and resins that impart delightful aromas and flavours to beer.
These can be detected in the form of pine, spice, sap and tart, citrus fruit. Fruit is often similar to lemon and orange, while some English hop varieties give powerful hints of apricots, blackcurrants and damsons. American hop varieties, the Cascade in particular, are famous for their grapefruit aroma and flavour.
Many British brewers now use hops from mainland Europe – such as Styrian Goldings from Slovenia and Saaz from the Czech Republic – that have been developed primarily for lager brewing. They impart a more restrained aroma and flavour, with a gentle, resinous character. Lager hops used in ale brewing are usually added late in the copper boil to give a fine aroma to the finished beer.
Kent is often thought of as the main hop-growing area of Britain but in 2004 it was overtaken by Herefordshire. The main hop varieties used in cask beer production are the Fuggle and Golding, but First Gold, introduced in the 1990s, is now a major variety. First Gold was one of the first dwarf or hedgerow hops that grow to only half the height of conventional varieties. As a result they are easier to pick, are less susceptible to disease and aphid attack, and therefore use fewer agri-chemicals. In 2004, a new hop variety called Boadicea was introduced: it is the first aphid-resistant hop and therefore needs fewer pesticides. The hop industry is working on trials of new varieties that need no pesticides or fertilisers and should gain Soil Association approval as organic hops.

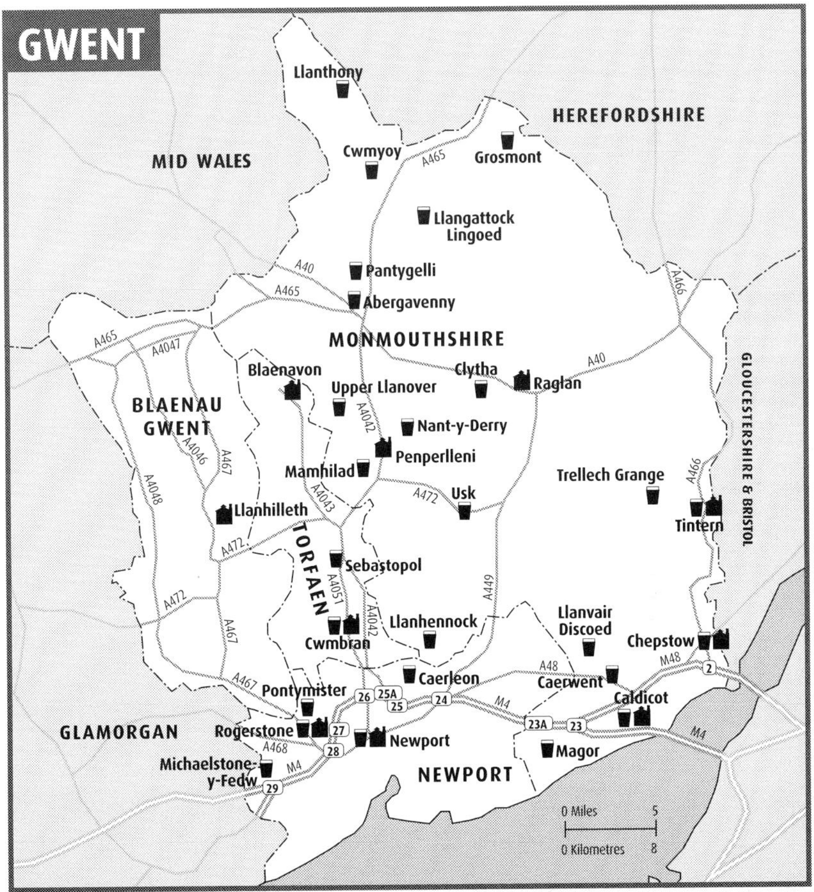

Authority areas covered: Blaenau Gwent UA, Caerphilly UA (part), Monmouthshire UA, Newport UA, Torfaen UA

Abergavenny

Cantreff Inn

61 Brecon Road, NP7 7RA

closed Mon; 12.30-11 ☎ (01873) 855888

Grey Trees Diggers Gold; Wye Valley Butty Bach; 1 changing beer (often Grey Trees) Ⓗ

Situated on the main road to Brecon, this pub started life in the late 1800s. It is divided into two: one half a cosy bar, the other a well-appointed dining room. Low ceilings, stone-flagged floors and a woodburner for cold days combine with a mixture of settees and tables of differing sizes to create a pleasant ambience. A sunny rear garden and a warm welcome for well-behaved dogs also add to the character.

Grofield Ⓛ

Baker Street, NP7 5BB

11-11 (11.30 Thu-Sat); 12-11 Sun ☎ (01873) 858939

grofield.com

Rhymney Bitter; Sharp's Doom Bar; 1 changing beer (sourced nationally; often Kingstone, Untapped) Ⓗ

This genuine, family-run free house is celebrating 10 consecutive appearances in the Guide. The licensee has spent many years in the trade and it shows in his eye for detail. Two permanent beers are joined by a regularly changing guest from an independent brewer, usually from Wales or the West Country. To the rear, a well-maintained garden is a suntrap on warm summer days. Lunches are popular (no food Mon). Sunday is quiz night. (47)

Station Hotel

37 Brecon Road, NP7 5UH

5 (2 Wed & Thu)-11; 12-midnight Fri; 1-midnight Sat; 11-11 Sun ☎ (01873) 854759

Draught Bass; Rhymney Bitter; Wye Valley HPA; 1 changing beer (sourced nationally) Ⓗ

The Abergavenny to Merthyr railway brought this pub into existence, but it is long gone while the pub continues to thrive as a local institution. On the

REAL ALE BREWERIES

Anglo Oregon Newport
Baa Chepstow
Brew Monster Cwmbran
Kingstone Tintern
Mad Dog Penperlleni
Rhymney Blaenavon
Tiny Rebel Rogerstone
Tudor Llanhilleth
Untapped Raglan
Zulu Alpha Caldicot (NEW)

one hand, it is fiercely traditional, with a separate bar and lounge, no slot machines or recorded music; on the other, it now hosts popular free live sessions with local musicians every Friday, and a quiz every Wednesday. The regularly changing guest beers are sourced nationally and include ales not common in the area. P

Caerleon

Bell Inn ✔

Bulmore Road, NP18 1QQ

closed Mon & Tue; 12-11 Wed & Thu (midnight Fri & Sat); 12-10.30 Sun ☎ (01633) 420613 thebellinncaerleon.co.uk

3 changing beers (sourced nationally; often St Austell, Wye Valley) H

An impressive-looking pub with solid stone walls, low-beamed ceilings and a great fireplace that provides welcome warmth on cold days. The menu offers a tempting range of dishes, making this a popular dining venue. The changing beer range is primarily from national brewers and is accompanied by a good selection of ciders. At the rear is a suntrap garden. A beer and cider festival is held during the Caerleon Arts Festival in July.
P (27,28)

Caerwent

Coach & Horses

Green Lane, NP26 5AX

12-11 ☎ (01291) 420352
caerwent-coachandhorses.co.uk

Wye Valley HPA, Butty Bach; 1 changing beer (sourced regionally; often Baa, Glamorgan, Kingstone) H

Popular two-bar inn in a village with Roman fortress remnants all around. A smart, dog-friendly public bar at the front links to a lounge behind, with comfortable space for all in a large new dining area. A recently installed fourth handpump expands choice to two Wye Valley ales and two guests. Conversation rules and this thriving pub is well established as the centre of village life. Three en-suite B&B rooms are available.
P (73)

Caldicot

Cross Inn

1 Newport Road, NP26 4BG

12-11 (midnight Fri & Sat) ☎ (01291) 409042
crossinncaldicot.co.uk

Sharp's Doom Bar; 2 changing beers (sourced nationally) H

Located in the pedestrianised centre of Caldicot, this pub has a large bar that is lively from late afternoon and at weekends. A central partition with a wall-mounted TV above a fireplace separates the open-plan bar from a secluded seating area. A large clock fixed to a pillar is useful if you have a bus to catch outside. A second, smaller bar has a pool table. Three real ales are served: Doom Bar plus two guests that change every few days. P (62,74)

Chepstow

Beaufort Hotel ✔

Beaufort Square, St Mary's Street, NP16 5EP

12-11 (1am Sat); 12-10.30 Sun ☎ (01291) 622497
beauforthotelchepstow.com

Butcombe Adam Henson's Rare Breed; St Austell Proper Job; Sharp's Doom Bar; 1 changing beer (sourced regionally) H

Popular with locals and business people, this relaxed town-centre hotel has a single L-shaped bar, recently refurbished, and a large side room for busy times. An air of reassuring continuity pervades here. Panels above the bar announce the Beaufort Hotel circa 1650, hinting at its longevity. Local scenes are framed in wall panels alongside a cabinet displaying racing colours and a picture of famed champion jockey Lester Piggot.
Q P (74)

Chepstow Athletic Club L

Mathern Road, Bulwark, NP16 5JJ (off Bulwark Rd)

7-11 (11.30 Fri); 12:30-11.30 (midnight winter) Sat; 12-4, 7-11 Sun ☎ (01291) 622126 chepstowac.co.uk

St Austell Cornish Best Bitter; Wye Valley Butty Bach; 2 changing beers (sourced regionally) H

This friendly club attracts sports players and supporters while also welcoming people from across the community and hosting local groups and organisations including Chepstow's male voice choir. Two changing guest ales complement two ever-presents, their high turnover ensuring beers are in top condition. Downstairs is a comfortable lounge bar, upstairs an equally popular function room that also serves real ale. A suntrap patio tempts customers into lazy summer Sunday supping while watching cricketers develop their thirsts. Visiting CAMRA members are particularly welcome. P

Queen's Head L

Moor Street, NP16 5DD

closed Mon; 5-11; 12-2.30, 5-11 Sat; 2-8 Sun
☎ 07793 889613

8 changing beers (sourced regionally; often Gower, Grey Trees, Untapped) H

Welcoming micropub that has achieved local CAMRA recognition. An eclectic range of furniture provides comfort while you sup your drink and absorb the atmosphere. Chatter and laughter dominate – there is no obtrusive noise from TV or electronic games here – and you cannot help but be drawn into friendly conversation with other drinkers. The beer and cider range is mainly from Wales although occasional themed weeks are held with ales from other regions. Local CAMRA Town Pub of the Year 2016-19. Q

Clytha

Clytha Arms L

Groesonen Road, NP7 9BW (on B4598 old road between Abergavenny and Raglan)

12-3.30 (not Mon), 6-11; 12-11 Fri-Sun ☎ (01873) 840206
clytha-arms.com

Felinfoel Double Dragon; Untapped Sundown; Wye Valley Bitter; 3 changing beers (often Untapped, Wye Valley) H

Multi award-winning pub, ever-present in this Guide for over a quarter of a century. It is renowned for its food as well as the range and quality of its beers – six are usually on offer at any one time. Since the Untapped Brewery opened along the road the pub has become an unofficial brewery tap. Extensive lawns are lovely for sitting out on warm days, while the rear garden is ideal for various outdoor events.
Q P (83)

Cwmbran

Bush Inn [L]
Graig Road, Upper Cwmbran, NP44 5AN
⏲ 4-11.30; 12-11.30 Fri-Sun ☎ (01633) 483764
🌐 thebushuppercwmbran.co.uk
3 changing beers (sourced regionally; often Tudor, Twt Lol) [H]
On the eastern flank of Mynydd Maen, with commanding views over Cwmbran and beyond, this cosy pub has a split-level interior reminiscent of two parlours. Old pictures of the locality recall that this was once an industrial community. Beers are mainly sourced from local or regional brewers; ciders are primarily from Welsh producers. Most evenings feature an attraction such as food or live music. Curry night on Wednesday is particularly popular. 🐴❀◗♣🍎P🚌(1,8)🐾📶

Mount Pleasant [L]
Wesley Street, Old Cwmbran, NP44 3LX
⏲ 4-7 Mon; 12-11 Tue-Thu; 12-12.30am Fri & Sat
☎ (01633) 712176 🌐 themountpleasantinncwmbran.co.uk
2 changing beers (sourced regionally; often Kingstone, Mumbles, Rhymney) [H]
The Mount attracts a good mix of regulars who visit just for a drink and others who come for a meal as well. A community hub in Old Cwmbran, it has a modern and comfortable interior. There are broadly three areas – the main section in front of the bar, a smaller area to the right and a raised area on the left, chiefly used for dining. The two handpumps serve ales primarily from Welsh breweries, with Kingstone and Rhymney beers particularly popular. 🐴❀◖◗♣🍎P🚌(6,6)🐾📶

Queen Inn
Upper Cwmbran Road, Upper Cwmbran, NP44 5AX
⏲ 12-11.30 (11 Sun) ☎ (01633) 484252
3 changing beers (sourced regionally) [H]
On the outskirts of Cwmbran in a countryside setting, the Queen is a popular destination for families, partly due to its excellent play area. The pub features a bar area to the left and a lounge to the right. Behind a central fireplace in the bar is a restaurant, though food can be eaten elsewhere. Up to three ales are served on tap from a restricted list; the licensees also have a choice of their own. Real cider is regularly available.
🐴❀◖◗♣🍎P🚌(1,8)🐾

Cwmyoy

Queen's Head
NP7 7NE SO311221
⏲ 12-2 (not Tue), 6-9; closed Wed; 6-10 Fri; 11-3, 6-9 Sat; 12-4 Sun ☎ (01873) 890241
Kingstone Classic [H]
This single-roomed pub is a local institution, known as Billy's in honour of its licensee of 40 years. It is situated in beautiful countryside in the Brecon Beacons, only a couple of miles from the main A465. Beams and a stone-flagged floor give character to the bar; outside a few benches allow visitors to soak up the glorious views. An all-day car park just past the pub can be used for a small charge. Q❀P

Grosmont

Angel Inn
NP7 8EP
⏲ 6-11 Mon; closed Tue; 6-11 (closed winter) Wed; 12-3, 6-11 Thu; 5-11 Fri; 12-11 Sat; 12-6 Sun ☎ (01981) 240646
🌐 angelinngrosmont.business.site
Wye Valley Butty Bach; 2 changing beers (sourced regionally) [H]
Perched high, almost on England's border, the Angel really is the village hub. The guitars on the wall reflect the influence of music on the pub's life; live music can be heard here on a monthly basis. The traditional bar, to the left as you walk in, has a rustic charm, with a selection of wooden tables, attractive benches and settles, as well as hop-decorated beams. Opening times vary, especially in winter – check before visiting. 🐴❀🛏◖◗♣🍎P🐾

Llangattock Lingoed

Hunter's Moon Inn
NP7 8RR SO361201
⏲ 12-11 (4-11 Mon-Fri winter) ☎ (01873) 821499
🌐 hunters-moon-inn.co.uk
Wye Valley HPA [H]/[G], Butty Bach [H]; 1 changing beer (sourced regionally) [H]/[G]
An ancient pub with a small bar and separate dining room. Two outside drinking areas give lovely views over the equally ancient church. The pub is at the heart of life in this hamlet, which is set in beautiful rolling countryside. The long-distance Offa's Dyke Path passes through the churchyard, making the pub popular with walkers. In summer the inn is open all day for food and drink, despite its rural location.
Q🐴❀🛏◖◗♣P🐾📶

Llanhennock

Wheatsheaf
NP18 1LT ST353927
⏲ 11-11; 2-11 Sat; 12-4, 8-11 Sun ☎ (01633) 420466
🌐 thewheatsheafatllanhennock.webs.com
Fuller's London Pride; 2 changing beers (sourced regionally) [H]
A Guide fixture for over 30 years, The Wheatsheaf has probably remained almost unchanged over that time. The main bar is to the right, with a slightly smaller and cosier bar to the left. The walls of both are festooned with old photographs, bric-a-brac and memorabilia. Outside, there are views of the hills miles away both front and back, plus a secluded garden. Boules is played seriously in the car park. There is usually a beer from a local brewery on sale. 🐴❀◖⛺♣P🐾📶

Llanthony

Half Moon
NP7 7NN SO286279
⏲ 12-11 (closed Wed) summer; closed Mon-Thu; 12-3, 6-11 Fri; 12-11 Sat; 12-10.30 Sun winter ☎ (01873) 890611
🌐 halfmoon-llanthony.co.uk
Wye Valley Butty Bach; 1 changing beer (sourced regionally; often Wye Valley) [H]
Situated in the heart of the Black Mountains between towering ridges and close to the ruins of a medieval priory, the Half Moon must be in one of the most idyllic pub settings anywhere. Its lawned rear garden is a suntrap for those who decline a walk in the stunning countryside. Nine basic but comfortable rooms are available all year. If you stay in winter, when the pub is normally closed outside weekends, it will open especially for you.
Q🐴🛏◖◗⛺♣P🐾📶

Llanvair Discoed

Woodlands Tavern
NP16 6LX

🌀 closed Mon & Tue; 12-3, 6-11 Wed-Fri; 12-11 Sat; 12-6 Sun
☎ (01633) 400313 ⊕ thewoodlandstavern.co.uk
Felinfoel Best Bitter; Wye Valley Butty Bach; 2 changing beers (sourced regionally; often Evan Evans) Ⓗ
Just north of the A48 main road and well worth seeking out, this smart pub reflects the pride in ownership of the long-established proprietors. A comfortable bar caters for drinkers and their dogs; a separate dining room provides popular home-cooked meals. Rugby memorabilia including Welsh international shirts and signed pictures adorn the bar's walls. The pub is a great place for slaking thirsts before or after an uplifting walk in the hilly expanse of ancient Wentwood forest, just up the lane. 🌣🕏🕼🕹♣️🐾P

Magor

Wheatsheaf Ⓛ ✓
The Square, NP26 3HN

🌀 11-11 (midnight Fri & Sat); 12-11 Sun ☎ (01633) 880608
⊕ wheatsheafinn.webeden.co.uk/home/4579955798
4 changing beers (sourced regionally; often Rhymney, Tiny Rebel) Ⓗ
A village pub with a sense of longevity about it. Within its whitewashed walls and beneath its old wooden beams are a public bar, lounge and restaurant. The pub's character extends to some of those who sup here, normally found near the handpumps in the lounge. The management team provide an interesting choice of ales from breweries near and far. A partly covered garden and patio can be enjoyed on warm days. 🌣🕏🕼🕹♣️P🚌(62,X74)🐾🛜

Mamhilad

Horseshoe Inn ✓
Old Abergavenny Road, NP4 8QZ

🌀 12-3, 5-11; 11.30-midnight Fri-Sun ☎ (01873) 880542
⊕ horseshoeinn.org
Sharp's Atlantic; Tiny Rebel Cwtch; house beer (by Mad Dog); 1 changing beer (sourced regionally) Ⓗ
A fine country inn and popular dining venue whose locally brewed house ale, served alongside other beers plus up to four ciders, provides a fine accompaniment to the excellent food. The menu offers a wide range of dishes, with a specials board adding further choice. Visitors can drink, dine and relax while enjoying the trappings of a typical country pub. The pleasant and hilly surrounding countryside delivers thirsty and hungry walkers seeking refreshment. Q🌣🕏🕼🕹Å🐾P🛜

Michaelstone-y-Fedw

Cefn Mably Arms ✓
CF3 6XS (N off A48 at Castleton, follow road for just over a mile)

🌀 12-midnight (10.30 Sun) ☎ (01633) 680347
⊕ cefnmablyarms.com
Wye Valley Bitter, HPA, Butty Bach Ⓗ
An upmarket, open-plan pub that is mainly aimed at diners but serves a selection of well-kept real ales and has plenty of room for those who pop in for a quiet drink. A small side room, the Cwtch, leads to the garden and smoking area. The pub is

off the beaten track, not easily accessible by public transport. Opening times are reduced between November and Easter, so check before visiting.
Q🌣🕏🕼🕹P🐾🛜

Nant-y-Derry

Foxhunter Inn
NP7 9DN SO331061

🌀 closed Mon; 12-3, 6-11; 12-11 Sat & Sun
☎ (01873) 881101 ⊕ foxhunterinn.com
Felinfoel Double Dragon; Untapped Whoosh; Wye Valley Butty Bach; 1 changing beer (sourced regionally; often Wadworth) Ⓗ
This fine old building once served as the tea rooms for Nant-y-Derry railway station; the former station house is opposite. A popular bar and restaurant for many years, the pub was revitalised by the current licensee in 2015. It offers good food and drink, with occasional entertainment and functions. Booking is advisable for the Tuesday curry night and Thursday seniors lunch. Well-behaved dogs are welcome. Accommodation is available in two adjoining cottages. 🌣🕏🏠🕹P🐾

Newport

Cellar Door
5 Clytha Park Road, NP20 4NZ

🌀 closed Mon-Wed; 5-11 Thu; 3-11 Fri; 12-11 Sat; 4-11 Sun
☎ 07930 857897
3 changing beers Ⓗ
Newport's first micropub, five minutes' walk from the railway station, opened in 2017 after extensive renovation of a former shop. It was soon judged CAMRA's Welsh Cider Pub of the Year and then one of the top four in Britain. Visitors can choose from three ales from mainly local or regional microbreweries, a selection of bottled beers, and up to eight chilled ciders. Whatever your tipple, you are guaranteed a warm welcome. There is no obtrusive noise from TV or games machines, although there is some background music.
Q🍺♣️🚌🐾

Godfrey Morgan Ⓛ ✓
158 Chepstow Road, Maindee, NP19 8EG

🌀 8am-midnight (1am Fri & Sat) ☎ (01633) 221928
Brains SA; Greene King Abbot; Ruddles Best Bitter; Sharp's Doom Bar; 2 changing beers (sourced nationally; often Rhymney) Ⓗ
Named after the 1st Viscount Tredegar, a survivor of the Charge of the Light Brigade, this large, open-plan Wetherspoon pub was once a cinema, and has numerous photos of erstwhile stars with local connections dotted around the walls. It stocks the firm's usual range of national and regional ales, plus one or two more interesting options. The pub has a small car park at the rear, with some or all of the charge refundable with your first purchase.
Q🌣🕏🕼🕹P🐾(8,73)🛜

Olde Murenger House
52-53 High Street, NP20 1GA

🌀 12-11; 12-3, 7.30-10.30 Sun ☎ (01633) 263977
Samuel Smith Old Brewery Bitter Ⓗ
The only Samuel Smith pub in Wales, this classic gem, whose walls could no doubt tell many a tale, dates back to the mid-16th century and is Grade II listed. High-back settles in a dark-wood, low-beamed interior offer the cosy backdrop for the hubbub of a traditional pub, with only chat and

laughter to disturb your thoughts. Popular and well run, with an appreciative clientele, this is a place to sit and sup while enjoying the atmosphere and character.

St Julian Inn

Caerleon Road, NP18 1QA
11.30-11.30 (midnight Thu-Sat); 12-11 Sun
(01633) 243548 stjulian.co.uk
Bombardier; Young's Bitter; 2 changing beers (sourced regionally; often Bath Ales, Ludlow, Wye Valley)
Perched high above a bend on the River Usk, this pub commands its scenic surroundings, which can be fully appreciated from its balcony. Inside is a smart lounge whose wood panelling was rescued from a former ocean liner. The central bar also serves the games room, small balcony bar and side area. Simple but tasty pub grub is complemented by a selection of well-known regular beers or, usually, a pale hoppy guest ale.
P (27,28)

Tiny Rebel

22-23 High Street, NP20 1FX
12-11 (1am Fri & Sat) (01633) 973934
Tiny Rebel Cwtch; 5 changing beers (sourced nationally; often Tiny Rebel)
Tiny Rebel's second pub was a welcome addition to Newport's thriving high-street pub scene when it opened at the front of the market in 2016. Its ground-floor bar is large and minimalist; the smaller downstairs Cwtch more plush and comfortable. Alongside a good selection of the brewery's own ales, the pub serves two or three ever-changing guests. It is not cheap for Newport, but real ale prices are much reduced on Monday.

Pantygelli

Crown Inn

Old Hereford Road, NP7 7HR
12-2.30 (not Mon), 6-11; 12-3, 6-11 Sat; 12-3, 6-10.30 Sun
(01873) 853314 thecrownatpantygelli.com
Draught Bass; Rhymney Best; Wye Valley HPA; 1 changing beer (sourced regionally; often Evan Evans, Grey Trees, Tomos Watkin)
While service to residents of the hamlet is crucial to this family-run gastro-pub, there is a genuinely warm welcome for visitors who come to enjoy the food, drink and hospitality. Inside, beams and a stone-flagged floor reflect the building's historic character; outside, the flower-decked patio provides glorious views over to Skirrid mountain. This is lovely countryside, yet only a couple of miles outside Abergavenny. Diners should always book ahead. P

Pontymister

Commercial Inn

Commercial Street, NP11 6BA
11-11.30; 10-11.30 Sat; 12-11.30 Sun (01633) 612608
thecommercialpontymister.com
3 changing beers (sourced nationally)
Large open-plan pub serving good-value meals but retaining a focus on beer, with three real ales always available. Its TV screens can dominate but are normally muted unless an important match is showing. The patio at the front is on the busy main road in the centre of Pontymister but can be inviting on a hot day. Buses and the local railway station are within easy walking distance.
(151,56)

Rogerstone

Tiny Rebel Brewery Bar

Wern Industrial Estate, Wern Terrace, NP10 9FQ (off Chartist Drive for vehicles)
12-11 (midnight Fri); 9.30am-midnight Sat; 9.30am-10 Sun
(01633) 547378 tinyrebel.co.uk/bars/brewery-bar
Tiny Rebel Cwtch; 2 changing beers (sourced locally; often Tiny Rebel)
Impressive new-build bar and dining area, with a shop on-site. A wide range of Tiny Rebel beers is available in cask, keg, bottles and cans, with Cwtch always on handpull. The bar has views of the brewery from the restaurant, while the front opens out onto a spacious south-facing veranda. A second drinking area is upstairs. Tiny Rebel graphics are on show throughout, as are pointers to merchandise available in the brewery shop.
P (151,56)

Sebastopol

Open Hearth

Wern Road, NP4 5DR
12-1am (2am Fri & Sat); 12-midnight Sun
(01495) 763752 theopenhearth.wales
Wye Valley HPA; 4 changing beers (sourced nationally; often Brains, Dartmoor, Sharp's)
Welcoming refreshment stop for regular customers, as well as those passing by on the tranquil Monmouthshire & Brecon canal. Entry via the towpath gives access to a traditional bar and small dining room. There is also a lounge/diner and function room. The towpath seating and decked areas are popular on warm days. A well-balanced beer range includes well-known brands and the occasional new ale; the menu offers a range of popular dishes. Last entry is 11pm.
P (X3,X24)

Sebastopol Social Club

Wern Road, NP4 5DU (on corner of Wern Rd with Austin Rd)
12-11 (midnight Fri & Sat); 12-10.30 Sun
(01495) 763808 sebastopolsocial.org.uk
Glamorgan Welsh Pale Ale; 3 changing beers (sourced regionally; often Grey Trees)
Real ale drinkers among the Social Club membership have enjoyed a terrific range of beers and ciders here over the years, as have visiting CAMRA members. The Club's commitment has earned many awards and is maintained today. It caters for many interests including various indoor sports plus those delivered by large TV screens. Live entertainment is hosted in the main room. A cosy lounge, upstairs function room and downstairs pool room are also put to good use.
P (X3,X24)

Tintern

Wye Valley Hotel

Monmouth Road, NP16 6SQ
11-3, 6-11; 12-3, 6.30-10.30 Sun (01291) 689441
thewyevalleyhotel.co.uk
Wye Valley Bitter; 1 changing beer (sourced locally; often Kingstone)

WALES

Here is a fine place to pause, drink and stay, whatever the weather in this beautiful valley, with a friendly welcome from the long-established owners. A guest ale from the nearby Kingstone Brewery often complements the Wye Valley beer. The comfortable single bar has a multi-angled shape matching the distinctive 1920s pub itself, while an array of commemorative beer bottles lines a shelf around the entire room. Home-cooked meals are available both in the bar and the traditional restaurant. (69)

Trellech Grange

Fountain Inn

NP16 6QW SO503011

closed Mon; 4-11 (9.30 Tue); 12-11 Sat; 12-9 Sun

(01291) 689303 fountaininntrellech.co.uk

Glamorgan Cwrw Gorslas/Bluestone Bitter; Wye Valley Butty Bach; 1 changing beer (sourced locally; often Kingstone) H

A fine traditional country pub, worth seeking out despite being off the beaten track a few miles from Tintern Abbey. Three well-kept ales are always available alongside one local cider. In winter two real fires keep the pub cosy. In summer the garden with its own brook is most welcoming. Please note that summer opening times can vary from those listed. Appealing menus and midweek darts, quiz and cribbage evenings help keep this venerable pub popular all year round. P

Upper Llanover

Goose & Cuckoo L

NP7 9ER (follow handwritten signs to the Goose) SO292073

closed Mon; 11.30-3, 7-11 Tue-Thu; 11.30-11 Fri & Sat; 12-10.30 Sun (01873) 880277

gooseandcuckooinn.wales

Rhymney Bitter; Untapped Monnow; 2 changing beers (sourced regionally; often Felinfoel, Wye Valley) H

The Goose has a reputation for being difficult to find but if you follow the signs you should eventually reach this comfortable pub that is seemingly stuck in a time warp. Its characterful interior has a flagged-stone floor with attractive benches and chairs. The use of mobile phones is discouraged. Quality local beers and a range of whiskies are served, along with local food. Customers can enjoy superb views across the valleys. Q P

Usk

King's Head Hotel

18 Old Market Street, NP15 1AL

11-11 (10.30 Sun) (01291) 672963

kingsheadusk.com

Fuller's London Pride; Timothy Taylor Landlord; Wye Valley Butty Bach H

A charming 16th-century hotel with a cosy lounge bar. Beneath its low beams the walls and ceilings are adorned with rural and music memorabilia, plus old books and other interesting artefacts. A large fireplace provides welcome warmth on cold days. The ale range reflects local choice and rarely changes. Diners are well catered for with a range of tasty dishes. En-suite accommodation is available. Q P (60,63)

New Court Inn

62 Maryport Street, NP15 1AD

12-11 (10.30 Sun) (01291) 671319

thenewcourthotel.co.uk

Sharp's Atlantic; Wye Valley Butty Bach; 3 changing beers (sourced regionally) H

A pleasant bar-restaurant with an attractive interior including a comfortable seating area near a warming fire. There is also a small snug with a TV and a restaurant with an eclectic mix of furniture. Seven handpumps dispense up to five real ales, often including local beers, and two ciders. The pub is popular with diners attracted by the tempting dishes on its award-winning menu. Q (60,63)

The language of beer

Nose: the aroma. Gently swirl the beer to release the aroma. You will detect malt: grainy and biscuity, often likened to crackers or Ovaltine. When darker malts are used, the nose will have powerful hints of chocolate, coffee, nuts, vanilla, liquorice, molasses and such dried fruits as raisins and sultanas. Hops add superb aromas of resins, herbs, spices, fresh-mown grass and tart citrus fruit – lemon and orange are typical, with intense grapefruit notes from some American varieties. Sulphur may also be present when waters are 'Burtonised', i.e. gypsum and magnesium salts have been added to replicate the famous spring waters of Burton upon Trent.

Palate: the appeal in the mouth. The tongue can detect sweetness, bitterness and saltiness as the beer passes over it. The rich flavours of malt will come to the fore but hop bitterness will also make a substantial impact. The tongue will also pick out the natural saltiness from the brewing water and fruit from darker malts, yeast and hops. Citrus notes often have a major impact on the palate.

Finish: the aftertaste, as the beer goes over the tongue and down the throat. The finish is often radically different to the nose. The aroma may be dominated by malt whereas hop flavours and bitterness can govern the finish. Darker malts will make their presence felt with roast, chocolate or coffee notes; fruit character may linger. Strong beers may end on a sweet or biscuity note but in mainstream bitters, bitterness and dryness come to the fore.

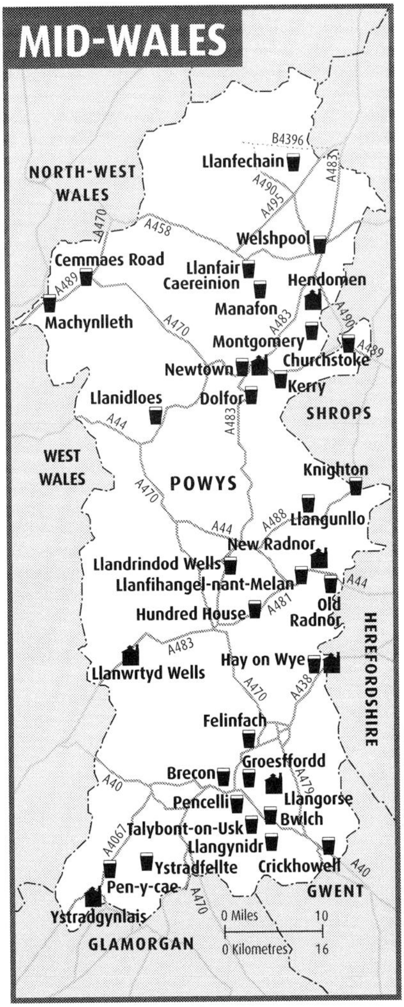

Authority area covered: Powys UA

Brecon

Brecon Tap

6 Bulwark, LD3 7LB

11-11 (midnight Fri & Sat); 12-11 Sun ☎ (01874) 623888

breconinns.co.uk

4 changing beers (sourced regionally) Ⓗ

In a prime town-centre location, this contemporary style bar has a light and airy feel, with comfortable seating throughout and walls lined with bottle-filled shelves. Three or four varying guest ales are served, often from Welsh breweries and sometimes from further afield. There is also an interesting range of international and UK craft ales, plus simple food including sandwiches and good-value pies. Bottled beers, wines, craft spirits and local artisan produce are available for off-sales.

Q (T4,X43)

Clarence

25 The Watton, LD3 7ED

12-midnight (2am Fri & Sat) ☎ (01874) 622810

clarenceinn.co.uk

Wye Valley Bitter, Butty Bach; 1 changing beer (often Wye Valley) Ⓗ

Two-roomed town-centre community pub with a contemporary, welcoming and relaxed atmosphere. The newly extended front bar tends to be frequented by locals; the larger back bar is more popular with diners. A large TV screen draws a crowd for big sporting events. The spacious garden is a major attraction, especially during the famous annual Brecon Jazz Festival. Guest beers are generally from local breweries.

(T4,X43)

Bwlch

New Inn

Brecon Road, LD3 7RQ (on A40 between Brecon and Crickhowell)

5-11; 12-11 Sat; 12-8 Sun ☎ (01874) 730215

beaconsbackpackers.co.uk

Wye Valley Butty Bach; 2 changing beers (sourced regionally; often Grey Trees, Oakham, Salopian) Ⓗ

Lively and cosy village pub popular with both locals and visitors. A comfortable dining area sits to the side of the stone-flagged bar, with armchairs around a huge fireplace. Two interesting guest beers supplement the regular ale, while excellent, good-value, home-cooked food is available at weekends – the pies are deservedly popular. An excellent base for exploring the surrounding Brecon Beacons and Black Mountains, with bunkhouse accommodation available. Local CAMRA Pub of the Year 2017-19.

Q P (43,X43)

Cemmaes Road

Dovey Valley Hotel ★

SY20 8JZ

5-11 ☎ (01650) 511335

1 changing beer (sourced locally; often Cader, Evan Evans, Monty's) Ⓗ

This gem of a pub was built to serve the nearby railway. Boasting a nationally important historic pub interior, it comprises a cosy main bar and snug room with traditional features from the 1870s, including the original slate floors and Edwardian tiled fireplace (with log fires in winter). The pub is furnished with a mix of mirrors, brewery memorabilia and other eclectic items. Live music sessions take place on occasion.

Q P (X85)

Churchstoke

Horse & Jockey

SY15 6AE

12 (4.30 Mon & Tue)-11 ☎ (01588) 620060

2 changing beers (sourced regionally) Ⓗ

A prominent stone-built pub on the edge of the village. It serves a changing range of guest ales, plus up to nine real ciders and perries during the

REAL ALE BREWERIES

9 Lives Ystradgynlais
Heart of Wales Llanwrtyd Wells
Left Bank Llangorse
Lucky 7 Hay On Wye
Monty's Hendomen
Radnorshire New Radnor
Wilderness Newtown

summer. The wood-beamed public bar hosts pool, darts and bar billiards. The carpeted lounge features comfortable armchairs and wall seating, and leads to a large, well-appointed restaurant. A stone fireplace with wood-burning stove provides winter warmth. ⚭❀◐♿▲♣●P🚌(81)🐾📶

Crickhowell

Bear Hotel

High Street, NP8 1BW
✪ 10-11; 11-10.30 Sun ☎ (01873) 810408
🌐 bearhotel.co.uk
Brains Rev James; Wadworth 6X; 2 changing beers (sourced regionally; often Caledonian) Ⓗ
Originally a 15th-century coaching inn, this is now an award-winning hotel and Guide regular. Its grand, multi-roomed bar features exposed beams, wood panelling, fine settles and an eclectic selection of furnishings and decorations. The two bar rooms have exposed fireplaces, as does one of the side rooms. Guest ales are often from smaller Welsh breweries. Food is excellent and the menu features much local produce. This is an excellent base for exploring the surrounding Black Mountains and Brecon Beacons National Park.
Q⚭❀🛏◐♿▲P🚌(43,X43)🐾

Dolfor

Dolfor Inn

SY16 4AA
✪ 6 (12 Thu)-11; 12-midnight Fri & Sat; 12-11 Sun
☎ (01686) 626531 🌐 thedolforinn.com
Ludlow Gold; 3 changing beers (sourced locally; often Clun, Six Bells, Wye Valley) Ⓗ
A former drovers' inn, this stone-walled, wooden-beamed rural pub has an intimate restaurant room with an inglenook fireplace. The bar area's settles and low ceiling create a cosy atmosphere. Adjacent to the well-stocked bar is a popular games area. Larger parties can use a room converted from the old stable block. The pub has a good local reputation for its food and is handy for walkers on the Kerry Ridgeway path. ⚭❀🛏◐♿♣P🚌(T4)📶

Felinfach

Griffin 𝕃

LD3 0UB (just off A470 3 miles NE of Brecon)
✪ 12-11.30 ☎ (01874) 620111
4 changing beers (sourced locally) Ⓗ
The Griffin's ethos – the simple things in life done well – says it all. This welcoming country pub, with restaurant and rooms, puts the emphasis on good beer and excellent food. Its multi-roomed layout allows for discrete areas for drinking and dining. The huge fireplace between the bar and main dining area dominates during winter, while an Aga lurks in a side room, providing warmth throughout. The garden affords superb views of the surrounding mountains. Q⚭❀🛏◐♿P🚌

Groesffordd

Three Horseshoes

LD3 7SN (just off B4558)
✪ 12-3 (not Mon), 5-11; 12-11 Fri-Sun ☎ (01874) 665672
🌐 threehorseshoesgroesffordd.co.uk
St Austell Tribute; 2 changing beers (sourced regionally) Ⓗ
Busy village-centre pub in the heart of the Brecon Beacons, boasting superb views from both the front and rear outdoor seating areas. The pub is only a 10-minute walk from the Brynich lock on the Monmouthshire & Brecon Canal and is a popular stop for boaters and other visitors. The emphasis here is very much on food, which is excellent, but the ales are always varied and interesting. Brynich caravan site and the Brecon YHA are nearby.
⚭❀◐♿▲♣●🐾📶

Hay on Wye

Blue Boar

Castle Street, HR3 5DF
✪ 9am-11 ☎ (01497) 820884
Brains Rev James; Timothy Taylor Landlord; 2 changing beers (sourced regionally) Ⓗ
Comfortable and friendly pub in the centre of the town famed for books. The Blue Boar has been owned and run by the same family for many years. It is dominated by a large central bar, around which are two separate seating areas, each with its own log fire. Two regular beers are usually supplemented by one or two guest ales. Food is available all day in the bar and the separate dining area. Q⚭◐♿🚌(T14)🐾📶

Hundred House

Hundred House

LD1 5RY (on A481, near Builth Wells)
✪ 12-2, 5.30-11; 11-11 Sat & Sun ☎ (01982) 570231
Sharp's Doom Bar; Wye Valley Butty Bach Ⓗ
Located among rolling Welsh hills, the Hundred House Inn takes its name from the Saxon hundred, which was an administrative area. At one time a drovers' inn, this is now a welcoming and friendly traditional pub, well patronised by the area's farming community. There is a lounge, locals' bar, pool room with TV (for rugby), restaurant area, conservatory and beer garden. Afternoon closing times are flexible so check before visiting.
Q⚭❀🛏◐▲♣P🐾

Kerry

Kerry Lamb

SY16 4NP
✪ 4-11 (midnight Thu & Fri); closed Tue; 12-midnight Sat; 12-11 Sun ☎ (01686) 670226 🌐 thekerrylambpowys.co.uk
Wye Valley Butty Bach; 2 changing beers (often Purple Moose, Three Tuns, Tudor) Ⓗ
Prominent red-bricked pub on the edge of the village, named after the Kerry Hill sheep. Locally owned, it seamlessly flits between its role as a community pub and restaurant, offering something for all tastes. It consists of a large lounge/bar, a games room and dining room. The St Michael and All Angels church backs onto the rear, giving a picturesque view from the beer garden during warmer weather. ⚭❀◐♿♣P🚌(81)🐾📶

Knighton

Watson's Ale House

24 High Street, LD7 1AT
✪ 4-10; 12-10 Sat & Sun ☎ (01547) 740017
🌐 watsonsalehouse.co.uk
3 changing beers Ⓗ
A former tea room near the clock tower, this is the home of Watson's Real Powys Farmhouse Cider.

The pub was also previously a butcher's – spot the hooks and cold-room door. It is next to a chip shop, where food can be ordered to eat with your drinks. Attractions include pizza nights and an occasional special offer price for three pints of beer – for each drinker. Walkers and dogs are welcome.
Q❀◐≠●🚌(46)🐾📶

Llandrindod Wells

Arvon Ale House 🏆 L

Temple Street, LD1 5DP

closed Mon & Tue; 4-10 Wed & Thu; 4-11 Fri & Sat; 4-10 Sun
☎ 07477 627267

5 changing beers (sourced regionally) H

Now an established highlight of the Llandrindod pub scene, this micropub offers sensibly priced beers sourced from Wales, the borders and the Midlands, plus at least four real ciders. Formerly shop premises, the pub is small and perfectly formed. It is a proper alehouse for the quiet enjoyment of beer with no distractions. Snacks are available. All-comers folk music sessions are held on the second and fourth Sunday of the month.
Q⛾≠♣●🚌(T4)🐾

Middleton Arms

Tremont Road, LD1 5EB (corner of Trefonen Lane)

11-3, 5-11.30 Mon; 12-3, 5-11.30 Tue; 2-11.30 Wed; 5-11.30 Thu; 11-1am Fri; 11-12.30am Sat; 11-11.30 Sun
☎ (01597) 822066

Worthington's; 1 changing beer (sourced regionally) H

A friendly street-corner local at the north end of town on the road to Newtown, named after one of the town's Victorian developers. The guest beer changes weekly. The pub supports four darts teams as well as pool and dominoes teams, and screens sports channels on TVs. There is an enclosed drinking area outside and families and dogs are welcome. Q⛾❀♿≠♣🚌(461,T4)🐾📶

Llanfair Caereinion

Black Lion

Parsons Bank, SY21 0RR

11-11 ☎ (01938) 810759

Purple Moose Cwrw Glaslyn/Glaslyn Ale; Worthington's; 1 changing beer (often St Austell, Wye Valley) H

Established in the 19th century, the Black Lion features a virtually unaltered public bar complete with period counter and even older wainscoting, plus quarry-tiled flooring and a 1930s brick inglenook fireplace. The pub once had a number of small rooms which have been converted into an open-plan drinking area while retaining a traditional feel. A large covered outside drinking area with a logburner also accommodates smokers.
⛾❀◐♿≠♣P🚌(87)🐾📶

Llanfechain

Plas-yn-Dinas Inn

SY22 6UJ (off B4393)

closed Mon & Tue; 12-2.30, 5-11 Wed-Fri; 12-11 Sat; 12-10.30 Sun ☎ (01691) 829055 🌐 plasyndinas.co.uk

3 changing beers (sourced locally; often Monty's, Purple Moose, Stonehouse) H

Early 18th-century, Grade II-listed public house which started life as a courthouse. Following a lengthy closure and a complete makeover, the Plas reopened in 2015. The interior features wooden beams and supports and has a number of handsome drinking spaces – the front area has tiled floors while the rear restaurant/lounge is carpeted. Outside is a patio with benches and a garden.
Q⛾❀◐♿P🚌(72,74)🐾📶

Llanfihangel-nant-Melan

Fforest Inn

LD8 2TN (jct of A44 and A481)

closed Mon; 12-11 ☎ (01544) 350526 🌐 thefforest.co.uk

3 changing beers (sourced nationally) H

Built in the 16th century as a drovers' inn, the pub is steeped in history and retains many original features. Three regularly changing real ales are served in summer, two in winter. The food menu features fresh local produce. Well-behaved dogs are welcome in the bar and, subject to prior arrangement, in the guest rooms. Open seven days a week July and August. Q⛾❀🛏◐P🚌(461)🐾

Llangunllo

Greyhound L

LD7 1SP (off A488 on B4356)

closed Mon & Tue; 4.30-11 Wed & Thu; 4.30-2am Fri; 2-2am Sat; 2-11 Sun ☎ (01547) 550400

2 changing beers (sourced regionally; often Six Bells) H

This unique 16th-century inn, set in picturesque countryside, is the first stop on the Glyndwr's Way long-distance trail. The beers are usually from Broughs and Six Bells breweries, and the cider is Westons Family Reserve. Regular music sessions are hosted. Opening times are approximate – ring the doorbell any time after midday and with luck you will be served. Q⛾❀⛺♣●P🐾

Llangynidr

Red Lion

Duffryn Road, NP8 1NT (off B4558)

12-11 ☎ (01874) 730223 🌐 theredlionpowys.co.uk

Wye Valley The Hopfather; 2 changing beers (sourced regionally) H

Popular village local, situated away from the main road, with a warm welcome for walkers, boaters, families and dogs – the Monmouthshire & Brecon Canal is a short walk away. The beer range changes regularly and good-value home-cooked food is served in the bar. A separate games area, outside seating and children's play area make this a pub for all. Regular quiz nights and live music also feature.
⛾❀🛏◐♣P🚌(43)🐾📶

Llanidloes

Old Mill

40-44 High Street, SY18 6BZ

closed Mon & Tue; 11-3, 5-11 Wed-Fri; 11-11 Sat; 12-3, 7-11 Sun ☎ (01686) 412008 🌐 oldmillbar.co.uk

3 changing beers (sourced regionally) H

Located in the old premises of the United Services Club, the building was previously a flannel mill. The bar has an eclectic mix of furniture including a baby grand piano and other curios. Subdued lighting and wall seating create a relaxed atmosphere. A second room to the left features a pool table and walls decorated with pages from encyclopedias. The pub hosts regular live music and other events.
Q⛾❀◐♿♣🚌(X75,525)🐾📶

Whistling Badger

4 Short Bridge Street, SY18 6AD
5-midnight Mon & Tue; 11-2, 5-midnight Wed-Fri; 11-midnight Sat; 12-midnight Sun ☎ (01686) 412583
thewhistlingbadger.co.uk
Wye Valley HPA, Butty Bach; 1 changing beer (sourced regionally) H
Renamed following a brief closure in 2017, this attractively refurbished pub was previously two – the Royal Oak and King's Head – which merged in the 1960s. It comprises two rooms, the larger of which retains its original beams and large stone inglenook. The smaller room is set up for eating in a wine-bar style. Tapas food is served daily in both bars 6-9pm. ❀ P (X75,525)

Machynlleth

Skinners Arms

Heol Penrallt, SY20 8AJ
12 (5.30 Mon)-midnight ☎ (01654) 703443
Banks's Amber Ale; 1 changing beer (sourced nationally; often Banks's, Marston's) H
The Skinners Arms is a cosy wood-panelled stone pub. Its bar is to the right on entering. To the left is a lounge where patrons can enjoy locally sourced home-cooked food next to the large stone fireplace. Home-made pasties are popular with locals on Thursday; booking is advised for Sunday lunch. The pub hosts a variety of entertainment including themed discos and quiz nights, plus bake-off competitions in winter. Q ❀ ⇌ ♣

Wynnstay Arms Hotel L

Heol Maengwyn, SY20 8AE
11-midnight; 12-midnight Sun ☎ (01654) 702941
wynnstay.wales
Cader Gold, Red Bandit; 1 changing beer (sourced locally; often Cader) H
This historic hotel in the centre of Machynlleth has operated for more than 200 years. Drinkers can enjoy a pint and a chat in the small, quiet bar or in the back room, the Cwtch, in front of a cosy log fire. The hotel is renowned for its locally sourced food, served in the dining area that covers most of the ground floor. Themed food nights are held regularly. Q ⇌ ♣ P

Manafon

Beehive Inn

SY21 8BL
7-11 Mon-Fri; 12-3, 7-11 Sat & Sun ☎ (01686) 651007
Stonehouse Station Bitter, Cambrian Gold H
A timbered black-and-white Rhiw Valley local in the heart of the village, established in the 1650s as a drovers' inn with original beams and settles throughout. It was originally a lot smaller – other rooms have been brought into pub use over the years. The room on the right was once a butcher's. There is a caravan park at the rear with the river running beside the large beer garden. The adjacent church creates a peaceful backdrop amid pleasant scenery. Q ❀ ♣ P

Montgomery

Dragon Hotel

Market Square, SY15 6PA
11-11 (10.30 Sun) ☎ (01686) 668359 dragonhotel.com
4 changing beers (sourced regionally; often Monty's) H
Dating from the mid-1600s, this former coaching inn has a distinctive Tudor black-and-white half-timbered frontage. The bar has been relocated to the rear of the hotel, giving more space to its clientele. There are patio areas outside to the front and rear for alfresco drinking. The hotel boasts an indoor swimming pool and a large function room. Q ❀ ♿ P (T12,81)

Newtown

Railway Tavern

Old Kerry Road, SY16 1BH (off A483)
11-2, 5-midnight Mon; 11-midnight Tue; 7-midnight Wed & Thu; 11-1am Fri & Sat; 11-midnight Sun ☎ (01686) 626156
3 changing beers (often Clun, Stonehouse, Three Tuns) H
This is the 25th consecutive year in the Guide for the Tavern. Two guest beers are always on offer, usually from regional or small breweries. The pub hosts darts and dominoes, and can get crowded on match nights. The interior is essentially divided in two – a lower bar area and a rear area with benches around the walls. Outside toilets are located through the passageway. Note the poster listing over 50 pubs that once operated in Newtown. Q ❀ ⇌ ♣

Sportsman L

17 Severn Street, SY16 2AQ (off A483)
closed Mon; 12-10 Tue (11 Wed & Thu; 11.30 Fri & Sat); 12-10 Sun ☎ (01686) 623978
Monty's Old Jailhouse, MPA, Sunshine, Masquerade, Mischief; 3 changing beers (sourced nationally; often Brains, Robinsons, Wychwood) H
Monty's taphouse, serving up to five of the brewery's beers alongside up to three guest ales and a varying number of ciders. The pub is divided into three areas – a snug with comfortable wall seating, a main bar area with a wood-burning stove and a rear tiled games area with pool table, TV and darts. There is a patio at the rear for summer drinking. A former local CAMRA Pub of the Year and Welsh Cider Pub of the Year.
Q ❀ ♿ ⇌ ♣

Old Radnor

Harp

LD8 2RH
closed Mon & Tue; 6-11 Wed & Thu; 12-3, 6-11 Fri & Sat; 12-3, 6-10.30 Sun ☎ (01544) 350655 harpinnradnor.co.uk
2 changing beers (sourced regionally) H
This early 15th-century Welsh longhouse commands a fine view over the Radnor Valley. The building was rescued and restored by the Landmark Trust in 1972, then sold on in 1983. The interior is a tasteful mix of old and new, including a modern restaurant. Beers are mainly from regional and local microbreweries. The food features locally sourced seasonal ingredients.
Q ❀ Λ ♣ P

Pen-y-cae

Ancient Briton

Brecon Road, SA9 1YY (on A4067 N of Abercrave)
12-midnight ☎ (01639) 730273 ancientbriton.co.uk
Wye Valley Butty Bach; 6 changing beers (sourced nationally; often Glamorgan, Kelham Island, Salopian) H

Attractive country inn situated on the main Swansea to Brecon road. It makes an ideal base for walkers, cyclists and cavers exploring the Brecon Beacons National Park, offering hotel accommodation plus full camping and caravanning facilities at the rear. An impressive array of 14 handpumps dispenses up to seven ales from regional and national sources plus two real ciders. A winner of local CAMRA Pub of the Year on numerous occasions. ➤✿✉◖❶▲◆P➡(T6)

Pencelli

Royal Oak
LD3 7LX
✪ 12-11 (10.30 Sun) ☎ (01874) 665396
Brains Rev James; 2 changing beers (sourced regionally; often Grey Trees, Tudor) Ⓗ
Comfortable and friendly family-run pub in a quiet village alongside the Monmouthshire & Brecon Canal. Its extended opening hours are welcome in this part of the Brecon Beacons. The regular ale is supplemented with two or three others, usually from independent Welsh breweries. The pretty garden next to the canal is a delight on a sunny day. Popular with walkers, cyclists and boaters, with moorings adjacent to the garden.
Q➤✿◖▲P➡✿

Talybont-on-Usk

Star Inn Ⓛ
LD3 7YX (on B4558 between Brecon and Crickhowell)
✪ 5-11; 12-11 Sat & Sun ☎ (01874) 676635
⊕ thestarinntalybont.com
4 changing beers (sourced regionally) Ⓗ
Traditional village pub tucked in alongside the Monmouth & Brecon Canal, popular with both locals and visitors. Two separate rooms with stone floors and log fires link to a small central bar, which usually offers up to four ales from local and regional breweries. The pub appeals particularly to boaters on the canal as well as walkers and cyclists taking advantage of the forest trails accessible from the village. The sunny garden is a popular spot when the weather is good.
➤✿✉◖&▲♣◆➡(43,X43)✿

Welshpool

Pheasant Inn
43 High Street, SY21 7JQ
✪ 1-11; 12-midnight Fri & Sat; 12-11 Sun ☎ (01938) 553104
3 changing beers (sourced locally; often Ludlow, Salopian, Three Tuns) Ⓗ
The Pheasant is a Grade II-listed building in a terrace of 18th-century former town houses. Much modified internally, it has one long room with a wooden floor, comfortable seating at the far end, and a pool table and dartboard. To the rear is a door leading to an outside drinking and smoking area. A third guest beer is often available at weekends; the ales are usually from small or regional breweries. ✿≈♣➡

Ystradfellte

New Inn
CF44 9JE
✪ closed Mon & Tue; 12-10; 12-6 Sun ☎ (01639) 721014
⊕ waterfallways.co.uk
2 changing beers (sourced locally; often Glamorgan, Grey Trees) Ⓗ
A 16th-century village pub in the middle of Waterfall Country, a popular walking area in the Brecon Beacons. With two log fires and a small beer garden, there's a welcome whatever the weather. Two local ales are kept on tap, usually from local breweries. There is a strong focus on local produce across the board, including spirits from Penderyn Distillery. Home-cooked food includes the popular Boozy Cow Pie, freshly made using the ale on tap. Friendly dogs and muddy boots are welcome. Q➤✿◖▲◆P✿

Skinners Arms, Machynlleth (Photo: Reading Tom/Flickr CC BY 2.0)

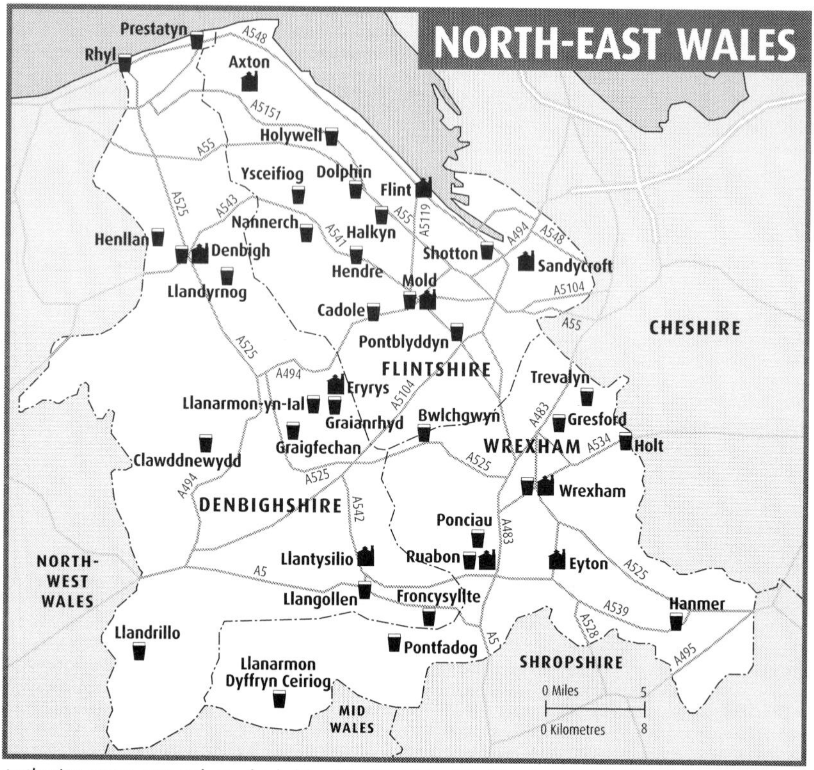

Authority areas covered: Denbighshire UA, Flintshire UA, Wrexham UA

Bwlchgwyn

King's Head Inn

Ruthin Road, LL11 5UT (on A525)

closed Mon & Tue; 5-11 Wed & Thu; 5-midnight Fri; 12-midnight Sat; 12-11 Sun (01978) 753089

2 changing beers (sourced locally; often Big Hand) H

A well-presented and friendly free house in one of the highest villages in Wales. It reopened in 2017 after an impressive modern refurbishment. A large woodburner features in the front room and a second warms the small side room which also has comfortable banquette seating. The bar offers two locally sourced beers on handpump, often from Big Hand Brewery. Hearty bar meals are available. Bus services are limited. P (X51)

Clawddnewydd

Glan Llyn Inn

Ruthin Road, LL15 2NA (on B5105)

5-11; 12-midnight Fri & Sat; 12-9 Sun (01824) 750754
clawddnewydd.org.uk/theglanllyninn

2 changing beers (sourced locally) H

This pub is now owned and run by the community, and a warm welcome is assured when you enter the lounge bar. Dating in parts back to the 16th century, it has been refurbished to include the lounge with a real fire and a stove, a dining room and a separate public bar. Another extension provides an additional dining area and a community shop. The Sunday carvery is popular. Two changing beers are always from Welsh brewers. Q P

Cadole

Colomendy Arms

Village Road, CH7 5LL (off A494 Mold-Ruthin road)

7-11 Mon-Wed; 6-11 Thu; 4-11 Fri; 2-11 Sat & Sun (01352) 810217

5 changing beers H

A wonderful pub in the middle of the village, run by the same family for more than 30 years and featuring in the Guide for most of that time. It has two cosy rooms warmed by real fires and festooned with local history and photographs. Conversation is king here. Five varied changing beers come from far and wide. A popular stop-off for walkers, with the Loggerheads Country Park close by. Q P

Denbigh

Y Goron Fach

6 Crown Lane, LL16 3SY (by town hall)

4-10 Thu-Sat; closed Sun-Wed 07850 687701

4 changing beers (sourced locally; often Dovecote, Heavy Industry) H

A small micropub opened in 2016 in a former hairdresser's by the local Denbigh Brewery. A single room with space for around 25 people, there are high chairs around the walls and a couple of tables. Pumps are room-side and serve four local changing beers. The Little Crown is just off Crown Square where the closed Crown Hotel once stood. Q

Dolphin

Glan yr Afon Inn

Milwr, CH8 8HE

12-11 (01352) 710052 glanyrafoninn.com

Facer's Dave's Hoppy Beer, Landslide; 1 changing beer

You can expect a warm welcome at this popular pub which first opened in the 16th century and is situated in an elevated position with views of the Dee Estuary and the Wirral Peninsula. A central bar serves four separate seating areas and the dining room, while the games room has its own bar. The inn also offers food and accommodation. Walkers and dogs are welcome and the fire is lit on cold days. **Q P**

Froncysyllte

Aqueduct Inn

Holyhead Road, LL20 7PY (on A5)

12 (5 Tue-Thu)-11 (01691) 777118

4 changing beers (sourced nationally; often Bathams, Slater's, Wood)

Friendly free house standing beside the busy A5. It is a simple three-roomed affair with a small central bar, games room with TV and a comfortable lounge with wood-burning stove. Up to four changing ales are available, often from Bathams. Food is served daily including the ever-popular Sunday roasts. There is some garden seating to the side and the rear veranda offers panoramic views, including the Llangollen Canal and the world-famous Pontcysyllte Aqueduct, a World Heritage site. There is limited parking adjacent. **P (64)**

Graianrhyd

Rose & Crown

Llanarmon Road, CH7 4QW (on B5430 off A5104)

4-11; 12-11 Sat; 12-10.30 Sun (01824) 780727

theroseandcrownpub.co.uk

Black Sheep Best Bitter; 2 changing beers

A traditional early 19th-century pub with a strong local following. The long bar serves two rooms – the main room has an open fire, copper-topped tables and a vast array of pumpclips. Guest beers are usually from local breweries. Popular with tourists, walkers, cyclists and fell runners keen to fuel up on post-race chip baps following the local Dash in the Dark. It is also a stop-off on the Three Taverns Tour taken by the local village choir each May. **Q P (2)**

Graigfechan

Three Pigeons Inn

LL15 2EU (on B5429 about 3 miles from Ruthin)

closed Mon; 5-11; 12-11 Sat; 12-10 Sun

(01824) 703178 threepigeonsinn.co.uk

4 changing beers

Fine old drovers' inn with parts originating from the 12th century. The interior is tastefully decorated, retaining the original features and open log fires. An extensive lounge area has a sports room to one side and a large dining area to the other. Cellars are ideal for keeping the cask ales that are still, on occasion, served in jugs. An outdoor area to the rear has great views over the Vale of Clwyd. Two self-catering apartments are available and a campsite is adjacent.

P (76)

Gresford

Griffin Inn

Church Green, LL12 8RG

4 (5 Tue & Wed)-11.30; 4-11 Sun (01978) 855280

Courage Best Bitter; 1 changing beer (sourced nationally; often Moorhouse's, Weetwood)

Friendly community pub built on a site that was a hostelry for pilgrims in the 14th century. The irregularly shaped open-plan bar area displays a variety of interesting pictures on the walls. A lawned area to the side has views of the 15th-century All Saints church whose bells are one of the Seven Wonders of Wales. The landlady has been working behind the bar since 1973. Beers are from the Punch Taverns list. **Q P (1)**

Pant-yr-Ochain

Old Wrexham Road, LL12 8TY (off A5156, E from A483, follow signs to The Flash)

11-11 (10.30 Sun) (01978) 853525

Purple Moose Cwrw Eryri/Snowdonia Ale; Stonehouse Off the Rails; Timothy Taylor Landlord; Weetwood Eastgate; house beer (by Phoenix); 4 changing beers (sourced regionally; often Big Hand, Castle Rock, Mobberley)

Impressive 16th-century dower house that retains many historic features and sits beside a small lake within extensive gardens. The central room, dominated by a large double-fronted bar, leads to a variety of seating areas including a garden room, a small snug behind the period inglenook fireplace, and the patio and lawn outside. Hugely popular with diners, food is served all day. Five regular beers are supplemented by four guests, often local, and draught cider, plus perry in summer.

Q P

Halkyn

Blue Bell Inn

Rhosesmor Road, CH8 8DL (on B5123)

4-midnight; 3-12.30am Fri; 12-12.30am Sat; 12-midnight Sun (01352) 780309

4 changing beers (sourced locally; often Facer's, JW Lees)

Situated on Halkyn Mountain, the Blue Bell is an excellent community pub with weekly events including free guided walks, conversational Welsh classes and trad jazz on Sunday afternoon. There are normally four real ales, two regulars from JW Lees and the local Facer's brewery, plus two guest ales, often from local producers. Real ciders feature strongly, with six usually available. Look for the display of beer mats and pumpclips on the roof beams in the bar. **Q P**

REAL ALE BREWERIES

Axton Axton (brewing suspended)
Big Hand Wrexham
Denbigh (Bragdy Dinbych) Denbigh
Dovecote Denbigh
Facer's Flint
Hafod Mold
Iâl Eryrys
Llangollen Llantysilio
Magic Dragon Eyton
McGivern Ruabon
Polly's Mold
Sandstone Wrexham
Top Rope Sandycroft

Hanmer

Hanmer Arms

SY13 3DE (just off A495, 1 mile from jct with A525)
⏲ 8am-11 ☎ (01948) 830458 🌐 hanmerarms.com
Hook Norton Hooky, Hooky Gold; Purple Moose Cwrw Ysgawen/Elderflower; 4 changing beers (sourced nationally; often Hobsons) 🄷
This attractive hotel-restaurant just off the main Wrexham to Whitchurch road makes an ideal base for exploring the north Welsh borderlands, Shropshire and Cheshire. The hotel is a short stroll from the picturesque Hanmer Mere and is adjacent to the charming 12th-century St Chad's church. Hook Norton ales are regular, alongside beers from Purple Moose and other changing guests. Lunchtime and evening meals are available from an extensive menu and accommodation is provided in 11 en-suite bedrooms.
Q❀♿♣P🚌(146)🐾📶

Hendre

Y Dderwen (The Oak) 🄻

Denbigh Road, CH7 5QE (on A541)
⏲ 7-11 (midnight Fri & Sat) ☎ (01352) 741466
2 changing beers (sourced locally) 🄷
A roadside pub with a central bar serving two rooms – a games room with pool table and a smaller cosy bar. The interior is adorned with an impressive collection of pottery including 1,666 mugs at the last count. The pub has a strong community focus, hosting several societies and holding regular folk nights, Welsh singing and bingo nights. There is an extensive beer garden for alfresco enjoyment on summer nights.
Q❀♿♣P🐾

Henllan

Llindir Inn 🄻

Llindir Street, LL16 5BH
⏲ 5 (12 Thu)-11; 12-midnight Fri & Sat; 12-11 Sun
☎ (01745) 812188
6 changing beers (sourced locally; often Heavy Industry) 🄷
Rambling 13th-century Grade II-listed thatched inn. On entry you are welcomed into a room with a long copper bar and an inglenook fireplace, with a comfortable TV lounge offset. Three steps take you up to another bar and a further three steps to a pleasant restaurant. The interior retains its character with old beams, tiled floors, copper and brassware. This is the home of Heavy Industry Brewing situated close by and serves up to six cask beers. Q❀♣P🚌(6)🐾📶

Holt

Peal o' Bells ✔

12 Church Street, LL13 9JP (400yds S of Holt-Farndon bridge)
⏲ 4 (12 Thu)-11; 12-1am Fri & Sat; 12-11 Sun
☎ (01829) 270411
House beer (by Marston's); 3 changing beers (sourced nationally; often Big Hand, Salopian, Stonehouse) 🄷
A popular community village pub situated next to the church and backing on to the River Dee. The house beer is supplemented by three guests, usually local, with one handpump free of tie. Food is served in one room but not in the dog-friendly bar. A large beer garden affords good views of the church and has a small play area. A recent refurbishment has added a woodburner and given a cosy, contemporary atmosphere.
❀♿♣P🚌(C56)🐾📶

Holywell

Market Cross 🄻 ✔

9-11 High Street, CH8 7LA (on main walkway)
⏲ 8am-midnight (1am Fri & Sat) ☎ (01352) 717800
Ruddles Best Bitter; Sharp's Doom Bar; 3 changing beers (often Big Bog, Purple Moose) 🄷
Converted in 2011 from a large retail outlet, this small Wetherspoon pub is in the middle of Holywell High Street and named after the obelisk of the same name that stood outside. There are many pictures of local interest on display remembering Holywell and the Greenfield Valley in times gone by. The regular beers are complemented by three guest ales, often from local breweries, and a real cider.
Q♿🍎🚌(X11,11)📶

Llanarmon Dyffryn Ceiriog

Hand at Llanarmon

LL20 7LD (end of B4500 from Chirk)
⏲ 11-11 (12.30am Fri & Sat); 12-11 Sun ☎ (01691) 600666
🌐 thehandhotel.co.uk
2 changing beers (sourced locally; often Big Hand, Weetwood, Stonehouse) 🄷
Cosy free house in a scenic location at the head of the delightful Ceiriog Valley and marked by a giant hand sculpture. Two real ales are available, usually sourced locally. Food and accommodation are both of a high standard (it is advisable to book at busy times). Dogs are welcome and the pub is popular with cyclists, walkers and tourists. Notaphilists will appreciate the collection of bank notes above the bar. Q❀♿♣P🚌(64)🐾📶

Llanarmon-yn-Ial

Raven Inn 🄻

Ffordd-Rhew-Ial, CH7 4QE (signed 500yds W of B5430)
⏲ closed Mon; 5-10.30 Tue-Thu; 5-11 Fri; 12-11 Sat; 12-9 Sun
☎ (01824) 780833 🌐 raveninn.co.uk
Purple Moose Cwrw Eryri/Snowdonia Ale; 2 changing beers (sourced locally) 🄷
Community-run by volunteers since 2009, this delightful old pub continues to go from strength to strength, with all profits used to benefit the community. There is a friendly and inviting ambience from the moment you enter. The bar serves two discrete carpeted areas and a tiled area to one side. The three guest beers are from local breweries. Excellent locally sourced home-cooked food is served Thursday to Sunday. Three self-catering bedrooms are available.
Q❀♿♣🍎P🚌(2)🐾📶

Llandrillo

Dudley Arms Hotel 🄻

High Street, LL21 0TL
⏲ 6-11; closed Tue; 12-midnight Sat; 12-10.30 Sun
☎ (01490) 440223 🌐 dudleyarms.wales
Stonehouse Station Bitter; 1 changing beer (sourced locally) 🄷
Traditional Welsh village inn nestling within the Berwyn mountains. The owners took over in 2015 and carried out extensive refurbishment to create a

pub full of charm, with many period features and exposed oak beams. There are several discrete areas including a lounge, dining area and pool room with stone walls, tiled floors and cosy fires. The guest beer is always from a local brewery. B&B accommodation is available upstairs and in an adjacent refurbished cottage.
P (T3)

Llandyrnog

Kinmel Arms

Waen, LL16 4HN
12-3, 5-9.30 (11 Wed-Fri); 12-11 Sat; 12-5 Sun
(01824) 790291 kinmelarms.com
Marston's Saddle Tank; Young's Special; 3 changing beers (often Big Hand, Heavy Industry) H
A warm and traditional pub on the edge of the Clwydian Range and close to Offa's Dyke path and Moel Arthur hill fort. The front bar area features a large woodburner. There is a separate dining space, children's play area and games room. The guest beers are usually from Heavy Industry, Cwrw Ial, Big Hand and Wild Horse breweries. Opening times are subject to change so check before visiting. Q P (76)

Llangollen

Chainbridge Hotel

Berwyn, LL20 8BS (off B5103)
9am-11 (01978) 860215 chainbridgehotel.com
Stonehouse Station Bitter; 2 changing beers (sourced locally; often Stonehouse) H
Historic country hotel in a splendid location between the Llangollen Canal and River Dee, close to the Horseshoe Falls. There are excellent views of the river and its rapids, with the Llangollen to Corwen heritage railway opposite. Travel by bus or steam train to Berwyn then cross the restored pedestrian chainbridge. A pleasant half-hour walk to Llangollen can be undertaken via the canal towpath. Up to three ales are available, often from Stonehouse Brewery.
Q P (T3)

Ponsonby Arms

Mill Street, LL20 8RY (near steam railway)
closed Mon; 12-midnight summer; closed Mon; 5-midnight Tue-Thu; 3-midnight Fri & Sun; 12-midnight Sat winter
(01978) 447985
Bollington Long Hop; Elland 1872 Porter; Ulverston Flying Elephants; 3 changing beers (sourced nationally; often Elland, Salopian, Saltaire) H
Rescued from closure and dereliction by the team from the nearby Sun, this is a community pub with an emphasis is on good beer and conversation. There is an ongoing restoration programme, with plans for increasing the food offering. The wide range of beers on offer is due to the use of small casks where possible. Outside, an extensive garden overlooks the River Dee. A free ticket for the nearby council car park can be obtained at the bar.
Q P (5,T3)

Sun Inn

49 Regent Street, LL20 8HN (400yds E of town centre on A5)
closed Mon; 7-2am; 7-3am Fri & Sat (01978) 860079
5 changing beers (often Bollington, Ulverston) H
A free house in which beer quality is important, with five changing real ales usually available and one cider. There is a large, open front room with an open fire, and a rear snug; outside is a covered seating area. The pub has a late licence, with live music Wednesday to Saturday evenings. Quieter in the early evening, it can get busy later on. Opening hours may vary; please check ahead if travelling.
(5,T3)

Mold

Fat Boar

17 Chester Street, CH7 1EG
11.30-11 (midnight Fri & Sat); 12-10.30 Sun
(01352) 759890 thefatboar.co.uk
2 changing beers (sourced locally) H
Formerly called the Boar's Head and closed for several years, the pub reopened as the Fat Boar in 2015 following an extensive renovation and contemporary refurbishment. As befits a food-led operation, the interior and upper floor is laid out for dining, with a large conservatory and additional seating outside at the rear of the building. Centrally situated in this market town, the pub is handy for local transport links to and from the surrounding areas.

Glasfryn

Raikes Lane, CH7 6LR (off A5119 ½ mile N of Mold)
11-11; 11-10.30 Sun (01352) 750500
glasfryn-mold.co.uk
Purple Moose Cwrw Eryri/Snowdonia Ale; house beer (by Brunning & Price); 6 changing beers H
Near to Theatre Clwyd and set in its own grounds opposite the Civic Centre, this large upmarket pub and restaurant was once the residence for circuit judges attending the nearby court. Operated by Brunning and Price, the interior decorated in their usual style, the emphasis is on food, served all day in three dining areas; the house beer is their Phoenix B&P Original. There are extensive views over the surrounding countryside from the large beer garden. Q P (28)

Mold Alehouse

Unit 2, Earl Chambers, Earl Road, CH7 1AL
closed Mon & Tue; 2-10 Wed; 4-10 Thu & Fri; 2-10 Sat; 4-9 Sun (01352) 218188 moldalehouse.co.uk
4 changing beers (sourced locally) H
Since opening in 2016, this micropub has won many CAMRA awards and gained a strong following based on sound principles of good beer, fellowship and conversation. It is centrally situated in a Grade II-listed building opposite Daniel Owen Square, named after the renowned Welsh novelist, and home to Mold museum and library. The cask ale range always features a dark beer, and two KeyKeg lines often include a beer from the nearby Polly's brewery. Q

Nannerch

Cross Foxes

Village Road, CH7 5RD
closed Mon; 6-11; 12-10.30 Sun (01352) 741464
nannerch.com
3 changing beers (sourced locally; often Big Hand, Cwrw Iâl) H
This delightful village pub close to the church was built in 1780 and originally also served as a pub and butcher's – the meat hooks still remain over the bar. The entrance leads to a main bar with a large fireplace. Off this is another small bar, a

lounge and a function room. Three pumps serve changing beers, usually sourced from local brewers including Big Hand and Cwrw Ial. Beer festivals are held in March and October.

Ponciau

Colliers Arms

Chapel Street, LL14 1SE (off B5426)

5 (7 Mon & Tue)-11; 2-11 Sat; 1-10.30 Sun

Tetley Bitter; 3 changing beers (sourced regionally) H

This splendid free house on a narrow terraced street is a rare cask ale outlet for the area. The front room has a slate floor, comfortable bench seating, stools and small cast-iron tables. There is also a tiny snug area and a rear room with a pool table and jukebox. To the rear is a pleasant decked area and lawn. Three of the four handpumps often feature beers from local microbreweries. Public parking is available nearby. A former local CAMRA Pub of the Year. (3,3E)

Pontblyddyn

Bridge Inn

Wrexham Road, CH7 4HN (on A541 3 miles S of Mold)

12-11 ☎ (01352) 770087

2 changing beers H

A fine historic building dating back to the 16th century, situated at a crossroads, with the River Alyn to the rear. The unspoilt interior comprises a warm and cosy front bar with a real fire, another room leading off it, and a separate restaurant. Outside, there is a courtyard at the front and an extensive riverside beer garden with a children's play area at the back. QP

Pontfadog

Swan Inn

Llanarmon Road, LL20 7AR (on B4500 next to post office)

11-11 ☎ (01691) 718273

2 changing beers (sourced locally; often Salopian, Stonehouse) H

Welcoming village free house in the scenic Ceiriog Valley which has been revitalised since new owners took over in 2017. The cosy red-tiled bar room, favoured by the locals, features a central fireplace which separates the TV and darts area from the servery. High-quality home-cooked food is available in the recently extended dining room, which leads to a pleasant outdoor area. The two cask beers are from local independent breweries. P(64,65)

Prestatyn

Bar 236

236 High Street, LL19 9BP

10.30 (5 Mon & Tue)-11; 10.30-12.30am Fri & Sat

☎ (01745) 850084 bar236.co.uk

4 changing beers (sourced locally; often Cwrw , Heavy Industry) H

This café bar is located at the top of the High Street. It opened in 2010 and was fully refurbished in 2014. The L-shaped room has a minimalist but pleasant feel with a wood-boarded floor and blue-tiled bar front. Glass-fronted on two sides, if offers open views inside and outside. TV sport is well catered for and there is live music at weekends, when it can be quite noisy.

Halcyon Quest Hotel

17 Gronant Road, LL19 9DT (on A547 just E of town centre)

3-11 (midnight Fri); 12-midnight Sat; 12-11 Sun

☎ (01745) 852442 halcyonquest-hotel.com

Facer's Flintshire Bitter; 3 changing beers (sourced nationally) H

A long-standing supporter of cask beer, the HQ, as it is known, is located at the southern end of town. It has just one room packed with sporting and other memorabilia, including a rowing boat suspended from the ceiling dedicated to JR Hartley of fly-fishing fame. The extensive garden patio at the rear has a covered area and is popular for drinking in the summer months.

P(35,36)

Rhyl

Cob & Pen

143 High Street, LL18 1UF

11-11 (midnight Fri & Sat); 12-11 Sun ☎ (01745) 350446

Facer's Mountain Mild, Flintshire Bitter; 3 changing beers H

A fine traditional town-centre pub close to the railway and bus stations with three separate areas to suit all tastes served from a central bar. The pub hosts darts, pool and dominoes teams and shows televised sports events, all adding to its popularity. Some of the beers are usually sourced from microbreweries and there is always a cask mild, a rarity for the area.

Dove at Rhyl

2 St Margarets Buildings, St Margarets Drive, LL18 2HT (on A525, ½ mile from centre)

closed Mon; 3-10; 12-10 Sat; 2-8 Sun ☎ 07908 957116

3 changing beers (sourced locally; often Dovecote) H

Situated on the outskirts of town, this welcome addition to the local pub landscape is the first in a small chain of pubs operated by Dovecote Brewery under the Dove umbrella. The interior is bright and airy, featuring a mural of Rhyl High Street, and the atmosphere is relaxed and friendly. The cask beer range includes at least two from Dovecote plus a guest, often from a local microbrewery.

Q(51)

Sussex

20-26 Sussex Street, LL18 1SG

8am-midnight (1am Fri & Sat) ☎ (01745) 362910

Greene King Abbot; Ruddles Best Bitter; 3 changing beers H

Located in the pedestrianised town centre in a building that has been both a Wesleyan chapel and an Old Comrades Club, this typical Wetherspoon outlet has a spacious, functional interior decorated with illustrated panels of local interest. Numerous gaming machines and TV screens provide in-house entertainment for locals and visitors. The guest beers are mainly from Wetherspoon's seasonal list but may also include beers from a local North Wales brewery. Q

Ruabon

Bridge End Inn

5 Bridge Street, LL14 6DA

5-11; 4-11 Fri; 12-11 Sat & Sun ☎ (01978) 810881

8 changing beers (sourced nationally; often Ossett, Rat, Salopian) H

This welcoming, traditional, community-focused local, close to Ruabon station, has three low-ceilinged rooms and a covered outside drinking area. It has deservedly won numerous awards since its revitalisation by the McGivern family, including CAMRA National Pub of the Year. The ever-changing range of cask ales often includes a brew from the on-site McGivern Brewery, plus porter, stout and real cider. Families and well-behaved dogs are welcome in the lounge.
Q

Shotton

Central Hotel

2-4 Chester Road West, CH5 1BX
8am-midnight (1am Fri & Sat) (01244) 845510
Greene King IPA, Abbot; Ruddles County; 3 changing beers (sourced nationally)
A local landmark built in the early 1920s beside the railway station. It had a major refurbishment in 2008 and reverted to its original name. The interior is typical Wetherspoon mock-Edwardian, with a large single bar partially separated into three similarly furnished areas. Three changing guest beers are served alongside the three Wetherspoon regulars. At the front is an open seating area overlooking the street. There are regular Meet the Brewer evenings. P

Trevalyn

Griffin

Rossett Road, LL12 0ER
12-11 (midnight Fri & Sat); 12-10.30 Sun
(01244) 570515 griffininn-trevalyn.co.uk
2 changing beers (sourced regionally)
This cosy, attractive whitewashed local, said to be 400 years old, stands in the heart of the village about a mile from Rossett. The golden griffin on the wall is particularly eye-catching. And look out for Phil, the bearded dragon. Outside is a grassed garden with trestles and to the rear a Camping and Caravanning Club site. Unusual fabricated handpumps dispense ales from the Marston's stable. P

Wrexham

Elihu Yale

44-46 Regent Street, LL11 1RR
8am-midnight (1am Thu-Sat) (01978) 366646
Greene King Abbot; Ruddles Best Bitter; Sharp's Doom Bar; 5 changing beers (sourced nationally)
Formerly the Majestic Cinema, this popular Wetherspoon town-centre pub is within walking distance of both the railway and bus stations. It serves three regular beers plus at least five guests, one of which will be from a Welsh brewery, and up to two real ciders. There are various seating areas in the large room – look for the interesting skylight in an area towards the front. Families are welcome until 10pm. Quiz night is Wednesday, poker night Sunday. Q(Central/General)

Fat Boar

11 Yorke Street, LL13 8LW
12-11 (midnight Fri & Sat); 12-10.30 Sun
(01978) 354201 thefatboarwrecsam.co.uk
4 changing beers (sourced locally; often Big Hand, Hafod)
A sister venue to the one of the same name in Mold, this stripped-down pub has a clean and bright feel with ceiling beams and exposed brick walls. It comprises a large L-shaped bar/lounge downstairs and a restaurant upstairs with a display of hanging potted plants. Up to four handpumps usually feature beers from local microbreweries. There is a large, stylish beer garden and smoking area at the rear.

Royal Oak

35 High Street, LL13 8HY
12-midnight (1am Fri & Sat) (01978) 364111
Joule's Blonde, Pale Ale, Slumbering Monk; 2 changing beers (sourced nationally)
A Grade II-listed building with a long and narrow interior. The real fire, wood panelling and etched brewery mirrors around the bar create a comfortable ambience – and the mounted eland antelope head is impossible to miss. Three beers from Joule's plus up to two changing guest ales are available. The small beer garden on the roof is open April to September. No food is served but you are welcome to bring your own. Darts and traditional pub games are played.
Q(Central/General)

Ysceifiog

Fox ★

Village Road, CH8 8NJ (signed from B5121)
4-11; 1-11 Sat & Sun (01352) 720241
foxinnysceifiog.co.uk
Tetley's Bitter; 2 changing beers
Built around 1730, the Fox is well worth seeking out, with a choice of four beers. The interior comprises four small rooms, two of them for dining. The bar has a sliding door that takes you back to the 1930s. A children's playground is adjacent to the outside drinking area. Identified by CAMRA as having a nationally important historic interior, this is a rare classic. QP

Learned drinker

He was a learned man, of immense reading, but is much blamed for his unfaithfull quotations. His manner of studie was thus, he wore a long quilt cap, which came two or rather three inches at least over his eies, which served him as an umbrella to defend his eies from the light. About every three houres his man was to bring him a roll and a pot of ale to refocillate (refresh) his wasted spirits so he studied, and dranke, and munched some bread and this maintained him till night, and then he made a good supper.

An Oxford man, William Prynne (1600-69), as described by John Aubrey in Brief Lives, ed. John Buchanan-Brown, 2000

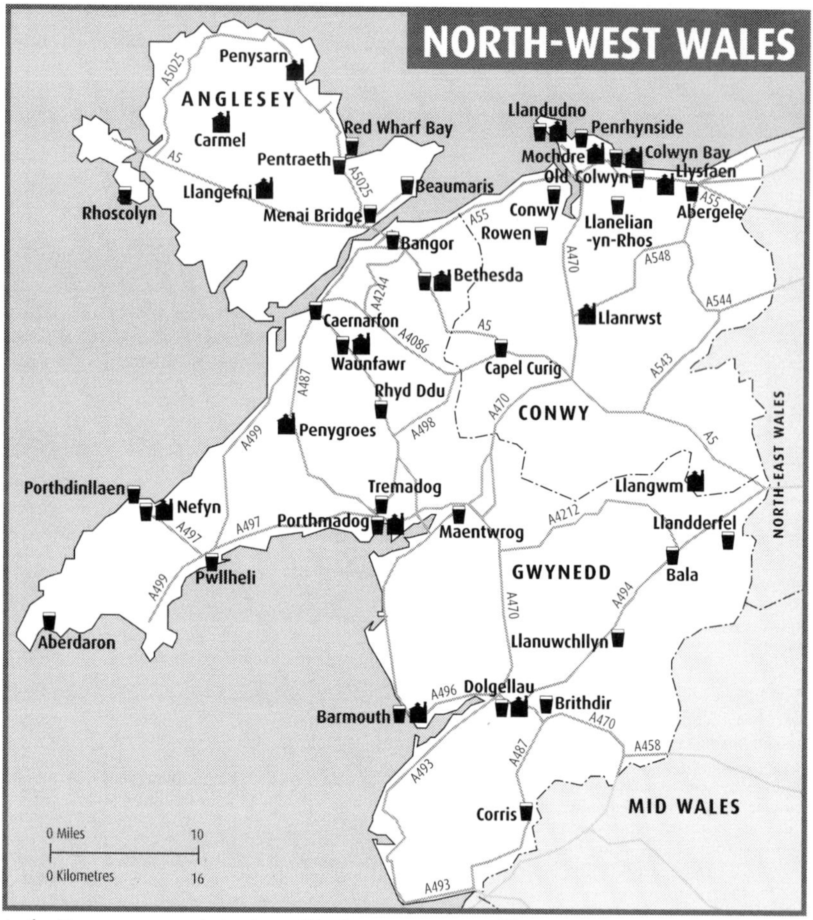

Authority areas covered: Anglesey UA, Conwy UA, Gwynedd UA

Aberdaron

Ty Newydd

LL53 8BE

11-midnight (10.30 Sun) (01758) 760207

gwesty-tynewydd.co.uk

Purple Moose Calon Lan; 2 changing beers (sourced locally) H

The hotel is at the centre of a picturesque and historic village at the end of the Llyn Peninsula. Beers are from two local breweries. Freshly caught Bardsey lobster and crab are on the menu, as well as afternoon teas. Eleven en-suite bedrooms are available, with stunning sea views. The Wales coastal footpath passes through the village. Bus services run from Pwllheli. Dog are welcome in the Yellow Room and on the Terrace, but are not permitted in bar/restaurant. **Q**

Abergele

Hoptimist

32 Market Street, LL22 7AA

closed Mon; 3-10; 12-10 Sat; 12-7 Sun

5 changing beers (sourced regionally; often Cwrw Iâl, Dovecote) H

An innovative conversion of a former building society has provided Abergele with its first micropub, a joint venture between Cwrw Ial and Dovecote breweries, which opened in 2018. Information regarding the beers and ciders, along with their prices and strengths, is clearly displayed on a large blackboard on the back wall. The bank of 13 taps offers five cask, five keg beers and three ciders, served in third-pint glasses on request. The large rear courtyard offers views into the small cellar. **Q** (12,43)

Bala

Stori

101 High Street, LL23 7AE (opp Old Bull's Head and Co-op)

10.30-8 (9 Fri & Sat) (01678) 520501

storibeers.wales

3 changing beers (sourced locally; often Geipel) G

This bottle shop and taproom is centrally situated in the popular town of Bala close to the lake and other attractions. The shop offers a wide range of beers and beer-related merchandise, with the emphasis on local products, and to the rear is the taproom. Cask and craft keg beers are available to either take away or enjoy in the cosy tasting room. Opening hours may be subject to seasonal variation. **Q** (T3)

Bangor

Patricks

59 Holyhead Road, LL57 2HE

⏲ 11-2am (2.30am Wed & Thu; 3am Fri & Sat)

☎ (01248) 353062 🌐 patricksbar.com

4 changing beers (sourced regionally) 🄷

Situated in upper Bangor, this lively Irish-themed bar is popular with both the locals and students of Bangor University. Numerous TVs display sporting events. There are usually two locally sourced ales and one regional beer on the bar. Note the extended opening hours for sports and late-night drinking. On the bus route towards the Menai Straits and near the railway station. ◑≹🚌(5C,T2)

Barmouth

Royal Hotel

LL42 1AB

⏲ 12-11 (midnight Sat) ☎ (01341) 406214

4 changing beers 🄷

Located beneath the main hotel with access from the main road, the hotel has had a major structural refurbishment including the kitchens. The pub is on two levels, with the main bar next to the entrance, and the lower level primarily for playing pool. There is a beer garden to the rear. Beers are usually from Welsh breweries but occasionally come from just over the border. 🐴◑⛺≹♣🚌🐾📶

Beaumaris

Castle Court Hotel ✔

Castle Square, LL58 8DA

⏲ 12-11 ☎ (01248) 810078 🌐 castlecourtbeaumaris.co.uk

Facer's This Splendid Ale; 1 changing beer (sourced regionally) 🄷

In the centre of this historic town and overlooking the castle, this was originally called the White Lion Hotel. The owners have renovated the reception and dining areas. It has a small beer garden to the rear, and in spring and summer the courtyard outside the main door provides more seating. Facer's Splendid Ale is always available plus one guest beer from a small independent brewery. Lunchtime meals are served 12-3pm during school holidays only. 🐴❀🛏⛺🚌📶

Bethesda

Y Sior

35-37 Carneddi Road, LL57 3SE

⏲ 7-midnight; 5-1am Fri; 1-1am Sat; 1-midnight Sun

☎ (01248) 600072

4 changing beers (sourced locally) 🄷

A friendly locals' pub in the village of Carneddi just outside Bethesda. A few minutes' drive from the A5, there is plenty of parking nearby. Free of tie, the pub offers a variety of ales from the Marston's range as well as locally brewed beers. There are views across the valley to the local slate quarry, which has the longest zip wire in Britain.

Q🚌(6,7)🐾

Brithdir

Cross Foxes

LL40 2SG (jct of A470 and A487)

⏲ 11-midnight ☎ (01341) 421001 🌐 crossfoxes.co.uk

Cader Gold; 2 changing beers (sourced regionally) 🄷/🄶

A newly refurbished Grade II-listed building situated near the foot of Cader Idris mountain and four miles from the historic town of Dolgellau. Beers are usually from Cader Ales and other local microbreweries. Breakfast is served from 8am and meals are available all day until 9pm. Dogs are welcome in the bar area. The hotel has Welsh Tourist Board 5-star grading. Bus service T2 passes by, but please check times.

Q🐴❀🛏◑⛺P🚌(T2)🐾📶

Caernarfon

Bar Bach

Tan y Bont, LL55 2NF (just off square, behind Caffi Maes)

⏲ 11.30-1.30am

3 changing beers (sourced regionally) 🄷

Under the looming shadow of Caernarfon's imposing castle lies the self-proclaimed smallest bar in Wales. Part of Caffi Maes, its narrow entrance is found around the corner. A charmingly intimate place, it does indeed occupy a small area but it is deceptive in that the bar leads to another longer room on a lower level. Plenty of exposed stonework, a small fireplace and a mix of dark-wood furniture give it a lived-in feel.

Q◐≹(WHR)🚌(5C,S4)🐾📶

Black Boy Inn 🏆 ✔

Northgate Street, LL55 1RW

⏲ 11-11 (11.30 Fri & Sat); 12-10.30 Sun ☎ (01286) 673604

🌐 black-boy-inn.com

Draught Bass; 5 changing beers (sourced regionally) 🄷

The pub is set within the town walls between the marina and castle. This historic town, a World Heritage Site, is well worth a visit, ending with a welcome pint at the Black Boy. The public bar and small lounge are warmed by roaring fires. Good-value food is served and a Purple Moose beer is often among the guest ales. There is a drinking area outside on the traffic-free street. A former local CAMRA Pub of the Year, and again for 2019.

🐴❀🛏◑♿≹(WHR)♣P🚌(5C,S4)📶

Tafarn Y Porth ✔

5-9 Eastgate Street, LL55 1AG (just off Bangor Rd near Barclays Bank)

⏲ 9am-midnight ☎ (01268) 662920

Big Bog Bog Standard Bitter; Draught Bass; Greene King Abbot; Ruddles Best Bitter; 5 changing beers (sourced nationally) 🄷

REAL ALE BREWERIES

Anglesey Brewhouse Llangefni
Anglesey Brewing Carmel
Black Cloak 🛢 Colwyn Bay (NEW)
Cader Dolgellau
Conwy Llysfaen
Druid Penysarn
Geipel Llangwm
Llŷn Nefyn
Lleu Penygroes
Myrddins Barmouth
Nant Llanrwst
Ogwen Bethesda
Purple Moose Porthmadog
Snowdon Craft Mochdre
Snowdonia Parc 🛢 Waunfawr
Wild Horse Llandudno

Friendly, welcoming Wetherspoon pub opposite the town walls and close to the castle. It has a large open-plan interior and a spacious, partly covered courtyard outside with plenty of seating. The real ale range often includes a beer from the Big Bog Brewing Company. The pub's location is handy for the Welsh Highland Railway, which takes you to the heart of Snowdonia. A rare conversion of a supermarket to a pub.
Q ☕ ☻ ⓓ ♿ ▲ ≠ (WHR) ☲ ♣ ● ⌷ (5C,S4) ☞

Capel Curig

Tyn-y-Coed Inn ⓛ
Holyhead Road, LL24 0EE
🕓 3-11; 12-11 Fri & Sat; 12-10.30 Sun ☎ (01690) 720331
⊕ tyn-y-coed.co.uk
Purple Moose Cwrw Eryri/Snowdonia Ale, Cwrw Madog/Madog's Ale; 2 changing beers (sourced regionally) Ⓗ
A spacious old multi-roomed pub with a hotel extension overlooking Moel Siabod. To mark its historic past on the coaching route, the Tyn-y-Coed has a majestic stagecoach opposite the entrance on the A5. It is popular with outdoor enthusiasts owing to its location in the Snowdonia National Park, with welcoming log fires in three of the bar areas in the winter months. Locally sourced food, ales and a good selection of whiskies are available. Dogs are admitted on leads.
☕ ☻ ⌂ ⓓ ♣ P ⌷ (S2) ☻ ☞

Colwyn Bay

Bay Hop ☗ ⓛ
17 Penrhyn Road, LL29 8LG
🕓 closed Mon; 2 (4 Tue & Wed)-10; 4-8 Sun
⊕ thebayhop.co.uk
5 changing beers (sourced regionally) Ⓗ
Opened in 2016, this is a welcome addition to the Bay drinking experience. Two large barrel tables are available for vertical drinkers and attractive high-backed wooden settles for those who prefer to sit down. Five ciders and perries are offered from a fridge behind the bar. Third-pint glasses and two-pint take-out cartons are available. Thursday is cheese night. Local CAMRA Pub of the Year 2017-2019 and Cider Pub of the Year 2018.
Q ☕ ≠ ♣ ● ⌷ (12,13) ☻

Black Cloak Taproom ⓛ
71 Abergele Road, LL29 7RU
🕓 closed Mon; 4 (2 Thu & Fri; 12 Sat)-10.30; 12-9.30 Sun
☎ (01492) 330274
3 changing beers (sourced locally) Ⓗ
This new brewpub was opened in December 2018 by two former employees of Heavy Industry Brewing, who are now brewing their own beer on-site using a one-barrel plant. The taproom has comfortable seating and a convivial atmosphere. Beers are available on cask, keg and direct from a brite tank, and served in thirds, halves, two-thirds or pint measures. Guest beers are sourced from quality breweries throughout the UK and bottled beers are also on offer. ☕ ≠ ⌷ (12,13) ☻ ☞

Pen-y-Bryn ⓛ
Pen-y-Bryn Road, LL29 6DD
🕓 11-11; 12-10.30 Sun ☎ (01492) 533360
⊕ penybryn-colwynbay.co.uk

Purple Moose Cwrw Eryri/Snowdonia Ale; house beer (by Phoenix); 4 changing beers (sourced regionally) Ⓗ
Large open-plan pub with bookcases, old furniture and real fires during the winter. The walls are decorated with photographs and memorabilia from the local area. Panoramic views of the Bay of Colwyn and the Great Orme can be admired from the terrace and garden. A changing menu of good food is served throughout the day. A boardroom-style function room for celebrations and meetings has been created in the cellar, opening onto the garden. Q ☕ ☻ ⓓ ♿ P ⌷ (23) ☻ ☞

Picture House ⓛ ✔
24-26 Prince's Drive, LL29 8LA
🕓 8am-midnight (1am Fri & Sat) ☎ (01492) 535286
Greene King Abbot; Ruddles Best Bitter; 4 changing beers (sourced regionally) Ⓗ
A Wetherspoon pub in the former Princess Cinema, now a Grade II-listed building, next to Colwyn Bay railway station. The building is on three levels, with an upper balcony, and the walls are adorned with theatre memorabilia. There are eight handpumps featuring at least one beer from a local brewery such as Conwy, Purple Moose or Snowdon Craft, with guest ciders on offer from a fridge behind bar. Local Meet the Brewer promotions, in addition to Wetherspoon's national events, are held throughout the year. Q ☕ ⓓ ♿ ≠ ⌷ (12,13) ☞

Station
Abergele Road, LL29 8BP
🕓 11-11; 12-11 Sun ☎ (01492) 532818
⊕ thestationcolwynbay.co.uk
5 changing beers (sourced regionally) Ⓗ
Large town-centre pub originally built around 1870 and reopened in 2015 by the management team from the successful Albert in Llandudno, following an extensive modern refurbishment and change of name. Food is served throughout the day. Beers are displayed on blackboards near the bar, with third-pint glasses available. With many tables overlooking the street, it is handy for a quick drink while waiting to travel home from the adjacent bus stop. ☕ ⓓ ♿ ≠ ⌷ (12,13) ☞

Conwy

Albion Ale House ★ ⓛ
Upper Gate Street, LL32 8RF
🕓 12-11 (midnight Fri & Sat) ☎ (01492) 582484
⊕ albionalehouse.weebly.com
9 changing beers (sourced locally; often Conwy, Nant, Purple Moose) Ⓗ
Multi-room pub on CAMRA's National Inventory of Historic Pub Interiors superbly refurbished by the current owners. Each room retains original 1920s features and several have wonderful fireplaces. There is no music or TV, just pleasant conversation. The pub is managed by four local brewers – Conwy, Nant, Purple Moose and Snowdon Craft – and showcases their beers as well as guests. There are up to 10 ciders and a good selection of wines and malt whiskies. CAMRA awards include local and Welsh Pub of the Year. Q ☻ ≠ ♣ ● ⌷ (5,19) ☻ ☞

Bank of Conwy ⓛ
1 Lancaster Square, LL32 8HT
🕓 9am-11 (midnight Fri & Sat) ☎ (01492) 573741
⊕ bankofconwy.com
4 changing beers (sourced regionally) Ⓗ

The Bank of Conwy is a modern continental-style craft beer bar which opened in 2015 in a Grade II-listed former bank. It uses many fittings from the original building – the bar used to be the counter and the manager's office is now a snug with a fire. The basement, which was formerly the vault, is available for private hire. Breakfast is served 9am-noon. Tuesday is jam night, Wednesday and Friday are music nights. ♘◐⇌🚌(5,19)🐾📶

Erskine Arms Ⓛ

Rosehill Street, LL32 8LD

⏲ 11.30-11 ☎ (01492) 593535 🌐 erskinearms.co.uk

Black Sheep Best Bitter; Conwy Clogwyn Gold; Timothy Taylor Boltmaker; 2 changing beers (sourced regionally; often Heavy Industry Brewing) Ⓗ

Reopened in 2017 following a major refurbishment, the pub's name was changed back to the Erskine Arms – the family name of the owners. It was previously the Malt Loaf, in keeping with its sister pub the Cottage Loaf in Llandudno. The inn has two distinct dining areas, one on an upper floor, and there is a snug to the left and an outside drinking area. The decor includes traditional wooden features, open fires and pictures on the walls portraying local history. ❀🛏◐◑⇌●🚌(5,19)🐾📶

Corris

Slaters Arms 🏆

Bridge Street, SY20 9SP

⏲ 5-midnight; 12-8 Sun ☎ (01654) 761324

3 changing beers (sourced nationally) Ⓗ

Named after what used to be the main trade in Corris, this Grade II-listed three-roomed village pub is popular with locals and visitors staying nearby. The main bar has traditional slate flooring and a decorative mantelshelf above a large inglenook fireplace. A smaller lounge is to the left and a pub games room is to the rear. Walkers, families and well-behaved dogs are welcome. A three third-pint platter is available for the price of a pint, and food is available to take away. ♘◑⛺♣●🚌🐾📶

Dolgellau

Torrent Walk Hotel Ⓛ

Smithfield Street, LL40 1AA

⏲ 11-midnight ☎ (01341) 422858

Purple Moose Cwrw Eryri/Snowdonia Ale; Wychwood Hobgoblin; 3 changing beers (sourced nationally) Ⓗ

An 18th-century hotel in the narrow streets of the town centre, retaining most of its multi-roomed interior and old fireplaces, although the bar fittings date from circa 1970. Note the Coffee Room etched panel in the door from the lobby to the room on the right. A real cider is always served and up to five ales, mostly from local breweries. An ideal base for walking in the Cader Idris area. 🛏◐◑♣●🚌🐾📶

Llandderfel

Bryntirion Inn Ⓛ

LL23 7RA (on B4401 4 miles E of Bala)

⏲ 11-11; 12-11 Sun ☎ (01678) 530205

🌐 bryntirioninn.co.uk

Purple Moose Cwrw Eryri/Snowdonia Ale; 1 changing beer (sourced locally) Ⓗ

Dating back to 1695, this former hunting lodge and coaching inn overlooks the Dee Valley. The cosy and comfortable bar area with a log fire is open all day. There are a number of other rooms to accommodate diners and families including a large function room for special events. There is also a small covered and heated courtyard at the rear. The guest beer varies and may be from a local or national brewer. Two en-suite guest rooms are available upstairs. Q♘❀🛏◐◑♣P🚌(T3)🐾📶

Llandudno

Albert Ⓛ ✔

56 Madoc Street, LL30 2TW

⏲ 11-11; 12-10.30 Sun ☎ (01492) 877188

🌐 albertllandudno.co.uk

5 changing beers (sourced regionally) Ⓗ

Just off the town centre and close to the railway station, this popular pub-restaurant has a modern decor with a range of interesting photographs and pictures on display. It offers five handpulled ales from local and independent breweries and a range of meals throughout the day. Current beers are displayed on blackboards above and beside the L-shaped bar, with third-pint glasses available. There is a heated and covered verandah with seating at the front. Q♘❀◐◑♿⇌●🚌(5,12)🐾📶

Links Hotel

77 Conwy Road, LL30 1PN

⏲ 12-11 (10.30 Sun) ☎ (01492) 879180

🌐 linkshotelllandudno.co.uk

JW Lees Manchester Pale Ale, Bitter, Dragon's Fire; 1 changing beer (sourced nationally; often JW Lees) Ⓗ

The Links is a family pub with large rooms and good car-parking facilities off the A470, enjoying a consistent local trade and also popular with holidaymakers. It was purpose-built in 1898 near two golf courses, hence the name. It reopened in 2017 following a lengthy and extensive refurbishment. The conservatory is used for dining and functions, and there is an enclosed outdoor play area adjacent to the patio decking. Third-pint taster glasses are available. Q♘❀🛏◐◑♿⇌P🚌(5)🐾📶

Snowdon

11 Tudno Street, LL30 2HB

⏲ 12-11 (11.30 Fri & Sat) ☎ (01492) 872166

🌐 the-snowdonhotel.co.uk

Draught Bass; house beer (by Coach House); 3 changing beers (sourced regionally) Ⓗ

One of the oldest pubs in Llandudno, just off the town centre and near the tram station. The beer range includes the house beer, Blue Sky from Coach House Brewing, and tasters of three third-pints are available for the price of a pint. An attractive Snowdon mirror features above the fireplace, and the small side snug has a dartboard and displays autographed celebrity photographs. The roadside garden, with fine views of the Great Orme, has won Llandudno in Bloom for its floral displays. ♘❀🚋(Great Orme)♣●🚌(5,12)🐾📶

Tapps Ⓛ

35 Madoc Street, LL30 2TL

⏲ 12-11 (9 Mon; 10 Tue & Wed); 12-10 Sun

☎ (01492) 870956

Conwy Welsh Pride; 4 changing beers (sourced regionally) Ⓗ

This micropub opened in October 2017 in a former cake shop and has an open-plan bar at the front with a small snug to the rear. Welsh beer is to the fore and there is a large bottled beer selection.

Vinyl music is played on an old record player. One of the tables is a chessboard that transforms into a backgammon or card table, other board games are provided and there are books to borrow.
🔥❀≋♣🍎🚌(5,12)🐾📶

Llanelian-yn-Rhos

White Lion Inn ✔

LL29 8YA

🕓 closed Mon; 11.30-3, 6 (5 Fri)-11; 11.30-4, 5-11.30 Sat; 12-10.30 Sun ☎ (01492) 515807 🌐 whitelioninn.co.uk

Marston's Saddle Tank; 2 changing beers (sourced regionally) [H]

A regular in the Guide for 28 years, this 16th-century inn situated in the hills above Old Colwyn, next to St Elian's Church, offers a warm welcome. Gracing the entrance are two white stone lions, leading into the bar area with slate-flagged flooring and large comfortable chairs around the log fires. Decorative stained glass is mounted above the bar in the tiny snug. The restaurant serves home-cooked food. Jazz night is Tuesday and quiz night Thursday. Q🔥❀◑⛺🍎P🐾📶

Llanuwchllyn

Eagles Inn (Tafarn Yr Eryrod) [L]

LL23 7UB

🕓 11-11 (midnight Thu-Sat); closed Sun ☎ (01678) 540278 🌐 yr-eagles.co.uk

6 changing beers (sourced locally; often Cader, Purple Moose) [H]

An old stone-built village local opposite the church, this is a little gem with a friendly welcome for all. The bar doubles as a shop and is open all day. It retains plenty of historic features including a wonderful stone floor. The adjacent restaurant serves highly rated locally produced food. The patio garden has good mountain views. It is a 10-minute walk to Llanuwchllyn station on the Bala Lake Railway. Opening times and beer range are reduced in winter.
🔥❀◑⛺≋(Bala Lake)♣P🚌(T3)🐾📶

Maentwrog

Grapes Hotel [L]

LL41 4HN (on A496 near A487 jct)

🕓 12-midnight ☎ (01766) 590365 🌐 grapeshotelsnowdonia.co.uk

Purple Moose Cwrw Eryri/Snowdonia Ale; Sharp's Doom Bar; 1 changing beer (sourced locally) [H]

A former coaching inn, this hotel dates back to the 17th century and overlooks the Vale of Ffestiniog. The interior comprises a lounge, public bar, verandah and large dining room; outside there is a sheltered beer garden to the rear. Most of the beers are sourced locally. Plas Halt railway station nearby is on the scenic Ffestiniog line. The village is an ideal base for visiting this beautiful area.
Q🔥❀🛏◑♿⛺♣🍎P🚌

Menai Bridge

Liverpool Arms ✔

St George's Pier, LL59 5EY

🕓 12-2, 5-11.30; 12-11.30 Fri-Sun ☎ (01248) 712453

Facer's Flintshire Bitter; Purple Moose Cwrw Eryri/ Snowdonia Ale [H]/[G], Ochr Tywyll y Mws/Dark Side of the Moose; 1 changing beer [H]

Refurbished to a high standard, the Livvy has four cask ales on offer and serves good-quality home-cooked food. This nautically themed pub is frequented by locals, students in term time and the local sailing fraternity. A short walk takes you beneath the famous suspension bridge and it is close to the quay for seasonal tourist boats. The Anglesey and Welsh Coast footpaths are nearby.
🔥◑♿🚌📶

Nefyn

Bragdy Llyn

Ffordd Dewi Sant, LL53 6EG

🕓 12-5; closed Sun ☎ (01758) 721981 🌐 cwrwllyn.cymru

Cwrw Llyn Brenin Enlli, Cwrw Glyndwr, Seithenyn; 1 changing beer (sourced locally) [H]

A friendly bar located within the Cwrw Llyn Brewery, open to the public all year round. Closing time may be later on Friday and Saturday depending on customer demand. Brewery tours are available on request which include a short film and tasters of the core range of ales. Near the coast and the National Trust village of Porthdinllean. ♿P

Old Colwyn

Crafty Fox [L]

355 Abergele Road, LL29 9PL

🕓 4-9 (10 Wed; 11 Thu & Fri); 2-11 Sat; 2-9 Sun ☎ 07733 531766

5 changing beers (sourced regionally) [H]

This micropub opened in 2018 in a former tattoo parlour and butcher's shop. The main entrance leads to the bar, with hops draped across the ceiling. The lounge is furnished with a mixture of leather sofas and stools. On the bar wall is an interesting set of photographs comparing the present street scene with a century ago. Cider and Welsh gin are also sold. Loyalty cards are available for regular drinkers. Q🔥♣🍎🚌(12)🐾

Red Lion

385 Abergele Road, LL29 9PL

🕓 5-11; 4-midnight Fri; 12-midnight Sat; 12-11 Sun ☎ (01492) 515042

Courage Best Bitter; changing beers (sourced nationally) [H]

In the Guide for 25 years, this free house serves up to five guest ales from independent and national brewers. It has an L-shaped lounge featuring antique brewery mirrors and other memorabilia. There is a traditional public bar with a pool table, dartboard and TV. To the rear is a Victorian-style covered and heated smoking conservatory. The real ale club held every Thursday offers nine beers at reduced prices. The pub sign is worth a look.
Q❀♣🍎🚌(12,13)🐾📶

Penrhynside

Penrhyn Arms [L]

Pendre Road, LL30 3BY

🕓 5 (4 Thu)-11; 4-midnight Fri; 12-midnight Sat; 12-11.30 Sun ☎ (01492) 549060

Banks's Amber Ale; 3 changing beers (sourced regionally) [H]

Reopened in 2017 following a major refurbishment, this welcoming free house offers up to four guest beers, concentrating on new breweries and new beers. The spacious L-shaped bar has pool, darts and a wide-screen TV. To the

rear is a conservatory with views of the cliff face behind. As well as its ales, the pub is renowned for its range of real ciders and perries. Thursday is cheese night. Live music plays on Saturday.
🛋❀♣●🚌(14,15)🐾

Pentraeth

Panton Arms ✔

The Square, LL75 8AZ
☉ 12-11 ☎ (01248) 450959
Purple Moose Cwrw Glaslyn/Glaslyn Ale; 2 changing beers Ⓗ
A spacious 18th-century Grade II-listed coaching inn with a long lounge bar and separate taproom, popular with locals and tourists alike. Set in the centre of the village, the location is ideal for walks in the nearby forest. Purple Moose Glaslyn is available all year round. Mid-week opening times can vary in the winter months.
Q🛋❀◐◑♿P🚌(62)🐾📶

Porthdinllaen

Ty Coch Inn

LL53 6DB (access by foot only)
☉ 11-11; 12-5 Sun ☎ (01758) 720498 🌐 tycoch.co.uk
Cwrw Llyn Brenin Enlli; Purple Moose Cwrw Ysgawen/Elderflower; 1 changing beer (sourced regionally) Ⓗ
The building, in an iconic position on the beach, opened as a pub in 1842 to serve the local fishermen. It can only be reached on foot either along the beach or across the golf course, and is rated one of the top 10 beach bars in the world. The single open-plan room is served by a central bar. Parking is available at the NT car park or the golf clubhouse. Check for out-of-season opening times. 🛋◐🐾

Porthmadog

Australia

31-35 High Street, LL49 9LR
☉ 12-11 (midnight Fri & Sat) ☎ (01766) 515957
Purple Moose Cwrw Eryri/Snowdonia Ale, Cwrw Ysgawen/Elderflower, Cwrw Glaslyn/Glaslyn Ale, Ochr Tywyll y Mws/Dark Side of the Moose; 2 changing beers (sourced locally) Ⓗ
A pub since 1864, the Australia was taken over by the Purple Moose Brewery and is now its taphouse. Most of the core real ale range is available as well as seasonal and special occasion beers. Two rooms are served by a long wooden bar with eight handpumps. There is a small outdoor seating area at the back. It is situated in the centre of town next to the bus stops and near the Ffestiniog & Welsh Highland Railways station. 🛋◐◑♿⇌🚌🐾📶

Royal Sportsman Hotel

131 High Street, LL49 9HB
☉ 12-11 (10 Sun) ☎ (01766) 512015
Purple Moose Cwrw Eryri/Snowdonia Ale, Cwrw Glaslyn/Glaslyn Ale; Sharp's Doom Bar Ⓗ
Built in 1862 as a staging post for coaches on the turnpike road to Porthdinllaen, the hotel is situated near the centre of town and the station for the Cambrian Coast railway. With a welcoming real fire, Gelerts Bar is a comfortable place to enjoy a drink or a bar meal, and attracts both locals and tourists. It hosts a popular quiz on Sunday evening. Also convenient for visiting the Ffestiniog & Welsh Highland Railways. 🛋❀🛏◐◑⇌♣P🚌🐾

> Bread is the staff of life, but beer is life itself. **Traditional**

Spooner's Bar

Harbour Station, LL49 9NF
☉ 9am-11; 12-10.30 Sun ☎ (01766) 516032 🌐 festrail.co.uk
Purple Moose Cwrw Eryri/Snowdonia Ale; 5 changing beers (sourced nationally) Ⓗ
Spooner's beer range varies, but there are always at least two ales from the local Purple Moose Brewery. Situated in the terminus of the world-famous Ffestiniog & Welsh Highland Railways, steam trains are outside the door most of the year. Food is served every lunchtime, evening meals Tuesday to Saturday, but check first out of season. A former local CAMRA Pub of the Year award winner. Q🛋◐◑⛺⇌(Ffestiniog)●🚌📶

Pwllheli

Pen Cob ✔

Station Square, LL53 5HG
☉ 7am-11 ☎ (01758) 704970
Greene King Abbot; Ruddles Best Bitter; 4 changing beers Ⓗ
Wetherspoon pub opened in 2013 opposite the railway station at the start/end of the scenic Cambrian Coast Line. Formerly a Bon Marche shop, it has been attractively refurbished and is now a light and airy venue popular with all ages. It gets especially busy with locals and tourists at weekends and during the holiday season. The area is popular for sailing. 🛋◐◑♿⇌🚌📶

Red Wharf Bay

Ship Inn ✔

LL75 8RJ (off A5025 between Pentraeth and Benllech)
☉ 11-11 (10.30 Sun) ☎ (01248) 852568
🌐 shipinnredwharfbay.co.uk
Adnams Broadside; Brains SA; 2 changing beers Ⓗ
Red Wharf Bay was once a busy port exporting coal and fertilisers in the 18th and 19th centuries. Previously known as the Quay, the Ship enjoys an excellent reputation for its bar and restaurant. It gets busy with locals and visitors in the summer. The garden has panoramic views across the bay to south-east Anglesey. The resort town of Benllech is two miles away and the coastal path passes the front door. Q🛋❀◐◑♿P

Rhoscolyn

White Eagle

LL65 2NJ (off B4545 signed Traeth Beach)
☉ 12-11 (10.30 Sun) ☎ (01407) 860267
🌐 white-eagle.co.uk
Marston's 61 Deep, Pedigree; Weetwood Ambush; 2 changing beers Ⓗ
Saved from closure by new owners, this pub has been renovated and rebuilt with an airy, brasserie-style ambience. It has a fine patio enjoying superb views over Caernarfon Bay and the Llyn Peninsula to Bardsey Island. The nearby beach offers safe swimming with a warden on duty in the summer months. The pub is also close to the coastal footpath. Excellent food is available lunchtimes and evenings, all day during the school holidays.
Q🛋◐◑♿⛺♣P

Rhyd Ddu

Cwellyn Arms

LL54 6TL

11-11 ☎ (01766) 890321 snowdoninn.co.uk

Conwy Welsh Pride; 5 changing beers (sourced regionally) Ⓗ

A traditional Welsh country inn, in a fabulous situation in the village of Rhyd Ddu at the foot of Snowdon. The pub's boast that it has nine real ales nine days a week is only slightly exaggerated. There are usually four handpulls in use, dispensing ales from local breweries. The lovely log fire makes the pub cosy and welcoming after a walk on Snowdon, or after a ride on the nearby Welsh Highland Railway. ❀🛏◑♿⛺⇌(WHR)P🚌(S4)🐾

Rowen

Ty Gwyn

High Street, LL32 8YU

4-11 (1am Fri); 12-11 Sat; 12-10 Sun ☎ (01492) 650232

JW Lees Bitter; 1 changing beer (often JW Lees) Ⓗ

Community village inn in an idyllic setting with a warm welcome for locals and visitors alike. There are two walled gardens, one with a stream running by. The comfortable lounge has horse brasses and old pictures on the walls, and there is a small restaurant area serving good food made with locally sourced ingredients. Traditional Welsh singing features on Friday evenings, live entertainment most Saturdays and charity quiz nights on occasion. Opening times may vary seasonally. ❀◑⛺♣P🚌(19)🐾📶

Tremadog

Union Inn ✓

7 Market Square, LL49 9RB

12-2, 5.30-12.30am; 12-2, 5.30-11 Sun ☎ (01766) 512748 union-inn.com

Big Bog Bog Standard Bitter; Purple Moose Cwrw Eryri/Snowdonia Ale; 1 changing beer Ⓗ

Friendly local situated in the village square, with two separate cosy bars and a restaurant at the rear. The pub has a policy of using locally sourced produce, and the ale range mainly features local beers. Children are welcome and there are board games available. Excellent food is served in the bar and restaurant. Tremadog was the birthplace of Thomas Edward Lawrence (Lawrence of Arabia) in 1888. Frequent bus services pass the building. Q❀◑♿⛺⇌🍎🚌(1A,T2)

Waunfawr

Snowdonia Park

Beddgelert Road, LL55 4AQ

11-11 (10.30 Sun) ☎ (01286) 650409 snowdonia-park.co.uk

House beer (by Snowdonia Parc); 5 changing beers Ⓗ

Home of the Snowdonia Brewery, this is a popular pub for walkers, climbers and families, with children's play areas inside and out. Meals are served all day. The pub adjoins Waunfawr station on the Welsh Highland Railway – stop off here before continuing on one of the most scenic sections of narrow gauge railway in Britain. There is a large campsite adjacent on the riverside. A frequent local CAMRA Pub of the Year. Q❀◑♿⛺⇌♣🍎P🚌(S4)🐾📶

Liverpool Arms, Menai Bridge (Photo: Reading Tom/Flickr CC BY 2.0)

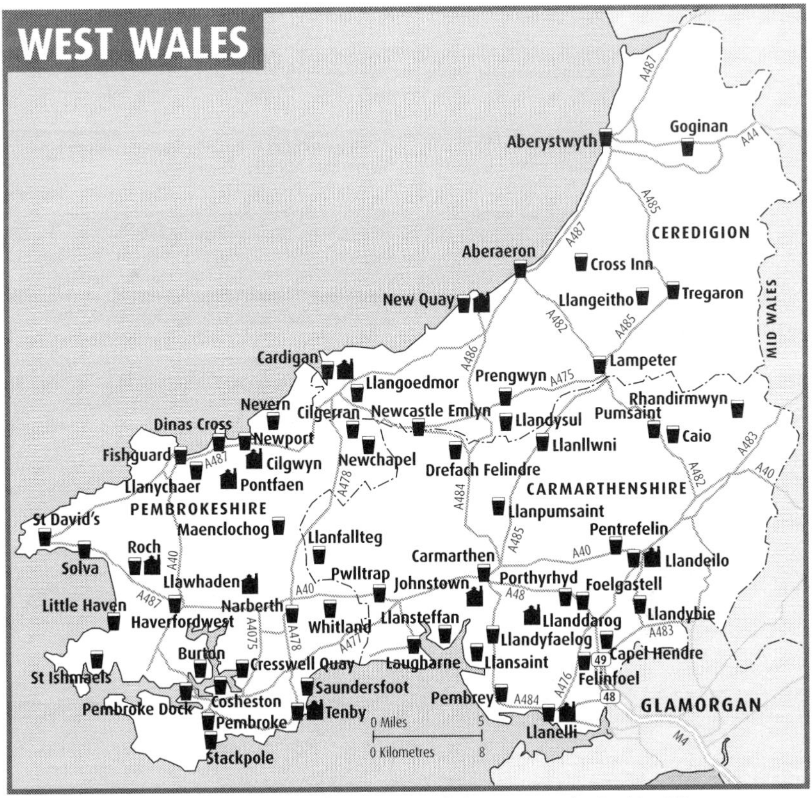

Authority areas covered: Carmarthenshire UA, Ceredigion UA, Pembrokeshire UA

Aberaeron

Cadwgan Inn

10 Market Street, SA46 0AU (off A487, overlooking harbour)
❂ 12 (5 Mon)-11; 12-midnight Fri & Sat; 12-5 Sun
☎ (01545) 570149
Hancocks HB; 2 changing beers (sourced nationally; often Bluestone, Evan Evans, Oakham) Ⓗ
Named after the last ship to be built in this attractive Regency town, this old-fashioned single-bar pub offers a friendly welcome and lively conversation. It is popular for its sports coverage, mainly rugby and racing. The guest beers are chosen from a wide range of small and regional breweries. Gwynt y Ddraig bottled ciders are available. There is a colourful hidden garden at the rear, and the small pavement drinking area at the front is a suntrap. Opposite is a free but busy harbourside public car park. ❀Ѧ🚌(T1,T5)🐾📶

Aberystwyth

Glengower Hotel 🄻 ✔

3 Victoria Terrace, SY23 2DH (on seafront at N end of promenade)
❂ 12-11 ☎ (01970) 626191 🌐 glengower.co.uk
Mantle Rock Steady; Wye Valley Butty Bach; 3 changing beers (sourced regionally; often Evan Evans, Harbwr, Purple Moose) Ⓗ
Excellent coastal views of Cardigan Bay can be enjoyed from the suntrap front terrace at this seafront hotel. The central front bar is the main drinking area, with a logburner for the winter months. There is also a quieter dining area and a large rear games room. An annual beer festival is held over the May bank holiday weekend. Food is locally sourced wherever possible. Up to five ciders come from Gwynt y Ddraig, plus regional guests.
Q🐴❀🛏◐Ѧ♣●🚌(03)🐾📶

Ship & Castle

1 High Street, SY23 1JG
❂ 2 (4 Mon)-midnight; 2-1am Fri & Sat ☎ 07773 778785
Wye Valley HPA, Butty Bach; 3 changing beers (sourced nationally; often Oakham, Salopian, Tiny Rebel) Ⓗ
Aberystwyth's flagship pub offers microbrewery guests from the UK and Ireland. Small amounts of excellent beer in other formats are also on offer including craft keg, bottles (eg Kernel, Tiny Rebel) and even cans, plus cider and perry from Gwynt y Ddraig. A five-pump platter of third-pint measures is available. Beer festivals in spring and autumn offer extended choice. The well-considered décor reflects the pub's name and history. The venue can be very busy on rugby days, but is welcoming at all times. Ѧ⥃♣●P🚌🐾📶

Burton

Jolly Sailor

SA73 1NX
❂ 11:30-3, 5 (6 winter)-11 ☎ (01646) 600378
🌐 jollysailorburton.co.uk
Brains Rev James; Draught Bass; Morland Old Speckled Hen Ⓗ

Overlooking the River Cleddau and in the shadow of the toll bridge that traverses it, there has been a public house here for over 150 years. It was from this point that travellers would come to Burton to cross by rowing boat to Pembroke Dock. They would leave their supply donkeys outside the Jolly Sailor until their return. The family- and food-oriented pub has a huge garden with a children's play area and an aviary. Winter opening times can vary – check ahead. ⏰❀◑P🖵(308)

Caio

Brunant Arms

Church Street, SA19 8RD (off A482 near Pumsaint Gold Mines)
🔆 closed Mon; 6-10 Tue; 12.30-3, 6-10 Wed; 12.30-10 Thu & Fri; 12.30-11 Sat; 12-3 Sun ☎ (01558) 650483
2 changing beers (sourced locally; often Evan Evans) 🅗
Friendly village pub on a historic drovers' route opposite an interesting church where a legendary Welsh wizard is buried. A hub for local societies and pool and darts teams, live music is hosted on occasion. The central bar serves a games room and seating areas divided by movable pews, warmed by a wood fire. One real ale is sold in winter, two in summer. Excellent food is served and the pub attracts caravanners, Caio Forest walkers and horse trekkers. Children's games and rare quoits can be played. Q⏰❀🛏◑▲♣●P🖵🤚

Capel Hendre

King's Head Hotel 🅛

Waterloo Road, SA18 3SF
🔆 4-11 Mon; 11-2.30, 5-midnight Tue-Sat; 11-3, 5-11 Sun
☎ (01269) 842377
Glamorgan Cwrw Gorslas/Bluestone Bitter, Jemimas Pitchfork; 2 changing beers (sourced regionally; often Bluestone) 🅗
A village pub tucked away just three miles from junction 49 of the M4, and a couple of miles from the former mining town of Ammanford. It has a main bar and dining room, with a sliding door leading to a separate snug. Outside there is a garden and a large car park. Two or sometimes three real ales are sourced from Wales, with Glamorgan, Bluestone and Neath breweries often represented. ⏰❀🛏◑🅶●P🖵(128,129)🤚🤚

Cardigan

Grosvenor

Bridge Street, SA43 1HY SN177459
🔆 11.30-11 ☎ (01239) 613792
Greene King Abbot; Sharp's Doom Bar; 1 changing beer (sourced nationally) 🅗
Situated on the edge of the town centre next to Cardigan Castle and the River Teifi, this large pub offers a good choice of ales, including a selection of bottled beers. The large open-plan bar/lounge provides various areas to relax, eat and drink, and there is an extra room upstairs for dining and functions. Good-value food is served lunchtimes and evenings every day. An outdoor patio area overlooks the river and the revamped quay. ⏰❀◑🅶♣●🤚🤚

Carmarthen

Coracle Tavern

1 Cambrian Place, SA31 1QG
🔆 12-11 Mon; 9am-11 Tue (midnight Wed-Sat); 12-11 Sun
☎ (01267) 468180
2 changing beers (sourced regionally; often Glamorgan, Mantle, Wye Valley) 🅗
In the centre of town, close to the main shopping area, this friendly free house offers a warm welcome to locals and visitors alike. Breakfast is served Tuesday to Saturday 9-11am. The large open-plan bar area has comfy sofas, and there is a separate restaurant upstairs. Darts is popular and a number of teams play here. ◑♣🖵

Friends Arms

Old St Clears Road, SA31 3HH
🔆 11-11 (midnight Fri & Sat) ☎ (01267) 234073
Mantle MOHO; Thornbridge Jaipur IPA; 2 changing beers (sourced locally; often Friends Arms) 🅗
Excellent hostelry half a mile from the town centre with a cosy and friendly atmosphere and a warm welcome, enhanced by two open fires. Popular with sports fans, it has Sky and BT Sports, plus darts. Four real ales are usually offered. The pub has its own microbrewery which regularly produces good beer. An outbuilding on two floors has function rooms for meetings and parties. Twice a local CAMRA Pub of the Year, the CAMRA branch meets here occasionally. ⏰❀●🖵🤚🤚

Queen's Hotel

10 Queen Street, SA31 1JR
🔆 10-10 (11 Thu-Sat); 11-7 Sun ☎ (01267) 231800
3 changing beers (sourced regionally; often Evan Evans, Glamorgan) 🅗
A busy town-centre pub near Carmarthenshire county hall with a bar and lounge. Locally sourced ales are always available. The public bar is popular with locals and has TV for sporting events. There is a patio area that nestles beneath the castle walls and is a suntrap during the summer months. The local CAMRA branch occasionally meets in the upstairs function room. ⏰❀🛲●🤚🤚

Yr Hen Dderwen ✅

47-48 King Street, SA31 1BH
🔆 8am-midnight (1am Sat) ☎ (01267) 242050
Greene King Abbot; Ruddles Best Bitter; 8 changing beers (sourced nationally; often Castlegate, Glamorgan, Kelham Island) 🅗
Named after the local legend of Merlin and an ancient oak which is depicted throughout the premises. Local Welsh ales are always available alongside a good selection of beers from around the world, including bottled and canned craft ale.

REAL ALE BREWERIES

Bluestone Cilgwyn
Caffle Llawhaden
Coles Family 🍺 Llanddarog
Evan Evans Llandeilo
Felinfoel Llanelli
Friends Arms 🍺 Johnstown
Gwaun Valley Pontfaen
Harbwr Tenby Tenby
Mantle Cardigan
Penlon Cottage New Quay
Seal Bay Cardigan
Tenby Tenby
Victoria Inn 🍺 Roch

There are international beer festivals in the spring and autumn and a cider festival in the summer. Meet the Brewer sessions feature throughout the year. Food is served all day. Q🐴◐♿🍎P🚌🐾📶

Cilgerran

Masons Arms

Cwnce, SA43 2SR

🕒 1 (4 Mon)-11; 12-11 Fri & Sat; 11-11 Sun ☎ 07989 990461

Hancocks HB; Sharp's Doom Bar; 1 changing beer (often Mantle) [H]

Also known as the Rampin, this venue was thought to have opened in 1836. It is a small, cosy and friendly village pub with an open fire (an old kitchen range). Many local characters can be found here and a great atmosphere awaits your visit. Three real ales are on offer, one changing regularly, usually from a local brewery. Various charity events are held during the year along with an occasional musical evening. Winter opening times may vary – check ahead. 🐴❀▲♣P🐾

Cosheston

Brewery Inn

SA72 4UD

🕒 closed Mon; 12-3, 6-11; 12-11 Sat; 12-6 Sun

☎ (01646) 686678 🌐 thebreweryinn.com

Brains Rev James; Coles Family Cwrw Blasus; 1 changing beer [H]

This Grade II-listed free house was once accommodation for monks, with its own brewhouse in outbuildings behind (brewing ceased in 1889). The light and airy stone-built inn has a traditional slate floor and beamed ceiling. To one side is a cosy area for drinkers to enjoy a chat in front of the log fire. Ingredients for the extensive menu are sourced locally, including fresh fish. The pub has a solid reputation for good food and ales. Q🐴❀🛏◐♿▲🍎P🚉🐾📶

Cresswell Quay

Cresselly Arms [L]

SA68 0TE

🕒 12-11 ☎ (01646) 651210

Sharp's Doom Bar [H]**; Worthington's Bitter** [G]**; house beer (by Caffle); 2 changing beers (sourced locally; often Bluestone, Mantle)** [H]

Situated on the Cresswell River, this 250-year-old ivy-covered hostelry is a throwback to the Victorian age. The homely farm kitchen interior, where a roaring fire burns in the hearth, is a haven for locals and visitors alike. Accessible by boat from the Milford Haven estuary at high tide, the pub also lies on a series of interesting walking routes. The house beer from Caffle is complemented by Worthington's Bitter dispensed from the barrel by jug. Q🐴❀♿▲🍎P🚌(361)

Cross Inn

Rhos yr Hafod Inn [L]

SY23 5NB (at B4337/B4577 crossroads)

🕒 5-11; closed Sun & Mon ☎ (01974) 272644

2 changing beers (sourced regionally; often Bluestone, Evan Evans, Mantle) [H]

This friendly, family-run pub offers an ever-changing range of guest ales and a warm welcome. A choice of drinking areas includes the front bar, popular in the early evening with lively locals, and the comfortable rear bar. Sunny days can be enjoyed in the roadside drinking area or in the large rear garden. A traditional turntable and vinyl collection are available for customers to peruse. There is ample parking both sides of the pub. Varied events are held throughout the year. CAMRA branch Pub of the Year 2018. 🐴❀♣P📶

Dinas Cross

Freemasons Arms

Spencer Buildings, SA42 0UW (on A487 coast road midway between Fishguard and Newport)

🕒 12-2.30 (not Mon), 4-11; 12-midnight Fri & Sat; 12-11 Sun

☎ (01348) 811674

Gower Gold; 1 changing beer (often Coles Family) [H]

Traditional sea captains' meeting place in the Pembrokeshire Coast National Park. This pub is conveniently placed for those who like to visit attractive beaches, walk the coastal path or enjoy sailing. It also has the advantage of being on a main bus route. Tastefully refurbished while retaining its original character, the main bar with a cosy open fire has a dining area at the side. Please check winter opening times before venturing forth. Q🐴❀◐♿▲♣P🚌(T5)🐾📶

Drefach Felindre

John Y Gwas

SA44 5XG SN354383

🕒 5-11; 4-midnight Fri; 12-midnight Sat; 12-11 Sun

☎ (01559) 370469

2 changing beers (sourced nationally; often Brains, Courage, Marston's) [H]

Early 19th-century village tavern with a striking yellow and black livery, attracting locals and tourists alike with snugs, a wood-burning stove, quality beer and cider, and a warm welcome, especially for dogs. Two ales are generally offered, alongside a wide variety of bottled beers and ciders. A beer festival, showcasing more than 10 different ales, is held over the August bank holiday weekend. 🐴❀◑♣🍎P🚌(460)🐾📶

Red Lion

SA44 5UH (1 mile off A484 Llandysul to Newcastle Emlyn road) SN354388

🕒 4-11 (midnight Fri & Sat); 12-10 Sun ☎ (01559) 371677

Draught Bass; Mantle Cwrw Teifi; 1 changing beer (sourced nationally) [H]

Located in this small village near the National Wool Museum, a warm welcome is assured at this 19th-century pub, which has been renovated in recent years. It is mostly open plan but with a separate dining room and a large outside drinking area. Community focused, it hosts regular fundraising events for charity. The car park is small but there is on-street parking. The original tiled entrance porch is worthy of note. Q🐴❀◐♿♣P🚌(460)📶

Felinfoel

White Lion Inn

Parkview, SA14 8BH (on main A476)

🕒 closed Mon; 12-11 ☎ (01554) 776644

Gower Gold; 4 changing beers (sourced nationally) [H]

A family-friendly split-level hostelry with defined drinking and dining spaces as well as a function room. There are covered and open drinking areas outside. A selection of well-kept real ales is available, and a good-value carvery. Quiz nights

are Sunday and Wednesday. National cycle and walking paths to the Swiss Valley and beyond are nearby. There is ample parking on the roadside.
P

Fishguard

Royal Oak Inn

Market Square, SA65 9HA
11-11 (01348) 218632
Brains Rev James; Glamorgan Jemimas Pitchfork; 1 changing beer (sourced locally; often Bluestone) H
This Grade II-listed building is famous for its place in history – a French invasion attempt on the west coast of Wales in 1797 was thwarted by locals in the Battle of Fishguard; this was known as the last invasion attempt on Britain. A peace treaty was signed between the British and the French in the Royal Oak's bar area. The interior is sparingly decorated with exposed stone and wooden beams, but with little reference to its historic past.
Q

Foelgastell

Smiths Arms

Heol y Foel, SA14 7EL
12-11 (11.30 Fri & Sat) (01269) 842213
thesmithsarms.co.uk
2 changing beers (sourced nationally; often Cottage, Marston's, Rhymney) H/G
A friendly locals' pub which also provides a handy stopping-off point for travellers on the A48, as well as visitors to the nearby National Botanic Garden of Wales. Open all day from midday, with food service lunchtimes and evenings except Sunday evening, there is a choice of bar or restaurant menus. The beer selection varies but usually includes one or two real ales from local and national breweries. Real cider is often available.
P (166)

Goginan

Druid Inn L

SY23 3NT (on A44 6 miles E of Aberystwyth)
12-midnight (1am Fri & Sat) (01970) 880650
Mantle MOHO; Wye Valley Bitter; 3 changing beers (sourced nationally; often Purple Moose, Tenby, Wood) H
A welcoming pub celebrating its 45th year in the Guide. The dining room and pool room flank an L-shaped main bar where dogs are welcome. Up to four real ales and four ciders are served, plus interesting bottles and craft beers on draught. Occasional music nights (sometimes with acts of more than local renown) and beer festivals are hosted. Food is popular and high quality. Buses run until early evening Monday to Saturday. A pub-owned B&B can be found next door. Wales CAMRA Pub of the Year 2017.
P (525,X47)

Haverfordwest

Pembroke Yeoman

11 Hill Street, SA61 1QQ
11-11 (01437) 762500
Draught Bass; 2 changing beers (sourced nationally) H
A little off the beaten track, conversation rules at this recently refurbished local pub, though there is a well-stocked jukebox should it flag. Guest ales come from small breweries and change often. Food is served in generous portions on special themed evenings. Known as the Upper Three Crowns until the 1960s, the pub's name was changed in recognition of the local yeomanry headquarters nearby. Q (301)

William Owen L

6 Quay Street, SA61 1BG
8am-midnight (1am Fri & Sat) (01437) 771900
Greene King IPA, Abbot; Sharp's Doom Bar; 5 changing beers (sourced regionally; often Bluestone, Boss, Caffle) H
Pembrokeshire's first and only Wetherspoon pub occupies a handsome 19th-century building, formerly a shop, hotel and restaurant, with a spacious extension to the rear. It was reputedly built in 1856 for Joseph Thomas, a corn and manure merchant, by local architect William Owen. It has also been a saddler's and more recently the Wilton House Hotel. Beer from one of the county's breweries is regularly available. The pub offers the chain's standard menu and promotional deals, and opens from 8am for breakfast.
Q

Lampeter

Nag's Head

14 Bridge Street, SA48 7HG
11-1.30am (2.30am Thu-Sat) (01570) 218517
2 changing beers H
This town-centre pub has recently been refurbished, and has a modern and bright horseshoe-shaped bar area. Friendly and fun, it attracts a good mix of customers – locals, students and tourists. Most live sports events are screened, and live music often features. It also offers B&B, evening and lunchtime meals, and a function room.

Royal Oak Hotel

38 High Street, SA48 7BB
9am-11 (1am Fri); 9am-midnight Sat (01570) 218615
2 changing beers (sourced nationally; often Sharp's) H
This is a new addition to the local CAMRA branch's choice of real ale pubs. Records of the building as a hotel pre-date 1800; originally the hotel only occupied the part to the right-hand side of the archway, but expanded to include the restaurant, now known as the Stables. The interior was refurbished in November 2018.

Laugharne

New Three Mariners Inn L

Victoria Street, SA33 4SE
3-11 (midnight Fri); 12-1am Sat; 6-11 Sun
(01994) 427426 newthreemarinersinn.co.uk
1 changing beer (often Evan Evans)
The building is in the centre of this historic town and only yards from its early 11th-century castle. Dylan Thomas lived in Laugharne for a number of years and he and his wife Caitlin are laid to rest in the graveyard of St Martin's Church. The pub moved to its current site when the original ale house opposite was converted to a carpentry shop. Popular with locals, it serves evening meals and hosts a weekly quiz night. P

Little Haven

Saint Brides Inn L
St Brides Road, SA62 3UN
11-midnight ☎ (01437) 781266 saintbridesinn.co.uk
Brains Rev James; Hancocks HB; 2 changing beers (sourced regionally; often Brains) H
Little Haven is a quaint old fishing village in a conservation area of the Pembrokeshire Coast National Park. This family-run pub in the centre of the village is open all year round, selling a range of Welsh, often local, Pembrokeshire ales. It is noted for the ancient well in the cellar. The attractive interior includes a separate dining area, and there are heaters on the patio in the pretty suntrap garden for outdoor drinking.
QAP (311,400)

Llandeilo

Salutation Inn
33 New Road, SA19 6DF
12-11 (10.30 Sun) ☎ (01558) 824255
Gower Gold; Sharp's Atlantic; Timothy Taylor Landlord; 2 changing beers (sourced nationally; often Mantle) H
A locals' pub near the town centre. The landlord is a cask beer enthusiast and friendly staff dispense five rapidly changing ales. The interior is divided into two areas, with a pool table on one side and a wood fire on the other. Live music often features at weekends. There is a garden and function area to the rear. The pub hosts a beer festival in the summer.

White Horse
Rhosmaen Street, SA19 6EN
11-11; 12-10.30 Sun ☎ (01558) 822424
Evan Evans Best Bitter, Cwrw, Warrior; 2 changing beers H
Grade II-listed coaching inn dating from the 16th century. The tap for the local Evan Evans Brewery, this multi-roomed hostelry is popular with all ages. There is a small outdoor drinking area to the front and a large council car park to the rear with access to the pub down a short flight of steps. A covered area is available for smokers with its own TV showing sport. A former local CAMRA Pub of the Year winner. (103,X13)

Llandybie

Ivy Bush
18 Church Street, SA18 3HZ (100yds from church)
12-11 Mon; 12-midnight Tue-Fri; 11-midnight Sat & Sun
☎ (01269) 850272
Timothy Taylor Landlord; 1 changing beer (sourced regionally; often Exmoor) H
This friendly local pub, modernised several years ago, has a single bar with two comfortable seating areas. Games and quizzes are held weekly and a large-screen TV shows sport. Timothy Taylor Landlord is usually joined by at least one regularly changing guest beer. The local birdwatching group holds its meetings here. The railway station nearby is on the scenic Heart of Wales line.
P (103,X13)

Red Lion Hotel
6 Llandeilo Road, SA18 3JA (near railway station)
12-3, 6-11; 12-11 Sat; 12-8 Sun ☎ (01269) 851202
redlionllandybie.com
2 changing beers (sourced regionally; often Gower, Timothy Taylor) H
Former coaching inn dating back to 1786 in parts, with an old painted coat of arms on display inside the main front door. The family-run pub serves food and quality beers in a convivial atmosphere. There is a comfortable enclosed seating area for drinking, and food is served in separate dining areas. Outside, there are benches in the garden. Handy for the railway station on the popular Heart of Wales line. P

Llandyfaelog

Red Lion
SA17 5PP (300yds off A484)
11-midnight ☎ (01267) 267530
redlionllandyfaelog.co.uk
3 changing beers (sourced regionally; often Butcombe, Evan Evans, Glamorgan) H
This family-run village hostelry can truly be described as at the heart of the community. It has a separate annexe staging concerts and functions for the surrounding area, and hosts the local choir practice evenings. The large public bar, with darts and a pool table, is complemented by a restaurant and a family room. Food is served in the bar and restaurant. Q (198,X12)

Llandysul

Porth Hotel
Church Street, SA44 4QS SN418407
12-11 (5.30 Sun) ☎ (01559) 362202 porthhotel.co.uk
2 changing beers (sourced locally) H
Set on the banks of the River Teifi, this 17th-century coaching inn is now a family-run village hotel with a bar, restaurant and function room. The public rooms still retain the original oak beams and panels. Food and drink is sourced locally, where possible. At the rear of the hotel is a car park and lawned garden beside the river, with access to walks and fishing. P

Llanelli

Stradey Arms
1 Stradey Road, SA15 4ET
12-11 (midnight Fri & Sat); 12-10.30 Sun
☎ (01554) 753332
Brains Bitter, SA, Rev James; 1 changing beer (sourced nationally) H
A busy Brains pub situated on the outskirts of the town, with a comfortable bar and separate restaurant. Real ale is available on up to four handpumps in the bar. A varied menu of freshly prepared food is served all day except on Sunday when there is a lunchtime carvery. Friendly and welcoming staff add to the pleasant ambience in this pub. It is a popular venue for sporting events, especially rugby internationals.
P

Llanfallteg

Plash
SA34 0UN (off A40 at Llanddewi Velfrey)
12 (4 Mon & Tue)-11; 3-9 Sun ☎ (01437) 563472
theplashinn.co.uk
Wye Valley Butty Bach; 2 changing beers H
At the centre of village life, this terrace-style cottage pub has been an inn for more than 180

years, and has featured in this Guide for more than 10 continuous years. It holds a quiz night on Tuesday, a regular monthly folk night and other special nights. The guest beers are usually from small, independent breweries. Home-made food using locally sourced ingredients is available on Wednesday, Friday and Saturday. An accessible entrance is to the rear. A former local CAMRA Pub of the Year. Q P

Llangeitho

Three Horseshoe

SY25 6TW

5.30-11; 12-2 Sun ☎ (01974) 821244

2 changing beers (sourced regionally; often Evan Evans, Ludlow, Mantle) [H]

A traditional, family-run pub in an historic village. It has a main bar, dining area, function room and sunny outside seating. The friendly landlord is a keen supporter of real ale and offers a constantly changing range, with up to three real ales and two or three bag-in-box ciders from Welsh producers including Gethins and Marcherman. Excellent-value, home-cooked meals are served, with a popular special offer menu on Wednesday. Pool and darts are played, and there is a big screen for sporting events. Live music is hosted, and an annual beer and music festival.
P (585)

Llangoedmor

Penllwyndu

SA43 2LY (on B4570 4½ miles from Cardigan) SN240458

12 (3 Mon)-11; 11-11 Sat & Sun ☎ (01239) 682533

Hancocks HB; 2 changing beers (sourced regionally; often Brains) [H]

Old-fashioned ale house standing at an isolated crossroads where Cardigan's evildoers were once hanged – the pub sign is worthy of close inspection. The cheerful and welcoming public bar retains its quaintness, with a slate floor and inglenook with wood-burning stove. Good home-cooked food including traditional favourites is available all day in the bar and the separate restaurant. Free live music plays on the third Thursday evening of the month. P

Llanllwni

Talardd Arms

SA39 9DX SN487392

6-10 Mon; 6-11 Tue & Wed; 12-2.30, 6-11 Thu-Sun

☎ (01559) 395633 talardd.co.uk

1 changing beer (sourced regionally) [H]

There are records of this old inn dating back to 1626, when drovers would stop for refreshments for man and beast before driving their livestock over Llanllwni Mountain on their way to markets over the border. Now sympathetically modernised, Tafarn y Talardd continues to offer a traditional warm and friendly welcome. Live music, quizzes and film nights are organised most Mondays.
P

Llanpumsaint

Railway Inn

SA33 6BU (by old railway bridge on main road through village)

4-11; 12-11 Sat & Sun ☎ (01267) 253643

2 changing beers (sourced nationally; often Brains, Mantle, Wye Valley) [H]

The Railway is at the centre of the village next to the former railway line. Now fully refurbished, it is a thriving hub for villagers and visitors alike. The warm and friendly little pub has a cosy interior with comfortable sofas, decorated with old railway memorabilia. It comes highly recommended for home cooking using local Welsh ingredients, and offers a great selection of home-made desserts. Food is served each evening except Sunday, with lunches on Saturday and Sunday.
P (215)

Llansaint

King's Arms

13 Maes yr Eglwys, SA17 5JE

closed Mon; 6-11; 12-11 Sat; 12-6.30 Sun

☎ (01267) 267487

Glamorgan Cwrw Gorslas/Bluestone Bitter, Jemimas Pitchfork; Young's Special [H]

A former local CAMRA Pub of the Year, this friendly village hostelry has been a pub for more than 200 years. Situated near an 11th-century church, it is reputedly built from stone recovered from the lost village of St Ishmaels. There is live music every Thursday and a TV/big screen for major sporting events. Good-value home-cooked food is served (book ahead, especially Sunday). Carmarthen Bay Holiday Park is a few miles away.
P (198)

Llansteffan

Castle Inn

The Square, SA33 5JG

12 (5 Wed)-11; 12-midnight Fri & Sat; 12-10.30 Sun

☎ (01267) 241225 thecastleinnpub.com

Sharp's Doom Bar; house beer (by Evan Evans); 2 changing beers (often Castlegate, Evan Evans) [H]

The Castle is a traditional inn committed to real ale, with a welcoming atmosphere and friendly staff. The interior has been completely redecorated and the toilets renovated. It has an open-plan layout but also plenty of cosy corners for customers to relax and unwind in relative peace and quiet. The pub hosts a number of local community groups, and provides bar snacks from an uncomplicated menu. There is an outside seating area overlooking the village square where locals and tourists mingle.
Q (227)

Llanychaer

Bridge End Inn

SA65 9TB (on B4313, 2 miles SW of Fishguard)

4-9 Mon & Tue; 12-11 ☎ (01348) 872545

Mantle Rock Steady, Cwrw Teifi, Dark Heart [H]**; 1 changing beer (sourced locally; often Bluestone, Evan Evans)** [H]/[G]

Known locally as the Bont, this friendly country pub, over 150 years old, nestles in the beautiful Gwaun Valley at a bridging point across the river. The cosy bars with log fires serve mainly local real ales. The dining room is housed in the smithy, once run as a complementary business to the inn, and features an external water wheel. Home-made food includes popular Sunday lunches. Check ahead for winter hours and food service.
Q (345)

Maenclochog

Globe Inn

SA66 7LE

4-11; 12-11 Sat; 7-10 Sun ☎ (01437) 532269

1 changing beer (sourced regionally) H

In the 19th century, Maenclochog was an important trading centre for slate from nearby quarries, and held a monthly livestock market – because of this trade there were once 19 public houses in the village. The Globe, run by the same family for over 150 years, is now the only survivor, and has become the social centre for villages in the surrounding area. P

Narberth

Eagle Inn

Water Street, SA67 7AT

12-11 ☎ (01834) 860769

1 changing beer (sourced nationally; often Bluestone) H

An unpretentious pub tucked away at the end of Water Street behind the Old Town Hall, offering something for everyone. Fairly basic, with wooden floors and exposed beams, it does not take many to fill the bar. Open mic nights and live bands draw a crowd at the weekend. Outside is a heated smoking area. No food is served except during sporting events. Please check opening times before visiting. (381)

Nevern

Trewern Arms

SA42 0NB (off A487, 2 miles N of Newport)

11-11 ☎ (01239) 820395 trewernarms.com

3 changing beers (sourced nationally; often Bluestone, Harbwr, Mantle) H

A picturesque 16th-century pub deep within a secluded valley astride the banks of the River Nevern. The village of Nevern is less than a mile from the beautiful fishing town of Newport. This multi-roomed pub caters for all, from those who just want a drink to large parties and wedding receptions. A great place to stay to experience some of the best walks in West Wales. Q P (T5)

New Quay

Black Lion L

Glanmor Terrace, SA45 9PT

12-11 ☎ (01545) 560122 blacklionnewquay.co.uk

Mantle MOHO; 2 changing beers (sourced locally; often Gower, Sharp's) H

Perched atop a steep street, this striking pub has Dylan Thomas connections. Refurbished in a contemporary style, it has separate dining areas and a main bar that gets busy when big games are screened on TV. The large garden has a play area and stunning sea views (dogs welcome in the garden). Mantle's MOHO is joined by another Welsh ale in busier months, and bottled cider comes from Gwynt y Ddraig. Excellent food is served. Live music is hosted during New Quay's August festival.

Newcastle Emlyn

Bunch of Grapes

Bridge Street, SA38 9DU

11-midnight (2am Fri & Sat); 10-10 Sun

☎ (01239) 711185 bunchofgrapes.net

2 changing beers H

The Bunch of Grapes dates back to the 17th century. The Grade II*-listed building is reputed to have been built from the ruins of the nearby 13th-century castle. Set in the heart of the community, the pub offers a warm and welcoming place to eat, drink and relax. The enclosed rear garden is complete with a children's play area and a covered smoking shelter. P (460)

Newchapel

Ffynnone Arms L

SA37 0EH

5-11; 1-1am Sat; 12-11 Sun ☎ (01239) 841800

ffynnonearms.co.uk

Hancocks HB; Wye Valley Butty Bach; 1 changing beer (sourced locally; often Mantle) H

This charming traditional 18th-century pub has been attractively refurbished. Local ales are often available alongside the regional and national beers. Welsh cider Gwynt y Ddraig is also sold. The landlady prides herself on good food using locally sourced ingredients where possible, with gluten-free, dairy-free and sugar-free options. Fish and chips night is Wednesday, on Sunday there is a carvery. The Ffynnone Arms sits on the borders of three counties – Pembrokeshire, Carmarthenshire and Ceredigion. Welsh and English are spoken. Q P

Newport

Royal Oak

West Street, SA42 0TA

11-midnight ☎ (01239) 820632

theroyaloaknewport.co.uk

Felinfoel Best Bitter; Gower Gold; 1 changing beer (sourced nationally) H

A warm welcome awaits you at the Royal Oak, a traditional Welsh country pub which retains all the charm and atmosphere of its roots, with oak beams, a tiled bar area and many original features. As well as the quality real ales, the pub is renowned for its Sunday roasts, curries and fish and chips. A pensioners' lunch is served on Tuesday. Q P

Pembrey

Ship Aground Inn

Ashburnham Road, SA16 0TL (on B4311 between Pembrey and Burry Port)

closed Mon & Tue; 12-11 Wed & Thu (midnight Fri & Sat); 12-10 Sun ☎ (01554) 835724

4 changing beers (often Sharp's, Tiny Rebel) H

Refurbished pub with the provision of real ale being a cornerstone of the premises. Four changing beers are served alongside a wide range of locally sourced home-cooked meals. A warm welcome is offered by this friendly husband and wife team. Popular with locals and visitors alike, there is an open-plan bar area with a separate restaurant space. P

Pembroke

Old King's Arms L

Main Street, SA71 4JS

11-11 ☎ (01646) 683611 oldkingsarmshotel.co.uk

Felinfoel Double Dragon; Marston's Old Empire; 2 changing beers (sourced locally; often Bluestone, Evan Evans) H
This former coaching inn is allegedly the oldest inn in Pembroke, dating from around 1520. The hotel's Kings Bar is a small room with exposed stone walls, beams and a real fire. It has four handpumps serving local, regional and national beers. There is a separate lounge with a dining area, and a restaurant with room for larger groups. Locally sourced meat and fish products feature on the menu. Q ☕ 🏠 🚪 ◑ 🕑 ♿ P 🚃 🐾 📶

Pembroke Dock

First & Last
London Road, SA72 6TX (on A477)
🕐 10-1am (1.30am Thu-Sat) ☎ (01646) 682687
Brains Rev James; Worthington's White Shield; 1 changing beer (sourced nationally; often Skinner's) H
Friendly single-bar local pub run by the same family for more than 50 years. Formerly the Commercial, it acquired its more distinctive name in 1991 to reflect its edge-of-town location. The walls display an eclectic mix of photos and prints. The food is good pub fare. There is a popular quirky Sunday evening quiz. It is handy for the Cleddau Bridge, giving easy access to Haverfordwest, and close to the historic naval dockyard and Irish Ferries. Q ☕ 🏠 ◑ ◑ ≈ P 🚃 📶

Red Rose Inn
113 High Street, SA72 6PA
🕐 4-11; 12-1am Fri & Sat; 12-11 Sun ☎ (01646) 622919
Brains Rev James; 1 changing beer (often Butcombe) H
A small locals' pub on the south-east limits of Pembroke Dock near the fire station. A converted cottage in a predominantly residential area, this pub could be quite easily be passed by, but is worth a visit. Exposed beams add to the character and atmosphere. Some unusual beers, sometimes German, are occasionally on draught. Real cider is available at times. Simple food is served when live sport is on TV. The pub can be busy at weekends when live music plays. 🏠 ▲ ≈ 🚃

Pentrefelin

Cottage Inn
SA19 6SD (on A40, 3 miles W of Llandeilo)
🕐 10.30-11 ☎ (01558) 824645 ⊕ cottageinnbandb.co.uk
3 changing beers (sourced regionally; often Glamorgan) H
A popular family-run community pub dating back to the 1850s, it was formerly a coaching inn and drovers' hostelry. Sky TV is screened and the pub gets busy during major sporting events. It has a separate restaurant/function room area. At the rear is a covered smoking area and outside a large car park with caravanning and camping space. Beer festivals are held the last week of January and over the August bank holiday weekend. Q ☕ 🏠 🚪 ◑ 🕑 ♿ ▲ P 🚃 🐾 📶

Porthyrhyd

Mansel Arms 🍷 ✓
Banc y Mansel, SA32 8BS (on B4310 between Porthyrhyd and Drefach)
🕐 3-11 (midnight Sat); 12-8 Sun ☎ (01267) 275305

3 changing beers (sourced regionally; often Courage, Glamorgan, Young's) H/G
Friendly 18th-century former coaching inn with wood fires in each room. The original limestone flags have been broken up and used in the fireplace, and low beams have been added to create atmosphere, with numerous jugs hanging from them. There is a saloon bar and separate restaurant serving home-cooked food. The landlord is keen to promote real ale and encourages customers to experience a variety of flavours. Two cask ales are on handpump, with another on gravity towards the weekend. Q ☕ ◑ 🕑 ♿ P 🚃 (129) 🐾 📶

Prengwyn

Gwarcefel Arms
SA44 4LU (on A475/B4476 crossroads) SN424442
🕐 4-midnight; 12-midnight Sat & Sun ☎ (01559) 363126
Sharp's Doom Bar; 1 changing beer (sourced nationally) H
A traditional country inn with a friendly atmosphere where everyone is welcome, including families and dogs. Situated at the junction of five roads in Prengwyn, three miles north of Llandysul, the pub has a main bar with a wood-burning stove, cosy seating, a pool table and a dartboard. A separate restaurant area, which caters for functions and parties, offers evening meals and Sunday lunches. The beer garden and large car park are to the rear. ☕ 🏠 ◑ ♣ P 🐾

Pumsaint

Dolaucothi Arms
SA19 8UW (on A482 midway between Llanwrda and Lampeter)
🕐 closed Mon; 12 (5 Tue)-11; 12-8 Sun ☎ (01558) 650237
2 changing beers (sourced regionally; often Evan Evans, Purple Moose, Wye Valley) H
A friendly welcome is assured at this substantial stone-built inn, owned by the National Trust and tastefully restored in traditional style. Real cider and real ales are offered, usually two beers sourced from Welsh breweries. The excellent food menu features seasonal ingredients. The National Trust's Dolaucothi Gold Mines are well worth visiting nearby. Opening times may vary so it is advisable to check ahead before travelling. ☕ 🏠 🚪 ◑ 🕑 ♿ ▲ ♣ 🕑 P 🚃 🐾 📶

Pwlltrap

White Lion
SA33 4AT
🕐 10.30-11; 11-10.30 Sun ☎ (01994) 230370
Courage Directors; Greene King Abbot; Shepherd Neame Bishops Finger; Young's Bitter; 1 changing beer (sourced locally) H
This roadside pub, just outside St Clears on the road to Whitland, is warm and welcoming with a real fire in winter. It has an old-world charm with oak beams and panelled walls, and boasts a large restaurant serving good food. Pool and darts are played and a large-screen TV shows regular sporting fixtures. The pub organises a range of events throughout the year. Two cask beers are available in winter, four in summer. Q ◑ 🕑 ♿ ♣ P 🚃 (224,322) 🐾 📶

WALES

Rhandirmwyn

Royal Oak

SA20 0NY
closed Mon; 12-2, 6-11; 12-2 Sun (01550) 760201
theroyaloakinn.co.uk
3 changing beers (sourced nationally)
Remote stone-flagged inn with excellent views of the Towy Valley and close to an RSPB bird sanctuary. Originally built as a hunting lodge for the local landowner, it is now a focal point for community activities and popular with fans of outdoor pursuits. The village shop is alongside. Two or three guest beers are offered and the good wholesome food is recommended. There are panoramic views from the beer garden at the side of the pub. Five times local CAMRA Pub of the Year. **Q P**

Roch

Victoria Inn

SA62 6AW (on A487)
11.30-11 (01437) 710426 thevictoriainnroch.com
Victoria Inn NewgAle, Fine & Dandy; 1 changing beer (sourced locally; often Victoria Inn)
A little gem with views across St Brides Bay, this locals' pub offers a warm welcome. The inn was established in 1851, although parts are older, and it has retained much of its old-world charm, with beamed ceilings and low doorways. Food is available every day except Monday. Curry and a pint night is Friday. The real ales are produced in the pub's on-site microbrewery. For those in a hurry there is a beer carry-out service. Live music features occasionally. **Q P** (411)

St David's

Farmers Arms

14-16 Goat Street, SA62 6RF
11-midnight (01437) 721666 farmersstdavids.co.uk
Brains Rev James; Felinfoel Double Dragon; house beer (by Hancocks); 2 changing beers (sourced nationally; often Evan Evans, Sharp's, Wychwood)
A traditional city pub with three rooms – the top bar, mainly for dining, the smaller Coxswains room, which is the social meeting place for the St David's lifeboat crew, and the Glue Pot bar, where the locals tend to gather around the fire. Outside, the patio offers views of the cathedral and has a seasonal bar. Winter opening times vary so please check before you visit. **Q**

St Ishmaels

Brook Inn

Brookside, SA62 3TE
12-11 (1am Fri & Sat) (01646) 636277
brookinnpembs.co.uk
3 changing beers (often Purple Moose, Tetley, Wadworth)
Located in the centre of St Ishmaels on the National Trails Pembrokeshire Coast Path, the Brook has been at the heart of the community since the 1880s. Previously brewery-owned, it became a free house when it was purchased by the current owner in 2014. Recently refurbished, stone-flagged floors and exposed brick walls help to create a cosy and comfortable atmosphere. It is reputedly haunted by Gladys and Tom, who may or may not pull you a pint! **P** (315)

Saundersfoot

Royal Oak Inn

Wogan Terrace, SA69 9HA
10-11 (01834) 812546
theroyaloaksaundersfoot.co.uk
Courage Best Bitter; Sharp's Doom Bar; 3 changing beers (sourced nationally; often Courage, Mantle)
An old pub and restaurant in the centre of town offering a wide selection of real ales. On entering the pub, to the right is a cosy drinkers' bar where locals and visitors are made welcome. To the left is another bar and a further dedicated restaurant with an extensive menu. Food is available throughout the day during the summer. At the front is a heated terrace with harbour views. (381)

Solva

Royal George

13 High Street, SA62 6TF
3-11; 2-11 Fri; 11.30-11 Sat & Sun (01437) 720002
theroyalgeorgesolva.co.uk
Marston's Pedigree; Ringwood Boondoggle
Set on the main road to St David's in Upper Solva, this friendly, imposing community pub commands stunning views over St Brides Bay. The one-roomed bar has a busy, homely feel with rugby memorabilia on the walls. The furniture is both rustic and eclectic which adds to the ambience. In winter a guest beer is only available on big occasions. A beer festival is held at least once a year. Chinese food is cooked to order, 12-9.30pm weekends. **P** (411)

Stackpole

Stackpole Inn

Jasons Corner, SA71 5DF (on B4319)
12-3, 6-11; 12-11 Sat; 12-4 Sun (01646) 672324
stackpoleinn.co.uk
Brains Rev James; Felinfoel Best Bitter, Double Dragon; 1 changing beer (sourced regionally; often Mantle)
Set just three miles south of the historic town of Pembroke, this is a multi award-winning pub in the Pembrokeshire Coast National Park. The Stackpole has a restaurant that focuses on local seafood dishes, and offers superb B&B accommodation. It is a short walk to the beautiful Pembrokeshire Coast Path and when visiting you can also explore the Stackpole Estate, the amazing Barafundle Bay and Broad Haven beach. **P**

Tenby

Buccaneer Inn

St Julian Street, SA70 7AS
11-12.30am (11 Sun) (01834) 842273
Harbwr MV Enterprise, Caldey Lollipop, RFA Sir Galahad; 1 changing beer (sourced locally; often Harbwr)
The Buccaneer is in quaint St Julian Street which links the town square to the harbour and beaches. The bar area is large but has a cosy feel with beams, stove and Tenby memorabilia adorning the walls. A sunny walled beer garden is to the rear. The pub is the brewery tap for the adjacent Tenby Harbour Brewery, showcasing its full range of beers. Food is served all day with locally sourced produce including fresh fish on the menu.

Hope & Anchor

St Julian Street, SA70 7AS

11-midnight (10.30 Sun) (01834) 842131

Felinfoel Double Dragon; Harbwr MV Enterprise, North Star, Caldey Lollipop; Sharp's Atlantic; 2 changing beers (sourced nationally; often Bluestone, Mantle)

Set in the old town on the way down to the harbour, this welcoming pub offers four guest beers and ciders. Food is important and specials supplement the standard menu. The convivial atmosphere and interesting local decor make it an excellent place to relax over a beer. Beers are sourced mainly from Welsh breweries including Evan Evans, Mantle and Purple Moose, while Wye Valley sometimes sneaks over the border. Ciders include Westons Old Rosie and Somerset Tree Shaker West Country Cider.

Tregaron

Talbot

The Square, SY25 6JL

11-11 (10.30 Sun) (01974) 298208 ytalbot.com

3 changing beers (sourced regionally; often Evan Evans, Ludlow, Mantle)

A former drovers' inn of immense character in an unspoilt town on the edge of the Cambrian Mountains. It has a cosy front bar with a real fire, a beamed and flagstoned snug with an inglenook fireplace, a rear bar with TV and a contemporary restaurant. Two real ales are available in winter, three in summer, and three real ciders. Quality food includes locally reared meat and tempting desserts. The beautiful landscaped rear garden has fine views and a memorial to a circus elephant reputedly buried here.

Q P (585,588)

Whitland

Station House Hotel

St Johns Street, SA34 0AP

9am-1am (2am Fri & Sat); 10-midnight Sun

(01994) 240556 stationhousewhitland.co.uk

Courage Directors; 2 changing beers (often Sharp's, Wye Valley)

A smile and a warm welcome are always on tap at this friendly hostelry. Very much a locals' pub for all ages, there is something for everyone here, with pool and darts teams and bingo on Sunday evening. A small room is available for people looking for a quiet corner. The outside drinking area is partly under cover. Car parking is to the rear and the railway station is close by.

P

Ship & Castle, Aberystwyth (Photo: Reading Tom/Flickr CC BY 2.0)

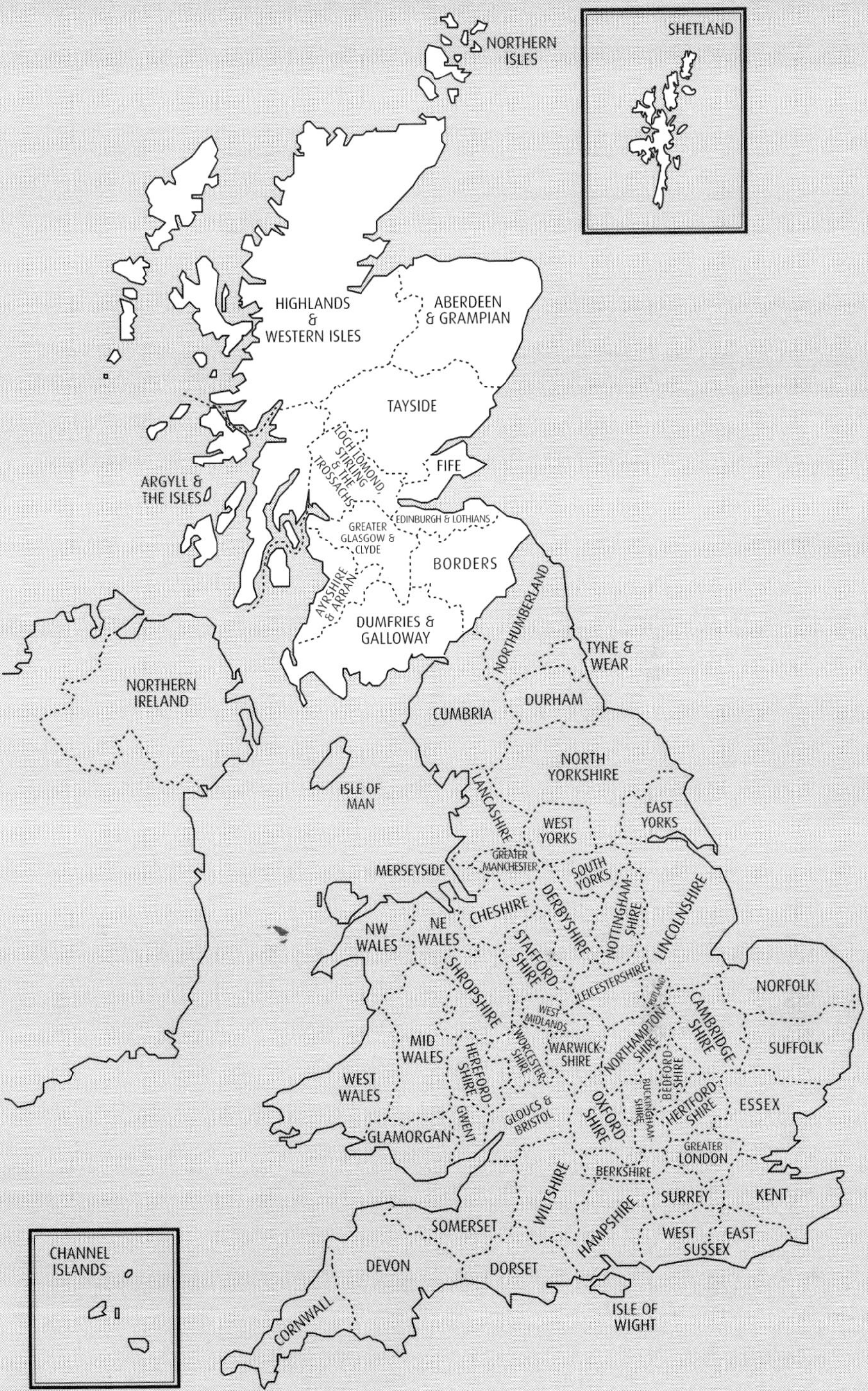

NORTHERN ISLES
SHETLAND
HIGHLANDS & WESTERN ISLES
ABERDEEN & GRAMPIAN
TAYSIDE
LOCH LOMOND, STIRLING & THE TROSSACHS
FIFE
ARGYLL & THE ISLES
EDINBURGH & LOTHIANS
GREATER GLASGOW & CLYDE
BORDERS
AYRSHIRE & ARRAN
DUMFRIES & GALLOWAY
NORTHUMBERLAND
TYNE & WEAR
NORTHERN IRELAND
DURHAM
CUMBRIA
NORTH YORKSHIRE
ISLE OF MAN
LANCASHIRE
WEST YORKS
EAST YORKS
GREATER MANCHESTER
MERSEYSIDE
SOUTH YORKS
CHESHIRE
DERBYSHIRE
NOTTINGHAM-SHIRE
LINCOLNSHIRE
NW WALES
NE WALES
STAFFORD SHIRE
SHROPSHIRE
LEICESTERSHIRE
RUTLAND
NORFOLK
WEST MIDLANDS
CAMBRIDGE-SHIRE
MID WALES
HEREFORD SHIRE
WORCESTER-SHIRE
WARWICK-SHIRE
NORTHAMPTON-SHIRE
BEDFORD SHIRE
SUFFOLK
WEST WALES
BUCKINGHAM-SHIRE
HERTFORD SHIRE
ESSEX
GWENT
GLOUCS & BRISTOL
OXFORD SHIRE
GLAMORGAN
GREATER LONDON
BERKSHIRE
WILTSHIRE
SURREY
KENT
SOMERSET
HAMPSHIRE
WEST SUSSEX
EAST SUSSEX
CHANNEL ISLANDS
DEVON
DORSET
ISLE OF WIGHT
CORNWALL

Scotland

ABERDEEN & GRAMPIAN

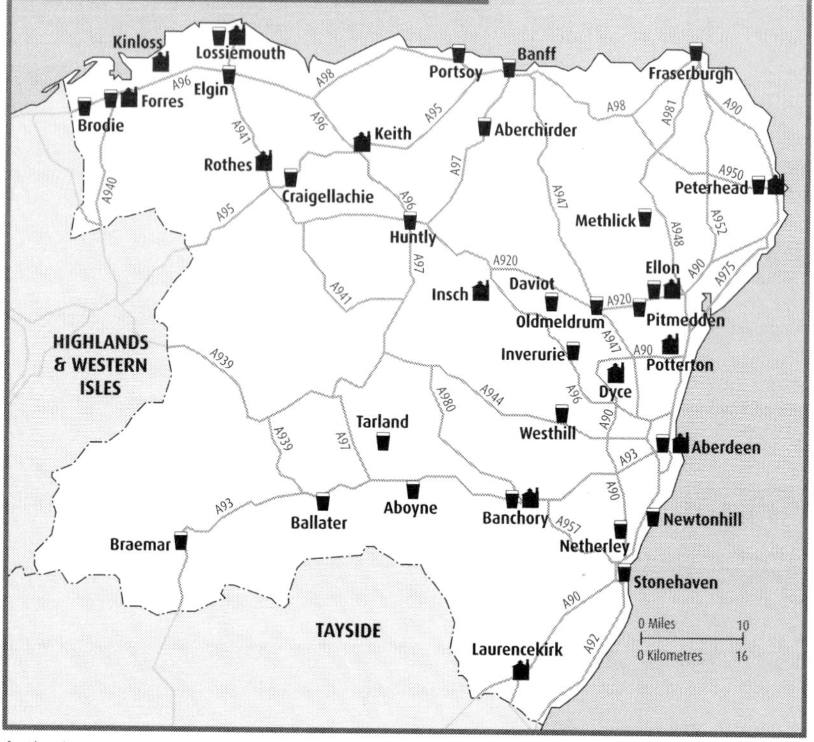

Authority areas covered: Aberdeenshire UA, City of Aberdeen UA, Moray UA

Aberchirder

New Inn

79 Main Street, AB54 7TB

12 (5 Mon)-12.30am; 12-11 Sun (01466) 780633

newinnaberchirder.co.uk

Windswept Wolf; 4 changing beers (sourced nationally; often Caledonian, Hambleton, Orkney) H

Traditional, friendly inn with wood-burning stoves, candlelit areas and a vintage atmosphere. It offers a good selection of quality ales from local and national breweries, often featuring Hambleton beers. A separate dining area provides locally sourced home-made food prepared by the owner/chef – the pork pies are highly recommended. Families are welcome in the dining room until 9pm (booking recommended). Dogs are permitted in the bar but should be kept on a lead at busy times.

Q P (301)

Aberdeen

Archibald Simpson

5 Castle Street, AB11 5BQ (E end of Union Street)

8am-midnight (1am Fri & Sat) (01224) 621365

Caledonian Deuchars IPA; Greene King Abbot; 9 changing beers (sourced nationally; often Orkney, Windswept) H

The former local headquarters of Clydesdale Bank, this Wetherspoon is in a magnificent granite building designed by local architect Archibald Simpson. It has a pillared entrance and retains many original architectural features – the main room is a central hall with a high ceiling and additional seating areas to the sides. The long bar has up to 12 handpumps offering a variety of beers, frequently from Scottish breweries. The usual beer festivals and Meet the Brewer nights are held. There is a narrow outside drinking area on the pavement on Union Street corner.

Grill ★

213 Union Street, AB11 6BA

10-midnight (1am Fri & Sat); 12.30-midnight Sun

(01224) 573530 thegrillaberdeen.co.uk

5 changing beers (sourced regionally; often Cromarty, Orkney, Windswept) H

REAL ALE BREWERIES

Beer Story Insch (NEW)
Bodachra Potterton (NEW)
Brew Toon Peterhead
Brewdog Ellon
Burnside Laurencekirk
Deeside Banchory
Fierce Dyce
Keith Keith
Quiet Banchory
Rothes Rothes
six°north Laurencekirk
Speyside Forres
StoatCraft Aberdeen (NEW)
Windswept Lossiemouth
Wooha Kinloss

With an exquisite interior redesigned in 1926 and remaining largely unchanged since, this is the only pub in the area listed on CAMRA's National Inventory of Historic Pub Interiors. It was male-only until 1975 when this was outlawed by legislation, following a famous women's protest that inspired the movie No Ladies Please. A ladies' toilet was eventually provided in 1998. Its beer, mainly from Scottish breweries, is complemented by a huge and award-winning selection of whiskies. Bar snacks are available. A former local CAMRA Pub of the Year. Now part of the local McGinty's Group after 48 years in the Watson family. ⇌🚌📶

Krakatoa

2 Trinity Quay, AB11 5AA (facing quayside at bottom of Market St)

🕒 2pm-midnight (3am Fri & Sat) ☎ (01224) 587602

🌐 krakatoa.bar

Windswept Weizen; changing beers (sourced regionally; often Cromarty, Spey Valley, Windswept) [P]

This historic harbourside bar, formerly the Moorings and then rebranded as Krakatoa, changes character from a friendly, laid-back local to a raucous rock bar on weekend evenings, when there may be a cover charge. The eclectic jukebox is popular with the varied clientele. A wide selection of Scottish ales is served on up to 12 American-style fonts to the far left of the bar, and a varied selection of Belgian beers and ciders is also available. Local CAMRA City Pub of the Year 2019 and overall branch winner in 2018. ♿⇌♣🍎▯🚌🐾📶

Ma Cameron's

6-8 Little Belmont Street, AB10 1JG

🕒 11-midnight; 10-1am Fri & Sat ☎ (01224) 644487

🌐 macamerons-aberdeen.co.uk

2 changing beers (sourced nationally; often Belhaven, Greene King, Inveralmond) [H]

Known simply as Ma's, this is one of Aberdeen's oldest pubs. Its snug bar at the front has a serving hatch and opens for limited hours on weekends only; drinks can be brought there from the back bar at other times. Sport is screened on TV in the large, modern rear lounge. Ales served in both bars are mainly from Greene King's Belhaven range. Meals are available until 9pm every day. A quiz is held every Monday; live music plays one Friday each month. ❀◑♿⇌♣🚌📶

Prince of Wales ✔

7 St Nicholas Lane, AB10 1HF (lane opp Marks & Spencer)

🕒 10-midnight (1am Fri & Sat) ☎ (01224) 640597

🌐 princeofwales-aberdeen.co.uk

8 changing beers (sourced nationally; often Cromarty, Swannay, Windswept) [H]

Refurbished in late 2016, the Prince is one of Aberdeen's oldest bars and features in Scotland's True Heritage Pubs, with possibly the longest bar counter in the city. It has a friendly atmosphere and a large following of regulars. It offers eight ales, mainly from Scottish breweries and from the owners Belhaven/Greene King, plus three craft beers. Sunday is folk music night and a prize quiz is held on Wednesday. This is a quiet pub whose only background noise is conversation. Good-value food is served daily until 9pm including filled rolls. Q◑⇌🚌📶

Queen Vic

126 Rosemount Place, AB25 2YU (10 mins' walk from W end of Union St along Rose St)

🕒 11-midnight (1am Fri & Sat); 12.30-midnight Sun

☎ (01224) 638500 🌐 pbdevco.com/queenvic.html

Timothy Taylor Landlord; 3 changing beers (sourced nationally; often Harviestoun, Spey Valley, Windswept) [H]

A cosy one-room locals' lounge bar slightly off the beaten track in a converted shop in a highly populated tenement area. Sporting events are frequently shown, when the pub gets extremely busy and noisy. Four cask ales are available including interesting guests often picked by the locals, alongside an extensive range of locally brewed bottled beers. A popular quiz is held on Monday evening, live bands play occasionally at weekends and there is live jazz on one Sunday a month. Snacks include sandwiches, wraps and local Big Beefys Biltong. 🚌(3,3G)🐾📶

St Machar Bar

97 High Street, AB24 3EN

🕒 11-midnight; 12.30-11 Sun ☎ (01224) 483079

🌐 adamsfamilypubs.com

Inveralmond Ossian; 2 changing beers (sourced regionally; often Stewart, Inveralmond) [H]

Located in the photogenic and historic Old Aberdeen conservation area amid the university buildings and close to King's College, this friendly and historic pub is frequented by academia and locals alike. A splendid mirror from the long-gone local Thomson Marshall Aulton Brewery and one from the original Devanha Brewery adorn the walls. Guest beers, frequently from Scottish micros, are available alongside a selection of whiskies and gins. The bar is home to a darts team, university football team and rugby team. Flippin' Bun & Wing food is served. ❀◑♣🚌(20)📶

Under the Hammer

11 North Silver Street, AB10 1RJ (off Golden Square)

🕒 5-11 (midnight Wed & Thu); 4-1am Fri & Sat; closed Sun

☎ (01224) 640253

Cromarty Happy Chappy; Fyne Jarl; 2 changing beers (sourced nationally; often Cromarty, Fyne) [H]

Located in a quiet side street near Golden Square just minutes from Union Street, this popular pub is in a basement next to Milne's auction house – hence the name. It is convenient for the Music Hall and His Majesty's Theatre. Guest beers come from a wide variety of Scottish breweries including Fyne Ales and Cromarty. Unobtrusive background music plays. Works by local artists displayed on the walls are for sale. Open mic sessions are held every Wednesday from 8pm. Q⇌🐾📶

Aboyne

Boat Inn

Charleston Road, AB34 5EL (N bank of River Dee next to Aboyne Bridge)

🕒 11-11 (midnight Fri & Sat) ☎ (01339) 886137

🌐 theboatinnaboyne.co.uk

3 changing beers (sourced nationally; often Belhaven, Cairngorm) [H]

Popular riverside inn with a food-oriented lounge. Junior diners (and adults) may request to see the model train, complete with sound effects, traverse the entire pub at picture-rail height upon completion of their meal. The public bar has a recess at the back for musicians on live music nights. The local Rotary Club regularly meets here. Three ales are served in summer, often reduced to two in winter. Breakfast is served 7.30-11.30am. Accommodation comprises seven twin rooms plus a family room. Q P

Ballater

Alexandra Hotel

12 Bridge Square, AB35 5QJ
11-2.30, 5-midnight; 11-midnight Fri; 11-midnight Sun
(01339) 755376 alexandrahotelballater.co.uk
Cairngorm Trade Winds; 2 changing beers (sourced regionally; often Cairngorm) H
Originally built as a private home in 1800, this smart, family-owned lounge bar became the Alexandra Hotel in 1915. Easily spotted when entering Ballater from the east side, it is popular both with local drinkers and those visiting for its excellent bar suppers. Ales are exclusively from Cairngorm, and may be drunk outside on benches in front of the pub. A handy stop-off on your way to Braemar for the Highland Games or on a visit with the royals at Balmoral. P

Glenaden Hotel

6 Church Square, AB35 5NE
11-1am (midnight Mon-Wed) (01339) 755488
3 changing beers (sourced regionally; often Windswept) H
Situated on the far side of the picturesque town square, this small hotel displays a prominent external sign for its Barrel Lounge. It normally serves three beers in busy periods, usually Scottish, mostly from Windswept. Darker ales are apparently favoured by the locals. A large function suite is at the rear of the hotel. Q P

Banchory

Ravenswood Club (Royal British Legion)

25 Ramsay Road, AB31 5TS
11-11 (midnight Fri & Sat) (01330) 822347
banchorylegion.co.uk
2 changing beers (sourced nationally) H
Large British Legion club with a comfortable lounge adjoining the pool and TV room and a spacious function room well-used by local clubs and societies as well as members. Darts and snooker are popular and played most evenings. The two handpumps offer excellent value and the beer choice changes constantly. An elevated terrace has fine views of the Deeside hills. Show a copy of this Guide or your CAMRA membership card for entry. P

Banff

Market Arms

5 High Shore, AB45 1DB
11-midnight (1am Fri); 10-1am Sat (01261) 818616
1 changing beer (sourced nationally; often Morland, Ruddles, Timothy Taylor) H
This fine building is one of the oldest in historic Banff, dating back to 1585. The courtyard, at the back, retains many original features. The long public bar has several fine examples of historic brewery and distillery mirrors. One of the two handpumps serves an ever-changing beer. The impressive upstairs lounge is used mainly for meals.

Braemar

Moorfield House Hotel

19 Chapel Brae, AB35 5YT (signposted from village centre)
4-10 (11 Fri); 12-11 Sat; 12-4 Sun (01339) 741244
moorfieldhousehotel.com
4 changing beers (sourced regionally; often Cairngorm, Orkney, Strathbraan) H
Small family-run hotel – the current owners took over in 2016 – overlooking the Highland Games ground at the edge of this historic village and close to the new heritage centre. Opening hours vary depending on the season and the weather – check ahead if you are travelling. If required, meals can be provided outside official times by prior arrangement. Four varying ales are served, sometimes three in winter. The local ukulele club meets here on Friday nights.
Q P (201)

Brodie

Old Mill Inn

IV36 2TD (on A96 between Forres and Nairn)
12-4, 5-11 (10.30 Sun) (01309) 641605
oldmillinnspeyside.co.uk
4 changing beers (sourced locally; often Spey Valley, Strathbraan, Windswept)
Under new ownership since autumn 2018, this gem is a spacious family-friendly pub-restaurant with a cosy fireside area, smart dining room, function room and a charming conservatory with views of the old watermill and garden. Up to four ales are available, mainly from Scottish micros. An excellent range of food is served with specials changing daily. A full restaurant menu is offered along with light lunches and traditional Scottish high teas. Live Scottish/Irish instrumental music plays on Sunday evening. Brodie Castle is nearby and Brodie Countryfare is opposite. A beer festival is normally held in June.
Q P (10,10A)

Craigellachie

Copper Dog (Craigellachie Hotel)

Victoria Street, AB38 9SR
12-11; 12-1am Fri & Sat; 1-11 Sun (01340) 881204
craigellachiehotel.co.uk/copper-dog
3 changing beers (sourced locally; often Spey Valley, Windswept) H
Situated in a beautiful village, the impressive Victorian building boasts picturesque views across the forests and mountains, and is next to the Fiddich and Spey rivers. The bar is beneath the hotel and while mostly given over to dining, it has a cosy, dimly lit area dedicated to drinking. There are over 800 whiskies in the Quaich Bar, with tasting sessions available. It can be busy, especially during whisky festivals. Booking is recommended if you wish to eat here. P (36)

Highlander Inn

10 Victoria Street, AB38 9SR (on A95, opp post office)
12-11 (12.30am Fri & Sat) (01340) 881446
whiskyinn.com
3 changing beers (often Rothes, Spey Valley, Windswept) H
Picturesque whisky and cask ale bar on Speyside's Whisky Trail, close to the Speyside Way. Popular with tourists, walkers and fishermen, it is very busy during whisky festivals and the tourist season.

Twinned with the Highlander Whisky Bar in Tokyo, it offers a fine selection of malts including many from Japan. Three ales are served, two in winter. CRAC (Craigellachie Real Ale Club) meets on the first Wednesday of the month and its members help to choose the guest ales. An outside decked area is a delight on a sunny afternoon. P (36)

Daviot

Smiddy

Main Street, AB51 0HZ

5-10; 4-1am Fri; 11.30-midnight Sat; 12.30-10 Sun
(01467) 671300

1 changing beer (sourced nationally; often Ruddles, Timothy Taylor)

Schmiede in German, Smiddy in Scots; this pub was once the village blacksmith's. It is very much a feature of village life, offering pool, darts and occasional live music in addition to a single well-presented ale. Nearby is the Loanhead of Daviot Stone Circle, one of the best examples of the numerous neolithic stone circles in the North-East. P

Elgin

Drouthy Cobbler

Shepherd's Close, 48a High Street, IV30 1BU

10-12.30am (1.30am Fri & Sat) (01343) 596000
thedrouthycobbler.co.uk

3 changing beers (sourced nationally)

This small, long, elegant pub is named after John Shanks, who was a shoemaker and an important figure in the conservation of Elgin Cathedral. Breakfast is available from 10am and meals are served for most of the day. A growing whisky collection stands at around 100, alongside a large gin and cocktail selection. Real ales at premium prices are supplemented by many local bottled beers. There are benches outside in the lane with awnings and heaters. Alcohol is served from 11am. Q

Muckle Cross

34 High Street, IV30 1BU

8am-midnight (1am Fri & Sat); 9am-11.45 Sun
(01343) 559030

Caledonian Deuchars IPA; Greene King Abbot; Sharp's Doom Bar; 4 changing beers (sourced nationally; often Windswept)

Typical small Wetherspoon pub converted from what was once a bicycle repair shop, then a Halfords branch. The pleasant long room has ample seating and a family area. Deservedly popular, it can be busy, particularly at weekends. Eight handpumps offer a wide range of beers from national and Scottish microbreweries. The pub also stocks a wide range of malt whiskies from more than 20 local distilleries. A cider festival and usually two beer festivals are held each year. Coffee and breakfast are served from 8am, alcohol from 11am. Q

Ellon

Tolbooth

21-23 Station Road, AB41 9AE (across road from public library)

12-11 (midnight Thu; 12.30am Fri & Sat); 12.30-11.30 Sun
(01358) 721308 thetolbooth.co.uk

Greene King Abbot; 2 changing beers (sourced regionally; often Cairngorm, Cromarty, Strathbraan)

A large pub, popular with all ages, close to the centre of the town and just a short walk from the bus stops on Market Street. There are separate seating areas on split levels as well as an airy conservatory with barrel tables. One Scottish and one English guest ale are usually available. No food is served. Several National Trust Scotland properties are nearby.

Forres

Mosset Tavern

Gordon Street, IV36 1DL

11-12.30am (1.30am Fri & Sat); 12-midnight Sun
(01309) 672981 mossettavern.com

6 changing beers (sourced locally; often Speyside, Swannay, Windswept)

Described as 'the country pub in the heart of Forres', this smart, extremely popular Scottish lounge bar/restaurant is situated next to the Mosset burn and pond, with swans and ducks. Friendly, efficient staff serve ale from a single handpump in the lounge and up to five in the spacious, comfortable public bar, where there are pool tables and large screens showing sport. A large function room is also available, home to the Foot Tapper beer festival in April. Live music plays on Friday evening, and there is a pub quiz every Tuesday. P (10)

Fraserburgh

Elizabethan Bar & Lounge

36 Union Grove, AB43 9PH (10 mins' walk from A90)

10-1am (01346) 510464

3 changing beers (sourced regionally; often Kelburn, Spey Valley, Windswept)

Set in the middle of a housing estate, with a mock-Tudor exterior, the large bar and lounges are in three distinct sections, with sport on TV in two of them. The bar has a formidable reputation for offering a wide range of quality ales sourced from throughout the country and also features well over 200 malts, the largest collection in the area. Approximately one mile from the beach, harbour and lighthouse museum. P

Saltoun Inn

Saltoun Square, AB43 9DA

7am-midnight; 7am-1am Fri & Sat (01346) 519548

Greene King Abbot; Sharp's Doom Bar; 4 changing beers (sourced nationally)

A Wetherspoon renovation of the historic Saltoun Arms Hotel, built in 1801, comprising several interconnecting low-ceiling rooms, including a lounge area to the left of the entrance. A garden area has been created to the rear which is surprisingly and pleasantly no smoking. Accommodation is also offered in 11 rooms, with reduced rates at weekends. The Scottish Lighthouse Museum is close by, as is the main fishing harbour. Alcohol sold from 10am. Q

Huntly

Crown Bar

4 Gordon Street, AB54 8AJ

11-11 (11.30 Sat); closed Sun (01466) 792244

Windswept Blonde, Wolf; 1 changing beer (sourced locally; often Keith) ℗

Situated just off the main square in the centre of Huntly, the Crown Bar was taken over in 2017 by the legendary Harry Halkett, late of the Clifton Bar in Lossiemouth and then the short-lived Imperial in Elgin. The pub has an original open, airy public bar and a small lounge at the rear. Beer is served on KeyKeg and can be classed as real ale – Windswept brews are all unfined and unfiltered. No food is served, except toasties sometimes. The small beer garden, which closes at 10pm, is accessed from lounge. ♿👪▲⇄♣🚲(10)

Inverurie

Gordon Highlander ✓
West High Street, AB51 3QQ
🕐 9am-11.30 (1am Fri & Sat) ☎ (01467) 626780
Sharp's Doom Bar; 4 changing beers (sourced nationally; often Cairngorm, Inveralmond, Strathaven) Ⓗ

A fine Wetherspoon conversion of a splendid Art Deco building which used to be the Victoria Cinema. The name refers to a locomotive built at the now defunct Inverurie Locomotive Works and there are many references to this throughout the pub. The famous Gordon Highlander Regiment also features prominently, with displays and a large mural. The books on the shelves are free to read and take home, with donations welcome. There are at least three guest ales and two real ciders, and the usual Wetherspoon beer festivals feature. Alcohol is served from 11am.
♿◑&⇄🚲(10,37)🛜

Lossiemouth

Windswept Tap Room
13 Coulardbank Industrial Estate, IV31 6NG
🕐 10-5 (8 Fri); closed Sun ☎ (01343) 814310
🌐 windsweptbrewing.com/tap-room
2 changing beers (sourced locally; often Windswept) ℗

This small bar, decked out with basic wooden furniture, is now the only outlet for ale in Lossie after one pub burnt down and the other changed ownership and ceased serving beer. Two varying Windswept ales on cask are supplemented by eight KeyKeg beers. The pub also serves coffee, tea, soft drinks, cakes and snacks, making it the perfect pit stop. The usual range of bottled beers and brewery merchandise is sold. The Tap Room is available for private hire. It may host the occasional beer festival. 👪P🚲(33A,33C)🛜

Methlick

Ythanview Hotel
Main Street, AB41 7DT
🕐 11-2.30, 5-11; 11-2.30, 4.30-1am Fri; 11-1am Sat; 12-11 Sun ☎ (01651) 806235 🌐 ythanviewhotel.co.uk
Harviestoun Bitter & Twisted; 2 changing beers (sourced regionally; often Fyne, Swannay) Ⓗ

Traditional inn in the village centre, home to the MCC (Methlick Cricket Club) at nearby Lairds. Log fires warm both the lounge bar at the front and the friendly sports-themed public bar at the rear. Beers are exclusively from Scottish micros. The pub is famous for the owner's special chicken curry, and Thursday's steak night is popular. Meals are served all day at weekends. Live music and quiz nights

take place on most Saturdays. Haddo House, Tolquhon Castle and Pitmedden Garden are nearby. ♿👪🏠◑♣P🚲(290,291)🐾🛜

Netherley

Lairhillock Inn
AB39 3QS (signposted off B979, 3 miles S of B9077) NO854952
🕐 11-11 (midnight Fri & Sat) ☎ (01569) 730001
🌐 lairhillock.co.uk
Timothy Taylor Landlord; 1 changing beer (sourced regionally; often Burnside, Strathbraan, Windswept) Ⓗ

This former coach house is a rambling, family-run building in attractive open countryside. Its traditional wood-panelled bar is warmed by a log fire in winter. The lounge, with its central open fireplace and large conservatory, is popular for dining. Coffee, scones and shortbread are served 2pm-5pm. Two function rooms of different size are available. The pub is convenient for the attractions of Stonehaven and Royal Deeside, and sometimes closes early in winter – phone to check.
Q♿👪🏠◑&♣P🐾🛜

Newtonhill

Newton Arms
10 Old Mill Road, AB39 3TZ
🕐 11-midnight; 12.30-midnight Sun ☎ (01569) 730227
Sharp's Doom Bar; 1 changing beer (sourced nationally; often Cromarty, Timothy Taylor, Windswept) Ⓗ

Traditional village local with a classic, dark-wood-panelled public bar featuring 1950s bar counters and intriguing under-counter shelves for drinks. The side lounge has light-wood panelling and tables; you can bring your own food, with plates and cutlery provided on request. An occasional guest beer is served when Sharp's is not available. A small, east-facing rear patio allows alfresco drinking. Neighbouring buildings spoil its sea view but provide protection from the onshore wind. ♿👪◑♣🚲🐾🛜

Oldmeldrum

Redgarth ▼
Kirk Brae, AB51 0DJ (on outskirts of village, signposted off A947)
🕐 11-3, 5-11 (11.45 Fri & Sat); 12-11 Sun ☎ (01651) 872353
🌐 redgarth.com
3 changing beers (sourced locally; often Cromarty, Fyne, Swannay) Ⓖ

A local inn that celebrates 30 years under the same ownership in 2020, and which provides excellent views of the eastern Grampian mountains. It retains a reputation for an imaginative choice of beers, sourced from many Scottish micros. They are served on gravity, with handpumps remaining on the bar to advertise the ales. Extra choice is offered during occasional Brewer in Residence nights. Food ranges from lunchtime bar meals to a more extensive menu in the evening. Winner of many local CAMRA awards including 2019 Country Pub of the Year and overall branch winner.
♿👪🏠◑▲♣P🚲(35,X35)🛜

Peterhead

Cross Keys

23-27 Chapel Street, AB42 1TH
7am-11 (midnight Thu; 1am Fri & Sat); 9am-11 Sun
(01779) 483500
Greene King Abbot; Sharp's Doom Bar; 3 changing beers (sourced nationally) H
A typical Wetherspoon outlet in the centre of a bustling port, close to the local museum where you can learn about the town's maritime history. The pub is named after the chapel dedicated to St Peter that previously stood on the site. The long single room has the bar towards the front and a large seating area at the rear. A sheltered and heated area outside caters for hardy souls and smokers. Alcohol is served from 9am; children are welcome until 9pm if dining. Q (66,69)

Pitmedden

Craft Bar

Tarves Road, AB41 7NX
4 (11 Wed & Thu)-11; 11-midnight Fri & Sat; 12-11 Sun
(01651) 842049
2 changing beers (sourced regionally; often Orkney, Spey Valley, Windswept)
A one-room corner pub run by a local CAMRA member. Old church pews provide seating for some of the tables around the walls; other tables have bench seating. Two handpumps serve ales from varying breweries, supplemented by KeyKeg beers from Windswept. There is also a comprehensive range of bottled and canned beer in the fridge. Occasional Brewer in Residence evenings are held. P

Portsoy

Shore Inn

Church Street, AB45 2QR (overlooking harbour)
11-11 (midnight Thu; 1am Fri & Sat); 12-11 Sun
(01261) 842831
2 changing beers (sourced locally; often Spey Valley, Windswept) H
Cosy, comfortable, coastal howff with a warm welcome in winter and scenic outdoor views in summer. The pub overlooks the oldest harbour on Moray coast which was recently a location for the remake of Whisky Galore. The L-shaped room with low ceilings is a fine example of a nautical bar. Expect the pub to be very busy each June during the Scottish Traditional Boat Festival.

Stonehaven

Marine Hotel

9-10 Shorehead, AB39 2JY (overlooking harbour)
11-midnight (1am Fri & Sat) (01569) 762155
marinehotelstonehaven.co.uk
Timothy Taylor Landlord; house beer (by six°north); 4 changing beers (sourced regionally; often Cairngorm, Cromarty, Windswept) H
Now the only outlet in the six°north empire that serves real ale, this is a former Scottish CAMRA Pub of the Year and a multiple branch winner. The small harbourside hotel features simple wood panelling in the bar and a rustic lounge with an open fireplace. Seating outside offers a splendid view of the harbour. Ales from six°north are served plus numerous Belgian beers and up to 18 craft keg beers. Historic Dunnottar Castle is one mile south and an open-air bathing pool one mile north.
(747,X7)

Ship Inn

5 Shorehead, AB39 2JY (on harbour front)
11-midnight (1am Fri & Sat) (01569) 762617
shipinnstonehaven.com
2 changing beers (sourced regionally; often Strathbraan) H
Built in 1771, this harbour-front hotel has a maritime-themed, wood-panelled bar featuring a mirror from the defunct Devanha brewery, and a seating area outside overlooking the water. Two beers are offered, at least one from a Scottish microbrewery, and an extensive range of malt whiskies is stocked. A modern restaurant with panoramic harbour views is adjacent to the bar – food is served all day at the weekend. Accommodation is available in 11 guest rooms.
(747,X7)

Tarland

Aberdeen Arms

31 The Square, AB34 4TX
4-11 (1am Tue); 12-1am Sat; 12-11 Sun
(01339) 881225 aberdeenarmstarland.co.uk
Cairngorm Trade Winds H
Part of a 300-year-old Grade B-listed building in the village centre, this traditional inn has a wood-lined bar area, stripped wooden floors, low ceilings and a real fire. Live music is performed on Tuesday night. There are rooms for hire in same building; the former restaurant is now a Chinese takeaway. Craigievar Castle, the Grampian Transport Museum at Alford and the Queen's View beauty spot are nearby, as are stone circles, which attract a lot of tourist interest. Closed winter Mondays and midweek lunchtimes. The bus service is infrequent.
P (210)

Westhill

Shepherds Rest

10 Straik Road, Arnhall Business Park, AB32 6HF
11-11; 12-11 Sun (01224) 740208
pub-explorer.com/nscotland/pub/shepherdsrestwesthill.htm
Belhaven 1719; Greene King IPA; Morland Old Speckled Hen; 3 changing beers (sourced nationally) H
Half a mile from the village across the busy A944, this pub features a large, rustic-style interior with plenty of nooks and crannies for privacy when required. Part of the Belhaven/Greene King empire, it serves the expected range of beers plus an occasional guest. Popular with families, it offers an extensive all-day food menu. Breakfast is available before alcohol sales commence. A Premier Inn next door provides accommodation.
P

For we could not now take time for further search (to land our ship) our victuals being much spent especially our beer. **Log of the Mayflower**

SCOTLAND

ARGYLL & THE ISLES

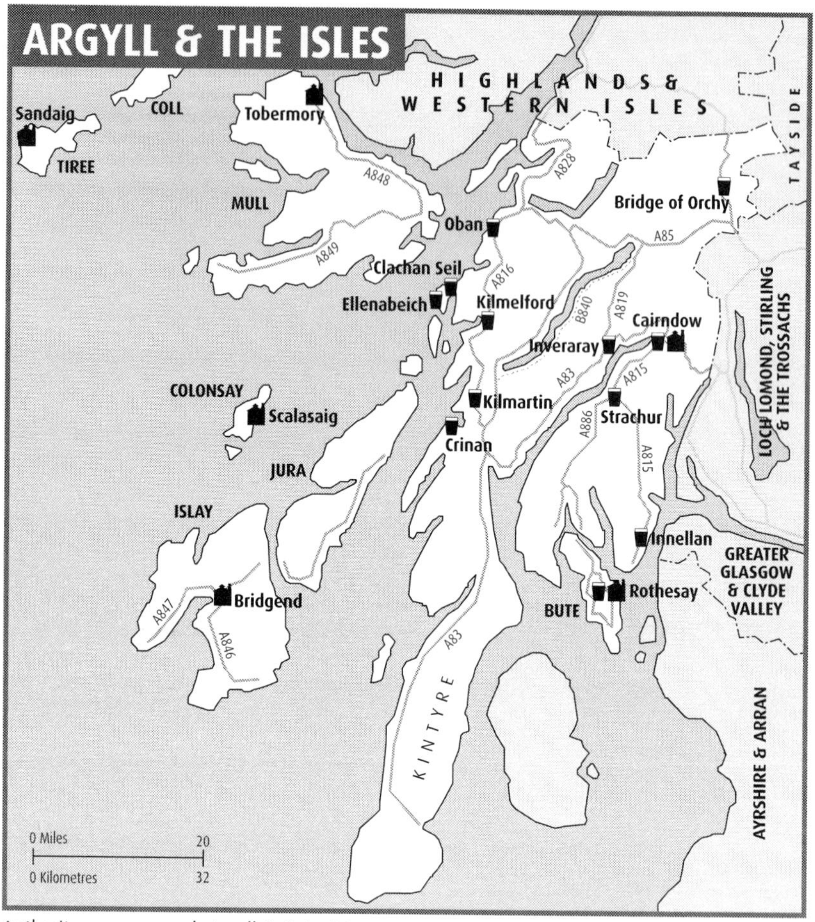

Authority area covered: Argyll & Bute UA

Bridge of Orchy

Bridge of Orchy Hotel

PA36 4AD

7-10 summer; 8-9 winter ☎ (01838) 400208
bridgeoforchy.co.uk

Harviestoun Bitter & Twisted; 1 changing beer (sourced regionally; often Harviestoun) H

Situated on the A82 that leads north to Glencoe, Fort William and Skye, and with a nearby railway station, this remote hotel is surprisingly accessible. With mountains and glens nearby it is popular with walkers, climbers and other outdoor types. The bar faces the road and features an iron stove, as does the comfortable lounge. The restaurant offers a panoramic view of the mountains. The menu includes local Scottish produce; meals are served midday-9pm. P (915)

Cairndow

Fyne Ales Brewery Tap L

Achadunan, PA26 8BJ (up side road at head of Loch Fyne)

10-6 ☎ (01499) 600120 fyneales.com/brewery-tap

Fyne Ales Jarl; 4 changing beers (sourced locally; often Fyne Ales) H

The brewery tap and shop opened in 2012 in what was originally a farm building. The bar, with its fine polished granite front, supports five handpumps selling a range of ales from the brewery along with a varied selection of bottled beers. Meat produced on the farm is available to buy and is also used to fill the excellent pies, which can be enjoyed in the bar or the courtyard looking across to the brewery. Q P

Stagecoach Inn L

PA26 8BN (on slip road off A83)

11-11 (1am Fri & Sat; midnight Sun) ☎ (01499) 600286
cairndowinn.com

2 changing beers (sourced regionally; often Fyne Ales, Loch Lomond) H

Down a loop road, formerly the main road and signed on the current A83 section, this former coaching inn offers a pleasant spot to break a

REAL ALE BREWERIES

Argyll Tobermory: Isle of Mull
Bun Dubh Sandaig: Isle of Tiree (NEW)
Bute Rothesay: Isle of Bute
Colonsay Scalasaig: Isle of Colonsay
Fyne Cairndow
Islay Bridgend: Isle of Islay

journey through Argyll. The bar has up to two handpumps dispensing mainly beers from nearby Fyne Ales and occasionally other Scottish breweries. Arches lead to the dining room and a comfortable lounge with log fire. In summer the attractive views over Loch Fyne can also be enjoyed from the lochside garden. Opening times may change in winter.
P (926,976)

Clachan Seil

Tigh-an-Truish Inn

PA34 4QZ
11 (12 Sun)-11 summer; 5-8 Mon; closed Tue & Wed; 5-8 Thu; 11-11 Fri (9 Sat); 12-8 Sun winter (01852) 300242
2 changing beers (sourced nationally; often Caledonian, Fyne Ales, Orkney)
This charming inn is worth veering off the A816 to visit. Its rustic wooden interior has an L-shaped counter with an unusual high bench seat, the Perch. Two handpumps (one in winter) serve Scottish ales from a range of breweries. A stone fireplace harbours a coal-burning iron stove, with a Highland sword and enigmatic wooden carving above. In summer the garden and patio are a delight. Check hours on weekdays and in winter before travelling any distance.
Q P (418)

Crinan

Crinan Seafood Bar

Crinan Hotel, PA31 8SR (at most westerly point of Crinan Canal)
12-11 (01546) 830261 crinanhotel.com
2 changing beers (sourced locally; often Fyne Ales)
The Seafood Bar is within the Crinan Hotel, overlooking the entry of the canal into the sea. It has two bars, the larger used mostly for meals. The smaller bar has interesting wooden panels and a fireplace with the head of a highland cow above it. Real ale pumps from Fyne Ales, located in the larger bar, can serve drinkers in either. Two ales are normally available in summer, one in winter. The pub also offers a large selection of whiskies.
P

Ellenabeich

Oyster Bar & Brewery

PA34 4RQ (by harbour)
10.30-11 summer; 10.30-3, 5-9 Mon-Thu; 10.30-11 Fri; 10.30-9 Sat & Sun winter (01852) 300121
oysterbareasdale.com
2 changing beers (often Fyne Ales, Orkney, Williams Bros)
Set on an island, this little bar no longer has a brewery but retains a reputation for good food and a unique view. It is not the easiest place to get to but is worth the effort. The pub is situated by the harbour at the end of a row of low whitewashed cottages once occupied by workers in the slate quarries around this historic village. Ale is generally from Scottish micros, often featuring unusual brews. Alcohol is available after 11am.
Q (418)

> How easy can the barley-bree
> Cement the quarrel.
> It's aye the cheapest lawyer's fee
> To taste the barrel.
> **Robert Burns**

Innellan

Osborne

44 Shore Road, PA23 7TJ
11.30-midnight (1am Fri & Sat) (01369) 830820
theosborneinnellan.co.uk
St Austell Tribute; 2 changing beers (sourced nationally)
This whitewashed seafront hotel a few miles south of Dunoon was built in 1869 and has been completely refurbished in the past few years. The comfortable bar has a pool table to one side and a cosy lounge with a log fire. At the front a conservatory acts as the dining room and provides excellent views across the Firth of Clyde. Any good weather can be enjoyed in a small outdoor area to one side. (489)

Inveraray

George Hotel

Main Street East, PA32 8TT
11-midnight; 12-midnight Sun (01499) 302111
thegeorgehotel.co.uk
3 changing beers (sourced regionally; often Caledonian, Fyne Ales, Inveralmond)
Attractive hotel developed from two private houses in 1860 by the Clark family, who still own it. The restaurants and bars have been completely restored but retain the original ambience with an abundance of dark wood, flagstone floors throughout and four roaring log and peat fires. Food has an emphasis on quality local produce, and the beers are mainly local too, served both in the main restaurant and the lively public bar (open from 5pm) alongside.
Q P (926,976)

Kilmartin

Kilmartin Hotel

PA31 8RQ (on A816 10 miles N of Lochgilphead)
12-midnight (1am Sat) summer; 5-11 Mon-Thu; 12-midnight Fri; 12-1am Sat; 12-11 Sun winter
(01546) 510250 kilmartin-hotel.com
3 changing beers (sourced regionally; often Fyne Ales, Loch Lomond, Orkney)
Whitewashed hotel on a promontory overlooking Kilmartin Glen and many sites of historic and religious significance. The small public bar to one side provides a cosy fireside nook and offers a good selection of whiskies to complement the real ale. To the rear, a pool and games room leads to a beer garden and smoking shed. Good home-made food is available in the evenings and some lunchtimes in the adjacent dining room, or in the garden in summer. P (423)

Kilmelford

Cuilfail ★

PA34 4XA
11-1am (01852) 200274 cuilfail.co.uk
2 changing beers (sourced nationally; often Box Steam, Loch Lomond)
An old former coaching inn, now an established hotel with a welcoming bar which is virtually unaltered since being refitted in 1957. Its interior

features the exposed boulders of the wall, an idea taken up in the facing of the counter (which also incorporates parts of whisky casks) and the wall just inside the entrance. Two real ales are served, one in winter. Enjoy a drink while you are warmed by the large wood-burning stove.
(423)

Oban

Corryvreckan

The Waterfront Centre, Railway Pier, PA34 4LW
7am-midnight (1am Fri & Sat) (01631) 568910
Caledonian Deuchars IPA; Greene King Abbot; Sharp's Doom Bar; 6 changing beers (sourced nationally) H
Excellently located Wetherspoon pub named after the famous whirlpool between Jura and Scarba. It lies alongside the fishing boat berth, next door to both the rail station and ferry terminal and with views across Oban Bay. The interior has a wood-panelled roof and is open and spacious. The pub is enlivened by much nautical ephemera including a casting of a sea eagle. Opening time for breakfast is 7am but you will need to wait until at least 11am to sample the ale.

Oban Inn

1 Stafford Street, PA34 5NJ
11-1am (01631) 567441
3 changing beers (often Fyne Ales) H
This traditional corner local by the old harbour pier was shut for many years before being reopened in 2016. The public bar remains unspoilt and retains its dark wood panelling and stone floors of Easdale slate. Maritime artefacts decorate the walls, and banknotes from many nations cover the wooden beams. Real ale is only occasionally available in the comfortable lounge upstairs but it is still possible to admire the stained-glass panels acquired from an Irish monastery.

Rothesay

Black Bull Inn

West Princes Street, Isle of Bute, PA20 9AF (opp harbour)
11-11; 11-midnight Fri & Sat; 12.30-11 Sun
(01700) 502366 theblackbullrothesay.com
3 changing beers (sourced regionally; often Fyne Ales) H
A pleasant ferry trip from Wemyss Bay rail station brings you to this well-known landmark, situated opposite the marina and within walking distance of all amenities including the Victorian toilets. The pub has two bars, a front and rear entrance and a separate dining area. It is always busy with yachtsmen and others looking for a meal.

Strachur

Creggans Inn

PA27 8BX (on A815 at N end of village)
11 (12 Sun)-11; closed Mon & Tue winter
(01369) 860279 creggans-inn.co.uk
2 changing beers (sourced locally; often Fyne Ales) H
Dating from the middle of the 19th century, this inn sits on the east shore of Loch Fyne. MacPhunn's Bar, named after a half-hung sheep rustler of yore, is comfortable with a real fire and plenty of room for dining. The exploits of the local shinty team are recorded around the walls and a pool table provides entertainment on winter evenings. There is a separate restaurant and accommodation is available. **Q** **P** (484,486)

Kilmartin Hotel, Kilmartin (Photo: Christian Hacker/Flickr CC BT 2.0)

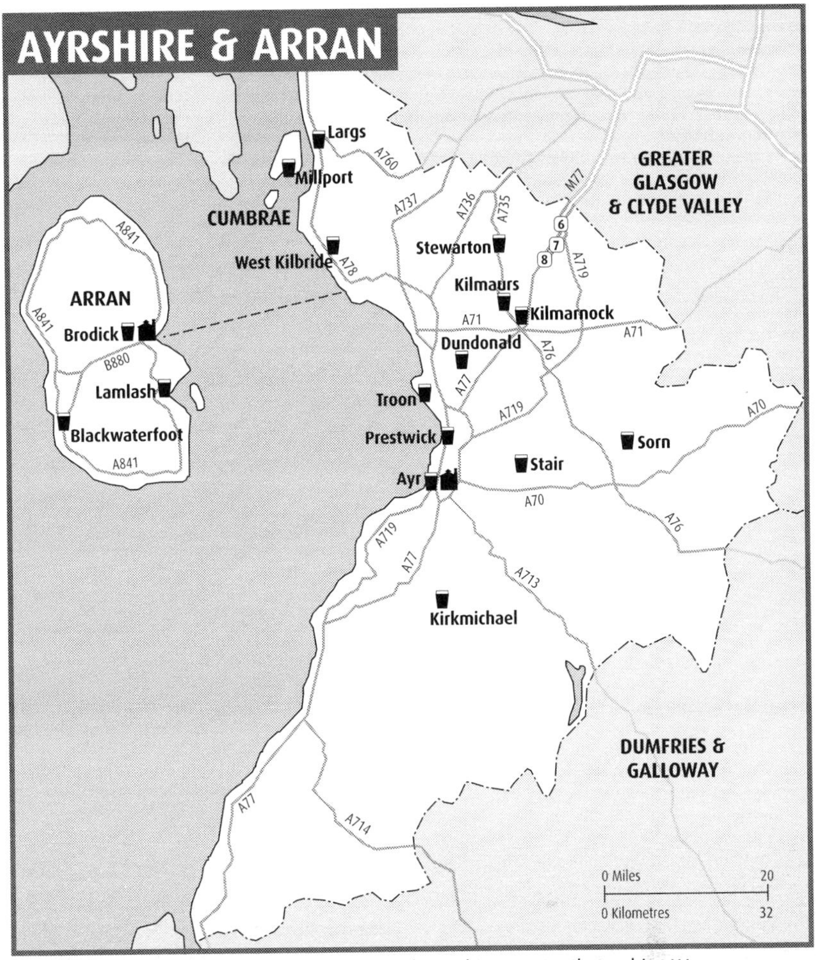

Authority areas covered: East Ayrshire UA, North Ayrshire UA, South Ayrshire UA

Ayr

Abbotsford Hotel

14 Corsehill Road, KA7 2ST (20-min walk from station)
10-12.30am (midnight Sun) (01292) 261506
abbotsfordhotel.co.uk
2 changing beers (often Fyne Ales, Hop Back, Wainwright)
A fine Scottish baronial-style building, in the same ownership since 1966, just under a mile south of Ayr town centre. The delightful and aptly named Copper Bar has the real ale. There is a pleasant dining room and a games room with TV showing sports. Book ahead for meals. P (57,361)

Chestnuts Hotel

52 Racecourse Road, KA7 2UZ (on A719, 1 mile S of centre)
10-11 (12.30am Fri & Sat) (01292) 264393
chestnutshotel.com
3 changing beers (sourced nationally)
Ales from a range of breweries are offered in The 19th Hole, a delightful oak-beamed hall with an interesting history and a huge collection of whisky water jugs. The family-run hotel serves excellent food in its bar and separate restaurant. Open log fires add to the comfortable atmosphere in winter and a pleasant beer garden is popular when the weather allows. P (9)

Glen Park Hotel

5 Racecourse Road, KA7 2DG
10-midnight; 12-midnight Sun (01292) 263891
glenparkhotel.co.uk
Ayr Leezie Lundie, Jolly Beggars; 2 changing beers (often Ayr)
This comfortable lounge bar, in an attractive 1860s B-listed Victorian building, is the brewery tap for Ayr Brewing Company who brew in the rear of the building. The guest ales usually include a seasonal from the brewery. Beers are usually also available to take away from a shop/bar at the rear of the dining room. Bar and restaurant meals are served daily except Monday. P (9)

REAL ALE BREWERIES

Arran Brodick: Isle of Arran
Ayr Ayr

SCOTLAND

Wellingtons Bar

17 Wellington Square, KA7 1EZ
🕓 11-12.30am; 12-midnight Sun ☎ (01292) 262794
🌐 welliesbar.weebly.com
3 changing beers (often Born in the Borders, Kelburn, Loch Lomond) Ⓗ
This basement bar attracts tourists and office workers alike. The Wednesday evening quiz is popular and weekend entertainment includes live music or a DJ on Saturday and an acoustic session on Sunday evening. The three changing ales constantly vary. ◖≠🖃🐾🛜

Blackwaterfoot: Isle of Arran

Kinloch Hotel

KA27 8ET
🕓 11-midnight; 12-midnight Sun ☎ (01770) 860444
🌐 bw-kinlochhotel.co.uk
Ayr Uisge Dubh; 1 changing beer (often Ayr, Belhaven, Greene King) Ⓗ
This family hotel offers coastal comfort and spectacular scenery. Fabulous local fare includes fish and seafood. The hotel has 37 bedrooms, a restaurant, three refurbished bars and a variety of facilities including a heated indoor swimming pool. A beer festival is held in August.
🛏🏠🍴◖🕭♣Å♣🚲🖃🐾🛜

Brodick: Isle of Arran

Ormidale Hotel

Knowe Road, KA27 8BY (off A841 at W end of village)
🕓 4-midnight; 12-12.30am Sat; 12-midnight Sun
☎ (01770) 302293 🌐 ormidale-hotel.co.uk
Arran Guid Ale; 2 changing beers (often Arran) Ⓗ
Set in seven acres of grounds, this hotel provides views across Brodick Bay from its attractive beer garden. Beers are now served from handpumps rather than tall founts on the boat-shaped bar, although one original fount is retained unused. Arran Blonde is often available in summer. The home-cooked meals are recommended. Discos and folk nights are held, and accommodation is available all year round.
🛏🏠🍴◖♣🖃(322,324)🐾🛜

Dundonald

Auchans

29-31 Main Street, KA2 9HH (on B730)
🕓 10-11 (12.30am Thu-Sat) ☎ (01563) 851472
🌐 theauchans.co.uk
2 changing beers (often Ayr, Fyne Ales, Kelburn) Ⓗ
Friendly family-run restaurant bar with a varied choice of food appealing to all tastes, including bar snacks, tapas and pizzas. The restaurant is to the rear and the comfortable and attractive lounge bar is next to the car park, with views of the historic castle. The two beers on handpump change regularly and tend to come from local and regional breweries. Q🛏◖🕭♣🖃(10,21,110)🐾🛜

Kilmarnock

First Edition ✓

50 Bank Street, KA1 1HA
🕓 9am-11 (1am Fri & Sat); 11-11 Sun ☎ (01563) 528833
🌐 firsteditionkilmarnock.co.uk
Caledonian Deuchars IPA; Harviestoun Bitter & Twisted; 2 changing beers (often Strathaven) Ⓗ

Four ales are served here, usually including two from a Scottish regional brewer. Food is available all day in bright surroundings. There are 16 TV screens showing sports, and the recently revamped beer garden houses table tennis and pool tables under a roof. A DJ performs on Friday to Sunday evenings. 🛏🏠◖🕭♣≠●🖃🛜

Wheatsheaf Inn ✓

70 Portland Street, KA1 1JG
🕓 8am-midnight (1am Fri & Sat) ☎ (01563) 572483
Greene King Abbot; Sharp's Doom Bar; 6 changing beers Ⓗ
This sizeable town-centre Lloyds No.1 bar is famous for its links to Robert Burns, who was first published in Kilmarnock. The bar is divided into various seating areas. Nine handpumps dispense a range of ales plus real cider; food is standard Wetherspoon fare. DJs entertain on Friday and Saturday, with karaoke early Friday evening. Licensed from 11am. 🛏🏠◖🕭♣≠●🖃🛜

Kilmaurs

Weston Tavern

27 Main Street, KA3 2RQ
🕓 8am-midnight (1am Thu-Sat) ☎ (01563) 538805
🌐 westontavern.co.uk
1 changing beer (often Ayr, Kelburn) Ⓗ
Housed in the former manse of reformist minister David Smeaton, this classic country pub and restaurant has a tiled floor, stone walls and a wood-burning fire. It sits beside the Jougs, a former jailhouse and tollbooth. A single pump dispenses ale from a rotating list of local breweries. The pub holds regular live music and quiz nights.
🛏🏠◖🕭♣♣🖃🐾🛜

Kirkmichael

Kirkmichael Arms

3-5 Straiton Road, KA19 7PH
🕓 12-midnight (12.30am Fri & Sat) ☎ (01655) 750200
🌐 kirkmichaelarms.co.uk
2 changing beers (often Ayr) Ⓗ
A friendly country pub with a lounge bar and separate dining room. Two handpumps dispense an Ayr Brewing Co beer plus a guest. This pub serves excellent meals. Walkers and dogs are made welcome, and small functions are catered for. Well placed for accessing Galloway Forest Park to the south. Q🛏🏠◖🕭♣♣🖃(358,361)🐾🛜

Lamlash: Isle of Arran

Pierhead Tavern

Shore Road, KA27 8JN
🕓 11-midnight (1am Thu-Sat) summer; 12-1am (midnight Sun) winter ☎ (01770) 600418 🌐 thepht.co.uk
3 changing beers (often Kelburn, Loch Lomond, Williams Bros) Ⓗ
Three handpumps serve a variety of rotating ales from breweries such as Kelburn, Loch Lomond and Williams, in addition to local Arran ales in the summer season. The pub grub is all home made and chef's specials change weekly. Live music is performed on Saturday, Sunday afternoon and some Fridays. The views from the roof terrace across to Holy Isle are spectacular.
🛏🏠◖🕭Å♣🖃(323)🐾🛜

Largs

JG Sharps Bar

34-36 Nelson Street, KA30 8LW (turn off seafront at Nardini's)

11-midnight (1am Fri & Sat); 12.30-midnight Sun

(01475) 675515 jgsharps.co.uk

Sharp's Sea Fury; 1 changing beer [H]

A large traditional pub with several drinking areas and an open fire in the bar area. Good-quality pub meals are served lunchtimes and Friday to Sunday evenings. Games and sport are shown on TV and live music is occasionally performed. The beer garden has space for smokers. Q

Millport: Isle of Cumbrae

Fraser's Bar

7 Cardiff Street, KA28 0AS

11-midnight (1am Thu-Sat) (01475) 530518

2 changing beers (often Ayr, Jaw, Kelburn) [H]

Well maintained and tidy, this pub caters for visitors to the island as well as locals. Buses meet every ferry from Largs and terminate just across the road. Two handpumps serve mostly light-coloured ales, usually including one from a local brewery. Good-value pub food is available lunchtimes and early evenings. Children are welcome in the rear lounge until 8pm. There is an open fire in the main bar. Q (320)

Prestwick

Prestwick Pioneer

87 Main Street, KA9 1JS

8am-midnight (12.30am Fri & Sat) (01292) 473210

Greene King Abbot; Sharp's Doom Bar; 8 changing beers [H]

Modern Wetherspoon outlet named after the first Scottish Aviation Pioneer light aircraft, built in 1947 at the nearby international airport. The pub has an airy feel with a light-wood decor, and features photos of Elvis at the airport, the only place in the UK that he set foot on. Ten handpumps serve local and national ales and food is available all day. Licensed from 10am.

Sorn

Sorn Inn

35 Main Street, KA5 6HU

closed Mon; 12-2.30, 6-10 (midnight Fri); 12-midnight Sat; 12-10 Sun (01290) 551305 sorninn.com

1 changing beer (often Orkney) [H]

The inn has an award-winning restaurant with a menu that offers a mix of fine dining and brasserie-style food. The cosy bar has one handpump and a selection of bottled ales. The pub offers accommodation in four rooms with en-suite facilities but is no longer served by public transport. P

Stair

Stair Inn

KA5 5HW (on B730 7 miles E of Ayr)

12-11 (1am Fri & Sat) (01292) 591650 stairinn.co.uk

1 changing beer (often Broughton, Inveralmond, Stewart) [H]

This family-run hotel on the banks of the River Ayr is not accessible by public transport but is well worth seeking out. The menu focuses on local produce, with fish from the inn's own smokehouse a speciality. Booking is recommended for weekend meals. Q P

Stewarton

Mill House

4 Dean Street, KA3 5EQ (on Glasgow road N of the cross)

12-midnight (1am Fri & Sat) (01560) 482255

themillhouse-stewarton.co.uk

3 changing beers (often Harviestoun, Inveralmond, Kelburn) [H]

The Mill House is located in a 400-year-old former mill building in Stewarton, known locally as the Bonnet Toun due to its bonnet-making heritage. Two or three cask ales are normally available at the bar. The full restaurant menu is also available in the bar. P

Troon

Cheeky Charlie's

47 Templehill, KA10 6BQ

10.30-1am; 12-2.30am Thu-Sun (01292) 312814

Cairngorm Wildcat; 3 changing beers (often Belhaven, Harviestoun, Inveralmond) [H]

A long single-room bar on one of the town's main routes. One real ale is discounted Sunday to Tuesday, and over-60s get a permanent discount. The pool table and jukebox are good value, with the former free on Wednesday. Thursday is quiz night; Friday and Saturday entertainment is a DJ from 10pm into the early hours.

McKay's

69 Portland Street, KA10 6QU

10-12.30am (midnight Sun) (01292) 737372

3 changing beers (often Fyne Ales, Inveralmond, Stewart) [H]

A popular town-centre bar with a large, well-furnished beer garden that gets busy in the summer. The bar hosts various food specials nights including burgers and steak. Local dominoes competitions are held here.

West Kilbride

Twa Dugs

71 Main Street, KA23 9AW

closed Mon; 3-10 Tue; 1-11 Wed & Thu; 12-1am Fri; 11-1am Sat; 11-10 Sun (01294) 822524

2 changing beers (often Ayr, Five Kingdoms, Kelburn) [H]

A welcoming village pub patronised by all age groups, refurbished to a high standard. Two handpulls dispense beers from mostly local breweries; bar snacks are served until 7pm Thursday to Sunday. Attractions include a pool table, fortnightly quiz and live music at weekends. The pub is opposite a bus stop and five minutes from the railway station. Local CAMRA Pub of the Year 2019. (585,585A)

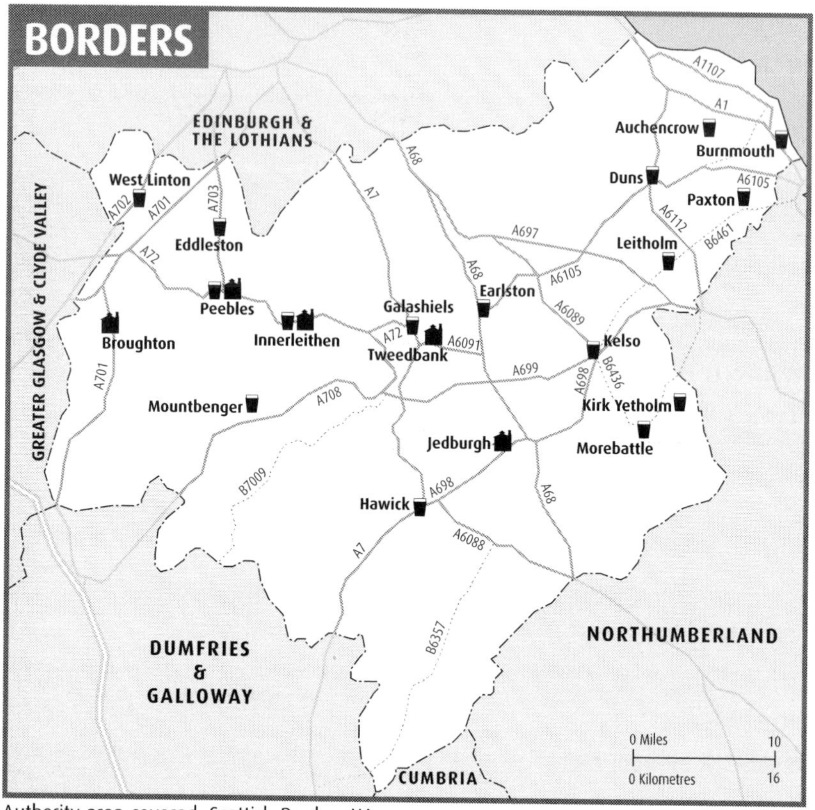

Authority area covered: Scottish Borders UA

Auchencrow

Craw Inn

TD14 5LS (signed from A1)
12-11 (midnight Fri & Sat) (01890) 761253
thecrawinn.co.uk
2 changing beers (sourced nationally; often Arbor, Cheviot, Swannay) H
A revitalised and friendly 18th-century Grade C-listed country inn. The real ales (three in summer) are usually from smaller breweries, as can be seen from the many pumpclips festooning the beams. A good selection of bottled beers is also available. The bar has a wood-burning stove and tables for dining and drinking. There is also an attractive little snug. Excellent home-cooked food is served in both the bar and well-appointed restaurant, with takeaways available. Q P (34)

Burnmouth

First & Last

Upper Burnmouth, TD14 5SL
3-11; 12-1am Fri & Sat; 12.30-11 Sun (01890) 781306
thefirstandlastpub.co.uk
2 changing beers (sourced locally; often Born in the Borders, Cheviot) H
This comfortable pub near the English border is frequented by locals and travellers on the adjacent A1. Its bar area, with a real fire and sports TV, is decorated with old photographs and nautical artefacts. The pub is carpeted throughout, apart from a small dance floor in the dining/function area. Meals are served all day but note the restricted opening hours. Handy for a walk down the steep hill to the charming little harbour at Lower Burnmouth. P

Duns

Black Bull Hotel

15 Black Bull Street, TD11 3AR (between town square and A6109)
11-midnight (1am Fri & Sat); 12-midnight Sun
(01361) 883379
3 changing beers (sourced regionally; often Born in the Borders, Credence, Tempest) H
This family-run 200-year-old hotel is well worth seeking out. The cosy wood-panelled bar is popular with locals while the lounge is well suited to families. The restaurant specialises in fresh local produce, with an intimate, relaxed, candlelit atmosphere. The secluded beer garden is lovely in good weather, with a gazebo and play area. No food is available on Monday or on winter Sunday evening. P (60,260)

REAL ALE BREWERIES

Born in the Borders Jedburgh
Broughton Broughton
Campbells Peebles
Freewheelin' Peebles
Old Worthy Broughton
Tempest Tweedbank
Traquair House Innerleithen

Earlston

Red Lion

The Square, TD4 6DB
9am-11 (midnight Fri) (01896) 848994
redlionearlston.co.uk
2 changing beers (sourced locally; often Born in the Borders) H
Dating from the 1800s, this former coaching inn stands well back from the main street in this small town. It boasts a spacious bar with a community noticeboard, huge fireplace and open fire, and a pool table and dartboard in the far corner. Food is available in the bar and attractive dining room, served all day on Saturday and Sunday. A children's menu and games are provided. Alcohol is sold from 11am. P

Eddleston

Horseshoe Inn

EH45 8QP
11-11 (1am Fri & Sat; midnight Sun) (01721) 730225
horseshoeinn.co.uk
3 changing beers (sourced nationally; often Campbells, Orkney, Stewart) H
A large and welcoming free house with a separate dining room and snug, plus eight B&B rooms in an annexe. The owners have returned this former restaurant to a cosy village inn serving decent beer and food. The bar and snug feature flagstone floors, exposed beams and characterful old timber furniture; the quiet dining room has very fancy decor. Q P (X62,X70)

Galashiels

Ladhope Inn

33 High Buckholmside, TD1 2HR (on A7, ⅓ mile N of centre)
4-11 (midnight Thu; 1am Fri); 3-1am Sat; 12-11 Sun
(01896) 752446
1 changing beer (sourced regionally; often Black Sheep, Born in the Borders) H
A friendly local with a vibrant Borders atmosphere, this pub is a community hub for locally arranged golf, horse racing and fishing trips. Originating circa 1792, it has been altered considerably over the years and comprises one long single room, decorated with a large inked map of the area. Two changing real ales are sometimes offered. Three TVs ensure the pub is busy during sporting events. Live music is hosted on occasion. Children are not allowed.

Hawick

Exchange Bar (Dalton's)

1 Silver Street, TD9 0AD (off SW end of High St)
11-11 (1am Fri & Sat); 12.30-11 Sun (01450) 376067
2 changing beers (sourced regionally; often Belhaven, Born in the Borders, Orkney) H
Tucked away between St Mary's Kirk and the Heart of Hawick Heritage Centre, the pub used to overlook the Corn Exchange, hence the name – however, a previous owner was called Dalton and that name has stuck. It is a Victorian gem with original dark-wood panelling and ornate cornice work. The bar is popular with locals and there is a comfy lounge used for parties, Friday karaoke, Sunday folk sessions and music nights. Children are not admitted.

Innerleithen

St Ronan's Hotel

High Street, EH44 6HF
12-midnight (12.45am Fri & Sat) (01896) 831487
stronanshotel.co.uk
2 changing beers (sourced regionally; often Broughton, Inveralmond, Traquair House) H
A village hotel with a blue-and-white exterior, named after a local saint. The long, thin public bar is warmed by a wood-burning stove. Two alcoves in differing styles provide extra seating and a darts area. A restaurant serves evening meals. The pub offers a pick-up service and packed lunches for walkers on the nearby Southern Upland Way, and has indoor games and a garden play area for children. P (X62)

Traquair Arms Hotel

Traquair Road, EH44 6PD (on B709, off A72)
11-11 (midnight Fri & Sat); 12-11.30 Sun
(01896) 830229 traquairarmshotel.co.uk
Traquair House Bear Ale; 2 changing beers (often Campbells, Tempest) H
Elegant 18th-century hotel in the scenic Tweed Valley. The comfortable lounge bar features a welcoming real fire, and a flagstoned sports bar with logburner provides a great thawing-out space for mountain bikers, walkers and anglers. A bistro area and separate restaurant provide plenty of room for diners. Meals are served all day at weekends and there is a menu for children. One of the few outlets for draught real ale from Traquair House. The bar may close earlier if quiet.
P (X62)

Kelso

Cobbles Freehouse & Dining

7 Bowmont Street, TD5 7JH (off NE side of town square)
11.30-11; 11-1am Fri; 11-midnight Sat; 12-11 Sun
(01573) 223548 thecobbleskelso.co.uk
2 changing beers (sourced locally; often Tempest) H
Diners and drinkers are equally well catered for at this long-established gastro-pub. The bright and welcoming interior includes a cosy bar on the right and a dining area to the left, with food served throughout. There is a menu to suit all tastes including children's, available lunchtime and evening during the week, all day at the weekend. The handpumps are dedicated solely to Tempest beers. Please ask before bringing in your dog.

Rutherfords

38 The Square, TD5 7HL
12-10 (11 Fri & Sat) summer; 3-10 Mon-Fri; 12-11 Sat; 12-10 Sun winter 07803 208460
rutherfordsmicropub.co.uk
4 changing beers (sourced nationally; often Firebrick, Fyne Ales, Stewart) G
At the time of writing, this tiny shop conversion is the only micropub serving real ale in Scotland. With no TV or music to distract, it is the ideal place to visit for a friendly chat or to play board games. All real ales are served directly from the cask and third-pint paddles are available. A selection of locally produced charcuterie, pies and cheeses is served all day. Winter hours apply from November to March, when cider may not be available. Children are welcome until 3pm. CAMRA Borders Pub of the Year 2018 and runner-up in 2019.
Q

Kirk Yetholm

Border

The Green, TD5 8PQ

11.30-midnight (1am Fri & Sat) ☎ (01573) 420237
borderhotel.co.uk

Hadrian Border Tyneside Blonde; 2 changing beers (sourced nationally; often Belhaven, Born in the Borders, Greene King) H

An attractive 260-year-old coaching inn with bar areas and a conservatory restaurant. It is popular with walkers, being at the confluence of several long-distance footpaths. Photos and pictures depict items of local interest. In a tradition from Wainwright's time, those completing the Pennine Way are awarded a free half of Pennine Pint. The hearty food, served all day on Sunday, is home cooked and features locally sourced ingredients. There is a menu for children, who can also enjoy games and a garden play area.
P (81)

Leitholm

Plough Inn

Main Street, TD12 4JN

closed Mon & Tue; 5.30-10 Wed; 12-3, 5.30-10 Thu; 12-3, 5.30-11 Fri & Sat; 12-10 Sun ☎ (01890) 840408
theploughinnleitholm.co.uk

House beer (by Born in the Borders); 2 changing beers (sourced nationally; often Cheviot, Greene King, Hetton Law) H

A charming family-run inn whose wood-floored bar is decorated and furnished to create a bright, modern and welcoming ambience. A massive clock dominates the fireplace. The accommodation is of a high standard and includes one dog-friendly room. Opening hours may be extended in summer. Local CAMRA Real Ale Quality Award winner 2018.
P (85)

Morebattle

Templehall Hotel

Main Street, TD5 8QQ

12-11 (1am Fri & Sat) ☎ (01573) 440249
templehallhotel.com

2 changing beers (sourced regionally; often Born in the Borders, Inveralmond) H

Templehall started life as part of the Temple Dairy back in 1812 and is now a small, family-owned village hotel, popular with walkers on the St Cuthbert's Way. The hub of the hotel is Cubby's, a cosy L-shaped bar. The adjacent lounge also functions as the dining room, and as a tea room in the summer months. Accommodation packages are offered to walkers. In winter the hotel opens at 4pm Monday-Thursday. P (81)

Mountbenger

Gordon Arms

TD7 5LE (at A708/B709 crossroads)

11-11 ☎ (01750) 82261 thegordonarms.com

1 changing beer (sourced locally; often Belhaven, Born in the Borders) H

Dating from 1828 and a former literati haunt for Walter Scott, James Hogg, Robert Burns and William Wordsworth among others. It reopened in 2012 and now doubles as a recording studio, hosting frequent folk music weekends. Walkers on the nearby Southern Upland Way are welcomed. The real ale is often local with two offered at busier times. Despite the remote location the hotel is open all year round, with food served all day and B&B accommodation available.
Q P

Paxton

Cross Inn

TD15 1TE (off B6461)

11.30-11 Mon-Sat; 12-10 Sun summer; closed Mon & Tue; 12-2.30, 5.30-10 Wed-Fri; 12-10 Sun winter
☎ (01289) 384877 thecrossinn.co.uk

Timothy Taylor Landlord; 2 changing beers (sourced regionally; often Firebrick, Hetton Law, Rigg & Furrow) H

An appealing 19th-century village local with friendly staff. Its small, welcoming bar is stone-floored; the attractive larger dining and function area has floorboards and carpeting. Real cider is occasionally available. Food is very much part of the pub's offering, with a menu that should appeal to most tastes, supplemented by daily specials (no food Sun eve). A children's menu helps make families welcome. P (32,87)

Peebles

Bridge Inn (Trust)

Portbrae, EH45 8AW

11-midnight (1am Thu-Sat); 12-midnight Sun
☎ (01721) 720589

Fyne Ales Jarl; 3 changing beers (sourced nationally; often Born in the Borders, Stewart, Tempest) H

Cheerful, welcoming pub also known as the Trust and once called the Tweedside Inn. The bright, comfortable bar is decorated with jugs, bottles, pictures of old Peebles and displays relating to outdoor pursuits. There is a cosy corner with a logburner and a small room to the rear. The suntrap patio overlooks the river and hills beyond. The Gents has superb old fittings. Children are not admitted. Local CAMRA Pub of the Year 2019.

West Linton

Gordon Arms Hotel

Dolphinton Road, EH46 7DR (on A702)

11-midnight (1am Fri & Sat); 12-11 Sun
☎ (01968) 660208 thegordon.co.uk

4 changing beers (sourced nationally; often Belhaven, Black Sheep, Stewart) H

Situated in a picturesque village on the road from Edinburgh to Biggar. The large L-shaped, airy bar has stone walls and cornicing more reminiscent of an Edinburgh pub than a village local. There is a roaring log fire in winter and you can relax in comfortable seating. Meals including a children's menu are served in the bar, restaurant and covered outdoor area, and are available all day on Sunday.
P

Is there anywhere in this damned place where we can get a decent bottle of Bass?
Alfred, Lord Tennyson, during a public performance of one of his poems, 1862

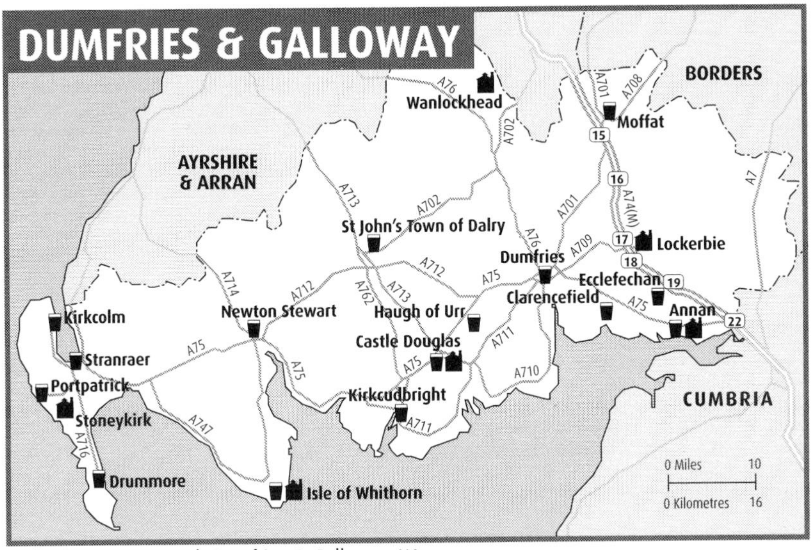

Authority area covered: Dumfries & Galloway UA

Annan

Blue Bell Inn

10 High Street, DG12 6AG

11-11 (midnight Thu-Sat); 12.30-11 Sun

(01461) 202385

Caledonian Deuchars IPA; 3 changing beers (sourced nationally; often Carlisle, Kelburn, Strathaven) H

Former coaching inn dating from 1770 where Hans Christian Andersen is said to have stayed, and part of the Gretna State Management Scheme from 1917 to 1972 when it was owned by the government. The pub is home to many community activities along with annual beer and cider festivals. The red sandstone building houses some traditional features, notably the panelled interior and rear stables. The on-site Motte & Bailey brewery range is only available in this pub and may include one-off brews.
P (79,383)

Castle Douglas

Sulwath Brewery Tap Room L

209 King Street, DG7 1DT

11-6; closed Sun (01556) 504525

sulwathbrewers.co.uk

Sulwath Black Galloway; 5 changing beers (sourced locally; often Sulwath) H

The visitor centre for Sulwath Brewery is a showcase for the brewery's beers although not all are conditioned. At times there may be guest beers from elsewhere. One draught cider, usually from Westons, is also stocked. Dried hop bines decorate the walls and old wooden casks of various sizes provide some of the furniture. Brewery tours are available and there is an annual beer festival.
Q P

Clarencefield

Farmers Inn

Main Street, DG1 4NF

12-2.30, 6-midnight (12.30am Fri); 12-12.30am Sat; 12-midnight Sun (01387) 870675 farmersinn.co.uk

2 changing beers (sourced nationally; often Born in the Borders) H

A 300-year-old village inn, run personally by its proprietors, located close to the Savings Bank Museum at Ruthwell. It is a real village pub with a good atmosphere and service. The building has a small bar and lounge with a separate games room that also houses the village post office. The bar has a cosy feel, enhanced by a warming stove in winter. Robert Burns visited here during his ill-fated attempt to recuperate at nearby Brow Well in July 1796. Q P (79)

Drummore

Clashwhannon

DG9 9QE (on A716 S from Stranraer)

12-midnight summer; closed Mon & Tue; 4-11 Wed & Thu; 12-11 Fri-Sun (01776) 840632 clashwhannon.co.uk

3 changing beers (often Fyne Ales, Hadrian Border, Portpatrick) H

This friendly and relaxing bar serves the adjacent caravan park and is open all year round. Demand from visitors and locals alike has seen the emergence of real ale in this remote location close to the Mull of Galloway. There is a bar area plus a large family room and restaurant where local produce is served at reasonable prices. Three handpumps are used in summer, one in winter. Music and variety events feature during the summer. P (407)

Dumfries

Cavens Arms

20 Buccleuch Street, DG1 2AH

REAL ALE BREWERIES

Five Kingdoms Isle of Whithorn
Lola Rose Wanlockhead
Lowland Lockerbie (NEW)
Mote & Bailey Annan (NEW)
Portpatrick Stoneykirk
Sulwath Castle Douglas

11-11 (midnight Wed, Fri & Sat) (01387) 252896
cavensarms.com
Fyne Ales Jarl; Greene King Abbot; Morland Old Speckled Hen; Swannay Orkney IPA; 4 changing beers (sourced nationally)
Busy food-oriented pub that is popular with diners for its range of good-value meals. A separate restaurant area has been created to cope with demand at peak times. Drinkers are welcomed in the bar area but seating can be limited during food service times. Guest ales are from a wide range of breweries, including some rarely seen in this locality. There are regular charity quizzes and other theme nights. Local CAMRA Pub of the Year 2017.

Coach & Horses

66 Whitesands, DG1 2RS
closed Mon; 11-11 (midnight Sat); 12.30-11 Sun
07746 675349
Draught Bass
A small, lively former coaching inn overlooking the River Nith. Situated next to the Tourist Information Centre, the pub is handy for local attractions. The small bar can feel cramped but service is always quick. The bar features a flagstone floor with a warming open fire during the colder months. There is a great atmosphere in this gem of a pub, enhanced by regular live music sessions. Winter opening times may vary. P

New Bazaar

39 Whitesands, DG1 2RS
11-11; 12-8 Sun (01387) 268776
Theakston XB; 3 changing beers (sourced nationally; often Fuller's, Greene King, Timothy Taylor)
Former coaching inn beside the River Nith with an attractive airy bar featuring a splendid Victorian gantry that displays an impressive malt whisky collection. The cosy lounge provides a quiet retreat and has a warming coal fire in winter. A small room is available for meetings. The pub is a favourite with football supporters attending nearby Palmerston Park and is ideally situated for car parking, local buses and tourist attractions. Winter opening times may vary. P

Riverside Bar

Dock Park, DG1 2RY
12-11 (midnight Thu; 1am Fri & Sat); 12.30-11 Sun
(01387) 254477
Morland Old Speckled Hen; 3 changing beers (sourced nationally)
The Riverside Bar is now an established venue on the Dumfries real ale scene. Comfortable and friendly, it has seating on two levels and a large conservatory. Two outside seating areas include a terrace with open views over the Dock Park and down to the River Nith. The pub is accessible from the St Michaels area near Robert Burns Mausoleum or from Dock Park. Guest beers can be sourced from local brewers as well as from further afield.

Robert the Bruce

81 Buccleuch Street, DG1 2AB
8am-midnight (1am Fri & Sat) (01387) 270320
Caledonian Deuchars IPA; Greene King Abbot; Sharp's Doom Bar; 4 changing beers (sourced nationally)
This former Methodist church, sensitively converted by Wetherspoon in 2001, has a relaxed atmosphere and is a popular meeting place in the town centre. There is a pleasant outside seating area to the rear. The pub stands near the site where Robert the Bruce killed John Comyn in 1306 in an incident linked to Scotland's fight for independence. The food menu offers a range of good-value meals all day, every day. Alcohol is served from 11am. P

Tam o' Shanter

113-117 Queensberry Street, DG1 1BH
11-11 (midnight Fri & Sat); 12-10 Sun (01387) 267880
Broughton Clipper IPA, Proper IPA; 4 changing beers (sourced nationally; often Broughton, Sulwath)
Established in 1630, this 17th-century coaching inn with a connection to Robert Burns has been a mainstay of the Dumfries beer scene for many years. It is a small traditional pub with a main bar and a couple of quiet cosy rooms including a games area behind. An upstairs room hosts live music and other functions. It is well positioned just off the High Street. Two of the guest beers are usually from local breweries. P

Ecclefechan

Ecclefechan Hotel

High Street, DG11 3DF
4-11 (midnight Fri); 12-midnight Sat; 12-11 Sun
(01576) 300213 ecclefechanhotel.co.uk
2 changing beers
Family-run hotel in a Grade C-listed building dating from the 1730s. Close to the M74, it is a convenient stop for travellers and offers a varied selection of real ales plus home-cooked meals and B&B accommodation. It has undergone a major refurbishment, with two real fires ensuring a cosy welcome. The picturesque village of Ecclefechan is the birthplace of Thomas Carlyle and was visited by Robert Burns. Q P (384,383)

Haugh of Urr

Laurie Arms Hotel

11-13 Main Street, DG7 3YA
12-2, 5-midnight (10 Mon & Tue); 12-midnight Sat & Sun
(01556) 660246 haugh-of-urr.co.uk
4 changing beers (sourced nationally; often Caledonian, Fyne Ales, Strathaven)
Welcoming family-run pub and restaurant in a charming, quiet village, popular for its range of beers and freshly cooked food featuring local produce. It has a good village-pub atmosphere, enhanced on winter nights by a warming log fire in the bar. Up to four beers are available depending on the season, mainly from independent breweries. National Cycle Route 7 passes nearby. A former local CAMRA award winner. Winter opening times may vary. P (501)

Isle of Whithorn

Steam Packet Inn

Harbour Row, DG8 8LL (on B7004 from Whithorn)
11-11; 12-11 Sun (01988) 500334
thesteampacketinn.biz
Morland Old Speckled Hen; 7 changing beers (often Five Kingdoms, Fyne Ales, Kelburn)
Traditional and historic family-run hotel overlooking the harbour, welcoming to all including families and pets. The public bar has stone walls and a multi-fuel stove, and there are pictures of the village and maritime events throughout. Four guest ales from a wide variety of

breweries are available in both bars, along with up to four beers plus bottle-conditioned ales from Five Kingdoms, the in-house brewery. The extensive food menu features local produce and includes a Sunday hot buffet and various themed food nights. Q🥾❀🛏◐◑♣🍎P🚌(415)🐾📶

Kirkcolm

Blue Peter Hotel

23 Main Street, DG9 0NL (on A718 5 miles N of Stranraer)

⏲ closed Mon, Wed & Thu; 7-11 Tue; 4-midnight Fri & Sat; 2-9 Sun ☎ (01776) 853221

2 changing beers (often Born in the Borders) Ⓗ

A small family-run hotel featuring two bars packed with memorabilia, and a decked patio for viewing the abundant wildlife, which includes red squirrels. Two handpumps dispense a constantly changing range of ales. Home-cooked food is served using fresh local produce, with takeaways available. The hotel is popular with real ale enthusiasts as well as walkers and wildlife watchers, and opens on Wednesday and Thursday evenings if darts or dominoes matches are being held. Good-value B&B is available. Q🥾❀🛏◑⛺♣🚌(408)🐾

Kirkcudbright

Selkirk Arms Hotel

High Street, DG6 4JG

⏲ 11-11 ☎ (01557) 330402 🌐 selkirkarmshotel.co.uk

2 changing beers (sourced nationally; often Sulwath) Ⓗ

Refurbished 18th-century hotel with a restaurant, bistro and lounge bar, renowned for locally sourced food, highlighted by the menus and photos of suppliers on the walls. The large garden area with tables is popular in summer. Robert Burns wrote his famous Selkirk Grace at the hotel in 1794. Kirkcudbright is notable for its artistic heritage and houses a number of interesting galleries and museums. One or two real ales are available in winter, three in summer. Q🥾❀🛏◐◑♿⛺P🚌🐾📶

Moffat

Black Bull Inn

Church Gate, DG10 9EG

⏲ 11-11 (midnight Fri & Sat) ☎ (01683) 221150
🌐 theblackbullmoffat.co.uk

Timothy Taylor Landlord; 1 changing beer (often Sulwath) Ⓗ

Recently reopened under new ownership following extensive renovations. The open-plan bar and dining area is light and airy with a small snug away from the restaurant. This historic hotel dating from 1568 is the oldest building in Moffat still in use and possibly one of the oldest hotels in Scotland. It was a centre for government troops during the time of the Covenanters and a visiting place for Robert Burns during his time as an excise officer.
Q🥾❀🛏◐◑♿⛺♣🚌🐾📶

Newton Stewart

Crown Hotel

102 Queen Street, DG8 6JW

⏲ 11-11.30 (1am Thu-Sat); 12-11.30 Sun ☎ (01671) 402727
🌐 the-crown-hotel.com

1 changing beer (often Caledonian, Greene King, Morland) Ⓗ

A well-established hotel on the outskirts of town, popular with visitors and locals. The hotel, bar and restaurant have recently been modernised. The bar, which has sports and seating areas, serves a weekly changing real ale from the Belhaven list. The restaurant offers à la carte, bar food and a Sunday carvery. To the rear are a patio, decked area and beer garden. Accommodation comprises 15 en-suite rooms.
🥾❀🛏◐◑♿⛺♣P🚌(359,500)🐾📶

Portpatrick

Crown Hotel

9 North Crescent, DG9 8SX (facing harbour)

⏲ 11-midnight (1am Fri & Sat); 12-midnight Sun
☎ (01776) 810261 🌐 crownhotelportpatrick.com

2 changing beers (often Hadrian Border, Portpatrick) Ⓗ

Hotel overlooking the picturesque and historic Portpatrick harbour with views on a clear day across to Ireland. The large comfortable bar area at the front of the building is adorned with fine pictures and ornaments and warmed by an open fire. Two regularly changing ales are sourced from breweries across the UK, including the local Portpatrick Brewery. Live music plays on Friday and Saturday nights, featuring both local and visiting musicians and groups.
🥾❀🛏◐◑♿⛺♣🚌(367)🐾📶

St John's Town of Dalry

Clachan Inn 🏆

8-10 Main Street, DG7 3UW

⏲ 12-midnight ☎ (01644) 430241 🌐 theclachaninn.co.uk

2 changing beers (sourced regionally; often Ayr, Fallen, Fyne Ales) Ⓗ

The Clachan has a reputation for excellent food, cosy, well-equipped bedrooms and a welcoming atmosphere. The menu is varied with excellent daily specials, and the kitchen makes use of local produce including organic lamb and venison. The pub has an attractive traditional main bar, a relaxing lounge bar and a separate restaurant – both bars have wonderfully warming open log fires in winter. A handy stop for walkers on the Southern Upland Way. Local CAMRA Pub of the Year 2018 & 2019. Q🥾❀🛏◐◑♿⛺♣🍎P🚌(520,521)🐾📶

Stranraer

Grapes

4-6 Bridge Street, DG9 7HY

⏲ 11-11.30 (midnight Thu-Sat); 12.30-11.30 Sun
☎ (01776) 703386 🌐 thegrapes1862.co.uk

2 changing beers (often Portpatrick) Ⓗ

Popular historic public bar, with an impressive mirror and gantry, which has altered little in over 50 years. It has a refurbished snug bar downstairs, an upstairs Art Deco lounge/function room, and a courtyard area with seating. Local musicians play in the public bar most Friday evenings, and touring American-style bands often perform upstairs. There is a strong commitment to real ales sourced both locally and from all over the UK. Mini beer festivals are held twice yearly. 🥾❀🚆♣🚌🐾📶

SCOTLAND

EDINBURGH & THE LOTHIANS

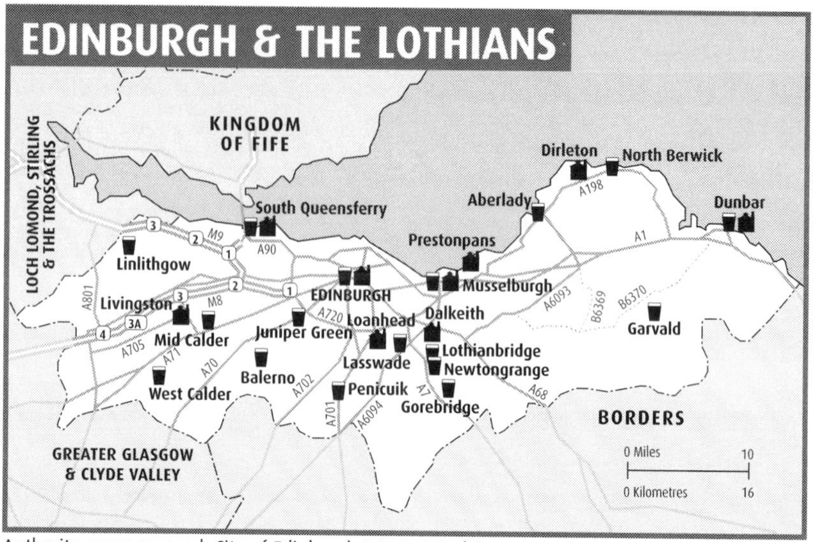

Authority areas covered: City of Edinburgh UA, East Lothian UA, Midlothian UA, West Lothian UA

Aberlady

Ducks Inn

Main Street, EH32 0RE

12-11 (1am Thu-Sat; midnight Sun) (01875) 870682

ducks.co.uk

Sharp's Doom Bar; 1 changing beer (sourced nationally; often Knops) H

Decorated with sporting and brewing memorabilia, this hotel hosts bar games including the unique Ducks Challenge putting contest. Three real ales are available in summer. Meals are served all day and families are welcome until 8pm. The place is closed Monday and Tuesday in winter and may shut early at other times if quiet. **Q P**

Balerno

Grey Horse

20 Main Street, EH14 7EH (off A70, in pedestrian area)

12-11 (midnight Fri & Sat) (0131) 449 2888

greyhorsebalerno.com

Fyne Ales Jarl; 4 changing beers (sourced regionally; often Alechemy, Orkney, Stewart) H

Traditional stone-built village pub, dating from the 18th century. The cosy public bar retains original features including wood panelling and a fine Bernard's mirror. The lounge is furnished with tables and chairs and offers a gastro-pub-style menu, with a children's option and occasional Chinese specials (no food Mon). Attractions include a monthly Sunday folk evening and major sports events shown on TV in the function room. Dogs are allowed in the bar, with biscuits and water provided. **Q**

Dunbar

Volunteer Arms

17 Victoria Street, EH42 1HP

12-11 Mon-Wed; 11-midnight Thu; 11-1am Fri & Sat; 12.30-midnight Sun (01368) 862278

volunteerarmsdunbar.co.uk

2 changing beers (sourced nationally; often Harviestoun, Orkney, Tryst) H

Close to Dunbar harbour, this is a friendly, traditional locals' pub. The cosy wood-panelled bar is decorated with lots of fishing and lifeboat-oriented memorabilia. The two real ales are often from smaller breweries. Upstairs is a restaurant serving an excellent, good-value range of food including a children's menu, with an emphasis on seafood. Meals are available all day, newspapers are provided and there is live music on Wednesday. Dogs must be on a lead.

Edinburgh: Central

Abbotsford Bar & Restaurant ★

3-5 Rose Street, EH2 2PR

11-11 (midnight Fri & Sat) (0131) 225 5276

theabbotsford.com

6 changing beers (sourced regionally; often Cromarty, Fyne Ales, Swannay) H/A

A traditional Scottish bar featuring a magnificent island bar and gantry in dark mahogany that have been fixtures since 1902. There is an extensive food menu, available all day in the bar. Children over five are permitted in the restaurant upstairs, where real ale can be ordered from downstairs. Closing times are later during festivals in August and December. **Q** (Waverley)

Blue Blazer

2 Spittal Street, EH3 9DX

11-1am; 12.30-1am Sun (0131) 229 5030

theblueblazer.co.uk

Stewart Jack Back, Pentland IPA A**; 6 changing beers (sourced regionally; often Cromarty, Edinbrew, Kelburn)** H

Two-roomed pub with wooden floors, high ceilings and old brewery window panels giving an old-fashioned feel, complemented by candles in the evening. Named after a local school uniform, it features a tiled blue blazer inlaid on the floor. The pub specialises in real ales from smaller Scottish breweries. Snacks are available all day. Close to theatres and cinemas, the pub stays open later in August and December. Children are not admitted.

Bow Bar

80 West Bow, EH1 2HH (Old Town, off Grassmarket)
12-midnight; 12.30-11.30 Sun (0131) 226 7667
thebowbar.co.uk
Fallen Oddysey; Stewart 80/-; Tempest Armadillo; 5 changing beers (sourced nationally; often Cromarty, Fallen, Swannay) A
A re-creation of a classic Scottish one-roomed ale house, dedicated to traditional Scottish air pressure dispense and upright drinking. The walls are festooned with original brewery mirrors and the superb gantry does justice to an award-winning selection of almost 400 single malt whiskies and international bottled beers. The real ales can be from anywhere in the UK. Beer festivals are held in January and July along with frequent tap takeovers. Gourmet pies are available 12-4pm. Children are not admitted. Q(Waverley)

Cafe Royal ★

19 West Register Street, EH2 2AA (off E end of Princes St)
11-11 Mon-Wed (midnight Thu; 1am Fri & Sat); 11-midnight Sun (0131) 556 1884
caferoyaledinburgh.co.uk
Greene King IPA; Stewart Pentland IPA; 5 changing beers (sourced regionally; often Belhaven, Kelburn, Stewart) H
One of the finest Victorian pub interiors in Scotland, dominated by an impressive oval island bar with ornate brass light fittings. It also features magnificent ceramic tiled murals of innovators, and sporting windows in the adjacent Oyster Bar/Restaurant. The real ales are mainly from Scottish breweries. Meals are served all day. Children are only allowed in the restaurant.
Q(Waverley)

Caley Picture House

31 Lothian Road, EH1 2DJ (W edge of centre)
8am-1am (0131) 656 0752
Caledonian Deuchars IPA; Greene King Abbot; 9 changing beers (sourced nationally) H
A stunning renovation of a Grade B-listed former cinema, originally opened in 1923. The main bar has a superb screen backdrop and is complemented by a smaller bar up in the gods, complete with plush cinema seating. A queue forms at the bar at busy times. Meals are served all day and there is a children's menu.

Guildford Arms

1 West Register Street, EH2 2AA (off E end of Princes St)
11-11 (midnight Thu-Sat) (0131) 556 4312
guildfordarms.com
Bombardier; Fyne Ales Jarl; Orkney Dark Island; Stewart Pentland IPA; Swannay Orkney IPA; 4 changing beers (sourced nationally; often Alechemy, Loch Lomond) H
A large hostelry built in the golden age of Victorian pub design. There is a large standing space around the canopied bar plus extensive seating areas. The diverse range of real ales includes many from Scottish micros, and real cider is occasionally available. Bar snacks are on offer all day. Children over five are allowed in the noteworthy upstairs gallery restaurant. (Waverley)

Halfway House

24 Fleshmarket Close, EH1 1BX (up steps opp Waverley Station Market St entrance)
11-11 (midnight Fri & Sat) (0131) 225 7101
4 changing beers (sourced nationally; often Broughton, Stewart, Strathbraan) H
Cosy, characterful bar hidden halfway down an Old Town close. Railway memorabilia decorate the interior of this small, often busy, bar. At the front are tables with window seats and stools. The rear area has more comfortable semicircular booth seating where children may be allowed if the pub is quiet. There are usually four interesting real ales from smaller Scottish breweries. Meals and bar snacks are served all day. The bar may stay open until 1am during busy times of year.
(Waverley)

Haymarket

11-14A West Maitland Street, EH12 5DS (W edge of centre)
12-11; 11-midnight Thu; 11-1am Fri & Sat
(0131) 228 2537
St Austell Nicholson's Pale Ale; Stewart Jack Back; 8 changing beers (sourced nationally; often Brew York, St Austell, Stewart) H
A large, busy pub whose comfortable interior is decorated with historic prints of the building and locality. An island bar overlooks the large central area with a raised mezzanine floor to one side and arches leading through to a restaurant. Twelve handpumps dispense a varied and interesting range of real ales and occasionally a real cider. Food is served all day from the Nicholson's and Pie House menus. Children are permitted if dining. May close earlier if quiet.
(Haymarket)

Jolly Judge

7 James Court, 493 Lawnmarket, EH1 2PB
12-midnight (11 Tue, Wed & Sun) (0131) 225 2669
jollyjudge.co.uk
3 changing beers (sourced nationally; often Cromarty, Tempest) H
Comfortable bar with an attractive painted ceiling hidden down an Old Town close just off the Royal Mile. This is a welcome spot for refreshment after visiting the castle. There are steps down to the entrance, as was common in the past. The real ales are usually from smaller breweries UK wide. This is one of Edinburgh's top pubs for cider, selling a varying selection of four types. Dogs are permitted after 3pm, but no children inside. Local CAMRA Cider Pub of the Year 2019.
Q(Waverley)

REAL ALE BREWERIES

Alechemy Livingston
Barney's Edinburgh
Belhaven Dunbar
Bellfield Edinburgh
Black Metal Edinburgh
Caledonian Edinburgh
Campervan Edinburgh
Cross Borders Dalkeith
Edinbrew Livingston
Eyeball Dunbar
Faking Bad Prestonpans (NEW)
Ferry South Queensferry
Hanging Bat Edinburgh
Hurly Burly Musselburgh
Knops Dirleton
Pilot Edinburgh
Stewart Loanhead
Top Out Loanhead

Monty's

185 Morrison Street, EH3 8DZ (W edge of centre)
4-11 Mon; 12-midnight Tue-Thu; 12-1am Fri; 12.30-midnight Sun ☎ (0131) 629 1104 montys.bar
Fyne Ales Hurricane Jack; Swannay Orkney IPA; 4 changing beers (sourced nationally; often Alechemy, Cross Borders, Oakham) H
Busy street-corner bar favoured by a younger clientele but welcoming to all. Its wood-panelled interior has large windows and a varied range of comfortable seating. There is also an upstairs area with cosy seating. Cask ale is featured on the bar counter with keg beer consigned to the back wall, along with impressive laddered and back-lit glass spirit shelves. Children are not allowed.
(Haymarket)

Oxford Bar ★

8 Young Street, EH2 4JB (New Town, off Charlotte Sq)
12-midnight; 11-1am Fri & Sat; 12.30-11 Sun
☎ (0131) 539 7119
Caledonian Deuchars IPA; 3 changing beers (sourced regionally; often Fyne Ales, Inveralmond, Stewart) H
A simple, vibrant drinking shop that is little changed since the late 19th century. The bar counter nearly fills the small front room but the side room is more spacious, and enhanced by a real fire. The pub is renowned as a favourite of Rebus and his creator Ian Rankin. Its real ales are normally from Scottish breweries. Children are not admitted. Q

Teuchters

26 William Street, EH3 7NH (W edge of centre)
10.30-1am ☎ (0131) 225 2973 teuchtersbar.co.uk
Fyne Ales Jarl; Stewart Pentland IPA; Swannay Dark Munro; Timothy Taylor Landlord; 1 changing beer (sourced regionally; often Fyne Ales, Inveralmond) H
A cosy but deceptively roomy bar with a rustic feel, wooden beams and original stone walls. Small place name plates from Teuchterland create a frieze along the walls. Real ales are usually from Scottish micros. The gantry has an impressive range of single malt whiskies and an explanation of the pub's name. Bar snacks are offered and the restaurant serves fresh local produce. Alcohol is available from 11am.
(Haymarket)

Edinburgh: East

Regent ✔

2 Montrose Terrace, EH7 5DL (1 mile E of centre)
12-1am; 12.30-1am Sun ☎ (0131) 661 8198
Caledonian Deuchars IPA; 2 changing beers (sourced nationally; often Edinbrew, Inveralmond, Stewart) H
Large tenement bar with two rooms, popular with LGBT real ale drinkers. The comfortable seating includes banquettes, leather sofas and armchairs. Real ales are served without sparklers on request. The cider is Westons Old Rosie. Bar snacks and simple meals are served all day, with good vegetarian and vegan options. Children over five are permitted until 8pm.

Edinburgh: North

Brass Monkey

362 Leith Walk, EH6 5BR (1 mile SE of centre)
12-1am; 12.30-1am Sun ☎ (0131) 554 5286
brassmonkeyleith.com
2 changing beers (sourced nationally; often Cross Borders) H
A friendly howff with a varied clientele, this is a welcome addition to the real ale scene on Leith Walk. Its large, three-sided traditional bar has a mix of seating including comfy leather sofas, high bar stools and tables and chairs. Two handpumps serve an ever-changing selection of real ales, backed-up by a good range of bottled beers. The varied menu is available all day, featuring vegetarian and vegan options with a home-made twist.

Dreadnought

72 North Fort Street, Leith, EH6 4HL (2 miles N of centre)
5-midnight; 2-1am Fri & Sat; 2-midnight Sun
☎ 07876 351535 dreadnoughtleith.com
4 changing beers (sourced nationally; often Brass Castle) H
A welcoming one-roomed pub with big picture windows, a high ceiling with plaster cornicing, sports TV screens and an attractive old-fashioned bar gantry. The Brass Castle beers are all vegan. No food is prepared on-site but pizza can be ordered 5-10pm from Origano. A wheelchair ramp is available but there is no toilet access.

Stockbridge Tap

2-4 Raeburn Place, Stockbridge, EH4 1HN (N of centre)
12-11.30 (midnight Thu-Sat); 12.30-11.30 Sun
☎ (0131) 343 3000
Swannay Island Hopping; 5 changing beers (sourced nationally; often Alechemy, Cross Borders, Cromarty) H
A multi CAMRA award-winning specialist real ale house, the pub offers unusual and interesting ales from all over the UK and holds occasional beer festivals. The L-shaped room, with a bright bar area and ample seating, boasts mirrors from lost breweries including Murray's and Campbell's. Cold snacks are served outside of main food times. Children are not admitted. Closing time may be a little earlier if quiet. Joint CAMRA Edinburgh Pub of the Year 2019.

Teuchters Landing

1C Dock Place, Leith, EH6 6LU (2 miles N of centre)
10.30-1am ☎ (0131) 554 7427 teuchtersbar.co.uk/teuchters-landing-bar-edinburgh
Fyne Ales Jarl; Inveralmond Ossian; Timothy Taylor Landlord; 3 changing beers (sourced regionally; often Cromarty, Fallen, Swannay) H
Once the waiting room for the Leith to Aberdeen ferry, the attractive front bar has a wood-panelled ceiling edged with tiles featuring Scottish place names from Teuchterland. To the rear are smaller rooms and a large conservatory extension opening out onto a pontoon floating on the Water of Leith. The varied food menu, available all day, features meals served in mugs. An excellent selection of malt whiskies is available. Children are allowed in the back rooms. Alcohol is served from 11am.

Windsor

45 Elm Row, EH7 4AH (N of centre)
12-midnight (1am Wed-Sat); 12.30-midnight Sun
☎ (0131) 556 4558 windsoredinburgh.co.uk
Caledonian Deuchars IPA; 3 changing beers H
This late-Victorian locals' bar retains a traditional look and fine ceiling cornices but is now brighter and more open plan. Comfortable green leather armchairs and bench seating complement the

extensive wood panelling; a raised rear area features a mirror and window with the pub logo. The three changing real ales come from a range of Scottish and north-east English breweries. Simple bar snacks are served. Children are not admitted.

Edinburgh: South

Cask & Barrel (Southside)

24-26 West Preston St., EH8 9PZ (1m S of centre)
12-midnight; 12-1am Fri; 11-1am Sat ☎ (0131) 667 0856
Swannay Orkney Best; Tryst Drovers 80/-; 6 changing beers (sourced nationally; often Cross Borders, Fyne Ales, Loch Lomond Brewery) Ⓗ
Modern re-creation of a Scottish city or tenement bar. The single room, with windows front and back, is divided by a horseshoe bar with a dark-wood gantry adorned with decorative wooden casks. Sport is screened on multiple TVs with the sound off. A good place to try real ales from interesting breweries UK-wide. Children are not admitted.

Cloisters Bar

26 Brougham Street, EH3 9JH (SW edge of centre)
12-midnight (1am Fri & Sat); 12.30-midnight Sun
☎ (0131) 221 9997 cloistersbar.com
Stewart Pentland IPA, Holy Grale; 7 changing beers (sourced nationally; often Alechemy, Swannay, Thornbridge) Ⓗ
Established in 1995 in the former All Saints Parsonage, this warm and friendly bar retains many traditional features. Its real ales are generally from interesting breweries UK wide. Frequent tap takeovers and Meet the Brewer events are held. The wide range of single malt whiskies, gins and rums does justice to the outstanding gantry. Freshly prepared meals are served all day, except on Mondays. Under-16s are not admitted.
Q

Dagda Bar

93-95 Buccleuch Street, EH8 9NG (S of centre)
12.30-1am; 1-1am Sun ☎ (0131) 667 9773
4 changing beers (sourced regionally; often Cromarty, Ferry, Oakham) Ⓗ
Small ground-floor bar in an 18th-century tenement terrace, in the heart of a university area. A stone-flagged floor surrounds the large rectangular counter which takes up at least a third of the room. Children are not admitted.

Edinburgh: West

Athletic Arms (Diggers) ✓

1-3 Angle Park Terrace, EH11 2JX (1 mile SW of centre)
11-1am ☎ (0131) 337 3822 athleticarms.com
Caledonian Deuchars IPA; Stewart Diggers 80/- Ⓐ; 4 changing beers (sourced nationally; often Alechemy, Caledonian, Edinbrew) Ⓗ
Dating from 1897, this legendary Edinburgh pub gained the name Diggers due to its location between two graveyards. Quieter now than in its heyday, though packed when Hearts are at home, it continues to extend a warm welcome to locals and visitors alike. Banquette seating lines the walls, and a compass drawing in the floor aids the geographically challenged. Children are allowed in the two smaller back rooms if eating; the pies are outstanding. There is further seating here, and the larger room also hosts a dartboard.

Golden Rule ✓

30 Yeaman Place, EH11 1BT (1 mile W of centre)
12-midnight; 12-1am Fri & Sat; 12.30-midnight Sun
☎ (0131) 229 3413 goldenruleedinburgh.co.uk
Stewart Jack Back; 4 changing beers (sourced nationally; often Arran, Cromarty, Swannay) Ⓗ
A split-level Victorian tenement bar close to the Union Canal and the Fountain Park entertainment complex. The pub is a real ale showcase, with a great selection from breweries around the UK. The upstairs bar is pleasantly furnished with bench seating, tables and stools. The downstairs bar comes into its own at weekends, but real ale has to be carried down the steps. There is live music most Saturday evenings and a quiz on Tuesday evening. Children are not admitted.

Roseburn Bar ✓

1 Roseburn Terrace, EH12 5NG (1½ mile W of centre)
9am-11 (midnight Thu-Sat); 11-11 Sun
☎ (0131) 337 1067 roseburnbar.co.uk
Caledonian Deuchars IPA; Fyne Ales Jarl; 2 changing beers (sourced nationally; often Edinbrew, Tryst) Ⓗ
A traditional pub that is popular with locals, and close to Murrayfield for rugby and Tynecastle for football. It boasts high ceilings and a largely wooden interior, with interesting mirrors and period photos on the walls. There are numerous comfortable booths along the walls and two separate lounge areas. Three TVs show sporting events, though the volume is typically kept low. Live music plays on Friday and Saturday evenings. Children are not admitted.

Winstons ✓

20 Kirk Loan, Corstorphine, EH12 7HD (3 miles W of centre, off St Johns Road)
11-midnight (1am Fri & Sat); 12.30-midnight Sun
☎ (0131) 539 7077 winstonslounge.co.uk
Stewart Pentland IPA Ⓟ; 3 changing beers (sourced regionally; often Harviestoun, Kinneil, Swannay) Ⓗ
A comfortable lounge bar in Corstorphine, just over a mile from Murrayfield stadium and half a mile from the zoo. The small, modern building houses a warm and welcoming community pub frequented by old and young alike. Real ales are usually from a variety of Scottish breweries. Wonderful home-made pies are a highlight on the lunchtime menu. Attractions include sports TV and monthly live music. Children are not admitted.

Garvald

Garvald Inn

EH41 4LN
closed Mon; 12-11 (midnight Fri & Sat); 12.30-7.30 Sun
☎ (01620) 830311
1 changing beer (sourced regionally; often Stewart) Ⓗ
A family-run 18th-century pub in a pretty village by the Lammermuir Hills. The bar is cosy and welcoming with half-panelled walls, a crimson colour scheme and an exposed stone wall with a large wood-burning stove. The inn is popular for food, served in both the bar and tiny dining room. Families are welcome, with a children's menu, garden play area and toys. Live music plays on occasion. Q P

SCOTLAND

Gorebridge

Stobsmill Inn (Bruntons)

25 Powdermill Brae, EH23 4HX (500yds S of centre)
12-11.30 Mon; 5-11 Tue; 12-11 Wed; 12-11.30 Thu; 12-midnight Fri & Sat; 12.30-11 Sun ☎ (01875) 820202
1 changing beer (often Born in the Borders, Cross Borders, Stewart) H
Built in 1866, the pub is distinguished from neighbouring houses only by a large red T and two small signs. The wooden-floored single room has a long L-shaped bar counter lined with stools in one area. There is also bench seating, tables and chairs. Downstairs is an attractive lounge. Entry is restricted to those over 21, apart from weekend afternoons for meals. P (29,33)

Juniper Green

Juniper Green Inn

542 Lanark Road, EH14 5EL
11-11 (midnight Thu-Sat); 12.30-11 Sun
☎ (0131) 458 5395
Caledonian Deuchars IPA; Timothy Taylor Landlord; 2 changing beers (sourced nationally; often Alechemy, Broughton, Stewart) H
Well-appointed single-room lounge bar in a late-1800s building, with a strong community spirit. The varied food menu includes light meals (no food Sun & Mon). The secluded patio and garden are popular in summer. Children over 12 are permitted if dining. Q

Lasswade

Laird & Dog Inn

5 High Street, EH18 1NA (on A768 near river)
9am-11 (midnight Thu; 1am Fri & Sat; 12.30am Sun)
☎ (0131) 663 9219 lairdanddoginn.co.uk
3 changing beers (sourced regionally; often Ferry, Fyne Ales, Stewart) H
Comfortable village local just five miles from central Edinburgh. It caters for all tastes, offering different areas for a quiet drink, a meal or a game of pool accompanied by music. The walls are decorated with old photographs and a possible explanation of the origin of the village name. The conservatory restaurant, which has an unusual bottle-shaped well by its entrance, serves meals all day, breakfast until noon. Alcohol is available from 11am. P

Linlithgow

Four Marys

65-67 High Street, EH49 7ED
11-11 (11.30 Wed & Thu; 1am Fri & Sat); 12.30-11 Sun
☎ (01506) 842147 fourmarys-linlithgow.co.uk
Belhaven St Andrew's Ale; Caledonian Deuchars IPA; 6 changing beers (sourced regionally; often Fyne Ales, Swannay) H
A stone's throw from Linlithgow Palace, birthplace of Mary Queen of Scots, the building dates back to around 1500 and is named after the Queen's ladies-in-waiting. It has had several changes of use over the years – at one time it was a chemist's run by the Waldie family whose most famous member, David, helped establish the anaesthetic properties of chloroform in 1847. The pub serves good-quality food and at least six real ales from breweries far and wide. Local CAMRA Pub of the Year 2018.
Q

Platform 3

1A High Street, EH49 7AB
10.30-midnight (1am Fri & Sat); 12.30-midnight Sun
☎ (01506) 847405 platform3.co.uk
Stewart Pentland IPA; 2 changing beers (sourced regionally; often Cairngorm, Harviestoun, Tryst) H
Small, friendly hostelry on the railway station approach, originally the public bar of the hotel next door and renovated in 1998 as a pub in its own right. Look out for the goods train that journeys from the station above the bar, with ducks waiting for a train that never comes. Two Scottish beers are served in addition to the regular ale. Dogs are welcome with biscuits 'on tap'. A live departures board keeps travellers informed. Alcohol is served from 11am (12.30pm Sun). Local CAMRA Pub of the Year 2019.

Lothianbridge

Sun Inn

EH22 4TR (on A7, near Newtongrange)
8am-11 (midnight Fri & Sat) ☎ (0131) 663 2456
thesuninnedinburgh.co.uk
2 changing beers (sourced regionally; often Ferry, Stewart, Tryst) H
Award-winning gastro-pub overlooked by the 23-span Waverley Line viaduct. The front area is for dining; to the rear is a modern bar area for drinkers and a coffee shop/function room. Meals are served all day on Sunday until 7pm, breakfast until 11am during the week. The bar may close earlier if quiet. Alcohol is available from 11am.
P (29,339)

Mid Calder

Black Bull

Market Street, EH53 0AA
11-11 (midnight Wed & Thu; 1am Fri & Sat); 12.30-midnight Sun ☎ (01506) 882170
blackbullmidcalder.co.uk
Caledonian Deuchars IPA; 2 changing beers H
Established in 1747, the Black Bull features a fine L-shaped public bar with a wooden interior and coal fire. Families are welcome in the open-plan lounge where food is popular and served all day. Both bars are decorated with country photos and prints. The changing real ales are chosen by customers. The public bar is open all day Saturday and Sunday, from 3pm Friday, and evenings only the rest of the week.

Musselburgh

Levenhall Arms

10 Ravensheugh Road, EH21 7PP (on B1348 1 mile E of centre)
12-11 (midnight Thu; 1am Fri & Sat); 12.30-midnight Sun
☎ (0131) 665 3220
Inveralmond Ossian A**; 2 changing beers (sourced regionally; often Knops, Sonnet 43, Strathaven)** H/A
A three-roomed hostelry dating from 1830 and close to the racecourse. Expect to find some interesting real ales from smaller, mainly Scottish breweries. The lively, cheerfully decorated public bar is half timber panelled and carpeted. Dominoes is popular here and there is a TV for sporting events. A smaller area leads off, with a dartboard and pictures of old local industries. It has a pleasant lounge, where familes are welcome until 8pm.
Q P

Volunteer Arms (Staggs)

81 North High Street, EH21 6JE (behind the Brunton)
12-11 (11.30 Thu; midnight Fri); 11-midnight Sat; 12.30-11 Sun (0131) 665 9654 staggsbar.com
Loch Lomond Silkie Stout; Oakham JHB, Bishops Farewell; 4 changing beers (sourced nationally; often Fyne Ales, Loch Lomond, Swannay)
Superb pub run by the same family since 1858. Its bar and snug are traditional, with wooden floors, wood panelling and mirrors from defunct local breweries. The more modern lounge opens at the weekend. Beers change regularly and are mostly pale and hoppy. Black Rat real cider is also served. CAMRA National Pub of the Year finalist 2019, and winner of many awards.

Newtongrange

Dean Tavern

80 Main Street, EH22 4NA
11-11; 10-midnight Fri & Sat; 10-11 Sun
(0131) 663 2419 deantavern.co.uk
1 changing beer (sourced regionally; often Born in the Borders, Cross Borders, Stewart)
Superb pub run by trustees on Gothenburg principles, with profits returned to the local community. The light and spacious bar was designed to help miners recover from their day in darkness, with roof lights in a high ceiling supported by arched iron beams. There is also the Lamp Room restaurant and a function room whose large mural depicts the town's mining past. Meals are available all day. Children are permitted until 8pm if dining. Alcohol is served from 11am (midday Sun).

North Berwick

Auld Hoose

19 Forth Street, EH39 4HX
11-11 (1am Thu-Sat; midnight Sun) (01620) 892692
auldhoosenorthberwick.co.uk
2 changing beers (sourced nationally; often Cairngorm, Greene King, Orkney)
An interesting traditional Scottish drinking shop with high ceilings, bare floorboards around a mahogany bar, carpeted areas and a welcoming atmosphere enhanced by a real fire in winter. Built in 1896 and said to be the oldest pub in town, it is certainly the closest to the sea.

Nether Abbey Hotel

20 Dirleton Avenue, EH39 4BQ (on A198 W of centre)
9am-11 (midnight Thu; 1am Fri & Sat) (01620) 892802
netherabbey.co.uk
Knops East Coast Pale; 3 changing beers (sourced nationally; often Stewart, Timothy Taylor, Williams Bros)
Busy, family-run hotel in a stone-built villa with a bright, contemporary, open-plan interior. The Fly Half Bar is in a split-level glass extension; large folding doors open out on to the patio. Real ales are often from Scottish breweries – sparklers can be removed on request. The upper central area is an award-winning restaurant. The Nethers is famous for its good, freshly cooked and locally sourced food, available all day Friday to Sunday. Alcohol is served from 11am.

Ship Inn

7-9 Quality Street, EH39 4HJ
11-11 (1am Thu-Sat) (01620) 890699
Fyne Ales Jarl; Harviestoun Schiehallion; 1 changing beer (sourced nationally; often Greene King, Orkney, Stewart)
Friendly and often lively bar with a spacious open-plan interior offering a wide variety of seating and tables. The pub is popular for food, with good vegetarian options, served all day until 8pm. Sparklers are happily removed on request. Try the suntrap rear patio garden in summer.

Penicuik

Navaar House Hotel

23 Bog Road, EH26 9BY (400yds W of centre)
12-midnight (01968) 672683 navaarhouse.co.uk
Stewart Jack Back; 1 changing beer (sourced regionally; often Fyne Ales)
A lively pub with a strong community spirit, in what was the home of zoologist James Cossar Ewart. The large bar is open plan with a log/coal stove, a pool table and TV screens. Real ale is more expensive in the pleasantly decorated restaurant which serves locally sourced food throughout the day at the weekend. Children are permitted in the restaurant and garden.

South Queensferry

Ferry Brewery Tap Bar & Shop

Bankhead Farm Steading, Bankhead Road, EH30 9TF
(just off B924, SE of Hawes Pier out of town)
closed Mon; 10-5 (7 Fri & Sat); 12-5 Sun
(0131) 331 1851 ferrybrewery.co.uk
4 changing beers (sourced locally)
The only brewery in Queensferry since 1851, with some of its beers brewed from historic recipes. A changing range of Ferry Brewery ales is served on four handpumps and seasonal beers are brewed for festivals such as the Loony Dook, Ferry Fair and Christmas. The small Tap Bar and shop is warm and friendly, with welcoming staff, great conversation and a relaxed atmosphere. Children and dogs are welcome. Open Friday and Saturday 10am-7pm only in January.

West Calder

Railway Inn ★

43 Main Street, EH55 8DL
11-11 (1am Fri & Sat); 12.30-11 Sun (01506) 871691
2 changing beers (sourced nationally; often Black Sheep, Inveralmond, Timothy Taylor)
A Grade C-listed building dating from around 1895 with a prominent octagonal turret. The atmospheric main bar has a large U-shaped timber counter and ornamental tiered wooden gantry. The coffered ceilings have elaborate cornicing and plastering and there are ornate coloured glass window panels. Plenty of TVs, with the sound kept low, enable customers to follow the sports action.

A glass of bitter beer or pale ale, taken with the principal meal of the day, does more good and less harm than any medicine the physician can prescribe. **Dr Carpenter, 1750**

GREATER GLASGOW & CLYDE VALLEY

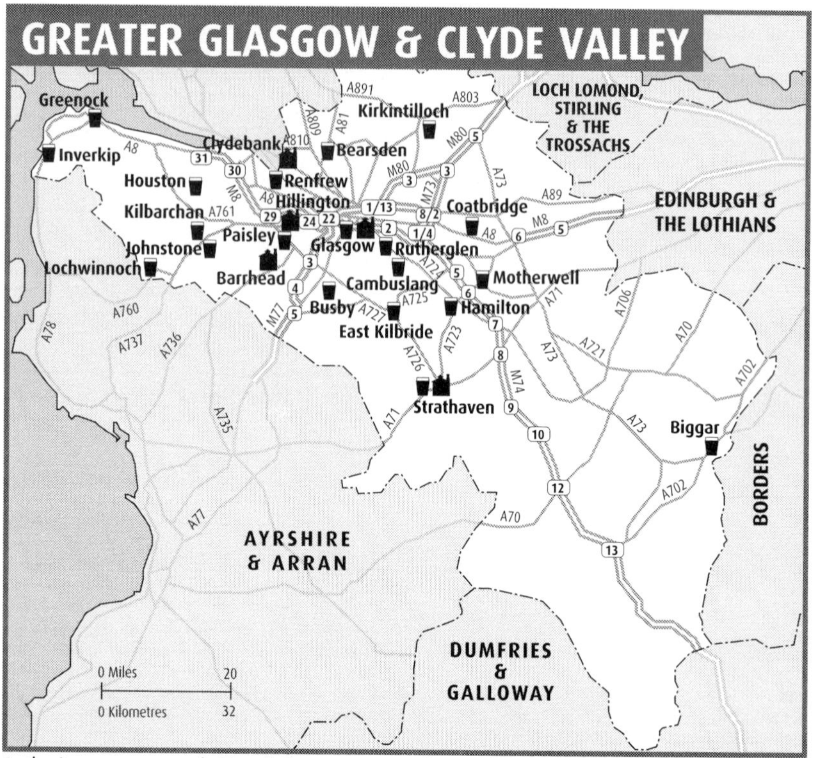

Authority areas covered: City of Glasgow UA, Dunbartonshire UAs, Inverclyde UA, Lanarkshire UAs, Renfrewshire UAs

Bearsden

Burnbrae ✔

281 Milngavie Road, G61 3DQ (next to Premier Inn)
9am-11 (midnight Fri); 10-11 Sat & Sun
☎ (0141) 942 5951
6 changing beers (sourced nationally; often Greene King) Ⓗ
Relatively recently built but old-world-style family-friendly pub restaurant with real fires and oak beams. The interior is open plan with several different areas mostly for dining, as well as a bar space for drinkers. Six handpumps supply beer from various breweries. Opens early for breakfast; alcohol is served from 11am (12.30pm Sun).
❀◐♿P (60A,B10)

Biggar

Crown Inn ✔

109-111 High Street, ML12 6DL
11-1am ☎ (01899) 220116 thecrownbiggar.co.uk
House beer (by Broughton); 5 changing beers (sourced nationally; often Broughton, Strathaven) Ⓗ
A pleasant and friendly inn in the centre of this market town, the Crown has years of tradition behind it, officially dating from the mid-17th century. The bar area is directly accessed from the street and there is a small, quiet room, conservatory and beer garden to the rear. Six handpumps offer beers from a range of breweries, including local ones. Beer festivals are held in May and October, the latter coinciding with the Biggar Festival. ❀◐ (91,191)

Elphinstone Hotel ✔

145 High Street, ML12 6DL
11-1am ☎ (01899) 220044 elphinstonehotel.co.uk
2 changing beers (sourced regionally; often Broughton, Fyne Ales) Ⓗ
An old coaching inn dating from the 18th century with a bright, modern public bar, a lounge bar, guest rooms and a large outdoor drinking area. There are four handpumps but in winter only two are in use to ensure that quality is maintained. The beers come in rotation from Fyne Ales, Broughton, Kelburn, Redcastle, Orkney and Strathaven. The bar has a pool table and dartboard and features live music on a Saturday. ❀◐ (91,191)

Busby

White Cart ✔

61 East Kilbride Road, G76 8HX
11.30-11; 12-10 Sun ☎ (0141) 644 2711

REAL ALE BREWERIES

Clockwork Glasgow
Drygate Glasgow
Jaw Hillington
Kelburn Barrhead
Late Night Hype Clydebank
Merchant City Glasgow
Ride Glasgow (NEW)
Shilling Glasgow
Strathaven Strathaven
WEST Glasgow

Greene King IPA, Abbot ⊞
A friendly welcome awaits you at this large Chef &
Brewer pub, with roaring fires in winter. The
emphasis is on food service but there are four
handpumps with three guest beers and one cider.
A patio area at the front is popular in the summer
and there is an area for families inside. Located in
the Busby conservation village, this pub is very
bright and spacious. ♿🏠🕪▸🍴🚆🍷P🚃☀️📶

Cambuslang

John Fairweather ✅
50-60 Main Street, G72 7EP
🕐 11-midnight ☎ (0141) 646 2411
Caledonian Deuchars IPA; Greene King Abbot; Sharp's
Doom Bar; 3 changing beers (sourced nationally) ⊞
A Wetherspoon pub opened in 2015 in the old
Savoy Cinema. The cinema dates back to 1929 and
was designed in a neo-classical style by John
Fairweather, after whom the pub is named. Many
of the old features have been retained and
restored. A choice of beers is available from both
local and national breweries. Food is served from
an open-plan kitchen. The pub is watched over by
old movie stars sitting in the balcony.
♿🏠🕪▸🍴🚆🍷🚃📶

Coatbridge

Vulcan ✅
181 Main Street, ML5 3HH (jct with Dunbeth Rd)
🕐 8am-midnight (1am Fri & Sat) ☎ (01236) 437972
Greene King Abbot; 5 changing beers (sourced
regionally; often Broughton, Kelburn, Stewart) ⊞
This pub is named after the first iron ship that used
to sail on the Monkland Canal. One of the smaller,
if not the smallest, Wetherspoon pubs, it has the
feel of a local pub. The five changing beers are all
from Scottish micros. There is a quiz on the first
Thursday of every month. Alcohol is available from
11am. (The pub is currently for sale.)
♿🏠🕪▸🍴🚆(Sunnyside)P🚃📶

East Kilbride

Hay Stook ⅃ ✅
26 Princes Avenue, G74 1JU
🕐 8am-midnight ☎ (01355) 244323
Caledonian Deuchars IPA; Greene King Abbot; Sharp's
Doom Bar; 5 changing beers (sourced nationally;
often Broughton, Strathaven) ⊞
This Wetherspoon pub is situated at the Brouster
Gate entrance in Princes Mall, a large shopping
mall, which makes it handy for shoppers and for
the nearby cinema complex. The staircase up to the
toilets neatly divides the room, with the bar area to
one side and family area to the other. It has a small
beer garden at the side overlooking the mall
entrance. Scottish beers are well represented
among the five guests. Alcohol is available from
11am. ♿🏠🕪▸🍴🚆🍷🚃📶

Glasgow

Babbity Bowster
16-18 Blackfriars Street, Merchant City, G1 1PE
🕐 11-midnight; 12.30-midnight Sun ☎ (0141) 552 5055
🌐 babbitybowster.com
Caledonian Deuchars IPA; Fyne Ales Jarl; 1 changing
beer (sourced regionally) ⊞

A unique establishment off the High Street, which
has been providing the services of pub, café,
restaurant and hotel since 1985. The bar room has
functional tables with some wall seating, and in
winter offers the radiance and aroma of a peat fire.
A French chef prepares meals for the upstairs
restaurant using Scottish produce including fish/
seafood, game and other meats. Acoustic music
sessions usually take place on Wednesday and
Saturday afternoons. In summer the garden has
barbecues and boules.
Q🏠🛏️🕪▸🚆(High St)🏨P🚃📶

Blackfriars ⅃
36 Bell Street, Merchant City, G1 1LG
🕐 11-midnight; 12.30-midnight Sun ☎ (0141) 552 5924
🌐 blackfriarsglasgow.com
5 changing beers (sourced nationally; often
Kelburn) ⊞
Popular Merchant City bar attracting a varied
clientele finding their own niche in either the
corner overlooking the streets, the bar room or the
dining area to the rear. Five handpumps dispense
at least one beer from the local Kelburn Brewery
plus some Scottish ales and others from further
afield. There is a good selection of foreign beers in
bottle and draught and a variety of tasty food – try
the beer-battered haddock. Live music plays on
Sunday and Tuesday nights. ▸🍴🚆(High St)🏨🚃📶

Bon Accord ⅃
153 North Street, Charing Cross, G3 7DA
🕐 11-midnight; 12.30-11 Sun ☎ (0141) 248 4427
🌐 bonaccordpub.com
Caledonian Deuchars IPA, Edinburgh Castle 80/-; 8
changing beers (sourced nationally) ⊞
One of the pioneers of the real ale scene in
Glasgow, the Bon serves over 800 different beers
each year. A dining area at the rear also hosts quiz,
poker and live music nights. As well as ensuring
there is a good choice of ale, the owner is
passionate about malt whisky – the pub stocks 400
varieties on the bar and there is a whisky club and
an online shop. Good-value food is served until
7.45pm. ♿🏠🕪▸🍴🚆(Charing Cross)🏨🍷🚃📶

Clockwork Beer Co ⅃ ✅
1153-1155 Cathcart Road, Mount Florida, G42 9HB
🕐 11-midnight ☎ (0141) 649 0184
🌐 newclockworkbeer.ltpubs.co.uk
Clockwork Oregon IPA, Hampden Roar; 6 changing
beers (sourced nationally; often Clockwork) Ⓐ
Up to four Clockwork and four guest ales, often
chosen as a result of customer feedback, are
available at this spacious brewpub. The pub gets
busy when there are football matches or other
events at nearby Hampden Park, and it is also
popular for watching live sport on several screens
dotted about the room. There is a dining area with
table service - food is served all day. A popular quiz
is hosted on Thursday and occasional live music.
Dogs are welcome except in the dining area.
♿🏠🕪▸🚆(Mount Florida)P🚃☀️📶

Counting House ✅
2 St Vincent Place, G1 2DH
🕐 8am-midnight ☎ (0141) 225 0160
Caledonian Deuchars IPA; Greene King Abbot; Sharp's
Doom Bar; 12 changing beers (sourced nationally) ⊞
A busy pub on George Square with a good view of
the City Chambers. In addition to the cask beers,
there are up to 12 guest ales, sourced UK wide. A
bottle store in one of the bank's old strong rooms

holds a large range of bottled and canned beers. Meet the Brewer nights are held regularly.
◑♿⇌(Queen St)🚇🍎🚌📶

Crystal Palace ✔

Jamaica Street, G1 4QD (close to Central Station)
⏲ 8am-midnight ☎ (0141) 221 2624
Caledonian Deuchars IPA; Greene King Abbot; Sharp's Doom Bar; 8 changing beers (sourced nationally) Ⓗ
Inspired by London's Crystal Palace, this Wetherspoon pub is in what was a Victorian iron-framed furniture house. There are two bars, one on each floor, offering different guest beers. The ground floor has a typical Wetherspoon layout and the upper floor is more relaxed, with large sofas. The original lift serves all floors.
🔥◑♿⇌(Central)🚇🚌📶

Curlers Rest ✔

256-260 Byres Road, Hillhead, G12 8SH
⏲ 12-midnight ☎ (0141) 341 0737
🌐 thecurlersrestglasgow.co.uk
Stewart Jack Back; 4 changing beers (sourced nationally) Ⓗ
Originally a conversion from two 18th-century cottages, this is a large open-plan pub spreading over two floors. The real ales are complemented by a selection of world beers, with a more limited range available in the upstairs bar with its open fire. A mix of classic pub food and modern dishes is served all day. 🔥◑♿🚇🚌🐾📶

Drum & Monkey ✔

91-93 St Vincent Street, G2 5TF (at Renfield St jct)
⏲ 12-11 (midnight Fri & Sat) ☎ (0141) 221 6636
St Austell Nicholson's Pale Ale; 5 changing beers (sourced nationally; often Inveralmond) Ⓗ
This corner pub housed in a former American-style bank has an opulent marble and wood-panelled interior and ornate ceilings. Convenient for both main railway stations and numerous bus routes, it is usually busy with a varied clientele. Family groups are welcome until 8pm when dining. The large P-shaped central bar features six handpulls offering a wide variety of styles, from local and national favourites to contemporary microbrews.
🔥◑♿⇌(Central)🚇🚌🐾📶

Drygate L

85 Drygate, Dennistoun, G4 0UT (off John Knox St)
⏲ 11-midnight ☎ (0141) 212 8815 🌐 drygate.com
Drygate Pale Duke, Seven Peaks; 2 changing beers (sourced nationally; often Drygate) Ⓗ
Situated on the historic Wellpark Brewery site, this brewpub offers numerous cask, keg and bottled beers, firmly positioned towards the craft beer market and younger drinkers. Lively with an industrial aesthetic, there are two bars over the ground and first floors, an outside terrace and a panoramic view of the brewery. Food is served throughout the day – the menu varies from modern British to street-inspired. Live music and comedy feature regularly in the upstairs beer hall.
🔥❀◑♿⇌(High St)P🚌🐾📶

Esquire House ✔

Great Western Road, Anniesland, G12 0AU
⏲ 8am-midnight ☎ (0141) 229 5480
Caledonian Deuchars IPA; Greene King Abbot; 3 changing beers (sourced nationally; often Williams Bros) Ⓗ
Unusually for a Wetherspoon establishment, this is a new-build on the site of a pub of the same name. It is a relatively small pub for this chain and has a friendly ambience. The family area is to the right of the bar, and there is a raised area handy for party groups. Five of the ten handpumps are normally in use. As well as the regular beers, the popular Williams Joker is on most of the time. Alcohol is served from 11am.
🔥❀◑♿⇌(Anniesland)🍎P🚌📶

Henglers Circus ✔

351-363 Sauchiehall Street, Charing Cross, G2 3HU
⏲ 8am-midnight ☎ (0141) 331 9810
Caledonian Deuchars IPA; Greene King Abbot; Sharp's Doom Bar; 7 changing beers (sourced nationally; often Broughton, Kelburn, Loch Lomond) Ⓗ
A spacious pub in a vibrant part of the city, popular with students and close to a wide selection of bars, restaurants and entertainment venues. As well as the regular cask ales, there are up to seven guest beers, often from Scottish breweries. A range of bottled and canned beers is available and Meet the Brewer events are held from time to time. Alcohol is served from 11am.
Q🔥◑♿⇌(Charing Cross)🚇🍎🚌📶

Inn Deep

445 Great Western Road, Hillhead, G12 8HH
⏲ 12-midnight (11 Sun) ☎ (0141) 357 1075 🌐 inndeep.com
3 changing beers (sourced nationally; often Williams Bros) Ⓟ
Below Great Western Road on the banks of the River Kelvin, Inn Deep is set in the arches of an old railway station. The middle arch houses the bar, which stocks three guest cask ales. There is an extensive range of keg beers. The pub offers good food and hosts regular poetry nights and occasional music sessions. The outdoor seating beside the river and in the adjacent arch is handy for the many passing walkers and cyclists.
🔥❀◑🚇🍎🚌(20,6)🐾📶

Laurieston Bar 🏆 ★

58 Bridge Street, Tradeston, G5 9HU
⏲ 11-11; 12.30-11 Sun ☎ (0141) 429 4528
Fyne Ales Jarl; 2 changing beers (sourced locally; often Fyne Ales, Jaw) Ⓗ
Probably Glasgow's friendliest pub, owned and run by two brothers, whose family has been in the pub trade for generations. It is situated 10 minutes' walk from Central Station and handy for some excellent curry houses. The bar is surrounded by formica-top tables and the walls covered in vintage photographs, mirrors, memorabilia and the occasional painting. Dogs are very welcome. Pies are available. Listed on CAMRA's National Inventory of Historic Pub Interiors. ⇌(Central)🚇🚌🐾📶

Pot Still

154 Hope Street, G2 2TH
⏲ 11-midnight ☎ (0141) 333 0980 🌐 thepotstill.co.uk
4 changing beers (sourced regionally; often Ayr, Broughton) Ⓗ
Near both main rail stations and major bus routes, this classic city-centre split-level bar is one of Scotland's leading whisky pubs, with a collection of around 300 malts. Listening to the staff describe the virtues of various drams to appreciative visitors is an education. Four handpumps offer Scottish beers, some not often seen in Glasgow. Food of the 'pie and beans' school is available during the day.
🔥◑⇌(Central)🚇🚌🐾📶

Raven

81-85 Renfield Street, G2 1LP
12-11 (midnight Thu-Sat) ☎ (0141) 332 6151
theravenglasgow.com
3 changing beers (sourced nationally) Ⓗ
Modern city-centre bar and restaurant close to the Royal Concert Hall, theatres and cinemas. Three real ales, which might come from Redcastle or Stewart but could come from anywhere, are found towards the end of the bar. A selection of craft and bottled beer is also available. The bar area opens out to a restaurant on two levels, with a small function room on the top floor. Dogs are permitted in the bar until 9pm. Children are allowed in the restaurant only. ≋(Queen St)

Scotia Bar

112-114 Stockwell Street, G1 4LW
11-midnight; 12.30-midnight Sun ☎ (0141) 552 8681
Greene King IPA; house beer (by Greene King); 2 changing beers (often Broughton, Edinbrew, Strathaven) Ⓗ
One of several pubs which claim to be the oldest in Glasgow, the Scotia certainly looks the part with its half-timbered frontage, wood panelling, dark wooden benches and low ceilings. It has been a firm fixture on the folk music scene for decades – the likes of Hamish Imlach and Billy Connolly performed here – and there are still regular sessions and live bands. There are three distinct areas: one closer to the band, one to the bar, and the cosy snug. ≋(Argyle St)

Sir John Moore ✔

260-292 Argyle Street, G2 8QW
7am-midnight; 7.30am-midnight Sat & Sun
☎ (0141) 222 1780
8 changing beers (sourced nationally) Ⓗ
Close to Central Station's lower level Hope Street exit, this busy Wetherspoon pub is a convenient place to wait for a train and has a screen showing departures. Converted from several shops, it has a number of distinct areas on different levels, and a pavement area outside. Opens at 7am for breakfast Monday-Friday (alcohol served from 11am).
≋(Central)

Sir John Stirling Maxwell ✔

136-140 Kilmarnock Road, Shawlands, G41 3NN
8am-midnight ☎ (0141) 636 9024
Caledonian Deuchars IPA; Greene King Abbot; 4 changing beers (sourced nationally; often Broughton, Kelburn) Ⓗ
Converted from an old Safeway supermarket, the pub has typical Wetherspoon touches: bookcases, pictures of historical figures related to the area and photographs of long-gone local cinemas. It has the feel of a local pub, with a good mix of clientele. There is a screen-free family area a few stairs up at the back. Real ales are normally available on at least six of the ten handpumps. Alcohol is served from 11am. ≋(Pollokshaws E)

Society Room ✔

151 West George Street, G2 2JJ
7.30am-midnight; 8am-midnight Sat & Sun
☎ (0141) 229 7560
Caledonian Deuchars IPA; Greene King Abbot; 4 changing beers (sourced nationally) Ⓗ
Wetherspoon's only Lloyds No.1 in Glasgow. However the music doesn't start until 8pm on weekdays and Sunday, and the pub is very popular with older people during the day. On Saturday there is music from 5pm, with a DJ from 9pm. Its low ceiling and lack of windows at the back give it a cavernous feel. Alcohol is available from 11am.
≋(Central)

State Bar

148 Holland Street, Charing Cross, G2 4NG (just off Sauchiehall St, opp Henglers Circus)
11-midnight ☎ (0141) 332 2159
House beer (by Stewart); 6 changing beers (sourced nationally; often Oakham) Ⓗ
A regular winner of CAMRA branch Pub of the Year, this popular town-centre establishment gets busy at lunchtimes and weekends. The pub has a traditional island bar offering changing beers rarely seen in Glasgow, including at least one from Oakham. Its proximity to the King's Theatre is reflected by old pictures and show bills displayed round the walls. There is a blues session on Tuesday in the main bar and a comedy club downstairs on Saturday.
≋(Charing Cross)

SCOTLAND

Tennent's ✔

191 Byres Road, Hillhead, G12 8TN
10-11 (midnight Thu-Sat) ☎ (0141) 339 7203
thetennentsbarglasgow.co.uk
Caledonian Deuchars IPA; Draught Bass; Fuller's London Pride; Harviestoun Bitter & Twisted; Marston's Pedigree; Timothy Taylor Landlord; 6 changing beers (sourced nationally) Ⓗ
Since opening in the 1880s, Tennent's has been at the heart of the community and has kept its traditional character. The large open bar with a small lounge to one side is frequented by many locals and not a few staff and students from the neighbouring university. The pub offers many regular and guest beers and a good-value range of food at all times. Several TV screens show mainly sports. Alcohol is served from 11am.

Three Judges L ✔

141 Dumbarton Road, Partick, G11 6PR
11-midnight ☎ (0141) 337 3055 threejudges.co.uk
9 changing beers (sourced nationally) Ⓗ
Traditional corner tenement pub on a busy junction at the bottom of Byres Road. Many customers come from the local community to watch the racing or listen to live jazz on the last Sunday afternoon of the month. But others come from further afield to enjoy the range of beers which has been a feature here for nearly 30 years, or sample the ciders, particularly during the annual cider festival. No food is available but it can be brought in. Q≋(Partick)

Greenock

James Watt ✔

80-92 Cathcart Street, PA15 1DD
8am-midnight (1am Fri & Sat); 9am-midnight Sun
☎ (01475) 722640
Greene King Abbot; Sharp's Doom Bar; 4 changing beers Ⓗ
Across the road from Greenock Central Station and 200 yards from the bus station, this large open-plan Wetherspoon, in a former post office, is named after one of Greenock's famous sons. The chain's standard value-for-money food is available all day and beer festivals are hosted at various times throughout the year. This pub is an oasis in a beer desert. ≋

Willow
203 Roxburgh Street, PA15 4DA
11-midnight (12.30am Thu; 1am Fri & Sat); 12.30-midnight Sun ☎ (01475) 791775
2 changing beers (sourced nationally)
Located in the busy West Station area of Greenock, across from Greenock West railway station, this friendly and welcoming free house is a recent addition to the CAMRA branch's recommended real ale pubs. Two handpumps dispense beers from across the UK, with an emphasis on Scottish ales including several local breweries. The pub is community focused, supporting a number of local causes and charities. A quiz night is held every Wednesday.

Hamilton

George Bar
18 Campbell Street, ML3 6AS
12-midnight (1am Fri); 12.30-midnight Sun
☎ (01698) 424225
3 changing beers (sourced nationally; often Strathaven)
This traditional, family-run pub is situated in a pedestrianised area just off the inner ring road in the town. The single bar room is quite small but full of character, decorated with hundreds of pumpclips celebrating many of the beers enjoyed over the years. The three handpumps usually offer at least one ale from the nearby Strathaven Brewery. Tasty home-cooked meals are available until 6pm. In warmer weather café-style seating provides extra space outside. (Central)

Houston

Fox & Hounds
South Street, PA6 7EN
9am-midnight (1am Fri & Sat) ☎ (01505) 808604
foxandhoundshouston.co.uk
Kelburn Goldihops; 4 changing beers (sourced nationally; often Fyne Ales, Kelburn, Tiny Rebel)
Excellent traditional village pub established in 1779. The bar, lounge and restaurant are downstairs, a cocktail bar upstairs. A range of beers on five handpumps is available alongside a selection of canned and bottled craft beers and an excellent choice of spirits including 130 whiskies. Gastro-pub food made wholly on the premises is served throughout the pub. An annual beer festival is held on the late May bank holiday weekend. There is a pool table upstairs and board games are played every Wednesday. Q P

Inverkip

Inverkip Hotel
Main Street, PA16 0AS
11-11 (11.30 Thu-Sat); 12.30-11 Sun ☎ (01475) 521478
inverkip.co.uk
Fyne Ales Jarl; 1 changing beer (sourced regionally; often Fallen, Fyne Ales)
Small family-run hotel located in the heart of a conservation village and just a short walk from the large Inverkip Marina, making it an ideal staging post for those just messing about on the river or passing through on the way to Largs and the Ayrshire coast. Food options range from snacks to special occasion dining. Battle of the Brewer nights are extremely popular. P (578,580)

Johnstone

Callum's
26 High Street, PA5 8AH
11-midnight (1am Fri & Sat); 12.30-midnight Sun
☎ (01505) 322925
Kelburn Pivo Estivo, Jaguar; 5 changing beers (often Orkney)
A popular town-centre pub offering a friendly welcome and a comfortable atmosphere. A large TV screen shows sporting events. The lounge is set for dining, with themed nights including curry on Thursday. Occasional live music features at weekends. Three regular beers are offered alongside four changing guests.
(36,38)

Kilbarchan

Trust Inn
8 Low Barholm, PA10 2ET
11-midnight; 12-1am Fri & Sat ☎ (01505) 702401
thetrustinn.com
3 changing beers
Small, popular, single-roomed pub in the centre of a conservation village, with old village photographs adorning the walls. A superior bar meal menu and special promotions mean it can be busy at mealtimes. Children are welcome until 9pm if dining. Regular live events including local bands and other entertainment are advertised via social media. (38)

Kirkintilloch

Kirky Puffer
1-11 Townhead, G66 1NG (by canal)
8am-midnight (1am Fri; 11.45 Sat) ☎ (0141) 775 4140
Caledonian Deuchars IPA; Sharp's Doom Bar; 3 changing beers (sourced nationally; often Kelburn, Loch Lomond, Oakham)
This large Wetherspoon pub is named after the small steamboats that were built nearby and worked the adjacent canal and further to the Argyll coast. It has a spacious feel with various nooks and crannies offering different areas in which to enjoy a drink or a meal, including a separate family space. The pub is well used by travellers on the canal and Antonine Trail, though it has a very local feeling and hosts various community events. Alcohol is served from 11am.

Lochwinnoch

Brown Bull
32 Main Street, PA12 4AH
12-11 (midnight Fri & Sat); 12.30-11 Sun
☎ (01505) 843250
Harviestoun Bitter & Twisted; 3 changing beers (sourced regionally; often Ayr, Merchant City)
More than 200 years old, this family-run village free house attracts locals and visitors alike. Quiz night is Tuesday and live music features every second Sunday. An ever-changing choice of four ales is offered, mainly from Scottish breweries. At the rear is a quirky outdoor seating area and garden. The popular upstairs restaurant uses local produce and bar meals are also available. Located close to Lochwinnoch RSPB nature reserve and Castle Semple visitor centre. Q

Motherwell

Brandon Works ✓
45-61 Merry Street, ML1 1JJ
8am-midnight (1am Fri & Sat) ☎ (01698) 210280
Caledonian Deuchars IPA; Greene King Abbot; Sharp's Doom Bar; 2 changing beers (often Loch Lomond , Strathaven) H
This busy town-centre bar, handy for buses and the main train station, is named after the works that previously occupied this site, in a town once known as Steelopolis. There are 10 handpumps with five beers usually available, often from Scottish breweries – check the blackboards to see what is on. Seating is split into two areas, with wooden fencing separating the dining space from the lively bar area. Alcohol is available after 11am.

Paisley

Bull Inn ★ ✓
7 New Street, PA1 1XU
11-11 (1am Fri & Sat) ☎ (0141) 849 0472
4 changing beers (sourced regionally; often Jaw, Kelburn, Loch Lomond) H
Established in 1901 and identified by CAMRA as having a nationally important historic interior, this is the oldest inn in Paisley. The pub retains many original features including stained-glass windows, three small snugs and a spirit cask gantry, and boasts the only original set of spirit cocks left in Scotland. Four changing guest ales are from the likes of Kelburn, Jaw, Loch Lomond, Orkney, Stewart and Strathaven breweries. Live sport is shown on large screens in the main bar and the snugs.

Canal Station
1 Stow Brae, PA1 2HF
11-11 (1am Fri & Sat); 12.30-11 Sun ☎ (0141) 848 1362
canalstation.co.uk
2 changing beers (often Clockwork, Stewart)
Housed in the original Canal railway station, the venue has a spacious lounge bar, a separate contemporary restaurant and a conservatory to the rear available for private functions. The beer garden gets the sun most of the day. There is a large off-street car park. Located next to Canal Street station and a five-minute walk to Paisley town centre. Closed Monday and Tuesday in winter. P (101)

Last Post L ✓
2 County Square, PA1 1BN
8am-midnight ☎ (0141) 849 6911
Caledonian Deuchars IPA; Greene King Abbot; Sharp's Doom Bar; 6 changing beers H
Large Wetherspoon pub converted from the town's main post office. Open plan in design on two levels, there is plenty of seating and good wheelchair access. The standard Wetherspoon food menu is served and six guest ales are usually available. Next to Gilmour Street railway station and close to the bus station, it is handy for a pint between trains or buses. (9,36)

Sandpiper ✓
Glasgow Airport, PA3 2SW
5-9 ☎ (0141) 842 7858
Greene King Abbot; 4 changing beers H
Positioned on the ground floor, in the public area of the airport, the Sandpiper is ideal if you are looking for an ale before heading through security, waiting for family or friends arriving on an incoming flight, or if you are a plane spotter in need of refreshment. With six handpumps you are spoilt for choice and can relax watching one of the many TV screens showing 24-hour news and sporting events. Opening hours are slightly longer in the summer season. Q P

Renfrew

Lord of the Isles ✓
Unit 21 Xscape, Kings Inch Road, PA4 8XQ
8am-midnight (1am Fri & Sat) ☎ (0141) 886 8930
Caledonian Deuchars IPA; Greene King Abbot; Sharp's Doom Bar; 3 changing beers (sourced nationally) H
Large, purpose-built Wetherspoon establishment attached to the Soar leisure complex with its cinema, ski slope and rock climbing at the Braehead shopping centre. The walls display photographs depicting the history of industry on the River Clyde. The south-facing outside seating area is a suntrap on summer days. Food is available all day and three varying guest ales are on handpump. A short stroll allows you to view the ships docked at Yarrow Shipyard. P

Rutherglen

An Ruadh Ghleann ✓
40-44 Main Street, G73 2HY
8am-11.45 (midnight Fri & Sat) ☎ (0141) 613 2370
Caledonian Deuchars IPA; Greene King Abbot; Sharp's Doom Bar; 4 changing beers (sourced nationally) H
Contemporary Wetherspoon pub at the west end of the high street of one of the oldest royal burghs in Scotland. The small shop frontage leads to a long narrow room brightened up by large windows down one side. The bar is towards the middle. At the far end the room opens up, with windows providing a view of the cellar and, to the rear, the split-level garden and smoking area. Alcohol is served from 11am. Q

Strathaven

Weavers L ✓
1-3 Green Street, ML10 6LT
11-midnight Mon; 4.30-midnight Tue & Wed; 4.30-1am Thu; 11-1am Fri & Sat; 2-1am Sun
4 changing beers (sourced nationally; often Strathaven) H
A family-run pub in the centre of a small historic town with links to the 19th-century weaving industry. A community hub, where local groups and clubs meet, it is comfortably furnished and decorated with an assortment of black and white pictures of film stars. Three handpumps offer beers from a varying range, the fourth provides beers exclusively from the nearby Strathaven Brewery. A selection of imported bottled beers is also available. (254,256)

Beer is proof that God loves us and wants us to be happy. **Benjamin Franklin**

SCOTLAND

HIGHLANDS & WESTERN ISLES

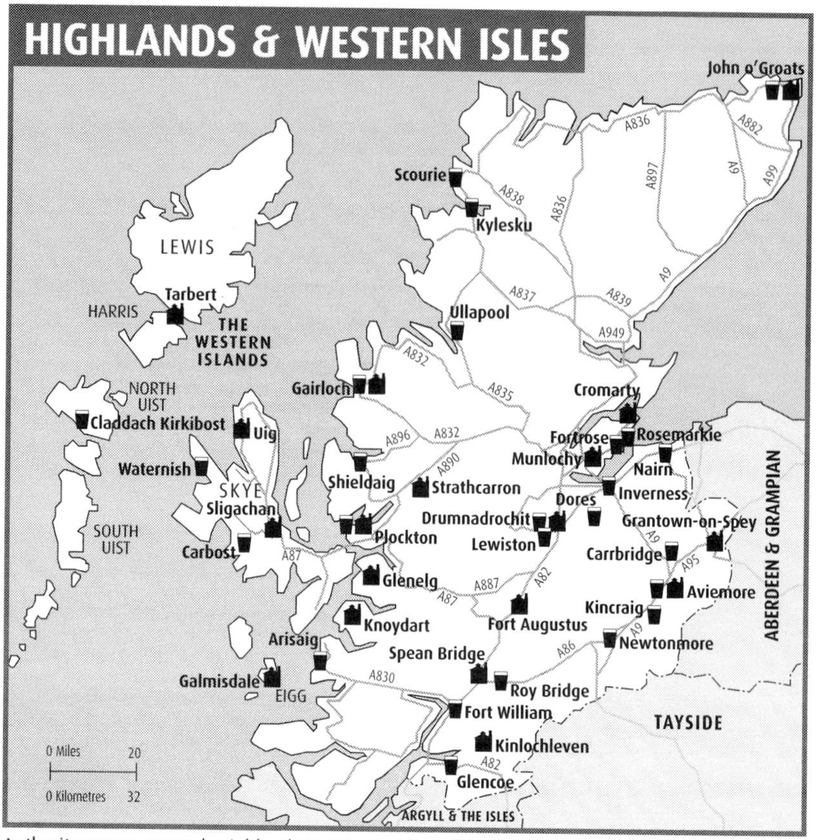

Authority areas covered: Highland UA, Western Isles UA

Arisaig

Arisaig Hotel (Crofters Rest)

Main Road, PH39 4NH (on B8008 off A830)
NM65808650
12-11 (11.45 Fri & Sat); 12-11 Sun (01687) 450210
arisaighotel.co.uk
2 changing beers (often Cromarty)
An old coaching inn built around 1720, the Arisaig Hotel is just off the main road to Mallaig and overlooks the turquoise waters of the bay towards Eigg, Rum and Skye. The Crofter's Bar offers up to two Cromarty beers. Locally caught seafood dominates the lunch and dinner menus, with vegetarian options. Music is hosted on Friday nights and Sunday afternoons, as well as two music festivals. For trainspotters, the Jacobite Steam Special chugs through the local station during the season. There are many scenic costal walks nearby. Q

Aviemore

Old Bridge Inn

23 Dalfaber Road, PH22 1PU
12-midnight (1am Fri & Sat) (01479) 811137
oldbridgeinn.co.uk
4 changing beers (sourced locally; often Cairngorm, Caledonian, Windswept)
Close to the gently flowing River Spey, this gem of a pub is worth seeking out and is an ideal place to relax after a busy day on the hills, or even just touring in the area. Four handpumps offer a mix of local and regional beers. Booking is recommended for the restaurant, with a menu using produce with low food miles. Local entertainment is hosted most nights, and there is a selection of games and books to pass away the time over a pint. Handy for the Strathspey Steam Railway.

Winking Owl

123 Grampian Road, PH22 1RH (N end of village)
12-11; 11-1am Fri & Sat; 12-11 Sun (01479) 812368
thewinkingowl.co
6 changing beers (sourced locally; often Cairngorm, Caledonian)
The Winky has been the brewery tap for the Cairngorm Brewery since 2014, with the addition of the Bothy Bar downstairs in 2018 massively increasing its popularity. Both bars have six handpumps offering four Cairngorm beers, two from the Caledonian stable, and an array of font beers. Hearty pub grub and international and Scottish dishes, including children's, vegetarian, gluten- and dairy-free are served throughout. Live music plays in the Bothy. The rustic courtyard has a covered seating area.

Carbost: Isle of Skye

Old Inn

IV47 8SR (on B8009) NG379318

◉ 11-1am; 12-12.15am Sun ☎ (01478) 640205
🌐 theoldinnskye.co.uk
3 changing beers (often Cuillin, Isle of Skye) Ⓗ
On the shores of Loch Harport, the Old Inn nestles on the tideline. Outside, trestle tables take advantage of the views that Skye is famous for – there can be no better place to enjoy a pint. Three handpumps offer beers from Skye and Cuillin breweries. The pub is busy all year round with an eclectic mix of outdoor folk, and those touring Skye or visiting the Talisker Distillery close by. Seafood is top of the menu, most of it coming from the loch.
Q ➷ ⊛ ⇦ ◑ ● P ⊟ ☀

Carrbridge

Cairn Hotel Ⓛ
Main Road, PH23 3AS (just off A9 on B9153 to N of village)
◉ 12-midnight (1am Fri & Sat); 12.30-midnight Sun
☎ (01479) 841212 🌐 cairnhotel.co.uk
3 changing beers (sourced regionally; often Cairngorm, Cromarty, Orkney) Ⓗ
The Cairn Hotel is very much the hub of the small village of Carrbridge, with the lure of excellent food and a warming open fire. The licensee is passionate about the beer he selects for his three handpumps and the bar is popular with loyal locals and the many visitors to the area. Close to Landmark Forest Adventure Park and busy when porridge-making or chainsaw-carving events are on. ➷ ⊛ ⇦ ◑ ● ♣ P ⊟ ☀ 🛜

Claddach Kirkibost: North Uist

Westford Inn
HS6 5EP (2½ miles NW of Clachan on A865)
NF7751066195
◉ 12-11 (midnight Fri; 1am Sat); 12.30-11 Sun
☎ (01876) 580653 🌐 westfordinn.com
Isle of Skye Red; 3 changing beers (sourced regionally; often Fyne, Isle of Skye) Ⓗ
The owners took on the Westford Inn in 2015 and have turned around its fortunes. Very much the hub of the community, it hosts live music and an annual beer festival. A second Skye ale is on rotation in winter, with three ales in summer, as well as a range of bottled beers. Good-quality pub food is served, also available to take away. Although probably one of the most remote pubs in the Guide, it is well worth making the effort to visit. The Bothy provide accommodation.
Q ➷ ⊛ ⇦ ◑ ▲ ♣ P ⊟ ☀ 🛜

Dores

Dores Inn Ⓛ
IV2 6TR (on B862) NH59753476
◉ 10-11 (midnight Fri & Sat); 10-11 Sun summer; closed Mon; 10-11 Tue-Thu (midnight Fri & Sat); 10-11 Sun winter
☎ (01463) 751203 🌐 thedoresinn.co.uk
4 changing beers (sourced regionally; often Cairngorm, Cromarty, Inveralmond) Ⓗ
Set on the shores of Loch Ness and featuring in an Old Speckled Hen commercial, the location offers excellent Nessie-spotting opportunities, and is popular all year round – a must-stop, just for the views. The cosy wood-finished bar has up to four ales from a selection of local and regional independents, and occasionally an English ale. During the summer, the OutDores Inn bar opens in the beer garden. Great food is available all day. The

pub opens from 10am, with full bar service from 11 (12 Sun). A free minibus service is provided to/from Inverness. Q ➷ ⊛ ◑ P ⊟ (301,302) ☀ 🛜

Drumnadrochit

Benleva Hotel Ⓛ
Kilmore Road, IV63 6UH (signed 800 yards from A82) NH513295
◉ 11-midnight (1am Fri & Sat); 12.30-midnight Sun
☎ (01456) 450080 🌐 benleva.co.uk
Hanging Tree First Light, After Dark, Hangmans IPA; 1 changing beer (sourced regionally) Ⓗ
The 400-year-old sweet chestnut outside the Benleva was once a hanging tree, hence the name of the brewery in the bothy just outside. The bar in this 300-year-old former manse offers four Hanging Tree beers and a guest ale. Classic home-made dishes have a Scottish twist. Regular music and themed nights are held throughout the year and an annual beer festival in September. Handy for Urquhart Castle and all Loch Ness attractions.
➷ ⊛ ⇦ ◑ ▲ ♣ P ⊟ ☀ 🛜

Fort William

Ben Nevis Inn Ⓛ
Achintee Road, Claggan, PH33 6TE NN12477293
◉ 12-11 summer; winter hours vary ☎ (01397) 701227
🌐 ben-nevis-inn.co.uk
3 changing beers (sourced locally; often Cairngorm, Isle of Skye, River Leven) Ⓗ
Traditional stone-built barn at the start of the Ben Nevis mountain path, popular with outdoor enthusiasts. The small bar counter has three handpumps offering beers from local breweries. The barn, with long beer hall-style tables and a beckoning stove, decorated with mountaineering and skiing paraphernalia, is a warm, informal and friendly setting, an ideal venue for the regular live music. A hearty food menu is available until 9pm and changes daily. The adjacent bunkhouse sleeps 24 people. Check ahead for opening hours in winter. Q ⊛ ⇦ ◑ & ▲ P

Garrison West
4 Cameron Square, PH33 6AJ
◉ 12-midnight Mon-Fri; 11-midnight Sat; 11-11 Sun summer; 12-11 winter ☎ (01397) 701873 🌐 garrisonwest.co.uk
2 changing beers (sourced regionally; often Belhaven, Glen Spean) Ⓗ

REAL ALE BREWERIES

Black Isle Munlochy
Cairngorm Aviemore
Cromarty Cromarty
Cuillin 🍺 Sligachan: Isle of Skye
Dun Glenelg
Glen Spean Spean Bridge (NEW)
Hanging Tree 🍺 Drumnadrochit
Isle of Skye Uig: Isle of Skye
John O'Groats John O'Groats
Knoydart Knoydart (NEW)
Laig Bay Galmisdale: Isle of Eigg
Loomshed Tarbert: Isle of Harris (NEW)
Nessie Fort Augustus
Old Inn 🍺 Gairloch
Plockton Plockton
River Leven Kinlochleven
Strathcarron Strathcarron
Two Thirsty Men Grantown-on-Spey

This cosy and agreeable bar has a welcoming stove and two handpumps serving beers from the local Glen Spean brewery and through a Belhaven link. A selection of beer on fonts and in bottles is also available, many real ale in a bottle, plus something for the designated driver. Plenty of whiskies and gins are also stocked, often local. The food, featuring many dishes with a Scottish nod, is well reviewed and worth trying out. Regular music and quiz nights are hosted. ◑≈🚌📶

Great Glen ✔

104 High Street, PH33 6AD

⏲ 7am-midnight (1am Fri & Sat) ☎ (01397) 709910

Changing beers (often Adnams, Caledonian, Strathaven) Ⓗ

Purpose-built in 2013, with a spacious and modern interior, this Wetherspoon pub is named after the 78-mile Great Glen (An Gleann Mor), the geological feature that runs up to Inverness. The decor is very much linked to local attractions, businesses and people. Up to 10 handpumps offer mostly local and regional beers. The roof garden is reached by an internal staircase. Alcohol is served from 11am (midday Sunday). There is a Travelodge immediately above. ⛑❀🛏◑♿⛺≈P🚌📶

Grog & Gruel 𝕃 ✔

66 High Street, PH33 6AE

⏲ 12-midnight Mon-Thu (1am Fri & Sat); 12.30-midnight Sun summer; 12-11.30 Mon-Wed (12.30am Thu-Sat); 5-11.30 Sun winter ☎ (01397) 705078 🌐 grogandgruel.co.uk

6 changing beers (sourced locally; often Loch Lomond, River Leven) Ⓗ

There is no better place to end the 96-mile walk along the West Highland Way. A regular in the Guide since 1997, and justifiably so, the pub is busy all day every day with a mix of locals and tourists. Beers on up to six handpumps, including many local brews, make it a draw for the real ale connoisseur. A newly refreshed food menu is available downstairs; the upstairs restaurant opens in the evening. Open mic features on most Friday evenings. CAMRA branch runner-up Pub of the Year 2019. ⛑◑⛺≈🍎🚌🐾📶

Fortrose

Anderson

Union Street, IV10 8TD

⏲ 4-11 summer; 4-11.30 Thu-Sat; closed Sun-Wed winter ☎ (01381) 620236 🌐 theanderson.co.uk

2 changing beers (sourced nationally; often Cromarty, Inveralmond) Ⓗ

With three handpumps, one offering cider, you can tour the whole of Scotland and parts of the UK from a bar stool, sampling exceptionally well-chosen beers, lovingly kept in the natural 200-year-old cellar. Award-winning home-cooked food, including vegetarian, is served in the busy restaurant, bar and whisky lounge with 250 single malts. The play-your-own radiogram is popular. Regular music, quiz and knitting evenings feature throughout the year and occasional food nights and themed weekend mini festivals. Closed for five weeks before Christmas. Q⛑❀🛏◑♿⛺♣🍎P🚌🐾📶

Gairloch

Old Inn 𝕃

Flowerdale, IV21 2BD (opp harbour)

⏲ 11-1am (11.45 Sat); 12-11.15 Sun summer; winter hours vary ☎ (01445) 712006 🌐 theoldinn.net

6 changing beers (often Old Inn, Orkney) Ⓗ

Once a Highland drovers' inn, the Old Inn offers a selection of up to six ales, including some from its own nano brewery, now including a North Coast 500 ale. The bar has a mix of seating and an all-important open fire for the winter. On warmer days there is shaded seating under the tree just in front of the burn. With an emphasis on seafood, there is something on the menu for everyone. Gairloch has many walks including the Flowerdale Glen opposite and two golden beaches. ⛑❀🛏◑♿⛺♣P🚌📶

Glencoe

Clachaig Inn 𝕃 ✔

PH49 4HX (3 miles SE of village, off A82) NN12705668

⏲ 11-11 (midnight Sat); 12.30-11 Sun ☎ (01855) 811252 🌐 clachaig.com

10 changing beers (sourced locally; often Cairngorm, Orkney, River Leven) Ⓗ

The Clachaig is a must for outdoor enthusiasts and beer lovers alike, set in a remote location among the spectacular hills and scenery of Glencoe. Having worked up a hunger on the hills, a huge choice of well-kept beers and hearty grub will replenish your energy. There are also more than 360 whiskies and 100 gins to distract you. On cooler days, wood-burning stoves keep the three bars and snugs warm. Beer festivals are held during the year and it has regular music nights. ⛑❀🛏◑♿♣P📶

Inverness

Black Isle Bar 𝕃

68 Church Street, IV1 1EN

⏲ 11-1am ☎ (01463) 229920 🌐 blackislebar.com

Black Isle Yellowhammer, Red Kite; 4 changing beers (sourced locally; often Black Isle) Ⓟ

The Black Isle Bar opened in 2016, offering up to six real ales and 20 font beers. Two big screens show the eclectic beer menu, mostly from Black Isle but some guests, with prices for pints, halves and thirds. The open-plan bar area offers a mix of seating. Upstairs, the secret garden utilises upcycled cable drums, pallet tables and stools under a cover of reclaimed corrugated iron. Organic ingredients from the brewery farm are used in an interesting food menu which features pizzas, salads and soups. Q🛏◑♿≈P🚌🐾📶

Castle Tavern 𝕃

1 View Place, IV2 4SA (top of Castle St)

⏲ 11-1am (12.30am Sat); 12-midnight Sun ☎ (01463) 718178 🌐 castletavern.pub

5 changing beers (sourced regionally; often Cromarty, Isle of Skye, Windswept) Ⓗ

A short walk from the centre of town will take you to the Castle Tavern, a pub popular with tourists visiting the castle opposite and locals who know their beer. Six handpumps offer an interesting rolling selection of beers, mostly from Scottish independents, and a changing cider. There is plenty of seating inside but the covered canopy area outside is always busy, even in winter, with panoramic views along the River Ness. Bar meals are available all day; the restaurant upstairs is open in the evening. Local CAMRA Cider Pub of the Year 2019. ⛑❀◑♿⛺≈🍎P🚌🐾📶

Clachnaharry Inn 🏆

17-19 High Street, Clachnaharry, IV3 8RB (on A862 Beauly road)
11-11 (1am Fri & Sat); 12-11 Sun ☎ (01463) 239806
clachnaharryinn.co.uk
Fyne Jarl; Harviestoun Bitter & Twisted; Inveralmond Ossian; 2 changing beers (sourced nationally; often Cairngorm, Greene King) H
The Clach has featured in the Guide for more than 30 years and is where many have discovered the joys of real ale. The 17th-century coaching inn is a must-visit location, with a friendly welcome for all. The bar oozes heritage, with an open fire on cooler days. Food is available in the bar area and the quieter dining area. Quiz and music nights feature regularly. On warmer days, the view from the terrace over the Beauly Firth and Black Isle, with Ben Wyvis beyond, never fails to satisfy.
QP (28,28A)

King's Highway ✔

72-74 Church Street, IV1 1EN
7am-1am ☎ (01463) 251830
Adnams Broadside; Caledonian Deuchars IPA; Fuller's London Pride; Greene King Abbot; Sharp's Doom Bar; changing beers H
Situated centrally, the King's Highway offers good-value Wetherspoon fare and is a popular and busy meeting point, handy for the town's bus and train stations. By virtue of its previous incarnation, it has separate seating areas and some quieter corners. Up to 10 handpumps feature mainly Scottish beers, many of them local to the area. Open from 7am for breakfast, full bar service from 11am. Accommodation is available. P

MacGregor's

109-113 Academy Street, IV1 1LX (on corner with Friars Lane)
11-1am; 12-midnight Sun ☎ (01463) 719629
macgregorsbars.com
2 changing beers (often Cromarty, Spey Valley, Swannay)
Crowdfunding allowed Blazin' Fiddles musician Bruce MacGregor's pub to become an instant hit on opening in 2017, winning many business innovation and tourist awards, and offering an insight into Scottish history, culture, food and drink. Two handpumps and a font gantry offer beers from local breweries, alongside an extensive menu of bottled beers, gins and whiskies. There is seating in the main bar, whisky room and outside. Music abounds – if not, make your own at the piano! An interesting food menu with a Scottish theme is served all day. P

Number 27 L

27 Castle Street, IV2 3DU (opp castle)
11-11 (12.30am Fri & Sat); 12.30-11 Sun
☎ (01463) 241999 number27inverness.uk
4 changing beers (sourced regionally; often Speyside, Windswept) H
The number 27 sign is hard to miss above the entrance to this bar and restaurant. Four handpumps normally offer beers from the much-respected Windswept Brewery, with beers from other local breweries making an appearance occasionally alongside an extensive selection of keg and bottled beers. Menus cater for a quick pub lunch and a more substantial offering in the evening, including an all-day children's menu.
P

John o' Groats

Seaview Hotel L

County Road, KW1 4YR (A99/A863 jct) ND380727
11-midnight (1am Fri & Sat); 11-midnight Sun
☎ (01955) 611220 seaviewjohnogroats.co.uk
John o' Groats Swelkie; 1 changing beer (sourced locally; often John o' Groats) H
The family-run Seaview Hotel has got to be the most northerly pub on the UK mainland and is the tap for the nearby John o' Groats Brewery. The 26 rooms, in the hotel itself, the cottage or the annexe over the road, are well used by End to Enders, either beginning the John o' Groats to Lands End (JoGLE) route or ending (LEJoG) the 838-mile journey by road or 1,200 miles on foot. Meals are served throughout the day. P

Kincraig

Suie Bar L

PH21 1NA (at head of Loch Insh on B9152) NH829057
5-11 ☎ (01540) 651788
Cairngorm Trade Winds; 2 changing beers (sourced regionally; often Orkney) H
It is worth pulling off the busy A9 and following the old road to seek out this wee gem. The outside may not look much, but inside you will find a warm Highland welcome and four handpumps offering Cairngorm and local beers. Sadly, the much-loved old stove has been replaced with a more modern, efficient model. The pub hosts a beer festival in late February and music most weekends. Handy for the Highland Wildlife Park. P

Kylesku

Kylesku Hotel

IV27 4HW NC229337
11 (12.30 Sun)-11; closed Dec-Feb ☎ (01971) 502231
kyleskuhotel.co.uk
3 changing beers (sourced regionally; often Isle of Skye, Orkney) H
Kylesku Hotel offers spectacular views of the loch and mountains. The hotel entrance is adorned with awards for its food over the years – this is a foodies' paradise. The crystal clear waters yield all the seafood, the venison is wild and the lamb and beef are also local. Food is served 8am-9pm. Four handpumps dispense the ales alongside an excellent selection of bottles. On the North Coast 500 route, accommodation tends to be booked months in advance. QP

Lewiston

Loch Ness Inn

IV63 6UW (W of A82)
11.30-11 ☎ (01456) 450991 staylochness.co.uk
3 changing beers (sourced locally; often Cairngorm, Cromarty, Windswept)
This traditional inn, dating from 1838, has rooms and a bunkhouse. The restaurant is fiercely proud of the local provenance of its ingredients. The comfy bar with a welcoming stove has up to three handpumps offering beers from mainly local breweries, occasionally Applecross. Set in a central location, the inn is an ideal base for visiting Loch Ness, local Nessie tourist haunts or nearby Urquhart Castle, or walking the Great Glen Way. A free courtesy bus is available for pick-ups within five miles. P

SCOTLAND

Nairn

Braeval Hotel L

Crescent Road, IV12 4NB (E end of town, near beach)
12-11 (midnight Fri & Sat) summer; 4-11; 12-12.30am Fri; 12-1am Sat winter ☎ (01667) 452341 braevalhotel.co.uk
6 changing beers (sourced nationally; often Cairngorm, Cromarty, Orkney) H
Set overlooking the green, beyond the beach and Moray Firth, the Bandstand Bar in the Braeval Hotel has six handpumps offering a great selection of local and regional Scottish ales and the occasional English one. The annual beer festival in early May is possibly one of the biggest in the UK, with around 200 ales and 10 ciders from all over, accompanied by themed food and live bands over three days. The Seaview Restaurant offers great food at a keen price. Live music features every weekend.
Q P

Newtonmore

Glen Hotel L

Main Street, PH20 1DD (S of village)
11-11 (midnight Fri & Sat); 12.30-11 Sun
☎ (01540) 673203 theglenhotel.co.uk
4 changing beers (often Cairngorm, Caledonian, Cromarty) H
Featuring in the Guide since 2005, the Glen was a trailblazer in the Highlands for real ale, with four handpumps offering Scottish beers from near and far. Cider is also available in the summer. The small cluster of CAMRA members in the locality have made the comfy bar their home. Good honest pub grub is served in the bar, restaurant and outside on trestle tables. Quiz nights and a games room make this a popular evening retreat for locals and visitors alike. Opens at 7.30am every day for breakfast. Bar service starts at 11 (12 Sun). P

Plockton

Plockton Hotel

41 Harbour Street, IV52 8TN NG80293343
11-midnight; closed Jan; 12-midnight Sun
☎ (01599) 544274 plocktonhotel.co.uk
4 changing beers (sourced regionally; often Cromarty, Fyne, Swannay) H
Plockton was the setting for TV's Hamish Macbeth, which is a draw for visitors to this pretty village, many of whom arrive by train on the picturesque Kyle Line. The bar proudly offers four handpumps dispensing both local and regional beers as well as a tempting food menu featuring locally sourced seafood, beef and venison. Take your beer onto the terrace and from the shade of the palm trees watch the tide. A real ale and gin festival is held in May.
Q P

Rosemarkie

Plough Inn ★

48 High Street, IV10 8UF (on A832)
11-midnight (1am Fri & Sat); 12-midnight Sun summer; closed Mon winter ☎ (01381) 620164
Cromarty Happy Chappy; 1 changing beer (sourced locally; often Cromarty) H
The licensees have worked hard to put the Plough back on the must-visit map. Walking in through the narrow double swing doors reveals a cosy wood-lined bar identified by CAMRA as having a nationally important historic pub interior. There is an ancient marriage stone lintel dated 1691 over the fireplace. Two handpumps offer beers from the local Cromarty brewery, less than six miles away. There are trestle tables outside in a small enclosed suntrap grassed area, and the walls of the pub give off their heat long after the sun has moved round.
Q P

Roy Bridge

Stronlossit Inn L

Main Street, PH31 4AG (on A86) NN27228117
11-11.45 (1am Thu-Sat); 12.30-11.45 Sun
☎ (01397) 712253 stronlossit.co.uk
3 changing beers (sourced locally; often Cairngorm, Isle of Skye, Orkney) H
The location of the Stronlossitt makes it attractive to those keen on the outdoors, and with the railway station just over the road, you can abandon the car and arrive by train from Fort William or London. The train can also take you for a day trip to Corrour to walk around Loch Ossian. Four handpumps spoil real ale fans, with beers from Scottish breweries including Glen Spean – more real ale is thought to be sold here than keg. Great food is available all day as well as rooms for all budgets. Q P

Scourie

Scourie Hotel L

IV27 4SX (on A894 between Laxford Bridge and Kylesku) NC156447
12-11; 12.30-11 Sun summer; 5-8.30 Mon-Fri; 12-2.30, 5-11 Sat; 6-9 Sun winter; closed Oct-Mar ☎ (01971) 502396
scouriehotel.com
2 changing beers (sourced regionally; often Caledonian, Orkney) H
A converted 1640 coaching inn in the heart of the wonderland wilderness of north-west Sutherland. It is popular with fishermen who enjoy access to around 300 lochs. Close to the Handa Island ferry, and a short drive to the peaks of Arkle and Foinaven, this is an ideal base for exploring. A bar menu is available and the dining room offers high-quality meals featuring seafood. Two handpumps serve Orkney and Caledonian ales.
Q P (806)

Shieldaig

Tigh an Eilean Hotel

IV54 8XN (off A896) NG815540
11-11 (midnight Fri & Sat) ☎ (01520) 755251
shieldaigbarcoastalkitchen.co.uk
Strathcarron Golden Cow, Red Cow H
Tigh an Eilean, House of the Island, nestles in the picturesque 200-year-old fishing village of Shieldaig in a line of whitewashed cottages strung out along the seafront. The menu features locally caught seafood, daily specials and pizzas from the wood-fired pizza oven. Two Strathcarron ales are offered, with seating in the bar area and views of the bay from the first floor and open-deck balcony. The Strathcarron bus runs to Shieldaig three times daily. Q P

Ullapool

Arch Inn

10-11 West Shore Street, IV26 2UR (on seafront)

11-11.30 summer; 11-11.30; 12-11.30 Sun winter
(01854) 612454 thearchinn.co.uk
2 changing beers (often Cairngorm)
The Arch Inn opened in 1973 and was originally an inn and store for fishermen and fish curers. It is popular with locals and visiting tourists either staying in Ullapool or passing through, the busy bar offering a warm welcome and two Cairngorm handpumps. The menu is complemented by a daily specials board featuring locally sourced seafood. There is seating over the road by the sea. Regular entertainment includes Scottish folk music, local bands and stand-up acts.

Morefield Motel

North Road, IV26 2TQ (signposted off A835)
12-11 (01854) 612000 morefieldmotel.co.uk
3 changing beers (sourced regionally; often Cairngorm)
There is room at the bar for a beer at this restaurant and everyone is welcome. The three handpumps offer a selection of Scottish ales. In late October the licensees host a popular beer and cider festival, with music in the evenings. Locally landed seafood is a speciality in the lounge and conservatory restaurants. The motel rooms are an ideal base for exploring the spectacular and dramatic west coast of Scotland. Q

Waternish: Isle of Skye

Stein Inn

MacLeod's Terrace, IV55 8GA (N of Dunvegan, on B886)
NG26255643
11-midnight; 12-11 Sun summer; closed Mon & Tue winter
(01470) 592362 stein-inn.co.uk
3 changing beers (often Caledonian, Isle of Skye)
Set on the picturesque shores of Loch Bay, the Stein Inn is one of the oldest hostelries on Skye. Two beers are on offer throughout the year, with a third during busy times. Given that it is landed 100 yards away, local seafood is the speciality. The low-beamed bar has a double-sided stove for cooler days, and when the sun shines trestle tables invite you outside. This has to be one of the most picturesque places in the UK to enjoy a pint.
Q

SCOTLAND

Waternish Isle of Skye, Stein Inn (Photo: Bryan Ledgard/Flickr)

KINGDOM OF FIFE

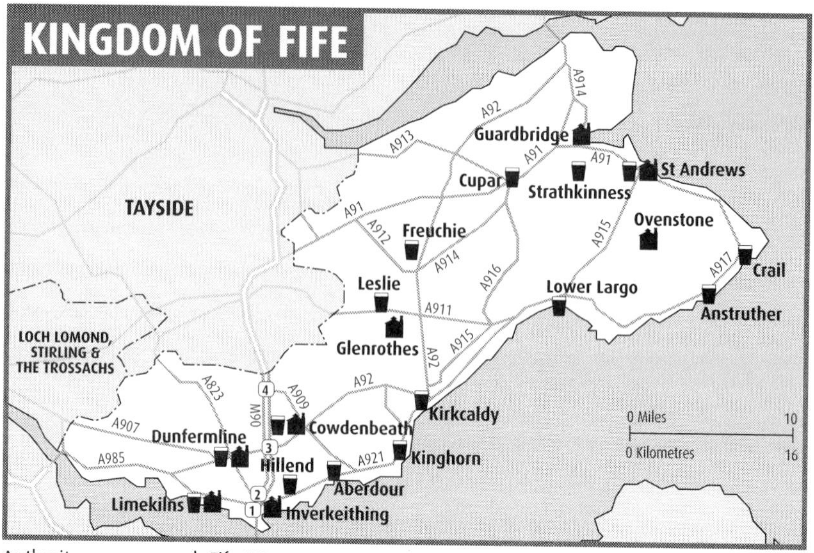

Authority area covered: Fife UA

Aberdour

Foresters Arms ✔

35 High Street, KY3 0SJ

☼ 11-midnight (1am Fri); 10-1am Sat ☎ (01383) 861245

🌐 theforestersarms.pub

4 changing beers (sourced nationally; often Adnams, Theakston, Young's) Ⓗ

Situated in the centre of the village, convenient for the railway station, castle, beaches and harbour. Bingo is played every Sunday afternoon and there is a monthly quiz. The pub has a jukebox and pool table. It serves breakfast and lunchtime meals, and is a popular stop-off for walkers on the Fife Coastal Path. A monthly meat raffle is held in aid of local good causes. A repeat winner of local CAMRA Pub of the Year. ❀♿⇌♣🚌(7)🐾📶

Anstruther

Boathouse ✔

28 Shore Street, KY10 3AQ

☼ 12-11 (midnight Fri & Sat) ☎ (01333) 312105

🌐 at-the-shore.co.uk

3 changing beers (sourced nationally) Ⓗ

Fomerly an 18th-century coaching inn, the Boathouse can be found in the middle of town by the harbour. It has two main rooms – the main bar area and a bistro where you can enjoy fresh locally prepared meals while taking in views of the sea. The food menu changes with the seasons, and uses East Neuk suppliers to feature specialities of the region. Breakfast is available from 9am daily, with the full menu from noon.
🛏🍴◐⛺♣P🚌(X60,95)🐾📶

Ship Tavern 🄻

49 Shore Street, KY10 3AQ

☼ 11-midnight (1am Fri & Sat) ☎ (01333) 310347

2 changing beers (sourced regionally; often Eden Mill) Ⓗ

Newly refurbished, the Ship is a traditional pub and a poplar meeting place for fishermen, locals and visitors to the waterfront. It is located right on the harbour front, next door to the fishery museum and across from the historic Reaper, a two-masted sailing lugger. The bar has all the character you would expect from a historic fishing village inn. Two changing ales come from regional or national brewers. Q❀⛺♣P🚌(X60,95)🐾📶

Cowdenbeath

Woodside Hotel 🄻

109 Broad Street, KY4 8JR

☼ 11-midnight; 12.30-midnight Sun ☎ (01383) 511598

1 changing beer (sourced nationally; often Beath, Kelburn, Swannay) Ⓗ

Large single-roomed bar with two handpumps serving ales from local and north of England microbreweries in lined glasses. One side of the room has a pool table and dartboard, and four plasma screens show sport. A warm, friendly atmosphere prevails, with live entertainment at the weekend. A separate lounge is available for functions. Outside, a covered and decked area with seating is a lovely suntrap in summer.
🛏❀🍴♿⇌♣P▯🚌(19,33)🐾📶

Crail

Golf Hotel ✔

4 High Street, KY10 3TD

☼ 11-11 (midnight Sat & Sun) ☎ (01333) 450206

🌐 thegolfhotelcrail.com

3 changing beers (sourced nationally; often Adnams, Eden Mill, Harviestoun) Ⓗ

REAL ALE BREWERIES

Beath Cowdenbeath
Brew Shed Limekilns
Coul Glenrothes (NEW)
Eden St Andrews Guardbridge
Inner Bay Inverkeithing
Ovenstone 109 Ovenstone (NEW)
Seven Kings Dunfermline (NEW)
St Andrews St Andrews

Grade A-listed 16th-century coaching inn in a picturesque village. The historic bar is one of the oldest in Scotland. The room retains the original low-beamed ceiling, wooden floor and a 16th-century fireplace with a marriage lintel over it bearing the initials of the owners. Relax with a beer in the garden or enjoy a meal in the restaurant after walking the coastal path. ➠✿🛏️◗P🖥️(95)🐾☕

Cupar

Boudingait 🅛
43 Bonnygate, KY15 4BU

🕐 11-10 Mon (11 Tue & Wed; midnight Thu; 1am Fri & Sat); 11-midnight Sun ☎ (01334) 654681

🌐 theboudingaitcupar.co.uk

2 changing beers (sourced nationally; often Eden Mill) 🅗

A wee gem hidden away in the centre of Cupar. It offers a varied menu of food daily, featuring a specials board. A loyalty card is available and booking is advised. Weekly activities include live music and a quiz night. Well-behaved dogs are welcome. ➠◗&🚲🖥️☕

Dunfermline

Commercial Inn 🅛
13 Douglas Street, KY12 7EB

🕐 10-11 (midnight Fri & Sat); 12.30-11 Sun

☎ (01383) 733876

8 changing beers (sourced nationally; often Beath, Redcastle, Tryst) 🅗

A warm, welcoming hostelry in a historic building dating back to the 1820s and just a short walk from the High Street across from the old post office. This classic wood-panelled pub has a homely feel, with good food and friendly service attracting an eclectic clientele. A great variety of ales is available on seven handpulls, along with a real cider. A Scottish Pub of the Year finalist. ➠◗🚲🍺🖥️☕

East Port Bar ✅
7 East Port, KY12 7JG

🕐 11-11 (midnight Fri & Sat); 12-11 Sun ☎ (01383) 736678

3 changing beers (sourced nationally; often Moorhouse's, Stewart, Timothy Taylor) 🅗

The East Port Bar is a terrific place to visit during a day out in Dunfermline. This busy town-centre bar has cosy sofas and booths in which to enjoy a drink or two. The interior features wood panelling and a wood bar and gantry, with soft background music usually playing. Value-for-money food is served at lunchtime. Sport from football to golf is shown on plasma screens. ✿◗&🚲🖥️☕

Guildhall & Linen Exchange ✅
79-83 High Street, KY12 7DR

🕐 7am-midnight; 8am-1am Fri & Sat ☎ (01383) 625960

Caledonian Deuchars IPA; Greene King Abbot; 6 changing beers (sourced nationally; often Redcastle, Rooster's) 🅗

Located on the High Street in the middle of Dunfermline's busy retail area, this split-level Wetherspoon establishment is a great place to hide for a quick half or two and a bite to eat. The Category A-listed building is decorated with a mixture of modern and Art Deco features. The pub also displays numerous pictures highlighting the historic past of Dunfermline and the Guildhall. ➠✿🛏️◗&🚲🖥️☕

Freuchie

Albert Tavern
2 High Street, KY15 7EX

🕐 5-midnight; 12-1am Fri & Sat; 12.30-midnight Sun

☎ 07876 178863 🌐 alberttavern.wixsite.com/albert

5 changing beers (sourced nationally; often Harviestoun, Hawkshead, Salopian) 🅗

A cosy two-roomed local with a low-beamed ceiling reminiscent of an English village pub. The bar's six handpumps dispense ales sourced from throughout the UK alongside up to four real ciders. The lounge hosts a malt whisky club and also has regular gin nights, plus a popular pie night on Thursday. A multi award-winning local CAMRA Pub of the Year and twice the Scottish Pub of the Year winner. Q✿♣🚲🖥️☕

Hillend

Hillend Tavern 🅛 ✅
37 Main Street, KY11 9ND

🕐 4-midnight; 3-midnight Fri; 1-midnight Sat & Sun

☎ (01383) 415391 🌐 hillendtavern.co.uk

4 changing beers (sourced nationally; often Loch Leven, Stewart, Timothy Taylor) 🅗

A small, welcoming pub with two real fires. Not far from Dalgety Bay, it has a spacious room at the back and a large covered area outside. At the heart of the village community, the Hillend offers numerous attractions including live music, quizzes, karaoke and televised sport including rugby. Four handpulls dispense a wide range of local, regional and national ales. Local CAMRA Pub of the Year 2017 and 2018. ➠✿🚲♣🖥️(7,87)🐾☕

Kinghorn

Crown Tavern 🅛 ✅
55-57 High Street, KY3 9UW

🕐 11-midnight (1am Fri & Sat); 12-midnight Sun

☎ (01592) 890340

2 changing beers (sourced nationally; often Inveralmond, Sharp's) 🅐

This lively two-roomed local, affectionately known as the Middle Bar by its patrons, is very much a community hub of this pleasant coastal village. The building features fine stained-glass windows. Two real ales are served through a pair of tall fonts, alongside two real ciders. There is a pool table to the rear, and TV screens show a wide variety of sporting events. Sunday is quiz night. 🚲♣🍺🖥️(7)🐾☕

Kirkcaldy

Betty Nicols 🅛
297 High Street, KY1 1JL

🕐 12-8 Mon (8.30 Tue & Wed; 11 Thu; midnight Fri); 11-midnight Sat; 1-8 Sun ☎ (01592) 642083

🌐 bettynicolsbarandbistro.co.uk

Fyne Ales Jarl; 1 changing beer (sourced regionally; often Fuller's, Orkney, Timothy Taylor) 🅗

A longstanding real ale venue on the High Street in Kirkcaldy, serving quality drinks in a relaxing and comfortable atmosphere. The traditional bar attracts a varied clientele; the modern bistro serves lunchtime meals. Live music is a popular attraction, as is the quiz evening on alternate Thursdays. ➠◗&🚲🖥️☕

Harbour Bar

471-475 High Street, KY1 2SN

5-midnight Mon & Tue; 12-3, 5-midnight Wed & Thu; 12-midnight Fri-Sun ☎ (01592) 264270

6 changing beers (sourced nationally; often Fyne Ales, Mallinsons, Oakham) H

This Grade C-listed building dates from around 1870 and became a pub in 1924. It has a public bar, lounge and rare Jug Bar. Handpulls serve changing real ales from a list of up to 20, sourced all over the UK, along with a real cider. Now included in the Guide for the 27th consecutive year, the pub is a previous winner of local CAMRA and Scottish Pub of the Year awards. Q♿🍎🚌 (X60)🐾

Leslie

Burns Tavern

184 High Street, KY6 3DB

11-midnight (1am Fri & Sat); 12.30-midnight Sun ☎ (01592) 741345

Timothy Taylor Landlord; 1 changing beer (sourced nationally; often Stewart) H

A friendly two-roomed local pub in a small former paper-making town north of Glenrothes. Very much a hub of the community, the pub hosts functions including a Thursday night quiz. Its public bar shows sport on TV and is split-level, with a pool table on the upper level. Timothy Taylor Landlord, the longstanding regular beer, is served alongside a guest ale usually from Stewart Brewing. Q❀🛏⛺♣P🚌 (39A)🐾

Limekilns

Ship Inn L

Halketts Hall, KY11 3HJ

10-11 (midnight Fri & Sat); 11-11 Sun ☎ (01383) 872247

3 changing beers (sourced nationally; often Blue Monkey, Kent) H

This pub sits on the River Forth with views of the three bridges spanning the river. It serves three different ales, which can be enjoyed by the bar or in the cosy alcove. Numerous ship-related artefacts displayed around the pub include an engine order telegraph, a communication device that takes pride of place on the bar. Meals are served lunchtimes, with fish and seafood the speciality (booking is essential). Q❀◐P🚌 (6)

Lower Largo

Railway Inn 🏆 L

1 Station Wynd, KY8 6BU

11-midnight (1am Thu-Sat) ☎ (01333) 320239

railwayinnlargo.co.uk

5 changing beers (sourced regionally; often Eden Mill, Fyne Ales, St Andrews) H

This friendly and traditional village pub has been established in Lower Largo, close to the picturesque harbour, since 1749. Its small two-roomed interior is warmed by a cosy real fire. Five handpumps serve beers from all over the UK. The pub is a champion of LocAle, stocking beers from the smaller Fife breweries on a regular basis. Situated near the East Neuk section of the Fife Coastal Path, it is a firm favourite with ramblers, dog walkers and locals. Q❀🚌 (95)🐾📶

St Andrews

Central Bar L ✔

77 Market Street, KY16 9NU

11-midnight (1am Fri & Sat) ☎ (01334) 478296

centralbar-standrews.co.uk

8 changing beers (sourced nationally; often Eden Mill, Greene King, Redcastle) H

As its name suggests, this large bar is centrally located in the cobbled market place of this historic university town. Inside, it features a Victorian-style island bar, an ornate ceiling and a collection of historical brewery mirrors, giving a traditional feel. A fine selection of beers is always available and the pub has a good atmosphere, generated by its unique blend of customers including students, tourists, golfers and locals. ❀◐◑🚌🐾📶

Criterion L ✔

99 South Street, KY16 9QW

10-midnight (1am Fri & Sat) ☎ (01334) 474543

criterionstandrews.co.uk

Caledonian Deuchars IPA, Edinburgh Castle 80/-; 3 changing beers (sourced nationally; often Eden Mill, Stewart) H

This traditional Scottish local, located in the centre of the bustling town, attracts a varied clientele. Opened in 1874, it is now among the area's few remaining family-run pubs. It serves a wide range of home-made food, including the famous Cri Pies which are available all day. Quiet background music contributes to the atmosphere by day, and regular live music and open mic nights are hosted. ❀◐◑🍎🚌🐾📶

Whey Pat Tavern L ✔

1 Bridge Street, KY16 9EX

11-midnight (1am Thu-Sat); 12-midnight Sun ☎ (01334) 477740 wheypat-standrews.co.uk

5 changing beers (often Eden Mill, Greene King, Timothy Taylor) H

A busy street-corner drinkers' pub, located just outside the ancient city walls opposite the West Port. Inside, it has a front bar with a dartboard and a spacious rear lounge with roof lights. A small courtyard caters for outdoor drinkers. The original birthplace of the Fife branch of CAMRA, the pub is now popular with locals, golfers and tourists alike. ❀◐◑♿♣🚌📶

Strathkinness

Tavern

4 High Road, KY16 9RS

5-11; 12-1am Fri & Sat; 12-midnight Sun ☎ (01334) 850085 strathkinnesstavern.co.uk

2 changing beers (sourced nationally; often Cromarty, Stewart) H

A family-owned community local at the heart of this quiet village, the Tavern is renowned for its friendly hosts, excellent food and varied beer selection. Lunches and evening meals are served in the bar and restaurant; the cosy lounge offers traditional pub games. The pub hosts regular live music and quiz nights. Its outdoor seating area provides wonderful views over the Eden estuary and north to the Grampian mountains. Q❀◐◑⛺♣P🚌 (64,64A)📶

LOCH LOMOND, STIRLING & THE TROSSACHS

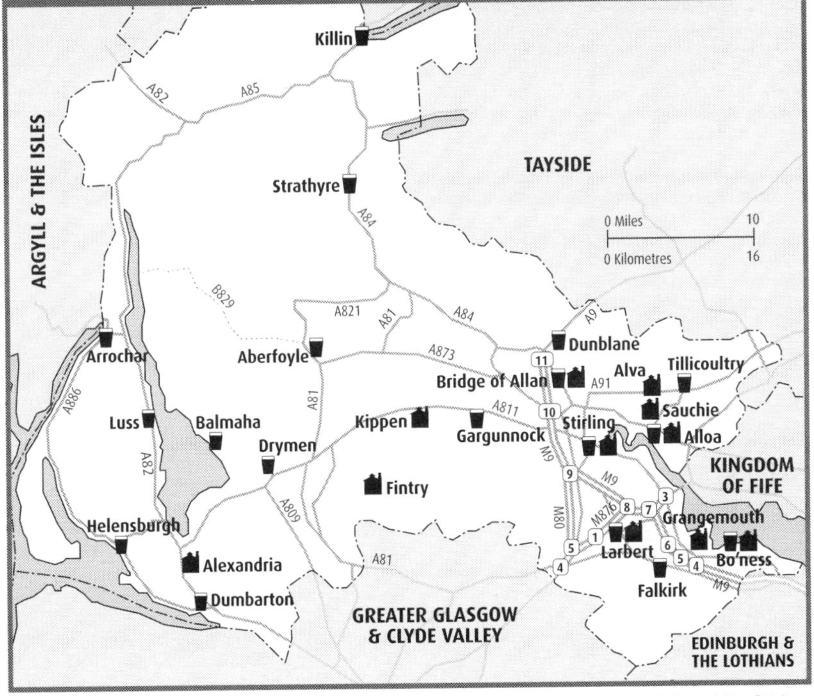

Authority areas covered: Argyll & Bute UA (part), Clackmannanshire UA, Falkirk UA, Stirling UA, West Dumbartonshire UA

Aberfoyle

Forth Inn ✅
Main Street, FK8 3UQ
☼ 10-midnight (1am Fri & Sat) ☎ (01877) 382372
⊕ forthinn.com
Harviestoun Schiehallion; 4 changing beers (sourced regionally; often Belhaven, Cairngorm, Fallen) Ⓗ
This 100-year-old inn is situated by the River Forth within the Trossachs National Park. The cosy wood-panelled bar is decorated with old photographs of the area and is a magnet for tourists and locals alike. The innovative landlord is proud to serve only Scottish ales from up to eight handpumps, with third-pint taster glasses available, and wholesome food featuring locally sourced produce. There is a separate dining room and a 'baronial' dining hall.
Q ☆ ❀ ◑ & ▲ ● P ⋤ (C11)

Alloa

Bobbing John ✅
46 Drysdale Street, FK10 1JL
☼ 8am-midnight (1am Fri & Sat) ☎ (01259) 222590
Caledonian Deuchars IPA; Greene King Abbot; Sharp's Doom Bar; changing beers (sourced nationally) Ⓗ
The pub is in a traditional three-storey sandstone building, purpose-built in 1895 for the Alloa Co-operative Society. Its name refers to locally born John Erskine who created industrial Alloa, developing the town as a coal-mining centre. He was twice Secretary of State for Scotland under Queen Anne; however, his frequent changes of political allegiance earned him the nickname

'Bobbing John'. Much of the building's original stone has been retained and a Victorian shop front reintroduced. Alcohol is served from 11am. Local CAMRA Pub of the Year 2019. ☆ ❀ ◑ & ⋤ ⋤ ☍

Arrochar

Village Inn ✅
Shore Road, G83 7AX (down A814 from A83 jct)
☼ 11-11 (midnight Fri & Sat); 12-11 Sun ☎ (01301) 702279
⊕ villageinnarrochar.co.uk
5 changing beers (sourced nationally; often Fallen, Fyne Ales, Loch Lomond) Ⓗ
Attractive pub set back from the road, originally built in 1827 as the local manse. A popular haven for walkers to the Arrochar Alps, it affords great views of Loch Long and the Cobbler. The bar to the left is welcoming and warm, and serves a wide range of ales from both local and more distant breweries. Food is offered and accommodation is

REAL ALE BREWERIES

Allanwater Bridge of Allan
Black Wolf Stirling
Devon 🍺 Sauchie
Fallen Kippen
Fintry Fintry
Harviestoun Alva
Hybrid Grangemouth
Kinneil Bo'ness
Loch Lomond Alexandria
Tryst Larbert
Williams Bros Alloa

available. The pub can be reached by rail or bus, and the journey is well worth the effort. ♘✿🛏◑♿⛺♣P🚌(926,976)🐾📶

Balmaha

Oak Tree Inn

Main Street, G63 0JQ
🕘 11-midnight (1am Fri & Sat); 12.30-midnight Sun
☎ (01360) 870357 🌐 theoaktreeinn.co.uk
4 changing beers (often Fallen, Jaw, Loch Lomond) [H]
Balmaha is a picturesque village on the quieter eastern shore of Loch Lomond, on the route of the famous West Highland Way and close to the statue of climber and broadcaster Tom Weir. This award-winning pub/restaurant has four handpumps dispensing Scottish ales, and serves food all day. There is a large outdoor drinking area under the eponymous oak tree. Licensed from 11am (12.30pm Sunday). Local CAMRA branch Pub of the Year 2019. ♘✿🛏◑♿P🚌(309)📶

Bo'ness

Corbie Inn

84 Corbiehall, EH51 0AS
🕘 12-11; 12.30-10 Sun ☎ (01506) 825307
🌐 corbieinn.co.uk
Changing beers (sourced nationally; often Kinneil) [H]
This pub opened in 2011 and has been handcrafted by the owners. Six ales are usually on handpump, including one from the Kinneil Brew Hoose at the back of the premises. An ideal refreshment stop after a visit to the Bo'ness & Kinneil Railway or the Bo'ness Motor Museum, the pub is also handy for the Hippodrome, Scotland's oldest purpose-built picture house. It is a community venue and involved in local charity projects. Local CAMRA Pub of the Year 2017. Q♘✿◑P🚌

Bridge of Allan

Allanwater Brewhouse [L]

Queens Lane, FK9 4NU
🕘 12-11 (midnight Fri & Sat) ☎ (01786) 834555
🌐 bridgeofallan.co.uk
Allanwater Gold Pot 70/-, Czech Pot, Pot Black, Procrastination [H]
A small, unique brewpub tucked away behind the main street in the lovely Bridge of Allan. Its single L-shaped room features breweriana, barrel seating and a collection of bottles. Ten handpumps dispense up to eight ales, all brewed on the premises. The candlelit interior makes for a warm, welcoming pub that attracts a cosmopolitan mix of students, walkers, cyclists and locals. Well-behaved children and dogs are welcomed. Q♘⇌P🍺🚌🐾

Drymen

Clachan Inn

2 The Square, G63 0BL
🕘 11-midnight (1am Fri & Sat); 12-midnight Sun
☎ (01360) 660824 🌐 clachaninndrymen.co.uk
2 changing beers (sourced regionally; often Belhaven) [H]
This popular free house dates from 1734 and is the oldest licensed premises in Scotland. It has recently been maintained, preserving many original features. Two handpumps dispense a changing selection of excellent local and Scottish beers. Good-quality food is served all day in both the bar and restaurant. A warm welcome is provided for all, including dog owners, walkers on the West Highland Way and tourists visiting Loch Lomond & The Trossachs National Park. ♘◑⛺🚌(309)🐾📶

Dumbarton

Captain James Lang [L] ✔

97-99 High Street, G82 1PH
🕘 8am-midnight (1am Fri & Sat) ☎ (01389) 742112
Greene King Abbot; 4 changing beers (sourced nationally; often Loch Lomond) [H]
Few pubs in the Glasgow area boast a beer garden but this well-designed Wetherspoon features a large outdoor area overlooking the River Leven. The pub was converted from a Woolworths store and has a light, open layout with a variety of seating options. It is named after the renowned captain of the paddle steamer Leven, which was built in the town. The area can be accessed via regular trains and buses. Alcohol is served from 11am. ♘✿◑♿⇌(Central)🚌📶

Dunblane

Tappit Hen ✔

Kirk Street, FK15 0AL
🕘 11-midnight (1am Fri & Sat) ☎ (01786) 825226
🌐 thetappithen-dunblane.co.uk
Belhaven IPA; 4 changing beers [H]
A traditional single-room pub that has had a recent tasteful refurbishment inside and out. The Tappit Hen is a cosy meeting point for local people as well as a delightful discovery for visitors, overlooking the magnificent Dunblane castle. It hosts a real ale festival once or twice a year. Fundraising events in support of local charities are held regularly at this hospitable and generous community venue. Dogs are welcome. ⇌🚌🐾📶

Falkirk

Carron Works [L] ✔

Bank Street, FK1 1NB
🕘 8am-midnight (1am Fri & Sat) ☎ (01324) 673020
Caledonian Deuchars IPA; Greene King Abbot; 3 changing beers [H]
An excellent Wetherspoon venue in a converted cinema. Centrally situated with a spacious interior, it is popular with locals and CAMRA members. The chain's regular and guest beers are served along with at least one real cider. Helpful staff are keen to promote real ale, hosting frequent beer festivals and regular Meet the Brewer nights. The standard Wetherspoon menu is available all day. Licensed from 9.30am (11am Sunday). ♘◑♿⇌🍎🚌📶

Wheatsheaf Inn ✔

16 Baxters Wynd, FK1 1PF
🕘 11-midnight (1am Fri & Sat); 12.30-midnight Sun
☎ (01324) 638282 🌐 wheatsheaffalkirk.co.uk
Caledonian Deuchars IPA; 3 changing beers (sourced nationally) [H]
A must-visit venue, this pub dates from the late 18th century. Reached from the High Street via one of the vennels, or alleys, it retains much of its original character. The wood-panelled bar is furnished in traditional style with numerous interesting features. Guest beers come from microbreweries in Scotland and England, with two on offer midweek and three at the weekend. Tea, coffee and snacks are served daily. ✿⇌🚌

Gargunnock

Gargunnock Inn

Main Street, FK8 3BW

12-10 (11 Thu; 12.30am Fri & Sat) ☎ (01786) 860333

gargunnockinn.co.uk

House beer (by Fintry); 2 changing beers H

Dating from the 1700s, this building has been extensively modernised to create a roomy, cosy pub/restaurant incorporating exposed original features. The single bar's two handpumps serve at least one Scottish ale. The restaurant rooms and seating areas are warmed by two wood-burning stoves in winter. An extensive menu of high-quality food (notably chicken with haggis and Aberdeen Angus steaks) is available throughout. The pub hosts an annual beer festival on the second Sunday in August. Popular local walks abound. Q♣P(12)

Helensburgh

Ashton

74 West Princes Street, G84 8UG

11-midnight (1am Fri & Sat) ☎ (01436) 675900

Stewart Pentland IPA; 2 changing beers (sourced nationally) H

A warm welcome awaits at this genuine local. The bar has been tastefully modernised and decorated with a nautical theme while retaining its original charm. During the work a set of tiles depicting scenes from Sir Walter Scott's Waverley novels was revealed. There is a small room for playing darts. A changing selection of ales from Scottish microbreweries is supported by quality English beers. Live music is a regular Saturday night feature. (Central)♣(1B,316)

Henry Bell

19-29 James Street, G84 8AS

8am-midnight (1am Fri & Sat) ☎ (01436) 863060

Greene King Abbot; changing beers (sourced nationally; often Loch Lomond) H

Close to the recently revamped town centre and esplanade, this sympathetic conversion of an old furniture showroom is a busy venue attracting both locals and visitors. At the heart of the town, it has established itself as an important real ale outlet in the area and a wide range of beers from across Britain can be found here. The interior is in the style of Charles Rennie Mackintosh and the walls are adorned with TVs in homage to Helensburgh-born John Logie Baird. Alcohol is served from 11am. Q(Central)(1B,316)

Killin

Coach House Hotel

Lochay Road, FK21 8TN

11-11 (1am Fri & Sat); 12.30-11 Sun ☎ (01567) 820349

hotelkillin.co.uk

2 changing beers (sourced regionally) H

Small family-owned hotel frequented by locals and tourists. The comfortable bar has a wood-burning stove, a large selection of board games and a pool table, not forgetting the parrot! Two handpumps, supplied by Scottish breweries, serve two real ales in summer and one the rest of the year. The gantry boasts a large selection of whiskies. Good, reasonably priced food is available 11am-8pm. The bar hosts live music on Friday or Saturday night between March and October. Children are welcome until 8pm and dogs are allowed. There are eight recently-refurbished bedrooms, and there is a Caravan and Motorhome Club site opposite the hotel. ÅP

Larbert

Station Hotel

2 Foundry Loan, FK5 4AW

12-11 (midnight Thu; 1am Fri & Sat); 12.30-11 Sun

☎ (01324) 557186 thestationhotellarbert.co.uk

5 changing beers (sourced nationally; often Cairngorm, Greene King, Strathaven) H

A popular local situated next to the railway station and on a regular bus route. The pub prides itself on the support it gives to a number of community groups. Three to five cask ales are usually on offer and efforts are made to provide a variety of local, regional and national ales. Large-screen TVs show sporting events. The Station is a sponsor of CAMRA's Larbert Real Ale Festival in nearby Dobbie Hall. P(6,7)

Luss

Loch Lomond Arms Hotel

G83 8NY

11-11; 12.30-11 Sun ☎ (01436) 860420

lochlomondarmshotel.com

3 changing beers (often Loch Lomond) H

A tastefully refurbished hotel, restaurant and bar in the popular tourist village of Luss on the bonnie banks of Loch Lomond. Local buses from Alexandria, Balloch and Helensburgh, or the express bus from Glasgow, allow pub visitors to enjoy ales from Loch Lomond Brewery at their leisure. A trip to Luss to visit the Arms and take in the magnificent scenery makes a great day out. QP(302,305)

Stirling

Birds & Bees

Easter Cornton Road, FK9 5PB

11-midnight (1am Fri & Sat) ☎ (01786) 473663

thebirdsandthebees-stirling.com

2 changing beers (sourced regionally) H

Welcoming pub in a converted farmstead, a stone's throw from the historic Wallace Monument in a residential area on the outskirts of north Stirling. Two handpumps dispense a variety of good-quality real ales. Excellent, locally sourced food is served both in the bar area and the separate restaurant. This appealing venue attracts a good mix of locals and tourists. P

Portcullis Hotel

Castle Wynd, FK8 1EG (adjacent to castle esplanade)

11.30-11 (midnight Fri & Sat) ☎ (01786) 472290

theportcullishotel.com

2 changing beers (sourced regionally; often Isle of Skye, Orkney) H

Popular pub at the top of town, originally the old grammar school building. Exposed stone walls and an open fireplace with ornate surround create a warm welcome in the heart of old Stirling. Frequented by tourists and supported by locals, the pub is renowned for its food and regularly changing selection of Scottish ales from the far north and west. Always busy, so diners are advised to reserve a table. QP

SCOTLAND

Settle Inn

91 St Marys Wynd, FK8 1BU

🕒 3-midnight (1am Fri & Sat) ☎ (01786) 463403

3 changing beers (sourced nationally) H

Warm, friendly and atmospheric inn frequented by a mixed clientele of locals, students and tourists. Situated on a route descending from Stirling Castle, it was built in 1733 and is the oldest pub in Stirling. The Settle Inn lives up to its name – settle down in front of the cosy fire and you may not want to leave, ghosts or no ghosts. There is music on Monday, Wednesday, Friday and Saturday evenings, and a quiz on Sunday. ☺≠🐾 ᯤ

Strathyre

White Stag

Main Street, FK18 8NA

🕒 3-midnight; 1-1am Sat; 1-midnight Sun

☎ (01877) 384224 🌐 thewhitestagfk18.uk

3 changing beers (sourced nationally; often Inveralmond, Joseph Holt, Tryst) H

Cosy pub that serves meals in its bar or bistro, with an emphasis on local produce. The beers are mainly Scottish. The raised beer garden enjoys panoramic views. Accommodation is available and dogs and children are welcome in the bar. Hill walking, fishing, golf and watersports are all close at hand, and Stirling, Callander and the Trossachs are within easy travelling distance. Opening hours are reduced in winter – check ahead before travelling. Local CAMRA Rural Pub of the Year 2018. Q☺❀🛏◑◐♣P🚌(C60)🐾 ᯤ

Tillicoultry

Royal Arms

2 High Street, FK13 6AE

🕒 11-midnight (1am Fri & Sat) ☎ (01259) 753037

Morland Old Speckled Hen; 1 changing beer H

This unpretentious, drinks-only pub has been given a new lease of life by enthusiastic tenants. Its functional bar caters mainly for local trade, with a dartboard, large sports TV and fruit machine, but also has comfortable seating, bar stools and a Victorian fireplace with logburner. A quieter side room with service via a small counter is ideal for families and small meetings. Three handpumps are in use, one dispensing the regular Old Speckled Hen and one a guest ale. The pub is well served by regular bus routes to Stirling and Alloa. ☺❀♣🚌🐾 ᯤ

Village Inn, Arrochar (Photo: David Jones/Flickr CC BY 2.0)

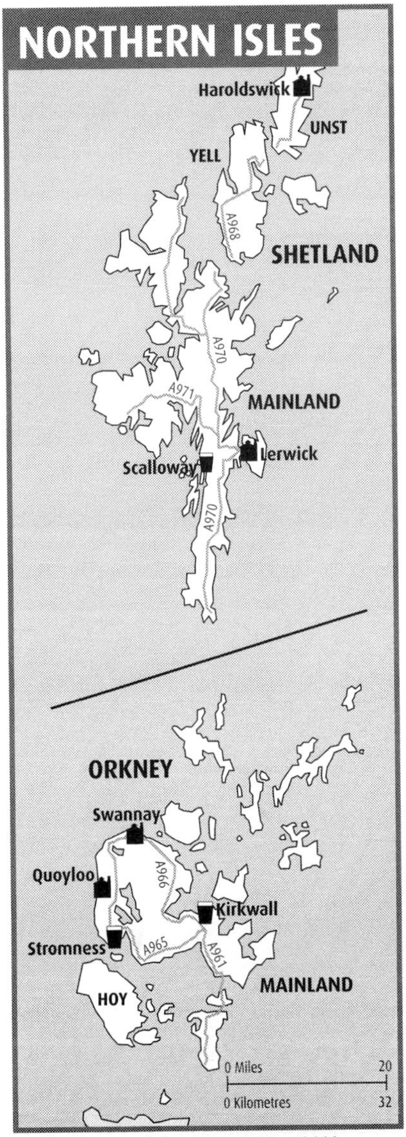

Authority area covered: Highland UA

Kirkwall: Orkney

Auld Motor Hoose

26 Junction Road, KW15 1AB
11-midnight (1am Thu-Sat) (01856) 871422
auldmotorhoose.co.uk
Swannay Scapa Special H
A welcoming and friendly motor-themed pub with a single bar room, featuring lots of motoring memorabilia and car parts scattered throughout. The jukebox tends to blast out rock classics. There is regular live music, mainly at weekends, and the Moho is one of the venues for the Orkney Rock Festival. Outside, the patio has a smoking area. It is the sister bar to the Torvhaug in Bridge Street and convenient for the bus station nearby. Local CAMRA Pub of the Year 2019. (X1)

Bothy Bar (Albert Hotel)

Mounthoolie Lane, KW15 1HW (lane connecting jct Lane and Bridge St)
11-midnight (1am Thu-Sat); 12-midnight Sun
0800 050 9037 hotelorkney.co.uk
Swannay Scapa Special; 2 changing beers (sourced locally; often Orkney, Swannay) H
Reconstructed following a fire some years ago using many of the original materials, the Bothy has more space than previously and is a popular town-centre local handy for buses, North Isles ferries and the shops. Frequented by locals, after-work drinkers and as part of the weekend circuit, it has several intimate alcoves, and a roaring fire that is welcoming in colder months. Historic St Magnus Cathedral is close by. A premium is paid when buying half pints. Only Scapa Special is served in winter.

Helgi's Bar

14 Harbour Street, KW15 1LE (by harbour)
11-midnight (1am Thu-Sat); 12.30-midnight Sun
(01856) 879293 helgis.co.uk
Swannay Scapa Special; 2 changing beers (sourced locally; often Swannay) H
Converted from a former shipping office, this small, smart bar has the look of a modern café with wood panelling and a floor of local stone. There is always one dark beer available and often some of the rarer Swannay varieties. Look out for the occasional food and drink evenings. Regular music sessions and a Thursday quiz night also feature. Set on the harbour front where seafood is landed daily, this is a handy place to fill in time before island hopping on the many ferries to outlying parts. No under-18s.

Kirkwall Hotel

Harbour Street, KW15 1LE (on corner with Bridge St)
11-midnight (1am Thu-Sat); 12-midnight Sun
(01856) 872232 kirkwallhotel.com
Swannay Scapa Special H
A smart and modern family-owned hotel on the harbour front. It has two bars connected by a corridor, both serving real ale. The large lounge area in the main part of the hotel often hosts wedding parties. The separate Skippers Bar, which has an entrance on the corner with Bridge Street, is vibrant and busy in the evenings with a mainly youngish clientele.

St Ola Hotel

Harbour Street, KW15 1LE
11-11.30 (midnight Thu); 10-1am Fri & Sat; 10-midnight Sun (01856) 875090 stolahotel.co.uk
Swannay Scapa Special; 1 changing beer (sourced locally; often Swannay) H
Built on the site of the Inns of Sinclair dating back to the 14th century, the Ola overlooks the harbour and is a short walk from all Kirkwall's major attractions. It has a public bar at the front complete with a roaring fire in winter and a larger lounge to the rear where food is served. An extensive range of whiskies is available alongside the ales. A music session is held on the last Sunday afternoon of the month.

REAL ALE BREWERIES

Lerwick Lerwick: Shetland
Orkney Quoyloo: Orkney
Swannay Swannay: Orkney

Scalloway: Shetland

Scalloway Hotel

Main Street, ZE1 0TR (on A970)
11-11 ☎ (01595) 880444 scallowayhotel.com
Swannay Scapa Special; 1 changing beer (often Lerwick) H
Harbourside hotel in the centre of the village with tremendous views. Refurbished a few years ago, it has a small lounge bar where sport is sometimes shown and an award-winning restaurant. It is the keyholder for the neighbouring Scalloway Castle, a listed ancient monument. The Scalloway Museum is also close by, providing an interesting insight into life in the village through the ages. Both loch and sea fishing can be arranged, and there are 9-hole and 18-hole golf courses within three miles.

Stromness: Orkney

Ferry Inn

10 John Street, KW16 3AD (across from ferry terminal)
9-11; 9.30-11 Sun ☎ (01856) 850280 ferryinn.com
Swannay Scapa Special; 2 changing beers (sourced locally; often Orkney, Swannay) H
An easy walk from the harbour front, the Ferry is handy for buses to Kirkwall and the ferry from Scrabster. It is popular with locals and visitors, including divers who come to Orkney to explore the sunken German fleet at Scapa Flow. Various attractions nearby include the Ring of Brodgar and Skara Brae village. Annual folk and blues festivals are held, with a marquee erected outside complete with an ale pump. Joint local CAMRA Pub of the Year 2018.

Stromness Hotel

15 Victoria Street, KW16 3AA (opp pier head)
1-11 Mon-Thu; 12-1am Fri & Sat; 1-11 Sun; closed winter
☎ (01856) 850298 stromnesshotel.com
Swannay Scapa Special; 2 changing beers (sourced locally; often Swannay) H
On the first floor of this imposing hotel you will find the Hamnavoe Lounge, with windows and a small balcony giving commanding views of the harbour. The lounge is mainly used for dining and there is a separate whisky bar with over 100 bottles to choose from. The Flattie Bar downstairs, open all year round, is complete with a 'flattie' hanging from the ceiling (a small boat, unique to Stromness) and serves a Swannay ale. Jazz, blues and beer festivals are held throughout the year. The hotel and upstairs bars are closed November to March.

Kirkwall Hotel, Kirkwall Orkney (Photo: Reading Tom/Flickr CC BY 2.0)

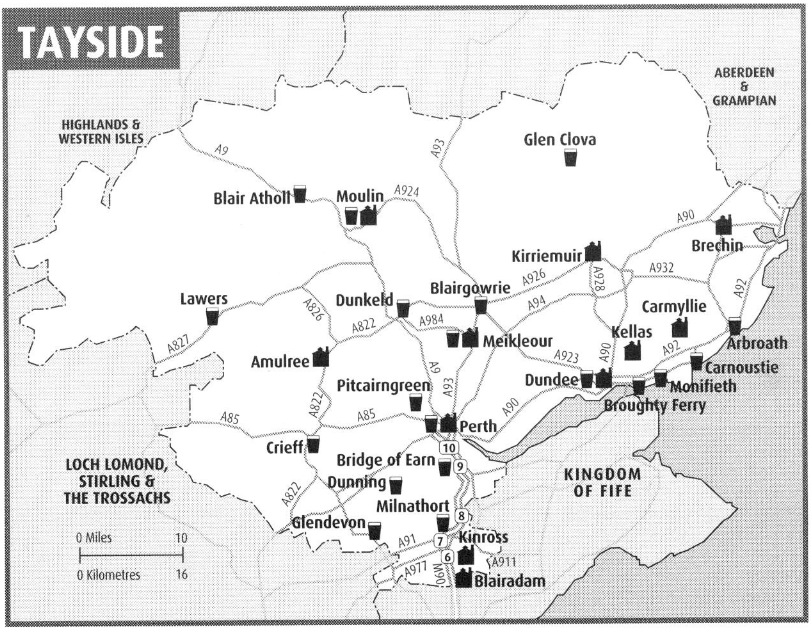

Authority areas covered: Angus UA, City of Dundee UA, Perth & Kinross UA

Arbroath

Corn Exchange

14 Olympic Centre, Market Place, DD11 1HR

8am-midnight (1am Fri & Sat) (01241) 432430

Caledonian Deuchars IPA; Greene King Abbot; Sharp's Doom Bar; 3 changing beers (sourced nationally)

Located just off the High Street, this Wetherspoon pub occupies a 19th-century former corn exchange. Although it is largely open plan there are a number of booths providing some privacy. A varied selection of real ales is always available. Boat trips offering fishing or a visit to the 200-year-old Bell Rock lighthouse can be taken from the nearby harbour.

Blair Atholl

Atholl Arms Hotel

PH18 5SG

11-11; 12-midnight Fri & Sat (01796) 481205

athollarmshotel.co.uk

Moulin Light, Braveheart, Ale of Atholl, Old Remedial

A characterful hotel with an imposing façade in the traditional Highland style. Its Bothy Bar serves four ales produced by the local Moulin Brewery, as well as freshly cooked food that is available all day. Blair Atholl and the surrounding area are popular for walking, climbing, biking and sightseeing. The Bothy Bar's opening hours may be shorter out of season but all four ales can be brought through to the lounge bar. Q P (M91,87)

Blairgowrie

Ericht Alehouse

13 Wellmeadow, PH10 6ND

1.30-11.30 (12.30am Sat) (01250) 872469

6 changing beers (sourced nationally)

Classic town-centre pub with a friendly atmosphere, close to the River Ericht. It has two seating areas separated by a well-stocked bar. A wide range of ever-changing ales and ciders is served, alongside increasing numbers of Scottish gins, malts and rums. No food is available but customers are welcome to bring their own. A winner of local CAMRA Pub of the Year several times over the past decade. Q

Stormont Arms

101 Perth Street, PH10 6DT (10 mins' walk from town centre)

2-11; 11-11 Fri; 12-midnight Sat; 12.30-10 Sun

(01250) 873142

1 changing beer (often Kelburn, Strathaven, Strathbraan)

Real ale is served from two handpulls in this traditional Scottish two-roomed pub, with StrathBraan ales featuring more than most. The friendly bar has wooden bench seating and a dartboard, and hosts a darts league during the week. A small seating area outside includes space for smokers. The pub may close early if quiet so check before travelling. Q

REAL ALE BREWERIES

71 Dundee
Blunt Chisel Blairadam (NEW)
Dalrannoch Meikleour
Inveralmond Perth
Kirrie Kirriemuir (brewing suspended)
Law Dundee
Loch Leven Kinross
MòR Kellas
Moulin Moulin
Park Brechin (brewing suspended)
Redcastle Carmyllie
Strathbraan Amulree

Bridge of Earn

Cyprus Inn

Back Street, PH2 9AB
11-11 (midnight Fri & Sat) ☎ (01738) 812313
1 changing beer (sourced locally; often Loch Leven, StrathBraan) H
A friendly wee pub with a great community atmosphere, in a Category C-listed building that dates back to around 1790. Rings on its outside walls, originally for securing horses, are now used for bicycles. The small bar area features fixed bench seating and a low ceiling. There is also a separate lounge/function room and a large beer garden. StrathBraan beer is usually available on handpull. Q

Broughty Ferry

Fisherman's Tavern

12-16 Fort Street, DD5 2AD
11-midnight (1am Thu-Sat) ☎ (01382) 775941
fishermanstavern-broughtyferry.co.uk
Greene King IPA; house beer (by Belhaven); 4 changing beers (sourced nationally) H
Licensed since 1857, this famous hostelry was originally three fishermen's cottages, later converted into a small hotel. The bar is to the right of the entrance, and a snug is to the left, leading to the dining room/lounge, warmed by a real fire. The lounge to the rear has wheelchair access from Bell's Lane. This Belhaven/Greene King-managed house serves ales from Scottish and English breweries. It hosts an annual beer festival in July.

Jolly's Hotel

43A Gray Street, DD5 2BJ
7am-midnight (1am Fri & Sat) ☎ (01382) 734910
Caledonian Deuchars IPA; Greene King Abbot; Sharp's Doom Bar; 3 changing beers (sourced nationally) H
Named after John Jolly, its proprietor for two decades in the late 19th century, this Wetherspoon hotel has expanded considerably over the years. It features two large areas, one for drinking and dining, the other principally for dining. Up to a dozen handpulls serve a wide selection of ales. The TV screens are usually muted. An outdoor patio area has a number of tables.

Royal Arch

285 Brook Street, DD5 2DS
11-midnight (1am Fri & Sat); 12.30-11 Sun
☎ (01382) 779741 royal-arch.co.uk
3 changing beers (sourced nationally) H
A popular locally owned pub in the centre of the Ferry. There are three TVs in the public bar for the many sports fans, and good-quality meals are served in the Art Deco lounge. Three handpulls dispense ales from local brewers as well as from all over Britain. The gantry in the public bar was rescued long ago from the demolished Craigour Bar in Dens Road, and the exterior was refurbished in 2014.

Ship Inn

121 Fisher Street, DD5 2BR
11-midnight; 12.30-midnight Sun ☎ (01382) 779176
theshipinn-broughtyferry.co.uk
Timothy Taylor Landlord; 2 changing beers H
Traditional free house on the waterfront, giving views over the Tay towards Fife. Dating back to 1847, this cosy retreat is atmospheric and interesting, with several nautical features. Three real ales are usually served. A range of tasty bar meals is on offer and there is a restaurant upstairs. Pavement seating outside the pub is available for fine weather.

Carnoustie

Stag's Head

61 Dundee Street, DD7 7PN
11-midnight (1am Fri & Sat); 12.30-midnight Sun
☎ (01241) 858815
1 changing beer (sourced nationally) H
This friendly pub has a large open-plan bar and lounge/function area where live music plays on most Saturdays. Two handpulls enable a swift changeover, ensuring that one widely sourced changing beer is always available. Situated a 10-minute walk from the championship golf links, the pub is home to a number of games and sports teams including football, pool and dominoes.
P (73,73A)

Crieff

Quaich

47 High Street, PH7 3HT
11-9 Mon, Wed & Thu; closed Tue; 11-midnight Fri & Sat; 1-7 Sun ☎ (01764) 656136 thequaichbar.co.uk
2 changing beers (often Inveralmond, Strathbraan) P
Relaxed and informal family-run bar, grill and coffee house on the High Street in Crieff. It is named after the traditional Scottish friendship cup. The atmosphere is quiet, with no TV or jukebox – just a log-burning stove that is more than welcome in the winter months. Two ales are usually available on electric pump. Food is described as 'NYC grill meets Scottish kitchen'. Families are welcome and a selection of books is provided.
Q

Dundee

Bank Bar

7-9 Union Street, DD1 4BN
11-midnight (10 Mon & Tue); 12.30-11 Sun
☎ (01382) 205037 thebankbardundee.com
Fyne Ales Jarl; house beer (by Marston's); 2 changing beers (sourced nationally) H
A former bank with bare-board floors, wooden furnishings and a series of alcoves with tables, in the tradition of older Scottish city pubs. A collection of themed pictures decorates the walls. Up to four ales are usually available and food is served until 7pm every day. Quality live music features on most Friday and Saturday nights.

Phoenix

103 Nethergate, DD1 4DH
11-midnight ☎ (01382) 200014
Caledonian Deuchars IPA; Timothy Taylor Landlord; 3 changing beers (sourced nationally) H
One of Dundee's oldest pubs, this traditional inn has a great atmosphere. Subdued lighting, sturdy wooden tables and chairs, green leather benches and a rare Ballingall Brewery mirror give the place character. Five ales are on offer, along with excellent pub food at sensible prices. The location is handy for the Rep Theatre, Dundee Contemporary Arts and Bonar Hall. Warm and cosy, like pubs used to be. (73)

Speedwell Bar (Mennie's) ★ ✓
165-167 Perth Road, DD2 1AS
11-11; 12.30-11 Sun ☎ (01382) 667783
speedwell-bar.co.uk
3 changing beers (sourced nationally) H
Built in 1903 for James Speed, the bar is known as Mennie's after the family who ran it for more than 50 years. The L-shaped bar is divided by a part-glazed screen and has a magnificent mahogany gantry and counter, dado-panelled walls and an anaglypta Jacobean ceiling. There are usually three ales to choose from, alongside a selection of Belgian bottled beers and around 150 malt whiskies. You can take in your own food. Local CAMRA Pub of the Year 2017. (73)

Dunkeld

Perth Arms
High Street, PH8 0AJ (close to cathedral)
11-11 (midnight Fri & Sat); 12-11 Sun ☎ (01350) 727270
StrathBraan Due South, Head East H
Cosy one-room establishment on the High Street, serving a mix of locals and tourists. This friendly place has been in the same family for almost 50 years and is the area's oldest trading pub, dating back to 1795. Its two handpulls dispense ales that are mostly from local breweries. There is a beer garden at the back with an area for smokers.

Royal Dunkeld Hotel
Atholl Street, PH8 0AR
11-11 (midnight Fri & Sat); 12-11 Sun ☎ (01350) 727322
royaldunkeld.co.uk
3 changing beers (sourced regionally; often StrathBraan) H
On the main street, this former coaching inn is now a comfortable hotel featuring a restaurant, lounge bar and public bar with an open fire. A pool room with dartboard is adjacent. Two local and one changing guest ale are available on three handpumps. Good food is served in the bar and restaurant. The large beer garden is a suntrap in summer. The hotel is an ideal base for outdoor activities including walking, fishing and golf. ♣P

Dunning

Kirkstyle Inn
Kirkstyle Square, PH2 0RR
5-midnight Mon; 12-3, 5-midnight Tue; 12-midnight Wed-Sat; 12-10 Sun ☎ (01764) 684248
thekirkstyleinn.co.uk
House beer (by Marston's); 2 changing beers (sourced nationally) H
A traditional village inn dating from 1760, overshadowed by the impressive Norman steeple of St Serf's Church, home to the ancient Dupplin Cross and other Pictish relics. One or two ales in the cosy public bar come from a variety of Scottish independents, as well as English and Welsh regional breweries. There is a separate restaurant. Around a mile west of the village stands a 20-foot high stone cross, a memorial to Maggie Wall who was burned here as a witch in 1657.
(17)

Glen Clova

Glen Clova Hotel
DD8 4QS
11-11 (1am Fri & Sat); 12-11 Sun ☎ (01575) 550350
clova.com
2 changing beers H
Situated near the head of one of Scotland's most beautiful glens, this hotel is popular with walkers after a day on the hills. Its bar has a large log-fired stove and plenty of character. Two handpumps supply the ales, usually from Scottish breweries. Local food, including lamb and venison, is served in both the bar and adjoining restaurant. The hotel offers a range of accommodation from bunkhouse to self-catering luxury lodge. P

Glendevon

Tormaukin Hotel
FK14 7JY
12-10 (11 Sat & Sun) ☎ (01259) 781252
thetormaukin.co.uk
2 changing beers (often Harviestoun) H
This 18th-century drovers' inn is on the Yetts o' Muckhart to Gleneagles road in a peaceful setting surrounded by the Ochil Hills. Popular with hill walkers and fishermen, it has a comfortable, relaxed atmosphere, enhanced by an open fire in winter. Soup, sandwiches, scones and other snacks are available throughout the day. Q

Lawers

Ben Lawers Hotel
Loch Tay, PH15 2PA
12.30 (5 Wed)-11 ☎ (01567) 820436
benlawershotel.co.uk
3 changing beers (often Strathbraan)
In the heart of one of Scotland's most beautiful and accessable unspoilt areas, this small hotel is popular with walkers and provides fantastic views over Loch Tay. In addition to the beer on handpull it has a large selection of bottled and canned Tempest ales. The staff can provide a tasting of an ale on request. Good food and accommodation are always available. Closes Tuesdays and Wednesdays during winter. P

Meikleour

Meikleour Hotel
PH2 6EB
11-11 ☎ (01250) 883206 meikleourarms.co.uk
House beer (by Inveralmond); 2 changing beers (sourced locally; often Strathbraan) H
Originally a coaching inn and posting house dating back to 1820, now a country inn with a flagstone floor in an informal bar and a comfortable lounge/dining room with a log fire. Up to three ales are available including a house beer, The Lure of Meikleour. Excellent quality food is served using locally sourced ingredients. Nearby is the worlds tallest beech hedge, which was planted in 1745 and is a third of a mile long. Q

Milnathort

Village Inn
36 Wester Loan, KY13 9YH
2-11 (midnight Fri); 12-midnight Sat; 12.30-11 Sun
☎ (01577) 863293

SCOTLAND

3 changing beers (sourced nationally) Ⓗ
Friendly local with a semi open-plan interior featuring classic brewery mirrors and local historic photographs. The comfortable lounge area has low ceilings, exposed joists and stone walls, and the bar area is warmed by a log fire. At the rear is a games room with a pool table. This pub has been family-owned since 1985 and usually serves three beers from Scottish and, often, English breweries. Milnathort links some great cycling routes through the Ochils, via Burleigh Castle, to the more leisurely Loch Leven Heritage Trail. ❀♣🚌🐾📶

Monifieth

Milton Inn ✔

Grange Road, DD5 4LU
closed Mon; 12-2.30, 5-11 Tue-Thu; 12-midnight Fri & Sat; 12-11 Sun ☎ (01382) 532620 🌐 themiltoninn.co.uk
3 changing beers (sourced nationally) Ⓗ
The only premises in Monifieth serving real ale, which it does with a passion. There are usually three beers to choose from, alongside good home-made food at fair prices. The pub is set back from the road, with large gardens and a sunny decked area to the rear providing a nice sheltered spot for a pint in the fresh air. Entertainment features regularly. Q❀🛏◐⇌P🚌(75)📶

Moulin

Moulin Inn

11-13 Kirkmichael Road, PH16 5EH
11-11 ☎ (01796) 472196 🌐 moulininn.co.uk
Moulin Light, Braveheart, Ale of Atholl, Old Remedial Ⓗ
First opened in 1695, the inn is the oldest part of the Moulin Hotel, situated within the village square at an ancient crossroads just east of Pitlochry. Full of character and charm, it is traditionally furnished and has two log fires. A good choice of home-prepared local fare is available, along with four Moulin beers, brewed in the old coach house behind the hotel. There is an area outside for dining and drinking in good weather. An ideal base for outdoor pursuits, with several marked walks nearby. Q⚇❀🛏◐♣P🚌🐾📶

Perth

Capital Asset ✔

26 Tay Street, PH1 5LQ
11-11 (12.30am Thu-Sat) ☎ (01738) 580457
Caledonian Deuchars IPA; Greene King Abbot; Sharp's Doom Bar; 3 changing beers (sourced nationally) Ⓗ
A Wetherspoon pub that was formerly a savings bank and is now run by real ale enthusiasts. High ceilings and ornate cornices have been retained; pictures of old Perth adorn the walls of the open-plan lounge which overlooks the River Tay. A large safe from the building's banking days can be seen in the family area. Six ales are dispensed, with food available all day. Local ale drinkers enjoy the beer festivals held twice a year. Q⚇❀◐♿🍎🚌(7)📶

Cherrybank Inn

210 Glasgow Road, PH2 0NA
11-11 (12.30am Thu-Sat); 12-midnight Sun
☎ (01738) 624349 🌐 cherrybankinn.co.uk
Harviestoun Bitter & Twisted; Inveralmond Ossian; 3 changing beers (sourced nationally) Ⓗ
This 250-year-old former drovers' inn is a popular watering hole and stopover for travellers. Ales from Inveralmond and other Scottish independents are dispensed from five handpulls in the multi-roomed public bar or the larger L-shaped lounge, with views up to a woodland walk. It has large, sunny elevated wooden decking to the rear. Good bar lunches and evening meals are served. The inn has seven en-suite rooms, and golf can be arranged for residents. ⚇❀🛏◐🍎P🚌(7)🐾📶

Green Room Wee Bar 🏆 Ⓛ

97 Canal Cres, PH2 8HX
12-11 (12.30am Fri & Sat); closed Sun ☎ (01738) 248121
🌐 thegreenroomperth.co.uk
5 changing beers (sourced nationally; often Inveralmond, Strathbraan) Ⓗ
This establishment has three bars, one with five handpulls, plus a large selection of bottled beers from around the world. It is a must-visit venue in Perth for ale enthusiasts, in a convenient city-centre location near the railway station. Live entertainment plays seven nights a week, pulling in plenty of customers. ⇌🐾📶

Greyfriars Ⓛ

15 South Street, PH2 8PG
4-11; 12-midnight Fri & Sat; 12-11 Sun ☎ (01738) 633036
🌐 greyfriarsbar.co.uk
Timothy Taylor Landlord; 3 changing beers (often Eden Mill, Loch Leven, Strathbraan) Ⓗ
Compact city-centre lounge bar with a small upstairs seating area. Up to four ales are served, often including a local Inveralmond beer. The pub takes its name from the former Greyfriars monastery. Nearby attractions include a Victorian theatre, art gallery, museum and concert hall. This may well be the smallest lounge bar in the Fair City but it has an enviable reputation among locals and visitors as one of the friendliest. 🚌🐾📶

Old Ship Inn ✔

31 High Street (Skinnergate), PH1 5TJ
11-11 (midnight Fri & Sat); 12.30-11 Sun ☎ 07956 924767
🌐 oldshipinnperth.co.uk
House beer (by Belhaven); 2 changing beers (often Belhaven, Fyne Ales, Harviestoun) Ⓗ
Said to be the oldest pub in Perth, having traded under the same name since 1665. This was Perth's oasis for real ale in the 1980s, and now serves one regular beer and two changing ales. A large oil painting of a sailing ship adds interest in the timber-lined bar, which is lightened by a frieze and white-painted ceiling. It has an outside seating area. The upstairs lounge was closed for 20 years before reopening in 2018. 🐾📶

Pitcairngreen

Pitcairngreen Inn

PH1 3LP
12-11 (midnight Fri); 11-midnight Sat ☎ (01738) 583022
🌐 pitcairngreeninn.co.uk
2 changing beers (sourced locally; often StrathBraan) Ⓗ
A fairly large establishment with several different areas including a snug warmed by an open log fire. The inn has a real enthusiasm for good beer, served on three handpulls. This is also the finest place in Tayside to enjoy real ciders and perries, presented professionally and with passion. The car park is just across the road. Local CAMRA Cider Pub of the Year. Q❀◐🍎P🚌(14,15)🐾📶

SHETLAND
NORTHERN ISLES
HIGHLANDS & WESTERN ISLES
ABERDEEN & GRAMPIAN
TAYSIDE
LOCH LOMOND, STIRLING & THE TROSSACHS
FIFE
ARGYLL & THE ISLES
EDINBURGH & LOTHIANS
GREATER GLASGOW & CLYDE
BORDERS
AYRSHIRE & ARRAN
DUMFRIES & GALLOWAY
NORTHUMBERLAND
TYNE & WEAR
NORTHERN IRELAND
DURHAM
CUMBRIA
ISLE OF MAN
NORTH YORKSHIRE
LANCASHIRE
WEST YORKS
EAST YORKS
GREATER MANCHESTER
MERSEYSIDE
SOUTH YORKS
CHESHIRE
DERBYSHIRE
NOTTINGHAM-SHIRE
LINCOLNSHIRE
NW WALES
NE WALES
STAFFORD SHIRE
SHROPSHIRE
LEICESTERSHIRE
RUTLAND
NORFOLK
WEST MIDLANDS
CAMBRIDGE SHIRE
MID WALES
HEREFORD SHIRE
WORCESTER-SHIRE
WARWICK-SHIRE
NORTHAMPTON-SHIRE
SUFFOLK
WEST WALES
BEDFORD SHIRE
BUCKINGHAM-SHIRE
HERTFORD SHIRE
ESSEX
GWENT
GLOUCS & BRISTOL
OXFORD SHIRE
GLAMORGAN
GREATER LONDON
BERKSHIRE
WILTSHIRE
SURREY
KENT
SOMERSET
HAMPSHIRE
WEST SUSSEX
EAST SUSSEX
CHANNEL ISLANDS
DEVON
DORSET
ISLE OF WIGHT
CORNWALL

Northern Ireland
Channel Islands
Isle of Man

NORTHERN IRELAND

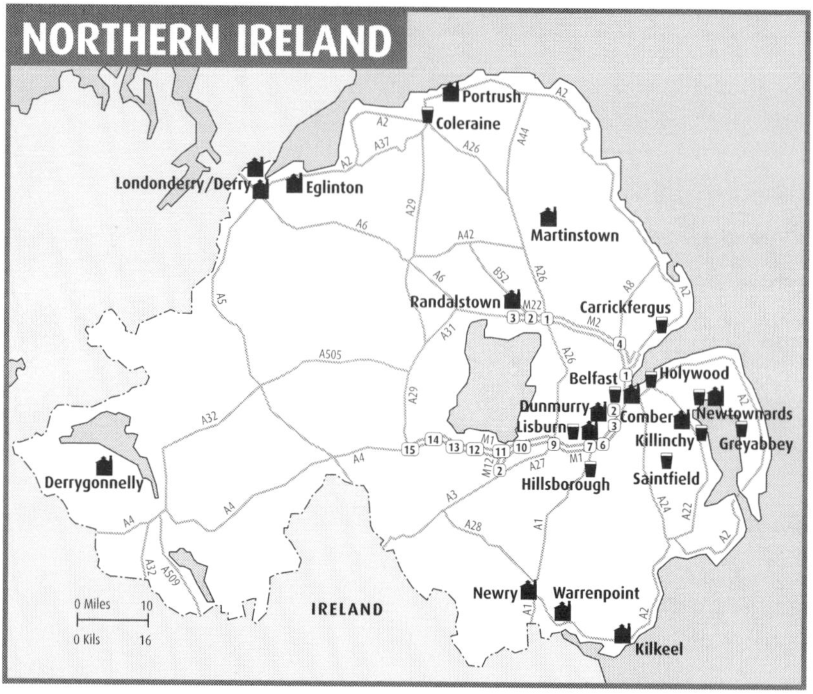

Belfast

Bridge House ✔

37-43 Bedford Street, BT2 7EJ

8am-midnight (1am Fri & Sat) ☎ (028) 9072 7890

Greene King Abbot; Sharp's Doom Bar; changing beers (sourced nationally) H

Reputed to be one of Wetherspoon's busiest bars, it sells a wide choice of real ale from eight handpumps. In a recent makeover, the beer lines have been changed and the bar given a brighter look. Upstairs is a dining area, and a beer terrace has been added. A two-times winner of CAMRA Northern Ireland Pub of the Year. Alcohol is served from 11.30am (12.30pm Sun). Q

Crown ★ ✔

46 Great Victoria Street, BT2 7BA (opp Europa Hotel and Great Victoria St station)

11.30-11; 12.30-10 Sun ☎ (028) 9024 3187

Mourne Mountains Mourne Gold; St Austell Nicholson's Pale Ale; 4 changing beers (sourced nationally) H

Dating back to the 1880s, the Crown is a gem of the Victorian era. This Grade A-listed building, owned by the National Trust, is unique in the province. It has also become a top spot for quality real ale under the watchful eye of the bar manager. The six handpumps serve Nicholson's Pale Ale and a mixture of local and national ales. Good food is available in the main bar and upstairs is the Crown Dining Rooms where there are three more handpumps. A former CAMRA Northern Ireland Pub of the Year. Q

Errigle Inn 🏆

312-320 Ormeau Road, BT7 2GE

11.30-1am; 10-midnight Sun ☎ (028) 9064 1410

errigle.com

5 changing beers (sourced locally; often Farmageddon, Knockout, Whitewater) H

The Errigle Inn is a real ale and craft brewery haven. Ale and food can be enjoyed in peace in the quiet back bar, the Oak Lounge. It has five handpumps mainly supporting local breweries – beers from Hilden, Whitewater, Farmageddon, Knockout, Bullhouse and Lacada are frequently available along with some national brands. There are also tap takeovers and occasional beers from the wood. Current CAMRA Northern Ireland Pub of the Year. Q

John Hewitt

51 Donegal Street, BT1 2FH (100yds from St Anne's Cathedral)

11.30-1am; 12-1am Sat; 7-midnight Sun

☎ (028) 9023 3768 thejohnhewitt.com

Shepherd Neame Master Brew H

Named after the poet, this is a busy single-room bar with a large snug in one corner and a stage area in another. It differs from most bars in that it is run by the Belfast Unemployed Resource Centre, and profits fund the centre's charitable work. It is also a popular venue for live music and art exhibitions. High-quality food is served at lunchtime with specials on the blackboard. A single handpump dispenses Shepherd Neame beers or an occasional guest such as Hercules Belfast Pale Ale. Q

McHughs

29-31 Queens Square, BT1 3FG (near Albert Clock)

12-1am (midnight Sun) ☎ (028) 9050 9999

mchughsbar.com

Whitewater Maggie's Leap IPA H

Housed in Belfast's oldest building, McHughs is a lively pub with several different drinking and dining areas. The main public bar has a handpump exclusively dispensing ales from Whitewater

Brewery. Next to it is the restored old bar where wall paintings depict scenes from Belfast's history. Good food is served in the restaurant upstairs as well as in the bars. Music is a regular feature – often folk or traditional – while the basement hosts a variety of acts. Q◑◗♿⇌(Central)🂠🚌📶

Northern Lights

451 Ormeau Road, BT7 3GQ
⏲ 12-midnight (1am Fri & Sat) ☎ (028) 9029 0291
🌐 galwaybaybrewery.com/northernlights
1 changing beer (sourced regionally) Ⓗ
This is the first pub owned by Galway Bay Brewery in the north of Ireland. It is very much a modern craft beer bar with up to 20 changing beers on draught; around 10 are from its own portfolio and the rest from a variety of craft producers. An impressive selection of bottles and canned beer is also available. A handpump has been added to the bar which dispenses cask ales from a number of Irish breweries. Q◑◗♿♣🚌🐾📶

Sunflower

65 Union Street, BT1 2JG
⏲ 11.30-midnight (1am Thu-Sat); 5-11 Sun
☎ (028) 9023 2474 🌐 sunflowerbelfast.com
1 changing beer (sourced locally; often Hilden)
A lively and welcoming corner bar with a selection of craft brews and a handpump offering a changing beer from Hilden. It is one of the few bars in the north that has replaced Ireland's famous stout with a local one from Hercules Brewery. There is music seven days a week, beer events are hosted, and the beer garden is a popular attraction, with pizza available Thursday, Friday and Saturday evenings. Q❀◗🚌🐾📶

Carrickfergus

Central Bar ✔

13-15 High Street, BT38 7AN (opp castle)
⏲ 8am-midnight (1am Fri & Sat) ☎ (028) 9335 7840
Greene King Abbot; Sharp's Doom Bar; 3 changing beers (sourced nationally) Ⓗ
Lively market-town community local with a loyal clientele. This Wetherspoon pub has a ground-floor public bar of robust character and a quieter family-friendly first-floor loggia-style sitting room with exposed timber trusses, affording fine views from its many windows over Belfast Lough and the adjacent 12th-century castle. Handpumps on both levels serve two house beers and three guest ales, usually from mainland micros, or seasonal specials from various breweries. Alcohol is served from 11.30am (12.30pm Sun). Q🐎❀◑◗♿⇌🚌(563)

Coleraine

Fairley's Bar

62-64 Railway Road, BT52 1PF
⏲ 11.30-11; closed Sun ☎ (028) 7032 0047
1 changing beer (often Lacada)
Fairley's Bar is a bar and off-licence situated very near Coleraine's railway station. The real ale is exclusively sourced from the Lacada Brewery in Portrush and dispensed from KeyKegs. Drinks can also be purchased from the well-stocked off-licence and consumed in the bar. This long-established venue is popular with locals and visitors alike. ♿⇌🚌📶

Greyabbey

Wildfowler Inn

1 Main Street, BT22 2NE (6 miles S of Newtownards on the A20)
⏲ 12-11; 12.30-10 Sun ☎ (028) 4278 8234
🌐 wildfowlerinn.co.uk
Ards Scrabo Gold; 1 changing beer (sourced locally; often Ards) Ⓗ
This is a restaurant with a small public bar situated on the east coast of the Ards Peninsula. It has a tiled and stone floor, exposed oak beams and stained-glass windows. The real ale is on two handpumps, one in the public bar and one in the restaurant, offering a changing choice of ales from Ards Brewing Company, less than two miles away. Phone ahead to find out which beers are on. Q🐎❀◑◗♿P🚌🐾

Hillsborough

Hillside

21 Main Street, BT26 6AE
⏲ 12-11.30 (12.30am Fri & Sat); 12-11 Sun
☎ (028) 9268 9233 🌐 hillsidehillsborough.co.uk
Hilden Ale, Twisted Hop Ⓗ
The Hillside is a bar and restaurant. It has a number of drinking and dining areas, with two handpumps in the front bar. Beers are mainly from Hilden Brewery, often including the house ale, Hillside Embers, and newer beers such as Irish Red Ale. The late summer beer festival is popular, and the bar hosts musical acts and charity quizzes throughout the year. It is notably dog-friendly. Q🐎❀◑◗♿🚌(38,238)🐾📶

Holywood

Dirty Duck Ale House

3 Kinnegar Road, BT18 9JN
⏲ 12-11 (1am Thu-Sat); 12.30-11 Sun ☎ (028) 9059 6666
🌐 thedirtyduckalehouse.co.uk
House beer (by Hilden); 3 changing beers (sourced nationally; often Inveralmond, Sharp's, Shepherd Neame) Ⓗ
A former CAMRA Northern Ireland Pub of the Year, this is a single-room bar with a restaurant upstairs. Three ales are usually on and the range changes regularly. Good food is also available. There is much to admire here – a great view over Belfast Lough, collections of pumpclips and plastic ducks,

REAL ALE BREWERIES

Ards Newtownards
Barrahooley Craft Martinstown
Beer Hut Kilkeel (NEW)
Boundary Belfast
Bullhouse Newtownards
Dopey Dick Derry
Farmageddon Comber
Fermanagh Derrygonnelly
Hercules Belfast
Hilden Lisburn
Hillstown Randalstown
Knockout Belfast
Lacada Portrush
Mourne Mountains Warrenpoint
Norn Iron Dunmurry (NEW)
Northbound Eglinton
Station Works Newry
Whitewater Kilkeel

and a corner in honour of golfer Rory McIlroy. A summer beer festival is held every year in the roomy beer garden. Q

Killinchy

Daft Eddy's

Sketrick Island, BT23 6QH (2 miles N of Killinchy at Whiterock Bay)
11.30-11.30 (1am Fri); 12-10.30 Sun (028) 9754 1615
dafteddys.co.uk
1 changing beer (sourced locally; often Farmageddon)
Set in glorious surroundings, this old favourite has been renovated with a log cabin-style public bar inside the restaurant, while the old public bar has been replaced with Little Eddy's coffee bar. The restaurant continues to serve quality local food, with oysters and lobster among the specialities. An alfresco dining area has been added. There is one handpump on the restaurant side of the bar serving a variety of beers from Farmageddon Brewery. Q P

Lisburn

Tuesday Bell

4 Lisburn Square, BT28 1TS
8am-11 (midnight Thu; 1am Fri & Sat) (028) 9262 7390
Greene King Abbot; Sharp's Doom Bar; 3 changing beers (sourced nationally)
A city-centre Wetherspoon pub spread over two floors, close to the bus station. It is well established as a part of Lisburn's social life, and a popular location for eating and drinking, especially at the weekend. There are five handpumps downstairs and three upstairs dispensing a changing range of beers. Real cider is served, often Old Rosie or Black Dragon. Alcohol is available from 11.30am (12.30pm Sun). Q P

Newtownards

Spirit Merchant

54-56 Regent Street, BT23 4LP (next to bus station)
8am-midnight (028) 9182 4270
Greene King Abbot; Sharp's Doom Bar; 2 changing beers (sourced nationally)
About 10 miles east of Belfast, this is a large single-bar Wetherspoon pub on the main street, near to the bus station. It has five handpumps that dispense up to three changing beers in addition to the regular ones. The real ale is always kept in good order by the manager and her dedicated staff. Popular with local people, it features a large heated courtyard/beer garden at the side. Alcohol is available from 11.30am (12.30pm Sun). Q (7)

Saintfield

White Horse

49-53 Main Street, BT24 7AB
11.30-1am; 12-10 Sun (028) 9751 1143
whitehorsesaintfield.com
Whitewater Copperhead, Maggie's Leap IPA
This place is about 11 miles from Belfast. It comprises a bar, restaurant and pizza parlour, housed in a bright white-painted building at the end of the main street. A former coaching inn and Whitewater brewery tap, it is now a busy food-oriented establishment. Although it no longer belongs to the brewery, two Whitewater ales are on handpump, often Copperhead and Maggie's Leap. A former CAMRA Northern Ireland Pub of the Year. Q (15,215)

Dirty Duck Ale House, Holywood (Photo: David Blaikie/Flickr CC BY 2.0)

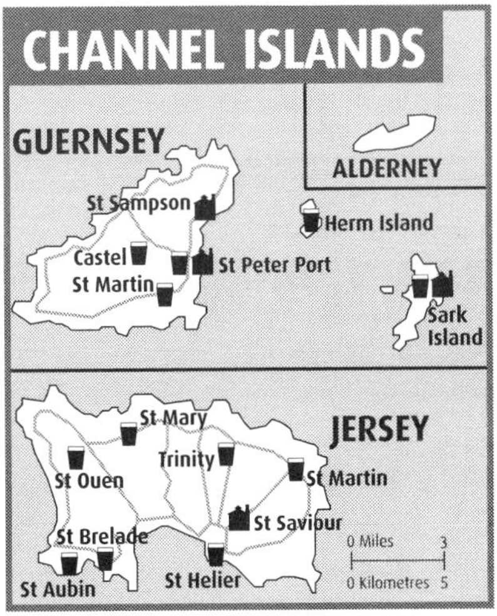

GUERNSEY

Castel

Fleur du Jardin

Kings Mills, GY5 7JT

10.30-11.45 (01481) 257996 fleurdujardin.com

2 changing beers

A building of unique charm with two bars – one traditional, small and cosy, attached to the restaurant, the other renovated in a more contemporary style to create a comfortable, relaxing area to enjoy a beer. A door from here leads to a large covered patio and out to the garden. Menus in both the bar and restaurant feature fresh local produce. The car park can be busy during the summer months.

Q P

Rockmount Hotel

Cobo, GY5 7HB

10.30-midnight (12.45am Fri & Sat) (01481) 252778

therocky.gg

3 changing beers

The pub has a taproom with sport on TV and a large lounge bar. The lounge has an emphasis on food, served lunchtimes and evenings, but there are comfy chairs near the fire for drinkers. Five handpumps offer a changing range of beers and you can also try a tasting paddle of different ales. Two ciders are available. Q

Herm Island

Mermaid Tavern

GY1 3HR (ferry from St Peter Port)

11-10.30; 12-10.30 Sun (01481) 750050 herm.com/mermaid

House beer (by Liberation); 2 changing beers

A short trip by ferry from Guernsey takes you to Herm. A large courtyard acts as a suntrap in the summer while in winter an open fire creates a cosy atmosphere. Real ale and cider festivals are held twice a year. The house beer is 4.2% ABV Herm Island Gold. A trip to Herm to discover the island's tranquillity and outstanding natural beauty is a must for any visitor to Guernsey.

St Martin

Captain's Hotel

La Fosse, GY4 6EF

11-11 (midnight Fri & Sat); 12-4 Sun (01481) 238990

thecaptainshotel.co.uk

Butcombe Original; Sharp's Doom Bar

In a secluded location down a country lane, this is a popular locals' pub with a lively, friendly atmosphere. It has a small, raised area in front of the bar furnished with a sofa to make a comfy zone. Good-quality meals can be eaten in the bar or bistro area, or you can take away a pizza. A meat draw is held on Friday. The car park to the rear fills up quickly. P

Les Douvres Hotel

La Fosse, GY4 6ER

10.30-12.30am (01481) 238731

lesdouvreshotel.co.uk

2 changing beers (often Black Sheep, Timothy Taylor)

Former 18th-century manor house, set in private gardens in St Martin near the south coast, two and a half miles from St Peter Port, with cliff walks and a tiny fishing harbour. A well-maintained, changing range of beers is offered on two handpumps, and real cider during the season. Excellent meals are served in the bar and separate restaurant. Live music features on Friday nights and occasional Wednesdays. The venue is popular with locals and visitors. P

St Peter Port

Cock & Bull

Lower Hauteville, GY1 1LL

11-12.45am; closed Sun (01481) 722660

cockandbullguernsey.com/home

5 changing beers

Just up the hill from the town church, the pub has five handpumps providing a changing range of beers, and real cider during the summer months. Seating is on three levels, with a pool table on the lower level. Live music features throughout the week, with open mic on Tuesday, Irish on Thursday, baroque monthly on a Monday, and on Saturday a silent set – gentle music that will not hinder conversation. A meat draw is held on Friday. The pub opens on Sundays when rugby is on.

Cornerstone

2 La Tour Beauregard, GY1 1LQ

11-12.30am; 12-11 Sun (01481) 713832

White Rock Wonky Donkey; 6 changing beers

The Cornerstone has a small bar area to the front and further seating to the rear, with a large screen for sporting events. White Rock beer is always on handpump together with a varying range of other ales. Gluten-free beer in bottles is stocked and gluten-free meals are available with advance notice. There is a meat draw on a Sunday.

REAL ALE BREWERIES

Isle of Sark La Seigneurie: Sark (NEW)
Liberation St Saviour: Jersey
Randalls St Peter Port: Guernsey
White Rock St Sampson: Guernsey

Golden Lion 🏆

7 Market Street, GY1 1HF
✪ 10-12.30am; 12-11 Sun ☎ (01481) 726634
⊕ thegoldenlion.gg
White Rock Wonky Donkey; 10 changing beers Ⓗ
Town-centre pub opposite the former market. The single room has a long bar selling 10 real ales at times, three of which are normally from White Rock. The pub has the modern feel of a craft beer bar. Live music plays on occasion in the downstairs bar. The first floor has been renovated and is now the Lions Den, open in the evenings and available for private hire. Gluten-free beer is available in bottles. Guernsey CAMRA Pub of the Year 2019.
◑🖫🛜

Pickled Pig (Duke of Normandie Hotel)

Lefebvre Street, GY1 2JP
✪ 11-12.45am (11 Sun) ☎ (01481) 721431
⊕ dukeofnormandie.com
2 changing beers Ⓗ
Town-centre hotel just off the High Street accessed through an arch near the Smith Street junction. The Pickled Pig pub is on the ground floor and has been refurbished, with three rooms offering different seating areas but easily accessible to each other. There is an emphasis on dining, but you are welcome to come in just for a drink, with stools and armchairs available. Outside is a courtyard beer garden. Gluten-free beer is available in bottles and gluten-free food is on the menu. 🛏◑Ⓟ🖫🛜

Red Lion

Les Banques, GY1 2RX (on seafront to N of St Peter Port)
✪ 11-11 (midnight Fri & Sat) ☎ (01481) 724042
3 changing beers Ⓗ
On the outskirts of St Peter Port, the pub has two bar areas – a lounge overlooking Belle Greve Bay to the front and a public area at the rear. Large-screen TVs show sport in both bars – just ask if there is something you would like to view. Meat draws are held on Friday and Saturday evenings. A changing variety of beers is offered on handpump and gluten-free beer in bottles. Real cider is available in the summer months. The pub is on several bus routes and on the cycle route between St Peter Port and St Sampson. 🚌❀◑🖤🖫🐾🛜

Ship & Crown ✅

North Esplanade, GY1 2NB
✪ 10-12.45am; 12-12.45am Sun ☎ (01481) 721368
Liberation Ale; 3 changing beers Ⓗ
A traditional local in the heart of the town, in the same family for more than 30 years, with fantastic views of the harbour, neighbouring islands and Castle Cornet. A friendly pub with welcoming staff, it is a popular spot to enjoy a pint and a good-value meal, attracting locals, yachtsmen and tourists. The walls are decorated with photos of local shipwrecks, Guernsey and the pub under German occupation. All major sports events are shown in a lively atmosphere. ◑🖤🖫🛜

JERSEY
St Aubin

Trafalgar ✅

Charing Cross, JE3 8AA
✪ 11-11 ☎ (01534) 741334
5 changing beers (often Liberation) Ⓗ

A traditional community pub with a strong nautical theme. There are two bars – a saloon bar at the front and a sports bar with pool, darts and TV behind. The handpumps are in the sports bar. Popular with rugby fans, the Jersey Reds often come here after Saturday home matches. The ale selection changes regularly, chosen from a list of about 200 different beers. Open mic and jam nights feature. 🚫❀🖫🐾

St Brelade

Old Smugglers Inn ✅

Le Mont du Ouaisne, JE3 8AW
✪ 11-11 ☎ (01534) 741510 ⊕ oldsmuggersinn.com
Draught Bass; house beer (by Liberation); 2 changing beers (often Skinner's) Ⓗ
Perched on the edge of Ouaisne Bay, the Smugglers has been the crown jewel of the Jersey real ale scene for many years. Steeped in history, dating back to when pirates came to enjoy an ale or two here, it is set within granite-built fishermen's cottages with foundations reputedly from the 13th century. Up to four ales are available including one from Skinner's, and mini beer festivals are regularly held. The pub is known for its good food including fresh daily specials.
Q🌳◑🖤Ⓟ🐾

St Helier

Lamplighter 🏆 Ⓛ ✅

9 Mulcaster Street, JE2 3NJ
✪ 11-11 ☎ (01534) 723119
8 changing beers Ⓖ
A traditional pub with a modern feel. The gas lamps that gave the pub its name remain, as does the original antique pewter bar top. An excellent range of up to eight real ales is available – the largest selection on the island – including one from Skinner's. All real ales are served direct from the cellar. A real cider is sometimes also on offer. A repeat winner of local CAMRA Pub of the Year.
◑🖤🖫🐾🛜

Post Horn Ⓛ ✅

Hue Street, JE2 3RE
✪ 10-11; 11-11 Sun ☎ (01534) 872853
Butcombe Original; Draught Bass; Liberation Ale, IPA; 1 changing beer (often Liberation) Ⓗ
Busy, friendly pub adjacent to the precinct and five minutes' walk from the Royal Square. It is particularly popular at lunchtimes with its own nucleus of regulars but all are welcomed. The large L-shaped public bar extends into the lounge area where there is an open fire and sports TV. A good selection of freshly cooked food is served. There is a large function room on the first floor, a drinking area outside and a public car park nearby.
🐾◑♿🖫🐾🛜

Prince of Wales Tavern

Hillgrove Street, JE2 4SL
✪ 10-11; 12-3 Sun ☎ (01534) 737378
Courage Directors; Fuller's London Pride; Ringwood Boondoggle; Sharp's Doom Bar; Wadworth Bishops Tipple; 3 changing beers (sourced nationally; often Bombardier, Shepherd Neame) Ⓗ
A traditional pub, situated next to the market, offering a large selection of up to eight cask ales advertised on blackboards. The Victorian-style interior features a bright and sparkling bar back

displaying a large selection of whiskies. The beer garden at the rear is a pleasant spot to relax with a pint.

St Martin

Royal

La Grande Route de Faldouet, JE3 6UG

11-11 (01534) 856289 randallsjersey.com

Draught Bass; Ringwood Razorback; 1 changing beer H

Originally a coaching inn, this large country-style hostelry is located at the centre of St Martin with sizeable public and lounge bars, a restaurant area and a spacious alfresco area. The interior features traditional furnishings, cosy corners and a real fire in colder months. Owned by Randalls Brewery, it serves guest ales from the Marston's, Sharp's and Skinner's stables. Quality food is popular with locals and visitors alike, with a good menu available lunchtimes and evenings until 8.30pm (no food Sun eve). P (3)

Rozel Bar & Restaurant

La Valle de Rozel, JE3 6AJ

10-11; 11-11 Sun (01534) 863438

rozelpubanddining.co.uk

Draught Bass; Fuller's London Pride; Liberation Ale; 1 changing beer H

A charming hostelry tucked away in the north-east corner of the island in the picturesque fishing village of Rozel. Bar meals are served in the public bar and snug, where there is a wood-burning stove in the winter. The excellent restaurant upstairs can be hired for private functions. Outside is a delightful beer garden. A Liberation Group partner pub, guest ales from Skinner's and Ringwood are often available. P (3)

St Mary

St Mary's Country Inn

La Rue des Buttes, JE3 3DS

11-11 (01534) 482897

Liberation Ale, IPA; 1 changing beer (often Butcombe) H

An archetypal country inn from the outside, this 17th-century farmhouse is opposite the 13th-century parish church. The interior is contemporary with a main bar and an extensive dining area. Three handpumps serve Liberation ales and a guest beer. Reasonably priced good food is available daily. The inn has a comfortable and relaxed atmosphere, with seating outside at the front and rear for when the sun shines. The north coast is a half-hour walk away, including the Devil's Hole blow hole. P

St Ouen

Farmers Inn

La Grande Route de St Ouen, JE3 2HY

10-11; 11-11 Sun (01534) 485311

Draught Bass; 2 changing beers H

Situated in the hub of St Ouen, near the war memorial and parish hall, the rustic Farmers Inn is a typical country pub offering up to three ales as well as a locally made cider when available (usually April to July). Traditional pub food is served in generous portions. Best described as a friendly community local, there is a good chance of hearing Jersey French (Jerriais) spoken at the bar. There is seating outside at the front of the pub. P

Moulin de Lecq

Le Mont de Ste Marie, JE3 2DT

11-11 (01534) 482818 moulindelecq.com

House beer (by Liberation) H**; 2 changing beers (often Greene King)** G

A free house on the island offering a range of real ales, the Moulin is a converted 12th-century watermill situated in the valley above the beach at Greve de Lecq. The waterwheel is still in place and the turning mechanism can be seen behind the bar. A large restaurant adjoins the mill and can be hired for functions. The children's play space and a barbecue area are used extensively in the summer. There is a pool table in the second floor games room. Q P

Trinity

Trinity Arms

La Rue es Picots, JE3 5JX

10-11; 11-11 Sun (01534) 864691

Liberation Ale H

Sporting the parish's ancient symbol of the Trinity, this 1976-built pub is modern by Jersey country pub standards but has plenty of character. Owned by the Liberation Group, it is central to and popular within village community life. It has a public bar and restaurant where food is served lunchtimes and evenings. There is seating outside, a children's play area and car parking. Breakfast is served from 10am. Close to Jersey Zoo. P (4)

SARK

Sark

Bel Air

Harbour Hill, GY10 1SB (top of Harbour Hill)

10-11.45 (01481) 832052

Shepherd Neame Spitfire; 1 changing beer (sourced locally) H

Open every day all year round, the Bel Air Inn offers a selection of traditional ales and ciders, and is a favourite pub among locals and tourists alike. Good food is served throughout day. There is a large sheltered beer garden for sunny days and a cosy fire for when it is cold outside. On summer weekends there is live music and barbecues. Families and dogs are welcome.

The Pub Manifesto
A Comedian Stands Up For Pubs

James Dowdeswell

Twenty-one pubs close per week in the UK. Award-winning stand-up and pub aficionado James Dowdeswell – who grew up in a West Country pub – believes humour is the best way to make the plight of the pub public and to generate a response.

To source the roots of the problem and to help crystallise what makes the perfect pub, James dissects, discusses and waxes lyrical on every aspect of pub culture. Dowdeswell's conversational prose style means reading this book is like sitting down with the author and discussing your ultimate pub over a beer. He champions many quirks and causes including: Interior design; Pub toilets; Beer, both real and crafty; Wine in pubs; Soft drinks and the designated driver; Pub games & entertainment; Pub dogs and other animals – and more. It concludes with his own take on George Orwell's *Moon Under Water* essay and a call to arms.

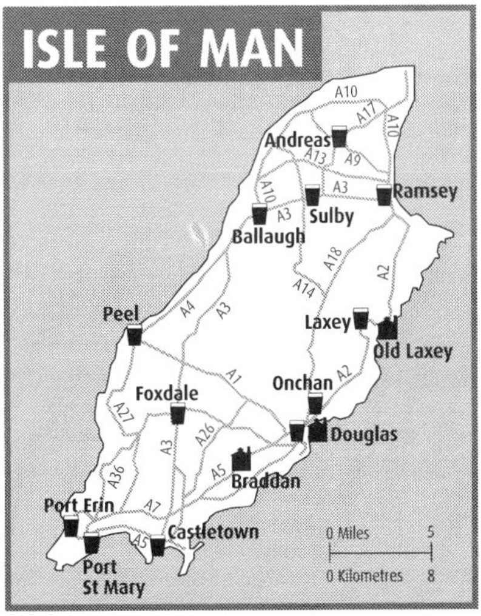

Andreas

Grosvenor Country Inn

Andreas Road, IM7 4HE

⏲ closed Mon; 12-2.30, 6-11 (midnight Fri & Sat); 12-4 Sun ☎ (01624) 888007

Okell's Bitter; 1 changing beer (sourced nationally) Ⓗ

Everyone is welcome at the Isle of Man's most northerly pub, which is equally popular for drinking and dining. The Tap Room public bar has a real sense of period charm and timeless character. There is a separate dining section and function room. Darts is played and a quiz night is held one Sunday evening a month. Beers come from the island's largest brewery, Okell's, including a guest ale. 🐴❀◐♣P🐾📶

Ballaugh

Raven ✔

The Main Road, IM7 5EG

⏲ 12-11 (midnight Fri & Sat) ☎ (01624) 896128

Okell's Bitter; house beer (by Okell's); 2 changing beers (sourced nationally) Ⓗ

Village-centre pub next to Ballaugh Bridge on the Isle of Man TT race course. There is a comfortable main bar area with dining areas off to the right and left. To the rear is a separate darts, pool and TV room. Seating areas outside the pub are heavily used in summer months, especially during race periods, when motorbikes leap over the bridge. The house brew is Ravens Claw, a rare Okell's beer exclusively available in this pub.
Q🐴❀◐♿♣P🚌(5,6)🐾📶

Castletown

Castle Arms ✔

The Quay, IM9 1LD

⏲ 12-11 (midnight Fri & Sat) ☎ (01624) 824673

Okell's Bitter, Dr Okell's IPA; 2 changing beers Ⓗ

Also known locally as the Glue Pot, the Castle Arms is a two-roomed pub in a superb location between the castle and harbour in Castletown. One room features nautical memorabilia while the other celebrates the TT races with many photographs and paintings. The pub famously features on the Manx £5 note – the only pub in the British Isles to appear on a banknote. There is a patio area used widely in summer overlooking the picturesque historic harbour. Q🐴❀⛺⇌♣🚌(1,2)🐾📶

Sidings

Victoria Road, IM9 1EF (next to railway station)

⏲ 11.30-11 (midnight Fri & Sat) ☎ (01624) 823282

Bushy's Castletown Bitter, Ruby (1874) Mild, Bitter; Okell's Bitter; 8 changing beers (sourced nationally) Ⓗ

The former ticket office for the Heritage Steam Railway Station, the pub is handily placed for visitors to the many Manx National Heritage attractions in Castletown including Castle Rushen, Old House of Keys, Old Grammar School and Nautical Museum. There is a large bar area with a real fire in winter, an adjacent dining area, a separate games and TV room, and a beer garden at the rear. An unashamedly beer-oriented traditional pub with unpretentious food on offer daily.
Q🐴❀◐♿⇌♣P🚌(1,2)🐾📶

Douglas

Albert Hotel ✔

3 Chapel Row, IM1 2BJ

⏲ 10-11 (midnight Fri & Sat); 12-11 Sun ☎ (01624) 673632

Bushy's Castletown Bitter; Okell's Bitter; 2 changing beers (sourced locally) Ⓗ

The Albert is a traditional and well-maintained pub close to Douglas Harbour and the nearest pub to the sea terminal. It has an interior recognised by CAMRA as being of regional historic importance. A central bar area serves two rooms – the one to the right features pool, darts and Sports TV, the one to the left is a quieter bar with photographs of Steam Packet boats adorning the walls. The cellar areas are thought to be some of the oldest structures in Douglas. Q⇌♣🚌🐾📶

Hooded Ram

North Quay, IM1 4LH

⏲ 3-11; 12-midnight Sat; closed Sun & Mon ☎ (01624) 612464 🌐 hoodedram.com

Hooded Ram Amber Ram, Jack The Ram Stout, Mosaic Single Hop Pale Ale; 3 changing beers (often Hooded Ram) Ⓗ

An interesting pub recently modernised, the Hooded Ram is also known as Clinch's and once housed the historic Clinch's Brewery. Up to six Hooded Ram beers and a cider from the Manx Cider Co are available. The main bar area has extensive seating, a shuffleboard and screens showing sporting fixtures. There is a further seating area for dining. The pub is next to the Steam Railway Station and within sight of the Hooded Ram Brewery. 🐴◐⇌♣🍎🚌📶

Horse & Plough ✔

Isle of Man Business Park, IM2 2QZ (in Bradden at jct with Vicarage Rd)

⏲ 12-11 (midnight Fri & Sat); 12-10 Sun ☎ (01624) 626060

Okell's Manx Pale Ale, Bitter, Dr Okell's IPA; 1 changing beer (often Okell's) Ⓗ

REAL ALE BREWERIES

Bushy's Braddan
Hooded Ram Douglas
Okell's Douglas
Old Laxey 🛢 Old Laxey

ISLANDS

Superbly designed Heron & Brearley business park pub near a housing estate. The spacious interior comprises a large conservatory, a dining area, a comfortable lounge with sports TV and a quieter raised area. There is a beer garden outside. The pub is a popular venue for functions and uses in-house catering for both formal and informal occasions, serving good-value food to a high standard. There is occasional live music. The four real ales are always from Okell's Brewery. P

Old Market Inn

Chapel Row, IM1 2BJ

10-11 Mon; 9am-11 Tue-Thu; 9am-midnight Fri & Sat; 10-11 Sun ☎ (01624) 675202

2 changing beers (often Bushy's) H

Under the same ownership for many years, the Market has the smallest bar on the island, serving two separate rooms. The landlord is a keen TT supporter and the pub's walls are adorned with photos of the races. Two ales are normally on offer, usually from Bushy's. Friendly and very popular with locals, the pub is close to both the bus station on Lord Street and the ferry terminal, so it makes an ideal waiting room. Q

Prospect Hotel

Prospect Hill, IM1 1ET

12-11 (midnight Fri); 5-midnight Sat; closed Sun ☎ (01624) 616773

Okell's Manx Pale Ale, Bitter; 6 changing beers (often Okell's) H

Opened in 1857 in the finance sector of the island's capital, this large single-room pub has different areas, some decorated with pictures of the law profession, reflecting its proximity to the law courts. There are eight handpumps in two banks of four on separate sides of the bar. Guest ales change regularly and occasionally real cider and perry are available. Wednesday is quiz night. The rear area known as the Library is full of bookshelves and can be quieter.
(3,11)

Queens Hotel

Queens Promenade, IM2 4NL (N end of promenade)

12-midnight ☎ (01624) 674438

Okell's Bitter; 5 changing beers (sourced nationally; often Okell's) H

Situated towards the north of the promenade, this popular pub has two bars and a separate pool and darts area. Food is served daily. Outside is a seating area with heating and large parasols where you can view the seasonal passing horse trams and get a year round vista of the bay. Live music plays at weekends. At least one guest beer is available, often many more during the summer to complement the Okell's regulars.
Q

Rosemount Hotel

Woodbourne Road, IM1 3HH

12-midnight ☎ (01624) 618500

Okell's Bitter; 2 changing beers (sourced nationally; often Okell's) H

The Rosemount has three large rooms all served from a central area with separate bar counters. The back room has darts and there is a front room with a pool table. A variety of entertainment includes karaoke on Sunday afternoon and live music on Friday and Saturday nights. There is a renewed focus on real ale from the current landlord with three ales now usually available. Q (2)

Rovers Return

11 Church Street, IM1 2AG

12-11 (midnight Fri & Sat) ☎ (01624) 676459

Bushy's Ruby (1874) Mild, Bitter; 5 changing beers H

The Rovers is a fascinating pub, with handpumps fashioned from fire hoses, a traditional coal fire, and a shrine to Blackburn Rovers in a back room. The almost warren-like series of rooms are frequented by a truly eclectic and loyal clientele. Famously large food portions are available at lunchtimes, and rare and unusual guest ales complement the Bushy's regular and seasonal ales. Real cider is also always on sale. The pub is tucked away down a narrow street behind Douglas Town Hall.

Terminus Tavern

Strathallan Crescent, IM2 4NR

12-11 (midnight Fri & Sat) ☎ (01624) 624312

Okell's Bitter; 3 changing beers (sourced nationally; often Okell's) H

Found at the Manx Electric Railway station at the northern end of the prom, the Terminus has an extensive and comfortable front bar with large bay windows, and another bar for games at the rear. Decoration in the front bar illustrates interesting architectural features. Outside at the front is a large patio with views over Douglas Bay. Excellent food is served and the pub is often busy. Okell's Bitter is offered alongside guest beers.
Q P (1,10)

Woodbourne Hotel

Alexander Drive, IM2 3QF (in Woodbourne area of Douglas)

3-midnight; 12-midnight Fri-Sun ☎ (01624) 676754

Adnams Broadside; Bombardier Colonel's Reserve; Okell's Manx Pale Ale, Bitter, Dr Okell's IPA; Rudgate Ruby Mild; 3 changing beers (sourced nationally) H

Built in 1895, the Woodbourne is a fantastic example of a large Victorian pub, set in a residential area within walking distance of Douglas town centre. It has three bars ready to serve a wide range of cask ales. The Woody has recently been refurbished to a high standard, with sports TV in two bars, Wi-Fi and disabled toilets. A former local CAMRA Pub of the Year. Q

Foxdale

Baltic Inn

1 Glentramman Terrace, IM4 3EE

4-midnight; 2-midnight Sat & Sun ☎ (01624) 801305

balticinn.pub

Okell's Manx Pale Ale, Bitter; 1 changing beer (sourced nationally) H

The only pub in a former mining town, with one main room divided into separate seating areas. A roaring real fire in winter adds to the atmosphere. Up to three real ales are now on handpump along with Okell's IPA and Maclir in bottles. There are some fascinating historic photos on the walls of Foxdale during the mining boom. This friendly village pub is unlike any other on the island, and has undergone a significant revival in recent years without losing any of its local character.
Q (4)

Laxey

Bridge Inn

6 New Road, IM4 7BE

⏲ 12-11 (midnight Fri & Sat) ☎ (01624) 862414
🌐 bridgeinn.im
Bushy's Bitter; 2 changing beers (sourced nationally) Ⓗ
The Bridge, a traditional pub in the heart of Laxey, dates back to at least 1857. It has two bars, the main one to the right on entering, with pool, darts and a large TV screen for sport. The separate bar room to the left is used at busier periods. In 1897 after the Snaefell mining disaster, in which 20 men perished, the cellars were used as a temporary morgue. The pub is reputedly haunted.
Q🍼❀🛏⛺⇌♣⧫🚌🐾📶

Mines Tavern

Captains Hill, IM4 7AY
⏲ 12-11 (midnight Fri & Sat); 12-10.30 Sun
☎ (01624) 861484
Okell's Manx Pale Ale, Bitter; 1 changing beer (sourced locally) Ⓗ
This former mine captain's home is beside the picturesque setting of Laxey's historic tram station, with an unusual bar made from a 1902 tram car. A warming fire in winter welcomes visitors and, outside, the garden is well used in good weather. Trams run to Douglas, Ramsey and the summit of Snaefell, the island's mountain. Closest to the famous Laxey Wheel, there is local memorabilia here from the mines and local railways. In winter opening time is 4pm on weekdays; food is available summertime only. ❀◐◑⛺⇌♣🚌(3A,3)

Onchan

Manx Arms ✔

Main Road, IM3 1BE
⏲ 12-11 (midnight Fri-Sun) ☎ (01624) 675484
Okell's Manx Pale Ale, Bitter; 2 changing beers (sourced nationally) Ⓗ
Traditional village pub on the main road with two separate bar areas. There are large TV screens for sporting fixtures, live music most Saturday evenings and occasional karaoke. Pub games are played including pool, darts and dominoes. This pub is on the former motorcycle racing Clypse Course and displays racing photographs from the 1950s on the walls. There are attractive heated patios at the front and rear. An extensive choice of real ciders is available. Q❀♿♣⧫P🚌(3,23)🐾📶

Peel

Royal Hotel

Atholl Street, IM5 1HG
⏲ 4-midnight; 12-midnight Fri-Sun ☎ (01624) 842217
Okell's Bitter; 4 changing beers (often Bushy's, Okell's) Ⓗ
For those entering for the first time, the layout of the Royal comes as a surprise. The bar is set deeply to the rear of the building, at the end of a long, narrow corridor within the well-furnished drinking area. Beyond that is a beautiful walled beer garden. Although guest ales have come from breweries from all over in the past, the landlord's intention is to source all beers from island brewers Bushy's and Okell's. ❀♣🚌(5,6)📶

White House Hotel ✔

2 Tynwald Road, IM5 1LA (150yds from bus station)
⏲ 11-midnight ☎ (01624) 842252
Bushy's Ruby (1874) Mild, Bitter; Okell's Bitter, Dr Okell's IPA; Timothy Taylor Landlord; 3 changing beers (sourced nationally) Ⓗ
The White House has a public bar area, multiple pool tables, darts and a larger room for TV sport plus live music at the weekend. Through an unusual sliding door is a cosy snug with its own bar. Now under new management, the pub remains a heavily community-focused stalwart, with a vast malt whisky collection to complement the real ales. A prolific winner of Isle of Man CAMRA Pub of the Year over many years.
Q❀⛺♣⧫P🚌(5,6)🐾📶

Port Erin

Falcon's Nest Hotel

Station Road, IM9 6AF
⏲ 11-11 (midnight Fri & Sat) ☎ (01624) 834077
🌐 falconsnesthotel.co.uk
Bushy's Bitter; 3 changing beers (sourced nationally) Ⓗ
The Falcon's Nest Hotel on the south-west coast is in a spectacular location overlooking the beautiful crescent-shaped bay of Port Erin, which is visible from the bar conservatory area. The hotel has two bars and a separate restaurant area. The lounge bar is where visitors can relax in front of an open fire and enjoy a varied range of guest beers and local real ales. The second bar has games and multiple TVs, usually showing sport.
Q🍼🛏◐◑⇌♣P🚌(1,12)🐾📶

Station Hotel ✔

Station Road, IM9 6AE
⏲ 10.30-11 (midnight Fri & Sat); 12-11 Sun
☎ (01624) 838991
Okell's Manx Pale Ale, Bitter, Dr Okell's IPA; 1 changing beer (sourced nationally) Ⓗ
Opposite the steam train station and near bus stops only a hundred yards from the stunning bay, the Station is an ideal first or last pub to visit in Port Erin. Traditionally and informally furnished, it has a relaxed atmosphere and offers the town's largest Okell's beer selection. Diners and drinkers mingle comfortably in the spacious main bar area, also using the large function room at busier times.
🍼◐◑♿⇌P🚌🐾📶

Port St Mary

Albert Hotel

Athol Street, IM9 5DS (opp harbour)
⏲ 12-midnight ☎ (01624) 832118
Bushy's Bitter; Okell's Bitter; 2 changing beers (sourced nationally) Ⓗ
A hidden gem in the heart of this coastal village, the Albert boasts impressive views over the harbour. It has a public bar with games area, a cosy lounge bar complete with wood-burning stove, and an overflow area of tables and seating. Immaculately decorated and furnished, it features walls adorned with many paintings by local artists who frequent the pub. An upstairs apartment is available for hire. A former Isle of Man CAMRA Pub of the Year. Q❀🛏♣P🚌📶

Shore Hotel

Shore Road, Gansey, IM9 5LZ
⏲ 12-11 (midnight Fri & Sat) ☎ (01624) 832269
🌐 theshore.im

Bushy's Old Bushy Tail; Okell's Bitter; 1 changing beer (sourced nationally) Ⓗ
A prominent building with stunning views over Gansey or Carrick Bay. The hotel has a wooden bar area fashioned from ship timbers and door panelling, with mixed seating and tables. The outside seating area is sheltered from the wind, which can be biting. The Gents incorporates some interesting fittings. Food is served throughout the day. This is a rare permanent outlet for Old Bushy Tail. ❀🛏◑◐⇌●P🚌🐾ᯤ

Ramsey

Central Hotel ✔
Bowring Road, IM8 2LL
✪ 2-11 (1am Fri & Sat) ☎ (01624) 813177
Okell's Bitter; house beer (by Okell's) Ⓗ
A traditional drinkers' pub externally decorated as a house for Castletown Brewery, which closed in 1986. Its central bar area serves two rooms, the front featuring a TV and the rear which leads to outside seating and the car park. Pool and darts are played in the games room behind. Okell's Bitter is served out of season, with additional guest beers added at busier periods. Popular at TT time due to its location on the outside of the course.
Q⇌(Plaza)♣P🚌ᯤ

Mitre
16 Parliament Street, IM8 1AP
✪ 10-11 (1am Fri & Sat); 10.30-11 Sun ☎ (01624) 813045
Okell's Bitter; house beer (by Okell's); 2 changing beers (sourced locally) Ⓗ
Welcoming pub that gives its friendly clientele a fine view of Ramsey's quayside and illuminated swing bridge. The first-floor Harbour Bar serves Okell's Jough; the refurbished basement Schooner Bar opens on Saturday night 10pm-1am. Food includes a Sunday lunchtime carvery – booking advised (no food Mon). The pub can also be accessed from the quay, which has ample parking. ◑⇌(Plaza)♣🚌(3,3A)🐾ᯤ

Trafalgar Hotel ✔
West Quay, IM8 1DW
✪ 11-11 (12.15am Fri & Sat); 11.30-11 Sun
☎ (01624) 814601
Moorhouse's Black Cat; Okell's Bitter; house beer (by Joseph Holt); 2 changing beers (sourced nationally) Ⓗ
Traditional twin-room pub on the harbour, offering a warm welcome and a choice of excellent beers. The house ale is a rebadged Manchester beer, unusually for the island. A mild is normally available, usually Moorhouse's Black Cat. Sport is shown on TVs downstairs; an upstairs room with fruit machines is open only during the day. Well-behaved dogs are welcome. Q⇌(Plaza)●🚌🐾ᯤ

Sulby

Sulby Glen Hotel ✔
Main Road, IM7 2HR
✪ 12-midnight (1am Fri & Sat); 12-11 Sun
☎ (01624) 897240 🌐 sulbyglen.net
Bushy's Bitter; Okell's Bitter; 2 changing beers (sourced locally) Ⓗ
Situated on the TT circuit's Sulby straight, this is a friendly and popular pub with accommodation and camping nearby. Interesting local and TT photos help attract motorcycle fans. A motorcycle engine set up on the main bar dispenses four keg beers. The home-cooked food uses local ingredients. Other features include a sports TV, pool table and warming open fire. Buses to Ramsey and Peel stop outside. Q🐎❀🛏◑◐♿⛺♣P🚌(5,6)

Shore Hotel, Port St Mary (Photo: Rick Pickup)

The Breweries

BREWERIES OVERVIEW

Roger Protz takes a look at what's been happening in the brewing industry.

The shock event of 2019, which rocked the brewing industry to its core, was the sale of Fuller's brewery and brands to the Japanese brewer Asahi. Fuller, Smith & Turner, to give the company its full title, has deep roots in London brewing. The three families joined forces in 1845 but brewing has been going on at the Chiswick site since the 1600s. While there are now more than 125 breweries in London, all the famous historic family brewers have thrown in the towel. Young's of Wandsworth, much loved by real ale drinkers, was the last to go and has been a pub company since 2006. Now Fuller's has followed in its arch rival's wake, with a huge estate of 385 pubs and hotels – but no longer with a brewery.

Asahi paid £250 million for Fuller's and the sale poses the key questions: who is next, is anybody safe, and what are the implications for quality beer, cask ale in particular?

The purchase of Fuller's was prompted by the 2016 takeover of SABMiller by AB InBev, the world's two leading brewing groups. It cost AB $100 billion and was the third biggest takeover in corporate history. It gives the group – which owns such leading brands as American Budweiser and Stella Artois – control of 30 per cent of all the beer brewed and sold throughout the world.

AB's dominant position means it can buy raw materials such as grain and hops at enormous discounts. It uses this muscle to brew beer more cheaply and undercut its rivals in both the pub and take-home sectors.

Since 2016, the other global giants – Asahi, Carlsberg, Heineken, Kirin and Molson Coors – have been rushing to catch up. As well as Fuller's, Asahi now owns Meantime in Greenwich, Heineken runs Caledonian in Scotland and has an undisclosed stake – thought to be 50 per cent – in another London brewery, Beavertown, which will move to a new and bigger plant. Fourpure in South-east London was bought in 2018 by the Australian group Lion, which is part of the Japanese Kirin group, while Carlsberg bought London Fields Brewery in 2017. In 2019 Lion/Kirin added the highly-regarded Magic Rock Brewery in Huddersfield to its acquisitions.

Fuller's brewery in Chiswick, London, was sold to Japanese brewer Asahi in early 2019

AB InBev owns Camden Town Brewery, which it bought for £80 million in 2016, and has moved the plant to a new, much enlarged site in Ponders End. As an indication of the marketing strength of the global brewers, Camden beers are now widely available in most major supermarkets at prices smaller independents would consider unprofitable. The trend of buying independent breweries was set in 2011 when Molson Coors paid £20 million for Sharp's in Cornwall. Sharp's had a modest output of 1,500 barrels a year but under new ownership that grew to 60,000. An injection of £7.5 million has enabled Sharp's to produce 200,000 barrels a year and Doom Bar is now Britain's biggest ale brand, overtaking Greene King's IPA.

All these acquisitions are small beer compared to the Fuller's sale, which brings in to sharp focus a problem that bedevils middle-ranking British breweries: excise duty, the tax levied on production. In its last full year, Fuller's made healthy profits of £45 million – but 90 per cent came from retailing. In common with many other breweries with large pub estates, Fuller's has seen income from brewing falling year upon year. With the exception of Finland, Britain pays the highest levels of beer duty in Europe. As a result, a number of 'squeezed middle' breweries have either become pub companies, such as Fuller's and Young's, or in the case of Batemans, Brains, Everards, McMullen, Thwaites and Charles Wells, have either drastically cut production levels or built new and much smaller breweries to qualify for Small Brewers Relief (SBR).

DUTY REFORM

SBR was first called Progressive Beer Duty and was introduced in 2002 to aid the growing number of micro brewers. It was an absurd anomaly that brewers producing a few hundred barrels a year should pay the same level of duty as larger companies making thousands of barrels. The bigger brewers benefit from 'economies of scale', meaning they are able to buy malt and hops in bulk with generous discounts, and in most cases can sell beer direct to their substantial pub estates. The problem with SBR is the cut-off level. At present, brewers producing up to 5,000 hectolitres a year have a 50 per cent cut in duty. There is then tapered relief up to 60,000 hectos. But there is no relief above 60,000 hectos – which explains the problems of the 'squeezed middle'. A Treasury review of SBR is now underway and SIBA, the Society of Independent Brewers, which campaigned vigorously for many years to introduce duty reform, agrees there should be relief for brewers above the present cut off as long as those currently benefitting from SBR don't have to pay more.

Artist's impressions of the proposed Truman's site

Fuller's, with a capacity of 200,000 barrels a year, would make only marginal gains from any changes to SBR. There are other reasons for its exit from brewing, including rumours of disputes at board level about the future of the company. But that is history. The main concern is possible changes to the beer range and their quality.

Asahi says it wants to turn London Pride, the brewery's main beer, into an 'international brand'. That should set alarm bells tolling. Pride is a cask ale with many awards to its name, but in 'international' format it would become keg, not cask. Could the same fate await the equally popular and garlanded ESB premium bitter?

Will short-run beers such as Chiswick Bitter and Gale's Prize Old Ale be dropped? And will the superb bottle-conditioned beers Vintage Ale and 1845 survive under the new owners? The jury is out and it will also have to monitor any changes in the ingredients used to make Fuller's beers. As AB InBev proves with the label for Budweiser, which lists rice before barley malt, global brewers have a habit of cheapening production to maximise profits.

NEW INVESTMENT

It's not all doom and gloom in London. There are remarkable success stories such as that of the Truman's brewery in Hackney Wick. It opened in 2013, reviving the name of the giant London brewery founded in 1666 and which closed in 1989. The new Truman's has a capacity of 45 barrels but the owners plan to move to a much bigger site in Walthamstow in 2020 where they can produce 150,000 barrels a year, of which around 40 per cent will be in cask form.

There are similar success stories in other parts of the country. Hawkshead in Cumbria has a large and successful brewery at Staveley but in 2019 it opened a second plant at Flookburgh at a cost of £175,000. The new brewery can produce 360 barrels a week and 70 per cent of the beers from the combined sites are in cask form.

In Gloucestershire, the Stroud Brewery also moved to a new site in 2019. It produces all organic beers in cask, keg, can and bottle. The capacity of the new plant is 20 barrels a week but this will grow to 40 barrels and 50 per cent of production will be in cask form.

These success stories get little media coverage. More attention was given in 2019 to Marston's decision to remove cask beer from all but one of its 22 managed pubs in Scotland. It was suggested in some media outlets that this marked a crisis for real ale north of the border. But with more than 100 breweries in Scotland, the more likely reason is that beer lovers there prefer to drink local ales to those from England. One Scottish wholesaler reports that sales of real ale are doing well.

Following the undoubted fall in sales of cask beer in 2018, there are signs of a recovery in the sector. That recovery would be all the greater if the British put aside their ingrained habit of attacking the things this country does well and proclaimed the pleasures of our national drink.

As Alex Brodie, the founder of Hawkshead, says: "Cask beer is unique to Britain and it needs to be treasured."

Former editor of the *Good Beer Guide*, **Roger Protz** is considered one of the leading beer writers in the world, with a long career in journalism and publishing, and having won multiple awards. Roger has authored many books on beer and pubs, including *300 Beers to Try Before You Die*. Follow him on Twitter **@RogerProtzBeer** and **protzonbeer.co.uk**.

How to use the Breweries section

This section lists breweries operating in the United Kingdom, the Isle of Man and the Channel Islands. Breweries are listed in alphabetical order. They include independent companies (regional, family, micro-brewers and brewpubs), national brewers and global groups. If a brewery owns more than one site, these are cross-referenced. Within each brewery entry, regular beers are listed in increasing order of strength. Websites should be consulted when breweries produce occasional or seasonal beers that are available for less than six months of the year. We mention when breweries produce bottle-conditioned beers but do not list or evaluate them.

KEY TO BREWERY ENTRIES

BREWERY SYMBOLS

Brewpub: a pub that brews beer on the premises.

CAMRA tasting notes, supplied by a trained CAMRA tasting panel. Beer descriptions that do not carry this symbol are based on more limited tastings or have been obtained from other sources.

A CAMRA Beer of the Year in 2018.

One of CAMRA's Beers of the Year 2019: a finalist in the Champion Beer of Britain competition held during the Great British Beer Festival in London in August 2019, or in the Champion Winter Beer of Britain competition held earlier in the year.

Serve with tight sparkler: the brewery's beers can be acceptably served through a 'tight sparkler' attached to the nozzle of the beer pump, designed to give a thick collar of foam on the beer.

Do not serve with tight sparkler: the brewery's beers should NOT be served through a tight sparkler. CAMRA is opposed to the growing tendency to serve southern-brewed beers with the aid of sparklers, which aerate the beer and tend to drive hop aroma and flavour into the head, altering the balance of the beer achieved in the brewery. When neither symbol is used it means the brewery in question has not stated a preference.

Brewery tours available: check with individual breweries for details.

Brewery shop: beer available to take away. Check opening hours in advance.

RAIB **Real Ale in a Bottle:** the brewery produces bottle-conditioned beer (known by CAMRA as Real Ale in a Bottle).

◆ **Seasonal beers:** the brewery produces seasonal beers in addition to its regular range.

V **Vegan:** the brewery produces vegan beers (check with brewery for further details. Not all beers produced may be vegan).

GF **Gluten free:** the brewery produces gluten-free beers (check with brewery for further details. Not all there beers may be gluten free).

ABBREVIATIONS

OG Stands for Original Gravity, the measure taken before fermentation of the level of 'fermentable material' (malt sugars and added sugars) in the brew. It is only a rough indication of strength and is no longer used for duty purposes.

ABV Stands for Alcohol by Volume, which is a more reliable measure of the percentage of alcohol in finished beer. Many breweries now only disclose ABVs but the Guide lists OGs where available. Often the OG and the ABV of a beer are identical, i.e. 1035 and 3.5 per cent. If the ABV is higher than the OG, i.e. OG 1035, ABV 3.8, this indicates that the beer has been 'well attenuated' with most of the malt sugars turned into alcohol. If the ABV is lower than the OG, this means residual sugars have been left in the beer for fullness of body and flavour: this is rare but can apply to some milds or strong old ales, barley wines and winter beers.

SIBA Indicates a member of the Society of Independent Brewers.

IFBB Indicates a member of the Independent Family Brewers of Britain.

NOTE: The Breweries section was correct at the time of going to press and every effort has been made to ensure that all regularly-available cask-conditioned beers are included.

The Breweries

The breweries listed in this section include micro, small, family, regional, national and global companies. Please use the Beer index (p1013) to help locate beers.

1086 (NEW)

Old Brewhouse, Cusworth Hall, Cusworth Lane, Doncaster, South Yorkshire, DN5 7TU

1086 was established in 2018, in the original brewhouse of Cusworth Hall, an 18th century, Grade I country house in Cusworth, near Doncaster. The beers are available at the Old Brewhouse on-site bar.

1648 SIBA

Old Stables Brewery, Mill Lane, East Hoathly, East Sussex, BN8 6QB
☎ (01825) 840830 🌐 1648brewing.co.uk

⊗ The 1648 brewery, set up in the old stable block at the King's Head pub in 2003, derives its name from the year of the deposition of King Charles I. One pub is owned and more than 40 outlets are supplied. ‼ ♦ RAIB

Hop Pocket (OG 1039, ABV 3.7%)

Triple Champion (OG 1041, ABV 4%)
A chestnut-coloured traditional ale, deep-flavoured and full-bodied.

Signature (OG 1044, ABV 4.4%)
Pale, light, crisply refreshing ale, with a bitter aftertaste.

Laughing Frog (OG 1052, ABV 5.2%)
Dark golden-coloured, full-bodied ale. Lightly-hopped, with a full malty flavour.

22 Bake & Brew

Platform 22, Station Road, Torphins, AB31 4JF
☎ (01339) 882807 🌐 22bakeandbrew.co.uk

Brewery adjacent to Platform 22 café/bar. No real ale.

3 Brewers of St Albans SIBA

The Potato Shed, Symonds Hyde Farm, Symonds Hyde Lane, Hatfield, Hertfordshire, AL10 9BB
☎ (01707) 271636 ☎ 07941 854615
🌐 3brewers.co.uk

⊗ Launched in 2013 by three brewers from St Albans who turned a potato shed into an eight-barrel brewery. Spent malt becomes compost for the farm. Its range of seven permanent beers is supplied to pubs, beer festivals, markets and other events in Hertfordshire and surrounding counties. ‼

Dark Mild (OG 1036, ABV 3.6%)
Dark ruby-coloured, this smooth and creamy mild combines a malty sweetness with a touch of liquorice bitterness to make a well-balanced ale.

Golden English Ale (OG 1038, ABV 3.8%)
A light golden-coloured ale, with a subtle citrus flavour, and a hint of sweetness.

Classic English Ale (OG 1040, ABV 4%)
Deep amber-coloured, with a light hoppy aroma. A rich, rounded malty taste is balanced by subtle hoppiness, giving a clean, smooth and refreshing ale.

Blonde (OG 1042, ABV 4.2%)
A light golden-coloured ale, with a hoppy aroma and a refreshing smack of fruity citrus flavours.

Ruby English Ale (OG 1043, ABV 4.3%)

IPA (OG 1046, ABV 4.6%)
Golden-coloured IPA, with a clean, dry finish.

Special English Ale (OG 1048, ABV 4.8%)
A deep copper-coloured, robust and full-bodied premium ale. Well-balanced, smooth and moreish, with a hint of berries.

3 Piers

19 Cocker Avenue, Poulton Industrial Estate, Poulton-le-Fylde, Lancashire, FY6 8JU ☎ 07977 469326
🌐 3piersbrewery.com

Brewing began in 2017 using a 15-barrel plant. A wide range of beers is produced and delivered direct all over the UK. ‼ ♦

Northern Monkey (ABV 3.8%)
A golden amber-coloured session ale brewed with a range of three hops.

Golden Smiler (ABV 4%)
Pale-coloured and hoppy, some fruit in the taste, and a long bitter finish.

Old Station Porter (ABV 4.5%)
A rich, dark-coloured porter that packs a punch.

West Coast Blonde (ABV 4.6%)
Pleasantly-hopped golden ale with a citrus bite.

Central Citra (ABV 5%)
Fresh IPA with a great hit of hops.

3D Beer

See Epic Beers

360° SIBA

Unit 24b, Bluebell Business Estate, Sheffield Park, East Sussex, TN22 3HQ
☎ (01825) 722375 🌐 360degreebrewing.com

⊗ Brewing began in 2013, adjacent to the famous Bluebell Railway at Sheffield Park, East Sussex, using a six-barrel plant. Its goal is to produce as wide a range of beers as it can with the best ingredients, brewing in small batches and ensuring quality is the priority. Beers are available across Sussex, the South East, and London. ‼ ♦

Pale (ABV 3.9%)
Light-bodied, fully-flavoured, zesty golden ale.

Best (ABV 4.2%)
A copper-coloured, aromatic best bitter, with a clean bitterness.

American Pale Ale (ABV 5%)
A contemporary pale ale, heavily-hopped to produce intense tropical fruit flavours and a long bitter finish.

4 Mice (NEW)

Coach & Horses, Main Street, Bolton-by-Bowland, Lancashire, BB7 4NW
☎ (01200) 447331
coachandhorsesribblevalley.co.uk

A four-barrel brewery in a gastro-pub, situated in the Trough of Bowland.

4Ts

Unit 20, Manor Industrial Estate, Lower Wash Lane, Latchford, Warrington, Cheshire, WA4 1PL
☎ (01925) 417820 ☎ 07917 730184
4tsbrewery.co.uk

Brewing returned to Warrington in 2015. The core range of eight beers can usually be found in the Tavern, Warrington. ‼♦

EPA (OG 1037, ABV 3.7%)
A well-balanced, pale-coloured, refreshing session ale with spicy notes.

Angels Mild (OG 1038, ABV 3.8%)
A dark mild, faithfully brewed from the old Walkers recipe.

APA (OG 1040, ABV 4%)
An American-style pale ale, hoppy, with spicy and citrus hints throughout with a hint of bitterness at the end, leaving a burst of citrus flavour.

WSB (ABV 4.2%)
Crisp and refreshing with a malty base and aromas of blackcurrant and citrus.

George Shaws Premium (OG 1043, ABV 4.3%)
An amber-coloured, complex and well-balanced bitter.

IPA (OG 1046, ABV 4.6%)
Hints of citrus and passion fruit, with a punch of bitterness.

Panzer Pils (ABV 4.8%)
A Czech-style pilsner. Earth and fresh bread aromas with hints of honeysuckle followed by malty sweetness and a pleasing bitterness.

English Stout (OG 1050, ABV 5%)
Well-balanced and smooth stout with biscuit, chocolate and burnt notes to start, then a burst of flowery tones.

Angels Folly (OG 1052, ABV 5.2%)
A strong, dark-coloured, complex beer, rich in texture with a strong malty aroma and subtle mouthfeel.

Taipur (OG 1059, ABV 5.9%)

Big Daddy DIPA (ABV 7.2%)
Clean and crisp double IPA with an intense amount of resinous, citrus and grapefruit aroma.

40FT

Bootyard, Abbott Street, Dalston, London, E8 3DP

Office: The Printhouse, 18-20 Ashwin Street, Dalston, London, E8 3DL 40ftbrewery.com

Six-barrel microbrewery 40FT began brewing in 2015. It is located in a 40-ft shipping container in a disused car park close to Ridley Road Market. Beers are produced for its brewery tap room as well as pubs, bars, restaurants and off-licences. Output is nearly all keg and cans. Expanded taproom open every Thursday-Saturday (5-11pm).

#alesnotdead (OG 1045, ABV 4.5%)
An amber-coloured, hoppy ale.

71

30/34 Reform Street, Dundee, DD1 1RJ

Brewing began in 2016, principally brewery-conditioned lagers. In 2018 71 Brewing was commissioned to produce a cask-conditioned festival ale and is now producing a range of cask-conditioned beers. A taproom and bottle shop is open daily. ‼

8 Sail SIBA

Heckington Windmill, Hale Road, Heckington, Lincolnshire, NG34 9JW
☎ (01529) 469308 ☎ 07866 183479
8sailbrewery.co.uk

8 Sail Brewery was established in 2010 and operates on a six-barrel brew plant. The brewery nestles in the shadow of Heckington Windmill, Britain's only eight-sailed windmill, from where the brewery gets its name. The mill is now working and helping to mill malted grain for the brewery. The brewery shop stocks bottle-conditioned beers alongside local ciders. The front of the brewery has been converted into a Victorian-style bar. ♦RAIB

8 Sail Ale (OG 1040, ABV 3.8%)
A traditional, easy-drinking session pale ale, lightly hopped.

Windmill Bitter (OG 1040, ABV 3.8%)
An amber-coloured session bitter with a good blend of malt and hops.

Blonde (OG 1042, ABV 4%)
A blonde beer, gently-hopped to create a refreshing taste.

Millwright (OG 1042, ABV 4%)
A mild with rich flavours, lightly-balanced with hops. The aroma is chocolate with a dry roast and liquorice flavour.

Fenman Bitter (OG 1043, ABV 4.1%)
A traditional, copper-coloured best bitter with well-balanced flavours from the English malt and hops.

Rolling Stone (OG 1044, ABV 4.3%)
A pale ale hopped with new British hop varieties.

Red Windmill (OG 1045, ABV 4.4%)
A red-coloured ale brewed with a spicy rye malt and complemented with fruity hops.

King John's Jewels (OG 1045, ABV 4.5%)

Millstone (OG 1046, ABV 4.5%)
A premium bitter with a good balance of malt and hops.

Windy Miller (OG 1047, ABV 4.6%)
A rich, dark-coloured, smooth-flavoured stout.

Fen Slodger (OG 1047, ABV 4.8%)

Damson Porter (OG 1053, ABV 5%)
Full-bodied, fruity, rich, complex flavours from the addition of damsons. A bitter aroma with caramel tones, and a malty, slightly fruity taste, with a bitter finish.

Victorian Porter (OG 1053, ABV 5%)
An aroma of berries, sour fruits and roasted malts, and deep, intense, chocolatey flavours give this dark beer a rich and full-bodied flavour. Brewed to a Victorian recipe.

Old Colony – Deacon John Ales (OG 1052, ABV 5.3%)
An American-style pale ale.

Black Widow (OG 1054, ABV 5.5%)
A strong, dark ruby-coloured mild. Dark malt and liquorice flavours dominate.

John Barleycorn IPA (OG 1053, ABV 5.5%)

81 Artisan

The Courtyard, Crowshall Farm, Chilgrove Road, West Dean, West Sussex, PO18 9HP
☎ (01243) 527444 🌐 81artisan.com

Brewing began in 2017 using a 10-barrel plant.

9 Lives

Unit 303, Ystradgynlais Workshops, Trawsffordd Road, Ystradgynlais, SA9 1BS ☎ 07743 559736
🌐 9livesbrewing.co.uk

9 Lives was established in 2017 by Robert Scott, formerly the brewer at the now defunct Bryncelyn Brewery, using the same six-barrel plant. A number of beers are replications of former Bryncelyn recipes, which have been renamed. !! ♦ RAIB

Amber (OG 1039, ABV 4%)
Pale amber in colour with a hoppy aroma. A refreshing hoppy, fruity flavour with balancing bitterness; a similar lasting finish. A beer full of flavour for its gravity.

Dark (OG 1040, ABV 4%)
Dark brown-coloured ale with an inviting aroma of malt, roast and fruit. A gentle bitterness mixes roast with malt, hops and fruit, giving a complex, satisfying and lasting finish.

Gold (OG 1045, ABV 4.5%)
An inviting aroma of hops, fruit and malt, and a golden colour. The tasty mix of hops, fruit, bitterness and background malt ends with a long, hoppy, bitter aftertaste. Full-bodied and drinkable.

Hot Tin Roof (OG 1045, ABV 4.5%)
A smooth-tasting copper red-coloured ale, with caramel malt, juicy fruit aromas, and a dry hoppy finish.

Pale (OG 1045, ABV 4.7%)
A light amber-coloured ale with a citrus hop aroma and tropical fruit flavour. Hoppy with a dry, bitter finish.

Special (OG 1050, ABV 5%)
A premium chestnut-coloured extra special bitter with a fruity aroma. Full-bodied, with hop balanced bitterness.

A-B InBev UK

Porter Tun House, 500 Capability Green, Luton, Bedfordshire, LU1 3LS
☎ (01582) 391166 🌐 inbev.com

No real ale.

Abbey SIBA

Abbey Brewery, Camden Row, Bath, BA1 5LB
☎ (01225) 444437 🌐 abbeyales.co.uk

Founded in 1997 Abbey Ales was the first brewery in Bath for more than 50 years. It supplies more than 80 regular outlets within a 20-mile radius and its beers are more widely available in the South West via wholesalers. Four pubs are operated in Bath. ♦

Bath Best (OG 1040, ABV 4%)
A good balance of malt and hops. Sweet on the nose, with a bitter finish.

Bath Pale Ale (ABV 4.2%)

Bellringer (OG 1042, ABV 4.2%)
A notably hoppy ale, light to medium-bodied, clean-tasting, refreshingly dry, with a balancing sweetness. Citrus, pale malt aroma and a dry, bitter finish.

Abbey Grange

See Llangollen

Abbeydale SIBA

Unit 8, Aizlewood Road, Sheffield, South Yorkshire, S8 0YX
☎ (0114) 281 2712 🌐 abbeydalebrewery.co.uk

Established in 1996, Abbeydale, the second oldest brewery in Sheffield, produces more than 220-barrels a week. Substantial recent investment and expansion has enabled growth and a new on-site events space. In addition to the core range, the brew team produce at least one new beer weekly. While many are widely available, some small batch brews are subsequently barrel-aged in Abbeydale's 'Funk Dungeon' project. Two pubs are owned; the Rising Sun, Nether Green, and the Devonshire Cat, Sheffield. ♦ GF

Daily Bread (OG 1037, ABV 3.8%)
A classic copper-coloured English bitter. Well-balanced with a smooth finish.

Deception (OG 1043, ABV 4.1%)
A pale-coloured beer with aromas of elderflower and grapes. Strong citrus flavours, especially grapefruit, and a long-lasting bitter finish.

Heathen (OG 1040, ABV 4.1%)
Refreshing American-style pale ale with tropical fruit flavours and a pleasant citrus bitterness.

Moonshine (OG 1041.2, ABV 4.3%)
A well-balanced pale ale with a full hop aroma and pleasant grapefruit traces.

Absolution (OG 1050, ABV 5.3%)
A fruity pale ale, deceptively drinkable for its strength. Sweetish but not cloying.

Black Mass (OG 1065, ABV 6.7%)
A strong, black-coloured stout with complex roast flavours and a lasting bitter finish.

Abernyte

South Latch Farm, Abernyte, Perthshire, PH14 9SU
☎ 07827 715915 🌐 abernytebrewery.com

Brewing began in 2016. No real ale.

Abington

Buckingham Garden Centre, Tingewick Road, Buckingham, MK18 4AE 🌐 abingtonales.com

Started by Peter Brown as a home brewery, commercial production began in 2016 in 50-litre batches at the family garden centre in

Buckingham. Beer is sold in bottles exclusively at the garden centre. ☞ RAIB

Abstract Jungle

Unit 14, Bailey Brook Industrial Estate, Amber Drive, Langley Mill, Derbyshire, NG16 4BE ☎ 07481 849332

Office: 2 Manor Farm Mews, Brinsley, Notts, NG16 5AG ✉ simon@abstractjunglebrewery.co.uk

Set up in 2016 by experienced head brewer Simon King, Abstract Jungle is a husband-and-wife team. A range of core beers is brewed on a custom-built six-barrel plant along with occasional beers that stretch the boundaries of modern day brewing. Its taphouse is the Bunny Hop, Langley Mill. ‼☞

Abstract Bitter (OG 1041, ABV 3.9%)
Copper-coloured bitter, traditional malt base and a soft hop profile.

Foolish (OG 1040.5, ABV 3.9%)
An easy-drinking session pale ale.

Pride (OG 1040, ABV 3.9%)
Crisp and clean pale ale, low mellow bitterness and a tropical aroma.

Jackal (OG 1043, ABV 4.2%)
Traditional-style porter with a subtle, spicy aroma.

Easy American Brown (OG 1045, ABV 4.4%)
Biscuit, caramel and chocolate notes with subtle hop flavours.

Restless (OG 1045, ABV 4.5%)
A hoppy session ale, resinous and fruity.

Casual (OG 1048, ABV 4.6%)
A bold, complex stout, using unrefined chocolate and with a hint of blueberries.

Sturdy (OG 1054, ABV 5.6%)
A classic hoppy IPA. Pine resinous and citrus fruits.

Abyss SIBA

Unit 12, Squires Farm Industrial Estate, Palehouse Common, Framfield, East Sussex, TN22 5RB
☎ (01825) 840561 ☎ 07919 445 345
⊕ abyssbrewing.co.uk

⊠ This small two-man brewery started in 2017 and moved into its present premises later the same year, using an eight-barrel plant purchased from Black Cat when it ceased brewing. As well as a core range, the brewery often produces experimental brews. Beers are only available in KeyKeg and cans at present, but the intention is to produce cask beers as the business develops.

Accidental (NEW)

☒ The Old Stables, Bulk Street, Lancaster, LA1 1PU
⊕ accidentalbrewery.com

Brewpub located on the edge of Lancaster city centre in an 18th century converted stable block. A 140-litre brewplant is used.

Acorn SIBA

Unit 3, Aldham Industrial Estate, Mitchell Road, Wombwell, Barnsley, South Yorkshire, S73 8HA
☎ (01226) 270734 ⊕ acorn-brewery.co.uk

☺Acorn was set up in 2003 with a 10-barrel expanding to a 20-barrel plant when the brewery moved to larger premises. It currently has a 160-barrel a week capacity. All beers are produced using the Barnsley Bitter yeast strain, dating back to the 1850s. ‼☞♦RAIB

Yorkshire Pride (OG 1037, ABV 3.7%) ◆
This session beer is golden in colour with pleasing fruit notes. A mouth-watering blend of malt and hops create a fruity taste which leads to a clean bitter finish.

Barnsley Bitter (OG 1038, ABV 3.8%) ⊡ ⊟ ◆
This brown-coloured bitter has a smooth, malty bitterness throughout, with notes of chocolate and caramel. Fruity bitter finish.

Blonde (OG 1040.5, ABV 4%) ◆
A clean-tasting, golden-coloured hoppy beer with a refreshing bitter and fruity aftertaste.

Barnsley Gold (OG 1041.5, ABV 4.3%) ◆
This golden ale has fruit in the aroma, with a hoppy and fruity flavour throughout. A well-hopped, clean, dry finish.

Old Moor Porter (OG 1045, ABV 4.4%) ◆
A rich-tasting, moreish porter, smooth throughout with a hint of chocolate and liquorice.

Gorlovka Imperial Stout (OG 1058, ABV 6%) ⊟ ◆
This black-coloured stout is rich, smooth and full of chocolate and liquorice flavours, with a fruity creamy finish.

Ad Hop

18 Severs Street, Liverpool, L6 5HJ ☎ 07957 165501

Ad Hop started life in 2014 at the Clove Hitch pub, moving a couple of times before ending up in much larger premises in 2017 where a 5.5-barrel plant was added to its existing 2.5-barrel one. ♦RAIB V

Liver Bird (OG 1042, ABV 4.2%)
A pale ale with slight pine notes leading to a crisp finish and a hint of a pepper bite.

Merseyful (OG 1042, ABV 4.2%)
A rich bitter with a fruity nose.

Paddy's Wigwam (OG 1045, ABV 4.6%)
Pale ale with a bitter mouthfeel leading to a sharp, hoppy finish.

Robusta (OG 1052, ABV 5%)
A full-bodied, rich and robust porter with deep roast flavours and rich coffee notes.

Enigma (OG 1053, ABV 5.5%)
An unfined, single-hopped IPA with fruity hop notes.

Equinox (OG 1052, ABV 5.5%)
A single-hopped, American-style IPA. Floral and citrus notes with a hint of pine lead to a crisp, peppery finish.

Adnams SIBA

Sole Bay Brewery, East Green, Southwold, Suffolk, IP18 6JW
☎ (01502) 727200 ☎ 07787 151311
⊕ adnams.co.uk

⊠ Established in 1872 and still based in Southwold, Suffolk. More than 35 pubs are owned around East Anglia, with national distribution. Beers are from a 300-barrel plant within the confines of the present site. ‼☞♦

Lighthouse (OG 1037, ABV 3.4%) ◆

A quaffable beer with bitterness predominating.

Southwold Bitter (OG 1037, ABV 3.7%) ◆
Aromas of toffee apple, caramel and sulphur. Taste is a complex mix of malt toffee and roast bitterness with hops. Malty bitter and apple flavours linger into the aftertaste.

Mosaic (OG 1041, ABV 4.1%) ◆
Tropical fruit on the nose and an intensely fruity flavour with complex hop characteristics, which linger in the aftertaste.

Ghost Ship (OG 1046, ABV 4.5%)
A pale ale with an assertive pithy bitterness, biscuit flavours and a fresh citrus aroma.

Broadside (OG 1049, ABV 4.7%) ◆
Rich, malty aroma with blackberries and dried fruit. Rich and full flavours of malt and fruit with roast and caramel notes and subtle hops. Well-balanced, long-lasting aftertaste.

Adur

Brick Barn, Charlton Court, Mouse Lane, Steyning, West Sussex, BN44 3DG
☎ (01903) 867614

Office: 2 Sullington Way, Shoreham-by-Sea, BN43 6PJ
adurvalleycoop.com

Adur Brewery, nestled in the heart of the South Downs, was launched in 2008 on a 5.5-barrel plant, marking the return of brewing to the Adur Valley after an interval of nearly 100 years. The brewery was sold to the Adur Valley Co-Operative in 2012, including the Adur Brewery name and recipes. A large part of the output is sold as bottle-conditioned beer. !! ♦ RAIB

Ropetackle Golden Ale (OG 1036, ABV 3.4%)
A light, golden ale with an initial sweetness and delicate aroma balanced by a dry finish.

Hop Token: Amarillo (OG 1040, ABV 4%)
An amber-coloured bitter with notes of peach and grapefruit in both aroma and taste, a good bitterness and a long, dry finish.

Hop Token: Summit (OG 1040, ABV 4%)
Hints of tangerine in the aroma and flavour.

Velocity (OG 1044, ABV 4.4%)
Traditional best bitter with a hoppy aroma and a hint of marmalade in the taste.

Black William (OG 1055, ABV 5%)
A rich, black-coloured stout with dark chocolate aromas and roasted flavours.

Robbie's Red (OG 1050, ABV 5.2%)
A strong, red-brown-coloured ale with an aroma of malt and hops. Slight initial sweetness leads into complex flavours including smoky orange peel, and a satisfying bitterness which persists into the long finish.

Affinity

Arch 7, Almond Road, South Bermondsey, London, SE16 3LR affinitybrewco.com

Established in 2016 using a 2.5-barrel plant, Affinity moved from Tottenham to South Bermondsey in 2017 becoming part of the popular Bermondsey Beer Mile. Beers are mainly available in keg format and they organise a cask ale festival each March. Taproom open at weekends.

Ainsty SIBA

Manor Farm, Intake Lane, Acaster Malbis, York, North Yorkshire, YO23 3UJ
☎ (01904) 703233 ☎ 07983 604989
ainstyales.co.uk

Established in 2014 as a cuckoo brewery, its own 10-barrel brewery opened in 2016 in the ancient York and Ainsty Wappentake, a few miles south-west of York. Homegrown hops are used in the beers, which can be found in York, across Yorkshire and as distant as the South of England. !! ♦

Ainsty Angel (ABV 3.7%)
An easy-drinking, session pale ale with a refreshing clean and smooth finish.

Flummoxed Farmer (ABV 4%)
A light blonde ale with a grapefruit and tropical nose, giving a refreshing and slightly hoppy, dry finish.

Bantam Best (ABV 4.2%)
Slightly sweet with a crisp bitter finish.

Ainsty Assassin (ABV 4.9%)
Oatmeal stout with a smooth and slightly sweet finish.

AJ's

Unit 12, Ashmore Industrial Estate, Longacre Street, Walsall, West Midlands, WS2 8QG ☎ 07860 585911
ajs-ales@hotmail.com

AJ's was established in 2015 and use a four-barrel plant with three fermenting vessels and a cool room. It brews three times a week and mainly supplys local Black Country pubs, local wholesalers and Wetherspoon pubs. ♦

Blackjack Mild (ABV 3.6%)

Stuck on Blondes (ABV 3.9%)

Best Bitter (OG 1040, ABV 4%)

Dukey's Delight (ABV 4.1%)

Go-a-ld (ABV 4.1%)

SPA (OG 1042, ABV 4.2%)

Stuck in the Mud (ABV 4.3%)

Ruby (OG 1044, ABV 4.4%)

IPA (ABV 4.6%)

Stuck in the Doghouse (ABV 4.7%)

Alcazar

See Shipstone's

Aldwark Artisan

Lydgate Farm, Aldwark, Matlock, Derbyshire, DE4 4HW
☎ (01629) 540720 ☎ 07834 353807
aaabrewery.co.uk

Housed in an old milking shed on a rural working farm, this 10-barrel plant produced its first beers in 2017 using water from the farm's own borehole.

Aldwark Pale IPA (OG 1046, ABV 4.8%)

Alechemy SIBA

Unit B, 1 Gregory Road, Kirkton Campus, Livingston, EH54 7DR
☎ (01506) 413634 ☎ 07748 156973
alechemy.beer

Dr James Davies, a keen traditional brewer and chemist, started brewing in 2012. A 12-barrel plant is used. New beers are being produced regularly. Beers can be found in shops and pubs across the UK. Alechemy is now part of the Consolidated Craft Breweries group, which opened its first bar in 2019, the Froth & Flame in Edinburgh. ♦RAIB

Charisma (OG 1036, ABV 3.7%)
A pale-coloured session IPA.

Ritual (OG 1042, ABV 4.1%)
Well-balanced golden ale. A strong hop character, balanced by malt and fruit with a long and dry finish.

Photon (OG 1043, ABV 4.2%)
Light pale ale with lots of American hops.

Five Sisters (OG 1045, ABV 4.3%)
Flavoursome tawny-coloured beer with an excellent balance of malt, hops and fruit plus hints of roast and caramel. Lingering distinctive finish.

10 Storey Malt Bomb (OG 1049, ABV 4.5%)
Modern take on a traditional 80/- using 10 different malts.

Bad Day at the Office (OG 1047, ABV 4.5%)

Secret Citra (OG 1056, ABV 5.7%)
Heavily-hopped pale ale, bursting with grapefruit and tangerine aromas. A pleasant bitter aftertaste.

Ales of Scilly

2b Porthmellon Industrial Estate, St Mary's, Isles of Scilly, TR21 0JY ☎ 07737 721599 alesofscilly.co.uk

Opened in 2001, Ales of Scilly is the most south-westerly brewery in Britain. Several island pubs are supplied, plus a number of outlets on the mainland and beer festivals across the country. Special one-off beers are produced in celebration of significant island events. !! ♦

Schiller (OG 1038, ABV 3.9%)
A hoppy session pale ale.

Challenger (OG 1039, ABV 4.2%)
Amber-coloured best bitter with faint malt and hop nose. A refreshing, light beer with apricot flavours throughout and gentle malty bitterness.

Association (OG 1045, ABV 4.5%)
A fruity and hoppy IPA.

Nancy (OG 1046, ABV 4.6%)
Full-flavoured, mid-amber coloured bitter.

Alfred's

Unit 6, Winnall Farm Industrial Estate, Easton Lane, Winchester, Hampshire, SO23 0HA
☎ (01962) 859999 alfredsbrewery.co.uk

Alfred's is a nine-barrel, state-of-the-art brewery, located close to the centre of Winchester. Production of Saxon Bronze is complemented by returning favourites and experimental beers. !! ♦

Saxon Bronze (OG 1038, ABV 3.8%)
A well-balanced, crisp and refreshing session ale.

All Day

Salle Brewery Barns 14-16, Salle Moor Hall Farm, Wood Dalling Road, Salle, Norfolk, NR10 4SB
☎ (01603) 327656 ☎ 07825 604887
alldaybrewing.co.uk

Located in a 400-year-old barn, the brewery also has its own hop garden on the farm site and an adjoining organic orchard. Its taproom bar and kitchen – serving vegan beer, fermented foods, real cider, and raw kombucha – are open throughout the spring and summer months, culminating in the Norfolk Hop Festival in September. !! ♦RAIB V

All Hallows

Main Street, Goodmanham, East Yorkshire, YO43 3JA
☎ (01430) 873849 goodmanhamarms.co.uk

Abbie Logozzi, landlady of the Goodmanham Arms, started brewing in 2012 in outbuildings behind the pub. The ex-Goodmanham Brewery buildings were purchased and a five-barrel plant installed. The brewery name comes from the adjacent 12th-century All Hallows Church. Local legendary characters are used in the naming of some of the beers. Brews are supplied to the pub and its sister pub, the Bay Horse, Burythorpe. ♦

All Nations (NEW)

20 Coalport Road, Madeley, Telford, TF7 5SU
☎ (01952) 585747 allnationsinn@btinternet.com

A famous brewpub established in 1832 and run by just two families for the first 151 years. The latest 10-barrel plant has brewed since 2016.

Bitter (ABV 3.8%)

Eliza Lewis (ABV 4.2%)

Traction Bitter (ABV 4.6%)

Allanwater

Queens Lane, Bridge of Allan, FK9 4NY
☎ (01786) 834555 ☎ 07831 224242
allanwaterbrewhouse.co.uk

Originally named Tinpot and then Wash House, the brewery was established in 2009 using a one-barrel plant designed to brew speciallity beer. From 2018 all beers and branding are under the Allanwater Brewhouse name. The beer range varies depending on season and demand, which is increasing every year. !! ♦RAIB GF

Allendale SIBA

Allen Mill, Allendale, Northumberland, NE47 9EA
☎ (01434) 618686 allendalebrewery.com

Established in 2006, the brewery is a 20-barrel plant in a historic lead smelting mill in the heart of the North Pennines Area of Outstanding Natural Beauty. Many of the beers reflect the heritage and identity of the local area. !! ♦GF

Wagtail Best Bitter (OG 1037, ABV 3.8%)
Amber-coloured bitter with spicy aromas and a long, bitter finish.

Golden Plover (OG 1039, ABV 4%)

Light, refreshing, easy-drinking blonde beer with a clean finish.

Pennine Pale (OG 1040, ABV 4%)
Pale ale with a full fruity aroma and flavour, and a refreshing citrus finish.

GFPA (Gluten Free Pale Ale) (ABV 4.7%)

Wolf (OG 1053, ABV 5.5%) ◆
Full-bodied, red-coloured ale with bitterness in the taste giving way to a fruity finish.

AllGates

See Wigan

Almasty

Unit 11, Algernon Industrial Estate, New York Road, Shiremoor, NE27 0NB
☎ (0191) 253 1639 🌐 almasty.co.uk

⊗ Opened in 2014, this two-man operated, 10-barrel plant produces an ever-changing range of unfined, unfiltered beers. A barrel-ageing programme is also in place. Twice yearly open days are held (spring and summer). Pumpclips are made from screen-printed, hand-sawn logs. The brewery tap is the Free Trade Inn, Byker, while the beers are supplied nationwide. ‼ ♦

Alpha State (NEW)

The Heath, Horsmonden, Kent, TN12 8JE

Alpha State was founded in 2012 by brewer Jonathan Queally, producing mainly bottled beer. In 2019 it launched a range of beer produced in collaboration with comedian Bob Mortimer. RAIB

Alphabet SIBA

99 Northern Western Street, Ardwick, Manchester, M12 6JL
☎ (0161) 272 6532 🌐 alphabetbrewing.co.uk

Alphabet began brewing in 2014 and is situated in Manchester city centre under railway arches. It has a 1,344-barrel capacity, with a 15-barrel kit, and 11 fermenting vessels. It focuses mainly on keg and KeyKeg beers, which are unflitered and unpasteurised. The brewery also cans its own beers on site. A brewery tap is open every Friday and Saturday.

Alphabeta

Pittcue, 1 The Avenue, Devonshire Square, Aldgate, London, EC2M 4YP
☎ (020) 7324 7770 🌐 pittcue.co.uk/bar

⊗ Alphabeta is a small in-house brewery at the front of the Pittcue restaurant, visible behind the bar. A wide range of small-batch beers is available on cask and keg. Brewing suspended after closure of the Pittcue restaurant. ♦

Altarnun

Inner Trenarrett, Altarnun, Launceston, Cornwall, PL15 7SY
☎ (01566) 86069 🌐 penpontbrewery.co.uk

⊗ Formerly known as Penpont, Altarnan began brewing in 2008 and has steadily increased its range and production since then. The award-winning brewery currently uses a 25-barrel plant, with an eight-barrel plant for special brews. Beers are available in pubs across Cornwall. Beer is also brewed under the Firebrand Brewing label.
‼ 🛒 ♦ RAIB

St Nonna's (OG 1037, ABV 3.7%) ◆
Tawny-coloured session bitter with floral nose and balanced malt and hop bitterness throughout, with roast and sweet notes. Bitter finish.

Cornish Arvor (OG 1040, ABV 4%) ◆
Golden-coloured bitter with good malt and pine/resin/earth hop presence. Complex mix of stone fruit and esters. Dry finish.

Creation Pale Ale (OG 1039.2, ABV 4.2%) ◆
Gold-coloured bitter with hop aroma. Quite hoppy taste with sweet peach, citrus zing and roast malt. Bitter, slightly dry finish.

Shipwreck Coast (OG 1044, ABV 4.4%) ◆
Gold-coloured best bitter with sweet malt well-balanced by citrus/tropical fruits hop flavour. Dry finish.

Roughtor (OG 1047, ABV 4.7%) ◆
Copper-coloured strong bitter with malt and citrus hop aroma. Hop bitterness balanced by malt, plum and marmalade. Bitter, dry finish.

Beast of Bodmin (OG 1046.5, ABV 5%) ◆
Tawny-coloured strong ale. Burnt sugar, tobacco, leather and stone fruit flavours. Mellow toffee/caramel and earthy hop finish.

Stormer IPA (OG 1046.7, ABV 5.2%)
A full-bodied, American-style IPA.

Brewed under the Firebrand Brewery name:

Big Hop, Little Beer (OG 1035, ABV 3.6%)
A golden-coloured malty ale, with a fruity aroma and taste.

Cross Pacific Pale Ale (ABV 4%)
This pale ale has a malty taste, which gives way to a burst of flavour.

Graffiti IPA (ABV 5%)
A smooth, malty body, generously hopped, leading to a fruity finish.

Amazing

Ship Inn, 65 High Street, Sandgate, Kent, CT20 3AH
☎ (01303) 248525

⊗ Amazing was set up in 2016 using a four-barrel plant and is situated at the Ship Inn, Sandgate. The pub and local beer festivals are supplied. The brewery can be viewed from inside the pub. ‼

Amber SIBA

Unit 7, Outram Business Centre, Whiteley Rd, Ripley, Derbyshire, DE5 3QL
☎ (01773) 512864 🌐 amberales.co.uk

⊗ Amber Ales began production in 2006 on a five-barrel plant from the Firkin brewpub chain. Around 100 outlets are supplied in the Derby/Nottingham/Chesterfield area, further afield via distributors. ‼ ♦ RAIB

Sunrise (ABV 3.8%)

Chocolate Orange Stout (OG 1040, ABV 4%)
Stout, with additional chocolate malt and Curacao orange peel. Vanilla pods are added during

fermentation, and yet more orange is added into each cask.

Original Black Stout (OG 1040, ABV 4%)
Traditional stout, full-flavoured, yet smooth and easy-drinking base, with a subtle hop aroma.

Barnes Wallis (OG 1040, ABV 4.1%)
A copper-coloured, easy-drinking, IPA-style bitter, with a full malt flavour.

Revolution (OG 1047, ABV 4.5%)
Spicy golden ale with a touch of rye, and a hoppy, citrus-packed flavour explosion

Dambuster (OG 1051, ABV 5.5%)
Well-hopped golden ale.

Imperial IPA (OG 1058, ABV 6.5%)
Traditional IPA with a substantial malty base and a big hop profile.

Ambridge

Unit 2a, Priory Piece Business Park, Priory Farm Lane, Inkberrow, Worcestershire, WR7 4HT ☎ 07500 046391 ⊕ ambridgebrewery.co.uk

⊛Ambridge commenced brewing in 2013, initially for the family pub, The Bulls Head in Inkberrow. Expansion was achieved by acquiring the Wyre Piddle Brewery. The range of beers has continued to change with specials brewed especially to support charity/events. Some small run bottling is also carried out. ‼♦RAIB

Flower Power (OG 1040, ABV 4%)

Sticky Dog (OG 1040, ABV 4%)
Smooth and easy-drinking ale with a citrus hop aroma and a refreshing, not too bitter finish.

Best Bitter (OG 1043, ABV 4.3%)

Ampersand SIBA

Camphill Farm, Middle Road, Earsham, Norfolk, NR35 2AH ☎ 07791 086689 ⊕ ampersandbrew.co

A small batch brewery established in 2017 and based on a family farm in South Norfolk.

Amwell Springs SIBA

Westfield Farm House, Cholsey, Oxfordshire, OX10 9LS ☎ 07812 396619 ⊕ asbco.co.uk

Brewing began in 2017 on a 70-litre plant using water from a spring in the farmhouse grounds. Capacity expanded in 2019 to six barrels. Beers are available in local pubs. RAIB

Chairman Dave (ABV 3.5%)
Sweet, crisp, session pale ale with a zesty bitterness complemented by a floral hop flavour.

Stay Jammy (ABV 3.8%)
Soft sweetness with mint and berry hops bursting through.

Easy Geez (ABV 4.5%)
Well-balanced, amber-coloured ale with a subtle pine and citrus aroma that complements the malty caramel tones.

Mad Gaz (ABV 5.2%)
IPA packed full of grapefruit and resinous flavours. Floral aroma with a refreshing, bitter finish.

Anarchy SIBA

Unit A1, Benfield Business Park, Newcastle upon Tyne, NE6 4NQ
☎ (0191) 380 4028 ☎ 07702 810111
⊕ anarchybrewco.com

Originally a 10-barrel plant based on the outskirts of Morpeth, the brewery moved to new premises in 2018, upgrading to a 30-barrel plant with a taproom. Run by an enthusiastic team producing a range of hand-crafted beers and lagers with big, bold flavours. RAIB

Smoke Bomb (OG 1043, ABV 3.9%)
Unfined and unfiltered bitter with a light, smoky nose and Bavarian smoked ham, and citrus flavours matched with dark, smooth toffee malts.

Blonde Star (OG 1041, ABV 4.1%)
Lemon, grapefruit, passion fruit flavours from the hops combine with pale malts to give a crisp, and fresh light-bodied session blonde.

Citra Star (OG 1041, ABV 4.1%)
Citrus, grapefruit, lemon, lime and passion fruit hop flavours give a clean, crisp, light-bodied blonde.

Boot Boys (OG 1049, ABV 5%)
Enjoy a kick in the taste buds from this classic northern brown ale. Laced up with rich caramel malt flavours and a nutty finish.

Urban Assault (OG 1050, ABV 5%)
Medium-bodied, light red-coloured pale ale with heavy notes of lemon, orange and passion fruit in the flavour, followed by a bitter finish.

Crime Scene (OG 1056, ABV 5.5%)
Fruit-flavoured, medium-bodied, amber-coloured beer, with a long-lasting bitter aftertaste.

Anti-venom (OG 1057, ABV 6%)
A strong IPA with tropical fruit notes.

Quiet Riot (OG 1063, ABV 6.6%)
Kiwi fruit, lime & orange zest flavours combine to give a big bitterness that is balanced with sweet malts.

Sublime Chaos (OG 1075, ABV 7%)
Liquorice, chocolate and caramel flavoured breakfast stout, infused with Ethiopian Guji natural coffee beans.

Knuckle Dragger (OG 1075, ABV 8.3%)
A double IPA with big tropical fruit flavours and resinous hops.

Andwell SIBA

Andwell Lane, Andwell, Hampshire, RG27 9PA
☎ (01256) 761044 ⊕ andwells.com

⊗Brewing commenced in 2008 on a 10-barrel plant. The brewery relocated and expanded in 2011 to an idyllic riverside location with a new bespoke 20-barrel plant. Beer is distributed within a 40-mile radius to Hampshire, Surrey, Wiltshire, Berkshire, Greater London and the Isle of Wight. More than 200 outlets are supplied. ‼🛒♦

Resolute Bitter (OG 1038, ABV 3.8%) ◆
An easy-drinking session bitter. A malty aroma, leads into an initially malty flavour with some bitterness and sweetish finish.

Gold Muddler (OG 1039, ABV 3.9%) ◆
Light golden-coloured standard bitter. Aroma of hops and malt, which carries into the flavour with solid bitterness and a dry, biscuity finish.

King John (OG 1042, ABV 4.2%) ◆
Malty best bitter, low in hops with short initial bitterness and underlying sweetness, leading to some dryness in the finish.

Ruddy Darter (OG 1047, ABV 4.6%)
A ruby chestnut-coloured ale with a hoppy, spicy aroma. This beer has a full bodied and fruity taste with a dry finish.

Angel

Angel, 7 Stoney Street, Nottingham, NG1 1LG
☎ (0115) 948 3343 🌐 angelmicrobrewery.com

Situated inside one of Nottingham's oldest pubs, the Angel Microbrewery is a 2.5-barrel plant nestled in the taproom. Beers are only available in the pub. Vegan and gluten-free beers are planned.

Angel Ales SIBA

62a Furlong Lane, Halesowen, West Midlands, B63 2TA ☎ 07986 382919 🌐 angelales.co.uk

Angel Ales began commercial brewing in 2011 and is expanding outlets. The brewery building has been a chapel of rest, a coffin makers' workshop and a pattern makers before becoming a brewhouse. Beers are produced using organic materials where possible. ♦ RAIB V

Angel Ale (OG 1042, ABV 4.1%)
Pale-coloured and intensely hopped bitter with a citrus aroma and lingering bitter finish.

Ginger Stout (OG 1048, ABV 4.8%)
A dark-coloured but light-bodied ginger stout brewed with root ginger.

Angels & Demons SIBA

Great Cauldham Farm, Cauldham Lane, Capel-le-Ferne, Kent, CT18 7HQ
☎ (01303) 255666 🌐 fantasticbeer.co.uk

Brewing began in 2016 using a 20-barrel plant. The brewery produces two ranges of beers, the McCanns range of traditional ales and the Angels & Demons range of more experimental brews.

49 Horses (ABV 2.8%)

Bombay Social (ABV 3.8%)

Racing Tiger (ABV 4.2%)

Panama Jazz (ABV 4.8%)

I Spy Dragonfly (ABV 5%)

ADH Me (ABV 5.2%)

Goldilocks is Dead (ABV 5.3%)

Black Taxi to the Moon (ABV 5.4%)

Brewed under the McCanns brand name:

Harry Hop (ABV 3.7%)

Grahams (ABV 4.2%)

Hockley Soul (ABV 4.2%)

Anglesey Brewhouse SIBA

Unit 12, Pen Yr Orsedd, Industrial Estate Road, Parc Bryn Cefni, Llangefni, LL77 7AW
☎ (01248) 345506 ☎ 07748 650368
🌐 angleseybrewhouse.co.uk

Microbrewery established in 2017 in the centre of Anglesey by a former home brewer. Currently producing bottle-conditioned beers sold direct from the brewery or in shops around North Wales. A five-gallon plant is used, but there are plans for expansion. RAIB

Anglesey Brewing

Chwaen Ddu, Carmel, LL71 7DE
☎ (01248) 717734
🌐 angleseybrewingcompany.co.uk

Brewing began in 2014 in Llanbadrig as Bragdy'r Bwthyn, producing bottle-conditioned beers. In 2017 the brewery relocated to Carmel under the Anglesey Brewing Co name and cask production began. Beers are mostly sold at events and outlets across Anglesey. RAIB

Anglo Oregon

3 Traston Lane, Newport, NP19 4RR ☎ 07854 194966
✉ aobrewingco@gmail.com

Originally in Parkend (Forest Of Dean) the brewery moved to its current location in Nash, on the eastern outskirts of Newport, a few years ago. The name comes from the fact one of the owners is English and the other (in whose garage the brewery is located) is from Oregon. Brewing capacity is just 100 litres and only bottle-conditioned ale is brewed (every few weeks, when necessary).

Animal

See XT

Anomaly (NEW)

59 Glebe Gardens, Old Malden, KT3 5RU ☎ 07903 623993 🌐 anomalybrewing.co.uk

Founded in 2017, brewing takes place on a 100-litre home kit. Most production is available locally in bottles but cask is sometimes available at beer festivals.

Witch Doctor (ABV 4.6%)
A breakfast porter with massive coffee and dark chocolate flavours with hints of peanut butter.

Luna-tic (OG 1062, ABV 7%)
A malty blonde beer with hints of passion fruit, thyme and banana.

Anspach & Hobday

118 Druid Street, Bermondsey, London, SE1 2HH
☎ (020) 8617 9510 🌐 anspachandhobday.com

Anspach & Hobday began brewing in 2014, eventually upgrading to its current seven-barrel kit in 2016. It is based in a railway arch along the Bermondsey Beer Mile. The vegan-friendly beers are available bottle-conditioned, in KeyKeg and increasingly in cask. There are plans for expansion. RAIB V

The Smoked Brown (OG 1061, ABV 6%) ◆
Smoked aroma with traces of coffee. Flavour has damsons, toffee, dark chocolate, an underlying smoked character and a lasting dry roastiness.

The Porter (OG 1062, ABV 6.7%) ◆

Black/brown-coloured beer with roasted notes throughout. Caramel, dark fruit and hops in the flavour and finish, which is slightly dry.

The Stout Porter (OG 1080, ABV 8.5%)

Anstey Ale

46a Albion Street, Anstey, Leicestershire, LE7 7DE
☎ 07960 776843 🌐 ansteyale.co.uk

Anstey Ale Brewery started as a one-barrel garage plant in 2015 brewing on a part-time basis. In 2017 it became full-time and upgraded some of the equipment. It moved to new premises in 2017 and increased plant size to 2.5-barrels. An on-site taproom opened in 2019 (open Thu-Sun). Monthly one-off brews are being released under the Anstey and Hijacked Brands. Beers are occasionally available in Leicestershire micropubs and regularly at the Stadon Sports & Social Club. ♦

Daydreamer (OG 1037, ABV 3.7%)
A light pale ale with a smooth mouthfeel and a spicy, floral, grapefruit character.

Bradgate Park Pale Ale (ABV 4%)
A pale ale with a citrus aroma and flavour.

Fluthered (ABV 4.5%)
A caramel and oatmeal Irish-style red-coloured ale. A fruity start gives way to a satisfying, smooth bitterness.

Darkroom (OG 1048, ABV 4.7%)
Well-rounded, triple-hopped stout made with six grain types.

Nook IPA (OG 1051, ABV 5%)

Anthology

Unit 6, Armley Link, Armley Road, Leeds, West Yorkshire, LS12 2QN ☎ 07594975245
🌐 anthologybrewing.co.uk

Established in 2018, Anthology is a small batch brewery based in Leeds with an ever evolving range of beers, and a focus on bold flavours.

Appleby

Unit 10, Castle Mills, Aynam Road, Kendal, Cumbria, LA9 7DE ☎ 07885 171210 🌐 applebybrewery.co.uk

Established by Fred Mills in 2015, the brewery outgrew its original premises in Appleby within a year and moved to a former horse stable in an Eden Valley village in 2016. The beers are available at selected pubs across Cumbria, but mainly in the Eden Valley area. The brewery was taken over in 2018 and moved to shared premises at Bowness Bay Brewery (qv). !! ♦ RAIB

Senior Moment (OG 1039, ABV 3.9%)

Vanya Yam (ABV 4%)
Amber-coloured IPA with a malty taste and a hoppy, citrus finish.

Midlife Crisis (OG 1042, ABV 4.2%)

Middle Aged Spread (OG 1052, ABV 5.2%)
A rich, dark-coloured stout. Nutty, chocolaty and lightly-hopped.

Applecross

c/o Applecross Inn, Shore Street, Applecross, IV54 8LR
☎ (01520) 744262 🌐 applecross.uk.com/inn

A microbrewery co-funded by 14 stakeholders. Brewing is currently suspended.

Arbor SIBA

181 Easton Road, Easton, Bristol, BS5 0HQ
☎ (0117) 329 2711 🌐 arborales.co.uk

Founded in 2007, Arbor has a brew length of 20 barrels and 10 fermenting vessels. Willing to experiment, more than 300 beers have been produced. The current range reflects modern tastes and leans towards hoppy pale ales and IPAs plus some interesting red and dark ales. ♦ RAIB

Pocket Rocket (OG 1038, ABV 3.7%)

Shangri La (OG 1040, ABV 4.2%)
Yellow-coloured best bitter with a hoppy aroma, light malt and tropical fruit on the palate, and a clean, refreshing bitter finish.

Blue Sky Drinking (OG 1043.5, ABV 4.4%)
Malty aroma and background flavour with hints of berry fruits and spice. Hop bitterness increases in the short, balanced finish.

Oz Bomb (OG 1045, ABV 4.7%)
Very hop-forward nose. Citrus and tropical fruit flavours with a powerful bitterness which lingers in the aftertaste.

The Devil Made Me Brew It (OG 1056, ABV 5.5%)
A velvety, stout-style speciality beer. Floral and citrus hops in the aroma, coffee and slightly burnt toffee flavours, sweet but with a bitter finish.

Why Kick A Moo Cow (OG 1052, ABV 5.5%)
A strong, amber-coloured ale with malt and hops on the nose, flavours of tropical fruit, and a dry bittersweet aftertaste.

Yakima Valley (OG 1067, ABV 7%)
A strong, full-bodied IPA. Hoppy and very fruity. Sweetness is well-balanced with bitterness, lasting into a soft bitter aftertaste.

Arcadian

Bridge Studios, 454 Western Avenue, Cardiff, CF5 3BL
☎ 07468612225 🌐 arcadianbrewing.com

Arcadian began brewing in 2018 using a 2.5-barrel brew plant. All beers are unfiltered and unpasteurised and available in keg and bottle.

Archerfield

See Knops

Archers

See Evan Evans

Ards

34B Carrowdore Road, Greyabbey, Newtownards, Co Down, BT22 2LX ☎ 07515 558406
✉ ardsbrewing@blackwood34.plus.com

Ards began brewing in 2011 using a 100-litre plant. A five-barrel plant is now in operation, allowing cask production in addition to the increasing range of bottle-conditioned and KeyKeg beers. Very much a local brewery with beers generally only supplied within a 15-mile radius. RAIB

Citra (OG 1042, ABV 4.8%)

Scrabo Gold (OG 1042, ABV 4.8%)

Hip Hop (OG 1050, ABV 5%)

Pig Island (OG 1052, ABV 5.2%)

Argyll

Unit 8a, Baliscate Industrial Estate, Tobermory, Isle of Mull, PA75 6QA
☎ (01688) 302821
✉ Isleofmullbrewing@btinternet.com

Argyll Breweries was formed in 2010 following the merger of Oban Bay and Isle of Mull breweries, continuing to trade under those names. A small brewing plant now supports the Isle of Mull beers in Tobermory, primarily producing bottles but some cask-conditioned ale is still available.

Brewed under the Isle of Mull Brewery name:

Island Pale Ale (OG 1038, ABV 3.9%)

Galleon Gold (OG 1041, ABV 4.1%)

Red Monk of Iona (OG 1042, ABV 4.2%)

Terror of Tobermory (OG 1045, ABV 4.6%)

Brewed under the Oban Bay Brewery name:

Kilt Lifter (ABV 3.9%)

Skinny Blonde (ABV 4.1%)

Ginger Jakey (ABV 4.2%)

Skelpt Lug (ABV 4.2%)

Fair Puggled (ABV 4.6%)

Arkell's SIBA IFBB

Kingsdown, Swindon, Wiltshire, SN2 7RU
☎ (01793) 823026 🌐 arkells.com

Arkell's Brewery was established in 1843 by John Arkell, and the Arkell family still brew beer in the original Victorian brewhouse. The brewery owns nearly 100 pubs across Wiltshire, Gloucestershire, Oxfordshire, Berkshire, and Hampshire. In 2018 a brewery shop and visitor centre was opened on-site to mark their 175th anniversary. Seasonal beers are brewed frequently, often linked to sporting and other national events. !! ♦

Wiltshire Gold (OG 1038, ABV 3.7%)
A light golden-coloured ale with a satisfyingly sweet, malty flavour. The use of traditional hops give the beer a mellow floral hop aroma, followed by a distinctive hoppy taste.

3B (OG 1040, ABV 4%)
A medium brown-coloured beer with a strong, sweetish malt/ caramel flavour. The hops come through strongly in the aftertaste, which is lingering and dry.

HOPeration IPA (OG 1041, ABV 4.2%)
A powerfully hoppy pale ale with a smooth, rounded finish.

Bee's Organic (OG 1045, ABV 4.5%)
A golden ale with a light, fresh taste, and a hint of honey..

Moonlight (OG 1046, ABV 4.5%)
Auburn-coloured ale with a warm, toasty aroma and distinctive citrus hoppy flavour.

Arran SIBA

Cladach, Brodick, Isle of Arran, KA27 8DE
☎ (01770) 302353

Office: 100 Wellington Street, Glasgow, G2 6DH
🌐 arranbrewery.com

The brewery opened in Brodick in 2000 using a 20-barrel plant with water sourced from the nearby mountains. In 2019 an additional 27-barrel plant was also acquired for installation at its proposed Loch Earn Brewery site. Around 400 outlets around the UK are supplied direct. Beers are also produced under the Devil's Dyke Brewery name. !! ♦ RAIB GF

Guid Ale (OG 1038, ABV 3.8%)
A golden-coloured, refreshing session ale with a delicate balance of malt and fruit

Dark (OG 1042, ABV 4.3%)
A well-balanced, malty beer with plenty of roast and hop in the taste and a dry, bitter finish.

Sunset (OG 1042, ABV 4.4%)
An amber-coloured ale with a light perfumed aroma, good balance of malt, fruit and hops and a pleasant, dry finish.

Blonde (OG 1048, ABV 5%)
A hoppy beer with substantial fruit, balanced taste and an increasingly bitter finish. An aromatic, strong bitter that drinks below its weight.

Brewery Dug (OG 1055, ABV 5.5%)
An American-style IPA with a refreshing citrus body and a dry, lemon zest, bitter finish.

Brewed under the Devil's Dyke Brewery name:

Devil's Blonde (ABV 4%)

Pale Ale (ABV 5%)

Arrow

c/o Wine Vaults, 37 High Street, Kington, Herefordshire, HR5 3BJ
☎ (01544) 230685 ✉ deanewright@yahoo.co.uk

Brewer Deane Wright built this five-barrel brewery at the rear of the Wine Vaults and started brewing in 2005. The Wine Vaults is the only pub outlet for Arrow Bitter.

Art Brew SIBA

Art Brew Barn, Brightwater Farm, Sutcombe, Holsworthy, Devon, EX22 7QE ☎ 07881 783626
✉ artbrewdorset@googlemail.com

Brewing started in 2008 on a five-barrel plant near the Jurassic Coast in Dorset. In 2016, the brewery relocated to a new site in Devon, with a brewery tap, using a 2.5-barrel plant. In addition to its core ales, a rolling programme of seasonal and one-off beers is also available. ♦ RAIB V

Baby Anarchist (OG 1034, ABV 3.2%)

Pale (OG 1034, ABV 3.2%)

Outsider Ale (OG 1042, ABV 4.4%)

Milk Stout (OG 1045, ABV 4.5%)
A sweet stout with added lactose.

Ab6 (OG 1045, ABV 4.6%)

Ginger & Chilli IPA (OG 1055, ABV 6%)

THE BREWERIES

Love Or Nothing (OG 1055, ABV 6%)
Dry-hopped with a bitter finish.

Orange IPA (OG 1055, ABV 6%)
Brewed with orange peel for bitterness.

Anarchist Party Bitter (OG 1068, ABV 7.2%)

Artisan (NEW)

Building 1a, Aston Down Business Park, Minchinhampton, Gloucestershire, GL6 8GA ☎ 07780 449102 🌐 artisan-ales.co.uk

⊗ Artisan Ales is located in a former fire station. Brewing began in 2018. ‼

PA03 (ABV 3.6%)

BB01 (ABV 3.7%)

PA02 (ABV 3.9%)

BB02 (ABV 4.2%)

PA04 (ABV 4.7%)

PA01 (ABV 4.9%)

DB01 (ABV 5.2%)

Arundel SIBA

Unit C7, Ford Airfield Industrial Estate, Ford, Arundel, West Sussex, BN18 0HY
☎ (01903) 733111 🌐 arundelbrewery.co.uk

⊗ Founded in 1992, Arundel Brewery is the historic town's first brewery in 70 years. A brewery shop opened in 2014 by the quayside with a good selection of beers, both its own and from other breweries. It also brews for the Bison Crafthouse, Brighton. ‼ ♦

Black Stallion (OG 1037, ABV 3.7%)
A dark mild with well-defined chocolate and roast character. The aftertaste is not powerful, but the initial flavours remain in the clean finish.

Castle (OG 1038, ABV 3.8%)
A pale tawny-coloured beer with fruit and malt noticeable in the aroma. A good balance of malt, fruit and hops in taste, with a dry, hoppy finish.

Sussex Gold (OG 1042, ABV 4.2%)
A golden-coloured best bitter with a strong floral hop aroma. The ale is clean-tasting and bitter for its strength, with a tangy citrus flavour. The initial hop and fruit die to a dry and bitter finish.

Sussex IPA (OG 1045, ABV 4.5%)
Formerly known as Heritage IPA. A special bitter with a complex roast malt flavour leading to a fruity, hoppy, bittersweet finish.

Stronghold (OG 1047, ABV 4.7%)
A smooth, full-flavoured premium bitter. A good balance of malt, fruit and hops comes through in this rich, chestnut-coloured beer.

Wild Heaven (OG 1052, ABV 5.2%)
A full-flavoured, American-style pale ale with strong grapefruit, orange and lime notes resulting in a lingering, dry, bitter finish.

Ascot SIBA

Unit 5, Compton Place Business Centre, Surrey Avenue, Camberley, Surrey, GU15 3DX
☎ (01276) 686696 🌐 ascotbrewing.co.uk

⊗ Ascot started production in 2007 on a four-barrel plant in a small industrial unit. The brewery has successfully expanded over the years and 2017 saw the brewery with new owners. ‼ ♦ RAIB

Starting Gate (OG 1038, ABV 3.8%)
A pale brown-coloured session bitter with malt flavours present throughout. Dry with a lasting sharp and bitter finish.

Gold Cup (OG 1039, ABV 4%)
A lemony aroma leads to a dry, bitter taste, with more citrus flavours. Hoppy finish with a hint of sweetness.

Final Furlong (OG 1042, ABV 4.2%)
A best bitter with balancing biscuity malt sweetness. Some citrus fruitiness and a clean hoppy aftertaste.

5/4 Favourite (OG 1047, ABV 4.6%)
Some grapefruit in the aroma, hop and bitterness in the taste, and plenty of balancing biscuit in the aroma and aftertaste.

Anastasia's Stout (OG 1049, ABV 5%)
Burnt coffee aromas lead to a roast malt flavour in this black-coloured beer. Notably fruity throughout, with a bittersweet aftertaste.

Yankee (OG 1049, ABV 5%)

Ash Valley

Prince of Wales, Green Tye, nr Much Hadham, Hertfordshire, SG10 6JP
☎ (01279) 842139 ☎ 07966 474730
🌐 thepow.co.uk

⊗ The brewery is part of the Prince of Wales pub in Green Tye, run by the landlord. Most of the beer is sold at the pub and occasional CAMRA beer festivals, and a small amount is swapped with other brewers. A micro pilot brewery is used to produce one-off experimental beers. Brewing is currently suspended.

Ashley Down

c/o 15 Wathen Road, St Andrews, Bristol, BS6 5BY
☎ (0117) 983 6567 ☎ 07563 751200
✉ ashleydownbrewery@gmail.com

⊗ Ashley Down began brewing in 2011 using a 5.5-barrel plant in the owner's garage. It suffered a major fire in 2017 so used spare capacity at other breweries while looking for new premises. Brewing is to restart in the owner's garage during the currency of this Guide. ♦ RAIB

Ashover SIBA

Unit 1, Derby Road Business Park, Clay Cross, Derbyshire, S45 9AG
☎ (01246) 251859 🌐 ashoverbrewery.co.uk

⊗ Brewing began in 2007 on a 3.5-barrel plant in the garage of the cottage next to the Old Poets' Corner, Ashover. Since its acquisition of a 10-barrel brewery in the neighbouring village of Clay Cross in 2015, Ashover now brews at both sites. The brewery serves local freehouses across Derbyshire and further afield as well as the Poets' Corner. ‼ ♦ RAIB

Font (OG 1037, ABV 3.8%)
Thirst-quenching, golden-coloured session beer.

Liquorice (OG 1037, ABV 3.8%)
Dark-coloured stout infused with liquorice root.

Poets Tipple (OG 1041, ABV 4%) ◆
Complex, tawny-coloured beer that drinks above its strength. Predominantly malty in flavour, with increasing bitterness towards the end.

Littlemoor Citra (OG 1041, ABV 4.1%) 🔲
Citra-hopped, pale-coloured session beer.

The Fabrick (OG 1042, ABV 4.4%)
Golden ale with a soft, fruity flavour, full mouthfeel and a crisp, clean finish.

Rainbows End (OG 1045, ABV 4.5%) ◆
Slightly smooth, bitter, golden-coloured beer with an initial sweetness. Grapefruit and lemon hop flavours come through strong. Increasingly dry towards the finish, ending with a bitter, dry aftertaste.

Red Lion (OG 1044, ABV 4.6%)
A full-bodied, red-coloured ale with well-balanced malt complementing the fruity hops.

Coffin Lane Stout (OG 1050, ABV 5%) ◆
Chocolate and coffee flavour is balanced by a little sweetness, with a long and quite dry finish.

Butts Pale Ale (OG 1055, ABV 5.5%) ◆
Pale-coloured and strong, yet easy-drinking, golden-coloured bitter. Combination of bitter and sweet flavours mingle with an alcoholic kick, leading to a warming yet bitter finish and aftertaste.

Zoo (OG 1050, ABV 5.5%)

Milk Stout (OG 1060, ABV 6%)
Smooth, rich, chocolate roasted notes with hints of coffee and caramel. Brewed with the addition of lactose.

Atlantic

Treisaac Farm, Treisaac, Newquay, Cornwall, TR8 4DX
☎ (01637) 880326 ⊕ atlanticbrewery.com

⊠ Specialist microbrewery producing organic and vegan ales. All ales are unfiltered and finings-free. There are nine core brews including four food-matched dining ales developed with Michelin chef Nathan Outlaw. Casks are supplied locally and to London, with bottle-conditioned beers available nationally. ◆RAIB

Azores (OG 1042, ABV 4.2%) ◆
Unfined golden ale. Citrus and resinous hops dominate the aroma and taste, with tropical fruits. Refreshing bitter and dry finish.

Earl Grey PA (OG 1045, ABV 4.5%) ◆
Cloudy amber-coloured organic speciality ale. Hop aroma leads to powerful citrus fruit flavours becoming intense. Fairly bitter and dry.

Elderflower Blonde (OG 1045, ABV 4.5%) ◆
Yellow-coloured, light, crisp floral beer. Floral elderflower and melon nose, and elderflower and gooseberry fruits with soft citrus/ pine hops flavours.

Mandarina Cornovia (OG 1045, ABV 4.5%) ◆
Pale gold-coloured speciality beer with full mandarin citrus fruit flavour matched by firm biscuit malt and resin/ earthy hop notes.

Masala Chai PA (OG 1045, ABV 4.5%)
Classic Indian roadhouse spices and black tea tannings in this pale session ale.

Simcotica (OG 1044, ABV 4.5%)

Vibrant passionfruit and grapefruit throughout this balance pale ale.

Gold (OG 1043, ABV 4.6%) ◆
Golden speciality beer with added ginger. Light aroma of malt. Refreshing hop bitter flavour dominated by strong zingy ginger.

Blue (OG 1045, ABV 4.8%) ◆
Smooth, rich porter with heavy roast malt aroma and taste. Smoky liquorice, bitter coffee and chocolate flavours with sweet fruit.

Honey Ale (OG 1046, ABV 4.8%)
A smooth, balanced golden-coloured honey beer.

Red (OG 1047, ABV 5%) ◆
Ruby tawny-coloured strong bitter with natural cloudiness. Complex nutty malt, bitterness and light roast followed by hedgerow fruits. Long bittersweet finish.

Fistral (OG 1048, ABV 5.2%) ◆
Full-flavoured, copper-coloured wheat beer. Sweet, stone fruit flavours blend with biscuit malt and citrus hops. Malt finish with hops and dryness.

Atlas

See Orkney

Atom

Unit 4, Food & Tech Park, Malmo Road, Sutton Fields Industrial Estate, Hull, East Yorkshire, HU7 0YF
☎ (01482) 820572 ⊕ atombeers.com

⊠ Atom Brewing Co, a science-focused brewery, has an ethos built on science and education, working with local colleges to inspire the next generation of scientists with brewing schools and classes. All beers are unfined, and unfiltered (so naturally hazy). ‼◆V

Schrodingers Cat (OG 1035, ABV 3.5%)
An American-style, amber-coloured beer with a big hop hit.

Blonde Ale (OG 1040, ABV 4%)
A fresh, smooth, easy-drinking, pale-coloured beer with citrus notes.

Quantum State (OG 1040, ABV 4.2%)
A session IPA, light, drinkable and full of citrus flavours.

Dark Matter (OG 1045, ABV 4.5%)
A rich and smooth oatmeal stout, brewed with Peruvian cacao nibs and sea salt, with notes of milk chocolate, coffee and soft roast.

Atomic

⧓ c/o Alexandra Arms, 72-73 James Street, Rugby, Warwickshire, CV21 2SL
☎ (01788) 578660 ☎ 07876 195895
⊕ atomicbrewery.com

Founded in 2006, by Nick Pugh and Keith Abbis, Atomic is located in the Alexandra Arms' outbuildings. The six-barrel plant, supplied by David Porter Brewing, was initially leased to them by the pub landlord, who also brewed Alex Ales on it. They acquired the Victoria Inn in 2007. At the end of 2010 the Alexandra Arms was put up for sale, threatening the existence of Atomic, but after some bargaining they bought their second freehold property including the brewery. ‼◆

Attic (NEW)

29b Mary Vale Road, Stirchley, Birmingham, B30 2DA
🌐 atticbrewco.com

A natural progression from homebrewing, Attic Brewery Co was launched in 2018 by two friends. Its taproom is open Friday evening and all day Saturday. Beer is mostly available in the tap but there are plans to expand into the local trade market. **V**

Aurora

Unit 6, Gallows Industrial Park, off Furnace Road, Ilkeston, Derbyshire, DE7 5EP ☎ 07740783631

Aurora was established in 2016. Joint owner Mark Derbyshire, formerly of Hardy & Hanson's, brews on a 10-barrel plant. Many local outlets, and a few further away, are supplied direct. The brewery swaps beers with other breweries throughout the UK, many of which can be found in its micropub, the Ilson Tap.

Austendyke

The Beeches, Austendyke Road, Weston Hills, Spalding, Lincolnshire, PE12 6BZ ☎ 07866 045778

Austendyke Ales began brewing in 2012 using a seven-barrel plant. The brewery is operated on a part-time basis by brewer Charlie Rawlings and business partner Nathan Marshall, who handles sales. The brewery owns and runs micropub the Prior's Oven, Spalding.

Long Lane (OG 1039, ABV 4%)

Sheep Market (OG 1040, ABV 4%)

Bakestraw Bitter (OG 1041, ABV 4.1%)

Holbeach High Street (OG 1045, ABV 4.5%)

Hogsgate (OG 1050, ABV 5%)

Autumn

8 East Cliff Road, Spectrum Business Park, Seaham, County Durham, SR7 7PS 🌐 autumnbrewing.co.uk

Autumn produce keg and bottled gluten free beers. No real ale. **GF**

Avid SIBA

Red Moss Farm, Quernmore Brow, Quernmore, LA2 0QW ☎ 07814 206881 🌐 avidbrewing.co.uk

Avid was established in 2015 by two experienced homebrewers. The 7.5-barrel microbrewery is based in picturesque Quernmore, near Lancaster. Water is used from a local borehole.

Golden Ale (OG 1039, ABV 3.9%)
A light bitter with caramel flavours and an earthy, spicy aroma.

American Pale (OG 1040, ABV 4%)
A session ale with refreshing citrus flavours and floral aromas.

New Zealand Pale (OG 1040, ABV 4%)
Well-balanced pale ale with lingering flavour and bitterness, and gooseberry aromas.

Milk Stout (OG 1048, ABV 4.5%)
Well-balanced, smooth, sweet stout with a hint of smokiness and added lactose.

IPA (OG 1050, ABV 5%)
Traditional IPA with strong, resin hop flavours and increased bitterness which are balanced by the sweet malt content.

TropicAle (OG 1050, ABV 5%)
A pale ale with subtle tropical fruit flavours which are more pronounced in the aroma. The inclusion of rye adds a gentle spicy note.

Whisky Vanilla Stout (OG 1070, ABV 7.4%)
Well-balanced stout with added vanilla to soften the finish. The whisky aroma comes from conditioning the beer with whisky-soaked oak cubes.

Axholme SIBA

7 Lakes Country Park, Wharf Road, Crowle, Lincolnshire, DN17 4JS
☎ (01724) 781804

Office: The Church, King Edward Street, Grimsby, Lincolnshire, DN31 3JD 🌐 axholmebrewing.co.uk

Brewing began in 2012 in Scunthorpe using a 2.5-barrel plant. The brewery is now housed at a four-barrel exhibition brewery at 7 Lakes Country Park. Due to rapid expansion a second site opened in 2018. This site, Docks Beers, an exhibition 15-barrel, or 30-hectolitre craft brewery and taproom, is housed in a converted Edwardian Church in Grimsby. Beers are distributed through East Midlands and South Yorkshire. **!! ♦ RAIB**

Magnitude (ABV 3.9%)
A light amber-coloured IPA, robust and well-rounded with heaps of tropical and citrus flavours.

Hard Graft (ABV 4%)
A punchy, piny pale ale underpinned by barley and rye malt, with bold hop flavours.

Cleethorpes Pale Ale (OG 1042, ABV 4.2%)
A refreshing pale ale with crisp, citrus hops and a sweet undertone from sea buckthorn berries.

Lightning Pale Ale (OG 1041, ABV 4.3%)
A refreshing pale ale with heaps of hops and an explosion of fresh citrus flavour notes.

Graveyard Shift (ABV 4.5%)
Chocolate malt and coconut flavours. Lactose additions boost texture and body making for a rich, smooth finish.

Never Say Die (ABV 6%)
A robust, amber-coloured IPA with a tropical and citrus hop kick.

Special Reserve (OG 1066, ABV 7.2%)
Powerful, amber-coloured old ale with flavours of brandy and dried fruits.

Axton

Pentre Lane, Axton, CH8 9DH
☎ (01745) 855657 ☎ 07756 636415

Office: Archies Bar, 151 High Street, Prestatyn, LL19 9AS ✉ jamesmcgeown@live.co.uk

Axton commenced brewing in 2015 on a 1.5-barrel plant, supplying only the brewery tap at Archies Bar, Prestatyn. It specialises in one-off brews at the rate of about a dozen each year. Brewing is currently suspended.

Aylesbury

83 Bicester Road, Aylesbury, Buckinghamshire, HP19 9AZ
(01844) 239237 aylesburybrewhouse.co.uk

Established in 2011 at the Hop Pole as a sister brewery to Vale (qv). One-off beers are brewed on a weekly basis using a 12-barrel kit. !! ♦

Ayr

5 Racecourse Road, Ayr, KA7 2DG
(01292) 263891
info@ayrbrewingcompany.com

Ayr began brewing in 2009 on a five-barrel plant and is located at the Glenpark Hotel. As well as the hotel, around 50 other outlets are supplied throughout Scotland and England. ♦ RAIB

HipHopopotamus (OG 1039, ABV 3.8%)
Dry-hopped pale ale with caramel malts, bitter oranges and green hops.

Leezie Lundie (OG 1037.5, ABV 3.8%)
A pale golden-coloured session ale with hints of grapefruit and a dry, lingering finish.

Otto & Griselda (OG 1004, ABV 4%)

Five of Diamonds (OG 1041, ABV 4.2%)

Jolly Beggars (OG 1041, ABV 4.2%)
A complex best bitter with plenty of character and a lingering malty aftertaste.

Complicated Maisie (OG 1042, ABV 4.3%)

Rabbie's Porter (OG 1042.5, ABV 4.3%)
Robust, full-bodied porter with well-balanced toffee, fruity maltiness and a slightly smoky finish.

Rhapsody (OG 1042, ABV 4.3%)

Fair Jennys Jig (OG 1044, ABV 4.4%)

Dunkel (OG 1046, ABV 4.8%)

Burning Gull (OG 1048, ABV 5%)
A strong bitter with toffee, caramelised oranges and grapefruit on the palate, leading to a creamy, rich bitter finish.

Betty & the Gardens (OG 1049.5, ABV 5.2%)
A blonde ale with hints of pineapple, passion fruit and strawberries leading to a smooth, fruity finish.

B&T SIBA

The Brewery, Shefford, Bedfordshire, SG17 5DZ
(01462) 815080 banksandtaylor.com

Banks & Taylor – now just B&T – was founded in 1982. It produces 13 regular beers, plus monthly specials and occasional beers, in an industrial unit close to the town centre. There are five tied houses. !! ♦

Two Brewers Bitter (OG 1036, ABV 3.6%)
Bronze-coloured bitter with citrus hop aroma and taste, and a dry finish.

Plum Mild (OG 1038, ABV 3.8%)
A rich, dark mild with a strong malty aroma, hints of plum flavour on the tongue, and a fruity plum finish.

Shefford Bitter (OG 1038, ABV 3.8%)
A pale brown-coloured beer with a light hop aroma and a hoppy taste leading to a bitter finish.

Shefford Dark Mild (OG 1038, ABV 3.8%)
A dark beer with a well-balanced taste. Sweetish, roast malt aftertaste.

Golden Fox (OG 1041, ABV 4.1%)
A golden, hoppy ale, dry-tasting with a fruity aroma and citrus finish.

Black Dragon Mild (OG 1043, ABV 4.3%)
Black-coloured with a toffee and roast malt flavour, and a smoky finish.

Dunstable Giant (OG 1044, ABV 4.4%)
Dark tawny-coloured bitter with a subtle blend of malt and hops.

Dragon Slayer (OG 1045, ABV 4.5%)
A golden-coloured beer with a malt and hop flavour and a bitter finish. More malty and less hoppy than is usual for a beer of this style.

Edwin Taylor's Extra Stout (OG 1045, ABV 4.5%)
A complex black-coloured beer with a bitter coffee and roast malt flavour and a dry bitter finish.

Fruit Bat (OG 1045, ABV 4.5%)
A warming straw-coloured beer with a taste of apricots and a bitter finish.

Shefford Pale Ale (SPA) (OG 1045, ABV 4.5%)
A well-balanced beer with hop, fruit and malt flavours. Dry, bitter aftertaste.

SOD (OG 1050, ABV 5%)
SOS with caramel added for colour.

SOS (OG 1050, ABV 5%)
A rich mixture of fruit, hops and malt is present in the taste and aftertaste of this beer. Predominantly hoppy aroma.

Baa SIBA

Unit 4, Station Rd Industrial Estate, Chepstow, NP16 5PF baabrewing.com

Located adjacent to Chepstow Railway Station, the brewery was established in 2015 using an eight-barrel plant with five fermenters and a bright beer tank. It claims to be the only brewery in Chepstow since the 12th century. !!

Baa B-Q Blonde (ABV 3.7%)
A light golden-coloured blonde summer ale, with a refreshing hint of fruity sweetness and a mild malty taste.

Best Bitter (ABV 4%)
Well-balanced with fruity, floral and aromatic hop notes. Smooth, mellow maltiness is followed by a crisp bitterness.

Hopping (ABV 4.2%)
A double-hopped ale with a light, refreshing taste.

Two Bridges (ABV 4.5%)
Smooth and full-bodied, a satisfying taste, with a gentle citrus hoppy aftertaste.

IPA (ABV 5%)
Strong, fully matured ale packed with character.

Bacchus

Bacchus Hotel, 17 High Street, Sutton-on-Sea, Lincolnshire, LN12 2EY
(01507) 441204 bacchushotel.co.uk

Bacchus began brewing in 2010 and now has a two-barrel plant supplying the Bacchus Hotel. !! RAIB

THE BREWERIES

Backyard SIBA

Unit 8a, Gatehouse Trading Estate, Lichfield Road, Brownhills, Walsall, West Midlands, WS8 6JZ
☎ (01543) 360145 🌐 tbb.uk.com

Backyard began brewing in 2008 and expanded to a 12-barrel plant in 2012, brewing up to 50 barrels a week. Two pubs are owned: the Fountain, Walsall and the Saddlers Arms, Solihull. A half-barrel experimental plant is also in operation and a tap house is open every Friday (1-8pm). ‼ ♦

Bitter (OG 1038, ABV 3.8%)
Blond style ale, slightly sweet with hints of tangerine and fruit salad.

The Hoard (OG 1040, ABV 3.9%)
Refreshing, dry golden-coloured bitter. Light malt flavour with hint of lemon on the palate.

Blonde (OG 1041, ABV 4.1%)
Platinum blonde bitter. Citrus and pine smell, with a dry, crisp and hoppy taste.

Americana (ABV 4.3%)
Light, fruity pale ale with powerful orange and lemon aromas and malty biscuit, fruity hops and vanilla flavours.

Gold (OG 1045, ABV 4.5%)
Golden-coloured bitter, with tropical fruit hop notes.

IPA (OG 1049, ABV 5%)
Intense floral, herbal smell. Strong, rich, fruity bitterness.

Antipodean (OG 1052, ABV 5.6%)
Full-bodied pale ale. Complex flavours of exotic fruits apricot and pine, and an undercurrent of spicy cedar and oak.

BAD

Unit 3, North Hill Road, Dishforth, North Yorkshire, YO7 3DH
☎ (01423) 324005 🌐 wearebad.co

Brewing commenced in 2014, originally using a 13-barrel plant, since upgraded to cope with demand. A new and evolving Off Tempo range has been developed, focusing on experimental and radical brews. ‼

Pale Aura (ABV 3.8%)
Fruity and slightly bitter ale, hoppy with notes of tangerine, mango, grapefruit and pineapple.

Yorkshire Bitter (ABV 3.8%)

Love Over Gold (ABV 4.1%)
A blonde ale, light, hoppy and well-balanced with grapefruit and grassy notes.

Summer Breeze (ABV 4.5%)

Wild Gravity (ABV 5.2%)
An IPA with a malty backbone and tropical hop flavours.

Dark Necessities (ABV 5.5%)
Dark-coloured, rich milk stout with hints of cherry, chocolate, coffee and almond.

Boston Tea Party (ABV 5.8%)

Bad Joke (NEW)

Unit 2Ca, Penn Street Works, Penn Street, Amersham, Buckinghamshire, HP7 0FA ☎ 07791 937737
✉ badjokebrewco@gmail.com

Production started in 2018. A variety of styles of bottle-conditioned beers are produced, which can only be obtained at the brewery, by prior arrangement. RAIB

Bad Seed

7 Rye Close, York Way Industrial Estate, Malton, North Yorkshire, YO17 6YD
☎ (01653) 695783 🌐 badseedbrewery.com

Launched in 2013 by James Broad and Chris Waplington, the four-barrel brewery was increased to a 12-barrel plant in 2015. Brewing 2-3 times a week, the beers are unfined and unfiltered. The core beers are complemented with up to 100 brews per year including regular and one-off specials. ‼ ♦

Kiwi (ABV 3.8%)
New Zealand-hopped pale ale with zesty freshness.

Dalliance (ABV 4%)
Pale ale with lychee, grapefruit and citrus flavours.

Session IPA (ABV 4%)

Badger

See Hall & Woodhouse

Bakehouse

See Warwickshire

Bakers Dozen

Unit 5 Ketton Business Estate, Pit Lane, Ketton, PE9 3SZ
☎ (01780) 238180 🌐 bakersdozenbrewing.co.uk

Brewing takes place on a five-barrel plant installed in 2015 by the owners of the Jolly Brewer, Stamford, where the beers are always available. ♦

Jentacular (OG 1033, ABV 3.5%)

Magic Potion (OG 1035, ABV 3.8%)

Stamford Pale (OG 1037, ABV 4%)

System of a Brown (OG 1038, ABV 4.1%)

Straight Outta Ketton (OG 1040, ABV 4.5%)
Hop-forward, oatmeal pale ale.

Electric Landlady (OG 1044, ABV 5%)

Bale

Janie Craig Cottage, Liddaton, Devon, EX20 4AD
☎ 07540 283014 🌐 baleale.com

Bale Ale is a nanobrewery established in 2016 situated near Dartmoor National Park. Only bottle-conditioned beers are produced at present. RAIB

Ballard's

See Greyhound

Bang the Elephant

17 Craig Street, Long Eaton, Nottinghamshire, NG10 1ET ☎ 07539 652055
✉ bangtheelephantbrewing@hotmail.com

⊗ Bang The Elephant are a Long Eaton based neo-Victorian, steampunk-inspired, nanobrewery, creating small batch beers.

Half Rats (ABV 4.4%)

Sons of Liberty APA (ABV 5%)

Kali Yuga (ABV 5.9%)

Odissi (ABV 6%)
Juicy IPA with flavours of tangerine and grapefruit.

Bang-On

Unit 3, George Street, Bridgend Industrial Estate, Bridgend, CF31 3TS
☎ (01656) 760790 🌐 bangonbrewery.beer

Established in 2016, this five-barrel plant produces a variety of unique beers. An on-site taproom offers tours and brew day experiences. A bespoke beer service is offered where beers are available with personalised labels. ‼ V

Doris (OG 1031, ABV 3.4%)
A heavily-hopped session IPA, with a fruity and fragrant taste.

Cariad (OG 1039, ABV 4.1%)
An easy-drinking, fresh, crisp session Welsh ale.

Arthur (OG 1039, ABV 4.4%)
Lightly-hopped, amber-coloured ale with floral notes and berries on the nose.

Trev (OG 1053, ABV 4.8%)
A ruby-coloured IPA with subtle hoppy notes.

Bank Top SIBA

The Pavilion, Ashworth Lane, Bolton, BL1 8RA
☎ (01204) 595800 🌐 banktopbrewery.com

Bank Top was established in 1995. Since 2002, the brewery has occupied a Grade II listed tennis pavilion housing an 11-barrel plant. Bank Top Brewery Estates was formed in 2010 and now owns three pubs, Bank Top Brewery Tap, Bank Top Ale House and Olde England Forever. ‼ ♦

Draymans Draught (OG 1037, ABV 3.6%)
A pale ale with a strong citrus flavour and bitter, hoppy aftertaste.

Bad to the Bone (OG 1040, ABV 4%)
A tan-coloured beer with floral qualities and delicate citrus notes.

Dark Mild (OG 1040, ABV 4%)
Coffee roast aroma, smooth mouthfeel, with roasted malt prominent throughout and some fruit. Moderate bitterness in aftertaste.

Flat Cap (OG 1040, ABV 4%)
Amber-coloured ale with a modest fruit aroma leading to a beer with citrus fruit, malt and hops. Good finish of fruit, malt and bitterness.

Pavilion Pale Ale (OG 1045, ABV 4.5%)
A yellow-coloured beer with a citrus and hop aroma, big fruity flavour with a peppery hoppiness, and a dry, bitter yet fruity finish.

Palomino Rising (OG 1049, ABV 5%)
A pale-coloured, refreshing bitter with a tropical fruit aroma and a dry, bitter, citrus finish.

Port O Call (OG 1050, ABV 5%)
Dark brown-coloured beer with a malty, fruity aroma. Malt, roast and dark fruits in the bittersweet taste and finish.

Banks's

Park Brewery, Wolverhampton, West Midlands, WV1 4NY
☎ (01902) 711811 🌐 bankssbeer.co.uk

Banks's was founded as a firm of maltsters in 1840, commencing brewing in 1874; and moved to the current Park Brewery the following year. It became the principal brewery of the Wolverhampton & Dudley Breweries, founded in 1890 by an amalgamation with two other local companies. Several other breweries were later acquired, notably Hanson's of Dudley in 1943, which continued brewing until 1991. Following the takeover of Marston's of Burton on Trent in 1999, W&DB subsequently adopted this name for the PLC in 2007. Whilst continuing to produce the original Banks's Mild and Bitter beers (for which they gained fame throughout the Midlands), many new beers have been developed, notably Sunbeam, introduced in 2011 to mark the 10th anniversary of Wolverhampton's city status. In recent years, Marston's PLC has taken on contract brewing of several well-known national ales, many at the Banks's site (including Tetley Bitter, for Carlsberg, and the principal Thwaites' brands, which were brewed under licence from 2014, and purchased outright by Marston's the following year). Under the terms of the purchase of Thwaite's principle brands, in 2016 Marston's were required to drop the Thwaite's name from all advertising, so Wainwrights and Lancaster Bomber carry no brewery name at point of sale. Part of Marston's PLC. ‼

Mild (OG 1036, ABV 3.5%)
An amber-coloured, well-balanced, refreshing session beer.

Amber Ale (OG 1038, ABV 3.8%)
A pale brown-coloured bitter with a pleasant balance of hops and malt. Hops continue through to a bittersweet aftertaste.

Sunbeam (OG 1042, ABV 4.2%)
Zesty, golden-coloured beer with refreshing gooseberry and grapefruit citrus hops. A vibrant hop aroma leads to a long clean finish.

Brewed under the Mansfield brand name:

Cask Ale (OG 1038, ABV 3.9%)
A copper-coloured bitter with fruity notes from the Mansfield yeast, subtle hop aromas, and a restrained bitterness.

Contract brewed for Carlsberg:

Tetley Mild (OG 1034, ABV 3.3%)

Tetley Bitter (OG 1035, ABV 3.7%)
Brewed with the Tetley yeast strain and brewing materials. A classic, dry northern session bitter. A distinct dry hop character prevails, with a subtle clove-like note derived from the yeast.

Gold (OG 1041, ABV 4.1%)
A straw-coloured golden ale. A dry, refreshing citrus/herbal hop character predominates.

Contract brewed for Marston's:

Wainwright (OG 1042, ABV 4.1%)
Refreshing golden ale with gentle bitterness and a sweet lemon hop finish.

Lancaster Bomber (OG 1044, ABV 4.4%)
Full-bodied, deep amber-coloured beer with a raisin-like sweetness and a noticeable dry hop character.

Barefaced

7 Norwich Road, Bournemouth, Dorset, BH2 5QZ ☎ 07435 157767 🌐 barefacedbrewing.co.uk

Barefaced Brewing was started in 2017 by two friends, Nick Horne and Tom Cooper, in one of their garden sheds in Wimborne. The brewery has since expanded and moved to Bournemouth using a 3.5-barrel plant. !! ♦ RAIB

Big Bang Blueberry Cream Ale (ABV 4.4%)
Speciality beer with blueberries.

So You've Travelled (ABV 4.4%)

Heartbreak Stout (ABV 5.4%)
Stout with plenty of bitterness.

Flash IPA (ABV 6.2%)

Sucker punch Saison (ABV 6.4%)
A spicy wheat beer.

Barn Owl

Buildings Farm, Faringdon Road, Gozzard's Ford, Oxfordshire, OX13 6QH ☎ 07724 551086

Located in a spacious barn on a farm just outside Abingdon, brewing began in 2016 using a four-barrel plant. Beers can often be found in the Black Horse, Gozzard's Ford, and other local free trade outlets.

Old Scruttock's Inscrutable (ABV 3.9%)

Golden Gozzard (OG 1040, ABV 4%)
A light, refreshing golden ale with soft bitterness and fruity finish.

Gozzard's Guzzler (OG 1044, ABV 4.4%)
A dark-coloured best bitter with a sweetish nose and fruity tones.

Old Scruttock's Dirigible (ABV 5%)
A rich, dark-coloured porter.

Barnaby's

The Old Stable, Hole Farm, Staverton, Devon, TQ11 0LA ☎ (01803) 762730 🌐 barnabysbrewhouse.com

Soil Association-certified organic brewery established in 2016. Occasional cask ale production. Expansion is planned. ♦

Barnard Castle SIBA

Quaker Yard, rear of 24 Newgate, Barnard Castle, Durham, DL12 8NG ☎ 07591 236210 ✉ barnardcastlebrewing@gmail.com

Brewing commenced in July 2017 on a 3.6-barrel plant, situated in one of the many yards in Barnard Castle. A tap room was incorporated at the brewery in 2019, and a mobile bar enables the brewery to take its beers to events further afield. Beers are named after local themes. Deliberation is sold as Barny Bitter at the Old Well Inn in Barnard Castle.

Quaker Yard (ABV 3.5%)

Deliberation (ABV 3.7%)

Mechanical Swan (ABV 4.5%)

Peg Powler (ABV 5.6%)

Barnet

Barnet Brewery, C/O The Black Horse, 80 Wood Street, High Barnet, Hertfordshire, EN5 4BW ☎ (0208) 449 2230 🌐 blackhorsebarnet.co.uk

The brewery opened in 2013 using a 2.5-barrel plant located behind the Black Horse pub. Four beers are regularly in production and brewed on a rotating basis. Two or three seasonal beers are also produced where the brewer trials new recipes. The beers are mainly supplied to the Black Horse, but small quantities may be found in other local pubs.

Barney's SIBA

Summerhall Brewery, 1 Summerhall, Edinburgh, EH9 1PL ☎ 07512 253 660 🌐 barneysbeer.com

The only microbrewery in Edinburgh's city centre, Barney's Beer was founded in 2010 and now brews on the site of the original 1800s Summerhall Brewery. Summerhall is Edinburgh's centre for the arts and science. !! RAIB

Good Ordinary Pale Ale (OG 1038, ABV 3.8%)
A gold-coloured, full-bodied, English-style bitter.

Barney's Extra Pale (OG 1040, ABV 4%)
Light and refreshing beer.

Red Rye (OG 1044, ABV 4.5%)
Warming spicy notes from the rye malt create an interesting twist.

Volcano IPA (OG 1049, ABV 5%)
Nice floral aroma to this moderately bitter IPA.

Barngates SIBA

Barngates, Cumbria, LA22 0NG ☎ (01539) 436575 🌐 barngatesbrewery.co.uk

Barngates was established in 1997 to supply only the Drunken Duck Inn. It became a limited company in 1999. Expansion over the years, plus a new purpose-built 10-barrel plant in 2008, means it now supplies more than 150 outlets throughout Cumbria, Lancashire and Yorkshire. !!

Pale (OG 1036, ABV 3.3%)
A well-balanced, fruity, hoppy bitter with plenty of flavour for its strength.

Cat Nap (OG 1037, ABV 3.6%)
Pale beer, unapologetically bitter, with a dry astringent finish.

Cracker (OG 1038, ABV 3.9%)
A full-bodied, hoppy beer with some balancing sweetness and fruit. There is plenty of taste in this brown beer.

Brathay Gold (OG 1042, ABV 4%)
Attractive sweet and rich aroma is followed by plenty of fruit and hops then a long bitter finish.

Goodhew's Dry Stout (OG 1045, ABV 4.3%)
A roast aroma leads to an easy-drinking, full-bodied, and well-balanced, roasty stout.

Tag Lag (OG 1044, ABV 4.4%)
Full on traditional bitter, with noble hops, malt balance, good body, with a crisp clean finish.

Red Bull Terrier (OG 1048, ABV 4.8%)
An assertive, roasted red-coloured beer with full mouthfeel. Initial sweetness and luscious fruit, give way to a lingering bitter finish.

Barrahooley Craft

122 Glenravel Road, Martinstown, BT43 6QL
⊕ barrahooleybrewery.com

Located in the heart of the Glens of Antrim, Barrahooley started brewing in 2014 producing a range of bottle-conditioned beers. RAIB

Barsham

Estate Office, West Barsham, Norfolk, NR21 9NR
☎ (01328) 864459 ☎ 07760 551056
⊕ barshambrewery.co.uk

⊠ Barsham Brewery purchased Jo C's Brewery business in 2017 and continues to brew the beers to Jo Coubrough's recipes. Maris Otter is grown on-site and a private bore hole supplies water for the brewery. Jo is still on board as consultant. RAIB

Oaks (ABV 3.6%)
An amber-coloured, easy-drinking bitter with a balanced hop finish.

Norfolk Kiwi (ABV 3.8%)
Straw-coloured, easy-drinking session bitter with a floral, citrus flavour.

Bitter Old Bustard (ABV 4.3%)
A russet-coloured best bitter with a malty biscuit flavour and well-balanced taste.

Knot Just Another IPA (ABV 5%)
Golden-coloured, hoppy IPA with a good blast of hops.

Bartleby's

Coachwerks, 19 Hollingdean Terrace, Brighton, East Sussex, BN1 7HB
☎ (01273) 275012 ☎ 07518 485 342
⊕ bartlebysbrewery.com

Bartleby's began trading in 2014 in Brighton. Since opening it has expanded its distribution to local pubs and has established an on-site shop with home deliveries by veloelectric tricycle. An on-site venue is used for music, community events and art shows. ‼◆

Barum SIBA

▤ c/o Reform Inn, Pilton High Street, Pilton, Barnstaple, Devon, EX31 1PD
☎ (01271) 329994 ⊕ barumbrewery.co.uk

⊠ Barum was established in 1996 by Tim Webster and is housed in a conversion attached to the Reform Inn, which acts as the brewery tap and main outlet. Distribution is exclusively within Devon. ‼◆RAIB

Bason Bridge (NEW)

Unit 1 & 2, 129 Church Road, Bason Bridge, Somerset, TA9 4RG

Established in 2018 using a 10-barrel plant. Further beers are planned.

Somerset Best Bitter (ABV 4%)

Somerset IPA (ABV 5%)

Batemans SIBA IFBB

Salem Bridge Brewery, Mill Lane, Wainfleet, Lincolnshire, PE24 4JE
☎ (01754) 880317 ⊕ bateman.co.uk

⊚Bateman's Brewery is one of Britain's few remaining independent family-owned and managed brewers. Established in 1874, it has been brewing award-winning beers for four generations. All 62 tied and managed houses serve cask-conditioned beer. ‼▦◆

XB (OG 1037, ABV 3.7%) ▣ ◄
A well-rounded, smooth, malty beer with a blackcurrant fruity background. Hops flourish initially before giving way to a bittersweet dryness that enhances the mellow malty ending.

Gold / Yella Belly Gold (OG 1039, ABV 3.9%)
A golden-coloured, refreshing beer with a citrus flavour and aroma, which is quite dry.

Salem Porter (OG 1048, ABV 4.8%) ◄
A black-coloured, complex mix of chocolate, liquorice and cough elixir.

XXXB (OG 1048, ABV 4.8%) ▣ ◄
A brilliant blend of malt, hops and fruit on the nose with a bitter bite over the top of a faintly banana maltiness that stays the course. A russet-coloured classic.

Bath Ales

Hare Brewery, Southway Drive, Warmley, Bristol, BS30 5LW
☎ (0117) 947 4797 ⊕ bathales.com

⊠ Established in 1995, Bath Ales was taken over by St Austell in 2016. Since 2018 Bath Ales beers have been brewed in a new high-tech brewery with a state-of-the-art bottling line in the headquarters building. The two remaining Beerd brews have been rebranded as Bath Ales beers. Eight venues are operated in the Bristol/Bath area, all serving cask ale. ‼▦◆RAIB

Prophecy (OG 1040, ABV 3.9%) ◄
Straw-coloured, refreshing bitter with a fruity aroma. Bittersweet taste blends subtle citrus fruits with pine notes. Crisp, dry bitter finish.

Gem (OG 1042, ABV 4.1%) ▢ ▣ ◄
Pale brown-coloured best bitter with sweet fruit and malt flavours, and a hint of caramel. Little aroma, but a balanced taste with a short bitter finish.

Barnsey (OG 1045, ABV 4.5%) ◄
A dark brown-coloured old ale with a grainy mouthfeel. Malt, dark fruits and toffee flavours combine to give sweetness before a lingering, bitter finish.

Lansdown (ABV 5%) ◄
Hop-forward IPA with some light malt balancing citrus, pine and grassy notes which continue into the satisfying bitter finish.

Bath Brewhouse

▤ City Pub Company, 14 James Street West, Bath, BA1 2BX
☎ (01225) 805609

Office: City Pub Group PLC, Essel House, 2nd Floor, 29 Foley Street, London, W1W 7TH
⊕ thebathbrewhouse.com

⊗ Previously known as the James Street Brewery, Bath Brewhouse opened in 2013 and is owned by the City Pub Company, which owns several other pubs and brewpubs around the country. The compact brewery is on the ground floor, with the fermenting vessels and conditioning tanks on the first floor. The on-site brewer produces a wide range of beers. The company's other pub, the Cork, Bath, is also supplied. !! ♦

Bathams IFBB

Delph Brewery, Delph Road, Brierley Hill, West Midlands, DY5 2TN
☎ (01384) 77229 bathams.com

A classic Black Country small brewery established in 1877. Tim and Matthew Batham represent the fifth generation to run the company. The Vine, one of the Black Country's most famous pubs, is also the site of the brewery. The company has 10 tied houses and supplies around 30 other outlets. Batham's Best Bitter is delivered in 54-gallon hogsheads to meet demand. ♦

Mild Ale (OG 1036.5, ABV 3.5%)
A fruity, dark brown-coloured mild with malty sweetness and a roast malt finish.

Best Bitter (OG 1043.5, ABV 4.3%)
A pale yellow-coloured light, refreshing ale. Fruity, sweetish bitter, with a dry, hoppy finish.

Battersea (NEW)

12-14 Arches Lane, Battersea Power Station, Nine Elms, London, SW11 8AB batterseabrew.co.uk

Opening in 2018, the brewery consists of two railway arches, one for the brewery and one for the taproom. A changing range of beers is produced.

Battle

The Calf House, Beech Farm, North Trade Road, Battle, East Sussex, TN33 0LL
☎ (01424) 772838 battlebrewery.co.uk

Battle Brewery is an eight-barrel brewery with on-site taproom and bottle shop, located at the heart of 1066 country in the historic town of Battle, East Sussex. Starting up in 2017 they now supply local pubs, cafés, and shops with a range of cask and bottle-conditioned beers.

Conquest (ABV 4%)
Well-balanced, premium copper-coloured ale, with a hop finish.

Black Arrow (ABV 4.5%)
Smooth, full-bodied porter, chocolatey with hints of liquorice, roasted malt, and a hoppy finish.

Abbey Pale (ABV 5%)
Refreshingly hoppy pale ale, complex, tropical fruit aroma and citrus flavours are balanced with biscuit malt.

Battledown SIBA

Dowdeswell Park,, London Road, Charlton Kings,, Cheltenham, Gloucestershire, GL52 6UT ☎ 07734 834104 battledownbrewery.com

⊗ Battledown was established by Roland and Stephanie Elliot-Berry in 2005, and were joined by Ben Jennison-Phillips the following year. The brewery relocated to new premises in 2016, and again in 2018. It supplies around 250 outlets. !! ♦ RAIB

Pale Ale (OG 1037, ABV 3.8%)
A golden-coloured pale ale with a refreshing aroma and sharp, but smooth taste, leaving a dry, hoppy aftertaste which lingers on the palate.

Amber Ale (OG 1041, ABV 4.2%)
A deep golden beer, the malts evident, but gives way to the triple hop addition giving a spicy and slightly citrus finish.

Original (OG 1046, ABV 4.6%)
A rich amber-coloured ale. A malty aroma and taste with a deep satisfying, full-bodied fruit and malt texture leaving a well-rounded mellow aftertaste.

Four Kings (OG 1066, ABV 7.2%)
A strong ale with a heady aroma.

Battlefield

See Tunnel

Bays SIBA

Aspen Way, Paignton, Devon, TQ4 7QR
☎ (01803) 555004 baysbrewery.co.uk

Bays Brewery is a multiple award-winning, family-run business based in Torbay on the Devon coast. Its passion is to brew premium ales using the finest local ingredients whilst also supporting the community and protecting the environment. !! ♦

Topsail (OG 1040, ABV 4%)
A tawny-coloured session bitter with a complex aroma. Malty, bitter taste leading to a long, dry and refreshing aftertaste.

Gold (OG 1042, ABV 4.3%)
Smooth, golden ale, with a light aroma, and taste of hops, malt and caramel. Lingering hoppy aftertaste.

Trunk Ale (ABV 4.5%)

Devon Dumpling (OG 1048, ABV 5.1%)
Strong ale, easily drinkable. Light aromas of hops and fruit continue through taste and lingering aftertaste.

Beach

See Milton

Beacon Brauhaus

Pilgrims Coffee, Falkland House, Marygate, Holy Island, TD15 2SJ
☎ (01289) 389109 pilgrimscoffee.com

Nanobrewery situated on Holy Island, the first brewery to be based there in around 500 years. Local outlets are supplied.

Bear Claw

Unit 3 Meantime Workshops, Spittal, Northumberland, TD15 1RG ☎ 07919 276715 bearclawbrewery.weebly.com

Bear Claw began brewing in 2012 using a two-barrel plant, producing a variety of mainly highly-hopped, cask-conditioned ales and many bottle-conditioned beers, including continental styles. Beers are available in the Green shop and Curfew pub in Berwick upon Tweed. RAIB

Beartown

Bromley House, Spindle Street, Congleton, Cheshire, CW12 1QN
☎ (01260) 299964 ⊕ beartownbrewery.co.uk

⊙Beartown began brewing in 1994 and uses a 25-barrel plant. It supplies more than 250 outlets. It is now in partnership with Manning Brewers (qv), also of Congleton. !! ⛟ ♦

Glacier (ABV 3.6%)
A light session ale with a delicate hop finish.

Best Bitter (OG 1037, ABV 3.7%)
A lightly-hopped, amber-coloured session ale with toffee notes.

Bluebeary (ABV 4%)
A pale-coloured session beer delicately infused with Canadian blueberries.

Ginger Bear (OG 1040, ABV 4%)
The flavours from the malt and hops blend with the added bite from the root ginger to produce a superbly quenching blonde ale.

Kodiak (OG 1040, ABV 4%) ◆
Hops and fruit dominate the taste of this crisp yellow-coloured bitter, following through to a dryish aftertaste. Biscuity malt also comes through on the aroma and taste.

Bearskinful (OG 1042, ABV 4.2%) ◆
Biscuity malt dominates the flavour of this amber-coloured best bitter. Hops and a hint of sulphur on the aroma. A balance of malt and bitterness follow through to the aftertaste.

Peach Melbear (ABV 4.4%)
A peach and elderflower pale-coloured beer.

Lit (OG 1045, ABV 4.5%)
Golden-coloured pale ale. Floral scented and packed with the flavours of summer fruits and lemon, ending with a smooth dryness.

Atlas (ABV 4.8%)
Smooth, golden-coloured, citrus beer with a mellow, sweet finish.

Creme Bearlee (ABV 4.8%)
A velvety stout with burnt cream, Madagascan vanilla and molasses.

Polar Eclipse (OG 1048, ABV 4.8%) ◆
Classic black-coloured, dry and bitter stout, with roast flavours to the fore. Hops on the nose, into the taste and a long, dry finish.

Quantock (OG 1050, ABV 5%)
Dark ruby-coloured strong mild ale. Subtle roast and malt flavours fill the taste, complemented by a mellow sweetness.

Wotjek (ABV 5.5%)
Deep golden-coloured, dry beer with a finish of citrus fruit and juniper berry.

Beat SIBA

9 Old Forge Trading Estate, Dudley Road, Lye, West Midlands, DY9 8EL ☎ 07821 132297

Office: 11 Sydenham Hill, Bristol, BS6 5SL
⊕ beatales.com

⊗Beat Ales has been re-marketed as Beat Brewery. It was brewing in North Curry but has since moved to Lye in the Black Country. Beer names reflect the owners musical inspiration, taking in different genres. Music can be played from the pumpclips. ♦RAIB

Raver (OG 1034, ABV 3.8%)
A light pale ale that is clean and hoppy with citrus aromas.

Ska Burst (ABV 4%)

New Wave (ABV 4.5%)
Golden ale with fruit flavours of tangerine, melon and apricot.

Metal Head (OG 1042, ABV 4.8%)
Blend of six malts giving flavours of vanilla, chocolate and blackcurrant.

Rocka (OG 1044, ABV 5.3%)
Huge citrus and tropical fruit notes combined with a touch of pine and spice.

Funk (ABV 5.5%)
A dry-hopped IPA with tropical hop flavours.

Cosmic Pop (ABV 6%)
A black IPA with hop flavours of grapefruit, lemon and pine, offset against a dark malt centre.

Beath SIBA

The Rectory, Foulford Road, Cowdenbeath, KY4 9AP
☎ 07792 369678 ⊕ beathbrewing.com

⊙Beath began brewing in 2016, originally with a 20-litre capacity upgraded to 100-litre within a few months. There are plans for a further expansion. The beer range varies from week to week. RAIB

Mad World (ABV 4%)

Are You With Me (ABV 4.5%)

Ella Ella Ella (ABV 4.5%)

Funkytown (ABV 5%)

Beatnikz Republic

Unit 15, Redbank Court, Green Quarter, Manchester, M4 4HF ☎ 07825 077832 ⊕ beatnikzrepublic.com

⊙Microbrewery Beatnikz Republic brews out of a railway arch near Manchester Victoria Station. Beers are available unfined in KeyKeg, can and cask. Its brewery tap opened in Manchester's Northern Quarter in 2018. ⛟ ♦

Midtown

2am Poet (ABV 3.8%)

DDH Tropic Fiesta (ABV 4%)

Leather Soul (ABV 4.3%)

Beach Bum (ABV 5%)

Kentucky Rye (ABV 5%)

Beavertown

Units 17 & 18, Lockwood Industrial Park, Mill Mead Road, Tottenham Hale, London, N17 9QP
☎ (020) 8525 9884 ☎ 07976 984173

Tottenham Hotspur: Stadium, 748 High Road, Tottenham, London, N17 0AP
⊕ beavertownbrewery.co.uk

⊗ Beavertown began brewing in 2014. Beers are mostly sold in KeyKeg, can and keg without filtration or pasteurisation. The brewery is open to visit most Saturday afternoons. After selling a large minority stake to Heineken in 2018, expansion is planned for 2019 including moving to 'Beaverworld' in Ponders End. In 2019 a new brewery and bar opened in the newly built Tottenham Hotspur's football ground (no real ale). ♦ RAIB

Beckstones

Upper Beckstones Mill,, The Green, Millom, Cumbria, LA18 5HL
☎ (01229) 314900 🌐 beckstonesbrewery.co.uk

⊗ On the site of an 18th-century mill, with its own water supply, this five-barrel operation continues to win awards. Beer names have connections to the long-closed Millom Iron Works or local characters, and the brewer designs the distinctive pump clips. ♦

Leat (OG 1036, ABV 3.6%)
Rich and fruity light mild with refreshing hops in the finish.

Barley Blonde (ABV 3.7%)
Full-flavoured, well-balanced, fruity, hoppy beer.

Black Dog Freddy Mild (OG 1038, ABV 3.9%)
A full-bodied, well-balanced ruby-coloured dark mild, replete with fruit and roast malt.

Border Stones (OG 1040, ABV 4.1%)
An old-fashioned style tawny bitter with a sweet start, some bitter notes and plenty of aftertaste.

Iron Town (ABV 4.1%)
Creamy, sweet, amber-coloured ale which fills the mouth with well-balanced fruit and hop.

Rev Rob (OG 1044, ABV 4.6%)
Very well-balanced and distinctive best bitter, fills the mouth with sweet malt fruit and complementary hops leaving a pleasing finish.

Hematite (OG 1054, ABV 5.5%)

Bedlam SIBA

St Helena Farm, St Helena Lane, Plumpton Green, East Sussex, BN7 3DH
☎ (01273) 978015 ☎ 07801 822645
🌐 bedlambrewery.co.uk

Eco-friendly Bedlam Brewery operates from the heart onf the South Downs on a farm with solar power. All spent grain is donated to cattle on the farm and hops are composted. More than 1,000 pubs and bars are supplied across London and the South of England. !! RAIB

Benchmark (OG 1040, ABV 4%)
A classic English amber-coloured best bitter, full of old-style, roasted barley malts and bittering hops.

Golden (OG 1042, ABV 4.2%)
An alternative to the contemporary American-styled golden ales, with a fuller bitterness and mouthfeel.

Beer Brothers SIBA

335 Ranglet Road, Walton Summit Centre, Bamber Bridge, Lancashire, PR5 8AR ☎ 07921 519129
🌐 beerbrothers.co.uk

Brewing began in 2015, before moving in 2017 and expanded to a 10-barrel European-style brew plant. The brewery has since expanded from two full-size fermenting vessels to nine. Several limited edition experimental beers are brewed. Its busy tap opens from 12pm on Fridays and Saturdays. Bottled beers are available in local Booths and Spar stores. !!

Gold (OG 1037, ABV 3.8%)
A bright golden-coloured session ale.

IPA (OG 1035, ABV 3.8%)
A full-bodied, full-flavoured, hoppy IPA.

True Brit (OG 1042, ABV 3.8%)
A smooth, amber-coloured, full-bodied, malty session ale.

Milk Stout (OG 1058, ABV 4.2%)
A dark-coloured, sweet and creamy ale, smooth on the palate with a gentle bitterness from the dark roasted barley.

Hop Chocolate (OG 1056, ABV 4.3%)
Full-bodied and well-balanced with notes of roasted coffee and dark chocolate. Made with real cocoa.

Gunslinger (OG 1044, ABV 4.7%)
Fruity, punchy ale with smacks of citrus to the fore and pine down the backbone.

Interstellar Pale Ale (OG 1066, ABV 5.6%)

Beer Engine SIBA

Newton St Cyres, Devon, EX5 5AX
☎ (01392) 851282 🌐 thebeerengine.co.uk

⊗ The Beer Engine was established in 1983 and is the oldest working microbrewery in Devon. The brewery is visible downstairs in the pub through multiple viewing windows. Several outlets are supplied, as well as local beer festivals. !! ♦

Beer Hut (NEW)

6 Riverside Park, Kilkeel, BT34 4NA
✉ andrew@beerhutbrewing.co.uk

Microbrewery situated near Kilkeel harbour. Established in a flat pack hut using a 100-litre kit, it has since upscaled twice and now operates using a 1,000-litre plant. Further expansion is planned. RAIB V

Pale Ale (ABV 4.5%)
Bright, hazy and juicy pale ale with flavours of orange and pineapple on the palate.

Fluffy Bunny (ABV 5%)
A dark-coloured marshmallow milk stout with flavours of roasted coffee, vanilla, dark chocolate and raisins, giving a silky texture and smooth mouthfeel.

Wahey IPA (ABV 5.6%)
Refreshing IPA packed full of powerful floral hop and grapefruit flavours.

Ahoy Captain (ABV 7.4%)
An IPA flavoured with Irish sea salt, providing salted caramel flavours.

Beer Ink

Plover Road Garage, Plover Road, Lindley, Huddersfield, West Yorkshire, HD3 3PJ

☎ (01484) 655262 ☎ 07885 676711 ✉ ryan@beer-ink.co.uk

The Beer Ink Brewery Company is based in Lindley and opened in 2015 using an eight-barrel plant. It specialises in barrel-aged beers. Regularly collaborates with other forward looking breweries. A small on-site brewery tap opened in 2016. ♦

Avant Garde (OG 1041, ABV 4%)

Pin Up (OG 1040, ABV 4%)

Flagship (OG 1050, ABV 5%)

Noire (OG 1050, ABV 5%)

Two Faced (OG 1075, ABV 7.5%)

Beer Me

The Belgian Café, 11/23 grand Parade, Eastbourne, East Sussex, BN21 3YN
☎ (01323) 729967 🌐 thebelgiancafe.co.uk

⊗ Beer Me was launched in 2014 by the owners of the Belgian Café in Eastbourne, building on 10 years in the catering industry. It uses a 2.5-barrel plant and produces continental-style beers which are served direct from the brewery. ‼♦

Beer Monkey SIBA

Unit 3 & 4, Enterprise Way, Airedale Business Centre, Skipton, North Yorkshire, BD23 2TZ
☎ (01756) 701289 🌐 beermonkeybrewco.com

The Beer Monkey Brew Co is based in Skipton in a modern brewery on the southern edge of town. Brewing takes place on a 30-barrel plant, using water from its own borehole. The core beer range is supplemented by limited edition brews. ‼ ♦

Bitter Revival (ABV 3.9%)

Blond (ABV 3.9%)
Fruity, hoppy bitter, with a grapefruit aroma. The taste develops into a dry, bitter grapefruit peel finish.

Evolution Pilsner (ABV 4%)
Light, straw-coloured, Pilsner-style beer.

Uncle Monk's IPA (ABV 4.5%)
Full-bodied best bitter. Malty and nutty with an orange citrus edge, leading into a bittersweet finish.

Beer Nouveau

75 North Western Street, Ardwick, Manchester, M12 6DY

75 North Western Street, Manchester, M12 6DY
🌐 beernouveau.co.uk

Beer Nouveau has expanded from a small kit in the owner's garage to occupying two railway arches, opened up into a single area. A small core range of beers is complemented by numerous one-off and special beers including barrel-aged beers and some based on historic recipes. The brewery has a bar enabling brew tap events to take place each weekend offering cask, keg and beers from the wood. RAIB

Beer Refinery

Chapel Court Enterprise Centre, Wervin Road, Wervin, Chester, CH2 4BP ☎ 07939 875308
✉ enquiries@thebeerrefinery.co.uk

⊗ The Beer Refinery is a partnership of 10 engineers, some homebrewers and some just beer lovers, with a locally-built four-barrel plant. They are not reliant on the brewery for an income so are able to brew the beers they want to drink rather than the ones they think will sell the best. ‼♦

Beer Story (NEW) SIBA

Unit 5, Insch Business, Muiryheadless Road, Insch, AB52 6TA
☎ (01464) 821595 ☎ 07714 995163
🌐 beerstory.co.uk

Beer Story was established in 2017 by Philip Anderson. Recent expansion has involved the purchase of 18-barrel fermentation vessels. Beers are available in bottles and cans. ♦

Beer Studio

See Hydes

Beerblefish SIBA

Unit 6, Georgiou Business Park, Second Avenue, Edmonton, London, N18 2PG ☎ 07946 634555
🌐 beerblefish.co.uk

Starting at UBrew in Bermondsey in 2015, the Edmonton site began production in Autumn 2016. Bottled beers were the main output, but cask has appeared in some North London pubs and CAMRA festivals. A range of Victorian heritage beers in bottles launched in 2018 comprising an IPA, an ESB and a Porter with strengths to match.

Goldfish (ABV 4.2%)
A pale-coloured ale, simple and delicious, great on a summer evening.

Pan Galactic Pale (ABV 4.6%)
Bright, smooth and fruity.

Beercraft Brighton

See Brewery at the Watchmaker's Arms

Beermats SIBA

New Yard, Winkburn, Nottinghamshire, NG22 8PQ
☎ (01636) 639004 🌐 beermatsbeer.co.uk

Brewing began in 2017 on the Winkburn Estate in old dairy buildings using a 10-barrel kit. The brewery was established by three friends with experience in the trade. Beers are named around the theme of the humble beermat. ‼ V

Charismatic (OG 1039, ABV 3.8%)

Pragmatic (OG 1039, ABV 3.8%)

Format (OG 1040, ABV 3.9%)

Team Mates (OG 1040, ABV 3.9%)
Pale ale with citrus notes.

Soul Mate (OG 1043, ABV 4.2%)
Golden ale with fruity notes.

Diplomat (OG 1047, ABV 4.6%)

Smooth stout with chocolate notes.

Ultimate (OG 1050.5, ABV 4.9%)
Fruity, red-coloured ale.

BeerRiff

Pilot House Wharf, Swansea, SA1 1UN ☎ 07897 895511 🌐 beerriffbrewing.com

⊗ The proprietors of Pilot Brewery, Mumbles set up this four-barrel brewery mainly producing beer in keg and can. All beers are unfined, unfiltered. The taphouse bar offers great views over Swansea Marina. No real ale.

BEEspoke

Fox, 41 Briggate, Shipley, West Yorkshire, BD17 7BP
☎ (01274) 594826 🌐 thefoxshipley.co.uk

Brewing began in 2015 in the cellar of the Fox pub using a one-barrel plant. Beers are available in the pub and at local beer festivals. Shiny Cowbird Gin now also produced. ♦

Beeston SIBA

Fransham Road Farm, Beeston, Norfolk, PE32 2LZ
☎ (01328) 700844 ☎ 07768 742763
🌐 beestonbrewery.co.uk

⊗ The brewery was established in 2006 in an old farm building using a five-barrel plant. Brewing water comes from a dedicated borehole and raw ingredients are sourced locally whenever possible. !! RAIB

The Squirrels Nuts (OG 1035, ABV 3.5%)
Cherry, chocolate and vanilla aroma. A malt and cherry sweetness comes to the fore but quickly fades, with a short finish.

Worth the Wait (OG 1041, ABV 4.2%)
Hoppy throughout with a growing dryness. Complex and grainy with fruit notes, malt and understated bitterness.

Stirling (OG 1045, ABV 4.5%)
Rich, malty, red-coloured bitter with toffee notes.

The Dry Road (OG 1048, ABV 4.8%)

Village Life (OG 1047, ABV 4.8%)
Copper-coloured with a nutty character. Malty throughout, a bittersweet background giving depth, and a strong toffee apple finish.

On the Huh (OG 1048, ABV 5%)
A fruity raisin aroma, with a bittersweet maltiness which jousts with caramel and roast notes. A dry hoppiness adds to a strong finale.

Old Stoatwobbler (OG 1065, ABV 6%)

Contract brewed for Brancaster Brewery:

Best (ABV 3.8%)
A refreshing session ale with a touch of citrus on the finish.

Malthouse Bitter (ABV 4.2%)
A mid amber-coloured ale with malty character with distinct bitterness on the finish.

Beeston Hop

Windmill Lane, Sneinton, Nottingham, NG2 4QB
🌐 beestonhop.co.uk

A nanobrewery launched in 2015 producing mainly bottle-conditioned beers. Cask beers are occasionally produced for festivals using capacity at other breweries. The beers are unfined, unfiltered and unpasteurised. RAIB

Belgian Brewer (NEW)

Unit 11, The Links Business Centre, Raynham Road, Bishop's Stortford, Hertfordshire, CM23 5NZ
☎ (01279) 507515 🌐 thebelgianbrewer.co.uk

Situated just outside Bishop's Stortford town centre, the Belgian Brewer is a small brewery and taproom. Established in 2018 it produces Belgian-style beers brewed to traditional Belgian methods using family recipes. Currently producing 1,000 litres per month, demand is increasing week by week, especially for its speciality fruit beers. !!

Belhaven

Brewery Lane, Dunbar, EH42 1PE
☎ (01368) 862734

Office: Spott Road, Dunbar, EH42 1RS
🌐 belhaven.co.uk

Belhaven brewery is one of the oldest brewing sites in Scotland. Established in Dunbar in 1719, it brews beers made with water from its own well and local Scottish barley. Part of Greene King PLC. !!

60/- Ale (OG 1030, ABV 2.9%)
A fine example of a Scottish light. This bittersweet, reddish-brown-coloured beer is dominated by fruit and malt with a hint of roast and caramel, and increasing bitterness in the aftertaste.

IPA (OG 1038, ABV 3.8%)
A golden-coloured ale with refreshing floral and citrus tones produced by a well-balanced fusion of malt and hops giving a clean, crisp flavour.

80/- Ale (OG 1040, ABV 4.2%)
One of the last remaining original Scottish 80 Shillings. Malt is the predominant flavour characteristic, though it is balanced by fruit and a little hop. A complex ale, true to the style.

Black (OG 1041, ABV 4.2%)
A smooth, balanced dry stout with malty body and roast notes of dark chocolate and coffee.

St Andrew's Ale (OG 1046, ABV 4.9%)
A bittersweet beer with lots of body. The malt, fruit and roast mingle throughout with hints of hop and caramel.

Bell Street

57-59 Bell Street, Henley-on-Thames, Oxfordshire, RG9 2BA
☎ (01491) 570200 🌐 bellstreetbrewery.co.uk

Bell Street Brewery opened in 2013 at the rear of Brakspear pub company's Bull on Bell Street. A four-barrel plant is used. The beers are sold at the pub and through the Brakspear estate. ♦

Brakspear Special (OG 1043, ABV 4.3%)
Tawny-coloured, full-bodied beer with a well-balanced aroma and a hint of sweetness, which gives way to a dry hop bitterness.

Belleville

36 Jaggard Way, Wandsworth Common, London, SW12 8SG ☎ 07712 298273
⊕ bellevillebrewing.co.uk

Belleville began brewing in 2012. It was formed by a group of parents who met in the playground at a local primary school. It specialises in American-style beers, and currently only occasionally brews cask-conditioned beer. Its nearby taproom is open Wednesday-Sunday. **‼◆**

Bellfield SIBA

46 Stanley Place, Edinburgh, EH7 5TB
☎ (0131) 656 9390

Office: 6 Logie Mill, Beaverbank Business Park, Edinburgh, EH7 4HG ⊕ bellfieldbrewery.com

☺Founded by two coeliacs, Bellfield Brewery is the UK's first dedicated gluten-free microbrewery, with the first beers launched in 2016. Accredited by Coeliac UK. **GF**

Lawless Village IPA (ABV 4.5%)

Bellinger's SIBA

Station Road, Grove, Oxfordshire, OX12 0DH
☎ (01235) 772255 ⊕ bellingersbrewery.co.uk

⊠Established in 2011 by the late Mike Bellinger and now run by his nephew and son-in-law, Bellinger's is a five-barrel plant producing mainly bottled beer with the occasional cask-conditioned ale. All beers, when available, are sold in the garage forecourt shop and other local farm shops. **‼ ⊫◆RAIB**

Original Bitter (OG 1040, ABV 4.1%)
A light and refreshing, easy-drinking beer with a delicate malt flavour.

Arnhem (ABV 4.4%)

Cavalry (OG 1045, ABV 4.6%)
A malty, robust bitter. Originally a 1st World War centenary brew.

IPA (OG 1050, ABV 5%)
Gently hoppy with a lingering bitter taste.

Gallipoli Stout (OG 1053, ABV 5.3%)
A stout with a big beautiful chocolate taste. Originally a 1st World War centenary brew.

Belrose (NEW)

⊟ Belrose Public House, 94 Haverstock Hill, Belsize Park, London, NW3 2BD ⊕ belrose.co.uk

Originally home of the Haverstock Brewery until the pub closed in 2017, the pub opened again in 2018 as the Belrose with an in-house brewery. At present one beer is produced, brewed at the London Beer Lab in Brixton. No real ale.

Belvoir SIBA

Crown Park, Station Road, Old Dalby, Leicestershire, LE14 3NQ
☎ (01664) 823455 ⊕ belvoirbrewery.co.uk

Belvoir (pronounced 'beaver') Brewery was set up in 1995 by former Shipstone's and Theakstons brewer Colin Brown. Long-term expansion has seen the introduction of a 25-barrel plant that can produce 120 barrels a week. The visitors centre incorporates brewery memorabilia, a bar, restaurant and shop. Around 150 outlets are supplied direct. **‼◆RAIB**

Dark Horse (OG 1034, ABV 3.4%)

Whippling (OG 1037, ABV 3.6%)

Star Bitter (OG 1039, ABV 3.9%) ◆
Reminiscent of the long-extinct Shipstone's Bitter, this mid-brown-coloured bitter lives up to its name as it is bitter in taste but not unpleasantly so.

Gordon Bennett (OG 1041, ABV 4.1%)
Light chestnut-coloured beer with a biscuity character and a pleasant hop finish.

Beaver Bitter (OG 1043, ABV 4.3%) ◆
A light brown-coloured bitter that starts malty in both aroma and taste, but soon develops a hoppy bitterness. Appreciably fruity.

Oatmeal Stout (OG 1044, ABV 4.3%)

Old Dalby (OG 1050, ABV 5.1%)
A rich, smooth ruby red-coloured strong ale with pleasant hop character.

Contract Brewed for Hoskins Brothers:

Hob Bitter (OG 1040, ABV 4%)

IPA (OG 1040, ABV 4%)

Contract Brewed for Steamin' Billy:

Tipsy Fisherman (OG 1036, ABV 3.6%)
Traditional light amber-coloured bitter, mellow crisp flavour with a hoppy aftertaste. A quaffing ale that tastes more robust than its strength suggests.

Bitter (OG 1043, ABV 4.3%)
Light golden-coloured bitter, pronounced floral flavour and aroma followed by a lingering aftertaste.

1485 (OG 1050, ABV 5%)

Skydiver (OG 1050, ABV 5%)
Mahogany-coloured beer, a fine balance of malty sweetness and hop bitterness.

Bentley Brook (NEW)

Unit 3, Lumsdale Mill, Lumsdale, Matlock, Derbyshire, DE4 5EX ☎ 07483 831640

Office: 1 Hilltop Terrace, The Cliff, Matlock, Derbyshire, DE4 5FY ⊕ bentleybrook.co.uk

⊠ Formed in 2018, this 1.5-barrel brewery is located in the heart of Lumsdale Valley and named after the local brook. It offers unfined, small batch beers available to purchase in the local area. **RAIB**

Beowulf

Forest of Mercia, Chasewater Country Park, Pool Lane, Brownhills, Staffordshire, WS8 7NL
☎ (01543) 454067 ☎ 07714 291226
⊕ beowulfbrewery.co.uk

Beowulf Brewing Company is based at the Chasewater County Park. Beers appear as guest ales across the country. **‼◆RAIB**

Beorma (OG 1038, ABV 3.9%) ◆
A well-balanced session ale with a malty hint of fruit giving way to a lingering bitterness. Background spice excites the palate.

Black & Blueberry (OG 1048, ABV 4.5%)

A dark-coloured ale with a fruity aroma. Sweet and smooth on the palate with a gentle bitter finish.

Chase Buster (OG 1045, ABV 4.5%)

Dark Raven (OG 1048, ABV 4.5%) 🍷 ◆
Dark in colour with apple and bonfire in the aroma. Sweet and smooth like liquid toffee apples, with a sudden bitter finish.

Swordsman (OG 1045, ABV 4.5%) ◆
Pale gold-coloured, light fruity aroma, tangy hoppy flavour and a faintly hoppy finish.

Folded Cross (OG 1045, ABV 4.6%) ◆
Malt and caramel aromas and tastes with hints of fruity biscuits are nudged aside by the robust hops, which give lingering bitter edges.

Hurricane (OG 1041, ABV 4.6%)

Dragon Smoke Stout (OG 1048, ABV 4.7%) ◆
Black-coloured with a light brown creamy head. Tobacco, chocolate, liquorice and mixed fruity hints on the aroma. Bitterness fights through the sweet and roast flavours and eventually dominates. Hints of a good port emerge.

Finn's Hall Porter (OG 1049, ABV 4.7%) ◆
Dark chocolate aroma, after dinner mints, coffee and fresh tobacco. Good bitterness with woodland hints of Autumn. Long late bitterness with lip drying moreishness.

Heroes Bitter (OG 1046, ABV 4.7%) ◆
Gold-coloured, malt aroma, hoppy taste but sweetish finish.

Mercian Shine (OG 1048, ABV 5%) ◆
Amber to pale gold-coloured with a good bitter and hoppy start, with a hint of nutmeg. Plenty of caramel and hops with background malt leading to a good bitter finish with caramel and hops lingering in the aftertaste.

Nordic Noir (OG 1063, ABV 6%)

IPA (OG 1067, ABV 7.2%)

Killer Stout (OG 1080, ABV 7.3%)
Black-coloured, smooth ale with dark chocolate and coffee hints in the aftertaste.

Bere

Bere Brewery, Homefield, Bere Alston, Devon, PL20 7JA
☎ (01822) 840382 ⊕ berebrewery.co.uk

Established in 2016 by growers Jerry and Buffy on their smallholding on the Bere Peninsula in the Tamar Valley. The brewery produces bottle-conditioned beers using hops grown on the holding, with a 1.3-barrel plant and a 50-litre small batch kit. Building on its horticultural background, the brewery is working towards being self-sufficient in hops. Beers are sold at Tavistock Farmers' Market, by arrangement from the brewery, and at the Olde Plough Inn, Bere Ferrers.
🛒 ◆ RAIB

Bespoke SIBA

Unit 5, The Mews, Mitcheldean, Gloucestershire, GL17 0SL
☎ (01594) 546426 ⊕ bespokebrewery.co.uk

⊗ Brewing commenced in 2012 on a 5.5-barrel plant on the site of the former Wintles Brewery, which closed in the early 1900s. In 2014 capacity was increased to 12 barrels. Speciality-labelled bottles are offered for celebratory occasions. An on-site brewery tap opens Friday and Saturday.
‼ 🛒 ◆

Saved by the Bell (OG 1037, ABV 3.8%)
A light, refreshing session bitter with a spicy hop bite and a light floral aroma from the late hop addition.

Golden Rule (OG 1041, ABV 4%)
A light golden-coloured session ale with a subtly refreshing and fruity finish.

Running the Gauntlet (OG 1046, ABV 4.4%)
Full malty-flavoured bitter with rich roasted undertones balanced with good hop bitterness with spicy blackcurrant aromas from late hopping.

Going off half-cocked (OG 1043, ABV 4.6%)
A spicy, hopped golden ale.

Money for Old Rope (OG 1050, ABV 4.8%)
Classic stout with rich dry flavours of malt and grain, with deep hop bitterness.

Over a Barrel (OG 1052, ABV 5%)
A richly coloured, fruity strong ale with a generous peppery finish.

Bestens (NEW)

Unit 17, Church Lane Farm Estate, Church Lane, Lower Beeding, West Sussex, RH13 6LU
☎ (01403) 892556 ⊕ bestensbrewery.co.uk

After moving back to Britain in 2017 following a period of globetrotting, owner Paul Swaffield establised a brewery in a 0.5-barrel brewhouse in Cuckfield. In 2018 it relocated to Lower Beeding, doubling capacity. Further expansion is planned.
🛒 ◆ V

Betteridge's SIBA

Coopers Barn, The Dene, Hurstbourne Tarrant, Hampshire, SP11 0AG ☎ 07771 966058
⊕ betteridgesbrewery.co.uk

Microbrewery trading since 2014 using a 2.5-barrel plant. The founder and brewer, Mark Betteridge, brews four core beers using principally English hops and traditional floor-malted barley. Beers are supplied to beer festivals, private events and to a growing number of pubs in the Test Valley area and occasionally further afield. RAIB

Old Chap (ABV 3.8%)
An easy-drinking amber-coloured session bitter, with good malt flavour and hopped lightly.

Jenny Wren (ABV 4.2%) ◆
A dark golden-coloured single-hopped beer, with initial fruit in aroma and taste leads to a bitter finish.

Private Sector (ABV 4.2%)
A full-flavoured, amber-coloured ale.

Serious Black (ABV 4.2%)
A complex enriched stout with coffee, chocolate notes and roast flavours but with some underlying sweetness from added lactose.

Bewdley SIBA

Unit 7, Bewdley Craft Centre, Lax Lane, Bewdley, Worcestershire, DY12 2DZ
☎ (01299) 405148 ⊕ bewdleybrewery.co.uk

⊠ Bewdley began brewing in 2008 on a six-barrel plant in an old school. This was upgraded to a 10-barrel plant in 2014. Beers are brewed with a railway theme for the nearby Severn Valley Railway. The brewery has an on-site tap and shop. Element gin is also produced. ☒◆RAIB

Worcestershire Way (OG 1036, ABV 3.6%) ◄
Refreshing golden ale with a citrus, faintly orange peel aroma, which leads to a balanced hop, malt and grapefruit taste and a lingering hoppy finish.

Jubilee (OG 1043, ABV 4.3%) ◄
Pale colour, fruit and citrus aroma, sweet malt with underlying citrus taste.

Sir Keith Park (OG 1045, ABV 4.5%) ◄
Pale amber-coloured, full fruity and balanced flavour followed by a long hoppy finish.

2857/ Worcestershire Sway (OG 1050, ABV 5%) ◄
Complex amber-coloured bitter with a fragrant, malty aroma, well-balanced slightly sweet malt and hops with hints of toffee and marmalade, malt with citrus and meadow grass finish.

William Mucklows Dark Mild (OG 1060, ABV 6%) ◄
Dark in colour, malty, sweetish fruity flavour with slight liquorice finish.

Bexar County

8 Belgic Square, Padholme Road, Peterborough, Cambridgeshire, PE1 5XF ☎ 07934 722584 ⊕ bexarcountybrewery.com

Bexar was established in 2012, brewing an ever-changing range of American-style beers.

Poquito Pequeno (OG 1040, ABV 3.5%)
A standard bitter using the same malt and hop bill each time but with varying brew temperatures and times to produce a different beer yet the same each time.

Prospect (OG 1048, ABV 4.5%)

Phantasmagorical (OG 1075, ABV 7.4%)

Bexley SIBA

18 Manford Industrial Estate, Erith, Kent, DA8 2AJ ☎ (01322) 337368 ⊕ bexleybrewery.co.uk

Bexley Brewery was founded in 2014. Brewers Cliff and Jane Murphy produce regular, seasonal and experimental brews as well as selling own-brand beer mustard from the Bird & Barrel, opened in 2018, providing a local outlet for their beer. The premises also houses a chilli jam producer and some brewing kit for Clarkshaws Brewery (qv). ‼☒◆

Session Golden Ale (OG 1042, ABV 3.6%) ◄
Refreshing golden ale with grapefruit and some honey notes, and a little peppery hop and a bitter finish.

Session Ruby Ale (OG 1042, ABV 3.7%) ◄
Malt and dark fruit on the nose, taste is malty, biscuity with hints of smoke, and there is a hoppy, long and dry aftertaste.

Session Pale Ale (OG 1044, ABV 3.8%) ◄
Refreshing beer with a zesty, citrus flavour. Limited sweetness and some bitterness in the taste.

Golden Acre (OG 1042, ABV 4%) ◄

Smooth golden ale with citrus aroma. Flavour is of grapefruit, hops and a strong bitterness, continuing in the dry, fruity finish.

Bexley's Own Beer (OG 1044, ABV 4.2%) ◄
Pale brown-coloured beer with a balance of fudge, floral hop, stone fruit and some bitterness growing in the dry finish.

Redhouse Premium (OG 1042, ABV 4.2%) ◄
Copper-coloured best bitter with roast and sweet orange marmalade. Dry finish with a touch of chocolate in finish and aroma.

Anchor Bay IPA (ABV 4.8%)
A deep golden-coloured beer with a fruity, citrus taste and a floral, spicy aroma

Bianca Road

83-84 Enid Street, Bermondsey, London, SE16 3RA ☎ (020) 7732 2587 ⊕ biancaroad.com

After starting in 2016 in Peckham, the brewery moved to a bigger site in 2017 and again in 2019 to two arches along the Bermondsey Beer Mile, one of which forms the taproom. Output is mostly keg and cans. The Cellar Boys brewery from New Cross use the kit for some of their production.

Bicester

▤ Angel, 102 Sheep Street, Bicester, Oxfordshire, OX26 6LP ☎ (01869) 360410 ⊕ theangelbicester.co.uk

Brewing commenced in 2017 in an outhouse behind the Angel, Bicester. Beers are supplied solely to the pub.

Big Bog SIBA

74 Venture Point West, Evans Road, Speke, Merseyside, L24 9PB ☎ (0151) 558 0290 ☎ 07867 792466 ⊕ bigbog.co.uk

Big Bog started life in Waunfawr, Wales in 2011, sharing its site with the Snowdonia Parc brewpub. Due to growth and expansion in 2016, the brewery moved to its present location in Speke, Liverpool, into a custom-built plant with a 10-barrel brew length. The brewery has its own licenced bar and is open to the public on Fridays. ◆

Bog Standard Bitter (OG 1035, ABV 3.6%)
A light-coloured session ale with a medium bitterness and a refreshing hoppy, malty finish.

Mire (OG 1035, ABV 3.8%)
A tawny-coloured session ale with fruity notes.

Pride of England (OG 1036, ABV 3.8%)
A well-balanced, traditional English ale, brewed with Muscovado sugar.

Blonde Bach (OG 1037, ABV 3.9%)
A light-coloured ale with citrus/grapefruit notes.

Hinkypunk (OG 1039, ABV 4.1%) ◄
An appealing fruity aroma, then some citrus hop flavours lead to a bitter finish.

Stog (OG 1040, ABV 4.1%)
A milk stout, brewed using chocolate and milk sugars to give a creamy, bittersweet taste.

Jack O Lantern (OG 1041, ABV 4.2%)
A spicy, chestnut-coloured ale.

Welsh Pale Ale (OG 1041, ABV 4.2%)
Copper-coloured classic ale with a medium bitterness and dry finish.

Morast (OG 1041, ABV 4.3%)

Billabong (OG 1042, ABV 4.4%)
A single-hopped brew with a subtle note of light caramel.

Blueberry Hill Porter (OG 1046, ABV 4.5%)
A dark-coloured, rich porter made with real blueberries to give a subtle, smooth blueberry taste.

Swampy (OG 1046, ABV 4.7%)
Ruby-coloured ale with a robust bitterness, offset by a slightly sweet finish due to the added Muscovado sugar.

Will O the Wisp (OG 1045, ABV 4.7%)
A golden-coloured premium ale with a strong, fruity and hoppy character.

Peat Bog Porter (OG 1048, ABV 4.9%)
A dark-coloured, rich porter made with liquorice root.

Bayou (OG 1047, ABV 5%)
An intensely hoppy American-style pale ale.

Quagmire (OG 1058, ABV 6%)
A strong but deceptively easy-drinking beer. Mid-brown in colour with a medium to high bitterness.

Big Clock

Grants, 1 Manchester Road, Accrington, Lancashire, BB5 2BQ
☎ (01254) 393938 thebigclockbrewery.co.uk

Brewing commenced in 2014. A 6.5-barrel plant is used.

Big Drop SIBA

Office: 46 St Nicholas Street, Ipswich, Suffolk, IP1 4TT
bigdropbrew.com

Established in 2016 this company contract brews low-alcohol bottled beers of no more than 0.5% ABV at a variety of breweries around the country. No real ale.

Big Fish (NEW)

c/o 45 Glenury Crescent, Stonehaven, AB39 3LF
info@brewscotland.com

A gypsy brewery established in 2017.

Big Hand SIBA

Unit A1, Abbey Close, Redwither Business Park, Wrexham, LL13 9XG
☎ (01978) 660709 ☎ 07946 514238
bighandbrewing.co.uk

Big Hand began brewing in 2013 and operates a 10-barrel plant on the outskirts of Wrexham. Now well established in the North Wales brewing scene, it has won many awards in recent years. !! ♦

Seren (OG 1037, ABV 3.7%)
Pale, full-flavoured and hoppy with a fruity aroma and taste.

Gold (ABV 3.9%)
Golden session ale with citrus hints.

Pendragon (OG 1039, ABV 3.9%)
Copper-coloured and well-balanced, with a smooth rich taste, juicy mouthfeel and hints of spice in the finish.

Little Monkey (OG 1039, ABV 4%)
A malty mild, mahogany-coloured, with a dry roasty taste. Some initial sweetness balanced by hoppy bitterness in the finish.

Super Tidy (OG 1040, ABV 4%)
A pale brown-coloured bitter beer with some citrus notes in the taste and peppery hops in the finish.

Bastion (OG 1041, ABV 4.2%)
A dry, malty best bitter, mahogany-coloured with a full mouthfeel. Biscuity flavours and faint roast notes feature throughout

Appaloosa (OG 1045, ABV 4.5%)
A full-bodied pale ale, some initial sweetness with strong new world hop flavours in the taste and spicy finish.

Spectre (OG 1045, ABV 4.5%)
A smooth, dry and satisfying stout with a good roast aroma, hoppy and bitter with hints of liquorice.

Havok (OG 1049, ABV 5%)
A powerfully-hopped American IPA with strong and tangy citrus fruit bitterness throughout.

Big Lamp

Grange Road, Newburn, Newcastle upon Tyne, NE15 8NL
☎ (0191) 267 1689 biglampbrewers.co.uk

Big Lamp started in 1982 and relocated in 1997 to a 55-barrel plant in a former water pumping station. It is the oldest microbrewery in the North-east of England. Around 160 outlets are supplied and two pubs are owned, one of which (the Keelman) is attached to the brewery. !! ♦ RAIB

Sunny Daze (OG 1036, ABV 3.6%)
Golden, hoppy session bitter, with a clean taste and finish.

Bitter (OG 1039, ABV 3.9%)
A clean-tasting bitter, full of hops and malt. A hint of fruit with a good, hoppy finish.

Lamplight Bitter (OG 1042, ABV 4.2%)
Crisp, light, refreshing ale, with a dry aftertaste.

Summerhill Stout (OG 1044, ABV 4.4%)
A rich, tasty stout, dark in colour with a lasting rich roast character. Malty mouthfeel with a lingering finish.

Prince Bishop Ale (OG 1048, ABV 4.8%)
A refreshing, easy-drinking bitter. Golden-coloured, full of fruit and hops. Strong bitterness with a spicy, dry finish.

Premium (OG 1052, ABV 5.2%)
Hoppy ale with a good bitter finish.

Keelman Brown (OG 1057, ABV 5.7%)
A full-bodied ale with a hint of toffee.

Big River (NEW)

c/o 12 Lewis Lane, Cirencester, Gloucestershire, GL7 1EA ☎ 07939 273697 bigriverbrew.co

Formed in 2018, using spare capacity at the now closed Ciren Ales. Three core beers are available, all of which are brewed with a gluten-reducing enzyme. The brewery will relocate during the currency of this Guide. ♦RAIB

Pale Ale (OG 1034, ABV 3.6%)

All About Citra (OG 1041, ABV 4%)

Rolling Hills (OG 1041, ABV 4%)

Big Smoke SIBA

Unit D3, Sandown Industrial Estate, Esher, Surrey, KT10 8BL
☎ (01372) 469606 ☎ 07859 88419030/05
🌐 bigsmokebrew.co.uk

⊗ Brewing began at the Antelope, Surbiton, in 2014. In 2019 Big Smoke moved to a new purpose-built 30-hectolitre brewery in Esher. A taproom is open Friday-Sunday. ♦

Solaris Session Pale Ale (ABV 3.8%) ◈
Unfined golden ale with a bitter grapefruit flavour, some malt and a long, dry bitter finish. Hoppy, fruity nose.

Dark Wave Porter (ABV 5%) ◈
Creamy, black-coloured porter with a dry roast bitter character balanced by a caramelised sweetness.

Electric Eye Pale Ale (ABV 5%)

Underworld Milk Stout (ABV 5%) ◈
Sweet, smooth stout with hints of chocolate and coffee in the aroma and taste coupled with toasted nuts and vanilla.

Biggar

Queens Arms Courtyard, Biggar Village, Cumbria, LA14 3YG
☎ (01229) 474335 🌐 biggarbrewing.co.uk

This 2.5-barrel brewery, an independent co-operative of several shareholders, opened in 2015 in the courtyard of the Queens Arms, Biggar Village on Walney Island. The beer names are themed on Barrow's shipbuilding heritage, and the brewery logo features a representation of Barrow's dockside cranes, a strong visual motif of the town's history.

Mikasa (OG 1035, ABV 3.6%)
Dark mild with mellow maltiness and a light body.

Vanguard (OG 1041, ABV 3.8%)
A traditional amber-coloured bitter with light hoppiness.

Oriana (OG 1039, ABV 4%)
A pale golden-coloured, lager-style beer with a fruity hop aroma.

Agamemnon IPA (ABV 6%)
A dry-hopped, stronger version of Vanguard.

Bilbrough Top

St James House, Main Street, Bilbrough, North Yorkshire, YO23 3PH

A one-person microbrewery, Bilbrough began brewing in 2016. It produces only one beer on a six-barrel plant, regularly available at its unofficial tap, the Three Hares at Bilbrough.

Top Beer (ABV 3.9%)
A golden ale with refreshing citrus flavours.

Billericay SIBA

Essex Beer Shop, 54c Chapel Street, Billericay, Essex, CM12 9LS
☎ (01277) 500121 ☎ 07788 373129
🌐 billericaybrewing.co.uk

Billericay Brewing opened at its present site in 2014, using a 4.5-barrel plant. A micropub and beershop are next door. ‼ 🛒 ♦RAIB

Zeppelin (OG 1037, ABV 3.8%)
Easy-drinking session ale with slight smoky notes.

Blonde (OG 1040, ABV 4%)

Dickie (OG 1041, ABV 4.2%)
A well-balanced, amber-coloured ale with biscuit notes.

Vanilla Woods (OG 1042, ABV 4.2%)

Woody's Wag (OG 1042, ABV 4.2%)

Rhythm Stick (OG 1047, ABV 4.8%)
Hoppy, rich ale with caramel flavours.

Sex & Drugs & Rock & Roll (OG 1050, ABV 5%)

Chapel Street Porter (OG 1059, ABV 5.9%)
Rich, dark-coloured, complex porter with chocolate and coffee flavours.

Chilli Porter (OG 1059, ABV 5.9%)
Porter with the addition of green chillies.

Mayflower Gold (OG 1064, ABV 6.5%)

Binghams SIBA

Unit 10, Tavistock Industrial Estate, Ruscombe, Berkshire, RG10 9NJ
☎ (0118) 934 4376 🌐 binghams.co.uk

⊗ Binghams began brewing in 2010, producing 40 firkins in each batch. The brewery is situated in an industrial unit on the site of a former brickworks – hence the name of one of the beers. Head brewer Chris Bingham is a member of the local CAMRA branch and had extensive experience in homebrewing and working at a local brewery prior to starting up. All stouts and porters are vegan-friendly. ‼ 🛒 RAIB V

Twyford Tipple (OG 1040, ABV 3.7%)
Tawny-coloured bitter with a good balance of malt and hops in the flavour and a citrus hop finish.

Brickworks Bitter (OG 1047, ABV 4.2%)
Chestnut-coloured best bitter with a sweetish, malty nose. Hops balance the maltiness to give a well-rounded flavour with a slightly nutty hint and a sweet, earthy aftertaste.

Hop Project (ABV 4.5%)

Coffee Stout (OG 1056, ABV 5%)
A mellow beer with dark malt notes that complement the coffee flavour.

Doodle Stout (OG 1056, ABV 5%)
A blend of dark malts provide a complex character.

Hot Dog Chilli Stout (OG 1056, ABV 5%)
Doodle Stout with a hint of chilli, providing a warm glow in the aftertaste.

Macchiato Stout (ABV 5%)
Dark-coloured stout infused with vanilla and coffee.

Space Hoppy IPA (OG 1052, ABV 5%)
Pale golden-coloured ale with a complex hoppy flavour and a long citrus finish.

Vanilla Stout (OG 1052, ABV 5%)
Infused with vanilla pods that complement the dark malts to create a smooth-drinking, dark stout.

Bingley SIBA

Unit 2, Old Mill Yard, Shay Lane, Wilsden, West Yorkshire, BD15 0DR
☎ (01535) 274285 🌐 bingleybrewery.co.uk

Bingley is a small, family-run brewery that opened in 2014 using a six-barrel plant. It is located in a rural setting in the village of Wilsden, part of Bingley Rural Ward. Beers are distributed coast to coast and as far south as Derby. ‼

Endeavour (ABV 3.7%)
Soft bitter blonde ale with grapefruit and lime flavours coupled with aromas of blackcurrant, loganberry and spice notes.

Goldy Locks Blonde (ABV 4%)
A refreshing citrus aroma and delicate toffee aftertaste.

Azacca (ABV 4.1%)
Slightly bitter taste with citrus, mango and pine characteristics in flavour and aroma.

Session IPA (ABV 4.2%)
An IPA with sharp citrus and spicy notes.

Steady State (ABV 4.2%)
A smooth caramel and toffee flavour, floral and sweet aroma and a tinge of elderberry.

Centennial (ABV 4.4%)
Golden-coloured ale with a subtle malty base and a delicate floral, tangy aftertaste.

Tri State (ABV 4.5%)
Golden-coloured beer with flavours of citrus, pine and spice. A bitter and tart dry finish.

1848 Stout (ABV 4.8%)
Creamy stout with hints of chocolate and liquorice and a pleasant bitter finish.

Jamestown APA (ABV 5.4%)
American-style pale ale, slightly spicy with distinct piny notes, an aroma of grapefruit and a hint of apricot.

Birch Cottage

Birch Cottage, Wilne Road, Sawley, Derbyshire, NG10 3AP ☎ 07966 757407
✉ birchcottagebrewery@outlook.com

Birch Cottage is a nanobrewery established in 2018 brewing small batch beers. Its brewery tap, Sawley Junction, opened in 2018.

Birchover

Red Lion, Main Street, Birchover, Derbyshire, DE4 2BN
☎ (01629) 650363 🌐 red-lion-birchover.co.uk

⊗ The enthusiastic Sardinian born brewery/ pub owner started brewing in 2016 at the Red Lion pub which is in the picturesque Peak District village of Birchover. Upgraded in 2017 to a five-barrel plant. Several of the core range are named after local landmarks in and around the adjacent historic Stanton Moor, and are usually available at the pub. ♦ RAIB

Birmingham SIBA

Unit 15, Stirchley Trading Estate, Hazelwell Road, Birmingham, B30 2PF ☎ 07717 704929
🌐 birminghambrewingcompany.co.uk

Birmingham Brewing Co was established in 2016 and is based in a small unit on a trading estate outside the city. ‼♦

Pale Brummie (ABV 4%)

Bitter Brummie (ABV 4.1%)

Bishop Nick SIBA

33 East Street, Braintree, Essex, CM7 3JJ
☎ (01376) 349605 🌐 bishopnick.com

⊗ Bishop Nick was launched in 2011 by Nelion Ridley, a member of the family that started Ridley's brewery near Chelmsford in 1842. In 2013 a new brewery was established in Braintree using a 20-barrel plant. ♦ RAIB

Ridley's Rite (OG 1036, ABV 3.6%)
A classic bitter with a floral aroma and a subtle but long-lasting bitter aftertaste.

Heresy (OG 1041, ABV 4%)
Refreshing golden ale with a spicy bitterness before the hops deliver citrus and floral notes.

1555 (OG 1043, ABV 4.3%)
Full-bodied, rich, tawny-coloured ale with a sweet, nutty taste underlined by ginger and fruit.

Martyr (OG 1049, ABV 5%)
Full-flavoured, spicy and floral bitterness supported by a sweet, malty backbone.

Divine (OG 1051, ABV 5.1%)
Dark amber-coloured ale with a warming malt aroma and spice, nuttiness and caramel. Well-balanced with a mellow hoppiness.

Bitter End

See Tirril

Black Bear SIBA

c/o Bear Inn, 8-10 North Street, Wiveliscombe, Somerset, TA4 2JY
☎ (01984) 623537 🌐 blackbearbrewery.co.uk

Originally established in 2014 at the Northbrook Arms, East Stratton, Hampshire, before relocating to the Bear Inn, Wiveliscombe, Somerset in 2015. Five beers are currently regularly brewed for the pub and a small but growing number of other local outlets. ♦

Black Cloak (NEW)

71 Abergele Road, Colwyn Bay, LL29 7RU ☎ 07701 031121

A brewpub opened in 2018 in a former café using a one-barrel plant. The core range and regular specials are usually only available at the Black Cloak taproom. ♦

Black Country

Rear of Old Bulls Head, 1 Redhall Road, Lower Gornal, West Midlands, DY3 2NU
☎ (01384) 401820

Office: 69 Third Avenue, Pensnett Trading Estate, Kingswinford, DY6 7FD 🌐 blackcountryales.co.uk

Brewery located at the rear of the Old Bulls Head. Brewing on the site began in the 1830s and continued until 1934, recommencing in 2002. In 2012 much of the brewing equipment was replaced or refurbished. Its sister company, Black Country Inns/Taverns, own 35 pubs across the West Midlands. Beers are also brewed under the Thomas Guest Brewing Company name. ‼♦

Bradley's Finest Golden (OG 1040, ABV 4.2%)
A straw-coloured beer with a bold citrus hop aroma, fruity, balanced sweetness and a lingering, refreshing aftertaste.

Pig on the Wall (OG 1042, ABV 4.3%)
A refreshing chestnut brown-coloured beer with a complex flavour of light hops giving way to a bittersweet blend of roasted malt. Suggestions of chocolate and coffee undertones.

Fireside (OG 1047, ABV 5%)
A well-rounded premium bitter, amber in colour and clean in taste leading to a pleasant, dry finish.

Black Dog

See Hambleton

Black Fall

See Neath

Black Flag

Unit 4D Bridge Road Industrial Estate, Goonhavern, Cornwall, TR4 9QL
☎ (01872) 858004 🌐 blackflagbrewery.com

⊗ Black Flag began brewing in 2013 using an eight-barrel plant. Much use is made of New Zealand and American hops. ♦RAIB

Chameleon (OG 1038, ABV 3.8%) ◆
Golden ale with crisp, lemon sherbet and grapefruit/ tropical fruits flavour, matched by grassy/floral hops and a full, hoppy finish.

Fang (OG 1040, ABV 4%) ◆
Crisp golden ale with citrus, marmalade and resin, matched by caramel toffee and hints of stone fruits, and a long, bitter finish.

Naughty Pilchard (OG 1040, ABV 4%) ◆
Copper-coloured bitter with malt aroma. Dominant biscuit malt flavour with a sharp bite of crisp hops, and a short malty, bitter finish.

Crab Claw (OG 1050, ABV 5%) ◆
Red-coloured, strong bitter with intense hop fruit nose. Powerful citrus hop flavour, lightly bittersweet. Dry hop and sweet finish.

Galaxy & Amarillo Pale Ale (OG 1055, ABV 5.5%)
Malty golden ale with mango and orange hops throughout.

Mosaic IPA (OG 1055, ABV 5.7%) ◆
Smooth, easy-drinking golden ale with heady citrus hop nose. Powerful grassy and citrus hop flavours throughout, with mango fruit and bitterness.

White Cross IPA (OG 1057, ABV 5.7%) ◆
Amber-coloured, strong bitter with full malty fruit aroma and flavours. Vibrant citrus and tropical fruits hops, and a crisp, bitter finish.

Black IPA (OG 1060, ABV 6%)
Smooth coffee and chocolate maltiness with a punchy, hoppy finish.

Export Stout (OG 1063, ABV 6.3%)
Smooth, rich imperial stout.

Captain Haddock (OG 1056, ABV 6.5%)
Smooth, Belgian-style ale, with vibrant mango and banana tones with a prolonged rich finish.

Black Hole SIBA

Unit 3a, Old Hall Mill Business Park, Alfreton Road, Little Eaton, Derbyshire, DE21 5EJ
☎ (01283) 619943 ☎ 07812 812953
🌐 blackholebrewery.co.uk

⊗ Black Hole was established in 2007 with a 10-barrel plant in the former Ind Coope bottling stores in Burton-on-Trent, but moved to its current location in 2017. Fermenting capacity of 36-barrels enables the production of up to four brews per week, some of which are marketed under the Little Eaton Brewery name. Around 600 outlets are supplied direct, and many more via wholesalers. Since 2014 the brewery has been owned by GHH Llp, which also owns Mr Grundy's Brewery (qv). ‼♦

Golden Ale (OG 1040, ABV 3.8%)
A fresh, lively session beer, hopped to give a clean, crisp finish of hoppy dryness and a touch of astringency. It has an amber-coloured glow and a malt and spicy hop aroma.

Cosmic (OG 1044, ABV 4.2%) ◆
Almost golden-coloured with an initial malt aroma. Complex balance of malt and hops give lingering tastes of nuts, fruit and dry, hoppy bitterness.

Supernova (OG 1048, ABV 4.8%) ◆
Marmalade-like, made from Seville oranges and grapefruit, the aroma mimics the sweet start but gives into the hops which deliver a dry, lingering bitter finish.

Milky Way (OG 1059, ABV 6%) ◆
Honey and banana nose advises the sweet taste but not the sweet, dry spicy finish from this wheat beer.

Brewed for Little Eaton:

Bates' Pale Ale (OG 1036, ABV 3.8%)
Light in colour and gently-hopped, giving a slight citrus flavour.

Bagnall Bros Bitter (OG 1041, ABV 4.2%)
Amber-coloured beer with a fruity hoppiness and a slightly sweet, malty aroma.

Delver's Drop IPA (OG 1047, ABV 4.8%)
An IPA-style ale with elderberry fruit flavours.

Old Mill Stout (OG 1049, ABV 5%)
Dark-coloured, strong stout with a hint of plum.

Brewed for Small Beer:

Lincoln Imperial Ale (OG 1036, ABV 3.8%)

Black Iris SIBA

Unit 1 Shipstone Street, New Basford, Nottingham, NG7 6GJ
☎ (0115) 979 1936 ✉ blackirisbrewery@gmail.com

Black Iris began brewing in 2011 using a six-barrel plant behind the Flowerpot pub in Derby. It expanded to a brand new 10-barrel plant in 2014 and relocated to premises in Nottingham. ‼♦

Snake Eyes (OG 1038, ABV 3.8%)
Golden-coloured ale with intense, hoppy aroma and taste with lingering, bitter finish.

Bleeding Heart (OG 1044, ABV 4.5%)
Red-coloured, malty rye ale, balanced with roast and hops, with a bitter finish.

Endless Summer (OG 1041.9, ABV 4.5%)
Golden-coloured with a tropical citrus fruit presence throughout, from aroma to aftertaste with a gentle bitter finish.

Better the Devil You Know (OG 1053, ABV 5.5%)
Pale, citrusy Australian IPA, with big fruity aromas and a lingering bitterness.

Black Isle

Old Allengrange, Munlochy, IV8 8NZ
☎ (01463) 811871 🌐 blackislebrewery.com

Black Isle Brewery was set up in 1998 in the heart of the Scottish Highlands. It expanded substantially in 2011 with a new brewhouse and bottling line. All beers are organic with Soil Association certification. ‼♦

Yellowhammer (OG 1038, ABV 3.9%)
A refreshing, hoppy golden ale with light hop and peach flavours throughout and a short, bitter finish.

Red Kite (OG 1042, ABV 4.2%)
Tawny-coloured ale with light malt on the nose and some red fruit on the palate. Slight sweetness in the taste.

Heather Honey (OG 1045, ABV 4.6%)
Very sweet, honey-flavoured brew.

Porter (OG 1046, ABV 4.6%)
A hint of liquorice and burnt chocolate on the nose and a creamy mix of malt and fruit in the taste.

Blonde (OG 1046, ABV 5%)

Hibernator (OG 1068, ABV 7%)
Strong-tasting, warming, malty and fruity dark brown-coloured brew.

Black Lodge

Kings Dock Street, Baltic Triangle, Liverpool, L1 8JU
☎ 07565 299879 🌐 blacklodgebrewing.co.uk

Small-batch and one-off brewery producing beers in cask, keg, bottle and can formats that can be drunk in its own taproom. It moved premises in 2019 and now uses the ex-Mad Hatter brewery kit. Collaboration and special brews are frequent.

Black Market

The Workman's, 43 High Street, Warsop, Nottinghamshire, NG20 0AE ☎ 07824 363373

Beers first appeared from Black Market in 2016. The 2.5-barrel plant is situated in the basement of the brewery tap, the Workman's/ Black Market Venue in Warsop. There are three regular beers brewed. Nearly all the brews are consumed on-site, though a few go to pubs and beer festivals in the locality.

Black Metal

Unit 3, 6b Dryden Road, Loanhead, EH20 9LZ
☎ (0131) 623 3411 ☎ 07711 295385
🌐 blackmetalbrewery.com

Black Metal Brewery was established in 2012 by two old friends – metalheads and inspired brewers. Equipment was shared with Top Out (qv) brewery but it has now moved next door to its own site. ♦RAIB

Will-o'-the-Wisp (OG 1060, ABV 6%)

Blood Revenge (OG 1066, ABV 6.6%)

Yggdrasil (OG 1066, ABV 6.6%)

Black Rock

Unit 6c, Empire Way, Tregoniggie Industrial Estate, Falmouth, Cornwall, TR11 4SN
☎ (01326) 379477 🌐 blackrockbrewing.com

Black Rock began brewing in 2013, producing just one beer. It now has a core range of six beers, which are available in the brewery's first pub, the Small Ship, Falmouth plus a number of other local outlets. Relocation to larger premises within Falmouth is planned. Brewing is currenlty suspended. ♦RAIB

Black Sheep SIBA

Wellgarth, Masham, North Yorkshire, HG4 4EN
☎ (01765) 689227 🌐 blacksheepbrewery.co.uk

Established in 1992 by Paul Theakston, a member of Masham's famous brewing family, the brewery operation is now run by his two sons. It is situated in the former Wellgarth Maltings and uses the traditional Yorkshire Square fermenting system. The company supplies the free trade across Yorkshire and the North, with national supply through pubcos and wholesale channels. Acquired York Brewery in 2018. Six pubs/bars are owned in Yorkshire. ‼♦

Best Bitter (OG 1038, ABV 3.8%)
A hoppy and fruity beer with strong, bitter overtones, leading to a long, dry, bitter finish.

Pale Ale (ABV 4%)
Straw-coloured, hoppy pale ale with citrus and delicate fruit flavours.

Special Ale (OG 1044, ABV 4.4%)
A robust, premium amber-coloured ale with fruit overtones leading to a clean, bittersweet finish.

Riggwelter (OG 1059, ABV 5.9%)
A fruity bitter with complex underlying tastes and hints of liquorice and pear drops leading to a long, dry, bitter finish.

Brewed for Ember Inns:

Ember Pale Ale (ABV 4%)

Black Storm

See Hadrian Border

Black Tor SIBA

Units 5-6, Gidley's Industrial Estate, Christow, Exeter, Devon, EX6 7QB
☎ (01647) 252120 🌐 blacktorbrewery.com

This independent, family-run brewery is located on the eastern edge of the beautiful Dartmoor National Park, and has been under the current family ownership since 2015. Several changes of ownership and brewery name have occurred since brewing began on-site in 1998, with the present Black Tor name established in 2013. ◆

Pride Of Dartmoor (OG 1040, ABV 4%)
This mid-brown-coloured session bitter has a gentle floral aroma and pleasant taste.

Raven (OG 1042, ABV 4.2%)

Devonshire Pale Ale (OG 1044, ABV 4.5%)

Black Wolf SIBA

Unit 7c, Bandeath Industrial Estate, Throsk, Stirling, FK7 7NP
☎ (01786) 817000 ⊕ blackwolfbrewery.com

☺Established in 2005, and now owned by VC2 Brands, the brewery is located in a former torpedo factory on the shores of the River Forth. In 2014 the brewery changed its name from Traditional Scottish Ales to Black Wolf Brewery, and rebranded its range of beers. ◆

Nevis (OG 1040, ABV 4%)

Rok (OG 1040, ABV 4%)

Florida Black (OG 1045, ABV 4.5%)

Glencoe (OG 1045, ABV 4.5%)

William Wallace (OG 1045, ABV 4.5%)

Lomond Gold (OG 1050, ABV 5%)

Valente's double espresso (OG 1060, ABV 6%)

Blackedge SIBA

Moreton Mill, Hampson Street, Horwich, BL6 7JH
☎ (01204) 692976 ☎ 07795 654895
⊕ blackedgebrewery.co.uk

☒ Blackedge Brewery, established in 2011, has expanded to a 10-barrel plant visible through a viewing window on the ground floor beneath the brewery bar. Its CAMRA and SIBA award-winning beers are influenced by both British traditions and modern hop flavours. ‼ ⌸ ◆ RAIB

Zinc (OG 1038, ABV 3.5%)
Refreshing golden ale with citrus notes.

HoP (OG 1039, ABV 3.8%)
Generously-hopped with a clean, dry, refreshing and hoppy citrus, floral flavour.

Dark Mild (ABV 3.9%) ⬥
Lightly-hopped ale with a chocolate roast aroma, smooth, roast malt chocolate taste, sweet with some blackcurrant fruitiness, and a dry, bitter roast aftertaste.

Black (OG 1047, ABV 4%)
A velvety stout with intense roasted barley flavours, rich undertones of chocolate and coffee and a liquorice finish.

Cascade (ABV 4%)
Golden ale with citrus and floral notes.

Pike (OG 1042, ABV 4%)
A pale ale with plenty of sweet citrus hop flavour.

West Coast (ABV 4.1%)
A golden ale with a clean, fresh flavour of tropical fruit and grapefruit and a light floral aroma.

American (OG 1043, ABV 4.2%)
Light, hoppy beer with intense citrus aromas.

Platinum (OG 1046, ABV 4.4%)

Blonde ale, lightly-hopped to give a clean, citrus flavour and sweet citrus aroma.

Blonde (OG 1046, ABV 4.5%)
Full-flavoured, full-bodied blonde ale. Well-hopped to give a clean, crisp, fruit-like flavour and aroma.

Ginger (ABV 4.5%)
A deep golden-coloured ale brewed using fresh ginger to give a spicy orange and ginger flavour.

Dark Rum (OG 1045, ABV 4.6%) ⬥
Rich roast aroma and strong dry roast flavour. Accompanying taste of dried fruit and a long-lasting, sweet finish.

IPA (OG 1047, ABV 4.7%)
Generously-hopped, full-bodied, full-flavoured and well-balanced, hoppy and intensely citrus with a grapefruit aroma.

Black Port (OG 1045, ABV 4.9%) ⬥
Black-coloured beer with a malty, fruity aroma. Rich, with chocolate and dark fruit flavours and a slightly drier finish.

Blackened Sun

3 Heathfield, Stacey Bushes, Milton Keynes, Buckinghamshire, MK12 6HP ☎ 07963 529859
⊕ blackenedsunbrewing.co.uk

☒ Blackened Sun began brewing unpasteurised, unfiltered beers in 2017, available in cask, KeyKeg and bottles. ◆RAIB

Blackhill SIBA

Unit 14, Stella Gill Industrial Estate, Pelton Fell, Chester-le-Street, County Durham, DH2 2RG ☎ 07905 778286 ⊕ blackhillbrewery.com

☒ Blackhill began brewing in 2012 using spare capacity at Geltsdale Brewery. In 2013 it moved to its own premises in Stanley using a 10-barrel plant, before relocating again in 2018 to a more convenient site at Chester-le-Street. Beers are named after Durham coal mining seams and are available on rotation. ‼◆

70 Fathom (OG 1039, ABV 4%)
Single-hop, blonde-coloured golden ale.

Blackjack SIBA

36 Gould Street, Manchester, M4 4RN
☎ (0161) 819 2767 ⊕ blackjack-beers.com

☺Blackjack began brewing in 2012 on a 4.5-barrel plant, expanding to a 10-barrel plant in 2017. Beers are widely available across the North West and in specialist beer outlets nationally. It brews a large range of regular beers from pale ales to specialist styles, many using Belgian and farmhouse yeasts. Glassworks Drinks, a distribution business specialising in craft breweries, is also owned. ◆RAIB

Table Beer (ABV 3.2%)
A small beer with a big, hoppy taste.

Mosaic Light (ABV 3.6%)
Big hop punch that belies its strength.

Pokies (OG 1036, ABV 3.6%)
Pale-coloured session ale with grapefruit, citrus and a punchy floral aroma, and clean bitterness.

Euchre Pale (ABV 3.9%)

Bramling Cross (OG 1040, ABV 4%) ◆
Amber-coloured beer, hops and tart fruit in the
aroma and taste, with a good bitterness
throughout.

Pale (ABV 4%)

You Bet (ABV 4%)
A heavily-hopped, pale-coloured bitter, with a
varying hop profile in each brew.

Dead Man's Hand (ABV 4.1%) ◆
Fruity and citrus hop aroma. Bitter citrus hops
balanced with malt in initial taste, with bitterness
more prominent in aftertaste.

Jabberwocky (ABV 4.1%)
A hoppy pale ale with a bit of rye.

New Deck (OG 1042, ABV 4.2%) ◆
Citrus hop aroma, sharp hop bitterness balanced
with sweet malt, and a dry bitter finish.

Pokerface (ABV 4.2%)

Rabbit Hunt (ABV 4.5%)

Small Saison (OG 1042, ABV 4.5%)
Spicy and dry ale.

Double Bluff (OG 1048, ABV 4.8%)
An amber-coloured ale with a rich aroma and bitter
notes.

Brown Ale (ABV 5%)

Devil's Bedpost (ABV 5%)

Stout (OG 1050, ABV 5%) ◆
Moderate chocolate aroma and caramel malt. Dark
chocolate with sweet malt taste. Sustained and
increasing bitterness and a dry aftertaste.

NZIPA (ABV 5.4%)

Aces High (OG 1055, ABV 5.5%)
Aroma has some ripe citrus notes of melon and
orange. Flavour is sweet with mild grass and pine,
along with ripe tangerine and melon.

Black Maria (OG 1057, ABV 5.8%)
A dark-coloured ale with a hoppy aroma and light
body.

Dragon's Tears (OG 1054, ABV 5.8%)
Jasmine tea-infused golden saison.

Blackpit

**Blackpit Farm, Silverstone Road, Stowe,
Buckinghamshire, MK18 5LJ**
☎ (01280) 827244 ⊕ blackpitbrewery.co.uk

⊗ Brewing began in 2017 in a converted stable
yard on Blackpit Farm, one mile south of
Silverstone. ‼◆

Best (ABV 3.4%)
An amber-coloured bitter with a malty and slightly
hoppy flavour.

Cloud Nine (ABV 3.9%)
A blonde-coloured beer with hints of lemon zest
and pine kernels.

Loosehead (ABV 4.2%)
Mid to light brown-coloured ale, with butterscotch
and a touch of barley sugar on the nose.

Goshawk (ABV 4.4%)
A chestnut-brown bitter with earthy and malty
flavours.

Sky Rocket (ABV 5.5%)

An amber-coloured, American-style IPA. An
aromatic nose with hints of nettles and
elderflower, and an earthy flavour leads to a long,
lingering finish.

Blackwater

See Maldon

Blimey!

**Branksome House, 166 St Clements Hill, Norwich,
NR3 1RS ☎ 07775788299**
✉ adriankbryan@googlemail.com

⊗ Brewing began in 2017.

Son of Pale Face (OG 1040, ABV 4%)

Eleven APA (OG 1042, ABV 4.5%)

TEN DDH APA Cryo (OG 1042, ABV 4.5%)

The Pale Face (OG 1045, ABV 4.5%)

Thirteen (OG 1042, ABV 4.5%)

First Born IPA (OG 1052, ABV 5.2%)
An American-style IPA with notes of citrus and
tropical fruit.

Blindmans SIBA

Talbot Farm, Leighton, Frome, Somerset, BA11 4PN
☎ (01749) 880038 ⊕ blindmansbrewery.co.uk

Established in 2002 in a converted milking parlour
and purchased by its current owners in 2004, this
five-barrel brewery has its own water spring. The
range of ales is regularly on tap at the
Cornerhouse, Frome. ‼◆

Buff Amber (OG 1036, ABV 3.6%)
Amber-coloured, smooth session beer.

Funny Farm (ABV 4%)
Pale, light golden-coloured ale, with a crisp and
hoppy finish.

Golden Spring (OG 1040, ABV 4%)
Fresh and aromatic straw-coloured beer.

Mine Beer (OG 1042, ABV 4.2%)
Full-bodied, copper-coloured, blended malt ale.

Icarus (OG 1045, ABV 4.5%)
Fruity, rich, dark ruby-coloured ale.

Block

⬛ **Wenlock Arms, 26 Wenlock Road, Hoxton, London,
N1 7TA**
☎ (020) 7608 3406 ⊕ wenlockarms.com

⊗ Block is based in the cellar of the award-winning
Wenlock Arms. Launched at the end of 2016, the
beer is available at the pub.

Blonde Brothers (NEW) SIBA

Great Bathampton Farm, Wylye, Wiltshire, BA12 0QD
☎ 07538 872379 ⊕ blondebrothers.beer

Established in 2019 on an organic family farm, it
uses home-grown barley and water drawn from its
own chalk borehole.

Bloomfield

Bloomfield Brewhouse, 47 Ansdell Road, Blackpool, FY1 6PW
(01253) 693219 bloomfield-brewhouse.co.uk

Brewery set up in 2015. The beers are produced using wort from a third-party brewery.

Blue Anchor

50 Coinagehall Street, Helston, Cornwall, TR13 8EL
(01326) 562821 spingoales.com

A 15th-century thatched brewpub, the oldest continuously brewing plant in the country. Home of the famous Spingo ales, which are made with water from the pub's well. !! ♦ RAIB

Blue Bear

See Davenports

Blue Bee SIBA

Unit 29-30, Hoyland Road Industrial Estate, Sheffield, South Yorkshire, S3 8AB 07375 659349
bluebeebrewery.co.uk

Originally established in 2010, this independently-owned, 10-barrel brewery supplies the free trade throughout Yorkshire and the East Midlands, although it is often seen further afield. Blue Bee regularly produces both innovative specials and collaborations with other like-minded breweries. A single-hopped IPA is always available. ♦

Hillfoot Best Bitter (OG 1039, ABV 4%)
Traditional, dark chestnut-coloured, fruity best bitter.

Reet Pale (OG 1038, ABV 4%)
Pale-coloured ale with floral and citrus flavours leading to a dry bitter finish.

American 5 Hop (OG 1041, ABV 4.3%)

Triple Hop (OG 1041, ABV 4.3%)

Ginger Beer (OG 1043, ABV 4.5%)
A pale ale with the addition of fiery ginger.

Tempest Stout (OG 1048, ABV 4.8%)
Rich, well-balanced stout with hints of coffee and chocolate leading to a bitter finish.

Blue Bell

Cranesgate South, Whaplode St Catherine, Lincolnshire, PE12 6SN
(01406) 540300 07788136663
thebluebell.net

Founded in 1998 behind the Blue Bell Pub. The brewery is owned by the pub after previously operating as a separate business. Beers are only available at the pub and to private customers. !! ♦ RAIB

Blue Bell Brewhouse

Warings Green Road, Warings Green, Warwickshire, B94 6BP 07922 554181
rnrbrewhouse@outlook.com

A two-barrel plant set up in 2013 by Mark Shepherd to resurrect on-site brewing at the Blue Bell Cider House (brewing ceased in 1968). Brewster Lynn Crossland, who joined in 2014, continues the tradition of female brewers in the original brewhouse, producing solely for the Blue Bell and local festivals. The brewery likes to experiment with unusual flavours, and using ingredients foraged from local hedgerows. ♦

Blue Monkey SIBA

10 Pentrich Road, Giltbrook Industrial Park, Giltbrook, Nottinghamshire, NG16 2UZ
(0115) 9385899 bluemonkeybrewery.com

Blue Monkey was established in 2008 as a 10-barrel plant but moved in 2010 to a bigger site to meet increasing demand. It now brews around 15,000 pints a week to supply more than 200 local outlets and selected national distributors. The brewery has four pubs called the Organ Grinder, in Nottingham, Arnold, Loughborough, and Newark. !!

BG Sips (OG 1041, ABV 4%)
Pale golden-coloured, hoppy beer. Very fruity and bitter.

Funky Gibbon (OG 1042, ABV 4.1%)
Tawny-coloured malty ale, dried fruit aroma and a gentle bitter finish.

99 Red Baboons (OG 1042, ABV 4.2%)
Red-coloured with a malty fruitiness. Not overly hoppy.

Infinity (OG 1045.7, ABV 4.6%)
Hoppy golden ale.

Chocolate Guerilla (OG 1052, ABV 4.9%)

Guerrilla (OG 1052, ABV 4.9%)
A creamy stout, full of roast malt flavour and a slightly sweet finish.

Ape Ale (OG 1052, ABV 5.4%)
Intensely-hopped, strong golden ale with dry, bitter finish.

Blue Square

See Truth Hurts

Blueball

The Old Bakery, 31-33 Ashridge Street, Runcorn, Cheshire, WA7 1HU
(01928) 775628

Blueball began brewing in 2010. After a short closure in 2017 the brewery reopened and continues to brew the beers listed. Owner Alex Haycraft has entered into a collaboration business arrangement with Heavy Industry Brewery (qv) by opening a bar called STR (Society LTD Taprooms, Runcorn) in the brewery building. Beers are also available in the free trade and at Kash 22 Bar, Frodsham.

Indie Girl (OG 1036, ABV 3.8%)
A gold hue, aroma of citrus and tropical fruits, with a clean, dry finish, and a long hoppy aftertaste.

Gold Digger (ABV 4%)

Communion (OG 1040, ABV 4.1%)

Ruby O'Reilly (OG 1040, ABV 4.3%)

Penny Black (OG 1045, ABV 4.5%)

Spank (OG 1059, ABV 6%)
Sweetish strong ale.

Bluestone (Lancashire)

Unit 6, Daniel Street Industrial Estate, Whitworth, Lancashire, OL12 8BX
☎ (01706) 853009 ☎ 07802 792536
bluestonebrewery.co.uk

A small 3.5-barrel brewery using traditional methods including double dropping. Brewing takes place mainly at the weekend.

Quarrymans Stout (OG 1041, ABV 4%)
A traditional, double-dropped, black-coloured stout.

EPA (English Pale Ale) (OG 1042, ABV 4.2%)
A traditional, dry pale ale with strong malt and hop flavours.

Night Hops Stout (OG 1043, ABV 4.2%)
Dark-coloured, dry stout with a good hop flavour through the roasted malt, liquorice and spice.

AKA (Amber Kitchen Ale) (OG 1043, ABV 4.4%)
A brown-coloured ale, lightly-hopped with a caramel and liquorice, malty flavour.

Spodden Pilsner (OG 1048, ABV 4.4%)
A full-bodied, full-flavoured, hoppy, bohemian-style Pilsner.

Bluestone (Pembrokeshire) SIBA

Tyriet, Cilgwyn, Newport/ Trefdraeth, Pembrokeshire, SA42 0QW
☎ (01239) 820833 bluestonebrewing.co.uk

A family-run business established in 2013 on a working hill farm in the Preseli Hills within the Pembrokeshire Coast National Park. The 10-barrel brewery has been installed in a renovated 200-year-old stone barn, which doubles as a visitor facility and office, with the surrounding yard becoming an events venue throughout the summer months. The brewery uses water from a private supply which filters down through the Preseli Hills. Numerous local outlets are supplied as well as wholesalers around the UK. !! ♦ RAIB

Rockhopper (OG 1039, ABV 3.9%)
Classic pale amber-coloured bitter with a light malt base and a spicy fruitiness.

Bedrock Blonde (OG 1040, ABV 4%)
A straw-coloured blonde ale with creamy, soft and malty flavours.

Elderflower Blonde (OG 1040, ABV 4%)
Straw-coloured, delicately-hopped and finished with a delicate hint of elderflower.

Hammerstone IPA (OG 1044, ABV 4.5%)
Modern IPA providing a fruity, effervescent and refreshing golden-coloured ale.

Rocketeer (OG 1046, ABV 4.6%)
A traditional, full-bodied bitter with a rich, malty base.

Fossil Fuel (ABV 4.8%)
A full-bodied, creamy stout with a shot of espresso coffee.

Blunt Chisel (NEW)

Phoenix Mill, Sawmill Road, Blairadam, KY4 0JG
thebluntchisel.co.uk

A nanobrewery set up in a former sawmill on the north bank of the Kelty Burn. A range of bottle-conditioned beers is on sale at the monthly Kinross Farmers' Market, and at Leith Market. RAIB V

Blythe SIBA

Blythe House Farm, Lichfield Road, Hamstall Ridware, Staffordshire, WS15 3QQ
☎ (01889) 504661 ☎ 07483 248723
blythebrewery.co.uk

⊗ Blythe began brewing in 2003 using a 2.5-barrel plant in a converted barn. A change of ownership occurred in 2017. 15 outlets are supplied direct. !! ♦ RAIB

Bagot's Bitter (OG 1040, ABV 3.8%)
A lightly-hopped, easy-drinking, amber-coloured ale with a fruit start and sweetness, which develops to a smooth, bitter finish.

Ridware Pale (OG 1042, ABV 4.3%)
Bright and golden-coloured, with a bitter floral hop aroma and citrus taste. Hop-sharp, bitter and refreshing. Long, lingering bite with ripples of citrus across the tongue.

Staffie (OG 1044, ABV 4.4%)
Hoppy and grassy aroma with hints of sweetness from this amber-coloured beer. A touch of malt at the start is soon overwhelmed by hops. A full hoppy, mouth-watering finish.

Palmers Poison (OG 1045, ABV 4.5%)
Refreshing beer, tawny in colour, with a light head. Coffee truffle aroma, pleasingly sweet to start but with a good hop mouthfeel.

Johnsons (OG 1056, ABV 5.2%)
Black-coloured with a thick head. Refreshingly hoppy and full-bodied with lingering bitterness of chocolate, dates, coal smoke and liquorice.

Boat Lane

Unit 3, Streamside Business Park, Boat Lane, Offenham, Worcestershire, WR11 8RS
☎ (01386) 48212 boatlanebrewery.co.uk

A microbrewery established in 2017 in a small village near Evesham.

Bodachra (NEW) SIBA

57 Denview Road, Potterton, AB23 8ZL

Bodachra is a small batch craft brewery established in 2018. ♦

Formantine (ABV 3.8%)
Pale gold-coloured session IPA with a subtle hoppiness.

Citrus Gold (ABV 4.9%)
A Belgian-style IPA.

Bog Brew SIBA

On the Green, 11 High Street, Old Town, Stevenage, Hertfordshire, SG1 3BG ☎ 07973 573040
bogbrew.co.uk

⊗ Paul Clinton started brewing as a hobby, then began brewing for his restaurant, On the Green, in 2017. Currently using a 1.5-barrel plant, there are plans for expansion. Beers are available in the restaurant, at local beer festivals and at free houses around Hertfordshire and Bedfordshire. !! RAIB V

Barking Spider (OG 1039, ABV 3.8%)

An easy-drinking session ale with hints of chocolate and coffee.

Bottoms Up (OG 1039, ABV 3.8%)
An easy-drinking, mid-gold-coloured ale with pear and grapefruit notes.

Porter Potty (OG 1040, ABV 4.1%)
A deep, dark-coloured stout with hints of chocolate and a rich, silky mouthfeel.

Pail Ale (OG 1049, ABV 5.3%)
An IPA with peppery, citrus hop notes, a bitter, long-lasting finish and a crisp mouthfeel.

2mhaard Blonde Ale (OG 1043, ABV 5.4%)
A saison-style blonde ale with classic sour notes from the Belgian yeast strain. Dry and crisp with hints of sage and pepper.

Bombs Away (OG 1057, ABV 6.3%)
A complex double IPA with peppery, citrus and fruity notes.

Bohem

Unit 5, Littleline House, 41-43 West Road, Tottenham, London, N17 0RE
☎ (020) 8617 8350 ☎ 07548 793771
bohembrewery.com

Traditional Bohemian lagers brewed by Czech expats in North London who moved to larger premises in 2018. Beers are supplied to local outlets, including the taproom near the original brewery site. No real ale and cans are becoming a popular choice.

Boilerhouse

See JW Lees (under L)

Bollington SIBA

Adlington Road, Bollington, Cheshire, SK10 5JT
☎ (01625) 575380 bollingtonbrewing.co.uk

Bollington began brewing in 2008 with the Vale Inn, Bollington, as its brewery tap. The Park Tavern, Macclesfield, and the Cask Tavern, Poynton, are also owned. Around 40 outlets are supplied direct. !! ♦ RAIB

Chinook & Grapefruit (OG 1036, ABV 3.6%)
Fresh grapefruit zest and juice paired with punchy hops.

Ginger Brew (OG 1041, ABV 3.6%)
A pale bitter, with a hoppy, bitter flavour, and a smooth taste with fresh root ginger added.

White Nancy (OG 1038, ABV 3.6%)
Very pale, light bitter, with a good hoppiness and light body.

Long Hop (OG 1039, ABV 3.9%)
Pale lager-style bitter with fruity refreshing hops.

Bollington Best (OG 1041, ABV 4.2%)
A delightfully hoppy bitter. Clean and crisp with a very light golden colour and a refreshing bitter aftertaste.

Dinner Ale (OG 1042, ABV 4.3%)
Deep copper-coloured, traditional-style bitter, with a fresh slightly fruity nose, and a dry, hoppy finish.

Oat Mill Stout (OG 1049, ABV 5%)
An oatmeal stout with a twist. A hoppy, bitter taste keeps the sweetness in check.

Eastern Nights (OG 1056, ABV 5.6%)
A pale gold-coloured balanced IPA, with a modest hop content. Very drinkable for its strength.

Bond Brews

Units 3 & 4, South Barns, Gardeners Green Farm, Heathlands Road, Wokingham, Berkshire, RG40 3AS
☎ (01344) 775450 bondbrews.co.uk

Bond Brews was established in 2015 using a six-barrel plant. Beers are delivered to pubs within a 30-mile radius. Brewery experience days are available by arrangement with the brewer. !! ♦ RAIB

Goldi-hops (OG 1039, ABV 3.9%)
A refreshing, amber-coloured pale ale with a malty and delicately citrusy nose, followed by a bitter flavour, and a long, dry, bitter finish.

Best of British (OG 1040, ABV 4%)
A tawny-coloured best bitter with malt and fruit on the nose, dry fruity flavours balancing the bitterness, followed by a touch of blackcurrant aftertaste.

Bengal Tiger (OG 1043, ABV 4.3%)
A pale golden-coloured IPA with a hoppy, fruity aroma. Initially fruity flavour leads to an earthy bitterness and a long, dry, bitter finish.

Railway Porter (OG 1045, ABV 4.5%)
An easy-drinking, dark brown-coloured porter with a reddish tint. Subtle toasty maltiness, with a gently-lingering fruity finish.

Bone Idle (NEW)

28 The Green, Idle, West Yorkshire, BD10 9PX
☎ 07525 751574

Established in 2018 in a converted barn situated in the heart of Idle village. The brewery offers the public the opportunity to try brewing. All beers produced are sold exclusively in the Idle Draper pub next door. A mezzanine floor has a mini cinema/function room.

Bone Machine (NEW)

20 Pier Street, Hull, East Yorkshire, HU1 1ZA ☎ 07931 313438

Office: Unit 1E, Hampden Road, Pocklington Industrial Estate, York, YO42 1NR
beer@bonemachinebrewing.com

Originally set up in Pocklington in 2017, Bone Machine have transferred operations to Hull's Fruit Market. The brewery operates on an eight-barrel plant. Finnish brothers Marko and Kimmo previously worked at Atom and Brass Castle Brewery before setting up on their own. V

Back Bone (OG 1037, ABV 3.7%)

Cloud Piercer (OG 1047, ABV 4.7%)

Dream Machine (OG 1052, ABV 5.2%)

Boot

12 Boot Hill, Repton, Derbyshire, DE65 6FT
☎ (01283) 346047
Office: 11 The Green, Willington, DE65 6BP
thebootbeer.co.uk

An eight-barrel brewery installed at the rear of the Boot Inn, Repton, home of the eponymous

THE BREWERIES

public school, during 2015. The brewery supplies the three pubs within the group and to free trade outlets across the Midlands. !! ♦ RAIB

Clod Hopper (OG 1038, ABV 3.9%)
Golden-coloured beer with hints of caramel in this citrus hop dominated ale that has a dry, soft, refreshing and finish.

Bitter (OG 1045, ABV 4.3%)

Tuffer's Old (OG 1047, ABV 4.6%)
Velvety, rich porter exudes notes of dark fruit, hazelnut and coffee with cocoa in the finish.

ESB (OG 1047, ABV 4.8%)
A refreshing, strong, amber-coloured and full-bodied ale with moderate bitterness packing floral, fruity hops and toasty malt flavour.

ReBoot (OG 1048, ABV 5.2%)
An orange citrus dominated pale ale loaded with hops. Citrus and floral aromas are balanced by a malty backbone. Smooth hop flavours linger in the aftertaste.

Beast (OG 1067, ABV 6.7%)
A dark mahogany-coloured, strong ale with rich, dark fruit, light spice and chocolate roast aromas, coupled with bitter fruit, raisin, fruit cake, gentle liquorice, toffee and some spice on the palate.

Boot Town

c/o Copper Kettle Brewing, Bosworths Garden Centre,, 110 Finedon Road, Burton Latimer, Northamptonshire, NN15 5QA
☎ (01536) 725212 boottownbrewery.co.uk

A microbrewery established in 2017 and based on the old Copper Kettle Brewery site, producing an ever-changing range of beers.

Bootleg IFBB

Horse & Jockey, 9 The Green, Chorlton-cum-Hardy, M21 9HS bootleg-brewingco.com

Nestled within the old brewery tower of a 200-year-old village inn, the microbrewery produces a range of regular beers. !! ♦

Born in the Borders SIBA

Lanton Mill, Jedburgh, TD8 6ST
☎ (01835) 830495 ☎ 07802 416494
bornintheborders.com

Scotland's original plough-to-pint brewery, it started brewing as Scottish Borders Brewery in 2011 using barley from its own farm before changing name. Beyond its core range of ales, projects have included the 'Wild Harvest' initiative, which sources locally-foraged ingredients for its ales. The brewery has a visitor centre, offering brewery tours, a café/restaurant and retail units featuring Borders beer, produce and food. !! ♦

Foxy Blonde (OG 1037.5, ABV 3.8%)
Invigorating golden ale bursting with citrus and floral flavours.

Game Bird (OG 1039.5, ABV 4%)
An amber-coloured ale with a moreish balance of malty sweetness and late summer fruit with a long, easy finish.

Holy Cow (OG 1041, ABV 4.2%)
Hints of dark malt combine with a long floral finish.

Gold Dust (OG 1041.5, ABV 4.3%)
A light IPA with a big burst of hop aroma.

Dark Horse (OG 1044, ABV 4.5%)
A classic dark ale with overtones of coffee and chocolate, and a spicy finish that lingers on the tongue.

Borough

33 Earle Street, Crewe, Cheshire, CW1 2BG
☎ (01270) 254999
info@borougharmscrewe.co.uk

A two-barrel brewery opened in 2005 to supply the pub but with beers occasionally available at festivals. Regular brewing restarted in 2019 with the intention of offering a variety of beer styles. !! ♦

Borough Arms

2 New Henry Street, Neath, SA11 2PH
☎ (01639) 644902 ☎ 07577 461915
boroughbreweryneath.com

Opened in 2014, the brewery was built by the landlord in a converted outbuilding at the rear of the pub. By 2016 it had expanded to 10-barrels and relocated to a nearby industrial estate. In 2019 the 10-barrel brewery and pub were sold to new owners. The kit is back at the pub in an outbuilding. !! RAIB

Iron Runner (OG 1042, ABV 4.3%)
Best bitter with a roasted, nutty aftertaste.

IPA (OG 1044, ABV 4.4%)
Strong-tasting with a crisp, clean mouthfeel.

Full Blast (OG 1050, ABV 4.7%)
Golden-coloured, fruity and zesty ale.

Nut Red Coke (OG 1051, ABV 4.9%)
Chestnut-coloured ale with malt overtones.

Boss SIBA

176 Neath Road, Landore, Swansea, SA1 2JT
☎ (01792) 450978 ☎ 07825 525735
bossbrewing.co.uk

The brewery opened in 2015 by Roy Allkin and Sarah John, using a 10-barrel plant. It relocated in 2017 to larger premises opposite the Liberty Stadium which now includes an on-site brewery tap – the Brewery Bar. Expansion has resulted in bottling, canning, kegging as well as casking. 250 outlets are supplied, bottles and cans are distributed to national retailers. In a further trade expansion, exports to France and Germany commenced in 2017. Boss established a bar, Copper, in Swansea city centre. !! ♦ RAIB

Blonde (OG 1040, ABV 4%)
Aroma of pine forest, exotic spice, grapefruit peel, followed by taste of grapefruit, resinous pine, clean bitterness to finish.

Blaze (OG 1045, ABV 4.5%)
Floral, herbal aroma gives way to a zingy citrus, spicy flovour.

Bix (ABV 4.6%)
Belgian witbier-style ale, with orange peel and coriander seeds.

Bare (OG 1050, ABV 5%)

Lager-style beer, lemony zest with a malty biscuit undertone, hints of caramel leading to a clean spicy finish.

Black (OG 1050, ABV 5%)
Aroma of roasted coffee and warm chocolate, with flavour of fire roasted nuts, toffee and chocolate.

Brave (OG 1055, ABV 5.5%)
Initial tropical fruit cocktail, elderflower and rose, with a grapefruit, citrus, piney kick to finish.

Bosun's SIBA

Unit 4, Prospect Business Centre, Prospect Street, Huddersfield, West Yorkshire, HD1 2NU
☎ (01484) 412300 ☎ 07513 112188
bosunsbrewery.co.uk

The first brew was produced in 2013 by a father-and-son team who had both served in the armed forces. The brewery relocated from Horbury to Huddersfield in 2018. The regular beers are produced on a 10-barrel plant with some given military themed names. The brewery tap is open Friday-Sunday. ‼ ♦

Tell No Tales (OG 1038, ABV 3.8%)

Blonde (OG 1039, ABV 3.9%)

Maiden Voyage (OG 1039, ABV 3.9%)
Chestnut brown-coloured traditional ale, gently bittered.

Down the Hatch (OG 1040, ABV 4%)

King Neptune (OG 1043, ABV 4.3%)

IPA (OG 1056, ABV 5.6%)

Botley SIBA

Botley Mills, Mill Hill, Botley, Hampshire, SO30 2GB
☎ (01489) 784867 ☎ 07909337212
botleybrewery.com

Botley Brewery was established in 2010 and uses a five-barrel plant. A recently added small bar next door, appropriately named the Hidden Tap, serves three of its ales Thu-Sat. ♦RAIB

Hampshire Pale Ale (OG 1038, ABV 3.8%)
Yorkshire-style amber-coloured session bitter.

Pommy Blonde (ABV 4.3%)

English IPA (ABV 5.1%)

Stinger Porter (ABV 5.2%)

Bottle Brook

Church Street, Kilburn, Belper, Derbyshire, DE56 0LU
☎ (01332) 880051 ☎ 07971 189915

A sister brewery to Leadmill (qv), Bottle Brook was established in 2005 using a 2.5-barrel plant on a tower gravity system. New World hops are predominantly used. The core range of beers is supplemented by one-off brews.

Columbus (OG 1040, ABV 4%)

Heanor Pale Ale (OG 1041, ABV 4.2%)

Roadrunner (OG 1047, ABV 4.8%)

Mellow Yellow (OG 1054, ABV 5.7%)

Rapture (OG 1058, ABV 5.9%)

Sand in the Wind (OG 1060, ABV 6.1%)

Boudicca

The Old Store, Walsingham Road, West Barsham, Norfolk, NR21 9NP
☎ (01328) 863854 ☎ 07864 321732
boudiccabrewing.co.uk

Established in 2015, Boudicca Brewery moved to its current premises on an estate in North Norfolk in 2017. It is an award-winning, independent brewery exclusively producing vegan beers, supplied to free trade outlets across East Anglia, including cafés, delis and off licences. ‼♦RAIB V

Queen of Hops (OG 1036.5, ABV 3.7%)
Refreshing pale ale, soft, rounded grassy and fruity aroma with hints of marmalade, tangy and fruity hop hit, with with some underpinning malt and bitterness. Zesty, citrus hop notes in the finish.

Three Tails (OG 1036.5, ABV 3.9%)
Classic amber-coloured bitter but with a touch of peppery spiciness. Gentle on the nose, with sweet fruit, malt and hops. Well-balanced with a pleasant, lasting finish of gently tangy hops and bitterness.

Golden Torc (OG 1039.5, ABV 4.3%)
Subtle on the nose, hops start to come through in the mouth, and burst out into a lasting finish, with a steady base of malt and bitterness and a hint of grapefruit/ citrus.

Spiral Stout (OG 1045, ABV 4.6%)
Dark autumnal berry aroma, full-bodied, with undertones of coffee and dark chocolate. A gentle, lingering, dry roast finish, with a hint of smoke.

Prasto's Porter (OG 1053.5, ABV 5.2%)
Dark fruit and hops on the nose, with hints of roast malt and smoke. Full-bodied and smooth with dark malt and dark fruit. A dry and subtle, smoky finish with fruit and hop notes.

Boundary

Unit A5, 310 Portview Trade Centre, Newtownards Road, Belfast, BT4 1HE boundarybrewing.coop

Boundary is a cooperative brewery based in Belfast, established in 2014. A taproom is open to the public. ♦

APA (OG 1035, ABV 3.5%)

Export Stout (OG 1070, ABV 7%)

IPA (OG 1070, ABV 7%)

Boutilliers

The Hop Shed, Macknade Fine Foods, Selling Road, Faversham, Kent, ME13 8XF ☎ 07743372434 or 07766 boutilliers.com

Founded in 2016, Boutilliers is a small brewery specialising in left field brews. Its beers are mainly bottled or canned. Cask-conditioned beers are supplied to a few local pubs and are sometimes available at the brewery on open days.

Bowland SIBA

Holmes Mill, Greenacre Street, Clitheroe, Lancashire, BB7 1EB
☎ (01200) 443592 bowlandbrewery.com

Founded in 2003, this family-run business uses a 30-barrel plant together with a nanobrewery for experimental brews. The site features a beer shop and beer hall with 42 handpumps featuring beers from Lancashire and beyond. 'Ales of Outstanding Natural Beauty' is named after the Forest of Bowland AONB nearby. ‼ ♦ RAIB

Pheasant Plucker (OG 1038, ABV 3.7%)
A copper-coloured bitter with rounded blackcurrant flavours and a malty aftertaste.

Gold (OG 1039, ABV 3.8%)
A hoppy, golden bitter with intense grapefruit flavours and aromas.

Boxer Blonde (OG 1040, ABV 4%)
Straw-coloured, refreshing ale, with gooseberry flavour and aroma.

Bumble (OG 1042, ABV 4%)
Lightly-hopped ale finished with a late addition of locally-sourced honey.

Hen Harrier (OG 1040, ABV 4%)
The malty start belies what comes next: fruity, sweet, hoppy bitter with a long-lasting finish comprising of all the previous elements.

Buster IPA (OG 1046, ABV 4.5%)
Well-balanced, medium-bodied and rounded, with long, tropical undertones.

Bowman SIBA

Wallops Wood, Sheardley Lane, Droxford, Hampshire, SO32 3QY
☎ (01489) 878110 bowman-ales.com

Brewing started in 2006 in converted farm buildings. The brewery supplies more than 100 outlets. A new 40-barrel plant came on stream in 2013, which is now working alongside the original 20-barrel plant. Bowman also brew the Suthwyk Ales range of beers. ‼ ♦ RAIB

Swift One (OG 1038, ABV 3.8%)
Easy-drinking bitter, well-balanced with sweet maltiness leading to a bittersweet finish and slightly dry, hoppy aftertaste.

Meon Valley Bitter (OG 1040, ABV 3.9%)
Well-balanced, copper-coloured bitter, sweet with an initial maltiness in taste and aroma leading to a more biter finish.

Yumi (OG 1039, ABV 3.9%)
A rich, amber-coloured, fairly bitter beer.

Wallops Wood (OG 1040, ABV 4%)
Malt flavours throughout balanced by toffee notes, sweetness and a slightly dry finish.

Contract brewed for Suthwyk Ales:

Old Dick (OG 1038, ABV 3.8%)
Easy-drinking, well-balanced, clean-tasting, pale brown-coloured bitter.

Liberation (OG 1042, ABV 4.2%)
Light-coloured with a soft, berry fruit flavour.

Skew Sunshine Ale (OG 1046, ABV 4.6%)
An amber-coloured beer, initial hoppiness leads to a fruity taste and finish.

Palmerston's Folly (OG 1050, ABV 5%)
A clear wheat and barley beer, slightly dry with a hint of honey in the aftertaste.

Bowness Bay SIBA

Unit 10, Castle Mills, Aynam Road, Kendal, Cumbria, LA9 7DE ☎ 07885 171210
bownessbaybrewing.co.uk

Bowness Bay Brewery moved to Kendal in 2015, increasing capacity from five to 15-barrels. The original five-barrel plant is used for small experimental brews. The brewery now has its own taphouse, the Barrel House. In 2019 grant funding allowed further expansion to quadruple capacity. ‼ ♦

Lakeland Blonde (ABV 3.7%)

Amazon Amber (OG 1038, ABV 3.8%)
A golden brown-coloured ale with a sweet grainy mouthfeel and a fruity nose, continues with some hops and a bitter finish.

Swift Best (OG 1044, ABV 3.8%)
A tawny-coloured bitter, caramel sweetness dominates, leading to a gentle bitter finish.

Swallow Gold (OG 1039, ABV 3.9%)
Golden ale, smooth floral hints of apricot, lime and peach.

Swan Blonde (OG 1039, ABV 4%)
A sweet, light session blonde with distinct citrus notes and flavour and light bitterness.

Swan Black (OG 1046, ABV 4.6%)
Stout-like beer with a fruity, raisiny middle, grainy mouthfeel and roast bitter finish.

Tern IPA (OG 1043, ABV 5%)
Well-balanced IPA with some sweet malt and fruit to balance the lingering hoppy finish.

Box Social SIBA

18 Riverdale Court, Newburn, NE15 8SG
☎ (0191) 340 4394 ☎ 07803 791761
boxsocial.pub

Launched in 2015, this family-run brewery has a licence and is open to the public most days (12-9pm). In 2016 it opened a micropub-cuterie based in Forth Street, Newcastle. ‼ ♦ RAIB

Hybrid Theory (ABV 3.5%)

Gentlemans Nectar Pale Ale (ABV 4.2%)

Sticky Beak (ABV 4.2%)

Kaffir Lime (ABV 4.3%)

A Certain Shade of Green (ABV 6%)

Box Steam SIBA

15 The Midlands, Holt, Wiltshire, BA14 6RU
☎ (01225) 782700 boxsteambrewery.com

Founded in 2004, the brewery boasts a Fulton steam-fired copper, hence the name. New ownership since 2006 meant expansion and increased capacity with the brewery moving to larger premises in Holt in 2011. Two pubs are owned and more than 100 outlets supplied. ‼ ♦

Golden Bolt (OG 1037.5, ABV 3.8%)
A straw-coloured bitter, full-flavoured with a slightly dry, hoppy aftertaste.

Tunnel Vision (OG 1040.5, ABV 4.2%)
A well-rounded light amber-coloured bitter. Clean tasting, with a slight bitterness on the finish.

Funnel Blower (OG 1045, ABV 4.5%)
A porter with vanilla sweetness and bitter chocolate.

Piston Broke (OG 1045, ABV 4.5%)

Full-bodied, deep golden-coloured ale with a refreshing hoppy, citrus palate and a subtle fruit-hop aroma.

Derail Ale (OG 1052, ABV 5.2%)
Hoppy traditional IPA. Full-flavoured with an intense floral aroma, finished with well-balanced bitterness.

Boxcar

Unit 1, Birkbeck Street, Bethnal Green, London, E2 6JY
boxcarbrewery.co.uk

Having started at Homerton, 2019 saw a move to bigger premises in Bethnal Green. No real ale.

Br3wery (NEW)

57 Mackenzie Road, Clock House, BR3 4RY
br3wery.com

Established in 2019 producing bottle-conditioned beers, available from the nearby Three Hounds bottle shop. RAIB

Brack'N'Brew

Brackenrigg Inn, Watermillock, Cumbria, CA11 0LP
(01768) 486206 brackenrigginn.co.uk

Brewing started in 2015, set up in the old stable block at the rear of the Brackenrigg Inn, on the shores of Ullswater in the Lake District. A four-barrel plant is used to produce cask and bottled beers, which are sold across Cumbria and the north of England.

Alfred's Golden Ale (OG 1032, ABV 3.2%)
A mildly bitter, light and crisp golden ale packed with citrus aroma and a hint of spice.

Boathouse Blonde (OG 1039, ABV 3.8%)
Hoppy nose with hints of grapefruit, bitter but refreshing taste.

The Rambling Bookkeeper Bitter (OG 1042, ABV 4.1%)
Mellow honey aroma and moderate hop bitterness with a sweet roasted malt taste.

The Steamer Stout (OG 1044, ABV 4.4%)
Uses espresso beans to makes a rich stout with notes of chocolate, caramel and dark fruits.

Aira Force IPA (OG 1054, ABV 5.9%)

Bradfield SIBA

Watt House Farm, High Bradfield, Sheffield, South Yorkshire, S6 6LG
(0114) 285 1118 bradfieldbrewery.co.uk

Established in 2005, Bradfield is a family-run business, based on a working farm in the Peak District using pure Millstone Grit spring water. The direct delivery distribution area covers the North of England from Northumberland to Northampton, East to West Coast. Beer is also supplied to outlets outside this area. The Nag's Head in nearby Loxley, has been the brewery tap since 2009. In 2018 the brewery obtained the King & Miller, Deepcar, as its second pub. Monthly specials are also available. ♦ RAIB

Farmers Bitter (OG 1039, ABV 3.9%)
A traditional, copper-coloured malt ale with a floral aroma.

Farmers Blonde (OG 1041, ABV 4%)
Pale, blonde beer with citrus and summer fruits aromas.

Farmers Brown Cow (OG 1042.5, ABV 4.2%)
A rich, deep chestnut-coloured ale, with a smooth creamy head. A citrus aftertaste gives way to a long dry finish.

Farmers Steel Cow (OG 1045, ABV 4.5%)
A light, fruity, full-bodied beer with a sharp, dry aftertaste.

Farmers Stout (OG 1045, ABV 4.5%)
A dark stout with roasted malts and flaked oats and a subtle, bitter hop character.

Farmers Belgian Blue (OG 1048, ABV 4.9%)
Berry overtones and a slight blue tint.

Farmers Pale Ale (OG 1049, ABV 5%)
A fruity pale ale, well-balanced with a powerful floral bouquet, full-bodied and a predominantly dry aftertaste.

Farmers Sixer (OG 1058, ABV 6%)
A strong lager-type ale with a fruity finish.

Brains IFBB

Dragon Brewery, Pacific Road, Cardiff, CF24 5HJ
(029) 2040 2060 sabrain.com

Brains was established in 1882 at the city centre-located Old Brewery, moving to the former Hancock's brewery site in 1999. The Craft Brewery remains at that site, which is within the Central Quay development area, and will be enhanced with a pub and visitor's centre, while the new Dragon Brewery and head office in Cardiff Bay commenced brewing in 2019. The company has remained in family ownership and runs more than 160 pubs throughout Wales. It is heavily involved in sponsoring charities and Welsh sport. ♦

Dark (OG 1035.5, ABV 3.5%)
A tasty, classic dark brown-coloured mild. Bittersweet, mellow and with a lasting finish of malt and roast.

Bitter (OG 1036, ABV 3.7%)
Amber-coloured with a gentle aroma of malt and hops, with a bitter finish.

Rev James Gold (OG 1041, ABV 4.1%)

SA (OG 1042, ABV 4.2%)
A mellow, full-bodied beer. Gentle malt and hop aroma leads to a malty, hop and fruit mix with a balancing bitterness.

SA Gold (OG 1042, ABV 4.2%)
A golden beer with a hoppy aroma. Well-balanced with a zesty hop, malt, fruit and balancing bitterness.

Rev James Rye (OG 1043, ABV 4.3%)

Rev James (OG 1045.5, ABV 4.5%)
A faint malt and fruit aroma with malt and fruit flavours in the taste, initially bittersweet. Bitterness balances the flavour.

Contract Brewed for Molson Coors:

M&B Brew XI (OG 1036, ABV 3.6%)
Crisp, Moreish, Citric.

Hancock's HB (OG 1037, ABV 3.7%)

Worthington's Bitter (OG 1037, ABV 3.7%)

Brakspear

Eagle Maltings, The Crofts, Witney, Oxfordshire, OX28 4DP
☎ (01993) 890800 ⊕ brakspear-beers.co.uk

Brakspear beers have been brewed in Oxfordshire since 1779. They continue to be traditionally crafted at the Wychwood Brewery (qv) in the historic market town of Witney using the original Victorian square fermenters and the renowned double drop fermenting system. Part of Marston's PLC. ‼ ☛ ◆ RAIB

Bitter (OG 1035, ABV 3.4%)
A classic, copper-coloured pale ale with big hop resins, juicy malt and orange fruit aroma, intense hop bitterness in the mouth and finish, and a firm maltiness and tangy fruitiness throughout.

Oxford Gold (OG 1040, ABV 4%)
A golden-coloured ale with a zesty aroma and full, fruity flavour.

Brampton SIBA

Units 4 & 5, Chatsworth Business Park, Chatsworth Road, Chesterfield, Derbyshire, S40 2AR
☎ (01246) 221680 ⊕ bramptonbrewery.co.uk

☺The original Brampton Brewery closed in 1955. In 2007 a new brewery was established, and brewing commenced on an eight-barrel plant. Three tied houses are situated close to the brewery. ‼ ☛ ◆ RAIB

Golden Bud (OG 1037, ABV 3.8%) ◄
Crisp and refreshing, golden-coloured bitter with a pleasant balance of citrus, sweetness and bitter flavours.

1302 (OG 1040, ABV 4%)
A sweet-tasting pale ale.

Griffin (OG 1040, ABV 4.1%)
A pale, slightly-sweet summer ale.

Best (OG 1041, ABV 4.2%) ◄
Classic, drinkable bitter with a predominantly malty taste, balanced by caramel sweetness and a developing bitterness in the aftertaste.

Impy Dark (OG 1047, ABV 4.3%) ◄
Mild ale with a strong, roasted coffee aroma and a rich flavour of vine fruit and chocolate.

Jerusalem (OG 1046, ABV 4.6%)
Traditional bitter ale with a pale colour and rich maltiness.

Tudor Rose (OG 1045, ABV 4.6%)
Well-balanced, creamy pale ale with a great hop nose and mouthfeel. Dominated by citrus hops.

Mild (OG 1054, ABV 4.9%) ◨
Warming, rich and roasted dark mild.

Wasp Nest (OG 1049, ABV 5%) ◄
Strong and complex with malt and hop flavours and a caramel sweetness.

Speciale (OG 1056, ABV 5.8%)
An IPA-style ale, the fruity hoppiness is balanced by the residual sweetness of such a strong ale.

Brancaster

See Beeston

Branscombe Vale SIBA

Branscombe, Devon, EX12 3DP
☎ (01297) 680511 ⊕ branscombevalebrewery.co.uk

⊗ The brewery was set up in 1992 in cowsheds at the back of a National Trust-owned farm, overlooking the sea at Branscombe. The brewery owners converted the sheds, digging their own well. In 2008 a new 25-barrel plant was shoehorned in through the roof to increase capacity. ◆ RAIB

Branoc (OG 1038, ABV 3.8%) ◄
Amber-coloured session bitter. Hops and malt throughout with good bitterness in taste and aftertaste.

Golden Fiddle (OG 1040, ABV 4%)
Effervescent golden ale with a citrus and butterscotch aroma with hints of peach and grapefruit and a dry finish.

Summa This (OG 1040, ABV 4.2%)
Amber-coloured, with digestive biscuit notes with a floral hop.

BVB White Label (OG 1045, ABV 4.6%) ◄
Red/brown-coloured beer with a fruity aroma and taste, and bitter/dry finish.

Summa That (OG 1049, ABV 5%)
Light golden beer, with a clean, refreshing taste, and a long, hoppy finish.

Brass Castle SIBA

10a Yorkersgate, Malton, North Yorkshire, YO17 7AB
☎ (01653) 698683 ☎ 07740 336851
⊕ brasscastlebrewery.co.uk

The brewery is based in the centre of Malton with a 12-barrel plant, having begun life in 2011 on a one-barrel kit in the owner's garage. It has an on-site taproom with up to eight beers available for on and off sales. ‼ ☛ ◆ RAIB

Northern Blonde (OG 1040, ABV 3.9%)

Misfit (OG 1043, ABV 4.3%)

Bad Kitty (OG 1061.5, ABV 5.5%) ◨
A chewy chocolate, vanilla dream of a porter.

Sunshine (OG 1061, ABV 5.7%)

Disrupter (OG 1075, ABV 7.4%)
Hazy, hoppy New England-style IPA.

Breakwater

St Martin's Yard, Lorne Road, Dover, Kent, CT16 2AA
☎ (01304) 700043 ☎ 07979 867045
⊕ breakwater.beer

⊗ Breakwater is a brewery and taproom established in 2016 behind Buckland Corn Mill in former industrial premises and on the site of the former Wellington Brewery. ◆ RAIB

HMS Minnow (ABV 2.8%)

Dover Pale Ale (ABV 3.5%)

Hellfire Corner (ABV 4.1%)

Castle on the Hill (ABV 4.4%)

Cowjuice Milk Stout (ABV 4.4%)

Mogul West Country IPA (ABV 5.6%)

Brecon

See Cold Black Label

Brentwood SIBA

Calcott Hall Farm, Ongar Road, Brentwood, Essex, CM15 9HS
☎ (01277) 200483 🌐 brentwoodbrewing.co.uk

Since its launch in 2006 Brentwood has steadily increased its capacity and distribution, relocating to a new purpose-built brewery unit in 2013 with a visitor centre. Seasonal and special beers are also available including more unusual beer styles under the Elephant School brand name. !! ♦ RAIB

BBC2 (OG 1030, ABV 2.5%)
Full-bodied, mid-brown-coloured bitter with dry, tropical citrus flavour.

IPA (OG 1039, ABV 3.7%)
A lightly-hopped, pale-coloured session beer.

Marvellous Maple Mild (OG 1038, ABV 3.7%)
Dark brown-coloured mild with a hint of maple syrup.

Legacy (ABV 4%)
Easy-drinking pale ale with citrus notes.

Best (OG 1042, ABV 4.2%)
A traditional, light-coloured best bitter with a well-rounded flavour and aroma.

Gold (OG 1043, ABV 4.3%)
A heavily-hopped, golden-coloured beer with a fruity taste and bitter finish.

Hope & Glory (ABV 4.5%)
Full-bodied, red-coloured premium bitter. Well-balanced with full malt flavours, a hoppy end note and lingering bitterness.

Lumberjack (ABV 5.2%)
Strong, slightly sweet, full-bodied bitter with a rounded, hoppy finish.

Chockwork Orange (OG 1067, ABV 6.5%)
A chocolaty, malty beer brewed with oranges.

Brewed under the Elephant School brand name:

Mallophant (OG 1048, ABV 4.1%)

Cheru Kol (ABV 4.5%)
A Belgian-style beer with fig and rosemary notes.

Sombrero (ABV 4.5%)
A saison-style beer with chia and passion fruit notes.

Brew Buddies

Unit 14, Highlands Farm Business Park, Highlands Hill, Swanley Village, Kent, BR8 7NA ☎ 07962 369717
🌐 brew-buddies.co.uk

Owned and run by husband and wife Simon and Rebecca, Brew Buddies Brewery are brewing for cask, keg, bottle and can. Beers range from traditional to modern, and are unfined and vegan-friendly. Beers are available in the new brewery tap room as well as venues across London and the South of England. !! V

Brew By Numbers

79 Enid Street, Bermondsey, London, SE16 3RA
☎ (020) 7237 9794 🌐 brewbynumbers.com

Brew By Numbers was established in 2012, specialising in saisons and hop-forward pale beers. All beers are named by a two digit number system, denoting the style of the beer, with a description of the recipe. As well as the popular taproom(s) along the Bermondsey Beer Mile, another opened in Peckham in 2019. RAIB

Brew Foundation

c/o Wincle Brewery, Toll Barn, Wincle, Cheshire, SK11 0QE
☎ (0114) 282 3098 ☎ 07545 618894

Office: 18 Jarrow Road, Sheffield, S11 8YB
🌐 thebrewfoundation.co.uk

A father-and-son brewery, currently using spare capacity at Wincle Brewery (qv). Beer is distributed both east and west of the Pennines.

Pop (ABV 3.6%)
A session pale ale with a tropical hop 'pop'.

Little Bitter That (ABV 3.8%)

Hops & Dreams (ABV 4%)
Session IPA, with a citrus, floral and tropical hoppy flavour and aroma.

Laughing Water (ABV 4.3%)
A tropical, fruity pale ale, with a subtle citrus base.

First Light (ABV 4.6%)

Janet's Treat Porter (ABV 4.8%)
Brewed in collaboration with Wincle Brewery. Cherry balances against the chocolate malt's bitterness and provides a subtle, dark cherry aroma.

Hop & Glory (ABV 4.9%)

Bitter That (ABV 5%)

Brew Monster SIBA

Unit C, Avondale Business Park, Avondale Road, Cwmbran, NP44 1XE ☎ 07772 869856
🌐 brewmonster.co.uk

Set up in 2017, the core range of four IPAs has a monster naming theme. Success has meant the purchase of new brewing vessels to meet demand, the recruitment of a second brewer, a collaboration to open a new micropub, the opening of a brewery tap and the introduction of a series of one-off beers. ♦

Leviathan IPA (ABV 4%)
Light and mellow session IPA with an aroma of citrus, pine and grapefruit.

Daemon Red IPA (ABV 4.6%)
Red-coloured IPA, with caramel and a subtle roast finish, a punchy citrus aroma and hints of fruit, with balanced bitterness.

Tiamat IPA (ABV 5%)
Special IPA, with biscuit and caramel undertones, floral notes, citrus and a dry, spicy finish.

Mephisto IPA (ABV 5.6%)
Premium, traditional-style IPA, full-bodied and biscuity, with hints of spice and a floral aroma.

Brew Shack

Sixpenny Handley, Dorset, SP5 5NU ☎ 07580 120258
🌐 thebrewshack.co.uk

⊗ Brewing began in 2015 on a 1.5-barrel plant in purpose-built premises, later upgraded to 10-barrels. All its beers are produced unfined and are suitable for vegans. The brewery is located on a working farm so there is no access for the general public. **V**

Pale Ale (ABV 4.5%)
Crisp, refreshing hoppy pale ale with a smooth bitterness.

Eight Grain Porter (ABV 5%)
Sweet, brown-coloured porter with a complex roasted malt flavour.

Sump Oil Stout (ABV 6%)
Rich, full-bodied stout with big roasted flavours and a smooth, hoppy, bitter finish.

Brew Shed

Wellheads House, Sandilands, Limekilns, KY11 3JD ☎ 07484 727672 🌐 brewshedbeers.wordpress.com

Brewing began in 2016 in a tiny brewery behind the owner's house, the first brewery in Limekilns since 1849. Brew Shed Beers revives a tradition of local breweries serving the neighbourhood.

Brew Studio

39 Meadowview Road, Sompting, West Sussex, BN15 0HU ☎ 07890 978350

⊗ Brew Studio started off as a 0.5-barrel nanobrewery in 2017 and has recently upgraded to a 2.5-barrel plant. Around 20 outlets are supplied direct.

Brew Toon SIBA

72a St Peter Street, Peterhead, AB42 1QB ☎ (01779) 560948 🌐 brewtoon.co.uk

Established in 2017, beers are brewed in small batches in the nautical town of Peterhead. An on-site café/bar is open Wed-Sun 4-8.30 (hours may vary at weekends due to events such as quizes or music nights). The five core beers are available on tap and bottles. All available in bottles for in-house and carry-out, look at the font for tap versions. Three other taps feature seasonal beers or guests.

Brew York SIBA

Enterprise Complex, Walmgate, York, YO1 9TT ☎ (01904) 848448 🌐 brewyork.co.uk

☺Established in 2016, Brew York was born out of two friends passion for beer and brewing. The brewery is located within York's historic city walls, a 15-minute walk from the station. A unique tap room and beer hall (including kitchen) with riverside beer garden has been constructed alongside the brewhouse. **!! ♦ GF**

JARSA (ABV 3.7%)
Refreshing, sessionable pale with hints of orange and sherbet.

Glutenous Minimus (ABV 3.9%)
Refreshing, crisp, traditional, gluten-free, West Coast pale ale.

Tonkoko (ABV 4.3%)
Creamy, easy-drinking ale, with huge coconut and chocolate flavours with a tonka and vanilla finish.

X-Panda (ABV 4.5%)
Sessionable IPA with big hop flavour and creaminess.

BrewBoard SIBA

Unit B3, Button End Industrial Estate, Harston, Cambridgeshire, CB22 7GX 🌐 brewboard.co.uk

Brewing began in 2017 using a 30-hectolitre brew plant. No real ale. **!!**

BrewDog

Balmacassie Industrial Estate, Ellon, AB41 8BX ☎ (01358) 724924

Tower Hill: Unit 3, Minster Building, 21 Great Tower Street, Tower Hill, London, EC3N 4DR ☎ (020) 7929 2545 🌐 brewdog.com

Established in 2007 by James Watt and Martin Dickie. Most of the production goes into bottles and keg. In 2016 a KeyKeg initiative began, described as 'real ale for modernists'. 48 bars now exist in the UK. Beer is now also served as 'Cask', conditioned in a KeyKeg. **!!**

Dead Pony (OG 1040, ABV 3.8%)

5am Saint (OG 1048, ABV 5%)

Brewers Folly

Ashton Farm House, Stanbridge, Wimborne, Dorset, BH21 4JD 🌐 brewersfolly.co.uk

Eric, Dean and Rufus were long-time avid homebrewers. They began brewing on a 1.4-barrel system brought from The Brew Shack in 2017. They currently work full-time and brew part-time, but hope to go full-time and expand the range in the future. **!! ♦**

Brewery at the Watchmaker's Arms (NEW)

84 Goldstone Villas, Hove, East Sussex, BN3 3RU ☎ (01273) 776307

Hove's first micropub has its own 100-litre microbrewery, producing under the Beercraft Brighton brand name. Beer is primarily for the Watchmakers but is available in other local pubs.

Brewery58 (NEW)

58 Wantage Road, Wallingford, Oxfordshire, OX10 0LY ☎ 07798 674724 ✉ brewery58@yahoo.com

A nanobrewery that started when the owner was given a brewing kit as a retirement present. Commercial production began in 2018. Bottle-conditioned ales are available at several local outlets. Cask-conditioned ales are available at beer festivals across southern England. **RAIB**

Brewheadz

Unit 16a, Rosebery Industrial Park, Rosebery Avenue, Tottenham Hale, London, N17 9SR 🌐 brewheadz.com

Brewheadz was established in 2016 and bought out by Ora (qv) in 2019, but still cuckoo brews on the now Ora-owned kit. The range is available bottle-conditioned and in KeyKeg from some speciality pubs, beer shops and online retailers. A taproom shared with Ora is open on Saturdays. RAIB

Brewhouse & Kitchen SIBA

Bedford: 115 High Street, Bedford, MK40 1NU ☎ (01234) 342931

Bournemouth: 154 Commercial Road, Bournemouth, Dorset, BH2 5LU ☎ (01202) 055221

Bristol: 31-35 Cotham Hill, Bristol, BS6 6JY ☎ (0117) 973 3793

Cardiff: Sophia Close, Pontcanna, Cardiff, CF11 9HW ☎ (029) 20371599

Cheltemham: Unit 7, The Brewery, St. Margaret's Road, Cheltenham, GL50 4EQ ☎ (01242) 509946

Chester: Forest House, Chester, CH1 1QY ☎ (01244) 404990

Dorchester: 17 Weymouth Avenue, Dorchester, DT1 1QY ☎ (01305) 265551

Gloucester Quays: Unit R1 St. Anne Walk, Gloucester, GL1 5SH ☎ (01452) 222965

Highbury: 2a Corsica Street, Highbury, London, N5 1JJ ☎ (0207) 226 1026

Horsham (NEW): 38 East Street, Horsham, RH12 1HL ☎ (01403) 788140

Hoxton (NEW): 397-400 Geffrye Street, Hoxton, London, E2 8HZ ☎ (020) 3861 8920

Islington: 5 Torrens Street, London, EC1V 1NQ ☎ (0207) 837 9421

Lichfield: 1 Bird Street, Lichfield, WS13 6PW ☎ (01543) 224740

Milton Keynes: 7 Savoy Crescent, Milton Keynes, MK9 3PU ☎ (01908) 049032

Nottingham: Trent Bridge, Nottingham, Nottinghamshire, NG2 2GS ☎ (0115) 986 7960

Poole: 3 Dear Hay Lane, Poole, Dorset, BH15 1NZ ☎ (01202) 771246

Portsmouth: 26 Guildhall Walk, Portsmouth, PO1 2DD ☎ (02392) 891340

Southampton: 47 Highfield Lane, Southampton, SO17 1QD ☎ (023) 8055 5566

Southbourne: 147 Parkwood Road, Southbourne, Bournemouth, Dorset, BH5 2BN ☎ (01202) 055209

Southsea (NEW): 51 Southsea Terrace, Portsmouth, Hampshire, PO5 3AU ☎ (023) 9281 8979

Sutton Coldfield: 8 Birmingham Rd, Sutton Coldfield, West Midlands, B72 1QD ☎ (01217) 966838

Wilmslow: 6-12 Swan Street, Wilmslow, Cheshire, SK9 1HE ☎ (01625) 441850 🌐 brewhouseandkitchen.com

Brewing started in 2013 in Portsmouth, the first in the growing Brewhouse & Kitchen chain. There are now 22 brewpubs, each producing its own particular range of beers and with its brewery on open display in the bar area. Local freehouses and beer festivals can be supplied. Carry outs and brewery experience days are available at all venues.

Brewing Brothers

Imperial, 119 Queens Road, Hastings, East Sussex, TN34 1RL 🌐 brewingbrothers.org

⊗ Brewing began in 2016 in the Imperial, Hastings. The brewery has a 2.5-barrel capacity with four fermenting vessels. A wide range of brother themed beers have been brewed to date, including a core range of seasonal beers, and a collaboration with Half Man Half Burger. ♦

Brewshed SIBA

Place Farm, Ingham, Suffolk, IP31 1NQ ☎ (01284) 848066 🌐 brewshedbrewery.co.uk

⊗ Brewshed began brewing in 2011 using a five-barrel plant in buildings located behind the Beerhouse, one of its outlets. It's now located in the nearby village of Ingham, using a 12-barrel plant, resulting in greater capacity and a wider beer range. The brewery continues to increase production and supplies bottled beers to Hotel Chocolat. ♦

Pale (OG 1040, ABV 3.9%)

Best (OG 1044, ABV 4.3%)

New England Pale Ale (ABV 4.4%)
Unfined, well-hopped, East Coast-style pale ale.

American Blonde (OG 1055, ABV 5.5%)

Brewsmith

Unit 11, Cuba Industrial Estate, Stubbins, BL0 0NE ☎ (01706) 829390 🌐 brewsmithbeer.co.uk

Brewsmith is a 10-barrel microbrewery established in 2014 by the Smith family – James, Jennifer and Ted. It produces a range of cask and bottle-conditioned ales in traditional British beer styles. !! ♦ RAIB

Mosaic (ABV 3.5%)

Amarillo (ABV 3.8%)
Light golden-coloured beer with floral, citrus and orange tones.

Bitter (OG 1039, ABV 3.9%)
A pale-coloured session bitter with moderate bitterness and pronounced floral/citrus hop aromas.

New Zealand Pale (ABV 4.2%)
Pale ale with pronounced floral and pine aromas and assertive bitterness.

Pale (OG 1042, ABV 4.2%)
A refreshingly bitter and hoppy pale ale.

APA (ABV 5%)
Pale ale with resinous pine, grapefruit and floral aromas.

Oatmeal Stout (OG 1052, ABV 5.2%)
A full-bodied, richly-textured stout.

IPA (OG 1060, ABV 6%)
Rich mouthfeel, big hop aromas and a long, dry, bitter finish.

Brewster's SIBA

Unit 5, Burnside, Turnpike Close, Grantham, Lincolnshire, NG31 7XU ☎ (01476) 566000 🌐 brewsters.co.uk

⊗ Brewster is the old English term for a female brewer and Sara Barton – who was named Brewer of the Year by the All Party Parliamentary Beer Group 2018 - is a modern example. Originally established in the Vale of Belvoir in 1998, moving to Grantham in 2006, Brewster's produces a range of traditional and innovative beers with two regularly-changing ranges; Women of Wonder (4.8% ABV) and WhimsicAles (4.0% ABV). ‼️🍴◆

Hophead (OG 1036, ABV 3.6%) 🍺
Amber-coloured beer, with a floral/ hoppy character, hops dominate throughout before yielding to grapefruit in the lasting, dry finish.

Marquis (OG 1038, ABV 3.8%)
A well-balanced, refreshing session bitter with maltiness and a dry, hoppy finish.

Aromantica (OG 1042, ABV 4.2%)
Amber-coloured brew, with a touch of roast malt, slight sweet nuttiness, tropical hop notes and aromas of lime and passion fruit, with a refreshingly, long, aromatic finish.

Hop A Doodle Doo (OG 1043, ABV 4.3%)
A copper-coloured ale with a rich, full-bodied feel and fruity hop character.

Decadence (OG 1044, ABV 4.4%)
A golden ale with a hint of malt sweetness, with passion fruit and grapefruit aromas on the nose. A complex zesty hop palate leads to a fresh herby finish.

Aromatic Porter (OG 1045, ABV 4.5%)
A rich, roasty dark porter with citrus and tropical fruit hop flavours.

Stilton Porter (OG 1049, ABV 4.9%)
A rich, roast-flavoured porter with spicy rich hop flavours.

Rutterkin (ABV 5%)
A premium bitter with a golden colour. A zesty hop flavour and a touch of malt sweetness to give a rich, full-bodied beer.

Briarbank

📦 70 Fore Street, Ipswich, Suffolk, IP4 1LB
☎ (01473) 284000 ⊕ briarbank.org

The Briarbank Brewing Company was established in 2013, and is situated on the site of the old Lloyds Bank on Fore Street. The brewery is a small two-barrel plant, and the bar above offers a core range of beers – including some speciality ales, as well as vegan-friendly ales. ‼️◆

Brick SIBA

Units 13-14, Deptford Trading Estate, Blackhorse Road, Deptford, SE8 5HY ☎ 07747 787636
⊕ brickbrewery.co.uk

Established by owner and former homebrewer Ian Stewart in 2013. Due to continued expansion, the brewing operation relocated from Peckham to larger premises in nearby Deptford in 2017. The original Peckham railway arch site is retained as an expanded taproom. Numerous local and regional outlets are supplied. Frequent one-off and collaboration brews are produced. 🚚◆

Kinsale (ABV 4%) 🍺
Fruity, tawny-coloured best bitter with a little nutty, roast character and hops throughout. Sweetish with a little honey on the palate.

Peckham Pale (ABV 4.5%) 🍺
Dark gold-coloured beer with hoppy, floral aroma. Malt, hops, bitterness, citrus and floral flavours. Long bitter, fruity, hoppy, dryish finish.

Blenheim Black (OG 1053, ABV 5.3%) 🍺
Roasted notes throughout with black cherry and blackcurrant and a trace of hops. Finish is bitter, dry and some malt.

Brick House

Patcham, East Sussex, BN1 8HQ ☎ 07708 384604
✉ brickhousebrewingco@gmail.com

☺Brick House has grown organically from humble homebrewing beginnings and plans to continue in this vein. Brewing is currently suspended. RAIB

Bricknell

Bricknell Avenue, Hull, East Yorkshire, HU5 4ET
☎ (07729) 722953 ☎ 07729 722953
⊕ bricknellbrewery.co.uk

Bricknell's range comprises 12 bottle-conditioned, vegan-friendly, higher strength ales. With some hops also grown on-site or locally, everything is completely hands-on from brewing through to hand bottling and labelling, to delivering. Around 150 litres, mainly developed from 19th-century recipes, is created each week. Casks for local beer festivals and a select number of local pubs are made available. 🚚 RAIB V

Bridgehouse SIBA

Airedale Heifer, Bradford Road, Sandbeds, Keighley, West Yorkshire, BD20 9LY
☎ (01535) 601222

Office: Unit 1, Aireworth Mills, Aireworth Road, Keighley, BD21 4DH ⊕ bridgehousebrewery.co.uk

☺Bridgehouse began brewing in 2010 using a 10-barrel plant. The brewery purchased the recipes and branding of Old Bear Brewery in 2014 and moved into its premises in Keighley. In 2015 the brewery relocated again to its present address behind the Airedale Heifer pub in Sandbeds, which it also operates. A bespoke 15-barrel brewery is used and the site includes a visitor centre. ‼️◆

Tequila Blonde (OG 1038, ABV 3.8%) 🍺
Refreshing blonde ale, initially sweet with hints of lime, finishing with a slight tingling aftertaste.

Blonde (ABV 4%)
A modern blonde ale with complex spicy, floral flavours.

Aired Ale (OG 1042, ABV 4.1%) 🍺
Brown-coloured beer with a malty aroma. Malt, hops and fruit in equal balance with lingering fruitiness in a long, bitter finish.

Porter (ABV 4.5%)
Ruby-coloured porter with strong toffee and malt flavours. Smooth with a long-lasting aftertaste.

Holy Cow (ABV 5.6%)
Amber-coloured beer with a sweet, fruity start balanced by a warming, hoppy finish.

Bridgetown

Albert Inn, Bridgetown Close, Totnes, Devon, TQ9 5AD
☎ (01803) 863214 ⊕ albertinntotnes.com/ bridgetown-brewery

⊠ Bridgetown started brewing in 2008 using a two-barrel plant in the outbuildings of the Albert

Inn, Totnes. Beers are available in an increasing number of local outlets. ‼♦RAIB

Albert Ale (OG 1039, ABV 3.8%) ◆
Pale bitter, malt dominating throughout. Roast and caramel in aroma, taste and aftertaste with a little bitterness on the tongue.

Bitter (OG 1042, ABV 4.2%)
Traditional bitter. Malt and slight fruit nose, bitter with slight fruit taste, and a bitter, dry, slight fruit aftertaste.

Shark Island Stout (OG 1044, ABV 4.5%) ◆
Smooth stout with strong malt and roast throughout. Touches of liquorice and chocolate lead to a bitter finish.

West Coast IPA (OG 1047, ABV 4.7%)
Fruity citrus nose, a dry, heavy citrus taste with a powerful citrus, dry finish.

Bridlington

10 Prospect Street, Bridlington, East Yorkshire, YO15 2AL

The brewery, founded in 2014 in the grounds of the Telegraph Inn, Bridlington, later moved to the rear of the Pack Horse, supplying the pub. It relocated again in 2019 to the former Half Moon pub, Bridlington. The beers and beer styles regularly change. Brewing is currently suspended but expected to recommence during the currency of this guide.

Briggs Signature

c/o Unit 1, Waterhouse Mill, 65-71 Lockwood Road, Huddersfield, West Yorkshire, HD1 3QU ☎ 07427 668004 🌐 briggssignatureales.weebly.com

⊗ Briggs Signature Ales started brewing in 2014 using spare capacity at Mallinsons (qv). Nick Briggs, also a member of the Mallinsons brewing team, produces a number of modern, hop-forward beers. RAIB

Northern Soul (OG 1038, ABV 3.8%)
Pale-coloured bitter with a citrus and zesty aroma.

Rock & Roll (OG 1040, ABV 4%)
A red-coloured ale, heavily hopped to give a fruity flavour and aroma, with a long bitter finish.

Hip Hop (OG 1042, ABV 4.2%)
Golden-coloured pale ale with a zesty lemon and ripe mango aroma, tropical fruit flavour and crisp bitter finish.

Brighton Bier

Unit 10, Bell Tower Industrial Estate, Roedean Rd, Brighton, East Sussex, BN2 5RU ☎ 07967 681203 🌐 brightonbier.com

Brighton Bier was established in 2012. It operates a 15-barrel brewery close to the centre of the city and also owns the Brighton Bierhaus pub, Brighton. Beers are available throughout the UK and exported to Europe and Asia.

Thirty Three (OG 1035, ABV 3.3%)

Brighton Bier (ABV 4%)

West Pier (OG 1042, ABV 4%)

Underdog (ABV 4.2%)

IPA (OG 1062, ABV 5%)

No Name Stout (ABV 5%)

Grand Porter (ABV 5.2%)

Brightside SIBA

Unit 10, Dale Industrial estate, Radcliffe, M26 1AD ☎ (0161) 725 9644 ☎ 07870 207442 🌐 brightsidebrewing.co.uk

⊗ Brightside is a 20-barrel family run brewery based in Greater Manchester focusing on brewing great beer to be enjoyed in pints. Around 20-25 beers (core range, seasonal specials and bespoke house beers) are brewed across cask, keg, can and bottle, including those from Wildside (one-off unusual experimental beers). Brightside prides itself on working as sustainably as possible, by limiting energy expenditure, recycling and reusing waste. ♦

Odin Blonde (OG 1038, ABV 3.8%) ◆
Refreshing, bitter hops, with bitterness carrying into finish. Peachy hop aroma with some malt.

B-Side Gold (OG 1042, ABV 4.2%)
A refreshing session ale, pale golden-coloured with a mild bitterness and a vibrant fruity hop flavour.

Brightside Best Bitter (OG 1043, ABV 4.3%)
A mid-amber-coloured bitter with subtle fruit and citrus flavours as well as earthy and spicy notes.

Academy Ale IPA (OG 1044, ABV 4.5%)
A moderately malty base allows the hops to shine through.

Manchester Skyline Gold (OG 1045, ABV 4.6%)
A full-flavoured golden ale with fresh, fruity, floral aromas and moderate bitterness.

Maverick IPA (OG 1047, ABV 4.8%)
An American-style IPA with bold grapefruit and floral aromas, finishing with a clean, refreshing bitterness.

Topaz IPA (OG 1049, ABV 5%)
A light amber-coloured beer with delicate caramel and light, toasty malt notes. Tropical hop overtones with fresh, resinous aromatics.

Brightwater

9 Beaconsfield Road, Claygate, Surrey, KT10 0PN ☎ (01372) 462334 ☎ 07802 316389 🌐 brightbrew.co.uk

⊗ Established in 2013 at Claygate in Surrey, Brightwater is a five-barrel brewery producing traditional beers. The range is available at its brewery tap, Platform 3, outside Claygate Station, and other Surrey and South London pubs.

Little Nipper (OG 1033, ABV 3.3%) ◆
A rather thin, hoppy bitter with a hint of a citrus taste and a bitter, slightly dry finish.

Top Notch (OG 1036, ABV 3.6%) ◆
Citrus notes dominant the aroma of this mid brown-coloured bitter.Well-balanced taste with some bitterness in the finish.

Ernest Pale IPA Bitter (OG 1037, ABV 3.7%)
Sessionable, fresh ale.

Daisy Gold (OG 1040, ABV 4%) ◆
Golden-coloured ale with a moderate tropical fruit hoppy character and some balancing malt leading to a bittersweet finish.

Liquorice & Blackcurrant Stout (OG 1040, ABV 4%)

Wild Orchid (OG 1040, ABV 4%)
Dark, oatmeal porter with a Madagascan vanilla pod in each cask giving vanilla undertones.

All Citra (OG 1043, ABV 4.3%)
Bitter with bite due to hops, resulting in a distinctly citrus flavour.

Lip Smacker (OG 1043, ABV 4.3%)
Golden-coloured bitter.

Coal Porter (OG 1049, ABV 4.9%)
A classic porter with well-balanced dryness, a clean hop taste, and a delicate hazelnut flavour.

Brimstage SIBA

Home Farm, Brimstage, Merseyside, CH63 6HY
☎ (0151) 342 1181 🌐 brimstagebrewery.com

Neil Young began brewing in 20016 using a 10-barrel plant in the heart of the Wirral countryside. Wirral's first brewery since the closure of the Birkenhead Brewery in the late 1960s. Since Neil passed away in 2018, his two sons now own the brewery. Outlets are supplied across the Wirral, Merseyside, Cheshire and North Wales. ‼♦

Sandpiper Light Ale (OG 1036.5, ABV 3.6%)
Moreish session beer, well-balanced, light and refreshing, with tropical fruit flavours.

Trapper's Hat Bitter (OG 1037.5, ABV 3.8%)
Gold-coloured, refreshingly hoppy session brew with a complex bouquet. A mouthful of fruit zest, with hints of orange and grapefruit.

Rhode Island Red Rye (OG 1039, ABV 4%)
Red-coloured, smooth and well-balanced malty beer with a good dry aftertaste. Some fruitiness in the taste.

Elderflower Wheat (ABV 4.1%)
Light, refreshing wheat beer brewed with dried elderflower. A delicate vanilla and honey-like aroma.

Scarecrow Bitter (OG 1041, ABV 4.2%)
Orange marmalade-coloured, well-balanced session brew with a distinct citrus fruit bouquet and a bitter finish.

Oyster Catcher Stout (OG 1043, ABV 4.4%)
Chocolate and vanilla flavours with a rich smoothness from the addition of oatmeal.

IPA (OG 1055.5, ABV 6%)
Modern IPA with a floral aroma and a dry, bitter finish.

Brinkburn Street SIBA

1a Ford Street, Byker, Newcastle upon Tyne, NE6 1LN
☎ (0191) 338 9039

Office: Quayside i4, Ouseburn Building, Albion Row, Newcastle upon Tyne, NE6 1LL
🌐 brinkburnbrewery.co.uk

Brewing began in 2015, much influenced by West Coast US beer styles. Citrus flavours and highly-hopped bitterness is a feature of many of its beers. The brewery relocated to a new site in 2018, which also incorporates a brewery tap.

Fools Gold (ABV 3.8%)

The Pursuit of Hoppiness (ABV 3.9%)

Byker Brown Ale (ABV 4.8%)

Briscoe's

16 Ash Grove, Otley, West Yorkshire, LS21 3EL
☎ (01943) 466515 ✉ briscoe.brewery@talktalk.net

The brewery was launched in 1998 by microbiologist/chemist Dr Paul Briscoe in the cellar of his house with a one-barrel brew length. Dr Briscoe is currently producing one brew per week on his original plant, several beers are produced on an irregular basis.

Otley Gold (OG 1040, ABV 3.9%)

Bristol Beer Factory SIBA

Unit A, The Old Brewery, Durnford Street, Ashton, Bristol, BS3 2AW
☎ (0117) 902 6317

Office: 291 North Street, Ashton, Bristol, BS3 1JP
🌐 bristolbeerfactory.co.uk

A 30-barrel microbrewery in a part of the former Ashton Gate Brewing Co, which closed in 1933. 50 outlets are supplied, with output and brewing capacity steadily increasing. Focusing on cask ale, it produces specials every 2-3 weeks. A brewery visitor centre opened in 2016. ‼ ♦ RAIB

Nova (OG 1040, ABV 3.8%)
Straw-coloured, light-bodied, bitter session ale with a citrus aroma. Hop-led taste with lemon fruit and pale malt following into a bitter hop aftertaste.

Fortitude (OG 1041, ABV 4%)
Amber-coloured ale with a light malt and hop nose, mildly fruity flavours balanced with hop bitterness and a short, dry finish.

Milk Stout (OG 1049, ABV 4.5%)
Very sweet, full-bodied, black-coloured stout with lactose creaminess and a smoky, roast bitter finish.

Independence (OG 1046, ABV 4.6%)
Initial hop aroma, well-balanced flavours blend the fruity citrus hops with a malty backbone leaving a clean, bittersweet aftertaste.

BritHop (NEW)

c/o 133 Parsonage Manorway, Belvedere, DA17 6NG
☎ 07883 223127 ✉ info@brithopbeer.com

Started in 2018, with Franklins Brewery (qv), beers are available around South East London and further afield. A penchant for the Britpop music scene of the 90s comes through in the beer names. There are plans for a move to its own plant. **V**

King of the Kerb (ABV 3.2%)

Sandstorm (ABV 3.8%)

Sweet Symphony (ABV 4.2%)

Shakermaker (ABV 4.4%)

Britman

The Stables, Atelier Suite, Burton Manor, Burton, Cheshire, CH64 5SJ ☎ 07925 875836
🌐 burtonmanorgardens.org.uk/whats-here/britman-craft-beers

Britman Craft Beers is a small, quirky independent brewery established in 2013. It brews to the Reinheitsgebot German purity law, and produces vegetarian-friendly beers. The brewery has been recognised by the Sustainable Restaurants Association as a sustainable product; all spent grain is sent to happy pigs locally. Brewing is currently suspended. ♦

Britt

See Pig Iron

Brixton

Arch 547, Brixton Station Road, Brixton, London, SW9 8PF
☎ (020) 3609 8880 🌐 brixtonbrewery.com

The brewery opened in 2013 in a railway arch in central Brixton, and beer names and branding reflect this. An investment by Heineken in 2017 enabled a major expansion into a nearby industrial unit. The original arch is now used for seasonal and experimental brews, while an adjacent arch houses the taproom. The bulk of production is in KeyKeg, cans and bottles. ‼ ♦ RAIB

Reliance Pale Ale (OG 1042, ABV 4.2%)
Tropical notes and a little malt are noticeable in this refreshing amber-coloured beer. A gentle bitterness grows on drinking.

Low Voltage Session IPA (ABV 4.3%)

Effra Ale (OG 1045, ABV 4.5%)
Dry, copper-coloured best bitter with peppery hops and fruit in flavour and bitter finish.

Windrush Stout (OG 1050, ABV 5%)
Smoky roast and blackcurrant aroma and flavour with sweet chocolate and liquorice and a dry, dark roast aftertaste.

Atlantic APA (OG 1054, ABV 5.4%)
Strong aroma of flowery hops, melon and citrus, biscuit, grapefruit and melon flavours with a little bitterness and a dry, complex finish.

Electric IPA (OG 1065, ABV 6.5%)
Sweet biscuit balances the bitterness in this golden ale. Strong citrus, passion fruit and melon with spicy hop flavours and a dry, hoppy aftertaste.

Brockenhurst

Balmer Lawn Hotel, Lyndhurst Road, Brockenhurst, Hampshire, SO42 7ZB

A microbrewery located in the grounds of the Balmer Lawn Hotel & Spa.

Smokin Deer (ABV 3.8%)

Brockley SIBA

31 Harcourt Road, Brockley, London, SE4 2AJ
☎ 07814 584338 🌐 brockleybrewery.co.uk

Established in 2013 by a group of local beer enthusiasts who installed a five-barrel plant in a converted builder's workshop. The brewery concentrates on supplying outlets within a six-kilometre radius. An on-site bar is open on Fridays and Saturdays. A second, off-site brewery will be brought on stream in 2019. ♦

Golden Ale (OG 1038, ABV 3.8%)
Easy-drinking beer with some earthy hops on the palate and finish, overlaid with biscuity sweetness and a pleasant fruitiness.

Pale Ale (OG 1041, ABV 4.1%)
Hints of citrus and lychee in the flavour with a sweetness and slight notes of spice in the bitterish finish.

Porter (OG 1043, ABV 4.3%)
Roast malt with a hint of blackcurrant becoming more hoppy and bitter late in the taste and aftertaste.

Red Ale (OG 1048, ABV 4.8%)
Well-balanced, sweet, fruity red-coloured ale, smoky aroma, a growing spiciness overlaid with dry-roasted bitter character.

Brodie's

Office: Unit 40, 4 Lammas Road, Fairways Business Park, Leyton, E10 7QT ☎ 07828 498733
🌐 brodiesbeers.com

⊗ Established in 2008 by James Brodie, beers are brewed using spare capacity at Rhymney Brewery (qv) in South Wales. ♦ RAIB

Broken Bridge

Hampshire ☎ 07493 114423
✉ richard@brokenbridgebrewing.co.uk

⊗ Established in 2016 in a small farm industrial unit, using a 2.5-barrel plant. Brewing is currently suspended. ♦ V

Broken Drum (NEW)

Heron Hill, Upper Belvedere, DA17 5ER
🌐 thebrokendrum.co.uk

Homebrewer that started trial brewing for the Broken Drum micropub in Blackfen, going commercial in 2018, brewing small batches. Phone ahead for availability.

Brolly

Lowfold Farm, Wisborough Green, West Sussex, RH14 0ES 🌐 brollybrewing.co.uk

Brolly was established in 2017 by keen homebrewer Brook Saunders. Beers are available in local pubs and at the brewery's on-site bar (open Fri-Sun). V

Little Pearl (ABV 3.5%)

New England Pale Ale (OG 1037, ABV 3.6%)
Smooth and juicy session pale ale.

Lowfold Wissy (OG 1037, ABV 3.8%)
A smooth, traditional Sussex bitter; well-balanced, earthy and floral.

Chub IPA (OG 1041, ABV 4.3%)
A well-balanced, American-style IPA with clean and fresh citrus flavours. Unfined and slightly hazy.

COW (OG 1048, ABV 4.8%)
A pale ale with citrus flavours of melon, lychee and lemon and a smooth mouthfeel.

Natural Spring Water (OG 1051, ABV 5%)
Dank, juicy, tropical fruit flavours with lots of body. Hazy and almost orange in colour.

Brooks

17 Birkenhead Road, Hoylake, Merseyside, CH47 5AE
🌐 brooks-brewhouse.co.uk

Brewing starting in 2017 at this nanobrewery, which predominately produces bottle-conditioned beers. RAIB

Brotherhood SIBA

Oakfield Business Centre, Northacre Industrial Park, Westbury, Wiltshire, BA13 4WF
☎ (01373) 823250 🌐 brotherhood.co.uk

⊗ This 10-barrel brewery was founded in 2016 by three brothers in Westbury, just south of Bath. A growing number of local outlets are supplied. ‼♦

Session Pale Ale (OG 1038, ABV 3.8%)
Thirst-quenching pale ale, a pleasant citrus and spice nose with a hint of grapefruit.

Dry Hopped Pale Ale (OG 1040, ABV 4%)
A refreshingly bitter, golden ale, with floral flavours and a big floral aroma.

Mango Pale Ale (OG 1042, ABV 4.2%)
A really fruity beer with strong mango flavours. Sweet and easy-drinking.

Double Dry Hopped IPA (OG 1043, ABV 4.3%)

American Red (OG 1044, ABV 4.5%)
Citrus notes of orange and tangerine, topped off with a huge kick of zesty grapefruit.

GIPA (OG 1050, ABV 5.2%)
A tangy bitter with strong grapefruit flavours.

IPA (OG 1053, ABV 5.6%)
A fruity floral IPA with hints of pine nuts.

Broughton SIBA

Main Street, Broughton, ML12 6HQ
☎ (01899) 830345 🌐 broughtonales.co.uk

Founded in 1979, Broughton Ales was then one of the first microbreweries. Broughton has developed since then and though more than 60% of production goes into bottle for sale in Britain and abroad, it retains a sizeable range of cask ales. All beers are suitable for vegetarians. ‼♦

Broughton Pale Ale (ABV 3.6%)

Hopopotamus (OG 1038, ABV 3.8%)

Greenmantle (OG 1038, ABV 3.9%)
A dark, bittersweet ale with a pleasant hop aftertaste.

Clipper IPA (OG 1042, ABV 4.2%)
A light-coloured, crisp, hoppy beer with a clean aftertaste.

Merlin's Ale (OG 1042, ABV 4.2%)
A well-hopped, fruity flavour is balanced by malt in the taste. The finish is bittersweet, light but dry.

Exciseman's 80/- (OG 1046, ABV 4.6%)
A traditional 80/- cask ale. A dark, malty brew. Full-drinking with a good hop aftertaste.

Jeddart Justice (OG 1046, ABV 4.7%)

Dark Dunter (OG 1050, ABV 4.8%)
Bursting with oatmeal and chocolate aromas complemented by dark roasted malts and a rich aftertaste.

Proper IPA (OG 1050, ABV 5%)

6.2 IPA (OG 1060, ABV 6%)
Hoppy, chestnut brown-coloured ale, with a bold citrus aroma and a biscuit, bitter aftertaste.

Old Jock (OG 1070, ABV 6.7%)

Strong, sweetish and fruity in the finish.

Brown Cow

Brown Cow Road, Barlow, Selby, North Yorkshire, YO8 8EH
☎ (01757) 618947 🌐 browncowbrewery.co.uk

Brewing since 1997, Brown Cow has won awards at many festivals. Keith and Sue Simpson operate a six-barrel plant. Handcrafted cask beers brewed using traditional methods are delivered to the local area direct from the brewery. ♦

Sessions (OG 1033, ABV 3.6%)
A very pale, hoppy session beer with a refreshing finish and citrus notes in the aftertaste.

Bitter (OG 1038, ABV 3.8%)
Copper-coloured, classic bitter. Full-flavoured with a smooth finish.

White Dragon (OG 1039, ABV 4%)
A pale, aromatic beer with a good level of bitterness, citrus undertones and a clean finish.

Scruff's Gold (OG 1041, ABV 4.2%)
Well-balanced,traditional, golden-coloured ale, full-flavoured, and a smooth finish.

Captain Oates Mild (OG 1044, ABV 4.5%)
Well-balanced dark mild with undertones of coffee and chocolate.

Mrs Simpsons Thriller in Vanilla (OG 1049, ABV 5.1%)
A rich porter brewed with fresh vanilla pods complementing the dark malts.

Broxbourne

See Fallen Angel

Brumaison SIBA

Unit 7 Crest Industrial Estate, Pattenden Lane, Marden, Kent, TN12 9QJ ☎ 07831704089
🌐 brumaison.beer

⊗ The name Brumaison came about from ideas to set up in a small village in France. However, Peter and Caroline decided to keep their 'Brewing Maison' in England after another brewery got there first. Trading since 2016 using a 10-barrel plant, Peter started brewing full time in 2017.

BB Traditional Ale (OG 1036, ABV 3.6%)
Easy-drinking, traditional bitter with plenty of malt and subtle hop flavour.

GB Golden Blonde Ale (OG 1042, ABV 4.4%)
Refreshing ale with the bitterness of a golden and the fruit spice of a blonde.

Bullion (OG 1041, ABV 4.5%)
Refreshing, single hop pale ale with a delicate zesty, spicy flavour.

Beulter (OG 1043, ABV 4.6%)
Deep copper-coloured best bitter.

1770 (OG 1054, ABV 4.7%)
Dark brown-coloured London porter with reddish hues. Full malt flavour, warm with hints of coffee and chocolate.

Brunning & Price

See Phoenix, St Austell & Tombstone

Brunswick SIBA

1 Railway Terrace, Derby, DE1 2RU
☎ 07534401352
brunswickbrewingcompany.co.uk

Derby's oldest brewery. It is a 10-barrel tower plant built as an extension to the Brunswick Inn in 1991. Bought by Everards in 2002, the brewery is now run separately yet in conjunction with the pub. It supplies the Brunswick Inn, Everards, wholesalers and the free trade within 100 miles. Brunswick also swaps with other breweries. Beers are also produced under the Engine Shed Project brand name. !! ♦ RAIB

White Feather (OG 1038, ABV 3.6%)
Pale-coloured, full-bodied session beer, easy-drinking with a citrus twist.

Triple Hop (OG 1040, ABV 4%)
Straw-coloured ale with a bitter astringency.

The Usual (OG 1042, ABV 4.2%)
A traditional, smooth, malty best bitter with hints of toffee.

Railway Porter (OG 1045, ABV 4.3%)
A classic dark-coloured porter, lightly-hopped with chocolate and coffee notes.

Rocket (OG 1047, ABV 4.7%)
An IPA with citrus, apricot and mango flavours.

Black Sabbath (OG 1058, ABV 6%)
Strong, dark-coloured ale with finely balanced liquorice, coffee and chocolate flavours.

Brewed under the Engine Shed Project brand name:

Ubiquitous (OG 1058, ABV 6%)
A single-hopped pale ale.

Brythonic

Tyersall Annexe, The Hudnalls, St Briavels, GL15 6RT
☎ 07766 652837 ✉ doug.morgan@hotmail.co.uk

One of the new breed of nanobreweries, having begun brewing in a Bristol suburb on a small scale in 2015, the brewery relocated to the Gloucestershire/Welsh border village of St Briavels. Beers can be found at the Doghouse, Coleford. There are plans for the brewery to move again. RAIB

Raven (OG 1048, ABV 5.3%)

Spark (OG 1048, ABV 5.3%)

Buccaneer

Sycamore House, Sutton Quays Business Park, Sutton Weaver, Cheshire, WA7 3EH
✉ buccaneerbreweryltd@gmail.com

Buccaneer began brewing in 2016. Beers are usually named with a pirate theme.

Buckland

Higher Thornhill Head, Bideford, Devon, EX39 5NU
☎ (01805) 601625 ☎ 07882 019255
thebucklandbrewers.co.uk

Brewing began in 2016. The original plant was then replaced in early 2018 with a new purpose-built microbrewery. It specialises in Belgian-style bottle-conditioned beers, which are now supplied to more than 40 local pubs, farm shops, restaurants and visitor attactions. RAIB

Bucks Star

23 Twizel Close, Stonebridge, Milton Keynes, Buckinghamshire, MK13 0DX
☎ (01908) 590054 bucksstar.beer

A solar-powered brewery, Bucks Star opened in 2015 using a 10-barrel, purpose-built plant. Only organic malt is used and no sugars or syrups are added. The beers are primarily available through Bucks Star's own zero-waste drinks innovation, called Growler Swap, where its range of beers are conditioned inside reusable glass growlers.
!! RAIB

Copernicus (ABV 3.8%)
A copper-coloured ale with earthy notes and hints of citrus and caramel.

No. 1 (OG 1040, ABV 4%)
A deep golden-coloured beer with a good balance between malt and hops. It has a light, dry and refreshing character with a lingering bitter finish.

Waltone (OG 1041, ABV 4%)
A refreshing wheat beer, with a strong, distinctive taste.

Magiovinium (OG 1045, ABV 4.5%)
Dark-coloured, sweet stout.

Bull of the Woods

Brook Farm, Kirby Cane, Norfolk, NR35 2PJ
☎ (01508) 518080 ☎ 07833 702658
✉ info@botwbc.co.uk

After 10 years of planning Bull of the Woods started brewing in 2017 using a four-barrel plant.
♦ RAIB

Rock Steady (ABV 3.8%)
A malty, amber-coloured session ale with a biscuity, caramel taste and fruity floral notes.

Vapour Trail (ABV 4.3%)
A pale ale with citrus fruits giving a clean, fresh taste and an assertive bitter finish.

Inca Gold (ABV 4.4%)
A smooth, malty, quaffable golden ale with subtle citrus hops.

Twisted Wheel (ABV 4.5%)
A session IPA with sweet orange marmalade hoppiness, a quick flash of pink grapefruit, and an easy, dry bitter finish.

Bullards

See Redwell

Bullen (NEW)

Bullen Lodge, Ledbury Road, Ledbury, Herefordshire, HR8 2JE ☎ 07878 200574

Set up as a one-barrel pilot brewery in 2017 by Adrian Whiles, Bullen launched commercial sales in 2018. It is located just outside of Ledbury in an old hunting lodge.

Best Bitter (ABV 3.8%)

Oh Well English Pale Ale (ABV 3.9%)

Ruby Special Ale (ABV 4.4%)

Bullfinch

Arches 886 & 887, Rosendale Road, Herne hill, London, SE24 9EH ☎ 07899795823
🌐 thebullfinchbrewery.co.uk

Bullfinch began brewing in 2014 using a 2.5-barrel plant. Production is mainly keg but cask and bottle-conditioned beers are available. The on-site taproom is open six days a week. In 2019 the brewery opened a pub called the Bull & Finch, which is located opposite Gypsy Hill station.
!! RAIB

Swift (OG 1042, ABV 4%)

Bullhouse

10 Greengraves Rd, Newtownards, BT23 5AG
☎ 07562 702825

Bullhouse was set up in 2016 by beer enthusiast and homebrewer William Mayne. It has since expanded from a 2.5-barrel plant to a custom-built 1,000-litre brewhouse with a fermentation capacity of 25,000 litres per year.

Small Axe (ABV 4.3%)

P45 (ABV 4.8%)

The Darkness (ABV 5.5%)

Bullmastiff SIBA

14 Bessemer Close, Leckwith, Cardiff, CF11 8DL
☎ (029) 2066 5292

Office: Units 7-8, Curran Rd Industrial Estate, Cardiff, CF10 5DF ✉ bob.bullmastiff@live.co.uk

The brewery was purchased by the present owners following the retirement of the founders Bob and Paul Jenkins. The beers, which replicate former owner recipes as a condition of brewery purchase, are available in South East Wales with the J D Wetherspoon Bears Head, Penarth serving as the informal brewery tap. The owners have recently secured an interest in the Traders Tavern, City Centre and some of the beers are featured there. ♦

Slobberchops (OG 1046, ABV 4.6%)

Welsh Red (OG 1048, ABV 4.8%)

Olde Snarler (OG 1053, ABV 5.1%)

Son of a Bitch (OG 1062, ABV 6%)
A complex, warming, amber-coloured ale with a tasty blend of hops, malt and fruit flavours, with increasing bitterness.

Special Reserve (OG 1068, ABV 6.5%)

Bumbling

See Xtreme

Bun Dubh (NEW) SIBA

Ceabhar, Sandaig, Isle of Tiree, PA77 6XG
☎ (01879) 220684

Duncan Castling began brewing on his picobrewery in 2016 catering solely for his restaurant, Ceabhar. Beer is produced in 200-litre batches. With an enviropunk ethos all production goes into reuseable containers, no bottles or cans, and distribution remains exclusive to the island. Expansion into the adjoining guesthouse is planned.

Buntingford

Greys Brewhouse, Therfield Road, Royston, Hertfordshire, SG8 9NW
☎ (01763) 250749 ☎ 07851 743799
🌐 buntingfordbrewery.com

Brewing commenced on the current site in 2005 and has expanded to a capacity of around 60 barrels per week. Two regular beers are brewed year round alongside seasonal/occasional brews and various themed specials. The beers are brewed using water from an on-site well and all liquid waste is treated in a reed bed. The brewery is located on a conservation farm and there is a wide variety of bird life visible from the doors of the brewhouse, often including rare and endangered species. ♦

Twitchell (OG 1038, ABV 3.8%)

Single Hop varieties (OG 1040, ABV 4%)

Hurricane (OG 1044, ABV 4.3%)

Polar Star (OG 1045, ABV 4.4%)

Burley Street

Fox & Newt, 7-9 Burley Street, Leeds, West Yorkshire, LS3 1LD
☎ (0113) 245 4527 🌐 burleystreetbrewhouse.co.uk

Burley Street Brewhouse is in the cellar of the Fox & Newt pub where the first brewery was installed by Whitbread in the 1980s. The freehold was purchased by the current owners and brewing recommenced in 2010 and then, following a two-year break, again in 2015.

Burning Sky SIBA

Place Barn, The Street, Firle, East Sussex, BN8 6LP
☎ (01273) 858080 🌐 burningskybeer.com

Burning Sky started brewing in 2013 using a 15-barrel plant, based on the Firle Estate in the South Downs. It is owned and run by Mark Tranter (ex-Dark Star head brewer). The brewery has its own yeast strains suited to the beer styles. It specialises in pale ales and Belgian-inspired farmhouse beers and has an extensive barrel-aging programme. RAIB

Plateau (OG 1035, ABV 3.5%)
Pale gold-coloured, with a crisp malt edge and sharp bitterness. Full-flavoured, zesty and refreshing.

Aurora (OG 1056, ABV 5.6%)
Premium strength, well-balanced, pale amber-coloured pale ale, with a juicy backbone, resinous mouthfeel, big citrus and tropical fruit flavours.

Devil's Rest IPA (OG 1070, ABV 7%)
Full-strength, full-flavoured, burnt orange-coloured IPA.

Burning Soul

Unit 1, 51 Mott Street, Hockley, Birmingham, B19 3HE
☎ (0121) 439 1490 ☎ 07793 026624
🌐 burningsoulbrewing.com

Established in 2016 by Chris Small and Richard Murphy who chose the name Burning Soul to reflect their passion for beer and brewing. A five-barrel, full mash brewery with an on-site brewery tap less that one mile from Birmingham City centre, offering key keg beer on tap. The core range is always available along with various special brews. Beers may be released into the trade in cask form at times. ‼ ♦

Low Clarity (ABV 3%)

Mosaic Session IPA (ABV 4.5%)

OCT IPA (ABV 6.7%)
Pale gold-coloured, with a fruity hop aroma, hoppy taste and a long, hoppy, bitter aftertaste.

Belgian IPA (ABV 6.8%)

Coconut Porter (ABV 6.9%)
Dark brown-coloured ale, with coconut in the aroma. A good balance of malt and hops in the taste leading to a fruity aftertaste.

Burnside SIBA

Laurencekirk Business Park, Laurencekirk, AB30 1EY
☎ (01561) 377316 burnsidebrewery.co.uk

Burnside began brewing in 2010 using a 2.5-barrel plant and by 2012 had expanded to a 10-barrel plant. Since then the focus has been to establish the brand and range of cask-conditioned ales locally and to develop a range of bottle-conditioned beers. Further expansion is planned. ‼ RAIB

Black Katz (OG 1036, ABV 3.6%)

No 1 Pale Ale (OG 1036, ABV 3.6%)
A well-balanced pale ale.

3-BULLZ (OG 1038, ABV 3.8%)

Mad Dogz (OG 1038, ABV 3.8%)
Season brew with a light mix of roasted malt and citrus hop flavours.

Golden X (OG 1042, ABV 4.1%)
Easy-drinking best bitter.

Wild Rhino (OG 1045, ABV 4.5%)

Chieftains Export (OG 1048, ABV 4.6%)
A classic export 80/- ale.

India Pale Ale (OG 1049, ABV 4.8%)
Full on citrus hop aroma declining through the taste.

After Dark (OG 1050.5, ABV 5%)
A double chocolate oatmeal stout.

M-PIRE (OG 1052, ABV 5.2%)
Very warming, sweetish peachy hoppy brew.

Stealth (OG 1058, ABV 6%)
A full-bodied, rich dark ale.

Burnt Mill

Unit 10, Woodlands Dairy, Badley, Suffolk, IP6 8RS
burntmillbrewery.com

Brewing began in 2016 in a former grain shed. Beers are available in KeyKeg and cans.

Burscough

See Hop Vine

Burton Bridge SIBA

24 Bridge Street, Burton upon Trent, Staffordshire, DE14 1SY
☎ (01283) 510573 burtonbridgebrewery.co.uk

The brewery was established in 1982 by Bruce Wilkinson and Geoff Mumford and owns three pubs in the local area, including its award-winning brewery tap. More than 300 outlets are supplied direct. ‼ ♦ RAIB

Golden Delicious (OG 1037, ABV 3.8%)
Burton classic with a sulphurous aroma and well-balanced hops and fruit. An apple fruitiness, sharp and refreshing start leads to a lingering mouth-watering bitter finish with a hint of astringency. Light, crisp and refreshing.

Sovereign Gold (OG 1040, ABV 4%)
Sweet, caramel aroma with a grassy hop start with malt overtones. Fresh and fruity with a bitterness that emerges and continues to develop.

XL Bitter (OG 1039, ABV 4%)
Burton classic with sulphurous aroma. Golden-coloured with fruit and hops and a lingering hint of toffee apple aftertaste.

XL Mild (OG 1040, ABV 4%)
Black treacle initial taste after liquorice aroma. Sweet finish with a touch of bitterness

Bridge Bitter (OG 1041, ABV 4.2%)
Gentle aroma of malt and fruit. Well-balanced start finishing with a robust hop mouthfeel.

Burton Porter (OG 1044, ABV 4.5%)
Chocolate aromas and sweet, smooth taste of smoky, roasted grain and coffee.

Damson Porter (OG 1044, ABV 4.5%)
Faint roast, caramel and dark fruit nose. Cough mixture and blackjack start. Uncomplicated profile with a mix of bitter fruitiness and yeasty maltiness.

Draught Burton Ale (OG 1048, ABV 4.8%)
Fruity, orange aroma leads to hoppy start, hop and fruit body, then fruity aftertaste. Dry finish with fruity hints.

Bramble Stout (OG 1049, ABV 5%)
Black-coloured ale, with a smoky aroma and fruit hint. Roast start with briar dry fruit, then a sharp black fruit taste balances the burnt note. Sweetish, dry blackberry finish. Prolonged mouthwatering.

Stairway to Heaven (OG 1049, ABV 5%)
Well-balanced, golden-coloured bitter. The fruity, hoppy start leads to a hoppy body and a mouthwatering finish.

Top Dog Stout (OG 1049, ABV 5%)
Black-coloured, rich ale with a roast and malty start, fruity and abundant hops give a fruity, bitter finish with a mouth-watering edge. Also available as Bramble Stout.

Festival Ale (OG 1054, ABV 5.5%)
Caramel aroma with plenty of hop taste balanced by a full-bodied malty sweetness.

Thomas Sykes (OG 1095, ABV 10%)
Sweet aroma, rich, fruity spirited tastes, warming and moreish.

Burton Road

See Mobberley

Burton Town

Unit 8, Falcon Close, Burton upon Trent, Staffordshire, DE14 1SG
☎ (01283) 510839 ☎ 07428 968702 🌐 burton.town

Open since 2015, Burton Town is run by head brewer Steve Haynes from converted premises off Hawkins Lane. Currently using a six-barrel plant, there are plans for expansion. An on-site tap is open to the public on Saturdays and before Burton Albion home games. !!

Lazy Hazy (OG 1036, ABV 3.5%)
A tropical, hazy New England-style IPA.

Swan/Albion (OG 1040, ABV 3.9%)
Layers of toasted malt and a balanced hop finish in this pale ale.

Scorned Woman (OG 1040, ABV 4%)

Kolsch (OG 1046, ABV 4.5%)
A bright lager, with a crisp, spicy and floral taste.

Modwena (OG 1052, ABV 4.8%)
Thick, velvet oatmeal stout with chocolate character.

Thomcat (OG 1051, ABV 5.1%)
Unfined, deep amber-coloured ale with a hop haze, and a strong, citrus hop aroma. High citrusy hop flavour, low malt, a hint of biscuit, high, lingering bitterness with a dry finish. Medium body, and high carbonation.

Burton IPA (OG 1054, ABV 5.6%)
A traditional, strong IPA. Full-flavoured, with a hint of toffee and a long-lasting bittersweet finish.

Burtonwood

Bold Lane, Burtonwood, Warrington, Cheshire, WA5 4TH
☎ (01925) 220022 🌐 thomashardybrewery.co.uk

Thomas Hardy's only brewery was acquired by Molson Coors in 2015. Currently producing no real ale, and operating solely as a contract brewer.

Bushy's SIBA

Mount Murray Brewery, Mount Murray, Braddan, Isle of Man, IM4 1JE
☎ (01624) 661244 🌐 bushys.com

Launched in 1986 as a brewpub, Bushys relocated in 1990 when demand outgrew capacity. Bushys goes one step further than the Manx Pure Beer Law preferring the German Reinheitsgebot (Pure Beer Law). The brewery hosts a successful festival during the TT period at Villa Marina Gardens, Douglas. !! ♦

Castletown Bitter (OG 1035, ABV 3.5%)
A light, refreshing, golden-coloured session beer full of floral and citrus hints.

Ruby (1874) Mild (OG 1035, ABV 3.5%)
Classic, full-bodied, malty, ruby mild with sweet caramel flavours throughout and well-balanced hops.

Bitter (OG 1038, ABV 3.8%)
A traditional malty and hoppy beer with good balance, and the fruit lasts through to the bitter finish.

Old Bushy Tail (OG 1045, ABV 4.5%)
A reddish brown-coloured beer with a pronounced hop and malt aroma, the malt tending towards treacle. Slightly sweet and malty on the palate with distinct orange tones. The full finish is malty and hoppy with a hint of toffee.

Red (OG 1047, ABV 4.7%)
Mahogany-coloured ale with a full mouthfeel, traditional dry, hoppy bitterness and a rich, dark fruit aroma.

Buswells (NEW)

Lime Kilns Pub, Watling Street, Burbage, Leicestershire, LE10 3ED ☎ 07754 711041

Office: 25 Bunneys Meadow, Hinckley, Leicestershire, LE10 0FQ 🌐 limekilnsinn.co.uk

Brewing started at the Lime Kilns pub Burbage in 2016 as a small batch brewery. The brewery is a two-barrel plant and provides up to 14 ales for the pub and other outlets, on demand. Bespoke brews are provided for events including several local beer festivals.

Butcombe SIBA

Cox's Green, Wrington, Somerset, BS40 5PA
☎ (01934) 863963 🌐 butcombe.com

Originally established in 1978, Butcombe moved to a purpose-built brewery with a 150-barrel plant in 2005. The brewery was bought by the Jersey-based Liberation Group for a reported £15m in 2015. Around 500 outlets are supplied direct and similar numbers via wholesalers and pub companies. Butcombe opened a new distribution centre with a bottling line in Bridgewater in 2018. The brewery has an estate of around 20 managed and 20 tenanted pubs. !! ♦

Adam Henson's Rare Breed (OG 1038, ABV 3.8%)
Subtle aroma of unripe fruit with sulphurous hints. Malty flavour is masked by dry bitterness which continues into the finish.

Original (OG 1039, ABV 4%)
A brown bitter with little aroma. Sweet and malty taste with faint fruit notes. The hop gradually asserts itself leaving a slightly bitter finish.

Gold (OG 1045, ABV 4.4%)
Amber-coloured golden ale with light aroma of fruit and hops, leading to well-balanced flavours of malt, pale fruit and hops. Bitter aftertaste.

Bute

15-17 Columshill Street, Rothesay, Isle of Bute, PA20 0DN
☎ (01700) 504260 ☎ 07980 259511
🌐 butebrewco.co.uk

Situated in the centre of Rothesay on the Isle of Bute, brewing began in 2015. Beers are supplied to several local outlets, and further afield. Beer festivals are also supplied. !!

Scalpsie Blonde (OG 1038, ABV 3.8%)

Red (OG 1042, ABV 4.2%)

The Maids (OG 1043, ABV 4.3%)

Butts

Northfield Farm, Wantage Road, Great Shefford, Berkshire, RG17 7BY
☎ (01488) 648133 🌐 buttsbrewery.com

The brewery was set up in a converted barn in 1994. In 2002 the owners took the decision to become dedicated to organic production; all the beers brewed use organic malted barley and organic hops and are certified by the Soil Association. ♦RAIB

Jester (OG 1036, ABV 3.5%)
A pale brown-coloured, session bitter with a hoppy aroma and a hint of fruit. The taste balances malt, hops, fruit and bitterness with a hoppy aftertaste.

Traditional (OG 1040, ABV 4%)
A pale brown-coloured bitter, soft on the tongue, hoppy citrus flavours, with a gentle bittersweetness, and a long, dry aftertaste dominated by fruity hops.

Barbus Barbus (OG 1046, ABV 4.6%)
Golden ale with a fruity, hoppy aroma and a hint of malt. Hops dominate taste and aftertaste, accompanied by fruitiness and bitterness, with a hint of balancing sweetness.

Buxton

Units 4 A & B, Staden Business Park, Staden Lane, Buxton, Derbyshire, SK17 9RZ
☎ (01298) 244200 buxtonbrewery.co.uk

Set up in 2009 as a five-barrel plant, Buxton now uses a 20-barrel plant. Its brewery tap is in Buxton and there is a tasting room at the brewery with views of the Derbyshire countryside. A wide range of small-batch beers is brewed throughout the year. ♦RAIB

SPA (OG 1041, ABV 4.1%)
Dry-hopped, fruity, session IPA-style beer

Pale (ABV 5.2%)
Amber-coloured beer with a bold aroma of citrus fruit and a slightly dry, bitter finish.

Wild Boar (OG 1057, ABV 5.7%)
Pale straw-coloured ale. Aromas of spicy lime and mango with distinct flavours of honey malt and fruit punch followed by a dry bitter finish.

Bwthyn

See Anglesey Brewing

By The Horns SIBA

Units 21-27, Summerstown, London, SW17 0BQ
☎ (020) 3417 7338 bythehorns.co.uk

By the Horns began in 2012 with a 5.5-barrel plant, since upgraded to 12-barrels. Output was expected to increase in 2019 to over 4,000 hectolitres. Located in industrial units near Wimbledon Stadium, the Brewery Tap opens six days a week (Tue-Sun) and regularly shows TV sporting events. Beers are available in cask, keg and cans.

Giggle Mug (ABV 3.5%)
Malty, sweetish amber-coloured ale, with fruity hops and a clean, bitter finish.

Stiff Upper Lip (OG 1038, ABV 3.8%)
A classic, amber-coloured bitter, well-balanced, hops to the fore, a hint of citrus, and a dry, bitter finish.

Hopadelic (ABV 4.3%)
A light and sessionable IPA, bursting with citrus and passionfruit notes. Hoppy yet also very balanced with bitterness and malt body

Lambeth Walk (OG 1051, ABV 5.1%)
Well-balanced, black-coloured porter with hops and a little fruit throughout. The roasted bitterness is complemented by the malt notes.

By The Mile

22 Detling Avenue, Broadstairs, Kent, CT10 1SL
☎ 07900 954680 jon@bythemilebrewery.co.uk

By the Mile began brewing in 2016 in domestic premises. Brewing is currently suspended.

Byatt's SIBA

Unit 7-8, Lythalls Lane Industrial Estate, Lythalls Lane, Coventry, CV6 6FL
☎ (024) 7663 7996 byattsbrewery.co.uk

Byatt's was established in 2011, and expanded in 2016. An extensive beer list is brewed throughout the year together with seasonal beers. A brewhouse bar with six handpulls also serves ciders on draught (open Thu-Sat, sometimes Sun). Tours and tasting sessions can be booked and private hire is available. Beer festivals are held during the year. Ricoh arena is nearby. !! ♦RAIB

XK Dark (OG 1038, ABV 3.5%)
Liquorice aroma, soft smoky tastes, sweet but giving hoppy sides.

Coventry Bitter (OG 1039, ABV 3.8%)
Smooth, light amber-coloured session ale. Earthy, grassy with hints of citrus and a lingering hop bitterness.

Platinum Blonde (OG 1039, ABV 3.9%)
Extra pale blonde ale with zesty, citrus flavours. Refreshing and hoppy.

Brewhouse Best (OG 1042, ABV 4.1%)
Chestnut-coloured ale. Rich malt, toffee flavour with a balanced bitter finish.

Phoenix Gold (OG 1042, ABV 4.2%)
Golden ale with initial malt sweetness. Crisp, fresh and hoppy with a rounded bitterness.

Crystal Cookie (OG 1044, ABV 4.4%)
A copper-coloured ale with light biscuit malt sweetness leading to minty, grassy hop flavours with hints of blackcurrant and a balanced bitterness.

Urban Red (OG 1047, ABV 4.5%)
Premium ruby-coloured ale, rich malt flavours, floral, fruity with spicy overtones and a well-balanced finish.

Playtime Chocolate Milk Stout (OG 1053, ABV 5%)
A traditional-style milk stout made with cocoa nibs, has a background malty sweetness and notes of dark chocolate and coffee.

Regal Blond (OG 1052, ABV 5.2%)
Strong golden ale with citrus, vanilla and lemongrass notes. Powerful and hoppy, smooth and refreshing.

Cader SIBA

Unit 4, Marian Mawr Enterprise Park, Dolgellau, LL40 1UU

☎ (01341) 388080 ☎ 07546 272372
🌐 caderales.com

Cader Ales was founded in 2012 by a husband-and-wife team. It was expanded in 2013 to its present five-barrel capacity The brewery is situated close to the centre of the picturesque market town of Dolgellau Deliveries are made to the licensed trade in North and Mid-West Wales and beers in cask or bottle are available to the general public direct from the brewery. ‼

Cader Gold (OG 1038, ABV 3.8%)
A light, hoppy golden ale with a subtle aroma of honey, lemon and tarragon.

Cwrw Cregennan (ABV 3.8%)
A golden ale with citrus notes and a soft malt flavour enhanced by local honey.

Machlyd Mawddach (ABV 3.9%)
A very light and refreshing ale. Added kaffir lime leaves give a fruity citrus aroma.

Idris Bitter (OG 1041, ABV 4.1%)
Traditional bitter with caramel and spicy notes.

Tallyllyn Pale Ale (OG 1044, ABV 4.4%)
A classic IPA, refreshingly bitter, with citrus floral notes.

Red Bandit (OG 1050, ABV 5%)
A warm ruby-coloured ale based on a traditional recipe with spicy berry aromas.

Caffle

The Old School, Llawhaden, Narberth, SA67 8DS
☎ (01437) 541502 🌐 cafflebrewery.co.uk

Started in 2013, Caffle is a four-barrel brewery which produces small-batch crafted ales, mainly for the local market. Production consists of a range of core and seasonal ales in cask and bottle-conditioned, with an annual green hop ale produced using Pembrokeshire grown hops via the brewery's hop co-op. ‼ RAIB

Skirp Gold (OG 1039, ABV 3.8%)
Golden ale with fruity, spicy aromas and a bitter, grapefruit flavour.

Quay Ale (OG 1044, ABV 4%)
A medium, amber-coloured ale, caramel with light hoppy citrus flavour. Balanced slightly to the malty side.

Sholly Amber (OG 1044, ABV 4%)
Light chestnut in colour with a good malt/hop balance.

Sprilly Maid (OG 1044, ABV 4%)
Light chestnut-coloured ale infused with rosemary to give a slight ginger finish.

Kift Blonde (OG 1044, ABV 4.3%)
Straw-coloured, with citrus and floral notes, flavoured with nettle tips.

In The Grip (OG 1052, ABV 4.7%)
Ruby-red in colour, malty caramel, slightly sweet, and warming.

Skaddly Pluck (OG 1048, ABV 4.8%)
IPA using a blend of hops to give a distinctive, hoppy, citrus flavour.

Drop Squint (OG 1052, ABV 5.2%)
Light golden in colour, smooth, clean-tasting with honey, malt and biscuit flavours.

Cairngorm SIBA

Unit 12, Dalfaber Industrial Estate, Aviemore, PH22 1ST
☎ (01479) 812222 🌐 cairngormbrewery.com

Cairngorm brews using a 20-barrel plant. Now with its own bottling line, it supplies the free trade as far south as the central belt and nationally via wholesalers. In 2016, in partnership with the Cobbs Group, it bought the brands of the Loch Ness Brewing Co and now brews selected beers under the Loch Ness brand name. ‼ ♦

Nessies Monster Mash (OG 1040, ABV 4.1%)
Best bitter with plenty of bitterness and malt flavour and a fruity background. Lingering bitterness in the aftertaste with diminishing sweetness.

Stag (OG 1040, ABV 4.1%)
Best bitter with plenty of roast and hop throughout. This tawny-coloured brew also has plenty of malt in the lingering bittersweet aftertaste.

Trade Winds (OG 1043, ABV 4.3%)
Citrus fruity hop and elderflower nose, follows through to the bittersweet finish.

Black Gold (OG 1044, ABV 4.4%)
Roast malt dominates throughout, slight smokiness in aroma leading to a liquorice and blackcurrant, sweet background. Very long, dry, bitter finish.

Cairngorm Gold (OG 1044, ABV 4.5%)
Fruit and hops to the fore with a hint of caramel in this sweetish brew. Also known as Sheepshaggers Gold.

Highland IPA (OG 1049, ABV 5%)
Refreshing, light-coloured citrus IPA. Some background biscuit and caramel.

Wildcat (OG 1049.5, ABV 5.1%)
A full-bodied, warming, strong bitter. Malt dominates but there is an underlying hop character through to a well-balanced aftertaste.

Caledonian

42 Slateford Road, Edinburgh, EH11 1PH
☎ (0131) 337 1286 🌐 caledonianbeer.com

The brewery was founded by Lorimer and Clark in 1869 and was sold to Vaux of Sunderland in 1919. In 1987 the brewery was saved from closure by a management buy-out and became independent. The brewery was purchased by S&N in 2004 and became part of Heineken in 2008. Guest beers, sometimes of an unusual style, are produced for occasions throughout the year, and there is a rolling programme of special beers covering each of the seasons. A pilot brewery 'Wee George' named after the founding father George Lorimer, was opened in 2015 to allow small scale brews of new recipes. ♦

Deuchars IPA (OG 1039.5, ABV 3.8%)
Well-balanced, golden session ale with hop aroma, malt-fruitiness, balanced sweetness and dry, bitter finish.

Edinburgh Castle 80/- (OG 1042.4, ABV 4.1%)
Predominantly malty, brown-coloured beer with soft roast and caramel throughout. Fruit gives sweetness, typical of a Scottish 80/-.

Brewed for Heineken:

John Smith's Bitter (ABV 3.5%)

Calverley's SIBA

23a Hooper Street, Cambridge, CB1 2NZ
☎ (01223) 312370 ☎ 07769 537342
🌐 calverleys.com

This small central Cambridge brewery was started in 2013 by Sam Calverley and his brother Tom. It is located in an old industrial unit close to the city centre. The brewery is open to the public for on and off sales (Thu-Sat). The majority of production is sold on the premises, but it will supply beer festivals and local pubs on demand. A proportion of the beers are keg (various styles), but the brewery remains committed to cask ale and their porter is usually available. ‼

Porter (ABV 5%)

Calvors SIBA

Home Farm, Coddenham Green, Suffolk, IP6 9UN
☎ (01449) 711055 🌐 calvorsbrewery.com

Calvors Brewery was established in 2008 and brews three craft lagers, as well as cask-conditioned beers.

Lodestar Festival Ale (OG 1038, ABV 3.8%)
Well-balanced, lightly hopped, rich, golden straw-coloured ale with a gentle sweetness and honey aroma.

Smooth Hoperator (OG 1040, ABV 4%)
A well-rounded, copper-coloured pale ale with background sweetness.

Cambridge

Cambridge Brew House, 1 King Street, Cambridge, CB1 1LH
☎ (01223) 858155 🌐 thecambridgebrewhouse.com

Brewing began in 2013 on an on-site microbrewery in the Cambridge Brew House. ♦

Camden Town

Unit 1, Navigation Park, Morson Road, Ponders End, London, EN3 4NQ
☎ (020) 7485 1671 🌐 camdentownbrewery.com

No real ale. Bought by A-B InBev in 2016. A modern, automated brewhouse situated in five railway arches underneath Kentish Town West railway station with an onsite brewery tap. A second brewery in Ponders End opened in 2017. ‼

Camerons

Lion Brewery, Stranton, Hartlepool, County Durham, TS24 7QS
☎ (01429) 852000 🌐 cameronsbrewery.com

Camerons was founded in 1865, and is a family-owned business. The brewery is also producing a range of cask ales throughout the year in association with the RNLI. The brewery also does a number of limited run ales through their Tooth & Claw pilot brewery. The brewing is done by various members of the Camerons team from office staff to brewery staff. It has a pub estate of more than 70 pubs including the Head of Steam pubs. ‼ ♦

Strongarm (OG 1041, ABV 4%)
A well-rounded, ruby red-coloured ale with a distinctive, tight creamy head. Initially fruity, but with a good balance of malt, hops and moderate bitterness.

A-Hop-Alypse Now (ABV 4.3%)
Golden ale with a citrus aroma and satisfying full hop flavour. Initial citrus flavour followed by bitterness.

Road Crew (ABV 4.5%)
Crisp, refreshing, American-style pale ale packed full of hoppy citrus and blackcurrant flavours.

Campbells

Unit 9, Southpark Industrial Estate, Peebles, EH45 9ED
☎ 07899 653151 🌐 campbells-brewery.com

Campbells was established in 2017 in Peebles, supplying pubs in the Borders, Edinburgh and the Lothians. The brewery has three fermentation vessels, using local malt from East Lothian, and has also invested in a bottling plant, which has an initial capacity of 3,000 bottles per week. ‼

Flintlock Golden Ale (OG 1035, ABV 3.7%)
Golden ale with a fruity and citrus hop flavour.

Gunner (OG 1039, ABV 4.3%)
Well-balanced, refreshing blonde ale.

Campervan

Unit 4, Bonnington Business Centre, 112 Jane Street, Edinburgh, EH6 5HG
☎ (0131) 553 3373 ☎ 07786 566000
🌐 campervanbrewery.com

Campervan began brewing in 2016 in a private garage but also in a 1973 VW campervan, hence the name. The van is used as a mobile sales outlet at beer festivals and other outdoor events. It expanded to a new 10-barrel facility in Edinburgh in 2017. A taproom is open Thursday-Saturday.

Blonde Voyage (OG 1038, ABV 3.8%)
Light blonde ale with zesty citrus aromas and a hint of fresh lemongrass together with a crisp, natural sweetness from the malt.

All Shook Up (OG 1040, ABV 4%)
A pale-coloured beer with tropical fruit flavours and bitter hops.

Mutiny on the Bounty (OG 1042, ABV 4.2%)
Milk stout with a coconut aroma, rich chocolate and coffee flavour and a subtle vanilla finish.

Cannon Royall IFBB

Unit 15a, Weston Industrial Estate, Honeybourne, Worcestershire, WR11 7GB 🌐 cannonroyall.co.uk

Cannon Royall's first brew was in 1993 in a converted cider house behind the Fruiterer's Arms. In 2018 the brewery plant relocated and now shares premises with White Rabbit Brewery (qv). ‼ ♦ RAIB

Black Betty (OG 1037, ABV 3.5%)
Dark brown-coloured mild with a toffee aroma. Gentle caramel taste with bitterness in the finish.

Black Coffee (OG 1039, ABV 3.7%)
Dark brown-coloured mild with a distinctive coffee aroma and taste and a subtle bitterness.

Fruiterers Mild (OG 1037, ABV 3.7%)
Fruity aroma with a hint of damsons, slightly sweet, fruity taste balanced with roasted malt and a fruity finish with smoky malt undertones.

Hunny Bear (OG 1038, ABV 3.8%)
Dark golden-coloured beer with a thin head and sweet aroma. Sweet honey taste with a hint of caramel. A gentle bitter finish balances the sweetness.

King's Shilling (OG 1038, ABV 3.8%)

Light Beer (OG 1040, ABV 3.8%) ◆
Amber-coloured session bitter, malty aroma with hints of toffee, initial hoppiness revealing a biscuit malt base, a slight grassiness and a lingering bitter finish.

Arrowhead Bitter (OG 1039, ABV 3.9%) ◆
Well-balanced, fruity aroma with hints of banana, fruit and hops with mango and peach on the palate, followed by a long, sweet, hoppy finish.

Best Bitter (OG 1043, ABV 4.2%) ◆
Amber-coloured best bitter, floral caramel aroma, initial hints of grapefruit and apple give way to complex hoppy bitterness then an initially flowery hoppiness in a long bitter finish.

Muzzle Loader (OG 1043, ABV 4.2%) ◆
Flavoursome, full-bodied, amber-coloured best bitter. A fruity nose with hints of butterscotch and apple continues into the taste, with a long, bitter finish.

Arrowhead Extra (OG 1043, ABV 4.3%)
A hop punch leads to a smooth palate and pleasant finish with a good malt balance.

Foxy Lady (OG 1044, ABV 4.3%) ◆
Light-bodied, amber-coloured bitter, sweet shop aroma, moderate sweet malt taste with faint hops and a short bitter finish.

Love Is Ale You Need (OG 1044, ABV 4.3%)
Pale golden-coloured beer with a tight, creamy head. Fruity aroma. Well-balanced session ale with a gentle bitterness.

Paddington (OG 1044, ABV 4.3%)

Silver Fox (OG 1044, ABV 4.3%)
Pale golden-coloured beer with a creamy head and a smooth mouthfeel. Biscuity aroma. Subtle fruit taste with a mellow bitterness.

Teddy Bear (OG 1044, ABV 4.3%)
Dark golden-coloured ale with a creamy head. Gentle bitterness with a medium finish.

Jeff's Old Ale (OG 1046, ABV 4.6%) ◆
Full-flavoured, fruity, copper-coloured ale with hints of plum, banana and molasses, balanced sweetness and hops leading to a fruity, lightly-hopped finish.

Son of Bertie (OG 1052, ABV 5%)

Bertie's Stout (OG 1068, ABV 6.7%)

Canopy

Arch 1127 Bath Factory Estate, 41 Norwood Road Herne Hill, London, SE24 9AJ ☎ 07792 463386
🌐 canopybeer.com

⊗ Canopy started brewing in a railway arch in Herne Hill in late 2014 with the taproom following in 2015 (open five days a week). Mostly available in keg and bottles, cask does get out into pubs around south London and the taproom is the best place to get the widest range including the regular specials. ‼ ♦ RAIB

Sunray Pale Ale (ABV 4.2%) ◆
Unfined, zesty, fruity refreshing golden-coloured pale ale with a building bitter hoppiness.

Snapper (ABV 4.8%) ◆
Refreshing, smooth, yellow-coloured beer. Mango, lemon and green pine notes lead to a dry, bitterish aftertaste, with hints of tobacco/ smokiness.

Full Moon Porter (ABV 5%) ◆
Strong malt aroma with raisins, figs, dark vintage marmalade and coffee. Roasted flavour with dark treacle, and dark chocolate sweetness.

Canterbury Ales SIBA

Unit 7 Stour Valley Business Park, Ashford Road, Chartham, Kent, CT4 7HF
☎ (01227) 732541 ☎ 07944 657978
🌐 canterbury-ales.co.uk

⊗ Brewing commenced in 2010. An eight-barrel plant is used. ‼ ♦

The Wife of Bath's Ale (OG 1038, ABV 3.9%) ◆
A golden ale with strong bitterness and grapefruit hop character, leading to a long, dry finish.

The Reeve's Ale (OG 1040, ABV 4.1%)

The Miller's Ale (OG 1044, ABV 4.5%)

Canterbury Brewers SIBA

Foundry Brew Pub, 77 Stour Street, Canterbury, Kent, CT1 2NR
☎ (01227) 455899 🌐 thefoundrycanterbury.co.uk

⊗ Canterbury Brewers started brewing in the Foundry Brewpub in the heart of Canterbury in 2011. The eight-barrel plant is purpose-built. Popular events are held there including the Kent Green Hop Festival (late Sep/early Oct). A wide range of spirits is now distilled in the brewpub and three ciders are produced. ‼ ♦ RAIB

Cap House

444-446 Bradford Road, Batley, West Yorkshire, WF17 5LW
☎ (01924) 479909 ☎ 07981 858270
🌐 caphousebrewery.co.uk

Cap House was established in 2011 using a 2.5-barrel plant as a joint venture between Peter Lister, who has a plastics business at the location, and Gary Wardman of the Reindeer Inn in Overton, which is the brewery tap. ♦

Miners A Pint (OG 1038, ABV 3.8%)
A tangy session bitter with a smooth mouthfeel balanced by toffee undertone and a deep, dry finish with lingering fruit notes.

Hey Blondie (OG 1044, ABV 4.2%)

Hoppylicious (OG 1040, ABV 4.2%)
A light, hoppy beer with a well-balanced fruity taste, refreshing citrus and grapefruit flavours and a bittersweet finish.

Temptress (OG 1054, ABV 5.6%)
A rich ruby-coloured brew with a smooth finish, fruity nut/toffee aroma and tangy palate.

Captain Cook

White Swan, 1 West End, Stokesley, North Yorkshire, TS9 5BL
☎ (01642) 714985 🌐 whiteswanstokesley.co.uk

Celebrating its 20th anniversary in 2019, the Captain Cook Brewery is located behind the 18th-century White Swan pub. The brewery, which supplies the pub, uses a four-barrel plant. Under new ownership since 2018 but with the same brewer. !! ♦

Navigator (OG 1040, ABV 4%)
A light-coloured ale with a hint of grapefruit and spruce.

Sunset (OG 1040, ABV 4%)
A smooth, light-coloured ale with a hint of citrus.

Slipway (OG 1042, ABV 4.2%)
A light-coloured, full-flavoured, hoppy ale with a smooth, malty aftertaste.

Endeavour (OG 1043, ABV 4.3%)
Brown-coloured ale with a bitter finish.

Skippy (OG 1043, ABV 4.3%)
A refreshing, golden-coloured pale ale with late bitterness.

Black Porter (OG 1044, ABV 4.4%)
Chocolate notes and dominant roast flavours lead to a dry, bitter finish.

APA (OG 1047, ABV 4.7%)
Fruity, bitter, American-style pale ale.

Schooner (OG 1047, ABV 4.7%)

IPA (OG 1051, ABV 5.1%)

Carlisle SIBA

Unit2, 12a Kingstown Broadway, Kingstown Industrial Estate, Carlisle, Cumbria, CA3 0HA
☎ (01228) 594959 ☎ 07979 728780
carlislerealale.com

Carlisle Brewing Company is a family-run brewery established in 2013. Initially using a 2.5-barrel plant in a shed behind the owner's freehouse, by 2015 it had expanded to a 10-barrel plant in an industrial unit. Beer is available in the Spinners Arms and other local outlets. !! ♦

Cumbrian Bitter (ABV 3.7%)
Light gold-coloured, session ale. Hoppy with light herbal, floral and caramel flavours and a long-lasting, bitter finish.

Carlisle Bell (ABV 3.8%)
Gluten-free, pale ale, with a light citrus and tropical fruit flavour.

Citadel (ABV 3.8%)
Light, aromatic bitterness with spicy and earthy notes.

Porter (ABV 3.8%)
Porter with a punchy, fruit flavour.

Spun Gold (OG 1043, ABV 4.2%)
Red gold-coloured, sweet beer. The hops follow on to build on the flavour and complement the balanced finish.

Flaxen (OG 1042, ABV 4.5%)
Flavours mingle in the mouth, well-balanced, with a hoppy bouquet.

Magic Number (OG 1045, ABV 4.5%)
A premium bitter, soft, smooth with indulgent caramel and toffee flavours, lightly bittered to give a refreshing, malty beer.

Carlisle Nut Brown (OG 1048, ABV 4.7%)
Sweet, mild, characterful amber-coloured ale, with predominately nutty and roasty flavours.

Oatmeal Stout (OG 1048, ABV 4.7%)
Well-balanced, soft, coating mouthfeel, creamy head, with coffee, chocolate, and smoke aromas.

Herkules (ABV 4.8%)
Kolsch lager-style, pale-coloured beer with a citrus and fruity taste and a lovely floral note.

The Carlisle Experiment (ABV 5.6%)
Pale ale with a fresh, citrus taste.

Carlsberg-Tetley

Jacobson House, 140 Bridge Street, Northampton, NN1 1PZ
☎ (01604) 668866 carlsberg.co.uk

International lager brewery, which whilst brewing no real ales is a major distributor of cask beer. The Tetley-owned real ales are mostly brewed by Marstons. Some Tetley beers are brewed at Leeds Brewery.

Castle SIBA

Unit 9a-7, Restormel Industrial Estate, Liddicoat Road, Lostwithiel, Cornwall, PL22 0HG ☎ 07880 349032
castlebrewery.co.uk

The brewery was established in 2007 using a one-barrel plant. It was re-equipped in 2016 with a new 200-litre plant. All brews are unfined, and are suitable for vegans. The brewery carries out its own bottling, and some for other breweries. The brewery offers off-sales of both draught and bottled beers on Friday afternoons. ♦ RAIB V

Once A Knight (OG 1048, ABV 5%)
A strong bitter.

Castle Combe

See Flying Monk

Castle Eden

8 East Cliff Road, Spectrum Business Park, Seaham, SR7 7PS
☎ (0191) 581 5711 ☎ 07768 044484
castleedenbrewery.com

Using the name of the former Castle Eden Brewery having acquired the intellectual rights and recipes, a new 20-barrel commercial plant was installed in 2015 along with a bottling/kegging plant. Besides its own brand production, the brewery also contract bottles for several local and national breweries. ♦

Ale (ABV 4.2%)
Light, creamy golden ale with a contrast between an initial sweet surge of flavour followed by a slight bitter aftertaste.

Contract brewed for HB Clark Brewery:

Classic Blonde (OG 1039, ABV 3.9%)

English Pale Ale (ABV 4%)

Merrie City Atlantic Hop (OG 1040, ABV 4%)

Merrie City Crystal Gold (OG 1042, ABV 4.2%)

Castle Rock SIBA

Queensbridge Road, Nottingham, NG2 1NB
☎ (0115) 985 1615 castlerockbrewery.co.uk

☺Castle Rock was established in 1998. Aside from its core range of beers it also produces a variety of seasonal and special brews throughout the year, including experimental beer under the banner of Traffic Street Specials. ‼◆RAIB V

Black Gold (OG 1037, ABV 3.8%) 🍷

Harvest Pale (OG 1037, ABV 3.8%) ◢
Pale yellow-coloured beer, full of hop aroma and flavour. Refreshing with a mellowing aftertaste.

Session IPA (ABV 4%)
Pale golden in colour with aromas of citrus and grapefruit. Juicy, fruity and moreish with a soft bitterness.

Preservation Fine Ale (OG 1044, ABV 4.4%) ◣◢
A traditional copper-coloured best bitter with malt predominant. Fairly bitter with a residual sweetness.

Sherwood Reserve (OG 1045, ABV 4.5%) ◢
An earthy yet smooth-tasting, dark-coloured stout with a smoked roastness through to a roast, bitter finish.

Elsie Mo (OG 1045, ABV 4.7%) ◢
A strong, golden ale with floral hops evident in the aroma. Citrus hops are mellowed by a slight sweetness.

Midnight Owl (OG 1055, ABV 5.5%) ◢
Black-coloured IPA with roast malts, fruity hops and a slightly sweet finish.

Screech Owl (OG 1055, ABV 5.5%) ◢
A classic, golden-coloured IPA with an intensely hoppy aroma and bitter taste with a little balancing sweetness.

Castor SIBA

30 Peterborough Road, Castor, Cambridgeshire, PE5 7AX
☎ (01733) 380337 ⊕ castorales.co.uk

This three-barrel brewery, established in 2009, is located in a specially converted outhouse in the garden of the founder brewer. Several local outlets feature the beers as well as many national beer festivals. ‼◆

Roman Gold (OG 1037, ABV 3.7%)
Golden-coloured session bitter with refreshing citrus and fruit notes.

Hopping Toad (OG 1040, ABV 4.1%)
A light golden-coloured bitter, well-balanced with a refreshing citrus flowery finish and a fruity aftertaste.

Old Scarlett (OG 1045, ABV 4.6%)
Ruby-coloured malty beer balanced by subtle hops with a fine aroma and citrus finish.

Cat Asylum

12 Besthorpe Road, Collingham, Nottinghamshire, NG23 7NP
☎ (01636) 892229 ☎ 07773502653
✉ henry.bealby@lineone.net

Established in 2017, Cat Asylum is a microbrewery specialising in historic recipes from Britain and around the world.

Cellar Boys

⊟ c/o White Hart, 184 New Cross Road, New Cross Gate, London, SE14 5AA ⊕ whitehartse14.com/beer

Starting out as PWA (Paddies With Attitude), the name was changed to Cellar Boys in 2018. Brewing in the cellar occasionally, most production is using spare capacity at Bianca Road (qv). Only available in keg, the pub is the main place to find it along with Howl at the Moon, Hoxton, N1.

Cellar Head SIBA

The Barn, Pillory Corner, Flimwell, East Sussex, TN5 7QG ☎ 07391557407 ⊕ cellarheadbrewing.com

⊠ Cellar Head is a microbrewery in the heart of the Weald countryside. ‼🍴

Sub Three (OG 1027, ABV 2.7%)

Session Bitter (OG 1036, ABV 3.5%)

Amber Ale (OG 1040, ABV 4%)

Session Pale Ale (OG 1042, ABV 4.2%)

Single Hop Pale (OG 1046, ABV 4.6%)

India Pale Ale (OG 1050, ABV 5%)

Celt Experience

See Evan Evans

Cerddin

⊟ c/o Cross Inn, Maesteg Road, Cwmfelin, CF34 9LB
☎ (01656) 732476 ☎ 07949 652237
⊕ cerddinbrewery.co.uk

Established in 2010 using a 2.5-barrel plant in a converted garage adjacent to the owner's pub, now enlarged to a four-barrel plant. Beer is usually only available in the pub. ‼◆RAIB

Cerne Abbas SIBA

Chescombe Barn, Barton Meadows Farm, Cerne Abbas, Dorset, DT2 7JS
☎ (01300) 341999 ☎ 07506 303407

Office: Cerne Abbas Brewery, The Mill House, Mill Lane, Cerne Abbas, DT2 7LB
⊕ cerneabbasbrewery.com

⊠ Established in 2014 by Vic Irvine and Jodie Moore. Operating on a five-barrel plant, the beers are made as naturally as possible using chalk-filtered water from its own spring. All beers are brewed with organic, locally sourced barley. Some non-conventional ingredients are used in seasonal brews. On the last Saturday in September, a community brew is produced using hops grown by people living in the village and surrounding area. ‼🍴◆

Responsibly (OG 1035, ABV 3.2%)

Ale (OG 1040, ABV 3.8%)
Well-balanced, tawny-coloured ale. Supple middle, full mouthfeel and refreshing finish.

Blonde (OG 1042, ABV 4.2%)
Heavily-hopped, easy-drinking blonde ale.

Tiger Tom Ruby Mild (OG 1044, ABV 4.4%)

Watercress Warrior (OG 1042, ABV 4.5%)

A pale ale made using local watercress, crisp with distinct spicy and mineral tones.

Gurt Stout (OG 1058, ABV 6.2%)
Silky smooth, full-bodied and rich stout.

Gurt Coconut Rum Stout (OG 1070, ABV 7.2%)
Robust, strong stout with a coconut sweetness and a rich, full body. Occasionally brewed at 6.2% ABV.

Chadlington

Chapel Road, Chadlington, Oxfordshire, OX7 3LZ
☎ 07931 482807 🌐 chadlingtonbrewery.com

Chadlington began brewing in 2015 on an occasional basis. Beers are supplied to the local area and a taproom is now open.

Golden Ale (OG 1040, ABV 4%)
A light, fruity and refreshing golden ale.

Oxford Blonde (OG 1041, ABV 4%)
A blonde beer with light, citrus notes and a crisp, dry finish.

Chain House

20 Brookdale, New Longton, Lancashire, PR4 4XL
☎ 07732 688121 🌐 chainhousebrewingco.uk

Brewing began in 2017. There is limited availability of the beers at present but there are plans for expansion.

Lit By Gas (OG 1038, ABV 3.8%)
Tropical fruit flavour and aroma.

Two Coffins (OG 1057, ABV 5.7%)
American-style IPA, with a fruity and citrus aroma.

Chalk Hill

Rosary Road, Norwich, NR1 4DA
☎ (01603) 477078 🌐 thecoachthorperoad.co.uk

Chalk Hill began production in 1993 on a 15-barrel plant. It supplies local pubs and festivals. A small plant is used to brew experimental beers. !! ♦

Tap Bitter (OG 1036, ABV 3.6%)
A biscuity backbone throughout, hints of hops and red fruits before a dry, watery astringency finish.

Black Anna (ABV 4%)
Well-balanced and complex with a sweet, roasty character. Echoes of caramel, coffee and chestnut in a long, smooth finale.

CHB (OG 1042, ABV 4.2%)
Yeasty aroma with malt and hop. Light biscuity airs flow over malt and floral hoppiness. Good balance, gentle finish.

Gold (OG 1043, ABV 4.3%)
A light, hoppy nose. Grapefruit, banana and hops mingle in a well-balanced beginning. The finish develops a growing bitterness.

Dreadnought (OG 1049, ABV 4.9%)
Red brown-coloured beer with a malty, sulphurous nose. Malty with fruit and nut notes. Full-bodied with a long finish.

Flintknapper's Mild (OG 1052, ABV 5%)
Malt and caramel on the nose. Watery mix of sweet fruitiness with a gentle nutty overhang. Short drying finish.

Chantry SIBA

Units 1 & 2, Callum Court, Gateway Industrial Estate, Parkgate, Rotherham, South Yorkshire, S62 6NR
☎ (01709) 711866 ☎ 07815 727285
🌐 chantrybrewery.co.uk

Brewing returned to Rotherham with the opening of Chantry in 2012 using the latest brewing technology in a 20-barrel plant built by Sheffield-based Moeschle UK. As well as the brewery tap, Cutlers Arms, two other pubs are owned; New York Tavern, Rotherham, and Chantry Inn, Handsworth. !!

New York Pale (OG 1039, ABV 3.9%)
Pale-coloured session bitter with a refreshing citrus taste and crisp bitter finish.

Iron & Steel Bitter (OG 1040, ABV 4%)
Chestnut-coloured with complex spicy flavours of dark fruits and a clean finish. An easy-drinking, Yorkshire-style session bitter.

Steelos (ABV 4.1%)
Fresh, easy-drinking ale with light, subtle citrus aromas of sweet orange, apricot and blackcurrant.

Full Moon (ABV 4.2%)
Delicately balanced flavours of lemon, blackberry, pine and grapefruit.

Diamond Black Stout (OG 1045, ABV 4.5%)
Full-bodied, dry stout, spicy with hints of liquorice and dark berries and a bitter finish.

Kaldo (ABV 5.5%)
A well-balanced pale ale with a subtle citrus taste and hints of orange and grapefruit.

Mighty Millers (ABV 5.5%)
Amber-coloured ale, light and refreshing with hints of citrus.

Special Reserve (ABV 6.3%)
Dark-coloured, rich, malty and full-bodied with undertones of liquorice and toffee.

Chapeau

Unit 8 Redkiln Close, Horsham, West Sussex, RH13 5QL
☎ (01403) 252459 🌐 chapeaubrewing.com

Chapeau Brewing is a microbrewery based in Horsham, West Sussex. Beers are available direct from the brewery and in local pubs.

Slip Stream (ABV 3.5%)
Amber-coloured, session bitter, with caramel malt flavours, and a zesty, bitter finish.

Rouleur (ABV 4%)

Summit (ABV 4%)
Golden pale ale with a passion fruit aroma.

Open Road (ABV 4.5%)
Milk stout with rich roasted coffee and chocolate aromas, lactose sweetness balanced by dark malts and hop finish.

Hard Yards (ABV 4.6%)
Best bitter with a strong malt profile and a hint of chocolate, and a fruit finish.

Chapel

Dinesfield, Chapel Lane, Criftins, Shropshire, SY12 9LZ
☎ (01691) 690412 ☎ 07928 682174
🌐 chapelbrewery.co.uk

Chapel began brewing in 2013 using a one-barrel plant behind the owner's bungalow. In 2016 the brewery expanded to larger premises. Occasional specials are brewed for festivals.

Angels Share (OG 1040, ABV 4%)
Session beer with a delicate, floral nose and a herbal, spicy flavour.

Miracle (OG 1044, ABV 4.4%)
Floral blonde ale with grapefruit, lychee and pine flavours.

Babylon (OG 1048, ABV 5%)
Traditional, dark-coloured, malty English ale.

Chapel Street

Thatched House, Ball Street, Poulton-le-Fylde, Lancashire, FY6 7BG
☎ (01253) 891063 thatchedhousepoulton.co.uk

This four-barrel plant is situated in the coach house of the award-winning Thatched House pub in Poulton-le-Fylde and has been brewing since 2014. The beers are only available in the pub.

Chapel-en-le-Frith

5, Market Place, Chapel-en-le-Frith, Derbyshire, SK23 0EW ☎ 07951 524003
timboothman@aol.com

Opened in 2016, this is a small operation located at the rear of Chapel-en-le-Frith Post Office. The brewing kit consists of a single 200-litre capacity integrated system supplemented by a 60-litre trial kit. Beers are available in bottles and five-litre minicasks from Chapel-en-le-Frith and Whaley Bridge Post Offices. Cask ales are available from a limited number of local outlets.

Siena (OG 1041, ABV 4.1%)
A crisp, light, Italian-inspired ale.

Busted Monkey (ABV 4.6%)

Isambard (ABV 4.6%)

Leningrad (OG 1052, ABV 5%)
A strong, ruby-coloured ale full of malt character.

Elysium Amber Ale (OG 1056, ABV 5.4%)
A full-bodied, rich, sweet and malty amber-coloured ale with a clean, crisp bitter finish.

Acadian (OG 1057, ABV 5.6%)
A New England-style IPA with a delicate malt character and a crescendo of tropical and citrus fruit hop flavours.

Hoppy as Funk (OG 1055, ABV 5.8%)
A light ale with a strong malt backbone, finished with a citrus flavour.

Sinamarian Black IPA (OG 1060, ABV 6%)
A smooth, dry black IPA with rich roast flavours and hints of chocolate, finished with a tropical fruit flavour.

Chapter

Unit 2a, Sutton Quays Business Park, Clifton Road, Sutton Weaver, Cheshire, WA7 3EH ☎ 07791 516948

Office: 38 Swanlow Lane, Winsford, CW7 1JE
chapterbrewing.co.uk

Chapter Brewing was established in 2016 using a 10-barrel plant. It produces diverse 'fictional beers' inspired by literature. ♦RAIB

02. Bread & Circuses (OG 1042, ABV 3.8%)

17. Taller than a House (OG 1042, ABV 3.9%)
Soft fruit aromas and a soft oat body allow the hops to shine, with a light bitterness at the finish.

18. Unconsenting Soul (OG 1048, ABV 4.2%)
Copious amounts of wheat and oats give a full-bodied, juicy session IPA with a fruity yeast profile and soft mouthfeel.

09. Temos Tanta (OG 1045, ABV 4.4%)
Pale ale with a marmalade bitterness and a juicy, citrus lift from freshly crushed coriander and zingy orange zest.

08. Parabola (OG 1047, ABV 4.7%)
Punchy American-style pale ale bursting with hoppy freshness.

11. That Old Rope (OG 1051, ABV 5.4%)
A chunky malt backbone supports the hop boost and bitterness.

03. Dead Man's Fist (OG 1056, ABV 5.5%)
Smoked porter with black pepper for a fiery hit after a gentle, sweet smokiness.

14. Her Musket (OG 1062, ABV 5.7%)
A deep, rich stout with lingering dark chocolate notes.

04. I Said Doctor (OG 1063, ABV 6%)
Milk stout with flakes of hand-toasted coconut throughout, with the bite and sharpness of lime zest lifting the finish.

01. As Lazarus (OG 1062, ABV 7.2%)
American-style IPA bursting with a double dry-hopped punch. Brewed using a different aroma hop each time.

Charnwood SIBA

22 Jubilee Drive, Loughborough, Leicestershire, LE11 5XS
☎ (01509) 218666 ☎ 07872 651561
charnwoodbrewery.co.uk

Family-run 10-barrel brewery established in 2014. Three core beers are complemented by three monthly specials with a wide range of styles. All beers are widely available locally, including at their newly opened micropub, the Sorrel Fox, in Mountsorrel. The front of the brewery has been fitted out with a shop, selling brewery merchandise, bottled beers, and local gins, and as well as a bar with three hand pumps and large glass windows giving a good view into the brewery. !! ♦

Salvation (OG 1038, ABV 3.8%)
A light refreshing golden beer, with tropical fruit, citrus, and floral flavours, a citrus aroma, and crisp, clean bitterness on the finish.

Vixen (OG 1040, ABV 4%)
A well-balanced, copper-coloured best bitter with subtle hints of honey, spice and hedgerow fruits. Fruity nose and finish.

APA (American Pale Ale) (OG 1048, ABV 4.8%)
A straw-coloured beer with wonderful tropical fruit aromas, and a spicy, fruity, hoppy finish.

Chasing Everest (NEW)

15 Ponteland Square, Blyth, NE24 4SH
chasingeverestbrew.com

Founded in 2018 by Zak Everest, focusing on small batch brews. Many of the beers are dry hopped, giving bold, hoppy flavours.

Cheadle (NEW)

George & Dragon, 1 High Street, Cheadle, SK8 1AX

Using the former Hogarth's kit from Bolton, the brewery was established in 2018. Brewer Jonathan Winchcombe is still in charge and Amber Inn pubs are supplied.

Checkstone

First & Last Inn, 10 Church Street, Exmouth, Devon, EX8 1PE
☎ (01395) 263275

Checkstone Brewery, named after the Checkstone reef outside the Exe Estuary, is a one-barrel plant inside the First & Last pub, Exmouth, established in 2016. Like the brewery, the beers are named after various sea features around Exmouth. ♦

Cheddar SIBA

Winchester Farm, Draycott Road, Cheddar, Somerset, BS27 3RP
☎ (01934) 744193 ⊕ cheddarales.co.uk

Established in 2006 in the heart of the Mendips, Cheddar Ales has expanded capacity to enable it to brew up to 100 barrels a week. Production is split approximately 75% cask-conditioned ale with the remaineder bottle conditioned. Its bottling plant produces around 120,000 bottles annually. Around 450 outlets are supplied including pubs, clubs and the off trade. A visitor centre and brewery tap opened in 2019. !! ♦ RAIB

Bitter Bully (OG 1038.5, ABV 3.8%)
Light session bitter with flowery hops on the nose and a dry, bitter finish.

Gorge Best (OG 1040, ABV 4%)
Malty bitter with caramel and fruit notes, followed by a short, bittersweet aftertaste.

Potholer (OG 1043.5, ABV 4.3%)
A well-balanced golden ale with fruit and sweetness throughout and some bitterness to finish.

Hardrock (OG 1044, ABV 4.4%)
Light gold-coloured, very hoppy pale ale with spicy, herbal notes and a floral, citrus finish.

Totty Pot (OG 1044.5, ABV 4.5%)
Roasted malts dominate this smooth, well-flavoured porter. Hints of coffee and rich fruits follow with a well-balanced bitterness.

Crown & Glory (OG 1045, ABV 4.6%)

Goat's Leap (OG 1054.5, ABV 5.5%)
Light malt aroma with enticing toffee and red liquorice hints. Traditional hop flavours and fruity sweetness, clean bitter finish.

Cheeky Imp

The Old Dairy Monson Farm, Jerusalum Road, Skellingthorpe, Lincolnshire, LN6 4RP ☎ 07884 022236 ⊕ cheekyimp.com

Brewing began in 2015 in Waddington using a 0.5-barrel plant. The brewery relocated and upgraded to a 2.5-barrel unit in Skellingthorpe in 2017. Emphasis is on quality and the brewer is developing collaborations with several landlords in the Lincoln area. RAIB

Chelmsford

2 Brewery Fields, Church Street, Great Baddow, Essex, CM2 7LE ☎ 07972 145611 ⊕ blueshackbeers.com

Chelmsford was established in 2017 by a former homebrewer who used to brew in a little blue shack at the end of his garden.

Cheshire Brew Brothers

See Oaks

Cheshire Brewhouse SIBA

Units 13, Daneside Business Park,, River Dane Road, Congleton, Cheshire, CW12 1UN
☎ (01260) 274788 ⊕ cheshirebrewhouse.co.uk

Cheshire Brewhouse was established in 2012 using a five-barrel plant, expanding in 2014 to a 10-barrel one. The brewery moved to a larger unit in 2018. !! ♦

Cheshire Gap (ABV 3.8%)
Light pale ale.

Cheshire Set (ABV 4%)
Pale and refreshing.

Engine Vein (ABV 4.2%)
A traditional, copper-coloured best bitter.

Lindow (ABV 4.5%)
A lighter take on stout – malty, easy-drinking, with a hint of espresso and dark chocolate, balanced with vine fruits.

DBA (ABV 4.6%)
Burton-style ale, strong, malty, with a peppery finish.

Dane'ish (ABV 5%)
A refreshing lager.

Chevin (NEW)

Office: 1 Mount Pisgah, Otley, West Yorkshire, LS21 3DX

Chevin is a co-operative brewery based in Otley and set up in 2018 by five homebrewers. Beers are primarily available in bottles.

Cheviot (NEW)

Ford & Etal Estate, Slainsfiield, Northumberland, TD12 4TP ☎ 07778 478943 ⊕ cheviotbrewery.co.uk

Brewing commenced in 2018 on a 7.5-barrel plant acquired from Goose Eye Brewery in West Yorkshire. The beers are named after local landmarks.

Upland Ale (ABV 3.8%)
Smooth, refreshing, copper-coloured best bitter. Rich malt tones, well-balanced with a floral citrus flavour.

Harbour Wall (ABV 4.3%)
An easy-drinking, light session pale ale with floral, tropical fruit and pine notes.

Trig Point (ABV 4.5%)

Aromatic, hoppy, citrus pale ale with a grapefruit finish.

Holy Bounty (ABV 4.8%)
Stout brewed with Lindisfarne oysters.

Menhir (ABV 5.1%)
Roast malt, dark chocolate, burnt caramel and a good hit of coffee in this bitter stout.

Flodden Thirst (ABV 5.4%)
A zesty, refreshing pale ale with citrus and tropical fruit notes.

The Schil (ABV 6%)
Smooth, traditional, copper-coloured bitter with floral aroma and plenty of roast malt flavours.

Chickenfoot (NEW)

Barley Mow Inn, The Dale, Bonsall, Derbyshire, DE4 2AY
☎ (01629) 825685 barleymowbonsall.co.uk

A purpose-built 2.5-barrel plant housed in the car park of the Barley Mow Inn in the picturesque rural village of Bonsall. The brewery supplies a range of hen-named ales for the pub which is famed as the Home of the World Hen Racing Championship. ♦

Chiltern SIBA

Nash Lee Road, Terrick, Aylesbury, Buckinghamshire, HP17 0TQ
☎ (01296) 613647 chilternbrewery.co.uk

Founded in 1980, Chiltern was one of the first microbreweries in the country. It is the oldest independent brewery in Buckinghamshire and the Chiltern Hills, growing from a capacity of five to its present 10-barrel plant. Now run by the second generation of the Jenkinson family, George and Tom, it supplies around 100 outlets including its own brewery tap, the Farmers' Bar, at the historic King's Head in Aylesbury. !! ♦ RAIB GF

Chiltern Pale Ale (OG 1037, ABV 3.7%)
An amber-coloured, refreshing beer with a slight fruit aroma, leading to a good malt/bitter balanced mouthfeel. Bitter, dry aftertaste.

Chiltern Black (OG 1040, ABV 3.9%)
Dark treacle tones, hints of roast barley and well-hopped. Rich, smooth flavours abound leading to a light finish.

Beechwood Bitter (OG 1043, ABV 4.3%)
This pale brown-coloured beer has a balanced butterscotch/toffee aroma, with a slight hop note. Balanced bitterness and sweetness, leading to a long, bitter finish.

Chin Chin

Unit 53F, Lidgate Crescent, Langthwaite Grange Industrial Estate, South Kirkby, West Yorkshire, WF9 3NS ☎ 07896 253650
david@chinchinbrewing.co.uk

Chin Chin was established in 2016 by brothers David and Andrew Currie. Brewing began on a one-barrel plant based in a domestic garage, relocating to larger premises in 2018. An expanding range of small batch brews is supplied across Yorkshire and to beer festivals nationwide. !!

Chorlton

69 North Western Street, Ardwick, Manchester, M12 6DX chorltonbrewingcompany.com

Founded in 2014 by Londoner Mike Marcus, Chorlton has grown a significant reputation for its sour and wild beers, some inspired by classic European styles. Mostly draught beer via KeyKeg but some bottle-conditioned beers are produced. RAIB

J Church

See Potbelly

Church Aston (NEW)

Church Aston, Shropshire, TF10 9EJ ☎ 07806 671436
beer@churchastonbrewery.co.uk

A small indepedent brewery established in 2013. In addition to the regular beers, bespoke brews are available on request.

Lower Bar Bitter (ABV 3.8%)

Upper Bar Bitter (ABV 4.5%)

Church End

Ridge Lane, Nuneaton, Warwickshire, CV10 0RD
☎ (01827) 713080 churchendbrewery.co.uk

The brewery started in 1994 in an old coffin shop in Shustoke. It moved to its present site in 2001 and has expanded over the years, it currently operates a 24-barrel purpose-built plant. Many one-off specials and old recipe beers are produced. Its award-winning beers are available throughout the Midlands. !! ♦ RAIB

Brewers Truth (OG 1036, ABV 3.6%)
Bright gold-coloured beer, hoppy and aromatic.

Cuthberts (OG 1038, ABV 3.8%)
A refreshing, hoppy beer, with hints of malt, fruit and caramel taste and a lingering, bitter aftertaste.

Goat's Milk (OG 1038, ABV 3.8%)

Gravediggers Ale (OG 1038, ABV 3.8%)

What the Fox's Hat (OG 1044, ABV 4.2%)
Malty aroma, hoppy, malty taste, and some caramel flavour.

Vicar's Ruin (OG 1044, ABV 4.4%)
A straw-coloured, best bitter with an initially hoppy, bitter flavour, softening to a delicate malt finish.

Stout Coffin (OG 1046, ABV 4.6%)

Fallen Angel (OG 1050, ABV 5%)

Church Farm SIBA

Church Farm, Budbrooke, Warwickshire, CV35 8QL
☎ (01926) 411084 ☎ 07939 607027
churchfarmbrewery.co.uk

Brewing began in 2012 using converted dairy equipment from the farm. In 2016 it moved to a purpose built brewery unit with a 20-barrel gas-fired plant. Beers are mostly brewed from local ingredients, some of the barley is grown on the farm and the water comes from its own well. Approximately 140 regular outlets spread across the South Midlands from Birmingham to Bristol.

Look out for the portable bar at food festivals and outdoor events in and around Warwickshire. RAIB

Pale Ale (OG 1041, ABV 3.8%)
Lightly-hopped, crisp, golden-coloured bitter with a tangy finish.

Session IPA (OG 1039, ABV 3.8%)
Refreshing, straw-coloured, light IPA. Hoppy in both aroma and flavour, with a pronounced citrus taste.

The Imp (OG 1041, ABV 3.8%)

Ren's Pride (OG 1044, ABV 4%)
An amber-coloured best bitter with a slightly sweet taste. The distinctive initial flavour comes from a complex array of malts.

Brown's Porter (OG 1042, ABV 4.2%)
A porter with a smooth, coffee taste and a long-lasting, creamy aftertaste.

Harry's Heifer (OG 1044, ABV 4.2%)
A light amber-coloured, quaffable best bitter with slight floral notes.

IPA (OG 1052, ABV 5%)
A light amber-coloured hoppy IPA. Easy-drinking, but full of flavour. Tangy citrus notes in the finish.

Church Hanbrewery SIBA

Unit F2, New Yatt Business Centre, New Yatt, Oxfordshire, OX29 6TJ
☎ (01993) 774986 ☎ 07907 272617

Office: Tithe Barn South, Church Hanborough, OX29 8AB 🌐 churchhanbrewery.com

⊗ Brewing commenced in 2016 on a small scale in the owner's kitchen. A year later, a 2.5-barrel plant was installed in a small industrial unit in New Yatt. Some beers are brewed for keg and bottling only. The brewery now runs a nano bar in Oxford's Indoor Market and supports local community festivals. RAIB

Ale X IPA (ABV 4.5%)
A powerful, complex IPA with citrus, pine, spice and herbal notes.

Rauk (ABV 5%)
Inspired by Rauchbier (smoked lager) from Bamberg.

Red Beetter (ABV 5%)
Brown-red in colour from a small amount of organic beetroot juice. Very malty and smooth, with low hop aroma and a balanced, hop bitterness.

Bluenette (ABV 5.5%)
A smooth porter with the addition of Scottish rolled oats, a delicate sweetness from organic honey and rich, roasted chocolate flavours.

Mat Black (ABV 5.5%)
A black-coloured IPA, with a strong lemon and herbal hop aroma, and the smoothness of a stout.

City of Cambridge

See Wolf

Clanconnel

Unit 5, 2 New Line, Gibson's Hill, Co Armagh, BT66 8TA ☎ 07711 626770

Office: PO Box 316, BT65 9AZ
🌐 clanconnelbrewing.com

Beers are contract brewed by the Rye River Brewery in Co Kildare in the Republic of Ireland under the McGraths Craft Beer brand. No real ale.

Clark's

See Castle Eden

Clarkshaws SIBA

Arch 497, Ridgway Road, Loughborough Junction, London, SW9 7EX ☎ 07989 402687
🌐 clarkshaws.co.uk

Clarkshaws, established 2013, is a small brewery focusing on using UK ingredients and reducing beer miles. The beers are suitable for vegetarians and are accredited by the Vegetarian Society. All beers are unfined and may be hazy. Some beers are brewed on a Clarkshaws-owned brewing kit inside the Bexley Brewery site. A taproom operates on the premises for most of the year.

Gorgon's Alive (OG 1040, ABV 4%)
Unfined, golden-coloured beer with spicy hops throughout. The flavour has hints of orange and peach with a dry bitterness.

Phoenix Rising (OG 1040, ABV 4%)
Tawny-coloured beer with a creamy toffee nose. Bananas, pineapple, hops and caramel flavours. Dryish, short, fruity, biscuit finish.

Strange Brew No. 1 (OG 1040, ABV 4%)
Easy-drinking, yellow-coloured pale ale. Peppery hops, tropical fruits and biscuit sweetness with a trace of bitterness.

Coldharbour Hell Yeah Lager (ABV 5.3%)
Hops and mango notes with some butterscotch. Dry palate.

Hellhound IPA (OG 1056, ABV 5.5%)
Spiced and citrus notes in this unfined, amber-coloured beer with a bitterness in the flavour and a dry finish.

Clavell & Hind

The Old Haulage Yard, Old Cirencester Road, Birdlip, Gloucestershire, GL4 8JL
☎ (01452) 238050 🌐 clavellandhind.co.uk

Clavell & Hind is a 20-barrel brewery based in the Cotswold countryside. A tap room is open Friday afternoon and Saturday daytime.

Coachman (ABV 3.8%)
Golden-coloured ale, well-balanced, citrus and marmalade hops, and fresh ginger.

Blunderbuss (ABV 4.2%)
An explosion of citrus and tropical hops.

Rook Wood (ABV 4.4%)
Traditional best bitter with a smooth blend of aromatic malts and dark hops.

Clay Brow (NEW)

256 Carfield, Skelmersdale, WN8 9DW ☎ 07769 581500

Nanobrewery that started production in 2017.

Eclipse (ABV 5.4%)

THE BREWERIES

Mr P's (ABV 5.7%)

Mrs P's (ABV 6%)

Clearsky

See Hilden

Clearwater SIBA

Unit 1, Little Court, Manteo Way, Gammaton Road, Bideford, Devon, EX39 4FG
☎ (01237) 420492 🌐 clearwaterbrewery.co.uk

⊗ Established in 1999, Clearwater is a 10-barrel brewery regularly supplying more than 250 outlets across the South-west and nationally with its Devon's Own labelled beers. Beers are also available at the brewery tap, the Champ, Appledore. ‼♦RAIB

Expedition Ale (OG 1037.3, ABV 3.5%)
Well-balanced, traditional, brown-coloured ale, hints of blackcurrant, hoppy, with a bitter finish.

Real Smiler (OG 1037, ABV 3.7%)
Golden-coloured, crisp, hoppy and refreshing.

Broad Reach (OG 1039, ABV 4%) ◆
Fruity aroma leads to crisp and fruity yet bitter taste. The aftertaste continues a balanced sweet fruit bitterness, which is slightly dry.

Mariners (OG 1042.9, ABV 4.2%)
Pale golden in colour. Clean, crisp and hoppy with a fresh grapefruit zestiness and lingering hint of bitterness.

Proper Ansome (OG 1041, ABV 4.2%)
Full-flavoured, dark ale, full of malty notes.

Riff (ABV 4.2%)
A hoppy session IPA.

Voyager (OG 1043, ABV 4.5%)
Copper-coloured ale, with aroma of grapes, nutty taste, and tongue-tingling light bitterness.

Cliff Quay

Unit 1 Meadow Works Kenton Road, Kenton Road, Debenham, Suffolk, IP14 6RT
☎ (01728) 861213 🌐 cliffquay.co.uk

⊗ Cliff Quay was established in 2008 by Jeremy Moss (former Wychwood brewer) and John Bjornson (owner of Earl Soham Brewery) in part of the historic Tolly Cobbold brewery in Ipswich. In 2012 the brewery relocated to Debenham, a small, picturesque market town, due to redevelopment of this brewery site. Re-established alongside Earl Soham brewery, with shared shop, offices and distribution. ‼🛒♦

Bitter (OG 1034, ABV 3.4%) ◆
Pleasantly drinkable, well-balanced, malty, sweet bitter with a hint of caramel, followed by a sweet/malty aftertaste.

Anchor Bitter (OG 1040, ABV 4%)

Black Jack Porter (OG 1042, ABV 4.2%) ◆
Unusual dark porter with a strong aniseed aroma and rich liquorice and aniseed flavours, reminiscent of old-fashioned sweets. Long, increasingly sweet aftertaste.

Tolly Roger (OG 1042, ABV 4.2%) ◆
Well-balanced, highly-drinkable, mid gold-coloured beer with a bittersweet hoppiness, some biscuity flavours and hints of summer fruit.

Tumble Home (OG 1047, ABV 4.7%) ◆
Aroma of marzipan and dried fruit. Flavour reminiscent of Amaretto, leading to a short, bitter, slightly spicy aftertaste.

Sea Dog (OG 1053, ABV 5.5%)
Strong, hoppy, bursting with the flavours of lemon and grapefruit, and a full maltiness.

Dreadnought (OG 1065, ABV 6.5%)

Clockwork

1153-1155 Cathcart Road, Glasgow, G42 9HB
☎ (0141) 649 0184 🌐 clockworkbeercompany.co.uk

Established in 1997. The beers are stored in cellar tanks where fermentation gases from the conditioning vessel blanket the beers (but not under pressure). A wide range of ales, lagers and specials is produced. Most beers are naturally gassed while the Craft Lager is pressurised. The establishment parted ways with its previous managing company, Maclays, and in 2014 the pub underwent a full refurbishment. ‼♦

Clouded Minds

Unit 5B Brailes Industrial Estate, Winderton Road, Lower Brailes, Warwickshire, OX15 5JW ☎ 07530 998149 🌐 cloudedminds.co.uk

Brewing began in 2013 using spare capacity at various breweries around London and Derbyshire. In 2015 the brewery moved to its own site near Banbury using a 10-barrel plant. The London area is mainly supplied but also some outlets in Birmingham, Nottinghamshire, Warwickshire and Oxfordshire. Wholesalers also distribute the beers more widely. RAIB

N29 (OG 1036, ABV 3.7%)
Light to medium-bodied, citrus pale ale, with a small amount of rye.

N253 (OG 1037, ABV 3.9%)
Light to medium-bodied oatmeal American-style pale ale. Fruity and resiny.

99 steps (ABV 4%)

N18 (OG 1038, ABV 4%)
Light to medium-bodied pale ale. Mild citrus, pine and resin.

Luppol (OG 1040, ABV 4.2%)
Light to medium-bodied, refreshing, with a bitter finish.

Clout Stout (OG 1048, ABV 4.5%)
Velvet mouthfeel with an aroma of roasted malts, cocoa, dried fruits and figs. Mildly sweet and sour with a smoky and bitter finish.

Hazelnutter (OG 1048, ABV 5%)
Well-balanced, smooth, American-style, brown-coloured ale brewed with organic Italian hazelnuts.

Elisir (OG 1052, ABV 5.3%)
Caramel and biscuit taste from the malts balanced by a lots of hops. Very fruity.

Black Pike (OG 1057, ABV 6.1%)
Medium-bodied, highly-hopped, black-coloured IPA.

Dolce Vita (OG 1058, ABV 6.2%)

Medium bodied, West Coast-style IPA, fruity and mildly spicy, with a dry finish.

Double Clout Stout (OG 1064, ABV 6.6%)
Rich and smooth coffee stout.

Cloudwater

Units 7-8, Piccadilly Trading Estate, Manchester, M1 2NP
☎ (0161) 661 5943 🌐 cloudwaterbrew.co

Cloudwater specialises in making modern, seasonal beers and also produce collaborative brews. One-off specials for beer festivals, experimental, canned and bottled beers are also available. Its beers now travel far and wide, from the UK to the US. The modern brewery tap is adjacent. !! ♦

Clueless

See RedWillow

Clun SIBA

White Horse Inn, The Square, Clun, Shropshire, SY7 8JA
☎ (01588) 640021 🌐 whi-clun.co.uk

Formerly a tiny brewery, capacity was increased to 2.5-barrels in 2010. Established behind the White Horse in Clun, beers (including specials such as Green Man in Spring and Green Hop in Autumn) are produced for the pub and, increasingly, the local trade. ♦

Loophole (OG 1035, ABV 3.5%)
Dry, hoppy, light-coloured beer with a crisp, hoppy flavour.

Clun Pale (OG 1040, ABV 4.1%)
Pale-coloured, clean-tasting bitter.

Solar (OG 1043, ABV 4.3%)
A fruity, smooth speciality ale with a hint of elderflower.

Citadel (OG 1065, ABV 5.9%)
Strong, hop-foward ale, with a hefty bitterness. Golden-coloured with rich and fruity malt flavours, an intense hop bitterness and aroma, and a long-lasting, dry finish.

Coach (NEW)

37 Cowbridge Road, Bridgend, CF31 3DH

Office: 2 Oldfield Road, Bocam Park, Bridgend, CF35 5LJ

Coach began brewing in 2018 in the award-winning freehouse of the same name. The equipment is clearly visible from the bar. Collaboration beers are brewed, including with Tiny Rebel and Grey Trees (qv).

Coach House SIBA

Wharf Street, Howley, Warrington, Cheshire, WA1 2DQ
☎ (01925) 232800 🌐 coachhousebrewery.co.uk

Established in 1991 by three former employees of Greenall Whitley Brewery, Coach House was bought by Martin Bailey in 2015. The 40-barrel plant produces up to 240-barrels per week. ♦

Coachman's Best Bitter (OG 1037, ABV 3.7%)
A well-hopped, malty bitter, moderately fruity with a hint of sweetness and a peppery nose.

Gunpowder Mild (OG 1037, ABV 3.8%)
Biscuity dark mild with a blackcurrant sweetness. Bitterness and fruit dominate with some hints of caramel and a slightly stronger roast flavour.

Honeypot Bitter (OG 1037, ABV 3.8%)
A medium-bodied, lightly-hopped, golden-coloured bitter. Silkiness from the addition of honey.

Farrier's Best Bitter (OG 1038, ABV 3.9%)
A smooth, tawny-coloured beer, slightly sweet but with rich hop flavours developing on the palate.

Cromwells Best Bitter (OG 1040, ABV 4%)
Amber-coloured, well-balanced beer with a smooth, clean-hopped finish.

Blonde (OG 1041, ABV 4.1%)
A thirst-quenching blonde ale with hints of citrus and grapefruit.

Cheshire Gold (OG 1042, ABV 4.1%)
A pale golden-coloured beer with a pine, lemon crispness.

Dick Turpin (OG 1042, ABV 4.2%)
Malty, hoppy, pale brown-coloured beer with some initial sweetish flavours leading to a short, bitter aftertaste. Sold under other names as a pub house beer.

ClIPAty Hop (OG 1043, ABV 4.3%)
IPA, light in colour with a hoppy aroma and flavour but a well-balanced, malty finish.

Flintlock Pale Ale (OG 1044, ABV 4.4%)
A pale golden-coloured beer, light on the palate with a touch of sweetness in the finish.

Innkeeper's Special Reserve (OG 1045, ABV 4.5%)
A dark-coloured, full-flavoured bitter. Quite fruity with a strong, bitter aftertaste.

Postlethwaite (OG 1045, ABV 4.6%)
A distinctive dry and fruity pale ale. Traditionally dry hopped to give a fine hop aroma.

Blueberry Classic Bitter (OG 1050, ABV 5%)
A straw-coloured beer with a light, hoppy aroma and a distinct blueberry aftertaste.

Posthorn Premium (OG 1050, ABV 5%)
A rich, straw-coloured, smooth premium ale. The beer has a robust, malty palate and well-balanced bitterness with a complexity of flavours.

Blunderbus (OG 1053, ABV 5.3%)
A dark-coloured ale with a full, malty flavour.

Brewed for 16 Hospitality:

16v9 (OG 1041, ABV 4.1%)
Flavour and aroma of tropical fruit. Well-balanced bitter aftertaste.

Cobbydale

Red Lion, 47 Kirkgate, Silsden, West Yorkshire, BD20 0AQ
☎ (01535) 930884 ☎ 07965 569885
🌐 cobbydalebrewery.co.uk

Brewing began in 2017 at the Red Lion, Silsden. Originally only brewing one beer, others are now brewed on an occasional basis.

Cocksure SIBA

Unit B, Totterdown Bridge Industrial Estate, Albert Road, St Philips, Bristol, BS2 0XH ☎ 07787 453222 🌐 cocksurebrewing.com

Established in 2017, this 10-barrel brewery moved from the Severn Vale to Bristol in 2018. Occasional specials and collaboration brews with other breweries complement the core range. An on-site taproom is open on Friday and Saturday. !! RAIB

Amber Session (OG 1038, ABV 3.9%) ◆
Slight citrus aroma, background sweet biscuit flavours overlaid with pine and citrus hoppiness, which fade during the short finish.

Pale (OG 1042, ABV 4.2%)
A fruity pale ale with complex flavours.

African Hibiscus & Honey Golden Ale (ABV 4.8%)
An easy-drinking, pale golden-coloured beer with subtle floral flavours. African honey imparts some sweetness.

Session IPA (OG 1046, ABV 4.8%) ◆
Piny hops on the nose combining on the palate with light malt and tropical fruit hints, lingering dry bitter ending.

African Mango & Orange Pale Ale (ABV 5%)
A cloudy, unfined beer brewed with African mangoes and oranges . Fruit flavours are strong without being unbalanced, with a subtle bitterness.

Nitro Cold Brew Stout (OG 1046, ABV 5%)
A smooth, rich and chocolaty stout, with cold-infused coffee added.

African Blackberrry, Raspberry & Gooseberry Stout (ABV 5.4%)
A tasty, full-bodied stout with subtle fruity flavours complemented by bitterness from the roasted malts.

IPA (OG 1056, ABV 6.5%)
A strong IPA-style bitter.

Colchester SIBA

Viaduct Brewhouse, Unit 16, Wakes Hall Business Centre, Wakes Colne, Essex, CO6 2DY ☎ (01787) 829422 🌐 colchesterbrewery.com

⊠ Set up in 2012 by three friends, Tom Knox, Roger Clark and Andy Bone, using the double drop process. Popular during the early 20th century this process requires additional brewing vessels in a two-tier system resulting in clean beer with pronounced flavours. !! ◆ RAIB

AKA Pale (OG 1039, ABV 3.7%)
1900s pale ale, mildly-hopped, fresh and fruity.

Metropolis (OG 1040.5, ABV 3.9%)
A golden-coloured hoppy beer, with enormous depth of flavour and a long spicy finish.

Jack Spitty's Smuggler's Ale (OG 1041.5, ABV 4%)
Golden-coloured, easy-drinking summer ale. Full of hop flavor with delicate bitterness and light aroma.

Colchester No 1 (OG 1042.5, ABV 4.1%)
A classic best bitter, copper in colour.

Red Diesel (OG 1043.5, ABV 4.2%)
Red-coloured, well-balanced best bitter, with a long, rich finish.

Brazilian Coffee & Vanilla Porter (OG 1048, ABV 4.6%)
Full-flavoured porter.

Cat's Whiskers (OG 1050, ABV 4.8%)
Smooth-drinking, full-bodied cream stout with a slight sweetness.

Old King Coel London Porter (OG 1052, ABV 5%)
Rich, classic, dark porter.

Cold Bath (NEW)

46 Kings Road, Harrogate, North Yorkshire, HG1 5JW ☎ 0330 880 7009

Cold Bath Brewing Co was established in 2018. The brew plant can be viewed on the mezzanine level of the pub. No real ale. **V**

Cold Black Label SIBA

Guardian House, 5 Squire Drive, Brynmenyn Industrial Estate, Bridgend, CF32 9TX ☎ (01656) 728081 🌐 coldblacklabel.co.uk

Beginning as a wholesale drinks company, Cold Black Label expanded its portfolio to include a range of cask-conditioned beers that were contract brewed at other breweries. In 2018 a six-barrel brewery came on stream, so all beers are now brewed in-house. The range of beers from the now closed Brecon Brewery are brewed here. In 2019, the Brecon Brewing element took over the recipes of the former Lithic brewery, and its beers are now also brewed here.

Glyder Fawr (ABV 4.2%)

Singing Sword (ABV 4.2%)
A lime-infused, dry-hopped pale ale.

Harlech Castle (ABV 4.4%)

Uncle Phil's Ale (ABV 4.4%)
Coffee-infused, amber-coloured ale.

Bwlch Passage (ABV 4.5%)
Tea-infused, fruity, amber-coloured ale.

Miners Ale (ABV 4.5%)

Chirk Castle (ABV 4.6%)

Sand Storm (ABV 4.6%)

Guardian (ABV 4.7%)

Crib Goch (ABV 5%)

Nutty Ale (ABV 5%)

Pirate Bay (ABV 5%)

Red Beast (ABV 6%)

Miners Imperial Ale (ABV 7.5%)

Brewed under the Brecon Brewing name:

Three Beacons (ABV 3%)
Full-bodied, hoppy, American-style, golden-coloured pale ale.

Welsh Beacons (ABV 3.7%)
Welsh-style pale ale, golden-coloured with a gentle, floral bitterness.

Dark Beacons (ABV 3.8%)
A full-flavoured, yet light and refreshing, dark-coloured beer.

Copper Beacons (ABV 4.1%)
A copper-coloured best bitter, smooth and well-balanced with fruit and hop flavours.

Gold Beacons (ABV 4.2%)
A golden ale with a soft, well-defined bitterness, balanced by a blend of malts.

Orange Beacons (ABV 4.3%)

Red Beacons (ABV 5%)
A well-hopped premium red-coloured ale, complex and smooth.

Mind Bleach (ABV 10%)

Cold Town

8-10 Dunedin Street, Edinburgh, EH7 4JB

A Signature Pubs venture that began brewing lager in 2018. A brewpub has been opened at Cold Town House, Grassmarket, Edinburgh. No real ale.

Coles Family

White Hart Thatched Inn and Brewery, Llanddarog, SA32 8NT
☎ (01267) 275395 thebestpubinwales.co.uk

The brewery is based at the ancient White Hart Inn, built in 1371 and which historically had an on-site brewery. Brewing started again in 1999 on a nine-gallon plant. A one-barrel plant was fitted in 2000. In 2012 the brewery was opened to the public. Cider is also produced. ♦

Collyfobble SIBA

Peacock, Hackney Lane, Barlow, Derbyshire, S18 7TD
☎ (0114) 289 0340 collyfobblebrewery.com

Collyfobble began brewing in 2018.

Colomendy

See Dovecote

Colonsay

The Brewery, Scalasaig, Isle of Colonsay, PA61 7YT
☎ (01951) 200190 colonsaybrewery.co.uk

Colonsay began brewing in 2007 on a five-barrel plant. Beer is mainly bottled or brewery-conditioned for the local trade. RAIB

Concertina SIBA

9a Dolcliffe Road, Mexborough, South Yorkshire, S64 9AZ
☎ (01709) 580841 concertina@btconnect.com

Concertina started in 1992 in the cellar of a club once famous as the home of a long-gone concertina band. The plant produces up to eight barrels a week for the club and other occasional direct outlets and the wider trade, via beer wholesalers. ‼♦

Concrete Cow

59 Alston Drive, Bradwell Abbey, Milton Keynes, Buckinghamshire, MK13 9HB
☎ (01908) 316794 ☎ 07889 665745
concretecowbrewery.co.uk

Concrete Cow opened in 2007 on a 5.5-barrel plant. The beers are named after aspects of local history. The brewery supplies pubs, farmers' markets, local shops and restaurants. English single malt whisky is also available, produced from the brewery's own malt at a local distillery. ‼ ♦ RAIB

Pail Ale (OG 1036, ABV 3.7%)
A light-coloured, easy-drinking ale.

Fenny Popper (OG 1039, ABV 4%)
A golden-coloured, single-hopped, zesty, citrusy ale with a sherbet aroma, and bitter finish.

Cock 'n' Bull Story (OG 1041, ABV 4.1%)
A dark amber-coloured, malty beer.

Cloven Hoof (OG 1045, ABV 4.5%)
A dark vanilla stout flavoured with natural vanilla pods.

Old Bloomer (OG 1045, ABV 4.7%)
A dark ruby-coloured, strong bitter with a spicy, earthy flavour.

Coniston

Coppermines Road, Coniston, Cumbria, LA21 8HL
☎ (01539) 441133 conistonbrewery.com

A 10-barrel plant started in 1995 behind the Black Bull Inn in Coniston, it now brews 40 barrels a week and supplies numerous outlets locally and nationally. Some bottle-conditioned Coniston beers are brewed using Ridgeway Brewery (qv). ‼ RAIB

Oliver's Light Ale (OG 1035, ABV 3.4%)
A fruity, hoppy, straw-coloured bitter with plenty of flavour for its strength.

Bluebird Bitter (OG 1036, ABV 3.6%)
A yellow gold-coloured, predominantly hoppy and fruity beer. Well-balanced with some sweetness and a rising bitter finish.

Asrai (OG 1039, ABV 4%)
Crisp on the palate, a gently hopped beer with a full-bodied finish.

Bluebird Premium XB (OG 1040.5, ABV 4.2%)
Well-balanced, hoppy and fruity golden bitter. Bittersweet in the mouth with dryness building.

Old Man Ale (OG 1040.5, ABV 4.2%)
Delicious fruity, wine-like beer with a complex, well-balanced richness.

Special Oatmeal Stout (OG 1045, ABV 4.5%)
A well-balanced, easy-drinking stout, fruity with a balanced ratio of malt to hop bitterness.

Coniston K7 (OG 1045, ABV 4.7%)
Balanced, fruity, hoppy bitter, plenty of body and a long, hoppy, bitter finish.

Thurstein Pilsner (OG 1044.5, ABV 4.8%)
True to style. Mild but unusually sweet, with a hoppy fruitiness.

Blacksmiths Ale (OG 1047.5, ABV 5%)
A tawny-coloured ale which holds both roastiness and fruitiness in a pleasing balance.

Infinity I P A (OG 1055, ABV 6%)
High impact strong bitter. Fruity aromas persist in the powerful but well-balanced hoppiness and sweetness with nothing lost in the finish.

No 9 Barley Wine (OG 1087.5, ABV 8.5%)
Hops and alcohol dominate with appropriate sweetness and fruit on the tongue. A full-bodied and well-balanced beer.

Connoisseur

(Rear of) Wolverhampton House,, 121-125 Church Street, St Helens, Merseyside, WA10 1AJ ☎ 07921 838831 connoisseurales.com

Launched in 2014 by a family team of award-winning licencees, the brewery was run by Mark Yates until his death in 2017. The torch has now been passed to son Kevin who has reinvigorated the range with a selection of new recipes to complement existing brews. Tasting days with free brewery tours are held monthly.

Bloody Mild (ABV 3.7%)
Well-balanced dark mild with aromatic hops.

The Usual (ABV 3.8%)
A traditional ale with characteristic bitterness.

Ruby Ruby Ruby Ruby (ABV 4.1%)
Well-balanced, ruby-coloured, malty ale.

Phi (ABV 4.2%)
Big bitterness atop a crisp, smooth blend of malts.

Lucem Light Ale (ABV 4.3%)
Packs a hop punch, distinctive nose and floral citrus taste.

Sparkling WIT (ABV 4.6%)
Complex malt flavours and a hint of chocolate. Hoppy aroma and flavour.

Bete Noir Dry Stout (ABV 5%)
Full-flavoured, dry stout with coffee, chocolate and a hint of smoke. Creamy oatmeal-like body, delicate molasses and spice nose.

Ex Terra Lupus IPA (ABV 5.6%)
A strong beer with a pronounced and well-balanced hop profile atop a clean, crisp pale ale.

Consall Forge

3 Railway Cottages, Consall Forge, Staffordshire, ST9 0AJ

A one-barrel brewery set in the heart of the Staffordshire Moorlands adjacent to the Churnet Valley Railway. The Black Lion at Consall Forge is a regular outlet.

Dark Ruby Mild (OG 1050, ABV 5.2%)

Equilibrium (OG 1054, ABV 6%)
Traditional stout with flavours of coffee and molasses.

Consett Ale Works SIBA

Grey Horse Inn, 115 Sherburn Terrace, Consett, County Durham, DH8 6NE
☎ (01207) 591540 thegreyhorse.co.uk

The brewery opened in 2006 in the stables of a former coaching inn at the rear of the Grey Horse, Consett's oldest pub. The name and branding commemorates the former steel work which closed in 1980. The brewery expanded in 2006 and 2017 to supply regionally and nationally. !! ♦

Steel Town Bitter (OG 1039, ABV 3.8%)
Moreish traditional copper-coloured bitter with a pronounced maltiness.

Steelworkers Blonde (ABV 4%)
Golden-coloured bitter with a grassy citrus aroma. Medium sweet with a dry and light bitter finish.

White Hot (OG 1040, ABV 4%)
Pale-coloured, highly-hopped session bitter with cereal characteristics.

Cast Iron (OG 1040, ABV 4.1%)
Golden-coloured bitter with good hoppiness balanced by a light malt base.

Consett Stout (OG 1045, ABV 4.3%)
Smooth, slightly sweet stout with coffee flavours and a hint of smokiness.

Men of Steel (OG 1045, ABV 4.3%)
A full-flavoured, golden-coloured, hoppy ale.

Red Dust (OG 1045, ABV 4.5%)
Rich, robust, ruby-coloured ale with a malty and fruity flavour.

Consortium

Consortium 13c Cornmarket, 13c Cornmarket, Louth, Lincolnshire, LN11 9PY ☎ 07717201724
theconsortiumlouth.co.uk !! ♦

Lincolnshire Traditional Bitter (OG 1038, ABV 3.8%)
A traditional session bitter, with a smooth finish.

Wheres My Fiorucci (OG 1038, ABV 3.8%)
Amber-coloured, session beer with delicate malt flavours and a slightly spicy aroma.

Aisey Dubitz (OG 1042, ABV 3.9%)
Very light blonde ale.

Farming County (OG 1040, ABV 4%)

Saturdays blonde (OG 1042, ABV 4%)
Delicate pale ale, bittered with citrus hops, leaving a subtle, yet refreshing aftertaste.

Wet Pocket (OG 1041, ABV 4.1%)
Amber-coloured rye beer.

Best Bitter (OG 1046, ABV 4.2%)

Pleasant Blonde (OG 1042, ABV 4.2%)
Refreshing, blonde ale with a clean citrus hop flavour and flowery grapefruit aroma.

Executioners Assistant (OG 1044, ABV 4.3%)

Obliging Blonde (OG 1044, ABV 4.3%)
Blonde, hoppy ale.

Black Frog (OG 1044, ABV 4.4%)
Very dark ale with complex malt flavours, nicely bittered with a slight smoky aroma.

Queens (OG 1040, ABV 4.4%)
Full-bodied, golden-coloured ale.

Willy Wickams Posthumous Ale (OG 1044, ABV 4.4%)

Englands Finest hour (OG 1046, ABV 4.5%)
A golden ale.

Fat Cat Fuller (OG 1052, ABV 5%)

Nicholas De Luda (OG 1050, ABV 5.4%)
A rich, dark, old style English stout, full bodied and packed with flavour.

Seek medical Help (OG 1057, ABV 5.5%)
Zesty IPA full of hops.

Thanks Pa (OG 1057, ABV 6%)
Traditional strength Indian pale ale with a floral bouquet and citrus finish.

Conwy SIBA

Unit 2, Ty Mawr Enterprise Park, Tan y Graig Road, Llysfaen, LL29 8UE
☎ (01492) 514305 conwybrewery.co.uk

Conwy started brewing in 2003, and was the first brewery in Conwy for at least 100 years. In 2013 it increased capacity and moved to bigger premises in Llysfaen with its own brewery tap. Around 100 outlets are supplied. Monthly seasonals are available as well as the West Coast range showcasing American-style beers. ‼ 🛒 ♦ RAIB

Clogwyn Gold (OG 1037, ABV 3.6%) ◆
A full-flavoured, golden ale, with strong citrus fruit flavours throughout. Hoppy bitterness dominates the full mouthfeel and lasting finish.

Welsh Pride (OG 1040, ABV 4%)
A clean-tasting, malty bitter. Fruit in aroma and taste with a crisp, grainy mouthfeel and a lingering hoppy, bitter aftertaste.

Beachcomber Blonde (OG 1042, ABV 4.2%) ◆
A pale-coloured beer with a citrus taste, initially sweetish with delicate hoppiness in the lingering, bitter finish.

Honey Fayre (OG 1044, ABV 4.5%)
Golden-coloured best bitter with a hint of honey sweetness balanced by an increasingly hoppy, bitter finish. Slightly watery mouthfeel for its strength.

Rampart (OG 1045, ABV 4.5%) ◆
A dark-coloured, fruity beer with a sweetish initial taste. Fruit flavours accompanied by the underlying hoppiness continue into the bittersweet aftertaste.

San Francisco (OG 1054, ABV 5.5%)
American-style IPA with a big hop hit and a strong, robust bitter finish.

Telford Porter (OG 1053, ABV 5.6%)

Cooper Hill (NEW)

Highcliffe Industrial Estate, Bruntcliffe Lane, Morley, Leeds, LS27 9LR
☎ (0800) 783 2989 ☎ (0113) 307 4585

Commenced brewing in 2018 on equipment from the former Trinity Brewery now relocated to Morley.

Copper Dragon

Lee Mills, St Pauls Road, Keighley, West Yorkshire, BD21 4QW
☎ (01756) 243243 🌐 copperdragon.co.uk

Copper Dragon are now brewing back in Yorkshire on a 15-barrel plant with the original team of brewers, Gordon Wilkinson, Matt Taylor and Dave Sanders. As well as the core range of Copper Dragon beers, Recoil Craft beers are also brewed.

Penny Pale (OG 1037.5, ABV 3.5%)

Best Bitter (OG 1036, ABV 3.8%) ◆
A traditional Yorkshire bitter with a malty aroma, a hoppy bitter taste with hints of fruit and a bitter finish.

Golden Pippin (OG 1037, ABV 3.9%) ◆
This golden ale has a citrus aroma and flavour. The dry, bitter astringency increases in the aftertaste.

Black Gold (ABV 4%)
Rich, dark-coloured and malty ale.

Silver Myst (OG 1040, ABV 4%)
Pilsner-style ale, crisp, smooth and refreshing.

Scotts 1816 (OG 1041, ABV 4.1%) ◆
Fruity, malty best bitter with a bitter finish. Hints of nuts, tropical fruits and vanilla in the aroma and taste.

Sidewinder (ABV 4.2%)
An American-style pale ale that is light in colour. Bold and aromatic finish.

Brewed under the Recoil Craft brand name:

Boom Slang (OG 1042, ABV 3.7%)

Back to Best (OG 1038, ABV 3.8%)

Blonde Avenger (OG 1040, ABV 3.9%)

Collision (OG 1040, ABV 4%)

Copper Street (NEW)

8 Copper Street, Brewery Square, Dorchester, DT1 1GH ☎ 07970 766622
✉ copperstreetbrewery@outlook.com

Anthony and Ann Buckton established Copper Street Brewery in 2018 using a 2.5-barrel plant. They were the previous owners of King Alfred Ales (now closed). The brewery is fully visible as part of a bottled ale shop in the new Brewery Square development, previously the Eldridge Pope brewery. It is the only brewery in Dorchester. 🛒 ♦

871 (ABV 4.3%)

Shield Wall (ABV 4.3%)
A full-flavoured, ruby-coloured bitter.

Saxon Gold (ABV 4.7%)
A refreshing, well-hopped, golden-coloured ale.

Corinium

Unit 1a, The Old Kennels, Cirencester Park, Cirencester, Gloucestershire, GL7 1UR ☎ 07716 826467 🌐 coriniumales.co.uk

Established in 2012, Corinium Ales brew classic and contemporary award-winning ales on a 2.5-barrel plant located in the small historic Old Kennels in Cirencester Park, just outside the town centre. The brewery tap is open on a Friday afternoon and occasional Saturdays. Beers are available at a growing number of local outlets and events. ‼ 🛒 ♦ RAIB

Firebird VI (OG 1042, ABV 4%)
Traditional deep, malty, red-coloured beer.

Corinium Gold I (OG 1043, ABV 4.2%)
An easy-drinking, fruity ale with a mellow blend of malt and hops and a soft bitter finish.

Plautus V (OG 1042, ABV 4.5%)
Fruity pale ale bursting with hops.

Bodicacia IV (OG 1045, ABV 4.7%)
A full-bodied pale ale with a long-lasting citrus finish.

Centurion II (OG 1051, ABV 4.7%)
A rich, malty stout with toasty chocolate undertones. Lightly-hopped leaving a well-rounded aftertaste.

Ale Caesar III (OG 1050, ABV 5%)
A well-hopped IPA with a tropical fruit aroma balanced with a pleasing bitterness.

Corless

c/o Station Road, Scorton, Lancashire, PR3 1AN
☎ 07983 563917

Brewing began in 2018 using spare capacity at other brewers.

Cornish Crown SIBA

End Unit, Badger's Cross Farm, Badger's Cross, Penzance, Cornwall, TR20 8XE
☎ (01736) 449029 ☎ 07870 998986
cornishcrown.co.uk

Cornish Crown began brewing in 2012 on a six-barrel plant and is based on a farm high above Mounts Bay. It was established by the brewer and landlord of the Crown Inn in Penzance, which acts as the brewery tap. Beer is available in local outlets and can be found as far away as the Southampton Arms in London. RAIB

Golden (OG 1038, ABV 4%)

Causeway (OG 1041, ABV 4.1%)
Amber-coloured, well-balanced best bitter. Fruity/molasses malts matched by citrus/resin hops, sultanas and hints of pear drops.

One Hop One Grain (OG 1041, ABV 4.1%)
Amber-coloured best bitter. Fresh bread/marmalade aroma, roast malt and citrus hop flavours with pear drops and honey hints, and a long, dry finish.

Helter Skelter (OG 1042, ABV 4.2%)
Fruity, hoppy, golden-coloured beer. Biscuit malt, pine hops and a touch of caramel honey provide a refreshing bitterness.

Honeyfuggle (OG 1043, ABV 4.5%)
Golden-coloured speciality honey beer. Light, subtle honey and caramel flavours evolving into a refreshing, sweet yet bitter beer.

SPA (OG 1048, ABV 4.8%)
Amber-coloured strong ale. Well-hopped with citrus, peach and grassy notes. Hints of honey leading to dry bitter finish.

Porter (OG 1053, ABV 5.2%)
Dark-coloured vanilla porter. Roasted malt aromas, molasses, treacle, liquorice flavours with raisin, fig/plum fruits and earthy hops, and a roast, dry finish.

IPA (OG 1055, ABV 5.5%)
Amber-coloured IPA with a hop aroma. Powerful, earthy hop bitter and persistent malt flavours. Kaleidoscope of fruitiness. Long bitter finish.

Red IPA (OG 1057, ABV 5.9%)
Copper-coloured speciality ale. Biscuit, molasses, liquorice malt with resiny hops, stone and tropical fruit flavours and a long, fruity, dry finish.

Corvedale SIBA

Sun Inn, Corfton, Shropshire, SY7 9DF
☎ (01584) 861239 corvedalebrewery.co.uk

Brewing started in 1999 behind the pub. Landlord Norman Pearce is also the brewer and uses only British malt and hops, with water from a local borehole. Beers are brewed for the pub and wider distribution. !! ♦ RAIB

Bitter (OG 1037, ABV 3.7%)
An amber-coloured beer with a refreshing, slightly hoppy taste and a bitter finish.

Dale Ale (OG 1040, ABV 4%)
Aromas of smoky molasses, dates and fruity, nutty, toffee tastes.

Fuggles Gold (OG 1042, ABV 4.2%)

Golden Dale (OG 1043, ABV 4.2%)

Norman's Pride (OG 1043, ABV 4.3%)
A golden-coloured beer with a refreshing, slightly hoppy taste and a bitter finish.

Farmer Ray (OG 1045, ABV 4.5%)
A ruby-coloured bitter with a smooth, malty taste.

Oatmeal Stout (OG 1045, ABV 4.5%)

Pax Ale (OG 1045, ABV 4.5%)

Dark & Delicious (OG 1045, ABV 4.6%)
A dark ruby-coloured beer with hops on the aroma and palate and a sweet aftertaste.

Cosmic

13 Glaisdale Road, Fishponds, Bristol, BS16 2HY
☎ 07713 475551 cosmicbrewingco@gmail.com

Brewing began in 2018 in the Fishponds area of Bristol. Owner and brewer, Pete Livingstone, predominantly uses American hops and yeast to produce American beer styles. Beers are available in local pubs and micropubs. ♦

Cotleigh SIBA

Ford Road, Wiveliscombe, Somerset, TA4 2RE
☎ (01984) 624086 cotleighbrewery.com

Established in 1979, Cotleigh is based in the historic town of Wiveliscombe. It supplies direct to 750 pubs, 200 retailers and selected wholesalers and is contracted to supply South West region Co-ops. A visitor centre is now established and available for functions. Monthly events include folk, jazz, open mic and curry nights. !! ♦ RAIB

Harrier (OG 1035, ABV 3.5%)
A light and golden-coloured beer with a delicate floral and fruity aroma for a refreshing sweet and slightly hoppy finish.

Tawny Owl (OG 1038, ABV 3.8%)
Well-balanced, tawny-coloured bitter with malt and fruity aroma, major malt taste followed by hop fruit, developing to satisfying bitter finish.

Cotleigh IPA (OG 1039, ABV 3.9%)

Commando Hoofing (OG 1040, ABV 4%)
A pale golden-coloured beer, refreshing and slightly sparkling.

Cotleigh 25 (OG 1040, ABV 4%)
Pale golden-coloured beer, fresh aroma, and fruit-filled finish.

Golden Seahawk (OG 1042, ABV 4.2%)
Gold-coloured, well-hopped golden ale with flowery hop aroma and fruity hop flavour. Clean mouthfeel, leading to a dry, hoppy finish.

Barn Owl (OG 1045, ABV 4.5%)
Mid-brown-coloured beer with a well-balanced malt and hop aroma. Smooth, full-bodied taste where hops dominate, balanced by malt.

Honey Buzzard (OG 1045, ABV 4.5%)
Local honey infused brew, giving a smooth, creamy and chocolate palate offering a subtle, bittersweet finish.

Old Buzzard (OG 1048, ABV 4.8%)
A traditional dark ale, deep copper red in colour with a dry, nutty flavour and hints of amarone biscuit. Dry, smoky, smooth finish.

Cotswold SIBA

College Farm, Stow Road, Lower Slaughter, Bourton-on-the-Water, Gloucestershire, GL54 2HN
☎ (01451) 824488 ☎ 07760 889100
🌐 cotswoldbrewco.uk

An independent producer of craft lager and speciality beers. The brewery was established in 2005 and expanded in 2010. More than 150 outlets are supplied, mainly in the Cotswolds and London. ‼ ♦ RAIB

Cask (OG 1040, ABV 4%)
Copper-coloured, well-hopped, easy-drinking ale.

Cotswold Lion SIBA

Grain Store 5, Dowmans Farm, Coberley, Gloucestershire, GL53 9QY
☎ (01242) 870164 🌐 cotswoldlionbrewery.co.uk

⊗ The 10-barrel plant is located in a grain store on a farm in the Cotswolds, but may relocate during the currency of this Guide. RAIB

Shepherd's Delight (OG 1036, ABV 3.6%)
A light session ale, crisp and full of citrus flavours.

Hogget (OG 1039, ABV 3.8%)
A copper-coloured best bitter. Fruit, light on the citrus, with a hint of spice.

Best in Show (OG 1042, ABV 4.2%)
Plenty of blackberry fruit with a hint of honey.

Golden Fleece (OG 1044, ABV 4.4%)
A not-so-traditional IPA, filled with Jamaican fruit.

Drover's Return (OG 1050, ABV 5%)
A strong, ruby-coloured bitter. Just enough hop to keep it interesting, but let's the malt shine through.

Cotton End

The Pomfret Arms, 10 Cotton End, Northampton, NN4 8BS
☎ (01604) 765544 🌐 facebook.com/thepomfretarms

⊗ Established in 2015, Cotton End Brewery is located in the garden of the Pomfret Arms, Northampton. A one-barrel plant, it brews specialist beers on sale at the pub as well as other local outlets.

Coul (NEW)

22 Laggan Crescent, Glenrothes, KY7 6FY
🌐 coulbrewing.co.uk

Coul is a family owned and run brewery in the heart of Fife producing small batch craft beers.

Country Life SIBA

The Big Sheep, Abbotsham, Bideford, Devon, EX39 5AP
☎ (01237) 420808 ☎ 07971 267790
🌐 countrylifebrewery.co.uk

⊗ Country Life is based at the Big Sheep tourist attraction. The brewery offers a beer show and free samples in the shop during the peak season (Apr-Oct). A 15.5-barrel plant was installed in 2005, making Country Life the biggest brewery in north Devon. Around 100 outlets are supplied. ‼ ♦ RAIB

Old Appledore (OG 1037, ABV 3.7%)
Classic, sessionable beer.

Reef Break (OG 1039, ABV 4%)
Gentle, sweet, malty taste.

Shore Break (OG 1042, ABV 4.4%)
Very light, easy-drinking, refreshing ale.

Black Boar/Board Break (OG 1044, ABV 4.5%)
Complex, well-balanced aromas, unusual dry, bitter hop taste leading to softer aftertaste with unexpected roasted malt and caramel.

Golden Pig (OG 1046, ABV 4.7%)

Country Bumpkin (OG 1058, ABV 6%)
A malty, full-flavoured, smooth taste.

Courtyard (NEW)

Gosfield Cottage, The Street, Gosfield, Essex, CO9 1TP
☎ (01787) 475993 ☎ 07710 230662
🌐 courtyardbrewery.co.uk

Courtyard Brewery uses a six-barrel plant designed to perfectly fit into a 19th century coachhouse in the north Essex village of Gosfield. It is run by two brewers passionate about producing ales traditionally, but with a 21st century twist.

IPA (ABV 3.8%)
A well-balanced session ale with subtle hop aromas and a light caramel taste.

Gold (ABV 4.1%)
A light golden-coloured ale with a crisp, fresh taste and smooth, balanced bitterness.

Dark (ABV 5%)
A porter with hints of coffee, chocolate and molasses.

CrackleRock

The Old Cooperage, High Street, Botley, Hampshire, SO30 2EA ☎ 07733 232806 🌐 cracklerock.co.uk

⊗ Cracklerock began brewing in 2014 at the Old Cooperage in the centre of Botley. Its taproom moved to larger premises near the brewery in 2018. ‼ ♦

Crackerjack (OG 1039, ABV 3.8%)
Full-flavoured, clean-tasting, light and hoppy ale with slight citrus notes.

Fire Cracker (OG 1043, ABV 4.2%)
Well-balanced, traditional bitter.

Gold Rush (OG 1046, ABV 4.5%)
A slightly sweet, premium golden ale with a full, deep, malty flavour and good hop balance.

Dark Destroyer (OG 1049, ABV 4.9%)
A rich, strong, dark-coloured, porter-style beer. A little caramel but not too burnt. Well-balanced with chocolate malt flavours.

Crafty Shag (OG 1050, ABV 5%)
A smooth, strong, full-bodied, well-balanced ale.

Crackatoa IPA (OG 1060, ABV 6.2%)
A pale ale with characteristics of an IPA. An enticing aroma of hops and overtones of citrus.

Craddock's

Duke William, 25 Coventry Street, Stourbridge, West Midlands, DY8 1EP
☎ (01384) 440202 🌐 craddocksbrewery.com

⊗ Craddock's began brewing at the rear of the Duke William pub in Stourbridge, though the brewing is now also carried out in the courtyard of the Stable Bar, Bridgnorth. It is an eight-barrel plant selling exclusively to its four pubs; the Duke William and the Plough & Harrow, Stourbridge, the King Charles, Worcester, and the Talbot, Droitwich. !! ♦ RAIB

Craft, The

29a Part Street, Southport, Merseyside, PR8 1HY
☎ 07870 160934 🌐 thecraftbrewery.com

The Craft is a small-batch, independently owned microbrewery producing vegan-friendly, unfined, hand-crafted ales using traditional techniques. ♦V

Crafty Gold (OG 1045, ABV 4%)
Very smooth, single malt beer, slight fruit flavours, and a refreshing finish.

Crafty Ale (OG 1055, ABV 4.5%)
A rich, dark ale with chocolate undertones and a malty finish.

Crafty IPA (OG 1055, ABV 4.5%)
A full-flavoured Indian Pale Ale, slightly bitter with citrus notes, great mouthfeel and a clean, dry finish.

Crafty Devil (OG 1062, ABV 5%)
A dark, rich traditional porter with a hint of cherry.

Crafty Smoke (OG 1064, ABV 5%)
A pale ale with a pleasant, smoky aftertaste.

Craft Academy

Florence, 131-133 Dulwich Road, Herne Hill, London, SE24 0NG 🌐 unbottlingpotential.co.uk/at-the-florence

Craft Academy was set up by Greene King in 2016 as an apprentice-led scheme offering young people the chance to learn the art of brewing. The brewery was installed at the Florence in 2017 and the beers are brewed by the students. Beer on cask and keg is only available in the pub. Beer found elsewhere is most likely to have been brewed at Greene King.

Crafty Beers

The Stables, Hall Farm, Stetchworth, Cambridgeshire, CB8 0TY
☎ (01223) 813938 🌐 craftybeers.co.uk

⊗ Crafty Beers have been brewed by Robert Beardsmore since 2012. Production moved to an old stable building near Stetchworth in 2016 in order to increase capacity. The beers are available at pubs in the Cambridge and Newmarket areas. RAIB

Carpenter's Cask (OG 1038, ABV 3.8%)
A well-balanced, amber-coloured brew with biscuit malt character giving way to hops on the palate and long finish.

Incognito (OG 1040, ABV 4%)
Dark copper-coloured ale with a malty flavour and refreshing, subtle dry hop finish.

Wilbraham (OG 1041, ABV 4.1%)
Amber-coloured ale with rich malt flavours and good balancing bitterness. Subtle hop aroma with earthy hop notes.

Sauvignon Blonde (OG 1042, ABV 4.4%)
An aromatic golden ale.

APA (OG 1045, ABV 4.6%)
Abundantly dry-hopped American-style pale ale with plenty of hops.

Crafty Brewing SIBA

Thatched House Farm, Loxhill, Dunsfold, Surrey, GU8 4BW
☎ (01483) 276300 ☎ 07702 305 595
🌐 craftybrewing.co.uk

⊗ Opened in 2014 and situated on Luke Herman's family farm behind Dunsfold aerodrome, Crafty's base has a historic connection with the Canadian troop presence during WWII. The five-barrel plant supplies more than 175 pubs across the region plus local events and markets. RAIB

Loxhill Biscuit (OG 1038, ABV 3.8%)
Golden-coloured bitter which belies its strength. Initial malty aroma and taste with a dry bitter finish.

Dark Sessions (OG 1040, ABV 4%)
A light-bodied, darker beer with hints of chocolate and orange.

Dunsfold Best (OG 1040, ABV 4%)
A deep red-coloured bitter, with initial toffee and caramel aromas, which leads to a slightly vinous flavour and a sweetish taste. Short finish with caramel notes.

Crafty One (OG 1042, ABV 4.2%)
Golden yellow-coloured beer, tropical fruits aroma, leads to a full bitterness, with a dry finish.

Hop Tipple (OG 1042, ABV 4.2%)
Thirst-quenching beer with a hoppy finish.

Crafty Devil

Stone Yard, Ninian Park Road, Cardiff, CF11 6HE
☎ (029) 2021 8099 ☎ 07766 014550
🌐 craftydevilbrewing.co.uk

⊗ Crafty Devil began brewing in 2014, and moved to new premises in 2017 to increase capacity. Currently only regularly produce bottled, canned and keg beer, supplying to markets and a number of other outlets in the city. Brewery will will arrange cask-conditioned beer by special request particularly for local beer events. !!

Crafty Dragon

8 Castell Morlais, Ponsticill, CF48 2YB

Crafty Dragon began brewing in 2017 and is situated within the Brecon Beacons National Park. Its brewery tap is the Butchers Arms in Pontsticill. ♦

Goldings Bitter (OG 1039, ABV 3.8%)

Session IPA (ABV 3.8%)

Pen Y Fan Chocolate & Rum Porter (ABV 4.5%)

Cwrw Coch (OG 1049, ABV 5%)

Crafty Little SIBA

Building 40, British Aerospace Business Park, Saltgrounds Road, Brough, East Yorkshire, HU15 1EQ
☎ (01482) 661393 🌐 thecraftylittlebrewery.co.uk

Crafty Little is an East Yorkshire family business. Extra fermenting vessels have helped the brewery meet demand. !! RAIB

Apex Predator (OG 1033, ABV 3.8%)

ChamALEon (OG 1036, ABV 4%)

Red Tale (OG 1042, ABV 4.5%)
Well-balanced with toasted malt notes, earthy undertones and a light burst of passion fruit, pine and forest berries.

Silk Stout (OG 1046, ABV 4.5%)

Black Ryeno (OG 1043.5, ABV 4.6%)
Well-balanced and delicate with lightly toasted liquorice, citrus and stone fruit flavours.

Perky Porter (OG 1046, ABV 4.8%)
Slightly sweet, velvety rich, roasted coffee porter.

Wolf Bite APA (OG 1048, ABV 4.8%)
An intense blend of refreshing fruit, heady with citrus, a touch of pine and a powerful, lingering aftertaste.

Snake Charmer (OG 1060, ABV 5.5%)

Brewed for Three Sisters Brewing Co:

Session Ale (OG 1043, ABV 4%)

Crafty Monkey SIBA

Benknowle Farm Elwick, Elwick, Hartlepool, TS27 3HF
craftymonkey.beer

Brewing commenced in 2018 on a plant supplied by Oban Ales.

Crafty Pint

c/o Half Moon, 130 Northgate, Darlington, County Durham, DL1 1QS
☎ (01325) 469965 ☎ 07804305175

Established in 2013 in the cellar of the Half Moon in Darlington. Originally a 10-gallon brew length, it was upgraded to a one-barrel plant in 2015. One-off beers are produced solely for the pub. ♦

Crankshaft

17e Boxer Place, Leyland, Lancashire, PR26 7QL
☎ 07827 289200 crankshaftbrewery.co.uk

The brewery launched in 2016, moved to new premises in 2017, and expanded into the next unit in 2018. A number of special occasional beers are brewed. A microbar, Cann Bridge Ale House, Higher Walton, has opened and a taproom at the brewery is planned. ♦

Propshaft (OG 1038, ABV 3.8%)
Classic, pale golden-coloured session beer. Refreshing grassy, earthy taste.

Ribble 100 (OG 1045, ABV 4.2%)

Crankcase (OG 1046, ABV 5%)

Ribble Red (OG 1047, ABV 5%)

Leyland Tiger Cub (OG 1052, ABV 5.5%)

Leyland Badger (OG 1058, ABV 5.8%)
Caramelised treacle toffee flavour and a dry taste with a hint of hops. Plenty of body and a smooth mouthfeel.

Sumners Steam (OG 1068, ABV 6.6%)

Crate SIBA

Unit 7 White Building, Queens Yard, Hackney Wick, London, E9 5EN ☎ 07834 275687
cratebrewery.com

Crate is a brewery and pizzeria opened in 2012 and situated in a canalside former print factory. The kit has moved and expanded into a unit across the yard from the bar. Available widely on cask, keg, bottles and cans. Crowdfunding was launched 2019. RAIB

IPA (ABV 6%)
Smooth, gold-coloured beer, Very bitter, fragrant, hoppy beer with distinctive citrus, tangerine aromas. Lingering hoppy, fruity bitter finish.

Creaton Grange

Old Wash House, Creaton Grange, Grooms Lane, Creaton, Northamptonshire, NN6 8NN ☎ 07943 595829 creatongrangeales.co.uk

Microbrewery started in 2017 and based in a converted disused building on a family farm in rural Northamptonshire. !! RAIB

Four Sons (ABV 3.5%)
A traditional beer with light roasted notes combined with a floral aroma and hints of sweet spice.

Pheasant Tale (OG 1038, ABV 3.8%)
A refreshing and lightly-hopped session golden ale.

March Yard (ABV 4.2%)
A pale ale with an aromatic and nutty hop flavour and a refreshing finish.

Credence SIBA

Unit 16B Coquet Enterprise Park, Amble, Northumberland, NE65 0PE
☎ (01665) 714855 credencebrewing.co.uk

Credence began brewing in 2015. A barrel-aging programme is being established and a new trade counter is the first step in opening up the brewery to the public. Around 100 outlets are supplied direct. ♦

Blonde (OG 1040, ABV 4%)

Croft

32 Upper York Street, Stokes Croft, Bristol, BS2 8QN
☎ (0117) 214 1990 ☎ 07480 624212
croftales.com

Croft began brewing in 2017 in a former faggot factory in Bristol's vibrant Stokes Croft area, from which the brewery takes its name. The brewery also serves as a taproom, which holds regular tasting events and launches of its seasonal ales, which are often accompanied by DJs and pop-up food vendors. !! ♦ V

BS2 (OG 1042, ABV 4%)
Hazy, unfined, golden ale with grassy hop aroma, clean yet slightly sweet citrus flavours, and balanced somewhat dry, bitter finish.

Beast (OG 1042, ABV 4.2%)
Hint of malt on the nose with some added hop bitterness on the tongue, slightly tart, bittersweet aftertaste.

Backjump (OG 1046, ABV 4.5%)

THE BREWERIES

Hazy, straw yellow-coloured with a citrus aroma, grapefruit flavours dominate with hints of pineapple, which both fade in the short finish.

Westide (OG 1045, ABV 4.5%) ◆
Copper-coloured ale with earthy hops on the nose, fresh tasting bitterness on the palate and a lingering, balanced aftertaste.

Deep Red (OG 1055, ABV 5.5%) ◆
Hoppy, red-coloured ale combining rye with sweetish malt and pine notes on the palate, finishing with a lingering bitterness.

Cromarty

Davidston, Cromarty, IV11 8XD
☎ (01381) 600440 ⊕ cromartybrewing.co.uk

Cromarty began brewing 2011 in a purpose-built brewhouse, installed another two large fermenters during 2014, and further fermenter/conditioning tanks in 2015. A fully automatic bottling line was commissioned in 2017 and a warehouse was built on-site in 2018 to help cope with demand. ‼ ▦ ♦

Atlantic Drift (OG 1035, ABV 3.5%) ◆
Good golden amber-coloured beer with a grapefruit hop flavour throughout. Tasty for its strength.

Whiteout (ABV 3.8%)

Happy Chappy (OG 1040, ABV 4.1%) ◆
Golden ale with plenty of hop character. Floral citrus hop aroma with a good bitter taste, which increases in aftertaste and balanced with malt.

Red Rocker (OG 1048.5, ABV 5%) 🗇 ◆
Red-coloured rye speciality hop monster with a malty background leading to a bitter finish.

Rogue Wave (OG 1052, ABV 5.7%) ◆
Easy-drinking, strong, peachy, hoppy bitter.

Ghost Town (OG 1058, ABV 5.8%) ◆
Classic dark roasted malty porter with a blackcurrant and liquorice background.

AKA IPA (OG 1067, ABV 6.7%) ◆
Strong IPA with a smooth, citrus, hoppy taste.

Cronx SIBA

Unit 6, Vulcan Business Centre, Vulcan Way, New Addington, Croydon, CR0 9UG
☎ (01689) 809093 ☎ 07793974395 ⊕ thecronx.com

▨ Cronx began brewing in 2012 and is the first commercial brewery in the area since 1954. The standard range and specials are available in cask, keg and bottles. The taproom was opened in 2016 at BOXPark Croydon. ‼ ▦ ♦

Standard (ABV 3.8%) ◆
Easy-drinking brown-coloured bitter with sweetish fudge and spicy hoppiness notes throughout. A malty, bitter finish with a dryness that remains.

Kotchin (ABV 3.9%) ◆
Grapefruity beer with pleasant hoppy notes. A little sweetness is balanced by a crisp, bitter finish that grows on drinking.

Nektar (ABV 4.5%) ◆
Full-bodied, dark gold-coloured best bitter. Peach with citrus, sweet biscuit and floral hops, gently fade in the lingering bitter finish.

Pop Up! (ABV 5%) ◆

Smooth, amber-coloured APA. Bitter and hoppy with hints of fruit in the aroma and taste and a dry finish.

Entire (ABV 5.2%) ◆
Dark brown-coloured porter with chocolate roast notes in the aroma, flavour and finish. The fruit character is of caramelised raisins.

Crooked

Units 12-15 The Garages, Leeds East Airport, Church Fenton, LS24 9SE ☎ 07890 526505
⊕ crookedbrewing.co.uk

Steve, Andy, Hudson and Mark started brewing in 2017. Beers are available in a number of city centre bars in York and Leeds.

Spokes (ABV 4%)
Well-balanced, session beer. Bitterness and a subtle blend of orange and grapefruit.

The Lash (ABV 4.4%)
An ocean of juicy hops with bitterness in this pale ale.

Rufus (ABV 4.8%)
Hoppy, red-coloured, naturally hazy ale.

Cropton

See Great Yorkshire

Cross Bay

Unit 1, Newgate, White Lund Industrial Estate, Morecambe, Lancashire, LA3 3PT
☎ (01524) 39481 ⊕ crossbaybrewery.co.uk

☺Cross Bay commenced brewing in 2011 on a 28-barrel brew plant. In 2017 it rebranded its core range introducing a couple of brand new ales. An on-site taproom opened in 2018. The beers are widely available across North-west England. ‼ ▦ ♦

Eazy (ABV 3%)
A session ale with flavours of grapefruit and lemon rind.

Halo (OG 1037, ABV 3.6%) ◆
A crisp and hoppy, pale bitter.

Vesper (ABV 3.8%)
Bright, tropical fruit hop flavours dominate this crisp, smooth beer.

RIPA (ABV 4%)

Omega (ABV 4.2%)
An American-style pale ale with grapefruit, citrus and spice notes.

Sunset (OG 1043, ABV 4.2%) ◆
Sweet best bitter with a rising bitter finish.

Zenith (OG 1050, ABV 5%) ◆
Gentle bitterness and fruity sweetness, with some dryness in the finish.

Guell (ABV 5.1%)
Light malt flavours, aromas of blueberry, tangerine, papaya and bubble gum.

Cross Borders SIBA

28-1, Hardengreen Industrial Estate, Dalkeith, EH22 3NX
☎ (0131) 629 3990 ⊕ crossborders.beer

Ⓧ Established in 2016 by childhood friends Jonathan Wilson and Gary Munckton. Cross Borders brews BRAW traditional Scottish ales without pretension. The brewery has an on-site tap open Fridays and Saturdays. !! ➤

Hop Series Pale (OG 1040, ABV 3.8%) ◣
Notes of citrus on the nose with a balanced, bitter finish.

Wee BRAW (ABV 4%)
Session IPA; juicy and refreshing with hints of tangerine and mango.

Heavy (OG 1046, ABV 4.1%)
Malt-forward ale with slight hoppy bite in the finish.

Bill's Beer (OG 1045, ABV 4.2%)
Session IPA, full-flavoured with zesty fruits and a clean finish.

Porter (OG 1045, ABV 4.2%) ◣
Flavours of coffee and chocolate come through in the finish of this easy-drinking porter.

IPA (OG 1044, ABV 4.5%)
Aromas of pear and pineapple tickle the nose, followed by a pine, resinous, bitter finish.

BRAW (OG 1055, ABV 5.2%) ◣
Enticing citrus and tropical notes in the aroma of this juicy, refreshing golden ale.

Crossed Anchors

▤ c/o Grapevine, 2 Victoria Road, Exmouth, Devon, EX8 1DL
☎ (01395) 222208 ☎ 07843 577608
⊕ crossedanchors.co.uk

Ⓧ Crossed Anchors was established in 2015. In 2016 a six-barrel plant became operational in the old stables of the Grapevine in Exmouth town centre. Beers are available across Devon and the South-west, as well as in the Grapevine. !! ➤ ◆ RAIB

CSH (OG 1038, ABV 3.8%)
A yellow-coloured, aroma-filled beer, less bitter than you would expect.

Bitter Exe (OG 1041, ABV 4%)
Deep brown in colour with a light citrus aroma and taste, and hints of marmalade.

Three Cs Gold (OG 1040, ABV 4.3%)
Pale gold in colour with a strong hop aroma. Well-balanced and easy-drinking with a hoppy bitterness in the taste and aftertaste.

American Pale Ale (OG 1045, ABV 4.6%)
A copper-coloured ale with a citrus hop and stone fruit aroma. The fruit and hops continue in the taste and aftertaste.

Weisse Guy (OG 1047, ABV 5%)
A naturally hazy German-style wheat beer. It has an aroma of banana and lemon with a crisp, malty taste with a hint of cloves and a long finish.

Crosspool Ale Makers

442 Manchester Road, Sheffield, South Yorkshire, S10 5DR ✉ crosspoolalemakers@gmail.com

Ⓧ Crosspool Ale Makers Society (previously Hopscotch Craft Brewery) began brewing in 2018. Recent equipment upgrades have increased capacity. A number of specials with locally-themed names are planned. The beers are regularly

available in an increasing number of Sheffield pubs, and at open brewery events. ◆ RAIB

Sandygate (ABV 3.6%)
Light-coloured session beer flavoured with maple and lemon peel.

Crosspale (ABV 4%)

Crouch Vale SIBA

23 Haltwhistle Road, South Woodham Ferrers, Essex, CM3 5ZA
☎ (01245) 322744 ⊕ crouchvale.co.uk

Ⓧ Founded in 1981 by two CAMRA enthusiasts, Crouch Vale is well established as a major player in Essex brewing, having moved to larger premises in 2006. The company is also a major wholesaler of cask ale from other independent breweries, which it supplies to more than 100 outlets, as well as beer festivals throughout the region. A tap room (Tap Room 19) is on the brewery site. One tied house, the Queen's Head in Chelmsford, is owned. !! ➤ ◆ RAIB

Blackwater Mild (OG 1037, ABV 3.7%) ◣
A dark bitter rather than a true mild. Roasty and very bitter towards the end.

Essex Boys Best Bitter (OG 1038, ABV 3.8%)
Full-bodied, traditional-style, mid-brown-coloured best bitter.

Brewers Gold (OG 1040, ABV 4%) ▣ ◣
Pale golden ale with a striking citrus nose. Sweet fruit and bitter hops are well-balanced throughout.

Yakima Gold (OG 1042, ABV 4.2%)
Golden-coloured, earthily aromatic and highly drinkable.

Amarillo (OG 1050, ABV 5%)
Premium, light-bodied golden ale with hoppy aroma, and a lasting spicy and orangey flavour.

Crown

▤ Crown, Green End, Little Staughton, Bedfordshire, MK44 2BU
☎ (01234) 376260 ⊕ thecrownstaughton.com

Brewing began in 2017 in a building behind the Crown public house in Little Staughton. The brewery is owned and run by the landlord of the Crown with the beers only being produced for the pub and local beer festivals. ◆

Crown Brewhouse

▤ The Square, Elford, Staffordshire, B79 9DB
☎ (01827) 383602 ⊕ none

A one-barrel brew plant, established in 2017 and housed in a former store room attached to the Crown pub. The pub and a limited number of local outlets are supplied.

Cuillin

▤ Sligachan Hotel,, Sligachan, Carbost, Isle of Skye, IV47 8SW
☎ (01478) 650204 ☎ 07795 250808
⊕ cuillinbrewery.com

☺The five-barrel brewery opened in 2004 and is situated in central Skye at the foot of the Cuillin mountains. The water from the Cuillins provides a

distinctive colour and taste to the ales. Beers are available on-site at the Sligachan Hotel and at several other pubs and hotels on the Isle of Skye. The brewery is open by appointment only in winter (Nov-Mar). ‼♦

Cullercoats SIBA

Westfield Court, 19 Maurice Road Industrial Estate, Wallsend, Tyne & Wear, NE28 6BY
☎ (0191) 252 8765 ☎ 07895 692881

Office: 17 St Oswins Avenue, Cullercoats, NE30 4PH
🌐 cullercoatsbrewery.co.uk

Established in 2011 with brewing taking place twice a week. The brewery champions English hops. ♦

Shuggy Boat Blonde (OG 1039, ABV 3.8%)
A refreshing, blonde beer, smooth and drinkable.

Lovely Nelly (OG 1039, ABV 3.9%)
Full-bodied, amber bronze-coloured session beer. Biscuit malt flavour balanced with a smooth hop bitterness.

Jack the Devil (OG 1045, ABV 4.5%)
Delicious and rich, a dark chestnut-coloured ale, well-balanced malty, nuttiness and a fresh, hoppy aroma.

Grace Darling Gold (OG 1050, ABV 5%)

Rocket Brigade (OG 1054, ABV 5.5%)
Classic pale ale, strong and bitter yet easy-drinking.

Cumberland

See Great Corby

Cumbrian Legendary SIBA

Old Hall Brewery, Hawkshead, Cumbria, LA22 0QF
☎ (01539) 436436 🌐 cumbrianlegendaryales.com

First established in 2003, the brewery is located in an idyllic position in a renovated barn on the shores of Esthwaite Water. The success of Loweswater Gold has meant the brewery is thriving. ‼♦

Esthwaite Bitter (OG 1038.5, ABV 3.8%)
Robust, refreshing bitter with plenty of hops, lasting well into the finish.

Langdale (OG 1040, ABV 4%)
Fresh grapefruit aromas with hoppy, fruity flavours and crisp, long hop finish, make for a well-balanced beer.

Grasmoor Dark Ale (OG 1043, ABV 4.3%)
Dark-coloured, fruity beer with complex character and roast nutty tones leading to a short, refreshing finish.

Loweswater Gold (OG 1041, ABV 4.3%)
A dominant fruity body develops into a light bitter finish. A beer that belies its strength.

American Dry Hopped Pale Ale (OG 1042, ABV 4.5%)
American-style, well-balanced, big flavour pale ale.

Curious (NEW)

Unit 1, Victoria Road, Ashford, Kent, TN23 7HQ
☎ (01580) 763033

Office: Level 2, Civic Centre, Tannery Lane, Ashford, Kent, TN23 1PL 🌐 curiousbrewery.com

Situated in the centre of Ashford, this multi-million pound investment by parent company Chapel Down opened in 2019. A modern state-of-the-art brewery with a shop and tasting room on the ground floor and a bar and 120-seat restaurant upstairs, which offers the Curious Brew core range of beers and cider, as well as special and seasonal brews. The Curious Brew products have been widely available in keg, bottle and can for some eight years but up until now have been contract brewed. Brewing now takes place on the Ashford site. Fresh beer from the brewery will be served from tanks above the bar; this will be unpasteurised but will be filtered. ‼

Custom Head

Unit 20-21, Grendon House Farm, Grendon, Warwickshire, CV9 3DT ☎ 07858 753653

Office: 8 Rocklands Crescent, Lichfield, Staffordshire, WS13 6DH

Formerly known as Hippy Killer Brewery, established in 2016, it relaunched as Custom Head in 2018. KeyKeg beers are produced under the Grendon Wave brand name.

Jonny Always Gets There in the End (ABV 4.3%)

Trent Valley Best (ABV 4.3%)

Trent Valley Gold (ABV 4.5%)

Cwm Rhondda

Fforch Farm, Cemetry Road, Treorchy, CF42 6TF
☎ (01443) 777491 🌐 cwmrhonddaales.co.uk

Cwm Rhondda Ales is a family-run brewery, situated on a farm in the Rhondda Valleys. Brewing commenced in a 2015 on a 2.5-barrel plant, using the brewery's spring water, which gives a unique taste to the ales. A farm shop, café and bar are situated in the nearby village.

Shwmae But (OG 1039, ABV 3.8%)

Boyo (OG 1044, ABV 4.5%)

Tommy Box (OG 1044, ABV 4.5%)

Afon Aur (OG 1046, ABV 4.6%)

Daleside SIBA

Camwal Road, Starbeck, Harrogate, North Yorkshire, HG1 4PT
☎ (01423) 880022 🌐 dalesidebrewery.com

Daleside was established in the mid 1980s, and moved to its current site at Starbeck in 1992. Daleside Brewery beers are sold to local, regional and national customers and export markets include Denmark, Sweden and Australia. ♦

Bitter (OG 1039, ABV 3.7%)
Pale brown-coloured, well-balanced, hoppy beer complemented by fruity bitterness and a hint of sweetness, leading to a long, bitter finish.

Blonde (OG 1040, ABV 3.9%)
A pale golden-coloured beer, predominantly hoppy aroma and taste, leading to a refreshing hoppy, bitter but short finish.

Old Leg Over (OG 1043, ABV 4.1%)

Well-balanced, mid brown-coloured, refreshing beer with a fruity, bitter aftertaste.

Monkey Wrench (OG 1055, ABV 5.3%)
Premium, chestnut-coloured ale with a spicy fruit aroma and warming spicy flavour.

Dalrannoch

Unit 16, The Old Dairy, Meikleour, Perth, PH2 6FB
dalrannochbrewing.co.uk

Brewing began in 2016 using a five-barrel plant.

Dancing Cows

Sadlers Farm Workshops, Lower Pennington Lane, Lymington, Hampshire, SO41 8AL
(01590) 676071 07952 639465
dancingcows.co.uk

Dancing Cows is a small-batch brewery and distillery close to Ancient Causeway and Pennington & Keyhaven Nature Reserve, sourcing local grains, hops, herbs and spices. Operated by the former owner of Bowland Brewery in Lancashire and inspired by a trip to Lake Michigan to bring a fresh outlook on brewing. New recipes are being developed constantly. !! ♦ RAIB

Dancing Duck SIBA

1 John Cooper Buildings, Payne St, Derby, DE22 3AZ
(01332) 205582 07581 122122
dancingduckbrewery.com

Dancing Duck was established in 2010 by Rachel Mathews using a 10-barrel brew plant. Its name comes from the local greeting 'ay up me duck'. The Exeter Arms in Derby is the brewery tap. !! ♦

Ay Up (OG 1040.5, ABV 3.9%)
A session pale ale with subtle malt and floral notes, matched with citrus hop and rounded off with a slightly dry finish.

Waitangi (OG 1041.3, ABV 4%)
An easy-drinking, crisp, clean pale ale. Subtle malt character is balanced with zesty lemon and lime hops.

Ginger Ninja (OG 1042, ABV 4.1%)
Quaffable, refreshing ale. Well-balanced, citrus notes from the hops and a subtle ginger flavour.

Nice Weather (OG 1042, ABV 4.1%)
Refreshing, copper-coloured, fruity ale packed full of blackberry, strawberry and floral rose notes. Well-balanced with just the right amount of malt character.

Back, Sack & Quack (ABV 4.2%)
A traditional, full-bodied mild with bags of malty flavour. Black cherry, cola and toffee notes with a caramel finish and berry aroma.

22 (OG 1044.1, ABV 4.3%)
A well-balanced best bitter with a malty flavour and dark fruit notes, offset by a strong hop character and clean finish.

DCUK (OG 1042, ABV 4.3%)
A session pale ale with a fruity aroma and juicy citrus flavour with hints of orange, mango, lemon and pine.

Dark Drake (OG 1051, ABV 4.5%)
Malty, caramel and liquorice flavours combine in a smooth-drinking, velvety oatmeal stout with a freshly roasted coffee and tea finish.

Waddle It Be? (OG 1045.2, ABV 4.5%)
Pale ale with a complex mouthfeel and intense fruity flavours of oranges, peaches and blackcurrants, a spicy, black pepper kick and balanced bitterness.

Indian Porter (OG 1051.8, ABV 5%)
Smoky bonfire flavours with a spicy hop and warming afterglow. Very moreish.

Quack Me Amadeus (ABV 5%)
Refreshing, Vienna-style lager.

Abduction (OG 1053, ABV 5.5%)
Tropical flavours in balance with hoppy bitterness, a good malt character and clean finish.

Imperial Drake (ABV 6.5%)
Rich, strong oatmeal stout.

Dancing Man

Wool House, Town Quay, Southampton, Hampshire, SO14 2AR
(023) 8083 6666 dancingmanbrewery.co.uk

Dancing Man began brewing in 2011 in the Platform Tavern. In 2015 the brewery moved to the historic Wool House, the only surviving freestanding medieval building in Southampton, in order to expand and include an on-site bar and restaurant. One-off and rare brews are available throughout the year. !! ♦ RAIB

Dancing Men

Hill House Inn, The Hill, Happisburgh, Norfolk, NR12 0PW
(01692) 650004 07818 038768
hillhouseinn.co.uk

Brewing began in 2014 at the 16th-century Hill House Inn on Happisburgh's fast-eroding clifftop. The microbrewery is named in honour of a Sherlock Holmes story by Sir Arthur Conan Doyle after he visited the pub in 1903. The five-barrel plant was acquired from Bees Brewery after its partial destruction during the tidal surge events in Walcott in 2013. New recipes have been crafted using exclusive hops and barley including locally-grown Norfolk varieties. !! ♦

After The Storm (OG 1038, ABV 3.8%)
Easy-drinking session beer with a slightly peaty finish.

Famous Norfolk Broads (OG 1037, ABV 3.8%)
Amber-coloured, session beer with well-balanced sweetness and bitter flavours leave the palate refreshed and cleansed.

Soggy Seagull (OG 1042, ABV 4.2%)
Well-balanced, fruity and refreshing, clean-tasting ale.

Knight's Noggin (OG 1044, ABV 4.8%)
A dark-coloured porter-style beer packed with toasted toffee malt flavours.

Cliffhanger (OG 1049, ABV 5.1%)
A pale-coloured, single-hop, premium ale. Easy-drinking with a smooth honey finish.

Dark Horse SIBA

Coonlands Laithe, Hetton, Nr. Skipton, North Yorkshire, BD23 6LY
☎ (01756) 730555 🌐 darkhorsebrewery.co.uk

Dark Horse began brewing in 2008. The brewery is based in an old hay barn within the Yorkshire Dales National Park. Around 50 outlets are supplied direct.

Craven Bitter (OG 1038, ABV 3.8%)
Well-balanced bitter with biscuity malt and fruit on the nose continuing into the taste. Bitterness increases in the finish.

Blonde Beauty (OG 1040, ABV 3.9%)

Hetton Pale Ale (OG 1041, ABV 4.2%)
Golden-coloured, well-balanced, full-bodied, with hoppy bitterness on the palate overlaying a malty base and a spicy citrus character.

Night Jar (OG 1042, ABV 4.2%)
A malty, fruity bitter in aroma and taste. Caramel and dark fruits lace the finish.

Dark Revolution SIBA

Unit 3-5 Lancaster Road, Salisbury, Wiltshire, SP4 6FB
☎ (01722) 411179 🌐 darkrevolution.co.uk

Dark Revolution started commercial brewing in 2015 using a one-barrel plant; the owner had been home-brewing for the previous decade. It upgraded to a 15-barrel brew plant in 2017, with more fermenting vessels added in 2019 retaining the smaller plant for trial brews and short runs. A canning line is now operational. An on-site taproom is also now open Fridays and Saturdays. Barrel-aging is a speciality. ♦ RAIB

Luminous (ABV 4.2%)

So.LA (ABV 4.5%)

Velveteen (ABV 4.8%)
A smooth, rich, black-coloured, unfined stout. Malt and roasted notes in the taste with balanced bitterness through to the finish.

Sonic (ABV 4.9%)

Deviant (ABV 5.6%)

ViPA (ABV 6%)

Dark Star

22 Star Road, Partridge Green, West Sussex, RH13 8RA
☎ (01403) 713085 🌐 darkstarbrewing.co.uk

The Dark Star Brewing Co is named after a Grateful Dead song and was established in the cellar of the Evening Star in Brighton back in 1994, moving to its current home in Partridge Green in 2010. Originally owned by Fuller's but now by Asahi, the 45-barrel plant produces a wide range of beers. !! ♦ RAIB

The Art of Darkness (OG 1040, ABV 3.5%)
Classic roast flavours along with a hint of sweetness. Fruit and spicy favours in perfect balance.

Hophead (OG 1040, ABV 3.8%)
A golden-coloured bitter with a fruity, hoppy aroma and a citrus, bitter taste and aftertaste. Flavours remain strong to the end.

Partridge Best Bitter (OG 1042, ABV 4%)
Traditional Sussex-style best bitter.

Espresso (OG 1048, ABV 4.2%)
Rich, black-coloured beer, with the addition of freshly ground Arabica coffee beans.

American Pale Ale (OG 1048, ABV 4.7%)
American-style pale ale, full of the aroma of hops.

Dark Star Original (OG 1052, ABV 5%)
Dark, strong and bitter beer.

Festival (OG 1052, ABV 5%)
A chestnut, bronze-coloured bitter with a smooth mouthfeel and freshness. Classic-style, strong bitter brewed as a version of Festive (King & Barnes recipe).

Revelation (OG 1057, ABV 5.7%)

Imperial (OG 1070, ABV 10.5%)
A densely rich beer with a dark brown head. It has toffee and berry-like aromas and a velvet-like mouthfeel with complex burnt flavours and a strong alcohol glow.

Dark Tribe

Dog and Gun, High Street, East Butterwick, Lincolnshire, DN17 3AJ
☎ (01724) 782324 🌐 darktribe.co.uk

Situated on the banks of the River Trent in the Dog & Gun pub, this 2.5-barrel brewing plant produces beers for the pub and local outlets. The award-winning brewery has been established since 1996. A range of one-off beers is produced throughout the year. !! ♦

Darkland (NEW)

Unit 4c, Ladyship Business Park, Mill Lane, Halifax, HX3 6TA
☎ (01422) 320100 🌐 darklandbrewery.co.uk

A microbrewery hidden away in a corner of an industrial estate. Regular and seasonal beers are named after ancient runes and are available at the brewery tap, Pallet Bar, Boothtown (open Friday 5pm-9pm, Saturday 5pm-10pm).

Isa (OG 1038, ABV 3.8%)
An easy-drinking, session blonde ale. Dry-hopped for a light finish.

Othala (OG 1038, ABV 3.8%)
An amber-coloured ale, malty and well-balanced. A smooth, session ale.

Drakkar (OG 1045, ABV 4.5%)
A dark and rich ale with complex toasted, rich malt flavours. It has a robust and bitter finish.

Jera (OG 1050, ABV 5.2%)
Refreshing, well-balanced, strong pale ale. Crisp and fruity with a developing bitter finish.

Darkplace

6a Wheelers Yard, Colyton Business Park, Colyton, Devon, EX24 6DT
☎ (01297) 551583

Microbrewery established in Colyton in 2017 using a four-barrel plant. The brewer is frequently trialling new recipes. The majority of current production is bottle-conditioned but cask ales are produced for some local pubs and for festivals. All beers are unfiltered, unfined and unpasteurised. An on-site brewery bar is planned. RAIB

Darkwave

52-54 Aqueduct Street, Preston, Lancashire, PR1 7RE
☎ 07970 110459 ✉ darkwave-ale@outlook.com

Previously known as Arkwrights Brewery, it began brewing at the rear of the Real Ale Shop on Lovat Road in 2010. In 2014 the plant was upgraded to a 10-barrel plant and moved to the current premises. Darkwave have a range of 19 beers, all of which are described as modern artisan beers, always unfined and vegan. ♦ V

Dartford Wobbler SIBA

St Margaret's Farm, St Margaret's Road, South Darenth, Kent, DA4 9LB
☎ (01322) 866233 ⊕ dartfordwobbler.com

☺John and Miriam Millis started with a 0.5-barrel plant at their home in Gravesend. Demand outstripped the facility and Millis moved in 2003 to its current location – a former farm cold store – using a 10-barrel plant. It supplies around 40 outlets within a 50-mile radius. ♦ RAIB

Curiously Dark (OG 1036, ABV 3.6%)
A dark mild with a roasted malt flavour and some background fruit notes, leading to a dry aftertaste.

Guinea Guzzler (OG 1037, ABV 3.7%)
An amber-coloured ale with a malty, fruity taste and a dry finish.

Peddler's Best (OG 1040, ABV 4%)
A copper-coloured bitter with floral fruit notes and an oaky, dry flavour.

Golden Wobbler (OG 1041, ABV 4.1%)
A pale golden-coloured malty beer with complex citrus and lightly-spiced flavours.

Dartford Wobbler (OG 1043, ABV 4.3%)
A full-bodied, russet brown-coloured premium bitter with a dark malt profile, fruit notes and a dry finish.

Thieves 'n' Fakirs (OG 1043, ABV 4.3%)
A dark-coloured porter with a full-bodied malt and hop base, and a long, dry aftertaste.

Penny Red (OG 1044, ABV 4.4%)
A red-coloured beer that has pungent hop notes, a dry finish and a malty base.

Country Wobbler (OG 1048, ABV 4.8%)
Bold flavours of malt and hops with a long, clean and dry finish.

Dartmoor SIBA

The Brewery, Station Road, Princetown, Devon, PL20 6QX
☎ (01822) 890789 ⊕ dartmoorbrewery.co.uk

⌧ Formerly named Princetown, Dartmoor Brewery was established in 1994 and is the highest brewery in England at 1,465 feet above sea level. In 2006 the brewery moved to a purpose-built building, and in 2012 capacity was increased to 360 barrels a week by the addition of another 60-barrel fermenter with a further increase in 2013. All beer is brewed using locally grown barley. ‼ ⬛♦

Dartmoor Best (OG 1037, ABV 3.7%)
Amber-coloured ale, drinkable, with a dry, citrus fruit character.

Dartmoor IPA (OG 1039.5, ABV 4%) ◆

Flowery hop aroma and taste, with a bitter aftertaste to this full-bodied, amber-coloured beer.

Legend (OG 1043.5, ABV 4.4%) ◆
Well-rounded, complex beer full of aromas and flavours. Malt and caramel dominate, and are balanced in an aftertaste of bitter hops.

Jail Ale (OG 1047.5, ABV 4.8%) ◆
Strong session ale, with complex notes dominated by malty, sweet bitterness. Well-rounded caramel and fruit with a pleasant aftertaste.

Darwin SIBA

1 West Quay Court, Sunderland Enterprise Park, Sunderland, SR5 2TE
☎ (0191) 549 9450 ⊕ darwinbrewery.com

☺Established in 1994, Darwin Brewery is based in purpose-built premises in Sunderland with a 3.5-barrel brew plant. The brewery supports students on Brewlab brewing courses at the university, who produce many unique specialist and international beers, often available locally. A range of established Darwin beers is also produced on demand, some based on analysis of historic recipes or student initiatives. Courses in distilling are now available. ‼♦ RAIB

Davenports SIBA

Unit 5, Empire House, 11 New Street, Smethwick, West Midlands, B66 2AJ
☎ (0121) 565 5622 ✉ info@bluebearbrewery.com

☺Formerly known as Blue Bear, Davenports occupies part of a distribution warehouse in an industrial unit in Smethwick on the outskirts of Birmingham. The 7.5-barrel plant produces a selection of beers with some occasional beers from the range of the now defunct Highgate brewery of Walsall. ♦

Mild (OG 1036.8, ABV 3.5%)

Gold (OG 1038, ABV 3.9%)

Original Bitter (OG 1041.8, ABV 4.2%)
A copper-coloured premium ale with a good balance between malt and fruity bitterness.

IPA (OG 1044, ABV 4.4%)

Dawkins

Unit 2, Lawnwood Industrial Units, Lawnwood Road, Easton, Bristol, BS5 0EF
☎ (0117) 955 9503 ⊕ dawkinsales.com

⌧ The established Dawkins Taverns group of independent Bristol pubs bought the Somerset-based Matthews Brewery in 2009. New premises in Easton, Bristol, opened in 2015 with a 20-barrel plant. The brewery distributes to its own five pubs and directly to another 80 outlets in the area. A sister company was set up in Edinburgh in 2017, reviving the long-defunct Steel Coulson brewing name for a bar in Leith with an on-site microbrewery planned. ‼ ⬛♦ RAIB

Bristol Blonde (OG 1036, ABV 3.8%) ◆
Pale yellow-coloured golden ale, citrus aroma, refreshing lemon taste with grassiness, which fades to astringent bitterness.

Bristol Best (OG 1040, ABV 4%) ◆
Copper-coloured bitter with a malty aroma and taste. Hints of apple and an astringent aftertaste.

Tremendous Delicious (OG 1042, ABV 4.2%) ◆
Amber-coloured ale with a malty base balanced with soft apple fruit and a background hop bitterness that lingers in the aftertaste.

Bristol Gold (OG 1043, ABV 4.4%)
Golden ale with a slightly spicy, fruity aroma and flavour.

Easton IPA (OG 1041, ABV 4.4%) ◆
Hazy, golden yellow-coloured unfined ale. Hop and ripe apple aroma, slightly sour citrus on the palate and a dry, bitter aftertaste.

Resolution IPA (OG 1046, ABV 5%) ◆
Naturally hazy, golden yellow-coloured ale with aromas of tropical fruit. Flavours of grapefruit and lemon continue into the bitter finish.

Dead Parrot

44 Garden Street, Sheffield, South Yorkshire, S1 4BJ

Established in 2018. An on-site taproom is planned.

Deben Peninsular

9 Rendlesham Mews, Rendlesham, Woodbridge, Suffolk, IP12 2SZ ☎ 07825 670865 🌐 redwalds.co.uk

Nanobrewery a few doors down from the owner's micropub, Redwalds Ale House.

Deeply Vale

Unit 25, Peel Industrial Estate, Chamberhall Street, Bury, BL9 0LU
☎ (0161) 761 7334 ☎ 07749 856043
🌐 deeplyvalebrewery.com

Deeply Vale is a family-run business established in 2012. The brewery's name immortalises the Deeply Vale area near Bury, famed for legendary 1970s music festivals. The range of traditional beers with a modern twist produced from the 6-barrel plant are distributed throughout North West England and West Yorkshire. ♦RAIB

Equilibrium (OG 1036, ABV 3.8%)
A finely-balanced golden ale. A malty base topped with just the right amount of bitterness.

Hop (OG 1036, ABV 3.8%)
A session bitter, pale gold in colour, complex in flavour.

Obsession (ABV 3.9%)
A malty session ale.

Citra Storm (OG 1038, ABV 4%)
Refreshing pale ale, bursting with the flavours and aromas of lemon and grapefruit.

Discovery (ABV 4%)
Smooth, easy-drinking, malty and bitter beer.

Ripper (OG 1038, ABV 4%)
A New Zealand-style pale ale, clean and fresh-tasting with hints of peaches and apricots.

Optimum (ABV 4.2%)
Classic golden-coloured best bitter. Satisfying bitterness and a slight caramel taste topped off with a subtle aroma of tropical fruit.

Deeply Blonde (OG 1043, ABV 4.5%)
An easy-drinking with a citrus and tropical fruit explosion.

DV8 (OG 1050, ABV 4.8%) ◆
Supple, fruity sweetness, accompanying luscious coffee roast. Clean, gentle malt finish, with lingering sweetness. Coffee and raisin aroma.

Deeside

The Steading Lochton of Leys, Lochton of Leys, Banchory, AB31 5QB
☎ (01330) 825598 🌐 deesidebrewery.co.uk

First established in 2005, a change of ownership and location in 2012 led to substantial growth in the Scottish retail sector as well as export markets in Europe, USA, the Middle East and Asia, while maintaining its independent status. RAIB

APA (OG 1038, ABV 3.8%) ◆
Light, citrus, hoppy session ale.

Blonde (OG 1038, ABV 3.8%) ◆
Grapefruit hoppy bitter, with a slight malt background.

Macbeth (OG 1042, ABV 4.1%) ◆
Roasted malt and hops coming through in the taste in this best bitter.

80/- (OG 1048, ABV 4.5%) ◆
Sweet malty brew in the traditional Scottish 80/- style.

IPA (OG 1054, ABV 5.2%) ◆
Slightly sweet, with a mix of malt and hops, and a slight raspberry background.

Denbigh

Crown Workshop, Crown Lane, Denbigh, LL16 3SY
☎ (0174) 817021 ☎ 07850 687701
🌐 bragdybinbych.co.uk

Brewing commenced in 2012 at the rear of the Hope & Anchor pub, relocating in 2015 to a dedicated brew house in the town. Output is cask and bottle in equal proportions. A tied micro pub, Y-Goron-Fach, is located next to the brewery. ♦RAIB

Dent SIBA

Hollins, Cowgill, Dent, Cumbria, LA10 5TQ
☎ (01539) 625326 🌐 dentbrewery.co.uk

Dent was set up in 1990 in a converted barn next to a former farmhouse in the Yorkshire Dales National Park. In 2005 the brewery was completely refurbished and capacity expanded. One pub is owned. More than 150 outlets are supplied direct. !!

Golden Fleece (OG 1035, ABV 3.7%) ◆
Light, hoppy and fruity, with a bitter aftertaste.

Dent Station Porter (OG 1042, ABV 3.8%) ◆
A veritable malt feast for the strength. A complex porter ending with roast highlights.

Aviator (OG 1039, ABV 4%) ◆
This amber-coloured ale is characterised by citrus, caramel and hop flavours that evolve into a bitter finish.

Rambrau (OG 1042, ABV 4.5%)
A clean, crisp and refreshing cask-conditioned lager.

Ramsbottom Strong Ale (OG 1042, ABV 4.5%) ◆
A well-balanced, malty best bitter.

Kamikaze (OG 1047, ABV 5%) ◆

Hops and fruit dominate this full-bodied, golden, strong bitter, with a dry bitterness growing in the aftertaste.

T'owd Tup (OG 1056, ABV 6%) ◆
A rich, full-flavoured, strong stout with a coffee aroma. The dominant roast character is balanced by a warming sweetness and a raisin, fruitcake taste that lingers into the finish.

Derby SIBA

Masons Place Business Park, Nottingham Road, Derby, DE21 6AQ
☎ (01332) 365366 ☎ 07887 556788
derbybrewing.co.uk

A family-run microbrewery, established in 2004 in the old Masons paintworks varnish shed by Trevor Harris, founder and former brewer at the Brunswick Inn, Derby (qv). The business has grown over the years and four venues are now owned across Derbyshire and Staffordshire. More than 400 outlets are supplied including major retailers. In addition to the core range there are at least three new beers each month. !! ♦

Hop Till You Drop (OG 1039, ABV 3.9%)
Blonde beer with fruity overtones and dry finish.

Triple Hop (OG 1041, ABV 4.1%)

Business As Usual (OG 1044, ABV 4.4%)
An easy-drinking, copper-coloured beer, well-balanced, smooth and malty with a satisfying finish.

Double Mash (OG 1046, ABV 4.6%)

Penny's Porter (OG 1046, ABV 4.6%)
A rich, dark-coloured beer with a fine hop balance.

Dashingly Dark (OG 1048, ABV 4.8%)
A smooth, dark-coloured beer with complex flavours and a chocolate roasted finish.

Mercia IPA (OG 1050, ABV 5%)

Quintessential (OG 1058, ABV 5.8%)
Complex and well-rounded with fruit and citrus flavours.

Derventio SIBA

The Brew Shed, Darley Abbey Mills, Darley Abbey, Derbyshire, DE22 1DZ
☎ (01332) 380199 ☎ Pete:07975 944242
derventiobrewery.co.uk

Established in 2005 and commercial brewing in 2006 at Trusley Brook Farm, Derventio moved to a Grade I listed mill complex in 2011, which is part of the Derwent Valley Mills World Heritage site. During 2019 a change in ownership took place with Nine Reigns taking over the company. Pete and John continue to brew the beers so there is no change to the award-winning recipes, just more inspiration and wider distribution of bottled beers. !! ♦

Gold (OG 1040.7, ABV 4.2%)
A pale bitter with subtle character and a hoppy finish, with lemon and pine notes.

Cleopatra (OG 1048.4, ABV 5%)
A complex beer with a hint of apricot.

Barbarian Stout (OG 1053.3, ABV 5.5%)
Dark, smooth, with a lingering finish of a subtle hop character.

Lucretius (ABV 5.5%)
Cherry-flavoured stout.

Derwent

Units 2a-2c, Station Road Industrial Estate, Silloth, Cumbria, CA7 4AG
☎ (01697) 331522 derwentbrewery.co.uk

Derwent was set up in 1996 in Cockermouth and moved to Silloth in 1998. Owners Mark and Allie Johnston bought the brewery in 2013. ♦RAIB

Cote Light (OG 1034, ABV 3.6%)
A pale-coloured, easy-drinking ale.

Carlisle State Bitter (OG 1036, ABV 3.7%) ◆
Malty, biscuity, hoppy beer with a gold colour.

W&M Mild (OG 1036, ABV 3.7%)
A dark mild with hints of fruit, a chocolate/caramel body and a nutty malt finish.

Parsons Pledge (OG 1039, ABV 4%) ◆
Amber-coloured ale with a biscuity tang, and a slightly fruity finish.

Blonde (OG 1039, ABV 4.2%)

Hudson Bay (OG 1043, ABV 4.2%)
A golden-coloured, hoppy pale ale.

Reaper (OG 1042, ABV 4.3%)
A dark ruby-coloured, well-hopped ale.

Mutineer (OG 1043, ABV 4.4%)
Golden amber-coloured ale with hints of caramel and a rich mouthfeel.

W&M Pale Ale (OG 1042, ABV 4.4%) ◆
A sweet, fruity, hoppy beer with a bitter finish.

Silloth Porter (OG 1046, ABV 4.5%)
A rich, dark-coloured porter with hints of chocolate and orange.

Grune Point (OG 1045, ABV 4.6%)
A single-hopped pale ale, full of citrus aroma and flavour.

Marshall Port Stout (OG 1054, ABV 5.2%)
Half a bottle of fine ruby port into each firkin makes for a smooth, dark-coloured ale.

Deva Craft

See Top Rope

Deviant & Dandy

Arch 165, Nursery Road, Hackney, London, E9 6PB
deviantanddandy.com

Initially cuckoo brewed at Enfield Brewery for the Off Broadway bar in London Fields, brewing started at its current premises in 2018. Beer is available in bars and bottle shops and at the on-site taproom, open at the weekend. No real ale.

Devil's Dyke

See Arran

Devon

Mansfield Arms, 7 Main Street, Sauchie, FK10 3JR
☎ (01259) 722020 devonales.com

Established in 1992 to produce cask ales for the Mansfield Arms, Sauchie, Devon is the oldest

THE BREWERIES

operating brewery in the county. A second pub, the Inn at Muckhart, was purchased in 1994 and the only beers sold there are from the Devon Ales brewery. The brewery also sells beer to the open market. ‼

Devon Earth SIBA

Buckfastleigh, Devon ☎ 07927 397871

Office: 7 Fernham Terrace, Torquay Road, Paignton, TQ3 2AQ ✉ info@devonearthbrewery.co.uk

Devon Earth brewery is located on the banks of the River Dart on the edge of Dartmoor and is run on a part-time basis. The brewery is proud to support local charities and supplies local and national beer festivals and free houses. ♦

Devon Earth (OG 1042, ABV 4.2%)
A light, refreshing summer ale with a bitter finish.

Grounded (OG 1047, ABV 4.7%)
A well-rounded, traditional session ale.

Lost in the Woods (OG 1052, ABV 5.2%)
A dark, full-flavoured porter, with roasted malt flavours and a touch of liquorice.

Devon's Own

See Clearwater

DEYA

33-34 Lansdown Industrial Estate, Gloucester Road, Cheltenham, Gloucestershire, GL51 8PL
☎ (01242) 269189 ☎ 07887 537356
deyabrewing.com

DEYA Brewing Company was established in 2016. It brews innovative, hop-forward beers, all of which are unfiltered, unfined and unpasteurised and available in keg and cans, with occasional casks. The taproom is open Thursday to Sunday. Expansion plans are underway and a range of barrel-aged beers is being developed.

Dhillon's SIBA

14a Hales Industrial Estate, Rowleys Green Lane, Longford, West Midlands, CV6 6AL
☎ (024) 7666 7413 dhillonsbrewery.com

Originally named Lion Heart, the brewery was established in 2014. It relaunched as Dhillon's in 2016 with a new range of beers brewed on a five-barrel plant. The main focus is on craft bottled beers but cask ales are also brewed. The Brewery Tap is open Friday evenings and before rugby and football matches at the nearby Ricoh Arena. ♦

Bright Eyes GPA (ABV 3.8%)

The Ambler Gambler (OG 1048, ABV 4.5%)

Red Rebel IPA (ABV 6.2%)

Dig

43 River Street, Digbeth, Birmingham, B5 5SA
☎ (0121) 773 2111

Dig Brew Company is a craft brewing project founded by Oliver Webb and Peter Towler of Mad O'Rourkes Pie Factory. The brewery and taproom is housed within a repurposed industrial unit in Digbeth, Birmingham.

Digfield SIBA

Lilford Lodge Farm, Barnwell, Northamptonshire, PE8 5SA
☎ (01832) 273954 digfield-ales.co.uk

Digfield Ales started brewing in 2005 and has continually expanded brewing capacity to keep up with demand. In 2012 they moved to a larger premises near Barnwell, where a reed bed was installed and the brewhouse was equiped with a new 15-barrel plant. More than 40 free houses are supplied. ♦

Fools Nook (OG 1037, ABV 3.8%)
Lavender and honey dominate the floral aroma and belies the hoppy bitterness that comes through in the taste of this golden ale. A fruity balance lasts.

Chiffchaff (OG 1038, ABV 3.9%)
An amber gold-coloured pale ale with a distinct, hoppy aroma.

Barnwell Bitter (OG 1039, ABV 4%)
A fruity aroma, and a sharp bitterness balanced by dry, biscuity malt.

Old Crow Porter (OG 1042, ABV 4.3%)
A rich, full-bodied porter with a balanced, roasted malt finish.

Shacklebush (OG 1044, ABV 4.5%)
Amber-coloured, with malt and hop on the nose which develops on the palate, complemented by a mounting bitterness. Dry finish with lingering malt notes.

Mad Monk (OG 1047, ABV 4.8%)
Fruity beer with bitter, earthy hops in evidence.

Dock Beer

See Axholme

Dog & Rabbit

Dog & Rabbit Micro Brew Pub, 36 Park View, Whitley Bay, Tyne & Wear, NE26 2TH ☎ 07944 552716 dogandrabbitbrewery.co.uk

The Dog & Rabbit Brewery was established in 2015 and relocated to new premises as a small one-barrel micro brewpub in 2016. Extra fermenters are planned. RAIB

Dog's Window

8 Nant-Yr-Adar, Llangewydd Court, Bridgend, CF31 4TY ☎ 07929 292930
✉ info@dogswindowbrewery.com

Dog's Window is a small batch brewery, which started production in 2018. It has a core range of eight beers with an ever-changing list of limited editions under the banner of the Experimental Series. The mainstay of production is bottle-conditioned beers, with the occasional keg. Bottles are available direct to the public by appointment (see website). ♦ RAIB

Dogbreath

52 Hyde Lane, Kinver, Staffordshire, DY7 6AF
☎ 07729121362 dogbreathbrewery.co.uk

Brewing began in 2016 using a 350-litre brew plant. Production is mainly bottled although a small number of cask-conditioned ales are available.

Doghouse SIBA

Unit 6 Watery Lane Industrial Estate, Watery Lane, Darwen, Lancashire, BB3 2EB
☎ (01254) 366338 ☎ 07860 913679
doghousebrewery.co.uk

First brewed in 2016 having purchased the equipment from the brewery of the same name based in the Isle of Man.

Cappuccino Stout (ABV 4%)
Dark and packed with roasted malt. Added lactose gives a smooth, cappuccino effect.

Cats Whiskers (ABV 4%)
A classic milk stout, smooth and rounded.

Centennial (ABV 4%)
A session ale, bitter and very moreish.

Citra (ABV 4%)
A citric, light pale ale.

UPA (ABV 4%)
Light session ale.

Mosaic (ABV 4.2%)
Full-bodied, darker pale ale.

Chinook (ABV 4.4%)
Single-hopped pale ale.

Pale Ale (OG 1045, ABV 4.6%)
A light gold-coloured ale, with floral, citrus, hoppy aromas and citrus and soft fruit taste.

Ekuanot (ABV 5%)
Strong and dry pale ale.

New England IPA (ABV 5%)
Very hoppy pale ale.

IPA (ABV 5.5%)
A true IPA, hoppy and bitter.

Dominion

c/o Red Fox Brewery, Upp Hall Farm, Salmons Lane, Coggeshall, Essex, CO6 1RY

Office: Queen Street Brewhouse, Colchester, Essex, CO1 2PG dominionbrewerycompany.com

Dominion Brewery was established in 2012 by Andy Skene. He was renting the premises and Pitfield brand names from the founder of Pitfield, Martin Kemp. In 2018 Dominion Brewery moved and is now using spare capacity at Red Fox Brewery. Dominion beers are available in cask, natural-conditioned keg and bottle, and are vegan. RAIB V

Pitfield Shoreditch Stout (OG 1040, ABV 4%)

Woodbine Racer (OG 1042, ABV 4.2%)

Woodbine Racer Turbo (ABV 6.2%)
Aroma of oranges, malty sweet and a juicy bitterness.

Yukon Gold (OG 1090, ABV 9.7%)

Mad Trappiste (OG 1095, ABV 10%)
Belgian Trappist-inspired, red-coloured ale. Aged in cognac casks and deliberately soured. Complex flavour.

Contract brewed for Billericay Brewery:

A Mild With No Name (OG 1055, ABV 5.5%)

Don Valley SIBA

Unit 3, Canalside Industrial Estate, Cliff Street, Mexborough, South Yorkshire, S64 9HU
☎ (01709) 580254 donvalleybrewery.co.uk

The brewery was established in 2016 and is based in an old rustic building alongside the Don Navigation in Mexborough. Its brewery tap is open daily in Doncaster Wool Market. !! ♦

Bit o'That (ABV 4%)
Dark chestnut-coloured bitter with hints of toffee and biscuit on the nose, giving way to pleasant bitterness.

Atomic Blonde (ABV 4.3%)
Light blonde bitter with floral and citrus aroma.

Gongoozler (OG 1044, ABV 4.5%)
Dark-coloured stout, roasted malt flavours with hints of citrus and honey.

Go Your Own Way (ABV 5%)
Golden-coloured IPA with undertones of sweet caramel and tropical citrus aromas.

Doncaster

7 Young Street, Doncaster, South Yorkshire, DN1 3EL
☎ (01302) 376436 ☎ 07921 970941
doncasterbrewery.co.uk

Established in 2012 and initially based at an industrial unit in Kirk Sandall, Doncaster, the brewery moved to new premises in 2014 using a 15-barrel plant, and opened a micropub taproom. ♦

Sand House (OG 1038, ABV 3.8%)
Golden straw-coloured beer with a citrus aroma and a refreshing, tangy bitter flavour.

Cheswold (OG 1042, ABV 4.2%)
A fruity and spicy aroma with a lingering spicy bitter finish define this deep copper-coloured beer.

Donkeystone SIBA

Units 17-18, Boarshurst Business Park, Boarshurst Lane, Greenfield, OL3 7ER
☎ (01457) 238710 donkeystonebrewing.co.uk

Donkeystone is a 10-barrel brewery set up in 2017 at the edge of the Peak District National Park featuring an on-site brewery tap. Former homebrewers Richard Thomas and Stephen James use a custom-built stainless steel plant supplied by Oban Ales. Brewing for the Pickled Pheasant, Holmbridge since 2019. !! ♦

Hoppinsesh (OG 1041, ABV 3.7%)
Crisp, clean, full-bodied, hoppy session beer.

APA (OG 1042.5, ABV 3.8%)

Bad Ass Blonde (OG 1039, ABV 3.8%)

Bray (OG 1040, ABV 4%)
Deep amber-coloured session bitter with residual sweetness and fruitiness.

Cotton Clouds (OG 1042.5, ABV 4%)
Session pale ale. Light and refreshing with slight hoppy flavours.

DPA (OG 1053, ABV 4.7%)
Pale ale with citrus, grapefruit and pine flavours and an exceptional hoppy finish.

Javanilla (OG 1057, ABV 5%)

Coffee and vanilla stout with a rich body and a rounded, complex flavour.

Vanilla Stout (OG 1051, ABV 5%)

Ponui (OG 1060, ABV 6.5%)
A fruity New Zealand-style pale ale.

DAPA Donkey (OG 1068, ABV 6.9%)
Full-bodied, bitter, American-style double IPA with a malty backbone.

Brewed for the Pickled Pheasant, Holmbridge:

Blonde (ABV 3.8%)

American Pale (ABV 4%)

Bitter (ABV 4%)

Donnington

Upper Swell, Stow-on-the-Wold, Gloucestershire, GL54 1EP
☎ (01451) 830603 🌐 donnington-brewery.com

Thomas Arkell bought a 13th-century watermill in 1827 and began brewing on-site in 1865. The waterwheel is still in use. Thomas's descendant Claude owned and ran the brewery until his death in 2007, supplying 20 outlets direct. It has now passed to Claude's cousin, James Arkell, also of Arkells Brewery, Swindon (qv). RAIB

BB (OG 1035, ABV 3.6%)
Amber-coloured bitter with a slight hop aroma, a good balance of malt and hops in the mouth and a bitter aftertaste.

Donnington Gold (OG 1041, ABV 4%)
A golden ale with a citrus flavour, followed by a rounded malt finish.

SBA (OG 1045, ABV 4.4%)
Malt dominates over bitterness in the subtle flavour of this premium bitter, which has a hint of fruit and a dry, malty finish.

Donzoko (NEW)

Hartlepool, County Durham ☎ 07463 863647 🌐 donzoko.org

Donzoko Brewing Company, founded by Reece Hugill in 2017, takes its inspiration and influences from Germany and translates this beer tradition, combined with techniques from modern UK and US craft brewing, into its beers. It is a cuckoo brewery that has teamed up with Gipsy Hill (qv) to produce its flagship lager in London. Other beers are brewed at various breweries in the north east. No real ale.

Dopey Dick

Skeoge Industrial Estate, Derry, BT48 8SE
☎ (028) 71418920 🌐 facebook.com/pg/dopeydickbrewingco

A microbrewery founded by the proprietors of the Grand Central Bar in Londonderry.

Dorking SIBA

Aldhurst Farm, Temple Lane, Capel, Surrey, RH5 5HJ
☎ (01306) 877988 🌐 dorkingbrewery.com

⊗ Dorking started brewing in 2008 at premises in Dorking. In 2017 production moved to a new, larger site in Capel with a 30-barrel brew plant capable of producing 35,000 pints per week. Beers can be found in Surrey, West Sussex and South London. ‼ ♦

Washington Gold (OG 1042, ABV 3.8%)

Pilcrow Pale (OG 1043, ABV 4%)

Smokestack Lightnin' (OG 1043, ABV 4%)

DB One (OG 1043, ABV 4.2%)
Hoppy best bitter with underlying orange fruit notes. Some balancing malt sweetness in the taste leads to a dry, bitter finish.

Black Noise (OG 1045, ABV 4.5%)

Lunar White (OG 1045, ABV 4.6%)

Red India (OG 1052, ABV 5%)

Buffalo Buffalo (OG 1050, ABV 5.1%)

Dorset (DBC) SIBA

Unit 7, Hybris Business Park, Warmwell Road, Crossways, Dorset, DT2 8BF
☎ (01305) 777515 🌐 dbcales.com

⊗ Founded in 1996, Dorset Brewing Company started in Hope Square, Weymouth, which was once the home of the Devenish and Groves breweries. In 2010 it moved to purpose-built premises near Dorchester. Here spring water is used in its state-of-the-art brewing equipment. Beers are available in local pubs and selected outlets throughout the South West. ‼ ♦

Dorset Knob (OG 1039, ABV 3.9%)
Complex, bitter ale with strong malt and fruit flavours, despite its gravity.

Jurassic (OG 1040, ABV 4.2%)
Clean-tasting, easy-drinking bitter. Well-balanced, with lingering bitterness after moderate sweetness.

Origin (ABV 4.3%)
Pale gold-coloured, clean, fruity and citrus IPA with a hoppy, sweet finish.

Yachtsman (OG 1048, ABV 4.7%)
A pale golden-coloured, bitter-tasting beer, with hints of vanilla and honey in the aroma and aftertaste.

Durdle Door (OG 1046, ABV 5%)
A tawny-coloured hue and fruity aroma, with a hint of pear drops and a good malty undertone, joined by hops and a little roast malt in the taste. Lingering bittersweet finish.

Double-Barrelled

Unit 20, Stadium Way Industrial Estate, Tilehurst, Reading, Berkshire, RG30 6BX
☎ (0118) 942 8390 🌐 doublebarrelled.co.uk

Brewing began in 2018 on a 15-barrel plant, focusing on stouts, sours and session beers. An on-site taproom opened later the same year.

Dove Street SIBA

82 St Helens Street, Ipswich, Suffolk, IP4 2LB
☎ (01473) 211270 ☎ 07880 707077
🌐 dovestreetbrewery.co.uk

⊗ Dove Street began brewing in 2011 using a 2.5-barrel plant in a garage opposite the Dove Street Inn. The pub, its sister pub and beer festivals are supplied. ‼

Underwood Mild (OG 1033, ABV 3.2%)
Dark-coloured, traditional mild with a fresh, spicy aroma and taste.

Gladstone Guzzler (OG 1037, ABV 3.6%)
Easy-drinking, light-coloured bitter with a hoppy flavour.

Clitra (OG 1039, ABV 3.9%)

Incredible Taste Fantastic Clarity (OG 1041, ABV 4%)
Golden-coloured, hoppy, session beer; clean, clear and crisp.

Dove Elder (OG 1042, ABV 4.1%)
A speciality ale brewed with elderflower.

Apples & Pears (OG 1043.5, ABV 4.2%)

Ed Porter (OG 1046.5, ABV 4.5%)

Thirsty Walker (OG 1047, ABV 4.6%)

Dovecote

Unit 2, Denbigh Enterprise Centre, Colomendy Industrial Estate, Denbigh, LL16 5TA
✉ dovecote.brewery@gmail.com

⊗ Also known as Bragdy Colomendy, named after the industrial estate where it is located. Owner and head brewer Richard Green commenced brewing in 2017 on a five-barrel plant. All beers are unfined and unfiltered. RAIB

Dove Dark (OG 1034, ABV 3.6%)
Dark-coloured, full-flavoured ale with subtle hints of toasted nuts, chocolate and liquorice on the palate, leading to a creamy, caramel, malt finish.

Dove Ale (OG 1038, ABV 4%)

Dove From Above (OG 1040, ABV 4.2%)
Gold-coloured IPA with bold hops and aromas of pine and tropical fruits. A fresh citrus finish.

Dove Down Under (OG 1045, ABV 4.8%)
A light amber-coloured, New World-style ale. Huge flavours of grapefruit and peppery, pine needle flavours. Well-balanced with caramel malts.

Dove Pale (OG 1044, ABV 4.8%)

Dovedale (NEW) SIBA

Damgate Farm, Stanshope, Derbyshire, DE6 2AD
☎ 07714 105035 ✉ info@dovedalebrewing.co.uk

Dovedale is a microbrewery sitauted on a farm, established in 2019. It is undergoing expansion to larger buildings to increase capacity.

Dow Bridge

2-3 Rugby Road, Catthorpe, Leicestershire, LE17 6DA
☎ (01788) 869121 ☎ 07790633525
🌐 dowbridgebrewery.co.uk

Dow Bridge commenced brewing in 2001 and takes its name from a local bridge where Watling Street spans the River Avon. The brewery uses English whole hops and malt with no adjuncts or additives. Seasonal and bottle-conditioned beers are also available. ♦RAIB

Bonum Mild (OG 1035, ABV 3.5%)
Complex, dark brown-coloured, full-flavoured mild. Strong malt and roast flavours which continue into the aftertaste. A long, satisfying finish.

Acris (OG 1037, ABV 3.8%)
Classic, session bitter, packed with flavour.

Centurion (OG 1039, ABV 4%)
Copper-coloured, well-rounded, best bitter. Well-balanced malt and hop flavour.

Legion (OG 1039.5, ABV 4.1%)
Golden-coloured, hoppy ale. A good balance of malt and fruity hop on the nose and palate.

Ratae'd (OG 1041, ABV 4.3%)
Tawny-coloured, full-bodied beer with bitter hop flavours against a grainy background, leading to a long, bitter and dry aftertaste.

Dow Bridge Dark (OG 1042, ABV 4.4%)
A strong, dark, full-bodied ale with roast malt giving hints of chocolate.

Gladiator (OG 1042.5, ABV 4.5%)
Ruby chestnut-coloured, well-balanced beer. Smooth and malty, but with a bitter, dry finish. Some fruit aroma and slight toffee sweetness.

Fosse Ale (OG 1046, ABV 4.8%)
Well-balanced, premium beer with caramel and burnt toffee flavours. Hoppy, dry finish.

Praetorian Porter (OG 1046.5, ABV 5%)
Dark, rich, full-bodied porter. Slightly sweet with hoppy undertones.

Onslaught (OG 1049, ABV 5.2%)
A deep ruby-coloured, strong ale. A good balance of fruit and hops with rich flavours and aroma.

Downham Isle

1 Matthew Wren Close, Little Downham, Cambridgeshire, CB6 2UL
☎ (01353) 699695 ☎ 07732 927479
🌐 downhamislebrewery.co.uk

⊗ Downham Isle began brewing in 2016. Artisan small-batch brewing methods are used to produce flavoursome, aromatic ales available across the Isles of Ely, Cambridge (and in Dusseldorf). There are opportunities to take part in brewery days. An on-site bar and taproom offers one or two of ales at a time (ring for opening times). !! ♦RAIB

Downham Isle (ABV 4.5%)

Downlands SIBA

Unit Z (2a), Mackley Industrial Estate, Small Dole, West Sussex, BN5 9XE
☎ (01273) 495596 🌐 downlandsbrewery.com

⊗ A 10-barrel brewery set up in 2012 distributing beers across the South-east of England. !!♦

Root Thirteen (OG 1033, ABV 3.6%)
Crisp, light, golden ale that layers floral, zesty aromas over a grapefruit and citrus flavour.

Best (OG 1042, ABV 4.1%)
A traditional and interesting malty, fruity best bitter.

Bramber (OG 1047, ABV 4.5%)
Powerfully-hopped, American-style, amber-coloured ale.

Devils Dyke Porter (OG 1052, ABV 5%)
Toffee, chocolate and smoky flavours are complemented by a subtle hint of marmalade.

Devils Dyke Salted Caramel (OG 1052, ABV 5%)
Caramel sweetness enriches chocolate and coffee flavours, with a hint of salt in the finish.

THE BREWERIES

Downton SIBA

Unit 11, Batten Road, Downton Industrial Estate, Downton, Wiltshire, SP5 3HU
☎ (01725) 513313 ⊕ downtonbrewery.com

⊗ Downton was set up in 2003. The brewery has a 20-barrel brew length and produces around 1,500 barrels a year. Around 100 outlets are supplied direct. A range of regular beers is produced together with speciality and experimental beers. The brewery offers an off-site mobile bar service and has an online shop. A regular bar is open on Friday (4-9pm) and sales are available on-site. ⊨RAIB

New Forest Ale (OG 1037, ABV 3.8%) ◆
An amber-coloured, bitter with subtle aromas leading to good hopping on the palate. Some fruit, and predominate hoppiness in the aftertaste.

Quadhop (OG 1038, ABV 3.9%) ◆
Pale golden-coloured session beer, initially hoppy on the palate with some fruit and a strong hoppiness in the aftertaste.

Elderquad (OG 1039, ABV 4%) ◆
Golden yellow-coloured bitter with a floral, fruity aroma, leading to a well-hopped taste with hints of elderflower. Dryish finish with good fruit and hop balance.

Honey Blonde (OG 1041, ABV 4.3%) ◆
Straw-coloured golden ale, easy-drinking with initial bitterness giving way to slight sweetness and a lingering balanced aftertaste.

Nelson's Delight (OG 1044, ABV 4.5%) ◆
An amber-coloured bitter full of hoppy character and a rich resinous aroma. Underlying sweetness and strength provided by the addition of navy rum.

IPA (OG 1063, ABV 6.8%) ◆
Golden yellow-coloured, strong bitter with good balance of hops and fruit, slight sweetness and some malt notes, all through to the aftertaste.

Dowr Kammel

Deaconstowe, Lower Lank, Cornwall, PL30 4PW
☎ 07774 427635

Office: 9 Tregarne Terrace, St Austell, Cornwall, PL25 4DD ✉ dowrkammel@btinternet.com

⊗ Brewing began in 2016. A small number of local free houses are supplied.

Blisland Dark (ABV 3.5%)

Blisland Gold (ABV 3.6%) ◆
Light golden ale with a strong citrus aroma. Dominant citrus and grassy hops with faint fruit sweetness. Very bitter and fairly dry finish.

Amber Rambler (ABV 4%)

Demelza (ABV 4.2%)

Devil's Jump (ABV 4.6%) ◆
Balanced, golden-coloured best bitter with malt and hops aroma. Assertive malt and bitterness in the mouth with smooth, zesty lemon hops.

Delank Dynamite (ABV 5.1%) ◆
Dark brown-coloured porter with chocolate and stone fruit aroma. Roast coffee/chocolate/smoky malt balanced by stone fruit flavour. Dry finish.

Brewards Droop IPA (ABV 6%) ◆

Golden-coloured IPA with a citrus aroma. Overpowering citrus hop with bitterness, balanced by malt and strong orange fruit through to the end.

Big Cat (ABV 7.7%)

Dragonfly (NEW)

George & Dragon, 183 High Street, Acton, London, W3 9DJ
☎ (020) 8992 3712 ⊕ georgeanddragonacton.co.uk

Dragonfly began brewing in 2014 for Remarkable Restaurants and subsequently brewed for Portobello Brewery between 2018 and 2019. Brewing is currently suspended pending a new brewing partner.

Draycott (Cambridgeshire)

Low Farm, 30 Mill Road, Buckden, Cambridgeshire, PE19 5SS
☎ (01480) 812 404 ☎ 07740 374710
⊕ draycottbrewery.co.uk

The brewery was set up in 2009 by Jon and Jane Draycott and is located in an old farm complex where they live. Only bottle-conditioned beers are produced and are available in 1pt traditionally shaped bottles. RAIB

Draycott (Derbyshire) SIBA

Ladywood Lodge Farm, Spondon Road, Dale Abbey, Derbyshire, DE7 4PS ☎ 07834 728540
⊕ facebook.com/draycottbrewingcompany

⊗ Microbrewery established in 2014, supplying local pubs and beer festivals. Relocation to new premises in 2015 saw beer range and capacity increased. A tap house in Draycott village is also operated.

Top Of The Hops (OG 1042, ABV 3.8%)
Single-hopped pale ale with good hop/malt balance.

Lamb & Flag (ABV 4%)
Traditional porter, with chocolate and coconut notes in the background.

Butcher's Bitter (OG 1042, ABV 4.2%)
Traditional bitter with caramel notes and a hint of nut.

California Steam Beer (OG 1042, ABV 4.2%)
American-style red-coloured beer, dry and refreshing, with a hint of citrus.

Piano Man Blues (ABV 4.2%)
An American-style, ruby-coloured ale with great malt tones. Clean taste and finish.

Obsidian (ABV 4.5%)
Dark lager-style ale

Tap House Tipple (ABV 4.5%)

Minnesota North Star American Red Ale (ABV 4.7%)
American-style, red-coloured bitter. Very complex in taste.

Irish Red Ale (ABV 5%)
Traditional Irish-style red-coloured ale. Very fruity.

Driftwood Spars SIBA

≡ **Driftwood Spars Hotel, Trevaunance Cove, Cornwall, TR5 0RY**

☎ (01872) 552591 🌐 driftwoodsparsbrewery.co.uk

⊗ Established in 2000, production on the custom-built five barrel plant expanded with the installation of additional fermentation and conditioning capacity. Annual production now stands at 1,500 barrels. The brewery has recently entered into cider production. ‼ ♦ RAIB GF

Bawden Rocks (OG 1037, ABV 3.8%)
Refreshing, amber-coloured bitter, with grassy, honey aromas, a malt and citrus, resin hop taste, honey and stone fruits, and a long, dry finish.

Blackheads Mild (OG 1037, ABV 3.8%)
Dark mild with coffee aroma. Silky, smoky roast malt, raisins and liquorice flavours persist to the finish with dry bitterness.

SPARS (OG 1038, ABV 3.8%)
Refreshing, copper-coloured session bitter with a balance of sweet malt and earthy hops, plum and orange flavours. Rising bitter finish.

Blue Hills Bitter (OG 1039, ABV 4%)
Pale brown-coloured, session bitter. Aroma of orange/marmalade, peach, grapefruit and floral hop flavour, and a long, bitter finish.

Booskor (OG 1042, ABV 4.2%)
Smooth, red-coloured, strong mild. Malt and fruit nose. Roasted malt/caramel, blackberry and light hop flavour. Rich malt/dried fruits finish.

Forest Blond (OG 1044, ABV 4.3%)
Light, refreshing golden ale. Citrus fruit aroma, tropical fruits, grapefruit and gentle hop flavours provide a balanced and easy-drinking beer.

Sundrift (OG 1046, ABV 4.5%)
Copper best bitter packed full of fruit and hop flavours with malt and spices. Bitter finish with persistent sweet malt.

Bolster's Blood (OG 1049, ABV 4.8%)
Full-bodied, dark brown-coloured porter. Coal-smoke and peaty malt flavour with dark chocolate and dried fruits. Bitterness and burnt malt persist.

Red River Rye (OG 1048, ABV 4.8%)
Tawny-coloured, speciality rye beer with spicy hops and hedgerow fruits. Lasting spicy and peppery finish, with a hint of liquorice.

Lou's Brew (OG 1049, ABV 5%)
Golden-coloured beer laden with orange and grapefruit flavours, with spice and pepper notes. Tropical fruit aromas give way a long-lasting, tangy grapefruit bitterness.

JSB (OG 1050, ABV 5.2%)
Full-flavoured, copper-coloured, strong bitter, with perfumed hop aroma. Assertive bitterness, woody malt and spicy hops, marmalade and pears, and a lasting bitterness.

Alfie's Revenge (OG 1060, ABV 6.5%)
Red-coloured, strong old ale, with malt, sweet fruit aroma and flavours, balanced by spicy hop bitterness and a malt and fruit finish.

Drone Valley SIBA

Unstone Industrial Complex, Main Road, Unstone, Derbyshire, S18 4AB ☎ 07794277091
🌐 dronevalleybrewery.com

☺ Community-owned, five-barrel brewery that began brewing commercially in 2016. All the brewing is carried out by volunteers under the supervision of qualified, experienced brewers. Profits go to local good causes. New owner members are always welcome. The brewery is open every Saturday and holds open days throughout the year. Additional seasonal and special brews enhance the regular offering and a full range of bottled-conditioned beers is available. ‼ ♦ RAIB

Dronny Bottom Bitter (ABV 3.7%)
A traditional bitter.

Gosforth Gold (ABV 4%)
A pale, straw-coloured beer, with a full body for its strength. Well-balanced, with a citrus hop finish.

Dronfield Best (ABV 4.3%)
Bright, amber copper-coloured best bitter, full of flavour and depth.

Coal Aston Porter (ABV 4.5%)
Traditional, smooth, fruity porter.

Fanshaw Blonde (ABV 4.8%)
An American-style, well-hopped IPA.

Stubley Stout (ABV 5%)
A rich, smooth stout.

IPA (ABV 5.2%)
Classic, old-fashioned IPA. Deep, amber-coloured, with a rich, malt base and generously-hopped giving a full mouthfeel, and a dry, bitter finish.

Candelriggs (ABV 5.8%)

Carr Lane Black Label (ABV 6%)

Drop The Anchor

Christchurch Emporium, Bridge Street, Christchurch, Dorset, BH23 1DY ☎ 07806 789946
🌐 droptheanchorbrewery.co.uk

⊗ Neil Hodgkinson began brewing in 2017 using a 2.5-barrel plant situated in the loft area of the Christchurch Emporium. Beer is available in a number of local pubs and a small bar and shop is situated in the brewery (open Fri-Sun). All beers are unfined. ♦ RAIB

Silent Stones (ABV 4.7%)
Hoppy, IPA-style, amber-coloured ale.

Tucktonia (ABV 4.7%)
Fruity pale ale.

Priest Hole Porter (ABV 4.9%)
Rich porter with prominent chocolate notes.

Fusee Chain (ABV 5%)
Full-flavoured, amber-coloured, American-style IPA.

Druid

4 Dinorben Terrace, Penysarn, LL69 9YR ☎ 07766 608889 ✉ alan@druidbrewery.co.uk

Microbrewery in the north of the Isle of Angelsey. It is fitted into a 19th century cottage that was built to house miners working in the historic copper mines of the nearby Parys Mountain and is also the home of the brewery's owners. The beers and ciders are produced in a purpose-built brew room using the latest German and British fermenters. ‼ RAIB

British Summer Time (ABV 3.8%)
A light and refreshing session IPA with a satisfying bitter finish.

Golden Venture (ABV 6.5%)

An IPA-style brew with satisfying bitterness and a hint of orange marmalade in the finish.

Drygate SIBA

🍴 85 Drygate, Glasgow, G4 0UT
☎ (0141) 212 8810 ⊕ drygate.com

Restaurant, bar and microbrewery, Drygate is a joint venture of Tennent's and Williams Bros, though operationally independent. The on-site brewery began production in 2014. ‼ ◆ RAIB

Dukeries

🍴 18 Newcastle Avenue, Worksop, Nottinghamshire, S80 1ET
☎ (01909) 731171 ☎ 07500 119299
⊕ dukeriesbrewery.co.uk

☺Founded in 2012, the brewery is located in the Dukeries tap premises using a five-barrel plant. Brewing capacity is restricted to three brews each week. ◆

Dun

Corrary Farm, Glen Beag, Glenelg, IV40 8JX
☎ (01599) 522333 ⊕ dunbrewing.co.uk

☺Established in 2018, this four-barrel brewery is named after the two neighbouring Iron Age brochs (forts) – Dun Telve and Dun Trodden. Using its own spring water and organic ingredients, the ales are unfiltered and naturally carbonated. Beers are only available locally at present. 🍺 RAIB

Dunham Massey

100 Oldfield Lane, Dunham Massey, WA14 4PE
☎ (0161) 929 0663 ⊕ dunhammasseybrewing.co.uk

☺Opened in 2007, Dunham Massey brews traditional North-western ales using only English ingredients. Around 30 outlets are supplied direct, along with the brewery tap, Costello's Bar, Altrincham. A sister brewery, Lymm (qv), opened in 2013 with Costello's Bar in Stockton Heath tied to both breweries. 🍺 ◆ RAIB

Castle Hill (OG 1036, ABV 3.5%)
Quaffable, session pale ale, with aromas of grapefruit and tropical fruits.

Walker's Bitter (OG 1036, ABV 3.5%)
Amber-coloured, session bitter.

Little Bollington Bitter (OG 1037, ABV 3.7%) ◀
Straw-coloured, light ale, with malt and citrus fruit taste, and a dry, bitter finish.

Chocolate Cherry Mild (OG 1040, ABV 3.8%)
Dark chocolate, coffee and liquorice flavours of a dark mild, with a dry bitter-sweet cherry flavour.

Dunham Dark (OG 1040, ABV 3.8%) ◀
Dark brown-coloured beer with malty aroma. Fairly sweet, with malt, some roast, hop and fruit in the taste and finish.

Big Tree Bitter (OG 1041, ABV 3.9%)
Classic-style, session bitter, golden in colour, full-bodied, with a good balance of hops and malt.

Obelisk (OG 1040, ABV 3.9%)
Light and hoppy, but not too bitter, with hints of citrus and grapefruit.

Dunham Milk Stout (OG 1051, ABV 4%)
A classic, full-bodied, sweet stout with a creamy, roast malt character. Brewed with lactose giving a sweet flavour.

Landlady (OG 1040, ABV 4%)
A light, refreshing, biscuit, dry ale, with a spicy hop finish.

Dunham Stout (OG 1046, ABV 4.2%)
A creamy, full-bodied, all English dry stout, with a classic bitter, burnt, dark roast flavour.

Stamford Bitter (OG 1045, ABV 4.2%)
A golden, full bodied bitter, with a complex blend of hops giving a slightly dry finish.

Deer Beer (OG 1047, ABV 4.5%)
A clean, full bodied, malty English ale, with a hint of toffee, and a distinct hop finish.

Cheshire IPA (OG 1047, ABV 4.7%)
Traditional-style, fairly strong, pale, hoppy and bitter.

Dunham Porter (OG 1056, ABV 5.2%) ☐
A classic, old-style porter, creamy, full-bodied and packed with flavour.

East India Pale Ale (OG 1062, ABV 6%)
A stronger, traditional-style IPA. Light and hoppy.

Dunham Gold (OG 1070, ABV 7.2%)
A Belgian-style ale, strong, light and fruity, with a hoppy finish.

Durham SIBA

Unit 6a, Bowburn North Industrial Estate, Bowburn, County Durham, DH6 5PF
☎ (0191) 3771991 ⊕ durhambrewery.com

☺Established in 1994, County Durham's oldest brewery has a portfolio of around 40 beers, some permanent, some on rotation and with new beers appearing regularly. Beers are available throughout the North East. ‼ 🍺 RAIB

Magus (OG 1036, ABV 3.8%) ◀
Straw-coloured, fruity aroma, a clean bitter mouthfeel, and a lingering dry, citrus-like finish.

Citra Nova (OG 1039, ABV 3.9%)
Massive hop bouquet, with a lively fresh, grapeful bitterness. Very drinkable with lots of character.

Pale Ice (OG 1039, ABV 3.9%)
A very refreshing, bitter pale beer. Clean bitterness and a floral aroma.

Apollo (OG 1040, ABV 4%)
Pale and aromatic, very hoppy, American-style IPA. Full, grapefruity and refreshing.

White Gold (OG 1040, ABV 4%)
Very satisfying, floral hop aroma, and grapefruit body.

White Amarillo (OG 1041, ABV 4.1%)
Easy-drinking, clean and satisfying.

Columbus IPA (OG 1042, ABV 4.2%)
Full- bodied, American-style IPA with mountains of hops, peachy aroma, and a full, grapefruity body

White Velvet (OG 1042, ABV 4.2%)
Smooth and clean.

Evensong (OG 1050, ABV 5%)
Traditional character.

White Stout (OG 1072, ABV 7.2%)
Very pale, full-bodied, strong beer. Massive floral and resinous character.

Dynamite Valley

Unit 6, Viaduct Works, Frog Hill, Ponsanooth, Cornwall, TR3 7JW
☎ (01872) 864532 ☎ 07775 570235
dynamitevalley.com

Dynamite Valley was set up in 2015 following a successful crowdfunding campaign and is located close to a historic gunpowder site near Falmouth. Beers are influenced by European and US beer styles. The brewery has broadened its horizons by expanding into bottling. It also acquired the Rebel Brewery brand name and beers.

Gold Rush (OG 1040, ABV 4%)
Smooth, gold-coloured bitter with a light malt nose. Malt dominates throughout with bitterness, honey, lemon and apricot flavours. Long malty, bitter finish.

Kennall Vale Pale (ABV 4.3%)
Session ale, with lemon and peach flavours.

TNT IPA (OG 1048, ABV 4.8%)
Robust, amber-coloured, American-style IPA with malt and fruity hop aroma. Heavy hop bitter taste, with sweet toffee apples, and malt balance.

Black Charge (OG 1050, ABV 5%)
Creamy, black-coloured stout in the sweet, oatmeal-style. Powerful roast coffee and dark chocolate throughout. Malt presence and prune hints.

Brewed under the Rebel Brewery brand name:

Surf Bum IPA (OG 1034, ABV 3.5%)
Golden ale with fruity, hop nose, dominant, grassy hop bitterness, with grapefruit, apples and apricots. Lingering, hop bitterness and a little dryness.

Gold (OG 1038, ABV 3.8%)
Refreshing, golden ale, with light, grassy hop and fruit nose. Sweet grapefruit and citrus marmalade throughout. Bitter and hoppy finish.

Bal Maiden (OG 1041, ABV 4%)
Tawny-coloured best bitter with a malty aroma. Full malt and bitter ale with apple and lemon flavours. Lingering bitter finish. Dry throughout.

Penryn Pale Ale (OG 1043, ABV 4.3%)
Pale brown-coloured best bitter with mainly hop aroma. Bitter taste, citrus fruit, and biscuit malt. Short fresh hop bitter finish.

Red (OG 1045, ABV 4.5%)
Red-coloured best bitter, with biscuit malt and toffee dominating the taste, with bitter hop and light fruit. Light bitter finish.

80/- Scotch Ale (OG 1051, ABV 5%)
Dark brown-coloured porter with roast malt aroma. Smoky roast and biscuit malt balanced by sweet plum and bitterness. Long finish.

Eagle

Havelock Street, Bedford, MK40 4LU
☎ (01234) 272766 eaglebrewery.co.uk

Founded as Charles Wells in Bedford in 1876 and remained in family hands until 2017 when the brewery and its brands were sold to Marston's (qv) and renamed. Wells itself had acquired full ownership of Young's of Wandsworth, brands in 2014; the Courage brands from Scottish & Newcastle —now Heineken in 2007, and the former McEwan's brands in 2011. Marston's supply the Wells pub estate with beers from the Eagle Brewery and from the other Marston's Breweries portfolios. Part of Marston's PLC. ‼ ♦

Brewed under the Bombardier brand name:

Pale Ale (OG 1033, ABV 3.6%)
Golden-coloured, pale ale with a hoppy aroma and notes of grapefruit and honey, balanced with a gentle, sweet maltiness and dry finish for a moreish and refreshing beer.

Bombardier (OG 1041, ABV 4.1%)
A heavy aroma of malt and raspberry jam. Traces of hops and bitterness are quickly submerged under a smooth, malty sweetness. A solid, rich finish.

Burning Gold (OG 1037, ABV 4.1%)
Zesty aromas, dry, crisp flavour with more than a hint of citrus on the palate, and a smooth, lasting finish.

Brewed under the Courage brand name:

Best Bitter (OG 1038, ABV 4%)
Full-bodied beer with a bitter/fruity palate, and a pleasant mouthfeel.

Directors (OG 1043, ABV 4.8%)
A rich, fruity and full-bodied, chestnut-coloured classic ale.

Brewed under the Young's brand name:

Bitter (OG 1034, ABV 3.7%)
Light-drinking, amber-coloured bitter has initial citrus on the palate with sweet malt and a hint of hops that linger into a slightly dry, bitter finish.

London Gold (OG 1037, ABV 4%)
A dark gold-coloured beer with a smooth mouthfeel. Citrus and malt in the low aroma, coming through more strongly on the palate and aftertaste with a little peach. Dry finish.

Special (OG 1043, ABV 4.5%)
Pale brown-coloured, well-rounded best bitter, with citrus throughout, some slight creamy toffee, which balances the bitterness that grows in the aftertaste.

Eagles Crag

Unit 21, Robinwood Mill, Todmorden, West Yorkshire, OL14 8JA
☎ (01706) 810394 eaglescragbrewery.com

Eagles Crag is named after and overlooked by a prominent landmark, famous in local folklore. Its eight-barrel plant is situated in a former textile mill and expansion has led to an large range of beers. Commercial brewing began in 2017 and the two founders both have over 30 years of brewing experience. Beers are delivered direct to 80 outlets in Lancashire, Yorkshire and Manchester. ♦

The Eagle's Feather (OG 1036, ABV 3.8%)
An amber-coloured, refreshing bitter. Piny, floral hop flavours with well-balanced malts lead to a refreshing and quaffable pint.

Pale Eagle (OG 1038, ABV 4%)
Easy-drinking, well-balanced pale ale. Light, citrus notes, offset by a touch of sweetness, giving a smooth, bitter finish.

Eye of the Eagle (OG 1041, ABV 4.3%)
An amber-coloured, traditional-style best bitter with malt and fruit to the fore, and a lingering, dry finish.

Eagle of Kindness (OG 1040, ABV 4.4%)

THE BREWERIES

Pale ale with a golden hue, its hoppy character is balanced with notes of malt, packing a lot of flavour into a rounded body.

Black Eagle (OG 1045, ABV 4.6%)
A stout with chocolate smoothness discernible within roasted malts.

The Eagle has Landed (OG 1046, ABV 4.6%) ◆
An amber-coloured best bitter with a good balance of fruit and malt. Moderate bitterness with a lingering, malty finish.

Eagle of Darkness (OG 1047, ABV 5%) ◆
Refreshing, dark brown-coloured porter. A subtle blend of chocolate malt and raisin-like fruit develops into a mellow, sweet aftertaste.

Bald Eagle (OG 1061, ABV 6.9%)
A big IPA with plenty of bitterness. Hoppy citrus aromas with plenty of fruit, balanced by the malt flavours.

Earl Soham SIBA

Meadow Works, Cross Green, Debenham, Suffolk, IP14 6RP
☎ (01728) 861213 ⊕ earlsohambrewery.co.uk

⊗ Earl Soham was set up behind the Victoria pub in 1984 and continued there until 2001 when the brewery relocated, moving again in 2013 to Debenham. Around 30 outlets are supplied and two pubs are owned. ‼ ⋤ ◆ RAIB

Gannet Mild (OG 1034, ABV 3.3%) ◆
Well-balanced mild, sweet and fruity flavour with a lingering, coffee aftertaste.

Victoria Bitter (OG 1037, ABV 3.6%) ◆
A light, fruity, amber-coloured, session beer with a clean taste and a long, lingering, hoppy aftertaste.

Elizabeth Ale (OG 1040, ABV 4%)
A clean, bitter, premium beer.

Sir Roger's Porter (OG 1042, ABV 4.2%) ◆
Roast/coffee aroma and berry fruit introduce a full-bodied porter with roast/coffee flavours. Dry roast finish.

Albert Ale (OG 1045, ABV 4.4%)
Hops dominate every aspect of this beer, but especially the finish. A fruity, astringent beer.

Brandeston Gold (OG 1045, ABV 4.5%) ◆
Sharp, clean flavour, malty/hoppy and heavily laden with citrus fruit. Malty finish.

Earth Ale

Unit A007, The Chocolate Factory, 5 Clarendon Road, Wood Green, London, N22 6XJ ☎ 07508 553546
⊕ earthale.com

A cuckoo brewery which has previously brewed at Oddly in Hampton and also at Bohem in Tottenham. It took on a unit in Wood Green in 2019. Its main outlet and notional home is a converted London bus, the Earth Tap, at Blue House Yard in Wood Green.

East London SIBA

Unit 45, Fairways Business Centre, Lammas Road, London, E10 7QB
☎ (020) 8539 0805 ⊕ eastlondonbrewing.com

⊗ East London Brewing Company is an award-winning 10-barrel brewery established in 2011 by Stu and Claire. Seven regular ales are brewed and are available in cask, keg, bottles and cans. A green hopped beer is produced each September in collaboration with Walthamstow Beer, a collective of small-batch hop growers. ◆ RAIB

Orchid (OG 1040, ABV 3.6%) 🗇 ◆
Smooth dark mild with caramelised toffee, damsons, and a dose of vanilla. Spicy notes on the dry, lingering, roasty finish.

Pale Ale (OG 1040, ABV 4%) ◆
Amber-coloured best bitter with spicy hops, bitter lemon, tropical fruits and biscuit that are there in the dry aftertaste.

Foundation Bitter (OG 1044, ABV 4.2%) ◆
Well-balanced, brown-coloured best bitter, with a fresh, green, fruity hop aroma and flavour, with caramelised pineapple. Short, bitter, marmalade finish.

Nightwatchman (OG 1046, ABV 4.5%) ◆
Dark, ruby brown-coloured, complex best bitter. Peach, caramelised fruit, toffee balanced by bitter, nutty and roasted malt flavours. Dry aftertaste.

Cowcatcher American Pale Ale (OG 1044, ABV 4.8%) ◆
Fruity, hoppy, rich golden ale with honey sweetness, mango and hints of passion fruit lingering in the dry, bitter finish.

Jamboree (OG 1045, ABV 4.8%) ◆
Golden-coloured, strong bitter with grassy and woody hop aroma. Spice with kiwi and sweet biscuit flavours. Dry, bitter finish.

Quadrant Oatmeal Stout (OG 1058, ABV 5.8%) ◆
Smooth, rich, oatmeal stout with liquorice, mocha and caramelised fruit. Roasted coffee aroma. A dry, slightly roasty bitter finish lingers.

East Yorkshire

2a, The Courtyard, Tokenspire Business Park, Hull Road, Woodmansey, East Yorkshire, HU17 0TB
☎ (01482) 873382 ☎ 07456 063670
⊕ eastyorkshirebeer.co.uk

☺East Yorkshire Beer Company is a family-run, licenced brewery with a local and environmentally friendly ethos. Ingredients are sourced as locally as possible, grains malted in Bridlington and Castleford and UK hops used where possible. Spring water is drawn from an underground aquifer. Beers are named after Hull and East Yorkshire pubs. ‼ ⋤

Top House Mild (OG 1041, ABV 3.8%)

King Billy Bitter (OG 1045, ABV 4.2%)

Earl de Grey IPA (OG 1047, ABV 4.5%)

Full Measure English Porter (OG 1049, ABV 4.5%)

Star of the West Pilsner (OG 1046, ABV 4.6%)

Odd Fellows (OG 1052, ABV 4.8%)
Bitter with a sweet and malty taste.

Eccleshall

See Slater's

Eden River SIBA

Hawksdale House, Hartness Road, Penrith, Cumbria, CA11 9DB

☎ (01768) 210565 ☎ 07729 677692
🌐 edenbrewery.com

Originally named Eden Brewery, the name changed to Eden River in 2018. Set up in 2011, the brewery is run by Jason Hill, assisted by Linda and Chris. The five-barrel plant was located at historic Brougham Hall but moved in 2017 to premises on a Penrith industrial estate. ‼ ♦ RAIB

Eden Best (OG 1039, ABV 3.8%) ◆
A traditional bitter, with a hoppy beginning, malty, bitter-sweet middle, and a gentle finish.

Eden Fuggle (OG 1039, ABV 3.8%) ◆
Initially sweet, a gently hopped pale beer, with a more bitter finish.

Blonde Knight (OG 1040, ABV 4%)
Crisp, clean refreshing taste.

Eden Dynamite (OG 1040, ABV 4%)
Distinctive, American-style pale ale. Very hoppy blonde ale with good flavour and aroma.

Eden Atomic Blonde (OG 1041, ABV 4.1%) ◆
Initial aroma of hops, followed by an intense hop flavour, with some fruitiness.

Eden Gold (OG 1042, ABV 4.2%) ◆
Gentle, fruity and honey aromas to start, lead to a well-balanced sweet beer, with a lasting, hoppy finish.

Eden First Emperor (OG 1046, ABV 4.6%) ◆
Fruity beer with balanced malt and hops, and a hint of butterscotch combining to a rich, bitter finish.

Eden St Andrews SIBA

Main street, Guardbridge, KY16 0UU ☎ 07786 060013
🌐 edenbrewerystandrews.com

The brewery was established in 2012 using a five-barrel plant in part of the former Guardbridge paper mills. In 2014 a new 20-barrel plant and distillery was installed. ‼ RAIB

St Andrews Blonde (OG 1040, ABV 3.8%)

19th (OG 1041, ABV 3.9%)

Clock Brew (OG 1045, ABV 4.3%)

1882 Lager (OG 1048, ABV 4.5%)

Seggie Porter (OG 1053, ABV 5.5%)

Shipwreck IPA (ABV 6%)
Refreshing, tropical fruit aroma, with a mellow, floral hop character, which leads to a dense hoppy body. A good bitterness develops alongside ripe, fruity notes, mellowing into a gentle, sweet finish.

Edinbrew SIBA

Unit 5, Knightsridge East Industrial Estate, Livingston, EH54 8RA ☎ 07736 680755 🌐 edinbrew.beer/index

Edinbrew opened in 2015 within a small industrial estate in the Knightsridge area of Livingston. The brewery, operated by Ross Hamilton, who trained at the Milestone Brewery, uses a 5.5-barrel plant.

Little Monster (OG 1040, ABV 3.7%)

The Good Stuff (OG 1039, ABV 3.9%)

Mid Atlantic (ABV 4%)

85 Shilling (OG 1043, ABV 4.1%)

Black Current (OG 1043, ABV 4.2%)

Citra Pale (ABV 4.2%)

CommRed (OG 1043, ABV 4.2%)

Luxury IPA (OG 1041, ABV 4.2%)
Dry, citrus flavour.

Friendly Fire (OG 1045, ABV 4.3%)
American-style, golden-coloured pale ale.

Super Stout (ABV 4.6%)

Industrial (OG 1054, ABV 5%)
Traditional IPA with soft fruit and a gentle malt taste.

Edinburgh Beer Factory SIBA

Unit 15, Bankshead Industrial Estate, 7 Bankhead Crossway North, Edinburgh, B3 2ES

Brewing began in 2015. No real ale.

Eel Pie (NEW)

Ricardo's Cellar, 44-45 Church Street, Twickenham, TW1 3NT 🌐 ricardoscellar.com

Eel Pie is located in Ricardo's Cellar bottle shop and runs courses teaching brewing on the in-house kit. Students get their beers bottled to take away. Some brews are sold through the shop from time to time (although it has been reported that these may be cuckoo brewed elsewhere).

Eight Arch SIBA

Unit 3a, Stone Lane Industrial Estate, Wimborne, Dorset, BH21 1HB
☎ (01202) 889254 ☎ 07554 445647
🌐 8archbrewing.co.uk

This award-winning brewery commenced in 2015 on a five-barrel plant on a small industrial estate on the outskirts of Wimborne. It has recently expanded into the unit next door and has increased capacity. The ales are distributed to local pubs and clubs as well as nationally. A brewery bar opens from 4pm-8pm on Fridays, with street food available. ‼ ♦ RAIB

Square Logic (ABV 4.2%)
A golden ale with a tangerine character.

Trefoil (ABV 4.5%)
Moreish golden ale packed full of hops.

Easy Life (ABV 5%)
An American-style pale ale.

Corbel (ABV 5.5%) ◆
Strong, golden ale with hops dominating, yet balanced with bitterness.

Electric Bear SIBA

Unit 12, Maltings Trading Estate, Locksbrook Road, Bath, BA1 3JL
☎ (01225) 424088 🌐 electricbearbrewing.com

Electric Bear began brewing in 2015 using a purpose-built 18-barrel plant, expanding capacity in 2016 and 2018. Its brewery tap showcases a selection of the range, including exclusive one-offs. Beers are available in cans, kegs or casks and all are unfiltered, unfined and unpasteurised.
‼ ♦ RAIB GF

Zorbing (ABV 4.1%)

Werrrd! (ABV 4.2%)

A well-balanced, session, American-style pale ale.

Inspector Remorse (ABV 4.7%)

Howdy Ho (ABV 5.1%)
An unfined, American-style, brown-coloured ale.

Whirly Bird (ABV 5.2%)

Elements (NEW)

Upton Downs Farm, Upton, Oxfordshire, OX18 4LY
☎ 07384 308670 🌐 elementsbrewery.co.uk

Began brewing in 2018 on a six-barrel plant, producing small-batch, hop-forward beers initially in keg. A taproom opened in 2019. No real ale.

Elephant School

See Brentwood

Elgood's SIBA

North Brink Brewery, Wisbech, Cambridgeshire, PE13 1LW
☎ (01945) 583160 🌐 elgoods-brewery.co.uk

The North Brink brewery was established in 1795. Owned by the Elgood family since 1878, the fifth generation are now involved in running the business. Elgood's has approximately 30 tied pubs within a 50-mile radius of the brewery and a substantial free trade. Lambic style beers are produced using the brewery's old open cooling trays as fermenting vessels. Off sales are available all year round from the shop in the brewery office when the visitor centre is closed. ‼ ♦

Black Dog (OG 1036.8, ABV 3.6%)
Black/red-coloured mild with liquorice and chocolate. Dry roasty finish.

Cambridge Bitter (OG 1037.8, ABV 3.8%)
Fruit and malt on the nose with increasing hops and balancing malt on the palate. Dry finish.

Golden Newt (OG 1041.5, ABV 4.1%)
Golden ale with floral hops and sulphur aroma. Floral hops and a fruity presence on a bittersweet background lead to a short, muted hoppy and fruity finish.

Blackberry Porter (ABV 4.5%)
A rich, full-bodied, dark-coloured porter with roast malt complemented by sweet, juicy blackberry fruit.

Plum Porter (ABV 4.5%)
A dark-coloured, rich porter with a note of roast malt, plum flavours and a fresh fruit aroma.

Elixir

Unit 2c, Brucefield Industry Park, Livingston, EH54 9BX ☎ 07760 330122 🌐 elixirbrew.com

Elixir Brew Company is an award-winning experimental brewery that produces beers using New World hops, unusual ingredients and novel techniques. Established in 2012, Elixir beers are produced at a variety of breweries throughout the UK, including frequent collaborations with the host brewers.

Elland SIBA

Units 3-5, Heathfield Industrial Estate, Heathfield Street, Elland, West Yorkshire, HX5 9AE
☎ (01422) 377677 🌐 ellandbrewery.co.uk

Orginally formed in 2002 as Eastwood & Sanders by the amalgamation of the Barge & Barrel and West Yorkshire Breweries, the company was renamed Elland in 2006 to reinforce its links with the town. The brewery has a capacity of 50 barrels (200 firkins) a week with further expansion planned. A brewery tap in Elland has been recently opened. ‼ ♦ RAIB

White Prussian (OG 1039, ABV 3.9%)
A straw-coloured, lightly-flavoured, easy-drinking, refreshing, lager-style speciality beer.

Elland Blonde (OG 1041, ABV 4%)
Creamy yellow-coloured, hoppy ale with hints of citrus fruits. Pleasantly strong bitter aftertaste.

Beyond the Pale (OG 1042, ABV 4.2%)
Gold-coloured, robust, creamy beer with ripe aromas of hops and fruit. Bitterness predominates in the mouth and leads to a dry, fruity and hoppy aftertaste.

Nettlethrasher (OG 1044, ABV 4.4%)
Smooth, amber-coloured beer. A rounded nose with some fragrant hops notes, followed by a mellow, nutty and fruity taste, and a dry finish.

1872 Porter (OG 1065, ABV 6.5%)
Creamy, full-flavoured porter. Rich, liquorice flavours with a hint of chocolate from roast malt. A soft, but satisfying aftertaste of bittersweet roast and malt.

Elliswood SIBA

Unit 3, Southways Industrial Estate, Coventry Road, Hinckley, Leicestershire, LE10 0NJ ☎ 07795 954392

Office: 24 Leicester Road, Hinckley, Leicestershire, LE10 1LS 🌐 elliswoodbrewery.co.uk

Founded in 2013 by Tracy Ellis and Phil Woodward and taken over in 2016 by Darren and Louise Lavender, who continue to brew using the David Porter 5.5-barrel system with a capacity to brew twice weekly. Beers are available across the Midlands.

Flaming Star (OG 1039, ABV 3.8%)

Hansom Pale (ABV 3.9%)

X Porter (OG 1038, ABV 4%)
Rich, smooth porter with coffee undertones.

Barrel of Laughs (OG 1042, ABV 4.2%)
Copper-coloured, spicy vanilla undertones, slight bitterness all the way through, with a sweet, pleasant aftertaste.

Just One More (OG 1042, ABV 4.2%)
A citrus flavoured beer with blackberry and grapefruit undertones.

Black Rose (OG 1045, ABV 4.5%)
Mild porter with a subtle chocolate aftertaste.

Fosse 107 (OG 1047, ABV 4.5%)
IPA with a crisp finish and good bitterness.

Nelson's Right Arm (OG 1044, ABV 4.5%)
Deep mahogany-coloured beer, spicy with heavy hints of autumn fruits.

Royal Standard 1485 (OG 1047, ABV 4.8%)

Deep red-coloured bitter with a sweet toffee taste and caramel undertones.

Legless (OG 1048, ABV 4.9%)
Gold in colour, easy on the palate and full-bodied with undertones of blackberry and spice.

Elmesthorpe

Church Farm, Station Road, Elmesthorpe, Leicestershire, LE9 7SG ☎ 07754 321283

Brewing began in 2017.

Elmtree SIBA

Unit 10, Oakwood Industrial Estate, Harling Road, Snetterton, Norfolk, NR16 2JU
☎ (01953) 887065 🌐 elmtreebeers.co.uk

⊗ Established in 2007, Elmtree brews on a six-barrel plant. More than 120 free trade outlets are supplied directly. The brewery specialises in high quality ales made with the best ingredients. All the dark cask beers, and all the bottled beers, are suitable for vegans. Some of the strongest beers are only available in bottled-conditioned form. Bespoke beers for individual pubs are also brewed. !! ♦ RAIB V

Burston's Cuckoo (OG 1038, ABV 3.8%) ◆
Gentle malt airs. Biscuity sweet beginning with delicate lime hints. Full-bodied, short, sweet finish.

Bitter (OG 1041, ABV 4.2%)
A well-balanced, copper-coloured, crisp beer. Early malt notes give way to a complex, hoppy finish.

Norfolk's 80 Shilling Ale (OG 1044, ABV 4.5%) ◆
Mixed fruit aroma, sweet, fruity, bitter balanced taste. Short, dry finish.

Dark Horse Stout (OG 1050, ABV 5%) ◆
Solid coffee and malt aroma. Vanilla, dark chocolate, and roast, with a sweet foundation. Long, strong finale.

Golden Pale Ale (OG 1048, ABV 5%) ◆
Full-bodied, with a swirling malty aroma. Lime fruit adds depth to the sweet, malty character. Short, sweetening finish.

Nightlight Mild (OG 1057, ABV 5.7%) ◆
A heavy mix of liquorice, roast and malt infuses aroma and first taste. A sweet spiciness slowly develops.

Elusive

Unit 5, Marino Way, Hogwood Lane Industrial Estate, Finchampstead, Berkshire, RG40 4RF ☎ 07917 541718 🌐 elusivebrewing.com

Established in 2016, Elusive is a five-barrel brewery located in Finchampstead, near Wokingham. It produces a diverse range of cask, KeyKeg and bottled beers. Elusive has and continues to be involved in many collaborations. In 2019 the brewery plans to expand, providing additional capacity and a Tap Room.

Sunset Rider (OG 1038, ABV 3.8%)

Sphere of Destiny (OG 1044, ABV 4.4%)
An American-style IPA with rotating hop varieties.

Level Up (OG 1051, ABV 5%)
An American-style, red-coloured ale, with rotating hop varieties.

Overdrive (OG 1054, ABV 5.5%)
An American-style pale ale, with rotating hop varieties.

Empire SIBA

The Old Boiler House, Unit 33, Upper Mills, Slaithwaite, West Yorkshire, HD7 5HA
☎ (01484) 847343 ☎ 07966 592276
🌐 empirebrewing.com

⊛ Empire Brewing was set up 2006 in a mill on the bank of the scenic Huddersfield Narrow Canal, close to the centre of Slaithwaite. In 2011 the brewery upgraded from a five-barrel to a 12-barrel plant. Beers are supplied to local free houses and through independent specialist beer agencies and wholesalers. !! ♦ RAIB

Golden Warrior (OG 1039.5, ABV 3.8%)
Pale-coloured bitter, quite fruity with a sherbet aftertaste and moderate bitterness.

Moonrakers Mild (ABV 3.8%)
Malt and chocolate prominent in this dark mild.

Strikes Back (OG 1041, ABV 4%)
Pale golden-coloured session bitter with a hoppy aroma, good hop and malt balance, citrus flavours and light palate.

Smoking Pistol (ABV 4.3%)

Porter (ABV 5%)
Dark-coloured and rich with a dry finish.

Emsworth Brewery

Rear of 16 West Street, Emsworth, Hampshire, PO10 7DY ☎ 07717 510294
🌐 theemsworthbrewery.co.uk

⊗ Michael and Hilary Bolt began their family-run brewery in 2011 on a 2.5-barrel plant, obtained from Oban Ales, in a shed behind an antiques shop in Emsworth. ♦ RAIB

Slipper (OG 1040, ABV 3.9%)

Wayfarer (OG 1042, ABV 4.1%)

Fairfield (OG 1042, ABV 4.2%)

Emsworth Brewhouse

Unit 45, Basepoint Business Centre, Havant, Hampshire, PO9 1HS ☎ 07828 799885
🌐 theemsworthbrewhouse.co.uk

Launched in 2015 as a half-barrel plant, it upgraded to 1.5-barrels in 2016. It was sold in 2017 and is now in the capable hands of Jonathan Khoo, who has moved it to larger premises in Havant with a shop and taproom. RAIB

Mainsail (OG 1038, ABV 3.8%)
Floral aroma with hints of citrus peel and tangerine and a refreshing, crisp taste.

Starboard (OG 1038, ABV 4%)
Hoppy, citrus pale ale with zesty lemon flavours and a fruity, tropical aroma.

Flotilla (OG 1044, ABV 4.4%)
A dark amber-coloured ale with fruity flavours and hints of sultana in the finish.

Wodehouse (OG 1048, ABV 4.8%)
A rich, dark chestnut-coloured ale delivering a smooth, full-bodied taste. A slight hint of Christmas cake.

Portside (OG 1052, ABV 5.2%)
Smoked porter with a rich, smoky flavour with molasses, coffee notes and a smooth finish.

SkIPA (OG 1047, ABV 5.4%)
Hoppy, American-style IPA with a rounded, full mouthfeel.

Enfield SIBA

Unit 17A, Eley Road, Edmonton, N18 3BB
☎ (020) 8807 1533 🌐 enfieldbrewery.co.uk

Brewing started in 2015 concentrating on bottled and keg beers with cask beers following in 2017. The beers use the brewery's well water and are sold under the Enefeld name, the Saxon spelling for Enfield. The range has been expanded during 2018 with availability increasing around North London and beyond, the beers proving popular in local Wetherspoon pubs.

Enefeld EB (ABV 4%)
Well-balanced, smooth, clean beer. Initial hop note leads to a flavour rainbow of light malts combined with a soft bitterness. Lingering, floral aftertaste.

Enefeld Iron Brew (ABV 4.2%)
A ruby red-coloured bitter, with a rich malt character that belies its ABV, and floral flavour notes.

Enefeld Speculation (ABV 4.8%)
Rich, dark, smooth, complex beer. Hops assert themselves in the finish.

Enefeld London Pale Ale (ABV 5%)
Light, refreshing beer. Hop-lead bitterness with a notable, but not overstated, aromatic finish.

Enefeld London Porter (ABV 5.5%) ◆
Ovaltine and cocoa aroma, chocolate flavour with damsons and a little apple. Dark chocolate with a little fruit that fades.

Enefeld London IPA (ABV 6.5%) ◆
Smooth, gold-coloured beer with spicy hops. A developing bitterness overlaid with sweet honey and tangerine in the lingering, dry aftertaste.

Engine Shed Project

See Brunswick

Engineer

Russetts, Burnt Oak Road, High Hurstwood, East Sussex, TN22 4AE ☎ 07841 669096
🌐 theengineerbrewery.co.uk

⊗ A tiny brewery that provides cask ales to a small number of local pubs, beer festivals and special events as well as bottled beers to nearby retail outlets. Special events include regular tap take-overs at the Coopers Arms in Crowborough (see website for details).

English Pale Ale (OG 1044, ABV 4.2%)
Sessionable pale ale, with refreshing citrus notes.

Milk Stout (OG 1051, ABV 4.2%)
Light milk stout, with a bit more hop character than typical for the style.

Golden Ale (OG 1045, ABV 4.4%)
Delicate fruit flavours.

Steam Beer (OG 1049, ABV 4.5%)
Amber-coloured ale/lager cross, subtle malt and lightly-hopped.

Altbier (OG 1051, ABV 5%)
Rich, caramel and biscuit malt body, balanced with a moderate and lingering bitterness.

US Amber Ale (OG 1049, ABV 5%)
Caramel maltiness, with a subtle hop character.

Ennerdale SIBA

Chapel Row, Rowrah, Cumbria, CA26 3XS
☎ (01946) 862977 ☎ 07918 626652
🌐 ennerdalebrewery.co.uk

This family-owned brewery began brewing in 2010 as a 10-barrel brewery in a converted barn. In 2016 the brewery moved to larger premises with plans for expansion. It distributes throughout Cumbria and the North of England. The brewery tap is open daily. ‼ ♦

Blonde (OG 1039, ABV 3.8%) ◆
A sweet, fruity, light-coloured beer with gentle bitterness.

Darkest (OG 1042, ABV 4.2%) ◆
Sweet, roasty, black-coloured mild with a fruity, hoppy flavour.

Ennerdale Wild (OG 1042, ABV 4.2%)
Amber-coloured ale with a hop aroma, well-rounded bitterness, fruity base and spicy finish.

Enville SIBA

Coxgreen, Hollies Lane, Enville, DY7 5LG
☎ (01384) 873728 🌐 envilleales.com

⊗ Enville Brewery is sited on a picturesque Victorian, Grade II-listed farm complex, using natural well water, traditional steam brewing and a reed and willow effluent plant. Enville Ale is infused with honey and is from a 19th-century recipe for beekeeper's ale passed down from the former proprietor's great-great aunt. ♦

Nailmaker Mild (OG 1041, ABV 4%)
A well-defined hop aroma and underlying caramel sweetness give way to a dry finish.

Simpkiss (OG 1039, ABV 4%) ◆
Caramel-smooth start, caramel body with sweet malt and hop bite. Fruity hop finish.

Cherry Blonde (OG 1042, ABV 4.2%)
A light, blonde-coloured bitter, delicately infused with essence of cherry to produce a Belgian-style fruit beer. Bitter, dry, hoppy and refreshing finish.

White (OG 1041, ABV 4.2%) ◆
Yellow-coloured ale with a malt, hops and fruit aroma. Hoppy but sweet finish.

Ale (OG 1044, ABV 4.5%) ◆
Sweet, malty aroma and taste, honey becomes apparent before bitterness finally dominates.

Old Porter (OG 1044, ABV 4.5%) ◆
Black-coloured ale with a creamy head and sulphurous aroma. Sweet and fruity start with touches of spice. Good balance between sweet and bitter, but hops dominate the finish.

Ginger Beer (OG 1045, ABV 4.6%) ◆
Golden-coloured, bright ale, with gently gingered tangs. Sweet hoppiness in aftertaste.

Brewed for the Stourton Brewing Co:

American Pale Ale (OG 1043, ABV 4.3%)

Classic, American-style pale ale. Creamy, smooth and bursting with citrus hops. Bold, refreshing, full-flavoured, hoppy session beer.

Epic Beers

The Brewery, West Huish, BS24 6RR
☎ (01934) 384044 🌐 pitchforkales.com / 3d-beer.com

⊗ Epic Beers, formed in 2017 from the ashes of RCH brewery, trades under two distinct brands, Pitchfork Ales and 3D Beer. The former produces cask-conditioned ales only and includes many of the former RCH brands, plus many experimental recipes. 3D Beers is aimed at a more modern market, often seen in keg but also occasionally available cask conditioned. !! ♦

Brewed under the 3D Beer brand name:

Hop Gun (OG 1043, ABV 4.3%)
Pronounced hoppy aroma. Pale fruit balance the hoppiness on the tongue, leading to a dry, bitter finish.

Brewed under the Pitchfork Ales brand name:

Goldbine (OG 1039, ABV 3.8%)
Grassy hops on the nose of this light-bodied golden ale precede a notably dry hop taste and increasingly bitter finish.

PG Steam (OG 1039, ABV 3.9%)
Light malt and faint hop aroma. Pale fruit combines with dry bitterness in the flavour, before a lasting, dry aftertaste.

Pitchfork (OG 1043, ABV 4.3%)
Light malt and faint hop aroma. Pale fruit combines with dry bitterness in the flavour, before a lasting dry aftertaste.

Old Slug Porter (OG 1046, ABV 4.5%)
Smoky, full-bodied porter with dark fruits and roast malts, leaving a short, bitter, dry aftertaste.

Epic Brewing (NEW)

Unit 2, Ty Mawr Enterprise Park, Tan Y Graig Road, Conwy, LL29 8UE

Office: Beehive Mill, Jersey Street, Manchester, M4 6JG ☎ (0161) 468 2775 🌐 epicbrewing.co.uk

Epic Brewing is a cuckoo brewery using spare capacity at Conwy Brewery (qv). Outlets are supplied throughout North Wales and North-west England.

Baby IPA (OG 1037, ABV 3.5%)
A session IPA with a big citrus hit.

Epic Pale (OG 1045, ABV 4%)
An easy-drinking, juicy pale ale with added crushed pineapple and lactose to give a fruity sweetness.

Beehive Blonde (OG 1042, ABV 4.2%)
Refreshing blonde ale with delicate grapefruit flavours and a crisp, dry finish.

Black IPA (OG 1043, ABV 4.3%)
Hoppy aroma with a little bitterness and dark malt character.

Marshmallow Porter (OG 1050, ABV 4.5%)
A smooth, dark-coloured, rich and chocolaty porter with slight sweetness from marshmallows.

Red (OG 1046, ABV 4.5%)
A bittersweet red-coloured ale; malty flavours packed with hops.

Errant

Arch 8 King Edward Bridge, off Pottery Lane, Newcastle upon Tyne, NE1 3TQ ☎ 07736 333303
🌐 errantbrewery.com

⊗ Brewing began in 2015 in an old Victorian railway arch. A range of speciality beers is available seasonally or on request. ♦

Essex Street

46 Essex Street, Temple, London, WC2R 3JF
☎ (020) 7936 2536 🌐 templebrewhouse.com

Opened in 2014 within the Temple Brew House pub. Beers are neither filtered nor pasteurised. The City Pub Group also operates sister brewpubs in London, Bath, Bristol, Cambridge and Norwich. !! ♦

Evan Evans SIBA

The New Brewery, 1 Rhosmaen Street, Llandeilo, Carmarthenshire, SA19 6LU
☎ (01558) 824455 🌐 evanevansbrewery.com

⊗ Evan Evans opened in 2004. The range of beer brands produced includes Evan-Evans, J Buckley which focusses on hop flavour, Artisan, a US-style craft beer brand, Fire-Island, a brand specialises in organic and gluten-free beers, Celt Experience and Archers. The brewery also bottles its own brands as well as bottling product of other independent breweries. In 2019 the brewery will be marketing its own traditional and berry versions of standard and low-alcohol cider lines. !! ♦ RAIB

BB/Best Bitter (OG 1036, ABV 3.6%)
A light, malty character with a dry, hop palate.

Welsh Pale Ale (WPA) (OG 1040, ABV 4%)
A golden ale, with hints of tropical fruits, and a malty finish.

Cwrw (OG 1043, ABV 4.2%)
Rich, malty flavour, and a distinct fruity palate.

J Buckley Brewer Original Best (ABV 4.4%)
A rich, malty bitter, with a fruit aroma.

Warrior (OG 1046, ABV 4.6%)
Full-bodied and malty, with a fruity flavour and dry, hop finish.

Everards

Office: Devana Avenue, Optimus Point, Glenfield, Leicester, LE3 8JS
☎ (0116) 201 4100 🌐 everards.co.uk

Everards was established in 1849 by William Everard and remains an independent family-owned company. It has a pub estate of more than 170 tenanted houses throughout the East Midlands. It plans to build a new brewery, offices and beer hall at Everards Meadows, opposite its old Castle Acres site. Work on this commenced in early 2019. For the duration of this Guide, its seasonal beers will be brewed by a range of brewing partners while Tiger and Beacon Hill are being brewed by Robinsons of Stockport (qv), and Sunchaser and Old Original by Purity (qv).

Evolution (NEW) SIBA

The Sidings, Harlescott Lane, Shrewsbury, Shropshire, SY1 3AH
☎ (01743) 465000 🌐 evolutionbeerco.com

Evolution is an independent craft brewery established in 2019.

Exe Valley SIBA

Land Farm, Silverton, Devon, EX5 4HF
☎ (01392) 860406 ⊕ exevalleybrewery.co.uk

⊠ Exe Valley was established as Barron's Brewery in 1984. The brewery is located in a converted barn overlooking the Exe Valley and Dartmoor hills. Locally sourced malt and English hops are used, along with the brewery's own spring water. Around 100 outlets are supplied within a 45-mile radius of the brewery. Beers are also available nationally via wholesalers. ♦ RAIB

Bitter (OG 1036, ABV 3.7%) ◆
Mid-brown-coloured bitter, pleasantly fruity with underlying malt through the aroma, taste and finish.

Barron's Hopsit (OG 1040, ABV 4.1%) ◆
Straw-coloured beer with a strong hop aroma, hop and fruit flavour and a bitter hop finish.

Dob's Best Bitter (OG 1040, ABV 4.1%) ◆
Delicate aroma, well-balanced taste with malt, hops and sweet fruit continuing into a bitter, hoppy aftertaste.

Fryer's Thirst (OG 1041, ABV 4.3%)
Golden-coloured ale with a fruity, malty aroma, well-balanced with a good body and a dry, hoppy, bitter finish.

Devon Glory (OG 1046, ABV 4.7%)
Mid-brown-coloured, fruity-tasting ale, with a sweet, fruity finish.

Mr Sheppard's Crook (OG 1046, ABV 4.7%) ◆
Smooth, full-bodied, mid-brown-coloured beer with a malty, fruit nose and a sweetish palate leading to a bitter, dry finish.

Exeter Old Bitter (OG 1046, ABV 4.8%) ◆
Mid-brown-coloured old ale with a rich, fruity taste, slightly earthy aroma and bitter finish.

It's Phil's Ale (OG 1046, ABV 4.8%)
Deep golden-coloured beer with intense hop flavours. Long, dry, bitter aftertaste.

Exeter SIBA

Unit 1, Cowley Bridge Road, Exeter, Devon, EX4 4NX
☎ (01392) 259059 ⊕ exeterbrewery.co.uk

⊠ Exeter began brewing in 2003 and is the largest brewery in the city, supplying more than 600 outlets in Devon, Cornwall, Dorset and Somerset. It moved to its present site in 2012, having outgrown its previous location. !! ☰ ♦ RAIB

Lighterman (OG 1036, ABV 3.5%)
A light copper-coloured ale, fruity, malt flavour, with a traditional bitter finish.

Avocet (OG 1038.5, ABV 3.9%) ◆
A lager-coloured bitter, fruity and sweet from nose to aftertaste. Slight maltiness balances pineapple. Light session ale.

'fraid Not (OG 1040, ABV 4%)
A golden-coloured, hoppy beer. A distinct clean, citrus bitterness and lasting, dry finish.

Ferryman (OG 1041, ABV 4.2%)
Classic copper-coloured session ale. Well-balanced, sweet, warm malt flavour. Crisp, bitter finish.

County Best (OG 1045, ABV 4.6%)
Premium best bitter. Rich malt fruity flavour. Smooth bittersweet finish.

Darkness (OG 1050, ABV 5.1%) ◆
Full-bodied stout. Roasted malt dominates the aroma. Complex taste with roast chocolate. Hints of licorice in a bitter finish.

Exile

See Exmoor

Exit 33

Unit 7, 106 Fitzwalter Road, Sheffield, South Yorkshire, S2 2SP
☎ (0114) 270 9991 ⊕ exit33.beer

☺This eight-barrel brewery was founded in Sheffield in 2008 as Brew Company but rebranded in 2014. The brewer is also a joint partner at the Harlequin pub. Regular house beers are brewed for local pubs. Beers are available nationally. ♦

Blonde (OG 1038.8, ABV 4%)
Pale-coloured, easy-drinking and fruity, session blonde ale.

Thirst Aid (OG 1038.8, ABV 4%)
A light, clean session beer with juicy, hoppy flavours.

Mosaic (OG 1039.7, ABV 4.1%)

Northern Best (OG 1040.7, ABV 4.2%)
Traditional-style, premium bitter with a smooth, well-balanced malty base, a rich flavour and dark colour.

Hop Monster (OG 1043.6, ABV 4.5%)
Golden ale with resinous pink grapefruit, biting citrus, soft floral characters and a long, bitter, hoppy finish.

Oat Stout (OG 1048.4, ABV 5%)
A dark-coloured, roasted, traditional stout. Initial hints of cocoa followed by delicate coffee and molasses and a silky, thick mouthfeel.

Exmoor SIBA

Golden Hill Brewery, Old Brewery Road, Wiveliscombe, Somerset, TA4 2PW
☎ (01984) 623798 ⊕ exmoorales.co.uk

Somerset's largest independent brewery was founded in 1980 in the old Hancock's brewery, which closed in 1959. In 2015 it moved to new, larger premises within 100 yards of the original site, doubling capacity. Over 250 outlets in the South West are supplied, plus others nationwide via wholesalers and pub chains. In 2017 it developed a new sub-brand, Exile Ales, to represent a new, modern breed of beers. !! ♦

Ale (OG 1039, ABV 3.8%) ◆
Mid-brown-coloured, medium-bodied, session bitter. Mixture of malt and hops in the aroma and taste lead to a hoppy, bitter aftertaste.

Fox (OG 1043, ABV 4.2%)
Mid-brown-coloured beer. Slight maltiness followed by a burst of hops with a lingering, bittersweet aftertaste.

Gold (OG 1045, ABV 4.5%) ◆

Golden-coloured best bitter, with a balance of malt and fruity hop on the nose and palate with sweetness following. Bitter finish.

Stag (OG 1050, ABV 5.2%) ◆
A pale brown-coloured beer with a malty taste and aroma and a bitter finish.

Beast (OG 1066, ABV 6.6%) 🍷
A dark-coloured brew, similar to a strong porter, with a complex, long aftertaste.

Eyam

Unit 4, Eyam Hall Craft Centre, Main Road, Eyam, Derbyshire, S32 5QW ☎ 07976 432682
⊕ eyamrealalecompany.com

Brewing began in 2017 using a 1.5-barrel plant producing keg and bottle-conditioned beers. Most output goes to its shop and events but 10 local outlets are also supplied. **RAIB**

Eyeball SIBA

The Works, Implement Road, West Barns, Dunbar, EH42 1UN ☎ 07764 606510 ⊕ eyeballbrewing.co.uk

Eyeball Brewing was established in 2016 by James Dempsey, who developed a passion for lager while travelling through Germany. Inspired, he built a brewery in his home and began to experiment. Now housed in a new brewery on the East Lothian coast, Eyeball produces three lagers in cask, keg and bottle.

Eyes

22-24 Rawson Road, Bradford, West Yorkshire, BD1 3SQ

Office: 54 Eden Crescent, Leeds, LS24 2TW
⊕ eyesbrewing.com

⊚Brewing began in 2016 using spare capacity at Ainsty Ales in York. In 2018 Eyes took over the former Bradford brewery and is developing its range and distribution, as well as producing more collaboration beers with other breweries. The UK's first and only wheat brewery, all beers are unfiltered. Its brewery tap is open on a Wednesday to Saturday. **V**

Fable

c/o George's Brewery, Common Road, Great Wakering, Southend-on-Sea, Essex, SS3 0AG
⊕ fablebrewery.com

A cuckoo brewery specialising in vegan beers. **V**

Genesis Pale Ale (OG 1038, ABV 3.8%)
Brewed using Chinook, Cascade and Columbus hops, and then dry-hopped with Huell Melon. Unfined.

Facer's

A8-9, Ashmount Enterprise Park, Aber Road, Flint, CH6 5YL ☎ 07713 566370 ⊕ facers.co.uk

Set up in 2003 by the now retired Dave Facer, it is now operated by long time employee Toby Dunn, It is the oldest brewery in Flintshire. Sales average some 30-barrels per week to around 100 outlets in North Wales and north west England. ‼◆

Mountain Mild (OG 1035, ABV 3.3%) ◆

A fruity, dark mild. Not too sweet, with underlying roast malt flavours and a full mouthfeel for its ABV.

Clwyd Gold (OG 1034, ABV 3.5%) ◆
Clean-tasting, session bitter, mid-brown in colour, with a full mouthfeel. Malty flavours are accompanied by increasing hoppiness in the bitter finish.

Flintshire Bitter (OG 1035, ABV 3.7%) ◆
Well-balanced, session bitter with a full mouthfeel. Some fruitiness in aroma and taste, with increasing hoppy bitterness in the dry finish.

Abbey Blonde (OG 1037, ABV 4%)

Abbey Original (OG 1038, ABV 4%) ◆
A sweetish, golden-coloured beer, with a good hop and fruit aroma, juicy taste, and a dry, hoppy finish.

Abbey Red (OG 1038, ABV 4%) ◆
Copper-coloured ale with a sweet, malty taste, and a bittersweet aftertaste.

North Star Porter (OG 1042, ABV 4%) ◆
Dark, smooth, porter-style beer, with good roast notes, and hints of coffee and chocolate. Some initial sweetness and caramel flavours followed by a hoppy bitter aftertaste.

Sunny Bitter (OG 1040, ABV 4.2%) ◆
An amber-coloured beer with a dry taste. Hop aroma continues into the taste, with some faint fruit notes. Lasting, dry finish.

DHB (Dave's Hoppy Beer) (OG 1041, ABV 4.3%) ◆
A dry-hopped version of This Splendid Ale. Some sweet flavours coming through in the mainly hoppy, bitter taste.

This Splendid Ale (OG 1041, ABV 4.3%) ◆
Refreshing tangy best bitter, yellow in colour with a sharp, hoppy, bitter taste. Good citrus fruit undertones with hints of grapefruit throughout.

Landslide (OG 1047, ABV 4.9%) ◆
Full-flavoured, complex, premium bitter, with tangy orange marmalade fruitiness in aroma and taste. Long-lasting, hoppy flavours throughout.

Fairy Glen (NEW)

5 The Corn Store, Heol Ty Gwyn, Maesteg, CF34 0BG
☎ 07968 847878

Office: 60 Oaklands Avenue, Bridgend, CF31 4ST
⊕ fgbltd.co.uk

Brewing began in 2018.

Faithless

See RedWillow

Faking Bad (NEW)

🖢 Prestoungrange Gothenburg, 227-229 High Street, Prestonpans, EH32 9BE ⊕ fakingbadbrewery.co.uk

Faking Bad was established in 2018 by Chemistry teachers Gareth Evans and Gordon Kidd.

Fallen

Kippen Station, Kippen, FK8 3JA ☎ 07507 862167
⊕ fallenbrewing.co.uk

Fallen began brewing in 2014 using a 10-barrel plant and now brews four times a week. The brewery has also installed a canning line. Electricity

is from 100% renewable sources and all waste malt goes to local farmers for cattle feed, while waste hops are composted for the garden. Beers are supplied throughout central Scotland (and further afield) and its beer can always be found at the Cross Keys in Kippen. ◆ RAIB

Local Motive (OG 1038, ABV 3.9%)
A session beer, turbo-charged with hops.

Oddysey (OG 1040, ABV 4.1%)
A refreshing, slightly spicy and citrus pale ale with a fruity aroma.

Grapevine (OG 1054, ABV 5.4%)
Big tropical and citrus fruit flavours and aromas develop into a lasting bitterness.

Chew Chew (OG 1060, ABV 6%)
A sweet milk stout, brewed with dark Belgian candy syrup, lactose and Hebridean sea salt.

Fallen Acorn

Unit 7, Clarence Wharf Industrial Estate, Mumby Road, Gosport, Hampshire, PO12 1AJ
☎ (023) 9307 9927 ⊕ fallenacornbrewing.co

⊗ Fallen Acorn is a 15-barrel microbrewery based in Gosport, resurrected from the ashes of the Oakleaf brewery in 2016. With 25 years experience in brewing, the brewing team is able to explore a multitude of styles and flavours whilst retaining an ethos of ensuring a proper balance is maintained. Repertoire includes traditional ales of all styles, real lagers and flavoured beers. !! ⚒ ◆ RAIB

Mumby's Ginger Pale (ABV 3.9%)
This pale ale is infused with ginger root.

Twisted Oak (ABV 4%)
A mid-brown-coloured, session ale with complex malt sweetness. Toffee, fruity caramel notes. Initially malty giving way to a lingering bitterness and a long hoppy finish.

Black Hearted (ABV 4.7%)
A dark version of Hole Hearted. Tropical flavour.

Hole Hearted (ABV 4.7%) ◥
Amber-coloured, with a strong, floral hop aroma, continuing into the flavour, with some malt, leading to a long, bittersweet finish.

Double Tide (ABV 5%)
A pilsner-style ale. Hoppy flavours and a light pale amber colour.

Expedition IPA (ABV 5.5%)
Dry, marmalade with a lingering bitterness. Initially dry and bitter, full-flavoured and complex grapefruit and citrus notes follow. Lingering bitterness.

Fallen Angel SIBA

Unit 21c, Reeds Farm Estate Roxwell Rd, Writtle, CM1 3ST
☎ (01245) 767220 ⊕ fallenangel-brewery.co.uk

Formerly known as the Broxbourne Brewery, a name change to Fallen Angel occured in 2017. Brewing began in 2013 using a 12-barrel plant. A 15-barrel plant has been in operation since the brewery's move from Hertfordshire to Essex in 2015.

Falstaff SIBA

⬛ 24 Society Place, Normanton, Derby, DE23 6UH
☎ (01332) 342902 ☎ 07947 242710
⊕ falstaffbrewery.co.uk

⊗ Attached to the Falstaff freehouse, the brewery dates from 1999 but was refurbished and re-opened in 2003 under new management. More than 30 outlets are supplied. ◆

3 Faze (OG 1040, ABV 3.8%)
Light gold in colour with a malt and honey nose. Smooth malt flavours lead to a clean, balanced malt and hop finish.

Fist Full of Hops (OG 1044, ABV 4.5%)
Golden amber in colour, powerful hop aromas with citrus undertones. Complex mouth-filling hop flavours and a long, hop-filled aftertaste.

Phoenix (OG 1045, ABV 4.7%) ◥
A smooth, tawny-coloured ale with fruit and hop, joined by plenty of malt in the mouth. A subtle sweetness produces a drinkable ale.

Smiling Assassin (OG 1050, ABV 5.2%)
Dark amber in colour with a fruity malt nose. Fruity malt flavours and a fruity finish with hops coming through at the end.

Darkside (OG 1056, ABV 6%)
A strong, black-coloured mild with ruby tones. Dark chocolate and plum aromas, with fruity, bitter chocolate flavours, and hints of coffee in the finish.

Good Bad & Drunk (OG 1057, ABV 6.2%)
Tawny in colour, full-bodied with a fruity, bittersweet aftertaste. Hints of caramel and a satisfying fruity aftertaste.

Faringdon

⬛ 1 Park Road, Faringdon, Oxfordshire, SN7 7BP
☎ (01367) 241480

⊗ Faringdon brewery opened in 2010 using a one-barrel plant with brewing on a larger scale beginning in 2011. After a period of closure, brewing restarted in 2019. All beers are supplied to the brewery tap, the Swan, when available. ◆

Farm Yard

Gulf Lane, Cockerham, Lancashire, LA2 0ER
☎ (01253) 799988 ☎ 07717 081170
⊕ farmyardales.co.uk

⊙ Situated on a family-run farm, this 10-barrel plant began brewing in 2017. A canning plant was added in 2018. The addition of four new tanks has meant an increase in capacity, enabling contract brewing. !! ⚒ ◆

Holmes Stead (OG 1033, ABV 3.4%)
Easy-drinking, classic beer with a caramel and biscuit flavour.

TVO 54 (OG 1036, ABV 3.7%)
Blonde beer, clean and crisp in malt, with fruity aromas.

Haybob (OG 1041, ABV 3.9%)
Session, golden-coloured, malty, and hints of caramel.

Sheaf (OG 1040, ABV 4.1%)
A fragrant, easy-drinking, well-balanced pale ale.

Hoof (OG 1042, ABV 4.3%)
A smooth, rich coffee stout.

Chaff (OG 1046, ABV 4.6%)
A hoppy session IPA.

Gulf IPA (OG 1057, ABV 5.8%)
Premium IPA with a tropical and pine aroma.

Farmageddon

25 Ballykeigle Road, Comber, BT23 5SD
☎ 07885442307 🌐 farmageddonbrewing.com

Co-operative brewery, formed in 2014. All beers are unfiltered with no preservatives and are suitable for vegans. As well as the core range, monthly specials are brewed throughout the year (available on request). ♦RAIB V

Session Pale Ale (ABV 3.8%)

California Common (ABV 4%)
Refreshing, session beer, initial malt sweetness balanced by bitterness. Light toffee notes followed by a lingering citrus bitterness.

Gold Pale Ale (ABV 4.2%)
A light, but well-hopped pale ale.

IPA (ABV 5.5%)
A big, hoppy American-style IPA.

Mosaic IPA (ABV 6.3%)
A light-bodied, straw-coloured, dry IPA. Tropical fruit, citrus and resinous pine, with a lasting bitterness.

Farmer's

See Maldon

Farr Brew SIBA

Unit 7, The Courtyard, Samuels Farm, Coleman Green Lane, Wheathampstead, Hertfordshire, AL4 8ER
☎ 07967 998820 🌐 farrbrew.com

⊗Farr Brew began brewing in 2014. The beers proved popular necessitating a move to a brand new 10-barrel brewery in 2016. Ecological and environmental concerns are at the forefront of everything Farr Brew creates. A micropub and bottle shop, the Reading Rooms, opened in Wheathampstead in 2018 and the Rising Sun, Slip End, in 2019. ‼♦

Chief Jester (OG 1036, ABV 3.6%)
An easy-drinking, pale-coloured session ale with fragrant, punchy hop aromas.

Our Greatest Golden (OG 1041, ABV 4.1%)
Dark golden-coloured ale with a well-rounded hoppiness.

Our Most Perfect Pale (OG 1042, ABV 4.2%)
A complex, pale-coloured, refreshing golden ale, packed full of tropical and citrus flavours, with a fine, crisp, bitter finish.

The Best Bitter (OG 1042, ABV 4.2%)
Dark-coloured, traditional bitter with a hint of caramel.

Black Listed IBA (OG 1045, ABV 4.5%)
Smoky, powerfully-hopped Indian black ale. Well-rounded, punchy flavour.

Our Most Potent Porter (OG 1050, ABV 5%)
Honey and treacle notes in a complex porter with a deep chocolate nose and a rich, fruity, well-hopped flavour. Made with local honey.

Farriers Arms

The Forstal, Mersham, Kent, TN25 6NU
☎ (01233) 720444 🌐 thefarriersarms.com

Brewing commenced in 2010 in this brewpub owned by a consortium of villagers. ‼♦

Fat Belly

Unit 8, Commercial Point, Mullacott Cross Industrial Estate, Ilfracombe, Devon, EX34 8PL
☎ (01598) 753496 🌐 thecottageinnlynton.co.uk

⊗Established in Lynbridge in 2016 at the Cottage Inn, using a three-barrel plant located at the rear of the pub. It relocated to its current premises in 2018, installing a new 10-barrel plant. As well as the pub it also supplies a growing number of outlets in the Exmoor area. Further beers are planned. ♦RAIB V

FPA Pale Ale (OG 1038, ABV 3.8%)
A fruity, American-style IPA.

Guzzler (OG 1038, ABV 3.8%)
A well-balanced, light bitter. Pale tawny in colour with a good hop finish with a hint of malt.

Ocean Gold (OG 1042, ABV 4.2%)
A well-balanced, golden-coloured ale with a light, fruity mouthfeel and citrus flavours. A light, fruity hop taste and finish.

Carver Doone (OG 1047, ABV 4.7%)
Stour with creamy head and mouthfeel. Good clarity, slight treacle, toffee and liquorice taste. Slow, gradual mild hop finish.

Fat Cat

Fat Cat Brewery Tap, 98-100 Lawson Road, Norwich, NR3 4LF
☎ (01603) 788508 ☎ 07795 633368
🌐 fatcatbrewery.co.uk

⊗Established in 2005 by the mini pub chain's founder, the brewery is based at the Fat Cat in Norwich. ‼♦RAIB

Norwich Bitter (OG 1038, ABV 3.8%) ◆
Malt and sulphur in aroma and taste. Initial hops fade beneath a growing bitter astringency. Short, defined finish.

Hell Cat (OG 1041, ABV 4.1%) ◆
A sulphurous, hoppy nose. An astringent hop character with a biscuity background, and a grainy mouthfeel with some grapefruit emerging.

Coffee Cream Stout (ABV 4.6%)
A smooth, creamy milk stout brewed with Fairtrade Peruvian coffee beans.

Top Cat (OG 1047, ABV 4.7%) ◆
A complex malt, caramel, and blackberry aroma leads into a similarly creamy beginning which continues to a rich finish.

Totally Tropical (ABV 5%)
A gold-coloured ale packed with tropical fruit flavours.

Wild Cat (ABV 5%)
A full-bodied, well-balanced extra pale ale.

Marmalade Cat (OG 1054.5, ABV 5.5%) ◆
Orange and malt pervades both aroma and taste. Full-bodied, balanced flavours, and a bittersweet finish with hoppiness.

DIPA (Dave's IPA) (ABV 6.1%)
A light but strong ale, packed full of hops.

Fat Pig

Railway Arches 17 & 18, St Thomas Court, Exeter, Devon, EX4 1AJ ☎ 07909 520580
🌐 fatpig-exeter.co.uk

⊗ Brewing commenced in 2013 using a 2.5-barrel plant to supply the Fat Pig pub and its sister pub, Tabac, Exeter. It is run as an experimental brewery, constantly playing with combinations of malts, hops and temperatures to improve the range of beers and push the boundaries. Grain liquor is also produced for its in-house gin and whisky distillery. The brewery relocated to its current address in 2018. ♦V

Tiny Small Ale (OG 1038, ABV 3.8%)

Pigmalion Bitter (OG 1039, ABV 3.9%)
Modern, golden-coloured, session ale, with a nice citrus finish.

Pigasus Brown Ale (OG 1040, ABV 4%)
Classic, brown-coloured ale with a refreshing, slightly sweet finish.

Ham 69 ESB (OG 1042, ABV 4.2%)
A spicy dark-coloured ale with a bitter edge.

John Street Ale (OG 1043, ABV 4.3%)
A classic, slightly dark-coloured best bitter.

Phat Nancys IPA (OG 1044, ABV 4.4%)
Pale amber in colour with a hoppy and fruity taste, leading to a spicy bitter aftertaste.

Steam King (OG 1045, ABV 4.5%)
An American-style, amber-coloured ale with a hoppy and fruity taste, leading to a spicy bitter aftertaste.

Faultline

Office: 87 Nower Road, Dorking, Surrey, RH4 3BY
✉ matt@faultlinebrew.co.uk

Cuckoo brewery set up in 2018 by Antoine Josserand and Matt Gillam. Brewing has mainly taken place on the Leith Hill Brewery (qv) plant. Brewing is currently suspended.

Faversham Steam

See Shepherd Neame

Federation

48 Greenwood Street, Altrincham, WA14 1RZ
☎ (0161) 696 6870 🌐 conclubuk.com

Located in the Con Club, a pub with restaurant that was formerly Altrincham Working Mens Conservative Club, this is a small 2.4-barrel plant that began brewing in 2017. Several new seasonal and speciality beers have been produced in addition to the core range.

Felday

Royal Oak, Village Green, Felday Glade, Holmbury St. Mary, Surrey, RH5 6PF
☎ (01306) 730654 🌐 feldaybrewery.co.uk

Brewing began in 2017 on a custom-made plant in a small, purpose built, building next to the Royal Oak pub car park. Almost all of the beer is supplied to the pub although it may very occasionally be seen in a free house or Big Smoke pub. ♦

Felinfoel SIBA

Farmers Row, Felinfoel, Llanelli, SA14 8LB
☎ (01554) 773357 🌐 felinfoel-brewery.com

Founded in the 1830s, the company is still family-owned and is now the oldest brewery in Wales. The present buildings are Grade II*-listed and were built in the 1870s. It supplies cask ale to half its 84 houses (though some use top pressure dispense), and to approximately 350 free trade outlets. ‼♦

Felinfoel IPA (OG 1036, ABV 3.6%)
A golden-coloured pale ale.

Celtic Pride (OG 1045, ABV 3.9%)
A light, golden-coloured, premium ale with a bright, clean flavour and citrus overtones.

Double Dragon (OG 1042, ABV 4.2%)
This pale brown-coloured beer has a malty, fruity aroma and taste. Background hop presence throughout, and a malty and fruity finish.

Stout (OG 1048, ABV 5%)
A Welsh stout, with a roast barley flavour and a rich, creamy head.

Fell

Unit 27, Moor Lane Business Park, Flookburgh, Cumbria, LA11 7NG
☎ (01539) 558980 ☎ 07967 503689
🌐 fellbrewery.co.uk

⊗ Fell Brewery was founded in 2012 by homebrewer Tim Bloomer and friend Andrew Carter, brewing beers inspired by their travels in the US and Belgium. Originally a five-barrel plant it recently expanded to 12 barrels.

Ghyll (OG 1035, ABV 3.7%)
A yellow-coloured, hoppy session bitter with a long, drying, bitter finish.

Tinderbox IPA (OG 1059, ABV 6.3%)
A strongly-hopped IPA with an initial sweetness leading to a lingering bitter aftertaste.

Fellows

2 Leopold Walk, Cottenham, Cambridgeshire, CB24 8XS
☎ (01954) 250262 🌐 fellowsbrewery.co.uk

⊗ Fellows began production in 2010 though brewer Mark Burton had been developing recipes for a year or so before. Five regular beers are available with plans for a series of special ales. Beers are increasingly visible in the local free trade.

Cambridge Fellow (OG 1038, ABV 3.8%)
A golden-coloured, session ale. Light and clean-tasting.

Gulping Fellow (OG 1042, ABV 4.2%)
Well-balanced best bitter with a spicy hop character and a dry, bitter finish.

Burton Snatch (OG 1048, ABV 4.8%)
Blonde ale with a citrus aroma and refreshing mouthfeel. A hint of wet leather completes the finish.

Jolly Fellows (OG 1050, ABV 5%)
Full-bodied, clean-tasting, premium bitter.

Clever Fellow (OG 1052, ABV 5.2%)
Malt loaf and toffee flavours combine with back of the tongue bitterness to achieve a balanced richness.

Fengate (NEW)

23 Fengate, Marsham, Norfolk, NR10 5PT
☎ (01263) 479953 ☎ 07884 960697
✉ fengatebrewery@gmail.com

Fengate Brewery was established in 2019.

Sunstone Pale Ale (ABV 3.8%)
Rich and smoky with dark roasted flavours. Sweet aromas of blackcurrant infused with chocolate malt to give a bold, well-balanced porter.

Three Threads (ABV 4%)
An easy-drinking, pale golden-coloured ale with light bitterness and a striking lemon and herbal flavour and aroma.

John Barleycorn Bitter (ABV 4.4%)
A best bitter with floral notes of spice and red berry giving way to a slight liquorice aftertaste balanced by malty sweetness.

Jamadhar (ABV 5.5%)
A strong, hoppy ale. Full-flavoured and refreshing.

Fermanagh

75 Main St, Derrygonnelly, BT93 6HW
☎ (028) 6864 1254 ✉ gordyfallis@hotmail.com

Now known as Fermanagh Beer Company but still using the Inishmacsaint brand, this small-scale brewery has been producing a range of bottle-conditioned beers since 2009. RAIB

Fernandes

5 Avison Yard, Kirkgate, Wakefield, West Yorkshire, WF1 1UA
☎ (01924) 291709 🌐 ossett-brewery.co.uk

Opened in 1997 and housed in a 19th-century malthouse, Ossett Brewing Company purchased the brewery and tap in 2007 but independent brewing continues. Around 90 different beers are brewed each year. The tap sells Fernandes and Ossett beers as well as guest ales; the former are more widely available through Ossett's supply chain. !! ♦

Malt Shovel Mild (OG 1038, ABV 3.8%)
A dark-coloured, full-bodied, malty mild with roast malt and chocolate flavours, leading to a lingering, dry, malty finish.

Polaris (OG 1041, ABV 3.9%)
A golden-coloured session beer with resinous, hoppy, grapefruit flavours.

Black Voodoo (OG 1050, ABV 5.1%)
Smooth, full-bodied, black-coloured stout with a chocolate, orange and vanilla flavour.

Ferry Ales SIBA

Ferry Hill Farm, Ferry Road, Fiskerton, Lincolnshire, LN3 4HU ☎ 07790 241999 🌐 ferryalesbrewery.co.uk

Ferry Ales began brewing in 2016 using a five-barrel plant. It is situated just outside Fiskerton, Lincolnshire. Beers can be found in the Lincoln area and beyond. ♦ V

Just Jane (ABV 3.8%)
Amber-coloured session ale with a fruity finish.

Spirit of Jane (ABV 3.8%)
Amber-coloured session bitter with a fruity finish.

Lincoln Lager (ABV 4.3%)

Golden Fleece (ABV 4.5%)

Witham Shield (ABV 4.5%)
An American-style pale ale, aromatic with a pleasant aftertaste.

Slippery Hitch (ABV 4.7%)

49 SQN (ABV 4.9%)
A pale amber-coloured beer. A well-balanced beer of malt, fruit and citrus hop flavour.

Smokey Joe (ABV 4.9%)
A classic porter with a hint of smokiness in the finish.

Ferry Brewery SIBA

Bankhead Farm Steading, Bankhead Road, South Queensferry, EH30 9TF
☎ (0131) 331 1851 🌐 ferrybrewery.co.uk

The first brewery in South Queensferry since 1851, Ferry Brewery was established in 2016 by Mark Moran and has an onsite tap room. Its beers combine traditional and historic beer recipes with a contemporary twist as well as modern-style beers. ♦ RAIB

Ferry Fair (OG 1038.8, ABV 4%)
Complex, golden-coloured session ale. Light and fruity with some bitterness.

Smokey Jack (OG 1040, ABV 4%)
Rauchbier-style taste, initial sweetness, followed by a smoky bitter aftertaste.

40/- Fine (OG 1040.7, ABV 4.2%)
A light take on a traditional 80/- style. Malty with a balance of sweetness and bitterness.

Ferry Crossing (OG 1043.6, ABV 4.5%)
Refreshing, fruity, golden ale with good malt balance. A fruity aroma and taste, with increasing bitterness.

Ferry Witches Brew (OG 1043.6, ABV 4.5%)
A reddish-copper-coloured, well-balanced ale, with a well-hopped flavour.

Three Bridges (OG 1043, ABV 4.5%)
Hoppy IPA, strong citrus flavours and aroma.

Ferry Stout (OG 1055, ABV 4.9%)
Well-balanced stout with hints of chocolate and subtle roast coffee flavours.

FNIPA (ABV 5.5%)
Juicy, fruity, creamy, naturally hazy, New England-style IPA. Bursting with citrus flavours and aromas.

Thomas Miller 1785 (OG 1054.2, ABV 5.5%)
A smooth, smoky, bitter coffee porter, with a sweet liquorice finish, and aromas of smoke and coffee.

Fierce

Unit 45-46, Howe Moss Avenue, Dyce, AB21 0GP
☎ (01224) 729131 🌐 fiercebeer.com

Initially started by an enthusuastic homebrewer, the brewery relocated to a factory unit in 2016.

Fierce & Noble

25 Mina Road, St Werburgh's, Bristol, BS2 9TA
☎ (0117) 955 6666 🌐 fierceandnoble.com

This eight-barrel microbrewery was established in 2017 by the owner of a small café chain in Bristol to supply beer to his cafés. Fierce & Noble's beers can now be found across Bristol, the south west and London. There is a licensed tap room on-site open year round (Fri/Sat/Sun), which regularly holds events and is available for private hire. RAIB

Noble Bitter (OG 1038, ABV 3.7%)

Session (OG 1042, ABV 4.2%)

American Pale Ale (OG 1050, ABV 5%)
Abundant powerful hop flavours add pine and tropical fruit to the slightly sweet malt background, before a lingering bitter aftertaste.

Black IPA (OG 1060, ABV 6%)
Hop laden aroma, initial roast malt flavour gives way to hop bitterness with forest fruits impressions. Slightly dry, bitter aftertaste.

West Coast IPA (OG 1065, ABV 6.5%)
Pine needles on the nose, fruity hop bitterness with spirit undertones on the palate and a dry bitter fruit finish.

FILO

The Old Town Brewery, Torfield Cottage, 8 Old London Road, Hastings, East Sussex, TN34 3HA
☎ (01424) 420212 🌐 filobrewing.co.uk

⊗ The brewery at the First In Last Out public house was established in 1985, with the current owners taking over in 1988. In 2011 the brewery relocated two minutes' walk away, remaining in the Old Town. The First In Last Out (FILO) is still supplied direct together with pubs throughout Sussex and Kent. !! ♦

Crofters (OG 1037, ABV 3.8%)

Churches Pale Ale (OG 1042, ABV 4.2%)

Old Town Tom (OG 1044, ABV 4.5%)

Gold (OG 1050, ABV 4.8%)

Fine Tuned SIBA

Unit 16, Wessex Park, Bancombe Trading Estate, Bancombe Road, Somerton, Somerset, TA11 6SB
☎ (01458) 897273 ☎ 07872 139945
🌐 finetunedbrewery.com/

Established in Langport, Somerset in 2016, but relocated to its current site in 2017. ♦ RAIB

Pitch Perfect (ABV 3.8%)

Langport Bitter (OG 1040, ABV 4%)
A traditional bitter, amber in colour.

Rack and Roll (OG 1041, ABV 4%)
Hoppy, very drinkable, amber-coloured ale.

Sunshine Reggae (OG 1043, ABV 4.2%)
An American-style pale ale, refreshing and very hoppy.

Finney's (NEW)

51 Wrockwardine Road, Wellington, Shropshire, TF1 3DA
☎ (01952) 412224 ✉ finney@blueyonder.co.uk

A microbrewery of a half-barrel capacity, which supplies local pubs.

Fintry SIBA

23 Main Street, Fintry, G63 0XA
☎ (01360) 860224 ☎ 07833 662820
✉ bill@fintrymusos.co.uk !! ♦

Kiltrochan Ale (OG 1038, ABV 3.6%)
Citrus, lemon, lime, mandarin sweetness from oats and rye. Spicy orange and lemon finish.

Clachertyfarlie (OG 1039, ABV 3.9%)
Mellow, easy-drinking, light-amber-coloured ale.

Firebird SIBA

Old Rudgwick Brickworks, Lynwick Street, Rudgwick, West Sussex, RH12 3UW
☎ (01403) 823180 🌐 firebirdbrewing.co.uk

⊗ Firebird began brewing in 2013 and has grown rapidly with new beers, new vessels, an extended warehouse and an expanded team. There is a comfortable upstairs bar on site, open until 9.30pm on Friday evenings. !! ♦ RAIB GF

Two Horses (OG 1038, ABV 3.8%)

Heritage XX (OG 1041, ABV 4%)

Old Ale XXXX (OG 1045, ABV 4.5%)
A smooth, bittersweet, dark-coloured ale with hints of roasted chocolate.

Parody (OG 1045, ABV 4.5%)
A pale-coloured, full-bodied and fruity golden ale.

Festive 51 (OG 1048, ABV 4.8%)
A dark amber-coloured, malty beer with moderate bitterness.

Firebrand

See Altarnun

Firebrick SIBA

Units 10 & 11, Blaydon Business Centre, Cowen Road, Blaydon, Tyne & Wear, NE21 5TW
☎ (0191) 447 6543 🌐 firebrickbrewery.com

Firebrick began brewing on a 2.5-barrel plant in 2013, expanding to a 15-barrel plant in 2014. Beers are mostly available in pubs within the Tyne & Wear area and a few outlets further afield. ♦

Blaydon Brick (OG 1038, ABV 3.8%)
Well-rounded, golden-coloured session beer. Toffee and fresh hop on the nose, biscuity with some spice in the taste.

Coalface (OG 1039, ABV 3.9%)
Dark-coloured session beer with a delicate blackcurrant taste and light coffee notes.

Elder Statesman (OG 1043, ABV 3.9%)
Dark amber-coloured bitter. Malt, biscuit and orange fruit in the taste, orange blossom and spice on the nose.

Tyne 9 (OG 1039, ABV 3.9%)
A black lager. Smooth maltiness and a hint of coffee are balanced by restrained resinous hopping.

Pagan Queen (OG 1040, ABV 4%)

Trade Star (OG 1041, ABV 4.2%)

Amber-coloured pale ale. Flavours of tropical fruit, lemon, lime and spice.

Stella Spark (OG 1043, ABV 4.4%)
Light malt and plentiful hops combine in this golden-coloured, citrus beer.

Toon Broon (OG 1046, ABV 4.6%)
Deep amber-coloured beer with a malty sweetness and nutty liquorice flavour.

Cushie Butterfield (OG 1050, ABV 5%)

Wey-Aye PA (OG 1058, ABV 5.8%)

Firehouse

13 Thames Street, Louth, Lincolnshire, LN11 7AD
☎ (01507) 608202 ☎ 07961 772905
firehouse-brewery.co.uk

Firehouse was founded by Jason Allen along with Louise Darbon in 2014 in the village of Manby using a 2.5-barrel plant. In 2016 the Fulstow Brewery in Louth was purchased and the brewery was relocated there. Beers from the Fulstow range are also produced. Beers are available in the free trade and from the bar located at the brewery, the Gas Lamp Lounge. ♦

Mainwarings Mild (ABV 3.6%)
A dark-coloured, malty mild based on a wartime recipe.

Marsh Mild (ABV 3.8%)
Traditional, ruby red-coloured mild ale with a rich, roast, full-bodied flavour.

FGB (ABV 3.9%)
An amber-coloured, session pale ale.

Northway IPA (OG 1042.5, ABV 4.2%)
Pale-coloured beer with a clean, citrus flavour and a dry finish.

Woodman Pale Ale (ABV 4.4%)
Pale yellow-coloured, fruity, sweetish session bitter with a dry, hoppy finish.

Pride of Fulstow (OG 1044, ABV 4.5%)
Premium pale ale. Full-bodied flavour with a rich mouthfeel.

Wobbly Weasel (ABV 4.9%)
Complex ale, rich and fruity in the mouth with an intense bittersweet finish.

Lincolnshire Country Bitter (ABV 5.1%)
A smooth, full-bodied, dark-coloured ale with fruity flavours. Intense bitter aftertaste that lingers.

FireRock (NEW)

20-24 Outram Street, Sutton-in-Ashfield, Nottinghamshire, NG17 4FS ☎ 07875 331898
firerock@mail.co.uk

FireRock Brewing Co is an independent microbrewery and craft beer bar specialising in hop-forward craft beers.

Firs

Station Road, Codsall, Staffordshire, WV8 1BX
☎ (01902) 844674 thefirscodsall.com

Beers are brewed on-site in the CAMRA award-winning Firs club and are exclusive to the club. The Firs specialise in unique seasonal beers and have increased production for 2019-20.

First & Last SIBA

Bird in Bush, Village Green, Elsdon, NE19 1AA
☎ (01830) 520804 ☎ 07757 286357
firstandlastbrewery.co.uk

First & Last was established in 2016 by Red Kelly, a founder member of Stu Brew (qv) in Newcastle upon Tyne. It was upgraded to a five-barrel plant in 2018, relocating from Rochester to the Bird in Bush, Elsdon. Other outlets in Northumberland and the Scottish Borders are supplied.

First Chop SIBA

B2, Barton Hall Business Park, Hardy Street, Eccles, M30 7NB ☎ 07970 241398
firstchopbrewingarm.com

Brewing began at Outstanding Brewery (qv) in Bury in 2012 before transferring to Salford in 2013. The brewery relocated again to Eccles in 2017 with increased capacity. It specialises in producing gluten-free beers. **GF**

AVA (OG 1034, ABV 3.5%)
A hoppy, session blonde. Strength belies its flavour and character.

POD (ABV 4.2%)
A classic oatmeal stout with vanilla and chocolate flavours, balanced bitterness and peppery, spicy hopping with hints of citrus.

SYL (OG 1064, ABV 6.2%)
A black-coloured IPA.

Fisher's SIBA

Unit 8, Central Park Business Centre, Bellfield Road, High Wycombe, Buckinghamshire, HP13 5HG
☎ (01494) 520038 ☎ 07789 007876
fishersbrewingcompany.com

Established in 2013, brewing at home and at Ubrew (qv), Fisher's began brewing commerically in 2017 and expanded further in 2019. Beers are supplied to an ever-increasing number of local pubs and restaurants and nationally via SIBA's Beerflex scheme. An on-site taproom is open on selected Friday evenings and event nights. !! RAIB

Blonde Ale (ABV 3.5%)

Honey Amber (ABV 4.2%)

Smoked Porter (ABV 4.4%)

APA (ABV 4.8%)

Dunkel (ABV 5%)

English Pale (ABV 5%)

Fishponds (NEW)

539 Fishponds Road, Fishponds, Bristol, BS16 3AF

Brewing since 2018, brothers Eimhin and Cillian look after the brewery while their father, Eimear, runs the attached pub. Further beers are planned.

The Old Mahony (ABV 4.1%) ◆
Malt and hop aroma, biscuit malt on the palate with a hop bitterness, which continues in the clean, lasting finish.

Oisin's 11 (ABV 4.4%)

The Red October (ABV 5%) ◆

Sweetish, red-coloured ale with subtle flavours of chocolate, vanilla and almonds and a hint of spiciness in the short aftertaste.

Five Kingdoms SIBA

Steam Packet Inn, Harbour Row, Isle of Whithorn, DG8 8LL
☎ (01988) 500334 🌐 thesteampacketinn.biz

Five Kingdoms was established in 2015 by Alastair Scoular, owner of the Steam Packet Inn, using a 2.5-barrel plant. It is situated in the harbourside village of Isle of Whithorn, the most southerly point of the Wigtownshire peninsular in Galloway and a tourist and sailing hotspot. The pub, selected beer festivals and a few local outlets are supplied. ♦

Five Points SIBA

3 Institute Place, Hackney Downs, London, E8 1JE
☎ (020) 8533 7746 🌐 fivepointsbrewing.co.uk

Five Points commenced brewing in 2013 on a 10-barrel plant in a railway arch under Hackney Downs Railway Station. Expansion has been continuous including an off-site depot used for events. 2018 saw successful crowdfunding to continue expanding and to buy the Pembury Tavern, over the road from the brewery (now considered the brewery tap). RAIB

XPA (ABV 4%)
Golden ale with strong citrus fruitiness, a developing bitterness and a sweet biscuity flavour providing balance. Lingering dry, bitter finish.

Pale (OG 1044, ABV 4.4%)
Strong, fruity, bitter, golden-coloured ale, with citrus and tropical fruit fading in the aftertaste where the bitterness lingers.

Railway Porter (ABV 4.8%)
Roasted black malt throughout creating a dry, roasted finish, softened by a treacly sweetness. Some caramelised fruit and peppery hops.

Brick Field Brown (ABV 5.4%)
Complex, dark brown-coloured beer. Fruit dominates the flavour with nutty chocolate and some sweet toffee character. Long, dry, bitter aftertaste.

Hook Island Red (ABV 6%)
Treacle notes on nose and flavour linger in the dry bitterness, which builds on drinking. The mouthfeel is creamy.

Five Towns

651 Leeds Road, Outwood, Wakefield, West Yorkshire, WF1 2LU
☎ (01924) 781887
✉ malcolmbastow@googlemail.com

Five Towns began production on a 2.5-barrel plant in 2008, supplying outlets mainly in Yorkshire but as far afield as Berkshire and the North East. As well as the standard beers a range of themed and speciality brews are also produced. ♦RAIB

Mi Usual (ABV 3.7%)

Middle Un (ABV 4.6%)
Strong session beer.

Owt'll Do (ABV 4.6%)
An easy-drinking, dark-coloured mild, with added Rum.

Nowt (ABV 6.7%)
A full-bodied stout, with an intense roasted malt and coffee flavour.

One At T'End (ABV 6.7%)
American-style IPA with tropical, citrus and grapefruit flavours.

Summat Else (ABV 7.2%)
An IPA with a strong, tropical fruit nose, biscuit malt with gooseberry flavour and a hoppy, maple syrup aftertaste.

Fixed Wheel SIBA

Unit 9, Long Lane Trading Estate, Long Lane, Blackheath, West Midlands, B62 9LD ☎ 07766 162794 🌐 fixedwheelbrewery.co.uk

Set up in 2014 by cycling and brewing enthusiasts Scott Povey and Sharon Bryant, this full mash brewery is situated on a trading estate on the Blackheath/Halesowen border. It brews three times a week using an eight-barrel plant. Alongside the core range, there are regular single hop and other specials brewed. As well as the taproom at the brewery two other bars are owned in Lye and Old Hill. !! ♦RAIB

Through & Off (OG 1038, ABV 3.8%)
Ever-changing session IPA concentrating on big fruity hops.

Wheelie Pale (OG 1041, ABV 4.1%)
Easy-drinking pale ale with sweet malts and hints of citrus and melon.

Chain Reaction Pale Ale (OG 1042, ABV 4.2%)
American-style pale ale with orange and citrus flavours.

Century Gold (OG 1048, ABV 4.8%)
A bright golden ale with a big hop presence, firm lemon bitterness and a big orange aroma.

Blackheath Stout (OG 1050, ABV 5%)
Full-bodied, fruity stout, oaky bitterness,and a big, lush, smooth, creamy dark fruit finish.

Mild Concussion (OG 1055, ABV 5.5%)
Ruby in colour with a creamy head. Aroma is red fruit with a rich, balanced taste and satisfying finish.

No Brakes IPA (OG 1059, ABV 5.9%)
American-style IPA, packed full of hops and fruity, citrus flavours. Malts add some balance to the hops, with a touch of sweetness.

Fizzy Moon

Fizzy Moon, 35 Regent Street, Leamington Spa, Warwickshire, CV32 5EE
☎ (01926) 888715 🌐 fizzymoonbrewhouse.com

Fizzy Moon is a bar and microbrewery in the heart of Leamington, brewing a range of small batch beers. Expansion is planned.

Flack Manor SIBA

8 Romsey Industrial Estate, Greatbridge Road, Romsey, Hampshire, SO51 0HR
☎ (01794) 518520 🌐 flackmanor.co.uk

Flack Manor commenced brewing in 2010 using a 20-barrel plant purchased from Canada. The brewery employs the double drop method of fermentation. Beers are supplied to local outlets within 30 miles of Romsey and may also be found in Wetherspoon pubs. ‼ ♦ RAIB

Flack's Double Drop (OG 1037, ABV 3.7%)
Classic, amber-coloured, session bitter. Hops, malt and some bitterness in the taste, with more hop and some malt in the finish.

Flack Catcher (OG 1045, ABV 4.4%)
A well-balanced, amber-coloured best bitter with some fruit aroma throughout, with good hop bitterness in the balanced taste and finish.

Hedge Hop (OG 1050, ABV 4.9%)
Amber-coloured best bitter, some fruit and hop in the aroma with biscuit malt balanced with fruit and spice flavours right through in the taste.

Flagship

c/o Ship & Mitre, 133 Dale Street, Liverpool, L2 2JH
☎ (0151) 236 0859

Launched in 2016, the Ship & Mitre Brewing Co rebranded as Flagship Beer in 2017, and primarily supplies the iconic city centre pub, the Ship & Mitre, with some sales locally and nationally. Beers are brewed using spare capacity at other breweries. ♦

Sublime (OG 1036, ABV 3.7%)
Light, session pale ale with a citrus tang.

Lupa (OG 1037, ABV 3.8%)
Sweeter, balanced pale ale with citrus peel notes.

Silhouette (OG 1048, ABV 4.5%)
Dry Irish-style stout with plenty of roasted, toasted richness.

Jar (OG 1047, ABV 4.7%)
Warming, sweet, light-bodied ale with roasted notes.

Century (OG 1046, ABV 5%)
West Coast-style IPA, solid bitterness with juicy hops.

Flash

Moss Top Farm, Moss Top Lane, Flash, Staffordshire, SK17 0TA ✉ flashbrewery@hotmail.com

The brewery is located high in the Peak District and was founded by two friends who brew on a part-time basis. All natural ingredients are used including spring water and seaweed finings which make the beer suitable for vegans. Three bottle-conditioned beers are produced and are sold at Leek Market, which is the only sales outlet. RAIB V

Flash House

Unit 1A Northumberland Street, North Shields, NE30 1DS ☎ 07481901875
flashhousebrewing.co.uk

Set up by Jack O'Keefe in 2016, after a life-long appreciation of ale, influenced by family associated with North East real ale pubs. Flash House aims to bring the best beer styles the world has to offer to the North East, and continues to produce new guest ales. The brewery and taproom are popular (open Fri 4pm-10pm, Sat 2pm-10pm Apr-Sep). ‼

KOLSCH (OG 1040, ABV 4.4%)

Tiny Dancer Pale Ale (OG 1051, ABV 5.4%)

Flipside

c/o Magpie Brewery, Unit 4, Ashling Court, Iremonger Road, Nottingham, NG2 3JA
☎ (0115) 987 7500 ☎ 07958 752334

Office: Old Volunteer, 35 Burton Road, Carlton, NG4 3DQ flipsidebrewery.co.uk

Andrew and Maggie Dunkin established their six-barrel brewery in an industrial unit in Colwick in 2010, expanding to 12-barrels in 2013 in a larger adjacent unit. The brewery opened its own tap, the Old Volunteer, Carlton, in 2014. In 2016 it relocated again to share the plant at Caythorpe Brewery (qv). With the closure of that brewery it now shares with Magpie Brewery (qv). ♦ RAIB V

Sterling Pale (OG 1039, ABV 3.9%)
Golden ale with a citrus aroma and hoppy taste, leading to a bitter and peppery finish.

Dark Denomination (OG 1041, ABV 4%)
Well-rounded, mildly-hopped beer. Chocolate and caramel malt flavours combined delicately with blackcurrant hop flavours.

bitcoin (OG 1041, ABV 4.1%)
Pale-coloured session beer.

Copper Penny (OG 1043, ABV 4.2%)
An easy-drinking, session bitter. Light brown-coloured, moderately bitter, with good hop flavours, ending with a hint of tangerine.

Golden Sovereign (OG 1043, ABV 4.2%)
A golden session ale. Refreshingly bitter, with dry, biscuit flavours, and citrus and grapefruit in the finish.

Franc in Stein (OG 1043, ABV 4.3%)
Golden ale with a floral hop aroma, leading to a hoppy and bitter finish.

Random Toss (OG 1044, ABV 4.4%)
A refreshing, light golden-coloured pale ale with lemon and lime tropical fruit flavours.

Kopek Stout (OG 1046, ABV 4.5%)
Full-bodied, dark-coloured stout with a coffee aroma and assertive roast flavours throughout and a balanced bitterness.

Flipping Best (OG 1046, ABV 4.6%)
Brown-coloured, malty, strong bitter with lasting malt, bitterness and subtle hop flavours.

Dusty Penny (OG 1052, ABV 5%)
A full-bodied, black-coloured porter. Bursting with chocolate and caramel malt flavours, rounded off with bitterness.

Clippings IPA (OG 1062, ABV 6.5%)
A traditional IPA, golden in colour with crushed gooseberry and bitter white wine hop flavours.

Russian Rouble (OG 1072, ABV 7.3%)
Strong, dark stout with balanced malt, roast and fruit flavours.

Flowerpots SIBA

Brandy Mount, Cheriton, Hampshire, SO24 0QQ
☎ (01962) 771534 flowerpotscheriton.co.uk

Flowerpots began production in 2006. The brewery is in a pretty Hampshire village, and stands across the car park from the pub of the same name. Its beers are supplied direct to the Flowerpots, its two sibling pubs, and many other local outlets. ♦

Perridge Pale (OG 1035.5, ABV 3.6%) 🏷 ◆
Pale-coloured, easy-drinking golden ale. Honey-scented, with grapefruit and bitterness throughout. Crisp with some citrus notes.

Bitter (OG 1038, ABV 3.8%) ◆
Dry, earthy hop flavours balanced by malt. Good bitterness with some hop in aroma and a sharp, bitter finish. Refreshing bitter.

Goodens Gold (OG 1046, ABV 4.8%) ◆
Complex, full-bodied golden ale bursting with hops and citrus fruit and a snatch of sweetness, leading to long, dry finish.

Flying Monk SIBA

Unit 1, Bradfield Farm, Hullavington, Wiltshire, SN14 6EU
☎ (01666) 838553 ⊕ flyingmonk.beer

⊠ Established in 2014 in a former farm building near Malmesbury, Flying Monk uses a 20-barrel plant and supplies more than 500 outlets regionally and utilises national wholesalers and retail contracts. The brewery uses only the best local ingredients including barley grown on its landlord's farm and English hops from Worcestershire. The brewery operates the Flying Monk Tavern, Chippenham. ‼ ☛ ◆

Elmers (OG 1040, ABV 3.8%) ◆
A refreshing, session beer with floral and citrus aromas, followed by an encouraging bitter finish.

Pendulum Pale Ale (OG 1037, ABV 3.8%)
A well-hopped, full-bodied, golden-coloured bitter.

Habit (OG 1045, ABV 4.2%) ◆
An amber-coloured, traditional best bitter, with a contrast of sweet and bitter flavours.

Circuit Bitter (OG 1043, ABV 4.3%)
A chestnut-coloured, well-balanced premium bitter.

Jackdaw (OG 1045, ABV 4.3%)
Rich, dark porter with subtle bittersweet overtone ending with plum and berry highlights.

Mighty Monk (ABV 4.3%)
Crisp, refreshing summer blonde beer. Subtle tropical fruit and citrus notes.

Fonthill (NEW)

🯄 c/o George, 29 Mount Ephraim, Tunbridge Wells, Kent, TN4 8AA
☎ (01892) 539492
⊕ thegeorgepubtunbridgewells.co.uk

⊠ Fonthill is a small batch brewery located in the George pub. Beers are available in the pub as well as its two sister pubs in Tunbridge Wells.

Fool Hardy SIBA

🯄 Hope Inn, 118 Wellington Road North, Heaton Norris, SK4 2LL
☎ (0161) 637 6191 ⊕ foolhardyales.co.uk

☺ Martin Wood bought the Hope Inn in 2012 and installed the brewery in the cellar. The beers first went on sale in 2013. In 2014 the brew kit was upgraded, almost doubling capacity to 4.5-barrels. Beers are supplied to the free trade, local pubs and festivals. ‼ ☛ ◆ RAIB

Jack's Ripper (OG 1034, ABV 3.4%)

Smooth, complex and dark-coloured oatmeal stout.

Rhidonkulous (OG 1037, ABV 3.7%)
A pale-coloured session ale with zesty, citrus notes.

Rash Dash (OG 1038, ABV 3.8%) ◆
Pale brown-coloured beer with a hoppy aroma, a balance of hops and malt in the taste and good bitterness throughout.

Ravenous Romp (OG 1038, ABV 3.8%)

Rendezvous #5 (OG 1037, ABV 3.8%)
A full-flavoured golden ale with fresh citrus notes and aroma.

Rise (ABV 3.9%)
A clean, easy-drinking pale ale. Quite hoppy and fruity for its strength.

Rival Blond (OG 1039, ABV 4%)
Extra pale-coloured blonde session ale. Hoppy and zesty with distinct fruit flavours.

Rude Vagablond (OG 1041, ABV 4.2%)
Pale-coloured blonde session ale with fruit flavours.

Rou Shou (OG 1042.4, ABV 4.3%)
Clean-drinking, sweet, refreshing pale ale with a strong floral aroma and elderflower notes.

Risky Blond (OG 1042, ABV 4.4%)
An easy-drinking golden ale with a good balance of hops, subtle hints of citrus and a well-rounded finish.

Oozy Rat in a sanitary Zoo (ABV 5%)
An incredibly hoppy and well-balanced IPA.

Reckless Danger (OG 1054, ABV 5%)
A sweet-tasting beer with hints of bitterness.

Riptide (ABV 5%)
Blood orange and Ceylon orange pekoe leaf tea IPA.

Russian Roulette (OG 1049, ABV 5%)
A crisp, hoppy and bitter IPA.

Rankenstein (ABV 5.5%)
A golden-coloured, American-style pale ale, packed full of hops. Full of hop taste and aroma.

Foraged & Found

See Welbeck Abbey

Foragers

🯄 Verulam Arms, 41 Lower Dagnall Street, St Albans, Hertfordshire, AL3 4QE
☎ (01727) 836004 ⊕ the-foragers.com

Brewing began in 2015. Four base beers are brewed with different wild ingredients added throughout the year.

Forge

Wilderland, Woolley, Cornwall, EX23 9PW
☎ (01288) 331669 ☎ 07837 487800
⊕ forge-brewery.co.uk

⊠ This multi-award-winning brewery was set up near Bideford in Devon by Dave Lang, who commenced brewing in 2008 using a five-barrel plant. The brewery relocated to Cornwall in 2017. ◆ RAIB

Discovery (OG 1039, ABV 3.8%) ◆

Gold-coloured bitter bursting with hops throughout. Subtle hints of fruit.

Hartland Blonde (OG 1040, ABV 4%) ◆
A golden ale with a light straw hop aroma. Moderate hop with gentle fruit, malt and bitterness in the mouth.

Litehouse (OG 1042, ABV 4.3%)
Golden in colour, hints of elderflower, with a citrus bite.

IPA (OG 1044, ABV 4.5%)
A light, hoppy beer with grapefruit and citrus notes.

Rev Hawker (OG 1046, ABV 4.6%)

Tamar Source (OG 1046, ABV 4.6%)
An amber-coloured beer, with complex hop notes.

Handsome (OG 1048, ABV 5.1%)
A light brown-coloured, well balanced, hoppy beer.

Fosse Way (NEW) SIBA

Unit 5a, Manor Farm, Hunningham Lane, Offchurch, Warwickshire, CV33 9AG ☎ 07956 179999 ⊕ fossewaybrew.co.uk

⊠ Housed in a converted barn on Manor Farm, near Offchurch, is the 5.5-barrel plant now operated by Fosse Way Brewing Co. Originally established in 2013, the new owner has made continued improvements to the equipment. The core beer range includes a lager influenced by the owner's extensive experience in South Africa.

Aurora (ABV 3.6%)
A golden ale with exotic fruit flavours.

Josse Gold Lager (ABV 4.2%)
A South African-style lager; light and crisp.

Sentinel (ABV 4.5%)
Malty and fruity, copper-coloured ale.

Dark Side (OG 1048, ABV 4.8%)
A roast malt chocolate porter.

Four Candles

≣ 1 Sowell Street, St Peters, CT10 2AT ☎ 07947 062063 ⊕ thefourcandles.co.uk

⊠ Based in the cellar of the micropub of the same name, Four Candles uses a 2.5-barrel plant and produces up to 10 nine-gallon casks with each brew. Never brewing the same ale twice, the brewery supplies the micropub, which is named after the well known Two Ronnies sketch. ‼

Four Kings

Unit 15g, Newton Moor Industrial Estate, Lodge Street, Hyde, SK14 4LD ☎ 07951 699428 ⊕ fourkingsbrewery.com

☺Four Kings is a six-barrel brewery established by five friends with a mutual love of beer. Only British ingredients are used and all beers are vegan. Regular open days are held at the brewery's on-site bar, which is also available for private functions and ad-hoc visits. Beers can be found in Hyde, Denton and Glossop. ‼🍺RAIB V

Gold (ABV 4%)
Golden-coloured beer with hop bitterness and tart fruit.

IPA (ABV 4%)

Pale in colour with a fresh, hoppy aroma and a malty, hoppy flavour. Well-balanced with an intense bitterness, leading to a long, dry finish.

Bitter (ABV 4.5%)
Bitter taste with a slight sweetness and moderate bitter finish. Light-bodied with a toffee aftertaste.

Porter (ABV 5.2%)
Smooth, dark brown-coloured ale with a rich, chocolaty character, bitter taste and slight sweetness. Moderate bitter finish and roasted coffee in the aftertaste.

Fourpure

22 Bermondsey Trading Estate, Rotherhithe New Road, South Bermondsey, London, SE16 3LL ☎ (020) 3744 2141 ⊕ fourpure.com

Fourpure began brewing in 2013. Beers are available in cans and kegs, unfiltered, unpasteurised and unfined. In 2018 the brewery was bought by Lion of Australia, part of Kirin of Japan. Business continues as normal so far but with an increased emphasis on canning. 🍺RAIB

Fowey

Unit 3F, 3-4 Restormel Industrial Estate, Liddicoat Road, Lostwithiel, Cornwall, PL22 0HG ☎ (01208) 871385 ☎ 07443 504644

Office: Pawton Mill, St Breock, PL27 7LH ⊕ foweybrewery.co.uk

Fowey began brewing in 2016, initially producing bottle-conditioned beers only. It relocated to a larger unit on the same industrial estate in 2017, allowing for a new eight-barrel plant. Cask-conditioned ales are occasionally available. ◆RAIB

Fownes

25 Clarence Street, Upper Gornal, West Midlands, DY3 1UL ☎ 07790 766844

Office: 42 The Ridgeway, Sedgley, DY3 3UR ⊕ fownesbrewing.co.uk

☺The brewery was established in 2012 by James and Tom Fownes in premises to the rear of the Jolly Crispin in Upper Gornal. It expanded to a three-barrel plant in 2014. Beers are available in the Jolly Crispin and a number of free houses in the Midlands. Frequent specials along a 'Dwarfen Ales' theme are brewed in addition to the core range. ‼◆RAIB

Elephant Riders (OG 1040, ABV 4%)

Gunhild (OG 1041, ABV 4%) ◆
Bright with a creamy head. Smooth mouthfeel, earthy aroma with hints of blackcurrants and honey, peardrops and caramel with some malt and blackcurrant flavour, and a dry malty aftertaste.

Crispin's Ommer (OG 1038, ABV 4.1%)

Frost Hammer (OG 1047, ABV 4.6%) ◆
Blonde and bright with a clingy head. Pine resin, nutmeg, malt, lemon and floral aroma. Dry mouthfeel with coffee, sweet malt and grapefruit flavours. Grapefruit and hoppy aftertaste.

Firebeard's Old Favourite No. 5 Ruby Ale (OG 1051, ABV 5%) ◆
Rich, red-coloured ale with a creamy head and smooth mouthfeel. Malty, fresh earth, rhubarb and

some coffee in the aroma. Dark chocolate and plum dominate the flavour with hints of malt and coffee. Pleasant dryness in the aftertaste, with hints of coffee, plum and cocoa.

King Korvak's Saga (OG 1058, ABV 5.4%) ◆
Peardrop and cocoa aroma with hints of coffee. Coffee, toasted malt, blackcurrant and slight cocoa taste, with rich malty tones in the aftertaste.

Fox

☷ 22 Station Road, Heacham, Norfolk, PE31 7EX
☎ (01485) 570345 ⊕ foxbrewery.co.uk

⊠ Based in an old cottage adjacent to the Fox & Hounds pub, Fox Brewery was established in 2002 and now supplies around 30 outlets as well as the pub. All the beers are brewed using malt from Crisps in Great Ryburgh. A hop garden next to the brewery, trialled during 2009, has been enlarged. ‼ ☛ ◆ RAIB

Best (OG 1037, ABV 3.9%)

Heacham Gold (ABV 3.9%)
A well-balanced, fruity golden ale.

Red Knocker (OG 1037, ABV 3.9%)
A copper-coloured, malty ale.

Norfolk Nectar (OG 1043, ABV 4.3%)
A slightly sweet beer.

Grizzly Bear (ABV 4.8%)
Well-hopped, dry honey ale.

Cascade (OG 1051, ABV 5%)
A light beer with a hoppy flavour.

Nelson's Blood (OG 1049, ABV 5.1%)
A red-coloured, full-bodied beer brewed with Nelson's Blood rum.

IPA (OG 1051, ABV 5.2%)
An easy-drinking IPA based on a 19th-century recipe.

Fox Meadow

23 Courtauld Road, Braintree, Essex, CM7 9BD
☎ 07932 420708 ⊕ foxmeadow.net

Fox Meadow is a small batch nanobrewery in Braintree, brewing just two firkins at a time. Brewing is currently suspended.

Foxfield SIBA

☷ Prince of Wales, Foxfield, Broughton in Furness, Cumbria, LA20 6BX
☎ (01229) 716238 ⊕ princeofwalesfoxfield.co.uk

☺Foxfield is a 4.5-barrel plant in old stables attached to the Prince of Wales. Several other outlets are supplied. Tiger Tops in Wakefield is also owned. The beer range constantly changes. ‼ ◆

Framework

The Old City Depot, 72-74 Friday Street, Leicester, LE1 3BW ⊕ frameworkbrewery.com

⊠ Framework is a six-barrel brewery in an historic Victorian red brick City Centre building that started brewing in 2016. Alongside its core range of ales it also offers changing seasonal beers, collaboration and one-off experimental brews. Both traditional and modern hop forward beers are available. Its

brewery tap bar opens on the third weekend of the month on a Friday and Saturday. ‼ ◆ V

Fosse Golden Bitter (ABV 3.7%)
A golden-coloured bitter with a traditional malt profile and a modern hop flavour. Subtle citrus lemon aromas meld with a complex and refreshing bitter finish.

Jackpin (ABV 3.9%)
A hop-forward, well-balanced pale ale.

Fox Paw (ABV 4%)
A smooth ale with a complex malt profile offering hints of dark hedgerow fruits.

16 Needles (ABV 4.2%)
A hoppy, pale-coloured golden ale with a crisp nose and traditional bitterness.

Friday St IPA (ABV 4.5%)
A dry-hopped session beer with a citrus hit.

ESB (ABV 4.9%)

Franklins SIBA

Highfields Farm, The Broyle, Ringmer, East Sussex, BN8 5AR ☎ 07900 218584 ⊕ franklinsbrewery.co.uk

⊠ Owned by Steve Medniuk, Franklins moved to a new site in Ringmer in order to aid expansion. A 10-barrel brew plant is currently used. Beers are also brewed under the Hastings Brewery name. Beers are available throughout the South East, London and beyond. ‼

English Garden (OG 1042, ABV 3.8%)
A hoppy, session golden ale.

Mama Knows Best (OG 1043, ABV 4.1%)
A refreshing, traditional best bitter, rich in mango, lemon and earthy pine.

Resurrection Stout (ABV 5.3%)

Citra IPA (OG 1056, ABV 5.5%)
Single-hopped IPA, bursting with citrus and lychee flavours and aroma.

North Shore IPA (ABV 5.5%)

Smoked Porter (OG 1052, ABV 5.5%)
A rich, intense porter made with oatmeal. Added chipotle chillies accentuate the smokiness and add a touch of heat.

Freedom SIBA

1 Park Lodge House, Bagots Park, Abbots Bromley, Staffordshire, WS15 3ES
☎ (01283) 840721 ⊕ freedombrewery.com

No real ale. Freedom specialises in producing hand-crafted English lagers, all brewed in accordance with the German Reinheitsgebot purity law. ‼ ☛

Freestyle

☷ Church Road, Shustoke, Warwickshire, B46 2LB
☎ (01675) 481205 ⊕ griffininnshustoke.co.uk

Griffin Inn started brewing in 2008 in the old coffin shop adjacent to the pub. In 2017 the brewery was updated to a modern, more efficient 2.5-barrel plant. At this time the name was changed to Freestyle though the business is still owned by the Pugh family who run the Griffin. Beers are available for the free trade as well as selling through the pub. ‼ ◆

Griffin Dark (ABV 3.8%)

Black-coloured mild with a roast palate and a long, dry finish.

Griffin Pale Ale (ABV 3.8%)
Crisp and hoppy with a rich, fruity malt finish.

Shawbury Blonde (ABV 4.2%)

Bullion (ABV 4.4%)
Golden bitter with moderate bitterness and balancing sweetness.

Yeti IPA (ABV 4.5%)
A hoppy pale ale with a fruity finish.

Black Magic Woman (ABV 4.8%)
Rich, dark-coloured and smooth porter.

Muzungu (ABV 5.5%)
A light gold-coloured ale with a hoppy bitter taste, malty body and sweet finish.

Freetime

19 St Lukes Court, Clarke Way, Winch Wen, Swansea, SA1 7ER
☎ (01792 713731) 07291 253227
✉ hello@freetimebeer.co

Formerly known as West by Three, brewing operations began in 2016 producing small batches of beer. All beers are unfined.

Freewheelin'

Peebles Hydro, Innerleithen Road, Peebles, EH45 8LX
☎ 07802 175826 🌐 freewheelinbrewery.co.uk

Freewheelin' began brewing in 2013 and is based in Peebles. It is located in a former joiners shed in the grounds of the Peebles Hydro Hotel. Local spring water is used in the brewing process. ‼♦

Blonde (OG 1040, ABV 3.8%)

IPA (OG 1043, ABV 4.2%)

Dizzy Blonde (OG 1045, ABV 4.3%)

Ruby (OG 1046, ABV 4.4%)

Stout (OG 1047, ABV 4.4%)

Frensham

The Old Dairy, Pierrepont Home Farm, The Reeds, Frensham, Surrey, GU10 3BS
☎ (01252) 793956 ☎ 07774 982174
🌐 craftbrews.uk

⊗ Set in the Surrey countryside, Frensham is a microbrewery founded in 2014 and situated in a 17th-century restored barn, on a working dairy farm. 🛒♦

Soul (OG 1038, ABV 3.8%)
A light, floral, session beer, with biscuit, orange notes.

Rambler (OG 1039, ABV 3.9%)
A golden-coloured, light, refreshing, session ale. Fruity hops with an oak edge give rise to a satisfying bitterness. Well-rounded, floral and hop aromas.

Silent Flight (ABV 4.2%)
A ruby-coloured ale with some bitterness and a spicy, floral aroma.

Forager (OG 1045, ABV 4.5%)
Rich golden/copper-coloured ale. A complex floral aroma with subtle oak/vanilla oaks, offset with a caramel/spicy hop balance. Lingering bitter finish.

Owlswood (OG 1057, ABV 6%)
A rich, dark-coloured porter with hints of coriander, juniper berries and orange peel, giving a fine, roasted flavour.

Friday Beer SIBA

Unit 4, Link Business Centre, Link Way, Malvern, Worcestershire, WR14 1UQ
☎ (01684) 572648 🌐 thefridaybeer.com

Founded in 2011, the Friday Beer Co primarily produces bottle-conditioned ales. The range of bottles now sells across the region and to a growing number of outlets from Birmingham to London and south of the M4 corridor (including local restaurants and venues). Cask-conditioned ales are only available in a few pubs local to the brewery or from the brewery for events. ‼🛒RAIB

Jubilee (OG 1034, ABV 3.1%)
A medium, dark-coloured session ale.

Summer Hill Blonde (OG 1043, ABV 4.3%)
Pale-coloured golden ale with a higher malt profile than expected. Hints of pineapple or blackcurrant.

Pinnacle (OG 1046, ABV 4.5%)

WR14 (OG 1057, ABV 4.7%)
Sweet, hoppy ale, with a full-bodied texture and citrus and spice aromas.

Friday Gold (OG 1054, ABV 5.6%)
Refreshing, golden ale, with a smooth texture and flavour and a slight citrus taste.

Friends Arms

Old St Clears Road, Johnstown, SA31 3HH
☎ (01267) 234073 🌐 thefriendsarms.co.uk

⊗ Friends Arms Brewery opened in 2011 on the premises of the Friends Arms, a traditional local community pub, which acts as the brewery tap. Brewing is now on a more consistent basis due to the brewery teaming up with a local brewer. ♦

Frisky Bear

Oscars Bar, 2a Queen Street, Morley, Leeds, West Yorkshire, LS27 9DG 🌐 friskybear.com

Established in 2016 using a one-barrel plant. Capacity was increased in 2018 with the addition of extra fermenters. Oscar's Bar is the main outlet but beers are available around West Yorkshire.

Frome SIBA

Unit L13, Marshall Way, Commerce Park, Frome, Somerset, BA11 2FB
☎ (01373) 467766 🌐 fromebrewingcompany.com

⊗ Formerly Milk Street Brewery, the business changed its name to Frome Brewing Company in 2018. The brewery was established in 1999 behind the Griffin in Frome before moving to an industrial unit on the edge of town in 2016 and increasing its capabilities to 60 barrels. Beer is supplied direct to local outlets and wholesalers are used to distribute further afield. ‼♦

Same Again (OG 1039, ABV 3.9%)

Funky Monkey (OG 1040, ABV 4%)

Copper-coloured ale with fruity flavours and aromas. A dry finish with developing bitterness and an undertone of citrus fruit.

Ra (OG 1041, ABV 4.1%)

Taiheke (OG 1043, ABV 4.3%)
A pale-coloured wheat beer with citrus and tropical notes.

The Usual (OG 1045, ABV 4.4%)
Aromas of pear drops and orange marmalade give way to a well-rounded fruitiness and hints of caramel in the taste. Slight sweetness is balanced by a dry, bitter, grainy finish, with hints of raspberry.

Zig-Zag Stout (OG 1046, ABV 4.5%)
A dark ruby-coloured stout with characteristic roastiness and dryness. Bitter chocolate and citrus fruit in the background.

Gulp IPA (OG 1048, ABV 4.8%)
A session beer, lemon and citrus aroma, full-mouthfeel, and a good hop balance. Clean bitter finish with spicy and blackcurrant notes.

Beer (OG 1049, ABV 5%)
A blonde beer with musky hoppiness and citrus fruit on the nose, while more fruit surges through on the palate, before the bittersweet finish.

Front Row SIBA

Unit A3, The Old School, Outclough Road, Brindley Ford, Staffordshire, ST8 7QD ☎ 07861 718673
🌐 frontrowbrewing.co.uk

After starting operations in Congleton in 2012 on a 2.5-barrel plant, Front Row expanded to an eight-barrel plant in 2014 and moved to its current location at the end of 2018 to allow for further increase in capacity. Phone for on-site brewery tap opening times. ‼♦

Number 8 (OG 1036, ABV 3.7%)

Crouch (OG 1039, ABV 3.8%)

LOHAG (Land of Hops & Glory) (OG 1036, ABV 3.8%)

Touch (OG 1037, ABV 4%)

Sin Bin (OG 1042, ABV 4.2%)

Try (ABV 4.2%)

Half-Time (OG 1049, ABV 4.5%)
A chocolate stout with a hint of bitter orange.

Pause (OG 1049, ABV 4.5%)

Red Roses (OG 1049, ABV 4.5%)

Pride (ABV 4.6%)

Blindside (ABV 4.7%)

Crafty Flanker (ABV 4.7%)

Rucked (OG 1052, ABV 5.2%)

Converted (ABV 5.4%)

Lomu (ABV 5.4%)

Oblensky (ABV 7.3%)

Froth Blowers SIBA

Unit P35, Hastingwood Industrial Park, Wood Lane, Erdington, West Midlands, B24 9QR ☎ 07966 935906
🌐 frothblowersbrewing.com

⊗ Froth Blowers began brewing in 2013. The brewery now has the capacity to brew 20 barrels at a site only metres away from its original one. ♦

Piffle Snonker (OG 1038, ABV 3.8%)
Straw-coloured ale with an almost jammy aroma with a little malt and hop. Well-balanced taste, with a slightly hoppier aftertaste.

Bar-King Mad (OG 1042, ABV 4.2%)

Wellingtonian (OG 1043, ABV 4.3%)

John Bull's Best (OG 1044, ABV 4.4%)
A golden-coloured, well-balanced bitter.

Gollop With Zest (OG 1045, ABV 4.5%)
A blonde beer with a floral start and a citrus finish.

Hornswoggle (OG 1050, ABV 5%)
A full-bodied, blonde beer with a floral nose and sweetish start, followed by a dry and satisfying bitterness.

Fuddy Duck

Unit 12, Kirton Business Park, Willington Road, Kirton, Lincolnshire, PE20 1NN ☎ 07881 818875
🌐 thefuddyduckbrewery.co.uk

Small brewery based in Kirton near Boston, where brewing commenced in 2016.

Pale Ale (ABV 4%)
Golden ale with a grapefruit citrus flavour.

American Red Ale (ABV 4.5%)

Blonde Ale (ABV 4.5%)
Blonde ale with flavours and aromas of banana and clove.

Dark Porter (ABV 4.5%)
Flavours of chocolate and liquorice.

German Ale Altbier (ABV 4.5%)

Biere De Garde (ABV 6.5%)

Fuggle Bunny SIBA

Unit 1, Meadowbrook Park Industrial Estate, Station Road, Holbrook, Sheffield, South Yorkshire, S20 3PJ
☎ (0114) 248 4541 ☎ 07813 763347
🌐 fugglebunny.co.uk

⊗ Fuggle Bunny was established in 2014 and is an independent family-run brewery. The plant, originally obtained from Flipside Brewery, has since been expanded. The core range is supplemented by occasional seasonal and special brews. Beers are delivered direct within a 40-mile radius of the brewery and are available nationally through wholesalers. Its first pub opened in Worksop in 2017. ‼

Chapter 5 Oh Crumbs (OG 1038, ABV 3.8%)
Amber-coloured ale with hints of spice cedar and pine. Sweet caramel and biscuity flavours gives this a distinctive finish.

Chapter 9 La La Land (ABV 3.9%)
An American-style pale ale. Refreshingly tropical with citrus and passion fruit flavours and a fresh, floral aroma.

Chapter 2 Cotton Tail (OG 1040, ABV 4%)
Fruity aromas of lychees and citrus with a dry, hoppy finish.

Chapter 6 Hazy Summer Daze (OG 1042, ABV 4.2%)

Tropical with mango, lime, apricot, melon, lychees and grapefruit with fresh, floral aromas.

Chapter 8 Jammy Dodger (OG 1045, ABV 4.5%)
A ruby red-coloured ale with hints of blackcurrants, liquorice and caramel and a malty undertone.

Chapter 1 New Beginnings (OG 1049, ABV 4.9%)
Amber-coloured, classic bitter, with a sweet edge of honey and spice leading to a dry, hoppy aftertaste.

Chapter 3 Orchard Gold (OG 1050, ABV 5%)
Golden ale with hints of spice and honey, and an earthy undertone.

Chapter 7 Russian Rare-Bit (OG 1050, ABV 5%)
Dark-coloured, malty, complex ale, with chocolate, coffee and liquorice aromas.

Chapter 4 24 Carrot (OG 1060, ABV 6%)
Smooth aromas of citrus and blackberry, with a spicy blanket of malt-flavoured hoppiness.

Full Mash

17 Lower Park Street, Stapleford, Nottinghamshire, NG9 8EW
☎ (0115) 949 9262 🌐 fullmash.net

Brewing commenced in 2003 and has grown steadily since, with a gradual expansion in outlets and capacity. ♦

Horse & Jockey (OG 1039, ABV 3.8%)
Easy-drinking golden ale with moderate hoppy aroma and finish.

Whistlin' Dixie (OG 1040, ABV 3.9%)

Séance (OG 1041, ABV 4%)
Predominantly hoppy golden-coloured beer with a refreshing bitter finish.

Illuminati (OG 1043, ABV 4.2%)
Gently-hopped golden ale with initial hops and bitterness giving way to a short, bitter finish.

Wheat Ear (OG 1043, ABV 4.2%)
Pale-coloured, clear wheat beer, fruity and aromatic.

Warlord (OG 1045, ABV 4.4%)
Amber-coloured beer with an initial malt taste leading to a dry bitter finish.

Apparition (OG 1046, ABV 4.5%)
A pale-coloured, hoppy bitter.

Northern Lights (OG 1048, ABV 4.7%)
Smooth, chocolaty ale with a slight roast flavour.

Manhattan (OG 1053, ABV 5.2%)
Refreshing, pale-coloured, American-style IPA with a complex citrus aroma and big hop finish.

Bhisti (OG 1063, ABV 6.2%)
Strong IPA with a kick of bitterness.

Fuller's

Griffin Brewery, Chiswick Lane South, Chiswick, London, W4 2QB
☎ (020) 8996 2000 🌐 fullers.co.uk

The Griffin brewery has stood for more than 360 years with the Fullers name coming from the partnership formed in 1845. Gales of Horndean was bought in 2005 and closed a year later, the beers are now brewed at Chiswick. Dark Star of Sussex was bought in 2018 and brewing continues there. Fullers sold its brewing interests to Asahi in April 2019 but will keep its pubs and hotels. !! ♦ RAIB

London Pride (OG 1040.5, ABV 4.1%)
Well-balanced, smooth best bitter with orange citrus fruit, malt and hops in aroma and flavour, which linger into a slightly bitter aftertaste. Honey and toffee develop as the beer matures.

Bengal Lancer (OG 1049.5, ABV 5%)
Rich, creamy, well-balanced, pale brown-coloured IPA with a gold hue. Hops with a dryish bitterness harmonise with the fruit and malty sweetness that linger into the aftertaste.

ESB (OG 1054, ABV 5.5%)
Bitter orange marmalade with hops, creamy toffee and some raisins are all present in this multifaceted, strong, brown-coloured bitter. A satisfying long, bitter, dry finish is balanced by a malty sweetness.

Brewed under the Gale's brand name:

Seafarers Ale (OG 1037, ABV 3.6%)
A pale brown-coloured bitter, predominantly malty, with a refreshing balance of fruit and hops that lingers into the aftertaste where a dry bitterness unfolds.

HSB (OG 1050, ABV 4.8%)
Dates and dried fruit with some spicy hops in the nose adding to the caramelised orange and treacle in the flavour of this smooth, brown-coloured beer. Malty throughout with a bittersweet finish.

Fulstow

See Firehouse

Funky Hop Donkey

See Silver

Furnace (NEW)

9 Duke Street, Derby, DE1 3BX
☎ (01332) 385981

Six-barrel brewhouse in the beer garden of the Furnace Inn on Duke Street. Three core beers are produced year round, plus lots of seasonal specials. Supply is mainly for the pub but beers can be seen at beer festivals and specialist pubs across the UK. ♦

Reprazent! (OG 1042, ABV 4.2%)
Kaffir lime pale ale.

Fun Sponge (OG 1043, ABV 4.3%)
A pale ale packed with hops.

My Milk Stout (OG 1049, ABV 4.9%)

Fuzzchat

Jolly Coopers, 84 Wheelers Lane, Epsom, Surrey, KT18 7SD
☎ (01372) 723222 🌐 fuzzchatbrewery.co.uk

Fuzzchat is Epsom's first brewery in more than 90 years. Housed behind the Jolly Coopers, it used to be an old blacksmith's cottage, recently restored after being derelict for several years. A Fuzzchat is anyone born on Epsom Common. !! ♦

Fuzzy Duck SIBA

18 Wood Street, Poulton Industrial Estate, Poulton-le-Fylde, Lancashire, FY6 8JY ☎ 07904 343729
fuzzyduckbrewery.co.uk

Fuzzy Duck was established in 2006. It relocated to Poulton-le-Fylde later that year, expanding capacity to an eight-barrel plant. The brewery delivers over a wide area of North-west England and Yorkshire. !! ♦ RAIB

Golden Cascade (OG 1038, ABV 3.8%)
Golden-coloured ale, with a citrus flavour and a floral aroma.

Mucky Duck (OG 1042, ABV 4%)
Dark stout, slightly sweet with chocolate and coffee notes.

Pheasant Plucker (OG 1042, ABV 4.2%)
Amber-coloured beer with a slightly spicy taste and a citrus finish.

Cunning Stunt (OG 1044, ABV 4.3%)
Amber-coloured beer with a blackcurrant and herbal aroma.

Ruby Duck (OG 1053, ABV 5.3%)
Dark ruby-coloured beer with a rich, full body and complex fruit flavours.

Fyne SIBA

Achadunan, Cairndow, PA26 8BJ
☎ (01499) 600120 fyneales.com

Fyne Ales has been brewing since 2001 and is situated at the head of Loch Fyne. In 2012 an on-site brewery tap was added. Expansion has allowed for the production of experimental brews. FyneFest runs annually, celebrating local fare and showcasing other breweries. !! ♦ RAIB

Jarl (OG 1038, ABV 3.8%)
A light golden ale with strong citrus notes.

Maverick (OG 1040.5, ABV 4.2%)
Full-bodied, roasty, tawny-coloured best bitter. It is balanced, fruity and well-hopped.

Hurricane Jack (OG 1042.5, ABV 4.4%)
Smooth golden ale, deep citrus flavours, which mellow to a lingering, citrus bitter finish.

Vital Spark (OG 1042.5, ABV 4.4%)
A rich, dark-coloured beer with glints of red. Clean taste, slightly sharp with a hint of blackcurrant.

Avalanche (OG 1043.5, ABV 4.5%)
True golden ale, citrus hops on the nose, well-balanced, good body, and fruit balancing a refreshing hoppy taste. Long, bittersweet aftertaste.

Highlander (OG 1046, ABV 4.8%)
Full-bodied, bittersweet ale with a good, dry hop finish. In the style of a Heavy, but malt is less pronounced and the sweetness ebbs away to leave a bitter, hoppy finish.

Sublime Stout (OG 1067, ABV 6.8%)
Stout with a hint of liquorice on the aftertaste.

Superior IPA (OG 1070, ABV 7.1%)
IPA with an oily mouthfeel, aromas of apricot and pine resin, a dusty, hoppy bitterness and a dry, fruity and hoppy aftertaste.

Gadds

See Ramsgate

Gale's

See Fuller's

Garden City

22 The Wynd, Letchworth Garden City, Hertfordshire, SG6 3EN ☎ 07932 739558
gardencitybrewery.co.uk

A brewbar established in 2016 using a 2.5-barrel plant, serving a selection of its own ales plus guests on gravity.

Gasworks

First Street, Manchester, M15 4FN

Gasworks is a six-barrel brewpub from the team behind Dockyard, opened in 2016. It supplies Gasworks Tap, Dockyard, Salford Quays and Dockyard, Spinningfields.

Gates Burton

Reservoir Road, Burton upon Trent, Staffordshire, DE14 2BP
☎ (01283) 532567
gatesburtonbrewery@talktalk.net

The Gates Burton Brewery was established in 2011 using a one-barrel plant. This has now expanded to a three-barrel plant. !! ♦

Reservoir (OG 1048, ABV 4.6%)
Pale brown-coloured ale with a malty aroma and roast hint. Caramel and malt lead to a sweet hop balanced taste. Hops arrive late on the palate.

Gates Burton Ale (GBA) (OG 1048, ABV 4.8%)
Robust, amber in colour, floral aroma and a sweet finish.

Damn (OG 1050, ABV 5%)
Smooth-drinking ale, with chocolate malt tones, delicately hopped, and a subtle, sweet finish.

Reservoir Gold (OG 1075, ABV 7.5%)
Full-bodied, smooth, amber-coloured, balanced with roast barley, subtly-hopped, and a sweet finish.

Geeves SIBA

Unit 12, Grange Lane Industrial Estate, Carrwood Road, Stairfoot, Barnsley, South Yorkshire, S71 5AS
☎ 07859 039259 geevesbrewery.co.uk

Geeves began brewing in 2011 using a 5.5-barrel plant with recipes developed when the owners lived on a narrow boat !! ♦ RAIB

Rococo (OG 1037, ABV 3.6%)
A smooth, dark-coloured mild with a hint of chocolate. Aromas are cocoa, dark fruits and berries with a subtle but lingering, bitter finish.

Evolver (OG 1037, ABV 3.8%)
A light, single-hopped pale ale.

Renaissance (OG 1040, ABV 4.1%)
Deep red-coloured ale packed with sweet malts giving dark fruits and molasses flavour. The hops

bring spicy earthiness, lemon citrus and hints of floral apricot and peach.

Aurelian (OG 1043, ABV 4.2%)
Golden ale with sweet, tangy orange citrus and a refreshingly crisp and bitter finish.

Cadenza (ABV 4.3%)

Captain Gingerbread (OG 1043, ABV 4.3%)
Hazy wheat beer infused with ginger. Spicy, refreshing and a hint of citrus.

Clear Cut (OG 1044, ABV 4.4%)
An extra pale ale with bags of hops for a citrus kick.

Oaty McOatface (ABV 4.5%)
A rich and full stout packed with malted oats giving a smooth and silky mouthfeel balanced by a lightly spicy hop character.

Smokey Joe Stout (OG 1050, ABV 5%)
Rich, bold stout, with black coffee, dark chocolate and a lingering smokiness, and a spicy, oaky finish.

Fully Laden (OG 1060, ABV 6%)
An IPA with strength and a juicy, citrusy, sweet floral taste and aroma, with a satisfying bitterness.

Geipel SIBA

Pant Glas, Llangwm, LL21 0RN
☎ (01490) 420838 ☎ 07549 526287 🌐 geipel.co.uk

Geipel commenced brewing in 2013 producing unpasteurised and unfiltered beers. The brewery specialises in lagers drawing inspiration from the classic styles of Germany and beyond. Available in keg, KeyKeg and bottle. RAIB

Aloha from Bala (OG 1047, ABV 4.4%)

Pilsner (OG 1046, ABV 4.6%)

Golden Gate (OG 1050, ABV 5%)
California-style lager with assertive hops.

Dunkelweizen (OG 1057, ABV 5.4%)
Amber brown-coloured Bavarian-style wheat beer.

Zoigl (OG 1053, ABV 5.4%)
An unfined, malty, amber-coloured, Bavarian-inspired lager.

Hefeweizen (OG 1054, ABV 5.6%)
A golden-coloured, cloudy, Bavarian-style, wheat beer.

Bock (OG 1066.9, ABV 6.5%)

Gemstone

See Nelson

Gentlewood (NEW)

Fir Tree Cottage, Tithe Barn, Gentleshaw, Staffordshire, WS15 4LR ☎ 07544 146900

Gentlewood began in 2018 and is co-owned and run by Darren Williams and Ben Colthorpe.

Heritage (ABV 4.2%)
A slightly hoppy golden ale with caramel overtones.

George Wright

See under W

George's SIBA

Common Road, Great Wakering, Essex, SS3 0AG
☎ (01702) 826755 ☎ 07771 871255
🌐 georgesbrewery.com

⊠ George's Brewery and Hop Monster Brewing Company (qv) are owned by the same brewer, using the same plant. George's concentrates on traditional styles and Hop Monster on the more unusual. !! ♦ RAIB

Wallasea Wench (OG 1036, ABV 3.6%)
Pale copper-coloured, easy-drinking ale with low bitterness.

Wakering Gold (OG 1038.5, ABV 3.8%)
Bursting with fresh hop aromas.

8-Bit Bitter (OG 1040, ABV 4%)

Best (OG 1041, ABV 4%)
Copper-coloured session bitter with a huge hop flavour.

Cockleboats (OG 1040, ABV 4%)

Empire (OG 1040, ABV 4%)

Figaro (OG 1038.5, ABV 4%)
Pale ale with tropical fruit flavours and a floral aroma.

Broadsword (OG 1047, ABV 4.7%)
Ruby-coloured ale with a malty, smooth start and a well-balanced, dry finish.

Excalibur (OG 1051.5, ABV 5.4%)

Merry Gentlemen (OG 1058, ABV 6%)
Dark chocolate, black cherries and old port flavours dominate this warming, velvety old ale.

Excalibur Reserve (OG 1067, ABV 7.2%)
Warming ale, full on citrus rush with fruit overtones and the warmth of Armagnac.

Brewed under the Hop Monster Brewery name:

Rakau (ABV 4.2%)

Snake Oil (OG 1048, ABV 5%)

German Kraft (NEW)

Mercato Metropolitano, 42 Newington Causeway, Borough, London, SE1 6DR 🌐 germankraftbeer.com

Initally beer was imported from its German brewery in Bavaria, Steinbach in 2017. By 2018 the brewery officially opened and beers are replicated on-site. The keg beers are of the usual German styles. No real ale.

Ghost

Unit D, Tong Business Centre, Otley Road, Baildon, West Yorkshire, BD17 7QD
☎ (0113) 418 2002 ☎ 01896 097882
🌐 ghostbrew.co.uk

Ghost Brew Co is the creation of Steve Crump and James Thompson.

Wraith (ABV 3.8%)
A pale ale with aromas of citrus peel and passion fruit and a smooth mouthfeel.

Spectre (ABV 4.4%)
Fruity, hoppy beer with spiced lemon and strawberry notes.

Phantom (ABV 5.2%)

Chewy, resinous hops dominate this golden-coloured IPA.

Gibberish

🏠 15 Caryl Street, Liverpool, L8 5AA ☎ 07871 645864

Gibberish is a brewpub that opened in 2017 in Liverpool's Baltic Triangle.

Gil's (NEW)

9 Ashcroft Crescent, Cardiff, CF5 3RJ ☎ 07882 076321
✉ gilsbrewery@gmail.com

Brewing began in 2018. Beer is available in kegs and bottles.

Gipsy Hill SIBA

Unit 11, Hamilton Road Industrial Estate, 160 Hamilton Road, West Norwood, London, SE27 9SF
☎ (020) 8761 9061 ⊕ gipsyhillbrewing.com

Founded in 2014, Gipsy Hill is an independent microbrewery producing mainly for the local market in London. A taproom is open to the public Thursday to Sunday. ◆RAIB

Wayfarer (ABV 4.6%) 🍺
Well-balanced porter with dark roast and spicy hop aroma. Roast continues in the taste, with sweetness is balanced by bitterness.

Glamorgan SIBA

Unit J, Llantrisant Business Park, Llantrisant, CF72 8LF
☎ (01443) 406080 ⊕ glamorganbrewingco.com

☺This family-owned and run brewery moved to its present site in 2013. Production capacity was increased in 2017 and again in 2018. A range of year-round and seasonal ales are produced, with additional special brews to mark notable events.The brewery tap is open for special events and tours and the brewery shop is open daily. Direct deliveries are made throughout Wales and distributed further afield by selected wholesalers and breweries. 🛒◆

Cwrw Gorslas/Bluestone Bitter (OG 1040, ABV 4%)
Well-rounded bitter, softly roasted undertones to a malty body complemented by a smooth and robust hoppiness from nose to finish.

Welsh Pale Ale (OG 1042, ABV 4.1%)
A crisp pale ale, light gold in colour and full of bright citrus aromas and flavours. Finishes dry, fruity and hoppy.

Jemimas Pitchfork (OG 1044, ABV 4.4%)

Thunderbird (OG 1045, ABV 4.5%)

Glasshouse (NEW)

Unit 6b, Waterside Business Park, Stirchley, B30 2DR

Glasshouse opened in 2018 run by Josh Hughes. Brewing mainly keg and keykeg beers in a broad range of exciting new styles. Some occasional casks will be sold to the local trade.

Glastonbury

Unit 11, Wessex Park, Somerton Business Park, Somerton, Somerset, TA11 6SB
☎ (01458) 272244 ⊕ glastonburyales.com

Established in 2002 as Glastonbury Ales on a five-barrel plant. In 2006 the brewery changed ownership and moved to Somerton, increasing capacity to a 20-barrel plant. Cider is also produced. ‼◆RAIB

Mystery Tor (OG 1040, ABV 3.8%) 🍺
Full-bodied, golden-coloured bitter with floral hop and fruit on the nose and palate, sweetness giving way to bitter hop finish.

Lady of the Lake (OG 1042, ABV 4.2%) 🍺
Full-bodied, amber-coloured best bitter with hops balanced by fruity malt flavour and a hint of vanilla. Clean, bitter hop aftertaste.

Love Monkey (OG 1042, ABV 4.2%)
Golden ale loaded with zesty, fruity hops.

Black As Yer 'At (OG 1043, ABV 4.3%)

Hedge Monkey (OG 1048, ABV 4.6%)
A well-rounded, deep amber-coloured bitter. Malty, rich and hoppy.

Golden Chalice (OG 1048, ABV 4.8%)
A powerful, golden-coloured ale with well-balanced malt and fragrant hops. A robust bitterness and lingering bittersweet finish.

Thriller Cappuccino Porter (OG 1050, ABV 5%)
Dark-coloured, richly roasted porter with hints of coffee.

Glede SIBA

Unit 1, Tweed Road Trading Estate, Clevedon, Somerset, BS21 6RR ☎ 07802 702367

Founded in the Chilterns by Howard Tucker in 2016 as Red Kite, the brewery relocated to Clevedon in 2017, changing its name to Glede. The names of the beers usually have significance to the Tucker family. Howard is traditional in his methods; all of the malts used are British, as are most of the hops. ◆

Golden Dawn (ABV 3.9%)

Tucker's Tipple (ABV 4%) 🍺
Background malt, initial hoppy bitterness fades as sweeter flavours come to the fore, melding into a short, balanced, bittersweet finish.

Percy's Porter (ABV 4.4%)

JPA (ABV 5%)

Tucker's Luck (ABV 5.2%)

Glen Affric

Unit 2 & 3 Lightbox, Knox Street, Birkenhead, Merseyside, CH41 5JG ☎ 07742 020275

Office: 53 Wood Street, Ashton-under-Lyne, OL6 7NB
⊕ glenaffricbrewery.com

⊠ Established in 2016, a small batch brewery producing only keg beers. ‼🛒

Glen Spean (NEW) SIBA

Tirindrish Steading, Spean Bridge, PH34 4EU ☎ 07467 953714 ⊕ glenspeanbrewing.com

Based in a converted steading, brewing began in 2018.

Globe

144 High Street West, Glossop, Derbyshire, SK13 8HJ
☎ (01457) 852417 ⊕ globepub.co.uk

Globe was established in 2006 by Ron Brookes on a 2.5-barrel plant in an old stable behind the Globe pub. Grandson Toby now has a major role in the brewery under the watchful eye of Ron. The beers are mainly for the pub but special one-off brews are produced for beer festivals. ◆

Gloucester SIBA

Fox's Kiln, West Quay, The Docks, Gloucester, GL1 2LG
☎ (01452) 668043 ☎ 07503 152749
⊕ gloucesterbrewery.co.uk

⊠ Situated in the historic Gloucester Docks, brewing began in 2011. The brewery expanded into larger premises in the docks area to cope with increased demand while retaining and sympathetically restoring its original converted stables site for experimental brews and a bar named Tank. The full range of beers is regularly available in pubs throughout Gloucestershire and beyond. Beers are brewed in cask, keg and bottled format, most are unfined. ‼ ₩ ◆ RAIB V

Session Pale (OG 1037, ABV 3.7%)
A pale ale with a fresh, zingy fruit taste and aroma of light citrus hops.

Gloucester Gold (OG 1040, ABV 3.9%)
A golden ale with a crisp, fruity and bitter taste, and luscious, tropical fruit aroma.

Cascade (OG 1042, ABV 4.2%)
Best bitter with a full-bodied, fruity, bitter taste, and aroma of bold, spicy, floral hops.

Session IPA (OG 1045, ABV 4.5%)
Session IPA with a resinous, full-bodied taste and aroma of juicy tropical fruit.

Six Malt Porter (OG 1045, ABV 4.5%)
A full-bodied, smooth porter, with aromas of roasted malt and dark fruits.

Dockside Dark (OG 1052, ABV 5.2%)
A silky, rich ale, warm and chocolaty with subtle sweetness.

Goacher's

Unit 8, Tovil Green Business Park, Burial Ground Lane, Tovil, Maidstone, Kent, ME15 6TA
☎ (01622) 682112 ⊕ goachers.com

A traditional brewery that uses only malt and Kentish hops for all its beers. Phil and Debbie Goacher have concentrated on brewing good wholesome beers without gimmicks. Two tied houses and around 30 free trade outlets in the mid-Kent area are supplied. Special is brewed for sale under house names. ‼◆

Real Mild Ale (OG 1033, ABV 3.4%) ◀
A rich, flavoursome mild with moderate roast barley and a generous helping of chocolate malt.

Fine Light Ale (OG 1036, ABV 3.7%) ◀
A pale, golden brown-coloured bitter with a strong, floral, hoppy aroma and aftertaste. A hoppy and moderately malty session beer.

Special/House Ale (OG 1037, ABV 3.8%)

Best Dark Ale (OG 1040, ABV 4.1%) ◀
Dark in colour but light and quaffable in body, this ale features hints of caramel and chocolate malt throughout.

Crown Imperial Stout (OG 1044, ABV 4.5%) ◀
A well-balanced, roasty stout, dark and bitter with just a hint of caramel and a lingering creamy head.

Gold Star Strong Ale (OG 1050, ABV 5.1%) ◀

Goddards SIBA

Barnsley Farm, Bullen Road, Ryde, Isle of Wight, PO33 1QF
☎ (01983) 611011 ⊕ goddardsbrewery.com

⊠ Anthony Goddard established what is now the oldest active brewery on the Isle of Wight in 1993. Originally occupying an 18th-century barn, a new brewery was built in 2008, quadrupling its capacity, which has since been further increased. Goddard's remain a locally-focused business distributing ales on the Isle of Wight and the easily accessible counties of southern England. ◆

Ale of Wight (OG 1037, ABV 3.7%)
An aromatic, fresh and zesty pale beer.

Special Bitter (ABV 4%)
A clean, easy-drinking bitter with an aroma of freshly rubbed hops that carries into the aftertaste.

Starboard (ABV 4%)
A golden-coloured session beer with an aromatic nose.

Wight Squirrel (OG 1042.5, ABV 4.3%)
Russet-coloured best bitter with an initial dry taste on the palate.

Fuggle-Dee-Dum (OG 1047, ABV 4.8%) ◀
Brown-coloured strong ale with plenty of malt and hops.

Godstone SIBA

Flower Farm, Oxted Road, Godstone, Surrey, RH9 8BP
☎ 07791 570731

Office: 3 Willow Way, Godstone, RH9 8NQ
⊕ thegodstonebrewers.com

⊠ The Godstone Brewers was established in 2015 using a one-barrel plant but moved to larger premises on a farm in Godstone with a five-barrel plant. Beers are named with local themes. Local outlets are supplied. Fresh Beer Fridays take place weekly (5-8pm) in the farm tearooms, with a larger event held most months using the historic barn, and some in conjunction with the farmer. ₩◆RAIB

Not So Black & White (ABV 3.7%)
A creamy, amber-coloured ale with fruity and refreshing hops.

Trenchman's Hop (OG 1041, ABV 3.8%)
A session IPA with well-balanced of malt and hops.

Redgate (ABV 4%)
Well-balanced malt and hops.

Pondtail Pale (OG 1044, ABV 4.1%)
Pale ale with lemon and grapefruit flavours without being over-poweringly hoppy.

Junction 6 (ABV 4.2%)
Refreshing, New World-style pale ale with a mandarin and orange character.

Oishi (ABV 4.2%)
Smooth and refreshing citrus character.

Rusty's Ale (ABV 4.4%)
Traditional, malty best bitter.

Buzz (ABV 4.7%)
Dry honey ale with a lime blossom character.

Dunkel (ABV 4.7%)
German-style, dark-coloured ale, low in bitterness with smooth, malty flavours.

Horse & Carter (ABV 4.7%)
An amber-coloured ale; sweet, creamy and fruity.

Bitter Entropy (ABV 5.3%)
Malty, caramel flavours dominate, with a hint of added rye.

Dubbel (ABV 5.5%)
German-style malt beer, slightly sweet with a fruit and caramel character.

Polly Paine's Porter (OG 1070, ABV 6.5%)
Full-bodied, complex ale with caramel, coffee and chocolate notes.

Dipa (ABV 7.4%)
New World-style double IPA with a mandarin and orange character.

Goff's SIBA

9 Isbourne Way, Winchcombe, Gloucestershire, GL54 5NS
☎ (01242) 603383 🌐 goffsbrewery.com

⊗ Goff's is a family concern that has been brewing cask-conditioned ales since 1994. The ales are available regionally in more than 200 outlets and nationally through wholesalers. ♦

Lancer (ABV 3.8%)
A zesty, golden-coloured ale.

Jouster (OG 1040, ABV 4%) ◆
A drinkable, tawny-coloured ale, with a light hoppiness in the aroma. Well-balanced malt and bitterness in the mouth, underscored by fruitiness. Clean, hoppy aftertaste.

Tournament (OG 1038, ABV 4%) ◆
Dark golden in colour, with a pleasant hop aroma. A clean, light and refreshing session bitter with a pleasant hop aftertaste.

Fallen Knight (ABV 4.4%)
Deep mahogany in colour, a rich and malty best bitter.

Cheltenham Gold (ABV 4.5%)

White Knight (OG 1046, ABV 4.7%) ◆
A well-hopped bitter with a light colour and full-bodied taste. Bitterness predominates in the mouth and leads to a dry, hoppy aftertaste.

Golcar

60a Swallow Lane, Golcar, Huddersfield, West Yorkshire, HD7 4NB
☎ (01484) 644241 ☎ 07970 267555
🌐 golcarbrewery.co.uk

☺Golcar started brewing in 2001 and production has increased from 2.5 barrels to five barrels a week. The brewery owns one pub, the Rose & Crown at Golcar, and occasionally supplies other outlets in the local area. ‼

Dark Mild (OG 1034, ABV 3.4%) ◆
Dark-coloured mild with a light roasted malt and liquorice taste. Smooth and satisfying.

Town End Bitter (OG 1039, ABV 3.9%) ◆
Amber-coloured bitter with a hoppy, citrus taste, with fruity overtones and a bitter finish.

Pennine Gold (OG 1038, ABV 4%)
A hoppy and fruity session beer.

Guthlac's Porter (OG 1047, ABV 5%)
A robust, malty porter.

Golden Duck

Unit 2, Redhill Farm, Top Street, Appleby Magna, Leicestershire, DE12 7AH ☎ 07846 295179
🌐 goldenduckbrewery.com

Golden Duck began brewing in 2012 using a five-barrel plant. It is run by the father-and-son team of Andrew and Harry Lunn. Beers have a cricket-related theme and are always available in Mushroom Hall, Albert Village and Cellar Bar, Sir John Moore Hall, Appleby Magna (Fri evenings only). ♦RAIB

LFB (Lunns First Brew) (OG 1043, ABV 4.3%)
Traditional, golden-coloured, hoppy session ale with citrus overtones.

Wristy Fitzy (OG 1046, ABV 4.6%)
Deceptively smooth and rich, chestnut-coloured ale. Hoppy with slight malty overtones.

Lunnys No. 8 (OG 1048, ABV 4.8%)
Hoppy bitter with a fruity and lasting aroma.

Golden Triangle SIBA

Unit 9, Watton Road Industrial Estate, Norwich, NR9 4BG
☎ (01603) 757763 ☎ 07976 281132
🌐 goldentriangle.co.uk

⊗ Golden Triangle, named after an area of Norwich, has been brewing modern, hop-forward ales on a 10-barrel plant since 2011. The brewery continues to add new beers to its range. Beers are mainly found in pubs across Norwich. The Artichoke, Norwich, purchased by owner and brewer Kevin Tweedy in 2018, is the brewery tap (two beers permanently available). ♦

City Gold (OG 1038, ABV 3.8%) ◆
A lemony hop aroma introduces a mix of citrus, hop, and bitterness. Dry, astringent finish.

Mosaic City (OG 1038, ABV 3.8%)
Light golden ale, distinctive hop flavour, and plenty of body for the ABV.

Citropolis (OG 1039, ABV 3.9%)
Light, refreshing and zesty golden ale, with citrus hop notes and fruity aroma.

Equinoxity (ABV 3.9%)
Classic pale ale, well-balanced, with a soft citrus hop note on a good biscuity malt base.

Hoptriptic (OG 1040, ABV 4%)

Black Hops IBA (OG 1047, ABV 4.6%) ◆
Intense hop and cherry aroma. Complex mix of malt, cherry and bitterness dominated by hops. Challenging, increasingly bitter ending.

Red Square (OG 1046, ABV 4.6%)
A red-coloured ale, balanced, complex flavour, develops into a strong hoppy finish.

Shenanigans (ABV 5%) ◆

Roasty throughout. A soft roast chestnut aroma introduces a charcoal biscuit beginning with caramel and blackcurrant. Short, increasingly bitter finish.

Hop Lobster (OG 1053, ABV 5.5%)
A strong golden ale with plenty of citrus hop character.

Goldmark SIBA

Unit 23, The Vinery, Arundel Road, Poling, West Sussex, BN18 9PY
☎ (01903) 297838 ☎ 07900 555415
goldmarks.co.uk

Ex-biochemist and homebrewer Mark Lehmann began commercial brewing in 2013 using an 11-barrel plant. !! RAIB

Ebony Mild (OG 1035, ABV 3.5%)
Black-coloured, spicy mild with hints of chocolate, coffee and toffee.

Liquid Gold (OG 1040, ABV 4%)
A refreshing, full-bodied, golden-coloured beer with bursts of fruit and citrus.

Pheonix (OG 1041, ABV 4.1%)
A brown-coloured ale with hints of toffee and caramel and a smooth hop finish.

Red IPA (OG 1043, ABV 4.3%)

American Hop Idol (OG 1040, ABV 4.4%)

Warrior (OG 1046, ABV 4.6%)
A brown-coloured ale with hints of honey and caramel with a smooth hop note to finish.

Black Lion Porter (OG 1048, ABV 4.8%)
A rich, smooth, black-coloured porter with chocolate hints and a coffee end note.

Vertigo Craft Lager (OG 1048, ABV 4.8%)

Good Chemistry

Unit 2, William Street, St Philips, Bristol, BS2 0RG
☎ (0117) 9039930 goodchemistrybrewing.co.uk

Good Chemistry was established in 2015 in a warehouse in St Philips, Bristol by Bob Cary and Kelly Sidgwick, using a 10-barrel plant. As the name suggests, all brewery and beer logos have a scientific theme. Frequent brewery open days are held. RAIB

Natural Selection (OG 1038, ABV 4%)
Hops and pale malt aromas, initially sweet body, followed by hoppy bitterness, which continues into the short, dry finish.

Kokomo Weekday (OG 1044, ABV 4.3%)
Hazy, golden-coloured ale with hop and sweet fruit aroma which continues onto the palate before a short, bitter finish.

Good Stuff

Abdication, 89 Mansfield Road, Daybrook, Arnold, Nottingham, NG5 6BH theabdication.co.uk

A nanobrewery located inside the Abdication micropub. Capacity is 0.5 barrels so occasional beers can only be found at the pub and local beer festivals.

Good Things (NEW) SIBA

The Brewery, Rendlye Farm, Sandhill Lane, Eridge, East Sussex, TN3 9LP ☎ 07837 910008
goodthingsbrewing.co

Brewing began in 2018. Good things is a sustainable brewery, meaning that its aim is to be energy-efficient, with everything recycled and reused. Beer is available in kegs and cans in more than 100 outlets. No real ale. **V**

Goodalls

The Lodge, 88 Crewe Road, Alsager, ST7 2JA
☎ (01270) 873669
goodalls.brewery@hotmail.co.uk

Goodall's began brewing in 2010 at the Lodge in Alsager using a 2.5-barrel plant. Mainly seasonal ales are brewed. !! ♦

Goodwood (NEW)

The New Brewery, Stane Street, North Heath, West Sussex, RH20 1DJ goodwood.com/estate/home-farm/goodwood-brewery

Beers are available in bottle and keg in restaurants and bars across the Goodwood estate. The beer is brewed by Hepworth (qv) using ingredients grown on the estate.

Goody SIBA

Bleangate Brewery, Braggs Lane, Herne, Kent, CT6 7NP
☎ (01227) 361555 goodyales.co.uk

Goody Ales began brewing in 2012 using a 10-barrel plant. A wood-burning boiler is used to heat the water for the brews using wood from its copse, thereby minimising the use of non-renewable fuel. An on-site bar and shop, the Cathedral, is now open (limited hours). ♦ RAIB

Good Evening (OG 1034, ABV 3.4%)
A smooth, dark-coloured mild with a tinge of chocolate.

Genesis (OG 1035, ABV 3.5%)
A dark ruby-coloured, single-hop ale with a full flavour and lasting, bitter finish.

Good Health (OG 1038, ABV 3.6%)
A honey-coloured golden ale with a fresh hoppy finish and undertone of zesty orange.

Good Life (OG 1040, ABV 3.9%)
Fresh-tasting pale ale, bursting with citrus, hoppy flavours.

Good Heavens (OG 1042, ABV 4.1%)

Good Sheppard (OG 1045, ABV 4.5%)
Deep amber-coloured ale with a warm vanilla twist on the palate and a soft mouthfeel.

Goodness Gracious Me (OG 1047, ABV 4.8%)
Robust, citrus flavoured, highly-hopped IPA.

Good Lord (OG 1050, ABV 5%)
Rich porter with a smooth, roasted coffee tinge and silky bitter finish.

Goose Eye SIBA

Unit 5, Castlefield Industrial Estate, Crossflatts, Bingley, West Yorkshire, BD16 2AF

☎ (01274) 512743 ⊕ goose-eye-brewery.co.uk

☺Goose Eye is a family-run brewery supplying 60-70 regular outlets, mainly in North and West Yorkshire and Lancashire. The beers are available through national wholesalers and pub chains. The brewery moved to a new custom-built brewery in 2017, which has enabled it to increase production. Its on-site brewery bar is open on a Friday and Saturday. ♦

Springwell (OG 1036, ABV 3.6%)

Bitter (OG 1038, ABV 3.9%) ◆
Traditional Yorkshire, brown-coloured, session bitter, well-balanced malt and hops with a pleasingly bitter finish.

Blackmoor (OG 1040, ABV 4%)
Dark-coloured, easy-drinking session beer.

Chinook Blonde (OG 1042, ABV 4.2%) ◆
Assertive grapefruit hoppiness in the aroma, tropical flavours and an increasingly tart, bitter finish.

Golden Goose (OG 1045, ABV 4.5%)
A straw-coloured beer, light on the palate with a smooth and refreshing, hoppy finish.

Over & Stout (OG 1052, ABV 5.2%) ◆
A full-bodied stout with roast and malt flavours mingling with hops, dark fruit and liquorice on the palate. Tart fruit on the nose, and a growing bitter finish.

Pommies Revenge (OG 1052, ABV 5.2%) ◆
Golden-coloured, strong bitter combining grassy hops, a cocktail of fruit flavours, a peppery hint and a hoppy, bitter finish.

Goose Island (NEW)

⌷ 222 Shoreditch High Street, Shoreditch, London, E1 6PJ ⊕ gooseislandshoreditch.com

The Chicago-based Goose Island opened its London brewpub in 2018. The on-site kit brews a range of special beers not seen elsewhere, including a bourbon barrel-aged version of the Shoreditch Porter (the barrel can be seen behind the bar). No real ale.

Gorgeous Brewery

⌷ Bull, 13 North Hill, Highgate, London, N6 4AB
☎ 07754 925562 ⊕ gorgeousbrewery.com

⊠ Formerly the home of London Brewing (qv), Gorgeous inherited the brewing kit on the purchase of the pub in 2017. At the beginning of 2018 a newly built brewhouse at the rear of the pub came on stream. This extra capacity has seen a wider range of beers including collaborations.

Gower SIBA

Unit 25, Crofty Industrial Estate, Crofty, SA4 3RS
☎ (01792) 850681 ⊕ gowerbrewery.com

⊠ Established in 2011 on a five-barrel brew plant at the Greyhound Inn, Llanrhidian, the brewery moved to a new 20-barrel brewery in Crofty, Gower in 2015. ‼🍴♦

Brew 1 (OG 1039, ABV 3.8%)
Honey-coloured ale with a pronounced floral aroma.

Gower Best Bitter (OG 1045, ABV 4.5%)

A traditional, honey-coloured ale with a full-bodied, balanced malty flavour and crisp, lingering hop bite.

Gower Gold (OG 1045, ABV 4.5%)
Thirst-quenching golden ale, refreshing citrus flavours and a hoppy aroma.

Gower Rumour (OG 1050, ABV 5%)
Strong, ruby red-coloured ale, with complex tastes and aromas, produced from a delicate mix of malts and hops.

Shipwreck (ABV 5.1%)
A pale straw-coloured beer with a refreshing bitter taste of grapefruit.

Gower Power (OG 1052, ABV 5.5%)

Grafton SIBA

Walters Yard, Unit 4, Claylands Industrial Estate, Worksop, Nottinghamshire, S81 7DW
☎ (01909) 476121 ☎ 07436 282779

Office: 8 Oak Close, Crabtree Park Estate, Worksop, S80 1BH ⊕ graftonbrewing.co.uk

☺Grafton is a 12-barrel brewery established in 2007. In 2017 the brewery took over the operation of the former Hale's Brewery, which was based in an adjacent unit, but utilised the Grafton plant, and now produces Hale's beers as a sub-brand within its portfolio. ‼♦

Framboise (OG 1038, ABV 4%) ◆
Golden ale with a raspberry aroma and taste, leading to a sweet and slightly bitter finish.

Silhouette (OG 1038, ABV 4%)
A pale-coloured beer with the addition of vanilla pods gives a vanilla flavour.

Lady Julia (OG 1041, ABV 4.3%)
A crisp, golden ale with a floral hop aroma.

Bananalicious (OG 1043, ABV 4.5%)
Mid-brown-coloured ale with a delicious banana and toffee aftertaste.

Lady Catherine (OG 1043, ABV 4.5%)
Well-balanced, easy-drinking, golden-coloured beer, with a gentle bitterness, and an enticing malty, slightly sweet biscuit flavour.

Lady Ruby (OG 1043, ABV 4.5%)
An easy-drinking, dark ruby-coloured ale made with cherries. Hint of cherries on the nose, on the palate a bitter start, which then finishes with a cherry bomb on the back of the tongue.

Apricot Jungle (OG 1046, ABV 4.8%)
A fruity, golden beer with honey, apricot and almond notes. Sweetness is balanced by hop bitterness.

Blondie (OG 1046, ABV 4.8%)
A strong, golden-coloured beer. Aroma is dominated by citrus notes. Hops and fruit on the palate are balanced by malt, leading to a hoppy finish, with soft fruit flavours.

Mint Chocolate Stout (OG 1046, ABV 4.8%)
Dark black-coloured ale brewed with the addition of mint. Mint chocolate flavour.

Caramel Stout (OG 1048, ABV 5%)
A black-coloured ale with caramel and dark roast notes.

Coco Loco (OG 1048, ABV 5%) ◆
Dark-coloured, smooth-drinking ale, infused with coconut, gentle bitterness.

Grain SIBA

South Farm, Tunbeck Road, Alburgh, Harleston,
Norfolk, IP20 0BS
☎ (01986) 788884 ⊕ grainbrewery.co.uk

⊠ Grain Brewery was launched in 2006 by Geoff
Wright and Phil Halls in a converted dairy in the
Waveney Valley. It upgraded to an 18-barrel plant
in 2012. Four pubs are owned: the Plough and the
Cottage, Norwich, the Locks Inn, Geldeston, and
the Spread Eagle, Ipswich. ‼ ☙ ◆ RAIB

Oak (OG 1038, ABV 3.8%) ◄
Balanced malt and hops, with marmalade
overtones. A hint of molasses in the short, sharp
ending.

ThreeOneSix (OG 1039, ABV 3.9%) ◄
Strong, citrus notes throughout. Tangerine, lemon
and lime mix with a solid hoppy base, and a well-
balanced bitter finish.

Best Bitter (OG 1042, ABV 4.2%) ◄
Well-balanced, complex bitter. Brazil nut and malt,
bittersweet caramel notes, a malty finish.

Redwood (OG 1043, ABV 4.3%) ◄
A fruity aroma introduces a smooth, full-flavoured
bitter. A malty fruit base defined by bitter
undertones. Lingering bitter finish.

Slate (OG 1060, ABV 6%) ◄
Coffee, caramel and plum on the nose. Dried fruit
and sweet maltiness dominate a creamy roast
background. Long, strong finish.

Lignum Vitae (OG 1065, ABV 6.5%) ◄
Solid orange and hops throughout. Imposing oily
character with a definite marmalade bias. A
bittersweet blast enlivens the towering finale.

Grainstore SIBA

Station Approach, Oakham, Rutland, LE15 6RE
☎ (01572) 770065 ⊕ grainstorebrewery.com

☺Grainstore, the smallest county's largest
brewery, has been in production since 1995,
founded by Tony Davis and Mike Davies. After 45
years in the industry Tony decided to retire,
handing the reins to his son, William. More than
200 outlets are supplied. ‼◆

Rutland Bitter (OG 1032, ABV 3.4%)
Light-coloured, light, well-balanced session beer.

Rutland Panther (OG 1034, ABV 3.4%) ▨ ◄
Reddish-black-coloured mild that punches above
its weight. Malt and roast flavours deliver a brew
that can match the average stout for intensity of
flavour.

Cooking (OG 1036, ABV 3.6%) ◄
Tawny-coloured beer with malt and hops on the
nose and a pleasant grainy mouthfeel. Hops and
fruit flavours give a bitterness that continues into a
long finish.

Red Kite (OG 1038, ABV 3.8%)
Malty, sweet beer with a good body.

**Stoney Ford Sheepmarket Supernova
(OG 1040, ABV 3.8%)**

Rutland Osprey (OG 1040, ABV 4%)
A refreshing, light, golden-coloured brew.
Complex, mellow flavour with a finely balanced
floral aroma and smooth bitterness.

Stoney Ford PE9 Paradise Pale (OG 1041, ABV 4%)

Steelback IPA (OG 1042, ABV 4.2%)
A golden-coloured, full-bodied IPA.

**Stoney Ford All Saints Almighty
(OG 1044, ABV 4.2%)**

Triple B (OG 1042, ABV 4.2%) ◄
Initially hops dominate over malt in both the
aroma and taste, but fruit is there, too. All three
linger in varying degrees in the sweetish aftertaste
of this brown-coloured brew.

GB Best (OG 1043, ABV 4.3%) ◄
Pronounced floral aroma and flavour. Light, well-
balanced, smooth beer.

Ten Fifty (OG 1050, ABV 5%) ◄
Pungent banana and malt notes on the nose. Rich
malt, fruit, and subtle hop taste on a bittersweet
base. Dry malt aftertaste with some fruit.

Rutland Beast (OG 1053, ABV 5.3%)
Strong mild ale. Complex flavour of chocolate/
coffee notes, raisins and autumn fruits.

Nip (OG 1073, ABV 7.3%) ◄
A well-balanced blend of flavours, sweetness and
hop bitterness. Smooth and warming with raisins
and winter fruit as the dominant flavor notes.

Grampus

⊟ Grampus Inn, Lee Bay, Devon, EX34 8LR
☎ (01271) 862906 ⊕ thegrampus-inn.co.uk

⊠ Grampus was established in 2014 at the back of
the Grampus Inn by Bill Harvey, the pub owner and
brewer. It is a small plant using traditional brewing
methods, but combining unique and unusual
ingredients. All beers are available in the local
area. ◆ RAIB

Bitter (OG 1039, ABV 4%)
A traditional session bitter with a good hop finish.

Ale (OG 1042, ABV 4.4%)
A best bitter with a slightly fuller hop feel and
increased hop finish.

Hoppy Dog (OG 1043, ABV 4.5%)
A pale-coloured, IPA-style beer with a soft flowery
taste and mild hop finish.

Kraken (OG 1047, ABV 4.7%)
A dark-coloured beer with spicy notes and a soft
mouthfeel.

Granite Rock

Unit 19, Kernick Road Industrial Estate, Penryn,
Cornwall, TR10 9EP
☎ (01326) 379251 ☎ 07436 817974
⊕ graniterockbrewery.co.uk

⊠ Granite Rock was established in 2013 as a
brewery and homebrew shop. Located on an
industrial estate in Penryn, the two-barrel plant
currently supplies the free trade in west Cornwall.
‼ ☙ ◆ RAIB

Penryn Company Pale Ale (OG 1040, ABV 4%) ◄
Copper-coloured bitter with fruity hop and malt
nose. Assertive bitterness, resinous hops, spicy
notes. Lasting bitterness with vine fruit hints.

Summer Solstice (OG 1040, ABV 4%) ◄
Golden ale with a citrus and pineapple aroma.
Refreshing orange, citrus and pineapple notes,
honey flavours leading to dry finish.

Granite IPA (OG 1040, ABV 4.3%)

Aroma of orange and grapefruit with a bitter citrus finish.

Penryn Pride (OG 1042, ABV 4.5%) ◆
Tawny-coloured best bitter. Grainy mouthfeel with biscuit malt. Complex flavours, traces of toffee and caramel, hoppy bitterness and spice notes.

Driller IPA (OG 1055, ABV 5.1%) ◆
Refreshing, golden-coloured IPA, apricot and orange peel aromas. Citrus hops with hints of pine and resin balanced with honey notes.

Bronescombe's Vision (OG 1048, ABV 5.2%) ◆
Well-balanced, red-coloured strong bitter with malt and hop bitterness. Pronounced malt flavour with prunes and a lingering, dry malt finish.

Glasney College Porter (OG 1050, ABV 5.4%) ◆
Black-coloured porter with roast malt aroma. Full-bodied taste of mocha coffee and dark chocolate, liquorice and pear drops. Light finish.

Grasmere SIBA

Lake View Country House, Lake View Drive, Grasmere, Cumbria, LA22 9TD
☎ (015394) 35572 🌐 grasmerepub.com

Brewing began in 2017 in old farm buildings at Lake View Country House. Beers are available at its nearby taproom and restaurant, the Good Sport.

Pale Ale (ABV 4%)

Stout (ABV 5%)

Grasshopper

Unit F2, Langley Bridge Industrial Estate, Linkmel Road, Langley Mill, Derbyshire, NG16 3RZ
☎ (01773) 530224 ☎ 07900 806277
🌐 grasshopperbrewery.co.uk

Grasshopper commenced brewing in 2017 using a purpose built 10-barrel plant. Beers started appearing in local pubs shortly after and have been well received. Its core range (five beers) can be found in pubs and at festivals throughout Nottinghamshire, Derbyshire, Leicestershire, Staffordshire and beyond.

Knee High (ABV 3.8%)
Thirst-quenching, citrus session pale ale.

Nymph (ABV 4.2%)
Copper red-coloured, rye bitter.

Cricket (ABV 4.5%)
Premium, American-style. pale amber-coloured ale.

Devil's Horse (ABV 4.8%)
Full-bodied, creamy, Irish-style stout.

Kung Fu (OG 1052, ABV 5.8%)
Deceptively powerful, hoppy and bitter IPA.

Gravity Well (NEW)

Arch 142, Tilbury Road, Leyton, London, E10 6RE
☎ 07833 226373 🌐 gravitywellbrewing.co.uk

The brewery was installed during 2018 in a railway arch under the Gospel Oak to Barking line. A taproom is open at weekends. No real ale.

Great British Breworks

Brew House, Black Swan, 18 Birdgate, Pickering, North Yorkshire, YO18 7AL
🌐 blackswan-pickering.co.uk/breworks

Brewing started on a permanent basis in the rear yard of the Black Swan in 2016, using a 2.5-barrel plant. ♦

Great Central (NEW)

Unit B, Marlow Road Industrial Estate, Leicester, LE3 2BQ ☎ 07584 435332 🌐 gcbrewery.co.uk

Brewing re-started in 2019 on a two-barrel plant primarily to supply the brewery tap, the Wheeltapper, Loughborough. Beers are named with a railway theme. ♦

Great Corby SIBA

The Forge, Great Corby, Cumbria, CA4 8LR
☎ (01228) 560899 🌐 greatcorbybrewing.co.uk

Established in 2009, with a bespoke 10-barrel plant, the brewery was situated in The Old Forge (originally a farriers shop, dating back to 1833). Alltech purchased the brewery in 2015 and, in 2017, brewing operations moved across the village green, to a former honey factory. The Forge buildings were retained for office space and cask washing. Monthly special beers commenced during 2018. ‼♦

Corby Ale (OG 1038, ABV 3.8%) ◆
A fruity session beer with sweetness leading to gentle bitterness in the aftertaste.

Corby Blonde (OG 1042, ABV 4%)
Pronounced hop character with clean hop flavours and aromas. Well-balanced flavour, full-bodied drink with a pleasant hoppy aftertaste.

Lakeland Summit (OG 1040, ABV 4%)

Corby Signal Peak APA (ABV 4.4%)
A light-bodied, amber-coloured, American-style pale ale, strong on grapefruit and stone fruit flavours with a hint of vanilla in the aroma.

Corby Stout (OG 1044, ABV 4.5%) ◆
Fruity aroma, sweet roast middle and dry finish.

Corby Fox (OG 1048, ABV 4.6%) ◆
A pleasant, brown-coloured ale with a slight bitter finish.

Great Heck SIBA

Harwinn House, Main Street, Great Heck, North Yorkshire, DN14 0BQ
☎ (01977) 661430 ☎ 07723 381002
🌐 greatheckbrewery.co.uk

Great Heck began production in 2008 in a converted slaughterhouse. The brewery moved across the road to a converted cottage in 2012 and now produces its regular beers on a 15-barrel plant with capacity for 45 barrels per week. ‼♦

Chopper (OG 1037, ABV 3.8%)
Pale-coloured, session beer with a hop hit.

Dave (OG 1038, ABV 3.9%)
Dark-coloured session bitter with a roasty taste

Mercy (OG 1039, ABV 3.9%)

Navigator (OG 1039, ABV 3.9%)

Traditional, mahogany-coloured session bitter with subtle yet exotic hop aromas.

Trafalgar (ABV 4%)

Blonde (OG 1043, ABV 4.3%)
A delicious, richly-balanced blonde beer, with a zesty finish.

Voodoo Mild (OG 1043, ABV 4.3%)
Rich, very black-coloured mild bursting with roasted malt flavour.

Christopher (OG 1043, ABV 4.5%)
A very clean, dry, moderately-bittered pale ale with loads of aroma hops.

Divine Intervention (ABV 4.5%)

Hapi (ABV 4.5%)

Mount Hood (OG 1043, ABV 4.5%)

Amish Mash (OG 1045, ABV 4.7%)
A cloudy wheat beer with notes of fruit, banana and clove.

Treasure IPA (OG 1045, ABV 4.8%)
Smooth, golden-coloured IPA with moderate bitterness and distinctive tropical fruit notes.

Shankar IPA (OG 1055, ABV 5.9%)
A pale-coloured, hoppy, fruity beer with a clean, zesty finish.

Black Jesus (OG 1060, ABV 6.5%)

Yakima IPA (OG 1070, ABV 7.4%)
Deep golden in colour, very low in bitterness, well-balanced alcohol and luscious fruity hop flavours and aromas.

Great Newsome SIBA

Great Newsome Farm, South Frodingham, East Yorkshire, HU12 0NR
☎ (01964) 612201 🌐 greatnewsomebrewery.co.uk

Nestled in the Holderness countryside, Great Newsome began brewing in 2007 in renovated farm buildings. A range of beers is now brewed using barley from the farm and brewing can be seen from a viewing area. Expansion into another farm building increased capacity in 2018. Beer is distributed throughout the UK and overseas. !! ♦

Sleck Dust (OG 1037, ABV 3.8%)
Straw-coloured, refreshingly bitter session beer with a floral aroma and subtle, dry finish.

Ploughman's Pride (OG 1042, ABV 4.2%)
Easy-drinking, moderately bitter ale, deep chestnut in colour. Malty with liquorice tones.

Pricky Back Otchan (OG 1042, ABV 4.2%)
Golden-coloured bitter with a nutty, toffee aroma. Complex with mild citrus notes.

Frothingham Best (OG 1042, ABV 4.3%)
Dark amber-coloured best bitter. Fruit and nut aroma with hop resin and peach notes leading to a sweetish finish.

Holderness Dark (OG 1042, ABV 4.3%)
Dark-coloured, strong mild. Chocolate malt and hazelnut notes with a hint of sweetness in a long, satisfying finish.

Jem's Stout (OG 1044, ABV 4.3%)
Dark-coloured, smooth beer with smoky, roasted malt flavours and aroma.

Liquorice Lads Stout (OG 1044, ABV 4.3%)
Black-coloured stout flavoured with real liquorice.

Great North Eastern SIBA

Contract House, Wellington Road, Dunston, Gateshead, NE11 9HS
☎ (0191) 447 4462 ☎ 07514 787483 🌐 gnebco.com

Brewing began in 2016 on a 10-barrel plant. In 2017 the brewery expanded into the adjacent premises and a tap and shop was opened, with an events space for live entertainment. Beers are supplied direct throughout the North-East, and nationally via wholesalers. ♦

Claspers Citra Blonde (OG 1038, ABV 3.8%)
A light pale-coloured ale with strong citrus notes.

Styrian Blonde (OG 1038, ABV 3.8%)

Great North Eastern Gold (OG 1039, ABV 4%)
Single-hopped golden ale, pungent hop flavours dominate.

Rivet Catcher (OG 1039, ABV 4%)
A light, smooth, golden-coloured, hoppy bitter with subtle fruity hops.

Delta APA (OG 1045, ABV 4.5%)
A pale golden-coluored, generously-hopped, American-style pale ale. Pungently hopped, with good bitterness and orange and citrus notes.

Graphite (OG 1046, ABV 4.6%)
A black IPA with complex hop notes.

Minnikins Stout (OG 1045, ABV 4.6%)
A rich, creamy stout with a long, lingering liquorice and pale chocolate finish.

Great Oakley SIBA

Ark Farm, High Street South, Tiffield, Northamptonshire, NN12 8AB
🌐 greatoakleybrewery.co.uk

Award-winning brewery established in 2005 in Great Oakley, relocating to Tiffield in 2012. It is run by Guy Jenkins who took over in 2017. More than 60 outlets are supplied, including brewery tap, the George, Tiffield. !! ♦ RAIB

Welland Valley Mild (OG 1037, ABV 3.6%)
A dark-coloured, traditional mild, full of flavour.

Egret (OG 1038, ABV 3.8%)

Wagtail (OG 1040, ABV 3.9%)

Wot's Occurring (OG 1040, ABV 3.9%)
A mid-golden-coloured session bitter with a subtle hop finish.

Tiffield Thunderbolt (OG 1043, ABV 4.2%)

Harpers (OG 1044, ABV 4.3%)
Traditional mid-brown-coloured bitter with a malty taste and slight hints of chocolate and citrus in the finish.

Gobble (OG 1045, ABV 4.5%)
Straw-coloured ale with a pleasant hop aftertaste.

Delapre Dark (OG 1047, ABV 4.6%)
A dark-coloured, full-bodied, malty ale.

Abbey Stout (OG 1051, ABV 5%)
A dark-coloured, rich stout.

Tailshaker (OG 1051, ABV 5%)
A complex golden ale with a great depth of flavour.

Great Orme

See Snowdon Craft

Great Western SIBA

Stream Bakery, Bristol Road, Hambrook, Bristol, BS16 1RF
☎ (0117) 957 2842 🌐 gwbrewery.co.uk

⊗ Great Western is a 12-barrel brewery set up in 2008 by Kevin Stone in a former bakery. The property has been renovated resulting in a bespoke showpiece brewery retaining many of the building's original features. The brewery owns a single pub – the Rising Sun, Frampton Cotterell – and 500 outlets are supplied. ‼ ♦

HPA (OG 1040, ABV 4%)
Hoppy, yellow-coloured bitter with zesty, citrus flavours and hints of tropical fruit, leading to a moreish, bittersweet finish.

Maiden Voyage (OG 1040, ABV 4%)
An amber-coloured bitter with a light aroma of malt and fruit which continues to the palate before leading to a strong, bitter finish.

Old Higby (OG 1045, ABV 4.8%)
Full-bodied, malty bitter with roast notes on the nose. Hints of fruit flavour give way to a bitter hop finish with some astringency throughout.

Moose River (OG 1047, ABV 5%)
Light citrus aroma, delicate hop taste with a long-lasting, bitter finish.

Great Yorkshire

New Inn, Cropton, North Yorkshire, YO18 8HH
☎ (01751) 417330
🌐 thegreatyorkshirebrewery.co.uk

Established in 1984, the brewery was built behind the New Inn in 1994. In 2010 Cropton Brewery rebranded as Great Yorkshire for its export markets. Beers are available throughout Yorkshire and nationally through wholesalers. ‼ ♦ RAIB

Yorkshire Classic (OG 1043.5, ABV 4%)
Light chestnut-coloured beer with a smooth, malty taste, balanced with complex biscuity flavours.

Yorkshire Golden (OG 1045, ABV 4.2%)
A refreshing, golden-coloured beer with hints of caramel and honey-like sweetness.

Yorkshire Blackout (OG 1051, ABV 5%)

Green Dragon

Green Dragon, 29 Broad Street, Bungay, Suffolk, NR35 1EF
☎ (01986) 892681

The Green Dragon is Bungay's busiest pub and oldest existing brewery, established in 1991 by brothers Robert and William Pickard. In 1994 the plant was expanded and moved to a converted barn. The doubling of capacity allowed the production of a larger range of ales. ‼ ♦

Chaucer Ale (OG 1037, ABV 3.8%)

Gold (OG 1045, ABV 4.4%)

Bridge Street Bitter (OG 1045, ABV 4.5%)

Strong Mild (OG 1054, ABV 5.5%)
A dark, ruby-coloured ale. Plum and dark chocolate on the nose, with a rich and smooth taste full of dark malt notes. Mildly-hopped to allow the malt character to prevail.

Green Duck SIBA

Unit 13, Gainsborough Trading Estate, Rufford Road, Stourbridge, West Midlands, DY9 7ND
☎ (01384) 377666 🌐 greenduckbrewery.co.uk

Green Duck began brewing in 2012 and relocated to its present site in Stourbridge in 2013. Experimental beers are brewed alongside a core range. The brewery has an on-site brewery tap, the Badelynge Bar, where the brewing equipment is visible through a glass partition. Private events and quarterly beer festivals are hosted as well as being open to the public at weekends (check social media for times). ‼ ♦

Duck & Cover (OG 1041, ABV 4%)
Pale gold-coloured ale with a tropical aroma. Refreshing with a dry pine and resin aftertaste.

Duck Blonde (OG 1042, ABV 4.2%)
Gold-coloured with a sharp fruity aroma. Lots of passion fruit flavour. Aftertaste is balanced with fruit sweetness and hops.

Sitting Duck (OG 1045, ABV 4.5%)
A hoppy and straw-like pale ale.

Duck & Dive (OG 1056, ABV 5.9%)
Amber-coloured ale with a fruity aroma. Citrus hop and spicy orange peel sweetness taste, with a long bitter finish.

Green Jack SIBA

Argyle Place, Love Road, Lowestoft, Suffolk, NR32 2NZ
☎ (01502) 562863 ☎ 0044 7902219459
🌐 green-jack.com

⊗ After 10 years at Oulton Broad, Green Jack moved to the Triangle Tavern, Lowestoft in 2003 and then to a nearby 35-barrel plant in 2009. One pub is owned and more than 150 outlets supplied. ‼ ♦ RAIB

Golden Best (OG 1037, ABV 3.8%)

Trawlerboys Best Bitter (OG 1045, ABV 4.6%)
Tawny-coloured beer with aroma of apple, sultana and malt plus hints of caramel and hops. Rich fig and plum base with malt and roast overtones. Strong finish with a sticky mouthfeel.

Lurcher Stout (OG 1046, ABV 4.8%)
Pleasant malt, roast and fruit aromas. Blackberry, raisin and port flavours. Long, dry, bitter roast finish.

Rising Sun (OG 1047, ABV 4.8%)

Red Herring (OG 1048, ABV 5%)

Gone Fishing ESB (OG 1052, ABV 5.5%)

Mahseer IPA (OG 1056, ABV 5.8%)

Ripper Tripel (OG 1074, ABV 8.5%)

Baltic Trader Export Stout (OG 1092, ABV 10.5%)

Green Mill SIBA

Harewood Arms, 2 Market Street, Broadbottom, SK14 6AX ☎ 07967 656887 🌐 greenmillbrewery.com

Green Mill started brewing in 2007 on a 2.5-barrel plant and moved in 2010 to the Cask & Feather in Rochdale. The brewery relocated again in 2013 to the Harewood Arms in Broadbottom. A number of occasional beers are brewed. Around 40 outlets are supplied. ♦GF

Gold (OG 1035, ABV 3.6%)

Chief (OG 1041, ABV 4.2%)

Citrus Snap (OG 1040, ABV 4.2%)
A copper-coloured bitter with citrus notes.

Old Git (OG 1040, ABV 4.2%)
A refreshing, complex, well-hopped, golden-coloured pale ale.

Talisman (OG 1040, ABV 4.2%)
A straw-coloured golden ale with tropical fruit notes.

Flavia (OG 1042, ABV 4.5%)
A blonde beer with a fresh hop aroma and a clean, dry finish.

Northern Lights (OG 1045, ABV 4.5%)
A pale-coloured, well-hopped premium bitter.

Big Chief (OG 1052, ABV 5.5%)
An aggressively-hopped premium bitter.

Greene King

Westgate Brewery, Westgate Street, Bury St Edmunds, Suffolk, IP33 1QT
☎ (01284) 763222 🌐 greeneking.co.uk

Greene King has been brewing in the market town of Bury St Edmunds since 1799. It brews its beers using water drawn from artesian chalk wells below its brewhouse as well as local East Anglia malt. Beers are also brewed under the Tolly Cobbold brand name. ‼ ♦RAIB

XX Mild (OG 1035, ABV 3%)
A dark-coloured mild with a sweet and roast flavour.

IPA (OG 1036, ABV 3.6%)
Hop-infused fruit cake aromas. Complex flavours of malt, caramel and hop with both sweetness and bitterness. A lingering mellow aftertaste with blackberries.

London Glory (OG 1041.1, ABV 4%)
Rich, fruity and full of flavour.

Yardbird (OG 1043.6, ABV 4%)
Inspired by bold American IPAs, full of hops with a lasting, fruity flavour.

IPA Gold (OG 1041, ABV 4.1%)
A deep golden-coloured ale, with a blend of tropical fruits, mango and spicy notes.

St Edmunds (OG 1038.6, ABV 4.2%)
A golden-coloured beer with an intense hop aroma and fruity character.

Abbot (OG 1049, ABV 5%)
Strong malt, toffee and caramel aromas. Rich, malty caramel flavours with vine fruit and a little hop bite. Heavy sweet finish, with a subtle hint of bitterness in the aftertaste.

IPA Reserve (OG 1055.5, ABV 5.4%)
A full-bodied amber-coloured ale. Grapefruit and orange citrus tones combine with floral and herbal notes. Dry, bitter finish.

Brewed for the Taylor Walker pub chain:

1730 (ABV 4%)

Brewed under the Hardy & Hansons brand name:

Bitter (OG 1038, ABV 3.9%)
A balance of sweetness and bitterness that combines with a subtle hop character. A distinctive beer with a full finish.

Olde Trip (OG 1043, ABV 4.3%)
A rich toffee-flavoured beer with a fruity character and a clean, bitter finish.

Brewed under the Morland brand name:

Original Bitter (OG 1039, ABV 4%)
A subtle malt and fruit character and a pronounced bitter finish.

Old Golden Hen (OG 1038.6, ABV 4.1%)
Light, golden-coloured beer, with tropical fruit notes.

Old Speckled Hen (OG 1045, ABV 4.5%)
Smooth, malty and fruity with a short finish.

Brewed under the Ruddles brand name:

Best Bitter (OG 1037, ABV 3.7%)
An amber/brown-coloured beer. Strong on bitterness, with some initial sweetness, fruit and subtle, distinctive hop note. Dryness lingers in the aftertaste.

County (OG 1043, ABV 4.3%)
Sweet, malty and bitter with a dry and bitter aftertaste.

Greenfield SIBA

Unit 8, Waterside Mills, Greenfield, Saddleworth, OL3 7NH
☎ (01457) 879789 ☎ 07716 239883
🌐 greenfieldrealale.co.uk

Greenfield was launched in 2002 and is situated in an old spinning mill next to the River Chew on the edge of the Peak District National Park. Spring water from the National Park is used for brewing. It is open to the public and supplies beer to more than 100 outlets. New owner Tony Pye took over in 2017. ‼ ♦

Black Five (OG 1041, ABV 4%)

Silver Owl (OG 1042, ABV 4%)
A golden-coloured beer with aromas of citrus fruits and hints of vanilla and oranges. Lightly-hopped with a dry finish.

Dobcross Bitter (OG 1041, ABV 4.2%)
A full-bodied, amber-coloured beer with lemon flavours and a dry finish.

Genesis (OG 1046, ABV 4.6%)

Greenodd

Ship Inn, Main Street, Greenodd, Cumbria, LA12 7QZ
☎ (01229) 861553 ☎ 07782 655294
🌐 theshipinngreenodd.co.uk

Established in 2010 at the Ship Inn on a two-barrel plant. The majority of production goes to the Ship with the remainder going to the local free trade. ‼♦

Greenwich (NEW)

Up The Creek Comedy Club, 302 Creek Road, Greenwich, London, SE10 9SW
☎ (020) 8858 4581

Greenwich Brewery Co began brewing in 2018 using a three-barrel plant and is situated in the front part of the bar area of the Up the Creek Comedy Club. The beers are available in the bar. Please note that entrance may be restricted to ticket holders for some events in the club area. RAIB

Greg's

Dambusters Inn, 23 High Street, Scampton, Lincolnshire, LN1 2SD
☎ (01522) 730123

Established in 2013, the microbrewery is situated on the premises of the Dambusters Inn. A number of house ales are produced by publican Greg Algar. ♦

Grendon Wave

See Custom Head

Grey Friars

Featherstone Hall Farm, New Road, Featherstone, Staffordshire, WV10 7NW
☎ (1785) 840093 ☎ 07966 361443

Office: 17 Cranbrooks, Wheaton Aston, ST19 9PZ
greyfriarsbrewery.co.uk

Established in 2014 and using equipment originally from Upham Brewery in Hampshire, the three-barrel plant is installed in a barn, formerly used as a snooker room and which still contains the original wood panelling. Brewing is currently suspended.

Grey Trees SIBA

Unit 5-6, Gasworks Road, Aberaman, CF44 6RS
☎ (01685) 267077 greytreesbrewing.com

The Award-winning Grey Trees brewery was established at the Red Cow Inn in 2011 on the outskirts of Aberdare and relocated to its present location in the Cynon Valley in 2013, upgrading to a 10-barrel plant. It supplies an increasing number of local outlets, as well as those in other parts of South Wales. !! ♦ RAIB

Caradog (OG 1038, ABV 3.9%)
Copper in colour with a crisp flavour and dry finish.

Black Road Stout (OG 1040, ABV 4%)
Dark-coloured, smooth stout with delicate roasted flavours and a bittersweet aftertaste.

Diggers Gold (OG 1040, ABV 4%)
A modern golden ale with fresh citrus aromas, which leave a subtle bitterness.

Drummer Boy (OG 1042, ABV 4.2%)

Mosaic Pale Ale (OG 1042, ABV 4.2%)
Crisp and refreshing pale ale, generously-hopped.

Chinookan VPA (OG 1043, ABV 4.3%)
Pale ale with a spicy and subtle grapefruit character.

Valley Porter (OG 1046, ABV 4.6%)
Warming and rich with notes of dark fruits, coffee, chocolate and hazelnuts.

JPR Pale (OG 1046, ABV 4.7%)

Afghan Pale (OG 1054, ABV 5.4%)
American-style pale ale, full-flavoured, crisp and thirst-quenching.

Greyhound SIBA

Watershed, Smock Alley, West Chiltington, West Sussex, RH20 2QX ☎ 07973 625510
greyhoundbrewery.co.uk

Established in 2015 by husband-and-wife team Nick and Sarah Allen, Greyhound is a 7.5-barrel brewery. In 2017 the brewery took over production of Ballard's Brewery beers, and continue to make its traditional ales alongside the Greyhound range. !! ♦ RAIB

Good Ordinary Bitter (OG 1038, ABV 3.8%)
Conker brown-coloured, classic-style, session bitter, nutty flavour, subtle bitterness.

Blonde Bird (OG 1039, ABV 3.9%)
Refreshing pale ale, with a well-rounded, dry finish, and a subtle lemon-fresh aroma.

Amber Eyes (OG 1040, ABV 4.2%)
A rich, well-balanced, golden amber-coloured ale with complex floral aromas, rounded light biscuit malt flavours, and a bitter finish.

Ballards Best Bitter (ABV 4.2%)
Amber-coloured ale with a malty aroma. Well-balanced fruit and malt in the flavour gives way to a dry, hoppy after taste.

B-46 (OG 1044, ABV 4.6%)
A rich, dark amber-coloured ale. Warm, biscuity malt flavours move towards toast and blackberry, which linger on the palate. Clean, hoppy finish.

Tree Frog (OG 1047, ABV 4.9%)
Fresh grassy ale, with a incredibly zesty spin.

Ballards Nyewood Gold (ABV 5%)
Auburn bronze-coloured, premium ale with malty sugar and spicy hop aromas. A smooth creamy flavour with soft fruits throughout, with a balanced finish.

White Bird (ABV 5.2%)

Gribble

Gribble Inn,, Oving, West Sussex, PO20 2BP
☎ (01243) 786893 gribbleinn.co.uk

Established in 1980 using a five-barrel plant, the Gribble Brewery is the longest-serving brewpub in the Sussex area, independently owned and run by the licensees since 2005. A number of local outlets are supplied. ♦

Griffin

See Freestyle

Gritchie SIBA

Ashgrove Farm, Ashmore, Wiltshire, SP5 5AW
☎ (01747) 828996 gritchiebrewingcompany.co.uk

Owned by the film director Guy Ritchie, this 20-barrel brewery in converted farm buildings on the Ashcombe Estate commenced brewing in 2017, using its own borehole water and estate-grown barley. Expansion to 40-barrel capacity is planned. Both cask and KeyKeg beers are produced, with new beers are being developed regularly. It is currently distributing locally with plans to expand nationally. The Lore of the Land in Fitzrovia, London, is the brewery tap. !! ♦

Moon Lore (ABV 3.6%)

Summer Lore (ABV 3.6%)
A golden-coloured, hoppy ale.

English Lore (OG 1040, ABV 4%) ◆
A copper-coloured bitter with some hint of fruit in the aroma. A sweet, slightly bitter taste, which diminishes quickly.

Grounding Angels (NEW)

6 Rear Battle Hill, Hexham, Northumberland, NE46 1BB ☎ 07508 175512 ⊕ grounding-angels.com

Brewing commenced in 2018.

Little Wing (ABV 3.8%)

Lazy Rider (ABV 4.3%)
A hazy, hop-forward pale ale.

Chasing the Horizon (ABV 5.3%)

Happy Accident Red Porter (ABV 5.5%)

Mr Stouty Pants (ABV 5.8%)

Snazzberry Juice (ABV 5.8%)
A full-bodied IPA with a kick of mango, grapefruit and guava. A smooth mouthfeel with rounded bitterness.

Black IPA (ABV 6%)
A rich, malty beer with chocolate roast notes and hints of orange, peach, lime and vanilla to finish.

The Sequence of Ninkasi (ABV 6.2%)

GT SIBA

Unit 5, The Old Aerodrome, Chivenor Business Park, Braunton, Devon, EX31 4AY
☎ (01271) 267420 ☎ 07909 515170 ⊕ gtales.co.uk

⊠ GT Ales was established in Barnstaple in 2013, producing only bottle-conditioned beers, before relocating to larger premises in Braunton in 2015. All six regular award-winning ales are now available in cask. One-off specials of 20 barrels are regularly produced. ‼◆RAIB

Thirst of Many (OG 1043, ABV 4.2%)
Amber-coloured best bitter with a slight caramel and fruity taste. Good medium hop finish and slight malty aftertaste.

North Coast IPA (OG 1045, ABV 4.3%)
American-style IPA with strong fruity aroma, sweet taste, hints of tropical fruits and a complex, lingering hop finish.

Blonde Ambition (OG 1044, ABV 4.5%)
Pale gold-coloured ale, good hop and citrus/gooseberry notes, with a floral aroma.

Dark Horse (OG 1048, ABV 4.5%)
Smooth, slightly sweet mouthfeel, fruity taste with hints of blackcurrant and slight coffee bitterness in the finish.

Battleaxe (OG 1046, ABV 4.7%)
Distinctly red in colour, brewed with rye malt. Fruity aroma with apricot and peach notes and some woody aromas. Malted taste with good, fruity, medium hop finish.

Crimson Rye'd (OG 1048, ABV 4.8%)
A red-coloured ale brewed with rye malt. Strong fruity and malty taste, with a good fruity, residual hop finish.

Gun

Hawthbush Farm, Gun Hill, East Sussex, TN21 0JY
☎ (01323) 700200 ☎ 07900 683355
⊕ gunbrewery.co.uk

⊠ Gun Brewery is located on a beautiful 140-acre organic mixed farm in the Sussex Weald. It generates much of its own power from a 15-kW solar array and heating comes from a wood-powered boiler. Spent grains keep the local livestock happy and all the water used for brewing comes from the brewery's spring. More than 30 outlets are supplied. RAIB V

Scaramanga Extra Pale (OG 1038, ABV 3.9%)
A refreshing, extra pale session ale with a hoppy finish.

Parabellum Milk Stout (OG 1057, ABV 4.1%)
A rich, jet black-coloured milk stout with a balance of coffee, vanilla and chocolate notes and a full malt base.

Chummy Bluster Best Bitter (ABV 4.4%)

Project Babylon Pale Ale (OG 1044, ABV 4.6%)
A classic American-style pale ale, vibrant and refreshing with citrus notes and dry finish.

Base Ejection Smoked Rye (OG 1046, ABV 4.7%)
A pale ale with a balance of spiciness from the rye and a subtle smokiness.

Zamzama IPA (OG 1060, ABV 6.5%)
Modern take on an IPA. Rounded malt body meets an avalanche of hops.

Gun Dog SIBA

Unit 5b, Great Central Way, Woodford Halse, Northamptonshire, NN11 3PZ
☎ (01327) 264095 ☎ 07834 374751
⊕ gundogales.co.uk

Gun Dog is a family-run brewery established in 2012. A six-barrel plant is used to brew modern crafted ales with a nod to brewing traditions of the past. Beers are available in a number of pubs and shops locally. ‼🛒◆RAIB

Jack's Spaniels (OG 1038, ABV 3.8%)
Well-balanced, floral, refreshing blonde ale.

Scrum Dog (OG 1040, ABV 4%)
An amber-coloured beer with a taste of fruit and hops.

Booze Hound (OG 1042, ABV 4.2%)
A copper-coloured IPA with a slightly sweet taste and a hoppy, bitter twist.

Lord Barker (OG 1042, ABV 4.2%)
Rich, dark-coloured, well-balanced stout. Chocolate nose, rounded taste in the mouth and a clean finish.

Bad to the Bone (OG 1045, ABV 4.5%) ◆
A light brown-coloured bitter with a fruity nose, biscuit malt flavour and a bitter finish.

Yankee Poodle (OG 1047, ABV 4.7%) ◆
A golden-coloured beer with a citrus hop aroma, citrus bitter flavour and a bitter finish.

Gwaun Valley

Kilkiffeth Farm, Pontfaen, SA65 9TP
☎ (01348) 872451 ☎ 07854 767383
⊕ gwaunvalleybrewery.co.uk

Gwaun Valley began brewing in 2009 on a four-barrel plant in a converted granary. The brewery offers views of the Preseli Hills and has a campsite, a holiday cottage and pitches for five caravans. Folk music sessions are held every Saturday evening. The owners retired early in 2019 and the business is being relaunched by a new tenant brewer who will retain some core range of beers and add others. !! ⛟

Farmhouse Ale (OG 1040, ABV 4%)
A malty ale with a smooth, balanced character.

St Davids Special (OG 1040, ABV 4%)
A light, fruity beer with a refreshingly citrus flavour.

Blodwen (OG 1043, ABV 4.3%)
Creamy, full-bodied bitter, ruby red in colour, with a hint of caramel.

Cascade (OG 1043, ABV 4.3%)
Refreshing, clear, hoppy pale ale.

Cwm Gwaun Porter (OG 1050, ABV 4.3%)
Rich, malty ale with medium body and a bittersweet aftertaste.

King of the Road (OG 1045, ABV 4.5%)
A full-bodied, smooth, classic, light chestnut ale, with a well-balanced finish.

Pembrokeshire Best Bitter (OG 1045, ABV 4.7%)
A full-flavoured, malty bitter ale, with a delightfully hoppy finish

Gyle 59 SIBA

The Brewery, Sadborow Estate Yard, Thorncombe, Dorset, TA20 4PW
☎ (01297) 678990 ☎ 07508 691178 🌐 gyle59.co.uk

⊗ Gyle 59 is a 10-barrel brewery that began commercial production in 2014. Bottling takes place on-site with bottles being available by mail order. !! ⛟ ♦ RAIB

Take It Easy (OG 1029, ABV 2.5%)
Light, refreshing session beer.

Freedom Hiker (OG 1038, ABV 3.7%)

Thoroughbred (OG 1037, ABV 3.7%)
Citrus, pale-coloured session beer.

Legless Liz (ABV 3.8%)

Toujours (OG 1042, ABV 4%)

C59's Special (OG 1044, ABV 4.2%)

Vienna Session Lager (ABV 4.2%)

Brad's Coffee Stout (OG 1045, ABV 4.5%)
A gentle stout with a subtle coffee aroma and taste.

Capitalist Hippie Far-Out (ABV 5%)
A New England-style IPA with flavours of pink grapefruit, mango and pineapple and a zingy, pithy aftertaste.

Halcyon Daze (OG 1046.5, ABV 5%)

IPA (OG 1050, ABV 5.3%)

Nettle IPA (OG 1050, ABV 5.3%)

Dorset GIPA (OG 1050, ABV 5.4%)
A ginger-infused IPA.

Starstruck (OG 1060, ABV 6.6%)
A fruity porter with the addition of star anise.

The Favourite (OG 1060, ABV 6.6%)
A smooth, rich porter.

Double IPA (OG 1063, ABV 7.3%)

Hackney Church

Arches 16 & 17, Bohemia Place, Hackney, London, E8 1DU
☎ (020) 8985 3496 🌐 hackneychurchbrew.co

Formerly known as St John at Hackney Brewery. Comprising two railway arches, the brewery almost fills one arch, the other being the taproom. With an experienced brewing team, the recipies are being continually refined. Available only in the tapoom for quality control, beers come from kegs or the tanks above the bar. All profits are used by the trust for worthy church based projects at St John at Hackney.

Hackney SIBA

Arch 358, Laburnum Street, Haggerston, London, E2 8BB
☎ (020) 3489 9595 🌐 hackneybrewery.co.uk

⊗ Founded in 2011, Hackney Brewery is the oldest brewery in the area. Cask is getting increasingly rare as the emphasis moves towards keg and canned beer. RAIB

Golden Ale (OG 1041, ABV 4%) ◆
Perfumed hops, honey and fruit balanced by a dry, pleasant bitterness that builds as the fruit and hops diminish.

Best Bitter (OG 1044, ABV 4.4%) ◆
Pale brown-coloured beer with a sweet citrus aroma and full, smooth mouthfeel. Citrus and floral hops on the palate.

American Pale Ale (OG 1045, ABV 4.5%) ◆

Hadham SIBA

Unit 6C Hadham Industrial Estate, Church End, Little Hadham, Hertfordshire, SG11 2DY
☎ (01279) 771916 ☎ 07770 766376
🌐 hadhambrewery.co.uk

⊗ Hadham began brewing in 2015 with a 10-barrel plant, using its own spring water found on site. Outlets are supplied within a 25-mile radius of the brewery.

Gold (OG 1038, ABV 3.7%)
Golden ale with a light citrus and fresh hops character; crisp and lightly bitter with some sweetness developing

Oddy (OG 1039, ABV 3.9%)
Copper-coloured ale with a rounded citrus aroma, splashes of grapefruit and lychee, and a smooth bitterness.

First (OG 1040, ABV 4%)
Reddish-brown-coloured best bitter, fruity, bitter body, with caramel notes and a full finish.

Hadrian Border SIBA

Unit 5 The Preserving Works, Newburn Industrial Estate, Shelley Road, Newburn, NE15 9RT
☎ (0191) 264 9000 🌐 hadrian-border-brewery.co.uk

Based in Newburn near Newcastle-upon-Tyne using a 40-barrel plant, the brewery can produce up to 200 barrels per week. Beer is delivered directly to the area between Edinburgh, North Yorkshire, Carlisle and the East Coast, and is also available nationally through wholesalers. A three-barrel plant is used for experimental craft brews.

Two pubs are run – the John Bull Inn, Alnwick, and Station East, Gateshead. ‼♦RAIB GF

Tyneside Blonde (OG 1039, ABV 3.9%) ◈
Refreshing blonde ale with zesty notes and a clean, fruity finish.

Farne Island Pale Ale (OG 1040, ABV 4%) ◈
A copper-coloured bitter with a refreshing malt/hop balance.

Northern Pale (OG 1041, ABV 4.1%)
A crisp, light pale ale delivering mellow citrus and grapefruit tones.

Secret Kingdom (OG 1042, ABV 4.3%)
Dark-coloured, rich and full-bodied, slightly roasted with a malty palate ending with a pleasant bitterness.

Coast to Coast (OG 1043, ABV 4.4%)
Light amber-coloured, hoppy beer with a good malt balance.

Reiver's IPA (OG 1043, ABV 4.4%)
Golden-coloured bitter with a clean citrus palate and aroma, with subtle malt flavours at the end.

Northumbrian Gold (OG 1044, ABV 4.5%)
Light golden-coloured ale with a biscuit malt flavour countered with floral and aromatic hops.

Grainger Ale (OG 1045, ABV 4.6%)
A pale-coloured ale, well-balanced, gluten free ale, with a refreshing bitter finish.

Ouseburn Porter (OG 1052, ABV 5.2%) ◈
Traditional robust porter with a distinct, bitter coffee finish.

Contract brewed for Black Storm Brewery:

Blonde (ABV 4%)
A refreshing, hoppy blonde beer with a subtle biscuit malt flavour and a strong hoppy backbone.

Gold (ABV 4.3%)

Porter (ABV 5.2%)

IPA (ABV 5.5%)

Hafod

Old Gas Works, Gas Lane, Mold, CH7 1UR
☎ (01352) 750765 ☎ 07901 386638
🌐 welshbeer.com

☺Hafod began brewing in 2011 on a small scale and relocated to the current premises in 2014, whilst retaining the original kit at the old site for low volumes. A number of one-off special brews are produced on a regular basis, and also on a limited basis using ingredients from the local upland areas. ‼♦RAIB

Sunrise (OG 1037, ABV 3.8%) ◈
A pale and refreshing golden ale with citrus fruit bitterness throughout, and a mouthwatering astringent finish.

Moonlight (OG 1039, ABV 3.9%)
A roasty porter with subtle notes of coffee and burnt toast.

Landmark (OG 1046, ABV 4.6%) ◈
Copper-coloured ale, with a malty, juicy mouthfeel. Fruit and faint roast flavours.

Moldbreaker (OG 1046, ABV 4.6%)
A crisp, smooth pilsner-style lager.

Clwydian Black (OG 1047, ABV 4.7%) ◈
A dry, roasty stout with a mellow, sweetish initial taste, accompanied by roast coffee bitterness in the finish.

Hal's

22a Woodmancote, Dursley, Gloucestershire, GL11 4AF ☎ 07765 890946 🌐 halsales.uk

Hal's is a one-barrel microbrewery established in Dursley in 2016, occasionally producing a number of small-batch beers for the New Inn, Woodmancote, Dursley and beer festivals. ♦

HHH (ABV 3.6%)
Hoppy, session pale ale.

Mick's Mild (ABV 3.8%)

What Sony's Havin (ABV 4.2%)
Amarillo-flavoured pale ale.

Hal's Gold (ABV 4.4%)
A classic golden ale with a slightly sweet finish.

Black Jack (ABV 4.5%)
A delicious blackcurrant and vanilla stout.

Hal's New Inn Chestnut Bitter (ABV 4.6%)
A balanced, malty, brown-coloured ale.

Hale

39a Markfield Road, Tottenham Hale, London, N15 4QA 🌐 hale.beer

Hale started in 2017 using the kit left behind by Affinity when it moved to Bermondsey. It is situated inside a shipping container outside the Five Miles bar which acts as its taproom. An ever-changing range of keg beers is available there and a growing number of bars and events around London.

Hale's

See Grafton

Half Moon SIBA

Forge House, Main Street, Ellerton, East Yorkshire, YO42 4PB
☎ (01757) 288977 ☎ 07741 400508
🌐 halfmoonbrewery.co.uk

Established in 2013 by Tony and Jackie Rogers, the brewery is situated in a former blacksmith's forge with a capacity of 5.5-barrels. Brewing takes place 2-3 times a week. ♦

Dark Masquerade (OG 1038, ABV 3.6%)
Rich, warm and smoky ruby-coloured ale packed with dark chocolate and liquorice.

Old Forge Bitter (OG 1040, ABV 3.8%)
Bright amber-coloured bitter with soft spiced lemon and honey flavours.

F'Hops Sake (OG 1039, ABV 3.9%)
Pale-coloured session bitter with a fruity and hoppy aftertaste.

Mount Hood (ABV 4.2%)

Session IPA (OG 1041, ABV 4.3%)
Crisp, session pale ale with citrusy aromas and juicy flavours.

Port Out (OG 1050, ABV 4.6%)

Classic porter, dark in colour and soft on the palate.

Lunar (OG 1047, ABV 5.5%)
A refreshing, golden-coloured bitter with an intense hop aroma and fine malt flavour. Hints of caramel are followed by a floral hop aftertaste.

Halfpenny

Crown Inn, High Street, Lechlade, Gloucestershire, GL7 3AE
☎ (01367) 252198 halfpennybrewery.co.uk

Halfpenny was established in 2008 on a four-barrel plant at the Crown at Lechlade, visible in a glazed outbuilding. It has since expanded to a third fermentation vessel. Beers are brewed mainly for the pub and the Swan at Radcot. ‼

Halifax Steam

The Conclave, Southedge Works, Brighouse Road, Hipperholme, West Yorkshire, HX3 8EF
☎ 07506022504 halifax-steam.co.uk

Brewing since 1999, the five-barrel plant supplies only the brewery tap, the Cock o' the North. It is now reputedly the oldest brewery in Calderdale. A range of permanent beers and around 200 different rotating beers are brewed, including the only rice beers in the country. 10-12 Halifax Steam beers are available in the pub at any one time, plus occasional guests on a fair trade basis. ♦

Hall & Woodhouse (Badger) SIBA IFBB

Bournemouth Road, Blandford St Mary, Blandford Forum, Dorset, DT11 9LS
☎ (01258) 452141 hall-woodhouse.co.uk

Hall & Woodhouse has been brewing in the heart of the Dorset countryside since 1777. Owned and run by the seventh generation of the Woodhouse family, it brews with local spring water filtered through the Cretaceous chalk downs and drawn up 120ft from its wells. A leading, independent UK brewer, its well-known range of Badger ales is award-winning, and has an estate (around 200 pubs) across southern England. Its ales are available exclusively in Hall & Woodhouse public houses. ‼ ♦

Badger Best Bitter (OG 1037, ABV 3.7%)
Well-balanced bitter with malt caramel sweetness and hop fruitiness.

Fursty Ferret (OG 1041.5, ABV 4.1%)
Easy-drinking best bitter with sweet bitterness that lingers into a dry aftertaste, with a hint of orange.

Tanglefoot (OG 1047, ABV 4.9%)
Relatively sweet-tasting and deceptive, given its strength. Caramel overtones and a bittersweet finish.

Halton Turner (NEW)

Lakey Lane, Hall Green, Birmingham, West Midlands, B28 2QT ☎ 07821 447329

Established in 2018, Halton Turner is a brewery and taproom based in Hall Green, Birmingham.

Hambleton SIBA

Melmerby Green Road, Melmerby, North Yorkshire, HG4 5NB
☎ (01765) 640108 hambletonales.co.uk

Established in 1991 in a farm shed on the banks of the River Swale in the Vale of York, Hambleton now occupies purpose-built premises with capacity for 100-barrels a week. The core range of beer is supplemented by monthly and seasonal specials. Village Brewer, Black Dog and Wharfe Brewery beers are contract brewed and a bottling line handles brands for other brewers. The brewery tap is the King William IV, Ripon. ‼ ♦

Session Pale (OG 1036, ABV 3.6%)
Straw-coloured, session pale ale, not too hoppy, with a citrus aroma.

Bootleggers Pale Ale (OG 1037, ABV 3.8%)

Pink Grapefruit (OG 1041, ABV 4.1%)
Pale ale brewed with grapefruit.

Stallion Amber (OG 1041, ABV 4.2%)
A premium bitter, moderately hoppy throughout, well-balanced malt and fruit. Robust bitterness, with earthy hops drying the aftertaste.

Stud Blonde (OG 1042.5, ABV 4.3%)
Easy-drinking, smooth, golden-coloured beer with pronounced fruit notes in the aroma and flavour.

Black Forest (OG 1050, ABV 5%)
A smooth porter with a black cherry twist.

Nightmare Porter (OG 1050, ABV 5%)
Strong roast malts dominate, but hoppiness rears out of this complex blend.

Contract brewed for Black Dog Brewery:

Whitby Abbey Ale (OG 1037.5, ABV 3.8%)

Schooner (OG 1041.5, ABV 4.2%)

Rhatas (OG 1045, ABV 4.6%)

Contract brewed for Village Brewer:

White Boar (OG 1037.5, ABV 3.8%)

Bull (OG 1039, ABV 4%)

Contract brewed for Wharfe Beers:

Verbeia (OG 1035, ABV 3.6%)

Tether Blond (OG 1039, ABV 3.8%)

Hammerpot SIBA

Unit 30, The Vinery, Arundel Road, Poling, West Sussex, BN18 9PY
☎ (01903) 883338 hammerpot-brewery.co.uk

Hammerpot started brewing in 2005 using a five-barrel plant, which was upgraded to 10 barrels in 2011. The brewery supplies as far as London and Southampton. ♦ RAIB

Shooting Star (OG 1038, ABV 3.8%)

HPA (OG 1044, ABV 4.1%)
A light, golden-coloured, tangy pale ale with a full, fresh hop flavour.

Red Hunter (OG 1046, ABV 4.3%)
A ruby red-coloured, smooth bitter with a full-bodied, rich character.

Woodcote (OG 1047, ABV 4.5%)
A tangy, amber-coloured bitter with a pleasant dry finish.

Brighton Belle (ABV 4.6%)

Pale amber-coloured bitter. Fresh, floral hop notes, spicy orange, crisp grapefruit and a hint of caramel.

Bottle Wreck Porter (OG 1047, ABV 4.7%)
A traditional, pitch black-coloured porter with coffee, chocolate and rich roast malt flavours.

Madgwick Gold (OG 1050, ABV 5%)
A golden ale with a fresh, citrus spice hop aroma. Very drinkable with a refreshing, thirst-quenching finish.

Hammerton SIBA

Unit 8 & 9, Roman Way Industrial Estate, 149 Roman Way, Barnsbury, London, N7 8XH
☎ (020) 3302 5880 🌐 hammertonbrewery.co.uk

Hammerton began brewing in London in 1868. It ceased brewing in the 1950s; the brewery was later demolished. In 2014, a member of the Hammerton family resurrected the family name in brewing. The brewery is currently undergoing major expansion to increase capacity and expand tap room opening hours. RAIB

N1 (OG 1044, ABV 4.1%) ◆
Refreshing, smooth pale ale. Honey, some citrus and pineapple flavours, fading in the finish where a spicy, hoppy bitterness builds.

Life on Mars (OG 1045, ABV 4.6%) ◆
Ruby-coloured ale with roast, toffee and fruit aroma. Peppery hops, nutty roasty flavour with dark bitter marmalade. Dry, lingering finish.

N7 (OG 1052, ABV 5.2%) ◆
Cocoa throughout with a pleasant sweetness, balanced by a lingering dark roast dryness and a raisin fruitiness. A trace of liquorice.

Pentonville Oyster Stout (OG 1057, ABV 5.3%) ◆
Liquorice and fruit on the palate. Dry finish with a little dark roast character and a touch of caramelised fruit.

Hand SIBA

▮ 33 Upper St James's Street, Kemptown, Brighton, East Sussex, BN2 1JN
☎ (07508) 814541 ☎ 07508 814541
🌐 handbrewpub.com/brew

⊙Founded in 1989, the brewery is the smallest commercially operating tower brewery in the world. Originally operating under the Kemptown Brewery name before being used as a gypsy brewery by Brighton Bier for four years. Now operating as the Hand Brew Co since 2016. Around 10 other outlets are supplied. ‼

Handley's

▮ Willow Tree, Front Street, Barnby in the Willows, Newark, Nottinghamshire, NG24 2SA
🌐 willowtreebarnby.co.uk

⊙Handley's began brewing in 2011 on a 0.5-barrel plant installed behind the Willow Tree pub. Beer is mostly sold in the pub, with at least two being on pump at all times, and can occasionally be found at local beer festivals.

Handsome SIBA

Bowstone Bridge Garage, Bowston, Cumbria, LA8 9HD
☎ 0344 848 0888 🌐 handsomebrew.co.uk

Originally Houston Brewery in Renfrewshire, it was re-established as Handsome in 2016 in the Lake District. It is situated on the River Kent in an old MOT garage, formerly the blacksmith's for James Cropper's paper mills.

Top Knot (ABV 3.7%)
A fruity beer with a gentle malt finish.

Stranger (ABV 4.2%)
Refreshing best bitter with a floral hop aroma and clean fruit taste.

Bar Steward (ABV 4.8%)
Premium bitter with with a hoppy taste.

Blacksmith (ABV 4.8%)
Rich and full bodied, bursting with strong flavours.

Contract brewed for Winster Valley Brewery:

Dark Horse (OG 1035, ABV 3.5%)
A dark-coloured, warming mild with a soft mouth feel and roasted malt aromas.

Hurdler (OG 1035, ABV 3.5%)
A golden ale with a hint of sweetness on the nose tilted towards the hops and soft malty flavour.

Best Bitter (OG 1036, ABV 3.7%)
Smooth, full-bodied best bitter with a roasted malt flavour and a hint of caramel.

Lakes Blonde (OG 1037, ABV 3.7%) ◆
An uncomplicated fruity, hoppy bitter

Old School (OG 1037, ABV 3.9%)
Full-bodied pale ale with a floral aroma on the finish.

Chaser (OG 1041, ABV 4.1%)
Smooth, chestnut-coloured ale with caramel and toffee notes and a bittersweet finish.

Handyman

▮ 461 Smithdown Road, Liverpool, L15 3JL
☎ (0151) 222 7422 🌐 handymansupermarket.co.uk

Handyman Brewery is based within the Handyman Supermarket. For years this was a hardware store but has now been refurbished into the Handyman Pub, which opened in 2017. Its 400-litre brew kit is situated on a mezzanine floor above the bar. ♦

Hanging Bat

▮ c/o Hanging Bat 133 Lothian Rd, Edinburgh, EH3 9AB
☎ (0131) 229 0759
🌐 hangingbatbrewco.tumblr.com

⊗Brewing began in 2012 from within the Hanging Bat bar using a 50-litre brew kit from the United States.

Hanging Tree

▮ Benleva Hotel, Kilmore Road, Drumnadrochit, IV63 6UH

⊙Hanging Tree began brewing in 2017 using a two-barrel brew plant in an old bothy in the grounds of the Benleva Hotel. Named after the 400-year-old chestnut tree growing in the garden, which was used as the hanging tree for the local area. Beers are available in the pub and a few other local outlets.

Hanlons SIBA

Hill Farm, Half Moon Village, Devon, EX5 5AE
☎ (01392) 851160 🌐 hanlonsbrewery.com

⊗ Hanlons, one of Devon's largest brewers since 2013, supply a range of award-winning ales nationwide. The purpose-built brewery also has a shop, bar and restaurant. ‼ ♦

Firefly (OG 1038, ABV 3.7%) ◆
Malty, fruity, light bitter with hints of orange.

Citra IPA (OG 1039, ABV 4%)
Golden-coloured IPA with a sweet, malty taste and a clean citrus finish.

Yellow Hammer (OG 1041, ABV 4.2%) ◆
Golden ale dominated by hops and fruit throughout. Sweetness develops into a lingering aftertaste.

Brewers Blend (OG 1045, ABV 4.5%)
An amber-coloured ale with a malty biscuit palate. Sweet and fruity with a tangy orange aftertaste.

Port Stout (OG 1048, ABV 4.8%) ◆
Strong, black-coloured, speciality ale. Mild coffee and chocolate with fruity port notes. Lots of body.

Stormstay (OG 1050, ABV 5%) ◆
Tawny-coloured, full-bodied ale. Caramel with hints of malt on the nose. Malt, caramel, and hops develop into lingering bitterness.

Hapax

See Kingstone

Happy Valley

73 Oxford Road, Macclesfield, SK11 8JG
☎ (01625) 618360 ☎ 07758 512080
🌐 happyvalleybrewery.co.uk

⊗ Happy Valley was established in 2010 using a 2.5-barrel plant located in Bollington. In 2018 the brewery was sold and relocated to Macclesfield. ♦

Little Mill Town (OG 1036, ABV 3.6%)

Small & Mighty (OG 1036, ABV 3.6%)
A clean, full-flavoured, crisp and refreshing ale. Lasting floral, citrus aroma with a hint of lemon.

Sworn Secret (OG 1038, ABV 3.8%)
Pale straw-coloured ale. Strong hop character, pleasant, hoppy nose with a citrus aftertaste.

Little Rascal (OG 1039, ABV 3.9%)
A light, golden-coloured session ale. Hops are well-balanced with a lingering citrus and grapefruit aftertaste.

Five Rings (OG 1040, ABV 4%)

Lazy Daze (OG 1042, ABV 4.2%)
Golden-coloured ale with a hoppy finish.

Black Out XO Rum Porter (OG 1044, ABV 4.4%)
A dark-coloured, full-bodied porter with a deep, intense malty flavour and lingering aroma of oak-aged rum.

Black Magic (OG 1046, ABV 4.6%)

Tie the Knot (OG 1050, ABV 5%)
A straw-coloured, strong, IPA-style bitter. Malty with a big hop character.

Dangerously Dark (OG 1056, ABV 5.6%)
Black-coloured, IPA-style beer brewed with lots of malt and hops.

Bollywood IPA (OG 1058, ABV 5.9%)
A full-bodied, straw-coloured, strong bitter. Rounded malt flavours blended with bitterness and a big hop character. Deep, intensely rich taste.

Harbour SIBA

Trekillick Farm,, Kirland, Bodmin, Cornwall, PL30 5BB
☎ (01208) 832131 ☎ 07870 305063
🌐 harbourbrewing.com

⊗ Harbour is an innovative brewery founded on the outskirts of Bodmin in 2011. Brewed using local spring water, the regular beers are established in an increasing number of outlets. A new 30-barrel plant was installed in 2016, and more conditioning tanks in 2017. The brewery produces cask and keg beers. Bottling and canning is done on-site (no RAIB). ♦

Light (OG 1037, ABV 3.7%) ◆
Yellow-coloured golden ale with citrus hop aroma. Dominant, zesty citrus hops with some pineapple and pear drops. Long, hoppy finish.

Daymer Extra Pale (ABV 3.8%)

Amber (OG 1037.5, ABV 4%) ◆
Pale brown-coloured bitter with a floral hop aroma and malt. Biscuit malt throughout with apple, peach and plum, balanced by hops.

Cornish Bitter (ABV 4%)

New Zealand Gold (ABV 4.2%) ◆
Golden Ale with light hop nose. Strong pine needle hop flavour. Bitter, sweet and dry throughout.

Ellensberg (ABV 4.3%) ◆
Amber-coloured golden ale with a powerful citrus aroma. Strong, grapefruit citrus hop flavour leading to a crisp, long-lasting bitter finish.

Session IPA (OG 1043, ABV 4.3%)

India Brown Ale (OG 1049, ABV 4.9%) ◆
Smooth, copper-coloured, strong bitter. Heavy body and balanced sweet malt and bitter hop flavour, with plums, prunes and some butterscotch.

IPA (OG 1048.5, ABV 5%) ◆
Amber-coloured, American-style IPA, with powerful, citrus hop aroma and taste. Marmalade, red grapefruit and orange flavours with assertive bitterness.

Cascadia (ABV 5.2%)

Light no2 (ABV 5.2%)

Antipodean IPA (ABV 5.5%)

Little Rock IPA (ABV 5.5%)

Porter (OG 1055, ABV 5.5%) ◆
Smooth, creamy, black-coloured porter with roast malt aroma. Malty, smoky and sweet followed by a bitter tang. Sweet finish.

Harbour Pale (OG 1059, ABV 6%) ◆
Golden ale with powerfull citrus hop aroma. Intense citrus hop flavour with marmalade, orange and bitterness. Hoppy, slightly dry finish.

Harbwr Tenby SIBA

Sargeants Lane, St Julian Street, Tenby, SA70 7BU
☎ (01834) 845797 🌐 harbwr.wales

Brewing commenced in 2015 on a five-barrel plant in an outbuilding of the Buccaneer Inn, Tenby. Beers are available in the pub, at the nearby

Hope & Anchor and further afield. A mezzanine bar area is available for tastings, tapas and tours. ‼♦

MV Enterprise (OG 1040, ABV 4%)
A refreshing, citrus pale ale with spicy, herbal bitterness finished with a floral and zesty aroma.

North Star (OG 1042, ABV 4.2%)
Smooth, malty, amber-coloured ale with a herbal bitterness and a spicy blackcurrant and lemon aroma.

Caldey Lollipop (OG 1044, ABV 4.5%)
Hoppy, golden-coloured IPA with hints of pine and grapefruit.

RFA Sir Galahad (OG 1046, ABV 4.6%)
A rich, ruby-coloured ale with a deep, complex malt character and cider, grapefruit and floral aromas.

Harby

Bottle & Glass,, 5 High Street, Harby, Nottinghamshire, NG23 7EB
☎ (01522) 703438
🌐 wigandmitre-lincoln.blogspot.co.uk

Harby Brewstore is a four-barrel malt extract brewery established in 2015 and located at the Bottle & Glass in Harby. Most output goes to the three pubs in the small Wig & Mitre pub group; the Wig & Mitre, Lincoln, Caunton Beck, Caunton and the Bottle & Glass itself.

Hardys & Hansons

See Greene King

Haresfoot

Global Infusion Court, Nashleigh Hill, Chesham, Buckinghamshire, HP5 3FE
☎ (01494) 790783 🌐 haresfoot.com

Established in Berkhamsted in 2014, the brewery moved to its current site in 2017. A range of short-run, limited edition beers are brewed using a dual-channel 12 and 2.5-barrel plant. Beers are delivered to pubs across the Chiltern area and London. ♦

Sundial Golden Ale (OG 1038, ABV 3.8%)
A refreshing, light golden ale with generous late hopping leading to an undercurrent of exotic fruits.

Lock Keeper's Launch Ale (OG 1039, ABV 3.9%)
A complex blend of malts with a hoppy edge and delicate fruit notes, leading to a long, bittersweet aftertaste.

New Moon (OG 1042, ABV 4%)
A hoppy pale ale packed full of citrus, pineapple, grapefruit and resinous flavours with a crisp, dry finish.

Dragon's Bane (OG 1044.5, ABV 4.5%)
A well-rounded, tawny-coloured bitter with a fruity flavour and a well-balanced finish.

Harrison's (NEW)

Unit 1, 108 Carolgate, Retford, Nottinghamshire, DN22 6AS ☎ 07850 228383 🌐 harrisonsbrewery.com

A three-barrel brewery built completely from scratch by the brewer, Christopher Harrison-Hawkes. The first brew was in 2018, and shortly after four beers were available at its own pub, the Brew Shed. ‼♦

Harrison's Vacant Gesture (OG 1037, ABV 3.8%)
Hop-forward blonde ale with tropical aromas.

Harrison's Best Bitter (OG 1041, ABV 4%)

Harrison's Stout (OG 1049, ABV 4.8%)
A dry, full-bodied, complex stout with tastes of roast coffee and chocolate.

Harrogate SIBA

Unit 7, Hookstone Centre, Hookstone Chase, Harrogate, North Yorkshire, HG2 7HW ☎ 07774 891664 🌐 harrogatebrewery.co.uk

Established in 2013, the brewery also uses the names Spa Town Ales and It's Quicker By Ale on its logo and pumpclips. The brewery has a capacity of four barrels and brews several times each week.

Pale (OG 1040, ABV 4.2%)

Cold Bath Gold (OG 1042, ABV 4.4%)

Pinewoods Pale Ale (OG 1042, ABV 4.4%)
Pale-coloured beer with citrus flavours.

Plum Porter (OG 1048, ABV 4.8%)
Porter made with local plums.

Vanilla Porter (OG 1048, ABV 4.8%)
Rich porter made with vanilla pods.

Beeching Axe (OG 1050, ABV 5.2%)

Kursaal Stout (OG 1071, ABV 6.7%)
A rich, bittersweet stout with espresso, liquorice and chocolate flavours.

Hart Family

The Old House, 29 Sheep Street, Wellingborough, Northamptonshire, NN8 1BS
☎ (01933) 225932 ☎ 07891 212476
🌐 hartfamilybrewers.com

Hart Family Brewers was established in 2012 using an eight-barrel plant. The brewery opened its first pub, the Old House, in 2017 in the centre of Wellingborough. The brewery relocated to be on-site at the pub, using a brand new 10-barrel plant in 2019. ‼ RAIB

House Beer (OG 1036, ABV 3.6%)
A classic bitter with straightforward malt and hops flavours.

Harts No 1 (OG 1043, ABV 4.1%)
A tawny-coloured, premium bitter with fruity, malty aromas and grassy citrus notes. Fresh and fruity on the palate with spicy bitterness and citrus, hay-like aromas on the refreshing finish.

Harts No 9 (OG 1044, ABV 4.3%)
A golden-coloured beer, light and refreshing with spicy grapefruit aromas. Fresh and light on the palate with pithy grapefruit flavours supported by biscuity malt.

Harts No 3 (OG 1047, ABV 4.7%)
A fruity, ruby-coloured beer with full malty, spicy aromas. Full and forward on the palate with rounded, rich malty flavours supported by gentle spicy hoppiness,

Harts No 8 (OG 1052, ABV 5%)
A dark-coloured beer with bold, toasted fruit aromas and hints of espresso. Full and warming

roasted fruit and molasses flavours balanced by bitter coffee, chocolate and spice aromas over a long finish.

Pale (OG 1052, ABV 5%)
Strong bitter beer. Biscuity malt complemented by an orange-scented bitterness.

1833 India Pale Ale (ABV 6.6%)
An golden amber-coloured beer with a honey malt and orange marmalade hop aroma, a strong malt, marmalade and spice taste, with a dry, bitter finish.

Hart of Stebbing

White Hart, High Street, Stebbing, Essex, CM6 3SQ
☎ (01371) 856383 ✉ nickeldred@hotmail.com

The brewery was established in 2007 by Nick Eldred, who is also the owner of the White Hart pub where the brewery is based. At present only the White Hart and local beer festivals are supplied. ♦

Hartlebury (NEW)

Station Park, Station Road, Hartlebury, Worcestershire, DY11 7YJ
☎ (01299) 253617 ☎ 07831 570117
✉ davehiggs@dhcommercials.co.uk

Hartlebury Brewing Co was established in 2019 by David Higgs, the owner of the Tap House pub. It supplies the Tap House and local free trade.

Crusader (ABV 4.2%)

Off the Rails (ABV 4.2%)
A smooth, golden ale with a balanced sweetness and bitterness.

APA (ABV 4.5%)
An American-style pale ale with a light, hoppy aroma and clean bitter finish.

Hartshorns

Unit 4, Tomlinsons industrial estate, Alfreton Road, Derby, DE21 4ED ☎ 07830 367125
hartshornsbrewery.com

Hartshorns began brewing in 2012 using a six-barrel plant installed by brothers Darren and Lindsey Hartshorn. In 2015 the brewery acquired its first pub, the Little Chester Ale House, Derby.

Ignite (OG 1039, ABV 3.9%)

Highgate (OG 1044, ABV 4.3%)
Smooth, easy-drinking, pale copper-coloured ale. Well-balanced malt sweetness with fruity hop flavour and a well-rounded bitterness.

Porter (OG 1045, ABV 4.5%)

Brooklyn Nights (OG 1052, ABV 5.4%)
A punchy, American-style brown-coloured ale with a complex malt base. Abundant flavour and aroma, with an assertive bitterness, with a clean, dry finish.

Shakademus (OG 1052, ABV 5.4%)
Full-bodied, premium golden ale with a citrus hop bite.

Apocalypse (OG 1055, ABV 6.2%)
Easy-drinking golden ale with a clean, bitter finish. Refreshingly crisp and packed with hop character.

Harvey's IFBB

Bridge Wharf Brewery, 6 Cliffe High Street, Lewes, East Sussex, BN7 2AH
☎ (01273) 480209 harveys.org.uk

Established in 1790, this independent family brewery operates from the banks of the River Ouse in Lewes. A major development in 1985 doubled the brewhouse capacity to more than 38,000 barrels a year. There are plans to re-establish a microbrewery on-site to brew special beers, including replicating old recipes using the 'County Town Beers' name. Harvey's supplies real ale to all its 48 pubs and about 550 free trade outlets in the south-east. !! ♦ RAIB

R (ABV 2.8%)

Sussex XX Mild Ale (OG 1030, ABV 3%)
A dark copper-brown coloured ale. Roast malt dominates the aroma and palate leading to a sweet, caramel finish.

IPA (OG 1033, ABV 3.5%)

Sussex Wild Hop (OG 1037, ABV 3.7%)

Sussex Best Bitter (OG 1040, ABV 4%)
Full-bodied brown-coloured bitter. A hoppy aroma leads to a good malt and hop balance, and a dry aftertaste.

Old Ale (OG 1043, ABV 4.3%)

Olympia (OG 1042, ABV 4.3%)

Armada Ale (OG 1045, ABV 4.5%)
Hoppy, amber-coloured best bitter. Well-balanced fruit and hops dominate throughout with a fruity palate.

Harviestoun SIBA

Alva Industrial Estate, Alva, FK12 5DQ
☎ (01259) 769100 harviestoun.com

Harviestoun has grown from one-man brewing in a bucket in the back of a shed in 1983 to a 60-barrel, multi-award-winning brewery today. With a reputation for experimentation, the brewery adds around eight to ten short-run seasonals to its core range. !! ♦ RAIB

Bitter & Twisted (OG 1039, ABV 3.8%)
Refreshing, golden-coloured, hoppy session beer, with fruit throughout. A bittersweet taste with a long, bitter finish.

Old Engine Oil (OG 1045, ABV 4.5%)
Dark chocolate, creamy coffee, burnt toast, and sweet caramel.

Schiehallion (OG 1048, ABV 4.8%)
A Scottish cask lager. A hoppy aroma, with fruit and malt, leads to a malty, bitter taste with floral hoppiness and a bitter finish.

Harwich Town

c/o Unit 1, Upp Hall Farm, Salmons Lane, Coggeshall, Essex, CO6 1RY ☎ 07723 607917
harwichtown.co.uk

Founded in 2007 with a five-barrel plant in premises next to Harwich Town railway station. In 2018 it moved out of its original home and became a cuckoo brewery, using spare capacity at Red Fox Brewery (qv). The owner/brewer, a former customs officer, names the beers after local characters and landmarks. Local pubs and beer festivals are supplied, with reciprocal trading with other breweries. It organises the Harwich Redoubt Beer Festival in a Napoleonic fort in July each year. ♦RAIB

EPA Centenary (ABV 3.8%)

SS Brussels (ABV 3.8%)

Ganges (ABV 4%)

Bathside Battery Bitter (ABV 4.2%)

Lighthouse Best Bitter (ABV 4.8%)

Phoenix (ABV 5%)

Hastings

See Franklins

Hattie Brown's

Swanage, Dorset
☎ (01929) 439229

Office: Square & Compass, Worth Matravers, BH19 3LF
⊕ hattiebrownsbrewery.co.uk

⊗ Hattie Brown's began brewing in 2014 at the Wessex brewery. In 2015 it moved to its present location. It is owned by the manager of the Square & Compass, Worth Matravers, and partner, Jean, the brewer.

HBA (OG 1039, ABV 3.8%)
Well-balanced, copper-coloured, lightly-malted ale.

Moonlite (OG 1039, ABV 3.8%)
Hoppy pale ale with strong citrus notes and a big finish.

Kirrin Island (OG 1045, ABV 4.5%)

Spangle (OG 1046, ABV 4.6%)
Dark gold-coloured ale with strong hints of marmalade.

Crowblack (OG 1052, ABV 5.1%)
Classic, full-flavoured porter. Rich and dark-coloured with hints of chocolate and molasses.

Dog on the Roof (ABV 6%)
Dark gold-coloured ale with a fruity finish.

Hawk Wing SIBA

Unit E, Hawkshill Business Park, Lesbury, Northumberland, NE66 3PG

Brewing began in 2012 as VIP Brewery, using a five-barrel plant to serve the owner's pub, the Village Inn in Longframlington, and the local free trade. In 2018 the brewery changed its name to Hawk Wing.

One (ABV 4.3%)

Hawkshead

Mill Yard, Staveley, Cumbria, LA8 9LR
☎ (01539) 822644 ⊕ hawksheadbrewery.co.uk

⊚Established in 2002, the brewery takes its name from the village it was founded in. It outgrew its original barn and moved to Staveley in 2006 to a purpose-built 20-barrel brewery. Capacity has been increased several times since, a new micro packaging plant was added and the Beer Hall, brewery tap, developed as a showcase for real ale. In 2018 production of the core range of beers was transferred to a brand new brewery in Flookburgh, with the Stavely plant continuing to produce small batch beers. !! ☞ ♦RAIB

Iti (OG 1036, ABV 3.5%) ◆
Packed with grapefruit aroma and taste. Well-balanced with a long-lasting, hoppy bitter finish.

Windermere Pale (OG 1036, ABV 3.5%) ◆
Crisp, fruity, yellow-coloured beer with hints of melon and grapefruit and a strong bitter aftertaste.

Bitter (OG 1037, ABV 3.7%) ◆
Well-balanced, thirst-quenching beer with fruit and hops aroma, leading to a lasting bitter finish.

Mosaic Pale (OG 1040, ABV 4%)
A pale ale brewed using only Mosaic hops.

Red (OG 1042, ABV 4.2%) ⊡ ◆
Rich beer, lots of fruitiness and good hop flavour with a lingering aftertaste.

Lakeland Gold (OG 1043, ABV 4.4%) ◆
Dry, refreshing beer with good body and bitterness to the end.

Dry Stone Stout (OG 1044, ABV 4.5%) ◆
Black-coloured, dry, bitter stout with an astringent, roast finish.

Session IPA (OG 1046, ABV 4.7%)

Great White (OG 1048, ABV 4.8%)
Spiced, cloudy wheat beer. Brewed with coriander seeds, and Seville orange peel.

Brodie's Prime (OG 1048, ABV 4.9%) ▨ ◆
Complex, dark brown-coloured beer with plenty of malt, fruit and roast taste. Satisfying full body, with a clean finish.

Cumbrian Five Hop (OG 1050, ABV 5%) ⊡ ◆
A robust, hoppy bitter with citrus hops and fruity middle.

Lakeland Lager (OG 1045, ABV 5%)

NZPA (OG 1056, ABV 6%) ◆
A very hoppy bitter with a sweet, fruity taste and a dry, bitter finish.

IPA (OG 1065, ABV 7%)
A modern IPA, amber in colour, with huge hop flavours.

Brodie's Prime Export (OG 1075, ABV 8.5%)
Fruity and sweet with powerful roast and hop flavours.

Haworth Steam

⚏ Rose & Crown, 2 Westgate, Cleckheaton, West Yorkshire, BD19 5ET
☎ (01535) 646059 ☎ 07974 483310
⊕ haworthsteambrewery.co.uk

⊚Established in 2011, the five-barrel brewery is located at the Rose & Crown, Cleckheaton, this being the main outlet for the beers along with the Haworth Steam Bistro, Haworth. Beers are also sold under the Whitechapel brand name. ☞

Hay Rake

⚏ Rake Tapas Bar, Blackstone Edge Old Road, Littleborough, OL15 0JX
☎ (01706) 379689 ☎ 07775 792684
⊕ hayrakebrewery.info

Mark Wickham, the landlord of the Rake Tapas Restaurant, resurrected the Hay Rake microbrewery in 2013. The Rake brewed its own beer during the reign of Queen Victoria but stopped in 1901. Beers are available in the restaurant, occasionally the nearby White House and at local beer festivals.

Haywood Bad Ram SIBA

Callow Top Holiday Park, Buxton Road, Sandybrook, Ashbourne, Derbyshire, DE6 2AQ
☎ (01335) 344020 ☎ 07974 948427
callowtop.co.uk/ccallow-top-brewery

Established in 2003, the brewery was based in a converted barn but a new brewery and bottling plant became operational in 2012. One pub is owned (on-site) and several other outlets are supplied. !! RAIB

Thoroughbred Bad Ram (OG 1038, ABV 3.8%)
A refreshing, straw-coloured ale with a crisp bite, spice and flowery notes.

Dr Samuel Johnson (OG 1044, ABV 4.5%)
A slightly fruity and refined spicy flavour.

Callow Top Imperial IPA (OG 1050, ABV 5.2%)
A full-bodied, rich ale with a fruity and slightly citrus aftertaste.

Headcorn Hop (NEW)

Shenley Road, Headcorn, Kent, TN27 9HX
headcornhop.weebly.com

Headcorn Hop is a picobrewery producing small batch beers. Originally brewed in France, the owners now brew both in France and Kent.

Headstocks (NEW)

Unit 2, Meden Road, Boughton, Nottinghamshire, NG22 9ZD ☎ 07557 049120
sales@headstocksbrewery.co.uk

Headstocks was originally established in 2017 to brew Prussia Lager in collaboration with a partner brewery in Kaliningrad on the Lithuania/Poland border. In 2018 cask-conditioned beer was added to the range. !! RAIB

Brakeman Best Bitter (OG 1039, ABV 4%)
Warming, traditional best bitter with subtle caramel and nutty undertones.

Canary Pale Ale (OG 1038.5, ABV 4%)
A light session pale ale with floral hints of citrus and bitterness.

Healey's

Wellington Inn, Main Street, Loppergarth, Cumbria, LA12 0JL
☎ (01229) 582388

Healey's began brewing in the Wellington in 2012 using a custom-made 2.5-barrel stainless steel plant, which can be viewed through full-length windows in the pub. A range of different beer styles is brewed, available in more than 15 pubs.

Heaney Farmhouse

c/o Boundary Brewing, Portview Trade Centre, Newtownards Road, Belfast, BT4 1HE
heaneyfarmhousebrewing.com

Founded in 2014. Bottled beers are currently brewed at Boundary (qv) in Belfast while its brewhouse project is underway at a farm in Bellaghy, Co Londonderry. No real ale.

Heart of Wales

Stables Yard, Zion Street, Llanwrtyd Wells, LD5 4RD
☎ (01591) 610236 heartofwalesbrewery.co.uk

The brewery was set up with a six-barrel plant 2006, in old stables at the rear of the Neuadd Arms Hotel. Beers are brewed using water from its own borehole. Seasonal brews celebrate local events such as the World Bogsnorkelling Championships. Cambrian Heart Ale was commissioned by and is brewed for the Cambrian Mountains Initiative, inspired by the Prince of Wales, which aims to promote and support rural producers and communities in the region. !! ♦ RAIB

Heathen

Grape & Grain, 51 The Broadway, Haywards Heath, West Sussex, RH16 3AS
☎ (01444) 456217 ☎ 07825 429428
heathenbrewers.co.uk

Located in the basement of the Grape & Grain off-licence and delicatessen, brewing began in 2014 using a full mash, two-barrel plant. Local outlets and beer festivals are supplied. !! ♦ RAIB

ISA (OG 1040, ABV 3.9%)

Black Eye PA (OG 1048, ABV 4.9%)

Stout (OG 1052, ABV 5%)
Soft, full-bodied and rich stout.

Pale (OG 1050, ABV 5.3%)
A hop-led pale ale.

West Coast (OG 1049, ABV 5.4%)
A honeyed, West Coast-style IPA.

Hoppler Effect (OG 1058, ABV 5.8%)
A hoppy, full-bodied pale ale.

Mocha (OG 1074, ABV 7%)
Rich, dark-coloured and full-bodied chocolate stout.

Heathton

c/o Old Gate, Heathton, Shropshire, WV5 7EB

This brewery is planned to be resurrected at the Old Gate pub, but its three beers are produced at present in three different breweries, and served only in the Old Gate. Brewing is currently suspended.

Heidrun

Inn House Brewery, 449 Great Western Road, Glasgow, G12 8HH hello@valhallasgoat.com

A small batch brewery with beers contract brewed by Drygate Brewery (qv). RAIB

Heineken Royal Trafford

Royal Brewery, 201 Denmark Road, Manchester, M15 6LD

No real ale.

Helm Bar

Ellerholme, Appleby-in-Westmorland, Cumbria, CA16 6JG ☎ 07736 364478 🌐 helmbarbrews.com

Inspired by a passion for strong, distinctive beers from the US Pacific North West and Belgium, Helm Bar currently brews small batch beers using the highest quality grain and hops. RAIB

Jabberwock (ABV 5.2%)

Ghost Tractor (ABV 5.3%)
Robust porter, finished with a hint of vanilla.

Jub Jub (ABV 5.5%)

Bandersnatch (ABV 6%)
American-style IPA. Mid brown-coloured, bitter and dry-hopped.

Vorpel Blade (ABV 6.4%)

Helmsley SIBA

18 Bridge Street, Helmsley, North Yorkshire, YO62 5DX
☎ (01439) 771014 ☎ 07525 434268

Located within the North York Moors National Park, brewing began in 2014. The brewery has a viewing gallery, tasting room and brewery tap. Local pubs are supplied. RAIB

Yorkshire Legend (ABV 3.8%)

Striding the Riding (ABV 4%)

Howardian Gold (ABV 4.2%)

Helmsley Honey (ABV 4.5%)

H!PA (ABV 5.5%)

Hemlock

37 Main Street, Hemington, Derbyshire, DE74 2RB ☎ 07791 057994 ✉ hembrew@yahoo.com

Established in 2015 on the borders of Derby, Leicester & Nottingham, this two-barrel plant is located in the outbuildings of a 17th Century thatched cottage. The brewery originally supplied beers in its local area, but in 2018, branched out further into north Derbyshire, Leicestershire and Staffordshire. !! ♦ RAIB

California Dreaming (OG 1042, ABV 4.3%)
Light-coloured pale ale featuring a refreshing fruity and crisp hoppiness.

Hoptimystic (OG 1042, ABV 4.3%)
Golden in colour, packed with hops for a grapefruit flavour and aroma.

Village Idiot (OG 1043, ABV 4.3%)

Six Pistols (ABV 6%)
Belgian/Dutch-style, strong, light pale ale.

Henry Smith (NEW)

Robin Hood, 4 Wakefield Road, Pontefract, West Yorkshire, WF8 4HN ☎ 07547 573378

Set up behind the Robin Hood pub in Pontefract by Dean Smith in 2019 with the help of Revolutions Brewery (where Head Brewer, Paul Windmill, learned to brew). The plant is the former James & Kirkman kit with a few tweaks. One beer is brewed at Revolutions Brewery due to high demand. Small batch specials for Revolutions will be brewed in Pontefract.

Hepworth SIBA

Stane Street, North Heath, West Sussex, RH20 1DJ ☎ (01403) 269696 🌐 hepworthbrewery.co.uk

Hepworth's was established in 2001. 274 outlets are supplied. Originally situated in Horsham, a new brewery site in North Heath opened in 2016. Its organic status is ratified by the Soil Association. !! ♦ RAIB

Traditional Sussex Bitter (OG 1035, ABV 3.5%)
A clean-tasting, amber-coloured session beer. Pleasant fruity and hoppy aroma. Crisp, bitter, tangy taste and a long, dry finish.

Dark Horse (OG 1038, ABV 3.8%)
Nutty and roasted malt characters with a complementary bitterness.

Summer Ale (OG 1038, ABV 3.8%)

Pullman First Class Ale (OG 1041, ABV 4.2%)
A sweet, nutty maltiness and fruitiness are balanced by hops and bitterness in this easy-drinking, pale brown-coloured best bitter. A subtle bitter aftertaste.

Prospect Organic (OG 1045, ABV 4.5%)

Classic Old Ale (OG 1046, ABV 4.8%)
A traditional brew, rich with balanced malt sweetness and bitter hops.

Iron Horse (OG 1048, ABV 4.8%)
Fruity, toffee aroma to this light brown-coloured, full-bodied bitter. A citrus flavour balanced by caramel and malt leads to a clean, dry finish.

Hercules

Unit 5b, Harbour Court, Heron Road, Sydenham, Holywood, Belfast, BT3 9HB
☎ (028) 9036 4516 ✉ niall@herculesbrewery.com

The original Hercules Brewing Company, founded in the 19th century, was one of 13 breweries in Belfast at the time. The company has been re-established to produce small batch brews using old brewing traditions. Its output is all under the Yardsman brand name.

Yardsman IPA (OG 1043, ABV 4.3%)

Yardsman Lager (OG 1048, ABV 4.8%)

Yardsman Belfast Pale Ale (OG 1056, ABV 5.6%)

Hereford

88 St Owen Street, Hereford, HR1 2QD
☎ (01432) 342125 ✉ jfkenyon@aol.com

Hereford began life as the Spinning Dog Brewery in 2000, changing its name in 2010. After a period as primarily a brewpub, in 2017 it began to expand its distribution to pubs in Herefordshire and Pembrokeshire. !! ♦ RAIB

Heritage SIBA

National Brewery Centre, Horninglow Street, Burton upon Trent, Staffordshire, DE14 1NG
☎ (01283) 777006
🌐 heritagebrewingcompany.co.uk

Heritage Brewing Company (formerly William Worthington's Brewery) was established in 2015 by Planning Solutions Limited, operators of the National Brewery Centre (NBC). They purchased the 25-barrel brewery and nearby bottling plant from the previous owners, Molson Coors. The team has set out to utilise the resources, history and knowledge available at the NBC to breathe new life into heritage beers, including those produced 10-15 years ago by the former Museum Brewing Co. !! ☞ ♦ RAIB

Victoria Pale Ale (OG 1034, ABV 3.8%)
A rich, golden-coloured ale; light but full-flavoured.

Charrington Oatmeal Stout (OG 1041, ABV 4%)
An oatmeal stout with a nutty flavour, slight bitterness and a hint of treacle.

Massey's Original Mild (OG 1041, ABV 4%)

Offilers' Best Bitter (OG 1038, ABV 4%)
Light, amber-coloured best bitter with a medium bitterness and a light hop finish.

St Modwen Golden Ale (OG 1040, ABV 4.2%)
Blonde beer, not too bitter with a subtle malted wheat biscuit taste.

Charrington IPA (OG 1046, ABV 4.5%)
Deep amber in colour with a pleasant hoppy bite leading to a smooth, malty flavour and balanced, lingering bitterness.

Masterpiece IPA (OG 1055, ABV 5.6%)
Aromatic hops, toasted cereal notes and hints of smoke and spice enhanced by fragrant, fruity character and a top note of fresh bread. A full mouthfeel combined with subtle peppery hints.

Hermitage

Heathwaite, Slanting Hill, Hermitage, Berkshire, RG18 9QG
☎ (01635) 200907 ☎ 07980 019484
⊕ hermitagebrewery.co.uk

⊠ Hermitage is a small 0.5-barrel plant which began brewing in 2013. The owner, Richard Marshall, taught degree-level food science, and has been homebrewing for more than 40 years. It produces a range of bottle-conditioned beers which are sold in local shops. Production is about 250 bottles per week. Casks are sometimes supplied to local pubs and beer festivals. RAIB

Tom Herrick's

The Stable House, Main Street, Carlton on Trent, Nottinghamshire, NG23 6NW ☎ 07877 542331
✉ tomherricksbrewery@hotmail.com

Tom Herrick installed his bespoke 2.5-barrel stainless steel brewery at the front of his premises during 2014 and began small scale commercial brewing the following year. The brewery is only operated on a part-time basis with output going to festivals and local pubs.

Bomber Command (OG 1045, ABV 4.2%)
A pale copper-coloured ale, full-bodied and malty with a delicate, well-balanced hop profile.

Hesket Newmarket SIBA

Old Crown Barn, Back Green, Hesket Newmarket, Cumbria, CA7 8JG
☎ (01697) 478066 ⊕ hesketbrewery.co.uk

☺Founded in 1988, and bought by a co-operative in 1999 to preserve a community amenity. Originally beers were named after Cumbrian fells, however a recent rebranding exercise has led to

the introduction of American hops and fruitier brews with the names reflecting this. !! ♦

Haystacks (OG 1037, ABV 3.7%) ◆
Light, easy-drinking, thirst-quenching blonde beer.

Skiddaw Special Bitter (OG 1037, ABV 3.7%)
An amber-coloured session beer, malty throughout, well-balanced with a dryish finish.

Red Pike (OG 1038, ABV 3.8%)
A dark red-coloured ale with complex malty backbone, plenty of hop flavour, balanced with a big hit of hops. Resin, pine, citrus and fruit.

Black Sail (OG 1042.1, ABV 4%) ◆
A sweet stout with roast flavours

Helvellyn Gold (OG 1039, ABV 4%) ◆
Complex, hoppy, fruity beer with malt presence and a refreshing finish.

High Pike (OG 1042, ABV 4.2%) ◆
A traditional-style bitter; fruity with a dry finish.

Doris' 90th Birthday Ale (OG 1045, ABV 4.3%)
Fruity, premium best bitter.

West Coast Red (OG 1046, ABV 4.3%)
Moreish and easy-drinking with initial bitterness giving way to biscuity malt flavours before leaving a long, dry bitter finish with notes of pine and grapefruit.

Scafell Blonde (OG 1043, ABV 4.4%) ◆
A hoppy, sweet, fruity, pale-coloured bitter.

Brim Fell (OG 1047, ABV 4.5%)
A light copper-coloured IPA, generously, but not overly-hopped. Well-balanced with malt body to back up hop bitterness, and a little residual sweetness. Light malt gives way to floral and citrus hops.

Catbells Pale Ale (OG 1050, ABV 5%) ◆
Golden ale with a nice balance of fruity sweetness and bitterness, almost syrupy but with a dry finish.

Smoked Porter (OG 1056, ABV 5.4%)
Dark roasted malts and a combination of citrus hops lend a balanced bitterness complemented by a subtle smokiness.

Old Carrock Strong Ale (OG 1060, ABV 6%) ◆
Reddy brown-coloured, strong ale. Vine fruit flavour and slightly astringent finish.

Double IPA (OG 1072, ABV 7.4%)
Initially bitter with flavours dominated by orange peel and citrus fruit, leaving a long bitter finish.

Hetton Law

Hetton Law Farm, Lowick, Northumberland, TD15 2UL
☎ (01289) 388558 ☎ 07889 457140
⊕ hettonlawbrewery.co.uk

Brewing began in 2015 using a 2.5-barrel plant. Run by retired dentists Judith and Nicholas Grasse, it uses local spring water and locally grown malt which gives the beers a distinctive character. Due to the size of the brewery availability on draught and in bottles is effectively limited to the local area on both sides of the border. ♦

Hetton Hermit (ABV 3.8%)

Hetton Harvest (ABV 4.2%)

Hetton Howler (ABV 4.2%)

Hetton Harlot (ABV 4.8%)

Hare Raiser (ABV 5.2%)

Hexhamshire SIBA

Dipton Mill Road, Hexham, Northumberland, NE46 1YA
☎ (01434) 606577 🌐 hexhamshire.co.uk

Hexhamshire is Northumberland's oldest brewery and is run by the same family since it was founded in 1993. The Brooker family also run the brewery tap, the Dipton Mill. Outlets are supplied direct and via the SIBA Beerflex scheme.

Devil's Elbow (OG 1036, ABV 3.6%) ◆
Amber-coloured brew full of hops and fruit, leading to a bitter finish.

Shire Bitter (OG 1037, ABV 3.8%) ◆
Amber-coloured, easy-drinking, session bitter. Well-balanced hops and fruity overtones.

Blackhall English Stout (OG 1040, ABV 4%)
A pleasant bitter beer with a strong roast malt flavour.

Devil's Water (OG 1041, ABV 4.1%) ◆
Copper-coloured best bitter, well-balanced with a slightly fruity, hoppy finish.

Whapweasel (OG 1048, ABV 4.8%) ◆
An interesting smooth, hoppy beer with a fruity flavour. Amber in colour, the bitter finish brings out the fruit and hops.

Old Humbug (OG 1055, ABV 5.5%)

High House Farm SIBA

Matfen, Newcastle upon Tyne, NE20 0RG
☎ (01661) 886192/886769
🌐 highhousefarmbrewery.co.uk

The brewery was founded in 2003 by a Brewlab graduate on a working farm, with visitor centre, brewery shop and function room. This has now expanded to include a restaurant and wedding venue. More than 350 regional outlets are supplied. !! ⛟ ♦

Sundancer (OG 1036, ABV 3.6%)

Pullet Please (OG 1037, ABV 3.7%)
A pale golden-coloured, refreshing ale with a delicate grapefruit nose and a crisp dry finish. An easy-drinking bitter.

Auld Hemp (OG 1038, ABV 3.8%) ◆
Tawny-coloured ale with hop, malt and fruit flavours and a good bitter finish.

Nel's Best (OG 1041, ABV 4.2%) ◆
Golden-coloured, hoppy ale full of flavour with a clean, bitter finish.

Matfen Magic (OG 1046.5, ABV 4.8%) ◆
Well-hopped, brown-coloured ale with a fruity aroma. Malt and chocolate overtones with a rich, bitter finish.

High Peak

41A Market Street, Chapel-en-le-Frith, Derbyshire, SK23 0HP ☎ 07936 174364 🌐 highpeakbrewco.com

High Peak is a microbrewery based in Chapel-en-le-Frith on the edge of the Peak District that specialises in hand-crafted, unfined, unfiltered and unpasteurised beers in small batches of 600 litres. There is no core range of beers as set recipes are not followed.

High Weald

Unit 24, Bassetts Manor, Butcherfield Lane, Hartfield, East Sussex, TN7 4LA ☎ 07836 291430

Office: 23 Hermitage Road, East Grinstead, RH19 2BP
🌐 highwealdbrewery.co.uk

⊗ Established in 2013, High Weald Brewery has grown from its home-brew origins to a four-barrel, purpose-built plant, which moved to Hartfield in 2017. The brewery supplies local (and not so local) free houses, shops and festivals.

Chronicle (OG 1038, ABV 3.8%)

Greenstede (OG 1040, ABV 4%)

Mosaic Pale (OG 1044, ABV 4.2%)
A single-hopped best bitter, with a zingy hop note.

Charcoal Burner (OG 1043, ABV 4.3%)
Traditional, rich, quenching stout. Velvety smoothness from the addition of oats.

Off the Chart (OG 1049, ABV 5%)

Highgate

See Davenports

Higsons

▤ 62-64 Bridgewater Street, Liverpool, L1 0AY
☎ (0151) 305 1292 🌐 h1780tapstill.co.uk

Established in 2017 in the Baltic Triangle area of Liverpool, the 30-barrel plant can be seen from the Higsons 1780 tap pub. Also trades under the name Love Lane.

Hilden

Hilden House, Hilden, Lisburn, Co Antrim, BT27 4TY
☎ (028) 9266 0800 🌐 hildenbrewery.co.uk

⊛ Established 1981, Hilden is Ireland's oldest independent brewery. Now in the second generation of family ownership, the beers are widely distributed across the UK. The beers are regularly available in Wetherspoon outlets in Northern Ireland. !! ⛟ ♦

Nut Brown (OG 1038, ABV 3.8%)

Ale (OG 1038, ABV 4%) ◆
An amber-coloured beer with an aroma of malt, hops and fruit. The balanced taste is slightly slanted towards hops, and hops are also prominent in the full, malty finish.

Barney's Brew (OG 1043, ABV 4.2%)
Wheat beer spiced with cardamon, coriander and black pepper.

Irish Stout (OG 1043, ABV 4.3%)

Scullion Irish Ale (OG 1046, ABV 4.6%)

Scullion's Irish (OG 1045, ABV 4.6%)
A bright amber-coloured ale, initially smooth with a slight taste of honey that is balanced by a long, dry aftertaste that lingers on the palate.

Twisted Hop (OG 1047, ABV 4.7%)

Halt (OG 1058, ABV 6.1%)
A premium, traditional Irish-style, red-coloured ale with a malty, mild hop flavour.

Brewed under the Clearsky name:

Rowlock (OG 1045, ABV 4.5%)

Fulcrum (OG 1050, ABV 5%)

Brewed under the College Brewery brand name:

Headless Dog (OG 1042, ABV 4.3%)
A well-hopped, bright amber-coloured ale.

Hill Island

Unit 7, Fowlers Yard, Back Silver Street, Durham, DH1 3RA ☎ 07740 932584
✉ **hillisland73@gmail.com**

Established in 2002, Hill Island is a literal translation of Dunholme, from which Durham is derived. It is part of Fowler's Yard Craft Workshops on the banks of the River Wear and can be reached by steps down from Silver Street. A pop-up bar operates at the brewery on the first and third Saturday each month, plus other weekends coinciding with Durham events such as the Durham Fire & Ice Festival and the Durham Miner's Gala. ‼ ♦

Peninsula Pint (OG 1036.5, ABV 3.7%)
Blonde and hoppy with a zesty aroma.

Bitter (OG 1039, ABV 3.9%)
A red gold-coloured bitter with pronounced caramel flavor and zesty bitterness.

Stout for the Count (OG 1040, ABV 4%)
A traditional, full-bodied stout. Almost black in colour with roast coffee flavors and a clean hop bitterness.

Neptune's Gold (OG 1042, ABV 4.2%)
Subtle bitterness balanced with hop flavours and hints of tropical fruit.

Cathedral Ale (OG 1042, ABV 4.3%)
Ruby-coloured ale with hints of roast malts and crisp bitterness.

THAIPA (OG 1043, ABV 4.3%)
Speciality ale with the addition of lemon grass.

Griffin's Irish Stout (OG 1045, ABV 4.5%)
Traditional Irish-style, black-coloured, bitter stout.

Hillfire SIBA

23 Edison Road, Aylesbury, Buckinghamshire, HP19 8TE
☎ **(01296) 338521** 🌐 **hillfirebrewing.com**

Hillfire commenced brewing in 2016 using a 2.5-barrel plant. Sole owner and CAMRA member Neil Coxhead brews once a week.

California Gold (OG 1043, ABV 4.3%)
A well-balanced, golden-coloured beer with subtle citrus, resin notes and hints of biscuit malt.

Hillside SIBA

Holly Bush Farm, Ross Road, Longhope, Gloucestershire, GL17 0NG
☎ **(01452) 830222** 🌐 **hillsidebrewery.com**

A six-barrel plant in a reconstructed farm dairy that started in 2011. A 60 metre bore hole produces pure water rich in minerals ideally suited to brewing. The regular beers are supplemented by limited run specials that explore different styles and flavours. An on-site brewery tap, the Hop Barn, is now open, which holds monthly events and can be hired privately. ‼ ♦RAIB

Over the Hill (OG 1042, ABV 3.5%)
Full-bodied, single-hopped, dark-coloured mild. Cocoa and roast malt character.

Pinnacle (OG 1038, ABV 3.8%)
A well-balanced session beer with a fresh, fruity finish.

Legless Cow (OG 1043, ABV 4.2%)
A well-balanced, full-flavoured best bitter. Rich caramel flavour with a smooth and citrus hop finish.

HCL (OG 1038, ABV 4.3%)
A clean and crisp lager with a subtle honey flavour, and a refreshing peach and zesty finish.

Legend of Hillside (OG 1046, ABV 4.7%)
A traditional IPA with a subtle honey flavour and a strong hop finish.

Summit Ruby Ale (OG 1050, ABV 4.9%)
Packed with rich, malty flavours, deep caramel notes and hints of chocolate and toffee to finish.

Hillstown

128 Glebe Road, Randalstown, BT41 3DT
🌐 **hillstownbrewery.com**

Brewing began in 2014 in a converted barn on a farm in Randalstown producing bottle-conditioned beers. ♦RAIB

Hilltop

Sheffield Road, Conisbrough, South Yorkshire, DN12 2AY
☎ **(01709) 868811** ☎ **07947 146746**
🌐 **thehilltophotel.co.uk**

Established in 2016, Hilltop Brewery is a 3.5-barrel plant situated in the outbuildings of the Hilltop Hotel in Conisbrough. Beers are available in the hotel and other local outlets. ‼♦RAIB

Hippy Killer

See Custom Head

Hitchin (NEW)

The Outhouse, 16 Thatchers End, Hitchin, Hertfordshire, SG4 0PD
✉ **hitchinbrewery@gmail.com**

Small brewery using a 100-litre brew kit. Established in 2018 it currently supplies three outlets with bottle-conditioned beers although cask and keg production is planned. RAIB

Hiver (NEW)

56 Stanworth Street, Bermondsey, London, SE1 3NY
🌐 **hiverbeers.com**

Hiver specialises in honey beers, sourcing its honey from British beekeepers. The brewery ethos is to use British suppliers for ingredients. A taproom and shop are open at the weekend. RAIB

Hobsons SIBA

Newhouse Farm, Tenbury Road, Cleobury Mortimer, Shropshire, DY14 8RD
☎ **(01299) 270837** 🌐 **hobsons-brewery.co.uk**

Established in 1993 in a former sawmill, Hobsons relocated to a farm site with more space in 1995. A second brewery, bottling plant and a warehouse have been added along with significant expansion to the first brewery. Beers are supplied within a 50-mile radius. The brewery utilises environmental sustainable technologies where possible. A visitor centre was added in 2014, with plans to open this as a brewery tap. ‼ ▆ RAIB

Mild (OG 1034, ABV 3.2%) ◆
A classic mild. Complex malt layers predominate.

Twisted Spire (OG 1036, ABV 3.6%)
Vibrant blonde ale with a sweet floral aroma, bursts of refreshing flavour and a crisp, dry finish.

Best (OG 1038.5, ABV 3.8%) ◆
A pale brown to amber-coloured, medium-bodied beer with strong hop character throughout. Bitter, but with malt discernible in the taste.

Old Prickly (OG 1042, ABV 4.2%)
Pale ale full of hop flavour with complex floral and citrus notes and a lingering but subtle bitterness.

Town Crier (OG 1044, ABV 4.5%)
A full-flavoured, crisp, straw-coloured golden ale. A hint of sweetness complemented by subtle hop flavours, leading to a dry finish.

Hogs Back SIBA

Manor Farm, The Street, Tongham, Surrey, GU10 1DE
☎ (01252) 783000 ⊕ hogsback.co.uk

⊠ This traditionally-styled brewery, established in 1992, boasts an extensive range of award-winning ales. The shop sells all the brewery's beers and related merchandise plus over 400 beers and ciders from around the world. In 2014 the brewery planted hops on neighbouring farmland, restoring the ancient Farnham White Bine variety. The brewery is building a new on-site hop kiln to dry its own hops. ‼ ▆ ◆ RAIB

HBB (OG 1039, ABV 3.7%) ◆
Biscuity aroma with some hops and lemon notes. Well-balanced, plenty of hops, with a long-lasting, dry, bitter aftertaste.

Surrey Nirvana (OG 1039, ABV 4%)
A well-balanced golden beer with a good bittersweet balance and a strong citrus aroma.

TEA (OG 1044, ABV 4.2%) ◆
A tawny-coloured best bitter with toffee and malt present in the nose. A well-rounded flavour with malt and a fruity sweetness.

Hop Garden Gold (OG 1048, ABV 4.4%) ◆
Full-bodied with an aroma of malt, hops and fruit. Hoppy bitterness grows in an dry aftertaste, with a hint of sweetness.

Rip Snorter (OG 1052, ABV 5%) ◆
Well-balanced sweet and malty bitter. Red brown-coloured, with a moderate bitterness that grows into the aftertaste.

Hogs Head

▤ 1 Stanley Street, Sowerby Bridge, West Yorkshire, HX6 2AH
☎ (01422) 836585
⊠ hogsheadbrewpub@outlook.com

⊕The Hogs Head Brewery opened in a huge 18th century former malthouse at the end of 2015. The twelve-barrel brew house, increased from eight-barrels in 2018, is situated at the back of the accompanying bar with the handsome copper and stainless steel brewing vats on display at the back of the building. Almost all the production is sold on the premises with occasional casks being provided to beer festivals. ◆

Holcot Hop-Craft (NEW)

Chequers Row, Main Street, Holcot, NN6 9SP
⊠ roger@gunnett.co.uk

This small brewery started brewing in 2017 and is located in the tiny village of Holcot, Northamptonshire. It is a one-hectolitre brewery, brewing once a week producing 180 pints either in pins or firkins. The beer is usually on tap at the Queens Arms at Orlingbury and is available in other pubs, clubs and beer festivals within a 10 mile radius of the brewery.

Holden's SIBA IFBB

George Street, Woodsetton, West Midlands, DY1 4LW
☎ (01902) 880051 ⊕ holdensbrewery.co.uk

⊕A family brewery spanning four generations, Holden's began life as a brewpub in 1915. Continued expansion means it now has 21 tied pubs in its estate. ‼ ▆ ◆

Black Country Mild (OG 1037, ABV 3.7%) ⌂ ◆
A good, red/brown-coloured mild. Refreshing, light blend of malt, hops and fruit, dominated by malt throughout.

Black Country Bitter (OG 1039, ABV 3.9%) ▮ ◆
A medium-bodied, golden ale. Light, well-balanced bitter with a subtle, dry, hoppy finish.

Golden Glow (OG 1045, ABV 4.4%)
A pale golden-coloured beer with a subtle hop aroma plus gentle sweetness and a light hoppiness.

Special (OG 1052, ABV 5.1%) ◆
A sweet, malty, full-bodied, amber-coloured ale with hops to balance in the taste and in the good, bittersweet finish.

Holler SIBA

19-23 Elder Place, Brighton, East Sussex, BN1 4BZ
☎ (01273) 894563 ☎ 07786 830368
⊕ hollerbrewery.com

Holler was established in 2017. ‼

Cheat Mode (ABV 3.8%)
Fruity, easy-drinking pale ale. Naturally hazy.

Extra Pale (ABV 4%)

Mr Best (ABV 4.4%)
Seven types of malt provide a comforting and luxurious best bitter

Juicy Pale (ABV 4.5%)

Steam Beer (ABV 4.5%)

Loot (ABV 5.5%)
A juicy, hazy and peachy IPA.

West Coast IPA (ABV 5.5%)

Hollow Stone

See Shipstone's

Holsworthy

Unit 5, Circuit Business Park, Clawton, Devon, EX22 6RR
☎ (01566) 783678 ☎ 07879 401073
🌐 holsworthyales.co.uk

⊗ Holsworthy Ales began brewing in 2011 using a six-barrel plant, serving the local rural community. **!! ♦ RAIB V**

Mine's A Mild (OG 1035, ABV 3.5%)
A traditional, thirst-quenching mild. Malty, lightly-hopped, good balance and finish.

Sunshine (OG 1040, ABV 4%)
Smooth golden ale. Hops overwhelm all else. Hints of fruit. Fresh and bitter hoppy aftertaste.

Green Hop (ABV 4.3%)
Light ale brewed with green, fresh hops.

Muck 'n' Straw (OG 1044, ABV 4.4%)
Hops dominate with hints of malt in aroma and taste. Well balanced with slight dryness in aftertaste

Make Me Hoppy (OG 1046, ABV 4.7%)
Classic, modern IPA with a big flavour.

Tamar Black (OG 1048, ABV 4.8%)
Dark-coloured stout with hints of liquorice and coffee. A complex mix full of malt, roast, fruit, hops and caramel.

Dark Bomb (OG 1050, ABV 5%)
Pleasant porter. Smoky chocolate aroma, caramel throughout, with complex sweet flavours of liquorice, malt and chocolate. Short bittersweet, dry finish.

Hop on The Run (ABV 5%)
An American-style IPA, packed full of vibrant hops. Good body and lasting flavour.

Proper Lager (ABV 5%)

Old Market Monk (OG 1059, ABV 6.1%)
A Belgian-style, full-flavoured ale. It has a deep rich tone with hints of coriander. Subtly-hopped for a smooth finish.

Joseph Holt SIBA IFBB

The Brewery, Empire Street, Cheetham, Manchester, M3 1JD
☎ (0161) 834 3285 🌐 joseph-holt.com

Founded in 1849, Joseph Holt is one of the UK's leading independent family breweries. Now in its sixth generation the business operates 127 pubs across Manchester and the North West and supplies more than 20 ales to over 500 outlets nationally.

Mild (OG 1033, ABV 3.2%)
A dark brown/red-coloured beer with a fruity, malty nose. Roast, malt, fruit and hops in the taste, with strong bitterness for a mild, and a dry malt and hops finish.

IPA (OG 1038, ABV 3.8%)
Golden-coloured bitter with biscuity malt, hops and restrained lemony notes. Dry, bitter finish.

Bitter (OG 1040, ABV 4%)
Pale brown-coloured beer with malt and hops in the aroma. Bitter taste with balanced malty flavour. Increased bitter finish.

Two Hoots (OG 1043.8, ABV 4.2%)
Light, refreshing and well-balanced golden ale. Citrus, fruity, floral aroma. Fruity, refreshing, zesty taste.

Holy Well

4 Barnfield Close, Egerton, Bolton, BL7 9UP ☎ 07949 179338 🌐 holywellbrewing.com

A nanobrewery specialising in small batch brews celebrating different styles and traditions. These are sold mostly in bottle-conditioned form at local farmers markets plus a few local outlets. The owners have strong links with Halliwell, an ancient township of Bolton whose name derives from the original Holy Well. **RAIB**

Hooded Ram SIBA

Shepherds Lodge, Leigh Terrace, South Quay, Douglas, Isle of Man, IM1 5AL
☎ (01624) 612464 🌐 hoodedram.com

Brewing began in 2013 on a 2.5-barrel plant. Expansion in 2014 saw an increase to a 10-barrel plant. A 100-litre pilot plant added in 2016. Relocation in 2017 to larger premises saw increased production. Beers are available across the island. A tied pub in the old Clinch's Brewery building, North Quay, Douglas, has opened, where all beer and merchandise are available. A further pub has opened in Wolverhampton. The brewery holds a multi-bar festival on Douglas Promenade at the Isle of Man TT. **!! RAIB**

Rams Head Bitter (OG 1037, ABV 3.7%)
A classic, amber-coloured bitter with a balanced hop and malt mouthfeel.

Amber Ram (OG 1038, ABV 4.3%)
Inviting fruity aromas, followed by sweet malty and slightly roasty taste, balanced by a lasting hop finish.

Jack the Ram Stout (OG 1044, ABV 4.7%)
Roast dominates the aroma and taste, with bitterness coming through in the finish. Plenty of body from the sweetness and fruit, make this an easy-drinking stout.

Mosaic Single Hop Pale Ale (OG 1044, ABV 5%)
Hoppy aroma, hop-led taste complemented with plenty of fruitiness, underlying sweetness, bitterness and a touch of malt.

Hook Norton SIBA IFBB

Brewery Lane, Scotland End, Hook Norton, Oxfordshire, OX15 5NY
☎ (01608) 737210 🌐 hooky.co.uk

⊗ One of the finest examples of a Victorian tower brewery, and the oldest independent brewery in Oxfordshire. Hook Norton began brewing in 1849. The current premises were built in 1900 and still house much of the original machinery, including a 25hp steam engine, which operates occasionally. Shire horses are used to make deliveries to local pubs and the surrounding area. Remaining family-owned, it combines its brewing heritage with a modern approach. The boardroom and Cellar Bar are available for hire. Customers can spend a day brewing their own beer. **!! ♦ RAIB**

Hooky Mild (OG 1033, ABV 2.8%)

A chestnut brown-coloured, easy-drinking mild. A complex malt and hop aroma give way to a well-balanced taste, leading to a long, hoppy finish.

Hooky (OG 1036, ABV 3.5%) ◆
A classic, golden-coloured session bitter. Hoppy and fruity aroma followed by a malt and hops taste and a continuing hoppy finish.

Hooky Gold (ABV 4.1%)
A very pale, crisp beer, with a hoppy character. A fruity aroma and a pleasant light taste.

Old Hooky (OG 1048, ABV 4.6%) ▢ ◆
A strong bitter, tawny in colour. A well-rounded fruity taste with a balanced bitter finish.

Hop & Stagger SIBA

The Old Cow Shed, Astol Farm, Norton, Shropshire, TF11 9EW
☎ (01952) 730737 ☎ 07487 898151
⊕ hopandstaggerbrewery.co.uk

Hop & Stagger began brewing in 2011 having set up a 2.5-barrel plant at the White Lion Inn in Bridgnorth. In 2015 the brewery relocated to a farm between Bridgnorth and Telford, with all new brewing equipment and an increase in capacity to six barrels. ◆

Shropshire Pale Ale (OG 1040, ABV 3.6%)

Golden Wander (OG 1042, ABV 4.1%)
A hoppy ale with citrus notes and a slightly spicy finish.

Beckbury Bitter (OG 1045, ABV 4.2%)
A traditional-style, full-flavoured, amber-coloured bitter.

Strategic Blonde (OG 1041, ABV 4.3%)

Bridgnorth Porter (OG 1055, ABV 5%)
Well-balanced porter with layers of chocolate, caramel and dark fruit flavours, topped with a tight, creamy head.

Triple Hop IPA (OG 1052, ABV 5%)

Hop Back SIBA

Units 22-24, Batten Road Industrial Estate, Downton, Wiltshire, SP5 3HU
☎ (01725) 510986 ⊕ hopback.co.uk

⊠ Founded in 1987, Hop Back owns 10 pubs and distributes nationally. The flagship beer, Summer Lightning, has won numerous CAMRA awards.
‼ ➠ ◆ RAIB

GFB (OG 1035, ABV 3.5%) ◆
A light gold-coloured, refreshing session bitter. The hoppy aroma leads to bitterness lasting through to the finish with some fruit.

Citra (OG 1040, ABV 4%) ◆
Pale yellow/ straw-coloured with lemon and grapefruit on the aroma and taste, rapidly developing a balanced hoppy aftertaste.

Fuggle Stone (OG 1040, ABV 4%)

Crop Circle (OG 1041, ABV 4.2%) ◆
A pale yellow-coloured best bitter with a fragrant hop aroma, complex hop, fruit and citrus flavours with a balanced hoppy, bitter/sweet aftertaste.

Taiphoon (OG 1041, ABV 4.2%) ◆
A clean-tasting, light fruity beer with hops and fruit on the aroma, complex hop character and

lemongrass notes in the taste, slight sweetness balanced with some astringency in the aftertaste.

Entire Stout (OG 1044, ABV 4.5%) ◆
A smooth, rich, ruby-black-coloured stout with strong roast and malt aromas and flavours, with a long bittersweet, malty aftertaste.

Summer Lightning (OG 1048, ABV 5%) ◆
Golden-coloured, strong bitter with a hoppy aroma and slightly astringent bitterness in the taste, balanced with some fruit sweetness, in the dry aftertaste.

Hop Fuzz SIBA

Unit 8, Riverside Industrial Estate, West Hythe, Kent, CT21 4NB
☎ (07730) 768881 ☎ 07858 562878
⊕ hopfuzz.co.uk

Hop Fuzz was started by two friends in 2011 and is situated on an industrial estate next to the Royal Military Canal at West Hythe. The brewery tap, Unit Number One, has been open from Thursday to Sunday since 2016 and is popular with locals. ◆

Martello (OG 1038, ABV 3.8%)

Northern Star (OG 1044, ABV 4.4%)

Bullion (OG 1050, ABV 5%)

Hop Kettle SIBA

🏠 Cricklade: Red Lion, 74 High Street, Cricklade, Wiltshire, SN6 6DD
☎ (01793) 750776

Swindon: Unit 4, Hawksworth Industrial Estate, Newcombe Drive, Swindon, Wiltshire, SN2 1DZ
☎ (01793) 490556 ⊕ theredlioncricklade.co.uk

Brewing began in a barn behind the Red Lion Inn, Cricklade, in 2012, using a one-barrel plant. Due to demand a larger four-barrel plant followed, which supplies the pub and is also used for experimental brews. A new 10-barrel plant was installed in an old Royal Mail warehouse in Swindon in 2016. ◆

Ordinary (ABV 3.8%)

Chameleon (ABV 4%)

Lode Star (ABV 4.3%)
An English pale ale with a complex combination of bright fruits, spice and pine.

North Wall (ABV 4.3%)
A traditional English best bitter with a mildly bitter finish.

Rising Star (ABV 4.8%)

East Star (ABV 5%)

Red Star (ABV 5.2%)

Evening Star (ABV 5.5%)

Hop Monster

See George's

Hop Shed SIBA

Old Chicken Shed, Stocks Farm, Suckley, Worcestershire, WR6 5EQ
☎ (01886) 884110 ☎ 07484 688026
⊕ hopshed.co.uk

Originally named Unity Brew House, brewing began in 2016 using a 10-barrel plant. It is the only brewery in the UK located on a commercial hop farm. Based in an old chicken shed, the beers are named after breeds of chicken. An on-site bar is open on Fridays and Saturdays.

Wybar (OG 1037, ABV 3.6%)
An easy-drinking, amber-coloured beer, full of flavour that belies its strength.

Sebright Golden Ale (OG 1039, ABV 3.8%)
Straw-coloured, thirst-quenching ale with fruity hop aromas and flavours.

Pekin (OG 1040, ABV 4%)
A refreshing pale ale with hints of tropical fruit.

Sultan (OG 1042, ABV 4.2%)
A rich, well-rounded, golden-coloured beer with apricot and gentle citrus aromas and flavours.

Frizzle British IPA (OG 1048, ABV 4.5%)
Golden in colour with a fruity, floral hop aroma and a slight malty presence, followed by a significant hoppy bitterness.

Hop Studio SIBA

3 Handley Park, Elvington Industrial Estate, York Road, Elvington, North Yorkshire, YO41 4AR
☎ (01904) 608029 🌐 thehopstudio.co.uk

Founded in 2012 the Hop Studio brews on a 10-barrel plant in an industrial unit just outside York. Some barrel-aged specials are produced. Outlets in Yorkshire are supplied direct and the rest of the UK via wholesalers. ♦ RAIB

Blonde (ABV 3.5%)
Refreshing, pale-coloured blonde ale with gooseberry grapefruit and citrus aroma and flavour.

Bitter (ABV 3.9%)

Pale (ABV 4%)
Hops pack a punch in this pale session ale. Grapefruit, lemons and tropical fruits linger into a dry finish.

Porter (ABV 4.3%)
A dark-coloured vanilla porter. Intense chocolate malt and berry flavours.

Gold (ABV 4.5%)
Juicy, easy-drinking golden ale, soft, rounded bitterness and citrus, peach and tropical fruit flavours.

XS (ABV 5.5%)
Strong complex chestnut-coloured ale. Spicy dark fruit flavours. Malty and bitter with hints of floral and citrus aroma

Avenoir (ABV 6%)
Rich, velvety oatmeal stout. Coffee, chocolate and oat, with subtle blackcurrant and cherry flavours.

Hop Stuff SIBA

Unit 35.9 Cobalt, White Hart Triangle Estate, White Hart Avenue, Thamesmead, London, SE28 0GU
☎ (020) 3247 4118 ☎ 07850 086461
🌐 hopstuffbrewery.com

Hop Stuff began brewing in 2013. After crowdfunding success it moved to a new 65-hectolitre brewhouse in Thamesmead in 2018. Brewing is currently suspended. In July 2019 the brewery, brand and taprooms were transferred to the ownership of Molson Coors. ♦

Hop Vine

Hop Vine, Liverpool Road North, Burscough, Lancashire, L40 4BY
☎ (01704) 893799 ☎ 07920 002783
✉ mikejulie6465@gmail.com

Hop Vine began brewing in 2017 using the four-barrel plant of the defunct Burscough Brewery. It is situated in old stable buildings in the courtyard to the rear of the Hop Vine. Beer is usually only supplied to the pub and the Legh Arms, Mere Brow. ♦

Hopburst

80 Grange Road, Darlington, DL1 5NP
☎ (01325) 787912 ☎ 07929 007509
🌐 hopburstbrewing.com

Focussing on small batch ales, commercial brewing began in 2016. A micropub is planned.

Hopcraft

See Team Toxic

Hopdaemon SIBA

Unit 1, Parsonage Farm, Seed Road, Newnham, Kent, ME9 0NA
☎ (01795) 892078 🌐 hopdaemon.com

Tonie Prins originally started brewing in Tyler Hill near Canterbury in 2000 and moved to a new site in Newnham in 2005. The brewery currently supplies more than 100 outlets. !! ♦ RAIB

Golden Braid (OG 1039, ABV 3.7%)
A refreshing, golden-coloured, session bitter with a good blend of bittering and aroma hops underpinned by malt.

Incubus (OG 1041, ABV 4%)
A well-balanced, copper-hued best bitter. Malts are blended with bitter and slightly floral hops to give a lingering, hoppy finish.

Skrimshander IPA (OG 1045, ABV 4.5%)
An aromatic, copper-coloured pale ale with a refreshing taste and a fruity finish.

Green Daemon (OG 1048, ABV 5%)
A golden-coloured, Bavarian helles-style beer with tropical fruit aromas and a crisp, clean finish.

Leviathan (OG 1057, ABV 6%)
Is a strong, ruby-coloured ale with spicy hop aromas and a rich malty finish.

Hophurst SIBA

Unit 8 Hindley Business Centre, Platt Lane Hindley, Wigan, WN2 3PA
☎ (01942) 522333 🌐 hophurstbrewery.co.uk

Hophurst Brewery was started in 2014 by Stuart Hurst, whose passion for producing craft ales combined with 20 years of supporting businesses and re-skilling unemployed people created a unique social enterprise brewery that employs people over the age of 50 and guides them through their training programme in the Wigan area. A microbar in Ashton-in Makerfield opened in 2018. ♦

2 Rounds of 6 Before Breakfast (OG 1035, ABV 3.5%)
A refreshing, American-style IPA, with tropical fruit and citrus flavours.

Flaxen (OG 1038, ABV 3.7%)
Easy-drinking, pale-coloured, session golden ale. Fresh, earthy hoppy aroma, with hints of honey and a long, refreshing finish.

Mellors (OG 1039, ABV 3.8%)
A citrus blonde ale with hop flavours of lemon and blackcurrant.

Quench (OG 1038, ABV 3.8%)
Citrus pale ale with tropical fruit and citrus flavours.

Campfire (OG 1042, ABV 3.9%)
A dark-coloured mild with a smoky, malt taste, and aromas of roasted coffee and chocolate.

Twisted Vine (OG 1041, ABV 4.1%)
A hoppy American-style, amber-coloured ale. Citrus, hoppy aromas of grapefruit and passion fruit.

Cosmati (OG 1042, ABV 4.2%)
Hoppy, citrus golden ale. Blueberry, citrus and tropical fruit flavours.

Arlo (OG 1047, ABV 4.7%)
West Coast-style pale ale. Mango, grapefruit and tropical fruit flavours.

Debonair (OG 1052, ABV 4.9%)
Robust stout with flavours of roasted coffee, liquorice and an aftertaste of pleasant bitterness.

Incognito (OG 1054, ABV 4.9%)
Black-coloured IPA with blueberry and tropical fruit flavours.

Porteresque (OG 1065, ABV 5.5%)
Full-bodied milkshake porter with flavours of chocolate and a smooth, milky sweetness to finish.

Hopper House Brew Farm (NEW)

Racecourse Road, Sedgefield, TS21 2HL
🌐 hopperhousebrewfarm.co.uk

Brewing commenced in 2019 on a 4.5-barrel plant situated on a working dairy farm. An on-site taproom showcases its beers along with guest beers from other breweries.

Hoppy Family

Harcourt Street, Kettering, Northamptonshire, NN16 0RS ☎ 07986 019579 🌐 hfbrewery.com

Microbrewery established in 2017 brewing a range of bottled-conditioned beers using ingredients such as blueberries, raspberries and chillies.

Hops & Dots (NEW)

8 Orchard Road, Linthorpe, Middlesbrough, TS5 5PW
✉ john@hopsanddots.com

The brewery was established in 2019 by a teacher of the visually impaired and a solicitor. Hops & Dots believe that craft beer should always be accessible to all, which is why it will try to promote braille alongside its beers. RAIB V

Fat Fingers (ABV 5.1%)
A dry-hopped, pale-coloured wheat ale with a full flavour.

Vienna Smog (ABV 5.6%)
A malt-forward, Vienna-style lager.

Oatie Dokie (ABV 6%)
A smooth, well-balanced, New England-style IPA.

Sim Specs (ABV 6.4%)
A smooth pale ale, dry-hopped with low bitterness.

Dimmer Switch (ABV 6.8%)
A smooth, full-bodied milk stout. Brewed with molasses and speciality malts, it offers notes of coffee to complement the sweetness provided by the addition of lactose.

IPA (ABV 7.1%)

Cognitive Overload (ABV 8.2%)

In the Dark (ABV 8.4%)
An imperial stout brewed with cocoa nibs and coffee beans.

Black Out (ABV 8.9%)
A strong stout brewed with treacle, dark sugar, a hint of vanilla, golden syrup and salt.

Hopscotch Craft

See Crosspool Ale Makers

Hopshackle

Unit F, Bentley Business Park, Blenheim Way, Northfields Industrial Estate, Market Deeping, Lincolnshire, PE6 8LD
☎ (01778) 348542 🌐 hopshacklebrewery.co.uk

Hopshackle was established in 2006 using a five-barrel plant. A 10-barrel plant was installed in 2015. More than 40 outlets are supplied direct. !! ♦ RAIB

Simmarillo (OG 1037, ABV 3.8%)
Burnished gold-coloured with an aroma of citrus and soft fruits. Tangy fruit taste with blackberry, plum and pineapple.

Zen (OG 1037, ABV 3.8%)
Brown-coloured, traditional, full-flavoured, full-bodied bitter, malty, fruity with a bittersweet finish.

American Pale Ale (OG 1042, ABV 4.3%)
An amber-coloured ale with a fruity zesty aroma. Citrus hop taste with background gooseberry and lychees, and a dry, bitter finish.

Hopnosis (OG 1050, ABV 5.2%)
Golden-coloured beer with a strong aroma of sweet malt and fruit. Strong citrus and tropical fruits taste, with a dry finish.

Hopstar SIBA

Unit 9 Rinus Business Park, Grimshaw Street, Darwen, BB3 2QX ☎ 07933 590159 🌐 hopstarbrewery.co.uk

Hopstar first brewed in 2004 on a 2.5-barrel plant and expanded in 2010 to a new unit with a six-barrel plant. More than 100 outlets are supplied around Lancashire and the Greater Manchester area. The brewery tap is Number 39 in Darwen. !! ♦ RAIB

Chilli (OG 1039, ABV 3.8%)

Dizzy Danny Ale (OG 1039, ABV 3.8%)

Dark Knight (OG 1041, ABV 3.9%)

Off T'Mill (ABV 3.9%)

Smokey Joe's Black Beer (OG 1041, ABV 3.9%)
Black-coloured beer, slightly smoky with tonnes of chocolate in the finish.

Darwen Spitfire (ABV 4%)
A true best bitter with a hint of caramel.

JC (OG 1041, ABV 4%)
A well-balanced beer, copper in colour and a real thirst-quencher.

Lancashire Gold (OG 1041, ABV 4%)
A light, session beer with a good combination of malt and hops.

Lush (OG 1041, ABV 4%)

Saaz Blonde (OG 1038, ABV 4%)

Horbury

The Brewhouse, Cherry Tree Inn, 19 Church Street, Horbury, West Yorkshire, WF4 6LT ☎ 07970 299292

Following the closure of Bob's Brewing Co, Horbury Ales took over the plant in 2016 and transferred production to the rear of the brewery tap, Cherry Tree Inn. Beers are available locally, regionally and nationally.

Now Then (ABV 3.9%)

5 Hop (ABV 4.1%)

First Light (ABV 4.1%)

Tiramisu (ABV 4.3%)

Horncastle

Old Nicks Tavern, 8 North Street, Horncastle, Lincolnshire, LN9 5DX
☎ (01507) 526862 horncastleales.co.uk

Brewing began in 2014 using a 3.75-barrel plant. The brewery is situated in Old Nicks Tavern with beer available in the pub plus other Lincolnshire outlets. It has its own bottling plant and a beer in box scheme is also available for pre-ordering. !!

Horner Bros (NEW)

Rear of Brook Street, Lancaster, LA1 1SL ☎ 07809 086851 ✉ lewis@hornerbros.co.uk

Started brewing in 2018 following the demise of the former Borough Brewery. Initially only keg beers were produced with cask beers becoming available.

Hornes SIBA

19b Station Road, Bow Brickhill, Buckinghamshire, MK17 9JU
☎ (01908) 647724 hornesbrewery.co.uk

A purpose-built, six-barrel brewery established in 2015 and producing a range of beers called Triple Goat after the three goats kept in a paddock at the brewery. A taproom and shop were added in 2018. ♦

Featherstone Amber Ale (OG 1037, ABV 3.6%)
A robust, traditional bitter with a soft, fruity finish.

Dark Fox (OG 1039, ABV 3.8%)
A rich, malty, brown-coloured brew with burnt notes and a lasting, dry bitter finish.

Triple Goat Pale Ale (OG 1039, ABV 3.9%)
Easy-drinking golden-coloured beer, bitter with hints of grapefruit.

Ryestone (OG 1042, ABV 4%)
A deep ruby-coloured rye ale with a spicy and fruity flavour.

Triple Goat Porter (OG 1047, ABV 4.6%)
Dark brown-coloured ale. Sweet and fruity notes give way to a lasting bitterness with hints of liquorice.

Triple Goat IPA (OG 1049, ABV 5%)
Deep golden-coloured beer, well-balanced with notes of orange and a touch of spice.

Horsforth

Horsforth, Leeds, West Yorkshire ☎ 07854 078330
horsforthbrewery.co.uk

Brewing began on a part-time basis on a one-barrel plant in 2017 in the owner's garage. In addition to the flagship beer an ever-changing range of specials is produced. The taproom is open on the first Saturday of the month. **V**

Pale (ABV 4.5%)
A hoppy, hazy pale ale with strong tropical citrus notes.

Aubretia (ABV 5.5%)
Black IPA with roasted notes and plenty of hop character.

Hoskins Brothers

See Belvoir

House

Prince, 1 Finsbury Road, Wood Green, London, N22 8PA
☎ (020) 8888 6698 housebrewery.co.uk

Brewing began in 2017 in the Prince public house in Wood Green. Beers are available in the pub and at the sister pubs, the Dukes Head in Highgate and Small Beer in Crouch End. It supports cask and keg equally and brews an annual green hop beer every September with the Wood Green Hopping hop collective. Brewing is currently suspended.

Howard Town SIBA

Hawkshead Mill, Hope Street, Glossop, Derbyshire, SK13 7SS
☎ (01457) 869800 howardtownbrewery.co.uk

Established in 2005, this award winning brewery moved to its current location in 2007. In 2019 they moved into the premises next door, increasing the capacity of the brewery from eight-barrel to 15-barrels. Six core beers are brewed for the free trade, along with seasonal beers. An on-site bar caters for members evenings and open days.
!! ♦ RAIB

Mill Town Mild (OG 1038, ABV 3.5%)
Dark-coloured, lightly-hopped ale with hints of toffee and coffee.

Longdendale Lights (OG 1039, ABV 3.9%)
A light-bodied, blonde, refreshing ale.

Monk's Gold (OG 1040, ABV 4%)
A golden-coloured session ale with subtle orange notes.

Wren's Nest (OG 1041, ABV 4.2%)
Citrus and floral hops dominate this bitter.

Super Fortress (OG 1044, ABV 4.4%)
Well-balanced, premium, chestnut-coloured bitter with malty, caramel notes and fruity hops.

Dark Peak (OG 1064, ABV 6%)
Strong, dark-coloured beer with a hint of liquorice and a warming rum kick.

Howfen (NEW)

66 Green Meadows, Westhoughton, BL5 2BN
howfenbrew.co

Howfen began brewing in 2018 and is situated in the owner's garage. It is named after the dialect word for Westhoughton.

Howling Hops

Unit 9a, Queen's Yard, White Post Lane, Hackney Wick, London, E9 5EN
(020) 3583 8262 howlinghops.co.uk

Brewing began in 2012. Originally brewing at the Cock Tavern in Hackney, a new plant opened in 2015 in Hackney Wick. Beers are available at the on-site taproom, the Tank Bar, the Cock and more increasingly in local free houses and at beer festivals. RAIB

Mild (ABV 3.3%)

Pale Ale (ABV 3.8%)
Citrus, pine and tropical fruit aroma and flavour, which is balanced by a light maltiness. Long, slightly bitter, dry finish.

Tropical Deluxe (ABV 3.8%)
Smooth, gold-coloured beer with hop and tropical fruit flavours, which subtly linger into the bitterish aftertaste.

Light Ale (ABV 4.2%)

Pale XX (ABV 5%)
Strong grapefruit and resinous hop aroma. Hops and fruit dominate with a biscuit sweetness lingering in the bitter, dry finish.

Really Red (ABV 5%)
Rye beer with chocolate aroma with fruit, fudge and a little spicy hop that is present throughout. Growing dry bitterness.

Smoked Porter (ABV 5.2%)

IPA (ABV 6%)
American-style, yellow-coloured IPA with a distinct aroma and taste of peach and orange. Fairly sweet with some underlying bitterness.

Old London Stout (ABV 6%)

Sarah Hughes

Beacon Hotel, 129 Bilston Street, Sedgley, West Midlands, DY3 1JE
(01902) 883381 sarahhughesbrewery.co.uk

Traditional Black Country Victorian tower brewery, taken over by Sarah Hughes in 1921. Brewing ceased in the 1950s and recommenced in 1987. The original grist case and rare open-topped copper give a unique character to the brews. The Beacon Hotel is the brewery tap. Famous for its Dark Ruby, the beers can be found far and wide.
!! ♦

Pale Amber (OG 1038, ABV 4%)
A well-balanced beer, initially slightly sweet but with hops close behind.

Sedgley Surprise (OG 1048, ABV 5%)
A bittersweet, medium-bodied, hoppy ale with some malt.

Dark Ruby Mild (OG 1058, ABV 6%)
A dark ruby-coloured strong ale with a good balance of fruit and hops, leading to a pleasant, lingering hops and malt finish.

Humpty Dumpty SIBA

Church Road, Reedham, Norfolk, NR13 3TZ
(01493) 701818 07843 248865
humptydumptybrewery.co.uk

Established in 1998, this 11-barrel, award-winning brewery continues to grow and expand its range of beers, including a new Norfolk Broads Brewing series of occasional one-off brews.
!! ♦ RAIB

Little Sharpie (OG 1039, ABV 3.8%)
Fruity aroma with malt and hop. Bitter throughout with balanced malt and hop in the background. Crisp, slightly astringent finish.

Branch Line Bitter (OG 1040, ABV 3.9%)
A light chestnut-coloured bitter brewed with a rich body, and spicy and fruity aroma.

Lemon & Ginger (OG 1041, ABV 4%)
An amber-coloured, crisp ale with a ginger and lemon tang.

Swallowtail (OG 1041, ABV 4%)
Full-bodied ale with a marmalade and biscuit aroma with matching beginning. Grainy texture is enhanced by solid bitter notes flowing onward.

Ale (OG 1042, ABV 4.1%)
A hoppy vanilla fudge edge in both nose and taste. Malt provides balance as a gentle bitterness quickly recedes. Lengthy finish.

Broadland Sunrise (OG 1043, ABV 4.2%)
Crisp red-orange-coloured ale brewed with additions of rye for a dry finish, with citrus hop notes.

Red Mill (OG 1045, ABV 4.3%)
A peppery redcurrant nose and grainy mouthfeel. Bittersweet base with vine fruit adding depth and gravity. Long sherry-like finish.

Reedcutter (OG 1045, ABV 4.4%)
A sweet, malty beer. Golden-hued with a gentle malt background. Smooth and full-bodied with a quick, gentle finish.

Cheltenham Flyer (OG 1047, ABV 4.6%)
A full-flavoured golden-coloured, earthy bitter with a long, grainy finish. A strong hop bitterness dominates throughout. Little evidence of malt.

EAPA (East Anglian Pale Ale) (OG 1047, ABV 4.6%)
Amber gold-coloured with an orange marmalade nose. A bittersweet caramel beginning slowly dries out as malty nuances fade away.

Hungry Bear

10-14 Stonegate Road, Leeds, West Yorkshire, LS6 4HY
(0113) 274 0241
hungrybearbrewingcompany.com

Hungry Bear began brewing in 2013 in the upstairs rooms of the Hungry Bear restaurant. A wide range of ales are produced in batches of about 70 litres, with a constantly evolving selection available either via the two taps on the draught dispense system, or as bottle-conditioned ale. ‼ ♦ RAIB

Hunters SIBA

Bulleigh Barton Farm, Ipplepen, Devon, TQ12 5UA
☎ (01803) 873509 ☎ 07540 657115
⊕ thehuntersbrewery.co.uk

⊗ Hunters began brewing in 2008. The award-winning brewery has a 60-barrel brew length and 4,000 gallon fermenting capacity. A bottling, labelling and packing plant means it can turn out 3,000 bottle-conditioned beers per hour; this, coupled with a dedicated conditioning room, is enabling Hunters to bottle for others as well as itself. ‼ ☛ ♦ RAIB

Old Charlie (OG 1038, ABV 3.8%)
Good malt feel in the mouth, with a dry, tangy bitter finish.

Crispy Pig (OG 1042, ABV 4%)
Speciality beer with a hint of apples, refreshingly sharp and hoppy.

Half Bore (OG 1040, ABV 4%) ◆
Light colour and body. Malt dominates from start to finish. Lots of flavour and slightly flowery.

Devon Dreamer (OG 1042, ABV 4.1%) ◆
Amber-coloured best bitter with hop aroma and undertones of caramel. Hops in the taste and slight bitterness develops later.

Pheasant Plucker (OG 1044, ABV 4.3%)
Luscious, full-flavoured with a bittersweet finish.

Hunters Premium (OG 1048, ABV 4.8%)
Zesty, refreshing, well-balanced ale.

Royal Hunt (OG 1055, ABV 5.5%) ◆
An easy-drinking, strong ale. Malt dominates, with rich roast and caramel tones bursting through.

Black Jack (OG 1062, ABV 6%)
Premium, strong but light stout made with Devon honey.

Full Bore (OG 1070, ABV 6.8%)
Lovely malt flavours, made with Devon honey.

Hurly Burly

Unit 1, Block 4, Inveresk Industrial Estate, Musselburgh, EH21 7UL
☎ (0131) 665 8135

Office: 15 Glenorchy Road, North Berwick, EH39 4P4
⊕ hurlyburlybrewery.co.uk

Small, family-run brewery producing bottle-conditioned ales. Originally based in the brewer's kitchen the brewery moved in 2019 to larger premises. RAIB

Hurns

See Tomos Watkins (under W)

Hurst SIBA

Highfields Farm, Hurstpierpoint, West Sussex, BN6 9JT
☎ 07866 438953 ⊕ hurstbrewery.co.uk

Hurst was founded in 2012, but reviving a name dating back to 1862.

700 (ABV 3.9%)
A hoppy blonde ale with light floral, citrus and herbal notes and a satisfying mouthfeel.

Founder's Best Bitter (ABV 4.2%)
A rich, dark amber-coloured beer with a rounded, malty palate and subtle caramel and orange flavours.

Keepers Gold (ABV 4.4%)
A golden ale with aromas of grapefruit, citrus and spice. Hoppy notes are balanced by a simple malt profile and a subtle infusion of South Downs honey.

Watchtower (ABV 5.5%)
A black-coloured London-style porter. Strong, with a distinctive earthy bitterness.

Husk SIBA

Unit 58a, Railway Arches, North Woolwich road, West Silvertown, London, E16 2AA
☎ (020) 7474 3827 ☎ 07803 271160
⊕ huskbrewing.com

Brewing in West Silvertown, along from the Royal Docks, since 2015. The first brewery in the area now has its taproom open every Friday and Saturday. Beers available in cask, keg and bottles with eye-catching clip and label designs. RAIB

Milk Stout (ABV 4.5%)
Dark roast and chocolate milk stout. Addition of oats gives a silky feel.

Pale Ale (OG 1050, ABV 5.1%) ◆
Light citrusy, hoppy, bready aroma. Taste is slightly sweet, balanced with lemon peel, slight spiciness and tangerines becoming more bitter.

Mandarin & Earl Grey IPA (ABV 5.5%)
Light malt base, loaded with hops and infused with Earl Grey tea.

Saison (ABV 6.3%)
Belgian farmhouse-style beer with a twist of ginger and juniper.

Hybrid SIBA

unit 14c, Abbotsinch Industrial Estate, Abbotsinch Road, Grangemouth, FK3 9UX
✉ contact@hybridbrewing.com

Hybrid began brewing in 2016 using a 10.5-barrel dual train brewplant, allowing for two different beers to be brewed at a time. Up to 40 outlets are supplied direct mostly in the Forth Valley. Six core beers are brewed all year round and seasonal and special beers are brewed throughout the year.

Ctrl Alt Delete (OG 1038, ABV 3.8%)
Amber-coloured ale with pronounced malt topped with a twist of fruit.

Groat (OG 1038, ABV 3.8%)

Apex (OG 1038, ABV 4.1%)
Straw-coloured, hoppy bitter with a slightly tropical and floral taste.

Hindsight (OG 1045, ABV 4.4%)
A biscuity backdrop underpins the citrus berry twang of hops in this IPA.

Magic Porridge (OG 1052, ABV 4.7%)
Dark-coloured, silky smooth oatmeal stout featuring full roasted chocolate flavours.

Street Legal (OG 1045, ABV 4.7%)
Heavily-hopped pale ale with punchy citrus, pine and tropical fruit notes.

Hydes SIBA IFBB

The Beer Studio, 30 Kansas Avenue, Salford, M50 2GL
☎ (0161) 226 1317 ⊕ hydesbrewery.com

☺Hydes Brewery has been in the Manchester area since 1863. In 2012 it relocated to Salford's Media City area. The new plant brews four traditional beers and over fifty seasonal beers (three or four each month). 15 recipes are brewed under the banner of the Beer Studio, 12 are marketed as Provenance, reflecting different international beer styles, and beers also appear under the Kansas Avenue Brewing Co brand. ‼◆

1863 (OG 1033.5, ABV 3.5%) ◆
Lightly-hopped, pale brown-coloured session beer with some hops, malt and fruit in the taste and a short, dry finish.

Old Indie (OG 1033.5, ABV 3.5%) ◆
Dark brown/red in colour, with a fruit and malt nose. Taste includes biscuity malt and green fruits, with a satisfying aftertaste.

Hydes Original (OG 1036.5, ABV 3.8%) ◆
Pale brown-coloured beer with a malty nose, malt and an earthy hoppiness in the taste, and a good bitterness through to the finish.

Lowry (ABV 4.7%) ◆
Citrus taste with increasing bitterness. Quite sweet. Dry citrus finish.

Iâl

Pant Du Road, Eryrys, CH7 4DD ☎ 07956 440402
⊕ cwrwial.com

Cwrw Iâl Community Brewery is run as a social enterprise assisted by EU funding with all profits used for local community projects. The 10-barrel plant brews a core range as well as regular specials. It supplies outlets along the North Wales coast and the North West.

Pocket Rocket (OG 1040, ABV 4%) ◆
Yellow in colour with citrus fruit prominent in the aroma and sharp, hoppy taste.

Kia Kaha! (OG 1043, ABV 4.3%) ◆
A dry, bitter beer, gold in colour with a fruity aroma leading to a good hoppy taste and finish

Lager (OG 1043, ABV 4.3%)
Crisp and clean, unfiltered, unpasteurised session lager.

Limestone Cowboy (OG 1045, ABV 4.5%) ◆
A copper-coloured best bitter, malty with faint roast notes and fruit flavours. Hops dominate in the dry bitter finish.

The Apache Line (OG 1050, ABV 5%)
An IPA with big mango fruit aromas, with a smooth bitterness, tropical fruits and hoppy awesomeness.

Pothole Porter (OG 1054, ABV 5.1%) ◆
A rich and fruity porter with a smooth mouthfeel and good roast notes in aroma and taste.

Iceni

The Walled Garden, Elveden Courtyard, London Road, Elveden, Suffolk, IP24 3TQ

☎ (01842) 878922 ☎ 07949 488113

Office: **70 Risbygate Street, Bury St Edmunds, Suffolk, IP33 3AZ** ⊕ icenibrewery.co.uk

The Iceni brewery is owned by Brendan Moore, who set it up in 1995. ‼◆RAIB

Fine Soft Day (OG 1038, ABV 4%) ◆
Golden-hued with toffee notes throughout. A creamy, lightly-hopped backdrop softly sinks into a pleasant sweetness.

Idle

⚑ **White Hart Inn, Main Street, West Stockwith, Nottinghamshire, DN10 4EY**
☎ (01427) 892672 ☎ 07949 137174
✉ theidlebrewery@btinternet.com

The brewery began production in 2007 and is situated in a converted stable to the rear of the White Hart Inn. The property borders the banks of the Rive Idle, from which the brewery takes its name. Total production is provided for the sole use of the White Hart Inn. ◆

Ignition

44a Sydenham Road, Sydenham, London, SE26 5QX
☎ (020) 8852 4100 ⊕ ignition.beer

Ignition is a South London brewery, which employs and trains people with learning disabilities to brew beer. Beers are available in keg and bottles. An on-site taproom was opened in 2018, providing the staff with customer-facing experience. RAIB

Ilkley SIBA

The New Brewery, Ashlands Road, Ilkley, West Yorkshire, LS29 8JT
☎ (01943) 604604 ⊕ ilkleybrewery.co.uk

☺Ilkley Brewery was founded in 2009 and has expanded rapidly since. Ilkley beers can be found throughout the UK and are now exported into Europe as far as Russia. The brewery is a frequent sponsor of local beer festivals and also holds regular on-site social events and brewery tours. ‼◆RAIB

Mary Jane (OG 1036, ABV 3.5%)
A crisp, pale ale with citrus aromas.

Blonde (ABV 3.9%)

Ruby Jane (ABV 4%)

Fireside (ABV 4.2%)
A smoky porter.

Pale (ABV 4.2%)

Rombald (ABV 4.6%)
American-style, amber-coloured ale with crisp and fruity hop flavours.

Hanging Stone (ABV 5%)
Rich and creamy with a bitter finish of forest fruits and coffee.

Crossroads IPA (ABV 5.4%)
Aromas of orange rind and citrus peel with dry, spicy finish.

Imperial

⚑ **Arcadia Hall, Cliff Street, Mexborough, South Yorkshire, S64 9HU**

☎ (01709) 584000 ☎ 07428 422703
✉ impbrewery@gmail.com

Brewing began in 2010 using a six-barrel tower brewery system located in the basement of the Imperial Club, Mexborough. Beer is available in the club as well as local outlets. ‼♦RAIB

Inadequate

Holy Inadequate, 67 Etruria Old Road, Stoke-On-Trent, ST1 5PE
☎ (01782) 915170 ☎ 07771358238
✉ paulcope.cope@gmail.com

This one-barrel brewery commenced brewing behind the Holy Inadequate pub in 2018. It mainly supplies the pub with an ever-changing range of beers (up to four can be found on the bar at any one time). Other local pubs are sometimes supplied, along with local beer festivals.

Incredible SIBA

Unit 1, 214-224 Broomhill Road, Brislington, Bristol, BS4 5RG ☎ 07780 977073
incrediblebrewingcompany.com

This microbrewery specialises in producing small batches of beer using a 2.5-barrel plant. It was established in 2014 by head brewer Stephen Hall with the aim of promoting experimental beers and traditional recipes. ‼♦RAIB

Milk Stout (OG 1044, ABV 4.4%)

Pale Ale (OG 1043, ABV 4.4%)

Amber Ale (OG 1052, ABV 5.2%)

Black IPA (OG 1056, ABV 5.6%)

Grapefruit IPA (OG 1054, ABV 5.6%)

Indian Pale Ale (OG 1063, ABV 6.6%)
Powerfully-hopped IPA with a robust maltiness.

Independent Lakeland

See Strands

Indian

119b Baltimore Trading Estate, Baltimore Road, Great Barr, B42 1DD
☎ (0121) 296 9000 indianbrewery.com

This six-barrel brewery, established in 2005 as the Tunnel Brewery at the Lord Nelson Inn, relocated to the picturesque stable block at Red House Farm in 2011. In 2015 the owners of Tunnel Brewery went their separate ways, with Mike Walsh retaining the brewery and renaming it the Indian Brewery. Later that year it was sold to new owners and relocated to the outskirts of Birmingham. ‼

Summer (ABV 4%)
Full-flavoured beer with a distinct citrus hop aroma. Light-bodied and well-balanced.

IPA (ABV 4.9%)
A traditional, well-rounded IPA with a citrus punch and tropical fruit.

Bombay Honey (ABV 5%)
A blonde beer, brewed with real honey.

Peacock (ABV 5%)
Vibrant amber-coloured ale with sweet mellow and spiced berry notes.

Indigenous

Peacock Cottage, Main Street, Chaddleworth, Berkshire, RG20 7EH
☎ (01488) 505060 indigenousbrewery.co.uk

An occasional and informal microbrewer for many years, Kevin Brady established Indigenous in 2014, increasing production using a 2.5-barrel plant. Availability is restricted to local pubs, shops and an increasing number of regional beer festivals. ‼♦RAIB

Baldrick (ABV 3.4%)
A smooth mild ale with plenty of malty flavours.

Forager's Gold (OG 1038, ABV 4%)
A crisp golden ale. Smooth and refreshing with caramel notes.

Summer Solstice (OG 1042, ABV 4.1%)
A straw-coloured pale ale with a fresh, hoppy aroma coupled with a subtle bitterness and a long, dry finish.

BillyNoMates (OG 1050, ABV 4.2%)
A well-hopped, American-style pale ale, with a slightly hazy appearance, good malt balance and a slightly bitter finish.

Frisky Mare (ABV 4.2%)
A generously-hopped golden-coloured ale with notes of gooseberry, grape and floral accents, leading to a long dry finish.

Silly Moo (ABV 4.2%)
A very smooth, well-balanced milk stout.

Monocle (OG 1049, ABV 4.5%)
A smooth stout with a malty aroma and a slightly dry finish.

Nutcracker (ABV 4.5%)
A brown-coloured ale with a good mix of roasted malts and fruity hops.

Old Cadger (OG 1046, ABV 4.5%)
Balanced, full-flavoured beer with rich malts and fruity hops.

Moonstruck (OG 1051, ABV 4.8%)
A porter with plenty of chocolate and coffee notes, complemented by a subtle bitterness and smooth finish.

Nosey Parker (OG 1058, ABV 5.5%)
A strong ruby-red-coloured mild, with a sweet malty base and a hint of hops.

AMMO Belle (OG 1055, ABV 5.6%)
A well-hopped, American-style pale ale that delivers lots of fruity notes, a floral aroma and a moderately dry finish.

Double Warp (ABV 5.8%)
A rich, dark-coloured, full-flavoured stout with plenty of deep chocolate notes and a hint of spice.

Industrial

See Silver

Inferno (NEW)

17 Station Street, Tewkesbury, GL20 5NJ
☎ (01684) 294873 ☎ 07854 949731
✉ cbowley3@yahoo.co.uk

Inferno began in 2018, after many years of home brewing, using a 2.5-barrel kit which was installed in 2019. Four regular ales and a number of well-received seasonal ales are brewed. The beers are available in local Gloucestershire pubs, clubs and at beer festivals. ♦

Inishmacsaint

See Fermanagh

Inkspot

Rookery Barn, The Rookery, 40 Streatham Common South, Streatham, London, SW16 3BX ☎ 07787 832292 🌐 theinkspotbrewery.com

Started in 2012 as Perfect Blend after a bar in Streatham, the brewery changed its name to Inkspot a few years later. Originally cuckoo brewing at various other brewereis, brewing began on its own premises in Streatham in 2018. Its Art & Craft bottle shops are the best place to find the beers.

Inner Bay SIBA

Seacliffe Villa, Hill Street, Inverkeithing, KY11 1AB 🌐 innerbay.co.uk

Brewing began in 2016. Inner Bay is a family-run brewery using traditional ingredients and methods producing bottle-conditioned beers in small batches.

INNformal

Five Bells Baydon Road, Baydon Road, Wickham, Berkshire, RG20 8HH ☎ (01488) 657300 🌐 fivebellswickham.co.uk

⊗ INNformal was established in 2015 in a purpose-built building behind the Five Bells pub in Wickham. A bore hole in the pub garden supplies water for the 2.5-barrel plant. A secondary 0.5-barrel kit is used for experimental brews. Beers are supplied mainly to the Five Bells and the John O'Gaunt, Hungerford. ‼♦

Innis & Gunn

See Inveralmond

Instant Karma

4 John Street, Clay Cross, Derbyshire, S45 9NQ ☎ (01246) 250 366 🌐 instantkarmabrewery.co.uk

Instant Karma began brewing in 2012 using a five-barrel plant with a brew length of 15 barrels per week. The brewery is part of the Rykneld Turnpyke brewpub.

Interbrew UK

Porter Tun House, Capability Green, Luton, Bedfordshire, LU1 3LS ☎ (01582) 391166

Interbrew (Magor): Magor Brewery, Magor, NP26 3DA

Interbrew (Samlesbury): Cuerdale Lane, Samlesbury, PR5 0XD

UK subsidiary of A-B InBev. No real ale.

Intrepid SIBA

Unit 12 Vincent Works, Brough, Bradwell, Derbyshire, S33 9HG ☎ (01433) 621851 ☎ 07870777594 ✉ info@intrepidbrew.co.uk

Based in the Hope Valley in the Peak District, Intrepid commenced brewing in 2014 using an eight-barrel plant. ‼

Intrepid Explorer (OG 1038, ABV 4%)
A refreshing blonde beer with fruity aromas and a crisp, dry finish.

Intrepid St. Bernard (OG 1044, ABV 4.4%)
A malty ale with oak and vanilla aromas, and caramel and biscuit flavours.

Intrepid Porter (OG 1049, ABV 4.8%)
A traditional East India-style porter using modern hops for a less bitter finish.

Traveller (OG 1049, ABV 5.4%)
American-style IPA with a fruity flavour, and a bitter finish.

Inveralmond SIBA

22 Inveralmond Place, Inveralmond, Perth, PH1 3TS ☎ (01738) 449448 ☎ 441738552872 🌐 inveralmond-brewery.co.uk

Established in 1997, Inveralmond was the first brewery in Perth for more than 30 years. Around 250 outlets are supplied. In 2016, Innis & Gunn bought Inveralmond after a successful crowdfunding scheme. I&G had planned to build a new brewing operation but decided to buy the Perth brewery, where the current 30-barrel plant will be expanded, with a new maturation plant for the I&G beers. I&G makes no real ale but the Inveralmond range will continue. ‼♦

EPA (ABV 3.8%)

Ossian (OG 1042, ABV 4.1%)
Well-balanced, full-bodied, amber-coloured best bitter. Fruit and hops dominate with a bittersweet character although excessive caramel can distract from this. Dry finish.

Lia Fail (OG 1048, ABV 4.7%)
A dark-coloured, robust, full-bodied beer with a deep malty taste. Smooth texture and balanced finish.

Daracha (ABV 5.2%)
Oak-matured, ruby-coloured Scotch ale.

Iron Pier

Units 6 & 7, May Industrial Estate, May Ave, Northfleet, Gravesend, Kent, DA11 8RU 🌐 ironpier.beer

⊗ Iron Pier Brewery was established in 2017 using a 15-barrel plant. It takes its name from the oldest iron pier in existence residing on the River Thames at Gravesend. An on-site tap room offers the brewery's beers plus other local brews. ‼

Perry St. Pale (OG 1035, ABV 3.7%)
Refreshing, light-bodied pale ale. Heavily-hopped for a nose full of fruit tones, with a smooth bitterness.

English Pale (OG 1040, ABV 3.9%)
A hoppy pale ale with herbal, floral and fruit notes.

Bitter (OG 1040, ABV 4%)

A traditional bitter with smooth bitterness, dark fruit and toffee flavours and honey and spice.

Wealdway (OG 1045, ABV 4.5%)
A pale amber-coloured ale with hints of pine and a citrus hop character.

Cast Iron Stout (OG 1046, ABV 4.7%)
A smooth chocolate character with a hint of roast coffee, full mouthfeel, and a balanced bitterness.

Porter (OG 1052, ABV 5.3%)
Rich porter with notes of chocolate and coffee. Balanced bitterness with dark fruits in the finish.

Irving SIBA

Unit G1, Railway Triangle, Walton Road, Portsmouth, Hampshire, PO6 1TQ
☎ (023) 9238 9988 🌐 irvingbrewers.co.uk

⊗ Established in 2007 by former Gale's brewer Malcolm Irving using a 15-barrel plant. Around 120 outlets are supplied in Hampshire, Sussex and Surrey with beers available further afield through beer swaps with other breweries. Speciality beers may be ordered for festivals. ‼ ♦

Frigate (OG 1039, ABV 3.8%)
Satisfying session bitter. Hoppy, with a floral aroma and initial sweetness, leading to bitterness and a smooth, slightly dry finish.

Type 42 (OG 1042, ABV 4.2%)
A robust best bitter with a deep ruby red hue. Sweet hedgerow berry notes are balanced by a long, roasted malt finish and a deep bitterness.

Admiral Stout (OG 1042.5, ABV 4.3%)
Well-balanced stout, with plenty of fruit and roast, together with pleasant hint of coffee, and short bitter finish.

Invincible (OG 1048, ABV 4.6%)
Tawny-coloured strong bitter. Sweet and fruity with underlying maltiness throughout and gradually increasing dryness, contrasting with the sweet finish.

Iron Duke (OG 1053, ABV 5.3%)
A refreshing, well-balanced strong IPA. Hoppy – but not overly so.

Irwell Works SIBA

Irwell Street, Ramsbottom, BL0 9YQ
☎ (01706) 825019 🌐 irwellworksbrewery.co.uk

Irwell Works has been brewing since 2010 in a building that once housed the Irwell Works steam, tin, copper and iron works. It changed hands in 2018. The brewery operates a six-barrel plant. A brewery tap on the first floor serves most of the brewery's beers. ‼ GF

Lightweights & Gentlemen (OG 1031, ABV 3.2%)
Light, refreshing pale ale with some fruitiness and a hoppy, bitter finish.

Breadcrumbs (ABV 3.6%)
A light, session strength pale ale. A good bitterness followed by a spicy, yet pleasant hoppiness.

Tin Plate (OG 1033, ABV 3.6%)
Traditional dark-coloured mild with a rich, creamy flavour and a slight bitterness to contrast.

Copper Plate (OG 1036, ABV 3.8%)
Traditional Northern bitter. Copper-coloured with a satisfying blend of malt and hops and good bitterness.

Costa Del Salford (OG 1039, ABV 4.1%)
A hoppy, light-coloured ale with bags of flavour.

Steam Plate (OG 1042, ABV 4.3%)
Golden-coloured best bitter. Medium bitterness balanced with a slight sweetness. Slightly nutty flavour and a pleasant hop aroma.

Iron Plate (OG 1043, ABV 4.4%)
Roast malt in the aroma is joined by hop and a toasty bitterness in the taste and finish.

Marshmallow Unicorn (ABV 4.4%)
Traditional milk stout using lactose to temper any bitterness from the roasted barley. Dark-coloured and creamy.

Mad Dogs & Englishmen (OG 1052, ABV 5.5%)
Strong pale ale. Little sweetness for its strength and a strong hop character. Smooth and easy-drinking.

Isaac Poad SIBA

Office: Axholme Croft, Chapel Street, Cattal, York, North Yorkshire, YO26 8DY
☎ (01423) 358114 🌐 isaacpoad.co.uk

Established in 2016, this is a subsidiary of a long established grain merchant known for supplying malting barley to many local maltsters. Currently using spare capacity at another local brewery pending the construction of its own plant, the emphasis is on using local Yorkshire malt and British hops. The regular beer range continues to expand and is supplemented by seasonal specials. ♦

No. 86 Golden Ale (ABV 3.6%)

1863 Best Bitter (ABV 3.8%)

No.91 Craft Ale (OG 1039, ABV 3.9%)
Ale with light citrus flavours.

All Four Yorkshire Red Ale (OG 1041.5, ABV 4.2%)
Biscuit flavours with hints of caramel and burnt toffee.

No.84 India Pale Ale (ABV 4.5%)
Pale-coloured, strong beer with a huge hop aroma overlaying malt.

Piccadilly Porter (OG 1047.5, ABV 4.8%)
Dark brown-coloured bitter beer with big hop notes.

Isca SIBA

Court Farm, Holcombe Village, Dawlish, Devon, EX7 0JT ☎ 07773 444501 🌐 iscaales.co.uk

⊗ Established in a disused milking parlour in 2009, Isca has developed a large range of ales. Seasonal and special brews are often available at beer festivals, including outside of the region. ♦RAIB

Citra (OG 1038, ABV 3.8%)
Light, refreshing beer with grapefruit aroma leading to a dry bitter finish.

Dawlish Summer (OG 1038, ABV 3.8%)
Light beer with hoppy aroma.

Golden Ale (OG 1038, ABV 3.8%)
A golden bitter with a hoppy aroma.

Dawlish Bittter (OG 1042, ABV 4.2%)

Glorious Devon (OG 1044, ABV 4.4%)
Grassy hop aroma with a hoppy aftertaste.

Holcombe White (OG 1045, ABV 4.5%)
Cloudy wheat with hints of banana, oranges and spice.

ISCA Gold (OG 1045, ABV 4.5%)
Golden beer full of hops, with a dry, bitter finish.

Dawlish Pale (OG 1050, ABV 5%)
Grassy hop aroma, with an intense hoppy aftertaste.

Black IPA (OG 1060, ABV 6%)
Strong, hoppy, black-coloured beer, packed with hops.

Devon Pale (OG 1068, ABV 6.8%)

Isla Vale

17 Westbrook Gardens, Margate, Kent, CT9 5DJ
☎ (01843) 292451 ☎ 07980 174616
🌐 islavalealesmiths.co.uk

⊗ Isla Vale was established in 2014 from a residential address in Westbrook (Margate). Along with its core range, specially commissioned beers are brewed for the Wheel Alehouse, Birchington, and the London Tavern, Margate. Outlets are supplied locally and across the South-East of England. ♦

Golding Delicious (OG 1038, ABV 3.8%)
A light, copper-coloured session ale, with a slight malty sweetness.

Hopping Mad (OG 1042, ABV 4%)
A tradional session bitter with a variety of hops, complex aromas and malty flavours.

Two Halves (OG 1040, ABV 4%)

Ninkasi Pale Ale (OG 1045, ABV 4.5%)
A hoppy pale ale with added elderflower.

Big Red Beer (OG 1046, ABV 4.6%)
A red-coloured session beer. Fruity, with plenty of hops and a hint of honey.

Cock-A-Snook (OG 1045, ABV 4.6%)
A dark golden-coloured session ale, with good hop aroma and hints of fruit.

Natural Blonde (OG 1046, ABV 4.7%)
A refreshing blonde ale, initial floral notes with a lasting hoppy bitterness.

Befuggled (OG 1052, ABV 5.2%)
A rich malty ESB-style ale, with plenty of hops.

IPA (OG 1058, ABV 5.5%)
A modern take on an IPA. A hint of fruit with an intense hoppy aroma and flavour.

Island SIBA

Dinglers Farm, Yarmouth Road, Newport, Isle of Wight, PO30 4LZ
☎ (01983) 821731 🌐 islandbrewery.co.uk

⊗ Island Brewery is the realisation of Tom Minshull's ambition to brew real ales to complement the existing family-owned drinks distribution business. Brewing commenced in 2010 using a 12-barrel brewery. More than 100 outlets are supplied direct. !!♦

Nipper Bitter (OG 1038, ABV 3.8%)
Straw-coloured, light and refreshing with a distinguishable balance of malt and hops and a satisfying afterbite.

Wight Gold (OG 1040, ABV 4%)
Golden brown in colour with rounded malt and hops throughout.

Yachtsmans Ale (OG 1042, ABV 4.2%)
Chestnut-coloured ale with a rich, malty mouthfeel and hop aroma.

Wight Diamond (OG 1046, ABV 4.4%)

Wight Knight (OG 1045, ABV 4.5%)
Strong, full-bodied beer.

Vectis Venom (OG 1048, ABV 4.8%)
Malty, dark ruby-coloured ale with an easy-drinking, underlying smooth characteristic.

Earls RDA (OG 1052, ABV 5%)
Rich yet understated stout, with espresso aftertaste.

Islay SIBA

The Brewery, Islay House Square, Bridgend, Isle of Islay, PA44 7NZ
☎ (01496) 810014 🌐 islayales.beer

☺ The only brewery on an island famous for its malt whiskies, Islay Ales started brewing in 2004 and continues to use a four-barrel plant. Situated in converted farm buildings, including a visitor centre and shop. The brewery tap is the only outlet for the brewery's cask-conditioned beers. !! 🛒 ♦ RAIB

Finlaggan Ale (OG 1039, ABV 3.7%)
A mid-brown-coloured beer with a gentle, rounded bitterness and a fresh, fruity and hoppy flavour.

Black Rock Ale (OG 1040, ABV 4.2%)
A reddish-coloured beer with a soft, nutty flavour, a robust body and a floral, grassy and herbal nose.

Saligo Ale (OG 1044, ABV 4.4%)
A golden ale with a rounded bitterness and a refreshing citrussy, lemon and grapefruit nose and taste.

Angus Og Ale (OG 1045, ABV 4.5%)
Mid-brown in colour with the balanced flavour similar to a traditional IPA.

Isle of Avalon SIBA

Stagman Lane, Ashcott, Somerset, TA7 9QW
☎ (01458) 210050 ☎ 07809 056855
🌐 avalonwholesaleandbrewing.co.uk

⊗ Brewing began in 2008. Isle Of Avalon is a five-barrel plant brewing for the parent company Avalon Wholesale, and occasionally for one-off events and local supply.

Isle of Mull

See Argyll

Isle of Purbeck SIBA

Manor Road, Studland, Dorset, BH19 3AU
☎ (01929) 450227 🌐 isleofpurbeckbrewery.com

⊗ Founded in 2003, the brewery is situated in the grounds of the Bankes Arms Hotel, overlooking Studland Bay on the Jurassic Coast. A 10-barrel plant is used. The core beers are available locally as

THE BREWERIES

well as nationwide via exchange swaps with other microbreweries, and at local beer festivals. ♦RAIB

Purbeck Best Bitter (OG 1036, ABV 3.6%) ◆
A classic, malty best bitter with rich malt aroma and taste, and a smooth, malty bitter finish.

Force Four (OG 1040, ABV 4%)
A balanced, smooth-drinking beer packed with sweet roasted malt flavours, and a subtle whisper of spicy hops.

Fossil Fuel (OG 1040, ABV 4.1%) ◆
Amber-coloured bitter with complex aroma with a hint of pepper. Rich malt dominates the taste, leading to a smooth, dry finish.

Solar Power (OG 1043, ABV 4.3%) ◆
Tawny-coloured, mid-range ale. Well-balanced flavours combine to give a strong, bitter taste but short, dry finish.

Studland Bay Wrecked (OG 1044, ABV 4.5%) ◆
Deep red-coloured ale with a slightly sweet aroma, and a dry, malty finish.

Purbeck IPA (OG 1047, ABV 4.8%) ◆
Mid-brown-coloured beer with hop/malt balance in the flavour and a long, dry aftertaste.

Isle of Sark (NEW)

La Seigneurie, Sark, GY10 1SF ☎ 07781 439881
✉ sarkbrewing@gmail.com

A nanobrewery established in 2016.

Isle of Skye SIBA

The Pier, Uig, Isle of Skye, IV51 9XP
☎ (01470) 542477 🌐 skyeale.com

The Isle of Skye Brewery was established in 1995. Originally a 10-barrel plant, it was upgraded to 20 barrels in 2004. !! ♦

Skyelight (OG 1038, ABV 3.8%) ◆
A slightly hoppy nose leads to a powerful hop and fruit taste, and a sharp finish.

Tarasgeir (OG 1040, ABV 4%) ◆
The peat-roasted barley dominates giving a mellow, peaty whisky taste.

Tiny Angels (OG 1040, ABV 4%)

YP (Young Pretender) (OG 1039, ABV 4%) ◆
A refreshing, amber-coloured, hoppy grapefruit bitter. Some sweetness in the taste, with a lingering, bitter finish.

Skye Red (OG 1041, ABV 4.2%) ◆
A light, fruity nose with a hint of caramel leads to a hoppy, malty, fruity flavour and a dry, bittersweet finish.

Skye Gold (OG 1041.5, ABV 4.3%) ◆
Well-balanced, refreshingly soft lemon, bitter flavour, with an oaty background due to the addition of porridge oats.

Skye Black (OG 1044, ABV 4.5%) ◆
Full-bodied, Scottish old ale. Malty richness holds sway, with plenty of hops and fruit.

Skye IPA (OG 1046, ABV 4.5%) ◆
Well-balanced, good malty background and flavoursome hops.

Blaven (OG 1047, ABV 5%) ◆
A well-balanced, strong, amber-coloured bitter, with kiwi fruit and caramel in the nose, and a lingering, sharp bitterness.

Skye Blonde (ABV 5.5%) ◆
Citrus hoppy brew, with some caramel sweetness.

Cuillin Beast (OG 1066, ABV 7%) ◆
Sweet, fruity, and drinkable. Plenty of caramel throughout with a variety of fruit on the nose.

It's Quicker by Ale

See Harrogate

Itchen Valley SIBA

Unit D, Prospect Commercial Park, Prospect Road, Alresford, Hampshire, SO24 9QF
☎ (01962) 735111 🌐 itchenvalleybrewery.com

Established in 1997, Itchen Valley moved to new premises in 2006 with a 20-barrel plant. More than 350 pubs are supplied, with wholesalers used for further distribution. !! ♦RAIB

Pride of the valley (ABV 3.8%)
Easy-drinking session bitter. Hazel-coloured with orange, coffee and honey notes.

Hampshire Rose (OG 1042, ABV 4.2%)
Amber-coloured ale, fruit and hops dominate the taste throughout, with a good mouthfeel.

New Hampshire (ABV 4.3%)
A light, refreshing, American-style pale ale, with peach, pear and citrus.

Pure Gold (OG 1046, ABV 4.8%) ◆
Aromatic hoppy, strong bitter. Golden-coloured, with initial maltiness and grapefruit counter-balanced with some sweetness, leading to dry finish.

Izaak Walton

See under W

James Street

See Bath Brewhouse

Jaw SIBA

Unit 9, The Centre Point, 67b Montrose Avenue, Hilington Industrial Estate, Hillington, G52 4LA
☎ (0141) 237 5840 🌐 jawbrew.co.uk

After 20 years as a homebrewer Mark Hazell together with wife Alison launched Jaw Brew in 2014. Using a five-barrel plant, beers are available in cask, bottle and can. Bespoke beers can be produced. !! RAIB

Fathom (ABV 4%)
Dark-coloured beer with deep flavours.

Drop (OG 1042, ABV 4.2%)
Session ale with a hoppy aroma and a smooth bitter finish.

Surf (OG 1043, ABV 4.3%)
Dry-hopped, tangy, naturally hazy beer.

Drift (OG 1047, ABV 4.6%)
A mellow golden ale with notes of biscotti.

Spinnaker (ABV 4.7%)

Clear, straw-coloured lager with a lemon hit behind the malt.

Wave (OG 1048, ABV 4.7%)
Sweet banana to start with a smooth finish.

Jeffersons

Brew Shed, 84 Verdun Road, Barnes, London, SW13 9AX ☎ 07960 597311
jeffersonsbrewery.co.uk

Brewing began in 2017 at this nanobrewery in Barnes. Output is mostly bottle-conditioned, some keg can be found locally at markets and craft beer festivals, and there has been the occasional trial with cask. RAIB

Jennings

Castle Brewery, Cockermouth, Cumbria, CA13 9NE
☎ (01900) 820362 jenningsbrewery.co.uk

Jennings Brewery was established as a family concern in 1828 in the village of Lorton. The company moved to its present location in 1874. Pure Lakeland water is still used for brewing, drawn from the brewery's own well. Part of Marston's PLC. !! ♦

Bitter (OG 1035, ABV 3.5%)
A malty beer with a good mouthfeel that combines with roast flavour and a hoppy finish.

Cumberland Ale (OG 1038, ABV 4%)
Fruit and caramel in the aroma gives way to a sweet middle, balanced by a gentle bitter finish.

Cocker Hoop (OG 1044, ABV 4.6%)
Full-bodied complex bitter beer with plenty of hops and a rising bitter finish.

Sneck Lifter (OG 1051, ABV 5.1%)
A strong, dark brown-coloured ale with a complex balance of fruit, malt, sweet and roast flavours through to the finish.

Jesus College

Jesus College, Cambridge, CB5 8BL

In-house brewery for Jesus College at the University of Cambridge. Beers are produced for college use only and are not available to the general public.

John O'Groats

County Road, John O'Groats, KW1 4YR
☎ (01955) 611220 ☎ 07842 401571
johnogroatsbrewery@gmail.com

Brewing began in 2015 with a four-barrel plant. It is housed in the old John O'Groats Fire Station almost opposite its tap, the Seaview Hotel. Tours are not formally offered but if brewing is taking place guests can be shown the process.

Swelkie (ABV 4%)
Slight honey taste in this hoppy, citrus brew.

Deep Groat (ABV 4.8%)
Nearly black-coloured brew full of chocolate and coffee, with some background roast.

John Smith's

See under S

John Thompson

See under T

Jolly Boys

Unit 16a Redbrook Business Park, off Wilthorpe Road, Redbrook, South Yorkshire, S75 1JN ☎ 07939 439166
jollyboysbrewery.co.uk

Jolly Boys started brewing using spare capacity at another brewery in 2016. Brewing began on its own plant later the same year. One pub in Wakefield, the Jolly Tap, is owned. !! ♦

Jolly Yorkshire Bitter (ABV 3.8%)

Blonde (OG 1041, ABV 4%)

Jolly Cascade (ABV 4%)

La Joll'a Blonde (OG 1041, ABV 4%)

Golden Best (OG 1042, ABV 4.5%)

Jolly YPA (ABV 4.8%)

Jolly Collier Porter (OG 1052, ABV 5%)

Jolly IPA (ABV 5.5%)

Jolly Sailor SIBA

Olympia Hotel, 77 Barlby Road, Selby, North Yorkshire, YO8 5AB
☎ (01757) 707564 ☎ 07923 635755
jolly-sailor-brewery.webplus.net

Jolly Sailor is a family-owned microbrewery situated in the quaint market town of Selby. A six-barrel plant is used. ♦

Bullseye Bitter (OG 1039, ABV 3.8%)

Jolly Blonde (OG 1036.5, ABV 3.8%)

Jolly Scotsman's Bitter (OG 1038, ABV 3.8%)
A fruity, amber-coloured ale with citrus notes.

Yellow Jersey (OG 1036, ABV 3.8%)

Cue Brew (OG 1040, ABV 4%)

Jollyboat SIBA

The Coach House, Buttgarden Street, Bideford, Devon, EX39 2AU
☎ (01237) 424343

Established in 1995, the brewery is named after a sailor's leave vessel and all the beers have a nautical theme. Most outlets supplied are in Devon. !! ♦

Mainbrace (OG 1042, ABV 4.2%)
Pale brown-coloured brew, with a rich, fruity aroma, and a bitter taste and aftertaste.

Plunder (OG 1049, ABV 4.8%)
Red/brown-coloured beer with an aromatic nose, a good balance of malt, hops and fruit present throughout, leading to a bitter finish.

Joseph Holt

See under H

Joule's SIBA

The Brewery, Great Hales Street, Market Drayton, Shropshire, TF9 1JP
☎ (01630) 654400 joulesbrewery.co.uk

Re-established in 2010, following a break of 40 years, Joule's is situated in Market Drayton and uses its own mineral water. It runs a collection of 40 pubs across Shropshire, Staffordshire and Cheshire. ‼◆

Blonde (OG 1038, ABV 3.8%)
Light, refreshing and aromatic straw-coloured ale. Well-balanced, crisp, clean palate with a pleasing aroma of citrus fruit.

Pale Ale (OG 1042, ABV 4.1%)
Fresh, clean, full-bodied, well-balanced beer with a pleasant bitter finish.

Slumbering Monk (OG 1045, ABV 4.5%)
Full-bodied, bright copper-coloured ale with a complex malt and nut character. Hints of caramel, round, soft smoothness in the palate, with complementary bitter notes.

Junction

🍴 1 Baildon Road, Baildon, West Yorkshire, BD17 6AB
☎ (01274) 582009 ☎ 07539 923744
✉ andydoug48@gmail.com

Junction is a microbrewery established in 2012 in the cellar of the Junction pub in Baildon, brewing around 300 gallons a week. Beer is sold in the pub and other local outlets. RAIB

Kansas Avenue

See Hydes

Keep

🍴 Village Inn, The Cross, Nailsworth, Gloucestershire, GL6 0HH
☎ (01453) 835715 ☎ 07963 200768
✉ paul@dropinpubs.com

After a break of 96 years, brewing returned to Nailsworth in 2004 at the Village Inn. The pub and brewery were sold in 2016 to Paul Sugden and Adam Pavey, who changed the brewery name from Nailsworth to Keep Brewing. Expansion is being considered. ◆RAIB

Keith SIBA

Unit R, Isla Bank Mills, Keith, AB55 5DD
☎ (01542) 488006 ⊕ keithbrewery.co.uk

Formerly known as Brewmeister and established in 2012, the brewery was renamed Keith Brewery in 2015. Beer is mainly available in bottles in selected specialist off-licenses but cask-conditioned beer is available to a few outlets and beer festivals. The Brewmeister brand name is kept for export-only orders. Spey Valley Brewery merged with Keith in 2018 and became a wholly owned subsidiary of Keith Brewery Holding Ltd. Its range has been retained but it shares staff and facilities. It is now part of the Consolidated Craft Breweries group along with Alechemy Brewing (qv). ◆RAIB

Herr Keith (OG 1044, ABV 4.5%) ◤
Cloudy white/yellow-coloured wheat beer with hints of coriander.

Larger Keith (OG 1048, ABV 4.5%)

Pale Keith (OG 1048, ABV 5%) ◤
Grapefruit hoppy bitter.

Stout Keith (OG 1048, ABV 5%)

Coffee stout made with chocolate and coffee beans.

Sir Keith (OG 1096, ABV 10.1%)
Slightly sweet but hoppy with a fruity aroma and complex malty character.

Brewed under the Spey Valley Brewery brand name:

Sunshine on Keith (OG 1036, ABV 3.5%) ◤
A golden-coloured beer with light citrus bitter hop notes.

David's Not So Bitter (OG 1046, ABV 4.4%) ◤
Light-brown-coloured beer with a good mix of malts, hops and red fruits.

Stillman's IPA (OG 1047.6, ABV 4.6%) ◤
Amber-coloured hoppy bitter with a whisky background.

1814 (OG 1050, ABV 5%)

Spey Stout (OG 1055, ABV 5.4%) ◤
A thick, dark-coloured, malty stout with a smoky blackcurrant background.

Spey's Hardware (ABV 6.4%)

Kelburn SIBA

10 Muriel Lane, Barrhead, G78 1QB
☎ (0141) 881 2138 ⊕ kelburnbrewery.com

⊠ Kelburn is an award-winning family business established in 2002. ‼◆

Sunriser (OG 1034, ABV 3.4%)
A well-balanced, hoppy, refreshing beer with a touch of rye. Long-lasting biscuit and grapefruit finish.

Goldihops (OG 1038, ABV 3.8%) ◤
Well-hopped session ale with a fruity taste and a bitter finish.

Pivo Estivo (OG 1038, ABV 3.9%)
A pale, dry, citrus, hoppy session ale.

Misty Law (OG 1040, ABV 4%)
A dry, hoppy amber-coloured ale, with a long-lasting bitter finish.

Red Smiddy (OG 1040, ABV 4.1%) ⊡ ◤
Bittersweet ale with an intense citrus hop character that assaults the nose and continues into the flavour, balanced perfectly with fruity malt.

Regnitz (OG 1042, ABV 4.4%)

Dark Moor (OG 1044, ABV 4.5%)
A dark, fruity ale with undertones of liquorice and blackcurrant.

Jaguar (OG 1043, ABV 4.5%) ⊡
A golden-coloured, full-bodied ale with undertones of grapefruit and a long-lasting citrus, hoppy aftertaste.

Cart Noir (OG 1046, ABV 4.8%)

Cart Blanche (OG 1048, ABV 5%) ◤
A golden, full-bodied ale. The assault of fruit and hop camouflages the strength of this easy-drinking ale.

Kelchner SIBA

Unit D, The Sidings, Station Road, Ampthill, Bedfordshire, MK45 2QY ☎ 07508305754
✉ kelchnerbrewery@gmail.com

Brewing began in 2018 using a six-barrel brew plant. ‼ RAIB

Local is Lekker (ABV 3.9%)

Ampthill Gold (ABV 4.1%)
Subtle biscuit flavours with a delicate hop aroma.

Ampthill IPA (ABV 4.5%)
Pale-coloured ale with a well-balanced hoppy and malty character.

After Dark (ABV 4.8%)
Black-coloured IPA with dense citrus, coffee and chocolate notes with a dry and resinous finish.

Kelham Island SIBA

23 Alma Street, Sheffield, South Yorkshire, S3 8SA
☎ (0114) 249 4804

Office: Prospect House, 17 Alma Street, Sheffield, S3 8RY ⊕ kelhambrewery.co.uk

☺Opened in 1990 behind the Fat Cat pub, the brewery moved to new purpose-built premises in 1999. The old building is used as a visitor centre, and there is a separate brewery shop together with offices and a function room in nearby Prospect House. ‼ ⏛ ♦ RAIB

Best Bitter (OG 1038, ABV 3.8%)
Classic, amber-coloured Yorkshire bitter with spicy, earthy aromas and a sweet, refreshing, malty finish.

Pride of Sheffield (OG 1040.5, ABV 4%)

Easy Rider (OG 1041.8, ABV 4.3%) ◆
A straw-coloured beer with a sweetish flavour and delicate hints of citrus fruits. A beer with hints of flavour rather than full-bodied.

Riders on the Storm (OG 1045, ABV 4.5%)
A robust, golden-coloured pale ale with berry notes and very slight roasted notes.

Pale Rider (OG 1050, ABV 5.2%) ◆
A full-bodied, straw-coloured pale ale with a good fruity aroma and a strong fruit and hop taste. Well-balanced sweetness and bitterness continue in the finish.

Keltek SIBA

Candela House, Cardrew Way, Redruth, Cornwall, TR15 1SS
☎ (01209) 313620

Office: Unit 5, Kernick Business Park, Annear Rd, Penryn, TR10 9EW ⊕ keltekbrewery.co.uk

⊠ Keltek, meaning Celtic in Cornish, began brewing award-winning ales in 1997, and was founded by Stuart Heath. It started as a 2.5-barrel plant in Stuart's disused stable block on the Roseland Peninsula. Several moves and expansions mean its now based in Redruth, and can brew more than 250 barrels a week. In 2013 Keltek acquired four pubs in south-west Cornwall (the second brewery in Cornwall to own its estate of pubs). Two more pubs were acquired in 2016. ⏛ ♦ RAIB

Even Keel (OG 1034, ABV 3.4%) ◆
Pale brown-coloured session bitter. Refreshing malt and hop taste with apple, plum and pear drops. Gentle dry and bitter finish.

Golden Lance (OG 1038, ABV 4%) ◆

Gold-coloured bitter with light fruity aroma. Grassy citrus hops, apples, malt and hints of elderflower and butterscotch. Long bitter finish.

Magik (OG 1040, ABV 4%) ◆
Pale brown-coloured bitter with gentle malt and hop aroma. Full malt balanced by citrus and marmalade hops with earthy notes.

Phoenix (OG 1045, ABV 4.5%) ◆
Golden-coloured best bitter. Powerful fruity hops with high bitterness but backed with solid malt which lingers well in the finish.

Wayward Knight (OG 1045, ABV 4.5%)

King (OG 1049, ABV 5.1%) ◆
Copper-coloured, strong bitter with a mix of malt and hop aromas. Biscuit malt balanced by tropical and citrus hops.

Gatekeeper (OG 1056, ABV 5.6%)
Rich, malty porter brewed with foraged kelp.

Beheaded (OG 1068, ABV 7.5%) ◆
Tawny-coloured, strong old ale with a balanced heavy body. Rich vine fruit accompanied by plum, raisin, apple and sherry flavours.

Kent SIBA

The Long Barn, Birling Place Farm, Stangate Road, Birling, Kent, ME19 5JN
☎ (01634) 780037 ⊕ kentbrewery.com

Kent Brewery was founded in 2010 by Toby Simmonds (ex-brewer from Dark Star) and Paul Herbert. Originally brewed at Larkins, a 10-barrel plant has been in operation at the Birling site since 2011. More than 300 outlets are supplied direct, mainly throughout Kent, Sussex and London. ♦ RAIB

Session Pale (OG 1037, ABV 3.7%)
A light, hoppy session beer with hints of citrus and elderflower.

Black Gold (OG 1040, ABV 4%)
Dark-coloured, easy-drinking, with qualities of a golden ale.

Pale (OG 1040, ABV 4%)
A full-flavoured and aromatic pale ale.

Cobnut (OG 1041, ABV 4.1%)
Generously-hopped, dark-coloured, and nutty.

KGB – Kent Golding Bitter (OG 1041, ABV 4.1%)

Single Hop (ABV 4.5%)
A strong citrus flavour and aroma.

Prohibition (ABV 4.8%) ▮
A citrusy pale ale, highly-hopped.

Brewers Reserve (OG 1050, ABV 5%)
A strong hop flavour of citrus and resin.

Kentish Town (NEW)

Ingestre Road, Kentish Town, London, NW5 1UF
⊕ kentishtownbrewery.com

Fleet Lager is partly brewed on site and cuckoo brewed at various London breweries for bigger batches. Sometimes available at the Pineapple and Rose & Crown, Kentish Town. No real ale.

Keppels SIBA

The Workshops, Little Stambridge Hall Lane, Rochford, Essex, SS4 1EW ☎ 07912251278
⊕ keppelsbrewery.co.uk

THE BREWERIES

⊗ Keppels was established in 2016. In 2018 it moved to new premises in Stambridge. Further expansion took place in early 2019. Pubs throughout Essex are supplied with cask ales. Bottled beers are available to purchase (two raise money for the Vulcan Trust). Regular updates on Twitter and Facebook.

Crows by the Crouch (OG 1038, ABV 3.8%)
Blonde beer; light and hoppy.

New Beginnings (ABV 3.8%)

Golden Crow (ABV 4%)

Home to Roost (ABV 4.2%)

Tipsy Crow Stout (ABV 5%)
A dark-coloured, strong stout with a smoky flavour. Thin liquorice taste with a mild bitterness.

Two Crows (OG 1057, ABV 5.7%)
Strong, ruby red-coloured old ale, with a malty finish.

Christmas Crow (ABV 6%)
Dark brown-coloured, with a malty aroma.

One of those days (OG 1068, ABV 6.8%)
Imperial stout; malty and dark with a pleasant finish.

Kernel SIBA

Arch 11, Dockley Road Industrial Estate, Dockley Road, Bermondsey, London, SE16 3SF
☎ (020) 7231 4516

Office: 01 Spa Business Park, Spa Road, London, SE16 4QT 🌐 thekernelbrewery.com

Kernel was established in 2009 by Evin O'Riordain and moved to larger premises in 2012 to keep up with demand. The brewery produces bottle-conditioned and keg beers, and has won many awards for its wide, ever-changing range. Bottles are available from the brewery on a Saturday as well as a selection of pubs around the country. RAIB

Keswick SIBA

The Old Brewery, Brewery Lane, Keswick, Cumbria, CA12 5BY
☎ (01768) 780700 🌐 keswickbrewery.co.uk

Keswick, owned by Sue Jefferson, began brewing in 2006 using a 10-barrel plant on the site of a brewery that closed in 1897. The brewery is set up to be environmentally friendly using sheeps wool insulation in the vessels and reducing its environmental impact. Outlets include the Fox bar at the brewery, the Dog & Gun, Keswick, and many other pubs across Cumbria. !! ♦

Black Star (OG 1034, ABV 3.5%)

Gold (OG 1035, ABV 3.6%)
Simple, slightly sweet light ale, with some bitterness in the finish.

Bitter (OG 1036, ABV 3.7%)
Gentle bitter with hints of roasted malt and a sweetness which fades.

Thirst Rescue (OG 1037, ABV 3.8%)

Park Your Thirst (OG 1038, ABV 3.9%)

Thirst Run (OG 1041, ABV 4.2%)
A well-balanced, golden-coloured beer that maintains its fruitiness from start to finish.

Waimia Pale (OG 1041, ABV 4.2%)
A pale-coloured, hoppy ale.

Thirst Quencher (OG 1042, ABV 4.3%)
Refreshing pale ale with an exotic fruit and citrus aroma.

Thirst Quencher (OG 1042, ABV 4.3%)

Special (OG 1047, ABV 4.8%)
Full malt flavour with notes of chocolate and roast barley.

Dark Horse (OG 1057, ABV 6%)
Rich, dark-coloured ale.

Thirst Celebration (OG 1065, ABV 7%)

Kettlesmith SIBA

Unit 16, Treenwood Industrial Estate, Bradford-on-Avon, Wiltshire, BA15 2AU
☎ (01225) 864839 🌐 kettlesmithbrewing.com

⊗ Kettlesmith is an independent microbrewery established in 2016. It brews modern interpretations of a wide variety of beer styles, drawing inspiration from its background in America and England, as well as a love of Belgian beer. !! ♦ RAIB V

Outline (OG 1040, ABV 3.8%)
An amber-coloured session ale with hints of chocolate and molasses, balanced with floral and pine hops.

Faultline (OG 1043, ABV 4.1%)
A hoppy pale ale with resinous floral citrus notes of grapefruit.

Streamline (OG 1040, ABV 4.2%)
Blonde ale with a white grape and pineapple aroma.

Plotline (OG 1047, ABV 4.4%)
Flavours of dark chocolate, rich coffee and roast barley, with fruity hops.

Fogline (OG 1046, ABV 4.7%)
A Belgian-style ale with hints of clove and honey and a subtle tart finish.

Coastline (ABV 4.9%)
Honey-like malt sweetness balanced with flavours of tangerine and lemon zest.

Ridgeline (OG 1051, ABV 5%)
A rich, American-style, red-coloured IPA. Subtle peppery, nutty rye malt is balanced by juicy, resinous hops.

Timeline (OG 1055, ABV 5.4%)
Hop-driven IPA with malty undertones. Herbal, berry and citrus flavours.

Skyline (OG 1051, ABV 5.6%)
A Belgian saison-style beer. Spicy, earthy with hints of orange and lemon with a refreshing tart finish.

Kew

477 Upper Richmond Road West, East Sheen, Richmond, SW14 7PU
☎ (020) 878 9415 🌐 kewbrewery.co.uk

⊗ Kew was established in 2015 and acquired by Jana Gray and Jonathan Sumner in 2018. It is a family-run, independent brewery, situated less than a mile from (and inspired by) the world-famous Royal Botanic Gardens at Kew. !! ♦ RAIB

Botanic (OG 1038, ABV 3.8%) ◆
Chocolate, grapefruit, juniper and unripe apricots in aroma. Toffee sweetness and a peppery, dry, bitter finish.

Camellia (ABV 4%)

Nightshade (OG 1045, ABV 4.2%) ◆
Chilli porter with cacao nibs creating a smooth balance. Earthy hops, chocolate and fruity flavours. Dry, roasty lingering chilli finish.

Petersham Porter (OG 1045, ABV 4.3%) ◆
Dark chocolate character in the aroma and flavour. Malty with toffee, treacle and blackberry notes and a dry, bitter finish.

Richmond Rye (OG 1045, ABV 4.3%) ◆
Dark gold-coloured beer with typical tart rye aroma and flavour. Earthy hops, orange and honey flavours. Dry, spicy, hoppy finish.

Pagoda Pale (OG 1052, ABV 4.5%) ◆
Unfined dark gold-coloured beer, with biscuit sweetness balancing the citrus fruit and dryness that builds in a long, bitter finish.

Keystone SIBA

Old Carpenters Workshop, Berwick St Leonard, Wiltshire, SP3 5SN
☎ (01747) 820426 ⊕ keystonebrewery.co.uk

⊗ Set up in 2006 with a 10-barrel plant, the brewer aims to be as sustainable and efficient as possible, brewing traditional southern English-style beers using local ingredients whenever possible. The beers are available in the brewery-run Benett Arms, Tisbury. Around 150 other outlets are also supplied. ‼ ◆

Bedrock (OG 1035, ABV 3.6%) ◆
Copper-coloured bitter, hops and malt in the aroma, followed by fruit and bitterness in the taste. Long, lingering aftertaste.

Large One (OG 1041, ABV 4.2%) ◆
Copper-coloured malty best bitter, fruit and bitterness to the fore initially, long fruit and bitter hop flavours to the finish.

Kiln SIBA

Chiddinglye Farm, West Hoathly, RH19 4QS
☎ 07800556729

Office: 1st Floor, 30 Church Road, Burgess Hill, RH15 9AE ⊕ thekilnbrewery.co.uk

Kiln brewery was set up by two friends in 2014. Following a search for new premises, they have joined forces with Missing Link brewery. Although Kiln's website is focusing on keg and canned beer, they are continuing to produce cask beers, but are no longer sticking with a core range.

King Street SIBA

Riverside House, Welsh Back, Bristol, BS1 4RR
☎ (0117) 405 8948

Office: City Pub Group Plc., Essel House, 2nd Floor, 29 Foley Street, London, W1W 7TH
⊕ kingstreetbrewhouse.co.uk

⊗ The King Street Brew House is owned by The City Pub Group, which has several pubs and brewpubs around the country. The compact brewery is on the ground floor, with the fermenting vessels and conditioning tanks in the basement. The enthusiastic on-site brewer produces a wide range of beers, from regular favourites, available all year, to one off/seasonal specials. Guest beers are also available. The Group's other pub in Bristol, The Prince Street Social, is also supplied. ‼ ◆ RAIB

King's Cliffe

Unit 10 Kingsmead, Station Road, King's Cliffe, Northamptonshire, PE8 6YH ☎ 07843 288088
⊕ kcbales.co.uk

⊗ In 2014, exactly 100 years after the last brewery in King's Cliffe ceased brewing, village resident Jeremy O'Neill set up this new venture. It currently produces five barrels a week. ‼ ◆

5C (OG 1038, ABV 3.8%) ◆
A light bitter with balanced taste of malt and hops, and a refreshing, bitter finish.

No. 10 (OG 1040, ABV 4%) ◆
Amber-coloured beer with a clean, malty taste, and a long, bitter finish.

66 Degrees (OG 1046, ABV 4.6%) ◆
Amber-coloured beer with a floral aroma, a balanced taste of malt and hops, and a long, bitter finish.

Kings Clipstone

Keepers Bothy, Kings Clipstone, Nottinghamshire, NG21 9BT
☎ (01623) 823589 ☎ 07790190020
⊕ kingsclipstonebrewery.co.uk

Located close to the heart of Sherwood Forest, Kings Clipstone began brewing in 2012 using a five-barrel plant. The owners, David and Daryl Maguire, produce a range of core beers plus one-off brews and seasonals. Beers are available to freehouses, festivals and wholesale markets. ◆

Palace Pale (OG 1036, ABV 3.6%)
Light and crisp golden ale with a refreshing taste.

Hop On (OG 1039, ABV 3.8%)
A pale, refreshing session beer with fruity aroma hops.

Amazing Gazing (OG 1040, ABV 4%)
A reddish-coloured, easy-drinking bitter with a floral aroma and moreish aftertaste.

Tabaknakas (OG 1041, ABV 4.1%)
A golden ale with overtones of spiced berries with floral characteristics.

Moonbeam (OG 1042, ABV 4.2%)
A chestnut-coloured bitter with a full flavour and well-rounded finish.

Sire (OG 1043, ABV 4.2%)
Well-rounded beer with a clean, bitter finish.

Royal Stag Stout (OG 1045, ABV 4.5%)
Dark-coloured with a creamy head, full of taste of roasted and dark chocolate malts.

Queen Bee (OG 1051, ABV 5.1%)
A ruby red-coloured strong ale, classically rich and smooth.

Kings Head

Kings Head, 132 High Street, Bildeston, Suffolk, IP7 7ED
☎ (01449) 741434 ⊕ bildestonkingshead.co.uk

⊗ Kings Head has been brewing since 1996 in an old cart lodge at the back of the pub. Under new ownership since 2008, the 2.5-barrel plant brews fortnightly. !!♦

Kingstone

Tintern, NP16 7NX
☎ (01291) 680111 🌐 kingstonebrewery.co.uk

Kingstone Brewery is located in the Wye Valley close to Tintern Abbey. Brewing began on a four-barrel plant in 2005. Special brews are marketed under the Hapax Brewing Co label. !! RAIB

Tewdric's Tipple (OG 1038, ABV 3.8%)
An ale with a dry, bitter character and tangy core.

Challenger (OG 1040, ABV 4%)
A smooth, richly-hopped ale with a malty nose and toffee undertones.

Gold (OG 1040, ABV 4%)
A straw-coloured, smooth ale with citrus notes and a balanced, hoppy finish.

Llandogo Trow (OG 1042, ABV 4.2%)
A ruby-coloured ale with a smooth, black fruit finish.

Premium Stout (OG 1044, ABV 4.4%)
A smooth, rich stout with a bitter finish.

Classic (OG 1045, ABV 4.5%)
A balanced, distinctly hoppy, dry ale with a floral nose and smooth, well-balanced finish.

1503 (OG 1048, ABV 4.8%)
A deep chestnut-coloured, lightly-hopped ale bursting with complex, rich flavours.

Abbey Ale (OG 1051, ABV 5.1%)
An amber-coloured, full-flavoured ale. The hoppy edge is balanced by a smooth, malty richness.

Humpty (OG 1058, ABV 5.8%)
An IPA with a slightly sweet, floral nose, a balanced level of malt supporting the hops and finally a subtle, but slightly citrus finish.

Kinneil

84 Corbiehall, Bo'ness, EH51 ☎ 07789204008
🌐 kinneilbrew.co.uk

Kinneil began brewing in 2011 using a 2.5-barrel plant. The brewery is adjacent to the Corbie Inn but separately owned.

Wonderfu' Jake (OG 1037, ABV 3.6%)

Katie Wearie's (OG 1039, ABV 3.8%)

Wayfinder (OG 1038, ABV 3.8%)

Pennvael Amber (OG 1042, ABV 4%)

Kincardine Sunset (OG 1042, ABV 4.1%)

Caer Edin Dark (OG 1044, ABV 4.2%)

Kinver SIBA

Unit 1, Britch Farm, Rocky Wall, Kinver, Staffordshire, DY7 5NW ☎ 07715 842676 🌐 kinverbrewery.co.uk

Established in 2004, Kinver produces a wide range of different beer styles including one-off specials. The brewery relocated in 2012 to a new 10-barrel plant on the edge of Kinver due to increased demand. Around 30 outlets are supplied direct including several in Kinver. !!♦RAIB

Light Railway (OG 1038, ABV 3.8%)
Straw-coloured session beer. A fruity and malty start quickly gives way to well-hopped bitterness and lingering, hoppy aftertaste.

Cavegirl Bitter (OG 1040, ABV 4%)
Very pale straw-coloured, balanced bitter.

Edge (OG 1041, ABV 4.2%)
Amber-coloured, with a malty aroma. Sweet, fruity start with a hint of citrus marmalade in the spicy edged malt. Lasting, hoppy, satisfyingly bitter finish.

Noble (OG 1043, ABV 4.5%)
Fruity hop aroma, very fruity start then grassy hops give a sharp, bitter finish with malt support.

Maybug (OG 1045, ABV 4.8%)

Half Centurion (OG 1047, ABV 5%)
A golden-coloured best bitter. Malty before hops take command giving a balanced, hoppy finish, and great aftertaste.ô

Black Ram Stout (OG 1048, ABV 5.2%)
Full-bodied, roasty, dark-coloured stout.

Khyber (OG 1054, ABV 5.8%)
Golden-coloured, strong bitter with a hop bite that overwhelms fleeting malty sweetness and drives through to a long, dry finish.

Over the Edge (OG 1068, ABV 10.5%)
Amber look, barley sugar aroma. Sweet sticky start, hop sharp and sugary. Warming and mind numbing sensational liquid. Long bitter finish.

Kirkby Lonsdale SIBA

Unit 2F, Old Station Yard, Kirkby Lonsdale, Cumbria, LA6 2HP
☎ (01524) 272221 ☎ 07793 149999
🌐 kirkbylonsdalebrewery.com

Kirkby Lonsdale is a family-run business established in 2009 on a six-barrel plant. In 2016 a further six-barrel plant was installed in its new brewery tap, the Royal Barn, Kirkby Lonsdale. !!♦

Crafty Mild (OG 1036, ABV 3.6%)
Typical mild with powerful malty aromas and some caramel, which follows through in the taste and finish.

Tiffin Gold (OG 1036, ABV 3.6%)
A full-flavoured, grapefruit-hoppy and bitter beer, with a dry finish.

Stanley's Pale Ale (OG 1038, ABV 3.8%)
Hops dominate this sweet and fruity, well-balanced beer.

Ruskins Bitter (OG 1039, ABV 3.9%)
A tawny-coloured bitter with a distinctive aroma of fruit and malt. The clean, hoppy flavour is well-balanced with fruity sweetness leading to a sustained bittersweet finish.

Singletrack (OG 1040, ABV 4%)
Crisp, citrus hops predominate in a well-balanced beer with a pleasant, bitter finish.

Pennine Ambler (OG 1040, ABV 4.1%)

Radical Red (OG 1042, ABV 4.2%)
Malty beer with a caramel sweetness, balanced by a bitter finish.

Monumental Blonde (OG 1045, ABV 4.5%)
Distinctly hoppy, a fruity, sweet, pale-coloured, full-bodied bitter.

Jubilee Stout (OG 1055, ABV 5.5%) ◆
Rich, well-balanced stout with malt. A long aftertaste retains this complexity and is surprisingly refreshing.

Imperial Dragon (OG 1080, ABV 8.2%)

Kirkstall SIBA

100 Kirkstall Road, Leeds, West Yorkshire, LS3 1HJ ☎ (0113) 898 0280 🌐 kirkstallbrewery.com

The brewery was established in 2011 a few yards from the original Kirkstall Brewery beside the Leeds-Liverpool canal. In 2017 it moved to a new state of the art brewery incorporating a 60-barrel plant, malting unit and bottling line. Nearby Kirkstall Abbey, which had its own brewhouse, and lost local industries are the inspiration for the beer names. The range can be sampled in the Kirkstall Bridge Inn, the brewery tap, as well as its other pubs, the Cardigan Arms and the Sparrow. !! ♦

Kirkstall Pale Ale (OG 1040, ABV 4%)
Session ale with floral, citrus and herbal hop character, backed up by a malty and balanced finish.

Three Swords (OG 1045, ABV 4.5%) ◆
Light-coloured golden ale, pithy grapefruit flavours, and plenty of hops from the start to the lingering finish.

Dissolution IPA (OG 1050, ABV 5%) ◆
Full-flavoured IPA with hops leading the charge and bitter fruit just behind.

Black Band Porter (OG 1055, ABV 5.5%) ◆
Dark-coloured, smooth and complex. Fruit cake flavours, hints of malted chocolate, coffee and liquorice plus occasional smokiness.

Kirrie

Bon Scott Brewery, 8 Bon Scott Place, Kirriemuir, DD8 4LD ☎ 07855 808975 🌐 kirrie-ales.co.nf

Established in 2014, Kirrie Ales is situated in the picturesque town of Kirriemuir, birthplace of JM Barrie, creator of Peter Pan, and gateway to the Angus Glens. The brewery space measures only 8 by 9 feet. Brewing is currently suspended. RAIB

Kissingate

Pole Barn, Church Lane Farm Estate, Church Lane, Lower Beeding, West Sussex, RH13 6LU ☎ (01403) 891335

Office: 2 Drury Close, Maidenbower, Crawley 🌐 kissingate.co.uk

Kissingate Brewery was founded in 2010 by husband-and-wife team Gary and Bunny Lucas. Current production capacity is eight barrels. The brewery building is a converted barn set in a wooded valley near the village of Mannings Heath. It has a taproom and minstrels gallery. The brewery is available to hire for private events. !! ♦ RAIB

Storyteller (OG 1036, ABV 3.5%)

Sussex (OG 1040, ABV 4%)

Moon (OG 1045, ABV 4.5%)
Golden-coloured ale, with lightly roasted malts, apples, and lingering bitterness.

Old Tale Porter (OG 1045, ABV 4.5%)
A classic porter, with full (slightiy tannin) flavours.

Pernickety Pale (OG 1045, ABV 4.5%)

Mandarina Red (OG 1048, ABV 4.8%)
A complex, red-coloured IPA with multiple flavour layers of malt and prominent citrus fruits. A piney and citrus bitter finish.

Chennai (OG 1050, ABV 5%)

Smelter's Stout (OG 1052, ABV 5.1%)

Powder Blue (OG 1058, ABV 5.5%)

Stout Extreme Jamaica (OG 1060, ABV 6%)

Mary's Ruby Mild (OG 1064, ABV 6.5%)
Deep ruby in colour, gentle aromas of well-aged Port, intense, rounded malt flavours, and a light, floral hop aftertaste.

Six Crows (OG 1068, ABV 6.6%)
A rich, dark and decadent stout with intense notes of molasses, oak and woodsmoke.

Murder of Crows (OG 1110, ABV 10%)

Kitchen

Putney, London, SW15

Kitchen is a homebrewer, originally selling bottled beers at the nearby Beer Boutique in 2015. Its first commercial brew was completed at Rocky Head Brewery (qv) in 2017. Brewing is currently suspended.

Knight Life (NEW)

44a-46a Shelbourne Road, Bournemouth, Dorset, BH8 8QY 🌐 knightlifebrewing.com

Established in 2018 using a 20-litre Braumeister plant. No real ale.

Knockout

Unit 10, Alanbrooke Park, Alexander Road, Belfast, BT6 9HB.

Founded in 2009 by Joseph McMullan, Knockout produces a range of bottle-conditioned beers. Each brew is usually in small 900-litre batches. RAIB

Knops SIBA

The Walled Garden, Archerfield Estate, Dirleton, EH39 5HQ ☎ 07949 879147 🌐 knopsbeer.co.uk

Knops began brewing in 2010 under contract. In 2013 it moved to new premises on the Archerfield Estate at Dirleton on the East Lothian coastline with an 11-barrel plant. Beers are based on modern interpretations of traditional styles and are bottled in-house. Cask-conditioned beers are available in Eastern Scotland and the Glasgow area. !! RAIB

East Coast Pale (OG 1039, ABV 3.8%) ◆
A light, aromatic session beer.

Musselburgh Broke (OG 1045, ABV 4.5%)
Full malt flavour with a clean, brisk finish.

California Common (OG 1048, ABV 4.6%) ◆
Deep gold in colour with a clean hop finish and light toffee notes, followed by a lingering bitterness.

India Pale Ale (OG 1047, ABV 5%)
Light golden ale with a citrus and apricot aroma. Well-balanced by a smooth, honeyed malt backbone.

THE BREWERIES

Black Cork (OG 1066, ABV 6.5%)
Dark-coloured beer with a prominent chocolate/coffee bitterness and hop aroma.

Contract brewed for Archerfield Fine Ales:

Golden Ale (OG 1039, ABV 3.8%)

Dark Ale (OG 1046, ABV 4.7%)

India Pale Ale (OG 1047, ABV 5%)

Knoydart Brewery (NEW)

St Agathas Chapel & Manse, Knoydart, PH41 4PL
☎ (01687) 462372 🌐 knoydartbrewery.co.uk

Knoydart is one of the most remote breweries on mainland Britain, there are no road links so access is by ferry boat or on foot over mountain passes. Beers are brewed in part of an old chapel using a 60-litre electric brewery and a five-barrel plant with four fermenters.

Korruptd (NEW)

Wheatcroft Gardens, Penistone, South Yorkshire, S36 6GA ☎ 07463 863647

Established in 2019, Korruptd is a nanobrewery producing craft and continental style beers, available in bottles.

Krafty Braumeister (NEW) SIBA

Unit 4a, Eastlands Industrial Estate, Leiston, Suffolk, IP16 4LL ☎ 07508 435893 🌐 kraftybraumeister.co.uk

Krafty Braumeister was established in 2018 and produces historic German beer styles, matured naturally in bottles and kegs. RAIB

Kult

See Plain

Lacada

7a Victoria Street, Portrush, BT56 8DL
☎ (028) 7082 5684 🌐 lacadabrewery.com

Lacada was established in 2015 and produces its Salamander series alongside three core beers.

Giant's Organ (OG 1045, ABV 4.5%)

Sorley Boy's Stash (OG 1045, ABV 4.5%)

Stranded Bunny (OG 1045, ABV 4.5%)

Lacons SIBA

The Courtyard, Main Cross Road, Great Yarmouth, Norfolk, NR30 3NZ
☎ (01493) 850578 🌐 lacons.co.uk

⊗ Lacons Brewery has a rich history dating back to 1760, but was closed by Whitbread in the 1960s. It relaunched in 2013 and the Falcon Brewery is now nestled in a courtyard in Great Yarmouth. Beers are available across East Anglia and use the original Lacons yeast. A range of Heritage seasonal ales is also produced, based on the brewery's original recipes from the archives. !! ♦ RAIB

Encore (OG 1038, ABV 3.8%) ◆
Balanced, hoppy bitter beginning. Strong, citrus and hop notes throughout, full-bodied with a claggy mouthfeel and a strong, bitter finish.

Patriot (OG 1038, ABV 4%) ◆
A powerful hop presence from the nose to the long, dry finish. Citrus notes and malt give balance and depth.

Falcon Ale (OG 1042, ABV 4.2%) ◆
Complex with malt, caramel, hop and plum. Smooth and grainy with a well-rounded, bittersweet finale.

Legacy (OG 1043, ABV 4.4%) ◆
Strong grapefruit aroma. Well-balanced mix of malt, citrus and bittersweet hoppiness. Full-bodied with a lemony malt finish.

Affinity (OG 1046, ABV 4.8%) ◆
A bouncy citrus nose. Orange notes soar over an astringent hoppiness softened by a gentle malt background. A growing hop finish.

Audit (OG 1072, ABV 8%)
Strong, dark copper-coloured barley wine. Prominent berry fruit flavour laced with pronounced spice and a warming, smooth and sweet finish.

Lady Luck

Little Angel, 18 Flowergate, Whitby, North Yorkshire, YO21 3BA
☎ (01947) 602899 ☎ 07920 282506

◎Lady Luck is a 0.5-barrel brewery situated at the back of the Little Angel, Whitby. Brewing began in 2018 and takes place twice a week. Beers, some infused with spirits, are exclusive to the Little Angel (with the exception of some beer festivals). ♦ RAIB

Laig Bay

Galmisdale, Isle of Eigg, PH42 4RL
🌐 laigbaybrewing.com

Brewing began in 2014. !!

Laine SIBA

Brighton: North Laine Bar & Brewhouse, 27 Gloucester Place, Brighton, East Sussex, BN1 4AA
☎ (01273) 683666

Battersea: Four Thieves, 51 Lavender Gardens, London, SW11 1DJ ☎ (020) 7223 6927

Victoria Park: People's Park Tavern, 360 Victoria Park Road, London, E9 7BT ☎ (020) 8533 0040

⊗ Laine launched its first brewery in 2012, in Brighton, using a five-barrel plant based within the North Laine pub, which is owned by the drinkinbrighton pub group. The brewing equipment and process can be viewed from the bar. In 2013 a sister brewery was opened in Acton, London (now closed). Since then two more Laine breweries have been established in London, in Hackney (2014) and Battersea (2015). The beer range varies in each establishment. !!

Lakehouse

Lake House, Peachfield Rd, Malvern, Worcestershire, WR14 3LE ☎ 07532 440634
🌐 lakehousebrewery.com

◎Lakehouse was established in 2016 by Dan Frost and Graeme Gordon on a 2.5-barrel plant. Situated below the Malvern Hills, within the grounds of a country house and fishing lake, from which it takes its name. Beers can be found at food & drink festivals, Farmers' Markets, and in trade outlets. ‼ RAIB

Amber Session Ale (OG 1038, ABV 3.9%) ◆
Golden-coloured session beer, aroma of hops and citrus fruits, complex slightly citrus taste with grassy undertones followed by a pleasant hoppy finish.

Citrus Pale Ale (OG 1039, ABV 4%) ◆
Pale amber-coloured, aroma of hops with hints of apple and grapefruit, pronounced hoppy taste with lemon and orange peel, followed by a lingering, citrus, then bitter, hoppy aftertaste.

Cherry-Chocolate Porter (OG 1061, ABV 5.5%) ◆
Dark ruby brown-coloured, creamy head, aromas of stone fruits with roast malt and chocolate. Taste initially of chocolate and coffee, soft velvety mouthfeel with hints of bitter cherry, and a fruity finish with hints of chocolate.

LAMB (NEW)

Queens Arms, Litton, North Yorkshire, BD23 5JQ
☎ (01756) 770096 ⊕ queensarmslitton.co.uk

Littondale Ale Mild & Bitter (LAMB) was established by brewer Thomas Crapper in 2019. It uses the old Littondale brewery plant at the Queens Arms following its sale to new owners.

Lancaster SIBA

Lancaster Leisure Park, Wyresdale Road, Lancaster, LA1 3LA
☎ (01524) 848537 ⊕ lancasterbrewery.co.uk

Lancaster began brewing in 2005. The brewery moved to new premises in 2010 and installed a larger 60-barrel brewing plant. As well as the regular beers, seasonal beers are brewed under the T'ales from the Brewhouse name. ‼ ◆

Amber (OG 1037, ABV 3.6%) ◆
Amber-coloured ale with malt flavours leading to an increasingly astringent, bitter finish.

Blonde (OG 1041, ABV 4%) ◆
A pale-coloured, gently-hopped, easy-drinking bitter with a drying finish.

Black (OG 1045, ABV 4.5%) ◆
A satisfying and robust, roast bitter beer, with hints of sweet fruitiness.

Red (OG 1047, ABV 4.8%) ◆
Sweet start with lasting roast malts, leading to a satisfying bitter finish.

Langdale (NEW) SIBA

Cross Houses Farm, Docker, Cumbria, LA8 0DE

Brewing began in 2017.

Gold (ABV 3.8%)

Pale (ABV 3.9%)

Blonde (ABV 4.2%)

Langham SIBA

Old Granary, Langham Lane, Lodsworth, West Sussex, GU28 9BU
☎ (01798) 860861 ⊕ langhambrewery.co.uk

Langham Brewery was established in 2006 in an 18th-century granary barn and is set in the heart of West Sussex with fine views of the rolling South Downs. It is owned by Lesley Foulkes and James Berrow who brew and run the business. The brewery is a 10-barrel, steam-heated plant and more than 200 outlets are supplied. ‼

Halfway to Heaven (OG 1035, ABV 3.5%)
A chestnut-coloured beer with a balanced biscuit maltiness and citrus and fruit hop character, with a hint of spice.

Saison (OG 1039, ABV 3.9%)
A zesty, unfined, saison-style, light, well-hopped beer.

Hip Hop (OG 1038, ABV 4%)
A blonde beer; clean and crisp. Aroma is loaded with floral hop while the pale malt flavour is overtaken by a dry and bitter finish.

Sundowner (OG 1042, ABV 4.2%)
A deep golden-coloured beer. Tropical fruit, pineapple and citrus aroma with a smooth maltiness in the background. Balanced, dry bitter finish with floral hop aroma.

Triple XXX (OG 1042, ABV 4.4%)

Best (OG 1043, ABV 4.5%)
A tawny-coloured classic best bitter with well-balanced malt flavours and bitterness.

Arapaho (OG 1046, ABV 4.9%)

LSD (Langham Special Draught) (OG 1049, ABV 5.2%)
An auburn-coloured beer with rich, complex flavours and a deep red glow. The sweet maltiness is balanced with spicy hop aromas and a dry finish.

Black Swallow (OG 1055, ABV 6%)

Langton SIBA

Grange Farm, Welham Road, Thorpe Langton, Leicestershire, LE16 7TU
☎ (01858) 540116 ☎ 07840 532826
⊕ langtonbrewery.co.uk

Established in 1999 in outbuildings behind the Bell Inn, East Langton, the brewery relocated in 2005 to a converted barn at Thorpe Langton, where a four-barrel plant was installed. Further expansion in 2010 and 2016 significantly increased capacity. ‼ ◆ RAIB

Caudle Bitter (OG 1039, ABV 3.9%) ◆
Copper-coloured. session bitter, similar to a pale ale. Flavours are relatively well-balanced throughout with hops slightly to the fore.

Inclined Plane Bitter (OG 1042, ABV 4.2%)
A straw-coloured bitter with a citrus nose and long, hoppy finish.

Hop On (OG 1044, ABV 4.4%)
A premium bitter, deep chestnut-coloured, with a good balance of flavours and aroma.

Bowler Strong Ale (OG 1048, ABV 4.8%)
A strong, traditional ale with a deep red colour and a hoppy nose.

Bullseye (OG 1050, ABV 4.8%)
Intensely dark stout with flavours of liquorice and chocolate.

Larkins SIBA

Larkins Farm, Hampkins Hill Road, Chiddingstone, Kent, TN8 7BB
☎ (01892) 870328

⊗ Larkins brewery was founded by the Dockerty family in Rusthall in Kent in 1986, on the site of the original Royal Tunbridge Wells Brewery. In 1988 the brewery relocated to Larkins Farm in Chiddingstone. All beers include hops grown on the farm itself. The brewery delivers direct to around 40-50 pubs and restaurants within a 20-mile radius. **!! ♦**

Traditional Ale (OG 1035, ABV 3.4%)
Tawny in colour, a full-tasting hoppy ale with plenty of character for its strength.

Pale (ABV 4.2%)
Pleasantly hoppy pale ale with a soft, fruity aftertaste.

Best (OG 1045, ABV 4.4%) ◈
Full-bodied, slightly fruity and unusually bitter for its gravity.

Late Night Hype

Unit 17, Andrew Court, South Douglas Street, Clydebank, G81 1PD 🌐 latenighthypebrewing.com

Late Night Hype is owned and operated by two friends. Around 25 outlets are supplied direct. There are plans for expansion.

Laverstoke Park

Laverstoke Park, Overton, RG25 3DR

A bottle-conditioned beer is contract brewed for Laverstoke Park by an unnamed brewery. **RAIB**

Law

Unit 17, Mid Wynd, Dundee, DD1 4JG ☎ 07893 538277 🌐 lawbrewing.co

Law was established in 2016 and is named after Dundee's most distinctive landmark; the volcano-like slopes of the Law.

Lazy Bay (NEW)

89 Julian Road, Lady Bay, Nottingham, NG2 5AL
🌐 lazybaybrewery.co.uk

Lazy Bay was established in 2018 by ex-teacher and homebrewer Brett Philips. **V**

Lazy Turtle (NEW)

Meadowbeck, Barnside Lane, Hepworth, West Yorkshire, HD9 1TN
☎ (01484) 680589 ☎ 07590 532880
✉ info@lazyturtlebrewing.com

Founded in 2018 by Dave Bore, a member of the Penistone Homebrew Collective, after he decided to move into commercial brewing. Production is mostly bottled but cask-conditioned beers are occasionally available.

Leadmill

Unit 3, Heanor Small Business Centre, Adams Close, Heanor, Derbyshire, DE75 7SW ☎ 07971 189915
✉ leadmill@fsmail.net

⊗ Set up in Selston in 1999, Leadmill moved to Denby in 2001 and again in 2010 to Heanor. A sister brewery to Bottle Brook (qv), the brewery tap is at the Old Oak, Horsley Woodhouse. ♦

Langley Best (OG 1036, ABV 3.6%)

Mash Tun Bitter (OG 1036, ABV 3.6%)

Old Oak Bitter (OG 1037, ABV 3.7%)

B52 (OG 1050, ABV 5.2%)

Slumdog (OG 1058, ABV 5.9%)

Leatherbritches

Brewery Yard, Tap House, Annwell Lane, Smisby, Derbyshire, LE65 2TA ☎ 07976 279253
🌐 leatherbritches.co.uk

The brewery, founded in 1993 in Fenny Bentley, has relocated and expanded over the years, moving to its current address in 2011 where it effectively took over the existing Tap House Brewery (established 2010) but continued to brew the latter's beers. Since 2015, however, Tap House beers have become re-badged Leatherbritches products. **!! ♦ RAIB**

Bounder (OG 1040, ABV 3.8%)
A light, golden-coloured beer with a flowery, hoppy aroma and a bitter finish.

Lemongrass and Ginger (OG 1036, ABV 3.8%)
Pale-coloured and hoppy ale infused with lemongrass and ginger. Crisp and refreshing.

Ashbourne Ale (OG 1040, ABV 4%)
A pale-coloured bitter with a crisp, lasting taste.

Cad (OG 1040, ABV 4%)

Dr Johnson (ABV 4%)
A smooth, chestnut-coloured, well-rounded, mellow and malty bitter.

Scoundrel (OG 1040, ABV 4.1%)
Full-bodied porter with a well-rounded, sweet finish.

Mad Ruby (ABV 4.4%)
Deep ruby brown in colour with a sweet finish.

Raspberry Belter (ABV 4.4%)

Ashbourne IPA (OG 1047, ABV 4.7%)
Pale ale with a flowery, hoppy aroma, and a strong bitter finish. Crisp and refreshing.

Hairy Helmet (OG 1047, ABV 4.7%)
Pale-coloured bitter, well-hopped but with a sweet finish.

Spitting Feathers (ABV 4.8%)

Bespoke (OG 1048, ABV 5%)
Full-bodied, well-rounded premium bitter.

Game Over (ABV 5%)

Bohemian Dark (ABV 5.9%)
Rich, full-bodied porter. Caramel, liquorice and toffee flavours.

Madder Ruby (ABV 6%)
Dark brown-coloured old ale. Sweet, malty tones and full-bodied.

Ledbury SIBA

Gazerdine House, Hereford Road, Ledbury, Herefordshire, HR8 2PZ
☎ (01531) 671184 ☎ 07957 428 070
ledburyrealales.co.uk

Established in 2012, Ledbury Real Ales uses hops grown in Herefordshire and Worcestershire with other materials sourced locally where possible. The beers are sold mainly within a 15-mile radius of the brewery. ‼♦

Bitter (OG 1038, ABV 3.8%)
A traditional, copper-coloured beer, with a noticeably bitter start and an enjoyable finish with hints of spice and citrus.

Dark (OG 1039, ABV 3.9%)
Chocolate and coffee start with a smooth, mellow finish with notes of spice, marmalade and honey.

Gold (OG 1040, ABV 4%)
Golden-coloured bitter, well-balanced with a honey and fruit finish.

Dr Rudi's Extra Pale (OG 1041, ABV 4.1%)
Light beer with a slight bitter finish.

Phoenixx (OG 1045, ABV 4.5%)
A dark-coloured beer brewed with a complex mix of malts and hops giving chocolate, spice and molasses.

Leeds SIBA

3 Sydenham Road, Holbeck, Leeds, West Yorkshire, LS11 9RU
☎ (0113) 244 5866 leedsbrewery.co.uk

Production began in 2007 and Leeds Brewery is now one of the largest in the city. It uses a unique strain of yeast originally taken from a now defunct West Yorkshire brewery. Beer is supplied directly across the region and as far as Nottinghamshire, Lancashire and the North East. It formerly ran an estate of pubs, still trading, across Leeds and York. In 2018 Leeds Brewery was selected to brew a series of heritage beers for former Yorkshire brewing giant Tetley's. ♦

Pale (OG 1037.5, ABV 3.8%)
Light gold-coloured ale with hops and fruit, citrus/lemony last to the bitter, dry, hoppy finish.

Yorkshire Gold (OG 1040, ABV 4%)
Refreshing beer with plenty of zesty citrus flavours, a wallop of hops and a long-lasting, bitter finish.

Best (OG 1041, ABV 4.3%)
Pleasing mix of malt and hops in this smooth, amber-coloured, bittersweet beer.

Midnight Bell (OG 1047.5, ABV 4.8%)
A full-bodied, strong mild. Deep red to dark brown in colour, chocolate and strong malt flavours throughout.

Brewed for Carlsberg-Tetley:

Tetley's No. 3 Pale Ale (ABV 4.2%)

Contract brewed for Suddaby's:

Double Chance (ABV 3.8%)

JW Lees IFBB

Greengate Brewery, Middleton Junction, M24 2AX
☎ (0161) 643 2487 jwlees.co.uk

Family-owned since its foundation by John Lees in 1828 (the current head brewer is a family member). It has a tied estate of around 150 pubs, mostly in north Manchester, Cheshire, Lancashire and North Wales. The vast majority serve cask beer. A new in-house microbrewery, Boilerhouse, came on stream in 2018. ‼

Dark (OG 1032, ABV 3.5%)
Dark brown-coloured beer with a malt and caramel aroma. Creamy mouthfeel, with malt, caramel and fruit flavours and a malty finish.

Supernova (OG 1035, ABV 3.5%)

Manchester Pale Ale (OG 1038, ABV 3.7%)
Yellow in colour, with malt, hops and a good bitterness throughout.

Cosmic Brew (ABV 3.9%)
An amber-coloured ale with crisp citrus flavours and a lemon, tropical aroma.

Bitter (OG 1037, ABV 4%)
Copper-coloured beer with malt and fruit in aroma, taste and finish.

Dragon's Fire (OG 1037, ABV 4%)

Game On (OG 1042, ABV 4.2%)

Stout (OG 1041, ABV 4.2%)

Founder's (OG 1041, ABV 4.5%)
A well-balanced, full-bodied premium bitter.

Gold (OG 1045, ABV 4.5%)

Moonraker (OG 1073, ABV 6.5%)
A reddish-brown-coloured beer with a strong, malty, fruity aroma. The flavour is rich and sweet, with roast malt, and the finish is fruity yet dry.

Brewed under the Boilerhouse Brewery name:

Craft Pale (OG 1042, ABV 4.2%)
Hints of passion fruit and pineapple to the fore, and grapefruit and lime in the finish. Perfectly balanced with moderate bitterness.

Left Bank

Ty Newydd Farm, Llangorse, LD3 7UA ☎ 07815 849523 leftbankbrewery.co.uk

Some earlier batches of beers were produced on a cuckoo basis at various north London breweries. The brewery moved to its current location, the site of the former Lithic Brewery, and commenced brewing in 2019. The 400 litre (2.5-barrel) plant produces cask, bottled and canned beers.

Left Handed Giant

Unit 8-9, Wadehurst Industrial Park, St Philips Road, St Philip's, Bristol, BS2 0JE lefthandedgiant.com

Originally launched in 2015 as a cuckoo brewery using spare capacity at other local breweries, Left Handed Giant has operated since 2017 using its own 15-barrel plant in premises shared with Big Beer Distribution. The head brewer, Richard Poole, is a former homebrewer who previously had his own nanobrewery, Rocket Science. Expansion is planned, with the addition of a 15-barrel brewpub in Bristol city centre. ♦RAIB

Legitimate Industries

10 Weaver Street, Leeds, West Yorkshire, LS4 2AU
legitimateworldwide.com

THE BREWERIES

Founded in 2016, the 30-barrel plant is at capacity with nearly all production being keg beer for the company's seven restaurants in the Red's True Barbecue chain, but a limited amount of cask-conditioned beer is available in the local free-trade. Extra brewing capacity will be installed in 2019 to enable canning.

Leigh on Sea SIBA

35 Progress Road, Leigh-on-Sea, Essex, SS9 5PR
☎ (01702) 817255 🌐 leighonseabrewery.co.uk

Ⓧ Established in 2017 to produce vegan-friendly beer, which is unfiltered, unpasteurised, and unfined. Initially brewing on a one-barrel kit, Leigh on Sea rapidly progressed to a 10-barrel plant. The names of the beers are based on Leigh's rich maritime heritage. The brewery has its own licensed taproom. ‼ 🛒

Legra Pale (OG 1038, ABV 3.8%)
A light and fresh session golden ale with a clean, citrus flavour.

Boys of England (OG 1039, ABV 3.9%)

Brhubarb (OG 1039, ABV 3.9%)

Renown (OG 1040, ABV 4%)

Six Little Ships (OG 1042, ABV 4.2%)

Two Tree Island Red (OG 1045, ABV 4.5%)
A spicy, red-coloured ale with a blend of malts and a big hop hit.

Crowstone (OG 1055, ABV 5.5%)
Dark-coloured beer with a rich blend of malts and lots of hop flavour and aroma.

Cockle Row Spit (OG 1056, ABV 5.6%)

SS9 (OG 1090, ABV 9%)

Leighton Buzzard SIBA

Unit 31, Harmill Industrial Estate, Grovebury Road, Leighton Buzzard, Bedfordshire, LU7 4FF
☎ (01525) 217736 ☎ 07538 903753
🌐 leightonbuzzardbrewingcompany.co.uk

The first brewery to operate in Leighton Buzzard for over 100 years. Established in 2014 by local CAMRA member and homebrew enthusiast Jon d'Este-Hoare, the first beers were upscaled versions of his homebrews. ‼ 🛒 ♦

Cuckoo (OG 1039, ABV 3.8%)
Traditional, malty bitter.

Nimbus (ABV 3.8%)
Golden-coloured and fruity, with a hint of melon and strawberry in the aftertaste.

Narrow Gauge (OG 1040, ABV 3.9%)
Light, refreshing golden ale, with a dry, bitter taste and crisp, citrus finish.

Alto (ABV 4%)

Restoration Ale (OG 1049, ABV 4.6%)
A mid brown-coloured beer, similar to a bet bitter but with generous hop fruitiness.

Rebel Yell (OG 1053, ABV 5%)
A black-coloured IPA with a smooth, malt richness and sharp, dry hops.

Train Robber (OG 1053, ABV 5%)
Pale and hoppy IPA.

Black Buzzard (OG 1061, ABV 5.8%)
Complex, robust porter.

Leila Cottage SIBA

🛢 Countryman,, Chapel Road, Ingoldmells, Skegness, Lincolnshire, PE25 1ND
☎ (01754) 872268
✉ countryman_inn@btconnect.com

Brewing began in 2007. The brewery is situated at the Countryman pub – Leila Cottage was the original name of the building before it became a licensed club and more recently a pub. The history of the Countryman and the brewery is on display in the pub. ‼ 🛒 RAIB

Leith Hill

🛢 c/o Plough Inn, Coldharbour Lane, Coldharbour, Surrey, RH5 6HD
☎ (01306) 711793 🌐 ploughinn.com

Ⓧ Leith Hill was established in 1996 at the Plough Inn and was moved to converted storerooms at the rear in 2001, increasing capacity to 2.5 barrels in 2005. New owners took over in 2016. ‼

Lenton Lane SIBA

Unit 5G The Midway, Lenton Industrial Estate, Nottingham, NG7 2TS
☎ (0333) 003 5008 ☎ 0333 003 5008
🌐 lentonlane.co.uk

Ⓧ Lenton Lane began brewing in 2014 under the name Frontier, after taking over the brewing plant at the Flower Pot pub in Derby. Lenton Lane changed its name in 2016 and relocated to a purpose-built brewery in Nottingham using a 10-barrel plant. The brewery has a range of SM&SH (single malt & single hops) beers. 🛒 ♦ RAIB

Bluebird (OG 1035, ABV 3.8%)
Refreshing and hoppy pale ale.

36 North (OG 1035.6, ABV 3.9%)

3x2 (OG 1036, ABV 3.9%)
Session pale ale with wild berry and fruit flavours.

Atlas Stout (OG 1039, ABV 4.2%)
Classic dry stout, full-bodied, rich and satisfying. Complex malt bill is well-balanced giving roasted and chocolate notes.

Gold Rush (OG 1037, ABV 4.2%)
Easy-drinking, session golden ale. Zesty and crisp. ABV belies the malt flavour.

Pioneer (OG 1039, ABV 4.3%)
Crisp, golden-coloured pale ale that packs a hoppy punch and delivers a dry, satisfying finish.

Jester SM&SH (OG 1042, ABV 4.5%)

Mosaic SM&SH (OG 1040, ABV 4.5%)

Outpost (OG 1041, ABV 4.5%)

Summit SM&SH (OG 1041, ABV 4.5%)

Amarillo (OG 1043.1, ABV 4.7%)

Motueka SM&SH (OG 1040.4, ABV 4.7%)

Vanguard (OG 1040.5, ABV 4.7%)
Pale-coloured, hoppy ale with citrus flavours and aroma.

Calibration (OG 1042, ABV 4.8%)
Zesty, citrus, crisp golden ale.

Centennial SM&SH (OG 1041.6, ABV 4.8%)

THE BREWERIES · L

Mandabav SM&SH (OG 1040.5, ABV 4.8%)

Nelson SM&SH (OG 1041.6, ABV 4.8%)

Citra SM&SH (OG 1044, ABV 5%)

Richard 1 (OG 1043.8, ABV 5%)
Hoppy pale ale with fresh, tropical fruit aroma.

American Pale Ale (OG 1048, ABV 5.3%)
A hazy, unfined, hoppy pale ale.

Explorer IPA (OG 1051, ABV 5.5%)
A strong, hoppy IPA. Plentiful hops give citrus fruits
and a clean, bitter finish.

Long White Cloud IPA (OG 1053.4, ABV 5.7%)

Lerwick SIBA

Staneyhill, North Road, Lerwick, Shetland, ZE1 0QA
☎ 07738948336 ⊕ lerwickbrewery.co.uk

Lerwick Brewery was established in 2011 using a
12-barrel plant and sits at the very edge of the
North Atlantic. Originally only brewing keg beer, a
cask-conditioned range was launched in 2015. ☛◆

Azure (ABV 4.3%) ◆
Refreshing, grapefruity, peachy, hoppy, golden-
coloured bitter.

Lerwick IPA (ABV 5%) ◆
Grapefruity, hoppy bitter, with a slight biscuit
background.

Tushkar (ABV 5.5%) ◆
Dark brown-coloured, roasted, malty stout with
chocolate, coffee and liquorice.

Leviathan (NEW)

Unit 4, 17 Reddicap Trading Estate, Sutton Coldfield,
West Midlands, B75 7BU ☎ 07983 256979
⊕ leviathanbrewing.co.uk

Established in 2018 by keen homebrewer Chris
Hodgetts. Initial production was keg and bottle-
conditioned ales only but there are plans for cask-
conditioned beers with an upgrade of the brewery
to a five-barrel plant. A shop and taproom are also
planned. RAIB

Liberation

Tregar House, Longueville Road, St Saviour, Jersey,
JE2 7WF
☎ (01534) 764089 ☎ 07911 744568
⊕ liberationgroup.com

▣ The Liberation Brewery (owned by the
Liberation Group, which also owns Butcombe
Brewery) is located at Longueville, just outside St
Helier. Its multi-award winning flagship beer
Liberation Ale can be found in many of the Group's
predominantly freehold Pubs, 43 located in Jersey,
26 in Guernsey, 3 in Alderney and 44 in the UK. ‼◆

Liberation Ale (OG 1039, ABV 4%)
Golden-coloured beer with a hint of citrus on the
nose.

Herm Island Gold (ABV 4.2%)

Liberation IPA (OG 1047, ABV 4.8%)
Rich, traditional, golden-coloured IPA. A coriander,
citrus hop flavour with a crisp, balanced finish.

Lincoln Green SIBA

Unit 5, Enterprise Park, Wigwam Lane, Hucknall,
Nottingham, NG15 7SZ
☎ (0115) 963 4233 ☎ 07748 111457
⊕ lincolngreenbrewing.co.uk

⊛Anthony Hughes established the Lincoln Green
Brewing Company in 2012 using a 10-barrel plant.
The brewery takes its name from the colour of
dyed woollen cloth associated with the legend of
Robin Hood. Locally sourced ingredients are used to
create the beer range, in addition to occasional,
seasonal and special edition brews linked to local
and national events. A range of craft beers is
available in KeyKeg. ☛◆RAIB

Marion (OG 1038, ABV 3.8%) ◆
Subtly-hopped golden ale with a citrus aroma and
a dry, bitter finish.

Archer (OG 1040, ABV 4%) ◆
Citrus golden ale with a moderately bitter finish.

Hood (OG 1042, ABV 4.2%) ◆
Tawny-coloured ale with balanced hops and
bitterness.

Bowman (ABV 4.3%)

Arrow (ABV 4.5%)

Shot Firer (ABV 4.5%)
Unfined, pale-coloured stout brewed with oatmeal,
cacao nibs and coffee beans.

Tuck (OG 1047, ABV 4.7%) ◆
Full-bodied, rich, dark-coloured ale with roast and
malt flavours throughout.

Gin & Beer It (OG 1047, ABV 5%)
A pale-coloured, light citrus ale, brewed with
juniper berries, coriander seeds and citrus peel. Gin
is added to casks.

Quarterstaff (OG 1053, ABV 5%) ◆
Black in colour with roasty aromas and taste,
leading to a dry coffee and bitter finish.

Shackler (ABV 5%)
Black-coloured IPA, few roasted malt notes leading
to a hoppy aroma and flavour.

Buttermuch (OG 1057, ABV 5.5%) ◆
Dark brown-coloured beer with a strong
butterscotch caramel taste throughout and a
gentle, bitter finish.

Sheriff (OG 1055, ABV 5.5%) ◆
Golden-coloured, full-bodied IPA, citrus hop taste
and bitterness balanced throughout.

Lincolnshire SIBA

The George, 15 Main Road, Langworth, Lincoln,
Lincolnshire, LN3 5BJ
☎ (0845) 094 5784 ☎ 07508554890
⊕ lincolnshirebrewingco.co.uk

An events company that operates mobile bars, in
2014 it started brewing for its own bars and has
since expanded into the free trade. An eight-barrel
plant brews both cask and bottle-conditioned
beers, with bottling carried out in-house. Beers can
be found at local fairs, shows, markets and free
houses and nationally via wholesalers. ◆RAIB

Great Tom (OG 1037, ABV 3.7%)
A dark-coloured ale with elements of chocolate
and coffee in the nose. A fruity and dark malt
mouthfeel with a long, but soft, bitter finish.

Yeast Coast Blonde (ABV 3.7%)
Easy-drinking blonde ale, zesty with a clean, fresh finish.

Don't be Bitter (OG 1040, ABV 4%)
A bitter with a tropical fruit nose and roast malt flavours.

Impaled Up (OG 1040, ABV 4%)
IPA with a lively hop character and malt flavourings, followed by an intense bitterness.

Spicy Sausage (OG 1041, ABV 4.1%)
A Lincolnshire amber-coloured ale, with a sharp bitterness and dry finish.

1215 Magna Carta Ale (OG 1043, ABV 4.3%)
Nice, fruity nose, then malt flavours come to the fore. Bursting fruity aftertaste and a gentle bitterness.

Friendly Rottweiler (OG 1045, ABV 4.5%)
A light, crisp ale with a subtle, hoppy taste.

Medicinal Purposes (OG 1045, ABV 4.5%)
A satisfying stout with malt chocolate flavour.

Cheeky Imp (OG 1046, ABV 4.6%)
A malty ale with caramel notes and hoppy aromas. Good mouthfeel and slightly sweet taste.

Angry Rottweiler (OG 1060, ABV 6%)
A strong pale ale brewed with lots of malts and hops.

Lincolnshire Craft SIBA

Race Lane, Melton Ross, Lincolnshire, DN38 6AA
☎ (01652) 680001 🌐 lincolnshirecraftbeers.com

Lincolnshire Craft Beers is the company formed by Mark Smith who bought the Tom Wood Brewery in 2017. It continues to brew the Tom Wood range of beers on the 60-barrel Melton Ross plant. ♦

Best Bitter (OG 1037, ABV 3.7%)
A good citrus, passion fruit hop dominates the nose and taste, with background malt. A lingering hoppy and bitter finish.

Lincoln Gold (OG 1041, ABV 4%)
Pale-coloured bitter, fruity aroma, slightly zesty flavour but retaining malt characteristics.

Bomber County (OG 1046, ABV 4.8%)
An earthy malt aroma, with a complex underlying mix of coffee, hops, caramel and apple fruit. The beer starts bitter and intensifies.

Linear

Bingham, Nottinghamshire, NG13 8EU 🌐 linear.beer

Small-scale, 50-litre brewery, started production in 2016 and is located at the owner's home. Currently focussing on a series of one-offs in a range of styles (sometimes in collaboration). These are supplied to three local pubs. Limited capacity restricts the supply of cask beers to others, but they have appeared at several local beer festivals in the recent years. A core range of bottle-conditioned beers is also available at several outlets.

Linfit

Sair Inn, 139 Lane Top, Linthwaite, Huddersfield, West Yorkshire, HD7 5SG
☎ (01484) 842370

A 19th-century brewpub that started brewing again in 1982. The beer is only available at the Sair Inn.

Liquid Light (NEW)

125 Sneinton Boulevard, Nottingham, NG2 4FN
☎ 07530 737842 🌐 liquidlightbrewco.com

The beer range has been named with a strong heavy rock and psychedelic influence, referencing the likes of Frank Zappa and Black Sabbath. It has an emphasis on pale-coloured, hoppy beers and fruit beers. ♦

Lister's SIBA

The Old Dairy, Ford Lane, Ford, West Sussex, BN18 0DF
☎ (01903) 739117 ☎ 07775853412
🌐 listersbrewery.com

Brewing began in 2012 using a 0.25-barrel kit. The brewery relocated in 2014 and expanded to a five-barrel plant. Lister's donates 5p from every pint and bottle sold to the Battersea Dogs & Cats Home.

Lister's Best Bitter (ABV 3.9%)

Limehouse Porter (ABV 4.1%)

Lister's Golden Ale (ABV 4.1%)

American Pale Ale (ABV 4.2%)

Lister's IPA (ABV 4.3%)

Lister's Special (ABV 4.6%)

Litchborough Artisan (NEW)

Unit 12, Northampton Road, Litchborough, Northamptonshire, NN12 8JB
☎ (01327) 831308
✉ info@litchboroughbrewery.co.uk

Formerly Merrimen Brewery, the name changed along with all the beers in May 2019 following the acquisition of Merrimen by Richard Bustin in 2018. The name change reflects the importance of the village of Litchborough, which in 1974 became the home to the first small scale brewing enterprise, which we now call a microbrewery.

Atomic (ABV 4%)

Monroe (ABV 4%)
Blonde beer with tropical fruit flavours and a light floral aroma.

DNA (ABV 4.1%)
Golden-coloured beer with tastes of honey, spice and blackberry.

Nubru (ABV 4.1%)
Golden-coloured beer with a smooth citrus flavour.

Infinity (ABV 4.2%)
Amber-coloured beer with a slightly spicy and fruity flavour.

Liberty (ABV 4.2%)
Amber-coloured beer with spice, blackcurrant and orange flavours.

Black Beauty (ABV 4.5%)
A dark-coloured IPA with hints of orange and lychee on the palate.

Galaxy (ABV 4.5%)
A dry-hopped, dark-coloured IPA with spice and tropical fruit flavours.

Lithic

See Cold Black Label

Little Black Dog

Carlton Towers Brewery, Carlton Towers, Carlton, North Yorkshire, DN14 9LZ ☎ 07495026173
🌐 littleblackdogbeer.com

Established in 2015, a small batch, family-run brewery based in the village of Carlton in North Yorkshire. All beer is unfined, unpasteurised and unfiltered.

Yorkshire Bitter (ABV 3.8%)
A traditional bitter, with malty notes of toffee over a light chocolate and biscuit base, gently-hopped giving delicate floral aromas, and a light, bitter finish.

India Pale Ale (ABV 3.9%)
A session pale ale, with a delicate citrus note over a light caramel base, and a good bitter finish.

New World Pale Ale (ABV 4%)

American Pale Ale (ABV 4.1%)
A light amber-coloured pale ale, with citrusy flavour, and a good, thirst-quenching bitterness.

Black IPA (ABV 4.5%)

Oatmeal Stout (ABV 4.5%)
A creamy, dark stout, lightly-hopped. Coffee and chocolate flavours are prominent without the dry, burnt roasted flavour of a traditional stout.

Little Creatures (NEW)

1 Lewis Cubitt Walk, King's Cross, London, N1C 4DL
☎ (020) 8161 4446 🌐 littlecreatures.co.uk

Brewing began in 2019 and is run by the UK arm of the Australian brewery, owned by Lion. Operating from the ground floor of an office block, beers are called Regent's Canal brews and are served from large tanks behind the bar. No real ale.

Little Critters SIBA

80 Parkwood Road, Sheffield, South Yorkshire, S3 8AG
☎ (0114) 2763171

Office: Horizon House, 2 Whiting Street, Sheffield, S8 9QR 🌐 littlecrittersbrewery.com

A small batch, family-owned microbrewery, opened in 2016 operating on a 10-barrel brewing plant. It runs one pub in Sheffield; the Doctor's Orders. Pubs are supplied throughout Yorkshire, the East Midlands, and increasingly nationally, through a collaboration with BrewDog. ♦RAIB

Little Hopper (OG 1038, ABV 3.6%)
Golden session ale, with a malty, refreshing finish.

Blonde Bear (OG 1040, ABV 4.2%)
Smooth blonde ale, with a balanced taste and tropical notes.

Shire Horse (OG 1043, ABV 4.3%)
Chestnut brown-coloured best bitter, with strong bread and toffee tastes, and a floral nose,

Sleepy Badger (OG 1043, ABV 4.5%)
Stout brewed with oatmeal and locally sourced honey.

White Wolf (OG 1048, ABV 5%)
A refreshing, extra pale ale with bitterness and a citrus finish.

Chameleon Series (OG 1052, ABV 5.5%)
Single-hopped pale ale with a strong, bitter finish.

Nutty Ambassador (OG 1059, ABV 6%)
Smooth stout with a hazelnut nose, supported by coffee and chocolate notes for a well-balanced taste.

Sultanas of Swing (ABV 6%)
Chocolate and raisin stout made with real raisins and cacao nibs. Rich chocolate taste with a fruit finish.

C Monster (OG 1060, ABV 6.5%)
Citrus IPA made with lime leaves and fresh citrus peel for a bold, refreshing taste.

King Crow (OG 1068, ABV 7.2%)
Smooth imperial stout with a strong coffee taste, brewed with ethically-sourced espresso coffee.

Little Earth Project

Mill Green, Edwardstone, Suffolk, CO10 5PX
☎ (01787) 211118 🌐 littleearthproject.com

Established as Mill Green Brewery in 2008, becoming Little Earth Project in 2016. The brewery is built on the site of an old stable behind the White Horse Inn. A green brewery, it has its own borehole for water and was built using local wood, reclaimed bricks, sheeps wool and lime plaster. Brewing liquor is heated using bio and solar power and its 3,000-litre storage is constantly heated by solar panels, topped up by a wood boiler. Barley and hops are grown nearby.

Little Eaton

See Black Hole

Little Giant SIBA

Unit 3, Stoke View Business Park, Fishponds, Bristol, BS16 3AE
☎ (0117) 939 2589 🌐 littlegiantbrewery.co.uk

⊗ Microbrewery established in the Fishponds area of Bristol in 2017. Its fully programmable 600-litre brew plant was commissioned in 2018. Its parent company Reyam Ltd. manufacture these microbreweries which can be supplied to pubs, bars or restaurants. Four core beers are produced, along with occasional one-off specials. !! RAIB

Fi (OG 1040, ABV 4.1%)
Zesty aroma and rich, balanced flavours of malt with hoppy bitterness.

Fo (OG 1040, ABV 4.1%)
Pale ale, with a citrus hit of lemon and grapefruit.

Fe (OG 1050, ABV 5%)
Rich, golden brown-coloured ale, with pungent aromas, malty base and fruity hop flavours leaving a clean, bitter aftertaste.

Fum (OG 1052, ABV 5%)
Clean, crisp, refreshing, pilsner-style beer, with a spicy note, and a complex malt background.

Little Goat (NEW)

70 New Rd Ynysmeurdy, Ynysmeurdy, Pontardawe, SA8 4PP

☎ (01639) 641823 🌐 littlegoatbrewery.co.uk

The 10-barrel brewery opened in 2018 in a converted back garden outbuilding.

Scapegoat (ABV 4.3%)

Golden Goat (ABV 4.4%)

Jumping Jack (ABV 4.9%)

Little London SIBA

Unit 6b, Ash Park Business Centre, Ash Lane, Little London, Hampshire, RG26 5FL
☎ (01256) 533044 ☎ 07785 225468
🌐 littlelondonbrewery.com

⊗ Brewing began in 2015 using a six-barrel plant. Three fermentation vessels ensure a production capability of 60 firkins per week, with capacity for expansion.

Doreen's Dark (OG 1035, ABV 3.2%)
Treacle-coloured beer with a creamy contrasting head, hints of liquorice and coffee and a dry finish.

Blacksmith's Gold (OG 1035, ABV 3.5%)
A light, dry, session beer with an instant hoppy hit, then a smooth hint of grapefruit.

Red Boy (OG 1036, ABV 3.7%)
A light, balanced session bitter with a delicate hop aroma and subtle hop flavours on the palate.

Hoppy Hilda (OG 1039, ABV 3.8%)

Luvly (OG 1040, ABV 3.9%)
A traditional-style bitter with a pronounced, hoppy flavour.

Pryde (OG 1040.5, ABV 4.2%)
A fruity, dark amber-coloured best bitter with caramel and toffee aromas and spicy hop notes.

Ash Park Special (OG 1048, ABV 4.9%)
A tawny-coloured ale with malt and raisin on the nose, slightly sweet with a long finish.

Little Monster (NEW)

Petworth, West Sussex 🌐 littlemonsterbrew.com

Brewing began in 2018. Owner Brenden collaborates with other breweries to produce his beers.

Little Ox SIBA

Unit 6, Wroslyn Road Industrial Estate, Freeland, Oxfordshire, OX29 8HZ
☎ (01993) 881941 ☎ 07730 496525

Office: 25 Castle Road, Wootton, OX20 1EQ
🌐 littleoxbrewery.co.uk

⊗ Little Ox began production in 2016 using a 10-barrel plant. Beer is regularly supplied to the White Horse, Stonesfield, plus other local pubs, shops and off licences. Contract bottling is conducted on-site. Oxbrew (qv) moved to Little Ox's premises in 2019. Although they are trading separately the production plant is shared. Total joint capacity is now 56 barrels. 🛒♦

Goldilox (ABV 3.9%)
A balanced, golden-coloured session ale with a malty-sweet aroma and a complex floral and fruity hoppiness. Finishes crisp and dry.

Oddbod (OG 1040, ABV 4%)
A characterful bitter with a malty backbone and a floral, bitter finish with hints of orange marmalade.

Wipeout (OG 1042, ABV 4.2%)
A zesty pale gold-coloured ale with generous amounts of hops giving a full-bodied, fruity flavour with citrus and tropical notes.

Ox Blood (OG 1042, ABV 4.3%)
A malty, red-coloured IPA with toffee and fruit overtones balanced by a big hit of zesty hops, and a fruity dry finish.

Filthy Rich (OG 1044, ABV 4.5%)
A porter with a rich, smooth body, balanced with hops. Finishes smooth and creamy with berry notes.

Yabba Dabba Doo (OG 1045, ABV 4.8%)
A strong bitter with intense tropical and stone fruit flavours and light bitterness.

Little Valley SIBA

Unit 3, Turkey Lodge Farm, New Road, Cragg Vale, Hebden Bridge, West Yorkshire, HX7 5TT
☎ (01422) 883888 🌐 littlevalleybrewery.co.uk

◎ Little Valley began brewing in 2005 on a 10-barrel plant. All beers are organic and vegan, and Radical Roots uses Fairtrade ingredients. Around 300 outlets are supplied. Several beers are contract brewed for Suma Wholefoods. 🛒♦ RAIB V

Withens Pale (OG 1037, ABV 3.9%) ◆
Creamy, light gold-coloured, refreshing ale. Fruity hop aroma, flavoured with hints of lemon and grapefruit. Clean, bitter aftertaste

Radical Roots (OG 1037, ABV 4%) ◆
Full-bodied speciality ale. Ginger predominates in the aroma and taste. Pleasant, powerful, fiery, spicy finish.

Cragg Bitter (OG 1039, ABV 4.2%) ◆
Tawny-coloured best bitter with a creamy mouthfeel. Malt and fruit aromas move into the palate, followed by a bitter finish.

Dark Vale (ABV 4.5%) ◆
Dark roast and fruit blend with vanilla to create a smooth, mellow, dark brown-coloured porter.

Hebden's Wheat (OG 1043, ABV 4.5%) ◆
A pale yellow-coloured, creamy wheat beer with a good balance of bitterness and fruit, a hint of sweetness but with a lasting, dry finish.

Stoodley Stout (OG 1044, ABV 4.8%) ◆
Very dark brown-coloured, creamy stout, with a rich roast aroma and luscious fruity, chocolate, roast flavours. Well-balanced with a clean bitter finish.

Tod's Blonde (OG 1045, ABV 5%) ◆
Bright yellow-coloured, smooth beer with a citrus hop start and a dry finish. Fruity, with a hint of spice. Similar to a Belgian blonde.

Moor Ale (OG 1051, ABV 5.5%) ◆
Tawny in colour, full-bodied, strong malty nose and palate, with hints of heather and peat-smoked malt. Well-balanced with a bitter finish.

Python IPA (OG 1055, ABV 6%) 🍺 ◆
Amber-coloured creamy beer with a complex bitter fruit palate subtly balanced by a malty sweetness, leading to a strong, lingering bitter aftertaste.

Littleover

Unit 9, Robinson Industrial Estate, Shaftesbury Street, Derby, DE23 8NL
☎ (01332) 987100 ☎ 07449 586811
🌐 littleoverbrewery.co.uk

Littleover was established in 2015 using a six-barrel plant.

Gold (OG 1038, ABV 3.8%)
Pale, golden-coloured session ale with a subtle, hoppy aroma.

8 O'Clock Bus (OG 1038, ABV 3.9%)

King George's Bitter (ABV 4%)
Traditional bitter, subtle, malty bitterness leads to a refreshing, crisp finish.

Epiphany Pale Ale (OG 1040, ABV 4.1%)

The Panther Oatmeal Stout (OG 1049, ABV 4.2%)

Dazzler IPA (OG 1043, ABV 4.5%)

Hollow legs Pale Ale (OG 1050, ABV 5.2%)

Liverpool Brewing (NEW)

39 Brasenose Road, Liverpool, L20 8HL
☎ (0151) 933 9660
🌐 liverpoolbrewingcompany.com

Liverpool Brewing Co purchased the brewing set-up of what was the Liverpool Organic Brewery including the recipes, names and branding. It is owned by seven local businessmen. A 12.5-barrel plant is used with six fermenters. Finings are added at racking giving the opportunity for all beers to be unfined, if requested. !!

Cascade (OG 1038, ABV 3.8%)
Hoppy, American-style session ale.

Pale Ale (OG 1039, ABV 4%)
A clean, sharp pale ale with dry hoppy notes and a floral complexity, giving way to citrus tones and a bitter finish.

24 Carat (ABV 4.1%)
Well-hopped with a balanced bitterness and lingering finish with notes of orange zest and a slight sweetness.

Bier Head (OG 1040, ABV 4.2%)
A best bitter with a hoppy foretaste, complex spice and crisp malt tones.

Stout (OG 1048, ABV 4.7%)
Strong, dark-coloured and dry stout with a smooth, spicy finish.

IPA (ABV 5.7%)
An intensely hopped, West Coast-style IPA

Lizard

The Old Nuclear Bunker, Pednavounder, Coverack, Cornwall, TR12 6SE
☎ (01326) 281135 🌐 lizardales.co.uk

Launched in 2004 in St Keverne, Lizard Ales is now based at former RAF Treleaver, a massive disused nuclear bunker in the countryside near Coverack on the Lizard Peninsula. Specialising in bottle-conditioned ales, it mainly supplies Asda and is available as far as Bristol. !! RAIB

Llangollen

Abbey Grange Brewing Ltd, Abbey Grange Hotel, Horseshoe Pass Road, Llantysilio, LL20 8DD
☎ (01978) 861916 🌐 llangollenbrewery.com

Brewing began in 2010 on a 2.5-barrel plant. The brewery was updated and upgraded in 2014 to a 10-barrel plant. !! RAIB

Grange No.1 (OG 1032, ABV 3.2%)
Light brown-coloured pale ale, fruity aroma with a slight hoppy finish.

Wrexham Borders Bitter (OG 1039, ABV 3.9%)
A pale ale, fruity notes, hay-like and distinctively hoppy.

Bitter (OG 1042, ABV 4.2%)
Medium brown-coloured pale ale, fruity aroma with a distinctive, hoppy finish.

Holy Grail (OG 1043, ABV 4.3%)
Light, citrus pale ale.

Welsh Black (OG 1055, ABV 5.5%)
Chocolate and toffee notes with a hoppy finish.

Lleu

Unit A9, Penygroes Industrial Estate, Caernarfon, LL54 6DB ☎ 07724 902532 🌐 bragdylleu.cymru

Brewing began in 2014 using a 1.25-barrel plant. The beer reflects the Welsh folklore tales of the Mabinogi in both name and character. Capacity was upgraded to six barrels in 2016 to meet demand. !!

Blodeuwedd (OG 1036, ABV 3.6%)
Refreshing, easy-drinking golden ale.

Lleu (OG 1040, ABV 4%)
Full-bodied, easy-drinking bitter with a good mouthfeel and a lasting, satisfying hoppy aftertaste.

Gwydion (OG 1047, ABV 4.7%)
Modern, dark chestnut-coloured bitter. Malty bitter with a subtle hop character and lasting aftertaste.

Bendigeidfran (OG 1050, ABV 5%)
A red-coloured IPA, combining bitterness, balanced malt flavours, and sweet hoppiness.

Llŷn

1 Parc Eithyn, Fford Dewi Sant, Nefyn, Gwynedd, LL53 6EG ☎ 07792 050134 🌐 cwrwllyn.cymru

Brewing began in 2011. In 2016 the brewing moved into a new purpose built 15-barrel brewery that includes a brewery shop, tap house and a visitor's gallery for tours. !! ♦

Y Brawd Houdini (OG 1040, ABV 3.5%)
An aromatic pale ale with citrus flavours.

Brenin Enlli (OG 1041, ABV 4%)
A fruity bitter, the initial malty taste leads to a hoppy, bitter aftertaste.

Cwrw Glyndwr (OG 1041, ABV 4%)
A full-bodied, well-balanced, amber-coloured beer, quite fruity with a good hoppy finish.

Seithenyn (OG 1042, ABV 4.2%)
A fruity golden ale with a tangy citrus taste and a dry hoppy finish.

Tria Hon (ABV 4.2%)

Porth Neigwl (OG 1044, ABV 4.5%)

Loch Leven SIBA

The Muirs, Kinross, KY13 8AS
☎ (01577) 864881 🌐 lochleven.beer

Based opposite the Green Hotel in Kinross, the brewery started production in 2017. Brewing plant and casks have been acquired from the former Loch Leven Brewery in Fife. ‼ 🛒

Warrior Queen (OG 1037.5, ABV 3.8%)
A refreshing, amber-coloured, relatively malty version of an IPA.

Shining Knight (OG 1040, ABV 4%)
A refreshing, well-balanced, pale yellow-coloured, malty lager.

Outlaw King (OG 1048.8, ABV 5%)
A well-balanced, golden-coloured, lightly-malt flavoured ale.

King Slayer (OG 1050.3, ABV 5.2%)
A traditional, dark amber-coloured Scottish ale.

Loch Lomond SIBA

Unit 5, Block 1, Lomond Industrial Estate, Alexandria, G83 0TL
☎ (01389) 755 698 ☎ 07891920213
🌐 lochlomondbrewery.com

Established in 2011 by Fiona and Euan MacEachern, Loch Lomond is the first brewery to be established in the area. ‼ 🛒 ♦ RAIB

Bonnie'n' Bitter (OG 1036, ABV 3.6%)
Pale-coloured bitter, easy-drinking with citrus flavours and a full, rounded bitterness.

West Highland Way (OG 1037, ABV 3.7%)
A light ale with fruity flavours.

Bonnie & Blonde (OG 1040, ABV 4%)
Light, refreshing ale with a well-rounded citrus flavour.

Southern Summit (OG 1040, ABV 4%)
Light, pale-coloured, highly-hopped ale. Fresh and fruity palate with hints of grapefruit and lemon, leading to a crisp, light bitter finish.

The Ale of Leven (OG 1045, ABV 4.5%)
An amber-coloured ale with a spicy citrus aroma and a well-rounded bitterness.

Bonnie 'n' Clyde (OG 1046, ABV 4.6%)
Amber-coloured ale with a big citrus hit on the nose that follows into the rich, bitter finish.

Silkie Stout (OG 1050, ABV 5%)
Black-coloured stout with chocolate orange spicy notes.

Kessog Dark Ale (OG 1052, ABV 5.2%)
Dark-coloured ale with warm, spicy flavours.

Bravehop Amber IPA (OG 1060, ABV 6%)
IPA with up-front hop bite and lots of sweetness to give balance.

Bravehop Dark IPA (OG 1060, ABV 6%)
A black-coloured IPA with upfront hop bite balanced with roasted malt and a long, dry bitter finish.

Loch Ness

See Cairngorm

Loddon SIBA

Dunsden Green Farm, Church Lane, Dunsden, Oxfordshire, RG4 9QD
☎ (0118) 948 1111 🌐 loddonbrewery.com

This family-run brewery was established in 2002 in a brick-and-flint barn that was originally a grain store. The custom-built 17-barrel plant typically produces 120 barrels per week and supplies more than 700 outlets far and wide. Popular open evenings are held quarterly and Beer Club members' evenings twice yearly. An on-site taproom opened in 2018, open to the public six days a week (not Sun). ‼ 🛒 ♦

Hoppit (OG 1036.2, ABV 3.5%)
Hops dominate the aroma of this drinkable, light-coloured session beer. Malt and hops create a balanced taste and a pleasant bitterness that carries into the aftertaste.

Reading Best (OG 1041.5, ABV 4%)
A dark golden-coloured best bitter with a smooth, nutty body and a lingering, bitter aftertaste.

Hullabaloo (OG 1043.8, ABV 4.2%)
A hint of fruit in the initial taste develops into a balance of hops and malt in this well-rounded, medium-bodied bitter, with a bitter aftertaste.

Ferryman's Gold (OG 1045.8, ABV 4.4%)
Golden-coloured with a strong hoppy character throughout, accompanied by fruit in the taste and aftertaste.

NOTUS (OG 1048.1, ABV 4.7%)
An amber-coloured, American-style pale ale with a good balance between malt and hops. Some biscuity notes accompany a fruity taste, leading to a bitter finish.

Forbury Lion (OG 1056.5, ABV 5.5%)
A malty IPA with a strong, complex hop finish.

Logan Beck (NEW)

The Barn at Beckfoot Farm, Duddon Bridge, Cumbria, LA20 6EU ☎ 07926 179749
✉ loganbeckbrewing@gmail.com

Brewing began in 2019 using a 0.5-barrel plant. There are plans for expansion.

Prime (ABV 3.7%)

Loka Polly

See Polly's

Lola Rose

Wanlockhead Inn, Wanlockhead, ML12 6UZ
☎ (01659) 74535 ☎ 07500 663405
🌐 lola-rose-brewery.co.uk

Lola Rose is based in the family-run Wanlockhead Inn, situated in the scenic Lowther Hills of the Scottish Lowlands. Local outlets only are supplied at present. RAIB

London Beer Factory SIBA

Unit 4, 160 Hamilton Road, West Norwood, London, SE27 9SF ☎ 07760 290489
🌐 thelondonbeerfactory.com

London Beer Factory started brewing in 2014 using a 20-barrel plant on the same estate and at the same time as Gipsy Hill. The taproom is open at weekends and it also runs the Barrel Project along the Bermondsey Beer Mile, showcasing its range and providing an impressive display of barrels used for aging beer. 360-degree cans are a popular innovation.

Beyond the Pale (ABV 4.2%) ◆
Easy-drinking, unfined pale ale with some malt and fruit to provide balance. Slightly bitter aftertaste.

Chelsea Blonde (ABV 4.3%) ◆
Grapefruit dominates the flavour and aroma with trace of spiciness and a dry bitterness balanced by a little honey sweetness.

Paxton Pale Ale (ABV 5%)

London Beer Lab

Arch 283, Belinda Road, Brixton, London, SW9 7DT
☎ (020) 8396 6517

Office: Arch 41, Nursery Road, Brixton, SW9 8BP
⊕ londonbeerlab.com

Opened in 2013 as a bottle shop and homebrew supplies outlet, also offering brewing workshops and tastings. Commercial brewing began in 2015 at a separate site with the focus on small batch production and collaborations. The shop now has a 14-line taproom. 🍺

Tip Top Citra (ABV 5%)
A pale ale with a slightly sweet malt base.

London Brewing SIBA

🍺 Bohemia, 762-764 High Road, North Finchley, London, N12 9QH
☎ (020) 8446 0294 ⊕ londonbrewing.com

⊠ London Brewing Co began brewing in 2011 at the Bull in Highgate using a 2.5-barrel plant. In 2014 it acquired its second pub, the Bohemia in North Finchley, at which brewing began in 2015 in a new 6.5-barrel brewhouse. The Bull was sold in the summer of 2016 to concentrate all production at the North Finchley site. Beer is now supplied widely. ◆

London Fields

365-366 Warburton Street, London Fields, London, E8 3RR ⊕ londonfieldsbrewery.co.uk

After brewing was suspended in 2014 beers were brewed at Tom Woods. Taken over by Carlsberg UK in 2017, the company was relaunched in 2018 with the main brands brewed at Trumans and smaller batches at other breweries. The London Fields brewery has been re-developed and will be brewing on site during the currency of this Guide.

London Road Brew House

🍺 67-75 London Road, Southampton, Hampshire, SO15 2AB
☎ (023) 8098 9401 ☎ 07597 147321
⊕ londonroadbrewhouse.com

⊠ Brewing commenced in 2017 in the London Road Brew House using a six-barrel plant. Beer is brewed for the pub, the City Pub Co estate and the trade.

Lonesome

36 Streatham Vale, Streatham, London, SW16 5TD
⊕ facebook.com/Lonesomebrewco

Small batch home brewer started in 2016. Beer available in bottles at the Railway in Streatham SW16 when brewed. Advised to contact the pub ahead to see if any in stock.

Long Arm

🍺 Long Arm, 20-26 Worship Street, London, EC2A 2DX
☎ (020) 3873 4065 ⊕ longarmpub.co.uk

Opening in 2017, this brewpub took over all Long Arm beers when the Ealing Park Tavern kit was suspended. No real ale.

Long Man SIBA

Church Farm, Litlington, East Sussex, BN26 5RA
☎ (01323) 871850 ☎ 07976 777992
⊕ longmanbrewery.com

⊠ Long Man began brewing in 2012 using a 20-barrel stainless steel plant. Hops and grain are sourced locally with a view to using homegrown barley, as well as a traditional strain of Sussex yeast. ‼

Long Blonde (OG 1039, ABV 3.8%)
A light-coloured golden ale with a distinctive hoppy aroma and crisp, clean bitterness on the finish. Smooth, light and refreshing.

Best Bitter (OG 1040, ABV 4%)
Traditional, well-balanced, Sussex-style best bitter with a complex, bittersweet malty taste, fragrant hops and a long, deep finish.

Copper Hop (ABV 4.2%)

Old Man (OG 1048, ABV 4.3%)
Dark-coloured beer with soft malt notes of coffee and chocolate combined with a pleasant, light hoppiness creating a rich, full-tasting old ale.

Sussex Pride (OG 1045, ABV 4.5%)
A classic, strong pale ale. Bronze-coloured with a fruity nose and full, rounded flavours. A perfect balance between malt and hops.

American Pale Ale (OG 1046, ABV 4.8%)
Pleasant citrus fruit aroma and characteristic robust bitterness.

Longdog SIBA

Unit A1, Moniton Trading Estate, West Ham Lane, Basingstoke, Hampshire, RG22 6NQ
☎ (01256) 324286 ☎ 07827 618733
⊕ longdogbrewery.co.uk

⊠ Longdog was established in 2011 using a six-barrel plant. The name is inspired by the owner's lurcher. ‼ 🍺 ◆ RAIB

Bunny Chaser (OG 1036, ABV 3.6%)
A mid-copper-coloured session bitter with plenty of malt in the mouth and a big hit of bitterness.

Golden Poacher (OG 1039, ABV 3.9%) ◆
A fruity nose with plenty of hops, balanced by a malty sweetness in the flavour. Hops build to a faint, astringent finish.

Red Runner (OG 1041, ABV 4.2%)
A fruity, hoppy, mahogany-coloured best bitter.

Kismet (OG 1045, ABV 4.5%)

A pale ale with assertive hop bitterness, flavour and aroma.

Lamplight Porter (OG 1048, ABV 5%) ◈
Porter, smoky and drier than many, with strong roast flavours giving way to blackberry taste and slightly vinous finish.

Longhill

Longhill Cottage, Whitstone, Holsworthy, Cornwall, EX22 6UG
☎ (01288) 341466

⊗ Longhill began brewing in 2011 using a 0.5-barrel plant, upgraded in 2012 to a four-barrel plant to meet demand. The beers are named with a wind theme. Eight outlets are supplied direct.

Whistler (OG 1038, ABV 3.8%) ◈
Smooth, pale brown-coloured bitter with little aroma. Gentle balance of caramel malt, bitter hops and sweet fruit. Slowly fading bittersweet finish.

Westerly (OG 1040, ABV 4%) ◈
Copper-coloured best bitter with malt and toffee aroma. Mainly malt and caramel flavour. Light finish with malt, fruit and bitterness.

Gale Force (OG 1048, ABV 4.8%) ◈
Copper-coloured, strong bitter. Malt and almonds aroma, malty flavours with toffee and nuts, and a short, malty, dry finish with stone fruit.

Hurricane (OG 1048, ABV 4.8%)
Smooth, initially sweet, with a full, rounded bitter aftertaste and the beer has distinct fruity and earthy flavours.

Loomshed (NEW)

Iomairt an Obain, Tarbert, Isle of Harris, HS3 3DS
☎ 07808 098860 🌐 loomshed.scot

Brewing commenced in 2019 on the outskirts of Tarbert. The brewery backs onto the Minch, with views of the Scottish mainland. An eco-friendly approach to brewing extends to the on-site taproom.

Crofter (ABV 3.5%)
The depth of flavour comes from the malt base overlaid with hoppiness. Earthy pine cones and green tea followed by fruity citrus and blackcurrant.

Loose Cannon SIBA

Unit 6, Suffolk Way, Abingdon, Oxfordshire, OX14 5JX
☎ (01235) 531141 🌐 lcbeers.co.uk

Brewing began in 2010 using a 15-barrel plant, reviving Abingdon's brewing history after the Morland Brewery closed in 2000. Beers can be found in an increasing number of local pubs and within 50 miles of the brewery. Popular brewery evenings take place on the first Tuesday of the month. ‼ ♦

Gunners Gold (OG 1034.5, ABV 3.5%)
Golden-coloured, easy-drinking, session ale with a subtle peach flavour.

Abingdon Bridge (OG 1041, ABV 4.1%)
Full-flavoured, smooth, with well-rounded bitterness and a floral aroma.

Detonator (OG 1044, ABV 4.4%)
Dark chestnut-coloured ale, malty and slightly sweet with hints of tropical fruit.

Porter (OG 1054, ABV 5%)
Moderately sweet with hints of dark chocolate, and a smooth, espresso finish.

India Pale Ale (OG 1053, ABV 5.4%)
Balanced floral aroma and fruity taste with a smooth, bitter kick and a warming quality.

Lord Conrad's

Unit 21, Dry Drayton Industrial Estate, Scotland Road, Dry Drayton, Cambridgeshire, CB23 8AT ☎ 07736 739700 🌐 lordconradsbrewery.co.uk

⊗ Lord Conrad's was established in 2007 and moved to Dry Drayton in 2011 using a 2.5-barrel plant. One permanent outlet is supplied, the Black Horse, Dry Drayton, along with other local free houses and beer festivals. The brewery adheres strongly to green principles, using low energy systems, recycled materials and local ingredients. ‼

Zulu Dawn (OG 1037, ABV 3.5%)

Hedgerow Hop (OG 1039, ABV 3.7%)

Her Majes Tea (OG 1038, ABV 3.8%)
Speciality ale infused with Earl Grey tea.

Lickety Split (OG 1038, ABV 3.8%)
Sweet, malty, brown-coloured ale, light but not overly hoppy.

Tangerine Dream (OG 1038, ABV 3.8%)
Warm, golden-coloured ale heavily-infused with tangerine and bitter orange.

Spiffing Wheeze (OG 1040, ABV 3.9%)
Pale-coloured beer with lemongrass and a peppery bitterness.

Big Bad Wolf (OG 1042, ABV 4%)
A pale-coloured ale with citrus and pine hints in the taste.

Conkerwood (OG 1044, ABV 4%)
Dark-coloured porter with hints of liquorice.

Fools Gold (OG 1042, ABV 4%)
Gold-coloured ale with subtle pear and watermelon tones in the taste.

Gubbins (OG 1040, ABV 4%)
An old ale with a hint of warming spice.

Lobster Licker (OG 1043, ABV 4.2%)
Red-coloured, malty bitter with strong, hoppy undertones.

Slap N' Tickle (OG 1042, ABV 4.3%)
A blonde ale with a hit of bitterness and a hint of hops.

Zulu (OG 1047, ABV 4.5%)
A strong, black-coloured bitter.

Horny Goat (OG 1048, ABV 4.8%)
A bitter brewed with nettles.

Pheasant's Rise (OG 1050, ABV 5%)
Smoky, woody, traditional, strong ale.

Stubble Burner (OG 1050, ABV 5%)
A straw-coloured beer with a good, earthy nose and a well-balanced, fruity bitterness.

Lord Randall's (NEW)

Holme View Farm, High Street, Laxton, Newark, NG22 0NX ☎ 07712078346

New brewery using equipment purchased from the defunct Market Harborough Brewery.

Lord's SIBA

Unit 15, Heath House Mill, Heath House Lane, Golcar, West Yorkshire, HD7 4JW ☎ 07976 974162
🌐 lordsbrewing.com

Established in 2015, Lord's is the brain child of three brothers-in-law, Ben, John and Tim. A picturesque 19th-century mill houses their eight-barrel plant, large tap room and gift/bottle shop. ♦

1895 Golden Ale (OG 1036, ABV 3.8%)
Crisp, pale-coloured bitter. Citrus notes and good malt character.

Tithe House Bitter (OG 1037, ABV 3.9%)
Light copper-coloured bitter with subtle malt flavours balanced by hops. Soft malt and caramel base, with a mellow pine and grapefruit flavour.

Expedition Blonde (OG 1038, ABV 4%)
Pale and delicately-hopped. Refreshing, with citrus notes.

The Bandon Car Porter (OG 1048, ABV 4.8%)
Irish-style porter. Subtle roast flavour, chocolatey with a sweet toasty finish.

Mount Helix West Coast Pale (OG 1047, ABV 5%)
American-style ale bursting with citrus, pine and floral overtones, which give way to a lightly-toasted, crisp malt base.

Havelock IPA (OG 1055, ABV 5.9%)
IPA with an abundance of hops, a touch of coriander seed and a hint of curacao orange peel.

Lost + Found

12-13 Ship Street, Brighton, East Sussex, BN1 1AD
🌐 lostandfoundbrewery.com

Brewing began in 2016. No real ale.

Lost & Grounded SIBA

Barley Mow, 91 Whitby Road, Bristol, BS4 4AR
☎ (0117) 332 7690 🌐 lostandgrounded.co.uk

Brewing began in 2016 at the Barley Mow. No real ale.

Lost Industry

14a Nutwood Trading Estate, Sheffield, South Yorkshire, S6 1NJ
☎ (0114) 2316393 🌐 lostindustrybrewing.com

Lost Industry is run by a family of beer enthusiasts and was established in 2015. A wide range of beer styles is brewed with no core range, although favourites may be repeated from time to time. A barrel aging programme began in 2018. Spare brewing capacity is utilised by Steel City (qv).

Loud Shirt SIBA

Unit 5, Bell Tower Industrial Estate, Roedean Road, Brighton, East Sussex, BN2 5RU
☎ (01273) 087077 ☎ 07901 856436
🌐 loudshirtbeer.co.uk

The brewery was set up by two old friends, Martyn and Mike. Established in 2017 using a 10-barrel plant. Regular monthly events are held at the brewery, look out for its psychedelic van at festivals. Around 30 outlets are supplied direct.

Love Lane

See Higsons

LoveBeer SIBA

95 High Street, Milton, Oxfordshire, OX14 4EJ
☎ 07889 455845 🌐 lovebeerbrewery.com

Established in a garage in 2013, LoveBeer's original 0.5-barrel plant grew to six barrels in 2017. The brewery supplies local pubs including the Plum Pudding, Milton, as well as beer festivals and farm shops. RAIB

Doctor Roo (OG 1038, ABV 4%)
A well-balanced, light pale ale with a zesty tropical flavour.

Molly's (OG 1041, ABV 4%)
A well-hopped, amber-coloured ale with a caramel biscuit aroma and hints of citrus.

OG (OG 1042, ABV 4.1%)
A pale-coloured ale. Light citrus flavour with hints of tropical fruit or rose petals.

Bonnie Hops (OG 1048, ABV 4.6%)
A hoppy, pale-coloured ale, full-flavoured and hoppy.

Lovibonds

Rear of 19-21 Market Place, Henley-on-Thames, Oxfordshire, RG9 2AA
☎ (01491) 576596 🌐 lovibonds.com

Lovibonds was founded by Jeff Rosenmeier in 2005 and is named after Joseph William Lovibond, who invented the Tintometer to measure beer colour. The beers are unfiltered and unpasteurised. In 2017 brewing moved from the kit at Old Luxters Brewery (qv) to a purpose-built brewery on the outskirts of Henley, which has a steam-heated mash tun and copper. The revamped website proclaims the American style of Lovibonds craft beers. !!

Lowland (NEW) SIBA

8 Well Street, Lockerbie, DG11 2EY
☎ (01576) 203999 🌐 lowlandbrewery.co.uk

This five-barrel brewery was established in 2018. The brewery is located in converted premises in the town centre and supplies direct to pubs in Dumfries & Galloway, Scottish Borders and north Cumbria. Further beers are planned.

Twa Dugs (ABV 4%)

Wee Tam (ABV 4%)

Loxley

539 Loxley Road, Sheffield, South Yorkshire, S6 6RR
☎ (0114) 233 4310 🌐 loxleybrewery.co.uk

Established in 2018, Loxley Brewery uses an eight-barrel plant located in the cellar of the Wisewood Inn. Beers are becoming increasingly available locally. Branded merchandise is available from the Wisewood Inn.

Wisewood Five (OG 1040, ABV 3.9%)

THE BREWERIES

Wisewood Three (OG 1040, ABV 3.9%)

Wisewood One (OG 1041, ABV 4%)

Wisewood Six (OG 1042, ABV 4.2%)

Wisewood Two (OG 1043, ABV 4.3%)
A bright golden-coloured ale with well-balanced malts and hops.

Wisewood Four (OG 1049, ABV 5%)

Lucky 7

Hay On Wye, HR3 5AW
☎ (01497) 822778 ☎ 07815 853353
lucky7beer.co.uk

Producer of small-batch craft and bottled beers, mainly sold through local stockists in Hay on Wye, Brecon, Hereford and Cardiff.

Luddite (NEW)

Calder Vale Hotel, Millfield Road, Horbury Junction, West Yorkshire, WF4 5EB

Brewing began in 2019 at the Calder Vale pub in Horbury Junction. The pub was shut for five years until being re-opened by a group of three former Horbury School friends, Ian Sizer, Tim Murphy and Gary Portman. The six-barrel plant brews, on average, once per week.

Ludlow SIBA

The Railway Shed, Station Drive, Ludlow, Shropshire, SY8 2PQ
☎ (01584) 873291
theludlowbrewingcompany.co.uk

Established in 2006, the brewery occupies a converted railway sidings shed. Beers are produced using a 20-barrel plant and a recently installed pilot plant for one-off beers. The premises also function as a brewery tap, visitor centre and event's area. **!!**

Best (OG 1037, ABV 3.7%)
Golden-coloured, well-balanced session beer with a banana, pineapple and toffee aroma and a resinous, dry finish.

Blonde (OG 1040, ABV 4%)
A pale-coloured, blonde ale; aromatic and well-hopped.

Gold (OG 1041, ABV 4.2%)
A yellow-coloured ale with a papaya, pineapple and lemon aroma and a soft, full-bodied, creamy taste.

Black Knight (OG 1045, ABV 4.5%)
A ruby black-coloured stout with a smoky, liquorice aroma and sweet, roasted nutty flavour.

Boiling Well (OG 1046, ABV 4.7%)
An auburn-coloured beer with a grassy aroma of autumn frui and a full-bodied sweet, then dry taste.

Stairway (OG 1048.5, ABV 5%)
A honey-coloured beer with a grassy, citrus floral aroma and a sharp, sweet, full-bodied taste.

Luna

See White Horse

Lydbrook Valley

Forge Row, Lydbrook, Gloucestershire, GL17 9NP
☎ (01594) 860310

Brewing commenced in 2018 in the Forge Hammer pub in Lydbrook. Alison and Andrew Jopson use full mash to produce beers for sale in the pub.

Lymestone SIBA

The Brewery, Mount Road, Stone, Staffordshire, ST15 8LL
☎ (01785) 817796 ☎ 07891 782652
lymestonebrewery.co.uk

Lymestone commenced brewing in 2008. Based in the old Bents Brewery, it uses a 10-barrel plant. A family-run business, daughter Sarah has joined the brew team as one of the UK's youngest brewsters. The brewery delivers in a 50-mile radius, works with national wholesalers and owns three pubs. **!!** ♦

Stone Cutter (OG 1037, ABV 3.7%)
Hoppy and grassy aroma, clean, sharp and refreshing. A hint of caramel start then intense bitterness emerges with a good bitter aftertaste and touch of mouthwatering astringency.

Stone Faced (OG 1040, ABV 4%)
Subtle citrus and toffee flavours, balanced by a hoppy aroma and bitter finish.

Foundation Stone (OG 1047, ABV 4.5%)
An IPA-style beer. Faint biscuit and chewy, juicy fruits burst on to the palate then the spicy hops pepper the palate, with a dry, bitter finish.

Ein Stein (OG 1052, ABV 5%)
A pale-coloured, citrus, hoppy ale.

Stone the Crows (OG 1056, ABV 5.4%)
A rich, dark-coloured beer. Fruit, roasts and hops abound, with a deep, lingering bitterness.

Abdominal Stoneman (OG 1072, ABV 7%)
Powerful hops dominate this American-style pale ale. Huge hoppy finish.

Lymm

18 Bridgewater Street, Lymm, Cheshire, WA13 0AB
☎ (0161) 929 0663 lymmbrewing.co.uk

Lymm is a small, family-run brewery, launched in 2013. Located in an old post office, the brewing equipment is downstairs in what used to be the mess rooms with a brewery tap upstairs in what was the sorting office/post office counter. A sister brewery to Dunham Massey (qv), a joint bar opened in 2013, Costello's Bar, Stockton Heath. ♦

Dark (OG 1035, ABV 3.4%)
An easy-drinking dark mild. Smooth and nutty with a hint of caramel.

Bitter (OG 1040, ABV 3.8%)
A light, refreshing, medium-bodied session bitter, with a good balance of malt and hops.

Bridgewater Blonde (OG 1041, ABV 4%)
Light, delicate, hoppy, subtle and refreshing.

Heritage Trail Ale (OG 1046, ABV 4.5%)
An easy-drinking, well-balanced best bitter, fruity with a light, crisp hop.

IPA (OG 1048.5, ABV 4.8%)
Traditional hoppy pale ale with hints of tropical fruit.

Dam Strong Ale (OG 1071, ABV 7.2%)
Belgian-style ale. Strong, malty and fruity with a dry finish.

Lytham SIBA

8 Cambell's Court, Lord Street, St Annes, Lancashire, FY8 2DF
☎ (01253) 725440 ⊕ lythambrewery.co.uk

⊚Lytham is a well-established, family-run brewery that began brewing in 2007. In 2018 they opened the Tap & Vent Brewhouse in Kirkham with plans to brew there in the future. ‼◆

Amber (OG 1037, ABV 3.6%)
A traditional, malty bitter.

Blonde (OG 1038, ABV 3.8%) ◖
Smooth, golden ale with a dry finish.

Gold (OG 1042, ABV 4.2%)
A golden-coloured beer with a fruity aroma and lasting, bitter finish.

Royal (OG 1044, ABV 4.4%)
A full-bodied ale with a crisp fruity aroma and a smooth, dry finish.

Stout (OG 1046, ABV 4.6%)
Dark-coloured, rich, roasty, full-bodied stout. Roasted barley blends with a touch of sweet, fruity flavours.

IPA (OG 1054, ABV 5.6%)
A pale-coloured bitter with a fresh, sweet, hoppy flavour leading to a long, dry finish.

McColl's

Unit 4, Randolph Industrial Estate, Evenwood, DL14 9SJ
☎ (01388) 417250 ⊕ mccollsbrewery.co.uk

Brewing commenced in 2017 using a 20-barrel plant. Outlets are supplied across the North-east and further afield. A brewery tap is open on the last Friday and Saturday of each month.

Golden Ale (OG 1040, ABV 3.8%)
Delicate, light malt and citrus hop flavours with lemon and floral aromas building to soft bitterness and a medium dry finish.

Best Bitter (OG 1045, ABV 4.4%)
Rich and resinous malts with spicy marmalade hop flavours and deep citrus aromas leading to an assertive bitterness balanced by a sweet body.

Pale Ale (OG 1044, ABV 4.5%)
Smooth, full-bodied pale ale with light spicy notes leading to citrus and soft fruit aromas.

IPA (OG 1050, ABV 5%)
Full-bodied IPA with earthy, rich hop flavours and punchy citrus and grapefruit aromas. Well-balanced with a firm bitterness and lingering dry finish.

McGivern

🏠 c/o Bridge End Inn, 5 Bridge Street, Ruabon, LL14 6DA
☎ (01978) 810881 ☎ 07891 676614
⊕ mcgivernales.co.uk

⊚The brewery was established in 2008 and was originally based at the brewer's home in Wrexham but moved in 2011 to the award-winning Bridge End Inn in Ruabon using a 2.5-barrel plant. Production is on an occasional basis. ◆

McMullen SIBA IFBB

26 Old Cross, Hertford, SG14 1RD
☎ (01992) 584911 ⊕ mcmullens.co.uk

⊚McMullen, Hertfordshire's oldest independent brewery, was founded in 1827 – its famous brew, AK, is traceable back into the 19th century. The 'Authentic Heritage' tag promotes its core beers. Additional seasonal ales are produced throughout the year, sometimes produced under the Rivertown Brewing name. A microbrewery supplements the main plant. All 125 tied pubs, spread across South-east England, serve cask beer. ‼◆

AK (OG 1035, ABV 3.7%) ◖
A pleasant mix of malt and hops leads to a distinctive, dry aftertaste that isn't always as pronounced as it used to be.

Cask Ale (OG 1039, ABV 3.8%)
A well-balanced, refreshing ale with subtle biscuit and citrus hop flavours.

Country Bitter (OG 1042, ABV 4.3%) ◖
A full-bodied beer with a well-balanced mix of malt, hops and fruit throughout.

IPA (OG 1047, ABV 4.8%)
A strong bitter with deep, rich flavours.

Mabby's

🟰 Mabby Brew Pub & Kitchen, Forest Road, Treforest, CF37 1SY
☎ (01443) 402033

A microbrewery situated in the cellar of the Otley Arms supplying the pub and a few other local outlets. The name is derived from a partnership between brewer Matt Otley and his wife Gabby. The beers have no names and each recipe is referred to as a colour, with the colour being reflected on the pumpclip. V

Mad Cat SIBA

Brogdale Farm, Brogdale Road, Faversham, Kent, ME13 8XZ
☎ (01795) 597743 ☎ 07960 263615
⊕ madcatbrewery.co.uk

Established in 2012 by Peter Meaney in a refurbished cold store using an eight-barrel plant. Beers are distributed to local pubs. Bottles and polypins are available from the brewery and Peter often attends local markets, festivals and events. ‼◆

Red Ale (ABV 3.9%)

Crispin Ale (ABV 4%)

Crispin Amber (ABV 4%)

Golden IPA (ABV 4.2%)

Platinum Blonde (ABV 4.2%)

Emotional Blackmail (ABV 4.5%)

Mad Dog SIBA

Shed 4, Unit 9, Park Farm, Plough Road, Penperlleni, NP4 0AL ☎ 07703 731197 ⊕ maddogbrew.co.uk

Brewing began 2014 at the brewer's home in Cwmbran. In 2018 brewing capacity increased to twelve barrels with six fermenting vessels and the brewery opened its first bar, the Dog House, Caerleon. !! ♦ RAIB

Third Eye Blind (ABV 3.8%)
A pale ale with tropical and citrus flavours.

Now in a Minute (ABV 4.2%)
A traditional Welsh red-coloured ale with flavours of sweet chocolate and citrus.

Marmarlade IPA (ABV 4.5%)
A smooth pale ale with a punch of sweet orange flavour.

Stouty McStoutface (ABV 4.5%)
Full-bodied, smooth ale with chocolate and roast flavours.

Mad Scientist

c/o the Quakerhouse, 2-3 Mechanics Yard, Darlington, DL3 7QF
☎ (01325) 245052

Brewing commenced in 2017 on a half-barrel plant situated in the cellar of the Quakerhouse.

Mad Squirrel SIBA

Unit 18, Boxted Farm, Berkhamsted Road, Potten End, Hertfordshire, HP1 2SG
☎ (01442) 256970 madsquirrel.uk

Situated on the outskirts of Hemel Hempstead, brewing began in 2004. Formerly called Red Squirrel, the company changed name in 2017 to coincide with the installation of a larger brew kit. Beer is distributed to venues throughout the South-east, including to its own chain of venues. !! ♦ RAIB

Hopfest (OG 1037.5, ABV 3.8%)
A pale-coloured golden ale with a floral, citrus aroma and elderflower notes.

Mister Squirrel (OG 1040, ABV 4%)
A chestnut-coloured bitter, lightly-hopped with a creamy texture. Hints of caramel and vanilla complement the slightly hoppy and malty overtones.

Resolution (OG 1045, ABV 4.2%)
Pale golden-coloured ale. Subtle fruit with some caramel on the nose. Lightly-hopped with a soft malt finish.

De La Crème (OG 1046, ABV 4.5%)
A smooth milk stout, full-bodied with hints of caramel, cream and chocolate.

$umo (OG 1046, ABV 4.7%)
An American-style pale ale with tropical fruit notes and some bitterness.

London Porter (OG 1052, ABV 5%)
Dark brown/black-coloured porter with a good balance of chocolate and roasted barley. Full-bodied on the palate with bittersweet liquorice, rich chocolate flavours and a creamy finish.

Roadkill (OG 1060, ABV 6.5%)
A yellow-coloured, American-style IPA. The hop varieties change with every batch and so will the flavour.

Mad Yank (NEW) SIBA

Alandale Drive, Northwood Hills, HA5 3UP
madyank.com

Brewing began in 2019. Beers can be found at Beer Asylum in Pinner. No real ale.

Made of Stone (NEW)

8 Woodford Road, Bramhall, SK7 2JJ

Nanobrewery situated at the back of the Mounting Stone.

Madrigal

The Manor House, Manor Green, Lynmouth, Devon, EX35 6EN ☎ 07857 560677 madrigalbrewery.co.uk

The brewery was established in 2014 in the village of Combe Martin. It relocated to larger premises in Lynmouth in 2016 to help meet increased demand. !! ♦ RAIB V

Garland (OG 1036, ABV 3.5%)
A wheat beer with hints of tropical fruit.

Surfer Rosa (OG 1036, ABV 3.6%)
A spicy, hoppy, red rye ale.

Burning House (OG 1042, ABV 4%)
A dark brown-coloured speciality beer with a smooth mouthfeel and a gradual smoke and hop finish.

Fossil (OG 1043, ABV 4%)

Hanged Man (OG 1042, ABV 4.2%)
Well-balanced stout made with raw cacao nibs. A smooth, soft taste with slight spicy notes.

Severed Hand (OG 1043, ABV 4.3%)
A velvety porter.

Monkey's Fist (OG 1048, ABV 5%)
Smooth, dark-coloured old ale with strong fruit and roast from start to lingering, slightly sour finish. Heavy and sweet but satisfying.

North Coast Voodoo (OG 1050, ABV 5%)
An aromatic IPA made with a mixture of hops, with a fruity aroma and a gradual hop finish.

Wheatear (OG 1048, ABV 5.1%)
Wheat beer made with fresh ginger and coriander.

Magic Dragon SIBA

Plassey Brewery, Eyton, LL13 0SP
☎ (01978) 781675 magicdragonbrewing.co.uk

Originally named Plassey then New Plassey, brewing began in 1985 on the 250-acre Plassey Estate. New owners in 2017 have renamed to Magic Dragon Brewing.

Border Bitter (ABV 3.8%)

Ice Dragon (ABV 3.8%)
A blonde ale with citrus and mango notes.

Eyton Gold (OG 1040, ABV 4%)

American Dragon (ABV 4.2%)

Obsidian (ABV 4.2%)
A dark, rich stout with roast notes.

Eyton Bitter (OG 1045, ABV 4.5%)
Smooth and malty best bitter, reddish brown in colour, with a good hop and fruit balance and a dry finish.

Magic Rock

Units 1-4, Willow Lane, Huddersfield, West Yorkshire, HD1 5EB
☎ (01484) 649823 🌐 magicrockbrewing.com

Magic Rock began brewing in 2011. The brewery is located about half a mile walk from Huddersfield town centre on an industrial estate. The site also houses a tap room and distribution centre. In 2019 Magic Rock was bought by Lion of Australia, who in turn are owned by Kirin of Japan. ♦RAIB

Hat Trick (OG 1041, ABV 3.7%)

Ringmaster (OG 1038, ABV 3.9%)
Pale ale with a floral, grassy aroma and citrus hops.

Inhaler (OG 1044, ABV 4.5%)

Rapture (OG 1044.5, ABV 4.6%)
Full-bodied, red-coloured ale with grapefruit and pine aromas, pithy orange, and a rich, malty body.

Common Grounds (OG 1063, ABV 5.4%)

High Wire (OG 1051, ABV 5.5%)
American-style pale ale with mango, lychee and grapefruit flavours.

Dark Arts (OG 1057, ABV 6%)
Chocolate, liquorice, blackberry and fig flavours with a long roasted bitter finish.

Magic Spells

24 Rigg Approach, Leyton, London, E10 7QN
☎ (020) 3475 1781 ☎ 07740 428952
🌐 magicspellsbrewery.co.uk

Magic Spells is an independent brewery located in East London, owned and operated by Jas Hare. Brewing takes place on a 10-barrel plant with a half-barrel kit used for experimental brews. RAIB

Magpie SIBA

Unit 4, Ashling Court, Ashling Street, Nottingham, NG2 3JA ☎ 07419 991310 🌐 magpiebrewery.com

Launched in 2006 using a six-barrel plant, the brewery upgraded to 17.5-barrels in 2017. Only British hops and malt are used in the core range, with the Wanderlust range taking more worldly influences and ingredients. ♦

Hoppily Ever After (OG 1035, ABV 3.8%)
Golden bitter, gently hopped with biscuit malt flavours and a bitter finish.

Best (OG 1040.7, ABV 4.2%)
A malty, traditional pale brown-coloured best bitter, with balancing hops giving a bitter finish.

Cherry Raven (OG 1044, ABV 4.4%)
Natural dark cherry fruit flavour added to a rich smoky stout, packed full of roasted malt flavour.

Raven Stout (OG 1044, ABV 4.4%)
Dark-coloured stout with roast coffee aroma and taste leading to a dry bitter finish.

Thieving Rogue (OG 1042, ABV 4.5%)
A hoppy golden ale with a long-lasting, bitter finish.

Jay IPA (OG 1048.6, ABV 5.2%)
Mature hops, citrus fruit nose with a balance of hops and malt in the mouth with a smooth, hoppy aftertaste.

Maldon

Stable Brewery, Silver Street, Maldon, Essex, CM9 4QE
☎ (01621) 851000 🌐 maldonbrewing.co.uk

Established in 2002, this family-run brewery is tucked away behind the 14th-century Blue Boar Hotel. The six-barrel plant is at full production serving more than 50 outlets including the brewery's micropub on the High Street. Also produces the Blackwater Brewhouse brand. ♦RAIB

Farmer's IPA (OG 1036, ABV 3.6%)
A crisp IPA based on an old Ridley's recipe.

A Drop of Nelson's Blood (OG 1038, ABV 3.8%)
An easy-drinking bitter. A tot of brandy is added to each cask.

The Hotel Porter (OG 1041, ABV 4.1%)
A classic stout with a smoky tang produced by a good amount of roast barley.

Pucks Folly (OG 1038, ABV 4.2%)
A pale golden-coloured ale with a spicy character and pineapple in the aroma and taste.

Farmer's Golden Boar (OG 1050, ABV 5%)
An amber-coloured ale with a hoppy aroma.

Dark Horse (OG 1064, ABV 6.6%)
A chestnut-coloured bitter, smooth but with spice in the finish.

Mallard

Unit A, Maythorne, Nottinghamshire, NG25 0RS
☎ 07811 193930 ✉ stevenhussey@tiscali.co.uk

Mallard is a 2.25-barrel brewery run by Steve Hussey and Alison Ryan, brewing for their own pub, the Cross Keys in Upton, and local outlets in and around the county. !! ♦RAIB

Duck 'n' Dive (OG 1039, ABV 3.7%)
A bitter, pale golden beer, with a dry finish.

Greet Ale (OG 1037, ABV 3.7%)
A copper-coloured traditional malty ale, pleasantly bitter on the palate.

Golden Duck (OG 1039, ABV 3.9%)
Golden-coloured bitter brewed with a combination of four hops.

Quacker Jack (OG 1040, ABV 4%)
Copper-coloured bitter with a well-balanced hop/malt bitterness.

Feather Light (OG 1040, ABV 4.1%)
A straw-coloured, lager-style beer with a hoppy taste and aroma.

Duckling (OG 1041, ABV 4.2%)
A dry-hopped golden ale. Very bitter; hops dominate in the aroma and aftertaste.

Specduckular (OG 1042, ABV 4.2%)
A refreshing golden ale full of fruity hops with a malty undertone.

Mallinsons

Unit 1, Waterhouse Mill, 65-71 Lockwood Road, Huddersfield, West Yorkshire, HD1 3QU
☎ (01484) 654301 ☎ 07850 446571
🌐 drinkmallinsons.co.uk

Mallinsons was originally set up in 2008 on a six-barrel plant by CAMRA members Tara Mallinson and Elaine Yendall. The company moved to new premises in 2012 with a 15-barrel plant and specialises in hop-forward and single hop beers. Its first tap house, the Corner, opened in Huddersfield in 2016. !! ♦ RAIB

Wappy Nick (OG 1038, ABV 3.8%)

Malt SIBA

Collings Hanger Farm, 100 Wycombe Road, Prestwood, Buckinghamshire, HP16 0HW
☎ (01494) 865063 🌐 maltthebrewery.co.uk

⊗ Family-owned brewery, founded in 2012 using a 10-barrel plant. Based on a dairy farm in the heart of the Chiltern Hills, it has sustainability built into its brewing with spent grains going to feed the pigs on the farm and spent hops being composted. The brewery tasting bar stocks bottled beers that are suitable for vegans alongside local ciders. In-house deliveries are made to trade and direct customers in six surrounding counties. National distribution is through leading distributors and wholesalers. !! ♦ RAIB

Moderation (ABV 3.4%)
A golden-coloured beer with a light, fruity flavour.

Missenden Pale (OG 1035, ABV 3.6%)
Light amber-coloured, hoppy session ale.

Golden Ale (OG 1038, ABV 3.9%)
Light and refreshing with a citrus finish.

Starry Nights (OG 1040, ABV 4%)
Light and fruity amber-coloured ale.

Voyager (OG 1048, ABV 5%)
Amber-coloured IPA with aromatic hop notes.

Malt Brewhouse (NEW)

166 Town Street, Horsforth, Leeds, West Yorkshire, LS18 4AQ
☎ (0113) 467 2001 🌐 themaltbrewhouse.co.uk

Established in 2019, this microbrewery also supplies the other bars in the pub group, Granvilles, Horsforth, and Parkside Tavern, Leeds.

Malt Coast

Branthill Farm, Wells-next-the-Sea, Norfolk, NR23 1SB ☎ 07881 378900 🌐 maltcoast.com

Brewing began in 2016. It grows its own barley on the farm. !!

Malvern Hills SIBA

15 West Malvern Road, Malvern, Worcestershire, WR14 4ND
☎ (01684) 560165 🌐 malvernhillsbrewery.co.uk

⊗ Founded in 1998 in an old quarrying dynamite store and an established presence in the Three Counties, Birmingham and the Black Country. Seasonal and special beers are directed more by ad-hoc requests from publicans rather than a planned brewery timetable apart from green-hopped beers in September. !! ♦

Beacon Gold (OG 1036, ABV 3.7%)
Pale-coloured golden ale, hoppy and full-flavoured with a good bitterness.

Feelgood (OG 1037, ABV 3.8%)
Golden-coloured beer with a floral spicy aroma and bitter notes.

Bertie's Best (OG 1040, ABV 4.2%)
Amber-coloured bitter with New World hops giving a flowery, spicy and citrus taste and a distinct orange bouquet.

Malvern Spring (OG 1040, ABV 4.2%)
Golden-coloured ale packed with soft caramel flavours leading to a sweet finish.

Priessnitz Plzen (OG 1040, ABV 4.3%)
Straw-coloured Pilsner-style cask lager having a mix of soft fruit and citrus. Well-balanced and light in colour with a resinous, aromatic finish.

Black Pear (OG 1042, ABV 4.4%)
Citrus hoppiness is the main constituent of this golden-coloured best bitter that has a long, dry aftertaste.

Manchester

66 North Western Street, Manchester, M12 6DX
☎ (0161) 273 6167 🌐 manchesterbrewing.co.uk

Brewing commenced in 2016. The eight-barrel brew plant is housed in a railway arch in the Ardwick district of Manchester. ♦

Factory Pale Ale (OG 1040, ABV 4%)
Dry, straw-coloured pale ale.

Some Might Say Session IPA (ABV 4.4%)

Elephant Juice NE Pale (OG 1045, ABV 4.5%)

Manchester Union (NEW)

96d North Western Street, Manchester, M12 6JL
🌐 manchesterunionbrewery.com

Manchester Union is a Czech-style lager brewery co-founded by former Six O'clock brewer Ian Johnson, using a decoction technique in the mash and German lager malts. The beers undergo several weeks conditioning in tanks. Beers are unfiltered and unpasteurised. The brewery tap is open every Saturday. V

Manning SIBA

Spindle Street, Congleton, Cheshire, CW12 1QN
☎ (01260) 299964 🌐 manningbrewers.co.uk

A family-owned and run brewery using only British hops, opened in 2015. It has now joined forces with the established Beartown Brewery (qv), also of Congleton.

Woah Man (ABV 3.8%)
A clean-drinking, golden-coloured session pale ale with a floral aroma.

Man Up! (ABV 4%)
A bronze-coloured malty session beer, lightly hopped allowing the sweetness of the malt to come through.

Cave-Man (ABV 4.2%)
A well-balanced bitter with a refreshing hop character. Light caramel in colour with a bitter, crisp finish, some blackberry aromas and a lasting gentle bitterness.

Mantle SIBA

Unit 16, Pentood Industrial Estate, Cardigan, SA43 3AG
☎ (01239) 623898 ☎ 07552 609909
🌐 mantlebrewery.com

From start-up in 2013 on a 10-barrel plant, Mantle has become a major player in the West Wales area. Engineer Ian Kimber and his scientist wife Dominique, formerly homebrewers, have built a sound reputation for consistent quality. More than 200 outlets are supplied direct with wider distribution via selected wholesalers. ‼ ⊵ ♦

Rock Steady (OG 1038, ABV 3.8%)
Golden-coloured session ale with great depth of flavour.

MOHO (OG 1041.5, ABV 4.3%) ⬚
Robust and aromatic Welsh pale ale with a full flavour.

Cwrw Teifi (OG 1045, ABV 4.5%)
A full-bodied, malt-driven best bitter with a well-balanced hop finish.

Dark Heart (OG 1052, ABV 5.2%)
Rich, dark-coloured and smooth porter with a hint of spice.

Many Hands (NEW)

Dunkeswell Airfield, Dunkeswell, Devon, EX14 4LF
⊕ manyhandsbrew.com

Many Hands Brew Co began brewing in 2017 producing small batch bottled beers. Each bottle sold gives a contribution to charity.

Marble SIBA

Unit 7, Boston Court, Salford, M50 2GN
⊕ marblebeers.com

Originally based at the Marble Arch pub in 1997, Marble Beers have recently moved to a new 15-barrel plant in Salford and opened a taproom (Thu-Sun) on site. Vegetarian beers are available in both its core and speciality ranges. It supplies its own two pubs and more than 70 other outlets. ♦

Table Beer (ABV 2.7%)

Pint (OG 1038.5, ABV 3.9%) ⬚ ◆
Fresh hop aroma of grapefruit. Clean citrus hop flavour with pale malt base. Dry bitter aftertaste and lasting hop.

Manchester Bitter (OG 1040.5, ABV 4.2%) ⬚ ◆
Peachy hop aroma. Balanced bitter hop and malt taste. Full fruity palate. Dry bitter finish.

Lagonda IPA (OG 1047, ABV 5%) ◆
Golden yellow-coloured beer with a spicy, fruity nose. Fruit, hops and malt in the mouth, with a dry fruitiness continuing into the bitter aftertaste.

Uppe Hela Natten (ABV 5.1%)
A porter with coffee and a dash of lactose. The Espresso coffee lends a subtle hit of sweet caramel and honeydew on the nose while adding a rich depth to the complex malt base.

Pale (ABV 5.4%) ◆
Bitter orange taste, lasting with dryness. Fruity aroma. Lingering dry bitter.

Earl Grey IPA (OG 1065, ABV 6.8%) ◆
Bold bitter bergamot flavour. Balanced and lasting hoppiness with a sweet taste.

Maregade

Arch 214, Ponsford Street, Homerton, London, E9 6JU
☎ 07833 765572 ⊕ maregade.com

Microbrewery originally based in the basement of the Cock Tavern in Hackney, it moved to its present address in 2017. Brews mainly keg beers but will provide cask-conditioned ale upon request. Brewing is currently suspended. ♦ V

Market Bosworth

Unit 10, Willow Farm Business Centre, Stoke Golding, Leicestershire, CV13 6EU
☎ (01455) 377855 ⊕ marketbosworthbrewery.co.uk

⊠ The brewery was set up by Jon Skinner in 2016 as a natural progression from his homebrew retail business. Rich Brine joined in partnership in 2017 and the kit was doubled in size to two barrels to meet demand. Its two main outlets are the Gate Hangs Well, Carlton, and the Horse & Hockey, Congerstone.

Stout (ABV 4.2%)
A stout with roasted notes.

Best Bitter (ABV 4.8%)
Dark copper in colour with a malty mouthfeel and a lingering bitter finish.

Porter (ABV 5%)

Pale Ale (ABV 5.2%)
A golden-coloured pale ale, hoppy and punchy with citrus aromas.

Marko Paulo

⊟ Owl & The Pussycat, 106 Northfield Avenue, Northfields, London, W13 9RT ⊕ markopaulo.co.uk

A 1.25-barrel brewpub opened in 2016 in a former bookshop by two ex-teachers. The beer travels about 20 feet from mash tun to glass. Cask-conditioned beers are complemented by a wide range of European-style keg beers. An additional four-barrel brewery is being set up in Brentford to increase capacity.

Marlpool

⊟ 5 Breach Road, Marlpool, Derbyshire, DE75 7NJ
☎ (01773) 711285 ☎ 07963 511855
⊕ marlpoolbrewing.co.uk

Marlpool was founded in 2010 by brothers Andy and Chris McAuley. The two-barrel brewery is situated behind the Marlpool Ale House. The brewery yard doubles up as a beer garden and the majority of the beer is sold through the Ale House and served unfined. The remainder is sold to reputable outlets. ‼ ♦ RAIB

Marston's

Shobnall Road, Burton upon Trent, Staffordshire, DE14 2BW
☎ (01283) 531131 ⊕ marstons.co.uk

☺Marston's has been brewing cask beer in Burton since 1834 and the current site is the home of the only working Burton Union fermenters, housed in rooms known as the Cathedral of Brewing. Burton Unions were developed in the 19th century to cleanse the new style of pale ale yeast. Only Pedigree is fermented in the unions but yeast from the system is used to ferment the other Marston's branded beers. In 2016 a 2.5-barrel nanobrewery was installed within the DE14 visitors centre. Beers from this nanobrewery are available

locally. Marston's continues to take contract brewing, and brews the iconic cask beer Draught Bass on behalf of AB Inbev. ‼ ♦ RAIB

EPA (OG 1036, ABV 3.6%)

61 Deep (OG 1038, ABV 3.8%) ◈
Light amber-coloured ale with intense tropical fruit aroma. Sweet tropical start with hints of spice. Hoppy bitterness overcomes the fruit and leaves a pleasant mouthfeel.

Saddle Tank (OG 1037, ABV 3.8%) ◈
Overwhelming sulphurous aroma supports a scattering of hops and fruit with an easy-drinking sweetness. The taste develops from the sweet middle to a satisfyingly hoppy finish.

Pedigree (OG 1043, ABV 4.5%) ◈
Pale brown in colour with a sweet, hoppy aroma. Malt with a dash of hop flavours give a satisfying tasty finish.

Old Empire (OG 1057, ABV 5.7%) ◈
Sulphur dominates the gentle malt aroma. Malty and sweet to start but developing bitterness with fruit and a touch of sweetness. A balanced aftertaste of hops and fruit leads to a lingering bitterness.

Brewed for AB InBev:

Draught Bass (OG 1043, ABV 4.4%) ◈
Hints of caramel aroma and taste, lightly hopped for a short bitter finish.

Martland Mill SIBA

Unit 5, Otterwood Square, Martland Mill, Wigan, WN5 0LF
☎ (01942) 665656 🌐 martlandmillbrewery.co.uk

Established in 2014, Martland Mill Brewery is a family-run business based just outside of Wigan town centre using a six-barrel plant. Beers are available throughout the North-west region, as well as at its brewery tap, the Tap 'n' Barrel, Wigan. ‼ ♦

Chonkin Feckle (OG 1038, ABV 3.8%)
A golden yellow-coloured ale with a citrus hop aroma, floral notes and a pine finish.

Spinner's Gold (OG 1038, ABV 3.8%)
An easy-drinking golden ale with a well-balanced hoppiness, pleasant citrus taste and a hint of spiciness.

Knocker Upper (OG 1040, ABV 3.9%)
Straw-coloured ale with a floral aroma, rich honey taste and hints of fruit.

Clogmaker (OG 1043, ABV 4%)
A rich, golden-coloured, full-bodied ale with a refreshing fruity flavour and an inkling of cedar and honey.

Lancashire Loom (OG 1046, ABV 4%)
A light golden ale bursting with a real fruit punch of grapefruit, lychees and lemon with a slight floral note.

D Day Dodger (OG 1046, ABV 4.1%) ◈
Brown in colour with a subtle malty aroma. Malt dominates throughout with hop notes. Initial sweetness gives way to a bitter, dry finish.

Wobbly Weaver (OG 1043, ABV 4.3%)
Quaffable golden ale with hints of citrus on the nose and an explosion of tropical fruits and blueberry flavours.

Bomber's Blonde (OG 1053, ABV 4.4%)
A pale blonde ale with an intense hoppy aroma and a crisp, refreshing citrus taste, leading to a slightly dry finish.

George 'n' Dragon (OG 1052, ABV 4.8%)
A smooth, full-bodied ale with honey flavours and a well-balanced pine hop aroma.

Marts

Marts Brewhouse & Tap, 66-68 Piccadilly, Hanley, Stoke-on-Trent, ST1 1HX ☎ 07709 110251

Brewing began in 2016 in a small unit. In 2018 Marts opened its first tap house with a five-barrel brew plant on the premises. Beers are available in the taphouse and at beer festivals.

Masquerade (NEW)

c/o 25 Mina Road, Bristol, BS2 9TA
✉ masqueradebrewing@gmail.com

Tom Hebden and Sam Hipwell of Masquerade Brewing met at university where they laid plans to produce full-on juicy beers, which they started doing in 2017 on a custom-built one-barrel plant in temporary premises. In 2018 the brewery moved and is now co-located at the Fierce & Noble Brewery (qv) in St Werburgh's.

Matlock Wolds Farm SIBA

South Barn, Cavendish Road, Farm Lane, Matlock, Derbyshire, DE4 3GZ
☎ (01629) 697989 ☎ 07852 263263
🌐 woldsfarm.co.uk

This family-run brewery started in 2014 and after several expansions now produces a full range of vegan-friendly ales on its five-barrel plant housed in a converted barn at the owners 17th-century farm. RAIB V

The Bitter End (OG 1030, ABV 3.4%)
Ruby-coloured ale with a rich, malty background. Earthy, grassy flavours from the hops with notes of chocolate, nuts and pine. A long, bitter finish.

Apogee (OG 1033, ABV 3.8%)
Amber-coloured ale with fruit and citrus aromas and a light bitterness. Orange peel and toasted coriander seeds are used to flavour.

Simcoe (OG 1033, ABV 3.8%)
Aromas of pine and apricot with earthy citrus flavours and hints of tropical fruit leading to a strong bitter finish.

High Tor (OG 1035, ABV 4%)
A pale ale made with a citrus flavour and aroma.

Riber Gold (OG 1038, ABV 4.3%)
Traditional golden ale with floral and apricot aromas, hints of tropical fruit and a complex finish.

100cc (OG 1042, ABV 4.9%)
Well-rounded, light chestnut-coloured ale with a malty aroma complemented by orange and pine. Huge citrus flavours with orange and lemon coming through and a good hop bitterness.

Classic Porter (OG 1042, ABV 4.9%)
Full-bodied, dark-coloured porter with a chocolate aroma and hint of vanilla. Full of roasted malt and coffee flavours with a lingering bitterness.

Mauldons SIBA

Black Adder Brewery, 13 Church Field Road, Sudbury, Suffolk, CO10 2YA
☎ (01787) 311055 🌐 mauldons.co.uk

The Mauldon family started brewing in Sudbury in 1795. The brewery with 26 pubs was bought by Greene King in the 1960s. The current business, established in 1982, was bought by Steve and Alison Sims in 2000. They relocated to a new brewery in 2005, with a 30-barrel plant that has doubled production. One pub is owned and around 200 outlets are supplied. !! ♦ RAIB

Micawber's Mild (OG 1035, ABV 3.5%)
Light, easy-drinking mild. Malty smoothness with a rich roast flavour turns into a caramel liquorice aftertaste.

Moletrap Bitter (OG 1038, ABV 3.8%)
Plum and toffee on the nose. A good balance of malt, hops and fruit, leading to an increasingly bitter aftertaste.

Christies Golden Ale (OG 1040, ABV 3.9%)
A light, golden-coloured, hoppy and refreshing beer.

Silver Adder (OG 1042, ABV 4.2%)
Lightly fruity aroma, dry hoppiness and citrus fruit with rich honey in the taste and a long, fruity, sweet aftertaste. Refreshing and well-balanced.

Blackberry Porter (OG 1048, ABV 4.8%)
A full-bodied, black-coloured porter with balanced hop aroma and a rich blend of chocolate and roast flavours, giving way to a subtle sweet fruit finish.

Suffolk Pride (OG 1048, ABV 4.8%)
A full-bodied, copper-coloured beer. A bubblegum nose leads to a spicy taste, with mild astringency in the aftertaste.

Black Adder (OG 1053, ABV 5.3%)
Malty, roasty aroma leads to a well-balanced, full-bodied beer. Malty with roast and dark soft fruit overtones.

Maule SIBA

Rothersthorpe Trading Estate, Northampton, NN4 8JH
🌐 maulebrewing.com

Brewing began in 2014 on a self-built plant. Production is mainly unfiltered keg and bottle-conditioned beers, but cask-conditioned ales are occasionally produced for festivals. The beers are available from various local stockists as well as featuring on the London craft beer scene. RAIB

Maxim SIBA

1 Gadwall Road, Rainton Bridge South, Houghton-le-Spring, DH4 5NL
☎ (0191) 584 8844 🌐 maximbrewery.co.uk

Rising from the ashes of Sunderland brewer Vaux, Maxim was set up with a 20-barrel plant in Houghton-le-Spring in 2007. More than 100 outlets are supplied direct and two pubs are owned. !! ♦

Lambtons (OG 1039, ABV 3.8%)
Smooth golden ale with citrus and hoppy flavours.

Samson (OG 1040, ABV 4%)
Traditional best bitter, chestnut brown in colour with caramel flavours and balanced bitter hops.

Ward's Best Bitter (OG 1040, ABV 4%)
A copper-coloured best bitter with a sweet, toasted biscuit flavour. Slightly hoppy, slightly fruity.

Swedish Blonde (OG 1042, ABV 4.2%)
A smooth, pale-coloured beer. Refreshingly hoppy with complex grapefruit flavours.

Double Maxim (OG 1048, ABV 4.7%)
A brown-coloured ale with a fruity, caramel, malty taste and a hint of sweetness. Well-balanced and smooth.

Raspberry Porter (OG 1050, ABV 5%)

Maximus (OG 1062, ABV 6%)
Ruby-coloured premium ale. Sweet with a liquorice, caramel and dark fruit flavours.

Mayflower SIBA

2 Woodford Street, Hindley, WN2 4UR ☎ 07703 816183 🌐 mayflowerbrewery.com

Originally established in Standish in 2001. The brewery was mothballed in 2018, but has now been re-established behind the old police station in Hindley, Wigan. It remains a five-barrel plant. ♦

Swinley Gold (ABV 3.6%)

Pie PA (ABV 3.9%)
A hoppy, pale-coloured session IPA.

Douglas Valley (ABV 4%)
A rich, pale-coloured, dry bitter.

Lancashire Stout (ABV 4%)
A traditional stout with a smooth, smoky finish.

Wigan Bier (ABV 4.2%)
A delicately-hopped beer, easy-drinking with an underlying sweetness.

Maypole

North Laithes Farm, Wellow Road, Eakring, Nottinghamshire, NG22 0AN ☎ 07971 277598
🌐 maypolebrewery.co.uk

The brewery opened in 1995 in a converted 18th-century farm building. After changing hands in 2001 it was bought by the former head brewer, Rob Neil, in 2005. ♦

Midge (OG 1035, ABV 3.5%)
Pale-coloured ale with a lasting bitter finish.

Monterey Hop (ABV 3.7%)
A pale ale packed with hops.

Little Weed (OG 1037, ABV 3.8%)
Deep golden in colour, subtle bitterness from a blend of hops.

Celebration (OG 1038, ABV 4%)
Amber-coloured traditional ale with slightly nutty overtones.

Gate Hopper (OG 1040, ABV 4%)
A golden ale with a floral aroma and lingering hoppy bitterness.

Hop Fusion (OG 1040, ABV 4.2%)

Major Oak (OG 1042, ABV 4.4%)
A well-balanced, full-bodied bitter with hints of fruit and burnt malt.

Wellow Gold (OG 1044, ABV 4.6%)
Refreshing blonde ale, citrus flavours on the nose and aftertaste.

Meantime

Lawrence Trading Estate, Blackwall Lane, East Greenwich, London, SE10 0AR
☎ (020) 8293 1111

Head Office: Norman House, 110-114 Norman Road, London, SE10 9EH 🌐 meantimebrewing.com

⊗ Founded in 2000, Meantime brews a wide range of continental-style beers. Two pubs are owned. In 2010 the brewery relocated to larger premises in Greenwich. Taken over by SABMiller in 2015 and now owned by Asahi UK. No real ale. !!

Meanwood

Stonegate Road, Meanwood, Leeds, West Yorkshire, LS6 4HZ 🌐 themeanwoodbrewery.com

The Meanwood Brewery was started by brothers Baz and Graeme Phillips in 2017 and focusses on brewing beer styles from around the world. The Terminus Tap Room & Bottle Shop opened in 2018. V

Herald (OG 1038, ABV 3.9%)

Black Goddess (OG 1049, ABV 4.9%)
A rich porter with flavours of biscuit, chocolate, caramel and liquorice.

Heroic (OG 1046, ABV 5%)
An English IPA with earthy, floral and honey hop flavours against a strong malt backbone, with a touch of caramel.

Shapeshifter (OG 1054, ABV 5.1%)
A steam beer with a bold malt body.

Mechanic (NEW)

22a Curdworth Street, Bethnal Green, London, E1 5QU
☎ 07410 910810 🌐 mechanicbrewery.co.uk

⊗ Brewing began in 2017, with the brewery moving to its current location, using a five-barrel plant, in 2018. The brewer, Olga, is orginally from Poland and likes to experiment with more adventurous beers. All beers are unflitered and unpasteurised. A brewery tap is open Friday to Sunday and several local outlets are supplied. RAIB

Melbourn

All Saints Brewery, All Saints Street, Stamford, Lincolnshire, PE9 2PA
☎ (01780) 752186

No real ale. A famous Stamford brewery that opened in 1825 and closed in 1974. It re-opened in 1994 and is owned by Samuel Smith of Tadcaster (qv). !!

Melwood SIBA

The Kennels, Knowsley Park, Merseyside, L34 4AQ
☎ (0151) 214 3340 ☎ 07545 265283
🌐 melwoodbeer.co.uk

Melwood began brewing in 2013 using a five-barrel plant in an old dairy. In 2016 the brewery moved to bigger premises in nearby old kennels on the Earl of Derby's Knowsley Estate. In 2019 it rebranded to add a small range of core beers, a series of modern beers, one-off specials and began experimenting with new styles and yeasts. ♦

Lovelight (OG 1038, ABV 3.8%)
Light, hoppy blonde beer with a big hop aroma and crisp, biting flavour.

Father Ted (ABV 4.2%)
A traditional English bitter with floral notes.

High Time (ABV 4.3%)
A hoppy, pale amber-coloured session ale.

Knowsley Blonde (OG 1043, ABV 4.3%)
Crisp, refreshing pale ale with a fresh, hoppy aroma and a pleasant bitter taste.

Moondance (ABV 4.3%)
A hoppy beer with wine-like flavours.

Stanley Gold (ABV 4.3%)
Triple-hopped beer with a crisp, hoppy flavour and citrus aroma. Well-balanced and refreshing.

Merchant City SIBA

Block 5, Unit 1, Oakbank Trading Estate, Glasgow, G20 7LU
☎ (0141) 258 1661

Office: Unit 10, Italian Centre, 168 Ingram Street, Glasgow, G1 1DN 🌐 merchantcitybrewing.com

Brewing began in 2017 using a 12-barrel plant. 25 outlets are supplied direct plus specialist off-licences across central Scotland. RAIB

Session Ale (OG 1040, ABV 3.9%)
A golden-coloured session beer with a biscuit malt flavour and light floral hop aroma.

Unit 1 Red Ale (OG 1040, ABV 4%)
An Irish-style red-coloured session beer with pronounced hop character, balanced with a caramel malt flavour and roasted grain aromas.

American Pale Ale (OG 1045, ABV 4.7%)
A pale ale with citrus aromas, refreshing bitterness and orange and lemon peel flavours from an infusion of tea.

Vienna Lager (OG 1049, ABV 5%)
A dark-coloured European-style lager with toasted malt flavours and hoppy aroma.

IPA (OG 1055, ABV 5.8%)
An IPA with a bold citrus character and a strong bitterness, balanced by a robust malt body.

Merlin SIBA

3 Spring Bank Farm, Congleton Road, Arclid, Cheshire, CW11 2UD
☎ (01477) 500893 ☎ 07812 352590
🌐 merlinbrewing.co.uk

Established in 2010 using an eight-barrel plant in a farm unit just outside Sandbach, the brewery is gently expanding now that daughter Sarah has joined the family firm. The beers are normally supplied to outlets within a 30-mile radius. Merlin is environmentally friendly, with power from solar panels and a wind turbine. Spent grain and hops are used on the farm. !! ♦ RAIB

Merlin's Gold (OG 1038, ABV 3.8%)
Light golden ale with rounded floral citrus flavours.

Excalibur (OG 1039, ABV 3.9%)
A light-coloured session ale. Bitter, hoppy flavours are accompanied by a faint sweetness.

Spellbound (OG 1040, ABV 4%)
A full-flavoured bitter, light chestnut in colour with a dry finish.

Avalon (OG 1041, ABV 4.1%)
A pale ale with grapefruit, lemon and spicy hop flavours.

The Wizard (OG 1042, ABV 4.2%)
A hoppy, bitter, golden-coloured ale with generous hints of grapefruit flavour.

Castle Black (OG 1044, ABV 4.4%)
Smooth, creamy stout with a hint of sweetness.

Dark Magic (OG 1048, ABV 4.8%)
A strong, full-bodied dark mild with a caramel aftertaste.

Dragonslayer (OG 1056, ABV 5.6%)
A dark-coloured brew with complex flavours.

Merrimen

See Litchborough Artisan

Mersea Island

Rewsalls Lane, East Mersea, Essex, CO5 8SX ☎ 07970 070399 🌐 merseabrewery.co.uk

⊗ The brewery was established at Mersea Island Vineyard in 2005. It supplies several local pubs on a guest beer basis as well as beer festivals. It holds its own festival of Essex-produced ales over the four-day Easter weekend. RAIB

Mersea Mud (OG 1036, ABV 3.8%)
An easy-drinking mild with a refreshing malty flavour.

Yo Boy! (OG 1038, ABV 3.8%)
A session bitter with a long-lasting bitterness on the finish.

Gold (OG 1043, ABV 4.4%)
A refreshing, golden-coloured, Pilsner-style ale.

Monkeys (OG 1044, ABV 4.4%)
Sweet, lightly smoky and lightly roasted aromas with smoky, fruity and herbal flavours.

Skippers (OG 1047, ABV 4.8%)
A dark amber-coloured best bitter with a good malty flavour and smooth hop bitterness.

Oyster Stout (OG 1048, ABV 5%)
A traditional oyster stout with local Mersea Island oysters.

Middle Earth

Rowditch Inn, 246 Uttoxeter New Road, Derby, DE22 3LL ☎ 07504 304564

Office: 53 Springfield Road, Etwall, DE65 6JZ 🌐 mebrewco.com

⊗ Middle Earth was set up utilising spare capacity at the Rowditch Inn, Derby. Operations are currently suspended but the brewer (Steve Twells) intends to resume as soon as personal circumstances permit.

Mighty Medicine

Unit 4, Daniel Street, Whitworth, Lancashire, OL12 8BX
☎ (01706) 558980 🌐 mightymedicine.com

Established in 2016 this brewery is committed to using the finest ingredients to produce an eclectic range of beers. A tap room is attached to the brewery.

Stunning Blonde (ABV 3.9%)
An easy-drinking, fruity blonde ale.

Greedy Boy (ABV 4%)

Madchester Cream (ABV 4.2%)
A creamy and smooth pale ale.

Magic Malt (ABV 4.5%)
A malty and hoppy red-coloured ale.

Mighty Oak

14b West Station Yard, Spital Road, Maldon, Essex, CM9 6TW
☎ (01621) 843713 🌐 mightyoakbrewing.co.uk

⊗ Mighty Oak was formed in 1996 and has expanded considerably following a move to Maldon in 2001. Current capacity is 8,000 barrels a year following the acquisition of two adjacent buildings and enlarged plant. Around 450 outlets are supplied. A popular free festive beer tasting day takes place each year in early December.
!! ♦

Oscar Wilde (OG 1039.5, ABV 3.7%)
Roasty dark mild with suggestions of forest fruits and dark chocolate. A sweet taste yields to a more bitter finish.

Captain Bob (OG 1039.5, ABV 3.8%)
A traditional deep amber-coloured bitter with a fruity and hoppy aroma. A slight sweet maltiness balances an easy going bitterness, followed by hints of gooseberry, elderflower and grape in the finish.

Maldon Gold (OG 1039.5, ABV 3.8%)
Pale golden ale with a sharp citrus note moderated by honey and biscuity malt.

Jake the Snake (OG 1041, ABV 4%)
Pale golden-coloured session ale with a subtle floral hop aroma and balanced maltiness.

Old Man and the Sea (OG 1045, ABV 4.1%)
Rich, black-coloured, creamy stout with flavours of espresso coffee, dark chocolate and a hint of dark fruit.

Kings (OG 1042.6, ABV 4.2%)
A deep golden-coloured beer bursting with hoppy fruitiness with orange, nectarine and passion fruit flavours lasting into the finish.

Mile Tree SIBA

29 Alfric Square, Woodston, Peterborough, Cambridgeshire, PE2 7JP ☎ 07858 930363
🌐 miletreebrewery.co.uk

⊗ Mile Tree was established in 2012 at the Secret Garden Touring Park in Wisbech, Cambridgeshire and moved to Peterborough in 2018. Beer is brewed on a five-barrel plant. It serves the local area and beer festivals. ♦RAIB

Meadowgold (ABV 3.8%)
A pale-coloured, hoppy ale.

Mosaica (ABV 4.2%)
A blonde, hoppy ale.

Larksong (ABV 4.5%)
An amber-coloured ale with tropical fruit flavours.

Wildwood (ABV 4.9%)
A spiced, brown-coloured ale.

Porter (ABV 5.2%)

A black-coloured, full-bodied and malty porter with a deep bittersweet finish.

Milestone SIBA

Great North Road, Cromwell, Nottinghamshire, NG23 6JE
☎ (01636) 822255 🌐 milestonebrewery.co.uk

Established in 2005, Milestone currently brews on a 12-barrel plant. More than 150 outlets are supplied. ‼ ♦ RAIB

Liberty Ale (OG 1037, ABV 3.7%)
A hoppy, straw-coloured session ale.

Lion Bitter (OG 1038, ABV 3.8%)
A copper-coloured session ale.

Sherwood Pale Ale (OG 1039, ABV 3.9%)

Classic Dark Mild (OG 1040, ABV 4%)

Shine On (OG 1039, ABV 4%)
A straw-coloured session ale with floral and citrus notes.

Azacca Gold (OG 1042, ABV 4.2%)

Loxley Ale (OG 1042, ABV 4.2%)
A golden-coloured ale with a subtle hint of honey.

Black Pearl (OG 1043, ABV 4.3%)
A traditional Irish-style stout.

Cromwell Best (OG 1044, ABV 4.4%)
An amber-coloured traditional bitter.

Crusader (OG 1044, ABV 4.4%)
Belgian-style blonde ale with a zesty, clean finish.

Rich Ruby (OG 1044, ABV 4.5%)
Rich, smooth and creamy red-coloured ale.

Olde English (OG 1049, ABV 4.9%)
Full-bodied winter warmer with a pleasing nutty finish.

Raspberry Wheat Beer (OG 1055, ABV 5.6%)
Continental-style ale infused with fresh fruit.

Milk Street

See Frome

Mill Valley

The Brewhouse, 589 Halifax Road, Hightown, West Yorkshire, WF15 8HQ ☎ 07565 229560
🌐 millvalleybrewery.co.uk

Launched in 2016 on a three-barrel plant in Cleckheaton, the brewery relocated to Liversedge in 2019, taking over the former Partners brewery site together with its 12-barrel plant. More than 40 outlets are supplied as well as numerous beer festivals. Two brewery taps are owned, one at both the new and old brewery sites, which hold regular events. ‼ ♦ V

Luddite Ale (ABV 3.8%)
Amber-coloured session ale with a smooth body and sweet finish.

Panther Ale (ABV 4%)
A session beer, crisp and refreshing with mellow tropical fruit flavours.

Yorkshire Bitter (ABV 4%)
Traditional bitter, chestnut in colour with a sweet caramel and toffee flavour.

Mill Blonde (ABV 4.2%)
A blonde ale with a fruity and light spice finish.

Yorkshire Rose (ABV 4.2%)
An American-style, hoppy pale ale with a bitter taste and grapefruit and citrus finish with floral notes.

Black Panther (ABV 4.6%)
Stout with a light vanilla and liquorice malt flavour and berry and light spice notes.

XTRA Fudge Stout (ABV 4.6%)
Smooth, rich stout with chocolate brownie flavours and a lightly roasted hint to balance out the sweetness.

Millis

See Dartford Wobbler

Mills

c/o Salutation Inn, Ham, Gloucestershire, GL13 9QH
☎ 07848 922558

Office: Jumpers Lane Yard, Berkeley, Gloucestershire, GL13 9BW ✉ millsbrewing@gmail.com

Mills was established in Berkeley in 2016 by Genevieve Kaye and Jonny Mills. Wort is produced in multiple locations, which is then fermented in wooden vessels at its premises in Berkeley using 100% wild yeasts and bacteria from the local surroundings. The Lambic-style beers are mostly available in bottles (bottle conditioned). RAIB

Millstone SIBA

Unit 4, Vale Mill, Micklehurst Road, Mossley, Lancashire, OL5 9JL
☎ (01457) 835835 🌐 millstonebrewery.co.uk

Established in 2003 by Nick Boughton and Jon Hunt, the brewery is located in an 18th-century textile mill and uses an eight-barrel plant. More than 30 regular outlets are supplied. ♦

Vale Mill (OG 1039, ABV 3.9%)
A pale gold-coloured session bitter with a floral and spicy aroma building upon a crisp and refreshing taste.

Three Shires Bitter (OG 1040, ABV 4%)
Yellow-coloured beer with a hop and fruit aroma. Fresh citrus fruit, hops and bitterness in the taste and aftertaste.

Tiger Rut (OG 1040, ABV 4%)
A pale-coloured, hoppy ale with a distinctive citrus/grapefruit aroma.

Stout (OG 1045, ABV 4.5%)
A traditional dry stout; pale chocolate malt, roasted barley and hint of sweetness to the aroma.

Rising Sunsation (OG 1047, ABV 4.7%)
A pale-coloured, dry bitter with hints of pine.

True Grit (OG 1050, ABV 5%)
A well-hopped strong ale with a mellow bitterness and a citrus/grapefruit aroma.

Milltown SIBA

The Brewery, The Old Railway Goods Yard, Scar Lane, Milnsbridge, West Yorkshire, HD3 4PE ☎ 07946 589645 🌐 milltownbrewing.co.uk

⊚Milltown began brewing in 2011 using a four-barrel plant. Two pubs are owned, the Dusty Miller at Longwood, which acts as the official brewery tap, and the Traveller's Rest, Meltham. ‼◆RAIB

Spud's (OG 1038, ABV 3.8%)
A pale-coloured, citrus, hoppy session bitter.

American Pale Ale (ABV 3.9%)
A light and hoppy pale ale.

Platinum Blonde (OG 1039, ABV 4%)
A refreshingly spicy blonde ale with floral notes.

Tiger's Tail (OG 1042, ABV 4.1%)
A session IPA with fruity citrus notes.

Black Jack Porter (OG 1049, ABV 4.5%)
A dark-coloured, velvety and chocolaty porter.

Weaver's Bitter (OG 1040, ABV 4.5%)
An amber-coloured traditional bitter.

Milton SIBA

Pegasus House, Pembroke Avenue, Waterbeach, Cambridgeshire, CB25 9PY
☎ (01223) 862067 ⊕ miltonbrewery.co.uk

⊠ The brewery has grown steadily since it was founded in 1999, moving to larger premises in the village of Waterbeach in 2012. It now operates three pubs in Cambridge through a sister company. In 2016 a separate brand, Beach Brewery, was created to market unpasteurised and unfiltered keg beers. ‼

Minotaur (OG 1035, ABV 3.3%) ◆
A dark ruby mild with liquorice and raisin fruit throughout. Light dry finish.

Dionysus (OG 1037, ABV 3.6%) ◆
Yellow-coloured bitter with a good balance of biscuity malt and citrus hop. Some malt and hops linger on the long, dry aftertaste.

Justinian (OG 1039, ABV 3.9%) ◆
Straw-coloured bitter with pink grapefruit hop character and light malt softness. Very dry finish.

Pegasus (OG 1043, ABV 4.1%) ◆
Malty, amber-coloured, medium-bodied bitter with faint hops. Bittersweet aftertaste.

Sparta (OG 1043, ABV 4.3%) 🍷 ◆
A yellow/gold-coloured best bitter with floral hops, kiwi fruit and balancing malt softness, which fades to leave long, dry finish.

Medusa (OG 1047, ABV 4.6%) 🍷

Minerva (OG 1046, ABV 4.6%)
A powerfully-hopped ale with a satisfying bitterness.

Nero (OG 1050, ABV 5%) 🍷 ◆
A complex black-coloured beer comprising a blend of milk chocolate, raisins and liquorice. Roast malt and fruit completes the experience.

Cyclops (OG 1055, ABV 5.3%)
Deep copper-coloured ale with a rich, hoppy aroma and full body; fruit and malt notes develop in the finish.

Marcus Aurelius (OG 1075, ABV 7.5%) ◆
A powerful black-coloured brew brimming with raisins and liquorice. Big balanced finish.

Missing Link

The Old Dairy, Chiddinglye Farm, West Hoathly, West Sussex, RH19 4QS ⊕ missinglinkbrewing.com

Missing Link was established in 2017 by Jeremy Cook using a five-barrel plant. No real ale.

Mission:Creep

See Team Toxic

Mitchell's Hop House

352-354 Meadowhead, Sheffield, South Yorkshire, S8 7UJ
☎ (0114) 274 5587 ⊕ mitchellswine.co.uk

Brewing began in 2016 in a converted space at the back of Mitchell's Wine Merchants. Beers are available from the brewery shop and a growing number of local pubs and beer retailers. All production is now bottled.

Mithril

Aldbrough St John, North Yorkshire, DL11 7TL
☎ (01325) 374817 ☎ 07889 167128
⊕ mithrilales.co.uk

⊚Mithril started brewing in 2010 in old stables opposite the brewer's house on a 2.5-barrel plant. Owner/brewer Pete Fenwick, a well-known craft brewer, brews twice a week to supply the local area of Darlington and Richmond. A new beer is brewed every week. ◆

Dere Street (OG 1039, ABV 3.8%)
Amber-coloured bitter with a fruity, malty sweetness and a smooth, hoppy finish.

Flower Power (OG 1040, ABV 3.9%)
A pale ale with a massive citrus, fruity hop flavour. Hints of grapefruit and floral on the tongue from the late addition of elderflower.

A66 (OG 1041, ABV 4%)
A crisp, refreshing, golden-coloured beer with a dry bitterness and lingering citrus and spicy hop taste and aroma.

Black Elf (ABV 4.4%)

Mix

3 Cemmaes Court Road, Hemel Hempstead, Hertfordshire, HP1 1ST ⊕ mixbrewery.co.uk

⊠ A small brewery established in 2013 and based in a domestic garage. Beer is produced in small batches allowing for an ever-changing range.

Mobberley SIBA

Unit 2, Barncroft Farm, Woodend Lane, Mobberley, Cheshire, WA16 7LZ
☎ (01565) 873601 ☎ 07879 771209
⊕ mobberleybrewhouse.co.uk

⊠ Mobberley began brewing in 2011 in an old milking parlour on a working farm in the heart of the Cheshire countryside. Expansion is planned. ◆

HedgeHopper (OG 1039, ABV 3.8%)
A golden-coloured, refreshing ale, light and aromatic.

RoadRunner (OG 1039, ABV 3.8%)

A pale ale with a delicate, lightly spicy finish and a sweet hop aroma.

Mandalay (OG 1040, ABV 4%)

Maori (OG 1040, ABV 4%)
A fresh, clean and fruity pale ale.

WhirlyBird (OG 1040, ABV 4%)
A sweet yet full-bodied pale ale with a smooth, subtle, zesty finish.

Red Vienna (ABV 4.2%)

Legacy (ABV 4.4%)
A zesty pale ale.

1924 (ABV 4.5%)
An amber-coloured, powerful and fruity ale.

Solstice (ABV 4.5%)

Elysium (ABV 4.7%)
A pale, well-balanced and fruity session IPA.

Origin (ABV 4.7%)

Contract Brewed for Burton Road Brewing Co:

Mosaic Pale (ABV 4.2%)

Pale Ale (ABV 4.8%)

Moles

See Wickwar

Molson Coors

Molson Coors (Burton): 137 High Street, Burton upon Trent, Staffordshire, DE14 1JZ
☎ (01283) 511000

Molson Coors (Tadcaster): Tower Brewery, Wetherby Road, Tadcaster, LS24 9SD
⊕ molsoncoorsbrewers.com

Molson Coors is the result of a merger between Molson of Canada and Coors of Colorado, US. Coors established itself in Europe in 2002 by buying part of the former Bass brewing empire, when Interbrew (now AB InBev) was instructed by the British government to divest itself of some of its interests in Bass. Coors owns several cask ale brands. It brews 110,000 barrels of cask beer a year (under licensing arrangements with other brewers) and also provides a further 50,000 barrels of cask beer for other breweries. In 2011 Molson Coors bought Sharp's brewery in Cornwall (qv) in a bid to increase its stake in the cask beer sector. No cask ale is produced in Burton or Tadcaster.

Moncada SIBA

37 Humber Road, Dollis Hill, London, NW2 6EN
☎ (020) 8964 0829 ⊕ moncadabrewery.co.uk

⊠ Established in 2011, Moncada was originially based in Kensal Town, but moved in 2018. The larger premises includes a taproom and bigger brew plant. ♦ RAIB

Notting Hill Bitter (ABV 3.7%) ◆
A fruity, biscuity sweet beer with a gentle lingering bitterness and spicy hops. Aroma is of biscuit and fruit.

Notting Hill Blonde (ABV 4.2%) ◆
Continental-style, golden-coloured beer with a smooth mouthfeel, sweetish with a touch of honey and fruity hops. Short, crisp finish.

Notting Hill Pale (ABV 4.5%) ◆
Unfined yellow-coloured beer with sweet biscuit, grapefruit and earthy hops on the palate fading slowly in the spicy, dry finish.

Notting Hill Amber (ABV 4.7%) ◆
Full-bodied, creamy, amber-coloured beer with a citrus peel aroma and flavour, well-balanced by the sweet biscuit character.

Notting Hill Porter (ABV 5%)

Notting Hill Stout (ABV 5%) ◆
A dry, malty beer with roast, caramel and a little malty sweetness. The pleasant aftertaste is long and lingering.

Notting Hill Ruby Rye (ABV 5.2%) ◆
Sweetish ruby red-coloured beer with a full, fruity aroma, a creamy mouthfeel and a little roast throughout.

Mondo

86-92 Stewarts Road, South Lambeth, London, SW8 4UG
☎ (020) 7720 0782 ☎ 07453 312170
⊕ mondobrewingcompany.com

⊠ Mondo began brewing in 2015. An on-site taproom (open Wed-Sun) showcases its wide range of beer styles. A cask collaboration in 2019 renewed enthusiasm for real ale with some of the main range possibly being produced in this format. ‼♦

Monty's

Unit 1, Castle Works, Hendomen, SY15 6HA
☎ (01686) 668933 ⊕ montysbrewery.co.uk

Monty's began brewing in 2009. It leases one pub, the Sportsman in Newtown, through its sister company, Hophouse Inns. The Cottage Inn in Montgomery is owned and acts as the brewery's visitor centre. It also houses a 250-litre plant producing small runs of experimental beers. ♦ RAIB GF

Old Jailhouse (OG 1039.5, ABV 3.9%)
Copper-coloured bitter with a good blend of malt and hops.

Best Offa (OG 1040, ABV 4%)
A golden-coloured, toasty bitter.

Moonrise (OG 1040, ABV 4%)
A copper-coloured, gently malty, well-balanced traditional brew.

MPA (OG 1040.5, ABV 4%)
Pale ale with a good bitter character.

Sunshine (OG 1041, ABV 4.2%) 🍺
A golden-coloured, hoppy, floral/citrus ale with a pleasantly dry finish.

Masquerade (OG 1046, ABV 4.6%)
A premium golden-coloured bitter with tropical fruit flavours and hoppy aroma.

Mischief (OG 1050, ABV 5%)
Strong golden ale with a good balance of malt and hop bitterness

Eastbound (OG 1073, ABV 7.3%)
A strong IPA with hoppy bitterness and aroma.

Moody Fox

Hilcote Country Club, Hilcote Lane, Hilcote, Derbyshire, DE55 5HR ☎ 07702 253235
✉ moodyfoxbrewery@gmail.com

Established in 2016, Moody Fox is a microbrewery specialising in traditional ales using the finest hops and barley from around the world. One micropub is owned, the Garrison, Mansfield.

Cub (ABV 3.8%)
Smooth session bitter with a slightly dry finish.

Vixon (ABV 4.5%)
A fruity, full-flavoured ale.

Blinder (ABV 5.4%)
A hoppy, citrus IPA.

Black Dog (ABV 5.5%)
A full-bodied porter with hints of chocolate and coffee.

Moody Goose

King William IV, 114 London Road, Braintree, Essex, CM77 7PU
☎ (01376) 567755 🌐 moodygoosebrewery.co.uk

A three-barrel brewery, brewing approximately 15 times a year. The beers are currently only available in the King William IV, where the brewery is located, and select beer festivals.

moogBREW

Meads End, Ye Meads, Taplow, SL6 0DH ☎ 07941 241954 🌐 moogbrew.co.uk

⊗ The brewery was set up in 2016 and moved to new premises in 2019. The majority of the output is bottle-conditioned. The focus of this tiny brewery is serving the local community and distribution is targeted to within a 10-mile radius. !! ♦ RAIB

Moon Gazer SIBA

Moon Gazer Barn, Harvest Lane, Hindringham, Norfolk, NR21 0PW
☎ (01328) 878495 🌐 moongazerale.co.uk

⊗ Brewing began in 2012 using a 10-barrel plant. The brewery is owned and run by Rachel and David Holliday. Chalk-filtered water is used from the brewery's own well. !! ♦

Jumper (OG 1040, ABV 3.9%) ◆
Smooth and easy drinking with a sweet malty intro. Full-bodied with a growing hoppy bitterness.

Jigfoot (OG 1040, ABV 4%) ◆
Orange peel and honey nose. Marmalade intro bolstered by well-defined bitterness. Initial sweetness fades into a sharp, astringent bitterness.

Nibbler (OG 1040, ABV 4%) ◆
Roasty dark fruit nose flows through into the first taste. Increasing malt and caramel. Smooth grainy mouthfeel. Short bitter finish.

Bouchart (OG 1051, ABV 4.9%) ◆
Savoury smoky bacon character throughout. Bittersweet dark chocolate nuances give depth. A smooth and creamy finish with hints of blackcurrant.

White Face (OG 1050, ABV 5%) ◆
Full-bodied with a rich tropical fruit aroma. Oranges in the taste, mixing well with a piquant hoppy bitterness.

Moonchild

18 The Village, Petrockstow, Devon, EX20 3HL
☎ 07773 367155

Moonchild was established in 2016 by Fred and Sophie Caure. All beers are unfined, unfiltered and unpasteurised and are only available in bottle-conditioned format. ♦ RAIB

Moonshine

Hill Farm, Shelford Road, Fulbourn, Cambridgeshire, CB21 5EQ ☎ 07906 066794

Office: 28 Radegund Road, Cambridge, CB1 3RS
🌐 moonshinebrewery.co.uk

⊗ Established in 2004, the brewery produces up to 20 barrels a week. Locally-produced ingredients are used including water from the brewery's own well and barley grown on the farm where the brewery is based. CAMRA beer festivals are supplied throughout the country, with 30 local outlets supplied direct. ♦ RAIB

Sundowner (OG 1036, ABV 3.6%)
Light amber-coloured session beer with balanced malt and a rounded hop finish.

Trumpington Tipple (OG 1036, ABV 3.6%)
Deep amber-coloured ale with malt flavours and a fragrant hop aroma.

Cambridge Pale Ale (OG 1038, ABV 3.8%)
Golden-coloured beer, light with a dry, citrus finish.

Shelford Crier (OG 1038, ABV 3.8%)
A light-bodied, amber-coloured beer with a citrus fruit aroma and taste that continues through to a refreshing clean and dry finish.

Spiritual Matter (OG 1037, ABV 3.8%)
A light and hoppy, straw-coloured beer.

Harvest Moon Mild (OG 1040, ABV 3.9%)
A well-balanced dark mild. Slightly sweet with smooth fruit notes combining with coffee and chocolate flavours.

Heavenly Matter (OG 1041, ABV 4.1%)
A huge, hoppy, citrus, straw-coloured beer. Tropical fruit notes with a generous bitter finish.

Cambridge Best Bitter (OG 1041, ABV 4.2%)
A copper-coloured best bitter; the malt and hop aromas carry through to the taste. The finish is rounded with a growing hop bitterness.

Nightwatch Porter (OG 1043, ABV 4.5%)
A well-rounded, sweet-starting and dry-finishing porter brewed with locally produced honey.

Raspberry Porter (OG 1043, ABV 4.5%)
A mellow, fruity porter.

Black Hole Stout (OG 1048, ABV 5%)
Full-bodied stout with a complex malt profile. The roasted flavours are rich, smooth and long-lasting.

Hot Numbers Coffee Stout (OG 1057, ABV 5.5%)
Dark roasted coffee milk stout with balanced coffee and hops.

Chocolate Orange Stout (OG 1068, ABV 6.7%)
A full-bodied, soft stout loaded with chocolate and coffee flavours. A good hop balance with a hint of orange on the nose.

Moonstone

☰ Ministry of Ale, 9 Trafalgar Street, Burnley, Lancashire, BB11 1TQ
☎ (01282) 830909 ⊕ moonstonebrewery.co.uk

⊛A small, three-barrel brewery, based in the front room of the Ministry of Ale pub. Brewing started in 2001 and beer is only available in the pub. ‼

Moor SIBA

Days Road, Bristol, BS2 0QS
☎ (0117) 941 4460 ⊕ moorbeer.co.uk

⊗ Starting out in Somerset in 1996, Moor is an established part of the Bristol beer scene. It also exports throughout the UK and around the world. The central Bristol brewery features a brewery tap and a shop, while there is also a Moor London Vaults in Bermondsey, which doubles as a tap room and facility for ageing beers. All beers are unfined and naturally hazy. Moor's canned beers were the first in the UK to be recognised as real ale by CAMRA. ‼ ⛟ ◆ RAIB V

All-Dayer (ABV 3.5%)
A session IPA with pronounced bitterness.

Revival (OG 1038, ABV 3.8%) ◆
Cloudy orange in colour with a peachy aroma, flavours of slightly resinous hops and a gentle bitterness in the short finish.

Lager (ABV 4%)
Unfined and unfiltered, clean and refreshing lager-style beer.

Nor'Hop (OG 1041, ABV 4.1%) □ ■ ◆
Golden yellow-coloured beer with spicy hops on the nose. Citrus flavours of grapefruit and lemon, short bitter aftertaste.

So'Hop (OG 1041, ABV 4.1%) ◆
Straw yellow-coloured beer with hop forward nose, hints of tropical fruit within powerful hop flavours, and long bitter finish.

Union Hop (ABV 4.1%)
A pale ale, zingy, citrus and refreshing with some sweet malt to balance.

Raw (OG 1043, ABV 4.3%) ◆
Amber-coloured best bitter with a pineapple aroma. Hoppy bitterness on the tongue balanced with malty sweetness leads to a subtle bitter finish.

Amoor (OG 1045, ABV 4.5%) ◆
Roasted malt and coffee aroma and taste adds chocolate and vanilla impressions before a smooth and almost spicy finish.

Claudia (ABV 4.5%)
Hoppy wheat beer. Flavours of banana, lemon and cloves together with a herbal and citrus hop character.

Dark Alliance (OG 1045, ABV 4.5%)
A hoppy coffee stout.

Illusion (OG 1045, ABV 4.5%) ◆
Black IPA with roast aroma, flavours of rich dark malt overlaid with hoppy bitterness, which lingers in the dry aftertaste.

Confidence (OG 1046, ABV 4.6%) ◆
A red-coloured ale with a spicy, peppery flavour. A rustic quality to its taste, with a sweetness given by hints of stone fruit. Pleasant short bitter finish.

Ported Amoor (OG 1047, ABV 4.7%)
Amoor with added reserve port.

Radiance (OG 1048, ABV 5%) ◆
Golden ale with floral aromas of citrus fruit and blossom. Grapefruit palate with an initial tanginess, becoming more sweet. The grapefruit is present in the pleasant, lingering aftertaste.

Smokey Horyzon (OG 1050, ABV 5%) ◆
A speciality beer made using smoked rye. Hoppy, pale brown-coloured strong ale with plenty of body, balanced by sweetness of unfermented rich dry rye malt and very smoky.

Stout (OG 1050, ABV 5%) ◆
A classic black-coloured stout. Smoky roast malt and dark fruit aroma with hints of vanilla. Prunes and liquorice notes follow into the taste. Pleasant dark chocolate aftertaste.

Do It Together (ABV 5.2%) ◆
Pronounced hoppy tropical fruit aroma. Flavours of sweet mango with a tart hop bitterness, which lingers in the prolonged finish.

Pils (ABV 5.2%)
A crisp, dry, full-flavoured, Pilsner-style lager with a traditional herbal flavour and citrus notes.

PMA (ABV 5.3%) ◆
Aroma and flavours are both well-balanced with biscuity malt, hops and tropical fruit before a short, bittersweet ending.

Return of the Empire (OG 1057, ABV 5.7%)
Modern English IPA. Light caramel honey malt with honeydew melon, citrus, apricot and peach flavours.

B-Moor (OG 1060, ABV 6%) ◆
Aromas of roasted malt and fruit, bitter chocolate and rich, dark fruit on the palate, with a dry bitter aftertaste.

Hoppiness (OG 1065, ABV 6.5%) ◆
Hop-forward nose with hints of honey. Full-bodied with tropical fruit flavours and bitterness, which increases into the finish.

Old Freddy Walker (OG 1073, ABV 7.3%) ■ ◆
Roasted malt and dark fruit aromas, flavours balance roasted malt with liquorice treacle and blackberry before a slightly dry finish.

Moorhouse's SIBA

The Brewery, Moorhouse Street, Burnley, Lancashire, BB11 5EN
☎ (01282) 422864 ⊕ moorhouses.co.uk

Established in 1865 as a soft drinks manufacturer, the brewery started producing cask-conditioned ale in 1978. A new brewhouse and visitor centre opened in 2012. Three pubs are owned. ‼◆

Black Cat (OG 1036, ABV 3.4%) ◆
A dark mild-style beer with delicate chocolate and coffee roast flavours and a crisp, bitter finish.

Premier Bitter (OG 1036, ABV 3.7%) ◆
A clean and satisfying bitter aftertaste rounds off this well-balanced, hoppy, amber-coloured session bitter.

White Witch (OG 1039, ABV 4%) ◆
Delicate citrus aroma. Sweet, fruity taste balanced with gentle bitterness. Increased bitterness in crisp citrus finish.

Pride of Pendle (OG 1040, ABV 4.1%) ◆
Well-balanced, amber-coloured best bitter with a fresh initial hoppiness and a mellow, malt-driven body.

Scaredy Cat (OG 1043, ABV 4.3%)

Blond Witch (OG 1045, ABV 4.5%) ◆
Pronounced sweet taste with gentle pithy bitterness and touch of citrus fruit. Dry finish. Slight fruity hop aroma.

Pendle Witches Brew (OG 1050, ABV 5.1%) ◆
Well-balanced, full-bodied, malty beer with a long, complex finish.

Moot Oak (NEW)

c/o Red Lion Inn, Matlock Green, Matlock, Derbyshire, DE4 3BT
☎ (01629) 584888 redlionmatlock.co.uk

Established in 2018, Moot Oak brewery is named after the original name for Matlock, which dates back to the medieval period. Beers are available in the pub and other local outlets.

MòR

Old Mill, Kellas, DD5 3PD ☎ 07884 346351
morbrewing.co.uk

Retired lifeboat coxswain Jim Hughan teamed up with family friend Ross Niven to establish the 2.5-barrel brewery in 2012. Just over a year later it expanded to a 4.5-barrel plant. In 2016 Matt Forrest joined the business as a co-director following Ross' retirement. !! ◆ RAIB

Tea Vicar? (OG 1038, ABV 3.8%)
A pale amber-coloured bitter with a pleasant balance of malt and hops, a malty, fruity aroma and a pronounced bitter finish.

Ish! (OG 1042, ABV 4.2%)
A bright amber-coloured ale with a malty, fruity aroma and a well-balanced and controlled bitter finish.

Please! (OG 1045, ABV 4.5%)
A clean-tasting, full-bodied, golden-coloured session bitter; bursting with malt and hops with a hint of honey and a good hoppy finish.

Morland

See Greene King

Morton

Unit 10, Essington Light Industrial Estate, Essington, Staffordshire, WV11 2BH ☎ 07988 69647

Office: 96 Brewood Road, Coven, WV9 5EF
mortonbrewery.co.uk

This family-run brewery was established in 2006 on a three-barrel, purpose-built plant. Beers are supplied locally, further afield by reciprocal arrangements, to various beer festivals and a selection is always available at the brewery's own micropub, Hail to the Ale. !! ◆

Essington Dark Mild (OG 1036, ABV 3.6%)

Essington Bitter (OG 1037, ABV 3.8%)
Fruity, hoppy session ale.

Merry Mount (OG 1037, ABV 3.8%)

Essington Blonde (OG 1039, ABV 4%)

Essington Ale (OG 1041, ABV 4.2%)

Jelly Roll (OG 1041, ABV 4.2%)

Essington Gold (OG 1044, ABV 4.4%)

Essington Supreme (OG 1046, ABV 4.6%)
A dark-coloured and sweet premium ale.

Scottish Maiden (OG 1045, ABV 4.6%)

Essington IPA (OG 1046, ABV 4.8%) ◆
Yellow in colour with lots of hop and fruit aromas. A good mouthful of bitterness with hops and fruit jostling for taste. Great lingering bitter finish.

Morton Collins

Star, Standbridge Lane, Sandal, Wakefield, West Yorkshire, WF2 7DY
☎ (01226) 728746 ☎ 07812 111960

Office: 49 Willow Garth, Durkar, Wakefield, West Yorkshire, WF4 3BX ged.morton@aol.com

Set up in 2016 by Ged Morton and Sam Collins using a 100-litre plant in Ged's garage. The brewery produces to demand but can brew every day if required. It took over the lease of the Star, Sandal, in 2016. Several of the beers are named after the nearby Nature Reserve at Wintersett. The brewery kit was upgraded to 200 litres per brew in 2017.

Magna (OG 1040, ABV 4%)

Star Bitter (OG 1040, ABV 4%)

Amber No. 9 (OG 1048, ABV 4.8%)

Stanley's Delight (OG 1048, ABV 4.8%)

Morwell

Morwellham Quay, Morwellham, Devon, PL19 8JL
☎ (01822) 832766 morwellham.org

Established in 2017 at Victorian tourist attraction Morwellham Quay, near Tavistock, by brewer George Lister. Using a 100-litre plant, three bottle-conditioned beers are brewed, which are available in the on-site shop and the Ship Inn, the on-site café, and a growing number of local outlets. RAIB

Moseley

14 Cleveland Court, St Agnes Road, Moseley, B13 9PR
moseleybeercompany.co.uk

Moseley Beer Company began brewing in 2016, set up by a family of four brothers.

Sightseer Wheat Beer (ABV 4.5%)
A bright, hoppy and refreshing beer with a citrus aftertaste.

Pale Ale (ABV 5%)

Marianna Porter (ABV 8%)
A dark and roasty porter with a sweet honey kick, based on a Victorian recipe.

Iron Man Stout (ABV 9%)

Mote & Bailey (NEW)

Blue Bell Inn, 10 High Street, Annan, DG12 6AG

Brewing began in 2018 in the cellar of the Blue Bell Inn, Annan, using equipment from Andrews Ales. Brewing capacity is one barrel. The range varies and is only available at the pub. ◆

THE BREWERIES

Moulin

2 Baledmund Road, Moulin, PH16 5EL
☎ (01796) 472196

Office: Moulin Hotel, 11-13 Kirkmicheal RoadMoulin, Pitlochry, PH16 5EH moulinhotel.co.uk

The brewery opened in 1995 to celebrate the Moulin Hotel's 300th anniversary. Two pubs are owned and four outlets are supplied. **!! RAIB**

Mount St Bernard SIBA

Mount St Bernard Abbey, Oaks Road, Charley, Coalville, Leicestershire, LE67 5UL
☎ (01530) 832298
brewery@mountsaintbernard.org

Monks at this Cistercian abbey launched a beer in 2017, the first monastic beer brewed in England since the Reformation. Tynt Meadow (7.4% ABV) is bottle-conditioned and brewed with all English ingredients. It is available commercially in selected outlets. **RAIB**

Mountain Hare

Mountain Hare Inn, Brynna Road, Brynnau Gwynion, CF35 6PG
☎ (01656) 860453 mountainhare.co.uk

Paul Jones, licensee of the Mountain Hare, finally realised his ambition of installing a brewery in his family-owned pub. A 1.5-barrel custom-built brewing plant was installed in 2013, supplying only the pub itself. There are plans for expansion to a six-barrel plant to meet demand. **V**

Mourne Mountains

Milltown East Industrial Estate, Upper Dromore Road, Warrenpoint, BT34 3PN
☎ (028) 4175 2299
mournemountainsbrewery.com

Brewing since 2015 with an extensive and varying range of seasonals, specials and one-off brews produced throughout the year – some may appear in cask format. **♦V**

Mourne Gold (ABV 4%)

Mouselow Farm

3 Mouselow Farm, Dinting, Derbyshire, SK13 7QQ
☎ 07920 048252 glossopowl@btinternet.com

Mouselow Farm began brewing in 2013 using a 2.5-barrel plant housed in a converted barn. Brewing is on a part-time basis. Local free houses, clubs and beer festivals are supplied. ♦

Mild (ABV 3.4%)

Golden Gosling (OG 1037, ABV 3.6%)

Orpingtons Buff (ABV 3.9%)

Udder the Influence (OG 1041, ABV 4%)

Flying Goose (ABV 4.2%)
Premium bitter with a hoppy character.

Mr Bees

Unit D, Searsons Farm, Cordys Lane, Trimley, Suffolk, IP11 0UD ☎ 07503 773630 mrbeesbrewery.co.uk

Mr Bees is based on the beautiful Suffolk Coast. All beers contain honey direct from the brewery's own beehives. Around 30 outlets are supplied direct including the Shannon Inn, Bucklesham, Felsto Arms, Felixstowe and the Ramsholt Arms.

Pollen Power (ABV 3.8%)

Best Bee-r (ABV 4%)

Bee Lightful (ABV 4.3%)

Black Bee (ABV 4.5%)

Mr Grundy's SIBA

Georgian House Hotel, 34 Ashbourne Road, Derby, DE22 3AD
☎ (01332) 349806 ☎ 07812 812953
mrgrundysbrewery.co.uk

Named after a local WW1 veteran who once resided on the site, the brewery opened in 2010 using a purpose-built 3.5-barrel plant fitted inside a former hotel bedroom. Beers are produced for the two hotels owned by the parent company, GHH Llp, and the free trade. Sales are handled by sister brewery Black Hole (qv). ♦

Mr Majolica

Units 7a & 15, Thurrock Enterprise Centre, Maidstone Road, Grays, Essex, RM17 6NF ☎ 07834 539761
mrmajolica.co.uk

A family-run microbrewery situated in Grays town centre, Mr Majolica began brewing in 2014 on a 2.5-barrel plant. Brewing is currently suspended.

Muckle SIBA

3 Bellister Close, Park Village, Haltwhistle, Northumberland, NE49 0HA ☎ 07711 980086
mucklebrewing.co.uk

Established in 2016, Muckle Brewing is a tiny brewery in rural Northumberland, close to Hadrian's Wall. Beers are influenced by the local landscape.

Whin Sill Blonde (ABV 3.5%)

Tickle (OG 1039, ABV 4%)

Chuckle (OG 1040, ABV 4.2%)

Moss Stout (OG 1042, ABV 4.3%)

Buster (OG 1043, ABV 4.5%)

Kings Crag (ABV 5.4%)

Muirhouse

Unit 1, Enterprise Court, Manners Avenue, Manners Industrial Estate, Ilkeston, Derbyshire, DE7 8EW
☎ 07916 590525 muirhousebrewery.co.uk

Muirhouse was established in 2009 in a domestic garage in Long Eaton. It expanded in 2011 to its present location in Ilkeston and the plant was upgraded in 2016 to 7.5 barrels. **!!♦**

Shopping for Hops (OG 1040, ABV 3.9%)
Pale-coloured session beer with a citrus bitterness.

Summit Hoppy (OG 1041, ABV 4%)
Pale-coloured session beer packed with hops.

Blueberry Porter (ABV 4.1%)

Magnum Mild (OG 1047, ABV 4.5%)

Pirate's Gold (OG 1045, ABV 4.5%)
A pale golden-coloured ale with a hint of caramel.

Hat Trick IPA (OG 1052, ABV 5.2%)
A bitter, citrus hop IPA.

Mumbles SIBA

Unit 14, Worcester Court, Swansea Enterprise Park, Swansea, SA7 9FD
☎ (01792) 792612 ☎ 07757 109938
mumblesbrewery.co.uk

Mumbles Brewery Ltd was established in 2011 and began brewing in 2013. In 2014 brewing took place using spare capacity at other local breweries but a permanent home was found in 2015, using a 10-barrel plant. Director/brewer Rob Turner supplies numerous pubs in South Wales and the Bristol area. Collaborative projects with other breweries are undertaken regularly. ♦

Hop Kick (OG 1038, ABV 4%)

Mile (OG 1039, ABV 4%)

Malt Bitter (ABV 4.1%)

Murmelt (ABV 4.2%)

Gold (OG 1042, ABV 4.3%)
A refreshing pale ale with bold lemon and lime hop flavours.

Oystermouth Stout (OG 1043, ABV 4.4%)
A rich, creamy head and dark roasted malt flavours distinguish this classic oyster stout.

Lifesaver Strong Bitter (OG 1048, ABV 4.9%)
A smooth, malty, bronze-coloured ale with a clean hop finish.

India Pale Ale (OG 1052, ABV 5.3%)
A light gold-coloured IPA with a distinct marmalade taste and aroma.

Albina New World Pale (ABV 5.7%)
A strong, hoppy pale ale with a clean citrus finish.

Musket SIBA

Unit 7, Loddington Farm, Loddington Lane, Linton, Kent, ME17 4AG
☎ (01622) 749931 ☎ 07967 127278
musketbrewery.co.uk

Launched in 2013 with a five-barrel plant, this family-owned brewery is based at Loddington Farm, Linton, in the heart of the Kent countryside. Expanding to a 15-barrel plant with on-site brewery tap, Musket Brewery now supplies more than 300 pubs, micropubs and clubs throughout Kent and Medway. ♦

Trigger (OG 1032, ABV 3.6%)
A hoppy, easy-drinking session pale ale.

Fife & Drum (OG 1034, ABV 3.8%)
A golden ale with flavours and aromas of spice, honey, marmalade, floral and a hint of wild blackcurrant.

Matchlock (OG 1034, ABV 3.8%)
A rich, dark-coloured mild with a full flavour.

Ball Puller (ABV 4%)
A smooth premium bitter with a hoppy aroma.

Flintlock (OG 1037, ABV 4.2%)
A best bitter with spicy orange undertones and a hint of marmalade.

Muzzleloader (OG 1039, ABV 4.5%)
A dark-coloured, smoky ale with a faint, spicy aroma of orange.

Muswell Hillbilly

Mews Workshops, 24-26 Avenue Mews, Muswell Hill, London, N10 3NP muswellhillbillybrewers.co.uk

Originally homebrewers, premises were acquired in Muswell Hill in 2017. Beers are brewed in small batches using the 100-litre brew kit formerly used by Oddly Ltd (qv) and are named after the local area. A nearby taproom opened in 2018.

Mutineers (NEW)

Bromley, BR1 4HE mutineers.beer

Established in 2018, Mutineers produce occasional small batch brews, which can be found at the One Inn the Wood micropub, Petts Wood, when available.

Myrddins

Church Street, Barmouth, LL42 1EH
☎ (01341) 388060 ✉ myrddins@talktalk.net

Established in 2016 within a café bar in the centre of Barmouth, the brewery relocated a short distance away in 2018.

Nailmaker

Unit 9, Darton Business Park, Barnsley Road, Darton, South Yorkshire, S75 5NH
☎ (01226) 380893 ☎ 07973 824790
nailmakerbrewing.co

Previously known as Two Roses Brewery before being purchased by its current owners in 2017, Nailmaker is located in an old carpet mill using an eight-barrel plant. Nailmaking was one of the largest occupations in the local area in the early 19th century. The core range of beers is supplemented by a limited edition range throughout the year named Shuffle. The brewery has two taphouses in the neighbouring village of Mapplewell, the Talbot Inn and Wentworth Arms. ♦

Wapentake (OG 1040, ABV 3.8%)

Auckland (OG 1040, ABV 4%)
A fruity ale brewed with New Zealand hops.

Chinook (OG 1040, ABV 4%)
A single-hopped pale ale with a clean bitterness and flavours of citrus, grapefruit and a hint of pine.

Cascade (OG 1040, ABV 4.2%)
Single-hopped pale ale bursting with citrus, floral and lychee aromas.

Anvil Porter (OG 1045, ABV 4.4%)
A dark-coloured porter with a generous addition of chocolate malt.

Wentworth (OG 1047, ABV 4.8%)
Tropical flavours with hints of grapefruit, mango and passion fruit.

Clout Stout (OG 1046, ABV 5%)
A rich stout with dark chocolate and coffee flavours.

Nant SIBA

Pen Y Bryn, Llanddoged, Llanrwst, LL26 0UA ☎ 07723 036862 ⊕ bragdynant.strikingly.com

⊗ Nant commenced brewing in 2007 with a plant purchased from the Yorkshire Dales Brewery. Capacity is currently 15-20 nine gallon firkins a week. ◆RAIB

Brenin (OG 1038, ABV 3.8%)
A light golden-coloured session ale with balanced hops and malt.

Prop Hop (OG 1036, ABV 3.8%)
Pale gold-coloured, hoppy session ale.

Cwrw Coryn (OG 1042, ABV 4.2%)
A traditional amber-coloured beer, slightly malty with good bitter overtones.

Chwaden Aur (OG 1043, ABV 4.3%)
Golden-coloured ale with a citrus aroma and full mouthfeel. Grapefruit and lemon citrus taste balance with biscuity malt for a long, fruity finish.

Mwnci Nel (OG 1055, ABV 5.5%)
A special dark-coloured ale, not excessively sweet but dominated by burnt chocolate flavours, balanced with hops.

NauticAles

Sowell Street, St Peters, Broadstairs, Kent, CT10 2AT ☎ 07552 600919

Office: 347 Margate Road, Ramsgate, Kent, CT12 6SG ✉ nauticales@outlook.com

⊗ Beers are only available at the brewery's micropub in Ramsgate and at local beer festivals. ◆

Maiden Voyage (ABV 4.4%)
A full-flavoured, ruby-coloured ale with hops to the fore and a rounded malt backbone.

Navigation SIBA

🍺 Trent Navigation Inn, 17 Meadow Lane, Nottingham, NG2 3HS
☎ (0115) 986 9877 ⊕ navigationbrewery.com

Brewing began in 2012 in the old stable block of the Trent Navigation Inn. The brewery is owned by sister company Great Northern Inns and supplies cask beers to the pubs in its estate. ‼

Patriot (OG 1038, ABV 3.8%) 🍺
Tawny-coloured, malty bitter.

New Dawn Pale (OG 1039, ABV 3.9%) 🍺
Golden-coloured ale with initial fruit and hops and a bitter finish.

Rebel (ABV 4.2%)

Splendor (OG 1041.8, ABV 4.3%)

Eclipse (OG 1043.5, ABV 4.4%) 🍺
A stout with a roast aroma and aftertaste with bitterness and some sweetness.

Saviour (OG 1054, ABV 5.5%) 🍺
Golden in colour with an assertive hop aroma and citrus fruit taste throughout and a balanced bitterness.

Naylor's SIBA

Midland Mills, Station Road, Cross Hills, North Yorkshire, BD20 7DT
☎ (01535) 637451 ⊕ naylorsbrewery.com

☺The Naylor brothers started brewing in 2005 at the Old White Bear pub in Cross Hills. The brewery moved to Midland Mills in 2006 and transferred to a larger unit on the same site in 2012. 100 outlets are regularly supplied and around 1,200 on an occasional basis. The on-site bar is open on Friday and Saturday evenings. ‼🍴◆

Yorkshire Ale (OG 1037, ABV 3.8%) 🍺
Predominantly malty traditional brown-coloured bitter with subtle fruit and hops in the nose and taste and a growing bitter finish.

Gold (OG 1040, ABV 4%)
Golden-coloured ale with a grapefruit hop finish.

Velvet (OG 1040, ABV 4%) 🍺
Chocolate and roast aromas and flavours predominate in this dark brown-coloured mild, which has an increasingly roast bitter finish.

Pinnacle Blonde (OG 1041.5, ABV 4.3%) 🍺
Hoppy, fruity aroma followed by grassy hop and tropical fruit flavours. The finish remains hoppy with a bitter, fruity edge.

Black & Tan (OG 1042, ABV 4.4%) 🍺
Dark brown-coloured best bitter with a roast edge and a hop hit. Liquorice and a malty sweetness lead to a bitter finish.

Old Ale (OG 1054, ABV 5.9%)
A smooth beer with sweet maltiness balanced by subtle bitterness.

Neath

Endeavour Close, Port Talbot, SA12 7PT ☎ 07772 468436 ⊕ neathales.co.uk

Neath Ales was established in 2009 and produces a range of single hop variety beers. Some beers are released under the Black Falls brand name. ◆RAIB V

Deliverance (OG 1045, ABV 4.5%)

Welsh Amber Ale (OG 1045, ABV 4.5%)

Dewi Sant (OG 1048, ABV 4.8%)
A pale ale with a well-balanced fruity hop flavour.

Neatishead

🍺 White Horse Inn, The Street, Neatishead, Norfolk, NR12 8AD
☎ (01692) 630828
⊕ thewhitehorseinnneatishead.com

⊗ Brewing began in 2015 at the White Horse Inn. The brew kit can be viewed through glass from the restaurant. Beer is only available in the White Horse and the owner's other pub, the Lion at Thurne. A range of semi-regular beers is brewed with at least one ever-changing ale.

Neckstamper SIBA

Unit 3, Cromwell Industrial Estate, Staffa Road, Leyton, London, E10 7QZ
☎ (020) 7018 1760 ☎ 07968 150075
⊕ neckstamper.com

Neckstamper began brewing in 2016 using a 10-barrel plant. No real ale. ◆

Neepsend

Units 1-3, Lion Works, Mowbray Street, Sheffield, South Yorkshire, S3 8EN

☎ (0114) 276 3406 ☎ 07545 323427
✉ gavin@neepsendbrewco.com

Established in 2015 by James Birkett and Gavin Martin after taking over Little Ale Cart Brewery and moving to new premises in Sheffield's Valley of Beer. A 10-barrel plant is used, supplying beers locally, including to the company's own pubs, Sheaf View, the Blake Hotel and the Wellington. Despite only having one core beer, the brewery produces an ever-changing range of hop-forward seasonal ales. There is an on-site taproom that opens occasionally. ♦

Blonde (OG 1039, ABV 4%)
An easy-drinking session pale ale with low bitterness and a short finish.

Nelson SIBA

Unit 2, Building 64, The Historic Dockyard, Chatham, Kent, ME4 4TE
☎ (01634) 832828 🌐 nelsonbrewery.co.uk

Based in Chatham's Historic Dockyard. The brewery supplies award-winning ales direct to more than 330 outlets. Gemstone Ales are brewed on site for its own pub, the Fisherman's Arms, Maidstone, and available to the free trade.
!! ♦ RAIB

Admiral IPA (OG 1040, ABV 4%)
A traditional IPA with citrus flavours on the palate.

Midshipman Dark Mild (OG 1040, ABV 4%)
A dark mild with a roasted aftertaste.

Trafalgar Bitter (OG 1040, ABV 4.1%)
A hoppy, easy-drinking golden ale.

Powder Monkey (OG 1043, ABV 4.3%)
A golden ale with a smooth aftertaste, which leaves a sweetness on the palate.

Press Gang (OG 1044, ABV 4.3%)
Zesty flavours burst in the mouth, giving a refreshing aftertaste.

Friggin' in the Riggin' (OG 1046, ABV 4.5%)
A premium bitter with a smooth malt flavour and bittersweet aftertaste.

Pursers Pussy Porter (OG 1051, ABV 4.8%)

Nelsons Blood (OG 1062, ABV 6%)
A strong, malty ale with mellow roast tones. Slightly nutty and fruity.

Nene Valley (NVB) SIBA

Oundle Wharf, Station Road, Oundle, Northamptonshire, PE8 4DE
☎ (01832) 272776 🌐 nenevalleybrewery.com

Established in 2011, a bespoke 15-barrel plant was installed in former Water Board premises on expansion in 2012. Further expansion in 2016 has doubled the floorspace. A brewery tap, Tap & Kitchen, opened on the same site in 2014.
!! ♦ RAIB GF V

Simple Pleasures (OG 1036, ABV 3.6%) ◆
A light, clean and refreshing beer with a pleasing citrus hop aroma and flavour.

Blonde Session Ale (OG 1036, ABV 3.8%)
A light golden session ale with a refreshing citrus hop finish.

Manhattan Project (OG 1037, ABV 4%)
A light and refreshing beer with lots of citrus and tropical flavours.

Bitter (OG 1038, ABV 4.1%) ◆
Floral hop and malt aroma introduces a full, clean biscuit malt taste balanced by bitterness and some fruit, ending with a long malt and bitter finish.

Starless Stout (OG 1042, ABV 4.2%)
Smooth oat stout, refreshing dark grain flavours with a slight hop bite to finish.

Australian Pale (OG 1041, ABV 4.4%)
A rich golden ale with a floral aroma preceding citrus and tropical fruit flavours.

Release the Chimps (OG 1043, ABV 4.4%)
An IPA with a crisp mouthfeel and clean, punchy bitterness.

Egyptian Cream (OG 1053, ABV 4.5%)
A milk stout with a velvety mouthfeel and a deep, full richness.

Dick's Extraordinary Bitter (OG 1045, ABV 4.6%)
Chestnut in colour with plenty of maltiness, balanced with a spicy character.

Hop Stash (OG 1046, ABV 5%)
A series of heavily-hopped beers.

Pulp Fiction (OG 1042, ABV 5.2%)
A refreshing, hoppy beer brewed with fresh whole grapefruits.

Big Bang Theory (OG 1048, ABV 5.3%) ◆
Well-balanced pale ale with a huge hop aroma giving way to malty sweetness and a gentle bitter finish.

A Beer Named LEEROY (ABV 5.5%)
Hugely hoppy and fruity pale ale. Lots of oats and aromatic malt give a big mouthfeel with a hint of maltiness.

Jim Irving Pale (OG 1053, ABV 5.6%)
Full-bodied pale ale with a big malty taste backed with heaps of zesty hop flavour.

Supersonic (OG 1055, ABV 6%) ◆
A pale wheat beer brewed with botanicals including lemons, juniper and cardamom.

Bible Black (OG 1063, ABV 6.5%) ◆
An inviting aroma of malt and fruit leads to a rich-tasting beer where blackberry dominates but is balanced by malt, hops and some bitterness. The lingering finish is bittersweet, with fruit assertive.

Fenland Farmhouse Saison (OG 1057, ABV 7.2%)
A complex and extremely refreshing beer with spicy clove notes and a fruity citrus aroma.

Mid-Week Bender (OG 1072, ABV 7.4%)
Dark amber-coloured beer with flavours of rich malt, molasses and candied orange and a big hop hit throughout.

Neon Raptor

Unit 14, Avenue A, Sneinton Market, Nottingham, NG1 1DT ☎ 07821 586342
🌐 neonraptorbrewingco.com

Established in 2016 Neon Raptor is a small independent brewery that utilised spare capacity at neighbouring breweries. Production commenced in 2018 in a brand new 10-barrel plant in the Sneinton Market area of Nottingham, which also has a licensed taproom. All beers are unfiltered, unfined and unpasteurised.

Neptune

Unit 1, Sefton Lane Industrial Estate, Maghull, Merseyside, L31 8BX
☎ (0151) 222 3908 🌐 neptunebrewery.com

Neptune began brewing in 2015 and uses a six-barrel plant.

Riptide (OG 1038, ABV 3.7%)

Ezili (OG 1040, ABV 4%)

Shifting Sands (OG 1043, ABV 4.3%)

King of the Sea (OG 1044, ABV 4.4%)

Triton (OG 1044, ABV 4.4%)

Mosaic (OG 1045, ABV 4.5%)

Abyss (OG 1058, ABV 5%)
Rich, roasted fruity aroma, sweet fruity oatmeal stout with dry roast finish.

On the Bounty (OG 1064, ABV 5.8%)
A chocolate and coconut stout.

Amarillo & Citra IPA (OG 1060, ABV 6.5%)

Nessie

Westoaks, Fort William Road, Fort Augustus, PH32 4BH

Set up in 2017 this nanobrewery markets to the tourist trade around Fort Augustus. ♦

Nethergate SIBA

The Brewery, Rodbridge Corner, Suffolk, CO10 9HJ
☎ (01787) 377087 🌐 nethergate.co.uk

Nethergate was formed in 1986 by Dick Burge and Ian Hornsey in Clare, Suffolk, and was one of the original UK microbreweries. Dick Burge remains the Chairman but it is now owned by a group of local beer lovers and moved to its new site at Rodbrdige Corner in 2017. The brand new brewery and visitor centre is only a couple of miles from its original home and produces both traditional recipes and more modern beers. !! ♦

Melford Mild (OG 1038, ABV 3.7%)
A traditional dark mild with a fresh bitterness.

Umbel Ale (OG 1039, ABV 3.8%)
Pleasant, easy-drinking bitter, infused with coriander, which dominates.

Venture (OG 1039, ABV 3.8%)
Light-tasting, sweetish and fruity session beer.

Suffolk County Best Bitter (OG 1041, ABV 4%)
Dark-coloured bitter with roast grain tones off-setting biscuity malt and powerful, hoppy, bitter notes.

Stour Valley Gold (OG 1042, ABV 4.2%)
A light and refreshing golden ale with fragrant citrus hops, a floral aroma and a mellow bitterness to finish.

Old Growler (OG 1051, ABV 5%)
Well-balanced porter in which roast grain is complemented by fruit and bubblegum.

Umbel Magna (OG 1051, ABV 5%)
Old Growler flavoured with coriander. The spice is less dominant than in Umbel Ale, with some of the weight and body of the beer coming through.

New Bristol

20a Wilson Street, Bristol, BS2 9HH ☎ 07837 976871
🌐 newbristolbrewery.co.uk

Having started out in 2013 with his brother Tom, Noel James, wife Maria and assistants now brew on a 15-barrel plant in spacious premises, which house the brewery tap and the Bristol Brewery School. The core range is supplemented by regular brew series based on common but varying themes. All beers are unfined, unfiltered and unpasteurised. !! ♦ RAIB

Joy of Sesh (OG 1040, ABV 4.2%)
A session ale with tropical, citrus and stone fruit notes.

Oolala (OG 1040, ABV 4.2%)
Fruit and hop aromas, initial flavours of fruity sweetness blend with a background hoppiness leading to a bittersweet ending.

New Lion SIBA

Station Road, Totnes, Devon, TQ9 5JR
☎ (01803) 226277 🌐 newlionbrewery.co.uk

Established in 2013 and named after Lion Brewery, renowned for Totnes Stout but closed in the 1920s. It is a modern five-barrel brew-house producing a range of core ales, seasonals and dozens of one-off white label beers annually, many in collaboration with local producers and businesses. It runs a popular membership scheme and is expected to move premises and become 100% community-owned in the near future. ♦ RAIB

Mane Event (OG 1039, ABV 3.8%)
A bronze-coloured, well-balanced, modern session bitter.

Totnes Stout (OG 1045, ABV 4.4%)
Full-bodied stout with roasted malts and some smoky chocolate and liquorice. Dry bitterness finishes.

Pandit IPA (OG 1046, ABV 4.9%)
A citrus and floral nose. These flavours are complemented on the palate by a well-defined, biscuity malt character.

Scorpion (OG 1046, ABV 4.9%)
A light, strong and fresh ale with a chilli bite.

Smokestack Lightning Porter (OG 1067, ABV 6.8%)
A rich, dark-coloured porter with hints of smoke, chocolate, plums and liquorice.

New Plassey

See Magic Dragon

New River SIBA

Unit 47, Hoddesdon Industrial Centre, Pindar Road, Hoddesdon, Hertfordshire, EN11 0FF
☎ (01992) 446200 🌐 newriverbrewery.co.uk

New River commenced brewing in 2015 on a brand new 10-barrel plant. ♦

London Tap (OG 1038, ABV 3.8%)
A refreshing pale ale with hints of toffee and light citrus with a dry, hoppy finish.

Twin Spring (OG 1039, ABV 4%)

A mellow golden ale with caramel malt flavours.

Riverbed Red (OG 1041, ABV 4.2%)
A copper-coloured ale with a resinous, earthy aroma and complex malt flavours.

Blind Poet (OG 1045, ABV 4.5%)
A smooth, dark-coloured, lightly smoked porter.

Five Inch Drop (OG 1044, ABV 4.6%)
A triple-hopped IPA with a toffee, malty aroma and pine resin and citrus flavours.

Isle of Rye (OG 1048, ABV 5.2%)
A light amber-coloured rye pale ale with distinctive aromas of orange and mango, a smooth mouthfeel and a long, peppery finish.

New Wharf SIBA

Hyde Farm, Marlow Road, Maidenhead, Berkshire, SL6 6PQ ☎ 07815 717251 🌐 newwharfbrewing.co.uk

A 20-barrel brewery set up in 2017 and producing a range of cask-conditioned and KeyKeg beers, which are distributed nationwide. RAIB

Wildflower (ABV 3.8%)
Delicately-hopped ale with a light, gentle finish.

Pale (ABV 4.3%)
A light-brown-coloured, fruity beer with a light finish.

Erin's (ABV 4.5%)
A full-bodied American-style pale ale with tropical fruit flavours.

Voyage (ABV 5.5%)
A full-bodied American-style beer with hints of caramel and chocolate, tinged with citrus and berry flavours.

Newark

77 William Street, Newark, Nottinghamshire, NG24 1QU ☎ 07804 609917 🌐 newarkbrewery.co.uk

Established in 2012 on the site of a former maltings using an eight-barrel plant. The bulk of production is supplied to local pubs. Its brewery tap is the Ram in Castle Gate, Newark. ♦

Best (OG 1038, ABV 3.8%)
Deep copper in colour with a biscuity malt nose. Sweet toffee dominates the palate with a long fruity finish.

NPA (Newark Pale Ale) (OG 1039, ABV 3.8%)
Pale gold in colour, citrus lemon on the nose, leading to a fruity finish.

BLH4 (OG 1040, ABV 4%)

Norwegian Blue (OG 1040, ABV 4%)
Deep gold-coloured ale with grapefruit and citrus on the nose, malty lemon on the palate and a long finish.

Pure Gold (OG 1045, ABV 4.5%)
A rich gold in colour with biscuit and burnt orange on the nose, leading to a soft biscuit finish.

Summer Gold (OG 1045, ABV 4.5%)
Deep gold in colour with a strong, sweet citrus nose. The lime character and light malt balance produce a lasting finish.

Phoenix (OG 1048, ABV 4.8%)
Russet brown in colour, slight spice and roasted malt on the nose with a fruity treacle, full-bodied finish.

5.5 (OG 1055, ABV 5.5%)
Deep gold-coloured strong ale. Strong honey on the nose with sweet soft fruits on the finish.

Newbridge

Unit 3, Tudor House, Moseley Road, Bilston, West Midlands, WV14 6JD ☎ 07970 456052 🌐 newbridgebrewery.co.uk

First established in 2014, the five-barrel plant incorporates six original Grundy cellar tanks. Occasional specials are brewed to complement the regular beers. ♦

Little Fox (OG 1042, ABV 4.2%)

Solaris (OG 1045, ABV 4.5%)

Indian Empire (OG 1051, ABV 5.1%)

Newby Wyke SIBA

Unit 24, Limesquare Business Park, Alma Park Road, Grantham, Lincolnshire, NG31 9SN ☎ (01476) 565682 🌐 newbywyke.co.uk

⊗ The brewery is named after a Hull trawler skippered by brewer Rob March's grandfather. It started life in 1998 as a 2.5-barrel plant in a converted garage then moved to premises behind the Willoughby Arms, Little Bytham. In 2009 it moved back to Grantham. ‼♦

Banquo (OG 1036, ABV 3.8%)
Pale-coloured blonde ale with a full hoppy taste and a long fruity finish.

Orsino (OG 1037, ABV 4%)
A blonde ale with a bright, fruity citrus and mango taste moving to a soft citrus hop finish.

Comet (OG 1039, ABV 4.1%)
Single-hopped, amber-coloured ale with slight malt undertones and a gooseberry citrus fruit finish.

Kingston Topaz (OG 1039, ABV 4.2%)
A single-hopped ale with floral undertones.

Black Beerd (OG 1040, ABV 4.3%)
A malty oat stout with a fruit undertones.

Bear Island (OG 1043, ABV 4.6%)
A blonde beer with a hoppy aroma and a crisp, dry finish.

White Squall (OG 1044, ABV 4.8%) ◆
Blonde-hued with a hoppy aroma. Generous amounts of hop are well-supported by a solid malty undercurrent. An increasingly bittersweet tang makes itself known towards the finish.

Newcastle

Arch 2, Stepney Bank, Ouseburn, Newcastle upon Tyne, NE1 2NP ☎ 07446 011941 🌐 newcastlebrewingltd.co.uk

⊗ Mike and Leo Bell initially founded the brewery in the Quayside Development Centre in Ouseburn before moving to new premises under Byker Bridge. ‼ RAIB

Newtown

25 Victoria Street, Gosport, Hampshire, PO12 4TX ☎ (023) 9250 4294 🌐 newtownbrewery.co.uk

THE BREWERIES

Brewing commenced in 2016 in this nanobrewery with just a half-barrel plant, although the brewer has had many years previous experience of homebrewing. Full mash beers are produced on demand for local pubs and beer festivals. ♦

Rev Bingham (OG 1044, ABV 4.3%)

Victorian Porter (OG 1047, ABV 4.6%)

Nightjar

2 Richmond House, Caldene Business Park, Mytholmroyd, West Yorkshire, HX7 5QL ☎ 07412 008221 🌐 nightjarbrew.co.uk

Nightjar Brew Co was initially established in 2011 and re-branded in 2018. The 10-barrel brewery is located in an industrial building in Mytholmroyd and supplies around 90 free trade outlets, mainly in Yorkshire and Lancashire. Its extensive beer swaps with other breweries means that its beers can also be found in more distant parts of the country. ♦

Hebden Hop (OG 1039, ABV 3.9%)
Blonde, easy-drinking, hoppy ale with a fruity aroma that leads to a thirst-quenching bitterness.

Haka Pale (OG 1040, ABV 4%)
A dry-hopped pale ale with gooseberry and fresh apple notes.

Klondike (OG 1042, ABV 4.2%)
A golden-coloured session bitter with fresh fruit notes.

Cosmonaut (OG 1044, ABV 4.4%)
A velvety and smooth milk oatmeal Irish-style stout.

Kalifornia (OG 1044, ABV 4.4%)
A West Coast-style dry-hopped pale ale with tropical fruit notes.

Bollywood IPA (OG 1050, ABV 5%)
A classic, punchy and fresh IPA.

Supernova (OG 1069, ABV 6.9%)
A dark-coloured, rich, chocolate milk stout with espresso and dark chocolate flavours.

Nine Standards

See Settle

Nirvana SIBA

Unit T6, Leyton Industrial Village, Argall Avenue, Leyton, London, E10 7QP
☎ (020) 3417 5580 🌐 nirvanabrewer.com

Established in 2017 producing a range of non-alcoholic beers. No real ale.

No. 18 Yard Brewhouse

See Shepherd Neame

No Frills Joe

50 Wakefield Road, Greenhithe, Kent, DA9 9JE
☎ 07516 725577

Established in 2015, No Frills Joe is a five-barrel microbrewery. The beer is always unpasteurised, unfiltered and unfined and therefore may be cloudy. The range is available in a small on-site taproom (its restricted opening hours are advertised on social media). RAIB V

Hefeweizen (ABV 4%)

Sour (ABV 4%)

Brainwash Bitter (ABV 4.4%)

Simcoe Pale Ale (ABV 4.5%)

Manderina-B IPA (ABV 4.8%)

Jerry Juice IPA (ABV 5%)

Stout (ABV 6.5%)

Nobby's SIBA

Unit 2, Cottingham Way, Thrapston, Northamptonshire, NN14 4PL
☎ (01832) 730800 🌐 nobbysbrewery.co.uk

Paul 'Nobby' Mulliner started commercial brewing in 2004 on a 2.5-barrel plant at the rear of the Alexandra Arms, Kettering. The brewery relocated to Guilsborough in 2007 and again in 2014 to larger premises in Thrapston. Brewing now takes place on a 12-barrel plant. !! ♦ RAIB

Claridges Crystal (OG 1036, ABV 3.6%)
An ultra pale ale, crisp and fresh with a slightly citrus hop finish.

The Guzzler (OG 1036, ABV 3.6%)
An easy-drinking, malty, auburn-coloured ale with a gentle hop finish.

Best (OG 1037, ABV 3.8%)
A session ale with a big hop finish.

Goldings (OG 1041, ABV 4%)
A full-bodied and well-balanced golden ale with a traditional hop finish.

Swift Nick (OG 1042, ABV 4.2%)

Plum Porter (OG 1044, ABV 4.4%)
A dark brown-coloured porter with bitterness from hops and plums.

Tow'd Navigation (OG 1067, ABV 6.1%)
Dark-coloured, strong ale with rich malt and hop flavours.

Nomadic

Unit 11, Sheepscar House, 15 Sheepscar Street, Sheepscar, Leeds, West Yorkshire, LS7 1AD ☎ 07868 345228 🌐 nomadicbeers.co.uk

Established in 2017, beers were originally produced using spare capacity at other breweries. Following an expansion in 2018, Nomadic Beers has emerged from the basement of the Burley Street Brewhouse and found a new home in Sheepscar. A taproom is open on the third Saturday of the month.

Pale (OG 1035, ABV 3.8%)

Strider (ABV 4.4%)

Bandit (ABV 4.8%)

Nook SIBA

Riverside, 7b Victoria Square, Holmfirth, West Yorkshire, HD9 2DN
☎ (01484) 682373 🌐 thenookbrewhouse.co.uk

The Nook Brewhouse is built on the foundations of a previous brewhouse dating back to 1754, next to the River Ribble. Two brewery taps are supplied, one with a restaurant whose dishes are matched with the beer brewed on site. A history room with renovated archives dating back to the 1700s and a brewery shop are planned. ‼♦RAIB

Norfolk Broads

See Humpty Dumpty

Norn Iron (NEW)

Unit 30, The Cutts, Dunmurry, BT17 9HN
✉ nornironbrewcoltd@outlook.com

Brewing began in 2018. RAIB

North SIBA

Unit 6, Taverner's Walk Estate, Sheepscar Grove, Leeds, West Yorkshire, LS7 1AH
☎ (0113) 345 3290 🌐 northbrewing.com

North Brewing is a 15-barrel brewery established in 2015, originally supplying the North Bar group of bars in and around Leeds. It has since grown and supplies other outlets. Collaborations with national and international breweries are common. An on-site tap is open on Friday evenings and all day Saturday. ‼♦

North Cotswold SIBA

Unit 3, Ditchford Farm, Stretton-on-Fosse, Warwickshire, GL56 9RD
☎ (01608) 663947 🌐 northcotswoldbrewery.co.uk

North Cotswold started in 1999 as a 2.5-barrel plant, which has since been upgraded to 10-barrel capacity. Beers are also produced under the Shakespeare brand name. ♦RAIB

Windrush Ale (OG 1036, ABV 3.6%)
A thirst-quenching, amber-coloured session bitter with a malty, slightly sweet taste.

Fosseway Flanker (OG 1038, ABV 3.8%)
A refreshing, pale-coloured, hoppy session ale.

Moreton Mild (OG 1038, ABV 3.8%)
A classic dark mild with a nutty palate.

Cotswold Best (OG 1040, ABV 4%)

Shagweaver (OG 1045, ABV 4.5%)

Hung, Drawn 'n' Portered (OG 1050, ABV 5%)
Strong, dark-coloured porter with a malty finish.

North Riding (Brewery)

Unit 6, Barkers Lane, Snainton, North Yorkshire, YO13 9BD
☎ (01723) 864845 🌐 northridingbrewery.com

Having outgrown the brewpub in Scarborough, Stuart Neilson established a 10-barrel brewery in East Ayton on the outskirts of Scarborough in 2015. In 2019 operations moved to much larger premises in Snainton, enabling further expansion of brewing capacity. Concentrating on hop-forward beers, distribution is throughout Yorkshire and further afield. ♦RAIB

US Session IPA (OG 1037, ABV 3.8%)

Cascade Pale Ale (OG 1040, ABV 4%)
A pale ale with citrus flavours.

Mosaic Pale Ale (OG 1042, ABV 4.3%)
A pale ale packed with blueberry and citrus flavours.

Citra Pale Ale (OG 1043, ABV 4.5%)
Easy-drinking premium pale ale with a grapefruit, mango and lemon taste and aroma.

North Riding (Brewpub)

North Marine Road, Scarborough, North Yorkshire, YO12 7HU
☎ (01723) 370004 🌐 northridingbrewpub.com

Brewing commenced in 2011 using a two-barrel plant situated in the cellar of the pub, which is now brewing to capacity with three fermenting vessels. ♦

North Yorkshire SIBA

Unit 7, South Gare Court, Tod Point Road, Warrenby, North Yorkshire, TS10 5BN
☎ (01642) 497298 ✉ sales@nybrewery.co.uk

Founded in Middlesbrough in 1989 the brewery moved to Pinchinthorpe Hall, Guisborough in 1998. In 2017, following the purchase of the brewery, the new owner moved the entire operation to new premises on an industrial estate in Warrenby near Redcar, North Yorkshire. ♦RAIB

Northern Navigator (OG 1036, ABV 3.6%)
A chestnut-coloured, nutty session ale. Medium-bodied and quite hoppy.

Old Jacks Tipple (OG 1038, ABV 3.8%)

Temptation (OG 1038, ABV 3.8%)
A refreshing beer with a pleasant bitterness and citrus and grapefruit aromas.

Yorkshire Coble (OG 1038, ABV 3.8%)

Beckwatter (OG 1040, ABV 4%)
Dark ruby-coloured ale with balanced notes of hops and malt. Full-bodied with a thick creamy head.

Yorkshire Porter (OG 1044, ABV 4.4%)

NYPA (OG 1046, ABV 4.6%)
IPA with an earthy, grassy character.

Flying Herbert (OG 1047, ABV 4.7%)
Smooth, full-flavoured premium bitter with a malty, fruity and dry finish.

White Lady (OG 1047, ABV 4.7%)
A hoppy, strong, pale-coloured beer.

Northbound SIBA

Campsie Industrial Estate, McLean Road, Eglinton, BT47 3XX ☎ 07512 198686
🌐 northboundbrewery.com

Established in 2015, Northbound produce a range of bottle-conditioned beers named after their measurement of bitterness (IBUs). ♦RAIB

Northdown

Unit J1C/A, Channel Road, Westwood Industrial Estate, Margate, Kent, CT9 4JS ☎ 07791 441219
🌐 northdownbrewery.co.uk

Northdown began brewing in 2018 using a seven-barrel plant. It is run by Jonny and Katie Spanjar and takes its name from their original intention to run out of the Northdown area of

Margate. The origins of a Northdown brewery date back to the 1600s. ‼ 🛒 ♦ RAIB

Pale Ale Mary (OG 1040, ABV 4%)
A pale ale with subtle tastes of apricot and a citrus and floral aroma. A slight bitterness with biscuit and malt overtones and a crisp finish that is gentle on the palate.

Papworth Victory Best Bitter (OG 1042, ABV 4.2%)
A well-balanced ale with a floral, pine and peach aroma. A fruity flavour leads to a balanced, dry finish with a hint of raisin.

HE-BRU IPA (OG 1048, ABV 4.8%)

Muggy Porter (OG 1054, ABV 5%)
A full-bodied oatmeal porter with dark chocolate, rich fruit and coconut flavours and a roasted coffee aroma.

Northern Alchemy

The Old Coal Yard, Elizabeth Street, Byker, Newcastle upon Tyne, NE6 1JS ☎ 07834 386333
🌐 wearenorthernalchemy.com

Brewing began in 2014. The brewery was situated in a converted shipping container, known as the Lab, just behind the Cumberland Arms. In 2017 it moved to larger premises in a former coal depot. All beers are unfined and unfiltered.

Northern Monk SIBA

The Old Flax Store, Marshalls Mill, Holbeck, Leeds, West Yorkshire, LS11 9YJ
☎ (0113) 243 6430

Unit 7, Sydenham Road, Holbeck, Leeds, West Yorkshire, LS11 9RU 🌐 northernmonkbrewco.com

Northern Monk started brewing using spare capacity at other breweries in 2013. It set up at its own Grade II-listed mill building in the centre of Leeds in 2014 using a 10-barrrel plant. In 2017 it expanded by opening a much larger second site, capable of producing 24,000 hectolitres per week, and installing a canning line. 18 beers are brewed across the two sites weekly. A taproom is open Tue-Sun at the old Flax Mill and another in Manchester. Although most of the production is keg, a small amount of cask-conditioned beer is available. ‼ 🛒 GF

Northern Monkey SIBA

Pack Horse, Nelson Square, Bolton, BL1 1AQ ☎ 07737 125629 🌐 northernmonkeybrew.co.uk

Established in 2016 and based in Bolton town centre, Northern Monkey Brew Co is a six-barrel brewery with an on-site tap bar. It brews a variety of ales, maintaining a traditional edge but with a modern twist. The ales rotate regularly so no core range is available. ♦

Northern Whisper

Hill End Mill, Hill End Lane, Cloughfold, Lancashire, BB4 7RN
☎ (01706) 230082
🌐 northernwhisperbrewingco.co.uk

Brewing began in 2017.

Blighty (ABV 3.8%)

Oppenchops (ABV 4%)

Yammerhouse (ABV 4.5%)

Beltie (ABV 4.8%)

Norton

Norton Priory, Tudor Road, Manor Park, Runcorn, Cheshire, WA7 1SX
☎ (01928) 716971 ☎ 07767 354674
🌐 nortonbrewing.com

Situated within the grounds of Norton Priory, the brewery was created as a social enterprise by Halton Borough Council to provide employment opportunities for people with learning disabilities, autism and other disabilities. It opened in 2011 with a 2.5-barrel plant.

Noss Beer Works SIBA

Unit 6, Ash Court, Pennant Way, Lee Mill, Devon, PL21 9GE ☎ 07977 479634 🌐 nossbeerworks.co.uk

Noss Beer Works, based in Lee Mill, was formed in 2012 using a six-barrel plant. The beers are made from only the finest locally sourced hops and malts. ‼ RAIB

Black Rock (ABV 4%)
A black IPA with liquorice, citrus and caramel notes and a slightly bitter aftertaste.

Church Ledge (OG 1040, ABV 4%) ◆
Bitter dominated by hops and fruit throughout. Hoppy and citrus, slight caramel balances bitter dryness. Slight kick at the end.

Mew Stone (OG 1043, ABV 4.3%)
A copper-coloured, refreshing and well-balanced best bitter.

Ebb Rock (OG 1049, ABV 4.9%)
A dark copper-coloured, full-bodied strong bitter.

Nottingham SIBA

Plough Inn, 17 St Peter's Street, Radford, Nottingham, NG7 3EN
☎ (0115) 942 2649 ☎ 07815 073447
🌐 nottinghambrewery.co.uk

The former owners of the Bramcote and Castle Rock Breweries re-established the Nottingham Brewery in 2000 in a purpose-built brewhouse behind the Plough Inn. Philip Darby and Niven Balfour set out to revive the brands of the original Nottingham Brewery, closed by Whitbread in the 1950s. Within the LocAle ethos, beers are supplied widely to the local trade including the brewery tap house, the Plough Inn, and its other tied house the Frame Breakers, Ruddington. ‼

Rock Ale Bitter Beer (OG 1038, ABV 3.8%) ◆
A pale-coloured and bitter, thirst-quenching, hoppy beer with a dry finish.

Rock Ale Mild Beer (OG 1038, ABV 3.8%) ◆
A reddish-black-coloured malty mild with some refreshing bitterness in the finish.

Legend (OG 1040, ABV 4%) ◆
A fruity and malty pale brown-coloured bitter with a touch of sweetness and bitterness.

Extra Pale Ale (OG 1042, ABV 4.2%) ◆
A hoppy and fruity golden ale with a hint of sweetness and a long-lasting bitter finish.

Broadway Reel Ale (OG 1044, ABV 4.4%) ◆
Hoppy golden ale with a lingering bitter finish.

Dreadnought (OG 1045, ABV 4.5%) ◆
Well-balanced best bitter. Blend of malt and hops give a rounded, fruity finish.

Bullion (OG 1047, ABV 4.7%) ◆
A refreshing premium golden ale. Brewed with a single malt variety, it is triple-hopped and exceptionally bitter.

Supreme (OG 1052, ABV 5.2%) ◆
A strong, amber-coloured, fruity ale. A touch of malt in the taste is followed by a sweet and slightly hoppy finish.

Brewed for the Trent Bridge Inn, Nottingham:

Trent Bridge Inn Ale (OG 1038, ABV 3.8%)
Tawny-coloured, traditionally-hopped bitter.

Nutbrook

6 Hallam Way, West Hallam, Derbyshire, DE7 6LA
☎ 0800 458 2460 ⊕ nutbrookbrewery.com

Nutbrook was established in 2007. In addition to a regular range, special beers are brewed to order for domestic and corporate clients. The brewery's unique Design-a-Beer system allows customers to design and brew their own beer. On Saturdays cask-conditioned beer is sold at Oakfield Farm, Stanley Common. !! RAIB

The Mild Side (OG 1036, ABV 3.6%)
A golden-coloured mild with a traditional malty taste and fruit tones.

Responsibly (OG 1041, ABV 4%)
A light bronze-coloured, crisp beer with a fruity flavour.

Banter (OG 1040.8, ABV 4.5%)
A golden yellow-coloured beer with a hoppy taste and floral notes.

Daft Apeth (OG 1050, ABV 4.5%)

More (OG 1047, ABV 4.8%)
Dark-coloured beer with a subtle red tint, burnt roasted barley taste and a sweet bitterness.

Black Beauty (OG 1054, ABV 5%)
A traditional milk stout with undertones of chocolate, honey and nuts.

Perfect 5th (OG 1047.8, ABV 5%)
A strong pale ale with honey tones.

Moderation (OG 1057, ABV 5.5%)
A golden ale with subtle hop flavours.

O'Connor

12 Lime Road, Faughanvale, Greysteel, BT47 3EH
☎ 07748 004065 ⊕ oconnorbrewing.com

Brewing began in 2013. No real ale.

Oakham SIBA

2 Maxwell Road, Woodston, Peterborough, Cambridgeshire, PE2 7JB
☎ (01733) 370500 ⊕ oakhamales.com

⊗ The brewery started in 1993 in Oakham, Rutland, and moved to Peterborough in 1998. The brewery's main production site is a 75-barrel plant. An additional six-barrel plant is located at its city-centre brewpub, which makes special and one-off brews. Around 350 outlets are supplied and four pubs are owned. !! ◆ RAIB

JHB (OG 1038, ABV 3.8%) ◆
Straw-coloured golden ale dominated by citrus hop character throughout. Long, dry, slightly astringent finish.

Inferno (OG 1039, ABV 4%) ◆
The citrus hop character of this straw-coloured brew begins on the nose and builds in intensity on the palate. Clean, dry citrus finish.

Citra (OG 1042, ABV 4.2%) ◆
Refreshing grapefruit and peach aroma and flavour characterise this golden ale. Bittersweet palate gives way to a long, dry aftertaste.

Scarlet Macaw (OG 1043, ABV 4.4%)
Tart gooseberry and soft peach on the nose and an intense bitter finish.

Bishops Farewell (OG 1046, ABV 4.6%) ◆
Powerfully citrus, the hops and fruit on the aroma of this golden/yellow-coloured beer become bittersweet on the palate. Zesty citrus aftertaste.

Oaks SIBA

Unit 6, Stanney Mill Industrial Estate, Dutton Green, Ellesmere Port, Cheshire, CH2 4SA ☎ 07890 567582 ⊕ oaksbrewing.co.uk

Founded as Cheshire Brew Brothers in 2013 and was taken into new ownership in 2017. The beers can be found in free and tied trade across North-west England and West Yorkshire.

Chester Gold (ABV 3.6%) ◆
A fruity, hoppy bitter with a pleasant sweet finish.

Cascade Pale Ale (ABV 4%)
A well-balanced American-style pale ale with a stone fruit aroma and flavour and a smooth finish.

Delamere Blonde (ABV 4%)
A blonde ale with soft hints of citrus and orange and a delicate finish.

Oakwood

c/o Northfield Crescent, Wells-next-the-Sea, Norfolk, NR23 1LP ☎ 07512 111211 ⊕ oakwoodbrewery.com

Oakwood was established in 2015. After producing beers on a small scale from home the brewer decided to turn his hobby into a full-time job. Barley is locally-grown by Teddy Maufe at Branthill Farm on the Holkham Estate in Norfolk. Beer is contract brewed elsewhere. RAIB

Oban Bay

See Argyll

Odcombe

Masons Arms, 41 Lower Odcombe, Odcombe, Somerset, BA22 8TX
☎ (01935) 862591 ⊕ masonsarmsodcombe.co.uk

Odcombe opened in 2000, but closed a few years later. It re-opened in 2005 with assistance from Shepherd Neame (qv). Brewing takes place once a week and beers are available only in the Masons Arms. !! ◆ RAIB

Oddly

Unit 6, Triumph Trading Estate, Tariff Road, Tottenham, London, N17 0EB
☎ (020) 3741 7717 🌐 oddlybeer.com

⊗ Oddly Beer is a one man operation using a five-barrel plant. Founded in 2017 on an island in the River Thames at Hampton, the plant was relocated in 2019 to Tottenham, North London. The brewery premises includes a tap room. ‼ ♦ RAIB

Rhia (ABV 4%)

Sumac (ABV 4.6%)

Empathy (ABV 5%)

Poppy (ABV 6%)

VIPA (ABV 6%)

Odyssey

Brockhampton Brewery, Oast House Barn, Whitbourne, Herefordshire, WR6 5SH
☎ (01885) 483496 ☎ 07918 553152
🌐 odysseybrewco.com

⊗ This six-barrel brewery was bought in 2014 by Alison and Mitchell Evans, who also own the Beer in Hand, Hereford. The original building, a restored barn on a National Trust estate, has been retained.

Syren (OG 1039, ABV 3.9%)

Mo' Citra (OG 1040, ABV 4%)

Little India Pale Ale (OG 1045, ABV 4.5%)

Latte Stout (OG 1062, ABV 5.4%)

Nirvana (OG 1052, ABV 5.4%)

31st State (OG 1049, ABV 5.8%)

Crowd Control (OG 1060, ABV 6%)

Cookie Monster (OG 1045, ABV 6.5%)
An oatmeal stout with chocolate, raisin and cinnamon flavours.

Offa's Dyke

Chapel Lane, Trefonen, Shropshire, SY10 9DX
☎ (01691) 656889 🌐 trefonen.org/offas-dyke-brewery.html

Established in 2007, the brewery and adjoining pub straddle the old England/Wales border, Offa's Dyke. The Olde Vaults and adjacent Ironworks in Oswestry serve as alternative brewery taps. ‼

Ogwen

5 Rhes Ogwen, Bethesda, LL57 3AY
☎ (01248) 605715 ☎ 07545 684752
🌐 cwrwogwen.cymru

The first brewery in the Ogwen valley for over a century. A local community venture, a group of shareholders perform all brewing operations. ‼ RAIB

Cwrw Caradog (OG 1039, ABV 3.9%)
Smooth, easy-drinking session pale ale.

Ryc (ABV 4%)

Tryfan (ABV 4.2%)

Chwalfa (OG 1046, ABV 4.5%)

Okell's SIBA

Kewaigue, Douglas, Isle of Man, IM2 1QG
☎ (01624) 699400 🌐 okells.co.uk

Founded in 1874 by Dr Okell, this is the main brewery on the island and moved in 1994 to a new, purpose-built plant at Kewaigue. All the beers are produced under the Manx Brewers' Act. ‼ ♦

MPA (Manx Pale Ale) (OG 1036, ABV 3.6%)
A golden-coloured fruity, session bitter with background sweetness and a rising hoppy finish.

Bitter (OG 1035, ABV 3.7%)
A gently-bittered, sweet beer with some fruit and malt flavours.

Dr Okell's IPA (OG 1044, ABV 4.5%)
A clean, fruity, sweetish bitter with an alcoholic bite.

Old Cannon

86 Cannon Street, Bury St Edmunds, Suffolk, IP33 1JR
☎ (01284) 768769 🌐 oldcannonbrewery.co.uk

⊗ The St Edmunds Head pub opened in 1845 with its own brewery. Brewing ceased in 1917, and Greene King closed the pub in 1995. It re-opened in 1999 as the Old Cannon Brewery complete with a unique state-of-the-art brewery housed in the bar area. A growing number of local outlets are supplied. ‼ ♦

Best Bitter (OG 1037, ABV 3.8%)
Traditional East Anglian bitter. Rich, hoppy aroma and bitterness dominate throughout with just a hint of sweetness in the aftertaste.

Elveden IPA (OG 1038, ABV 3.9%)

Hornblower (OG 1038, ABV 4%)
Very light in colour with an IPA hoppiness.

Black Pig (OG 1042, ABV 4.2%)

Blonde Bombshell (OG 1042, ABV 4.2%)
Subtle citrus flavours with a pleasant bitterness and astringency that grows on the aftertaste. Hoppy, well-balanced and quaffable.

Gunner's Daughter (OG 1052, ABV 5.5%)
A well-balanced strong ale with a complexity of hop, fruit, sweetness and bitterness in the flavour and a lingering hoppy, bitter aftertaste.

Old Chimneys

Suffolk, IP22 2NX 🌐 oldchimneysbrewery.com

Old Chimneys was established in 1995, moving to a converted farm building in 2001. In 2019 Alan Thompson ceased brewing at Market Weston to concentrate on collaborative brewing projects with other breweries.

Old Cross

Old Cross Tavern, 8 St Andrew Street, Hertford, SG14 1JA
☎ (01992) 583133

⊗ The microbrewery was set up in 2008 and is located within the pub. Beers of varying styles are brewed on an occasional basis and appear solely at the Old Cross Tavern. ♦

Old Dairy SIBA

Tenterden Station Estate, Station Road, Tenterden, Kent, TN30 6HE
☎ (01580) 763867 🌐 olddairybrewery.com

Old Dairy was founded in 2009. It relocated from Rolvenden in 2014 to larger premises near the Kent & East Sussex Railway in Tenterden in order to increase capacity. !! ♦ RAIB

Red Top (OG 1038, ABV 3.8%)
A sweetish copper-coloured bitter with hints of caramel and a subtle hop character.

Uber Brew (OG 1038, ABV 3.8%)
Full-bodied hoppy pale ale with a strong floral aroma.

Copper Top (OG 1041, ABV 4.1%)

Blue Top (OG 1048, ABV 4.8%)
Rich and full bodied, this pale brown-coloured ale has a long bittersweet finish and a hint of aroma hop.

Snow Top (OG 1060, ABV 6%)

Old Friends (NEW)

Old Friends Inn, 49 Soutergate, Ulverston, Cumbria, LA12 7ES
☎ (01229) 208195 🌐 oldfriendsulverston.co.uk

Brewing began in 2019 in a room to the rear of the Old Friends pub in Ulverston. Beers are currently only available at the pub.

Old Inn

Old Inn & Brewpub, Flowerdale Glen, Gairloch, IV21 2BD
☎ (01445) 712006 🌐 theoldinn.net

Brewing began in 2010 using a 150-litre plant. ♦

Old Laxey

Shore Hotel Brew Pub, Old Laxey, Isle of Man, IM4 7DA
☎ (01624) 863214 🌐 shorehotel.im

Beer brewed on the Isle of Man is brewed to a strict Beer Purity Act. Additives are not permitted to extend shelf life, nor are chemicals allowed to assist with head retention. Old Laxey's beer is sold mostly through the adjacent Shore Hotel. !!

Old Luxters

Old Luxters Vineyard, Dudley Lane, Hambleden, Buckinghamshire, RG9 6JW
☎ (01491) 638330 🌐 chilternvalley.co.uk

Situated in a 17th-century barn beside the Chiltern Valley Vineyard, Old Luxters is a traditional brewery established in 1990 and was awarded a Royal Warrant of Appointment in 2007. The core range is bottle-conditioned beers. !! ♦ RAIB

Old Mill SIBA

Mill Street, Snaith, East Yorkshire, DN14 9HU
☎ (01405) 861813 🌐 oldmillbrewery.co.uk

Opened in 1983 in a 200-year-old former malt kiln and corn mill, the brew-length is 60 barrels. The brewery is building a tied estate, now standing at 16 houses. Beers can be found nationwide through wholesalers and around 80 free trade outlets are supplied direct. The RT Brew Co range is produced for HB Clark (qv). !! ♦

Bullion IPA (OG 1037, ABV 3.7%)

Jacks' Batch (OG 1034, ABV 3.8%)

Traditional Bitter (OG 1039.5, ABV 3.9%)
A malty nose is carried through to the initial flavour. Bitterness runs throughout.

Blonde Bombshell (OG 1041, ABV 4%)
A straw-coloured beer, easy-drinking due to delicate and refreshing fruity flavours.

Yorkshire Elixir (OG 1040, ABV 4%)

12th Man (OG 1042, ABV 4.2%)

La Bolsa (OG 1045, ABV 4.5%)
A rich, dark-coloured chocolate porter with a smooth coffee aftertaste.

Old Pie Factory

4 Montague Road, Warwick, CV34 5LW ☎ 07816 413026 ✉ josh@oldpiefactorybrewery.co.uk

Brewing began in 2011 using a 5.5-barrel plant and is a joint venture between Underwood Wines, Stratford upon Avon, and the Case is Altered, Five Ways.

Case Bitter (OG 1036, ABV 3.9%)
Classic English session bitter with only English ingredients.

Pie in the Sky (OG 1042, ABV 4.1%)

Humble Pie (OG 1045, ABV 4.2%)

I Pie A (OG 1040.3, ABV 4.5%)

American Pie (OG 1051, ABV 5.5%)

Old Sawley SIBA

Old Sawley Brewing Co, 352a Tamworth Road, Sawley, Derbyshire, NG10 3AT ☎ 07722 311209 🌐 oldsawley.com

Established in 2013, initially on a 0.5-barrel plant, upgraded to a 10-barrel plant in 2016. Beers are available in the White Lion, at Midlands beer festivals and in outlets across the East Midlands. !! ♦

Jobber (OG 1042, ABV 4.2%)
Traditional amber-coloured session bitter with a good balance of malt and hops.

Little Jack (OG 1043, ABV 4.3%)
Crisp, refreshing pale ale with a fruity citrus taste.

Plummeth the Hour (OG 1045, ABV 4.5%)
A full-bodied plum porter.

Tollbridge Porter (OG 1045, ABV 4.5%)
A dark-coloured porter with smooth, subtle flavours of chocolate, coffee and vanilla.

Old School SIBA

Holly Bank Barn, Crag Road, Warton, Lancashire, LA5 9PL
☎ (01524) 740888 ☎ 07515 376700
🌐 oldschoolbrewery.co.uk

A 12-barrel brewery, founded in 2012, located in a renovated 400-year-old former school outbuilding overlooking the picturesque village of

Warton. Beer is mainly sold to free houses within a 40-mile radius. ‼♦

Hopscotch (OG 1037, ABV 3.7%)
Initially hoppy, astringency builds in this satisfying beer, ending with a bitter finish.

Textbook (OG 1039, ABV 3.9%)
Pale-coloured beer with malt and hops in the taste, a creamy texture and a dry bitter finish.

Detention (OG 1041, ABV 4.1%)
Light amber-coloured, hoppy best bitter with a lingering aftertaste.

Headmaster (OG 1045, ABV 4.5%)
A dark-coloured, strong best bitter. It mixes a complex malty flavour with a blackcurrant aroma leaving a subtle, sweet, nutty aftertaste.

Old Spot SIBA

Manor Farm, Station Road, Cullingworth, West Yorkshire, BD13 5HN ☎ 07496 092655
oldspotbrewery.co.uk

Old Spot, named after the owner's sheepdog, started brewing in 2005. The beers are available in several outlets in West Yorkshire. The acting brewery tap is the George Hotel in Cullingworth. ♦

Light But Dark (OG 1043, ABV 4%)
Chestnut-coloured bitter with a slight malty taste and pleasant bitter finish. An ideal session beer.

OSB (OG 1042, ABV 4%)
A golden-coloured, full-bodied bitter.

Spot Light (OG 1040, ABV 4.2%)
This smooth-drinking golden ale has a slightly fruity, hoppy aroma leading to a well-balanced fruit, hop flavour with hints of pineapple and a long bittersweet finish.

Spot O'Bother (OG 1060, ABV 5.5%)
Complex porter with a chocolate ice cream taste and slight liquorice bitterness to finish.

Old Street

Arch 11, Gales Gardens, Bethnal Green Road, Bethnal Green, London, E2 0EJ ☎ 07491 990970
oldstreet.beer

Originally situated in the basement of the Queen's Head pub in King's Cross, brewing began in 2013. In 2018 the brewery moved to a railway arch in Bethnal Green with an on-site taproom. No real ale.

Old Tree

Old Tree, Yachtwerks, 28-29 Richmond Place, Brighton, East Sussex, BN2 9NA ☎ 07413 064346
oldtree.house

A co-operative based in Brighton producing a unique range of small-batch, probiotic and celebration drinks. It supplies its own zero-waste Silo restaurant. Brewing and gardening are combined and a production process is used that contributes to land regeneration. RAIB

Old Vault

Old Vault, 12 Market Place, Thorne, South Yorkshire, DN8 5DP ☎ 07809 471355

Production began in 2017. The brewing equipment is in a room at the back of the Old Vault Brewery & Tap micropub in Thorne. Brewing is currently suspended.

Old Vicarage (NEW)

Old Vicarage, Walton, Cumbria, CA8 2DH
☎ (01697) 543002 oldvicaragebrewery.co.uk

A microbrewery, bar and B&B accommodation in North Cumbria. Brewing experience days are offered.

Old Windsor (NEW)

68 Straight Road, Old Windsor, SL4 2RX
owbrewery.com

Run by an enthusiastic homebrewer who went commercial in 2016, brewing takes place in his garage and the beers are sold locally to a couple of regular outlets. Each batch is unique and custom made in small quantities. The majority of the output is bottle-conditioned, with just a few cask-conditioned ales being provided on request. RAIB

Old Worthy

Broughton, ML12 6HQ ☎ 07955 113083
oldworthybeer.co.uk

Brewing takes place on a 10-barrel plant. The beers are designed to be drunk as a half 'n' half, a beer served with a dram of whisky on the side. The malt used is sourced from Scottish whisky distilleries. Around 200 outlets are supplied.

Wee XP (OG 1045, ABV 4.4%)

Wee Blonde (OG 1048, ABV 4.7%)

The Old Worthy (OG 1050, ABV 5%)

Wild Bill's Aces & Eights (OG 1050, ABV 5%)

A Midnight Caper (OG 1050, ABV 5.5%)

Mighty XP (OG 1060, ABV 6%)

Olde England

See Potbelly

Olde Potting Shed

See TOPS

Olde Swan

Old Swan, 89 Halesowen Road, Netherton, West Midlands, DY2 9PY
☎ (01384) 253075

A famous brewpub best known as Ma Pardoe's after the matriarch who ruled it for years. The pub has been licensed since 1835 and the present brewery and pub were built in 1863. Brewing continued until 1988 and restarted in 2001. ‼♦

Original (OG 1034, ABV 3.5%)
Straw-coloured light mild, smooth but tangy and sweetly refreshing with a faint hoppiness.

Dark Swan (OG 1041, ABV 4.2%)
Smooth, sweet dark mild with late roast malt in the finish.

Entire (OG 1044, ABV 4.4%) ◆
Faintly hoppy, amber-coloured premium bitter with sweetness persistent throughout.

NPA (Netherton Pale Ale) (OG 1048, ABV 4.8%)

Bumble Hole Bitter (OG 1052, ABV 5.2%) ◆
Sweet, smooth, amber-coloured ale with hints of astringency in the finish.

Oldershaw SIBA

Heath Lane, Barkston Heath, Lincolnshire, NG32 2DE ☎ (01476) 572135 🌐 oldershawbrewery.com

Oldershaw Brewery has been brewing since 1997. Owned and run by brewster Kathy Britton, the brewery produces around 20 different beers of varying styles. Bespoke beers can be created to order. !! ◆

Heavenly Blonde (OG 1038, ABV 3.8%)
Pale-coloured session ale packed with zesty tropical fruit flavours. A crisp, dry finish.

Newton's Drop (OG 1041, ABV 4.1%) ◆
Balanced malt and hops but with a strong bitter, lingering taste in this mid-brown-coloured beer.

Grantham Stout (OG 1043, ABV 4.3%)
Smooth, dark brown-coloured ale with rich roast malt notes and complex, warming, fruity flavours.

Mosaic Blonde (OG 1041, ABV 4.3%)
A powerfully citrus, tropical beer packed with hops.

Old Boy (OG 1047, ABV 4.8%) ◆
A full-bodied, amber-coloured ale, fruity and bitter with a hop/fruit aroma. The malt that backs the taste dies in the long finish.

American Hopquad (ABV 5%)
A fresh IPA with sharp citrus and herbal notes on a warm toasted malt base. A distinct orange aroma leads to a crisp finish.

Blonde Volupta (OG 1050, ABV 5%)
Straw gold-coloured, zesty premium beer packed with complexity. Intense tropical fruit flavours lead to a crisp, dry finish.

On the Edge

Sheffield, South Yorkshire ☎ 07854 983197 🌐 ontheedgebrew.com

On the Edge started brewing commercially in 2012 using a 0.5-barrel plant in the brewer's home. Brewing takes place once a week. Three local pubs are supplied as well as beer festivals. There is no regular beer list as new brews are constantly being tried. **V**

One Mile End SIBA

Unit 2, Compass West Estate, West Road, Tottenham, London, N17 0XL
☎ (020) 7998 0610 ☎ 07912 411147

Office: White Hart, 1-3 Mile End Road, London, E1 4TP 🌐 onemileend.com

One Mile End took over the former premises of the Redemption Brewery (qv) using a 12.5-barrel plant brewing up to four times a week. A three-barrel plant is also occasionally in operation at the White Hart in Whitechapel, its original home. Beer is sometimes brewed using the Under the Street brand name. !!

Great Tom Mild (ABV 3.8%) ◆
Complex dark mild with hints of coffee, cocoa and vanilla in the taste. Slightly roasty bitter finish.

Hospital Porter (ABV 5.2%) ◆
Dark brown-coloured porter with a smoky, roasty nose. Sweet mocha, roast and nuts on the palate. Dry, dark roast finish.

Opa Hay's

Glencot, Wood Lane, Aldeby, Norfolk, NR34 0DA ☎ (01502) 679144 ☎ 07916 282729 🌐 engelfineales.com

Opa Hay's began brewing in 2008. It is a small, family-run brewery, taking its name from the brewer's great grandfather. Only traditional brewing methods are used, with ingredients that are, where possible, sourced locally. ◆RAIB

Engels Fruity Little Number (ABV 3.6%) ◆
Powerful citrus/grapefruit aroma with malt and hops. Smoky, sweetish flavours with fruit notes, and a fruity, hoppy aftertaste.

Engel's Best Bitter (ABV 4%)
A triple-hopped aromatic beer.

Hop Hop Hooray (ABV 4.3%)

Matilda's Revenge (ABV 4.3%)

SEMP (Samuel Engels Meister Pils) (ABV 4.8%)
A pale-coloured, Pilsner-style beer with a hoppy aroma.

Liquid Bread (ABV 5.2%)
Bavarian-style wheat beer with an aroma of cloves and banana. Naturally cloudy.

Bavarian Breakfast Beer (ABV 5.4%)
A real lager with a malty body.

Ora (NEW) SIBA

Unit 16a, Rosebery Industrial Estate, Rosebery Avenue, Tottenham, London, N17 9SR ☎ 07703 563559 🌐 orabeer.com

Originally split between Italy and cuckoo brewing at Ubrew (qv), Ora took over Brewheadz in Tottenham, who now cuckoo on its kit. A variety of hop-forward beers are brewed complemented with styles incorporating classic Italian ingredients such as lemons, balsamic vinegar and vanilla.

Orbit

Arches 225 & 228, Fielding Street, Walworth, London, SE17 3HD ☎ 07885 663842 🌐 orbitbeers.com

Established in 2014 in a railway arch in Walworth, Orbit produces keg and bottle-conditioned beers. Its core range is supplemented by White Label specials. The design work and beer names relate to the brewer's love of vinyl. RAIB

Origami

75 Temperance Street, Manchester, M12 6HU

Office: 23 Bradshaw Lane, Stretford, Manchester, M32 8WF 🌐 http://origamibrewingcompany.com/

Brewing began in 2016 on the premises of Beer Nouveau (qv) where Origami has its own brew plant but also uses the larger plant of Beer Nouveau as required. 2019 saw a change of focus, with most of the brewery's output being bottled.

THE BREWERIES

Fortune Teller (ABV 4%)

1000 Cranes (ABV 5%)

Valley Fold (ABV 5.3%)

Rabbit Ear (ABV 5.5%)

Arctic Fox (ABV 7%)

Orkney SIBA

Quoyloo, Orkney, KW16 3LT
☎ (01667) 404555 ☎ 07721 013227
Office: Sinclair Breweries Ltd, Cawdor, IV12 5XP
⊕ orkneybrewery.co.uk

☺Orkney was established in 1988 in an old village school building. Having incorporated sister brewery Atlas (qv), it moved next door in 2010 to enable an increase in capacity and the completion of an award-winning visitor centre in 2012. !!☰♦

Raven (OG 1038, ABV 3.8%) ◆
A well-balanced quaffable bitter. Malty fruitiness and bitter hops last through to the long, dry aftertaste.

Dragonhead (OG 1040, ABV 4%) ◆
A strong, dark roasted malt aroma flows into the taste. The roast malt continues to dominate the aftertaste, and blends with chocolate to develop a strong, dry finish.

Northern Light (OG 1040, ABV 4%) ◆
A well-balanced golden ale with a real smack of fruit and hops in the taste and an increasing bitter aftertaste.

Red MacGregor (OG 1040, ABV 4%) ⊟ ◆
This tawny red-coloured ale has a well-balanced mix of red fruit, malt and hops. Slight sweetness throughout.

Corncrake (OG 1042, ABV 4.1%) ◆
A straw-coloured beer with soft citrus fruits and a floral aroma.

Puffin Ale (OG 1045, ABV 4.5%) ◆
Bittersweet mix of malts and plenty of hops.

Dark Island (OG 1045, ABV 4.6%) ⊟ ◆
A sweetish roast chocolate malt taste leads to a long-lasting roasted, slightly bitter, dry finish.

Skull Splitter (OG 1080, ABV 8.5%) ◆
An intense velvet malt nose with hints of apple, prune and plum. The hoppy taste is balanced by satiny smooth malt with sweet fruity spicy edges, leading to a long, dry finish with a hint of nut.

Brewed for Atlas Brewery:

Wayfarer (OG 1044, ABV 4.4%) ◆
Full of citrus fruits and hops with a bitter finish.

Golden Amber (OG 1045, ABV 4.5%) ◆
Refreshing hops, honey, marmalade and grapefruit to the fore with a dry, hoppy finish.

Blizzard (OG 10477, ABV 4.7%) ◆
Light on malts and hops with ginger and spices coming through.

Oscars

Unit 1, Riverside Works, Brunswick Street, Nelson, Lancashire, BB9 0HZ ⊕ oscarsbrewery.co.uk

Originally based in Preston, the brewery was taken over in 2017 by the Lancashire Beer Co, a pub supplies wholesaler in Nelson. In 2018 the brewery name was changed to Oscars and a new range of

beers introduced. Production moved to purpose-built premises in Nelson at the parent company in 2019. ♦

Top Dog (ABV 3.8%)

Dogfather (ABV 3.9%)

Gun Dog (ABV 4%)

Golden Retriever (OG 1042, ABV 4.2%)

Ossett SIBA

Kings Yard, Low Mill Road, Ossett, West Yorkshire, WF5 8ND
☎ (01924) 261333 ⊕ ossett-brewery.co.uk

☺Brewing began in 1998, moving to a new site in 2005. 2017 saw significant investment in brewery improvements and expansion to bring total brewing capacity up to 360 barrels per week. In addition a brand new warehouse and packaging facility was constructed. A visitor centre is planned. The brewery owns 26 pubs, three of which are Hop-branded bars – larger city centre venues based around a concept of real ale and live music. !!☰♦

Yorkshire Brunette (ABV 3.7%)
An easy-drinking session bitter with aromas of spice and citrus fruit.

Yorkshire Blonde (OG 1040, ABV 3.9%)
A pale-coloured, full-bodied and well-rounded ale. Slightly sweet on the palate with a hoppy aroma.

Silver King (OG 1041, ABV 4.3%)
A lager-style beer with a crisp, dry flavour and citrus fruity aroma.

Excelsior (OG 1051, ABV 5.2%)
A strong pale ale with a full, mellow flavour and a fresh, hoppy aroma with citrus/floral characteristics.

Ostlers

🞮 White Horse, 2 York Street, Harborne, West Midlands, B17 0HG
☎ (0121) 427 8004 ⊕ whitehorseharborne.com

Situated at the rear of the White Horse in Harborne, the brewery was in occasional production for a few years. It now has a 4.5-barrel plant brewing a small range of core beers alongside frequent specials and seasonal beers.

Other Monkey

Three Wise Monkeys, 60 High Street, Colchester, Essex, CO1 1DN
☎ (01206) 543014 ⊕ othermonkeybrewing.com

⊗ Other Monkeys is located in the basement of the Three Wise Monkeys pub. The brewery and pub are separately owned but beer is only brewed for the Three Wise Monkeys and two other outlets in Colchester.

Pale Ale (ABV 4.4%)

Otter SIBA

Mathayes, Luppitt, Devon, EX14 4SA
☎ (01404) 891285 ⊕ otterbrewery.com

⊗ A family-run brewery set high up in the Blackdown Hills. Environmental responsibility lies at the heart of its ethos. Otter's eco cellar has been built underground and is naturally chilled. The beers are made from the brewery's own springs and locally-sourced ingredients. ♦

Bitter (OG 1036, ABV 3.6%)
Well-balanced, amber-coloured session bitter with a fruity nose, bitter taste and aftertaste.

Amber (OG 1038.5, ABV 4%)
Light, refreshing and mellow with hints of citrus hoppiness. Creamy and delicate with hops and fruit.

Bright (OG 1039, ABV 4.3%)
A light and refreshing golden ale with delicate malt and fruit leading through hops to a lingering bitter aftertaste.

Ale (OG 1043, ABV 4.5%)
Malt dominates from nose to throat. Sweet fruit, toffee and caramel with a dry aftertaste, full of flavour.

Head (OG 1054, ABV 5.8%)
Smooth, strong ale. Caramel malt throughout. Full-bodied with rich, malty fruitiness and a chocolate hint, leaving a bitter aftertaste.

Out There SIBA

Unit 4, Foundry Lane Industrial Estate, Newcastle upon Tyne, NE6 1LH ☎ 07946 579534
outtherebrewing.com

Out There was established in 2012 by Steve Pickthall. Branding and beer names are themed around the 1950s space race.

Space is the Place (OG 1034, ABV 3.5%)
An amber-coloured table beer with a cream head. The aroma is digestive biscuits and brown bread with a sweet malt flavour and floral notes.

Laika (OG 1049, ABV 4.8%)
A straw-coloured cloudy ale. The aroma is citrus with a hint of custard cream biscuits. Flavours of orange peel and spices liven the malt base.

Celestial Love (OG 1051, ABV 5.1%)
A rich red-coloured ale with aromas of caramel. The taste is sweet malt with floral and grapefruit hop flavours.

Outgang

Kinsley Hotel, Wakefield Road, Kinsley, West Yorkshire, WF9 5EH ☎ 07747 694611
kinsleyhotel.com/Outgang-Brewery.html

Originally established in 2011, brewing resumed in 2017 after a period of inoperation. Local outlets are supplied as are outlets further afield due to increased production.

Tailgate Ripper (OG 1039, ABV 3.9%)

Pit Bottom (OG 1040, ABV 4%)

Button Man (ABV 4.3%)

Outhouse (NEW)

c/o Unit 16a, Redbrook Business Park, off Wilthorpe Road, Redbrook, Barnsley, South Yorkshire, S75 1JN ☎ 07572 164446

Office: Henry Morgan House, Industry Road, Carlton, Barnsley, S71 3PQ outhousebrewing.co.uk

After a 13 year teaching career Andy Jones established Outhouse in 2018 using spare capacity at Jolly Boys (qv). !! GF V

Ged (OG 1038, ABV 3.8%)

Henry (OG 1042, ABV 4.1%)

Ollie (OG 1042, ABV 4.3%)

Bikeshed (OG 1039, ABV 4.5%)

Edd (OG 1048, ABV 4.5%)

Outlaw

See Rooster's

Outstanding SIBA

Units 1 & 2, Foundry, Ordsall Lane, Ordsall, Manchester, M5 3AN
☎ (0161) 873 8090 outstandingbeers.com

Established in 2008, the brewery operates a dual system, brewing on a 15-barrel plant and using a 2.5-barrel plant for special and experimental brews. Originally based in Bury, it moved to Ordsall in 2017. Selected free trade accounts are supplied nationally. ♦

3.9 (OG 1036, ABV 3.9%)

UltraPale (OG 1041, ABV 4.1%)
Straw in colour, with a light citrus aroma. Lemony fruit with hop bitterness to taste and a bitter, astringent finish.

Red (OG 1045, ABV 4.4%)
A copper-coloured, mellow ale with biscuit notes.

Blond (OG 1044, ABV 4.5%)
A pale, refreshing blonde ale with citrus flavours.

IPA (OG 1058, ABV 5.5%)
A golden-coloured, dry and bitter IPA.

Stout (OG 1061, ABV 5.5%)
A jet black-coloured, roasty stout with liquorice notes.

Imperial IPA (OG 1065, ABV 7.4%)
A massively-hopped, golden-coloured, strong IPA.

Ovenstone 109 (NEW) SIBA

Ovenstone Works, Ovenstone, KY10 2RR
☎ (01333) 311394 ovenstone109.com

Established in 2018, Ovenstone 109 is a microbrewery in the East Neuk of Fife. The brewer aims to use renewable and sustainable technology in the brewing process.

Overtone (NEW) SIBA

Unit 19, New Albion Industrial Estate, Halley Street, Yoker, Glasgow, G13 4DJ overtonebrewing.com

Established in 2018. No real ale.

Oxbrew SIBA

Unit 6, Wroslyn Road Industrial Estate, Freeland, Oxfordshire, OX29 8HZ
☎ (01993) 881941 ☎ 07789 241084
oxbrew.co.uk

Brewing began in 2017 on an eight-barrel plant in Enstone and moved to share the same premises as Little Ox (qv) in 2019. Although trading separately, the production plant is shared, with some of Oxbrew's kit being used and some sold. Total joint capacity is now 56 barrels. ♦ RAIB

THE BREWERIES

Amber Ale (OG 1045, ABV 4.5%)

Red (ABV 5%)

Oxted

Oxted, Surrey ☎ 07867 541700
🌐 theoxtedbrewery.co.uk

⊗ Oxted Brewery was established in 2015 using a two-barrel plant and occupies a purpose-built extension at the owner's home. Beers are regularly available in the Crown and Wheatsheaf pubs, Old Oxted, and the Hatch, Redhill. Bottles can be found in local off-licences and farm shops. Occasional events are held locally. RAIB

Hop'dfather (OG 1038, ABV 3.8%)
A hoppy pale ale.

Amber Ale (OG 1039, ABV 3.9%)
Citrus and grapefruit flavours with a light, malty finish.

Single Hop (OG 1039, ABV 3.9%)
Light, fresh, mildly-hopped session beer, which may use a different hop for each brew.

BOB (Best Oxted Bitter) (OG 1041, ABV 4%)
Biscuity, mildly chocolate ale with a smooth finish.

The Black Perle (OG 1044, ABV 4.4%)
Dark roasted flavour with a hint of coffee and a clean aftertaste.

Treehouse IPA (OG 1048, ABV 4.9%)
Well-balanced IPA with citrus and grapefruit to the fore.

Padstow SIBA

The Brewery, Unit 4a, Trecerus Industrial Estate, Padstow, Cornwall, PL28 8RW
☎ (01841) 532169 ☎ 07834 924312
🌐 padstowbrewing.co.uk

⊗ Owners Des & Caron Archer established the brewery in 2013, using a 0.5-barrel plant, which has since been upgraded to 10 barrels. Besides the integral brewery shop, a town-centre off-licence shop with tasting room has been established. !! ♦ RAIB

Pale Ale (OG 1037, ABV 3.6%) ◆
Golden-coloured beer with an assertive hop aroma. Citrus hops dominate the taste with bitterness and dryness. Hoppy, refreshing and crisp finish.

Stowe Away IPA (OG 1041, ABV 4.1%)
A light and refreshing IPA-style beer.

Windjammer (OG 1042, ABV 4.3%) ◆
Copper-coloured best bitter. Light malty, hop aromas leading to a combination of biscuit malt pine and resin hops. Lasting bitterness.

Pride (OG 1044, ABV 4.5%) ◆
Balanced copper-coloured beer. Fruity aromas lead to nutty malt complemented by stone and summer fruit. Crisp malt, slightly sweet finish.

IPA (OG 1046, ABV 4.8%) ◆
Refreshing IPA. Fully hopped on the nose and taste with orange bitterness. Sweet finish with citrus hops and faintly dry.

May Day (OG 1048, ABV 5%) ◆
Golden ale with an aromatic citrus hop aroma and flavour. Powerful grapefruit and moderate bitterness. Strong grassy hop finish with dryness.

Palmers SIBA IFBB

Old Brewery, West Bay Road, Bridport, Dorset, DT6 4JA
☎ (01308) 422396 🌐 palmersbrewery.com

⊗ Palmers is one of Britain's only thatched breweries and dates from 1794. It is situated in Bridport, the heart of the Jurassic Coast in south-west Dorset. The company continues to make substantial investment in its 54 tenanted pubs, all serving cask ale. An additional 400 outlets are supplied within the free trade. !!

Copper Ale (OG 1036, ABV 3.7%) ◆
Beautifully-balanced, copper-coloured light bitter with a hoppy aroma.

IPA (OG 1040, ABV 4.2%) ◆
Hop aroma and bitterness stay in the background in this predominately malty best bitter, with some fruit on the aroma.

Dorset Gold (OG 1046, ABV 4.5%) ◆
More complex than many golden ales thanks to a pleasant banana and mango fruitiness on the aroma that carries on into the taste and aftertaste.

200 (OG 1052, ABV 5%) ◆
This is a big beer with a touch of caramel sweetness adding to a complex hoppy, fruit taste that lasts from the aroma well into the aftertaste.

Tally Ho! (OG 1057, ABV 5.5%) ◆
A complex, dark-coloured old ale. Roast malts and treacle toffee on the palate lead in to a long, lingering finish with more than a hint of coffee.

Panther

Unit 1, Collers Way, Reepham, Norfolk, NR10 4SW
☎ 07766 558215 🌐 pantherbrewery.co.uk

⊗ Panther began brewing in 2010 on an industrial estate near the old railway station, formerly the home of Reepham Brewery. !! ♦ RAIB

Mild Panther (OG 1035, ABV 3.3%) ◆
A smooth, malty character with notes of chocolate, which gives this beer plenty of flavour and aroma.

Ginger Panther (OG 1037, ABV 3.7%) ◆
Refreshingly clean ginger wheat beer with a distinct fiery kick.

Golden Panther (OG 1039, ABV 3.7%) ◆
Refreshing orange and malt notes flow through this well-balanced, easy-drinking bitter. Hops and a soft bitterness add depth.

Honey Panther (OG 1044, ABV 4%) ◆
A gentle, flowing brew with honey and malt throughout. Amber coloured with a tapering bittersweet finale.

Red Panther (OG 1041, ABV 4.1%) ◆
Full-flavoured brew. Solidly malty in both aroma and taste. Hops, and a residual sweetness, provide balance.

American Pale Ale (OG 1044, ABV 4.4%)
A light malt base lets tropical flavours and aromas shine through, with a crisp, dry finish.

Black Panther (OG 1050, ABV 4.5%) ◆
This dark-coloured ale is full flavoured, smooth and complex. It has a bittersweet balance that leads to a dry finish.

Beast of the East (OG 1052, ABV 5.5%)
An amber-coloured IPA, refreshing with floral and grapefruit hop notes.

Papworth SIBA

24 Earith Business Park, Meadow Drove, Earith, Cambridgeshire, PE28 3QF
☎ (01487) 842442 ☎ 07835 845797
papworthbrewery.com

Brewing began in 2014 in Papworth Everard. The brewery moved to new premises in Earith in 2017 and acquired an 11-barrel plant, significantly increasing its production. The new brewery site is licensed for on and off-sales. !!

Mild Thing (OG 1037, ABV 3.5%)
A traditional conker-coloured mild with a light roasted malt flavour.

Mad Jack (OG 1039, ABV 3.8%)
A well-balanced session bitter with a light copper colour and gentle citrus aroma. Caramel overtones lead to a long and delightfully hoppy finish.

The Whitfield Citrabolt (OG 1038, ABV 3.8%)
A refreshing, pale-coloured golden ale with a long citrus bitter finish.

Whispering Grass (OG 1038, ABV 3.8%)
A subtle malt aroma and strong hop finish.

Tooty Frooty Too (OG 1038, ABV 4%)
A pale-coloured, hoppy golden ale with strong tropical fruit flavours and aromas.

Papillon (OG 1042, ABV 4.1%)
Combines sweet malty notes with a lingering and fruity hop finish, leaving a hint of strawberry.

Crystal Ship (OG 1040, ABV 4.2%)
An amber-coloured ale with a light body and strong citrus finish.

Half Nelson (OG 1039, ABV 4.2%)
A well-balanced, ruby-coloured IPA with a fresh and zesty finish.

Red Kite (OG 1048, ABV 4.7%)
Well-balanced ale with a long, strong hop finish bursting with tropical fruit flavours.

Big Sur (OG 1053, ABV 5%)
A West Coast-style pale ale with a light malt body and floral and citrus flavours on the finish.

Robin Goodfellow (OG 1054, ABV 5.4%)
A dark-coloured and full-bodied ale with a strong hop aroma. Heavy and complex malts softened with dark fruit flavours give way to a smooth yet hoppy finish.

Koura (OG 1058, ABV 5.7%)
Golden-coloured, cloudy wheat beer with a delicate banana aroma. Well-balanced bitterness with sweet tropical fruit flavours leading to a lasting, zesty finish.

Paradigm

4d Green End Farm, 93a Church Lane, Sarratt, Hertfordshire, WD3 6HH
☎ (01923) 291215 paradigmbrewery.com

Founded by two friends, Neil Hodges and Rob Atkinson, Paradigm went into production in 2015. Its five-barrel plant is located in an industrial unit on a farm. One-off beers are also brewed. The brewery and beer names are based on corporate jargon and buzzwords. !! ♦ RAIB

Watercress Ale (OG 1036, ABV 3.6%)
Produced with locally grown watercress to add a peppery flavour to this bitter, amber-coloured beer.

Low Hanging Fruit (OG 1038, ABV 3.7%)
Refreshing with citrus flavours, particularly tangerine and grapefruit.

Fake News (OG 1036.5, ABV 3.8%)
A pale-coloured session beer with citrus flavours.

Touch Point (OG 1039, ABV 3.9%)

Juxtaposition (OG 1041, ABV 4%)
An amber-coloured, hoppy beer with a hint of blueberries in the aroma.

Heads Up (OG 1041, ABV 4.1%)
A light golden-coloured beer, full of fruity flavours with peppery hop notes developing and a dry aftertaste.

Win Win (OG 1042, ABV 4.2%)

Best Practice (ABV 4.5%)
A dark ruby-coloured, malty beer with a vanilla flavour.

Zeitgeist (OG 1048, ABV 4.5%)

Synergy (OG 1052, ABV 5.1%)
A full-bodied, fruity IPA.

Black Friday (OG 1062, ABV 6%)
A dark-coloured, strong mild. Smooth and sweetish with a hint of smoked malt.

Parish

6 Main Street, Burrough on the Hill, Leicestershire, LE14 2JQ
☎ (01664) 454801 ☎ 07715 369410
bazbrewery@gmail.com

Parish began in 1983 and now operates on a 20-barrel plant, with capacity to brew a further 12 barrels. The brewery is located in a 400-year-old building next to Grants Freehouse, which stocks the full range of beers. Other local outlets are also supplied and one-off brews are produced for beer festivals. !! RAIB

PSB (OG 1038, ABV 3.9%)
Hoppy session beer with a malty aftertaste.

Burrough Bitter (OG 1047, ABV 4.8%)
Darker version of PSB with a good balance of malt and hops. Reddish brown in colour.

Poachers Ale (OG 1060, ABV 6%)
A ruby-coloured, full-bodied, malty beer.

Baz's Bonce Blower (OG 1098, ABV 12%)
Strong, dark-coloured beer with a rich, malty character. A Christmas pudding ale.

Park Brew

Unit 10, Brechin Business Centre, Brechin, DD9 6DY
☎ 07905 998740 info@parkbrew.com

Established in 2016 by John Leatherbarrow and Andrew Donald. Brewing is currently suspended.

Park Brewery SIBA

Unit 7, Hampden Road, Norbiton, Surrey, KT1 3HG
☎ 07949 574618

Office: 38 St Georges Road, Kingston, KT2 6DN
theparkbrewery.com

The Park Brewery was founded in 2014 in a former greengrocer's premises, using a one-barrel plant, increasing in 2015 to four barrels. Beers are available locally as well as across London and are named after locations in Richmond Park. After a year cuckoo brewing at Reunion, brewing at its new site commenced in 2019. ‼◆RAIB

Killcat Pale (OG 1037, ABV 3.7%) ◀
Unfined golden-coloured bitter with grapefruit throughout and a strong hoppy bitter flavour and finish, which is dry and slightly tart.

Gallows Gold (OG 1044, ABV 4.4%) ◀
Unfined hoppy golden ale with citrus notes. Bitterness develops in the taste and finish, which has some pineapple fruitiness.

Spankers IPA (OG 1055, ABV 5.5%) ◀
An amber-coloured, hoppy, citrus, dry golden ale with a similar finish and a touch of dry bitterness.

Parker

Unit 3, Gravel Lane, Banks, Lancashire, PR9 8BY
☎ (01704) 620718 ☎ 07949 797889
⊕ theparkerbrewery.co.uk

☺Parker was established in 2014 using a 25-litre plant, and has since expanded to a five-barrel plant. ‼RAIB

Centurion Pale Ale (OG 1040, ABV 3.9%)
A light, refreshing pale ale with zesty fruit flavours and a crisp, dry and hoppy finish.

Barbarian Bitter (OG 1041, ABV 4.1%)
Amber-coloured traditional ale with notes of caramel. Smooth and well balanced.

Saxon Red Ale (OG 1046, ABV 4.5%)
Ruby-coloured, smooth ale with warm fruit flavours and a subtle hint of spice on the finish.

Viking Blonde (OG 1042, ABV 4.5%)
A blonde ale with subtle hints of blackcurrant and summer berry fruit flavours and a refreshing, full, crisp finish.

Dark Spartan Stout (OG 1052, ABV 5%)
A smooth, silky, dark-coloured stout with hints of chocolate and coffee.

Partizan

34 Raymouth Road, South Bermondsey, London, SE16 2DB
☎ (020) 8127 5053 ⊕ partizanbrewing.co.uk

Partizan began brewing in 2012. Each brew is different, but is based on a variety of international styles. ☛◆V

Partridge

Dog & Partridge, Hesketh Lane, Chipping, Lancashire, PR3 2TH
☎ (01995) 61201 ⊕ dogandpartridgechipping.co.uk

Established in 2017, Partridge is a nanobrewery located at the now closed Dog & Partridge Pub, which is situated between Thornley and Chipping, near Preston. Brewing is currently suspended.

Peak SIBA

Barn Brewery, Chatsworth, Derbyshire, DE45 1EX
☎ (01246) 583737 ⊕ peakales.co.uk

☺Opened in 2005 in former derelict farm buildings on the Chatsworth estate aided by a DEFRA Rural Enterprise Scheme grant and support from trustees of Chatsworth Settlement. Main beer production

moved to a new facility at Ashford in the Water in 2014 to increase capacity. A new shop and visitor centre opened in 2017 at the original site on the Chatsworth Estate where a pilot brewery for experimental and occasional brews is now operational with its own gin distillery. ‼☛◆

Swift Nick (ABV 3.8%) ◀
Easy-drinking, copper-coloured bitter with balanced malt and hops and a gentle hoppy bitter finish.

Bakewell Best Bitter (ABV 4.2%) ◀
Full-bodied, tawny-coloured bitter with a hoppy bitterness against a malty background, leading to a hoppy dry aftertaste.

Chatsworth Gold (ABV 4.6%) ◀
Speciality beer made with honey, which gives a pleasant sweetness leading to a hop and malt finish.

Black Stag (ABV 4.8%)
A roasted coffee and chocolate base with a spicy blackcurrant and liquorice finish.

IPA (ABV 6%)
A classic IPA, bold and hoppy with a modern citrus twist.

Peakstones Rock SIBA

Peakstones Farm, Cheadle Road, Alton, Staffordshire, ST10 4DH ☎ 07891 350908 ⊕ peakstonesrock.co.uk

☒ Peakstones Rock was established in 2005 with a five-barrel plant located on a farm in the Peak District National Park. The brewery was expanded to 10-barrel capacity in 2009. It supplies an expanding free trade market in the North Midlands and surrounding areas. ‼◆RAIB

Nemesis (OG 1042, ABV 3.8%) ◀
Biscuity aroma with some hop background. Sweet start, sweetish body then hops emerge to give a fruity middle. Bitterness develops slowly to a tongue-tingling finish.

Pugin's Gold (OG 1043, ABV 4%)

Chained Oak (OG 1045, ABV 4.2%)
A copper-coloured beer with a bitter finish and hop aroma.

Alton Abbey (OG 1051, ABV 4.5%)

Black Hole (OG 1048, ABV 4.8%) ◀
Grassy aroma with malt background. Hops hit the mouth and intensify. Bitterness lingers with some mouthwatering astringency.

Submission (OG 1048, ABV 5%) ⌐

Oblivion (OG 1055, ABV 5.5%)

Peerless SIBA

The Brewery, 8 Pool Street, Birkenhead, Merseyside, CH41 3NL
☎ (0151) 647 7688 ⊕ peerlessbrewing.co.uk

Peerless began brewing in 2009 and is under the directorship of Steve Briscoe. Beers are sold through festivals, local pubs and the free trade. ‼◆

Pale (OG 1036, ABV 3.8%)
Pale-coloured session ale. Good initial bitterness and a hint of grapefruit on the finish.

Deadbeat (ABV 4%)
A toasted wheat backbone leads to a fruity hop finish.

Triple Blond (OG 1040, ABV 4%)
A blonde ale with a fruity citrus hop finish.

Lottie Dod (ABV 4.2%)
An amber-coloured ale with a good malt backbone and a hint of bitterness.

Langton Spin (ABV 4.4%)
A well-balanced, dry-hopped golden ale. Initial hop bitterness leads to a citrus, crisp, dry finish.

Oatmeal Stout (OG 1050, ABV 5%)
Full-bodied stout with toffee and caramel tones.

Red Rocks (OG 1047, ABV 5%)
Full-bodied, ruby-coloured ale. Rich malt flavours combine with the hops to give fruity overtones.

Knee-Buckler IPA (ABV 5.2%)
Initial hop bitterness is balanced by malty sweetness. A blend of hops gives the distinct fruity finish.

Full Whack (OG 1054, ABV 6%)
A strong beer, bitter with a fruity hop finish.

Tectonic (ABV 6.2%)
A deep honey-coloured ale with lots of hop aroma and flavour.

Penistone SIBA

White Heart, 77 Gate Bridge Street, Penistone, South Yorkshire, S36 7AH ☎ 07885 251603
✉ chrisward41@btinternet.com

Brewing began in 2017 at the back of the White Heart pub, which dates back to 1377. Initially set up to provide cask-conditioned ales for the pub, the brewery now supplies other local outlets and beer festivals. ♦

Ambers Brew (OG 1042, ABV 4.3%)

Blonde Bombshell (OG 1046, ABV 4.7%)

Queen Bee (OG 1046, ABV 4.7%)
A blonde ale brewed with honey.

Back Oil Tap (OG 1048, ABV 4.9%)

Penlon Cottage

Panteg Farm, New Quay, SA45 9TL
☎ (01545) 561492 🌐 penlonbrewery.co.uk

Established in 2004, Penlon is a six-barrel, farm-based brewery situated on the Cardigan coast above New Quay. In 2017 it opened the Granary tap room with stunning views across the Cardigan coastline. In 2018 the range of ales increased with a likelihood of brewery expansion. !! RAIB

Cardi Bay Best Bitter (OG 1036, ABV 4%)

Hidden Howler (OG 1038, ABV 4.3%)

RSA (OG 1055, ABV 6.2%)

Pennine SIBA

Well Hall Farm, Well, North Yorkshire, DL8 2PX
☎ (01677) 470111 🌐 pennine-brewing.co.uk

Located in the village of Well near Masham, the brewery has been in production on this site since 2013 using an 18-barrel plant complete with lauter tun. Beer is supplied to pubs throughout the north of England as well as to beer festivals and local outdoor events. !!♦

Amber Necker (OG 1039, ABV 3.9%)
A session beer with a smooth and creamy texture and hoppy aftertaste.

Hair of the Dog (OG 1039, ABV 3.9%)
Refreshing, easy-drinking blonde ale with a good hop aroma and gentle bitter aftertaste.

Heartland (OG 1040, ABV 3.9%)
Dark copper-coloured ale with a toffee, malted caramel aroma and a rich, smooth flavour.

Natural Gold (OG 1043, ABV 4.2%)
Sweet palate and subtle aroma with hoppy, smooth aftertaste.

IPA (OG 1045, ABV 4.4%)
A crisp, golden-coloured IPA with a balanced fruitiness, mild liquorice notes and peppery undertones.

Penton Park (NEW) SIBA

Penton Park, Penton Mewsey, Hampshire, SP11 0RD
☎ (01264) 773845 ☎ 07764 691771
🌐 pentonparkbrewery.com

Started from homebrew equipment, this brewery has now expanded to five barrels and is located in the historic early Georgian kitchen of Penton Park. The room is nearly 300 years old and the brewery draws water from the nearby well. !!♦

The Duke (ABV 4%)
Light golden ale, lightly-hopped with rich biscuit background.

50 Not Out (ABV 4.5%)
Malty best bitter with delicate floral spicy notes.

Colonel Bob (ABV 4.5%)
Fruity blonde ale with hints of summer fruits and blackberry.

Pentrich SIBA

Unit B, Asher Lane Business Park, Asher Lane, Pentrich, Derbyshire, DE5 3RB
☎ (01773) 741700
✉ pentrichbrewingco@gmail.com

Two former homebrewers began producing beer for sale in their garage in Pentrich, before moving to share the plant of the Landlocked Brewing Co (qv) at the Beehive Inn, Ripley, in 2014. In 2016 the brewery moved into its own premises. ♦

Shoot the Servant (OG 1038, ABV 3.8%)
A malt-driven, dark-coloured bitter with flavours of toasted caramel and subtle chocolate. English hops add blackcurrant aromas and an understated spicy character.

Soma (OG 1041, ABV 4.1%)
A session pale ale, golden in colour with vibrant citrus and floral flavours.

Eighteen Seventeen (OG 1045, ABV 4.5%)
A full-bodied, amber-coloured ale with a dry fruit aroma and a pleasing bitter finish.

Kiama (OG 1047, ABV 5%)
A vibrant, hoppy pale ale with punchy citrus flavours and huge stone fruit aromas.

Death Valley (ABV 5.2%)
A subtle caramel malt character with huge citrus and tropical flavours alongside subtle floral and pine notes.

Dry River (ABV 5.8%)

Huge pine, grapefruit and orange flavours of tropical fruit fuse with punchy citrus notes. A delicate malt backbone complements the hops.

Three Graves (OG 1060, ABV 6%)

Northfield Garage (ABV 6.5%)

Black Ale (ABV 7.4%)
A black IPA with a silky texture and pungent pine and stone fruit flavours.

Penzance

Star Inn, Crowlas, Cornwall, TR20 8DX
☎ (01736) 740375
penzancebrewing.wordpress.com

Owner Peter Elvin began brewing in 2008 on a self-built five-barrel plant in the old stable block of the Star Inn. The fermentation capacity has since been expanded, increasing the volume and range of beer produced. Production is now at full capacity of 1,400 barrels a year. Besides the pub, selected outlets and beer festivals are supplied. !! ♦

Mild (OG 1042, ABV 3.6%)
Creamy dark brown-coloured mild, chocolate and roast aroma. Coffee and chocolate dominate the taste with fruit notes, bittersweet balanced finish.

Crowlas Bitter (OG 1037, ABV 3.8%)
Refreshing copper-coloured session bitter with a light malt aroma. Light biscuit maltiness and hops. Lingering finish of malty bitterness with dryness.

Potion No. 9 (OG 1039, ABV 4%)
Refreshing golden ale with stone fruit aromas. Grapefruit and tropical fruit dominate the taste with resin notes, pleasant hoppy finish.

Crows-an-Wra (OG 1041, ABV 4.3%)
Straw-coloured golden ale with a grassy, hoppy aroma. Bitter hops dominate throughout, balanced by grapefruit and some malt. Long, clean finish.

Brisons Bitter (OG 1043, ABV 4.5%)
Brown-coloured best bitter, pleasant malt and hop balance. Biscuit malt accompanies bitter orange fruit with a lasting bitter, dry finish.

Trink (OG 1048, ABV 5.2%)
Pale golden ale with a grapefruit nose. Punchy pine-resin hop flavours with grapefruit, marmalade and peaches. Bittersweet and hoppy finish.

IPA (OG 1058, ABV 6%)
Smooth, golden-coloured IPA with a hoppy aroma. Powerful hop bitterness with light malt and tropical fruits, finishing bitter and dry.

Scilly Stout (OG 1067, ABV 7%)
Black-coloured, full-bodied, creamy stout with a chocolate aroma. Chocolate roast malt with liquorice and plums. Long finish with strong roast malt.

People's

Mill House, Mill Lane, Thorpe-next-Haddiscoe, Norfolk, NR14 6PA
☎ (01508) 548706 ✉ peoplesbrewery@mail.com

A one-barrel brewery associated with the community-owned Queen's Head pub in Thurlton, which takes most of its draught output. Beers are also available at the Thurlton Community shop.

Northdown Bitter (OG 1035, ABV 3.8%)

Raveningham Bitter (OG 1036, ABV 3.9%)

Thurlton Gold (OG 1038, ABV 4.2%)
A golden ale with a citrus edge.

Norfolk Cascade (OG 1042, ABV 4.5%)

Northern Brewers (OG 1043, ABV 4.6%)

Perivale (NEW)

Horsenden Farm, Horsenden Lane North, Perivale, UB6 7PQ perivale.beer

Estabished in 2019, the brewery is based at a farm looked after by the Friends of Horsenden Hill. As well as other events, monthly taproom openings are hosted selling beers using hops grown on the farm and other local foraged ingredients.

Pershore SIBA

Unit 5, Lyttleton Road, Pershore, Worcestershire, WR10 2DF
☎ (01386) 561578 ☎ 07495 578397
pershorebrewery.com

Husband and wife team Sean and Elizabeth Barnett set up the 10-barrel plant in an industrial unit on the outskirts of Pershore in 2015. Its extensive range of beers is supplied to local and regional pubs and festivals in the West Midlands area. ♦RAIB

Summertime (OG 1038, ABV 3.8%)

Croft (OG 1042, ABV 4.2%)

Pale Ale (ABV 4.5%)
Amber-coloured IPA with a light floral aroma and refreshing hoppy taste.

Black Moon (ABV 5%)
A light porter with deep roasted and dark chocolate maltiness. A hoppy aftertaste and light glow of ginger and lemongrass lift the taste.

Oh Betty (ABV 5%)
Amber-coloured ale with a distinct floral aroma and a delicate citrus bitterness, finishing with a dry juniper aftertaste.

Pheasantry SIBA

High Brecks Farm, Lincoln Road, East Markham, Nottinghamshire, NG22 0SN
☎ (01777) 872728 ☎ 07984 976749
pheasantrybrewery.co.uk

Pheasantry began brewing in 2012 using a new 10-barrel plant from Canada. Situated in a listed barn on a farm, the brewery incorporates a wedding and events venue, with the brewery visible through glass partitions. It supplies more than 200 pubs and retail outlets in Nottinghamshire, Lincolnshire, Derbyshire and South Yorkshire. A bottling line was installed in 2018 and contract bottling takes place for other breweries. ♦

Best Bitter (OG 1038, ABV 3.8%)
A well-balanced, copper-coloured beer with fruity highlights and a hoppy finish.

Pale Ale (OG 1040, ABV 4%)
A light, slightly dry modern pale ale with a touch of vanilla and a subtle floral aroma.

Ringneck Amber Ale (OG 1041, ABV 4.1%)
Amber-coloured best bitter, initial malt and caramel leading to a brief bitter, dry finish.

Black Pheasant (OG 1042, ABV 4.2%)

A smooth, soft. satisfying dark-coloured ale with malty flavours, balanced bitterness and a velvety texture.

Lincoln Tank Ale (OG 1042, ABV 4.2%)
A classic English amber-coloured ale; malty, hoppy and soft.

Excitra (OG 1043, ABV 4.5%)
A bright orange-coloured ale with a pungent hop punch. Bold but well balanced.

Dancing Dragonfly (OG 1042, ABV 5%)
A pale golden-coloured ale packed with peachy, exotic fruit flavours.

Philsters

Unit 16, Camp Industrial Estate, Rycote Lane, Milton Common, Oxfordshire, OX9 2NP ☎ 07747 827489

Office: Beehive Cottage, Little Hazeley, Oxfordshire, OX44 7LH 🌐 philsters.co.uk

⊗ Named after the owner/brewer's nickname, this small brewery, established in 2015 at the brewer's home, expanded with a 4.5-barrel plant into new premises in 2019. It supplies local pubs, including the Plough, Great Haseley and the Bull, Great Milton. ♦

Glass Blower (OG 1035, ABV 3.6%)

Haseley Gold (OG 1039, ABV 4.1%)
A light golden ale with a good balance of malt and hops, giving an initial bright, fresh bitterness, with soft woody, honey notes following.

Oxford Red (OG 1045, ABV 4.2%)
A deep ruby-coloured ale with a smooth bitterness and a fruity, pine aroma.

Boosh (OG 1041, ABV 4.5%)
A light copper-coloured best bitter with an easy-drinking, crisp, dry bitter finish to balance the rich malts.

Rising (OG 1040, ABV 4.5%)
A pale-coloured IPA with an earthy bitterness and a citrus and resinous hop hit.

Phipps SIBA

Albion Brewery, 54 Kingswell Street, Northampton, NN1 1PR
☎ (01604) 946606 ☎ 07717 078402
🌐 phipps-nbc.co.uk

Originally founded in Towcester in 1801, Phipps had been brewing in Northampton since 1817 until taken over by Watney Mann, who closed the brewery in 1974. The company name and recipes were acquired and in 2008 the first Phipps draught beer reappeared after 40 years, brewed to the original recipe at Grainstore Brewery (qv) in Oakham. The Albion Brewery site, once owned by Phipps, was acquired and a new 15-barrel brewing plant installed in 2014 to enable Phipps beers to be once again brewed in the town. !! ♦ RAIB

Diamond Ale (OG 1037, ABV 3.7%)

Red Star (OG 1038, ABV 3.8%)
A deep red-coloured, nutty bitter based on an original recipe.

Cobbler's Ale (ABV 4%)
A chestnut-coloured session bitter, full-flavoured with a dry finish.

India Pale Ale (OG 1043, ABV 4.3%)
A pale amber-coloured best bitter recreated from an old Phipps recipe. A residual malt sweetness and grapefruit notes from the hops give a fresh, crisp finish.

Ratliffe's Celebrated Stout (OG 1043, ABV 4.3%)
A creamy, well-balanced stout with just a hint of bitterness.

Becket's Ale (ABV 4.5%)
A sweet, dark-coloured, malty beer with honey notes.

Bison Brown (OG 1046, ABV 4.6%)
A strong, smooth and sweet brown-coloured ale.

Cascadia (OG 1050, ABV 5%)

Gold Star (OG 1050, ABV 5.2%)

Phoenix SIBA

Green Lane, Heywood, OL10 2EP
☎ (01706) 627009 ✉ tony@phoenixbrewery.co.uk

Established in Ellesmere Port in 1982, Oak Brewery moved to the old Phoenix Brewery in Heywood and adopted the name in 1991. It now supplies more than 400 outlets plus wholesalers. Restoration of the old brewery, built in 1897, is ongoing. ♦

Hopsack (OG 1038, ABV 3.8%)
A light-drinking, hoppy session beer.

Navvy (OG 1039, ABV 3.8%) ◆
Amber-coloured beer with a citrus fruit and malt nose. Good balance of citrus fruit, malt and hops with bitterness coming through in the aftertaste.

Monkeytown Mild (OG 1039, ABV 3.9%) ◆
Light roast aroma. Mild creamy roast flavour with sweet malt and some astringency. Lasting dry bitter finish.

Arizona (OG 1040, ABV 4.1%) ◆
Yellow in colour with a fruity and hoppy aroma. A refreshing beer with citrus, hops and good bitterness, and a shortish dry aftertaste.

Spotland Gold (OG 1041, ABV 4.1%)
A pale-coloured, hoppy beer with a lingering bitter finish.

Pale Moonlight (OG 1042, ABV 4.2%)
Quite bitter with lingering grassy hop finish.

Black Bee (OG 1045, ABV 4.5%)
Brewed with honey this porter has a malty aroma, which tastes of dark fruit, honey and a hint of coffee.

White Monk (OG 1045, ABV 4.5%) ◆
Yellow-coloured beer with a citrus fruit aroma, plenty of fruit, hops and bitterness in the taste, and a hoppy, bitter finish.

Thirsty Moon (OG 1046, ABV 4.6%) ◆
Tawny-coloured beer with a fresh citrus aroma. Hoppy, fruity and malty with a dry, hoppy finish.

West Coast IPA (OG 1046, ABV 4.6%) ◆
Golden in colour with a hoppy, fruity nose. Strong hoppy and fruity taste and aftertaste with good bitterness throughout.

Double Gold (OG 1050, ABV 5%)

Wobbly Bob (OG 1060, ABV 6%) ◆
A red/brown-coloured beer with malty, fruity aroma and creamy mouthfeel. Strongly malty and fruity in flavour, with hops and a hint of herbs. Both sweetness and bitterness are evident throughout.

Brewed for Brunning & Price Pub Co:

Original (ABV 3.8%)

Pictish

Unit 9, Canalside Industrial Estate, Woodbine Street East, Rochdale, OL16 5LB
☎ (01706) 522227 🌐 pictish-brewing.co.uk

The brewery was established in 2000 and supplies free trade outlets in the North-west and West Yorkshire. Famed for the consistency and clarity of its brews and its ever-changing single hop series of beers. ♦

Brewers Gold (OG 1038, ABV 3.8%)
Yellow in colour with a hoppy, fruity nose. Soft maltiness and a strong hop/citrus flavour lead to a dry, bitter finish.

Talisman IPA (OG 1042, ABV 4.2%)
Strong hoppy aroma; hops and fruit in the taste. Some initial sweetness but with hoppy bitterness throughout.

Alchemists Ale (OG 1043, ABV 4.3%)
Sweet malt balanced with fruity hops and moderate bitterness. Increased lasting bitterness in aftertaste.

Piddle SIBA

Unit 24, Enterprise Park, Piddlehinton, Dorset, DT2 7UA
☎ (01305) 849336 ☎ 07730 436343
🌐 piddlebrewery.co.uk

Established in 2007, with new owners in 2014. The brewery produces a broad range of beers from their location in the Piddle valley in Dorset. Some beer names reflect this unusual name. Beers are available in pubs and retail outlets across Dorset and beyond. ♦

Dorset Rogue (OG 1038, ABV 3.9%)
A balanced, complex, chestnut-coloured best bitter. Malty and fruity with a hint of caramel and toffee.

Piddle (OG 1043, ABV 4.1%)
Easy-drinking, amber-coloured session ale. A full-bodied beer, slightly sweet but malty with a fruity nose and citrus twist.

Cocky (OG 1047, ABV 4.3%)
A golden-coloured, hoppy IPA with a refreshing hoppy zing and crisp grapefruit finish with pine and floral notes.

Bent Copper (OG 1050, ABV 4.8%)
Smooth, strong bitter with a herbal and grassy aroma.

Slasher (OG 1053, ABV 5.1%)
A strong, lager-style ale with floral aromas and flavours. Slightly sweet with a refreshing dry finish.

Pied Bull

Pied Bull Hotel, 57 Northgate Street, Chester, CH1 2HQ
☎ (01244) 325829 🌐 piedbull.co.uk

Pied Bull began brewing in 2011 using a one-barrel plant. Beer is mainly for in-house consumption but local beer festivals are supplied and occasional brewery swaps occur. ♦

Pig & Porter

9 Chapman Way, Tunbridge Wells, Kent, TN2 3EF
☎ (01892) 615071 🌐 pigandporter.co.uk

Originally brewing at several microbreweries in Sussex and Kent, brewing has taken place on its own plant in Tunbridge Wells since 2013 using a 10-barrel plant. ♦

Blackbird (ABV 4%)

Skylarking (ABV 4%)

Slave to the Money (ABV 4.1%)

Red Spider Rye (ABV 4.8%)

All These Vibes (ABV 5.3%)

Pig Iron

Rowley Village, Rowley Regis, B65 9AT ☎ 07816 018777 🌐 pigironbrewingco.co.uk

Set up in 2015, this three-barrel plant has relocated and is now sited to the rear of the Britannia pub in Rowley Regis. The brewer, from a former baking family, acquired the kit from Brewmeister in Scotland. The brewery supplies free trade outlets within 15 miles of the brewery and the brewers home, as well as Weavers Real Ale House, Kidderminster. ♦

Blonde (OG 1038, ABV 3.8%)

EPA (OG 1042, ABV 4.2%)
A golden-coloured ale with floral, grapefruit, pine and cedar flavours and a spicy honey aroma.

IPA (OG 1042, ABV 4.2%)

Unbeweavable (OG 1042, ABV 4.2%)

APA (OG 1045, ABV 4.5%)
An American-style IPA with pronounced citrus, blackcurrant and grapefruit flavours.

Brewed under the Britt Brewery brand name:

Brew Britannia

Pop (OG 1049, ABV 4.9%)

Pig Pub

Pig In Muck, Manor Road, Claybrooke Magna, Leicestershire, LE17 5AY
☎ (01455) 202859 🌐 piginmuck.com/brewery

Brewing began in 2013 using a two-barrel plant, upgraded to a five-barrel plant built by head brewer Kev Featherstone. RAIB

Pilgrim SIBA

11 West Street, Reigate, Surrey, RH2 9BL
☎ (01737) 222651 ☎ 07973 297410 🌐 pilgrim.co.uk

Pilgrim was the first microbrewery in Surrey, set up in 1982 in Woldingham before moving to its current premises in Reigate in 1984. New owners from 2017 are developing new ales to complement the current selection and have enlarged to a 12-barrel brew length and opened a taproom. Beers are available in around 40 local outlets. !! ♦

Surrey (OG 1038, ABV 3.7%)
Pineapple, grapefruit and spicy aromas. Biscuity maltiness with a hint of vanilla balanced by a hoppy bitterness and refreshing bittersweet finish.

Session IPA (OG 1040, ABV 3.9%)

Clean, crisp bitterness and a hoppy fruity flavour. The hops produce prominent and complex tropical fruit aromas, notes of sherbet, orange and passion fruit.

Progress (OG 1041, ABV 4%) ◆
Well-rounded, tawny-coloured bitter. Predominantly sweet and malty with an underlying fruitiness and hint of toffee, balanced with a subdued bitterness.

Quest (OG 1043, ABV 4.3%)
Light on the palate with a mix of hops giving the beer floral and lime notes.

Saracen (OG 1047, ABV 4.5%)
Complex beer with coffee undertones and roast nut characteristics.

Wheat Beer (OG 1050, ABV 5.2%)
A full-bodied, crisp and clean wheat beer. Biscuity malts combine with floral hops along with notes of banana and clove in this complex beer.

Pillars SIBA

Unit 2, Ravenswood Industrial Estate, Shernhall Street, Walthamstow, London, E17 9HQ
☎ (020) 8521 5552 ⊕ pillarsbrewery.com

Brewing began in 2016 and is the only exclusively lager brewery and taproom in London. No real ale.

Pilot Beer

4b Stewartfield, Edinburgh, EH6 5RQ
☎ (0131) 561 4267 ⊕ pilotbeer.co.uk

Pilot began brewing in 2013 in an industrial unit in Leith using a five-barrel plant. A recent move to larger premises has allowed for expansion. Beers are unfined and unfiltered. Almost all output is keg or can but cask-conditioned ale is occasionally available. RAIB

Pilot Brewery

🛏 **726 Mumbles Road, Mumbles, Swansea, SA3 4EL**
☎ 07897 895511 ⊕ thepilotbrewery.co.uk

☺The Pilot Brewery began production on its 2.5-barrel plant in 2013. It is located at the rear of the Pilot Inn on the Mumbles sea front. The output is mainly for the Pilot Inn but can be found at festivals and other select outlets. A sister brewery, BeerRiff (qv) was established in 2017 (no real ale).

Pin-Up SIBA

Unit 3, Block 3, Chalex Industrial Estate, Manor Hall Road, Southwick, West Sussex, BN42 4NH
☎ (01273) 411127 ☎ 07888 836892
⊕ pinupbrewingco.com

⊠ Pin-Up began brewing in 2011, initially having its beers contract brewed at an Essex brewery. In 2014 it obtained its own plant and began brewing in Southwick, expanding from a five-barrel to a 10-barrel plant in 2015. Its first pub, the United Brethren, Chelmsford, opened in 2016. ◆RAIB

Session IPA (OG 1040, ABV 4.1%)

Gold Rush (OG 1041, ABV 4.2%)

Fernie Red (OG 1046, ABV 4.7%)

White IPA (OG 1047, ABV 4.8%)

Oatmeal Stout (OG 1049, ABV 5%)

Pale Ale (OG 1050, ABV 5.1%)

Pinnora (NEW)

Unit 2, Rear of Jubilee Parade, West End Avenue, Pinner, HA5 1BB ☎ 0845 474 2337
⊕ pinnorabrewing.com

Pinnora, named after the 13th century village, was founded by two local brothers. It moved into its first commercial premises in 2018. The beers are named after local landmarks and traditions. No real ale.

Pipes

183a Kings Road, Cardiff, CF11 9DF ☎ 07776 382244
⊕ pipesbeer.co.uk

Formerly known as Artisan, the brewery was established in 2008. All beers are unfiltered, without additives or preservatives. The main output is bottled and keg beers, although cask-conditioned beers are occasionally produced. ⛟◆V

Pit Top

See Wrytree

Pitchfork

See Epic Beers

Plain SIBA

17c Deverill Trading Estate, Sutton Veny, Wiltshire, BA12 7BZ
☎ (01985) 841481 ⊕ plainales.co.uk

⊠ Plain Ales started production in 2008 on a 2.5-barrel plant in a garage, and expanded to a 10-barrel plant in 2010 to keep up with demand for its award-winning ales. 2018 saw the introduction of its Kult Brewing Co beer brand to brew edgier beers. ‼◆

Sheep Dip (OG 1040, ABV 3.8%)
A session ale with a zesty start leading to a dry and hoppy finish.

Innocence (OG 1042, ABV 4%)
A straw-coloured, fragrant bitter.

Innspiration (OG 1042, ABV 4%)
A traditional, copper-coloured, easy-drinking bitter.

Inntrigue (OG 1044, ABV 4.2%)
Ruby-coloured best bitter with flavours of woodland berries and a whisper of dark chocolate.

Inncognito (OG 1053, ABV 4.8%) 🍺
A flavoursome stout with sweet, roasted malt, aged port and mature fruits of the vine.

India Plain Ale (OG 1052, ABV 5.2%)

Inndulgence (OG 1055, ABV 5.2%)
A dark ruby-coloured porter with coffee and chocolate notes and a hint of smoke.

Plan B

Audley Avenue Enterprise Park, Newport, TF10 7DW
☎ (01952) 810091

☺Plan B is a family-run brewery set up in 2016 using a 10-barrel plant. Beers are distributed within a 30-mile radius of the brewery and are available from the shop or on-site bar. ‼ RAIB

New Alchemy (ABV 3.9%)

New Session IPA (ABV 4%)

Newport Pale Ale (ABV 4.4%)

Boscobel Bitter (ABV 4.8%)

Steam Stout (ABV 4.8%)

Platform 5 SIBA

Railway Brewhouse, 197 Queen Street, Newton Abbot, Devon, TQ12 2BS
☎ (01626) 437140 ⊕ platform5brewing.co.uk

⊗Established in 2013 using a six-barrel plant. The Railway Inn is supplied along with Molloys in Teignmouth and Torquay. This family-run brewery is situated in part of an enclosed alley under the disused Platform 5 of Newton Abbot station.

The Coaster (OG 1040, ABV 4%)

The Antelope (OG 1043, ABV 4.3%)

American Pale Ale (OG 1046, ABV 4.6%)
A refreshing, light-bodied beer, golden in colour with a clean malt character, moderate bitterness and a long, smooth finish.

The Whistleblower (OG 1046, ABV 4.6%) ◆
Complex nose with roast and caramel leading to fruit and sweet hops with bitterness on the tongue. Dry aftertaste.

Western Gold (OG 1048, ABV 4.8%)

Blitzen (OG 1050, ABV 5%)

IPA (OG 1050, ABV 5%)

Plockton

5 Bank Street, Plockton, IV52 8TP
☎ (01599) 544276 ☎ 07823 322043
⊕ theplocktonbrewery.com

The brewery started trading in 2007 and expanded to a 2.5-barrel plant in 2009. ‼♦RAIB

Bay (OG 1047, ABV 4.6%) ◆
A well-balanced, tawny-coloured best bitter with plenty of hops and malt, which give a bittersweet, fruity flavour.

Fiddlers Fancy (OG 1046, ABV 4.6%) ◆
Refreshing grapefruit aroma and taste turning to a more malty finish.

Starboard! (OG 1052, ABV 5.1%) ◆
A fine, fruity golden ale with a light citrus bitterness. Hop and spicy fruit feature on the nose with a smack of grapefruit in the taste. The bitterness holds well into the aftertaste.

Ring Tong (OG 1056, ABV 5.6%)
A hoppy IPA with a full, fruity flavour.

Poachers

439 Newark Road, North Hykeham, Lincolnshire, LN6 9SP
☎ (01522) 807404 ☎ 07954 131972
⊕ poachersbrewery.co.uk

☺Brewing started in 2001 on a five-barrel plant. In 2006 it was downsized to 2.5-barrel and relocated to outbuildings at the rear of the brewer's home. 2011 saw capacity returned to five barrels. Regular outlets in Lincolnshire and surrounding counties are supplied direct; outlets further afield via wholesalers. An on-site bar is open to public on a Friday evening. ‼♦

Trembling Rabbit Mild (OG 1034, ABV 3.4%)
Rich, dark mild with a smooth, malty flavour and a slightly bitter finish. Local honey used.

Shy Talk Bitter (OG 1037, ABV 3.7%)
A pale golden-coloured, crisp session beer, refreshing with citrus overtones.

Rock Ape (OG 1038, ABV 3.8%)

Poachers Pride (OG 1040, ABV 4%)

Tedi Boy (OG 1040, ABV 4%)

Bog Trotter (OG 1042, ABV 4.2%)
An amber-coloured, full-flavoured, malty beer with a bitter hop aftertaste.

Lincoln Best (OG 1042, ABV 4.2%)
A brown-coloured beer with a flowery hop nose and well-balanced but bitter taste that stays with the malt, becoming more apparent in the drying finish.

Billy Boy (OG 1044, ABV 4.4%)

Imp Ale (OG 1044, ABV 4.4%)
Copper-coloured, fruity and floral ale with a bitter finish.

Black Crow Stout (OG 1045, ABV 4.5%)
A full-bodied stout with a lingering aftertaste. Burnt toffee and caramel flavours come to the fore.

Hykeham Gold (OG 1045, ABV 4.5%)

Monkey Hanger (OG 1045, ABV 4.5%)
A ruby-coloured bitter with a smooth, fruity flavour balanced by hop bitterness.

Jock's Trap (OG 1050, ABV 5%)
A strong, pale brown-coloured bitter, well-balanced and hoppy with a slightly dry fruit finish.

Trout Tickler (OG 1055, ABV 5.5%)
A strong, ruby-coloured bitter with intense flavour and character, sweet undertones with a hint of chocolate. A rich, malty beer.

Polarity

5 Abbotts Close, Worthing, West Sussex, BN11 1JB
☎ 07872 105300 ⊕ polaritybrewing.co.uk

A small brewery established in 2016 by two homebrewing enthusiasts, focusing on small batch cask-conditioned beers. They now work full time as brewer's for other established breweries and come together at weekends to brew Polarity beers. ♦

Rosetta's Comet (OG 1052, ABV 5.4%)
A traditional IPA with a malt-forward flavour, balanced with hops to give a lasting bitter, fruity finish.

Polly's

Holland Farm, Blackbrook, Mold, CH7 6LU
☎ (01244) 940621 ⊕ lokapolly.co.uk

Established in 2016 inside the stable of an old horse called Polly as Black Brook Brewery, it rebranded in 2018 to Loka Polly. It concentrates on keg/KeyKeg and canned beer widely distributed via wholesalers. The beer range changes constantly. The brewery rebranded again to Polly's Brew Co in 2019.

Pomona Island

Unit 33, Waybridge Enterprise Centre, Daniel Adamson Road, Salford, M50 1DS
☎ (0161) 637 2140 ☎ 07972 445474
pomonaislandbrew.co.uk

Brewery set up in 2017, part owned by the people behind the Gas Lamp in Manchester city centre. Head brewer James Dyer is formerly of Tempest Brew Co (qv). All beers are vegetarian. A brewery tap opened in 2019 at 41 Waybridge Enterprise Centre. **V**

Pale (ABV 3.8%)
Pungent fruity hop aroma. Sweet, fruity taste with some bitterness. Gentle and balanced. Lasting delicate bitter finish.

Session IPA (ABV 4.5%)

Stout (ABV 4.5%)

APA (ABV 5.3%)

Pope's Yard

Cutter Room, Frogmore Mill, Apsley, Hertfordshire, HP3 9RY
☎ (01442) 767790 popesyard.co.uk

Pope's Yard began commercial brewing in 2012 using a one-barrel plant. Relocation in 2015 also meant expansion to a five-barrel plant with a one-barrel pilot plant. In 2018 the brewery relocated to Apsley, Hemel Hempstead. **RAIB**

Luminaire (OG 1041, ABV 3.9%)
Hints of citrus, passion fruit and pineapple with a bitter finish.

Quartermaster (OG 1044, ABV 4.4%)

Club Hammer Stout (OG 1060, ABV 5.5%)
Chocolaty sweetness and roast richness balanced by hop bitterness and aroma.

Strong Dark Mild (OG 1063, ABV 6.8%)

Poppyland

46 West Street, Cromer, Norfolk, NR27 9DS
☎ (01263) 515214 ☎ 07802 160558
poppylandbeer.com

Established in 2012 by museum curator and geologist Martin Warren as a working retirement project. The two-barrel brewery, which produces adventurous, unfiltered and vegan-friendly beers, was bought in 2019 by Dave Cornell, who with the help of Martyn to start with, will carry on with a similar style of brewing. Beers are on sale at the brewery and at numerous specialist beer shops across East Anglia and the Midlands. Cask ales available in some Norwich free houses. **RAIB GF V**

East Coast IPA (OG 1069, ABV 7%)

Portobello SIBA

Unit 6, Mitre Bridge Industrial Estate, Mitre Way, North Kensington, London, W10 6AU
☎ (020) 8969 2269 portobellobrewing.com

Starting in 2012, brewing continues at the original site but with an updated and modern theme to its branding. The beers are widely available around London. ♦

Westway Pale Ale (OG 1040, ABV 4%)
Refreshing yellow-coloured beer with a tart lemon flavour. Sweet biscuit, soft citrus and earthy hops aroma. Bitter, dry, lingering, spicy aftertaste.

Star (OG 1044, ABV 4.3%)
Pale brown-coloured malty best bitter with a sweetish nose, a fruity flavour and bitter finish. Hints of nut on the palate and some hops throughout.

APA (OG 1050, ABV 5%)
Full-bodied, straw-coloured strong ale. The honey sweetness and soft citrus fruit balanced by a bitter hops. Dry aftertaste.

Portpatrick

The Neuk, Stoneykirk, DG9 9EF ☎ 07826 542149
portpatrick-brewery.co.uk

The brewery opened in 2015 using a 1.5-barrel plant in converted space in outbuildings. A number of local pubs are supplied. **♦RAIB**

16-21 (OG 1040, ABV 3.8%)

Beltie Blonde (OG 1042, ABV 4%)

Rhins Ruby (OG 1043, ABV 4%)

Dark Skies (OG 1045, ABV 4.2%)

Dorn Rock (OG 1046, ABV 4.3%)

Fog Horn (OG 1049, ABV 4.8%)

Potbelly SIBA

Sydney Street Entrance, Kettering, Northamptonshire, NN16 0JA
☎ (01536) 410818 ☎ 07834 867825
potbelly-brewery.co.uk

Potbelly started brewing in 2005 on a 10-barrel plant and supplies around 200 outlets. Beers are also contract brewed for J Church and under the Olde England Ales brand name. **‼ ♦RAIB GF V**

Best (OG 1036.9, ABV 3.8%)

A Piggin' IPA (OG 1040, ABV 4%)

Hop-Trotter (OG 1041, ABV 4.1%)
Golden-coloured ale with spicy aromas and citrus notes.

Piggin' Saint (OG 1042, ABV 4.2%)

Beijing Black (OG 1045, ABV 4.4%)

Pigs Do Fly (OG 1041, ABV 4.4%)

Hedonism (OG 1045, ABV 4.5%)
A light-coloured bitter with a citrus, hoppy finish.

SOAB (OG 1050, ABV 5%)
Chestnut-coloured bitter with a warm, malty taste that gives way to a lightly-hopped finish.

Crazy Daze (OG 1050, ABV 5.5%)

Contract brewed for J Church Brewing:

Gold Testament (OG 1036, ABV 3.9%)

Potton (NEW)

Unit 3, 8 Market Square, Potton, Bedfordshire, SG19 2NP ☎ 07789 680049
pottonbrewingcompany.com

THE BREWERIES

⊗ Potton Brewing Company was founded in 2017 by the current owner in order to return brewing to the community after the previous local brewery shut down a few years before. The brewery uses an Oban Ales 2.5-barrel plant, brewing 1-2 times a week. The brewery has a strong social ethic and gives 1p from every pint sold to charity. All bottled beers are unfined and suitable for vegans. RAIB V

South of the Border (OG 1037, ABV 3.6%)
Session bitter with robust biscuit and caramel flavours. Spicy, fresh hop aroma.

West of the Sun (OG 1036, ABV 3.6%)
Light, refreshing golden ale brewed with a crisp taste and aroma of orange citrus.

Holly Pup (OG 1038, ABV 3.8%)
Smooth mild with flavours of chocolate and coffee.

Widdershins (OG 1040, ABV 4.1%)
An unusual dark-coloured session bitter. Aromas of chocolate and caramel flavours lead to a delicate finish of blackberries.

Republic IPA (OG 1042, ABV 4.2%)
An American-style IPA with light citrus and soft fruit aromas.

Nice Pint of Beer (OG 1046, ABV 4.6%)
Traditional best bitter with strong malt, biscuit and caramel flavours.

Black Cat (OG 1048, ABV 4.7%)
A robust yet smooth porter with deep, complex flavours of chocolate, coffee and dark fruit.

Nightspear (OG 1046, ABV 4.8%)
A dark-coloured ale with juicy, soft fruit hop aromas. Big flavours of passion fruit and citrus are complemented by a slight late roasted hint.

Powderkeg SIBA

10 Hogsbrook Units, Woodbury Salterton, Devon, EX5 1PY
☎ (01395) 488181 🌐 powderkegbeer.co.uk

⊗ Powderkeg was established in 2015 brewing small batches of beer. It combines International beer styles with new ingredients sourced from around the world. ♦

Speak Easy Transatlantic Pale Ale (OG 1041.5, ABV 4.3%)
Uniting robust malt and epic fruitiness with balanced bitterness and a clean finish.

Poynton

Royal British Legion Club, St George's Road West, Poynton, Cheshire, SK12 1JY ☎ 07771 722403

◎ The Poynton Brewery was established in 2015 by Colin Bavens and Andy King, located at the Poynton Legion Club. Around 20 pubs, clubs and bars are supplied in the Stockport, Altrincham, East Cheshire and Macclesfield areas. In 2018 the brewery opened its first pub, the Flute & Firkin, Poynton. ♦

Hoppy Daze (ABV 3.8%)
A hoppy beer with a zesty aroma and crisp, dry finish.

Kiwi (ABV 4%)
A light golden-coloured beer with mellow fruit flavours.

Viaduct (ABV 4.1%)
A golden ale with an upfront hoppy bitterness and fruity finish.

Idaho (ABV 4.2%)
A robust, fruity and thirst-quenching pale ale.

Session IPA (ABV 4.2%)
An easy-drinking IPA with citrus fruit and pine flavours.

Vulcan (ABV 4.2%)

Slow Boat IPA (ABV 4.8%)

Dark Side (ABV 5.2%)

Prescott

Unit 1, The Bramery Business Park, Alstone Lane, Cheltenham, Gloucestershire, GL51 8HE ☎ 07526 934866 🌐 prescottales.co.uk

Established in 2008, Prescott Ales brews on a 25-barrel plant, clad in wood, brass and copper. It takes its name from the famous Prescott Hill Climb, which is also the home of the UK Bugatti Owners Club. In 2015, a range of craft ales brewed under the Super-6 banner was introduced. ‼♦

Hill Climb (OG 1039.5, ABV 3.8%)
A late-hopped, straw-coloured session beer with a refreshing fruity finish.

Chequered Flag (OG 1042, ABV 4.1%)
A generously-hopped, amber-coloured ale with a malty finish.

Track Record (OG 1044, ABV 4.4%)
A fruity, copper-coloured best bitter with a slightly sweet finish.

Grand Prix (OG 1050, ABV 5.2%)
A dark amber-coloured strong ale with a rich, smooth finish.

Pressure Drop

Unit 6, Lockwood Industrial Estate, Mill Mead Road, Tottenham Hale, London, N17 9QP
☎ (020) 8801 0616 🌐 pressuredropbrewing.co.uk

Run by three partners who were homebrewers but began commercial brewing in 2013, using a five-barrel plant and a small pilot kit. Moving to Tottenham in 2017, the original location is now a bar called the Experiment, operated with Verdant Brewery (qv). An on-site brewery tap is open at weekends and both bars are the best places to find the usual range plus specials. Beers are mostly sold in KeyKeg, bottles and cans. Cask-conditioned versions are produced occasionally for beer festivals. RAIB

Pretty Decent

Arch 338, Sheridan Road, Forest Gate, London, E7 9EF
☎ 07825 381346 🌐 prettydecentbeer.co

Brewing began in 2017 in a railway arch in Forest Gate. Production is mostly keg and KeyKeg but some bottle-conditioned beers are available. An on-site taproom is open Thursday-Sunday and the beers are available in other local bars, several in nearby railway arches. RAIB

Priest Town

139 Ribbleton Avenue, Preston, Lancashire, PR2 6YS
🌐 priesttownbrewing.com

Priest Town is a craft microbrewery, operational since 2017. Originally using a 2.5-barrel plant, it has recently acquired a larger kit and plans to increase production. RAIB

Prior's Well SIBA

Unit 8, Block 22, Farm Way, Old Mill Lane Industrial Estate, Mansfield Woodhouse, Nottinghamshire, NG19 9BQ
☎ (01623) 632393 ☎ 07970 885204
🌐 priorswellbrewery.co.uk

Originally established in a National Trust building on the Clumber Park Estate, but brewing ceased there in 2014. The brewery was subsequently sold and the five-barrel plant modernised and relocated to a new site in Mansfield Woodhouse in 2016 with an on-site bar. ‼

Citra (ABV 3.9%)

Incensed (ABV 4%)

Silver Chalice (OG 1014.7, ABV 4.2%)
A straw-coloured ale with a balanced hop flavour and good bitterness. Orange peel and coriander seeds add further layers of flavour.

Blade (OG 1043.1, ABV 4.7%)

Priory Gold (OG 1045.2, ABV 4.7%)
Pale gold in colour with a citrus aroma, pleasant hop flavours and an intense bitter finish.

Prior's Pale (OG 1047.1, ABV 4.8%)
A full-flavoured pale ale with a lingering bitter finish.

Resurrected (OG 1046.7, ABV 4.8%)
Dark ruby in colour with complex nutty overtones and a dry finish.

Wolfcatcher (OG 1047.1, ABV 4.8%)
American-style pale ale with intense citrus, grapefruit tones.

Dirty Habit (OG 1054.4, ABV 5.8%)
An American-style IPA with a complex hop profile and a pleasant maltiness.

Problem Child

Wayfarer Inn, Alder Lane, Parbold, Lancashire, WN8 7NL
☎ (01257) 464600 ☎ 07588 736926
🌐 problemchildbrewing.co.uk

Problem Child began brewing in 2013 using a five-barrel plant at the Wayfarer Inn, Parbold, where two beers from the range are always available. ‼

Project 88

Beer + Burger, 88 Walm Lane, Willesden Green, London, NW2 4QY
☎ (020) 3019 7575 🌐 beerandburgerstore.com

Established in 2017, Project 88 is a nanobrewery at the Beer + Burger bar in Willesden Green. Beers under the Project 88 name are also available at the three other branches plus two pubs in the chain but are most likely produced elsewhere under contract. No real ale.

Prospect SIBA

Unit 10a, Great George Street, Off Wallgate, Wigan, WN3 4DL
☎ (01257) 421329 🌐 prospectbrewery.com

Prospect was founded as a five-barrel plant in 2007 in the Prospect Hill area of Standish, hence the name, relocating to its current town centre premises in 2017. The brewery owns a popular local bar, Wigan Central, across the road. ‼ ♦

Silver Tally (OG 1037, ABV 3.7%)
A clean, pale golden-coloured bitter with citrus aromas, a full hop flavour and a dry bitter finish.

Whatever! (OG 1040, ABV 3.8%)
Yellow-coloured beer with a light malt/hop aroma. Some malt in taste, but hop and bitterness dominate. Dry, bitter finish.

Nutty Slack (OG 1039, ABV 3.9%)
Dark brown-coloured mild ale with malt and fruit in the aroma. Creamy and chocolaty on the palate, with both malt and fruit in evidence. Malty and moderately bitter finish.

Pioneer (OG 1040, ABV 4%)
A light-bodied, amber-coloured beer with aromas of dry pale malt and earthy hops.

Whatever Next! (ABV 4%)

Cascade Blonde (OG 1039, ABV 4.1%)
A yellow/gold-coloured beer with zesty citrus notes and a clean, refreshing lemon taste.

Blinding Light (OG 1042, ABV 4.2%)
A pale-coloured, refreshing beer with citrus and spicy notes.

Gold Rush (OG 1045, ABV 4.5%)
A deep golden-coloured ale with hoppy and bitter flavours, light fruity notes and a grassy floral finish.

Big John (OG 1047, ABV 4.8%)
Pronounced roast flavour with highlights of blackcurrant and hops. Moderate hoppy bitter aftertaste. Fruit in aroma with malt.

Provenance

See Hydes

Providence

Unit 51, Old Mill Industrial Estate, Bamber Bridge, Lancashire, PR5 6SY ☎ 07811 599147
✉ anne.graham.driver@btinternet.com

Brewing began in 2017 using a 3.25-barrel plant.

Gold Standard (ABV 4.1%)

Pumphouse Community

Green Man, Church Lane, Toppesfield, Essex, CO9 4DR
☎ 07421 994518
🌐 pumphousecommunitybrewery.com

Pumphouse is the first community-owned brewery in the UK. Established in 2015 it uses a two-barrel plant and specialises in session beers with occasional one-off, experimental brews. Pubs, clubs, special events and festivals are supplied within a 10-mile radius as well as its Green Man tap outlet. ‼ ♦

Toppesfied Tap (OG 1037, ABV 3.6%)

Golden Duck IPA (OG 1040, ABV 3.7%)

St Margaret's Ale (OG 1040, ABV 3.8%)

Gold (OG 1041, ABV 4.2%)

Punchline

Unit 13, Monmore Road, Wolverhampton, WV1 2TZ
☎ (01902) 213063 ⊕ punchlinebrewery.co.uk

Launched in 2017, this 200-litre nanobrewery is run by a group of beer-loving friends. All brews are named after the punchline to jokes. RAIB

Purity SIBA

The Brewery, Upper Spernal Farm, Spernal Lane, Great Alne, Warwickshire, B49 6JF
☎ (01789) 488007 ⊕ puritybrewing.com

Brewing began in 2005 in a purpose-designed plant housed in converted barns. The brewery incorporates an environmentally-friendly effluent treatment system. It supplies the free trade within a 70-mile radius, plus London postcodes, and delivers to more than 500 outlets. !! ♦

Bunny Hop (OG 1037, ABV 3.5%)

Pure Gold (OG 1039.5, ABV 3.8%)
An easy-drinking beer with a dry and bitter finish.

Mad Goose (OG 1042.5, ABV 4.2%)
A light copper-coloured ale with a zesty hop character and citrus overtones.

Pure UBU (OG 1044.8, ABV 4.5%)

Purple Cow

Alexandra Arms, 39 Victoria Street, Kettering, Northamptonshire, NN16 0BU ☎ 07507 398353
⊕ purplecowbrewing.co.uk

Purple Cow was established in 2017. It is owned by David Burns, who is also the brewer. ♦RAIB

Purple Moose SIBA

Madoc Street, Porthmadog, LL49 9DB
☎ (01766) 515571 ⊕ purplemoose.co.uk

Established in 2005, Purple Moose is a 40-barrel brewery housed in former iron works in the coastal town of Porthmadog. It owns a brewery shop on Porthmadog High Street plus the Australia pub. The names of the beers reflect local history and geography. !! ♦

Cwrw Eryri/Snowdonia Ale (OG 1035.3, ABV 3.6%)
Golden-coloured, refreshing bitter with citrus fruit hoppiness in aroma and taste. The full mouthfeel leads to a long-lasting, dry, bitter finish.

Cwrw Madog/Madog's Ale (OG 1037, ABV 3.7%)
Full-bodied session bitter. Malty nose and an initial nutty flavour but bitterness dominates. Well-balanced and refreshing with a dry roastiness on the taste and a good dry finish.

Cwrw Ysgawen/Elderflower Ale (OG 1039, ABV 4%)
A pale-coloured and refreshing elderflower beer with a good citrus fruit aroma, bittersweet taste, and a zesty, hoppy, mouthwatering finish.

Cwrw Glaslyn/Glaslyn Ale (OG 1040.5, ABV 4.2%)
Refreshing, light and malty, amber-coloured ale. Plenty of hop in the aroma and taste. Good smooth mouthfeel leading to a slightly chewy finish.

Ochr Dywyll Y Mws/Dark Side of the Moose (OG 1045, ABV 4.6%)
A dark-coloured, complex beer, quite hoppy and bitter with roast undertones. Malt and fruit flavours also feature in the smooth taste and dry finish.

Q Brew (NEW)

58 Lower North Road, Carnforth, Lancashire, LA5 9LJ
☎ 07971 073835

Q Brew started brewing in 2019 and is Carnforth's first microbrewery.

Citra Glow (ABV 3.9%)

Golden Ale (ABV 4.5%)

Q Brewery

16 The Ringway, Queniborough, Leicestershire, LE7 3DL ☎ 07762 300240 ⊕ qbrewery.co.uk

A microbrewery situated in a converted building behind the house of head brewer Tim Lowe. It was established in 2014 and uses a 0.5-barrel brew kit. Beers are brewed on demand.

Quantock SIBA

Westridge Way, Broadgauge Business Park, Bishops Lydeard, Somerset, TA4 3RU
☎ (01823) 433812 ⊕ quantockbrewery.co.uk

Quantock is a family-run brewery that started trading in 2008 on an eight-barrel plant, which has since been expanded. The brewery supplies beers to outlets throughout the South-west and further afield via wholesalers. The brewery taproom is open six days and three evenings a week. ♦RAIB

Ale (OG 1036, ABV 3.8%)
Amber-coloured ale with a fruity, full-bodied flavour and dry finish. The hop blend creates a balanced, fruity character with a delicate, spicy aroma.

Ralehead (OG 1037, ABV 3.9%)
An amber-coloured bitter with a full-flavoured taste for its strength.

QPA (OG 1040, ABV 4%)
A pale ale with a citrus aroma.

Sunraker (OG 1039, ABV 4.2%)
A pale straw-coloured beer, light and refreshing with a delicate, clean grassy hop aroma.

Wills Neck (OG 1040, ABV 4.3%)
A bright golden ale with a rich, malty flavour and lasting bitterness on the palate. A prominent aroma with hints of grapefruit and cherries.

Stout (OG 1044, ABV 4.5%)
A full-bodied, traditional dry stout, dark ebony in colour. The blend of hops gives an aroma of liquorice and citrus fruits. Chocolate and coffee flavours.

Plastered Pheasant (OG 1045, ABV 4.8%)
Rich ale, dark amber in colour with a fruity aroma and smooth coffee and toffee flavours.

Titanium (OG 1050, ABV 5.1%)
A West Coast US-style IPA with tropical hop flavours.

Stag (OG 1056, ABV 6%)

A copper-coloured IPA with a malty and fruity flavour. Generously-hopped it has a smoky aroma with hints of banana and toffee.

Quartz SIBA

Archers, Alrewas Road, Kings Bromley, Staffordshire, DE13 7HW
☎ (01543) 473965 ⊕ quartzbrewing.co.uk

Quartz was established in 2005 by Scott and Julia Barnett. Around 50 outlets are supplied direct. ‼ ♦

Blonde (OG 1038, ABV 3.8%)
Little aroma, gentle hop and background malt. Sweet with unsophisticated sweetshop tastes.

Crystal (OG 1040, ABV 4.2%)
Sweet aroma with some fruit and yeasty, Marmite hints. Hoppiness begins but dwindles to a bittersweet finish.

Extra Blonde (OG 1042, ABV 4.4%)
Sweet, malty aroma with a touch of fruit. Sweet start, smooth with a hint of hops in the sugary finish.

Heart (OG 1045, ABV 4.6%)
Pale brown in colour with some aroma of fruit and malt. Gentle tastes of fruit and hops eventually appear to leave a bitter finish.

Cracker (OG 1050, ABV 5%)
Chestnut in colour with a slight roasted aroma, smooth fruit notes leaving a dry hop finish.

Queen Inn

28 Kingsgate Road, Winchester, Hampshire, SO23 9PG
☎ (01962) 853898 ⊕ thequeeninnwinchester.co.uk

Brewing began in 2013 using a 2.5-barrel brew plant. Currently brewing once or twice a month and nearly always just for the pub.

Quiet

Buchanan's Bistro, Banchory, AB31 5QA
☎ (01330) 826530 ✉ bistro@buchananfood.com

Quiet Brewery is situated at Buchanan's Bistro. Beers are available bottle-conditioned and are only supplied to the bistro. ♦RAIB

Quirky

Unit 3, Ash Lane, Garforth, Leeds, West Yorkshire, LS25 2GA
☎ (0113) 286 2072 ☎ 07425 133199
⊕ quirkyales.com/home.html

Established in 2015, Quirky Ales brews two or three times a week on its 2.5-barrel plant. Its on-site taproom is open every weekend from Thursday evening.

Porter (ABV 3.5%)
A smooth, dark-coloured ale with a malty finish.

2 Islands (ABV 3.8%)
A refreshing pale ale with a spicy bitterness and citrus fruit finish.

Blonde (ABV 3.8%)
A light, crisp, refreshing beer with a tropical citrus finish.

Bitter (ABV 4%)
An easy-drinking session bitter with well-balanced malt and hops.

Ruby (ABV 4%)
A ruby-coloured ale with a smooth finish.

Hip Hop (ABV 5.5%)
A full-bodied, hoppy beer with a dry, clean malt base.

Radnorshire SIBA

Timberworks, Brookside Farm, Mutton Dingle, New Radnor, LD8 2SU
☎ (01544) 350456 ☎ 07789 909748
✉ info@radnorhillsholidaycottages.com

Set up in 2012 in a barn on the grounds of a farm offering holiday cottage accommodation, Radnorshire uses its own spring water. Drinkers staying at the cottages are supplied as well as a few local pubs. ‼

Whimble Gold (OG 1038, ABV 3.8%)

Four Stones (OG 1040, ABV 4%)
A light amber-coloured ale with a subtle maltiness.

Smatcher Tawny (OG 1042, ABV 4.2%)

Water-Break-Its-Neck (ABV 5.7%)

Ralph's Ruin

c/o Royal Oak, Lower Bristol Road, Bath, BA2 3BW
☎ (01225) 481409

Brewing commenced in 2017 using a two-barrel plant in the old kitchen of the Royal Oak. Beer is only available in the pub.

Ramsbury SIBA

Stockclose Farm, Aldbourne, Wiltshire, SN8 2NN
☎ (01672) 541407 ☎ 07843 289527
⊕ ramsbury.com/brewery

The Ramsbury Brewing & Distilling Company started brewing in 2004 using a 10-barrel plant, situated high on the Marlborough Downs in Wiltshire. The brewery uses home-grown barley from the Ramsbury Estate. Expansion in 2014 saw an upgrade to a 30-barrel plant with a visitor centre and a well to provide the water. A distillery that uses grains grown on the estate became operational in 2015. ‼ ♦

Farmer's Best (OG 1036, ABV 3.6%)
Dark amber-coloured ale with subtle floral notes and a delicate rounded flavour.

Same Again (ABV 3.8%)
Pale amber-coloured ale with a citrus finish.

Deerstalker (OG 1040, ABV 4%)
Amber in colour with a pleasing hoppy aroma.

RPA (Ramsbury Pale Ale) (ABV 4%)

Flint Knapper (OG 1042, ABV 4.2%)
A smooth, rich, amber-coloured ale with malty overtones.

Gold (OG 1045, ABV 4.5%)
A rich, golden-coloured beer with a light hoppy aroma and taste.

Red Ram (OG 1045, ABV 4.5%)

Chalk Stream (OG 1050, ABV 5%)

Belapur IPA (OG 1055, ABV 5.5%)
A well-hopped IPA with a fruity, citrus finish.

Ramsgate (Gadds') SIBA

1 Hornet Close, Pyson's Road Industrial Estate, Broadstairs, Kent, CT10 2YD
☎ (01843) 868453 ⊕ ramsgatebrewery.co.uk

Ramsgate was established in 2002 at the back of a Ramsgate seafront pub. In 2006 the brewery moved to its current location, allowing for increased capacity and bottling. A 25-hectolitre brew plant is used. !! ♦ RAIB

Gadds' No. 7 Bitter Ale (OG 1037, ABV 3.8%)

Gadds' Seasider (OG 1042, ABV 4.3%)

Gadds' No. 5 Best Bitter Ale (OG 1043, ABV 4.4%)

She Sells Sea Shells (OG 1042, ABV 4.7%)
A light, refreshing, straw-coloured ale, bitter but with sweet notes.

Gadds' No. 3 Kent Pale Ale (OG 1047, ABV 5%)

Gadds' Faithful Dogbolter Porter (OG 1054, ABV 5.6%)

Gadds' Black Pearl (OG 1062, ABV 6.2%)

RAN

Unit 8, Ormonde Street, Fenton, Stoke-on-Trent, Staffordshire, ST4 3NP ☎ 07843 092620
⊕ ranales.co.uk

Brewing began in 2014 using a one-barrel kit in the garage to the rear of the owner's house. It relocated in 2015 to larger, purpose-built premises nearby, increasing capacity to 2.5 barrels. ♦

Coppa Flya (OG 1040, ABV 4%)
A copper-coloured bitter with a dry finish and a complementary caramel aftertaste.

American Pale Ale (OG 1045, ABV 4.5%)

Flya (OG 1045, ABV 4.5%)
Easy-drinking session ale. Amber in colour with a malty bitterness.

Hedge Hopper (OG 1045, ABV 4.5%)
A light golden-coloured bitter with refreshing fruity notes.

Owd Flya (OG 1050, ABV 5%)
Malt and roast aromas. Liquorice flavours, sweet finish with gentle hops.

Cherry Chilli Stout (OG 1053, ABV 5.3%)

Rum 'n' Raisin Stout (OG 1053, ABV 5.3%)
Chocolate aroma with cocoa. Sweet fruity start with a hoppy background, which develops to a mouthwatering finish.

Stout (OG 1053, ABV 5.3%)
Rich and flavoursome, dark-coloured ale with hints of coffee and chocolate.

Randalls

La Piette Brewery, St Georges Esplanade, St Peter Port, Guernsey, GY1 3JG
☎ (01481) 720134 ⊕ randallsbrewery.com

Randalls has been brewing in Guernsey since 1868. The company was bought out in 2006 and moved into a modern, purpose-built brewery in 2008. 19 pubs are owned and a further 70 outlets are supplied. !! ♦

Range SIBA

Unit N4, Lympne Industrial Estate, Otterpool Lane, Lympne, Kent, CT21 4LR
☎ (01303) 230842 ☎ 07912 207775
⊕ rangealesbrewery.co.uk

Range Ales was planned and set up in 2016 by two friends over a few pints in their local. The brewery name comes from associations with the Hythe small arms ranges nearby, which provides the names of the beers. A four-barrel plant is used to supply pubs and clubs in the Hythe and Folkestone areas. !!

Golden Shot (ABV 3.7%)
A hoppy beer with citrus flavours.

CQB (ABV 4%)
English pale ale with a sharp, hoppy note to the nose and flavours of lemon sorbet.

One in the Chambers (ABV 4%)

Double Tap (ABV 4.1%)
Based on an original Burton recipe, this ale has a sweetish, gentle hop aftertaste.

Black 'Ops (ABV 4.8%)
A modern black IPA with a smooth coffee-like finish.

Rat

Rat & Ratchet, 40 Chapel Hill, Huddersfield, West Yorkshire, HD1 3EB
☎ (01484) 542400 ✉ ratandratchet@ossett-brewery.co.uk

The Rat & Ratchet was originally established as a brewpub in 1994. Brewing ceased and it was purchased by Ossett Brewery (qv) in 2004. Brewing re-started in 2011 with a capacity of 30 barrels per week. A wide range of occasional brews with rat themed names supplement the regular beers. ♦

Rat Attack (OG 1038, ABV 3.8%)
A pale golden-coloured session beer with a powerful citrus aroma.

White Rat (OG 1040, ABV 4%)
A pale-coloured, hoppy ale. Intensely aromatic with a resinous finish.

Black Rat (OG 1047, ABV 4.5%)
Porter with a burnt, coffee and chocolate malt character. Slightly sweet on the palate with a fruity, spicy aroma.

King Rat (OG 1050, ABV 5%)
A highly bitter beer with a white wine aroma. The bitterness is balanced by a residual malty sweetness.

Rat Against the Machine (OG 1071, ABV 7%)

Raven Hill (NEW)

Raven Hill Farm, Kilham, East Yorkshire, YO25 4EG
☎ 07979 674573

Raven Hill Brewery started trading in 2018 and is based on a farm near Kilham. The nearby Old Star pub is owned by the brewer's family and regularly stocks the ales. RAIB

Summit (ABV 3.6%)
An easy-drinking ale with a burst of tropical fruit flavours.

Chalk Stream (ABV 4%)

Crisp and refreshing beer with a good balance of malt and hops.

Brook (ABV 4.3%)
A thirst-quenching ale with citrus flavours.

Ridge Way (ABV 5.5%)
Full of smooth chocolate flavours from the combination of malt and flaked oats.

Elevation (ABV 6.2%)
A hoppy, punchy IPA with complex flavours.

RAW

See Silver

Reality

127 High Road, Chilwell, Nottingham, NG9 4AT
☎ 07801 539523
✉ alandenismonaghan@hotmail.com

⊗ Since starting in 2010, the brewery has built up a loyal following of pubs locally, while supplying beer festivals across the country, functions and individual customers. ♦

Virtuale Reality (OG 1039, ABV 3.8%)

No Escape (OG 1043, ABV 4.2%)

Bitter Reality (OG 1044, ABV 4.3%)

Stark Reality (OG 1046, ABV 4.5%)
Amber-coloured bitter with a hint of rum.

Reality Czech (OG 1047, ABV 4.6%)

Rebel

See Dynamite Valley

Rebellion SIBA

Rebellion Brewery, Bencombe Farm, Marlow Bottom, Buckinghamshire, SL7 3LT
☎ (01628) 476594 🌐 rebellionbeer.co.uk

⊗ Established in 1993, Rebellion has grown steadily with one site move and several expansion projects, including an on-site shop. It currently brews approximately 100,000 pints per week, supplying more than 600 local pubs and clubs within a 30-mile radius of Marlow. Its ever-popular membership club now has over 4,500 active members. ‼ ♦

IPA (OG 1039, ABV 3.7%) ◆
Copper-coloured bitter, sweet and malty with resinous and red apple flavours. Caramel and fruit decline to leave a dry, bitter and malty finish.

Smuggler (OG 1042, ABV 4.2%) ◆
A red-brown-coloured beer, full-bodied and bitter with an uncompromisingly dry, bitter finish.

Roasted Nuts (OG 1046, ABV 4.6%)
A deep ruby-coloured, complex beer packed with intense malt and hop character.

Zebedee (OG 1047, ABV 4.7%)
A clean and fresh, straw-coloured pale ale with a crisp bitterness and tropical fruit aroma.

Recoil

See Copper Dragon

Rectory SIBA

Streat Hill Farm, Streat Hill, Streat, East Sussex, BN6 8RP
☎ (01273) 890570 ✉ rectoryales@hotmail.com

⊗ Rectory was founded in 1995 by the Rev Godfrey Broster to generate funds for the maintenance of his three parish churches. 107 parishioners are shareholders. ‼♦

Rector's Pleasure (OG 1037, ABV 3.7%)

Rector's Light Relief (OG 1045, ABV 4.5%)
Golden ale with a fresh, floral aroma and distinctly hoppy, bitter characteristics.

The Rector's Revenge (OG 1050, ABV 5%)
Traditional-style, mid-brown-coloured, strong bitter with a good balance of malt and hops and a long bitter finish.

Red Cat SIBA

Unit 10, Sun Valley Business Park, Winnall Close, Winchester, Hampshire, SO23 0LB
☎ (01962) 863423 ☎ 07824 876489
🌐 redcatbrewing.co.uk

Red Cat Brewing Company was established in 2014 using an 11-barrel plant. It supplies Hampshire and bordering counties. A small bar and shop in the brewery sells a range of products. ‼

Art of T (OG 1033, ABV 3.6%) ◆
Easy-drinking speciality pale ale with a slight fruit aroma. Refreshing dry astringency and bitterness in the taste and lingering aftertaste.

Prowler Pale (OG 1034.5, ABV 3.6%) ◆
Pale yellow-coloured session bitter with dominant hop flavours and some fruit in the taste and aftertaste. Pale yellow session bitter with dominant hop flavours and some fruit in the taste and aftertaste.

Scratch (ABV 4%) ◆
Session pale golden-coloured bitter, low aroma but well-balanced hop, malt and fruit flavours in the taste and aftertaste.

Mr M's Porter (OG 1050, ABV 4.5%) ◆
A rich, fruity porter, complex flavours with good roast aroma and taste, well-balanced with fruit flavours throughout.

Mosaic Pale (OG 1050, ABV 4.9%) ◆
American-style pale ale with a rich, floral aroma leading to balanced fruit and hop flavours fading to a hop, fruit and bitter finish.

Red Dragon

Office: Unit 24, Ard Business Park, New Inn, NP4 0SW
☎ (01495) 788477 ✉ marc@reddragon.beer

Director Marc Hillman commutes to the UK a couple of times a year. There are plans to ship his plant from Australia but in the meantime an un-named local brewery contract brews the beers.

Red Fox SIBA

The Chicken Sheds, Upp Hall Farm, Salmons Lane, Coggeshall, Essex, CO6 1RY
☎ (01376) 563123 🌐 redfoxbrewery.co.uk

Red Fox began brewing in 2008 and has continued to expand in line with increasing demand. Brewery

THE BREWERIES

experience days are available and contract brewing services are offered. ‼ ♦ RAIB

Mild (OG 1037, ABV 3.6%)
A classic dark-coloured, full-flavoured mild with hints of chocolate and a deep roast barley flavour.

IPA (OG 1038, ABV 3.7%)

Bitter (OG 1039, ABV 3.8%)
A traditional-style bitter with well-balanced malt and fruit flavours.

Hunter's Gold (OG 1040, ABV 3.9%)
A golden-coloured beer with a delicate citrus aroma.

Best Bitter (OG 1040, ABV 4%)
A light brown-coloured best bitter with a full flavour and malty backbone.

Coggeshall Gold (OG 1041, ABV 4%)
An aromatic, golden-coloured beer, packed full of citrus and exotic fruit flavours.

Surrex Gold (OG 1041, ABV 4.1%)
An insanely-hopped, aromatic beer. Pink grapefruit and peach aromas abound leading to a slightly bitter finish.

Black Fox Porter (OG 1046, ABV 4.8%)
A rich-flavoured, black-coloured beer packed with malty flavour and undertones of chocolate.

Wily Ol' Fox (OG 1050, ABV 5.2%)
An aromatic, amber-coloured traditional IPA with a soft, fruity palate.

Ruby Red Mild (OG 1065, ABV 6.9%)
A full mash dark ruby-coloured mild, full-bodied and well-rounded.

Red Moon

25 Holder Road, Yardley, West Midlands, B25 8AP
☎ 07825 771388

Office: 39 Kimberley Road, Solihull, B92 8PU
redmoonbrewery.co.uk

Red Moon Brewery was started in 2015 by two friends. Beer names are inspired by their own life events. The bulk of their production is bottled, however some cask beer finds its way into the local free trade.

Back Yard BBQ (ABV 4.5%)

Poisons Pleasure (ABV 4.5%)
A red-coloured ale, full-bodied with good hop bitterness and a hoppy finish.

Screaming Dwarf (ABV 4.5%)
A pale amber-coloured ale with sweet candy caramel notes, a full, rich hop flavour and a citrus finish.

Red Rock SIBA

Higher Humber Farm, Bishopsteignton, Devon, TQ14 9TD
☎ (01626) 879738 redrockbrewery.co.uk

Red Rock first started brewing in 2006 with a four-barrel plant and upgraded in 2011 to a 7.5-barrel one. It is based in a converted barn on a working farm using locally sourced malt, fresh hops and the farm's own spring water. It has a bar and can accommodate private functions. ‼ ♦ RAIB

Lighthouse IPA (OG 1038, ABV 3.9%)
A pale ale with a dry finish, floral hop nose and a citrus palate.

Red Rock (OG 1041, ABV 4.2%)

Break Water (OG 1046, ABV 4.6%)
Roasted malt flavours balanced with a heavy hop finish.

Red Shoot

Toms Lane, Linwood, Hampshire, BH24 3QT
☎ (01425) 475792 redshoot.co.uk

The 2.5-barrel brewery was commissioned in 1998 and can be viewed from inside the pub. Most of the output is sold in the pub, but sometimes the beers are made available to Wadworth outlets.

Red Star SIBA

54b Stephenson Way, Formby Business Park, Formby, Merseyside, L37 8EG
☎ (01704) 461120 ☎ 07899 904270
redstarbrewery.co.uk

Production started in 2015 using a 10-barrel plant. Pubs and bars are supplied in Merseyside and the wider North-west region. ‼

Formby Blonde (ABV 3.9%)
Sweet, hoppy-tasting light golden-coloured bitter with a dry hoppy finish.

Formby IPA (ABV 4%)
A session IPA with a hint of elderflower.

Lakota (ABV 4.1%)
An amber-coloured ale with a smooth, sweet edge.

Coney Island (ABV 4.2%)
A traditional malty ale.

Havana Moon (ABV 4.2%)
An oatmeal stout with notes of chocolate, coffee and raisins.

Samba (ABV 4.7%)

Hurricane (ABV 4.8%)
A premium copper-coloured ale with a bittersweet finish.

Weissbier (ABV 5.3%)
A naturally cloudy wheat beer with big orange and coriander flavours.

Partisan (ABV 5.4%)
A dark chestnut-coloured ale with a smooth, malty finish and flavours of mocha and caramel.

Redcastle SIBA

Drummygar Mains, Carmyllie, DD11 2RA
☎ (01241) 860516 ☎ 07967 226357
redcastlebrewery.co.uk

Established by local farmer and Clydesdale horse breeder John Anderson, Redcastle started brewing in rural Angus in 2016 in a purpose-built brewery on the family farm. The brewery takes its name from the nearby ruined red castle at Lunan Bay and the beers are named accordingly with a historic theme. In addition to the 10-barrel plant, the brewery also includes a bottling line.

Crusader (OG 1043, ABV 4%)

Red Lady (OG 1044, ABV 4%)

Nobleman (OG 1042, ABV 4.2%)

Tower IPA (OG 1046, ABV 4.8%)

An American-style IPA with a fruity aroma and a hint of toffee on the palate.

Redchurch

15-16 Mead Park Industrial Estate, Harlow, Essex, CM20 2SE
☎ (01279) 626895 ☎ 07968 173097
theredchurchbrewery.com

Redchurch was established in 2011 using an eight-barrel plant and was situated in a pair of railway arches at Bethnal Green. Expansion took place in 2016 with most of the production moving to Harlow. The Bethnal Green site entered administration in 2019 with brewing ceasing there altogether, although the taproom continues under different ownership. All beers are now brewed at the Harlow site. No real ale. Brewing is currently suspended. ♦ RAIB

Redemption SIBA

Unit 16, Compass West Industrial Estate, 33 West Road, Tottenham, London, N17 0XL
☎ (020) 8885 5227 redemptionbrewing.co.uk

Redemption began brewing in 2010 on a 12-barrel plant. In 2016 it moved into a larger unit with a 30-barrel plant. Most of the beer is supplied to pubs in north and central London and to beer festivals. Successful crowdfunding in 2018 means there are plans for expansion. !! ♦ RAIB

Trinity (OG 1037, ABV 3%)
Refreshing golden-coloured beer with strong citrus notes throughout. The strong bitterness is softened by a little sweet malt character.

Pale Ale (OG 1038, ABV 3.8%)
Well-balanced, amber-coloured bitter with peppery hops and citrus throughout. Sweet toffee and fruit fades in the slightly dry bitter finish.

Hopspur (OG 1045, ABV 4.5%)
Smooth, brown-coloured best bitter. Sweet coffee roast notes and a little nuttiness with resinous hops on the flavour. Dry bitter finish.

Urban Dusk (OG 1045, ABV 4.6%)
Full-bodied, brown-coloured best bitter; chocolate and fudge in the aroma and flavour overlaid with citrus. Lingering dry bitter finish.

Fellowship Porter (OG 1052, ABV 5.1%)
Sweetish, smooth porter. Liquorice, treacle and caramelised fruit balances the dry, dark roast coffee and chocolate notes in the flavour.

Big Chief (OG 1053, ABV 5.5%)
Golden ale with a smooth mouthfeel and strong fruity aroma, flavour and finish, which is also dry and bitter.

Redhouse

44 Sandhill, Newcastle upon Tyne, NE1 3JF
☎ (0191) 261 1037

Established in 2014 the brewery is situated in the Redhouse pub, where the brewing equipment is on view. Its constantly changing beer range is supplied solely to the pub. ♦

Redscar SIBA

c/o Cleveland Hotel, 9-11 High Street West, Redcar, North Yorkshire, TS10 1SQ
☎ (01642) 513727 ☎ 07828 855146
redscar-brewery.co.uk

Redscar first brewed in 2008. In 2014 it increased its capacity to a five-barrel plant. The brewery supplies the hotel, local pubs and beer festivals. !! ♦

Blonde (ABV 3.8%)

Poison (OG 1040, ABV 4%)

Beach (OG 1050, ABV 5%)

Redwell SIBA

7 The Arches, Bracondale, Trowse Millgate, Norwich, NR1 2EF
☎ (01603) 624072 redwellbrewing.com

Redwell was started in 2013 by a group of beer lovers, tracing their beery influences from England and Scotland to Canada, Sweden, Norway, New Zealand and America. It is now under new ownership and has recently appointed Belinda Jennings as its head brewer. !!

Brewed under the Bullards Brewery name:

No. 4: Session IPA (OG 1041.8, ABV 3.8%)
A golden-coloured, juicy session beer packed with hops.

No. 5: Best Red Bitter (OG 1040, ABV 4%)
A deep red-coloured, malty bitter.

No. 1: East Coast Pale Ale (OG 1042, ABV 4.2%)
Punchy tropical fruit nose. Well-balanced with grapefruit, lemon, biscuit and citrus hoppiness. Smooth finish dominated by marmalade and maltiness.

No.6: Rye Pale Ale (OG 1045, ABV 4.4%)
A brown-coloured rye ale with spicy hop notes.

No. 3: Amber Ale (OG 1047, ABV 4.7%)
A malty, amber-coloured ale with hints of caramel as well as peppery and fruity hops.

No. 2: India Pale Ale (OG 1058, ABV 6%)
An IPA full of rich caramel and burnt brown sugar flavours with a bitter orange aroma.

RedWillow SIBA

The Lodge, Sutton Garrison, Byrons Lane, Macclesfield, Cheshire, SK11 7JW
☎ (01625) 502315 redwillowbrewery.com

Established in 2010 by homebrewer Toby McKenzie and his wife Caroline. In 2015 brewing moved to a larger, purpose-built unit on the same site. The award-winning beers are distributed nationwide and are available from the brewery's own RedWillow bars in Macclesfield and Buxton. Experimental brews are branded under the Faithless and Clueless labels. ♦

Effortless (OG 1035, ABV 3.7%)
A crisp, zesty pale ale.

Headless (OG 1037, ABV 3.9%)
A moderately hoppy bitter with plenty of fruit in the aroma and taste, all of which is retained in the finish with the hops still in charge.

Feckless (OG 1040, ABV 4.1%)

THE BREWERIES

A classic best bitter, rich toffee and malt balanced with subtle hop flavours.

Weightless (OG 1044, ABV 4.2%) ◆
Well-rounded best bitter with a promise of fruit and hop at the start, full-bodied, bittersweet middle and a quick finish.

Wreckless (OG 1046, ABV 4.8%)
A pale ale with tropical fruit flavours and a clean finish.

Heartless (OG 1048, ABV 4.9%)
A bold, complex beer with Colombian chocolate, which provides a dry, balanced bitterness and long espresso finish.

Sleepless (OG 1052, ABV 5.4%)
An American-style rye IPA, amber in colour with rich toffee malt, juicy hops and a long bitter finish.

Smokeless (OG 1055, ABV 5.7%)
A smooth, smoky porter infused with chipotles.

Shameless (OG 1054, ABV 5.9%)
A big, juicy, American-hopped IPA with tropical fruit flavours and a clean, grapefruit finish.

Restless (OG 1096, ABV 8.5%)
A milk coffee porter. Rich, dark coffee and chocolate flavours with a little residual sweetness.

Reedley Hallows SIBA

Unit B3, Farrington Close, Farrington Road Industrial Estate, Burnley, Lancashire, BB11 5SH ☎ 07749 414513 🌐 reedley-hallows-brewery.co.uk

Brewing started on this four-barrel plant in 2012. Having moved to larger premises the brewery now has nine fermenters to cope with demand. ‼

Old Laund Bitter (OG 1038, ABV 3.6%)
A session beer, smooth and creamy with a distinctive hoppy aftertaste.

Filly Close Blonde (OG 1040, ABV 3.9%)
A well-balanced ale, bitter and spicy with a good fruity finish.

Pendleside (OG 1042, ABV 4%)
A light-coloured beer with hints of tropical fruits and a spicy aftertaste.

Monkholme Premium (OG 1042, ABV 4.2%)
A premium golden ale, smooth with a hoppy taste throughout.

New Laund Dark (OG 1044, ABV 4.4%)
A dark-coloured stout, sweet with a smoky, bitter finish.

Griffin IPA (OG 1045, ABV 4.5%)
Well-hopped classic IPA balanced with traditional malty sweetness.

Nook of Pendle (OG 1050, ABV 5%)
An amber-coloured, warming ale with a dried fruit and malty aroma. Tropical fruits in the taste with a bittersweet finish.

Regather

57-59 Club Garden Road, Sheffield, South Yorkshire, S11 8BU
☎ (0114) 273 1258 🌐 regather.net/food-drink/regather-brewery

Regather Brewery is one of Sheffield's smallest breweries. It runs as a part of the Regather Co-op. Brewer Dan Robinson has created a series of bottle-conditioned beers that range from traditional favourites to more inventive brews. Beers are available at all Regather events, in local bottle shops and to order online. Brewing is currently suspended. RAIB

Reids Gold (NEW)

61 Provost Barclay Drive, Stonehaven, AB39 2GE
🌐 reidsgold.com

Reids Gold was established in 2018. It is a small-batch microbrewery with an average weekly production of five barrels. No real ale.

Remedy

10-11 Market Place, Stockport, SK1 1EW
☎ (0161) 477 1842
🌐 remedybarandbrewhouse.co.uk

Opened in 2016, the three-barrel plant is located in a glazed partition in the main bar of the Remedy pub, situated in the historic market place in the heart of the old part of Stockport. Every beer is a one-off recipe, available in the pub only.

Reunion SIBA

Units 16 & 17, Vector Park, Forest Road, Feltham, TW13 7EJ
☎ (020) 8890 8309 🌐 reunionales.com

Reunion Ales was founded in 2015 by Francis Smedley using a Moeschle 16.5-hectolitre plant. Beers are available across London, from the taproom at the brewery and sometimes further afield. ‼ ◆

Opening Gambit (OG 1038, ABV 3.8%) ◆
Traditional bitter with pleasant balance of biscuit, hop and bitter orange. Bitterness builds strongly in the lingering finish.

Beardtongue (OG 1044, ABV 4.5%) ◆
Reddish-brown-coloured best bitter with a chocolate and damson aroma and flavour with some honey. Lingering sweet finish with dry cocoa.

Talwar (OG 1042, ABV 4.5%) ◆
Yellow-coloured beer with sweet earthy hops overlaid with a lemony fruitiness and a touch of spice from the added coriander.

Incredible Pale Ale (OG 1047, ABV 5%) ◆
Smooth amber-coloured beer with honey sweetness overlaid with a mix of fruits. Earthy hop character is present throughout. Bitter finish.

Revolutions SIBA

Unit B7, Whitwood Enterprise Park, Speedwell Road, Whitwood, West Yorkshire, WF10 5PX
☎ (01977) 552649 ☎ 07503 007470
🌐 revolutionsbrewing.co.uk

Revolutions began brewing in 2010. All beers are musically inspired. The Rewind 33 series of bi-monthly specials references music from 33 years ago. ‼◆

Candidate Session Pale (OG 1039, ABV 3.9%)

Clash Porter (OG 1048, ABV 4.5%)
A complex dark malty beer rounded off with a smooth hop finish.

Switch (OG 1044, ABV 4.5%)

Light golden-coloured ale with a hop bill that switches every two months.

Swoon Chocolate Fudge Milk Stout (OG 1053, ABV 4.5%)
Milk stout with flavours of chocolate and fudge.

Marquee US IPA (OG 1053, ABV 5.4%)
Rich, golden-coloured, well-hopped IPA.

Manifesto Stout (OG 1059, ABV 6%)
Stout with berry fruit hop notes.

Rhymney SIBA

Gilchrist Thomas Industrial Estate, Blaenavon, NP4 9RL
☎ (01495) 790456 🌐 rhymneybreweryltd.com

Award-winning brewery established in 2005 and based at the World Heritage Site at Blaenavon, where the world's first steel was developed. Proud of its Welsh industrial heritage, beers are widely available throughout the Valleys and South Wales, and through the free trade. Capacity at the 75-hectolitre plant is sufficient for brewing all its own beers and to support contract brewing for a number of other breweries. It takes its name from the major brewery once based in the Valleys town of Rhymney, which was bought and closed by the Whitbread empire nearly half a century ago. ‼ ♦ RAIB

Best (OG 1037, ABV 3.7%)

Hobby Horse (OG 1038, ABV 3.8%)

Dark (OG 1040, ABV 4%)

Bevans Bitter (OG 1042, ABV 4.2%)
A well-balanced beer, hoppy beer with malts coming through initially.

General Picton (OG 1043, ABV 4.3%)

Bitter (OG 1045, ABV 4.5%)

King's Ale (OG 1047, ABV 4.7%)

Export (OG 1050, ABV 5%)
A sweet, strong bitter in which malts dominate, but with the hops coming through in the aftertaste.

Richmond SIBA

Station Brewery, Station Yard, Richmond, North Yorkshire, DL10 4LD
☎ (01748) 828266 🌐 richmondbrewing.co.uk

Richmond opened in 2008 in the renovated Victorian station complex beside the River Swale. Producion is split 50/50 between cask-conditioned and bottled beers. The former are available in the local area at the Hildyard Arms, Colburn, and the Castle Tavern, Richmond, as well as direct from the brewery. ‼ ♦ RAIB

SwAle (OG 1035, ABV 3.7%)
Dark mild brewed using chocolate malt with slightly more bitterness than a traditional mild.

Station Ale (OG 1039, ABV 4%)
Light golden-coloured bitter brewed using hedgerow hops.

Greyfriars Stout (OG 1042, ABV 4.2%)

Dale Strider (OG 1043, ABV 4.5%)

Stump Cross Ale (OG 1046, ABV 4.7%)
Dark-coloured, malty and full-flavoured beer.

Ride (NEW) SIBA

Unit 1, Bridge Court, 12 Cook Street, Glasgow, G5 8JN
☎ 07463 667097

Ride Brew Co is a social enterprise brewery established in 2017. ♦

Charon (OG 1045, ABV 4.5%)

Ridgeside SIBA

Unit 24, Penraevon 2 Industrial Estate, Meanwood, Leeds, West Yorkshire, LS7 2AW ☎ 07595 380568
🌐 ridgesidebrewery.co.uk

Ridgeside began brewing in 2010 using a four-barrel plant. Regular outlets are supplied around Leeds and beers can be found across West and North Yorkshire. Cask beers are unfiltered and unfined. A taproom is open on the first Saturday of the month. ‼ ♦ V

Objects in Space (ABV 4.8%)
Pale ale, generously hopped with low bitterness.

Equator (ABV 5.6%)
An IPA packed with tropical pineapple and grapefruit flavours.

Milky Joe (ABV 5.6%)
A rich, dark-coloured milk stout brewed with real coffee.

Ridgeway SIBA

Stane Street, North Heath, West Sussex, RH20 1DJ
☎ (01491) 873474

Office: Ridgeway Brewing Ltd, South Stoke, RG8 0JW
🌐 ridgewaybrewery.co.uk

Set up by ex-Brakspear head brewer Peter Scholey, Ridgeway specialises in bottle-conditioned beers, although cask beers are occasionally available at beer festivals and locally. A new brewery has been operational since 2016, located within Hepworth Brewery's new premises near Pulborough, sharing some facilities. RAIB

Rigg & Furrow

Acklington Park Farm, Acklington, Northumberland, NE65 9AA 🌐 riggandfurrow.com

Brewing commenced in 2017 in a former milking parlour. It is a family-run business celebrating the best of home-grown Northumbrian and British produce. More than 60 outlets are supplied direct.

The Pale Ale (ABV 3.8%)

Owl Porter (ABV 4%)

Run Hop Run (ABV 4.2%)

Trickster (ABV 4.3%)

Ringwood

Christchurch Road, Ringwood, Hampshire, BH24 3AP
☎ (01425) 471177 🌐 ringwoodbrewery.co.uk

Ringwood was bought in 2007 by Marston's for £19 million. Production has been increased to 50,000 barrels a year. Some 750 outlets are supplied. Ringwood beers are now available in Marston's pubs all over the country. Part of Marston's PLC. ‼ ♦

Razorback (OG 1038, ABV 3.8%)

A malty session bitter with strong toffee notes in the aroma, leading to a short, bittersweet finish. Malt tends to dominate throughout.

Boondoggle (OG 1042, ABV 4.2%)
A golden-coloured beer, full of zesty hop flavours and hop aromas.

Fortyniner (OG 1049, ABV 4.9%) ◆
A caramel, biscuity aroma, with hints of damson, lead to a sweet but well-balanced taste with malt, fruit and hop flavours.

Old Thumper (OG 1055, ABV 5.1%) ◆
A powerful, sweet, copper-coloured beer. A fruity aroma preludes a sweet, malty taste with fruit and caramel and a bittersweet aftertaste.

Rising Sun

Rising Sun, 235 Stockport Road, Mossley, OL5 0RQ
☎ (01457) 238236 🌐 risingsunmossley.co.uk

Brewing began in 2016 using a two-barrel plant at the side of the Rising Sun. The beers are primarily produced for sale in the pub. In addition to the regular beer, various other brews are produced on demand.

Rival

60 Theobald Road, Cardiff, CF5 1LQ ☎ 07889 596306
✉ rivalbrewingcompany@gmail.com

Brewing began in 2017 using a one-barrel plant in a residential garage. No real ale.

River Leven

Lab Road, Kinlochleven, PH50 4SG
☎ (01855) 831519 ☎ 07901 873273
🌐 riverlevenales.co.uk

Established in 2011, River Leven Ales is situated among stunning scenery on the West Highland Way in Kinlochleven. Beers are produced using the pure Kinlochleven water with no added sugars or unmalted grain.

Blonde (OG 1040, ABV 4%)
A clean-tasting, pale golden-coloured beer with hints of citrus.

Traditional IPA (OG 1040, ABV 4%)
A copper-coloured ale with traditional hop and nutty malt flavours.

Riverhead

2 Peel Street, Marsden, West Yorkshire, HD7 6BR
☎ (01484) 841270 (pub) 🌐 ossett-brewery.co.uk

Riverhead is a brewpub that opened in 1995. Ossett Brewing (qv) purchased the site in 2006 but runs it as a separate brewery. It has since opened the Dining Room on the first floor, which uses Riverhead beers in its dishes. Many different beers are produced on a rotating basis. !!◆

Riverside

Unit 6, Beeding Court Business Park, Shoreham Road, Upper Beeding, West Sussex, BN44 3TN
☎ (01903) 898030 🌐 riversidebreweryltd.co.uk

Riverside began brewing in 2015 using a five-barrel plant. Beers are available locally. RAIB

Rambling Monarch (OG 1035, ABV 3.6%)
A floral, citrus/spicy hop aroma is followed by classic bitter tastes.

Steyning Stinker (OG 1042, ABV 4%)
A slight fruity/spicy edge from the hops is complemented by earthy, smoky notes.

Beeding Best Bitter (OG 1038, ABV 4.2%)
Pine and floral characteristics with just a hint of liquorice.

Sneaky Steamer (OG 1050, ABV 5.1%)
Pine and floral characteristics with a hint of grapefruit.

Tubbers' Tipple (OG 1051, ABV 5.6%)
A premium bitter with earthy/spicy notes and a tinge of honey.

Rivertown

See McMullen

Riviera

4 Yonder Meadow, Stoke Gabriel, Devon, TQ9 6QE
☎ 07857 850110 🌐 rivierabrewing.co.uk

Riviera started brewing commercially in 2015 using a one-barrel plant. ◆

RBC Best (ABV 3.8%)

Devonian (OG 1039, ABV 4.1%)
A lightly-hopped, amber-coloured ale with a floral finish.

Gold (OG 1040, ABV 4.2%)
A refreshing golden ale with citrus notes.

Torbay Express (OG 1046, ABV 4.8%)
A copper-coloured premium ale with fruity, spicy notes and citrus and pine aromas.

Rivington

Cunliffe Farm, New Road, Anderton, Lancashire, PR6 9EY ☎ 07989 165370 🌐 rivingtonbrewing.co.uk

Established in 2015 using a three-barrel plant, a number of local outlets are supplied direct from the brewery. Approximately 20% of production is supplied in cask form, but all beers are unpasteurised, unfiltered and unfined. Experimental brews and collaborations are regularly available. ◆RAIB V

Roa Island (NEW)

Belfast Pier, Roa Island, Cumbria, LA13 0PN
☎ (01229) 825291

Brewing commenced in 2017 in a small room at the back of the Roa Island Boat Club. Beers are brewed once a week in 50-litre quantities and are only available on site.

Roam SIBA

Unit 9, Porsham Close, Beliver Industrial Estate, Plymouth, Devon, PL6 7DB
☎ (01752) 396052 ☎ 07971 411727
🌐 roambrewco.uk

Formerly known as Tavy Ales, Roam Brewing Co produces small batch beers using a combination of traditional and modern brewing techniques and local ingredients. A six-barrel plant is used. The brewery may relocate during the currency of this Guide. ‼♦RAIB

Tavy Gold (ABV 4%)
Clean, bright session ale, this balanced beer has a solid hoppy flavour and aroma, backed up with nicely balanced malt.

Hometown Pale (OG 1042, ABV 4.1%)
This session pale ale takes ingredients from across the globe to produce this full-on flavour fest. Don't let this sessionable ABV fool you, this beer packs a punch.

Tavy Best Bitter (OG 1043, ABV 4.3%) ◆
Malt dominates the nose and taste with caramel, roast and hops overpowering a subtle hint of fruit. A complex aftertaste.

Sound Bitter (OG 1045, ABV 4.5%)

Tavy IPA (OG 1048, ABV 4.8%) ◆
Gold ale dominated by hops and fruit from start to finish. Slight fruit/straw aroma. Citrus/hoppy dry taste. Dry/bitter finish.

Tavy Porter (OG 1052, ABV 5.2%) ◆
Full bodied porter. Malt, liquorice, chocolate nose. Slightly bitter fruity taste. Roasted coffee and touch of vanilla in the aftertaste.

Robinsons SIBA IFBB

Unicorn Brewery, Lower Hillgate, Stockport, SK1 1JJ ☎ (0161) 612 4061 🌐 robinsonsbrewery.com

Brewing since 1838, the business is now run by the sixth generation of the Robinson family. The tied estate, stretching from Cumbria to Cheshire and out to North Wales has reduced to 260 pubs in recent years. The regular range is supplemented by seasonals, one-off white label specials and occasional additions to the 'Trooper' range brewed in conjunction with Iron Maiden's Bruce Dickinson. ‼♦

Wizard (OG 1037, ABV 3.7%)
A well-balanced, crisp and refreshing, mid-brown-coloured session beer.

Dizzy Blonde (OG 1037, ABV 3.8%) ◆
A light-bodied beer, yellow in colour. It has malt and hops in the taste and a dry bitter finish.

Cumbria Way (OG 1040, ABV 4.1%) ◆
Pale brown in colour with a malty aroma, this beer has a balance of malt, some hops and a little fruit, with sweetness and bitterness throughout.

Cwrw'r ddraig aur (OG 1041, ABV 4.1%)

Unicorn (OG 1041, ABV 4.2%) ◆
Amber-coloured beer with a fruity aroma. Malt, hops and fruit in the taste with a bitter, malty finish.

Cascade IPA (ABV 4.8%)
Pale brown-coloured beer with malt and fruit on the nose. Full hoppy taste with malt and fruit, leading to a hoppy, bitter finish.

Trooper (OG 1048, ABV 4.8%) ◆
Well-balanced, amber-coloured beer with malt and hops in aroma and taste.

Old Tom (OG 1079, ABV 8.5%) ◆
A full-bodied, dark-coloured beer with malt, fruit and chocolate on the aroma. A complex range of flavours includes dark chocolate, full maltiness, port and fruits leads to a long, bittersweet aftertaste.

Contract brewed for Everards Brewery:

Beacon Hill (OG 1036, ABV 3.8%) ◆
Light, refreshing, well-balanced pale amber-coloured bitter in the Burton style.

Tiger (OG 1041, ABV 4.2%) ◆
A mid-brown-coloured, well-balanced best bitter crafted for broad appeal, benefiting from a long, bittersweet finish.

Rock & Roll

Unit 2, 60 Regent Place, Hockley, Birmingham, B1 3NJ ☎ 07922 554181
✉ rnrbrewhouse@outlook.com

Rock & Roll started life as Birmingham's only rooftop pub brewery, set up by experienced brewer Mark Shepherd using a two-barrel plant. In 2014 brewster Lynn Crossland joined and now does all of the brewing. In 2016 the brewery moved and expanded to a six-barrel plant in Birmingham's historic Jewellery Quarter in order to increase capacity. A brewhouse bar is open at weekends. ‼♦V

Brew Springsteen (OG 1042, ABV 4.2%)

Thirst Aid Kit (OG 1042, ABV 4.2%)

Mash City Rocker (OG 1045, ABV 4.5%)

Voodoo Mild (OG 1052, ABV 5%)

Rock Mill

1b Rock Mill Lane, New Mills, Derbyshire, SK22 3BN ☎ 07971 747050

Office: 81-83 Bridge Street, New Mills, SK22 4DN ✉ rbpine@Hotmail.co.uk

Rock Mill is a microbrewery established by Ray Barton, a former homebrewer, in 2016. An on-site bar is open Monday and Tuesday evenings. ♦

Mermaids Pool (OG 1035, ABV 3.5%)

Strange Ways (OG 1038, ABV 3.8%)

Back to the Future (OG 1040, ABV 4%)

Cotton Spinner (OG 1040, ABV 4%)

Toffee Town (OG 1041, ABV 4%)

Orangeytang (OG 1044, ABV 4.3%)
A golden-coloured bitter with a hint of orange.

Rock Solid

Office: 25 Thornebank, Blackpool, FY3 8QE ☎ 07963 860080 ✉ rocksolidbrewingcompany@gmail.com

This brewery, based at the owner's home, started brewing in 2017 using a one-barrel plant. ♦

Blonde (ABV 3.9%)

Amarillo Gold (ABV 4%)

American Pale (ABV 4.5%)

Rock the Boat SIBA

6 Little Crosby Village, Little Crosby, Merseyside, L23 4TS
☎ (0151) 924 7936 ☎ 07727 959356
🌐 rocktheboatbrewery.co.uk

Rock the Boat began brewing in 2015 in a converted 16th-century wheelwright's workshop in Little Crosby. Beer names relate to a local theme, often reflecting the brewer's musical tastes and local landmarks. Specials are often brewed for Market Town Taverns pubs in Liverpool. A green hop beer is produced each year. ♦RAIB V

Liverpool Light (OG 1033, ABV 3.4%)
A blonde ale with subtle bitterness and a delicate hop flavour.

(Sittin' on) The Dock (OG 1039, ABV 3.5%)
A beer with nutty and chocolate flavours.

Dazzle (OG 1035, ABV 3.6%)
Pale golden-coloured beer bursting with hop flavour. Smooth in the mouth with a long bitter finish.

Bootle Bull (OG 1040, ABV 3.8%)
A traditional, light brown-coloured bitter. Smooth and malty, balanced with a good hop character.

Mussel Wreck (OG 1040, ABV 3.9%)
A subtle blend of malt and hops creates an easy-drinking, deep golden-coloured ale. Fruity hop flavours with a short bitter finish.

Yellow Submarine Special (OG 1038, ABV 3.9%)
Golden ale brewed with a different British hop each time.

Faith Hope & Charity (OG 1041, ABV 4%)
A copper-coloured traditional bitter. A little malt flavour with a bitter edge.

Waterloo Sunset (OG 1044, ABV 4.2%)
Biscuit and toasted malt flavours with a subtle orange marmalade hint.

Dragon's Teeth Chocolate Stout (OG 1045, ABV 4.3%)
A stout with a chocolate edge.

Fab Four Liverpool IPA (OG 1043, ABV 4.4%)
Golden ale with a fruity richness leading to a hoppy finish.

Maple Dog (ABV 4.4%)
Dark brown-coloured ale with hints of maple syrup.

Lift Off (ABV 4.5%)
Caramel and chocolate flavours with a bitter aftertaste.

Rookie (ABV 4.6%)

DPA (ABV 4.8%)
A pale ale with floral notes.

Rockhopper

1 Forrest Crescent, Luton, Bedfordshire, LU2 9AR
☎ 07879 810558 🌐 rockhopperbrew.co

Rockhopper began brewing in 2016 using a two-barrel plant.

Rockin' Robin SIBA

c/o Old Dairy Brewery, Tenterden Station Estate, Station Road, Tenterden, Kent, TN30 6HE ☎ 07779 986087

Office: 6 Pickering Street, Loose, ME15 9RS
🌐 rockinrobinbrewery.co.uk

Brewing began in 2011 using a one-barrel plant in a garden shed. It moved to Boughton Monchelsea in 2014 and in 2019 began cuckoo brewing at Old Dairy (qv). Outlets throughout Kent, Sussex and South-east London are supplied, including several micropubs. ♦

Reliant Robin (OG 1036, ABV 3.7%)
An auburn-coloured classic session bitter with a fresh, spicy finish.

RPA (OG 1038, ABV 3.9%)
An American-style pale ale with a rich lemon flavour.

Rock A Hula (OG 1039, ABV 4%)
A pale ale with a fruity and slightly spicy taste.

Blizzard of Oz (OG 1046, ABV 4.5%)
Rich dark malts and a blend of English hops create a full-bodied, mahogany-coloured old ale.

Reckless Robin (OG 1044, ABV 4.5%)
A strong bitter that delivers a fresh, hoppy punch. Well-balanced with soft fruit malt.

Stoutly Robin (OG 1046, ABV 4.5%)
A rich, creamy stout with a smooth burnt roasted character.

Portly Robin (OG 1049, ABV 5%)
Full-bodied, deep ruby-coloured porter. Rich fruits promote a vinous character with liquorice undertones.

Really Rockin (OG 1052, ABV 5%)
A full-bodied pale ale with tropical fruit flavours.

Rocket

The Orchard, Garden Farm, Great Staughton, Cambridgeshire, PE19 5BE
☎ (01733) 390828 ☎ 07747 617527
✉ mikeblakesley@virginmedia.com

Originally using spare capacity at King's Cliffe Brewery (qv), Rocket Ales relocated to its own site in 2017.

Atlas IPA (ABV 5.8%)

Rocket Town

c/o Unit 1, Cleveland Industrial Estate, Darlington, DL1 2PB ☎ 07964 301040
✉ info@rockettownbrewing.com

Rocket Town began brewing in 2015 using spare capacity at Schoolhouse Brewery (qv).

Rocket Blonde (ABV 3.6%)
Smooth blonde ale with grapefruit notes.

Black India Pale Ale (ABV 3.8%)
Dark-coloured session beer with roasted, malty flavours and a hoppy finish.

Rocket Kolsch (ABV 4%)

Dirty Bumble (ABV 4.2%)
Roasted chocolate flavours with hints of honey lead to a rounded finish.

Second Burn (ABV 4.2%)

Rockingham SIBA

Blatherwycke, Northamptonshire, PE8 6YN
☎ (01832) 280722

Office: 25 Wansford Road, Elton, PE8 6RZ
🌐 rockinghamales.co.uk

⊗ Rockingham is a small brewery established in 1997 that operates from a converted farm building near Blatherwycke, Northamptonshire, with a two-barrel plant producing a prolific range of beers. It supplies half a dozen local outlets. ♦

Forest Gold (OG 1039, ABV 3.9%)
A hoppy blonde ale with citrus flavours. Well-balanced and clean finishing.

Hop Devil (OG 1040, ABV 3.9%)
Six hop varieties give this golden ale a bitter start and fruity finish.

White Rabbit (OG 1040, ABV 4%)
Light golden ale with a bitter start and tropical fruit finish.

Saxon Cross (OG 1041, ABV 4.1%)
A golden red-coloured ale with a nutty coffee aroma and fruit and blackcurrant undertones.

Fruits of the Forest (OG 1043, ABV 4.3%)
A multi-layered beer in which summer fruits and several spices compete with a big hop presence.

Dark Forest (OG 1050, ABV 5%)
A dark-coloured and complex beer with malty/smoky flavours that give way to a fruity bitter finish.

Roebuck SIBA

Roebuck, Tobys Hill, Draycott-in-the-Clay, Staffordshire, DE6 5BT
☎ (01283) 703411 ☎ 07757 503851
roebuckdraycott.co.uk

Brewing begain in 2017 using a six-barrel plant. Although situated adjacent to the Roebuck pub the brewery is a separate business. Head brewer Steve Topliss has more than 45 years experience in the industry. The Roebuck and its sister pub, the Hawk & Buckle, Etwall, are supplied. ‼

Blonde (OG 1038, ABV 3.7%)

Hopzester (OG 1041, ABV 4.2%)
A sharp lemon hit with lingering aftertaste.

Bitter (OG 1045, ABV 4.5%)
A mellow bitter with a good balance of sweetness and bitterness.

Porter (OG 1047, ABV 4.6%)
Dark-coloured ale with plenty of chocolate malt and roasted barley in the mash.

IPA (OG 1052, ABV 5.2%)
Straw-coloured IPA with an orange citrus flavour and aroma.

Romney Marsh SIBA

Unit 7, Jacks Park, Cinque Ports Road, New Romney, Kent, TN28 8AN
☎ (01797) 362333 ☎ 07796 176011
romneymarshbrewery.com

An award-winning, 12-barrel, family-run brewery founded in 2015 by former Come Dine with Me executive producer Matt Calais. Beer is supplied to outlets throughout Kent and East Sussex. A pop up pub called Ales by the Rails is operated for special occasions on the grounds of the Romney Hythe & Dymchurch Railway station in Dungeness, Kent. ‼ RAIB

Mellow (OG 1036, ABV 3.6%)
American-style session pale ale with creamy hop flavours.

Romney Best (OG 1039, ABV 4%)
Biscuit and chocolate malts with blackcurrant hop notes.

Romney Amber Ale (OG 1042, ABV 4.4%)
Tropical hop flavours with a hint of caramel.

Rooster's SIBA

Unit H5, Fifth Avenue, Hornbeam Park, Harrogate, North Yorkshire, HG2 8QT
☎ (01423) 865959 roosters.co.uk

Founded in 1993 by Sean and Alison Franklin, Rooster's is now owned and operated by Ian Fozard and his sons, Tom and Oliver. Having relocated from Knaresborough to a larger site in Harrogate, 60 barrels per week are now produced. One-off experimental beers are also brewed under the Outlaw Brewing Co name. An on-site taproom is open Wednesday to Sunday. ♦V

Buckeye (OG 1035.5, ABV 3.5%)
An easy-drinking ale with orange citrus fruit aromas and a refreshing level of bitterness.

Highway 51 (OG 1036.5, ABV 3.7%)
Juicy tropical fruit flavours to the fore, backed with a hint of citrus and a grapefruit finish.

Capability Brown (ABV 4%)
A classic best bitter, deep amber in colour with hedgerow hop characteristics.

YPA (Yorkshire Pale Ale) (OG 1039.5, ABV 4.1%)
A pale-coloured, aromatic ale with delicate peach and berry fruit flavours.

London Thunder (ABV 4.2%)
Roasted malt and chocolate flavours in a smooth, dark-coloured porter.

Yankee (OG 1041, ABV 4.3%)
A straw-coloured beer with a delicate, fruity aroma leading to a well-balanced taste of malt and hops with a slight evidence of sweetness, followed by a refreshing, fruity/bitter finish.

TwentyFourSeven (OG 1043, ABV 4.7%)
Aromas of lemon, tangerine and gooseberry are followed by a balanced grapefruit bitterness.

Baby-Faced Assassin (OG 1058, ABV 6.1%)
An IPA with aromas of mango, apricot, grapefruit and mandarin with a lasting, juicy, tropical fruit bitterness.

Rossendale

Griffin Inn, 84 Hud Rake, Haslingden, Lancashire, BB4 5AF
☎ (01706) 214021 rossendalebrewery.co.uk

The brewery acquired the brew plant previously used by Porter Brewing Co in 2007 and is based in the cellar of the Griffin Inn in Haslingden. The Sportsman in Hyde and many other local outlets are also supplied.

Floral Dance (OG 1040, ABV 3.8%)
A pale-coloured and fruity session beer.

Hameldon Bitter (OG 1040, ABV 3.8%)
A dark-coloured, traditional bitter with a dry and assertive character that develops in the finish.

Ale (OG 1045, ABV 4%)
A malty aroma leads to a complex, malt dominated flavour, supported by a dry, increasingly bitter finish.

Glen Top Bitter (OG 1040.5, ABV 4%)

THE BREWERIES

A citrus, full-bodied, pale-coloured beer with a dry aftertaste.

Halo Pale (OG 1045, ABV 4.5%)
A citrus pale ale with a slightly bitter aftertaste.

Pitch Porter (OG 1050, ABV 5%)
A full-bodied, rich beer with a slightly sweet, malty start, balanced with sharp bitterness and a roast barley dominance.

Sunshine (OG 1055, ABV 5.3%)
A hoppy and bitter golden-coloured beer with a citrus character. The lingering finish is dry and spicy.

Rother Valley SIBA

Gate Court Farm, Station Road, Northiam, East Sussex, TN31 6QT
☎ (01797) 252922 ☎ 07798 877551
rothervalleybrewery.co.uk

⊠ Rother Valley Brewey was established in Northiam in 1993, overlooking the Rother Levels and the Kent & East Sussex Railway. Brewing on a 10-barrel plant, around 100 outlets are supplied direct. Established and new hop varieties are sourced locally. ♦

Black Ops (OG 1037, ABV 3.8%)
A black IPA with hints of fruit.

Smild (OG 1038, ABV 3.8%)
A full-bodied, dark-coloured, creamy mild with hints of chocolate.

Valley Bitter (OG 1037, ABV 3.8%)
A traditional copper-coloured bitter. A sound bitterness is mixed with soft caramel notes.

Level Best (OG 1040, ABV 4%)
Full-bodied, tawny-coloured session bitter with a malt and fruit aroma, malty taste and a dry, hoppy finish.

Copper Ale (OG 1041, ABV 4.1%)
A copper-coloured ale with a good balance of malt and hops.

Hoppers Ale (OG 1044, ABV 4.4%)
A copper-coloured ale. The initial burst of hop is followed by a pleasant caramel taste.

Boadicea (OG 1045, ABV 4.5%)
A straw-coloured beer with a delicate, fruity flavour.

Blues (OG 1050, ABV 5%)
Black-coloured ale with notes of roast malt and chocolate.

Exit (OG 1055, ABV 5.7%)
A strong IPA with complex fruity notes.

Rothes

77 New Street, Rothes, AB38 7BJ ☎ 07336 233634
therothesbrewery@sky.com

⊠ Situated in the heart of the Spey Valley, Rothes began producing commercially in 2014. Initially producing only bottle-conditioned beers, cask ales are now also available. RAIB

BlackHall Bitter (ABV 4%)

Roughacre (NEW)

Castle Camps, Cambridgeshire, CB21 4TA
☎ (01799) 585956 roughacre.com

Roughacre Brewery was established in 2018 in Castle Camps. It produces small batch brews in a wide range of styles. Beers are available across South Cambridgeshire, West Suffolk and North Essex. RAIB V

Zestival (OG 1036, ABV 3.6%)
A thirst-quenching, zesty pale ale with orange, apricot and melon flavours and a refreshing grapefruit aroma.

Red (OG 1038, ABV 3.8%)
A ruby-coloured mild with a chocolaty, malty flavour and a subtle, spicy yet fruity aroma.

Alliance TPA (OG 1040, ABV 4.2%)
A pale ale with citrus hop flavours and a powerful, fruity aroma.

Ashdon Amber (OG 1042, ABV 4.4%)
Amber-coloured ale with a refreshing bitterness and delicate hoppy finish.

Nighthawker (OG 1046, ABV 4.6%)
Complex porter brewed with freshly ground coffee delivering a balanced bitterness with a hint of red berries.

All Saints (OG 1046, ABV 4.8%)
Tawny-coloured beer with a satisfying malt flavour, delicate spiciness and a hoppy aroma.

Mosquito (ABV 5.2%)
A hoppy IPA with a citrus aroma and refreshing flavour with hints of grapefruit and lychee.

Round Corner (NEW)

Melton Mowbray Market, Scalford Road (Gate 2), Melton Mowbray, Leicestershire, LE13 1JY
☎ (01664) 569855

Round Corner was launched after 15 years of planning by city director Combie Cryan and brewer Colin Paige. The state-of-the-art 20-hectolitre brewery and its taproom can be found in the old sheep shed at the heart of Melton Mowbray Market. Single batch releases began in 2019 and include cask-conditioned ales. Beers are available in several outlets around the East Midlands as well as further afield via Small Beer Ltd.

Roundhill SIBA

Unit 1, Lagonda Court, Cowpen Lane Industrial Estate, Cowpen Bewley, TS23 4JF ☎ 07910 567847

Office: 9 Trevine Gardens, Ingleby Barwick, Stockton-on-Tees, TS17 5HD
✉ roundhillbrewery@outlook.com

Brewing commenced in 2016 on a five-barrel plant. Along with the core and seasonal beers, collaboration brews are produced with local bars. !! ♦ RAIB

Billa's Bitter (OG 1035, ABV 3.6%)

Cowpen Pale (OG 1036, ABV 3.8%)

Bewley Blonde (OG 1041, ABV 4.3%)

Midnight Slug (OG 1047, ABV 4.8%)
A dark-coloured, rich and creamy porter.

Rowditch

Rowditch Inn, 246 Uttoxeter New Road, Derby, DE22 3LL
☎ (01332) 343123

⊗ The Rowditch Brewery was established in 2010 and is a 3.75-barrel plant situated on the premises of the Rowditch Inn, where all of the production is currently consumed. Several regular ales and some one-off specials are brewed by the publican, Steve Birkin. ♦

Rowton SIBA

Stone House, Rowton, Shropshire, TF6 6QX ☎ 07854 885870 🌐 rowtonbrewery.com

Rowton Brewery is family-run and was established in 2008 in a converted Victorian cowshed on a farm. The brewing operation is split over two locations, the original brewery is still in the village of Rowton and uses water from a borehole on the farm. A second brewery has been installed at the Pheasant Pub, Wellington. Combined brew length over the two plants is 10 barrels. ♦

Moonstruck Mild (OG 1033, ABV 3.3%)

Star Light (OG 1036, ABV 3.6%)

Pure Gold (OG 1038, ABV 3.8%)

Bitter (OG 1040, ABV 3.9%)

Meteorite (OG 1042, ABV 4.2%)

Portly Stout (OG 1045, ABV 4.5%)
A smooth, flavoursome stout fortified with port.

Area 51 (OG 1051, ABV 5.1%)

Ruddles

See Greene King

Rudgate SIBA

2 Centre Park, Marston Moor Business Park, Tockwith, York, North Yorkshire, YO26 7QF ☎ (01423) 358382 🌐 rudgatebrewery.co.uk

◎ Rudgate Brewery was established in 1992 and is situated in the heart of Yorkshire in the Vale of York on the old RAF Marston Moor airfield. The old Roman road of Rudgate runs through the airfield and led the Vikings into Jorvik (York), which is what inspires many of the beer names. ♦

Jorvik Blonde (OG 1036, ABV 3.8%)
Blonde ale with a balanced hoppy bitterness and a crisp, fruity finish.

Viking (OG 1036, ABV 3.8%) ◈
An initially warming and malty, full-bodied beer, with hops and fruit lingering into the aftertaste.

Battleaxe (OG 1040, ABV 4.2%) ◈
A well-hopped bitter with a slightly sweet initial taste and light bitterness. Complex fruit character gives a memorable aftertaste.

Ruby Mild (OG 1041, ABV 4.4%) ◈
Nutty, rich, ruby-coloured ale, stronger than usual for a mild.

Valkyrie APA (ABV 5%)
A gold-coloured, American-style pale ale with a tropical hop finish.

York Chocolate Stout (OG 1049, ABV 5%)
Deep, rich stout with complex balanced flavours and a subtle chocolate finish.

Runaway

Unit 4, Millgate, Dantzic Street, Manchester, M4 4JW ☎ (0161) 832 2628 ☎ 07505 237078 🌐 therunawaybrewery.com

Runaway is located in a railway arch outside Manchester Victoria station. It began brewing in 2014 producing KeyKeg and bottle-conditioned beers. All core range beers are unfiltered and unpasteurised, with many available locally. ‼ ♦ RAIB

Running Man (NEW)

26 Greenway, Davis Estate, Chatham, Kent, ME5 9UX ✉ runningman.brewery@yahoo.com

Running Man began brewing in 2018.

Ryedale SIBA

Roseberry, Moor Lane, Sinnington, North Yorkshire, YO62 6SE ☎ 07850 510859 🌐 ryedalebrewing.co.uk

◎ Rydale began brewing in 2013 using a four-barrel plant. In 2016 it relocated to Cross Hills and again in 2019 to Sinnington.

Angler (ABV 3.8%)
Blonde ale with light bitterness and a pleasant hoppy aftertaste.

Gold (ABV 3.8%)
Golden ale with a hoppy taste.

Pale (ABV 3.8%)
Light-coloured, clean and refreshing ale with a slightly hoppy taste.

Rambler (ABV 3.8%)
Dark chestnut-coloured bitter, creamy with a well-balanced, smooth, hoppy aftertaste.

Bitter (ABV 4%)

Stout (ABV 4.3%)

S&P

Homestead, Brewery Lane, Horsford, Norfolk, NR10 3AN ☎ 07552 300768 🌐 spbrewery.co.uk

⊗ Production commenced in 2013 using a 10-barrel plant constructed upon land once owned by prominent Norfolk brewers Steward & Patteson (1800-1965), hence the name. Locally produced malts are used, as is water from the brewery's own borehole. ‼

Topaz Blonde (OG 1038, ABV 3.7%)
A golden-coloured beer with a citrus aroma and grapefruit taste. A crisp bitter finish.

Blackberry Porter (OG 1044, ABV 4%)
Dark-coloured porter with fruity, blackberry notes.

First Light (OG 1042, ABV 4.1%)
A light golden-coloured beer with a pleasing citrus aroma and deep hoppy flavour, complemented by a lingering bitter finish.

Dennis (OG 1042, ABV 4.2%)
A rich, amber-coloured bitter with a malty sweetness.

Darkest Hour (OG 1047, ABV 4.4%) ◈
Smoky, roasty and bitter throughout. Full-bodied, the sweet malty undertones wane leaving a notable liquorice finish with dark fruit hints.

NASHA IPA (OG 1050, ABV 5%) ▮ ◈

Strong banana and grapefruit character throughout. A good balance of malt and hop with a bittersweet background.

S43 SIBA

Durham Road, Coxhoe, County Durham, DH6 4HX
☎ (0191) 3773039 ⊕ sonnet43.com

☺Previously known as Sonnet 43, S43 began brewing in 2012. The name is inspired by the famous works of the poet Elizabeth Barrett-Browning, who was born nearby. The brewery owns seven outlets and supplies the free trade in Northern England and Southern Scotland. ◆RAIB

Abolition (OG 1038, ABV 3.8%)
Amber-coloured ale with sourdough and nutty aromas and a slightly bitter aftertaste.

Seraphim (OG 1041, ABV 4.1%)
A straw-coloured beer with a sweet, delicate, floral aroma.

The Raven (OG 1046, ABV 4.3%)
Bourbon, cocoa and oats give this dark-coloured beer a rich, full-bodied, chocolaty bitterness.

Aurora (OG 1044, ABV 4.4%)
A strong pale ale with a complex hop aroma and delicate fruity malt tastes.

Impressment (OG 1055, ABV 5.4%)
Bronze-coloured ale with a spicy, peppery aroma and a fruity, malty, spicy flavour.

St Andrews Brewhouse

🔳 City Pub Co, 41 St Andrews Street, Norwich, NR2 4TP
☎ (01603) 305995 ☎ 07976 652410
⊕ standrewsbrewhouse.com

⊗A city centre brewpub opened in 2015 in the premises formerly occupied by Delaney's Irish Bar. ‼◆GF

St Andrews Brewing

Unit 7, Bassaguard Business Park, St Andrews, KY16 8AL
☎ (01334) 208586
⊕ standrewsbrewingcompany.com

Established in 2012 the brewery is a four-barrel plant producing bottle-conditioned, cask and eco-keg beers. In addition to its own five outlets (in St Andrews, Edinburgh and Dundee), beers are supplied to a number of supermarket chains, local retailers and outlets. ◆RAIB

The Wee Blonde (OG 1035, ABV 3.7%)
Gentle blonde ale with light citrus hops, hints of fruit and a floral aroma.

Fife Gold (OG 1040, ABV 4.2%)
Straw yellow in colour with a fresh floral aroma backed up with a citrus punch of lemon, lime and grapefruit.

Crail Ale (OG 1043, ABV 4.5%)
A bright golden ale with long-lasting citrus and floral flavours.

Oatmeal Stout (OG 1043, ABV 4.5%)
A smooth, full-bodied Scottish oatmeal stout. Strong coffee, chocolate and dark fruit flavours balanced against a blend of hops to create a rich, silky aftertaste.

Eighty Bob (OG 1046, ABV 4.8%)
A traditional Scottish 80/- ale. Complex malt flavours dominate.

India Pale Ale (OG 1048, ABV 5%)
Bold IPA with a big hop kick and depth of orange and tropical fruit flavours.

Mocha Porter (ABV 6%)
A coffee and chocolate porter.

Notorious BIPA (ABV 6%)
A strong, smoky IPA with dark stone fruit flavours, particularly cherry.

Yippie IPA (ABV 6%)

St Annes SIBA

St Annes Church, Lea Cross, Shropshire, SY5 8JE
☎ (01743) 860296 ☎ 07505 56951

Office: 38 Hafren Road, Shrewsbury, Shropshire, SY3 8NQ ⊕ shropshirebeers.co.uk

⊗ Brewing began in 2017, this independent brewery is in the quirky location of a restored and occasionally functioning church. Recipes are Scandinavian influenced. A broad range of beers styles is produced. ‼◆

Three Erics (ABV 3.7%)

Golden Dart (ABV 3.8%)

Bad Bad Lea Cross Brown (ABV 3.9%)

Lea Cross Dark (ABV 3.9%)

Tumbledown Dick (ABV 4.1%)

Round the Wrekin (ABV 4.7%)

Iron & Fire (ABV 7.5%)

St Austell

63 Trevarthian Road, St Austell, Cornwall, PL25 4BY
☎ (01726) 74444 ⊕ staustellbrewery.co.uk

☺Founded in 1851, St Austell Brewery remains fully independent and family owned. Cask ale is available in all its pubs, and is widely available nationally. A ten-barrel, small batch plant is used to brew monthly specials, including beers for its annual Celtic beer festival in November. These beers are available in 40 selected outlets, and at Hicks Bar at the Brewery. In 2016 it purchased Bath Ales (qv). ‼🍺◆RAIB

Cornish Best Bitter (OG 1036, ABV 3.5%) 🍺
Light, refreshing copper-coloured bitter with a hop aroma. Gentle biscuit malt and hops flavour with fruity bitterness. Dry, malty, bitter finish.

Trelawny (OG 1039, ABV 3.8%) 🍺🍺
Light tawny-coloured bitter with an aroma of malt and hops. English hop bitterness develops into toffee-malt sweetness. Rising malty, fruity finish.

Nicholson's Pale Ale (OG 1040, ABV 4%) 🍺
Copper-coloured bitter. Hops dominate the taste with citrus, tropical fruits and malt. Dry bitterness rises in the finish.

Tribute (OG 1043, ABV 4.2%) 🍺🍺
Amber-coloured best bitter with a malt and fruity hop aroma. Dominant hop bitterness with sweet malt, ending refreshingly bitter and fruity.

Proper Job (OG 1046, ABV 4.5%) 🍺

Golden ale with resinous hop aroma. Copious citrus fruits with bitterness and a crisp hop bitter and grapefruit finish.

HSD (OG 1051, ABV 5%) ◆
Tawny-coloured strong bitter with a malt nose. Powerful malt and vine fruit flavour with balancing bitterness. Long malty and floral finish.

Contract brewed for Brunning & Price:

Traditional Bitter (OG 1036, ABV 3.5%)
An easy-drinking ale with a touch of bitterness complemented by a smooth, malty finish.

St Ives SIBA

Trewidden Road, St Ives, Cornwall, TR26 2BX
☎ (01736) 793467 ☎ 07702 311595
🌐 stives-brewery.co.uk

⊗ The two-storey brewhouse with 10-barrel plant, integral visitor centre, gift shop and 60-seater café was built in 2015. Owner Marco Amura started brewing commercially in 2016 with production steadily increasing since then. Bottled beers are the highest seller due to strong demand from local restaurants and cafés. The brewery's café, which enjoys a panoramic view of St Ives Bay, is a popular venue. ‼ ♦ RAIB

Harbourside Light Ale (OG 1038, ABV 3.8%) ◆
A golden ale with a citrus hop aroma. Fresh grassy hop, grapefruit and gooseberry flavours with moderate and rising bitterness.

Boilers Golden Ale (OG 1040, ABV 4%) ◆
Amber-coloured bitter with an earthy, hoppy aroma. Strong, bitter citrus hop flavours balanced by nutty, biscuit malt. Bitter, hoppy finish.

XPA (OG 1048, ABV 4.8%) ◆
Golden ale with grapefruit and lemon aroma and dominant taste. Assertive bitterness and hops throughout with kiwi fruit and peach.

Porthminster Porter (OG 1049, ABV 4.9%)
Smooth and full flavoured with a slightly bitter finish.

IPA (OG 1051, ABV 5%) ◆
Yellow-coloured beer with a grapefruit and pine aroma. Bitter and powerfully-hopped with zesty grapefruit citrus flavours. Faintly sweet and dry.

Knill by Mouth (OG 1048, ABV 5%) ◆
Pale brown-coloured strong bitter with a citrus hop and malt aroma. Pine, grassy citrus hop flavour with stone fruits and bitterness.

Brewhouse Belgian Golden Ale (OG 1076, ABV 7.3%) ◆
Smooth, copper-coloured barley wine. Oily and alcoholic. Complex flavours of vine and stone fruits, cloves, light malt and a rising dry bitterness.

St John at Hackney

See Hackney Church

St Judes

▤ 2 Cardigan Street, Ipswich, Suffolk, IP1 3PF
☎ (01473) 413334 ☎ 07879 360879
🌐 stjudestavern.com

⊗ The brewery resumed brewing in 2015 on a newly installed 10-barrel plant. Run by Frank Walsh and Colleen Seymour, the beers are sold mainly through their Ipswich tavern, but can occasionally be found further afield through a distribution agreement with Nethergate Brewery (qv). A core range of beers is offered, but the emphasis is on a wide range of one-off and special brews.

Hoppy Jude (OG 1042, ABV 4.2%)

Lemon Grass (OG 1042, ABV 4.2%)

Gainsborough Bitter (OG 1044, ABV 4.4%)
Satisfying amber-coloured bitter. Good body with a hoppy aftertaste.

Honey Slip (OG 1044, ABV 4.4%)
Light, hoppy bitter with good flavour for its strength.

St Marys Stout (OG 1058, ABV 5.5%)
Smooth, malty, dark-coloured stout. Full-flavoured with a long finish.

St Mars of the Desert (NEW)

90 Stevenson Road, Attercliffe, Sheffield, South Yorkshire, S9 3XG ☎ 07365 222101
🌐 beerofsmod.co.uk

With over 20 years of brewing experience, Dann Paquette, together with partner Martha Holley, relocated from Boston, Massachusetts to the UK and established their brewery in 2018. The brewery is located in an industrial area of Sheffield and consists of two buildings around a courtyard – one containing the brewery, the other the taproom which opens most Fridays and Saturdays, plus selected additional days.

St Mary's

St Mary the Virgin, Elsworthy Road, Primrose Hill, London, NW3 3DJ
☎ (020) 7722 3238 🌐 stmarysbrewery.co.uk

Based in the church crypt, this nanobrewery produces small batch bottled beers sold in aid of the church's youth projects. Larger batches are produced at UBrew (qv), the bottle label will show origin. The first pint was blessed by the Bishop of Edmonton and the names have an ecclesiastical bias.

St Peter's SIBA

St Peter's Hall, St Peter South Elmham, Suffolk, NR35 1NQ
☎ (01986) 782322 🌐 stpetersbrewery.co.uk

⊗ The brewery, built in 1996, is housed in traditional former agricultural buildings adjacent to moated medieval St Peters Hall, dating from 1280. Brewing makes use of the water from an on-site bore hole combined with locally malted barley. Beer is distributed nationally across the UK and exported to more than 40 countries worldwide. ‼ ♦ GF

Best Bitter (OG 1037, ABV 3.7%) ◆
A complex but well-balanced, hoppy brew. A gentle hop nose introduces a singular hoppiness with supporting malt notes and underlying bitterness. Other flavours fade to leave a long, dry, hoppy finish.

EPA (OG 1038, ABV 3.8%)
A session beer with a robust bitterness. Clean-tasting and relatively dry.

Golden Ale (OG 1040, ABV 4%) ◆

THE BREWERIES

Amber-coloured, full-bodied, robust ale. A strong hop bouquet leads to a mix of malt and hops combined with a dry, fruity hoppiness. The malt quickly subsides, leaving creamy bitterness.

Organic Best (OG 1041, ABV 4.1%) ◈
A dry and bitter beer with a growing astringency. Pale brown in colour, it has a gentle hop aroma which makes the definitive bitterness surprising.

Ruby Red (OG 1043, ABV 4.3%)
A tawny red-coloured ale with subtle malt undertones and a distinctive spicy hop aroma.

Organic Ale (OG 1045, ABV 4.5%) ◈
A rich toffee apple aroma and a smooth grainy feel. Malt and caramel initially match the dry hoppy bitterness. As the flavours mature, liquorice dryness develops. Full-bodied.

Plum Porter (OG 1046, ABV 4.6%)
A dark, full-flavoured porter with distinctive fruity plum notes.

Grapefruit Beer (OG 1047, ABV 4.7%) ◈
Fudge as well as grapefruit on the nose. A refreshing fruit flavour, with hints of grapefruit peel in the aftertaste.

IPA (OG 1055, ABV 5.5%)
A full-bodied, highly-hopped pale ale with a zesty character.

Cream Stout (OG 1065, ABV 6.5%)
Strong, dark-coloured and aromatic stout with coffee and vanilla notes, smooth, creamy chocolate flavours and a satisfying bittersweet aftertaste.

Sabrina

See Worcester

Saddleworth

Church Inn, Church Lane, Uppermill, OL3 6LW
☎ (01457) 820902 🌐 churchinnsaddleworth.co.uk

Saddleworth started brewing in 1997 in a 120-year old brewhouse at the Church Inn. Brewery and inn are set above a valley overlooking Saddleworth Moor. Brewing capacity was significantly expanded in 2011 with a new 13-barrel plant. ♦

Mild (OG 1038, ABV 3.6%)

St George's Bitter (OG 1038, ABV 3.8%)
Quite dry and bitter with some citrus and nutty notes.

The Notorious IPA (OG 1045, ABV 4.5%)

Shaftbender (OG 1060, ABV 5.4%)

Bitter & Twisted IPA (OG 1065, ABV 6.2%)

Taking the Pith (OG 1065, ABV 6.2%)

Sadler's

Unit 2, Conyers Trading Estate, Station Drive, Lye, West Midlands, DY9 8ER
☎ (01384) 895230 🌐 sadlersales.co.uk

Third and fourth generation brewers John and Chris Sadler re-opened this historic brewery in 2004. Having moved to larger premises in 2015, the brewery is situated next to Lye train station and incorporates a 30-barrel plant, shop and bar. More than 1,000 outlets are supplied nationwide with beers also exported overseas. ‼ ♦

JPA (OG 1036, ABV 3.6%)
A pale-coloured, hoppy bitter with a crisp and zesty lemon undertone.

Mellow Yellow (OG 1039, ABV 3.9%)
A pale-coloured ale with an uplifting hop character, balanced with a sweet honey finish.

Thin Ice (OG 1042.5, ABV 4.3%)
A pale ale, bitter with an orange and lemon finish.

Worcester Sorcerer (OG 1041.5, ABV 4.3%)
Brewed with English hops and barley with hints of mint and lemon, creating a floral aroma and crisp bitterness.

Peaky Blinder (OG 1044, ABV 4.4%) ◈
Black in colour with malt and fruit in the aroma. Smoky bitterness and toffee in the taste with powerful hops lingering.

Boris Citrov (OG 1045, ABV 4.5%)
A punchy orange marmalade ale with a sweet, crisp and fruity finish.

Hop Bomb (OG 1046, ABV 4.6%)
An American-style pale ale with a sweet malt base lifted by a powerful hop character.

Red IPA (OG 1050, ABV 5%)

Mud City Stout (OG 1061, ABV 6%) ◈
Dark brown-coloured stout with a soft fruity aroma and malty taste with caramel and raisins. A lingering sweet aftertaste with a hint of bitterness.

Saeburh

Long Lane, Tendring, Essex, CO16 0BG 🌐 saeburh.com

Saeburh was established in 2015 by two horticulturalists with a passion for beer. Hops and fruit are grown on the grounds of the estate where the brewery is based. Expansion is planned.

Amber No. 1 (OG 1040, ABV 4%)

Citrus Isles (OG 1040, ABV 4%)

Blacksails Treacle Stout (OG 1048, ABV 5%)

Cannonball (ABV 5%)

Saffron

The Cartshed, Parsonage Farm, Henham, Essex, CM22 6AN
☎ (01279) 850923 ☎ 07980 972067
🌐 saffronbrewery.co.uk

Founded in 2005, the brewery was upgraded to a 15-barrel plant in early 2008 and re-located to a converted barn at Parsonage Farm, with a purpose-built reed bed for environmentally-friendly disposal of waste products. 40 outlets are supplied direct. ‼ ♦ RAIB

IPA (OG 1036, ABV 3.6%)

Citra (ABV 3.8%)
Light golden ale with grapefruit aromas and a crisp gooseberry finish.

Dawn Til Dusk (ABV 3.8%)
Traditional copper-coloured bitter with hints of citrus and biscuit maltiness.

Ramblers Tipple (OG 1040, ABV 3.9%)
A rich, copper-coloured bitter with toffee and caramel flavours.

Brewhouse Bell (OG 1041, ABV 4%)

Golden amber in colour with citrus and hop flavours balancing well for a clean, fresh finish.

Royal Blue (ABV 4.1%)

Littlebury Lighthouse (OG 1043, ABV 4.2%)

Blonde (OG 1044, ABV 4.3%)
A light golden ale with a delicate balance of citrus and smooth, malty flavours. A crisp finish.

Squires Gamble (OG 1044, ABV 4.3%)
Traditional copper-coloured ale; soft, mellow, full-flavoured and hoppy with citrus and biscuit hints.

Turpins Temptation (ABV 4.8%)
Warming malty beer with nutty and bittersweet toffee flavours.

Tiddly Vicar (OG 1051, ABV 5.1%)
Traditional dark copper-coloured, nutty beer with a light spicy finish.

Porter (ABV 5.2%)
Ruby-coloured porter with rich chocolate and coffee aromas. Ruby port and red grape juice create a soft fruit and spice finish.

Saints Row

Unit 1, Cleveland Industrial Estate, Darlington, DL1 2PB ☎ 07922 617622

Office: 18 Maude Street, Darlington, DL3 6PW ⊕ saintsrowbrewing.com

Formerly known as Hells Kettle, Saints Row commenced brewing in 2017 using equipment at Three Brothers Brewing (qv). In 2019 the brewery moved to its own premises in Darlington.

The Catcher (ABV 4%)

The Moth (ABV 4%)

Even Drop (ABV 4.2%)

Wellspring (ABV 5%)

Salcombe SIBA

Estuary View, Ledstone, Devon, TQ7 4BL
☎ (01548) 854888 ⊕ salcombebrewery.com

⊗ Formerly known as Quercus, brewing began in 2007 using an eight-barrel plant, before being sold to local residents John Tiner and Mike George in 2012. A complete rebranding occurred in 2016, with the brewery relocating to a new purpose-built 20-barrel brewery and visitor centre in 2017. ‼🍽◆

Devon Amber (OG 1038, ABV 3.8%)
A classic bitter. Amber in colour with a dry, hoppy aroma and flavour and a sweet malt backbone.

Gold (OG 1042, ABV 4.2%)
A light, refreshing, straw-coloured ale with a good hop aroma and taste and long, hoppy finish.

Shingle Bay (OG 1042, ABV 4.2%)
A light, easy-drinking ale with a fruity aroma and flavour. Smooth to the taste with a crisp finish.

Seahorse (OG 1044, ABV 4.4%) ◆
Toffee malt is evident throughout this complex yet subtle mix of everything you would expect from a best bitter.

Lifesaver (OG 1048, ABV 4.8%)
A refreshing ale, deep copper in colour with a smack of citrus and orange peel and a malty flavour. A dry citrus finish with a taste of liquorice.

Salopian SIBA

The Old Station Yard, Station Road, Hadnall, Shropshire, SY4 3DD
☎ (01743) 248414 ⊕ salopianbrewery.co.uk

☺The brewery was established in 1995 in an old dairy on the outskirts of Shrewsbury but moved in 2014 to its new location in an industrial unit in the village of Hadnall, where it now produces more than 150 barrels a week. ‼🍽◆RAIB

Shropshire Gold (OG 1037, ABV 3.8%)
A light, copper-coloured ale with an unusual blend of body and dryness.

Oracle (OG 1040, ABV 4%) 🍷🍴◆
Citrus aromas lead to an impressive dry and increasing citrus taste.

Darwins Origin (OG 1042, ABV 4.3%) 🍷🍴◆
Pale brown-coloured ale in which hops and fruit are dominant. Hops top the aftertaste with a pleasing lingering bitterness. Well-balanced with a moreish finish.

Hop Twister (OG 1044, ABV 4.5%) 🍷
A premium bitter with a citrus flavour and complex hop finish. Refreshing and crisp.

Lemon Dream (OG 1043.5, ABV 4.5%) 🍷
A light gold-coloured ale subtly flavoured with fresh lemons.

Golden Thread (OG 1048, ABV 5%)
A bright gold-coloured ale; strong and quite bitter but well balanced.

Kashmir (OG 1053.5, ABV 5.5%)

Automaton (OG 1068, ABV 7%) ◆
Gold in colour with pine forest aromas and peaches. Syrup with a kick. Dry hints and exotic astringency as hops give a dry finish but sweet balance.

Salt (NEW)

199 Bingley Road, Shipley, West Yorkshire, BD18 4DH
☎ (01274) 533848 ⊕ saltbeerfactory.co.uk

Housed in a Grade II-listed Edwardian tramshed, Salt is a state of the art 200-hectolitre brew plant and one of the Ossett group of independently run breweries. The site includes a taproom (open at the weekend) and live music space. Two bars, branded as Craft Asylum, are operated. ‼🍽◆

Saltaire SIBA

103 Dockfield Road, Shipley, West Yorkshire, BD17 7AR
☎ (01274) 594959 ⊕ saltairebrewery.com

☺ Launched in 2006, Saltaire is an award-winning brewery based in a former Victorian power station. A brewery tap and shop opened in 2014. A period of major upgrade and development took place in 2018, with expansion to the brewing capacity and the addition of a packaging and bottling plant. More than 600 pubs are supplied across West Yorkshire and the north of England and beer is exported to more than ten countries. ‼🍽◆

South Island (OG 1035, ABV 3.5%)
A clean, crisp beer with subtle hop fruitiness.

Titus (OG 1039, ABV 3.9%)
Traditional bitterness meets a twist of citrus in this clean bitter.

THE BREWERIES

Blonde (OG 1040, ABV 4%) ◆
Thirst-quenching and quaffable, this straw-coloured beer is slightly sweet and well rounded with fruit, malt and hops in the taste and a fruity, hoppy finish.

No. 5 (ABV 4.2%)
A stout with creamy, smooth roasted malts and a hint of smoke on the finish.

Best (ABV 4.4%)
Classic best bitter, a good balance of rich malt backbone with fruity hop notes.

Cascade (OG 1046, ABV 4.8%)
Punchy citrus flavours with a distinctive bitterness.

Triple Choc (OG 1048.5, ABV 4.8%) ◆
A creamy, dark brown-coloured, roast, chocolate stout with a dry bitter finish and a rich chocolate aroma.

Sambrook's SIBA

Units 1-3, Yelverton Road, Battersea, London, SW11 3QG
☎ (020) 7228 0598 sambrooksbrewery.co.uk

Sambrook's was founded in 2008 and supplies its award-winning ales throughout London. The brewery tap hosts various events, is available for private booking and is open as a pub Thursday to Saturday. Sambrook's brews the Watneys range of beers for Watneys Beer Company, now widely available around London. There are plans for a move to the old Young's Brewery site in Wandsworth with a taproom and visitors centre. !! ♦ RAIB

Wandle Ale (OG 1038.5, ABV 3.8%) ◆
Dryness balances the rounded sweetish malt flavour of this fruity, quaffable, pale brown-coloured bitter. Some peach and citrus notes.

Pumphouse Pale Ale (OG 1041.5, ABV 4.2%) ◆
Refreshing golden-coloured beer with a hint of citrus aroma becoming more pronounced on the palate, lingering into the bitter finish.

Junction Ale (OG 1045.5, ABV 4.5%) ◆
Smooth, full-bodied, brown-coloured best bitter. Fruit and spicy hoppy aroma and flavour, lingering in the dry, slightly bitter finish.

Powerhouse Porter (OG 1050, ABV 4.9%) ◆
Dark brown-coloured porter with a pleasant roasted malt nose with some sultana, blackcurrant and treacle character. Dry roasted finish.

Sandbanks

Unit 6, 4-6 Abingdon Road, Nuffield Industrial Estate, Poole, Dorset, BH17 0UG
☎ (01202) 671950 sandbanksbrewery.net

Opened in 2018 on the same site as the old Bournemouth Brewery with a new plant. Most of the beer is sold from the brewery bar although a big push is underway to get into the local free trade. !! ♦

Sandbanks Bitter (OG 1038, ABV 3.9%) ◆
Session bitter with lingering aftertaste.

Wessex Wobble (OG 1041, ABV 4.3%)
Traditional English ale with a mildly hoppy taste.

Sandiway

Blakemere Village, Chester Road, Sandiway, Cheshire, CW8 2EB
☎ (01606) 301000 ☎ 07543 623152
sandiwayales.co.uk

Sandiway began brewing in 2015 using a five-barrel plant in the premises of the former Blakemere Brewery at Blakemere Village Craft Centre. Aimed at local trade, outlets include the on-site shop called Wee Howff. Beers are also available at the No. 4 Bar in Winsford and limited outlets throughout Cheshire and surrounding areas. Brewing is currently suspended. !!

Sandstone

Unit 5, Wrexham Enterprise Park, Preston Road, off Ash Road, North Wrexham Industrial Estate, Wrexham, LL13 9JT
☎ (01978) 664805 ☎ 07851 001118
sandstonebrewery.co.uk

Sandstone Brewery was established as a four-barrel plant in 2008. The brewery was taken over by the current owners in 2013. The beers are available at around 50 outlets in North-west England and North Wales. !! ♦

Edge (OG 1039, ABV 3.8%) ◆
A satisfying session ale, this pale-coloured, dry, bitter beer has a full mouthfeel and a lingering hoppy finish that belies its modest strength.

Steam Dragon (ABV 3.9%)

Celtic Pride (ABV 4%)

Onyx Dragon (OG 1040, ABV 4%)
Coal black in colour with hints of chocolate, toffee and caramel.

Post Mistress (OG 1046, ABV 4.4%) ◆
A full-bodied, smooth premium bitter, ruby-red in colour, with a rich, mellow taste.ôGood combination of malt, hops and fruit in aroma and initial taste leading to a lasting, satisfying finish.

Twisted Dragon (OG 1058, ABV 5.8%)

Sarah Hughes

See under H

Saviour (NEW)

White Hart Inn, Hamstead Marshall, Berkshire, RG20 0HW
☎ (01488) 657545 info@saviourwhitehart.co.uk

Brewing began in 2019 on a four-barrel plant in an outbuilding in the grounds of the White Hart pub in Hamstead Marshall. Beers are only available in the pub.

Sawbridgeworth

81 London Road, Sawbridgeworth, Hertfordshire, CM21 9JJ
☎ (01279) 722313 ☎ 07446 960409
thegatepub.net

Set up in 2000 by owners Tom and Gary Barnett, the brewery is situated behind the Gate Inn. Tom is a former professional footballer whose clubs included Crystal Palace. Special and one-off beers are regularly brewed by Bob Renvoise (ex-Nethergate). ‼♦

Scarborough SIBA

Unit 21b, Stadium Works, Barry's Lane, Scarborough, North Yorkshire, YO12 4HA
☎ (01723) 367500 🌐 scarboroughbrewery.co.uk

Scarborough is a family-run brewery established in 2010, now using a 10-barrel plant. Beers can be found in the family-owned Valley Bar and Rivelyn Hotel as well as being the sole suppliers to Merchant Bar in Scarborough. ♦

Trident (ABV 3.8%)
Pale-coloured session beer with refreshing flavours of lemon and passion fruit.

Citra (OG 1042, ABV 4.2%)
Refreshing and light pale golden-coloured beer with light citrus aromas.

Sealord (OG 1043, ABV 4.3%)
Golden ale with subtle hints of lime, grapefruit and melon.

Stout (OG 1046, ABV 4.6%)
Full-bodied, dark-coloured stout brewed using five malts giving depth of flavour and a bitter chocolate aroma.

Hello Darkness (ABV 5%)
Dark-coloured, rich porter. Pronounced malty flavours along with chocolate, caramel notes and a subtle hop kick.

Scribbler's

7 Lime Grove, Stapleford, Nottinghamshire, NG9 7GF
☎ (0115) 875 1759 ☎ 07780 662244
🌐 scribblers-ales.com

Scribbler's was established in 2014 by Richard Nettleton, an author (hence the name) and Roger Frost. The 4.5-barrel plant was constructed by the owners, the fermentation and mash tun converted from old ice cream vessels. Beer names are based on classic book titles.

Beerfest at Tiffanys (OG 1046, ABV 3.8%) ◆
Golden-coloured ale with a citrus fruit aroma and taste and a dry bitter finish.

Hoppy Potter & the Goblet of Ale (OG 1048, ABV 4.2%)
Light-coloured ale with citrus hop aromas.

Life of IPA (OG 1053, ABV 4.7%)

Masher in the Rye (OG 1053, ABV 4.8%) ◆
Golden-coloured, delicately-hopped beer with subtle malt, a hint of fruit and soft bitterness.

Rubecca (OG 1053, ABV 4.8%) ◆
Dark ruby-coloured ale with a mixture of roast malt, raisin, fruit and chocolate, leading to a gentle bitter finish.

Beyond Reasonable Stout (OG 1068, ABV 6%) ◆
Initial roast malt and coffee giving way to moderate bitterness and a dark fruit finish.

Scruffy Dog (NEW)

94 Station Road, Sutton-in-Ashfield, Nottinghamshire, NG17 5HF
☎ (01623) 550826 🌐 thescruffydog.co.uk

Microbrewery at the Scruffy Dog pub in Sutton-in-Ashfield.

Seal Bay

Parc-y-Pratt Farm, Fishguard Road, Cardigan, SA43 3DR ☎ 07969 420501
✉ colintmathew@yahoo.com

Seal Bay was established in 2016 in a farm outbuilding using a one-barrel plant. Beer is supplied to local pubs and parties on an occasional basis.

Craig (OG 1042, ABV 4.2%)
Straw-coloured best bitter with distinctive malt and hop flavours.

Secret Herb Garden

See Top Out

Serious

Unit C5, Fieldhouse Industrial Estate, Fieldhouse Road, Rochdale, OL12 0AA ☎ 07840 301797
✉ jenny@seriousbrewing.co.uk

Established in 2015 and run by husband an wife team Ken and Jenny Lynch. The beers are brewed using a six-barrel plant supplied by Vincent Johnson. The focus is on producing high quality beers drawing influences from traditional British ales, US craft beers and artisanal Belgian beers. Many outlets are supplied direct and the beers are available nationwide via wholesalers. A taproom opened at the brewery in 2019. ♦RAIB

Arboria (OG 1036, ABV 3.6%)
A pale ale with a spicy, earthy bitterness and pleasant aroma with floral and pine overtones.

Evergreen (OG 1045, ABV 4.5%) ◆
Hoppy aroma. Taste of fruit and bitter hops, with lasting bitterness. Crisp and bitter throughout. Background of sweet malt.

Moonlight (OG 1045, ABV 4.5%)
Silky smooth stout with chocolate notes and a bitter hop finish.

Redsmith (OG 1045, ABV 4.5%)

Arrakis (OG 1051, ABV 5.1%)
A Belgian-style IPA with a dry, spicy finish.

Goldrush (OG 1056, ABV 5.6%)

Settle SIBA

Unit 2b, The Sidings, Settle, North Yorkshire, BD24 9RP
☎ (01729) 824936 🌐 settlebrewery.co.uk

Settle Brewery is located in an industrial unit adjacent to Settle railway station. Brewing started in 2013 using a 12-barrel plant. More than 40 outlets across Cumbria, the Yorkshire Dales, West Yorkshire and North Lancashire are supplied. The beers are also available through wholesalers. ‼♦

Blonde (OG 1036, ABV 3.6%)
A delicate straw-coloured beer with a subtle blend of fruit and spice flavours and citrus overtones.

Jericho Blonde (OG 1036, ABV 3.6%)
Light and refreshing ale with notes of honey and a subtle floral aroma. A crisp, clean finish.

Mainline (OG 1037.5, ABV 3.8%) ◆
Creamy traditional Yorkshire Bitter. Good balance of rich malt and bittering hops, giving a pronounced raspberry fruitiness and hints of nuts in both aroma and taste.

Ribblehead Bitter (OG 1037.5, ABV 3.8%)
Traditional copper-coloured Yorkshire bitter, a perfect balance of malt and subtle hops.

Epic IPA (OG 1043, ABV 4.4%)
Crisp and fruity IPA with a big hop hit.

Ernie's Milk Stout (OG 1045, ABV 4.5%)
Full-bodied, malty and creamy stout with roast coffee and chocolate tones.

Brewed under the Nine Standards brand name:

No. 4 Amber Ale (OG 1037, ABV 3.7%) ◆
Rich biscuity, malty taste balanced by bitter hops and a dry finish. Malty aroma and gentle fruitiness.

No. 1 Golden Ale (OG 1040, ABV 4.1%)
A golden ale with a hint of blackcurrant.

No. 2 Pale Ale (OG 1042, ABV 4.3%)
A classic pale ale with a strong hoppy aroma.

No. 3 Porter (OG 1048, ABV 4.7%) ◆
Roasty porter with coffee and dark fruits. Hints of liquorice and plums in the aroma. The finish is bitter & roasty.

Seven Bro7hers SIBA

Unit 63, Waybridge Enterprise Centre, Daniel Adamson Road, Salford, M50 1DS
☎ (0161) 228 2404 ☎ 07902 199822
🌐 sevenbro7hers.com

Brewing began in 2014 using a 10-barrel plant. A new brewhouse and fermentation tanks doubled brewing capacity in 2017 and allowed for the brewing of speciality and one-off beers plus a brewery tap. The Seven Bro7hers Beerhouse in Ancoats opened in 2016 and a new Beerhouse opened in 2019 in the Middlewood Locks area near Salford Central station. Further outlets are planned in Leeds and Liverpool. !! 🛒

Session (ABV 3.8%) ◆
Fruity hop taste of tropical fruit, well balanced with bitter and pale malt. Citrus hop aroma. Refreshing bitter finish.

Ruby (ABV 4%)
A ruby-coloured beer with aromas of tropical fruit, grapefruit and champagne followed by tangerine, spiced cherry and herbal vanilla flavours.

EPA (ABV 4.8%) ◆
Pleasant and balanced. Fruity aroma, sweet and peachy taste with background bitterness. Delicate dry hop finish.

Seven Kings (NEW)

Wymet House, 87 New Row, Dunfermline, KY12 7DZ
☎ 07909 015606
✉ jonathan@sevenkingsbrewery.co.uk

Brewing began in 2019.

Fallen King (ABV 3.8%)

Hero King (ABV 4.2%)

King's Bane (ABV 5%)

Severn SIBA

The Brewery, Tortworth Business Park, Tortworth, Gloucestershire, GL12 8HQ
☎ (01454) 269421 🌐 s7n.co.uk

⊗ Following a short period of closure, the assets of Combined Brewers were purchased by a drinks distribution company, Foxstead Ltd, in 2017. Steve McDonald, the brewer from Combined, was brought in to set up the brewing operation. A new range of beers is brewed using the 30-barrel plant, with experimental beers brewed using a smaller five-barrel plant. !! 🛒 ♦ GF

Copper Ale (OG 1038, ABV 3.8%)
A classic English ale with a subtle bitterness balanced with smooth malt notes and fruity hops on the finish.

Chocolate Stout (OG 1043, ABV 4.1%)
Full-bodied chocolate stout. Deep roasted flavours with big hits of chocolate and coffee.

Double Hopped Pale Ale (OG 1042, ABV 4.2%)
A session pale ale, well-balanced with a smooth hoppy finish and aroma.

Golden IPA (OG 1045, ABV 4.5%)
Rich and full-bodied IPA with fruity flavours.

Ruby Porter (OG 1048, ABV 4.8%)
Dark-coloured porter with deep roasted malt flavours, balanced with traditional English hops.

Extra Special (OG 1052, ABV 5.2%)
A complex, smoky and strong ale with a subtle hop balance and deep fruity flavour.

Severn Valley (NEW)

Unit 5, Churchill Court, Faraday Drive, Bridgnorth, Shropshire, WV15 5BB ☎ 07402 636482
🌐 severnvalleyales.co.uk

Brewing began in 2019.

Cartway Gold (ABV 4.2%)

Shadow (NEW)

44 Whiteley Croft Rise, Otley, West Yorkshire, LS21 3NR

Established by Ian Shutt, one of the founders of the Chevin brewing collective, in 2019.

Shakespeare

See North Cotswold

Shalford SIBA

PO Box 10411, Braintree, Essex, CM7 5WP
☎ (01371) 850925 ☎ 07749 658512
🌐 shalfordbrewery.co.uk

Shalford began brewing in 2007 on a five-barrel plant at Hyde Farm in the Pant Valley in Essex. More than 50 outlets are supplied direct. ♦ RAIB

1319 Mild (OG 1037, ABV 3.7%)
Roast malt and chocolate sweetness with a slight bitter finish.

Barnfield Pale Ale (OG 1038, ABV 3.8%) ◆
Pale-coloured but full-flavoured, this is a traditional, hoppy bitter rather than a golden ale.

Malt persists throughout, with bitterness becoming more dominant towards the end.

Braintree Market Ale (OG 1040, ABV 4%)
Traditional, easy-drinking session ale with a hoppy, lingering, dry finish.

Levelly Gold (OG 1040, ABV 4%)
Golden-coloured bitter with a pleasant finish.

Stoneley Bitter (OG 1042, ABV 4.2%) ◆
Dark amber-coloured session beer with a vivid hop character supported by a juicy, malty body. A dry finish.

Hyde Bitter (OG 1047, ABV 4.7%) ◆
Stronger version of Barnfield, with a similar but more assertive character.

Levelly Black (OG 1048, ABV 4.8%)
A dark-coloured, heavy, well-hopped ale with a grainy toffee taste.

Rotten End (OG 1065, ABV 6.5%)
Strong beer with slightly sweet, nutty undertones and a bitter edge to finish.

Shardlow

The Old Brewery Stables, British Waterways Yard, Cavendish Bridge, Leicestershire, DE72 2HL
☎ (01332) 799188 ✉ nev@shardlowbrewery.co.uk

On a site associated with brewing since 1819, Shardlow delivers to more than 100 outlets throughout the East Midlands and is also one of the largest UK cider distributors. Reverend Eaton is named after a scion of the Eaton brewing family, Rector of Shardlow for 40 years. The brewery tap is the Blue Bell Inn at Melbourne, Derbyshire. Prolific supplier of beers to local beer festivals. !! ◆ RAIB

Chancellors Revenge (OG 1036, ABV 3.6%)
A light-coloured, refreshing, full-flavoured and well-hopped session bitter.

Cavendish Dark (OG 1037, ABV 3.7%)
A mild, well-balanced beer with a hoppy aftertaste.

Golden Hop (OG 1041, ABV 4.1%)
Golden-coloured, sweet-tasting beer with a hoppy aroma.

Kiln House (OG 1041, ABV 4.1%)
A refreshing golden ale with a lingering bitter finish.

Narrow Boat (OG 1043, ABV 4.3%)
A pale amber-coloured bitter with a short, crisp hoppy aftertaste.

Cavendish Bridge (OG 1045, ABV 4.5%)
Pale amber-coloured premium bitter. Refreshing, clean and fruity with a pleasing bitter finish.

Cavendish Gold (OG 1045, ABV 4.5%)
Pale gold in colour, bright and clean tasting. A full-bodied ale with pronounced bitterness and complexity.

Reverend Eaton (OG 1045, ABV 4.5%)
A smooth bitter, full of malt and hop flavours with a sweet aftertaste.

Mayfly (OG 1048, ABV 4.8%)
Fruit notes predominate together with a pronounced malty aroma. Easy-drinking but strong.

Five Bells (OG 1050, ABV 5%)
Rich ruby-coloured ale, powerful and bittersweet to the palate. Coffee notes complete the profile.

Whistlestop (OG 1050, ABV 5%)

Sharp's

Pityme Business Centre, Rock, Cornwall, PL27 6NU
☎ (01208) 862121 🌐 sharpsbrewery.co.uk

Sharp's was bought for £20 million by Molson Coors in 2011. The brewery was founded in 1994 and within 15 years had grown from producing 1,500 barrels a year to 60,000. £7.5 million of investment from Molson Coors has brought the capacity up to 200,000 barrels a year. The company owns no pubs and delivers beer to more than 1,200 outlets across the south of England via temperature-controlled depots in Bristol and London. Molson Coors has stressed that it will maintain production in Cornwall. Part of Molson Coors PLC. ◆ RAIB

Cornish Coaster (OG 1035.2, ABV 3.6%) ◆
Refreshing tawny-coloured bitter with a malt and tropical fruit nose. Stone fruit and tropical fruit with biscuit malt and caramel notes.

Doom Bar (OG 1038.5, ABV 4%) ◆
Copper-coloured bitter with gentle fruit and hop aroma. Clean, balanced taste of biscuit malt, hops and plum fruit. Bittersweet finish.

Atlantic (OG 1043, ABV 4.2%) ◆
Amber-coloured best bitter with a light citrus hop aroma. Malt sweetness balanced by grapefruit, resin and pepper notes. Refreshing bitter finish.

Original (OG 1042.5, ABV 4.4%) ◆
Mid brown-coloured best bitter with pleasant hop and malt aroma. Prune and berry fruits on the palate with smoky malt.

Sea Fury (OG 1050, ABV 5%) ◆
Smooth, red-coloured strong bitter with malt and fruit aromas. A combination of berry, stone and dried fruits with spice hints.

Shed

Broadfields, Pewsey, Wiltshire, SN9 5DT
☎ (01672) 564533 ☎ 07769 812643
🌐 shedales.com

Shed Ales was launched in 2012 operating from a one-barrel plant in a converted garden shed. The brewery currently produces three core ales and several bespoke beers, available at selected local outlets including the brewery-owned Shed Alehouse, a micropub in Pewsey. ◆

Dig It (OG 1037.5, ABV 3.7%)

Shed Some Light (OG 1041, ABV 3.8%)
A refreshing blonde beer made with a light earthy hop aroma and flavour.

Dibber (OG 1042.5, ABV 4.2%)
Light amber in colour with a biscuit malt and citrus hop aroma. Easy-drinking with a good balance of malt and fruity hop notes and dry finish.

Sheelin

178 Derrylin Road, Bellanaleck, County Fermanagh, BT92 2BA ☎ 07730 432232 🌐 sheelin.com

Sheelin was established by brewer and chemist Dr George Cathcart in 2013. Beer is mainly available in bottles.

Sheffield SIBA

Unit 111, JC Albyn Complex, Burton Road, Sheffield, South Yorkshire, S3 8BT
☎ (0114) 272 7256 🌐 sheffieldbrewery.com

Established in 2006, Sheffield Brewery Company is situated in a former Victorian factory, originally known for making Blanco polish. The 10-barrel plant operates on a gravity-fed tower based system. The brewery has its own on-site tap room. !!

Crucible Best (OG 1038, ABV 3.8%)

Five Rivers (OG 1038, ABV 3.8%)
Easy-drinking, straw-coloured pale ale with a hoppy aroma and finish.

Blanco Blonde (OG 1042, ABV 4.2%)

Sheffield Porter (OG 1045, ABV 4.4%)
A classic, dark-coloured porter with a rich chocolate, malty and caramel flavour.

Shepherd Neame IFBB

17 Court Street, Faversham, Kent, ME13 7AX
☎ (01795) 532206 🌐 shepherdneame.co.uk

Shepherd Neame traces its history back to 1698, making it the oldest continuous brewer in the country, though brewing probably began even earlier. The company has 300 tied houses in the South-east, nearly all selling cask ale. More than 2,000 other outlets are also supplied. The cask beers are made with mostly Kentish hops, and water from the brewery's own artesian well. There is a microplant within the brewery to produce speciality ales for special occasions and product development. A Cask Club offers a new, different cask ale every month. The company also brews cask ales under the Faversham Steam Brewery and No. 18 Yard Brewhouse names. !! ♦RAIB

Master Brew (OG 1032, ABV 3.7%)
A distinctive bitter, mid-brown in colour, with a hoppy aroma. Well-balanced with a nicely aggressive bitter taste from its hops, it leaves a hoppy/bitter finish, tinged with sweetness.

Whitstable Bay Pale Ale (OG 1038, ABV 3.9%)
A full-bodied, fruity ale with a subtle bitterness and glorious grapefruit and pine aromas.

Spitfire Gold (ABV 4.1%)
A well-balanced golden ale with tropical fruit and pine aromas, and a subtle bitterness.

Spitfire (OG 1036, ABV 4.2%)
A well-balanced bitter. Hints of marmalade, red grapes and pepper, with warm, mellow malts. A fruity finish with hints of spice and raspberry.

Bishops Finger (OG 1046, ABV 5%)
A strong ale with a complex hop aromas of lemons, oranges and bananas combined with malt, molasses and toffee. Refreshing with a good malt character tinged with a lingering bitterness.

Sherfield Village SIBA

Goddards Farm, Goddards Lane, Sherfield on Loddon, Hampshire, RG27 0EL ☎ 07906 060429
🌐 sherfieldvillagebrewery.co.uk

Production started in 2011 in a converted barn on a working dairy farm. Using a five-barrel plant, the brewery supplies local pubs and regional festivals. Extensive use is made of New World hops, particularly those from New Zealand. All beers are unfined. ♦RAIB

TBA (OG 1037, ABV 3.9%)
Copper-coloured session beer with a long hoppy finish.

Best of Both Worlds (OG 1040, ABV 4.1%)
A well-balanced, light-coloured bitter.

Green Bullet (OG 1042, ABV 4.3%)
A strong lemony nose, with hops dominating the taste building to a strong aftertaste with a big astringent hit at the end.

Single Hop (OG 1042, ABV 4.3%)
A golden ale which uses a single hop variety that changes every month, thereby subtly changing the beer characteristics.

Pioneer Stout (OG 1048, ABV 5%)
A black-coloured stout, chocolaty with a hint of vanilla.

Pendragon Porter (OG 1053, ABV 5.4%)
A rich, smooth, dark-coloured porter with a well-rounded flavour.

Shilling

92 West George Street, Glasgow, G2 1PJ
☎ (0141) 353 1654 🌐 shillingbrewingcompany.co.uk

Brewing began in 2016.

ShinDigger

Office: 170 Vie Building, 185 Water Street, Manchester, M3 4JU 🌐 shindiggerbrewing.co

Established in 2012, ShinDigger's output is predominantly keg and cans supplied to outlets such as restaurants and music venues around Manchester. Music, beer and food events are run. Beers are contract brewed in Cumbria and Lancaster.

Shiny SIBA

Unit 10, Old Hall Mill Business Centre, Little Eaton, Derbyshire, DE21 5EJ
☎ (01332) 902809

Brewing commenced in 2012 using a six-barrel plant sited in the beer garden of the Furnace Inn, Derby. After initially brewing solely for the pub, 2014 saw an increase in scale and output, with beers distributed across most of the country. A second 12-barrel brew plant was built in 2015 to increase capacity and host a visitor centre, tap and shop. ♦RAIB GF V

New World (OG 1039, ABV 3.7%)
Golden in colour with powerful citrus hop flavours.

Happy People (OG 1042, ABV 4.1%)

Wrench (OG 1045, ABV 4.4%)

4 Wood (OG 1045, ABV 4.5%)
Traditional, well-balanced, light chestnut-coloured ale with a delicate hop finish.

Affinity (OG 1046, ABV 4.6%)
Strong golden-coloured bitter with lots of fruity hops.

Disco Balls (OG 1055, ABV 5.3%)
Refreshing American-style IPA with citrus flavour and aroma.

Ship Inn

Ship Inn, Low Newton-by-the-Sea, Northumberland, NE66 3EL
☎ (01665) 576262 shipinnnewton.co.uk

Brewing commenced in 2008 on a 2.5-barrel plant. The brewery now produces 7.5 barrels per week. All regular beers are brewed in constant rotation but are only available on the premises. A special beer (4.2% ABV) is brewed for every 100 brews. ♦RAIB

Shipstone's SIBA

Little Star Brewery, Fox & Crown, Church Street, Old Basford, Nottingham, NG6 0GA
☎ (0115) 837 4200 shipstones.com

Set up in 1996, originally as Fiddlers Ales. In 1999 it became Alcazar Brewery on change of ownership. A full mash brewery with a 10-barrel brew length, it is located behind the Fox & Crown. The brewery changed hands in early 2016, when the name of the brewery was changed again and a new portfolio of beers established but this was short lived and it soon reverted back to the name Alcazar. In late 2016 Shipstone's took over brewing, producing its range of beers that had previously been contract brewed at Belvoir Brewery (qv). Beers are also brewed under the Hollow Stone Brewing Co name. !!♦

Original (OG 1040, ABV 3.8%)
Pale brown-coloured, malty traditional bitter, well-balanced in both hops and bitterness without either becoming overpowering.

Nut Brown (OG 1042, ABV 4%)
Full-bodied ale with a rich nut brown colour and malty finish. Hints of butterscotch and mild liquorice, caramel and roasted cacao flavours.

Gold Star (OG 1043, ABV 4.2%)
Golden in colour with a delicate citrus hop and slight dry bitter finish.

IPA (OG 1054, ABV 5.5%)

Brewed under the Hollow Stone Brewing Co name:

Oligo Nunk (OG 1041, ABV 4%)
An amber-coloured ale with a sharp cranberry, hop finish.

Pale Ale (OG 1043, ABV 4.2%)
A session pale ale with a hoppy finish.

Waitomo (OG 1045, ABV 4.5%)
A pale ale with a grapefruit hoppy flavour.

Short Stack (NEW)

Cock, 315 Mare Street, Hackney, London, E8 1EJ
howlinghops.co.uk

Brewing began in 2018. Beers are only available in the pub. The brewery name reflects the limited headroom in the cellar where it is situated. No real ale.

Shortts SIBA

Shortts Farm, Thorndon, Suffolk, IP23 7LS ☎ 07900 268100 shorttsfarmbrewery.com

An award-winning brewery established in 2012 by Matt Hammond on what has been the family farm for over a century. Ales are produced using carefully selected ingredients to create both traditional and more complex contemporary flavours. The beer names are based around a musical theme and can be found throughout East Anglia. RAIB

The Cure (ABV 3.6%)
A malty best bitter.

Strummer (OG 1038, ABV 3.8%)
An amber-coloured ale. Easy-drinking, light and hoppy bitter with a good moreish malt character.

Two Tone (ABV 3.8%)
A sweet, dark mild with roasted malt and chocolate flavours.

Blondie (OG 1040, ABV 4%)
A golden-coloured IPA. Subtle but refreshing citrus fruit followed by a spicy and almost honey-like lingering bitter finish.

Rockabilly (ABV 4.3%)
An American-style pale ale with a citrus hop character.

Skiffle (OG 1047, ABV 4.5%)
Chestnut in colour. A complex and malty rich bitter with a great balance of hops over malt, creating a full-flavoured premium ale.

Black Volt (ABV 4.8%)
A silky, smooth, sweet and chocolaty milk stout.

Indie (OG 1048, ABV 4.8%)
A golden-coloured IPA with subtle but refreshing citrus fruit followed by a spicy, almost honey-like lingering bitter finish. Hints of citrus and lemongrass.

Darkside (ABV 5%)
A traditional, smooth, dark-coloured and rich porter.

Shotover SIBA

Coopers Yard, Manor Farm Road, Horspath, Oxfordshire, OX33 1SD
☎ (01865) 604620 ☎ 07710 883273
shotoverbrewing.com

A family-owned and run brewery four miles from Oxford city centre. It began brewing in 2009 and supplies outlets in the Oxford area. !! ♦RAIB

Prospect (OG 1040, ABV 3.7%)

Trinity (OG 1040, ABV 4.2%)
Pale gold in colour with an intense grapefruit hop character.

Scholar (OG 1047, ABV 4.5%)
Deep copper-coloured premium bitter combining a silky malt base with a mixture of oranges, grapefruit and spiciness. It delivers a satisfying bitter finish.

Shottle Farm

c/o School House Farm, Lodge Lane, Shottle, Derbyshire, DE56 0DS
☎ (01773) 550056 ☎ 07877 723075

Located in the hills above Belper, the Grade II-listed farm is part of the Chatsworth Estate. Established in 2011 with a 10-barrel plant, beers are now contract brewed elsewhere. Shottle Farm has an on-site bar (limited opening hours), the Bull Shed, which is the only outlet for its beers.

Shugborough

Shugborough Estate, Milford, Staffordshire, ST17 0XB
☎ (01782) 823447 🌐 shugborough.org.uk

Brewing in the original brewhouse at Shugborough, home of the Earls of Lichfield, restarted in 1990, but a lack of expertise led to the brewery being a static museum piece until Titanic Brewery of Stoke-on-Trent (qv) began helping in 1996. Brewing is currently suspended.

Signal SIBA

8 Stirling Way, Beddington Farm Road, Beddington, CR0 4XN
☎ (020) 8684 6111 🌐 signallager.com

Starting in 2016, Signal Brewery's lager was the staple product in keg and cans. 2018 saw a change and a small range of cask ale is now produced.

Absolutely Fuggled (ABV 4%) ◆
Grassy, malty nose. Taste is bitter initially, offset slightly by a little kiwi fruit sweetness. Fairly short and bitter finish.

Signature SIBA

Unit 25, Leyton Business Centre, Etloe Road, Leyton, London, E10 7BT
☎ (020) 7684 4664 🌐 signaturebrew.co.uk

Signature Brew has been brewing beer inspired by music since 2011. Originally using spare capacity at a number of breweries, a successful crowd funding initiative has resulted in it owning its own brewery in Leyton. Special seasonal beers are brewed in collaboration with music artists. ♦RAIB

Session (OG 1042, ABV 4%) ◆
Refreshing bitter with spicy hop on the nose and palate balanced by a malty sweetness and a lingering bitterness.

Pale (OG 1033, ABV 4.1%) ◆
Golden-coloured beer using pale malts with a little wheat. The American hops give the beer its fruity character.

Black Vinyl Stout (OG 1046, ABV 4.2%) ◆
Rich cocoa roasted notes predominate on the palate balanced by some sweetness and hops, giving lightness to the flavour.

Red Wedge (OG 1047, ABV 4.7%) ◆
Reddish brown-coloured beer with a hoppy, fruity aroma. Flavour is dominated by hops with bitterness coming through later. Tangerine fruit notes

Backstage IPA (OG 1054, ABV 5.6%) ◆
Amber-coloured, unfined IPA with fruity hops and a bitterness overlaid with some banana and biscuity malty notes. Lingering, dry finish.

Silhill SIBA

Oak Farm, Hampton Lane, Solihull, West Midlands, B92 0JB
☎ (0845) 519 5101 ☎ 07977 444564

Office: PO Box 15739, Solihull, B93 3FW
🌐 silhillbrewery.co.uk

⊗ Established in 2010, Silhill is a small independent brewery based in premises just outside Solihull town centre using a 10-barrel plant. Bottling operations commenced in 2015. Beers are available in Solihull, Birmingham and Stratford-upon-Avon as well as in Malmaison restaurants. !! RAIB

Gold Star (OG 1039, ABV 3.9%)
A golden amber-coloured ale. Malty and smooth, finishing with a delicate honey note.

Blonde Star (OG 1041, ABV 4.1%)
A refreshing, sweet citrus pale ale.

HOP star (OG 1041, ABV 4.2%)
A golden-coloured, American-style IPA with flavours of grapefruit, lemon and tropical fruit zest.

Pure Star (OG 1043, ABV 4.3%)
A chestnut-coloured ale, warm and well-balanced with a hint of chocolate.

Super Star (OG 1051, ABV 5.1%)

Silks SIBA

Wash Farm, Queen Street, Sible Hedingham, Essex, CO9 3RH
☎ (01787) 275513 ☎ 07921 654910
🌐 silksbrewery@co.uk

Silks is a five-barrel microbrewery producing hand-crafted ales in small batches. Established in 2015, it is based on a North Essex farm in a converted grain store. ♦RAIB

Molly's Jolly Mild (OG 1036, ABV 3.6%)
A dark-coloured, mellow mild with a hint of dark chocolate and roasted coffee.

Veteran Campaigner (OG 1037, ABV 3.7%)
An amber-coloured session ale with a spicy finish.

Whacker Payne (OG 1037, ABV 3.8%)
A crisp, golden-coloured ale with subtle fruity citrus hints.

Old Man Shirv (OG 1043, ABV 4.5%)
A smooth and full-bodied, copper-coloured premium ale with a rich malt flavour.

Pegstar Porter (OG 1048, ABV 4.8%)

Silver (NEW)

Units 3 & 4, Silver House, Adelphi Way, Staveley, Derbyshire, S43 3LJ
☎ (01246) 470074 ☎ 07496 757619
🌐 silverbrewhouse.com

⊗ Silver Brewhouse took over the units and 12-barrel brewery from the RAW Brewing Company in 2018 and still brews the RAW branded beers as well as the Funky Hop Donkey range to complement their own brand, Industrial Ales.

Brewed under the Industrial Ales brand name:

Brickworks Bitter (OG 1040, ABV 4%)

Stephensons Pale (OG 1040, ABV 4%)

Coal Face Stout (OG 1044, ABV 4.5%)

Brewed under the RAW Brewing Co brand name:

West Coast Pale Ale (OG 1037, ABV 3.7%)

Baby Ghost (OG 1039, ABV 3.9%)

Independence American IPA (OG 1041, ABV 4.1%)

New World Pale Ale (OG 1042, ABV 4.2%)

Grey Ghost IPA (OG 1054, ABV 5.9%)

Silver Street SIBA

Britannia Mill, Cobden Street, Bury, BL9 6AW
☎ 07515 651874
silverstreetbrewingcompany.com

Brewing began in 2014 at the Clarence on Silver Street, Bury. The brewery has since expanded to a 15-barrel plant at Britannia Mill. !! ♦

Session (OG 1039, ABV 3.9%)

Fire Island (OG 1040, ABV 4%)

One (OG 1040, ABV 4%)
An ever-changing pale ale showcasing hops from around the world.

Ruby, Ruby, Ruby, Ruby (OG 1047, ABV 4.7%)
Deep ruby-coloured ale with a slight treacle undertone and a strong floral aroma.

Porter (OG 1053, ABV 5%)
Pronounced chocolate roast and raisin in aroma and taste. Moderate bitter caramel finish with some dark chocolate roast.

Red (OG 1055, ABV 5.5%)
An IPA with biscuity flavours, floral hops and an intense maltiness.

USA IPA (OG 1056, ABV 5.7%)
Malty caramel undertones and bold hops.

Silverstone

Office: Shacks Barn Farm, Silverstone, Northamptonshire, NN12 8TB
☎ (01280) 860288 ☎ 07918 031464
silverstonerealale.com

This traditional tower brewery, which is located near the celebrated motor racing circuit, opened in 2008. It changed hands in 2015 and again in 2019. !! ♦

Ignition (OG 1036, ABV 3.4%)
Floral, hoppy blonde ale which delivers a zesty powerful taste for its strength.

Pitstop (OG 1040, ABV 3.9%)
Session bitter with mellow bitter flavour and undertones of lime.

Polestar (OG 1042, ABV 4.1%)
Amber-coloured ale with hints of caramel toffee and a long bittersweet finish.

Chequered Flag (OG 1043, ABV 4.3%)
Full-bodied, amber-coloured IPA with a complex taste and citrus finish.

Octane (OG 1047, ABV 4.8%)
A strong ale, rich with hints of honey and toffee. A mellow, slightly coffee aroma.

Classic IPA (OG 1057, ABV 5.6%)
A mildly hoppy IPA with a touch of bitter honey.

Simpsons

White Swan, Eardisland, Herefordshire, HR6 9BD
☎ (01544) 388635 simpsonsfineales.co.uk

Tim Simpson acquired the White Swan in 2011 and set up the brewery at the rear of the pub in 2013. Beers are currently served in the White Swan, and locally to the free trade. A bottling facility is now in operation to supply local county shows. ♦

Golden Cock (OG 1037, ABV 3.7%)

Red Leg (OG 1043, ABV 4.3%)

Black Grouse (OG 1045, ABV 4.5%)

Old English (OG 1047, ABV 4.7%)

Timmy's Tipple (OG 1050, ABV 5%)

Siren Craft SIBA

Unit 1, Hogwood Industrial Estate, Weller Drive, Finchampstead, Berkshire, RG40 4QZ
☎ (0118) 973 0929 sirencraftbrew.com

Established in 2013, this is a state-of-the-art, 40-barrel craft brewery, which produces a range of cask, keg and bottled beers that are distributed throughout Europe. 2018 saw the first anniversary of the opening of the Siren Tap Yard at the brewery in Finchampstead. Siren have expansion plans funded by a successful crowdfunding project, including rolling out the Tap Yard concept to city centre locations. !! ♦ RAIB

Yu Lu (OG 1041, ABV 3.6%)
A pale ale made with lemon zest and loose leaf earl grey tea with bergamot orange and lemon notes. A surprising hoppy bitterness and a peach and apricot finish.

Undercurrent Oatmeal Pale Ale (OG 1042, ABV 4.5%)
A pale ale with spicy, grassy aromas and grapefruit and apricot flavours.

Soundwave IPA (OG 1056, ABV 5.6%)
An American-style IPA; golden in colour and immensely hoppy with grapefruit, peach and mango flavours.

Liquid Mistress Red IPA (OG 1061, ABV 5.8%)
An American-style red-coloured ale with burnt raisins and crackers balanced by a citrus grapefruit and peach spark.

Broken Dream Breakfast Stout (OG 1072, ABV 6.5%)
A breakfast stout with a gentle touch of smoke, coffee and chocolate. Deep and complex.

six°north

Reekie House, Aberdeen Road, Laurencekirk, AB30 1AG
☎ (01561) 377047 ☎ 07840 678243
sixdnorth.co.uk

Established in 2013, the brewery brews beers in the Belgian tradition, using a purpose-built 470-hectolitre plant. Depending on beer style, the beers are supplied as cask or keg. !! ♦ RAIB

Chopper Stout (ABV 4.1%)
Roasted coffee malted, with background liquorice.

Six Towns

Wheatsheaf, 234 High Street, Tunstall, Staffordshire, ST6 5TT
☎ (01782) 922628 sixtownsbrewery.com

Previously known as Sunset Taverns, Six Towns is a small independent brewery at the rear of the Wheatsheaf pub in the Potteries.

Sixpenny SIBA

The Old Dairy, Holwell Farm, Cranborne, Dorset, BH21 5QP
☎ (01725) 762006 sixpennybrewery.co.uk

⊗ Founded in 2007, Sixpenny Brewery increased capacity to a 20-barrel plant by moving in 2016 to its present home in renovated Victorian farm buildings near Cranborne. This has allowed for the expansion of the brewery bar and shop (the Sixpenny Tap), which is located next to the brewery in converted stables. More than 50 outlets are supplied. ‼ ♦

6d Best Bitter (OG 1042, ABV 3.8%)
A well-balanced ale with a rounded malt flavour that leads to a pleasantly bitter and hoppy finish.

6d Gold (OG 1043, ABV 4%)
A golden ale, slight citrus flavours with a distinct hoppy floral aroma.

6d IPA (OG 1053, ABV 5.2%)
Traditional IPA with a powerful hop character and a long, rounded malt finish.

Skinner's SIBA

Riverside, Newham Road, Truro, Cornwall, TR1 2DP
☎ (01872) 271885 🌐 skinnersbrewery.com

⊗ Award-winning brewery established in 1997. The brewery moved to bigger premises in 2003, opening a shop and visitor centre. The 25-barrel plant produces more than 26,000 hectolitres per year, using local Cornish barley. Quarterly small batch brews have been introduced, with limited availability. ‼ ♦

GTA (OG 1038, ABV 3.8%) ◆
A golden speciality honey ale. Citrus hop aroma and powerful flavour balanced by bitterness. Lingering bitter finish with some fruitiness.

Sennen (OG 1038, ABV 3.8%)
Pale straw-coloured session ale, full-flavoured with zingy citrus finish.

Betty Stogs (OG 1040, ABV 4%) ◆
Amber-coloured bitter with a gentle hop aroma. Light citrus hops are balanced by peach and blackcurrant fruits. Lasting pleasant bitterness.

Hops 'n' Honey (OG 1040, ABV 4%) ◆
A gold-coloured speciality beer containing Cornish honey. Balance of light citrus, grassy hops, apple and sweet malt. Pleasing long finish.

Lushingtons (OG 1041, ABV 4.2%) ◆
Smooth golden ale with a citrus hop aroma. Lemon zest and marmalade citrus hop flavours with bitterness and tropical fruits.

Cornish Knocker (OG 1044, ABV 4.5%) ◆
Refreshing amber-coloured ale with fragrant hop and malt aromas. Balanced citrus and floral hops with biscuit malt and caramel hints.

Pennycomequick (OG 1046, ABV 4.5%) ◆
Creamy, dark brown-coloured, sweet stout with a roast grain aroma. Heavy roast coffee, malt, fig and cherry flavours. Roast, dry finish.

Porthleven (OG 1048, ABV 4.8%) ◆
Refreshing golden ale with a citrus hop and pine nose. Assertive citrus hop, bitter and fruity flavour. Bitter citrus hop finish.

Seven Hop (OG 1050, ABV 5%) ◆
Smooth golden ale. Strong hop aroma and heavy punch of grapefruit citrus hops throughout. Marmalade and stone fruits. Bitter, dry finish.

Skippool Creek

Alexandra Road, Thornton-Cleveleys, Lancashire, FY5 5DB
☎ (01253) 858904 ☎ 07446 219497
🌐 skippoolcreek.co.uk

⊚ Nanobrewery based in Thornton-Cleveleys on the Fylde coast with a 100-litre brewing capacity. Brewing began in 2016, supplying local pubs and clubs. RAIB

Skippers Dark Ale (ABV 3.2%)
A dark-coloured ale with a delicate, slightly floral aroma. The balanced malt flavour has overtones of caramelised toffee with a hint of nuts.

Top Sail Pale Ale (ABV 4.2%)
Pale ale with complex blackcurrant, loganberry and spice notes to the aroma and a gentle grapefruit and lime flavour.

Black Oar Stout (ABV 4.9%)
Rich, full-bodied stout with an aroma that carries hints of coffee, chocolate, liquorice and molasses.

Slater's SIBA IFBB

St Albans Road, Common Road Industrial Estate, Stafford, ST16 3DR
☎ (01785) 257976 🌐 slatersales.co.uk

⊚ The brewery was opened in 1995 and in 2006 moved to new, larger premises. It has won numerous awards from CAMRA and SIBA and supplies a large number of outlets. ‼

Ultra (OG 1035.5, ABV 3.7%)
Amber in colour with a hop and malt aroma. Hoppiness develops into a long dry finish.

Rye IPA (OG 1038.5, ABV 3.8%)

Top Totty (OG 1039, ABV 4%) ◆
Yellow-hued with a fruit and hop nose. Big malty start leads to citrus hints with mouthwatering edges. Dry finish with tangs of lingering lemon bitterness.

Premium (OG 1042.5, ABV 4.4%) ◆
Pale brown-coloured bitter with a malt and caramel aroma. Malt and caramel taste supported by hops and some fruit provide a warming descent and satisfyingly bitter mouthfeel.

Smoked Porter (OG 1046, ABV 4.8%) ◆
Nose full of smoke, bonfire tastes with bacon. Hops break out to a bitter finish.

Western (OG 1048, ABV 4.9%)
A pale ale with a heady hop aroma and chewy aromatic finish.

Haka (OG 1049, ABV 5.2%) ◆
Exotic aromas of tropical fruits lead to a sweet, fruity start with background bitterness. This erupts into a mouthy bitterness with a long finish.

Slaughterhouse SIBA

Bridge Street, Warwick, CV34 5PD
☎ (01926) 490986 ☎ 07951 842690
🌐 slaughterhousebrewery.com

⊚ Production began in 2003 on a four-barrel plant in a former slaughterhouse. Around 30 outlets are supplied. The brewery premises are licensed for off-sales direct to the public. In 2010 Slaughterhouse opened its first pub, the Wild Boar in Warwick, adding a two-barrel plant. ‼

Saddleback Best Bitter (OG 1038, ABV 3.8%)
Amber-coloured session bitter with a distinctive hop flavour.

Extra Stout Snout (OG 1044, ABV 4.4%)

Boar D'eau (OG 1045, ABV 4.5%)

Wild Boar (OG 1052, ABV 5.2%)

Small Beer

70-72 Verney Road, South Bermondsey, London, SE16 3DH theoriginalsmallbeer.com

Small Beer Brewery was set up in 2017 as the world's first to specialise exclusively in the production of low strength beers (0.5-2.7% ABV). No real ale.

Small Paul's

27 Briar Close, Gillingham, Dorset, SP8 4SS
☎ (01747) 823574 smallbrewer@btinternet.com

Launched in 2006, this half-barrel brewery is located in the owner's garage. There are usually two brews a month. A small number of local pubs, clubs and beer festivals are supplied direct and beers can be designed and brewed to order. ♦

Small World SIBA

Unit 10, Barncliffe Business Park, Near Bank, Shelley, West Yorkshire, HD8 8LU
☎ (01484) 602805 smallworldbeers.com

The brewery is situated in the former Barncliffe Mill near the picturesque village of Shelley. The beers are brewed on a 20-barrel plant using spring water from an on-site bore hole. !! ♦

Barncliffe Bitter (OG 1037, ABV 3.7%)
Pleasant, easy-drinking bitter with fruit and citrus notes and a lasting bitterness through the finish.

Long Moor Pale (OG 1039, ABV 3.9%)
Pale ale with grapefruit and citrus notes and a light bitter finish.

Spike's Gold (OG 1043, ABV 4.4%)
Smooth, well-balanced golden ale with fruit and hop flavours through to the finish.

Thunderbridge Stout (OG 1051, ABV 5.2%)
Traditional dry stout with roast flavours giving way to smooth coffee undertones and a sharp, dry finish.

Twin Falls (OG 1051, ABV 5.2%)
Full-bodied pale ale with a fruity aroma and strong tropical fruit and hop taste.

Samuel Smith

The Old Brewery, High Street, Tadcaster, North Yorkshire, LS24 9SB
☎ (01937) 832225 samuelsmithsbrewery.co.uk

Fiercely independent, family-owned company. Tradition, quality and value are important, resulting in brewing without any artificial additives. All real ale is supplied in traditional wooden casks. RAIB V

Old Brewery Bitter (OG 1040, ABV 4%)
Malt dominates the aroma, with an initial burst of malt, hops and fruit in the taste, which is sustained in the aftertaste.

John Smith's

The Brewery, Tadcaster, North Yorkshire, LS24 9SA
☎ (01937) 832091 heineken.com

No real ale. The brewery was built in 1879 by a relative of Samuel Smith (qv). John Smith's became part of the Courage group in 1970 before being taken over by S&N and now Heineken UK. John Smith's cask Magnet has been discontinued. John Smith's Bitter in cask form is brewed by Caledonian Brewery (qv) in Edinburgh.

Snaggletooth

c/o Rear of 11 Pole Lane, Darwen, Lancashire, BB3 3LD ☎ 07810 365701
snaggletoothbrewing.com

Snaggletooth was established in 2012 by three beer geeks with a passion for crafting ales. A 2.5-barrel plant is used at the Hopstar Brewery (qv) in Darwen, Lancashire. Beers are available throughout East Lancashire and Manchester. ♦

Allotropic (ABV 3.8%)
A pale ale with floral and citrus notes.

BeEr (ABV 3.9%)

I Ain't Afraid of Noh Ghost (ABV 3.9%)

Three Amigos (ABV 3.9%)

Déjà Brewed (OG 1040, ABV 4%)
Refreshing ale with floral, spicy and citrus flavours.

Rolling Maul (ABV 4.1%)
Pale ale with bursts of floral flavours and a citrus finish.

'Cos I'm a Lobster (OG 1044, ABV 4.2%)
A red-coloured ale with subtly roasted malts.

Avonaco (ABV 4.3%)

Snowdon Craft

Quinton Hazell Enterprise Parc, 55 Glan-y-Wern Road, Mochdre, LL28 5BS
☎ (01492) 545143
sales@snowdoncraftbeer.co.uk

Formerly known as Great Orme Brewery, which was established in 2005. In 2019 it relocated to new modern premises, still using an 18-barrel plant, with a new range of beers. It owns or part owns three pubs but supplies many more in the area. !! ♦

Base Camp Session Pale (OG 1037, ABV 3.7%)

Nomad All-Night-Stout (OG 1038, ABV 3.8%)

Driftwood Dry-Hopped Amber (OG 1045, ABV 4.5%)

Summit Blond IPA (OG 1052, ABV 5.2%)

Snowdonia Parc

Snowdonia Parc Brewpub & Campsite, Waunfawr, LL55 4AQ
☎ (01286) 650409 snowdonia-park.co.uk

Snowdonia Parc started brewing in 1998 in a two-barrel brewhouse. The brewing is now carried out by the owner, Carmen Pierce. The beer is brewed solely for the Snowdonia Parc pub and campsite.

Snowhill

Snowhill Cottage, Snow Hill Lane, Scorton, Lancashire, PR3 1BA
☎ (01524) 791352

☺Snowhill was established in 2015 by Nigel Stokes following several years of small scale brewing. It uses a 1.5-barrel plant. A one-man operation, Nigel brews 3-4 times per month to supply pubs in North-west Lancashire and South Cumbria. An environmentally-friendly set-up sees the spent grain feeding local cattle and waste water treated through a small reed bed. ◆

Pale (OG 1037, ABV 3.7%)
A fruity, pale yellow-coloured beer with a pronounced citrus aftertaste.

Copy Cat (ABV 3.8%)

Retro Bitter (ABV 3.8%)
A well-balanced session bitter with a clean finish.

Target (ABV 3.8%)
A fruity, hoppy golden ale with a long-lasting bitterness.

Blonded (ABV 3.9%)
A light, fruity, well-hopped blonde ale with a bitter, slightly astringent finish.

Gold (OG 1039, ABV 3.9%)
Fruit and malt dominate, with a dry bitter finish.

Best Bitter (OG 1042, ABV 4.2%)
Smooth, rich and malty with caramel notes leading to a pronounced bitter finish.

Black Magic IPA (OG 1042, ABV 4.2%)
A complex black IPA with a hoppy aroma and taste and hints of roast.

Porter (OG 1048, ABV 4.8%)
Dark-coloured and smooth with a liquorice, malty and dry hop taste.

Winter Porter (OG 1050, ABV 4.8%)
Rich and black in colour, the initial roast and malty taste leads to a bitter, fruity and hoppy aftertaste.

Sociable SIBA

6-8 Britannia Road, Worcester, WR1 3BQ ☎ 07957 583984 ⊕ thesociablebeercompany.com

☺ A small craft brewery just outside Worcester city centre, established in 2017. An on-site taproom is open on Fridays.

Shindig (OG 1039, ABV 3.6%)

Bash (OG 1042, ABV 4%)
Traditional English ale with subtle hints of pine and a dry finish.

Wingding (OG 1042, ABV 4.2%)
American-style, pale-coloured IPA with a citrus aroma.

Solvay Society

Unit 8, Aldborough Hall Farm, Aldborough Hatch, Essex, IG2 7TD
☎ (020) 7226 2277 ⊕ solvaysociety.com

Solvay Society began brewing in 2014 in the cellar of a Walthamstow pub using a small 0.5-hectolitre kit. In 2015 it transferred the equipment to the Hops & Glory pub in North London. In 2016 the brewery moved again, taking over the old equipment from the Ha'penny Brewery in Aldborough Hatch. A taproom in Leytonstone is open at weekends. Production is mostly keg but bottle-conditioned beer is also available. RAIB

Son of Sid

⊟ Chequers, 71 Main Road, Little Gransden, Cambridgeshire, SG19 3DW
☎ (01767) 677348 ⊕ sonofsid.co.uk

⊠ Son of Sid was established in 2007. The three-barrel plant is situated in a room at the back of the pub and can be viewed from a window in the lounge bar. It is named after the father of the current landlord, who ran the pub for 42 years. His son has carried the business on as a family-run enterprise. Beer is sold in the pub and at local beer festivals. ‼ ⊟ RAIB

Sonnet 43

See S43

Soul

Correspondence: 18 Broomfield Road, Heaton Moor, Stockport, SK4 4ND ☎ 07718 155191

⊠ Brewing commenced in 2017 using spare capacity at Manchester Brewing (qv). Beers are supplied to outlets in Greater Manchester and are inspired by Northern Soul music. A move to its own premises is planned. ‼◆

All Nighter (OG 1038, ABV 3.8%)
Lemon citrus hoppiness with floral notes and a bitter finish.

Magic Touch (OG 1046, ABV 4.7%)

The Snake (OG 1052, ABV 5.8%)
Grapefruit and citrus flavours with an earthy spiciness and malty finish.

Double-O Soul (OG 1060, ABV 5.9%)
A big, juicy IPA with bags of citrus, peach and tropical fruit flavours.

South Hams SIBA

Stokeley Barton, Stokenham, Devon, TQ7 2SE
☎ (01548) 581151 ⊕ southhamsbrewery.co.uk

⊠ The brewery moved to its present site, a milking parlour, in 2003, with a 10-barrel plant and plenty of room to expand. It supplies more than 60 outlets in Plymouth and South Devon. Wholesalers are used to distribute to other areas. The brewery is run by Sam Brooking, the owner's youngest son. ‼ ⊟ ◆ RAIB

Devon Pride (OG 1039, ABV 3.8%)
A dark amber-coloured beer, smooth to drink with a malty palate.

Wild Blonde (OG 1044, ABV 4.4%) ◆
Subtle notes of malt, roast and caramel, dominated by fruity hops. These persist to a refreshing hint of lemon.

Hopnosis (OG 1046, ABV 4.5%)

Eddystone (OG 1050, ABV 4.8%) ◆
Strong, amber-coloured, summery ale. Hoppy, caramel, slightly citrus nose. Dry taste with light fruit and hops. Dry yet fruity finish.

Pandemonium (OG 1054, ABV 5%)

South Lakes

Unit 30, Ulverston Auction Mart, North Lonsdale Road, Ulverston, Cumbria, LA12 0AU ☎ 07795 363523 ✉ aaronpos1@hotmail.com

South Lakes began brewing on a 1.5-barrel plant in 2016, in a part of the Auction Mart in Ulverston.

4Cs Extra Pale (OG 1040, ABV 3.8%)
An American-style pale ale with hints of grapefruit.

Lucky Dip (OG 1040, ABV 3.8%)
Blonde ale with a simple malt backbone and plenty of hops.

Amacoe (OG 1042, ABV 4%) ◆
Pronounced hoppiness in both the aroma and taste combines with a balancing sweetness and lasting bitter finish.

Poison Dwarf (OG 1043, ABV 4.1%) ◆
Hoppy and fruity aromas are followed by a full-bodied and lasting bitter finish.

Rakau (OG 1048, ABV 4.7%) ◼ ◆
A bitter beer with lots of hops, backed by fruit sweetness and some malt in the background. A well-constructed bitter with full mouthfeel and lasting bitter finish.

American Pale Ale (OG 1050, ABV 4.8%)
A rich golden ale with lots of citrus.

Ripe (OG 1055, ABV 5.5%)

Southbourne SIBA

41-43 Poole Hill, Bournemouth, Dorset, BH2 5PW ☎ (01202) 421190 ☎ 07845 795464 ⊕ southbourneales.co.uk

⊗ Jennifer Tingay, former technologist and brewer for Ringwood, began brewing in 2013 using spare capacity at Town Mill brewery. The brand quickly became established and a successful crowdfunding campaign allowed her to purchase the lease of a former car showroom on Bournemouth's West Cliff. The tap opened in 2017 and the brewery started production in 2018 using an 80-barrel plant. Beers are also available under the name Tingay Ales. ‼ ☛ ◆

Paddlers (OG 1037, ABV 3.6%)
A light but balanced session bitter with moderate hop characteristics.

Sunbather (OG 1040, ABV 4%) ◆
Dry red-coloured ale with some caramel sweetness and a lingering nutty aftertaste.

Headlander (OG 1043, ABV 4.2%)
Floral aroma and a full hop bitterness balanced with malt.

Beachcomber (OG 1058, ABV 5.7%)
A full-flavoured, brown-coloured ale with a good malt and hop balance.

Brewed under the Tingay Ales brand name:

Tingay's No. 1 (OG 1046, ABV 4.5%)

Southey

21 Southey Street, Penge, London, SE20 7JD ☎ 07450 573577 ⊕ southeybrewing.co.uk

⊗ Southey took over the premises formerly used by Late Knights Brewery in 2017. An on-site tap opens at weekends and its three other outlets are also supplied in Brockley, Dulwich and Brighton. A range of green hop beers is produced in the autumn in association with Palace Pint, the Crystal Palace based hop collective. ◆

Crack of Dawn (ABV 3.7%) ◆
Amber-coloured hoppy beer with strong citrus notes. Flavour has a faint maltiness and bitterness. Aftertaste is bitter and fractionally dry.

Pale Ale (ABV 3.8%) ◆
A fairly bitter, hoppy citrus beer balanced with some sweetness. A subtle aroma of citrus fruit and spices. Dry taste and aftertaste.

Hop of the Morning (ABV 4.2%) ◆
Strong, black-coloured, roast bitter character in the aroma and flavour with some coffee notes and fruit. Long bitter, dry finish.

Old Red Eyes (ABV 4.5%) ◆
Reddish brown-coloured beer with a clean hop flavour and hints of citrus and butterscotch. Finish is hoppy and dryish.

Worm Catcher (ABV 5%) ◆
Amber-coloured beer with a honey marmalade sweetness and a bitterness that builds and lingers in the slightly dry finish.

Southport SIBA

Unit 3, Enterprise Business Park, Russell Road, Southport, Merseyside, PR9 7RF ☎ 07748 387652 ⊕ southportbrewery.co.uk

☺ Southport Brewery was established in 2004 on a five-barrel plant. Outlets are supplied in Southport, North-west England and nationally. ◆

IPA (ABV 3.6%)
A pale-coloured, hoppy session IPA.

Sandgrounder Bitter (OG 1039.5, ABV 3.8%)
Pale-coloured, hoppy session bitter with a floral character.

Dark Night (OG 1040.5, ABV 3.9%)

Golden Sands (OG 1041.5, ABV 4%)
A golden-coloured, triple-hopped bitter with a citrus flavour.

Southsea

Southsea Castle, Clarence Esplanade, Southsea, Portsmouth, Hampshire, PO5 3PA ☎ 07939 063970 ⊕ southseabrewing.co.uk

⊗ Launched in 2016, Southsea Brewing is located in an old ammunition storage room within the walls of a coastal defence fort built by Henry VIII in 1544. All beers are unfined, unfiltered and unpasteurised and bottled on site. ‼ ☛ RAIB

Southwark SIBA

46 Druid Street, Bermondsey, London, SE1 2EZ ☎ (020) 3302 4190 ⊕ southwarkbrewing.co.uk

⊗ Established in the Bermondsey brewing scene, Southwark Brewing Co opened in 2014. Focusing on cask-conditioned ales, the range of Big Bear craft keg ales is also available. A tap room is open most evenings. ☛ ◆ RAIB

London Pale Ale (OG 1038.5, ABV 4%) ◆
Pale golden-coloured, smooth beer. Sweet biscuity malt is balanced by pineapple and pithy citrus. Dry aftertaste with a building bitterness.

Potters' Fields Porter (OG 1040, ABV 4%) ◆
Dark brown-coloured porter. Raisins, prunes and cocoa in the flavour and aroma, fading in the dry roast bitter aftertaste.

Bermondsey Best (OG 1042, ABV 4.4%) ◆
A well-balanced best bitter with the fruity notes developing in the finish, which is bitter. Some malty notes on the palate.

Harvard (OG 1049, ABV 5.5%) ◆
Honey with sweet orange and grapefruit marmalade character are present in this rich, smooth pale brown-coloured beer. Dry bitter finish.

Spa Town

See Harrogate

Spartan

Arch 8, Almond Road, South Bermondsey, London, SE16 3LR ⊕ spartanbrewery.com

Spartan began brewing at UBrew (qv) in 2017 until moving in 2018 to premises vacated by Partizan Brewery, becoming a part of the Bermondsey Beer Mile. Beer is available in its on-site taproom and an increasing number of other outlets.

Son of Zeus (OG 1037, ABV 3.6%)

River Styx (OG 1037, ABV 3.7%)

Hoplite (OG 1039, ABV 3.8%)

Phalanx (OG 1049, ABV 5%)

Sperrin

Lord Nelson Inn, Birmingham Road, Ansley, Warwickshire, CV10 9PQ
☎ (024) 7639 2305 ☎ 07917 772208
⊕ sperrinbrewery.co.uk

Sperrin began brewing in 2012 and is situated by the side of the Lord Nelson Inn. A brewery was first established there in 1868. Beers are also available at its sister pub, the Blue Boar, Mancetter. !! ◆ RAIB

Ansley Mild (OG 1035, ABV 3.5%)
A traditional mild giving a rich, roast, malty flavour.

Full Mortis (OG 1085, ABV 8.5%)

Spey Valley

See Keith

Speyside SIBA

2 Greshop Road, Forres, IV36 2GU
☎ (01309) 358082 ☎ 07854 053277
⊕ speysidecraftbrewery.com

Based in a traditional whisky-producing area, Speyside Brewery uses the same water that goes into the region's whisky. A number of local outlets are supplied. A donation from sales of Bottlenose Bitter goes to help support the work of the Whale & Dolphin Conservation Society. ◆

Bow Fiddle Blonde (OG 1038, ABV 3.8%)

Bottlenose Bitter (OG 1041, ABV 4.1%) ◆
Slightly citrus hoppy bitter.

Randolph's Leap (OG 1049, ABV 4.9%)

Moray IPA (OG 1055, ABV 5.5%)

Findhorn Killer Red IPA (OG 1056, ABV 5.6%)

ScotcHop IPA (ABV 8.5%)

Spitting Feathers SIBA

Common Farm, Waverton, Cheshire, CH3 7QT
☎ (01244) 332052 ☎ 07974 348325
⊕ spittingfeathers.co.uk

Spitting Feathers was established in 2005. The brewery is located in a sandstone building set around a cobbled yard. Around 200 local outlets are supplied. Monthly Brewbarn sessions throughout the year include a brewery tour but tickets must be purchased in advance. !! ◆

Session Beer (OG 1035, ABV 3.6%)

Thirstquencher (OG 1038, ABV 3.9%) ◆
Powerful hop aroma leads into the taste. Bitterness and a fruity citrus hop flavour fight for attention. A sharp, clean, golden-coloured beer with a long, dry, bitter aftertaste.

Brainstorm (ABV 4%)
A citrus pale ale with a dry, zesty finish.

Special Ale (OG 1041, ABV 4.2%) ◆
Complex tawny-coloured beer with a sharp, grainy mouthfeel. Malty with good hop coming through in the aroma and taste. Hints of nuttiness and a touch of acidity. Dry, astringent finish.

Old Wavertonian (OG 1043, ABV 4.4%) ◆
Creamy and smooth stout. Full-flavoured with coffee notes in the aroma and taste. Roast and nut flavours throughout, leading to a hoppy, bitter finish.

Rush Hour (ABV 4.5%)
A pale ale bursting with citrus fruit flavours.

Empire IPA (ABV 5.2%)

Spotlight

The Goddards, Goole Road, West Cowick, East Yorkshire, DN14 9DJ ☎ 07713 477069
⊕ spotlightbrewing.co.uk

Spotlight is a social enterprise. All beers are brewed, packaged and delivered by people with learning disabilities. A taproom is planned. !! ◆

One More (OG 1038, ABV 3.9%)
An American-style pale ale with biscuity malt flavours complemented by a citrus, fruity aroma.

Bollingham Bitter (OG 1045, ABV 4.4%)
Well-balanced, malty ale with pronounced bitterness and a gentle hop kick.

Fragile X (OG 1057, ABV 5.8%)
Slightly smoked porter with a subtle hop aroma.

Sprey Point

Unit 10, Helmores Yard, Exeter Street, Teignmouth, Devon, TQ14 8JW ☎ 07917 434859
⊕ spreypointbrewery.com

Established in 2017, this microbrewery specialises in small batch beers using a wide variety of ingredients, sourced locally and organic where possible. Output is mostly keg but some cask conditioned beer is available. Brewing is currently suspended.

Springhead SIBA

Robin Hood Site, Main Street, Laneham, Nottinghamshire, DN22 0NA
☎ (01777) 228080 ☎ 07720 461655
springhead.co.uk

Springhead Fine Ales opened in 1990, expanding and moving to bigger premises three years later to meet increased demand. In 2011 the brewery relocated to its current address. The brewery went into self administration in 2017 and re-opened in 2018 as Springhead Ales, with a new owner. ‼ ♦

Outlawed (OG 1040, ABV 3.8%)
A triple-hopped, easy-drinking, American-style pale ale with a citrus aroma.

Drop o' the Black Stuff (OG 1041, ABV 4%)

Robin Hood (OG 1041, ABV 4%)
A chestnut brown-coloured traditional bitter with a good head and plenty of hops.

Maid Marian (OG 1045, ABV 4.5%)
A pale golden-coloured beer with a fruity orange aroma and a dry finish.

The Leveller (OG 1047, ABV 4.8%)
A dark-coloured ale with a smoky flavour and toffee finish.

Roaring Meg (OG 1052, ABV 5.5%)
A smooth, classic IPA. Golden in colour with a citrus honey aroma and dry finish.

Squawk

Unit 4, Tonge Street, Ardwick, Manchester, M12 6LY
☎ 07590 387559 ✉ sales@squawkbrewingco.com

Squawk initially cuckoo-brewed on the Hand Drawn Monkey plant in Huddersfield in 2013, with the first brew from the Manchester site being in 2014. The eight-barrel plant is located in a railway arch in Ardwick. Beers are widely available in the North West and Yorkshire but can be found further afield. RAIB V

Pavo (ABV 3.8%)
A golden ale with blossom and bubblegum on the nose, a delicate mouthfeel and a yellow fruit tang.

Crex (ABV 4.5%)
A golden-coloured session IPA with dried apricot, peach and pink grapefruit notes, flavours of tropical fruit and a rounded bitterness.

Pica (ABV 4.9%)
A golden-coloured pale ale with traces of spiced orange and mango. Oats give a silky and delicate mouthfeel.

Milvus (ABV 6.3%)
An IPA with a passion fruit, pine and berry aroma, lightly bitter with citrus fruit on the palate. Oats and wheat balance the medium body.

Corvus (ABV 7.4%)
A bitter chocolate, roasted hazelnut and burnt cherry stout. Crushed pepper and wild flowers on the nose.

Stables

Beamish Hall Country House Hotel, Beamish, DH9 0YB
☎ (01207) 288750 beamish-hall.co.uk/stables

Stables was established as part of a £1 million development of an old stable block of Beamish Hall, converting a disused building to a restaurant and eight-barrel microbrewery. The hotel is supplied plus the Sun Inn at Beamish Museum. ‼♦

Beamish Hall Best Bitter (OG 1038, ABV 3.8%)

Old Miner Tommy (OG 1037, ABV 3.8%)

Bobby Dazzler (OG 1042, ABV 4.2%)

Coppy Lane (OG 1043, ABV 4.2%)

Silver Buckles (OG 1044, ABV 4.4%)

Beamish Burn (OG 1045, ABV 4.5%)

Bell Tower (OG 1052, ABV 5%)

Staffordshire

12 Churnet Court, Cheddleton, Staffordshire, ST13 7EF
☎ (01538) 361919 ☎ 07971 808370
staffordshirebrewery.co.uk

No real ale. Brewing started in 2002. The brewery was renamed from Leek Brewery in 2013 at which time cask production ceased, being replaced by filtered, pasteurised bottled beers only. A small pilot plant is sometimes used to contract brew for Wicked Hathern (qv) when time permits. ‼

Contract brewed for Wicked Hathern Brewery:

Albion Special (OG 1042, ABV 4%)
Light copper in colour with a nutty aroma and a smoky malty taste.

Hawthorn Gold (OG 1045, ABV 4.6%)
A light golden-coloured, easy-drinking beer with a good balance of hops and malt.

Stag (Cheshire)

Stag at Walton, Chester Road, Walton, Cheshire, WA4 6EG
☎ (01925) 261680 thestagatwalton.co.uk

Nanobrewery based at the Stag at Walton, near Warrington. Beers are available in the pub and occasionally at local beer festivals.

Stag (Kent)

Little Engeham Farm, Woodchurch, Kent, TN26 3QY
☎ 07539 974068 stagbrewery.co.uk

Stag began brewing in 2016. RAIB

Jane Doe (ABV 4%)

Screeming Sika (ABV 5%)

Staggeringly Good SIBA

Unit 3, St Georges Industrial Estate, Rodney Road, Portsmouth, Hampshire, PO4 8SS
☎ (023) 9229 7033 staggeringlygood.com

Brewing began in 2014, originally using spare capacity at other breweries. In 2015 a 10-barrel plant at its own premises came on stream. There is an on-site shop and taproom with limited opening hours. No real ale. ‼ ♦

Stamps

St Mary's Complex, Waverley Street, Liverpool, L20 4AP ☎ 07779 000094 stampsbrewery.co.uk

Brewing began in 2012, producing beers named after famous world postage stamps. The brewery moved to its new site in 2017 on a temporary basis. There are plans to build a brand new brewery and pub. ‼ 🛒

Blond Moment (OG 1037, ABV 3.6%)
A pale-coloured beer with a smooth floral and citrus aroma and flavour.

Bondi Blond (OG 1037, ABV 3.7%)
A pale-coloured, full-flavoured blonde beer. Floral and citrus notes evident.

Ahtanum (OG 1039, ABV 3.9%)

First Class (OG 1039, ABV 3.9%)

Mail Train (OG 1042, ABV 4.2%)
A traditional bitter with a noticeable bitterness and good malt character.

Swedish Blond (OG 1041, ABV 4.3%)
A session blonde ale with a strong hint of citrus.

Inverted Jenny (OG 1046, ABV 4.6%)
Golden in colour with a grassy and floral bouquet and a noticeable tinge of caramel.

Penny Black (OG 1055, ABV 5.5%)

Stancill SIBA

Unit 2, Oakham Drive, off Rutland Road, Sheffield, South Yorkshire, S3 9QX
☎ (0114) 275 2788 ☎ 07809 427716

Stancill began brewing in 2014 and is named after the first head brewer and co-owner. It is situated on the doorstep of the late Stones' Cannon Brewery, taking advantage of the soft Yorkshire water. ‼

Barnsley Bitter (OG 1037.5, ABV 3.8%)

Blonde (OG 1038.5, ABV 3.9%)

India (ABV 4%)

No. 7 (OG 1042, ABV 4.3%)

Stainless (ABV 4.3%)

Porter (OG 1042.5, ABV 4.4%)

Black Gold (ABV 5%)

Stannary

Unit 6, Pixon Trading Centre, Tavistock, Devon, PL19 8DH
☎ (01822) 258130 ☎ 07971 238758
stannarybrewing.co.uk

Stannary began operating in 2016 using a 2.5-barrel plant, moving to larger premises with a six-barrel plant in 2018. The brewery tap is open on Friday evenings, showcasing its many unfined and unfiltered craft beers inspired by ingredients from around the world.

Stansfield (NEW)

Stansfield Compasses, High Street, Stansfield, CO10 8LN
☎ (01284) 789263 stansfieldcompasses.co.uk

Microbrewery operating at the Compasses pub using locally grown barley.

Stanway

Stanway House, Stanway, Gloucestershire, GL54 5PQ
☎ (01386) 584320 stanwaybrewery.co.uk

Stanway is a small brewery founded in 1993 with a five-barrel plant that confines its sales to the Cotswolds area (15 to 20 outlets). The brewery uses wood-fired coppers for all its production. ♦

Stanney Bitter (OG 1042, ABV 4.5%)
A light, refreshing, amber-coloured beer dominated by hops in the aroma, with a bitter taste and a hoppy, bitter finish.

Star Wing SIBA

Unit 6, Hall Farm, Church Road, Redgrave, Suffolk, IP22 1RJ
☎ (01379) 890586 starwingbrewery.com

Brewing began in 2017 after converting an old sawmill into a brewery. Half an acre of hops have been planted with plans to grow more. Part of the sawmill has been converted into a taproom, which opened in 2019. Around 75 outlets are supplied direct. 🛒

Dawn on the Border (ABV 3.6%)
A dry-hopped pale ale; crisp and aromatic.

Gospel Oak (OG 1038, ABV 3.8%)
A copper-coloured session ale, well-balanced with slight esters and biscuit undertones matched with a smooth bitterness and fruity aroma.

Spire Light (OG 1041, ABV 4.2%)
A light, refreshing golden ale with hops to the fore.

Red at Night (ABV 4.5%)
A rich, red-coloured ale with a sweet malt character and fruity aromas giving a refreshingly balanced flavour.

Four Acre Arcadia (OG 1048, ABV 5%)
A hoppy, crisp IPA.

Stain Glass Blue (OG 1055, ABV 5.4%)
A dark-coloured, complex porter with notable bitterness. Full-bodied and malty.

Stardust SIBA

Unit 5, How Lane Farm Estate, Howe Lane, White Waltham, Berkshire, SL6 3JP
☎ (01628) 947325 stardustbrewery.co.uk

An independent, family-owned and run brewery, Stardust was established in 2016. Tucked away towards the back of a farm estate, brewing takes place on a six-barrel plant. There is a brewery shop and taproom on site. ‼ 🛒 ♦ RAIB

Easy Pale Citra (OG 1038, ABV 3.8%)
A refreshing beer with citrus fruit aromas, including grapefruit and lime.

English Bitter (OG 1041, ABV 4%)
Notes of roasted caramel balanced by a clean bitter finish with a classic hop aroma.

Optic (OG 1041, ABV 4.2%)
An American-style golden ale with aromatic notes and tropical fruit flavours.

PK3 (OG 1051, ABV 5.6%)
An American-style IPA with a complex tropical, spicy and fruity hop profile.

Station 119

Unit 4, Progress Way, Eye, Suffolk, IP23 7HU
☎ (01379) 882230 station119.co.uk

Brewing started in 2014 using a two-barrel plant, upgraded in 2018 to a 12-barrel one to meet demand. Beers are available locally. RAIB

Station Works

Camlough Road, Newry, Northern Ireland, BT35 6JP

A sister brewery to Cumberland Breweries/Great Corby Brewery, Station Works was bought by the US firm Alltech in 2015.

The Foxes Rock (OG 1042, ABV 4.2%)

Finn (OG 1045, ABV 4.5%)

Stealth

34 Old Broughton Road, Melksham, Wiltshire, SN12 8BX
☎ (01225) 707111 ☎ 07917 272482
stealthbrew.co

Brewing began in 2014 under the name of Kennet & Avon, with beer brewed by Wessex Brewery (qv) while the plant was under construction. It relocated to its current site in 2015 and changed its name to Stealth in 2018. It now brews a range of hop-forward pale ales and dark beers, all of which are unfined and hazy. A microbar in Melksham is planned. !! ♦ RAIB GF

Hush (OG 1040, ABV 3.8%)
A single-hopped pale ale with aromas of grapefruit and tropical fruits.

Covert (ABV 3.9%)
A pale-coloured session ale with grapefruit, lime and mango flavours.

Ambush (ABV 4.5%)
Unashamedly bitter with notes of pepper, herbs, pine and stone fruits in the aroma.

Camouflage (ABV 4.7%)

Conceal (ABV 4.8%)
A dark brown-coloured porter infused with raw liquorice root. Well-balanced with a slight sweetness.

Solitude (OG 1053, ABV 5.3%)
Full-bodied, black-coloured beer with aromas of liquorice, roast coffee and chocolate and a delicate pleasant aftertaste.

Seclusion (ABV 5.5%)
Full-bodied, pale-coloured ale with aromas of grapefruit, mango and passion fruit.

Steam Town SIBA

1 Bishopstoke Road, Eastleigh, Hampshire, SO50 6AD
steamtownbrewco.co.uk

Steam Town is a five-barrel microbrewery with its own craft beer bar and restaurant, established in 2017. Other local pubs, clubs and micropubs are also supplied as well as beer festivals and outlets further afield by special arrangement.

Stoke Pale (OG 1040, ABV 3.8%)
Crisp pale ale with fruity flavours.

Barton Bitter (OG 1042, ABV 4%)

Reefer (OG 1045, ABV 4.2%)
Amber-coloured session IPA with citrus fruit flavours.

Steam Stout (OG 1051, ABV 4.5%)
Milk stout with complex chocolate malt bitterness balanced with lactose and spicy hop notes.

Steamin' Billy

See Belvoir

Steel City

c/o Lost Industry Brewing, 14a Nutwood Trading Estate, Sheffield, South Yorkshire, S6 1NJ
steelcitybrewing.co.uk

Steel City was established in 2009 and operates on a cuckoo basis, brewing once or twice a month. Brewing now takes place at Lost Industry Brewing (qv). Much of the Steel City output is collaborations with other like-minded brewers having a little fun producing interesting and experimental beers. ♦

Stewart SIBA

26a Dryden Road, Bilston Glen Industrial Estate, Loanhead, EH20 9LZ
☎ (0131) 440 2442 stewartbrewing.co.uk

Established in 2004 by Steve and Jo Stewart, the brewery moved to a larger, custom-built brewery in 2013 with a brand new 50-hectolitre plant. It produces a wide portofolio of beers including collaborations such as the Natural Selection Brewing partnership with the brewing school at Heriot Watt. The on-site Craft Beer Kitchen is a small 80-litre plant providing a brew-it-yourself facility. !! ♦ RAIB

Jack Back (OG 1039, ABV 3.7%)
A pale-coloured, hoppy beer with strong citrus and tropical fruit aromas. The taste is light, crisp and refreshing.

Pentland IPA (OG 1040, ABV 3.9%)
A pleasing, hoppy, golden-coloured session ale. The dry bitter taste is well balanced by sweetness from the malt, and fruit flavours. The aftertaste is dry with a lingering bitterness.

80/- (OG 1044, ABV 4.4%)
Traditional Scottish heavy. The complex profile is dominated by malt with fruit flavours giving the sweetish character typical of this beer style. Hops provide a gentle balancing bitterness that intensifies in the dry finish.

Radical Road Reverse (OG 1046, ABV 4.6%)
A triple-hopped pale ale with a good malty body along with grapefruit, citrus and pine hop aromas and taste, giving a good balance of flavours.

Edinburgh Gold (OG 1048, ABV 4.8%)
A full-bodied but easy-drinking continental-style golden ale. Bitterness from the hop character is strong in the finish and complemented in the taste by a little sweetness from malt, and fruit flavours.

Sticklegs

Primrose Farm, Hall Road, Great Bromley, Essex, CO7 7TR ☎ 07971 138038
waterhouse.philip@btinternet.com

Sticklegs was established in 2008 at the Cross Inn, Great Bromley. The brewery expanded and relocated to Elmstead Market, where it continued to grow. In 2016 it moved to Primrose Farm. The brewery is owned and run by Phil Reeve and his wife Linda, the brewster. Brewing is currently suspended.

StoatCraft (NEW)

Stoneywood, Aberdeen, AB21 9UG ☎ 07738 256780 🌐 stoatcraftbeer.com

Founded in 2017 in Stoneywood, Aberdeen, this brewery produces limited amounts of beer available in a small number of outlets.

Stockport SIBA

Unit 16, The Gate Centre, Bredbury Parkway, Stockport, SK6 2SN
☎ (0161) 637 0306 ☎ 07961 056198
🌐 stockportbrewingcompany.com

◎A former cuckoo brewery, Stockport Brewing installed its own eight-barrel plant initially under the iconic Stockport Viaduct in 2014. It then moved to a larger, modern facility in the Bredbury Industrial Estate north of Stockport. The beers are widely available throughout the UK through a trading agreement with other breweries. ‼🛒♦

Cascade (ABV 4%)
Light-coloured ale with a slight citrus flavour.

Crown Best Bitter (ABV 4.2%)
Amber-coloured ale with a smooth, hoppy taste and a dry finish.

Stock Porter (ABV 4.8%) ◆
Malty flavour and aroma with some treacle toffee. Coffee and chocolate roast notes and hint of dark fruit.

Stocks

See Welbeck Abbey

Stockton

28 Light Pipe Hall Road, Stockton on Tees, County Durham, TS18 4AH
☎ (01642) 678334
🌐 stocktonbrewingcompany.co.uk

Stockton started production in 2015 based in an industrial unit. It uses a 2.5-barrel plant. RAIB

Stod Fold

Stod Fold Farm, Hays Lane, Halifax, West Yorkshire, HX2 8UL
☎ (01422) 245951 ☎ 07568 487182
🌐 stodfoldbrewing.com

The 10-barrel Stod Fold Brewery is located on the edge of the moors in a renovated farm building. It supplies around 300 free trade outlets each year, mainly in Yorkshire, but occasionally distributes out of the region via nationwide brewing partners on the swaps scheme. Beers can always be sampled at the Stod Fold Brewery Tap at Dean Clough Mills, Halifax. ♦

Gold (OG 1038, ABV 3.8%) ◆
A refreshing golden-coloured and fruity session ale with a smooth, hoppy aftertaste

Best Yorkshire Bitter (OG 1038, ABV 3.9%) ◆
Well-rounded, traditional, tawny-coloured bitter. Lightly-hopped with a lingering malty and bitter aftertaste.

The West American Pale (OG 1042, ABV 4%) ◆
A light, hoppy, citrus pale ale.

Yorkshire Blonde (OG 1041, ABV 4.3%) ◆
Smooth-tasting, fruity beer with a lingering dry finish.

Dark Porter (OG 1048, ABV 4.8%) ◆
Easy-drinking, well-balanced, dark brown-coloured porter. Smooth and mellow with roast to the fore.

Stonehenge SIBA

The Old Mill, Mill Road, Netheravon, Wiltshire, SP4 9QB
☎ (01980) 670631 🌐 stonehengeales.co.uk

⊗The brewery was founded in 1984 in what was originally a water-driven mill built in 1914. In 1993 the company was bought by Danish master brewer Stig Andersen and now supplies more than 300 outlets. From 2013 a new borehole, accessing the Salisbury Plain aquifer, has been supplying the brewery's water. It is of such pristine quality that the brewery now bottle and sell it under the Stonehenge name. ‼♦

Spire Ale (OG 1037, ABV 3.8%) ◆
A pale golden-coloured session bitter with an initial bitterness giving way to a well-rounded bitter aftertaste with discernible fruit balance.

Pigswill (OG 1039, ABV 4%) ◆
A tawny-coloured session bitter with an initial pleasant hop aroma and slight bitterness to the taste moving to a well-rounded, bitter finish with slight malt and fruit in the finish.

Heel Stone (OG 1042, ABV 4.3%) ◆
A copper-coloured best bitter with some malt and fruit in the aroma, continuing into the initial taste along with pleasant hoppiness. Medium-bodied with plenty of flavour in the aftertaste with noticeable malt, fruit and hops.

Great Bustard (OG 1046, ABV 4.8%) ◆
A copper-brown-coloured strong bitter. Complex malt and fruit flavours at first with a long fruit and bitter aftertaste.

Danish Dynamite (OG 1048, ABV 5%) ◆
Golden-coloured, strong bitter with good hop and fruit aromas. Complex flavours in the initial taste with a well-balanced, full-bodied aftertaste with hops and fruit to the fore.

Stonehouse SIBA

Stonehouse, Weston, Shropshire, SY10 9ES
☎ (01691) 676457 🌐 stonehousebrewery.co.uk

Stonehouse is a family-run brewery, established in 2007, operating a 22-barrel plant. It is next to the preserved Cambrian railway line and includes a shop, bar and visitor centre. Direct delivery is within 30 miles of the brewery. ‼🛒

Sunlander (OG 1037, ABV 3.7%)
Pale-coloured ale with a good balance of citrus and floral hops.

Station Bitter (OG 1041, ABV 3.9%)
A traditional, amber-coloured bitter. A full-bodied session beer with a perfect balance of fruity hops and roasted malt.

Zaffir (OG 1038, ABV 4%)
Pale in colour and balanced with hints of tropical fruit hops.

Cambrian Gold (OG 1042, ABV 4.2%)
A deep golden-coloured, fruity beer with a subtle dry finish.

Ballast (ABV 4.4%)

Off the Rails (OG 1048, ABV 4.8%)
A rich and malty premium bitter with a classic British hop flavour.

Storm SIBA

2 Waterside, Macclesfield, Cheshire, SK11 7HJ
☎ (01625) 431234 🌐 stormbrewing.co.uk

Storm Brewing was founded in 1998. In 2001 it moved to its current location, an old riverside pub building, which until 1937 was called the Mechanics Arms. More than 60 outlets are supplied. ♦RAIB

Beauforts Ale (OG 1038, ABV 3.8%)
Golden brown-coloured, full-flavoured session bitter with a lingering hoppy taste.

Desert Storm (OG 1040, ABV 3.9%)
Amber-coloured beer with a smoky flavour of fruit and malt.

Bosley Cloud (OG 1041, ABV 4.1%)
Dry, golden-coloured bitter with peppery hop notes throughout. Some initial sweetness and a mainly bitter aftertaste. Soft, well-balanced and quaffable.

Ale Force (OG 1042, ABV 4.2%)
Amber-coloured, smooth-tasting, complex beer that balances malt, hop and fruit on the taste, leading to a roasty, slightly sweet aftertaste.

Dexter (OG 1040, ABV 4.2%)

Downpour (OG 1043, ABV 4.3%)
A pale ale with a full, fruity flavour, a hint of apple and a sightly hoppy aftertaste.

PGA (OG 1044, ABV 4.4%)
Light, crisp, lager-style beer with a balance of malt, hops and fruit. Moderately bitter and slight dry aftertaste.

Hurricane Hubert (OG 1045, ABV 4.5%)
A dark-coloured beer with a refreshing full, fruity hop aroma and a subtle bitter aftertaste.

Silk of Amnesia (OG 1047, ABV 4.7%)
Smooth, premium, easy-drinking bitter. Fruit and hops dominate throughout. Not too sweet, with a good lasting finish.

Red Mist (OG 1049, ABV 4.8%)
A dark red-black-coloured porter with fruity notes and a hoppy finish.

Stourton

See Enville

Stowey

Old Cider House, 25 Castle Street, Nether Stowey, Somerset, TA5 1LN
☎ (01278) 732228 🌐 stoweybrewery.co.uk

Somerset's smallest brewery was established in 2006, primarily to supply the owners' guesthouse and to provide beer to participants at events run from the accommodation. The small quantities of beer produced are also supplied to the George, Nether Stowey. ‼♦

Strands

Strands Inn, Nether Wasdale, Cumbria, CA20 1ET
☎ (01946) 726237 🌐 strandshotel.com

Strands Brewery is a ten-barrel plant with a 5,000-litre fermentation capacity. Six of the beers are available on the bar of the Strands Inn at all times or in the Screes, across the road. ‼♦RAIB

Pied Piper (OG 1030, ABV 2.7%)
Lots of traditional mild characteristics: malty, caramel, roast, sweet and fruity.

Green Bullet (OG 1037, ABV 3.5%)
High impact hop, so bitterness dominates this low strength golden ale. Loads of finish, good for hopheads.

Responsibly (OG 1038, ABV 3.7%)
Clean-tasting, heavily-hopped and lightly smoked beer.

Brown Bitter (OG 1039, ABV 3.8%)
A complex-tasting, brown-coloured beer with a lingering bitter aftertaste.

Errmmm... (OG 1038, ABV 3.8%)
A complex, traditional bitter.

Best Bitter (ABV 4.3%)

Red Screes (OG 1047, ABV 4.5%)
A rich-tasting, smooth, strong bitter; full-flavoured with plenty of roast and malt tastes.

T'errmmm-inator (OG 1052, ABV 4.9%)
A smooth, dark brown-coloured, roast-led beer. Full-bodied and well-balanced.

Traditional IPA (OG 1060, ABV 6%)

Contract brewed for Independent Lakeland Breweries:

Gold Wing (OG 1040, ABV 4%)
A full-bodied, hoppy, bitter beer with a malty start.

Dark Knight (OG 1050, ABV 5%)

Strata (NEW)

c/o Unit 4, Daniel Street, Whitworth, Lancashire, OL12 8BX 🌐 stratabrewing.co.uk

Brewing began in 2019 using spare capacity at Mighty Medicine (qv). The name comes from the owner's background in geology.

Thalweg (ABV 4%)

Tekapo (ABV 4.5%)

Strathaven SIBA

Craigmill Brewery, Sandford Road, Strathaven, ML10 6PB
☎ (01357) 520419 🌐 strathavenales.com

Strathaven Ales is a 10-barrel brewery on the River Avon close to Strathaven and was converted from the remains of a 16th-century mill. The range is distributed throughout Scotland and the north of England. ‼♦

Craigmill Mild (OG 1035, ABV 3.5%)
A black-coloured ale with a chocolate aroma and subtle orange zest aftertaste.

Clydesdale (OG 1038, ABV 3.8%)
A pale ale with a grapefruit aroma and sweet malt finish.

Duchess Anne (ABV 3.9%)

THE BREWERIES

A straw-coloured wheat beer with a floral aroma.

Avondale (OG 1048, ABV 4%)
An amber-coloured ale with a floral aroma and subtle bitter finish.

Line Out (ABV 4%)
An amber-coloured ale with a floral aroma and a subtle spicy aftertaste.

Old Mortality (OG 1046, ABV 4.2%)
A chestnut-coloured ale with a well-rounded malty aroma and a rich dried fruit flavour.

Claverhouse (OG 1046, ABV 4.5%)
A burnished red-coloured ale with a sweet citrus aroma and lingering malt finish.

Teuchter (ABV 5.6%)
A strong, dark-coloured ale with a chewy toffee aroma, citrus hop flavour and a satisfying dry finish.

500 (ABV 7%)
A smooth, full-flavoured, amber-coloured ale with subtle tropical fruit and lemon zest tones balanced by malt.

Usquebae Ale (ABV 7%)
A rich, honey-coloured ale, matured in oak casks, exuding a vanilla aroma, chewy toffee palate and a lasting, warming finish.

Strathbraan SIBA

Deanshaugh, Amulree, PH8 0EB
☎ (01350) 725264 ☎ 07747 857908
✉ strathbraan.bry@btinternet.com

Strathbraan began brewing in 2012 using a 10-barrel plant. RAIB

Due South (OG 1038, ABV 3.8%)

Head East (OG 1042, ABV 4.2%)

Strathcarron

Arinackaig, Strathcarron, IV54 8YN
☎ (01599) 577236 🌐 strathcarronbrewery.com

⊗ Brewing began in 2016 using a 2.5-barrel plant. Fresh West Highland water is used from an on-site spring. Beer is only available locally. RAIB

Golden Cow (OG 1038, ABV 3.8%)

Black Cow (OG 1042, ABV 4.2%)
A traditional dark-coloured stout with a toasty malt flavour.

Red Cow (OG 1042, ABV 4.2%)

Stringers

Unit 3, Low Mill Business Park, Ulverston, Cumbria, LA12 9EE
☎ (01229) 581387 🌐 stringersbeer.co.uk

Stringers is a family-run, small craft brewery. Brewing started 2008 on a five-barrel plant run on 100% renewable energy. ♦RAIB GF V

Furness Gold (OG 1036, ABV 3.5%)
A hoppy aroma and a fruity, full-bodied taste of hops, finishes with a drying bitterness.

Plan B (OG 1036, ABV 3.7%) ◈
An easy-drinking, zingy, pale-coloured thirst quencher.

No. 2 Stout (OG 1042, ABV 4%) ◈
A robust drying stout full of roast and hop bitterness.

Yellow Lorry (OG 1037, ABV 4%)

Landlord's Tipple (OG 1041, ABV 4.2%)
A copper-coloured beer with a sweet, soft aroma leading to a full mouthfeel and a soft bitter finish.

Blonde (OG 1042, ABV 4.4%)
A rich, golden-coloured beer with floral hops.

The North (OG 1046, ABV 4.9%)
An amber/red-coloured beer with a herbal hop aroma, touch of sweetness and a tangy bitter finish.

Turbine Porter (OG 1057, ABV 5.1%)
A lightly-smoked, dark ruby-coloured beer with hints of dried fruit.

IPA (OG 1052, ABV 5.5%)
A spicy beer with fruit from the hops leading to a lasting bitter finish.

Stripey Cat

Tiger Inn, 14-16 Barrack Street, Bridport, Dorset, DT6 3LY
☎ (01308) 427543 🌐 tigerinnbridport.co.uk/the-stripey-cat-craft-brewery

Brewing began in 2017 at the Tiger Inn producing ales exclusively for the pub.

Stroud SIBA

Kingfisher Business Park, London Road, Thrupp, Gloucestershire, GL5 2BY
☎ (01453) 887122 🌐 stroudbrewery.co.uk

⊗ Established in 2006, Stroud Brewery supports the local economy and does not sell its beers through supermarkets. The ales are sold in 40-50 pubs, independent retailers and its brewery shop. All beers have full organic status. A brewery bar is open every day and Wednesday to Saturday evenings. ‼ ♦RAIB

Tom Long (OG 1039, ABV 3.8%)
An amber-coloured session bitter. Full-bodied with caramel notes and a spicy orange aroma.

OPA (Organic Pale Ale) (OG 1041, ABV 4%)
An easy-drinking, golden-coloured pale ale. Refreshing and soft on the palate with hints of caramel and a delicate apple aroma.

Budding (OG 1045, ABV 4.5%)
Complex pale ale with aromatic citrus hop notes, a sweet malt backbone and a balanced, grassy bitterness.

Contract brewed for Yubberton Brewing Co:

Yubbie (ABV 3.8%)
A copper-coloured, traditional bitter. Strong caramel malty notes carry through to a fruity hop character, with a pleasant bitter finish.

Goldie (ABV 4%)
A refreshing ale with a strong hoppy character.

Stu Brew

Newcastle University, Merz Court, Newcastle upon Tyne, NE1 7RU 🌐 stubrew.com

Stu Brew is Europe's first student-run microbrewery based at Newcastle University. The brewery was set up as part of a research project aimed at reducing waste and costs in all parts of brewing. The university and local pubs are supplied. V

VMS (Vanilla Milk Stout) (ABV 3.8%)

Lab Session (ABV 4.3%)

Textbook IPA (ABV 4.5%)

Extended Overdraft (ABV 5.2%)

Into the Black (ABV 5.6%)

Stubborn Mule

Unit 2, Radium Works, Bridgewater Road, Altrincham, WA14 1LZ ☎ 07730 515251
⊕ stubbornmulebrewery.com

Brewing began in 2015 producing mainly bottled beers distributed to micropubs, beer shops and restaurants in the Manchester area. In 2016 the brewery relocated to new premises in Altrincham and expanded to a 10-barrel plant. Regular tap events and tastings are held (last Sat of the month and other one-off events). ‼ ♦ RAIB

The Mandarin Candidate (OG 1032, ABV 3.4%)
A pale ale packed with mandarin citrus flavours.

Li'l Napoleon Pale Ale (OG 1038, ABV 3.9%)
A session pale ale with a tropical, citrus orange finish and fruity bitterness.

Absolute Banker (OG 1047, ABV 4.7%)
An American-style pale ale with resinous, earthy hop flavours, some spiciness and citrus characteristics.

Donkey Punch NEIPA (OG 1054, ABV 5.5%)
A highly-hopped beer with a bitter zing.

Pre-Prohibition Cream Ale (OG 1050, ABV 5.5%)
A light, crisp beer with flavours of citrus, grapes, peaches and vanilla. Hoppy with a drop of honey and a clean finish.

Single Hop IPA (OG 1054, ABV 5.7%)
Smooth caramel notes with hints of tangerine, orange, citrus, tropical fruit and grapefruit.

Original Chocolate Stout (OG 1052, ABV 5.8%)
A dark-coloured chocolate stout, not too sweet.

WA15 Magnum Red IPA (OG 1066, ABV 7.2%)
A highly-hopped IPA with a powerful, complex and well-balanced flavour and aroma.

Stumptail

North Street, Great Dunham, Norfolk, PE32 2LR
☎ (01328) 701042 ✉ stumptail@btinternet.com

⊠ Stumptail began commercial homebrewing in 2011 using a 100-litre plant. Bottle-conditioned beers are produced with cask-conditioned versions brewed to order. Only the West Norfolk area is supplied. RAIB

Suddaby's

See Half Moon and Leeds

Sulwath SIBA

The Brewery, 209 King Street, Castle Douglas, DG7 1DT
☎ (01556) 504525 ⊕ sulwathbrewers.co.uk

⊕Sulwath started brewing in 1995. The beers are supplied to markets as far away as Devon in the south and Aberdeen in the north. The brewery has a fully licensed tap. Cask ales are sold to around 100 outlets and four wholesalers. ‼ ➔ ♦ RAIB

Cuil Hill (OG 1039, ABV 3.6%) ◆
Distinctively fruity session ale with malt and hop undertones. The taste is bittersweet with a long-lasting dry finish.

Tri-ball (OG 1039, ABV 3.9%)

The Grace (OG 1044, ABV 4.3%)
A refreshing, rich ale with a full-bodied flavour that balances the caramel undertones.

Black Galloway (OG 1046, ABV 4.4%)

Criffel (OG 1044, ABV 4.6%) ◆
Full-bodied beer with a distinctive bitterness. Fruit is to the fore with hops becoming increasingly dominant in the taste and finish.

Galloway Gold (OG 1049, ABV 5%) ◆
A cask-conditioned lager that will be too sweet for many despite being heavily hopped.

Knockendoch (OG 1047, ABV 5%) ◆
Dark copper-coloured ale, reflecting a roast malt content, with bitterness from Challenger hops.

Solway Mist (OG 1052, ABV 5.5%)
A naturally cloudy wheat beer. Sweetish and fruity.

Summer Wine

The Old Furnace, Unit 15, Crossley Mills, New Mill Road, Honley, West Yorkshire, HD9 6QB
☎ (01484) 665466 ⊕ summerwinebrewery.co.uk

⊕Brewing commenced in 2006 on a 10-gallon kit. A 2007 upgrade saw a 0.5-barrel plant installed and in 2008 the brewery expanded to a six-barrel plant. More than 500 outlets are supplied direct. ➔♦

Resistance (OG 1037, ABV 3.7%)
Dark ruby-coloured mild with a malty body and hints of caramel, cocoa and bitter roasted barley combined with a light, fruity hop character.

Zenith (OG 1040, ABV 4%)
Pale golden-coloured beer with floral aroma and a crisp bitter finish.

Barista (OG 1048, ABV 4.8%)
A rich coffee-flavoured stout.

Teleporter (OG 1050, ABV 5%)
A malty porter with a creamy body and cocoa, caramel and vanilla flavours.

Oregon (OG 1055, ABV 5.5%)
American-style pale ale with a grapefruit, sherbet, spicy and floral aroma, malty body and moreish hop finish.

Rogue Red Hop Ale (OG 1058, ABV 5.8%)
Deep ruby red in colour with good body and moreish flavour and finish.

Diablo (OG 1060, ABV 6%)
A strong IPA with tropical fruit aroma and flavours.

Summerskills SIBA

15 Pomphlett Farm Industrial Estate, Broxton Drive, Billacombe, Devon, PL9 7BG
☎ (01752) 481283 ⊕ summerskills.co.uk

⊠ Established in a vineyard in 1983 at Bigbury-on-Sea, Summerskills moved to its present site in 1985 and is the oldest brewery in Plymouth. Wholesalers and pub companies provide national distribution and the beers regularly appear in a selection of local outlets. In recent times the number of beers has increased and the brewer has won many awards. Locally sourced ingredients are used wherever possible. ◆RAIB

Start Point (OG 1036, ABV 3.7%)
Golden ale with a clean and fresh nose. Sweet up front with a delicate bitter finish.

Westward Ho! (OG 1040, ABV 4.1%) ◆
Malt dominates a light nose. Gentle bitterness introduces its malty-fruit friends. Malt and bitterness remain, with bitterness dominating the conversation.

Best Bitter (OG 1042, ABV 4.3%) ◆
A mid-brown-coloured beer with plenty of malt and hops through the aroma, taste and finish. A good session beer.

Tamar (OG 1042, ABV 4.3%)
A tawny-coloured bitter with a fruity aroma and a hoppy taste and finish.

Stout (OG 1044, ABV 4.4%)

Devon Dew (OG 1044, ABV 4.5%)
Honey yellow in colour with a floral, clean, malty aroma. Sweet lemon up front, with a long grapefruit finish.

Devon Frost (OG 1044, ABV 4.5%)
A lighter, slightly more hoppy version of Devon Dew.

Menacing Dennis (OG 1045, ABV 4.5%)
Golden amber in colour with aromas of dark malt and hops, and a slight hint of liquorice.

Bolt Head (OG 1046, ABV 4.7%) ◆
Fruit-hop nose has roast-malt hints. Bitter flavours with sweet malt, roast and hoppiness. Lingering bitter finish with background malt and fruit.

Whistle Belly Vengeance (OG 1047, ABV 4.7%) ◆
Full-flavoured, strong, red-coloured ale. Roast and malt aroma with roasted chestnut taste. Sweetness and bitterness mingle in the aftertaste.

Ninja (OG 1049, ABV 5%)

Plymouth Porter (OG 1050, ABV 5%)
A lightly-hopped, dark-coloured beer with a malty taste.

First Light (OG 1054, ABV 5.5%) ◆
Strong golden ale. Fruity, hoppy aroma. Sweet grapefruit and hops on the palate. Aftertaste continues with fruit and hops.

Indiana's Bones / South Star (OG 1055, ABV 5.6%) ◆
Old ale with good body. Rich malty roast aroma bursting with strong, sweet flavours on the tongue. Slightly dry finish.

Sunbeam

52 Fernbank Road, Leeds, West Yorkshire, LS13 1BU
☎ 07772 002437 ⊕ sunbeamales.co.uk

☺Sunbeam Ales was established in a house in Leeds in 2009, with commercial brewing beginning in 2011. Since moving, capacity has increased to a two-barrel plant based in a garage. The core range of ales, available in West and North Yorkshire at present, are brewed on rotation up to twice weekly with occasional brews every six weeks or so. ◆

Eclipse (ABV 3.8%)

A stout infused with ground coffee and orange peel. Robust roasted malts makes for a full bodied beer.

Blinded by the Light (ABV 4%)
A session IPA with fruity flavours and a hoppy aroma.

New Dawn (ABV 4.1%)
A golden-coloured session ale with well-balanced malt and hops.

White Chocolate Pale Mild (ABV 4.2%)

Tropical Rain (ABV 4.3%)

Rain Stops Play (ABV 4.5%)
A classic, single-hopped, English pale ale with a crisp, lemony finish.

Nigel's Plum Porter (ABV 4.8%)

Helios (ABV 5.8%)
An American-style IPA with a tropical fruit flavour and aroma.

Sunset

Office: 63 The Hurlings, St Columb Major, Cornwall, TR2 4TB
☎ (01637) 881798 ☎ 07702 087256
⊕ sunsetbrewingcompany.co.uk

Established in 2017 by Dan Piper, a bottled beer is contract brewed to Dan's own recipe. Brewing is currently suspended.

Sunset Taverns

See Six Towns

Super-6

See Prescott

Surrey Hills SIBA

Denbies Wine Estate, London Road, Dorking, Surrey, RH5 6AA
☎ (01306) 883603 ⊕ surreyhills.co.uk

⊗ Surrey Hills began brewing in 2005 near Shere, moving to Dorking in 2011. Nearly 95% of production is sold within 15 miles of the brewery. The beers have won several local and national awards. ‼️🍺◆

Ranmore (OG 1039, ABV 3.8%) ◆
A light, flavoursome session beer. An earthy hoppy nose leads into a grapefruit and hoppy taste and a clean, bitter finish.

Shere Drop (OG 1043, ABV 4.2%) 🍺 ◆
A hoppy ale with some balancing malt. A pleasant citrus aroma and a noticeable fruitiness in the taste, with some sweetness.

Gilt Complex (OG 1047, ABV 4.6%)

Greensand IPA (OG 1047, ABV 4.6%) ◆
A bold IPA with intense grapefruit and hops in the aroma and taste and a soft citrus finish.

Collusion (OG 1053, ABV 5.2%)

Sussex Small Batch (NEW)

c/o 23 The Vinery, Poling, West Sussex, BN18 9PY
☎ 07718 22425

Office: 48 Henty Road, Worthing, BN14 7HE
ssbbrewery@outlook.com

Jim Brown started the Sussex Small Batch Brewery in 2018, focusing on producing quality stouts with a difference. Brewing takes place using spare capacity at Goldmark Brewery (qv).

Tiramisu Stout (ABV 5.5%)

Zucotto Stout (Chocolate & Raspberry) (ABV 5.5%)

Smoked Chili Chocolate Stout (ABV 5.8%)

Vegan Raspberry Wheat Rye (ABV 5.8%)

Suthwyk

See Bowman

Swan Brewery SIBA

Unit 17, Brunel Road, Enterprise Park, Leominster, Herefordshire, HR6 0LX
☎ (01568) 617709 ☎ 07377 728822
swanbrewery.co.uk

Swan Brewery was established in 2016 by Jimmy Swan and partner Gill Bullock using a 10-barrel plant in Leominster. A 1.3-barrel plant is used to brew bespoke beers for local pubs.

Ruffled Feathers (OG 1040.5, ABV 3.8%)
A session ale with a clean, crisp hop flavour that lingers.

Gold (OG 1042, ABV 4.2%)
A golden ale with floral, herbal and zesty notes.

Swan on the Green

Swan on the Green, West Peckham, Kent, ME18 5JW
☎ (01622) 812271 swan-on-the-green.co.uk

The brewery was established in 2000 in an old coal shed behind the Swan on the Green pub using a two-barrel plant. !! ♦

Swannay SIBA

Swannay Brewery, Swannay by Evie, Orkney, KW17 2NP
☎ (01856) 721700 swannaybrewery.com

Brewing began in 2006 at the redundant Swannay dairy on Orkney mainland's exposed north-western tip. Two brewing plants are utilised, a five and a twenty barrel. Founder Rob is assisted by son Lewis plus a further small team of passionate beer lovers. !! ♦

Orkney Best (OG 1038, ABV 3.6%)
A refreshing, light-bodied, golden-coloured beer bursting with hop, peach and sweet malt flavours. The long, hoppy finish leaves a dry bitterness.

Island Hopping (OG 1039, ABV 3.9%)
Passion fruit hoppiness with some caramel and a lasting bitter aftertaste.

Dark Munro (OG 1040, ABV 4%)
The nose presents an intense roast hit which is followed by plums and blackcurrant in the mouth. The strong roast malt continues in the aftertaste.

Scapa Special (OG 1042, ABV 4.2%)
A good copy of a typical Lancashire bitter, full of bitterness and background hops, leaving your mouth tingling in the lingering aftertaste.

Sneaky Wee Orkney Stout (OG 1044, ABV 4.2%)
Bags of malt and roast with a mixed fruit berry background. Dry bitter finish.

Pale Ale (OG 1047, ABV 4.7%)

Orkney IPA (OG 1048, ABV 4.8%)
A traditional bitter with light hop and fruit flavour throughout.

Duke IPA (OG 1053, ABV 5.2%)
Good, refreshing citrus fruit IPA with background malt.

Orkney Blast (OG 1058, ABV 6%)
Plenty of alcohol in this warming strong bitter/barley wine. A mushroom and woody aroma blossoms into a well-balanced smack of malt and hop in the taste.

Swansea SIBA

Joiners Arms, 50 Bishopston Road, Bishopston, SA3 3EJ
☎ (01792) 232658

Opened in 1996, Swansea was the first commercial brewery in the area for almost 30 years. Beers are regularly available at the Joiners and also at the Railway Inn, Killay. !! ♦

Deep Slade Dark (OG 1034, ABV 4%)
A dark brown-coloured beer with a reddish hue and a nutty, malty taste. The aroma is malty with a little roast.

Bishopswood Bitter (OG 1043, ABV 4.3%)
A delicate aroma of hops and malt in this pale brown-coloured ale. The taste is a balanced mix of hops and malt with a growing hoppy bitterness ending in a lasting bitter finish.

Three Cliffs Gold (OG 1042, ABV 4.7%)
A golden-coloured beer with a hoppy and fruity aroma, a hoppy taste with fruit and malt, and a quenching bitterness. The pleasant finish has a good hop flavour and bitterness.

Original Wood (OG 1046, ABV 5.2%)
A full-bodied, pale brown-coloured beer with an aroma of hops, fruit and malt. A complex blend of these flavours with a firm bitterness ends with increasing bitterness.

T'ales from the Brewhouse

See Lancaster

Taddington

Blackwell Hall, Blackwell, Buxton, Derbyshire, SK17 9TQ
☎ (01298) 85734

Taddington started brewing in 2007, and brews one Czech-style unpasteurised lager in two different strengths. No real ale.

Tally Ho!

14 Market Street, Hatherleigh, Devon, EX20 3JN
☎ (01837) 810306 ☎ 07730 972980
info@tallyhobrewery.co.uk

Having stood idle at the rear of the Tally Ho! pub for 14 years, the brewery was recommissioned in 2015 by four brewing enthusiasts. The current owner and brewer, Bradley Horn, took over in 2018. As well as the pub, local free houses and other establishments are supplied. ♦

Pale Ale (OG 1040, ABV 4%)

Tamworth

29 Market Street, Tamworth, Staffordshire, B79 7LR ☎ (01827) 319872 🌐 tamworthbrewing.co.uk

Owner/brewer George Greenaway has brought brewing back to Tamworth town centre after a gap of 70 years. Brewing started in 2017. The showcase five-barrel plant sits on open view in a former shop, which dates from Tudor times and also serves as a taproom. Around 25 outlets are supplied. ‼ ♦

Hopmaster (ABV 4.2%)
Single-hopped golden ale with overtones of coconut.

Big Game (ABV 4.5%)
Pale-coloured, warming beer with subtle hoppiness and balancing malty sweetness.

Ethelfleda (ABV 4.5%)
Straw-coloured ale with robust citrus notes, grapefruit to the fore.

Hoppy Poppy (ABV 4.5%)
Golden-coloured beer with a gentle malty sweetness and a well-defined citrus bitterness.

Our Aethel (ABV 4.8%)
Easy-drinking, black-coloured ale with roasty flavours and a good hit of hops on the palate. The finish has a pleasant touch of smokiness.

Whopper (ABV 6.5%)
Strong IPA-style golden ale with an assertive resin hoppiness and a dry bitter finish.

Tankleys

Correspondence: 33 Beech Avenue, Sidcup, Kent, DA15 8NH ☎ 07901 333273 🌐 tankleysbrewery.com

Tankleys is a cuckoo brewery based in South-east London using spare capacity at Beerblefish Brewing (qv). Its Australian brewer has been brewing for 17 years and produces small batch brews, available occasionally around the local area.

English Golden Strong Ale (OG 1040, ABV 4.5%)

TAP

Marsden Estate, Rendcomb, Gloucestershire, GL7 7EX ☎ 07931 920988 ✉ tapbrewery@hotmail.com

⊗ TAP is a microbrewery established near Cirencester in 2015. It prides itself on sourcing materials and services locally, with malt from Warminster, hops from Worcester and the beer labels produced in Cirencester. Twelve local pubs are regularly supplied. ‼ ♦ RAIB

Old Dairy Mild (OG 1038, ABV 3.2%)

Old Dairy Gold (OG 1040, ABV 3.9%)
A golden ale with a zesty finish.

Old Dairy Bronze (OG 1043, ABV 4.2%)

Tap East SIBA

7 International Square, The Great Eastern Market, Westfield Stratford City, Montfichet Road, Stratford, London, E20 1EE
☎ (020) 8555 4467 🌐 tapeast.co.uk

⊗ Tap East is located in Westfield Stratford City shopping centre opposite the main entrance to Stratford International Station. Brewing began in 2011 using a 2.5-barrel plant. One-off and collaborative beers with other breweries are also produced. Bottle-conditioned beers are planned. ♦

Tap House

See Leatherbritches

Tap It SIBA

Unit 6, Muira Industrial Estate, William Street, Southampton, Hampshire, SO14 5QH ☎ 07484 649425 🌐 tapitbrew.co.uk

The first brew by enthusiastic homebrewer Rob Colmer was in 2018. Tap It is an eight-barrel plant producing eight regular beers mainly in KeyKeg and bottles, but occasional cask-conditioned beers are available. There is an on-site brewery tap and a bar in Southampton is planned. ‼

Tap Social Movement

27 Curtis Industrial Estate, North Hinksey Lane, Oxford, OX2 0LX
☎ (01865) 236330 🌐 tapsocialmovement.com

A 1,000-litre brewery, situated in an old warehouse. It was founded in 2016 to provide training and opportunities for effective rehabilitation for people serving prison sentences. The three co-founders all have a background in the criminal justice system. A good proportion of the beer is now brewed on the kit at the no-longer trading LAM brewery site in nearby Kennington. A popular taproom is open from Thursday to Sunday. Cask beer is available from collaboration brews and on request for beer festivals. Beers are supplied in KeyKegs to some local outlets. RAIB

Tapped

Sheffield: Sheffield Tap, Platform 1b, Sheffield Station, Sheaf Street, Sheffield, South Yorkshire, S1 2BP
☎ (0114) 273 7558

Leeds: Leeds Tap, 51 Boar Lane, Leeds, West Yorkshire, LS1 5EL ☎ (0113) 244 1953
🌐 tappedbrewco.com

Brewing began in 2013 after the old Edwardian dining rooms were converted into an on-site brewery with a viewing gallery at the Sheffield Tap pub. The beer is supplied via the company's specialist beer wholesale business, Pivovar. A further on-site brewery opened at the Leeds Tap in 2014.

Ale (OG 1035, ABV 3.5%)

Mojo (OG 1036, ABV 3.6%)
A clear, crisp and light pale ale.

SMASH (Single Malt and Single Hop) (ABV 3.9%)

A pale-coloured, crisp beer with light and hoppy flavours.

Rodeo (OG 1039, ABV 4%)
Fruity and light session pale ale.

Stout (OG 1041, ABV 4%)
A dry stout with hints of coffee and dark chocolate.

Bramling (OG 1042, ABV 4.2%)

Pegler (ABV 4.4%)

USP (ABV 4.5%)

Porter (ABV 5%)

IPA (ABV 5.3%)

Tapstone

11 Bartlett Park, Millfield, Chard, Somerset, TA20 2BB
☎ (01460) 929156 ☎ 07969 651998
tapstone.co.uk

Founded in 2015, the brewery was custom built around a brewing process that preserves delicate hop oils – making beers with a saturated hop flavour. It is growing Centennial hops about two miles from the brewery. A small on-site taproom recently opened. All beers are unfined and hazy. ‼

Sea Monster (ABV 4.2%)
Fresh and fruity pale ale with tropical flavours of blueberry, mango and lime.

Soma (OG 1046, ABV 4.6%)
Brewed with plenty of oats so the fruity hops come to the fore.

Hop Wire (OG 1048, ABV 4.8%)
A golden-coloured ale with the appearance of orange juice. Intensely fruity with a bitter aftertaste.

Kush Kingdom (OG 1050, ABV 5%)
An orange-coloured beer with a heavy mix of hops giving fruity, citrus flavours and a complex resin mouthfeel.

Tarn Hows

Low Bield, Knipe Fold, Outgate, Cumbria, LA22 0PU
☎ 07852 881105 tarnhowsbrewery.com

A microbrewery near Hawkshead specialising in stouts and hoppy pale ales. Oak casks may be used for barrel-aging and occasional seasonal beers. ♦

Beertrix Porter (OG 1042, ABV 4%)
A well-balanced, fruity beer with some liquorice aromas and a lasting finish of bitterness and roast.

Pale (OG 1042, ABV 4.6%)
Lemon sherbet, grapefruit and citrus flavours. Unfined and naturally hazy.

Blueberry & Vanilla Oatmeal Stout (OG 1054, ABV 5%)
Easy-drinking, dark-coloured beer with fruity aromas and sweet fruity taste. The finish lasts well with roast malt flavours coming through.

Tarn51

Robin Hood, 10 Church Road, Altofts, West Yorkshire, WF6 2NJ
☎ (01924) 891234

Tarn51 uses a three-barrel plant situated at the Robin Hood in Altofts. Expansion is planned. Five other outlets are supplied.

Tatton SIBA

Unit 7, Longridge Trading Estate, Knutsford, Cheshire, WA16 8PR
☎ (01565) 750747 ☎ 07738 150898
tattonbrewery.co.uk

Tatton is a family-owned business based in the heart of Cheshire. Brewing commenced in 2010 using a steam-fired, custom-built 15-barrel brewhouse. It supplies pubs throughout Cheshire and the North-west. ‼ ♦

Blonde (OG 1039, ABV 4%)
A clean-tasting, smooth pale ale with a fine hop aroma.

Best (OG 1040.5, ABV 4.2%)
A classic light amber-coloured best bitter with a clean malt flavour and fine hop character.

Gold (OG 1044, ABV 4.5%)
A golden-coloured special ale with a maltiness backed by a robust hop character.

Malted Milk Chocolate Stout (OG 1050, ABV 4.6%)
A luxurious, full-bodied, silky-smooth, malty, chocolaty beer.

VIPA Pale Ale (OG 1058, ABV 6.3%)

Tavernale

Bridge Tavern, 7 Akenside Hill, Newcastle upon Tyne, NE1 3UF
☎ (0191) 232 1122 thebridgetavern.com

A two-barrel plant supplying beers to the Bridge Tavern only. All beers brewed are one-offs. ♦

Taw Valley (NEW)

Westacott Farm, Westacott Lane, North Tawton, Devon, EX20 2BS ☎ 07900 002299
tawvalleybrewery.com

Established in 2017 in a Grade-II listed 17th century thatched barn. Beer is delivered in the brewery dray, a VW camper van. ♦RAIB

Black Ops (ABV 3.9%)
A dark-coloured, full-flavoured, hoppy ale with a good balance of fruit and herbal characteristics.

Tawton Session Ale (ABV 4%)
A session ale with a subtle grapefruit taste, well-balanced hoppiness and a fresh floral aroma.

Kennard's Steam (ABV 4.3%)
A traditional best bitter with a fruity blackcurrant finish and a balanced bitterness.

Taw Golden Brown (ABV 4.5%)
A full-bodied, golden brown-coloured ale with a depth of malt flavour.

Timothy Taylor SIBA IFBB

Knowle Spring Brewery, Keighley, West Yorkshire, BD21 1AW
☎ (01535) 603139 timothy-taylor.co.uk

An independent, family-owned company established in 1858, it has occupied the Knowle Spring site since 1863. Pennine spring water is used to brew its award-winning ales on both the established main plant and a 10-barrel plant introduced in 2017 to develop new beers, including occasional specials. ♦

Dark Mild (OG 1034, ABV 3.5%)

Malt and caramel dominate throughout in this sweetish beer with background hop and fruit notes.

Golden Best (OG 1033, ABV 3.5%)
Refreshing, amber-coloured traditional mild. A delicate fruity, hoppy aroma leads to a fruity taste with underlying hops and malt. Fruity finish.

Boltmaker (OG 1038, ABV 4%)
Tawny-coloured bitter combining hops, fruit and biscuity malt. Lingering, increasingly bitter aftertaste. Formerly and sometimes still sold as Best Bitter.

Knowle Spring (OG 1041, ABV 4.2%)
A golden ale with a floral aroma, malty with grassy hops and a finish of bitter lemon.

Landlord (OG 1042, ABV 4.3%)
A moreish bitter combining citrus peel aromas, malt and grassy hops, marmalade sweetness and a long bitter finish.

Ram Tam (OG 1043, ABV 4.3%)
A black-coloured beer with red highlights topped by a coffee coloured head. Burnt caramel on the nose, sweetish caramel taste, leading to a light, sweet finish.

Taylor Illingworth

21 Harwood Court, Riverside Park Industrial Estate, Middlesbrough, TS2 1PU ☎ 07562 248707

Having honed his skills at other local microbreweries Ben Taylor, together with owners the Illingworth brothers, launched Taylor Illingworth in 2017 using a four-barrel plant. The beers are named after sections of the former Redcar steelworks.

Stock Yard (ABV 3.9%)
Straw-coloured beer with a moderate hop aroma and fruity, citrus flavour.

Blast Furnace (ABV 4.1%)
Red-coloured ale with earthy spice maltiness coupled with floral herb aromas and caramel toffee flavours.

Beam Mill (ABV 5%)
Dark-coloured, roasted stout. Sweet plums lead to pronounced bitterness in the finish.

Bunker 241 (ABV 5%)
Amber-coloured, traditional IPA with fruit notes.

Taylors

London Tavern, Church Street, Attleborough, Norfolk, NR17 2AH ☎ 07871 773206
taylorsbrewery@gmail.com

Brewing began in 2014, primarily to supply the London Tavern. The brewery was upgraded in 2019 and relocated from an outbuilding to the inside of the pub.

Number One (ABV 3.9%)
A hoppy ale with a dry finish.

Second Coming (ABV 3.9%)

Dogtooth (ABV 4%)
A reddish brown-coloured beer, malty with fruity notes.

English Pale Ale (OG 1040, ABV 4%)

Remember Me (OG 1044, ABV 4.4%)
A malty beer with caramel notes and a dry finish.

Stitched Up (ABV 4.7%)

Team Toxic (NEW)

Office: A13/A14 Champions Business Park, Arrow Brook Road, Birkenhead, CH49 0AR ☎ 07981 535024
sue@theteamtoxic.co.uk

The relocated and renamed Hopcraft Brewery produces a range of one-off beers led by Gazza Prescott and Sue Hayward. Beers from Gazza will appear under the name Mission:Creep and those from Sue will continue to use the Waen identity. Some output is made in collaboration with other breweries. ♦

Teignworthy SIBA

The Maltings, Teign Road, Newton Abbot, Devon, TQ12 4AA
☎ (01626) 332066 teignworthybrewery.com

Teignworthy Brewery opened in 1994 within the historic Tucker's Maltings building. The 20-barrel plant produces 50 barrels a week and supplies around 300 outlets in Devon and Somerset. It diversified in 2017 with the addition of the Black Dog gin distillery. !! ♦ RAIB

Neap Tide (OG 1038, ABV 3.8%)
A pale-coloured, fruity bitter.

Reel Ale (OG 1039.5, ABV 4%)
Subtle aromas. The taste is gentle with malt and fruit dominating the hops. The aftertaste is dry.

Gun Dog (OG 1043.5, ABV 4.3%)
Easy-drinking session best bitter. Fruity throughout. Dry aftertaste lingers; sweetness and fruit over malt and caramel, progressing into hoppiness.

Spring Tide (OG 1043.5, ABV 4.3%)
A full-bodied and well-rounded, mid-brown-coloured beer with a dry, bitter taste and aftertaste.

Old Moggie (OG 1044.5, ABV 4.4%)
Best bitter. Hoppy and bitter with fruity undertones. Complex aftertaste with a balance of malt, hops and fruit.

Beachcomber (OG 1045.5, ABV 4.5%)
A pale brown-coloured beer with a light, refreshing fruit and hop nose, grapefruit taste and a dry, hoppy finish.

Teme Valley SIBA

Talbot, Bromyard Road, Knightwick, Worcestershire, WR6 5PH
☎ (01886) 821235 ☎ 07792 394151
temevalleybrewery.co.uk

Teme Valley was established in 1997 to brew beer for the Talbot, Knightwick. Only hops grown in Herefordshire and Worcestershire are used in brewing. Beers are supplied throughout the West Midlands and Marches. !! ♦ RAIB

T'Other (OG 1035, ABV 3.5%)
A pale-coloured beer with a delicate aroma and gentle bitterness. Amber malt contributes a light biscuit flavour.

This (OG 1037, ABV 3.7%)
Easy-drinking, light ale with a vivid hop aroma.

That (OG 1041, ABV 4.1%)

A chestnut-coloured best bitter with a robust malt flavour and potent bitterness to balance any sweetness.

Talbot Blonde (OG 1042, ABV 4.4%)
A smooth, rich and hoppy, golden-coloured beer.

Talbot Porter (OG 1042, ABV 4.4%)
A traditional, dark-coloured porter with roasted notes.

Wotever Next? (OG 1045, ABV 5%) ◆
Roasted malt and toffee aromas lead to a complex taste of stone fruits, dark malt, hops and melon. The finish is at first of slightly smoky malt and fruits fading into lingering dry hops.

Tempest SIBA

Block 11, Units 1 & 2, Tweedbank Industrial Estate, Tweedbank, TD1 3RS
☎ (01896) 759500 🌐 tempestbrewingco.com

Based in a former dairy, Tempest was set up in 2010 by Gavin Meiklejohn, brewer and co-proprietor of the Cobbles Inn in Kelso, which is the brewery tap. In 2015 the brewery moved from Kelso to new premises at Tweedbank. !! ♦ RAIB

Pemberton Pale (OG 1037, ABV 3.7%)
An American-style pale ale, straw-coloured with a refreshing hop character. Aromas of lemon and lime, some tropical notes and subtle spice.

Armadillo (OG 1039, ABV 3.8%) ◆
After a hoppy aroma, a well-balanced and complex beer emerges.

Cascadian (OG 1039, ABV 3.9%)
A light, citrus, hoppy session ale.

White Light (OG 1047, ABV 4.7%)
American-style hop hitter with a smooth citrus finish.

Tenby

Unit 15, The Salterns, Tenby, SA70 8EQ
☎ (01834) 218090 ☎ 07410 169447
🌐 tenbybrewingco.com

Formerly known as Preseli, Tenby Brewing Co uses a six-barrel plant. Beer is supplied to outlets in Pembrokeshire, neighbouring counties and further afield. Spent grain is fed to animals at a local eco-farm and through energy savings the brewery plans to become carbon neutral. RAIB

Son of a Beach (OG 1049, ABV 4.2%)
A citrus nose with a smooth fruit balance gives way to a hoppy, slightly dry finish.

Hang Ten (OG 1050, ABV 4.3%)

Barefoot (OG 1041, ABV 4.7%)
A refreshing, clean, crisp blonde ale, infused with kaffir lime leaves.

Black Flag Porter (OG 1055, ABV 5.6%)
Full of character, with coffee and chocolate and a hint of vanilla spiced rum.

Tenby Harbour

See Harbwr Tenby

Test

Old Stables, Greyhound Inn, High Street, Broughton, Hampshire, SO20 8AA
☎ (01794) 301573 ☎ 07831 746725
🌐 testbrewing.co.uk

⊗ Brewing started in 2017 in redundant stables behind, and independent of, the Greyhound Inn, using a four-barrel plant. There are four part-time brewers. Two local pubs as well as around 20 pubs in North Hampshire and the Test Valley are supplied. RAIB

Anton Bitter (OG 1037, ABV 3.8%)
An easy-drinking, malty, brown-coloured session bitter.

Red Fox Ale (OG 1038, ABV 3.8%)
A red-hued, malty session bitter.

Wallop Gold (OG 1042, ABV 4.3%)
A golden ale with a gentle hop aroma and flavour.

Thame

East Street, Thame, Oxfordshire, OX9 3JS
☎ (01844) 218202
✉ thamebrewery@btinternet.com

⊗ This one-barrel brewery was set up in 2009 by Peter Lambert and Oak Taverns in the old stables at the Cross Keys. Beer is produced from time to time for the Cross Keys.

Thames Side SIBA

Unit 7, Tims Boatyard, Timsway, Staines-upon-Thames, Surrey, TW18 3JY
☎ (01784) 409887 ☎ 07749 204242
🌐 thamessidebrewery.co.uk

⊗ Thames Side was founded in 2015 by CAMRA member Andy Hayward using a four-barrel plant situated in an old boatyard on the banks of the river. Beer is supplied to the local area as well as into central London. Beers are named after birds found on or near the River Thames. ♦

Harrier Bitter (ABV 3.4%)
A traditional session bitter with punch hop flavours.

Heron Ale (ABV 3.7%)
A smooth, easy-drinking bitter, well-balanced and malty.

White Swan (OG 1041, ABV 4.2%)
An American-style pale ale bursting with hoppy citrus flavours.

Egyptian Goose (ABV 4.8%)
A full-bodied IPA, hoppy, well-balanced and complex.

Wryneck Rye (OG 1055, ABV 5.6%)
A spicy but hoppy IPA.

Theakston

The Brewery, Masham, North Yorkshire, HG4 4YD
☎ (01765) 680000 🌐 theakstons.co.uk

⊚ After several years under the control of other companies Theakston is now owned by four brothers, grandsons of Thomas Theakston, the son of the company's founder who built the brewery in 1875. A new fermentation room was built in 2004 to provide additional flexibility and capacity, and further capacity was added in 2006. All Theakston beers are now brewed in Masham. ‼♦

Best Bitter (OG 1038, ABV 3.8%)
A golden-coloured beer with a full flavour that lingers pleasantly on the palate. With a good bittersweet balance, this beer has a robust hop character, citrus and spicy.

Black Bull Bitter (OG 1037, ABV 3.9%) ◆
A distinctively hoppy aroma leads to a bitter, hoppy taste with some fruitiness and a short bitter finish.

Lightfoot (OG 1041, ABV 4.1%)
Refreshing, golden-coloured pale ale with a light, fruity flavour and honeyed aroma.

XB (OG 1044, ABV 4.5%)
A sweet-tasting bitter with background fruit and spicy hop. Some caramel character gives this ale a malty dominance.

Old Peculier (OG 1057, ABV 5.6%) 🗐 🖢 ◆
A full-bodied, dark brown-coloured, strong ale. Slightly malty but with hints of roast coffee and liquorice. A smooth caramel overlay and a complex fruitiness leads to a bitter chocolate finish.

Thirst Class

Unit 16, Station Road Industrial Estate, Reddish, Stockport, SK5 6ND
☎ (0161) 431 3998 ⊕ thirstclassale.co.uk

⊛Thirst Class opened in 2014 in the centre of Stockport using a purpose-built two-barrel plant. In 2016 the brewery relocated to larger premises and installed a 10-barrel plant. ◆RAIB V

High Five (OG 1053, ABV 4.2%)
A session pale ale; light, hoppy and moreish with a citrus aroma and flavour.

Stocky Oatmeal Stout (ABV 4.7%)
Smooth, full-bodied oatmeal stout with notes of coffee and chocolate.

Any Porter in a Storm (ABV 4.8%)
Smooth, full-bodied porter with a rich taste and finish.

Green Bullet Pale Ale (ABV 4.8%)
A traditional English pale ale with earthy hop and floral flavours.

American Brown Ale (ABV 5.6%)
A brown-coloured ale, hoppy with a pronounced roasted maltiness.

Hoppy Couple IPA (ABV 6.2%)
American-style IPA. Rich copper in colour with a big citrus hop aroma and flavour.

Thomas Guest

See Black Country

John Thompson

Ingleby, Derbyshire, DE73 7HW
☎ (01332) 862469 ⊕ johnthompsoninn.com

⊠ Established by John Thompson in 1977 as an addition to the John Thompson Inn, which he converted from a 15th-century farmhouse in 1968, and is now run by his son Nick. John Thompson Special (formerly JTS XXX) is Derbyshire's longest continuously brewed ale. ‼

Thorley & Sons

30 East Street, Ilkeston, Derbyshire, DE7 5JB ☎ 07899 067723 ⊠ dylan.thorley1@yahoo.co.uk

Thorley & Sons began brewing commercially in 2016 on a 1.5-barrel plant located in an old coach house at the rear of brewer Dylan Thorley's house.

Pale & Interesting (ABV 4.5%)
Easy-drinking pale ale with a subtle hint of citrus in the taste.

Thornbridge SIBA

Riverside Business Park, Buxton Road, Bakewell, Derbyshire, DE45 1GS
☎ (01629) 815999 ⊕ thornbridgebrewery.co.uk

⊛The first Thornbridge craft beers were produced in 2005 using a 10-barrel brewery, housed in the grounds of Thornbridge Hall. The beers have gained considerable success with over 300 consumer and industry awards won. A 30-barrel brewery opened in Bakewell in 2009. The original site continues to develop new, seasonal and speciality beers. 200 outlets are supplied direct. 12 pubs are managed and owned. ‼ ▦ ◆RAIB

Wild Swan (OG 1035, ABV 3.5%) ◆
Extremely pale yet flavoursome and refreshing beer. Plenty of lemon citrus hop flavour, becoming increasingly dry and bitter in the finish and aftertaste.

Brother Rabbit (OG 1035, ABV 4%)
Yellow-coloured beer with a clean, hoppy aroma. A resinous finish and some bitterness.

Lord Marples (OG 1041, ABV 4%) ◆
Smooth, traditional, easy-drinking bitter. Caramel, malt and coffee flavours fall away to leave a long, bitter finish.

Ashford (OG 1043, ABV 4.2%)
A brown-coloured ale with floral hoppiness, a smooth, malty kick and a delicate coffee finish.

Kipling (OG 1050, ABV 5.2%) ◆
Golden-coloured bitter with aromas of grapefruit and passion fruit. Intense fruit flavours continue throughout, leading to a long bitter aftertaste.

Jaipur IPA (OG 1055, ABV 5.9%) ◆
Flavoursome IPA packed with citrus hoppiness that's nicely counterbalanced by malt, underlying sweetness and robust fruit flavours.

Saint Petersburg Imperial Russian Stout (OG 1073, ABV 7.4%) 🗐 ◆
Smooth and easy to drink with raisins, bitter chocolate and hops throughout, leading to a lingering coffee and chocolate aftertaste.

Three B's SIBA

▤ Black Bull, Brokenstone Road, Blackburn, Lancashire, BB3 0LL
☎ (01254) 581381 ☎ 07563 573199
⊕ threebsbrewery.co.uk

Robert Bell acquired the Black Bull in 2011 and the brewpub now supplies 50 outlets. ‼ ◆RAIB

Bee Thrifty (OG 1036, ABV 3.4%)

Stoker's Slake (OG 1038, ABV 3.6%) ◆
Lightly roasted coffee flavours are in the aroma and the initial taste. A well-rounded, dark brown-

coloured mild with dried fruit flavours in the long finish.

Honey Bee (OG 1039, ABV 3.7%)
A golden-coloured beer with honey apparent in both aroma and taste.

Bobbin's Bitter (OG 1038, ABV 3.8%)
A golden-coloured bitter with warm aromas of nutty grain and a full, fruity flavour with a light, dry finish.

Bee Blonde (OG 1041, ABV 4%)
A distinctive, pale-coloured bitter with a light, dry, balance of grain and hops and a delicate finish with citrus fruits.

Black Bull (OG 1042, ABV 4%)
Dark ruby-coloured ale with a bitter, rich character and a hint of chocolate.

Tackler's Tipple (OG 1044, ABV 4.3%)
A dark-coloured best bitter with a full hop flavour, biscuit tones on the tongue and a deep, dry finish.

Black Bull Lager (ABV 4.5%)

Doff Cocker (OG 1045, ABV 4.5%) ◆
Yellow in colour with a hoppy aroma and initial taste giving way to subtle malt notes and orchard fruit flavours. Crisp, dry finish.

Pinch Noggin (OG 1046, ABV 4.6%)
A dark-coloured, strong best bitter with a full hop flavour and long aftertaste.

Knocker Up (OG 1047, ABV 4.8%) ◆
A smooth, rich, creamy porter. The roast flavour is foremost without dominating and is balanced by fruit and hop notes.

Shuttle Ale (OG 1050, ABV 5.2%)

Three Blind Mice

Unit W10, Black Bank Business Park, Black Bank Road, Little Downham, Cambridgeshire, CB6 2UA
☎ (01353) 864438 ☎ 07912 875825
threeblindmicebrewery.com

Award-winning, seven-barrel brewery, established in 2014. Beer is supplied regularly to the Drayman's Son micropub, Ely, plus other outlets in Ely, Cambridgeshire and further afield. The name comes from the three owners/brewers, who reckoned they didn't have a clue what they were doing when they first started brewing. ♦

Lonely Snake (ABV 3.5%)

Juice Rocket (ABV 4.5%)

Old Brown Mouse (ABV 4.7%)

Milk Worm (ABV 5.3%)

Three Brothers SIBA

Unit 4, Clayton Court, Bowesfield Crescent, Stockton on Tees, TS18 3QX
☎ (01642) 678084 threebrothersbrewing.co.uk

The brewery is the vision of Kit Dodd after brewing for five years with another local brewery. He established it in 2016, together with his brother Dave and brother-in-law Chris. !! ♦ RAIB

The Ex Wife (OG 1037, ABV 3.7%)
A bitter beer brewed in a traditional way with a modern, slightly fruity twist.

Trilogy (OG 1039, ABV 3.9%)
A pale-coloured, blonde, hoppy bitter.

Honeysuckle Smash (OG 1040, ABV 4%)
A delicate golden ale brewed with honey.

ThaIPA (OG 1041, ABV 4.1%)
A full-flavoured, hoppy pale ale infused with lemongrass.

Au (OG 1042, ABV 4.2%)
A refreshingly crisp, lightly-hopped golden ale with light citrus notes.

Ruby Revolution (OG 1046, ABV 4.6%)

Short & Stout (OG 1050, ABV 5%)

Three Castles SIBA

Unit 12, Salisbury Road Business Park, Pewsey, Wiltshire, SN9 5PZ
☎ (01672) 564433 ☎ 07725 148671
threecastlesbrewery.co.uk

Three Castles is an independent, family-run brewery established in 2006. It delivers direct to around 80 pubs and independent retailers. Wholesalers and beer festivals are also supplied. !! ♦ RAIB

Chain Mail Pale (OG 1038, ABV 3.8%)
A clean, zesty pale ale with a citrus fruit cocktail flavour and a clean, bittersweet finish.

Barbury Castle (OG 1039, ABV 3.9%)
A balanced, easy-drinking pale ale with a hoppy, spicy palate.

Armour Plated (OG 1040, ABV 4%)

Saxon Archer (OG 1040, ABV 4%)
A balanced, easy-drinking session ale with a hoppy, fruity palate.

Heritage (OG 1042, ABV 4.2%)
A bronze-coloured best bitter with a smooth taste.

Uffington Castle (OG 1042, ABV 4.2%)
A dark brown-coloured ale with a malty, nutty palate and a pleasant bitterness. The hop comes through well with a big spicy aroma.

Vale Ale (OG 1043, ABV 4.3%)
Golden-coloured with a fruity palate and strong floral aroma.

Corn Dolly (OG 1047, ABV 4.7%)
Honey-coloured, easy-drinking, slightly floral, delicate aroma with a unique blend of malt and hops.

Three Daggers SIBA

Westbury Road, Edington, Wiltshire, BA13 4PG
☎ (01380) 830940 threedaggersbrewery.com

⊗ Three Daggers Brewery was established in 2013 using a 2.5-barrel brew plant in a farm shop next to a popular roadside pub. Malt is sourced locally from Warminster Maltings and hops from Charles Faram in Herefordshire. Hops are grown on-site for use in seasonal beers. !! ♦ RAIB

Daggers Blonde (OG 1037, ABV 3.6%)

Daggers Ale (OG 1041, ABV 4.1%)
A refreshingly malty ale with a dry hoppy finish.

Daggers Edge (OG 1047, ABV 4.7%)

Three Engineers

c/o Little Giant Brewery, Bristol

THE BREWERIES

Office: Winterbourne Medieval Barn, Church Lane, Winterbourne, Bristol, BS36 1SE
threeengineersbrewery.co.uk

Nanobrewery established near Bristol in 2017. Beers are brewed on demand. Due to major renovations at the brewery's home, Winterbourne Medieval Barn, it is currently cuckoo brewing at Little Giant Brewery (qv).

Three Fiends

Brookfield Farm, 148 Mill Moor Road, Meltham, West Yorkshire, HD9 5LN ☎ 07810 370430
threefiends.co.uk

The brewery was set up by three friends in 2015 and is based in one of the outbuildings at Brookfield Farm. The current two-barrel plant is being upgraded to an eight-barrel plant. Beers are available around Huddersfield and at CAMRA beer festivals.

Two Face (OG 1041, ABV 4%)
An easy-drinking session ale with floral, citrus and honey-like tones.

Bad Uncle Barry (OG 1042, ABV 4.2%)

Boomer (OG 1043, ABV 4.3%)

Bandito (ABV 4.5%)

Moko Titi (OG 1045, ABV 4.6%)

Dark Side (OG 1053, ABV 5.3%)
A black IPA with a smooth chocolaty start, leading to an increasingly bitter finish.

Little Devil (OG 1051, ABV 5.3%)

Punch Drunk (ABV 5.5%)

Voodoo (OG 1061, ABV 6%)

Panic Attack Espresso Stout (OG 1071, ABV 6.8%)

Bukowski (OG 1065, ABV 7%)

Three Hills

4 Thrapston Rd, Woodford, Northamptonshire, NN14 4HY ☎ 07400 706884 threehillsbrewing.com

Named after the ancient communal tombs that stand on the outskirts of the village of Woodford, Three Hills is a small batch brewery established in 2016. Initially producing only in bottle, can and KeyKeg, it, now produces a monthly series of varying styles of cask-conditioned ales called the Woodford Experiment. ♦

Three Kings SIBA

14 Prospect Terrace, North Shields, NE30 1DX
☎ 07580 004565 threekingsbrewery.co.uk

Three Kings started in 2012 using a 2.5-barrel plant, and have steadily upgraded it to its current 25 barrel capacity. Two house beers are brewed for local pubs. As well as the regular beers it typically brews two one-off beers each month. ♦

Shieldsman (ABV 3.8%)
Easy-drinking session ale with medium bitterness and tropical fruit flavours.

Billy Mill Ale (OG 1040, ABV 4%)

Dark Side of the Toon (OG 1042, ABV 4.1%)
A dry, dark-coloured, roasty and bitter stout with hints of chocolate and coffee.

Ring of Fire (OG 1045, ABV 4.5%)
A golden-coloured, American-style IPA with strong floral, citrus and grapefruit tones.

Silver Darling (OG 1053, ABV 5.6%)
A strong pale ale with a long-lasting bitterness and a spicy, pine, citrus and grapefruit aroma.

Three Legs

Unit 1, Burnt House Farm, Udimore Road, Broad Oak, East Sussex, TN31 6BX ☎ 07939 997622
thethreelegs.co.uk

Three Legs Brewing Company was started in 2014 by two friends who met studying viticulture and oenology at university. Initially a nanobrewery in a shipping container, it has expanded through a four-barrel plant onto a 12-barrel plant, in a converted farm barn. Serving pubs, restaurants and bottle shops across Kent and Sussex. The brewery is also home to a thriving brewery bar. !! RAIB

Table Pale (OG 1025, ABV 2.8%)
Refreshing minerality with a citrus nose.

Three Peaks

Scar Top, Buck Haw Brow, Settle, North Yorkshire, BD24 0DJ
☎ (01729) 822939 ☎ 07795 358932

Office: 7 Craven Terrace, Settle, BD24 9DB
threepeaksbrewery.co.uk

Formed in 2006 using a five-barrel plant, Three Peaks is run by husband and wife team Colin and Susan Ashwell assisted by Andrew Murphy. ♦

Fell Walker (OG 1035, ABV 3.5%)

Pen-y-Ghent Bitter (OG 1040, ABV 3.8%)
The malty character of this mid-brown-coloured session bitter is balanced by fruit in the aroma and taste. The finish is malty and hoppy.

Ingleborough Gold (OG 1041, ABV 4%)
This golden-coloured best bitter is hoppy throughout with fruit in the aroma and taste and a hoppy bitter finish.

Whernside Pale Ale (OG 1042, ABV 4.2%)

Three Sisters

See Crafty Little

Three Sods SIBA

Bethnal Green Working Men's Club, 42 Pollard Row, Bethnal Green, London, E2 6NB ☎ 07554 457868
threesodsbrewery.com

Based in a working men's club in East London, Three Sods specalise in small batch beers produced using a range of malt and hops from around the world. There are plans to move and expand in the near future. RAIB

Three Tuns SIBA

Salop Street, Bishop's Castle, Shropshire, SY9 5BN
☎ 07973 301099

Office: 16 Market Square, Bishops Castle, SY9 5BW
threetunsbrewery.co.uk

Brewing on this site started in the 16th century and was licensed in 1642. A small-scale tower brewery from the late 19th century survives. Three Tuns was one of only four pub breweries still running in the 1970s. ‼ ☕ ◆RAIB

Mild (OG 1040, ABV 3.4%)
Tawny-coloured beer of rich maltiness with burnt and roasted flavours.

Rantipole (OG 1036, ABV 3.7%)

1642 Bitter (OG 1042, ABV 3.8%)
A golden ale with a light, nutty maltiness and spicy bitterness.

Best (OG 1038, ABV 3.8%)

Solstice (OG 1037, ABV 3.9%)
Pale straw-coloured beer with a light malty quality, crisp, fruity bitterness and citrus and straw flavours.

XXX (OG 1046, ABV 4.3%) ▤ ◣
A pale-coloured, sweetish bitter with a light hop aftertaste that has a honey finish.

Stout (OG 1048, ABV 4.4%) ◣
Dark brown to black in colour. Mixed dried fruit aroma with yeast. Bitter start, fruity with roast. Balanced finish with fruit and sweetness among the hops.

Cleric's Cure (OG 1059, ABV 5%)
A light tan-coloured ale with a malty sweetness. Strong and spicy with a floral bitterness.

Old Scrooge (OG 1065, ABV 6.5%)
Rich, dark-coloured and fiery, smooth barley wine with flavours of liquorice, ginger, caramel and roasted malts lasting through into a strong bitter finish.

Steampunk (OG 1065, ABV 6.5%)
Rich, dark-coloured, smooth barley wine with flavours of liquorice, ginger, caramel and roasted malts, lasting through to a strong bitter finish.

Three Valleys

290-292 Rochdale Road, Todmorden, West Yorkshire, OL14 7PD ☎ 07736 061150
⊕ threevalleysbrewery.co.uk

☺This five barrel brewery is located in the building previously occupied by Bare Arts Brewery. It started selling beers to other outlets in 2018 and is run by Chris Duerden and Chris Leyland, two enthusiastic and accomplished homebrewers. New beers are planned. ◆RAIB

Paradisi (ABV 3.2%)
Well-balanced beer with mellow citrus notes.

Cascade (ABV 3.8%)
Light citrus notes give a clean, crisp ale with mild sweetness.

Stout (ABV 4.3%)
Smooth, dark-coloured, well-balanced ale with a subtle malty finish.

Pennine Mystic (ABV 4.5%)

Gold (ABV 4.7%)
Silky smooth golden ale with honey and caramel notes.

Walsden Brown (ABV 5.5%)
Brown-coloured IPA with burnt caramel notes followed by a lasting savoury finish.

Brew Long (ABV 7.9%)

Thurstons

The Courtyard, 102c High Street, Horsell, Surrey, GU21 4ST
☎ (01483) 729555 ☎ 07789 936784
⊕ thurstonsbrewery.co.uk

⊠ Originally based in the Crown, Horsell, Thurstons moved next door in 2014 when the brewery upgraded to a 4.5-barrel plant. The brewery supplies pubs across Surrey. ◆RAIB

Horsell Best (OG 1038.5, ABV 3.8%) ◣
Traditional, well-balanced bitter, initially malty with strong caramel flavours throughout and balancing bitterness, becoming drier in the finish.

Horsell Gold (OG 1038.5, ABV 3.8%) ◣
Light fruit and slightly nutty aroma lead to some bitterness and malt, which soon fades into a light bitter finish.

Milk Stout (OG 1055, ABV 4.5%) ◣
Smooth, sweet stout with a chocolaty flavour. A sweet malty flavour with a pleasant sharpness and a slightly dry finish.

Un-American Pale Ale (OG 1044, ABV 4.6%)
An American-style pale ale with grapefruit and pineapple on the nose and palate. This is balanced by a strong malt backbone and a good bitter finish.

Thwaites IFBB

Myerscough Road, Mellor Brook, Lancashire, BB2 7LB
☎ (01254) 686868 ⊕ thwaites.co.uk

☺Founded in 1807, Thwaite's brewed in Blackburn until 2018 when it moved to a rural site some five miles away in the Ribble Valley. A 20-barrel plant brews exclusively for the company's 240 or so pubs, 11 managed Inns of Character, eight hotels and two lodges. All properties can sell the regularly-brewed cask beers plus members of the company's 1807 Cask Club can sell the seasonal ales. Marston's, owner of the Wainwright and Lancaster Bomber brands, continues to sell these beers into Thwaites' outlets. TBC (Thwaites Best Cask) appears largely as a house beer with the name chosen by the outlet. ◆RAIB

Mild (OG 1036, ABV 3.3%)
Traditional, malty dark mild with caramel notes and a slightly bitter finish.

Original (OG 1039, ABV 3.6%)
A classic copper-coloured session bitter with a good balance between malt flavour and hop bitterness.

Gold (OG 1043, ABV 3.8%)
A refreshing, gold-coloured ale with citrus notes.

TBC (Thwaites Best Cask) (OG 1040, ABV 3.8%)
A well-balanced, traditional amber-coloured bitter.

IPA (OG 1042.5, ABV 4%)
A light, amber-coloured bitter with a zesty citrus flavour.

Amber (ABV 4.4%)
Well-balanced, full-bodied bitter with a floral hop aroma.

Tigertops

22 Oakes Street, Flanshaw, Wakefield, West Yorkshire, WF2 9LN
☎ (01229) 716238 ☎ 07951 812986
⊠ tigertopsbrewery@hotmail.com

☺Tigertops was established in 1995 by Stuart Johnson and his wife Lynda who, as well as owning the brewery, run the Foxfield brewpub in Cumbria (qv). The brewery is run on their behalf by Barry Smith, supplying five regular outlets. ◆

Tiley's

🍴 Salutation Inn, Ham, Gloucestershire, GL13 9QH
☎ (01453) 810284 ⊕ sallyatham.com

⊠ This 2.5-barrel microbrewery was established in an outbuilding of the award-winning Salutation Inn in 2015. It concentrates on producing small batches of award-winning beer, predominantly in cask with some in KeyKeg. Most of the brewery's output is sold on-site at the Salutation Inn and at the Butcher's Hook, Thornbury, with the rest going to selected pubs in the local area.

Tilford

🍴 Duke of Cambridge, Tilford Road, Tilford, Surrey, GU10 2DD ☎ 07710 500967
✉ genesiscraftales@hotmail.com

⊠ Tilford Brewery was started in 2017 using a 2.5-barrel plant in an old coaching house on the site of the Duke of Cambridge pub. A shop, tasting room and mini maltings are planned for the upstairs of the building. Beer is supplied to pubs in Surrey and Hampshire. ‼🍺

Red Mist (ABV 3.7%)

Rushmoor Ripper (OG 1044, ABV 4.4%)
Chestnut-coloured bitter, malty and sweet balanced by delicate but not overpowering hops.

Wit (OG 1045, ABV 4.5%)

Tillingbourne SIBA

Old Scotland Farm, Staple Lane, Shere, Surrey, GU5 9TE
☎ (01483) 222228 ⊕ tillybeer.co.uk

⊠ Tillingbourne was established in 2011 on a farm site previously used by Surrey Hills Brewery using its old 17-barrel plant. Around 25 local outlets are supplied. ‼🍺◆

The Source (OG 1033, ABV 3.3%) 🍺
Light and crisp golden ale with strong grapefruit flavours. Packed full of hops and drinking well above its strength.

Black Troll (OG 1035, ABV 3.7%) 🍺
A black-coloured bitter in which initial roast notes are eventually overpowered by citrus hop through to the finish.

Bouncing Bomb (ABV 3.8%)
A light, easy-drinking, traditional ale with subtle malty tones throughout.

Dormouse (ABV 3.8%)
A chestnut-coloured, traditional English ale with a malty sweetness balanced by hops.

AONB (OG 1036, ABV 4%) 🍺
Golden ale in which citrus hop dominates throughout. Some balancing malt in the aroma and taste, however.

Falls Gold (OG 1037, ABV 4.2%) 🍺
Whilst hops dominate, balancing malt is evident throughout. Hints of grapefruit in the aroma and taste lead to a dry finish.

Whakahari (ABV 4.6%)
A straw-coloured, refreshing, single-hopped pale ale.

Hop Troll (OG 1045, ABV 4.8%) 🍺
Golden ale with big hop flavours together with peach and apricot. Sweet, fruity taste leads to a floral bitter finish.

Summit (ABV 6%)

Time & Tide

Statenborough Farm, Felderland Lane, Eastry, Kent, CT14 0BX ☎ 07739 868256
⊕ timeandtidebrewing.co.uk

Time & Tide began brewing in 2013 using spare capacity at Ripple Steam Brewery (qv). In 2015 it obtained its own 20-barrel brewhouse. No real ale. ◆

Tin Head (NEW)

Unit 22f, Bradley Fold Trading Estate, Bradley Fold Road, Radcliffe, BL2 6RT ☎ 07980 263766
✉ beer@tinheadbrewery.co.uk

Established in 2017 as a beer canning factory, the site has been expanded and now operates a brewery with a large taproom. No real ale. ‼

Tindall

Toad Lane, Seething, Norfolk, NR35 2EQ

Tindall Ales began brewing in 1998. It was originally based in Ditchingham but moved to its current location towards the end of 2001. ◆

Best Bitter (OG 1037, ABV 3.7%)

Fuggled Up (OG 1037, ABV 3.7%)

Mild (OG 1037, ABV 3.7%)

Liberator (OG 1038, ABV 3.8%)

Alltime (OG 1040, ABV 4%)

Mundham Mild (OG 1040, ABV 4%)

Ditchingham Dam (OG 1042, ABV 4.2%)

Seething Pint (OG 1043, ABV 4.3%)

Norwich Dragon (OG 1046, ABV 4.6%)

Honeydo (OG 1050, ABV 5%)

Tingay

See Southbourne

Tintagel SIBA

Condolden Farm, Tintagel, Cornwall, PL34 0HJ
☎ (01840) 213371 ⊕ tintagelbrewery.co.uk

⊠ Established in 2009 in a redundant milking parlour on the highest farm in Cornwall, using a 7.5-barrel plant. A new purpose-built brewery, shop, restaurant and visitor centre opened in 2017. Around 80 outlets are supplied direct. ‼🍺◆

Castle Gold (OG 1038, ABV 3.8%) 🍺
Refreshing golden ale with little aroma. Citrus hop dominates taste with other fruit flavours and faint malt. Bitter hop finish.

Cornwall's Pride (OG 1040, ABV 4%) 🍺

Pale brown-coloured bitter with a malt aroma. Sweet, grainy malt with toffee and summer fruits. Late dried fruit and coffee hints.

Arthur's Ale (OG 1044, ABV 4.4%) ◆
Pale brown-coloured, complex beer with a balance of sweet toffee, malt and earthy hops. Hints of figs, vine fruits and liquorice.

Pendragon (ABV 4.5%) ◆
Amber-coloured beer with a citrus hop nose. Refreshing, strong citrus hop bitterness, grapefruit tang and hints of toffee, honey and malt.

Poldark Ale (OG 1045.8, ABV 4.5%) ◆
Brown-coloured mild with a malt aroma. An assertive malty flavour with stone fruits, dates, sweet caramel, smokiness and a citrus edge.

Harbour Special (OG 1048.9, ABV 4.8%) ◆
Tawny-coloured strong bitter with a ripe fruity, malty aroma. Rich nutty malt, stone fruits and esters taste, finishing bitter and malt.

Merlins Muddle (OG 1052, ABV 5.2%) ◆
Copper-coloured, smooth strong bitter. Malt dominates the taste throughout with hop bitterness and a complex mixture of fruit flavours.

Excalibur (OG 1058, ABV 5.8%) ◷ ▣ ◆
Dark-coloured old ale. Smoky, roast malt and Christmas pudding fruits with rich and complex flavours including treacle and earthy hops.

Tinworks

Llys Cerdd, Heol Gelli Fawr, Llanelli, SA15 5EQ
☎ 07595 841958 ⊕ tinworksbrewery.co.uk

Tinworks commenced brewing in 2018. Bottled beers are produced, named after the local industry.

Tiny Rebel SIBA

Wern Industrial Estate, Rogerstone, NP10 9FQ
☎ (01633) 547378 ⊕ tinyrebel.co.uk

☺Established in 2012, Tiny Rebel moved to new, bespoke premises in 2017 having outgrown its previous site. Originally using a 12-barrel plant, the brewery now operates a dual-stream 30-barrel plant, and consists of 23 fermentation tanks and four conditioning tanks, supplying its three tied pubs as well as numerous outlets across the UK. ‼▤◆

Dutty (OG 1052, ABV 4.2%)
A full-flavoured session IPA with a smooth texture and mouthfeel.

Cwtch (OG 1045, ABV 4.6%) ◷ ▣
A well-balanced, red-coloured ale that combines caramel malt flavours with citrus hops.

Stay Puft (OG 1053, ABV 5.2%)
This marshmallow porter has the classic roasty qualities of a dark-coloured ale with a smooth sweetness.

Tiny Vessel

Unit 505, Platts Eyot, Hampton, TW12 2HF ☎ 07888 730210 ⊕ tinyvessel.co.uk/home.html

☒ Tiny Vessel is a 1.5-barrel brewery established in 2016 on Platts Eyot, an island on the River Thames near Hampton. All beers are unfiltered and unfined, mostly available bottled or in keg,

although at least one beer is usually available on cask in the Northumberland Arms, Brentford. RAIB V

Tipples

Unit 3, The Mill, Wood Green, Salhouse, Norfolk, NR13 6NY
☎ (01603) 721310 ⊕ tipplesbrewery.com

☒ Tipples was established in 2004 on a six-barrel brew plant. In addition to a full range of cask ales, an extensive range of bottled beers is produced, which can be found in some farmers markets and supermarkets in Norfolk. ◆RAIB

Bowline (ABV 3.8%)

Ginger (OG 1038, ABV 3.8%) ◆
A spicy aroma introduces this yellow-coloured brew. Ginger dominates with supporting malty bitterness. Quick ginger nut finish.

Hanged Monk (OG 1038, ABV 3.8%) ◆
Strong roast and malt notes dominate the aroma and taste. A grainy mouthfeel with caramel and a growing vinous finish.

Sundown (OG 1040, ABV 3.9%) ◆
Berries and malt introduce this smooth, creamy bitter. Bitterness gives depth to the fruity malt core as it slowly sweetens.

Lady Evelyn (OG 1041, ABV 4.1%) ◆
A crisp, hoppy aroma. Bitterness and hops throughout. Some malt and sweetness take the edge off a smoky finish.

Redhead (OG 1042, ABV 4.2%) ◆
Malt and hops in both nose and palate. Toffee in the initial taste gives way to an increasing bitterness.

Malten Copper (ABV 4.4%)

Topper (OG 1045, ABV 4.5%) ◆
Coffee and dark chocolate to the fore throughout. Just enough malt sweetness and bitterness to provide balance. Strong, big-hearted finish.

Brewers Progress (OG 1046, ABV 4.6%) ◆
Solid and malty with strong caramel and vanilla support. Smooth and creamy with added depth by a bitter blackcurrant fruitiness.

Moonrocket (OG 1050, ABV 5%) ◆
A complex golden-coloured brew. Malt, hop, bitterness and a fruity sweetness swirl round in an ever-changing kaleidoscope of flavours.

Jack's Revenge (OG 1058, ABV 5.8%) ◆
An explosion of malt, chocolate, roast and plum pudding. Full-bodied with a deep red hue and a strong, solid finish.

Indian Hill (ABV 6.5%)

Tír Dhá Ghlas

▤ Cullins Yard, 11 Cambridge Road, Dover, Kent, CT17 9BY
☎ (01304) 211666 ⊕ cullinsyard.co.uk

☒ Brewing began in 2012 using a two-barrel plant. Beers are only available in the bar/restaurant and occasionally at the nearby Royal Cinque Ports Yacht Club.

Tirril SIBA

Red House, Long Marton, Cumbria, CA16 6BN

☎ (01768) 361846 🌐 tirrilbrewery.co.uk

Established in 1999, Tirril Brewery has twice outgrown its premises. It delivers to more than 170 outlets, 100 of which regularly stock the beer. One pub is owned. Contract brewing is also carried out for Bitter End Brewery. !! ♦

Original Bitter (OG 1038.5, ABV 3.8%)

Ullswater Blonde (OG 1038.5, ABV 3.8%)

Grasmere Gold (OG 1039, ABV 3.9%)

Kirkstone Gold (OG 1039, ABV 3.9%)

Old Faithful (OG 1040, ABV 4%)
Initially bitter, gold-coloured ale with an astringent finish.

1823 (OG 1041, ABV 4.1%)
A full-bodied session bitter with a gentle bitterness.

Academy Ale (OG 1041.5, ABV 4.2%)
A dark-coloured, full-bodied, traditional rich and malty ale.

Borrowdale Bitter (OG 1041.5, ABV 4.2%)

Windermere IPA (OG 1043, ABV 4.3%)

Red Barn Ale (OG 1043, ABV 4.4%)
A ruby red-coloured ale with a strong hop finish.

Titanic SIBA

Callender Place, Burslem, Stoke-on-Trent, Staffordshire, ST6 1JL
☎ (01782) 823447 🌐 titanicbrewery.co.uk

Titanic is one of the earliest microbreweries, founded in 1985. Now owned by two brothers, it has grown from a seven-barrel brewery to producing more than four million pints per year. With an expanding fleet of tied pubs and café bars, it also supplies free trade customers in the Midlands, North-west and further afield. The brewery is named after Captain Smith, a Potteries man and captain of the ill-fated Titanic. !! ♦ RAIB

Mild (OG 1036, ABV 3.5%)
Fresh, fruity hop aroma leads to a caramel start then a rush of bitter hoppiness ending with a lingering dry finish.

Steerage (OG 1039.5, ABV 3.8%)
Pale yellow-coloured bitter. Flavours start with hops and fruit but become zesty and refreshing in this light session beer with a long, dry finish.

Lifeboat (OG 1040, ABV 4%)
Dark brown in colour with fruit, malt and caramel aromas. Sweet start, malty and caramel middle with hoppiness developing into a fruity and dry lingering finish.

Anchor Bitter (OG 1042, ABV 4.1%)
Amber-coloured beer with a spicy hint to the fruity start that says go to the rush of hops for the dry bitter finish.

Iceberg (OG 1042, ABV 4.1%)
Yellow gold-coloured sparkling wheat beer with a flowery start leading to a big hop crescendo.

Cherry Dark (OG 1045, ABV 4.4%)

Cappuccino Stout (OG 1046, ABV 4.5%)

Chocolate & Vanilla Stout (OG 1047, ABV 4.5%)
Chocoholic paradise with real coffee and vanilla support. Cocoa, sherry and almonds lend depth to this creamy, drinkable stout.

Stout (OG 1046, ABV 4.5%)
Roasty, toasty with tobacco, autumn bonfires, chocolate and hints of liquorice; perfectly balanced with a bitter, dry finish, reminiscent of real coffee.

White Star (OG 1048, ABV 4.5%)
Hints of cinnamon apple pie are found before the hops take over to give a bitter edge to this well-balanced, refreshing and fruity beer.

Plum Porter (OG 1051, ABV 4.9%)
Dark brown in colour with a powerful fruity aroma. A sweet plum fruitiness gives way to a gentle bitter finish.

Captain Smith's Strong Ale (OG 1054, ABV 5.2%)
Red brown in colour and full bodied, lots of malt and roast with a hint of honey but a strong bittersweet finish.

Titsey SIBA

Botley Hill Farmhouse, Limpsfield Road, Titsey, Surrey, CR6 9QH ☎ 07850 914189
🌐 titseybrewingco.com

A microbrewery established in 2017 on the Titsey Estate, it has recently moved to larger premises, still on the estate, using a five-barrel plant purchased through crowdfunding. It supplies two associated pubs, the Botley Hill Farmhouse and the White Bear, Fickleshole, as well as an increasing number of local outlets. The beers are named after historic owners of the Titsey Estate. RAIB

Gresham Hopper (OG 1040, ABV 3.7%)
Golden ale with refreshing citrus and pine notes and some bitterness.

Leveson Buck (OG 1040, ABV 3.7%)
Session IPA with citrus, passion fruit and grapefruit notes.

Gower Wolf (OG 1042, ABV 4%)
Caramel and honey sweetness contrast with spicy flavours.

Toll End

c/o Waggon & Horses, 131 Toll End Road, Tipton, West Midlands, DY4 0ET ☎ 07903 725574

The four-barrel brewery opened in 2004. With the exception of Phoebe's Ale, named after the brewer's daughter, all brews commemorate local landmarks, events and people. !! RAIB

Tollgate SIBA

Unit 1, Southwood House Farm, Staunton Lane, Calke, Derbyshire, LE65 1RG
☎ (01283) 229194 🌐 tollgatebrewery.co.uk

This six-barrel brewery was founded in 2005 on the site of the old Brunt & Bucknall Brewery in nearby Woodville, but relocated to new premises on the National Trust's Calke Park estate in 2012. Around 180 outlets are supplied direct, mainly in the North Midlands. The brewery operates three micropubs: Queens Road Tap, Leicester, Tap at No.76, Ashby-de-la-Zouch, and Town Street Tap, Duffield. !! ♦ RAIB

Stand & Deliver (OG 1036, ABV 3.8%)
Traditional session bitter; medium malts with a smooth finish.

Hackney Blonde (OG 1036, ABV 3.9%)
Crisp, pale-coloured, lager-style session ale, refreshing with a citrus finish.

Melbourne Bitter (OG 1038, ABV 4%)
A golden-coloured, mellow bitter with a hint of citrus in the finish.

California Steam (OG 1041, ABV 4.2%)
A US West Coast inspired lager-style beer.

Eclipse BIPA (OG 1040, ABV 4.2%)
A dark-coloured IPA with malted rye.

Red Storm (OG 1040, ABV 4.2%)
A red-coloured ale with soft malts and complex hops.

Duffield Amber (OG 1042, ABV 4.4%)
A traditional amber-coloured bitter with English malt and hops.

Ashby Pale (OG 1043, ABV 4.5%)
A light, refreshing traditional English pale ale with a citrus finish.

Old Rasputin (OG 1043, ABV 4.5%)
Dark in colour with a hint of sweet creaminess, balanced with a smooth, slightly bitter finish.

Red Star IPA (OG 1043, ABV 4.5%)
Traditional IPA with smooth, hoppy flavours.

Billy's Best Bitter (OG 1044, ABV 4.6%)
An easy-drinking, smooth, dark amber-coloured best bitter with good malt flavours balanced with fruity hops.

High Street Bitter (OG 1045, ABV 4.7%)
A dark-coloured, strong, smooth English bitter, brewed with rich malts.

Spark IPA (OG 1050, ABV 5.6%)
A dark-coloured, hoppy and strong golden ale.

Tolly Cobbold

See Greene King

Tom Herrick's

See under H

Tom's Tap (NEW)

4-6 Thomas Street, Crewe, Cheshire, CW1 2BD
☎ 07931 573425
🌐 tomstapandbrewhouse.wordpress.com

Tom's Tap & Brewhouse consists of three units; brewery equipment in the first, live music and special events in the middle, including meet the brewer events, and a taproom in the third, which is open to the public Thursday to Sunday. Beer is also distributed to four other outlets and local beer festivals. ‼

Tombstone

6 George Street, Great Yarmouth, Norfolk, NR30 1HR ☎ 07584 504444
🌐 tombstonebrewery.co.uk

⊗ Established in 2013, the brewery is run by former homebrewer Paul Hodgson. The original brewery backed onto the town cemetery, inspiring the name, but it has now relocated to the rear of its brewery tap, the Tombstone Saloon. Around 30 outlets are supplied around Norwich. ♦

Ale (OG 1038, ABV 3.7%)
Banana toffee aroma. Piquant bitter hoppy beginning softened by a biscuity maltiness. Dry bitter finish.

Arizona (OG 1040, ABV 3.9%)
Malt and lemon nose. Initial lemongrass and sweet biscuit beginning quickly fades. Sweet watery finish enhanced by malt.

Texas Jack (OG 1040, ABV 4%)
Toffee apple and vanilla aroma. Caramel leads the smooth complex mix of flavours. A bittersweet fruitiness continues to the end.

Regulators (OG 1040, ABV 4.1%)
Golden-coloured, hoppy ale with a bitter, dry finish.

Gunslinger (OG 1044, ABV 4.3%)
Golden in colour with a caramel, nutty finish.

Lone Rider (OG 1044, ABV 4.3%)

Stagecoach (OG 1044, ABV 4.4%)
A rich caramel and treacle aroma. Malt, roast and caramel dominate a hoppy, bittersweet foundation. Short, increasingly dry finish.

Cherokee (OG 1045, ABV 4.5%)
Malty nose with plum and cherry. Initial mix of biscuit and roasty bitterness gently changes to a slightly spicy maltiness.

Santa Fe (ABV 5%)
A sweet and fruity ale.

Big Nose Kate (OG 1054, ABV 5.3%)
Ruby-coloured ale. Malty and fruity with a subtle passion fruit taste.

6 Shooter (ABV 6.6%)
Fresh orchard fruits, floral with citrus undertones.

Brewed for Brunning & Price Pub Co:

Blackfoot (ABV 4.8%)

Tomos a Lilford SIBA

Unit 11b, Vale Business Park, Llandow, CF71 7PF
☎ (01446) 796905 ☎ 07779 132647

Office: 117 Boverton Road, Llantwit Major, CF61 1YA
✉ tomos.lilford@gmail.com

⊗ Tomos a Lilford was launched in 2013 by homebrewers Rolant Tomos and brothers Rob and James Lilford. The brewery supplies pubs and clubs across the Vale of Glamorgan and further afield. All point of sale material is bilingual. ♦

Cob (OG 1040, ABV 4%)
Malty session beer with creamy, nutty notes.

Annwyl (OG 1050, ABV 5%)

Gaucho (OG 1050, ABV 5%)
An IPA with a long, smooth finish.

OPA (OG 1050, ABV 5%)

Rosemary Ale (ABV 5%)
Pale-coloured, refreshing ale bursting with the flavours of honey and rosemary.

Hay (OG 1052, ABV 5.2%)
An English-style IPA with added hay for sweetness and aroma.

Tonbridge SIBA

Unit 19, Branbridges Industrial Estate, East Peckham, Kent, TN12 5HF
☎ (01622) 871239 🌐 tonbridgebrewery.co.uk

⊗ Tonbridge Brewery was launched in 2010 using a four-barrel plant, expanding in 2013 to a 12-barrel plant. It is owned and run jointly by Paul Bournazian and Mark Gardner. Pubs, clubs and shops are supplied throughout Kent and also parts of Surrey, Sussex, Essex and South-east London. ‼

Golden Rule (OG 1036.5, ABV 3.5%)
Hoppy golden ale with a light, crisp body and delicate floral aroma.

Traditional Ale (OG 1038, ABV 3.6%)
Easy-drinking and refreshing ale with a light fruity taste and hoppy aroma.

Coppernob (OG 1039.5, ABV 3.8%)
A fairly dry, rich copper-coloured ale with a robust, fruity hop flavour.

Countryman (OG 1041, ABV 4%)
Classic best bitter with a light malty taste and refreshing spice and fruit finish.

Rustic (OG 1041.5, ABV 4%)
Deep bronze-coloured, rich-tasting ale with a delicate spicy taste and aroma.

Blonde Ambition (OG 1043.5, ABV 4.2%)
Crisp, refreshing blonde ale, hoppy with spicy and citrus notes.

Old Chestnut (OG 1045, ABV 4.4%)
Full-bodied, chestnut-coloured ale with a malty base and a berry and honey finish.

American Pale (OG 1050, ABV 5%)
Classic, full-bodied, American-style pale ale with a distinct, refreshing citrus finish.

Toolmakers SIBA

6-8 Botsford Street, Sheffield, South Yorkshire, S3 9PF
☎ 07956 235332 🌐 toolmakersbrewery.com

Toolmakers is a family-run brewery established in 2013 in an old tool-making factory. Beers are brewed on a five-barrel plant and are available within a 40-50 mile radius of the brewery. The adjoining Forest pub is owned. ‼♦

Lynch Pin (OG 1038, ABV 4%)
A dark-coloured best bitter with chocolate and caramel undertones.

Pull Saw (ABV 4.4%)
A blonde beer with citrus overtones.

Tooth & Claw

See Camerons

Top-Notch

Haywards Heath, West Sussex, RH16 1UQ ☎ 07963 829368 ✉ topnotchbrewing@hotmail.com

This 0.5-barrel brewery is situated in a converted residential outbuilding in Haywards Heath. RAIB

Hop Festival (OG 1039, ABV 3.9%)

Royal Fanfare (OG 1046, ABV 4.6%)

Top Out SIBA

Unit 3, 6b Dryden Road, Loanhead, EH20 9LZ
☎ (0131) 440 0270 ☎ 07742 234970
🌐 topoutbrewery.com

Brewing began in 2013 using a six-barrel plant. Initially focusing on bottle-conditioned beers, the brewery has expanded into brewing cask beer for the on-trade. Branding has a topographical theme. Top Out also contract brews for Secret Herb Garden, a visitor attraction in Edinburgh. ♦RAIB

Copperheid (ABV 3.4%)
A well-balanced ale with spices, gooseberry and a bitter finish with a long ginger twist.

Eldorado (ABV 3.6%)

Staple (OG 1037, ABV 4%)
A smooth session pale ale with a dry finish.

Altbier (ABV 4.5%)
A dark-coloured, malty beer brewed with German hops.

Schmankerl (ABV 4.9%)
A Bavarian-style wheat beer with notes of banana and cloves.

Simon Says-on (ABV 5.1%)
A pink-coloured berry saison fruit beer.

Smoked Porter (OG 1060, ABV 5.6%)
A full-flavoured porter with smoked beechwood and peaty notes.

South Face IPA (ABV 5.9%)

The Cone (OG 1058, ABV 6.8%)
An intensely hoppy IPA with lots of grapefruit notes.

Top Rope

Unit 14, Engineer Park, Babbage Road, Sandycroft, CH5 2QD ☎ 07581 483075 🌐 topropebrewing.com

Top Rope commenced brewing on a small scale in Merseyside in 2016 and expanded in 2018, moving to the former Deva Craft brewery in North East Wales. Output is mainly keg but some cask-conditioned beer is also produced, including some of the original Deva Craft range. ‼

TOPS (The Olde Potting Shed)

High Spen, NE39 2EQ

TOPS began brewing in 2013 using a five-barrel plant with a small test kit for experimental beers. Pubs are supplied direct within a 30-mile radius of the brewery.

Blondie (ABV 3.8%)

Topsham (NEW)

The Warehouse, Haven Road, Exeter, Devon, EX2 8GR

The Topsham-based owners started up the brewery in 2018 and moved to the current location at the end of the year using a 3.5-barrel plant. There is a taproom next to the brewery that is open four days a week (more in summer), and the beers are also available in the local free trade.

Ten (ABV 3.8%)
A light, floral ale with citrus, gooseberry and blackcurrant flavours.

Goat Walk (ABV 4.6%)

Session IPA with tropical fruit, citrus and pine flavours.

Mud Monster (ABV 5%)
A stout brewed with lactose and cacao nibs. Smooth with chocolate, coffee, caramel and vanilla flavours.

Ice Works (ABV 6%)
IPA featuring tropical fruit, citrus pine and peach flavours.

Torrside

New Mills Marina, Hibbert Street, New Mills, Derbyshire, SK22 3JJ
☎ (01663) 745219 ☎ 07539 149175
torrside.co.uk

Established by three friends in 2015, Torrside brews a wide range of beers on a 10-barrel plant, under the tagline Hops, Smoke, Monsters. A changing line-up of largely hop-driven, smoked and strong beers are sold to pubs, bars and bottle shops within a 50-mile radius. All beers are unfined. Brewery tap events usually take place one weekend each month (Apr-Sep) and there's a smoked beer festival in early November. !! RAIB

Candlewick (OG 1047, ABV 4%)

Mam Tor (OG 1039, ABV 4%)

Euro-Hop (ABV 4.5%)

West of the Sun (OG 1046, ABV 4.5%)

I am Curious Lemon (OG 1045, ABV 4.8%)

Franconia (OG 1051, ABV 5.2%)

I'm Spartacus (OG 1063, ABV 6.8%)

Totally Brewed

Units 8 & 9, Meadow Lane Fruit & Veg Market, Clarke Road, Nottingham, NG2 3JJ ☎ 07702 800639
totallybrewed.com

Totally Brewed began brewing in 2014 using a seven-barrel plant previously used at White Dog Brewery. A diverse range of hop-forward beers are produced. ♦

Guardian of the Forest (OG 1037, ABV 3.8%)

Slap in the Face (OG 1040, ABV 4%)
Golden-coloured ale with a citrus fruit hop aroma and taste and a dry bitter finish.

Crazy Like a Fox (OG 1045, ABV 4.5%)
Copper-coloured, malty best bitter with a caramel aroma and gentle bitter finish.

Papa Jangle's Voodoo Stout (OG 1046, ABV 4.5%)
Full-bodied, dark-coloured stout oozing complex malt tastes throughout.

Punch in the Face (OG 1047, ABV 4.8%)
Golden-coloured ale, assertive hop aroma leading to a grapefruit and malt taste with a hoppy bitter finish.

Four Hopmen of the Apocalypse (OG 1047, ABV 5.2%)
Immense, hugely-hopped, fruity golden ale, moderate bitterness with a lasting hoppy finish.

Captain Hopbeard (OG 1050, ABV 5.5%)
Amber-coloured ale with citrus hops aplenty and a strong bitter finish.

Totnes

59a High Street, Totnes, Devon, TQ9 5PB
☎ (01803) 849290 ☎ 07974 828971
richard.kidd@idnet.net.uk

Brewing began in 2014 at a family-run pub at the foot of Totnes Castle. The brewery is situated immediately behind the bar. An increase in the portfolio of the brewery has also meant a greater emphasis on keg and KeyKeg output. Beers are available almost exclusively at the pub. All ales are unfined and unfiltered. ♦V

Towcester Mill SIBA

The Mill, Chantry Lane, Towcester, Northamptonshire, NN12 6AD
☎ (01327) 437060 towcestermillbrewery.co.uk

A five-barrel brewery situated at the Grade II listed Old Mill in Towcester. There is a brewery tap on site and a shop off site at the Bell Plantation Garden Centre in Towcester. !! ♦

Crooked Hooker (OG 1038, ABV 3.8%)
Amber-coloured session ale with a satisfying bitter finish.

Mill Race (OG 1040, ABV 3.9%)
Blonde ale with a herbal and grapefruit finish.

Bell Ringer (OG 1044, ABV 4.4%)
Golden ale with subtle malt tones and orange and citrus hop notes.

Black Fire (OG 1050, ABV 5.2%)

Tower

Old Water Tower, Walsitch Maltings, Glensyl Way, Burton upon Trent, Staffordshire, DE14 1PZ
☎ (01283) 562888 ☎ 07771 926323
towerbrewery.co.uk

Tower was established in 2001 by John Mills, formerly a brewer at Burton Bridge, in a converted derelict water tower, originally built for Thomas Salt's Brewery in the 1870s. The conversion was given a Burton Civic Society award for the restoration of an industrial building. Tower has 20 regular outlets. !! ♦

Salt's Burton Ale (OG 1035, ABV 3.5%)

Bitter (OG 1042, ABV 4.2%)
Gold-coloured bitter with a malty, caramel and hoppy aroma. A full hop and fruit taste with the fruit lingering. A bitter and astringent finish.

Gone for a Burton (OG 1046, ABV 4.6%)
An amber-coloured beer with a malty and hoppy aroma.

Imperial IPA (OG 1050, ABV 5%)
A premium IPA, light golden in colour, with a rich, citrus fruity flavour and floral hop aroma.

Townes

Speedwell Inn, Lowgates, Staveley, Derbyshire, S43 3TT
☎ (01246) 472252

Townes Brewery, which started in 1994, has been situated in the rear of the Speedwell Inn at Staveley since 1997. After the retirement of brewer Alan Wood in 2013, Lawrie and Nicoleta Evans have continued brewing to the same recipes on the five-barrel plant. Beers are rarely found outside the Speedwell Inn, other than occasional swaps and beer festivals. ♦

Townhouse

Units 1-4, Townhouse Studios, Townhouse Farm, Alsager Road, Audley, Staffordshire, ST7 8JQ ☎ 07976 209437 ✉ j.nixon2@btinternet.com

Townhouse was set up in 2002 with a 2.5-barrel plant. In 2004 the brewery scaled up to five barrels and in 2006 two further fermenting vessels were added. Bottling is planned. ♦

Enigma (OG 1035, ABV 3.5%)

Styrian Pale (OG 1035, ABV 3.5%)

Rye Pale Ale (OG 1035, ABV 3.6%)

Flowerdew (OG 1039, ABV 4%)
Golden in colour with a floral aroma. Flavours of flowery hops delivering a crisp, hoppy bite and presenting a lingering taste of flowery citrus waves.

Meridian Mild (OG 1039, ABV 4%)

Barney's Stout (OG 1043, ABV 4.5%)
Roast chocolate and toffee nose atop this black-coloured stout. Sweet to start becoming bitter at the end, with velvety roast throughout.

Armstrong Ale (OG 1045, ABV 4.8%)
A rich, fruity, ruby-coloured beer with a hoppy, dry finish.

Gladstone Strong Ale (OG 1048, ABV 5%)

Track

5 Sheffield Street, Manchester, M1 2ND ☎ (0161) 273 4832 ☎ 07725 692096 🌐 trackbrewing.co

Track Brewing Co was established in 2014 and is based in a railway arch underneath Manchester's Piccadilly railway station. Since its inception the brewery has expanded considerably in size and now produces a wide variety of beer styles. A taproom opened in nearby Crusader Mill in 2018 (Thu-Sun). ‼ V

Sonoma (OG 1040, ABV 3.8%)
Prominent fruit hop aroma. Balanced sweet, fruity taste. Moderate bitterness at first with punchy citrus hop after. Unfined.

Tractor Shed SIBA

Tractor Shed, Calva Brow, Workington, Cumbria, CA14 1DB ☎ (01900) 68860 🌐 tractor-shed.co.uk

Renamed from Mitchell Krause in 2014 and having previously had its beers brewed under contract, brewing started in an old tractor shed on the family farm in 2013. After initially focusing on bottled and kegged continental-style beers, the first cask-conditioned beer was produced in 2014. The brewery contract brews various beers for Shindigger (qv), mostly for bottle and keg. ‼ RAIB

Clocker Stout (OG 1043, ABV 4%)

Traffic Street Specials

See Castle Rock

Traquair House SIBA

Traquair House, Innerleithen, EH44 6PW ☎ (01896) 830323 🌐 traquair.co.uk/traquair-house-brewery

The 18th century brewhouse is based in one of the wings of the 1,000-year-old Traquair House, Scotland's oldest inhabited house. All the beers are oak-fermented and 60% of production is exported. ‼ ♦

Bear Ale (OG 1050, ABV 5%)
Malty aroma and a complex taste of malts, citrus fruit, sweetness and bitterness, all lasting into the aftertaste.

Treboom SIBA

Millstone Yard, Main Street, Shipton-by-Beningbrough, North Yorkshire, YO30 1AA ☎ (01904) 471569 ☎ 07761 608662 🌐 treboom.co.uk

Established in 2011 this 10-barrel plant brews using water from its own borehole, whole hops and locally malted barley. Its award-winning beers are distributed throughout Yorkshire. ‼ ♦ RAIB

Tambourine Man (OG 1038.5, ABV 3.9%)
A deep golden-coloured ale with a hint of maltiness complemented by fruity hop flavours.

Yorkshire Sparkle (OG 1039, ABV 4%)
A pale ale with a fresh citrus taste.

Kettle Drum (OG 1042, ABV 4.3%)
Copper-coloured ale with a distinct fruitiness and robust hop flavours leading to a clean finish.

Hop Britannia (OG 1047.5, ABV 5%)
A hoppy, strong pale ale, honey in colour with intense citrus fruit and spice notes.

Myricale (OG 1047.5, ABV 5%)
A golden-coloured wheat beer brewed with bog myrtle.

Baron Saturday (OG 1049, ABV 5.2%)
A strong, dark-coloured porter with flavours of coffee and liquorice.

Treen's

Unit 3, Viaduct Works, Frog Hill, Ponsanooth, Cornwall, TR3 7JW ☎ 07552 218788

Office: 18 St. Michael's Road, Ponsanooth, Cornwall, TR3 7EA 🌐 treensbrewery.co.uk

This family-run brewery was founded in 2016, initially using spare capacity at other local breweries. It now has its own premises using a 12-barrel plant. Bottling was introduced in 2018. Expansion is planned. ♦

Essential (ABV 3.8%)
Robustly bitter, gold-coloured beer with grassy, resinous hops and light malt flavours. Citrus and stone fruit notes. Long, bitter finish.

Classic (ABV 4.3%)
Tawny-coloured bitter with a malt aroma. Robust malt balanced by spicy hop bitterness. Coffee, molasses with light citrus and stone fruit.

Sunbeam (ABV 4.8%)
Smooth, golden-coloured beer. Refreshing spicy hop and malt flavours with hints of citrus and toffee. Pronounced bitterness. Long, bitter finish.

Resolve (ABV 5.2%)

Black-coloured stout with a dark chocolate aroma. Dominant smoky coffee, bitter chocolate, molasses flavours with malt and stone fruit. Dry finish.

Tremethick

Grampound, Cornwall, TR2 4QY ☎ 07726 427775
tremethick.co.uk

Tremethick began brewing in 2015. Having brewed in small batches in a garage or using spare capacity at other breweries, a new building was completed and 5.5-barrel plant commissioned in 2016. Regular brewery open evenings are held. !! RAIB

Pale Ale (OG 1043, ABV 4.3%) ◆
Yellow-coloured golden ale with aromas of cider and sherbet. Refreshing grassy citrus hops, bitterness and apple fruit. Lemon grainy aftertaste.

Dark Ale (ABV 4.6%) ◆
Dark brown-coloured strong mild. Nutty malt with vine fruit flavours. Quite sweet with hints of coffee roast. Faintly bitter and hoppy.

Red IPA (ABV 4.6%) ◆
Auburn in colour. Malt balanced by firm pine and gentle citrus hops. Spicy notes. Bitter throughout and a kaleidoscope of fruits.

Tring SIBA

Dunsley Farm, London Road, Tring, Hertfordshire, HP23 6HA
☎ (01442) 890721 tringbrewery.co.uk

Founded in 1992, Tring Brewery moved to its present site in 2010. It brews more than 130 barrels a week, producing an extensive core range of beers augmented by monthly and seasonal specials, most taking their names from local myths and legends. !! ◆ RAIB

Side Pocket for a Toad (OG 1035, ABV 3.6%)
A straw-coloured ale with citrus notes, a floral aroma and a crisp, dry finish.

Brock Bitter (OG 1036, ABV 3.7%)
A mid-brown-coloured ale with a hint of sweetness and caramel.

Mansion Mild (OG 1036, ABV 3.7%)
Smooth and creamy dark ruby mild with a fruity palate and gentle late hop.

Citra Session (OG 1039, ABV 3.9%)

Drop Bar Pale Ale (OG 1039, ABV 4%)
A dry-hopped pale ale with a biscuit malt base and citrus aroma.

Ridgeway (OG 1039, ABV 4%)
Balanced malt and hop flavours with a dry, flowery hop aftertaste.

Moongazing (OG 1042, ABV 4.2%)
Amber/red-coloured ale with a rounded bitterness and hoppy aftertaste.

Pale Four (OG 1048, ABV 4.6%)

Tea Kettle Stout (OG 1047, ABV 4.7%)
Rich, complex traditional stout with a hint of liquorice and moderate bitterness.

Colley's Dog (OG 1051, ABV 5.2%)
A dark-coloured ale with a long, dry finish and overtones of malt and walnuts.

Death or Glory (OG 1074, ABV 7.2%)
A strong, dark-coloured, aromatic barley wine.

Trinity SIBA

5 Church Road, Gisleham, Suffolk, NR33 8DS
☎ (01502) 743121 ✉ graham@trinityales.co.uk

Trinity Ales was launched in 2009 using a four-barrel plant. It uses pure spring water from its own ancient well along with locally-sourced ingredients. Pubs, restaurants, retail outlets and festivals are supplied throughout Suffolk and beyond. RAIB

Wishing Well (OG 1039, ABV 3.8%)

High Light (OG 1040, ABV 4%)

Black Street Smithy (OG 1045, ABV 4.5%)

Gisleham Gold (OG 1045, ABV 4.5%)

Gold (OG 1045, ABV 4.5%)

Triple fff SIBA

Magpie Works, Station Approach, Four Marks, Hampshire, GU34 5HN
☎ (01420) 561422 triplefff.com

Established in 1997 close to a stop on the Watercress Line, the brewery and all the beers except Alton's Pride are named following a musical theme. The fff refers to fortissimo, meaning louder or stronger. Brewing on a 50-barrel plant since 2006, multiple CAMRA awards have been won. Two pubs are owned: the Railway Arms, Alton, and the White Lion, Aldershot. !! ◆ RAIB

Alton's Pride (OG 1039, ABV 3.8%) ◆
Full-bodied session biter. An initially malty flavour fades as citrus notes and hoppiness take over, leading to a lasting hoppy/bitter finish.

Pressed Rat & Warthog (OG 1039, ABV 3.8%) ◆
Toffee aroma with hints of blackcurrant and chocolate lead to a well-balanced flavour with roast, fruit and malt vying with the hoppy bitterness.

Moondance (OG 1042, ABV 4.2%) ◆
An aromatic citrus hop nose, balanced by bitterness and sweetness in the mouth. Bitterness increases in the finish as fruit declines.

Triple Point (NEW)

178 Shoreham Street, Sheffield, South Yorkshire, S1 4SQ ☎ 07828 131423 triplepointbrewing.co.uk

Father and son operated modern brewery and bar conversion of what was formerly a carpet showroom. The brewery is clearly visible from the drinking area, which operates as the taproom for the brewery (open Thu-Sat). Convenient for Bramall Lane football ground. !!

S IPA (ABV 4.5%)
Citrus flavours with grapefruit and lemon undertones and a hint of mandarin and mango.

Debut (ABV 5.5%)
Thirst-quenching, smooth, American-style IPA.

Triumph (NEW)

39 Hawthorn Lane, Tile Hill, Coventry, CV4 9LB
☎ 07903 131512 ✉ triumphbrewing@aol.com

Triumph is a nanobrewery offering brew days to the public who want to try homebrewing with professional standard equipment.

THE BREWERIES

True North SIBA

47 Eldon Street, Sheffield, South Yorkshire, S1 4GY
☎ (0114) 272 0569

Office: 127-129 Devonshire Street, Sheffield, S3 7SB
🌐 truenorthbrewco.uk

True North began brewing in 2012 using spare capacity at Welbeck Abbey Brewery (qv). It opened its own plant in Sheffield in 2016. Dean Hollingworth is head brewer, supplying 11 pubs owned by the company plus other independent outlets. ♦

Best Bitter (ABV 3.8%)
A malty, sweet, traditional brown-coloured ale, balanced with spicy hop flavours.

Blonde Pale Ale (ABV 4%)
An easy-drinking golden ale with smooth vanilla and floral flavours.

Polaris Pale Ale (ABV 4.3%)
A smooth, golden-coloured beer with a juicy, fruity and pine character. Restrained bitterness and malt character balances the hops.

Truman's SIBA

The Eyrie, 2 & 3 Stour Road, Hackney Wick, London, E3 2NT
☎ (020) 8533 3575 🌐 trumansbeer.co.uk

From 1665 to 1989 Truman's produced one of the capital's most famous beers. Revived in 2013, it is just a stroll down the Roman Road from its original site. The original Truman's yeast, recovered from the National Collection of Yeast Cultures, is used. In 2020 it will relocate to a new 50,000 sq ft site in Walthamstow. ♦RAIB

Swift (OG 1040.5, ABV 3.9%) ◆
Well-balanced, golden-coloured bitter with hops and a trace of grapefruit on the nose and palate and a bitter finish.

Runner (OG 1040, ABV 4%) ◆
Traditional brown-coloured best bitter with a spicy, hoppy aroma and flavour fading in the dry aftertaste. Some marmalade fruity notes.

Lazarus (OG 1043, ABV 4.2%) ◆
Well-balanced, pale golden-coloured ale with a peaches and straw aroma, refreshing grassy and citrus flavour, continuing into the short finish.

Zephyr (OG 1044, ABV 4.4%) ◆
Pale brown-coloured, smooth beer with a slightly dry roasted character on palate and a bitter finish. Touch of orange and hops.

Roller IPA (OG 1010, ABV 5.1%)
A clean, refreshing ale with some caramel sweetness in the aftertaste.

Truth Hurts

c/o MSS City Mills, Peel Street, Morley, Leeds, West Yorkshire, LS27 8QL
☎ (0113) 238 0382 ☎ 07950 567341
🌐 truthhurts.co.uk

⊛Established in 2016 as Blue Square Brewery. It produces one-off brews from its four-barrel plant in a split level building that is part of a mill complex. 🛒

Tryst

Lorne Road, Larbert, FK5 4AT
☎ (01324) 554000 🌐 trystbrewery.co.uk

Tryst started production in 2003. A large range of beers is produced. !! 🛒 ♦RAIB

Brockville Pale (OG 1039, ABV 3.9%)
A pale golden-coloured session ale, smooth on the palate.

Hop Trial (OG 1040, ABV 3.9%)

Carronade Pale Ale (OG 1043, ABV 4.2%) 🍺
A pale ale bursting with citrus flavours.

Drovers 80/- (OG 1044, ABV 4.3%)

Double Chocolate Porter (OG 1044, ABV 4.4%)

Sherpa Porter (OG 1044, ABV 4.4%)

German Hops Pils (OG 1045, ABV 4.5%)

VIP (OG 1046, ABV 4.5%)
Light brown-coloured best bitter with a deep hop taste and floral aroma.

RAJ IPA (OG 1055, ABV 5.5%)
An English-hopped IPA with balanced flavours and a hoppy aroma and palate.

Tudor SIBA

Unit A, Llanhilleth Industrial Estate, Llanhilleth, NP13 2RX
☎ (01495) 214808 ☎ 07971 015844
🌐 tudorbrewery.co.uk

⊛Tudor is a family-run, four-barrel plant that began brewing in 2007 in Abergavenny before moving in 2012 to Llanilleth. Several local pubs are supplied, in addition to others further afield. RAIB

Blorenge (OG 1038, ABV 3.8%)
A session pale ale with fresh citrus undertones.

Black Mountain Stout (OG 1039, ABV 4%)

IPA (OG 1039, ABV 4%)
A classic IPA with a sharp, hoppy, grapefruit finish.

Skirrid (OG 1040, ABV 4.2%)
A full-bodied, dark-coloured beer with hoppy flavours.

Sugarloaf (OG 1044, ABV 4.7%)
A rounded, full-bodied ale with smooth caramel undertones.

Winter Cheer (OG 1046, ABV 5%)
A dark-coloured ale infused with ground ginger, lemon rind, honey, cinnamon and nutmeg.

Black Rock (OG 1050, ABV 5.6%)
A dark-coloured ale with a rich aroma and smooth chocolate/coffee aftertaste.

Tunnel SIBA

Correspondence: Red House Farm, Nuneaton Road, Ansley, Nuneaton, Warwickshire, CV10 0QU ☎ 07765 223110 🌐 tunnelbrewery.co.uk

Beers are brewed at various breweries under the Tunnel and Battlefield Brewery brand names. ♦RAIB

Percheron (OG 1037, ABV 3.7%)
A refreshing, golden-coloured ale with citrus notes.

Late Ott (OG 1040, ABV 4%)
An amber-coloured session bitter with a fruity, citrus aroma and bitter finish.

Trade Winds (OG 1045, ABV 4.6%)
A bright gold-coloured IPA with a refreshing, clean, crisp finish.

Shadow Weaver (OG 1046, ABV 4.7%)
Deep red-coloured beer. Chocolate and coffee give way to a mellow fruit finish.

Nelson's Column (OG 1051, ABV 5.2%)
A ruby red-coloured ale. A complex blend of fruit, malt and hops.

East India Pale Ale (OG 1056, ABV 5.6%)
Copper-coloured, full-bodied ale with a robust hit of hops and a caramel/toffee finish.

Brewed under the Battlefield Brewery name:

Let Battle Commence (OG 1041, ABV 4%)
Amber-coloured bitter with well-balanced malt and hops.

Richard III (OG 1042, ABV 4%)
A pale ale with a sweet start and dry finish.

Henry Tudor (OG 1050, ABV 5%)
A chestnut-coloured ale with a fruit and malt nose and a mellow hop finish.

Turning Point

34 Dove Way, Kirkby Mills Industrial Estate, Kirkbymoorside, North Yorkshire, YO62 6QR
☎ (01751) 431132 🌐 turningpointbrewco.com

Two friends, Cameron Brown and Aron McMahon, began brewing in 2017 on a 12-barrel plant, utilising the water from a well beneath the brewery. All beers are unfined and unfiltered.

Lucid Dream (ABV 5%)
Cookie cream stout with a smooth mouthfeel and body. Cacao nibs, chocolate and a touch of vanilla are added to give a unique taste.

Disco King (ABV 5.1%)
A pale ale with strong hop flavours on a clean malt base.

Turnstone

20 West Cliff, Whitstable, Kent, CT5 1DN ☎ 07807 262662 ✉ turnstoneales@outlook.com

⊗ Turnstone Ales is a small, home-based brewery set up in 2014. It has a regular stall at the Best of Faversham market (1st and 3rd Saturdays). Beers are supplied to a few local pubs and shops in Whitstable, Tankerton, Faversham and Canterbury.
RAIB V

Turpin

Turpins Lodge, Lodge Farm, Tadmarton Heath Road, Hook Norton, Oxfordshire, OX15 5DQ
☎ (01608) 737033
✉ turpinbrewery@btconnect.com

⊗ Brewing started in 2013. A number of local pubs are supplied regularly, as well as a few pubs further afield in Rugby and Birmingham. ♦

Golden Citrus (OG 1042, ABV 4.2%)
A bright golden-coloured beer with a pronounced citrus character and a strong, lasting, bitter hop finish.

Turpin's SIBA

Unit 13b, Sawston Trade Park, London Road, Pampisford, Cambridgeshire, CB22 3EE
☎ (01223) 833883 🌐 turpinsbrewery.co.uk

Turpin's is a vibrant, modern brewery based in Pampisford, near Cambridge, established in 2015 and brewing a wide variety of beers. Open days are planned. ♦

Dragon's Den (ABV 3.9%)
Light amber-coloured ale with a citrus and blueberry aroma, tropical fruit and pine with citrus flavours and a dry hoppy finish.

Single Hop Range (ABV 3.9%)
Each brew uses a single British hop to highlight its unique flavours and aromas.

Meditation (ABV 4.3%)
A pale ale with blackcurrant, grapefruit and tropical fruit flavours, complex bitter taste and hints of apricot, herbs and punchy floral notes.

Towen & Gown (ABV 4.5%)
Balanced malt profile highlighting biscuit and caramel notes, medium-bodied with hints of orange, marmalade and citrus.

Cambridge Black (ABV 4.6%)
A refreshing beer with a combination of coffee, cocoa and dark chocolate flavours.

NAPA (ABV 5%)
Hazy and creamy American-style pale ale with pine, tropical fruit and grapefruit flavours, a gentle malt background and assertive bitterness.

Tweed

Unit 1c, Grey Street, Denton, M34 3RU
☎ (0161) 336 9200 🌐 tweedbrewing.com

Tweed began brewing in 2014 and expanded to bottle production in 2015. Beers are available in Manchester, particularly the Northern Quarter. Its micropub opened in 2017 in Hyde town centre and serves as the brewery tap. The brewery relocated to Denton in 2018 and now occupies the site of the former Hornbeam/Epicurus Brewery. ♦

Sorachi (ABV 3.7%)

Pale Ale (ABV 3.8%)
A straw-coloured pale ale with delicate pine and cedar notes and a sweet honey finish.

Hopster (ABV 3.9%)
Pale golden in colour, this single-hopped, pineapple-infused pale ale delivers citrus flavour with a rounded body.

Orange County IPA (ABV 4.3%)
Well-balanced ale brewed with sweet oranges.

Black Shire Stout (ABV 4.5%)
Robust stout with smooth coffee, chocolate and sweet liquorice notes.

Twice Brewed SIBA

Twice Brewed Inn, Bardon Mill, NE47 7AN
☎ (01434) 344534 🌐 twicebrewedinn.co.uk

Brewing commenced on a five-barrel plant in 2017. Due to the close proximity of Hadrian's Wall, beer names have a Roman theme. Beers are available at the Twice Brewed Inn as well as other outlets. ♦

Best Bitter (ABV 3.8%)

A traditional best bitter, deep copper in colour with a rich, fruity aroma. Hints of tangerine and blackcurrant are balanced by a rich, malty sweetness.

Sycamore Gap (ABV 4.1%)
A light and refreshing pale ale with punchy citrus hop flavours.

Ale Caesar (ABV 4.2%)
An American-style, amber-coloured ale with toasted malt and toffee flavours combined with a spiced warmth and citrus notes.

Steel Rigg (ABV 4.9%)
A rich, full-bodied porter with an aroma of dried fruit and molasses and a complex malt character.

Vindolanda Excavation IPA (ABV 5.3%)
A golden-coloured IPA with light floral and citrus aromas and just a hint of spiciness.

Twickenham SIBA

Unit 6, 18 Mereway Road, Twickenham, TW2 6RG
☎ (020) 8241 1825 🌐 twickenham-fine-ales.co.uk

⊗ Established in 2004, Twickenham Fine Ales is London's oldest microbrewery. Operating a 25-barrel plant, it is the first brewery in Twickenham since the 1920s. It opens on match days for the rugby fans going to the nearby stadium. ‼ ♦

Grandstand Bitter (OG 1038, ABV 3.8%)
Pale brown-coloured beer with peach, citrus and malt on the palate, fading in the bitter, slightly dry finish.

Redhead (OG 1041, ABV 4.1%)
A creamy, chestnut brown-coloured best bitter with interesting sweet caramel hints and a mild, short, roasted bitter finish.

Naked Ladies (OG 1044, ABV 4.4%)
Refreshing dark golden-coloured ale with a touch of spicy hop in the flavour but fruit dominates with a lasting bitterness.

Twin Taff

5 John Street, Merthyr Tydfil, CF47 0AW ☎ 07564 187945 ✉ twintaffbrewery@outlook.com

Twin Taff was established in 2018 by twin brothers Darryl and Daniel Williams. It is Merthyr Tydfil's first town centre microbrewery. A brewpub opened in 2019.

Penydarren Mild (OG 1039, ABV 3.8%)
A malty mild with a clean finish.

Iron King Pale (OG 1040, ABV 4%)

Cyfarthfa Bitter (OG 1042, ABV 4.2%)

Twisted SIBA

Unit 8, Commerce Business Centre, Commerce Close, Westbury, Wiltshire, BA13 4LS
☎ (01373) 864441 🌐 twisted-brewing.com

⊗ Twisted began brewing in 2014. It is an independent brewery producing traditional ales with a modern twist. ♦

Three & Sixpence (OG 1036, ABV 3.6%)
A session pale ale dominated by American hops.

Rider (OG 1041, ABV 4%)
A triple-hopped, amber-coloured ale balanced with biscuit malt flavours.

Pirate (OG 1043, ABV 4.2%)
A classic, copper-coloured best bitter with aromas of roasted malt and coffee. Undertones of nutty fruit cake.

Urban Legend (OG 1045, ABV 4.3%)
A dark golden-coloured beer with a fruity aroma and palate.

Gaucho (OG 1048, ABV 4.6%)
Ruby-coloured ale with aromas of soft fruits, coffee and a hint of chocolate. A long-lasting finish.

Twisted Barrel

Unit 11, Fargo Village, Far Gosford Street, Coventry, CV1 5ED
☎ (024) 7610 1701 🌐 twistedbarrelale.co.uk

⊗ Commencing commercial production as a picobrewery in 2013, Twisted Barrel expanded to a six-barrel brewery and moved to Fargo Village in 2015 with an on-site taphouse open at weekends. Continued growth resulted in another move to larger premises on the same site in 2017 and increased opening hours. The brewery hosts a vibrant homebrew club. Beers are distributed throughout the UK and exported to Mainland Europe and further afield. ‼ ♦ RAIB V

Beast of a Midlands Mild (OG 1044, ABV 3.5%)
A traditional dark mild brewed with vanilla pods for a complex, nutty, roasted chocolate body.

The Great Went (ABV 4%)
A German-style Hefeweizen with a hint of orange.

Detroit Sour City (ABV 4.5%)
A dry, refreshing Berliner Weisse-style sour beer with a lemon sherbet character and juicy, mango flavour.

God's Twisted Sister (OG 1050, ABV 4.5%)
A smooth, roasted oatmeal stout with coffee and liquorice notes.

Inspired (OG 1046, ABV 4.5%)

Sine Qua Non (OG 1046, ABV 4.5%)
A well-balanced, West Coast-style session IPA with a complex malt base and citrus and pine hop profile.

The Morgul Path (ABV 4.5%)

Naido (ABV 5%)
A modern pale ale with low bitterness and notes of mango, grapefruit and tangerine.

Saison From Another Place (ABV 5.5%)

Twisted Oak SIBA

Yeowood Farm, Iwood Lane, Wrington, BS40 5NU
☎ (01934) 310515 🌐 twistedoakbrewery.co.uk

⊗ Twisted Oak began brewing in 2012 using a five-barrel plant, crafting small batches of unique ales. It is situated in a former agricultural building on a working farm in the North Somerset countryside. One pub is owned, the Fallen Tree, Clevedon. Beer is available in several local outlets. ♦ RAIB

Fallen Tree (OG 1038, ABV 3.8%)
Bittersweet session bitter. Aroma and flavour of hops and ripe fruit. Complex and satisfying bitter astringent finish.

Crack Gold (OG 1039, ABV 4%)

Balanced golden ale. Hints of honey on the nose, flavours of malt biscuit and hops, and a short hoppy ending.

Wild Wood (OG 1041, ABV 4%) ◆
Little aroma. Smooth, with flavours of hops and fruit and a little malt. Minimal aftertaste.

Crack Hops (OG 1040, ABV 4.2%) ◆
Hops on the nose, pale malt with fruity orange and grapefruit hints on the palate leaving a balanced, bittersweet aftertaste.

Junction Lock IPA (OG 1039, ABV 4.2%)

Old Barn (OG 1044, ABV 4.5%) ◆
Fruity red-coloured ale. Well-balanced flavour with a long bitter finish.

Spun Gold (OG 1043, ABV 4.5%) ◆
Classic golden ale with a soft mouthfeel. Spicy notes to the fruity malt aroma and flavour. Hops in the aroma develop into a bitter finish.

Leveret (OG 1043, ABV 4.6%) ◆
Amber-coloured best bitter with a light hop aroma. Initial pale malt flavours combine with hoppy bitterness that continues into the aftertaste

Sheriff Fatman (OG 1048, ABV 5%) ◆
Amber-coloured ale with hops dominant on both the nose and the slightly citrus palate, also in the bitter finish.

Slippery Slope (OG 1054, ABV 5.3%)

Two by Two

Unit 28, Point Pleasant Industrial Estate, Wallsend, NE28 6HA ☎ 07723 959168

Office: 14 Albany Gardens, Whitley Bay, NE26 2DY
✉ twobytwobrewing@gmail.com

Brewing began in 2014 using a five-barrel plant in Wallsend on Tyneside. At the end of 2018 an additional five-barrel plant was installed, increasing capacity to 10 barrels. RAIB

Session IPA (OG 1040, ABV 4%)
A light, zesty ale with a tropical aroma.

Leap Frog (OG 1041, ABV 4.1%)

Foxtrot Pale (OG 1045, ABV 4.5%)
A hoppy, pale-coloured and juicy beer with a big citrus hit.

Snake Eyes Pale (OG 1046, ABV 4.6%)
A single-hopped pale ale with a fruity tropical hop character.

Dragonfly (OG 1055, ABV 5.5%)
A pale ale, light and bitter with a fruity character.

Sitting Duck (OG 1057, ABV 5.7%)

American Pale Ale (OG 1058, ABV 5.8%)
A light, zesty, American-style pale ale with a citrus pine hop character.

South Paw IPA (OG 1062, ABV 6.2%)
A light, bitter IPA with a tropical fruit character.

Two Cocks

Church Lane, Enborne, Berkshire, RG20 0HB
☎ (01635) 37777 ☎ 07831 201533
🌐 twococksbrewery.com

⊗ The brewery was established in 2011 after wild hops were found growing in the farm's hedgerows. A 180-feet deep borehole supplies water for the brewery. During the English Civil War, the first Battle of Newbury (1643) was fought on the surrounding land and most of the beer names refer to it in some way.

Diamond Lil' (OG 1035, ABV 3.2%)
A light and fruity golden ale.

1643 Cavalier (OG 1039, ABV 3.8%)

1643 Leveller (OG 1040, ABV 3.8%)
A malty session bitter.

1643 Roundhead (OG 1042, ABV 4.2%)

1643 Puritan (OG 1049, ABV 4.5%)
A dark-coloured stout with notes of caramel and chocolate.

1643 Viscount (OG 1054, ABV 5.6%)
An unusually fruity strong beer.

Two Drifters

Unit 5, Skyways Business Park, Fair Oak Close, Exeter Airport, Exeter, Devon, EX5 2UL
☎ (01392) 445151 🌐 twodriftersbrewery.com

Husband and wife team Gemma and Russ produced their first beers from their Swansea premises, but have now set up a 10-barrel brewery in Exeter, which began production in 2019. A rum distillery is also on site. RAIB V

Two Finches

Finchley Cricket Club, 1 Arden Cottages, 33-45 East End Road, Finchley, London, N3 2TA
🌐 twofinchesbrewery.co.uk

Brewing began in 2015 on a small kit in the shed beside the clubhouse. The bottled beers are available at the bar (open to the public). No real ale.

Two Rivers SIBA

2 Sluice Bank, Denver, Norfolk, PE38 0EQ
☎ (01366) 858365 ☎ 07518 099868
🌐 denverbrewery.co.uk

Two Rivers was established in 2012 by John Nash. Bottled-conditioned ale has been available since the establishment of the brewery and cask ales have been produced since 2013. !! ♦ RAIB

Miners Mild (OG 1032, ABV 3.1%)
Easy-drinking, tawny-coloured mild with good malt character, light finish and chocolate notes.

Hares Hopping (OG 1041, ABV 4.1%)
Refreshing, clean-flavoured ale with a distinctive late bitterness and a dry finish.

Kiwi Kick (ABV 4.1%)
A golden-coloured bitter with a pleasant hop aroma and zesty hop finish.

Denver Diamond (OG 1047, ABV 4.4%)
A full-bodied, well-rounded ale with a malty, bitter taste and grassy, slightly floral aromatic character.

Porters Pride (OG 1050, ABV 5%)
A rich porter with a slight sweetness cutting through the smooth malt. Coffee and chocolate aromas and taste, with a liquorice and vanilla finish.

Norfolk Stoat (OG 1050, ABV 5.8%)
A full-bodied, silky oatmeal stout with a subtle burnt edge.

Two Thirsty Men SIBA

74 High Street, Grantown-on-Spey, PH26 3EL
☎ (01479) 872246 🌐 twothirstymen.com

Brewing began in 2016 in a garage at the back of a café bar.

Spey IPA (ABV 3.5%) ◈
Malt and hops with a slight citrus taste and a dry finish.

Angus Pale Ale (ABV 4%) ◈
Well-balanced bitter with a good mix of lemon and malt.

No. 74 (ABV 4.5%) ◈
Malty, red-coloured, fruited bittersweet brew.

Two Tone

Tor View, Hayes Cross, Shebbear, Devon, EX21 5SW
☎ 07450 745338

Home-based nanobrewery run by Gary Seaton, an ex Coventrian, hence the Two Tone record label connection, and Paul Scantlebury, originally from Bristol. Bottle-conditioned beer is produced in small batches. ♦ RAIB V

Two Towers SIBA

29 Shadwell Street, Birmingham, B4 6HB
☎ (0121) 439 3738 ☎ 07795 247059
🌐 twotowersbrewery.co.uk

⊗ Established in 2010, the 10-barrel brewery moved to its current location behind its taphouse, the Gunmakers Arms, in 2016 and is visible from the beer garden. The brewery also undertakes bespoke brewing for special events, mainly local in nature. ‼ 🛒 ♦ RAIB V

Baskerville Bitter (OG 1038, ABV 3.8%)
Full-bodied bitter with a blend of hops, providing a complex but well balanced ale.

Hockley Gold (OG 1041, ABV 4.1%)
A bitter with a fruity aroma and distinctive hoppy characteristics.

Complete Muppetry (OG 1043, ABV 4.3%)
An aromatic beer with powerful hop characteristics. Well-balanced with citrus, fruity notes.

Chamberlain Pale Ale (OG 1042, ABV 4.5%)
A crisp, light ale loaded with grapefruit flavours with a long, hoppy finish.

Peaky Blinders Mild (ABV 4.5%)

Jewellery Porter (OG 1049, ABV 5%)
A full-bodied stout with a thick and slightly chocolate texture underlined with hops.

Two Tribes SIBA

Tileyard Studios, Tileyard Road, King's Cross, London, N7 9AH
☎ (020) 3955 6782 🌐 twotribesbrewing.com

Two Tribes, formerly of Horsham, has moved into its new home in King's Cross using a 10-hectolitre brew kit. An on-site taproom is open daily. No real ale.

Twt Lol SIBA

Unit B27, Trefforest Industrial Estate, Pontypridd, CF37 5YB ☎ 07966 467295 🌐 twtlol.com

Established in 2015 using a 10-barrel plant, the brewery has a capacity of 80 firkins a week, with the potential to expand to 160. All of its branding is produced in both Welsh and English. The brewery is open the first weekend of each month. ‼ 🛒 ♦

Bwgan Brain / Scarecrow (OG 1034, ABV 3.5%)
A light amber-coloured beer with a mellow flavour. Peppery and hoppy with pine and mango notes.

Cuwch Goch Goata / Little Red Cow (OG 1036, ABV 3.7%)
An American-style red-coloured ale. Fruity, crisp and rich.

Glog (OG 1043, ABV 4%)
Smooth, malty and refreshing, copper-coloured ale.

Twti Ffrwti (OG 1040, ABV 4%)
A light, bitter, fruity ale with mango and grapefruit hop notes.

Cwrw'r Afr Serchog / Horny Goat Ale (OG 1039, ABV 4.2%)
A golden ale with pine and citrus flavours. A hint of Horny Goat Weed is also used in the brew.

Lol (ABV 4.4%)
A smooth golden ale with spicy hop flavours.

Glo in the Dark (OG 1045, ABV 4.5%)
A dark-coloured beer with crisp, fresh, hoppy notes.

Blwbri (OG 1042, ABV 4.6%)
A blonde, hoppy beer brewed with a small amount of blueberries.

Pewin Ynfytyn / Crazy Peacock (OG 1045, ABV 4.8%)
A powerful, earthy, American-style IPA with strong hoppy flavours.

Pyncio Pioden IPA / Pretty Fly for a Magpie (OG 1048, ABV 5%)
A dry-hopped IPA with hints of oat to soften the bitterness.

Dreigiau'r Diafol / Diablo Dragons (OG 1050, ABV 5.5%)

Tydd Steam SIBA

Manor Barn, Kirkgate, Tydd Saint Giles, Cambridgeshire, PE13 5NE
☎ (01945) 871020 ☎ 07932 726552
🌐 tyddsteam.co.uk

⊗ Established in 2007 in a converted agricultural barn, the brewery is named after two farm steam engines. A 15-barrel plant was installed in 2011. Around 70 outlets are supplied direct. ‼ ♦ RAIB

Barn Ale (OG 1038, ABV 3.9%) ◈
A golden-coloured bitter that has good biscuity malt aroma and flavour, balanced by spicy hops. Long, dry, fairly astringent finish.

Scoundrel (OG 1040, ABV 4%) ◈
A dry, pale amber-coloured bitter with a gentle malty and hoppy aroma with a sulphur edge, plenty of hop bitterness with fruity hints in the taste and a persistent dry aftertaste.

Piston Bob (OG 1044, ABV 4.6%) ◈
Malt and faint hops on the aroma progress through to a malty flavour complemented by a balance of hops and fruit. A long, dry finish rounds off this amber-coloured strong bitter.

Tyne Bank SIBA

375 Walker Road, Newcastle upon Tyne, NE6 2AB
☎ (0191) 262 2828 ☎ 07989 426604
tynebankbrewery.co.uk

Tyne Bank began brewing in 2011. It moved and expanded in 2016 due to a successful crowdfunding initiative. It features an on-site brewery tap. The SMaSH (Single Malt and Single Hop) series of ales is now available. ‼ ♦

Single Blonde (OG 1037, ABV 3.5%)
Light ale with a slightly dry bitterness and hints of vanilla.

EPA (OG 1040, ABV 3.8%)

Summer Breeze (OG 1040, ABV 3.9%)

West Coast IPA (OG 1040, ABV 4%)
A pale ale with a light citrus character.

Monument Bitter (OG 1041, ABV 4.1%)
Smooth, well-balanced bitter with a berry fruit character.

80 Degrees North (OG 1046, ABV 4.5%)
Rich, malty character with dry finish.

Northern Porter (OG 1047, ABV 4.5%)
A subtly smoky porter, aged on oak.

Northern Warmth (OG 1046, ABV 4.5%)
A cinnamon-spiced, dark-coloured session ale.

Silver Dollar (OG 1050, ABV 4.9%)
Hoppy American-style ale with lasting bitterness and a citrus kick.

Helix (OG 1050, ABV 5%)
Czech-style lager with a crisp, clean finish and bold malty taste.

Ubrew

Arches 29-30, Old Jamaica Business Estate, Old Jamaica Road, Bermondsey, London, SE16 4AW
ubrew.cc

Ubrew is a an open membership brewery where anyone can brew their own beer. Situated in a railway arch it also features an adjacent taproom. A large number of brewery businesses operate out of the premises. These breweries beers, along with Ubrew's own, are often available in the taproom.

Uffa

White Lion Inn, Lower Street, Lower Ufford, Suffolk, IP13 6DW
☎ (01394) 460770 uffordwhitelion.co.uk/brewery

Uffa began brewing in 2011 using a 2.5-barrel plant. It is situated next to the White Lion pub in a converted coach house. ♦

Uley

The Old Brewery, 31 The Street, Uley, Gloucestershire, GL11 5TB
☎ (01453) 860120 uleybrewery.com

Brewing at Uley began in 1833 as Price's brewery. After a long gap, the premises were restored and Uley Brewery opened in 1985. Now operating a 10-barrel plant, it uses its own spring water. Uley delivers to 40-50 outlets in the Cotswolds area. ♦

Hogshead Cotswold Pale Ale (OG 1035, ABV 3.5%)
A pale-coloured, hoppy session bitter with a good hop aroma and a full flavour for its strength, ending in a bittersweet aftertaste.

Bitter (OG 1040, ABV 4%)
A copper-coloured beer with hops and fruit in the aroma and a malty, fruity taste, underscored by a hoppy bitterness. The finish is dry, with a balance of hops and malt.

Laurie Lee's Bitter (OG 1045, ABV 4.5%)
A copper-coloured, full-flavoured, hoppy bitter with some fruitiness and a smooth, long, balanced finish.

Old Spot Prize Strong Ale (OG 1050, ABV 5%)
A ruby-coloured ale with an initial strong, malty sweetness that develops into a smooth, dry, malty finish. A beer that is deceptively easy to drink.

Pig's Ear Strong Beer (OG 1050, ABV 5%)
A golden-coloured pale ale with an initial refreshing taste and a hint of fruitiness that develops into a light malty finish. A smooth, quaffable strong ale.

Brewed for the Old Spot Inn, Dursley:

Old Ric (OG 1045, ABV 4.5%)
A full-flavoured, copper-coloured, hoppy bitter with some fruitiness and a smooth, balanced finish.

Ulverston

Lightburn Road, Ulverston, Cumbria, LA12 0AU
☎ (01229) 586870 ☎ 07840 192022
ulverstonbrewingcompany.co.uk

The brewery occupies the octagonal bullring of the old livestock market. There is a bar that overlooks the brew-plant, which opens by prior arrangement and during some local festivals. Some beers have a Laurel and Hardy theme: Stan Laurel was born in Ulverston. ‼ ♦

Flying Elephants (OG 1037, ABV 3.7%)
Clean, refreshing, yellow-coloured bitter, sweet and fruity with a dry citrus finish.

Celebration Ale (OG 1039, ABV 3.9%)
Yellow-coloured, fruity bitter with hints of tangerine and a notably sustained dry finish.

Harvest Moon (OG 1039, ABV 3.9%)
A well-balanced, pale-coloured, hoppy bitter.

Laughing Gravy (OG 1040, ABV 4%)
Smooth and grainy brown-coloured bitter with a good mix of flavours.

Lonesome Pine (OG 1042, ABV 4.2%)
A fresh and fruity pale gold-coloured beer; honeyed, lemony and resiny with an increasingly bitter finish.

Fra Diavolo (OG 1043, ABV 4.3%)

Unbarred

c/o The Old Dairy, Chiddinglye Farm, West Hoathly, West Sussex, RH19 4QS ☎ 07850 070471

Office: 33 Bolsover Road, Hove, BN3 5HQ
unbarredbrewery.com

UnBarred has upscaled from a purpose-built brewery in the owner's garden and has teamed up with Missing Link Brewing (qv) in West Hoathly. It has a core range of beers, almost exclusively in can and keg, but also brews small batches and occasional casks for festivals and a small number of local pubs. RAIB

Under the Street

See One Mile End

Unity

23-27 Princes Street, Northam, Southampton, SO14 5RP ⊕ unitybrewingco.com

Founded in 2016, Unity Brewing Co is a six-barrel brewery. It produces beers influenced by Belgian and North East American styles using traditional techniques and modern ingredients. Output is mainly keg or cans with occasional special releases in cask.

Unsworth's Yard SIBA

4 Unsworth's Yard, Ford Road, Cartmel, Cumbria, LA11 6PG ☎ 07810 461313 ⊕ unsworthsyard.co.uk

Unsworth's Yard opened in 2011, brewing on a five-barrel plant. The brewery produces beers named after historic figures and legends associated with the Cartmel area. Beers are available in Cartmel pubs and other local outlets as well as the brewery's tap bar. !!

Peninsula Best (OG 1039, ABV 3.8%)
A mellow and sweet bitter brewed with Kent hops.

Crusader Gold (OG 1041, ABV 4.1%)
A crisp and refreshing golden ale with subtle citrus finish.

Sir Edgar Harrington's Last Wolf (OG 1045, ABV 4.5%)
Well-balanced, rich, fruity, tawny-coloured ale with a gentle bitterness.

The Flookburgh Cockler (OG 1057, ABV 5.5%)
Smooth, rich and dark in colour, with roasted grain and mocha flavours.

Untapped

Unit 6, Little Castle Farm Business Park, Raglan, NP15 2BX
☎ (01291) 690074 ⊕ untappedbrew.com

Brewing started in 2009 at Newent but transferred to its current premises in Raglan in 2013. A wide range of beers is brewed, including a range primarily aimed at the bottled market. !! ♦RAIB

Border (OG 1036.8, ABV 3.8%)
An easy-drinking, session, amber-coloured bitter with distinct hop characteristics.

Sundown (OG 1038.8, ABV 4%)
A refreshing golden ale; a sweet aroma with a hint of spice and a dry, mellow finish.

Monnow (OG 1038.3, ABV 4.2%)
Traditional best bitter with a rich mouthfeel, well-balanced, sweetly hoppy flavours and a fruity finish.

Whoosh (OG 1038.3, ABV 4.2%)
Pale straw-coloured beer with a fruity aroma, bright, zesty flavours and a clean, dry finish.

UPA (OG 1043.6, ABV 4.5%)
A light straw-coloured beer with citrus flavours and a hoppy aroma.

Triple S (OG 1048.4, ABV 4.9%)
A black-coloured stout with a powerful malt profile and a long-lasting hop character.

Ember (OG 1050, ABV 5.2%)
A rich brown-coloured old ale with a chocolate biscuit aroma and well-balanced malt and hop profile.

Crystal (OG 1052.3, ABV 6%)

Up Front

Office: 1.1, 27 Skirving Street, Glasgow, G4 0UT ☎ 07526 088973 ⊕ upfrontbrewing.com

Established in 2016, Up Front is a gypsy brewery producing canned beers. Cask-conditioned beers are occasionally available.

Uprising

See Windsor & Eton

Urban Chicken

Ilkeston, Derbyshire, DE7 5EH ☎ 07976 913395 ⊕ urbanchickenale.co.uk

A nanobrewery producing small batches of beer for local pubs, restaurants, bottle shops and beer festivals. It was registered as a commercial brewery in 2016 and upscaled to a one-barrel plant in 2018. ♦RAIB

Rooster Juice (ABV 4.3%)

Urban Gold (ABV 4.5%)

Pit Pony (ABV 4.9%)

Take Me To The Circus (ABV 5.1%)
An American-style, brown-coloured ale; roast flavours with citrus hop finish.

Earthquake (ABV 5.2%)
An earthy, rich, oatmeal stout.

Bantam (ABV 5.4%)
Balanced American-style pale ale with tropical fruit flavours.

Urban Island SIBA

Unit 28, Limberline Industrial Estate, Limberline Spur, Portsmouth, Hampshire, PO3 5DZ
☎ (023) 9266 8726 ⊕ urbanislandbrewing.uk

Urban Island began production in 2015 on a bespoke five-barrel, purpose-built plant. The range is distributed throughout Hampshire and the South East and expanding further afield. The brewery also features an on-site taproom. !!

Urban Pale (OG 1040, ABV 3.8%)
Hoppy pale ale with aromas of orange and pink grapefruit.

Mosaic (OG 1041.3, ABV 4%)
Single hop ale with a huge amount of hops resulting in a tropical fruit bomb with aromas of blueberry and papaya and a slight bitter finish.

Ammo (OG 1046, ABV 4.5%)
A juicy ale with a fruity kick of apricot, peach and tangerine, a malty, sweet mouthfeel and gentle notes of honey.

DSB (Dolly's Special Beer) (OG 1045, ABV 4.6%)

A light, refreshing ale, slightly fruity with a bitter hop finish.

New England (OG 1050.6, ABV 5%)
A pale ale with an intense bouquet and flavour of tropical fruits complemented with a smooth malt finish.

Porter 28 (OG 1056, ABV 5%)
A combination of malts give gentle hints of smokiness and chocolate with a roasted finish.

Big City, Small Island (ABV 5.2%)
Hazy, smooth tropical pale ale with a fruity mouthfeel and citrus notes of lemon, lime and melon and a subtle coconut aftertaste.

High & Dry (OG 1056, ABV 5.5%)
A hoppy IPA with an earthy base and citrus finish.

Urban Graffiti (OG 1067, ABV 6%)
A smooth, dark-coloured beer with smoked and roast malts and a distinct hoppy flavour.

Utopian (NEW)

Unit 4, Clannaborough Business Units, Bow, Devon, EX17 6DA
☎ (01392) 769765 🌐 utopianbrewing.com

Utopian began brewing in 2019 producing craft lagers. No real ale.

Uttoxeter SIBA

26b Carter Street, Uttoxeter, Staffordshire, ST14 8EU
☎ 07734 392321 🌐 uttoxeterbrewingcompany.com

A nanobrewery set up in 2016, exploiting the famous Burton upon Trent hard water.

Full Gallop (ABV 4.4%)
A brown-coloured ale; malty and spicy, with slight sweetness and toffee notes.

Dr Johnson's Contrafibularity (ABV 4.5%)
A hoppy IPA with an orange citrus flavour and colour.

Earthmover (ABV 4.5%)
Traditional English bitter, quite hoppy with a good malty flavour and a fruity finish.

Final Furlong (ABV 4.5%)
A smooth best bitter, spicy and floral with a caramel flavour.

Uxonian (ABV 4.5%)
An amber-coloured ale with grape and tangerine flavours.

Earthmover Gold (ABV 4.7%)
A bright, light-coloured golden ale, hoppy yet fruity.

Ground Breaker (ABV 4.7%)
A golden-coloured beer, grassy aromas with some earthy notes, with pineapple flavours.

Paddock Porter (ABV 4.8%)
A chocolaty porter with a distinctive dark roasted grain flavour and a slight sweetness.

American IPA (ABV 5.6%)
An American-style IPA, strong, bitter and fruity.

Vadum (NEW)

Correspondence: 27 Burman Road, Wath-upon-Dearne, South Yorkshire, S63 7NE ☎ 07949 684633
✉ vadumbrewery@gmail.com

Vadum was established in 2018 by Roy Lomax with a focus on traditional ales. Beer names reference Wath-upon-Dearne's Roman history. Beers are brewed using spare capacity at Hilltop Brewery (qv). **V**

Centurion (ABV 4%)
A chestnut-coloured, malty best bitter.

Tribune Blonde (ABV 4.2%)
Moderately hopped, pine resin flavour with a dry finish.

Legate (ABV 4.6%)
Mellow, easy-drinking, citrus session IPA with a dry finish.

Commander (ABV 5.2%)
Full-bodied IPA with slight malt and sweetness in the flavour.

Vale SIBA

Tramway Business Park, Ludgershall Road, Brill, Buckinghamshire, HP18 9TY
☎ (01844) 239237 🌐 valebrewery.co.uk

⊗ Established in 1995 and initially based in Haddenham, Vale moved to Brill in 2007. In 2010 it expanded to a 20-barrel brew plant. Five pubs are owned, including the Hop Pole where sister brewery the Aylesbury Brewhouse (qv), opened in 2011. ‼ ♦ RAIB

Brill Gold (OG 1035, ABV 3.5%)
Golden-coloured session ale with a full malt flavour, well-balanced with fruity, slightly citrus hop aromas and a soft bitterness.

Best IPA (OG 1036, ABV 3.7%) ◆
This pale amber-coloured beer starts with a slight fruit aroma. This leads to a clean, bitter taste where hops and fruit dominate. The finish is long and bitter with a slight hop note.

Black Swan Mild (OG 1038, ABV 3.9%)
Dark-coloured and smooth with hints of chocolate and coffee on the nose and a malty, dry finish.

Wychert Ale (OG 1038, ABV 3.9%)
Woody flavours are notable in this malty beer with a finish of port and berries on the nose.

VPA (Vale Pale Ale) (OG 1042, ABV 4.2%)
An assertive, dry, hoppy ale with a citrus nose, combined with a pronounced malt background.

Red Kite (OG 1043, ABV 4.3%)
Refreshing, chestnut-coloured beer with a bitter finish.

Black Beauty Porter (OG 1044, ABV 4.4%) ◆
A dark-coloured ale, the initial aroma is malty. Roast malt dominates initially and is followed by a rich fruitiness, with some sweetness. The finish is increasingly hoppy and dry.

Gravitas (OG 1047, ABV 4.8%)
A strong pale ale packed with hop and citrus flavours, rounded off by a dry, malty, biscuit finish.

Vendetta (NEW)

Unit 42, Grainger Road, Southend-on-Sea, Essex, SS2 5DD
☎ (01702) 742033 ✉ info@vendettabrewing.co.uk

Microbrewery in the heart of Southend-on-Sea using both traditional and modern brewing methods.

Mild (ABV 3.8%)
Rich, smooth-tasting, black-coloured mild with a subtle sweet roasted flavour.

Gold (ABV 4%)
Easy-drinking, gold-coloured session ale with a tropical fruit and pine hop aroma.

Best Bitter (ABV 4.2%)
A classic reddish-brown-coloured best bitter with moderate bitterness and a well-rounded flavour.

Session IPA (ABV 4.5%)
An American-style IPA, full-bodied with a resinous fruity hop aroma.

Verdant

Unit 6, Tressidder Close, Tregoniggie Industrial Estate, Falmouth, Cornwall, TR11 4SP
☎ (01326) 619117 ☎ 07970 503574
verdantbrewing.co

Brewery established in 2014 by keen homebrewers using a 10-barrel plant. No real ale. ‼

Vibrant Forest

The Purlieu Centre, Units 3-6, Hardley Industrial Estate, Hardley, Hampshire, SO45 3NQ
☎ (023) 8200 2200 ☎ 07921 753109
vibrantforest.co.uk

Vibrant Forest Brewery started brewing commercially in 2011, as a one-barrel plant, this gradually increased to ten barrels over the next five years at Lymington. It has now relocated to a four unit brewery at Hardley and increased in size to a 12-barrel plant. ‼ ♦ RAIB

Summerlands (OG 1036, ABV 3.5%)
An IPA-style bitter, well-hopped with balanced malt flavours. An easy-drinking session beer.

Farmhouse (OG 1043, ABV 5%)
A light golden ale with slightly peppery and spicy aromas, subtle bitter and fruity flavours and a dry finish.

Single Hop Pale Ale (OG 1047, ABV 5%)
A golden ale that is brewed with a single rotating hop variety.

Kick-Start (OG 1060, ABV 5.7%)
A rich, black-coloured stout made with freshly roasted Colombian coffee beans. Oats add a smooth texture.

Metropolis (OG 1100, ABV 6%)
A hoppy black IPA with a balanced bitterness and flavours of citrus and tropical fruits with undertones of chocolate.

Kaleidoscope (OG 1060, ABV 6.5%)
Massively-hopped, American-style IPA with intense citrus hop flavours.

Umbral Abyss (OG 1086, ABV 8.8%)
A rich stout with coffee notes.

Victoria Inn

Roch, SA62 6AW
☎ (01437) 710426 ☎ 07814 684975
thevictoriainnroch.com

A microbrewery in a separate building on the same site as the pub. At present the only outlet for the beers is the pub itself. ‼

Village Brewer Brew 22

Number Twenty 2, 22 Coniscliffe Road, Darlington, DL3 7RG
☎ (01325) 354590 villagebrewer.co.uk

One-barrel microbrewery, established in 2013, which has been brewing on a regular basis since 2015. The plant is also used to produce the malt wash for the distilling of gin and vodka on site. The beer strength and style varies from brew to brew and complement the Village Brewer beers produced by Hambleton Ales (qv) since 1992.

Village Brewer

See Hambleton

Villages

21-22 Resolution Way, Deptford, London, SE8 4NT
☎ (020) 3489 1143 villagesbrewery.com

Established in 2016 by brothers Archie and Louis Village. Beers are currently only available in keg and can. An on-site tap room is open on at weekends.

Vine Inn

Vine Inn & Brewery, Sheep Fair, Rugeley, Staffordshire, WS15 2AT
☎ (01889) 574443 ✉ oli@thevinebrewery.com

Brewery based within the Vine Inn, parts of which date back to the 16th century. Its beers can be found in a number of pubs in the Cannock Chase area.

Session Ale (OG 1039, ABV 3.8%)
Light ale with subtle fruity hints.

EPA (OG 1045, ABV 4%)

Vanilla Porter (OG 1046, ABV 4.5%)
A dark-coloured porter with coffee undertones and a rising sweetness from the vanilla.

Grapefruit IPA (OG 1045, ABV 4.8%)
Well-hopped IPA with fresh grapefruit, giving it a balanced bitterness.

Vittles (NEW)

Hull Trinity Market, Trinity House Lane, Hull, East Yorkshire, HU1 2JH ☎ 07598 098632
vittlesandcompany.co.uk

Vittles & Co started brewing in 2018 at the Trinity Market, Hull. The site can produce just 50 litres at a time. The brewery name comes from the fact that the owner loves to pair beer and food, hence the old name for food, vittles.

Vocation

Unit 8, Craggs Country Business Park, New Road, Cragg Vale, Hebden Bridge, West Yorkshire, HX7 5TT
☎ (01422) 410810 vocationbrewery.com

Vocation began brewing in 2015 on a bespoke 20-barrel plant. The brewery is located high above Hebden Bridge. In 2017 it opened its first bar in Hebden Bridge called Vocation & Co and a second one, Assembly Underground, Leeds, in 2018. Brewing capacity trebled to 45 barrels in 2018 due to increased demand. ♦

Bread & Butter (ABV 3.9%) ◀
A feast of floral hops with citrus aromas and taste. Robust bitter aftertaste.

Heart & Soul (ABV 4.5%) ▣ ◀
A golden ale with a strong citrus aroma. Hops dominate taste and aftertaste.

Pride & Joy (ABV 5.3%) ◀
Flavoursome IPA packed with citrus hoppiness. A hint of sweetness gives way to a mellow aftertaste.

Life & Death (OG 1061, ABV 6.5%) ▢ ▣
American-style IPA with flavours of tropical and citrus fruits with a lingering bitterness set against a smooth, malty backbone.

VOG

Unit 8a, Atlantic Trading Estate, Barry, CF63 3RF
☎ (01446) 730757 ⊕ vogbrewery.co.uk

☺ Created in 2005, the founders handed over the reins to a new team in 2015 who have rebranded the brewery and refreshed the beer range. Beers can be found in a number of South Wales pubs as well as occasionally throughout the country due to brewery beer swaps. ◆RAIB

Paradigm Shift (OG 1042, ABV 4.2%)

South Island (OG 1042, ABV 4.2%)
A pale ale, dry, bitter and refreshing with big punchy hops.

Dark Matter (OG 1044, ABV 4.4%)
A blackcurrant porter, easy-drinking, rich and smooth with liquorice and chocolate notes.

Speak Easy IPA (OG 1046, ABV 4.6%)
A hoppy IPA underpinned by a big malt character and with a bitter tropical citrus finish.

Lady Liberty (OG 1048, ABV 4.8%)
An American-style pale ale with a refreshing, clean bitterness supporting a juicy, resinous hop character.

Volden SIBA

35a Neville Road, Croydon, CR0 2DS
☎ (020) 8684 4492 ⊕ volden.co.uk

▣ Volden produce beer for the Antic pub group with branches throughout London. ◆

Session Ale (OG 1037, ABV 3.8%) ◀
Amber-coloured bitter with a caramel and orange aroma. Lemon marmalade and sweetish malty biscuit that fades to a bitter, dryish finish.

Pale Ale (ABV 4.6%) ◀
Dry, bitter, floral hop flavour with a slight hint of fresh orange peel, becoming more bitter on drinking. A little malt.

Wadworth SIBA IFBB

Northgate Brewery, Devizes, Wiltshire, SN10 1JW
☎ (01380) 723361 ⊕ wadworth.co.uk

▣ Established in 1875 by Henry Alfred Wadworth, this impressive family-owned brewery has a modern brewhouse and a microbrewery, which enables it to create unique small batch beers. Its traditional horse-drawn drays deliver beer daily around Devizes. Wadworth has more than 200 pubs in the South-West of England. The brewery

also has an on-site bar, brewery shop and visitor centre. ‼ ➤ ◆RAIB

IPA (OG 1035, ABV 3.6%)
A classic session beer with malt-led flavours.

Horizon (OG 1039, ABV 4%)
A pale gold-coloured beer with zesty citrus and hop aromas and a crisp, tangy finish on the palate.

6X (OG 1040.5, ABV 4.1%) ◀
Copper-coloured ale with a malty and fruity nose, and some balancing hop character. The flavour is similar, with some bitterness and a lingering malty, but bitter finish.

Bishops Tipple (OG 1048, ABV 5%)
A golden-coloured brew giving well-balanced hop bitterness and a clean finish.

Swordfish (OG 1047.5, ABV 5%)
A full-bodied, deep copper-coloured ale flavoured with Pussers rum.

Waen

See Team Toxic

Wagtail

New Barn Farm, Wilby Warrens, Old Buckenham, Norfolk, NR17 1PF
☎ (01953) 887133
✉ wagtailbrewery@btinternet.com

Wagtail Brewery went into full-time production in 2006. All beers are only available bottle-conditioned. This is Britain's only chemical-free brewery. No chemicals are on site and all cleaning is done with hot water and 'elbow grease'. RAIB V

Walled City

70 Ebrington Square, Londonderry, BT47 6FA
☎ (028) 7134 3336 ⊕ walledcitybrewery.com

Restaurant-based brewery established in 2015. No real ale.

Izaak Walton (NEW)

Whitehouse Farm, Cold Norton, Staffordshire, ST15 0NS
☎ (01785) 760780

Brewing began in 2017.

Last Cast (ABV 4%)
A light, pale-coloured session beer with a hint of hops.

Last Drop (ABV 4%)
A dark-coloured mild with a stout finish.

Amber Nymph (ABV 4.5%)
A light copper-coloured traditional English bitter.

Wander Beyond

98 North Western Street, Manchester, M12 6HR
☎ (0161) 661 3676
✉ sales@wanderbeyondbrewing.com

Wander Beyond launched in 2017 in a railway arch under Piccadilly Station. The range of beer available can vary. ◆

Peak (ABV 3.8%)

Northern Night (ABV 4.1%)

A session porter with flavours of ginger cake and sweet malts.

Great Rift (ABV 6%)

Finders Keepers (ABV 6.2%)

Wanderlust

See Magpie

Wantage (NEW)

c/o Kings Arms, 39 Wallingford Street, Wantage, Oxfordshire, OX12 8AU
☎ (01235) 765465 🌐 kingsarmswantage.co.uk

Wantage is initially brewing on its sister Oak Taverns brewery plant in Faringdon. There are plans to install a small plant at the Kings Arms.

Wantsum SIBA

Kent Barn, St Nicholas Court Farm, Court Road, St Nicholas at Wade, Kent, CT7 0PT
☎ (01227) 910135 🌐 wantsumbrewery.co.uk

⊗ Wantsum Brewery, established by James Sandy in 2009, takes its name from the nearby Wantsum Channel. Previously located in Hersden near Canterbury, the brewery relocated to a farm site in 2017. It has an extensive range of beers, named after pivotal events in Kent's history. Outlets are supplied throughout the South of England. An on-site taproom showcases the beers. ‼ ♦ RAIB

More's Head (OG 1034, ABV 3.5%)
A chestnut-coloured bitter with malt and roasted grains balanced against fruit and floral hops with a hint of citrus.

1381 (OG 1036, ABV 3.8%)
A light amber-coloured IPA with delicate citrus and herbal aromas.

Black Prince (OG 1036.5, ABV 3.9%)
A rich, full-bodied mild, smooth on the palate with subtle hop notes.

Imperium (OG 1037, ABV 4%)
A deep amber-coloured best bitter; smooth biscuit malts and a rich hoppy nose balance this beer perfectly.

Montgomery (OG 1037, ABV 4%)
Amber in colour with spicy citrus aromas.

Fortitude (OG 1039, ABV 4.2%)
A full-bodied bitter with a pronounced hop finish.

One Hop (OG 1040, ABV 4.2%)

Dynamo (OG 1043, ABV 4.3%)
A crisp, light golden ale, fruity and floral with an orange citrus twist.

Turbulent Priest (OG 1041, ABV 4.4%)
A full-bodied best bitter offering chocolate and coffee notes on top of a sweet malt base. The hops give the beer bitterness tempered with deep fruity hop aromas.

Yellow Tail (OG 1043, ABV 4.5%)
Pale-coloured, hoppy ale with a sweet, floral taste. Fruity with a hint of vanilla.

Black Pig (OG 1044, ABV 4.8%)
A smooth, dark-coloured beer with burnt chocolate and smoky malt notes mixed with delicate hop bitterness and floral notes.

Hengist (OG 1045, ABV 5%)
A golden-coloured pale ale with flavours of biscuit malt balancing a deep, mellow, fruity nose.

Red Raddle (OG 1049, ABV 5%)
Ruby-coloured premium bitter, biscuit and toasted malt base supporting a broad, hoppy, smooth finish.

Golgotha (OG 1047, ABV 5.5%)
A rich, deep and broad malt base gives this stout a long, smooth finish. Hops are prominent on the nose with blackcurrant, liquorice and cedar.

Ravening Wolf (OG 1052, ABV 5.9%)
A light amber-coloured, strong pale ale; toasted biscuit and rye malt flavours support a pine lemon hop crispness with a hint of vanilla.

Warwickshire SIBA

Bakehouse Brewery, Queen Street, Cubbington, Warwickshire, CV32 7NA
☎ (01926) 450747 🌐 warwickshirebeer.co.uk

A six-barrel brewery in a former village bakery which has been in operation since 1998. Bottled beers are available from local farm shops, garden centres, wine specialists and supermarkets, as well as from the brewery direct and its four pubs. More unusual craft beers are available under the Bakehouse Brewery brand name. ♦ RAIB

SPA (Spa Pale Ale) (ABV 3.8%)

Darling Buds (OG 1041, ABV 4%)

Duck Soup (OG 1043, ABV 4.2%)
Copper-coloured brew with rich, malty overtones.

Lady Godiva (OG 1042, ABV 4.2%)
An aromatic golden ale, with honey and malt on the nose. Slightly sweet, biscuity maltiness is balanced by rounded hop bitterness.

Yer Bard (ABV 4.3%)

Two Castles Porter (ABV 4.4%)

Brewed under the Bakehouse Brewery name:

Liquid Bread (OG 1046, ABV 4.5%)

Wash House

See Allanwater

Watermill SIBA

Watermill Inn, Ings, Cumbria, LA8 9PY
☎ (01539) 821309 ☎ 07831 873300
🌐 lakelandpub.co.uk

Watermill was established in 2006 in a purpose-built extension to the inn. The beers have a doggy theme – dogs are allowed in the main bar. The brewery was extended in 2008 with a new brewery planned within the grounds. Also produces beers under the Windermere Brewery name. ‼ ♦

Tomos Watkin SIBA

Unit 3, Alberto Road, Century Park, Valley Way, Swansea Enterprise Park, Swansea, SA6 8RP
☎ (01792) 797280 🌐 tomoswatkin.com

Brewing began in 1995, originally in Llandeilo behind the Castle Hotel. The brewery moved to Swansea in 2000 and was taken over by Hurns

Water Mineral Company in 2002. More than 60% of production is bottled beers (not bottle conditioned). ‼ ♦

Delilah (OG 1040, ABV 4%)
Light blonde ale with zesty citrus flavours and a hint of spice.

OSB (Old Style Bitter) (OG 1045, ABV 4.5%)
Amber-coloured ale with an inviting aroma of hops and malt. Full-bodied; hops, fruit, malt and bitterness combine to give a balanced flavour continuing into the finish.

IPA (OG 1049, ABV 4.8%)
Full bodied, crisp IPA with floral bitterness and aromas of peach and mandarin.

Watling Street

Unit 2a, 6 Greycaine Road, Watford, Hertfordshire, WD24 7GP ☎ 07713 841936
watlingstreetbeer.com

Brewing began in 2015 in Aldenham and relocated to an old farm building on Hilfield Farm in 2016 to allow for expansion to a 10-barrel plant. The brewery relocated again to North Watford in 2017. An on-site tap room is open six days a week. ‼

Uncle Damn (ABV 3.7%)

Sir Newton Golden Ale (ABV 3.8%)

Queen Boudicca Premium Ale (ABV 4.2%)
A traditional English ale with rich undertones of toffee.

Miss Shelley Pale Ale (ABV 4.3%)

Salted Caramel Stout (ABV 4.4%)

Mr Ripper Red Ale (ABV 4.6%)

Wat Tyler Pale Ale (ABV 4.8%)

Watneys

See Sambrook's

Watson's

Old Heath, Colchester, Essex, CO1 2HD ☎ 07804 641267 watsonsbrewery.co.uk

Small batch home brewery set up in 2016 using a 100-litre brew plant. Local pubs, festivals and bottle shops are supplied with one-off beers.

Watts Brewing?

Magnet Freehouse, 51 Wellington Road North, Stockport, SK4 1HJ
☎ (0161) 429 6287 themagnetfreehouse.co.uk

Brewing began in 2014 on the premises of the Magnet freehouse. No regular beers. Speciality beers are brewed to suit the season, and are mostly sold in the pub. ♦

Waveney

Queen's Head, Station Road, Earsham, Norfolk, NR35 2TS
☎ (01986) 892623 lyndahamps@aol.com

Established at the Queen's Head in 2004, the five-barrel brewery produces three beers, regularly available at the pub along with other free trade outlets. ♦

Way Outback

144 Seabourne Road, Southbourne, Dorset, BH5 2HZ
thewayoutback.co.uk

Started in 2017 and born in a shed, Way Outback now has a taproom based in a lovingly restored building, with an adjacent dedicated brewery plant. It is run by owner and head brewer Rich Brown with help from his four legged assistant Arthur.

Working like a Dog (ABV 3.6%)
A session pale ale with fruity flavours.

Take Me to Valhalla (ABV 4%)
A pale ale with aromas of blueberry, citrus and tropical fruit.

Hopposites Attract (ABV 5.6%)
A double-hopped pale ale with aromas of passion fruit, grapefruit and gooseberry.

Weal SIBA

Unit 6, Newpark Business Park, London Road, Chesterton, Staffordshire, ST5 7HT
☎ (01782) 565635 ☎ 07980 606966
wealales.co.uk

Weal Ales is an award-winning microbrewery established in 2014 on a one-barrel plant. It expanded to a six-barrel plant in 2015 and is now also bottling its beers. Its first pub, Wellers, opened in Newcastle under Lyme in 2016. RAIB

This is the Modern Weal (OG 1038, ABV 3.8%)
A pale-coloured, hoppy session beer.

Wagon Weal (OG 1041, ABV 4.1%)
A smooth and creamy traditional bitter.

Weald Wood (OG 1040, ABV 4.1%)
A hoppy session beer with a refreshing tangerine taste.

Wealy Hopper (OG 1042, ABV 4.2%)
A light, refreshing pale ale with a floral and citrus aroma and a dry bitter finish.

Weller Weal (OG 1046, ABV 4.6%)
A hoppy pale ale with a citrus finish.

Weal Noir (OG 1048, ABV 4.8%)
A rich, warming porter with a roast malt flavour throughout and a subtle hint of spice.

Centwealial Milk Stout (OG 1059, ABV 4.9%)
A sweet, creamy milk stout with a rich chocolate taste and silky smooth finish.

Ginger Weal (ABV 5.5%)
A strong golden ale with added ginger to give a spicy kick.

Lemon & Ginger Weal (ABV 5.5%)
A strong golden ale with lemon and ginger, giving a distinctive citrus and spicy kick.

Weard'ALE

Hare & Hounds, 24 Front Street, Westgate, DL13 1RX
☎ (01388) 517212

Brewing commenced in the Hare & Hounds in 2010. The beers are mainly sold on the premises

THE BREWERIES

but some have found their way to nearby beer festivals and other local pubs.

Weatheroak

Unit 7, Victoria Works, Birmingham Road, Studley, Warwickshire, B80 7AP
☎ (0121) 445 4411 (eve) ☎ 07798 773894
weatheroakbrewery.co.uk

The brewery was set up in 1997 at Weatheroak Hill. It is now in a spacious factory unit in Studley. Around 40 outlets are supplied direct. Off sales are available for all beers at the Tap House on High Street, Studley. !!♦

St Udley Mild (OG 1034, ABV 3.4%)

Ale (OG 1041, ABV 4.1%)
The aroma is dominated by hops in this golden-coloured brew. Hops also feature in the mouth and there is a rapidly fading dry aftertaste.

Victoria Works (OG 1043, ABV 4.3%)
A pale-coloured, hoppy bitter with a citrus finish.

Redwood (OG 1047, ABV 4.7%)
A rich, tawny-coloured, strong but mellow beer with a short-lived sweet fruit and malt balance.

Keystone Hops (OG 1050, ABV 5%)
A golden yellow-coloured beer that is surprisingly easy to quaff given the strength. Fruity hops are the dominant flavour without the commonly associated astringency.

Weatheroak Hill

Coach & Horses, Weatheroak Hill, Worcestershire, B48 7EA
☎ (01564) 823386 ☎ 07496 289924
weatheroakhillbrewery@gmail.com

Weatheroak Hill Brewery is located at the busy Coach & Horses pub and restaurant near Alvechurch. !!♦

Websters

Graham's Place, 73 Bridgnorth Road, Wollaston, West Midlands, DY8 3PZ
☎ (01384) 440315 info@grahams-place.co.uk

Microbrewery set up to the side of Graham's Place in 2014. Currently brewing with malt extract, full mash beers are planned. All beers are sold though the pub including some one-off specials.

Weetwood SIBA

The Brewery, Common Lane, Kelsall, Cheshire, CW6 0PY
☎ (01829) 752377 weetwoodales.co.uk

Weetwood Ales, which originally began brewing in 1992 in a barn, now operates out of a modern 30-barrel plant close to Kelsall. A broad range of beers is produced and can be found in pubs across the North-west and North Wales. Besides monthly Thursday evening brewery tours and an on-site shop, a distillery was installed in 2018, which produces a range of spirits including gin and vodka. !!

Southern Cross (ABV 3.6%)
A hoppy session ale. Pale gold-coloured with pine and lemon hop flavours.

Bitter (OG 1038.5, ABV 3.8%)
Pale brown-coloured beer with an assertive bitterness and a lingering dry finish. Despite initial sweetness, peppery hops dominate throughout.

Mad Hatter (OG 1038.5, ABV 3.9%)
A red-coloured beer, malty aromas lead to a fruity, sweet middle, backed up with a bitter finish.

Cheshire Cat (OG 1040, ABV 4%)
Pale-coloured, dry bitter with a lemon zest and grape aroma. Hoppy aroma leads through to the initial taste before fruitiness takes over. Smooth, creamy mouthfeel and a short, dry finish.

Eastgate (OG 1043.5, ABV 4.2%)
Well-balanced, refreshing, clean, amber-coloured beer. Citrus fruit flavours predominate in the taste and there is a short, dry aftertaste.

Oregon Pale (ABV 4.3%)
Pale-coloured ale with big flavours of citrus and grapefruit.

Old Dog (OG 1045, ABV 4.5%)
Robust, well-balanced, amber-coloured beer with a slightly fruity aroma. Rich malt and fruit flavours are balanced by bitterness. Some sweetness and a hint of sulphur on nose and taste.

Revelry (OG 1050, ABV 5%)
A straw-coloured, crisp, full-bodied and fruity golden ale with a good dry finish.

Weighbridge

Penzance Drive, Swindon, Wiltshire, SN5 7JL
☎ (01793) 881500 weighbridgebrewhouse.co.uk

A microbrewery established in 2011 and based within the Weighbridge Brewhouse Restaurant & Bar, in the building which was formerly the home of Archer's brewery and once part of Swindon Railway Works. !!♦

Weird Beard SIBA

Unit 5, Boston Business Park, Trumpers Way, Hanwell, London, W7 2QA
☎ (020) 3645 2711 weirdbeardbrewco.com

Brewing began in 2013 on an industrial estate in Hanwell. The plant has expanded a few times, including into the adjacent unit. Bottle-conditioned beers are the mainstay but also widely available in keg and cask. RAIB

Dark Hopfler (OG 1043, ABV 2.5%)
A hoppy, dark-coloured beer with pine and chocolate on the nose. Roasted malt and sweet cocoa flavours are balanced by resinous hop bitterness.

Black Perle (OG 1053, ABV 3.8%)
Coffee milk stout with roast notes throughout in this full-favoured, sweetish, black-coloured beer. Finish has some roast bitter dryness.

Little Things That Kill (OG 1044, ABV 3.9%)
Hoppy, fruity golden ale which varies in flavour as the hops that are used can alter.

Hops Maiden England (OG 1047, ABV 4.5%)
An oatmeal pale ale with earthy hop aromas and flavours that change with the different hop varieties used.

Mariana Trench (OG 1048, ABV 5.3%)

Passion fruit and citrus are noticeable throughout this malty, sweet, golden-coloured beer. Bitterness builds and lingers, overlaid by dryness.

Decadence Stout (OG 1062, ABV 5.5%) ◆
Orange in colour with some black treacle sweetness balancing the dry chocolate and coffee character that lingers pleasantly with the bitterness developing.

K*ntish Town Beard (OG 1054, ABV 5.5%)

Fade to Black (OG 1063, ABV 6.5%) ◆
Balanced, black-coloured IPA with some fruitiness and roast coffee notes throughout.

Five O'Clock Shadow (OG 1065, ABV 7%) ◆
Golden ale with an apple nose and palate. Sweet biscuit and resinous spicy hops dominating. Dry, sweet aftertaste fading to spicy.

Weird Sisters (NEW)

24 Timworth Heath Cottages, Great Barton, Suffolk, IP31 2QH ☎ 07827 923923

A nanobrewery established by a father and three daughters (the weird sisters) in 2018. The brewery has one core beer and mainly produces seasonal beers to mark the eight seasonal festivals of the wheel of the year. The main outlets are at festivals, Morris dancing events and specialist beer shops. RAIB V

Slaphead (OG 1062, ABV 6.7%)
A full-flavoured, golden-coloured IPA with an intense tropical fruit taste and aroma.

Welbeck Abbey SIBA

Brewery Yard, Welbeck, Nottinghamshire, S80 3LT
☎ (01909) 512539 ☎ 07921 066274
welbeckabbeybrewery.co.uk

Welbeck Abbey opened in 2011. The microbrewery is housed in a listed barn at the centre of the traditional landed Welbeck estate. General manager Claire Monk trained at the Kelham Island Brewery after studying microbiology at Sheffield University. The brewery produces the Foraged & Found range of beers and contract brews for Stocks Brewing Co. !! ♦

Henrietta (OG 1034, ABV 3.6%)
A clean-tasting, delicate golden ale with notes of honeysuckle and fresh hay.

Red Feather (OG 1036, ABV 3.9%)
A robust, auburn-coloured ale with bold walnut and bittersweet caramel flavours.

Kaiser (OG 1038, ABV 4.1%)
A pale-coloured beer with a biscuity sweet but refreshingly herbal flavour.

Harley (OG 1039.5, ABV 4.3%)
A floral-tasting, honey-coloured ale. Orange blossom and fresh zest are at the forefront with subtle sweetness behind.

Portland Black (OG 1043, ABV 4.5%) ◆
Black-coloured ale with a roast malt aroma and taste throughout, and a well-balanced bitterness.

Cavendish (OG 1046, ABV 5%) ◆
Golden in colour with a smooth, hoppy and malt mouthfeel and a lingering, hoppy, bitter finish.

Weldon

Bencroft Grange, Bedford Road, Rushden, Northamptonshire, NN10 0SE
☎ (01536) 601016

Office: 12 Chapel Road, Weldon, NN17 3HP
weldonbrewery.co.uk

Weldon originally started brewing in 2014 on a two-barrel plant at the Shoulder of Mutton, after which the brewery was originally named. In 2016 the premises and 3.5-barrel kit of the former Copper Kettle brewery in Rushden were purchased and became the main production facility, with the brewery being renamed Weldon. The original plant at the Shoulder of Mutton has been retained and is used for small runs and test batches. ♦

Essanell (OG 1038, ABV 3.8%)
A dark mild with roasted malts, chocolate, coffee, nutty caramel and hints of raisin and stewed fruits.

Dragline (OG 1040, ABV 3.9%)
Golden ale, light and crisp with delicate fruit and floral notes.

Stahlstadt (OG 1040, ABV 4%)
A blonde ale, light and refreshing with delicate hints of lemon and fragrant herbs.

Galvy Stout (OG 1042, ABV 4.2%)
A classic stout with hints of coffee, chocolate and liquorice.

Rosie's Sweatbox (OG 1042, ABV 4.2%)
A deep ruby-coloured ale, fruity in character with hints of toffee and wood smoke.

Windmill (OG 1042, ABV 4.2%)

Mad Max (OG 1044, ABV 4.4%)
A tawny-coloured, American-style session ale with a dry finish complemented by delicate fruitiness.

Paradisium (OG 1044, ABV 4.4%)
An American-style pale ale with a fruity, long-lasting bitter finish and delicate hints of grapefruit.

Roman Mosaics (OG 1044, ABV 4.6%)
A robust, hoppy pale ale with deep, complex stone fruit flavours.

Well Drawn SIBA

Unit 5, Greenway Workshops, Bedwas House Industrial Estate, Caerphilly, CF83 8HW ☎ 07854 806617 welldrawnbrewing.co.uk

This six-barrel brewery opened in 2017 in a small industrial unit near Caerphilly, supplying direct to local pubs as well as through a number of regional wholesalers. ♦ RAIB

WD Pale Ale (ABV 3.8%)
Pale golden-coloured session ale with a floral aroma brought to life by hints of elderflower.

Bedwas Bitter (ABV 4.2%)
Classic bitter with a malty flavour coming through traditional bittering hops.

Caerphilly Pale (ABV 4.2%)
Bold and floral with a strong, aromatic aftertaste.

WD Gold (ABV 4.4%)
Golden-coloured session ale with a toffee hint and floral, hoppy aromas.

Welland (NEW)

Cradge Bank, Spalding, Lincolnshire, PE11 3AN
☎ 07732 033702 ✉ info@wellandbrewery.co.uk

Welland Brewery commenced in 2018 and was set up by Tom Bradshaw and Dave Jackson, assisted by the owner and brewer of nearby Austendyke Ales, Charlie Rawlings. A brewery taphouse is planned.

Sneaky Stoat (OG 1044, ABV 3.9%)
A velvety mouthfeel combines with mild roast flavours and hints of coffee and dark chocolate.

YFM (OG 1043, ABV 4.2%)
An easy-drinking pale ale with hints of tropical fruit.

Jack Rawlshaw (OG 1044, ABV 4.4%)
A floral aroma leads to a smooth, bitter finish.

Black Cow (OG 1057, ABV 4.7%)
A smooth milk stout, roasted malt flavours of coffee and chocolate combined with vanilla and berry notes.

Rusty Giraffe (OG 1050, ABV 5%)
Amber-coloured ale with hints of toffee and caramel leading to a crisp citrus finish.

Charles Wells

See Eagle

Weltons SIBA

1 Mulberry Trading Estate, Foundry Lane, Horsham, West Sussex, RH13 5PX
☎ (01403) 242901 🌐 weltonsbeer.co.uk

⊗ Ray Welton moved the brewery into a factory unit in 2003. More than 70 different beers are brewed every year. Pubs throughout the South-east and London are supplied. ‼ ♦ RAIB

Pride 'n' Joy (OG 1028, ABV 2.8%)
A light brown-coloured bitter with a slight malty and hoppy aroma. Fruity with a pleasant hoppiness and some sweetness in the flavour, leading to a short malty finish.

Horsham Pale (OG 1037, ABV 3.7%)
Amber-coloured ale, bitter but with a huge aroma.

Sussex Pride (OG 1040, ABV 4%)
A copper-coloured, malty ale with a hint of spiced rum aroma.

Old Cocky (OG 1043, ABV 4.3%)
A golden-coloured beer with a bittersweet flavour.

American Graffiti (OG 1045, ABV 4.5%)
A pale ale with citrus bitterness and a huge powerful aroma, which lingers.

Old Harry (OG 1051, ABV 5.2%)
Deep red-coloured beer with a malty, nutty flavour.

Churchillian Stout (OG 1066, ABV 6.6%)
Hints of burnt toast, balanced by good levels of hops, with a long finish.

Wensleydale SIBA

Unit 4, Badger Court, Leyburn, North Yorkshire, DL8 5BF
☎ (01969) 622463 ☎ 07765 596666
🌐 wensleydalebrewery.co.uk

Wensleydale was set up in 2003 and recently moved to larger premises in Leyburn with plans for further expansion. Around 100 outlets are supplied direct. ‼ ♦ RAIB

Pale (ABV 3.5%)
Pale-coloured session bitter, hoppy and aromatic.

Falconer (OG 1038, ABV 3.9%)
A fruity, malt-based session ale, copper in colour, with a long, bitter, dry finish.

Semer Water (OG 1040, ABV 4.1%)
Pale-coloured ale with citrus aromas balanced by a light, malty sweetness.

Gamekeeper (OG 1042, ABV 4.3%)
A copper-coloured best bitter with huge spicy hop flavours and a juicy malt flavour.

Black Dub (OG 1043, ABV 4.4%)
Oat stout with a sweet, rich, complex taste of roasted coffee and hints of chocolate.

Gold (OG 1044, ABV 4.5%)
A golden-coloured best bitter with aromatic and spicy hop flavours combined with light malts.

Weobley (NEW)

Jules, Portland Street, Weobley, Herefordshire, HR4 8SB
☎ (01544) 318206 🌐 theweobleybrewing.co

Brewing began in 2019 at this nanobrewery adjacent to Jules restaurant. Beers are initially available bottled for the restaurant and other local outlets.

Wessex

Rye Hill Farm, Longbridge Deverill, Wiltshire, BA12 7DE
☎ (01985) 844532
✉ wessexbrewery@tinyworld.co.uk

⊗ This four-barrel brewery went into production in 2001 and moved to its current location in 2004. Since then two new fermenters have been installed. Five local outlets are regularly supplied and beers are also available through selected wholesalers. Beers are occasionally contract brewed when capacity permits. ♦

Stourton Pale Ale (OG 1038, ABV 3.5%)
A pale-coloured, hoppy session beer with plenty of character.

Mild (OG 1038, ABV 3.9%)

Kilmington Best (OG 1041, ABV 4.2%)
Slightly sweet, amber-coloured best bitter with balanced malt and hop characteristics.

Maltings Gold (ABV 4.2%)

Warminster Warrior (OG 1045, ABV 4.5%)

Old Ale (OG 1047, ABV 4.6%)

Golden Apostle (OG 1048, ABV 4.8%)

Beast of Zeals (OG 1066, ABV 6.6%)

Russian Stoat (OG 1080, ABV 9%)

WEST

Templeton Building, Glasgow Green, Glasgow, G40 1AW
☎ (0141) 550 0135 🌐 westbeer.com

Brewery producing artisan lagers and ales in strict accordance with the German Purity Law of 1516, which also has an on-site beerhall, restaurant and

events venue. All beers are unpasteurised.
‼ 🍺 ◆ RAIB V

West Berkshire SIBA

The Old Dairy, Yattendon, Berkshire, RG18 0XT
☎ (01635) 767090 ⊕ wbbrew.com

⊠ West Berkshire was established in 1995. In 2018, following investment from new shareholders, capacity was increased tenfold. The new state-of-the-art brewery is located in a former dairy building. Plans have been approved for the brewery to take over the whole of the old dairy, which would effectively double its size again. The site also includes a shop, taproom and kitchen. Beers are available throughout the South of England. ‼ 🍺 ◆ RAIB

Mister Chubb's (ABV 3.4%)
A copper-coloured, well-balanced session bitter with spicy, fruit and floral flavours.

Maggs' Mild (ABV 3.5%) 🍺
A traditional, rich, dark-coloured mild with biscuit malt flavours, a light earthy hop aroma and a velvety smooth finish.

Mister Swift (ABV 3.7%)
A punchy pale ale with herbal and pine notes backed by subtle caramel maltiness.

Good Old Boy (OG 1043, ABV 4%) 🍺 🍂
Tawny-coloured bitter with a malty aroma, then a balanced flavour with hops and fruit, leading to a long, dry, bitter aftertaste.

Maharaja IPA (OG 1048, ABV 5.1%)
An IPA with tropical fruit flavours, full bitterness and a rich, earthy finish.

West by Three

See Freetime

West Coast

See Conwy

West Coast Rock

🏠 1877 The Brew Room, 137-139 Church Street, Blackpool, FY1 3NX
☎ (01253) 319165 ⊕ thebrewroom1887.co.uk

⊚Historic Blackpool pub, which reopened as a specialist beer outlet in 2017 and first brewed in 2018 using a six-barrel plant. Many of the beers have a Blackpool Football Club theme, the club being founded in the pub in 1887. ‼◆

West End

🏠 68-70 Braunstone Gate, Leicester, LE3 5LG
☎ 07875 745302 ⊕ thewestendbrewery.co.uk

⊚The West End Brewery is Leicester city centre's original brewpub, which opened in 2016 using a 2.5-barrel plant. Total capacity doubled to five barrels in 2019. Beers are available in the pub and occasionally in other local outlets. ◆ RAIB

Westerham SIBA

Beggars Lane, Westerham, Kent, TN16 1QP

☎ (01732) 864427 ⊕ westerhambrewery.co.uk

⊠ The brewery was established in 2004 at the National Trust's Grange Farm, and is housed in a former dairy. More than 500 outlets are supplied in Kent, Surrey, Sussex and London. In 2017 more than £1.6m was invested in a new building, which houses the brewery, taproom, shop and the tasting room for the Squerryes Estate Winery. ‼ 🍺 ◆ RAIB

Finchcocks Original (OG 1036.2, ABV 3.5%)
Mid-gold-coloured session beer. Citrus notes on the palate with a hint of biscuit and resin hoppiness.

Grasshopper Kentish Bitter (OG 1039, ABV 3.8%)
A dark-coloured, malty bitter with nutty, roasted notes from the chocolate malt.

Summer Perle (OG 1038.5, ABV 3.8%)
Golden ale with a spicy, refreshing finish.

Spirit of Kent (OG 1039.5, ABV 4%)
Crisp golden ale with floral and fruity notes. Complex tropical fruit and citrus flavours blend with the sweet malt. Assertive dry hop notes on the finish.

British Bulldog (OG 1040, ABV 4.1%)
A rich, full-bodied best bitter with a massive aroma and palate of jammy fruit, biscuity malt and bitter hop resins.

1965 Special Bitter Ale (OG 1047.5, ABV 4.8%)
A clean, refreshing bitter with a full-bodied flavour.

Audit Ale (OG 1061, ABV 6.2%)
Hoppy, strong and bitter.

Westmorland

Kendal, Cumbria ☎ 07554 562662
✉ westmorlandbrewery@gmail.com

Westmorland began brewing in 2016 using a one-barrel plant.

Wetherby

York Road Estate, York Road, Wetherby, West Yorkshire, LS22 7SU
☎ (01937) 584637 ⊕ wetherbybrewco.com

⊚Wetherby Brew Co was established in 2017 and is located a short walk from the town centre. It is independently owned and operated and brews on a 1.25-barrel plant. The brewery incorporates an on-site taproom and bottle shop. Regular events are held and half day brewing experiences are offered. ‼ 🍺 ◆ RAIB V

Bitter (ABV 3.8%)

Blonde (ABV 3.9%)

Gold (ABV 4%)

Porter (ABV 4.3%)

Classic (ABV 4.4%)

IPA (ABV 4.4%)

Wharfe

See Hambleton

Wharfedale

🏠 Back Barn, 16 Church Street, Ilkley, West Yorkshire, LS29 9DS
☎ (01943) 609587 ⊕ wharfedalebrewery.com

Wharfedale began brewing in 2012 using spare capacity at Five Towns brewery in Wakefield. Brewing moved to Ilkley in 2013 using a 2.5-barrel plant located at the rear of the Flying Duck pub, creating Wharfedale's first brewpub.

Whim SIBA

Whim Farm, Hartington, Derbyshire, SK17 0AX
☎ (01298) 84991 whimales.co.uk

Whim opened in 1993 in outbuildings at Whim Farm. The beers are available in 50-70 outlets and the brewery's tied house, Wilkes Head, Leek. ♦

Marynka (ABV 3.3%)

Arbor Light (OG 1035, ABV 3.6%)
Light-coloured bitter, sharp and clean with lots of hop character and a delicate light aroma.

Hartington Bitter (OG 1039, ABV 4%)
A light, golden-coloured, well-hopped session beer. A dry finish with a spicy, floral aroma.

Earl Grey Bitter (OG 1042, ABV 4.2%)
Traditional, full-bodied deep golden brown-coloured ale. Complex malt and dry hop flavours.

Hartington IPA (OG 1045, ABV 4.5%)
Pale-coloured ale, smooth on the palate allowing malt to predominate. Slightly sweet finish combined with distinctive light hop bitterness.

Flower Power (OG 1053, ABV 5.3%)
Light, golden-coloured beer with a flowery hop aroma, citrus with mild spice on the palate and a dry, bitter finish.

Whitacre

Dog Inn, Dog Lane, Nether Whitacre, Warwickshire, B46 2DU
☎ (01675) 481318 ☎ 07977 393833
thedoginnwhitacre.co.uk

Established in 2017 by licencees Gary and Joanne Webb to supply the adjacent Dog Inn. The nine-gallon brewery is situated in an outbuilding. All the beer names are dog themed as the owners are dog lovers with two Shih Tzus, Ted and Chicco.

Whitby SIBA

East Cliff, Whitby, North Yorkshire, YO22 4JR ☎ 07516 116377 whitby-brewery.com

Whitby Brewery was established in 2012 under the Conquest name by a local team who built the brewery from scratch. It expanded in 2016 to a new site in the shadow of Whitby Abbey, with a 20-barrel capacity and an on-site taproom. Local outlets are supplied. !!

Abbey Blonde (OG 1036, ABV 3.6%)
A golden-coloured blonde ale with a zesty finish and strong notes of toffee.

Whaler (OG 1040, ABV 4%)
A fruity pale ale with a malty, citrus flavour and a mild bitter finish.

Saltwick Nab (OG 1044, ABV 4.2%)
A full-bodied, ruby-coloured ale with a pleasantly fruity finish.

Black Death (OG 1045, ABV 4.5%)

Jet Black (OG 1047, ABV 4.5%)
A finely-balanced porter packed with liquorice, coffee and sweet toffee flavours.

Brewed for Station Inn, Whitby:

Platform 3 (OG 1038, ABV 3.6%)
Nutty pale ale with a smooth citrus finish.

White Hart

White Hart Hotel & Restaurant, 15 High Street, Halstead, Essex, CO9 2AP
☎ (01787) 475657 whitehartbrewery.co.uk

Brewing began in 2017 in old stables at the back of the White Hart. Both the brewery and pub are owned by father and son, Charles and Hugo Townsend. Beers are available in the pub and at local beer festivals.

White Hart Tap

White Hart Tap, 4 Keyfield Terrace, St Albans, Hertfordshire, AL1 1QJ
☎ (01727) 860974 whitehарttap.co.uk

Brewing began in 2015. Beers are only available in the pub.

White Horse SIBA

3 Ware Road, White Horse Business Park, Stanford in the Vale, Oxfordshire, SN7 8NY
☎ (01367) 718700 whitehorsebrewery.co.uk

White Horse was founded in 2004. The brewery has major outlets in Oxfordshire, as well as supplying other outlets nationally. In addition to its regular beers, a range of monthly beers is brewed as well as a number of one-off beers brewed under the Luna brand name. ♦

Oxfordshire Bitter (OG 1038.7, ABV 3.7%)
Golden-coloured bitter, well-hopped with a clean, fruity finish.

Black Beauty (OG 1043.2, ABV 3.9%)
Rich, deep, ruby-coloured mild.

Village Idiot (OG 1041.8, ABV 4.1%)
A blonde ale with a complex hop aroma and taste.

Dark Blue Oxford University Ale (OG 1045, ABV 4.3%)

Wayland Smithy (OG 1047.1, ABV 4.4%)
A red-brown-coloured ale with a biscuit flavour balanced with a spicy hop finish.

White Rabbit (NEW)

Unit 15a, Weston Industrial Estate, Honeybourne, Worcestershire, WR11 7GB ☎ 07713 952807
whiterabbit@aol.co.uk

Brewing began in 2018. The brewery incorporates Cannon Royall brewery, previously situated in Ombersley, and has upgraded and re-used some of the old equipment.

Brown Bess (OG 1036, ABV 3.5%)

Opal (OG 1042, ABV 4%)

Elwood's Dark (OG 1044, ABV 4.1%)
Dark brown-coloured porter, small creamy head, coffee and chocolate aromas continue with smoky stone fruit flavours finishing with a slightly sweet then peaty, slightly bitter finish.

Jammers Ale (OG 1044, ABV 4.3%)

Old Ale (OG 1048, ABV 4.6%)

White Rock SIBA

Units 6 & 7, Dysons Complex, Southside, St Sampson, Guernsey, GY2 4QJ
☎ (01481) 249920 ☎ 07911 760302
whiterockbrewery.gg

White Rock began brewing in 2013 in a modern industrial unit and supplies the limited free trade on the island as well as a small number of tied houses. ‼♦

Pushang (OG 1038, ABV 3.8%)
Golden ale with a light floral aroma and subtle sweetness.

Wonky Donkey (OG 1047, ABV 4.7%)
A distinctive hoppy bitter with hints of citrus.

Lost Tourist (OG 1050, ABV 5.3%)
A hoppy IPA with citrus and slight caramel flavours.

White Rose SIBA

7 Doncaster Road, Mexborough, South Yorkshire, S64 0HL
☎ (0114) 246 6334
whiterose.brewery@btinternet.com

Established in 2007 by Gary Sheriff, former head brewer at Wentworth Brewery. Formerly sharing premises with Little Ale Cart, White Rose then brewed in Mexborough, sharing premises with Imperial Brewery (qv). In 2018 it moved to its own premises using a new seven-barrel plant. ‼♦

Original Blonde (OG 1040, ABV 4%)
A golden ale with a citrus aroma and bitterness on the palate.

Stairlift to Heaven (OG 1042, ABV 4.2%)

Raven (OG 1048, ABV 4.9%)
A classic stout, well-balanced, dark-coloured, rich and fruity.

Whitechapel

See Haworth Steam

Whitefaced (NEW)

c/o 24 Ashfield Close, Penistone, South Yorkshire, S36 6EY ☎ 07894 532456

Established in 2017 producing bottled and keg beers, the brewery moved into cask production in 2019. Owner/brewer David Hampshaw operates from his residence on a 1.3-barrel kit and is looking to relocate. The brewery is named after the highly prized local whitefaced woodland sheep. ♦

Whitewater

40 Tullyframe Road, Kilkeel, Northern Ireland, BT34 4RZ
☎ (028) 4176 9449 whitewaterbrewery.com

Established in 1996, Whitewater is now the biggest brewery in Northern Ireland. One pub is owned, the White Horse in Saintfield, Co Down. ‼♦

Copperhead (OG 1037, ABV 3.7%)

Crown & Glory (OG 1038, ABV 3.8%)

Belfast Black (OG 1042, ABV 4.2%)

Belfast Ale (OG 1046, ABV 4.5%)

Maggie's Leap IPA (OG 1047, ABV 4.7%)
Triple-hopped IPA with powerful hop and fruit aromas.

Clotworthy Dobbin (OG 1050, ABV 5%)

Whitley Bay

The Brewery, 2-4 South Parade, Whitley Bay, NE26 2RG ☎ 07392 823480
whitleybaybrewingcompany@gmail.com

Brewing commenced in 2016 on a five-barrel plant and relocated to larger premises, a new brewery tap, in the centre of Whitley Bay in 2018. Around 40 local outlets are supplied. **V**

Slow Joe (ABV 3.9%)
Pilsner-style ale with a hint of magnolia.

Warrior (ABV 3.9%)
A well-balanced pale ale, an initial flavour of crystal malt followed by a pleasant bitter aftertaste.

Spanish City Blonde (ABV 4.2%)
A light golden-coloured ale with a hint of grapefruit and citrus.

Dark Knight (ABV 4.3%)

Ghost Ships (ABV 4.3%)

Equinox (ABV 5%)

55 Degrees North (ABV 5.5%)

Whitstable SIBA

Little Telpits Farm, Woodcock Lane, Grafty Green, Kent, ME17 2AY
☎ (01622) 851007 whitstablebrewery.co.uk

Whitstable Brewery was founded in 2003. It currently provides all the beer for the Whitstable Oyster Company's three restaurants, their hotel and a brewery tap as well as supplying pubs all over Kent, London and Surrey. ♦

Native Bitter (OG 1036, ABV 3.7%)
A classic copper-coloured Kentish session bitter with a hoppy aroma and a long, dry bitter hop finish.

Renaissance Ruby Mild (OG 1038, ABV 3.7%)
Deep ruby in colour, this classic mild has a nutty taste with a gentle roast malt aroma.

East India Pale Ale (OG 1040, ABV 4.1%)
A well-hopped, golden-coloured IPA with a good grapefruit aroma, hop character and lingering bitter finish.

Oyster Stout (OG 1045, ABV 4.5%)
Rich, dry deep chocolate, coffee and roast malt flavours.

Pearl of Kent (OG 1043, ABV 4.5%)
A well-rounded premium golden ale with a subtle bitterness and hints of tropical fruit.

Winkle Picker (OG 1042, ABV 4.5%)
A well-balanced, amber-coloured best bitter. A pleasant maltiness is offset by a firm but not overpowering bitterness and hints of orange.

Kentish Reserve (OG 1047, ABV 5%)
Reddish-amber-coloured premium bitter. Malty notes with flavours of peaches and plums, ending on a note of rich ruby port.

Whittington's

Three Choirs Vineyards, Newent, Gloucestershire, GL18 1LS
☎ (01531) 890555 🌐 whittingtonbrewery.co.uk

Whittington's started in 2003. Beers are contract brewed by an unnamed brewery. The legendary Dick Whittington came from nearby Pauntley, hence the name and feline theme. Five bottle-conditioned ales are available. RAIB

Why Not

27 Redfern Road, Thorpe St Andrew, Norwich, NR7 9RB
☎ (01603) 300786 🌐 thewhynotbrewery.co.uk

Why Not began brewing in 2005 on a 1.5-barrel plant located to the rear of the house of proprietor Colin Emms. In 2006 the brewery was extensively upgraded, doubling in capacity. In 2011 the brewery was moved to a new location in Thorpe St Andrew. RAIB

Wally's Revenge (OG 1040, ABV 4%)
An overtly bitter beer with a hoppy background. The bitterness holds on to the end as an increasing astringent dryness develops.

Roundhead Porter (OG 1045, ABV 4.5%)

Cavalier Red (OG 1047, ABV 4.7%)
Explosive fruity nose belies the gentleness of the taste. The summer fruit aroma dominates this red-gold-coloured brew. A sweet, fruity start disappears under a quick, bitter ending.

Norfolk Honey Ale (OG 1050, ABV 5%)
A golden-coloured beer with a honey nose. A definite hop edge leaves a honey aftertaste.

Chocolate Nutter (OG 1056, ABV 5.5%)

Whyte Bar (NEW)

Exeter, Devon 🌐 whytebarbrew.com

Whyte Bar (pronounced White Bear) began brewing in 2018 using spare capacity at other breweries. No real ale.

Wibblers SIBA

Goldsands Road, Southminster, Essex, CM0 7JW
☎ (01621) 772044 🌐 wibblers.com

⊠ Wibblers was established in 2007 and expanded to a 20-barrel plant in 2009. In 2016 the brewery moved to new premises in Southminster with a taproom. Last year the taproom was expanded four fold along with capacity. Craft beers and ciders are now produced as well as seasonal specials. Wibblers supply numerous outlets throughout East Anglia, London and Kent in addition to exporting to mainland Europe. !! ♦ RAIB

Dengie IPA (OG 1037, ABV 3.6%)
Malty and full flavoured with gentle bitterness and balanced sweetness.

Apprentice (OG 1039, ABV 3.9%)
Amber-coloured session beer with a hoppy aroma and light, malty taste.

Dengie Dark (OG 1039, ABV 4%)
Smooth, light, malty beer with subtle bitterness and balancing sweetness.

Dengie Gold (OG 1040, ABV 4%)
Golden in colour with a refreshing hop punch, providing a citrus aroma and balanced bitterness.

Hop Black (OG 1041, ABV 4%)
A dark-coloured bitter that tastes light and hoppy.

Crafty Stoat (OG 1056, ABV 5.3%)
A dark-coloured, malty stout.

Winter Wibble (OG 1062, ABV 6%)

Wicked Hathern

See Staffordshire

Wickwar SIBA

Old Brewery, Station Road, Wickwar, Gloucestershire, GL12 8NB
☎ (01454) 292000 🌐 wickwarbrewing.co.uk

Wickwar was established as a 10-barrel brewery in 1990. In 2004 it expanded to 50 barrels. Moles Brewery and pubs were acquired in 2017, bringing its pub estate up to 20. 350 outlets are supplied on a regular basis and the beers are available nationally through most distributors and SIBA. !! ♦

BOB (OG 1040, ABV 4%)
Amber-coloured, this has a distinctive blend of hop, malt and apple/pear citrus fruits. The slightly sweet taste turns into a fine, dry bitterness, with a similar malty, lasting finish.

Cotswold Way (OG 1042, ABV 4.2%)
Amber-coloured, it has a pleasant aroma of pale malt, hop and fruit. Good dry bitterness in the taste with some sweetness. Similar though less sweet in the finish, with good hop content.

Falling Star (OG 1045, ABV 4.2%)
A golden-coloured premium beer with a floral aroma and light malty finish.

Stand-Up IPA (OG 1047, ABV 4.6%)
An intense IPA with complex bitterness, a citrus twang and subtle herbal notes.

Station Porter (OG 1061, ABV 6.1%)
Aromas of roasted malt, coffee, chocolate and rich fruits, and flavours of chocolate, liquorice, coffee and smoke. Smooth and warming roast and slightly sweet finish.

Brewed under the Moles brand name:

Gold (OG 1038, ABV 3.8%)
Golden-coloured, hoppy beer with subtle citrus fruit aroma and flavour, with a malty background.

Best (OG 1040, ABV 4%)
An amber-coloured bitter, clean, dry and malty with some bitterness and delicate floral hop flavour.

Elmo's (OG 1044, ABV 4.4%)
Medium-bodied bitter with a subtle fruit aroma and flavours, leading to a long bitter finish.

Wigan

The Old Brewery, Brewery Yard, off Wallgate, Wigan, WN1 1JU
☎ (01942) 234976 🌐 wiganbrewhouse.co.uk

Local businessman Martin Blythe leased the now-defunct AllGates Brewery premises in 2018, including the acquisition of beers formerly brewed by AllGates. He will also be featuring some of his own beer recipes, developed by head brewer Jonathan Provost with Martin's input. ‼♦

Pretoria (OG 1036, ABV 3.6%)
A yellow gold-coloured ale with assertive lemon sherbet hops, juicy but dry and bitter. Pale malt to finish with a touch of balancing sweetness.

California (OG 1037, ABV 3.9%)
A pale yellow-coloured beer with a restrained hoppy and fruity aroma. It is clean and fresh-tasting, with hops and fruit in the mouth and a bitter hoppy finish.

Casino (ABV 3.9%)
A well-balanced session pale ale with aromas of stone fruit and citrus.

Wigan Junction (OG 1038, ABV 3.9%)
A deep copper-coloured traditional session bitter.

Dry Bones (OG 1040, ABV 4%)
Light golden in colour and hoppy, with tropical fruits and hints of melon.

Slider (ABV 4%)
A light and crisp pale ale brewed with lager and oat malts.

Tempo (ABV 4.1%)

Blue Sky Tea (ABV 4.2%)
A pale ale infused with Blue Sky blend tea.

Kicker IPA (OG 1042, ABV 4.2%)
Pale-coloured and fruity, single-hopped ale with fruit salad flavours.

All-Nighter (ABV 4.3%)
Black-coloured ale, bitter with strong roast malt flavours and a hoppy aroma.

Station Road Stout (ABV 4.5%)
Dark brown-coloured beer with a malty, fruity aroma. Creamy and malty in taste, with blackberry fruits and a satisfying aftertaste.

Wild Beer SIBA

Lower Westcombe Farm, Evercreech, Somerset, BA4 6ER
☎ (01749) 838742 ☎ 07968 721841
wildbeerco.com

Brewing began in 2012 using a 24-hectolitre plant. Set on a Somerset farm, the brewery shares premises with Westcombe Dairy in an adjacent building. A wide range of beers is produced, including sour beers using alternative fermentation methods and unusual yeasts, alongside barrel-aging and a blending programme. Seasonal wild ingredients are also foraged. Two pub restaurants are owned. ♦RAIB

Bibble (OG 1042, ABV 4.2%)
Pale ale with tropical fruits and mangoes. Unfined and naturally hazy.

Scarlet Fever (OG 1048, ABV 4.8%)
A classic ale, balancing hops with caramel and bready sweetness.

Fresh (OG 1055, ABV 5.5%)
A citrus ale with big hits of grapefruit.

Madness IPA (OG 1068, ABV 6.8%)

Wild Boar

Wild Boar, Crook Road, Bowness-on-Windermere, Cumbria, LA23 3NF ☎ 08458 504604
englishlakes.co.uk

Brewing began in 2013 at the Wild Boar, a large, traditional Lakeland luxury hotel. The hotel is part of the English Lakes Hotels group and supplies beers to hotels within the group. ♦

Wild Card SIBA

Unit 2, Lockwood Way, Blackhorse Road, Higham Hill, London, E17 5RB ☎ 07982 402650
wildcardbrewery.co.uk

Wild Card began brewing in 2013, initially using spare capacity at several breweries in and around London. After brewing at its Ravenswood site, production moved to Lockwood in 2018 along with increasing the capacity of the brewery. Both sites remain popular taprooms at the weekend.

Pale Amarillo (ABV 3.4%)

Jack of Clubs (ABV 4.5%)
Complex ruby-brown-coloured best bitter with malty nose. Flavour has hints of chocolate, citrus and malt and a slightly bitter finish.

King of Hearts (ABV 4.5%)
Easy-drinking beer with a lager character in the lemony flavour, which is sweet and biscuity. Clean, dry finish.

Ace of Spades (ABV 4.7%)
Black-coloured porter with a fruity nose overlaid with a little roast. Liquorice, caramelised fruit and roasted malt flavour. Lingering dryness.

Queen of Diamonds (ABV 5%)
Smooth golden ale with strong citrus aroma and flavour alongside biscuit notes. The finish is dry with a little bitterness.

Wild Horse SIBA

Unit 4, Cae Bach Builder Street, Llandudno, LL30 1DR
☎ (01492) 868292 wildhorsebrewing.co.uk

Small brewery concentrating on supplying KeyKeg and bottled beers to local bars and off-licences. All products are unfiltered and unpasteurised. ♦

Wild Weather Ales SIBA

Unit 19, Easter Park, Benyon Road, Aldermaston, Berkshire, RG7 2PQ
☎ (0118) 970 1837 wildweatherales.com

Established in 2012, this is a 15-barrel plant brewing a vast array of beer styles. Many of the beers are one-off collaborations. All beers are unfined and available in cask, can and KeyKeg and are distributed throughout the UK. The brewery shop has eight beers on tap, which can be consumed on site. ‼♦RAIB

Serendipity (OG 1037, ABV 3.9%)
A fruity golden ale.

Betrayal (OG 1039, ABV 4%)
Tropical fruity flavours of limes, pineapple, mango and orange, with a long hop finish.

Obscure 80's Reference (ABV 5%)
A smooth, hazy beer bursting with passion fruit, pine and berry flavours.

Shepherd's Warning (OG 1056, ABV 5.6%)
A smooth, rich IPA with strong hoppy flavours of grapefruit, peach and mango.

Wildcraft

Foragers' Rest, Buxton, Norfolk, NR10 5JD
☎ (01603) 278054 ☎ 07584 308850
wildcraftbrewery.co.uk

Wildcraft was set up in 2016 and uses as much foraged and locally sourced ingredients as possible to produce its beers.

Wilde Child

Unit 5, Armley Road, Leeds, West Yorkshire, LS12 2DR
☎ 07908 419028 wildechildbrewing.co.uk

Established as one of the smallest breweries in Leeds in 2016, Keir McAllister-Wilde took his operation from a one-barrel plant in a garage to a 10-barrel operation in a 2,000 square foot unit within two years. There are more than 60 different ales in Wilde Child's portfolio, all are unfined.

Opaque Reality (ABV 5.9%)

Wilderness

Unit 54, Mochdre Industrial Estate, Newtown, SY16 4LE
☎ (01686) 449020 wildernessbrew,co.uk

Wilderness began brewing in 2018 using a custom-made five-barrel plant. The brewery focuses on seasonal, barrel-aged and mixed fermentation beers. Belgian and farmhouse-style beers make up the majority of the range.

Motueka Grisette (ABV 3.8%)

Southern Pale (ABV 4.3%)

Keller Weiss (ABV 5.1%)

Equinox Saison (ABV 5.2%)

Wildside

See Brightside

Williams Bros SIBA

New Alloa Brewery, Kelliebank, Alloa, FK10 1NT
☎ (01259) 725511 williamsbrosbrew.com

A brotherhood of brewers, creating unique beers. Bruce and Scott Williams started brewing Heather Ale in 1988. A range of indigenous, historic ales have been added since. Hundreds of cask ale outlets are supplied worldwide. ‼♦

Fraoch Heather Ale (OG 1041, ABV 4.1%)
The unique taste of heather flowers is noticeable in this beer. A fine floral aroma and spicy taste give character to this drinkable speciality beer.

Birds & Bees (OG 1044, ABV 4.3%)
A bright golden ale with a late infusion of fresh elderflower and lemon zest. Fruity, aromatic and refreshing.

March of the Penguins (OG 1050, ABV 4.9%)
A dark-coloured, creamy stout with aromas of roast malts, coffee, liquorice and orange peel. The aromas carry on into the flavour with a smooth mouthfeel, rich malty start, fresh hoppy middle and a lingering orange aftertaste.

Joker IPA (OG 1050, ABV 5%)
A well-balanced, bittersweet IPA, golden in colour and fruity on the nose with hints of cedar.

Seven Giraffes (OG 1051, ABV 5.1%)
A classic IPA with a late infusion of elderflower and lemon. Deep gold in colour with aromas of elderflower and citrus hops, followed by sweet caramel. On the tongue the biscuity malts are balanced by the bitterness of the hops.

Willy's

17 High Cliff Road, Cleethorpes, Lincolnshire, DN35 8RQ
☎ (01472) 602145

The brewery opened in 1989 to provide beer mainly for its in-house pub in Cleethorpes, although some beer is sold in the free trade. It has a five-barrel plant with maximum capacity of 15 barrels a week. The brewery can be viewed at any time from pub or street. ‼♦

Willy's Brew

Rose & Crown, 2 Oxford Road, Stone, Buckinghamshire, HP17 8PB
☎ (01296) 749160 roseandcrownstone.co.uk

A microbrewery based at the Rose & Crown, Stone. Brewing began in 2017 on an 80-litre plant.

Wily Fox SIBA

1 Kellet Close, Wigan, WN5 0LP
☎ (01942) 215525 wilyfoxbrewery.co.uk

A bespoke 20-barrel brewery, set up in 2016. Head brewer Dave Goodwin previously worked for Thwaites and Samuel Smith. ‼

Blonde Vixen (OG 1039.5, ABV 3.8%)
A blonde session ale, light and refreshing with a spicy citrus character and grapefruit overtones.

Prohibition APA (OG 1041, ABV 3.9%)
A classic American-style pale ale with pungent grapefruit notes.

Crafty Fox (OG 1042.5, ABV 4%)
Well-balanced bitter and malty sweetness, with fruity hops. Creamy mouthfeel and bitter finish.

The Fox Hat (OG 1044, ABV 4.2%)
Fruity aroma. Citrus hop taste and bitter hoppy aftertaste.

Karma Citra (OG 1044.5, ABV 4.3%)
A golden ale with intense citrus and tropical flavours.

Wimbledon SIBA

8 College Fields, Prince George's Road, Colliers Wood, London, SW19 2PT
☎ (020) 3674 9786 wimbledonbrewery.com

Set up by Mark Gordon after a 23 year career in the City, Wimbledon began production in 2015 with former Young's and Fuller's brewer Derek Prentice at the helm of a brand new 30-barrel plant. The brewery expanded in 2017 with two new 60-barrel fermenters and further expanded in 2018 with an additional 60-barrel fermenter. ‼ ♦ RAIB

Common PA (ABV 3.7%)
Well-balanced, gold-coloured bitter with mandarin and hoppy flavours and aroma. Floral note in the lingering finish with some dry bitterness.

Copper Leaf (OG 1040, ABV 4%) ◆
Toffee, nuts, apricot and dark marmalade aroma. Chocolate, caramelised toffee, raisins and citrus, well-balanced by a growing dry, spicy bitterness.

Quartermaine IPA (ABV 5.8%) ◆
Amber-coloured beer with slight sweetness complementing citrus and summer fruits plus spicy hops. Fruit, spice and bittersweet finish. Hoppy nose.

Wincle SIBA

Tolls Farm Barn, Dane Bridge, Wincle, Cheshire, SK11 0QE
☎ (01260) 227777 🌐 winclebeer.co.uk

Wincle Beer Company was set up in 2008 in a redundant milking parlour on a working farm located within the Peak District National Park. The brewery now operates a 15-barrel plant in Wincle using water from its own borehole. A brewery shop and sampling room opened in 2017 in a converted stable next to the brewery. !! ◆

Waller (OG 1038, ABV 3.8%)
A pale-coloured and refreshing beer with a distinctive hop character.

Rambler (ABV 4%)
A well-balanced beer with autumn fruit hoppiness.

Sir Philip (OG 1041, ABV 4.2%)
Amber in colour, a premium bitter with a light malty overtone, balanced by hops.

Wibbly Wallaby (OG 1043, ABV 4.4%)
A full-bodied, golden-coloured beer with fruity hop overtones and a dry, slightly biscuity finish.

Burke's Special (ABV 5%)
A chestnut-coloured special bitter with a full malty and fruity taste.

Windermere

See Watermill

Windmill Hill SIBA

Garage Unit, 11 Williams Road, Radford Semele, Warwickshire, CV31 1UR
☎ (01926) 355450 🌐 whbrewery.co.uk

Windmill Hill is an independent microbrewery using a one-barrel plant brewing small batch beers. Around 30 outlets are supplied direct.

Windsor & Eton SIBA

Unit 1, Vansittart Estate, Duke Street, Windsor, Berkshire, SL4 1SE
☎ (01753) 854075 🌐 webrew.co.uk

Four friends, including two fully-qualified brewers, set up the brewery in 2010 though their brewing experience goes back to the original Courage Brewery. In 2018 it was granted a Royal Warrant as Brewer to Her Majesty the Queen. The purpose-built plant is 18 barrels, which supplies around 300 outlets in London and the Thames Valley area. Beers are also produced under the Uprising brand name. !! ◆ RAIB

Knight of the Garter (OG 1036.5, ABV 3.8%) ◆
Golden ale with a citrus hop aroma, joined by some sweetness in the taste, followed by bitterness in the finish.

Windsor Knot (OG 1039, ABV 4%)
Amber-coloured ale with a tropical fruit aroma. An initially sweet malt and fruit taste is followed by a mild bitter finish.

Guardsman (OG 1041, ABV 4.2%)
A tangy best bitter, tawny in colour with a fresh hoppy finish.

Conqueror (OG 1049, ABV 5%) ◆
A black IPA. Malty and hoppy with berry notes. A full, rounded, slightly dry finish.

Brewed under the Uprising brand name:

All Day Pale Ale (ABV 2.7%)
A pale ale with a huge hoppy character.

Windswept SIBA

Unit B, 13 Coulardbank Industrial Estate, Lossiemouth, IV31 6NG
☎ (01343) 814310 🌐 windsweptbrewing.co.uk

Windswept Brewing Co was established in 2012 and is situated near the gates of RAF Lossiemouth. It is run by two former Tornado pilots who are CAMRA members. The brewery has developed to include a bar, shop and regular tours. !! ◆ RAIB

Blonde (OG 1036, ABV 4%) ◆
Smooth, golden-coloured, citrus hoppy brew with hints of peach. Slight malty background.

Hurricane (OG 1041, ABV 4.5%)
A smooth, fruity IPA with a gentle, lingering bitterness. Tropical fruit on the nose with ripe stone fruits on the palate.

Lighthouse (OG 1043, ABV 4.7%)
A delicately-balanced, kolsch-style lager with subtle fruit aromas and clean malt flavours.

APA (OG 1045, ABV 5%) ◆
Good mix of malts and grapefruit hop throughout. Tangy finish.

Weizen (OG 1053, ABV 5.2%) ◆
Cloudy wheat beer full of bananas and pear drops with a hint of spices.

Wolf (OG 1062, ABV 6%) ◆
Dark-coloured, strong-tasting, slightly sweet, roasted malty brew with chocolate and a vanilla coffee background.

Typhoon (OG 1055, ABV 6.2%)
A refreshing IPA with citrus flavours, especially mandarin.

Tornado (OG 1065, ABV 6.7%)
Robust malt complements the tropical fruit and resinous pine hop flavours.

Windy

Volunteer Inn, New Road, Seavington St Michael, Somerset, TA19 0QE
☎ (01460) 240126 🌐 thevolly.co.uk

The brewery was established at the Volunteer Inn in 2011 using a four-barrel plant. The name stems from the time when alterations were carried out to the back of the pub and the workmen suffered extremes of varying weather conditions. All beers are named with a weather theme. !! ◆

Winster Valley

See Handsome

Winter's

8 Keelan Close, Norwich, NR6 6QZ
☎ (01603) 787820 🌐 wintersbrewery.com

Winter's was established in 2001 by David Winter, who had previous award-winning success as a brewer for both Woodforde's and Chalk Hill breweries. Winter's ales have won many awards, with David now passing his brewing knowledge to his son, Mark, an award-winning brewer in his own right. ♦

Mild (OG 1036.5, ABV 3.6%)
A long-lasting, biscuity roast backbone. Caramel notes give depth as a growing hoppy bitterness adds complexity to the finish.

Bitter (OG 1038.5, ABV 3.8%)
Gentle, easy-drinking brew with a soft strawberry bouquet. Sweet biscuity notes develop to augment the hoppy, increasingly citrus base.

Evolution APA (ABV 4%)

Geniuss (OG 1041.5, ABV 4.1%)
A dark brown-coloured stout that has a smooth mouthfeel with a grainy edge. Roast dominates throughout but is balanced by a mix of malt, a bittersweet fruitiness and an increasingly nutty finish.

Golden (OG 1041.9, ABV 4.1%)
Just a hint of hops in the aroma. The initial taste combines a dry bitterness with a fruity apple buttress. The finish slowly subsides into a long, dry bitterness.

Tranquility (ABV 4.2%)

Storm Force (OG 1053, ABV 5.3%)
A well-defined, sweetish brew. Hops and vine fruit give depth to the malty backbone of this pale brown-coloured strong beer. All flavours hold up well as the finish develops a warming softness.

Wintrip

7 Copenhagen Street, Worcester, WR1 2HB ☎ 07964 196194 🌐 wintripbrew.co

Wintrip began brewing in 2014 as Three Shires Brewery on a hand-built plant in Worcester before moving to new premises and subsequent name change. Local outlets are supplied.

Butchers Beastly Best (OG 1043, ABV 4%)
A russet-coloured best bitter with a punchy fruit aroma.

Salt Mine Stout (ABV 4.6%)
Stout brewed with salt chocolate and vanilla pods, with a hoppy bite.

Wiper and True SIBA

2 – 8 York Street, St Werburghs, Bristol, BS2 9XT
☎ (0117) 941 2501 🌐 wiperandtrue.com

Originally launched in 2012 by Michael Wiper as a cuckoo brewery, Wiper and True has operated since 2015 using its own 20-barrel plant. It produces an ever-changing range of bottle-conditioned beers, with a small amount going into casks. The beers are available locally in Bristol/Bath, nationally and internationally. !! ♦ RAIB

Wishbone

2a Worth Bridge Industrial Estate, Chesham Street, Keighley, West Yorkshire, BD21 4LG ☎ 07867 419445 🌐 wishbonebrewery.co.uk

Established in 2015 and run by a husband and wife team with many years previous experience in the brewing industry, beers are brewed on a modern 10-barrel brew plant. The on-site bar is open to the public two days each month.

Blonde (OG 1037, ABV 3.6%)
A hoppy golden ale with with a strong citrus character. A bitter, hoppy and slightly astringent finish.

Volk (OG 1038, ABV 3.9%)

Flux (OG 1041, ABV 4.1%)

Drover (OG 1043, ABV 4.2%)

Tiller Pin (OG 1041, ABV 4.2%)

Abyss (OG 1048, ABV 4.3%)
Caramel and coffee bean aroma in a stout of chocolate and liquorice, leading into a malty finish.

Gumption (OG 1046, ABV 4.5%)
Well-balanced, amber-coloured best bitter. Look for hints of dried fruit, biscuit and nuts, underpinned by dry hoppiness, leading to a bitter finish.

Witham

c/o The Chicken Sheds, Upp Hall Farm, Salmons Lane, Coggeshall, Essex, CO6 1RY
☎ (01376) 563123 ☎ 07824 698235
✉ glennackerman15@gmail.com

Brewing started in 2012, using a 0.5-barrel plant at the Woolpack Inn, Witham. In 2015 it began using spare capacity at the Red Fox Brewery (qv). The beer continues to be available at the Woolpack.

Scruffy (OG 1041, ABV 3.9%)

Gold (OG 1041, ABV 4.1%)
A light, refreshing, golden-coloured beer with a citrus aftertaste.

No Name (OG 1043, ABV 4.3%)
A best bitter with malty roasted flavours giving way to a surprisingly hoppy finish.

Withnell's SIBA

Unit 35, The Old Mill Industrial Estate, School Lane, Bamber Bridge, Lancashire, PR5 6SY
☎ (01254) 830989 ☎ 07787 567471
🌐 withnells.co.uk

Withnell's was established in 2016 using a five-barrel plant. Beers are supplied direct to pubs within a 20-mile radius of the brewery.

Invincibles Ale (ABV 3.7%)

Blonde Summit (ABV 4%)

Hoppy Fettler (ABV 4.3%)
A refreshingly hoppy pale ale, packed with tropical hops balanced against a malt background.

Push Iron (ABV 4.5%)

Wizard

Unit 4, Lundy View, Mullacott Cross Industrial Estate, Ilfracombe, Devon, EX34 8PY ☎ 07584 093470 ✉ wizardbrewery@gmail.com

⊠ Having closed for a period, new owner Carly O'Callaghan purchased the brewery in 2017. Beers are available in local pubs and restaurants. Further beers are planned. ‼◆

Lundy's Gold (OG 1042, ABV 4.1%)

Druid's Fluid (OG 1048.5, ABV 5%)

Wobbly

Unit 22c, Beech Business Park, Tillington Road, Hereford, HR4 9QJ ☎ (01432) 355496 ⊕ wobblybrewing.co

Wobbly began brewing in 2013 using a 2.5-barrel plant. A 30-barrel plant is now operational and an on-site taphouse is open on a Friday and Saturday. ‼🍴◆RAIB

Gold (OG 1036.5, ABV 4.2%)
A golden ale with well-balanced bitterness and aromas of lemon balm and spice.

Welder (OG 1046.5, ABV 4.8%)
A modern pale ale with a traditional English and sweet floral aroma. Winter fruit notes of loganberry and blackberry complement the malt background.

Wold Top SIBA

Hunmanby Grange, Wold Newton, East Yorkshire, YO25 3HS ☎ (01723) 892222 ⊕ woldtopbrewery.co.uk

☺An integral part of Hunmanby Grange Farm, Wold Top brewed its first ale in 2003 and uses home and Wolds-grown malting barley and chalk filtered water from the farm's own borehole. Now brewing on a 40-barrel plant, the range includes special edition cask and bottled beers plus three gluten-free beers. The brewery installed a bottling line in 2007 and contract bottles for other breweries. ◆GF

Bitter (OG 1036, ABV 3.7%)
A crisp, clean, aromatic session bitter. Full-flavoured with a long, hoppy finish.

Anglers Reward (OG 1039, ABV 4%)
A refreshing, golden-coloured pale ale with a fruity bitterness and lingering aftertaste.

Wolds Way (OG 1039, ABV 4%)
A golden-coloured pale ale with a fruity bitterness.

Headland Red (OG 1042, ABV 4.3%)
Red-coloured, well-balanced beer with slight peppery, toffee and rye flavours.

Against the Grain (OG 1044, ABV 4.5%)
Premium gluten free bitter, clean and refreshing with a pronounced hoppy lemon aroma and citrus aftertaste.

Wold Gold (OG 1046, ABV 4.8%)
A light-coloured beer with a soft, fruity flavour and a hint of spice.

Wolf SIBA

Decoy Farm, Old Norwich Road, Besthorpe, Norfolk, NR17 2LA ☎ (01953) 457775 ⊕ wolfbrewery.com

⊠ The brewery was founded in 1995 on a 20-barrel plant, which was upgraded to a 25-barrel plant in 2006. It moved to its current site in 2013. More than 300 outlets are supplied. 🍴◆

Edith Cavell (OG 1037, ABV 3.7%) 🍷◆
Hoppy, peppery nose flows into taste. Malt, caramel and bitterness give depth and complexity. Crisp finish with a hoppy edge.

Golden Jackal (OG 1039, ABV 3.7%) 🍷
A hoppy, citrus nose and first taste. Increasingly dry bitter ending as citrus notes fade.

Wolf in Sheep's Clothing (OG 1039, ABV 3.7%) 🍷
Strong, fruity nose with roast. A strong caramel beginning with a bitter roast counterpoint. Gently tapering finish. Increasing raspberry sweetness.

Lavender Honey (OG 1038, ABV 3.8%) 🍷
Malty caramel aroma leads into a bittersweet beginning with background honey notes. A long, drying finish.

Ale (OG 1039, ABV 3.9%)
A hoppy, copper-coloured, full-bodied ale.

Battle of Britain (OG 1039, ABV 3.9%)

Lupus Lupus (OG 1042, ABV 4.2%) 🍷
Hops, with a citrus edge, dominate both aroma and taste. A biscuity background disappears quickly in a short, sharp finish.

Sirius Dog Star (OG 1044, ABV 4.4%) 🍷
Roast, coffee and caramel aroma flows into a similar first taste. Big mouthfeel with a slightly sour, caramel enhanced finale.

Sly Wolf (OG 1041, ABV 4.4%)
A light-coloured blonde beer with lime flavours.

Straw Dog (OG 1045, ABV 4.5%) 🍷
Delicately-flavoured ale with a fruity character. A redcurrant aroma gives way to marmalade and hops. A strong, increasingly bitter finish.

Mad Wolf (OG 1048, ABV 4.7%)

Granny Wouldn't Like It (OG 1049, ABV 4.8%) 🍷
Complex, with a malty bouquet. Increasing bitterness is softened by malt as a gentle, fruity sweetness adds depth.

Woild Moild (OG 1048, ABV 4.8%) 🍷
Heavy and complex with malt, vine fruit, bitterness and roast notes vying for dominance. Increasingly dry finish.

Contract brewed for the City of Cambridge Brewery:

Boathouse (OG 1037, ABV 3.7%)
A light copper-coloured session bitter with a pleasant aroma from the unique blend of hops and malt.

Hobson's Choice (OG 1041, ABV 4.2%)
A light golden ale with a refreshing flowery nose and slightly citrus aftertaste.

Atom Splitter (OG 1045, ABV 4.5%)
An amber-coloured beer bursting with hoppiness and character.

Parkers Piece (OG 1050, ABV 5%)
A rich, ruby-coloured, fruity bitter.

Wood SIBA

Wistanstow, Shropshire, SY7 8DG ☎ (01588) 672523 ⊕ woodbrewery.co.uk

The brewery opened in 1980 in buildings next to the Plough Inn, the brewery's only tied house. Steady growth over the years included the acquisition of the Sam Powell Brewery in 1991. The brewery was sold to drinks firm Yarrawaddie in 2018 and continues to operate, supplying around 200 outlets. ‼◆

Parish Bitter (OG 1038, ABV 3.8%) ◣
A blend of malt and hops with a bitter aftertaste. Pale brown in colour.

Shropshire Lass (OG 1040, ABV 4%)
A golden ale with zesty bitterness.

Beauty (OG 1042, ABV 4.2%)
Mid amber in colour. A fusion of fruity hops give a lingering bitter aftertaste together with a well-rounded maltiness.

Shropshire Lad (OG 1045, ABV 4.5%)
Well-rounded malty flavour with sweetish overtones followed by a subtle bitterness and fruity notes.

Tom Wood's

See Lincolnshire Craft

Woodcote Manor

Kidderminster Road, Dodford, Worcestershire, B61 9DY
☎ (01527) 558141 ☎ 07779 166174
⊕ woodcotemanor.com

⊠ Opened in 2015 in former dairy outbuildings attached to the brewer's house. The one-barrel plant can produce 20 firkins a week. It is run by a keen homebrewer who turned his hobby into a business, using locally sourced ingredients including own grown hops. The regular beers are distributed to a number of local pubs. ◆ RAIB

SSS (OG 1038, ABV 3.8%) ◣
Lightly toasted malt with citrus hops notes and lingering light fruit. Well-balanced on the finish, leaving a lingering soft bitterness with fruity notes.

Half Cut (OG 1042, ABV 4.2%)
A pale ale with a slightly malty aroma with hints of citrus and mango. Malty biscuit tastes with a hint of passion fruit.

Single Hop (OG 1044, ABV 4.4%) ◣
Well-balanced, golden-coloured bitter, light hop aromas with subtle melon, the initial sweetness is followed by a hint of ginger with hops predominating. Long and smooth hoppy finish.

IPA (OG 1046, ABV 4.6%) ◣
Golden-coloured, well-balanced and hoppy. Grapefruit aromas are followed by a pronounced hop and slightly spicy taste, with a lingering bitter finish.

Oatmeal Stout (OG 1049, ABV 4.9%) ◣
Dark in colour, roasted malt, chocolate and coffee tones are evident in the aroma and flavour, leading to a satisfying, slightly bitter finish.

Cap'n Will's Rum & Raisin Stout (OG 1060, ABV 6%)
An initial sweetness followed by flavours of rum then roasted coffee and chocolate. A lingering sweetness and light bitter finish.

Brewed for the Weavers, Kidderminster:

Weavers Exclusive (OG 1044, ABV 4.4%)

Straw-coloured bitter with dry hop flavours, a noticeable grapefruit background and a long, dry finish.

Woodforde's SIBA

Broadland Brewery, Woodbastwick, Norfolk, NR13 6SW
☎ (01603) 720353 ⊕ woodfordes.co.uk

⊠ Founded in 1981 by two members of the Homebrewers' Society, Woodforde's is named after Parson Woodforde, the 18th century Norfolk diarist with a penchant for real ale. In 1989 the brewery moved to its current home at Woodbastwick, where it has its own boreholes and brews using locally-grown Maris Otter. Investment in 2001 and 2008 more than doubled the production capacity. The brewery tap, the Fur & Feather, is located next door, and more than 600 outlets are supplied on a regular basis. ‼ ▆ ◆ RAIB

Mardler's (OG 1036, ABV 3.5%) ◣
Full, malty aroma with hop and caramel. Sweet biscuit flavour with a bitter hoppiness. Caramel notes and sweet malty finish.

Wherry (OG 1037.5, ABV 3.8%) ◣
Malty aroma infused with summer fruits. Smooth and creamy with a huge biscuit base and peachy elements. Hoppy bittersweet ending.

West Coast Wherry (OG 1043.8, ABV 4.2%)
A fresh, zesty, crisp ale.

Bure Gold (OG 1043, ABV 4.3%) ◣
A bouncy orange and biscuit bouquet. A bittersweet hoppy beginning develops into a full-bodied marmalade ending.

Norada (OG 1043.8, ABV 4.3%)
A golden-coloured, hoppy pale ale with a tropical aroma. Hints of mango and papaya twist through the citrus.

Nelsons Revenge (OG 1045, ABV 4.5%) ◣
Malt aroma with hop. Initially malt and caramel float over a slightly hoppy, sweetish character. Tapering biscuity finish with caramel.

Volt (OG 1045.8, ABV 4.5%)
An IPA with tropical, citrus, floral and pine notes.

Norfolk Nog (OG 1047, ABV 4.6%) ◣
Echoes of Pontefract cake dominate. A plummy sweetness is aided by a dry bitterness and a hint of caramel.

Woodman's

Unit 5, Viaduct Works, Frog Lane, Ponsanooth, Cornwall, TR3 7JW ☎ 07941 069890
⊕ woodmanswildale.co.uk

Wild food forager Stuart Woodman started brewing in 2016. He brews a core range of speciality beers plus seasonal and special brews. Most feature fruits and herbs. ‼ ◆ RAIB

Wooha SIBA

Upper Hempriggs Farm, Kinloss, IV36 2UB
☎ (01667) 459929 ☎ 07811 260732
⊕ woohabrewing.com

Wooha opened in 2015 using a 10-barrel plant. It specialises in producing bottle-conditioned ales. Cask-conditioned beers are brewed on demand for beer festivals. Pubs and retail outlets are supplied locally, in Nairn, and across Scotland. In 2017 the brewery moved to larger premises. RAIB

IPA (ABV 6.2%) ◆
Malty background but with a strong peachy hop character in this pale brown-coloured IPA.

Wooly Butt (NEW)

31 Alexandra Road, Hull, East Yorkshire, HU3 2NS
☎ 07966 511242
✉ woolybuttbrewshed@hotmail.com

Wolly Butt Brew Shed is a two-barrel brewery. Rob Sutherland moved to commercial brewing after years of homebrewing experience.

English Pale Ale (Brew 31) (OG 1045, ABV 4.4%)

Worcester

Arch 49, Cherry Tree Walk, Worcester, WR1 3AU
☎ 07906 432049 🌐 worcesterbrewingco.co.uk

A small brewery in the heart of Worcester and home to Sabrina Ales. A range of beers brewed in rotation using traditional British hops, with a loose association to the English Civil War.

Holy Ground (OG 1042, ABV 4.2%)

Powick Porter (ABV 4.5%)

1651 (ABV 5.1%)

Sabrina's Dark Ruby Ale (ABV 5.5%)

Working Hand

Three Horseshoes, Pit House Lane, Leamside, DH4 6QQ
☎ (0191) 584 2394 ☎ 07703 337556
🌐 threehorseshoesleamside.co.uk

Brewing began in 2012 using a 2.5-barrel plant. Beers are available at the Three Horseshoes as well as the four other pubs in the group. The brewery was renamed the Working Hand Brewery in 2016 when Matthew Booth took over the brewing. In 2018 it upgraded to a seven-barrel plant.

World's End

Crown Inn, 60 Wilcot Road, Pewsey, Wiltshire, SN9 5EL
☎ (01672) 562653 🌐 thecrowninnpewsey.com

World's End Ales was established in 2009 on a one-barrel plant at the rear of the Crown Inn, Pewsey. World's End is the 18th-century name for the area in which the brewery is located. !! ◆

Worsthorne SIBA

Unit 11, Siberia Mill, Holgate Street, Briercliffe, Lancashire, BB10 2HQ
☎ (01282) 422588 ☎ 07815 708289
🌐 worsthornebrewingcompany.co.uk

Worsthorne began brewing in 2011 using a 5.5-barrel plant. The brewery moved to larger premises behind the original building in 2014. An expansion to a 10-barrel plant was carried out in 2016, including a licensed visitor centre. More than 150 outlets are supplied. !! ◆

Gold (OG 1036, ABV 3.6%)
Lightly bittered golden ale with a spicy aroma.

Packhorse (OG 1037, ABV 3.7%)
Pale amber-coloured ale with a subtle earthy bitterness and floral spicy finish.

Palamino (OG 1039, ABV 3.9%)

Some Like It Blonde (OG 1039, ABV 3.9%)
A blonde beer with a lingering dry aftertaste.

Chestnut Mare (OG 1040, ABV 4%)
Smooth, dark-coloured bitter, malty with liquorice overtones.

Great White (OG 1042, ABV 4.2%)
Single-hopped blonde beer, smooth with citrus overtones.

Red Man (OG 1042, ABV 4.2%)
Smooth, full-flavoured, light bitter. Overtones of honey and citrus with a satisfying aftertaste and subtle lingering bitterness.

Old Trout (OG 1045, ABV 4.5%)

Blackthorne Stout (OG 1049, ABV 4.9%)
Rich, dark-coloured stout with distinct chocolate and liquorice flavours. A hint of ripe berries and a smooth bitter aftertaste.

Colliers Clog (OG 1055, ABV 5.5%)
A strong pale ale, lightly bittered with spicy overtones and a citrus finish.

Worthington's

See Heritage

Wrexham Lager

42 St Georges Crescent, Wrexham, LL13 8DB
☎ (01978) 266222 🌐 wrexhamlager.co.uk

Brewing began in 2011. No real ale.

Wriggle Valley SIBA

Unit 4, The Sidings, Station Road, Stalbridge, Dorset, DT10 2RQ
☎ (01963) 363343 ☎ 07952 198777
🌐 wrigglevalleybrewery.co.uk

Wriggle Valley began brewing in 2014 based in a converted garage at the owner's house but relocated in 2017 to an industrial unit using a three-barrel plant. Beers are mainly supplied within a 15-mile radius of the brewery. ◆RAIB

Golden Bear (ABV 4%)

Ryme Rambler (OG 1040, ABV 4%)

Dorset Pilgrim (ABV 4.2%)
Session bitter with a good level of bitterness and some fruit.

Copper Hoppa (OG 1047, ABV 4.5%)
A full-bodied, dark copper-coloured ale with big fruit aromas and flavour.

Valley Gold (ABV 4.5%)

Wriggly Monkey

B.131 Motor Transport Yard, Bicester Heritage Centre, Bicester, Oxfordshire, OX26 5HA
☎ (01869) 246599 ☎ 07590 749062
🌐 wrigglymonkeybrewery.com

Established in 2018 on a 1.25-barrel kit, the brewery is based in an old motor transport workshop at an automotive centre and named after the compartment of a chain-drive mechanism of the Fraser Nash car.

Super Sports (ABV 3.2%)
Delicately-balanced, straw-coloured, light pale ale. Subtle floral hop notes balance lemony, crisp malt flavours, a gentle sweetness and a light, hoppy finish.

Full Tilt (ABV 4.2%)
A full-bodied, well-hopped, amber-coloured session bitter with a floral aroma, caramel maltiness and lasting bitterness.

Chara Banc (ABV 5.3%)
A rich, ruby-coloured premium bitter with sweet maltiness, subtle chocolate notes and a gentle, floral, medium dry bitterness in the finish.

George Wright SIBA

Unit 11, Diamond Business Park, Sandwash Close, Rainford, Merseyside, WA11 8LY
☎ (01744) 886686 ⊕ georgewrightbrewing.co.uk

George Wright started production in 2003. The original 2.5-barrel plant was replaced by a five-barrel one, which has since been upgraded again to 25 barrels. ‼ ♦

Drunken Duck (OG 1040, ABV 3.9%)
Fruity, gold-coloured bitter beer with good hop and a dry aftertaste. Some acidity.

Longboat (OG 1040, ABV 3.9%)
Good hoppy bitter with grapefruit and an almost tart bitterness throughout. Some astringency in the aftertaste. Well-balanced, light and refreshing with a good mouthfeel and long, dry finish.

Blonde Moment (OG 1040, ABV 4%)
A premium blonde beer. Light in colour with a herbal nose and sweet aftertaste.

Mild (OG 1042, ABV 4%)

Pipe Dream (OG 1044, ABV 4.3%)
Refreshing, hoppy best bitter with a fruity nose and grapefruit to the fore in the taste. Lasting dry bitter finish.

Pure Blonde (OG 1045, ABV 4.6%)
A premium blonde ale, light and hoppy with an earthy hop flavour.

Cheeky Pheasant (OG 1047, ABV 4.7%)
Light amber in colour, distinctive fruit, malty taste with a sweet aftertaste.

Roman Black (OG 1047, ABV 4.8%)
A dark-coloured premium ale, smooth and creamy with a long, malty, sweet taste.

Blue Moon (OG 1048, ABV 5%)
Easy-drinking, strong, gold-coloured beer. Good malt/bitter balance and well hopped.

Mocne Piwo (OG 1051, ABV 5%)
Strong ale, light amber in colour with a moreish hoppy aftertaste.

Northern Lights (OG 1049, ABV 5.1%)
Strong ale, amber in colour. A strong citrus taste balanced by the bitter hop.

Wrytree

Unit 1, Wrytree Park, Greenhead, Northumberland, CA8 7JA

Brewing commenced in 2015 as Pit Top Brewery. The name changed to Wrytree in 2019.

Gold (OG 1039, ABV 3.9%)

Copper (OG 1040, ABV 4%)

Wychwood

Eagle Maltings, The Crofts, Witney, Oxfordshire, OX28 4DP
☎ (01993) 890800 ⊕ wychwood.co.uk

Wychwood brewery is located in the Cotswold market town of Witney. The brewers take inspiration from the myths and legends associated with the ancient medieval Wychwood forest. Part of Marston's PLC. ‼ ♦ RAIB

Hobgoblin Gold (OG 1042, ABV 4.2%)
A golden-coloured beer full of malty flavours with a refreshing bitterness and zesty aroma.

Hobgoblin (OG 1045, ABV 4.5%)
A well-balanced, smooth, dark-coloured ale with a crisp, refreshing hop bitterness.

Wye Valley SIBA IFBB

Stoke Lacy, Herefordshire, HR7 4HG
☎ (01885) 490505 ☎ 07970 597937
⊕ wyevalleybrewery.co.uk

Founded in 1985 in the back of a village pub, this award-winning brewery is now producing around 250,000 pints per week and delivers direct to more than 1,200 pubs, including eight of its own. Its products are also available through selected wholesale and retail stockists. ‼ ♦ RAIB

Bitter (OG 1037, ABV 3.7%)
A beer whose aroma gives little hint of the bitter hoppiness that follows right through to the aftertaste.

The Hopfather (OG 1039, ABV 3.9%)
A smooth ale with a spicy honey, pine and grapefruit flavour.

HPA (OG 1040, ABV 4%)
A pale-coloured, hoppy, malty brew with a hint of sweetness before a dry finish.

Golden Ale (OG 1042, ABV 4.2%)

Butty Bach (OG 1046, ABV 4.5%)
A full-bodied, smooth and satisfying, gold-coloured premium ale.

Wholesome Stout (OG 1046, ABV 4.6%)
A smooth and satisfying stout with a bitter edge to its roast flavours. The finish combines roast grain and malt.

Wylam

Palace of Arts, Exhibition Park, Newcastle upon Tyne, NE2 4PZ
☎ (0191) 650 0651 ⊕ wylambrewery.co.uk

Wylam commenced brewing in 2000 on a 4.5-barrel plant. Originally brewing in Heddon-on-the-Wall in Northumberland, the brewery moved to Newcastle upon Tyne in 2016 with a new 30-barrel brew kit with an on-site brewery tap. ‼ ♦

Galatia (OG 1039, ABV 3.9%)
A light session pale ale with fresh orange shred flavours, stone fruit blasts and a clean, dry and fresh pine kick to the finish.

Gold Tankard (OG 1040, ABV 4%)

Fresh, clean flavour, full of hops. This golden ale has a hint of citrus in the finish.

Hickey the Rake (OG 1042.5, ABV 4.2%)
A pale ale with tropical flavours.

Jakehead IPA (OG 1058, ABV 6.3%)
A strong IPA, amber-coloured with a big hop aroma. Distinctly bittersweet on the palate with a massive hop complexity.

Macchiato (OG 1067.6, ABV 6.5%)
A hazelnut praline coffee porter with a complex grain bill, giving extra body and mouthfeel.

Imperial Macchiato (OG 1106.4, ABV 10%)
A double hazelnut praline coffee porter with additions of cacao and caramalt.

Wylde Sky (NEW)

Unit 8a, The Grip, Hadstock Road, Linton, Cambridgeshire, CB21 4XN
☎ (01223) 778350 🌐 wyldeskybrewing.com

⊗ Established in 2018, the brewery has a purpose-built 10-barrel plant brewing small batches of innovative beers in a range of styles from around the world. All beers are unfined, unfiltered and unpasteurised. A number of outlets are supplied in the area and an on-site taproom is open on Fridays and Saturdays. **V**

Wyre Piddle

See Ambridge

XT SIBA

Notley Farm, Chearsley Road, Long Crendon, Buckinghamshire, HP18 9ER
☎ (01844) 208310 🌐 xtbrewing.com

⊗ XT started brewing in 2011 using an 18-barrel plant. It supplies direct to pubs across southern England and the Midlands. The brewery taproom sells a range of draught beers along with bottles and other gifts. A range of limited edition, one-off brews is produced under the Animal Brewing Co name. **!! ♦ RAIB**

Four (OG 1037, ABV 3.8%)
A balanced, mellow, amber-coloured session ale with pine and citrus hop notes.

Hop Kitty (OG 1038, ABV 3.9%)
A hugely hoppy, golden-coloured ale, bursting with intense tropical and citrus flavours.

Nineteen (OG 1042, ABV 4.2%)
A hop-forward beer packed with five different malts and rye grains.

One (OG 1041, ABV 4.2%)
Blonde beer with dry citrus, lemon and spice notes.

Three (OG 1041, ABV 4.2%)
An American-style pale ale with citrus and pine flavours and a light biscuit malt character.

Eight (OG 1045, ABV 4.5%)
A full-bodied, dark-coloured porter with roast malt and bitter coffee notes.

Fifteen (OG 1044, ABV 4.5%)
A pale amber-coloured IPA with caramel malt notes and a lasting floral, grassy hop character.

Seventeen (OG 1044, ABV 4.5%)
A golden-coloured IPA, bursting with intense tropical and citrus flavours.

Thirteen (OG 1044, ABV 4.5%)
A red-coloured ale, brewed with a range of citrus aromatic hops.

Lion London Porter (OG 1047, ABV 4.6%)
A full-bodied porter with a rich character, matched with a toasty aroma and a hint of sweet earthy notes.

Squid Ink (OG 1055, ABV 5.5%)

Xtreme

Unit 21, Alfric Square, Maxwell Road, Woodston, Peterborough, Cambridgeshire, PE2 7JP ☎ 07427 661839 🌐 xtremeales.com

⊗ Family-run, small, independent brewery, which supplies a wide range of beers to local pubs and beer festivals. In addition to its regular beers, it specialises in developing one-off brews for different festivals and occasions including the annual Whittlesea Straw Bear festival in January. Bumbling Brewery beers are also brewed for the Bumble Inn micropub, Peterborough. **!! ♦**

Pigeon Ale (OG 1043, ABV 4.3%)

Chocolate Stout (OG 1050, ABV 5%)

Evil Pigeon (OG 1055, ABV 5.5%)

Yard of Ale

Surtees Arms, Chilton Lane, Ferryhill, DL17 0DH
☎ (01740) 655724 ☎ 07540 733513
🌐 thesurteesarms.co.uk

Established in 2008, the 2.5-barrel microbrewery supplies ales to its brewery tap, the Surtees Arms, beer festivals and to a growing number of pubs. **!! ♦ RAIB**

Reach for the Yard (ABV 3.8%)

Yard Dog Brown Ale (ABV 4%)

One Foot in the Yard (OG 1044, ABV 4.5%)
Premium golden ale. Fruity on the nose and palate with a sweet finish.

Yardsman

See Hercules

Yates' SIBA

Unit 4c, Langbridge Business Centre, Newchurch, Isle of Wight, PO36 0NP
☎ (01983) 867878 🌐 yates-brewery.co.uk

Brewing started in 2000 on a five-barrel plant at the Inn at St Lawrence. In 2009 it moved to Newchurch and upgraded to a 10-barrel plant. In 2015 the brewery was moved on to the same site as the wholesale unit at Newchurch. **!! ♦**

Golden Bitter (OG 1040, ABV 4%)
Light, refreshing, golden-coloured bitter with fruity notes, finished with a subtle bitter finish.

Islander (OG 1040, ABV 4%)

Beachcomber (OG 1043, ABV 4.3%)
A straw-coloured, easy-drinking ale with a distinctive fresh aroma and a crisp, clean, hoppy finish.

Holy Joe (OG 1050, ABV 4.9%)
Amber-coloured ale with a bittersweet aftertaste. Ground coriander is added to the brew to give it a citrus, spicy finish.

Dark Side of the Wight (OG 1049, ABV 5%)
Malty milk chocolate at first in the nose, then plenty of orange fruit. Bitter, malty and toasted to taste, with perfumed bitter orange notes always present. Bitter roasted finish.

Yelland Manor

Lower Yelland Farm, Yelland, Devon, EX31 3EN
☎ 07770 267592 ✉ yellandmanor@gmail.com

⊗ Located on the Taw Estuary and close to the Tarka Trail, this is a five-barrel plant in a converted milking parlour. The brewery began production in 2013 and supplies a small number of local pubs and hotels, although the majority of sales are now made from the premises, either as takeaways or for consumption as part of a brewery experience. ♦

The Tarka Special (OG 1040, ABV 4.1%)

Standard (OG 1043, ABV 4.2%)

Yeovil SIBA

Unit 5, Bofors Park, Artillery Road, Lufton Trading Estate, Yeovil, Somerset, BA22 8YH
☎ (01935) 414888 🌐 yeovilales.com

⊗ Yeovil Ales was established in 2006 using an 18-barrel plant. More than 300 pubs are supplied in the South West. ‼ ♦

Hopkandi (OG 1038, ABV 3.8%)
A pale-coloured bitter with citrus hops and a dry finish.

Star Gazer (OG 1042, ABV 4%)
Easy-drinking, tawny-coloured bitter. Malt and toffee in the aroma lead to a predominantly sweet flavour. Short bitter finish.

Summerset (OG 1041, ABV 4.1%)
Blonde ale with a fruity hop finish.

Kellerbier (OG 1043, ABV 4.3%)
A full-bodied, smooth, golden-coloured beer, lagered for more than 30 days for a crisp, fruity flavour.

Lynx Wildcat (OG 1044, ABV 4.3%)
A bronze-coloured, full-bodied, hoppy bitter. Specialist malt provides a sweetness, which is accompanied by grapefruit hop flavours.

Stout Hearted (OG 1045, ABV 4.3%)
A smooth, dark-coloured stout, full-bodied with rich roast flavours.

Ruby (OG 1047, ABV 4.5%)
Red-coloured bitter with rich malt depth.

POSH IPA (OG 1052, ABV 5.4%)
A strong IPA with a fruity body and hoppy finish.

Yetman's

Bayfield Farm Barns, Bayfield Brecks Farm, Bayfield, Norfolk, NR25 7DZ ☎ 07774 809016 🌐 yetmans.net

A 2.5-barrel plant built by Moss Brew was installed in restored medieval barns near Holt in 2005. The brewery supplies local free trade outlets. RAIB

Red (OG 1036, ABV 3.8%)
A plummy malt carapace with a balanced hop and caramel undercoat. Full-bodied and long-lasting. Bittersweet notes slowly intercede.

Orange (OG 1042, ABV 4.2%)
A dry, full-flavoured and hoppy beer.

Stout (OG 1042, ABV 4.2%)
Creamy, dry and full-bodied, with a toasted, malty nose.

Green (OG 1048, ABV 4.8%)
Strong, with a fruity sweetness and dark colour.

Yonder (NEW)

The Workshop, Rookery Farm, Binegar, Somerset, BA3 4UL 🌐 brewyonder.co.uk

Brewing began in 2018 producing small batch brews, often using foraged ingredients. A combination of modern and traditional brewing techniques are used including oak barrel ageing.

York

c/o Black Sheep Brewing, Wellgarth, Masham, North Yorkshire, HG4 4EN
☎ (01904) 621162 🌐 york-brewery.co.uk

York started production in 1996 and was bought out of administration by Black Sheep Brewery (qv) in 2018. Four pubs are owned in York and Leeds. Brewing of all York Brewery beers is temporarily taking place at Black Sheep until new premises can be found. ♦

Guzzler (OG 1036, ABV 3.6%)
Refreshing golden ale with dominant hop and fruit flavours developing throughout.

Hansom Blonde (OG 1039, ABV 3.9%)
Creamy, fruity ale with a light bitterness, hints of tropical fruit and citrus on the aftertaste.

Yorkshire Terrier (OG 1041, ABV 4.2%)
Refreshing and distinctive amber/gold-coloured brew where fruit and hops dominate the aroma and taste. Hoppy bitterness remains assertive in the aftertaste.

Otherside IPA (OG 1043, ABV 4.5%)
A host of tropical fruit notes against a background of citrus and pine.

Centurion's Ghost Ale (OG 1051, ABV 5.4%)
Dark ruby in colour, full-tasting with mellow roast malt character balanced by light bitterness and autumn fruit flavours that linger into the aftertaste.

Yorkshire SIBA

Brewery Wharf, 70 Humber Street, Fruit Market, Hull, East Yorkshire, HU1 1TU
☎ (01482) 618000 ☎ 07850 494990
✉ guy@yorkshirebrewing.co.uk

Brewing started in 2012 in the Fruit Market Arts Quarter of Hull using a six-barrel plant. A special commemorative beer is brewed in honour of Hull Minster once a year and showcased at the Real Ale & Cider festival within the Minster. A bottling plant along with tours and a retail outlet have been established. Festivals and local outlets are supplied. A tapas bar has opened next to the brewery.
‼ ♦ RAIB

Mutiny (OG 1036, ABV 3.6%)
A distinctive coffee aroma and chocolate flavour.

Lazy Days (OG 1040, ABV 4%)
A golden-coloured pale ale with a sweetish, clean, refreshing floral taste.

Supernatural Blonde (OG 1041, ABV 4.1%)

Mosaic (OG 1042, ABV 4.2%)
Easy-drinking session bitter with a mango, peach and tangerine finish.

Blackjack (OG 1046, ABV 4.5%)
A complex stout fortified with fresh blackberries, providing lasting fruit and chocolate characteristics.

Moondance (OG 1045, ABV 4.5%)
A blonde ale infused with passion fruit for a refreshing taste.

Oregon Gold (OG 1045, ABV 4.5%)
A cloudy, Belgian-style wheat beer brewed with coriander and curacao oranges.

Passion (OG 1045, ABV 4.5%)

Raspberry Tipple (OG 1048, ABV 4.8%)
A cloudy, Belgian-style wheat beer infused with raspberries.

Strawberry Blonde (OG 1048, ABV 4.8%)
A cloudy, Belgian-style wheat beer infused with strawberries.

Waverider (OG 1052, ABV 5.2%)

Shangri-la (OG 1067, ABV 6.7%)
A double IPA with tropical notes and a lingering grapefruit finish.

Yorkshire Brewhouse

The Brewery, Goulton Street, Hull, East Yorkshire, HU3 4DD
☎ (01482) 755199 🌐 yorkshirebrewhouse.com

Founded in 2017 by Jon Constable and Simon Cooke. Around 20 outlets are supplied direct. The beers are given names that mirror Yorkshire dialect or are representative of their Hull sporting roots. RAIB

YPA (OG 1037, ABV 3.4%)

1904 (ABV 3.7%)
A malty, golden-coloured bitter with a light fruity hop aroma and dry, nutty finish.

Ey Up (OG 1040, ABV 3.8%)
Spicy hop aroma and malty bitter finish.

Reet (OG 1039, ABV 3.8%)
Powerful peppery hops, light malt background and a long, dry bitter finish.

Red Robin (OG 1049, ABV 4.8%)
A ruby/black-coloured stout with a malty chocolate finish.

Faithful (OG 1050, ABV 4.9%)
Rich, dark-coloured, malty stout with a fruity bitter finish.

Yorkshire Dales

Abbey Works, Askrigg, North Yorkshire, DL8 4LP
☎ (01969) 622027 ☎ 07818 035592
🌐 yorkshiredalesbrewery.com

Situated in the heart of the Yorkshire Dales, brewing started in a converted milking parlour in 2005. In 2016 the brewery moved to larger premises. More than 150 pubs are supplied throughout the north of England. A tap and bottle shop opened at the brewery in 2017. ♦RAIB

Butter Tubs (OG 1037, ABV 3.7%)
A pale golden-coloured beer with a dry bitterness complemented by strong citrus flavours and aroma.

Askrigg Bitter (OG 1038, ABV 3.8%)

Bainbridge Blonde (OG 1038, ABV 3.8%)

Buckden Pike (OG 1040, ABV 3.9%)
A refreshing blonde beer with a crisp, fruity finish.

Nappa Scar (OG 1041, ABV 4%)
A golden ale with citrus and peach flavours throughout.

Muker Silver (OG 1041, ABV 4.1%)
A blonde, lager-style ale, crisp with a sharp, hoppy finish.

Askrigg Ale (OG 1043, ABV 4.3%)
A pale golden ale with an intense aroma that generates a crisp, dry flavour with a long, bitter finish.

Garsdale Smokebox (OG 1057, ABV 5.6%)
A complex ale created by smoked and dark malts. Deep, rich chocolate and coffee flavours are complemented by the smokiness.

Yorkshire Heart SIBA

The Vineyard, Pool Lane, Nun Monkton, North Yorkshire, YO26 8EL
☎ (01423) 330716 ☎ 07838 030067
🌐 yorkshireheart.com

Yorkshire Heart has been brewing since 2011 and is situated adjacent to the Yorkshire Heart vineyard and winery, not far from York. ‼ ♦ GF

Lightheart (OG 1033, ABV 3.3%)
A pale ale with citrus and spice flavours.

Off the Wheaten Path (OG 1035, ABV 3.5%)

Hearty Bitter (OG 1037, ABV 3.7%)
A chestnut-coloured bitter with toffee flavours.

Rhubarbeer (OG 1037, ABV 3.7%)
A rhubarb-flavoured, dark-coloured ale.

Dark Heart (OG 1039, ABV 4%)
Roasted coffee colour with a smooth treacle flavour.

SilverHeart IPA (OG 1039, ABV 4%)
Light amber in colour with a citrus and spice flavour.

JRT Golden Best Bitter (OG 1041, ABV 4.2%)
Golden ale with a caramel and citrus flavour.

Blackheart Stout (OG 1047, ABV 4.8%)
Stout with a roasted coffee flavour.

Platinum EPA (OG 1047, ABV 5%)
A pale ale with zest and spice flavours.

Young's

See Eagle

Yubberton

See Stroud

Zapato

Unit 1a, Holme Mills, West Slaithwaite Road, Marsden, West Yorkshire, HD7 6LS ☎ 07788 513432
🌐 zapatobrewery.co.uk

Small company, established in 2016, that cuckoo brewed in the Leeds area prior to establishing a permanent home in Marsden, brewing on a 15-barrel plant. It produces innovative beers based on traditional European styles. Collaboration brews are a staple part of its output.

Zepto

Graig Fawr Lodge, Blackbrook Road, Caerphilly, CF83 1NF ☎ 07951 505524 🌐 zeptobrew.co.uk

Established in 2016, Zepto is a 100-litre brewery set up by CAMRA member Chris Sweet. Although production is mainly bottled, cask-conditioned beers are occasionally brewed. RAIB

Zerodegrees SIBA

Blackheath: 29-31 Montpelier Vale, Blackheath, London, SE3 0TJ

Bristol: 53 Colston Street, Bristol, BS1 5BA ☎ (0117) 925 2706

Cardiff: 27 Westgate Street, Cardiff, CF10 1DD ☎ (029) 2022 9494

Reading: 9 Bridge Street, Reading, RG1 2LR ☎ (0118) 959 7959 🌐 zerodegrees.co.uk/blackheath

Brewing started in 2000 in Blackheath, London and now four brewpubs are owned, each incorporating a state-of-the-art, computer-controlled, German plant producing unfiltered and unfined ales and lagers. All beers use natural ingredients, are suitable for vegetarians, and are served from tanks using air pressure (not CO2). ♦V

Zulu Alpha (NEW) SIBA

51b Symondscliffe Way, Caldicot, NP26 5PW ☎ 07899 794294 ✉ info@zulualphabrewing.co.uk

Zulu Alpha Brewing occupies the former Castles brewery in Caldicot. It consists of a seven-barrel brewhouse with four fermenters. Production began in 2018.

New Horizon (OG 1039, ABV 4%)
A rich, amber-coloured session lager with a subtle but refreshing bitterness.

Voyager (OG 1043, ABV 4.8%)
A smooth pale ale with a vibrant citrus and tropical fruitiness to the flavour and aroma.

Evolution (OG 1049, ABV 5.2%)
A hoppy pale ale with a complex malt backbone against a mild but crisp bitterness.

Crush (OG 1052, ABV 5.4%)
An American-style IPA with crisp citrus hops and punchy, lingering bitterness.

Zymurgorium

Unit 19, Irlam Business Centre, Soapstone Way, Irlam, M44 6RA 🌐 zymurgorium.com

The UK's first craft meadery and Manchester's first distillery. In combination with the brewery it was established in Irlam in 2013. Most of its output is in bottled form.

Come on in, the water's lovely

The importance of water to the brewing process is often overlooked. Most people know that barley malt and hops are the main ingredients used in beer making and that yeast turns malt sugars into alcohol. But 93% of even the strongest beer is made up of water – and the quality of the water is essential to the taste and character of the finished product.

Brewers call the water they use in the brewing process 'liquor' to distinguish it from cleaning water. Brewing liquor, whether it comes from natural wells or the public supply, will be filtered and cleaned to ensure its absolute purity. Care will be taken, however, to ensure that vital salts and irons are not removed during the filtering process, as they are essential to the production of cask beer.

The benchmark for brewing liquor is Burton upon Trent in the English Midlands. The natural spring waters of the Trent Valley have rich deposits of calcium and magnesium sulphates – also known as gypsum and Epsom salts. Salt is a flavour-enhancer and the sulphates in Burton liquor bring out the finest flavours from malts and hops. Since the 19th century, ale brewers have added salts to 'Burtonise' their liquor.

It's fascinating to compare the levels of salts in the water of three famous brewing locations: Burton, London and Pilsen. Pilsen is the home of the first golden lager beer, Pilsner. Brewers of genuine lager beers want comparatively soft brewing liquor to balance the toasted malt and gentle, spicy hop nature of their beers. Pilsen water has total salts of 30 parts per million, with minute amounts of calcium and magnesium.

London, once celebrated as a dark beer region, famous for mild, porter and stout, has 463 total salts per million, with high levels of sodium and carbonate. Burton liquor has an astonishing level of total salts of 1,226 per million. If this figure is further broken down, Burton liquor is rich in magnesium, calcium, other sulphates and carbonate.

Closed breweries

The following breweries have closed or gone out of business since the 2019 Guide was published:

4Four, Bethesda, West Wales
7, Durris, Aberdeen & Grampian
Aire Heads, Goole, East Yorkshire
Albion, Bath, Somerset
An Teallach, Dundonnell, Highlands & Western Isles
Andrews, Cummertrees, Dumfries & Galloway
Angles, Peterborough, Cambridgeshire
Antoine's, Dorking, Surrey
Arcane Bridge, Newcastle upon Tyne, Tyne & Wear
Axiom, Wrexham, North-east Wales
Balmaha, Balmaha, Loch Lomond, Stirling & the Trossachs
Barlow, Barlow, Derbyshire
Battlefield, Shrewsbury, Shropshire
Beer Bores, Ashwicke, Gloucestershire & Bristol
Beercraft, Hove, East Sussex
Bishop's Crook, Penwortham, Lancashire
Black Paw, Bishop Auckland, County Durham
Blackbeck, Egremont, Cumbria
Bont, Bridgend, Glamorgan
Bootlegger, High Wycombe, Buckinghamshire
Bradford, Bradford, West Yorkshire
Brandon, Brandon, Suffolk
Brecon, Brecon, Mid Wales
BrewSaurus, Dinas Powys, Glamorgan
Brewshine, Kendal, Cumbria
Bridge, Holmbridge, West Yorkshire
Broughs, Wolverhampton, West Midlands
Bude, Bude, Cornwall
Butchers Arms, Woolhope, Herefordshire
Buzzard, Denbigh, North-east Wales
Castlegate, Johnstown, West Wales
Caveman, Swanscombe, Kent
Caythorpe, Caythorpe, Nottinghamshire
Ciren, Cirencester, Gloucestershire & Bristol
Co Pilot, Whetstone, Leicestershire
Cornish Chough, Lizard, Cornwall
Craft Originale, Markinch, Kingdom of Fife
Crafted, Bewdley, Worcestershire
Cricklewood, London, Greater London
Devitera, Rowde, Wiltshire
Double Top, Worksop, Nottinghamshire
Dunscar, Bolton, Greater Manchester
Edmunds, Birmingham, West Midlands
Epicurus, Bolton, Greater Manchester
Famous Railway Tavern, Brightlingsea, Essex
Fish Key, Looe, Cornwall
Force, Cirencester, Gloucestershire & Bristol
Frog Island, Northampton, Northamptonshire
G2, Ashford, Kent
Gaol, Wirksworth, Derbyshire
Gene Pool, Hull, East Yorkshire
George Samuel, Spennymoor, County Durham
Glens of Antrim, Ballycastle, Northern Ireland
Gorgeous Beer, Telford, Shropshire
Hairy Brewers, Holbrook, Derbyshire
Hamelsworde, Hemsworth, West Yorkshire
Hebridean, Stornoway: Isle of Lewis, Highlands & Western Isles
Hexagon, Marple, Greater Manchester
Hogarths, Bolton, Greater Manchester
Hope Sprints, Wendover, Buckinghamshire
Kendal, Kendal, Cumbria
Kentwood, Prestonpans, Edinburgh & the Lothians
King Alfred, Bourton, Dorset
Kingdom, Rosyth, Kingdom of Fife
Krafty Brew, Linlithgow, Edinburgh & the Lothians
Landlocked, Alfreton, Derbyshire
Lawman, Cumbernauld, Greater Glasgow & Clyde Valley
Leafy Hollow, Bodmin, Cornwall
Lines, Cardiff, Glamorgan
Lion's Lair, Arbroath, Tayside
Lithic, Llangorse, Mid Wales
Little Beer, Guildford, Surrey
Littondale, Litton, West Yorkshire
Liverpool Craft, Liverpool, Merseyside
Luckie, Leven, Kingdom of Fife
Macclesfield, Macclesfield, Cheshire
Mad Hatter, Liverpool, Merseyside
MASH, East Stratton, Hampshire
Melin Tap, Little Mill, Gwent
Merrimen, Litchborough, Northamptonshire
Merry Miner, Grendon, Warwickshire
Mordue, North Shields, Tyne & Wear
New Inn, Liversedge, West Yorkshire
North Blyth, Blyth, Northumberland
O'Brien, Leicester, Leicestershire
Ollie's, Cardiff, Glamorgan
Partners, Hightown, West Yorkshire
Patriot, Taunton, Somerset
Pigeon Fishers, Hollingwood, Derbyshire
Pirate, Fewcott, Oxfordshire
Ramsbottom Craft, Bolton, Greater Manchester
Raw, Staveley, Derbyshire
Rebel, Penryn, Cornwall
Red Hand, Donaghmore, Northern Ireland
Ripple Steam, Sutton, Kent
Roath, Cardiff, Glamorgan
Robin Hood, New Basford, Nottinghamshire
Round Tower, Chelmsford, Essex
RPM, Weston-super-Mare, Somerset
St George's, Callow End, Worcestershire
St Oswald's, Guiseley, West Yorkshire
Samphire, Folkestone, Kent
Savour, Windsor, Berkshire
Schoolhouse, Darlington, County Durham
Sentinel, Sheffield, South Yorkshire
Seren, Rosebush, West Wales
Six Bells, Bishop's Castle, Shropshire
Spencer's, Upper Norton, West Sussex
Stocklinch, Stocklinch, Somerset
Stratford upon Avon, Stratford upon Avon, Warwickshire

Closed breweries (continued)

Surfing Monkey, Cardiff, Glamorgan
Third Eye, Heskin, Lancashire
Thousand Trades, Birmingham, West Midlands
Tipsy Angel, Warrington, Cheshire
Titan, Derby, Derbyshire
Twisted Angel, Beverley, East Yorkshire
Two Beach, Devon
Upham, Upham, Hampshire
Valhalla, Unst: Shetland, Northern Isles
Velvet Owl, Gloucester, Gloucestershire & Bristol
Vision, Hull, East Yorkshire
Wainstones, Hutton Rudby, North Yorkshire
White Park, Bedford, Bedfordshire
Windmill, Standish, Greater Manchester

Future breweries

The following new breweries have been notified to the Guide and will start to produce beer during 2019/2020. In a few cases they were in production during the summer of 2019 but were too late for a full listing:

Anchor House, Plympton, Devon
Baronscourt, Newtownstewart, Northern Ireland
Cullach, Perth, Tayside
Emmanuales, South Yorkshire
Escape, Bolton, Greater Manchester
Fearless Nomad, Brentford, Greater London
GetSet, Milton Keynes, Buckinghamshire
Goodness, London, Greater London
Grafham, Grafham, Cambridgeshire
Lennox, Dumbarton, Greater Glasgow & Clyde Valley
Makemake, Southsea, Hampshire
Mashdown, Banbridge, Northern Ireland
Mashionistas, Coventry, West Midlands
Mona, Gaerwen, North-west Wales
Moonface, Loughborough, Leicestershire
Motley Hog, Ross on Wye, Herefordshire
New Invention, Walsall, West Midlands
New Union, Kendal, Cumbria
North Shore, Ardrossan, Ayrshire & Arran
Pig Beer, Brockenhurst, Hampshire
Pipeline, St Agnes, Cornwall
Scott's, Coventry, West Midlands
Second Wave, London, Greater London
Steel Brew, Sherford, Devon
Stratton Lane, East Stratton, Hampshire
Talke O' Th' Hill, Talke, Staffordshire
Urban Alchemy, New Barnet, Greater London
Wickham House, Conisholme, Lincolnshire

Breweries for sale

The following breweries are reported as being for sale:

Brigstock, Brigstock, Northamptonshire
Buffy's, Wicklewood, Norfolk
Burton Old Cottage, Burton upon Trent, Staffordshire
Coastal, Redruth, Cornwall
Heavy Industry, Henllan, North-east Wales
Hopjacker, Dronfield, Derbyshire
Hubsters, Bamber Bridge, Lancashire
Salamander, Bradford, West Yorkshire
Shropshire Brewer, Longden Common, Shropshire
Violet Cottage, Gwaelod y Garth, Glamorgan
Yaarbrew, Hickling, Norfolk

Indexes & Further Information

Places index

C

D

E

PLACES INDEX

T

PLACES INDEX

Beers index

These beers refer to those in bold type in the breweries section (beers in regular production) and so therefore do not include seasonal, special or occasional beers that may be mentioned elsewhere in the text.

A

D

E

F

G

H

BEERS INDEX

I

J

K

L

M

BEERS INDEX

N

O

BEERS INDEX

BEERS INDEX

S

BANKS'S
SPECIAL
SHARP'S
ST AUSTELL
TRIBUTE
YOUNG'S
BITTER
MARSTON'S
BODDINGTONS
ESTD.
1778
ENGLISH ALE
TRADE
BOMBARDIER
GLORIOUS
ENGLISH
From the Wells Brewery
ALC 4.1% VOL

AWARD-WINNING PUBS

The Pub of the Year competition is judged by CAMRA members. Each of the CAMRA branches votes for its favourite pub: criteria include the quality and choice of real ale, atmosphere, customer service and value. The pubs listed below are the current winners of the title; look out for the 🏆 next to the entries in the Guide.

ENGLAND

🏆 Bedfordshire
Engineers Arms, Henlow
Black Lion, Leighton Buzzard
Polhill Arms, Renhold

🏆 Berkshire
Bell Inn, Aldworth
Craufurd Arms, Maidenhead
Nag's Head, Reading
Crispin, Wokingham

🏆 Buckinghamshire
Rising Sun, Haddenham
Lamb, Stoke Goldington

🏆 Cambridgeshire
Drayman's Son, Ely
Frothblowers, Peterborough
Ale Taster, St Neots
Chestnut Tree, West Wratting

🏆 Cheshire
Bhurtpore, Aston
Olde Cottage, Chester
Helter Skelter, Frodsham
Bottle Bank, Holmes Chapel
Society Tap Rooms, Runcorn

🏆 Cornwall
White Hart, Chilsworthy

🏆 Cumbria
Manor Arms, Broughton-in-Furness
New Union, Kendal
Kirkstile Inn, Loweswater
Drovers Rest, Monkhill

🏆 Derbyshire
Smith's Tavern, Ashbourne
Rose & Crown, Chesterfield
Smithfield, Derby
Miners Arms, Hundall
Burnt Pig, Ilkeston
Colvile Arms, Lullington
Thorn Tree Inn, Matlock
Talbot, Ripley
Devonshire Arms, South Normanton
Three Stags' Heads, Wardlow Mires

🏆 Devon
Bell Inn, Chittlehampton
Royal Oak Inn, Meavy
Taphouse & Bottle Shop, Newton Abbott
Tom Cobley Tavern, Spreyton

🏆 Dorset
Ship Inn, Shaftesbury
White Hart Inn, Yetminster

🏆 Durham
Grey Horse, Consett
ORB Micropub, Darlington
Victoria Inn, Durham
Three Horseshoes, Leamside
Golden Smog, Stockton-on-Tees

🏆 Essex
Woolpack, Chelmsford
New Inn, Colchester
White Hart, Grays
Hanover Inn, Harwich
Farmers Yard, Maldon
Woodbine Inn, Waltham Abbey
West Road Tap, Westcliff-on-Sea
Fleur de Lys, Widdington

🏆 Gloucestershire & Bristol
Barley Mow, Bristol: St Philips
Craven Arms, Brockhampton
Kemble Brewery, Cheltenham
Fleece Inn, Hillesley
Berkeley Arms, Tewkesbury

🏆 Hampshire
Firkin Shed, Bournemouth
Steel Tank Alehouse, Chandler's Ford
Golden Pheasant, Lower Farringdon
Lawrence Arms, Portsmouth
Wonston Arms, Wonston

🏆 Herefordshire
Alma Inn, Linton

🏆 Hertfordshire
Valiant Trooper, Aldbury
Land of Liberty, Peace & Plenty, Heronsgate
Red Lion, Preston
Woodman, Wildhill

🏆 Isle of Wight
Railway, Ryde

🏆 Kent
Larkins' Alehouse, Cranbrook
Bowl Inn, Hastingleigh
Old House, Ightham Common
Admiral's Arm, Queenborough
10:50 From Victoria, Strood
George, Tunbridge Wells

Bhurtpore, Aston (p71)

Kirkstile Inn, Loweswater (p98)

Manor Arms, Broughton-in-Furness (p92)

Smith's Tavern, Ashbourne (p104)

Kent (continued)
Tyler's Kiln, Tyler Hill
Berry, Walmer
Bake & Alehouse, Westgate-on-Sea

Greater London
Star & Garter, Bromley
Hope, Carshalton
Penny Farthing, Crayford
North Star, E11: Leytonstone
Gidea Park Micropub, Gidea Park
Albion, Kingston
Little Green Dragon, N21: Winchmore Hill
Snooty Fox, N5: Canonbury
River Ale House, SE10: East Greenwich
Cask Pub & Kitchen, SW1: Pimlico
Masons Arms, Teddington
Owl & the Pussycat, W13: West Ealing

Greater Manchester
Old Packet House, Altrincham
Lamb Hotel, Eccles
Brewery Bar, Horwich
Bobbin, Leigh
Crown & Kettle, Manchester
Flying Horse Hotel, Rochdale
Station Buffet Bar, Stalybridge
Baker's Vaults, Stockport
Wigan Central, Wigan

Lancashire
Three Mariners, Lancaster
Craft House Beer Café, Lytham
Swan with Two Necks, Pendleton
Moorbrook, Preston

Leicestershire
Geese & Fountain, Croxton Kerrial
Pestle & Mortar, Hinckley
Blue Boar, Leicester
Organ Grinder, Loughborough
Real Ale Classroom, Lutterworth
Stilton Cheese, Somerby

Lincolnshire
No. 2 Refreshment Room, Cleethorpes
Sweyn Forkbeard, Gainsborough
Nobody Inn, Grantham
Ebrington Arms, Kirkby on Bain
Strugglers Inn, Lincoln
Consortium Micropub, Louth
Pooleys, Messingham

Merseyside
Sparrowhawk, Formby
Lazy Landlord Ale House, Liscard
Peter Kavanagh's, Liverpool: City Centre
Cricketers Arms, St Helens

Norfolk
Old King's Head, Brockdish
Rose & Crown, Harpley
Leopard, Norwich
Lion Inn, Thurne

Northamptonshire
St Giles Ale House, Northampton
Tap & Kitchen, Oundle

Nottinghamshire
Horse & Plough, Bingham
Old Green Dragon, Oxton
Brew Shed, Retford
Final Whistle, Southwell
Scruffy Dog, Sutton-in-Ashfield

Oxfordshire
Brewery Tap, Abingdon
Horse & Groom, Caulcott
Fleur de Lys, East Hagbourne
Royal Oak, Wantage

Rutland
White Lion Inn, Whissendine

Shropshire
Sandbrook Vaults, Market Drayton

Tom Cobley Tavern, Spreyton (p131)

Woolpack, Chelmsford (p158)

Hope, Carshalton (p312)

Snooty Fox, N5: Canonbury (p294)

White Hart, Shifnal
Prince of Wales, Shrewsbury

Somerset
Crossways Inn, West Huntspill

Staffordshire
Bull's Head, Alton
Swan Hotel, Brewood
Dog Inn, Burton upon Trent
Newhall Arms, Cannock
Cross Inn, Kinver
Fountain Inn, Leek
Hopinn, Newcastle-under-Lyme
Borehole, Stone
Tamworth Tap, Tamworth

Suffolk
Rose & Crown, Bury St Edmunds
Stanford Arms, Lowestoft
Wheatsheaf, Tattingstone

Surrey
Olde Swan, Chertsey
Crown, Horsell
Running Horse, Leatherhead
Surrey Oaks, Newdigate

East Sussex
Brighton Bierhaus, Brighton
King's Head, East Hoathly
Tower, St Leonards on Sea

West Sussex
Hornet Alehouse, Chichester
White Horse, Maplehurst
Green Man Ale & Cider House, Worthing

Tyne & Wear
Office, Morpeth
Ship Isis, Sunderland
Dog & Rabbit, Whitley Bay

Warwickshire
Turk's Head, Alcester
Seven Stars, Rugby
Lord Nelson Inn, Ansley
Angel Ale House, Atherstone
Old Bakery, Kenilworth
Old Post Office, Warwick

West Midlands
Lamp Tavern, Birmingham: Highgate
Broomfield Tavern, Coventry: Spon End
Plough & Harrow, Cradley Heath
Waggon & Horses, Halesowen
Ale Rooms, Knowle
Mare Pool, Mere Green
Fountain Inn, Walsall
Hail to the Ale, Wolverhampton

Wiltshire
Red Lion, Cricklade
Bell Inn, Lacock
Wyndham Arms, Salisbury
Organ Inn, Warminster

Worcestershire
Cross Inn, Finstall
King & Castle, Kidderminster
Dragon Inn, Worcester

East Yorkshire
Butcher's Dog, Driffield
Goodmanham Arms, Goodmanham
Whalebone, Hull

North Yorkshire
Mended Drum, Huby
George & Dragon, Hudswell
Sun Inn, Pickering
One-Eyed Rat, Ripon
North Riding Brew Pub, Scarborough
Talbot Arms, Settle
Waiting Room, Whitby

South Yorkshire
Hilltop, Conisbrough
Doncaster Brewery Tap, Doncaster
Gardeners Rest, Sheffield: North
Huntsman, Thurlstone
Wath Tap, Wath upon Dearne

Wonston Arms, Wonston (p200)

Land of Liberty, Peace & Plenty, Heronsgate (p208)

Swan With Two Necks, Pendleton (p251)

Redgarth, Oldmeldrum (p632)

West Yorkshire
Record Café, Bradford
Dunkirk, Denby Dale
West Riding Refreshment Rooms, Dewsbury
Fox & Goose, Hebden Bridge
Cricketers Arms, Horbury
Riverhead Brewery Tap, Marsden
Fleece, Pudsey

WALES

Glamorgan
Lansdowne, Cardiff
Brit Pub, Cwmafan
Cross Inn, Cwmfelin
Bunch of Grapes, Pontypridd
No Sign Bar, Swansea

Gwent
Queen's Head, Chepstow

Mid-Wales
New Inn, Bwlch
Arvon Ale House, Llandrindod Wells

North-East Wales
Mold Alehouse, Mold

North-West Wales
Black Boy Inn, Caernarfon
Bay Hop, Colwyn Bay
Slaters Arms, Corris

West Wales
Pembroke Yeoman, Haverfordwest
Mansel Arms, Porthyrhyd

SCOTLAND

Aberdeen & Grampian
Redgarth, Oldmeldrum

Ayrshire & Arran
Twa Dugs, West Kilbride

Borders
Bridge Inn (Trust), Peebles

Dumfries & Galloway
Clachan Inn, St John's Town of Dalry

Edinburgh & the Lothians
Platform 3, Linlithgow

Greater Glasgow & Clyde Valley
Laurieston Bar, Glasgow
Bull Inn, Paisley

Highlands & Western Isles
Clachnaharry Inn, Inverness

Kingdom of Fife
Railway Inn, Lower Largo

Tayside
Green Room Wee Bar, Perth

NORTHERN IRELAND

Northern Ireland
Errigle Inn, Belfast

CHANNEL ISLANDS

Jersey
Lamplighter, St Helier

Guernsey
Golden Lion, St Peter Port

Bull Inn, Paisley (p657)

Railway Inn, Lower Largo (p666)

Readers' recommendations

Suggestions for pubs to be included or excluded

All pubs are regularly surveyed by local branches of the Campaign for Real Ale to ensure they meet the standards required by the *Good Beer Guide*. If you would like to comment on a pub already featured, or on any you think should be featured, please fill in the form below (or a copy of it), and send it to the address indicated. Alternatively, email **gbgeditor@camra.org.uk**. Your views will be passed on to the branch concerned. Please mark your envelope/email with the county where the pub is, which will help us to direct your comments efficiently.

Pub name:

Address:

Reason for recommendation/criticism:

Pub name:

Address:

Reason for recommendation/criticism:

Pub name:

Address:

Reason for recommendation/criticism:

Your name and address:

Please send to: [Name of county] Section, Good Beer Guide,
230 Hatfield Road, St Albans, Hertfordshire AL1 4LW

Readers' recommendations

Suggestions for pubs to be included or excluded

All pubs are regularly surveyed by local branches of the Campaign for Real Ale to ensure they meet the standards required by the *Good Beer Guide*. If you would like to comment on a pub already featured, or on any you think should be featured, please fill in the form below (or a copy of it), and send it to the address indicated. Alternatively, email **gbgeditor@camra.org.uk**. Your views will be passed on to the branch concerned. Please mark your envelope/email with the county where the pub is, which will help us to direct your comments efficiently.

Pub name:

Address:

Reason for recommendation/criticism:

Pub name:

Address:

Reason for recommendation/criticism:

Pub name:

Address:

Reason for recommendation/criticism:

Your name and address:

Please send to: [Name of county] Section, Good Beer Guide,
230 Hatfield Road, St Albans, Hertfordshire AL1 4LW

CASK BREATHERS

At CAMRA's 2018 annual conference, members voted to adopt a 'neutral' position on cask breathers, overturning a policy which had been in place since the early 1980s. The motion arose from a recommendation of the Revitalisation Project.

So what does 'neutral' mean, and what is a cask breather?

Simply put, neutral means that CAMRA will neither promote the use of cask breathers nor campaign against their use. Before this motion was passed, pubs could not be put into this Guide if they used cask breathers on all their beers and, if cask breathers were used on some beers, those beers could not be listed.

A cask breather, also known as an aspirator, is a device which is fitted to the shive hole of a cask where a spile would normally be found. This device contains a valve and is connected to a cylinder of carbon dioxide (CO_2). When beer is drawn from the cask, a decrease in pressure inside is detected and CO_2 is admitted into it. This restores the pressure inside the cask to atmospheric pressure (1 Bar or 15psi). If a cask breather were not fitted, air would enter into the cask. Similarly, if the valve detects that the pressure inside the cask has increased above atmospheric pressure (as a result of secondary fermentation for example) then it allows CO_2 to escape until atmospheric pressure is reached again.

There has long been a myth that cask breathers can be misused and the valve can be 'turned up' so that more CO_2 is allowed into the cask making the beer fizzy. This is not, and never has been the case. Cask breathers can only be used to maintain atmospheric pressure, they only have one setting.

What effect does a cask breather have on the beer?

CO_2 is more soluble in beer than air is, so the beer will maintain its condition for longer (it will take longer to go flat). Also, as it prevents air from getting in, then those biochemical processes which result in beer spoilage (aerobic oxidation mainly) will be slowed down. This does not, however, mean that beer cannot spoil with a cask breather applied; anaerobic processes (without air) can cause the beer to go off too. The effect is the beer in the cask lasts longer. CAMRA's Technical Advisory Group is of the view that a cask of beer between 3 and 5 per cent ABV should be on sale for no more than three days. With a cask breather in use, this is five days. Some British breweries promoting the use of cask breathers in their tied houses agree with this (although some would say six days rather than five).

So, the effect of these devices on the beer should be beneficial, although many drinkers feel that the inhibition of aerobic oxidation can reduce the complexity of flavours in some beers. Many brewers describe oxygen (20 per cent of air, and what causes oxidation) as 'the enemy of the brewer'. You pays your money and you takes your choice!

Another myth is that using cask breathers makes a licensee lazy when it comes to looking after their real ales. The only difference a cask breather makes is extending shelf life, which may be important for some rural pubs wanting to stock a couple of cask beers; if all the other factors in keeping real ale properly are not observed the beer will still not be very good and will not trouble this Guide.

Some brewers mandate their use in tied houses, which is the reason for so few pubs owned by the likes of Hall & Woodhouse, Palmer's and McMullens appearing in this Guide in recent years.

It is also true that pubs using cask breathers have graced the pages of this Guide. Members carrying out surveys have not always asked to look in the cellar, and those who have probably wouldn't recognise a cask breather anyway. An unscientific poll of active members found about four per cent would go through the recommended procedure for finding out if a pub was using cask breathers.

Nick Boley is one of CAMRA's National Directors and a former Chair of CAMRA's Technical Advisory Group.

RETURN TRAYS

Also known as an Autovac or beer economiser, a return tray is a device that collects beer spilled in the pouring process, recycles it by mixing it with fresh beer, and returns it to the glass. It can be identified by a stainless steel drip tray below the nozzle on a handpump, with a pipe connected from the bottom of the tray to the draw line of the cask. They are commonly found in use in Yorkshire and parts of south-east Scotland and have been seen in north-east Scotland and north-west England. In accordance with Motion 15 carried at Conference 2018, a symbol ↺ will appear next to entries in the Guide where a return tray is in use on some or all of the beers.

ADDITIONAL RESOURCES

The *Good Beer Guide* is also available in digital formats, including a mobile app, an e-book (available on the Amazon Kindle store and iBooks store) and a sat-nav Points of Interest (POI) download. Together, these offer the perfect solution to pub-finding on the move. See **shop.camra.org.uk** for further information.

GOOD BEER GUIDE APP

The *Good Beer Guide* mobile app provides detailed information on the latest *Good Beer Guide* pubs, breweries and beers wherever you are or wherever you are going. It also provides information for more than 31,000 other real ale pubs all over the UK, collated by CAMRA. Social media integration lets you share your beer experiences with other users and you can record your pub visits, tasted beers and personal reviews. For more information visit **gbgapp.camra.org.uk**

CAMRA'S NATIONAL BEER SCORING SYSTEM

CAMRA's National Beer Scoring System (NBSS) is used by members across the country to help them identify outlets that serve consistently good beer. The system uses a 0–5 scale that can be submitted online. Any member can submit a beer score by logging in to CAMRA's **whatpub.com**, logging in as a member and selecting 'Submit Beer Scores' or by using the beer scoring function on the Good Beer Guide app.

The NBSS is also used to select beers for the annual Champion Beer of Britain competition.

See **camra.org.uk/NBSS** for details.

WhatPub

JOIN CAMRA'S GOOD BEER GUIDE PRIVILEGE CLUB

CAMRA members can take advantage of an even bigger discount on the *Good Beer Guide*, and get further benefits, by joining the Good Beer Guide Privilege Club.

- Pay just £11 (RRP £15.99) for your copy, with free p&p
- Receive your copy hot off the press and in advance of other purchasers
- Receive occasional special Club offers and discounts on other CAMRA books and merchandise
- Stay up-to-date every year with *CAMRA's Good Beer Guide* as everything is taken care of with one simple Direct Debit
- Help to fund CAMRA directly, allowing us to continue to campaign for real ale and community pubs

For further details and to sign up visit **camra.org.uk/gbg-privilege-club** and follow the online instructions.

BOOKS AND MERCHANDISE

CAMRA's online shop is the ideal place to visit for anyone looking for beer- and pub-related books, clothing or merchandise for themselves or fellow beer lovers.

With an ever-changing list of new and established titles from CAMRA Books and a carefully curated selection of titles from a variety of other publishers and authors, the CAMRA Shop is the go-to destination for anyone looking for books on pubs, beer bars, beer and brewing. Whether you are looking for a basic introduction to the world of beer or to deepen your knowledge, or whether you are after a consumer guide to the best local pubs or some authoritative industry insight, we have something for you on our shelves.

The shop also stocks a range of CAMRA-branded and beer-themed clothing and products, all chosen with the keen beer drinker in mind.

- Browse the full range of CAMRA Books titles within categories including beer knowledge; beer travel; history, heritage & culture; home brewing; and pub walks
- Discover our growing selection of beer-related titles from other publishers
- Shop among our expanding range of clothing and merchandise
- Get upcoming CAMRA titles in advance of publication at special pre-order prices
- As a CAMRA member, log in to receive further discounts

Visit us at: **shop.camra.org.uk**

JOIN THE CAMPAIGN

CAMRA, the Campaign for Real Ale, is an independent, not-for-profit, volunteer-led consumer group. We promote good-quality real ale and pubs, as well as lobbying government to champion drinkers' rights and protect local pubs as centres of community life.

CAMRA has over 190,000 members from all ages and backgrounds, brought together by a common belief in the issues that CAMRA deals with, and their love of good-quality British beer.

From just £26.50 a year, you can join CAMRA and enjoy the following benefits:

- A **welcome pack**, including membership card, to help you make the most of your membership
- Access to award-winning, quarterly **BEER magazine** and monthly **What's Brewing** newspaper
- **Free or reduced entry** to over 180 beer festivals
- £30 worth of **CAMRA real ale* vouchers**
- Access to the **Real Ale Discount Scheme**, where you receive discounts on pints at over 3,500 participating pubs nationwide
- **Learning resources** to help you discover more about beer and brewing
- The opportunity to **campaign for great real ale, cider and perry**, and to save pubs under threat from closure
- **Discounts on CAMRA books** including our best-selling Good Beer Guide
- Social activities in your local area and **exclusive member discounts online**

Whether you're a dedicated campaigner, a beer enthusiast looking to learn more about beer, or you just love to meet up with friends in your local, make sure to join the beer movement today!

Join the campaign at
www.camra.org.uk/join

CAMRA, 230 Hatfield Road, St Albans, Herts AL1 4LW.
Tel: 01727 798440
Email: camra@camra.org.uk

Rates and benefits are subject to change.
*real ale, cider and perry, subject to terms and conditions.

Campaign for Real Ale